PAGE
54

ON THE
ROAD

...TE DESTINATION GUIDE
..., detailed listings
and insider tips

C8 000 000 797175

Darwin &
Uluru (p798)

Queensland &
the Great
Barrier Reef
(p275)

Perth & Western
Australia (p891)

Adelaide &
South
Australia
(p704)

Sydney & New
South Wales
(p56)

Canberra &
Around (p243)

Melbourne &
Victoria
(p470)

Tasmania
(p613)

BIRMINGHAM LIBRARIES

919 404 72

TOWER HILL LIBRARY

SURVIVAL GUIDE

VITAL PRACTICAL INFORMATION TO
HELP YOU HAVE A SMOOTH TRIP

Transport

GETTING THERE
& AWAY

THIS EDITION WRITTEN AND RESEARCHED BY

Charles Rawlings-Way & Meg Worby,

Jayne D'Arcy, Peter Dragicevich, Sarah Gilbert, Paul Harding,

Nevez, Virginia Maxwell, Miriam Raphael, Regis St Louis,

Steve Waters, Penny Watson

welcome to
Australia

Hip Cities

Most Australians live along the coast, and most of these folks live in cities. In fact, Australia is the 18th-most urbanised country in the world, with around 70% of Australians living in the 10 largest towns. It follows that cities here are a lot of fun! Sydney, the sun-kissed Harbour City, is a glamorous collusion of beaches, boutiques and bars. Melbourne is all arts, alleyways and Australian Rules football. Brisbane is a subtropical town on the way up; Adelaide has festive grace and pubby poise. Boomtown Perth breathes west-coast optimism; Canberra transcends political agendas. If you're looking for contrast, the tropical northern frontier town of Darwin and

chilly southern sandstone city of Hobart couldn't be more different. But whichever city you're wheeling into, you'll never go wanting for a decent coffee, live band, art-gallery opening or music festival mosh-pit.

Food & Drink

Australia has broken the binds of its Anglo meat-and-two-veg culinary past, serving up a multicultural fusion of European techniques and fresh Pacific-rim ingredients. 'Mod Oz' (or Modern Australian) is what the locals call it. Seafood plays a starring role – 'Hardly surprising on an island this big!', we hear you say...but from succulent Moreton Bay Bugs to delicate King George Whiting, there's a lot of variety in

Island, country, continent... Australia is a big'un whichever way you spin it. The essence of the place is diversity: deserts, coral reefs, tall forests, snow-cloaked mountains and multicultural melting-pot cities.

(left) Pinnacles Desert (p962), Western Australia
(below) Sydney Opera House (p68)

the ocean's bounty. And of course, beer in hand, you'll still find beef, lamb and chicken at traditional Aussie BBQs. Don't drink beer? Australian wines are world-beaters: punchy Barossa Valley reds, McLaren Vale Shiraz, Hunter Valley Semillon and Sauvignon Blanc from Tasmania's cool-climate Tamar Valley. Need a caffeine hit? Italian cafes have always known how to make the perfect espresso, but now there are coffee machines in pubs and petrol stations, and baristas in downtown coffee carts – you're never far from a double-shot, day or night.

It's A Wide Open Road

There's a heckuva lot of tarmac across this wide brown land. From Margaret River to Cooktown, Jabiru to Dover, the best way to really appreciate Australia is to hit the open road. Car hire here is relatively affordable, road conditions are generally good, and outside of the big cities there's bugger-all traffic. If you're driving a campervan, you'll find well-appointed caravan parks in just about every town of any size. If you're feeling more adventurous, hire a 4WD and go off-road: Australia's national parks and secluded corners are custom-made for down-the-dirt-road camping trips. So embrace your inner road warrior and sing it loud: '*Get your motor runnin'... Head out on the highway...*'

›Australia

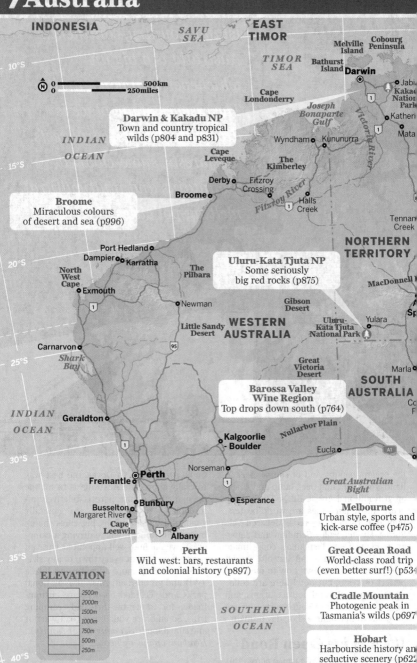

INDONESIA

EAST TIMOR

SAVU SEA

TIMOR SEA

Melville Island
Cobourg Peninsula

Bathurst Island

Darwin

Jabi
Kakad
Nation
Park

Katheri

Mata

Cape Londonderry

Joseph Bonaparte Gulf

Victoria River

Darwin & Kakadu NP
Town and country tropical
wilds (p804 and p831)

Wyndham
Kununurra

INDIAN OCEAN

Cape Leveque

The Kimberley

Derby
Fitzroy Crossing

Broome

Fitzroy River

Halls Creek

Broome
Miraculous colours
of desert and sea (p996)

Tennan
Creek

NORTHERN TERRITORY

Port Hedland
Dampier
Karratha

North West Cape

Exmouth

The Pilbara

Uluru-Kata Tjuta NP
Some seriously
big red rocks (p875)

MacDonnell

Sp

Newman

Gibson Desert

Carnarvon

Shark Bay

Little Sandy Desert

WESTERN AUSTRALIA

Uluru-Kata Tjuta National Park

Yulara

Marla

SOUTH AUSTRALIA

Great Victoria Desert

Barossa Valley Wine Region
Top drops down south (p764)

Co
F

INDIAN OCEAN

Geraldton

Nullarbor Plain

Kalgoorlie - Boulder

Eucla

C

Norseman

Great Australian Bight

Fremantle **Perth**

Busselton **Bunbury**
Margaret River
Cape Leeuwin

Esperance

Albany

Melbourne
Urban style, sports and
kick-arse coffee (p475)

Perth
Wild west: bars, restaurants
and colonial history (p897)

Great Ocean Road
World-class road trip
(even better surf!) (p53∢

Cradle Mountain
Photogenic peak in
Tasmania's wilds (p697)

SOUTHERN OCEAN

Hobart
Harbourside history an
seductive scenery (p62∷

ELEVATION

2500m
2000m
1500m
1000m
750m
500m
250m

500km
250miles

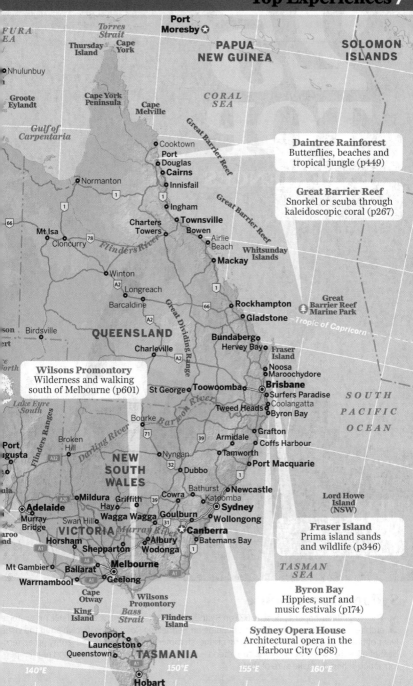

FURA EA

Nhulunbuy

Groote Eylandt

Gulf of Carpentaria

Torres Strait

Thursday Island

Cape York

Port Moresby ✪

PAPUA NEW GUINEA

SOLOMON ISLANDS

Cape York Peninsula

Cape Melville

CORAL SEA

Normanton

Great Barrier Reef

Cooktown

Port Douglas

Cairns

Innisfail

Ingham

Mt Isa

Cloncurry

Charters Towers

Townsville

Bowen

Airlie Beach

Whitsunday Islands

Mackay

Flinders River

Winton

Longreach

Barcaldine

QUEENSLAND

Great Dividing Range

Rockhampton

Gladstone

Great Barrier Reef Marine Park

Tropic of Capricorn

son ert

e orth

Birdsville

Charleville

Bundaberg

Hervey Bay

Fraser Island

Noosa

Maroochydore

Brisbane

Surfers Paradise

Coolangatta

Byron Bay

SOUTH PACIFIC OCEAN

Lake Eyre South

St George

Toowoomba

Tweed Heads

Bourke

Barwon River

Darling River

Armidale

Grafton

Coffs Harbour

Port

agusta

0

ula

roo nd

Flinders Ranges

Broken Hill

NEW SOUTH WALES

Nyngan

Dubbo

Tamworth

Port Macquarie

Mildura

Hay

Griffith

Cowra

Bathurst

Katoomba

Newcastle

Sydney

Wollongong

Lord Howe Island (NSW)

Adelaide

Murray Bridge

Swan Hill

Wagga Wagga

Goulburn

VICTORIA

Murray River

Canberra

Batemans Bay

Fraser Island
Prima island sands and wildlife (p346)

Horsham

Shepparton

Albury

Wodonga

TASMAN SEA

Mt Gambier

Ballarat

Melbourne

Geelong

Warrnambool

Cape Otway

Wilsons Promontory

King Island

Bass Strait

Flinders Island

Byron Bay
Hippies, surf and music festivals (p174)

Devonport

Launceston

Queenstown

TASMANIA

Sydney Opera House
Architectural opera in the Harbour City (p68)

Hobart

Daintree Rainforest
Butterflies, beaches and tropical jungle (p449)

Great Barrier Reef
Snorkel or scuba through kaleidoscopic coral (p267)

Wilsons Promontory
Wilderness and walking south of Melbourne (p601)

140°E   150°E   155°E   160°E

25 TOP EXPERIENCES

Sydney Opera House

1 The magnificent opera house (p68) on Sydney Harbour is a headline act in itself. An exercise architectural lyricism, Jørn Utzon's building on Bennelong Point holds its own amid the visua feast of the harbour's attention-grabbing bridge, shimmering blue waters and jaunty green ferri Best of all is the fact that everyone can attend – its bars, restaurant, daily tours and regular per formance schedule make sure of that.

reat Barrier Reef

Stretching over 2000km up the Queensland coastline, the awe-inspiring Great Barrier Reef (p267) is one of the world's great wonders. Among the best ways to experience it: donning a sk and fins and delving into the vivid undersea kingdom for a close-up view of dazzling corals, turtles, sharks, rays and tropical fish of every colour and size...or exploring the reef by sailboat, ing a scenic flight, gazing at marine life through a glass-bottomed semisubmersible and ering in a resort (or camp) on a remote coral-fringed island.

elbourne

Head down bluestone laneways in Melbourne's city centre (p475) to find the hidden restau-rants and bold street art that encapsulates the alternative vibe here. Take your place on a milk te in Degraves St and let a local barista change the way you think about coffee, then window pp for quirky 'only in Melbourne' crafts and clothes. Watch evening's arrival by the Yarra River, n head up some stairs or down to the very end of a graffiti-covered lane to find a smooth drink-establishment serving up quality Victorian wine, beer and music. Section 8 (p511), Melbourne

Uluru-Kata Tjuta National Park

4 No matter how many times you've seen it on postcards, nothing prepares you for the burnished grandeur of the Rock as it first appears on the outback horizon. With its remote dese location, deep cultural significance and spectacular natural beauty, Uluru is a pilgrimage well wor the many hundreds of kilometres it takes to get there. But Uluru-Kata Tjuta National Park (p875) offers much more than the chance to see the Rock. Along with the equally captivating Kata Tjuta (the Olgas), there are mystical walks, sublime sunsets and ancient desert cultures to encounter.

MONA

5 Occupying an improbable riverside location a ferry ride from Hobart's harbourfront, Moori Estate's Museum of Old & New Art (MONA; p627) is an innovative and truly world-class institution. Described by its owner, Hobart philanthropist David Walsh, as a 'subversive adult Disneyland', three levels of spectacular underground galleries showcase more than 400 often challenging and controversial works of art. Visitors may not like everything they see, but it's guaranteed that intense debate and conversation will be on the agenda after viewing one of Australia's unique arts experiences.

Fan palms, ferns and mangroves are just some of the 3000-plus plant species in the ancient, World Heritage–listed Daintree Rainforest (p449), which is alive with a chorus of birds, insects and frogs. Guided day walks, wildlife-spotting night tours, mountain treks, interpretive boardwalks, canopy walks, self-guided walking trails, 4WD trips, horse riding, kayaking, croc-spotting cruises, tropical-fruit orchard tours and tastings...there are many ways to experience one of the most extraordinary ecosystems on the planet. Mossman Gorge (p446), Daintree Rainforest

Great Ocean Road

7 The Twelve Apostles – rock formations jutting out of wild waters – are one of Victoria's most vivid sights, but it's the 'gett there' road trip that doubles their impact. Take it slow while driving along roads that c beside spectacular Bass Strait beaches, the whip slightly inland through rainforests alive with small towns and big trees. The secrets the Great Ocean Road (p534) don't stop he further along is maritime treasure Port Fairy and hidden Cape Bridgewater. For the ultim in slow travel, walk the Great Ocean Walk fro Apollo Bay to the Apostles. Twelve Apostles (p543), Port Campbell National Park

Byron Bay

8 Vibrant, laid-back and offbeat are words oft used to describe this small-time, big-heart, beachside destination. At first encounter, it might seem too touristy, too packed – but no matter how many bronzed shoulders you rub up against, Byron Bay (p174) tends to soften even the hardest critic. Long lazy stretches of beach and a cute undeveloped town centre help; so too does the eclectic food scene, where cheap, cheerful takeaway joints sit comfortably next to hip bars and restaurants. The town's infectious up-beat vibe puts a smile on your dial, no matter where you hail from. Cape Byron lighthouse (p175), Byron Bay

Gold Coast Surf Carnivals

9 They're the bronzed gods of the surf, the beefcakes of the sea and the uberfit icons of Australia's beach-crazed culture. From the first appearance of a surf belt in 1907, Australia's surf life-savers have evolved into superfit and superbuff athletes, pitting their skills against each other in seasonal surf carnivals on the Gold Coast (p317) – gruelling events involving ocean swimming, beach running and surf boat racing. It's hard work but makes for an extraordinary spectator sport for the rest of us limp squids. Surf life-saver, Surfers Paradise, Gold Coast

CHRISTOPHER GROENHOUT/LONELY PLANET IMAGES ©

The Whitsundays

10 Sailing across the shimmering blue water of the Coral Sea, lounging beside the pool in a luxury island resort, playing castaway on a secluded beach...there are so many ways to enjoy the beautiful Whitsunday Islands (p391). One of the best is from the deck of a sailing boat, basking in the warm sunshine and balmy sea air, savouring the dramatic tropical sunsets and star-studded night skies. Sailing through this island paradise brings the romance of the sea to life. Whitehaven Beach (p394), Whitsunday Island

HOLGER LEUE/LONELY PLANET IMAGES ©

Gourmet Food & Wine

11 Right across Australia you'll find gourmet offerings for all budgets: cool-climate wines and cheeses in Tasmania, coffee in Melbourne, oysters and seafood in Sydney, punchy red wines in South Australia, marron in WA, and native meats and bush tucker in the Northern Territory. Foodie heaven! One of our favourite spots is Victoria's prosperous King Valley, noted for its Italian wine varietals. You can also sample locally made cheese, olives, mustards and marinades here, and dine in some of the region's best pubs, cafes and winery restaurants.

JOHN HAY/LONELY PLANET IMAGES ©

Canberra

12 If there's one thing Canberra's got going for it, it's museums. Whether your passion is art, history, film or big guns, you'll find it in spades in the bush capital. Highlights include the National Gallery of Australia (p246), with its magnificent collection of Aboriginal and Torres Strait Islander, Australian and Asian art; the National Museum of Australia (p244), whose imaginative exhibits provide insights into the Australian heart and soul; and the War Memorial (p246) with its moving Hall of Memory and its fascinating displays. National Museum of Australia, Canberra

Wilsons Promontory

13 For sheer natural beauty, Wilsons Promontory (p601) has it all. This national park boasts sublime ocean beaches and some of the best wilderness hiking and camping in coastal Australia – you just need to grab a map and permit, strap on a pack and disappear into the wilds. The overnight walk across 'the Prom' from Tidal River to Sealer's Cove and back is a great way to get started. Serious hikers should tackle the three-day Great Prom Walk, staying a night in the gloriously isolated lighthouse keepers' cottage. Tidal River, Wilsons Promontory

GRANT DIXON/LONELY PLANET IMAGES ©

Cradle Mountain

14 A precipitous comb of rock carved out by millennia of ice and wind, crescent-shaped Cradle Mountain (p697) is Tasmania's most recognisable – and spectacular – mountain peak. It's an all-day walk (and boulder scramble) to the summit and back, for unbelievable panoramas over Tasmania's alpine heart. Or you can stand in awe below and fill your camera with the perfect views across Dove Lake to the mountain. If the peak has disappeared in clouds or snow, warm yourself by the fire in one of the nearby lodges... and come back tomorrow.

Perth & Fremantle

5 Perth (p897) may be isolated but it's far from being a backwater. Sophisticated restaurants fly the flag for modern Australian cuisine, while a new crop of chic cocktail bars lurks down likely laneways. In contrast to the flashy face that Perth presents to the Swan River, charmingly ungy inner suburbs echo with the thrum of guitars and the sizzle of woks. Just down the river, the ely port of Fremantle (p915) has a pub on every corner that doesn't already have a hostel on it, d a wealth of colonial buildings. Little Creatures Brewery (p920), Fremantle

Broome & the Kimberley

16 Like no other town in the country, Broome (p996) is a kinetic, postmodern pastiche of bars, beaches, nature, locals and every type of traveller. Turquoise waters melt with package tourists while red pindan earth blows into luxury spa resorts, and camels amble past a searingly beautiful sunset. Away from the bling, boabs roam the spinifex plains of the vast Kimberley (p993), as Wandjina and Gwion Gwion (Bradshaw) stand mute guard over hidden pools and gorges, and the melted-jaffa domes of Purnululu National Park crumble imperceptibly, as they've always done.

RICHARD I'ANSON/LONELY PLANET IMAGES ©

Southwest Coast WA

17 The joy of drifting from winery to winery along country roads shaded by gum trees is only one of the delights of Western Australia's southwest (p928). There are caves to explore, historic towns to visit and spring wildflowers to admire. Surfers flock to world-class breaks around Margaret River, but it's not unusual to find yourself on a white-sand beach with nobody else in sight. In late winter and early spring, look offshore and chances are you'll spot whales cruising on the coast-hugging 'Humpback Highway'. Twilight Cove (p950), Esperance

ORIEN HARVEY/LONELY PLANET IMAGES ©

AFL Grand Final

18 AFL Grand Final day in Melbourne (p495), on the last Saturday of September, is the perfect time to head to your local pub (or make it your local for the day) and get rowdy with footy supporters. In 2010 Melburnians loved it so much there were two grand finals: the first one was a draw, so they had to replay it the following week – another excuse to go to the pub! The regular season lasts the entire length of winter, so expect colourful beanies and scarves bobbing around the state as a sign of devotion.

© DAVID CALLOW/THE SLATTERY MEDIA GROUP

Indigenous Art in WA

19 Around 59,000 Aboriginal people call Western Australia home, comprising many different Indigenous peoples, speaking many distinct languages. The Art Gallery of Western Australia (p897) is a treasure trove of Indigenous art. In the state's north, the Kimberley (p1002) encompasses the art of the Wandjina, the Gwion Gwion (Bradshaw) images and contemporary Indigenous art. Gwion Gwion (Bradshaw) images, the Kimberley

MICHAEL GEBICKI/LONELY PLANET IMAGES ©

Darwin & Kakadu National Park

20 Levelled by WWII bombs and Cyclone Tracy, Darwin (p831) knows a thing or two about reinvention. This frontier city has emerged from the tropical steam to become a multicultural, hedonistic hotspot: the launch pad for trips into some of Australia's most remarkable wilderness. Two hours southeast down the highway, Kakadu National Park (p831) is the place to see Indigenous rock art under jagged escarpments and idyllic waterholes at the base of plummeting waterfalls. Raucous birdlife and saltwater crocodiles are guaranteed highlights. Gunlom (p837), Kakadu National Park

South Australian Wine Regions

21 Adelaide is drunk on the success of its three world-famous wine regions, all within two hours' (designated) drive: the Barossa Valley (p764) to the north, with its gutsy reds, old vines and German know-how; McLaren Vale (p737) to the south, a Mediterranean palette of sea, vines and Shiraz; and the Clare Valley (p770), known for Riesling and wobbly bike rides (in that order). Better-kept secrets are the cool-climate stunners from the Adelaide Hills (p734) and the country Cabernet Sauvignon of Padthaway and Coonawarra (p757). Clare Valley, South Australia

Fraser Island

22 Fraser Island (p346) is an ecological wonderland created by drifting sand, where wild dogs roam free and lush rainforest grows on sand. It's a primal island utopia, home to a profusion of wildlife including the purest strain of dingo in Australia. The best way to explore the island in a 4WD – cruising up the seemingly endless Seventy-Five Mile Beach and bouncing along sandy inland tracks. Tropical rainforest, pristine freshwater pools and beach camping under the stars will bring you back to nature. Seventy-Five Mile Beach (p347), Fraser Island

23 Furry, cuddly, ferocious – you can find all this and more on a wildlife-watching journey around Australia. Head south on the East Coast for adorable little penguins and fur seals, and north for otherworldly cassowaries and dinosaur-like crocodiles. In between, you'll find a panoply of extraordinary animals found nowhere else on earth: koalas, kangaroos, wombats and platypuses. There's great whale-watching along the coast, the awe-inspiring sight of nesting sea turtles (and later, hatchlings) on Queensland beaches, plus the omnipresent and unforgettable cackle of the laughing kookaburra.

˙anami Road & ˙anning Stock Route

˙4 Whether you're belting an old Falcon station-wagon along ˙ Tanami Road (p1011), or depreci-˙ng your new 4WD camper some-˙ere near Well 45 on the Canning ˙ck Route (p959), you know you're ˙ just visiting the outback, you've ˙ome part of it. The sky is bluer, the ˙st redder, and salt lakes whiter than ˙thing you've ever seen before. ˙s are measured in hundreds of ˙metres, spinifex and blowouts. ˙hts are spent in the five-zillion-star ˙el, waiting for one to fall... Canning ˙ck Route, Western Australia

Outback Horse Racing: Birdsville Races

25 What started in 1882 as a run for stock horses has today morphed into a massive event, attracting more than 6000 spectators who pile into the one-pub town for four days of dusty track racing and boozing. The race weekend is early September, though in recent years heavy rains have flooded out the event. But even when equine flu stopped the horses turning up in 2007, crowds still thronged to Birdsville (p380) to pitch tents in the dust, drink beer and see old mates.

need to know

Currency
» Australian dollars ($)

Language
» English

When to Go

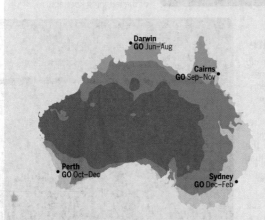

Darwin
GO Jun–Aug

Cairns
GO Sep–Nov

Perth
GO Oct–Dec

Sydney
GO Dec–Feb

Hobart
GO Jan–Mar

Desert, dry climate
Dry climate
Tropical climate, wet dry seasons
Warm to hot summers, mild winters

High Season
(Dec–Feb)

» Summertime: local holidays, busy beaches and cricket.

» Expect to pay up to 35% more for big-city accommodation.

» Winter (June to August) in Central Australia and the north – mild days and low humidity.

Shoulder Season
(Sep–Nov)

» Warm sun, clear skies, shorter queues.

» Local business people are relaxed, not yet stressed by summer crowds.

» Autumn (March to May) is also shoulder season – atmospheric in Melbourne.

Low Season
(Jun–Aug)

» Cool rainy days down south; mild sunny skies up north.

» Tourist numbers are down; restaurants and attractions keep slightly shorter hours.

» Head for the ski resorts in Victoria and NSW.

Your Daily Budget

Budget less than
$130

» Dorm beds: $25–$35 a night

» Big-city food markets for self-catering bargains

» Take public transport and visit free museums

Midrange
$130–$250

» Double room in a midrange hotel: $100–$150

» Midrange restaurants and a few beers at the pub

» Hire a car and explore further

Top end more than
$250

» Double room in a top-end hotel: from $200

» Three-course meal in a classy restaurant: $70

» Go clubbing, catch a show or hit the ritzy bars

Money

» ATMs widely available, especially in larger cities and towns. Credit cards accepted in most hotels and restaurants.

Visas

» All visitors to Australia need a visa, except New Zealanders. Apply for an ETA or eVisitor visa (apply online), each allowing a three-month stay.

Mobile Phones

» European phones will work on Australia's network, but not most American or Japanese phones. Use global roaming or a local SIM card and pre-pay account.

Driving

» Drive on the left; the steering wheel is on the right side of the car.

Websites

» **Lonely Planet** (www.lonelyplanet. com/australia) Destination information, hotel bookings, traveller forum and more.

» **Tourism Australia** (www.australia.com) Government tourism site with visitor info.

» **Bureau of Meteorology** (www. bom.gov.au) Nationwide weather forecasts.

» **The Australian** (www. theaustralian.com.au) National broadsheet newspaper online.

» **Parks Australia** (www. environment.gov.au/ parks) Info on national parks and reserves.

» **Coastal Watch** (www.coastalwatch. com) Surf condition reports and webcams.

Exchange Rates

Canada	C$1	$0.96
China	Y1	$0.14
Euro zone	€1	$1.31
Japan	¥100	$1.17
Korea	W100	$0.09
New Zealand	NZ$1	$0.79
UK	UK£1	$1.49
USA	US$1	$0.91

For current exchange rates see www.xe.com.

Important Numbers

Regular Australian phone numbers have a two-digit area code followed by an eight-digit number. Drop the initial 0 if calling from abroad.

Country code	☑61
International access code	☑0011
Emergency (ambulance, fire, police)	☑000
Road conditions	☑13 27 01
Directory assistance	☑1223

Arriving in Australia

» **Sydney Airport** (p121)

Trains – Every 10 minutes, 4.30am–12.40am
Shuttle buses – Prebooked services to city hotels
Taxis – $40–$50; 30 minutes to the city

» **Melbourne Airport** (p519)

Buses – SkyBus every 10 to 30 minutes, 24-hours
Taxis – $40–$50; 25 minutes to the city

» **Brisbane Airport** (p311)

Trains – Every 15–30 minutes, 5.45am–10pm
Shuttle buses – Prebooked services to city hotels
Taxis – $35–$45; 25 minutes to the city

Getting Around Australia

Australia is absolutely enormous –the sixth-largest country in the world – and while it's tempting to strap a surfboard onto the roof of a campervan, crank up the AC/DC as loud as hell and hit the open road, you might find yourself spending a lot of time getting not very far. Formula 1-wannabes can drive from Melbourne to Sydney or Adelaide in a day, but you won't see much. Sydney to Brisbane becomes a similar blur of road signs and trucks, and forget about Adelaide to Darwin or Perth unless you've got weeks up your sleeve. Passenger trains do ply these routes if you have plenty of time (and money), but you'll find internal flights are relatively cheap and, most importantly, fast. And you can usually carbon-offset your flights if you're feeling guilty.

if you like...

Beaches

On this big sandy island there's a lot of variety. The vast, damp stretch of Cable Beach in Western Australia is literally miles from the sheltered glow of Wineglass Bay, far south in Tasmania. Meanwhile, on urban beaches, locals mix up their morning macchiatos with a bit of bather-spotting...

Bondi Beach An essential Sydney experience: carve up the surf, watch the human race, or laze around on your fashionable patch of sand (p82)

Whitehaven Beach The jewel of the Whitsundays, and one of Australia's loveliest beaches, with powdery white sand and crystal-clear waters (p394)

Hellfire Bay Sand like talcum powder in the middle of Cape Le Grand National Park, which is precisely the middle of nowhere (p951)

Carrickalinga Beach A 1½-hour drive southeast of Adelaide, near the McLaren Vale wine region, is this underpopulated 2km beach all of your own: good fishing, refreshing winter walks, and shallow aquamarine swimming in summer (p740)

Islands

Home to hundreds of islands, Australia has spectacular getaways of the powdery sand and palm-fringed variety. Magical bushwalks, magnificent wildlife, deserted beaches and aquatic beauty (colourful coral reefs, whale and dolphin watching) are just a few draws...

Kangaroo Island An adventurous ferry-ride away, this is a great spot for South Australian wildlife watching and the place to feast on some of Australia's freshest seafood (p743)

Bruny Island A windswept, sparsely populated retreat where the coastal scenery is magical – there are countless swimming and surf beaches, plus good fishing (p644)

Fraser Island The world's largest sand island has giant sand dunes, freshwater lakes and abundant wildlife (p346)

Whitsundays Book in at one of the islands' top resorts, or board a sailboat and explore as many of these amazingly pristine islands as you can (p391)

Lady Elliott Island Ringed by the Great Barrier Reef and reachable by light aircraft, this remote island is a great place to play castaway (p362)

Wilderness

Australia is roughly 15 times the size of the United Kingdom, with a third as many people, so it's no surprise that there are plenty of wild places here. And what's more, many of them are just a short hop from the major cities.

Otways Two hours' drive from Melbourne you'll find a magnificent wild coastline cloaked with temperate rainforest inland. Look up and you'll see the rumps of multiple koalas in the tall eucalypts (p542)

Flinders Ranges Treading a line between desolation and beauty, the ancient outcrops of Wilpena Pound and the Flinders Ranges are mesmerising. Camping here is the best way to stumble on a 600-million-year-old fossil (p782)

Litchfield National Park Most people have heard of Kakadu, but just up the highway are some wild waterfalls that are more accessible, a couple of hours from Darwin. The termite mounds here look like an alien landscape (p828)

Cradle Mountain-Lake St Clair National Park There are few better places to immerse yourself in the Tasmanian landscape than the sometimes forbidding, ever-photogenic Cradle Mountain. The legendary Overland Track kicks off here (p697)

If you like...white-water rafting, Queensland's mighty Tully River has 44 rapids and makes for one great (and very wet) white-water journey (p410)

History

They say white Australia has a black history. This isn't an old country by most of the world's standards, but Indigenous history here dates back more than 50,000 years.

Ku-Ring-Gai Chase National Park This sprawling reserve north of Sydney shelters hundreds of important Aboriginal sites, including rock engravings and cave paintings (p87)

The Rocks Next to Sydney's Circular Quay, the Rocks were squalid, cramped and lawless. The site of Sydney's first white settlement is a bit touristy, but the old buildings and alleyways are hauntingly historic (p69)

Port Arthur Historic Site Tassie's big-ticket tourist destination, Port Arthur has seen a lot of sadness and not just in colonial times. Still, it's a fascinating window into Australia's convict past (p652)

Mintaro This heritage-listed Clare Valley hamlet (1849) was built to service copper carts travelling from the nearby Burra mines. Don't miss Martindale Hall (used in the classic film, *Picnic at Hanging Rock*) (p771)

Beechworth Victoria's high country was once home to bushrangers, including the infamous Ned Kelly and his gang. Now there's an illegally good bakery (p591)

Luxury Stays

If you've got money in your pocket and time on your hands, a growing number of first-rate hotels and resorts compete for top honours when it comes to guest pampering.

Paradise Bay This eco-resort has just 10 beautifully sited bungalows, and manages to deliver a heavy dollop of luxury while still doing good by the environment (p393)

Park Hyatt Drink in the majestic views at this opulent hotel facing the Sydney Harbour, just one of many excellent top-end hotels (p102)

Daintree Eco Lodge & Spa This splendid rainforest retreat has it all – boutique villas, a high-end spa and guided walks led by members of the Kuku Yalanji community (p447)

Valleys of Wine

Wherever there's a valley in Australia, someone admirable has climbed in and planted a grapevine. These wine regions cultivate a strong food culture and are home to some great restaurants.

Barossa Valley More than 80 wineries within a spittoon's dribble of each other in this German-settled enclave of villages, home to some of Australia's greatest reds (p768)

Clare Valley Clare Valley Riesling rocks. Skillogallee House is a favoured restaurant: delicious food and wines from the region, served in an old farmhouse, makes you feel that life is very agreeable (p771)

Tamar Valley One of Tasmania's key wine-producing areas, the dry premium wines created here have achieved international recognition (p673)

Yarra Valley Chase Melbourne's Yarra River an hour northeast and you'll bump into the cool-climate Yarra Valley. This is the place for syrupy whites and complex cabernets (p526)

Hunter Valley Dating back to the 1820s, the Hunter Valley is Australia's oldest wine region, bottling Australia's gift to the world – super Semillon (p134)

If you like...clambering over bridges, both Sydney and Brisbane offer bridge walks – a magnificent way to see the city from eagle's-nest heights (p101) and (p291)

Festivals

There's usually one massive annual art-and-culture fest in each major city, bringing a stellar program of music, theatre, dance, comedy, film, Indigenous art and public exhibitions – but we like these lesser-known events.

East Coast International Blues & Roots Festival Byron Bay's big jam fest is reason enough to venture to this lovely, chilled-out surf town (p178)

Laura Aboriginal Dance Festival Held every two years on odd-numbered years (2013, 2015...), this colourful dance festival celebrates Aboriginal culture through song, dance, ceremony and performance. Laura is 330km north of Cairns (p463)

WOMADelaide One of the world's best live-music events, with more than 300 musicians and performers from around the globe. Held over four days at the beginning of March, in Adelaide's Botanic Park (p718)

Woodford Folk Festival One of the Sunshine Coast's biggest gatherings, this festival hosts a diverse collection of performers playing world folk music. There's also dance, food, performance art, workshops, discussions and more; runs 27 December to 1 January (p342)

Live Music/Pubs

Even AC/DC had to start somewhere. Across the nation you'll find live rock rooms and acoustic beer gardens, perfect settings for a cold beer and some tunes. Even if there's no band, you can always count on a giant schnitzel for dinner.

Northcote Social Club One of Melbourne's best live-music spots, with a buzzing front bar and a spacious deck out the back (p514)

Venue 505 Sydney's best little jazz bar features top-notch performers in an edgy underground space (p116)

Railway Friendly Bar This sprawling indoor-outdoor pub features live music most nights and is a requisite stop in easy-going Byron Bay (p181)

Governor Hindmarsh Hotel All genres are represented at this sprawling old rocker where the pub grub is decent, drinks are cheap and the crowd is up for it (p727)

Knopwood's Retreat There's no sight more welcoming than the huge fire in 'Knoppie's' grate on a chilly Hobart evening, or the sound of summer revellers spilling out into Salamanca Place (p637)

Markets

There are reliably good markets in every state. Locals and artisans bring their fresh produce and handmade goods. You'll usually find in-season fruit, cut flowers, food from other cultures, cheeses, small goods, vintage and cotton clothes, and regional delicacies (honey in Tasmania or macadamia nuts in Queensland).

Queen Victoria Market A great place to start the gourmand's journey is this legendary market, over 130 years old (p478)

Sydney Markets You'll find lively farmers markets in the Rocks (Friday and Saturday), Bondi Junction (Thursday), Darlinghurst (Saturday) and Manly (Saturday) (p120)

Mindil Beach Sunset Markets The sound of the didgeridoo reverberates through the smoke from the satays. Most people head to the beach for sunset dinner on the sand before browsing myriad colourful stalls (p822)

Byron Farmers Market Typical of the clean-living northern New South Wales coast, you'll find this community treasure on Thursday mornings (p181)

WILL SALTER/LONELY PLANET IMAGES ©

» Queen Victoria Market (p478), Melbourne

Art Galleries

In addition to the big-ticket galleries listed here, there are some great regional galleries around Australia.

National Gallery of Australia This superb Canberra museum houses over 7500 works by Aboriginal and Torres Strait Islander artists, including the moving Aboriginal Memorial (p246)

Museum of Old and New Art (MONA) Cut into a sandstone peninsula at Moorilla Estate winery, Australia's newest fine-art gallery is the talk of Hobart town (p627)

National Gallery of Victoria International Home to travelling exhibitions par excellence (Dali, Caravaggio, Man Ray et al), you'll have to queue up with the rest of arts-mad Melbourne to get in (p480)

Art Gallery of NSW This old-stager keeps things hip with ever-changing national and international exhibitions, the always-controversial Archibald Prize (for portraiture) and architecturally challenging extensions (p75)

Art Gallery of South Australia A cultural high watermark on Adelaide's North Terrace, this art house does things with progressive style (p711)

Indigenous Culture

There are some fine ways to experience the age-old culture of the first Australians. You can take a Dreaming tour through spiritually rich native sites, gaze upon ancient rock art or hit the galleries where a new generation of Aboriginal artists is making its mark.

Dampier Peninsula Interact with remote communities from Western Australia and learn how to spear fish and catch mud crabs (p1004)

Carnarvon Gorge Get a close-up view of stunning rock art inside the twisted gorges of this ancient wonderland (p371)

Koorie Heritage Trust Unearthing the past in Melbourne, the Koorie Heritage Trust is a great place to discover south-eastern Aboriginal culture, with contemporary and traditional art on display and tours on offer (p479)

Kuku-Yalanji Dreamtime Walks Take a guided walk through lush Mossman Gorge, learning about bush-tucker sources and Dreaming legends from knowledgeable indigenous guides (p446)

Outback Adventure

Getting from point to point can be a big adventure in Australia. You can plan an itinerary by train, sailboat or even sky gondola, taking in some awe-inspiring scenery along the way. If you hire a 4WD, be well prepared; or take a tour with a well-informed guide.

4WD to Cape York One of Australia's great wilderness adventures is the off-road journey to the tip of Australia. Experienced drivers can go it alone; you can also join a tour (p469)

The Red Centre Explore Australia's desert heart via a Wayoutback two-day Red Centre Culture and Country Tour from Alice Springs, or a one-day Uluru tour with Emu Run Tours (p858)

Karijini National Park Western Australia's landscapes are awe inspiring. Scramble, abseil, slide and dive through the gorges on an adventure tour (p989)

Oodnadatta Track Head north from the Flinders Ranges along this historic former rail route, passing Lake Eyre, remote pubs and plenty of emus and lizards (p795)

month by month

January

January yawns into action as Australia recovers from its Christmas hangover, but then everyone realises: 'Hey, this is summer!' The festival scene ramps up with sun-stroked outdoor music festivals; Melbourne hosts the Australian Open tennis.

Big Day Out

(www.bigdayout. com) This touring one-day alt-rock festival visits Sydney, Melbourne, Adelaide, Perth and the Gold Coast. It features a huge line-up of big-name artists from all over the world (Metallica, Kings of Leon, Neil Young) and plenty of home-grown talent. Much head-banging, sun and beer.

Australia Day

(www.australia-day. com) Australia's 'birthday' (when the First Fleet landed in 1788) is 26 January, and Australians celebrate with picnics, barbecues, fireworks and, increasingly, much nationalistic flag-waving, drunkenness and chest-beating. In less mood to celebrate are the Aboriginal community, who refer to it as Invasion Day or Survival Day.

February

February is usually Australia's warmest month: hot and sticky up north as the wet season continues, but divine in Tasmania. Everywhere else, locals go back to work, to the beach or to the cricket.

Tropfest

(www.tropfest.com. au) The world's largest short-film festival happens on Sydney's grassy Domain on the last Sunday in February. To discourage cheating and inspire creativity, a compulsory prop appears in each entry (kiss, sneeze, key etc). Free screenings and celeb judges (Joseph Fiennes, Salma Hayek).

Adelaide Fringe

(www.adelaide fringe.com.au) All the acts that don't make the cut (and those that wouldn't want to) for the more highbrow Adelaide Festival end up in the Fringe. The hyperactive Garden of Unearthly Delights can barely contain itself; comedy, music and circus acts spill from the parklands.

March

March is harvest time in Australia's vineyards and in recent years it has been just as hot as January and February, despite its autumnal status. Melbourne's streets jam up with the Formula One Grand Prix.

Sydney Gay & Lesbian Mardi Gras

(www.mardigras.org.au) A month-long arts festival culminating in a flamboyant parade along Sydney's Oxford St on the first Saturday in March (700,000 people like to watch). Gyms empty out, solariums darken, waxing emporiums tally their profits. After-party tickets are gold.

Margaret River Wine Region Festival

(www.margaretriverfestival. com) This five-day festival titillates the tastebuds with the best of southwestern Western Australia's wine, food, art, music and outdoor adventures. It includes carnivals, master classes, the Slow Food Long Table Feast and a cricket match at Cowaramup Oval.

WOMADelaide

(www.womadelaide.com.au) Annual festival of world music, arts, food and dance, held over four days in Adelaide's luscious Botanic Park, attracting loyal crowds from around the country. Eight stages play host to hundreds of world-music acts, it's very family friendly, and you can get a cold beer too.

April

Melbourne and the Adelaide Hills are atmospheric as European trees turn golden then maroon. Up north the rain is abating and the desert temperatures are becoming manageable. Easter = pricey accommodation everywhere.

Ten Days on the Island

(www.tendaysontheisland.org) Every odd-numbered year from late March until early April, Tasmania's major cultural event takes the stage in venues around the state. Expect plenty of theatre, live music, offbeat film, dance, literature and kids' events.

May

The dry season begins in the Northern Territory, northern WA and Far North Queensland: relief from humidity. A great time to visit Uluru, before the tour buses arrive in droves.

Ord Valley Muster

(www.ordvalleymuster.com) For two weeks every May, Kununurra (WA) hits overdrive during the annual Ord Valley Muster, a collection of various sporting, charity and cultural events leading up to a large outdoor concert under the full moon on the banks of the Ord River.

Whale Watching

Along the southeastern Australian coast, migrating southern right and humpback whales come close to shore to feed, breed and calf. The whales are here between May and October; see them at Hervey Bay (New South Wales), Warrnambool (Victoria), Victor Harbor (South Australia) and Albany (WA).

June

Winter begins: snow falls across the Southern Alps ski resorts and football season fills grandstands across the country. Peak season in the tropical north: waterfalls and outback tracks are accessible (accommodation prices less so).

Laura Aboriginal Dance Festival

(www.laurafestival.tv) Sleepy Laura, 330km north of Cairns on the Cape York Peninsula in Far North Queensland, hosts the largest traditional Indigenous gathering in Australia. Communities from the region come together for dance, song and ceremony.

The Laura Races and Rodeo are held the following weekend.

Ski Season

(www.ski.com.au) When winter blows in (June to August), snow bunnies and powder hounds dust off their skis and snowboards and make for the mountains. Victoria and NSW have the key resorts, and there are a couple of small runs in Tasmania too.

July

Pubs with open fires, cosy coffee shops and empty beaches down south; packed markets, tours and accommodation up north. Pack warm clothes for anywhere south of Alice Springs. Don't miss 'MIFF'.

Melbourne International Film Festival

(MIFF; www.miff.com.au) Right up there with Toronto and Cannes, MIFF has been running since 1952 and has grown into a wildly popular event; tickets sell like piping-hot chestnuts in the inner city. Myriad short films, feature-length spectaculars and documentaries flicker across city screens every winter.

August

August is when southerners, sick of winter's grey-sky drear, head to Queensland for some sun. Last chance to head to the tropical Top End and outback before things get too hot and wet.

Cairns Festival

(www.festivalcairns.com.au) Running three weeks from late August to early September, this massive art-and-culture fest brings a stellar program of music, theatre, dance, comedy, film, Indigenous art and public exhibitions. Outdoor events held in public plazas, parks and gardens make good use of Cairns' tropical setting.

September

Spring heralds a rampant bloom of wildflowers across outback WA and SA and flower festivals happen in places like Canberra. Football finishes and the spring horse-racing carnival begins, culminating in the Melbourne Cup in November.

Brisbane Festival

(www.brisbanefestival.com.au) One of Australia's largest and most diverse arts festivals (p295) runs through 22 days in September and features an impressive line-up of concerts, plays, dance performances and fringe events around the city. It kicks off with 'Riverfire', an elaborate fireworks show over the river.

AFL Grand Final

(www.afl.com.au) The pinnacle of the annual Australian Rules football season is this show-stopping spectacle watched (on TV) by 4 million impassioned Aussies. Tickets to the game

(in Melbourne) are scarce, but at half-time everyone's neighbourhood BBQ moves to the local park for a little amateur kick-to-kick.

October

The weather avoids extremes everywhere: a good time to go camping. After the football and before the cricket, sports fans twiddle their thumbs, but the arts community enjoys international festivals in Melbourne and Brisbane.

Jazz in the Vines

(www.jazzinthevines.com.au) There are lots of food and wine festivals like this across Australia's wine regions (Barossa, McLaren Vale, Yarra Valley...). The Hunter Valley's proximity to the Sydney jazz scene ensures a top line-up at Tyrrell's Vineyard.

November

Northern beaches may be closed due to 'stinger season': jellyfish floating in the shallows of north Queensland, the Northern Territory and Western Australian waters. Outdoor events ramp up; the surf life-saving season flexes its muscles on beaches everywhere.

Melbourne Cup

(www.melbournecup.com) On the first Tuesday in November, Australia's (if not the world's) premier horse race chews up the

turf in Melbourne. Country towns schedule racing events to coincide with the day, and the nation does actually stop to watch the big race. Also see Horse Racing, p1044.

Sculpture by the Sea

(www.sculpturebythesea.com) In mid-November, the clifftop trail from Bondi Beach to Tamarama in Sydney transforms into an exquisite sculpture garden. Serious prize money is on offer for the most creative, curious or quizzical offerings from international and local sculptors. Bondi chefs cook gourmet BBQ edibles.

December

Ring the bell, school's out! Holidays begin two weeks before Christmas. Cities are packed with shoppers and the weather is desirably hot. Up north, monsoon season is underway: afternoon thunderstorms bring pelting rain.

Sydney to Hobart Yacht Race

(www.rolexsydneyhobart.com) On Boxing Day, Sydney Harbour churns with competitors and onlookers for the start of the world's most arduous open-ocean yacht race (628 nautical miles!). When the yachties hit Hobart (see the boxed text, p630) a few days later, this small city celebrates with feasting, drinking and dancing sea-legs.

Your Reef Trip

Best Wildlife Experience

Watching protected sea turtles hatch and make their first daring dash to the water on Lady Elliot Island or Heron Island, then, while snorkelling or diving, watching their older relatives glide gracefully through the ocean.

Best Snorkelling Experience

Taking a fast catamaran from Airlie Beach out to Knuckle Reef or a seaplane to Hardy Reef and immersing yourself in some of the word's best snorkelling spots.

Best View from Above

Soaring above the Great Barrier Reef on a scenic flight from Cairns and watching its huge and vivid mass carpet the sea that lies beneath you.

Most Tranquil Experience

Exploring the southern end of the Great Barrier Reef, especially Fitzroy Reef Lagoon.

Best Sailing Experience

Sailing from Airlie Beach through the Whitsunday Islands and exploring exquisite fringing reefs on the islands' perimeters.

The Great Barrier Reef is one of Australia's World Heritage areas and one of nature's richest realms. Stretching over 2000km from just south of the tropic of Capricorn (near Gladstone) to just south of Papua New Guinea, it is the most extensive reef system in the world, and made entirely by living organisms.

There are a multitude of ways to see the magnificent spectacle of the Reef. Diving and snorkelling are far and away the best methods of getting up close and personal with the menagerie of marine life and dazzling corals. Immersing yourself in the sea furnishes you with the most exhilarating appreciation of just how wonderful and rich this community is. The unremarkable surface of the water belies the colourful congestion less than a metre or so beneath.

You can also surround yourself with fabulous tropical fish without getting wet on a semisubmersible or a glass-bottomed boat, which provide windows to the underwater world below. Alternatively, you can go below the ocean's surface inside an underwater observatory, or stay up top and take a reef walk.

Another spectacular way to see the Reef while staying dry is on a scenic flight. Soaring high provides a macroperspective of the Reef's beauty and size and allows you to see the veins and networks of coral connecting and ribboning out from one another.

When to Go

High season on the Great Barrier Reef is from June to December. The best overall visibility is from August to January.

From December to March **northern Queensland** (north of Townsville) has a distinct wet season, bringing oppressive heat and abundant rainfall (from July to September it's drier and cooler). Cyclones can occur from November to March but are not common and shouldn't prevent you from going (an effective cyclone warning system is in place in the Pacific).

Anytime is generally good to visit the **Whitsundays**. Winter (June to August) can be pleasantly warm, but you will occasionally need a jumper during the day and a light jacket at night. South of the Whitsundays, summer (December to March) can be hot and humid, but the wet season doesn't extend as far south as the Whitsundays.

Southern and **central Queensland** experience mild winters (June to August) – pleasant enough for diving or snorkelling in a wetsuit.

Picking Your Spot

It's said you could dive here every day of your life and still not see all of the Great Barrier Reef. Individual chapters in this book provide in-depth information, but the following are some of the most popular and remarkable spots from which to access the Reef. Bear in mind that individual areas change over time, depending on the weather or any recent damage.

Mainland Gateways

There are several mainland gateways to the Reef, all offering slightly different experiences or activities. Deciding which to choose can be difficult – so here's a brief overview, ordered from south to north.

Agnes Water & Town of 1770 (p364) are small towns and good choices if you want to escape the crowds. From here tours head to Fitzroy Reef Lagoon, one of the most pristine sections of the Reef, where visitor numbers are still limited. The lagoon is excellent for snorkelling but also quite spectacular viewed from the boat.

Gladstone is a slightly bigger town but still a relatively small gateway. It's an excellent choice for avid divers and snorkellers, being the closest access point to the southern or Capricorn reef islands and innumerable cays, including Lady Elliot Island.

Airlie Beach (p385) is a small town with a full rack of sailing outfits. The big attraction here is spending two or more days aboard a boat and seeing some of the Whitsunday Islands' fringing coral reefs. The surrounding scenery is sublime, but you'll only see the edges of the Reef. There are, however, a number of fast-catamaran operators that zoom across 60km to reach reefs that provide outstanding snorkelling, swimming and diving.

Airlie is also friendly to all wallets, so whether you're a five- or no-star traveller, there'll be a tour to match your budget.

Townsville (p395) is a renowned gateway among divers. Whether you're learning or experienced, a four- or five-night onboard diving safari around the numerous islands and pockets of the Reef is a great choice. In particular, Kelso Reef and the wreck of the SS *Yongala* are teeming with marine life. There are also a couple of day-trip options on glass-bottomed boats, but for more choice you're better off heading to Cairns. **Reef HQ** (p395), which is basically a version of the Reef in an aquarium, is also here.

Mission Beach (p408) is closer to the Reef than any other gateway destination. This small, quiet town offers a few boat and diving tours to sections of the outer reef. Although the choice isn't huge, neither are the crowds, so you won't be sharing the experience with a fleet of other vessels.

Cairns (p414) is undeniably the main launching pad for Reef tours: there is a bewildering number of operators here. You can do anything from relatively inexpensive day trips on large boats to intimate five-day luxury charters. The variety of tours covers a wide section of the Reef, with some operators going as far north as Lizard Island. Inexpensive tours are likely to travel to inner reefs, ie those close to the mainland, which tend to be more damaged than outer reefs. Scenic flights also operate out of Cairns. Bear in mind, though, that this is the most popular destination, so unless your budget stretches to a private charter you'll be sharing the experience with many others.

Port Douglas (p440) is a swanky resort town and a gateway to the Low Isles and Agincourt Reef, an outer ribbon reef featuring crystal-clear water and particularly stunning corals. Although Port Douglas is

USEFUL WEBSITES

» **Dive Queensland** (www.dive -queensland.com.au) Queensland's dive tourism association, with info on dive locations, dive operators, live-aboards and diving schools.

» **Tourism Queensland** (www. queenslandholidays.com.au) Official state tourism portal with listings for accommodation and attractions.

» **Great Barrier Reef Marine Park Authority** (www.gbrmpa.gov.au) Reef-related info on climate change, conservation, tourism and fisheries.

» **Queensland Parks & Wildlife Services** (www.derm.qld.gov.au) Info, including permits and how to get there, for all national parks.

» **Australian Bureau of Meteorology** (www.bom.gov.au) The latest info (and annual statistics) on rainfall, temperatures and weather conditions.

smaller than Cairns, it's very popular and has a wealth of tour operators. Diving, snorkelling and cruising trips tend to be classier, pricier and less crowded than in Cairns. You can also take a scenic flight from here.

Cooktown (p454) is another one for divers. The town's lure is its close proximity to Lizard Island (see p457). Although you can access the island from Cairns, you'll spend far less time travelling by boat if you go from here. Cooktown's relatively remote location means there are only a handful of tour operators and small numbers of tourists, so your experience is not likely to be rushed or brief. The only drawback is that the town and its tour operators shut down between November and May for the wet season.

Islands

Speckled throughout the Reef is a profusion of islands and cays that offer some of the most stunning access to the Reef. Here is a list of some of the best islands, travelling from south to north.

For more information on individual islands, see the Whitsunday Coast (p381), Capricorn Coast (p361), Townsville to Mission Beach (p395), Cairns & Around (p414) and Port Douglas to Cooktown (p440)

sections of the Queensland & the Great Barrier Reef chapter.

The coral cay of **Lady Elliot Island** (p362) is the most southerly of the Reef islands. It's awe-inspiring for birdwatchers, with some 57 species living on the island. Sea turtles also nest here and it's possibly the best location on the Reef to see manta rays. It's also a famed diving spot. There's a simple, pricey camping resort here, but you can also visit Lady Elliot on a day trip from Bundaberg.

Heron Island (p363) is a tiny coral cay sitting amid a huge spread of reef. It's a diving mecca, but the snorkelling is also good and it's possible to do a reef walk from here. Heron is a nesting ground for green and loggerhead turtles and home to some 30 species of birds. It's an exclusive, utterly tranquil place, and the sole resort on the island charges accordingly.

Hamilton Island (p394), the daddy of the Whitsundays, is a sprawling resort laden with infrastructure. While this doesn't create the most intimate atmosphere, there is a wealth of tours going to the outer reef. It's also a good place to see patches of the Reef that can't be explored from the mainland. Families are extremely well catered for.

Hook Island (p393) is an outer Whitsunday Island surrounded by fringing reefs. There is excellent swimming and snorkelling here, and the island's sizeable bulk provides plenty of good bushwalking. There's affordable accommodation on Hook and it's easily accessed from Airlie Beach, making it a top choice for those on a modest budget.

Orpheus Island is a national park and one of the Reef's most exclusive, tranquil and romantic hideaways. This island is particularly good for snorkelling – you can step right off the beach and be surrounded by the Reef's colourful marine life. Clusters of fringing reefs also provide plenty of diving opportunities.

Green Island (p428) is another of the Reef's true coral cays. The fringing reefs here are considered to be among the most beautiful surrounding any island, and the diving and snorkelling are quite spectacular. Covered in dense rainforest, the entire island is national park. Bird life is abundant, with around 60 species to be found. The resort on Green Island is well set up for reef activities; several tour operators offer diving and snorkelling cruises and there's also an underwater observatory. The island is accessible as a day trip from Cairns.

Lizard Island (p457) is remote, rugged and the perfect place to escape civilisation. It has a ring of talcum-white beaches, remarkably blue water and few visitors. It's also world-renowned as a superb scuba-diving location, with what is arguably Australia's best-known dive site at Cod Hole, where you can swim with docile potato cod weighing as much as 60kg. Pixie Bommie is another highly regarded dive site on the island.

Snorkellers will also get an eyeful of marine life here all around the island, with giant clams, manta rays, barracudas and dense schools of fish abundant in the waters just offshore.

If you're staying overnight you need to have deep pockets or no requirements whatsoever – it's either five-star or luxury bush camping.

Diving & Snorkelling the Reef

Much of the diving and snorkelling on the Reef is boat-based, although there are some excellent reefs accessible by walking straight off the beach of some islands scattered along the Great Barrier. Free use of snorkelling gear is usually part of any cruise to the Reef and you can typically fit in around three hours of underwater wandering. Overnight or 'live-aboard' trips obviously provide a more in-depth experience and greater coverage of the reefs. If you want to do more than snorkel but don't have a diving certificate, many operators offer the option of an introductory dive, which is a guided dive where an experienced diver conducts an underwater tour. A solid lesson in safety and procedure is given beforehand and you don't require a five-day Professional Association of Diving Instructors (PADI) course or a 'buddy'.

Boat Excursions

Unless you're staying on a coral-fringed island in the middle of the Great Barrier Reef, you'll need to join a boat excursion – either on a day trip or on a multiday live-aboard – to experience the Reef's real beauty. Daytrips leave from many places along the coast, as well as from island resorts (see p28 for prime gateways) and typically include the use of snorkelling gear, snacks and a buffet lunch, with scuba diving an optional extra. Many boats also offer an introductory scuba dive on the Reef, escorted by a divemaster, which can be a great way to get a taste of diving. On some boats a naturalist or marine biologist presents a talk on the Reef's ecology.

Boat trips vary dramatically in passenger numbers, type of vessel and quality – which is reflected in the price – so it's worth getting all the details before committing to a particular trip. When selecting a tour, consider the vessel (motorised catamaran or sailing ship), the number of passengers (from six to 400), what extras are offered and the destination. The outer reefs are usually more pristine. Inner reefs often show signs of damage from humans, coral bleaching and coral-eating crown-of-thorns starfish. Some

TOP SNORKELLING SITES

Some nondivers may wonder if it's really worth going to the Great Barrier Reef 'just to snorkel'. The answer is a resounding yes. There are some fantastic sites for snorkellers – in fact, much of the rich, colourful coral lies just underneath the surface (as coral needs bright sunlight to flourish) and is easily accessible. Here's a round-up of the top snorkelling sites:

» Fitzroy Reef Lagoon
» Heron Island
» Keppel Island
» Lady Elliot Island
» Lady Musgrave Island
» Hook Island
» Hayman Island
» Lizard Island
» Border Island (Whitsundays)
» Hardy Reef (Whitsundays)
» Knuckle Reef (Whitsundays)
» Michaelmans Reef (Cairns)
» Hastings Reef (Cairns)
» Norman Reef (Cairns)
» Saxon Reef (Cairns)
» Opal Reef (Port Douglas)
» Agincourt Reef (Port Douglas)
» Mackay Reef (Port Douglas)

MOTION SICKNESS

If you're prone to motion sickness, be sure to bring medication or acupressure wristbands with you, as boat rides out to the Reef can be a little rough. Some swear by herbal ginger remedies, while others say they don't work. Take your tablets 30 minutes before boarding – once you're on the water, it's generally too late.

companies that are only licensed to visit the inner reef have cheaper tours; in most cases you get what you pay for. Some operators offer the option of a trip in a glass-bottomed boat or semisubmersible.

Many boats have underwater cameras for hire – although you'll save money by hiring these on land (better yet, purchase an underwater housing case for your digital camera if you plan to take a lot of pictures). Some boats also have professional photographers on board who will dive with you and take high-quality shots of you in action.

Live-Aboards

If you're eager to do as much diving as possible, a live-aboard is an excellent option. This allows reef-goers the chance to dive around three dives per day, plus the ocassional night dive, and visit more remote parts of the Great Barrier Reef. Trip lengths vary from one to 12 nights. The three-day/three-night voyages, which allow up to 11 dives (nine day and two night dives), are among the most common. Some go on exploratory trips, others run a set route and may use fixed moorings or pontoons, while others are more impromptu.

It is worth checking the various options as some boats offer specialist itineraries following marine life and events such as minke whales or coral spawning, or offer trips to more remote spots like the far northern reefs, Pompey Complex, Coral Sea Reefs or Swain Reefs.

It's recommended to go with operators who are Dive Queensland members: this ensures they follow a minimum set of guidelines. See www.dive-queensland.com.au for the latest membership list. Ideally, they are also accredited by the Ecotoursim Association of Australia (www.ecotourism.org.au).

Popular departure points for live-aboard dive vessels, along with the locales they visit:

» **Bundaberg** – the Bunker Island group, including Lady Musgrave and Lady Elliot Islands, possibly Fitzroy, Llewellyn and rarely visited Boult Reefs or Hoskyn and Fairfax Islands.

» **1770** – Bunker Island group.

» **Gladstone** – Swains and Bunker Island group.

» **Mackay** – Lihou Reef and the Coral Sea.

» **Airlie Beach** – the Whitsundays, Knuckle Reef and Hardy Reef.

» **Townsville** – *Yongala* wreck, plus canyons of Wheeler Reef and Keeper Reef.

» **Cairns** – Cod Hole, Ribbon Reefs, the Coral Sea and possibly the far northern reefs.

» **Port Douglas** – Osprey Reef, Cod Hole, Ribbon Reefs, Coral Sea and possibly the far northern reefs.

Dive Courses

In Queensland there are numerous places where you can learn to dive, take a refresher course or improve your skills. Dive courses in Queensland are generally of a high standard, and all schools teach either PADI or Scuba Schools International (SSI) qualifications. Which certification you choose isn't as important as choosing a good instructor, so be sure to seek local recommendations and meet with the instructor before committing to a program.

One of the most popular places to learn is Cairns, where you can choose between courses for the budget-minded (four-day courses from around $450) that combine pool training and reef dives, to longer, more intensive courses that include reef diving on a live-aboard (five-day courses including three-day/two-night live-aboard are around $825).

Other places where you can learn to dive, and then head out on the Reef include the following:

» Bundaberg

» Mission Beach

» Townsville

» Airlie Beach

» Hamilton Island

» Magnetic Island

» Port Douglas

For more details on Dive Courses, see p420.

KEY DIVING DETAILS

Diving & Flying

Remember that your last dive should be completed 24 hours before your flight – even in a balloon or for a parachute jump – in order to minimise the risk of residual nitrogen in the blood that can cause decompression injury. On the other hand, it's fine to dive soon after arriving by air.

Insurance

Find out whether or not your insurance policy classifies diving as a dangerous sport and excludes it. For a nominal annual fee, the **Divers Alert Network** (DAN; www.diversalertnetwork.org) provides insurance for medical or evacuation services required in the event of a diving accident. DAN's hotline for diving emergencies is ☑800 088 200.

Visibility

Coastal areas: 1m to 3m
Several kilometres offshore: 8m to 15m
Outer edge of the Reef: 20m to 35m
Coral Sea: 50m and beyond

Water Temperature

In the north, the water temperature is warm all year round, from around 24°C to 30°C. Going south it gradually gets cooler, dropping to 20°C to 28°C in winter.

Safety Guidelines for Diving

Before embarking on a scuba-diving, skin-diving or snorkelling trip, carefully consider the following points to ensure a safe and enjoyable experience:

» If scuba diving, make sure you have a current diving certification card from a recognised scuba-diving instructional agency.

» Ensure you're healthy and feel comfortable diving.

» Obtain reliable information from a reputable local dive operation about the physical and environmental conditions at the dive site, such as water temperature, visibility and tidal movements, and find out how local divers deal with these considerations.

» Be aware that underwater conditions vary significantly from one region, or even site, to another. Seasonal changes can significantly alter any site and dive conditions. These differences influence the way divers dress for a dive and what diving techniques they use.

» Be aware of local laws, regulations and etiquette with regard to marine life and the environment.

» Dive only at sites within your realm of experience. If available, engage the services of a competent, professionally trained dive instructor or divemaster.

Diving for Nondivers

Several operators from Cairns use systems that allow nondivers to 'dive' using surface-supplied air systems. With helmet diving, hoses provide fresh surface air to divers via astronaut-like helmets so you can breathe normally and your face and hair stay dry (you can even wear glasses). There's also no need to know how to swim as you'll be walking on a submerged platform, 4m to 5m below the surface. Walks typically last 15 to 20 minutes, and are conducted under the guidance of a qualified dive instructor. Prices start at around $140. Anyone older than 12 and over 140cm tall can participate, although as with scuba diving, certain medical conditions will prohibit participation (asthma, heart disease, pregnancy, epilepsy). For operators, see p417.

Picking the Right Resort

The Great Barrier Reef is home to over a dozen island resorts, offering varying levels of comfort and style. Although most options sit squarely in the luxury category, there are some affordable stays for those who are seeking a beautiful setting, but don't mind middle-of-the-road accommodation, like that offered on Lady Elliot Island.

Where to stay depends not only on your budget, but also what sort of activities you have in mind. Some resorts are small and secluded (and don't allow children), which can be ideal for a tropical getaway doing little more than swinging in a hammock, basking on powdery sand beaches and sipping tropical cocktails. If this sounds ideal, try Orpheus or Hayman Islands. Other resorts have a busier vibe and offer a wide range of activities, from sailing and kayaking to helicopter joy rides, plus restaurants and even some nightlife. If this is more to your liking, try Hamilton Island.

You'll find the widest selection of resorts in the Whitsundays (p391).

Camping on the Great Barrier Reef

Pitching a tent on an island is a unique and affordable way to experience the Great Barrier Reef. If you don't mind roughing it a bit, you can enjoy an idyllic tropical setting at a fraction of the price of the five-star island resort that may be located down the road from the campground. Camp-site facilities range from virtually nothing to showers, flush toilets, interpretive signage and picnic tables. Most islands are remote, so ensure you are adequately prepared for medical and general emergencies.

Wherever you stay, you'll need to be self-sufficient, bringing your own food and drinking water (5L per day per person is recommended). Weather can often prevent planned pickups, so have enough supplies to last an extra three or four days in case you get stranded.

As a general reminder, all the islands have fragile ecosystems, so camp only in designated areas, keep to marked trails and take out all that you brought in. Fires are banned so you'll need a gas stove or similar.

You'll need to reserve camp sites well in advance. National park camping permits can be reserved online through **QPWS** (⌂13 74 68; www.derm.qld.gov.au). Here are our top camping picks.

Whitsunday Islands (p391) Nearly a dozen beautifully sited camping areas, scattered on the islands of Hook, Whitsunday and Henning.

MAKING A POSITIVE CONTRIBUTION TO THE REEF

The Great Barrier Reef is incredibly fragile and it's worth taking some time to educate yourself on responsible practices while you're there. Here are a few of the more important sustainable practices, but this is by no means an exhaustive list.

» Whether on an island or in a boat, take all litter with you – even biodegradable material like apple cores – and dispose of it back on the mainland.

» Remember that it is an offence to damage or remove coral in the marine park.

» Don't touch or harass marine animals and be aware that if you touch or walk on coral you'll damage it. It can also create some nasty cuts. Never rest or stand on coral.

» If you have a boat, be aware of the rules in relation to anchoring around the reef, including 'no anchoring areas'. Be very careful not to damage coral when you let down the anchor.

» If you're diving, check that you are weighted correctly before entering the water and keep your buoyancy control well away from the reef. Ensure that equipment such as secondary regulators and gauges aren't dragging over the reef.

» If you're snorkelling (and especially if you are a beginner) practice your technique away from coral until you've mastered control in the water.

» Hire a wetsuit rather than slathering on sunscreen, which can damage the reef.

» Watch where your fins are – try not to stir up sediment or disturb coral.

» Do not enter the water near a dugong, including when swimming or diving.

» Note that there are limits on the amount and types of shells that you can collect.

TOP REEF DIVE SPOTS

The Great Barrier Reef is home to some of the world's best diving sites. Here are a few of our favourite spots to get you started:

» **SS Yongala** – a sunken shipwreck that has been home to a vivid marine community for more than 90 years.

» **Cod Hole** – go nose-to-nose with a potato cod.

» **Heron Island** – join a crowd of colourful fish straight off the beach.

» **Lady Elliot Island** – with 19 highly regarded dive sites.

» **Pixie Bommie** – delve into the after-five world of the Reef by taking a night dive.

Capricornia Cays Camping available on three separate coral cays including Masthead Island, North West Island and Lady Musgrave Island (p363) – a fantastic, uninhabited island that's limited to a maximum 40 campers.

Dunk Island (p412) Equal parts resort and national park with good swimming, kayaking and hiking.

Fitzroy Island (p428) Resort and national park with short walking trails through bush and coral just off the beaches.

Frankland Islands (p428) Coral-fringed island with white-sand beaches off Cairns.

Lizard Island (p457) Stunning beaches, magnificent coral and abundant wildlife, but generally you must arrive by plane.

Orpheus Island Secluded island (accessible by air) with pretty tropical forest and superb fringing reef.

Your Outback Trip

Best Season
Winter (June to August) Mild days, cool nights and low humidity. Summer (December to February) in the outback can be hellish, with 45°C temperatures, clouds of dust and masses of flies.

Best Things to Pack
Sunscreen, a hat, insect repellent, plenty of water and some good tunes for the car stereo.

Best Outback Road Trip
Stuart Hwy, Darwin to Uluru Epic journey from the tropical north to the parched central deserts.

Best Outback Track
Oodnadatta Track 620km of red dust, emus, lizards, salt lakes and historic railroad remnants.

Best for Indigenous Culture
Kakadu National Park Head into the tropical Top End wilderness for ancient rock art and cultural tours run by Indigenous guides.

Best Outback National Park
Uluru-Kata Tjuta National Park Uluru is simply unmissable: one of the biggest boulders you're ever likely to lay eyes on.

In 'Power & the Passion', Midnight Oil's damning ode to the Australian suburban condition, Peter Garrett sings, *'And no-one goes outback that's that.'* It really is amazing how few Australians have explored the outback. To many, it's either a mythical place inhabited by tourists and Indigenous Australians, or something for the too-hard basket – too hot, too far to drive, too expensive to fly, too many sand dunes and flies... But for those that make the effort, a strange awakening occurs – a quiet comprehension of the primal terrain and profound size of Australia that you simply can't fathom while sitting on Bondi Beach.

About the Outback

The Australian outback is vast, blanketing the centre of the continent. While most Australians live on the coast, that thin green fringe of the continent is hardly typical of this enormous land mass. Inland is the desert soul of Australia.

Weather patterns vary from region to region – from sandy arid deserts to semiarid scrublands to tropical savannah – but you can generally rely on hot sunny days, starry night skies and mile after mile of unbroken horizon.

When to Go
Best Times

» **June–August** When southeastern Australia (where most of the population lives) is sniffling through rainy, cloudy winter days, the outback comes into its own. Rain isn't unheard of in central Australia – in fact there's been a hell of a lot of it in recent years – but clear skies, moderate temperatures and good driving conditions are the norm.

» September–October Spring is also a prime time to head into the outback, especially if you're into wildflowers. Southwestern Western Australia (WA) and the Flinders Ranges in northern South Australia (SA) explode with colourful blooms, all the more dazzling in contrast with red-orange desert sands.

Avoid

» December–February Central Australia heats up over summer – temperatures approaching 50°C have been recorded in some desert towns – but that's just part of the picture. With the heat comes dusty roads, overheating cars, driver fatigue, irritating flies and the need to carry extra water everywhere you go.

Planes, Trains or Automobiles?

» Air If you want to access the outback without a long drive, the major airlines fly into Alice Springs (for the central deserts) and Darwin (for the tropical Top End) from Perth, Adelaide and the major east-coast cities. From Darwin or Alice you can join a guided tour or hire a 4WD and off you go.

» Train Unlike much of the world, train travel in Australia is neither affordable nor expedient. It's something you do for a special occasion or for the sheer romance of trains, not if you want to get anywhere in a hurry. That said, travelling on the *Indian Pacific* between Perth and Sydney or the legendary *Ghan* between Adelaide and Darwin takes you through parts of the country you wouldn't see otherwise, and it certainly makes for a leisurely holiday. Train travel is also a good way to beat the heat if you're travelling in summer.

So if you have time on your side, and you can afford it, give it a try because it could be perfect for you.

» Car You can drive all the way around Australia on Hwy 1 and through the centre from Adelaide to Darwin without leaving sealed roads. However, if you really want to see outback Australia, there are plenty of routes that breathe new life into the phrase 'off the beaten track'. Driving in the outback has its challenges – huge distances, difficult terrain and searing temperatures – but it's ultimately the most rewarding and intimate way to experience Australia's 'dead heart' (rest assured, it's alive and kicking!).

Essential Outback
The Red Centre: Alice Springs, Uluru & Kings Canyon

From Alice Springs (p853) it's a six-hour drive to Uluru-Kata Tjuta National Park (p875). The Alice is a surprising oasis: big enough to have some great places to eat and stay, as well as some social problems. Uluru is to tourists what half a watermelon is to ants at a picnic: people from all over the globe swarm to and from this monolith at all times of the day. But it's still a remarkable find. The local Anangu people would prefer that you didn't climb it. Kings Canyon (p873), north of Uluru, is a spectacular chasm sinking into the red desert landscape.

The Stuart Highway: Adelaide to Darwin

In either direction, from the north or south, this is one of Australia's greatest road trips: 3020km of red desert sands, flat scrublands and galloping roadside emus. Make sure you stop at spookily pock-marked Coober Pedy (p791) – the opal-mining capital of the world – and detour to Uluru on your way to the Al-

---

OUTBACK CYCLING

Pedalling your way through the outback is certainly not something to tackle lightly, and certainly not something you'd even consider in summer. But you do see the odd wiry, suntanned soul pushing their panniers along the Stuart Hwy between Adelaide and Darwin. Availability of drinking water is the main concern: isolated water sources (bores, tanks, creeks etc) shown on maps may be dry or undrinkable. Make sure you've got the necessary spare parts and bike-repair knowledge. Check with locals if you're heading into remote areas, and always tell someone where you're headed. And if you make it through, try for a book deal – this is intrepid travel defined.

On many outback highways you'll see thundering road trains: huge trucks (a prime mover plus two or three trailers) up to 50m long. These things don't move over for anyone, and it's like a scene out of *Mad Max* having one bear down on you at 120km/h. When you see a road train approaching on a narrow bitumen road, slow down and pull over – if the truck has to put its wheels off the road to pass you, the resulting barrage of stones will almost certainly smash your windscreen. When trying to overtake one, allow plenty of room (about a kilometre) to complete the manoeuvre. Road trains throw up a lot of dust on dirt roads, so if you see one coming it's best to just pull over and stop until it's gone past.

And while you're on outback roads, don't forget to give the standard bush wave to oncoming drivers – it's simply a matter of lifting the index finger off the steering wheel to acknowledge your fellow motorist.

ice. Nitmiluk (Katherine Gorge) National Park (p844) is also en route, a photogenic series of sheer rocky gorges and waterholes. Kakadu National Park (p831) is next, with World Heritage–listed tropical wetlands. When you get to Darwin, reward yourself with a cold beer and some nocturnal high jinks on Mitchell St.

The Northwest: Gibb River Road & the Kimberley

The rough-and-ready Gibb River Rd (aka the Gibb; p1006) is a northern classic. Wiggling through the exotic Kimberley region (captured in glorious CGI in Baz Luhrman's 2008 film *Australia*), it delivers swimming holes, hiking opportunities, outback campsites and regular flat tyres. The Kimberley is more famous for its extraordinary rock art and the bizarre landscape of Purnululu (Bungle Bungle) National Park (p1010). The pearling town of Broome (p996) lies to the west, with Cable Beach stretching toward the sunset.

The Tropics: Darwin, Kakadu & Katherine

The outback in the tropical Top End is a different experience to the deserts further south. Here, the wet and dry seasons determine how easy it is to get from A to B. In the Wet, roads become impassable and crocodiles move freely through the wetlands. But before you cancel your plans, this is also a time of abundance and great natural beauty in the national parks – plus Kakadu resorts approach half-price! Darwin (p804) isn't really an outback town these days, especially in the Dry when backpackers from around the world fill the bars and Mindil Beach market. Katherine

(p840), three hours to the south, is much more 'country', and the jumping-off point for the astonishing Nitmiluk (Katherine Gorge) National Park.

Cape York

Cape York (p461) is as far north as you can go without bumping into the Torres Strait Islands (that lie between Australia and Papua New Guinea). The landscape is tropical savannah: vast grasslands threaded with river systems, flowing into the Gulf of Carpentaria. Like in the Top End, the Wet and the Dry transform the scenery here. Most travellers find their way to Cairns and Port Douglas further south, but venture north along the Mulligan Hwy to explore remote national parks, Indigenous communities and mining towns.

Facilities

Outback roadhouses emerge from the desert heat haze with surprising regularity. It always pays to calculate the distance to the next fuel stop, but even on the remote Oodnadatta Track you'll find petrol and cold beer every few hundred kilometres. Most roadhouses (many of them open 24-hours) sell fuel and have attached restaurants where you can get a fry-up feed for very little cash. There's often accommodation for road-weary drivers – usually air-conditioned motel-style rooms or cabins out the back, going for around $120 a night.

Resources

» **Tourism NT** (www.travelnt.com) Bountiful info on the Northern Territory (NT) outback. Also produces *The Essential NT Drive Guide*, a great booklet with driving distances, national parks, and outback info and advice for 2WD and 4WD travellers.

» **Parks & Wildlife NT** (www.nreta.nt.gov.au) General advice on the NT's fabulous national parks.

» **South Australian Tourism Commission** (www.southaustralia.com) The lowdown on the South Australian (SA) outback, from Port Augusta to Oodnadatta.

» **Department for Environment & Natural Resources** (www.environment.sa.gov.au) Advice, maps and camping permits for SA's desert parks.

Organised Tours

If you don't feel like doing all the planning and driving, a guided tour is a great way to experience the outback. These range from beery backpacker jaunts between outback pubs, to Indigenous cultural tours and multiday bushwalking treks into remote wilderness. See destination chapters for listings of reliable operators.

Outback Tracks

The Australian outback is criss-crossed by sealed highways, but one of the more interesting ways to get from A to B is by following historic cattle and rail routes. While you may not necessarily need a 4WD or fancy equipment to tackle some of these roads, you do need to be carefully prepared for the isolation and lack of facilities.

Don't attempt the tougher routes during the hottest part of the year (December to February, inclusive); apart from the risk of heat exhaustion, simple mishaps can lead to tragedy in these conditions. There's also no point going anywhere on outback dirt roads if there's been recent flooding.

Oodnadatta Track

Mostly running parallel to the old *Ghan* railway line through outback SA, this iconic track (p795) is fully bypassed by the sealed Stuart Hwy to the west. Using this track, it's 429km from Marree to Oodnadatta, then another 216km to the Stuart Hwy at Marla. As long as there is no rain, any well-prepared conventional vehicle should be able to manage this fascinating route, but a 4WD will do it in comfort.

Birdsville Track

Spanning 517km from Marree in SA to Birdsville just across the border of Queensland, this old droving trail (p380) is one of Australia's best-known outback routes. It's generally feasible to travel it in any well-prepared, conventional vehicle. Don't miss a beer at the Birdsville Hotel!

Strzelecki Track

This track (p796) covers much the same territory through SA as the Birdsville Track. Starting south of Marree at Lyndhurst, it reaches Innamincka 460km northeast and close to the Queensland border. It was at Innamincka that the hapless explorers Burke and Wills died. A 4WD is a safe bet, even though this route has been much improved due to work on the Moomba gas fields.

Tanami Track

Turning off the Stuart Hwy just north of Alice Springs, this 1000km route (p853) runs northwest across the Tanami Desert to Halls Creek in WA. The road has received extensive work so conventional vehicles are normally OK, although there are sandy stretches on the WA side and it can be very corrugated if it hasn't been graded recently. Get advice on road conditions in Alice Springs.

Gibb River Road

This 'short cut' (p1006) between Derby and Kununurra runs through the heart of the spectacular Kimberley in northern WA – it's approximately 660km, compared with about 920km via Hwy 1. The going is much slower, but the surroundings are so beautiful you'll probably find yourself lingering anyway. Although badly corrugated in places, it can usually be negotiated by conventional vehicles in the Dry (May to October) without too much difficulty; it's impassable in the Wet.

Outback Way (Great Central Road)

This route (p959) runs west from Uluru to Laverton in WA, from where you can drive down to Kalgoorlie and on to Perth. The road is well maintained and is normally OK for conventional vehicles, but it's pretty remote. It passes through Aboriginal land, for which travel permits must be obtained in advance; contact the Department of Indigenous Affairs (p972) for details. It's almost 1500km from Yulara (the town nearest Uluru) to Kalgoorlie. For 300km, from near the Giles Meteorological Station, this road and the Gunbarrel Hwy run on the same route. Taking the old Gunbarrel (to the north of

You need to be particularly organised and vigilant when travelling in the outback, especially on remote sandy tracks, due to the scorching temperatures, long distances between fuel stops and isolation. Here are a few tips:

Communication

☐ Report your route and schedule to the police, a friend or relative.

☐ Mobile phones are practically useless in the outback. A safety net is to hire a satellite phone, high-frequency (HF) radio transceiver equipped to pick up the Royal Flying Doctor Service bases, or emergency position-indicating radio beacon (EPIRB).

☐ In an emergency, stay with your vehicle; it's easier to spot than you are, and you won't be able to carry a heavy load of water very far. Don't sit inside your vehicle as it will become an oven in hot weather.

☐ If you do become stranded, set fire to a spare tyre (let the air out first). The pall of smoke will be visible for miles.

Your Vehicle

☐ Have your vehicle serviced and checked before you leave.

☐ Load your vehicle evenly, with heavy items inside and light items on the roof rack.

☐ Check locations and opening times of service stations, and carry spare fuel and provisions; opportunities for fill-ups can be infrequent.

☐ Carry essential tools: a spare tyre (two if possible), a fan belt and a radiator hose, as well as a tyre-pressure gauge and an air pump.

☐ An off-road jack might come in handy, as will a snatchem strap or tow rope for quick extraction when you're stuck (useful if there's another vehicle to pull you out).

☐ A set of cheap, high-profile tyres (around $80 each) will give your car a little more ground clearance.

Supplies & Equipment

☐ Always carry plenty of water: in warm weather allow 5L per person per day and an extra amount for the radiator, carried in several containers.

☐ Bring plenty of food in case of a breakdown.

☐ Carry a first-aid kit, a good set of maps, a torch and spare batteries, a compass, and a shovel for digging if you get bogged.

Weather & Road Conditions

☐ Check road conditions before travelling: roads that are passable in the Dry (March to October) can disappear beneath water during the Wet.

☐ Check weather forecasts daily.

☐ Keep an eye out for potholes, rough sections, roads changing surfaces without notice, soft and broken verges, and single-lane bridges.

☐ Take note of the water-level markers at creek crossings to gauge the water's depth before you proceed.

☐ Don't attempt to cross flooded bridges or causeways unless you're sure of the depth, and of any road damage hidden underwater.

Dirt-Road Driving

☐ Inflate your tyres to the recommended levels for the terrain you're travelling on; on desert dirt, deflate your tyres to 25psi to avoid punctures.

☐ Reduce speed on unsealed roads, as traction is decreased and braking distances increase.

☐ Dirt roads are often corrugated: keeping an even speed is the best approach.

☐ Dust on outback roads can obscure your vision, so always stop and wait for it to settle.

☐ If your vehicle is struggling through deep sand, deflating your tyres a bit will help. If you do get stuck, don't attempt to get out by revving the engine; this just causes wheels to dig in deeper.

Road Hazards

☐ Outback highways are usually long, flat ribbons of tarmac stretching across the red desert flats. The temptation is to get it over with quickly, but try to keep a lid on your speed.

☐ Take a rest every few hours: driver fatigue is a real problem.

☐ Wandering cattle, sheep, emus, kangaroos, camels, etc make driving fast a dangerous prospect. Take care and avoid nocturnal driving, as this is often when native animals come out . Many car-hire companies prohibit night-time driving.

☐ Road trains are an ever-present menace on the main highways. Give them a wide berth, they're much bigger than you!

PERMITS FOR ABORIGINAL LAND

In the outback, if you plan on driving through pastoral stations and Aboriginal communities you must get permission first. This is for your safety; many travellers have tackled this rugged landscape on their own and required complicated rescues after getting lost or breaking down.

Permits are issued by various Aboriginal land-management authorities in each state and territory; see destination chapters for details. Processing applications can take anywhere from a few minutes to a few days.

Warburton) to Wiluna in WA is a much rougher trip, requiring a 4WD.

Canning Stock Route & Gunbarrel Highway

This old 2006km cattle-droving trail (see p959) runs southwest from Halls Creek to Wiluna in WA. The route crosses the Great Sandy Desert and Gibson Desert and, since the track is entirely unmaintained, it's a route to be taken very seriously. You should travel only in a well-equipped 4WD party of at least three vehicles, equipped with high-frequency (HF) radio or emergency position-indicating radio beacon (EPIRB). Nobody does this trip in summer.

From Wiluna, the 1000km Gunbarrel Hwy runs to Warakurna near the NT border (where it joins the Outback Way). Again, 4WDs only, with water and fuel for the entire journey.

Mulligan Highway

This road (p458) goes all the way up to the tip of Cape York and has a number of river crossings, such as the Jardine, that can only be made in the dry season. Only those in 4WD vehicles should consider the journey to Cape York, via any route. The shortest route from Cairns is 1000km, but a worthwhile alternative is Cooktown to Musgrave via Lakefield National Park, which then meets up with the main route.

Plenty & Sandover Highways

These remote routes run east from the Stuart Hwy, north of Alice Springs, to Boulia or Mt Isa in Queensland. They're normally suitable for conventional vehicles, but are often rough going.

Simpson Desert

The route crossing the Simpson Desert (p380) from the Stuart Hwy to Birdsville is a real test of both driver and vehicle. A 4WD is definitely required and you should be in a party of at least three vehicles equipped with HF radio or EPIRB.

Australia Outdoors

Best Bushwalks

Thorsborne Trail, Queensland
Great South West Walk, Victoria
Overland Track, Tasmania
Deep Creek Conservation Park, South Australia
Larapinta Trail, Northern Territory

Top Five for Daredevils

Rock climbing, Blue Mountains, New South Wales
Bungee jumping, Cairns, Queensland
Mountain biking, Mt Wellington, Tasmania
Diving, HMAS Hobart, SA
Speed-boating, Horizontal Waterfalls, Western Australia

Top Five Wildlife Encounters

Whales, Hervey Bay, Queensland
Grey kangaroos, Namadgi National Park, Australian Capital Territory
Penguins, Phillip Island, Victoria
Tasmanian Devils, Tasmania
Dolphins, Monkey Mia, WA

Hot Surf Spots

Avalon, NSW
Superbank, Queensland
Bells Beach, Victoria
Eaglehawk Neck, Tasmania
Margaret River, WA

Although Australia provides plenty of excuses to sit back and do little more than roll your eyes across some fine landscape, that same landscape lends itself very well to any number of outdoor pursuits – whether it's getting active on the rocks, wilderness trails and mountains on dry land, or on the swells and reefs offshore.

Following are some outdoor highlights; for more detail read the individual Activities sections at the start of state and territory destination chapters. See also Deadly & Dangerous (p1046) for info on environmental hazards while you're out and about.

Planning Your Outdoor Trip

When to Go

» **September–October** Spring brings the end of football season, which means a lot of yelling at the umpire/wayward full-forward from the grandstands. The more actively inclined rejoice in sunnier weather and warmer days, perfect for bushwalking, wildlife watching and rock climbing.

» **December–February** Australians hit the beach in summer. This isn't to say they're necessarily energetic once they get there, but at least they're not inside watching TV. Now is the time for surfing, sailing, swimming, fishing, snorkelling, skydiving, paragliding...

» **March–May** Autumn is a nostalgic time in Australia, with cool nights and wood smoke. Perfect weather for a bushwalk or perhaps a cycling trip – not too hot, not too cold.

SAFETY GUIDELINES FOR BUSHWALKING

Before embarking on a walking trip, consider the following points to ensure a safe and enjoyable experience:

» Pay any fees and possess any permits required by local authorities.

» Be sure you are healthy and feel comfortable walking for a sustained period.

» Obtain reliable information about physical and environmental conditions along your intended route (eg from park authorities).

» Be aware of local laws, regulations and etiquette about wildlife and the environment.

» Walk only in regions, and on tracks, within your realm of experience.

» Be aware that weather conditions and terrain vary significantly from one region, or even from one track, to another. Seasonal changes can significantly alter any track. These differences influence the way walkers dress and the equipment they carry.

» Ask before you set out about the environmental characteristics that can affect your walk and how local, experienced walkers deal with these considerations.

» **June–August** When winter hits, there are only two places you need to go: the outback and the snow. Pack up your 4WD and head into the desert for a hike or scenic flight, or grab your snowboard and head into the mountains for some powdery fun.

Organisations & Resources

» **Lonely Planet** (www.lonelyplanet.com) The *Walking in Australia* guide has detailed information about bushwalking around the country.

» **Bushwalking Australia** (www. bushwalkingaustralia.org) Website for the national body, with links to state/territory bushwalking clubs and federations.

» **Bicycles Network Australia** (www. bicycles.net.au) Information and news.

» **Ski.com.au** (www.ski.com.au) Links to major resorts and snow reports.

» **Dive-Oz** (www.diveoz.com.au) Online scuba-diving resource.

» **Fishnet** (www.fishnet.com.au) Devoted to all aspects of Australian fishing.

» **Surfer's Travel Guide** (www.thesurfers travelguide.com.au) Detailed description of just about every break along the Australian coast.

On The Land

The Australian landscape is ripe with outdoor opportunities: bushwalking is a prime pastime. Cycling is a great way to get around Australia, despite the mammoth distances sometimes involved. There's also skiing in the mountains and wildlife-watching.

Bushwalking

Bushwalking is supremely popular in Australia and vast tracts of untouched scrub and forest provide ample opportunity. The best time to go varies from state to state, but a general rule is that the further north you go the more tropical and humid the climate gets: June to August are the best walking months up north; in the south, summer and early Autumn (December to March) is better.

You can follow trails through many national parks. Notable walks include the Overland Track and the South Coast Track in Tasmania, and the Australian Alps Walking Track, Great Ocean Walk and Great South West Walk in Victoria. The Bibbulmun Track in Western Australia (WA) is great, as are the Thorsborne Trail across Hinchinbrook Island and the Gold Coast Hinterland's Great Walk in Queensland.

In New South Wales (NSW) you can trek between Sydney and Newcastle on the Great North Walk, tackle the Royal National Park's coastal walking trail, the 42km Six Foot Track or Mt Kosciuszko. In South Australia (SA) there's the epic 1200km Heysen Trail and in the Northern Territory (NT) the majestic, 233.5km Larapinta Trail and remote tracks in Nitmiluk (Katherine Gorge) National Park.

Cycling

Cyclists have access to lots of cycling routes and can tour the country for days, weekends or even multiweek trips. Or you can just rent a bike for a few hours and explore a city.

Standout routes for longer rides include the Murray to the Mountains Rail Trail and the East Gippsland Rail Trail in Victoria.

In WA, the Munda Biddi Mountain Bike Trail offers 900km of pedal power and you can tackle the same distance on the Mawson Trail in SA.

Individual chapters list bike-hire companies where relevant. Rates charged by most outfits for renting road or mountain bikes (not including the discounted fees offered by budget accommodation by their guests) are around $20 per hour and $40 per day. Deposits range from $50 to $200, depending on the rental period. Most states have bicycle organisations that provide maps and advice; see p1069 and destination chapters for more information.

Wildlife Watching

Wildlife is one of Australia's top selling points and justifiably so. The vast majority of national parks are home to native fauna, although much of it is nocturnal so you may need to hone your torch (flashlight) skills to spot it.

Australia is a twitcher's haven, with a wide variety of habitats and **bird life**, particularly water birds. Canberra has the richest bird life of any Australian capital city.

In the NT the best parks to spot wildlife are in the tropical north, particularly Kakadu National Park, where the bird life in particular is abundant. You've also got a good chance of spotting **crocodiles** up here.

In NSW there are **platypuses** and **gliders** to be found in New England National Park, and 120 bird species in Dorrigo National Park. The Border Ranges National Park is home to a quarter of all of Australia's bird species. Willandra National Park is World Heritage-listed and encompasses dense temperate wetlands and wildlife, and **koalas** are a dime a dozen around Port Macquarie. WA also has ample birdwatching hot spots.

In Victoria, Wilsons Promontory National Park teems with wildlife – in fact, **wombats** seem to have right of way.

In SA make a beeline for Flinders Chase National Park. In Queensland, head to Malanda

RESPONSIBLE BUSHWALKING

To help preserve the ecology and beauty of Australia, consider the following tips when bushwalking.

» Carry out all your rubbish. Never bury your rubbish: digging disturbs soil and ground cover and encourages erosion. Buried rubbish will likely be dug up by animals, who may be injured or poisoned by it.

» Sanitary napkins, tampons, condoms and toilet paper should be carried out despite the inconvenience.

» Where there is a toilet, please use it. Where there is none, bury your waste. Dig a small hole 15cm (6in) deep and at least 100m (320ft) from any watercourse. Cover the waste with soil and a rock. In snow, dig down to the soil.

» Don't use detergents or toothpaste in or near watercourses, even if they are biodegradable.

» For personal washing, use biodegradable soap and a water container at least 50m (160ft) away from the watercourse. Disperse the waste water widely to allow the soil to filter it fully.

» Wash cooking utensils 50m (160ft) from watercourses using a scourer, sand or snow instead of detergent.

» Stick to existing tracks and avoid short cuts.

» Don't depend on open fires for cooking. Cook on a lightweight kerosene, alcohol or Shellite (white gas) stove and avoid those powered by disposable butane gas canisters.

» In alpine areas, ensure that all members are outfitted with enough clothing so that fires are not a necessity for warmth.

» If you light a fire, use an existing fireplace. Don't surround fires with rocks. Use only dead, fallen wood. In huts, leave wood for the next person.

» Do not feed the wildlife as this can lead to animals becoming dependent on handouts, to unbalanced populations and to diseases.

» Seek advice from environmental organisations such as the **Wilderness Society** (www.wilderness.org.au), the **Australian Conservation Foundation** (ACF; www.acfonline. org.au) and **Planet Ark** (www.planetark.org).

Bells Beach, Cactus, Margaret River, the Superbank – mention any of them in the right company and stories of surfing legend will undoubtedly emerge. The Superbank hosts the first event on the Association of Surfing Professionals (ASP) World Tour calendar each year, and Bells Beach the second, with Bells having recently become the longest-serving host of an ASP event. Cactus dangles the lure of remote mystique, while Margaret River is a haunt for surfers chasing the bigger waves.

While the aforementioned might be jewels, they're dot points in the sea of stars that Australia has to offer. Little wonder – the coastline is vast, touching the Indian, Southern and South Pacific Oceans. With that much potential swell, an intricate coastal architecture and the right conditions, you'll find anything from innocent breaks to gnarly reefs not far from all six Australian state capitals.

New South Wales

» Manly through to Avalon, otherwise known as Sydney's Northern Beaches.
» Byron Bay, Lennox Head and Angourie Point on the far north coast.
» Nambucca Heads and Crescent Head on the mid-north coast.
» The areas around Jervis Bay and Ulladulla on the south coast.

Queensland

» The Superbank (a 2km-long sandbar stretching from Snapper Rocks to Kirra Point).
» Burleigh Heads through to Surfers Paradise on the Gold Coast.
» North Stradbroke Island in Moreton Bay.
» Caloundra, Alexandra Heads near Maroochy and Noosa on the Sunshine Coast.

Victoria

» Bells Beach (the spiritual home of Australian surfing; when the wave is on, few would argue, but the break is notoriously inconsistent).

for bird life, **turtles** and pademelons, Cape Tribulation for even better bird life, Magnetic Island for koala spotting, Fraser Island for **dingoes** and the Daintree for **cassowaries**. In Tasmania, Maria Island is another twitcher's paradise, while Mt William and Mt Field National Parks and Bruny Island teem with native fauna.

Skiing & Snowboarding

Australia has a small but enthusiastic skiing industry, with snowfields straddling the NSW–Victoria border. The season is relatively short, however, running from about mid-June to early September, and snowfalls can be unpredictable. The top places to ski are within Kosciuszko National Park in the Snowy Mountains in NSW, and Mt Buller, Falls Creek and Mt Hotham in Victoria's High Country.

On The Water

As Australia's national anthem will tell you, this land is 'girt by sea'. Indeed, there's a heckuva lot of coastline here, and beach culture infuses the national psyche. Surfing, fishing, sailing, diving and snorkelling are what people do here – national pastimes one and all. Marine-mammal-watching trips have also become popular in recent years. Inland there are vast lakes and meandering rivers, offering rafting, canoeing, kayaking and (yet more) fishing opportunities.

Diving & Snorkelling

The Great Barrier Reef has more dazzling dive sites than you can poke a fin at.

In WA the Ningaloo Reef is every bit as interesting as the east-coast reefs, without the tourist numbers, and there are spectacular artificial reefs created by sunken ships at Albany and Dunsborough.

The Rapid Bay jetty off the Gulf St Vincent coast in SA is renowned for its abundant marine life, and in Tasmania the Bay of Fires and Eaglehawk Neck are popular spots. In NSW, Jervis Bay and Fish Rock Cave off South West Rocks are popular spots.

See also p32 for tips on safe diving, and p31 for dive course info around the Great Barrier Reef.

» Smiths Beach on Phillip Island.

» Point Leo, Flinders, Gunnamatta, Rye and Portsea on the Mornington Peninsula.

» On the southwest coast, Barwon Heads, Point Lonsdale, Torquay, Bells Beach and numerous spots along the Great Ocean Road.

Tasmania
Be sure to pack a full-length wetsuit.

» Marrawah on the exposed northwest coast – can offer huge waves.

» St Helens and Bicheno on the east coast.

» Eaglehawk Neck on the Tasman Peninsula.

» Closer to Hobart, Cremorne Point and Clifton Beach.

South Australia

» Cactus Beach, west of Ceduna on remote Point Sinclair, is something of a bogey for surfers due to the odd shark attack. Internationally recognised for its quality and consistency.

» Streaky Bay and Greenly Beach on the western side of the Eyre Peninsula.

» Pennington Bay, which has the most consistent surf on Kangaroo Island.

» Pondalowie Bay and Stenhouse Bay on the Yorke Peninsula tip in Innes National Park.

» Victor Harbor, Port Elliot and Middleton Beach at Port Elliot.

Western Australia
Check out www.srosurf.com for more info.

» Margaret River, Gracetown and Yallingup.

» Trigg Point and Scarborough Beach, just north of Perth.

» Further north at Geraldton and Kalbarri.

» Down south at Denmark on the Southern Ocean.

Fishing

Barramundi fishing is hugely popular across the Top End, particularly around Borroloola in the NT, and Karumba and Lake Tinaroo in Queensland.

Ocean fishing is possible right around the country, from a pier or a beach, or on an organised deep-sea charter. There are magnificent glacial lakes and clear streams for fishing in Tasmania.

Before casting a line, be warned that strict limits to catches and sizes apply in Australia, and many species are threatened and therefore protected. Check local guidelines via fishing equipment stores or through individual state's government fishing bodies for information.

Whale, Dolphin & Marine-Life Watching

Southern right and humpback **whales** pass close to Australia's southern coast on their migratory route between the Antarctic and warmer waters. The best spots for whale-watching cruises are Hervey Bay in Queensland, Eden in southern NSW, the mid-north coast of NSW, Warrnambool in Victoria, Albany on WA's southwest cape, and numerous places in SA. Whale-watching season is roughly May to October on the west coast and in southwestern Victoria, September to November on the east coast, and July to September off the SA coast. For **whale sharks** and **manta rays** try WA's Ningaloo Marine Park.

Dolphins can be seen year-round along the east coast at Jervis Bay, Port Stephens and Byron Bay in NSW; off the coast of WA at Bunbury and Rockingham; and you can swim with them off Sorrento in Victoria. You can also see **fairy penguins** in Victoria on Phillip Island. Back in WA, **fur seals** and **sea lions** can variously be seen at Rottnest Island, Esperance, Rockingham and Green Head, and all manner of beautiful sea creatures can be seen at Monkey Mia (including **dugongs**!).

itineraries

Whether you've got six days or 60, these itineraries provide a starting point for the trip of a lifetime. Want more inspiration? Head online to lonelyplanet.com /thorntree to chat with other travellers.

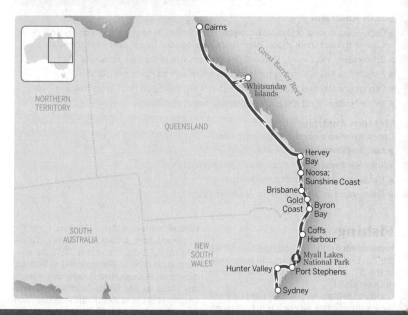

Four Weeks
Surf & Sun Run

On the east coast between Sydney and Cairns for 2864km, this is the most well-trodden path in Australia. You could do it in a fortnight, but why not take a month and chill out.

Start with the bright lights and glitz of **Sydney** and then meander north along the Pacific Hwy through central and northern New South Wales (NSW). Hang out in the **Hunter Valley** for vino-quaffing and national-park tramping, and stop for water sports in family-friendly **Port Stephens**, **Myall Lakes National Park** and **Coffs Harbour**. Skip up to **Byron Bay** for New Age indulgences and great beaches, then head over the Queensland border into the honey-hued, surf-addicted **Gold Coast**. Pause in **Brisbane** and then amble up through **Noosa** and the glorious **Sunshine Coast**.

The Bruce Hwy wends along the stunning coast into the far north. Nature lovers should visit the whale-watching haven of **Hervey Bay** and then make their way further north, up to the blissful **Whitsunday Islands**, the coral charms of the **Great Barrier Reef** and the scuba-diving nexus of **Cairns**.

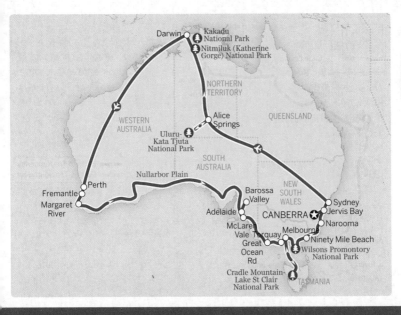

Four Weeks

The Giant Loop

> Bid a fond *au revoir* to the bright lights, bars and boutiques of **Sydney** and hop on an internal flight to **Alice Springs** in desert-hot Central Australia. Check out the outstanding **Alice Springs Desert Park**, then take a tour south to the awesome **Uluru-Kata Tjuta National Park**. Don't miss a guided walk around Uluru with the Anangu people, who have lived here for millennia.

Back in Alice, pick up a hire car and cruise north along the Stuart Hwy to youthful, exuberant **Darwin**. En route is the gorgeous **Nitmiluk (Katherine Gorge) National Park** (go canoeing or take a cruise), and **Kakadu National Park**, arguably the best place in Australia to see Aboriginal rock art and crocodiles.

From Darwin, hop another flight to the ebullient, 'life is a beach' city of **Perth** and the artsy old port town of **Fremantle**. Continuing south, wine away some hours at **Margaret River** until you're ready to tackle the flat immensity of the **Nullarbor Plain** – if you're not up for the epic drive to steadfast, smart-casual **Adelaide**, the *Indian Pacific* train ride is one you won't forget in a hurry.

Check out a few wine regions around Adelaide (the **Barossa Valley** and **McLaren Vale** are both an hour away, north and south respectively), or drive along the impossibly scenic **Great Ocean Road** to surf-town **Torquay** and sports-mad **Melbourne**. Don't miss a game of Australian Rules football at the cauldron-like Melbourne Cricket Ground.

If you have a few extra days, take the car ferry across to **Tasmania** – as 'English' as Australia gets. Australia's divine island state preserves some of the country's oldest forests and World Heritage–listed mountain ranges: **Cradle Mountain-Lake St Clair National Park** is easily accessible and absolutely beautiful.

From Melbourne, continue along the Victorian coast to the secluded wilderness of **Wilsons Promontory National Park**. Spend a couple of days somewhere along **Ninety Mile Beach**, then cruise around **Narooma** on the southern NSW coast and bask in idyllic **Jervis Bay** (spot any whales offshore?). After you've detoured to the national capital, **Canberra**, where the politics and nightlife are equally spicy, return to the big smoke of Sydney. There are so many beaches here, you're sure to find a patch of sand with your name on it.

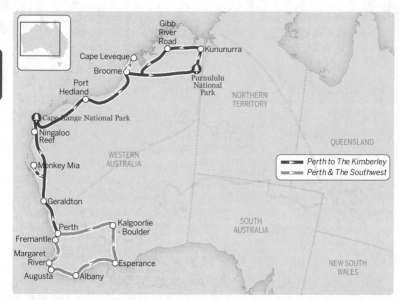

Perth to The Kimberley
Perth & The Southwest

Two Weeks
Perth & the Southwest

Three Weeks
Perth to the Kimberley

In Western Australia (WA), combine the best of the country's lush southwest with a taste of the bare and beautiful outback. Start in **Perth** and exhaust all of your urban urges in the great pubs, galleries, bars and restaurants. Be sure to fit in an afternoon in the cruisy port of **Fremantle**, south of the city. Then head south via the stunning beaches of Cape Naturaliste, before camping out in **Margaret River** (a three-hour hop from Perth) mixing wines with marinated marron in the surrounding wineries. Go surfing and winery-hopping before continuing south to **Augusta** and magnificent Cape Leeuwin, where whales drop by. Meander through the giant old-growth forests of the southwest and rest a while in **Albany** with its historic architecture and world-class diving. Follow the southern coast to **Esperance**, where you can visit seals, penguins and seabirds in the Archipelago of the Recherche.

Bid the coast farewell and head north to the iconic outback gold-mining town of **Kalgoorlie-Boulder**, roughly four hours away. Play 'wild west', succumb to hedonism and buy a miner a beer. From here it's under seven hours' drive along the Great Eastern Hwy back to Perth, where the ocean beckons beyond the beaches of **Scarborough** and **Cottesloe**.

In northern WA, the **Kimberley** region is a curious mix of seasonal extremes, rough outback towns and jaw-dropping scenery – the kind of place you think you'll trundle through in a day or two but can end up exploring for weeks. Pack a tent, do your homework and get ready for 3214km heading north from **Perth**.

Taking the inland Great Northern Hwy and National Hwy 1 might save you two hours, but the North West Coastal Hwy is more interesting. Be sure to check out the excellent museum in **Geraldton**, followed by a date with a bottlenose dolphin at **Monkey Mia**. Take a sidetrack to the snorkel-friendly **Cape Range National Park** and the marine brilliance of **Ningaloo Reef**.

The mining town of **Port Hedland** is south of the Kimberley gateway town of **Broome**, a multicultural pearl-diving town with ritzy resorts along Cable Beach. Head north from here to see **Cape Leveque**, or head east into the Kimberley proper: here you'll find the colossal domes of the **Bungle Bungles** in **Purnululu National Park**. The rugged **Gibb River Road** is a 4WD-only alternative to National Highway 1, both of which deliver you to pretty **Kununurra** near the Northern Territory border.

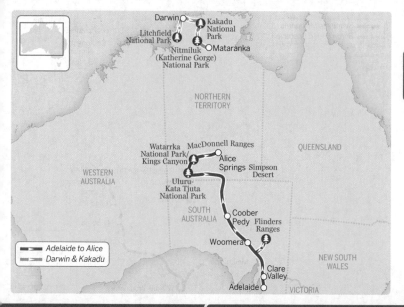

Legend:
- Adelaide to Alice
- Darwin & Kakadu

10 Days
Adelaide to Alice

From festival-frenzied **Adelaide** (March = festival madness), head two hours north to the **Clare Valley** for world-class Riesling and old stone mining towns. Next stop is the ragged **Flinders Ranges**, jagging up from the semidesert like a rust-coloured mirage. Rich in Indigenous culture, the Flinders and the amazing **Wilpena Pound** will etch itself into your memory.

Hit the Stuart Hwy – a must for avid road trippers – and journey to the mildly spooky rocket-testing town **Woomera** and the opal-tinted dugouts of **Coober Pedy**. You're now well and truly into an 'outback odyssey', entering the **Simpson Desert**.

The Lasseter Hwy turn-off takes you to weighty, awe-inspiring **Uluru** and the captivating **Kata Tjuta** rock formations. You've seen the photos and the TV shows, but there's nothing quite like seeing an Uluru sunset firsthand.

Located about 300km north of Uluru on the (usually) dry Kings Creek, the spectacular, vertigo-inducing **Watarrka (Kings Canyon) National Park** rewards intrepid travellers with eye-popping walks into and around the rim of this gaping desert chasm. Finish up in the desert oasis of **Alice Springs**, in the heart of the steep-sided **MacDonnell Ranges**.

Two Weeks
Darwin & Kakadu

Gone are the days when **Darwin** was little more than a brawling frontier town full of fishers, miners and truck drivers blowing off steam. These days there seem to be more backpackers here than anyone else, and Darwin is very multicultural, as a visit to the fabulous **Mindil Beach Sunset Market** will confirm. Grab some Thai stir-fry, Indonesian beef *rendang*, a Malaysian laksa or a Greek souvlaki and head for the beach. Don't miss the **Deckchair Cinema** and the excellent Aboriginal and Cyclone Tracy exhibits at the **Museum & Art Gallery of the Northern Territory**.

A few hours south on the Stuart Hwy you'll run into some superb national parks. **Litchfield National Park** is famous for plummeting waterfalls and cooling swimming holes. Spend a few days exploring World Heritage–listed **Kakadu National Park**, a wetland of international significance with amazing rock outcrops dappled with equally amazing Aboriginal rock art. Further south is **Nitmiluk (Katherine Gorge) National Park**, where the Katherine River cuts its way through 13 jagged ravines. There are also thermal springs nearby at **Mataranka** – soak off the road dust in a (free!) naturally heated swimming hole.

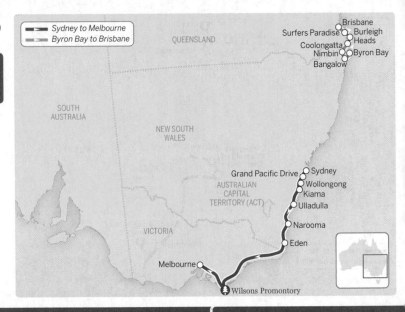

Legend:
- Sydney to Melbourne
- Byron Bay to Brisbane

10 Days

Sydney to Melbourne

> Most people fly in to Sydney, Australia's biggest and brightest city, but just under 1000km south in Victoria is Melbourne, Sydney's arty rival.

Check out **Sydney** from its sparkling harbour: the gorgeous **Sydney Opera House** and impressive **Sydney Harbour Bridge** are literally unmissable. For a bird's-eye view, tackle the **Bridge Climb** over the grey arch. If you feel like a swim, head to **Bondi Beach**: backpackers, beach breaks and bikinis make it the quintessential Australian experience.

Heading out of town, zip along the elevated **Grand Pacific Drive**, through **Wollongong** to the lovely coastal town of **Kiama**. Nearby, the **Illawarra Fly Tree Top Walk** jags through the rainforest canopy.

You'll meander through **Ulladulla**, **Narooma** and the aptly named **Eden** near the Victorian border. The road from here to Melbourne is low key: spice it up with a detour to **Wilsons Promontory National Park** for some beautiful bushwalking and beaches.

Melbourne lives up to the hype, a burgeoning bayside city famous for the arts, Australian Rules football and exemplary coffee. While you're here, explore its laneways, haunt the galleries and revel in its exalted shopping and food scenes.

10 Days

Byron Bay to Brisbane

> Strap your mini-mal to the roof rack, fire up the Kombi and cruise out into your very own *Endless Summer*: this stretch of Australia's east coast has the most consistent and challenging surf.

Despite big development arriving from the north and south, **Byron Bay** remains a happy hippie town with great pubs, restaurants, beaches and the famous Pass point break. Don't miss inland day-trips to pretty **Bangalow** and Australia's almost mythical alt-lifestyle hangout, **Nimbin**. After crossing into Queensland north of Tweed Heads, you'll hit the Gold Coast. First stop is surf life-saving mecca **Coolangatta**, then beautiful **Burleigh Heads** on a rocky headland (great surf and swimming). You'll soon catch sight of **Surfers Paradise**, a slightly unnerving cityscape on the horizon. There are as many apartment towers here as shades of fake tan. Check it out if you like casinos and theme parks, or head up the Pacific Hwy to the easy-going river city of **Brisbane**, 70kms north. Once a sleepy country town, 'Brisvegas' is now Boom Town, growing so fast that it can be difficult to navigate. Its urban charms (great dining, nightlife and the arts) meld seamlessly with the natural environment (riverside cliffs, parklands and botanic gardens).

regions at a glance

Sydney & New South Wales

Beaches ✓✓✓
Food ✓✓✓
National Parks ✓✓

Beaches
Australia claims to be the 'world's best' in a number of fields (sport and beer-drinking being two of the more credible), but we think there's one claim that is indisputable – Aussie surf beaches can't be beaten, particularly those in Sydney. From a plane, the coast of New South Wales (NSW) looks like one long beach with a few pointed headlines interrupting the tranquillity every now and then. Buy some boardies or a bikini and immerse yourself.

Food
Sydney used to come a very sluggish second to Melbourne in the culinary stakes, but in recent years a thoroughbred line up of chefs, restaurateurs and artisan producers have made the dining scenes in Sydney, the Blue Mountains and the Hunter Valley the most exciting in the country – make sure you celebrate their ascendancy.
In wider NSW you can wake up and smell the coffee almost anywhere. Sea-changers and tree-changers from the capital have transferred their culinary expertise to all corners of the state via gourmet restaurants, cafes, delis and farmers markets.

National Parks
New South Wales has some of the biggest and best in the country. Wollumbin National Park has the remnants of an ancient volcano and Border Ranges National Park has a forest of trees over 2000 years old. Others spread their green leaves over the hinterland and meet the beach in a vision splendid, kangaroos and all.

p56

Canberra & Around

Museums ✓✓✓
Wineries ✓✓
Politics ✓✓✓

Museums
If you want to take in Australia's history and culture in one giant gulp, Canberra offers the National Gallery, with its magnificent collections of Aboriginal and Torres Strait Islander, Australian and Asian art; the National Museum, whose imaginative exhibits provide insights into the Australian heart and soul; the moving and fascinating War Memorial and the evocative and often hilarious vintage reels on display at the National Film and Sound Archive.

Wineries
Canberra's wine industry is relatively new but it has proved itself with a consistent crop of very fine cold-climate wines, and vineyards are an easy and picturesque drive from downtown.

Politics
This is what really makes Canberra tick – find out for yourself at Parliament House's Question Time, or visit the Museum of Australian Democracy at Old Parliament House.

p243

Queensland & the Great Barrier Reef

Diving ✓✓✓
Beaches & Islands ✓✓✓
Outdoor Fun ✓✓✓

Diving
Blessed with the awe-inspiring Great Barrier Reef, Queensland is the place for world-class diving and snorkelling. There are countless ways to explore this dazzling aquatic wonderland, whether on a day trip, a live-aboard diving vessel, or staying on a reef-fringed island.

Beaches & Islands
With great surf along the south coast, rainforest-covered islands and picture-perfect white-sand beauties fronting turquoise seas, Queensland is pure bliss for beach- and island lovers. The Whitsundays are the place to start: get on a yacht and enjoy.

Outdoor Fun
You can go surfing, sea kayaking, whale-watching, bushwalking, skydiving, white-water rafting or take a 4WD island safari. Afterwards, take some much-needed R&R on an island resort.

p275

Melbourne & Victoria

History & Culture ✓
Sports ✓✓
Beaches ✓✓✓

History & Culture
Go back to pre-settlement time at Victoria's Indigenous centres. Walk the streets of towns that knew no bounds during the goldrush of the mid-1800s. Art hides in the state's art galleries and, in Melbourne itself, on its walls. Head Footscray- and Richmond-way for international flavours.

Sports
Victoria is the home of AFL and, come wintertime, everyone seems to have aligned themselves with a team. Summer means tennis, with international players bumping shoulders with cricket folk in their whites. If locals aren't watching it, they're in the streets or backyards playing it.

Beaches
Victoria's seascapes range from family-friendly to exceptionally rowdy. With its exposure to the relentless Southern Ocean swell, there's plenty of quality (if chilly) surf.

p470

Tasmania

Food ✓✓✓
Wildlife ✓✓
History ✓✓✓

Gourmet Travel
Australia's southern addendum to the 'Mainland' fits several return visits of attractions into its relatively small landmass. Chefs from all over Australia are increasingly besotted with Tasmania's excellent fresh produce, including briny fresh salmon and oysters, and plump and tasty fruit and vegetables.

Wildlife
Chances to interact with the island's wildlife abound. Witness the struggle of the iconic Tasmanian Devil. There's whale-, seal- and penguin-spotting in the cool southern waters.

History
Tasmania's – and Australia's – often tragic colonial history is on display in Port Arthur and up the Heritage Hwy, often with the background of dramatic landscapes seemingly out of proportion with the state's compact footprint.

p613

Adelaide & South Australia

Wine Regions ✓✓✓
Festivals ✓✓
Pubs ✓✓

Wine Regions
We challenge you to visit South Australia (SA) without inadvertently driving through an up-and-coming wine region. You'll have heard of the Barossa Valley and McLaren Vale but what about Langhorne Creek, Mt Benson, Currency Creek, Southern Fleurieu or Adelaide Hills? All top drops worth pulling over for.

Festivals
There's a reason SA number plates declare this the festival state. Adelaide erupts with visual arts, music, theatre, busking and the growl of V8 engines at the end of every summer...the question is, why do they do it all at the same time?

Pubs
Adelaide is supposedly the city of churches, but for every steeple there's a temple of tipple. Beyond the city, there are boutique beer halls, brews with a sea view and rambling outback boozers.

p704

Darwin & Uluru

Wildlife ✓✓✓
Indigenous Culture ✓✓✓
National Parks ✓✓

Wildlife
The further north you head in Australia, the more deadly, dangerous and just damn big the creatures become. Whopping crocs inhabit the waterways, while the country's largest snakes, scrub pythons, slither across the land. The Northern Territory is home to countless species of birds, including dancing brolgas, which are like pelicans on stilts.

Indigenous Culture
Meet Australia's first people. Tour Uluru with an Anangu elder; see Kakadu with an Indigenous guide. Hop over to the Tiwi Islands for the legendary Tiwi Grand Final and Art Show.

National Parks
Experience iconic Australian wilderness, from the deserts to the tropics. Uluru and Kata-Tjuta are the biggest boulders you'll ever see; West MacDonnell has gorgeous gorges. Kakadu and Litchfield have big waterfalls, crocs and ancient rock-art galleries.

p798

Western Australia

Beaches ✓✓✓
Adventure ✓✓✓
Wildlife ✓✓✓

Beaches
If you subscribe to the 'life's a beach' school of thought, you'll fall in love with Western Australia and its 12,500km of spectacular coastline. Superb isolated beaches lead down to shallow lagoons hemmed by World Heritage–nominated Ningaloo Marine Park.

Adventure
Bring it on: the Kimberley will provide the ride of your life along the bone-shaking Gibb River Road, to the exceptional Mitchell Falls, and remote Kalumburu. Jump on a speedboat and head full throttle for the Horizontal Waterfalls, then grab a canoe and paddle down the mighty Ord River.

Wildlife
Whale sharks, manta rays, turtles and migrating whales are just a few of the marine creatures along the central west coast, while inland birds flock to the oasis pools of Millstream-Chichester National Park, and pythons and rock wallabies hide in the shadows of Karijini.

p891

Look out for these icons:

 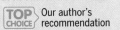 Our author's recommendation

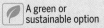 A green or sustainable option

 No payment required

See the Index for a full list of destinations covered in this book.

On the Road

Sydney & New South Wales

Best Places to Eat

» Icebergs Dining Room & Bar (p111)

» Margan (p138)

» Racine at La Colline Winery (p198)

» Seagrass Brasserie (p214)

» Solitary (p132)

Best Places to Stay

» Bondi Beach House (p105)

» Byron at Byron (p178)

» Petersons Guesthouse (p193)

» Sydney Harbour YHA (p102)

» Tower Lodge (p137)

Why Go?

The country's most populous state and the birthplace of the modern nation, New South Wales (NSW) is rich in history, landscapes and contrasts. It's also home to stunning Sydney, the nation's capital in all but name.

Diversity reigns supreme here. South of the harbour, languid coastal towns hug the rugged coastline and there's a profusion of beautiful beaches, many of which are idyllically deserted. Settlements founded by gold miners and graziers pepper the heart of the state, and to the far west the arid lunar landscape of the outback beckons and beguiles. In the north, classic Aussie surf culture dominates, tempered by the occasional outbreak of alternative hinterland lifestyle. In almost every corner you'll find incredible national parks to explore.

Wherever you choose to travel you can be certain of three things: the scenery will be spectacular, the road will be easy and the welcome will be warm – and it's hard to beat that.

When to Go

Sydney

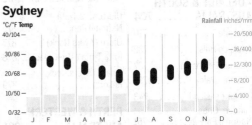

Feb Sydney's summer party season culminates with the Gay & Lesbian Mardi Gras.

Jul Enjoy wood fires and fine wine in the Blue Mountains, Central West and Hunter Valley.

Oct Creamy Sydney rock oysters come into season and are fresh and plentiful until March.

Farmers Markets

The state's growing reputation as an international culinary hot spot owes much to the stellar quality of the local produce, and a visit to a farmers market is becoming an increasingly popular activity for locals and visitors alike. Most of these markets feature organic, locally grown products; some also offer live music, buskers and special events such as cooking demonstrations. For a handy list, go to www.farmersmarkets.org.au/markets and www.organic foodmarkets.com.au.

In Sydney, a visit to the Sydney Fish Market (p78) and Eveleigh Market (p120) is highly recommended.

In country NSW, there are growers markets at Blackheath (p132), Newcastle (p144), Camden (p124), Bangalow (p186), Lismore (p187), Bellingen (p214), Byron Bay (p183), Nimbin (p187), Orange (p200) and Jervis Bay (p214).

DON'T MISS

Rural NSW offers a treasure trove of eccentric festivals. In January, the town of Parkes in the central west is inundated by hundreds of middle-aged, jumpsuit-clad men during the **Elvis Festival** (p203), and at Easter the opal town of Lightning Ridge stages its annual **Great Goat Race** (p196).

October sees the town of Deniliquin holding its famous **Ute Muster** (p237), where blokes and sheilas compete for titles such as 'Chick's Ute' and 'Feral Ute'. Also in October is Wooli's **Australian National Goanna Pulling Championships** (p171), in which grown men and women, squatting on all fours, attach leather harnesses to their heads and engage in a cranial tug of war. Go figure.

The biggest rural festival of all is a serious music event, but has pronounced eccentric characteristics. Tamworth's **Country Music Festival** (p191) stages more than 800 events every January including its exuberant 'Longest Line Dance', the world record for which was set in 2009 when 3392 bootscooters participated.

Top Five Beaches

» Main Beach, Byron Bay (p178) Chilled Byron vibe, with great fish-and-chip options.

» Northern Beaches, Sydney (p87) A 20km stretch of amazing urban surf.

» One Mile Beach, Anna Bay (p146) Secluded location, soft sand and great surf.

» Pebbly Beach, Murramarang National Park (p214) Kangaroos outnumber people on this idyllic beach.

» Pippi's Beach, Yamba (p173) Great surf with dolphins.

Fast Facts

» Population: 6.5 million
» Area: 800,642 sq km
» Telephone area code: ☎02 (Broken Hill ☎08)
» Number of patrolled surf beaches: 175

Planning Your Trip

» Visit the regions when they hold their annual festivals.

» Book your accommodation well in advance, particularly for the summer months.

» Make weekend fine-dining reservations well in advance and, in regional areas, call ahead to check opening hours.

Resources

» New South Wales (www.visitnsw.com.au) Covers Sydney and NSW.

» Environment & Heritage (www.environment.nsw.gov.au/nationalparks) Info about NSW national parks.

» Outback Beds (www.outbackbeds.com.au) Outback accommodation guide.

» NSW Government (www.nsw.gov.au) Check the 'Culture, Sport & Recreation' section.

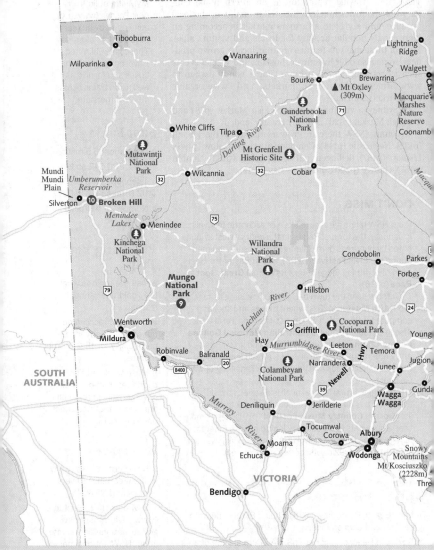

QUEENSLAND

Tibooburra

Milparinka

Wanaaring

Lightning Ridge

Walgett

Bourke

Brewarrina

▲ Mt Oxley (309m)

Macquarie Marshes Nature Reserve

Coonamb

White Cliffs

Tilpa

Darling River

Gunderbooka National Park

71

Mt Grenfell Historic Site

Mutawintji National Park

32

Wilcannia

Cobar

32

Macqu

Mundi Mundi Plain

Umberumberka Reservoir

Silverton

10 Broken Hill

Menindee Lakes

Menindee

75

Willandra National Park

Condobolin

Parkes

Forbes

Kinchega National Park

79

Mungo National Park

9

Lachlan River

Hillston

24

Griffith

Cocoparra National Park

Young

24

Wentworth

Mildura

Robinvale

Balranald

20

Hay

Murrumbidgee River

Leeton

Narrandera

Temora

Junee

Jugion

Newell Hwy

Wagga Wagga

Gunda

SOUTH AUSTRALIA

B400

Colambeyan National Park

39

Deniliquin

Jerilderie

Murray River

Tocumwal

Corowa

Albury

Snowy Mountains Mt Kosciuszko (2228m)

Thre

Moama

Echuca

Wodonga

VICTORIA

Bendigo

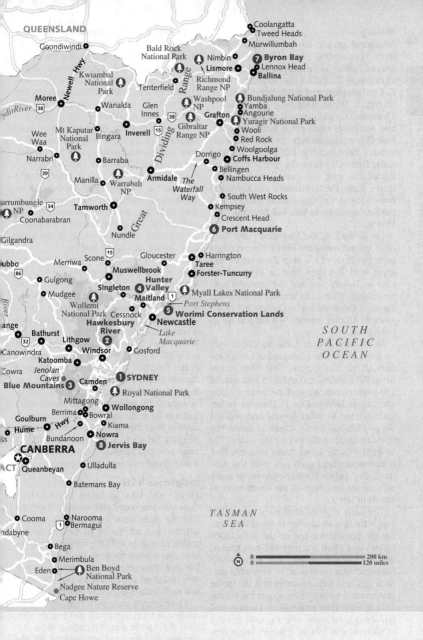

QUEENSLAND

Goondiwindi

Newell Hwy

Coolangatta
Tweed Heads
Murwillumbah
Nimbin
Bald Rock
National Park
7 **Byron Bay**
Lennox Head
Lismore
Ballina
Richmond
Range NP
Washpool
NP
Kwiambal
National
Park
Tenterfield
Moree
Warialda
Glen
Innes
38
Bundjalung National Park
Yamba
Angourie
Yuragir National Park
Wooli
Red Rock
Woolgoolga
6 **Coffs Harbour**
Grafton
Gibraltar
Range NP
Mt Kaputar
National Park
Bingara
Inverell
15
Wee
Waa
Narrabri
Barraba
Dorrigo
Bellingen
Nambucca Heads
39
Manilla
Warrabah
NP
Armidale
The
Waterfall
Way
South West Rocks
Kempsey
Crescent Head
rrumbungle
NP
34
Coonabarabran
Tamworth
Great
Nundle
6 **Port Macquarie**
Gilgandra
Harrington
Taree
Scone
15
Gloucester
Merriwa
ubbo
86
Forster-Tuncurry
Muswellbrook
Hunter
Valley
Myall Lakes National Park
Gulgong
Singleton
4 Maitland 1
Mudgee
Wollemi
National Park
Cessnock
Hawkesbury
River
Port Stephens
5 **Worimi Conservation Lands**
Newcastle
ange
Bathurst
32
Lithgow
2
Windsor
Gosford
*Lake
Macquarie*
SOUTH
PACIFIC
OCEAN
Canowindra
Katoomba
Jenolan
Caves
Blue Mountains **3**
Camden
1 SYDNEY
Royal National Park
owra
Mittagong
Berrima
Bowral
Wollongong
Goulburn
Hume
Kiama
Bundanoon
Nowra
CANBERRA
8 **Jervis Bay**
ACT
Queanbeyan
Ulladulla
Batemans Bay
TASMAN
SEA
Cooma
Narooma
1
Bermagui
dabyne
Bega
Merimbula
Eden
Ben Boyd
National Park
Nadgee Nature Reserve
Cape Howe
N
0   200 km
0   120 miles

7 Make a beeline for the
beautiful beaches and laid-
back organic lifestyle of
Byron Bay (p176)

8 Dip your toes in the pure
white sand and sapphire
waters of **Jervis Bay** (p214)

9 Encounter Aboriginal
history and the amazing Walls

of China in **Mungo
National Park** (p242)

10 Be inspired by the
dramatic scenery and empty
spaces of **Broken Hill** (p239)

History

Aboriginal people have lived in NSW for more than 40,000 years. The coastal area around Sydney is the ancestral home of the Eora people (including the Birrabirragal and Gadigal peoples), and the Anaiwan, Ngarigo, Dainggati, Darug, Badjalang, Kumbainggiri, Tharawal, Gandangara, Guringai, Worimi and Awabakal clans come from the southeast. Other clans include the Dharawal from around Berrima; the Bandjigali, Barindji, Kula, Barkindji, Parundji, Yorta Yorta and Baranbinja from the Darling Riverine; the Birpai from the northeast; the Kamilaroi from around the Queensland border; and the Karenggapa and Wadikali from the Lake Eyre area.

On 19 April 1770 Lieutenant (later Captain) James Cook of the British Navy climbed onto the deck of his ship *Endeavour* and spied land. Ten days later he dropped anchor at Botany Bay and declared the area New South Wales. His arrival caused much alarm to the Eora, for as Cook noted in his journal: 'All they seemed to want was for us to be gone.'

In 1788 the British came back, this time for good. Under the command of naval Captain Arthur Phillip, the 'First Fleet' numbered 751 convicts and children and around 250 soldiers, officials and their wives. Upon arriving at Botany Bay, Phillip was rather disappointed by what he saw and ordered the ships to sail north, where he found 'the finest harbour in the world'. The date of the landing was 26 January, an occasion that is commemorated each year with the Australia Day public holiday (known to many Indigenous members of the community as 'Invasion Day').

The early days of settlement were difficult, with famine and lawlessness threatening the population, but by the early 1800s Sydney was a bustling port with new houses, warehouses and streets. The surrounding bushland was overtaken by vegetable gardens and orchards, ensuring that the threat of starvation no longer hung over the colony.

In 1793 Phillip returned to London and self-serving military officers took control of Government House – the vigorous new society that the first governor had worked so hard to establish began to unravel. Fortunately, London swiftly took action, dispatching Governor Lachlan Macquarie to restore the rule of law. Under his guidance the colony flourished.

In 1813 the Blue Mountains were penetrated by explorers Blaxland, Lawson and Wentworth, opening the way for the colony to expand onto the vast fertile slopes and plains of the west. By the 1830s, the Lachlan, Macquarie, Murrumbidgee and Darling river systems had been explored and the general layout of NSW was determined.

Over the next 60 or so years, the rapid expansion of the NSW economy resulted in good wages, social mobility and increasingly strong unions, all of which fed the belief that Australia's first and largest colony might become 'the working man's paradise'. This belief was strengthened when, on 1 January 1901, NSW and the other colonies federated to form the nation of Australia, shrugging off the yoke of Britain whilst at the same time staying part of the Empire.

In 1914, thousands of Australian men volunteered to fight in the Australian Imperial Force when WWI broke out. They did the same again during WWII, after which the Australian government embarked on a massive immigration program, attracting migrants from Britain and mainland Europe. These 'new Australians' had a huge impact on NSW, especially in the irrigation farms of the Riverina, in the building of the great Snowy Mountains Hydro-Electric Scheme, in the large industrial centres and in Sydney itself. In recent decades, immigration patterns have changed, with most migrants coming from the Middle East and Asia (particularly Lebanon, China and Vietnam) to forge new and successful lives in one of the world's great multicultural societies.

Indigenous NSW

Indigenous clans or bands in NSW have their own languages and identity. Traditionally, the clans were semi-nomadic, moving within their territories to fish, hunt and gather plants. As well as providing food, the land also formed the basis for their spiritual life and Dreaming (belief system), which is why its forced acquisition by the Europeans had such catastrophic consequences.

The colonists were swift to subject the local people to kidnappings and punishment, with the explicit aim of terrifying them into submission. Smallpox, introduced by the Europeans, also decimated the local population, which had no resistance to such a disease. But there was resistance in other forms: Aboriginal freedom-fighting groups began to spring up, led by indigenous warriors including Pemulwuy (1750–1802), a member of the Bidjigal clan from around Botany Bay, and Musquito (c1780–1825), a member of the Eora from the north shore of Port Jackson. The freedom fighters were eventually crushed as the settlers resorted to ever more barbaric methods to achieve total domination.

At the most recent national census (2006) there were an estimated 152,685 Aboriginal people in NSW (29.5% of the country's Indigenous population and just over 2% of the total population of the state). This figure was predicted to grow to approximately 208,341 by 2021. Approximately 28% of the population lives in the Greater Sydney area.

There are a number of ways to gain an insight into the state's Indigenous culture when you are here.

In Sydney, the Australian Museum, Art Gallery of NSW, Museum of Sydney, Powerhouse Museum and Royal Botanic Gardens all have exhibits and programs relating to Aboriginal life and culture.

For information on the ancient Aboriginal rock paintings and engravings around the harbour, check with the Sydney Harbour National Parks Information Centre (p119). You can see rock engravings up close on the Manly Scenic Walkway and in the Ku-ring-gai Chase National Park.

Unfortunately, there are very few companies offering tours concentrating on Aboriginal culture. If you're lucky, you may be able to book a place on an Aboriginal heritage tour in the Sydney Royal Botanic Gardens. Another option is to take an Aboriginal culture tour on Sydney Harbour (p65).

Outside Sydney, there are many sites of Aboriginal heritage, including Brisbane Water National Park near Gosford; Gunderbooka National Park; the Pilliga Forest; the Murramarang Aboriginal Area in the national park of the same name; and the Mt Grenfell Historic Site.

Tour companies include Blue Mountains Walkabout, which runs guided adventurous treks with Aboriginal and spiritual themes, and Aboriginal Cultural Concepts in Ballina, which offers Aboriginal heritage tour along the Bundjalung Coast. Other options include Warrumbungle Tara Cave Walk (p195) in the wonderfully monikered Warrumbungle National Park, or visits to the remote Mungo National Park guided by the Indigenous owned and operated Harry Nanya Tours.

Cultural centres include the Muru Mittigar Aboriginal Cultural Centre (p127) in Penrith, the Aboriginal Cultural Centre & Keeping Place in Armidale, the Yarrawarra Aboriginal Cultural Centre in Red Rock, the Minjungbal Aboriginal Cultural Centre (p184) in Tweed Heads and the Umbarra Cultural Centre near Bermagui.

For more information about Indigenous NSW, go to www.visitnsw.com.au and follow the links to Aboriginal NSW under Things to Do/Attractions, or go to www.indigenoustourism.australia.com for links to Indigenous-owned and -operated tour and accommodation operators, as well as artists and art organisations.

National Parks

There are over 800 exceptionally diverse national parks and reserves in NSW, from the subtropical rainforest of the Border Ranges and white peaks of the Snowy Mountains to the haunting, fragile landscapes of the outback. In reasonable weather most of these parks and reserves are accessible by conventional vehicle; unfortunately, few can be accessed by public transport.

The **NSW National Parks & Wildlife Service** (NPWS; www.nationalparks.nsw.gov.au) does an excellent job. Many parks have visitor centres with detailed information on the area, walking tracks and camping options. Where there isn't one, visit the nearest NPWS office for information.

Forty-six of the parks charge daily entry fees, generally $7 per vehicle; check the NPWS website for a list. If you plan on visiting a number of parks, the annual multi-park pass ($65), which gives unlimited entry to all the state's parks and reserves except Kosciuszko National Park, the Chowder Bay precinct of Sydney Harbour National Park and the Worimi Conservation Lands is extremely worthwhile.

Many parks have camp sites with facilities; some are free, others cost between $5 and $10 a night per person. Popular sites are often booked out during holidays. Bush camping is allowed in some parks; contact the NPWS office for regulations.

Activities

The state offers a huge array of activities suiting every level of fitness and fearlessness.

BIRDWATCHING

Lord Howe Island is known for its bird life, as are Dorrigo National Park and the Macquarie Marshes Nature Reserve.

HAVE YOUR SAY

Found a fantastic restaurant that you're longing to share with the world? Disagree with our recommendations? Or just want to talk about your most recent trip?

Whatever your reason, head to lonelyplanet.com, where you can post a review, ask or answer a question on the Thorntree forum, comment on a blog, or share your photos and tips on Groups. Or you can simply spend time chatting with like-minded travellers. So go on, have your say.

BUSHWALKING

Almost every national park has marked trails or wilderness-walking opportunities; these range from gentle wanders to longer, more challenging treks.

Katrina O'Brien's *Sydney's Best Harbour & Coastal Walks (2nd Edition)* profiles 37 walks including the 6km Bondi to Coogee Coastal Walk (p93) and the 10km Manly Scenic Walkway (p85). Also look out for *Sydney's Best Bush, Park & City Walks* (Veechi Stuart), which includes 50 walks and covers most of the major national parks; the highly regarded *Blue Mountains: Best Bushwalks* is by the same author. Lonely Planet's *Walking in Australia* provides maps and descriptions of many major trails throughout NSW.

Near Sydney, the wilderness areas of Royal National Park hide dramatic clifftop walks including a 28km coastal walking trail. There are smaller bushwalks around the inlets of Broken Bay in Ku-ring-gai Chase National Park.

West of Sydney, the sandstone bluffs, eucalyptus forests and wildflowers of the Blue Mountains make for a breathtaking experience, as does the walk to the summit of Australia's highest peak, Mt Kosciuszko (2228m), in Kosciuszko National Park.

In the state's northwest, Warrumbungle National Park, with its volcanic peaks, has over 30km of trails to keep you hale and strong.

The Yuraygir Coastal Walk (p170) is a 65km signposted walk from Angourie to Red Rock following the path of the coastal emu over a series of tracks, trails, beaches and rock platforms, and passing through the villages of Brooms Head, Minne Water and Wooli.

Keen trampers should try the 15km Syndicate Ridge Walking Trail near Bellingen (p164), the 45km Six Foot Track (p129) from Katoomba to the Jenolan Caves and the 100km World Heritage Walk in Washpool National Park (p194) on the south coast. Those who can cope with steep ascents should consider taking the challenge of climbing the 980m-high Pigeon House Mountain.

There are also great walks on Lord Howe Island and Norfolk Island.

The NPWS website offers loads of information about walks within its parks and reserves.

CYCLING

Sydney's ever-growing network of cycling paths is a pivotal component of Sydney City Council's praiseworthy Sustainable City 2030 initiative. See www.cityofsydney.nsw. gov.au/aboutsydney/parkingandtransport/ cycling for details.

Other popular cycling destinations include the Blue Mountains and the Great North Road around the Hawkesbury River (p125). In the southeast, mountain biking is a warm-weather favourite in Kosciuszko National Park and at Mt Canobolas, southwest of Orange.

You can access cycling guides and maps, a handy bike-shop finder, past issues of *Australian Cyclist* magazine and a PDF of the Roads & Traffic Authority's *Handbook for Bicycle Riders* through the Resources pages of the Bicycle NSW website (www. bicyclensw.org.au). Another useful resource is Lonely Planet's *Cycling Australia*.

DIVING & SNORKELLING

North of Sydney, try Broughton Island near Port Stephens and Fish Rock Cave off South West Rocks (p160). You can swim with grey nurse sharks at Narooma (p216) and with leopard sharks at Julian Rocks Marine Reserve off Byron Bay (p178). Good dive schools can be found at Byron Bay and Coffs Harbour (p165); the Coffs Harbour ones can organise dives in Solitary Islands Marine Park, where warm tropical currents and cooler southern currents meet, resulting in a wonderful combination of corals, reef fish and seaweeds.

On the South Coast popular diving spots include Jervis Bay, Montague Island and Bass Point near Shellharbour.

There's also great diving and snorkelling on Lord Howe Island.

SCENIC DRIVES

Spectacular scenic drives include the Greater Blue Mountains Drive (p130); the Bells

Line of Road (p133) between Richmond and Lithgow; the Waterfall Way (p161) from just south of Coffs Harbour to inland Armidale; Loop Road (p164), which takes you from Gleniffer near Bellingen to the foot of the New England tableland; and the Alpine Way in the Snowy Mountains

SKIING & SNOWBOARDING

Snowfields criss-cross the NSW–Victoria border. The season is relatively short (early June to late August) and snowfalls can be unpredictable. Cross-country skiing is popular and most resorts offer lessons and equipment.

The Snowy Mountains boast popular resorts, including Charlotte Pass, Perisher Blue, Selwyn and Thredbo.

SURFING

For the low-down on Sydney's top surfing and swimming spots, see p98 and p99.

You can also fine-tune your surfing skills (or indeed learn some) at Newcastle, Port Macquarie and Coffs Harbour. Crescent Head is the longboarding capital of Australia, and the gnarly swells at Angourie Point (p170) are for seasoned surfers and/or nutcases only. Further north, you can hang ten at Lennox Head and Byron Bay.

The South Coast is literally awash with great surf beaches, particularly around Wollongong, Batemans Bay and Bermagui.

For surf forecasts and other information, go to www.coastalwatch.com.

WHALE & DOLPHIN WATCHING

Every year between late May and late November, southern right and humpback whales migrate along Australia's southern coast. Get up close to these magnificent creatures on a whale-watching cruise; good spots are Eden in southern NSW and along the mid-north coast at Coffs Harbour and Port Stephens. Eden even hosts a whale-watching festival in early November each year.

Dolphins can be seen year-round at many places along the NSW coast, including Jervis Bay, Port Stephens and Byron Bay. They're even occasionally seen off Sydney's Eastern Beaches.

WHITE-WATER RAFTING, KAYAKING & CANOEING

For rafting, try the upper Murray near Jindabyne.

There is stunning sea kayaking at Byron Bay, Lord Howe Island, Batemans Bay and Eden. You can also kayak around Sydney Harbour (p98).

For canoeing, head to Barrington Tops National Park, Myall Lakes National Park, Bellingen, Coffs Harbour and the Kangaroo Valley.

For more information, check the Paddle NSW (www.paddlensw.org.au) and River Canoe Club (www.rivercanoeclub.canoe.org.au) websites; you can purchase a copy of *The Canoeing Guide to New South Wales* from the latter.

YOGA & ALTERNATIVE THERAPIES

There's only one place to go if you're keen to indulge in a spot of yoga or investigate some alternative therapies: Byron Bay.

Wine Regions

The oldest and best-known wine region in NSW is the Hunter Valley, which is known for its Semillon and Shiraz. Though it has long held the reputation as the state's premier wine-growing area, its claim to this accolade has been seriously challenged in recent decades by the Central Ranges Region, which comprises Cowra, known for its Chardonnay; Mudgee, for its Cabernet Sauvignon and Shiraz; and Orange, for a number of varietals including Shiraz, Cabernet Sauvignon, Chardonnay and Sauvignon Blanc.

Other wine regions include the Southern New South Wales Zone, made up of Gundagai (known for its Chardonnay, Shiraz and Cabernet Sauvignon); Hilltops (for its Cabernet Sauvignon and Shiraz); and Tumbarumba (for its Pinot Noir, Chardonnay and sparkling wines).

Smaller and less-renowned regions include the Riverina, Perricoota, the Shoalhaven Coast, the Southern Highlands, the Hastings River, the Northern Slopes and the Western Plains.

The most exciting of the state's wine regions is undoubtedly Orange – oenophiles should consider visiting in late October for its Wine Week (www.tasteorange.com.au/wine week), 10 days of events and activities highlighting the region's premium wines. Other wine-related events include the Hunter Valley Harvest Festival (www.huntervalley.com/events) in April, the Mudgee Wine Festival (www.mudgeewine.com.au) in September and the UnWINEd in the Riverina Festival (www.unwined-riverina.com) held in Griffith in early June.

👉 Tours

NSW offers tours to suit all tastes and budgets: wineries, whale watching, bushwalking, Aboriginal heritage, surfing and more.

For details, look for listings under the Tours headings in destination sections throughout this chapter.

Seasonal Work

Most seasonal work is available in autumn, when the fruit and grapes harvests occur. For information about working in orchards and vineyards see p201, p236, p242) and p194. For information about cotton jobs in Narrabri see p196.

In winter, there are plenty of jobs available in the snowfields of the Snowy Mountains (see p225).

The Australian Government's **Harvest Trail** (☑1800 062 332; www.jobsearch.gov.au/harvesttrail) is an excellent resource for job hunters.

ℹ️ Getting There & Around

By car and motorcycle, you'll probably reach NSW via the Hume Hwy (Rte 31) if you're coming from the south, or via the Pacific Hwy (Rte 1) if you're coming from the north. The Princes Hwy heads south from Sydney along the state's southern coast.

AIR

Sydney Airport (code: SYD; Map p88; www.sydneyairport.com.au) is the main gateway for most visitors to Australia and is also the country's major domestic hub.

Qantas (☑13 13 13; www.qantas.com.au), **Jetstar** (☑13 15 38; www.jetstar.com.au), **Virgin Australia** (☑13 67 89; www.virginaustralia.com) and **Tiger Airways** (☑03-9335 3033; www.tigerairways.com/au/en) have frequent flights to/from Sydney. Qantas and smaller airlines, including **Regional Express** (Rex; ☑13 17 13; www.regionalexpress.com.au), fly to rural destinations throughout NSW.

BUS

Bus is the major form of transport to most towns in NSW. If you want to make multistop trips, look for cheap stopover deals rather than buying separate tickets. In remote areas school buses may be the only public-transport option; the drivers will usually pick you up, but they're not obliged to. Note that fares purchased online are marginally cheaper than over-the-counter tickets.

Bus companies servicing NSW (usually to/from Sydney) include the following:

Australia Wide (☑02-9516 1300; www.austwidecoaches.com.au) Orange and Bathurst

Busways (☑02-9625 8900; www.busways.com.au) Central Coast

Firefly (☑1300 730 740; www.fireflyexpress.com.au) Wagga Wagga, Albury, Melbourne and Adelaide

Greyhound (☑1300 GREYHOUND/1300 4739 46863; www.greyhound.com.au) Canberra, Melbourne, Tamworth and Byron Bay

Murrays (☑13 22 51; www.murrays.com.au) Canberra and the South Coast

Port Stephens Coaches (☑02-4982 2926; www.pscoaches.com.au) Newcastle and Nelson Bay

Premier (☑13 34 10; www.premierms.com.au) Coffs Harbour, Byron Bay, Brisbane and Cairns

TRAIN

CountryLink (☑13 22 32; www.countrylink.info), the state rail service, will take you to many sizeable towns in NSW, in conjunction with connecting buses. You need to book in advance by phone, online or in person at one of Sydney's CountryLink Travel Centres – these are listed on its website. CountryLink offers 1st- and economy-class tickets, as well as a quota of discount and multistop tickets: the Backtracker Pass, only available to international visitors, offers unlimited travel on the CountryLink network, including the Gold Coast, Tamworth and Albury, from $275 for one month.

CityRail (☑13 15 00; www.cityrail.info), the Sydney metropolitan service, runs frequent commuter-style trains south through Wollongong to Bomaderry; west through the Blue Mountains to Katoomba and Lithgow; north to Newcastle; and southwest through the Southern Highlands to Goulburn. For train information, visit the helpful **CityRail Information Booth** (Circular Quay; ⏰9.05am-4.50pm).

See p57 for information about discounted travel on public transport in Sydney and its surrounds.

SYDNEY

POP 4.5 MILLION

Sydney is the capital that every other Australian city loves to hate, but what that really means is that they all want to be just like her: sun-kissed, sophisticated and supremely self-confident. Built around one of the most beautiful natural harbours in the world, she has three of Australia's major icons – the Harbour Bridge, Opera House and Bondi Beach – and her attractions definitely don't stop there. This is the country's oldest, largest and most diverse city; home to magnificent museums, even more magnificent beaches and an edgy multiculturalism that injects colour and vitality into her inner neighbourhoods and outer suburbs.

Two Days

Start your first day by exploring **Circular Quay** and then follow the harbourside walkway to the **Art Gallery of NSW**. That night, enjoy a performance at the **Opera House**.

Next day, board a ferry and sail through the Heads to **Manly**, where you can swim at the beach, have a long lunch or brave the 10km Manly Scenic Walkway. That night, head to fashionable **Surry Hills** for drinks and dinner.

Four Days

On day three, energise yourself with yum cha in **Chinatown** before catching a ferry to genteel **Balmain** or shopping in pretty **Paddington**.

On day four, it's time to spend the day soaking up the sun and scene at **Bondi** – be sure to take the Coogee Clifftop Walk to Coogee and then make your way back to Bondi for a sunset drink at **Icebergs Dining Room & Bar**.

One Week

With a week, you can spare a couple of days to visit the majestic **Blue Mountains**, fitting in a full day of bushwalking before rewarding yourself with a gourmet dinner. Back in Sydney, get out on the water on a **yacht**, explore **The Rocks** or take a tour of **Sydney Harbour National Park**. On your last night, explore infamous **Kings Cross**.

◉ Sights

Sydney will keep you busy. If you plan on seeing an exceptional number of museums, attractions and tours, check out the discount passes offered by **Australian Travel Specialists** (ATS; ☑1800 355 537; www.atstravel.com.au; ticket booths at Wharf 6, Circular Quay & Harbourside Shopping Centre, Darling Harbour). These include the **See Sydney & Beyond Pass** (with/without travel on public transport adult from $183/149, child $122/109) – but be sure to work out whether purchasing the pass really will save you money. Other discount cards include the **Explore 4 Pass** (adult/child $50/30), which gives access to the Sydney Aquarium, Sydney Tower, Oceanworld in Manly and Sydney Wildlife World; and the excellent **Ticket Through Time** (☑02-8239 2211; www.hht.net.au/visiting/ticket_through_time; adult/concession & child $30/15), which gives access to 11 properties opened to the public by the Historic Houses Trust.

The vast majority of sights and museums in Sydney have good disabled access.

SYDNEY HARBOUR

Stretching 20km inland from the South Pacific Ocean to the mouth of the Parramatta River, this magnificent natural harbour is the city's shimmering soul and the focus of every visitor's stay. Providing a serene and picture-perfect backdrop to Sydney's fast-paced urban lifestyle, the harbour's beaches, coves, bays, islands and wildlife-filled pockets of national park offer locals innumerable options for recreation, relaxation and rejuvenation. Exploring this vast, visually arresting area by ferry (p121) is one of Sydney's great joys.

Forming the gateway to the harbour from the ocean are **North Head** (Map p66) and **South Head** (Map p66). The former fishing village of **Watsons Bay** (Map p66) nestles on South Head's harbour side, and the city's favourite day-trip destination, **Manly** (Map p66), occupies a promontory straddling harbour and ocean near North Head. Into the harbour and roughly equidistant between the heads is the North Shore's **Middle Head** (Map p66), characterised by sheltered coves and upmarket residential suburbs.

The focal point of the inner harbour and the city's major transport hub is **Circular Quay** (Map p70), home to one of the city's flamboyant visual signatures, the Sydney Opera House. From here, you are able to access the central business district and catch ferries to destinations along both shores of the harbour and to some of the harbour islands (see p65).

Sydney Harbour National Park   NATURE RESERVE

This national park (Map p66) protects scattered pockets of harbourside bushland incorporating walking tracks, scenic lookouts,

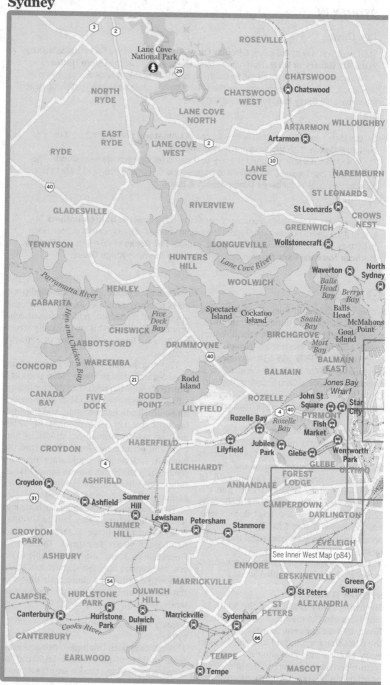

See Inner West Map (p84)

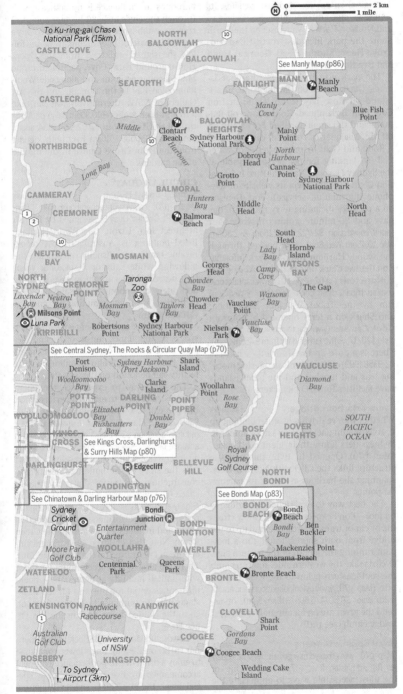

0 — 2 km
0 — 1 mile

To Ku-ring-gai Chase
National Park (15km)

NORTH
BALGOWLAH
10
BALGOWLAH
CASTLE COVE
SEAFORTH
FAIRLIGHT
CASTLECRAG
See Manly Map (p86)
MANLY
Manly
Beach
CLONTARF
Manly
Cove
Blue Fish
Point
BALGOWLAH
HEIGHTS
Middle
Clontarf
Beach
Sydney Harbour
National Park
Manly
Point
NORTHBRIDGE
10
Harbour
Dobroyd
Head
North
Harbour
Long Bay
Grotto
Point
Cannae
Point
Sydney Harbour
National Park
CAMMERAY
BALMORAL
Hunters
Bay
Middle
Head
North
Head
CREMORNE
1
2
Balmoral
Beach
South
Head
10
Georges
Head
Lady
Bay
Hornby
Island
NEUTRAL
BAY
MOSMAN
WATSONS
BAY
Camp
Cove
NORTH
SYDNEY
CREMORNE
POINT
Taronga
Zoo
Chowder
Bay
The Gap
Lavender
Bay
Neutral
Bay
Mosman
Bay
Chowder
Head
Watsons
Bay
Milsons Point
Taylors
Bay
Luna Park
KIRRIBILLI
Robertsons
Point
Sydney Harbour
National Park
Nielsen
Park
Vaucluse
Point
Vaucluse
Bay
See Central Sydney, The Rocks & Circular Quay Map (p70)
Fort
Denison
Sydney Harbour
(Port Jackson)
Shark
Island
VAUCLUSE
Woolloomooloo
Bay
Clarke
Island
Woollahra
Point
Diamond
Bay
POTTS
POINT
DARLING
POINT
POINT
PIPER
Rose
Bay
WOOLLOOMOOLOO
Elizabeth
Bay
Double
Bay
Rushcutters
Bay
ROSE
BAY
DOVER
HEIGHTS
SOUTH
PACIFIC
OCEAN
KINGS
CROSS
See Kings Cross, Darlinghurst
& Surry Hills Map (p80)
Royal
Sydney
Golf Course
DARLINGHURST
Edgecliff
BELLEVUE
HILL
NORTH
BONDI
PADDINGTON
See Chinatown & Darling Harbour Map (p76)
See Bondi Map (p83)
Sydney
Cricket
Ground
Bondi
Junction
BONDI
BEACH
Bondi
Beach
Entertainment
Quarter
BONDI
JUNCTION
Ben
Buckler
Moore Park
Golf Club
WOOLLAHRA
WAVERLEY
Bondi
Bay
Mackenzies Point
Centennial
Park
Queens
Park
Tamarama Beach
WATERLOO
BRONTE
Bronte Beach
ZETLAND
KENSINGTON
Randwick
Racecourse
RANDWICK
CLOVELLY
1
Shark
Point
Australian
Golf Club
University
of NSW
COOGEE
Gordons
Bay
ROSEBERY
KINGSFORD
Coogee Beach
Wedding Cake
Island
To Sydney
Airport (3km)

Aboriginal engravings and historic sites. Its southern side incorporates South Head and Nielsen Park in Vaucluse; on the North Shore the park includes North Head, Dobroyd Head, Middle Head, Georges Head and Bradleys Head.

The park also includes five harbour islands: Clark Island off Darling Point, Shark Island off Rose Bay, Rodd Island in Iron Cove near Birkenhead, Goat Island off Balmain, and the small, fortified Fort Denison off Mrs Macquaries Point. All can be visited – Rodd and Goat by private vessel or water taxi ($7 landing fee per person payable at the Sydney Harbour National Park Information Centre (p119) or via its website or telephone information service); Fort Denison on a package including ferry transport, day pass and 30-minute guided history tour (adult/concession $27/22; ☺12.15pm & 2.30pm, also 10.45am Wed-Sun), also booked through the Sydney Harbour National Park Information Centre; Clark on a two-hour Aboriginal culture tour (☎02-9206 1111; www.captaincook.com.au/tribal; adult/child $60/40; ☺Wed-Sun) run by the Tribal Warriors Association; and Shark on a ferry operated by Captain Cook Cruises (www.captaincook.com.au; adult/child $20/17; ☺five ferries daily from 9.45am-3pm). There is a cafe and restaurant (☎bookings 02-9358 1999) on Fort Denison offering morning teas and lunches and the other islands have facilities for BYO picnickers.

Sydney Harbour Bridge   LANDMARK
Whether they're driving over it, climbing up it, rollerblading across it or sailing under it, Sydneysiders adore their 'giant coathanger' (Map p70). Opened in 1932, this majestic structure links the CBD with North Sydney, spanning the harbour at one of its narrowest points.

The best way to experience the bridge is on foot – don't expect much of a view crossing by car or train. Staircases climb up to the bridge from both shores, leading to a footpath running the length of the eastern side. Cyclists take the western side. You can climb the southeastern pylon to the Pylon Lookout (Map p70; www.pylonlookout.com.au; adult/child/senior $9.50/4/6.50; ☺10am-5pm), or ascend the great arc on an adrenaline-charged bridge climb (see p101).

Royal Botanic Gardens   GARDEN
(Map p70; www.rbgsyd.nsw.gov.au; Mrs Macquaries Rd; admission free; ☺7am-sunset) One of the most accessible ways to appreciate the

harbour's magnificence is by taking a walk through the city's lush, 30-hectare botanical reserve, established in 1816 as the colony's vegetable patch. The highlight is to follow the signed walkways from the Opera House around Farm Cove, past picturesque Mrs Macquaries Point and alongside Woolloomooloo Bay to the Domain and the Art Gallery of NSW. Alternatively you can take a free guided walk (☺10.30am daily) or Aboriginal Heritage Tour (☎02-9231 8134; adult/concession $28/13; ☺10am Fri); both depart from the Palm Grove Centre in the middle of the gardens.

CIRCULAR QUAY

Sydney Opera House   LANDMARK
(Map p70; www.sydneyoperahouse.com; Bennelong Pt, Circular Quay E) Designed by Danish architect Jørn Utzon, this World Heritage listed-building is Australia's most recognisable landmark. Visually referencing the billowing white sails of a seagoing yacht (but described by some local wags as more accurately resembling the sexual congress of turtles), it's a commanding presence on Circular Quay.

The complex comprises five performance spaces hosting dance, music, opera and theatre – the most spectacular is the Concert Hall. Program details and an online booking facility can be found on the website.

The best way to experience the opera house is, of course, to attend a performance, but you can also take a guided tour (☎02-9250 7250). The one-hour Essential Tour (adult/concession $35/24.50, cheaper if booked in advance online; ☺every 30 minutes 9am-5pm) is an interactive audiovisual presentation that tells the story of the building's design and construction and visits one performance space. The two-hour Backstage Tour ($155; ☺daily at 7am) gives access to areas normally reserved for performers and production crews and includes a breakfast in the Green Room. Note that children 12 years and under are not permitted on the Backstage Tour. There are also special access tours for those with limited mobility at noon daily – bookings are essential for this and for the Backstage Tour. To purchase tickets on the spot, go to the Guided Tours desk in the Box Office Foyer.

Locals and visitors alike flock to the Opera Bar (p112) on the building's lower concourse to enjoy a drink or pre-performance bar meal accompanied by live jazz. And for a special meal, the supremely stylish Guillaume at Bennelong (p108) is hard to beat. Both venues offer extraordinary harbour views.

FREE **Museum of Contemporary Art**   MUSEUM
(Map p70; www.mca.com.au; 140 George St; admission free except for touring exhibitions; ☺10am-5pm) This spectacularly sited showcase for Australian and international contemporary art occupies a stately art deco building fronting Circular Quay West – the view from its ground-floor cafe is an artwork in itself. The constantly changing exhibition program has a particularly strong multimedia focus, but painting and sculpture also feature prominently. The annual 'Primavera' show held in spring showcases Australian visual artists under the age of 35 and offers a fascinating survey of the local art scene.

Customs House   LANDMARK
(Map p70; www.cityofsydney.nsw.gov.au/library; 31 Alfred St; admission free; ☺8am-midnight Mon-Fri, 10am-midnight Sat, noon-5pm Sun, library 10am-7pm Mon-Fri, 11am-4pm Sat & Sun) Opposite the unforgivably dishevelled Circular Quay transport hub, this handsome 1885 building reopened to the public in 2005 after a major renovation. It now houses a branch of the Sydney City Libraries where it's possible to access the internet via free wi-fi or on the library's own terminals ($2 per 30 minutes plus initial purchase of $1 access card), read a huge selection of international newspapers and magazines, use toilet facilities and admire a 1:500 model of Sydney displayed under the foyer's glass floor. The upmarket Café Sydney occupies the building's top floor, but its harbour view is considerably more impressive than its menu, so locals tend to patronise the ground-floor indoor/outdoor **Young Alfred Café** (cnr Alfred & Young Sts, Circular Quay; pizzas $24-32, pastas $22-26; ☺7am-11pm Mon-Sat) instead.

THE ROCKS
The site of Sydney's first European settlement, this historically rich enclave at the foot of the Harbour Bridge's southern pylon has evolved unrecognisably from the days when its residents sloshed through open sewers and squalid alleyways. Here, sailors, whalers and larrikins boozed and brawled shamelessly in countless harbourside pubs and nearly as many brothels and opium dens.

The Rocks remained a commercial and maritime hub until shipping services left Circular Quay in the late 1800s. A bubonic plague outbreak in 1900 continued the decline. Construction of the Harbour Bridge in the 1920s brought further demolition, entire streets disappearing under the bridge's southern approach.

It wasn't until the 1970s that The Rocks' cultural and architectural heritage was recognised. The ensuing tourism-driven redevelopment saved many old buildings, but has turned the area east of the bridge highway into a tourist trap where kitsch cafes and shops hocking stuffed koalas and ersatz didgeridoos reign supreme. Nevertheless, it's a fascinating area to explore on foot – see our walking tour (p72).

Cadmans Cottage (Map p70; www.national parks.nsw.gov.au; 110 George St; ☺9.30am-4.30pm Mon-Fri, 10am-4.30pm Sat & Sun), built on a buried beach, is Sydney's oldest house (1816). Water police detained criminals here in the 1840s and it was later converted into a home for retired sea captains; these days it functions as an information centre for the NSW National Parks and Wildlife Service.

The excellent **Rocks Discovery Museum** (Map p70; www.therocks.com; 2-8 Kendall Lane, The Rocks; admission free; ☺10am-5pm) digs deep into the area's artefact-laden history and provides interactive insights into the lives of its people, including the original Indigenous inhabitants.

Further up the hill is the **Susannah Place Museum** (Map p70; www.hht.net.au; 58-64 Gloucester St, The Rocks; 1hr guided tour adult/child & concession $8/4; ☺2-6pm Mon-Fri, 10am-6pm Sat & Sun, to 5pm Jun-Aug), a row of four terrace houses and a corner shop that has survived largely unchanged since it was built in 1844. After watching a documentary about the people who lived here (some until as recently as 1990), a guide will take you through the terraces, which are decorated to reflect different periods in their histories.

Beyond the **Argyle Cut** (Map p70), an impressive tunnel excavated by convicts, is **Millers Point**, a charming district of early colonial homes; stroll here to enjoy everything The Rocks is not. **Argyle Place** (Map p70) is an English-style village green overlooked by **Garrison Church** (Map p70), Australia's oldest house of worship (1848).

The Italianate **Sydney Observatory** (Map p70; www.sydneyobservatory.com; Watson Rd; free entry to building and grounds, daytime show adult/

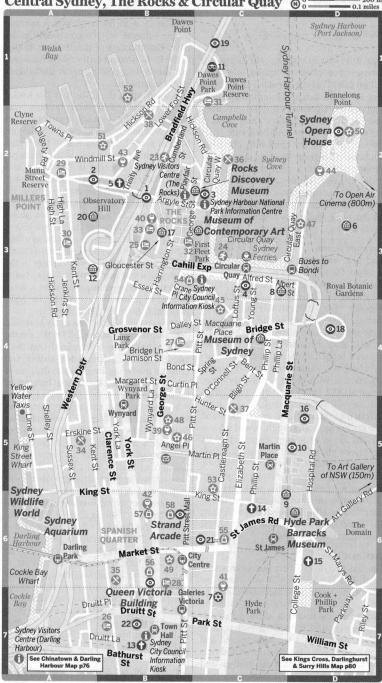

SYDNEY & NEW SOUTH WALES SYDNEY

child & concession $7/5, night viewings adult/child/concession $15/10/12; ◎10am-5pm), built from Sydney sandstone and sporting a copper-domed roof, sits atop Observatory Hill. You can visit the building and grounds, enjoy a celestial show in the 3-D theatre or see the stars and planets through the telescopes at night (note that the hours of night viewings vary and that booking for these is essential). Sessions for the daytime shows are at 2.30pm and 3.30pm on weekdays and at 11am, noon, 2.30pm and 3.30pm on weekends.

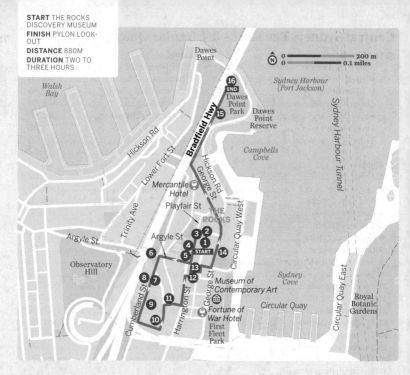

START THE ROCKS
DISCOVERY MUSEUM
FINISH PYLON LOOK-
OUT
DISTANCE 880M
DURATION TWO TO
THREE HOURS

Walking Tour
The Rocks

❯ This area was where European settlers landed on 26 January 1788, and it remains the first port of call for most visitors to Sydney. Start this walk at the ❶ **The Rocks Discovery Museum**, where the exhibits offer an excellent overview of the area's rich and often disreputable history. From the museum, walk north up Kendall Lane to its junction with ❷ **Mill Lane**, named after a steam-powered flour mill that was once located here. The mill was demolished around 1920, one of many 18th- and 19th-century buildings in The Rocks to suffer the same fate during the 20th century. Turn left (west) into Mill Lane and walk up to ❸ **The Rocks Square** on the corner of Playfair St where, in 1973, local residents, conservationists, social activists and members of trade unions clashed with police and put themselves in the path of bulldozers that were demolishing structures on this site. The protesters were intent on preserving the streets and buildings that had been home to local families for genera-

tions, and their fight became known in the national media as the 'Battle for The Rocks'. In 1975, the NSW State Government, which had initially backed the developers, bowed to popular opinion and declared that all remaining historic buildings north of the Cahill Expressway were to be retained, conserved and restored. In that same year, the federal parliament passed the Australian Heritage Commission Act, protecting built heritage across the nation – many believe that the fight to save The Rocks led to the development of a national heritage consciousness.

Turn left (south) into Playfair St and walk past the ❹ **Argyle Terrace** (1877) and ❺ **Argyle Stores** (1828–1913) on your right. Then turn right and walk west up Argyle St to the impressive ❻ **Argyle Cut**, a road cut through a sandstone ridge of rock to allow access between Circular Quay and the port at Millers Point. It was created between the 1830s and 1860s, initially by convicts and later by qualified stonemasons. The sandstone excavated here was used to construct local buildings, including parts of the Argyle Stores.

Turn left into Cumberland St until you see the 1914 **7** **Australian Hotel** on the corner of Gloucester St. The **8** **King George V Recreation Centre** opposite the hotel was designed by Lippmann Associates and opened in 1998; wedged between the historic street and the boundary wall of the elevated freeway, it's an interesting and popular contemporary architectural intervention in this historic precinct (look for the 1960s community mural from a previous structure that the architects were briefed to retain).

Continue along Cumberland St. On the left-hand side of the road is the newly built, ecofriendly **9** **Sydney Harbour YHA**, an impressive building that incorporates an archaeological dig site. In 1994, the remains of over 30 houses, two laneways, shops and pubs were excavated here, along with over 750,000 artefacts. All that remained after a huge demolition project in the early decades of the 20th century, the archaeological remains are preserved on the ground floor of the hostel and are open to the public. A number of the artefacts are on display at The Rocks Discovery Museum.

Veer left into Longs Lane, which will take you through to Gloucester St. On the northwest corner of the lane is **10** **Jobbins Terrace**, constructed between 1855 and 1857. A handsome row of housing, it is one of only two extant Greek Revival–style terraces in NSW. The modest 1844 terrace now functioning as the **11** **Susannah Place Museum**, opposite, presents an interesting contrast.

From the museum's shop, which sells a quirky range of Australiana souvenirs, walk down the stairs in Cumberland Pl to Harrington St, then veer left and walk north down to **12** **Suez Canal**, a narrow laneway on the right-hand side. In the 19th century, this was one of the most infamous locations in Sydney, frequented by prostitutes and members of the infamous 'Rocks Push'

larrikin gang that ruled the area from the 1870s to the end of the 1890s. Members were known for assault and battery against police and pedestrians; one of their tried and trusted techniques was to have female members of the gang entice drunks and seamen into dark areas to be assaulted and robbed.

Turn into Suez Canal and then left into the Well Courtyard, once used for dog baiting and cock fighting. Then walk down the steps to stone-paved Greenway Lane, named after famous convict architect Francis Greenway, who lived nearby on the corner of Argyle and George Sts.

Exit onto Argyle St; the building at No 45–47 is **13** **Gannon House**, built in 1839 as a residence and carpentry store by former convict Michael Gannon; he was known for the quality of his coffins. It's now home to a patisserie and a gallery selling Aboriginal and Torres Strait Islander art.

Turn right, towards the harbour, and walk down to George St. In the park opposite is diminutive **14** **Cadmans Cottage**, built in 1815–16 for John Cadman, the Government Coxswain. It is the only remaining element of the city's original dockyard precinct, and is Sydney's oldest house.

From here you can walk north to Dawes Point, stopping at the **15** **Dawes Point Battery**, where, in 1788, Second Lieutenant William Dawes built and operated the colony's first observatory; for a fictionalised account of his time in the colony, read Kate Grenville's *The Lieutenant*. In front of the battery, on the southeastern pylon of the Sydney Harbour Bridge, is the **16** **Pylon Lookout**, the end of this tour. After enjoying the view, head back to George St for a drink at the Mercantile Hotel (1915) or Fortune of War pub. Alternatively, make your way to the impressive Museum of Contemporary Art, where you can check out the exhibits or relax over lunch or a drink at the terrace cafe, which overlooks Circular Quay.

The old military hospital building nearby houses the state headquarters of the National Trust and is home to the trust's **SH Ervin Gallery** (Map p70; www.nsw.nationaltrust.org.au/ervin.html; Watson Rd; adult/child over 11 years $7/5; ◷11am-5pm Tue-Sun), which exhibits historical and contemporary Australian art.

The wharves around Dawes Point are rapidly emerging from prolonged decay. Walsh Bay's Pier 4 houses the renowned Sydney Theatre Company (p117) and several other performance troupes. The impressive Sydney Theatre (p117) is across the road.

CITY EAST

Narrow lanes lead southeast from Circular Quay up the hill towards Sydney's historic parliament precinct on Macquarie St.

Justice & Police Museum   MUSEUM

(Map p70; www.hht.net.au; cnr Albert & Phillip Sts; adult/child & concession $8/4; ◷10am-5pm) Occupying the old Water Police Station (1858) building opposite Circular Quay East, this small museum documents the city's dark and disreputable past through a constantly changing series of exhibitions.

Museum of Sydney   MUSEUM

(Map p70; www.hht.net.au; cnr Bridge & Phillip Sts; adult/child/family $10/5/20; ◷9.30am-5pm) Janet Laurence and Fiona Foley's evocative *Edge of the Trees* sculptural installation occupies pride of place in the forecourt of this sleek museum, marking the site of first contact between the British colonisers and Sydney's original inhabitants, the Gadigal people. It's one of a number of important artworks here, including Gordon Bennett's 1991 painting *Possession Island*, which greets visitors as they enter the foyer and presents a very different interpretation of Captain Cook's 1770 arrival and claim of British sovereignty to that presented in most history books. Built on the site of Sydney's first Government House (1788), the foundations of which can be spotted through panels of glass in the floor, the museum also offers a modest array of permanent exhibits documenting Sydney's early colonial history – brought to life through oral histories, artefacts and state-of-the-art interactive installations – as well as a changing exhibition program in its two temporary galleries.

Macquarie Street   HISTORIC PRECINCT

A swathe of splendid sandstone colonial buildings graces this street, defining the central city's eastern edge. Many of these buildings were commissioned by Lachlan Macquarie, the first NSW governor with a vision of Sydney beyond its convict origins. He enlisted convict architect Francis Greenway to help realise his plans, and together they set a gold standard for architectural excellence that the city has – alas – never since managed to replicate.

FREE **Government House** (Map p70; ☏02-9931 5222; www.hht.net.au; ◷10.30am-3pm Fri-Sun, grounds 10am-4pm daily), built between 1837 and 1845 in the Gothic Revival style, is just off Macquarie St in the Royal Botanic Gardens. The interior can only be visited on a tour, and bookings are essential.

At the top of Bridge St, the **Sydney Conservatorium of Music** (Map p70; www.usyd.edu.au/conmusic; Macquarie St) was the Greenway-designed stables and servants' quarters built to service an earlier Government House. Governor Macquarie was usurped as governor before the house could be finished, partly because of the project's extravagance.

Further south, the **State Library of NSW** (Map p70; www.sl.nsw.gov.au; ◷9am-8pm Mon-Thu, 9am-5pm Fri, 10am-5pm Sat & Sun) holds over five million tomes and hosts innovative exhibitions in its galleries. If you are travelling with a laptop, the State Reference Library is a great place to access free wi-fi – just ask for the day's password at the desk.

Next to the library are the deep verandas, formal colonnades and ochre tones of the twin 1816 **Mint** (Map p70; www.hht.net.au; admission free; ◷9am-5pm Mon-Fri) and **Parliament House** (Map p70; www.parliament.nsw.gov.au; admission free; ◷9am-5pm Mon-Fri) buildings, originally wings of the infamous Rum Hospital, built by two Sydney merchants and the colony's principal surgeon in 1816 in return for a three-year monopoly on the rum trade. At the rear of the Mint building is one of central Sydney's most thoughtful and attractive contemporary architectural interventions, the headquarters of the Historic Houses Trust, designed by FJMT Architects and built in 2002.

TOP CHOICE **Hyde Park Barracks Museum** (Map p70; www.hht.net.au; adult/child/family $10/5/20; ◷9.30am-5pm) is one of two nearby Greenway gems. Built in 1819, the barracks functioned as quarters for Anglo-Irish convicts (aka Oz pioneers) from 1819 to 1848, an immigrant depot (1848–86) and government courts (1887–1979) before its current incarnation as a museum offering an absolutely

The most recent Australian additions to the World Heritage List are 11 sites that are collectively known as the **Australian Convict Sites** (www.environment.gov.au/heritage/places/world/convict-sites). Four of these sites are in or around Sydney: Old Government House and Domain in Parramatta (p97); Hyde Park Barracks in Sydney (p74), Cockatoo Island at the junction of the Parramatta and Lane Cove Rivers in Sydney; and the Old Great North Road (p125), which you can visit on your way to the Hunter Valley.

These sites are among a number in NSW dating back to early colonial times, including examples in Port Macquarie, Norfolk Island and Windsor.

fascinating insight into everyday convict life through installations and exhibits.

Close by, the Greenway-designed **St James' Church** (Map p70), built in 1819, is Sydney's oldest church.

AROUND HYDE PARK

At the southern end of Macquarie St, this much-loved civic park (Map p70) has a grand avenue of trees and a series of delightful fountains. Its dignified **Anzac Memorial** (Map p80; www.rslnsw.com.au; admission free; ⊙9am-5pm) has an interior dome studded with one star for each of the 120,000 NSW citizens who served in WWI, and the pines near the entrance grew from seeds gathered at Gallipoli. **St Mary's Cathedral** (Map p70) overlooks the park from the east, while the 1878 **Great Synagogue** (Map p70; www.greatsynagogue.org.au; 187a Elizabeth St; adult/child & senior $8/5; ⊙tours noon Tue & Thu) is located off the park's western flank.

TOP CHOICE **Art Gallery of NSW**   ART GALLERY
(off Map p70; www.artgallery.nsw.gov.au; Art Gallery Rd, The Domain; admission free, varied costs for touring exhibitions; ⊙10am-5pm Thu-Tue, till 9pm Wed) Highlights at this impressive gallery include 19th- and 20th-century Australian art and Aboriginal and Torres Strait Islander art. There's also an excellent program of touring exhibitions from interstate and overseas. The controversial, much-discussed **Archibald Prize** (www.thearchibaldprize.com.au) exhibits here annually, with portraits of the famous and not-so-famous bringing out the art critic in everyone.

While here, consider having a drink in the cafe or eating in the restaurant, which has a lovely view across to Woolloomooloo Bay. See the website for details about guided tours, lectures, film screenings and the kids program.

Australian Museum   MUSEUM
(Map p80; www.australianmuseum.net.au; 6 College St; adult/child/concession $12/6/8; ⊙9.30am-5pm) Occupying a prominent position opposite Hyde Park on the corner of William St, this natural history museum stuffed its first animal just 40 years after the First Fleet dropped anchor and its curatorial philosophy and exhibits don't appear to have changed much in the intervening centuries. The only exceptions are the changing exhibits in the Indigenous Australians gallery, which often showcase contemporary Aboriginal issues and art.

CENTRAL SYDNEY

Sydney lacks a true civic centre, but **Martin Place** (Map p70) comes close. This grand pedestrian mall extends from Macquarie St to George St, and is lined with monumental financial buildings and the Victorian colonnaded general post office. There's a cenotaph commemorating Australia's war dead, an amphitheatre for lunchtime entertainment and plenty of places to sit and watch the weekday crowds. On weekends it's as quiet as a graveyard.

The 1874 **Town Hall** (Map p70) is a few blocks south of Martin Pl on the corner of George and Druitt Sts. The elaborate chamber room and concert hall inside match the fabulously ornate exterior. The neighbouring Anglican **St Andrew's Cathedral** (Map p70), built around the same time, is Australia's oldest cathedral. Next to St Andrew's, occupying an entire city block, the Queen Victoria Building (p118) is Sydney's most sumptuous shopping complex and a real highlight. Running a close second is the elegant Strand Arcade (p118) between Pitt St Mall and George St, which has a strong representation of Australian designer fashion. The newly opened Westfield Sydney (p118) is the city's glitziest shopping mall and has an excellent food hall on its 5th level. It's

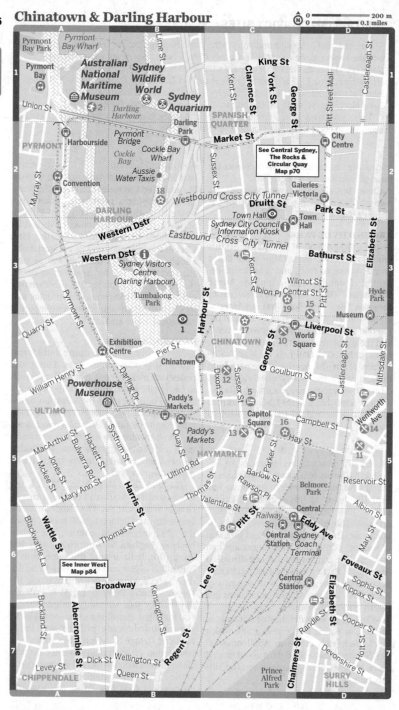

also the access point for **Sydney Tower** (Map p70; 86-100 Market St; adult/child/concession $25/15/20; ☺9am-10.30pm), where you can enjoy a stunning 360-degree view of the city.

Breathing life into the southwestern zone are Sydney's modest **Spanish Quarter** (Map p76) and thriving **Chinatown** (Map p76), an always-busy district of restaurants, shops and aroma-filled alleyways around Dixon St. Chinatown parties hard during Chinese New Year in late January/early February – streets throng with sideshows, digitally accompanied musicians and stalls selling everything from good-luck tokens to black-sesame ice-cream burgers (fear not: seeing jaunty, fire-breathing paper dragons after eating these is not a hallucinogenic effect).

DARLING HARBOUR & AROUND
Cockle Bay on the city's western edge was once an industrial dockland full of factories, warehouses and shipyards. These days it's a sprawling and exceptionally tacky waterfront tourist development (www.darlinghar-bour.com), the only redeeming features of which are an excellent aquarium and maritime museum.

Visitors are confronted with an architectural spoil of grotesque flyovers, an ugly convention centre, chain hotels and expensive eateries and shops – none will entice you to linger. If you're keen to find somewhere for a coffee or meal, we suggest skipping the overpriced and underwhelming outlets on **Cockle Bay Wharf** (Map p76) and **King St Wharf** (Map p70), instead making your way

to **Jones Bay Wharf** (Map p66), home to the excellent Flying Fish restaurant (p111) and reliable **Café Morso**. Both have great views.

Alternatively, stroll across the restored **Pyrmont Bridge** (Map p76), which cuts over this mess with a timeless dignity. It leads to **Pyrmont** (Map p66), home of the Sydney Fish Market.

Darling Harbour and Pyrmont are serviced by ferry, monorail and Metro Light Rail (MLR).

Sydney Aquarium AQUARIUM
(Map p70; www.sydneyaquarium.com.au; Aquarium Pier; adult/child $35/18; ☺9am-8pm) Celebrating the richness of Australian marine life, this phenomenally popular tourist attraction has three 'oceanariums' moored in the harbour: sharks, rays and humungous fish are in one; Sydney Harbour marine life and seals in the other two. Don't miss the kaleidoscopic colours of the Great Barrier Reef exhibit, platypuses and crocodiles at the Southern and Northern Rivers exhibits, and the cute penguins in the Southern Oceans section.

Sydney Wildlife World ZOO
(Map p70; www.sydneywildlifeworld.com.au; Aquarium Pier; adult/child $35/18; ☺9am-5pm) This indoor wildlife zoo next to the aquarium offers the chance to get up close to local critters, including koalas, red kangaroos, rock wallabies and scrub pythons. The displays of ants and other industrious bugs are unexpectedly intriguing.

CHAMPAGNE AT SUNSET

Instead of paying the steep admission price to visit the Sydney Tower's viewing platform, make your way to its Moët & Chandon Bar (☎02-8223 3800; www.sydneytower restaurant.com.au; flute of Moët & 4 canapés $26; ☺from 4.30pm). The view is the same, but for roughly the same amount of money you'll also get a glass of champagne and some canapés, enabling you to enjoy the sunset in style. Note: booking is advised and a strict dress code applies (no trainers, shorts or flip-flops). Sunset is around 5pm in winter and 7.30pm in summer.

Also here are the 360 Restaurant (2/3-course dinner excl drinks $85/90) and Sydney Tower Buffet (meals $49.50-85), both of which – like the bar – rotate 360 degrees over one hour.

Australian National Maritime Museum
MUSEUM

(Map p76; www.anmm.gov.au; 2 Murray St; general admission free; ☺9.30am-5pm) Beneath an Ut-zonlike roof, this museum examines Australia's inextricable relationship with the sea through exhibits that are arranged thematically. Exhibitions range from Aboriginal canoes to surf culture and the Navy. You'll need a Big Ticket (adult/child & concession $32/17, cheaper limited options available) to explore the destroyer HMAS *Vampire*, submarine HMAS *Onslow*, tall ship *James Craig* and replica of Captain Cook's *Endeavour*, all of which are docked here.

Powerhouse Museum
MUSEUM

(Map p76; www.powerhousemuseum.com; 500 Harris St, Ultimo; adult/child under 4/child 4-15 & student card holders $10/free/5, additional costs for special exhibits; ☺9.30am-5pm) Housed in the former power station for Sydney's defunct tram network, this sensational showcase for science and design is thought by many (including us) to be Australia's best museum. Visitors are encouraged to discover and be inspired by human ingenuity through exhibits that are always thoughtfully curated and often interactive.

Chinese Garden of Friendship
GARDEN

(Map p76; www.chinesegarden.com.au; adult/Australian student & child under 12 $6/3; ☺9.30am-5.30pm) Built according to the balanced principles of yin and yang, this garden is an oasis of tranquillity in otherwise hectic Darling Harbour.

Sydney Fish Market
MARKET

(Map p66; ☎02-9004 1122; www.sydneyfishmarket.com.au; cnr Pyrmont Bridge Rd & Bank St, Pyrmont; ☺7am-4pm) With over 15 million kilograms of seafood shipped through here annually, the city's cavernous fish market is the place to introduce yourself to a bewildering array of mud crabs, Balmain bugs, lobsters, oysters, mullet, rainbow trout and more. There are plenty of fishy restaurants (including an excellent yum cha venue), a deli, a wine centre, a sushi bar and an oyster bar. You can also picnic on the water. This is the world's second-largest largest fish market (after Tokyo) and the early morning auctions are exciting to watch – but the only way you can do so is on a Behind the Scenes Tour (adult/child 6-12 $20/10; ☺6.55-8.30am Mon & Thu). Note that reservations for this tour are essential and participants must wear closed-toe shoes. You can also book yourself in for a cooking class at the Sydney Seafood School (☎02-9004 1111; classes from $85); many of these are conducted by local celebrity chefs.

The market is west of Darling Harbour on Blackwattle Bay; get here on the MLR.

KINGS CROSS

Riding high above the CBD under the big Coca-Cola sign (Map p80) – Sydney's equivalent of LA's iconic Hollywood sign – 'the Cross' is a bizarre, densely populated dichotomy of good and evil. Once home to grand estates and stylish apartments, the neighbourhood took a left turn in the 1930s when wine-soaked intellectuals, artists, musicians, pleasure-seekers and ne'er-do-wells claimed the streets for their own. The neighbourhood's reputation for vice was sealed during the Vietnam War, when American sailors flooded the Cross with a tide of bawdy debauchery.

Today the streets retain an air of seedy hedonism, but along with the strip joints and shabby drinking dens there are classy restaurants, cool bars and boutique hotels. Sometimes the razzle-dazzle has a sideshow appeal;

sometimes walking up Darlinghurst Rd promotes pity. Either way, it's never boring.

The gracious, tree-lined enclaves of Potts Point (Map p66) and Elizabeth Bay have been popular residential enclaves ever since Alexander Macleay, Colonial Secretary of New South Wales, built the Greek revival–style Elizabeth Bay House here between 1835 and 1839. Once set in 54 acres of land, his charming residence overlooks the harbour and is now open to the public as a house museum (www.hht.net.au; 7 Onslow Ave, Elizabeth Bay; adult/concession $8/4; ☉9.30am-4pm Fri-Sun).

Possibly the only word in the world with eight 'o's, Woolloomooloo (Map p66), down McElhone Stairs from the Cross, was once a slum full of drunks and sailors (a fair few of whom were drunken sailors). Things are begrudgingly less pugilistic these days – the pubs are relaxed and Woolloomooloo Wharf is now home to the self-consciously hip BLUE Sydney (p104) and a swathe of upmarket restaurants. Outside the wharf is the famous Harry's Café de Wheels, where generations of Sydneysiders have stopped to sober up over a late-night 'Tiger' (beef pie served with mushy peas, mashed potato and gravy) on the way home from a big night at the Cross.

It's a 15-minute walk to the Cross from the city, or you could hop on a train. Buses 323-7, 324-5 and 333 from the city also pass through here.

INNER EAST
Once the heart of Sydney's entertainment and shopping scenes, Oxford Street (Map p80) is now sadly tawdry. Most shopping action has moved onto side streets such as Glenmore Rd in Paddington and Queen St in Woollahra, while bars and restaurants have migrated to neighbouring Surry Hills (Map p80). Despite this, the area around Taylor Square (Map p80) is still the decadent nucleus for the city's gay community – the Sydney Gay & Lesbian Mardi Gras (p101) famously gyrates through here every February, and gay-centric pubs and clubs do a brisk trade every weekend. To get here from the CBD, walk from Hyde Park or catch bus 378 from Railway Sq or bus 380, 389 or L82 from Circular Quay.

Wedged between Oxford and William Sts, the boho neighbourhood of Darlinghurst is home to cafes, boutique hotels and the Sydney Jewish Museum (Map p80; www.sydneyjewishmuseum.com.au; 148 Darlinghurst Rd; adult/child/concession $10/6/7; ☉10am-4pm Sun-Thu, to 2pm Fri, closed Jewish holidays).

LOCAL KNOWLEDGE

BRIDGET SMYTH – DIRECTOR, DESIGN, CITY OF SYDNEY

Major challenge: working with council to implement the Sustainable Sydney 2030 vision to make Sydney green, global and connected.

Exciting Architectural Project

Surry Hills Library and Community Centre at 405 Crown St by Francis-Jones Morehen Thorp (FJMT) sets a high benchmark in terms of sustainable and excellent design; it's also home to Robert Owen's artwork *Interlude*.

Green Initiatives

Council is building 200km of cycleways to link the city and suburbs (55km separated from traffic), plus dedicated pedestrian precincts. Our 2030 plan includes pedestrianising George St and building a public foreshore walk connecting Glebe with Woolloomooloo.

Arts Programs

I'm really excited by our City Art Program (www.cityofsydney.nsw.gov.au/cityart/). There are so many fabulous works on show in the city's streets, squares and laneways. Three of my favourites are Janet Laurence and Fiona Foley's *Edge of the Trees* (p74), Nigel Helyer's *The Wireless House* in Glebe's Foley Park and Michael Thomas Hill's *Forgotten Songs* in Angel Pl, off Pitt St.

Urban Design Development

Bars and cafes are finally starting to open in the city's laneways. One of my favourites is Grasshopper (p113) in Temperance Lane.

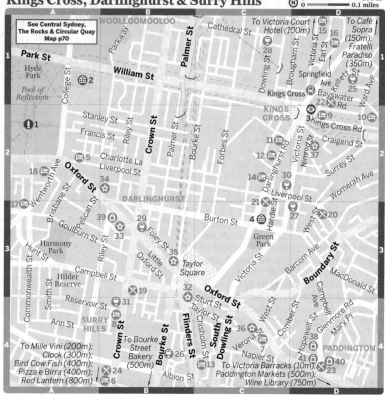

Paddington (Map p66), aka 'Paddo', is an upmarket residential suburb of restored Victorian-era terrace houses, many with attractive iron 'lace' detailing. It's home to one of the city's finest examples of Georgian architecture, **Victoria Barracks** (off Map p80; ☎02-8336 3330; cnr Oxford St & Greens Rd, Paddington). Built between 1840 and 1848, it's still in operation as the headquarters of the Australian Army's Training Command. You can visit on a two-hour guided tour (Thursdays at 10am, $2) or pop into the paraphernalia-packed NSW Army Museum on a Sunday (10am to 4pm, $2). It's a good idea to book for the tour.

The best time to explore Paddington's jacaranda-lined streets and laneways is on Saturday, when the Paddington Market (p120) is held.

FREE **Brett Whiteley Studio** (www.brett whiteley.org; 2 Raper St, Surry Hills; ⊙10am-4pm Sat & Sun) After braving the market's crowds, you can easily wander over to Surry Hills for lunch and a visit to this studio, where works by the talented and famously drug-addicted Sydney artist (1939–1992) are on show. The streets around here are home to a raffish mishmash of style-conscious urbanites and plenty of great pubs – be sure to sink a few schooners while you're in the area. Surry Hills is a short walk east of Central Station or south from Oxford St. Catch bus 301, 302 or 303 from Circular Quay.

Just southeast of Paddington, at the top end of Oxford St, is the 220-hectare **Centennial Park** (Map p66), which has running, cycling, skating and horse-riding tracks, duck ponds, barbecue sites and sports pitches.

Near Moore Park, much of the former Sydney Showgrounds has been converted into the private **Fox Studios**. Nearby are the Aussie Stadium and Sydney Cricket Ground.

EASTERN SUBURBS

Handsome **Rushcutters Bay** (Map p66) is a five-minute walk east of Kings Cross; its harbourside park is a lovely spot for a walk or jog. The eastern suburbs extend out from here – a conservative conglomeration of European sedans, overpriced boutiques and heavily mortgaged waterside mansions. The harbour-hugging New South Head Rd passes through **Double Bay** (Map p66) and **Rose Bay** (Map p66), and then climbs east into the gorgeous enclave of **Vaucluse** (Map p66), where shady **Nielsen Park** is home to one of Sydney's best harbour beaches, complete with a netted swimming enclosure, crescent-shaped stretch of sand, picnic facilities and a popular cafe/restaurant. It's an idyllic spot to spend a day, preferably during the week – crowds are inevitable on weekends.

From the park, you can take an easy 10-minute loop walk along Bottle and Glass Rocks or make your way to the public park in the grounds of nearby **Strickland House**, built in 1856. The harbour views from here are wonderful. Alternatively, you can visit **Vaucluse House** (www.hht.net.au; Wentworth Rd, Vaucluse; adult/child/family $8/4/17; ⊙9.30am-4pm Fri-Sun), an imposing, turreted specimen of Gothic Australiana set in gorgeous gardens. Explorer and political sabre-rattler William Charles Wentworth lived here from 1828 to 1862.

At the entrance to the harbour is **Watsons Bay** (Map p66), where you can enjoy blissful briny breezes and a postcard-perfect view of the city skyline while eating takeaway fish and chips at **Doyle's on the Wharf** (fish & chips $11.80-17.50; ⊙10am-6pm;) at Fisherman's Wharf. Nearby **Camp Cove** (Map p66) is a lovely beach, and there's a nude beach (mostly male) near South Head at **Lady Bay**. **South Head** (Map p66) has great views across the harbour entrance to North Head and Middle Head. The **Gap** (Map p66) is an epic clifftop lookout where sunrises, sunsets, canoodling and suicide leaps transpire with similar frequency.

Buses 324 and 325 from Circular Quay service the eastern suburbs via Kings Cross (grab a seat on the left heading east to snare the best views). The Watsons Bay ferry leaves from Wharf 4 at Circular Quay, stopping at Double Bay and Rose Bay en route.

BONDI

Bondi (Map p83) lords it over every other beach in the city despite the crowds, the crass boardwalk, the often-treacherous rips and the less-than-consistent surf breaks. Flanked by rugged rocks and multi-million-dollar apartments, the famous golden crescent attracts a daily cast of sunburned backpackers, bronzed locals, Botoxed mini-celebs and body-worshipping Sydneysiders who swarm over the sand, surrounding clifftop paths and beachfront park. Perhaps it's the contradictions of the place that make it so compelling – everyone fits into the Bondi scene as long as they're wearing swimmers, sunblock and a smile. The suburb itself has a unique atmosphere due to its eclectic mix of traditional Jewish community members, dyed-in-the-wool Aussies, tourists who never went home and socially aspirational young professionals.

The simply sensational 5.5km **Bondi to Coogee Clifftop Walk** leads south from Bondi Beach along the clifftops to Coogee via Tamarama, Bronte and Clovelly, interweaving panoramic views, patrolled beaches, sea baths, waterside parks and plaques recounting local Aboriginal myths and stories.

In Bondi, most of the decent pubs, bars and restaurants are found at the northern end of Campbell Pde, on Bondi Rd or on Glenayr Ave. Sunday's laid-back Bondi Markets (p120) are held in the grounds of the primary school on Campbell Pde, and the famous Bondi Icebergs Swimming Club, with its beachfront pool (p99), is at the southern end of the beach where the clifftop walk starts.

Catch bus 380 or 333 from Circular Quay to get to North Bondi (note that this service doesn't stop at Bondi Beach, which is a five-minute walk from the bus interchange at Brighton Blvd) or take a bus or train to the transport interchange at Bondi Junction, from where bus 389 or 333 will take you straight to the beach.

INNER WEST

West of the city centre is the higgledy-piggledy peninsula suburb of **Balmain** (Map p66), once a notoriously rough neighbourhood of dockyard workers but now an arty enclave flush with beautifully restored Victorian houses, welcoming pubs, cafes and trendy shops. The Saturday market (p120) is a popular drawcard, particularly when combined with a stop at Sydney's most famous patisserie, Adriano Zumbo (p111). Catch a ferry from Wharf 5 at Circular Quay, or bus 441/2 from the QVB.

Once a bohemian hot spot, the now-somnolent suburb of **Glebe** (Map p84) lies just southwest of the centre, close to Sydney University. There are a couple of good hostels here, as well as one of the city's best-loved bookshops, **Gleebooks** (Map p84; www.gleebooks.com.au; 49 Glebe Point Rd; ⊘9am-9pm). On Saturdays, **Glebe markets** (p120) overrun Glebe Public School. Glebe is a 10-minute walk from Central Station along side streets – avoid smoggy Broadway. Buses 431 and 433 run via George St along Glebe Point Rd; the 433 continues to Gladstone Park at the western end of Balmain. The MLR also stops here.

South of Sydney University is **Newtown** (Map p84), a melting pot of social and sexual subcultures. King St, its relentlessly urban main drag, is full of funky clothes stores, bookshops and cafes. Take the train, or bus 422, 423, 426 or 428 from Circular Quay or Castlereagh St to King St.

Southwest of Glebe is predominantly Italian **Leichhardt** (Map p66). Norton St is the place for pizza, pasta and debates about the relative merits and demerits of the Ferrari 430 Spider. Buses 436, 438 and 440 from Circular Quay service Leichhardt.

BOTANY BAY

In May 1787 the First Fleet left Britain for Australia, bound for Botany Bay, which Captain Cook had visited in 1770 and noted as an excellent site for settlement. On arrival, it was discovered that Cook had been mistaken – the sandy infertile soil was unsuitable for settlement. Arthur Phillip then made the decision to move north to the natural harbour of Port Jackson.

These days, Botany Bay, on the city's southern fringe, is a smoke-stacked industrial heartland that bears little resemblance to the landscape that first confronted Cook when he stepped ashore. However, it still has scenic stretches and continues to hold a special place in Australian history. Joseph Banks, the naturalist with Cook's expedition, named the bay for the many botanical specimens he found here.

Kamay Botany Bay National Park (Map p88; www.environment.nsw.gov.au/NationalParks; cars $7, pedestrians & cyclists free; ⊘7am-7.30pm Sep-May, to 5.30pm Jun-Aug) occupies both headlands of the bay – 458 hectares of bushland and coastal walking tracks, picnic areas, sheltered coves and beaches. A sandstone obelisk marks Cook's landing place in Kurnell, on the southern side of the park. The **Kurnell Visitor**

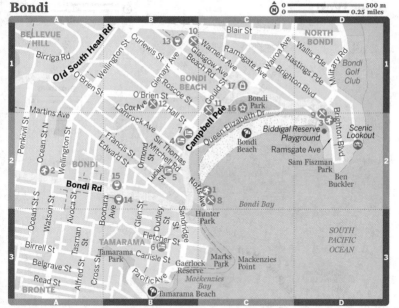

Bondi

Centre (Cape Solander Dr, Kurnell; admission free; ☾9.30am-4.30pm) focuses on the first contact between Aboriginal people and the crew of the *Endeavour*. There's also information on the geography of the region.

There are a number of walking tracks on this southern side of the park at Kurnell – consider doing the 1.1km **Burrawang Walk**, which lets you imagine what the park looked like in 1770 when the *Endeavour* arrived, or the spectacular 8km-long **Cape Baily Coast Walk**.

To get here via public transport, catch the train to Cronulla, where you can connect with bus 987 operated by **Veolia Transport** (www.veoliatransportnsw.com.au) going to Kurnell.

La Perouse, on the northern headland, is named after the French explorer who arrived in 1788, just six days after the arrival of the First Fleet. Lapérouse and his men camped at Botany Bay for a few weeks before sailing off into the Pacific, never to be seen again. The **Lapérouse Museum & Visitor Centre** (www.environment.nsw.gov.au; Cable

SYDNEY & NEW SOUTH WALES SYDNEY

Inner West

Station, Anzac Pde, La Perouse; adult/child/family $5.50/3.30/13.20; ⊙10am-4pm Thu-Sun), housed inside the old cable station (1882), charts the course of La Pérouse's fateful expedition, and also hosts changing exhibitions on local history and environment. It is well worth a visit.

About 50m offshore at La Perouse sits the strange **Bare Island** (www.nationalparks.nsw.

gov.au; tours adult/concession/family $10/8/25; ⊙tours 1.30, 2.30 & 3.30pm Sun), used as a set for *Mission: Impossible II*. Originally built in 1885 to discourage a sea attack (which never materialised), today the decaying concrete fort is a museum. A 45-minute guided tour is the only way to access the island.

Bus 394 runs from Circular Quay to La Perouse.

NORTH SHORE

At the northern end of the Harbour Bridge are the unexpectedly tranquil waterside suburbs of Milsons Point (Map p66) and McMahons Point (Map p66). Both command astonishing city views and also overlook the shimmering waters of Lavender Bay (Map p66).

FREE Wendy Whiteley's Secret Garden, on the shore of Lavender Bay, is one of Sydney's hidden treasures. This public garden was created by the widow of artist Brett Whiteley (an artist in her own right) on an old railway siding and is accessed through Clark Park, off Lavender St.

On the eastern shore of Lavender Bay is Luna Park (www.lunaparksydney.com; 1 Olympic Pl, Milsons Point; admission free, multiride passes from $20; ☺hours vary wildly, see website for details), a classic carnival in the Coney Island mould. Operating since 1935, it boasts a Ferris wheel, Rotor, Flying Saucer, Tumble Bug and other rides.

Just east of the bridge is the stately suburb of Kirribilli (Map p66), home to Admiralty House and Kirribilli House, the Sydney residences of the governor-general and prime minister respectively.

You can walk across the bridge to access Milsons Point, McMahons Point, Lavender Bay and Kirribilli, or take the short ferry ride from Wharves 4 and 5 at Circular Quay.

East of Kirribilli are the upmarket residential suburbs of Neutral Bay (Map p66), Cremorne (Map p66) and Mosman (Map p66), known for their coves, harbourside parks and ladies who lunch. On the northern side of Mosman is pretty-as-a-picture Balmoral (Map p66), the beach of which fronts Hunters Bay. There's a netted swimming enclosure here, as well as the much-loved Bather's Pavilion restaurant, cafe and kiosk (p112). The best way to visit all of these North Shore suburbs is by catching a ferry from Wharf 4 at Circular Quay.

Taronga Zoo   ZOO
(Map p66; www.taronga.org.au/taronga-zoo; Bradleys Head Rd, Mosman; adult/child 4-15/concession $43/21/30; ☺9am-5pm) Sydneysiders often joke that the animals here are housed on the best tract of real estate in the city. Unfortunately, the zoo's knock-'em-dead views and glorious profusion of trees go hand in hand with sadly cramped enclosures for the residents.

Twilight concerts take place during summer and you can even sign up for a 'Roar and Snore' overnight stay. Families can save money by taking advantage of the family tickets on offer.

Zoo ferries depart Circular Quay's Wharf 2 twice every hour – note that the entrance near the ferry stop doesn't open until 11am on weekdays. After alighting from the ferry, head to the ticket office and then to the nearby Sky Safari cable car (ticket included in admission), which will take you up the steep slope to the zoo's highest point. You'll look down onto a number of enclosures during the short trip. A ZooPass (adult/child 4-15 $49.50/24.50), sold at Circular Quay and elsewhere, includes return ferry rides and zoo admission and usually represents a 10% saving.

MANLY

Refreshingly relaxed Manly (Map p86) occupies a narrow isthmus between ocean and harbour beaches near North Head. It's the only place in Sydney where you can catch a harbour ferry to swim in the ocean. The scene here is radically different to that at Bondi – locals outnumber foreign tourists, and bodyboards are considered far more important accessories than designer bikinis or show-off budgie smugglers (tight-fitting mens' swimming costumes).

The helpful Manly Visitor Centre (☑9977 1430; www.manlytourism.com; Manly Wharf; ☺9am-5pm Mon-Fri, 10am-4pm Sat & Sun) is just outside the ferry wharf.

There's an array of cafes, pubs and restaurants at the wharf, the best of which is Hugos (p112). For something special, make your way to the close-by Manly Pavilion (p112), which offers a glorious view of the harbour and is a wonderful spot to enjoy a leisurely lunch or sunset drinks. Next to the pavilion is Oceanworld (Map p86; www.oceanworld.com.au; W Esplanade; adult/child/concession $20/10/14; ☺10am-5.30pm), a tired 1980s aquarium with underwater transparent tubes where you can see 3m sharks.

One of the most popular activities in Manly is to stroll along the Manly Scenic Walkway. This has two major components: the western stretch between Manly Cove and Spit Bridge, and the eastern stretch from Manly Cove to North Head.

The western walkway tracks around North and Middle Harbours, past waterside mansions, harbour beaches and viewpoints, an

SYDNEY & NEW SOUTH WALES SYDNEY

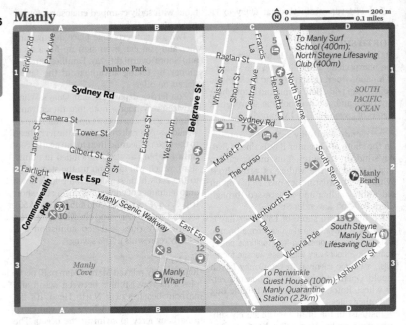

Manly

◎ Sights
1 Oceanworld A2

⊕ Activities, Courses & Tours
2 Dive Centre Manly B2
3 Skater HQ C1

🛏 Sleeping
4 Boardrider
   Backpacker C2
5 Manly Pacific C1

✕ Eating
6 Adriano Zumbo C3
7 BenBry Burgers C2
8 Hugos Manly B3
9 Manly Fish Market D2
10 Manly Pavilion A2

🍷 Drinking
11 Barefoot Coffee Traders C2
12 Manly Wharf Hotel B3
13 Manly Wine D3

Aboriginal engraving site and through rugged Sydney Harbour National Park. It ends at Spit Bridge on Fisher Bay, from where you can catch bus 160, 179 or 189 into the CBD.

The eastern walkway follows Eastern Esplanade and Stuart St to Spring Cove, heads into the North Head section of the Sydney Harbour National Park, and makes its way through the bush to the spectacular Fairfax Lookout on North Head. If you're here in the middle of the year, you may see migrating whales from this vantage point. From the lookout, walk the Fairfax Loop and then head back to the ferry wharf via the Cabbage Tree Bay Coastal Walk, which follows the sea-sprayed shoreline back to Manly via tiny Fairy Bower Beach and picturesque Shelly Beach.

The Manly Visitor Centre stocks a free brochure detailing the route; there's also a map on its website.

On North Head, you can also visit the Manly Quarantine Station (off Map p86; ☎02-9466 1500; www.qstation.com.au; 1 North Head Scenic Dr; ⊙Wed-Sun), where disease-riddled migrants were isolated between 1832 and 1984. The once-decaying station has been revamped and visitors can wander around part of the compound or sign up for a two-hour Quarantine Station Story Tour (adult/child/concession $35/25/29; ⊙3pm Sat & Sun), a spooky adults-only ghost tour (adult/concession $44/40; ⊗8pm Wed-Sun) or a **family ghosty tour** (adult/child/concession $34/26/30; ⊗7pm Fri & Sat). Bookings are essential for all three. For a full-immersion experience, you can even choose to overnight here. The website has details.

Free shuttle buses run between the quarantine station and the 'kiss and ride' bus stop on the corner of East Esplanade and Belgrave St in Manly (in front of the taxi rank) between 10.30am and 9.30pm Wednesday to Sunday (until midnight Friday and Saturday); see the website for a timetable.

To get to Manly, take the ferry from Circular Quay's Wharf 3 – it's one of Sydney's best-loved journeys.

NORTHERN BEACHES
The 20km-stretch of coast between Manly and well-heeled **Palm Beach** (where TV soap *Home and Away* is filmed) is often described as the most impressive urban surfing landscape in the world, and the locals who swim and catch the waves at Manly, Collaroy, Freshwater, Dee Why, Narrabeen, Mona Vale, Newport, Bilgola, Avalon, Whale and Palm Beaches would be quick to agree.

Each of these beaches has a markedly different atmosphere – for instance, Palm and Whale Beaches are glamorous and relatively secluded, Manly is egalitarian and ever-crowded, Avalon and Dee Why are favourites with families and Narrabeen is frequented by serious surfers.

To get to Collaroy, North Narrabeen (for Narrabeen), Mona Vale, Newport, Bilgola, Avalon, Whale and Palm Beaches from the CBD, catch bus L90 from Railway Sq. From Manly Wharf, bus 136 goes to Chatswood via Curl Curl and Dee Why; bus 156 goes to McCarrs Creek via Dee Why, North Narrabeen and Mona Vale.

Ku-ring-gai Chase National Park   PARK
(Map p88; www.nationalparks.nsw.gov.au; admission per car $11) This spectacular, 14,928-hectare park, 24km from the city centre, forms Sydney's northern boundary. It's a classic mix of sandstone, bushland and water vistas, taking in over 100km of coastline along the southern edge of Broken Bay where it heads into the Hawkesbury River.

Ku-ring-gai takes its name from its original inhabitants, the Guringai people, who were all but wiped out just after colonisation through violence at the hands of British settlers or introduced disease. It's well worth reading Kate Grenville's Booker-nominated

The Secret River for an engrossing but harrowing telling of this story.

Remnants of Aboriginal life are visible today thanks to the preservation of more than 800 sites, including rock paintings, middens and cave art. To learn about these sites and about the park's flora and fauna, enter the park through the Mt Colah entrance and visit the **Kalkari Discovery Centre** (✆02-9472 9300; Ku-ring-gai Chase Rd; admission free; ⊗10am-4pm Mon-Fri, to 5pm Sat & Sun), which has displays and videos on Australian fauna and Aboriginal culture. There is a short self-guided walk around the centre on which you can see swamp wallabies, bush turkeys, native ducks and goannas.

From the Resolute picnic area at **West Head** you can amble 100m to **Red Hands Cave**, where there are some very faint ochre handprints. About another 500m along **Resolute Track** (after a short steep section) is an Aboriginal engraving site. You can turn around or continue to one more site and make a 3.5km loop that takes in **Resolute Beach**. The view from the **West Head Lookout** is truly spectacular – don't miss it.

Less than 3km west of the picnic area, along West Head Rd, is the **Basin Track**, which offers an easy stroll to a good set of engravings. Approximately 2.5km further along the track is the **Basin** (day visit adult/child $3/2), a shallow round inlet where there is a **camping area** (✆02-9974 1011; www.basin campground.com.au; sites per adult/child $14/7) with BBQs, showers and toilets. Access is via the Basin Track or by ferry or water taxi from Palm Beach.

For information about the park, stop at the **Bobbin Head Information Centre** (✆02-9472 8949; Bobbin Inn, Bobbin Head; ⊗10am-4pm), which is operated by the NSW Parks and Wildlife Service. Also here are a marina, picnic areas, a cafe and a boardwalk leading through mangroves.

Access to the park is by car or the **Palm Beach Ferry** (www.palmbeachferry.com.au; adult/child $6.90/3.50; ⊗9am-7pm Mon-Fri, to 6pm Sat & Sun) run by Fantasea. This runs hourly from Palm Beach to Mackerel Beach, via the Basin. To get to Palm Beach from the CBD, catch bus L90 from Railway Sq or Bus 156 or 169 from Manly Wharf.

If you are arriving by car, enter Ku-ring-gai Chase Rd off Pacific Hwy, Mt Colah; Bobbin Head Rd, North Turramurra; or McCarrs Creek Rd, Terrey Hills.

continued on p97

Around Sydney

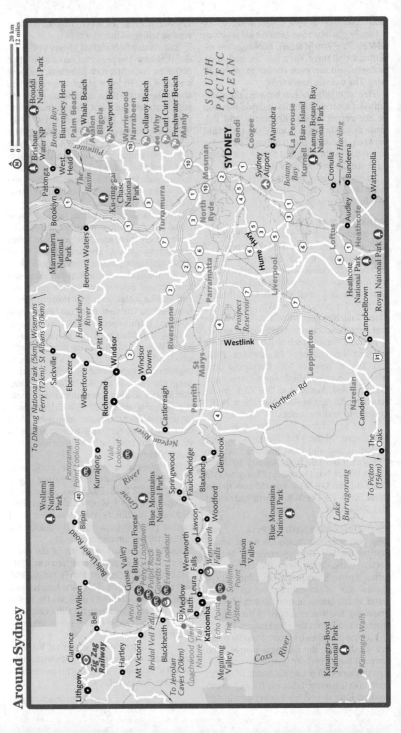

This is Sydney

Sydney Harbour »
Beaches »
After Dark »
National Parks »

Sydney Harbour Bridge (p68)

Sydney Harbour

It's called the Harbour City for good reason. Few places on earth are as defined by their geographical form as Sydney, and none are blessed with such a spectacular natural landscape.

Visitors have been writing odes to the harbour's beauty ever since the First Fleet landed here on 26 January 1788. Few have done it justice, though. After all, how can any writing match the exultation of a ferry trip across shimmering blue waters or the satisfaction of an afternoon spent lazing in a sheltered sandy cove?

Everything here revolves around this huge body of water – suburbs, recreation, traffic, even the collective consciousness.

The somewhat stolid North Shore is the location of choice for the city's conservative middle classes, whose leafy villas stretch from Neutral Bay to Manly. Traffic snarls are the norm here, as are the residents' aspirations to own a sailboat for weekends on the water.

Across the iconic Sydney Harbour Bridge is an altogether different Sydney. A ring of gregarious inner-city neighbourhoods surround the central business district and give the city its urban edge, albeit one with a magnificent harbour view around every corner.

ANDREW WATSON/LONELY PLANET IMAGES ©

1

To the east a genteel ribbon of suburbs unfurls, characterised by mansions, money and mindsets that are often as old as the colony itself. Harking west, towards the Parramatta River, are former working-class neighbourhoods that in recent years have been reinvented as arty residential enclaves.

At the centre of all this is Circular Quay, home to Sydney's two signature sights – the Opera House (p68) and Harbour Bridge (p68). From here, the city's famous flotilla of green-and-yellow ferries do five-minute dashes across to Milsons Point and Kirribilli, speedy sails to the Middle Harbour and majestic processions past the Heads to Manly.

The harbour's attractions are as entrancing as they are accessible – a rare and wonderful combination. Ferry trips are relatively inexpensive; and there's no charge to explore the scenic walking paths and bushwalking tracks scattered throughout Sydney Harbour National Park (p65), swim in a harbour cove or marvel at an extraordinary water view. When you're here, make sure you take advantage of them all.

TOP FIVE HARBOUR ACTIVITIES

» Take the ferry to **Manly** (p85)
» Enjoy a harbour view with your meal at **Quay** (p107), **Manly Pavilion** (p112) or the **Bather's Pavilion** (p112)
» Swim at **Nielsen Park** (p81), **Balmoral Beach** (p85) or **Camp Cove** (p81)
» Follow the **Manly Scenic Walkway** (p85)
» Explore the **harbour islands** (p68)

Clockwise from top left
1. Sydney Opera House (p68) **2.** Sydney Harbour Bridge climb (p101) **3.** Fishing, Sydney Harbour

Beaches

Here, nothing beats a day at the beach. Sun, sand and surf dominate the culture for six months of every year, and locals wouldn't have it any other way.

The city's magnificent string of ocean beaches stretches north from the Royal National Park to Palm Beach, luring surfers, scenesters, swimmers and sunbathers onto their golden sands and into the powerful waves of the South Pacific Ocean.

There's none of that horrible European habit of privatising the beach here. Lay down a towel and you've claimed a personal patch of paradise for as long as you want it. Some locals enjoy a quick dip before or after work, while the lucky ones stay on the sand for the whole day – everyone makes the most of what time they have.

Serious surfers head to Cronulla in the south; Maroubra, Bronte, Tamarama and North Bondi in the east; and Narrabeen, Queenscliff, Harbord (Freshwater) and Manly on the Northern Beaches. Of these, Bronte and Manly are also popular with swimmers, joining Coogee, Clovelly, Bondi, Whale and Palm as regular entries on 'Best Beaches' lists. Each of these beaches has a devoted crew of regulars – families flock to Clovelly, Bronte and Whale Beach, while bronzed singles strut their stuff at Coogee and Palm Beach. The best-known beaches – Bondi and Manly – host an incongruous mix of pasty-skinned foreigners, weather-wizened surf gurus, grommets (beginner surfers), camera-savvy minor celebrities and geriatric locals who have been perfecting their body-surfing techniques for more than half a century. Always crowded, these two beaches showcase the most endearing and eclectic aspects of Sydney's character, and shouldn't be missed.

Those who find surf off-putting have two excellent alternatives: ocean pools and harbour beaches. Of the many pools on offer, the most popular are the Bondi Icebergs Swimming Club (p99), the historic Wylie's Baths in Coogee (p99) and the

Clockwise from top left

1. Surfers, Manly (p85) **2.** Looking out to Bondi Beach (p82), from Bronte **3.** Coogee Beach

ocean pools at Bronte, Avalon, Bilgola, Newport, Freshwater, Manly, Palm and Whale beaches. In the harbour, there are netted swimming enclosures or pools at Cremorne Point, Nielsen Park and Balmoral Beach.

And the choices don't stop there. Aspiring skinny-dippers should make their way to Lady Bay near Watsons Bay; Obelisk and Cobbler's beaches in the Middle Harbour; and Werrong Beach in the Royal National Park (p123), all of which are official nudist beaches.

Our advice? Plunge in and enjoy yourself, regardless of whether you're wearing a swimsuit or not!

BONDI TO COOGEE CLIFF-TOP WALK

This 5.5km, 2.5-hour walk follows a cliff-top path from Bondi Beach to Coogee, and is one of the city's most exhilarating experiences. Start at the Bondi Icebergs Swimming Club and follow the signposts south toward the small reserve known as Mark's Park. Along the route there are scenic vantage points (look out for whales and dolphins) as well as plaques recounting local Aboriginal myths and stories.

Continue to diminutive Tamarama Beach. Walk around the grassed reserve and continue onto charming Bronte Beach with its Norfolk Island pines, picnic ground and popular children's playground.

Follow the cliff-top and continue along the boardwalk edging picturesque Waverley Cemetery, which will lead you to Clovelly (a popular snorkelling spot), Gordon's Bay and Coogee Beach.

The best time of year to do the walk is between late October and mid-November, when the wildly popular Sculpture by the Sea (www.sculpturebythesea.com) transforms the route between Bondi and Tamarama.

After Dark

Sydneysiders love nothing more than shimmying and shaking their way from performance to party, makin' plenty of friends along the way. And who's to blame them?

After all, the city has come a long way in the leisure stakes since its foundation as a penal colony. Back then, a beaker or two of rum was the only type of partying available to soldiers, convicts and emancipists. These days, the situation couldn't be more different.

The festival calendar is a good case in point. The year kicks off with a frenzy of fireworks over Circular Quay and doesn't calm down for months. No sooner has the Sydney Festival, with its associated openings and events, finished than the biggest party of all kicks off: the famous Gay & Lesbian Mardi Gras (p100). Winter brings fashion, literature, film and art to the fore, with opening nights, cocktail parties and literary soirées dominating everyone's datebooks. And then there's a slight hiatus until summer works its magic and everyone takes to the city's streets to make the most of daylight savings' long days and blissfully balmy nights.

Whatever your inclination, Sydney will indulge it. You can attend the theatre or the opera, take in a jazz performance or a drag show, watch films under the stars or

club late into the night. Sexy, sweaty and solipsistic, the social scene here is bigger and way better than those in the other states; ignore anyone who tries to convince you otherwise.

And lest you think that the only way to kick up your heels is to take to the dance floor or attend a star-studded concert, think again. For many locals, the best evening entertainment comes courtesy of the city's huge range of bars and restaurants – there truly is something for every budget and palate here.

Put simply, this is a town that well and truly lives up to its hype when it comes to partying. Enjoy!

DON'T MISS

» The restaurant and bar scene on **Crown Street, Surry Hills** (p109 and p113)
» Attending a performance at the **Sydney Opera House** (p68)
» Camping it up during the **Gay & Lesbian Mardi Gras** (p100)
» Spending a hot night chillin' to some **cool jazz** (p116)
» Watching a movie under the stars at an **open air cinema** (p115)

Clockwise from top left
1. City skyline from Darling Harbour 2. Mardi Gras (p100)
3. New Year's Eve fireworks, Sydney Harbour

2

National Parks

Sampling Sydney's sybaritic menu of sights, activities and entertainments can lead to sensory overload. When this happens, it pays to escape to one of the four national parks in the immediate area.

The most accessible of these is the Sydney Harbour National Park (p65), which includes islands and foreshore areas in and around the harbour. Rich in remnant bushland and cultural heritage, the park is one of the city's great – and refreshingly understated – tourist attractions.

A bit harder to access, but worth the effort, is Ku-ring-gai Chase National Park (p87), 150 sq km of forest located where the Hawkesbury River meets the South Pacific Ocean. A repository for millennia-old Aboriginal rock art, it also protects a wide array of native wildlife and plants.

Incongruously but wonderfully located in the midst of residential development on the North Shore, the Lane Cove National Park extends from East Ryde to Pennant Hills, protecting bushland and freshwater sectio of the Lane Cove River. It's the city's large and best-loved suburban back garden.

The greatest escape of all is the Royal National Park (p123). The world's second-oldest national park (after Yellowstone in the USA), it offers magnificent surf beache walks through cliff-top heathland and innumerable leisure activities.

TOP FIVE NATIONAL PARK ACTIVITIES

- » Enjoy a picnic, walk and swim at **Nielsen Park** (p81)
- » View Aboriginal rock paintings and engravings in the **Ku-ring-gai Chase National Park** (p87)
- » Camp overnight at the **Lane Cove River Tourist Park** (p106)
- » Surf at **Garie Beach** (p123)
- » Walk the Coast Track in the **Royal National Park** (p123)

Resolute Beach, Ku-ring-gai Chase National Park (p87)

continued from p87

PARRAMATTA

These days Sydney's most desirable residential locations are those with harbour views, but early colonists much preferred the fertile pastures of Parramatta (Map p88), 24km west of the city centre. By 1792 the area was home to 1970 people, compared with just 1170 on the coast.

More recently, however, folk living in Parramatta and other western Sydney suburbs have been labelled (usually by poncey central Sydneysiders) as flannel-shirt-wearing AC/DC fans. While this may have been true in the 1980s when the local rugby league team, the mullet-proud Parramatta Eels, topped the league tables, those stereotypes no longer hold any merit. Today Parramatta has successfully established itself as Sydney's second CBD and is fast developing its own art, theatre and festival scene to boot.

Parramatta is the traditional home of the Burramatta clan of the Darug people; its name means 'the place where the eels lie'.

Although modernity reigns, a clutch of colonial buildings remains; the visitor information desk in the Parramatta Heritage Centre (📞1300 889 714; www.parracity.nsw.gov.au; 346a Church St; ☺9am-5pm) can steer you towards the city's attractions. See www.discoverparramatta.com for more information. There's also a small exhibition – 'Parramatta: Past and Present' – at the heritage centre.

There are two heritage precincts in Parramatta that are of interest to visitors: Parramatta Park, where Old Government House is located; and Harris Park, where Experiment Farm Cottage, Hambledon Cottage and Elizabeth Farm are set. A free city bus service known as the Loop (www.parramattaloop.com.au; ☺7am-6.30pm Mon-Fri, 8am-4pm Sat & Sun) connects O'Connell St on the edge of Parramatta Park with Charles St, near Harris Park, with the ferry wharf and with Parramatta train station.

Established in 1799, Old Government House (www.nationaltrust.com.au; Parramatta Park; adult/child & concession $9/6, joint ticket with Experiment Farm Cottage $13/9; ☺1hr tours 10am-4pm Tue-Fri, 10.30am-4pm Sat & Sun) is Australia's oldest public building. For seven decades it was the country retreat of early colony governors looking to escape the bawdy, crime-ridden streets of Sydney. It is now a carefully maintained museum operated by the National Trust. Nearby on O'Connell St, St John's Cemetery dates back to 1790 and is the

» **Bondi Beach** (Map p82)
» **Camp Cove** (p81)
» **Manly Beach** (Map p85)
» **Palm Beach** (p87)

resting ground for many of Australia's earliest settlers: you'll find graves of governors' wives, notable citizens and First Fleet convicts.

In 1789 ex-convict James Ruse was chosen by Governor Phillip to run a trial in self-sufficiency, and was given a land grant of 30 acres. By 1791, Ruse had become Australia's first successful private farmer. In 1835 he sold the land to surgeon John Harris, who built Experiment Farm Cottage (www.nationaltrust.com.au; 9 Ruse St; adult/child & concession $7/5, joint ticket with Old Government House $13/9; ☺tours 10.30am-3.30pm Tue-Fri, 11am-3.30pm Sat & Sun).

Elizabeth Farm (www.hht.net.au; 70 Alice St, Rosehill; adult/child & concession $8/4; ☺9.30am-4pm Fri-Sun) is the oldest surviving homestead (1793) in Australia. Built by renegade pastoralist/rum trader/wool merchant John Macarthur, it is now a hands-on museum chock-full of history. It's an 'access all areas' house museum, meaning that visitors can recline on the furniture, thumb voyeuristically through Elizabeth Macarthur's letters and generally make themselves feel at home.

Nearby Hambledon Cottage (www.hotkey.net.au/~parramattahistry/hambledon.html; 63 Hassall St; adult/child/concession $4/2/3; ☺11am-4pm Thu-Sun) was built in 1824 for the Macarthurs' daughter's governess, and was later used as weekend lodgings.

The Paramatta Heritage Centre can give you details about the 2.4km, 45-minute Harris Park Heritage Walk, which begins at Parramatta Wharf and loops around Elizabeth Farm, Experiment Farm Cottage and Hambledon Cottage. It also has brochures about self-guided walking tours of Colonial Rose Hill, the former Governor's Domain in Parramatta Park.

The most pleasant way to get to Parramatta is by RiverCat from Wharf 5 at Circular Quay; the trip takes 55 minutes. Note that during low tides, the boat stops at Rydalmere and a bus transports passengers on to Parramatta. The train from Central Station takes 30 minutes. By car, exit the city via Parramatta Rd and detour onto the M4 at Strathfield.

☆ Activities

Canoeing & Kayaking

Natural Wanders   CANOEING, KAYAKING
(☑0427 225 072; www.kayaksydney.com; per person from $65) Offers exhilarating morning tours around the Harbour Bridge, Lavender Bay, Balmain and Birchgrove.

Cycling

Bicycle NSW (www.bicyclensw.org.au) publishes *Cycling Around Sydney*, which details city routes and paths; it also sells Bicycle Australia's *Where to Ride Sydney* and the NRMA's *Great Cycling Rides in NSW* from its online store. **Sydney City Council** (www.cityofsydney. nsw.gov.au) has information about inner-city maps and routes on its website, provides links to cycling information offered by other councils and publishes the hard-copy, free-of-charge *Sydney Cycling Guide + Map*.

Centennial Park Cycles   CYCLING
(www.cyclehire.com.au; per day/week from $50/110; ☺9am-5pm) Branches in Randwick and Centennial Park.

Diving

Sydney's best shore dives are at Gordons Bay, north of Coogee (Map p66); Shark Point, Clovelly (Map p66); and Ship Rock, Cronulla (Map p88). Popular boat-dive sites are Wedding Cake Island off Coogee (Map p66), Sydney Heads (Map p66), and off Royal National Park (Map p88).

Dive Centre Bondi   DIVING
(Map p83; ☑02-9369 3855; www.divebondi.com. au; 198 Bondi Rd, Bondi; ☺8.30am-6pm Mon-Fri, from 7.30am Sat & Sun) One-day PADI Discover Scuba course $225; shore and boat dives; rentals.

Dive Centre Manly   DIVING
(Map p86; ☑02-9977 4355; www.divesydney.com. au; 10 Belgrave St, Manly; ☺9am-6pm Mon-Wed & Fri, 9am-8pm Thu, 8am-6pm Sat & Sun) PADI Discover Scuba course $155; shore and boat dives; rentals.

Horse Riding

Centennial Parklands Equestrian Centre   HORSE RIDING
(☑02-9332 2809; www.cpequestrian.com.au; Lang Rd, Paddington; ☺9am-5pm) Several stables at the centre conduct lessons and rides for adults and children in tree-lined Centennial Park, Sydney's favourite urban green space (one-hour, 3.6km horse rides $70 to $80, one-hour lessons $100 to $135).

In-Line Skating

The beach promenades at Bondi and Manly and the paths of Centennial Park are the favoured spots for skating.

Rollerblading Sydney   IN-LINE SKATING
(☑0411 872 022; www.rollerbladingsydney.com. au; lessons per hr $50) Rentals, lessons and tours.

Skater HQ   IN-LINE SKATING
(Map p86; www.skaterhq.com.au; 2/49 North Steyne, Manly; ☺10am-7pm Mon-Thu, 10am-8pm Fri, 9am-8pm Sat, 9am-6pm Sun) Hires rollerblades, scooters and skateboards.

Sailing

Sydney has dozens of yacht clubs and sailing schools.

EastSail Sailing School   SAILING
(☑02-9327 1166; www.eastsail.com.au; d'Albora Marina, New Beach Rd, Rushcutters Bay; cruises per adult/child from $119/89, 2-day 'start yachting' course $575; ☺9am-6pm) A sociable outfit offering 'start yachting' courses, more advanced outings and morning/sunset cruises.

Sydney by Sail   SAILING
(Map p76; ☑02-9280 1110; www.sydneybysail. com.au; Festival Pontoon, National Maritime Museum, Darling Harbour) Daily harbour sailing tours (three hours, adult/child $150/75), introductory weekend sailing courses ($495), whale-watching cruises (six hours, $175) and plenty of other options.

Surfing

On the South Shore, get tubed at Bondi, Tamarama, Coogee, Maroubra and Cronulla. The North Shore is home to a dozen gnarly surf beaches between Manly and Palm Beach, including Curl Curl, Dee Why, Narrabeen, Mona Vale and Newport.

Let's Go Surfing   SURFING
(Map p83; ☑02-9365 1800; www.letsgosurfing. com.au; 128 Ramsgate Ave, Bondi; 2hr group lesson incl use of board & wetsuit adult/child from $89/79; ☺9am-5pm, later in summer) Also offers board and wetsuit hire ($30 for two hours).

Manly Surf School   SURFING
(off Map p86; ☑02-9977 6977; www.manlysurf school.com; North Steyne Surf Lifesaving Club, Manly; 2hr group lesson incl use of board & wetsuit adult/child $60/50; ☺9am-6pm) Lessons cater to all levels of fitness, ability and age.

Organised kids' activities ramp up during school holidays (December/January, April, July and September); check www.sydneyforkids.com.au, www.kidfriendly.com.au and the free *Sydney's Child* magazine for listings.

Most kids love the Sydney Aquarium (p77), Sydney Wildlife World (p77), Australian National Maritime Museum (p78) and Powerhouse Museum (p78) at Darling Harbour and neighbouring Ultimo. Also worth investigating is the Sunday afternoon GalleryKids program at the Art Gallery of NSW (), which includes dance, stories, magic, cartoons, Aboriginal performances, costumed tour guides and exhibition-specific events.

Elsewhere, Taronga Zoo (p85) and Luna Park (p85) are sure-fire entertainers. Visits to swimming pools (p99), surfing lessons (p98) and horse or pony rides (p98) are also popular.

Nielsen Park (p65) in Vaucluse is the perfect choice if the younger members of your entourage need to stretch their legs and burn up some energy. It's also a great spot for sandcastle building! Other kid-friendly beaches include Balmoral Beach, Shelly Beach and Dee Why on the North Shore, and Clovelly Beach, Bronte Beach and the North Bondi Children's Pool on the Eastern Beaches.

Swimming

There are 100-plus public swimming pools in Sydney, and many beaches have protected rock pools. Harbour beaches offer sheltered and shark-netted swimming, but nothing beats Pacific Ocean waves. Always swim within the flagged lifeguard-patrolled areas, and never underestimate the surf.

Some outdoor swimming pools:

Andrew 'Boy' Charlton Pool SWIMMING
(www.abcpool.org; 1c Mrs Macquaries Rd, The Domain; adult/child/locker $5.60/2/3; ⊙6am-7pm Sep-Apr, one hr later during daylight savings) A 50m outdoor saltwater pool and harbour-view cafe.

Bondi Icebergs Swimming Club SWIMMING
(Map p83; http://icebergs.com.au/; adult/child & senior $5/3; ⊙6am-6.30pm Mon-Wed & Fri, 6.30am-6.30pm Sat & Sun) Sydney's most famous swimming pool commands the best view in Bondi and has a cute little cafe.

Dawn Fraser Baths SWIMMING
(www.lpac.nsw.gov.au/Dawn-Fraser-Baths.html; Elkington Park, Glassop St, Balmain; adult/senior/child & student $4/2.10/2.80; ⊙7.15am-6.30pm Oct-Nov & Mar-Apr, 6.45am-7pm Dec-Feb) This magnificently restored late-Victorian tidal-flow seawater pool (1884) offers a small beach at low tide and yoga classes ($12.20) during summer.

North Sydney Olympic Pool SWIMMING
(www.northsydney.nsw.gov.au; 4 Alfred St South, Milsons Point; adult/child/senior $6.50/3.20/5.20; ⊙5.30am-9pm Mon-Fri, 7am-7pm Sat & Sun) Next to Luna Park, right on the harbour. A place of legends – many world records

have been set here. For $18 you can also use the gym, sauna and spa.

Wylie's Baths SWIMMING
(www.wylies.com.au; Neptune St, Coogee; adult/child/senior $4/0.50/1.50; ⊙7am-7pm daylight saving time, to 5pm rest of year) Superb seawater pool built in 1907. After your swim, take a yoga class ($14), enjoy a massage or have a coffee at the kiosk, which has magnificent views of the Pacific Ocean.

Tours

There are countless tours available in Sydney. You can book most of them at the visitor centres (p119).

City Bus Tours

City Sightseeing BUS TOURS
(www.city-sightseeing.com) Operates two sightseeing buses around Sydney. One ticket (adult/child/senior/student 24hr ticket $35/20/25/30, 48hr ticket $56/32/40/48, ⊙every 20 minutes from 8.30am to 7.30pm) covers both. Buses leave Central Station every 15 to 20 minutes and can be boarded at any stop. Buy your ticket on the bus. One of the two services is **Sydney Tour**, which has a 90-minute, 23-stop hop-on, hop-off loop from Central Station through Pyrmont, Darling Harbour, The Rocks, Circular Quay, the city centre, Kings Cross, the Domain, and Macquarie St. The other service is **Scenic Bondi & Bay Tour**, which runs a 90-minute nine-stop hop-on, hop-off loop starting at Central Station and stopping at Sydney Tower, Paddington, Bondi Beach, North Bondi, Rose Bay, Double Bay and the Australian Museum.

Gay and lesbian culture forms a vocal and vital part of Sydney's social fabric. **Taylor Sq** (Map p80) on Oxford St is the centre of arguably the second-largest gay community in the world after San Francisco; Newtown is home to Sydney's lesbian scene.

Sydney's famous **Gay & Lesbian Mardi Gras** (www.mardigras.org.au) draws over 300,000 spectators and involves over 10,000 participants; the Mardi Gras also runs the annual **Sleaze Ball** held in late September/early October at the Horden Pavilion in Moore Park (Map p66).

Free gay media includes *SX*. Online resources include www.ssonet.com.au (Sydney's main gay newspaper), www.lotl.com (Sydney's monthly lesbian magazine) and the G&L pages of the monthly *Time Out* magazine.

Most accommodation in and around Oxford St is very gay-friendly. For frolicking, go for a wander along the city end of Oxford St, or check out the following:

ARQ
NIGHTCLUB

(Map p80; www.arqsydney.com.au; 16 Flinders St, Darlinghurst; cover varies; ☺9pm-7am Thu, 9pm-9am Fri-Sun) This flash mega-club has a cocktail bar, a recovery room and two dance floors with high-energy house music and drag shows. The Moist night for gay girls is held on the last Friday of every month.

Imperial Hotel
CABARET

(Map p84; www.theimperialhotel.com.au; 35 Erskineville Rd, Erskineville; public bar free, cellar dance club $5, cabaret bar $10; ☺3-11.30pm Mon, 3pm-midnight Tue & Wed, 3pm-4am Thu, 3pm-6am Fri & Sat, 1pm-midnight Sun) The drag shows at this art-deco pub inspired *Priscilla, Queen of the Desert* (the opening scene was filmed here), and there's a Priscilla tribute show every Saturday night ($10). Any drag queen worth her sheen has played the Cabaret Bar.

Midnight Shift
NIGHTCLUB

(Map p80; www.themidnightshift.com.au; 85-91 Oxford St, Darlinghurst; video bar free, club cover varies; ☺noon-4am Mon-Wed, noon-6am Thu & Fri, 2pm-6am Sat & Sun) The grande dame of the Oxford St scene, the Shift has two quite distinct venues. The downstairs video bar attracts an unpretentious mix of blokes, twinks and bears; upstairs there's a club with grinding beats and lavish drag productions.

Oxford Hotel
NIGHTCLUB

(Map p80; www.theoxfordhotel.com.au; 134 Oxford St, Taylor Sq, Darlinghurst; admission free; ☺10am-late) Another year, another owner, another refit...another panic that this treasured venue might (shudder) go straight. Fortunately, so far, so gay. Three very different floors await.

Finally, if you simply must bring home a gift, the **Tool Shed** (Map p80; www.toolshed.com.au; level 1, 81 Oxford St; ☺24hr) has sex toys that will both fascinate and horrify airport screeners.

Eco Tours

Ecotreasures ECO TOURS

(☎0415 121 648; www.ecotreasures.com.au) Small group tours of Sydney's Northern Beaches and Ku-ring-gai Chase National Park. The nine-hour 'Sydney Coastal Experience Tour' (adult/child $135/85) includes stand-up paddling, guided bushwalks, a visit to a whale-watching viewing platform, a visit to an aquatic reserve and a swim at a secluded beach.

Harbour Cruises

Captain Cook Cruises HARBOUR CRUISES

(Map p70; ☎02-9206 1111; www.captaincook.com.au; Wharf 6, Circular Quay) Offers a 1¼-hour 'Harbour Highlights' cruise (adult/child 5-14 years/student $30/16/26) and a 24-hour hop-on hop-off 'Harbour Express' pass with entry to Fort Denison, Shark Island and Taronga Zoo (adult/child/student $58/32/36). Also at Aquarium Wharf, Darling Harbour.

Sydney Ferries
HARBOUR CRUISES

(Map p70; www.sydneyferries.nsw.gov.au) Visit the website or one of the Circular Quay ticket booths to find out everything there is to know about touring the harbour by ferry.

Scenic Flights

Sydney Seaplanes
SCENIC FLIGHTS

(☎02-9974 1455; www.seaplanes.com.au; 15/30min scenic flights $170/235, flight & lunch packages $460-555) Adrenalin-inducing excitement meets epicurean delight when you take a seaplane flight from Rose Bay to the Berowra Waters Inn (p125) on the Hawkesbury or Jonah's at Whale Beach (p112) on Sydney's Northern Beaches. Also offers scenic flights around Sydney Harbour and 30-minute flights to Newcastle ($175 to $225).

Walking Tours

Sydney Architecture Walks
WALKING TOURS

(☎02-8239 2211; www.sydneyarchitecture.org; adult/concession $35/25) These two-hour, architect-led tours run from September to May, departing from the Museum of Sydney. There's a tour of the city on most Wednesdays at 10.30am, one concentrating on the Opera House on Saturdays at 10.30am and an occasional tour focusing on the industrial heritage of The Rocks (various times).

BridgeClimb
WALKING TOURS

(Map p70; ☎02-9240 1100; www.bridgeclimb.com; 5 Cumberland St, The Rocks; adult $188-268, child 10-15 $128-188; ⊙3½hr tours around the clock) Don a headset, an umbilical cord and a naff grey jumpsuit and you'll be ready to embark on the climb of your life! Book well in advance.

★ Festivals & Events

Sydney has plenty of festivals and special goings-on year-round. Visitor centres will be able to advise you what's on when you're in town.

January

Big Day Out
MUSIC

(www.bigdayout.com) Open-air concert in January featuring many local and international performers and bands.

Sydney Festival
ARTS

(www.sydneyfestival.org.au) This massive event in January floods the city with art and includes free outdoor concerts in the Domain.

February

Chinese New Year
CULTURE

(www.cityofsydney.nsw.gov.au/cny) Colourful celebration featuring food, fireworks and much more. Actual dates vary according to the phases of the moon.

Sydney Gay & Lesbian Mardi Gras
GAY PRIDE

(www.mardigras.org.au) The highlight of this world-famous festival is the over-the-top, sequined Oxford St parade, culminating in a Bacchanalian party at the Entertainment Quarter in Moore Park.

Tropfest
FILM

(www.tropfest.com) The world's largest short-film festival takes over The Domain for one night.

March/April

Royal Easter Show
AGRICULTURE

(www.eastershow.com.au) Twelve-day agricultural show and funfair at Homebush Bay.

May

Sydney Writers' Festival
LITERATURE

(www.swf.org.au) The country's pre-eminent literary shindig is held at venues include Pier 4/5 at Walsh Bay.

June

Biennale of Sydney
ART

(www.biennaleofsydney.com.au) High-profile festival of art and ideas held every even-numbered year.

September

Rugby League Grand Final
SPORT

(www.nrl.com) The two teams left standing in the National Rugby League (NRL) meet to decide who's best.

December

Sydney to Hobart Yacht Race
SPORT

(www.rolexsydneyhobart.com) On 26 December Sydney Harbour is a sight to behold as hundreds of boats crowd its waters to farewell the yachts competing in this gruelling race.

New Year's Eve
FIREWORKS

(www.cityofsydney.nsw.gov.au/nye) The biggest party of the year, with a flamboyant firework display on the Harbour Bridge.

🛏 Sleeping

You'll sleep well (though not cheaply) in Sydney. The winter months sometimes deliver bargains, but between November and February you should expect prices to jump by as much as 40%. The reality is that the city is busy all year – we advise you to book ahead and shop around for the best price.

In this chapter, a budget room ($) is classified as costing under $110 per night. Midrange rooms ($$) cost between $110 and $200; top-end rooms ($$$) start at $200 a night. The prices we have given don't apply during the busy Christmas/New Year period, when rates skyrocket.

CIRCULAR QUAY & THE ROCKS

TOP CHOICE **Sydney Harbour YHA** HOSTEL $
(Map p70; ☑02-8272 0900; www.yha.com.au; 110 Cumberland St, The Rocks; dm $44-59, d $148-170, d with harbour view $165-185; ✳@🛜) The view from the rooftop terrace and deluxe rooms at this recently opened and exceptionally well-run YHA hostel is fabulous – right over Circular Quay to the Opera House. The modern dorms and private rooms are neat, comfortable and air-conditioned; all have private bathrooms. The building was designed to be environmentally sustainable and incorporates an archaeology education centre that reflects its location amid the archaeological remnants of the early colony.

Russell BOUTIQUE HOTEL $$$
(Map p70; ☑02-9241 3543; www.therussell.com. au; 143a George St, The Rocks; d $199-245, without bathroom $130-199; ✳) A recent renovation has seen this long-standing favourite divest itself of frills and furbelows and attain some contemporary style as well as a lift and a downstairs wine bar. The rooftop garden and location just minutes from Circular Quay are major drawcards, but only a few rooms have air-con.

Lord Nelson Brewery Hotel BOUTIQUE HOTEL $$
(Map p70; ☑02-9251 4044; www.lordnelson.com. au; 19 Kent St, The Rocks; d $190, without bathroom $130; ✳🛜) Built in 1841, this boutique sandstone pub has its own brewery (try a pint of 'Nelson's Blood') and offers elegantly understated rooms, many with walls of the original exposed stone. Bathrooms are regal – even those that are shared.

Park Hyatt HOTEL $$$
(Map p70; ☑02-9241 1234; www.sydney.park. hyatt.com; 7 Hickson Rd, The Rocks; r $695-1045; ✳@🛜) Luxury meets location at Sydney's most expensive hotel. Bookending Circular Quay with the Opera House, the rooms'

service levels and facilities are second to none, although the building itself lacks architectural grace (and then some).

Observatory Hotel HOTEL $$$
(Map p70; ☑02-9256 2222; www.observatory hotel.com.au; 89-113 Kent St, The Rocks; r $315-615; ✳@🛜) Giving the Park Hyatt a run for its money in the luxury stakes, this sleek operation is housed in an undistinguished building in The Rocks, but more than makes amends with its extremely elegant and comfortable rooms. There's a day spa, restaurant, gym, indoor pool and tennis court.

B&B Sydney Harbour B&B $$
(Map p70; ☑02-9247 1130; www.bedandbreakfast sydney.com; 140-142 Cumberland St, The Rocks; s $165-214, without bathroom $140-165, d $178-260, without bathroom $155-178; ✳) Rooms at this century-old guesthouse in The Rocks sport a pleasant traditional decor with an Australiana flavour; some have harbour views. The lavish breakfast can be enjoyed in the pretty courtyard. Not all rooms have air-con.

CITY CENTRE

Vibe Hotel HOTEL $$
(Map p76; ☑02-9282 0987; www.vibehotels.com. au; 111 Goulburn St; d $165-220, ste $220-300; ✳@🛜) The rooms are spacious and extremely well priced at this excellent choice near Central Station. All have a seating area, flat-screen TV, work desk and enormous closet. There's a ground-floor cafe and a gym, sauna and good-sized pool on the outdoor deck. Breakfast costs an extra $22 to $28.

Westend Backpackers HOSTEL $
(Map p76; ☑02-9211 4588; http://legendhasitwest end.com.au; 412 Pitt St; dm $19-35, s $85-95, d $87-97; ✳@🛜) For the cheapest sleep in Sydney, check into the 32-bed 'Church' dorm at this well-run hostel. You'll save even more money by taking advantage of the free pasta and rice supplied in the excellent communal kitchen, and the free wine and cheese served in the welcoming communal lounge on Friday nights. All this plus the fact that it's clean, comfortable and secure makes Westend a top choice.

Y Hotel HOSTEL $$
(Map p80; ☑02-9264 2451; www.yhotel.com. au; 5-11 Wentworth Ave; dm $35-65, s $70-202, d $70-250; ✳@🛜) Package tourists are in more evidence than party animals at this popular budget hotel. Perfectly located in a quiet pocket of the city close to Hyde Park,

Oxford St, train stations and bus stops, it offers simple, well-maintained and extremely clean sleeping options that span the gamut from small dorms to spacious studios with en suites and kitchenettes.

Bounce Hotel
HOSTEL $

(Map p76; ☎02-9281 2222, 1800 890 897; www.bouncehotel.com.au; 28 Chalmers St; dm $31-37, d/f $135/165; ✳@⑳) Bounce describes itself as a 'fresh, new and modern hotel providing upmarket accommodation for budget travellers', and we're pretty much in agreement. All dorms and rooms are air-conditioned, female-only dorms have private bathrooms, beds have inner-spring mattresses and bathrooms are sleek.

Pensione Hotel
BOUTIQUE HOTEL $$

(Map p76; ☎02-9265 8888; www.pensione.com.au; 631-635 George St; s/d from $100/135; ✳@⑳) This tastefully reworked post office features 68 smart, neutrally shaded rooms, some of which are tiny. There's also a communal lounge with kitchenette. Aim for a rear room away from traffic noise. Breakfast is an extra $10.

Medina Grand Sydney
APARTMENTS $$$

(Map p76; ☎02-9270 0000; www.medina.com.au/medina-grand-sydney/hotel; 511 Kent St; studio $160-430, 1-bed apt $210-500, 2-bed apt $280-650; ✳⑳⑳) Near both Chinatown and Darling Harbour but with double-glazed windows to ensure a good night's sleep, this apartment hotel offers spacious, fully equipped apartments and smaller studio rooms with kitchenettes. The apartments offer the best value.

Establishment Hotel
BOUTIQUE HOTEL $$$

(Map p70; ☎02-9240 3100; www.merivale.com; 5 Bridge Lane; r $445-800; ✳@⑳) Through this door pass discreet celebrities, style-conscious couples and execs hoping for a nooner with their assistant. What the hotel lacks in facilities is more than made up for in glamour, although light sleepers should beware – the hotel is in one of Sydney's most happening (and noisy) entertainment complexes.

Wake Up!
HOSTEL $

(Map p76; ☎02-9288 7888; www.wakeup.com.au; 509 Pitt St; dm $32-40, d & tw $112-132, without bathroom $98-118; ✳@⑳) This converted 1900 department store on top of Sydney's busiest intersection is a convivial, colourful, professionally run hostel with a tour desk, 24-hour check-in, sunny cafe, bar and pronounced party atmosphere. Dorms have four to 10 beds.

Travelodge Sydney
HOTEL $$

(Map p80; ☎02-8267 1700; www.travelodge.com.au/travelodge-sydney-hotel/home; cnr Wentworth Ave & Goulburn St; d from $99; ✳@⑳) A great location near Hyde Park (equidistant between Museum Station and Central Station) plus clean, comfortable and well-set-up rooms with basic kitchenette mean that this is a compelling choice, particularly if you can score one of the sensational internet specials (look for the five-night package).

Sydney Central YHA
HOSTEL $

(Map p76; ☎02-9218 9000; http://www.yha.com.au; 11 Rawson Pl; dm $36-45, d $108-132; ✳@⑳⑳) Near Central Station, this 1913 heritage-listed 556-bed monolith was renovated in recent years and is a safe if somewhat utilitarian choice. Rooms are brightly painted and the kitchens and cinema room are great, but the highlight is lazing in the heated rooftop pool.

Base Backpackers
HOSTEL $

(Map p70; ☎02-9267 7718; www.stayatbase.com; 477 Kent St; dm $28-35, d $120-125, d without bathroom $99; ✳@⑳) The flashpacker chain maintains its high standards (mostly) in this hostel near the Town Hall. The girls-only 'sanctuary' dorm is a winner, and some of the mixed dorms have their own bathrooms. Be warned that the downstairs Scary Canary bar can be noisy.

Hilton
HOTEL $$$

(Map p70; ☎02-9266 2000; www.sydney.hilton.com; 488 George St; d from $299; ✳@⑳) This Hilton is a whole lot classier than the one who used to adorn the pages of celebrity magazines. The rooms are contemporary, chic and surprisingly spacious, and the hotel's fabulous bars and Glass Brasserie are added fillips.

KINGS CROSS, POTTS POINT & WOOLOOMOOLOO

Original Backpackers
HOSTEL $

(Map p80; ☎02-9356 3232; www.originalbackpackers.com.au; 160-162 Victoria St, Kings Cross; dm $25-32, d $90-95, without bathroom $80-85; @⑳) Operating for over three decades, this exceptionally well-run hostel occupies two character-filled Victorian houses filled with contemporary art (the owners also run an art gallery). A new wing hosts double rooms with en suite bathrooms, fridge, TV and DVD; dorms and doubles with shared bathroom are in the original houses and feature polished floorboards and high ceilings.

Smack-bang in the middle of the party precinct, it runs a busy activities program and has a convivial courtyard area and excellent communal kitchen with food lockers.

Diamant Hotel
HOTEL $$$

(Map p80; ☑02-9295 8888; www.8hotels.com; 14 Kings Cross Rd, Kings Cross; d $165-350, ste $305-375; ❄@☎) Standing as proudly tall as the nearby Coca-Cola sign, this supersleek member of the 8 Hotels chain offers a choice of room styles, many complete with views and courtyards. King-size beds and quality linen feature in a seriously sophisticated package, with the only disappointment being the lack of wi-fi access in rooms (but available in the foyer and wine bar). The popular Time to Vino wine bar is on the ground floor. No breakfast.

Simpsons of Potts Point
B&B $$$

(☑02-9356 2199; www.simpsonspottspoint.com. au; 8 Challis Ave, Potts Point; r $235-335, ste $325-385; ❄@☎) An 1892 red-brick villa at the quiet end of a busy cafe strip, the perennially popular Simpsons looks towards Laura Ashley and her ilk for decorative flourishes. The downstairs lounge and breakfast room are lovely, and rooms are both comfortable and impeccably clean. An excellent, albeit conservative, choice.

Eva's Backpackers
HOSTEL $

(☑02-9358 2185; www.evasbackpackers.com.au; 6-8 Orwell St, Kings Cross; dm $30-34, d $80-92; ❄@☎) This long-running favourite offers a friendly communal kitchen, rooftop terrace and free wi-fi/internet. Though basic, the rooms and bathrooms are clean and well maintained. A few of the upstairs dorms have air-con, but the rest of the building gets hot in summer.

Victoria Court Hotel
B&B $$

(off Map p80; ☑02-9357 3200; www.victoriacourt. com.au; 122 Victoria St, Potts Point; s $99-132, d $110-280; ❄@☎) Chintzy charm reigns supreme at this faded but well-run B&B, which has 25 rooms in a pair of three-storey 1881 brick terrace houses. The more expensive rooms are larger and have balconies.

Hotel 59
B&B $$

(Map p80; ☑02-9360 5900; www.hotel59.com.au; 59 Bayswater Rd, Kings Cross; s $88, d $110-121, f $132; ❄☎) The nine rooms at this popular choice may hark back to a time when Wham! and crimped hair were in vogue, but they are spotless and oddly charming. The

central location and incredibly helpful staff add to the appeal. Free wi-fi.

BLUE Sydney
BOUTIQUE HOTEL $$$

(☑02-9331 9000; www.tajhotels.com/sydney; 6 Cowper Wharf Rd, Woolloomooloo; d from $200; ❄@☎) Stay here for the night and boast that you slept next to Russell Crowe (he owns one of the apartments at the end of the wharf). But even if he's not your cup of tea, you're sure to enjoy the boutique sensibilities and excellent location of this Taj-owned hotel. Breakfast costs a hefty $50 extra.

Sydney Central Backpackers
HOSTEL $

(☑02-9358 6600; www.sydneybackpackers.com. au; 16 Orwell St, Kings Cross; dm $25-28, d without bathroom $70-80; @☎) The run-down and slightly dingy rooms at this Kings Cross stayer contrast with the newly renovated downstairs kitchen and popular rooftop terrace. Breakfast is included but dorms are extremely cramped and there are no lockers.

Maisonette Hotel
HOTEL $$

(☑02-9357 3878; www.maisonettehotel.com; 31 Challis Ave, Potts Point; s $99-110, without bathroom $65-85, d $110-185; ☎) You get bang for your buck at the Maisonette, a cheery hotel in the heart of Potts Point's cafe scene. Sure, the carpet's a little frayed and a lick of paint is overdue, but the rooms are welcoming and the location rocks. There are considerable discounts for stays of a week or more.

Quest Potts Point
HOTEL $$$

(Map p80; ☑02-8988 6999; www.questpottspoint. com.au; 15 Springfield Ave, Kings Cross; d from $180; ❄@☎) Occupying an art-deco building in the thick of the Cross action, this branch of the franchised Quest operation offers 68 elegant and well-equipped studios and suites. Most have kitchenettes and the executive suites have stunning city-view terraces.

INNER EAST

TOP CHOICE Adina Apartment Hotel Sydney
APARTMENTS $$$

(Map p80; ☑02-9212 1111; www.adinahotels.com. au; 359 Crown St, Surry Hills; 1-bed apt $250-350, 2-bed apt $350-460; ❄@☎❄) In the heart of the Surry Hills entertainment precinct, the recently renovated Adina offers 85 exceptionally stylish and well-equipped apartments. Bills, one of Sydney's most famous cafes, is in the same building and will provide room service dinners on request. Ask for an upper-floor apartment, as those on the lower floors can be noisy.

Kirketon BOUTIQUE HOTEL **$$**
(Map p80; ☎02-9332 2011; www.8hotels.com; 229 Darlinghurst Rd, Darlinghurst; r $145-239; ❄@) The Kirketon's 40 designer rooms are as impeccably turned out as its hip clientele and hot staff. The stylishly sparse standard rooms are cramped – upgrade to premium, executive or superior if possible. If not, never fear – you can always hang out in the glam Eau de Vie bar.

Hotel Altamont BOUTIQUE HOTEL **$$**
(Map p80; ☎02-9360 6000; www.8hotels.com; 207 Darlinghurst Rd, Darlinghurst; r from $135; ❄@📶) The Rolling Stones have stayed in this Georgian pile, hence the name. It's been given a postmodern makeover since their stay, though, with the rooms now more Zen than rock-and-roll grunge. The foyer bar/breakfast room is a great spot to sit and watch the daily Darlinghurst parade go by. Excellent value.

150 Apartments APARTMENTS **$$$**
(Map p80; ☎1300 246 835; www.apartmenthotel.com.au; 150 Liverpool St, Darlinghurst; apt $249-599; ❄📶) Designed by minimalist masters Engelen Moore, these ferociously fashionable two-bedroom apartments near Hyde Park are fully equipped with designer furniture and appliances. There are discount rates for long-term stays.

Medusa BOUTIQUE HOTEL **$$$**
(Map p80; ☎02-9331 1000; www.medusa.com.au; 267 Darlinghurst Rd, Darlinghurst; r $310-420; ❄📶) There's not a serpent in sight at this theatrically decorated designer hotel. Eighteen seductive rooms open onto a tranquil courtyard with reflection pool or onto tree-lined Darlinghurst Rd. Staff will happily welcome your chihuahua, but aren't crazy about children.

City Crown Motel MOTEL **$$**
(Map p80; ☎02-9331 2433; www.citycrownmotel.com.au; 289 Crown St, Surry Hills; r $110-150, f $140-177; ❄@) In an unbeatable Surry Hills location, this nondescript three-storey motel has basic rooms with a bright colour scheme and so-so beds. Escape to the balconies (every room has one) or to the streetside cafe to plan your next fun foray. Breakfast costs extra.

Hughenden GUESTHOUSE **$$$**
(☎02-9363 4863; www.thehughendenhotel.com.au; 14 Queen St, Woollahra; r $148-328, apt $228-288; ❄@📶) This 1870s Italianate guesthouse is owned by a writer of children's novels, and has a cheerfully bohemian ambience that comes to the fore during the Thursday and Friday jazz nights. The well-worn rooms feature eclectic furnishings; some are small and dark but the best have balconies overlooking pretty Queen St. Pet friendly.

Manor House BOUTIQUE HOTEL **$$$**
(Map p80; ☎02-9380 6633; www.manorhouse.com.au; 86 Flinders St, Paddington; r $175-350, ste $400; ❄@🏊) Step off busy Flinders St and step back in time to 1850 as you enter this grand mansion, complete with extravagant chandeliers, moulded ceilings, Victorian tiling and enough brocade for a queen (many of whom stay here, especially during Mardi Gras).

Arts Hotel HOTEL **$$**
(Map p80; ☎02-9361 0211; www.artshotel.com.au; 21 Oxford St, Paddington; r $140-195; ❄📶🏊) Another choice popular with gay travellers, this well-run 64-room motel in 'Paddinghurst' has 64 bland but comfortable rooms that could do with a makeover. On the positive side, there's free car parking, bicycles are available for guest use and the garden courtyard has a good-sized solar-heated pool. Breakfast costs an extra $15 to $20.

BONDI

TOP CHOICE **Bondi Beach House** GUESTHOUSE **$$**
(Map p83; ☎0417 336 444; www.bondibeachhouse.com.au; 28 Sir Thomas Mitchell Rd; s $95-135, without bathroom $80-110, d $170-300, without bathroom $120-215, ste $185-325; ❄📶) Tucked away in a tranquil pocket behind Campbell Pde, this charming place offers a real home-away-from-home atmosphere. Though only a five-minute walk from the beach, you may well be tempted to stay in all day – the rear courtyard and front terrace are great spots for relaxing, and the rooms (particularly the suites) are conducive to long sleep ins. No children under 12, and DIY breakfast.

Bondi Beachouse YHA HOSTEL **$**
(Map p83; ☎02-9365 2088; www.yha.com.au; 63 Fletcher St; dm $33-50, d & tw $100-130, without bathroom $78-110; @📶) A short stroll from the beach, this 95-bed art-deco hostel is the best in Bondi. Dorms sleep between four and eight, and some of the double/twin rooms have ocean views – all are clean and well maintained. Facilities include a table-tennis table, games room, air-conditioned TV room, barbecue, free bodyboard and snorkel use, and a rooftop deck with views over to Tamarama Beach. Put simply, it's the sort of place where you keep telling the staff

'another night please'. Bus 380 from Circular Quay stops nearby.

Ravesi's
BOUTIQUE HOTEL $$$

(Map p83; ✆02-9365 4422; www.ravesis.com.au; 118 Campbell Pde; r weekdays $249-399, weekends $269-429; ✳🖥) To enjoy a sybaritic Bondi sojourn, claim one of the 12 spacious and stylish rooms above the famous Campbell Parade bar. Those celebrating a big occasion should consider booking the Deluxe Penthouse, which has a large private terrace overlooking the beach. No breakfast.

Bondi Backpackers
HOSTEL $

(Map p83; ✆02-9130 4660, 1800 304 660; www. bondibackpackers.com.au; 110 Campbell Pde, Bondi; dm $25-27, s without bathroom from $43, d without bathroom from $31, all incl breakfast; 🖥) Coming a distant second to the YHA in the quality stakes, this run-down joint opposite the beach gets a mention solely on account of its location. It's the only one of the budget sleeps on Campbell Pde worth considering. Dorms and rooms are clean(ish), and there's free internet.

COOGEE

Coogee Sands Hotel & Apartments
HOTEL $$$

(✆02-9665 8588; www.coogeesands.com.au; 161 Dolphin St; r $155-295; ✳🖥) The golden sands of Coogee Beach are across the street from this apartment hotel on Dolphin St (love that name!). The pick of the accommodation is a terrace studio with ocean view.

Dive Hotel
HOTEL $$$

(✆02-9665 5538; www.divehotel.com.au; 234 Arden St; r $150-310; ✳🖥) It seems strange to be recommending a hotel that describes itself as a dive, but so be it. Here's your chance to live the cheap-chic Ikea lifestyle without having to screw your furniture together. The smart and simple rooms have kitchenettes and blue-tile bathrooms; some have balconies with beach views.

GLEBE & NEWTOWN

Billabong Gardens
HOSTEL $

(Map p84; ✆02-9550 3236; www.billabonggardens. com.au; 5-11 Egan St, Newtown; dm $26-28, s & d $95, s/d without bathroom $55/75; @🖥🏊) This enduring motel/hostel near Sydney University offers a richer experience than most backpacker joints, with travellers, touring rock bands and anonymous others mixing by the jellybean of a pool. Rooms and six-bed dorms come with or without bathrooms;

dorms have up to six beds. Internet is free (wi-fi is charged).

Glebe Point YHA
HOSTEL $

(off Map p84; ✆02-9692 8418; www.yha.com.au; 262-264 Glebe Point Rd, Glebe; dm $28-32, s/d with shared bathroom $64/76.50; @🖥) A good example of what architect Robin Boyd called the 'Great Australian Ugliness', this utilitarian hostel on leafy Glebe Point Rd is best seen from the inside looking out. Rooms, dorms and shared bathrooms are basic but clean; a few dorms have no external windows. There's a large and well-equipped communal kitchen and a rooftop where barbecue nights are held.

Glebe Village
HOSTEL $

(off Map p84; ✆02-9660 8878; www.glebevillage. com; 256 Glebe Point Rd, Glebe; dm $23-27, s/d without bathroom $65/90; @🖥) The dorms here are hot and stuffy, the private rooms are basic and the place isn't as clean as the nearby YHA, but management is friendly, prices are low and there's a great garden entertainment area with table tennis, meaning that the party vibe is strong.

NORTH SHORE

🌲 Lane Cove River Tourist Park
CAMPGROUND $

(✆02-9888 9133; www.lcrtp.com.au; Plassey Rd, North Ryde; d powered/unpowered sites $37/35, cabins from $121, d luxury eco tent $390-450; ✳@🖥) This cheery place in the Lane Cove National Park lies 14km north of the city and has excellent facilities. The CBD is a 25-minute trip away by train or bus.

Big4 Sydney Lakeside Holiday Park
CAMPGROUND $

(✆02-9913 7845, 1800 008 845; www.sydneylakeside.com.au; Lake Park Rd, North Narrabeen; powered sites $60; @🖥) You're surrounded by 21 beaches at this popular place 17km north of Sydney's CBD. Forget about the cabins and lakeside 'villas' – they're overpriced for what they offer. Free wi-fi.

MANLY

101 Addison Road
B&B $$

(✆02-9977 6216; www.bb-manly.com; 101 Addison Rd; s/d $150/170) Owner Jill Caskey offers a B&B in the true sense of the word – two rooms of her charming Victorian cottage are available, but only one guest booking is accommodated. The private lounge comes complete with books, TV, DVD and grand piano. There are even beach towels and umbrellas for guests' use.

Boardrider Backpacker
HOSTEL $

(Map p86; ☑02-9977 6077; www.boardrider.com.au; Rear 63, The Corso; dm $26-47, d $90-162, without bathroom $65-132; @ 🛜) The best of the two hostels in Manly (by a long shot), Boardrider has a range of dorms and private rooms; the best options are the female-only eight-bed dorm and the deluxe en suite doubles. Be warned: cleanliness doesn't appear to be high on the priority list and the location right on the Corso will make noise a problem for light sleepers.

Manly Pacific
HOTEL $$$

(Map p86; ☑02-9977 7666; www.accorhotels.com.au; 55 North Steyne; d $209-419; ❋@🛜🛏) Right on Manly's ocean beach, this recently refurbished midrise hotel is managed by resort-brand Novotel. Its 214 rooms may be a quick ferry ride from the CBD but they are closer in holiday spirit to Coffs Harbour or even the Gold Coast. Lounge by the rooftop pool or on your ocean-view balcony.

Periwinkle Guest House
B&B $$

(off Map p86; ☑02-9977 4668; www.periwinkle.citysearch.com.au; 18-19 East Esplanade, Manly; s $154-174, s without bathroom $124-134, d $179-215, d without bathroom $149-159) Two Federation-style houses on Manly Cove have been combined to create this relaxed guesthouse with 18 pretty bedrooms. Our only quibble is that the prices are a bit steep considering the lack of amenities (eg, air-conditioning).

SOUTHERN BEACHES

Cronulla Beach YHA
HOSTEL $

(☑02-9527 7772; www.cronullabeachyha.com; level 1, 40-42 Kingsway, Cronulla; dm $32.50-34.50, s/d $75/100; @) Conveniently located 300m from the Cronulla train station, this is a top spot for honing your surfing skills or hooking up with fellow coastal-trail walkers. Travellers give the friendly staff a big thumbs-up, but warn not to expect too much when it comes to cleanliness. Bodyboard and sandboard use is free. The train trip to Central Sydney takes 55 minutes (Eastern Suburbs and Illawarra line), and Royal National Park is approximately 20km away.

✕ Eating

Abundant fresh produce, innovative chefs and a multicultural melange all combine to make eating out in Sydney an extremely pleasurable and popular activity.

In this chapter, budget options ($) are those offering main courses for under $20; midrange options ($$) charge between $20 and $50, and top-end options ($$$) charge over $50. Inclusion of a telephone number means that booking is advisable.

CITY CENTRE, THE ROCKS & CIRCULAR QUAY

TOP CHOICE Bécasse
MODERN AUSTRALIAN $$

(Map p70; ☑02-9283 3440; www.becasse.com.au; Westfield Sydney, Pitt St; mains $48, 9-course tasting menu $190; ☻lunch Mon-Fri, dinner Mon-Sat) Acclaimed chef Justin North takes inspiration from what's in season and at the markets, constructing French-influenced dishes with a deft and delicious touch. Recently, he took the bold step of relocating his flagship restaurant from Clarence St to the 5th floor of the new Westfield Sydney complex, and his new space accommodates a mere 25 diners. Those who don't manage to score a table (bookings are eagerly sought after) can instead try another of his new ventures, the adjacent **Quarter 21** (mains $32-39, 7-course tasting menu $90; ☻lunch daily, dinner Mon-Sat), a more casual and less pricey option. And the North empire at Westfield doesn't stop there – there's also a retail store selling ready-made meals, a bakery, a cooking school (classes $150 to $200) and a burger outlet called **Charlie & Co** (wagyu burgers $18, parmesan & truffle fries $8).

Rockpool Bar & Grill
MODERN AUSTRALIAN $$

(Map p70; ☑02-8078 1900; www.rockpool.com.au/sydney/bar-and-grill; cnr Hunter & Blight Sts, Sydney; mains $21-110; ☻lunch Mon-Fri, dinner Mon-Sat) You'll feel like a pampered 1930s Manhattan stockbroker when you dine at this sleek operation in the art-deco City Mutual Building. The bar is famous for its dry-aged, full-blood wagyu burger (make sure you also order a side of the hand-cut fat chips), but carnivores will be equally enamoured with the succulent steaks served in the grill. Both go down well with an expertly made martini. Owner/chef Neil Perry also runs the darkly atmospheric **Spice Temple** (☑02-8078 1088; www.rockpool.com.au/sydney/spice-temple; dishes $16-85) in the basement, which specialises in Chinese provincial dishes and has the same opening hours.

Quay
MODERN AUSTRALIAN $$$

(Map p70; ☑02-9251 5600; www.quay.com.au; upper level, International Passenger Terminal, Circular Quay; 3-course lunch $105, 3-course dinner $155, degustation menu $210; ☺lunch Tue-Fri, dinner daily) One of the big guns of the Sydney dining scene, Quay is known for its extraordinary harbour views, solicitous service and exquisitely presented dishes. Those who baulk at the prospect of the city's heftiest bill should instead purchase a copy of chef Peter Gilmore's cookbook, which discloses the secrets of the utterly extraordinary sea pearls entrée and snow egg dessert that grace the menu here.

Le Grand Café
FRENCH $

(Map p70; www.becasse.com.au; 257 Clarence St, Sydney; breakfast $4-12, lunch $9-12; ☺breakfast & lunch Mon-Sat) All we can say about Justin North's cafe in the foyer of the Harry Seidler–designed Alliance Française building is *ooh la la*. The classic French snacks (think rich soups, quiche and croque-monsieur) are delicious, and the surrounds are extremely smart. No bookings and cash only.

Central Baking Depot
BAKERY $

(Map p70; www.centralbakingdepot.com.au; 37-39 Erskine St, Sydney; pies & sandwiches $4-8, cakes & pastries $2.50-5; ☺7am-5pm Mon-Fri, 8am-2pm Sat) Once upon a time the best bakeries were confined to outside Sydney's business district, but fortunately all that has changed. Come for a savoury snack (pies, sausage rolls, quiches, pizzas, sandwiches), or a sweet treat with coffee.

Guillaume at Bennelong
FRENCH $$$

(Map p70; www.guillaumeatbennelong.com.au; ☏02-9241 1999; Bennelong Pt, Circular Quay East; mains $40-80; ☺lunch Thu & Fri, dinner Mon-Sat) Indulge in master chef Guillaume Brahimi's delectable creations under the sails of the city's most famous landmark. Snuggle into a chocolate-brown banquette or sit yourself next to the window (the views are extraordinary) to enjoy a memorable meal or nosh on tapas (four/six/eight dishes $35/40/45) at the bar. The pre-theatre dinner menu (two/three courses $66/78) offers excellent value.

CHINATOWN & DARLING HARBOUR

Din Tai Fung
TAIWANESE $

(Map p76; www.dintaifungaustralia.com.au; level 1, World Sq, 644 George St, Haymarket; dumplings $9-18, noodles $5-17; ☺lunch & dinner daily) Din Tai Fung's crabmeat, crab roe and pork dumplings deliver an explosion of fabulously flavoursome broth when you bite into their delicate casing. And the delights of this place don't stop there, with a huge choice of noodles, dumplings and buns to choose from. Come early, come hungry, come prepared to share your table.

Sydney Madang
KOREAN $

(Map p76; 371a Pitt St, Sydney; ☺11.30am-1am) Secreted in a somewhat dingy laneway off Pitt St, Sydney Madang serves spicy steam bowls, killer kimchi dishes and lavish BBQ arrays to a loyal coterie of locals and an appreciative cast of visiting Korean nationals. No reservations, so arrive early or expect to queue.

Mamak
MALAYSIAN $

(Map p76; www.mamak.com.au; 15 Goulburn St, Haymarket; satay $8-14, roti $5-10.50, mains $13-18; ☺lunch & dinner daily, to 2am Fri & Sat) Get here early (from 5.30pm) if you want to score a dinner table without queuing, because this eat-and-run Malaysian joint is one of the most popular cheap eateries in the city. The satays are cooked over charcoal and are particularly delicious when accompanied by a flaky golden roti. No bookings and BYO alcohol.

Marigold Restaurant
CHINESE $$

(Map p76; ☏02-9217 6090; www.marigold.com.au; levels 4 & 5, 683-689 George St, Haymarket; 4-5 serves yum cha $15-25, set lunch & dinner menus $33-48; ☺10am-3pm & 5.30pm-midnight) This vast yum-cha palace is a constant whirl of cheongsam-clad waitresses, waiters in bow ties and up to 800 diners tucking into some of the best dumplings in town.

KINGS CROSS, POTTS POINT & WOOLLOOMOOLOO

TOP CHOICE Fratelli Paradiso
ITALIAN $$

(off Map p80; 16 Challis Ave, Potts Point; mains $20-33; ☺7am-11pm Mon-Fri, to 6pm Sat & Sun) Challis Ave is one of the city's cafe hubs, and this bakery-bistro is in the thick of the action. The menu and atmosphere are 100% Italian, a theme that is maintained with excellent espresso and great service. Dishes change daily, and everything is delicious.

Café Sopra
ITALIAN $$

(off Map p80; 81 Macleay St, Potts Point; panini $10.50, salads $16-22, mains $16-24; ☺lunch & dinner daily) Attached to the mighty impressive Fratelli Fresh provedore, Sopra is quite possibly the most popular eatery in Sydney, and for good reason. It serves no-fuss, perfectly prepared Italian food in a bustling, friendly atmosphere. The huge menu changes seasonally, but some favourites (eg the fabulous rigatoni alla bolognese) are constants. There are other branches in Danks St, **Waterloo**

Many Sydneysiders consider a sprinkling of celebrity to be an essential ingredient when it comes to dining out – whether it be courtesy of a star-studded roll-call of regulars, or a celebrity chef at the restaurant's helm. Restaurants such as Armando Percuoco's Buon Ricordo (www.buonricordo.com.au) in Paddington fit perfectly into the former category, and there is a veritable constellation of chefs cooking around town who have attained local and international stardom courtesy of television cooking programs or cookbooks. These include the following:

» **Bill Granger**: Bills (below) Lifestyle chef and author of 12 cookbooks whose food and style are thought by many to be quintessentially Sydney.

» **Kylie Kwong**: Billy Kwong (p110) Presents her own television programs (*My China* etc) and has written a number of cookbooks.

» **Luke Nguyen**: Red Lantern (p110) Presents his own television program (*Luke Nguyen's Vietnam*) and has written the *Songs of Sapa* cookbook.

» **Neil Perry**: Rockpool Bar & Grill (p107), Rockpool and Spice Temple (www.rockpool.com.au) The city's original rock-star chef (with ponytail to match) has a long list of cookbooks and appearances on television cooking programs to his credit.

» **Adriano Zumbo**: Adriano Zumbo (p111) Everyone who watched the TV series about Sydney's hip pastry chef knows that Mr Zumbo takes his role as a celebrity chef very seriously – fortunately, his sweet concoctions live up to their hype.

(brunch & lunch daily) and at **Walsh Bay** (Map p70; lunch & dinner daily).

Fish Face SEAFOOD $$
(Map p80; 132 Darlinghurst Rd, Darlinghurst; mains $36-45; ☉lunch Sun, dinner daily) This sardine-sized hole in the wall is the place to come for fish so fresh it's almost wriggling. Plate after plate of exquisite preparations emerge from the constant drama of the open kitchen – the sushi and sashimi are particularly noteworthy.

Bills CAFE $
(Map p80; www.bills.com.au; 433 Liverpool St, Darlinghurst; breakfast $5.50-18.50, lunch $7.50-26; ☉7.30am-3pm Mon-Sat, 8.30am-3pm Sun) Bill Granger almost single-handedly kicked off the Sydney craze for stylish brunch. His two most famous dishes – ricotta hotcakes and sweetcorn fritters – have legions of fans, but we wish the coffee served at his three Sydney cafes was better. The other branches are in Woollahra and Surry Hills (Map p80).

Tilbury Hotel GASTROPUB $$
(www.tilburyhotel.com.au; 12-18 Nicholson St, Woolloomooloo; mains $26-38, daily lunch special incl glass of wine $30; ☉lunch & dinner Tue-Sat, brunch & lunch Sun) Once the dank domain of burly sailors and visiting ne'er-do-wells, the Tilbury now sparkles as one of the city's best gastropubs. It attracts a well-heeled crowd that

hangs out in the outdoor courtyard (lunch only) or indoor restaurant, cafe and bar.

SURRY HILLS

Bird Cow Fish MODERN AUSTRALIAN $$
(off Map p80; ☎02-9380 4090; www.birdcowfish.com.au; 4-5/500 Crown St, Surry Hills; brunch $15.50-18.50, mains $36-37; ☉lunch daily, dinner Mon-Sat, brunch Sat & Sun from 9am) The name sums up the ingredient list, but gives no hint of the excellence of the produce, dishes, wine list and service on offer at this terrific Surry Hills bistro. Brunch is a delight, particularly as the coffee is among the best in Sydney.

Spice I Am THAI $
(Map p76; www.spiceiam.com.au; 90 Wentworth Ave; mains $14-26; ☉lunch & dinner Tue-Sun) The signature dishes at this mega-popular BYO eatery on the city edge of Surry Hills are fragrant, flavoursome and cheap, meaning that queues are inevitable. Service is speedy, but if the tables aren't turning over fast enough, you can always try nearby **House** (Map p76; 202 Elizabeth St), a courtyard eatery in the Triple Ace Bar that is run by the same crew and serves Thai street food.

Porteño SOUTH AMERICAN $$
(☎02-8399 1440; 358 Cleveland St, Surry Hills; share dishes $4-48; ☉dinner Mon-Sat) The attitude-laden boys who made their mark with the wildly popular Bodega tapas bar in Commonwealth St have decided to move

their robust homage to the foods of South America to the western edge of Surry Hills, and they've taken loads of fans along for the gastronomically wild ride. Bring a huge appetite and at least four friends if possible, as you can only book for five or more. And don't miss the roast suckling pig – it's truly magnificent.

Bourke Street Bakery
BAKERY **$**

(off Map p80; www.bourkestreetbakery.com.au; 633 Bourke St, Surry Hills; pastries & cakes $3-5, pies & sandwiches $4-7.50; ☺7am-6pm Mon-Fri, 8am-5pm Sat & Sun) Surry Hill's much-loved corner bakery makes wonderful sandwiches with its sourdough, soy-loaves and crusty white *ficelles*. Its cakes, pastries, pies and quiches are equally delicious. Grab one of the hotly contested seats and enjoy your choice with a coffee.

Marque
MODERN AUSTRALIAN **$$$**

(Map p80; ☎02-9332 2225; www.marquerestaurant.com.au; 4-5 Crown St, Surry Hills; 3 courses $95, degustation $150; ☺lunch Fri, dinner Mon-Sat) Mark Best's cooking style is global in inspiration but has superbly executed French cuisine at its heart – after eating here you'll understand why Marque won the 2011 *Sydney Morning Herald Good Food Guide* restaurant of the year. There's an excellent-value, three-course set lunch on Fridays ($45).

Red Lantern
VIETNAMESE **$$**

(off Map p80; ☎02-9698 4355; www.redlantern.com.au; 545 Crown St, Surry Hills; mains $28-38; ☺lunch Tue-Fri, dinner daily) At the Cleveland St end of the gourmet mile-and-a-bit that is Crown St, this atmospheric eatery is run by television presenters Luke Nguyen *(Luke Nguyen's Vietnam)* and Mark Jensen *(Ready Steady Cook)* and sister/wife Pauline (author of the excellent *Secrets of the Red Lantern* cookbook-cum-autobiography). It serves modern takes on classic Vietnamese dishes, and is deservedly popular.

Bentley Restaurant & Bar
MODERN AUSTRALIAN **$$**

(Map p80; ☎02-9332 2344; Crown St, Surry Hills; mains $33-40; ☺lunch & dinner Tue-Sun) Almost as fashionable as Surry Hills itself, this converted corner pub has a down-to-earth bar where you can enjoy tasty tapas, but its main drawcard is the highly regarded restaurant, which serves beautifully presented and carefully prepared food in – alas – tiny portions. The eight-course tasting menu

($120) is the way to go, particularly with the $70 wine match.

Pizza e Birra
PIZZA **$$**

(off Map p80; 500 Crown St, Surry Hills; pasta $20-24, pizza $22-25; ☺lunch Thu-Sun, dinner Mon-Wed) Authentic, Neapolitan-style pizza goes down a treat with a well-chilled beer or excellent glass of wine at this perennially popular pizzeria. No bookings.

Billy Kwong
CHINESE **$$**

(Map p80; shop 3, 355 Crown St, Surry Hills; mains $26-48; ☺dinner) We're in two minds as to whether we should recommend Kylie Kwong's phenomenally popular eatery. The business strives hard to be sustainable, serving organic, seasonal and local produce wherever possible, and the results can be truly inspired (on our most recent visit, the crispy skin duck with orange was truly magnificent). However, the cramped, noisy and uncomfortable setting, sometimes lackadaisical service, lack of desserts and no-bookings policy don't seem to tally with the high prices. Make up your own mind.

PADDINGTON & WOOLLAHRA

Four in Hand
FRENCH **$$**

(☎02-9362 1999; 105 Sutherland St, Paddington; mains $36-42; ☺lunch & dinner Tue-Sun) You can't go far in Paddington and Woollahra without tripping over a beautiful old pub with amazing food. In this case, you'll be tripping over some of the best pub grub in Sydney. The restaurant here is famous for its slow-cooked meat dishes, and also offers fabulously fresh seafood dishes and a limited but delectable array of desserts. The bar menu (mains $15 to $18) is also a winner.

Bistro Moncur
FRENCH **$$**

(116 Queen St, Woollahra; mains $30-43; ☺lunch Tue-Sun, dinner daily,) For the city's best *steak frites*, you need look no further than the famous ground-floor bistro at the upmarket Woollahra Hotel. Its blue swimmer crab and sweetcorn omelette is pretty fabulous, too. There's live rock and roll on Thursday nights between 7.45pm and 10.45pm, and live jazz on Sunday from 6.30pm to 9.30pm. No bookings.

Jackie's Cafe
JAPANESE, MODERN AUSTRALIAN **$$**

(Map p80; 1c Glenmore Rd, Paddington; sandwiches $13-18, sushi from $15; ☺7.30am-4pm) Join the air-kissing, perennially dieting local ladies who lunch at this, their favourite cafe. The sushi is excellent, the sashimi salad looks lavish but is low-cal, and the coffee is consistently good.

The surrounding boutiques offer tempting après-lunch credit-card workouts.

Jones the Grocer DELI, CAFE $
(68 Moncur St, Woollahra; breakfast $5.50-16.50, baguettes $9-10; ☺8.30am-5.30pm Mon-Sat, 9am-5pm Sun) JTG offers high-end groceries, cookbooks and gourmet goodies. Enjoy a good coffee while you're here, then grab some provisions for a Centennial Park picnic. The next-door Woollahra Hotel has an excellent bottle shop (one of the best in Sydney), where you can choose a bottle of wine to accompany your repast.

BONDI

TOP
CHOICE **Icebergs Dining Room**
& Bar ITALIAN $$$
(Map p83; ☑02-9365 9000; www.idrb.com; 1 Notts Ave; mains $36-97; ☺lunch & dinner Tue-Sun) The magnificent view sweeps over Bondi Beach, making Icebergs Australia's most glamorous restaurant – bar none. The menu doesn't disappoint either, offering modern and delicious takes on classic Italian dishes and a choice of aged beef, perfectly cooked. Come for lunch so as to make the most of the view, or arrive in time to enjoy a sunset cocktail at the bar before your meal.

Pompei's PIZZA $$
(Map p83; ☑02-9365 1233; www.pompeis.com.au; 126-130 Roscoe St, Bondi Beach; pizzas $19-23, pasta $24-26; ☺11am-late Fri-Sun, 3pm-late Tue-Thu) Simply sensational Roman-style pizzas, homemade pasta and the best gelato in the city are devoured by locals and visitors alike at Bondi's busiest eatery. There's indoor and outdoor seating, but no views.

Organic Republic BAKERY $
(Map p83; cnr Glenayr & Warners Aves, Bondi Beach; pastries $3-4, sandwiches $7-10; ☺5am-6pm) Its motto 'let the bread speak' says it all – fabulous sandwiches on slabs of home-baked organic bread (including spelt) are the signature at this bakery cafe in a peaceful pocket of Bondi, but you can also enjoy delicious cakes, pastries, pies and biscuits accompanied by a free-trade coffee made with organic milk.

North Bondi Italian Food ITALIAN $$
(Map p83; www.idrb.com/northbondi; 118-120 Ramsgate Ave, North Bondi; pasta $27, mains $29; ☺dinner) As noisy as it is fashionable, this terrific trattoria in the North Bondi RSL building has a casual vibe, simple but *molto*

delizioso food and a democratic no-booking policy. Come early to snaffle a table overlooking the beach.

Sabbaba FAST FOOD $
(Map p83; 80-82 Hall St, Bondi Beach; falafel roll $8.50, kebap roll $9.50, kebap with dips & salad $17; ☺11am-10pm) There are more boardshorts than black coats on view at this friendly Middle Eastern joint in Bondi's main Hassidic strip. Choose from falafels and kebaps in pitta, vegetarian Moroccan soup, dips and salads – everything's fresh, well priced and tasty.

EASTERN BEACHES

Bronte Road Bistro FRENCH $$
(☑02-9389 3028; www.bronteroadbistro.com; 282 Bronte Rd, Charing Cross; mains $31; ☺lunch Thu-Sat, dinner Tue-Sat) This friendly neighbourhood bistro is the perfect reward/draw for the lovely clifftop walk from Bondi. The casual, always-bustling interior (half indoor, half outdoor) and the menu of French favourites are true crowd pleasers.

INNER WEST

Adriano Zumbo PATISSERIE $
(http://adrianozumbo.com; 296 Darling St; ☺8am-6pm Mon-Sat, to 5pm Sun) Look for the queue, and you'll find Sydney's most famous patisserie. Pastry chef Adriano Zumbo became an overnight star when he appeared on the *Masterchef* reality TV show, and he now leads a sugar-fuelled celebrity lifestyle. Try his signature macaroons (the passionfruit and basil ones are divine) and any of the cakes. Takeaway only here and at his shop in **Manly** (Map p86; cnr East Esplanade & Wentworth St; ☺7am-7pm Mon-Fri, 8am-5.30pm Sat & Sun), although there's a cafe in nearby **Rozelle** (114 Terry St; ☺6.30am-4pm Mon-Fri, 7.30am-4pm Sat & Sun).

Bloodwood INTERNATIONAL $$
(Map p84; 416 King St, Newtown; dishes $7-32; ☺lunch Fri-Sun, dinner Wed-Mon) Relax over a few drinks and a progression of small plates (we love those polenta chips!) in the front bar, or make your way to the rear dining spaces to enjoy expertly cooked and soundly conceived dishes from across the globe. The decor is industrial-chic and the vibe is alternative – very Newtown.

Flying Fish SEAFOOD $$
(☑02-9518 6677; www.flyingfish.com.au; Lower Deck, Jones Bay Wharf, Pyrmont; mains $38-48; ☺lunch Tue-Fri & Sun, dinner Mon-Sat) Chef Peter

Kuruvita is known for his aromatic Sri Lankan curries, but everything in this glamorous loft-style eatery is delicious. You can watch the action on the water as you sample sushi, freshly shucked oysters or sophisticated fish dishes. Kids' meals are $15.

Glebe Point Diner MODERN AUSTRALIAN **$$** (off Map p84; [☎]02-9660 2646; 407 Glebe Point Rd, Glebe; mains $26-34; ⊙lunch Fri-Sun, dinner Mon-Sat) A sensational neighbourhood diner, where only the best local produce is used and everything from the home-baked bread and hand-churned butter to the nougat finale is made from scratch. The food is creative and comforting at the same time – a rare combination.

NORTH SHORE & MANLY

Manly Pavilion ITALIAN **$$** (Map p86; [☎]02-9949 9011; West Esplanade; mains $40-45; ⊙lunch & dinner) Lingering over lunch on the waterfront terrace or water-facing dining room of Manly's best restaurant is one of the quintessential Sydney dining experiences. The 1930s building (an old bathing pavilion) has been stylishly restored and the view, modern Italian cuisine, wine list and service are all impressive. It's also a great choice for a sunset aperitivo with delectable *stuzzichini* (snacks, $10 to $15) or antipasti ($26 to $30).

Hugos Manly PIZZA **$$** (Map p86; ([☎]02-8116 8555; www.hugos.com.au; Shop 1, Manly Wharf, East Esplanade; pizzas $20-28; ⊙noon-late Mon-Fri, from 11.30am Sat & Sun) Glamour counts a lot in this town, and nowhere is this more the case than at Hugos. The location at the wharf is great and the pizzas are good, but the waiters often display more attitude than aptitude. There's another branch in **Kings Cross** ([☎]9332 1227; 33 Bayswater Rd; ⊙5pm-late Tue-Sat, 3pm-late Sun).

Bathers' Pavilion MODERN AUSTRALIAN **$$** ([☎]02-9969 5050; www.batherspavilion.com.au; 4 The Esplanade, Balmoral Beach) Gazing out over Balmoral Beach from within the confines of this iconic Spanish Mission–style building is a favourite Sydney pastime. The well-heeled North Shore crowd favours the **restaurant** (mains $48; ⊙lunch Mon-Sat, dinner daily), but the **cafe** (breakfast $7-25, mains $16-33, high tea $25; ⊙breakfast, lunch & dinner daily, afternoon tea Mon-Fri) serves equally impressive food with a more affordable price tag. There's also a **kiosk** (⊙from 7am daily) selling coffee, pastries and baguettes.

A somewhat scruffy pedestrian mall known as the Corso connects the suburb's ocean and harbour beaches. There are plenty of burger joints, juice bars and cafes along the Corso, but the quality is underwhelming and you're much better off buying a takeaway burger from **BenBry Burgers** (Map p86; www.benbryburgers.com.au; 5 Sydney Rd; burgers $7.50-14; ⊙7am-late) or fish and chips from **Manly Fish Market** (Map p86; 11-27 Wentworth St; fish & chips $11.50; ⊙8am-8pm) to eat on the beach.

PALM BEACH

Barrenjoey House MODERN AUSTRALIAN **$$** ([☎]02-9976 2051; www.barrenjoeyhouse.com; 1108 Barrenjoey Rd, Palm Beach; mains $25-39; ⊙lunch & dinner daily) Overlooking picturesque Pittwater from its location opposite the ferry wharf, Barrenjoey House is the perfect location for a leisurely weekend lunch. The menu is casual but assured, with a selection that will please most palates, even junior ones.

Boathouse CAFE **$$** (www.theboathousepb.com.au; Governor Phillip Park, Palm Beach; breakfast $5.50-15.50, lunch $12.50-34; ⊙7.30am-4pm) Sit on the large timber deck suspended over Station Beach or take a picnic blanket so that you can stretch out on the grass – either option is alluring at Palm Beach's most popular cafe. The food and coffee here are nearly as impressive as the views, and that's really saying something.

Jonah's Whale Beach MODERN AUSTRALIAN **$$$** ([☎]02-9974 5599; 69 Bynya Rd, Whale Beach; breakfast $45, mains $44-68; ⊙breakfast, lunch & dinner) Jonah's is more about the experience than the food, although you'll still eat well here. For the ultimate Sydney indulgence, take a seaplane from Rose Bay (see p146) and stay overnight in the **ocean-view rooms** (d $529-895; ✿).

🍸 Drinking

Pubs are a crucial part of the Sydney social scene, and you can down a glass or schooner (NSW term for a large glass) of amber nectar at elaborate 19th-century affairs, cavernous art-deco joints, modern and minimalist recesses, and everything in between. Bars are generally more stylish and urbane, sometimes with a dress code.

THE ROCKS & CIRCULAR QUAY

Opera Bar BAR (Map p70; www.operabar.com.au; Circular Quay East; ⊙11.30am-midnight Sun-Thu, to 1am Fri & Sat) The Opera Bar puts all other beer gardens to shame. Spilling into the harbour with the Opera House on one side and the Harbour Bridge on the other, this outdoor drinking den has it all. There's live music from 8.30pm Monday to Friday and from 2pm on weekends.

Hero of Waterloo
PUB

(Map p70; http://heroofwaterloo.com.au; 81 Lower Fort St, The Rocks; ☺9am-midnight Mon-Sat, noon-10pm Sun) Enter into the roughly hewn stone interior, meet some of the boisterous locals and enjoy the nightly music (piano, folk, jazz or Irish tunes) at this historic, old-time bar (established 1843).

Lord Nelson Brewery Hotel
PUB

(Map p70; www.lordnelson.com.au; 19 Kent St, Millers Point; ☺11am-11pm Mon-Sat, noon-10pm Sun) Built in 1841, the 'Nello' claims to be the oldest pub in this area (although the Fortune of War begs to differ). The on-site microbrewery produces some of Sydney's best ales.

Fortune of War Hotel
PUB

(Map p70; www.fortuneofwar.com.au; 137 George St, The Rocks; ☺9am-late) This 1828 drinking den retains much of its original charm and, by the looks of things, some of the original punters, too. There's live music on Friday and Saturday nights from 8pm and Sunday afternoons between 3pm and 6pm.

Australian Hotel
PUB

(Map p70; 100 Cumberland St, The Rocks; ☺11.30am-midnight Mon-Sat, to 10pm Sun) Beer geeks rejoice! Not only is this pub architecturally notable (c1914), it also boasts 10 Aussie beers on tap and around 50 in bottles; the majority are from NSW. Keeping with the antipodean theme, the kitchen also fires up pizzas topped with kangaroo, emu and saltwater crocodile ($23 to $25).

CITY CENTRE

Grasshopper
BAR

(Map p70; Temperance Lane; ☺noon-1am Mon-Fri) The first of what is bound to be many grungy laneway bars in the inner city (Ash Street Cellar doesn't count, as the laneway was created anew), Grasshopper is about as cool as the city centre gets. The food served in the upstairs restaurant is good, but the heart of the operation is the downstairs bar.

Bambini Wine Room
WINE BAR

(Map p70; www.bambinitrust.com.au; 185 Elizabeth St; ☺3-11pm Mon-Fri, 5.30-11pm Sat) This tiny darkwood-panelled room with a huge chandelier is the sort of place where you might

expect to see Oscar Wilde holding court in a corner. There's an extensive wine list and a classy array of bar food ($8 to $40). The excellent Bambini Trust restaurant is in the same building.

Ash Street Cellar
WINE BAR

(Mapp70;www.merivale.com/#/ivy/ashstreetcellar; 1 Ash St; tapas $8-32; ☺11am-late Mon-Fri) Part of the frighteningly fashionable Ivy complex, this European-flavoured wine bar in a pedestrianised laneway off George St largely caters to suits, but makes everyone feel welcome. There's excellent coffee during the day, and even better tapas and wine at night. Other bars in the complex include the Ivy Bar and Ivy Lounge.

Zeta Bar
BAR

(Map p70; www.zetabar.com.au; 4th fl, Hilton Hotel, 488 George St, Sydney; ☺5pm-late Mon-Sat) The Zeta is all about cocktails, but not the kind that come with paper umbrellas. There's a glam indoor lounge and a fabulous roof terrace. Downstairs in the basement is another Hilton watering hole, the ornate Marble Bar (www.marblebarsydney.com.au), which offers live music Wednesday to Saturday from 8pm.

WOOLLOOMOOLOO

Old Fitzroy Hotel
PUB

(Map p80; 129 Dowling St; ☺11am-midnight Mon-Fri, from noon Sat, from 3pm Sun) The Old Fitzroy has 13 beers on tap in the downstairs bar (six in the more intimate upstairs bar), a smokers' veranda and a resident theatre company that stages regular performances (http://rocksurfers.org).

KINGS CROSS, DARLINGHURST & SURRY HILLS

Shakespeare Hotel
PUB

(200 Devonshire St; ☺11am-11pm) Surry Hills' best-loved pub is everything a neighbourhood boozer should be, with ice-cold beer, cheap bar meals and laconic locals watching the gee-gees and chewing the fat.

Mille Vini
WINE BAR

(off Map p80; 397 Crown St; ☺6-11pm Tue-Thu, 6pm-midnight Fri, 2pm-2am Sat, 2-10pm Sun) Claim a seat at the downstairs bar or on the pavement, choose a glass of wine from a huge list of tipples (the name means 1000 wines), order a plate of antipasto and settle back for an hour or two of Italian-style R&R.

Aperitif
BAR

(Map p80; 7 Kellett St, Kings Cross; ☺6pm-3am Mon & Wed-Sat, to midnight Sun) Like a gently sloping mini Bourbon St, Kellett St is a snaky, sexy laneway with as many bars as brothels. Intimate Aperitif elevates the tone with an expertly constructed all-European wine list and a late-night kitchen (last orders 2am) serving fabulous French and Spanish food.

Gazebo Wine Garden   WINE BAR
(www.gazebowinegarden.com.au; 2 Elizabeth Bay Rd, Elizabeth Bay; ☺3pm-midnight Mon-Thu, from noon Fri-Sun) You've got to love a place that divides its wine list into sections including 'Unpronounceable', 'Opulent' and 'Slurpable'. Nocturnal garden parties at this bizarrely decorated Kings Cross oasis can be fantastic. The same crew operates the chichi Winery (Map p80; www.thewinerysurryhills.com.au; 285a Crown St; ☺noon-midnight) in Surry Hills and Manly Wine (Map p86; www.manlywine.com.au; 8-13 South Steyne; ☺noon-late) near the Manly Lifesaving Club.

Shady Pines Saloon   BAR
(Map p80; shop 4, 256 Crown St, Darlinghurst; ☺4pm-midnight) There's a boho buzz about 'Surryhurst' (the border of Darlinghurst and Surry Hills) at the moment, largely due to drinking dens like this one. Expect American pioneer memorabilia and Willie Nelson on the sound system. Yes, really.

Green Park Hotel   PUB
(Map p80; www.greenparkhotel.com.au; 360 Victoria St, Darlinghurst; ☺10am-2am Mon-Sat, noon-midnight Sun) This dolled-up corner pub is popular with Darlo locals and staff from the nearby St Vincent's Hospital. There's live music on Thursday nights.

Clock   PUB
(off Map p80; www.clockhotel.com.au; 470 Crown St, Surry Hills; ☺11.30am-midnight) The wraparound balcony bar at this iconic Surry Hills pub is always packed, as is the pool bar, which comes complete with pool table, lounges and big-screen TV screening sporting matches.

Victoria Room   BAR
(Map p80; www.thevictoriaroom.com; level 1, 235 Victoria St, Darlinghurst; ☺6pm-midnight Tue-Thu, 6pm-2am Fri, noon-2am Sat, 1pm-midnight Sun) Plush Chesterfields, art-nouveau wallpaper, dark-wood panelling and bamboo screens – this long-standing favourite is 1920s Bombay gin palace meets Hong Kong opium den. There's high tea complete with sparkling wine on Saturday and Sunday afternoons.

Beresford Hotel   PUB
(Map p80; www.theberesford.com.au; 354 Bourke St, Surry Hills; ☺noon-1am) A venue (with attitude) rather than a classic pub, the Beresford has a sleek public bar, Italian trattoria and beer garden where flicks are screened on occasional summer evenings.

PADDINGTON & WOOLLAHRA

TOP CHOICE Wine Library   WINE BAR
(off Map p80; 18 Oxford St, Woollahra; ☺9am-10pm Mon-Sat, to 6pm Sunday) This new wine bar is located at the top end of Oxford St, about halfway between the city and Bondi. It has an impressive range of wines by the glass and a stylish but casual feel. When it's time to eat you can choose from the Mediterranean-inclined bar menu or consider sauntering around the corner to Buzo (www.buzorestaurant.com.au; mains $26-35; ☺dinner Mon-Sat) in Jersey Rd, a much-loved local trattoria run by the same team.

Royal Hotel   PUB
(237 Glenmore Rd, Five Ways, Paddington; ☺11am-midnight) One of the points on the five-pointed junction star, this fine pub is spread over three floors. At the top, the Elephant Bar has views over the city skyline.

NEWTOWN & GLEBE

Courthouse Hotel   PUB
(Map p84; 202 Australia St, Newtown; ☺10am-midnight Mon-Sat, to 10pm Sun) Your drinking companions are a multifaceted lot – everyone from uni students enjoying a cheap meal in the beer garden to ferals hanging around the jukebox and nuggety locals who have propped up the front bar for half a century.

Madame Fling Flong   COCKTAIL BAR
(Map p84; www.madameflingflong.com.au; level 1, 169 King St, Newtown; ☺5pm-late) Newtown's best (and only) cocktail bar has got that scruffy Inner West thang going on with its retro lounge and shabby-chic decor. On Tuesday nights the Flong screens art-house movies from 7.30pm ($20 for a meze plate for one, glass of wine or beer and the movie); check the website for details.

Friend in Hand Hotel   PUB
(Map p84; www.friendinhand.com.au; 58 Cowper St, Glebe; ☺8am-midnight Mon-Sat, 10am-10pm Sun) Don't be surprised when the life-drawing classes, poetry readings, stand-up comedians, crab racing and raffles distract you from an investigation of the 11 local beers on tap.

BONDI & COOGEE

Corner House
GASTROPUB

(Map p83; www.thecornerhouse.com.au; 281 Bondi Rd, Bondi; ⊙from 5pm daily) Three spaces – the Kitchen (wine bar), Dining Room (restaurant) and Living Room (bar) – make this one house you'll be happy to visit. The Italian food served in all three is great, as are the cocktails.

Rum Diaries
COCKTAIL BAR

(Map p83; www.therumdiaries.com.au; 288 Bondi Rd, Bondi; ⊙6pm-midnight Mon-Sat, to 10pm Sun) A popular addition to the Bondi drinking scene, this dark (but far from dingy) place serves fusion tapas and lots of rum-based cocktails. There's live blues music every Monday from 7pm.

Beach Road Hotel
PUB

(Map p83; www.beachroadbondi.com.au; 71 Beach Rd, Bondi; ⊙10am-11pm Mon & Tue, 10am-midnight Wed-Fri, 9am-midnight Sat, 10am-10pm Sun) Weekends at this big, boxy pub see Bondi types (bronzed, buff and often brooding) sharing bar space with out-of-towners playing pool, drinking beer and partying to live bands and DJs.

Ravesi's
BAR

(Map p83; www.ravesis.com.au; cnr Campbell Pde & Hall St, Bondi; ⊙10am-1am Mon-Sat, to midnight Sun) At weekends, the crowd throbs in the downstairs Low Tide bar. The older set prefers the Drift Bar's upstairs balcony (Friday 6pm to late, Saturday 3pm to late, Sunday 2pm to late), which overlooks the beach and serves tasty tapas.

Coogee Bay Hotel
PUB

(www.coogeebayhotel.com.au; cnr Coogee Bay Rd & Arden St, Coogee; ⊙10am-late) The rambling, rowdy Coogee Bay complex has live music, a beer garden and views across the water.

MANLY

Manly Wharf Hotel
PUB

(Map p86; http://manlywharfhotel.com.au; East Esplanade, Manly; ⊙11.30am-midnight Mon-Fri, 11am-midnight Sat & Sun) Yep, it's on the wharf. And yep again, it's got great views. The perfect place to watch the ferries roll in while indulging in beer and pub grub.

Barefoot Coffee Traders
CAFE

(Map p86; cnr Sydney Rd & Whistler St; ⊙6.30am-5.30pm Mon-Fri, from 7.30am Sat & Sun) The suburb's best coffee (fair trade, organic beans from Toby's Estate) is served at this tiny space near the corner of Whistler St and Sydney Rd.

☆ Entertainment

Sydney has an eclectic and innovative arts, entertainment and music scene. Outdoor cinemas and sports stadiums cater to families, the city's theatre scene is healthy and dynamic, and live music is everywhere.

Pick up the 'Metro' section in Friday's *Sydney Morning Herald* for comprehensive entertainment details. Free weekly street magazines, including *The Brag* and *The Drum,* specialise in gig and club information. Tickets for most shows can be purchased directly from venues or through the Moshtix (☎1300 438 849; www.moshtix.com.au), Ticketmaster (☎1300 723 038; www.ticketmaster.com.au) or Ticketek (☎132 849; www.ticketek.com.au) ticketing agencies.

Cinemas

First-run cinemas abound; tickets generally cost $15 to $18 for an adult, $13 to $14 for a student and $10 to $12 for a child. Most cinemas have a cheap night when tickets are discounted by around a third. Sydney also has a huge following of indie and foreign films.

Open Air Cinema
CINEMA

(off Map p70; www.stgeorgeopenair.com.au; Mrs Macquaries Point, Royal Botanic Gardens; adult/concession $30/28; ⊙box office 6.30pm, screenings 8.30pm Jan & Feb) Right on the harbour, the outdoor three-storey screen here comes with surround sound, sunsets, skyline and swanky food and wine. Most tickets are purchased in advance, but a limited number of tickets go on sale at the door each night at 6.30 – check the website for details.

Bondi Open Air Cinema
CINEMA

(Map p83; ☎1300 438 849; www.bondiopenair.com.au; Bondi Pavilion, Bondi; ⊙dusk-late Jan-early Mar) Enjoy open-air screenings at the ocean's edge, with live bands providing prescreening entertainment. Bookings essential.

Dendy Opera Quays
CINEMA

(Map p70; www.dendy.com.au; shop 9, 2 Circular Quay E) A plush cinema screening first-run independent films from around the world.

Moonlight Cinema
CINEMA

(www.moonlight.com.au; Belvedere Amphitheatre, cnr Loch & Broome Aves, Centennial Park; adult/child/concession $18/14/16; ⊙box office 7pm, screenings 8-8.30pm Dec-Mar) Take a picnic and rug and enjoy a new-season release under the stars in magnificent Centennial Park. Enter via Woollahra Gate on Oxford St.

Palace Verona
CINEMA

(Map p80; www.palacecinemas.com.au/cinemas/verona/; 17 Oxford St, Paddington) The Verona screens international, art-house, documentary and independent films. There's also a wine and espresso bar, meaning that you can enjoy a drink before, during or after the film.

Nightclubs

GoodGod Small Club
NIGHTCLUB

(Map p76; www.goodgodgoodgod.com; 53-55 Liverpool St, Chinatown; cover charge varies, front bar free; ☺10pm-late Wed-Sat) In a defunct underground taverna in the Spanish Quarter, GoodGod's rear dancetaria hosts everything from live indie bands to Jamaican reggae, '50s soul, rockabilly and tropical house music. Its success lies in the focus on great music rather than glamorous surrounds.

Home
NIGHTCLUB

(Map p70; www.homesydney.com; Cockle Bay Wharf, Darling Harbour; admission varies; ☺Thu-Sat) Welcome to the pleasuredome: a three-level, 2000-capacity timber-and-glass extravaganza, home to a huge dance floor, countless bars, outdoor balconies and an amazing DJ booth. Top-name international DJs spin house; live bands amp it up.

Ivy
NIGHTCLUB

(Map p70; www.merivale.com; 330 George St, Sydney) Celebrities and wannabes flock to Justin Hemmes' Ivy complex to see and be seen. The main bar features a spacious dance floor and hosts Saturday's **Pure Ivy** ($20; ☺6pm-late), the **Tank** (☺from 10pm Fri, from 9pm Sat) dance floor glitters on weekends and the infamous rooftop **Pool Club** (☺4pm-late Mon, noon-late Tue-Fri) provides a place to aqua-boogie when the weather gets too hot. You'll need to finagle your way onto the guest list for all three.

Oxford Arts Factory
NIGHTCLUB

(Map p80; www.oxfordartsfactory.com; 38-46 Oxford St, Darlinghurst; cover charge & opening hours vary) The Darlo set parties against an arty backdrop at this two-room multipurpose venue modelled on Warhol's New York creative base. There's a gallery, bar and performance space that often hosts international acts and DJs. Check the website for a program.

Live Music
CLASSICAL

Sydney Opera House
CLASSICAL MUSIC

(Map p70; www.sydneyoperahouse.com; Bennelong Point) Yes, it's more than a landmark. As well as theatre and dance, the Opera House hosts performances by **Opera Australia** (☑tickets 02-9318 8200; www.opera-australia.org.au) and the **Sydney Symphony** (☑tickets 02-8215 4600; www.sydneysymphony.com).

City Recital Hall
CLASSICAL MUSIC

(Map p70; ☑02-8256 2222; www.cityrecitalhall.com; Angel Pl, Sydney; tickets free-$80; ☺box office 9am-5pm Mon-Fri & before performances) Classically configured, this custom-built 1200-seat venue boasts near-perfect acoustics. Top-billing companies here include the Sydney Conservatorium of Music and Sydney Symphony, plus touring international ensembles, soloists and opera singers. The Little Lunch Music concerts are excellent value ($12 per person).

JAZZ

TOP CHOICE Venue 505
JAZZ

(http://venue505.com; 280 Cleveland St, Surry Hills; cover varies; ☺from 7.30pm Mon-Sat) Focusing on jazz, world and classical music, this small and relaxed live venue is artist-run and thoughtfully programmed. The space features comfortable couches and murals by local artist Benjamin Yarrad.

Basement
JAZZ

(Map p70; www.thebasement.com.au; 7 Macquarie Pl, Circular Quay; admission varies; ☺noon-1.30am Mon-Thu, noon-2.30am Fri, 7.30pm-3am Sat, 7pm-1am Sun) Sydney's premier jazz venue presents headline touring acts and big local talent. A broad musical mandate also sees funk, blues and soul bands performing. Book a table by the stage.

ROCK

Annandale Hotel
ROCK

(off Map p84; www.annandalehotel.com; 17 Parramatta Rd, Annandale) 'F*ck this – I'm going to the Annandale!' is the motto at Sydney's premier rock venue. Loads of regulars follow its advice, enjoying live music most Wednesdays to Sundays and cult movies on Tuesdays; check the website for the program.

Vanguard
ROCK

(Map p84; ☑02-9550 3666; www.thevanguard.com.au; 42 King St, Newtown; ☺6.30pm-midnight Tue-Sun) The UK's *Independent* newspaper rates the Vanguard as one of the world's 10 best live-music venues, and the city's boho set would probably agree. An intimate, purpose-built space, it showcases everything from burlesque to blues, country to world. Most seats are reserved for dinner-and-show ($40 to $45) patrons; door entry is $15.

Enmore Theatre
ROCK
(off Map p84; ☑02-9550 3666; www.enmore theatre.com.au; 118-132 Enmore St, Newtown) Newtown is the centre of Sydney's music scene, and the Enmore is its mainstream heart, hosting big-name local and international acts.

Metro Theatre
ROCK
(Map p76; ☑02-9550 3666; www.metrotheatre. com.au; 624 George St) Big-name indie acts grace the Metro's stage. It has theatre-style tiers, air-con, super sound and good visibility.

Spectator Sports
On any given Sydney weekend there'll be all manner of balls being hurled, kicked and batted around. Sydneysiders are passionate about the National Rugby League (NRL; www.nrl.com.au; tickets through Ticketek from $25), the season kicking off in March in suburban stadia and the ANZ Stadium (www.anz stadium.com.au; Sydney Olympic Park, Olympic Blvd, Homebush Bay), with September finals.

Also from March right through to September, hometown favourites the Sydney Swans (www.sydneyswans.com.au) play in the Australian Football League (AFL; www.afl. com.au; tickets $20-40) at the Sydney Cricket Ground (SCG; www.sydneycricketground.com. au; Driver Ave, Moore Park). In 2012 they will be joined by a second Sydney-based team, Greater Western Sydney (the Giants), which will probably be based at the Sydney Showgrounds.

The cricket (http://cricket.com.au) season runs from October to March, the SCG hosting interstate Sheffield Shield and sell-out international Test, Twenty20 and One Day International matches.

Theatre

Sydney Theatre Company
THEATRE
(Map p70; ☑02-9250 1777; www.sydneytheatre. com.au; level 2, Pier 4, Hickson Rd, Walsh Bay; tickets $60-65) Sydney's premier theatre company performs at its Walsh Bay base and in the Drama Theatre at the Sydney Opera House. Artistic directors Cate Blanchett and Andrew Upton program work by local and international playwrights and draw actors and directors from around the world. There are heavily discounted tickets for under 30s.

BW Stables Theatre
THEATRE
(Map p80; ☑02-8019 0292; www.griffintheatre. com.au; 10 Nimrod St, Kings Cross; tickets $28-47) Home to the Griffin Theatre Company, this quirky, intimate theatre (it seats just 120) is the home for new writing. It's also where many actors started out – Cate Blanchett and David Wenham both trod the boards here early in their careers. Rush tickets ($15) are available on Monday evenings.

Company B
THEATRE
(☑02-9699 3444; www.belvoir.com.au; 25 Belvoir St, Surry Hills; tickets from $39) Stars such as Geoffrey Rush regularly perform at this innovative theatre space.

Sydney Comedy Store
THEATRE
(☑02-9357 1419; www.comedystore.com.au; Building 207, Entertainment Quarter, 122 Lang Rd, Moore Park; tickets $7.50-25) This purpose-built comedy hall lures big-time Australian and overseas comics, including Edinburgh Festival stand-ups.

Sydney Theatre
THEATRE
(Map p70; ☑02-9250 1999; www.sydneytheatre. org.au; 22 Hickson Rd, Walsh Bay; tickets $40-79) The resplendent Sydney Theatre at the base of Observatory Hill puts 850 bums on seats for specialist drama and dance.

The following theatres host local seasons of West End and Broadway musicals, as well as concerts (tickets from $50 to $200; bookings can be made through Ticketmaster or on websites):

Capitol Theatre
THEATRE
(Map p76; www.capitoltheatre.com.au; 13 Campbell St, Haymarket; ◉box office 9am-5pm Mon-Fri)

State Theatre
THEATRE
(Map p70; ☑02-9373 6655; www.statetheatre. com.au; 49 Market St)

Theatre Royal
THEATRE
(Map p70; www.theatreroyal.net.au; MLC Centre, 108 King St; ◉box office 9am-5pm Mon-Fri)

🛍 Shopping
Most shops are open from 9.30am to 6pm Monday to Wednesday, Friday and Saturday, and until 9pm Thursday. Sunday trading is common but expect shorter hours, such as noon to 4pm or 5pm. Exceptions are noted in reviews.

Serious shoppers should consider downloading the suburb-by-suburb shopping guides produced by Urban Walkabout (www. urbanwalkabout.com); free printed versions of the maps are also available at tourist information offices and booths across the city. There are dedicated guides (with handy map) covering the CBD, Paddington, Woollahra,

Surry Hills, Darlinghurst, Potts Point/Kings Cross, Balmain, Mosman, Newtown, Redfern/Waterloo, Glebe, Double Bay and Bondi.

Department Stores & Arcades

David Jones DEPARTMENT STORE
(Map p70; www.davidjones.com.au; cnr Market & Castlereagh Sts, Sydney; ⊙9.30am-7pm Mon-Wed, 9.30am-9pm Thu & Fri, 9am-9pm Sat, 10am-7pm Sun) DJs is Sydney's premier department store. The Market St store has menswear; Castlereagh St has womenswear and childrenswear and a friendly concierge to point you in the right direction. The Australian designer fashion and the food halls in the Market St basement are particularly impressive.

Queen Victoria Building MALL
(QVB; Map p70; www.qvb.com.au; 455 George St, Sydney) This high-Victorian masterpiece occupies an entire city block opposite the Town Hall, and though there are some inspiring retail offerings, they run a distant second to the magnificent wrought-iron balconies, stained-glass shopfronts and mosaic floors.

Strand Arcade MALL
(Map p70; www.strandarcade.com.au; 412 George St & 193-5 Pitt St Mall, Sydney) Constructed in 1891, the Strand competes with the QVB for the title of most gorgeous shopping centre in Sydney. It has a particularly strong range of Australian designer fashion, and is home to the famous Strand Hatters (Map p70; shop 8), which blocks and steams hats to customers' cranial requirements.

Westfield Sydney MALL
(Map p70; http://westfield.com.au/sydney; cnr Pitt St Mall & Market St, Sydney) The city's newest and largest shopping mall hosts main-street retailers such as Zara, as well as designer boutiques and an excellent food court.

Clothing & Accessories

Glenmore Rd in Paddington and Queen St in Woollahra are Sydney's premier fashion enclaves, but there are also plenty of boutiques in the CBD and in Newtown.

Akira Isagawa CLOTHING
(www.akira.com.au; 12a Queen St, Woollahra) Meticulously tailored ensembles featuring gorgeous fabrics. There's another store in the Strand Arcade.

Collette Dinnigan CLOTHING
(www.collettedinnigan.com.au; 104 Queen St, Woollahra) The queen of Aussie couture delivers fabulously feminine frocks with exquisite trimmings.

Dinosaur Design ACCESSORIES
(www.dinosaurdesigns.com.au; 339 Oxford St, Paddington) Fabulous jewellery and homewares made from richly coloured polyester resin. There's another store in the Strand Arcade.

Easton Pearson CLOTHING
(Map p80; www.eastonpearson.com; 30 Glenmore Rd, Paddington) Brisbane designers who popularised ethno-chic in Australia and are particularly beloved by women of a slightly fuller figure.

High Tea With Mrs Woo CLOTHING
(www.highteawithmrswoo.com.au; 72b Oxford St, Paddington) Natural fabrics and a Japanese sensibility characterise the stylish ensembles designed by the three Foong sisters.

RM Williams CLOTHING
(Map p70; www.rmwilliams.com.au; 389 George St, Sydney) Urban cowboys and country folk can't get enough of this hard-wearing outback gear. Favourites include oilskin jackets, Akubra hats, moleskin jeans and leather boots. There are other outlets scattered throughout the city.

Willow CLOTHING
(Map p80; www.willowltd.com.au; 3a Glenmore Rd, Paddington) Local designer Kit Willow Podgornik has made it big around the globe with her gorgeous clothes and lingerie.

Zambesi CLOTHING
(Map p80; www.zambesi.co.nz; 5 Glenmore Rd, Paddington) New Zealand outfit stocking an exciting range of men's and women's clothing.

Zimmermann CLOTHING
(Map p80; http://zimmermannwear.com; shop 2, 2-16 Glenmore Rd, Paddington). Chic and cheeky street clothes and swimwear from Nicky and Simone Zimmermann. There's another store in Westfield Sydney.

Wine

Australian Wine Centre WINE SHOP
(Map p70; shop 3, Goldfields House, 1 Alfred St, Circular Quay) This basement shop is packed with quality Australian and New Zealand wine, as well as a healthy dose of Aussie beer and spirits. There's something for every budget.

ℹ Information

Emergency
In the event of an emergency, call ☎000 to contact the police, ambulance and fire authorities.

There are plenty of shops and galleries around the state selling Indigenous-made artworks, artefacts and products, but it's sadly common to encounter Chinese-made fakes, works that breach the cultural copyright of Indigenous artists, and galleries that exploit artist poverty by buying their art unreasonably cheaply – wherever possible, look for products that are being produced and/or marketed by Indigenous-owned, not-for-profit operators.

If buying from a gallery, make sure that it's a member of the Australian Indigenous Art Trade Association or the Australian Commercial Galleries Association. Art and artefacts should be properly documented (ie by a certificate of authenticity from a reputable source, by photographs or by other evidence) and their provenance should be clearly stated (ie where, when and by whom was it made? How has it come onto the market?).

Lifeline (☑13 11 14; www.lifeline.com.au) Over-the-phone counselling services, including suicide prevention.

Police stations For a searchable list of all police stations in NSW, go to www.police.nsw. gov.au, then click on 'contact us', then 'click for police station search'.

Rape Crisis Centre (☑1800 424 017) Twenty-four-hour counselling.

Internet Access

Internet cafes are common in Sydney, especially in Kings Cross, Chinatown and Bondi. Rates are around $3 an hour. Hostels tend to use providers such as **Global Gossip** (http://globalgossip. com) for their guest wi-fi and broadband access; these charge approximately $3 per hour. The more expensive hotels can use providers charging up to $20 per hour. For a list of free wi-fi hot spots, go to www.unwired.com.au/get/store finder.php?p=3.

Medical Services

Kings Cross Travellers Clinic (☑02-9358 3066; www.travellersclinic.com.au; 13 Springfield Ave, Kings Cross; standard consultation $65; ☺9am-1pm & 2-6pm Mon-Fri, 10am-noon Sat) General medical, travel medical and vaccinations; bookings advised.

St Vincent's Hospital (☑02-8382 1111; www. stvincents.com.au; 390 Victoria St, Darlinghurst; ☺24hr emergency)

Sydney Hospital (☑02-9382 7111; www. sesahs.nsw.gov.au/sydhosp; 8 Macquarie St, Sydney; ☺24hr emergency)

Money

There are plenty of ATMs throughout Sydney; foreign exchange offices are found in Kings Cross and around Chinatown, Circular Quay and Central Station.

American Express city centre (☑1300 139 060; 296 George St, Sydney; ☺9am-5pm Mon-Fri); Haymarket (☑1300 139 060; 45 Sussex St, Sydney; ☺9am-5pm Mon-Fri)

Post

General post office (GPO; Map p70; ☑13 13 18; www.auspost.com.au; 1 Martin Pl; ☺8.15am-5.30pm Mon-Fri, 10am-2pm Sat)

Tourist Information

Sydney City Council Information Kiosks (www.cityofsydney.nsw.gov.au) Circular Quay (Map p70; cnr Pitt & Alfred Sts; ☺9.30am-3.30pm); Town Hall (Map p70; George St; ☺9.30am-3.30pm) Extremely friendly and helpful staff supply maps, brochures and information, including the free *Sydney Guide*, which includes information and discount vouchers and is available in English-, Chinese-, Japanese- and Korean-language editions.

Sydney Harbour National Parks Information Centre (Map p70; ☑02-9247 5033; Cadmans Cottage, 110 George St, The Rocks; ☺9.30am-4.30pm Mon-Fri, 10am-4.30pm Sat & Sun) Has maps of walks in different parts of the park and information on tours of the harbour islands.

Sydney Visitor Centres (☑02-9240 8788; www.sydneyvisitorcentre.com) Darling Harbour (Map p76; Palm Grove, behind Imax; ☺9.30am-5.30pm); The Rocks (Map p70; 1st fl, cnr Argyle & Playfair Sts; ☺9.30am-5.30pm) Both branches have a wide range of brochures and staff can book accommodation, tours and attractions. The Rocks location is part gift shop.

Websites

For more information on Sydney, check out the following websites:

Art Almanac (www.art-almanac.com.au) Comprehensive public and private gallery listings.

City of Sydney (www.cityofsydney.nsw.gov.au) Visitor information, disabled access, parking, history and downloadable walking tours.

RealSurf (www.realsurf.com) Local surf reports.

Sydney Events (www.timeoutsydney.com.au) Listings and articles from the monthly magazine.

Sydney Harbour Foreshore Authority (www. shfa.nsw.gov.au) Links to dedicated websites

MARVELLOUS MARKETS

Sydneysiders enjoy going to local markets nearly as much as going to the beach (and that's really saying something). Many inner-city suburbs host weekend markets in the grounds of local schools and churches, and these sell everything from organic food to original designer clothing. You'll inevitably encounter some tragic hippy paraphernalia, appalling art and overpriced tourist tat, but there are often exciting purchases to be made, too. The best of the markets:

Balmain Market

(www.balmainmarket.com.au; cnr Darling St & Curtis Rd, Balmain; ⊙8.30am-4pm Sat) This small market is set in the shady grounds of St Andrews Congregational Church. Stalls sell arts, crafts, books, clothing, jewellery, plants, and fruit and veg.

Bondi Markets

(Map p83; www.bondimarkets.com.au; Bondi Beach Public School, cnr Campbell Pde & Warners Ave, Bondi; ⊙10am-4pm Sun) The kids are at the beach on Sunday while their school fills up with Bondi characters rummaging through tie-dyed secondhand clothes and books, beads and earrings, aromatherapy oils, candles, old records and more. There's a farmers market in the school grounds on Saturdays between 9am and 1pm.

Eveleigh Market

(Map p84; www.eveleighmarket.com.au; 243 Wilson St, Darlington; ⊙farmers market 8am-1pm Sat, artisans market 10am-3pm 1st Sun of every month, closed 1st half of Jan) Over 70 regular stallholders sell their home-grown produce at Sydney's best farmers market, which is held in a heritage-listed railway workshop in the Eveleigh Railyards. When here, you can also visit the CarriageWorks arts and cultural precinct (www.carriageworks.com.au).

Glebe Markets

(Map p84; www.glebemarkets.com.au; Glebe Public School, cnr Glebe Point Rd & Derby Pl, Glebe; ⊙10am-4pm Sat) The best of the west; Sydney's dreadlocked, shoeless, inner-city contingent beats an aimless course to this crowded hippy-ish market.

Paddington Markets

(off Map p80; www.paddingtonmarkets.com.au; St John's Church, 395 Oxford St, Paddington; ⊙10am-4pm Sat) Sydney's most popular weekend market dishes up vintage clothes and hip fashions, jewellery, books, massage and palmistry. Just as your spirits flag, you'll find something special under a little awning.

---

about three Sydney Harbour Foreshore Authority precincts: The Rocks, Darling Harbour and soon-to-be-developed Barangaroo.

Sydney Morning Herald (www.smh.com.au) Good for upcoming events, restaurant and bar reviews, and to take the pulse of the city.

TwoThousand (www.twothousand.com.au) Snapshot of Sydney's subculture.

Getting There & Away

Air

Sydney Airport (code: SYD; Map p88; www.sydneyairport.com.au) is Australia's busiest, so don't be surprised if there are delays. It's only 10km south of the city centre, making access relatively easy. The T1 (international) and T2 and T3 (domestic) terminals are a 4km bus ($5.50, 10 minutes) or train ($5, 2 minutes) ride apart (the airport is privately run so transferring terminals – a service that's free in most of the world – is seen as a profit opportunity). If you are transferring from a Qantas international flight to a Qantas domestic flight (or vice versa), free transfers are provided by the airline. Virgin Australia offers a similar service.

You can fly into Sydney from all the usual international points and from within Australia. **Qantas** (⌨13 13 13; www.qantas.com.au), **Jetstar** (⌨13 15 38; www.jetstar.com.au), **Virgin Australia** (⌨13 67 89; www.virginaustralia.com) and **Tiger Airways** (⌨03-9335 3033; www.tigerairways.com/au/en) have frequent flights to other major cities. Smaller Qantas-affiliated airlines fly to less busy Oz destinations.

For further details on air travel within Australia, see p1068. For air travel to/from Australia, see p1067.

Bus

All private interstate and regional bus travellers arrive at **Sydney Coach Terminal** (Map p76; ☑02-9281 9366; Central Station, Eddy Ave; ☺6am-6pm Mon-Fri, 8am-6pm Sat & Sun). Sample destinations include Brisbane (from $88, 16 hours), Byron Bay (from $85, 12½ hours), Canberra (from $15, 3½ hours) and Melbourne (from $60, 14 hours). There are lots of discounted fares.

The government's CountryLink rail network is also complemented by coaches. Most buses stop in the suburbs on the way in and out of Sydney. The major bus companies using the depot are:

Australia Wide (☑02-9516 1300; www.aust widecoaches.com.au) Orange and Bathurst

Busways (☑02-9625 8900; www.busways. com.au) Central Coast

Firefly (☑1300 730 740; www.fireflyexpress. com.au) Wagga Wagga, Albury, Melbourne and Adelaide

Greyhound (☑1300 GREYHOUND/1300 4739 46863; www.greyhound.com.au) Canberra, Melbourne, Byron Bay and Tamworth

Murrays (☑13 22 51; www.murrays.com.au) Canberra and the South Coast

Port Stephens Coaches (☑02-4982 2926; www.pscoaches.com.au) Newcastle and Nelson Bay

Premier (☑13 34 10; www.premierms.com.au) Coffs Harbour, Byron Bay, Brisbane and Cairns

Train

Sydney's main rail terminus for CountryLink interstate and regional services is the huge **Central Station** (Map p76; ☑bookings 13 22 32, 24hr transport information 13 15 00; www.coun trylink.info; Eddy Ave; ☺staffed ticket booths 6.15am-8.45pm, ticket machines 24hr).

Sample train fares (without discount) include Brisbane ($92, 14½ hours) and Melbourne ($92, 11 hours).

❶ Getting Around

Your transport options may be many in Sydney but your journey won't always be easy. Spend more than a day in town and you won't be able to miss stories about the dire state of the over-patronised, underfunded system. Ferries, trains and many buses are operated by the same government department, but each mode seems to operate in blissful ignorance of the others, with only one integrated ticket, the MyMulti pass, available. And even this doesn't include the privately owned tram and monorail.

For information on government buses, ferries and trains try the **Transport Infoline** (☑13 15 00; www.131500.com.au).

To/From the Airport

One of the easiest ways to get to and from the airport is with a shuttle company such as **Kingsford Smith Transport** (KST; ☑02-9666 9988; www.kst.com.au; one-way/return from $12.60/20.70; ☺5am-7pm), which services central Sydney hotels. **Airport Shuttle North** (☑1300 505 100; www.airportshuttlenorth. com; one way from $35; ☺5am-11pm) and **Manly Express** (☑02-8065 9524; www.manly express.com.au; one-way from $30; ☺3am-11.30pm) service the North Shore and Northern Beaches. Bookings are essential for all.

Airport Link (☑13 15 00; www.airportlink. com.au; one-way/return from Central Sydney adult $15/25, child $10/15.50, ☺4.30am-12.40am) is a strange service: it's a normal commuter train line (with dirty cars) but you pay through the nose to use the airport stations (punters going to Wolli Creek, the next stop *beyond* the airport pay $3.20). The trip from Central Station takes a mere 10 minutes or so.

Taxi fares from the airport are approximately $39 to the city centre ($51 between 10pm and 6am), $43 to Bondi ($55 between 10pm and 6am) and $80 to Manly ($106 between 10pm and 6am).

Boat

FERRY Harbour ferries and RiverCats (to Parramatta) operated by **Sydney Ferries** (www. sydneyferries.info) depart from Circular Quay. Most ferries operate between 6am and midnight; those servicing tourist attractions operate shorter hours.

A one-way inner-harbour ride on a regular ferry costs adult/concession $5.30/2.60. A one-way ride to Manly or Parramatta costs $6.60/$3.30. Seniors are eligible for a $2.50 all-day excursion ticket and on Sundays families can take advantage of the 'Family Funday' ticket, which gives all-day travel on all Sydney transport for $2.50 per person (minimum one adult and one child).

The privately owned **Captain Cook Ferries** (www.captaincook.com.au) operates ferry services to Manly from Circular Quay (return adult/child $17/8.50) and Darling Harbour (return adult/child $24/12). It also runs a Zoo Express service to Taronga Zoo from Circular Quay and Darling Harbour (return adult/child $49.50/24.50 including entrance fee).

For information about harbour cruises see p100.

WATER TAXI Water taxis ply dedicated shuttle routes; rides to/from other harbour venues can be booked.

MYZONE TICKETS & PASSES

There are two discount options for travelling on Sydney's public transport network. You can purchase these passes and tickets at newsagencies, newsstands and bus/ferry/train ticket offices. For information, see www.myzone.nsw.gov.au.

» MyMulti Passes You can purchase a day pass ($20) or weekly pass (zone 1/2/3 $41/48/57) giving unlimited transport on government-operated buses, ferries and trains within Sydney, the Blue Mountains, Hunter Valley, Central Coast, Newcastle and Port Stephens.

» MyBus, MyTrain and MyFerry TravelTen Tickets These offer 10 discounted rides but can only be used on one mode of transport.

Aussie Water Taxis (Map p76; ☎02-9211 7730; www.aussiewatertaxis.com; Cockle Bay Wharf, Darling Harbour; ☺9am-10pm) Darling Harbour to Circular Quay single/return adult $15/25, child $10/15; Darling Harbour to Taronga Zoo single/return adult $25/40, child $15/25; 45-minute Harbour and Nightlights Tours adult/child $35/25.

Yellow Water Taxis (Map p76; ☎1300 138 840; www.yellowwatertaxis.com.au; King St Wharf, Darling Harbour; ☺7am-midnight) Circular Quay to Darling Harbour adult/child $15/10; 45-minute Harbour 'Hop On, Hop Off' Tour stopping at Sydney Aquarium, Luna Park, Taronga Zoo and Sydney Opera House adult/child $40/20.

Bus

Sydney Buses (www.sydneybuses.info) has an extensive network; you can check route and timetable information online. Nightrider buses operate infrequently after regular services cease around midnight.

The main city bus stops are Circular Quay, Wynyard Park (York St) and Railway Sq. Many services are prepay-only during the week – buy tickets from newsagents or Bus TransitShops. On weekends, you can usually purchase your ticket on the bus. There are three fare zones: $2/3.30/4.30. There's a **Bus TransitShop booth** (www.sydneybuses.info; cnr Alfred & Loftus Sts; ☺7am-7pm Mon-Fri, 8.30am-5pm Sat & Sun) at Circular Quay, and there are others at the Queen Victoria Building, Railway Sq and Wynyard Station.

Bus routes starting with an X indicate limited-stop express routes; those with an L have limited stops. A free CBD shuttle (bus 555) departs every 20 minutes between 9.30am and 3.30pm Monday to Wednesday and Friday, till 9pm on Thursday and between 9.30am and 6pm Saturday and Sunday. Its route travels between Circular Quay and Central Station, stopping at Martin Pl, St James and Museum railway stations, Chinatown, Town Hall, QVB and Wynyard railway station en route.

Car & Motorcycle

Cars are good for day trips out of town, but driving one in the city is like having an anchor around your neck. Heavy traffic, elusive and very expensive parking (even at hotels, expect $30 per day) and the extra costs just aren't worth the stress.

BUYING OR SELLING A CAR The second-hand car industry is a minefield of mistrust and dodgy wheelers and dealers, but with a bit of research you can still land yourself a decent deal. Parramatta Rd is lined with used-car lots, and the *Trading Post* (www.tradingpost.com. au), a weekly rag available at newsagents, lists secondhand vehicles. For more information on buying or selling a vehicle, see p1071.

The **Kings Cross Car Market** (☎1800 808 188; www.carmarket.com.au; 110 Bourke St, Woolloomooloo; ☺9am-5pm) is a good spot to buy and sell a car. It's potentially hit and miss, but always busy.

HIRE Major car-hire agencies with offices in Sydney:

Avis (☎13 63 33; www.avis.com.au)

Budget (☎13 27 27; www.budget.com.au)

Europcar (☎1300 13 13 90; www.europcar. com.au)

Hertz (☎13 30 39; www.hertz.com.au)

Thrifty (☎1300 367 227; www.thrifty.com.au)

The **Yellow Pages** (www.yellowpages.com.au) lists many other car-hire companies, some specialising in renting clapped-out wrecks at rock-bottom prices – read the fine print! For camper-van hire, head towards William St in Kings Cross, where companies such as **Jucy** (☎1800 150 850; www.jucy.com.au) are located.

ROAD TOLLS There's a $4 southbound toll on the Sydney Harbour Bridge and Tunnel; a $5.50 northbound toll on the Eastern Distributor; a $2.10 toll on the Cross City Tunnel; and a $2.83 toll on the Lane Cove Tunnel. Sydney's main motorways (M2, M5 and M7) are also tolled ($2.50 to $7). There are a few cash booths at toll gates, but the whole system is electronic, meaning that it's up to you to organise an electronic tag or visitor's pass through any of the following websites: www.roamcom.au, www.roamexpress.com.au or www.myRTA.com.au. For info, try www.sydneymotorways.com.

Monorail & Metro Light Rail (MLR)

The privately operated **Metro Monorail** (www.metromonorail.com.au; single circuit $4.90, day pass $9.50; ☺every 5min, 7am-10pm Mon-Fri, 8am-10pm Sat & Sun) travels in a loop from Galleries Victoria on the corner of Pitt and Park Sts through Chinatown and Darling Harbour.

Run by the same outfit, the **Metro Light Rail** (MLR; www.metrolightrail.com.au; zone 1 adult/concession $3.40/2.20, zone 1 & 2 adult/concession $4.40/3.40, day pass adult $9; ☺24hr, every 10-15min 6am-midnight, every 30min midnight-6am) is a tram running between Central Station and Pyrmont via Chinatown and Darling Harbour. The zone 2 service beyond Pyrmont to Lilyfield via the Fish Markets, Glebe and Rozelle operates from 6am to 11pm Monday to Thursday and Sunday, till midnight Friday and Saturday.

Taxi

Taxis and cab ranks proliferate in Sydney. Flag fall is $3.30, then it's $1.99 per kilometre (plus 20% from 10pm to 6am). The waiting charge is $0.86 per minute. Passengers must pay bridge, tunnel and road tolls (even if you don't incur them 'outbound', the returning driver will incur them 'inbound').

The major taxi companies offering phone bookings ($2.20 fee) are:

Legion (☏13 14 51; www.legioncabs.com.au)

Premier Cabs (☏13 10 17; www.premiercabs.com.au)

Taxis Combined (☏13 33 00; www.taxiscombined.com.au)

Train

Sydney's suburban rail network is operated by **CityRail** (☏13 15 00; www.cityrail.info). Lines radiate from the underground City Circle (seven city-centre stations) but don't service the northern and southern beaches, Balmain or Glebe. All suburban trains stop at Central Station, and usually one or more of the other City Circle stations, too.

Trains run from around 5am to midnight. After 9am on weekdays you can buy an off-peak return ticket, valid until 4am the next day, for little more than a standard one-way fare.

Twenty-four-hour ticket machines occupy most stations, but customer service officers are usually available if you need help with the fares. If you have to change trains, buy a ticket to your ultimate destination, but don't exit the transfer station en route or your ticket will be invalid.

For train information, visit the helpful **CityRail Information Booth** (Circular Quay; ☺9.05am-4.50pm).

AROUND SYDNEY

Sydney's extensive urban sprawl eventually dissolves into superb national parks and historic small towns. To the south, Royal National Park – the second-oldest national park in the world – hides lost-to-the-world beaches, rainforest pockets and precipitous cliffscapes. The wooded foothills of the Great Dividing Range sit to the west of Sydney and climb to the magnificent Blue Mountains. Inland, the rolling hills and fertile soils of Macarthur Country support towns established in the early days of settlement.

Royal National Park

The 15,080-hectare Royal National Park (www.environment.nsw.gov.au/nationalparks; pedestrians & cyclists free, cars $11; ☺gates to park areas open at sunrise and are locked at 8.30pm daily) was established in 1879, making it the oldest national park in the world after Yellowstone in the USA. Here you'll find pockets of subtropical rainforest, wind-blown coastal scrub, sandstone gullies dominated by gum trees, fresh- and saltwater wetlands, and isolated beaches. Traditionally the home of the Dharawal people, there are also numerous Aboriginal sites and artefacts.

The national park begins at Port Hacking, 32km south of Sydney, and stretches 20km further south. Its main road detours to Bundeena, a small town on Port Hacking, the starting point for kayaking tours of the park and the spectacular two-day, 26km-long Coast Track. See the website for details of other bushwalks in the park.

Within the park there's sheltered saltwater swimming at Wattamolla, Jibbon, Little Marley and Bonnie Vale, and freshwater swimming holes at Karloo Pool (around 2km east of Heathcote Station), Deer Pool and Curracurrang. Surfers should head for Garie Beach, North Era, South Era and Burning Palms on the park's southern coastline. At the historic Audley Boat Shed (www.audleyboatshed.com; Farnell Ave, Audley; ☺9am-5pm Mon-Sat, to 5.30pm Sun) you can hire rowboats, canoes and kayaks ($20/40 per hour/day), aqua bikes ($15 per 30 minutes) and bicycles ($16/34 per hour/day) and paddle up Kangaroo Creek or the Hacking River.

The park office (☏02-9542 0648; Farnell Ave, Audley Heights; ☺8.30am-4.30pm) can assist with maps, brochures, camping permits and bushwalking details.

There's a drive-in camp site at Bonnie Vale near Bundeena, for which you'll need to book in advance through the park office. If you're walking, you can camp along the coastal trail at North Era and at Uloola Falls on the western side of the park; organise permits (adult/child $5/3 per night) through the park office. The Cronulla Beach YHA (p107) is a 30-minute ferry ride from Bundeena.

ⓘ Getting There & Away

From Sydney, take the Princes Hwy south and turn off at Farnell Ave, south of Loftus, to the park's northern end – it's about a 45-minute drive from the city. If you're driving north from Wollongong, don't miss the famous 665m-long curving Sea Cliff Bridge section of Lawrence Hargrave Dr between Clifton and Coalcliff.

The most scenic route into the park is to take the CityRail train (Eastern Suburbs and Illawarra line) to Cronulla (one way adult/child $4.60/3.20), and then jump aboard a **Cronulla National Park Ferry** (☑02-9523 2990; www.cronullaferries.com.au; Cronulla Wharf) to Bundeena (one way adult/child $5.80/2.90, 30 minutes, hourly between 5.30am and 6.30pm, until 5.30pm Sun in winter). Cronulla Wharf is off Tonkin St just below the train station. This outfit also runs three-hour **Port Hacking Scenic Cruises** (adult/child $25/20; ◷10.30am daily Sep-May, 10.30am Sun, Mon, Wed & Fri Jun-Aug), for which bookings are recommended.

Alternatively, Loftus, Engadine, Heathcote, Waterfall and Otford train stations are on the park boundary and have trails leading into the park. Loftus is closest to the park office (6km).

Camden Area

About 50km southwest of Sydney, Camden (population 3166) is a peaceful agrarian town that played a pivotal role in the birth of the Australian wool, wine and wheat industries. Several heritage-listed buildings remain and there's a popular farmers market in John St every second and fourth Saturday of the month between 7am and noon.

Built in the 1890s as a workman's cottage, John Oxley Cottage (☑02-4658 1370; www.camden.nsw.gov.au/page/visitor_information_centre; Camden Valley Way, Elderslie; ◷9.30am-4pm) today houses the volunteer-staffed visitor centre. It's on the town's northern outskirts.

The 400-hectare Australian Botanic Garden (www.rbgsyd.nsw.gov.au/mount_annan; Mt Annan Dr, Mt Annan; admission car/pedestrian $9/2.50; ◷10am-5pm) at nearby Mt Annan is the native-plant branch of Sydney's Royal Botanic Gardens and describes itself as the largest botanic garden in the southern hemisphere. With 4000 species on 1000 acres, its claim seems entirely plausible.

North of Camden, pretty Cobbitty Village was first settled in 1812 and many of the original homes still stand. A craft and local-produce market (www.cobbittymarkets.com.au) is held on the first Saturday of every month (except January and February) between 8am and 1pm.

South of Camden is Picton (pop 4286), traditional land of the Gundangurra people. A handful of significant buildings remain, including the old post office where you'll find the Wollondilly Visitor Centre (☑02-4677 8313; www.visitwollondilly.com.au; cnr Argyle & Menangle Sts; ◷9am-5pm). The historic George IV Inn (☑02-4677 1415; www.georgeiv.com.au; 180 Argyle St; s/d/tw without bathroom $40/55/60) has simple pub-style accommodation.

ⓘ Getting There & Away

CityRail trains run from Sydney's Central Station to Picton (one way adult/child $7.80/3.90, roughly hourly). They also run to Campbelltown (one way adult/child $6/3, half-hourly).

Busways (☑Camden office 02-4647 7785; www.busways.com.au) buses 890 and 895 run from Campbelltown to Camden (one way adult/child $4.30/2.10, 35 minutes, half-hourly). Bus 891 runs from Cambelltown to Mt Annan (one way adult/child $4.30/2.10, 25 minutes, half-hourly) To get to the Australian Botanic Gardens, you'll need to get off bus 891 on the corner of Welling and Stenhouse Drs and walk up the hill.

You'll need a car to get to Cobbitty Village, as bus services are so infrequent as to be almost nonexistent.

Hawkesbury River

POP 60,600

Less than an hour from Sydney, the tranquil Hawkesbury River is a favourite weekend destination for stressed-out city folk. The river – one of the longest in eastern Australia – flows past honeycomb-coloured cliffs, historic townships and riverside hamlets into bays and inlets and between a series of national parks.

The fertile farming country around the Hawkesbury sustains vineyards, vegetable farms, flower acreages and alpaca studs. Contact Hawkesbury Harvest (☑0406 237 877; www.hawkesburyharvest.com.au) for information on wine and farm trails.

The Riverboat Postman (☎0400 600 111; www.riverboatpostman.com.au; Riverboat Postman Wharf, Brooklyn; adult/child/family $50/30/130; ◷9.30am Mon-Fri), Australia's last operating mail boat, departs from the Brooklyn Wharf, beside the Hawkesbury River Railway Station, and chugs 40km up the Hawkesbury as far as Marlow, returning to Brooklyn at 1.15pm. There are additional 'coffee cruises' towards the mouth of the river (adult/child/family $25/15/65) on Sundays at 11am and 1.30pm.

Near Brooklyn is the unique Peats Bite (☎02-9985 9040; www.peatsbite.com.au; Sunny Corner; set menu per person without wine $120; ◷lunch Sat & Sun, closed Jul & Aug), which has been operated by the same family since 1981. A truly laid-back place, it offers a four-course, four-hour set lunch and encourages guests to linger over their food, take a dip in the pool between courses and shimmy on the dance floor when owner Tammy gets up to sing. Access is by boat only, and you can book to stay overnight if you so choose (suite from $280). Boat transfers from the Kangaroo Point boat ramp in Brooklyn take 10 to 15 minutes; call for details.

Further upstream a narrow forested waterway diverts from the Hawkesbury and peters down to the chilled-out river town of Berowra Waters, where a handful of businesses, boat sheds and residences cluster around the free, 24-hour ferry across Berowra Creek. If you feel like exploring, rev the river in a tinny (outboard dinghy) from the Berowra Waters Marina (☎02-9456 7000; www.bbqboat. info; 199 Bay Rd, Berowra Waters; per half-day $85; ◷8am-5pm). Nearby, elegant Berowra Waters Inn (☎02-9456 1027; www.berowrawatersinn. com; 4/5/6 courses $130/145/160; ◷lunch Fri-Sun, dinner Fri & Sat), housed in a waterside pavilion designed by Australia's most acclaimed contemporary architect, Glenn Murcutt, is one of the state's best restaurants, offering a degustation-style men . The restaurant is only accessed by seaplane from Sydney (see p146) or via the restaurant's own ferry, which leaves from a wharf near the village of Berowra.

CityRail trains run from Sydney's Central Station to Berowra (one way adult/child $6/3, 45 minutes, roughly hourly) and on to Brooklyn's Hawkesbury River Station (one way adult/child $6/3, one hour). Berowra Station is a solid 6km trudge from Berowra Waters. Hawkesbury Water Taxis (☎0400 600 111; www.hawkesburycruises.com.au) will take you anywhere along the river.

The lively riverside hamlet of Wisemans Ferry spills over a bow of the Hawkesbury River where it slides east towards Brooklyn. The surrounding area retains remnants of the convict-built Great North Road, originally constructed to link Sydney with the Hunter Valley and now part of the Australian Convict Sites listing on Unesco's World Heritage List (see the boxed text, p75). Today the road is a pretty back route to the north. Some 15km of the original road has been preserved and offers an excellent mountain-bike trail. To download a self-guided tour brochure, go to www.rta.nsw.gov.au and type 'convict trail' into the search box.

The social hub at Wisemans Ferry is the historic sandstone Wisemans Ferry Inn Hotel (☎02-4566 4301; Old Northern Rd, Wisemans Ferry; ◷10am-before midnight Mon-Thu, to midnight Fri & Sat, to 10pm Sun), which has decent pub rooms (doubles $75) and a bistro (mains $13 to $28; open noon to 8.30pm). There's live music (mainly country) and dozens of bikies at weekends. The prettiest access is from the east, via Old Wisemans Ferry Rd, which is wedged between Dharug National Park and the river. Two free 24-hour ferries connect the Wisemans Ferry riverbanks.

Largely unsealed but photogenic roads on both sides of the Macdonald River run north from Wisemans Ferry to tiny St Albans in Darkinung tribal country.

Windsor & Richmond

POP 1670 (WINDSOR), 5560 (RICHMOND)

On the banks of the Hawkesbury River, Windsor is the third-oldest place of British settlement in Australia. The town still boasts a handful of original buildings, but there's no denying that much of its charm has been swallowed up by the ever-creeping urban sprawl. To download a heritage map or heritage walks brochures, go to www.hawkesburytourism.com.au.

Designed by convict architect Francis Greenway, the Windsor Courthouse on the corner of North Pitt and Court Sts was built in 1822. Nearby, the convict-built St Matthew's Anglican Church on Moses St was built between 1817 and 1820 and held its first service in September 1821. It remains the oldest Anglican church in Australia.

The reputedly haunted Macquarie Arms Hotel (www.macquariearms.com.au; 99 George St; ◷10am-midnight) has been calling last orders since 1815, and describes itself as Australia's

HAWKESBURY HOUSEBOATS

The best way to experience the Hawkesbury is on a fully equipped houseboat. Expect rates to skyrocket during summer and school holidays, but most outfits offer affordable low-season, midweek and long-term rental specials. To give a very rough guide, a two-/four-/six-berth boat for three nights costs from $650/720/1150 from September to early December, with prices doubling during the Christmas/New Year period and on weekends and holidays throughout the year.

Most companies are based in Brooklyn. The following are some of the main players:

Able Hawkesbury River Houseboats (☎02-4566 4308, 1800 024 979; www.hawkesburyhouseboats.com.au; 3008 River Rd, Wisemans Ferry)

Brooklyn Marina (☎02-9985 7722; www.brooklynmarina.com.au; 45 Brooklyn Rd, Brooklyn)

Holidays Afloat (☎02-9985 7368; www.holidaysafloat.com.au; 65 Brooklyn Rd, Brooklyn)

Ripples Houseboats (☎02-9985 5555; www.ripples.com.au; 87 Brooklyn Rd, Brooklyn)

oldest pub (surely we've heard that before?). The interiors retain much of their country-town charm; but the poker machines detract considerably from the historical ambience. Bar meals cost between $10 and $15 and there's live music on Saturday nights and Sunday afternoons.

Housed in a heritage building with a modern, purpose-built annexe, the Hawkesbury Regional Museum (www.hawkesbury.nsw.gov.au/services/hawkesbury-regional-museum; 7 Thompson Sq; admission free; ☺10am-4pm Wed-Mon) has a permanent exhibition around the theme 'River, Land, People' that includes information on the cultural heritage of the local Darug people. The relatively new Hawkesbury Regional Gallery (www.hawkesbury.nsw.gov.au/services/hawkesbury-regional-gallery; level 1, Deerubbin Centre, 300 George St; admission free; ☺10am-4pm Mon & Wed-Fri, to 3pm Sat & Sun) has a changing program of exhibitions in a variety of media, including visual art, craft, photography and design.

Five kilometres west of Windsor is Richmond, first settled in 1794. Like its neighbour the town has suffered from its now suburban location, but has managed to cling onto some noteworthy buildings, including the 1878 courthouse and police station on the corner of Market and Windsor Sts and St Andrew's Church (1845) on Market St.

Halfway between Richmond and Windsor (opposite the RAAF base), the Hawkesbury Visitor Centre (☎02-4578 0233; www.hawkesburytourism.com.au; Ham Common Park, Hawkesbury Valley Way, Clarendon; ☺9am-5pm Mon-Fri, to 4pm Sat & Sun) can supply information and help with accommodation bookings.

CityRail trains run from Sydney's Central Station to Windsor (one way adult/child $6/3, 70 minutes, every 30 minutes) and Richmond (one way adult/child $6/3, 80 minutes, every 30 minutes).

BLUE MOUNTAINS

POP 77,800

A region with more than its fair share of gorges, gum trees and gourmet restaurants, the spectacular Blue Mountains (Map p88) was an obvious contender when Unesco called for Australian nominations to the World Heritage List, and its inclusion was ratified in 2000. The slate-coloured haze that gives the mountains their name comes from a fine mist of oil exuded by the huge eucalyptus gums that form a dense canopy across the landscape of deep, often-inaccessible valleys and chiselled sandstone outcrops.

The foothills begin 65km inland from Sydney, rising to an 1100m-high sandstone plateau riddled with valleys eroded into the stone over thousands of years. There are eight connected conservation areas in the region, including the Blue Mountains National Park (www.environment.nsw.gov.au/nationalparks), which has some truly fantastic scenery, excellent bushwalks, Aboriginal engravings and all the canyons and cliffs you could ask for. It's the most popular and accessible of the three national parks in the area. Great lookouts include the Evan's and Govett's Leap lookouts near Blackheath, and Echo Point in Katoomba.

Wollemi National Park (www.environment.nsw.gov.au/nationalparks), north of the Bells Line of Road, is NSW's largest forested wilderness area, stretching all the way to Denman in the Hunter Valley.

Six Aboriginal language groups treasure connections with the area that reach back into ancient time. They are the Dharawal and Gundungurra people (in the south), the Wiradjuri (in the west and northwest), and the Wanaruah, Darkinjung and Darug (in the northeast).

Although it's possible to visit on a day trip from Sydney, we strongly recommend that you stay at least one night so that you can explore a few of the towns, do at least one bushwalk and enjoy a dinner at one of the excellent restaurants in Blackheath or Leura.

After the beaches of Bondi you may find the hills surprisingly cool, so bring a coat or wrap.

◉ Sights

GLENBROOK TO BLACKHEATH

Arriving from Sydney, the first of the Blue Mountains town you will encounter is Glenbrook (population 5138). From here, you can drive or walk into the Blue Mountains National Park (per car $7, walkers free; ☉8.30am-6pm, to 7pm during daylight savings); this is the only part of the park where entry fees apply. Six kilometres from the park entrance gate is the Mt Portal Lookout, which has panoramic views into the Glenbrook Gorge, over the Nepean River and back to Sydney.

Artist, author and bon vivant Norman Lindsay, infamous for his racy artworks (imagine an unfortunate conflation of Boucher and Beardsley) but much loved for his children's tale *The Magic Pudding*, lived in Faulconbridge, 14km up the mountain from Glenbrook, from 1912 until his death in 1969. His home and studio have been preserved and maintained by the National Trust as the Norman Lindsay Gallery &

Museum (www.normanlindsay.com.au; 14 Norman Lindsay Cres, Faulconbridge; adult/child/concession $10/5/7; ☉10am-4pm), with a significant collection of his paintings, watercolours, drawings and sculptures. There's a cafe (mains $19.50-24.50; ☉9am-4.30pm) on site, but its kitchen's enthusiasm is greater than its skill – we suggest sticking to scones, jam and tea ($7.50) or a sandwich.

Further up the mountain, the town of Wentworth Falls (population 5650) commands views to the south across the majestic Jamison Valley. Wentworth Falls themselves launch a plume of spray over a 300m drop – check them out from Falls Reserve. This is also the starting point for a network of walking tracks into the sublime Valley of the Waters, which has waterfalls, gorges, woodlands and rainforests. Many of these walks start from the Conservation Hut (www.conservationhut.com.au; Fletcher St; mains $23-30; ☉9am-4pm Mon-Fri, to 5pm Sat & Sun), where you can enjoy a coffee or meal on a deck overlooking the valley.

Nearby Leura (population 4385) is a genteel town of undulating streets, heritage houses and lush gardens. At its centre is The Mall, a tree-lined main street with boutiques, galleries and cafes. The town's major heritage property is the National Trust-owned Everglades (www.everglades. org.au; 37 Everglades Ave; adult/child/concession $8/4/6; ☉10am-5pm Oct-Mar, to 4pm Apr-Sep), which was built in the 1930s and has one of the country's foremost heritage gardens, designed by Danish landscaper Paul Sorensen.

Just outside town is Gordon Falls Reserve, an idyllic picnic spot. From here you can trek the steep Prince Henry Cliff Walk, or take the Cliff Drive 4km west past Leura Cascades to Katoomba (population 7623), the

---

MURU MITTIGAR ABORIGINAL CULTURAL CENTRE

If travelling from Sydney to the Blue Mountains, consider taking a few hours out in Penrith to visit the Muru Mittigar Aboriginal Cultural Centre (☎02-4729 3277; www. murumittigar.com.au; 89-151 Old Castlereagh Rd, Castlereagh; ☉9am-4pm Mon-Fri, 10am-2pm Sat, by appointment Sun), which was opened as an Aboriginal Meeting Place in 1998 to acknowledge the Darug people as the traditional custodians of the region. The Cultural Museum here showcases the art and stories of the Darug people as well as the rich diversity of Indigenous peoples throughout Australia. An outdoor amphitheatre plays host to traditional dance performances, where local guides also play the didgeridoo and explain the story of its creation and significance. Cultural tours are offered (adult/child from $45/34), and a cafe on site serves bush tucker, so you can scoff that side of roo or wallaby you've always wanted.

The centre is an hour's drive west of Sydney and an hour's drive east of Katoomba.

region's main town, where the often-misty steep streets are lined with art-deco buildings. The population here is an odd mix of country battlers, hippies, mortgage refugees from the big smoke (Sydney) and members of a Tennessee-based messianic Christian sect called the Twelve Tribes (aka the Community of Believers), who live communally, believe in traditional lifestyle and operate the Common Ground Café in the main street. Extraordinarily, all of these locals seem to live together harmoniously. They also seem to cope with the huge numbers of tour buses and tourists who come here to ooh-and-aah at the spectacular view of the Jamison Valley and Three Sisters rock formation towers from the Echo Point viewing platforms.

There are a number of short walks from Echo Point that allow you to escape the bulk of the crowds. Parking is expensive ($3.80 for first hour, $4.40 for subsequent hours); if you're walking here from the town centre, Lurline St is the most attractive route.

Three kilometres from the centre of Katoomba you'll find Scenic World (www.scenicworld.com.au; cnr Cliff Dr & Violet St; cable car/railway return adult/child $21/10; ⊙9am-5pm), with a megaplex vibe and an 1880s railway and modern cable car descending the 52-degree incline to the valley floor. Also here is the glass-floored Scenic Skyway (adult/child $16/8), a cable car floating out across the valley.

The next town to the west is neat and petite Blackheath (population 4177), which is a good base for visiting the Grose, Kanimbla and Megalong Valleys.

East of town are lookouts at Govetts Leap (comparable to the Three Sisters in terms of 'wow' factor), Bridal Veil Falls (the highest in the Blue Mountains) and Evans Lookout. To the northeast, via Hat Hill Rd, are Pulpit Rock, Perry's Lookdown and Anvil Rock. There are steep walks into the Grose Valley from Govetts Leap; experienced walkers may want to follow the 5km (5½ hours) route from Perry's Lookdown to the magical Blue Gum Forest; the easier 1.5km walk to Evans Lookout takes 1½ hours one way.

Crowds at Govetts Leap aren't as oppressive as at Echo Point, there's a branch of the excellent Gleebooks bookshop on Govetts Leap Rd and there are plenty of gourmet restaurants – in short, it's a great option if you're looking for somewhere to base yourself, particularly as the charming Glenella Guesthouse (p131) is located here.

MEGALONG VALLEY

Unless you walk in or take Katoomba's Scenic Railway, the only way you'll see a Blue Mountains gorge from the inside is in the Megalong Valley. This is straw-coloured rural Australia, a real departure from the quasi-suburbs strung along the ridgeline. The 600m Coachwood Glen Nature Trail features dripping fern dells, stands of mountain ash and sun-stained sandstone cliffs.

A 30-minute drive from Katoomba, the Megalong Australian Heritage Centre (☑02-4787 8188; www.megalong.cc; Megalong Rd; adult/child/family $8/6/20; ⊙8am-5pm) has a display farm that little tackers love – they can feed and pat sheep, ducks, chickens, donkeys and alpacas and enjoy a pony ride. There's also guided horse riding into the bush and along escarpments ($50/95 per person for one/two hours).

You can also go horse riding with Werriberri Trail Rides (☑02-4787 9171; www.australianbluehorserides.com.au; Megalong Rd; pony rides 20 minutes $33, 1/2/4hr trail rides $55/99/149; ⊙10am-5pm).

MT VICTORIA, HARTLEY & LITHGOW
POP 830 (MT VICTORIA), 19,800 (LITHGOW)

With a charming alpine air, Mt Victoria sits at 1043m and is the highest town in the mountains. Historic buildings dominate and include St Peter's Church (1874) and the Toll Keepers Cottage (1849).

Inside an old public hall, the 130-seat Mount Vic Flicks (www.bluemts.com.au/mountvic; Harley Ave; adult/child $10/8; ⊙Thu-Sun, from 10.30am Thu) is a wonderful step back in time. With ushers, a piano player and door prizes you'll soon forget what you came to see. On Thursdays, all tickets cost $7.

The best pub in the area by a mountain mile is the 1878 Imperial Hotel (1 Station St, Mt Victoria; ⊙10am-10pm), where you can enjoy a decent counter attack (pub meal; mains $14.50, kids meals $8). You can also overnight if need be (dorm $30), although the accommodation is very run down

About 12km past Mt Victoria, on the western slopes of the range, is the tiny, sandstone 'ghost' town of Hartley, which flourished from the 1830s but declined when bypassed by the railway in 1887. It's been well preserved and a number of historic buildings remain, including several private homes and inns.

A further 14km on from Hartley, in the western foothills of the Blue Mountains, is Lithgow, a sombre coal-mining town popular with trainspotters for its **Zig Zag Railway** (www.zigzagrailway.com.au; Clarence Station, Bells Line of Road; adult/child/family $28/14/70; ⊙11am, 1pm & 3pm), which sits just 10km east of town. Built in the 1860s to transport the Great Western Railway tracks down from the mountains into Lithgow, today it zigzags tourists gently down the precipice (1½-hour return trip).

JENOLAN CAVES

The story behind the discovery of **Jenolan Caves** (www.jenolancaves.org.au; Jenolan Caves Rd; admission with tour adult/child/family from $28/18.50/68; ⊙9am-5pm) is the stuff of legends: local pastoralist James Whalan stumbled across the prehistoric caves while tracking the escaped convict and cattle rustler James McKeown, who is thought to have used the caves as a hideout.

Originally named Binoomea or 'Dark Places' by the Gundungurra people, the caves took shape more than 400 million years ago and are one of the most extensive and complex limestone cave systems in the world.

There are over 350 caves in the region, although only a handful is open to the public. You must take a **tour** to see them; there's a bewildering array of options at different levels of difficulty; staff at the ticket office are happy to explain them all. You can also don a boiler suit and squeeze yourself through narrow tunnels with only a headlamp to guide you on a **'Plughole' Adventure Tour** ($70; ⊙1.15pm daily).

The caves are 30km from the Great Western Hwy (Rte 4), a 1¼-hour drive from Katoomba. The narrow Jenolan Caves Rd becomes a one-way system between 11.45am and 1.15pm daily, running clockwise from the caves out through Oberon.

Although there are a few accommodation options in Jenolan Village and the surrounding area, none are worthy of recommendation.

🏃 Activities

Bushwalking

Explorers Wentworth, Blaxland and Lawson set off a craze for exploring the area when they became the first Europeans to traverse these majestic mountains in 1813. Fortunately, there are walks of every possible duration and level of difficulty on offer, so everyone can participate. The two most popular bushwalking areas are the Jamison Valley, south of Katoomba, and the Grose Valley, northeast of Katoomba and east of

Blackheath. Other great walking opportunities can be found in the area south of Glenbrook, the Kanangra Boyd National Park (accessible from Oberon or Jenolan Caves) and the Wollemi National Park, north of Bells Line of Road. One of the most rewarding walks is the 45km, three-day **Six Foot Track** from Katoomba along the Megalong Valley to Cox's River and on to the Jenolan Caves. It has camp sites along the way.

The extraordinarily helpful **NPWS Visitor Centre** (☎02-4787 8877; www.nationalparks.nsw.gov.au; Govetts Leap Rd, Blackheath; ⊙9am-4.30pm) at Blackheath, about 2.5km off the Great Western Hwy and 10km north of Katoomba, can help you pick a hike, offer safety tips and will advise about camping; for information about shorter walks, ask at the Katoomba Visitor Centre (p134). Note that the bush here is dense and that it can be easy to become lost – there have been deaths as a consequence. Always leave your name and walk plan with the Katoomba Police, at the NPWS office or at one of the visitor centres; the Katoomba police station, Echo Point Visitor Centre and NPWS office also offer free use of personal locator beacons.

Also remember to carry clean drinking water with you – the mountain streams are polluted due to their proximity to urban areas.

A range of NPWS walks pamphlets and maps ($3 to $6) are available from the NPWS office and from the visitor information centres at Glenbrook and Katoomba. All three also sell the Hema *Blue Mountains* walking map ($8.95) and Veechi Stuart's well-regarded *Blue Mountains: Best Bushwalks* book ($29.95).

Cycling

The mountains are also a popular cycling destination, with many people taking their bikes on the train to Woodford and then cycling downhill to Glenbrook, a ride of two to three hours. Cycling maps ($7) are available from the visitor information centres at Glenbrook and Katoomba.

Driving

The **Greater Blue Mountains Drive** (www.greaterbluemountainsdrive.com.au) is a 1200km tour linking Sydney with the Blue Mountains region; it incorporates 18 'discovery trails' (stand-alone scenic drives), the most popular being the 36km, one hour 'Blue Mountains Drive Discovery Trail' that starts in Katoomba and finishes at the Valley of the Waters picnic area at Wentworth Falls.

SYDNEY & NEW SOUTH WALES BLUE MOUNTAINS

The best driving maps are Gregory's *Blue Mountains Touring Map* ($7.95) and the *Greater Blue Mountains Drive Touring Map* ($7.95). Both are available at the visitor information centres.

Adventure Activities & Tours

Most operators have offices in Katoomba – competition is steep, so shop around for the best deal.

Australian Eco Adventures ECOTOURS
(☑02-9971 2402; www.ozeco.com.au; adult/child $255/160; ⊘7am) Eco-certified deluxe day tours of the Blue Mountains departing from Sydney at 7am (maximum 16 people) and including short bushwalks. Prices drop if you choose an option without breakfast and lunch.

Australian School of Mountaineering ADVENTURE ACTIVITIES
(ASM; Map p130; ☑02-4782 2014; www.asmguides.com; 166 Katoomba St, Katoomba)

Rock climbing from $175, abseiling from $145 and canyoning from $175.

Blue Mountains Adventure Company ADVENTURE ACTIVITIES
(Map p130; ☑02-4782 1271; www.bmac.com.au; 84a Bathurst Rd, Katoomba) Abseiling from $110, abseiling and bushwalking combo from $180, canyoning from $165, bushwalking from $100 and rock climbing from $180.

Blue Mountains Walkabout INDIGENOUS TREKS
(☑0408 443 822; www.bluemountainswalkabout.com) Seven-hour/half-day Aboriginal-owned and guided adventurous treks with Aboriginal and spiritual themes ($95/75). Meets at Faulconbridge train station.

High 'n' Wild Mountain Adventures ADVENTURE ACTIVITIES
(Map p130; ☑02-4782 6224; www.highandwild.com.au; 3/5 Katoomba St) Half-/full-day

abseiling (from $99/145) and climbing ($159/179), and full-day canyoning ($179).

Tread Lightly Eco Tours   ECOTOURS
(☑02-4788 1229; www.treadlightly.com.au) Has a wide range of day and night walks ($65 to $135) that emphasise the ecology of the region.

✦ Festivals & Events

Every year between June and August, the Blue Mountains enjoy out-of-kilter Christmas-style celebrations with Yulefest (☑1300 653 408; www.bluemts.com.au). Festivities reach a pagan peak at Katoomba's Winter Magic Festival (www.wintermagic.com.au), held on the Saturday closest to 21 June and featuring a street parade, market stalls and general frivolity to welcome the winter solstice.

🛏 Sleeping

There's a good range of accommodation in the Blue Mountains, but you'll need to book ahead during winter and for every weekend during the year (Sydneysiders love coming here for romantic weekends away). Backpackers tend to stay in Katoomba, where the hostels are, but those with their own transport prefer Leura and Blackheath, where the restaurants and cafes are better.

Note that the famous Hydro Majestic Hotel (www.hydromajestic.com.au), an art-deco extravaganza at Medlow Bath, was undergoing a major renovation when this book was being researched and was due to reopen in late 2012.

TOP CHOICE Glenella Guesthouse   GUESTHOUSE $$
(☑02-4787 8352; www.glenellabluemountains hotel.com.au; 56-60 Govetts Leap Rd, Blackheath;

r $100-160, f $200-240; 🛜) Gorgeous Glenella has been functioning as a guesthouse since 1912 and is now operated with enthusiasm and expertise by a young British couple who make guests feel very welcome. There are seven comfortable bedrooms, an attractive lounge and a stunning dining room where a truly excellent breakfast is served.

Flying Fox   HOSTEL $
(☑02-4782 4226; www.theflyingfox.com.au; 190 Bathurst Rd, Katoomba; tent sites per person $19, dm $29, d without bathroom $79; @🛜) Owners Ross and Wendy are travellers at heart, and have endowed this unassuming hostel with an endearing home-away-from-home feel. There's no party scene here – just *glüwine* (mulled wine) and Tim Tams in the friendly lounge and a free pancake breakfast in the well-equipped communal kitchen. Internet and wi-fi are free, which is a plus, but there aren't many bathrooms.

Blue Mountains YHA   HOSTEL $
(☑02-4782 1416; www.yha.com.au; 207 Katoomba St, Katoomba; dm $29.50-31.50, d with/without bathroom $98.50/$88.50, f with/without bathroom $140/$126; @🛜) Behind the austere art-deco exterior of this popular 200-bed hostel is a selection of dorms and family rooms that are comfortable, light and spotlessly clean. Highlights include a lounge with open fire, central heating, a huge TV room, pool table, excellent communal kitchen and outdoor space with barbecues. You can organise plenty of activities from here. A DIY breakfast costs $6.50.

Jemby-Rinjah Eco Lodge   ECO LODGE $$$
(☑02-4787 7622; www.jembyrinjahlodge.com.au; 336 Evans Lookout Rd; cabins Mon-Thu $185-219,

Fri-Sun & holidays $240-265) These eco-cabins are lodged so deeply in the bottlebrush you'll have to bump into one to find it. All of the one- and two-bedroom weatherboard cabins are self-equipped; the deluxe model also has a Japanese hot tub.

Greens of Leura
B&B **$$**
(☎02-4784 3241; www.thegreensleura.com.au; 24-26 Grose St, Leura; r weekdays/weekends from $145/175; ❷❸) On a quiet street parallel to The Mall, this pretty timber house set in a lovely garden offers five rooms named after English writers (Browning, Austen etc). All are individually decorated; some have four-poster beds and spas.

Leura House
GUESTHOUSE **$$**
(☎02-4784 2035; www.leurahouse.com.au; 7 Britain St, Leura; s $145, d $170-190, ste $190-230; ❷❸) Occupying an 1880s mansion set in a splendid garden, this sprawling place has functioned in the past as a convent but has been a guesthouse for the past few decades. The 13 rooms are comfortable and extremely clean, if a tad faded (opt for number 11, which has a great view). Breakfast could be better.

Carrington Hotel
HOTEL **$$$**
(☎02-4782 1111; www.thecarrington.com.au; 15-47 Katoomba St, Katoomba; r $205-315, r without bathroom $129-149, ste $340-490; ❋❷❸) Katoomba's social and architectural highwater mark, the Carrington has been accommodating road-weary travellers since 1880. Though much of the building has been refurbished, its historical character remains intact. Throwback amenities include a library, a billiards room and stately gardens.

No 14
HOSTEL **$**
(☎02-4782 7104; www.no14.com.au; 14 Lovel St, Katoomba; dm $25-28, d $79-89, d without bathroom $69-75; ❷❸) Resembling a cheery share house, this small hostel has a friendly vibe but suffers from a lack of bathrooms (three showers for 30 beds). Dorms have three or four beds; attic-style doubles are comfy. A basic breakfast is included in the price and internet access on the in-house computer is free; wi-fi costs $5 per 24 hours.

Hawkesbury Heights YHA
HOSTEL **$**
(☎02-4754 5621; www.yha.com.au; 836 Hawkesbury Rd, Hawkesbury Heights; dm/d from $29/58, entire hostel from $270-395) This small, quiet and ecofriendly hostel sits tucked away in the bush 11km northeast of Springwood, at the foot of the mountains. It has solar power, comfortable rooms and sensational valley views. You need wheels to get here; the reception is in the red-brick house on the main road.

Megalong Ranch Guesthouse
GUESTHOUSE **$**
(☎02-4787 8188; www.megalong.cc; Megalong Rd) The basic farm accommodation offered at the Megalong Australian Heritage Centre (p128) comprises camp sites ($12 per person), dorm beds ($20) and B&B guesthouse rooms (adult $95 to $125, child $50 to $65, family $250 to $295).

✖ Eating

Despite being the major town in the mountains, Katoomba has a lacklustre array of restaurants and cafes – if you have transport you are better off eating elsewhere. Blackheath is the undoubted gastronomic centre of the region, with some excellent restaurants operating between Thursday and Sunday. Every second Sunday of the month, the **Blackheath Growers Market** (www.blackcastleevents.com.au) is held at the Blackheath Community Centre, on the corner of Gardiner Cres and the Great Western Hwy between 8am and noon. Note that the market isn't held in January.

⌐TOP⌐ Solitary
MODERN AUSTRALIAN **$$**
(☎02-4782 1164; www.solitary.com.au; 90 Cliff Dr, Leura Falls; lunch dishes $14-33.50, dinner mains $26-33.50; ☯lunch daily, dinner Sat, closed 2 weeks Jan) The magnificent views to Mt Solitary are the main event here, but the seasonally driven and totally delicious food lives up to this elegant restaurant's setting atop the Leura Cascades. Also serves Devonshire teas ($10).

Ashcrofts
MODERN AUSTRALIAN **$$**
(☎02-4787 8297; www.ashcrofts.com; 18 Govetts Leap Rd, Blackheath; 2/3 courses $68/85; ☯dinner Wed-Sun, lunch Sun, closed Feb & first half of Mar) Chef Corinne Evatt has been wooing locals

Bells Line of Road (Map p88) between Richmond and Lithgow is the most scenic route across the Blue Mountains and is highly recommended if you have your own transport. There are fine views towards the coast from Kurrajong Heights on the eastern slopes of the range, there are orchards around Bilpin and there's sandstone-cliff and bush scenery all the way to Lithgow.

Midway between Bilpin and Bell, the delightful **Blue Mountains Botanic Garden Mount Tomah** (www.mounttomahbotanicgarden.com.au; Bells Line of Road; adult/child/concession $5.50/3.30/4.40; ⊙10am-4pm Apr-Sep, to 5pm Oct-Mar) is a cool-climate annexe of Sydney's Royal Botanic Gardens. As well as native plants there are displays of exotic cold-climate species, including some magnificent rhododendrons. Parts of the park are wheelchair accessible.

If you're at Bilpin for lunch or dinner, make a beeline for **Apple Bar** (www.applebar.com.au; 2488 Bells Line of Road; pizzas $20-26; ⊙lunch & dinner Fri-Mon, lunch & coffee Tue-Thu), which is set in a weatherboard cottage amongst Bilpin's apple orchards and serves excellent pizzas and grills from its wood-fired oven. At other times, head to **Tutti Frutti** (http://tuttifruitti.com.au; 1917 Bells Line of Road; ⊙10am-4pm Thu & Mon, 9.30am-4pm Fri, 9.30am-5pm Sat & Sun), where you can enjoy Devonshire teas, coffee, homemade pies (including a sensational apple version) and berry ice cream in the charming rose courtyard.

To access Bells Line of Road, head out on Parramatta Rd from Sydney, and from Parramatta drive northwest on Windsor Rd to Windsor. Richmond Rd from Windsor becomes the Bells Line of Road west of Richmond.

and visitors alike with her flavoursome, globally inspired dishes for the past decade. The wine list is possibly the best in the mountains and service is exemplary.

Escarpment   MODERN AUSTRALIAN **$$**
(☑02-4787 7269; www.escarpmentblackheath.com; 246 Great Western Hwy, Blackheath; mains $28-34.50; ⊙dinner Thu-Mon, lunch Sat & Sun) The decor at this recently opened bistro near the railway station features attractive artwork and an old-fashioned espresso machine. There's nothing old-fashioned or overly arty about the menu, though – it changes with the season and makes the most of local produce.

Fresh Espresso & Food Bar   CAFE **$**
(www.freshcafe.com.au; 181 Katoomba St, Katoomba; breakfast $4.50-15, lunch $13-16; ⊙8am-5pm Mon-Sat, to 4pm Sun) The organic, rainforest-alliance and fair-trade coffee served at Fresh attracts a devoted local following. Excellent all-day breakfasts are popular, too. The Katoomba branch is small but the new cafe/roastery on the corner of Megalong St and The Mall in Leura has plenty of seats.

Silk's Brasserie   MODERN AUSTRALIAN **$$**
(☑02-4784 2534; www.silksleura.com; 128 The Mall, Leura; mains $24-37; ⊙lunch & dinner) The decor and staff are equally welcoming at Leura's long-standing fine diner. Dishes

can sometimes be overworked, but serves are generous and flavours generally harmonious.

Blue Mountains Food Co-op   SELF-CATERING **$**
(www.bluemtnsfood.asn.au; shops 1 & 2, Ha'penny Lane, Katoomba; ⊙9am-6pm Mon-Wed & Fri, 9am-6.30pm Thu, 8.30am-5pm Sat, 10am-4.30pm Sun) The perfect stop for hard-core self-caterers and bushwalkers in need of goodies for their backpacks, the Co-op stocks organic, vegan and gluten-free local foods and produce.

🍷 Drinking & Entertainment

Station Bar   BAR
(http://stationbar.com.au; 287 Bathurst Rd, Katoomba; ⊙daily till late) This new bar next to the train station is Katoomba's most popular drinking hole, but our experience would indicate that the pizzas are best avoided. There's live music on Sunday nights from 7pm.

Old City Bank Bar & Brasserie   BAR
(Katoomba St, Katoomba; ⊙7am-2am Mon-Thu, to 3am Fri & Sat, 10am-10pm Sun; 🛜) Run by the Carrington Hotel, this popular place has a pleasant bar on the ground floor and a dining room upstairs serving decent pub grub and pizzas (mains $14 to $24). There's live music most Friday and Saturday nights.

Edge Cinema CINEMA
(www.edgecinema.com.au; 225 Great Western Hwy, Katoomba; adult/child/concession $14/10/12.50; ⊕9.30am-late) A giant screen shows mainstream flicks plus a 40-minute Blue Mountains documentary (adult/child $15/10). Budget Tuesdays feature flicks for $8.50 per person.

❶ Information

There are **visitor information centres** (☑1300 653 408, 1800 641 227; www.visitbluemountains.com.au) on the Great Western Hwy at **Glenbrook** (⊕9am-4.30pm Mon-Fri, 8.30am-3.30pm Sat & Sun) and at Echo Point in **Katoomba** (⊕9am-5pm). Both can provide plenty of information and will book accommodation, tours and attractions.

The **Blue Mountains District Anzac Memorial Hospital** (☑02-4784 6500; www.wsahs.nsw.gov.au/bluemountains/index.htm; cnr Woodlands Rd & Great Western Hwy, Katoomba; ⊕24hr emergency). Katoomba has a 24-hour emergency department.

❶ Getting There & Around

To reach the Blue Mountains by road, leave Sydney via Parramatta Rd. At Strathfield detour onto the toll-free M4, which becomes the Great Western Hwy west of Penrith and takes you to all of the Blue Mountains towns. It takes approximately 1½ hours to drive from central Sydney to Katoomba.

Blue Mountains Bus (☑02-4751 1077; www.bmbc.com.au) Local buses travel from Katoomba to Wentworth Falls (buses 685 and 690K), Scenic World (bus 686), Leura (bus 690K) and Blackheath (bus 698). Fares cost between $2 and $4.30.

Blue Mountains Explorer Bus (☑1300 300 915; www.explorerbus.com.au; 283 Main St, Katoomba; adult/child $36/18; ⊕9.45am-4.54pm) Offers hop-on hop-off service on a Katoomba/Leura loop. Leaves from Katoomba station every 30 minutes to one hour.

Blue Mountains ExplorerLink (☑13 15 00; www.cityrail.info; 1-day pass adult/child from $46.80/23.40, 3-day pass adult/child from $66.80/33.40) Gives return train travel from Sydney to the Blue Mountains, plus access to the Explorer Bus service.

CityRail (☑13 15 00; www.cityrail.info) Runs to the mountains from Sydney's Central Station (one way adult/child $7.80/3.90, two hours, hourly). There are stations at towns along the Great Western Hwy, including Glenbrook, Faulconbridge, Wentworth Falls, Leura, Katoomba, Medlow Bath, Blackheath, Mt Victoria, Zig Zag and Lithgow.

Trolley Tours (☑02-4782 7999, 1800 801 577; www.trolleytours.com.au; 285 Main St, Katoomba; adult/family $20/60; ⊕9.45am-5.42pm) Runs a hop-on, hop-off bus barely disguised as a trolley. Twenty-nine stops in Katoomba and Leura.

HUNTER VALLEY

POP 50,900 (CESSNOCK SHIRE),
14,050 (UPPER HUNTER SHIRE)

A filigree of narrow country lanes crisscrosses this verdant valley, but a pleasant country drive isn't the main motivator for visitors – sheer decadence is. The Hunter is one big gorge-fest: fine wine, boutique beer, chocolate, cheese, olives, you name it. Bacchus would surely approve.

Going on the philosophy that good food and wine will inevitably up the odds for nookie, the region is a popular weekender for Sydney couples. Every Friday they descend, like a plague of Ralph-Lauren-Polo-shirt-wearing locusts. Prices leap up accordingly.

The oldest wine region in Australia, the Hunter is known for its Semillon and Shiraz. Vines were first planted in the 1820s and by the 1860s there were 20 sq km under cultivation. However, the wineries gradually declined, and it wasn't until the 1960s that winemaking again became an important industry. If it's no longer the crowning jewel of the Australian wine industry, it still turns in some excellent vintages.

The Hunter has an important ace up its sleeve: these wineries are refreshingly attitude-free and welcoming of viticulturists and novices alike. Staff will rarely give you the evil eye if you leadenly twirl your glass once too often, or don't conspicuously savour the bouquet. Even those with only a casual interest in wine should be sure to tour around – it's a lovely area, and a great direction to turn to if the weather drives you from the beaches.

◉ Sights & Activities

Most attractions lie in an area bordered to the north by the New England Hwy and to the south by Wollombi/Maitland Rd. The main town serving the area is Cessnock, to the south. Wine Country Dr heads straight up from Cessnock to Branxton, where there's a train station. To confuse matters, the bottom half of this route is sometimes labelled Allandale Rd and the top end Branxton Rd.

SYDNEY & NEW SOUTH WALES HUNTER VALLEY

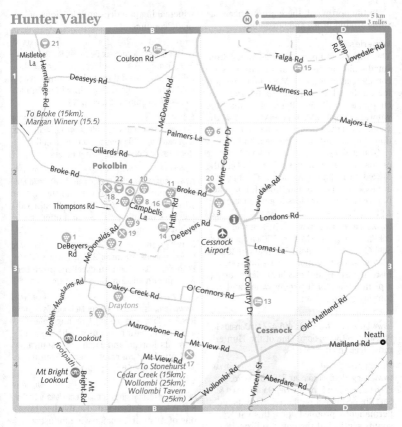

To the northwest, there are further vineyards around Broke and Singleton.

Wineries

The valley's 140-plus wineries range from small-scale family-run affairs to massive commercial operations. Most offer free tastings, although a couple of the glitzier ones charge a small fee. Remember that the vineyards don't offer this service out of the goodness of their hearts. It's poor form if you don't buy at least the occasional bottle.

Grab a vineyard map and plot your course or just follow your nose, hunting out the tucked-away small producers. The majority are located on or around Broke Rd in Pokolbin. Here are a few picks to get you started:

Audrey Wilkinson Vineyard VINEYARD
(www.audreywilkinson.com.au; DeBeyers Rd, Pokolbin; ☺9am-5pm Mon-Fri, 9.30am-5pm Sat & Sun) One of the oldies (first planted 1866), it's worth visiting more for its interesting historic display and excellent views (bring a picnic) than for its overcrowded and touristy tasting room.

Brokenwood VINEYARD
(www.brokenwood.com.au; 401-427 McDonalds Rd, Pokolbin; ☺9.30am-5pm) One of the Hunter's most acclaimed wineries.

Hungerford Hill VINEYARD
(www.hungerfordhill.com.au; 2450 Broke Rd, Pokolbin; ☺10am-5pm Sun-Thu, 9am-6pm Fri & Sat) Shaped like a big barrel, with its 'lid' permanently propped open, this winery stands sentinel at the entry to Broke Rd. It's home to the highly regarded **Muse restaurant** (☺lunch daily, dinner Wed-Sat; lunch mains $28-36, dinner mains $39-44, 5-course tasting menu $110).

Macquariedale Estate VINEYARD
(www.macquariedale.com.au; 170 Sweetwater Rd, Rothbury; ☺10am-5pm) A boutique winemaker that's certified organic and biodynamic. It also grows garlic.

Margan VINEYARD
(www.margan.com.au; 1238 Millbrodale Rd, Broke; ☺10am-5pm) Gorgeous setting, classy tasting room and the valley's best restaurant (see p138).

McWilliams Mount Pleasant VINEYARD
(www.mountpleasantwines.com.au; 401 Marrowbone Rd, Pokolbin; ☺10am-5pm) Guided wine tours at 11am ($5).

Moorebank Vineyard VINEYARD
(www.moorebankvineyard.com.au; 150 Palmers Lane, Rothbury; ☺10am-5pm) Sustainable winemaking practices and delicious homemade condiments.

Pooles Rock Wines VINEYARD
(www.poolesrock.com.au; DeBeyers Rd, Pokolbin; ☺9.30am-5pm) A big player, producing the midpriced Cockfighter's Ghost range as well as its excellent flagship wines. Fabulous cafe-restaurant (see p138).

Small Winemakers Centre CELLAR DOOR
(www.smallwinemakerscentre.com.au; McDonalds Rd, Pokolbin; ☺10am-5pm) Acts as a cellar door for six boutique winemakers.

Stonehurst Cedar Creek VINEYARD
(www.cedarcreekcottages.com.au; 1840 Wollombi Rd, Wollombi; ☺10am-5pm) One of the six wineries in the picturesque Wollombi Valley. Uses organic practices and offers basic cabin accommodation.

Tamburlaine VINEYARD
(www.tamburlaine.com.au; 358 McDonalds Rd, Pokolbin; ☺9am-5pm) An excellent producer focusing on sustainable viticulture.

Tempus Two VINEYARD
(www.tempustwo.com.au; cnr McDonald's & Broke Rds, Pokolbin; ☺9am-5pm) This huge place is a favourite with tour buses, who descend upon its Korean and Japanese restaurants and purchase gourmet goodies from its Smelly Cheese Shop (p138).

Tower Estate VINEYARD
(www.towerestatewines.com.au; cnr Halls & Broke Rds, Pokolbin; ☺10am-5pm) Established by one of Australia's major wine industry figures, the late Len Evans, Tower is the classiest winery in the valley and also offers its most sophisticated accommodation option (see p137).

Other Attractions

Hunter Valley Gardens GARDEN
(www.hvg.com.au; Broke Rd; adult/child/concession $23.50/12/18; ☺9am-5pm) Although there's something a little Disney about it, this relatively young 24-hectare garden has impressive floral and landscape displays. It's the home of the valley's famous **Christmas Lights Spectacular** (☺mid-Nov–early Jan), Australia's biggest Christmas lights display.

☞ Tours

If no one's volunteering to stay sober enough to drive, there are plenty of winery tours available. Some operators will collect you in Sydney or Newcastle for a lengthy day trip. Staff at visitor centres and accommodation providers should be able to arrange a book-

SENSIBLE SUPPING

If you are driving, remember to stay under the blood-alcohol limit of 0.05. Men can generally have two standard drinks in the first hour and one every hour after. Women can have one standard drink per hour. Wineries usually offer 20mL tastes of wine – five of these equal one standard drink.

ing that suits your needs. These are a few of the local operators:

Wine Rover WINE
(☎02-4990 1699; www.rovercoaches.com.au) Coaches connect at Morriset in the morning with trains coming from Sydney and drop passengers back at the station after a day of visiting wineries and attractions ($55). It also picks up passengers at Newcastle (weekdays/weekends $60/70) and Cessnock (weekdays/weekends $45/55).

Aussie Wine Tours WINE
(☎0402 909 090; www.aussiewinetours.com.au) You can determine your own itinerary if you take one of these private, chauffeur-driven tours.

Hunter Valley Tours WINE
(☎02-4990 8989; www.huntervalleytours.com. au) Small group local-run boutique tours; from $65 per person for a half-day tour and from $99 for a full day tour including lunch.

✬ Festivals & Events

During the warm months superstars regularly drop by for weekend concerts at the bigger vineyards. If there's something special on, accommodation books up well in advance. Check what's on at www.winecountry.com.au.

A Day on the Green MUSIC
(www.adayonthegreen.com.au) At Bimbadgen Estate during summer.

Lovedale Long Lunch FOOD
(www.lovedalelonglunch.com.au) Seven wineries and chefs produce gut-bursting lunches, served with music and art; May.

Hunter Valley Wine & Food Month WINE, FOOD
(www.hvwineandfood.hvva.com.au) In June.

Jazz in the Vines JAZZ
(www.jazzinthevines.com.au) At Tyrrell's Vineyard in October.

Opera in the Vineyards OPERA
(www.4di.com.au) At Wyndham Estate in October.

🛏 Sleeping

Prices shoot up savagely on Friday and Saturday nights and two-night minimum stays are common. It's best to time your trip for midweek.

TOP CHOICE **Tower Lodge** HOTEL $$$
(☎02-4998 7022; www.towerlodge.com.au; Halls Rd, Pokolbin; d midweek/weekends from $720/810; ✳@🛜🛒) There are 12 luxurious rooms to choose from at this vineyard hotel, each furnished with antiques, artworks and the biggest bathrooms in the world (or at least the Hunter). After a day spent touring the valley, you can enjoy a complimentary afternoon tea or aperitif in the magnificent lounge before kicking onto dinner in the intimate **Nine Restaurant** (degustation menu $180, with matched wines $250). The anti-children policy attracts some visitors while putting some offside.

Buffs at Pokolbin CABINS $$
(☎02-4998 7636; www.buffsatpokolbin.com.au; 47 Coulson Rd, Pokolbin; 1-bedroom cottage midweek/weekend $180/225, 2-bedroom cottage $250/350; ✳🛒) Set on a tranquil 40-hectare property where kangaroos hop under the gum trees and gentle cooling breezes come off the dam, Buffs' four spotlessly clean self-contained cottages are as comfortable as they are keenly priced. A fantastic choice for families and couples alike.

Peppers Convent BOUTIQUE HOTEL $$$
(☎02-4998 4999; www.peppers.com.au; Halls Rd; r from $372; ✳@🛜) Recently taken under the wing of the crew who run the luxe Tower Lodge, this grand former nunnery has been moved hundreds of kilometres, planted among the vineyards and thoroughly renovated in a French provincial style. It makes for a lovely, lavish retreat. Don't get it mixed up with the far-less-impressive Peppers Guest House.

Tonic BOUTIQUE HOTEL $$$
(☎02-4930 9999; www.tonichotel.com.au; 251 Talga Rd, Lovedale; d incl breakfast $425; ✳@🛒) Sydney style-meisters adore this boutique hotel, which has six double rooms and a two-bedroom apartment. The decor is self-avowedly anti-chintz, with polished concrete floors, a vivid colour scheme and

contemporary furnishings; toiletries are from Aesop. It's another anti-child venue.

Hunter Valley YHA HOSTEL $

(☑02-4991 3278; www.yha.com.au; 100 Wine Country Dr; site per person $10, dm $27-34, d $85.50-95, d without bathroom $73.50-82; @🐾) In late summer this newish, custom-built hostel is packed to the rafters with working-holidaymakers picking fruit on the vineyards. The reward at the end of a long day is a welcoming pool, clean facilities and plenty of bonhomie; on weekends the hostel's winery tours are popular. Be warned that the rooms can get stiflingly hot.

Eating

It seems that everyone expects wine lushes to also be gluttons and millionaires, as the Hunter is stuffed full of expensive restaurants offering huge set menus.

TOP CHOICE Margan MODERN AUSTRALIAN $$

(☑02-6579 1372; 1238 Milbrodale Rd, Broke; mains $22-36; ⊘breakfast Sun, lunch Fri-Sun, dinner Fri & Sat) Live up to the area's name and go for broke when it comes to ordering from the tempting array of dishes on offer at this vineyard restaurant. Much of the produce is sourced from the vineyard's kitchen garden; the rest comes from local providores whenever possible. Views are across the vines to the Brokenback Range.

Firestick Café & Rock Restaurant MODERN AUSTRALIAN $$$

(☑02-4998 6968; www.rockrestaurant.com.au; Pooles Rock Wines, DeBeyers Rd; pizzas $23-25, lunch mains $36-39, dinner mains $59-60; ⊘lunch daily, dinner Thu-Fri) By day, the restaurant at picturesque Poole Rock winery functions as the casual Firestick Café; at night, it morphs into the award-winning Rock. Both are terrific, albeit terrifically expensive. The delicious daytime-only crispy pizzas are an affordable route to sampling the Hunter's top foodie destination, although you run the risk of caving in once you peruse the innovative Mod Oz mains on the menu.

Café Enzo CAFE $

(www.enzohuntervalley.com.au; Peppers Creek, cnr Broke & Ekerts Rds, Pokolbin; breakfast dishes $8.50-22.50, lunch mains $22.50-36; ⊘breakfast & lunch) Claim a table by the fireside in winter or in the garden in summer to enjoy the rustic, generously sized dishes served at this popular place in the Pepper Creek Village. There's a tempting produce shop next door.

Bistro Molines FRENCH $$

(☑02-4990 9553; www.tallaveragrove.com.au; 749 Mt View Rd, Mt View; mains $40-45; ⊘lunch Thu-Mon, dinner Fri & Sat) Set in the Tallavera Grove winery, this French restaurant has a sensational, seasonally driven menu that is nearly as impressive as the view over the vines.

Providores

Hunter Valley Smelly Cheese Shop DELI $

(www.huntervalleysmellycheeseshop.com.au; Tempus Two Winery, 2144 Broke Rd, Pokolbin; ⊘9am-5.30pm) A hugely popular place that's full to the rafters with produce from local suppliers and elsewhere. The climate-controlled cheese room is stacked with smelly desirables, and you can also buy bread, relishes, meats and olives for Wine Country picnics. There's another branch at Pokolbin Village, 2188 Broke Rd.

Hunter Valley Cheese Company CHEESE SHOP $

(www.huntervalleycheese.com.au; McGuigans Complex, McDonalds Rd; platters $28; ⊘9am-5.30pm) 'Blessed are the cheesemakers' quote the staff T-shirts, and the people inside those shirts will chew your ear about cheesy comestibles all day long, especially during the daily 11am cheese talk. There's a bewildering variety of styles available for purchase.

Hunter Valley Chocolate Company CHOCOLATE SHOP $

(www.hvchocolate.com.au; Peterson's Champagne House, cnr Broke & Branxton Rds; ⊘9am-5pm) All manner of cacao derivatives.

Hunter Olive Centre OLIVE SHOP $

(www.pokolbinestate.com.au; Pokolbin Estate Vineyard, 298 McDonalds Rd; ⊘10am-5pm) Dozens of things to try on little squares of bread – oil, tapanade, *dukkah* (a blend of ground nuts and spices), chutney etc. If you're shameless, you could make it lunch.

Drinking

Wollombi Tavern PUB

(www.wollombitavern.com.au; Old North Rd, Wollombi; ⊘10am-late) Strategically located at the Wollombi crossroads, this fabulous little pub is the home of Dr Jurd's Jungle Juice, a dangerous brew of port, brandy and wine. The less adventurous (or should that read foolhardy?) can opt for a glass of excellent locally produced wine, including Stonehurst's Chambourcin and Undercliff's Semillon and Shiraz. On weekends, the tavern is a favourite pit stop for motorbike clubs (the nonscary sort).

Bluetongue Brewery MICROBREWERY
(www.huntervalley.com.au/bluetongue; Hunter Valley Resort, Hermitage Rd; ☺10am-late) Sample the creative and refreshing brews using the Tasting Paddle (six beers for $12). Also on offer are pies, sandwiches, cheese plates and a pool table.

Harrigan's PUB
(Broke Rd) A comfortable Irish pub with beef-and-Guinness pies on the menu, live bands most weekends and plenty of opportunities for a craic.

❶ Information

Visitor centre (☎02-4990 0900; www.wine country.com.au; 455 Wine Country Dr; ☺9am-5pm Mon-Sat, to 4pm Sun)

❶ Getting There & Away

If you're driving from Sydney, consider exiting north from the M1 at the Peats Ridge Rd exit and making your way along the convict-built Great North Rd (p125) to the charming colonial town of Wollombi and then heading north to Broke or east to Cessnock via Wollombi Rd. Pokolbin can be accessed from both.

CityRail has a line heading through the Hunter Valley from Newcastle (adult/child $6/3, 55 minutes). From Sydney (adult/child $7.80/3.90, 3¾ hours) you'll need to catch a train to Hamilton and then change for Branxton, which is the closest station to the vineyards.

Greyhound (☎1300 GREYHOUND/1300 4739 46863; www.greyhound.com.au) runs a daily bus from Sydney ($65, 4½ hours) to Branxton, departing outside Central Station at 6.30pm.

Rover Coaches (☎02-4990 1699; www.rover-coaches.com.au) has regular services between Cessnock and Newcastle ($4.30, 1½ hours).

Hunter Valley Day Tours (☎02-4951 4574; www.huntervalleydaytours.com.au) operates a shuttle service from Newcastle Airport to Hunter Valley hotels ($125 for one to two persons).

❶ Getting Around

Exploring without a car can be challenging. The YHA hostel hires bikes, as do **Grapemobile** (☎0418 404 039; www.pokolbinbrothers.com.au/grapemobile.htm; Pokolbin Brothers Vineyard, Palmers Lane; per day $25) and **Hunter Valley Cycling** (☎0418 281 480; www.hunter valleycycling.com.au; 2 days $45).

The **Vineyard Shuttle** (☎02-4991 3655; www.huntervalleyclassiccarriages.com.au) offers a door-to-door service from $15 per person per trip, which is perfect for trips to and from restaurants.

NORTH COAST

It's no wonder that the NSW north coast is one of the most celebrated road trips in Oz. This idyllic stretch of coastline from Sydney to Tweed Heads is a magical blend of sea and sand, sparkling lakes, enchanting national parks, rootsy towns and alternative lifestyles.

Leaving Sydney the coast rolls gently north. Craggy headlands and golden beaches dominate a landscape that's broken only by seaside towns and surf settlements, which become increasingly languorous the further north you travel. To the west, green fields roll inland, melting into the ancient forests and charming hill towns of the beautiful hinterland. Many travellers head straight to New Age Byron Bay, tempted by its organic, ecofriendly lifestyle, but take your time on the road and you'll discover that this corner of NSW has so much more to offer: from the deep-blue basins of the Myall Lakes to spectacular World Heritage rainforests and sun-blessed coastal parks peppered with idyllic coves and great surf.

At times you'll feel like the only person on the road, for despite the well-trodden path the trail only ever gets busy when passing through the inevitable network of urban centres (keep moving!). But whatever your final destination remember to occasionally put away the map, close your guidebook and see where the road takes you; it's unlikely you'll be disappointed.

Sydney to Newcastle

After struggling through the traffic of Sydney's northern suburbs, you can choose whether to motor straight up the freeway to Newcastle or meander along the coast. Truth be told, neither route will be a highlight of your trip, but if you've got time to kill there are some pleasant diversions along the coastal road.

The largest town in the area is hilly Gosford, an uninspiring place that serves as the transport and services hub for the surrounding beaches. The best place to access tourist information about the area is the **Central Coast Visitor Centre** (☎02-4343 4444; www.visitcentralcoast.com.au; The Avenue, Kariong; ☺9am-5pm Mon-Fri, 9.30am-3.30pm Sat & Sun), just off the F3 freeway at the entrance to town.

The **Australian Reptile Park** (www.reptilepark.com.au; adult/child/concession $24.50/12.50/17; ◔9am-5pm), well signposted from the freeway exit, offers a chance to get up close to koalas and pythons, watch funnel-web spiders being milked (for the production of antivenin) and learn about the plight of the Tasmanian devil (the park serves as a breeding ark). There's also a wonderfully craptastic *Lost Kingdom of Reptiles* Disney-style enclosure.

Southwest of Gosford, rambling trails run through rugged sandstone in **Brisbane Water National Park** (www.nationalparks.nsw.gov.au), which borders the Hawkesbury River and is known for its wildflowers. The **Bulgandry Aboriginal Engraving Site** is 3km south of the Central Coast Hwy on Woy Woy Rd.

A favourite retreat for actors, writers and other luvvies is the pretty village of **Pearl Beach**, on the eastern edge of the park. It has plenty of cafes and restaurants, including **Pearls on the Beach** (◔02-4342 4400; www.pearlsonthebeach.com.au; 1 Tourmaline Ave; mains $30-36; ◔lunch & dinner Thu-Sun), a stylish beach shack right on the water.

Southeast of Gosford, **Bouddi National Park** (www.environment.nsw.gov.au/nationalparks) extends from the north head of Broken Bay to MacMasters Beach, 12km south of Terrigal. Vehicle access is limited but there are short walking trails leading to wonderfully isolated beaches, including lovely **Maitland Bay**. The park is in two sections on either side of **Putty Beach**, which has vehicle access ($7). There are camp sites at **Little Beach** (site per adult/child $14/7), **Putty Beach** (site per adult/child $14/7) and **Tallow Beach** (site per adult/child $10/5); book through the office of the **National Parks & Wildlife Service** (NPWS; ◔02-4320 4200; 207 Albany St N; ◔8.30am-4.30pm Mon-Fri) in Gosford. Only the Putty Beach site has drinkable water and flush toilets.

East of Gosford the coast is heavily populated. The crescent-shaped beach at **Terrigal** is pleasant and the surf's good, so it's worth a pit stop. You can enjoy a meal or drink overlooking the water at **Cove Café** (http://covecafe.com.au; The Haven; mains $16-34; ◔breakfast & lunch daily, dinner Fri & Sat in summer) or grab some fish and chips to eat on the beach from Haven Seafoods on the waterfront or the Snapper Spot on The Esplanade. Attractive accommodation options are thin on the ground – try the cramped but clean **Terrigal Beach YHA** (◔02-4384 1919; www.yha.com.au; 9 Ocean View Dr; dm $30, d $85, without bathroom $75; ◈).

A series of saltwater 'lakes' spreads north up the coast between Bateau Bay and Newcastle, the largest of which, **Lake Macquarie**, covers four times the area of Sydney Harbour.

❶ Getting There & Away

Gosford has numerous CityRail connections to Sydney (adult/child $7.80/3.90, 1½ hours) and Newcastle (adult/child $7.80/3.90, 1½ hours). From Gosford station, **Busways** (◔02-9625 8900; www.busways.com.au) and **Redbus** (◔02-4332 8655; www.redbus.com.au) run services to Terrigal and neighbouring towns and beaches; these are less frequent on weekends.

CityRail trains stop at Wondabyne train station inside Brisbane Waters National Park upon request (rear carriage only). To access Bouddi National Park via public transport, take Busways bus 61 from Gosford.

Newcastle

POP 540,800

Sydney may possess the glitz and the glamour, but the state's second-largest city has down-to-earth larrikin charm instead. Newcastle is the kind of place where you can grocery shop barefoot, go surfing in your lunch hour and quickly become best buddies with the Novocastrian sitting next to you in the bar.

This easygoing, 'no worries' attitude has been shaped by Newcastle's rough-and-tumble past, shaped by a cast of convicts and coal miners. Today it continues to be the largest coal export harbour in the world, but the city is undergoing something of a renaissance. Wharf rejuvenation projects are breathing new life into the harbour and an eclectic and innovative arts scene is injecting colour and culture into the streets.

Swim or surf at the popular beaches and soak in ocean baths, explore the outstanding heritage architecture in the CBD and window shop along funky Darby St. Dine on fish and chips, watch the tankers chug along the horizon and catch some live music – Newcastle is easily worth a day or two of your time.

❍ Sights

Museums, Galleries & Historical Sites

Newcastle Regional Museum   MUSEUM
(www.newcastle.nsw.gov.au/discover_newcastle/regional_museum; Workshop Way, Honeysuckle Precinct; admission free; ◔10am-5pm Tue-Sun) Opened in May 2011 to great fanfare, the

city's flagship museum occupies the restored Honeysuckle rail workshops on the foreshore and focuses on the people, activities and places of the Hunter region.

FREE **Lock Up** CULTURAL CENTRE
(www.thelockup.info; 90 Hunter St; ☺10am-4pm Wed-Sun) These days, artists-in-residence are incarcerated in this former police station (1861) rather than prisoners. There's a contemporary art gallery, artists studios and an interesting law-and-order museum within the creepy, cramped cells of the heritage-listed prison cells.

Fort Scratchley HISTORIC SITE
(www.fortscratchley.org.au; Nobby's Rd; admission to top area free, guided tour of site & tunnels adult/child/concession $15/7.50/8; ☺10am-4pm Wed-Mon, guided tours weekends or by appointment) Originally constructed during the Crimean War to protect the city from possible invasion, this recently restored fort perched high above Newcastle Harbour was one of the few gun installations in Australia to fire a gun in anger during WWII. On 8 June 1942, a Japanese submarine suddenly surfaced, raining shells on the city. Fort Scratchley returned fire, negating the threat after just four rounds. Learn all about it on a guided tour.

FREE **Newcastle Region Art Gallery** ART GALLERY
(www.newcastle.nsw.gov.au/nag; 1 Laman St; ☺10am-5pm Tue-Sun) This excellent regional gallery has a permanent collection of works by revered Australian artists (Drysdale, Nolan, Whiteley) and hosts exciting temporary exhibitions.

Newcastle Maritime Centre MUSEUM
(Lee Wharf, 3 Honeysuckle Dr; adult/child/concession $10/5/7; ☺10am-4pm Tue-Sun) Learn all about Newcastle's nautical heritage – including its still-working harbour – at this new museum in a restored harbourfront wharf building.

Wildlife Reserves

FREE **Blackbutt Reserve** NATURE RESERVE
(www.newcastle.nsw.gov.au/recreation/blackbutt_reserve; Carnley Ave, Kotara; ☺9am-5pm) Sitting in a tract of bushland with plenty of walking trails and picnic areas, this council-run reserve has enclosures featuring native critters, including koalas, kangaroos, wallabies and wombats, along with a cacophonic chorus of native birds. Take bus 224 or 317 (30 minutes) to the park's edge then walk 1km to the entrance.

Hunter Wetlands Centre NATURE RESERVE
(www.wetlands.org.au; Sandgate Rd, Shortland; adult/child/concession $10/5/6.50; ☺9am-4pm Mon-Fri, to 5pm Sat & Sun) This swampy wonderland is home to over 200 bird and animal species. You can explore via canoe ($14.90 for two hours) or dip in a net and examine the results under a magnifying glass. Bring mosquito repellent if you don't want to contribute to the ecosystem in ways you hadn't intended. Take the Pacific Hwy towards Maitland and turn left at the cemetery, or catch bus 106 or 107 (40 minutes) from the train station.

Other Attractions
Queens Wharf Tower, on the waterfront, and the **obelisk**, above King Edward Park, provide commanding views of the city and the water. Across the river (about five minutes by ferry) is **Stockton**, a modest settlement with striking views back towards Newcastle and exposed shipwrecks in its waters.

Nobby's Head used to be an island until it was joined to the mainland in 1846 to create a singularly pretty sand spit; it was twice its current height before being reduced to 28m above sea level in 1855. The walk along the spit towards the lighthouse and meteorological station is exhilarating, with waves crashing about your ears and joggers jostling your elbows.

🏃 Activities
Swimming & Surfing
At the East End, the needs of surfers and swimmers are sated at **Newcastle Beach**, but if you're irrationally paranoid about sharks, the concrete **ocean baths** are a mellow alternative, encased in wonderful multicoloured 1922 architecture. There's a shallow pool for toddlers and a compelling backdrop of heaving ocean and chugging cargo ships. Surfers should goofy-foot it to **Nobby's Beach**, just north of the baths – the fast left-hander known as the Wedge is at its north end.

South of Newcastle Beach, below King Edward Park, is Australia's oldest ocean bath, the convict-carved **Bogey Hole**. It's an atmospheric place to splash about when the surf's crashing over its edge.

The most popular surfing break is at **Bar Beach**, 1km south. If your swimsuit is chafing, scramble around the rocks at the north end to the (unofficial) clothing-optional **Susan Gilmour Beach**, which is only accessible at low tide. At nearby **Merewether Beach** the opening of the winter swimming

Newcastle

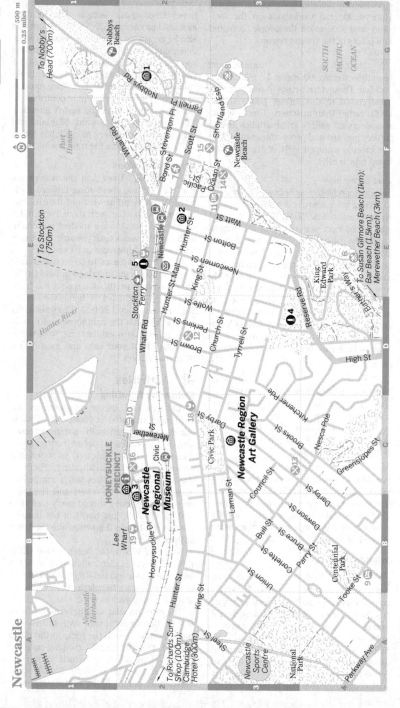

SOUTH PACIFIC OCEAN

Nobbys Beach

To Nobby's Head (700m)

Newcastle Beach

Port Hunter

To Stockton (750m)

Stockton Ferry

Newcastle

To Stockton (750m)

Hunter River

HONEYSUCKLE PRECINCT

Newcastle Regional Museum

Lee Wharf

Newcastle Harbour

Civic Park

Newcastle Region Art Gallery

King Edward Park

To Susan Gilmore Beach (1km); Bar Beach (1.5km); Merewether Beach (3km)

To Richards Surf Shop (100m); Cambridge Hotel (300m)

Newcastle Sports Centre

National Park

500 m
0.25 miles

season is heralded at its ocean baths, where blocks of ice are dumped into the water so that the cold-blooded freaks from the Merewether Mackerels Winter Swimming Club can strut their stuff. Frequent local buses from the CBD run as far south as Bar Beach, but only buses 201, 225 and 310 continue to Merewether.

For surfing supplies, head to **Richards Surf Shop** (☎02-4961 3088; 755 Hunter St). The **Jye Byrnes Surf School** (☎0409 227 407; jyebyrnes@hotmail.com; 80min group lesson per person $40, private lesson $70) specialises in individual coaching and small-group tuition.

The city's famous surfing festival, **Surfest** (www.surfest.com), takes place in March each year.

Walking Tours

The visitor centre has a map/brochure outlining two self-guided themed walking tours of the city. The **Bather's Way** leads between Nobby's and Merewether Beaches, with signs describing Indigenous, convict and natural history in between swims. The **Newcastle East Heritage Walk** heads past colonial highlights, including the **Convict Lumber Yard** opposite the Newcastle train station.

The *Newcastle By Design* brochure, available at the visitor centre, outlines a short stroll down and around Hunter St, covering some of the inner city's interesting architecture.

☞ Tours

Hunter Valley Day Tours   WINE, FOOD
(☎02-4951 4574; www.huntervalleydaytours.com.au) Visits four or five Hunter Valley

vineyards, the Hunter Valley Cheese Company and the Hunter Valley Chocolate Company; prices vary according to group numbers (from $95 per person).

Tex Tours   WINE
(www.textours.com.au; ☎0410 462 540) Offers entertaining full-day Hunter Valley winery tours ($65, backpacker discounts available) as well as dolphin and 4WD dune tours to Port Stephens ($75).

🛏 Sleeping

Newcastle Beach YHA   HOSTEL $
(☎02-4925 3544; www.yha.com.au; 30 Pacific St; dm/s/d $33/55/80; @🖥) This heritage-listed building is a bikini strap away from Newcastle Beach. Inside, it's a bit like an English public school (without the humiliating hazing rituals), featuring grand spaces and high ceilings. There's also free bodyboard use, surfboard hire, free pub meals and a free BBQ on Thursday nights.

Stockton Beach Tourist Park   CAMPGROUND $
(☎02-4928 1393; www.stocktonbeach.com; Pitt St, Stockton; unpowered site $24-37, powered site $29-46, d bunkhouse $59-86, d cabins $97-176; @🖥) The beach is at your doorstep (or should that be tent flap?) at this tourist park behind the dunes in Stockton. There are BBQs, a camp kitchen, kids' playground areas, a fully equipped laundry and free wi-fi and internet access. You'll need to hire linen if you stay in a bunkhouse.

Hamilton Heritage B&B B&B **$**
(☎02-4961 1242; colaine@iprimus.com.au; 178 Denison St, Hamilton; s $95-110, d $135-165; ✳🎧) It's all florals and frills in this Federation-era home near the Beaumont St cafe strip to the west of the city centre. Three rooms are reasonably sized and have en suites; one 'hobbit' room uses a shared bathroom (s/d $60/80). Child and pet friendly.

Backpackers Newcastle HOSTEL **$**
(☎1800 33 34 36, 02-4969 3436; www.backpack ersnewcastle.com.au; 42-44 Denison St; camp site per person $15, dm $26-29, d & tw $60-65; @🎧🏊) It's not a patch on the YHA but it's cheap and offers free surfing lessons (board and wetsuit hire $25 for two hours), free dinners on Monday and Wednesday and free pick-up from the train station.

Crowne Plaza HOTEL **$$$**
(☎02-4907 5000; www.crowneplaza.com.au /newcastle; cnr Merewether St & Wharf Rd; r $248-374; ✳@🎧🏊) This large, beige modern hotel is right on the waterfront and is easily the best sleeping option in town. Service is excellent and the pool is a real plus. Breakfast costs $40.

Cooks Hill Cottage RENTAL HOUSE **$$$**
(☎0401 269 863; www.cookshillcottage.com.au; 102 Dawson St, Cooks Hill; rates on application; ✳) Relax in the five-person hot tub on the deck or cook up a storm in the gourmet kitchen in this stylishly renovated two-bedroom house near Centennial Park.

✕ Eating

Darby and Beaumont are the main eat streets. There are also plenty of cafes and restaurants around Honeysuckle Wharf and along the foreshore. The Newcastle City Farmers Market (www.newcastlecityfarmer-smarket.com.au) is held at Newcastle Showground, Griffiths Rd, Broadmeadows most Sundays between 8am and 1pm.

Bacchus MODERN AUSTRALIAN **$$$**
(☎02-4927 1332; www.bacchusnewcastle.com.au; 141 King St; lunch 2/3 courses $48/60, dinner mains $44-49, degustation $110-120; ⊘lunch Thu & Fri, dinner Tue-Sat) A decadent Roman

god has transformed this former Methodist mission into a very atmospheric place to splurge (not purge – this isn't ancient Rome, after all). The surrounds are extremely elegant, dishes are assured and the wine list is excellent.

Jonah's on the Beach MODERN AUSTRALIAN **$$$**
(☎02-4929 5181; cnr Shortland Esplanade & Zara St; mains $35-57, set 2/3-course lunch $38/45; ⊘breakfast, lunch & dinner) In a four-star hotel overlooking Newcastle Beach, Jonah's offers magnificent views and a menu full of robustly flavoured delights. The wine list has a strong representation of Hunter Valley drops and there's live music on Thursday, Friday and Saturday evenings.

Estabar CAFE **$**
(61 Shortland Esplanade; ⊘7am-8pm) Start the day with an excellent coffee or a Spanish-style hot chocolate at this sun-drenched cafe overlooking Newcastle Beach. When the temperature soars, stop in for the best gelato in town.

Silo MODERN AUSTRALIAN **$$**
(www.silolounge.com.au; 1 Honeysuckle Wharf; lunch mains $19-25, dinner mains $32-39; ⊘breakfast Sat & Sun, lunch & dinner daily) One of the many places to have opened in the restored wharf precinct in recent times, Silo is a popular bar-restaurant with outdoor seating and pretensions to glamour. Pop in between 4pm and 6pm and you can enjoy $10 pizzas and $3.50 glasses of beer or sparkling wine.

Delucas Pizza PIZZA **$$**
(☎02-4929 3555; 159b Darby St, Cooks Hill; pizzas $18-25; ⊘dinner 5pm-late Tue-Sun) Delicious pizza and endearingly old-school decor make this Newcastle's most popular pizzeria. The pasta's good, too.

3 Bean CAFE **$**
(103 Tudor St, Hamilton; breakfast $7-16, lunch mains $18-21; ⊘7am-5pm Mon-Fri, to 3pm Sat) Serious foodie attention has been paid to the menu here, including notes on the provenance of the produce, much of which is biodynamic and organic. Enter off Beaumont St.

🍸 Drinking & Entertainment

Finnegans   PUB
(www.finneganshotel.com.au; 21-23 Darby St;
⊗Mon-Sat) The place for backpacker meals,
trivia, pool competitions and, on the weekends, live bands and DJs.

Brewery   MICROBREWERY
(http://qwb.com.au; 150 Wharf Rd) Perched on
Queens Wharf; the views and outdoor
tables are sought after by both Novocastrian office workers and uni students. Has
regular live music Wednesday to Sunday
and decent food.

Honeysuckle Hotel   PUB
(www.honeysucklehotel.com.au; Lee Wharf,
Honeysuckle Drive; ⊗10am-11pm Mon-Thu, to
midnight Fri & Sat, to 10pm Sun) The deck at
this waterfront place, located in the trendy
Honeysuckle precinct, is a perfect spot for
a sundowner. A DJ takes centre stage on
summer Sundays between 4pm and 9pm.

Cambridge Hotel   NIGHTCLUB
(www.yourcambridge.com; 789 Hunter St, Newcastle West) This backpacker favourite launched
Silverchair, Newcastle's most famous
cultural export, and continues to showcase
touring national bands and local acts in
live gigs from Wednesday to Sunday.

ℹ Information

If you've got a laptop with wireless capability,
head to Beaumont St in Hamilton where there's
free wi-fi broadband between Tudor and Donald
Sts. The airport also offers free wireless connections. You'll find banks and ATMs in Hunter St
Mall. Most have foreign exchange facilities.

John Hunter Hospital (📞02-4921 3000;
Lookout Rd, New Lambton) Has 24-hour
emergency care.

Post office (📞13 13 18; 1 Market St)

Visitor centre (📞02-4974 2999; www.visitnew
castle.com.au; Lee Wharf, 3 Honeysuckle Dr;
⊗10am-4pm Tue-Sun) Volunteer-operated and
while well-intentioned, not particularly useful.

ℹ Getting There & Away

Air

Newcastle Airport (📞02-4928 9800; www.
newcastleairport.com.au) is at Williamtown,
23km north of the city.

Virgin Australia (📞13 67 89; www.virgin
australia.com) and **Jetstar** (📞13 15 38; www.
jetstar.com) both fly to Brisbane, the Gold Coast
and Melbourne. **Brindabella Airlines** (📞1300
66 88 24; www.brindabellaairlines.com.au) services Brisbane, Coffs Harbour, Port Macquarie

and Canberra. **Aeropelican** (📞13 13 13; www.
aeropelican.com.au) flies to Sydney. **Norfolk Air**
(📞1300 669 913; www.norfolkair.com) has a
weekly link to its island home.

Sydney Seaplanes (📞1300 732 752; www.
seaplanes.com.au) operates a twice-daily weekday service between Honeysuckle Wharf and
Sydney's Rose Bay ($175 to $225, 45 minutes).

Bus

Nearly all long-distance buses stop behind the
Newcastle train station. **Greyhound** (📞1300
GREYHOUND/1300 4739 46863; www.grey
hound.com.au) heads to Forster ($39, three
hours, daily) and Port Macquarie ($59, four
hours, three daily). **Premier Motor Service**
(📞13 34 10; www.premierms.com.au) runs a
daily bus to/from Sydney ($34, 2½ hours) and
Brisbane ($76, 14 hours).

Rover Coaches (📞02-4990 1699; www.rov-
ercoaches.com.au) heads to Cessnock ($4.30,
1½ hours) in the Hunter Valley. **Port Stephens
Coaches** (📞02-4982 2940; www.pscoaches.
com.au) has regular buses between Nelson Bay
and Newcastle ($4.30, 1¾ hours). **Busways**
(📞1800 043 263; www.busways.com.au) operates services to/from Hawks Nest via Tea Gardens ($23, 1½ hours, three daily).

Train

A better option than the buses, **CityRail** (📞13
15 00; www.cityrail.info) has frequent trains to
Sydney (adult/child $7.80/3.90, three hours)
via Gosford (adult/child $7.80/3.90, 1½ hours).
A line also heads to Branxton (adult/child
$7.80/3.90, 55 minutes) in the Hunter Valley.

ℹ Getting Around

To/From the Airport

Port Stephens Coaches (📞02-4982 2940;
www.pscoaches.com.au) heads to Williamtown
airport frequently ($4.30, 40 minutes) en route
to Nelsons Bay.

Shuttle bus services from the airport to Newcastle cost approximately $35 per person ($45
for two people). To book these or shuttles to
other destinations in the area, contact **Newcastle Airport Information Services** (📞02-4928
9822; ⊗7am-7pm).

A taxi to Newcastle city centre will cost
around $65.

Bus

Newcastle has an extensive and reasonably
priced network of **local buses** (📞13 15 00;
www.newcastlebuses.info). There's a fare-free
bus zone in the inner city between 7.30am and
6pm. Other fares are time-based (one hour/
four hours/all day $3.30/6.40/9.80). The main
depot is next to Newcastle train station.

Ferry

The Stockton ferry (adult/child $2.30/1.10) leaves every half-hour from Queens Wharf between 5.15am and midnight on Friday and Saturday, until 11pm Monday to Thursday and until 10pm on Sunday.

Train

Services terminate at Newcastle station after stopping at Broadmeadow, Hamilton, Wickham and Civic.

Newcastle to Taree

From Newcastle and the nearby Hunter Valley, you can choose to zoom north along the Pacific Hwy or enjoy a far more pleasant trip by making a series of meandering diversions along the coast.

PORT STEPHENS
POP 27,600

This stunning sheltered bay is about an hour's drive north of Newcastle, occupying a submerged valley that stretches more than 20km inland. Framing its southern edge is the narrow Tomaree Peninsula, blessed with near-deserted beaches, national parks and an extraordinary sand-dune system. The main centre, Nelson Bay, is home to both a fishing fleet and an armada of tourist vessels, capitalising on its status as the 'dolphin capital of Australia'.

Just east of Nelson Bay, and virtually merged with it, is the slightly smaller Shoal Bay, with a long beach that's great for swimming (but only in the morning, as winds come up in the afternoon). The road ends a short drive south from here at Fingal Bay, with another lovely beach on the fringes of Tomaree National Park. The park stretches west around clothing-optional Samurai Beach, a popular surfing spot, and One Mile Beach, a gorgeous semicircle of the softest sand and bluest water favoured by those in the know: surfers, beachcombers, idle romantics.

The park ends at the somnolent surfside village of Anna Bay, which has as a backdrop the incredible Worimi Conservation Lands. Gan Gan Rd connects Anna Bay, One Mile Beach and Samurai Beach with Nelson Bay Rd.

◉ Sights

The Worimi Conservation Lands at Stockton Bight are the longest moving sand dunes in the southern hemisphere, stretching over 35km. The tourist board claims the dunes are Mad Max–style, but if you want to talk films, think Lawrence of Arabia – it's more Sahara than outback. In the heart of it, it's possible to become so surrounded by shimmering sand that you'll lose sight of the ocean or any sign of life. In short, it's incredibly evocative. At the far west end of the beach, the wreck of the Sygna founders in the water.

Thanks to the generosity of the Worimi people (see boxed text, p152), whose land this is, you're able to roam around (provided you don't disturb any Aboriginal sites), camp within 100m of the high-tide mark (you'll need a portable toilet), drive along the beach (4WD only; permit required) and mash up the sand dunes within the designated recreational-vehicle area. Get your permits ($10 for three days) from the Port Stephens Visitor Centre or NPWS office in Nelson Bay (p149) or by telephoning ☎02-4984 8200 (allow seven days for pass to be mailed to you).

Tomaree National Park (www.environ ment.nsw.gov.au/nationalparks; vehicle admission $7) is a wonderfully wild expanse harbouring several threatened species, including the spotted-tailed quoll and powerful owl. If you keep your eyes peeled you're bound to spot a koala or wallaby. At the eastern end of Shoal Bay there's a short walk to the surf at unpatrolled Zenith Beach (beware of rips and strong undercurrents), or you can tackle the strenuous Tomaree Head Summit Walk (1km, one hour return) and be rewarded by stunning ocean views. Longer walks are detailed in Bushwalks Around Port Stephens ($5.95), a pamphlet available from the NPWS Office and the visitor centre.

FREE The restored 1875 Heritage Light House Cottage (☎02-4984 2505; ⊙10am-4pm) at Nelson Head has a small museum with displays on the area's history and a tearoom. The views of Port Stephens are suitably inspiring.

🏃 Activities

There are dozens of operators offering action-packed ways to spend your day. Inquire and book at the visitor centre in Nelson Bay.

Imagine Cruises   DOLPHIN-WATCHING
(☎02-4984 9000; www.imaginecruises.com.au; Dock C, d'Albora Marinas, Nelson Bay) Eco-accredited trips, including 3½-hour Sail, Swim & Snorkel (adult/child/concession $50/30/45, December to March), two-hour Dolphin Watch cruises ($30/15/25, December

Norfolk Island (population 2120) is a pine-studded speck adrift in the South Pacific Ocean, 1600km northeast of Sydney and 1000km northwest of Auckland. It's the largest of a cluster of three islands emerging from the underwater Norfolk Ridge, which stretches from New Zealand to New Caledonia, the closest landfall, almost 700km north.

Recent excavations place Polynesians in Norfolk 800 years before it was first eyeballed by Captain James Cook in 1774. From 1788, only weeks after the First Fleet reached Port Jackson to settle Sydney, until 1855 it was twice used as a penal colony and became known as 'hell in the Pacific' after being declared 'a place of the extremest punishment short of death'.

After 1855, the prisoners were shipped off to Van Diemen's Land (Tasmania) and Queen Victoria handed the island over to the descendants of the mutineers from the HMS *Bounty*, who had outgrown their adopted Pitcairn Island. About a third of the present population is descended from the 194 Pitcairners and their Tahitian wives who arrived on 8 June 1856.

The island measures only 8km by 5km, with vertical cliffs defining much of the coastline. Kingston is on Slaughter Bay on the island's south coast. The service town of Burnt Pine is in the centre of the island, near the airport, while Norfolk Island National Park (www.environment.gov.au/parks/norfolk) encompasses the hillier northern part of the island.

Kingston, knocked up by convicts of the second penal colony, is Norfolk's star attraction. Many historic buildings have been restored – the best of these, along Quality Row, still house the island's administrators, as well as four small-but-engaging museums (www.museums.gov.nf; single/combined ticket $10/25; ⊙11am-3pm).

By the shore are the ruins of an early pentagonal prison, a lime pit (into which convict murder victims were sometimes thrown) and the convict cemetery.

Bounty Folk Museum (Middlegate Rd; admission $10; ⊙10am-4pm) is crammed with motley convict-era and *Bounty* souvenirs. Fletcher's Mutiny Cyclorama (www.norfolkcyclorama.nlk.nf; Queen Elizabeth Ave; per person from $11.50; ⊙9am-5pm Mon-Sat, 10am-3pm Sun) is a 360-degree painting depicting the *Bounty* mutiny and Norfolk Island history.

Covering 650 hectares of the island's north, the national park offers bushwalking, with awesome views from Mt Pitt (316m) and Mt Bates (318m). There's a sheltered beach at Emily Bay in the south, from where glass-bottom boats depart to ogle the coral below.

Snorkelling around the Kingston breakwall is worthwhile; hire gear in Burnt Pine. Alternatively, several companies arrange **snorkelling**, **diving** and **fishing** trips.

There is plenty of accommodation on Norfolk, though none of it is budget; check out www.norfolkisland.com.au for listings. All accommodation must be booked in advance. Most visitors come on package deals, sometimes including car hire and breakfast.

The visitor centre (☎6723-22 147; www.norfolkisland.com.au; Taylors Rd, Burnt Pine; ⊙8.30am-5pm Mon-Fri, to 3pm Sat & Sun) is next to the post office or check out the websites www.norfolkbedbank.com and www.gonorfolkisland.com.

The island is a 2½-hour flight from east-coast Australia, 1¾ hours from Auckland. Air New Zealand (☎in New Zealand 0800 737 000; www.airnewzealand.co.nz) flies from Auckland on Sunday. Return fares start at around NZ$208. Norfolk Air (☎1800 612 960; www.norfolkair.com) flies from Sydney and Brisbane on Wednesday, Thursday, Saturday and Sunday; from Melbourne on Friday; and from Newcastle on Monday. Return fares start at around $830 ex-Sydney, $730 ex-Brisbane.

There's a departure tax of $25, payable at Norfolk airport or in advance at the visitor centre. All visitors must have a valid passport and a return airline ticket. Australian and New Zealand passport holders don't require visas, but all other nationalities must obtain an Australian entry visa before flying. Australian citizens who don't have a passport can obtain a 'Document of Identity' through Australia Post.

Island time is GMT plus 11½ hours – 1½ hours ahead of Sydney (30 minutes ahead in summer).

to March), three-hour Whale Watch cruises ($60/25/50, May to November); two-hour Seafood Dinner Cruise ($35/20/30; December to April) and 3½-hour Swim with the Dolphins experience ($229; weekends only).

Anna Bay Surf School SURFING
(☑0411 419 576; www.annabaysurfschool.com.au; Hannah Pde, One Mile Beach Holiday Park; introductory/2-/3-day lessons $75/110/165) Surf lessons and board hire (per hour/day $17/50).

Moonshadow DOLPHIN-WATCHING
(☑02-4984 9388; www.moonshadow.com.au; shop 3, 35 Stockton St, Nelson Bay) Dolphin-watching (adult/child/concession $23/11.50/18), whale-watching ($51/22/43, May to November) and dinner cruises ($65/21.50/59). Eco-accredited.

Oakfield Ranch CAMEL RIDING
(☑0429 664 172; www.oakfieldranch.com.au; Birubi Pt car park, James Patterson Dr, Anna Bay) Twenty-minute camel rides along the beach on Sundays and school holidays.

Blue Water Sea Kayaking SEA KAYAKING
(☑0405 033 518; www.kayakingportstephens.com.au) Offers a range of paddle-powered excursions, including hour-long beginner tours (adult/child $25/20), 1½-hour champagne sunset tours ($35/25) and 2½-hour discovery tours ($45/35).

Port Stephens 4WD Tours 4WD
(☑02-4984 4760; www.portstephens4wd.com.au; shop 3, 35 Stockton St, Nelson Bay) Offers a 1½-hour beach and dune tour (adult/child/concession $49/29/46) and a sandboarding experience (adult/child $26/19).

🛏 Sleeping

Accommodation in both Nelson Bay and Shoal Bay is generally characterless and expensive – consider staying at Anna Bay or One Mile Beach instead so that you can take advantage of their tranquil settings near great beaches.

TOP CHOICE **Port Stephens YHA Samurai Beach Bungalows** HOSTEL $
(☑02-4982 1921; www.samuraiportstephens.com; Frost Rd, Anna Bay; dm $31-37, d $102-159, d without bathroom $82-117; @🛜🏊) These attractively furnished wooden-floored cabins are arranged around a swimming pool and set in koala-populated bushland dotted with Asian sculpture. There's a bush kitchen with BBQs and a ramshackle games shed with pool table. Fabulous.

TOP CHOICE **Melaleuca Surfside Backpackers** HOSTEL $
(☑02-4981 9422; www.melaleucabackpackers.com.au; 2 Koala Pl, One Mile Beach; camp sites per person $18-20, d $80-100; @🛜) Architect-designed wooden cabins are set amid peaceful scrub inhabited by koalas and kookaburras at this friendly, well-run place. There's a welcoming lounge area and kitchen, and the owners offer dune surfing and other day trips. Equally fabulous.

Wanderers Retreat HOTEL $$
(☑02-4982 1702; www.wanderersretreat.com; 7 Koala Pl, One Mile Beach; d cabin $125-250, treehouse d $195-270; ❄🏊) Guests can make like Robinson Crusoe in one of the three luxury treehouses at this tranquil retreat. For those who prefer to keep their feet on the ground, there are also seven two-bedroom cottages.

O'Carrollyn's APARTMENTS $$
(☑02-4982 2801; www.ocarrollyns.com.au; 5 Koala Pl, One Mile Beach; d weekdays $120-140, weekends $140-180, children extra $15 each; ❄🛜🏊) Nine two-bedroom self-contained cabins (two with spas and all wheelchair-accessible) in two hectares of landscaped garden are on offer here. A health and wellness centre shoud be open by the time you read this.

Bali at the Bay APARTMENTS $$$
(☑02-4981 2964; www.baliatthebay.com.au; 1 Achilles St, Shoal Bay; d $240-260; ❄) Two exceedingly beautiful self-contained apartments, chock-full of flower-garlanded Buddhas and carved wood, do a good job of living up to the name. The bathrooms are exquisite and spa treatments are available.

🍴 Eating

Yikes! The eating options on this part of the coast are either ridiculously pretentious (and overpriced) or pretty well inedible. Fortunately, all of the accommodation options we have recommended have self-catering facilities – do yourself a favour and pick up provisions in Nelson Bay so that you can eat well.

Point MODERN AUSTRALIAN $$
(☑02-4984 7111; www.thepointrestaurant.com.au; Soldiers Point Marina, Sunset Blvd, Soldiers Point; mains $34-38; ⊙lunch & dinner Tue-Sun) When locals celebrate romantic milestones, this restaurant on the marina at Soldiers Point is their number-one choice. Views from the balcony and glassed dining room are lovely, and the menu has loads of tempting seafood dishes. It's 9km west of Nelson Bay.

Red Ned's Pies

FAST FOOD $

(www.redneds.com.au; shop 3/17-19 Stockton St, Nelson Bay; pies $5.50-7; ⊙6am-5pm) Piemaker Barry Kelly learnt his trade in top-shelf international hotels and his philosophy is simple: he gets a kick out of watching people stare at his specials board, goggle-eyed (anyone for crocodile in parsley, shallot and white-wine sauce?).

❶ Information

NPWS office (☏02-4984 8200; www.npws.nsw.gov.au; 12b Teramby Rd, Nelson Bay; ⊙8.30am-4.30pm Mon-Fri)

Visitor centre (☏02-4980 6900; www.port-stephens.org.au; Victoria Pde, Nelson Bay; ⊙9am-5pm) Provides free copies of the useful *Port Stephens Visitors Guide*.

❶ Getting There & Around

Port Stephens Coaches (☏02-4982 2940; www.pscoaches.com.au) regularly zips around Port Stephens' townships heading to Newcastle and Newcastle Airport ($4.30, 1¾ hours). There's also a daily service to/from Sydney (adult/child $38/31, four hours) stopping at Soldiers Point, Nelson Bay and Shoal Bay.

Port Stephens Ferry Service (☏0412 682 117) chugs from Nelson Bay to Tea Gardens and back three times a day (return fare adult/child $20/10, one hour each way).

TEA GARDENS & HAWKS NEST

POP 2100 (TEA GARDENS), 1030 (HAWKS NEST)

Opposite Nelson Bay, on the north shore of Port Stephens, are Tea Gardens and Hawks Nest. Sporting the most quaintly evocative names on the coast, this tranquil pair of towns in the Great Lakes district straddle the mouth of the Myall River, linked by the graceful, curved Singing Bridge. Tea Gardens has a quiet, laid-back charm; it's a river culture here, older and genteel. At Hawks Nest it's all about the beaches. Jimmys Beach fronts a glasslike stretch of water facing Nelson Bay, while stunning Bennetts Beach looks to the ocean and Broughton Island.

🍴 Sleeping & Eating

Tea Gardens Hotel Motel

HOTEL $

(☏02-4997 0203; www.teagardenshotelmotel.com.au; cnr Marine Dr & Maxwell St; r from $55; ▨) On the riverfront, this popular watering hole offers basic rooms set around a rear garden.

Tea Gardens Boat Shed

CAFE $

(110 Marine Dr, Tea Gardens; breakfast dishes $5-16.50, sandwiches $7.50, mains $15-25; ⊙8.30am-9pm) You'll have to cope with a few shrieks from the local pelicans when you choose to

devour your meal at this former boatshed right on the water rather than sending the food their way. And it's no wonder they're miffed – everything's delicious. The coffee is good and the deck is a lovely spot for a sunset drink.

Nicole's

CAFE $

(81 Marine Dr, Tea Gardens; breakfast & lunch $5-17, dinner $15-27; ⊙breakfast & lunch daily, dinner Mon-Sat) Housed in a Victorian cottage, this seriously sweet cafe doubles as an art gallery and gift shop. The garden is seductive, with trickling water features, bird baths, much greenery and statues.

❶ Information

Tea Gardens Visitor Centre (☏02-4997 0111; www.greatlakes.org.au; Myall St; ⊙10am-4pm) Near the bridge.

❶ Getting There & Around

While only 5km from Nelson Bay as the cockatoo flies, the drive necessitates returning to the Pacific Hwy via Medowie and then doubling back – a distance of 81km. The alternative is the Port Stephens Ferry Service (this page).

If you're continuing north, take the stunning scenic route through Myall Lakes National Park; it involves a short ferry crossing at Bombah Point (see p151).

Busways (☏1800 043 263; www.busways.com.au) operates services to/from Newcastle ($23, 1½ hours, three daily).

MYALL LAKES NATIONAL PARK

On an extravagantly pretty section of the coast, this large national park (www.environment.nsw.gov.au/nationalparks; vehicle admission $7) incorporates a patchwork of lakes, islands, dense littoral rainforest and beaches. The lakes support an incredible quantity and variety of bird life, including bowerbirds, white-bellied sea eagles and tawny frogmouths. There are paths through coastal rainforest and past beach dunes at Mungo Brush in the south, perfect for spotting wildflowers and dingoes.

The best beaches and surf are in the north around beautiful, secluded Seal Rocks, a bushy hamlet hugging Sugarloaf Bay. It has a great beach, with emerald-green rock pools, epic ocean views and golden sand. Take the short walk to the Sugarloaf Point Lighthouse, where the views are sublime. There's a water-choked gorge along the way and a detour to lonely Lighthouse Beach, a popular surfing spot. The path around the lighthouse leads to a lookout over the actual Seal Rocks – islets that provide sanctuary for Australia's

WORTH A TRIP

BARRINGTON TOPS NATIONAL PARK

Lying on the rugged Barrington Plateau, this World Heritage–listed wilderness (www.environment.nsw.gov.au/nationalparks; vehicle admission $7) rises to a height of almost 1600m. Northern rainforest butts into southern sclerophyll here, creating one of Australia's most diverse ecosystems, with giant strangler figs, mossy Antarctic beech forests, limpid rainforest swimming holes and pocket-sized pademelons (note: it is illegal to put pademelons in your pocket).

Bushwalks, mountain biking, horse riding, canoeing, fishing and 4WDing are the order of the day here. The Barrington Trail is particularly popular for 4WDing, but it's closed from June to September. Be prepared for cold snaps, and even snow, at any time.

Barrington Outdoor Adventure Centre (☎02-6558 2093; www.boac.com.au; 126 Thunderbolts Way; 1-/2-day kayaking tours $140/360, 1-day mountain-biking tour $150, 2-day mountain-bike/kayak tour $370) specialises in downhill mountain-biking adventures and white-water kayaking trips. It also hires out mountain bikes, canoes and kayaks (one-day hire mountain bike/canoe/kayak $60/85/60).

Camping is possible throughout the park (adult per night $5 to $10, child $3 to $5). You can access the camping grounds at Devils Hole, Wombat Creek, Polblue, Horse Swamp and Gloucester River in a 2WD, but you'll need a 4WD for those at Little Murray, Gummi Falls and Junction Pools.

Full-day tours of the park are offered by Dam It Getaway Accommodation and Tours (☎02-6558 4272; www.damitgetaway.com; 81 Kia Ora Hill Rd, Gloucester; tour & lunch adult/child $95/45), which also offers accommodation in its homestead and cabin (d $150-220).

The park can be accessed from Scone, Dungog and Gloucester. For more information contact the NPWS office in Gloucester (☎02-6538 5300; 59 Church St; ⊙8.30am-4.30pm Mon-Fri) or Nelson Bay (p149).

---

northernmost colony of Australian fur seals. During summer breeding, the seals are out in abundance and you'll do well to bring binoculars. Humpback whales swim past Seal Rocks during their annual migration and can sometimes be seen from the shore.

About a half-hour by boat from Nelson Bay, Broughton Island is uninhabited except for muttonbirds, little penguins and an enormous diversity of fish species. The diving is tops and the beaches are incredibly secluded.

There are plenty of accommodation options in the park, the most atmospheric of which are the three historic stone lighthouse keepers' cottages (☎02-4997 6590; www.sealrockslighthouseaccommodation.com.au; cottage $300-450) at Sugarloaf Point. These self-contained cottages are fully refurbished and sleep between six and eight people each.

🖋 Bombah Point Eco Cottages (☎02-4997 4401; www.bombah.com.au; 969 Bombah Pt Rd; d $220-275; 🗶) is a cluster of architect-designed and attractive self-contained cottages. Each cottage sleeps between five and six guests; one cottage is suitable for wheelchair access and offers disabled-friendly facilities. The 'Eco' in the name is

well-deserved: sewage is treated on site using a bioreactor system, electricity comes courtesy of solar panels and filtered rainwater tanks provide water.

The park is well served with camp sites (www.npws.nsw.gov.au; sites per adult $7.50-10, child $3.50-5), most of which have composting toilets and water for boiling; none can be booked ahead of your visit. Also here is the excellent Seal Rocks Holiday Park (☎02-4997 6164; www.sealrocksholidaypark.com.au; Kinka Rd, Seal Rocks; unpowered camp sites $26-33, powered camp & caravan sites $30-37, cabins $70-185), offering a range of budget accommodation styles including grassed camping and caravan sites that are right on the water.

At Bombah Broadwater the Bombah Point ferry (per car $5) crosses every half-hour from 8am to 6pm; the trip takes five minutes. A 10km section of Bombah Point Rd, heading to the Pacific Hwy at Bulahdelah, is unsealed.

THE LAKES WAY

A recommended alternative to the Pacific Hwy, this scenic drive starts just after the small town of Bulahdelah and twists through Myall Lakes and Booti Booti National Parks, passing popular Pacific Palms en route. It then continues through the built-up regional centre of Forster-Tuncurry before rejoining the Pacific Hwy at Rainbow Flat, an 80km journey all up.

If you need to refuel your vehicle before veering off the highway, do so at Bulahdelah. And if you're hungry, grab one of the fabulous meat pies sold at the Bulahdelah Bakery (65 Stroud St; ☺daily).

PACIFIC PALMS
POP 680

Secreted between Myall Lakes and Booti Booti National Parks, Pacific Palms is one of those places that well-heeled city dwellers slink off to on weekends – which sounds perfectly dreadful, but is actually something that we'd all like to do if we had the chance. It's a hell of a lot nicer than Forster and Tuncurry up the road, which you should avoid at all costs. If you're camping in either of the parks you might find yourself here when the espresso cravings kick in – there are a couple of excellent cafes.

Most of the houses cling to Blueys Beach or Boomerang Beach, both long stretches of golden sand that are popular with surfers. The most popular swimming beach in the area (and the only one that's patrolled) is Elizabeth Beach, on the southern edge of nearby Booti Booti National Park. The volunteer-run visitor centre (☎02-6554 0123; Boomerang Dr; ☺10am-3pm) has internet access ($2.50 per 15 minutes) and some arts and crafts for sale.

For accommodation, try Mobys Beachside Retreat (☎02-6591 0000; www.mobys retreat.com.au; 4 Red Gum Rd, Boomerang Beach; 1-bedroom apartment $170-225, 2-bedroom $210-275, 3-bedroom $290-365; ❉☀), which lies directly opposite Boomerang Beach. This holiday resort crams 75 self-contained holiday apartments with sleek decor and excellent amenities into a relatively small area. There's a tennis court, swimming pool and children's playground on site, as well as the extremely popular M Bistro (☎02-6554 0766; www.mbistro.com.au; set lunch $17.50, dinner mains $22-29; ☺lunch & dinner Wed-Sun).

Five minutes' drive east of Blueys Beach is the laid-back restaurant Buddha on the Lake (☎02-6554 0877; www.thebuddhaonthelake.com.au; cnr The Lakes Way & Kookie Ave; breakfast dishes $5-15, mains $25-27; ☺breakfast Sat & Sun, lunch Wed-Sun, dinner Wed-Sat), where guests are greeted by Balinese statues and the evocative scent of spices when they arrive. There's

a dedicated vegetarian menu and $10 kids' meals. BYO alcohol. For a caffeine fix, head to Twenty by Twelve (shop 8, 207 Boomerang Dr; breakfast dishes $4-13, wraps $9.50, burgers & pies $14.50; ☺7.30am-3pm). Camping is all very well, but try getting a coffee like this out of a billycan. It also sells light meals, local organic produce and delicious deli treats. If you want to be formal, the Recky (The Lakes Way; mains $14-21; ☺11am-late) is actually the Pacific Palms Recreation Club. Yep, it's one of those sign-in clubs with cheap booze, a bistro and occasional live music. And be warned: its slogan is 'Get wrecked at the Recky'.

To get here, Busways (☎1800 043 263; www.busways.com.au) stops at Blueys Beach on its journey between Taree/Forster and Newcastle.

BOOTI BOOTI NATIONAL PARK

This 1567-hectare national park (www.environment.nsw.gov.au/nationalparks; vehicle admission $7) stretches along a skinny peninsula with Seven Mile Beach on its eastern side and Wallis Lake on its west. The northern section of the park is swathed in coastal rainforest and topped by 224m Cape Hawke. At the Cape Hawke headland there's a viewing platform, well worth the sweat of climbing the 420-something steps.

You won't really be darkening the door of a church if you visit the Green Cathedral, as there is no door. This interesting space (consecrated in 1940) consists of wooden pews under the palm trees, looking to the lake.

There's self-registration camping at the Ruins (camping per adult $10-14, child $5-7), at the southern end of Seven Mile Beach, with an NPWS office (☎02-6591 0300; ☺8.30am-4.30pm) nearby.

Lakeside Escape B&B (☎02-6557 6400; www.lakesideescape.com.au; 85 Green Point Dr, Green Point; s $140-155, d $165-195; @) is located in the Green Point fishing village on the park's western edge. All three rooms overlook Wallis Lake and there's a heated spa on the outdoor deck.

Taree to Port Macquarie

From Forster-Tuncurry the Pacific Hwy swings inland to Taree (population 20,000), a large town serving the farms of the fertile Manning Valley. The helpful Taree Visitor Centre (☎1800 182 733, 02-6592 5444; 21 Manning River Dr; ☺9am-5pm daily Sep-May, 9am-5pm Mon-Fri, 9am-4pm Sat & Sun Jun-Aug) is at the northern end of town.

Further west into the valley is Wingham Brush Nature Reserve, a patch of idyllic rainforest that is home to giant, otherworldly Moreton Bay figs and flocks of flying foxes. The nearby town of Wingham combines English county cuteness with a rugged lumberjack history. Consider stopping here for two reasons: to eat at Bent on Food (sandwiches & salads $12-16; ◷8am-5pm Mon-Fri, 8am-3pm Sat, 9am-3pm Sun), one of the best cafes in rural NSW, and to stay overnight at the Bank Guesthouse (✆02-6553 5068; www.thebankandtellers.com.au; 48 Bent St; s $155-175, d $165-185, cottage $110-120; ✻❖), a friendly place offering stylishly decorated rooms in a 1920s bank manager's residence, as well as a self-catering guesthouse cottage in the rear garden.

CountryLink (✆02-8202 2000; www.countrylink.info) trains from Sydney stop at Taree and Wingham ($47, 5½ hours, two daily). The train continues to Coffs Harbour ($32, 3½ hours, two daily).

Back on the Pacific Hwy, a half-hour drive north will bring you to the turn-off to the fishing village of Harrington, sheltered by a spectacular rocky breakwater and watched over by pelicans. It's a leisure-orientated hamlet popular with both holidaymakers and retirees – 30% of the population is over the age of 65. When not playing golf or fishing, the locals hang out at the Harrington Hotel (✆02-6556 1205; 30 Beach St; s/d $45/55), a spacious pub with a popular bistro and large waterside terrace.

Crowdy Head is an even smaller fishing village 6km northeast of Harrington at the edge of Crowdy Bay National Park (www.environment.nsw.gov.au/nationalparks; vehicle admission $7). It was supposedly named when Captain Cook witnessed a gathering of Aborigines on the headland in 1770. The views from the 1878 lighthouse are absolutely breathtaking – out to the limitless ocean, down to the deserted beaches and back to the apparent wilderness of the coastal plain and mountains. It's like Cook never arrived at all.

Known for its rock formations and rugged cliffs, the 10,001-hectare national park here backs onto a long and beautiful beach that sweeps from Crowdy Head north to Diamond Head. There's a lovely 4.8km (two-hour) loop track over the Diamond headland.

The roads running through the park are unsealed and full of potholes, but the dappled light of the gum trees makes it a lovely drive. There are basic camp sites (✆02-6582 3355; site per adult/child $10/5) at Diamond Head, Indian Head, Kylie's Hut and Kylie's Beach, as well as in the southern part of the park at Crowdy Gap (✆02-6552 4097; site per adult/child $10/5). You'll need to bring water in for all of them.

Leaving the national park via Diamond Head Rd, continue through to Laurieton and onto the tiny town of Kew, from where you can veer off the highway and follow Ocean Dr all the way to Port Macquarie. Along the way, you'll pass Dooragan National Park, dominated by North Brother Mountain with lookouts and incredible views. Nearby is Camden Haven, a cluster of sleepy villages around the wide sea entrance of Queens Lake, and North Haven, an absolute blinder of a surf beach. North of here, the road passes Lake Cathie (pronounced cat-eye), a shallow body of water perfect for kids to paddle in.

WORIMI COUNTRY

The area from the Tomaree Peninsula to Forster and as far west as Gloucester is the land of the Worimi people, who have lived in this region for thousands of years. Very little of it is now in their possession, but in 2001 the sand dunes of the Stockton Bight were returned to them, creating the Worimi Conservation Lands (p146). The Worimi people in turn entered an agreement to co-manage it with the NPWS.

Sacred places and occupation sites are scattered throughout the region. Dark Point Aboriginal Place in Myall Lakes National Park has been significant to the Worimi for around 4000 years. Local lore has it that in the late 19th century it was the site of one of many massacres of Aborigines at the hands of white settlers, when a group was herded onto the rocks and pushed off.

For more information, look out for the *Worimi Conservation Lands* brochure published by the NSW Department of Environment & Climate Change.

If you're fond of country drives, the 40km route from Wingham to these waterfalls shouldn't be missed. About 17km of it is unsealed and full of potholes, but the countryside is bucolic. As the road climbs steeply to the Bulga Plateau, farms give way to native bush once exploited for its cedar. The falls plunge 200m in one dramatic drop into a gorge below. The best view is from The Knoll, an easy short bushwalk. A more strenuous walk leads to the base, taking about 30 minutes down but 45 minutes back up.

Port Macquarie

POP 39,220

Pleasure has long replaced punishment as the main purpose of Port Macquarie. Formed in 1821 as a place of hard labour for those convicts who reoffended after being transported to Sydney, it was the third town to be established on the Australian mainland. These days, though, Port, as it's commonly known, is overwhelmingly holiday-focused, making the most of its position at the entrance to the subtropical coast, its beautiful surf beaches and its laid-back coffee culture.

◎ Sights

Beaches

Port is blessed with awesome beaches. Surfing is excellent at Town, Flynns and Lighthouse Beaches, all of which are patrolled in summer. The rainforest runs down to the sand at Shelly and Miners Beaches, the latter of which is an unofficial nude beach.

It's possible to walk all the way from the Town Wharf to Lighthouse Beach. Along the way, the breakwater at the bottom of town has been transformed into a work of community guerrilla art. The elaborately painted rocks range from beautiful memorials for lost loved ones to 'party hard'-type inanities.

Wildlife

Koala Hospital   NATURE RESERVE
(www.koalahospital.org.au; Lord St; admission by donation; ⊘8am-4.30pm) Koalas living near urban areas are at risk from traffic and domestic animals, and more than 200 each year end up in this shelter. You can walk around the open-air enclosures any time of the day, but you'll learn more during the tours (3pm). Some of the longer-term patients have signs detailing their stories. Check the website for details of volunteer opportunities.

Sea Acres Rainforest
Centre   NATURE RESERVE
(www.nationalparks.nsw.gov.au; Pacific Dr; adult/child $8/4; ⊘9am-4.30pm) This 72-hectare pocket of coastal rainforest (a candidate for national-park status) is alive with birds, goannas, brush turkeys and, so as to be truly authentic, mosquitoes (insect repellent is provided). While there's no charge for wandering through most of the paths here, it's worth paying the admission to the ecology centre and wheelchair-accessible 1.3km-long boardwalk. Fascinating one-hour guided tours by knowledgeable volunteers are included in the price. Call ahead for times of bush-tucker tours led by Aboriginal guides.

Billabong Koala & Wildlife
Park   NATURE RESERVE
(61 Billabong Dr; adult/child $18/11; ⊘9am-5pm) For more koala action head just west of the intersection of the Pacific and Oxley Hwys and make sure you're there for the 'koala patting' (10.30am, 1.30pm and 3.30pm). The park has a koala breeding centre, although if this facility is anything to go by, koala dating requires a lot of sitting around looking stoned. There are heaps of other Australian critters here, too.

FREE Kooloonbung Creek
Nature Park   NATURE RESERVE
(cnr Gordon & Horton Sts) Home to many bird species, this park close to the town centre encompasses 50 hectares of bush and wetland that can be explored via walking trails and wheelchair-accessible boardwalks. It includes the Port Macquarie Historic Cemetery (Gordon St).

Historic Buildings & Museums

Most of Port's historic buildings are in the city centre. The recently opened Glasshouse Cultural Centre (www.glasshouse. org.au; cnr Clarence & Hay Sts; ⊘9am-5.30pm Mon-Fri, to 4pm Sat & Sun) was built on the

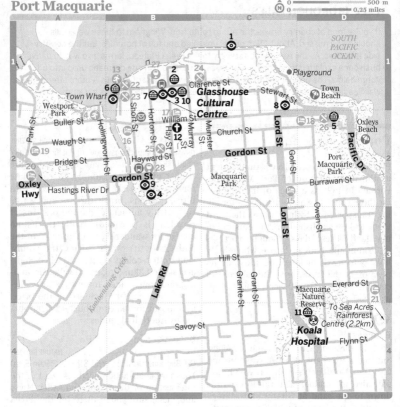

site of convict overseers' cottages and many archaeological artefacts from the original buildings are on display in the foyer. The city's major public building, it's home to the Newcastle Regional Art Gallery (admission free; ☺10am-5pm Tue-Fri, to 4pm Sat & Sun), a 600-seat theatre, the tourist information centre and a shop selling local arts and crafts.

The 1835 Garrison building (cnr Clarence & Hay Sts) is camouflaged by an uninspiring array of fast-food shops. Next door, the 1836 Port Macquarie Historical Society Museum (22 Clarence St; adult/child $5/2; ☺9.30am-3pm Mon-Sat) has fared better; its labyrinth of rooms includes a costume gallery. Opposite is an 1869 courthouse (adult/child $2/0.50; ☺10am-3.30pm Mon-Fri, to 1pm Sat).

The 1824, convict-built St Thomas' Anglican Church (Hay St; adult/child $2/1; ☺9.30am-noon & 2-4pm Mon-Fri) is one of Australia's oldest still-functioning churches. It still has its box pews and crenulated tower, echoing the Norman churches of southern England.

Roto House (Lord St; admission by gold coin donation; ☺10am-4pm subject to availability of volunteer staff), next to the Koala Hospital in Macquarie Nature Reserve, is a lovely Victorian villa (1890) with interesting displays about its original owners.

Between Miners and Lighthouse Beaches, little Tacking Point Lighthouse (1879) commands a headland offering immense views up and down the coast. It's a great spot to watch the waves rolling in to the long beautiful stretch of Lighthouse Beach.

The old pilot house above Town Beach has been converted into a small Maritime Museum (6 William St; adult/child $5/2; ☺10am-4pm). There's an even smaller extension of the museum in the 1890s Pilots Boatshed at the Town Wharf.

SYDNEY & NEW SOUTH WALES PORT MACQUARIE

Stargazers will enjoy the small **observatory** (www.pmobs.org.au; William St; adult/child $8/7; ⊙7.30-8.30pm Wed & Sun, 8.15-9.15pm during daylight saving) in Rotary Park.

Activities

Port Macquarie Surf School   SURFING
(⊡02-6585 5453; www.portmacquariesurfschool.com.au; lessons from $40) Offers a wide range of lessons and prices.

Port Sea Kayak Adventures   SEA KAYAKING
(⊡0409 776 566; www.portkayak.com.au; Buller St Bridge) Runs a two-hour River & Mangrove trip ($35) and a six-hour Freshwater Rapids trip ($70).

Port Macquarie Camel Safaris   CAMEL RIDING
(⊡0437 672 080; www.portmacquariecamels.com.au; Matthew Flinders Dr; ⊙9.30am-1pm Sun-Fri) Thirty-minute camel rides (adult/child $30/25) on the southern end of Lighthouse Beach.

Tours

Port Macquarie Cruise Adventures   CRUISES
(⊡1300 555 890; www.cruiseadventures.com.au; 74 Clarence St, Town Wharf; adult/child/concession

from $25/10/22) Offers dolphin-watching, whale-spotting, oyster-guzzling, lunch, sunset, river and everglades tours.

Sleeping

Port offers options ranging from a clutch of tidy hostels to a multitude of apartment-style resorts.

TOP CHOICE **Observatory**   HOTEL $$
(⊡02-6586 8000; www.observatory.net.au; 40 William St; r $129-199, apt $159-329; ❄@☎☲) A friendly welcome is the norm at this excellent modern hotel opposite Town Beach. Rooms and apartments are comfortable and well equipped; many have balconies overlooking the water. The close proximity to the beach, good cafes and the Stunned Mullet restaurant mean that you won't have to stray far from your room. Everyone loves the indoor pool, spa and sauna.

Port Macquarie Backpackers   HOSTEL $
(⊡02-6583 1791; www.portmacquariebackpackers.com.au; 2 Hastings River Dr; dm $26-30, d without bathroom $60-80; @☎☲) This heritage-listed house has pressed-tin walls, comfy bunks, a new shower/toilet block and an

enthusiastic owner-manager who sometimes takes guests on three-day camping/surfing trips to Crowdy Bay National Park ($195). Traffic can be noisy, but the freebies (including breakfast) compensate.

Ozzie Pozzie Backpackers HOSTEL $
(☑02-6583 8133; www.ozziepozzie.com; 36 Waugh St; dm $26-33, s without bathroom $45-65, d without bathroom $65-90; @☒) In a somewhat strange compound made up of three converted suburban houses, this hostel offers clean rooms, uncomfortable beds and a definite party atmosphere. There's a range of activities on offer, along with pool and table-tennis tables, free internet, free bodyboard use, bike hire ($5 per day) and surfboard/wetsuit hire ($20 per day).

Mantra Quayside APARTMENTS $$
(☑02-6588 4000; www.mantraquayside.com.au; cnr William & Short Sts; studios from $135, apt from $170; ✲@☎☒) This place joins the newly opened **Mercure Centro Hotel** (☑1300 786 989; www.centrohotel.com.au; 103 William St; r from $169) in being as slick as Port gets. It's a favourite with visitors wanting a self-contained bolthole close to both the beach and the cafe strip.

South Pacific Apartments APARTMENTS $$$
(☑02-6583 8033; www.southpacificpm.com.au; 37 Pacific Dr; apt $99-320; ✲☎☒) The upstairs apartments at this somewhat characterless block opposite Flynn's Beach have sea views and those downstairs have a small terrace; all sleep between four and six people and are clean and bright.

Eastport Motor Inn MOTEL $$
(☑02-6583 5850; www.hwmotel.com.au; cnr Lord & Burrawan Sts; s $95-105, d $130-140; ✲☎☒) At the cheaper end of the nonhostel scale, this place has smallish clean and well-equipped rooms with comfortable beds and crisp linen. Wi-fi is free.

✗ Eating

Port punches above its weight when it comes to food and coffee – you'll eat and drink well here.

TOP CHOICE Stunned Mullet MODERN AUSTRALIAN $$$
(☑02-6584 7757; www.thestunnedmullet.com.au; 24 William St; mains $26-49; ☺lunch & dinner) Australian idiom lesson: to look like a stunned mullet is to wear an expression of bewilderment. It's exactly the sort of look you might adopt while struggling to choose

between the delicious Mod Oz menu items and extensive wine-list offerings at Port's best restaurant.

Corner Restaurant Cafe CAFE $$
(cnr Clarence & Munster Sts; breakfast dishes $6-19, baguettes $16, dinner mains $27-34; ☺breakfast, lunch & dinner) On the ground floor of the Macquarie Waters Boutique Apartment Hotel (www.mwaters.com.au), this sleek operation has a definite Sydney-ish sheen and good cafe fare that could hold its own in Surry Hills (and that's a real compliment).

Milkbar Town Beach CAFE $
(shop 2, 40 William St; breakfast dishes $4.50-11.50, lunch dishes $9.50-14.50; ☺breakfast & lunch Mon-Fri, breakfast & brunch Sat & Sun) Another casually chic cafe on the ground floor of a modern apartment block (this time the Observatory), Milkbar is known for its homemade icy poles, Single Origin coffee and surfer clientele.

Fusion 7 MODERN AUSTRALIAN $$
(☑02-6584 1171; www.fusion7.com.au; 124 Horton St; mains $28-34; ☺dinner Tue-Sat) Chef Lindsey Schwab worked with the father of fusion cuisine, Peter Gordon, in London but returned to Port to be closer to his family. Despite this pedigree and the restaurant's name, the food is more Mod Oz than fusion. Desserts are particularly delicious.

Cedro CAFE $
(72 Clarence St; breakfast $6-18, lunch $12-18; ☺breakfast & lunch Mon-Sat) On a sunny day you can sit on the street between the palm trees, order the generous house breakfast, sip a good coffee and plan your next move: the beach, or another coffee stop?

Boardwalk TAPAS $$
(75 Clarence St; tapas dishes $8-22; ☺breakfast, lunch & dinner Sat & Sun, lunch & dinner Mon-Fri) Commanding lovely views over the Hastings River, this recently opened tapas and wine bar is just a castanet click away from Town Wharf. Locals love it.

♒ Drinking & Entertainment

Finnian's PUB
(97 Gordon St; ☺11am-late) The backpacker's boozer of choice, this Irish tavern near the new bus depot offers raffles and trivia nights midweek but cranks up the party atmosphere on Fridays and Saturdays with live music from 8pm.

Beach House PUB
(Horton St; ⊙11am-late) The enviable position right on the grassy water's edge makes this beautiful pub perfect for lazy afternoon drinks. As the wee hours draw near, folk fasten their beer goggles and mingle on black-leather couches inside.

ℹ Information
Port Macquarie Base Hospital (☑02-6581 2000; Wrights Rd)
Post office (Palm Court, cnr Short & William Sts)
Visitor centre (☑02-6581 8000; www.portmacquarieinfo.com.au; The Glasshouse, cnr Hay & Clarence Sts; ⊙9am-5.30pm Mon-Fri, to 4pm Sat & Sun)

ℹ Getting There & Around
Air
Port Macquarie Airport (☑02-6581 8111; Boundary St) is 5km from the centre of town ($17 in a taxi).

Both **Qantas** (☑13 13 13; www.qantas.com.au) and **Virgin Australia** (☑13 67 89; www.virginaustralia.com) have daily flights to Sydney. **Brindabella Airlines** (☑1300 66 88 24; www.brindabellaairlines.com.au) has services to Brisbane, Coffs Harbour and Newcastle.

Bus
Greyhound (☑1300 GREYHOUND/1300 4739 46863; www.greyhound.com.au) stops three times daily on its way between Sydney ($49 to $81, 6½ hours) and Brisbane ($55 to $110, 9½ hours).

Premier Motor Service (☑13 34 10; www.premierms.com.au) heads daily to Sydney ($60, 6½ hours), Newcastle ($47, four hours) and Brisbane ($67, 8½ hours).

ℹ Getting Around
Busways (☑02-6559 7712; www.busways.com.au) runs local bus services.

The **Settlement Point Ferry** (per car $3) operates 24 hours. A 10-minute trip on a flat punt gives you access to North Beach.

Port Macquarie to Coffs Harbour

KEMPSEY
POP 8140
About 45km north of Port Macquarie, Kempsey is a large rural town serving the farms of the Macleay Valley. It is home to the fabled Akubra (www.akubra.com.au) hat, the headwear of choice for a swag of Aussie

icons. The factory is not open to the public, but the local department store will happily fit out those wanting an iconic Aussie souvenir.

Country-music legend the late Slim Dusty (who also favoured an Akubra) was born here. The wheels are in (very slow) motion for the opening of a Slim Dusty Heritage Centre (www.slimdustycentre.com.au; Old Kempsey Showgrounds). The Kempsey visitor centre (☑02-6563 1555; Pacific Hwy) is at a rest stop on the south side of town, sharing space with a sheep shearer's museum (adult/child $4/2; ⊙10am-4pm).

The turn-off to Crescent Head is near the visitor centre in Kempsey. Alternatively, from the north take the very scenic Belmore Rd, which leaves the Pacific Hwy at Seven Oaks and follows the Macleay River.

Cavanaghs (☑02-6562 7800; www.cavanaghs.com.au) run buses to South West Rocks from Kempsey Medical Centre (Belgrave St).

CRESCENT HEAD & AROUND
POP 1080
This little hideaway, 18km southeast of Kempsey, is the kind of sleepy place you'd come to write a book. Failing that, how about learning to ride a longboard? The town is the surf longboarding capital, and it's here that the Malibu surfboard gained prominence in Australia during the '60s.

Today many come just to watch the longboard riders surf the epic waves of Little Nobby's Junction. There's also good short-board riding off Plomer Rd. Untrammelled Killick Beach stretches 14km north.

⭐ Bush and Beach Motel (Surfari Central; ☑1800 007 873; www.surfaris.com; 353 Loftus Rd; dm/d $25/60; @☒) is the perfect place for keen surfers to stay. These guys started the original Sydney-Byron surf tours and have now based themselves in Crescent Head because 'the surf is guaranteed every day'. The rooms are clean and comfortable with bathrooms and some wicked wall murals. Surf-and-stay packages are a speciality.

🏄 Sun Worship Eco Apartments (☑1300 664 757; www.sunworship.com.au; 9 Belmore St; apt $150-300; ☎) are new and funky rammed-earth villas featuring sustainable designs, including flow-through ventilation, solar orientation and solar hot water. They're spacious too.

For shorter stays Wombat Beach Resort (☑02-6566 0121; www.wombatresort.com.au; 30-34 Pacific St; d $95-115; ☀@☒) offers comfy

LORD HOWE ISLAND

Shhh! Lord Howe Island (population 350) is one of Australia's best-kept coastal secrets – Lord how we love it! About 600km northeast of Sydney, at the same latitude as Port Macquarie, this gorgeous subtropical island remains remarkably pristine. Listed on the World Heritage Register for its rare bird and plant life, the island is a haven for ecotourists and those seeking a *real* holiday. Many visitors (numbers are limited to 400 at any one time) are repeat customers, returning for a dose of the island's barefoot, first-name hospitality, empty beaches and balmy vibes.

The island is far from a budget destination, although prices fall considerably in winter. Unless you have a boat you'll have to fly here and both food and accommodation are limited and pricey. But there's plenty of family-friendly stuff to do here if you're feeling lively.

Crescent-shaped Lord Howe wraps itself around a lagoon, fringed by coral reefs. The island is lorded over by three peaks: **Mt Lidgbird** (777m) and **Mt Gower** (875m) in the south, and the astonishing spike of **Ball's Pyramid** (551m) jagging up from the sea 23km to the southeast. The island is about 11km long by 3km wide; most accommodation and services are located in the flat area north of the airport. Island time is GMT plus 10½ hours – 30 minutes ahead of Sydney (the same as Sydney in summer).

Between September and April, Lord Howe becomes a rabbling gaggle of nesting seabirds – a bird nerd's wonderland! Check out the bird life on **bushwalks** along the coast and through the hills and rainforest. The summit climb up Mt Gower (eight to 10 hours return) is one of Australia's best one-day walks. The steep hike will either cure or initiate vertigo; you must be accompanied by a licensed guide.

Fish feeding causes a splash in the Ned's Beach shallows, and you can **snorkel** among vivid tropical fish and coral just offshore. Hire a mask, snorkel, fins and wetsuit at the beach using an honesty-box system. There's good **surf** at Blinky Beach, and off the island's western shore is the world's southernmost **coral reef**, sheltered by a wide lagoon popular for **sea kayaking**. You can also inspect the sea life from above via a **glass-bottom boat** or immerse yourself completely on a **scuba dive**.

Camping is prohibited on the island, and all accommodation must be booked in advance. There are 18 lodge and self-contained apartment businesses here, some of which close in winter or lower their rates. Eating out is expensive; bookings are essential. Keep an eye out for 'Fish Fries' held on various nights at various resort restaurants, plus the bowls club and golf course – they offer all-you-can-eat seafood fresh off the boat (the local kingfish is brilliant). You can also have it delivered to your door.

You can hire bicycles and cars, but a bicycle is all you really need and most accommodation places will happily drive you anywhere. There's a 25km/h speed limit.

The **visitor centre** (☎1800 240 937, 02-6563 2114; www.lordhoweisland.info; cnr Lagoon & Middle Beach Rds; ◷9.30am-2.30pm Mon-Fri, to 2pm Sun; @) website has links to flight and accommodation packages. Winter prices start at $1100 for seven nights. The centre is inside the **Lord Howe Island Museum**, a good source of island geography and natural history. It has internet access.

Near the corner of Ned's Beach and Lagoon Rds there's a post office, general store and two banks (no ATMs). Some businesses have Eftpos facilities. **QantasLink** (☎13 13 13; www.qantas.com.au) has flights most days from Sydney (from $395 one way), and weekend flights from Brisbane (via Sydney). There are also seasonal weekly flights from Port Macquarie ($465 one way) and midweek flights from Brisbane from February to June, and September to December. Flight time from the mainland is around two hours.

rooms, lush gardens and a decent pizza restaurant.

Right on the beach, **Crescent Head Holiday Park** (☎02-6566 0261; Pacific St; camp sites/cabins from $20/87; @) is a lovely spot to pitch a tent. The reception doubles as Creso Cafe with espressos, wraps and sandwiches as well as a heart-starting breakfast egg-and-bacon roll for $5. It also rents out surfboards ($15/30/40 hour/half-/full-day).

TOP CHOICE **Mongrel's** (7 Main St) sells a dozen of the freshest Sydney Rock oysters you can eat for $6.50, $9 if you want them shucked – the perfect beach snack.

Crescent Tavern (2 Main St; ⊘lunch & dinner) has cold beer, a sun-soaked deck and excellent food – what else could you want? How about authentic rice paper rolls dished up by a Vietnamese chef at the weekend.

Busways (☎1800 043 263; www.busways.com.au) buses run from Crescent Head to Kempsey.

HAT HEAD NATIONAL PARK

This coastal park (per car per day $7) of 7458 hectares runs north from near Hat Head to Smoky Cape (south of Arakoon), protecting scrubland, swamps and some excellent beaches backed by one of the largest dune systems in NSW.

The wonderfully isolated village of Hat Head, surrounded by the national park, is much smaller and quieter than Crescent Head with its own natural beauty. At the end of town, a picturesque wooden footbridge crosses the aqua-green salt marsh ocean inlet. The water is so clear you can see fish darting around. Hat Head Holiday Park (☎02-6567 7501; www.4shoreholidayparks.com.au; camp sites from $22, cabins from $79) is close to the sheltered bay and footbridge and offers backpacker rates. You can camp (adult/child $5/3) at Hungry Gate, 5km south of Hat Head, or at Smoky Cape, just below Smoky Cape Lighthouse (this page).

Hat Head and the national park are accessible from the hamlet of Kinchela, on the road between Kempsey and South West Rocks.

SOUTH WEST ROCKS & AROUND
POP 4070

South West Rocks is at the end of a headland, ensuring only those willing to divert off the highway, then backtrack to it, end up here. Good for them. It's a pretty seaside place, perfect for weekenders, where brisk beach walks, bottomless bottles of red and top-notch food are the order of the day. The spectacular beach here is one of the few places on the east coast where you can watch the sun set over the water.

◉ Sights & Activities

Imposing and profoundly historic, Trial Bay occupies the west headland of the town and the Trial Bay Gaol (☎02-6566 6168; adult/child $8/5) dominates the area. Pity (or perhaps envy) the wretched souls incarcerated here during the 19th century; they had to endure breathtaking views of the ocean, forests and freedom. Actually it's been mostly unoccupied, aside from a brief interlude in WWII when it housed Germans. Today it's a worthwhile museum. The Arakoon State Conservation Area surrounds the gaol and has a popular campground.

From South West Rocks it's a 45-minute dawdle past the surf club along the beach to Trial Bay.

Southeast of South West Rocks, Smoky Cape Lighthouse (☎02-6566 6301), perched high above the ocean on a bracingly breezy cape, is a landmark that shouldn't be missed. Phone ahead for tours.

The South West Rocks area is great for divers, especially Fish Rock Cave, south of Smoky Cape. South West Rocks (☎02-6566 6474; www.southwestrocksdive.com.au; 5/98 Gregory St) and Fish Rock (☎02-6566 6614; www.fishrock.com.au; 134 Gregory St) dive centres both offer two dives for around $165. Both have accommodation.

Little Bay Beach is a good spot to have a swim with kangaroos looking on. It's the start of a couple of nice walks.

🛏 Sleeping & Eating

TOP CHOICE Smoky Cape Lighthouse   B&B $$
(☎02-6566 6301; www.smokycapelighthouse.com; d $198, cottages per 2 nights from $390) Romantic evenings can be spent hearing the wind whip around the sturdy white lighthouse-keeper's building just a few metres from the lighthouse itself. The views are also fuel for passion.

Seabreeze Hotel   PUB FARE, HOTEL $$
(☎02-6566 6909; www.seabreezebeachhotel.com.au; Livingstone St; mains $8-18; ⊘lunch & dinner; ❇@) This place serves scrubbed-up pub nosh on pleasant decks. The basic self-contained rooms (single/double from $80/105) with balconies don't have views and the rooms with views don't have balconies, but they're clean and spacious.

Heritage   GUESTHOUSE $$
(☎02-6566 6625; www.heritageguesthouse.com.au; 21-23 Livingstone St; d incl breakfast from $115; ❇) This renovated 1880s house has lovely, old-fashioned rooms, some with spas. Choose from the simpler rooms downstairs or the more lavish versions upstairs with ocean views.

TOP CHOICE Trial Bay Camping Area   CAMPGROUND $
(☎02-6566 6168; camp sites per night from $27) Behind the gaol, this magnificent camp site sits on the peninsula affording generous beach views from most sites.

WORTH A TRIP

DIRT ROADS & RIVERS

For a bit of adventure take the partly unsealed but well-kept Loftus Rd from Crescent Head to South West Rocks alongside the pretty-as-a-picture Belmore and Macleay Rivers. The road detours through gorgeous riverside **Gladstone**, which is worth a stop for a meal at **Heritage Hotel** (www.heritagehotel.net.au; 21 Kinchela St; ☺lunch & dinner), an excellent pub on the water's edge with an oasis-like beer garden. Nearby, the **Old Lodge Gallery & Riverbank Café** (www.riverbankcafe.com.au; 8 Kinchela St; ☺breakfast & lunch) does sumptuous scones.

Amenities include hot showers and coin-slot barbies.

South West Woks   ASIAN $
(☑02-6566 6655; Gregory St; mains $5-23; ☺dinner) This is a good option for a cheap night out. Take a bottle of wine (it's BYO) and choose from a varied Asian menu. Some tables are alfresco.

Geppys   MEDITERRANEAN $$
(☑02-6566 6169; cnr Livingstone & Memorial Sts; mains $30; ☺dinner) This cosmopolitan restaurant is signed up to the slow-food movement; tuck into veal medallions with a raspberry reduction or fresh fish with salsa verde. It's open for drinks, too.

🍷 Drinking

Surf Club   SURF CLUB $
(☺4-9pm Fri-Sun Dec-Feb) This club on Horseshoe Bay is the best place in town for a beer with an ocean view. Unpretentious meals, including roasts and shepherd's pie, are a Sunday must.

ℹ Information

Visitor centre (☑1800 642 480; The Boatman's Cottage) At the end of the main street.

ℹ Getting There & Away

Busways (☑1300 555 611; www.busways.com. au) runs two or three times daily Monday to Saturday to/from Kempsey (Belgrave St, $12, 50 minutes).

Cavanaghs (☑02-6562 7800; www.cavana ghs.com.au) runs to Kempsey, leaving from the town bus stop at Horseshoe Bay.

NAMBUCCA HEADS
POP 5880

Map reading around Nambucca's labyrinth of streets might be nauseating but that's a minor trade-off in a town idyllically strewn over a dramatically curling headland interlaced with the estuaries of the Nambucca River. It is spacious, sleepy and unspoilt with one of the coast's prettiest foreshores.

👁 Sights & Activities

From the visitor centre, **Gulmani Boardwalk** stretches 3km along the foreshore, through parks and bushland, and over pristine sand and waterways. It's the perfect introduction to the town.

Of the numerous lookouts, **Captain Cook Lookout**, with its 180-degree vista, best exploits the staggering views.

The only patrolled beach in town is **Main Beach**. **Beilby's** and **Shelly Beaches** are just to the south, closer to the river mouth – where the best surf is – and can be reached by going past the Captain Cook Lookout.

Located near the foreshore, the **V-Wall** is a clever snapshot of life. Here you can read graffitied memoirs from newlyweds, young people and travellers who have left their colourful mark. Pick up a paintbrush and make your mark.

Worth a visit is **Headland Historical Museum** (www.here.com.au/museum/; Liston St; adult/child $2/0.50; ☺2-4pm Wed, Sat & Sun) with local-history exhibits, including a collection of more than 1000 photos.

Nambucca Kayaks (☑0488 588 743; www. nambuccakayaks.com.au) has creek and inner-harbour tours, including a sunset tour (per person $33).

🛏 Sleeping

Nambucca Heads has a loyal cadre of sun-seekers and books out in summer.

Riverview Boutique Hotel   GUESTHOUSE $$
(☑02-6568 6386; www.riverviewlodgenambucca. com.au; 4 Wellington Dr; d $125-185; ❄) Built in 1887, this old pub was, for many years, one of only a few buildings on the rise of a hill overlooking the foreshore. Today the old two-storey wooden charmer has a colourful history the owners will happily share. The eight rooms have fridges; some have stunning views.

White Albatross Holiday
Resort   CARAVAN PARK
(☎02-6568 6468; www.whitealbatross.com.
au; Wellington Dr; camp sites/vans/cabins from
$35/45/90) Located near the river mouth
with an adjacent lagoon to swim in, this
large holiday park surrounds a sheltered
lagoon. Beaches and the V-Wall Tavern are
all close by.

Marcel Towers   APARTMENTS $$
(☎02-6568 7041; www.marceltowers.com.au;
Wellington Dr; d from $120; ❄@) The decor at
these holiday apartments might be somewhat passé, but the balcony views over a
restaurant-studded foreshore soon make up
for it. Apartments are clean and available for
overnight stays.

🍴 Eating
The bracing ocean breezes here put people
to bed early; the streets are mostly rolled up
by 10pm weeknights.

TOP / Matilda's   SEAFOOD $$$
CHOICE
(☎02-6568 6024; Wellington Dr; mains $25-39;
☺dinner Mon-Sat) Saved up for a seafood
feast? Go no further. This cute little shack
juggles good old-fashioned beachfront character with food and service know-how. A
front porch allows diners to catch a few rays
as they indulge in their favourite fish. BYO.

Ocean Chill   MODERN AUSTRALIAN $$$
(☎02-6568 8877; Ridge St; mains $35; ☺dinner
Wed-Sat) Set in the bushy urban streets, this
contemporary restaurant has all the telltale
signs of people who know food and service.
Mind the crisp white linen when you're
eating the likes of roast duck with cocotte
spuds, bok choy and beetroot.

V-Wall Tavern   PUB FARE, BRASSERIE $$
(1 Wellington Dr; mains $27; ☺lunch & dinner) A
big, modern place with classic water views
from its long patio on the upper floor.
There's pub food and a bistro called Bluewater Brasserie with more expensive fishy fare.
On weeknights the taps stop pouring their
mediocre selection of beer as early as 9pm.

Bookshop Café   CAFE $
(cnr Ridge & Bowra Sts; meals $8-16; ☺8am-5pm;
@) The porch tables here are *the* place in
town for breakfast. The fruit smoothies
are excellent.

❶ Information
Nambucca Heads visitor centre (☎02-6568
6954; cnr Riverside Dr & Pacific Hwy) doubles as

the main bus terminal and has a nice spot on the
estuary. The Bookshop Café has internet.

❶ Getting There & Away
Long-distance buses stop at the visitor centre.
Premier (☎13 34 10; www.premierms.com.au)
charges $63 to either Sydney or Brisbane (both
eight to nine hours). **Greyhound** (☎1300 GREY-
HOUND/1300 4739 46863; www.greyhound.
com.au) charges $96 to Sydney (nine hours) and
$110 for a slightly quicker run to Brisbane.

Busways (☎1300 555 611; www.busways.
com.au) runs two or three times Monday to
Saturday from Nambucca Heads to Bellingen
($9, one hour) and Coffs Harbour ($9, 50 minutes) via Urunga.

CountryLink (☎13 22 32; www.countrylink.
info) has three trains north to Coffs Harbour ($5,
40 minutes) and beyond, and south to Sydney
($67, eight hours).

The Waterfall Way
If you're into touring, point the car in this
direction. The Waterfall Way (www.visitwater
fallway.com.au) is an awe-inspiring scenic
drive from just south of coasty Coffs Harbour to inland Armidale – and what a ride.
Not only does the journey traverse the gamut of spectacular World Heritage–listed national parks, it passes through characteristic
old towns, including charm-your-socks-off
Bellingen (12km from the Pacific Hwy) and
sleepy hillside Dorrigo (a further 27km). You
can easily drive the 168km to Armidale in a
day but, as this is one of the loveliest parts of
NSW, why not take a few?

BELLINGEN
POP 2860
Buried in foliage on a hillside by the banks
of the Bellinger River, this gorgeous town
dances to the beat of its own bongo drum,
attracting a populace of artists, academics
and those drawn to a more organic lifestyle.
Thick with gourmet cuisine and accommodation, Bellingen has just a hint of unpretentious chic. As one visitor rightly stated,
it's hippie without the dippy. From December to March a huge colony of flying foxes
descends on Bat Island.

❂ Sights & Activities
Hammond & Wheatley
Emporium   HISTORIC BUILDING
(Hyde St) First up, head to this magnificent
shop, formerly an old department store. It
has been beautifully restored and now houses a shop selling stylish duds, as well as an
art gallery and cafe.

Markets
MARKET

(www.bellingenmarkets.com.au) On the third Saturday of the month the community market in Bellinger Park is a regional sensation, with over 250 stalls. On the second and fourth Saturday of the month there's a growers market at Bellingen showgrounds.

Heartland Didgeridoos
MUSIC

(www.heartlanddidgeridoos.com.au; 2/25 Hyde St) The first didg in space came from here. As such, the Indigenous owners have a growing international reputation.

Old Butter Factory
HISTORIC BUILDING

(1 Doepel St) This historic place houses craft shops, a gallery, opal dealers, a masseur and a great cafe.

Bellingen Canoe Adventures
CANOEING

(☑02-6655 9955; www.canoeadventures.com.au; 4 Tyson St, Fernmount; day tours per adult/child $90/60) This outfit has wonderful guided canoe tours on the Bellinger River, including full-moon tours (adult/child $25/20).

★ Festivals & Events

Camp Creative
ARTS

(www.campcreative.com.au) A week-long carnival of the arts in mid January.

Bellingen Jazz & Blues Festival
JAZZ

(www.bellingenjazzfestival.com.au) Features a strong line-up of jazz names in mid August.

Global Carnival
WORLD MUSIC

(www.globalcarnival.com) A multicultural mix of music and performances held in early October.

⌂ Sleeping

TOP CHOICE ⟩ Bellingen YHA
HOSTEL $

(☑02-6655 1116; www.yha.com.au; 2 Short St; dm/tw/d/f from $30/78/98/98; @) This renovated two-storey weatherboard, overlooking the pristine river valley, attracts backpackers via the grapevine and then keeps them here with its tranquil, engaging atmosphere. Camping also available.

Federal Hotel
PUB $

(☑02-6655 1003; www.federalhotel.com.au; 77 Hyde St; dm/s/d $40/65/80; ✱@) This beautiful old pub has refurbished weatherboard rooms that open onto a balcony with a sweeping view of the main street. Bathrooms are shared. Downstairs there is a lively pub scene, and excellent Relish Bar & Grill (meals $20; ⊘lunch & dinner).

Rivendell
GUESTHOUSE $$

(☑02-6655 0060; www.rivendellguesthouse.com.au; 12 Hyde St; s/d from $115/140; ✱) Unlike many, Rivendell is right in town. The three bedrooms have verandas fronting lush gardens surrounding a freshwater pool. Decor is restrained, always a plus with a B&B.

Maddefords Cottages
APARTMENTS $$

(☑02-6655 9866; www.maddefordscottages.com.au; 224 North Bank Rd; d $145; ✱) These polished mountain cabins have cosy interiors with country furnishings and big, sunny windows. Timber balconies overlook a tumbling private valley. Your first night includes a sizeable brekkie hamper.

✗ Eating & Drinking

There are plenty of excellent options to choose from in this hedonistic town except on Mondays and Tuesdays.

TOP CHOICE ⟩ Vintage Espresso
CAFE $

(62 Hyde St; sandwiches $9; ⊘breakfast & lunch) Sip on excellent coffee amid the eclectic curios of this vintage shop. One side is clothestastic, the other is a nudge at nostalgia with old books and records, used furniture and 70s kitchenware. Thankfully the hearty sandwiches are not preloved.

TOP CHOICE ⟩ Lodge 241
CAFE, BAR $$

(www.bellingen.com/thelodge; Hyde St; mains $12-25; ⊘8.30am-5.30pm Wed-Sun, dinner Fri & Sat) A pew at this excellent cafe is golden. Chess players gather here on a Sunday to soak up the atmosphere while locals line up along a communal table and imbibe great coffee. It has recently been licensed so is good for a tipple too.

No 2 Oak St
MODERN AUSTRALIAN, FRENCH $$

(☑02-6655 9000; www.no2oakst.com.au; 2 Oak St; mains $30-35; ⊘dinner Wed-Sat, Tue during holidays) The bounty of local produce is celebrated at this restaurant where host Toni Urquart provides the welcome while Ray Urquart works his kitchen magic. A table on the veranda in the 1910 country house is a magical place for the evening. Book ahead.

Tuckshop Bellingen
CAFE $

(www.tuckshopbellingen.com.au; 63 Hyde St; mains $8-15; ⊘7.30am-3.30pm Mon-Sat) Great coffee and a delicious line-up of breakfast and good vegetarian options.

Bellingen Gelato Bar
CAFE $

(101 Hyde St; ⊘10am-6pm) A 1950s-Americastyled cafe with homemade ice cream.

Little Red Kitchen ITALIAN $$
(111 Hyde St; mains $10-32; ⊗5-9pm Thu-Mon)
Gourmet pizza and pasta.

❶ Information
There's an excellent community website at www.
bellingen.com.

Bellingen Book Nook (25 Hyde St) Bookworm
heaven.

❶ Getting There & Away
Busways (☑1300 555 611; www.busways.com.
au) runs two or three times Monday to Saturday
from Nambucca Heads ($10, 40 minutes) and
Coffs Harbour ($9, 70 minutes) to Bellingen via
Urunga.
 Keans (☑1800 625 587) has buses west to
Dorrigo and Tamworth twice a week.

AROUND BELLINGEN
There are some beautiful spots waiting to be
discovered in the surrounding valleys. The
most accessible is the hamlet of Gleniffer,
6km to the north and clearly signposted
from North Bellingen. There's a good swim-
ming hole in the Never Never River be-
hind the small Gleniffer School of Arts at
the crossroads. Then you can drive around
Loop Road, which takes you to the foot of
the New England tableland – a great drive
for which words don't do justice.
 If you want to sweat, tackle the Syndi-
cate Ridge Walking Trail (www.environment.
nsw.gov.au/NationalParks) a strenuous 15km-
long, seven- to eight-hour walk from Gleniff-
er to the Dorrigo plateau following the route
of a tramline once used by timber cutters.
There's a very steep 1km climb on the way
up. To get to the start, take the Gordonville
Rd, turning into Adams Lane soon after
crossing the Never Never River. The walking
track commences at the first gate.

DORRIGO NATIONAL PARK
The most accessible of Australia's World
Heritage–listed rainforests, this 11,902-hect-
are national park is simply stunning,
encompassing around 120 bird species and
numerous walking tracks. The turn-off to
the park is just south of Dorrigo. The Rain-
forest Centre (Dome Rd; ⊗9am-4.30pm), at
the park entrance, has information about
the park's various ecosystems and can advise
you on which walk to conquer. The Walk
with the Birds Track is an easy 400m stroll
but the highlight is the Skywalk, a walkway
jutting over the rainforest canopy with jaw-
dropping views of the ranges beyond. Those
interested in dawn and dusk photography

WORTH A TRIP

DORRIGO TO COFFS

A partly sealed road continues north
from Dorrigo and swings east into Coffs
Harbour via beautiful winding rainforest
roads and a huge tallow wood tree,
56m high and more than 3m in diam-
eter. With time on your hands it's the
perfect detour.

should note that the skywalk is accessible
after hours.

DORRIGO
POP 2400
Set on the T-junction of two wider-than-wide
streets, Dorrigo is a pretty little place, home
to laid-back and affable locals. One gets the
sense that this might be the next Bellingen
in terms of food and wine, but it hasn't quite
happened yet. The winding roads that lead
here from Armidale, Bellingen and Coffs
Harbour, however, reveal rainforests, moun-
tain passes and waterfalls – some of the
most dramatic scenery in NSW.
 The visitor centre (☑02-6657 2486) is on
Hickory St. The town's main attraction is the
Dorrigo Rainforest Centre (this page) and
Dangar Falls, which cascade over a series of
rocky shelves before plummeting into a pris-
tine gorge. A lookout provides Kodak mo-
ments, and you can swim beneath the falls if
you have a yen for glacial bathing.
 In the heart of town, 33 on Hickory
(☑02-6657 1882; www.thirtythreeonhickory.com.
au; 33 Hickory St; mains $20; ⊗lunch Sun, dinner
Thu-Sun) is a gorgeous 1920s weatherboard
cottage with stained-glass windows, taste-
ful antiques and a blossoming garden. The
main game is organic sourdough pizza, but
it's served in style with white tablecloths,
sparkling silverware and a cosy wood fire.
The B&B accommodation (double $135) is
equally as stylish. David Scott, the owner of
the Red Dirt Distillery (☑02-6657 1373; 51-53
Hickory St; ⊗10am-4pm Mon-Fri, to noon Sat), gets
creative with a range of vodka and liqueurs
made with, for example, spuds grown in
Dorrigo's red dirt. Buy a bottle, plus some of
his deli snacks and you're talking picnic, or
sit in for an antipasto platter.
 The exterior charm of the almighty Dor-
rigo Hotel/Motel (☑6657 2017; www.hotel
moteldorrigo.com.au; cnr Cudgery & Hickory Sts;
dm $30, d $60-85, f $190) might not be echoed
in the public bar or the rear dining room.

DORRIGO TO ARMIDALE

Once you've travelled the 41km from the Pacific Hwy through Bellingen to Dorrigo, you've gone pretty far from the coast, although there's still another 124km of the Waterfall Way to go before you reach Armidale. Should you press on, these are the highlights:

» Forty-eight kilometres past Dorrigo (2km west of Ebor) there's a turn for Ebor Falls, where the Guy Fawkes River takes a big plunge.

» A further 7km on is Point Lookout Rd, which leads to New England National Park, another World Heritage site. There are numerous walks into this misty rainforest.

» After another 30km, look for Wollomombi Falls, a highlight of the World Heritage–listed Oxley Wild Rivers National Park. Here the water plunges down 260m.

Upstairs, however, the bedrooms, some with bathrooms, have been tastefully renovated to provide wholesome country hospitality. Double doors open onto the wide-girthed verandah for a sweeping main-street vista. There are motel rooms also.

The local foodies' hub and hangout is Dragonfly (18-20 Cudgery St; mains $10-20; ⊙breakfast & lunch Mon-Sat), a cafe-cum-bookshop set in a chic minimalist space with a large, sunny rear dining area. Creative salads, sandwiches and veggie specials entice even if service is a tad slow.

Twice a week Keans (🖉1800 043 339) buses run to Bellingen, Coffs Harbour and Armidale.

Coffs Harbour

POP 64,910

Coffs Harbour has always had to work hard to tart up its image. Where other coastal towns have the ready-made aesthetic of a main street slap-bang on the waterfront, Coffs has an inland city centre, a town 'jetty' (albeit with some great restaurants) that isn't actually on the water, and a semi-enclosed marina. On the flipside, the city has a string of fabulous beaches and a preponderance of water-based activities, action sports and wildlife encounters, making it hugely popular with families and the 'middle-Australian' market.

Orientation

The town is split into three areas – the jetty, the town centre and beaches – making it infamously tedious to navigate. Harbour Dr (aka High St) is the spine of main activity. It runs from the town centre to the jetty and marina. The Pacific Hwy turns into Grafton St and then Woolgoolga Rd on its run north through town.

◎ Sights

The city's beaches include Park Beach, a long and lovely stretch of sand which has a picnic ground and is patrolled at busy times. It is backed by dense shrubbery and dunes that conceal the urban blight beyond. Jetty Beach is more sheltered. Diggers Beach, reached by turning off the highway near the Big Banana, has a nude section. Surfers enjoy Diggers and Macauleys Headland where swells average 1m to 1.5m.

North Coast Botanic Gardens   GARDEN
(Hardacre St; admission by donation) Immerse yourself in the subtropical surrounds. Lush rainforest and numerous endangered species are some of the features. The 6km Coffs Creek Habitat Walk passes by, starting opposite the council chambers on Coff St and finishing near the ocean.

Muttonbird Island   NATURE RESERVE
Dramatically joined to Coffs Harbour by the northern breakwater in 1935, this eco treasure is occupied from late August to early April by some 12,000 pairs of muttonbirds, with cute offspring visible in December and January. The 500m walk to the top rewards with sweeping vistas along the coast. It marks the southern boundary of Solitary Islands Marine Park (p170), a meeting place of tropical waters and southern currents.

Big Banana   AMUSEMENT PARK
(www.bigbanana.com; Pacific Hwy; ☉9am-4.30pm)
Some see this as a national icon, others find
it ripe for abuse. Admission is free with
charges for individual attractions such as the
ice skating and snow-slope combo ($16/14).
Built in 1964, it actually started the craze for
'Big Things' in Australia (just so you know
who to blame or praise).

Galleries worth visiting:

Coffs Harbour Regional Gallery (www.
coffsharbour.nsw.gov.au; Rigby House, cnr Coff &
Duke Sts; ☉10am-4pm Wed-Sat) Regional art
and travelling shows.

Bunker Cartoon Gallery (www.coffs
harbour.nsw.gov.au; John Champion Way; adult/
child $2/1; ☉10am-4pm Mon-Sat) Rotating
selections from the permanent collection
of 18,000 cartoons on display in a WWII
bunker.

🏃 Activities

Coffs Harbour is a centre for activities in the
region, many involving the ocean. Pick up
the useful walking brochure from the visitor centre.

Promenade Canoes   CANOEING
(☑02-6651 1032; The Promenade, 321 Harbour Dr;
single/double/triple canoes per hr $15/22/27, 3rd hr
free; ☉9am-1pm Mon-Fri, to 5pm Sat & Sun) Grab
a canoe for a 5km, self-guided trip along
scenic Coffs Creek in the heart of town.

Jetty Dive Centre   DIVING
(☑02-6651 1611; www.jettydive.com.au; 398
Harbour Dr; double dives from $115) Great-value
PADI certification; the diving and snorkelling around Solitary Islands Marine Park
is pretty spectacular.

**Liquid Assets Adventure
Tours**   ADVENTURE TOURING
(☑02-6658 0850; www.surfrafting.com; 328 Harbour Dr; half-day tours from $50) Watery fun of
all kinds is on offer: surf-kayaking, white-
water rafting, kayaking in the marine
park, platypus tours and more.

East Coast Surf School   SURFING
(☑02-6651 5515; www.eastcoastsurfschool.com.au;
Diggers Beach; lessons from $55) This school is
particularly female-friendly as it is run by
noted east coast surfer Helene Enevoldson.

Crying Tiger Cooking School   COOKING
(☑02-6650 0195; http://thecryingtiger.com;
382 Harbour Dr; per person $110; ☉10am)
If you don't mind cooking on holiday,
brush up on Thai cooking at this popular

restaurant. The class finishes with a sit-
down feast.

Lee Winkler's Surf School   SURFING
(☑02-6650 0050; Park Beach; from $60)

Valery Horse Trails   HORSE RIDING
(☑02-6653 4301; www.valerytrails.com.au; 758
Valery Rd, Valery; 2hr ride $50) A stable of 60
horses and plenty of acreage

Coffs Jet Ski   JET SKIING
(☑0418 665 656; Park Beach; 15/30/60min
$60/100/160)

Coffs City Skydivers   SKYDIVING
(☑02-6651 1167; www.coffsskydivers.com.au;
Coffs Harbour airport; tandem jumps $325)
Satisfies all urges to fling yourself from a
plane.

👉 Tours

Spirit of Coffs Harbour Cruises   WHALES
(☑02-6650 0155; www.gowhalewatching.com.au;
shop 5, Coffs Harbour Marina) Whale watching
($45) and cruises.

Pacific Explorer Whale Watching   WHALES
(☑0422 210 338; www.pacificexplorer.com.au;
2-3hr from $30) A 10m catamaran limited to
23 passengers.

🎊 Festivals & Events

Pittwater to Coffs Yacht Race   YACHT RACE
(www.pittwatertocoffs.com.au) New Year. Starts
in Sydney, finishes here.

Sawtell Chilli Festival   CHILLI FESTIVAL
(www.sawtellchillifestival.com.au) Early July.

**Coffs Harbour International Buskers'
Festival**   MUSIC
(www.coffsharbourbuskers.com) Late September and not to be missed.

Gold Cup   HORSE RACE
(☑02-6652 1488) Early August. Coffs' premier horse race.

🛏 Sleeping

Motels cluster in two spots: out on the Pacific Hwy by the visitor centre where they
can suck in road-trippers, and down by Park
Beach where they can comfort beachgoers.

There's no real reason to stay out by the
Pacific Hwy. It's good to note that many
hostel prices remain consistent all year, but
book ahead.

One of many holiday-apartment agents
is **Pacific Property & Management** (☑02-
6652 1466; www.coffsholidayrentals.com.au; 101

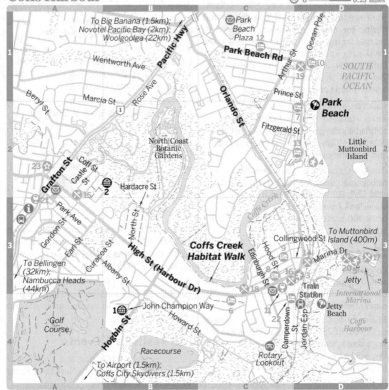

Park Beach Rd). The visitor centre has an accommodation booking service.

Observatory Holiday Apartments
APARTMENTS **$$**

(☎02-6650 0462; www.theobservatory.com.au; 30-36 Camperdown St; apt from $130; ❄🛜) The one-, two- and three-bedroom apartments in this attractive modern complex are bright and airy, with chef-friendly kitchens. Some have spas with window views and all have balconies with ocean views.

Caribbean Motel
MOTEL **$$**

(☎02-6652 1500; www.caribbeanmotel.com.au; 353 High St; r $100-180; ❄@🛜) Close to Coffs Creek and the jetty, this 24-unit motel has been tastefully renovated and features a breakfast buffet and tables outside by the pool. The best rooms have balconies, views and spas plus great-value one-bedroom suites with kitchenettes.

Coffs Harbour YHA
HOSTEL **$**

(☎02-6652 6462; www.yha.com.au; 51 Collingwood St; dm/d/f $31/86/132; @🛜) The dorms and doubles with bathrooms are spacious and modern here, and the TV lounge and kitchen are immaculate. You can hire surfboards and bikes.

Aussitel Backpackers
HOSTEL **$**

(☎1800 330 335, 02-6651 1871; www.aussitel. com; 312 Harbour Dr; dm/d $27/65; @🛜) Don't be put off by the exterior. This capacious brick house, with homely dorms and a shady courtyard, is a hub for backpackers of all shapes and sizes, codes and creeds. Diving specialists are on site (PADI courses from $295).

Hoey Moey Pub
HOSTEL **$**

(☎02-6652 3833; www.hoeymoey.com.au; 90 Ocean Pde; s/d $25/60) You can hear the waves roll in from these motel-style backpacker rooms nicely located between the pub and the main beach. You can also hear your mates in the beer garden. Renovated rooms are slightly pricier.

Aanuka Beach Resort RESORT **$$**
(☎02-6652 7555; www.aanuka.com.au; 11 Firman Dr; r from $123; ❀@❀) It might be out of town, but this luxurious resort, set amid luscious foliage, has excellent studios and apartments, all with spas and dishy interiors. It sits on a quiet neck of Diggers Beach and has tennis courts and an award-winning restaurant.

Novotel Pacific Bay RESORT **$$$**
(☎02-6659 7000; www.pacificbayresort.com.au; cnr Pacific Hwy & Bay Dr; r from $185; ❀❀❀) Has all the features of a large resort: tennis courts, a golf course, walking trails, a kids' club, a spa and a fitness centre. The grounds are large and the 180 rooms have balconies, many with kitchens. It's 3km north of Coffs.

Park Beach Holiday Park CARAVAN PARK **$**
(☎02-6648 4888; www.coffsholidays.com.au; Ocean Pde; camp sites/cabins from $27/61; @❀) Massive, with 332 sites and 55 cabins; ideally located at the beach. Kids are well catered for.

Bo'suns Inn Motel MOTEL **$$**
(☎02-6651 2251; www.motelcoffsharbour.com; 37 Ocean Pde; d from $80; ❀❀) One of many run-of-the mill places credited for its beachside locale rather than aesthetic.

✕ Eating

You can eat well down by the jetty. The strip of eateries on Harbour Dr is a hungry browser's delight. The downtown area is good for lunch, or for coffee all day, but most places are closed in the evening. The pedestrian area opposite Palm Mall (part of High St Pedestrian Mall) has a few pavement cafes.

As well as the listings here, you'll find budget Italian, Vietnamese, Indian, and fish and chips. Kitchens start closing around 8.30pm, so come early and make a reservation if you have your heart set on a particular place or a pavement table.

TOP CHOICE **Mangrove Jacks** MODERN AUSTRALIAN **$$**
(www.mangrovejackscafe.com.au; The Promenade Centre, Harbour Dr; mains $25; ⊙breakfast & lunch daily, dinner Tue-Sat) One of two restaurants wonderfully located on a quiet bend of Coffs Creek. This one serves sultry gourmet dinners and has Coopers on tap. Brekkie and lunch are more casual.

Urban Espresso Lounge CAFE $$
(www.urbanespressolounge.com.au; 384a Harbour Dr, Jetty; mains $8-17; ☺breakfast & lunch) A stylish little java outpost on the strip. Pancakes, fresh fruit and yogurt are some of the breakfast delights. Lunches include a Thai beef and prawn salad and a luscious roast-beef sandwich.

Caffé Fiasco ITALIAN $$$
(www.caffefiasco.com.au; 368 Harbour Dr, Jetty; mains $15-30; ☺brunch Sun, dinner Tue-Sat) Caffé Wonderful is more apt. Classic Italian fare is prepared in an open kitchen surrounded by widely spaced tables that flow from inside to out. The gardens' herbs are used in the dishes, which include some excellent local seafood. Bar open from 4pm.

Crying Tiger THAI $$
(http://thecryingtiger.com; 382 Harbour Dr, Jetty; mains $19-24; ☺dinner) Swimming in ambience and fragrant smells, the Crying Tiger keeps inquisitive diners happy with redduck curry and king prawns in lime leaf and coconut. You can turn the chilli gauge as high or low as you like.

YKnot Bistro BISTRO $$
(www.yknotbistro.com.au; 30 Marina Dr, Marina; mains $15-39; ☺breakfast, lunch & dinner) Part of the Coffs Harbour Yacht Club, this understated eatery has a bar serving pub-style seafood, steaks and pasta in a huge dining room. There's also plenty of outdoor seating. Best of all, it has an ocean view – rare in Coffs.

OP81 MODERN AUSTRALIAN $$
(81 Ocean Pde; mains $8-27; ☺breakfast & lunch Tue-Sun, dinner Fri) Modern decor, contemporary food and a big front deck.

Cocoa CAFE $
(36/35 Harbour Dr, City; mains $8-13; ☺breakfast & lunch) A hot spot for the business set and pram brigade. Great breakfast.

Foreshore Café CAFE $
(394 Harbour Dr, Jetty; ☺breakfast & lunch) Spacious cafe with menu to suit all tastes.

Fisherman's Co-op FISH & CHIPS $
(www.coffsfishcoop.com.au; 69 Marina Dr; mains $8-10; ☺9am-6pm winter, to 8pm summer) Fresh off the boats; perfect fodder for a Muttonbird Island picnic.

🍷 Drinking & Entertainment

See Thursday's edition of the *Coffs Harbour Advocate* for live-music listings.

Coast Hotel PUB
(www.coasthotel.com.au; 2 Moonee St; ☺11am-late) Formerly the Old Fitzroy Hotel, this place has been purpose-renovated to supply lovers of a lazy afternoon in a beer garden with a venue. It has landscaped decking and cool breakaway areas so you can kick back on a couch if the mood takes you. The food is great, too.

Hoey Moey Pub PUB
(www.hoeymoey.com.au; 90 Ocean Pde; ☺10amlate) The massive inner beer 'garden' gives a good indication of how much this place kicks off in the summer. Pool comps, live music (Wednesday to Sunday) and terrifying karaoke sessions are the norm.

Coffs Hotel PUB
(www.coffsharbourhotel.com; cnr Pacific Hwy & West Harbour Dr) Irish pub with bands, several bars, DJs and mad Friday nights.

Pier Hotel PUB
(www.pierhotelcoffs.com.au; cnr Hood St & Harbour Dr) Renovated with a sunny rear terrace, this place has live music on Wednesdays.

Plantation Hotel PUB
(www.plantationhotel.com.au; 88 Grafton St aka Pacific Hwy) The Plantation is a pub at heart, so beer, live rock and decent steak are mainstays.

ℹ Information

Jetty Dive (398 Harbour Dr; per hour $4) Internet.

Main post office (Park Beach Plaza shopping centre)

Visitor centre (☑1300 369 070, 02-6652 1522; www.coffscoast.com.au; Pacific Hwy)

ℹ Getting There & Away

Air

Coffs Harbour Airport (CFS) is just south of town. **Virgin Australia** (☑13 67 89; www.virginaustralia.com) and **Qantas** (☑13 13 13; www.qantas.com.au) fly to Sydney ($119, 1¼ hours).

Bus

Long-distance and regional buses leave from a shelter adjacent to the visitor centre.

Premier (☑13 34 10; www.premierms.com.au) has several services a day north, including Byron Bay ($50, 5¼ hours), and south to Sydney ($66, 8½ hours). **Greyhound** (☑1300 GREYHOUND/1300 4739 46863; www.greyhound.com.au) offers similar services in both directions.

Busways ([phone]1300 555 611; www.busways. com.au) runs two or three times daily Monday to Saturday to Nambucca Heads ($9, 70 minutes) and Bellingen ($8, 70 minutes) via Urunga.

Train

CountryLink ([phone]13 22 32; www.countrylink.info) has three trains daily all the way north to the non-thriving town of Casino (where the train used to branch off to Byron Bay) and Brisbane ($59, 5½ hours), and south to Sydney ($67, nine hours).

❶ Getting Around

Hostel shuttles meet all long-distance buses and trains.

Coffs Bike Hire ([phone]02-6652 5102; cnr Orlando & Collingwood Sts; per day $25) rents mountain bikes.

The major car-rental companies have offices in town and/or at the airport. Coffs District Taxi Network ([phone]13 10 08) operates a 24-hour cab service.

Coffs Harbour to Byron Bay

The Pacific Hwy runs near the coast – but not in sight of it – for 30km north of Coffs. Look for turn-offs to small beaches that are often quite uncrowded. The road then turns inland to Grafton, avoiding Yuraygir National Park and the isolated beach town of Wooli.

WOOLGOOLGA

POP 4360

Also known as Woopi, this coastal town, just north of Coffs, is a good small-town stop option. It's known for its surf-and-Sikh community. As you drive by on the highway you're sure to notice the impressive Guru Nanak Temple, a Sikh *gurdwara* (place of worship).

Drive straight through town for a magnificent view of the group of five islands in the Solitary Islands Marine Park, the meeting point of warm tropical currents and cooler southern currents, making for a wonderful combination of corals, reef fish and seaweeds. Dive shops in Coffs Harbour organise tours.

The Woolgoolga Beach Caravan Park ([phone]02-6654 1373; www.coffscoastholidayparks. com.au; Beach St; unpowered sites/cabins from $27/60) is right on the beach. Bluebottles Brasserie (cnr Wharf & Beach Sts; mains $24-28; ⊙breakfast & lunch daily, dinner Fri & Sat) is a happening place that serves fine seafood and hosts live jazz sessions.

RED ROCK

POP 280

Red Rock is a sleepy village with an inlet and surrounds so gorgeous it's worth trekking 3km off the highway. It is a site sacred to the Gunawarri people. Soak up the sun or catch a fish while camping at Red Rock Caravan Park ([phone]02-6649 2730; www.redrock. org.au; 1 Lawson St, Red Rock; camp sites/cabins from $19/94, cottages $105). The Yarrawarra Aboriginal Cultural Centre ([phone]02-6640 7100; http://yarrawarra.org; 170 Red Rock Rd, Corindi Beach) has bush-medicine tours, traditional-basket-weaving and art classes and a bush-tucker cafe with croc, roo and emu dishes. Ring ahead to see what's on.

The 53,502-hectare Yuraygir National Park (per car per day $7) covers the 60km stretch of coast north from Red Rock. The isolated beaches are best discovered on the Yuraygir Coastal Walk, a 65km signposted walk from Angourie to Red Rock following the path of the coastal emu over a series of tracks, trails, beaches and rock platforms, and passing through the villages of Brooms Head, Minne Water and Wooli.

Walkers can bush-camp at seven basic camping areas (per person from $17) along the route. It's best walked north to south with the sun at your back. Grafton NPWS ([phone]02-6641 1500; www.environment.nsw.gov.au) has info and a downloadable map.

WOOLI

POP 500

Wooli is on a long isthmus, with a river estuary on one side and the ocean on the other. This only adds to its isolated charm. It hosts the Australian National Goanna Pulling Championships (www.goannapulling. com.au). Rather than ripping the eponymous animal to shreds, participants, squatting on all fours, attach leather harnesses to their heads and engage in a cranial tug of war.

Solitary Island Marine Park Resort ([phone]1800 003 031, 02-6649 7519; North St; sites/ beach shack/cabins from $26/46/82) here has lovely cabins in a scrubby bush setting.

GRAFTON

POP 17,500

Grafton is not so much a blast from the past as a serene gust or a puff. Nestled into a quiet bend of the Clarence River, the town's charming grid of wide streets, grand pubs and splendid old houses capture an era that is hard to come by in beachside towns. It's also the 1963 founding home of hang-gliding, though you'll have to go elsewhere to partake in the sport.

Don't be fooled by the franchises along the highway, the main part of town is reached over an imposing 1932 double-decker (road and rail) bridge.

◉ Sights & Activities

Victoria St is the town's historical focal point, providing fascinating glimpses of 19th-century architecture, including the courthouse (1862), Roches Family Hotel (1870) and the Anglican Cathedral (1884).

The Grafton Regional Gallery (🖉02-6642 3177; www.graftongallery.nsw.gov.au; 158 Fitzroy St; admission by donation; ☺10am-4pm Tue-Sun) hosts quality works from galleries around NSW. Susan Island, in the middle of the river, is home to the biggest fruit-bat colony in the southern hemisphere. Their evening departure is a spectacular summer sight.

The local arts scene manifests itself in Grafton Artsfest (www.artsfestgrafton.com), held twice yearly with workshops and exhibitions.

🛏 Sleeping & Eating

Roches Family Hotel HOTEL $
(🖉02-6644 2866; www.roches.com.au; 85 Victoria St; s/d incl breakfast $30/50) This fantastic, historic hotel has spruced-up pub rooms, a cafe and a beer garden. It's worth calling in just for a peek at the croc in the public bar.

Annies B&B B&B $$
(🖉0421 914 295; www.anniesbnbgrafton.com; 13 Mary St; r $120-200) This beautiful big old Victorian house on a leafy corner has private rooms set apart from the family home.

Clocktower Hotel PUB $$
(www.clocktowerhotel.com.au; 93 Princes St; mains $12-32; ☺11am-late) Too young for old stuff? The Clocktower is Grafton's newest eating and drinking venue.

Georgies at the Gallery CAFE $$
(🖉02-6642 6996; 158 Fitzroy St; mains $8-25; ☺lunch Tue-Sat, dinner Wed-Sat) At the Grafton Regional Gallery; this is Grafton's best cafe by a long shot. It occupies the gallery's heaven-sent internal courtyard where Grafton's cultured folk sip on decent coffee and nibble on gourmet salads, quiche and cake.

❶ Information

Clarence River visitor centre (🖉02-6642 4677; www.clarencetourism.com; cnr Spring St & Pacific Hwy) South of town.

NPWS office (🖉02-6641 1500; level 3, 49 Victoria St)

❶ Getting There & Away

Busways (🖉1300 555 611; www.busways.com.au) runs to Yamba ($12, 1¼ hours, six times daily) and Maclean ($10, 45 minutes).

Greyhound (🖉1300 GREYHOUND/1300 4739 46863; www.greyhound.com.au) and **Premier** (🖉13 34 10; www.premierms.com.au) stop at the train station on runs south to Sydney ($67, 11 hours) and north to Byron ($47, 3½ hours).

CountryLink (🖉13 22 32; www.countrylink.info) stops here on its north coast route. Sydney is served three times daily ($72, 10 hours).

YAMBA & ANGOURIE
POP 5520 (YAMBA), 170 (ANGOURIE)

Once a sleepy little fishing town, Yamba is slowly distancing itself from this reputation by attracting a fan base that has cottoned on

---

RUSSELL CROWE'S CURIOS

What is Russell Crowe's *Gladiator* costume doing in an old wooden barn in the tiny town of Nymboida, 30 minutes southwest of Grafton? How about Johnny Cash's gold albums and Don Bradman's caps? The answer: this is the 'Museum of Interesting Things', and Crowe owns it.

The Aussie superstar grew up in nearby Nana Glen where his parents still live. When he bought the adjoining Coaching Station Inn (🖉02-6649 4126; www.coachingstation.com; 3970 Armidale Rd; s/d $90/120), he had the old barn pimped-up to house his considerable collection of boy's toys, from music and movie memorabilia to sporting paraphernalia and vintage motorbikes. The museum (☺11am-3pm Wed-Fri & Sun, to 5pm Sat) also acts as a repository for artefacts from local pioneering history, a nod to the day when horse-drawn Cobb & Co coaches stopped here on the woolpack road from Armidale to Grafton.

Don't get too excited, aside from the photos that dot the inn's main bar, you're not likely to see the man himself. Then again, the barman reckons he sometimes pops in unannounced. After all, 'it's only 11 minutes by chopper from his mum and dad's house'.

WORTH A TRIP

GRAFTON TO YAMBA

Heading north on the Pacific Hwy it's worth taking a small detour to Ulmarra (population 1586), a heritage-listed town with a river port. There's a quaint old corner pub (☑02-6644 5305; 2 Coldstream St; ⊙breakfast & lunch daily, dinner Fri & Sat) with a wrought-iron verandah, pub rooms (singles/doubles $40/65) and a greener-than-green beer garden that stretches down to the river, which can be crossed by car ferry 1km north of town. Further on, Maclean (population 3245) is a picturesque little town that takes its Scottish heritage seriously.

to the merits of beaches on three fronts, a relaxed pace and excellent food without too much encroaching development.

Its southern neighbour, Angourie, is home to NSW's first National Surfing Reserve and has always been a hot spot for experienced surfers (the type who were born on a board, wear helmets and leap off rocks). It complements Yamba's can-do attitude by remaining a small chilled-out place. Apart from the surf, the only sign of development is the Pacific St home (mansion) of Gordon Merchant, founder of the surf brand Billabong, who grew up here (and who, by all accounts, still gets around in boardshorts).

◉ Sights & Activities

Iluka Nature Reserve   NATURE RESERVE
World Heritage–listed Iluka is a short detour off the highway or a ferry ride away; it's the southern end of Bundjalung National Park (per car per day $7), largely untouched and best explored with 4WD. Highlights include the literally named Ten Mile Beach and the hopefully not-literally named Hell Hole Lagoon. The passenger-only Clarence River Ferry (☑02-6646 6423; www.clarenceriverferries.com; adult/child $8/3) runs four times daily.

Blue Pools   NATURE RESERVE
These spring-water-fed water holes are the remains of the quarry used for the breakwall. Locals and the daring climb the 'chalkline', 'tree-line' or 'death-line' cliff faces and plunge to their depths. The saner can slip silently into clear water, surrounded by bush, only metres from the surf.

Yamba-Angourie Surf School   SURFING
(☑02-6646 1496; www.yamba-angouriesurfschool.com.au; 2hr lessons $50) Classes here are run by an Australian surfing champion. To go it alone, rent boards of all shapes and sizes, including mini-mals, from the Plank Shop (☑02-6645 8362; Clarence St, Yamba).

Rockfish Cruises   CRUISING
(☑0447 458 153; www.rockfish.com.au; The Marina, Yamba Rd) Owners Di and Pete offer barbecue-lunch cruises on the Clarence River (11am to 2pm, budget/gourmet $55/75); passengers can swim clinging onto the boom nets. Also, romantic sunset cruises ($55, departures at sunset) and three-hour whale-watching cruises ($95, 9.30am late May to mid-November).

Yamba Kayak   KAYAKING
(☑02-6646 1137; www.yambakayak.com.au; Whiting Beach car park; 3hrs $70) Half- and full-day adventures are a speciality including multiday pub crawls – or pub paddles – stopping at heritage hotels along the Clarence River.

Xtreme Cycle & Skate   CYCLING, WALKING
(☑02-6645 8879; 34 Coldstream St; adult half/full day $15/25, child half/full day $10/15) Has bikes for rent. A walking and cycling track wends around the peaks and troughs of Yamba's coastline. The prettiest bit is from Pippi's Beach around Lovers Point to Convent Beach.

Yamba River Markets   MARKET
(www.rivermarkets.weloveyamba.com; Ford Park) Fourth Sunday of month on Clarence River.

Story House Museum   MUSEUM
(☑02-6646 2316; River St; adult/child $3/0.50; ⊙10am-4.30pm Tue, Wed & Thu, 2-4.30pm Sat & Sun) Maritime culture and shipwrecks.

Sunday Jazz Cruise   CRUISING
(☑0408 664 556; adult/child $30/15; ⊙11am-3pm) River cruise with licensed bar. Also, Hardwood Island cruise (adult/child $20/10; ⊙Wed & Fri 11am-3pm).

Surfing for the big boys is at Angourie Point but Yamba's beaches have something for everyone else. When the surf is flat Pippi's is decent, especially when dolphins hang around. Main Beach is the busiest with an ocean pool, banana palms and a grassy slope for those who don't want sand up their clacker. Convent Beach is a sunbaker's haven and Turner's, protected by the breakwall, is ideal for surf lessons.

The Yuraygir Coastal Walk (p170) begins in Angourie.

🛌 Sleeping

TOP CHOICE Yamba YHA
HOSTEL $

(☑02-6646 3997; www.yha.com.au; 26 Coldstream St; dm/d $30/80; ❄@🔊☃) Spankingly modern and groovy, this is a purpose-built hostel with an excellent downstairs bar and restaurant (mains $9 to $29). Upstairs there's a rooftop deck, pool and barbecue area. It's family run and extremely welcoming. After sampling one of Shane's '10 buck' welcome tours, you're guaranteed to extend your stay.

Pacific Hotel
PUB, HOTEL $

(☑02-6646 2466; www.pacifichotelyamba.com.au; 18 Pilot St, Yamba; dm $35, r with/without bathroom $120/60) This is a fabulous pub overlooking the ocean, with bright bunk rooms and handsome hotel rooms. It would be remiss to come to Yamba without sampling a beer with this kind of view but the food is also exceptional – a lofty step above the usual pub nosh.

Angourie Rainforest Resort
RESORT $$

(☑02-6646 8600; www.angourieresort.com.au; 166 Angourie Rd, Angourie; r $140-355; ❄@☃) A tiny piece of paradise sidled up to 600 hectares of flora. Luxuries include a pool, tennis court, restaurant and day spa. Extras include a pristine rainforest aroma and resident birds and lizards.

Surf Motel
MOTEL $$

(☑02-6646 2200; 2 Queen St, Yamba; r $120-300; ❄) On a bluff overlooking the main beach, this modern, seven-room place is across from a large green. Rooms are quite big and have balconies and kitchenettes. It's blissfully quiet, aside from the surf.

Calypso Holiday Park
CARAVAN PARK $

(☑02-6646 2468; www.calypsoyamba.com.au; Harbour St, Yamba; camp sites from $26, cabins from $77; @☃) The best-located camping place, Calypso is a short walk from the town centre and all the beaches. There are 162 sites and 32 cabins, some quite posh.

🍴 Eating & Drinking

TOP CHOICE Gormans Restaurant
SEAFOOD $$

(☑02-6646 2025; Yamba Bay; mains $30; ☺dinner) Tucked away behind Calypso Holiday Park, this seafood restaurant, hanging out

over the water, is a Yamba institution. The greenhouse decor is a flashback to the '70s. Happily, so is the menu – few places still do 'bugs thermidor' and 'garlic prawns' quite like this place.

El Pirata
TAPAS $$

(☑02-6646 3276; 6 Clarence St, Yamba; ☺dinner Tue-Sun) This is a fabulous tapas bar serving authentic hot and cold Spanish dishes, including *jamon* (ham), chorizo, oily garlic prawns and cheesy stuffed peppers ($9 to $18). It's at its best during summer when the Sydney owners are back in town.

Yamba Bar & Grill
STEAK $$

(☑02-6646 1155; 15 Clarence St; mains $14-34; ☺dinner Tue-Sun) This stylish food den is spacious with a great rear deck and view. The menu is for serious steak lovers with sides right from the gastropub playbook: chips and rocket salad. There are a couple of other restaurants on this little strip.

Sounds Lounge Café
CAFE $

(☑02-6646 3909; 16 Yamba Rd, Yamba; mains $5-18; ☺breakfast & lunch; @🔊) There's a funky collection of CDs for sale at this idiosyncratic place in the centre. Smoothies, burgers, juices and coffees highlight the menu. There are tables inside and out.

Frangipan
MEDITERRANEAN $$

(☑02-6646 2553; www.frangipan.com.au; 11-13 The Crescent, Angourie; mains $19-32; ☺dinner Tue-Sat) It has won awards but reviews are mixed.

Beachwood
MIDDLE EASTERN $$

(☑02-6646 9781; www.beachwoodcafe.com.au; 22 High St; mains $15; ☺breakfast & lunch) Tipped as the best breakfast in town.

ℹ Information

There is no visitor centre (yet), but **Yamba YHA** (☑02-6646 3997; www.yha.com.au; 26 Coldstream St) and http://weloveyamba.com have the low-down on everything.

ℹ Getting There & Away

Busways (☑1300 555 611; www.busways.com. au) buses go to Maclean ($6, 30 minutes) and Grafton ($11, 1¼ hours, several Monday to Saturday). **CountryLink** (☑13 22 32; www.countrylink.info) buses go to Byron Bay ($14, three hours, one daily) and to Grafton where they connect to Sydney ($75, 11½ hours). **Greyhound** (☑1300 GREYHOUND/1300 4739 46863; www. greyhound.com.au) stops on runs south to Sydney ($127, 11½ hours) and north to Byron ($54, two hours).

BALLINA

POP 16,480

At the mouth of the Richmond River, Ballina is spoilt for white sandy beaches and crystal-clear waters. If it were not so close to Byron it would be a tourist haven in its own right. Instead, it is somewhere between a commercial centre and a wannabe tourist lure, maintaining a coastal ambience without tarting itself up for the holiday bucks.

◉ Sights & Activities

For a good sampling of local history, stroll the length of Norton St, which boasts a number of impressive late-19th-century buildings from Ballina's days as a rich lumber town. For architecture of a different kind, the dilapidated Big Prawn is 1km west of town.

White and sandy, like all good beaches, Shelly Beach is patrolled. Calm Shaws Bay Lagoon is popular with families. South Ballina Beach is a good excursion option via the car ferry on Burns Point Ferry Rd.

Naval & Maritime Museum MUSEUM
(☑02-6681 1002; Regatta Ave; admission by donation; ☺9am-4pm) Behind the information centre, this museum is where you will find the amazing remains of a balsawood raft that drifted across the Pacific from Ecuador as part of the Las Balsas expedition in 1973.

Richmond River Cruises CRUISES
(☑02-6687 5688; Regatta Ave; 2hr trip adult/child $25/13; ☺noon & 2pm Wed, Sat & Sun) This is the most established cruise service and is also wheelchair friendly. It offers lunch and dinner cruises, as well as morning and afternoon tea cruises.

Aboriginal Cultural Concepts INDIGENOUS
(☑0405 654 280; www.aboriginalculturalcon cepts.com; from $80; ☺10am-1pm Wed-Sat) Get an indigenous insight into the local area on these heritage tours exploring mythological sights along Bundjalung Coast. The three-hour bush tucker tour is popular.

Jack Ransom Cycles CYCLING
(16 Cherry St) Ballina's many waterways are lined with paths. This place rents bikes from $20 per day.

🛏 Sleeping & Eating

TOP CHOICE Ballina Manor GUESTHOUSE $$$
(☑02-6681 5888; www.ballinamanor.com.au; 25 Norton St; r $165-375; ✻🐾) This grand old dame of hospitality was once a school but has since been converted to a luxurious guesthouse filled to the hilt with restored 1920s furnishings, carpets and curtains. Though antique in design, all rooms are indulgent: the best room has a four-poster bed and spa.

Ballina Heritage Inn HOTEL $$
(☑02-6686 0505; www.ballinaheritageinn.com. au; 229 River St; d $130; ✻🐾🐾) In the centre of town, this tidy inn has neat, bright and comfortable rooms that are a significant leap in quality from the nearby motels. Some rooms have spas.

Ballina Travellers Lodge HOTEL $
(☑02-6686 6737; www.ballinatravellerslodge. com.au; 36-38 Tamar St; s/d/tw $69/92/98; ✻@🐾🐾) In an urban street, this lodge combines motel and hostel guests. It is clean and comfortable and the owners are a good source of info.

La Cucina di Vino ITALIAN $$
(cnr Martin & Fawcett Sts; mains $15-30; ☺lunch daily, dinner Wed-Sun) Water views and an open corner locale make this Italian restaurant an excellent venue for a long lunch. Short on time? There's pizza too.

Evolution Espresso Bar CAFE, BAR $
(Martin St; mains $12-18; ☺breakfast & lunch, dinner Fri & Sat; @🐾) Sniff hard enough and the fresh coffee aroma emanating from this cool little cafe might lead you off the highway.

Healthy Noodle Bar ASIAN $
(216 River St; mains $10; ☺lunch & dinner) One of several cheap and cheerful takeaways on this little strip.

Shelly's on the Beach MODERN AUSTRALIAN $$
(Shelly Beach Rd; mains $16-36; ☺breakfast & lunch) Fine brekkies and lunchtime sambos.

Wicked MEDITERRANEAN $$
(37 Cherry St; mains $8-34; ☺lunch Tue-Fri, dinner Tue-Sat) Huge menu to suit all tastes.

❶ Information

Ballina visitor centre (☑02-6686 3484; www. discoverballina.com; cnr Las Balsas Plaza & River St) At the eastern end of town.

❶ Getting There & Away

If you're driving to Byron Bay, take the coast road through Lennox Head. It's much prettier than the Pacific Hwy and less traffic-clogged as well.

AIR

Ballina's airport (BNK) is the best way to reach Byron Bay – only 30km to the north. It has car-rental desks and plenty of local transport options. Airline service is increasing.

Jetstar (☑13 15 38; www.jetstar.com.au) Serves Sydney.

Regional Express (☑13 17 13; www.regional express.com.au) Serves Sydney.

Virgin Australia (☑13 67 89; www.virgin australia.com) Serves Melbourne via Sydney.

BUS

Greyhound (☑1300 GREYHOUND/1300 4739 46863; www.greyhound.com.au) heads north to Byron ($17, 40 minutes) and Brisbane ($55, three hours) and south to Sydney ($137, 12 hours). **Premier** (☑13 34 10; www.premierms. com.au) heads south to Sydney ($97, 11 hours).

Blanch's Bus Service (☑6686 2144; www. blanchs.com.au) operates several daily services from the airport and the Tamar St bus stop to Lennox Head ($6, 30 minutes), Byron Bay ($10, 70 minutes) and Mullumbimby ($10, 85 minutes). **CountryLink** (☑13 22 32; www.coun-trylink.info) has buses connecting to trains at the Casino train station (70 minutes).

SHUTTLE

Numerous shuttle companies meet flights and serve Ballina, Byron Bay and other nearby towns. Rates average $15 to $20.

Airport Express (☑0414 660 031; www. stevestours.com.au)

Byron Easy Bus (☑02-6685 7447; www. byronbayshuttle.com.au)

LENNOX HEAD
POP 6620

A protected National Surfing Reserve (à la the surfing mecca of Angourie), Lennox Head is home to picturesque coastline with some of the best surf on the coast, including long right-hander breaks. Its blossoming food scene combined with a laid-back atmosphere makes it an alternative to its boisterous well-touristed neighbour Byron, 17km north, although its small main street can get crowded.

Sights & Activities

Stunning Seven Mile Beach runs along parallel to the main street. The best places for a dip are at the north end near the surf club or at the southern end in The Channel. Port Morton lookout is a whale- and dolphin-spotting high point.

Lake Ainsworth, a lagoon just back from the surf club, is made brown by tannins from the tea trees along its banks, which also make swimming here beneficial to the skin. If the wind's up, Wind & Water Action Sports (☑0419 686 188; www.windnwater. net; from $80) has kite-boarding, windsurfing and surf lessons, plus hire equipment.

Seabreeze Hang Gliding (☑0428 560 248; www.seabreezehanggliding.com; from $95) offers tandem flights off Lennox Headland.

Sleeping & Eating

The **Professionals** (☑02-6687 7579; www. professionalslennoxhead.com.au; 66 Ballina St) is a good agent for holiday rentals.

Lennox Lodge HOSTEL $
(☑02-6687 7210; www.lennoxlodge.com.au; 20 Byron St; s/d $25/80; @≋) This motel-style backpackers is daubed in mustard paint and dotted with palm trees and frangipanis. The atmosphere is relaxed and with a maximum of four people to each room, with bathroom, it's comfortable.

Lennox Head Beach House HOSTEL $
(☑02-6687 7636; www.yha.com.au; 3 Ross St; dm/d $28/78) YHA-affiliated and only 100m from the beach, this place has immaculate rooms and a great vibe. For $5 you can use the boards, sailboards and bikes.

Lake Ainsworth Holiday Park CARAVAN PARK $
(☑02-6687 7249; www.ballinabeachside.com.au; Pacific Pde; unpowered/powered sites $27/29, cabins from $80) Family-friendly, just opposite the beach.

O-pes MEDITERRANEAN $$
(☑02-6687 7388; 90-92 Ballina St; ☺breakfast Sat & Sun, lunch & dinner daily) Comfy couches and low-slung tables mix it with a beach-front vibe and vista. The menu balances casual tapas with more formal à la carte dishes.

Lennox Bistro MODERN AUSTRALIAN $$
(☑02-6687 5769; 17-19 Pacific Pde; mains $22; ☺lunch & dinner) Gastro-bistro fare with your eye to a wave.

Getting There & Away

Blanch's Bus Service (☑02-6686 2144; www. blanchs.com.au) operates a service to Ballina ($7), Mullumbimby ($10) and Byron Bay ($8).

Byron Bay
POP 4990

Byron Bay's reputation precedes it like no other place in Australia: it's a gorgeous town where the trademark laid-back, New Age populace lives an escapist, organic lifestyle against a backdrop of evergreen hinterland and never-ending surfable coastline.

With such a heady high rap in mind, the pitfall lies in arriving in this utopia along with every other backpacker on the coast, and wondering what all the fuss is about. Never fear, the sensation doesn't last long. Byron's unique vibe has a way of converting even the most cynical with its long days, balmy weather, endless beaches, delightful accommodation, delectable food, delirious nightlife, ambling milieu and the charisma and hospitality of the local community.

It's an addiction that's hard to kick; many simply don't. A weekend turns into a week, a week into a month...Before you know it, dreadlocks are a serious consideration.

◉ Sights

Cape Byron

The grandfather of the 'mad, bad and dangerous to know' poet Lord Byron was a renowned navigator in the 1760s, and Captain Cook named this spot, Australia's most easterly, after him. (A star-struck clerk in Sydney thought the grandson was the one being honoured, and named the streets – and the town – after poets: Keats, Jonson, Shelley.)

The views from the summit are spectacular, particularly if you've just burnt breakfast off on the climbing track from Clarkes Beach. Ribboning around the headland, it dips and (mostly) soars its way to the lighthouse. The surrounding ocean also jumps to the tune of dolphins and migrating humpback whales in June and July. Towering over all is the 1901 lighthouse (②02-6685 6585; Lighthouse Rd; ⊙8am-sunset), Australia's most easterly and powerful. The Cape Byron Walking Track continues around the northeastern side of the cape, delving into Cape Byron State Conservation Park, where you'll stumble across bush turkeys and wallabies. En route, photo-hungry walkers can work the lens at Captain Cook Lookout. You can also drive right up to the lighthouse and pay $7 for the privilege of parking (or nothing at all if you park 300m below).

Beaches

Main Beach, immediately in front of town, is terrific for people-watching and swimming. At the western edge of town, Belongil Beach is clothing-optional. Clarkes Beach, at the eastern end of Main Beach, is good for surfing, but the best surf is at the next few beaches: Pass, Wategos and Little Wategos.

Tallow Beach is an amazing stretch that extends 7km south of Cape Byron to a rockier patch around Broken Head, where

a succession of small beaches dots the coast before opening onto Seven Mile Beach, which goes all the way to Lennox Head.

The suburb of Suffolk Park (with more good surf, particularly in winter) starts 3km south of town. Kings Beach, a popular gay beach, is just off Seven Mile Beach Rd near the Broken Head Holiday Park.

⚡ Activities

Adventure sports abound in Byron Bay and most operators offer a free pick-up service from local accommodation. Surfing and diving are the biggest draws.

Surfing

Byron Bay waves are often quite mellow. Most hostels provide free boards to guests.

Half-day classes typically start at $60.

Blackdog Surfing   SURFING
(②02-6680 9828; www.blackdogsurfing.com; shop 8, The Plaza, Jonson St) Intimate group lessons and women's courses.

Byron Bay Surf School   SURFING
(②1800 707 274; www.byronbaysurfschool.com; 127 Jonson St) Surf camps too.

Byron Surf Kool Katz   SURFING
(②02-6685 5169; www.koolkatzsurf.com) Half-day lessons $49.

Mojosurf Adventures   SURFING
(②1800 113 044; www.mojosurf.com; Marvell St) Epic surf trips.

Samudra   SURFING
(②02-6685 5600; www.samudra.com.au) Surf-and-yoga retreats.

Surfing Byron Bay   SURFING
(②02-6685 7099; www.gosurfingbyronbay.com; 84 Jonson St) Has courses for kids.

Diving & Snorkelling

About 3km offshore, Julian Rocks Marine Reserve blends cold southerly and warm northerly currents, attracting a profusion of marine species and divers alike.

Dive Byron Bay   DIVING
(②1800 243 483, 02-6685 8333; www.byronbay divecentre.com.au; 9 Marvell St) Rentals, sales, PADI courses from $495, dives from $95.

Sundive   DIVING
(②02-6685 7755; www.sundive.com.au; 8 Middleton St; ⊙tours 8am, 10.45am & 1pm) Scuba diving plus daily snorkelling tours ($50).

Alternative Therapies

Byron is the alternative-therapy heartland. The *Body & Soul* guide, available from the

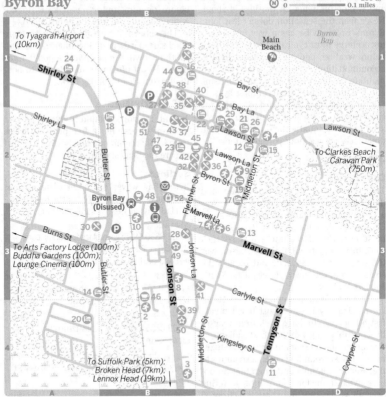

visitor centre, is a handy guide to therapies on offer.

Abundantia RELAXING
(☏02-6685 8008; www.ruthsmithhealing.com; 6-7 Byron St; treatments from $125) Connect with your spirit to bring about healing.

Bikram Hot Yoga RELAXING
(☏02-6685 6334; www.bikramyogabyronbay.com.au; 35 Childe St; casual 90min class $20)

Buddha Gardens RELAXING
(☏02-6680 7844; www.buddhagardensdayspa.com.au; Arts Factory Village, 21 Gordon St; treatments from $85; ☺10am-6pm) Balinese-style day spa.

Byron Ayurveda Centre RELAXING
(☏02-6632 2244; www.ayurvedahouse.com.au; shop 6, Middleton St; treatments from $45; ☺10am-5pm Wed-Sun) It's exfoliation over enemas at this restful place aimed at the masses.

Cocoon RELAXING
(☏02-6685 5711; www.cocoonbyron.com.au; 6/11 Fletcher St; massage from $65) Offers 'healthful retreats' from family holidays.

Relax Haven RELAXING
(☏02-6685 8304; www.belongilbeachouse.com; Belongil Beachouse, 24 Childe St; ☺10am-8pm) Flotation tanks (one hour $35) and massage (one hour $45). Female therapists.

Shambala RELAXING
(☏02-6680 7791; www.shambala.net.au; 4 Carlyle St; treatments from $50; ☺9am-7pm) Massage, reflexology and acupuncture.

Flying

Byron Airwaves HANG-GLIDING
(☏02-6629 0354; www.byronair.cjb.net) Tandem hang-gliding ($145) and courses (from $1500).

Byron Bay Ballooning   BALLOONING
(☎1300 889 660; www.byronbayballooning.com.
au; Tyagarah Airport; adult/child $325/175) Sunrise flights including gourmet breakfast.

Byron Bay Microlights   MICROLIGHTING
(☎0407 281 687; Tyagarah Airport) Whalewatching ($180) and scenic flights ($100).

Skydive Byron Bay   SKYDIVING
(☎02-6684 1323; www.skydivebyronbay.com; Tyagarah Airport) Tandem dives ($249 to $334) are priced depending on altitude and time of freefall (20 to 70 seconds).

Kayaking

Exhibitionist dolphins enhance scenic, halfday kayaking tours in and around Cape Byron Marine Park. Tours go for $60 to $65 per adult, less for children.

Cape Byron Kayaks   KAYAKING
(☎02-6680 9555; www.capebyronkayaks.com; ⊙tours 8.30am & 1pm)

Dolphin Kayaking   KAYAKING
(☎02-6685 8044; www.dolphinkayaking.com.au; ⊙tours 8.30am)

Gosea Kayaks   KAYAKING
(☎0416 222 344; www.goseakayakbyronbay.com. au; ⊙tours 9.30am & 2pm)

Other

Byron Surf & Bike Hire   CYCLING
(☎02-6680 7066; 1-3 31 Lawson St) Rents bikes ($20 per day), kayaks (half-day $45), surfboards ($25 per day) and other active gear.

Circus Arts
JUGGLING

(☑02-6685 6566; www.circusarts.com.au; 17 Centennial Circuit) About 2km west of town; Type A characters may find the juggling classes useful.

☞ Tours

Numerous operators run tours to Nimbin and other interesting places in the hinterland. Most tour companies will pick you up from where you're staying.

Aboriginal Cultural Concepts
INDIGENOUS

(☑0405 654 280; www.aboriginalcultural concepts.com; from $80; ⊙10am-1pm Wed-Sat) Heritage tours exploring mythological sights along Bundjalung Coast. Includes bush-tucker tour.

Byron Bay Eco Tours
ECOLOGICAL

(☑02-6685 4030; www.byron-bay.com/ecotours; tours $85; ⊙9am) Excellent commentary.

Byron Bay Wildlife Tours
WILDLIFE

(☑0429 770 686; www.byronbaywildlifetours.com; adult/child $70/35) Platypus and wildlife spottings guaranteed. Cheaper if booked online.

Happy Coach
HINTERLAND

(☑02-6685 3996; www.happycoach.com.au; $25; ⊙10am) Nimbin tours.

Jim's Alternative Tours
HINTERLAND

(☑0401 592 247; www.jimsalternativetours.com; tours $40; ⊙10am) Entertaining tours (with soundtrack!) to Nimbin.

Mountain Bike Tours
CYCLING

(☑1800 122 504, 0429 122 504; www.mountain biketours.com.au; tours $99; ⊙9.30am) Environmentally friendly bike tours.

Night Vision Walks
WILDLIFE

(☑02-6685 0059; www.visionwalks.com; adult/child from $40/25) See nocturnal animals in their natural habitat.

☆ Festivals & Events

East Coast International Blues & Roots Music Festival
BLUES

(www.bluesfest.com.au) Held over Easter, this international jam attracts high-calibre international performers and local heavyweights. Book early.

Byron Bay Writers Festival
LITERATURE

(www.byronbaywritersfestival.com.au) In late July/early August, this festival gathers together top-shelf writers and literary followers from across Australia.

🛏 Sleeping

There's every kind of accommodation you could hope for in and around Byron. Just don't be a bonehead and turn up in January without a reservation or you'll join the hordes of backpackers and jet-set models milling around the visitor centre with hangdog looks because they thought there would be just one more room.

Schoolies Week at the end of November is also one to avoid. During these periods, one-night-only bookings are rare.

Motels are clustered in town and south along Bangalow Rd. There are scores of B&Bs and apartments all along Belongil Beach.

The **accommodation booking office** (☑02-6680 8666; www.byronbayaccom.net), run by the visitor centre, is a great service for booking in advance.

For holiday houses check out **Professionals** (☑02-6685 6552; www.byronbaypro.com. au; cnr Lawson & Fletcher Sts).

TOP CHOICE Byron at Byron
RESORT $$$

(☑1300 554 362, 02-6639 2000; www.thebyron atbyron.com.au; r from $325; ❋@☞☎) For the ultimate in luxury this 92-suite resort is set within 45 acres of subtropical rainforest. It is a hive of wildlife and endangered species and the resort maintains its sympathy to the environment with eco credentials listed online. When you're not lounging by the infinity pool take the 10-minute stroll to Tallow Beach via a series of wonderful boardwalks.

Atlantic
GUESTHOUSE $

(☑02-6685 5118; www.atlanticbyronbay.com. au; 13 Marvell St; dm/d from $25/150; ❋☞☎) What a difference a facelift makes. This little residential compound has been transformed into a shiny white seaside haven with varying room combos to suit everyone. Rooms are bright and cheery; the cheapest share bathrooms and kitchens, and dorm rooms are bunk-free. Ask about sleeping in the retro polished aluminium caravan ($175).

Arts Factory Lodge
HOSTEL, CAMPGROUND $

(☑02-6685 7709; www.artsfactory.com.au; Skinners Shoot Rd; camp sites $17, dm/d from $34/80; @☎) For an archetypal Byron experience, bunker down here. The complex has didgeridoo lessons and yoga and meditation workshops delivered in a serene hippie-esque setting on a picturesque swamp. Choose from colourful six- to 10-bed dorms, a cottage, tepees or wagons. Couples can opt for aptly titled 'cube' rooms, island retreat canvas huts (both $90) or the pricier love shack with bathroom ($100).

Nomads   HOSTEL $
(☑02-6680 7966; www.nomadsbyronbay.com. au; 1 Lawson Lane; dm/d $30/89; @⊚) Byron's newest backpackers packs an edgy punch with its glossy designer-led decor and funky furniture. It is purpose-built so the 10 dorm rooms are squeaky clean, but they're not half as good as the king rooms ($140), which have bathrooms, fridges and plasma televisions. It adjoins Global Gossip in the heart of town.

Beach Hotel Resort   RESORT $$$
(☑02-6685 6402; www.beachhotelresort.com. au; Bay St; r incl breakfast from $260; ✻⊛) In Byron's hub, this beachfront icon attracts a classy crowd slightly more reserved than that of the massive hotel beer garden next door. Ground-floor rooms open onto lush gardens and a heated pool where a family of lizards sunbakes; rooms in the upper storeys have ocean views.

Bamboo Cottage   GUESTHOUSE $$
(☑02-6685 5509; www.byron-bay.com/bamboo cottage; 76 Butler St; r from $99) Featuring global charm and wall hangings, Bamboo Cottage treats guests to a choice of three individually styled rooms with Asian overtones in a home-away-from-home atmosphere. It's on the quiet side of the tracks.

Rae's on Watego's   HOTEL $$$
(☑02-6685 5366; www.raes.com.au; Marine Pde; price on application; ✻@⊚⊛) This dazzlingly white Mediterranean villa was once rated one of the world's top 25 hotels. It's definitely one of Australia's. Rooms here have an artistic and casual elegance that lets the luxury sneak up on you. The restaurant (p183) is worth the trip alone.

Oasis Resort & Treetop
Houses   APARTMENTS $$
(☑1800 336 129, 02-6685 7390; www.byronbayoasisresort.com.au; 24 Scott St; apt/treetop apt from $190/325; ✻⊛) Away from the town centre, this compact resort is engulfed by palms and has apartments with big balconies. Even better are those sitting atop the tree canopies with outdoor spas and ocean views.

Aquarius   HOSTEL $
(☑02-6685 7663; www.aquarius-backpackers. com.au; 14-16 Lawson St; dm/d/motel d from

$35/100/200; ✻@⊛) This motel-style backpackers overflows with the comings and goings of hyperactive, excitable travellers. There's plenty of communal space – including a bar – ensuring those going it solo can find mates. Self-contained apartments also available (doubles from $140).

Amigos   GUESTHOUSE $$
(☑0417 732 244; www.amigosbb.com; 32 Kingsley St; s/d from $88/108) Soaked in south-of-the-border flavours, this cute TV-free B&B has three bedrooms with crisp white linen and South American spreads. The owners *habla espanole* (the author tries).

Bay Beach Motel   MOTEL $$
(☑02-6685 6090; www.baybeachmotel.com. au; 32 Lawson St; r $155-180, 2-bed apt from $235; ✻⊛) Unpretentious but smart, this white-brick hotel with IKEA-esque furnishings is close to town and the beach, but not so close that party-goers keep guests awake.

Byron Bayside Motel   APARTMENTS $
(☑02-6685 6004; www.byronbaysidemotel.com. au; 14 Middleton St; d/f from $89/109) These spotless but basic rooms have small kitchenettes and full laundries; ideal for campers looking for downtime.

Outrigger Bay Resort   APARTMENTS $$$
(☑02-6685 8646; www.outriggerbay.com; 9 Shirley St; 2-/3-bedroom apt $206/267; ✻⊚⊛) This apartment complex has one-, two- and three-bedroom units with open kitchens on a shady site overlooking a pool. The beach is only 50m away.

Belongil Beachouse   HOSTEL $
(☑02-6685 7868; www.belongilbeachouse. com; Childe St; dm/d/self-contained cottages from $28/70/160; @) Across from Belongil Beach. Excellent cabins, spartan studio units and comfortable dorms.

Main Beach Backpackers   HOSTEL $
(☑02-6685 8695; www.mainbeachbackpackers. com; cnr Lawson & Fletcher Sts; dm/d from $27/70; ✻@⊚⊛) Ninety-four beds near the beach and town centre.

Cape Byron YHA   HOSTEL $
(☑02-6685 8788, 1800 652 627; www.yha. com.au; cnr Middleton & Byron Sts; dm/d from $34/115; ✻@⊛) Modern, tidy, central.

Clarkes Beach Caravan
Park   CARAVAN PARK $
(☑02-6685 6496; www.northcoastparks.com.au/ clarkes; off Lighthouse Rd; unpowered sites/cabins from $38/125) Tightly packed cabins and sites in a bush setting.

DON'T MISS

NAPPING IN NATURE

Located right at the Byron Bay Lighthouse (p177), the historic 1901 **Lighthouse Keepers Cottages** (☑02-6685 6552; www.byronbaypro.com.au; 3-day rentals from $900) have been renovated with polished wood floors and lovely furnishings so that guests can spend the night here. The views are swell and you have the place to yourself after dusk. If you miss out on this one don't sweat it. There is a booty of similar gems hidden in national parks, state conservation areas and nature reserves along the coast. You can hole up in a lighthouse; get back to nature in a beachfront cottage or bunker down in a hinterland cabin. The NPWS website (www.environment.nsw.gov.au/NationalParks) is a wealth of info.

Hibiscus Motor Inn   MOTEL **$$**
(☑02-6685 6195; www.hibiscusmotel.com.au; 33 Lawson St; d $165; ☀) Basic but central, with friendly owners.

Waves   APARTMENTS **$$$**
(☑1800 040 151; www.wavesresorts.com.au; 35 Lawson St; d apt from $300; ☀☎) Cushy, central boutique penthouse and studio apartments.

Glen Villa Resort   CARAVAN PARK **$$**
(☑02-6685 7382; www.glenvillaresort.com.au; Butler St; d cabin from $120; ☀@☎) Slightly militant 'two people only' rule, but well maintained. It's off the main traffic route so is last to fill up.

Byron Motor Lodge   MOTEL **$$**
(☑02-6685 6522; www.byronmotorlodge. com; cnr Lawson & Butler Sts; s/d/tw/tr/f from $110/120/130/150/160; ☀☎) Low-key, low-rise 14-room motel in perfect shape.

✖ Eating

You can eat well in Byron; there's a huge range of choices and many are excellent. Where phone numbers are included, booking is recommended in peak times.

TOP CHOICE **St Elmo**   MEDITERRANEAN/BAR **$$**
(☑02-6680 7426; www.stelmodining.com; cnr Fletcher St & Lawson Lane; mains $18-28; ⊙lunch & dinner) Kartell stools nod to just how much design work it takes to get bums on seats. Sit on one to be served gourmet cocktails by extremely fit bronzed and accented barmen, or settle in for dinner; the shared plates ($23) make great date fodder.

Kinoko Sushi Bar   JAPANESE **$$**
(7/23 Jonson St; mains $7-25; ⊙lunch & dinner) Choo choo choose something from the sushi train or let the Japanese chef slice up a plate of fresh sashimi. This is a lively place where the Asahi also goes down well. It's also one of the last places open for dinner.

Balcony   MEDITERRANEAN **$$**
(☑02-6680 9666; www.balcony.com.au; cnr Lawson & Jonson Sts; dinner $9-39; ⊙breakfast, lunch & dinner; ☎) The eponymous architectural feature here wraps around the building and gives you tremendous views of the passing Byron parade and the always-clogged traffic circle. The food is Mediterranean fusion, with global influences. The drink list is long.

Petit Snail   FRENCH **$$$**
(☑02-6685 8526; www.thepetitsnail.com.au; 5 Carlyle St; mains $31-39; ⊙dinner) This intimate restaurant is off the main beat and is more Bordeaux than Byron. French staff serve up traditional red-, white-and-blue fare such as steak tartare, wild rabbit terrine, duck *confit* and lots of fromage. There's outdoor dining on the verandah.

Bay Leaf Café   MODERN AUSTRALIAN **$**
(Marvell St; mains $10-18; ⊙breakfast & lunch daily, dinner Thu-Sat) This tiny wedge-shaped bohemian cafe has a small but excellent menu prepared in a busy open kitchen. Best meal of the day is breakfast. That is, unless fresh homemade pasta takes your fancy.

Fishheads   SEAFOOD **$**
(www.fishheadsbyronbay.com.au; 1 Jonson St; mains $6-27; ⊙breakfast, lunch & dinner; ☎) Right on the beach, this fabulous takeaway shop sells traditional battered fish and chips ($12.50) or take it up a notch with grilled prawns and salad ($18). The restaurant is fine too, but why wouldn't you dine on the beach?

Orient Express   THAI, VIETNAMESE **$$**
(☑02-6680 8808; www.orientexpresseatery.com. au; 1/2 Fletcher St; mains $20-34; ⊙lunch Fri-Sun, dinner Tue-Sun) Easily mistaken for an Asian decorator's shop, or a teahouse, this is actually one of the best restaurants in Byron, helmed by Tippy Heng. The modern menu

here is fairly brief but, you guessed it, full of flavour. Expect to wait.

Orgasmic
MIDDLE EASTERN $

(11 Bay Lane; mains $8-19; ☺10am-10pm) Plop your bum on a cube cushion at this alley eatery that's one step above a stall. Takeaways include big mezze plates, ideal for quick picnics.

One One One
MEDITERRANEAN $$

(☑02-6680 7388; 1/111 Jonson St; mains $10-25; ☺breakfast & lunch daily, dinner Fri & Sat; ☎) HQ for slow-food devotees locally, the ingredients here celebrate regional produce. The menu is mostly vegetarian save for some superb spiced prawns and other seafood. Plates are good for sharing.

Earth 'n' Sea
ITALIAN $$

(www.earthnsea.com.au; cnr Fletcher & Byron Sts; mains $14-34; ☺lunch & dinner) The pizza list at this old favourite is long and full of flavour. Pasta is on the menu too. Beers include several excellent microbrews from the Northern Rivers Brewing Co.

Rae's on Watego's
MODERN AUSTRALIAN $$$

(☑02-6685 5366; www.raes.com.au; Marine Pde; mains $40-45; ☺lunch & dinner) Exquisite cuisine on a terrace with the sound of surf providing background noise to your witticisms. The menu changes daily but always surprises with its unconventional pairings of ingredients and spices. Book ahead.

Fresh
CAFE $$

(☑02-6685 7810; www.byronfresh.com.au; 7 Jonson St; meals $13-31; ☺breakfast, lunch & dinner) Top spot for breakfast with excellent pancakes. At night, sit at open-air tables and chow down on a menu running the gamut of light (salads) or heavy (braised beef cheek) dishes. People-watching is half the appeal.

Twisted Sista
BAKERY $

(shop 1, 4 Lawson St; mains $9-18; ☺breakfast & lunch) Bounteous baked goods include huge muffins, cheesy casseroles and overstuffed sandwiches on beautiful bread. Outdoor tables add to the slightly happy hungover vibe.

Mary Ryan's
CAFE/BOOKSHOP $

(www.maryryans.com.au; shop 5, 21-25 Fletcher St; mains $8-18) Snuggled up to the ABC bookshop, this literary cafe provides coffee drinkers with a caffeine high. Speaking of high, the ceilings are, leaving plenty of wall space for artworks.

Mongers
FISH AND CHIPS $

(www.byron-bay.com/mongers; Bay Lane; mains $10-20; ☺lunch & dinner) Tucked behind the Beach Hotel, this fish-and-chips joint issues forth to tables of devotees. It's a narrow, back-alley space but the quality is all high-street.

Espressohead
CAFE $

(shop 13, 108 Jonson St) Tucked away behind Woolworths; locals flock to this place for its excellent coffees. See if you can count the number of dodgy vans for sale on the bulletin board.

Byron Farmers Market
SELF-CATERING $

(www.byronfarmersmarket.com.au; Butler St Reserve; ☺8-11am Thu) An open-air temple to regional food.

Dip
MEDITERRANEAN $

(21 Fletcher St; tapas $6-18; ☺breakfast & lunch daily) Groovy bar with inspired menu.

Mokha
MEDITERRANEAN, MIDDLE EASTERN $

(Shop 2, Lawson St; mains $6-27; ☎) Eclectic Euro-Middle Eastern menu and lengthy wine list.

Lemongrass
VIETNAMESE $$

(Lawson Arcade, 3/17 Lawson St; mains $15-20; ☺dinner Mon-Sat) All your favourites: rice-paper rolls, beef *pho*, pawpaw salad.

Blue Olive
DELI $$

(27 Lawson St; ☺10am-5.30pm Tue-Sat, to 4pm Sun) Deli and shady pavement tables.

Engine Room
CAFE $

(shop 1, Lawson Lane) Hole-in-the-wall coffee place that opens early.

🍷 Drinking

Byron Bay's nightlife is varied and runs late. Check the gig guide in Thursday's *Byron Shire News* or tune into Bay 99.9 FM.

TOP CHOICE Balcony
BAR

(www.balcony.com.au; cnr Lawson & Jonson Sts; ☺8am-11pm) With its verandah poking out amid the palm trees, this fine bar-cum-restaurant is the place to park yourself. Choose from stools, chairs or sofas while working through a cocktail list that will make you giddy just looking at it.

Railway Friendly Bar
PUB

(Jonson St; ☺11am-late) This indoor-outdoor pub, aka 'The Rails', draws everyone from grey pensioners and lobster-red British tourists to acid-soaked hippies and high-on-life earth mothers. Its cosy interior is the old railway station. The front beer garden, conducive to boozy afternoons, has live music every night. The pub grub is excellent, so too the St Arnou beer on tap.

Great Northern PUB
(www.thenorthern.com.au; Byron St; ☺noon-late) You won't need your fancy duds at this brash and boisterous pub. It's loud and beery with live music most nights and even louder when hosting headline acts. Live music almost nightly. Soak up the booze with a wood-fired pizza.

Beach Hotel PUB
(www.beachhotel.com.au; cnr Jonson & Bay Sts; ☺11am-late) The mothership of all pubs is close to the main beach and is shot through with a fabulously infectious atmosphere that makes everyone your best mate. There's live music and DJs some nights.

St Elmo BAR
(www.stelmodining.com; cnr Fletcher St & Lawson Ln) Gourmet cocktails.

☆ Entertainment

Arts Factory Lounge Cinema CINEMA
(☑02-6685 5828; www.loungecinema.com; Skinners Shoot Rd; admission $9) The Arts Factory Lodge (p181) has a 135-seat cinema that shows classic reruns and art-house flicks nightly.

Byron Theatre CINEMA
(☑02-6685 6807; www.byroncentre.com.au; 69 Jonson St) A 350-seat theatre and cinema showcasing art-house and foreign films and directors.

Cocomangas NIGHTCLUB
(www.cocomangas.com.au; 32 Jonson St; ☺9pm-late) Byron's oldest club. Mondays is backpacker night.

Cheeky Monkeys NIGHTCLUB
(www.cheekymonkeys.com.au; 115 Jonson St; ☺7pm-3am) A backpackers bonanza – with wet T-shirt comps.

Shopping

You can while away hours away from the beach in Byron's many shops. Broadly speaking, Fletcher St, north of Marvell St, has artsy boutiques; frock shops hover around the Lawson and Fletcher Sts traffic circle; west of here and south on Jonson St you'll find a huge range – everything from lingerie to New Age hokum.

Planet Corroboree INDIGENOUS ART
(1/69 Jonson St) Huge range of Aboriginal art.

Happy High Herbs HERBS
(www.happyhighherbs.com; 1/5-7 Byron St) Herbs and natural remedies. Adults only.

Information

In addition to the resources listed here, the website www.byron-bay.com is helpful. The *Pink Guide* is a local publication aimed at gay and lesbian tourists; have a look at its useful website (www.byronbaypinkguide.blogspot.com).

Internet Access

Byron has many internet-access places that cram customers together in tight, sweaty little pods to stare at tiny screens. The Balcony and One One One restaurants have wi-fi.

Global Gossip (☑02-6680 9140; 84 Jonson St; per hr $8; @) Internet access.

Laundry

Coin Laundry (cnr Jonson & Marvell Sts; ☺7am-7pm)

Medical Services

Bay Centre Medical Clinic (☑02-6685 6206; www.byronmed.com.au; 6 Lawson St; ☺8am-5pm Mon-Thu, to 5.30pm Fri, to noon Sat) Full-service general surgery.

Byron Bay Hospital (☑02-6639 6699; www.ncahs.nsw.gov.au; cnr Wordsworth & Shirley Sts; ☺24hr) For medical emergencies.

ChemCoast Pharmacy (☑02-6685 6274; 20 Jonson St; ☺8am-8pm)

Money

Byron Foreign Exchange (Central Arcade, 4/47 Byron St; @) Foreign exchange, cash and money transfers, internet access.

Tourist Information

Backpackers World (☑02-6685 8858; www.backpackersworld.com.au; shop 6, 75 Jonson St) Primarily a travel agent.

Byron Bus & Backpacker Centre (☑02-6685 5517; 84 Jonson St; ☺7.30am-7pm) Next to the coach stop; handles bus, train, accommodation and activity bookings. Has left-luggage lockers ($6).

Byron Environmental Centre (www.byron environmentcentre.asn.au; Mullumbimby Railway Station, 2 Prince St, Mullumbimby) The hours are highly sporadic but the passions of these local environmentalists are not.

Visitors centre (☑02-6680 9279; www.visitby ronbay.com; Stationmaster's Cottage, Jonson St) Ground zero for tourist information (and when it's busy this cramped office feels like it).

❶ Getting There & Away

Air

The closest airport is at Ballina and with its rapidly expanding service it is the best airport for Byron. It also has shuttle services and hire cars for Byron travellers.

Coolangatta airport on the Gold Coast has a greater range of services but can involve a traffic-clogged drive. **Byron Bay Shuttle** (www.byronbayshuttle.com.au) serves both Coolangatta ($37) and Ballina ($15) airports.

Bus

Long-distance buses for **Greyhound** (☑1300 GREYHOUND/1300 4739 46863; www.greyhound.com.au) and **Premier** (☑13 34 10; www.premierms.com.au) stop on Jonson St. Approximate times and fares for both are as follows: Brisbane ($30, 2¾ hours), Coffs Harbour ($50, 5¼ hours) and Sydney (friom $85, 12 to 14 hours). Services operate several times daily. Check the boards at the bus stop for other Queensland options.

Blanch's Bus Service (☑02-6686 2144; www.blanchs.com.au) operates several daily services from the airport to Lennox Head ($6, 25 minutes), Ballina (Tamar St stop, $10, 40 minutes) and Mullumbimby ($10, 35 minutes).

Train

People still mourn the loss of the popular CountryLink train service from Sydney. In fact a popular movie released in 2008, *Derailed*, documents this transport travesty. **CountryLink** (☑13 22 32; www.countrylink.info) has buses connecting to trains at the Casino train station (70 minutes). Get full details from the rather forlorn **train station** (◷10am-4pm Mon-Fri).

❶ Getting Around

Byron Bay Bicycles (☑02-6685 6067; The Plaza, 85 Jonson St) Hires mountain bikes for $28 per day.

Byron Bay RentaCar (☑02-6685 5517; 84 Jonson St) Rents a wide range of vehicles.

Byron Bay Taxis (☑02-6685 5008; www.byronbaytaxis.com.au) On call 24 hours.

Earth Car Rentals (☑02-6685 7472; www.earthcar.com.au; 3a/1 Byron St) 'Australia's first carbon-neutral car rentals'.

Hertz (☑02-6621 8855; 5 Marvell St) Ask about one-way rentals to Ballina airport.

FAR NORTH COAST HINTERLAND

Beach bums and surfers might not credit it, but there are people who not so secretly regard the hinterland – as opposed to Byron Bay – as the jewel in the Far North Coast crown.

Just minutes from Byron, the greener-than-green undulating landscape is a crocheted rug of lush rainforest, pastoral lands, striped orchards and stands of eucalypt, all navigable via pretty winding roads.

Characteristic towns hide in among the foliage offering an eclectic take on small-town life. The hippie haven of Nimbin is the most popular, but towns such as Bangalow, with its esteemed boutiques and gourmet restaurants, exemplify the trend for combining the laid-back lifestyle of the country with the cultural idiosyncrasies and creature comforts of the big smoke.

The hinterland also boasts the Border Ranges, Wollumbin (which now includes former Mt Warning National Park) and Nightcap National Parks, which form part of the World Heritage–listed rainforests of the Central Eastern Rainforest Reserves. With a combined total of 43,926 hectares, the parks are a haven for walking and camping, and a bounty of Aboriginal history and culture.

Bangalow

POP 1330

Boutiques, fine eateries, bookshops and an excellent pub – a mere 14km from Byron Bay. Beautiful Bangalow, with its character-laden main street, is the kind of place that turns Sydneysiders into tree-changers.

There's a good weekly farmers market (Byron St; ◷8-11am Sat) and a praised cooking school (☑02-6687 2799; www.bangalowcooking school.com).

Stately old Riverview Guesthouse (☑02-6687 1317; www.riverviewguesthouse.com.au; 99 Byron St; tw/d from $150/195) sits on the river's edge ensuring guests see platypuses and oversized lizards as they take on breakfast. It's the stuff of B&B dreams.

About 4km north, Possum Creek Eco Lodge (☑02-687 1188; www.possumcreeklodge.com.au; Cedarvale Rd; bungalows from $198; ☒) has views across the lush valleys. The 'eco' in the name is not green-washing – water is recycled, stored from rain and otherwise conserved. Power is partially solar.

Located at Bangalow Hotel, Bangalow Dining Rooms (www.bangalowdining.com; Byron St; mains $15-32; ◷lunch & dinner) is a classy place with just the right amount of cool. Reserve a table in the dining room or sit on the deck and order from the cheaper menu; gourmet burgers and the like.

WORTH A TRIP

TWEED HEADS

The Pacific Hwy continues north to the Queensland border at Tweed Heads. If it's a leisurely pace you're after take a detour through the towns of **Mullumbimby** ('Mullum'; population 3655) and **Brunswick Heads** (population 1614). The former is a serene coast-hinterland hybrid with lazy palms, typical tropical architecture and a cosmopolitan spread of cafes, bistros and pubs. One of the goodies is **Milk & Honey** (☑02-6684 1422; 59a Station St; mains $14-22; ⊙dinner Mon-Sat), an artisan pizza joint. Lines form early for the tables inside and out. Walk it off on a trail along the Brunswick River in town that passes through tropical forest and is lined with signs relating Aboriginal stories. The **Mullum Music Festival** (www.mullummusicfestival.com), at the end of November, is prime time to visit.

Only slightly north of Mullum on the Old Pacific Hwy, beautiful Brunswick Heads reaps a bounty of fresh oysters and mud crabs from its peaceful Brunswick River inlets and beaches. The 1940s **Hotel Brunswick** (☑02-6685 1236; www.hotelbrunswick.com.au; Mullumbimby St; s/d/f $55/85/110) is a sight to behold and a destination unto itself with a magnificent beer garden that unfurls beneath flourishing poincianas. It has decent pub rooms and there's live music on weekends. Similarly laudable but easy to miss in a daggie motel, **FatBellyKat** (☑02-6685 1100; www.fatbellykat.com; 26 Tweed St; mezze plates $4-26; ⊙dinner Wed-Mon) is a celebrated Greek restaurant that brings feta-fetishists and dolmade-adorers from afar.

Tweed Heads (population 51,788) marks the southern end of the Gold Coast strip. Before you cross into the 'Sunshine State' check out the **Minjungbal Aboriginal Cultural Centre** (☑02-5524 2109; cnr Kirkwood & Duffy Sts; ⊙9am-4pm Mon-Fri), set in a grove of old gum trees on the Tweed River. There's a Walk on Water Track and **boardwalk** through the mangroves.

Ate (☑02-6687 1010; www.ate.net.au; 33 Byron St; mains $23-36; ⊙breakfast & lunch) is great for sipping coffee on the verandah or dining in for inventive dishes. Upstairs, **Satiate** (degustation from $75; ⊙dinner Tue-Sat) does a designer set menu with seasonal local produce. Book ahead.

The interior at **Utopia** (☑02-6687 2088; 13 Byron St; meals $13-30; ⊙breakfast & lunch daily, dinner Fri & Sat; ✸) is like the foam on a rich latte. The long narrow space is open and airy; piles of stylish magazines provide diversions. Desserts are to die for.

Urban Café (37 Byron St; mains $10-25; ⊙breakfast & lunch), a haven for the hungry, changes its stripes at night to become **Bang Thai** (☑02-6687 2000; mains $20-32; ⊙dinner Thu-Sat), with all the faves including Mussuman curry.

Blanch's Bus Service (☑02-6686 2144; www.blanchs.com.au) operates a service to Ballina ($8) and Byron Bay ($7).

Lismore

POP 27,070

Lismore, the hinterland's commercial centre, appears to have been dropped into its green surroundings without ruffling the feathers of the pristine hinterland. The town itself sits on the Wilson River, though it has yet to take advantage of this, and is otherwise beautified by a liberal supply of heritage and art-deco buildings, and a thriving artistic community. Students from Southern Cross University add to the town's eclecticism.

◉ Sights & Activities

The diminutive **Lismore Regional Art Gallery** (www.lismoregallery.com.au; 131 Molesworth St; admission by donation; ⊙10am-4pm Tue-Sat, to 6pm Thu) has just enough space for two visiting exhibitions, but they're excellent.

The worthy **Koala Care Centre** (Range Rd; per person/family $5/10; ⊙tours 10am & 2pm Mon-Fri, 10am Sat) is home to recovering koalas. To get a glimpse of platypuses, head to the northern end of Kadina St and walk up to **Tucki Tucki Creek** at dawn or sunset. You can also spot fuzzy grey bums-in-the-gums at **Robinson's Lookout** (Robinson's Ave, Girards Hill).

Wilson River walking track starts in the CBD and skirts the river. Along the way you'll pass a **bush-tucker garden**, nurturing the once daily diet of the Widjabal people, the traditional owners of the land.

More than a half-dozen used book stores are within a block of the intersection of Carrington and Magellan Sts. Typical is Noahs Arc (66 Magellan St), which has a large selection in a heritage building.

The farmers market (⊗8-11am Sat) and Organic Market (⊗8-11am Tue) are held at the showground, off Nimbin Rd.

🛏 Sleeping

Lismore is not a motel mecca. Most people stay in the hinterland's villages or closer to the coast.

Lismore Palms CARAVAN PARK $
(☑02-6621 7067; 42 Brunswick St; camp sites/ cabins from $20/70; ⊛) The best of Lismore's caravan parks, this one is right on the river and has 13 self-contained cabins.

Karinga MOTEL $$
(☑02-6621 2787; www.karingamotel.com; 258 Molesworth St; s/d $95/105; ⊛@⊛) The pick of the litter, the Karinga has had a tasteful facelift: the rooms have been fully refurbished and a funky pool and spa installed.

🍴 Eating

Blue Tongue CAFE $
(43 Bridge St; mains $8-19; ⊗breakfast & lunch) One of a couple of worthy cafes on the quieter side of the river, this one is in a wonderfully worn building. Great BLATs, toasted Turkish sandwiches and fine coffee can be enjoyed in a sunny courtyard out the back.

Mecca CAFE, BAR $
(http://meccacafe.com.au/; 80 Magellan St; meals $8-16; ⊗7am-5pm Mon-Wed, to late Thu-Sat) A stodgy old caff has been reborn as a retro-hip scenester playground. Lots of local musicians hang out at the pavement tables sipping the excellent coffee by day and jamming till late weekend nights.

TOP CHOICE Howard's CAFE, DELI $
(106 Keen St; www.howardsdeli.com.au; mains $8-20; ⊗breakfast & lunch) Go no further than this deli-cum-cafe-cum-butchery, a *Babette's Feast* of wholesome salads, meaty lasagnes and hearty frittatas. For picnics: gourmet chutney, oil and coffee. For camping: house-made snags.

Lismore Pie Cart FAST FOOD $
(11 Magellan St; ⊗6am-5pm Mon-Fri) Serves homemade pies, mash, mushy peas and gravy.

Goanna Bakery & Café CAFE $
(www.goannabakery.com.au; 171 Keen St; mains $6-10; ⊗breakfast & lunch Mon-Sat) House-roasted coffee, veggie meals at tables inside or out.

ℹ Information

The **Lismore visitor centre** (☑1300 369 795; www.visitlismore.com.au; cnr Molesworth & Ballina Sts) has internet ($6 per hour) and a rainforest display ($1) and local Indigenonus art. Kids dig the Heritage Park playground and skate park, next to the centre.

ℹ Getting There & Away

Lismore may well have the most helpful transit centre in NSW. It's right on Molesworth St by the gallery.

Kirklands (☑02-6622 1499; www.kirklands. com.au) runs to Byron Bay ($15, 50 minutes, two to three times daily). **Waller's** (☑02-6687 8550) school buses run to Nimbin ($10, 70 minutes).

Nimbin

POP 350

A trip in Nimbin, or rather, a trip *to* Nimbin – is, erm, *high*-ly recommended for anyone visiting the Far North Coast. Wordplays aside, this strange little place, a hangover from an experimental 'Aquarius Festival' in the '70s, still feels like a social experiment where anything goes. Reefers included. But it's not all dreadlocks and tie-dye, or, for that matter, tourists. A day or two here will reveal there's a growing artist community, a New Age culture and welcoming locals.

◉ Sights & Activities

Despite the reticence of many locals to be pinned down on exact opening times, for fear of ruining Nimbin's image, generally everything is open 10am to 5pm. Every third and fifth Sunday, Nimbin has its own **market** (Nimbin Community Centre; ⊗8am-4pm), a spectacular affair of produce and art where locals revel in their culture. There's live music.

There's talk of a **skate park** being built in town.

Hemp Embassy NOVELTY SHOP
(www.hempembassy.net; 51 Cullen St) This place raises consciousness about marijuana legalisation, as well as providing all the tools and fashion items you'll need to get high (or at least attract more police raids). The embassy

leads the Mardi Gras festival each May. Smokers are welcome at the tiny Hemp Bar next door, which is like Haight-Ashbury in a bottle.

Nimbin Candle Factory CANDLE SHOP
(www.nimbincandles.com.au) Just 400m down the hill from town and off the Murwillumbah road, the Old Butter Factory incubates a number of little businesses, including the candle factory where thousands of hand-dipped paraffin candles are on display.

Nimbin Museum & Café MUSEUM
(www.nimbinmuseum.com; 62 Cullen St) An interpretive and expressionistic museum that packs an eclectic collection of local art into a modest space. It's far more a work of art than of history.

Nimbin Artists Gallery GALLERY
(47 Cullen St; ☺10am-4pm) There are even more artists than pot dealers and you can find their work on display here.

🛏 Sleeping

Given that some locals would have a hard time answering the question: 'Which came first, Nimbin or the organic farms?', it shouldn't surprise that there are nearly 100 local farms more than happy to host volunteers willing to yank weeds and perform other chores. The international Willing Workers on Organic Farms (www.wwoof.com.au) coordinates many such programs.

Nimbin Rox YHA Hostel HOTEL $
(☎02-6689 0022; www.nimbinrox.com; 74 Thornburn St; camp sites $10, dm/d from $28/60; @☀) Rox has hammocks, permaculture gardens, craft workshops, live bands, Thai massage, yurts ($72), tepees (per person $25) and camping and a heated pool. Check out the website, a trip in itself.

Rainbow Retreat Backpackers HOSTEL $
(☎02-6689 1262; www.rainbowretreat.net; 75 Thorburn St; camp sites/dm $10/20, d from $40) Very basic, but totally in the age-of-Aquarius spirit. Relax, chill out, sleep in a shack ($30), gypsy van ($30 to $50) or camp out. There's a free courtesy bus from Byron Bay.

Black Sheep Farm GUESTHOUSE $$
(☎02-6689 1095; www.blacksheepfarm.com.au; d $195; ☀) With a saltwater pool and Finnish sauna, guests might struggle to leave the self-contained cabin on the edge of a rainforest near Nightcap National Park. It sleeps up to seven people (per extra person $20).

There's also a smaller and cheaper cottage available.

Nimbin Hotel & Backpackers PUB $
(☎02-6689 1246; www.nimbinhotelandbackpackers.com; 53 Cullen St; dm/d $30/60 @) The two- and four-bed rooms in the town's veteran pub are tidy and open onto the classic shaded verandah.

🍴 Eating & Drinking

A number of coffee places tenuously exist along the pavement.

Nimbin Hotel MODERN AUSTRALIAN $
(☎02-6689 1246; Cullen St; meals $7-15; ☺lunch & dinner) The classic local boozer. A vast covered porch out back overlooks a verdant valley. Inside, artistic photos of regulars grace the walls and there's actually a slight hint of minimalist style. The fare is typical pub grub; there's live music many Friday nights.

Rainbow Café CAFE $
(☎02-6689 1997; 64a Cullen St; mains $6-13; ☺breakfast & lunch) Murals cover the walls of this thumping Nimbim institution serving generous burgers, wraps, nachos and salads. The leafy courtyard has a familiar whiff.

Nimbin Trattoria & Pizzeria ITALIAN $$
(☎02-6689 1427; 70 Cullen St; mains $10-20; ☺lunch Fri-Sun, dinner daily) You'll find outstanding pizzas ($3 a slice or $8 for three) and delicious pastas here plus live music every Thursday.

ⓘ Information

Visitor centre (☎02-6689 1388; Cullen St) Has great local info.

ⓘ Getting There & Away

The **Nimbin Tours & Shuttle Bus** (☎02-6680 9189; www.nimbinaustralia.com/nimbin-shuttle/nimbin.html) runs between Byron Bay, Nimbin and Uki with optional stops at Wollumbin-Mt Warning. The bus leaves from the visitor centre.

Several outfits run shuttles and tours for day trippers from Byron Bay; some include stops in the region.

Waller's (☎02-6687 8550; www.nimbingoodtimes.com) For a traditional trip (as it were), Waller's runs school buses to Lismore, Uki, Murwillumbah and the Wollumbin-Mt Warning turn-off.

Murwillumbah

POP 7950

Murwillumbah is gleefully free of precociousness. Sitting calmly, as it does, on the banks of the Tweed River, it's a great base for exploring the river country, Wollumbin-Mt Warning National Park and the surrounding NSW-Queensland Border Ranges. The town, an agricultural focal point for the region, is old school with a charming main street and hills flanked with heritage facades. Views of Wollumbin-Mt Warning peek around every corner.

Sights

Tropical Fruit World GARDEN
(☎02-6677 7222; www.tropicalfruitworld.com.au; Duranbah Rd; adult/child $37/20; ⏰10am-4.30pm) Just north of town, this place allegedly has the world's largest collection of tropical fruit, along with plantation safaris, tastings and a jungle cruise. Plan for at least half a day to make the most of the pricey entry.

FREE **Tweed River Regional Art Gallery** ART GALLERY
(www.tweed.nsw.gov.au/artgallery; cnr Mistral Rd & Tweed Valley Way; ⏰10am-5pm Wed-Sun) This exceptional gallery is an architectural delight, home to some of Australia's finest in a variety of media.

Murwillumbah Museum MUSEUM
(☎02-6672 1865; 2 Queensland Rd; adult/child $2/1.50; ⏰11am-3pm Wed-Fri & 4th Sun of month) This small museum is housed in a beautiful old building and features a solid account of local history and an interesting radio room.

Sleeping & Eating

Mount Warning-Murwillumbah YHA HOSTEL $
(☎02-6672 3763; www.yha.com.au; 1 Tumbulgum Rd; dm/d from $32/70) This former river captain's home now houses a colourful waterfront hostel with eight-bed dorms. There's free ice cream at night plus canoe and bike hire. Tours to Mt Warning are reason enough to bunk down here.

Murwillumbah Motor Inn MOTEL $$
(☎02-6672 2022; www.murwillumbahmotorinn.com.au; 17 Byangum Rd; s/d $96/106; ❄@≋) These clean and comfortable rooms are a great option away from the town centre. The deluxe rooms have flat-screen televisions. There's a pleasant courtyard out the back.

Sugar Beat CAFE $
(☎02-6672 2330; Shop 2, 6-8 Commercial Rd; mains $15; ⏰breakfast & lunch Mon-Sat) Park yourself by the sunny window, settle into a corner of the long bench seating or take in the scene from one of the pavement tables. There's cafe-style fusion fare and locally famous baked goods.

Modern Grocer DELI $$
(☎02-6672 5007; shop 3, 1 Wollumbin St; ⏰Tue-Sat) A foodie haven to turn everyday picnics into gluttonous feasts.

New Leaf Café VEGETARIAN $
(☎02-6672 2667; shop 10, Murwillumbah Plaza; meals $5-18; ⏰breakfast & lunch) The food here is creative and vegetarian, with plenty of Middle Eastern flavours and salads on offer. Dine inside, alfresco, or take away.

Information

Murwillumbah visitor centre (☎02-6672 1340; www.tweedcoolangatta.com.au; cnr Alma St & Tweed Valley Way) Has national park info.

Getting There & Away

Greyhound (☎1300 GREYHOUND/1300 4739 46863; www.greyhound.com.au) and **Premier** (☎13 34 10; www.premierms.com.au) have services several times daily on the Sydney ($92, 14 hours) and Brisbane ($27, two hours) route.

Waller's (☎02-6622 6266) has school-day buses to Nimbin (one hour) and Lismore.

NEW ENGLAND

New England misses out on the kind of exposure Australia's desert landscapes and vast coastlines attract, but the area's rolling green hills and farmland, autumnal foliage and vast tracts of bushland are at least as worthy of exploration.

The verdant scenery prompted the original settlers to name the area New England in 1839. In the northern 'highlands' especially, images of Britain still raise their head. Mist settles in the cool-climate hilltops and valleys, little churches sit in oak-studded paddocks and winding roads navigate impossibly green landscapes.

Curiously some of the small country towns along the New England Hwy, the region's main thoroughfare, show signs that this nostalgia might verge on obsession.

The bigger towns of Tamworth and Armidale, though resplendent with heritage architecture, are less enamoured with their past, more focused on a future that can draw tourists.

The region has a string of national parks including Bald Rock and Washpool National Parks in the north. On the Waterfall Way linking Armidale and Coffs Harbour, Guy Fawkes River, Cathedral Rock, New England and Oxley Wild Rivers National Parks feature granite outcrops, unforgettably deep gorges and waterfalls.

On the Fossickers Way, north of Tamworth, you'll need to get out the shovel and dig a little deeper, as each town carries its own signature gem.

Tamworth

POP 33,480

Country music kicks this town along like a line of boot-scooters but only for a couple of weeks a year. At other times don't expect much more than a regional town can offer: a marvellously tree-filled main street, an agricultural scene and country music. The wine scene is emerging but the food and cafe culture lags behind.

For live country music, check Thursday's *Northern Daily Leader*. Dress codes are stricter in Tamworth than elsewhere in the region.

◎ Sights & Activities

Australian Country Music Foundation   MUSEUM
(www.acmf.org.au; 93 Brisbane St; adult/child $6/4; ⊙10am-4pm Mon-Fri, to 2pm Sat) If the names Tex Morton, Buddy Williams and Smoky Dawson mean anything to you, then this will too. This is a country-music great Hall of Fame (in the making) with photographs, historic video and film footage, music and souvenirs.

Big Golden Guitar Tourist Centre   MUSEUM
(☑02-6765 2688; www.biggoldenguitar.com.au; New England Hwy) This info hub has a cafe and a shop where you can stock up on all-important golden-guitar snow cones. When you've finished, check out the Wax Museum (adult/child $10/4).

Oxley Scenic Lookout   LANDMARK
(Scenic Rd) Grab a bottle of wine and follow jacaranda-lined White St to the very top, where you'll reach this viewpoint. It is the best seat in the house as the sun goes down over Tamworth and the surrounding Liverpool Ranges.

Tamworth Regional Gallery   ART GALLERY
(www.tamworthregionalgallery.com.au; 466 Peel St; ⊙10am-5pm Tue-Fri, to 4pm Sat) In purpose-built premises next to the library, the gallery has some interesting local bequeaths and more modern roving exhibitions.

FREE **Oxley Marsupial Park**   ZOO
(Endeavour Dr; ⊙8am-4.45pm) Overfriendly cockatoos and other native animals live here alongside barbecues and picnic shelters. The park joins the Kamilaroi walking track.

Leconfield Jackaroo & Jillaroo School   FARMING
(☑02-6769 4328; 'Bimboola', Kootingal; www.leconfield.com; 5-day course $625) Keen on mustering, milking, shearing and shoeing? This school will have you sorting the cowboys from the girls' blouses in no time.

☆ Festivals & Events

Held at the end of January, New England's biggest annual party, the Country Music Festival, lasts 10 days. There are over 800 acts, of which 75% are free. If you missed it, get along to Hats Off to Country Music in July.

⎓ Sleeping

Unless you book years in advance, you'll be lucky to find a bed or camp site during the festival when prices skyrocket. However, the council makes large areas of river land available to campers, where it's rough and rowdy but fun.

Quality Hotel Powerhouse   HOTEL $$
(☑02-6766 7000, www.qualityhotelpowerhouse.com.au; New England Hwy; r from $185; ❋🐾🎧🕸) Mod cons and a flash restaurant called Monty's, open Tuesday to Saturday.

Tamworth YHA   HOSTEL $
(☑02-6761 2600; www.yha.com.au; 169 Marius St; dm/d $28/64.50; ❋@) On a busy street but neat as a pin. Contacts for Jackaroo & Jillaroo School (this page).

Austin Tourist Park   CARAVAN PARK $
(☑1800 826 967, 02-6766 2380; www.austintouristpark.com.au; 581 Armidale Rd; unpowered/powered sites $21/36, cabins $65-140; ❋🕸)

✕ Eating

Tamworth Hotel
PUB $

(☑02-6766 2923; 147 Marius St; mains $8-34) Heritage colours and a 1930s design make this one of Tamworth's more aesthetically pleasing pubs. Choose from a formal dining area with white tablecloths and shiny glasses, or cook your own meat in the bistro/brasserie. There's a great rear courtyard the kids will love. There are basic pub rooms upstairs (s/d $40/50).

Sleepy Monkey
CAFE $$

(www.thesleepymonkey.com; 403 Peel St; mains $16-19; ☺breakfast & lunch) A rather plain exterior belies the fun interior of this excellent food and coffee option. The menu is a cut above, with wagyu burgers and Vietnamese prawn salads, or just sip on a wine while flicking through magazines and newspapers on a long communal table. Call ahead for occasional dinners.

ℹ Information

To get into the string of things, drop into the guitar-shaped **visitor centre** (☑02-6767 5300; www.visittamworth.com.au; cnr Peel & Murray Sts) and check out the Walk a Country Mile Museum.

ℹ Getting There & Around

Qantas (☑13 13 13; www.qantas.com.au) flies to Sydney ($105, one hour).

Greyhound (☑1300 GREYHOUND/1300 4739 46863; www.greyhound.com.au) has daily services along the New England Hwy to Armidale ($47, 1½ hours) and through to Sydney ($40, 6½ hours). **Keans** (☑1800 043 339) runs to Coffs Harbour, Port Macquarie and south to Scone once a week. **CountryLink** (☑13 22 32; www.countrylink.info) runs daily to Armidale ($14, two hours) and Sydney ($59, 6¼ hours).

Tamworth Buslines (☑02-6762 3999; www.tamworthbuslines.com.au) operates extensively throughout town; stops are obvious.

Armidale

POP 19,490

Armidale's heritage buildings, gardens and moss-covered churches look like the stage set for a period drama. This olde-worlde scenery coupled with spectacular autumn foliage plays a big part in attracting people to this regional centre blessed with some of Australia's best grazing country. It also boasts private schools and the New England University, recession-proof institutions that attract professionals and ensure arts and culture prosper. Excellent delis and coffee shops point to a food scene worthy of exploring, too.

◎ Sights & Activities

There are some elegant old buildings around the town centre. Pick up the heritage-walking-tour pamphlet from the visitor centre.

New England Regional Art Museum
MUSEUM

(www.neram.com.au; Kentucky St; ☺10am-5pm Tue-Fri, to 4pm Sat & Sun) At the southern edge of town, 'Neram' has a sizeable permanent collection and good contemporary exhibitions in pleasant grounds. It also houses the **Museum of Printing** (☺10am-3pm Wed-Fri, to 4pm Sat & Sun), a cafe and souvenir shop.

Aboriginal Cultural Centre & Keeping Place
ART GALLERY

(www.acckp.com.au; 128 Kentucky St; art exhibits $2-5; ☺9am-4pm Mon-Fri, 10am-2pm Sat) Next door, this place will broaden your perception of Indigenous art, and enable the kids to make their own with the help of a resident artist.

Heritage Bus Tours
TOURING

(☑1800 627 736; ☺10am) Free tours of Armidale depart from the visitor centre; bookings essential. Better still, get on a bike from the Armidale Bicycle Centre (p191).

⌂ Sleeping

There are motels around the visitor centre and on Barney St. Head out of town on the Glen Innes Rd to find doubles under $70.

TOP CHOICE Petersons Guesthouse
GUESTHOUSE $$$

(☑02-6772 0422; www.petersonsguesthouse.com.au; Dangarsleigh Rd; r from $200; ❂) Beautifully restored to its former British opulence, this grand old estate has seven suites with period bathrooms and gorgeous antique furniture. The hosts wine and dine their guests fireside without impinging on privacy. Enjoy lunch under the trees at the weekends ($17).

Lindsay House
B&B $$

(☑02-6771 4554; www.lindsayhouse.com.au; 128 Faulkner St; s $140-190, d $140-$220, all incl breakfast; @) Immerse yourself in a past when beds were four-poster, ceilings were ornate, furniture was beautifully crafted and port was served in the evening. This lovely old home is as restful and recuperative as it is grand.

THE FOSSICKERS WAY

You're now heading into gemstone territory. This scenic route (www.fossickersway.com) begins about 60km southeast of Tamworth at Nundle and continues through Tamworth, 191km north to Warialda, then 124km east through Inverell to Glen Innes, 100km north of Armidale.

Nundle

This charming town (population 289) is coveted for its tranquil locale between the Great Dividing Range and Peel River. There is a mining museum, some cute little old wares shops and an intriguing **Woollen Mill** (1 Oakenville St; ⊙10am-4pm), one of only two in the country. Ask Nick for a tour. **Peel Inn** (☑02-6769 3377; www.peelinn.com.au; s $45-60, d $65-80) is an all-round great pub. Meals include delicious local trout. The **visitor centre** (☑02-6769 3026; www.nundle.info/nundle/) is on Jenkins St.

Manilla

Australia's **national paragliding championships** are held here in February. **Manilla Paragliding** (☑02-6785 6545; www.flymanilla.com) offers tandem flights. The town itself is a glimmer of its former glory, but the three remaining pubs stand defiantly on the main street. Grab your bait and licence from **North Manilla Store** just north of the bridge, before heading to **Lake Keepit** or north to **Warrabah National Park** (camp sites per adult/child $5/3) for the big bites. The **visitor centre** (☑02-6785 1207) is on Manilla St.

Barraba

Settled in the 1830s, Barraba, with its old wide streets and elegant awnings, was put on the map during the gold-feverish late 1800s. Travel 3km north, turn right onto Woodsreef Rd and you will come to **Ironbark Goldfield and Woodsreef Reserve**, where you too can use a shovel, pick and pan. **Millie's Park Vineyard**, also north of town, has wines, a barbecue and a nature walk. Drop-ins are welcome at **Andy's Backpackers** (☑02-6782 1916; www.andysbackpackers.com.au; 98 Queen St; dm $25; @), whether for a bed, meal, game of chess (Friday nights) or just a chat. Drop a few dollars on the counter and help yourself to a cold stubby! The **visitor centre** (☑02-6782 1255; www.barraba.org; 116 Queen St) has fossicking info.

Armidale Pines Motel MOTEL $$
(☑02-6772 0625; www.armidalepinesmotel.com; 141 Marsh St; r from $135; ❋❄) Slap bang in the middle of town, this spick-and-span motel has fresh decor with a contemporary colour scheme. Long-haulers will appreciate the kitchenettes and shared guest laundry.

Pembroke Tourist & Leisure Park & YHA HOSTEL $
(☑02-6772 6470; www.pembroke.com.au, www.yha.com.au; 39 Waterfall Way; unpowered/powered sites $23/28, dm $31.50, cabins $64-120; @❄) Friendly and leafy with a hostel wing.

🍴 Eating & Drinking

TOP CHOICE Goldfish Bowl BAKERY, CAFE $
(Jessie St; mains $10-17; ⊙breakfast & lunch) This popular spot is in addition to the original and truly excellent Dangar St coffee haunt. It has indoor and outdoor tables and some menu surprises such as snails in mushrooms caps with Pernod and hazelnut butter.

TOP CHOICE Bistro on Cinders EUROPEAN, ASIAN $$
(☑02-6772 4273; www.bistrooncinders.com; 14 Cinders Lane; mains $30; ⊙breakfast & lunch Mon-Sat, dinner Fri & Sat summer) Behind the post office, this plain brick building with a little courtyard houses a fantastic eatery. It's contemporary but not pretentious – have a quick coffee or sit around all night admiring the groovy chandeliers and artwork.

Bottega Café & Delicatezza CAFE, DELI $
(2/14 Moore St; mains $12-22; ⊙breakfast & lunch Tue-Sat) A haunt not just for foodies, but for hungries too. This cafe has tables and shelves stocked with gourmet produce and a deli full of charcuterie and cheese. Breakfast doesn't get much better.

Bingara

This small town straddling the Gwydir River is horse-riding country; try it at **Gwydir River Trail Rides** (☎02-6724 1562; www.gwydirrivertrailrides.com.au; 17 Keera St; 2hr trail ride $55, half-day canoe hire $30). For fair-dinkum Aussieness, complete the five-day Jackeroo/Jillaroo Adventure ($670). **Fossickers Way Motel** (☎02-6724 1373; www.bingaramotel.com.au; 2 Finch St; s/d $70/80; ✵) is one of the few hotels on the main road between Tamworth and Warialda. The **visitor centre** (☎02-6724 0066; www.bingara.com; 74 Maitland St) is in the Roxy Theatre, a Greek-influenced, refurnished art-deco cinema still used today. Ask about tours.

Warialda

Meaning 'place of wild honey'. Warialda was one of the earliest settled towns west of the Great Dividing Range. Quirky **Ceramic Break Sculpture Park** (☎02-6729 4147; www.cbreaksculpturepark.com.au) is 15km south of town. It has accommodation, sleeping six, in a basic but cute **cottage** (per night $50). The **visitor centre** (☎02-6729 0046; www.warialda nsw.com.au) is on the Gwydir Hwy.

Inverell

It might not be that aesthetically fabulous but its sapphires are. Pick up a fossicking map at the **visitor centre** (☎02-6728 8161; www.inverell.com.au; Campbell St) and sample olive oil at **Olives of Beaulieu** (439 Copeton Dam Rd; ⊙Wed-Sun). Built on an extinct volcano, **Blair Athol Estate B&B** (☎02-6722 4288; www.babs.com.au/blairathol; Warialda Rd; d from $130) has stunning grounds peppered with a rich mix of flora from Himalayan cedars to boabs.

Glen Innes

Businesses with names such as Glen This and Wee That hint at the Scottish heritage in Glen Innes (population 5944). The **visitor centre** (☎02-6730 2400; www.gleninnestourism.com) is on the New England Hwy and there are **standing stones** off the Gwydir Hwy. **Land of the Beardies History House** (www.beardieshistoryhouse.info; cnr West Ave & Ferguson St; ⊙10am-noon & 1-4pm Mon-Fri, 1-4pm Sat & Sun) fills an old hospital with eclectic artefacts. If you fancy saddling up, take a **pub crawl on horseback** (☎02-6732 1599; www.pubcrawlson horseback.com.au; Bullock Mountain Homestead; 2/4-day ride $395/1480, B&B s/d $45/80).

❶ Getting There & Around

The **visitor centre** (☎1800 627 736, 02-6772 3888; www.armidaletourism.com.au; 82 Marsh St) is at the bus station. The **library** (Faulkner St) has free internet.

❶ Getting There & Around

The airport is 5km southeast of town. **Qantas** (☎13 13 13; www.qantas.com.au) flies to Sydney ($105, 1¼ hours).

Greyhound (☎1300 GREYHOUND/1300 4739 46863; www.greyhound.com.au) runs to Glen Innes ($51, 1¼ hours), Tamworth ($47, 1½ hours) and Sydney ($55, eight hours). **Keans** (☎1800 043 339) runs to Coffs Harbour twice a week.

CountryLink (☎13 22 32; www.countrylink.info) runs daily to Tamworth ($14, two hours), Newcastle ($56, 5¾ hours) and Sydney ($66, 8¼ hours).

Edwards (☎02-6772 3116; www.edward-scoaches.com.au) runs a local bus service about town. For taxi services, call **Armidale Radio Taxis** (☎02-6771 1455). You can rent a bike from

Armidale Bicycle Centre (☎02-6772 3718; 244 Beardy St; per hr/day $5.50/22).

Around Armidale

The Caledonian-culture-consumed populace of Glen Innes (this page) is about 100km north on the New England Hwy.

Dramatic, forested and wild, **Gibraltar Range** and **Washpool National Parks** (per car per day $7) lie south and north of the Gwydir Hwy, about 80km east of Glen Innes on the road to Grafton. There are two camping areas; **Mulligans** (adult/child $10/5) is near Little Dandahra Creek, which is ideal for swimming. Of the many walks, the 100km **World Heritage Walk** is a standout.

About 66km west of Glen Innes is Inverell (this page). Further northwest, **Kwiambal National Park** (admission free), pronounced kigh-*am*-bal, sits at the junction of the Macintyre and Severn Rivers.

Largely undiscovered, it is an important conservation area for the tumbledown gum and Caley's ironbark.

Head east of Armidale on the road to Ebor to experience the beautiful Waterfall Way (p162) or south for a bit of bushranger history in Uralla.

Tenterfield & Around

POP 3130

At the junction of the New England and Bruxner Hwys, Tenterfield is the hub of a region boasting a smattering of characteristic villages and 10 national parks. In the town itself you can have fun wandering around historic buildings and getting an eyeful of Australia's oldest cork tree.

There is plenty of work fruit picking on farms near town from October through to May. To pick stone fruit, cherries, tomatoes and grapes, contact Barbara at **Tenterfield Lodge & Caravan Park** (☑02-6736 1477).

◉ Sights & Activities

Bald Rock National Park   NATURE RESERVE
(per car per day $7) About 29km northeast of Tenterfield, here you can hike to the top of Australia's largest exposed granite monolith (which looks like a stripy little Uluru) and camp (adult/child $10/5) near the base.

Richmond Range National Park   NATURE RESERVE
East of Tambulam, this 15,712-hectare park contains some of the best-preserved old-growth rainforest in NSW. It's part of a World Heritage–listed preserve showing off what this part of Australia looked like before settlement.

Tenterfield Saddler   LANDMARK/SHOP
(www.tenterfieldsaddler.com; 123 High St; ◷10am-4pm) Celebrated by Peter Allen (who was born here) in his eponymous song, the saddler is still open for business.

Thunderbolt's Hideout   LANDMARK
About 12km out on the road north to Lisbon, this is where bushranger Captain Thunderbolt did just that. On your way, check out the **Tenterfield Weather Rock** near the baths.

Kurrajong Downs Winery   WINE TASTING
(www.kurrajongdownswines.com; Kurrajong Downs Rd; ◷9am-4pm Thu-Mon) One of a handful of wineries in the district, Kurrajong has a restaurant and cellar door.

🛏 Sleeping & Eating

Deloraine B&B   B&B $
(☑02-6736 2777; 14 Clarence St; r from $95) Motels line Rouse St leading south out of town or try this characteristic old heritage roadhouse with some lovely antique-filled rooms. The owners – plus a resident kangaroo – are lovely and provide a cooked breakfast and tea and scones.

Tenterfield Lodge & Caravan Park   CARAVAN PARK $
(☑02-6736 1477; www.tenterfieldbiz.com/ten terfieldlodge; 2 Manners St; unpowered/powered sites $15/22, dm from $25, vans $45, cabins $55-70; ◉) This friendly place has a range of accommodation.

❶ Information

The **visitor centre** (☑02-6736 1082; www. tenterfieldtourism.com; 157 Rouse St) has bush-walking guides and can book tours to nearby national parks.

❶ Getting There & Away

Buses leave Tenterfield from the **Community Centre** (Manners St). **Greyhound** (☑1300 GREYHOUND/1300 4739 46863; www.grey hound.com.au) runs to Tamworth ($76, four hours) and Sydney ($123, 10½ hours). **Northern Rivers Buslines** (☑02-6626 1499; www. nrbuslines.com.au) has buses to Casino and Lismore ($34).

CountryLink (☑13 22 32; www.countrylink. info) buses run south to Glen Innes ($12, 1¼ hours), and to Armidale ($25, 2¾ hours) where you can change for Sydney ($66, 8¼ hours).

NORTHWEST

People tend to put pedal to the metal driving through this flat archetypal Australian landscape, possibly because they have Queensland beaches on their minds.

The Newell Hwy (Rte 39), the through-route from Victoria, passes through stargazing Coonabarabran, the cotton-picking centre of Narrabri, and the burgeoning Aboriginal art hub of Moree, before hitting the border at Goondiwindi. The roads in between are flanked by crops of cotton, canola and, increasingly, olive groves, offering a glimpse of an arid landscape worked for its agricultural rewards.

If Queensland isn't on the itinerary, chances are Lightning Ridge is. Like other

Australian mining communities, the town throws up as many characters as it does gems.

West of Coonabarabran, Warrumbungle National Park is one of the most popular in NSW with camping, walking, stargazing and a wealth of Aboriginal culture and history. Similarly, Moree has some intriguing Aboriginal sites, largely undiscovered by tourists. You'll have to be adventurous or curious to track them down.

Castlereagh Highway

The Castlereagh Hwy (Rte 55) forks off the Oxley Hwy at pretty Gilgandra then runs to the Queensland border through Walgett, Coonamble and the rugged opal country of Lightning Ridge.

Just north of Gilgandra, pull off the highway at the spot where, in 1818, John Oxley spat the dummy. Expecting to find a giant inland sea, he instead discovered that the Macquarie River petered out into a boggy marsh. The town was also the starting point for the Coo-ee March, a WWI recruiting drive to Sydney, led by a butcher and his brother.

West of here, the prolific bird life of 19,824-hectare Macquarie Marshes Nature Reserve is best seen during breeding season (usually spring, but it varies with water levels).

LIGHTNING RIDGE
POP 2750

Know what a 'ratter', a 'rough' and a 'blower' are? Opal lingo, that's what. Near the Queensland border, this strikingly imaginative mining community (one of the world's few sources of black opals) has real frontier spirit, home to eccentric artisans, true-blue bushies and a general unconventional collective.

The 'Ridge' (www.lighteningridgeinfo.com.au) was named after an unfortunate event in 1963 when a flock of sheep, their drover and his faithful dog were struck down by lightning. Their singed woolly carcasses were still wafting with smoke when the town took its name from the event.

Sights & Activities

In an example of the community's spirit, locals have mapped out four touring routes around town. Car doors were the original markers but now the routes are formally signposted. Get a map from the visitor centre.

Fossicking   INDUSTRIAL
Several underground mines and opal showrooms are open to the public.

Walk-In Mine
(02-6829 0473; www.walkinmine.com.au; Blue Car Door 4, Bald Hill; adult/child $20/6; 8.30am-12.30pm) Visit this mine to get a feel for the type of environment encountered by the average opal miner.

Black Opal Tours
(02-6829 0368; www.blackopaltours.com.au; adult/child $30/12; tours 8.30am, 9.30am & 1.30pm). You can do a bit of exploring with this outfit on its daily tours.

Black Queen   MUSEUM
(02-6829 0980; www.blackqueen.com.au; Red Car Door E; adult/family $25/75) This is a quirky antique lamp museum in a building built from 14,000 bottles, but the main attraction is the award-winning three-act 'outback theatre' performances (9am, 1pm and 3pm). Book ahead.

Chambers of the Black Hand   ART GALLERY
(www.wj.com.au/whatto/blackhand.html; 3 Mile Rd, Yellow Car Door 5) Similarly wacky is this creation by artist and miner Ron Canlin who has turned a 40ft-deep claim into a cavernous gallery of carvings: dinosaurs, Aboriginal scenes, pharaohs, you name it.

FREE Hot Artesian Bore Baths   RELAXING
(Pandora St; 24hr) Most visitors find time for a soak in the warm artesian water here. It is closed 10am to noon Monday, Wednesday and Friday for cleaning.

Festivals & Events

Though it's hard to work out how many – if any – opals are still being dug up, the town makes a show of it when fossicking season kicks off over the Easter long weekend. You can prove your worth at the Great Goat Race. Catch a feral beast, give it some racing lessons, let it go with 50 other goats, and bet money on it. There's a gem festival every July.

Sleeping & Eating

Glengarry Hilton   PUB $
(02-6829 3983; per person incl breakfast $16) About 80km south of town, the opal fields of Grawin and Glengarry are also part of the experience. The Hilton is a tin shed of a pub, frequented by lots of local characters. There are four bunk rooms and a double room. If you hadn't guessed, the name is tongue-in-cheek.

Lorne Station   CAMPGROUND $
(📞02-6829 1869; www.lornestation.com.au;
off Opal St; unpowered/powered sites $16/25,
bunkhouse r $42, self-contained cottages $60-165;
✳❄) This is a 10,000-hectare property
with an intriguing variety of accommodation. The lovely owner conducts free opal-
field walking tours.

Chats On Opal   CAFE $
(4 Opal St; mains $8-16; ⊙breakfast & lunch)
A colourful place serving gourmet sandwiches, cakes and decent coffee. It's a
good place to watch the world go by.

❶ Information

Visitor centre (📞02-6829 1670; www.lightning
ridge.net.au; Morilla St)

❶ Getting There & Away

Air Link (📞02-6884 2435; www.airlinkairlines.
com.au) has charter flights to Walgett, Coonamble and Sydney via Dubbo. **CountryLink**
(📞13 22 32; www.countrylink.info) buses run to
Dubbo ($47, 4½ hours).

Newell Highway

The Newell Hwy is the quickest route across
NSW between Victoria and Queensland. It
forks off the Oxley Hwy in Coonabarabran,
passing through Narrabri and Moree on its
way to Goondiwindi over the border.

COONABARABRAN

POP 2610

The Newell Hwy briefly joins the Oxley
Hwy from Tamworth at Coonabarabran, the
gateway to the Warrumbungles. The helpful
visitor centre (📞02-6842 1441; www.warrum
bunglesregion.com.au; Newell Hwy) is south of
the clock tower. Motels dot the highway.

Head 27km west of town in the Warrumbungle Range for some of the world's major,
and Australia's largest, telescopes at Siding
Spring Observatory (📞02-6842 6211; www.
sidingspringexploratory.com.au; National Park Rd;
activity centre adult/child $5.50/3.50). Access
to the telescope is free for tours call Donna
(📞02-6842 6255). Alternatively, phone local stargazer Peter Starr (seriously) who
conducts night-time telescopic viewings
(📞0488 425 112; www.tenbyobservatory.com;
adult/child/family $15/5/35; ⊙8.30pm).

Between Coonabarabran and Narrabri,
the Pilliga Forest springs either side of the
highway. For a closer look at this iconic semi-
arid landscape featuring sandstone caves
with Aboriginal rock engraving, contact the

new Discovery Centre (📞02-6843 4011; 50-58
Wellington St), west of the highway at Baradine.

NARRABRI

POP 6100

Narrabri is a major cotton-growing centre.
At time of writing the Australian Cotton
Centre (www.australiancottoncentre.com.au; Newell Hwy) was closed for business. Check website for updates.

The visitor centre (📞02-6799 6760; www.
narrabri.nsw.gov.au; Newell Hwy) has displays
and a shop and sits on the riverfront where
there's a swimming beach and picnic tables.
Joblink (📞02-6792 5188; 5/100 Maitland St)
can help with cotton jobs; also check out the
government's National Harvest Labour
Information Service (📞1800 062 332; www.
jobsearch.gov.au/harvesttrail).

Sawn Rocks, a pipe-organ formation
about 40km northeast of Narrabri (20km
unsealed), is the most accessible and popular part of Mt Kaputar National Park. The
southern part of the park has dramatic lookouts, climbing, bushwalking and camping.

MOREE

POP 8080

This large town on the Gwydir River has
the Hot Artesian Pool Complex (www.
mpsc.nsw.gov.au; cnr Anne & Gosport Sts; adult/
child $6/4; ⊙6am-8.30pm Mon-Fri, 7am-7pm Sat
& Sun), where locals frolic in 42°C water.
Many accommodation options also have
artesian pools. Ask at the visitor centre
(📞02-6575 3350; wwwmoreetourism.com.au) on
the highway.

Moree Plains Gallery (www.moreeplains
gallery.org.au; cnr Frome & Herber Sts; ⊙10am-
5pm Mon-Fri, to 1pm Sat) has an inspiring
collection of Aboriginal art by some of
the country's best artists, including Arone
Meeks, Dorothy Napangardi, Elizabeth
Nyumi Nungurrayi and Judy Watson.
For a more local take, check out Yaama
Maliyaa Arts (29 Herber St); the friendly
owner is also a good source of info on local
Aboriginal sites.

Café 2400 (123 Balo St; ⊙breakfast & lunch
Mon-Fri, breakfast Sat) would be at home in
Sydney's groovier suburbs.

Cotton-related work is available from
March to May for skilled workers. Anyone
can partake in cotton chipping from November to January or olive- and pecan-picking
from April to August. Contact Joblink (📞02-
6752 8488) or the National Harvest Labour
Information Service (www.jobsearch.gov.au/
harvesttrail).

WARRUMBUNGLES

When the Warrumbungle Volcano erupted more than 13 million years ago it formed the spectacular granite domes of the Warrumbungle National Park (www.warrumbungles. com.au; per car $7). Sitting 33km west of Coonabarabran, this 23,311-hectare park has 43km of bushwalking trails and explosive wildflower displays during spring. Park fees are payable at the NPWS visitor centre (☏02-6825 4364) in the park; some sights also have camp fees (adult/child from $5/3). Before you go, book ahead for the expensive but worthwhile Warrumbungle Tara Cave Walk (guide fee Mon-Fri $175, Sat & Sun $265), which is guided by local Kamilaroi people, including Aboriginal elders. The tour encompasses a walk through Tara Cave, a significant Aboriginal site that was occupied for over 4000 years.

For another real Australian experience, restored Mt Tenandra Homestead B&B (☏02-6825 4322 www.mttenandra.com.au; r $110), on the western side of the Warrumbungles, is an original pastoral settlement and Cobb & Co stop. It is self-contained with an old country kitchen, lounge and barbecue area and five glorious bedrooms that open onto an old bull-nose verandah.

CENTRAL WEST

The Central West's relative proximity to Sydney and its population of eager tree-changers, weekend-awayers and holiday-homers has no doubt given many of the agricultural cities and towns just beyond the Blue Mountains a leg-up.

The university city of Bathurst is also a rev-head's haven, Orange has an inordinate number of lauded chefs and restaurants, Mudgee is a small town with a big nose for wine, and Dubbo has joined the milieu with a newish cultural centre.

The stately buildings, grandiose wide streets, parks, and vivid and well-tended English gardens align these cities with a past built on gold-mining and bushranger folklore, but this history is best explored in the smaller hill towns where wide verandahs and old pubs are often coupled with a decent cafe or restaurant and local B&B.

Further west, Forbes and Parkes were united by the radio telescope made famous by the movie *The Dish* until Elvis fever gave the latter town something of its own to focus on. Drive further west and the rolling agricultural heartland transforms into vast plains and finally the harsher outback soil of the far west.

Bathurst

POP 29,000

There are two sides to Bathurst. Primarily, it is Australia's oldest inland settlement, boasting European trees, a cool climate and a beautiful manicured central square where formidable Victorian buildings can snap you back to the past. But it's also the bastion of Australian motor sport, hosting numerous events.

◉ Sights & Activities

Ask at the visitor centre for information about wineries in the region.

Australian Fossil & Mineral Museum MUSEUM
(www.somervillecollection.com.au; 224 Howick St; adult/child/family $9/7/23; ⊙10am-4pm Mon-Sat, 10am-2pm Sun) See Tyrannosaurus rex, Australia's only complete skeleton. You'll also see the internationally renowned Somerville Collection and over 6000 fossils from every period of the earth's history. It's fantastic.

Bathurst Regional Art Gallery ART GALLERY
(www.bathurstart.com.au; 70-78 Keppel St; admission free; ⊙10am-5pm Tue-Sat, 11am-2pm Sun) The gallery has a dynamic collection of work, featuring local artists as well as exciting touring exhibitions.

Courthouse HISTORIC BUILDING, MUSEUM
(Russell St) This 1880 building is the most impressive of Bathurst's historical buildings and houses the small Historical Museum (adult/child/family $4/2/10; ⊙10am-4pm Tue, Wed & Sat, 11am-2pm Sun).

Chifley Home HISTORIC BUILDING
(www.chifleyhome.org.au; 10 Busby St; adult/child/family $8/5/21; ⊙tours 10am & noon Sat-Mon) Ben Chifley, prime minister from 1945 to 1949, lived in Bathurst, and the

modest Chifley Home is on display. There's also a new **education centre**.

National Motor Racing Museum   MUSEUM (www.nmrm.com.au; Pit Straight, Murrays Corner, Mt Panorama; adult/child/family $9.50/3.50 /23.50; ☺9am-4.30pm) Rev-heads will enjoy the 6.2km Mt Panorama Motor Racing Circuit, the venue for the **Bathurst Motorsport Spectacular** in October. You can drive around the circuit, but only up to an unthrilling 60km/h.

🛏 Sleeping

Jack Duggans Irish Pub   PUB $ (☎02-6331 2712; www.jackduggans.com.au; 135 George St; dm/s/d $25/45/65) The recently renovated former Commerical Hotel, in the heart of town, has a lively restaurant and bar downstairs and small but inviting rooms upstairs, opening onto a verandah. Prices go up on weekends.

Accommodation Warehouse APARTMENTS $$ (☎02-6332 2801; www.accomwarehouse.com.au; 121a Keppel St; s/d $80/116) A soaring, historic brick building with arched windows and Juliet balconies, this place has three lovely self-contained apartments. Continental breakfast included.

Panorama Holiday Park   CARAVAN PARK $ (☎02-6331 8286; www.bathurstholidaypark.com.au; Sydney Rd; 2-person powered sites/cabins from $30/89; ✱☀) This well-equipped park with cute, red-topped, corrugated-iron miners cottages, is the main caravan and camping option. Prices increase when the races are on.

🍴 Eating

TOP
CHOICE **Church Bar**   PIZZA $$ (www.churchbar.com.au; 1 Ribbon Gang Lane; mains $14-25; ☺lunch & dinner Tue-Sat, lunch Sun) This restored 1850s church now attracts punters praying to a different deity: the god of wood-fired pizza. The soaring ceilings and verdant courtyard off William St make it one of the region's best eating and socialising venues.

Hub   CAFE $$ (52 Keppel St; mains $15; ☺breakfast & lunch Tue-Sun, dinner Thu-Sat) A canopy of red umbrellas and green leaves makes this busy spot the perfect place for alfresco lunch. The vego burgers and salads go down a treat as does live jazz on Thursday nights.

Yummy Noodle   FAST FOOD $ (96 William St; meals $9-11; ☺lunch & dinner) A variety of laksas, rice and noodles packaged ideally for eating in the park across the road.

❶ Information

The **visitor centre** (☎1800 681 000; www.visitbathurst.com.au; Kendall Ave) is helpful. Internet access is free at **Bathurst Library** (70-78 Keppel St).

❶ Getting There & Away

Rex (☎13 17 13; www.rex.com.au) flies to Sydney ($94, 45 minutes).

Australia Wide Coaches (☎02-6362 7963; www.austwidecoaches.com.au) Sydney Express leaves daily ($30, 3½ hours). **CountryLink** (☎13 22 32; www.countrylink.info) trains go to Sydney ($8, 4¼ hours) and Dubbo ($29, 2½ hours). CountryLink's XPT train also stops here on the daily Sydney ($32, 3¾ hours) and Dubbo ($29, three hours) service.

Around Bathurst

The region north of Bathurst is good driving territory with beautiful scenery, parks and reserves and a handful of quaint little towns – such as **O'Connell**, **Sofala** and **Hill End** – that owe their existence to the gold-mining days. While the populations have long since dwindled, the remaining old timbered houses, pubs and for that matter, locals, make for hospitable pit stops. For longer stays there are two **NPWS camping grounds** (☎02-6337 8206; unpowered sites adult/child $7/4, powered sites $10/5) and the **Royal Hotel** (☎02-6337 8261; Beyers Ave; r from $40) in Hill End. The **Old Sofala Gaol** (☎02-6337 7064; www.oldsofalagaol.com.au; Barkly St; d/tw $65/70) is a cafe and B&B.

The famous **Abercrombie Caves** (☎02-6368 8603; self-guided/guided tours $13/16) are south of Bathurst. The complex has one of the world's largest natural tunnels, the Grand Arch. The Jenolan Caves (p129) are also in the region. **Jenolan Adventure** (☎1300 763 311; www.jenolancaves.com.au) hosts caving and abseiling tours throughout the 40km of multilevelled caves and passages. There's **accommodation** (☎02-6368 8603) nearby from $100 per double.

Orange

POP 33,180

There might be pears, apples and stone fruit aplenty in the surrounding orchards, but it just so happens the town was named after Prince William of Orange. It's now a dedicated food-and-wine hub with four distinct seasons – and a food festival for each. The city's parks and gardens are a kaleidoscope of colours throughout the year, with cold winters bringing occasional snowfalls. Bush poet AB 'Banjo' Paterson was born here.

Sights & Activities

Wineries

Orange has a reputation for distinctive cool-climate wines, with many award-winning vineyards. Get info from the visitor centre or www.winesoforange.com.au. Word of Mouth Wines (www.wordofmouthwines.com.au; Pinnacle Rd; ⊙9am-5pm Fri-Sun) is highly recommended; after visiting pop across the road to Brangayne of Orange (www.brangayne.com; 837 Pinnacle Rd). Printhie (www.printhiewines.com.au; 439 Yuranigh Rd, Molong) is also on the hit list. Taxi Cab Co-op (☑02-6325 0004; 3hr tour per five people from $150) does wine tours in late-model taxis. Central West Getaways (☑0413 551 212; www.centralwestgetaways.com; half-/full day per person $45/65) also does tours.

Other Sights & Activities

Mt Canobolas   NATURE RESERVE

Southwest of Orange, this nature reserve forms part of an extensive volcanic chain stretching 3000km along Australia's eastern seaboard. The flora and fauna, waterfalls, views, walking trails and bike paths make this great exploratory territory. Kayaks, paddle boats and windsurfers are available for hire from Geoff at Lake Canobolas Reserve (☑0428 645 301; Lake Canobolas Rd; per hr from $10; ⊙dawn-dusk) off Cargo Rd. This is also a great place for swimming, or to have a picnic – the barbecues are clean and free.

Orange Regional Gallery   ART GALLERY

(www.org.nsw.gov.au; Civic Sq; admission free; ⊙10am-5pm Tue-Sat, 1-4pm Sun) Next to the visitor centre, the gallery has an ambitious, varied program of exhibitions and some Australian masters.

Festivals & Events

Testament to its 'foodie' reputation, Orange now has four seasonal festivals (www.tasteorange.com.au) where the region's producers make star appearances: Slow Summer, in early February, F.O.O.D Week (www.orangefoodweek.com.au) in mid-April, Frost Fest in early August and Wine Week in late October.

Local produce can be foraged at the popular farmers market (www.orangefarmersmarket.org.au; Orange Regional Gallery North Ct; ⊙8.30am-noon) held on the second Saturday of the month. From May to September, or when it's wet, the market is in the Orange Showground.

Sleeping & Eating

Accommodation in Orange is limited due to a surplus of miners and business people. Prices go up on weekends.

De Russie Suites   BOUTIQUE HOTEL **$$**

(☑02-6360 0973; www.derussiehotels.com.au; 72 Hill St; d from $158; ☎) As good as anything in Sydney, this hotel has boutique written all over it. It has all the luxurious cons expected in a hotel plus self-contained facilities. Breakfast is included and comes in hamper format.

Town Square Motel   MOTEL **$$**

(☑02-6369 1444; 246 Anson St; s/d $105/118; ❄@) Just off the main street, this clean and comfortable hotel, painted white and green, has fluffy pillows, doonas and a chock-full mini bar. The adjoining Balcony Restaurant (mains $15-30) is one of the few venues open Sunday night.

Arancia B&B   B&B **$$**

(☑02-6365 3305; www.arancia.com.au; Wrights Lane; r $150-195) Set in rolling green hills, this B&B has hotel-worthy facilities, including spacious rooms with big beds, en suites, cups of tea and classy furnishings. Breakfasts here are famous.

TOP CHOICE Union Bank   WINE BAR **$$**

(www.unionbank.com.au; cnr Sale & Byng Sts; mains $18-32; ⊙lunch & dinner Mon-Sat, lunch Sun) This upmarket and rather groovy cellar door and wine bar has more than 500 wine labels, any of which can be enjoyed with a cheese platter or antipasto plate. There's also a wine store.

Hotel Canobolas   PUB FARE **$$**

(cnr Summer St & Lords Pl; ⊙10am-late) A good pub for a relaxed beer and cook-your-own steak with park views and windows opening onto the footpath.

TASTE SENSATIONS

Orange is known for its great food. Try these on for size:

Mills Cafe (Byng St; ☺lunch & dinner) Take-away shop over the railway line. Best burgers (around $10) in town.

Lolli Redini (☎02-6361 7748; 48 Sale St; mains $35; ☺dinner Tue-Sat) The apple of Orange's eye.

Racine at La Colline Winery (☎02-6365 3275; www.racinerestaurant. com.au; 42 Lake Canobolas Rd; mains $36; ☺lunch & dinner Thu-Sun, cellar door Wed-Sun) Amid vines.

Old Convent (☎02-6365 2420; www. oldconvent.com.au; Convent Ln, Borenore; mains $20; ☺breakfast, lunch & arvo tea Sun) Sunday brunch.

Hawkes General Store   CAFE/GIFT SHOP **$** (www.hawkesgeneralstore.com.au; Sale St; ☺lunch & dinner) Great coffee and sublime melting moments.

❶ Information

Seasonal Work

The autumn apple-, cherry- and grape-picking season lasts for about six weeks. **Harvest Labour Services** (☎02-6382 9258, 0408 898 010; www.cwcc.nsw.edu.au) can help you find work or ask at the **visitor centre** (☎02-6393 8226; www.visitorange.com.au; Byng St) for orchards with accommodation.

❶ Getting There & Away

Rex (☎13 17 13; www.rex.com.au) flies to Sydney ($140, 50 minutes). The airport is 13km southeast of Orange. **Australia Wide Coaches** (☎02-6362 7963; www.austwidecoaches.com.au) Sydney Express leaves daily ($38, 4¼ hours). **CountryLink** (☎13 22 32; www.countrylink.info) trains go to Sydney ($27, five hours) and Dubbo ($19, 1¾ hours). CountryLink's XPT train also stops here on the daily Sydney ($38, five hours) and Dubbo ($19, 1¾ hours) service.

Canowindra

POP 1500

The teeny town of Canowindra, 32km north of Cowra, is the perfect laid-back weekender. It has a heritage-listed main street where a surprising number of art galleries and old wares shops make for a leisurely meander.

The new **visitor centre** (☎02-6344 1008; cnr Gaskill & Ferguson Sts) is in the same building as the **Age of Fishes Museum** (www. ageoffishes.org.au; adult/child $8.50/5.50), an intriguing exhibition unravelling the mysteries of a fossil site found nearby featuring the preserved remains of long extinct fish predating the dinosaurs.

The town is the self-proclaimed ballooning capital of Australia. **Aussie Balloontrek** (☎02-6361 2552; www.aussieballoontrek.com.au; Nanami Lane; flights from $160) can get you high with a champagne breakfast. **Balloon Joy Flights** (www.balloonjoyflights.com.au; adult/child $260/170) operates from Tom's Waterhole Winery.

The **Old Vic Inn** (☎02-6344 1009; www.oldvicinn.com.au; 56 Gaskill St; r with/without bathroom $120/90) serves as the town's information hub, with a cosy restaurant (open Thursday to Saturday) and B&B accommodation. For a little more space and romance, **Everview Retreat** (☎02-6344 3116; www.everview.com. au; 72 Cultowa Lane; d from $220; ❀) has luxury stone cottages equipped with spas, DVDs, the works.

Tom's Waterhole Winery (www.tomswaterhole.com.au; Longs Corner Rd; ☺10am-4pm) has a cellar door and a cafe serving ploughman's lunches.

Taste Canowindra (www.tastecanowindra. com.au; 42 Ferguson St; ☺10am-4pm) hosts regional wine tastings, art-and-craft exhibitions, and the occasional live band. Next door, the **Trading Post** (www.canowindratradingpost.com.au) is a lovely renovated building serving coffee in the garden.

Cowra

POP 8430

History buffs will be prone to various states of excitability in Cowra, a town with a unique story. Ever since August 1944, when 1000 Japanese prisoners broke out of a prisoner-of-war camp here (231 of them died, along with four Australians), Cowra has aligned itself with Japan and the cause of world peace.

The **visitor centre** (☎02-6342 4333; www. cowratourism.com.au; Olympic Park, Mid Western Hwy) shows an excellent nine-minute holographic film about the breakout scene. **Ideal Tours** (☎02-6342 1797; 1 Kendal St) runs tours of wineries and other local attractions.

DON'T MISS

MILLTHORPE

Only 20 minutes from Orange, this pioneering village with cobbled streets and heritage architecture is a little slice of the mid 1800s. Its cuteness is such that the National Trust has classified the whole place. Rather than stifle progress, the old stone pubs and antique weatherboard shops have become home to some of the country's best restaurants, cafes and accommodation options. Four of the best:

Hockeys B&B (☑02-6366 3643; www.hockeysaccomodation.com.au; 28 Park St) In the old chemist.

Tonic (☑02-6366 3811; www.tonicmillthorpe.com.au; cnr Pym & Victoria Sts, Millthorpe; mains $30; ⊘lunch Sat & Sun, dinner Thu-Sat) White tablecloths, shiny glassware, contemporary food.

La Boucherie (25 Victoria St; www.laboucherie.com.au; ⊘9am-5pm Fri-Sun, to 4pm Mon) Art, books, cakes and espresso.

Basalt (Commerical Hotel; mains $28; ⊘lunch Fri-Sun; dinner Wed-Sun) Fine dining plus tapas, bar, pool and darts.

The **Cowra Cork & Fork** (www.cowrashow.com) wine and food festival, held in early November, brings all the region's produce to the one place on the one day.

◉ Sights & Activities

Japanese Garden   GARDEN
(www.cowrajapanesegarden.com.au; Binni Creek Rd; adult/child $12/6; ⊘8.30am-5pm) Built as a token of Cowra's connection to Japanese POWs (but with no overt mention of the war or the breakout), the garden and attached cultural centre, with its collection of *ukiyo-e* paintings depicting everyday events in pre-industrial Japan, are well worth visiting. A *sakura matsuri* – cherry-blossom festival – is held around September/October.

Australian & Japanese War Cemeteries   MEMORIAL
About 5km south of town; many of those remembered here died very young. A nearby memorial marks the site of the breakout, and you can still see the camp foundations.

Darby Falls Observatory   OBSERVATORY
(☑02-6345 1900; Observatory Rd; adult/child $10/7; ⊘7-10pm, 8.30-11pm summer) This is one of the darkest places for stargazing in all of Australia. From town, head out Darby Falls Rd for 22km, then follow the signs.

Cowra Regional Art Gallery   ART GALLERY
(www.cowraartgallery.com.au; 77 Darling St; ⊘10am-4pm Tue-Sat, 2-4pm Sun) The gallery has a permanent collection and exhibitions. For art alfresco, take a peek beneath Lachlan River bridge to see murals painted by Aboriginal artist Kim Freeman.

🛏 Sleeping & Eating

In the heart of town, the **Mill** (www.windowrie.com.au; 6 Vaux St; ⊘11am-5pm) is Cowra's oldest building, where the millstone first turned in 1861. The region's Chardonnay has tickled many a palate; enjoy it here with a cheese platter. About 4km along Boorowa Rd, **Quarry** (☑02-6342 3650; ⊘lunch Thu-Sun, dinner Fri & Sat) cellar-door restaurant is set amid vineyards, and the cuisine is well regarded.

Vineyard Motel   MOTEL **$$**
(☑02-6342 3641; www.vineyardmotel.com.au; Chardonnay Rd; s/d from $115/130, d with spa $150; ❈🐾🛜❈) The Lachlan Valley vineyard views from this boutique hotel, 4km from town, are so mesmerising that the plastic flowers and lace doilies can be forgiven.

Neila   GREEK, CHINESE **$$**
(☑02-6341 2188; www.neila.com.au; 5 Kendal St; mains $35; ⊘dinner Thu-Sat) On Cowra's main drag, this small gem, with a contemporary Australian menu, is a tribute to the quality of food in the region and to the owners themselves who grow much of what ends up on the plate. It has received a chef's hat award nine years running. BYO.

Apsara   THAI **$**
(☑02-6342 2212; 69 Kendal St; mains $9-17; ⊘lunch & dinner Mon-Sat) It might look like one of the many takeaway shops on the main street, but Apsara serves up a mean selection of Thai dishes in a casual setting.

❶ Getting There & Away

CountryLink (☑13 22 32; www.countrylink.info) has daily services to Sydney ($32, 5¾ hours).

Young

POP 7140

Come to Young in spring and you'll be welcomed by the dazzling pink, red and green hues of the region's cherry orchards. On the edge of the western slopes of the Great Dividing Range, this is Australia's 'cherry capital'. Prunes are also an important local industry, but 'prune capital' doesn't have quite the same ring.

The visitor centre is housed in the old railway station and has a list of orchards where you can pick your own fruit. The cherry harvest is in November and December. In January other stone fruits are harvested and in February the prune harvest begins.

◎ Sights & Activities

Young hosts the Cherry Festival on the first weekend in December.

Wineries WINERIES

There are about 15 small vineyards producing award-winning cool-climate wines, including the excellent Lindsay's Woodonga Hill (www.lindsayswine.com.au; 1101 Cowra Rd;), northeast of Young, and Grove Estate Wines (www.groveestate.com.au; Murringo Rd), on the road to Cowra.

Lambing Flat Folk Museum MUSEUM

(Campbell St; adult/child $4/1; ⊙10am-4pm) Displays artefacts from the goldfields, including the remarkable 'Roll Up' banner carried by European miners in protest against the Chinese in 1861.

Chinese Tribute Garden GARDEN

(Pitstone Rd; admission free) The Sydney Chinese community raised money to build this tranquil spot featuring a pagoda and dam, to remember the contribution the Chinese miners made.

✕ Sleeping & Eating

Colonial Motel MOTEL $$

(☑02-6382 2822; Olympic Hwy; s/d/tw from $85/95/100) This place has decent-sized, clean and comfortable rooms, some of them with spa baths. The owners are exceptionally welcoming.

Young Affordable Accommodation HOSTEL $

(☑02-6382 2444; cnr Campbell St & Olympic Hwy; s from $150 per week) A decent option for cherry pickers, this place books out quickly during harvest season.

TOP CHOICE Art of Espresso CAFE $

(www.artofespresso.com.au; 35 Main St; ⊙breakfast & lunch Mon-Sat) Off Boorowa St, this funky place serves the obvious, plus cakes, Portuguese tarts and paninis ($8).

Café du Jour EUROPEAN $$

(cnr Lovell & Zouch Sts; mains $17-30; ⊙lunch & dinner Tue-Sat) Run by an amiable couple, this lovely restaurant with a bland exterior has stood the test of time.

Young Tourist Park CARAVAN PARK $

(☑02-6382 2190; Zouch St; camp sites per adult $25, cabins $70; ⊛) A comfortable camping option that has drive-through sites with bathrooms for caravans.

For fruit-inspired produce, head to Poppa's Fudge & Jam Factory (shop 1, Lovell St).

❶ Information

Harvest Labour Services (☑02-6382 9258, 0408 898 010; www.cwcc.nsw.edu.au) Can help you find work.

Visitor centre (☑02-6382 3394; www.visityoung.com.au; Lovell St) In the old railway station. Can tell you about orchards with accommodation.

❶ Getting There & Away

CountryLink (☑13 22 32; www.countrylink.info) has daily services to Sydney ($55, 8¼ hours).

Forbes

POP 9360

You might recognise Forbes from the popular Australian film *The Dish,* where much of the filming took place? Maybe not. Perched on the banks of the Lachlan River and Forbes Lake, Forbes is very pretty and has retained much of its 19th-century flavour.

The visitor centre (☑02-6852 4155; cnr Newell Hwy & Union St) is inside the old train station and has local art exhibits and a DVD about local legend Ben Hall, a landowner who became Australia's first official bushranger. He was betrayed and shot near Forbes and is buried in the town's cemetery; people still miss him, if the notes on his grave are anything to go by. The Forbes Museum (11 Cross St; adult/child $2/1; ⊙2-4pm) houses Ben Hall relics and other memorabilia.

The Newell Hwy has plenty of motels. To bunk down in a heritage building, try the Vandeberg Hotel (☑02-6852 2015; 7 Court St; s/d $35/45) with basic rooms that open onto a gorgeous wrought-iron balcony overlooking the park.

Mezzanine Style (www.mezzaninestyle.com; 23 Rankin St; breakfast $9.50-16, lunch $9-14; ⊘breakfast & lunch) has an unimpressive exterior but the spacious interior with a mezzanine level is relaxed with a hearty menu.

CountryLink (☑13 22 32; www.countrylink.info) has daily services to Sydney ($41, 7¼ hours).

Parkes

POP 9,830 (DOUBLES DURING THE ELVIS FESTIVAL)

Parkes was content being known as the home of the radio telescope made famous by the film *The Dish,* until hundreds of Elvis impersonators started coming to town. Now the King's birthday is the focal weekend for this sleepy town.

◉ Sights

Sir Henry Parkes Museum   MUSEUM
(cnr Newell Hwy & Thomas St; admission $5; ⊘9am-3.30pm Mon-Sat, 9am-2.30pm Sun) At the visitor centre. Here you can walk through the 'moat cottage', a replica of Sir Henry Parkes' birthplace, and the new **Kings Cottage Elvis Museum** (admission $5; ⊘9am-3.30pm Mon-Thu).

Radio Telescope   TELESCOPE
Built by the Commonwealth Scientific & Industrial Research Organisation (CSIRO) in 1961, this telescope is 6km east of the Newell Hwy, about 20km north of Parkes. As one of the world's most powerful telescopes it has helped Australian radio astronomers become leaders in their field, and brought pictures of the *Apollo 11* moon landing to an audience of 600 million people. Although the telescope is off limits, you can get close enough for a good look. The **Dish CSIRO visitor centre** (www.parkes.atnf.csiro.au; admission free; ⊘8.30am-4.15pm) has hands-on displays and visual effects; 3-D films (adult/child $6.50/5) screen throughout the day.

Holden Utes Art Installation ART INSTALLATION
(www.utesinthepaddock.com.au; Mulgutherie Ln) About 70km from Parkes on the Condobolin road, this is a peculiar tribute to life in the outback with the iconic vehicles given a creative makeover. Spot the bottle of Bundy and Dame Edna on the 'loo'.

⚑ Festivals & Events

Elvis Festival   ELVIS
(www.parkeselvisfestival.com.au) On the second weekend in January, this is one of the weirdest and wackiest festivals in the country. An influx of King lookalikes invade the town to celebrate his birthday with street parades, concerts, talent quests and busking. Don't forget your blue suedes!

🛏 Sleeping & Eating

Accommodation during the festival is booked out more than a year in advance.

Old Parkes Convent   B&B $$
(☑02-6862 2385; www.parkesconvent.com.au; 33 Currajong St; s/d $130/170) This lovely blast from the past has a huge studio in the old boarding house and another self-contained bedroom in the main heritage building. Both are clean and antique-filled.

Coachman Hotel Motel   MOTEL $
(☑02-6862 2622; www.coachman.com.au; 48-54 Welcome St; s/d $85/90; ❄@❄) Just off the main street, this white brick motel is a good option for Gen Y and Xers who prefer a bit of nightlife.

Bellas   CAFE $$
(45 Clarinda St; meals $20; ⊘breakfast & lunch Tue-Sat, dinner Wed-Sat) An excellent eatery. On-the-go brekkies include banana bread ($5) and paninis ($9) or sit in for heartier modern Oz-Italian fare and vino by the glass.

❶ Information

Visitor centre (☑02-6863 8860; www.visitparkes.com.au; cnr Newell Hwy & Thomas St) In a new purpose-built building along the Newell Hwy on the Dubbo side of town.

❶ Getting There & Away

CountryLink (☑13 22 32; www.countrylink.info) runs daily buses to Sydney ($52.45, 20 minutes).

Dubbo

POP 30, 580

Dubbo has long been known as the home of the Western Plains Zoo. Now the rural centre and transport crossroads on the northern fringe of the Central West region has another string to its bow – the Western Plains Cultural Centre. For locals it has inspired a new era of arts and culture and hard-to-come-by statewide attention.

◉ Sights

Western Plains Zoo   ZOO
(☑02-6881 1400; www.taronga.org.au; Obley Rd; 2-day adult/child/family pass $45/22/109;

⊙9am-4pm) With over 1500 animals, this is Dubbo's star attraction. You can walk the 6km trail, hire a bike ($15) or join the crawling line of cars. Guided walks (adult/child $10/5) start at 6.45am every weekend and Wednesday and Friday in school holidays. Book ahead (☎02-6881 1488) for special animal encounters: Wild Africa (adult/child $29/19, 10.45am), Big Cats ($59 per person, Thursday to Tuesday), Giraffes ($5 per person) and Meerkats ($39 per person).

Stay at a lodge within the zoo for **private encounters** (☎02-6881 1488; www.zoofari.com.au; adult/child from $309/55) or experience **Roar & Snore camping** (☎02-6681 1405; www.taronga.org.au; adult/child package $175/110). Book well ahead.

Western Plains Cultural Centre MUSEUM
(www.taronga.org.au; 76 Wingewarra St; admission free; ⊙10am-4pm Wed-Mon) Incorporating **Dubbo Regional Museum and Gallery**, the cultural centre is housed in a swanky architectural space cleverly incorporating the main hall of Dubbo's former high school. The combination befits the centre's exhibitions, both contemporary and historic. There's an innovative dedicated children's gallery, so mums and dads can wander the gallery sans sleeve-tugging.

Old Dubbo Gaol MUSEUM
(www.olddubbogaol.com.au; 90 Macquarie St; adult/child $15/5) This is now a museum where 'Animatronic' characters tell their stories – you hear from a condemned man due for a meeting with the gallows. Creepy but authentic.

Dubbo Observatory OBSERVATORY
(www.dubboobservatory.com.au; 17 Camp Rd; adult/child/family $20/10/50) Partake in a bit of stargazing. There are two sessions each evening.

Dundullimal HISTORIC BUILDING
(Obley Rd; adult/child $8/4; ⊙10am-4pm Tue-Thu) About 2km beyond the Western Plains Zoo, this is a National Trust timber-slab homestead built in the 1840s showcasing some of the earliest forms of permanent European housing in NSW.

🛏 Sleeping

There are plenty of hotels on Cobra St.

No. 95 Dubbo MOTEL $$
(☎02-6882 7888; www.no95.com.au; 95 Cobra St; r from $115/130; ❀@🛜🐕) This place has a hotel-standard facade but inside, the rooms are equipped with top-notch furniture,

linen and appliances. It's one of the nicer options in town.

Westbury Guesthouse GUESTHOUSE $$
(☎02-6884 9445; www.westburyguesthouse.com.au; cnr Brisbane & Wingewarra Sts; s/d $125/155; ❀) This lovely old heritage home (1910) has spacious rooms, all with bathrooms, and a shared lounge and kitchen. It doesn't have much competition so is overpriced.

Dubbo City Holiday Park CAMPGROUND $
(☎02-6882 4820; www.dubbocityholidaypark.com.au; Whylandra St; powered sites/cabins from $27/94; ❀🐕) On the riverbank with cabins nestled between trees.

🍴 Eating & Drinking

TOP
CHOICE **Two Doors Tapas & Wine Bar** TAPAS $$
(☎02-6885 2333; www.twodoors.com.au; 215b Macquarie St; tapas $7-27; ⊙lunch & dinner Wed-Sat) Kick back with a drink in a leafy courtyard below street level, while munching on, say, pan-fried whole prawns with fresh chilli and garlic ($20).

Artology + Café CAFE $
(209 Darling St; mains $11-15; ⊙breakfast & lunch Mon-Sat) A black-and-red-daubed terrace fronts Dubbo's latest ode to caffeine culture. Inside it's all funky spaces, Bodum coffee cups and cube stools. The fare is easy eats: rolls, quiches, muffins etc.

Red Earth Estate Vineyard VINEYARD
(www.redearthestate.com.au; 18 Camp Rd; ⊙10am-5pm Thu-Tue) Just past the zoo, Red Earth is one of four vineyards. It has lunchtime platters and free tastings.

Outlook Café CAFE $
(☎02-6884 7977; 76 Wingewarra St; mains $12-16; ⊙breakfast & lunch Wed-Mon) In the light and airy Western Plains Cultural Centre.

Sticks & Stones PIZZA $$
(215 Macquarie St; mains $18-29; ⊙dinner) Great pizzas, and one of the few places open on Sunday.

Grape Vine Café CAFE $
(☎02-6884 7354; 144 Brisbane St; mains $11-15; ⊙breakfast & lunch) In a cute two-storey terrace with a lovely courtyard.

ℹ Information

The **visitor centre** (☎1800 674 443, 02-6801 4450; www.dubbo.com.au; cnr Macquarie St & Newell Hwy) is in a park at the northern end of town. *Photo News* is a free Thursday paper with good local info.

Getting There & Around

Rex (☑13 17 13; www.rex.com.au) and **Qantas** (☑13 13 13; www.qantas.com.au) fly to Sydney ($133, one hour). **Air Link** (☑02-6884 2435; www.airlinkairlines.com.au) has charter flights to Cobar, Bourke and Lightning Ridge via Walgett and Coonamble.

The **CountryLink** (☑13 22 32; www.country link.info) XPT trains run to Sydney ($55, 6¾ hours).

Darrell Wheeler Cycles (25 Bultje St; ⊙Mon-Sat) rents out mountain bikes for $15 per day.

Mudgee

POP 8250

Mudgee is an Aboriginal word for 'nest in the hills', a fitting name for this quaint little grid of a town with vineyards on its edge and rolling hills wherever you turn. The wineries come hand in hand with excellent cuisine, making it a popular weekend getaway where gastronomic exploration is central to the experience.

◉ Sights

Wineries

Mudgee's 40-plus vineyards are clustered in two groups north and southeast of town. This makes them ideal for cycling between, as long as you don't get the wobbles. The vintage is later than the Hunter Valley because of Mudgee's higher altitude. The region is well known for its Shiraz, Cabernet Sauvignon and a blend of the two.

Logan (www.loganwines.com.au; 33 Castlereagh Hwy; ⊙10am-5pm) An impressive cellar door. Floor-to-ceiling windows, an extravagant deck, cheese platters and coffee, too.

Pieter Van Gent (☑02-6376 3030; www. pvgwinery.com.au; 141 Black Springs Rd; ⊙9am-5pm Mon-Fri, 10.30am-4pm Sun & public holidays) Heavenly Muscat, picnic-lunch wine tours by bike, tastings in the barrel room (11.30am Saturday) and accommodation.

Petersons of Mudgee (www.petersonswines. com.au; Black Springs Rd; ⊙10am-4pm Mon-Fri & Sun, to 5pm Sat) Smaller with a lovely deck overlooking vineyards.

Vinifera Wines (www.viniferawines.com.au; 194 Henry Lawson Dr; ⊙10am-5pm Mon-Sat, 11am-5pm Sun) Croquet days, barbecues and tapas. Good tunes too.

Burnbrae Winery (www.burnbraewines.com.au; 548 Hill End Rd; ⊙9am-5pm Mon-Fri, 10am-4pm Sun) Lunch platters under an old peppercorn tree ($20).

There's a **wine festival** (www.mudgeewine. com.au) in September.

⌁ Sleeping

Anne's Wildwood Guesthouse
GUESTHOUSE **$$**

(☑02-6373 3701; www.wildwoodmudgee.com. au; Henry Lawson Dr; r from $170) There are plenty of flash guesthouses and B&Bs in and around Mudgee. This luxury option, set amid the countryside, is highly recommended.

Mudgee Vineyard Motor Inn
MOTEL **$$**

(☑02-6372 1022; 252 Henry Lawson Dr; r from $90; ▣@☀) Located only a couple of minutes' drive from town, this is an attractive place in the heart of the vineyards with pretty rooms and great views.

Cobb & Co Boutique Hotel
BOUTIQUE HOTEL **$$**

(☑02-6372 7245; www.cobbandcocourt.com.au; 97 Market St; r from $170) In the centre of town, this place has mod cons elegantly suited to its heritage style.

✕ Eating & Drinking

TOP▸CHOICE Deebs Kitchen
MEDITERRANEAN **$$$**

(☑02-6373 3133; www.deebskitchen.com.au; Cassilis Rd; set menu $55; ⊙dinner Sat only) A lovely couple run this gorgeous, hidden-away restaurant where Mediterranean cuisine (with a Lebanese skew) and plenty of wine are served in the garden. BYO. Book ahead.

Butcher Shop Café
CAFE **$**

(49 Church St; mains $7-20; ⊙breakfast & lunch daily, dinner Fri & Sat) A hip eatery in an old butchery with stained glass and interesting artwork. The delicious fare is understated and the coffee is roasted in-house. Yumi, from northern Thailand, cooks on Saturday nights.

High Valley Wine & Cheese Co
CAFE, DELI **$$**

(www.highvalley.com.au; 137 Cassilis Rd; mains $18; ⊙breakfast & lunch) Located in a beautiful stone-and-corrugated-iron building, this foodie stop has a produce shop and a vine-laden verandah under which you can indulge in coffee and cake or cheese and antipasto plates for two.

Rajarani INDIAN **$$**
(75 Church St; mains $15-21; ⊘lunch Thu-Fri,
dinner Tue-Sun) Tikkas, tandooris, murghs,
masalas and vindaloo; this place has won
over the locals (and Sydneysiders) with its
Bollywood authenticity.

Sajo's MODERN AUSTRALIAN **$$**
(✐02-6372 2722; www.sajos.com.au; 22 Church
St; breakfast $5.50-19, lunch mains $13-23, dinner
mains $15-30; ⊘breakfast, lunch & dinner Wed-
Sun) Stained-glass window character. *Good
Food Guide* highly commended.

Mudgee Brewery MICROBREWERY
(www.mudgeebrewery.com.au; Church St;
⊘breakfast & lunch, dinner Thu-Sat) Beer *and*
Beaujolais. Live music Thursdays.

Roth's WINE BAR
(www.rothswinebar.com.au; 30 Market St; ⊘5pm-
late Wed-Sat) Oldest wine bar in NSW, plus
live acts, tapas and wood-fired pizza.

❶ Information

The **visitor centre** (✐02-6372 1020; www.
visitmudgeeregion.com.au; 84 Market St),
near the post office, can help with wine-tasting
jaunts. The **NPWS** (✐02-6372 7199) is in
Church St.

❶ Getting There & Around

CountryLink (✐13 22 32; www.countrylink.
info) buses to Lithgow connect with Sydney
trains ($38, five hours). **Aeropelican** (✐02-
4928 9600; www.aeropelican.com.au) has daily
flights to Sydney ($129, 50 minutes).

Countryfit (www.countryfitbicyclehire.com.
au; 6-42 Short St; 1-4hrs $25, 1 day $30) has
bikes for hire.

Gulgong

POP 1910

This gorgeous time-warped town (www.
gulgong.net) once featured alongside author
Henry Lawson on the $10 note. Today the
narrow, rambling streets, classified by the
National Trust, are not so done-up that they
have lost their charm.

The huge **Gulgong Pioneer Museum**
(www.gulgong.net/museum.htm; 73 Herbert St;
adult/child $10/3.50) has one of the most
eclectic and chaotic collections of artefacts
in the state.

Author Henry Lawson spent part
of his childhood here, and the **Henry
Lawson Centre** (www.henrylawsongulgong.
org.au; 147 Mayne St; adult/child/family $5/3/12;

⊘10am-3.30pm Wed-Sat, to 1pm Sun & Tue)
looks at his early memories of the town.

Originally built from bark, the **Opera
House** (✐02-6374 1162; 99-101 Mayne St) is one
of the oldest surviving theatres in Australia
and still holds several performances a year.

Cudgegong Gallery (www.cudgegong
gallery.com.au; 102 Herbert St; ⊘10am-5pm) has
the most beautiful ceramics collection you're
likely to see.

Ten Dollar Town (✐02-6374 1204; www.ten
dollartownmotel.com.au; cnr Mayne & Medley Sts; r
from $110) is a motel with a heritage facade
and a rear garden and sitting area to make
you feel at home.

Butcher Shop Café (113 Mayne St; mains
$8-21; ⊘lunch & dinner) is a delightful little,
erm, former butcher shop, cleverly transformed. It serves a hearty array of food all
chalked up on the blackboard. The melts
and toasties are especially good.

The **visitor centre** (✐02-6374 1202; 66
Herbert St; ⊘10am-3pm Thu-Mon) has guides to
some terrific walks.

CountryLink (✐13 22 32; www.countrylink.
info) runs daily buses to Mudgee ($5, 30
minutes).

SOUTH COAST

If a road trip takes your fancy you've come to
the right place. The South Coast, breathtaking in the extreme, stretches 400km by road
to the Victorian border through rolling dairy
country, blast-from-the-past heritage towns,
stunning national parks and rugged coastline. Though the main thoroughfare, the
Princes Hwy (Rte 66), projects a lot of this
scenery onto your windscreen, the South
Coast is undoubtedly best experienced by
dipping on and off the road well travelled.
It's on the back roads and byways that isolated beaches, pristine camp sites and remote
lighthouses reveal themselves.

The South Coast's pit stops hold their
own, too. The holiday-hectic, coastal hubs of
Wollongong, Kiama, Batemans Bay, Narooma and Merimbula cater to holidaymakers
of all budgets with restaurants and bars to
match. Alternatively put the brakes on the
pace in the beautiful little beachside nooks
of Jervis Bay, Bermagui and Eden, where
the comforts of the city cater to a quieter
crowd just as partial to a day's fishing as an
espresso coffee.

The inland towns of Berry and Kangaroo
Valley manage to compete with their coastal

counterparts with top-notch restaurants, heritage buildings and vineyards.

With time on your hands, the region is inundated with activities, be it kayaking and scuba diving, hiking and camping, bike riding and boating. If you pack one thing, make it your binoculars – whales are quite fond of the South Coast, too.

Wollongong

POP 93,850

The 'Gong', 80km south of Sydney, is the envy of many cities. Sure, it has restaurants, bars, arts, culture and entertainment, that's easy enough. But it also enjoys a laid-back, beachside lifestyle impossible to match anywhere inland. Just to rub it in, Sydney is easily accessible by local rail.

There are 17 patrolled beaches – all unique – and a spectacular sandstone escarpment that runs from the Royal National Park south past Wollongong and Port Kembla. The Grand Pacific Dr makes the most of the landscape and the whole combination makes for a host of outdoor activities: excellent surf, safe beaches, bushwalks and sky-high adventures to name a few.

Crown St is the main street in town. Between Kembla and Keira Sts is a two-block pedestrian mall, badly in need of an update. Keira St is part of the Princes Hwy. Through-traffic bypasses the city on the Southern Fwy.

◎ Sights

Wollongong's fishing fleet is based at the southern end of the harbour, Belmore Basin. There's a fishing cooperative here (with a fish market and a couple of cafes) and an 1872 lighthouse on the point. Nearby, on the headland, is the newer Breakwater Lighthouse.

Along the highway, Nan Tien Buddhist Temple (☎02-4272 0600; www.nantien.org. au; Berkeley Rd, Berkeley; ◎9am-5pm Tue-Sun) has weekend retreats, vegetarian cooking classes, meditation and t'ai chi.

Brand spanking new, the Jumbulla Aboriginal Discovery Centre (www.jumbulla.com. au; visitor centre, Pacific Hwy, Bulli Tops, adult/child $15/10.50) explores the social history and culture of the Illawarra Aboriginal people with the latest technology, including four theatre narrations.

🏃 Activities

Taupu Surf School (☎02-4268 0088; www. taupusurfschool.com; 1/3 lessons $59/149; ◎Mon-Sat) runs courses at Thirroul and North Wollongong.

A bird's-eye view of the coastline is perhaps the best. HangglideOz (☎0417 939 200; www.hangglideoz.com.au) and Sydney Hang Gliding Centre (☎0400 258 258; www.hanggliding.com.au) offer tandem flights ($220) from breathtaking Bald Hill at Stanwell Park. If the adrenalin still hasn't kicked in, you can skydive from 14,000ft and land in the sand with Skydive the Beach (☎02-4225 8444; www.skydivethebeach. com; Stuart Park; tandem jumps $285-339; ◎any day, any time).

Southwest of Wollongong, the Illawarra Escarpment is a state recreation area. There's no vehicle access, but the spot is good for bushwalking. The Wollongong NPWS office (p207) can provide information on bush camping.

Just south of Wollongong, Lake Illawarra is very popular for water sports, including windsurfing.

🛏 Sleeping

The visitor centre can make accommodation reservations.

Keiraleagh   HOSTEL $

(☎02-4228 6765; www.backpack.net.au; 60 Kembla St; dm $20-25, s/d $43/70) This rambling heritage house is clogged with atmosphere, with pressed metal ceilings, roses in the cornices and festively painted rooms. The basic

---

NORTH BEACH & WOLLONGONG CITY BEACH

North Beach and Wollongong City Beach have breaks suitable for all visitors and are walking distance from the city centre. Look for the Acids Reef break on North Beach for more of a challenge. Up the coast, the options are varied and less crowded, with fun beach breaks at Coledale and Bulli beaches, and reef breaks at Sharkies (also at Coledale) and Headlands. The risk of meeting a finned friend at Sharkies is minimal, but surfers have occasionally encountered humpback whales surfacing close to shore.

Check out www.wannasurf.com for a full rundown on local waves and a five-day forecast.

Wollongong

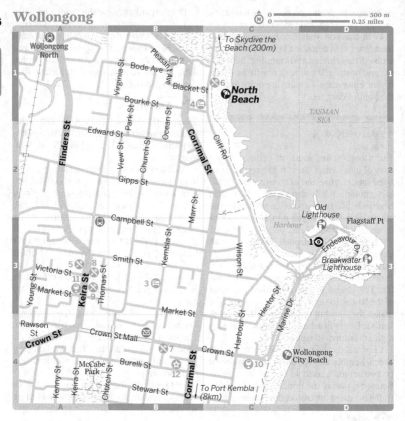

dorms are out the back, along with a sizeable patio and a BBQ.

**Coledale Beach Camping
Reserve** CAMPGROUND **$**
(☑02-4267 4302; Beach Rd, Coledale; unpowered/powered sites from $22/28) Small and right on the beach, this is one of the best urban camping spots on the coast.

Novotel Northbeach HOTEL **$$$**
(☑02-4226 3555; www.novotelnorthbeach.com.au; 2-14 Cliff Rd; r incl breakfast from $209; ✳@☲) Wollongong's flashiest joint is all class. The spacious and comfortable rooms have balconies with ocean or escarpment views.

Beach Park Motor Inn HOTEL **$$**
(☑02-4226 1577; 16 Pleasant Ave, North Beach; s $82-99, d $88-120; ✳) The friendly owners keep the slightly twee rooms in this white brick establishment spick and span. It's in an urban setting, a short walk from the beach.

✖ Eating

Keira St has the greatest concentration of restaurants, especially north of the mall.

TOP CHOICE Lee & Me CAFE **$**
(www.leeandme.com.au; 87 Crown St; mains $15; ⊗breakfast & lunch) A cafe and art-and-clothing store in a two-storey heritage building. There's nothing quite like dining on a mushroom and goats-cheese omelette on the sunny balcony, then shopping on a full stomach.

Diggies CAFE, BAR **$**
(www.diggies.com.au; 1 Cliff Rd, North Beach; tapas $7-11; ⊗breakfast & lunch daily, dinner Fri & Sat) With a view to the rolling waves, this is the perfect spot for feasting any time of day. Friday and Saturday evening is tapas time. From 4pm on Sunday arvo during summer, cocktails and tunes are let loose on the deck.

TOP CHOICE Caveau   MODERN AUSTRALIAN **$$$**

(☏02-4226 4855; www.caveau.com.au; 122-124 Keira St; 2-/3-/7-course degustation $60/77/95; ⊘dinner Tue-Sat) Sitting unpretentiously on Keira St, this lauded restaurant washed in a soft amber glow serves gourmet treats such as mushroom ravioli with asparagus and shaved truffle.

Lorenzo's Diner   ITALIAN **$$**

(☏02-4229 5633; www.lorenzosdiner.com.au; 119 Keira St; mains $19-34; ⊘lunch Thu & Fri, dinner Tue-Sat) Seriously nice people run this upmarket modern Italian restaurant. The food matches the excellent service. Bookings recommended.

Old Siam Style   THAI **$**

(157 Keira St; mains $14; ⊘lunch & dinner) One of the more sleek restaurants on the Keira St strip, this spacious place with all the trimmings serves up exquisite authentic Thai dishes, orchids and all.

🍷 Drinking & Entertainment

Hotel Illawarra   PUB

(www.hotelillawarra.com.au; cnr Market & Keira Sts; ⊘11am-late) Best suited to the cocktail-sipping funky set, this complex has the red-hued Amber bar and Cucina Illawarra, which dishes up Mediterranean fare, tapas-style.

Five Islands Brewing Company   BAR

(www.fiveislandsbrewery.com; WIN Entertainment Centre, cnr Crown & Harbour Sts; ⊘11am-1am) This slick bar has nine fine draught beers, including a Pig Dog Pilsner, named after the owner (an ex-St George rugby player).

Illawarra Performing Arts Centre   THEATRE

(IPAC; ☏02-4226 3366; www.ipac.org.au; 32 Burelli St) For a cultural injection here you'll find excellent theatre, dance and music, including topical productions.

ℹ Information

The **Wollongong visitors centre** (☏02-4227 5545; www.tourismwollongong.com) has moved to purpose-built premises inconveniently located 20 minutes from the CBD on the Princes Hwy at Bulli Tops.

NPWS office (☏02-4223 3000; ground fl, State Government Office Block, Market St; ⊘9am-3pm Mon-Fri)

ℹ Getting There & Away

All long-distance buses leave from the **long distance bus station** (☏4226 1022; cnr Keira & Campbell Sts). **Premier** (☏13 34 10; www.premierms.com.au) has buses to Sydney ($18, two hours) and Eden ($69, eight hours). **Murrays** (☏13 22 51; www.murrays.com.au) travels to Canberra ($33, 3½ hours). **CountryLink** (☏13 22 32; www.countrylink.info) runs buses to Moss Vale ($7.80, 1½ hours) from outside the train station, and links with **CityRail** (☏13 15 00; www.cityrail.info) to Sydney's Central Station ($8, 1½ hours). CityRail also runs south to Kiama, Gerringong and Bomaderry/Nowra.

ℹ Getting Around

Bringing a bike on the train from Sydney is a great way to get around; a cycle path runs from the city centre north to Bulli and south to Port Kembla.

Two local bus companies, **Premier Illawarra** (☏02-4271 1322; www.premierillawarra.com.au) and **Dions** (☏02-4254 4888; www.dions.com.au), service the local area. The main stops

HERE'S TO THE VIEW

Built in 1886 and now heritage-listed, the grand old Scarborough Hotel (www.scarbor oughhotel.com.au; 383 Lawrence Hargrave Dr, Scarborough) has recently been renovated, reopened and reinvigorated so that punters can once again take advantage of one of the best beer gardens in NSW, if not Australia. The ocean view from the wooden bench seats and tables is so spectacular it wouldn't matter if the beer was warm. It's not, thankfully, and the gastro food (mains $12 to $33) gets thumbs up too.

are on Marine Dr, and the corner of Crown and Keira Sts.

The number 55 **Gong Shuttle** (www.131500. com.au; ⊙7am-10pm Mon-Fri, to 6pm Sat & Sun) runs every 10 minutes from 7am to 6pm weekdays and every 20 minutes at other times.

For taxis, call ⊉02-4229 9311.

Wollongong to Nowra

This region has some great beaches, state forests and, in the ranges to the west, the big Morton National Park. It's a popular family-holiday area, but it isn't yet as crowded as parts of the north coast and much of the tourism is confined to weekenders from Sydney. Lake Illawarra is popular for water sports.

Further south is Shellharbour, a popular holiday resort and one of the oldest towns along the coast (its name comes from the number of shell middens, remnants of Aboriginal feasts, that the early Europeans found here). There are beaches on the Windang Peninsula north of the town and scuba diving off Bass Point to the south.

KIAMA & AROUND

Right on the water's edge with good beaches and surf, Kiama (population 12,286) hasn't had to work hard for its share of glory. What it has done is admirable and tasteful, making this one of the best stops on the South Coast. The visitor centre is on Blowhole Point, so called because of a blowhole that can spurt water 60m.

⊙ Sights & Activities

There's a good lookout from the top of Saddleback Mountain, and waves at Surf and Bombo Beaches. A new 6km coastal walk with the requisite boulders, beaches, sea caves and cliff faces stretches from Love's Bay in Kiama Heights to the north end of Werri Beach.

Amid the flora and fauna of the Southern Highlands, about 14km inland from Kiama, the fabulous Illawarra Fly Tree Top

Walk (⊉1300 362 881; www.illawarrafly.com.au; 182 Knights Hill Rd, Knights Hill; adult/child/family $22/9.50/55; ⊙9am-7pm) takes visitors on a 500m elevated walk to the edge of the forest with spectacular Illawarra and ocean views. Near the tree top walk, the Minnamurra Rainforest Centre has two stunning nature walks and a NPWS visitor centre (⊉02-4236 0469) in beautiful Budderoo National Park (per car $11). On the way you'll pass through the old village of Jamberoo, which has a nice pub.

✗ Sleeping & Eating

Kiama Harbour Cabins CABINS $$$
(⊉02-4232 2707; Blowhole Point, Kiama; 1/2/3-bedroom cabins from $205/220/280) These are in the best position in town and have barbecues on the front verandahs, which overlook the beach and the ocean pool.

Bellevue GUESTHOUSE $$
(⊉02-4232 4000; 21 Minnamurra St, Kiama; r from $180) This charming house hosts guests in luxury serviced apartments in a two-storey 1890s heritage manor. It has ocean views and is a short walk to the main street.

Grand Hotel PUB $
(⊉02-4232 1037; www.grandhotelkiama.com. au; 49 Manning St, Kiama; per person $35) The Grand caters to backpackers with basic but clean rooms. The self-contained studio apartment next door is $200 per night.

Chachi's ITALIAN $$
(⊉02-4233 1144; 32 Collins St; mains $14-34; ⊙dinner Mon-Sat, Sun during summer) Located in a historic strip of terraced houses, Chachi's is well loved among locals for its casual Italian alfresco dining. The smells wafting onto the pavement are irresistible.

ℹ Information
Visitor centre (⊉02-4232 3322, 1300 654 262; www.kiama.com.au) On Blowhole Point.

Getting There & Away

Premier (📞13 34 10; www.premierms.com.au) buses run twice daily to Berry ($18, 30 minutes), Eden ($69, 7½ hours) and Sydney ($25, 2½ hours). **Kiama Coachlines** (📞02-4232 3466; www.kiamacoachlines.com.au) runs to Gerroa, Gerringong and Minnamurra (via Jamberoo).

Frequent **CityRail** (📞13 15 00; www.cityrail.info) trains run to Wollongong, Sydney and Bomaderry/Nowra.

BERRY
POP 1490

Berry has metamorphosed from a small retiree kind of town into a popular inland South Coast stop. Is the chintz outweighing the heritage character these days? You decide. In any case, it has a plethora of great eating venues, an overdose of cafes (some good, some average), two pubs fit for shouting a round or two, and a smattering of National Trust–classified buildings.

⊙ Sights & Activities

There are several nearby wineries. **Hotel Berry** (📞02-4464 1011; 120 Queen St; ⊘11am Sat) runs a short-and-sweet wine tour ($30), but you need to book ahead.

Mild to Wild (📞02-4464 2211; www.m2w.com.au; 84 Queen St) offers adventure tours such as a pedal, picnic and plunge.

🛏 Sleeping & Eating

Accommodation is abundant in Berry, but prices rise at weekends. Holiday apartments can be booked through **Elders Real Estate** (📞02-4464 1600; 121 Queen St).

Hotel Berry   PUB $
(📞02-4464 1011; 120 Queen St; s/d without bathroom $50/80) This popular local watering hole has standard but large pub bedrooms. Its rear dining room serves grilled steaks and other pub grub.

Village Boutique   MOTEL $$
(📞02-4464 3570; www.berrymotel.com.au; 72 Queen St; r $155-235; ❋ ✿) Stylish rooms (some with a spa). The pool is more water-feature size.

Hungry Duck   ASIAN FUSION $$
(📞02-4464 2323; 85 Queen St; mains $9-28; ⊘lunch Sun, dinner Wed-Sat) Has a contemporary Asian menu served tapas-style. Fresh fish and meat are sourced locally and the eggs are from the chef's own chooks. Try the tempura zucchini flowers with aged soy and citrus. Book ahead.

Berry Woodfired Sourdough   BAKERY $
(Prince Alfred St; mains $5-17; ⊘breakfast & lunch Wed-Sun) Delicious bread is baked here, or sit down for a light meal.

🛍 Shopping

Treat Factory   FOOD
(www.treatfactory.com.au; Old Creamery Lane; ⊘9.30am-4.30pm Mon-Fri, 10am-4pm Sat & Sun) This place is chock-full of nostalgic favourites such as rocky road and liquorice.

ℹ Information

The main visitor centre is about 20km south in Nowra. Try www.berry.net.au.

Getting There & Away

There are scenic roads from Berry to pretty Kangaroo Valley. **Premier** (📞13 34 10; www.premierms.com.au) has buses to Kiama ($18, 30 minutes), Nowra ($18, 20 minutes) and Sydney ($25, three hours, twice daily).

Frequent **CityRail** (📞131 500; www.cityrail.info) trains go to Wollongong ($6, 1¼ hours) and Nowra ($4, 10 minutes) from **Berry station** (📞02-4464 1022; Station Rd), with connections to Sydney.

KANGAROO VALLEY
POP 320

Unbelievably picturesque Kangaroo Valley is pegged in by a fortress of rainforest-covered cliffs and the valley floor is carpeted by cow-dotted pasturelands, river gums and gurgling creeks. The slow country town of Kangaroo Valley itself has an excellent pub, bakery and general store, plus the odd feel-good shop and gallery to satiate wealthy Sydneysiders who populate the town at the weekend.

The formal entry to the valley is the castellated sandstone-and-iron **Hamden Bridge** (1898), a few kilometres north of the town. The beach just below the bridge is a good spot for a swim.

Next to the bridge, the walkabout **Pioneer Museum Park** (📞02-4465 1306; Hampden Bridge, Moss Vale Rd; adult/child/family $7/5/15; ⊘10am-4pm Fri-Mon Oct-Easter, 11am-3pm Fri-Mon Easter-Sep) provides a visual encounter with rural life in the late 19th century.

Kangaroo Valley Adventure Co (📞02-4465 1372; www.kvac.com.au; Glenmack Park camp site) offers combined hiking and biking (half-day $60), canoeing and camping (overnight $75) and biking, hiking and kayaking (full day $100).

Kangaroo Valley Safaris (📞02-4465 1502; www.kangaroovalleycanoes.com.au; 2210 Moss Vale Rd) rents canoes and bikes (half/full day

$35/50) and runs overnight canoe ($90) and sea-kayak ($130) camping trips.

Near the Hamden Bridge, the pretty little Hamden Cottage (☑02-4465 1502; 2210 Moss Vale Rd; d incl breakfast $245) has a rear garden that attracts wallabies.

There's a carpet of grass to pitch a tent on at Glenmack Park (☑02-4465 1372; www.glen-mack.com.au; 215 Moss Vale Rd; adult/child $10/7, cabins from $75) or take the more comfortable option of a cabin. You can light a campfire (such a rarity!). For a bush-camping experience head north out of town to Bendeela picnic spot. It's signed.

Friendly Inn Hotel (☑02-4465 1355; 159 Moss Vale Rd; mains $18; ⊙lunch & dinner) is Kangaroo Valley's heartbeat, a classic country boozer, ever-so-subtly renovated to retain its local character. The rear grassy beer garden has gorgeous views, or sit on the sunny pub verandah to people-watch.

A few doors up from the pub, Café Bella (151 Moss Vale Rd; mains $15-24; ⊙breakfast & lunch Thu-Sun, dinner Fri-Sun) has books, nooks and crannies and is a homely place for a no-fuss eggs-and-bacon breakfast.

Kennedy's Bus Service (☑1300 133 477; www.kennedystours.com.au) has daily buses to Moss Vale via Fitzroy Falls, and Nowra via Cambewarra.

Nowra

POP 27,480

Nowra sits about 17km from the coast and is the largest town in the Shoalhaven area. Although it's not top of the pops in terms of beach holidays, it is a handy base for excursions to beaches and villages around the region.

The 6.5-hectare Nowra Wildlife Park (☑02-4421 3949; www.nowrawildlifepark.com.au; Rock Hill Rd, North Nowra; adult/child $16/8), on the north bank of the Shoalhaven River, is a hangout for mammals, birds and reptiles. It has a fully catered camp site (adult/child $10/6).

The relaxing Ben's Walk starts at the bridge near Scenic Dr and follows the south bank of the Shoalhaven River (6km return). North of the river, the circular 5.5km Bomaderry Creek Walking Track runs through sandstone gorges from a trailhead at the end of Narang Rd.

Shoalhaven River Cruises (☑0429 981 007; www.shoalhavenrivercruise.com; 2hr cruise $26; ☒) has river tours that leave from the wharf, near the visitor centre.

George Bass Motor Inn (☑02-4421 6388; www.georgebass.com.au; 65 Bridge Rd; s $109-129, d $124-144) has decent motel rooms. Whitehouse (☑02-4421 2084; www.white houseguesthouse.com; 30 Junction St; s/d/tr from $90/110/130) is a homely and family-friendly guesthouse.

The old renovated Boatshed Restaurant (☑02-4423 4936; 10 Wharf Rd; mains $28; ⊙breakfast Sat & Sun, lunch Fri-Sun, dinner Thu-Sat) serves excellent food with a river view.

Red Raven (☑02-4423 3433; 55 Junction St; mains $26; ⊙lunch Tue-Fri, dinner Tue-Sat), in an old fire-brigade building, dishes up distinctly Aussie flavours such as roasted kangaroo fillets with polenta chips.

The Shoalhaven visitor centre (☑1300 662 808; www.shoalhavenholidays.com.au; Princes Hwy; @) is just south of the bridge. There's also a NPWS office (☑02-4423 2170; 55 Graham St).

Premier (☑13 34 10; www.premierms.com. au) coaches stop on the run between Sydney ($25, three hours) via Berry ($18, 20 minutes), and Melbourne ($82, 14 hours) via Ulladulla ($19, one hour).

The train station (☑4423 0141; Meroo St) is 3km north of town at Bomaderry. Frequent CityRail (☑131 500; www.cityrail.info) trains go to Wollongong ($7.80, 1¼ hours) via Berry ($4, 10 minutes), with connections to Sydney.

Jervis Bay

South of Nowra, Jervis Bay is a scenically opulent and unmissable stretch of coastline with white sandy beaches, bushland, forest and a protected marine park. Huskisson (population 1593), one of the oldest towns on the bay, is the main hub. It has a handful of excellent eating venues, plenty of adventure-based activity and delightful surrounds that make it a great place to spend a night or two.

◉ Sights & Activities

Lady Denman Heritage Complex   MUSEUM
(☑02-4441 5675; www.ladydenman.asn.au; Dent St; adult/child $10/5; ⊙10am-4pm) This complex has interesting history on Jervis Bay, a maritime museum and a small visitor centre. On the first Saturday of each month it hosts a growers market.

Dolphin Watch Cruises   DOLPHIN-WATCHING
(☑02-441 6311; www.dolphinwatch.com.au; 50 Owen St) June to November is prime whale time. This place has the best reputation for dolphin-watching (adult/child $35/20,

SURF & TURF

East of Nowra, the Shoalhaven River meanders through dairy country in a system of estuaries and wetlands, finally reaching the sea at Crookhaven Heads, aka Crooky, where there's good surf. Greenwell Point, on the estuary about 15km east of Nowra is a quiet, pretty fishing village specialising in **fresh oysters**. The little kiosk near the pier has fish and chips.

On the north side of the estuary is Shoalhaven Heads, where the river once reached the sea but is now blocked by sandbars. Just north of the surf beach here is stunning Seven Mile Beach National Park stretching up to Gerroa. It's an idyllic picnic spot.

Just before Shoalhaven Heads you pass through Coolangatta, the site of the earliest European settlement on this coast. Coolangatta Estate (☎02-4448 7131; www.coolangattaestate.com.au; s/d $120/140; ⊙winery 10am-5pm) is a slick winery with a golf course, a good restaurant and accommodation in convict-built buildings.

two hours) and whale-watching (adult/child $65/35, three hours, May to November) tours.

Dive Jervis Bay DIVING
(☎02-4441 5255; www.divejervisbay.com; 64 Owen St; 1/2 dives for $100/170)

Hire Au Go-Go CYCLING
(☎02-4441 5241; www.hireaugogo.com.au; 1 Tomerong St; 1hr/day $18/60) Electric bike for exploring pathways around the water's edge.

Jervis Bay Kayaks KAYAKING
(☎02-4441 7157; www.jervisbaykayaks.com; 13 Hawke St) Kayak rentals (two-hour/day $39/69) or guided half-day paddling ($96).

🛌 Sleeping & Eating

There's substantial accommodation in Huskisson and Vincentia; book ahead for weekends and holidays, when prices soar.

TOP CHOICE Paperbark Camp CAMPGROUND $$$
(☎1300 668 167; www.paperbarkcamp.com.au; 571 Woollamia Rd; d from $350; ⊙Sep-Jun) Ecotourism at its luxury best: this five-star accommodation includes 12 safari-style tents with outdoor showers, plus Gunyah Restaurant (☎02-4441 7299; mains $35; ⊙dinner), which sits among the treetops.

Jervis Bay Guesthouse GUESTHOUSE $$$
(☎02-4441 7658; www.jervisbayguesthouse.com.au; Owen St; r incl breakfast $235-255) This beautifully restored wooden manor opposite the beach has views and verandahs.

Huskisson B&B B&B $$
(☎02-4441 7551; www.huskissonbnb.com.au; 12 Tomerong St; r from $195; ❄) A quaint weatherboard with bright and airy eclectic rooms containing comfy beds and fluffy towels.

TOP CHOICE Seagrass Brasserie SEAFOOD $$
(☎02-4441 6124; www.seagrass.net.au; mains $34; ⊙dinner) With its wooden louver windows and white tablecloths, this eatery combines indoor and outdoor deck dining. Seafood with Asian ingredients is a stand out, so too the bloody Mary oyster shots.

Supply CAFE $
(☎02-4441 5815; shop 1, 54 Owen St; mains $8-15; ⊙breakfast & lunch) The fresh and healthy fodder and juices found here are echoed in the floor-to-ceiling shelves of produce.

ℹ Getting There & Around

Jervis Bay Territory (☎02-4423 5244) runs a bus around Jervis Bay communities, and from Huskisson to Nowra three times every weekday and once on Saturday and Sunday. **Nowra Coaches** (☎02-4423 5244; www.nowracoaches.com.au) runs a bus (route 733) around Jervis Bay and to Nowra (70 minutes) on Tuesdays and Fridays.

Around Jervis Bay

Ulladulla (population 10,300) itself doesn't have much to offer. There is, however, good swimming and surfing nearby at Mollymook beach, just north of town. Or head to Pigeon House Mountain/Didthul (p212), which has a fantastic walk.

If you do spend a night, try Traveller's Rest Accommodation (☎02-4454 0500; www.southcoastbackpackers.com; 63 Pacific Hwy, Ulladulla; dm/d/tw $30/65/65) aka Southcoast Backpackers. At the other end of the budget, welcoming Ulladulla Guest House (☎02-4455 1796; www.guesthouse.com.au; 39 Burrill St, Ulladulla; d $218-248; ❄❄) has art-lined walls and a fantastic French restaurant (open for dinner Thursday to Tuesday).

TOP CHOICE Cupitt's Winery & Restaurant (☎02-4455 7888; www.cupittwines.com.au; 60 Washburton Rd, Ulladulla; mains $32-37; ☺lunch Wed-Sun, dinner Fri & Sat) is a little piece of Provence with some of the most respected cuisine this side of Sydney. Wine tasting is in the restored 1851 creamery and there's boutique accommodation in the vineyard.

Premier (☎13 34 10; www.premierms.com.au) coaches stop on the run between Sydney ($35, five hours) and Melbourne ($82, 12 hours) via Batemans Bay ($16, 45 minutes) and Nowra ($19, one hour). Ulladulla Bus Lines (☎4455 1674; www.ulladullabus.com.au) services the local area, including Milton, Narrawallee and Mollymook.

Batemans Bay

POP 10,850

The good beaches and a luscious estuary in this fishing port have given it a leg-up to become one of the South Coast's largest holiday centres. But the town and waterfront are lacklustre, and the food scene is yet to take off.

⊙ Sights & Activities

Beaches

Corrigans Beach is the closest patch of sand to the town centre. South of here is a series of small beaches nibbled into the rocky shore. Surfers flock to Surf Beach, Malua Bay and Broulee, which has a small wave when everywhere else is flat. For the experienced, the best surfing in the area is at Pink Rocks (near Broulee). For amateurs Soulrider Surf School

(☎02-4478 6297; www.soulrider.com.au; 1hr adult/child $45/40) conducts lessons on Surf Beach.

Boats

On the north side of the Clyde River estuary, just across the bridge, there are a couple of boat-hire places. Several boats offer cruises up the estuary from the ferry wharf just east of the bridge, including Merinda Cruises (☎02-4472 4052; www.southcoast.com.au/tickets/merinda; Boatshed, Clyde St; 3hr cruise adult/child $27/14; ☺11.30am). Region X (☎0400 184 034; www.regionxrivers.com) hosts three-hour sea-kayak ($75), and morning or evening ($99) tours. Bay & Beyond (☎02-4478 7777; www.bayandbeyond.com.au) does similar.

🛏 Sleeping & Eating

Holiday apartments are profuse; letting agents include Nola Debney Real Estate (☎02-4472 1218; www.beachfrontholidays.com.au). Rates go up in summer.

Clyde River Motor Inn   MOTEL $$
(☎02-4472 6444; www.clydemotel.com.au; 3 Clyde St; s $90-136, d $100-157, f $136; ☀) This central motel is excellent value, with good river rooms and townhouses.

Esplanade Motor Inn   MOTEL $$$
(☎02-4472 0200; www.esplanade.com.au; 23 Beach Rd; d $130-230) If you're cashed up, try this place for river views that kick butt.

Shady Willow Holiday
Park   HOSTEL, CARAVAN PARK $
(☎02-4472 6111; www.shadywillows.com.au; cnr South St & Old Princes Hwy; dm/d $27/57; ☀☎☺) YHA set amid static caravans and shady palms, with a boho ambience.

PIGEON HOUSE MOUNTAIN

Climbing Pigeon House Mountain (720m) in the far south of Morton National Park might be the kind of upper-thigh workout that isn't called for on holiday, but the rewards make any huffing and puffing worthwhile.

The main access road leaves the highway about 8km south of Ulladulla, then it's a rough and rocky 26km drive to the picnic area at the start of the track. The return walk takes three to four hours but plan for longer; the summit is barbaric-yawp territory where the rest of the world rolls out from under your feet in all directions.

On a clear day, Gulaga (Mt Dromedary) sticks its head up in the south and to the northwest is Point Perpendicular. In between, a canopy of stunning national park vegetation spreads out like a blanket, occasionally making creases in the steep gorges carved by the Clyde River and flattening out over the elongated plateaus of Byangee Walls and the Castle.

People with a fear of heights should avoid the final section; and be sure to take water.

BOODEREE NATIONAL PARK

Occupying Jervis Bay's southeastern spit, this stunning **park** (2-day car entry $10) combines heathland, small rainforest pockets, sparkling water, white sandy beaches and a botanic garden. In 1995 the Wreck Bay Aboriginal community won a land claim and now jointly administers the vast park. There are walks aplenty, basic camp sites and beaches. Get maps and info from **Booderee visitor centre** (02-4443 0977; www.booderee.gov. au; Jervis Bay Rd) at the park entrance.

North Stg   CAFE & BAR **$**
(North St, Batemans Bay; ⊙breakfast & lunch)
This refreshingly funky little den has decent coffee and a tasty selection of salads and light lunches ($9 to $18). It's a neat place for a wine, too.

Monet's   CAFE **$$**
(www.monetscafe.com.au; 2/5 Orient St; mains $20; ⊙breakfast & lunch, tapas Thu-Sat). Also worth trying.

An alternative accommodation option is to gather your mates and hire a houseboat. **Bay River Houseboats** (02-4472 5649; www.bayriverhouseboats.com.au; Wray St) and **Clyde River Houseboats** (02-4472 6369; www.clyderiverhouseboats.com.au) lease six-/10-berth boats from $840 for four nights (Monday to Friday).

⊙ Information

The **visitor centre** (1800 802 528; Princes Hwy) has local art for sale. **Livefire** (02-4472 2006; shop 1, 6 Orient St; per 20min $2) has internet access.

⊙ Getting There & Away

Murrays (13 22 51; www.murrays.com.au) services Batemans Bay with daily services to Canberra ($22, 2½ hours), Moruya ($16, one hour) and Narooma ($24, two hours). **Premier** (13 34 10; www.premierms.com.au) coaches stop on the run between Sydney ($45, six hours) and Melbourne ($73, 11 hours) via Ulladulla ($16, 45 minutes) and Moruya ($11, 30 minutes).

Narooma

POP 3100

Narooma is a sleepy little seaside town with a large number of retiree residents adding to its snail-paced leisurely atmosphere. It's also one of the prettier coastal towns, boasting the attractive Wagonga River

inlet, a picturesque bridge and relatively little development.

The visitor centre, incorporating the Lighthouse Museum, is just south of the bridge.

⊙ Sights & Activities

Narooma is an access point for Deua, Gulaga and Wadbilliga National Parks.

Water Sports
Mystery Bay, between Cape Dromedary and Corunna Point, is rocky but good for **surfing**, as is Handkerchief Beach. More relaxing **swims** can be had at the south end of Bar Beach. On the other side of the Wagonga Inlet entrance, 400m as the crow flies, **Bar Rock Lookout** has views of Montague Island. The clear waters around the island are good for **diving**, especially from February to June when you can snorkel with the fur seals. **Boat hire** and **fishing charters** are available along Riverside Dr.

Other Sights & Activities
Island Charters
Narooma   DIVING, WHALE-WATCHING
(02-4476 1047; www.islandchartersnarooma. com) This popular company offers diving ($85), snorkelling ($75) and whale-watching ($80/55 adult/child). Attractions in the area include grey nurse sharks, fur seals and the wreck of the SS *Lady Darling*. For the cheapest deal, book tours at the visitor centre.

Wagonga Princess   CRUISING
(02-4476 2665; ; adult/child/family $33/22/100; ⊙3hr cruise departs 1pm Sun, Wed & Fri Feb-Dec, daily Jan) Cruise on this century-old electric ferry up the Wagonga River.

Mills Bay Boardwalk   WALKING
Heading north over the bridge, take the first two right turns to this 5km wheelchair- and pram-friendly walking track where you can spot large schools of fish and stingrays.

MURRAMARANG NATIONAL PARK

This beautiful, coastal **park** (per car per day $7) is home to wild kangaroos and lorikeets and the protected **Murramarang Aboriginal Area**, which contains ancient middens and other Indigenous cultural treasures. Inside the park, stunning **Pretty** (☎02-4457 2019; unpowered sites adult/child $10/5, powered sites $14/7), **Pebbly** (☎02-4478 6023; adult/child $10/5) and **Depot Beach** (☎02-4478 6582; unpowered sites adult/child $10/5, powered sites $14/7) camping grounds are idyllic locations close to the surf (Pebbly is the most popular for surfing). Pretty Beach is the most accessible. No caravans are allowed at Pebbly Beach.

🛌 Sleeping & Eating

Narooma Real Estate (☎02-4476 2169), opposite the visitor centre, rents holiday accommodation.

Narooma YHA   HOSTEL **$**
(☎02-4476 3287; www.yha.com.au; 243 Princes Hwy; dm/d $32/75; @) A YHA stalwart, this place has comfortable, clean motel-style rooms and fun hosts.

Whale Motor Inn   HOTEL **$$**
(☎02-4476 2411; www.whalemotorinn.com; 104 Wagonga St; d $120-205; ❄❀) This place offers the best all-round views of Narooma. It has large, clean renovated rooms with balconies, and an excellent **restaurant** (mains $34).

Lynch's Hotel   HOTEL **$**
(☎02-4476 2001; 135 Wagonga St; s/d without bathroom $50/80) This old-school place in the heart of town has lovely rooms, and shared kitchen and bathroom facilities. Downstairs is a cute French restaurant open for dinner.

Taylor's Seafood   FISH & CHIPS **$**
(Riverside Dr; mains $7-16; ⊙lunch & dinner Tue-Sun) Taylor's does cheap takeaways but why miss out on the chance to consume the grilled fish and nongreasy chunky chips while gazing at paradise.

Quarterdeck Marina   SEAFOOD **$$**
(13 Riverside Dr; mains $22; ⊙breakfast & lunch Thu-Mon) With its colourful, eclectic decor, Quarterdeck serves ah-me-hearties breakfasts and fresh seafood lunches on a great enclosed deck overhanging the river.

ℹ Information

NPWS office (☎02-4476 0800; www.national parks.nsw.gov.au; cnr Graham & Burrawang Sts)
Visitor centre (☎1800 240 003, 02-4476 2881; www.eurobodalla.com.au; Princes Hwy)

ℹ Getting There & Around

Premier (☎13 34 10; www.premierms.com. au) has buses to Melbourne ($67, 10 hours) via Eden ($27, 2½ hours), and Sydney ($58, seven hours) via Wollongong ($56, five hours). Buses stop outside Lynch's Hotel. **Murrays** (☎13 22 51; www.murrays.com.au) runs to Moruya ($17, one hour), Batemans Bay ($22, two hours) and Canberra ($33, 4½ hours).

Around Narooma

About 10km offshore from Narooma, **Montague Island** was once an important source of food for local Aborigines (who called it Barunguba) and is now a nature reserve. **Little penguins** nest here; the best time to see them is spring. Many other seabirds and hundreds of fur seals also call the island home, and there's a historic **lighthouse**.

Narooma Charters (☎0407 909 111; adult/child/family $130/99/430) operates a daily four-hour boat trip to Montague Island, including a NPWS tour. Take the afternoon trip if you want to see the little penguins.

Off the highway, 15km south of Narooma, **Central Tilba** is perched on the side of **Gulaga** (Mt Dromedary; 797m). It's a delightful 19th-century gold-mining boomtown. There's information and a town guide at **Bates Emporium** (Bates St; ⊙8am-5pm), at the start of the main street. Further along are several craft, antique and gift shops, galleries, and food venues, including the **ABC Cheese Factory** (⊙9am-5pm) where you can chow down on cheddar.

Nearby **Gulaga National Park** includes Gulaga Flora Reserve, a large portion of Gulaga and the former **Wallaga Lake** national park. Wallaga Lake is a worthy scenic drive in its own right.

On the Princes Hwy is **Cobargo**, another unspoilt old town. Near here is the main 2WD access point to rugged **Wadbilliga National Park**, a subalpine wilderness area of 98,530 hectares.

BERMAGUI

POP 1300

South of the beautiful bird-filled Wallaga Lake and off the Princes Hwy, Bermagui is a pretty fishing port with a main street that hums to the sound of small-town contentment. The visitor centre ([🖉]02-6493 3054; www.bermagui.net; Bunga St) was the first sign that tourists had cottoned on to the place. Now there's a new whiz-bang Fishermen's Wharf (Lamont St), designed by renowned architect and resident Philip Cox, with all the tempters city visitors expect.

There are several walks around Bermagui, including 6km north along the coast to Camel Rock and a further 2km to Wallaga Lake. There's good surfing at Camel Rock and Cuttagee beaches, or you could toss a mullet from the shops and hit Shelly Beach, a child-friendly swimming spot. A kilometre's wander around the point will bring you to the Blue Pool, a dramatic ocean pool built into the base of the cliffs.

🛏 Sleeping & Eating

TOP CHOICE Bermagui Beach Hotel   HOTEL $$
([🖉]02-6493 4206; 10 Lamont St; r 110-135; ❉) This is a gorgeous old place with the best balcony views in town. Stay here to tap into the local scene. The suites have spas.

Julie Rutherford Real Estate   RENTAL HOUSE $$
([🖉]02-6493 3444; www.julierutherford.com.au) Located at the wharf, this place can assist with lettings. One option is Seaview Flats (per week $385), a row of blue-and-white two-bedroom beach huts on the main road into town.

Zane Grey Park   CARAVAN PARK $
([🖉]02-6493 4382; www.zanegreytouristpark.com. au; Lamont St; powered/unpowered sites $27/22, cabins $47-95) This place has a prime position on Dickson's Point, a Frisbee throw from Horseshoe Bay.

TOP CHOICE Bluewave Seafoods   FISH & CHIPS $
(Fishermen's Wharf; fish & chips $10; ⊙lunch & dinner) Has the best fish and chips on the South Coast.

Il Passaggio   ITALIAN $$
(Fishermen's Wharf; mains $29; ⊙lunch Fri-Sun, dinner Tue-Sun) Dishes up excellent modern Italian in a contemporary dining room with white walls and red leather.

🍷 Drinking

TOP CHOICE Mister Jones   CAFE
(1/4 Bunga St; www.misterjones.com.au; ⊙7am-2pm Tue-Sat) This cool espresso bar–cum–art studio would go unnoticed if it weren't for the caffeine fiends sitting outside sipping on cappuccinos topped with choc chunks.

Horse & Camel Wine Bar   WINE BAR
(Fishermen's Wharf; www.horseandcamel.com. au; ⊙2-10pm Wed-Sun summer, Thu-Sun winter) Grab a vino here.

❶ Getting There & Away

Premier ([🖉]13 34 10; www.premierms.com. au) stops here once a day on the run between Sydney ($60, 10 hours) via Narooma ($13, 40 minutes), and Eden ($24, 1¾ hours) via Merimbula ($20, 45 minutes).

South to the Victorian Border

Running along 20km of beautiful coastline, Mimosa Rocks National Park (per car $7) is 5802 hectares of earthly paradise with dense and varied bush, caves, headlands and beaches with crystal-clear water. There are basic camp sites (adult/child $10/5) at Aragunnu Beach, Picnic Point, and Middle and Gillards Beaches. The Narooma NPWS office ([🖉]02-4476 0800; www.national parks.nsw.gov.au) has more info.

Taking in most of the coast from Merimbula north to Tathra (on beautiful Sapphire Coast Dr), Bournda National Park (per car $7) is a 2654-hectare park with good beaches, freshwater lagoons and several walking trails. Camping (adult/child $10/5) is permitted at Hobart Beach, on the southern shore of the big Wallagoot Lagoon. Contact the Merimbula NPWS office ([🖉]02-6495 5000) for more information.

MERIMBULA

POP 3850

The surplus of nondescript hotels and holiday apartments lining the sloping main street of Merimbula still manages to play second fiddle to the town's impressive inlet (or lake). The rocking boat masts and sky-blue water – catering to fisherfolk throwing in a line wherever they please – make this popular holiday place very easy on the eye.

◎ Sights & Activities

Boardwalk　　　　　　　　　　WALKING

West of the bridge, just off the causeway, a magnificent 1.75km boardwalk takes nature lovers and morning people hopping and skipping around mangroves, oyster farms and melaleucas. Pick up the useful brochure at the tourist information centre.

Merimbula Aquarium　　　　　AQUARIUM

(www.merimbulawharf.com.au; Lake St; adult/child $11.50/6.50; ☉10am-4pm) At the wharf on the eastern point is this small aquarium. There are good views across the lake from near here and the jetty is a popular fishing spot.

Merimbula Divers Lodge　　　　DIVING

(☎02-6495 3611; www.merimbuladiverslodge.com.au; 15 Park St) The lodge has PADI-certificate courses ($499), shore dives (one/two $77/99 plus $55 for gear), three wreck dives and a cave dive.

Coastlife Adventures　　　　　SURFING

(☎02-6494 1122; www.coastlife.com.au) This place does morning surf ($55) and stand-up paddle ($30) lessons as well as marine kayak tours ($55).

Merimbula Marina　　　　　　CRUISING

(Merimbula jetty) The small kiosk here runs five-hour reef cruises (adult/child $100/60), two-hour dolphin cruises ($30/25) and whale-watching cruises (from $40/25) from September to November. There's also boat hire ($35/90 per hour/per day).

🛏 Sleeping & Eating

Self-contained apartments are usually let on a weekly basis, particularly in summer when rates take a hike. Letting agents include **Fisk & Nagle** (☎02-6495 2000; www.getawaymerimbula.com.au; The Promenade, Market St).

Merimbula Lakeview Hotel　　MOTEL $$$

(☎02-6495 1202; www.merimbulalakeviewhotel.com.au; Market St; r from $79) This waterfront establishment has stylish rooms with all the motel trimmings. Come summertime, they're close to the beer garden...which may be good or bad. The **Lakeview bistro** (mains $12-30) has upmarket pub food and an open fire in winter.

Coast Resort　　　　　APARTMENTS $$

(☎02-495 4930; www.coastresort.com.au; 1 Elizabeth St; 1-/2-/3-bedroom apt from $160/180/240; ❋❋) You could describe the decor of this huge upmarket apartment-style complex as ultramodern, although stark might be more apt. Still, comfort's not a problem and the two pools, tennis court and proximity to the beach are all very appealing.

Wandarrah YHA Lodge　　　　HOSTEL $

(☎02-6495 3503; www.yha.com.au; 8 Marine Pde; dm/d from $24/60) This clean place, with a good kitchen and hanging-out areas, is near the surf beach and the bus stop. Pick-ups by arrangement or let the staff know if you're arriving late.

TOP CHOICE **Zanzibar**　　MODERN AUSTRALIAN $$

(☎02-6495 4038; cnr Main & Market Sts; mains $25-33; ☉dinner Tue-Sat) Don't leave town without an evening at this culinary gem, which prides itself on locally caught seafood and hand-picked produce. The seafood hot pot for two filled with king prawns, Eden black mussels and Balmain bugs is a menu stalwart.

Cantina　　　　　　　　SPANISH $$

(56 Market St; tapas $10-16, mains $18-30; ☉lunch & dinner) This atmospheric little hidey-hole in the centre of town dishes up tasty plates of salt-and-pepper calamari, fried chorizo and lamb souvlaki. Not hungry? The bar has a good vibe also.

Merimbula Beach Holiday Park

CAMPGROUND, CARAVAN PARK　　　　　　$

(☎02-6495 3381; www.merimbulabeachholidaypark.com.au; 2 Short Point Rd; camp sites $31-67, cabins $75-185; ❋🆖) At Short Point Beach. Leafy and kid-friendly.

Merimbula Divers Lodge　　　HOSTEL $

(☎02-6495 3611; www.merimbuladiverslodge.com.au; 15 Park St; dm $29) Clean, bunk-style accommodation. Linen $10.

Merimbula Gardens Motel　　HOTEL $

(☎02-6495 5900; 36 Merimbula Dr; r from $75; ❋@❋) Cheap option in the town centre.

Crown Apartments　　　APARTMENTS $$

(☎02-6495 2400; www.crownapartments.com.au; 23 Beach St; 1-/2-bedroom apt $135/165; ❋❋) Units come with kitchens, balconies and views.

❶ Information

NPWS office (☎02-6495 5000; cnr Merimbula & Sapphire Coast Drs).

Visitor centre (☎02-6495 1129; www.sapphirecoast.com.au; cnr Market & Beach Sts; per 15min $2) Has internet access.

ⓘ Getting There & Away

AIR

The **airport** (www.merimbulaairport.com.au) is 1km out of town on the road to Pambula. **Rex** (☑13 17 13; www.rex.com.au) flies daily to Melbourne ($143, 1½ hours), Moruya ($75, 30 minutes) and Sydney ($143, 1¾ hours).

BUS

Buses stop outside the Commonwealth Bank on Market St. **Premier** (☑13 34 10; www.premierms.com.au) has daily buses to Sydney ($69, 8½ hours) via Narooma ($25, two hours) and to Melbourne ($58, 8¼ hours). **CountryLink** (☑13 22 32; www.countrylink.com.au) runs a daily bus to Canberra ($33, four hours).

Deanes Buslines (☑02-6495 6452; www.deanesbuslines.com.au) runs to Bega ($10.60, one hour, six daily) and Eden ($8.80, 40 minutes, five daily). **Tathra Bus Service** (☑02-6492 1991; www.tathrabus.com.au) runs to Tathra ($8.40, 25 minutes) on Tuesdays and Thursdays.

EDEN
POP 3000

Eden lives up to its namesake. Once a haven for fisherfolk and woodchippers, this charming seaside town is now squarely on the itinerary for those looking to laze a day away on the town's 1.5km beach or explore the surrounding national parks and wilderness areas. Whale-watching is big on the agenda and you're likely to hear a bit about failed whaling-boom enterprise Boydtown.

The Killer Whale Museum (94 Imlay St; adult/child $7.50/2; ☺9.15am-3.45pm Mon-Sat, 11.15am-3.45pm Sun) is often derided as a little old hat. You decide. The skeleton of Old Tom, a killer whale and local legend, is housed there.

October and November, Cat Balou Cruises (☑0427 260 489; www.catbalou.com.au; Main Wharf; adult/child $70/60) runs whale-spotting cruises. At other times, dolphins, fur seals and seabirds can usually be seen during the shorter bay cruise ($32.50/20).

Ocean Wilderness (☑02-6495 3669; www.oceanwilderness.com.au) does half-day kayaking trips through Ben Boyd National Park and Twofold Bay ($80) and a day trip to Davidson Whaling Station ($125). Ask about overnight trips.

Off the highway 10km south of Eden, Boydtown has relics of Ben Boyd's stillborn empire.

See the sea through a rocky reef aquarium at the newish Sapphire Coast Marine Discovery Centre (www.sapphirecoastdiscovery.com.au; Main Wharf; ☺1-4pm Wed-Sun) and sign up for a rocky shore ramble or beachcombing walk (adult/child $5/2).

Eden comes alive at the start of November with the annual Whale Festival (www.edenwhalefestival.com).

The sturdy Great Southern Hotel (☑02-6496 1515; www.greatsoutherninn.com.au; 121 Imlay St; dm/s/d/f $20/30/60/80) has good-value shared pub rooms and nicely renovated backpacker accommodation. The pub grub downstairs is hearty and the rear deck is a winner.

At Boydtown, overlooking Twofold Bay, the lavish boutique Seahorse Inn (☑02-6496 1361; www.seahorseinn.com.au; d from $175) has all the trimmings. It's worth popping into the bar for a stickybeak.

Eden Tourist Park (☑02-6496 1139; Aslings Beach Rd; www.edentouristpark.com.au; unpowered/powered sites from $22/26, cabins from $63) is neat, trim and in a prime position on a spit separating stunning Aslings Beach from Lake Curalo.

Taste of Eden (Main Wharf; mains $10-28; ☺breakfast & lunch) is an atmospheric, tiny cafe with seafaring decor serving a good selection of seafood, including fresh local mussels with white wine, chilli and lemon.

The corner locale of Wharfside Café (www.wharfsidecafe.com.au; Main Wharf; mains $10-20; ☺8am-3pm) makes this place ideal for lazy coffee in the sun. For lunch try macadamia-and-parmesan-crusted fish or Sichuan fish and prawn salad.

The visitor centre (☑02-6496 1953; www.visiteden.com.au; Mitchell St) is in the same building as the library, which has internet access.

Premier (☑13 34 10; www.premierms.com.au) has buses to Melbourne ($58, eight hours) and Sydney ($71, nine hours). Deane's (☑02-6495 6452; www.deanestransitgroup.com.au) runs to Bega ($13.20, 1¼ hours) via Merimbula ($8.80, 40 minutes). It stops opposite the Caltex service station.

BEN BOYD NATIONAL PARK & AROUND

Protecting some relics of failed entrepreneur Ben Boyd's long-defunct whaling operations, this national park (10,485 hectares), stretching north and south along the coast on either side of Eden, has dramatic coastline, bush and walking territory. The southern access road is the sealed Edrom Rd, off the Princes Hwy 19km south of Eden.

Wonboyn Rd is 4km south of Edrom Rd, and gives access to Nadgee Nature Reserve,

20,671 hectares of remote wilderness stretching from the southern tip of Ben Boyd National Park to the Victorian border, and to **Wonboyn**, a small settlement on Wonboyn Lake at the northern end of the reserve. Many roads in the parks have unsealed sections that can be slippery after rain.

SNOWY MOUNTAINS

The Snowies, as they are known, form part of the Great Diving Range where it straddles the NSW–Victorian border and also the Australian Alps stretching north to the ACT border and south to the Victorian Alps. This larger region boasts five of the highest peaks on the mainland, and the Snowies themselves lays claim to *numero uno*, Mt Kosciuszko (koz-zy-*os*-ko), at 2228m. In its entirety, the region is mainland Australia's only true alpine area, and as such can expect snowfalls from early June to late August.

Kosciuszko National Park, NSW's largest at 673,492 hectares, dominates the Snowies in all seasons. The Snowy Mountains Hwy and Alpine Way worm their way through the park providing spectacular scenery and access to the tiny towns of the famed Snowy Mountain Scheme. In winter, the bigger towns of Jindabyne and Cooma become hives of activity when day trippers and holidaymakers pass through on their way to Thredbo and Perisher Blue.

❶ Getting There & Away

Cooma is the eastern gateway to the Snowy Mountains. The most spectacular mountain views can be enjoyed from the Alpine Way (sometimes closed in winter), running between Khancoban, on the western side of the national park, and Jindabyne. You'll need a car to use this road. There are restrictions on car use in the national park during the ski season; check with the NPWS or visitor centres at Cooma or Jindabyne before entering.

If you are just going to one place to ski, then public transport is an option. Otherwise, you'll need a car, which does let you fully appreciate the region.

The airport, about 10km southwest of Cooma on the Snowy Mountains Hwy, is running again. **Aeropelican** (☑02-4928 9600; www.aeropelican.com.au) has daily flights to Sydney ($149, 1¼ hours).

Murrays (☑13 22 51; www.murrays.com.au) buses run from Canberra via Cooma, Jindabyne and Bullocks Flat (all $50) to Thredbo ($55). It also has day returns to Thredbo ($75)

and Perisher Blue ($60), with lift passes and equipment packages available. **Transborder** (☑02-6241 0033; www.transborder.com.au) and **Greyhound Ski Express** (☑1300 GREYHOUND/1300 4739 46863; www.greyhound.com.au) have similar itineraries and package deals.

Snowliner Coaches (☑02-6452 1584; www.snowliner.com.au) does a public-accessible school run to Jindabyne (adult/child $15/8) and back.

CountryLink (☑132 232; www.countrylink.info) runs year-round to Canberra ($13, 1¼ hours) and Sydney Central ($53, seven hours). Snowboards and skis are not permitted on board.

Cooma

POP 6590

You could 'coo-ee' down the main street of Cooma in summer and not raise an eyebrow. But proximity to the snowfields keeps this little town punching above its weight during winter. It imbues the best of 'country town' and 'mountain momma', with good places to hang out, an attractive centre and a laid-back vibe.

◉ Sights & Activities

On the Monaro Hwy, 2km north of the town centre, the **Snowy Mountains Scheme Information Centre** (☑1800 623 776; www.snowyhydro.com.au; admission free) has the best info on this feat of engineering; the dams and hydroelectric plant took 25 years and more than 100,000 people to build.

Cooma Monaro Railway (☑02-6452 7791; www.cmrailway.org.au; Bradley St; ◷11am, 1pm & 2pm Sat & Sun summer, 1pm & 2pm Sun winter) runs train rides to Snowy Junction (adult/child $6/4), Bunyan ($12/8) and Chakola ($18/12) aboard restored 1923 CPH rail motors. Ring ahead for midweek rides.

Next to functioning Cooma Gaol is the **NSW Department of Corrective Services Museum** (www.correctiveservices.nsw.gov.au; 1 Vagg St; admission free; ◷12.30-3.30pm Tue-Fri, from 9.15am Sat), exhibiting artefacts from convict time through to the present prison system. Inmates conduct tours and sell their art and craft.

🍴 Sleeping & Eating

TOP CHOICE **Alpine Hotel**　　　　　HOTEL **$$**
(☑02-6452 1466; www.alpinehotel.com.au; 170 Sharp St; winter d $115, winter s/tw/d without

bathroom $60/85/90) This newly renovated art-deco pub is as comfortable as budget rooms get. Downstairs the bistro is equally clean with lovely wooden fittings, classic pub meals and outdoor seating. Room rates are $5 less in summer.

Royal Hotel
HOTEL $

(☑02-6452 2132; www.royalhotelcooma.com; 59 Sharp St; s/d $35/65) The oldest licensed hotel in Cooma is a beautiful old sandstone place with decent pub rooms, open fires, shared bathrooms and a great verandah. Refurbished Lambies Grill (⊙lunch & dinner) is a fine place for a grilled steak and a beer.

Snowtels
CARAVAN PARK $

(☑02-6452 1828; www.snowtels.com.au; 286 Sharp St; unpowered/powered sites $22/27, 1-/8-berth huts from $50, cabins from $65) On the highway, 1.5km west of town, this is a big, well-equipped place. Prices go up marginally in winter.

TOP CHOICE Lott
BAKERY, CAFE $$

(☑02-6452 1414; 177 Sharp St; ⊙breakfast & lunch daily, dinner Fri) In a kitted-out corner shop, Cooma's foodie hub has excellent coffee, hearty snacks, light lunches ($9 to $22) and pastries ($4 to $7) and is a provedore of all kinds of gourmet goodies perfect for picnics.

Kuma Pies & Pastries
BAKERY $

(180 Sharp St; ⊙breakfast & lunch Mon-Sat) This cosy slip of a cafe has bar stools where patrons can munch on a 'bushman' pie (cheese, bacon and beef) or a 'drover' (beef, mushy peas and bacon) for under $5. It does decent coffee.

ℹ Information
The **visitor centre** (☑02-6455 1742; www.visitcooma.com.au; 119 Sharp St; per hr $6) makes accommodation bookings and has internet access.

ℹ Getting There & Away
Victoria's **V/Line** (☑13 61 96; www.vline.com.au) has a twice-weekly run from Melbourne to Canberra via Cooma (9¼ hours). The trip from Melbourne takes you by train to Bairnsdale, then by bus.

Heading to Batemans Bay, you can travel via Numeralla to Braidwood on a partly sealed road skirting Deua National Park. If you're heading to Bega, be warned that there's no petrol until Bemboka.

Jindabyne
POP 1900

Jindabyne has a split personality. As the closest town to Kosciuszko National Park's major ski resorts, it sleeps more than 20,000 visitors in winter. But in summer the crowds go elsewhere and the town reverts to its relatively peaceful small-town self, where fishing is the mainstay activity.

🏃 Summer Activities

Jindabyne Adventure Booking
ADVENTURING

(☑1300 736 581; 2 Thredbo Tce) Has various tours and packages, including wake boarding, mountain biking, white-water rafting, abseiling and guided walks to the top of Mt Kosciuszko. It also rents bikes (adult/child per hour $15/10, per day $40/30).

Paddy Pallin
ADVENTURING

(☑1800 623 459; www.paddypallin.com.au; cnr Kosciuszko & Thredbo Rds; ⊙9am-5pm summer, 8am-6pm Mon-Thu, 7.30am-midnight Fri, to 7pm Sat & Sun winter) A kitted-out adventure centre 2.5km from Jindabyne, just past the Thredbo Rd turn-off.

Discovery Holiday Parks
BOATING

(☑02-6456-2099; www.discoveryholidayparks.com.au; cnr Kosciuszko Rd & Alpine Way) Has motorboats (two hours $45), canoes (first hour $20) and paddleboats (one hour $25) for hire.

Snowy River Horseback Adventure
HORSE RIDING

(☑02-6457 8393; www.snowyriverhorseback-adventure.com.au; half-/2-day rides $115/725) Experienced riders. Also two- to five-day treks.

Stone Bridge Tours
4WDING

(☑02-6456 6745; www.stonebridgetours.com.au; half-/full-day tours $75/150) Four-wheel-drive tours, including Matong Gorge visit.

Photography & Alpine Walks
WALKING

(☑02-6451 3000; www.lakecrackenback.com.au; Lake Crackenback Resort, Alpine Way; from $65) Overnight and day walks with experts.

🛏 Sleeping
The influx of snow bunnies in winter sends prices through the roof, so book ahead. Agents for holiday rental include Jindabyne & Snowy Mountains Accommodation Centre (☑1800 527 622; www.snowaccommodation.com.au) and Visit Snowy Mountains (☑02-6457 7132; www.visitsnowymountains.com.au).

Many lodges have ski gear and accommodation packages.

Snowy Mountains Backpackers   HOSTEL $
(⌀1800 333 468; www.snowybackpackers.com.au; 7-8 Gippsland St; summer dm/d $25/60, winter dm $35-50, d $90-140, family dm $100-240; @) Perhaps the best winter value in Jindabyne, this well-oiled machine has clean rooms, a cafe, internet ($3 per 20 minutes), rooms with bathrooms and service with a smile. The way a backpackers should be.

Banjo Paterson Inn   HOTEL $$
(⌀02-6456 2372; www.banjopatersoninn.com.au; 1 Kosciuszko Rd; summer r from s/d $69/84, winter $130-230) The best rooms at this lakefront place have balconies and lake views. Other facilities include a rowdy bar and brewery. It might look a little washed out in summer but it's a lively establishment come snowtime.

Carinya Alpine Village   SKI LODGE $
(⌀02-6456 2252; www.carinya-village.com.au; Carinya Lane; winter bunkrooms per person $27-47, apt per person from $168) Off the Snowy River Way, this budget abode with four- to 10-bed apartments has no pretensions. It's homely and basic – ideal for those who prefer boarding to critiquing furniture. Skis and boards available for rent.

Lake Jindabyne Hotel/Motel   HOTEL, MOTEL $$
(⌀1800 646 818; www.lakejindabynehotel.com.au; Kosciuszko Rd; s/d from $85/95; ☒) A big place by the lake in the centre of town, this has a heated pool, a spa, sauna and bar.

✕ Eating & Drinking

Angie's Italian Kitchen   ITALIAN $$
(⌀02-6456 2523; Snowy Mountains Plaza; mains $20; ⊙lunch & dinner) Ignore the nearby Italian competitors: this cosy eatery with an outdoor deck and water views has been around for over 20 years. Think black mussels with tomato and garlic, homemade ravioli and wood-fired pizzas.

Café Darya   MIDDLE EASTERN $$
(⌀02-6457 1867; Snowy Mountains Plaza; ⊙dinner Tue-Sat) Tucked away on the upper level, this Persian restaurant is a treat for those who find it. Fill up on slow-cooked lamb shank in Persian spices and rose petals or, for something lighter, a trio of dips.

Eboshi   JAPANESE $$
(⌀02-6456 1503; www.eboshi.com.au; Gippsland St; ⊙lunch & dinner) Japanese

beer, including Yebisu. Takeaway bento boxes from 11am.

Kosciuszko Brewery   MICROBREWERY, BAR
(www.banjopatersoninn.com.au; Banjo Paterson Inn, 1 Kosciuszko Rd) Sample Kosciuszko Pale, a slightly cloudy ale.

Lake Jindabyne Hotel/Motel   BAR
(www.lakejindabynehotel.com.au; Kosciuszko Rd) Massive bar, purpose-built for packing people in.

❶ Information

Koscom (⌀02-6456 2766; shop 17, Nugget's Crossing, per hr $10) Has internet access.

Nugget's Crossing (Kosciuszko Rd) is the town's main shopping centre. The post office is located behind the centre.

Snowy Region visitor centre (⌀02-6450 5600; www.nationalparks.nsw.gov.au; Kosciuszko Rd) Operated by the NPWS with display areas, a cinema and a good cafe.

❶ Getting There & Away

Several coach companies operate shuttle services from the **Snowy Region visitors centre** (⌀1800 004 439) to the ski fields.

Kosciuszko National Park

It would be short-sighted to visit the jewel in NSW's national-park crown – home to Australia's highest mountain, Mt Kosciuszko (2228m) – and to focus purely on the snow. Sure the mountain welcomes throngs of ski bunnies in winter, but this natural park, covering 673,492 hectares and stretching 150km from north to south, has so many varied attractions that it takes visits in all seasons to really gauge its full potential.

Scenic drives reveal a wonderland of alpine and subalpine flora and fauna. This is the only place on the planet, for example, where you'll find the rare mountain pygmy possum. Come spring and summer, pristine walking trails and camp sites can be appreciated when spectacular alpine flowers are in full bloom. Mystical caves, limestone gorges, historic huts and homesteads are also ripe for discovery.

In some parts, the ghostly dead-white trunks of eucalypts bare witness to a treacherous bushfire in 2003, from which a huge swath of land is still recovering.

Despite this, the park has been National Heritage listed. It has also lured pundits of another sport – cyclists addicted to the calf-burning sensation of those winding up-hill climbs, and mountain bikers, enjoying the same sensation in the other direction.

Mt Kosciuszko and the main ski resorts are in the south-central area of the park. From Jindabyne, Kosciuszko Rd leads to the resorts of Smiggin Holes (30km), Perisher Valley (33km) and Charlotte Pass (40km), with a turn-off before Perisher Valley to Guthega and Mt Blue Cow. From Jindabyne, the Alpine Way leads to Thredbo (33km) and on to Khancoban (103km). The Snowy Mountains Hwy runs from Cooma northwest to Tumut, dissecting the north of the park.

Skiing

With a short season (early June to late August) and unpredictable snowfalls, this is not the Swiss Alps. But don't be put off. Thredbo has just completed the final stage of its $6 million automated snowmaking machines (ensuring coverage across most of the middle and lower slopes), and Perisher Blue has upgraded its facilities to enable more reliable connections between major chairlifts. If the outcome is not exactly 100%-guaranteed snow, it's a pretty good start.

Off the slopes there's lively nightlife, excellent restaurants, and a plethora of facilities and activities catering for families. Both Thredbo and Perisher Blue have a designated kids' skiing program, crèches and day care.

On the downside, the resorts tend to be particularly crowded at weekends and the short season means operators have to get their returns quickly, so costs are high. (There's a running joke among Australians that it is cheaper to fly to New Zealand to ski).

North of the Park

The Snowy Mountains Hwy, stretching from Cooma northwest to the Hume Hwy, cuts a meandering path through the beautiful highland country of Kosciuszko's north.

The fishing reputation of Adaminaby (1017m) is trumped by its history as a town relocated when the Snowy Mountains Scheme dams were built. Relics of old can still be fished from the lake when water levels are low.

On the banks of Eucumbene River, Kiandra is an abandoned gold-mining town. Interpretive boards tell the story.

Yarrangobilly Caves (☎02-6454 9597; Jillabenan & Jersey cave tours incl in car entry of $3, South Glory cave self-guided tours adult/family

$13/30; ☺11am, 1pm & 3pm), 6km off the highway, shows off three caves, with the requisite stalactites, helictites and a remarkable 4m stalagmite, known as Cleopatra's Needle. There is also a 20m mineral thermal pool.

🛏 Sleeping

There's no longer a problem finding accommodation in summer, especially at the year-round resort of Thredbo. The Alpine Way between Jindabyne and Thredbo is similarly punctuated with cosy B&Bs and resorts. In all cases the off-season prices will be considerably lower, some less than half the peak-season prices.

Travel agents in most regions book accommodation and ski packages. Useful contacts:

Jindabyne & Snowy Mountains Accommodation Centre (☎1800 527 622; www.snowaccommodation.com.au)

Ski In Ski Out (☎02-6457 7030; www.skiinskiout.com.au)

Snowy Mountains Holiday Centre (☎1800 641 064; www.smhc.com.au)

Snowy Mountains Reservation Centre (☎1800 020 622; www.snowholidays.com.au)

Thredbo Accommodation (☎1800 801 982; www.accommodationthredbo.com.au)

Thredbo Resort Centre (☎1300 020 589; www.thredbo.com.au)

Visit Snowy Mountains (☎02-6457 7132; www.visitsnowymountains.com.au)

The only formal camping area is Kosciuszko Mountain Retreat (☎02-6456 2224; www.kositreat.com.au; unpowered/powered sites from $20/29, vans/cabins from $50/68), but there are 48 rough camp sites spread throughout the park, most of them accessible by 2WD and equipped with toilet, picnic and barbecue facilities.

For a real high-country experience, bunker down in one of the historic homesteads run by the NPWS (www.environment.nsw.gov.au).

❶ Information

The main NPWS visitor centre for the park is at Jindabyne (this spread). There's an education centre (☎02-6451 3700) at Sawpit Creek (15km from Jindabyne), which runs programs during school holidays, and visitor centres at Khancoban in the west of the park, and Yarrangobilly Caves and Tumut in the north.

SKI COSTS

During peak season at Thredbo, an adult two-/5½-/7½-day lift ticket costs $212/460/642. Children's tickets cost $116/264/368. Two-day group-lesson packages (including lift tickets) cost from $299/193 for adults/children.

During peak season at Perisher Blue an adult two-/five-day lift ticket costs $218/671, or $273/833 including return Skitube tickets (see p226). Children's tickets cost $120/370 or $150/460. Group lessons (including lift passes) for adults/children start at $310/212 per person, less for beginners.

During peak season at Charlotte Pass an adult one-/three-day lift ticket costs $93/267. Children's tickets cost $56/160.

Boots, skis and stocks, or snowboards and boots, can be hired for $49/39 per half-day rising incrementally to seven days $183/103 for adults/children.

For a great park map and information, pick up a free copy of *Kosciuszko Today* at the visitor centres.

Entry to the national park costs $27 a day per car in winter and $16 at other times. If you intend to stay a while, buy the $190 annual parks permit, which gives you unlimited access to every national park in NSW.

For snow and road reports, contact the visitor centres at **Thredbo** (☑1900 934 320) and **Perisher Blue** (☑1900 926 664) or try www.rta.nsw.gov.au, www.bom.gov.au and www.ski.com.au. Also tune into 97.7 Snow FM locally or 96.3FM in the north of the park.

Seasonal Work

Thredbo employs about 200 year-round full-time staff and close to 750 in winter. For job vacancies and info, **Snowy Staff** (☑02-6457 1950; www.snowystaff.com.au; Nuggets Crossing, Jindabyne) is a one-stop shop. Also check out www.thredbo.com.au/about-thredbo/snow-jobs. The noticeboard at Thredbo supermarket in the village centre also posts jobs and accommodation.

For seasonal job vacancies and information in Perisher Blue, check out www.perisherjobs.com.au. Foreign applicants need a **working visa** (www.immi.gov.au); however, Perisher Blue can apply for sponsored work visas. Winter job applications tend to close at the start of April.

Charlotte Pass also has jobs ops (www.charlottepass.com.au/read/103.html).

ℹ Getting There & Around

Several coach companies operate shuttle services from the **Snowy Region visitors centre** (☑1800 004 439) in Jindabyne to the ski fields.

In winter you can normally drive as far as Perisher Valley, but snow chains must be carried in 2WD vehicles – even when there's no snow – and fitted where directed. The penalty if you're caught without them is hefty. The simplest, safest way to get to Perisher Valley and Smiggin Holes in winter is to take the Skitube train (p226).

Thredbo

POP 480

Thredbo (☑1300 020 589; www.thredbo.com.au) is oft lauded as Australia's number-one ski resort. At 1370m it not only has the longest runs and some of the best skiing, the village itself is eye candy compared with other Australian ski villages, the blue, green and grey tones ensuring chalets and lodges blend with the surrounding snow gums and alpine flora. And, of course, Thredbo is an all-season resort, so if you can't afford it in winter, summer has a lot to offer, too. **Thredbo Blues Festival** (www.thredboblues.com.au) is held in mid January.

✦ Activities

Thredbo's skiing terrain is roughly 16% beginner, 67% intermediate and 17% advanced, with different snow 'parks' to suit each category. No matter what category you fit into you should try to have a crack at a long run. The **Supertrail** (3.7km) begins at Australia's highest lifted point, then drops 670m through some pretty awesome scenery. From up here you can also take the 5km easy **Village Trail** to Friday Flats, or black-run junkies can crank it up a notch on the 5.9km hair-raiser from **Karels T-Bar** right down to Friday Flats. These back-valley slopes are best in the morning; head to the front valley in the afternoon for more freestyle action. For lift ticket prices see this page.

There's free **twilight skiing** (with a valid lift ticket) from 4.30pm to 7.30pm on Thursdays and Saturdays during July and August at Friday Flats.

The slopes are also popular in summer when the **scenic chairlift** (adult/child return $29.50/15) and **Bobsled** (1/6/10 rides $7/32/46) are in action.

Thredbo Leisure Centre (02-6459 4138; Friday Dr) organises all sorts of activities, summer and winter, including hiking, mountain biking, canoeing, white-water rafting, abseiling and horse riding. **Thredbo Snow Sports Outdoor Adventures** (02-6459 4044; www.thredbo.com.au) has a diverse range of high-energy activities including snowshoeing, snow climbing, telemark and back-country alpine touring in winter, and abseiling, climbing, quad biking and scenic helicopter rides in summer.

You can conquer Mt Kosciuszko on a **guided walk** (1300 020 589; adult/child/family $38/24/90; 10am-3.30pm Sat, Sun, Tue & Thu Nov-Apr) or a once-in-a-lifetime **sunset tour** (adults only $77; selected Saturdays from Jan-Apr).

There are beautiful mountain-fed **rock pools** at Woodridge near the end of Mountain Dr. Take the track on your right after the gate, cross the bridge and the pool is on your left. Otherwise **Snowmakers Pond** is on the left when you enter the village. It's warmer and has a pontoon.

🛏 Sleeping

The following places are open in both summer and winter.

Thredbo YHA Lodge HOSTEL **$**
(02-6457 6376; www.yha.com.au; 8 Jack Adams Path; summer tw $88, dm/tw without bathroom $31/70; @) The best value on the mountain, this YHA is well appointed, with great common areas, a good kitchen and a balcony. Expect to pay five times this amount in peak season when adults must be full YHA members.

Candlelight Lodge LODGE **$$**
(1800 020 900; www.candlelightlodge.com.au; 32 Diggings Tce; s/d winter from $200/240, summer from $95/125) Founded by Hungarian immigrants, this Tyrolean lodge has great rooms, all with views. The restaurant's fondue (winter only) is fabulous.

Thredbo Alpine Hotel HOTEL **$$$**
(1800 026 333; Friday Dr; winter/summer d incl breakfast from $260/130; ❄@✉) Suitably flash rooms.

Aneeki Lodge LODGE **$$$**
(0417 479 581; www.aneeki.com.au; 9 Bobuck Lane, winter d $300-340, summer d $200) One of the cheapest lodges on the mountain.

🍴 Eating & Drinking

Knickerbocker MODERN AUSTRALIAN, BAR **$$**
(02-6457 6844; www.knickerbocker.com.au; Diggings Tce; mains $30; dinner) Thredbo's latest ode to good times; sit indoors for alpine cosiness or rug up on the deck with brilliant views and a 'log' fire. Seriously gourmet meals go down a treat after 'schnappy hour' (4pm to 6pm).

Aprés Bar BAR **$$**
(www.thedenman.com.au; The Denman Hotel, Diggings Tce; 6pm-late) Cosy couches and crimson leather poufs are crammed together in this cosy over-25s atmosphere. The tunes are spot-on and vino by the glass is affordable.

Berntis Bar BAR **$$**
(02-6457 6332; 4 Mowomba Pl; 6pm-late) The winter steakhouse and year-round tapas bar are the starting points for a good night out at this locals-recommend-it hang-out.

THREDBO TRAGEDY

On a winter's night in July 1997, when most of Thredbo's residents were sleeping soundly, the Kosciuszko Alpine Way embankment, running across the upper edge of the village, collapsed, taking with it two snow lodges and 2000 cu metres of liquefied soil. Courtesy of a media throng that engulfed the ski village, Australians sat around the breakfast table and watched as rescue teams, working around the clock, removed victims from the debris. The only survivor, Stuart Diver, lay trapped under the rubble next to his dead wife for 65 hours – nearly three days – before being miraculously rescued. His courageous story became the subject of endless tabloid coverage and somewhat inevitably, a TV movie. He remains the name and face of the first disaster of its kind in Australia.

For Thredbo folk, memories of that terrible night and the people who lost their lives remain in the tapestry of the landscape. The **Thredbo Landslide Memorial** can be seen along Bobuck Lane where the two lodges, Carinya and Bimbadeen, once stood. The 18 posts used in the construction of the platform signify the 18 lives lost. A **self-guided Memorial Walk** is available from the visitor centre.

Altitude 1380 CAFE $$
(☎02-6457 6190; Village Sq; mains $15; ☺breakfast & lunch) Reliable lively eatery.

Gourmet 42 CAFE $
(100 Mowamba Pl, Village Sq; mains $12; ☺breakfast & lunch) Hungover boarders and sleepy bar staff rock up here for excellent coffee, soup and pasta.

❶ Information

Hot Shots (☎02-6457 6422; 1st fl, Upper Concourse, Alpine Hotel; per 5min $1.50) Unfathomably expensive internet access.

Thredbo Leisure Centre (☎02-6459 4100/51; Friday Dr) The low-down on everything.

Thredbo visitor centre (☎02-6459 4294; Friday Dr) Good for accommodation.

Perisher Blue

ELEV 1680M

Perisher Valley, Smiggin Holes, Mt Blue Cow and Guthega make up the massive resort of Perisher Blue (☎02-6459 4495, 1300 369 909; www.perisherblue.com.au). Guthega (1640m) and Mt Blue Cow (1640m) are mainly day resorts, so they're smaller and less crowded. Mt Blue Cow is accessible via the Skitube (☎1300 655 822; same-day return adult/child/family $50/28/119, open return $55/37/141). The accessibility of the Skitube is Perisher's most underrated drawcard. Simply park the car at Bullocks Flat (Alpine Way), buy a ticket, board the train and within 15 minutes you're on the slopes. Blue Cow doesn't have the village ambience of Thredbo, but there are alpine and cross-country runs, valley and bowl skiing and snowboarding areas (dude!). For lift ticket prices see p222.

Intermediate and above skiers and boarders can get to know the slopes on a free tour (☺10am Mon, Thu & Sat) with an orange-jacket-clad mountain host. Meet under the Trail Guide sign at the mid-station of Perisher Quad Express.

For something adventurous, Wilderness Sports (☎02-6456 2966; www.wildernesssports.com.au) are the back-country experts, with tours including a Gourmet Snowshoeing Tour (three hours $149). Ask about the Indigenous Snowshoeing Tour every full moon.

Most accommodation is in Perisher Valley and Smiggin Holes. The following rates include either breakfast and lunch or breakfast and dinner. Winter only.

Sundeck Hotel (☎02-6457 5222; www.sundeckhotel.com.au; Kosciuszko Rd; d & tw per person $200-285), Australia's highest hotel and one of Perisher's oldest lodges, has a comfy bar and great views. It's blissfully ski-in, ski-out.

Book early at budget Aurora Ski Club (☎0412 363 206; www.ski.com.au; Perisher Valley; 2-night d per person $230-320). Heidi's Chalet (☎1800 252 668; www.heidis.com.au; Munyang Rd, Smiggin Holes; 2-night apt $1600-1800) has four-person apartments a short snowplough to the ski lifts.

Charlotte Pass

ELEV 1780M

At the base of Mt Kosciuzko, Charlotte Pass (www.charlottepass.com.au) is one of the highest, oldest and most isolated ski resorts in Australia, and in winter you have to 'snowcat' (use oversnow transport) the last 8km from Perisher Valley (about $50 each way; book ahead). Five lifts service rather short but uncrowded runs, and this is good ski-touring country. It's also marketing itself as a good base for summer activities.

Accommodation includes the grand Kosciuszko Chalet (☎1800 026 369; www.charlottepass.com.au; Fri & Sat r per person incl 2 meals, transfer & lift tickets $709-947) and the cheaper Alitji Alpine Lodge (☎02-6457 5024; www.ski.com.au; r per person $145-240).

The Alpine Way

From Jindabyne this spectacular route runs through Bullocks Flat, pretty Thredbo Valley, Thredbo ski village, and on through the dense forest around the southern end of Kosicuszko National Park to Khancoban.

The most southern tip is at Tom Groggin picnic and camping area.

Geehi camp site, right on Swampy Plain River, is one of the loveliest in the park with resident kangaroos.

Two of the best mountain views are from Scammell's Lookout, just off the Alpine Way at a good picnic spot, and Olsen's Lookout, 10km off the Alpine Way on the Geehi Dam dirt road.

All vehicles have to carry chains in winter, which can be hired at Margaritta Hire (☎02-6456 1959; 8 Kosciuszko Rd, Jindabyne) and dropped off at Khancoban Lakeside Caravan Resort (☎02-6076 9488; www.klcr.com.au; 1362 Alpine Way) or vice versa. Motorbikes are not permitted along the Alpine Way from June to October.

In winter, check conditions at Khancoban or Jindabyne. There's no fuel available between Thredbo and Khancoban (71km). If you're driving between Jindabyne and Khancoban you can get a free transit pass, but if you stop en route you must have a day pass (winter/nonwinter $27/16).

SOUTHWEST & THE MURRAY

This wide, endless country is rarely the first destination on a visitor's itinerary, but nor should it be the last. Between Sydney and Albury, a string of atmospheric old inland towns straddles the Hume Hwy, each of them with a claim to some kind of fame, be it bushrangers, drought, rich grazing land or old money.

Northwest of the highway, the land flattens out, becoming incrementally redder and drier. The Murray and Murrumbidgee Rivers that make up the Riverina district not only offer respite in a harsh landscape, but an income through farming and agricultural practices centred on irrigation. Success stories can be seen in the lush vineyards and orchards around the immigrant foodie hubs of Griffith and Mildura on the Victorian side.

In the eclectic collection of smaller towns, rural folk have a tougher time. Even so, curious travellers will find these places have a story to tell.

Hume Highway

Like all big swaths of four-lane bitumen, the Hume Hwy, running nearly 900km from Sydney to Melbourne, is somewhat lacking in aesthetic appeal. Sure, visitors will spot some of Australia's most beloved animals – kangaroos, wombats and koalas – but they're likely to be roadkill. Despite this, the highway is easily navigable and an effortless way to traverse the country by car. It also provides an opportunity, via myriad signposted scenic routes, to visit small towns.

Much of the highway is speed limited to 110km/h, which is rigorously enforced by speed cameras and roadside police cars. Take heed for safety reasons but also for the back pocket. Speeding fines are hefty.

The highway was named after Hamilton Hume, the first Australian explorer who, along with William Hovell, 'discovered' much of the land straddling the highway.

Sydney to Goulburn

MITTAGONG & BOWRAL
POP 7460 (MITTAGONG), 11,500 (BOWRAL)

The large towns of Mittagong and Bowral adjoin each other just off the Hume Hwy. Together with Moss Vale, they make up the main towns of the Southern Highlands, a pretty area still revelling in its Englishness.

Bowral is where the late great cricketer Sir Donald Bradman, undoubtedly Australia's greatest sporting hero, spent his boyhood. There's a cricket ground here and now fans worldwide can pay homage at the new International Cricket Hall of Fame (☑02-4862 1247; www.internationalcricket hall.com.au; St Jude St, Bowral; adult/child/family $18/8/45; ☺10am-5pm), which has an engrossing cricket-tragic collection of Ashes and Don-centric memorabilia that even cricket-loathers admit is worthwhile. It incorporates the old Bradman Museum of Cricket (www.bradman.com.au).

Catch Bowral Tulip Time Festival (www.tuliptime.net.au) in September and October.

This pocket of the Hume is popular with Sydney day trippers and overnighters, and has a good dining and B&B scene. Links Manor (☑02-4861 1977; www.linkshouse.com.au; 17 Links Rd, Bowral; r from $190) is a boutique guesthouse with a lovely library, drawing room, garden courtyard and staff straight out of Remains of the Day.

Striping the paddocks in the hilly countryside are about 15 vineyards. Top spots for lunch include Centennial Vineyards (☑02-4861 8700; www.centennial.net.au; Centennial Rd; lunch Mon-Fri 1/2/3 courses $28/55/70, Sat & Sun mains $35-40; ☺10am-5pm), which has a flash restaurant open 11am to 5pm (closed Tuesday) or Southern Highland Wines (☑02-4686 2300; www.shw.com.au; Oldbury Rd; mains $27-39; ☺10am-5pm Sat & Sun) with its tasty cafe. McVitty Grove Estate (☑02-4878 5044; www.mcvittygrove.com.au; Wombeyan Caves Rd; ☺10am-5pm Fri-Sun) scores points for its stunning views and weekend tapas from 6pm ($6 to $16).

The convoluted but spectacular limestone Wombeyan Caves (☑02-4843 5976; www.nationalparks.nsw.gov.au; Wombeyan Caves Rd; Figtree Cave adult/child/family $15/10/40, 2 caves & tour $27/20/65) are at the end of an unsealed mountain road 65km northwest of Mittagong. Nearby are walking trails, a campground with cabins ($68 to $90), a dormitory ($50), cottage ($85 to $100) and plenty of wildlife.

The **Southern Highlands Visitors Centre** (☑02-4871 2888; www.southern-highlands.com.au; 62-70 Main St, Mittagong) has comprehensive information on the area.

BERRIMA & BUNDANOON
POP 870 (BERRIMA), 2035 (BUNDANOON)

A little further south along the Hume, and also part of the Southern Highlands, is tiny but heritage-classified Berrima, founded in 1829. It's full of art galleries, tourist-trapping antique shops, historic buildings and fine food and wine. It's the best quick stop on this stretch of highway.

The Southern Highlands takes pride in its literary history and has plenty of bookshops to explore (www.booktown.com.au). One is 3km north of Berrima: **Berkelouw's Book Barn & Café** (☑02-4877 1370; www.berkelouw.com.au; Old Hume Hwy; ⊙9.30am-4.30pm Mon-Fri, to 5pm Sat & Sun) stocks over 200,000 second-hand and antiquated tomes.

South of Berrima is the small, appealing town of Bundanoon, one of the gateways to the vast and unruly **Morton National Park**, which has the deep gorges and high sandstone plateaus of the **Budawang Range**. The **NPWS visitor centre** (☑02-4887 7270; www.nationalparks.nsw.gov.au; Nowra Rd, Fitzroy Falls) is at the park entrance and has information on walking and hiking.

Bundanoon YHA (☑02-4883 6010; www.yha.com.au; 115 Railway Ave; unpowered sites $31, dm/d $28/67) occupies a fastidiously restored Edwardian guesthouse, complete with shady verandah. It's close to the village where **Ye Olde Bike Shoppe & Café** (☑02-4883 6043; www.wildhorizons.com.au; 9 Church St) has bikes for hire (per hr/half-/full day $20/37/50).

CountryLink (☑13 22 32; www.countrylink.info) runs from Bundanoon to Wollongong ($10, two hours) and Sydney Central ($21, two hours).

Goulburn & Around
POP 20,130

Goulburn lays claim to being Australia's first inland city and it now pats itself on the back for being one of the faster-growing regional centres. It's a feeling enhanced by the fact the drought has ended and residents can now take longer showers. The old town centre, studded with historic buildings, is worth a stroll. There are plenty of alfresco cafes to choose from but not many gourmet ones.

Your first stop should be **Old Goulburn Brewery** (☑02-4821 6071; http://goulburnbrewery.servebeer.com; 23 Bungonia Rd; adult/child $15/free; ⊙11am-4pm, tours 10am & 3pm Fri-Sun), where you can see the workings of a brewery and, more importantly, sip on a beer. It also has a restaurant and cheap and cheerful 1830s brewer's cottage accommodation (single $88, double adult/child $66/33).

The three-storey-high **Big Merino** (www.thebigmerino.com.au; cnr Hume & Sowerby Sts; admission free) is near Goulburn's southern exit.

The **Goulburn Club** (www.goulburnclub.com.au; 19 Market St; ⊙4pm-late Thu-Sat) is a groovy hub that prides itself on live music and boutique brewed beer rather than big screens and poker machines. Art and photography exhibitions line the walls.

The **Goulburn visitor centre** (☑02-4823 4492, 1800 353 646; www.igoulburn.com; 201 Sloane St) has regional information and free internet access. Ask about **cellar door wineries** out of town.

About 40km southeast of Goulburn and abutting Morton National Park, **Bungonia State Conservation Area** (☑02-4844 4277; www.nationalparks.nsw.gov.au; 838 Lookdown Rd) has a dramatic forested gorge, deep caves and a cool camping area with hot showers, toilets, a communal kitchen and gas barbecues. The easiest walk is the White Track (1.5km, one hour return) to **Mt Ayre** from David Reid car park.

Yass & Around
POP 5333

Yass is pretty and quiet (thanks to the highway bypass). But it's also atmospheric, laced with heritage buildings, and shops and pubs of the wide-verandah variety.

The **Yass Valley visitor centre** (☑02-6226 2557; www.yassvalley.nsw.gov.au; 259 Comur St) is in Coronation Park. Next door, the **Yass & District Museum** (☑02-6226 2577; adult/child $3/1; ⊙10am-4pm Sat & Sun summer) has a model reconstruction of the town in the 1890s. Check at the visitor centre for off-season opening hours. Hume's house, the 1835 **Cooma Cottage** (☑02-6226 1470; adult/child/family $7/5/15; ⊙10am-4pm Thu-Sun), is on the Yass Valley Way on the Sydney side of town.

The **Hume & Hovell Walking Track**, which follows the route chosen by Hume

HIGHWAY PIT STOP

Not so long ago when the Hume Hwy bypassed Jugiong, its shops shut their doors and the place looked largely forlorn. Then the coffee cultural revolution hit the countryside, allowing city slickers plying the road between Sydney and Melbourne to drink the coffee they've been used to in the big smoke. The protagonist in this caffeine love story is **Long Track Pantry** (www.longtrackpantry.com.au; Riverside Dr, Jugiong; ☺breakfast & lunch Wed-Mon), a rarefied country cafe in a renovated old general store. Its success has seen a wine shop open on one side. On the other, the old **Sir George** (☎02-6945 4207; www.sirgeorge. com.au; ☺4-11pm Thu & Fri, noon-11pm Sat & Sun) pub, owned by the Holm/Sheahan family since 1845, has reopened, serving top-notch pizzas and a pint ($16). Too many pints, or pizzas for that matter, and you might want to stay in the free camp site across the road.

and his sometime partner in exploration, William Hovell, has some half-day and longer walks that begin at Cooma Cottage.

At the start of November the **Wine, Roses & All That Jazz Festival** features live music, gourmet food and wine tasting at 25 cellar doors.

The best place to stay is undoubtedly the graceful old **Globe Inn** (☎02-6226 3680; www. globeinn.com.au; 70 Rossi St; s $110, d $140-160).

About 57km southeast of Yass, along some partly dirt roads, the limestone **Careys Cave** (☎02-6227 9622; www.weejaspercaves.com; adult/child $11/7) is at **Wee Jasper**. Phone ahead for tours.

Gundagai

POP 2000

Gundagai, on the Murrumbidgee River, is relaxed and one of the more interesting small towns along (or bypassed by) the Hume with fascinating bushranger and Aboriginal history.

The **Prince Alfred Bridge** (closed to traffic so you can walk it) is the star of Gundagai's sights. It crosses the flood plain of the Murrumbidgee River. Running alongside it is a stretch of the longest wooden railway track in NSW. There's a cute coffee kiosk in the **Gundagai River Caravan Park** (☎02-6944 1702; www.gunda gairivercaravanpark.com.au; sites $18-28, cabins $70) just below the bridge.

Green Dog Gallery (www.greendoggallery. com.au; Sheridan St; ☺10.30am-5.30pm Thu-Sat Sep-Jul) and **Lannigan Abbey & Bandamora Art Gallery** (☎02-6944 2852; www. laniganabbey.com.au; 72 First Ave) are worth a bo peep. The latter has B&B accommodation (doubles $200).

Gold rushes and bushrangers were part of the town's colourful early history. The notorious bushranger Captain Moonlight was tried in Gundagai's 1859 **courthouse** and is now buried in the town. While you're in the cemetery, check out the **monument to Yarri**, an Aborigine who saved dozens of locals when the area flooded in the early 1800s.

The **Mt Parnassus lookout** has picnic facilities and good 360-degree views over the town and surrounds; take the steep walk (or drive) up Hanley St.

About 8km east of town, the **Dog on the Tuckerbox** is Gundagai's most famous monument. A sculpture of a dog from a 19th-century bush ballad, it is well-known along the Hume Hwy. It is mostly a petrol-and-sausage-roll pit stop.

Just 6km out of town, **Gundagai Wines** (☎0419 220 711; www.gundagaiwines.com; Nangus Rd; ☺10.30am-4.30pm Fri-Sun) cellar door is in an old woolshed set within a rose garden. On the last Sunday of each month, it does lunchtime wood-fired pizza. Book ahead.

The **Snake Gully Cup**, in mid-November, is a highly prized local racing carnival that straddles two days. On a Celtic note, the **Turning Wave festival** (www.turningwave.org. au) in September is a folksy folk favourite.

Touches such as a swimming pool, spa and bar make **Poet's Recall** (☎02-6944 1777; cnr West & Punch Sts; s/d $80/95; ☒) the best motel in town. The restaurant is in a lovely old stone building.

The **visitor centre** (☎02-6944 0250; www. gundagai.nsw.gov.au; 249 Sheridan St) is on the grand main street. Housed within is Rusconi's Marble Masterpiece, a cathedral model that relentlessly plays 'Along the Road to Gundagai', so that you'll likely hum it mindlessly for days.

Albury

POP 43,790

This major regional centre on the Murray River, just below the big Hume Weir, sits on the state border opposite its Victorian twin, Wodonga. Given its history, heritage buildings and river orientation, Albury is the more interesting and aesthetically pleasing part of the conurbation. It's a good base for trips to the snowfields and high country of both Victoria and NSW; the vineyards around Rutherglen (Victoria); and for exploring the upper Murray River. It's also a good spot to break the journey between Sydney and Melbourne.

◉ Sights & Activities

There are 440km of bike tracks and walking tracks in and around Albury. Hire bikes (two hours/half-/full day $15/25/35) from the info centre and make use of bike lockers at the Dean St end of QEII Square. BYO lock.

Library Museum   MUSEUM
(☑02-6023 8333; cnr Kiewa & Swift Sts; admission free; ◷10am-7pm Mon, Wed & Thu, to 5pm Tue & Fri, to 4pm Sat, noon-4pm Sun) Albury's fabulous state-of-the-art showpiece, dubbed the 'living room', blends book borrowing, magazine browsing and net surfing with exhibitions and local history, including Aboriginal culture and 20th-century migration into the area.

Noreuil Park   PARK
For a cleansing river swim, turn right into Albury, just before the Lincoln Causeway, where there are beautiful shady plane trees and a river swimming pool. Try the **loop**, a magical 20-minute float (on your back) around a big bend that ends close to where you began. Also here is the tree marked by explorer William Hovell on his 1824 expedition with Hume from Sydney to Port Phillip.

Albury Art Gallery   ART GALLERY
(☑02-6051 3480; 546 Dean St; admission free; ◷10am-5pm Mon-Fri, to 4pm Sat, noon-4pm Sun) This gallery has a small permanent collection featuring works by Russell Drysdale and Fred Williams, contemporary Australian photography, a reading room and a shop.

Botanic Gardens   GARDEN
This 4-hectare garden, at the northern end of Wodonga Pl, is old, formal and beautiful – a heritage walk is available from the visitor centre.

Wonga Wetlands   NATURE RESERVE
(☑02-6051 3800; www.wongawetlands.nsw.gov.au; Riverina Hwy, Splitters Creek) See over 120 bird species and an Indigenous camp site established by local Wiradjuri people at this innovative project to restore local wetlands using treated waste water. Call for tour information.

FREE Cinema under the Stars   CINEMA
(☑02-6023 8111; www.alburycity.nsw.gov.au; ◷8pm). During summer at QEII Sq on Dean St.

Oz E Wildlife   ZOO
(www.ozewildlife.com.au; Wagga Rd, Ettamogah; adult/child $10/5) Sanctuary for sick and injured wildlife.

Ettamogah Pub   NOTABLE BUILDING
(☑02-6026 2366; www.ettamogahhotel.com.au; Wagga Rd, Tabletop) A real-life re-creation of a famous Aussie cartoon pub by Albury-born Ken Maynard.

Canoe Guy   CANOEING
(☑02-6041 1822; thecanoeguy@hotmail.com; 301 Macauley St; half/full day $25/35) Canoe trips on the Murray.

🛏 Sleeping

Motels line Hume and Young St, which are quieter now the internal freeway has been built.

New Albury Motel   MOTEL $
(☑02-6021 3599; www.newalburyhotel.com.au; 491 Kiewa St; s/d/f $60/70/130) Just off the main street, this multistorey place has clean and comfortable, if characterless, rooms with en suites and fridges. One has a spa. Downstairs Paddy's Irish bar has an excellent beer garden and serves food.

Chifley   MOTEL $$
(☑02-6021 5366; www.chifleyhotels.com; cnr Dean & Elizabeth Sts; r from $130; ✸) Albury's tallest building is also its most popular hotel. It has all the expected mod cons plus a restaurant and cocktail bar. It's on the main street.

Albury Motor Village YHA   HOSTEL $
(☑02-6040 2999; www.yha.com.au; 372 Wagga Rd; powered sites/dm/d/cabins $20/36/69/69; @✸) About 4.5km north of the centre on the road to Sydney, this is a tidy park with a range of cabins, vans and backpacker beds in clean dorms.

Eating & Drinking

Dean St is a long strip of takeaways, cafes, restaurants and nightlife.

TOP CHOICE Baan Sabai Jai THAI $
(☑02-6021 2250; 459 Smollett St; mains $9; ☺lunch & dinner Mon-Sat) This excellent restaurant with a traditional food cart on the front pavement has stolen the hearts and appetites of locals with its authentic Thai dishes. Fly by or eat in.

Kinross Woolshed HOTEL
(www.kinrosswoolshed.com.au; Old Sydney Rd, Thurgoona; ☺breakfast & lunch Mon-Sat) It's worth taking a drive (or get the shuttle bus, ☑02-6043 1155) to this excellent country pub in an old 1890s woolshed. It has live music on Saturday night and the area's cheapest breakfast: $2 bacon-and-egg rolls (☺7-11am Saturday).

Border Wine Room MODERN AUSTRALIAN $$
(www.borderwineroom.com.au; 492a Dean St; mains $27-33; ☺4pm-midnight Tue-Sat) Albury's funkiest restaurant is upstairs with a bay of windows overlooking the main street. It's more a restaurant than a bar.

Source Dining MODERN AUSTRALIAN $$$
(☑02-6041 1288; www.sourcedining.com.au; 664 Dean St; ☺lunch Thu & Fri, dinner Tue-Sat) Formal food, casual dining. The best in town.

Electra Café CAFE $$
(☑02-6021 0900; 492a Dean St; mains $17; ☺Wed-Sun) Excellent coffee and a sunny footpath eating area.

Information

Gateway visitor centre (☑1300 796 222; www.visitalburywodonga.com.au, www.albury wondongaaustralia.com.au; Lincoln Causeway) Part of a large 'island' between Albury and Wodonga.

Library Museum (☑02-6023 8333; cnr Kiewa & Swift Sts; admission free) Free internet access.

Getting There & Away

The **airport** (Borella Rd) is 10 minutes out of town. **Rex** (☑13 17 13; www.rex.com.au), **Brindabella** (☑1300 668 824; www.brindabel laairlines.com.au), **Virgin Australia** (☑13 67 89; www.virginaustralia.com) and **Qantas** (☑13 13 13; www.qantas.com.au) share routes to Sydney ($109, 1¼ hours), Melbourne ($189, one hour) and Canberra ($176, 45 minutes).

Greyhound (☑1300 GREYHOUND/1300 4739 46863; www.greyhound.com.au) has coaches to Melbourne ($20, 3¾ hours), Wagga Wagga ($31, 1½ hours) and Sydney ($35, 8½ hours).

The **CountryLink** (☑13 22 32; www.countrylink.info) XPT train runs north to Wagga ($19, 1¼ hours) and Sydney ($72, eight hours), and south to Melbourne ($47, 3½ hours). CountryLink buses run to Echuca ($32, 4¼ hours) three times a week (from the train station bus stop). **V/Line** (☑13 61 96; www.vline.com.au) trains run to Melbourne ($30).

Wagga Wagga

POP 46,740

The Murrumbidgee River squiggles around the northern end of 'Wagga' like a snake in an Aboriginal painting. Its wide-girthed eucalypts and sandy banks add an understated beauty to a place already prettied by wide tree-lined streets and lovely gardens. Meaning 'place of many crows' in the language of the local Wiradjuri people, 'Wagga' is the state's largest inland city.

Sights & Activities

Botanic Gardens GARDEN
(Macleay St; ☺sunrise-sunset) Has a small **zoo**, geese and peacocks roam free here, and there's a free-flight aviary. The entrance is just before the archway telling you you're entering Lord Baden Powell Dr, which itself leads to a good lookout and the scenic **Captain Cook Dr**.

Museum of the Riverina MUSEUM
(www.wagga.nsw.gov.au/museum; Baden Powell Dr; admission free; ☺10am-5pm Tue-Sat, noon-4pm Sun) The museum operates from both the Civic Centre and the Botanic Gardens; the latter site focuses on Wagga's people, places and events and includes a **Sporting Hall of Fame**. FYI many famous AFL players come from Wagga.

Wagga Wagga Art Gallery ART GALLERY
(☑02-6926 9660; www.waggaartgallery.org; Civic Centre, Morrow St; admission free; ☺10am-5pm Tue-Sat, noon-4pm Sun) This excellent gallery is also home to the wonderful **National Art Glass Gallery** (admission free).

Wagga Beach BEACH
At the end of Tarcutta St, this is a good swimming option by the river.

Livestock Sales AGRICULTURE
(Boman industrial area) Wagga is a major centre for livestock sales; you can watch farmers sell cattle on Monday in an amphitheatre-style ring, and sheep by the thousands on Thursday.

229

SYDNEY & NEW SOUTH WALES WAGGA WAGGA

Wiradjuri Walking Track WALKING
(www.lands.nsw.gov.au) This great 30km circuit beginning from the visitor centre (get your map there) includes some good lookouts and places of Aboriginal significance.

Out-of-town wineries and food producers include:

Harefield Ridge WINERY
(www.cottontailwines.com.au; 562 Pattersons Rd; ⊙10am-close Thu-Sun) Restaurant with woodfired pizzas.

Wagga Wagga Winery WINERY
(Oura Rd; ⊙11am-10pm Wed-Sun) Delicious barbecue meals.

Charles Sturt University Winery WINERY
(www.csu.edu.au/winery; McKeown Dr; ⊙11am-5pm Mon-Fri, to 4pm Sat & Sun) Award-winning wines, olive oil and cheese tastings.

Wollundry Grove Olives PRODUCE
(☎02-6924 6494; www.wollundrygroveolives.com.au; Mary Gilmore Rd) Phone ahead for tours and tastings.

🛏 Sleeping

There are many motels in town, especially along Tarcutta St.

Romano's Hotel HOTEL $
(☎02-6921 2013; www.romanoshotel.com.au; cnr Fitzmaurice & Sturt Sts; d $85, s/d/tw without bathroom $45/55/70) This is an airy old pub with high ceilings, quaint rooms, grand beds and old bathrooms; ask for a room on the quieter 2nd floor.

Dunns B&B B&B $$
(☎02-6925 7771; www.dunnsbedandbreakfast.com.au; 63 Mitchelmore St; r $130) A pristinely decorated federation home with three en suite rooms and the use of a private balcony and sitting room. It's out of the city centre near the Botanic Gardens.

Prince of Wales Motel MOTEL $$
(☎02-6921 7016; www.princeofwalesmotel.com.au; 143 Fitzmaurice St; r $120-195; @☷) This place is in the heart of town. The quaint pub facade is contrasted by the modern and clean interiors, some equipped with spas and minibars.

Wagga Wagga Beach Caravan Park CARAVAN PARK $
(☎02-6931 0603; www.wwbcp.com.au; 2 Johnston St; sites per adult $19, standard/deluxe cabins from $60/90; ❋☎) This park has a swimming beach fashioned from the riverbank and plenty of grassy knolls and cabins.

Eating

TOP CHOICE **Magpies Nest** MEDITERRANEAN $$
(☎02-6933 1523; 20 Pine Gully Rd; mains $22-33; ⊙lunch Wed-Sun, dinner Wed-Sat) A delightfully informal restaurant set in a restored 1860s stone stable overlooking the Murrumbidgee River flats and surrounded by olive groves and vineyards. The fare is regional with a hint of Tuscany, and my, it's good.

TOP CHOICE **Monastery Brasserie** MODERN AUSTRALIAN $$
(☎02-6931 8288; www.themonastery.com.au; 18 Morgan St; mains $28-37; ⊙breakfast & lunch daily, dinner Thu-Sat) The monastery's redbrick verandah and cool, lofty interior make ideal spaces for intimate meals and quick coffees alike. Book ahead for dinner, this is a local favourite.

Mates Gully Organics CAFE $
(32 Fitzmaurice St; dishes $7-15; ⊙breakfast & lunch daily, dinner Fri & Sat; ☎) Long wooden tables and wall art create a nice vibe in Wagga's newest cafe. The owners have a farm-to-plate approach and much the produce is home-grown.

Café Lulaba CAFE $
(www.cafelulaba.com.au; 10 Best St; mains $11-16; ⊙breakfast & lunch Tue-Sat) It's known for its dhal curry, but how could you go past the quiche? It's a cheery spot with a large zebra watching over you.

❶ Information

Visitor centre (☎1300 100 122; www.waggawaggaaustralia.com.au; Tarcutta St) Close to the river.

❶ Getting There & Away

Qantas (☎13 13 13; www.qantas.com.au) flies to Sydney ($116, one hour) and **Rex** (☎13 17 13; www.rex.com.au) flies to Melbourne ($144, 1¼ hours) and Sydney ($118, 1¼ hours).

CountryLink (☎13 22 32; www.countrylink.info) buses leave from **Wagga train station** (☎13 22 32, 02-6939 5488), where you can make bookings. CountryLink's XPT train runs to Albury ($19, 1¼ hours), Melbourne ($63, five hours) and Sydney Central ($63, 6¾ hours).

Greyhound (☎1300 GREYHOUND/1300 4739 46863; www.greyhound.com.au) runs to Sydney ($56, eight hours); Albury ($31, 2½ hours) and Melbourne ($45, six hours).

Junee

POP 3740

Once known as the 'Rail Centre of the South', Junee is a small, friendly country town with an extraordinary number of impressive buildings. Get info from the small visitor centre (Aquatic Centre, Lorne St) and from Broadway Museum (☑02-6924 1832; Broadway St; adult/child $5/free; ☺10am-4pm Wed-Mon) and coffee shop, where there's a collection of historical artefacts and some tasteful antiques.

Built in 1884, the mansion of Monte Cristo (☑02-6924 1637; www.montecristo.com.au; Monte Cristo Rd; adult/child $9.50/free; ☺10am-4pm) is open for self tours and Devonshire tea. It was the home of a shrewd landowner named Christopher Crawley who haunts the place apparently.

Built in 1947, the Railway Roundhouse (☑02-6924 2909; www.rhta-junee.org; Harold St; adult/child/family $6/4/16; ☺noon-4.30pm Mon-Fri, from 9.30am Sat & Sun), a giant turntable with 42 train-repair bays, is the only surviving, working one of its kind in Australia. Railway enthusiasts should visit the Roundhouse Museum in the same complex.

Junee Liquorice & Chocolate Factory (☑02-6924 3574; www.greengroveorganics.com; 45-61 Lord St; adult/child $4/2; ☺10am-4pm) makes a show out of creating liquorice and chocolate in the old Junee Flour Mill (1935). An excellent cafe and gift shop are all part of the fun.

Junee boasts some magnificent old pubs with massive verandahs dripping with iron lace. The 1915 Commercial Hotel (cnr Lorne & Waratah Sts) still has a busy bar crowded with after-work drinkers. The Loftus was the town's grandest hotel, with a frontage running for an entire block. The film *The Crossing*, starring Russell Crowe, was filmed there. It is now Loftus on Humphreys (☑02-6924 2555; 6 Humphreys St; ☺10.30am-late Tue-Sat, 11am-3pm Sun), complete with accommodation (room $85 to $150). Downstairs is a surprisingly upmarket restaurant, bar and cafe (mains $15 to $31), run by the same hard-working people.

Across the tracks, the Junee Hotel (☑02-6924 1124; Seignior St) was built in 1876. The pub hasn't had a lot done to it over the years, but that means the original fittings are still intact. Cheap pub rooms are available.

Griffith

POP 16,180

You're almost as likely to see Indians as Italians in Griffith, a tribute to the cultural eclecticism in this small agricultural town. Its wide leafy main street might lack the heritage architecture of other regional centres, but behind the urbane shopfronts there's a culinary world that has made Griffith the wine-and-food capital of the Riverina.

◉ Sights & Activities

In early June, UnWINEd (www.unwined-riverina.com) is a festival of food and wine with tutored tastings, languid lunches and live music at various venues. Griffith Day Tours (☑0418 696 280) runs winery tours with lunch at an Italian cafe.

Pioneer Park Museum MUSEUM
(☑02-6962 4196; cnr Remembrance & Scenic Drs; adult/child $10/6; ☺9.30am-4pm) High on a hill north of the town centre is a re-creation of an early Riverina village, with an old hospital, a music room and other fascinating displays in original old buildings.

Sir Dudley de Chair Lookout LOOKOUT
Further along Scenic Dr, this pretty spot has a panoramic view and is near the Hermit's Cave.

Riverina Grove FOOD
(☑02-6962 7988; www.riverinagrove.com.au; 4 Whybrow St) This produce mecca has everything from marinated feta to homemade jams and chutney.

Griffith Regional Art Gallery ART GALLERY
(☑02-6962 5991; 167-185 Banna Ave; admission by gold-coin donation; ☺during exhibitions only) Though small, this art-deco art hub has a lovely sense of space and excellent changing exhibitions.

Catania Fruit Salad Farm FOOD
(☑02-6963 0219; www.cataniafruitsaladfarm.com.au; Farm 43 Cox Rd, Handwood; ☺1.30pm) The friendly owners host enjoyable working farm tours that wind up with a session tasting pickles, relishes, plums and jam.

Altina Wildlife Park ZOO
(☑0412 060 342; www.altinawildlife.com; Waddi Roadhouse, 7 Sturt Hwy; ☺daily by appointment) Nearby at Darlington Point is 207 hectares of natural bush on the banks of the Murrumbidgee where the exotic residents, including giraffes, bison and camels, live in natural enclosures.

Australian Old Vine Wine WINE
(02-6963 5239; www.australianoldvinewine.
com.au; Farm 271 Rosetto Rd, Beelbangera;
⊙10am-4pm) Boutique – these guys still
hand-pick their grapes (and sometimes
need help).

McWilliam's Hanwood Estate WINE
(www.mcwilliamswine.com; Jack McWilliam Rd,
Hanwood; ⊙tastings 11am-4pm Tue-Sat) The
oldest winery (1913).

De Bortoli WINE
(www.debortoli.com.au; De Bortoli Rd) Also
serves locally brewed Red Angus beer.

🛏 Sleeping

TOP
CHOICE **Myalbangera Outstation** HOSTEL $
(0428 130 093; www.myalbangera.com; Farm
1646, Rankin Springs Rd, Yenda; dm $19-25, d $40-
45; ✳) An excellent backpacker option, located about 12km out of town in an iconic
Australiana setting. The owners know the
lay of the land and can assist with work and
transfers from town.

Grand Motel MOTEL $$
(02-6969 4400; www.grandmotelgriffith.com.
au; 454 Banna Ave; r from $130; ✳@) Griffith's
snazziest sleep option has lofty ceilings,
bright modern rooms and an impressive
foyer. Parking, gym and spa facilites are
nice extras, so too the in-room dining from
Marco's Restaurant. Avoid the room without
windows.

Hotel Victoria HOTEL $
(02-6962 1299; www.hotelvictoria.com.au; 384
Banna Ave; s/d incl breakfast $80/90; ✳@) The
Victoria features bright corridors, cheerful
rooms and good bathrooms. Downstairs
there is a bistro with a chargrill. Must be
booked through visitor centre.

Tourist Caravan Park CARAVAN PARK $
(02-6964 2144; 919 Willandra Ave; caravans
$30, camp sites $30, s cabins $45-70, d $55-80;
✳) This convenient caravan park is small
and organised, and has grassy sitting
areas.

Alberta Lodge HOSTEL $
(02-6964 6288; 87 Canal St; dm/d $30/35)
Closest to the city centre. Weekly rates
available.

**Shearer's Quarters at Pioneer Park
Museum** HOSTEL $
(0429 300 126; Remembrance Dr; s $18)
Cheapest nightly option. Weekly rates
available.

✗ Eating

Banna Ave is dotted with 'true-blue' Italian
pizza and pasta shops.

TOP
CHOICE **La Scala** ITALIAN $$
(02-6962 4322; 455b Banna Ave; dishes $26;
⊙dinner Tue-Sat) Hidden down steps and behind a couple of old brown doors, this huge
cellar, covered in murals, is one of Griffith's
institutions. There's nothing modern about
the menu either; expect old-school recipes
and house white for $5 a glass. Brilliant.

Marco's Restaurant MODERN AUSTRALIAN $$$
(02-6964 3438; www.marcosgriffith.com.au;
10/454 Banna Ave; ⊙dinner Mon-Sat) One of the
snazzier options in town with a menu that
includes chorizo-and-rocket risotto, salt-and-
pepper calamari, and bacon-wrapped eye-
fillet steak. It's hidden up a little staircase a
few metres from the affiliated Grand Motel.

La Tavola ITALIAN $$
(02-6962 7777; 188 Banna Ave; mains $25; ⊙
lunch & dinner) The tacky decor is all part of
the Italian experience at this restaurant
dishing up favourites such as chicken *al fun-
ghi*, pepper steak, saltimbocca, a darn good
La Tavola Special pizza and the like.

Miei Amici Café CAFE $
(02-6962 5999; 350 Banna St; dishes $6-12;
⊙breakfast & lunch Mon-Sat) This tiny place
has simple but delicious breakfasts; or
pull up a seat on the footpath for coffee
and one of the best carrot cakes around.

ℹ Information

Grapes and other crops provide year-round
harvest jobs, but some periods are slower than
others. Check first. Lack of transport around
Griffith's farms and orchards can make job seeking difficult. Having your own vehicle is a distinct
advantage. **Summit Personnel** (02-6964
2718; griffith@summitpersonnel.com.au; 86
Yambil St), **Skilled** (02-6964 2547; btaylor@
skilled.com.au; 102 Yambil St) and **Cozwine**
(02-6962 6315; jgavin@cozwine.com.au;
1/100 Yambil St) can sort you out. *Area News* is
also a good source for jobs.

Library (02-6962 2515; 449 Banna Ave; per
hr $1) Internet access.

Riverina NPWS office (02-6966 8100; www.
environment.nsw.gov.au/nationalparks; 200
Yambil St) Information on nearby national
parks.

Visitor centre (02-6962 4145; www.griffith.
com.au; cnr Banna & Jondaryan Aves) Has a
heritage map.

DON'T MISS

ITALIAN GREATS IN GRIFFITH

» Best cannoli pastry – **Bertoldo's Bakery** (324 & 150 Banna Ave; ☺breakfast & lunch).

» Best foccaccia – **La Piccola Italian Deli** (444a Banna Ave; ☺breakfast & lunch) Huge and stuffed with ham, cheese, olives and semidried tomatoes.

» Best cappuccino – **Dolce Dolce** (449 Banna Ave; ☺breakfast & lunch) In a row of art-deco inspired shops circa 1957.

» Best pizza – **Belvedere** (494 Banna Ave; ☺lunch & dinner Tue-Sun) Ignore the modern refit, these guys were behind one of Australia's first pizza shops.

ℹ Getting There & Around

Rex (☑13 17 13; www.rex.com.au) flies to Sydney ($145, 1¼ hours).

All buses, except CountryLink (which stops at the train station), stop at the **Griffith Travel & Transit Centre** (☑02-6962 7199; Banna Ave), which is in the same building as the visitor centre. Services run daily to Melbourne ($81, 9½ hours), Sydney ($72, 10¼ hours) and Mildura ($59, six hours).

There's **Griffith Taxis** (☑13 10 08) and an **airport express bus service** (☑0418 696 280).

Deniliquin & Around

POP 7430

Deniliquin, or 'Deni', as it's known, is an attractive old town, set on a grid beside a wide bend of the Edward River. It's the shopping, eating and drinking hub for the larger agricultural region and home to the famed and ever-growing local ute muster.

◉ Sights & Activities

The **visitor centre** (☑1800 650 712; www.deniliquin.nsw.gov.au; ☺9am-5pm) is part of the attractive **Peppin Heritage Centre** (☑1800 650 712, 03-5898 3120; George St; admission by gold coin donation; ☺9am-5pm), with historical displays devoted to the wool industry.

The **Island Sanctuary**, on the riverbank in town, has a pleasant walking track among the river red gums, which joins the historic town and heritage walk (maps available at the visitor centre). It's home to plenty of wildlife, including kangaroos, possums and birds.

For swimming, head to **McLean Beach**, one of Australia's finest river beaches, with sand, picnic facilities and a walking track.

✯ Festivals & Events

Deniliquin holds an annual **Ute Muster** (www.deniutemuster.com.au), which attracts people from across the country for an action-packed weekend in their utes – 10,152 of them at last record-breaking count! The event is part of the **Play on the Plains Festival**, held on the Labour Day long weekend in October, which celebrates Aussie culture with live music, celebrity guests, carnivals and bull-rides. If you're single get along to the four-day **Deni Matchmakers Festival** (www.denimatchmakers.com.au) in March.

🛏 Sleeping & Eating

Coach House   MOTEL **$$**
(☑03-5881 1011; www.coachhousedeniliquin.com.au; 99 End St; s/d $74/84; ☎❄) Considering its clean and spacious rooms, this place is very reasonably priced. Adjoining the motel is Taylors restaurant and bar, popular for having the best steak in town and a family-friendly atmosphere.

Riverside Caravan Park   CARAVAN PARK **$**
(☑03-5881 1284; www.deniliquinriversidecaravanpark.com.au; 20 Davidson St; cabins $75-130, unpowered/powered sites per person from $12/25; @❄) This camp site on the river bank has classy cabins and mod cons, including a swimming pool. It's a short walk from the main street.

Riverview Motel   MOTEL **$**
(☑03-5881 2311; www.riverviewmotel.com.au; 1 Butler St; s/d $78/88; ❄@) These spacious rooms have private porches overlooking speckled gum trees and the Edward River. It's a serene option away from the main street.

TOP CHOICE Crossing Café   MODERN AUSTRALIAN **$$**
(☑03-5881 7827; Peppin Heritage Centre; mains $25-30; ☺lunch Tue-Sun, dinner Fri & Sat) This place has an outdoor deck overlooking an idyllic riverside setting. The menu focuses on quality rather than quantity. Think: Thai beef salad, eggs Benedict, gourmet burgers.

CONARGO & JERILDERIE

Some 92km east of Deniliquin and on the Newell Hwy, Jerilderie is immortalised by the bushranger Ned Kelly, who held up the whole town for three days in 1879. Kelly relics can be seen in Willows Museum & Ned Kelly Post Office (☑03-5886 1511; Powell St; admission by donation; ☺9.30am-4pm). On your way be sure to stop at the marvellous Conargo Pub, 32km from Deni. It has a bar dotted with memorabilia and photos of local sheep history and out the back there's a restored old shearing shed than now serves as a loo!

❶ Getting There & Away

Long-distance buses stop on Whitelock St, opposite Gorman Park. **CountryLink** (☑13 22 32; www.countrylink.info) buses run to Wagga ($38, 3½ hours), linking with the XPT train to Sydney Central ($81, 11 hours). **V/Line** (☑13 61 96; www.vline.com.au) coaches run to Melbourne ($23, four hours).

Along the Murray

Most of the major river towns are on the Victorian side (see p555), but it's easy to hop back and forth across the river. You can cross the border at the twin towns of Moama (NSW) and Echuca (Victoria).

The visitor centre (☑1800 804 446, 03-5480 7555; www.echucamoama.com; 2 Heygarth St, Echuca) serves both towns and is located in Echuca beside the bridge that crosses into NSW. Ask about trips on the paddle steamers that ply these waters (reminders of when the Murray and Darling Rivers were the main highways of communication and trade).

Downstream from Albury is Corowa, a wine-producing centre, whose Lindemans winery dates from 1860. Tocumwal, on the Newell Hwy, is a quiet riverside town with sandy beaches and a big fibreglass Murray cod in the town square. The cod- and carp-stuffed Murray River has some good beaches.

Wentworth

POP 1300

Complete with a proud old wharf, the colonial river port of Wentworth lies at the impressive confluence of the Murray and Darling Rivers, 30km northwest of Mildura on the fringe of the desert. Enormous river red gums shade the banks, and there are numerous lookouts and walking tracks. The town's streets are dotted with restored colonial buildings.

You can see some local history in the Old Wentworth Gaol (☑03-5027 3327; Beverley St; adult/child/family $6/3/13; ☺10am-5pm) and across the road in the interesting Folk Museum & Pioneer World (☑03-5027 3160; adult/child $5/2; ☺10am-4pm). The latter has eclectic exhibitions, including a megafauna replica display and a collection of photos of the paddle steamers that once made this a major port.

Take a cardboard box for some desert tobogganing action at Perry Sand Hills, amazing orange sand dunes dating back 40,000 years. They're 6km north of town, off the road to Broken Hill.

Harry Nanya Tours (☑03-5027 2076; www.harrynanyatours.com.au; adult/child from $170/110) runs day (April to October) and sunset (November to March) tours with Aboriginal guides into Mungo National Park (p241). Pick-ups are available or tag along with your own car (adult/child $90/45).

Step back in time in a room at Avoca-On-Darling (☑03-5027 3020; www.users.bigpond.com/lawsavoca; off Low Darling Rd; homestead per person incl meals $125) guesthouse, an 1800s heritage homestead 26km from Wentworth on the gum-laden banks of the river junction. A self-contained cook's cottage ($150) and jackeroo's quarters ($15 to $25 per person) are also available. Alternatively, visit for a Devonshire tea and tour ($15).

Plenty of houseboats are available for long meanders down both rivers. Sunraysia Houseboats (☑03-5027 3621; www.sunraysia houseboats.com) has the biggest fleet or ask at the visitor centre (☑03-5027 3624; www.wentworth.nsw.gov.au; 66 Darling St), next to the old courthouse.

OUTBACK

Clumps of grey saltbush hole-punch the red landscape out here and if you concentrate hard enough you can imagine yourself superimposed onto the world's biggest Aboriginal dot painting, a canvas reaching as far as the eye can see.

If you've made it this far, you ought to be congratulated. NSW is rarely credited for its far-west outback corner but it should be. The harsh dry landscape either sucks you in or spits you out depending on its mood. Whatever it has in store, it is guaranteed to be an adventure.

The mining town of Broken Hill is its unique heart-centre, close to the much-photographed town of Silverton; handy for forays into national parks; and a good base for road trips to Tibooburra, the hottest town in the state, and beyond to Cameron Corner at the intersection of NSW, Queensland and South Australia (SA), a milestone of sorts marked by nothing but the feat of arriving there.

Further afield are the unique towns of White Cliffs and Lightning Ridge, where there is more to do underground than above. Like everywhere in the outback, the people here are larger than life, hardened as much by the intense summer heat as they are softened by the eccentricities of actually living here.

Seek local advice if you want to venture onto unsealed roads, even in a 4WD. Although the country is flat to the horizon there are plenty of birds, mobs of emus, cattle, feral goats and kangaroos along the roadside to watch – and to watch out for! Not to mention drifts of fine sand that can be as difficult to navigate as floodplains.

Broken Hill

POP 18,850

The massive silver skimp dump forming the background of Broken Hill's town centre accentuates the unique character of this desert location known as Silver City, and remains a stark reminder of the area's vibrant – if colossal – mining history. Though set in the barren and dry environment, at least a day's driving from the nearest capital city, Broken Hill is a fascinating destination for its comfortable, oasis-like existence.

Some of the state's best national parks are in the area, plus interesting near-ghost towns. Elements of 'traditional' Australian culture that are disappearing in other cities can still be found in Broken Hill, showing the sensibilities that come with access to a huge, unpopulated landscape. This has also inspired a major arts centre, with poets, writers, artists and sculptors offering a surprisingly different and delightful view of the great outback.

History

A boundary rider, Charles Rasp, laid the foundations in Broken Hill that took Australia from an agricultural country to an industrial nation. In 1885 he discovered a silver lode and formed the Broken Hill Proprietary Company (which now goes by the name of BHP Billiton). It ultimately became Australia's largest company and an international giant.

Early conditions in the mine were appalling. Hundreds of miners died and many more suffered from lead poisoning and lung disease. This gave rise to the other great force in Broken Hill, the unions. Many miners were immigrants, but all were united in their efforts to improve conditions. The Big Strike of 1919–20 lasted for over 18 months, but the miners achieved a 35-hour week and the end of dry drilling.

Today the world's richest deposits of silver, lead and zinc are still being worked here. However, all of the mining operations are slowly being wound down and the gold of tourism is replacing the silver of the ground.

PHONES, TIMES & FOOTBALL

When the NSW government refused to give Broken Hill the services it needed, saying the town was just a pinprick on the map, the Barrier Industrial Council replied that Sydney was also a pinprick from where it was, and Broken Hill would henceforth be part of South Australia (SA). Since the town was responsible for much of NSW's wealth there was an outcry, the federal government stepped in, and Broken Hill was told it was to remain part of NSW. In protest, the town adopted SA time, phone area code, and football, playing Australian Rules from then on.

Tourists beware: time in Broken Hill is Central Standard Time (CST), 30 minutes later than the surrounding area on Eastern Standard Time (EST); you're in the 08 phone code region; and don't talk about rugby in the pub.

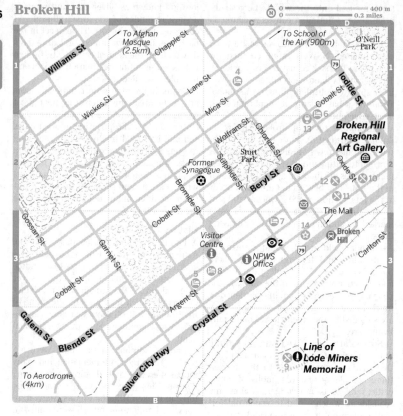

The city is laid out in a grid, with the streets named after metals and their compounds. Argent St is the main street.

☉ Sights

Many sights are closed sporadically during summer. The **St Pats Day Races** (www.st-patricks.org.au) in March is an iconic annual event. With its dramatic scenery and empty spaces, Broken Hill is an inspiring place, and, unsurprisingly, is home to an abundance of galleries.

Day Dream Mine   MINING
(☑08-8088 5682; underground tours adult/family $25/54, surface $7/3.50; ☺tours hourly 10am-3pm, 10am & 11.30am summer) The first mines were walk-in, pick-and-shovel horrors. For an amazing experience, tour this historic mine where you squeeze down the steps with your helmet-light quivering on your head. Sturdy footwear is essential. It's a scenic 20-minute dirt drive off the Silverton road, 28km from Broken Hill.

Line of Lode Miners Memorial   MINING
(www.brokenearthrestaurant.com.au; Federation Hill; adult/child $2.50/free; ☺10am-5pm, later summer) Teetering atop the huge silver skimp dump is this moving memorial. It houses the impressively stark Cor-Ten steel memorial to the 900 miners who have died since Broken Hill first became a mining town. Inside the monument, a sobering series of plaques for each year itemise an appalling litany of gruesome deaths. The neighbouring Line of Lode Visitor Centre makes an excellent sunrise or sunset vantage point over Broken Hill, and the Broken Earth Café & Restaurant is next door.

Broken Hill Regional Art Gallery   ART GALLERY
(www.brokenhill.net.au/bhart/main.html; 404-408 Argent St; admission by donation; ☺10am-5pm)

This must-see gallery is housed in the beautifully restored Sully's Emporium. It is the oldest regional gallery in NSW and holds 1500 works in its permanent collection. Tours on request.

Royal Flying Doctor Service MUSEUM
(☎08-8080 1714; www.flyingdoctors.org; aerodrome; adult/child $5.50/2.20; ☺9am-5pm Mon-Fri, 10am-3pm Sat & Sun) This iconic Australian Institution exhibition includes the fascinating Mantle of Safety Museum, with lots of quirky stories and things to see. Tours run during the week, or visit the museum at any time.

Mario's Palace Hotel HISTORIC BUILDING & MURALS
(☎08-8088 1699; cnr Argent & Sulphide Sts) Star of the hit Australian movie *The Adventures of Priscilla, Queen of the Desert,* Mario's is an impressive old pub (1888) with an elaborate cast-iron verandah – the longest in the state and now heritage listed by the National Trust. With the passing of the legendary Mario, the hotel has fallen into troubled times (and disrepair) but the extravagant murals can still be viewed. Anyone wanting an experience as opposed to comfort and service can try for a room ($37), although accommodation is usually reserved for workers. Ring the buzzer on the door for a peek at the murals.

Pro Hart Gallery ART GALLERY
(www.prohart.com.au; 108 Wyman St; adult/child $4/2; ☺9am-5pm Mon-Sat & school holidays, 10am-5pm Sun) Pro Hart, who died early in 2006, was a former miner and is Broken Hill's best-known artist. Aside from housing

his work, the gallery holds a superb collection of Australian art (such as Brett Whiteley's *Nude,* Norman Lindsay's *Selena* and Albert Tucker's *Australian Girl in Paris*) and several works by international artists such as Pablo Picasso and Salvador Dalí.

Bells Milk Bar & Museum MILK BAR & MUSEUM
(www.bellsmilkbar.com.au; 60 Patton St; ☎) On the other side of the hill, the old commercial hub of Patton St is a slice of 1950s nostalgia. Sip on a 'soda spider' in a high-topped glass.

School of the Air CULTURAL
(www.schoolair-p.schools.nsw.edu.au/; Lane St; admission $4.40; ☺broadcasts 8.30am school days) For a back-to-school experience, sit in on a class that broadcasts to kids in isolated homesteads.

GeoCentre MUSEUM
(cnr Bromide & Crystal Sts; adult/child $3.50/2.50; ☺10am-4.45pm Mon-Fri, 1-4.45pm Sat & Sun) This is an interactive geology museum, with beautiful and rare minerals and crystals on display and lots of touch-and-feel exhibits. It's also home to a 42kg silver nugget.

Photographic Recollections PHOTO GALLERY
(Old Central Power Station, Eyre St; adult/child $5/2.50; ☺10am-4pm Mon-Fri, 1-4pm Sat) This wonderful exhibition is a pictorial history of Broken Hill.

Silver City Mint & Art Centre ART GALLERY
(Chloride St; ☺10am-4pm Mon-Sat, 1-4pm Sun) This is home to a chocolate factory and

the Big Picture (admission $5), the largest continuous canvas in Australia, an amazing 100m-by-12m diorama of the Broken Hill outback.

Afghan Mosque MOSQUE
(cnr Williams & Buck Sts; admission $2.50; ⊘2-4pm Sun) This simple corrugated-iron building was erected around 1891. Afghani cameleers helped open up the outback; the mosque was built on the site of a camel camp.

☞ Tours

Two-hour guided walks (for a donation) of Broken Hill commence from the tourist centre at 10am Monday, Wednesday and Friday (April to November). Most tours can be booked at the visitor centre.

Broken Hill's Outback Tours 4WD
(✆1800 670 120; www.bhoutbacktours.com.au) Deluxe 4WD tours of the area for up to nine days.

Bush Mail Run 4WD
(✆0411 102 339; ⊘7am-4pm Wed & Sat) The 4WD outback mail-delivery service covers 550km, stopping at isolated homesteads for the occasional cuppa.

John Arnold's 4WD Tours 4WD
(✆0439 877 704; adult/child $200/150; ⊘7am Wed & Sat) Includes a one-day tour following the route of the Old Stage Coach mail run along the Darling River.

Mine Tours MINE
(✆08-8087 2484) Day Dream Mine ($65) and Silverton ($106) tours depart daily at 9.30am. Call ahead for reservation and pick-up.

Tri State Safaris OUTBACK
(✆08-8088 2389; www.tristate.com.au) Half- to 18-day tours to places such as Corner Country, Birdsville and the Simpson Desert.

⌂ Sleeping

TOP CHOICE Caledonian B&B B&B $
(✆08-8087 1945; www.caledonianbnb.com.au; 140 Chloride St; s/d $75/85; ❀) This B&B is in a refurbished pub (1898) known as 'the Cally'. The decor and garden are a little cluttered and the owner a tad chatty but the rooms are superclean and comfortable. Wake up and smell Hugh's espresso coffee!

Imperial GUESTHOUSE $$
(✆08-8087 7444; 88 Oxide St; r from $180; ❀⦿❀) One of Broken Hill's best, this converted

heritage pub, with a spectacular wrought-iron verandah, has been exquisitely renovated and doesn't skimp on creature comforts with a full-size billiard table in the 'main bar'.

Duke of Cornwall Inn MOTEL $$
(✆08-8087 8495; www.dukeofcornwallinn.com; 76 Argent St; s/d incl breakfast from $75/90; ❀) On the main street with terrific views across to the silver dump from the balcony, this two-storey, heritage hotel – in all its dated glory – is a repository for interesting artefacts, heirlooms and clippings of Broken Hill. The rooms have basic bathrooms.

TOP CHOICE Royal Exchange Hotel MOTEL $$$
(✆08-8087 2308; www.royalexchangehotel.com; 320 Argent St; d $205, with balcony $260; ❀⦿) This beautifully restored 1930s hotel with an art-deco bent is an accommodation oasis in the heart of town.

Tourist Lodge HOSTEL $
(✆08-8088 2086; www.thetouristlodge.com.au; 100 Argent St; dm/s/d $28/40/60; ❀⦿❀) This popular and central YHA has a laid-back atmosphere and is set around a charming courtyard with a small pool. Tours and bike rental can be arranged.

✗ Eating

Noodle Sushi Bar FAST FOOD $
(351 Argent St; mains $12; ⊘lunch & dinner) Every country town should have one of these. This clean and friendly eat-in or takeaway restaurant dishes up a vast array of noodles – Hokkien, Mongolian and Singapore to name a few – plus nasi goreng, curry laksa and stir-fried veg.

TOP CHOICE Broken Earth Café & Restaurant MODERN AUSTRALIAN $$
(✆08-8087 1318; www.brokenearthrestaurant.com.au; Line of Lode visitor centre; mains $18-34; ⊘breakfast, lunch & dinner) With its stunning views over Broken Hill, airy modern design and eclectic gourmet menu, this gets a big thumbs up. There's all-day coffee and cakes, too. Book ahead.

Thom, Dick & Harry's CAFE $
(www.thomdickharrys.com.au; 354 Argent St; ⊘breakfast & lunch Mon-Sat) A narrow shop cluttered with stylish kitchenware and gourmet produce. Sit in among it for a decent coffee and delicious baguette, sanger, wrap or Turkish (around $9).

One of the most brilliant experiences at Broken Hill is a sunset or sunrise at the Sculpture Symposium on the highest hilltop 9km from town. The sculptures are the work of 12 international artists who carved the huge sandstone blocks on site. The colours of the stone change constantly with the light, a vision matched by 360-degree views. The symposium is part of the 2400-hectare Living Desert, featuring a 2km cultural trail through protected native flora, a Sturt desert pea display, an Aboriginal story pole and picnic and barbecue area. The visitor centre has gate keys and directions to drive to the top (per car $10), where there's wheelchair access to the sculptures. Or take the second exit (also $10) through the Living Desert for a 20-minute climb to the sculpture site from the lower car park.

Café Alfresco's   MODERN AUSTRALIAN **$$**
(cnr Argent & Oxide Sts; mains $15; ☺lunch & dinner) The service ticks along at an outback pace but this place still pulls an unfussy crowd pining for plates of pancakes, roasts, salads, pasta dishes and gourmet pizzas.

Drinking & Entertainment

Broken Hill stays up late and people feel safe here, so you'll find pubs doing a roaring trade on Thursday, Friday and Saturday. The nightlife slows down considerably in summer.

Musicians Club   NIGHTCLUB
(http://musiciansclub.com.au/index.html; 267 Crystal St; ☺10am-midnight Mon-Thu, to 1am Fri & Sat, to 11pm Sun; @) A jolly place with a heaving mix of young and old. Country, blues and rock-and-roll music bands play at weekends while the drinks flow. Two-up (gambling on the fall of two coins) is played on Friday and Saturday night from 10pm to 2am.

Southern Cross Hotel   PUB
(www.southerncrosshotel.net.au; 357 Oxide St; ☺10am-midnight) Here you'll find a convivial atmosphere with '70s- and '80s-style music, a pool table and Dunes, a restaurant with a bushtucker menu including 'roo' and 'barra'.

ⓘ Information

Caledonian Inn Art Directory & Coffee Shop (☑08-8087 1945; www.caledonianbnb.com.au; 140 Chloride St; ☺10am-6pm) Local art hangings with mud maps to relevant galleries.
Library (Blende St; first hr free) Wi-fi and internet access.
NPWS office (☑08-8080 3200; 183 Argent St) Local national-park inquiries and bookings.
Royal Automobile Association of South Australia (RAA; ☑08-8088 4999; 320 Argent St) Reciprocal service to other auto-club members.

Visitor centre (☑08-8088 3560; www.visit-brokenhill.com.au; cnr Blende & Bromide Sts)

ⓘ Getting There & Around

Rex (☑13 17 13; www.rex.com.au) flies to Adelaide ($115, 1¼ hours), Sydney ($246, 2¾ hours) and Dubbo ($213, two hours).

Buses arrive at the visitor centre. **CountryLink** (☑13 22 32; www.countrylink.info) runs the *Broken Hill Outback Explorer* to Sydney ($97, 13½ hours). A coach departing from the visitor centre connects with the Dubbo XPT train to Sydney ($97, 16½ hours). The **CountryLink booking office** (☑08-8087 1400; ☺8am-5pm Mon-Fri) is at the train station.

The **Indian Pacific** (☑13 21 47; www.trainways.com.au) goes east to Sydney ($99, 16 hours), south to Adelaide ($99, 6¾ hours) and west to Perth ($304, 47 hours).

A free bus services some of the clubs from 6pm to midnight. **Murton's Citybus** (☑08-8087 3311; www.murtons.com.au) operates four routes around Broken Hill, or you can call a **taxi** (☑08-8087 2222).

The **Old Bike Shop** (29 Sulphide St) has bikes for hire.

Around Broken Hill

SILVERTON
POP ABOUT 90 PEOPLE & 2 DONKEYS

It's absolutely obligatory to visit Silverton (www.silverton.org.au), an old silver-mining town where you walk inside a Drysdale painting and discover the charm of the outback. Silverton's fortunes peaked in 1885, when it had a population of 3000, but in 1889 the mines closed and the people (and some houses) moved to the new boom town at Broken Hill.

Today it's a ghost town with a new lease of life due to the spirits at the pub (beer too) and a small community of artists, a couple of whom have studios here. The basic visitor centre (☑08-8088 7566) is in the Beyond 39 Dips shop, a reference to the roller-coaster road from Broken Hill. It has walking-tour maps.

Silverton is the setting of films such as *Mad Max II* and *A Town Like Alice*. The popular Silverton Hotel (☑08-8088 5313; Layard St; ◎9am-9pm) displays film memorabilia and a litany of miscellany typifying Australia's peculiar brand of larrikin humour. The replica *Mad Max* 'interceptor', which stood out the front for years, has moved down the road outside the souvenir shop.

It's hard to believe the Old Silverton Gaol (adult/child $3/0.50; ◎9.30am-4pm) housed 14 cells. Today the tiny building is home to a museum with photos and memorabilia of the early prison days. The School Museum (adult/child $4/0.50; ◎9.30am-3.30pm Mon, Wed, Fri & Sat) is another history pit stop.

Barrier Range Camel Safaris (☑08-8088 5316; www.silvertoncamels.com; 30/60min tours $25/35, 2hr sunset/sunrise treks $65/125), on the road to Silverton, runs a variety of camel tours from Silverton on friendly and quiet camels.

Silverton Tea Rooms (☑08-8088 6601; mains $8; ◎breakfast & lunch), with 'cafe' sprawled across the corrugated-iron roof, has a menu with staples such as Gun Shearers Pie and Bushman's Burger. It also has collections of old wares dug up in the area, and dolls. Next door, the new Mad Max Museum (adult/child $7.50/5) is the culmination of Englishman Adrian Bennett's lifetime obsession with the theme.

The road beyond Silverton becomes isolated and vast almost immediately, but it's worth driving 5km to Mundi Mundi Lookout where the view over the Mundi Mundi Plain is so extensive it reveals the curvature of the Earth. About 8km further, Umberumberka Reservoir is a popular picnic spot.

MUTAWINTJI NATIONAL PARK

This exceptional 69,000-hectare park lies in the Byngnano Range – the eroded and sculptured remains of a 400-million-year-old seabed. Its stunning gorges and rock pools teem with wildlife, and the mulga plains here stretch to the horizon.

The Malyangapa and Bandjigali peoples have lived in the area for more than 8000 years, and there are important rock engravings, stencils, paintings and scattered remains of their day-to-day life.

You can camp at Homestead Creek (adult/child $5/3), but you will need to bring your own food. Check road-closure info on ☑08-8082 6660, 13 27 01 or 08-8091 5155.

MENINDEE LAKES

Menindee Lakes are a series of nine natural, ephemeral lakes adjacent to the Darling River that have been dammed to ensure year-round water. There's a helpful visitor centre (☑08-8091 4274; www.outbacknow.com.au; 49 Yartle St). River Lady Tours (☑0427 195 336; from $32) has daytime cruises, sunset cruises and camp-oven dinner cruises, departing from Lake Wetherell weir.

Kinchega National Park (admission per car $7) is close to Menindee, and the lakes here are a haven for bird life. There are three well-marked driving trails through the park, or, during July, join the NPWS discovery tours (adult/child $8/4), including billy tea with Aboriginal elders. Accommodation is available at the shearers' quarters (adult/child $17/9), which can be booked at Broken Hill NPWS office (see p242). There are also four riverside camp sites (adult/child $5/3). Just south of Kinchega National Park, glorious old Bindara Station (☑02-8091 7412; www.bindarastation.com) is a working cattle property with B&B accommodation (double $95), camp sites, Jillaroo's quarters and a cottage (all $10 per person). Ring ahead for camp-oven meals. If you're driving, call roads info (☑08-8087 0660, 08-8091 5155)

WHITE CLIFFS

There are few stranger places in Australia than the tiny pock-marked opal-mining town of White Cliffs, located about 91km northwest of Wilcannia. Surrounded by some of the harshest country the outback has to offer, many residents in this pot-holed landscape have moved underground to escape temperatures that soar to 50°C.

There are opal showrooms, dug-out homes and old mines to explore. See all three (tours $8) at PJ's Underground B&B (☑08-8091 6626; www.babs.com.au; Dugout 72, Turley's Hill; s/d $125/160), a clean and comfortable desert oasis with a serene garden.

You can also try fossicking for the world-renowned local opals around the old diggings where you'll see interpretative signs, but watch the kids around those deep, unfenced holes.

White Cliffs Underground Motel (☑08-8091 6677; www.undergroundmotel.com.au; s/d $79/99; @☒) was custom built with a tunnelling machine. It has wide corridors, a lively dining room and delightfully comfortable silent rooms. Claustrophobes can stay in the two above-ground rooms.

The visitor centre is in the general store. Next door, the NPWS info centre (☏08-8083 7900; Keraro St; tours adult/child $8/4; ☉Jul only) conducts discovery tours of Paroo Darling National Park, east of town. Its 178,052 hectares includes picturesque catchment from the Paroo and Darling Rivers. There's camping (adult/child $5/3) near the ruins of the Coach and Horses Pub.

Mungo National Park

This remote, beautiful and important place covers 27,850 hectares of the Willandra Lakes World Heritage area. The echoes of over 400 centuries of continuous human habitation are almost tangible in Lake Mungo, a dry lake that is the site of the oldest archaeological finds in Australia as well as being the longest continual record of Aboriginal life (the world's oldest recorded cremation has been found here). A 25km semicircle ('lunette') of huge sand dunes has been created by the unceasing westerly wind, which continually exposes fabulously ancient remains. These shimmering white dunes are known as the Walls of China.

Mungo is 110km from Mildura and 150km from Balranald on good, unsealed roads that become instantly impassable after rain. These towns are the closest places selling fuel.

Harry Nanya Tours (☏03-5027 2076; www.harrynanyatours.com.au) runs daily tours (adult/child $170/110, tag-along $90/45) to Mungo National Park from Mildura and Wentworth, and employs Aboriginal guides who give cultural information. Indigenous-owned My Country Enterprise Tours (☏0401 919 275; www.mycountryenterprises.com) runs a five-day walking tour that includes a nocturnal tour of the Mungo lunette. Ring ahead for price and dates.

In June and July the NPWS conducts 'Discovery' foreshore walks, tag-along tours and starry night adventures (adult/child $8/4). The NPWS office (☏03-5021 8900), on the corner of the Sturt Hwy (Rte 20) at Buronga, near Mildura, has information. There's a visitor centre (not always staffed) in the park, by the old Mungo woolshed; pay your day-use fee here.

From here a road leads across the dry lake bed to the Walls of China, and you can drive a complete 70km signposted loop of the dunes when it's dry. There's a self-guided

drive brochure at the visitor centre. Alternatively take the 2.5km Grassland Nature Trail direct from Main Camp or the 2.5km Foreshore Walk from the visitor centre.

In school holidays accommodation fills up. Mungo Lodge (☏03-5029 7297; www.mungolodge.com.au; d from $250), on the Mildura road, about 4km from the visitor centre, has cute cabins and a flash restaurant (book ahead).

In the park, Main Camp (adult/child $5/3, car $7) is 2km from the visitor centre, and secluded Belah Camp (adult/child $5/3, car $7) is on the eastern side of the dunes. Bookings not required. Accommodation is also available at the shearers' quarters (adult/child $30/10), which has five rooms, a communal kitchen and bathroom, and barbecue area. It's BYO bed linen.

Corner Country

Ever read the classic Australian novel *Wake in Fright*? Perhaps you should. Or not, depending on your perspective. Out here, it's a different world; both harsh and peaceful, stretching forever to the endless sky. This far-western corner of NSW is a semidesert of red plains, heat, dust and flies. But it's also cattle and sheep country, where the properties are huge.

Tiny Tibooburra, the hottest town in the state, boasts two rough-around-the-edges sandstone pubs, a small drive-in cinema and a landscape of large red rock formations known as 'gibbers'. The Keeping Place (☏08-8091 3435) features Indigenous artefacts and art from the Wadigali, Wangkumara and Malyangaba peoples.

You can normally reach Tibooburra (driving slowly and carefully) from Bourke (395km via Wanaaring) or Broken Hill (336km via Milparinka) in a conventional vehicle, except after rain (which is pretty rare). The road from Broken Hill is partly sealed. It passes by the Packsaddle Roadhouse, providing petrol, food, beer and camping facilities ($15) to weary (or thirsty) travellers.

The large NPWS office (☏08-8091 3308; Briscoe St) with its adjoining Courthouse Museum is a good source of information on many things local, including Sturt National Park, covering 325,329 hectares of classic outback terrain. Just out of town in the park, glorious Mt Wood Historic Homestead provides the impetus for a real outback stay.

Dead Horse Gully (adult/child $5/3, car $7) is a basic NPWS camping ground 1km north of town; you'll need to bring drinking water (as you should everywhere).

The park stretches northeast to **Cameron Corner**, reached by a well-signposted dirt road (allow two hours). A post marks the spot where Queensland, SA and NSW meet. In the Queensland corner, vine-covered **Cameron Corner Store** (☑08-8091 3872) has fuel, meals, accommodation and good advice on road conditions.

North of Tibooburra on the Silver City Hwy (Rte 79) it's mostly sealed but monstrous after rain. Along the Queensland border is the 5400km dingo-proof fence, patrolled daily by boundary riders.

Bourke

POP 2150

Immortalised for Australians in the expression 'back of Bourke' (that is, anything in the middle of nowhere), this town sits on the edge of the outback, 161km north of Cobar. Beyond Bourke, green pastoral lands stop abruptly, settlements are few, and the country is flat, brown and alluring. Sprawled along the beautiful Darling River, Bourke is historic and quaint, but come 6pm, its metal-shuttered shop windows point to an element of social unrest.

The **visitor centre** (☑02-6872 1222; www.visitbourke.com; Anson St; ⊗closed Sun summer) has an excellent leaflet called *Bourke Mud Map Tours,* detailing walks and intriguing drives to smaller towns such as Brewarrina and Tilpa.

There's seasonal fruit- and cotton-picking work available November to January, and May to October; contact **Bourke Joblink** (☑02-6870 1041; www.joblinkplus.com.au; 26 Oxley St) for information.

The very worthwhile **Back O' Bourke Exhibition Centre** (www.backobourke.com.au; Kidman Way; adult/child/family $20/10/50) follows the legends of the back country – both Indigenous and settler – through interactive installations and innovative visuals.

The historical and agricultural **Mateship Country Tours** (☑02-6872 2280; www.visitbourke.com; adult/child $27.50/15; ⊗2pm Mon-Fri, 9.30am Sat) last 3½ hours.

The impressive **three-tiered wharf** at the northern end of Sturt St is a faithful reconstruction of the original (built in 1897). Nearby there's a coffee shop, internet cafe and men's shed where you can eye off some local art. On the river, the **PV Jandra** (☑02-6872 1321; Kidman's Camp Tourist Park; adult/child/family $16/10/35; ⊗9am & 3pm Mon-Sat, 2.30pm Sun) offers one-hour cruises on a replica of an 1895 paddle wheeler. Book at the visitor centre.

Contact the **NPWS office** (☑02-6872 2744; 51 Oxley St) for visits to the Aboriginal art sites at **Gunderbooka National Park**. There's camping at Dry Tank (adult/child $5/3) or try the shearer's quarters (doubles $80).

Bourke's Historic Cemetery (Kidman Way) is peppered with epitaphs saying 'perished in the bush', and tells a thousand stories about the many cultures and creeds buried here. Professor Fred Hollows, the eye surgeon who was determined to help restore the sight of people going needlessly blind, is buried here, after his decades of work in the region.

🛏 Sleeping & Eating

TOP CHOICE **Bourke Riverside Motel** MOTEL **$$**
(☑02-6872 2539; www.bourkeriversidemotel.com; 3 Mitchell St; s/d $105/110; ✸@☒) An oasis in the desert, this rambling historic motel with an enchanting riverside garden has eclectic rooms with antique furniture and an array of good and bad artwork.

Gidgee Guesthouse HOSTEL **$**
(☑02-6870 1017; www.gidgeeguesthouse.com.au; 17 Oxley St; dm/s/d $30/40/70; @) The tired old London Bank building is actually a guesthouse with homely rooms around a peaceful native garden. It has canoes for hire.

Port O'Bourke Hotel HOTEL **$**
(☑02-6872 2544; 32 Mitchell St; s/d $50/80; ✸) This cheerful place has a large grassy beer garden – with a pet rabbit – and OK pub meals that are included in the tariff.

Morrall's Bakery BAKERY, CAFE **$**
(☑02-6872 2086; 37 Mitchell St; ⊗6am-4pm Mon-Fri, to 2pm Sat) Tuck into a Back o' Bourke lamb pie ($5), a drover's breakfast or a cappuccino here.

❶ Getting There & Away

Air Link (☑02-6884 2435; www.airlinkairlines.com.au) has charter flights to Cobar and Dubbo. **CountryLink** (☑13 22 32; www.countrylink.info) buses run to Dubbo ($47, 4½ hours). **Bourke Courier Service** (☑02-6872 2092; cnr Oxley & Richard Sts) sells bus and plane tickets.

A **road condition report** (☑02-6872 2055, 0419 722 055) is posted at service stations. All unsealed roads are closed when wet.

Canberra & Around

POPULATION: 352,200
AREA: 2366 SQ KM

Includes »

Best Places to Eat

Best Places to Stay

Why Go?

The city of Canberra is a monument to the young country's aspirations, its urban landscape designed to show off the nation's democratic and cultural institutions. The city is an excellent destination for museum addicts, with wonderful fine-art and historical collections. Canberra is the nation's political heart – its restaurants buzz with power-lunchers, while at the city's bars political reporters hang about hoping for a bit of gossip or a wine-fuelled indiscretion. Canberrans are richer and better educated than the national average, and the Australian Capital Territory (ACT) is known for its liberal politics, becoming the first jurisdiction to vote a woman its head of government and enacting progressive legislation on everything from gay unions and women's rights to porn and marijuana.

The hyper-planned city is cradled by hilly wilderness, beyond which are several charming villages and a growing number of cold-climate wineries. Half of the territory is protected as national park or reserve, with plenty to attract hikers, campers and nature lovers of all kinds.

When to Go

Canberra

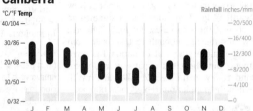

Feb-Mar (except Easter) Sun's still shining and kids are back at school.

May-Nov Spot whales along the coast.

Dec Enjoy Christmas Aussie-style on the coast – seafood for lunch and beach cricket.

CANBERRA

POP 347,000

A tranquil artificial lake, an enormous flag flying above and huge avenues fanning out from its centre: Canberra, like other purpose-built capitals, can seem big on architectural symbolism and low on spontaneity. But behind its slightly sterile exterior the city has plenty going on. Apart from its world-class museums and galleries – which alone justify a visit – the city boasts a lively bar scene (if only from Thursday to Saturday), and a vibrant live-music culture fuelled by the city's university students. Canberra's museums host gaggles of school kids, bussed in from all over the country to pay homage to the nation's icons, while the fine permanent collection and frequent international blockbuster exhibitions at the National Gallery draw visitors from around Australia. During parliamentary-sitting weeks the town hums with the business of national politics, but it can feel a bit dead during university holidays, especially around Christmas and New Year.

History

The Ngunnawal people called this place Kanberra, believed to mean 'meeting place' – a name the area may have earned for the huge intertribal gatherings that happened each year in Bogong moth season.

Like most of the first Australians, the Ngunnawal suffered a violent disruption to their way of life following European settlement around 1820, but they've survived to increase their profile and numbers in recent decades.

In 1901 Australia's separate colonies were federated and became states. The fierce rivalry between Sydney and Melbourne meant neither could become the new nation's capital, so a small chunk was carved out of New South Wales' Limestone Plains somewhere between the two cities. By 1927 Canberra was established enough to take over from Melbourne as the seat of national government, but the city's expansion really got under way in the decade following WWII, when the population trebled to 39,000.

⊙ Sights

Canberra's significant edifices, museums and galleries are dotted around Lake Burley Griffin. Wheelchair-bound visitors will find that most sights are fully accessible.

Those keen on visiting Questacon, the Australian Institute of Sport (AIS) and Cockington Green (p265) should pick up a 3-in-1 Ticket (adult/child/concession/family $47.50/27/33/128.50), which gives access to all three attractions; buy it at any of the sites or the visitors centre.

Lake Burley Griffin   LANDMARK
Named after Canberra's architect, the lake (Map p254) was filled by damming the Molonglo River in 1963 with the 33m-high Scrivener Dam. Around its 35km-long shore are many places of interest.

Built in 1970 to mark the bicentenary of Cook's landfall, the Captain Cook Memorial Water Jet (Map p254; ⊘10am-noon & 2-4pm, also 7-9pm daylight-saving months) flings a 6-tonne column of water up to 147m into the air, and sometimes gives free showers, despite its automatic switch-off in strong winds. There is a skeleton globe at nearby Regatta Point on which Cook's three great voyages are traced; also close is the National Capital Exhibition (Map p254; ☑02-6257 1068; Barrine Dr; admission free; ⊘9am-5pm), displaying the city's history. Further east is the stone-and-slab Blundells' Cottage (Map p254; ☑02-6257 1068; Wendouree Dr; adult/child/family $7/5/15; ⊘11am-4pm), built in 1860 to house workers on the surrounding estate and now a reminder of the area's early farming history.

On Aspen Island is the 50m-high National Carillon (Map p254; ☑02-6257 1068), a gift from Britain on Canberra's 50th anniversary in 1963. The tower has 55 bronze bells, weighing from 7kg to 6 tonnes each, making it one of the world's largest musical instruments. Daily recitals are held – call ahead or check www.nationalcapital.gov.au then hit 'visiting' to download the latest schedule.

On the northern shore fronting Old Parliament House is Reconciliation Place (Map p254), where artwork represents the nation's commitment to the cause of reconciliation between Indigenous and non-Indigenous Australians.

National Museum of Australia   MUSEUM
(Map p254; ☑1800 026 132, 02-6208 5000; www.nma.gov.au; Lawson Cres, Acton Peninsula; admission free; ⊘9am-5pm) This museum is one big abstract Australian storybook. Using creativity, controversy, humour and self-contradiction, the National Museum dismantles national identity and in the process provokes visitors to come up with ideas of their own. There are lots of attendants on hand to help you navigate exhibitions on environmental change, Indigenous culture,

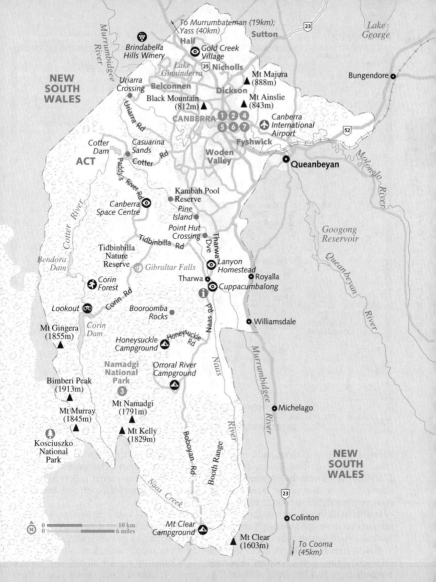

Canberra & Around Highlights

1 Stroll the corridors of creativity in the **National Gallery of Australia** (p246)

2 Lose yourself for days or silently stand for the last post at the **Australian War Memorial** (p246)

3 Spot kangaroos and Aboriginal rock art in **Namadgi National Park** (p265)

4 Marvel at Australia's moving-picture and sound-recording history at the **National Film & Sound Archive** (p247)

5 Negotiate the network of Australiana in the **National Museum of Australia** (p244)

6 Paddle, cycle, skate, walk or run around **Lake Burley Griffin** (p244)

7 Ogle at the architectural splendour of **Parliament House** (p247)

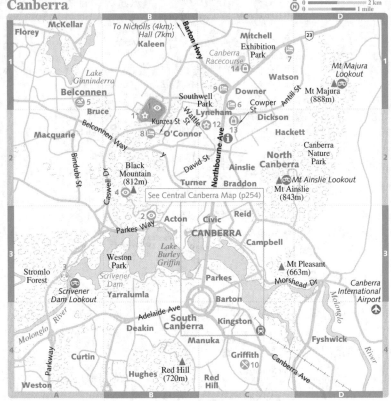

See Central Canberra Map (p254)

national icons and more, and you can take one-hour **guided tours** (adult/child $7.50/5.50). Don't miss the introductory film, shown in a small rotating theatre at the start of the exhibition rooms, which is an enjoyable audiovisual taste of the range of artefacts on show and how they form part of Australia's national identity.

Bus 34 runs here. There's also a free bus on weekends and public holidays, departing regularly from 10.30am from platform 7 in the Civic bus interchange (Map p254) along Alinga St, East Row and Mort St.

National Gallery of Australia   ART GALLERY
(Map p254; ☑02-6240 6502; www.nga.gov.au; Parkes Pl, Parkes; permanent collection admission free; ◷10am-5pm) The national gallery has a stunning collection of over 100,000 works of art representing four major areas: Aboriginal & Torres Strait Islander, Australian (from colonial to contemporary), Asian and international. Treasures range from traditional

Aboriginal art to the controversial *Blue Poles* by Jackson Pollock. The spectacular Art of the Indian Subcontinent gallery showcases one of the largest subcontinent collections outside of India.

There's also a striking Sculpture Garden, drawings, photographs, furniture, ceramics, fashion, textiles and silverware. Visiting exhibitions usually attract an admission fee. In addition to regular all-inclusive **guided tours** (◷11am & 2pm), there's also a **tour** (◷11am Thu & Sun) focusing on Aboriginal and Torres Strait Islander art. Visually impaired visitors should ask about the *Braille Guide.*

Australian War Memorial   MUSEUM
(Map p254; ☑02-6243 4211; www.awm.gov.au; Treloar Cres, Campbell; admission free; ◷10am-5pm) In a stately position, overlooking Anzac Pde and Lake Burley Griffin, the magnificent war memorial is Australia's most visited museum, and one of the finest in the country.

This genuinely moving memorial provides a fascinating insight into how battle forged Australia's national identity, with an enormous collection of pictures, dioramas, relics and exhibitions that detail and humanise wartime events. For military-history fans, there's also plenty of weaponry and uniforms – most of the heavy machinery is arrayed in Anzac Hall, which features an impressive sound-and-light show (⊙hourly from 10am). Entombed among the mosaics of the Hall of Memory is the Unknown Australian Soldier, whose remains were returned from a WWI battlefield in 1993 and who symbolises all Australian war casualties. Even if you're not a history buff, the engaging and affecting contents of this massive edifice are sufficient for two full days of exploration.

There are free 90-minute guided tours; alternatively, purchase the *Self-Guided Tour* leaflet ($3).

Along Anzac Pde, which is Canberra's broad commemorative way, there are 11 poignant memorials to various campaigns and campaigners.

The memorial's new cafe, next door to the main building, combines excellent food with a lovely view.

Parliament House   NOTABLE BUILDING
(Map p254; ☑02-6277 5399; www.aph.gov.au; admission free; ⊙9am-5pm) The symbolic and extravagant Parliament House opened in 1988 after a $1.1 billion construction project. The building is dug into Capital Hill, its roof covered in grass and topped by an 81m-high flagpole with a flag the size of a double-decker bus. The rooftop lawns are easily accessible, encompass 23 hectares of landscaped gardens, and provide superb 360-degree views of the city.

Free 45-minute guided tours (⊙every 30min 9am-4pm) are available on nonsitting days and 20-minute tours on sitting days, but you're welcome to self-navigate and watch parliamentary proceedings from the public galleries. Tickets for Question Time (2pm on sitting days) in the House of Representatives are free but must be booked through the Sergeant at Arms (☑02-6277 4889); tickets aren't required for the Senate chamber.

National Film & Sound Archive   MUSEUM, CINEMA
(Map p254; ☑02-6248 2000; www.nfsa.gov.au; McCoy Circuit, Acton; admission free; ⊙9am-5pm Mon-Fri, 10am-5pm Sat & Sun) This excellent archive, set in a delightful art deco building, preserves Australian moving-picture and sound recordings for posterity. Highlights include the absorbing permanent exhibition *Sights + Sounds of a Nation,* and 100 years of audio and visual recordings, from Norman Gunston's idiosyncratic interviews to the 1943 Oscar-awarded propaganda flick

A LONG WEEKEND IN CANBERRA

Saturday

After checking into your digs, get your fill of Australian art, stopping by the **National Gallery of Australia** and the **National Portrait Gallery**. Wander west along Lake Burley Griffin's foreshore, past the High Court and **National Library**, ending your walk with high tea at the historic **Hyatt Hotel**. Take in a classic or a modern masterpiece at the Arc Cinema before a late dinner at **Ottoman** or **Italian & Sons**. For something livelier, try a few rounds of tapas and drinks at the swish **Parlour Wine Room**.

Sunday

Have brunch at **Silo** or **Urban Pantry** then head to the **National Museum of Australia**, where you'll learn all you need to know about the country's fascinating Indigenous and postcolonial histories. If you have a car, take the afternoon to explore some of the region's excellent wineries (see www.canberrawines.com.au for details). Otherwise, jump on a bicycle and cycle around **Lake Burley Griffin** before exploring nearby Yarralumla, with its collection of quirky embassy buildings. Reward yourself with a tasty dinner at **Sammy's Kitchen** or **Portia's Place**.

Monday

If today's a sitting day, book a ringside seat at the only game in town – **Parliamentary Question Time**. On your way to the 2pm session, drop into the **Museum of Australian Democracy** at Old Parliament House and bone up on some political history before lunching in the pleasant courtyard cafe. Before leaving town, be sure to visit the moving and informative **Australian War Memorial**.

Kokoda Front Line. There are also temporary exhibitions, talks and film screenings (2pm and 7pm Thursdays, 2pm and 4:30pm weekends plus a 7:30 screening Saturday nights). Teatro Fellini Café serves excellent snacks in the sunny courtyard.

National Portrait Gallery ART GALLERY
(Map p254; ✆02-610 7000; www.portrait.gov.au; Parkes Pl, Parkes; admission free; ◷10am-5pm) This gallery tells the story of Australia through its faces – from colonial portraits of the nation's founding families to Bill Henson's photographs of Australian conductor Simone Young and shots of celebrities such as Cate Blanchett and AC/DC's Angus Young. The several hundred works on show also tell the story of the evolution of portraiture, from wax cameos of Aboriginal tribespeople to a Day-Glo Nick Cave. The collection used to be housed at Old Parliament House, and this beautiful new purpose-built gallery is a treat in itself – it's made from wood and stone from every state and territory and its gardens are planted with varieties from all over the country.

Australian National Botanic Gardens GARDEN
(off Map p246; ✆02-6250 9450; www.anbg.gov.au/anbg; Clunies Ross St, Acton; admission free; ◷8.30am-5pm Feb-Dec, to 6pm Mon-Fri & 8pm Sat & Sun Jan) Spread over 90 invigorating hectares on Black Mountain's lower slopes are these beautiful gardens, devoted to the growth, study and promotion of Australian floral diversity. While enjoying the gardens' tranquillity, take the Aboriginal Plant Use Walk (1km, 45 minutes), which passes through the cool Rainforest Gully. The Eucalypt Lawn is peppered with 600 species of this quintessential Aussie tree.

The visitors centre and bookshop (◷9.30am-4.30pm) is the departure point for free guided walks (◷11am & 2pm, also 10am summer). Nearby is Hudsons in the Gardens (✆02-6248 9680; mains $11-22; ◷breakfast & lunch), a pleasant cafe with a verdant aspect.

Museum of Australian Democracy MUSEUM
(Map p254; ✆02-6270 8222; www.moadoph.gov.au; King George Tce, Parkes; adult/concession/family $2/1/5; ◷9am-5pm) This museum is housed in the venerable Old Parliament House, which was the seat of government from 1927 to 1988 and is a great place to get a whiff of bygone parliamentary activity. As well as preserving the old Senate and House of Representatives chambers, the museum's

exhibits place Australia's tradition in the context of the broader history of democracy, spanning the globe over two millennia.

Old Parly's **Ginger Room** (☑02-6273 4366; 2 courses $59; ⊙dinner Tue-Sat) offers some of Canberra's best fine dining, while the more modest **Café in the House** (☑02-6270 8156; mains $8-18; ⊙9am-5pm) offers quick snacks and hosts an alfresco cocktail night on Fridays during summer.

Parked on the lawn in front of Old Parliament House is the **Aboriginal Tent Embassy** – an important site in the struggle for equality and representation for Indigenous Australians.

National Zoo & Aquarium ZOO
(Map p246; ☑02-6287 8400; www.nationalzoo. com.au; Lady Denman Dr, Yarralumla; adult/child/ concession/family $34/20/27.50/99; ⊙10am-5pm) Nestled behind Scrivener Dam is this wonderful zoo and aquarium, to which you should definitely devote a few hours. It has a roll call of fascinating animals, ranging from capuchins to sharks, and includes Australia's largest collection of big cats. Book ahead to cuddle a cheetah ($165) or take a **tour** (weekends/weekdays $135/110) behind the scenes to handfeed the lions and tigers and bears.

Questacon – National Science & Technology Centre MUSEUM
(Questacon; Map p254; ☑1800 020 603, 02-6270 2800; www.questacon.edu.au; King Edward Tce, Parkes; adult/child & concession/family $20/15/60; ⊙9am-5pm) The hands-on National Science & Technology Centre is a child magnet, with its lively, educational and just-plain-fun interactive science and technology exhibits. Kids can explore the physics of sport, athletics and fun parks, cause tsunamis and take shelter from cyclones and earthquakes. Exciting science shows, presentations and puppet shows are included in the admission price.

Canberra Museum & Gallery MUSEUM, ART GALLERY
(Map p254; ☑02-6207 3968; www.museumsand gallery.act.gov.au; Civic Sq, London Circuit, Civic; admission free; ⊙10am-5pm Mon-Fri, noon-4pm Sat & Sun) This stylish museum and gallery is ostensibly devoted to Canberra's social history and visual arts. The highlight is the Nolan Collection, a changing collection of the painter Sidney Nolan's work, including his wonderful paintings of Ned Kelly, Australia's most famous and beloved outlaw.

Lookouts LANDMARK
Black Mountain (812m), northwest of the city, is topped by the 195m-high **Telstra Tower** (Map p246; ☑02-6219 6111; Black Mountain Dr; adult/ child & concession $7.50/3; ⊙9am-10pm), which has a great vista from 66m up its shaft. In the northeast, 834m **Mt Ainslie** (Map p246) has fine views day and night; walking tracks start behind the War Memorial, climb Mt Ainslie and end at 888m **Mt Majura** (Map p246).

High Court of Australia NOTABLE BUILDING
(Map p254; ☑02-6270 6811; www.hcourt.gov. au; Parkes Pl, Parkes; admission free; ⊙9.45am-4.30pm Mon-Fri, closed public holidays) The grandiose High Court was dubbed 'Gar's Mahal' when it opened in 1980, a reference to Sir Garfield Barwick, chief justice during the building's construction.

The rarefied heights of the foyer (that's a 24m-high ceiling!) and main courtroom are in keeping with the building's name and position as the highest court in the Australian judicial system. Have a chat to a knowledgeable attendant about judicial life and check out the murals and paintings adorning the walls.

National Library of Australia NOTABLE BUILDING
(Map p254; ☑02-6262 1111; www.nla.gov.au; Parkes Pl, Parkes; admission free; ⊙main reading room 9am-9pm Mon-Thu, to 5pm Fri & Sat, 1.30-5pm Sun) The National Library was established in 1901 and has since accumulated over six million items, most of which can be accessed in the reading rooms. The library has been undergoing refurbishments over the past year or so, though the building has remained open and still hosts exhibits. Call ahead or check the website to find out what's on.

National Archives of Australia MUSEUM
(Map p254; ☑02-6212 3600; www.naa.gov.au; Queen Victoria Tce, Parkes; admission free; ⊙9am-5pm) Canberra's original post office now houses the National Archives, a repository for Commonwealth government records in the form of personal papers, photographs, films, maps and paintings. There are short-term special exhibits, but the centrepiece exhibit is the Federation Gallery and its original charters, including Australia's 1900 Constitution Act and the 1967 amendment ending constitutional discrimination against Aboriginal people.

Australian National University UNIVERSITY
(Map p254; ☑02-6125 5111; Acton; www.anu. edu.au) The attractive grounds of the ANU,

founded in 1946, lie between Civic and Black Mountain and make for a pleasant wander. Drop into the Drill Hall Gallery (☑02-6125 5832; Kingsley St; admission free; ⊗noon-5pm Wed-Sun) to see special exhibitions and paintings from the university's art collection; a permanent fixture is the near-phosphorescent hue of Sidney Nolan's *Riverbend*.

Australian Institute of Sport
SPORTS INSTITUTE

(Map p246; ☑02-6214 1444; www.ausport.gov.au/tours; Leverrier Cres, Bruce) The country's elite and aspiring-elite athletes hone their sporting prowess at the AIS. The 90-minute tours (adult/child/concession/family $16/9/11/44; ⊗10am, 11.30am, 1pm & 2.30pm) are led by resident athletes, with information on training routines and diets, displays on Australian champions and the Sydney Olympics, and interactive exhibits where you can publicly humble yourself at basketball, rowing and skiing.

Embassies
NOTABLE BUILDINGS

Being a relatively new capital, many nations have custom-built their embassies. The Yarralumla embassy zone is a fascinating place to explore if you're a fan of 20th-century architecture. Many incorporate somewhat quirky elements of their respective cultures.

Activities

Canberra's lakes, mountains and climate offer abundant bushwalking, swimming, cycling and other activities.

Boating

Lake Burley Griffin Boat Hire
BOAT HIRE

(Map p254; ☑02-6249 6861; www.actboathire.com; Acton Jetty, Civic; ⊗9am-5pm Mon-Fri, 8am-dusk Sat & Sun, closed May-Aug) Canoe, kayak and paddleboat hire ($30 per hour).

Bushwalking

Tidbinbilla Nature Reserve (p264), southwest of the city, has marked walking tracks. Another great area for bushwalking is Namadgi National Park (p265), one end of the challenging 655km-long Australian Alps Walking Track.

The *Namadgi National Park* map ($5.50), available from the Canberra and Namadgi Visitor Centres, details 22 walks.

Cycling

Canberra has one of the most extensive cycle-path networks of any Australian city, with dedicated routes making it almost possible to tour the entire city without touching a road. The visitors centre sells the *Canberra Cycleways* map ($6) and *Canberra & Queanbeyan Cycling & Walking Map* ($8), the latter published by Pedal Power ACT (www.pedalpower.org.au).

Canberra YHA Hostel (p253) and Victor Lodge (p257) rent out bikes, as do the following:

Mr Spokes Bike Hire
BIKE HIRE

(Map p254; ☑02-6257 1188; www.mrspokes.com.au; Barrine Dr, Civic; ⊗9am-5pm Wed-Sun, daily during school holidays) Near the Acton Park ferry terminal; bike hire per hour/half day/full day costs $15/25/35.

Row'n'Ride
BIKE HIRE

(☑0410 547 838) Delivers bicycles (hire per day/week $50/95) to your door.

Capital Bike Hire
BIKE HIRE

(☑02-6259 5335, 0412 547 387; www.capitalbikehire.com.au) Rents out mountain bikes (from $50 per day) and offers tours.

Swimming

See Murrumbidgee River Corridor (p264) for more on inviting waterholes around the city.

Canberra International Sports & Aquatics Centre
AQUATIC CENTRE

(Map p246; ☑02-6251 7888; www.cisac.com.au; 100 Eastern Valley Way, Bruce; adult/child $5.50/4; ⊗6am-9pm Mon-Fri, 7am-7pm Sat & Sun) With 25m and 50m heated indoor swimming pools.

Canberra Olympic Pool
SWIMMING POOL

(Map p254; ☑02-6248 6799; www.canberraolympicpool.com; cnr Allara St & Constitution Ave, Civic; adult/child $6/4; ⊗6am-8.30pm Mon-Thu, to 7.50pm Fri, 7am-6pm Sat, 8am-6pm Sun)

Manuka Swimming Pool
SWIMMING POOL

(Map p254; ☑02-6295 1349; www.manukapool.com.au; Manuka Oval, Manuka; adult/child $5/4; ⊗6.30am-7pm Mon-Fri, 8am-7pm Sat & Sun Nov-Mar, usually closed Apr-Oct) A National Trust–listed 75-year-old pool.

Tours

Aquila Helicopters
AERIAL TOUR

(☑0457 729 792; www.aquilahelicopters.com.au; Canberra International Airport; flights for 2 people $230) For aerial views.

Balloon Aloft
AERIAL TOUR

(☑02-6285 1540; www.canberraballoons.com.au; rides from adult/child $290/210) For quieter aerial views.

To look at them, Australia's politicians seem a respectable enough bunch, but a close examination of the parliamentary debating record tells a different tale. There it says the Senate is made up of 'unrepresentative swill', the opposition are a pack of 'dullards, mugs and scumbags', while the government is a 'conga line of suck-holes'.

Australia inherited its system of government from England, and along with it the daily spectacle known as Question Time. The idea is that the members ask questions of one another, illuminating for both the press gallery and the public the policies of the day. But a good day is when the political jousting switches to vaudeville and insults fly, roars of indignation rise up from the opposite benches, and suddenly the house is on fire.

Conservative Peter Costello (treasurer 1996–2007) addressed his colleagues thus: 'Let me remind the very voluble Leader of the Opposition, "The Skipper", and his crew on Gilligan's Island over there...'

Not even the press gallery is safe. 'In my experience,' declared James Killen (conservative member, 1955–83) of one hack, 'that journalist could not be relied upon to report accurately a minute's silence.'

But the undisputed king of the one-liner was Paul Keating (Labor prime minister 1991–96). 'Howard will wear his leadership like a crown of thorns, and in the parliament I'll do everything to crucify him', he warned his opposite number, John Howard (who eventually beat Keating to became prime minister himself in 1996). Keating welcomed Howard to the parliament with 'Come in, sucker', and accused him of 'slithering out of the Cabinet room like a mangy maggot'.

Howard's predecessors did even worse, with Keating calling one 'a gutless spiv', while declaring that debating another was 'like being flogged with a warm lettuce'.

While those on the other side of politics may prefer to find him entirely unfunny, Keating's lines were so legendary that they became the basis for a successful stage show, *Keating! The Musical*.

Canberra Day Tours CITY TOUR
(☏0418 455 099; www.canberradaytours.com.au; adult/child $30/20) This hop-on hop-off service on the Red Explorer bus leaves from the Melbourne Building, Northbourne Ave, Civic. The first service leaves at 9.30am, the last at 3.15pm. Check the website for the timetable.

Southern Cross Yacht Club CRUISE
(Map p254; ☏02-6273 1784; www.cscc.com.au; 1 Mariner Pl, Yarralumla) Provides lunch and dinner sightseeing cruises aboard the MV *Southern Cross,* departing noon and 7pm daily (adult/child $65/26), as well as a one-hour tour departing 3pm daily ($15/9).

Lake Burley Griffin Cruises CRUISE
(☏0419 418 846; www.lakecruises.com.au; adult/child $15/8) Runs several informative tours on the lake each day.

★ Festivals & Events

January

Summernats Car Festival MOTOR RACE
(www.summernats.com.au) Revs up over three days in January at Exhibition Park.

Australia Day Live LIVE MUSIC
(www.australiadaylive.gov.au) The annual 25 January live concert on the lawns of Parliament House, featuring the hottest names in Australian music.

February

National Multicultural Festival CULTURAL
(www.multiculturalfestival.com.au) Celebrated over 10 days in February.

Royal Canberra Show AGRICULTURAL SHOW
(www.rncas.org.au/showwebsite/main.html) The country meets the city at the end of February.

March & April

Canberra Festival ARTS & CULTURE
(www.events.act.gov.au) The city's extended birthday party, with a day-long food, drinks and arts festival, including free outdoor performances by Australian and international artists.

National Folk Festival ARTS & CULTURE
(www.folkfestival.asn.au) One of the country's largest folk festivals.

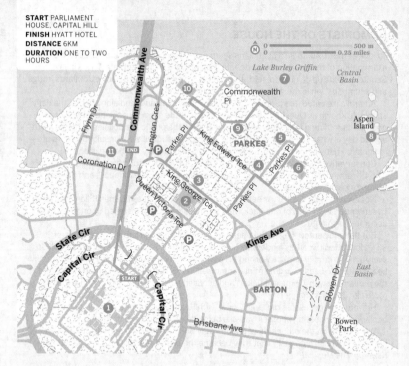

START PARLIAMENT
HOUSE, CAPITAL HILL
FINISH HYATT HOTEL
DISTANCE 6KM
DURATION ONE TO TWO
HOURS

Walking Tour
Canberra's Architecture

❯ As a purpose-built capital, Canberra's architectural environment is heavy on meaning. A stroll past the city's major institutional and cultural edifices is an excellent way to get a sense of what the city is trying to say and how it seeks to express Australia's history and aspirations.

Begin the walk at ❶ **Parliament House** on Capital Hill, and note how the building's colonnades gently echo those of its predecessor, ❷ **Old Parliament House**, which you'll reach after heading north along Commonwealth Ave towards the lake (passing by the Canadian, New Zealand, and UK high commissions on your way). Note the ❸ **Aboriginal Tent Embassy** parked on the lawn in front of Old Parliament House – an important landmark in the Aboriginal rights struggle.

Head southeast along King George Tce and turn left at Parkes Pl, across King Edward Tce, to the ❹ **National Portrait Gallery**, where you'll find plenty of famous faces. Just beyond it, towards the lake, you'll see the grand ❺ **High Court of Australia**,

with its ornamental watercourse burbling alongside the path to the entrance. Next door is the wonderful ❻ **National Gallery of Australia**, where you can imbibe caffeine as well as culture.

Follow Parkes Pl down to the shores of ❼ **Lake Burley Griffin** where you'll see and perhaps hear the ❽ **National Carillon** on Aspen Island. Turn left towards Commonwealth Pl where you can explore Indigenous issues through art at ❾ **Reconciliation Place**. Take time here to glance back towards Old Parliament House with the new Parliament and Capital Hill behind it, then across the lake to the War Memorial, and notice how the three connect.

Cross diagonally (northwest) over the lawns and cross Parkes Pl (heading northwest) to arrive at the ❿ **National Library of Australia**. Head back up Parkes Pl to Coronation Dr, crossing the busy Commonwealth Ave and heading north to the art nouveau classic ⓫ **Hyatt Hotel Canberra** for a well-earned refreshment.

Anzac Day
MEMORIAL

National holiday held on 25 April, commemorating the armed services. Dawn services and marches held at the Australian War Memorial.

June

National Capital DanceSport Championships
DANCE CONTEST

(www.ncdccanberra.com.au) Competition ballroom dancing at its glitziest best.

September–November

Floriade
FLOWER SHOW

(www.floriadeaustralia.com) Held in September/October and dedicated to Canberra's spectacular spring flowers.

SCOTT
BICYCLE RACE

(www.scott24hr.com.au) Largest mountain bike race in the southern hemisphere, held over two days in early to mid-October.

Stonefest
LIVE MUSIC

(www.stonefest.com.au) Big-time two-day music festival staged at the end of October at the University of Canberra.

Canberra International Film Festival
CINEMA

(www.canberrafilmfestival.com.au) A 10-day international film festival held in October/November.

🛏 Sleeping

Northbourne Ave is strung with nondescript but serviceable hotels, while the neighbourhoods around Capital Hill, particularly in the politician-favoured domains of Kingston and Barton, are within easy distance of the city's museums and other sights. Canberra's accommodation is busiest during parliamentary sitting days, which means booking ahead on weekdays and some great discounts on weekends. Many hotels offer special deals on internet bookings.

Most places can supply cots and a room or two suitable for a family-sized stay. Travellers with limited mobility will find that few places outside top-end accommodation have true barrier-free rooms.

NORTH OF LAKE BURLEY GRIFFIN

Canberra YHA Hostel
HOSTEL $

(Map p254; ☑02-6248 9155; www.yha.com.au; 7 Akuna St, Civic; dm $29-39, d & tw $89-99; ✲ 🕏 🖭) This bright, well-run hostel has an impressive list of services, including an indoor pool and spa, 24-hour reception, laundry,

bar, self-catering kitchen and cable TV. It remains fond of backpackers, but has all the facilities (except parking) to attract families seeking central, reasonably priced rooms.

Diamant
BOUTIQUE HOTEL $$$

(Map p254; ☑02-6175 2222; www.diamant.com.au; 15 Edinburgh Ave, Civic; r/ste from $180/295; ✲ 🕏) This hip boutique hotel is tucked away in a quiet corner of Civic, not far from the National Museum. Its 80 rooms have all been decorated with an eye for detail: printed wallpaper on the ceilings, mini fish-scale tiles in the bathrooms and flat-screen TVs. The restaurant offers fine contemporary Australian cuisine and the Parlour Wine Room (p260) has is its own buzzing little scene.

Olims Hotel Canberra
HOTEL $$

(Map p254; ☑1800 475 337, 02-6243 0000; www.olimshotel.com; cnr Ainslie & Limestone Aves, Braddon; r $85-350; ✲ 🕏) This 1927 National Trust–listed building and its later refurbishments look a little worse for wear on the outside, but the well-appointed rooms surround a nice, terraced courtyard garden. There are standard rooms, superior rooms and 1st-floor, self-contained 'loft' rooms with balconies overlooking the inner garden.

University House
HOTEL $$

(Map p254; ☑02-6125 5211; www.anu.edu.au/unihouse; 1 Balmain Cres, Acton; s with shared facilities $90, r with bathroom $134-149; ✲ @) This 1950s-era building, with furniture to match, resides in the bushy grounds of ANU and is favoured by some politicians during sitting weeks. The spacious rooms and two-bedroom apartments can be hired with or without breakfast and come with a small balcony from where you can watch donnish professors come and go. There's also a pleasant courtyard in which to let your thoughts wander, a fine restaurant, cafe and a good selection of wine in the cellar.

Quest
APARTMENTS $$$

(Map p254; ☑02-6224 2222; www.questapartments.com.au; 28 West Row, Civic; ste $200-350; ✲ 🕏) These apartments are spic and span and right in the heart of town – easy walking distance to the National Museum and all the bars, theatres and eateries of Civic. Each comes with a comfortable lounge, big TV, spacious balcony and modern kitchenette.

Blue & White Lodge
B&B $$

(Map p246; ☑02-6248 0498; www.blueandwhitelodge.com.au; 524 Northbourne Ave, Downer; s/d $110/130; ✲ 🕏) The Hellenic columns and

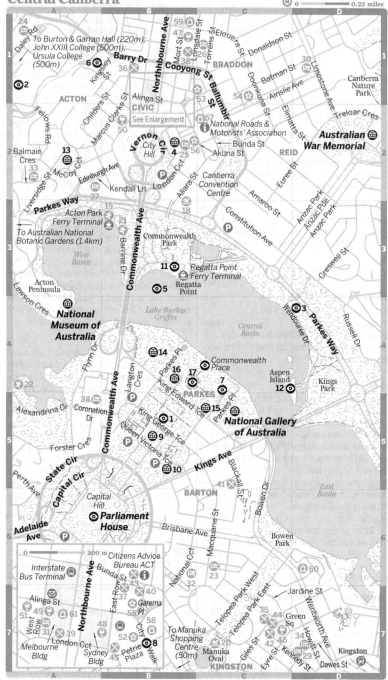

0   500 m
0   0.25 miles

A   B   C   D

24
Daley Rd
To Burton & Garran Hall (220m);
John XXIII College (500m);
Ursula College
(500m)   6   Kingsley St   Barry Dr   59   Mort St   Lonsdale St   Torrens St   Elouera St
47   26   Donaldson St
36   Cooyong St   BRADDON   30   Limestone Ave   Canberra
Nature
Park
2   ACTON   Kingsley St   Childers St   Marcus Clarke St   Alinga St   38   Batman St   Ainslie Ave   Doonkuna St   Elimatta St   Treloar Cres
CIVIC   53   Ballumbir   54   Ainslie Ave   Euree St   Australian
War Memorial
See Enlargement   57   National Roads &
Motorists' Association   Akuna St   REID   Anzac Park
50   Vernon   Bunda St   Amaroo St   Anzac Pde
13   City   4   56   Anzac Park
Balmain   Hill   25   Creswell St
Cres   33   Edinburgh Ave   London Cct   Canberra   Constitution Ave
McCoy   Convention   Anzac Park
Liversidge St   27   Allara St   Centre   18
Parkes Way   Kendall Ln   Amaroo St
19   Acton Park   Barrine Dr   Commonwealth   Constitution Ave
Ferry Terminal   21   Park
To Australian National   Commonwealth Ave   Regatta Point
Botanic Gardens (1.4km)   11   Ferry Terminal   Wendouree Dr   3   Parkes Way
West   5   Regatta   Russell Dr
Basin   Point
Acton
Peninsula   Lake Burley   Central
Lawson Cres   Griffin   Basin
National
Museum of   Flynn Dr   14   Parkes Pl   Commonwealth
Australia   Langton Cres   16   Place   Aspen   Kings
22   28   17   Island   Park
Alexandrina Dr   Coronation   King Edward Tce   PARKES   7   12
Dr   1   15   East
Forster Cres   King George Tce   National Gallery   Basin
9   of Australia
Queen Victoria Tce
10   Kings Ave
State Cir   Blackall St   BARTON   41   East
Perth Ave   Capital Cir   Basin
Adelaide   Capital   Brisbane Ave   Bowen Dr
Ave   Hill   Parliament   Bowen
House   BARTON   Park
0   200 m   Citizens Advice
Interstate   Bunda St   Bureau ACT   National Cct   23   60
Bus Terminal   43   40   32   Jardine St
Alinga St   37   Garema   35   44   Green
51   49   61   55   Pl   Telopea Park West   Sq
West   31   39   58   City   Telopea Park East   42   46   34   Howitt St   Kingston
Row   48   52   City   To Manuka   20   29   Wentworth Ave
Melbourne   London Cct   Walk   Shopping   Giles St   Eyre St   Kennedy St   Dawes St
Bldg   Sydney   45   Petrie   Centre   Manuka   KINGSTON
Bldg   Plaza   8   (50m)   Oval

CANBERRA FOR CHILDREN

The hyperactive demands of children are easily met in Canberra. There's lots of free stuff and outdoor activities; but beware, some of the big-ticket attractions have big-ticket prices and strategically placed souvenir shops. Also watch out for the family-ticket small print where more than two kids is considered a rort.

The visitors centre has the brochure **Kidfriendly** (www.kidfriendly.com.au), a *Parks & Playgrounds* leaflet and a map of skate parks.

For fresh air and exercise, stroll through the lovely Australian National Botanic Gardens (p248). Take budding Attenboroughs to the tooth-and-claw distractions of the National Zoo & Aquarium (p249). Or drape them in a python at the Australian Reptile Centre (p265). The littlest littlies will appreciate a spin on Civic's landmark **merry-go-round** (Map p254; cnr Petrie Plaza & City Walk; per child $5; ⏰10am-4pm Mon-Thu, 10am-7pm Fri, 9.30am-4pm Sat, 11am-3pm Sun).

Energy levels can also be accommodated by swimming at a pool or waterhole (see p250), or by hiring bikes (see p250).

For hands-on scientific fun, visit Questacon (p249), the interactive science museum.

Miniature steam-train rides can be taken at Cockington Green (p265). And there is a plethora of museums custom-built for active imaginations, including the National Dinosaur Museum (p265) and the brilliant National Museum of Australia (p244).

Mediterranean colour scheme at this impeccable B&B pay tribute to the friendly owners' Greek roots. The comfortable rooms, some with shared bathrooms, are neat as a pin and come with a delicious cooked breakfast for $10. The owners also manage the neighbouring Canberran Lodge.

Canberran Lodge B&B $$
(Map p246; 528 Northbourne Ave, Downer; s/d/f $95/110/130; ✷) Managed by the owners of neighbouring Blue & White Lodge, this is a similarly styled place, where the family-sized rooms are en suite. Make inquiries at the Blue & White Lodge, where you will also find your breakfast dining room.

Northbourne Lodge B&B $$
(Map p246; ☎02-6257 2599; www.northbourne lodge.com.au; 522 Northbourne Ave, Downer; s/d $110/130; ✷🛜) This terracotta-coloured B&B provides good-value accommodation and a $20 optional breakfast. The owners have a wealth of ideas for what to do in Canberra, and speak several languages, including French and Chinese.

Dickson Backpackers HOSTEL $
(Map p246; ☎02-6262 9922; www.dicksonbackpack ers.com.au; 4/14 Woolley St, Dickson; dm/r $35/99; ✷@) This new backpackers, in the heart of Canberra's Chinatown, boasts comfortable bunks (spring mattresses and warm coverings), a large kitchen and games room, and pleasing oriental decor. Go for a room

with windows – the ones without are a little dingy.

Canberra Motor Village CARAVAN PARK, CABINS $
(Map p246; ☎02-6247 5466; www.canberravillage. com; Kunzea St, O'Connor; camp sites per 2 people powered/unpowered $28/23, powered caravan sites $35, cabins $115-195; ✷🛋) Attractively positioned in a peaceful, bushy hillside setting 6km northwest of Civic, this place has an abundance of amenities, motel rooms and self-contained cabins ($97 to $170) in various sizes. Note no pets allowed.

Yowani Country Club APARTMENTS $$
(Map p246; ☎02-6241 3377; www.yowani.com. au; 455 Northbourne Ave, Lyneham; units $127-149, extra person $15; ✷🛜) This club, complete with golf course and bowling green, offers accommodation in spacious and comfortable, if somewhat characterless, apartments (one of which is wheelchair-accessible). The club has a restaurant and is also an easy walk from the Asian eateries of Dickson.

Canberra Carotel CARAVAN PARK, CABINS $
(Map p246; ☎02-6241 1377; www.carotel.com. au; Federal Hwy, Watson; unpowered/powered site $25/29, d cabins, units & motel rooms $89-195; ✷🛋) This is a large caravan park and motel complex on the northern outskirts of town. The complex looks a little ordinary on its 22 acres with not enough trees, but the reception-shop is friendly and the cabins

are good value, especially for larger families and groups.

Halls of Residence
Some of the ANU's halls of residence, nestled in the campus' leafy grounds, rent out rooms from late November to late February during uni holidays. Most offer similar facilities; room prices start around $60 ($15 more for B&B).

Bruce Hall (Map p254; 02-6267 4000) and Burton & Garran Hall (off Map p254; 02-6267 4333) are at the northern end of Daley Rd. The affiliated Ursula College (off Map p254; 02-6279 4303) and John XXIII College (off Map p254; 02-6279 4905) are opposite Sullivans Creek. Civic is a brisk 15-minute walk across campus.

SOUTH OF LAKE BURLEY GRIFFIN
Hyatt Hotel Canberra HOTEL $$$
(Map p254; 02-6270 1234; www.canberra.park.hyatt.com; Commonwealth Ave, Yarralumla; r from $250; 🅿🕸🛜🏊) This beautifully restored, luxurious, art-deco hotel boasts an impressive spa, gym and pool, a cigar bar, restaurant and round-the-clock room service. High tea in the hotel's elegant lounge is a Canberra institution. Try for a room with a view of the lake, and ask about the various B&B packages.

Brassey HOTEL $$
(Map p254; 02-6273 3766; www.brassey.net.au; cnr Belmore Gardens & Macquarie St, Barton; s $175-192, d $190-207, incl breakfast; 🕸🛜) This charming and historic hotel is an easy walk from Parliament House, the National Gallery and other museums. The rooms are spacious and decorated in a stately, mock-1920s style. Room rates include a buffet breakfast and free use of nearby tennis courts, while Manuka Pool is a short walk away.

Realm HOTEL $$$
(Map p254; 02-6163 1800; www.hotelrealm.com.au; 18 National Circuit, Barton; r/ste from $190/350; 🅿🕸🛜🏊) This flashy, high-rise ultramodern five-star joint aims to impress, from the soaring atrium lobby to the spacious double rooms overlooking Capital Hill. Mostly servicing business guests, it's an easy distance from the museums on King Edward Tce.

Victor Lodge GUESTHOUSE $
(Map p254; 02-6295 7777; www.victorlodge.com.au; 29 Dawes St, Kingston; s/d & tw $89/106, all with shared bathroom; 🕸🛜) This place makes a good option if you need to park a vehicle and it is very handy to the Kingston cafes and shops. The rooms are compact. There's linen provided, use of a commercial kitchen, a barbecue area, continental breakfasts and bicycle hire, plus a helping hand if you need info on local attractions.

AROUND CANBERRA
Ginninderry Homestead B&B $$$
(02-6254 6464, 0438 547 764; www.ginninderry.com.au; 468 Parkwood Rd via MacGregor; ste incl breakfast $195-335; 🕸🛜🏊) This award-winning and green-rated heritage B&B is a 20-minute drive out of town. Its gardens are quite magnificent and the airy rooms are all decorated with antique furniture. There are also tennis courts and some friendly dogs.

🍴 Eating
Canberrans fork in food and fork out cash at several hundred diverse eateries. Dining hubs include Civic, Kingston, Manuka and Griffith. There's also a fantastic Asian strip on Woolley St in Dickson and a growing trend of excellent options throughout the suburbs. Many of the town's museums and sights have their own excellent cafes – try Old Parliament House, the War Memorial, the High Court and the National Film & Sound Archive for some of the best.

On Monday and Sunday nights it can be hard to find a restaurant that's open.

CIVIC
Within and around Civic you'll find everything from burger joints to no-fuss Italian restaurants and trendy Asian eateries.

 Italian & Sons ITALIAN $$
(Map p254; 02-6162 4888; 7 Lonsdale St, Braddon; mains $23-32; ⊘lunch Tue-Fri, dinner Mon-Sat) This friendly new restaurant on the edge of Civic serves sophisticated yet hearty mains along with superlative pastas and wood-fired pizzas, all made from the best ingredients. There are plenty of vegetarian options and the cheese and wine lists are excellent.

Sammy's Kitchen MALAYSIAN $
(Map p254; 02-6247 1464; Canberra Centre, Bunda St; mains $9-23; ⊘lunch & dinner) This place, now in new digs, has been serving up delicious, cheap and plentiful Chinese and Malay dishes for years. Don't miss out on the prawn sambal ($18) or the Mongolian lamb ($15).

Dieci e Mezzo
ITALIAN $$$

(Map p254; ✆02-6248 3142; AGL House, cnr Bunda & Mort Sts; mains $30-45; ☺breakfast & lunch Mon-Fri, dinner Wed-Sat) This new entry on the Canberra dining scene sells killer coffee and scrumptious pastries at breakfast time, and serves a well-suited crowd at lunch. The $49 express lunch (three courses plus a glass of wine, or $39 for just two courses and wine) is terrific value.

Courgette
FRENCH $$

(Map p254; ✆02-6247 4042; 54 Marcus Clarke St, Civic; mains $23-32; ☺lunch Mon-Fri, dinner Mon-Sat) This fine French-influenced establishment may be named after a vegetable, but meat gets top billing here, from pan-seared calf liver to wonderful prawn ravioli. Frequented by an older clientele, this restaurant is earnest but low key and offers a splendid assortment of mature wines by the glass or bottle.

Lemon Grass
THAI $$

(Map p254; ✆02-6247 2779; 65 London Circuit; mains $14-18; ☺lunch Mon-Fri, dinner Mon-Sat) This dependable Thai institution offers a long list of vegetarian, stir-fry, curry and seafood dishes. You can bring your own wine and beer, and if you're a fan of king prawns order the *goong gratiam* (garlic prawns) with pepper and steamed vegetables.

Milk & Honey
MODERN AUSTRALIAN $$

(Map p254; ✆02-6247 7722; Garema Pl, Civic; breakfast $5-16, lunch & dinner $16-32; ☺breakfast, lunch & dinner) There are lots of long-standing cafes on this alley but this newcomer has the most interesting food. Try the breakfast trifle or, for something more substantial, the gypsy breakfast with eggs, chorizo and beans.

Tosolini's
ITALIAN $$

(Map p254; ✆02-6247 4317; cnr London Circuit & East Row; mains $25-34) This cafe has a loungey feel inside and plenty of alfresco tables, with a varied menu of pastas and rich, meaty dishes. Lighter meals include sandwiches and salads, and there are a few vegetarian dishes available. The cakes are scrumptious.

Fast food is on the menu at the Canberra Centre's **food hall** (Map p254; Bunda St; meals $6-12), including sushi, kebabs, burgers, laksa, gourmet rolls and smoothies.

MANUKA

Southeast of Capital Hill is the multicuisine culture of Manuka Shopping Centre (off Map p254), an upmarket hub for diplomats and other suits. Try French, Spanish, Turkish, Italian, Lebanese, Vietnamese, Indonesian and more in the local eateries.

Kushi
INDIAN $

(✆02-6295 7122; Style Arcade, Franklin St; mains $8-18; ☺lunch Tue-Fri & Sun, dinner Tue-Sat) Great-value Kushi specialises in South Indian cuisine and has a comprehensive menu of vegetarian and meat dishes from Goan vindaloo and Keralan fish curries to lamb Madras. There's a popular lunch buffet on Sunday ($17).

Alanya
TURKISH $$

(✆02-6295 9678; Style Arcade, Franklin St; mains $23-30; ☺lunch Tue-Fri, dinner Tue-Sat) This long-standing, award-winning Turkish restaurant has been feeding its fans authentic delights for over 20 years. The brief but tasty menu includes vegetarian options, plates to share and stand-alone mains such as the excellent *hünkar beğendi* (diced lamb on a bed of eggplant).

Urban Pantry
MODERN AUSTRALIAN $$

(✆02-6162 3556; 5 Bougainville St, Manuka; mains $12-38; ☺8am-late Mon-Sat, to 4pm Sun) This popular brunch spot boasts a chic bistro atmosphere inside and sunny tables in the small square outside. It serves excellent lunches and dinners, with dishes ranging from hearty soups to gourmet main courses. Its cakes are delicious, and on Friday nights during summer there's free jazz outside.

Emilio's Ocean Grill
SEAFOOD, STEAKHOUSE $$

(✆02-6295 1036; www.emiliosoceangrill.com.au; 36 Franklin St; mains $22-45; ☺lunch & dinner Tue-Sun) This family-run establishment has a Mediterranean flavour, and serves deliciously fresh fish as well as seafood pasta and grilled meats.

KINGSTON

Kingston's cafes, bars and restaurants surround the leafy Green Sq and continue right around the perimeter of the shopping centre.

Silo
BAKERY, CAFE $

(Map p254; ✆02-6260 6060; 36 Giles St; mains $7-22; ☺breakfast & lunch Tue-Sat) This accomplished bakery-cafe can be standing room only during the breakfast and lunch rushes, when locals line up to buy the exquisite homemade tarts and breads.

Portia's Place
CHINESE $$

(Map p254; ☑02-6239 7970; 11 Kennedy St; mains $22-35; ☺lunch Sun-Fri, dinner daily) During sitting weeks, you'll often find parliamentary powerbrokers fine-tuning their strategy over steaming noodles or Peking duck at this popular local Chinese restaurant.

La Capanna
ITALIAN $$

(Map p254; ☑02-6239 6712; 32 Giles St; mains $15-31; ☺lunch & dinner) This traditional trattoria serves classic pastas and stone-fired pizzas, along with a few meat and fish dishes. Try the pasta with king prawns and mussels.

Artespresso
MODERN AUSTRALIAN $$

(Map p254; ☑02-6295 8055; 31 Giles St; mains $15-34; ☺breakfast & lunch Mon-Fri, brunch Sat & Sun, dinner Mon-Sat) This sun-filled bistro-style eatery has contemporary art on the walls, but the paintings get scant attention from diners elbow-deep in decadent eggy breakfasts or supping on delicious dinners.

DICKSON

Dickson's eclectic shopping precinct is dominated by an Asian smorgasbord where Chinese, Thai, Laotian, Vietnamese, Korean, Japanese, Indian, Turkish and Malaysian restaurants compete with odd bedfellows as McDonald's and an Irish pub.

Dickson Asian Noodle House
THAI, LAOTIAN $

(Map p246; ☑02-6262 5903; 29 Woolley St; mains $12-15; ☺lunch & dinner) This perennially popular Laotian and Thai cafe is usually booked up towards the end of the week, though thankfully there's always takeaway. Within minutes of ordering, eat your fill of wok-fried, Hokkien-style or soup-laden noodles. Pick of the menu is the addictive combination laksa.

Fekerte's Ethiopian Cuisine
ETHIOPIAN $$

(Map p246; ☑02-6262 5799; 2 Cape St; mains $25; ☺lunch Wed-Fri, dinner Tue-Sat) This African gem weaves culinary magic with authentic Ethiopian cuisine along the lines of thick stews, spicy curries and moreish *injera* (Ethiopian flat bread). It's like comfort food, only far more interesting and from another continent.

Âu Lac
VIETNAMESE $

(Map p246; ☑02-6262 8922; 39 Woolley St; mains $10-14; ☺lunch Tue-Sun, dinner daily) This simple Vietnamese vegetarian restaurant employs soya bean as a culinary chameleon, making it pretend to be a beef curry, fried fish or honey-roast chicken. The meals are tasty and the service is quick. A good-value lunchbox special is $7.

Belluci's
PUB FARE, BISTRO $$

(Map p246; ☑02-6257 7788; cnr Cape & Woolley Sts; mains $12-37; ☺lunch & dinner) This slick, modern pub bistro offers casual dining (tapas, burgers, and fish and chips) at the bar and outside tables, as well as a slightly more sophisticated restaurant setting with menu to match (pasta, seafood and steaks). On Fridays and Saturdays there's live music and dancing.

Sfoglia
CAFE $

(Map p246; ☑02-6262 5538; 57 Woolley St; mains $9-16; ☺breakfast & lunch) A relaxed cafe where you'll find a hearty cooked breakfast and strong coffee to kick-start your day or a focaccia to give you a lunchtime boost.

AROUND CANBERRA

Ginger Room
MODERN AUSTRALIAN $$$

(Map p254; ☑02-6270 8156; Old Parliament House, King George Tce, Parkes; 2-course meal $59; ☺dinner Tue-Sat) The members of parliament could only have dreamt of being so well fed when this place was the humble parly dining room. These days white-linen service, sophisticated cuisine and a superb wine list make this one of Canberra's top restaurants. To enjoy the elegant surrounds of Old Parliament House on the cheap, try Ginger's little sister, Café in the House (open for lunch and snacks daily), or in the summer, head to the courtyard lawn for some cocktails and tunes.

Green Herring Restaurant
MODERN AUSTRALIAN $$

(☑02-6230 2657; Ginninderra Village, O'Hanlon Pl, Nicholls; mains $31; ☺dinner Tue-Sat) This place offers rustic cosiness in a 120-year-old slab hut. Don't be put off by the name – it serves Mod Oz with creative flourishes, exceptional desserts, and has a separate vegetarian menu. To get here, turn right off the Barton Hwy towards Gold Creek Village, then left at the roundabout.

Ottoman
TURKISH **$$$**

(Map p254; ☎02-6273 6111; cnr Broughton & Blackall Sts, Barton; mains $29-45; ⊘lunch Tue-Fri, dinner Tue-Sat) One of Canberra's finest restaurants, serving sophisticated Turkish cuisine to the city's hungriest power-lunchers.

Aubergine
MODERN AUSTRALIAN **$$$**

(☎02-6260 8666; 18 Barker St, Griffith; 2-course dinner per person $60; ⊘lunch Wed-Sun, dinner daily) Another fine-dining favourite, with fine ingredients artfully presented amid a refined atmosphere. It's worth saving room for the decadent desserts.

 Drinking

Pubs and bars are mostly concentrated in Civic, but there are also some in the northern suburbs of Dickson and O'Connor and across the lake in Kingston that merit a visit. During the summer, when the university students are out of town, the bar scene goes a bit limp, while between Christmas and New Year many places shut down for several days.

TOP CHOICE Parlour Wine Room
WINE BAR

(Map p254; ☎02-6162 3656; www.parlour.net. au; 16 Kendall Lane, Civic; ⊘noon-late Tue-Thu, to 3am Fri & Sat, to midnight Sun) Modern banquettes share the polished wood floor with well-stuffed chesterfield lounges in this contemporary take on the Victorian smoking lounge, located in the same building as the Diamant Hotel. Views over the lake complement the list of local, Australian and international wines, not to mention the killer cocktails.

Phoenix
PUB

(Map p254; ☎02-6247 1606; www.lovethephoenix. com; 21 East Row, Civic) Regulars don't think twice about coming back to this pub after rising from the ashes of the night before, and we love it too. It's a staunch supporter of new local musos, and has a mellow atmosphere, rustic decorations and armchairs that incline you towards pondering life for the night.

Knightsbridge Penthouse
COCKTAIL BAR, WINE BAR

(Map p254; ☎02-6262 6221; www.knightsbridge penthouse.com.au; 34 Mort St, Braddon) It's about as chic as Canberra gets – which is surprisingly chic. This opulent den of a bar is cleverly illuminated by optic fibres and serves dishy cocktails to dishy folk. It's New Orleans Gothic meets Bret Easton Ellis.

Wig & Pen
PUB

(Map p254; ☎02-6248 0171; www.wigandpen. au; cnr Alinga St & West Row, Civic) This little brewery and pub has its two-room interior packed out on Friday nights by thirsty office workers who also enjoy the hearty pub meals ($10 to $12). It produces several styles of beer, including real English ale.

Trinity Bar
COCKTAIL BAR

(Map p246; ☎02-6262 5010; www.lovetrinitybar. com; 28 Challis St, Dickson; ⊘3pm-late Tue-Sun) Sleek, DJ-equipped Trinity has fine vodkas, martinis and cocktails to sample, plus beer pulled from ceiling-hung taps. Look for the deep-red lighting and the tri-stripe symbol on the wall – they're the only signs directing strangers to this out-of-the-way haunt.

Muddle Bar
COCKTAIL BAR

(Map p254; ☎02-6262 7898; www.muddlebar. com; shop 8, West Row, Civic; ⊘4pm-late Mon-Sat) This bar in the Melbourne Building fills with lively after-office drinkers who get stuck into the happy-hour cocktails and the sophisticated bar snacks with alacrity.

Belgian Beer Cafe
PUB

(Map p254; ☎02-6260 6511; 29 Jardine St, Kingston) With 33 bottled Belgian beers and five on tap, this is the place to quench a thirst and educate a palate.

For a Guinness and Irish-themed schmaltz head to **PJ O'Reilly's** (Map p254; ☎02-6230 4752; www.pjoreillys.com.au; Melbourne Bldg, cnr Alinga St & West Row, Civic; ⊘10am-late), endearingly referred to by the locals as Plastic McPaddy's; the **Durham Castle Arms** (Map p254; ☎02-6295 1769; www.thedurham.com.au; Green Sq, Kingston; ⊘noon-late), a cosy village-pub wannabe in the middle of cafe-filled Kingston; or **King O'Malley's** (Map p254; ☎02-6257 0111; www.kingomalleys.com.au; 131 City Walk, Civic; ⊘11am-midnight), where there are cheap, hearty meals and free live music nearly every night.

☆ Entertainment

Canberra has always been curiously good at nurturing its music talent, and it pop up around town. You'll find entertainment listings in Thursday's *Canberra Times* and in the free monthly street mag *bma*. **Ticketek** (Map p254; ☎02-6219 6666; www.ticketek.com. au; Akuna St, Civic) sells tickets to all major events.

Nightclubs

Academy NIGHTCLUB
(Map p254; ☎6257 3355; www.academyclub.com.
au; Bunda St, Civic; admission $5-25; ☺9pm-late
Thu-Sat) The original movie screen of this former cinema dominates the crowded dance
floor of this nightclub with frenetic, larger-
than-life visuals. Head to the Candybar cocktail lounge if you want to take it easy.

Cube NIGHTCLUB
(Map p254; ☎02-6257 1110; www.cubenightclub.
com.au; 33 Petrie Plaza, Civic; ☺8pm-late Thu-
Sun) Revellers throw themselves onto the
bed-sized lounges to take a break from the
dance floor at this hetero-friendly gay club,
which goes from relaxed games of pool in
the early evening to riotous partying well
into the wee hours.

Uni Pub NIGHTCLUB, PUB
(Map p254; ☎02-6257 9090; www.unipub.com.au;
17 London Circuit, Civic; ☺noon-late Mon-Sat) The
four floors at this mega-venue offer, variously,
a basic pub bar, a grill, a pool bar, a cocktail
lounge and a nightclub. Cheap drinks keep
the uni crowd happy.

Cinemas

Dendy Canberra Centre CINEMA
(Map p254; ☎02-6221 8900; www.dendy.com.
au; 2nd fl, Canberra Centre, 148 Bunda St, Civic;
adult/concession $17/14.50) Canberra's newest
cinema is also the last bastion for independent and art-house cinema in the city.
Tuesday is discount day.

Greater Union CINEMA
(☎02-6295 9042; www.greaterunion.com.au; cnr
Canberra Ave & Furneaux St, Manuka; adult/child
$17/13) This venue screens mainstream
releases. Other multiplex cinemas can be
found within Canberra's various suburban
shopping malls.

Theatre

Canberra Theatre Centre THEATRE
(Map p254; ☎box office 1800 802 025, 02-6275
2700; www.canberratheatre.org.au; Civic Sq, London Circuit, Civic; ☺box office 9am-5.30pm Mon-
Sat) This centre is the hub of live theatre in
Canberra and the dramatic goings-on range
from Shakespeare to Circus Oz and Indigenous dance troupes. Information and tickets
are supplied by Canberra Ticketing in the
adjacent North Building.

Gorman House Arts Centre THEATRE
(Map p254; ☎02-6249 7377; www.gormanhouse.
com.au; Ainslie Ave, Braddon) This arts centre

hosts various theatre and dance companies
that regularly stage their own self-hatched
productions, including the innovative
moves of the **Australian Choreographic
Centre** (☎02-6247 3103).

Live Music

Many pubs have free live music.

Tilley's Devine Cafe Gallery BAR
(Map p246; ☎02-6249 1543; www.tilleys.com.
au; cnr Wattle & Brigalow Sts, Lyneham; admission
$20-40; ☺shows from 9pm) People of all ages
breeze in and out of Tilley's cool, clean-air
interior, with its scuffed furniture, dark
booths and eclectic menu of local and international musicians and comedians. It
also does poetry nights, writers sessions and
great cooked breakfasts.

ANU Union Bar PUB
(Map p254; ☎02-6125 2446; www.anuunion.com.
au; Union Court, Acton; admission $5-20; ☺gigs
from 8pm) A mainstay of Canberra's music
scene, the Uni Bar (on the ANU campus) has
energetic live music bouncing off its walls
and into the ears of sozzled students up to
three times a week during the semester. Significant student discounts usually apply to
gigs. It's also a good place for a game of pool
and a drink.

Transit Bar BAR
(Map p254; ☎02-6162 0899; 7 Akuna St, Civic;
☺noon-late Mon-Sat, 2pm-late Sun) Tucked
under the youth hostel, this bar stocks an
excellent range of international bottled
beers and live music from hip-hop to punk
by local bands and overseas acts.

Hippo Bar BAR
(Map p254; ☎02-6257 9090; 17 Garema Pl, Civic;
☺5pm-late Wed-Sat) This cosy lounge bar
is popular with young cocktail slurpers
who file in for Wednesday-night jazz – the
turntable rules other evenings.

Sport

The Canberra Raiders are the home-town
rugby league side and during the season
(from March to September) they play regularly at **Canberra Stadium** (Map p246; ☎02-
6256 6700; www.canberrastadium.com; Battye St,
Bruce). Also laying tackles at Canberra Stadium are the ACT Brumbies rugby union
team, who play in the international Super 14
competition (February to May). From October to February, catch the super-successful
women's basketball team, the Canberra Capitals, at **Southern Cross Stadium** (☎tickets

02-6253 3066; cnr Cowlishaw St & Athllon Dr, Greenway); their compatriots, the AIS, play at the AIS Training Hall (Map p246; ☑02-6214 1201; Leverrier Cres, Bruce).

 Shopping

Clothing shops for all budgets are concentrated in the city centre, but if you want to splash some cash in chic boutiques head to Manuka Shopping Centre (off Map p254) and Kingston, or try on some of the local designers who have shops along Lonsdale St in Braddon. For multicultural groceries and Asian goods head to Dickson Shopping Centre (Map p246). Canberra is a crafty city and a good place for picking up creative gifts and souvenirs from galleries, museum shops and markets. For Aboriginal art see Gold Creek Village (p265).

Canberra Centre   MALL
(Map p254; ☑02-6247 5611; Bunda St, Civic) The city's biggest shopping centre boasts numerous speciality stores, including fashion boutiques, food emporia, jewellery shops and several chain stores. The ground-floor information desk can help with wheelchair and stroller hire.

Craft ACT   CRAFT SHOP
(Map p254; ☑02-6262 9993; www.craftact.org.au; 1st fl, North Bldg, London Circuit, Civic) It's well worth visiting this venue for the wonderful exhibitions of contemporary work, including cutting-edge designs in the form of bags, bowls, pendants and prints.

Old Bus Depot Markets   MARKET
(Map p254; ☑02-6292 8391; www.obdm.com.au; Wentworth Ave, Kingston; ☺10am-4pm Sun) This popular, decade-old indoor market specialises in handcrafted goods and regional edibles, including the output of the Canberra district's 20-plus wineries.

Gorman House Arts Centre Markets   MARKET
(Map p254; ☑02-6249 7377; Gorman House Arts Centre, Ainslie Ave, Braddon; ☺10am-4pm Sat) Art, craft, tarot, massages, vintage goods and the odd burst of entertainment liven up the courtyards of this heritage precinct.

Kamberra Wine Company   WINE SHOP, GALLERY
(Map p246; ☑02-6262 2333; www.kamberra. com.au; cnr Northbourne Ave & Flemington Rd, Lyneham; ☺10am-5pm) A winery and part-time gallery, this complex showcases the district's fine cool-climate wines.

National Library Bookshop   BOOKSHOP
(Map p254; ☑02-6262 1424; Parkes Pl, Parkes) Stocks exclusively Australian books, including a superb range of fiction.

Electric Shadows Bookshop   BOOKSHOP
(Map p254; ☑02-6248 8352; 40 Mort St, Braddon; ☺9am-7pm Mon-Thu, 9am-8pm Fri & Sat, 11am-6pm Sun) This bookshop specialises in books on theatre and film, plus gay and lesbian books and rentable art-house DVDs.

Smiths Alternative Bookshop   BOOKSHOP
(Map p254; ☑02-6247 4459; 76 Alinga St, Civic) Sells everything from New Age 'science' to gay and lesbian literature.

Dymocks   BOOKSHOP
(Map p254; ☑02-6257 5057; 177 City Walk, Civic) Large, central bookshop with latest releases.

ℹ Information

Emergency

Dial ☑000 for ambulance, fire or police.
Canberra Rape Crisis Centre (☑02-6247 2525) Help 24 hours.
Lifeline (☑13 11 14) Crisis counselling available 24 hours.

Internet Access

Public libraries, the Canberra Centre (this page), the interstate bus terminal (this spread) at the Jolimont Centre and some hostels have public internet access.
Bytes Internet Cafe (☑02-6248 9155; 7 Akuna St, Civic; per hr $5; ☺7am-11pm) Underneath the YHA Hostel – coffee and food available.

Internet Resources

Canberra Arts Marketing (www.canberraarts. com.au) Comprehensive events listings.
Canberra Bed & Breakfast Network (www. canberrabandb.com) B&B options in and around Canberra.
Events ACT (www.events.act.gov.au) A guide to local festivals and events.
National Capital Authority (www.national capital.gov.au) Good for capital history and facts.
Visit Canberra (www.visitcanberra.com.au) What to eat, see, drink and do in Canberra.

Medical Services

Canberra Hospital (☑02-6244 2222, emergency dept 02-6244 2611; Yamba Dr, Garran)
Capital Chemist Kingston (☑02-6295 9146; 58 Giles St; ☺8.30am-7pm Mon-Fri, 10am-4pm Sat & Sun); O'Connor (☑02-6248 7050; Sargood St; ☺9am-11pm)

Travel Doctor (📞02-6222 2300; 5th fl, 8-10 Hobart Pl, Civic; ⏰8.30am-4.30pm Mon-Wed & Fri, to 7pm Thu) For all travel vaccinations – appointments essential.

Maps

The **National Roads & Motorists' Association** (NRMA; Map p254; 📞02-6240 4630; 6 City Walk, Canberra Centre, Civic; ⏰9am-5pm Mon-Fri) has the *Canberra & Southeast* map ($8; free if you belong to an affiliated motoring organisation), good for tours of the city and surrounding area. The Canberra Visitors Centre (this page) stocks good city maps and maps for bushwalking in Namadgi National Park ($4.50).

Money

Major banks and ATMs are abundant. Foreign exchange bureaus include the following:

American Express (Amex; 📞1300 139 060; cnr City Walk & Petrie Plaza, Civic; ⏰9.30am-4pm Mon-Thu, to 5pm Fri) Located inside a branch of the Westpac bank.

Travelex (📞02-6247 9984; Canberra Centre, Bunda St, Civic; ⏰9am-5pm Mon-Fri, 9.30am-12.30pm Sat) Inside the Harvey World Travel office.

Post

Main post office (Map p254; 📞13 13 18; 53-73 Alinga St, Civic) Pick up your poste restante here. Mail can be addressed: poste restante Canberra GPO, Canberra, ACT 2601.

Tourist Information

Canberra Visitors Centre (Map p246; 📞1300 554 114, 02-6205 0044; www.visitcanberra.com.au; 330 Northbourne Ave, Dickson; ⏰9am-5.30pm Mon-Fri, to 4pm Sat & Sun) For a wealth of information on the region, head to this centre, operated by the ACT's peak tourist information body, the Canberra Tourism & Events Corporation.

Citizens Advice Bureau ACT (Map p254; 📞02-6248 7988; www.citizensadvice.org.au; New Griffin Centre, Genge St, Civic; ⏰10am-4pm Mon, Tue, Thu & Fri, to 1pm Wed) The helpful people here can provide you with plenty of information on the community services and facilities available in the ACT.

❶ Getting There & Away

Air

Canberra International Airport (Map p246; 📞02-6275 2236) is serviced by **Qantas** (📞13 13 13, TTY 1800 652 660; www.qantas.com.au; Jolimont Centre, Northbourne Ave, Civic) and **Virgin Australia** (📞13 67 89; www.virgin australia.com), with direct flights to Adelaide, Brisbane, Melbourne and Sydney.

Brindabella Airlines (📞1300 668 824; www.brindabella-airlines.com.au) flies between Canberra, Albury-Wodonga, Brisbane, Port Macquarie, Coffs Harbour and Newcastle.

Bus

The **interstate bus terminal** is at the Jolimont Centre, and has showers, left-luggage lockers, public internet access and free phone lines to the visitor information centre and some budget accommodation.

Inside is **Greyhound Australia** (📞1300 GREYHOUND/1300 4739 46863; ⏰Jolimont Centre branch 6am-9.30pm) with frequent services to Sydney ($25 to $40, 3½ hours) and also runs to/from Adelaide ($180, 18 hours) via Melbourne ($50 to $80, nine hours). In winter there are services to Cooma, Jindabyne and Thredbo.

Also in the terminal is **Murrays** (📞13 22 51; www.murrays.com.au; ⏰Jolimont Centre branch 7am-7pm), which runs daily express services to Sydney (adult $36, 3¼ hours) and also runs to Batemans Bay ($24, 2½ hours), Narooma ($37, 4½ hours) and Wollongong ($31, 3½ hours) as well as the ski fields.

Transborder (📞02-6241 0033; www.transborder.com.au) runs daily to Yass ($14, 50 minutes). Its Alpinexpress service runs to Thredbo ($65, three hours) via Jindabyne ($45, 2½ hours) daily.

Car & Motorcycle

The Hume Hwy connects Sydney and Melbourne, passing 50km north of Canberra. The Federal Hwy runs north to connect with the Hume near Goulburn and the Barton Hwy (Rte 25) meets the Hume near Yass. To the south, the Monaro Hwy connects Canberra with Cooma.

Rental-car prices start at around $60 a day. Major companies with city-centre offices and desks at the airport include the following:

Budget (📞02-6257 2200; 17 Lonsdale St, Braddon)

Hertz (📞02-6257 4877; 32 Mort St, Braddon)

Thrifty (📞02-6247 7422; 29 Lonsdale St, Braddon)

Train

Kingston train station (Map p254; Wentworth Ave), is the city's rail terminus. You can book trains and connecting buses inside the station at the **CountryLink travel centre** (📞13 22 32, 02-6295 1198; ⏰6am-5pm Mon-Sat, 10.30am-5.30pm Sun).

CountryLink trains run to/from Sydney ($56, 4½ hours, two daily). There's no direct train to Melbourne, but a CountryLink coach to Cootamundra links with the train to Melbourne – though the trip takes considerably longer than a direct bus with Greyhound. A daily **V/Line** (📞13 61 96; www.vline.com.au) Canberra Link service involves a train between Melbourne and Albury-Wodonga, then a connecting bus to Canberra ($55, 8½ hours).

Getting Around

To/From the Airport

Canberra International Airport is in Pialligo, 8km southeast of the city. Taxi fares to the city centre cost around $35. **Airliner** (☎ 02-6299 3722; www.airliner.com.au) runs a regular bus service ($9, 20 minutes, 11 per day Monday to Friday) from bay 6 of the Civic bus interchange.

Car & Motorcycle

Canberra's road system is as circuitous as a politician's answer to a straight question. That said, the wide and relatively uncluttered main roads make driving easy, even at so-called 'peak-hour' times. A map is essential.

Public Transport

Canberra's public transport provider is the **ACT Internal Omnibus Network** (Action; ☎ 13 17 10; www.action.act.gov.au). The main bus interchange (Map p254) is along Alinga St, East Row and Mort St. Visit the **information kiosk** (East Row, Civic; ☉7.15am-5pm) for free route maps and timetables.

You can buy single-trip tickets (adult/concession $4/2), but a better bet for most visitors is to buy a daily ticket (adult/concession $7.60/3.80). Prepurchase tickets are available from Action agents (including the visitors centre and some newsagents). You can also buy them on board from the driver.

Action also offers several tourist routes (buses 33, 34, 40 and 80) that service most of Canberra's tourist attractions.

Taxi

Taxis Combined (☎ 13 22 27) has vehicles with access for wheelchairs. There's a convenient **taxi rank** (Bunda St) outside the Greater Union cinema.

AROUND CANBERRA

For information and maps on attractions around Canberra, including the unspoiled bushland just outside the outer urban limits, head to the visitors centre (p263).

South & West of the City – The Wild Side

MURRUMBIDGEE RIVER CORRIDOR

About 66km of the Murrumbidgee River flows through the ACT, and along with major tributaries of the Molonglo and Cotter Rivers, it provides great riverside picnic locations and swimming spots. Pick up a map and brochure at the Canberra Visitors Centre (p263) and explore the waters of: Uriarra Crossing, 24km northwest of the city, on the Murrumbidgee near its meeting with the Molonglo River; Casuarina Sands, 19km west of the city at the meeting of the Cotter and Murrumbidgee Rivers; Kambah Pool Reserve, another 14km upstream on the Murrumbidgee; Cotter Dam, 23km west of the city on the Cotter River and with a camping ground; Pine Island and Point Hut Crossing, upstream of Kambah Pool Reserve on the Murrumbidgee; and Gibraltar Falls, roughly 45km southwest of the city.

On the banks of the Murrumbidgee, 20km south of Canberra, is the beautiful Lanyon Homestead (Map p246; ☎02-6237 5136; Tharwa Dr; adult/concession/family $7/5/15; ☉10am-4pm Tue-Sun).

Near Tharwa is Cuppacumbalong (Map p246; ☎02-6237 5116; Naas Rd; ☉11am-5pm Wed-Sun & public holidays), a 1922 homestead and heritage garden reincarnated as a quality Australian craftware studio and gallery.

SPACE OBSERVATORIES

The Canberra Space Centre (Map p246; ☎02-6201 7880; www.cdscc.nasa.gov; off Paddy's River Rd; admission free; ☉9am-5pm) resides in the grounds of the Canberra Deep Space Communication Complex, 40km southwest of the city. Pride of place goes to Deep Space Station 43, a 70m-diameter dish that has communicated with the likes of *Voyager 1* and *2, Galileo* and various Mars probes. There are displays of spacecraft and deep-space tracking technology, plus a piece of lunar basalt scooped up by Apollo XI in 1969. A theatre continuously screens short films on space exploration.

TIDBINBILLA & NAMADGI

Tidbinbilla Nature Reserve (Map p246; ☎02-6205 1233; www.environment.act.gov.au; off Paddy's River Rd) is just 45km southwest of the city and is threaded with bushwalking tracks. There are kangaroos and emus and it's a great spot to view platypuses and lyrebirds at dusk. Call for information on ranger-guided activities on weekends and school holidays.

Corin Forest (Map p246; ☎02-6235 7333; www.corin.com.au; Corin Rd), roughly 50km southwest of the city, is a mountain recreation facility surrounded by Tidbinbilla Reserve. There's a 1.2km bobsled track and a flying fox,

It's been a slow and steady process but Canberra's wine region is finally attracting worldwide recognition for the cool-climate vinos produced here. In particular the area knocks out wonderful Riesling, Shiraz and Chardonnay.

There are over 30 cellar doors to go knocking on; click onto www.canberrawines.com.au or ask at the visitors centre (p263) for detailed information. Otherwise, these are a good start:

» **Brindabella Hills Winery** (Map p246; ☑02-6230 2583; www.brindabellahills.com.au; Woodgrove Cl, Hall; ⊙cellar door 10am-5pm Sat & Sun) This sizeable vineyard has been operating for more than 20 years. Set on a beautiful ridge, it has won awards for its Shiraz, Cabernet Sauvignon and Riesling.

» **Clonakilla Wines** (☑02-6277 5877; www.clonakilla.com.au; Crisps Lane, Murrumbateman; ⊙cellar door 11am-5pm) Boutique winery producing a handful of highly sought varieties.

» **Lake George Winery** (☑02-9948 4676; Federal Hwy, Lake George; www.lakegeorge winery.com.au; ⊙cellar door 9am-5pm) Overlooking the now drought-parched bed of Lake George, this winery produces fine Pinot Noir, Chardonnay, Pinot Grigio and Shiraz. It also has a restaurant, **grapefoodwine** (mains $23-28; ⊙9am-5pm Thu-Sun).

both open year-round; a water slide in summer; and a 'snowplay' area in winter. See the website for prices and special packages.

Namadgi National Park (Map p246; www.environment.act.gov.au) includes eight peaks higher than 1700m and offers excellent opportunities for bushwalking, mountain biking, fishing, horse riding and viewing Aboriginal rock art. For more information, visit the **Namadgi Visitor Centre** (☑02-6207 2900; Naas Rd, Tharwa; ⊙9am-4pm Mon-Fri, to 4.30pm Sat & Sun), 2km south of the Tharwa township. **Camping** (unpowered sites per person $3-5) is available at Honeysuckle Creek, Mt Clear and Orroral River; book through the visitor centre.

North & East of the City

GOLD CREEK VILLAGE

The attractions at **Gold Creek Village** (Map p246; ; ☑02-6253 9780; www.goldcreekvillage.com.au; Gold Creek Rd, Barton Hwy, Nicholls; admission free; ⊙10am-5pm) are a combination of colonial kitsch and genuinely interesting exhibits that will keep the kids occupied.

Little tackers will also ogle at the big bones at the **National Dinosaur Museum** (☑02-6230 2655; www.nationaldinosaurmuseum.com.au; adult/child/family $11.50/8.50/38; ⊙10am-5pm).

The **Australian Reptile Centre** (☑02-6253 8533; adult/child/concession/family $11/8/9/36; ⊙10am-5pm) is a fascinating showcase of reptilian life. Behind glass you can see tree skinks and scrub pythons, plus the world's four deadliest land snakes.

Cockington Green (☑02-6230 2273; www.cockingtongreen.com.au; adult/child/family $17.50/9.50/49; ⊙9.30am-5pm) is an immaculately groomed, too-quaint-for-its-own-good English village in miniature, coupled with miniature steam-train rides.

Nearby is the **Aboriginal Dreamings Gallery** (☑02-6230 2922; 19 O'Hanlon Pl, Nicholls; ⊙10am-5pm) with an excellent selection of Aboriginal artwork that includes didgeridoos and bark paintings.

Surrounding Towns & Villages

A number of NSW towns lie just over the border and are intrinsically linked to the national capital, many of them offering charming country-style accommodation as well as fine food and wine.

Just 15 minutes' drive from downtown Canberra along the Barton highway you'll find **Hall**, where the **Poacher's Pantry** (☑02-6230 2487; www.poacherspantry.com.au; Nanima Rd, Hall; ⊙10am-5pm daily for tastings and sales) attracts foodies from all over the region for its cured meats, which are best enjoyed before the pot-bellied stove in the attached **Smokehouse Café** (mains $18-33; ⊙brunch weekends, lunch Fri-Sun, dinner Fri & Sat), washed down with a wine from the neighbouring **Wily Trout Vineyard**.

At **Murrumbateman** (30 minutes' drive from Canberra along the Barton Hwy), there are wineries as well as chic B&Bs such as the

Schönegg Guesthouse (☎02-6227 0344; www.schonegg.com.au; 381 Hillview Dr, Murrumbateman; d weekdays from $150, weekends with a 2-night minimum $210; ❄) and ecofriendy **Redbrow Garden** (☎02-6226 8166; www.redbrowgarden.com.au; 1143 Nanima Rd, Murrumbateman; r for a 2-night minimum from $350; ❄).

Queanbeyan is a thriving country town to the southeast of Canberra with inexpensive motel accommodation; try the **Mid City Motor Inn** (☎02-6297 7366; www.midcitymotorinn.com.au; 215 Crawford St, Queanbeyan; s/d $95/110; ❄) if you run out of options in Canberra.

Bungendore is a very attractive village, 35km east of Canberra, which bustles on weekends but sleeps during the week.

There are galleries and antique stores aplenty to keep the cardigan crowd amused and bemused, but the highlight would have to be the **Bungendore Wood Works Gallery** (☎02-6238 1682; www.bwoodworks.com.au; cnr Malbon & Ellendon Sts, Bungendore). As well as showcasing superb works crafted from Australian timber there are changing exhibits of contemporary Australian artists.

The best place to stay in the region is the **Old Stone House** (☎02-6238 1888; www.theoldstonehouse.com.au; 41 Molonglo St, Bungendore; r incl breakfast $220; ❄), a charismatic 1867 granite-block house offering B&B in four antique-furnished rooms.

The Great Barrier Reef

Gateways to the Reef »
Top Reef Encounters »
Nature's Theme Park »
The Perfect Reef Trip »

ver explores the wonderland of Kelso Reef (p28), off Townsville

Gateways to the Reef

There are numerous ways to approach Australia's massive undersea kingdom. You can head to a popular gateway town and join an organised tour, sign up for a multiday sailing trip exploring less-travelled outer fringes of the reef, or fly out to a remote island, where you'll have the reef largely to yourself.

Port Douglas

1 An hour's drive north of Cairns, Port Douglas (p440) is a laid-back beach town with dive boats heading out to over a dozen sites, including more pristine outer reefs such as the Agincourt Reefs.

Townsville

2 Australia's largest tropical city (p395) is far from the outer reef (2½ hours by boat) but has some exceptional draws: access to Australia's best wreck dive, an excellent aquarium and marine-themed museums, plus multiday live-aboard dive boats departing from here.

Cairns

3 The most popular gateway to the reef, Cairns (p414) has dozens of boat operators offering both day trips and multiday reef explorations on live-aboard vessels. For the uninitiated, Cairns is a good place to learn to dive.

The Whitsundays

4 Home to turquoise waters, coral gardens and palm-fringed beaches, the Whitsundays (p391) have many options for reef-exploring: base yourself on an island, go sailing or stay on Airlie Beach and island-hop on day trips.

Southern Reef Islands

5 For an idyllic getaway off the beaten path, book a trip to one of several remote reef-fringed islands (p361) on the southern edge of the Great Barrier Reef. You'll find fantastic snorkelling or diving right off the island.

Clockwise from top left
1. A windswept vista at Port Douglas (p440) **2.** Marina at Townsville (p395) **3.** Cairns' northern beaches (p428)

Nature's Theme Park

Home to some of the greatest biodiversity of any ecosystem on earth, the Great Barrier Reef is a marine wonderland. It's home to 30-plus species of marine mammals along with countless species of fish, coral, molluscs and sponges. Above the water, 200 bird species and 118 butterfly species have been recorded on reef islands and cays.

Commonly encountered fish species include dusky butterfly fish, which are a rich navy blue with sulphur-yellow noses and back fins; large and lumbering graphic turkfish, with luminescent pastel coats; teeny neon damsels, with darting flecks of electric blue; and six-banded angelfish, with blue tails, yellow bodies and tiger stripes.

The reef is also a haven to many marine mammals, such as whales, dolphins and dugongs. Dugongs are listed as vulnerable, and a significant number of them live in Australia's northern waters; the reef is home to around 15% of the global population. Humpback whales migrate from Antarctica to the reef's warm waters to breed between May and October. Minke whales can be seen off the coast from Cairns to Lizard Island in June and July. Porpoises and killer and pilot whales also make their home on the reef.

One of the reef's most-loved inhabitants is the sea turtle. Six of the world's seven species (all endangered) live on the reef and lay eggs on the islands' sandy beaches in spring or summer.

LEONARD ZELL / LONELY PLANET IMAGES ©

BOB HALSTEAD / LONELY PLANET IMAGES ©

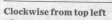

Clockwise from top left

1. Barracuda are among many fish species that inhabit the reef 2. Nesting turtle, Lady Elliot Island (p362) 3. Giant soft coral, Coral Sea

The Perfect Reef Trip

A Two-Week Itinerary

Along with experiencing the majesty of the Great Barrier Reef on snorkelling and diving trips, this itinerary includes a sailing excursion around coral-trimmed cays, rainforest walks and idyllic stays on tropical islands fronting white-sand beaches.

» After arriving in Bundaberg, take a seaplane to **Lady Elliot Island** (p362), an island resort with superb snorkelling and diving.

» Head north to the **Town of 1770** (p364) and day-trip out to **Lady Musgrave Island** (p363), for semisubmersible coral-viewing, plus snorkelling or diving in a pristine blue lagoon.

» Continue to **Airlie Beach** (p385) and book a two-night sailing cruise exploring the Whitsundays' white-sand beaches and coral gardens.

» Back at Airlie, board a catamaran to **Hardy Reef**, a spectacular 13km-long reef with a suspended lagoon and 'waterfalls' that drain it.

» Go north to **Townsville** (p395), visiting the excellent Reef HQ aquarium; if you're

an experienced diver, book a trip on a live-aboard boat to dive the **Yongala** (p398).

» Unwind on **Mission Beach** (p408), with rainforest walks, and overnight on nearby **Dunk Island** (p412), which has good bushwalking, swimming and snorkelling.

» Head to **Cairns** (p414) and take day trips to stunning **Green and Fitzroy Islands** (p428), both with rainforest and fringing coral.

» Pretty **Port Douglas** (p440) is next. From here visit the Agincourt Reefs, home to excellent diving and snorkelling sites.

» If time and money allow, add on a trip to **Lizard Island** (p457), gateway to some of Australia's best diving sites.

Above
1. Idyllic Lady Musgrave Island (p363) 2. Rainforest trek to Mt Kootaloo, Dunk Island (p412)

Queensland & The Great Barrier Reef

Best Places to Eat

» E'cco (p298)

» Oskars (p326)

» Fish D'vine (p390)

» Ochre (p423)

» Mojo's (p446)

Best Places to Stay

» Komune (p327)

» Islander Noosa Resort (p333)

» Kingfisher Bay Resort (p349)

» Paradise Bay (p393)

» Daintree Eco Lodge & Spa (p447)

Why Go?

From the surf-loving beaches of the Gold Coast to the wildlife-rich rainforests of the Daintree, Queensland spreads a dazzling array of wonders. The state's most famous attraction is the marine-rich kingdom of the 2000km-long Great Barrier Reef. Islands are also a Queensland speciality, and with over 1000 of them, you'll find everything from idyllic white-sand beauties ringed by coral reefs to rugged dune- and forest-covered locales ripe for adventure.

Speaking of adventure, the Sunshine State delivers the goods. You can snorkel or dive through underwater landscapes, go white-water rafting on grade-four rapids, kayak enchanting coastlines, or bushwalk (for the day or the week) through rainforests and gorges, up mountains and along lakes and rivers. Wildlife watching is superb, with tropical birds, whales, cassowaries and even crocs on Queensland's greatest-hits list.

When the sun sets, Queensland doesn't retire. Seafood feasts and drinks with new friends await. The hardest part is deciding where to begin...

When to Go

Cairns

°C/°F Temp — Rainfall inches/mm

Jan 'The Wet' brings heavy rains to the north; elsewhere there's high heat and humidity.

Jun Peak tourist season (through August), with mild days and cool nights (bring a jacket).

Sep Springtime sees warm, pleasant temperatures, blooming wildflowers and lively festivals.

Fast Facts

» Population: 4.5 million
» Area: 1,852,642 sq km (slightly larger than Alaska and Greece combined)
» Birds: 630 species

Top Tip

» Don't swim off northern beaches during stinger season (November to May).
» Don't forget your motion sickness tablets before boating on the Great Barrier Reef (if you need them).

Resources

» Lonely Planet (www.lonelyplanet.com/australia/queensland) is the best online travel forum.
» Courier Mail (www.couriermail.com.au) is Brisbane's daily.
» Queensland Holidays (www.queenslandholidays.com.au) is great for trip planning.

Best Wildlife Watching

» Humpback Whales: See them in Hervey Bay (p354) during their annual migration (late July to early November).
» Koalas: Spot them on Magnetic Island (p401).
» Cassowaries: Look for them around Mission Beach (p408) and Cape Tribulation (p452).
» Platypuses: See them in Eungella National Park (p385).
» Sea turtles: From November to March, witness nesting sea turtles lumbering up from the deep, followed weeks later by tiny hatchlings making a dash for the shore, on Mon Repos (p361).
» Crocs: Photograph estuarine (saltwater) crocodiles – the world's largest crocodile species – on a cruise along the Daintree River (p446).

Regional Tours

Plenty of operators offer 4WD tours of Cape York Peninsula, often with the option of driving one way and flying or boating the other.

Tours of Fraser Island from Noosa and Hervey Bay are a convenient way of seeing one of Queensland's natural wonders for those who don't wish to tackle the 4WD alone (and it's tough going even for experienced drivers).

For sailing, few places rival the Whitsunday Islands. Many operators based in Airlie Beach offer cruises, and if you want to do your own thing, you can get a group together and charter a yacht.

History

Europeans first arrived in Queensland in the 1600s with Dutch, Portuguese and French navigators exploring the north-eastern region, and then in 1770 Captain James Cook took possession of the east coast. By 1825 the area that is modern-day Brisbane's central business district (CBD) was established as a penal colony for the more intractable convicts. Despite fierce Aboriginal resistance, the area was later settled (Queensland's early white settlers indulged in one of the greatest land grabs of all time) and in 1859 the state became a separate colony independent of New South Wales (NSW). Since that time, Queensland has experienced dynamic growth and progress, aided by the discovery of gold and other minerals in the 1860s and '70s, and successful sugar-cane production. Mining and agriculture continue to form the state's economic backbone today. Queensland was one of the fastest-growing states in Australia until recently (growing more than 20% from 2000 to 2010). A souring state economy and natural disasters (devastating floods across the state followed by Cyclone Yasi in 2011) have slowed the immigration rate.

Indigenous Queensland

Before Europeans arrived, Queensland contained over 200 of Australia's 600 to 700 Aboriginal nations. Among them, they spoke at least 90 languages and dialects. Like many pre-colonial countries, the cultural and geographic boundaries of Indigenous Australia bore little resemblance to the state's borders as they are today. By the turn of the 19th century, the Aboriginal people who had survived the bloody settlement of Queensland, which saw some of the most brutal massacres in Australia, had been comprehensively run off their lands, and the white authorities had set up ever-shrinking reserves to contain the survivors. A few of these were run according to well-meaning (if misguided) missionary ideals, but the majority of them were strife-ridden places where people from different areas and cultures were thrown unhappily together and treated as virtual prisoners.

Today, 'Murri' is the generic term used to refer to the Indigenous peoples of Queensland. Indigenous Torres Strait Islanders come from the islands of the Torres Strait, located off the coast of Cape York. They are culturally distinct from the Aboriginal tribes that originated on Australia's mainland, having been influenced by indigenous Papua New Guineans and Pacific Islanders. Traditionally they were seafaring people, engaging in trade with people from the surrounding islands and Papua New Guinea, and with mainland Aborigines. Some 6800 Torres Strait Islanders remain on the islands in the strait; an estimated 42,000 live in northern Queensland.

EXPERIENCING ABORIGINAL CULTURE

Over the last few years there has been a tremendous surge in interest in Aboriginal Australia from local and international visitors, which has led to increased government funding for Indigenous tourism initiatives. As such, today there are great opportunities for contact with Aborigines. In addition to the beautiful rock-art sites at various locations, you can encounter living Aboriginal culture at the Hopevale community (see Guurrbi Tours, p455) north of Cooktown. There are Aboriginal-led tours at Mossman Gorge and Malanda Falls. The Gab Titui Cultural Centre (p469) on Thursday Island is a unique development by Torres Strait Islander communities, and at the Tjapukai Cultural Park (p415) near Cairns an award-winning Aboriginal dance group performs most days for tourists. The annual Dreaming festival, held as part of the Woodford Folk Festival (p342), is a colourful showcase of Indigenous arts from across the country.

Perhaps the most exciting event, however, is the Laura Aboriginal Dance Festival (p463) held every odd-numbered year in June on the Cape York Peninsula.

ABORIGINAL ROCK ART

Rock art is a diary of human activity by Australia's Indigenous peoples stretching over tens of thousands of years. Queensland has plenty of sites, especially splashed round the far north. Try to see some while you're here – the experience of viewing rock art in the surroundings in which it was painted is far more profound than seeing it in a gallery.

One of Queensland's most spectacular sites is inside the Carnarvon Gorge, with amazing rock and stencil art dating back 19,000 years.

Quinkan rock art is a very distinct style from northern Australia, and there are hundreds of ancient sites around Laura in Cape York. The most accessible is the Split Rock site (see p463).

Queensland & The Great Barrier Reef Highlights

1 Strolling the pretty riverside, followed by a memorable night out in buzzing **Brisbane** (p283)

2 Bushwalking through deep gorges and towering rainforests in **Springbrook National Park** (p328) and **Lamington National Park** (p329)

3 Chilling with a kangaroo at the eco-friendly **Australia Zoo** (p337)

4 Bushwalking, kayaking or surfing followed by wining and dining in lovely **Noosa** (p330)

5 Exploring the stunning scenery on **Fraser Island** (p346)

Crocodiles inhabit rivers and lakes in tropical areas; swimming is not recommended.

Torres Strait Islands

PAPUA NEW GUINEA (Mugie Daudai)

Boigu

Dauan · Saibai

Ugar (Stephen Is)

Erub (Darnley Is)

Mabuiag

Iama (Yam Is)

Poruma (Coconut Is)

Masig (Yorke Is)

Mer (Murray Is)

Great Barrier Reef

CORAL SEA

Badu

Moa

St Pauls

Warraber (Sue Is)

Muri (Mt Adolphus Is)

Kubin

Thursday Is

Horn Is

Muralag (Prince of Wales Is)

Cape York Peninsula

Adolphus Channel

Bamaga

0 — 40 km
0 — 20 miles

PAPUA NEW GUINEA

Torres Strait

See Torres Strait Islands Inset

Jardine River National Park

Weipa

ABORIGINAL LAND

Cape York Peninsula

Mitchell

CORAL SEA

Great Barrier Reef Marine Park

Lizard Island

Cooktown

Lakefield National Park

Laura

River

Daintree National Park (Cape Tribulation Section)

Bloomfield Track

Daintree National Park (Mossman Gorge Section)

Mossman

Port Douglas

Cairns

Chillagoe

Atherton Tableland

Innisfail

Mission Beach

Dunk Island

Tully

Cardwell

Hinchinbrook Island

Great Barrier Reef

Croydon

Normanton

Karumba

Gulf of Carpentaria

Mornington Island

Burketown

Boodjamulla (Lawn Hill) National Park

0 — 200 km
0 — 100 miles

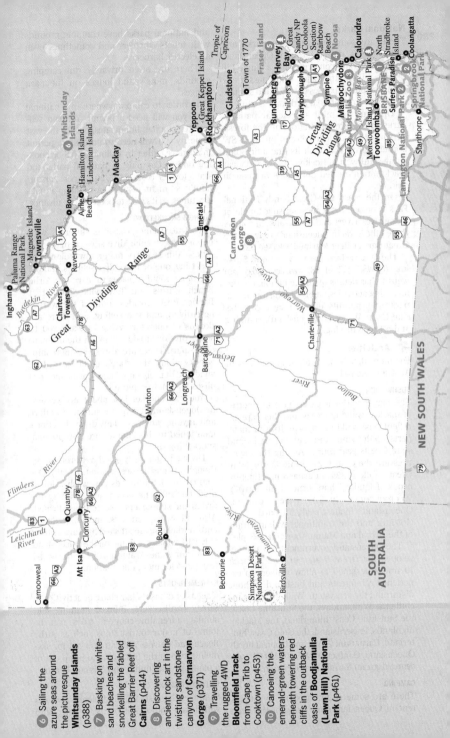

6 Sailing around the azure seas around the picturesque **Whitsunday Islands** (p388)

7 Basking on white-sand beaches and snorkelling the fabled Great Barrier Reef off **Cairns** (p414)

8 Discovering ancient rock art in the twisting sandstone canyon of **Carnarvon Gorge** (p371)

9 Travelling the rugged 4WD **Bloomfield Track** from Cape Trib to Cooktown (p453)

10 Canoeing the emerald-green waters beneath towering red cliffs in the outback oasis of **Boodjamulla (Lawn Hill) National Park** (p461)

National Parks

There are some 220 national parks and state forests dotted around Queensland, and while some comprise only a single hill or lake, others are major wilderness areas. Many islands, expanses of water and stretches of coast are national parks.

Three of the most spectacular national parks inland are Lamington, on the forested rim of an ancient volcano on the NSW border; Carnarvon, with its dramatic 30km gorge southwest of Rockhampton; and, near Mackay, rainforested Eungella swarms with wildlife.

On the coast, the Great Sandy National Park (Cooloola) is a mesmerising tangle of mangroves, rivers and forest; and, of course, there's the jewel in Queensland's crown – the Great Barrier Reef Marine Park (see p27).

The Queensland Parks & Wildlife Service (QPWS; ☎13 74 68; www.derm.qld.gov.au) website has details of all the national parks, including activities, safety and history of the parks, plus permits for multi-day bushwalks (the Great Walks of Queensland), camping and off-road driving.

🏃 Activities

For more details on outdoor adventures in Australia see p41.

BUSHWALKING

The bigger national parks have kilometres of marked walking tracks and there are excellent bushwalking opportunities in many parts of the state and national parks and state forests year-round. Among the favourites are the Gold Coast hinterland's 54km Great Walk (p329); Carnarvon; Hinchinbrook Island's Thorsborne Trail (p407); Wooroonooran (p413), which contains Queensland's highest peak, Mt Bartle Frere (1657m); and the traditional walking trails of the Jirrbal and Mamu Aboriginal people.

The Queensland government has also developed the Great Walks of Queensland: 10 tracks designed to allow walkers to experience rainforests and bushland without disturbing the ecosystem. Walk locations include the Whitsundays, the Sunshine Coast, the Sunshine Coast hinterland, the Mackay highlands, Fraser Island, the Gold Coast hinterland, Carnarvon Gorge and tropical north Queensland. Contact QPWS (☎13 74 68; www.derm.qld.gov.au) for more information.

CAMPING

There are some stunning spots to pitch a tent in Queensland and many of the state and national parks have camping grounds with toilets, showers and sometimes even an electric barbecue.

There are often privately run camping grounds, motels and lodges on the park fringes.

In order to camp anywhere in a national park you will need a permit. You can self-register at a handful of sites, but for the vast majority you will need to purchase a permit in advance, either by calling QPWS or booking online. Camping in national parks and state forests costs $5.15/20.60 per person/family per night. Popular parks fill up at holiday times, so it's wise to book well in advance.

DIVING & SNORKELLING

The Queensland coast is littered with enough spectacular dive sites to make you giddy. Almost every major town along the coast has one or more dive schools, though the most popular places to learn are Airlie Beach, Cairns and Townsville. The Great Barrier Reef provides some of the world's best diving and snorkelling, and there are dozens of operators vying to teach you to scuba dive or provide you with the ultimate dive safari. There are also some 1600 shipwrecks along the state's coast, providing vivid and densely populated marine metropolises for you to explore.

You can snorkel just about everywhere in Queensland; it requires minimum effort and anyone can do it. Many diving locations mentioned in this chapter are also popular snorkelling sites.

Diving is generally good year-round, although during the wet season, usually December to March, floods can wash a lot of mud out into the ocean and visibility for divers and snorkellers is sometimes affected. Also, all water activities, including diving and snorkelling, are affected by stingers (box jellyfish), which are found on the Queensland coast from Agnes Water north. See the boxed text, p364 for more information.

EXTREME SPORTS

Queensland has its fair share of activities to satisfy thrillseekers. Bungee jumping and similar adrenaline-charged rides can be found at major tourist stops such as Airlie Beach and Cairns. You can also opt for skydiving: two of the best spots to jump out of a plane are Caloundra and Mission Beach.

SAILING & FISHING

Sailing enthusiasts will find plenty of places with boats and/or sailboards for hire, both

SITE	DIVE OPERATORS	FEATURES
North Stradbroke Island	Manta Lodge (www.mantalodge.com.au)	manta rays, leopard & grey nurse sharks, humpback whales, turtles, dolphins, hard & soft corals
Moreton Island	Dive In Sports at Tangalooma (www.tangalooma.com)	Tangalooma Wrecks, good snorkelling site
South Port	Diving the Gold Coast (www.divingthegoldcoast.com.au)	abundant marine life, including rays, sharks, turtles & 200 fish species
Mooloolaba	Scuba World (www.scubaworld.com.au)	dive with sharks & rays at Underwater World; or wreck dive a sunken warship off the coast
Hervey Bay	Dive Hervey Bay (http://diveherveybay.com.au)	shallow caves, schools of large fish, wreck dives, turtles, sea snakes, stonefish, rays, trevally
Rainbow Beach	Wolf Rock Dive Centre (www.wolfrockdive.com.au)	one of Australia's top diving destinations, with grey nurse sharks, turtles, manta rays and giant groupers amid volcanic pinnacles
Bundaberg	Bundaberg Aqua Scuba (www.aquascuba.com.au)	wreck dives, groupers, turtles, rays, live-aboard dive boat

along the coast and inland. Manly (near Brisbane) and Airlie Beach – gateway to the Whitsunday Islands – are probably the biggest centres and you can indulge in almost any type of boating or sailing. The Whitsundays, with their plentiful bays and relatively calm waters, are particularly popular for sailing; day trips start at $100 and overnight trips from $250. Bareboat charters (sailing yourself) are also possible from $500 per day.

Fishing is one of Queensland's most popular sports and you can hire fishing gear and/or boats in many places. Fraser Island, Karumba, Cooktown and North Stradbroke Island are some good spots. The Great Barrier Reef has tight fishing regulations. For comprehensive information, contact the **Great Barrier Reef Marine Park Authority** (☐07-4750 0700; www.gbrmpa.gov.au), based at Reef HQ in Townsville.

SURFING
There are some fantastic breaks along Queensland's south-eastern coast, most notably at Coolangatta, Burleigh Heads, Surfers Paradise, North Stradbroke Island, Noosa and Town of 1770. Surf shops in these areas generally offer board hire, or you can buy secondhand ones. If you've never hit the surf before, it's a good idea to have a lesson or two.

SWIMMING
North of Fraser Island the beaches are sheltered by the Great Barrier Reef, so they're great for swimming, and the clear waters are deserving of their reputation. There is also a fantastic abundance of good freshwater swimming spots around the state. Box jellyfish are a serious problem from Rockhampton north between October and April; see the box, p364, for more information. Be careful of estuarine crocs ('salties') swimming in the coastal waters and rivers north of Rockhampton. Heed any warning signs.

WHITE-WATER RAFTING & CANOEING
The Tully and North Johnstone Rivers between Townsville and Cairns are the big ones for white-water rafting. You can do full-day rafting trips for about $130 on the Russell River, $185 on the Tully, including transfers.

Kayaking and canoeing are also popular activities in Queensland, and numerous operations offer paddling expeditions along idyllic waterways and lakes, or out through the calm Barrier Reef waters - sometimes from the mainland to offshore islands. There are also plenty of companies that operate guided tours off the waters of the Gold and Sunshine Coasts.

KAYAKING SITES

SITE	TYPE	OPERATOR	FEATURES
North Stradbroke Island	Kayaking	Straddie Adventures (www.straddie adventures.com.au)	mangroves & lovely coastline, dolphins, sea turtles, rays
Great Sandy National Park	Kayaking & canoeing	Elanda Point (www.elanda.com.au)	high-backed dunes, wildflowers, mangroves, rainforests
Whitsunday Islands	Sea kayaking	Salty Dog (www.saltydog.com.au)	day & multi-day trips exploring Molle Islands, amid coral reefs, dolphins, turtles, sea eagles
Noosa	Kayaking	Noosa Ocean Kayak (www.noosakayaktours.com)	sea-kayak tours amid dolphins, turtles on Laguna Bay; river kayaking on Noosa River
Magnetic Island	Kayaking	Magnetic Island Sea Kayaks (www.seakayak.com.au)	exploring the picturesque bays of the island
Mission Beach	Kayaking	Coral Sea Kayaking (www.coralseakayak.com.au)	day paddles to and around Dunk Island, multi-day trips to stunning Hinchinbrook Island

Wine Regions

Still under the radar in most parts of Australia (and virtually unknown abroad), the Granite Belt, located a few hours southwest of Brisbane, has slowly been carving a name for itself, buoyed by an excellent showing at international awards shows. The first vines were planted here by Sicilian immigrants in the 1800s, and some of the best-known wineries are still family-run affairs, with vines dating back many generations. Gateway town Stanthorpe lies amid 50-plus boutique wineries, which produce an impressive range of varietals. Grapes from Italy, South Africa, Portugal, Spain and France all do well in the diverse microclimates of the Granite Belt, which remains cooler than coastal Queensland owing to its higher elevations (topping out at 954m).

Tours

There are all sorts of specialised tours around Queensland. Most are connected with a particular activity (eg bushwalking or horse riding) or area (eg 4WD tours to Cape York).

There are many options for trips from the mainland out to the Great Barrier Reef. You can fly in a seaplane out to a deserted coral cay, take a fast catamaran to the outer reef and spend the day snorkelling, join a liveaboard dive boat to explore remote sections of the reef, or take a day trip to snorkel coral gardens and bask on pretty islands.

There are hundreds of tours operating out of Cairns and Port Douglas. As well as trips to the reef and islands, you can take the Kuranda Scenic Railway up to the Kuranda markets, tour the Atherton Tableland, visit Cape Tribulation on a 4WD tour, cruise along the Daintree River, go white-water rafting, and visit Aboriginal rock-art galleries in Cape York.

From the Gold Coast there are tours to Lamington and Springbrook National Parks, and numerous tours run out of Brisbane to the Sunshine and Gold Coasts, and the lovely sand islands of Moreton Bay.

Seasonal Work

There is seasonal fruit- and vegetable-picking work aplenty in Stanthorpe, Childers, Bundaberg and even Cairns, and during harvests these towns attract backpackers by the bucket load. Many are hoping to pick tomatoes in exchange for a bit of cash and, even better, a second holidaymaker visa.

Some popular destinations, such as Stanthorpe, are basically one-traffic-light villages with little to do as far as nightlife goes. If you're only coming to work, this is fine, but if you're also looking for a bit of atmosphere, it's probably best to head to Bundaberg.

Most backpackers are usually hooked up with farm work directly through their hostel, which also provides transport to and from the harvest site each day. This is a major plus, as there is no public transport to

the farms. Being connected to a hostel can also be helpful if you end up having a problem with your farm boss.

ⓘ Information

There are official tourist offices in almost every city and town in Queensland so you're never far from a helping hand. **Queensland Holidays** (www.queenslandholidays.com.au) is the official Queensland Tourism site, and a great resource for trip planning. **Sunlover Holidays** (☑13 88 33; www.sunloverholidays.com) offices are located in state capitals for booking accommodation and tours.

For comprehensive information about the state, it's worth picking up a copy of Lonely Planet's *Queensland & the Great Barrier Reef* guidebook.

Some other useful contacts are the **Department of Environment and Resource Management** (☑13 74 68; www.derm.qld.gov.au) and **Royal Automobile Club of Queensland** (RACQ; ☑13 19 05; www.racq.com.au).

ⓘ Getting There & Around

Brisbane is the main port of call for flights into Queensland and is the main international airport for the state, but Cairns and Gold Coast airports also receive international flights. For more information, see p1067.

AIR

National carriers **Qantas Airways** (☑13 13 13; www.qantas.com.au), **Jetstar** (☑13 15 38; www.jetstar.com.au) and **Virgin Australia** (☑13 67 89; www.virginaustralia.com) fly to Queensland's major cities. **Tiger Airways** (☑03-9999 2888; www.tigerairways.com) connects Melbourne with major Queensland cities.

There are also smaller airlines, including charter flights, operating up and down the coast, across the Cape York Peninsula and into the outback. **Skytrans** (☑1300 759 872; www.skytrans.com.au) serves smaller towns in northern Queensland.

BUS

Greyhound Australia (☑1300 473 946; www.greyhound.com.au), the largest bus company in Australia, has extensive coverage of Queensland and beyond. For extensive bus travel Greyhound has various travel passes to save money. See p1070 for more information.

Premier Motor Service (☑13 34 10; www.premierms.com.au) also covers the route between Melbourne, Sydney, Brisbane and Cairns, with fewer services than Greyhound but often cheaper fares.

CAR

The roads in Queensland are in good condition, particularly along the coastal highways and main thoroughfares in the hinterland and outback. However, they can often turn into badly maintained sealed roads or dirt tracks in the more remote areas of the state. For car-hire information see individual destinations. Brisbane generally has the cheapest rates.

TRAIN

Queensland Rail (☑13 16 17; www.queenslandrail.com.au) operates numerous services throughout Queensland. The main railway line is the Brisbane to Cairns run, which is serviced by the *Tilt Train*, a high-speed connection that operates three times weekly, and the *Sunlander*, a more leisurely option with three services weekly. There are also inland services from Brisbane to Charleville, Brisbane to Longreach and Charleville, and from Townsville to Mt Isa, plus a more regular *Tilt Train* service between Brisbane and Rockhampton. More detail is listed under the relevant destinations.

BRISBANE

POP 2 MILLION

One of Australia's most underrated destinations, Brisbane is an easy-going city with a vibrant arts scene, burgeoning nightlife and first-rate dining, with lush gardens, iconic sights and historic buildings all woven into the urban landscape.

Brisbanites are an active bunch and make good use of the temperate climate and lovely riverside setting. You can go jogging, cycling, kayaking and rock climbing, wander through outdoor markets or relax on palm-fringed artificial beaches just a short jaunt from the high-rises looming over the winding Brisbane River.

Brisbane's chefs cater to a global palate, and eating and drinking is all about the open-air experience. Many restaurants, bars and cafes have back gardens, riverside views, or sidewalk seating on tree-lined streets.

As an epicentre of the arts, Brisbane is no longer just the 'big country town' of decades past. Instead you'll find world-class museums, theatres, live-music venues, massive sporting events and heaps of unique fare – open-air cinema, outdoor concerts, colourful festivals and more.

When Brisbane suffered devastating floods in early 2011, Queenslanders came together to help the city's speedy recovery.

History

Aboriginal inhabitants knew the area later known as Brisbane as Mian-jin, meaning 'place shaped like a spike'. The first white settlement here was established at Redcliffe on Moreton Bay in 1824 – a penal colony for

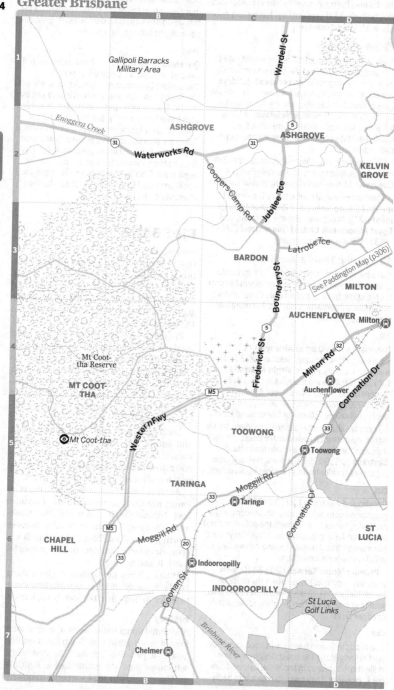

See Paddington Map (p306)

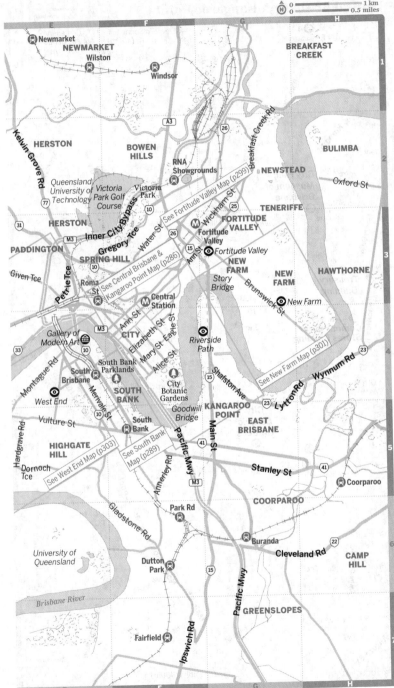

Map labels:

0 — 1 km
0 — 0.5 miles

285

QUEENSLAND & THE GREAT BARRIER REEF BRISBANE

Newmarket
NEWMARKET
Wilston
Windsor

BREAKFAST CREEK

A3

26

Breakfast Creek Rd

BULIMBA

HERSTON

BOWEN HILLS

RNA Showgrounds

NEWSTEAD

Oxford St

Kelvin Grove Rd

Queensland University of Technology

Victoria Park Golf Course

Victoria Park

See Fortitude Valley Map (p299)

TENERIFFE

77

31

10

Wickham St

25

FORTITUDE VALLEY

HERSTON

Inner City Bypass

Gregory Tce

Water St

26

M Fortitude Valley

Fortitude Valley

HAWTHORNE

M3

PADDINGTON

SPRING HILL

10

15

Ann St

NEW FARM

NEW FARM

Given Tce

Roma St

See Central Brisbane & Kangaroo Point Map (p286)

Story Bridge

Brunswick St

New Farm

Petrie Tce

M Central Station

Ann St

CITY

Elizabeth St

Mary St East St

Alice St

Riverside Path

23

Gallery of Modern Art

M3

33

10

South Bank Parklands

SOUTH BANK

City Botanic Gardens

See New Farm Map (p301)

Wynnum Rd

South Brisbane

Merivale St

15

Shafston Ave

23

Lytton Rd

West End

Vulture St

10

South Bank

Goodwill Bridge

KANGAROO POINT

EAST BRISBANE

Hardgrave Rd

HIGHGATE HILL

See West End Map (p303)

See South Bank Map (p289)

Pacific Mwy

41

Main St

Stanley St

41

Coorparoo

Dornoch Tce

Annerley Rd

M3

COORPAROO

Gladstone Rd

Park Rd

Buranda

Cleveland Rd

22

CAMP HILL

University of Queensland

Dutton Park

15

Pacific Mwy

GREENSLOPES

Brisbane River

Fairfield

Ipswich Rd

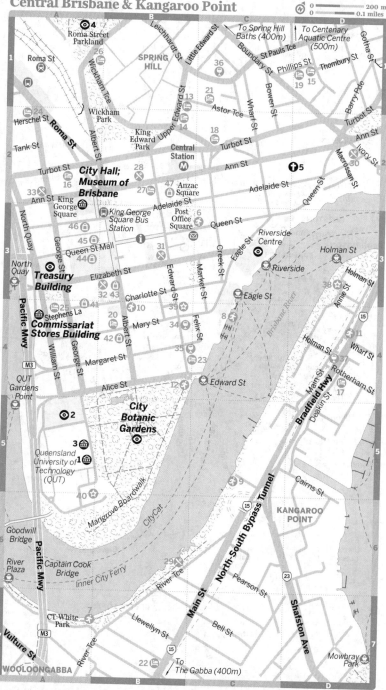

0 — 200 m
0 — 0.1 miles

Roma Street Parkland ●4
26
SPRING HILL
Leichhardt St
Little Edward St
To Spring Hill Baths (400m)
To Centenary Aquatic Centre (500m)
Gotha St
St Pauls Tce
Boundary St
Roma St
Wickham Tce
Phillips St
19 ● 15
Thombury St
Barry Pde
Turbot St
Herschel St
24
Roma St
Albert St
Wickham Park
13
21
Astor Tce
Upper Edward St
Wharf St
Bowen St
Ann St
Ivory St
30
Tank St
King Edward Park
14
18
Turbot St
Macrossan St
Turbot St
16
Central Station Ⓜ
Ann St
●5
33
City Hall; Museum of Brisbane
28
47 Anzac Square
Adelaide St
Queen St
Ann St King George Square
27
Adelaide St
Post Office Square
6
Holman St
46
King George Square Bus Station
Queen St
Riverside Centre
North Quay
45
Queen St Mall
31
Eagle St
Riverside
44
Elizabeth St
Holman St
North Quay
Treasury Building
32 43
Charlotte St
Edward St
Market St
Eagle St
8
38 Annie St
Pacific Mwy
25 Stephens La
41
20
10
39
34
Mary St
Felix St
Holman St
11
Wharf St
Commissariat Stores Building
42
35
23
37
Rotherham St
17
William St
George St
Margaret St
Edward St
Bradfield Hwy
Deakin St
QUT Gardens Point
Alice St
12
Edward St
Main St
●2
City Botanic Gardens
Cairns St
3
●3
KANGAROO POINT
Queensland University of Technology (QUT)
●1
North-South Bypass Tunnel
40
9
15
Goodwill Bridge
Pacific Mwy
Mangrove Boardwalk
CityCat
River Plaza
Captain Cook Bridge
Inner City Ferry
River Tce
29
Pearson St
23
River Tce
Llewellyn St
Main St
Bell St
Shafton Ave
CT White Park
15
Vulture St
M3
22
To The Gabba (400m)
Mowbray Park
WOOLLOONGABBA

QUEENSLAND & THE GREAT BARRIER REEF BRISBANE

difficult convicts from the Botany Bay colony in NSW. After struggling with inadequate water supplies and hostile Aboriginal groups, the colony was relocated to safer territory on the banks of the Brisbane River, before the whole colony idea was abandoned in 1839.

Moreton Bay was opened to free settlers in 1842. This marked the beginning of Brisbane's rise to prominence and the beginning of the end for the region's Aboriginal peoples.

◎ Sights

Most of Brisbane's historical and colonial sights are in the city centre (CBD). The surrounding inner-city suburbs offer loads of attractions and activities: South Bank's parkland, galleries and arts centres; Fortitude Valley and New Farm's cafes, bars and live-music venues; and West End's bohemian vibe.

CITY CENTRE

City Botanic Gardens PARK

(Map p286; Albert St; ◎24hr) On the river, Brisbane's favourite green space is a mass of lawns, towering Moreton Bay figs, bunya pines, macadamia trees and other tropical flora, descending gently from the Queensland University of Technology (QUT) campus. Its lawns are popular with lunching office workers, joggers and picnickers.

City Hall
HISTORIC BUILDING

(Map p286; btwn Ann & Adelaide Sts) Overlooking King George Sq, this 1930s sandstone building has an observation platform up in the bell tower, which affords brilliant views across the city. At research time, City Hall was undergoing extensive restoration and remained closed to visitors.

FREE Museum of Brisbane
MUSEUM

(Map p286; www.museumofbrisbane.com.au; 157 Ann St; ⊙10am-5pm) Around the corner from City Hall, this museum illuminates the city from a wide variety of viewpoints, with interactive exhibits that explore both social history and the current cultural landscape.

Treasury Building
HISTORIC BUILDING

(Map p286; Queen St Mall) At the western end of the Queen St Mall is the magnificent Italian Renaissance–style Treasury Building. Behind the lavish facade you won't find pin-striped bureaucrats and tax collectors, but rather spruikers and an entirely different kind of money spinner: Brisbane's 24-hour casino.

Opposite the casino across a grassy plaza stands the equally gorgeous former Land Administration Building, which has been converted to the five-star Treasury hotel.

Commissariat Stores Building
MUSEUM

(Map p286; 115 William St; adult/child $5/2.50; ⊙10am-4pm Tue-Fri) Built by convicts in 1829, the former government storehouse is one of Brisbane's oldest buildings and houses a museum devoted to Brisbane's convict and colonial history.

FREE QUT Art Museum
MUSEUM

(Map p286; 2 George St; ⊙10am-5pm Tue-Fri, noon-4pm Sat & Sun) In the grounds of QUT is this museum, which has regularly changing exhibits of contemporary Australian art and works by Brisbane art students. Next door is Old Government House, a beautiful colonnaded building dating from 1860 and now the home of the National Trust.

FREE Parliament House
HISTORIC BUILDING

(Map p286; cnr Alice & George Sts) This French Renaissance–style building dates from 1868 and is one of Brisbane's treasured historical landmarks. Free tours leave on demand from 9am to 4pm Monday to Friday.

Roma Street Parkland
PARK

(Map p286; 1 Parkland Blvd; ⊙24hr) The 16-hectare Roma St Parkland is one of the world's largest subtropical urban gardens. Formerly the site of a market and later a railway yard, the parkland features 40 varieties of Australian native trees, a lake, three waterfalls, a playground and public barbecues.

SOUTH BANK

TOP
CHOICE Queensland Cultural Centre
MUSEUMS, CONCERT HALL

On South Bank, just over Victoria Bridge from the CBD, the Queensland Cultural Centre is the epicentre of Brisbane's cultural confluence. It's a huge compound that includes a concert and theatre venue, four museums and the Queensland State Library.

LOADS OF TOADS

Queenslanders have several nicknames, but perhaps the most curious one is 'cane toad', after the amphibious critters that were introduced to Australia in 1935 in an attempt to control the native cane beetle. The toads are not a pretty sight: with dry, warty skin, heavy-ridged eyes and poisonous glands across their backs, they'd make any girl looking for her prince run a mile. But fairy tales aside, the cane toads have proved to be absolutely useless; they ignored the pesky cane grub and instead focused on reproducing. From an original batch of just 101 toads, there are now over 200 million of these long-legged creatures hopping around Australia – an invasion that has seen the populations of native snakes and goanna lizards decline. Indeed, the problem got so bad that a millionaire pub owner introduced a beer-for-a-bag-of-toads bounty that even got the support of the Royal Society for the Prevention of Cruelty to Animals (RSPCA). There's also a Stop the Toad Foundation in Western Australia, raising funds for barrier fencing to keep the state cane-toad free. But it seems that not everyone hates them; Queensland's representative rugby league team has chosen the cane toad as its unofficial mascot, and the toad has even been listed by the National Trust of Queensland as a state icon. Warts and all.

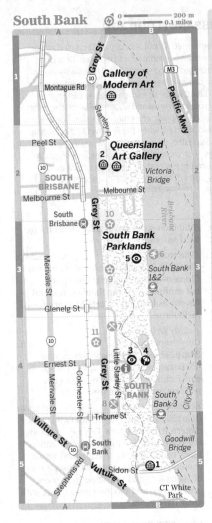

that delve into life science and technology in fun, thought-provoking ways.

Queensland Art Gallery

(Map p289; www.qag.qld.gov.au; Melbourne St, South Brisbane; admission free; ⊙10am-5pm Mon-Fri, 9am-5pm Sat & Sun) The gallery houses a fine permanent collection, mostly of domestic and European artists. The Australian art dates from the 1840s to the 1970s, and you can view works by celebrated masters including Sir Sydney Nolan, Arthur Boyd, William Dobell and George Lambert.

Gallery of Modern Art

(GoMA; Map p289; Stanley Pl; admission free; ⊙10am-5pm Mon-Fri, 9am-5pm Sat & Sun) GoMA displays Australian art from the 1970s to today in a variety of changing exhibitions and media: painting, sculpture and photography sit alongside video, installation and film.

South Bank Parklands   PARK

(Map p289; ⊙dawn-dusk) This beautiful smear of green park, skirting the western side of the Brisbane River, is home to cultural attractions, fine eateries, small rainforests, hidden lawns and gorgeous flora. The standout

Queensland Museum

(Map p289; www.southbank.qm.qld.gov.au; cnr Grey & Melbourne Sts; admission free; ⊙9.30am-5pm) This museum occupies imaginations with all manner of curiosities. Queensland's history is given a once-over with an interesting collection of exhibits, including a skeleton of the state's own dinosaur, *Muttaburrasaurus,* and the *Avian Cirrus,* the tiny plane in which Queensland's Bert Hinkler made the first England-to-Australia solo flight in 1928.

The museum also houses the **Sciencentre** (Map p289; adult/child/family $12/9/40), with over 100 hands-on, interactive exhibits

WHEN IT RAINS, IT POURS: BRISBANE FLOOD 2011

Wild weather in the Sunshine State in December 2010 and January 2011 caused major flooding throughout Queensland, with many towns inundated and isolated. Brisbane did not escape the onslaught, recording its biggest flood since 1974. The usually placid Brisbane River became a swirling torrent of brown water sweeping boats, pontoons and other debris downstream towards the sea. Flood water streamed into the CBD's riverfront areas, while in low-lying suburbs only rooftops remained above the waterline. More than 30,000 homes were affected by the floods. Popular attractions such as South Bank Parklands and the Riverside Centre were also affected, while the Riverwalk, the section of floating walkway of the riverside path, was destroyed. Along the riverfront, the city's ferry terminals suffered substantial damage, with many docks swept away, disrupting Brisbane's busy ferry services. After the clean-up, restoration and reconstruction of damaged areas proceeded rapidly. In many parts of the city little evidence of the floods remained a few months later.

attractions here are **Streets Beach** (Map p289), a funky artificial beach resembling a tropical lagoon, and, behind the beach, **Stanley Street Plaza** (Map p289), a renovated section of historic Stanley St, with shops, cafes and a tourist information centre.

On the eastern edge of the parklands is the **Queensland Maritime Museum** (Map p289; Sidon St, South Brisbane; adult/child $8/3.50, dry dock $4/2; ⊙9.30am-4.30pm), which has a wide-ranging display of maritime adventures (and misadventures) along the coast. It's worth shelling out a little extra to tour the dry dock – the museum highlight is clambering around the fascinating rooms of the HMAS *Diamantina,* a restored 1944 navy frigate.

The London Eye–style **Wheel of Brisbane** (Map p289; www.thewheelofbrisbane.com.au; Russell St, South Brisbane; adult/child $15/10; ⊙11am-9pm) offers 360-degree views from its 60m heights; rides last around 15 minutes and include audio commentary of Brisbane sights.

The South Bank Parklands are within easy walking distance of the city centre, but CityCat and Inner City Ferries also stop there; you can also get there by bus or train from Roma St or Central Station.

FORTITUDE VALLEY & NEW FARM

For over a decade the alternative neighbourhoods of Fortitude Valley and nearby New Farm have been the hub of all things contemporary and cool, thanks to a confluence of artists, restaurateurs and various fringe types flooding the area.

Institute of Modern Art ART GALLERY
(Map p299; www.ima.org.au; ⊙11am-5pm Tue-Sat, to 8pm Thu) In the Judith Wright Centre, this noncommercial gallery with an industrial

exhibition space has regular showings by local names.

Chinatown NEIGHBOURHOOD
(Map p299; Duncan St) Brisbane's very own Chinatown occupies only one street but exhibits the same flamboyance and flavour as its counterparts in Sydney and Melbourne.

Judith Wright Centre for Contemporary Arts ARTS CENTRE
(Map p299; www.judithwrightcentre.com.au; 420 Brunswick St, Fortitude Valley) The excellent Judith Wright Centre shows live performance of all genres.

Brisbane Powerhouse ARTS CENTRE
(Map p301; 119 Lamington St, New Farm) On the eastern fringes of New Farm Park stands the Powerhouse, a former power station that's been superbly transformed into a contemporary arts centre. It hosts a range of visual arts and music performances (many free), and has two restaurants with great river views.

GREATER BRISBANE

Newstead HISTORIC SITE
(⊋07-3216 1846; www.newsteadhouse.com.au; cnr Breakfast Creek Rd & Newstead Ave, Newstead; adult/child/family $6/4/15; ⊙10am-4pm Mon-Thu, 2-5pm Sun) On a breezy hill overlooking the river, Brisbane's best-known heritage site dates from 1846 and is beautifully fitted out with Victorian furnishings, antiques, clothing and period displays. It's surrounded by manicured gardens and has superb water vistas. It's located north of the centre, in Newstead Park. On Sunday, Devonshire tea is served on the verandah.

Mt Coot-tha Reserve
NATURE RESERVE

A short drive or bus ride from the city, this huge bush reserve and parkland (Map p284) has an excellent botanic garden, a planetarium, eateries and a superb lookout over the city. On a clear day you can see the Moreton Bay islands. The lookout is accessed via Samuel Griffith Dr and has wheelchair access.

Just north of the road to the lookout, on Samuel Griffith Dr, is the turn-off to JC Slaughter Falls, reached by a short walking track, plus a 1.5km Aboriginal Art Trail, which takes you past eight art sites with works by local Aboriginal artists.

The pleasant Brisbane Botanic Gardens (admission free; 8am-5pm, free guided walks 11am & 1pm Mon-Sat) has a plethora of mini ecologies, which include cactus, Japanese and herb gardens, rainforests, and arid zones, making you feel like you're traversing the globe's landscape in all its vegetated splendour.

Also within the gardens, the Sir Thomas Brisbane Planetarium (10am-4pm Tue-Fri, 11am-7.30pm Sat, 11am-4pm Sun) is Australia's largest planetarium. There's a great observatory here and the shows inside the Cosmic Skydome (adult $7-14, child $7-9) will make you feel like you've stepped on board the *Enterprise*. Outside of show times, you can explore the small space museum.

To get here via public transport, take bus 471 from Adelaide St, opposite King George Sq ($3.90, 25 minutes, hourly Monday to Friday, five services Saturday and Sunday). The bus drops you off in the lookout car park and stops outside the Brisbane Botanic Gardens en route.

D'Aguilar Range National Park
NATURE RESERVE

Brisbanites suffering from suburban malaise satiate their wilderness cravings at this 50,000-hectare park in the D'Aguilar Range, 10km north of the city centre. There are walking trails ranging from a few hundred metres to 13km, including the 6km Morelia Track at Manorina day-use area and the 5km Greene's Falls Track at Mt Glorious.

At the park entrance the Walkabout Creek Visitor Centre (camping permits 13 74 68; www.derm.qld.gov.au; 60 Mt Nebo Rd) has information about camping (per person $5.15) and maps of the park. If you plan to camp, keep in mind that these are remote, walk-in, bush campsites.

Beside the visitor centre is Walkabout Creek (adult/child/family $6/3/15), a wildlife centre where you can see a resident platypus up close, as well as turtles, green tree frogs, lizards, pythons and gliders. There's also a small but wonderful walk-through aviary. It's an outstanding alternative to a zoo.

To get here catch bus 385 ($5.30, 30 minutes), which departs from Roma Street Station hourly from 10.22am to 3.22pm (services start at 8.47am on weekends). The bus stops outside the visitor centre, and the last departure back to the city is at 4.48pm (3.53pm on weekends).

Lone Pine Koala Sanctuary
NATURE RESERVE

(07-3378 1366; Jesmond Rd, Fig Tree Pocket; adult/child/family $30/21/80; 8.30am-5pm) A 35-minute bus ride south of the city centre, Lone Pine Koala Sanctuary is set in attractive parklands beside the river. It is home to 130 or so koalas, as well as kangaroos, possums and wombats. The koalas are undeniably cute and most visitors readily cough up the $16 to have their picture taken hugging one.

To get here catch bus 430 ($4.70, 43 minutes, hourly), which leaves from the Queen St bus station. Alternatively, Mirimar II (1300 729 742; www.mirimar.com; incl park entry per adult/child/family $60/35/180) cruises to the sanctuary along the Brisbane River from North Quay, next to Victoria Bridge. It departs daily at 10am, returning from Lone Pine at 1.45pm.

🏃 Activities

The riverside paths are popular among runners, cyclists and walkers. There's also great rock climbing and kayaking on the river.

A good one-stop shop for a wide range of activities is Riverlife Adventure Centre (Map p286; 07-3891 5766; www.riverlife.com.au; Naval Stores, Kangaroo Point), located near the Kangaroo Point cliffs. It offers rock climbing ($45 per session), abseiling (rappelling, $39) and kayaking instruction ($39), and hires out bicycles ($15/30 per 1½ hours/four hours), kayaks ($25 per 1½ hours) and in-line skates ($20/40 per 1½ hours/four hours).

Story Bridge Adventure Climb
BRIDGE CLIMBING

(Map p286; 1300 254 627; www.storybridge adventureclimb.com.au; 170 Main St, Kangaroo Point; adult/child from $89/76) Fast becoming a Brisbane must-do, the bridge climb offers breathtaking views of the city. The 2½-hour climb takes place on the southern half of the bridge and reaches heights of 80m above the Brisbane River.

CityCat
FERRY RIDES

Ditching the tourist bus and catching one of the sleek CityCat ferries down the Brisbane River has become the sightseeing journey of choice for visitors to the city. Passengers can stand on the open-air front deck of the catamarans and glide under the Story Bridge to South Bank and the city centre. Ferries run every 15 to 30 minutes, between 5.40am and 11.45pm, from the University of Queensland in the southwest to Apollo Rd, Bulimba, stopping at 15 terminals, including New Farm Park, North Quay (for the Queen St Mall), Riverside (for the CBD) and West End.

Cycling

Brisbane has over 900km of bike trails, including scenic routes that follow the Brisbane River. Check out the city council **website** (www.ourbrisbane.com/transport/bicycles) for bike routes, maps and general information. Pick up free maps at the **Transport Information Centre** (cnr Ann & Albert Sts).

You can rent bikes from **Gardens Cycle Hire** (☑04-0800 3198; www.brisbanebicyclehire.com; cnr Albert & Alice Sts; per hr/day $15/35; ☺closed Tue) and **Bicycle Revolution** (Map p303; www.bicyclerevolution.org.au; 294 Montague Rd, West End; per day/week $35/150).

Brisbane also has bike-sharing program **City Cycle** (www.citycycle.com.au), but you'll need a helmet, and bikes aren't cheap for long rentals.

Rock Climbing & Abseiling

A spectacular sight at night with its floodlit vertical rock face, the 20m **Kangaroo Point Cliffs** (Map p286) on the southern banks of the Brisbane River offer outdoor climbing and abseiling during the day.

Near the cliffs, the **Riverlife Adventure Centre** (Map p286; ☑07-3891 5766; www.riverlife.com.au; Naval Stores, River Tce, Kangaroo Point) provides lessons. **Adventures Around Brisbane** (☑1800-689-453; www.adventuresaroundbrisbane.com.au; climbing $35), holds rock-climbing introductory courses and meets at the base of the cliffs. It also has an introductory abseiling course, and leads climbs to Glass House Mountains and Mt Tinbeerwah.

Adventure Seekers ROCK CLIMBING, ABSEILING
(☑1300 855 859; www.adventureseekers.com.au; half-day climb or abseil $110) Runs half-day abseiling and rock climbing (separately) at Kangaroo Point. Also offers two-hour abseiling sessions at dusk ($59).

Urban Climb ROCK CLIMBING, ABSEILING
(Map p303; ☑07-3844 2544; www.urbanclimb.com.

au; unit 2, 220 Montague Rd, West End; adult/child/family $18/16/88) Large indoor climbing wall.

Swimming

A good central place for a quick (and free) dip is the artificial **Streets Beach** (Map p289) on the banks of the Brisbane River at South Bank.

Centenary Aquatic Centre SWIMMING
(off Map p286; 400 Gregory Tce, Spring Hill; adult/child $5/4; ☺5.30am-7pm Mon-Fri, 7am-4pm Sat & Sun)

Spring Hill Baths SWIMMING
(off Map p286; 14 Torrington St, Spring Hill; adult/child $4.50/3.20; ☺6.30am-7pm Mon-Thu, to 6pm Fri, 8am-5pm Sat, 8am-1pm Sun)

Valley Pool SWIMMING
(Map p299; 432 Wickham St, Fortitude Valley; adult/child $4.50/3.20; ☺5.30am-7pm Mon-Fri, 7.30am-6pm Sat & Sun)

In-line Skating

Skaters reclaim the streets on Wednesday night with **Planet Inline** (☑07-3217 3571; www.planetinline.com) skate tours starting at 7.15pm from the top of the Goodwill Bridge ($15). It also runs a Saturday-morning breakfast-club tour ($15), and Sunday-afternoon tours that differ each week and last about three hours ($15).

You can hire skates and equipment from **Skatebiz** (Map p286; ☑07-3220 0157; www.skatebiz.com.au; 101 Albert St; per 2/24hr $13/20) or **Riverlife Adventure Centre** (Map p286; ☑07-3891 5766; www.riverlife.com.au; Naval Stores, River Tce, Kangaroo Point).

Skydiving & Ballooning

The **Brisbane Skydiving Centre** (☑1300 788 555; www.jumpthebeachbrisbane.com.au) picks up from the CBD and offers tandem skydives over Brisbane, landing on the beach in Redcliffe (from $310). **Ripcord Skydivers** (☑07-3399 3552; www.ripcord-skydivers.com.au; skydives from $295) does the same.

Fly Me to the Moon (☑07-3423 0400; www.brisbanehotairballooning.com.au) offers one-hour ballooning trips over Brisbane costing $298 per person on weekdays and $348 on weekends. Free pick-up and breakfast included.

👉 Tours

Castlemaine-Perkins
XXXX Brewery BREWERY
(Map p306; ☑07-3361 7597; www.xxxxalehouse.com.au; cnr Black & Paten Sts; adult/child $22/15; ☺hourly 11am-4pm Mon-Fri & 6pm Wed, 12.30pm,

1pm & 1.30pm Sat) If you're a fan of the golden nectar, you'll enjoy touring the XXXX brewery. Adult entry includes four ales to quench your thirst at the end of the tour, so leave the car at home. Also on offer are weekend beer and barbecue tours ($35), which include lunch. Call or go online for details. The brewery is a 20-minute walk west from the transit centre, or you can take the Citytrain to Milton Station. Wear enclosed shoes.

City Sights   CITY

(day tickets per adult/child $25/20) This hop-on-hop-off shuttle bus takes in 19 of Brisbane's major landmarks. Tours depart every 45 minutes between 9am and 3.45pm from Post Office Sq on Queen St (Map p286). The same ticket covers you for unlimited use of CityCat ferry services.

Ghost Tours   CITY

(☎07-3344 7265; www.ghost-tours.com.au; walking/coach tour $25/75) Guided 90-minute walking tours or 2½-hour bus tours of Brisbane's haunted heritage: murder scenes, cemeteries, eerie arcades and the infamous Boggo Road Gaol.

Brisbane Lights Tours   CITY

(☎07-3822 6028; www.brisbanelightstours.com; adult/child from $65/30) Tour departs at 6.30pm nightly (pick-up from your hotel included in price) and covers a dozen city

landmarks, dinner or refreshments at Mt Coot-tha Lookout, and a CityCat cruise.

Kookaburra River Queens   RIVER CRUISES

(Map p286; ☎07-3221 1300; www.kookaburrariver queens.com; lunch/dinner cruises per person from $39/75) Chug up and down the river in a restored wooden paddle steamer. Meals are a three-course seafood and carvery buffet, and there's live entertainment (bands, DJs, dancing) on evening cruises. Steamers depart from the Eagle Street Pier.

River City Cruises   RIVER CRUISES

(Map p289; ☎0428 278 473; www.rivercitycruises. com.au; South Bank Parklands Jetty A; adult/child/family $25/15/60) River City has 1½-hour cruises with commentary departing South Bank at 10.30am and 12.30pm (plus 2.30pm during summer).

Moreton Bay Escapes   HINTERLAND

(☎1300 559 355; www.moretonbayescapes.com. au; per person $109) Offers several day trips, including rainforest walks through Springbrook and Lamington National Parks. Overnight rainforest trips also available. See also p316.

Araucaria Ecotours   HINTERLAND

(☎07-5544 1283; www.learnaboutwildlife.com) Ecotours include birdwatching ($154), a three-day tour to World Heritage rainforests (from $462) and a weekend budget wildlife camp ($220).

293

QUEENSLAND & THE GREAT BARRIER REEF BRISBANE

BRISBANE FOR CHILDREN

From toddlers to teenagers, there's no shortage of places to keep youngsters busy (and parents happy) in Brisbane.

The spacious inner-city parks are your best place to start. **South Bank Parklands** have a smattering of playgrounds and the **Wheel of Brisbane** would be the highlight of any kids' day out. **Streets Beach** is also located here, with a shallow paddling pool for really small tots. The **Roma Street Parkland** and **New Farm Park** are other good spots to roam free.

One of the best attractions for children is the **Queensland Cultural Centre**. Here the Queensland Museum runs some fantastic, hands-on programs for little tackers during school holidays. The incorporated Sciencentre is made for inquisitive young minds and will keep them inventing, creating and discovering for hours. The Queensland Art Gallery has a Children's Art Centre in which it runs regular programs throughout the year.

C!RCA (Map p299; ☎07-3852 3110; www.circa.org.au; 420 Brunswick St; per day $80) offers action-packed 'circus classes' (tumbling, balancing, jumping, trapeze work) for budding young performers at the Judith Wright Centre in Fortitude Valley.

The river is a big plus. Many children will enjoy a river-boat trip, especially if it's to **Lone Pine Koala Sanctuary**, where they can cuddle up to one of the lovable creatures. If heading out Mt Coot-tha way, seeing a show at the **Sir Thomas Brisbane Planetarium** is recommended.

Day-care or babysitting options include **Dial an Angel** (☎1300 721 111; www.dialanangel. com) and **Care4Kidz** (www.careforkidz.com.au/brisbane/babysitting.htm).

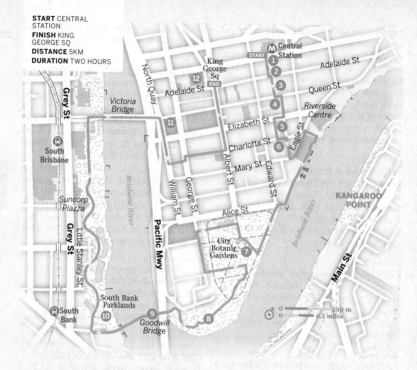

START CENTRAL STATION
FINISH KING GEORGE SQ
DISTANCE 5KM
DURATION TWO HOURS

Walking Tour
A Stroll from the CBD to South Bank

❯ Cross the road south of Central Station and descend the steps into ① **Anzac Sq**, with the ② **Shrine of Remembrance** at its north-western end.

Take the pedestrian bridge over the road at the south-western corner of the square, which leads into ③ **Post Office Sq**. Heading in the same direction, cross Queen St to Brisbane's historic ④ **GPO**. Walk down the small alley that skirts the eastern side of the post office through to Elizabeth St. Cross the road and explore the beautiful ⑤ **St Stephen's Cathedral**.

Walk through the grassy courtyard behind the cathedral until reaching Charlotte St. Take a left and the first right onto Market St, stopping to refuel at ⑥ **Market Street Cafe**. Continue to Eagle St, take a left, then walk to the first light and turn right. Cross the busy road, and walk through the high-rises of Eagle Street Pier until you reach the river. Take in the city views to your right and the river views to your left as you walk south along the waterfront.

When you get to Edward Street Pier take a stroll through the ⑦ **City Botanic Gardens**, winding your way to the ⑧ **Mangrove Boardwalk**, a wooden walkway with fine river views. When the boardwalk ends, get back on the main path and cross pedestrian-only ⑨ **Goodwill Bridge** to reach the pretty ⑩ **South Bank Parklands**, with numerous attractions and places to eat.

At the northern end of the parklands, cross Victoria Bridge back into central Brisbane. Just south of the ⑪ **Treasury Hotel** on William St, an unnamed alley cuts through to George St. Turn left on George St and then immediately right onto Charlotte St. Continue along Charlotte St and turn left onto Albert St to explore Brisbane's modern CBD.

At the top of Albert St, cross Adelaide St into King George Sq, with ⑫ **City Hall** anchoring the south-west side. After taking in the scene, head to one of the square's cafes for a much-deserved pick-me-up.

Bushwacker Ecotours HINTERLAND
(☎1300 559 355; www.bushwacker-ecotours.com.
au; adult/child from $115/95) Day tours and
overnight trips to southeast Queensland
national parks.

✯✯ Festivals & Events

Brisbane's most popular events and festivals
are listed on the city council's website
(www.ourbrisbane.com/whats-on).

Brisbane International TENNIS
(www.brisbaneinternational.com.au) Professional tennis tournament attracting the
world's best, held in January prior to the
Australian Open, at the new Queensland
Tennis Centre.

Cockroach Races COCKROACHES
(www.cockroachraces.com.au) A hilarious
Australia Day (January 26) tradition at the
Story Bridge Hotel. Entrants are encouraged to bring their own roach, or you can
choose from the house stable. Proceeds go
to charity.

Chinese New Year CHINESE NEW YEAR
Held in Fortitude Valley's Chinatown Mall
in February. Expect loads of firecrackers
and dancing dragons.

Tropfest FILM
(www.tropfest.com) Nationwide short-film
festival telecast live at the Suncorp Piazza
at South Bank in late February.

Brisbane Comedy Festival COMEDY
(www.briscomfest.com) Four-week festival in
March featuring local and international
comedians at the Brisbane Powerhouse.

**Queensland Winter Racing
Carnival** HORSE RACING
(www.queenslandracing.com.au) The state's
major horse-racing carnival held from
early April to mid-July. The biggest day is
the Stradbroke Handicap in early June.

Urban Country Festival COUNTRY MUSIC
(www.urbancountry.com.au) Four-day country-
music festival in May with up to 500
artists. Held 45 minutes north of Brisbane
in Caboolture.

Brisbane Pride Festival GAY & LESBIAN PRIDE
(www.pridebrisbane.org.au) Brisbane's annual
gay and lesbian celebration held over four
weeks. Fair Day in mid-June features a
parade through the city streets.

Out of the Box ARTS
(www.outoftheboxfestival.com.au) Biennial
festival of performing and visual art for
kids aged three to eight. Held in June in
even-numbered years.

Brisbane International Film Festival FILM
(www.biff.com.au) Ten days of quality films
starting in late July.

Queensland Music Festival MUSIC
(www.queenslandmusicfestival.com.au) State-
wide festival with styles ranging from
classical to contemporary, held over two
weeks in July in odd-numbered years.

**'Ekka' Royal National Agricultural
Show** AGRICULTURE
(www.ekka.com.au) Country and city come
together in August for Queensland's largest
annual event, the Ekka. Plenty of animal
pavilions, fun-park rides and fashion shows.

Brisbane Festival ARTS
(www.brisbanefestival.com.au) Brisbane's major
festival of the arts, held over three weeks
in September.

Brisbane Writers Festival WRITING
(www.brisbanewritersfestival.com.au)
Queensland's premier literary event; held
in September.

Valley Fiesta MUSIC
(www.valleyfiesta.com.au) Rock bands and dance
acts take over Fortitude Valley's Brunswick

QUEENSLAND & THE GREAT BARRIER REEF BRISBANE

BRISBANE FESTIVAL

Brisbane's streets become a hurly-burly of colour, flair, flavour and fireworks during the
city's biggest arts event of the year – the Brisbane Festival (formerly known as Riverfest;
www.brisbanefestival.com.au). Running over three weeks in September, the festival
is one of Australia's biggest with over 300 performances and 60-odd events, bringing
2000-plus artists from across the globe. Art exhibitions, dance, theatre, opera, sympho-
nies, circus performers and vaudeville all add to the eclectic scene, with street events
and free concerts around town.

The festival is opened each year with a bang – literally. Staged over the Brisbane River,
with vantage points from South Bank, the city and West End, Riverfire is a massive fireworks show with dazzling visual choreography and a synchronised soundtrack.

St and Chinatown malls in September for Brisbane's biggest free festival of music.

🛏 Sleeping

Brisbane has an excellent selection of accommodation options that will suit any budget. Most are outside the CBD, but more often than not they're within walking distance or have good public-transport connections.

The inner suburbs have their own distinct flavours. Spring Hill, just north of the CBD, is quiet and within easy striking distance of the CBD and Fortitude Valley. Petrie Tce and Paddington, just west of the city centre, combine trendy restaurants and rowdy bars. Staying in the alternative neighbourhoods of Fortitude Valley and nearby New Farm places you next door to Chinatown and in the city's most concentrated nightlife scene. West End, south of the river, has a decidedly chilled-out, slightly bohemian atmosphere and some great cafes and restaurants.

In a pinch, North Kangaroo Point has inexpensive motels lining the busy highway feeding into the Story Bridge.

Prices vary widely for midrange lodging. You can often score the best deals on www.wotif.com. Many places give cheaper rates on weekends.

CITY CENTRE

TOP CHOICE Treasury　　　HOTEL $$$

(Map p286; ☑07-3306 8888; www.treasurybrisbane.com.au; 130 William St; r $200-349; ❀@) Brisbane's classiest hotel is in the beautifully preserved former Land Administration Building. Every room is unique and awash with heritage features, with high ceilings, framed artwork on the walls and polished wood furniture and elegant furnishings. Even the standard rooms are quite spacious. The best rooms have river views.

Portal　　　BOUTIQUE HOTEL $$

(Map p286; ☑07-3009 3400; www.portalhotel.com.au; 52 Astor Tce; d from $160; ❀📶) Behind the ultra-modern black-and-white facade, Portal has contemporary rooms with a nice overall design and thoughtful touches (original artwork in each room, iPod docking stations, free wi-fi). There's also a women-only floor. The downside: some rooms are quite small. The bar-restaurant on the ground floor is an atmospheric spot for a drink.

Urban Brisbane　　　BOUTIQUE HOTEL $$

(Map p286; ☑07-3831 6177; www.hotelurban.com.au; 345 Wickham Tce; d from $170; ❀📶❄) Fresh from a $10-million makeover in 2008, the Urban Brisbane has stylish rooms kitted out in masculine tones with balconies and high-end fittings (super-comfortable beds, oversized LCD TVs, fuzzy bathrobes). There's a heated outdoor pool and a bar with live music on Friday night.

Stamford Plaza Brisbane　　　HOTEL $$$

(Map p286; ☑07-3221 1999; www.stamford.com.au; cnr Edward & Margaret Sts; r from $225; ❀@📶❄) At the southern end of the city, the Stamford has a historic facade in front of a modern tower. The indulgent rooms have antique touches, large beds and plenty of atmosphere. On site are a gym, an art gallery, a hair-and-beauty salon, a bar and several restaurants.

M on Mary　　　APARTMENTS $$

(Map p286; ☑07-3503 8000; www.monmary.com.au; 70 Mary St; apt from $170; ❀) Handily located a few blocks from the botanic gardens, this 43-storey building has modern, comfortably furnished one- and two-bedroom apartments. The best apartments have balconies. Some have poor layouts and are gloomy.

Annie's Inn　　　B&B $

(Map p286; ☑07-3831 8684; www.babs.com.au/annies; 405 Upper Edward St; s/d without bathroom $68/78, d with bathroom $88) In a central location within walking distance of the CBD, this budget-minded B&B has simple rooms with thin walls, tiny washbasins and frilly curtains and duvets. It can be noisy in the morning.

Tinbilly　　　HOSTEL $

(Map p286; ☑1800 446 646, 07-3238 5888; www.tinbilly.com; 466 George St; dm $22-30, d $100; ❀@) Tinbilly has a clean, modern interior and excellent facilities. The popular bar is one big party place – with live bands, DJs and open-mic nights.

Inchcolm Hotel　　　HOTEL $$$

(Map p286; ☑07-3226 8888; www.theinchcolm.com.au; 73 Wickham Tce; r $160-250; ❀❄) This elegant heritage hotel retains elements from its early-20th-century past, but the rooms have been renovated extensively. Those in the newer wing have more space and light, while rooms in the older wing have more character. There's also a rooftop pool and an in-house restaurant.

X-Base Brisbane Central　　　HOSTEL $

(Map p286; ☑1800 242 273, 07-3211 2433; www.stayatbase.com; 398 Edward St; dm $27-32, s/d/tw $27/49/80; ❀@📶) This colossal backpacker institution has basic rooms set in a heritage

QUEENSLAND & THE GREAT BARRIER REEF BRISBANE

building across from Central Station. There's a rooftop terrace with views over the CBD, and a bar on the ground floor. Its second branch, **X-Base Brisbane Embassy** (Map p296; 214 Elizabeth St) is nearby.

PETRIE TERRACE

Brisbane City YHA   HOSTEL $

(Map p306; ☑07-3236 1004; www.yha.com.au; 392 Upper Roma St; dm $32-40, tw & d $83-100; ❋@🛜≋) This clean and well-run hostel has a rooftop pool and sundeck with river views. Rooms range from three- to 10-bed dorms, and there's a cafe-bar on-site where you can meet other travellers. Several other hostels are along this street.

Aussie Way Backpackers   HOSTEL $

(Map p306; ☑07-3369 0711; 34 Cricket St; dm/s/d without bathroom $28/55/68; ❋@) Set in a picturesque, two-storey timber Queenslander, Aussie Way feels more like a guesthouse than a hostel, with spacious, nicely furnished rooms and a pleasant outdoor area. No children.

Chill Backpackers   HOSTEL $

(Map p306; ☑1800 851 875, 07-3236 0088; www.chillbackpackers.com; 328 Upper Roma St; dm $29-35, d/tr $89/105; ❋@) This garish aqua building on the CBD fringe has small, clean, modern rooms, and there's a fabulous deck with river views.

Banana Benders Backpackers   HOSTEL $

(Map p306; ☑1800 241 157, 07-3367 1157; www.bananabenders.com; 118 Petrie Tce; dm/d $30/72; ❋@🛜) This friendly, down-to-earth backpackers has basic rooms and a great deck with top city views. Owners can help you find work.

SPRING HILL

Spring Hill Terraces   GUESTHOUSE $$

(off Map p299; ☑07-3854 1048; www.springhillterraces.com; 260 Water St; r $85-110, studio/terrace units $130/160; ❋@🛜≋) Offering good old-fashioned service, Spring Hill has motel-style rooms and roomier terrace units with balconies and leafy courtyards. It's set amid greenery within 10 minutes' walk of Fortitude Valley.

Dahrl Court   APARTMENTS $$

(Map p286; ☑07-3830 3400; www.dahrlcourt.com.au; 45 Phillips St; apt from $155; ❋🛜) Tucked into a quiet, leafy pocket of Spring Hill, this boutique complex offers good value for its roomy accommodation. The sizeable apartments have heritage aesthetics throughout

and are fully self-contained (kitchens); two apartments have balconies.

Kookaburra Inn   GUESTHOUSE $

(Map p286; ☑07-3832 1303; www.kookaburra-inn.com.au; 41 Phillips St; s/d without bathroom $59/76; ❋🛜@) This small and friendly two-level guesthouse has simple rooms with a washbasin and fridge and shared clean bathrooms. There's a lounge, a guest kitchen and an outdoor patio. Overall, it's a good budget option for those looking to escape the dormitory experience.

FORTITUDE VALLEY

Limes   BOUTIQUE HOTEL $$$

(Map p299; ☑07-3852 9000; www.limeshotel.com.au; 142 Constance St; d from $229; ❋@🛜≋) A stylish newcomer to the Valley, Limes has handsomely outfitted rooms that make good use of tight space – each has plush furniture, kitchenettes and thoughtful extras (iPod docks, free wi-fi, a free gym pass). The rooftop bar is smashing.

Central Brunswick
Apartments   APARTMENTS $$

(Map p299; ☑07-3852 1411; www.centralbrunswickhotel.com.au; 455 Brunswick St; r $135-155; ❋) These modern serviced apartments, favourites with business travellers, have fully equipped kitchens and on-site gym, sauna and spa.

Bunk Backpackers   HOSTEL $

(Map p299; ☑07-3257 3644; www.bunkbrisbane.com.au; cnr Ann & Gipps Sts; dm $18-33, s/d $65/85; ❋@🛜≋) This party-minded hostel has generous dorms with bathrooms, good mattresses, gleaming kitchens and funky decor. It's steps to Brisbane's best nightlife, and weekends are noisy. There's also a fabulous bar (Birdee Num Num), a swimming pool and a spa.

City Palms Motel   MOTEL $

(off Map p299; ☑07-3252 1338; www.citypalmsmotel.com; 55 Brunswick St; d from $90; ❋) Fringed by palm trees on busy Brunswick St, this little motel has cool, dark rooms with kitchenettes. Some rooms are in better shape than others. It's a decent location if you want to be close to the Valley, but it can be noisy – request a room at the back.

NEW FARM

Bowen Terrace   GUESTHOUSE $

(Map p301; ☑07-3254 0458; www.bowentceaccommodation.com; 365 Bowen Tce; dm/s/d $35/60/85, deluxe r $99-145; P@≋) A beautifully restored Queenslander, this guesthouse

is tucked away in a quiet area of New Farm. The friendly owners have installed TVs and bar fridges in every room and there's a lovely back deck overlooking the pool. Excellent value for money.

Allender Apartments APARTMENTS $$
(Map p301; ☑07-3358 5832; www.allenderapart ments.com.au; 3 Moreton St; studio/1-bedroom apt $130/160; ❉☎) Allender's studios and one-bedroom apartments are a mixed bag. In the plain yellow-brick building are simply furnished but clean rooms in need of an update. More attractive are the heritage apartments in the adjoining Fingal House, a 1918 Queenslander with polished wood floors, oak furniture and access to a private verandah or courtyard.

SOUTH BANK & WEST END

Edmondstone Motel MOTEL $$
(Map p303; ☑07-3255 0777; www.edmond stonemotel.com.au; 24 Edmondstone St, South Bank; s/d $109/119; ❉☎☎☎) A 10-minute walk from both the South Bank Parklands and West End, the Edmondstone Motel has small, comfortable rooms with new mattresses, kitchenettes and LCD TVs – and yellow brick walls. Most have small balconies, and there's a small pool and BBQ.

Brisbane Backpackers Resort HOSTEL $
(Map p303; ☑07-3844 9956; www.brisbaneback packers.com.au; 110 Vulture St, West End; dm $25-32, d/tr $99/120; ❉☎☎) The best feature of this popular hostel is the pool and spa, with a tiled outdoor area and a bar. The rooms are basic but generally well maintained. It's a short stroll to the bars and cafes of West End.

Somewhere to Stay HOSTEL $
(Map p303; ☑1800 812 398, 07-3846 2858; www.somewheretostay.com.au; 47 Brighton Rd, West End; dm $19-27, s $44-49, d $54-74; ☎☎) Big and breezy, this enormous white Queenslander has more than 50 rooms and a very laid-back vibe.

KANGAROO POINT

Il Mondo BOUTIQUE HOTEL $$
(Map p286; ☑07-3392 0111; www.ilmondo.com. au; 25 Rotherham St; r/apt $160/250; ❉☎☎) In a fine location near the Story Bridge, this boutique hotel has handsome three- and four-star rooms with contemporary, minimalist design, high-end fixtures and plenty of space. The cheaper options are standard hotel rooms while the more expensive are self-contained apartments.

Queensland Motel HOTEL $
(Map p286; ☑07-3391 1061; www.queenslandmotel. id.au; 777 Main St; d/tr $98/109; ❉☎☎☎) The nicely maintained Queensland Motel offers large, brightly coloured rooms with good beds. Try to get a room on the top floor, where you'll be greeted by rustling palm trees while enjoying coffee on the balcony.

OUTER BRISBANE

Fern Cottage GUESTHOUSE $$
(☑07-3511 6685; www.ferncottage.net; 89 Fernberg Rd, Paddington; s/d $120/150; ❉@) Fern Cottage is a beautifully renovated Queenslander with a splash of Mediterranean ambience. The rooms are utterly cushy and there's a lush garden retreat out the back with a shady balcony.

Newmarket Gardens Caravan Park CAMPGROUND $
(☑07-3356 1458; www.newmarketgardens.com. au; 199 Ashgrove Ave, Ashgrove; powered/unpowered sites $33/31, cabins $95-116; ❉@) This clean site doesn't have many trees, but it is just 4km north of the city centre, accessible by several bus routes and Citytrain (Newmarket Station).

✖ Eating

Brisbane's restaurants make fine use of the temperate climate, with outdoor seating, spacious courtyards and concealed gardens all integral settings in the dining scene.

The CBD houses a number of fine eating options, including many riverside cafes and restaurants. In the Valley you'll find inexpensive cafes and a smorgasbord of Asian flavours, thanks to Chinatown. Nearby, stylish New Farm has superb dining with a large selection of multicultural eateries and award winners. West End is a distinctly cosmopolitan corner, with trendy cafes and eclectic cuisine.

CITY CENTRE

E'cco MODERN AUSTRALIAN $$$
(Map p286; ☑07-3831 8344; 100 Boundary St; mains $43; ⊙lunch Tue-Fri, dinner Tue-Sat) One of the finest restaurants in the state, award-winning E'cco is a must for any culinary aficionado. Masterpieces on the menu include Milly Hill lamb rump with baby beetroot, roast pumpkin, blue cheese and pine nuts. The interior is suitably swish and you'll need to book well in advance.

Cha Cha Char STEAKHOUSE $$$
(Map p286; ☑07-3211 9944; Eagle St Pier; mains $30-50; ⊙lunch Mon-Fri, dinner daily) Wallowing

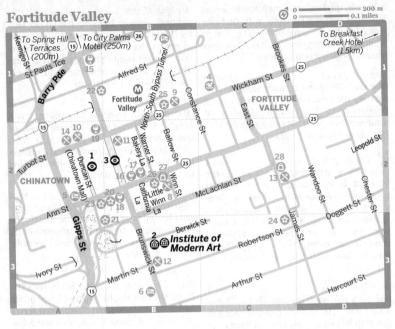

Fortitude Valley

in awards, this long-running favourite serves Brisbane's best steaks, along with first-rate seafood and roast game meats. The elegant semicircular dining room has floor-to-ceiling windows with waterfront views.

Embassy Hotel PUB FARE $
(Map p286; 188 Edward St; mains $10-18; ⊙lunch & dinner) With red tones, cubed seating and polished wood, this groovy hotel dishes out some excellent pub nosh and is popular with city folk and travellers alike.

✎ Bleeding Heart Gallery CAFE $
(Map p286; www.bleedingheart.com.au; 166 Ann St; mains $6-8; ⊙8am-5pm Mon-Fri; ☎) Set back from busy Ann St in a charming, two-storey Queenslander with verandah, this spacious cafe and gallery has a bohemian vibe and hosts art openings, occasional concerts and other events. All profits go into funding charitable and community enterprises.

Java Coast Cafe CAFE $
(Map p286; 340 George St; mains $9-14; ⊙7.30am-3.30pm Mon-Fri) Head to the peaceful back garden with its fountain, subtropical plants and Buddha statues for a quick escape from the bustling CBD. Good coffee, teas, sandwiches, salads and light meals with Asian accents.

CHINATOWN & FORTITUDE VALLEY

Vietnamese Restaurant VIETNAMESE $
(Map p299; 194 Wickham St; mains $8-15; ⊙lunch & dinner) Aptly if unimaginatively named, this is indeed *the* place in town to eat Vietnamese, with exquisitely prepared dishes served to an always crowded house. The real delights are to be found on the 'Authentic Menu'. The shredded beef in spinach rolls are tops, as is any dish containing the word 'sizzling'. BYO and licensed.

Kuan-Yin Tea House VEGETARIAN $
(Map p299; 198 Wickham St; mains $8-10; ⊙11.30am-5pm Mon & Sat, to 7pm Wed-Fri, to 3pm Sun) Kuan-Yin is a small, warmly lit BYO place with wood panelling and a bamboo-lined ceiling, where a wide crosssection of Brisbanites come for flavourful vegetarian noodle soups, dumplings and mock-meat rice dishes. Great tea selection.

Garuva FUSION $$
(Map p299; ☎07-3216 0124; 324 Wickham St; mains $24; ⊙dinner) Garuva's rainforested foyer leads to tables with cushioned seating concealed by silk curtains. There's a rather

Arabian Nights feel to the place, with dim lighting, loungey beats and subdued banter (more raucous on weekends). Plates are meant for sharing and lean toward Asian fusion – sweet-potato and bean curry, warm Thai beef salad, coconut prawns. Hunt out the cool, hidden cocktail bar.

Café Cirque CAFE $$
(Map p301; 618 Brunswick St; breakfast mains $14-17; ⊙8am-4pm) One of the best breakfast spots (served all day) in town, the buzzing Café Cirque serves rich coffees and daily specials, along with open-face sandwiches and gourmet salads for lunch.

Flamingo CAFE $
(Map p299; 5B Winn St; mains $9-15; ⊙7.30am-4pm) Tucked down a tiny lane off Ann St, the Flamingo is a buzzing little cafe with black and pink walls, a boho vibe and cheerfully profane wait staff.

Spoon Deli CAFE $$
(Map p299; 22 James St; breakfast $10-15, mains $14-21; ⊙5.30am-7pm Mon-Fri, to 6pm Sat & Sun) Inside James Street Market, this upscale deli serves deliciously rich pasta, salads, soup and colossal paninis and focaccias. The fresh juices are a liquid meal unto themselves. Diners munch their goodies amid the deli produce at oversized square tables or low benches skirting the windows, which flood the place with sunlight. You'll feel hungry as soon as you walk in.

Self-catering

The Asian supermarkets in Chinatown mall have an excellent range of fresh vegies, Asian groceries and exotic fruit.

James Street Market MARKET
(Map p299; James St) It's pricey, but the quality is excellent and there's a good seafood shop here.

McWhirters Marketplace MARKET
(Map p299; cnr Brunswick & Wickham Sts) Has a great produce market.

NEW FARM

Ortiga SPANISH $$
(Map p299; ☎07-3852 1155; 446 Brunswick St; sharing plates $18-36; ⊙dinner Tue-Sun) One of Brisbane's best new restaurants, Ortiga opened in 2010 to much fanfare. You can dine in the stylish upstairs tapas bar with rustic wood tables or head to the elegant subterranean dining room where chefs work their magic in an open kitchen. Top picks include *cochinillo* (slow-cooked suckling pig),

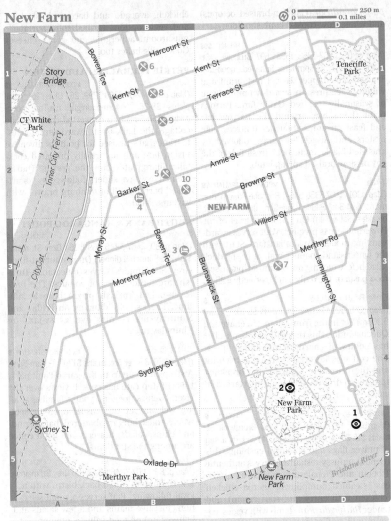

New Farm

◉ Sights
1 Brisbane Powerhouse D5
2 New Farm Park C4

🛏 Sleeping
3 Allender Apartments B3
4 Bowen Terrace B2

🍴 Eating
5 Anise B2
6 BurgerUrge B1
7 Cafe Bouquiniste C3
8 Café Cirque B1

9 Himalayan Cafe B2
Watt .... (see 1)
10 Wok On Inn B2

Drinking
Alto Bar .... (see 1)

Entertainment
Brisbane Powerhouse .... (see 1)
Moonlight Cinemas .... (see 2)

Shopping
Jan Power's Farmers Market .... (see 1)

pulpo a gallega (Galician-braised octopus) and whole slow-cooked lamb shoulder.

Anise
FRENCH $$$

(Map p301; ☑07-3358 1558; 697 Brunswick St; mains $36-42; ⊙5pm-1am Sun-Wed, noon-1am Thu-Sat) This dapper 21-seat restaurant and wine bar features an award-winning menu of seasonally inspired Gallic fare. Patrons plant themselves around the narrow bar and feast on amuse-bouches (entrees) like oysters and Alsace foie gras, followed by grass-fed black Angus beef, fresh fish of the day or slow-braised spring lamb.

Watt
MODERN AUSTRALIAN $$

(Map p301; ☑07-3358 5464; Brisbane Powerhouse; mains $24-34; ⊙lunch Tue-Sun, dinner Tue-Sat, breakfast Sat & Sun) On the lower level of the Powerhouse arts precinct, Watt serves award-winning modern Australian fare. Start with the Queensland spanner crab or crispy duck salad before moving on to lamb striploin, seafood pasta or the daily catch perfectly grilled.

Cafe Bouquiniste
CAFE $

(Map p301; 121 Merthyr Rd; mains $8-10; ⊙8am-5.30pm) Set in the front room of a charming Queenslander, this tiny cafe and bookseller has oodles of charm, if not much space. The coffee is fantastic, service is friendly, and the prices are right for the breakfast fare, toasted sandwiches, savoury tarts and cakes.

Himalayan Cafe
NEPALESE $

(Map p301; ☑07-3358 4015; 640 Brunswick St; mains $15-23; ⊙dinner Tue-Sat; ☑) Set in a sea of prayer flags and colourful cushions, this friendly, unfussy restaurant serves authentic Tibetan and Nepalese fare such as momo cha (steamed dumplings), sherpa chicken (chicken with curry and sour cream), and tender *fhaiya darkau* (lamb with vegies, coconut milk and spices). It gets rave reviews and kids are welcome.

Wok on Inn
ASIAN FUSION $

(Map p301; 728 Brunswick St; mains $11-14; ⊙lunch Sun-Fri, dinner daily) With a lovely shaded front courtyard, this industrious and popular noodle bar is the New Farm spot for some fast noodles. Choose your noodle, your cooking style (including Mongolian) and your meat/veg combo. Regular $7.50 lunch special.

BurgerUrge
BURGERS $

(Map p301; 542 Brunswick St; mains $9-13; ⊙lunch Fri-Sun, dinner Tue-Sun; ☑) Among the city's best burgers, with a wealth of options: lamb;

chicken, avocado and bacon; classic beef; and vegie options (grilled tofu, portabello mushroom, aubergine and goat's cheese). Good milkshakes too.

PETRIE TERRACE & PADDINGTON

Lark
MODERN AUSTRALIAN $$

(Map p306; ☑07-3369 1299; 267 Given Tce; small plates $8-26; ⊙4pm-midnight Tue-Thu, noon-midnight Fri-Sun) In a converted colonial-style cottage, the Lark is an award-winning restaurant that's praised for both its inventive fusion fare and its artfully prepared cocktails. Share plates from the 'grazing' (tapas) menu like wagyu sliders, followed by yogurt-baked barramundi or tempura prawns with wakame salad.

SOUTH BANK & KANGAROO POINT

Ahmet's
TURKISH $$

(Map p289; ☑07-3846 6699; 164 Grey St; mains $20-28; ⊙lunch & dinner) On restaurant-lined Grey St, Ahmet's serves delectable Turkish fare amid a riot of colours. The *pide* (oven-baked Turkish pizza) here is sublime. There's belly dancing on Friday and Saturday nights, plus live 'gypsy-jazz' on Thursday night.

Cliffs Cafe
MODERN AUSTRALIAN $

(Map p286; 3 River Tce; mains $12-17; ⊙7am-5pm) A steep climb up from Kangaroo Point park, this cliff-top cafe has superb views over the river. Cyclists, joggers, young families – all are welcome at this casual open-air spot, where thick burgers, battered barramundi and chips, salads, desserts and good coffee are among the standouts.

Piaf
FRENCH $$

(Map p289; ☑07-3846 5026; 186 Grey St; mains $22; ⊙7am-late) A laid-back bistro with a loyal following, Piaf serves a small selection (just five mains and a few salads and lighter fare) of good-value contemporary food.

WEST END

✐ Mondo Organics
MODERN AUSTRALIAN $$

(Map p303; ☑07-3844 1132; 166 Hardgrave Rd; mains $26-38; ⊙lunch Fri-Sun, dinner Wed-Sat, breakfast Sat & Sun) Using the highest-quality organic and sustainable produce, Mondo Organics earns top marks for its delicious seasonal menu. Recent hits include pumpkin, leek and ricotta tortellini; lamb rack with wild mushroom risotto; and ocean trout with shaved fennel and saffron-infused mashed potatoes.

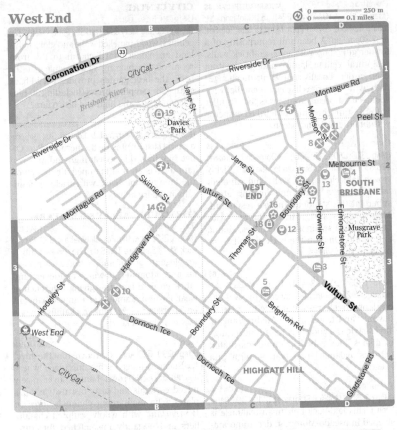

West End

🟢 Activities, Courses & Tours
1 Bicycle Revolution B2
   Mondo Organics Cooking
   Courses .... (see 10)
2 Urban Climb C1

🔵 Sleeping
3 Brisbane Backpackers Resort D3
4 Edmondstone Motel D2
5 Somewhere to Stay C3

🔴 Eating
6 Black Star C3
7 Caravanserai A3
8 Gunshop Cafe D2
9 Kafe Meze D2
10 Mondo Organics B3

11 Three Monkeys D2

🟡 Drinking
   Archive Beer Boutique & Bistro . (see 17)
12 Lock'n'Load C3
13 Lychee Lounge D2

🟠 Entertainment
14 Cafe Checocho B2
15 Hi-Fi D2
16 Music Kafe C2
17 Uber D2

🟣 Shopping
18 Avid Reader C3
19 West End Markets B1

Gunshop Cafe
MODERN AUSTRALIAN **$$**

(Map p303; ☑07-3844 2241; 53 Mollison St; mains $24-33; ⊙7am-2pm Mon, to late Tue-Sat, to 12.30pm Sun) A beautiful repurposing of a former gun shop with exposed-brick walls, sculptural ceiling lamps and an inviting back garden. Locally sourced menu changes daily, with favourites like eggs Benedict with vodka-cured ocean trout, grass-fed rib fillet with roast mushrooms, and grilled emperor with braised leek and bacon.

Caravanserai
TURKISH **$$**

(Map p303; ☑07-3217 2617; 1-3 Dornoch Tce; mains $25-33; ⊙lunch Thu-Sun, dinner Tue-Sun) Richly woven tablecloths, red walls and candlelit tables create a warm and inviting atmosphere at this standout Turkish restaurant. Meze platters are great for sharing (with hummus, babagounosh, artichokes, dolma and more). Dine on the back verandah for pleasant river views.

Kafe Meze
GREEK **$$**

(Map p303; ☑07-3844 1720; 56 Mollison St; mains $27-29; ⊙lunch & dinner) This indoor-outdoor Greek restaurant delivers fresh flavours and tastes of the Mediterranean. Tapas-style is a good way to sample a range of dishes, like grilled haloumi, marinated octopus, calamari and tzatziki with pita bread.

Three Monkeys
CAFE **$**

(Map p303; 58 Mollison St; mains $12-15; ⊙9.30am-10pm) This laid-back bohemian teahouse is steeped in pseudo-Moroccan decor and ambience. Low lighting, rustic wood furnishings and tiny nooks make a fine setting for delicious cake and coffee – or heartier pizzas, focaccia and panini. There's also a courtyard out the back.

Black Star
CAFE **$**

(Map p303; 44 Thomas St; ⊙7am-3pm Mon, to 5pm Tue-Fri, to late Sat, 8am-3pm Sun) A neighbourhood favourite, West End's most popular roastery has excellent coffee, outdoor tables, all-day breakfast and live music on Saturday night.

Drinking

The prime drinking destination in Brisbane is Fortitude Valley, with its lounges, live-music bars and nightclubs. New Farm also has fine nightlife, while the CBD attracts a bottoms-up after-work crowd. West End has some fine bars, attracting a mostly neighbourhood crowd.

CITY CENTRE

Belgian Beer Cafe
BAR

(Map p286; cnr Mary & Edward Sts; ⊙noon-late) Tin ceilings, wood-panelled walls and globe lights lend an old-fashioned charm to the front room of this buzzing space, while out the back, the beer garden provides a laid-back setting for sampling brews (including 30-plus Belgian beers) and high-end bistro fare.

Moo Moo
RESTAURANT-WINE BAR

(Map p286; cnr Margaret & Edward Sts; ⊙6pm-midnight Mon-Sat) Inside the heritage Port Office building, this stylish high-end grill restaurant has an inviting open-air lounge on the lane out the back, with trickling fountain and fairy lights.

FORTITUDE VALLEY & NEW FARM

Press Club
COCKTAIL BAR

(Map p299; www.thepressclub.net.au; 339 Brunswick St; ⊙5pm-late Thu-Sat) The Press Club is an elegant spot of amber hues, leather sofas and ottomans, glowing chandeliers and fabric-covered lanterns, giving it a touch of Near Eastern glamour. Live music happens on Thursday – jazz, funk, rockabilly – while DJs spin on weekends.

La Ruche
COCKTAIL BAR

(Map p299; 680 Ann St) French for 'the hive', La Ruche is indeed a buzzing place, where a well-dressed crowd banters over nicely mixed cocktails and tasty bistro-style tapas plates. The main room channels *Alice in Wonderland* with wildly sculpted chandeliers and elegantly mismatched furniture, while there's a spacious (smoker's) courtyard in the back and a small, cosy retreat upstairs.

Alloneword
BAR

(Map p299; www.alloneword.com.au; 188 Brunswick St) On a seedy stretch of Brunswick, this underground spot is the antidote to the sleek cocktail bars taking over the Valley. The front room is pure whimsy: vintage wallpaper, velvety banquettes and a mirrored ceiling, while the back patio has graffiti murals and DJs.

Sky Room
COCKTAIL BAR

(Map p299; level 2, 234 Wickham St; ⊙5pm-late Wed-Sun) The Sky Room is a rambling lounge of plants, lime-green couches and chairs, a long wooden bar and a balcony complete with flickering tiki torches. DJs play a mix of old-school rock. Bottled beer is served in a brown paper bag.

Bowery

COCKTAIL BAR

(Map p299; 676 Ann St) Exposed-brick walls, gilded mirrors and antique chandeliers lend a classy, old-fashioned vibe to this long, narrow bar. The cocktails are top-notch (and priced accordingly), and there's a tiny patio in the back. Live jazz Tuesday to Thursday; DJs spin on weekends.

Cru Bar & Cellar

WINE BAR

(Map p299; 22 James St, Fortitude Valley) A mindboggling menu of 400 wines (20 by the glass) is on offer at this classy bar, which also features a very impressive on-site cellar for connoisseurs. Sommeliers can help you with gourmet food and wine matching.

Sportsman's Hotel

BAR

(Map p286; 130 Leichhardt St, Spring Hill; ☺10am-late) A popular gay venue, this lively no-frills pub is famous for 'camp karaoke' and fabulous drag shows. There are also pool tables and hearty pub fare.

WEST END

Lychee Lounge

COCKTAIL BAR

(Map p303; 94 Boundary St) Sink into the lush furniture and stare up at the macabre dollhead chandeliers at this exotic oriental lounge bar, with mellow beats, mood lighting and an open frontage to Boundary St.

Lock 'N' Load

BAR-RESTAURANT

(Map p303; www.locknloadbistro.com.au; 142 Boundary St; ☺10am-late) This classic allwood two-storey gastro-pub gathers a friendly mixed crowd most nights. Bands play on the small front stage, and there's a leafy garden in the back.

NEW FARM & BREAKFAST CREEK

Alto Bar

BAR-RESTAURANT

(Map p301; www.brisbanepowerhouse.org; Powerhouse) Inside the arts-loving Powerhouse, this upstairs bar has an enormous balcony overlooking the river that makes a mighty fine vantage point, no matter what the weather.

Breakfast Creek Hotel

BAR-RESTAURANT

(off Map p299; 2 Kingsford Smith Dr; ☺lunch & dinner) In a great rambling building dating from 1889, this historic pub is a Brisbane institution. Built in French Renaissance style, the pub encompasses various bars (including a beer garden and an art-deco 'private bar' where you can still drink draft beer tapped from a wooden keg). The stylish, modern Substation No 41 bar serves boutique beers and cocktails.

KANGAROO POINT & SOUTH BANK

Story Bridge Hotel

BAR

(Map p286; 200 Main St, Kangaroo Point) Beneath the bridge at Kangaroo Point, this beautiful old pub with beer garden is the perfect place for a pint after a long day exploring. Live jazz on Sunday (from 3pm).

☆ Entertainment

Most touring international bands have Brisbane on their radar and the city's nightclubs regularly attract top-class DJs. Theatres, cinemas and other performing-arts venues are among Australia's biggest and best.

Pick up one of the free entertainment papers: Time Off (www.timeoff.com.au), Rave (www.ravemagazine.com.au) and Scene (www.scenemagazine.com.au). The fortnightly Q news (www.qnews.com.au) covers events on the gay and lesbian scene and Queensland Pride (www.qlp.e-p.net.au) takes in the whole of the state.

The Courier-Mail (www.news.com.au/courriermail) has daily arts and entertainment listings, or check the Brisbane Times (www.brisbanetimes.com.au).

Ticketek (☎13 19 31; www.ticketek.com.au) is a centralised phone-booking agency that handles bookings for many of the major events, sports and performances. You can pick up tickets from the Ticketek booth (Map p286; Elizabeth St), at the back of the Myer Centre, or at the South Bank visitor information centre.

Nightclubs

Spruce up and head straight to Fortitude Valley for Brisbane's multilevel superclubs. Most are open Wednesday to Sunday nights; some are free to enter, but others charge up to $20. Photo ID is an absolute must and remember that some places are sticklers for dress codes.

Cloudland

NIGHTCLUB

(Map p299; 641 Ann St, Fortitude Valley; ☺11.30am-late Wed-Sun) Like stepping into a cloud forest (or at least the Ann St version of it), this sprawling, multilevel nightclub has a huge, open, plant-filled lobby with a retractable roof, a wall of water and wrought-iron birdcage-like nooks sprinkled about; you'll also find a rooftop garden and a cellar bar.

Monastery

NIGHTCLUB

(Map p299; ☎07-3257 7081; 621 Ann St, Fortitude Valley) Monastery really does look like a monastery inside (apart from the heaving, sweaty

hordes churning up the dance floor), with its iconic, plush design and gothic lighting.

Family
NIGHTCLUB

(Map p299; ☑07-3852 5000; 8 McLachlan St, Fortitude Valley) One of Brisbane's best nightclubs, Family exhilarates dance junkies every weekend on four levels with two dance floors, four bars, four funky themed booths and a top-notch sound system.

Uber
NIGHTCLUB

(Map p303; ☑07-3846 6680; 100 Boundary St, West End) Uber is a bit decadent like an old-style boutique hotel, with its brushed steel and polished dark wood. The music varies, but weekends are dedicated to pure main-room house. There's a fine 'beer boutique and bistro' – called Archive – on the lower level.

Beat MegaClub
NIGHTCLUB

(Map p299; 677 Ann St, Fortitude Valley) Five dance floors, six bars and hardcore techno equals the perfect place for dance junkies who like their beats hard. It's popular with the gay and lesbian crowd, with regular drag performances.

Birdie Num Num
NIGHTCLUB

(Map p299; www.birdeenumnum.com.au; 608 Ann St, Fortitude Valley) Part of the Bunk Backpackers complex, it's filled with backpackers and students nightly.

Wickham Hotel
NIGHTCLUB

(Map p299; 308 Wickham St, Fortitude Valley) Brisbane's most popular gay and lesbian venue; drag shows Tuesday to Friday nights.

Paddington

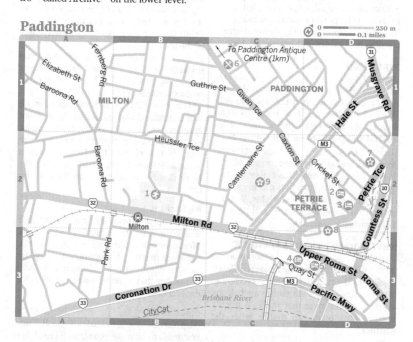

Paddington

⊕ Activities, Courses & Tours
1 Castlemaine-Perkins XXXX Brewery ... B2

🛏 Sleeping
2 Aussie Way Backpackers D2
3 Banana Benders Backpackers D2
4 Brisbane City YHA C3
5 Chill Backpackers D3

🍴 Eating
6 Lark C1

⊕ Entertainment
7 Brisbane Arts Theatre D2
8 Palace Barracks D2
9 Suncorp Stadium C2

BRIS-BAND'S WALK OF FAME

It won't ever match Hollywood Blvd for glamour, but Brisbane's Brunswick St Mall has its very own **Valley Walk of Fame** (Map p299) honouring the city's seminal and most successful musical acts. Located at the top of the mall, near the Royal George pub, are 10 plaques for bands that called Brisbane home, at least for the formative years of their careers. Long before the tight pants and disco beats of *Saturday Night Fever*, the **Bee Gees** lived just north of Brisbane in Redcliffe, where they honed their harmonies from 1958 until cracking the UK charts in the mid-'60s. Punk legends the **Saints** formed here in 1974, a band Bob Geldof is quoted as saying 'changed rock music in the '70s' along with the Sex Pistols and the Ramones. The **Go-Betweens** were an internationally influential rock band during the 1980s and were the first band chosen for the Walk of Fame following the untimely death of Brisbane-based singer Grant McLennan in 2006. Another singer not known for his Brisbane roots, **Keith Urban** grew up just north of the city in Caboolture. He started winning talent quests there at age eight; in 2008 he won a Grammy for best male country vocal performance. Popsters **Savage Garden** formed in 1993 after guitarist Daniel Jones placed an ad in a Brisbane street-press magazine. Singer Darren Hayes responded and together they went on to sell 25 million albums worldwide. Other bands on the Walk of Fame include 15-time ARIA award-winning rock band **Powderfinger**, electro-rockers **Regurgitator**, '90s indie band **Custard**, '70s group **Railroad Gin**, and local act **Blowhard**.

Live Music

Fortitude Valley has the majority of Brisbane's rock and dance venues, though there are a few others in West End, New Farm and Kangaroo Point. Smaller venues have free entry, but expect to pay anything from $6 to $30 for live gigs and significantly more for international touring bands.

Hi-Fi   ROCK
(Map p303; www.thehifi.com.au; 125 Boundary St, West End) In 2009 Melbourne's popular rock venue opened an outpost in Brisbane's hipster-loving West End. The modern, minimalist space has unobstructed sight lines and a decent line-up of local and international talent (hosting the likes of the Bronx, Guttermouth, Concrete Blond and the Charlatans).

Zoo   ECLECTIC
(Map p299; www.thezoo.com.au; 711 Ann St, Fortitude Valley; ☺Wed-Sat) The long queues at Zoo start early for a good reason: whether you're into hard rock, hip hop, acoustic, reggae or electronic soundscapes, Zoo has a gig for you. It's one of your best chances to hear some raw local talent.

Brisbane Jazz Club   JAZZ
(Map p286; ☎07-3391 2006; www.brisbanejazzclub.com.au; 1 Annie St, Kangaroo Point) Beautifully sited overlooking the river, this tiny club has been a beacon for jazz purists since 1972. The space is small and intimate, and anyone who's anyone in the jazz scene plays here

when they're in town. Sets happen Thursday to Sunday nights; there's usually a cover charge of $15 to $20.

Brisbane Powerhouse   ECLECTIC
(Map p301; www.brisbanepowerhouse.org; 119 Lamington St, New Farm) Has live music on Friday night and throughout Saturday and Sunday; many shows are free.

Cafe Checocho   JAZZ, BLUES, WORLD
(Map p303; 69 Hardgrave Rd, West End; ☺3-10pm Mon, 10am-10pm Tue-Sat; ☎) Serving up chess, coffee and chocolate (che-cocho), this charming, lived-in cafe also has live music most nights.

Music Kafe   ECLECTIC
(Map p303; www.themusickafe.com; 185 Boundary St, West End) Live music most days with blues, rock, jazz and folk, plus an open-mic night (currently Wednesday).

Globe   ROCK
(Map p299; www.globetheatre.com.au; 220 Brunswick St, Fortitude Valley) An old cinema converted into a live-music venue; gigs on weekends.

Cinemas

From March to April, you can see films in the open air at the South Bank Parklands (www.brisbaneopenair.com.au). New Farm Park also hosts alfresco cinema between December and February at the **Moonlight Cinema** (Map p301; www.moonlight.com.au; adult/child $15/11; ☺7pm Wed-Sun). Arrive early to get a spot.

QUEENSLAND & THE GREAT BARRIER REEF BRISBANE

Palace Centro
CINEMA

(Map p299; www.palacecinemas.com.au; 39 James St, Fortitude Valley) In the Valley, Palace Centro screens art-house films and has a Greek film festival at the end of November.

Palace Barracks
CINEMA

(Map p306; www.palacecinemas.com.au; Petrie Tce) Near Roma St Station, Palace Barracks shows a mix of Hollywood and alternative fare.

South Bank Cinema
CINEMA

(Map p289; www.cineplex.com.au; cnr Grey & Ernest Sts, South Bank) The cheapest for mainstream flicks.

Brisbane City Myer Centre
CINEMA

(Map p286; level 3, Myer Centre) On Queen St Mall; also shows mainstream blockbusters.

Performing Arts

Brisbane is well stocked with theatre and dance venues, most of them located at South Bank. For bookings at the Queensland Performing Arts Centre and all South Bank theatres, contact Qtix (☑13 62 46; www.qtix.com.au).

Brisbane Powerhouse
THEATRE, LIVE MUSIC

(Map p301; ☑07-3358 8600; www.brisbanepowerhouse.org; 119 Lamington St, New Farm) The former 1940 power station continues to bring electricity to the city – albeit in the form of nationally acclaimed theatre, music and dance productions. There are loads of happenings at the Powerhouse – many free – and the venue, with its several bar-restaurants, enjoys a beautiful setting overlooking the Brisbane River.

Queensland Performing Arts Centre
THEATRE, LIVE MUSIC

(QPAC; Map p289; ☑07-3840 7444; www.qpac.com.au; Queensland Cultural Centre, Stanley St, South Bank) This centre consists of three venues and features concerts, plays, dance and performances of all genres. Catch anything from flamenco to *West Side Story* revivals.

Queensland Conservatorium
LIVE MUSIC

(Map p289; ☑07-3735 6111; www.griffith.edu.au/concerts; 16 Russell St, South Bank; ☺Mar-Oct) South of the Queensland Performing Arts Centre, the Conservatorium hosts opera, as well as national and international artists playing classical, jazz, rock and world music. Many concerts are free.

Judith Wright Centre of Contemporary Arts
THEATRE, LIVE MUSIC

(Map p299; ☑07-3872 9000; www.judithwrightcentre.com; 420 Brunswick St, Fortitude Valley) A medium-sized (300 seats max) creative space for cutting-edge performances: contemporary dance and world music, Indigenous theatre, circus and visual arts.

Brisbane Arts Theatre
THEATRE

(Map p306; ☑07-3369 2344; www.artstheatre.com.au; 210 Petrie Tce, Petrie Tce) Small community theatre; catch improvisation troupes, children's theatre or classic plays.

QUT Gardens Theatre
THEATRE

(Map p286; ☑07-3138 4455; www.gardenstheatre.qut.com; Queensland University of Technology, 2 George St; ℗) Set within a university campus, but productions are anything but amateur. Expect to see Australia's best professional stage actors.

Sport

Like most other Australians, Brisbanites are sports-mad. You can see interstate cricket matches and international Test cricket at the Gabba (Brisbane Cricket Ground; off Map p286; www.thegabba.org.au; 411 Vulture St) in Woolloongabba, south of Kangaroo Point. If you're new to the game, try to get along to a Twenty20 match, which is cricket in its most explosive form. The cricket season runs from October to March.

The Gabba is also a home ground for the Brisbane Lions, an Australian Football League (AFL) team. Watch them in action, often at night under lights, between March and September.

Rugby league is also a big spectator sport. The Brisbane Broncos play home games at Suncorp Stadium (Map p306; www.suncorpstadium.com.au; 40 Castlemaine St, Milton).

Also calling Suncorp home are the Queensland Roar football (soccer) team, attracting massive crowds in recent years. The domestic football season lasts from August to February.

Shopping

Lovers of fashion can splash out at a range of high-end boutiques and designer stores in Brisbane. The Queen St Mall and Myer Centre in the CBD have large chain stores, upmarket outlets and the obligatory tourist tat.

Smaller independent and specialist shops are in Fortitude Valley.

Paddington Antique Centre
ANTIQUES

(off Map p306; 167 Latrobe Tce, Paddington) The city's biggest antique emporium houses over 50 dealers selling all manner of treasure/ trash from the past. Clothes, jewellery, dolls, books, artwork, lamps, musical instruments, toys and more.

Blonde Venus
CLOTHING

(Map p299; 707 Ann St, Fortitude Valley) One of the top boutiques in Brisbane, Blonde Venus has been around for 20-plus years, stocking a well-curated selection of both indie- and couture labels. Other great boutiques line this street.

Record Exchange
MUSIC

(Map p286; level 1, 65 Adelaide St) Record Exchange is home to an astounding collection of vinyl, plus CDs, DVDs, posters and other memorabilia.

Globe Trekker
OUTDOOR GEAR

(Map p286; 142 Albert St) Excellent selection of outdoor gear, including tents, sleeping bags, backpacks, and camping equipment.

Archives Fine Books
BOOKS

(Map p286; 40 Charlotte St) You could get lost in here for hours: fantastic range of secondhand books.

Avid Reader
BOOKS

(Map p303; www.avidreader.com.au; 193 Boundary St, West End) Diverse selection, excellent cafe and frequent readings and other events.

Folio Books
BOOKS

(Map p286; www.foliobooks.com.au; 80 Albert St) Small bookshop with eclectic offerings.

World Wide Maps & Guides
BOOKS

(Map p286; shop 30, Anzac Sq Arcade, 267 Edward St; ⊙closed Sun) Good assortment of travel guides and maps.

ⓘ Information

Emergency
Ambulance (✆000)
Fire (✆000)
Lifeline (✆13 11 14)
Police (✆000) city (✆07-3224 4444; 67 Adelaide St); headquarters (✆07-3364 6464; 200 Roma St); Fortitude Valley (✆07-3131 1200; Brunswick St Mall)
RACQ (✆13 19 05, breakdown 13 11 11) City (GPO Bldg, 261 Queen St); St Pauls Tce (300 St Pauls Tce) Roadside service.

Internet Access
Wireless internet access is widely available at many hotels and cafes, though it's rarely free.
Brisbane Square Library (266 George St) Free internet terminals and wi-fi access.
State Library of Queensland (South Bank; ⊙10am-8pm Mon-Thu, to 5pm Fri-Sun) Quick 20-minute terminals or free wi-fi.

Medical Services
Pharmacy on the Mall (141 Queen St)
Royal Brisbane & Women's Hospital (✆07-3636 8111; cnr Butterfield St & Bowen Bridge Rd, Herston) Has 24-hour casualty ward.

MARKET-LOVERS GUIDE TO BRISBANE

» **James Street Market** (Map p299; James St, New Farm; ⊙8.30am-6pm) Paradise for gourmands, this small but beautifully stocked market has gourmet cheeses, a bakery-patisserie, fruit, vegetables, and lots of gourmet goodies. The fresh seafood counter serves excellent sushi and sashimi.

» **Jan Power's Farmers Market** (Map p301; Brisbane Powerhouse, 119 Lamington St, New Farm; ⊙7am-noon 2nd & 4th Sat of month) Don't miss this excellent and deservedly popular farmers market if it's on when you're in town: over 120 stalls selling fresh produce, local wines, jams, juices, snacks (waffles, sausages, desserts, coffees) and much more. The CityCat takes you there.

» **West End Markets** (Map p303; Davies Park, cnr Montague Rd & Jane St; ⊙6am-2pm Sat) This sprawling flea market has loads of fresh produce, herbs, flowers, organic foodstuffs, clothing and bric-a-brac. It's an apt representation of the diverse West End and a good place for noshing, with stalls selling a wide range of cuisines; there's also live music in the park.

» **South Bank Lifestyle Markets** (Map p289; Stanley St Plaza, South Bank; ⊙5-10pm Fri, 10am-5pm Sat, 9am-5pm Sun) These popular markets have a great range of clothing, craft, art, handmade goods and interesting souvenirs.

Travel Clinic (☑1300 369 359, 07-3211 3611; 1st fl, 245 Albert St)

Travellers' Medical & Vaccination Centre (TMVC; ☑07-3815 6900; 75 Astor Tce, Spring Hill)

Money

There are foreign-exchange bureaus at Brisbane Airport's domestic and international terminals, as well as ATMs. ATMs are prolific throughout Brisbane.

American Express (☑1300 139 060; shop 3, 156 Adelaide St)

Travelex (☑07-3210 6325; shop 149F, Myer Centre, Queen St Mall)

Post

Main post office (GPO; Map p286; 261 Queen St; ⊙7am-6pm Mon-Fri)

Post office (Post Shop; Map p286; 2nd fl, Wintergarden Centre, 171 Queen St Mall)

Tourist Information

Brisbane Visitor Information Centre (Map p286; ☑07-3006 6290; Queen St Mall; ⊙9am-5.30pm Mon-Thu, to 7pm Fri, to 4.30pm Sat, 9.30am-4pm Sun) Located between Edward and Albert Sts. Great one-stop info counter for all things Brisbane.

Queensland Parks & Wildlife (☑1300 130 372; level 3, 400 George St; ⊙8.30am-4.30pm Mon-Fri) Pick up maps, brochures and books on national parks and state forests, as well as camping information and Fraser Island permits.

South Bank Visitors Centre (Map p289; www.visitsouthbank.com.au; Stanley St Plaza, South Bank Parklands; ⊙9am-5pm) Information on South Bank activities. The place to buy tickets for entertainment events.

ℹ Getting There & Away

Air

Brisbane's main airport (Map p312) is about 16km northeast of the city centre at Eagle Farm and has separate international and domestic terminals about 2km apart, linked by the **Airtrain** (per person $5, every 15 to 30min).

Bus

Brisbane's main terminus and booking office for all long-distance buses and trains is the **Brisbane Transit Centre** (Map p286; Roma St, Brisbane), about 500m west of the city centre.

On the 3rd level, you'll find booking desks for bus companies, including **Greyhound** (☑1300 473 946; www.greyhound.com.au) and **Premier Motor Service** (☑13 34 10; www.premierms.com.au), the big carriers.

Sample times and prices:

DESTINATION	DURATION	ONE-WAY FARE
Byron Bay	4hr	$30-45
Sydney	16-17hr	$90-200
Airlie Beach	18-20hr	$190-240
Cairns	29-34hr	$310-360
Hervey Bay	5½hr	$50-75
Mackay	16½-22hr	$200-230
Noosa Heads	2½hr	$21-35
Rockhampton	11-14hr	$138-170
Surfers Paradise	1½hr	$21-32
Townsville	23hr	$265-300

Car & Motorcycle

There are five major routes, numbered from M1 to M5, into and out of the Brisbane metropolitan area. If you're just passing through, take the Gateway Motorway (M1) at Eight Mile Plains, which bypasses the city centre to the east and crosses the Brisbane River at the Gateway Bridge ($3 toll).

HIRE All of the major companies – **Hertz** (☑13 30 39), **Avis** (☑13 63 33), **Budget** (☑1300 362 848), **Europcar** (☑13 13 90) and **Thrifty** (☑1300 367 227) – have offices at the Brisbane Airport terminals and throughout the city.

Smaller rental companies in Brisbane:

Abel Rent A Car (☑1800 131 429, 07-3236 1225; www.abel.com.au; Roma St) Attached to the Roma St Transit Centre.

Ace Rental Cars (☑1800 620 408; www.acerentals.com.au; 330 Nudgee Rd, Hendra)

East Coast Car Rentals (☑1800 028 881; www.eastcoastcarrentals.com.au; 76 Wickham St, Fortitude Valley)

Train

Brisbane's main station for long-distance trains is Roma St Station (also called Brisbane Transit Centre). For reservations and information visit the **Queensland Rail Travel Centre** (☑13 16 17; www.queenslandrail.com.au) Central Station (ground fl, Central Station, 305 Edward St); Brisbane Transit Centre (Brisbane Transit Centre, Roma St).

CountryLink (☑13 22 32; www.countrylink.info) Brisbane–Sydney (economy/1st class $92/130, 13 to 14½ hours, daily).

Spirit of the Outback Brisbane–Longreach (economy seat/economy sleeper/1st-class sleeper $190/250/385, 24 hours) via Rockhampton ($190/250/385, 10 hours) twice weekly.

Sunlander Brisbane–Cairns (economy seat/economy sleeper/1st-class sleeper $219/279/430, 31 hours, Tuesday, Thursday and Sunday) via Townsville. Queenslander class ($785) includes restaurant meals and historical commentary.

Tilt Train Brisbane–Cairns (business class $328, 24 hours). Departs Brisbane at 6.25pm Monday and Friday; returns from Cairns at 9.15am Wednesday and Sunday.

Westlander Brisbane–Charleville via Toowoomba and Roma (economy seat/economy sleeper/1st-class sleeper $106/187/274, 17 hours).

❶ Getting Around

Brisbane boasts an excellent public-transport network. Obtain bus, train and ferry info at the **Transit Information Centre** (www.translink. com.au; cnr Ann & Albert Sts) or call ☑13 12 30.

Fares on buses, trains and ferries operate on a zone system. There are 23 zones in total, but the city centre and most of the inner-city suburbs fall within zone 1, which translates into a single fare of $3.90/2 per adult/child. To save money (around 30% off individual fares), purchase a **Go Card** ($5), which is sold (and recharged) at transit stations and newsagents.

To/From the Airport

The easiest way to get to and from the airport is via the **Airtrain** (☑07-3215 5000; www.airtrain. com.au; adult/child $15/7.50; ☉6am-7.30pm), which runs every 15 to 30 minutes from the airport to Fortitude Valley, Central Station, Roma St Station (Brisbane Transit Centre) and other key destinations. There are also half-hourly services to the airport from Gold Coast Citytrain stops.

If you prefer door-to-door service, **Coachtrans** (☑07-3358 9700; www.coachtrans.com.au) runs regular shuttle buses between the airport and any hotel in the CBD (adult/child $15/8); it also connects Brisbane Airport to Gold Coast accommodation (adult/child $44/20).

A taxi into the centre from the airport will cost around $40.

Boat

In addition to the CityCats (p292), Inner City Ferries zigzag back and forth across the river between North Quay, near the Victoria Bridge, and Mowbray Park. Services start at 6am and run till about 11pm. There are also several cross-river ferries; most useful is the Eagle Street Pier to Thornton St (Kangaroo Point) service.

As with all Brisbane public transport, fares are based on zones (zone 1 adult/child $3.90/2).

Bus

The Loop, a free bus service that circles the city area, stops at QUT, Queen Street Mall, City Botanic Gardens, Central Station and Riverside. It runs every 10 minutes on weekdays between 7am and 6pm.

The main stop for local buses is in the underground Queen Street Mall bus station, where

there's an information centre, and King George Sq bus station (Map p286). You can also pick up many buses from the colour-coded stops along Adelaide St, between George and Edward Sts.

Buses generally run every 10 to 30 minutes Monday to Friday, from 5am till about 11pm, and with the same frequency on Saturday morning (starting at 6am). Services are less frequent at other times, and cease at 9pm Sunday and at midnight on other days.

Car & Motorcycle

There is ticketed two-hour parking on many streets in the CBD and in the inner suburbs, but the major thoroughfares become clearways (ie parking is prohibited) during the morning and afternoon peak hours. If you do park in the street, pay close attention to the times on the parking signs, as Brisbane's parking inspectors take no prisoners. Parking is cheaper around South Bank than in the city centre but is free in the CBD during the evening.

Taxi

It's easy to find a cab around the city centre during the day. There are taxi ranks at the transit centre and at the top end of Edward St, by the junction with Adelaide St. You might have a tough time hailing one late at night in Fortitude Valley. There's a rank near the corner of Brunswick St and Ann St, but expect longer queues the later it gets.

The major taxi companies are **Black & White** (☑13 10 08) and **Yellow Cab Co** (☑13 19 24).

Train

The fast Citytrain network has seven lines, which run as far as Gympie North in the north (for the Sunshine Coast) and Robina in the south (for the Gold Coast). All trains go through Roma St, Central and Brunswick St Stations; there's also a handy South Bank Station.

MORETON BAY

The patch of water lapping at Brisbane's urban edges is packed full of marine life, including whales, dolphins and dugongs. Moreton Bay also has some startlingly beautiful islands that are very accessible from the mainland. The most popular of these is North Stradbroke Island, with its great surfing beaches, visible marine life and nonchalant holiday air. On Moreton Island, wild dolphin feeding is the major attraction.

☞ Tours

Humpback whales are a regular sight in the bay between June and November when they migrate to and from their southern feeding

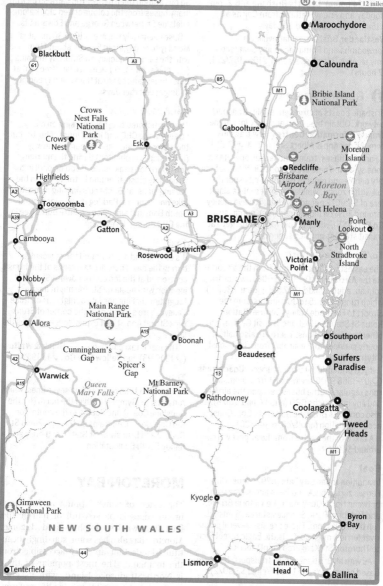

grounds. Moreton Bay also has the largest resident population of bottlenose dolphins in the world (more than 300).

Dolphin Wild BOAT
(☎07-3880 4444; www.dolphinwild.com.au; per adult/child/family incl lunch $110/60/290)

Departing from Redcliffe, these full-day ecotours include a cruise to Moreton Island with commentary from a marine naturalist and guided snorkel tours ($20/10 per adult/child) around the Tangalooma wrecks.

Manly Eco Cruises BOAT
(☎07-3396 9400; www.manlyecocruises.net; per adult/child $99/44) Ride on the catamaran boom nets, enjoy free canoe rides or sit back on the MV *Getaway* and spot marine life. The two-hour Sunday barbecue breakfast tour ($29/14 per adult/child) is especially popular.

North Stradbroke Island

POP 2100

Brisbanites are lucky to have such a brilliant holiday island on their doorstep. A mere 30-minute ferry ride from Cleveland, this sand island has a string of glorious powdery white-sand beaches. Surfers come for the awesome breaks around Point Lookout, which is also a regular spot for sighting dolphins, turtles and manta rays. Between June and November, hundreds of humpback whales can also be seen here.

Those seeking a freshwater dip venture to the lakes in the middle of the island, and the south-eastern coast is a playground for 4WD drivers.

There are only a few small settlements on the island, with a handful of accommodation and eating options – mostly near Point Lookout. Dunwich, on the western coast, is where the ferries dock. Amity Point is a small village on the north-western tip. The southern part of the island is closed to visitors because of sand mining.

◉ Sights & Activities

At Point Lookout, the breathtaking North Gorge Headlands Walk is an absolute must for any visitor to Straddie. Turtles, dolphins and manta rays can be spotted any time of year from the wooden boardwalk that skirts the rocky outcrops, and the view from the headland down Main Beach is sublime.

There are several gorgeous beaches huddled around Point Lookout. A patrolled swimming area, Cylinder Beach is popular with families and is flanked by Home Beach and Deadman's Beach. Further around the point, Frenchman's Beach is another peaceful, secluded spot if you don't mind the occasional nudist passing by. On the eastern side, surfers and bodyboarders descend on Main Beach in search of the ultimate wave, while fishing fanatics take their 4WD vehicles down the strip of beach that extends towards Eighteen Mile Swamp.

No trip to Straddie is complete without a refreshing swim in a freshwater lake. East of Dunwich, the aptly named Brown Lake is the colour of stewed tea owing to the native tea trees that line the waters. There are picnic tables, barbecues and a toilet at the lake.

It's well worth taking the 2.6km (40-minute) bush track to the sparkling Blue Lake. Wildlife such as forest birds and reptiles can be spotted on the way. Further north, The Keyholes is a freshwater system of lakes and lagoons where you can listen to the surf just metres away.

Used mainly for ferry access to the mainland, Dunwich is also a handy spot for picking up supplies at the convenience store and bakery. The small but impressive North Stradbroke Island Historical Museum (☎07-3409 9699; 15-17 Welsby St; adult/child $3.50/1.10; ⊙10am-2pm Tue-Sat) describes shipwrecks, harrowing voyages, life in the 'benevolent asylum' and an introduction to the rich Aboriginal history of the island. An oddball collection of island artefacts includes the skull of a sperm whale, washed up along Main Beach in 2004.

For a greater sense of seclusion, Amity Point is a lovely, quiet place for fishing and snorkelling in calmer waters.

Surfboards, snorkelling equipment and bicycles can be hired at Straddie Adventures (☎07-3409 8414; www.straddieadventures.com.au; 112 East Coast Rd, Point Lookout), which also offers sea-kayaking trips around Straddie for $60 and sandboarding for $30.

Based at Manta Lodge YHA, Manta Scuba Centre offers snorkelling for $85, inclusive of a two-hour boat trip and all the gear. Open-water three-day dive courses cost $520, while a trip with two dives for certified divers is $185. The centre also hires out snorkel gear ($25).

Across the road from the entrance to the North Gorge Headlands Walk, the fish-and-chips shop Fishes (East Coast Rd, Point Lookout) hires out bicycles ($22 for four hours) and binoculars ($10 for four hours). It also has free wi-fi.

Anglers can hire fishing gear from Straddie Super Sports (☎07-3409 9252; 18 Bingle Rd, Dunwich) for around $25 per day.

☞ Tours

A number of companies offer tours of the island. Generally the 4WD tours take in a strip of the eastern beach and several freshwater lakes.

North Stradbroke Island 4WD Tours & Camping Holidays (☑07-3409 8051; straddie@ecn.net.au) Generally, half-day tours cost $35/20 per adult/child.

Straddie Kingfisher Tours (☑07-3409 9502; www.straddiekingfishertours.com.au; adult/child $79/59) Operates six-hour 4WD and fishing tours; also has whale-watching tours in season.

Sleeping

Most accommodation is at Point Lookout, which is strung along 3km of coastline on the northern shore of the island.

Pandanus Palms Resort   APARTMENTS **$$$**
(☑07-34098106;www.pandanus.stradbrokeresorts. com.au; 21 Cumming Pde; apt $245-315; ☀) Perched high above the beach, with a thick tumble of vegetation beneath, the large two-bed townhouses here are a good size and boast modern furnishings; the best face the ocean, with private yards and barbecues. Excellent restaurant on site.

Straddie Views   B&B **$$**
☑07-3409 8875; www.northstradbrokeisland.com/straddiebb; 26 Cumming Pde; r from $150) Several spacious and comfortably furnished suites are available in this friendly B&B run by a Straddie couple. Breakfast is served on the upstairs deck with fantastic water views.

Stradbroke Island Beach Hotel   HOTEL **$$$**
(☑07-3409 8188; www.stradbrokeislandbeach hotel.com.au; East Coast Rd; d $230-310; ☀☀) Straddie's only hotel has an intriguing modern design, with 12 cool, inviting rooms in muted colour schemes, each with high-end fixtures and a balcony. The open bar downstairs with outdoor beer garden is a delight, and there's also a restaurant and spa.

Domain Stradbroke Resort   APARTMENTS **$$**
(☑07-3415 0000; www.stradbrokedomain.com; 43 East Coast Rd; villas from $167; ☀) Large ultra-modern villas are set in a leafy compound and backed by forest here. Each villa (or 'shack' as the one-bedrooms are called) features blond woods, original artwork and outdoor deck with barbecue. Unfortunately, there isn't much space between villas, and the layouts for two-bedrooms are a little zany, with a completely separate building for the master bedroom.

Anchorage on Straddie   APARTMENTS **$$**
(☑07-3409 8266; www.anchorage.stradbroke sorts.com.au; East Coast Rd; 2 nights $235-400; ☀)

The friendly managers of these large self-contained apartments with balconies keep the place shipshape and there's a boardwalk from the hotel grounds straight to the beach. For sea views, ask for a room on the third level.

Straddie Holiday Parks   CAMPGROUND **$**
(☑1300 551 253; unpowered/powered sites $35/40, cabins $109-165) There are seven camping grounds on the island operated by this outfit, but the most attractive are those grouped around Point Lookout. The **Adder Rock Camping Area** and the **Thankful Rest Camping Area** both overlook lovely Home Beach, while the **Cylinder Beach Camping Area** sits right on one of the island's most popular beaches. There are also several cheaper sites (from $15 per night) accessible by 4WD only. Book well in advance.

Manta Lodge YHA   HOSTEL **$**
(☑07-3409 8888; www.mantalodge.com.au; 1 East Coast Rd; dm/d $30/78; @☀) This large well-kept hostel near the beach has excellent facilities, including a dive school on the doorstep.

Eating

There are a couple of general stores selling groceries in Point Lookout, but it's worth bringing basic supplies.

TOP CHOICE **Amis**   MODERN AUSTRALIAN **$$**
(☑07-3409 8600; 21 Cummings Pde, Pandanus Palms Resort; mains $28-36; ☺dinner Wed-Sun) Combining north African and Asian accents with fresh local produce, Amis is one of Straddie's best. Standouts include Queensland kangaroo loin fillet, chargrilled prawns on bamboo, fish of the day and crispy duck confit.

Look   MODERN AUSTRALIAN **$$**
(☑07-3415 3390; 29 Mooloomba Rd; lunch mains $12-18, dinner mains $25-30; ☺breakfast & lunch daily, dinner Thu-Sat) This seems to be the hub of Point Lookout during the day, with funky tunes in the background and great outdoor seating with breezy water views. It's an elegant but relaxed affair.

Island Fruit Barn   CAFE **$**
(Bilinga Rd, Dunwich; mains $10-14; ☺7am-4pm) On the main road in Dunwich, the Island Fruit Barn is a casual and welcoming little spot that serves excellent breakfasts, smoothies, salads and sandwiches using high-quality ingredients. The tiny gourmet grocery is a good place to stock up on goodies.

Fishes

SEAFOOD **$$**

(East Coast Rd; mains $15-20; ⊙9am-7pm Sat-Mon, to 4pm Tue-Thu) True to its name, Fishes serves scrumptious fish and chips, with outdoor seating across the road from the North Gorge Headlands Walk.

Bowls Club

PUB FARE **$$**

(East Coast Rd; mains $10-26; ⊙lunch & dinner) For tasty, casual meals that won't break the budget head to the friendly Bowls Club, with pub fare and different baked meals nightly.

❶ Information

Although it's quiet most of the year, the population can swell significantly at Christmas, Easter and during school holidays, so book accommodation or camping permits well in advance.

You can get information and obtain a 4WD permit ($34) – if you plan to go off-road – on the way to the ferries at Cleveland's **Redlands on Moreton Bay Visitor Centre** (☑1300 667 386; www.more2redlands.com.au; 152 Shore St West, Cleveland; ⊙9am-5pm Mon-Fri, to 3pm Sat & Sun).

❶ Getting There & Away

The gateway to North Stradbroke Island is the seaside suburb of Cleveland. Regular **Citytrain** (www.translink.com.au) services run from Brisbane's Central and Roma St stations to Cleveland station ($6.70, one hour) and buses to the ferry terminals meet the trains at Cleveland station (10 minutes).

Stradbroke Ferries (☑07-3488 5300; www.stradbrokeferries.com.au) goes to Dunwich almost every hour from 6am to 6pm ($19 return, 25 minutes). It also has a slightly less frequent vehicle ferry ($135 return per vehicle including passengers, 40 minutes).

Gold Cat Stradbroke Flyer (☑07-3286 1964; www.flyer.com.au) runs an almost-hourly catamaran service from Cleveland to One Mile Jetty ($19 return, 25 minutes), 1km north of central Dunwich.

Sea Stradbroke (☑07-3488 9777; www.bigredcat.com.au) has a Big Red Cat vehicle and passenger ferry departing Cleveland daily from 5.30am to 7pm ($135 return per vehicle including passengers, $11 return walk-on, 45 minutes).

❶ Getting Around

North Stradbroke Island Bus Services (☑07-3415 2417; www.stradbrokebuses.com) meet the water taxis (not the vehicle ferries) at Dunwich and One Mile Jetty and run across to Point Lookout and Amity Point ($9.50 return). The last bus to Dunwich leaves Point Lookout around 6.15pm. There's also the **Stradbroke**

Cab Service (☑0408 193 685), which charges around $60 from Dunwich to Point Lookout.

Moreton Island

POP 250

City life rapidly fades from memory when you're cruising on the ferry from Brisbane out to this sand island north of Stradbroke. Day trippers, campers and folks staying at the island's resort love to explore its extremes, diving deep into crystal-clear waters to view marine life or rising to the summits of enormous sand dunes for tobogganing. It's comforting to know Moreton Island's miles of sandy beaches, prolific bird life, sparkling lagoons and precious bushland are well protected – more than 90% is designated national park. The island has a colourful history, from evidence of early Aboriginal settlements to being the site of Queensland's first and only whaling station, which operated between 1952 and 1962.

Tangalooma is the island's tourist resort, and there are three other small settlements on the west coast: Bulwer sits near the northwestern tip, Cowan Cowan between Bulwer and Tangalooma, and Kooringal is near the southern tip. There are a small convenience store and two cafes at the resort, but it's best to bring food supplies from the mainland.

❍ Sights & Activities

Tangalooma, halfway down the western side of the island, is a popular tourist resort sited at an old whaling station. The main attraction is the **dolphin feeding**, which takes place each evening around sunset. Between five and nine dolphins swim in from the ocean and take fish from the hands of volunteer feeders. Although you have to be a guest of the resort to participate, onlookers are welcome. The resort also organises **whale-watching** cruises (June to October), plus loads of other activities.

Just north of the resort, off the coast, are the **Tangalooma Wrecks**, which provide fine snorkelling. You can hire gear from Dive In Sports on the resort grounds. **Tangatours** (☑07-3410 6927; www.tangatours.com.au; Tangalooma) offers 1½-hour snorkelling trips around the Tangalooma Wrecks ($35) as well as kayaking tours ($35 to $45); Tangatours also offers self-guided combo packages of kayak and snorkelling gear (three hours for $35), and it has a kids club ($10 per hour).

Next to the resort near the ferry terminal is the **Marine Education & Conservation Centre** (◎10am-noon & 1-5pm), which has interesting displays of marine and bird life.

Walking trails include a desert trail (two hours) and a bushwalk (1½ hours), both leaving from the resort, as well as a longer walk to Water Point (four hours) on the east coast. It's also worth making the strenuous trek to the summit of Mt Tempest (280m), 3km inland from Eagers Creek, but you'll need transport to reach the start.

Built in 1857, **Cape Moreton Lighthouse** at the island's northern tip is the oldest operating lighthouse in Queensland, and is the place to come for great views if the whales are passing by.

🖙 Tours

Moreton Bay Escapes　　　ACTIVITIES, CAMPING
(☑1300 559 355; www.moretonbayescapes.com. au; 1-day tours adult/child from $165/125, 2-day camping tours $249/149) A certified ecotour, the one-day Moreton Island 4WD tour includes sand-boarding, tobogganing, marine-wildlife watching and a picnic lunch.

Micat　　　ACTIVITIES, CAMPING
(☑07-3909 3333; www.micat.com.au; 1-day tours adult/child from $155/95, 2-day camping tours from $299) Runs similar itineraries to Moreton Bay Escapes.

Sunrover Expeditions　　　CAMPING
(☑1800 353 717, 07-3203 4241; www.sunrover. com.au; adult/child $120/100) A friendly and reliable 4WD-tour operator with good day and camping tours.

🛏 Sleeping

There are a few holiday flats and houses for rent at Kooringal, Cowan Cowan and Bulwer. To browse listings, go to www.moreton island.com.au.

There are 10 national-park **camping grounds** (sites per person/family $6/21), all with water, toilets and cold showers; five campgrounds are on the beach. For information and camping permits, book online (www. derm.qld.gov.au), contact the DERM office in Brisbane (☑1300 130 372; level 3, 400 George St) or call ☑13 74 68. Camping permits must be arranged before you get to the island.

**Tangalooma Wild Dolphin
Resort**　　　HOTEL, APARTMENTS **$$$**
(☑1300 652 250, 07-3637 2000; www.tangalooma. com; 1-night packages from $310; ❄@☎) This beautifully sited but ageing resort is the only formal set-up on the island. There're a plethora of options, starting with pretty bland hotel-style rooms. A step up are the units and suites, where you'll get beachside access and rooms kitted out in cool, contemporary decor with good facilities. Look for online deals through www.wotif.com. The resort has several eating options.

Information

There are no paved roads on Moreton Island, but 4WDs can travel along the beaches and a few cross-island tracks. Vehicle permits for the island cost $40 and are available through the ferry operators, online (www.derm.qld.gov.au) or at a DERM office (in Brisbane: level 3, 400 George St). Note that ferry bookings are *mandatory* if you want to take a vehicle across.

ⓘ Getting There & Around

A number of ferries operate from the mainland. The **Tangalooma Flyer** (☑07-3268 6333; www. tangalooma.com; adult/child return day trips from $45/25) is a fast catamaran operated by Tangalooma Resort. It makes the 1¼-hour trip to the resort on Moreton Island daily from a dock at Eagle Farm, at Holt St off Kingsford Smith Dr. A bus (adult/child one way $19/9) goes to the *Flyer* from the CBD. Return service also available. Depending on group size, a taxi may be cheaper. Bookings essential (☑07-3637 2000).

The **Moreton Venture** (☑07-3909 3333; www.moretonventure.com; vehicle & passengers return $190-265; ◎8.30am daily) is a vehicle ferry that runs from Howard-Smith Dr, Lyton, at the Port of Brisbane, to Tangalooma. It returns from the island at 3.30pm daily. Additional departures on Friday and Sunday.

The new vehicle ferry **Amity Trader** (☑0487 227 437; www.amitytrader.com; vehicle & passengers return $100) sails between Amity and Kooringal on Moreton Island's southern tip. Call for times and to reserve a spot.

There is one 4WD taxi driver operating **Moreton Island Tourist Services** (☑07-3408 2661; www.moretonisland.net.au). One-way trips range from $40 to $180.

Bribie Island

POP 16,500

Queensland's only offshore island linked to the mainland by bridge, Bribie is 70km north of Brisbane at the top end of Moreton Bay. Like Stradbroke and Moreton, it is a sand island with protected bushland areas but is far more developed due to its easy accessibility. Popular with grey nomads and those seeking the laid-back island lifestyle, it

has some beautifully remote **QPWS camping areas** (☏13 13 04; www.derm.qld.gov.au; 4WD access only per person/family $5.15/21) on the western and northern coasts. You must book ahead before arriving.

There is no 4WD hire on the island and 4WD permits ($38 per week) can be purchased online (www.derm.qld.gov.au). You can also purchase permits at **Bribie Passage Kiosk and Boat Hire** (☏07-5497 5789; 23 Kalmakuta Dr, Sandstone Point). **Bribie Island visitor centre** (☏07-3408 9026; www.bribie.com.au; Benabrow Ave, Bellara; ⊙9am-4pm Mon-Fri, to 3pm Sat, 9.30am-1pm Sun) has more information.

If you're not camping, the **Inn Bongaree** (☏07-3410 1718; www.innbongaree.com.au; 25 Second Ave, Bongaree; s/d $50/65) is a great budget option two minutes' walk from the beach. Or you can stay at **Sylvan Beach Resort** (☏07-3408 8300; www.sylvanbeachresort.com.au; d from $170; ❋@✉), which has comfortable self-contained units across the road from the beach.

Bribie Island SLSC (☏07-3408 4420; Rickman Pde; mains $10-25; ⊙lunch & dinner), at the southern end of the beach, serves up good ol' Aussie tucker.

Frequent Citytrain services run from Brisbane to Caboolture, where a Trainlink bus connects to Bribie Island.

GOLD COAST

Behind the long, unbroken ribbon of sand of some of the world's best surfing beaches is a shimmering strip of high-rises, eateries, bars and theme parks that attracts a perpetual stream of sun-loving holidaymakers. The undisputed capital is Surfers Paradise, where the dizzying fun sucks you into a relentless spin and spits you back out exhausted. But the brash commercialism and relentless pace won't appeal to everyone. The hype diminishes drastically outside the epicentre; Broadbeach's beach chic and Burleigh Heads' seaside charm mellow into Coolangatta's laid-back surfer ethos.

ⓘ Getting There & Around

The Gold Coast international airport at Coolangatta is 25km south of Surfers Paradise.

The **Gold Coast Tourist Shuttle** (☏1300 655 655, 07-5574 5111; www.gcshuttle.com.au; one way per adult/child/family $18/9/45) will meet your flight and drop you at most Gold Coast accommodation.

Citytrain services link Brisbane to Helensvale, Nerang and Robina stations (approx $11, one hour) roughly every half-hour. **Surfside Buslines** (☏13 12 30; www.translink.com.au) runs regular shuttles from the train stations down to Surfers ($4 to $5) and beyond, and to the theme parks.

Coachtrans (☏1300 664 700, 07-3358 9700; www.coachtrans.com.au) runs transfers between Brisbane airport and most Gold Coast accommodation (one way adult/child $44/20). It also offers the Gold Coast Super Pass, which includes return airport transfers, unlimited coach transfers between Gold Coast accommodation and theme parks, and unlimited use of the Surfside bus network (three days adult/child $131/62).

Southport & Main Beach

POP 24,100

The northern gateway to the Gold Coast, Southport is a residential and business district known for its shopping centres and family-friendly vibe. It is sheltered from the ocean by a long sandbar known as the Spit, home to one of the big theme parks, Sea World. Directly southeast is Main Beach (population 3400), where apartment blocks

---

UNEXPECTED TREASURE: ABBEY MUSEUM

The impressive art and archaeology collection in the **Abbey Museum** (☏07-5495 1652; www.abbeytournament.com; 1 The Abbey Pl; adult/child $8.80/5; ⊙10am-4pm Mon-Sat) spans the globe and would be at home in any of the world's famous museums. Once the private collection of Englishman John Ward, the pieces – including Neolithic tools, medieval manuscripts and even an ancient Greek foot-guard (one of only four worldwide) – will have you scratching your head in amazement. The church has more original stained glass from Winchester Cathedral than what is actually left in the cathedral. In July you can make merry at Australia's largest medieval festival, held on the grounds.

The Abbey Museum is on the road to Bribie Island, 6km from the Bruce Hwy turn-off, where you'll find the **Caboolture Warplane Museum** (☏07-5499 1144; Hangar 104, Caboolture Airfield, McNaught Rd; adult/child/family $8/5/18; ⊙9am-3pm), which has a collection of restored WWII warplanes, all in flying order.

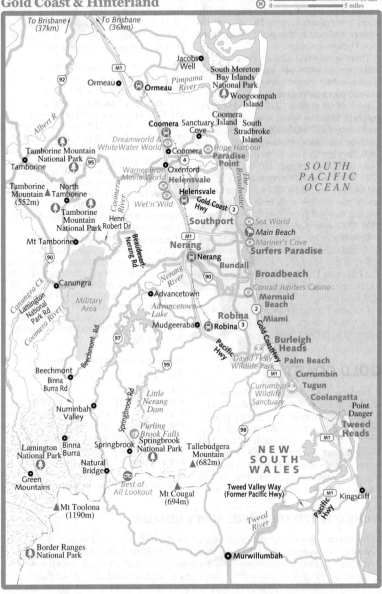

are many and golden sand stretches for miles.

◉ Sights & Activities

The ocean side of the Spit is a popular fishing spot and from here you can see across the channel to South Stradbroke Island. Opposite the entrance to Sea World, in the car park of Phillip Park, is the start of the **Federation Walk**, a pretty 3.7km trail that winds its way through patches of littoral rainforest and down to the Gold Coast Oceanway.

Near the start of the walk is the upmarket shopping and dining complex **Marina Mirage**; a **farmers market** is held at the nearby Mariner's Cove on the first and third Saturday of each month. **Tall Ship Cruises** (☏07-5532 2444; www.tallship.com.au; adult/child $129/79) runs day trips from Mariner's Cove to McLarens Landing Resort on South Stradbroke Island. Lunch is included.

At the **Mariner's Cove Booking Office** (☏07-5571 1711; ⏲8.30am-4.30pm) you can arrange most of the following activities:

Balunjali KAYAKING
(☏07-5533 8527; www.balunjali.com.au; half-day tours adult/child $89/77) Includes an interpretative Aboriginal cultural experience, kayaking to South Stradbroke Island, snorkelling, and traditional billy tea.

Gold Coast Helitours HELICOPTER FLIGHTS
(☏07-5591 8457; www.goldcoasthelitours.com.au; adult/child 5min rides $54/39) Departs from Mirage Heliport.

Spirit of Gold Coast WHALE WATCHING
(☏07-5572 7755; www.goldcoastwhalewatching.com; adult/child $89/59) Available June to November.

🛏 Sleeping

Harbour Side Resort MOTEL $$
(☏07-5591 6666; www.harboursideresort.com.au; 132 Marine Pde, Southport; studios $90, 1-/2-bedroom apt $120/160; ✳@🏊) Disregard the overwhelming brick facade and busy road; within this sprawling property you'll find pastel-hued units with oodles of room. The kitchens are well equipped and the complex also has a laundry and tennis courts.

Surfers Paradise YHA at Main Beach HOSTEL $
(☏07-5571 1776; www.yha.com.au/hostels; 70 Sea World Dr, Main Beach; dm/d & tw $25/69.50; @) In a great position overlooking the marina, here you only have to drop over the balcony to access the plethora of water sports, cruises and tours on offer. There're a free shuttle bus and barbecue nights every Friday, and the hostel is within staggering distance of the Fisherman's Wharf Tavern.

Trekkers HOSTEL $
(☏1800 100 004, 07-5591 5616; www.trekkersbackpackers.com.au; 22 White St, Southport; dm/d & tw $27/70; @🏊) You could bottle the friendly vibes of this beautiful Queenslander and make a mint. The building is looking a bit

tired, but the communal areas are homey and the garden is a mini-oasis.

Main Beach Tourist Park CARAVAN PARK $$
(☏07-5667 2720; www.gctp.com.au/main; Main Beach Pde, Main Beach; unpowered/powered sites from $33/36, cabins from $140; ✳🏊) Just across the road from the beach, this caravan park is a favourite with families. It's a tight fit between sites, but the facilities are good. Rates are for two people.

🍴 Eating

Saks ITALIAN $$$
(☏07-5591 2755; Marina Mirage, 74 Sea World Dr, Main Beach; mains $30-50; ⏲lunch & dinner) Head straight for the deck where tall glass windows offer uninterrupted views of the marina. The brief but sophisticated menu boasts seafood, steak and good Italian fare.

Sunset Bar & Grill MODERN AUSTRALIAN $$
(☏07-5528 2622; Marina Mirage, Main Beach; dishes $8-25; ⏲7am-6pm) This little place on the water serves reasonably priced steaks, burgers and seafood dishes.

Fisho's SEAFOOD $
(☏07-5571 0566; Mariner's Cove, Main Beach; dishes under $13; ⏲lunch & dinner Mon-Fri, breakfast Sat & Sun) Attached to the Fisherman's Wharf Tavern, Fisho's whips up reliable burgers and fish and chips. It transforms into a partying hotspot with live music on weekends.

Peter's Fish Market SEAFOOD $
(Sea World Dr, Main Beach; meals $10-16; ⏲9am-7.30pm) A no-nonsense fish market selling fresh and cooked seafood in all shapes and sizes at reasonable prices.

Surfers Paradise & Broadbeach

Some say the surfers prefer other beaches and the paradise is tragically lost, but there's no denying this wild and trashy party zone attracts phenomenal visitor numbers all year round. Spend-happy tourists flock to Surfers (population 19,000) for the dizzying mix of nightclubs, bars, shopping malls, fun rides and maybe a bit of beach time when the hangover kicks in.

Surfers' party scene happily caters to all demographics, from 40-somethings getting squiffy on martinis to gen Ys getting down on the dance floor and schoolies cutting loose on the beach. The backpacker places

LUKE EGAN: FORMER PRO SURFER

The Gold Coast is one of the top five surfing destinations in the world. The most unique thing about the Goldy is that the waves break mostly on sand, so for sandy bottoms we get some of the most perfect waves in the world.

Best Surf Beaches

The length of ride on the famous points of Burleigh Heads, Kirra, Rainbow Bay and Snapper Rocks make the Goldy a must for every passionate surfer.

Where to Learn

The waves at Greenmount Point and Currumbin allow first-timers plenty of time to get to their feet and still enjoy a long ride. Learning to surf at these two places would be close to the best place to learn anywhere in Australia, and probably the world.

Best Experience

There isn't a better feeling than being 'surfed out' – the feeling you have after a day of surfing. Even though I no longer compete on the world surfing tour I still surf every day like it's my last.

When not Surfing

I love mountain-bike riding in the hills close to Mt Warning, and catching up with friends at one of the Gold Coast's great cafes and restaurants.

particularly go all out to ensure that the town goes off every night of the week, but after a while the excessive party scene becomes repetitive.

Directly south is Broadbeach (population 3800), where the decibel level is considerably lower, but it offers some chic restaurants and a gorgeous stretch of golden beach.

⊙ Sights

Surfers' sights are usually spread across beach towels, but for an eagle-eye scope, zip up to the 230m-high **QDeck** (Q1 building, Hamilton Ave; adult/child/family $19/11/49; ⊗9am-9pm Sun-Thu, to midnight Fri & Sat), offering a spectacular 360-degree panorama of the Gold Coast and its hinterland. There's a cafe and bar so there's no need to hurry back to earth.

The **Gold Coast City Gallery** (☑07-5581 6567; www.gcac.com.au; Gold Coast Arts Centre, 135 Bundall Rd; ⊗10am-5pm Mon-Fri, 11am-5pm Sat & Sun), about 1.5km inland, displays excellent temporary exhibitions.

🏃 Activities

Most surf schools aim to have you standing up and catching waves in your first lesson. Surfboard and wetsuit hire is also available.

Cheyne Horan School of Surf   SURFING
(☑1800 227 873, 0403 080 484; www.cheyne horan.com.au; 2hr lessons $45) World

champion surfer Cheyne Horan offers excellent tuition.

Go Ride a Wave   SURFING
(☑1300 132 441, 07-5526 7077; www.gorideawave. com.au; Cavill Ave Mall; 2hr surfing or kayaking lessons from $55; ⊗9am-5pm) Also rents out surfboards, kayaks, beach chairs and umbrellas.

Splash Safaris Sea Kayaking   KAYAKING
(☑0407 741 748; half-day tours $85) Tour includes kayaking, snorkelling, fish feeding, bushwalking and morning or afternoon tea.

Movie Stunt Experience   STUNTS
(☑0415 999 626; www.moviestuntexperience. com; half/full day incl pick-up and drop-off $149/299) Be an action hero for the day, abseiling commando-style through windows, flying on wires, jumping from buildings and being set on fire.

Gold Coast Skydive   SKYDIVING
(☑07-5599 1920; www.goldcoastskydive.com.au; tandem dives from $325) Get a DVD of your experience for $115 extra.

Balloon Down Under   BALLOONING
(☑07-5593 8400; www.balloondownunder. com; 1hr flights adult/child $310/200) Early-morning flights ending with a champagne breakfast.

Gumnuts Horseriding
HORSE RIDING

(☎07-5543 0191; www.gumnutsfarm.com.au; Biddaddaba Creek Rd; adult/child $110/75) Damper, billy tea, lunch, and transfers to accommodation throughout the Gold Coast.

Numinbah Valley Adventure Trails
HORSE RIDING

(☎07-5533 4137; www.numinbahtrails.com; adult/child $75/65) Three-hour horse-riding treks through beautiful rainforest and river scenery in the Numinbah Valley, 30km south of Nerang.

Tours

Aquaduck
LAND, WATER

(☎07-5539 0222; www.aquaduck.com.au; 7A Orchid Ave, Surfers Paradise; adult/child/family $35/26/95) Explore Surfers by land and water in a boat with wheels. Tours depart from Appel Park every 75 minutes between 9am and 5.30pm.

Festivals & Events

Big Day Out
MUSIC

(www.bigdayout.com) Huge international music festival in late January.

Quicksilver Pro-Surfing Competition
SURFING

See some of the world's best surfers out on the waves in mid-March.

Surf Life-Saving Championships
SURF LIFE-SAVING

Also in mid-March, expect to see some stupidly fit people running about wearing very little.

Gold Coast International Marathon
MARATHON

July.

Gold Coast 600
MOTORSPORTS

(www.goldcoast600.com.au) For three days in October the streets of Surfers are transformed into a temporary race circuit for the high-speed V8 Supercars race.

Coolangatta Gold
SURF LIFE-SAVING

October; gruelling competition with surf-ski paddle, beach runs, ocean swim, board paddle and long beach run to finish.

Schoolies
SCHOOLIES

Month-long party by school leavers from mid-November to mid-December. Generally involves lots of alcohol and unruly behaviour.

The **Gold Coast Accommodation Service** (☎07-5592 0067; www.goldcoastaccommodationservice.com; shop 1, 1 Beach Rd) can arrange and book accommodation and tours.

TOP CHOICE Vibe Hotel
BOUTIQUE HOTEL $$

(☎07-5539 0444; www.vibehotels.com.au; d from $140; ❃@≋) You won't miss this chocolate and lime-green high-rise on the Nerang River, a vibrant gem amongst Surfers' bland plethora of hotels and apartments. The rooms are subtle-chic and the poolside is the spot for sundowners. The aqua-view rooms have superb views over the river.

Q1 Resort
APARTMENTS $$$

(☎07-5630 4500; www.q1.com.au; Hamilton Ave; 1-/2-/3-bedroom apt from $252/340/500; ❃@≋) Spend a night in the world's second-tallest residential tower. This stylish 80-storey resort is a modern mix of metal, glass and fabulous wrap-around views. All units have glass-enclosed balconies. There're a lagoon-style pool, a fitness centre and a day spa.

Surfers International Apartments
APARTMENTS $$

(☎1800 891 299, 07-5579 1299; www.surfers-international.com.au; 7-9 Trickett St; 1-/2-bedroom apt from $150/210; @≋) This high-rise just off the beach has large, comfortable apartments with full ocean views. The complex comes with a small gym and a rooftop pool. This is a good option, close to everything. Minimum three-night stay.

Chateau Beachside
APARTMENTS $$

(☎07-5538 1022; www.chateaubeachside.com.au; cnr Elkhorn Ave & Esplanade; d/studio/1-bedroom apt $145/160/175; ❃@≋) Right in the heart of Surfers, this seaside complex is an excellent choice. All the newly renovated studios and apartments have ocean views and the 18m pool is a bonus. Minimum two-night stay.

Trickett Gardens Holiday Inn
APARTMENTS $$

(☎07-5539 0988; www.trickettgardens.com.au; 24-30 Trickett St; s/d $150/185; ❃≋) This friendly low-rise block is great for families, with a central location and well-equipped, self-contained units. It's so tranquil it's hard to believe you're close to Surfers' frantic action.

International Beach Resort
APARTMENTS $$

(☎1800 657 471, 07-5539 0099; www.internationalresort.com.au; 84 Esplanade; apt $125-204; ❃@🛜≋) A seafront high-rise, this place is

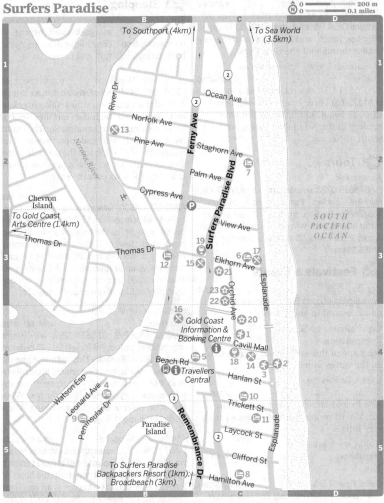

To Southport (4km)

To Sea World (3.5km)

River Dr

Ocean Ave

Norfolk Ave

Pine Ave

Staghorn Ave

Ferry Ave

Palm Ave

Surfers Paradise Blvd

Cypress Ave

Chevron Island
To Gold Coast Arts Centre (1.4km)

Thomas Dr

View Ave

Thomas Dr

Elkhorn Ave

Orchid Ave

Esplanade

SOUTH PACIFIC OCEAN

Gold Coast Information & Booking Centre

Cavill Mall

Beach Rd

Travellers Central

Hanlan St

Watson Esp

Leonard Ave

Peninsular Dr

Paradise Island

Remembrance Dr

Trickett St

Laycock St

Esplanade

Clifford St

To Surfers Paradise Backpackers Resort (1km); Broadbeach (3km)

Hamilton Ave

just across from the beach, and has good studios and one- and two-bedroom units.

Breakfree Cosmopolitan Resort   APARTMENTS $$

(☎07-5570 2311; www.breakfree.com.au; cnr Surfers Paradise Blvd & Beach Rd; 1-/2-bedroom apt from $119/189; ❄☎) Set back from the beach but still very central, this complex contains 55 privately owned, self-contained apartments, each uniquely furnished by the owners. There's also a barbecue area, a spa and a sauna. It can be noisy at night. Minimum two-night stay.

Sleeping Inn Surfers   HOSTEL $

(☎1800 817 832, 07-5592 4455; www.sleepinginn.com.au; 26 Peninsular Dr; dm $22-26, d with/without bathroom $78/68; @☎) The newly renovated rooms are comfortable and all dorms have their own en suite and well-equipped kitchen. Free limo pick-up from the transit centre. Movies are shown by the pool or, oddly enough, in an orange bus converted into a mini-cinema.

Surfers Paradise Backpackers Resort   HOSTEL $

(☎1800 282 800, 07-5592 4677; www.surfersparadisebackpackers.com.au; 2837 Gold Coast Hwy,

Surfers Paradise; dm/d $23/74; @🅿🛜🏊) This purpose-built hostel with sauna, tennis court, pool room and bar has newly renovated rooms and self-contained apartments. It's family-friendly and offers good security, free laundry facilities and a free courtesy bus to and from the transit centre.

Backpackers in Paradise   HOSTEL $
(⏚07-5538 4344; www.backpackersinparadise. com; 40 Peninsular Dr; dm/d from $20/65; @🏊) The mini-cinema is a major drawcard in this party hostel. At research time the rooms and bathrooms were all undergoing much-needed renovations, which should lift standards and make this a comfortable hostel. The on-site convenience store is a bonus.

Wave   APARTMENTS $$$
(⏚07-5555 9200; www.thewavesresort.com.au; 89-91 Surf Pde, Broadbeach; r $225-550; ✻@🛜🏊) You can't miss this spectacular high-rise with its wave-inspired design towering over glam Broadbeach south of Surfers. These luxury apartments make full use of the coast's spectacular views, especially from the sky pool on the 34th floor. Minimum three-night stay.

✗ Eating

Broadbeach's culinary scene is a class above Surfers' – where quantity often trumps quality. Self-caterers will find supermarkets in **Centro Surfers Paradise** (Cavill Mall), **Chevron Renaissance Shopping Centre** (cnr Elkhorn Ave & Surfers Paradise Blvd) and **Circle on Cavill** (cnr Cavill & Ferny Aves).

Moo Moo   STEAKHOUSE $$$
(⏚07-5539 9952; Broadbeach on the Park, 2685 Gold Coast Hwy, Broadbeach; mains $30-60; ☽lunch & dinner) A mecca for serious carnivores, Moo Moo's signature dish is a 1kg wagyu rump steak rubbed with spices, chargrilled until smoky, then roasted, and carved at the table. Less carnivorous diners will be happy with the seafood and pasta dishes on the menu.

Surfers Sandbar   MODERN AUSTRALIAN $$
(cnr Elkhorn Ave & Esplanade; dishes $8-20; ☽breakfast, lunch & dinner) The ocean view gives this cafe, bar and restaurant the edge over most Surfers eateries. The menu gravitates towards burgers, beer-battered fish and chips, and light seafood meals, but forgo the rather impersonal indoor restaurant and dine outdoors.

Baritalia   ITALIAN $$
(⏚07- 5592 4700; shop 15, Chevron Renaissance Bldg, cnr Elkhorn Ave & Surfers Paradise Blvd; mains $10-25; ☽breakfast, lunch & dinner) The perfect spot for people-watching, this alfresco Italian-style bar and restaurant has rustic wooden benches and an atmosphere to match.

Koi   FUSION $$
(⏚07-5570 3060; Wave Bldg, cnr Surf Pde & Albert Ave, Broadbeach; mains $24-40; ☽breakfast,

lunch & dinner) Cruisy cafe and lounge bar with gourmet pizzas, tapas and contemporary seafood dishes.

Kamikaze Teppanyaki
JAPANESE $$

(☑07-5592 0888; Circle on Cavill, Surfers Paradise Blvd; dishes $8-27; ☺lunch & dinner) Popular alfresco Japanese restaurant.

Bumbles Café
CAFE $$

(☑07-5538 6668; 21 River Dr; dishes $11-25; ☺7am-4pm) Peaceful cafe opposite the Nerang River with small global menu.

🍷 Drinking

Beer Garden
BAR

(Cavill Ave) A very popular watering hole, the upstairs Beer Garden isn't a garden but a huge barn-like affair overlooking Cavill Ave. It's the place to start a night of clubbing.

Clock Hotel
PUB

(cnr Elkhorn Ave & Surfers Paradise Blvd) Easily recognisable with its gaudy clock-tower exterior, this three-level pub is a good central meeting place for beer and cheap steak. There's outdoor seating and DJs on Friday and Saturday nights.

Northcliffe SLSC
SURF CLUB

(Garfield Tce) A little south of Cavill Mall, this surf club sits directly on the beach. It's large and modern with zero intimacy, but the expansive ocean views go well with a coldie on a hot day.

☆ Entertainment

Orchid Ave is Surfers' main bar and nightclub strip. Cover charges are usually between $10 and $20, and Wednesday and Saturday are generally the big party nights.

If you're up for partying with other backpackers, Wednesday, Friday and Saturday nights see the **Wicked Club Crawl**

GOLD COAST THEME PARKS

The roller coasters and water slides at these American-style theme parks offer so much dizzying action that keeping your lunch down can be a constant battle. Discount tickets are sold in most of the tourist offices on the Gold Coast; the 3 Park Super Pass (adult/ child $177/115) covers entry to Sea World, Movie World and Wet'n'Wild.

Australian Outback Spectacular (☑07-5519 6200; www.myfun.com.au; Entertainment Rd, Oxenford; adult/child incl dinner $99/69) Between Movie World and Wet'n'Wild, this is not actually a theme park but rather a 1½-hour dinner and show in a 1000-seat arena. The venue captures the spirit of the Australian outback with displays of brilliant horsemanship, stampeding cattle and even a little boot scootin' to music written by Australian country singer Lee Kernaghan. You're given a stockman's hat to keep; dinner is three courses of outback tucker.

Dreamworld (☑07-5588 1111; www.dreamworld.com.au; Pacific Hwy, Coomera; adult/child $72/47; ☺10am-5pm) Home to the Big 6 Thrill Rides, including the Giant Drop and Tower of Terror. Get your photo taken with a Bengal tiger at Tiger Island.

Sea World (☑07-5588 2222, show times 07-5588 2205; www.seaworld.com.au; Sea World Dr, The Spit, Main Beach; adult/child $75/50; ☺10am-5pm) See polar bears, sharks and performing dolphins at this aquatic park, or ride one of the original Gold Coast roller coasters, the Corkscrew. Catch up with Bert and Ernie at the new Sesame Street Beach.

Warner Bros Movie World (☑07-5573 8485; www.myfun.com.au; Pacific Hwy, Oxenford; adult/child $75/50; ☺10am-5pm) Movie-themed shows, rides and attractions, including the Batwing Spaceshot and Lethal Weapon roller coaster.

Wet'n'Wild (☑07-5573 2255; www.wetnwild.com.au; Pacific Hwy, Oxenford; adult/child $55/35; ☺10am-5pm Feb-Apr & Sep-Dec, to 4pm May-Aug, to 9pm 27 Dec-25 Jan) The ultimate water slide here is the Kamikaze, where you plunge down an 11m drop in a two-person tube at 50km/h. This vast water fun park also has slippery slides, white-water rapids and tube rides; latest-release films are shown at Dive'n'Movies.

WhiteWater World (☑07-5588 1111; www.whitewaterworld.com.au; Dreamworld Parkway, Coomera; adult/child $45/30; ☺10.30am-4.30pm) Connected to Dreamworld; features the Cave of Waves, Pipeline Plunge and more than 140 water activities and slides. A World Pass (adult/child one day $89/65, two days $109/75) ensures entry to Dreamworld and WhiteWater World.

07-5580 8422; www.wickedclubcrawl.com.au; tickets $30-50), **Plan B Party Tours** (0400 685 501; www.planbtours.com; tickets $30) or **Backpackers Big Night Out** (www.goldcoast backpackers.net; tickets $30; Wed & Sat). The teams organise a club crawl to five or six nightclubs (including free entry for the rest of the week), a free drink and pizza at each venue, party games and other goodies.

Vanity   NIGHTCLUB
(26 Orchid Ave) Formerly the Bedroom, Vanity is one of the hottest clubs in town, priding itself on beautiful people and upmarket glam.

Sin City   NIGHTCLUB
(22 Orchid Ave) A newcomer on the party scene, this Las Vegas–style nightclub is the place to be seen.

Cocktails & Dreams   NIGHTCLUB
(Orchid Ave) One of the oldest clubs in town, it still draws a regular crowd of party animals.

MP's   NIGHTCLUB
(Forum Arcade, 26 Orchid Ave) This popular gay club has cheap drinks and drag shows. On Friday and Saturday it fills with a happy, mixed crowd soaking up a generic nightclub atmosphere.

FREE **Conrad Jupiters Casino**   CASINO
(07-5592 8100; www.conrad.com.au; Broadbeach Island, Gold Coast Hwy, Broadbeach; 24hr) Live music and dinner shows.

Gold Coast Arts Centre   THEATRE
(07-5588 4000; www.gcac.com.au; 135 Bundall Rd) Beside the Nerang River, GCAC has two cinemas, a restaurant, a bar and a 1200-seat theatre, which regularly hosts impressive productions.

ⓘ Information

Between mid-November and mid-December tens of thousands of school leavers descend on the Gold Coast for Schoolies Week, a month-long party that's great fun for those celebrating but basically hell for everyone else.

Car theft is a problem around Southport and Surfers Paradise – park in well-lit areas and don't leave valuables in your vehicle.

The **Gold Coast Hospital** (07-5519 8211; 108 Nerang St, Southport) is in Southport.

The following are all based in Surfers Paradise.

Email Centre (Orchid Ave; 9am-10pm)

Gold Coast Information & Booking Centre (Cavill Mall; 8.30am-5pm Mon-Sat, 9am-4pm Sun) Information booth; also sells theme-park tickets.

Our High Speed Internet (3063 Surfers Paradise Blvd; 9am-11pm)

Paradise Medical Clinic (07-5592 3999; Centro Surfers Paradise, Cavill Mall; 8.30am-5pm Mon-Fri, 9am-12.30pm Sat)

Surfers Paradise Day & Night Medical Centre (07-5592 2299; 3221 Surfers Paradise Blvd; 7am-11pm)

Travellers Central (www.travellerscentral.com.au; Surfers Paradise Transit Centre, cnr Beach & Cambridge Rds; 9am-7pm) Help with accommodation and tours.

ⓘ Getting There & Around

Long-distance buses stop at the **Surfers Paradise Transit Centre** (Beach Rd). **Greyhound Australia** (1300 473 946, 07-5531 6677) and **Premier Motor Service** (13 34 10; www.premierms.com.au) have frequent services to/from Brisbane ($20 to $30, 75 minutes). The bus stops for Burleigh Heads and Southport are on Ferny Ave.

Car hire costs around $30 to $50 per day.

Avis (13 63 33, 07-5539 9388; cnr Ferny & Cypress Aves)

Budget (1300 362 848, 07-5538 1344; cnr Ferny & Palm Aves)

Getabout Rentals (07-5504 6517; shop 9, The Mark, Orchid Ave) Also rents scooters and bikes.

Red Back Rentals (07-5592 1655; Transit Centre, cnr Beach & Cambridge Rds)

Red Rocket Rent-A-Car (1800 673 682, 07-5538 9074; Centre Arcade, 16 Orchid Ave) Also rents scooters ($30 per day) and bicycles ($12 per day).

The major taxi companies servicing the area are **Regent Taxis** (13 62 94), **Gold Coast Taxis** (13 10 08) and **Silver Service Taxis** (13 31 00).

See p325 for more transport information.

Burleigh Heads

POP 7800

A little further south and the true essence of the Gold Coast – far removed from the frenzied party atmosphere of Surfers – permeates the chilled-out surfie town of Burleigh Heads. With its cheery cafes and beachfront restaurants overlooking a gorgeous stretch of white sand, and its small but beautiful national park on the rocky headland, Burleigh Heads charms everyone.

In the right weather conditions, the headland here produces a spectacular right-hand point break, famous for its fast, deep barrel rides, but it definitely isn't for beginners.

⊙ Sights & Activities

A walk around the headland through **Burleigh Heads National Park** is a must for any visitor – it's a 27-hectare eucalypt forest reserve with plenty of bird life and several walking trails. The natural rock slides and water cascades at the **Currumbin Rock Pools** are wonderful in the summer months.

There are two excellent wildlife sanctuaries in the vicinity. The **Currumbin Wildlife Sanctuary** (☎07-5534 1266; www.cws.org.au; Gold Coast Hwy, Currumbin; adult/child $49/31; ⊙8am-5pm) has Australia's biggest rainforest aviary, where you can hand feed rainbow lorikeets. There's also kangaroo feeding, photo opportunities with koalas, Aboriginal dance displays and the Snakes Alive show. One of the best ways to see the sanctuary is on a Wildnight Tour (adult/child $89/59), when the native nocturnal animals go about their business. To get here catch Surfside bus 700 from Surfers Paradise or 765 from Robina train station.

Opened by the doctor who first succeeded in breeding platypuses, the **David Fleay Wildlife Park** (☎07-5576 2411; West Burleigh Rd; adult/child/family $17/8/44; ⊙9am-5pm) has 4km of walking tracks through mangroves and rainforest and plenty of educational and informative shows throughout the day. It's an excellent opportunity to experience Australian fauna. The platypus was first bred in captivity here and the park still runs a research and breeding program for rare and endangered species.

The **Hot Stuff Surf Shop** (☎07-5535 6899; 1969 Gold Coast Hwy) rents out surfboards (mostly long boards) per half/full day for $30/40.

Surfing Services Australia (☎07-5535 5557; www.surfingservices.com.au; adult/child $35/25) has surfing lessons at Currumbin Alley every weekend at 8am and 10am.

🛏 Sleeping

Hillhaven Holiday Apartments
APARTMENTS **$$**

(☎07-5535 1055; www.hillhaven.com.au; 2 Goodwin Tce; d $170; ⊛) Situated on the headland adjacent to the national park, these upmarket apartments – the pick is the gold deluxe room at $300 per night – have a grand view of Burleigh Heads. There's no through traffic so it's ultra quiet, yet it's only 150m to the beach and cafe scene. Minimum three-night stay.

Burleigh Palms Holiday Apartments
APARTMENTS **$$**

(☎07-5576 3955; www.burleighpalms.com; 1849 Gold Coast Hwy; 1-bedroom apt per night/week from $130/550, 2-bedroom apt from $160/660; ⊛) Even though they're on the highway, these large and comfortable self-contained units, so close to the beach, are solid value. The owner is a mine of information and is happy to organise tours and recommend places to visit.

Wyuna
APARTMENTS **$$**

(☎07-5535 3302; http://wyunaapartments.com. au; 82 The Esplanade; 2-bedroom apt per week from $640; ☎) Large, old-fashioned apartments in a great location opposite the beach.

Burleigh Beach Tourist Park
CARAVAN PARK **$**

(☎07-5667 2750; www.goldcoasttouristparks. com.au; Goodwin Tce; unpowered/powered sites $29/36, cabins from $115; ✳@☎⊛) This council-run park is snug, but it's in a great spot near the beach.

🍴 Eating & Drinking

Oskars
SEAFOOD **$$$**

(☎07-5576 3722; 43 Goodwin Tce; dishes $20-50; ⊙lunch & dinner) One of the Gold Coast's finest, this elegant restaurant right on the beach serves award-winning seafood amid sweeping views of the coastline.

Elephant Rock Café
MODERN AUSTRALIAN **$$**

(☎07-5598 2133; 776 Pacific Pde, Currumbin; mains $16-34; ⊙breakfast & lunch daily, dinner Tue-Sat; ☎) A cool cafe specialising in Mod Oz and 'gourmet vegetarian' cuisine, this trendy cafe morphs from beach-chic by day to ultrachic at night. Great ocean views from the top deck.

Mermaids on the Beach
MEDITERRANEAN **$$**

(☎07-5520 1177; 31 Goodwin Tce; mains $23-36; ⊙breakfast, lunch & dinner) Another gem directly on the beach, Mermaids spreads delectable fruit platters for breakfast and Mediterr-asian dishes like prawn and lemon tortellini by night.

Pointbreak
BAR

(43 Goodwin Tce) Nothing beats a sundowner on the deck at this chic waterfront bar and restaurant.

Bluff Cafe
CAFE **$$**

(1/66 Goodwin Tce; dishes $10-30; ⊙breakfast, lunch & dinner) Popular and breezy cafe just opposite the beach. Excellent pizza.

Zullaz FUSION $$

(☑07-5535 3511; 50 James St; mains $11-28; ⊙lunch Fri, dinner Tue-Sat) With Polynesian, Moroccan and Indian dishes, the menu is as exotic as the decor in this funky bar-restaurant.

Coolangatta

POP 5000

A laid-back seaside resort on Queensland's southern border, Coolangatta is proud of its good surf beaches and tight community. With a sleek makeover transforming the esplanade, this once sleepy town is now the pick of the Gold Coast. If you want to bypass the glam and party scene, catch the best waves on the coast, or just kick back on the beach, you've found the spot. North of the point, Kirra has a beautiful long stretch of beach with challenging surf. Heading south, there are good views down the coast from Point Danger, the headland at the end of the state line.

Cooly Surf (cnr Marine Pde & Dutton St; ⊙9am-5pm) hires out high-performance surfboards as well as Malibu surfboards (half/full day $30/45) and stand-up paddleboards ($40/55). Learn to surf with **Walkin' on Water** (☑07-5534 1886, 0418 780 311; www.walkinonwater.com; 2hr group lesson per person $40) or **Gold Coast Surf Coaching** (☑0417 191 629).

Rainforest Cruises (☑07-5536 8800; www.goldcoastcruising.com; 2hr cruises from $35) has a number of options ranging from crab catching to surf 'n' turf lunches on rainforest cruises along the Tweed River.

🛏 Sleeping

TOP CHOICE **Komune** BOUTIQUE HOTEL $$

(☑07-5536 6764; www.komuneresorts.com; 146 Marine Pde; dm from $45, 2-bedroom apt $220, penthouses $695, penthouses incl Sky-House party room $1500; @🛜🏊)With beach-funk decor, tropical poolside and an ultra laid-back vibe, this is the ultimate surf retreat. The new concept in accommodation – from budget dorms (including a girls-only dorm), self-contained apartments, and a hip penthouse begging for a party – attracts a broad range of travellers, and fosters eclectic friendships.

Coolangatta Sands Hostel HOSTEL $

(☑07-5536 7472; www.coolangattasandshostel.com.au; cnr Griffith & McLean Sts; dm from $30, d $72) Above the Coolangatta Sands Hotel and directly opposite the beach, this clean, airy and pleasant hostel is a good choice. As

well as a free shuttle to and from the airport, there are plenty of incentives – free surf lessons and free trips to Nimbin, Mt Warning and Byron Bay.

Coolangatta YHA HOSTEL $

(☑07-5536 7644; www.coolangattayha.com; 230 Coolangatta Rd, Bilinga; dm $25-32, s $38-42, d $60-67; @🛜🏊) A looong 4km haul from the bustle, this well-equipped YHA is favoured by surf junkies, who overdose on the excellent breaks across the road. You can also hire boards ($25 per day) and bikes. Courtesy transfers from Coolangatta are available. All rates include breakfast.

Beach House Seaside Resort APARTMENTS $$

(☑07-5590 2111; www.classicholidayclub.com.au; 52 Marine Pde; s/d from $150/180; 🏊) A holiday apartment complex that often has rooms available to non-members. Bright, airy units sleep six, and there's a gym, spa and sauna.

Kirra Beach Tourist Park CARAVAN PARK $

(☑07-5667 2740; www.goldcoasttouristparks.com.au; Charlotte St, Kirra; unpowered/powered sites $29/34, cabins from $115; ❄@🛜🏊) Large council-run park has plenty of trees and a well-stocked open-air camp kitchen. Good-value self-contained cabins.

🍴 Eating & Drinking

Marine Pde is lined with alfresco cafes and restaurants.

Bread'n'butter TAPAS $$

(☑07-5599 4666; 76 Musgrave St, Kirra; tapas $14-19; ⊙dinner nightly, lunch Sat & Sun) Head upstairs to the balcony, where mood lighting and chill tunes make this tapas bar perfect for a drink or a light meal. The pizzas are tasty and the tapas are huge. On Friday and Saturday nights a DJ turns upstairs into a lively bar scene.

Mist MODERN AUSTRALIAN $$$

(☑07-5536 8885; cnr Douglas & Musgrave Sts, Kirra; tapas $10-23, mains $36-42; ⊙breakfast, lunch & dinner) The Mod Oz cuisine is creative, innovative and sassy, and the curtained alcoves, arty chandeliers and eclectic decor add up to stylish beach-chic.

Coolangatta Hotel PUB

(cnr Marine Pde & Warner St) One of the hottest spots on the Gold Coast, the 'Cooly' has legendary Sunday sessions, and the Balcony nightclub attracts some of the biggest acts in the music industry.

ℹ️ Information

Coolangatta visitor centre (shop 22, Showcase on the Beach, Griffith St; ⊘8.30am-5pm Mon-Fri, 9am-3pm Sat, 9am-noon Sun)

GOLD COAST HINTERLAND

Inland from the surf, sand and half-naked bods on the Gold Coast beaches, the densely forested and unspoilt mountains of the McPherson Range feel like a million miles away. The range forms a natural barrier between the eastern coastline and the rolling green hills of the Darling Downs, and is a subtropical paradise of rainforests, waterfalls, panoramic lookouts and amazing wildlife. Closest to the coast, Springbrook is arguably the wettest place in southeast Queensland and the villages that speckle this area are influenced by the cooler air and vast sea of dense forest. Lamington National Park attracts birdwatchers, nature lovers and serious hikers, while Tamborine Mountain lures the craft cottage set. In winter, cosy cabins and fireplaces attract romantic weekenders.

👉 Tours

Winding your way around the mountain and valley roads is great fun in a hire car, or take a tour if you'd prefer an experienced navigator. See p293 for hinterland tours departing from Brisbane.

Australian Day Tours SCENIC
(☑1300 363 436; www.daytours.com.au) A variety of tours, including day tours to Springbrook National Park (adult/child $105/62) and to O'Reilly's Rainforest Retreat (this spread) via Mt Tamborine (adult/child $93/57).

Tour Gold Coast GLOW-WORMS
(☑07-5532 8687; www.tourgc.com.au; adult/child $90/45, incl dinner $110/55) Runs glow-worm night tours to Natural Bridge, including a rainforest walk and stargazing with an Aboriginal tour guide.

🖊 Bushwacker Ecotours ECOTOUR
(☑07-3720 9020; www.bushwacker-ecotours.com. au; day trips adult/child $115/95) Has an extensive array of ecotours to the hinterland and includes rainforest walks.

Tamborine Mountain

Just 36km northwest from Southport stands Tamborine Mountain (525m), a small plateau community known for its quaint shops selling homemade sweets and Australiana-themed craft souvenirs. Grey nomads love this place for its kitschy offerings and heritage feel, and there are some beautiful natural settings in Tamborine National Park (1500 hectares). Spectacular cascades at Witches Falls, Cameron Falls and Curtis Falls are accessed via walking trails and the Cedar Creek Falls track (900m return) is one of the most popular in the area, leading you past gently tumbling falls and rock pools (some wheelchair access).

The visitor information centre (Doughty Park; ⊘10am-4pm Mon-Fri, 9.30am-4pm Sat & Sun) is located in North Tamborine.

Sample the good stuff at Tamborine Mountain Distillery (87 Beacon Rd, North Tamborine; ⊘10am-3pm Mon-Sat), a boutique distiller manufacturing schnapps, liqueurs and other spirits from organically grown fruits. Beer lovers will head straight for the Mt Tamborine Brewery (165-185 Long Rd, North Tamborine; ⊘10am-5pm), where a tasting tray gives you four beers to sample for $10.

Take a walk through the rainforest canopy at Skywalk (www.rainforestskywalk.com. au; 333 Geissman Dr, North Tamborine; adult/child/family $18.50/9.50/47; ⊘9.30am-4pm). The path descends to the forest floor and leads to Cedar Creek. Look out for the rare Richmond Birdwing butterfly.

You can overnight at the Polish Place (☑07-5545 1603; www.polishplace.com.au; 333 Main Western Rd, Tamborine Mountain; chalets from $249; 🌀) in European-style timber chalets with spectacular views.

Tamborine Mountain Caravan & Camping (☑07-5545 0034; www.tamborine. info; Thunderbird Park, Tamborine Mountain Rd, Mt Tamborine; unpowered/powered sites $18/24, safari tents $80-100) is a lovely wooded camping ground with a freshwater swimming creek.

Springbrook National Park

The breathtaking landscape of Springbrook is a remnant of the huge shield volcano that centred on nearby Mt Warning in NSW more than 20 million years ago. The national park is directly west of Coolangatta, just 29km from Mudgeeraba or 42km from Nerang. It's a natural wonderland for hikers, with excellent walking trails through cool-temperate and eucalypt forests offering a mosaic of gorges, cliffs and waterfalls.

The park is divided into four reserves. The **Springbrook Plateau** is a 900m-high section with numerous waterfalls and spectacular lookouts. The village of Springbrook is balanced right on the edge of the plateau and there are several places where you can get the giddy thrill of leaning right out over the edge, including Purling Brook Falls, Canyon Lookout and Best of All Lookout. The pathway to Best of All Lookout is home to several ancient Antarctic beech trees.

The beautiful **Natural Bridge** section, off the Nerang–Murwillumbah road, has a 1km walking circuit leading to a rock arch spanning a water-formed cave, which is home to a huge colony of glow-worms. (Swimming in the creek is no longer allowed and rangers do enforce fines.)

The **Mt Cougal** section, accessed via Currumbin Creek Rd, has several waterfalls and swimming holes. The **Numinbah** forest reserve was recently added as the fourth section of the national park.

There's a **ranger's office** (87 Carrick Rd; ⊙8am-3.30pm Mon-Fri) at Springbrook where you can pick up a copy of the national park's walking tracks. There's also an unstaffed **information centre** at the end of Old School Rd.

Those seeking a romantic retreat in the mountains will adore **Mouses House** (☑07-5533 5192; www.mouseshouse.com.au; 2807 Springbrook Rd, Springbrook; r from $240, 2 nights from $395). Linked by rainforest boardwalks, there are 12 luxury A-frame chalets here with double spas and wood fires, set amid enchanting greenery.

You can pitch a tent at the uninspiring, unshaded **Settlement Campground** (sites per person/family $4.85/19.40), off Carricks Rd, the only campground in the park. You need to book in advance through **QPWS** (☑13 74 68; www.derm.gov.au).

Lamington National Park

This precious ecological giant west of Springbrook is part of a Unesco World Heritage Site and is Queensland's best-known protected area. The 200-sq-km park covers much of the McPherson Range and adjoins the Border Ranges National Park in NSW. Most of the park is lying on a 900m plateau characterised by beautiful gorges, waterfalls, thick subtropical rainforests and stunning bushwalking trails.

The two most popular and accessible sections of the park are **Binna Burra** and **Green Mountains**, both reached via narrow, winding roads from Canungra. The drive to Green Mountains is a little challenging at times – due to blind curves around the mountains – but extremely rewarding. Binna Burra can also be reached from Nerang.

There are numerous walking tracks within the park. The latest attraction for experienced hikers is the **Great Walk**, a three-day trip along a 54km path to the Springbrook Plateau. Other favourites include the excellent **tree-top canopy walk** along a series of rope-and-plank suspension bridges at Green Mountains, and the 21km **Border Track** that follows the dividing range between NSW and Queensland and links Binna Burra to O'Reilly's Rainforest Retreat.

Walking trail guides are available from the **ranger stations** at Binna Burra and Green Mountains.

🛏 Sleeping & Eating

Binna Burra Mountain Lodge GUESTHOUSE $$
(☑1300 246 622; www.binnaburralodge.com.au; Binna Burra Rd, Beechmont; unpowered/powered sites $24/30, safari tents from $55, d incl breakfast with/without bathroom $250/190) Stay in the lodge, in rustic log cabins or in a tent surrounded by forest in this atmospheric mountain retreat. The central **restaurant** (mains $20-35; ⊙breakfast & dinner) has good views over the national park. While here, try the lodge's **senses trail** for the blind, indulge in the **Rejoove Day Spa**, or learn to abseil. Other activities include guided walks, flying-fox flights and free nightly nature documentaries. Transport to and from the lodge can be arranged upon request.

O'Reilly's Rainforest Retreat GUESTHOUSE $$$
(☑1800 688 722; www.oreillys.com.au; Lamington National Park Rd; s/d from $163/278, 1-/2-bedroom villas from $400/435; @ ≋) Established in 1926, this famous guesthouse at Green Mountains is still run by the O'Reilly family. The original guesthouse (looking dated and faded) still manages to retain its old-world rustic charm – and sensational views – but there's also a choice of luxury villas. The **Discovery Centre** runs daily activities, including guided rainforest walks, glow-worm walks, 4WD tours, flying-fox and giant swing rides (all at added cost), and free nightly nature documentaries. There's a day spa, a bar, and a plush **restaurant** (mains $25-40; ⊙breakfast, lunch & dinner).

There is a QPWS camping ground (☑13 13 04; www.derm.qld.gov.au; sites per person $5.15) as you head down the hill from O'Reilly's, and bush camping is also permitted in several areas of the park. But only a limited number of permits are issued. Reserve online or from the ranger at Green Mountains, or self-register on site.

ⓘ Getting There & Away

Mountain Coach Company (☑07-5524 4249) has a daily service from the Gold Coast to O'Reilly's via Tamborine Mountain (return day trip $69/39 per adult/child, one hour). To overnight at O'Reilly's, the transfer fee is $45 each way.

NOOSA & THE SUNSHINE COAST

If your idea of the perfect summer holiday involves lazy days in the sun, sand between your toes, and fish and chips on the beach then pack a smile, ditch the bling and immerse yourself in the laid-back beach-chic culture of the refreshingly natural and unaffected Sunshine Coast.

From the tip of Bribie Island, the 'Sunny Coast' stretches north for 100 golden kilometres to the Cooloola Coast, just beyond the exclusive, leafy resort town of Noosa. The coast is perfect for surfing and swimming, and Mooloolaba with its popular beach, outdoor eateries and cafes is a firm favourite with holidaying Australian families.

Forming a stunning backdrop to this spectacular coastline are the ethereal Glass House Mountains and, a little further north, the Sunshine Coast hinterland, home to the forested folds and ridges, gorges and waterfalls, lush green pastures and quaint villages of the Blackall Range.

The Sunshine Coast is also home to the one of the world's great wildlife sanctuaries, the iconic Australia Zoo.

ⓘ Getting There & Away

AIR

The Sunshine Coast Airport is at Mudjimba, 10km north of Maroochydore and 26km south of Noosa. **Jetstar** (☑13 15 38; www.jetstar.com.au) and **Virgin Australia** (☑13 67 89; www.virginaustralia.com) have daily flights from Sydney and Melbourne. **Tiger Airways** (☑03-9999 2888; www.tigerairways.com) has flights from Melbourne.

BUS

Greyhound Australia (☑1300 473 946; www.greyhound.com.au) has daily services from Brisbane to Caloundra ($30, two hours), Maroochydore ($30, two hours) and Noosa ($32, 2½ hours). **Premier Motor Service** (☑13 34 10; www.premierms.com.au) also services Maroochydore and Noosa from Brisbane.

Veolia (☑1300 826 608; www.vtb.com.au) has an express service from Brisbane to Noosa (one way/return $25/46) twice daily.

ⓘ Getting Around

Several companies offer transfers from Sunshine Coast Airport and Brisbane to points along the coast. Fares from Brisbane cost $40 to $50 for adults and $20 to $25 for children. From Sunshine Coast Airport fares are around $15 to $25 per adult and $7 to $12 per child. The following are recommended:

Col's Airport Shuttle (☑07-5450 5933; www.airshuttle.com.au)

Henry's (☑07-5474 0199; www.henrys.com.au)

Noosa Transfers & Charters (☑07-5450 5933; www.noosatransfers.com.au)

Sun-Air Bus Service (☑1800 804 340, 07-5477 0888; www.sunair.com.au)

The blue minibuses run by **Sunbus** (☑13 12 30) buzz frequently between Caloundra and Noosa. Sunbus also has regular buses from Noosa across to the train station at Nambour ($5, one hour) via Eumundi.

TRAIN

Citytrain has services from Nambour to Brisbane ($22, two hours). Trains also go to Beerwah ($12, 1½ hours), near Australia Zoo.

Noosa

POP 9110

Once a little-known surfer hang-out, gorgeous Noosa is now a stylish resort town and one of Queensland's star attractions. Noosa's stunning natural landscape of crystalline beaches and tropical rainforests blends seamlessly with its fashionable boulevard, Hastings St, and the sophisticated beach elite who flock here. On long weekends and school holidays, though, the flock becomes a migration and narrow Hastings St a slow-moving file of traffic.

Despite Noosa's designer boutiques, pricey restaurants and air of exclusivity, the beach and bush are still free, so glammed-up fashionistas simply share the beat with thongs, board shorts and bronzed bikini bods baring their bits.

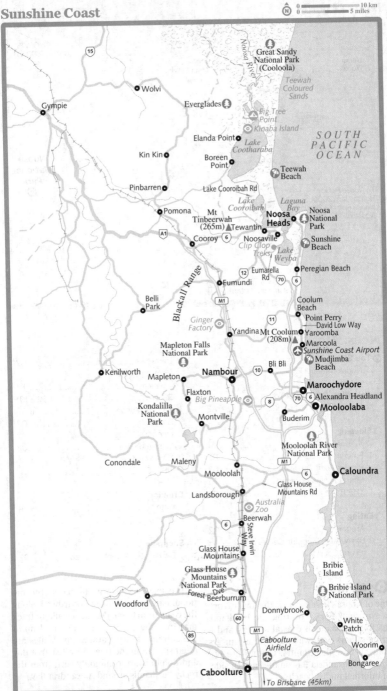

Great Sandy
National Park
(Cooloola)

Teewah
Coloured
Sands

**SOUTH
PACIFIC
OCEAN**

Wolvi

Gympie

15

Everglades

Big Tree
Point

Kinaba Island

Lake
Cootharaba

Elanda Point

Kin Kin

Boreen
Point

Teewah
Beach

Pinbarren

Lake Cooroibah Rd

Lake
Cooroibah

Laguna
Bay

Pomona

Mt
Tinbeerwah
(265m) ▲Tewantin

Noosa
Heads

Noosa
National
Park

A1

Cooroy

6

Noosaville

Clip Clop
Treks

Sunshine
Beach

Belli
Park

Eumundi

Ginger
Factory

Mapleton Falls
National Park

Kenilworth

Mapleton

Nambour

Flaxton

Big Pineapple

Kondalilla
National
Park

Montville

Conondale

Maleny

Mooloolah

Landsborough

Lake
Weyba

Eumarella
Rd

12

70

6

Peregian Beach

Coolum
Beach

11

Point Perry
David Low Way

Yandina Mt Coolum
(208m)

Yaroomba

Marcoola

Sunshine Coast Airport

Mudjimba
Beach

Bli Bli

10

Maroochydore

8

70

6

Alexandra Headland

Mooloolaba

Buderim

Mooloolah River
National Park

M1

6

Caloundra

Glass House
Mountains Rd

QUEENSLAND & THE GREAT BARRIER REEF NOOSA

Australia
Zoo

Beerwah

6

Steve Irwin
Way

Glass House
Mountains

Glass House
Mountains
National Park
Forest Dve
Beerburrum

Woodford

60

Donnybrook

Bribie
Island

Bribie Island
National Park

White
Patch

85

M1

Caboolture
Airfield

Woorim

85

Bongaree

Caboolture

↓To Brisbane (45km)

0 _____ 10 km
0 _____ 5 miles

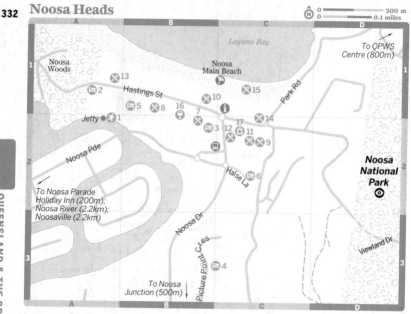

Noosa Heads

Sights

One of Noosa's best features, the lovely **Noosa National Park**, covering the headland, has fine walks, great coastal scenery and a string of bays with waves that draw surfers from all over the country. Clothes are optional at Alexandria Bay on the eastern side, an informal nudist beach.

The most scenic way to access the national park is to follow the boardwalk along the coast from town. Pick up a walking-track map from the **QPWS centre** (☺9am-3pm), at the entrance to the park. Sleepy koalas are often spotted in the trees near Tea Tree Bay and dolphins are commonly seen from the rocky headlands around Alexandria Bay.

For a panoramic view of the park, walk or drive up to **Laguna Lookout** from Viewland Dr in Noosa Junction.

🏃 Activities

Noosa River is excellent for canoeing and kayaking. It's possible to follow it north past beautiful homes through to Lakes Cooroibah and Cootharaba and the Cooloola section of the Great Sandy National Park to just south of Rainbow Beach Rd. **Noosa Ocean Kayak Tours** (☑0418 787 577; www.learntosurf. com; 2hr tours $66, kayak hire per day $55) hires kayaks and offers sea-kayaking tours around Noosa National Park and Noosa River.

For a more sedate experience, hop aboard the **Noosa Ferry** (☑07-5449 8442; per person $20), which cruises the waters of Noosa Sound on its popular BYO sunset cruise. It also has 90-minute round-trip cruises to Tewantin from the Sheraton jetty.

Numerous companies offer surf lessons and board hire, including **Merrick's Learn to Surf** (☑0418 787 577; www.learntosurf. au; 2hr lessons $60), **Go Ride A Wave** (☑1300 132 441; www.gorideawave.com.au; 2hr lessons $60, 2hr surfboard hire $25, 1hr stand-up paddleboard hire $25) and **Noosa Kite Surfing** (☑0458 909 012; www.noosakitesurfing.com.au; 2hr lessons $160).

👉 Tours

A number of tour operators offer trips from Noosa to Fraser Island via the Cooloola Coast.

Fraser Island Adventure Tours   4WD
(☑07-5444 6957; www.fraserislandadventure-tours.com.au; day tours $170) Has won several industry awards for its day tour to Eli Creek and Lake McKenzie and packs as much punch as a two-day tour.

Discovery Group   4WD
(☑07-5449 0393; www.thediscoverygroup.com.au; day tours adult/child $159/115) Visit the island in a big black 4WD truck. Guided rainforest walk at Central Station; visits to Lakes Birrabeen and McKenzie. Also offers day tours exploring the Noosa everglades by 4WD and boat.

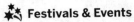
🎉 Festivals & Events

Noosa Food & Wine Festival   FOOD, WINE
(www.noosafoodandwine.com.au) May; a three-day tribute to great eating and drinking.

Noosa Long Weekend   FOOD, FASHION
(www.noosalongweekend.com) June or July; 10 days of fine food, fashion and frivolity.

Noosa Jazz Festival   JAZZ
(www.noosajazz.com.au) Late August; over four days, the festival draws talented musicians from across the globe.

🛏 Sleeping

Most accommodation in Noosa is in self-contained units, although there are several backpacker hostels and caravan parks. Accommodation prices soar around school holidays and Christmas; book ahead at these times.

Accom Noosa (☑1800 072 078; www.accomnoosa.com.au; shop 5, Fairshore Apartments, Hastings St, Noosa Heads) has an extensive list of private holiday rentals that are good for stays of three nights or more.

Islander Noosa Resort   RESORT $$
(☑07-5440 9200; www.islandernoosa.com.au; 187 Gympie Tce, Noosaville; 2-/3-bedroom villas $178/205; ❋@🛜🏊) Set on more than 1.5 hectares of lush tropical gardens, with a central tropical pool and wooden board-walks meandering through the trees to your comfortable bungalow, this resort is excellent value. It's bright and cheerful and packs a cocktail-swilling, island-resort ambience.

Picture Point Terraces   APARTMENTS $$$
(☑07-5449 2433; www.picturepointterraces. com.au; 47 Picture Point Cres, Noosa Heads; 2-/3-bedroom apt from $410/480; ❋@🛜🏊) On high ground behind Noosa, these ultrachic apartments with all the mod cons have fantastic views over the rainforest to Laguna Bay. The private spa bath on the balcony is the ideal spot for a sunset cocktail. There's a seven-night minimum stay in high season.

#2 Hastings St   APARTMENTS $$$
(☑07-5448 0777; www.2hastingsst.com.au; 2 Hastings St, Noosa Heads; units from $225; ❋🛜) These two-bedroom, two-bathroom units at the Noosa Woods end of Hastings St are great value as a four-share. Units overlook the river or the woods, and you're within a short walk of everything. Minimum two-night stay.

EUMUNDI

Sweet little Eumundi is a quaint highland village with a quirky New-Age vibe greatly amplified during its famous market days. The historic streetscape blends well with modern cafes, unique boutiques, silversmiths, crafts people and body artists doing their thing.

The **Eumundi markets** (⊙6.30am-2pm Sat, 8am-1pm Wed) attract thousands of visitors to their 300-plus stalls and have everything from hand-crafted furniture and jewellery to homemade clothes and alternative-healing booths, plus food and live music.

If you'd like to stay the night, **Hidden Valley B&B** (☑07-5442 8685; www.eumundibed. com; 39 Caplick Way; r $175-195; ☎☀) is an attractive Queenslander 400m from Eumundi on the Noosa road, with wildly designed thematic rooms with balconies.

Sunbus runs hourly from Noosa Heads ($3.20, 40 minutes) and Nambour ($4.10, 30 minutes). A number of Noosa tour operators visit the Eumundi markets.

Sheraton Noosa Resort
RESORT $$$

(☑07-5449 4888; www.starwoodhotels.com/ sheraton; 14-16 Hastings St, Noosa Heads; r $255; ☀@☎☀) As expected, this five-star hotel has tastefully decorated rooms with suede fabrics, fabulous beds, balconies, kitchenettes and spas. The hotel houses the popular Cato's cocktail bar as well as a day spa.

YHA Halse Lodge
HOSTEL $

(☑1800 242 567, 07-5447 3377; www.halselodge. com.au; 2 Halse Lane, Noosa Heads; members/ non-members dm $29/32, d $78/86, meals $10-15; @☎) Elevated from Hastings St by a steep driveway, this splendid colonial-era timber Queenslander is a legend on the backpacker route. There are three- and six-bed dorms as well as doubles, and a lovely wide verandah. The bar is a mix-and-meet bonanza and serves great meals.

Emerald
APARTMENTS $$$

(☑1800 803 899, 07-5449 6100; www.emerald noosa.com.au; 42 Hastings St, Noosa Heads; 1-bedroom apt from $255; ☀@☎☀) The stylish Emerald has indulgent rooms bathed in ethereal white and sunlight. Expect clean, crisp edges and exquisite furnishings. All one-, two- and three-bedroom apartments are fully self-contained, but ask for a balcony with a view.

Anchor Motel Noosa
MOTEL $$

(☑07-5449 8055; www.anchormotelnoosa.com.au; cnr Anchor St & Weyba Rd, Noosaville; r from $115; ☀☎☀) There's no escaping the nautical theme in this colourful motel. Blue-striped bedspreads, porthole windows and marine motifs will have you wearing stripes and cutoffs while grilling prawns on the barbie.

Noosa Parade Holiday Inn
APARTMENTS $$

(☑07-5447 4177; www.noosaparadeholidayinn. com; 51 Noosa Pde, Noosa Heads; r $125; ☀☎☀)

Not far from Hastings St, these large, bright apartments are good value. The pleasant and cool interiors are clad in bold colours and face away from the street and passing traffic.

Noosa River Retreat
APARTMENTS $$

(☑07-5474 2811; www.noosariverretreat.net; cnr Weyba Rd & Reef St, Noosaville; studios $110; ☀@☎☀) Your buck goes a long way at this orderly complex, which houses spick, span and spacious units. On site are a central barbecue and a laundry, and the corner units are almost entirely protected by small native gardens.

Nomads Backpackers
HOSTEL $

(☑07-5447 3355; www.nomadshostels.com; 44 Noosa Dr, Noosa Junction; dm from $26; @☎☀) One of the Nomad chain, this hostel has the usual trademarks – popular bar, central location and party atmosphere. You can't get less than an eight-bed dorm, but you'll be partying so hard it won't matter. There's a tour desk on site.

Noosa Backpackers Resort
HOSTEL $

(☑1800 626 673, 07-5449 8151; www.noosaback packers.com; 9-13 William St, Noosaville; dm/d $25/58; @☀) The concrete courtyard that greets you on arrival isn't particularly welcoming, but this is a quiet and pleasant hostel in the backstreets of Noosaville. It's looking decidedly tired, and the six-bed dorms and doubles all have shared bathrooms.

Noosa River Caravan Park
CARAVAN PARK $

(☑07-5449 7050; Russell St, Noosaville; unpowered/powered sites $31/39; ☎) On the banks of the Noosa River, this park has the closest camping facilities to Noosa. Although it's in a pretty spot, the regulations might make you think twice before pitching your tent.

Eating

Noosa has a fabulous dining scene. For quick bites, you can eat well for around $10 at the **Bay Village Shopping Centre food court** (Hastings St, Noosa Heads). Self-caterers can stock up at the Noosa Fair Shopping Centre.

NOOSA HEADS & HASTINGS STREET

Hastings St and the Noosa Heads area is where to head for sophisticated dining.

Berardo's on the Beach MODERN AUSTRALIAN **$$**
(☑07-5448 0888; On the Beach Resort, Hastings St; mains $20-36; ⊘breakfast, lunch & dinner) Reminiscent of the French Riviera, this stylish bistro is only metres from the waves. Classy without being pretentious, this is Noosa in a seashell. The Mod Oz menu uses local produce with a focus on seafood.

Gaston MODERN AUSTRALIAN **$$**
(5/50 Hastings St; mains $17-25; ⊘breakfast, lunch & dinner) This casual alfresco bar and bistro is highly recommended by the locals. It's also a great place to watch the passing parade of beautiful people.

Bistro C MODERN AUSTRALIAN **$$**
(☑07-5447 2855; On the Beach Resort, Hastings St; mains $25-35; ⊘breakfast, lunch & dinner) The menu at this yuppie beachfront brasserie is an eclectic blend of everything that seems like a good idea at the time. The legendary egg-fried calamari is still popular.

Café Le Monde MODERN AUSTRALIAN **$$**
(Hastings St; mains $15-28; ⊘breakfast, lunch & dinner) There's not a fussy palate or dietary need that isn't catered for on Café Le Monde's enormous menu. The large, open-air patio buzzes with diners digging into burgers, seared tuna steaks, curries, pastas, salads and plenty more. Come for daily happy-hour drinks from 4pm to 6pm.

Lindoni's ITALIAN **$$$**
(☑07-5447 5111; Hastings St; mains $20-50; ⊘dinner) Behind the gothic candelabra guarding the entrance, this romantic Italian restaurant has a Mediterranean courtyard for intimate candlelit dining. The cuisine favours the lighter southern Italian style – think Positano and the Amalfi coast – with lashings of *amore*.

Berardo's MODERN AUSTRALIAN **$$$**
(☑07-5447 5666; Hastings St; mains $30-42; ⊘dinner) Beautiful Berardo's is culinary Utopia, from the sun-dappled setting swimming in elegance to the heavenly food. Soft music from the grand piano and delicate dishes made from fresh local produce will have you swooning in gustatory ecstasy.

Aromas CAFE **$$**
(32 Hastings St; mains $10-28; ⊘breakfast, lunch & dinner) This European-style cafe is unashamedly ostentatious, with chandeliers, faux-marble tables and cane chairs deliberately facing the street so patrons can ogle the passing foot traffic. There's the usual array of panini, cakes and light meals, but most folk come for the coffee and the atmosphere.

Noosa Heads SLSC PUB FARE **$$**
(Hastings St; mains $10-28; ⊘breakfast Sat & Sun, lunch & dinner daily) Perfect beach views from the deck.

Massimo's GELATI **$**
(Hastings St; gelati $2-4; ⊘9am-10pm) Definitely one of the best *gelaterias* in Queensland.

NOOSAVILLE

Check out the strip along Thomas St or Gibson St. Many places here are BYO, so stock up on wine and beer beforehand.

Humid MODERN AUSTRALIAN **$$**
(☑07-5449 9755; 195 Weyba Rd; mains $25-30; ⊘lunch & dinner Wed-Sun) It might feel as though you're eating inside a designer warehouse in this high-ceilinged, two-storey restaurant, but the food begs to differ. The Italian influences are subtle and classy and Humid is consistently rated as one of the best restaurants in Noosa.

Wasabi JAPANESE **$$**
(☑07-5449 2443; 2 Quamby Pl; mains $20-33; ⊘dinner Tue-Sun, lunch Fri & Sat) The must-try is this award-winning Japanese restaurant's signature dish, hiramasa ponzu: kingfish sashimi slices on a long glass plank, drizzled with toasted sesame seeds, fried ginger chips, sliced green onions and citrusy soy ponzu dressing.

Red on Thomas FUSION **$$**
(4 Thomas St; mains $15-25; ⊘lunch & dinner Tue-Sun) A popular venue for Noosaville locals, this casual street eatery is always busy. Consistently good food with an emphasis on seafood and pizza and a large selection of cocktails is guaranteed to make anyone happy.

Thomas Corner MODERN AUSTRALIAN **$$**
(cnr Thomas St & Gympie Tce; mains $15-31; ⊘lunch & dinner) A newcomer to Noosaville's 'Eat Street', this casual alfresco restaurant oozes trendy-chic with its rough concrete

floor and concrete and wooden furnishings. The relaxed menu showcases simple dishes without fuss but with style.

Ricky's River Bar & Restaurant
MODERN AUSTRALIAN $$$

(☎07-5447 2455; Noosa Wharf, 2 Quamby Pl; mains $30-40; ☺lunch & dinner) In a perfect location on the Noosa River, this elegant restaurant has a simple, well-executed menu favouring local produce like Noosa spanner-crab spaghettini. The tapas menu is tantalising.

Burger Bar
BURGERS $

(4 Thomas St, Noosaville; burgers $10-15; ☺11am-9pm) This informal and quirky venue whips up hormone-free, vegetarian, and weird and wonderful burgerian delights.

Drinking & Entertainment

Zachary's
BAR

(30 Hastings St, Noosa Heads) This shabby-chic, 2nd-storey 'gourmet pizza bar' is a favourite meeting place and night-starter.

KB's
BAR

(44 Noosa Dr, Noosa Junction) Noosa's backpackers and other free spirits start their nightly revelry at this popular hostel bar. Live rock fills every crevice several nights a week; when it doesn't, the place hums to the harmony of beer jugs and beery banter.

Cato's
COCKTAIL BAR

(Sheraton Noosa Resort, 16 Hastings St, Noosa Heads) As well as a decadent cocktail list, Cato's boasts over 30 wines by the glass. The place can get noisy, especially on Friday nights when live music draws the crowds.

J
THEATRE

(☎07-5455 4455; www.thej.com.au; 60 Noosa Dr, Noosa Junction) The J, aka the Junction, showcases a broad range of artistic, cultural and musical performances from world and rock to classical. Check the website for event details.

Noosa 5 Cinemas
CINEMA

(☎07-5447 5130; www.noosacinemas.com.au; 29 Sunshine Beach Rd, Noosa Junction) This plush, comfortable cinema screens the latest blockbusters.

Shopping

Dwyer's Bookstore
BOOKSTORE

(shop 5, Laguna, Hastings St, Noosa Heads) Good range of new fiction.

ⓘ Information

Noosa has an amazing number of roundabouts and it's easy to get lost. Broadly speaking, Noosa encompasses three zones: Noosa Heads (around Laguna Bay and Hastings St), Noosaville (along the Noosa River) and Noosa Junction (the administrative centre).

Noosa visitor centre (☎07-5430 5020; www.visitnoosa.com.au; Hastings St, Noosa Heads; ☺9am-5pm)

Palm Tree Tours (☎07-5474 9166; www.palmtreetours.com.au; Bay Village Shopping Centre, Hastings St, Noosa Heads; ☺9am-5pm) Very helpful tour desk. Can book tours, accommodation and bus tickets.

Post office (91 Noosa Dr)

Urban Mailbox (Ocean Breeze, Noosa Dr, Noosa Heads; per 15min $3; ☺8am-8pm) Internet access.

ⓘ Getting There & Around

Long-distance buses stop at the bus stop near the corner of Noosa Dr and Noosa Pde; see p367 for fares. Most hostels have courtesy pick-ups, except YHA Halse Lodge, which is 100m away. At the time of research a new transit centre was under construction in Noosa Dr, Noosa Junction. Once completed, long-distance buses will arrive here.

Sunbus (☎13 12 30) has frequent services to Maroochydore ($5, one hour) and the Nambour train station ($5, one hour).

During peak holiday seasons (26 December to 10 January and over Easter), free shuttle buses travel between Weyba Rd, just outside Noosa Junction, to Tewantin, stopping just about everywhere in between.

Noosa Bike Hire (☎07-5474 3322; www.noosabikehire.com; per 4hr/day $23/39) hires bicycles from several locations in Noosa, including Nomads Backpackers. Alternatively, bikes are delivered free to your door.

Scooter Style (☎0404 861 322; www.scooterstyle.com.au; 175 Eumundi Rd, Noosaville; per day from $65) hires out zippy scooters.

Noosa Ferry (☎07-5449 8442) operates ferries between Noosa Heads and Tewantin (one way adult/child/family $13/4.50/30, all-day pass $19.50/5.50/45, 30 minutes).

Car rental starts at about $60 per day: **Avis** (☎07-5447 4933; shop 1, Ocean Breeze Resort, cnr Hastings St & Noosa Dr, Noosa Heads), **Budget** (☎07-5474 2820; 52 Mary St, Noosaville).

CREATURE FEATURE: AUSTRALIA ZOO

Just north of Beerwah is one of Queensland's, if not Australia's, most famous tourist attractions. **Australia Zoo** (📞07-5494 1134; www.australiazoo.com.au; Steve Irwin Way, Beerwah; adult/child/family $49/29/146; ⊗9am-4.30pm) is a fitting homage to its founder, zany celebrity wildlife enthusiast Steve Irwin. As well as all things slimy and scaly the zoo has an amazing wildlife menagerie complete with a Cambodian-style Tiger Temple, the Asian-themed Elephantasia, as well as the famous Crocoseum. There are macaws, birds of prey, giant tortoises, snakes, otters, camels, and more crocs and critters than you can poke a stick at. Plan to spend a full day at this amazing wildlife park.

Various companies offer tours from Brisbane and the Sunshine Coast. The zoo operates a free courtesy bus from towns along the coast, as well as from the Beerwah train station (bookings essential).

Glass House Mountains

Rising high above the green subtropical hinterland are the 16 volcanic crags known as the Glass House Mountains. Mt Beerwah (556m), the highest of these ethereal cornices, is the mother according to Dreamtime mythology. These stunning natural formations lend an eerie otherworldliness to a region brimming with life.

Reach the Glass House Mountains National Park via a series of sealed and unsealed roads off Steve Irwin Way. Coming from the Bruce Hwy (Rte 1), take the Landsborough exit.

Hikers are spoilt for choice here. If you're in a hurry, the **Glass House Mountains lookout** provides a fine view of the peaks and the distant beaches. The **lookout circuit** (800m) is a short and steep walking track that leads through open scribbly-gum forest and down a wet gully before circling back.

For something more intense, check out the 1.4km (return) hike to the summit of **Mt Ngungun** (253m). It has impressive views of the four major peaks and a bit of challenging hiking – keep the kids close as the steep trail passes close to the cliff line and can be slippery.

For some mountainside parkour, otherwise known as 'bouldering', leg it up **Tibrogargan** (3km return) and **Beerwah** (closed until further notice); you'll need good shoes and leg muscles to spring up the patches of loose rock.

Accommodation in the park is limited. **Glasshouse Mountains Holiday Village** (📞07-5496 9338; www.glasshousemountainsholidayvillage.com.au; 778 Steve Irwin Way, Glass House Mountains; unpowered/powered sites $25/35, cabins from $110; ✳✳) has comfortable, self-contained cabins, pretty sites and spectacular mountain views.

The fine country swill hall at **Glasshouse Mountains Tavern** (10 Reed St, Glass House Mountains; mains $15-25; ⊗lunch & dinner) serves good pub grub and icy-cold glasses of beer. Visiting in winter? Take your red wine and beef sausages by the fireplace.

Caloundra

POP 20,200

The Sunshine Coast's southernmost suburb is a sprawling beach community of seven surf beaches linked up by a fine promenade running north to Currimundi. With loads of beachfront cafes – and a grand backdrop of the Glass House Mountains – Caloundra makes an ideal base for beach-loving families and those wanting to keep life pretty simple.

👁 Sights & Activities

Caloundra's beaches curve around the headland so you'll always find a sheltered beach no matter how windy it gets. **Bulcock Beach**, just down from the main street and pinched by the northern tip of Bribie Island, captures a good wind tunnel, making it popular with kite surfers. There's a lovely promenade on the foreshore that extends around to **Kings Beach**, where there's a kiddie-friendly interactive water feature, and a free saltwater swimming pool on the rocks. Depending on the conditions, **Moffat Beach** and **Dickey Beach** have the best surf breaks.

Q Surf School (📞0404 869 622; www.qsurfschool.com; 1hr lessons $45, 3 lessons $120) offers surf lessons plus stand-up paddleboarding (one-hour lessons $55).

Blue Water Kayak Tours (📞07-5494 7789; www.bluewaterkayaktours.com; half/full-day tours minimum 4 people $75/150) runs an excellent

day trip for active souls to the northern tip of Bribie Island.

Caloundra Cruise (☎07-5492 8280; www.caloundracruise.com; adult/child/family $20/10/45) has a great 2½-hour eco-explorer cruise through the Pumicestone Passage.

Get a flightless bird's-eye view of Caloundra with the popular **Sunshine Coast Skydivers** (☎07-5437 0211; www.sunshinecoastskydivers.com.au; Caloundra Aerodrome; tandem jumps from $220).

🛏 Sleeping

There's often a minimum three- to five-night stay in high season.

Rolling Surf Resort APARTMENTS **$$$**
(☎07-5491 9777; www.rollingsurfresort.com; Levuka Ave, Kings Beach; 1-/2-bedroom apt $240/400; ❀@☎☎) This ultrachic resort directly on the beach has *très* modern furnishings, fantastic views and a heated pool.

City Centre Motel MOTEL **$$**
(☎07-5491 3301; 20 Orsovar Tce; d $100-119; ❀) The closest motel to the city centre holds no surprises, but it's a small complex and the rooms, although basic, are comfortable.

Caloundra Backpackers HOSTEL **$**
(☎07-5499 7655; www.caloundrabackpackers.com.au; 84 Omrah Ave; dm/d $28/65; @☎) A newcomer to Caloundra, the dorms here are adequate, there's a comfy lounge and two decent kitchens. Plus you get free bike, surfboard, and stand-up paddleboard hire.

Dicky Beach Family Holiday Park CARAVAN PARK **$**
(☎07-5491 3342; www.dicky.com.au; 4 Beerburrum St; unpowered/powered sites $32/35, cabins from $90; ❀☎☎) You can't get any closer to one of Caloundra's most popular beaches. The brick cabins are as ordered and tidy as the grounds and there's a small swimming pool for the kids.

Belaire Place APARTMENTS **$$**
(☎07-5491 8688; www.belaireplace.com; 34 Minchinton St; apt from $175; ❀☎☎) Overlooking Bulcock Beach, these spacious, one-bedroom apartments might have poky design, but you can watch the action on the beach from the large balcony. It's walking distance to the beach, cafes and restaurants.

✕ Eating & Drinking

The newly spruced up Bulcock Beach esplanade has a number of alfresco cafes and restaurants, all with perfect sea views.

Saltwater@Kings CAFE **$$**
(☎07-5437 2260; 8 Levuka Ave, Kings Beach; mains $16-35; ☺breakfast, lunch & dinner) The playful menu at this casual beachside cafe promises nude oysters, spiced chook salad and a range of 'voluptuous dishes'. Perfect for lunch straight off the beach.

La Dolce Vita ITALIAN **$$**
(☎07-5438 2377; shop 1, Rumba Resort, Esplanade, Bulcock Beach; mains $20-35; ☺breakfast, lunch & dinner) This modern Italian restaurant has a stylish black-and-white theme, but it's best to sit outdoors behind the large glass-windowed booth for alfresco dining with gorgeous sea views.

Tides SEAFOOD **$$$**
(☎07-5438 2304; 26 Esplanade, Bulcock Beach; mains $35-50; ☺lunch & dinner) For fine dining, exquisite seafood and stunning views of the Pumicestone Passage treat yourself to Tides. The non-fishy dishes are just as tempting as Neptune's bounty.

Chilli Jam Cafè CAFE **$**
(51 Bulcock St; mains $8-14; ☺breakfast & lunch) A friendly couple from Yorkshire runs this popular cafe where you can devour a range of gourmet sandwiches, wraps, salads and burgers.

CBX PUB
(12 Bulcock St) CBX works like a stock exchange, with beer prices rising and falling depending on demand. Live bands and DJs on weekends make this the local party scene.

❶ Information

Sunshine Coast visitor centre (☎07-5478 2233; 7 Caloundra Rd; ☺9am-5pm) On the roundabout at the entrance to the town. There's also a kiosk in the main street.

❶ Getting There & Away

The **bus terminal** (Cooma Tce) is one block back from Bulcock Beach. **Sunbus** (☎13 12 30) runs shuttles to Noosa ($6.70, 1½ hours) that stop in Maroochydore ($3.70, 50 minutes). **Greyhound** (☎1300 473 946; www.greyhound.com.au) has buses to/from Brisbane ($32, two hours).

Maroochy

POP 47,000

The Sunshine Coast suburbs of Maroochydore, Alexandra Headland and Mooloolaba, collectively known as Maroochy, were once bastions of the Australian surfing scene,

but these days their coastal charm is giving way to a steady suburban sprawl. The beaches themselves are still captivating, and the buzz in the ocean-front shops and cafes makes the district of Maroochy a reliable summer getaway. Try Cotton Tree Beach for a more chilled-out beach break, or wander inland to the ginger 'hood of Buderim for a taste of the 1950s.

Maroochydore takes its name from the local Aboriginal word, *murukutchi-da*, meaning 'home of the black swan'.

◉ Sights & Activities

Mooloolaba is perhaps the hippest of the bunch, having the longest beaches, the most consistent surf and a plethora of cafes, shops and colourful rental houses. If the surf's up, kiddies will find relatively calm water at the Spit at the southern end of the beach.

Swim with sloppy-kissing seals, dive with sharks and psyche out psychedelic fish at Underwater World (Wharf, Mooloolaba; www.underwaterworld.com.au; adult/child/family $32/22/90; ⊘9am-5pm), Queensland's largest oceanarium. The adjoining Scuba World (⏰07-5444 8595; www.scubaworld.com.au; Wharf, Mooloolaba; dives from $99; ⊘9am-5pm Mon-Sat, 10.30am-4pm Sun) arranges shark dives (certified/uncertified divers $195/225) at Underwater World, coral dives off the coast and a wreck dive of the ex-HMAS *Brisbane*. Professional Association of Diving Instructors (PADI) courses available.

The Aussie Sea Kayak Company (⏰0407 049 747; www.ausseakayak.com.au; Wharf, Mooloolaba; 4hr tours $65, 2hr sunset paddles $45) goes kayaking around Mooloolaba and the Noosa everglades, and arranges multiday trips to North Stradbroke, Fraser and Moreton Islands.

For those who can't make it north to Hervey Bay, Steve Irwin's Whale One (⏰1300 274 539; www.whaleone.com.au; adult/child/family $135/75/330) runs whale-watching cruises in September and October.

Pin Cushion, near the mouth of the Maroochy River, is probably the top **surfbreak** in this excellent stretch for surfing, but most visitors head to the more easily accessed Maroochy and Memorial Ave. For the inexperienced, Robbie Sherwell's XL Surfing Academy (⏰07-5478 1337; www.robbiesherwell.com.au; 1hr lessons private/group $95/45) runs popular introductory lessons.

Sunshine Coast Bike & Board Hire (⏰0439 706 206; www.adventurehire.com.au)

hires surfboards (per day $25), bikes (per day $30) and kayaks (per day $40).

Hire Hut (⏰07-5444 0366; www.oceanjetski.com.au; Wharf, Parkyn Pde, Mooloolaba) hires out kayaks ($25 per two hours), stand-up paddleboards ($35 per two hours), jet skis ($100 per hour) and boats ($42/75 per hour/half-day).

🛏 Sleeping

Landmark Resort RESORT **$$**
(⏰07-5444 5555; www.landmarkresort.com.au; cnr Esplanade & Burnett St, Mooloolaba; studios/1-bedroom apt from $175/195; ❄@⊛🌊) Nothing compares to the ocean views from these breezy apartments. The resort sits above Mooloolaba's trendy eateries and is only 20m from the beach. There's a heated lagoon-style pool, and a rooftop spa and barbecue.

Seamark on First APARTMENTS **$$**
(⏰07-5457 8600; www.seamarkresort.com.au; 29 First Ave, Mooloolaba; 1-bedroom apt from $180; ❄⊛🌊) One street back from Mooloolaba's fashionable Esplanade, this stylish and modern resort is bright, airy and spacious. Most apartments have ocean views and balconies.

Kyamaba Court Motel MOTEL **$$**
(⏰07-5444 0202; www.kyambacourtmotel.com.au; 94 Brisbane Rd, Mooloolaba; d Mon-Fri $95, Sat $130; ❄⊛🌊) Although this motel is on a busy road, it also fronts the canal and has large, comfortable rooms. It's a short walk into town and to the beach. Great value.

Coral Sea Apartments APARTMENTS **$$**
(⏰07-5479 2999; www.coralsea-apartments.com; 35-7 Sixth Ave, Maroochydore; 1-/2-bedroom apt from $160/190; ❄@🌊) These tastefully furnished apartments with balconies occupy a lovely spot close to Maroochy Surf Club and the beach.

Mooloolaba Beach Backpackers HOSTEL **$**
(⏰07-5444 3399; www.mooloolababackpackers.com; 75 Brisbane Rd, Mooloolaba, dm/d $28/70; @⊛🌊) The rooms look a bit tired, but loads of freebies (bikes, kayaks, surfboards, stand-up paddleboards and breakfast) more than compensate. It's only 500m from the beach and nightlife.

Cotton Tree Beach House Backpackers HOSTEL **$**
(⏰07-5443 1755; www.cottontreebackpackers.com; 15 Esplanade, Cotton Tree; dm/d $26/55) The vibe is warm and the atmosphere laid-back at this century-old Queenslander opposite a park and a river. Free surfboards, kayaks and bikes.

Cotton Tree Caravan Park CARAVAN PARK $
(☑07-5443 1253; www.maroochypark.qld.gov.au;
Cotton Tree Pde, Cotton Tree; unpowered/powered
sites from $25/28, cabins $125-160) Right on
the beach at the mouth of the Maroochy
River, this place gets packed in summer.

**Mooloolaba Beach Caravan
Park** CARAVAN PARK $
(☑07-5444 1201; www.maroochypark.qld.gov.au;
Parkyn Pde, Mooloolaba; powered sites from $35)
This little beauty fronts lovely Mooloolaba
Beach.

Eating

Bella Venezia ITALIAN $$$
(☑07-5444 5844; 95 Esplanade, Mooloolaba; mains
$25-38; ⊙lunch & dinner) This understated yet
casually chic restaurant with a funky wine
bar spreads across an arcade cul-de-sac. The
menu is extensive, and exclusively Italian,
with exquisite dishes such as Moreton Bay
bug ravioli.

Boat Shed SEAFOOD $$
(☑07-5443 3808; Esplanade, Cotton Tree; mains
$25-35; ⊙lunch daily, dinner Mon-Sat) A shabby-
chic gem on the banks of the Maroochy
River, great for sunset drinks beneath the
sprawling cotton tree. Seafood is the star
of the menu and a must-try is the coconut-
battered prawns with roasted banana and
caramelised rum syrup.

India Today INDIAN $$
(☑07-5452 7054; 91 Aerodrome Rd, Maroochydore;
mains $15-22; ⊙lunch Thu-Sat, dinner nightly) You
can't miss the masses of fairy lights deco-
rating this restaurant on Maroochydore's
main drag. Be prepared for the brightly and
chaotically coloured visual feast of Indian
cloths, textiles, paintings and wall hangings
waiting inside.

Nude CAFE $
(shop 3, Mooloolaba Esplanade, Mooloolaba; dishes
$6-18; ⊙breakfast & lunch) Occupying the prime
position on the Esplanade, this casual alfres-
co cafe is the ideal spot for people-watching,
and for ocean views with your latte. Salads,
wraps, gourmet sandwiches and cakes will
satisfy post-swimming munchies.

Karma Waters MODERN AUSTRALIAN $$
(Mantra, Esplanade, Mooloolaba; mains $21-32;
⊙breakfast, lunch & dinner) Another outdoor
eatery along the lively Esplanade, Karma
Waters dishes up Mod Oz cuisine with a Portuguese influence. Try the seared Atlantic
salmon with lemon caper butter sauce.

Raw Energy CAFE $
(Mantra, Esplanade, Mooloolaba; dishes $6-18;
⊙breakfast & lunch) In this popular beachside
cafe pretty young things serve up tofu, tem-
peh and gluten-free with 'zinger' juices. Muffin addicts will think they've found The One.

Drinking & Entertainment

Mooloolaba SLSC SURF CLUB
(Esplanade, Mooloolaba; ⊙10am-10pm Sun-Thu,
to midnight Fri & Sat) Right on the beach,
Mooloolaba's iconic surf club has floor-to-
ceiling windows affording stunning views
during the day and suntanned dance-floor
antics by night.

Fridays NIGHTCLUB
(Wharf, Parkyn Pde, Mooloolaba; ⊙Tue-Sat) It's
loud, tacky and incredibly popular with
backpackers and locals.

❶ Information

Sunshine Coast visitor information centre
(☑1800 644 969; www.maroochytourism.com;
⊙9am-5pm) Maroochydore (cnr Sixth Ave &
Melrose St, Maroochydore); Mooloolaba (cnr
Brisbane Rd & First Ave, Mooloolaba); Sunshine
Coast Airport (Friendship Dr, Marcoola)

❶ Getting There & Around

Long-distance buses stop in front of Maroochydore's **Sunshine Coast visitor information centre** (cnr Sixth Ave & Melrose St). **Sunbus** (☑13 12
30) has frequent services between Mooloolaba
and Maroochydore ($2) and on to Noosa. The
local bus interchange is at the Sunshine Plaza.

Around Maroochy

Coolum Beach and **Peregian Beach** are
both favourites with local surfers when
there's good swell. **Point Perry** is a wonderful vantage point for that quintessential
Aussie summer snap, while intrepid photographers (and anyone else for that matter)
can climb **Mt Coolum** (208m) for bird's-eye
vistas. Get details at the **visitor information
office** (David Low Way; ⊙9am-5pm Mon-Fri, 10am-
4pm Sat) – look for it off the main drag from
Maroochy towards Coolum and Peregian.

In Coolum, **Villa Coolum** (☑07-5446 1286;
www.villacoolum.com; 102 Coolum Tce, Coolum
Beach; r $79-99; ❄) has spacious motel-style
rooms fronting a long balcony.

On Peregian Beach, the best sleeping
bet is the crisp, clean and spacious **Pacific
Blue Apartments** (☑07-5448 3611; www.

pacificblueapartments.com.au; 236 David Low Way, Peregian Beach; apt from $130; ☀).

Just across the road from Coolum's main strip, **Coolum Beach Caravan Park** (☎1800 461 474; David Low Way, Coolum; unpowered/powered sites $32/35) is beachfront and basic.

For dinner, come to **My Place** (☎07-5446 4433; David Low Way, Coolum; mains $17-25; ☉7am-11pm) for the ocean views, cocktails and Mediterranean cuisine.

Cooloola Coast

Running from its southern tip at Noosa to Rainbow Beach in the north is 50km of gloriously undeveloped Cooloola Coast. Wildlife abounds, but a fair amount of 4WD through traffic means your starry nights are not always spent in silence.

Nevertheless, travelling north here is a real buzz, as you forgo the bitumen for low tidal highways, passing the Teewah Coloured Sands and the wreck of the *Cherry Venture*, swept ashore in 1973.

LAKE COOROIBAH

Where the Noosa River widens into the wondrous Lake Cooroibah, you'll find surprisingly thick bushland – a popular base for engaging with the natural environment.

Lake Cooroibah is about 2km north of Tewantin. From the end of Moorindil St in Tewantin, you can catch the **Noosa North Shore Ferry** (☎07-5447 1321; per pedestrian/car one way $1/6; ☉5.30am-10.20pm Sun-Thu, 5am-12.20am Fri & Sat) up to the lake in a conventional vehicle and camp along sections of the beach.

The refreshingly feral **Gagaju Backpackers** (☎1300 302 271, 07-5474 3522; www.travoholic.com/gagaju; 118 Johns Dr, Tewantin; unpowered sites/dm $10/15; @) is a riverside eco-wilderness camp with basic dorms constructed out of recycled timber. There's a somewhat hands-off managerial approach, unless a good party is involved! Don't forget to bring food and mozzie repellent. A courtesy shuttle runs to and from Noosa twice a day.

A touch more luxury is found at the **Noosa North Shore Retreat** (☎07-5447 1225; www.noosanorthshoreretreat.com.au; Beach Rd; unpowered/powered sites from $15/24, r from $145, cabins from $65; ✳@☀). Choose from a tent or a shiny motel room, then break up your day with stints paddling around the lake, bushwalking or tracking marsupials. There's also a **pub** (mains $10-20; ☉lunch & dinner).

LAKE COOTHARABA

A little further northwest of Tewantin is Lake Cootharaba, the gateway to the Noosa everglades, offering bushwalking, canoeing and bush camping. This pretty water reserve is some 10km long and 5km across. A good entry to the lake is at **Boreen Point**, a relaxed little community with several places to stay and to eat.

Kanu Kapers (☎07-5485 3328; www.kanukapersaustralia.com; 11 Toolara St, Boreen Point; kayak hire per day $65) offers guided or self-guided kayaking trips (per person $145, overnight trip $145) into the everglades.

Cooloola Adventures (☎07-5485 3164; www.cooloolaadventures.com.au; 20 Boreen Point Pde, Boreen Point; canoe hire per day per person $99, 3-day camping safaris $139) hires out canoes and kayaks for self-guided trips. The company also operates a water taxi to Kinaba (one way/return $15/30).

The two self-contained units at **Lake Cootharaba Gallery Units** (☎07-5485 3153; 64 Laguna St, Boreen Point; r from $99) are homey and practical.

On the river, the quiet and simple **Boreen Point Camping Ground** (☎07-5485 3244; Dun's Beach, Teewah St, Boreen Point; unpowered/powered sites $15/22) is dominated by large gums and native bush.

Apollonian Hotel (☎07-5485 3100; Laguna St, Boreen Point; mains $10-24; ☉lunch & dinner) is a gorgeous old pub with sturdy timber walls, shady verandahs and a beautifully preserved interior. The pub grub is tasty and popular. Come for the famous Sunday spit-roast lunch.

From Boreen Point, an unsealed road leads another 5km up to **Elanda Point**.

GREAT SANDY NATIONAL PARK (COOLOOLA)

This 54,000-hectare national park stretching east and north of the lakes sports a varied wilderness of mangroves, forest and heathland that is traversed by the Noosa River. It's great fun to explore the region with a 4WD (available in Noosa) and you can drive through the park all the way to Rainbow Beach to the north. Other activity options include kayaking and some fantastic walking trails starting from Elanda Point on the shore of Lake Cootharaba, including the 46km Cooloola Wilderness Trail to Rainbow Beach and a 7km trail to an unstaffed QPWS information centre at Kinaba.

Before you go, pop into the **QPWS Great Sandy Information Centre** (☎07-5449 7792;

240 Moorindil St, Tewantin; ⊘8am-4pm), which can provide information on park access, tide times and fire bans within the park. The centre issues car and camping permits for both Fraser Island and Great Sandy National Park, but these are best booked online (www.derm.qld.gov.au).

The park has a number of camping grounds, many of them along the river. The most popular (and best-equipped) camping grounds are Fig Tree Point (at the northern end of Lake Cootharaba), Harry's Hut (about 4km upstream) and Freshwater (about 6km south of Double Island Point) on the coast. You can also camp (per person/family $5.15/20.60) at designated zones on the beach if you're driving up to Rainbow Beach. Apart from Harry's Hut, Freshwater, and Tee-wah Beach, all sites are accessible by hiking or river only.

Sunshine Coast Hinterland

Inland from Nambour, the Blackall Range creates a scenic hinterland with rather chintzy rustic villages. The scenic Mapleton–Maleny road runs along the ridge of the range, past rainforests at Mapleton Falls National Park, 4km northwest of Mapleton. You can now walk all the way to the bottom of the falls – well worth it for a spectacularly refreshing swim.

Kondalilla National Park is 3km northwest of Montville. Both Mapleton and Kondalilla waterfalls plunge more than 80m, and their lookouts offer wonderful forest views.

The largest town in the region is Maleny, a green and scenic mountain town famous for its bohemian spirit. The Maleny Lodge Guest House (☑07-5494 2370; www.maleny lodge.com; 58 Maple St; s/d from $155/180; 🖥🕮) is a super-charming B&B.

For a memorable meal, visit the Up Front Club (☑07-5494 2592; 31 Main St; dishes $10-20;

⊘breakfast, lunch & dinner), with organic fare and live music on weekends.

Gourmet travellers should try the Terrace (☑07-5494 3700; cnr Mountain View Rd & Landsborough Hwy; mains $26-50) for award-winning seafood and views of the Glass House Mountains.

Midway between Mapleton and Maleny is Montville, a dinky trinket town popular with short-term visitors escaping the steamy coast. There's an antique-clock emporium, candy-making display centre, cafes, pubs and a contender for 'best view from a car park'. The area is brimming with B&Bs – ask the information centre (☑07-5478 5544; 198 Main St; ⊘10am-4pm) for up-to-date listings and vacancies. Particularly magical is Secrets on the Lake (☑07-5478 5888; www.secretsonthelake.com.au; 207 Narrows Rd; midweek/weekend from $200/250; 🖥) a handcrafted tree-house kingdom.

A little further west through the Blackall Ranges is Kenilworth, a friendly 'outdoorsy' village in the Mary River Valley.

DARLING DOWNS

Queensland's breadbasket is a rich pastoral tapestry of rolling greens and grainy hues that make a relaxing detour from the coast. The lush and picturesque countryside of the Granite Belt supports an up-and-coming wine region and a thriving fruit industry (ably supported by young itinerant workers). The dramatic boulder-and-bush landscapes of Girraween and Sundown National Parks attract walkers and wildflower hunters alike, while the stately city of Toowoomba is famed for its gardens.

Further north, the Bunya Mountains National Park is filled with high-altitude pines and prehistoric grasses that skirt the Great Dividing Range. Inland, huge sheep and cotton farms run west into the outback, where you can leave your ride in the highest gear and roll out into the great unknown.

NEW YEAR'S MUSIC AT WOODFORD

The famous Woodford Folk Festival (www.woodfordfolkfestival.com) features a huge diversity of over 2000 national and international performers playing folk, traditional Irish, indigenous and world music, as well as buskers, belly dancers, craft markets, visual-arts performances, environmental talks and a visiting squad of Tibetan monks. The festival is held on a property near the town of Woodford from 27 December to 1 January each year. Camping grounds are set up on the property but be prepared for a mud bath if it rains.

Woodford is 35km northwest of Caboolture. Shuttle buses run regularly from the Caboolture train station to and from the festival grounds.

🛈 Getting There & Away

Greyhound Australia (☑1300 473 946; www.greyhound.com.au) has connections from Brisbane to Toowoomba ($25, two hours), Roma ($80, eight hours) and Stanthorpe ($80, 4½ hours).

Crisps' Coaches (☑07-4661 8333; www.crisps.com.au) is the biggest local operator, offering services from Brisbane to Stanthorpe ($60, 3½ hours).

The **Queensland Rail** (☑13 22 32, 1300 131 722; www.traveltrain.com.au) *Westlander* runs twice weekly from Brisbane to Charleville (economy seat/sleeper $127/166, 17 hours) on Tuesday and Thursday, returning on Wednesday and Friday, stopping in Toowoomba (from $33, four hours) and Roma (economy seat/sleeper $106/155, 11 hours).

Stanthorpe

POP 4300

Queensland's coolest town (literally), at an altitude of 915m, Stanthorpe has a distinct four-season climate. It's a popular winter retreat where normally sweltering Queenslanders can cosy up in front of a fire or enjoy a fine red from one of the more than 50 boutique wineries in the region.

The annual **Brass Monkey Festival** is celebrated here from June to August with a parade of music events and food fiestas in town and at various wineries.

If you yawn at the whiff of a Chardonnay or Shiraz, perhaps the **Strange Bird Alternative Wine Trail** will sing a more palatable tune. Sample Tempranillo, Barbera, Viognier and other grapes more suited to the intense Granite Belt climate. Maps are available at the visitor centre, or check out www.granitebeltwinecountry.com.au.

Located 17km south of Stanthorpe, **Girraween National Park** is home to towering granite boulders, pristine forests and brilliant blooms of springtime wildflowers. There are a number of good trails here. The shortest path is a 3km walk and scramble up the 1080m Pyramids, while the granddaddy of Girraween walks is the 10.4km trek to the top of Mt Norman (1267m).

🛏 Sleeping

TOP CHOICE Happy Valley   CABINS **$$**
(☑07-4681 1370; www.happyvalleyretreat.com; Glenlyon Dr; cabins midweek $170, weekend $190-230) Some 4km west of Stanthorpe (signposted off the Texas road), this fine complex offers secluded, beautifully sited timber cabins, all

with wood fires and verandahs. There's a good restaurant.

Diamondvale B&B Cottages   B&B **$$**
(☑07-4681 3367; www.diamondvalecottages.com.au; 26 Diamondvale Rd; d from $180; 🐾) In a bucolic setting of bushland outside of Stanthorpe, Diamondvale is a friendly place with four lovely cottages, each with charming old-fashioned details. You can follow the creek 2km and stroll into town.

Murray Gardens   MOTEL, CABINS **$$**
(☑07-4681 4121; www.murraygardens.com.au; 10 Pancor Rd; motel r $80-120, cottages $120-240; ❄🐾) This good-value option is set on eight hectares of natural bushland on the outskirts of town. You can choose between a motel room or a fully self-contained cottage with a fireplace or gas heating. Except for the bird life, it's very quiet.

Country Style   CABINS, CAMPGROUND **$**
(☑07-4683 4358; www.countrystyleaccommodation.com.au; 27156 New England Hwy; campsites/caravan sites/cabins $20/25/90; @) Amid five hectares of bushland, Country Style has basic motel-style cabins with small kitchens and wood-burning fires. Peaceful, unpowered campsites overlook the Severn River. It's on the highway to Ballandean, 10km south of Stanthorpe.

Briar Rose Cottages   INN **$**
(☑07-4683 6334; www.briarrosecottages.com.au; 66 Wallangarra Rd; d Sun-Thu $95, Fri & Sat $110) These cute cottages are small in size but big on romance.

Girraween Environmental Lodge   CABINS **$$$**
(☑07-4684 5138; www.girraweenlodge.com.au; Pyramids Rd, Ballandean; cabins $260) An eco-friendly bushland retreat set on 162 hectares adjacent to the national park. There's an outdoor spa and plunge pool.

Girraween Country Inn   GUESTHOUSE **$$**
(☑07-4683 7109; www.girraweencountryinn.com.au; Eukey Rd; d incl breakfast from $115) A two-storey, chalet-style guesthouse with a welcoming restaurant downstairs and eight attractive guest rooms upstairs.

🍽 Eating

Shiraz   MODERN AUSTRALIAN **$$**
(☑07-4684 1000; 28200 New England Hwy, Ballandean; mains $33-35; ⏱lunch & dinner Wed-Sun) The menu is small but features exquisitely turned-out fare – black Angus rib fillet, rack of lamb and mouth-watering scallops. It's on

TOP VINEYARDS & GRANITE BELT DELICACIES

With dozens of wineries offering free tastings, you could easily spend a week or more sampling the great fruits of the region – and still just scratch the surface. All of the following are on the free map available at the tourist office.

» **Ravens Croft** (www.ravenscroftwines.com.au; 274 Spring Creek Rd, Stanthorpe; ⊗10.30am-4.30pm Fri-Sun Sep-Jan, Wed-Sun Feb-Aug) With its own resident koala ('Blinky') in the bush out back.

» **Ballandean** (www.ballandeanestate.com; Sundown Rd, Ballandean; ⊗9am-5pm) One of Queensland's oldest wineries, with free winery tours (11am, 1pm and 3pm) and a good restaurant.

» **Pyramids Road** (www.pyramidsroad.com.au; Pyramids Rd, Wyberba; ⊗10am-4.30pm) On the road to Girraween National Park.

» **Robert Channon** (www.robertchannonwines.com.au; 32 Bradley Lane, Stanthorpe; ⊗11am-4pm) Trophy-winning wines and a fine lunch restaurant with lake views.

» **Felsberg Winery** (www.felsberg.com.au; 116 Townsend Rd, Glen Aplin; ⊗9.30am-4.30pm) A hilltop Bavarian-style chalet with views; the restaurant serves seasonal fare (lunch daily, dinner Fridays and Saturdays).

» **Granite Belt Dairy Farmhouse** (cnr Amiens Rd & Duncan Lane, Thulimbah; ⊗10am-4pm) What's wine without cheese? It's all available for sampling, plus there are fantastic milkshakes, cheesecake, breads, chutneys and other picnic fare.

» **Heavenly Chocolate** (2117 Pyramids Rd, Wyberba; ⊗10am-4pm Fri-Mon) Decadent handmade chocolates and fudge – plus 21 different creamy hot chocolates.

» **Bramble Patch** (www.bramblepatch.com.au; 381 Townsend Rd, Glen Aplin; ⊗10am-4pm) Berry grower worth visiting for the ice cream with homemade berry compote, waffles with berries and fresh fruits (November to April).

the highway just north of Ballandean, opposite the dinosaur statue.

Patty's on McGregor MODERN AUSTRALIAN $$
(⊘07-4681 3463; 2 McGregor Tce; mains $28-36; ⊗dinner Thu-Sat) Patty's serves a changing selection of beautifully prepared dishes with Eastern accents. Candlelit tables and artwork on the walls set the scene inside the cosy dining room.

Queensland College of Wine Tourism MODERN AUSTRALIAN $$
(⊘07-4685 5050; cnr New England Hwy & Caves Rd; mains $15-34; ⊗10am-3pm Tue-Sun) The elegant Cellar Door Bistro features the delectable handiwork of student chefs at the college. The multi-course tasting menu ($38) is great value. Floor-to-ceiling windows overlook the vineyard.

Barrel Room MODERN AUSTRALIAN $$
(⊘07-4684 1326; Ballandean Estate Wines, Sundown Rd, Ballandean; mains $18-29; ⊗10am-4pm Wed-Mon, 6-8pm Fri & Sat) This cosy restaurant, framed by 140-year-old floor-to-ceiling wine barrels, makes a fine setting for a decadent meal and a bottle of the winery's excellent vintage.

Anna's Restaurant ITALIAN $$
(⊘07-4681 1265; cnr Wallangarra Rd & O'Mara Tce; mains $19-33; ⊗dinner Tue-Sat) A family-run Italian BYO restaurant set in a pretty Queenslander, Anna's is famous locally for its weekend buffets ($30 to $35).

Toowoomba

POP 129,000

It might sound like it belongs in the middle of nowhere, but Toowoomba (meaning 'reeds in the swamp') is a provincial town just 128km west of Brisbane. Queensland's largest inland city dangles on the edge of a plateau of the Great Dividing Range, some 700m above breathtaking Lockyer Valley. The cooler climate produces an array of dazzling gardens, which are celebrated with particular fervour during the fabulous **Carnival of Flowers** (www.tcof.com.au) in September.

◉ Sights

The ever-expanding **Cobb & Co Museum** (27 Lindsay St; adult/child $13/7; ⊗10am-4pm) is more than a collection of carriages and

traps from the horse-drawn age; it's also a showcase for Toowoomba's Indigenous and multicultural communities, and includes a children's play area. Queen's Park (cnr Lindsay & Campbell Sts) houses the botanic gardens, although some might prefer the beautiful Ju Raku En Japanese Garden (West St; ⊙7am-dusk), with its Zen-like beauty.

Picnic Point, on the eastern outskirts of town, offers outstanding views over the Lockyer Valley. There's a cafe and restaurant (⊙breakfast & lunch daily, dinner Fri & Sat) and a walking trail.

Sleeping

Book well ahead if visiting during September's Carnival of Flowers festival.

TOP CHOICE Vacy Hall GUESTHOUSE **$$**
(☑07-4639 2055; www.vacyhall.com.au; 135 Russell St; d $98-225; ☎) Just uphill from the town centre, this magnificent 1880s mansion offers 12 heritage-style rooms with loads of romantic old-world charm.

James Cottage B&B **$$**
(☑07-4637 8377; www.jamescottage.com; 128 James St; d $150-165) An elegant B&B in an early-20th-century Queenslander, James Cottage has two fine guest bedrooms and an open fireplace. It's a short walk into town.

Park Motor Inn MOTEL **$$**
(☑07-4632 1011; www.parktoowoomba.com.au; 88 Margaret St; s/d $96/108; ❋) This comfortably furnished motel has a handy location opposite leafy Queens Park. It's close to a couple of popular cafes.

Burke & Wills Hotel HOTEL **$$**
(☑07-4632 2433; www.burkeandwillshotel.com. au; 554 Ruthven St; d $140-220; ❋❋) A six-storey hotel with comfortable rooms in the centre of town.

Central Plaza Hotel HOTEL **$$**
(☑07-4688 5333; www.toowoombacentralplaza. com.au; 523 Ruthven St; apt from $175; ❋❋) Award-winning hotel complex with colourful, well-designed apartments.

Toowoomba Motor Village Tourist Park CAMPGROUND, CABINS **$**
(☑07-4635 8186; www.toowoombamotorvillage. com.au; 821 Ruthven St; campsites $20-31, cabins & units $55-100) Excellent, modern park 2.5km south of the centre, with terrific views.

Eating & Drinking

345

Park House Cafe MODERN AUSTRALIAN **$$**
(☑07-4638 2211; 92 Margaret St; mains $19-34; ⊙breakfast & lunch daily, dinner Wed-Sat) Facing Queens Park, this chic cottage cafe has a lovely verandah and front-patio seating for gourmet sandwiches, hearty salads, pastas, grilled meats, seafood and daily specials.

GPO Café & Bar MODERN AUSTRALIAN **$$$**
(☑07-4659 9240; 140 Margaret St; mains $30-40; ⊙breakfast & lunch Mon-Sat, dinner Wed-Sat) Set in a heritage building with a relaxing verandah and an intimate dining room, GPO serves flavourful dishes like herb-crusted Atlantic salmon, beautifully grilled steaks, and seafood dishes with Asian touches.

Oxygen Café CAFE **$**
(cnr Ruthven & Little Sts; mains $9-16; ⊙7.30am-2.30pm Tue-Sun; ☑) This colourful, breezy cafe serves organic fare: filling breakfasts (scrambled eggs and ocean-trout roe), juices and smoothies, burgers (vegetarian, grilled yellow fin tuna) and sandwiches.

Bon Amici CAFE, LIVE MUSIC **$**
(191 Margaret St; light meals $6-12; ⊙8am-late) For a stiff drink or a good coffee (with delectable cakes), settle down at this red-walled, cruisy cafe. There's often live music in the evenings.

Spotted Cow BAR
(cnr Ruthven & Campbell Sts) A lively spot for a drink or a bite, the Spotted Cow is a Toowoomba favourite for its extensive drinks menu (including 70 different beers) and tasty bistro fare (try the 1kg pot of mussels).

ⓘ Information

The heart of downtown Toowoomba is around Ruthven St (part of the north–south New England Hwy, Rte 61) and Margaret St.

Toowoomba visitor centre (86 James St) Located southeast of the centre, at the junction with Kitchener St. Very helpful.

West of Toowoomba

About 45km west of Toowoomba is the Jondaryan Woolshed Complex (☑07-4692 2229; www.jondaryanwoolshed.com; 264 Evanslea Rd; adult/child $13/8; ⊙10am-4pm), which displays antique tractors and obscure farm machinery. There are daily blacksmithing and shearing demonstrations – check the website for times. To really get into the pioneering spirit, try spending a night in the shearers'

quarters ($17) or one of the self-contained cabins ($95 to $150). Or you can pseudo-camp in pre-erected safari tents ($29 to $36), which come complete with mattress.

A further 167km west, on the main street in Miles, is **Dogwood Crossing** (☎07-4628 5566; www.dogwoodcrossing.com; ☺9am-5pm Mon-Fri, 10am-4pm Sat & Sun), a $1.6-million community project that combines visual arts, social history and literature into a museum, gallery, library and multimedia resource centre. You can bed down for the night in a refurbished underground bunker or a converted troop train at **Possum Park** (☎07-4627 1651; Leichhardt Hwy; d from $90). Munitions were stored in these bunkers during WWII as part of Australia's prepared last line of defence against the advancing Japanese. There's also a campground.

Some 350km west of Toowoomba lies Roma, an early Queensland settlement that is today the centre of a sheep- and cattle-raising district. The town's major landmark is the **Big Rig Complex** (☎07-4622 4355; www.thebigrig.com.au; Warrego Hwy; adult/child $10/7, combined entry & night show $16/11; ☺9am-5pm, night show 7pm daily Apr-Nov, Wed & Sun Dec-Mar), a museum of oil and gas exploration centred on the old steam-operated oil rig at the eastern edge of town. There's also a sound-and-light show. In the same spot, the **visitor information centre** (☎07-4622 8676; 2 Riggers Rd; ☺9am-5pm) can help with accommodation, especially handy if you're stopping here en route to Carnarvon Gorge (p371).

Easter in the Country is Roma's annual week-long celebration of country music and life in western Queensland. It's held in April.

FRASER ISLAND & THE FRASER COAST

Nature buffs will beeline it to World Heritage–listed Fraser Island, a mystical land of giant dunes, ancient rainforests and luminous lakes.

Across the calm waters of the Great Sandy Strait, Hervey Bay is the launching pad to Fraser. There's a whiff of burgeoning beach-cafe culture, but at heart it's a mellow coastal community riding on the back of the annual humpback-whale migrations. Further south, tiny Rainbow Beach is a refreshingly unaffected seaside village and an alternative departure point for Fraser Island. Fishing,

swimming, boating and camping are hugely popular along the entire stretch of coastline.

Inland, grazing and agricultural fields surround old-fashioned country towns steeped in history. Bundaberg, the largest city in the region, overlooks a sea of waving sugar cane and is famous for its golden rum – a fiery, gut-churning spirit guaranteed to scramble a few brain cells!

Fraser Island

POP 360

The region's Aborigines call it K'Gari (paradise). Sculpted from wind, sand and surf, the striking blue freshwater lakes, crystalline creeks, giant dunes and lush rainforests of this gigantic sandbar form an enigmatic island paradise unlike any other in the world. Created over hundreds of thousands of years from sand drifting off the east coast of mainland Australia, Fraser Island is the largest sand island in the world (measuring 120km by 15km) and the only place where rainforest grows on sand.

Inland, the vegetation varies from dense tropical rainforest and wild heath to wetlands and wallum scrub, with 'sandblows' (giant dunes over 200m high), mineral streams and freshwater lakes opening onto long sandy beaches fringed with pounding surf. The island is home to a profusion of bird life and wildlife, including the purest strain of dingo in Australia, while offshore waters teem with dugong, dolphins, sharks and migrating humpback whales.

This island Utopia, however, is marred by an ever-increasing volume of 4WD traffic tearing down the beach and along sandy inland tracks. With over 350,000 people visiting the island each year, Fraser can sometimes feel like a giant sandpit with its own peak hour and congested beach highway.

The 4WD rules the sandy tracks, and it's essential that all visitors have some understanding of how to drive one. Before crossing via ferry from either Rainbow Beach or Hervey Bay, ensure also that your vehicle has suitably high clearance and, if camping, that you have adequate food, water and fuel. Driving on Fraser all looks pretty relaxed in the brochure, but a sudden tide change or an unseen pothole can set your wheels spinning perilously. See the boxed text, p350 for more details.

History

Fraser Island takes its European name from James and Eliza Fraser. The captain of the

Stirling Castle and his wife were shipwrecked on the northwest coast in 1836. He died here, and she survived with help from the local Aboriginal people.

As European settlers awoke to the value of Fraser's timber, that same tribe of Aborigines was displaced (although not without a fight) and tracts of rainforest were cleared in the search for turpentine (satiny), a waterproof wood prized by shipbuilders. The island's mineral sands were also mined for many years.

In the late 20th century the focus shifted from exploitation to protection. Sand mining ceased in 1975 and logging ended in 1991. Fraser Island joined the World Heritage list in 1992.

◉ Sights & Activities

The aptly named Seventy-Five Mile Beach runs the length of the island's east coast and offers some captivating scenery along the way. From Fraser's southern tip, use the high-tide access track between Hook Point and Dilli Village, rather than the beach. From here on, the eastern beach is the main thoroughfare. Stock up at nearby Eurong, the start of the inland track, across to Central Station and Wanggoolba Creek (for the ferry to River Heads).

In the middle of the island is Central Station, the starting point for numerous walking trails. Signposted tracks head to the beautiful Lakes McKenzie, Jennings, Birrabeen (with fewer tourists) and Boomanjin, in effect giant rainwater puddles 'perched' atop a thin impermeable layer of decaying twigs and leaves. Lore has it that rich mineral sand lends the lakes anti-ageing properties.

About 4km north of Eurong along the beach is a signposted walking trail to Lake Wabby. An easier route is from the lookout on the inland track. Wabby is edged on three sides by eucalypt forest, while the fourth side is a massive sandblow, which is encroaching on the lake at a rate of about 3m a year. The lake is deceptively shallow and diving is extremely dangerous. You can often find turtles and huge catfish under the trees in the eastern corner of the lake.

Driving north along the beach you'll pass Happy Valley, with many places to stay, and Eli Creek. After rainfall this becomes a fast-moving, crystal-clear waterway that will carry you effortlessly downstream. Pretty much everyone wanders knee-deep along its pretty path. About 2km from Eli Creek is the wreck of the Maheno, a passenger liner that was blown ashore by a cyclone in 1935 while being towed to a Japanese scrapyard.

Roughly 5km north of the Maheno you'll find the Pinnacles (a section of coloured sand cliffs) and, about 10km beyond, Dundubara. Then there's a 20km stretch of beach before you come to the rocky outcrop of Indian Head, the best vantage point on the island. Sharks, manta rays, dolphins and (during the migration season) whales can often be spotted from the top of the headland.

From Indian Head the trail branches inland, passing the Champagne Pools, the only safe spot on the island for saltwater swimming. This inland road leads back to Waddy Point and Orchid Beach, the last settlement on the island. Many tracks north of this are closed for environmental protection. The 30km of beach up to Sandy Cape, the northern tip, with its lighthouse, is off-limits to hire vehicles. The beach from Sandy Cape to Rooney Point is closed to all vehicles, as is the road from Orchid Beach to Platypus Bay on the western coast.

On the island you can take a scenic flight with MI Helicopters (☎1800 600 345, 07-4125 1599; www.mihelicopters.com.au; 25min flights $240) or with Air Fraser (☎1800 600 345, 07-4125 3600; 10min flights from $70).

FRASER ISLAND GREAT WALK

Opened in 2004, the Fraser Island Great Walk is a stunning way to see this enigmatic island in all its diverse colours. The trail undulates through the island's interior for 90km from Dilli Village to Happy Valley. Broken up into sections of 6km to 16km, plus some side trails off the main sections, it follows the pathways of Fraser Island's original inhabitants, the Butchulla people, and passes underneath rainforest canopies, through shifting dunes and alongside some of the island's vivid lakes.

Before you go, pick up the Fraser Island Great Walk brochure from a QPWS office (or download it from www.derm.qld.gov.au) and seek updates on the track's conditions.

⌂ Sleeping & Eating

Camping is by far the best way to experience the island, but come prepared or pay through the nose for supplies. Permits are required at QPWS camping grounds and any public area (ie along the beach). Camping is permitted on designated stretches of the eastern beach, but there are no facilities.

Fraser Island

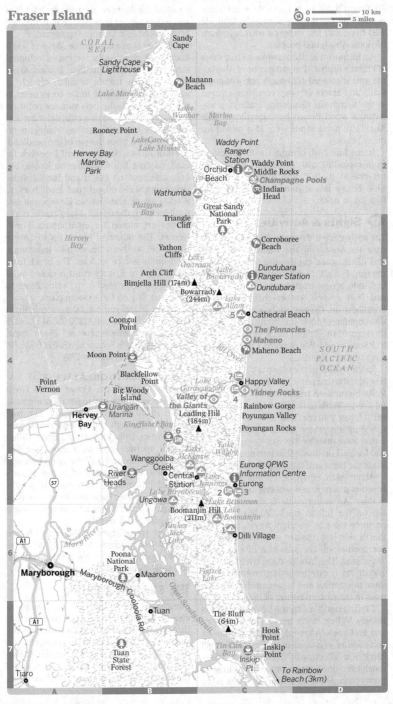

CORAL SEA

Sandy Cape

Sandy Cape Lighthouse

Manann Beach

Lake Marong

Lake Wanbar

Marloo Bay

Rooney Point

LakeCarrie
Lake Minka

Hervey Bay Marine Park

Waddy Point Ranger Station

Orchid Beach

Waddy Point Middle Rocks

Champagne Pools

Indian Head

Wathumba

Platypus Bay

Great Sandy National Park

Hervey Bay

Triangle Cliff

Yathon Cliffs

Lake Gnaraun

Corroboree Beach

Arch Cliff
Bimjella Hill (174m) ▲

Lake Bowarrady

Dundubara Ranger Station

Dundubara

Bowarrady ▲ (244m)

Lake Allom

Cathedral Beach

Coongul Point

The Pinnacles

Maheno

Hill Creek

Maheno Beach

SOUTH PACIFIC OCEAN

Moon Point

Point Vernon

Blackfellow Point

Big Woody Island

Lake Garawongera

Happy Valley

Valley of the Giants

Yidney Rocks

Urangan Marina

Hervey Bay

Leading Hill (184m) ▲

Rainbow Gorge
Poyungan Valley
Poyungan Rocks

Kingfisher Bay

Wanggoolba Creek

Lake McKenzie

River Heads

Central Station

Lake Jennings

Eurong QPWS Information Centre

Eurong

Ungowa

Lake Birrabeen

Lake Benaroon

Boomanjin Hill (211m) ▲

Lake Boomanjin

Dilli Village

Yankee Jack Lake

Mary River

Poona National Park

Maaroom

Maryborough

Maryborough Cooloola Rd

Fig tree Lake

Great Sandy Strait

Tuan

The Bluff (64m) ▲

Hook Point

Tin Can Bay

Inskip Point

Inskip Pt

Tuan State Forest

To Rainbow Beach (3km)

Tiaro

0 ———— 10 km
0 ———— 5 miles

Fraser Island

Fires are prohibited, except in communal fire rings at Waddy Point and Dundubara.

Sailfish on Fraser   APARTMENTS $$$
(☎07-4127 9494; www.sailfishonfraser.com.au; Happy Valley; d from $230-250, extra person $10; ✸) Any notions of rugged wilderness and roughing it will be forgotten quick smart at this plush, indulgent retreat. These two-bedroom apartments are cavernous and classy, with wall-to-wall glass doors, spas and mod cons; and there's an alluring pool.

✎Kingfisher Bay Resort   RESORT $$
(☎1800 072 555, 07-4194 9300; www.kingfisherbay.com; Kingfisher Bay; d $160, 2-bedroom villas $198; ✸@✸) This elegant eco-resort has hotel rooms with private balconies, and sophisticated timber villas, some with spas on their private decks. There's a three-night minimum stay in high season. The resort has restaurants, bars and shops and operates daily tours of the island (adult/child $169/99).

Fraser Island Beachhouses RENTAL HOUSE $$
(☎1800 626 230, 07-4127 9205; www.fraserislandbeachhouses.com.au; Eurong Second Valley; per 2 nights studio $300, 2-bedroom house from $700; ✸) Another luxury option, this complex contains sunny, self-contained units kitted out with polished wood, cable TVs and ocean views.

Eurong Beach Resort   RESORT $$
(☎1800 111 808, 07-4120 1600; www.eurong.com.au; Eurong; r $140, 2-bedroom apt $199, mains $18-50; ⊙breakfast, lunch & dinner; ✸@✸) Cheerful Eurong is the main resort on the east coast. The cheapest digs are in simple motel rooms and units; the comfortable apartments and A-frame chalets are a little pricier. There's also a restaurant, a lagoon-style pool and the popular Beach Bar, plus a bottle shop and petrol station.

Fraser Island Wilderness Retreat HOSTEL $
(☎07-4127 9144; Happy Valley; dm $30, mains $20-25; ⊙lunch & dinner; @✸✸) This wilderness-

retreat-turned-backpackers has dorms (sleeping up to six) in nine timber lodges. The cabins cascade down a gentle slope amid plenty of tropical foliage, and there's a bistro and bar on site.

Dilli Village Fraser Island CAMPGROUND $
(☎07-4127 9130; Dilli Village; unpowered sites $20, bunkrooms $40, cabins $100) This tidy site perched on a gentle slope is run by the University of the Sunshine Coast.

Frasers@Cathedral Beach CARAVAN PARK $$
(☎07-4127 9177; Cathedral Beach; unpowered sites $29-39, powered sites $39-49, cabins with/without bathroom $180/145; @) This spacious, privately run park with its abundant, flat, grassy sites is a fave with families.

The most developed **QPWS camping grounds** (per person/family $5.15/20.60), with coin-operated hot showers, toilets and barbecues, are at Waddy Point, Dundubara and Central Station. Campers with vehicles can also use the smaller camping grounds with fewer facilities at Lake Boomanjin, Ungowa and Wathumba on the western coast. Walkers' camps (for hikers only) are set away from the main campgrounds along the Fraser Island Great Walk trail. The trail map lists the campsites and their facilities.

❶ Information

General supplies and expensive fuel are available from stores at Cathedral Beach, Eurong, Kingfisher Bay, Happy Valley and Orchid Beach.

The main ranger station, **Eurong QPWS Information Centre** (☎07-4127 9128), is at Eurong. Others can be found at **Dundubara** (☎07-4127 9138) and **Waddy Point** (☎07-4127 9190).

The **Fraser Island Taxi Service** (☎07-4127 9188) operates all over the island. A one-way fare from Kingfisher Bay to Eurong is $80.

If your vehicle breaks down, call **Fraser Island Breakdown** (☎07-4127 9173) or the **tow-truck service** (☎07-4127 9449, 0428 353 164), both based in Eurong.

Permits

You will need permits for vehicles (per month/year $39.40/197.20) and camping (per person/family $5.15/20.60), and these must be purchased before you arrive. It's best to purchase the permits online at www.derm.qld.gov.au or contact **QPWS** (☎13 74 68). Permits aren't required for private camping grounds or resorts. Permit-issuing offices:

Bundaberg QPWS Office (☎07-4131 1600; 46 Quay St)

SAND SAFARIS: EXPLORING FRASER ISLAND

The only way to explore Fraser Island is with a 4WD vehicle. For most travellers there are three transport options: tag-along tours, organised tours or 4WD hire.

Please be aware of your environmental footprint. When choosing how to visit this precious natural landscape bear in mind that the greater the number of individual vehicles driving on the island, the greater the environmental damage.

Tag-Along Tours

Popular with backpackers, tag-along tours feature a group of travellers that pile into a 4WD convoy and follow a lead vehicle with an experienced guide and driver.

Advantages – flexibility; you can make new friends fast.

Disadvantages – if your group doesn't get along it's a loooong three days. Inexperienced drivers get bogged in sand all the time, but this can be part of the fun.

Rates hover around $300 to $320 for three-day/two-night packages and exclude food, fuel and alcohol. See p354 for operators.

Organised Tours

Package tours leave from Hervey Bay, Rainbow Beach and Noosa and typically cover rainforests, Eli Creek, Lakes McKenzie and Wabby, the coloured Pinnacles and the *Maheno* shipwreck.

Advantages – minimum of fuss, plus you can return to Rainbow Beach or Noosa, or vice versa. Expert commentary.

Disadvantages – during peak season you could share the experience with 40 others.

We've listed a few companies below (for options based in Hervey Bay, see p354):

Footprints on Fraser (☎1300 765 636; www.footprintsonfraser.com.au; 4-/5-day walks $1375/1825) Highly recommended guided walking tours of the island's natural wonders.

Fraser Explorer Tours (☎1800 249 122, 07-4194 9222; www.fraserexplorertours.com.au; 1-/2-day tours $175/312) Highly recommended.

Fraser Experience (☎1800 689 819, 07-4124 4244; www.fraserexperience.com; 2-day tours $295) Small groups and more freedom about the itinerary.

4WD Hire

Hire companies lease out 4WD vehicles in Hervey Bay, Rainbow Beach and on the island itself. When planning your trip, reckon on covering 20km an hour on the inland tracks and 40km an hour on the eastern beach. Most companies will help arrange ferries and permits and hire camping gear.

Advantages – complete freedom to roam the island and escape the crowds.

Disadvantages – you may find you have to tackle beach and track conditions even experienced drivers find challenging.

Rates for multiday rentals start at around $185 per day depending on the vehicle. On the island, **Kingfisher Bay 4WD Hire** (☎07-4120 3366) hires out 4WDs from $175/280 per half-/full day. Also see p359 and p353 for Hervey Bay and Rainbow Beach rental companies.

Great Sandy Information Centre (☎07-5449 7792; 240 Moorinidil St, Tewantin; ⊗8am-4pm) Near Noosa.

Marina Kiosk (☎07-4128 9800; Buccaneer Ave, Urangan Boat Harbour, Urangan; ⊗6am-6pm)
Maryborough QPWS (☎07-4121 1800; 20 Tennyson St; ⊗8.30am-5pm Mon-Fri)

Rainbow Beach QPWS (☏07-5486 3160; Rainbow Beach Rd)

River Heads Information kiosk (☏07-4125 8485; ⊙6.15-11.15am & 2-3.30pm) Ferry departure point at River Heads, south of Hervey Bay.

ⓘ Getting There & Away

Vehicle ferries connect Fraser Island with River Heads, about 10km south of Hervey Bay, or further south at Inskip Point, near Rainbow Beach.

Fraser Island Barges (☏1800 227 437; www.fraserislandferry.com.au) makes the crossing (vehicle and four passengers $150 return, 30 minutes) from River Heads to Wanggoolba Creek on the western coast of Fraser Island. It departs daily from River Heads at 8.30am, 10.15am and 4pm, and returns from the island at 9am, 3pm and 5pm.

Kingfisher Vehicular Ferry (☏1800 072 555; www.fraserislandferry.com) operates a daily vehicle and passenger ferry (pedestrian adult/child $50/25 return, vehicle and four passengers $150 return, 50 minutes) from River Heads to Kingfisher Bay, departing at 6.45am, 9am, 12.30pm, 3.30pm, 6.45pm and 9.30pm and returning at 7.50am, 10.30am, 2pm, 5pm, 8.30pm and 11pm.

Coming from Rainbow Beach, the operators **Rainbow Venture & Fraser Explorer** (☏07-4194 9300; pedestrian/vehicle return $10/80) and **Manta Ray** (☏07-5486 8888; vehicle return $90) both make the 15-minute crossing from Inskip Point to Hook Point on Fraser Island continuously from about 7am to 5.30pm daily.

Air Fraser Island (☏07-4125 3600; www.airfraserisland.com.au) charges from $125 for a return flight (20 minutes each way) to the island's eastern beach, departing Hervey Bay airport.

Gympie

POP 11,500

Gympie's gold once saved Queensland from near-bankruptcy, but that was in the 1860s and not much has happened since. A few period buildings line the main street, but most travellers on the Bruce Hwy bypass the town centre.

On the highway south of town, **Woodworks Forestry & Timber Museum** (cnr Fraser Rd & Bruce Hwy; adult/student $10/5; ⊙10am-4pm Wed-Sun) displays memorabilia and equipment from the region's old logging days.

The **Gympie Gold Mining & Historical Museum** (215 Brisbane Rd; adult/child/family $10/5/25; ⊙9am-4pm) holds a diverse collection of mining equipment and steam engines. There's also a week-long **Gold Rush Festival** (www.goldrush.org.au) every October.

The **Valley Rattler** (☏07-5482 2750; www.thevalleyrattler.com; half-day tours per adult/child $20/10, day tours $47/23.50) is a restored 1923 steam train that leaves from the old Gympie train station on Tozer St every Wednesday and Sunday morning at 10am and chugs through the pretty Mary Valley to the tiny township of Imbil 40km away. The return trip takes 5½ hours, with lunch, caffeine and souvenir stops. On Saturday, **half-day tours** (⊙9.30am, 11.30am & 1.45pm) only go as far as Amamoor, 20km away.

For lodging, the **Gympie Muster Inn** (☏07-5482 8666; 21 Wickham St; d $135; ❉❂⊛) is a large, central motel.

Greyhound Australia (☏1300 473 946; www.greyhound.com.au) and **Premier Motor Service** (☏13 34 10; www.premierms.com.au) serve Gympie from Noosa ($22, two hours) and Hervey Bay ($33, 1¼ hours). Long-distance coaches stop at the bus shelter in Jaycee Way, behind Mary St. **Polley's Coaches** (☏07-5480 4500; Pinewood Ave) has buses from Gympie to Rainbow Beach ($18, 1¾ hours), departing from the Sovereign Cinema on Monkland St (at O'Connell St) at 1.15pm on weekdays.

Rainbow Beach

POP 1100

Gorgeous Rainbow Beach is a tiny town at the base of the Inskip Peninsula with spectacular multicoloured sand cliffs overlooking its rolling surf and white sandy beach. Still relatively untouched, the town has friendly locals and a relaxed vibe. Convenient access to Fraser Island (only 15 minutes by barge) and the Cooloola section of the Great Sandy National Park has made it a rising star of Queensland's coastal beauty spots.

The town is named for the **coloured sand cliffs**, a 2km walk along the beach. A 600m track along the cliffs at the southern end of Cooloola Dr leads to the **Carlo Sandblow**, a spectacular 120m-high dune.

🏃 Activities

The Cooloola section of the **Great Sandy National Park** has a number of **national park campsites** (www.derm.qld.gov.au; per person/family $5.15/20.60), including a wonderful stretch of beach camping along Teewah Beach. Book permits online. You'll also need a **4WD permit** (www.derm.qld.gov.au; per day/week/month $10/25/40).

If you don't have camping gear, **Rainbow Beach Hire-a-Camp** (☑07-5486 8633; www.rainbow-beach.org) can get you set up.

Bushwalkers will find tracks throughout the national park, including the 46.2km **Cooloola Wilderness Trail**, which starts at Mullens car park (off Rainbow Beach Rd) and ends near Lake Cooloola. Maps are available from the **QPWS** (☑07-5486 3160; Rainbow Beach Rd).

Without a 4WD, beach options are limited to the patrolled surf beach at the end of town. For those not wishing to hire a 4WD, **Surf & Sand Safaris** (☑07-5486 3131; www.surfandsandsafaris.com.au; per adult/child $70/35) runs 4WD tours through the national park, and along the beach to the coloured sands and lighthouse at Double Island Point.

Rainbow Beach Dolphin View Sea Kayaking (☑0408 738 192; 4hr tours per person $85) operates kayaking safaris and rents kayaks ($65 per half-day). It also runs the **Rainbow Beach Surf School** (2hr session $55).

Rainbow Paragliding (☑07-5486 3048, 0418 754 157; www.paraglidingrainbow.com; glides $150) offers tandem glides above the Carlo Sandblow, where the state championships are held every December. For more airborne action, talk to **Skydive Rainbow Beach** (☑0418 218 358; 8000/14,000ft dives $260/334).

Nearby Wolf Rock is one of Queensland's finest scuba-diving sites. **Wolf Rock Dive Centre** (☑07-5486 8004; www.wolfrockdive.com.au; double dive charters from $160) offers courses and dives.

🛏 Sleeping

Beds are found on Spectrum St and up the hill towards Carlo Sandblow. The three main hostels arrange 4WD tours to Fraser Island.

TOP CHOICE **Debbie's Place** B&B $
(☑07-5486 3506; www.rainbowbeachaccommodation.com.au; 30 Kurana St; d/ste from $79/89, 3-bedroom apt from $99; ❄) Inside this beautiful timber Queenslander the charming rooms are fully self-contained and have private entrances and verandahs. The effervescent Debbie is a mine of information and makes this a cosy home away from home.

Rainbow Ocean Palms Resort APARTMENTS $$$
(☑07-5486 3211; www.rainbowoceanpalms.com; 105 Cooloola Dr; 1-/2-bedroom apt from $200/300; ❄⛱) Making the most of the panoramic ocean views, these luxury apartments have

a modern, contemporary design and feature loads of glass, light and space. They overlook the national park, you can see the ocean from your spa, and there's a great restaurant next door.

Plantation Resort APARTMENTS $$$
(☑07-5486 9000; www.plantationresortatrainbow.com.au; 1 Rainbow Beach Rd; apts from $260; ❄@⛱) These swish apartments have perfect ocean views, and the outdoor cane settings and white plantation-themed rooms will have you reaching for the nearest gin and tonic. It's classy beach-chic and smack bang in the middle of town.

Rainbow Shores Resort RESORT $$
(☑07-5486 3999; www.rainbowshores.com.au; 12 Rainbow Shores Dr; r from $140, villas & beach houses from $170; ❄⛱) For luxury in the bush, this is the place, with holiday units, three-bedroom beach houses and stylish split-level villas. On site you'll find a nine-hole golf course, tennis courts, barbecues, a restaurant and plenty of bush. Minimum five-night stay in high season.

Pippies Beach House HOSTEL $
(☑1800 425 356; www.pippiesbeachhouse.com.au; 22 Spectrum St; dm/d $24/65; ❄@⛱) With only 12 rooms, this small, super-chilled hostel is the place to relax between surfing, diving and bushwalking. Other bonuses include free breakfasts and water toys, and garden space for tents and vans ($12 per person).

Dingo's Backpacker's Resort HOSTEL $
(☑1800 111 126; www.dingosresort.com; 20 Spectrum St; dm/d $22/65; ❄@⛱) This party hostel with bar has live music every Wednesday and Saturday night, a Balinese-style gazebo for recovery, free tours to Carlo Sandblow, free pancake breakfasts, and cheap meals every night.

Fraser's on Rainbow YHA HOSTEL $
(☑1800 100 170; www.frasersonrainbow.com; 18 Spectrum St; dm/d from $25/65; @⛱) In a converted motel, this hostel has roomy dorms and a pleasant, relaxed atmosphere. Locals join guests for a tipple at the sprawling outdoor bar, and you can also buy cheap meals nightly.

Rainbow Beach Holiday Village CARAVAN PARK $
(☑1300 366 596; www.beach-village.com; 13 Rainbow Beach Rd; unpowered/powered sites from $27/34, cabins from $90; ❄⛱) This excellent and popular park spreads over two hectares overlooking the beach and ocean.

✕ Eating

Self-caterers will find a supermarket on Rainbow Beach Rd.

Waterview

Bistro   MODERN AUSTRALIAN **$$**
(☑07-5486 8344; Cooloola Dr; mains $26-35; ☺breakfast & lunch Sun, lunch & dinner Wed-Sat) Sunset drinks are a must at this swish restaurant with sensational views of Fraser Island from its hilltop perch.

Rainbow Beach Hotel   PUB FARE **$$**
(1 Rainbow Beach Rd; mains $20-35; ☺lunch & dinner) The spruced-up pub carries on the plantation theme with ceiling fans, palm trees, timber floors and cane furnishings. The restaurant is bright and airy and serves up traditional pub grub. Have a sunset drink on the upstairs balcony.

Shak   CAFE **$$**
(12 Rainbow Beach Rd; mains $10-30; ☺breakfast, lunch & dinner) This popular cafe perfectly encapsulates Rainbow's laid-back surfer chic, serving smoothies, vegie burgers, and fish in various guises.

ℹ Getting There & Around

Greyhound Australia (☑1300 473 946; www.greyhound.com.au) and **Premier Motor Service** (☑13 34 10; www.premierms.com.au) have daily services from Brisbane ($65, five hours), Noosa ($33, 2½ hours) and Hervey Bay ($30, 1½ hours).

Most 4WD-hire companies will also arrange permits, barge costs and hire out camping gear, including **All Trax 4WD Hire** (☑07-5486 8767; www.fraserisland4x4.com.au; Shell service station, Rainbow Beach Rd; per day from $120) and **Rainbow Beach Adventure Centre 4WD Hire** (☑07-5486 3288; www.adventurecentre.com.au; Rainbow Beach Rd; per day from $150).

Maryborough

POP 21,500

Born in 1847, Maryborough is one of Queensland's oldest towns, and its port was the first shaky step ashore for thousands of 19th-century free settlers looking for a better life in the new country. Heritage and history are Maryborough's fortes, the pace of yesteryear reflected in its beautifully restored colonial-era buildings and gracious Queenslander homes.

This big old country town is also the birthplace of PL Travers, creator of everyone's favourite umbrella-wielding nanny, Mary Poppins.

Thirteen heritage-listed buildings, parklands and museums in **Portside** (101 Wharf St; ☺10am-4pm Mon-Fri, to 1pm Sat & Sun) paint a different story from Maryborough's colourful past – ruffians, brothels, opium dens and all.

Brennan & Geraghty's Store (64 Lennox St; adult/child/family $5.50/2.50/13.50; ☺10am-3pm), which traded for 100 years before becoming a museum, is like a vintage graveyard of tins, bottles and packets, all crammed onto the ceiling-high shelves. Just look how far the happy little Vegemite has come.

Maryborough Riverboat Cruises (☑07-4123 1523; www.maryboroughrivercruise.com; 1hr tours $20, 2hr lunch cruises $35; ☺10am, noon & 2pm Tue-Sun) provides informed commentaries along the Mary River.

Free **guided walks** (☺9am Mon-Sat) depart from the city hall every morning and take in the town's sites.

On the last Saturday of each month you can get spooked on a torch-lit tour of the city's grisly murder sites, opium dens, haunted houses and cemetery with **Ghostly Tours & Tales** (☑1800 214 789; tours incl dinner $75).

Every Thursday and on the last Sunday of the month in Queen's Park you can take a ride (adult/child $3/2) on the **Mary Ann**, a full-sized replica of Queensland's first steam locomotive, built in Maryborough in 1873.

In the lovely **Eco Queenslander** (☑0438 195 443; www.ecoqueenslander.com; 15 Treasure St; house $120-140) you'll find a comfy lounge, a full kitchen, a laundry, a cast-iron bathtub and bikes to use. **McNevin's Parkway Motel** (☑1800 072 000; www.mcnevins.com.au; 188 John St; r from $110; ✳@⊜✷) has well-lit, comfortable motel rooms. **Wallace Caravan Park & Units Motel** (☑07-4121 3970; www.wallacecaravanpark.com; 22 Ferry St; unpowered/powered sites $20/25, cabins $75-85; ✳✷) is leafy, pleasant and very convenient.

For a meal, try the **Port Residence** (☑07-4123 5001; Customs House, Wharf St; mains $15-30; ☺breakfast, lunch & dinner Thu-Sun), an elegant restaurant and tea room overlooking the Mary River Parklands. **Basement** (☑07-4121 0002; 389 Kent St; tapas $9; ☺4.30pm-midnight Thu-Sat) is a chic underground tapas bar with Mediterr-asian-inspired tapas.

ℹ Information

Inside the 100-year-old city hall, the **Maryborough/Fraser Island visitor centre** (Kent St; ☺9am-5pm Mon-Fri, to 1pm Sat & Sun) is extremely helpful and has free copies of comprehensive self-guided walking tours.

ⓘ Getting There & Away

Maryborough's train station, Maryborough West, is 7km west of town on Lennox St. Here you'll find trains to Brisbane ($60, five hours, at least four weekly). The main bus station for long-haul trips north or south is next to the train station, but a shuttle connects both stations with town.

If you just need to get to Hervey Bay ($8, one hour), catch one of the frequently departing **Wide Bay Transit** (☏07-4121 3719) buses from outside city hall.

Hervey Bay

POP 54,000

Once the caravanning capital of Queensland, Hervey Bay has matured from a welfare-by-the-sea escape into a top tourist-dollar destination thanks to its lovely sandy bay (and soothing sea breezes, energetic resort development and huge pods of humpback whales.

As the main gateway to Fraser Island, the often sleepy, startlingly long Esplanade has an air of youthful anticipation as the bars and clubs crank come nightfall.

From July to October fishing boats are kitted out like assault vehicles to make way for the life-affirming migration of humpback whales. This is reputedly the best viewing region in the world.

The gentle, shallow bay itself is very safe for swimming and snorkelling (especially off the end of Zephyr St in Scarness), which means many mums, dads and kids also pay Hervey Bay a seasonal visit.

◉ Sights

Reef World (☏07-4128 9828; Pulgul St, Urangan; adult/child $18/9, shark dives $40; ⊗9.30am-4pm) is a small aquarium stocked with some of the Great Barrier Reef's most colourful characters. You can also take a dip with lemon, whaler and other nonpredatory sharks.

The **Botanic Gardens** (Elizabeth St, Urangan; ⊗6.30am-8.30pm) have dense foliage, walking tracks, a few lagoons and over 80 species of bird.

🏃 Activities

Fraser Island

Hervey Bay is great for arranging a 4WD adventure on Fraser Island. Some hostels put groups together in tag-along tours. A maximum of five vehicles follow a lead vehicle with an experienced guide and driver. Rates hover around $300 to $320 for a three-day/

two-night camping trip, and exclude food, fuel and alcohol.

Colonial Village YHA (☏1800 818 280; www.cvyha.com)

Fraser Roving (☏1800 989 811, 07-4125 6386; www.fraserroving.com.au)

Nomads (☏1800 354 535, 07-4125 3601; www.nomadshostels.com)

Next Backpackers (☏07-4125 6600; www.nextbackpackers.com.au)

Palace Adventures (☏1800 063 168; www.palaceadventures.com)

If you prefer to go on your own (not recommended for inexperienced off-road drivers), see p359 for car-hire information. For more Fraser Island options, see the boxed text, p350.

Water Sports

Aquavue   EQUIPMENT HIRE, TOURS
(☏07-4125 5528; www.aquavue.com.au; The Esplanade, Torquay) Hires out SeaKarts (somewhat of a cross between a windsurfer and a catamaran; $50 per hour), kayaks ($20 per hour) and jet skis ($50 per 15 minutes). Guided Fraser Island jet-ski tours for $320.

Enzo's on the Beach   EQUIPMENT HIRE, LESSONS
(☏07-4124 6375; 351a The Esplanade, Scarness) Kitesurfing ($130 per two-hour lesson), paddleboarding ($30/40 per hour/two hours). Also hires out kayaks and surf skis.

Cruises

Krystal Klear   CRUISES
(☏07-4128 9800; 5hr tours adult/child $90/50) Leaving from the Urangan marina, this day trip on a 40ft glass-bottomed boat includes snorkelling, coral viewing and an island tropical barbecue.

Fishing

The fishing in and around Hervey Bay is excellent and numerous vessels operate fishing safaris. **MV Fighting Whiting** (☏07-4124 6599; www.fightingwhiting.com.au; adult/child/family $70/35/170) and **MV Princess II** (☏07-4124 0400; adult/child $130/85) both offer expeditions that include lunch.

Other Activities

Air Fraser Island   SCENIC FLIGHTS
(☏1800 247 992; www.airfraserisland.com.au) Whale-watching flights and scenic flights over Fraser Island from $70.

Skydive Hervey Bay
SKYDIVING

(☎0458 064 703; www.skydiveherveybay.com.au) Tandem skydives for $250/270 from 10,000/14,000ft.

Susan River Homestead
HORSE RIDING

(☎07-4121 6846; www.susanriver.com; Hervey Bay-Maryborough Rd) Located halfway between Maryborough and Hervey Bay. Two-hour rides cost $85.

★ Festivals & Events

In early August, the Hervey Bay Whale Festival (www.herveybaywhalefestival.com.au) celebrates the return of the whales.

🛏 Sleeping

Quarterdecks Harbour Retreat
APARTMENTS $$

(☎07-4197 0888; www.quarterdecksretreat.com.au; 80 Moolyyir St, Urangan; 1-/2-/3-bedroom villas $150/195/225; ✳🤶🏊) Backing onto a nature reserve, these excellent villas are stylishly furnished with a private courtyard, all the mod cons you could wish for, and little luxuries like fluffy bathrobes. It's a short stroll to the beach.

Beachfront Tourist Parks
CARAVAN PARK $

(www.beachfronttouristparks.com.au; unpowered/powered sites $23/31); Pialba (☎07-4128 1399); Scarness (☎07-4125 1578); Torquay (☎07-4128 1274) Fronting Hervey Bay's exquisitely long sandy beach, all three of these shady parks have the best ocean views; the Torquay site is in the heart of the action.

Shelly Bay Resort
APARTMENTS $$

(☎07-4125 4533; www.shellybayresort.com.au; 466 The Esplanade, Torquay; 1-/2-bedroom units $125/170; ✳@🏊) The bold, cheerful self-contained units at this complex are clean and spacious. All rooms have water views, and with the beach just across the road this is one of the best options in town. There's also an Indian restaurant on site.

Bay B&B
B&B $$

(☎07-4125 6919; www.baybedandbreakfast.com.au; 180 Cypress St, Urangan; s $75, d $135-150; ✳@🏊) This great-value B&B is run by a friendly, well-travelled Frenchman. Guest rooms are in a comfy annexe out the back, and breakfast is served on an outdoor patio in a tropical garden surrounded by birds and masses of greenery.

Colonial Village YHA
HOSTEL $

(☎1800 818 280; www.cvyha.com; 820 Boat Harbour Dr, Urangan; unpowered/powered sites $18/24,

dm/d/cabins from $20/54/85; ✳@🏊) This excellent YHA is set on eight hectares of tranquil bushland, close to the marina and only 50m from the beach. It's a lovely spot, thick with ambience, possums and parrots. Facilities include a spa, tennis and basketball courts, and a funky bar. Breakfast is free and dinners cost $8 to $10.

Grange Resort
RESORT $$$

(☎07-4125 2002; www.thegrange-herveybay.com.au; cnr Elizabeth & Shell Sts, Urangan; 1-/2-bedroom villas $195/225; ✳🤶🏊) Reminiscent of a stylish desert resort with fancy split-level condos and filled with life's little luxuries, this place is close to the beach and to town.

Alexander Lakeside B&B
B&B $$

(☎07-4128 9448; www.herveybaybedandbreakfast.com.au; 29 Lido Pde, Urangan; r $140-150, ste $160-170; ✳🤶) In a quiet street, this warm and friendly B&B offers lakeside indulgence where turtles come a-visiting in the morning. There's a heated lakeside spa, two spacious rooms and two luxury self-contained suites.

Boat Harbour Resort
APARTMENTS $$

(☎07-4125 5079; www.boatharbourresort.net; 651-652 Charlton St, Urangan; studio from $120, bungalow from $150; ✳🤶🏊) Close to the Hervey Bay marina, these timber studios and bungalows are set on attractive grounds. The studios have sizeable decks out the front, and the roomy two-bedroom bungalows are great for families.

Palace Backpackers
HOSTEL $

(☎1800 063 168, 07-4124 5331; www.palaceadventures.com; 184 Torquay Rd, Scarness; dm/d $25/55; ✳@🏊) These self-contained units (with doubles as well as three-, four- and six-bed dorms) are set in tropical gardens only a short walk to the beach. Good deals for Fraser Island tours.

Happy Wanderer Village
CARAVAN PARK $

(☎07-4125 1103; www.happywanderer.com.au; 105 Truro St, Torquay; unpowered/powered sites from $30/35, cabins/villas from $64/121; ✳🤶🏊) The manicured lawns and profuse gum-tree cover at this large park make for great tent sites.

Next Backpackers
HOSTEL $

(☎07-4125 6600; www.nextbackpackers.com.au; 10 Bideford St, Torquay; dm $20-32, d $69; ✳@🤶) This modern hostel is a cut above the usual offerings, with polished wooden floors, ultraclean, roomy rooms and a well-equipped stainless-steel kitchen. There's a girls only dorm and a bar open until midnight.

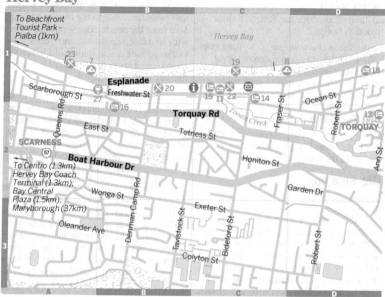

Hervey Bay

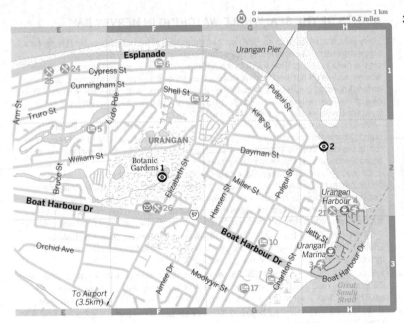

Nomads
HOSTEL $

(☎07-4125 3601; www.nomadshostels.com; 408 The Esplanade, Torquay; dm/d from $18/60; ❄@🛜🏊) Sprawling complex opposite the beach.

Fraser Roving
HOSTEL $

(☎1800 989 811, 07-4125 6386; www.fraserroving. com; 412 The Esplanade, Torquay; dm $23-25, d with/without bathroom $65/60; @🏊) Stark, spartan rooms but serious party vibe.

✖ Eating & Drinking

Self-caterers can stock up at the supermarkets inside the Centro, Urangan Central and Bay Central Plaza shopping centres.

Black Dog Café
FUSION $$

(☎07-4124 3177; 381 The Esplanade, Torquay; mains $14-33; ☉lunch & dinner) The ambience is funk, the menu is Zen. The East-meets-West dishes feature sushi, Japanese soup, fresh burgers, curries, club sambos and seafood salads.

Café Tapas
TAPAS $$

(417 The Esplanade, Torquay; tapas $7; ☉lunch & dinner) This slick venue has funky artwork, dim lighting, red couches, and low tables flickering with coloured lights. Come for Asian-inspired tapas, and linger longer for drinks and music.

Enzo's on the Beach
CAFE $

(351A The Esplanade, Scarness; mains $8-20; ☉6.30am-5pm) A shabby-chic outdoor cafe with a superb beachfront location where you can dine on focaccias, wraps, healthy salads and light meals or just sip a coffee and wallow in the perfect ocean views. Active sorts can hire kayaks, surf skis and paddleboards or learn kitesurfing.

Aquavue
CAFE $

(415 The Esplanade, Torquay; mains $8-13; ☉breakfast & lunch) Another outdoor cafe on the beachfront offering unbeatable sea views and the usual assortment of sandwiches and light meals. There are plenty of water toys for hire.

Café Balaena
CAFE $$

(shop 7, Terminal Bldg, Buccaneer Ave, Urangan; mains $10-25; ☉breakfast & lunch daily, dinner Thu-Mon) This waterfront cafe at the marina provides expansive views, atmosphere with a decidedly laid-back twist and wallet-friendly prices. The menu ranges across the board with a good dose of seafood.

Raging Bull Stonegrill
STEAKHOUSE $$

(☎07-4194 6674; 486 The Esplanade, Torquay; mains $20-40; ☉dinner) This interactive dining experience, whereby a slab of meat, chicken or fish cooks on a hot rock on your

GIANTS OF THE SEA: WHALE WATCHING IN HERVEY BAY

Every year, from August to early November, thousands of humpback whales (*Megaptera novaeangliae*) cruise into Hervey Bay's sheltered waters for a few days before continuing their arduous migration south to the Antarctic. Having mated and given birth in the warmer waters off north-eastern Australia, they arrive in Hervey Bay in groups of about a dozen (known as pulses), before splitting into smaller groups of two or three (pods). The new calves use the time to develop the thick layers of blubber necessary for survival in icy southern waters, by consuming around 600L of milk daily.

Viewing these majestic creatures is simply awe-inspiring. Showy aqua-acrobats, humpbacks wave their pectoral fins, slap their tails, breach and simply 'blow'. Many will roll up beside the whale-watching boats with one eye clear of the water, making those on board wonder who's actually watching whom.

Cruises go from the Urangan Marina out to Platypus Bay and then zip around from pod to pod to find the most active whales. In a very competitive market, vessels offer half-day (four-hour) tours that include breakfast or lunch and cost around $115 for adults and $60 for children. The larger boats run six-hour day trips and the amenities are better, but they take around two hours to reach Platypus Bay. Some recommended operators:

» **Spirit of Hervey Bay** (☑1800 642 544; www.spiritofherveybay.com; ◷8.30am & 1.30pm) The largest vessel with the greatest number of passengers. Has an underwater hydrophone and underwater viewing window.

» **That's Awesome** (☑1800 653 775; www.awesomeadventure.com.au; ◷7am, 10.30am & 2.30pm) This rigid inflatable boat speeds out to the whales faster than any other vessel. The low deck level means you're nearly eyeball-to-eyeball with the big mammals.

» **MV Tasman Venture** (☑1800 620 322; www.tasmanventure.com.au; ◷8.30am & 1.30pm) Maximum of 80 passengers; underwater microphones and viewing windows.

» **Blue Dolphin Marine Tours** (☑07-4124 9600; www.bluedolphintours.com.au; ◷7.30am) Maximum 20 passengers on a 10m catamaran.

plate, will make carnivores feel righteously healthy. Don't forget to eat your greens.

Pier Restaurant   SEAFOOD $$
(☑07-4128 9699; 573 The Esplanade, Urangan; mains $20-40; ◷dinner Mon-Sat) Although it sits opposite the water, à la carte Pier makes little use of its ocean views. It does have an interesting seafood menu (crocodile and Hervey Bay scallops), though, and is deservedly popular.

Hoolihan's   PUB $$
(382 The Esplanade, Scarness; mains $16-27) Like all good Irish pubs, Hoolihan's is wildly popular, especially with the backpacker crowd. Maybe it's got something to do with its hard-drinking ethos and carbo-laden meals.

ℹ Information

Hervey Bay visitor centre (☑1800 649 926; 401 The Esplanade, Torquay; internet per hr $4) Friendly, privately run booking office with internet access.

Hervey Bay Visitor Information Centre (☑1800 811 728; www.herveybaytourism.com. au; cnr Urraween & Maryborough Rds) Helpful tourist office on outskirts of town.

Mad Travel (☑07-4125 3601; 408 The Esplanade, Torquay; internet per hr $4) Located at Nomads. Offers internet access and is a booking agent for tours and activities.

ℹ Getting There & Away

Boat

Boats to Fraser Island leave from River Heads, about 10km south of town, and Urangan Marina; see p351. Most tours leave from Urangan Harbour.

Bus & Train

Long-distance buses depart **Hervey Bay Coach Terminal** (☑07-4124 4000; Central Ave, Pialba). Regular services head to/from Brisbane ($75, 5½ hours), Maroochydore ($50, 3½ hours), Bundaberg ($24, 1½ hours) and Rockhampton ($95, six hours). **Wide Bay Transit** (☑07-4121 3719) has hourly services from Urangan Marina to Maryborough ($8, one hour) every weekday, with fewer services on weekends.

Queensland Rail (☑13 12 30; www. queenslandrail.com.au) connects Brisbane with Maryborough West ($74, five hours), where a Trainlink bus ($8) transfers you to Hervey Bay.

ℹ️ Getting Around

Most places to stay will pick you up from the bus station if you call ahead. **Seega Rent a Car** (☎07-4125 6008; 463 The Esplanade) has small cars from $40 to $55 a day.

Plenty of rental companies make Hervey Bay the best place to hire a 4WD for Fraser Island:

Aussie Trax (☎1800 062 275; 56 Boat Harbour Dr, Pialba)

Fraser Magic 4WD Hire (☎07-4125 6612; www.fraser-magic-4wdhire.com.au; 5 Kruger Crt, Urangan)

Hervey Bay Rent A Car (☎07-4194 6626) Also rents out scooters ($30 per day).

Safari 4WD Hire (☎1800 689 819; www.safari 4wdhire.com.au; 102 Boat Harbour Dr, Pialba)

Childers

POP 1500

One of the sweeter stops on the heavily plied Bruce Hwy is pretty little Childers. This sugar-cane town, scattered with liquorice-coloured houses and fruit-picking youth, is used by most travellers to stretch the legs or take a cafe break in the country.

Sadly, Childers is widely known for a devastating fire at the Palace Backpackers Hostel in June 2000, in which 15 backpackers died. There is now a beautiful memorial, with moving dedications to those who perished, at the **Childers Palace Memorial Art Gallery and Information Centre** (72 Churchill St; ⊙9am-5pm Mon-Fri, to 3pm Sat & Sun), where you'll also find a good gallery.

🛏️ Sleeping & Eating

A little out of town, **Sugarbowl Caravan Park** (☎07-4126 1521; 4660 Bruce Hwy; unpowered/powered sites $20/22, cabins $66; @🏊) has spectacular views over the surrounding countryside. There's plenty of space and a good scattering of foliage between sites. Many farm-working backpackers stay here, but a better option is the very clean and friendly **Childers Tourist Park & Camp** (☎07-4126 1371; 111 Stockyard Rd; unpowered/powered sites $24/25, on-site vans $66) – you'll need a car. Rates are for two people.

For warm, country hospitality the cute cane-cutter cottages at **Mango Hill B&B** (☎07-4126 1311; www.mangohillcottages.com; 8 Mango Hill Dr; s/d $90/120; 🏊), 4km south of town, are decorated with handmade wooden furniture, country decor and comfy beds that ooze charm and romance. There's an on-site organic winery.

If you're stopping for lunch, **Kapé Centro** (65 Churchill St; mains $9-15; ⊙breakfast & lunch) in the old post office building dishes up light meals, salads and pizzas on the verandah. On your way out of town take a detour to **Mammino's** (115 Lucketts Rd; ⊙9am-5pm) for wickedly delicious homemade macadamia-nut ice cream. Lucketts Rd is off the Bruce Hwy just south of Childers.

ℹ️ Getting There & Away

Childers is 50km southwest of Bundaberg. **Greyhound Australia** (☎1300 473 946) and **Premier Motor Service** (☎13 34 10) both stop at the Shell service station north of town and have daily services to/from Brisbane ($75, 6½ hours), Hervey Bay ($18, one hour) and Bundaberg ($18, 1½ hours).

Bundaberg

POP 60,000

Boasting a sublime climate, coral-fringed beaches and waving fields of sugar cane, 'Bundy' should feature on the Queensland tourist hit parade. But this old-fashioned country town feels stuck in a centuries-old time warp and nothing much seems to happen here. The pleasant main strip is a wide, palm-lined street, and the surrounding countryside forms a picturesque chequerboard of rich, red volcanic soil, small crops and sugar cane stretching pancake-flat to the coastal beaches 15km away. Born out of these cane fields is the famous Bundaberg Rum, a potent and mind-blowing liquor bizarrely endorsed by a polar bear but as iconically Australian as Tim Tams and Vegemite.

Hordes of backpackers flock to Bundy for fruit-picking and farm work; others quickly pass through on their way to family summer holidays at the nearby seaside villages.

◎ Sights & Activities

Bundaberg's biggest claim to fame is the iconic Bundaberg Rum. Aficionados of the good stuff can see the vats where liquid gold is made at the **Bundaberg Rum Distillery** (☎07-4131 2999; www.bundabergrum.com.au; Avenue St; self-guided tours adult/child $15/7.50, guided tours $25/12.50; ⊙9am-3.30pm Mon-Fri, to 2.30pm Sat & Sun). Tours follow the rum's production from start to finish and, if you're over 18, you get to sample the final product. The one-hour, wheelchair-accessible tours run every hour from 10am to 3pm. Note that you must wear closed-toe shoes.

Two kilometres north of the town, the **Botanic Gardens** (Mt Perry Rd; ⊘6am-6.30pm) are an oasis of tropical shrubs, towering trees and flowering gardens surrounding a few small lakes. Within the grounds are a number of museums, including the **Hinkler Hall of Aviation** (www.hinklerhallofaviation. com; Botanic Gardens, Mt Perry Rd; adult/child/family $15/10/40; ⊘9am-4pm), which has multimedia exhibits, a flight simulator, and informative displays about Bert Hinkler, the first pilot to fly solo between England and Australia, in 1928.

Bundaberg Ferry Company (✆07-4152 9188; 3 Quay St; 2½hr tours adult/child/family $25/13/70; ⊘9.30am Wed & Fri, 1.30pm Tue & Fri-Sun) runs slow-paced tours to the mouth of the Burnett River.

About 16km east of Bundaberg the small beach hamlet of **Bargara** entices divers and snorkellers with a dazzling bank of coral near the Barolin Rocks and in the Woongarra Marine Park. There are some good surf breaks here too, especially to the south of Bargara. **Dive Musgrave** (✆1800 552 614; www.divemusgrave.com.au; 239 Bourbong St; per person $698) leads three-day trips for experienced divers to Lady Musgrave and the Bunker island group in the Great Barrier Reef.

🛌 Sleeping

There are plenty of midrange motels on the Bundaberg–Childers road into town. Bundaberg's hostels cater to working backpackers; most hostels arrange harvest work, and stays of one week or longer are the norm. Check the hostels carefully before deciding, as standards vary considerably.

Inglebrae B&B **$$**
(✆07-4154 4003; www.inglebrae.com; 17 Branyan St; r incl breakfast $110-140; ❋) For old-world English charm in a glorious Queenslander, this delightful B&B is just the ticket. Polished timber and stained glass seep from the entrance into the rooms, which come with high beds and small antiques. Big breakfasts are served on the verandah.

Quality Hotel HOTEL **$$**
(✆07-4155 8777; www.burnettmotel.com.au; 7 Quay St; r $185-200; ❋⊛❀) The rooms at this top-notch hotel are quite stylish, and there's a gym, a sauna, and a licensed restaurant and cocktail bar overlooking the Burnett River.

Bundaberg Spanish Motor Inn MOTEL **$**
(✆07-4152 5444; www.bundabergspanishmotorinn. com; 134 Woongarra St; s/d$85/95; ❋⊛❀) In a quiet side street off the main drag, this Spanish hacienda–style motel is great value. All units are self-contained and all rooms overlook the central pool.

Cellblock Backpackers HOSTEL **$**
(✆1800 837 773; cnr Quay & Maryborough Sts; dm per night/week from $27/160, d $66; ❋⊛❀) Doing time has never been so good! This arresting hostel in Bundy's heritage-listed former lock-up is a swish resort with a trendy pool bar and clean, modern facilities. The seven restored jail cells (grab the padded cell!) lack windows (of course) but are great for couples. The hostel arranges harvest work.

Feeding Grounds Backpacker HOSTEL **$**
(✆07-4152 3659; www.footprintsadventures.com. au; 4 Hinkler Ave; dm $30) The smallest hostel in Bundaberg is a friendly, family-run affair in a converted and extended house. The environmentally conscious owner of the hostel runs Footprints Adventures turtle tours (see this spread). Combined accommodation and tour packages are available.

🍴 Eating & Drinking

Self-caterers should head to the **IGA supermarket** (Woongarra St).

Les Chefs INTERNATIONAL **$$**
(✆07-4153 1770; 238 Bourbong St; mains $27; ⊘lunch Tue-Fri, dinner Mon-Sat) One for the carnivores, this upmarket, intimate restaurant goes global, treating diners to duck, veal, seafood, chicken and beef dishes à la Nepal, Mexico, France, India and more. It's immensely popular, so make a reservation.

Spinnaker Restaurant & Bar MODERN AUSTRALIAN **$$**
(✆07-4152 8033; 1A Quay St; dishes $10-40; ⊘lunch Tue-Fri, dinner Tue-Sat) With a picturesque perch above the Burnett River, this is a great choice for a long lunch, an intimate dinner or a sundowner at the bar.

Spicy Tonight FUSION **$**
(✆07-4154 3320; 1 Targo St; dishes $12-20; ⊘lunch & dinner Mon-Sat) Bundaberg's spicy little secret combines Thai and Indian cuisine, with hot curries, vindaloo, tandoori and a host of vegetarian dishes.

Restaurant MODERN AUSTRALIAN **$$**
(✆07-4154 4589; cnr Quay & Toonburra Sts; mains $25-35; ⊘dinner Tue-Sat) Once a rowing shed,

this riverside bar and restaurant serves up simple Mod Oz cuisine. The interior can be a bit dim, but the outdoor tables on the timber deck make a lovely spot for a quiet drink. Live music plays on weekends.

Indulge CAFE $
(80 Bourbong St; dishes $9-16; ⊘breakfast & lunch) Intoxicating pastries, fancy brekkies, decent coffee and consistently good food draw in the crowds.

Teaspoon CAFE $
(10 Targo St; mains $5-10; ⊘8am-5pm Mon-Sat) This funky little cafe has the best coffee in town.

Central Hotel PUB
(18 Targo St) Strut your stuff on the dance floor at Bundy's hottest nightclub.

Club Hotel PUB
(cnr Tantitha & Bourbong Sts) The lounge bar has laid-back lounges and chill-out music.

❶ Information

Bundaberg Email Centre (197 Bourbong St; per hr $4; ⊘10am-10pm)
Bundaberg visitor centre (☑1300 722 099, 07-4153 8888; www.bundabergregion.info; 271 Bourbong St; ⊘9am-5pm)
QPWS (☑07-4131 1600; Targo St)

❶ Getting There & Away

The coach terminal is in Targo St. Both **Greyhound Australia** (☑1300 473 946; www.greyhound.com.au) and **Premier Motor Service** (☑13 34 10; www.premierms.com.au) have daily services connecting Bundaberg with Brisbane ($95, seven hours), Hervey Bay ($24, 1½ hours), Rockhampton ($75, four hours) and Gladstone ($50, 2½ hours).

Duffy's Coaches (☑07-4151 4226) has numerous weekday services to Bargara ($5, 35

minutes), leaving from the back of Target on Woongarra St and stopping around town.

Queensland Rail (☑13 12 30; www.queenslandrail.com.au) *Sunlander* ($68, seven hours, three weekly) and *Tilt Train* ($68, five hours, Sunday to Friday) services travel from Brisbane to Bundaberg on their respective routes to Cairns and Rockhampton.

Bundaberg's **Hinkler Airport** (Takalvan St) is about 4km southwest of the centre. There are several Bundaberg–Brisbane flights daily with **QantasLink** (☑13 13 13; www.qantas.com.au).

CAPRICORN COAST

The stunning powdery white beaches and aqua-blue waters of the tropical islands and coral cays of the Capricorn Coast superbly fit the picture-postcard image. The peaceful islands of the southern Great Barrier Reef – Heron and Lady Elliot in particular – offer some of the best snorkelling and diving in Queensland, while remote beaches and windswept national parks can be found along the entire Capricorn coastline from lovely Byfield to charming 1770.

Rising above the inland plains, the weathered plateaus of the Great Dividing Range form spectacular sandstone escarpments, especially around the Carnarvon and Blackdown Tableland National Parks, where ancient Aboriginal rock art, deep gorges and waterfalls abound.

Southern Reef Islands

Some of the Capricorn Coast's finest moments lie 80km to the northeast of Bundaberg, on these lush green-and-gold islands atop a glassy azure sea. More and more savvy travellers are doing their Great Barrier Reef

GRAND DAMES OF THE DEEP

At the dead of night on the quiet beach of Mon Repos, 15km northeast of Bundaberg, female loggerhead turtles lumber laboriously up the sand, scoop a shallow hole with their flippers, lay 100 or so eggs, then cover them up before returning to the ocean deep. About eight weeks later the hatchlings dig their way to the surface, and under cover of darkness emerge en masse to scurry down to the water as quickly as their little flippers allow. Egg laying and hatching takes place at night from November to March. The **Mon Repos visitor centre** (☑07-4159 1652; ⊘7.30am-6pm Mon-Fri) has information on turtle conservation and organises nightly tours (adult/child $10/5.25) from 7pm during the season. Bookings are mandatory and can be made through the Bundaberg visitor centre or online at www.bookbundabergregion.com.au. Alternatively, you can take a turtle-watching tour with **Footprints Adventures** (☑07-4152 3659; www.footprintsadventures.com.au; adult/child incl transfers $48/30).

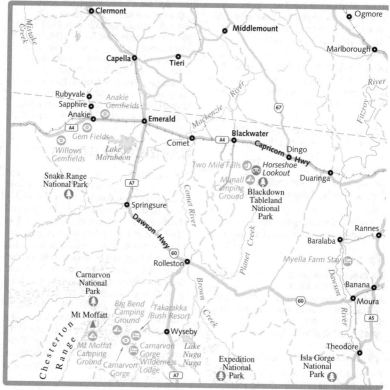

thing here – and for good reason. These sparkling coral cays are as good as it gets in Australia, without nearly the same crowds, storms or miles to travel. There's the diving wilderness of Lady Elliot and Lady Musgrave, while at secluded Heron Island you can literally wade into an underwater paradise.

The Town of 1770 is the most common stepping-off point (see p364); otherwise there's Hervey Bay or Bundaberg. Tours to the islands (from $175) stop at a number of beaches and snorkelling spots and include lunch. Alternatively, you can camp at Lady Musgrave, or stay overnight at the no-frills resort on Lady Elliot.

LADY ELLIOT ISLAND

On the southern frontier of the Great Barrier Reef, Lady Elliot is a 40-hectare vegetated coral cay popular with divers, snorkellers and nesting sea turtles. The island is a breeding and nesting ground for many species of tropical seabirds, but its stunning underwater landscape is the main attraction. Divers can walk straight off the beach to explore an ocean bed of shipwrecks, coral gardens, bommies (coral pinnacles or outcroppings) and blowholes, and abundant marine life including barracuda, giant manta rays and harmless leopard sharks.

Lady Elliot Island is not a national park, and camping is not allowed. Your only option is the low-key Lady Elliot Island Resort (☎1800 072 200; www.ladyelliot.com.au; per person $160-326). Accommodation at this basic resort is in tent cabins, simple motel-style units, or more expensive two-bedroom self-contained suites. Rates include breakfast and dinner, snorkelling gear and some tours.

Most resort guests travel to the island on light aircraft. Seair flies guests in from Bundaberg and Hervey Bay for $254/136 per adult/child return; book through the resort. Day trippers can visit the island on cruises from Bundaberg and Hervey Bay

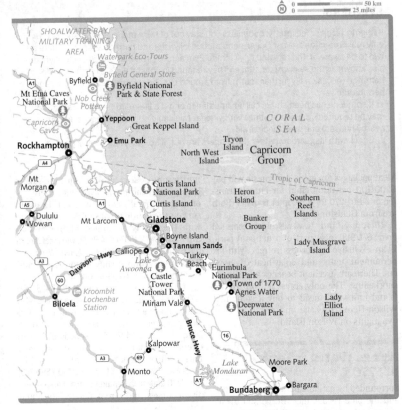

for $300/170, including tours and activities, lunch and snorkelling gear.

LADY MUSGRAVE ISLAND

Wannabe castaways look no further – this is the perfect desert island! This tiny 15-hectare cay 100km northeast of Bundaberg sits on the western rim of a stunning, turquoise-blue reef lagoon renowned for its safe swimming, snorkelling and diving. A squeaky, white-sand beach fringes a dense canopy of pisonia forest brimming with roosting bird life, including terns, shearwaters and white-capped noddies. Birds nest from October to April, green turtles from November to February.

The uninhabited island is part of the Capricornia Cays National Park and there is a QPWS camping ground on the island's west side. The camping ground has bush toilets but little else and campers must be totally self-sufficient, even bringing their own water. Numbers are limited to 40 at any one time, so apply well ahead for a permit with

the QPWS (☎13 74 68). Online bookings can be made through www.qld.gov.au/camping – search under Capricornia Cays National Park. Don't forget to bring a gas stove as fires are not permitted on the island.

Day trips to Lady Musgrave depart from the Town of 1770 marina (see p364).

HERON & WILSON ISLANDS

With the underwater reef world accessible directly from the beach, Heron Island is famed for scuba diving and snorkelling, although you'll need a fair amount of cash to visit. A true coral cay, it is densely vegetated with pisonia trees and surrounded by 24 sq km of reef. There's a resort and research station on the northeastern third of the island; the remainder is national park.

Heron Island Resort (☎07-4972 9055, 1800 737 678; www.heronisland.com; s/d incl buffet breakfast from $399/479) has comfortable accommodation suited to families and couples; the Point Suites have the best views.

It mightn't look or feel pretty, but unless you stay out of the water a 'stinger suit' is your only real protection against Queensland's lethal jellyfish (and harmful UV rays). There are two to be aware of: the rare and tiny (1cm to 2cm across) irukandji and the box jellyfish, also known as the sea wasp or stinger. They're found in coastal waters north of Rockhampton (occasionally further south) from around October to April, although the danger periods can vary.

If someone has been stung, call an ambulance or get a lifeguard (artificial respiration may be required), douse the stings with vinegar (available on many beaches or from nearby houses) and seek medical aid.

Check with lifeguards whether the stingers are out. If so, stick to the hotel pool.

Meal packages are extra, and guests will pay $200/100 per adult/child for launch transfer, or $440/270 for helicopter transfer. Both are from Gladstone.

Wilson Island (www.wilsonisland.com; s/d from $671/918), also part of a national park, is an exclusive wilderness retreat with six permanent tents and solar-heated showers. There are excellent beaches and superb snorkelling. The only access is from Heron Island and you'll need to buy a combined Wilson-Heron package and spend at least two nights on Wilson Island.

Agnes Water & Town of 1770

Surrounded by national parks, sandy beaches and the blue Pacific, the twin coastal towns of Agnes Water and Town of 1770 are among Queensland's most appealing seaside destinations. The tiny settlement of Agnes Water has a lovely white-sand beach, the east coast's most northerly surf beach, while the even tinier Town of 1770 (little more than a marina!) marks Captain Cook's first landing in Queensland. This area provides good access to the southern end of the reef, including the Fitzroy Reef Lagoon. The 'Discovery Coast' is a popular nook for surfing, boating and fishing away from the crowds. To get here, turn east off the Bruce Hwy at Miriam Vale, 70km south of Gladstone. It's another 57km to Agnes Water and a further 6km to the Town of 1770.

For info on the area, your best bet is **Agnes Water Visitor Information Centre** (☑07-4902 1533; Rural Transaction Centre, 3 Captain Cook Rd, Agnes Water).

🏃 Activities

The action around here happens on and in the water. Agnes Water is Queensland's northernmost **surf beach**. A surf life-saving club patrols the main beach and there are often good breaks along the coast. Learn to surf on the gentle breaks of the main beach with the highly acclaimed **Reef 2 Beach Surf School** (☑07-4974 9072; www.reef2beach surf.com; 1/10 Round Hill Rd, Agnes Water). A three-hour group surfing lesson is $17, and surfboard hire is $20 for four hours.

1770 Liquid Adventures (☑0428 956 630; www.1770liquidadventures.com.au; tours $40) runs a spectacular twilight kayak tour. You can also rent kayaks ($40 per half-day). **Dive 1770** (☑07-4974 9359; www.dive1770.com) offers PADI courses (from $250) and Great Barrier Reef dives (from $30). **1770 Underwater Sea Adventures** (☑1300 553 889; www.1770underseaadventures.com.au) also offers dive courses, and Great Barrier Reef and wreck dives.

You could also ride an automatic chopper down coastal tracks, past roos, wallabies and gorgeous sea-backed scrub. The laid-back South African guide at **Scooteroo** (☑07-4974 7696; www.scooterootours.com; 21 Bicentennial Dr, Agnes Water; 3hr chopper rides $55) makes the trip ultra-cool. Pick-ups are at around 2.45pm.

👉 Tours

1770 Larc Tours　　　　　　　AMPHIBIOUS
(☑07-4974 9422; www.1770larctours.com.au; adult/child $148/88) It might feel a touch A-Team, but these amphibious-vehicle tours to Bustard Head and Eurimbula National Park are eco-certified and heaps of fun. The outfit also runs daily one-hour sunset cruises ($35) and sandboarding safaris ($85 per person).

Lady Musgrave Cruises　　　　　　CRUISES
(☑07-4974 9077; www.1770reefcruises.com; Captain Cook Dr, Town of 1770; adult/child $175/85) Has excellent day trips to Lady Musgrave Is-

land aboard the *Spirit of 1770*. Trips include snorkelling, fishing gear, coral viewing in a semisubmersible, lunch and snacks. Island camping transfers are also available for $320 per person.

ThunderCat 1770 ADVENTURE, SIGHTSEEING
(☑0427 177 000; adult/child $85/65) Wide range of tours from adrenaline-fuelled wave jumping to more sedate Wilderness Explorer tours, where you visit secluded beaches, learn some local history and explore 1770's pristine waterways and national-park coastline.

🛏 Sleeping

Agnes Water Beach Caravan Park CARAVAN PARK, CABINS **$$**
(☑07-4974 9132; www.agneswaterfirstpoint.com.au; Jeffrey Ct, Agnes Water; unpowered sites $30, powered sites $59, cabins $120-$250) This park has tented cabins on stilts that offer excellent-value beachfront rooms. Each cabin comes with its own deck, equipped with gas barbecue.

Sandcastles 1770 Motel & Resort MOTEL, RESORT **$$**
(☑07-4974 9428; www.sandcastles1770.com.au; 1 Grahame Colyer Dr, Agnes Water; motel r from $120, villas/beach-home apt from $160-650; ❄@❄) Set on four hectares of landscaped gardens and subtropical vegetation, Sandcastles has a mix of motel-style rooms (from $90) luxury beach-home apartments and airy Balinese-themed villas. There's also a popular restaurant on site.

1770 Southern Cross Tourist Retreat HOSTEL **$**
(☑07-4974 7225; www.1770southerncross.com; 2694 Round Hill Rd, Agnes Water; dm/d incl breakfast $25/75; @❄) More of an eco-resort than a backpackers, this excellent retreat is set on 6.5 hectares of bushland 2.5km out of town. The three- and four-bed dorms are in clean, airy timber cabins, and there's an open-air meditation *sala*, a communal chill-out zone, kangaroos in the grounds, and a free shuttle bus to town. Bike hire is free, and you can swim or fish in the lake. There's a two-night minimum stay.

Cool Bananas HOSTEL **$**
(☑07-4974 7660; www.coolbananas.net.au; 2 Springs Rd, Agnes Water; dm $26; @) This funky Balinese-themed backpackers has roomy six- and eight-bed dorms and open and airy communal areas, and is only a five-minute walk to the beach and shops. Otherwise, you can laze the day away in a hammock in the tropical gardens.

Beach Shacks APARTMENTS **$$**
(☑07-4974 9463; www.1770beachshacks.com; 578 Captain Cook Dr, Town of 1770; d from $178) These delightful self-contained tropical 'shacks' are decorated in timber, cane and bamboo. They offer grand ocean views just a minute's walk from the water.

Mango Tree Motel MOTEL **$$**
(☑07-4974 9132; www.mangotreemotel.com; 7 Agnes St, Agnes Water; r from $135; ❄) Good-value motel with large rooms 100m from the beach.

Lodge GUESTHOUSE **$$$**
(☑07-4974 9257; www.1770sovereignlodge.com; 1 Elliot St, Town of 1770; d $165-280; ❄❄) Lovely boutique accommodation and spa with immaculate rooms, some with excellent views from its hilltop perch.

Agnes Water Beach Club APARTMENTS **$$**
(☑07-4974 7355; www.agneswaterbeachclub.com. au; 3 Agnes St, Agnes Water; 1-/2-bedroom apt from $145/190; ❄@❄) Brand-new luxury apartments with excellent facilities in a great location.

Backpackers 1770 HOSTEL **$**
(☑07-4974 9132; www.the1770backpackers. com; 7 Agnes St, Agnes Water; dm/d $25/55; @) Small friendly backpackers 700m from the beach.

1770 Camping Grounds CARAVAN PARK **$**
(☑07-4974 9286; www.1770campinggrounds. com; Captain Cook Dr, Town of 1770; unpowered/powered sites $33/38) A large peaceful park by the beach.

🍴 Eating

Deck MODERN AUSTRALIAN **$$**
(☑07-4974 9157; 584 Captain Cook Dr, Town of 1770; mains $20-30; ☉dinner Tue-Sun) Locally caught seafood is served inside or alfresco amongst the palms, accompanied by delicious sides or nestled in perfectly cooked pasta.

Tree Bar MODERN AUSTRALIAN **$$**
(☑07-4974 7446; 576 Captain Cook Dr, Town of 1770; mains $14-38; ☉breakfast, lunch & dinner) This little salt-encrusted waterfront diner has plenty of charm and an atmospheric bar. Seafood is a prime offering.

Getaway Garden Café MODERN AUSTRALIAN **$$**
(☑07-4974 9232; 303 Bicentennial Dr, Agnes Water; mains $8-27; ☉breakfast, lunch & dinner Sun-Thu, breakfast & lunch Fri) The airy outdoor cafe

serves delectable cakes for afternoon tea and is a short walk from several deserted beaches.

Kahunas Pizza Bar & Grill
MODERN AUSTRALIAN $$

(☎07-4974 9428; 1 Grahame Colyer Dr, Agnes Water; mains $15-38; ☯dinner) At Sandcastles, Kahunas is a popular choice, especially for beer and pizza on a hot night. There's plenty of meat on the chargrill and an excellent seafood plate.

ⓘ Getting There & Away
Only one of several daily **Greyhound** (☎13 20 30; www.greyhound.com.au) buses detours off the Bruce Hwy to Agnes Water; the direct bus from Bundaberg ($24, 1½ hours) arrives opposite Cool Bananas at 6.10pm. Others, including **Premier Motor Service** (☎13 34 10; www.premierms.com.au), drop passengers at Fingerboard Rd.

Rockhampton
POP 74,500

If the wide-brimmed hats, cowboy boots and V8 utes don't tip you off, the large bull statues around town let you know you're in the 'beef capital' of Australia. Despite the rough edges, there's something endearing about Rockhampton's crumbling deco and Queenslander buildings, cowboy-collared pub life and stiff tropical whiff along the mighty Fitzroy River. 'Rocky' has a smattering of attractions but is best seen as the gateway to the coastal gems of Yeppoon and Great Keppel Island.

Rockhampton Visitor Information Centre (208 Quay St) is in the beautiful former Customs House.

◉ Sights
Just south of town, Rockhampton's **Botanic Gardens** (☎07-4922 1654; Spencer St; ☯6am-6pm) are a beautiful oasis with tropical and subtropical rainforest, landscaped gardens and lily-covered lagoons. The **cafe** (☯8am -5pm) serves tea and cakes under a giant banyan fig, and the **zoo** (☯8.30am-4.30pm) has koalas, wombats, dingoes and a walk-through aviary.

The **Dreamtime Cultural Centre** (☎07-4936 1655; www.dreamtimecentre.com.au; Bruce Hwy; adult/child $14/6.50; ☯10am-3.30pm Mon-Fri, tours 10.30am & 1pm) is an easily accessible insight into Aboriginal and Torres Strait Islander heritage and history. The excellent 90-minute tours are hands on (boomerangs!) and appeal to all ages. It's about 7km north of the centre.

Rockhampton City Art Gallery (62 Victoria Pde; admission free; ☯10am-4pm Tue-Fri, 11am-4pm Sat & Sun) exhibits an impressive collection of Australian paintings, including works by Sir Russell Drysdale, Sir Sidney Nolan and Albert Namatjira.

🛏 Sleeping
Rockhampton has plenty of motels lining the highway, most with attached restaurants. Choose somewhere in the old centre, south of the river, if you want to stroll the elegant palm-lined streets overlooking the Fitzroy.

Criterion
HOTEL $$

(☎07-4922 1225; www.thecriterion.com.au; 150 Quay St; r $55-80, motel r $125-150; ✳) The Criterion is Rockhampton's grandest old pub, with an elegant foyer, a friendly bar and a great bistro. Its top two storeys have dozens of period rooms (with showers only), some of which have been lovingly restored. The hotel also has a few decent motel rooms.

Rockhampton YHA
HOSTEL $

(☎07-4927 5288; www.yha.com.au; 60 MacFarlane St; dm $22, d $50-67; ✳@☒) This well-maintained hostel has a spacious lounge and dining area, dorms, private doubles and cabins. The hostel arranges tours, has courtesy pick-ups from the bus station, and sells coach tickets.

Denison Hotel
BOUTIQUE HOTEL $$

(☎07-4923 7378; www.denisonhotel.com.au; 233 Denison St; r $165-200; ✳@) This freshly renovated 1885 Victorian home is an easy walk from Quay St. Its stately rooms come with four-poster beds and plasma TVs, and the hotel's Rolls Royce can pick you up from the airport or station.

Coffee House
MOTEL, APARTMENTS $$

(☎07-4927 5722; www.coffeehouse.com.au; 51 William St; r $160-189; ✳☒) The Coffee House features beautifully appointed motel rooms, self-contained apartments and spa suites. There's a popular and stylish cafe-restaurant–wine bar on site.

Southside Holiday Village
CARAVAN PARK, CABINS $

(☎1800 075 911; www.sshv.com.au; Lower Dawson Rd; sites unpowered/powered/with bathroom $25/32/42, cabins $62-102; ✳☒) This excellent caravan park has cabins, villas and

large grassy campsites about 3km south of the centre. There's a courtesy coach.

Eating

Saigon Saigon ASIAN $$
(☑07-4927 0888; www.saigonbytheriver.com; Quay St; mains $15-20; ☺lunch & dinner Wed-Mon) This two-storey bamboo hut near the corner with Denham St overlooks the Fitzroy River and serves pan-Asian food with local ingredients like kangaroo and crocodile served in a sizzling steamboat (pre-order required for these exotic treats). If you're not up for reptile, try the crispy chicken or the king prawns.

Pacino's ITALIAN $$
(☑07-4922 5833; cnr Fitzroy & George Sts; mains $19-39; ☺dinner Tue-Sun) This stylish Italian restaurant oozes Mediterranean warmth with its stone floors, wooden tables and potted fig trees.

Cassidy's SEAFOOD, STEAKHOUSE $$
(☑07-4927 5322; www.98.com.au; 98 Victoria Pde; mains $18-46; ☺breakfast daily, lunch Mon-Fri, dinner Mon-Sat) One of Rocky's finest, this licensed dining room features modern Australian versions of kangaroo, steak, lamb and seafood. Sit inside or on the terrace overlooking the river.

🍷 Drinking & Entertainment

Great Western Hotel BAR, RESTAURANT
(www.greatwesternhotel.com.au; 39 Stanley St) Looking like a spaghetti-western film set, this 116-year-old pub is home to Rocky's cowboys and -gals. Out back there's a rodeo arena where every Wednesday (which is also two-for-one meal night in the bistro) and Friday night you can watch poor brave fools try to ride bucking bulls and broncos. DJs and occasional live acts also feature on Friday night.

Heritage Hotel PUB
(☑07-4927 6996; cnr William & Quay St) This grand old pub with iron-lattice balconies has a stylish cocktail lounge with river views and outdoor tables. After-work drinks can linger on to dinner in the tavern (meals $7 to $21), where the extensive menu includes pizzas, burgers and lamb shank pie as well as the ubiquitous steak.

🛍 Shopping

Mavericks CLOTHING
(☑07-4921 0622; 33 Stanley St) Attached to the Great Western Hotel, Mavericks sells

quality belt buckles, Akubra hats, stockman whips and other countrified regalia.

❶ Getting There & Away

Air

Rockhampton is serviced by **Qantas** (☑13 13 13; www.qantas.com.au), **Virgin Australia** (☑13 67 89; www.virginaustralia.com) and **Tiger Airways** (☑03-9999 2888; www.tigerairways.com).

Bus

Greyhound Australia (☑13 20 30; www.greyhound.com.au) has regular services from Rocky to Mackay ($60, four hours), Brisbane ($114, 11 hours) and Cairns ($178, 18 hours). All services stop at the **Mobil roadhouse** (91 George St). **Premier Motor Service** (☑13 34 10; www.premierms.com.au) operates a Brisbane–Cairns service, stopping at Rockhampton.

Young's Bus Service (☑07-4922 3813) to Yeppoon ($12.10, 45 minutes) includes a loop through Rosslyn Bay and Emu Park. Young's also has buses to Mt Morgan ($12.10, 50 minutes) Monday to Friday. Buses depart the Kern Arcade in Bolsover St.

Train

Queensland Rail (☑1800 872 467; www.queenslandrail.com.au) runs the *Tilt Train*, which connects Rockhampton with Brisbane (from $119, 7½ hours, Sunday to Friday) and Cairns (from $266, 16 hours, twice weekly). The slower *Sunlander* also connects Brisbane with Rockhampton three times a week and has a sleeper service between Rockhampton and Cairns (sleepers from $252, 20 hours). The *Spirit of the Outback* also connects Rockhampton with Brisbane (from $119, twice weekly), Emerald ($65, five hours, twice weekly) and Longreach ($130, 14 hours, twice weekly). The train station is 450m southwest of the city centre.

Around Rockhampton

About 24km north in the Berserker Range are the impressive **Capricorn Caves** (☑07-4934 2883; www.capricorncaves.com.au; Caves Rd; adult/child $26/13; ☺9am-4pm). These deeply illuminated limestone passages are particularly spectacular during the summer solstice period (1 December to 14 January), when the sun beams vertical light through the roof of the Belfry Cave. The informative one-hour Cathedral Tour is an easy guided walk that leaves on the hour.

Myella Farm Stay (☑07-4998 1290; www.myella.com; Baralaba Rd; 3/7 days $360/750, day trips $110; ❋@❋) offers a chance to stay at an authentic cattle station without having

to travel all the way to whoop-whoop. This 1040-hectare beef property 120km south-west of Rockhampton is a fully renovated homestead, fitted with hardwood floors and pine-scented mod cons. There's plenty to do – including exploring the bush on horseback, motorcycle or 4WD and caring for orphaned joeys at the on-site kangaroo rehab centre – but some prefer just unwinding in the almost outback. Prices include free transfers from Rockhampton.

Another fine farmstay is at **Kroombit Lochenbar Station** (07-4992 2186; www.kroombit.com.au; dm $27, d with/without bathroom $84/68, 2-day & 2-night packages per person incl r, meals & activities $280; ❋@❄), 35km east of Biloela.

Yeppoon

POP 13,300

The gateway to Great Keppel Island, Yeppoon is an attractive seaside village with pleasant beaches giving way to untapped rainforest around Byfield. Travelling south, you pass Rosslyn Bay, the departure point for Great Keppel, and lovely little Emu Park, before winding your way along similarly scenic coastline.

For information on the area, head to **Capricorn Coast Information Centre** (1800 675 785; www.capricorncoast.com.au; Scenic Hwy; ⊙9am-5pm).

🛏 Sleeping

Surfside Motel MOTEL $
(07-4939 1272; 30 Anzac Pde; r $90-95; ❋@❄❄) Across the road from the beach and close to town, this 1950s strip of lime-green motel units epitomises summer holidays at the beach. And it's terrific value – the rooms are spacious and unusually well equipped, complete with free wi-fi.

Driftwood Motel & Holiday Units MOTEL $$
(07-4939 2446; www.driftwoodunits.com.au; 5-7 Todd Ave; r $99-130; ❋❄) Driftwood has huge self-contained units at motel prices with absolute beach frontage. There are good family units with separate bedrooms and a children's playground, but be aware that there's a four-night minimum stay in high season.

Emu's Beach Resort & Backpackers HOSTEL $
(1800 333 349; www.emusbeachresort.com; 92 Pattison St, Emu Park; dm $24-27, d/tr/q $75/90/100; ❋@❄) This low-key, welcoming place sits across the road from Emu Beach, 19km south of Yeppoon. The central pool and barbecue are a major draw and dorms are self-contained and spacious (if a touch stuffy).

While Away B&B B&B $$
(07-4939 5719; www.whileawaybandb.com.au; 44 Todd Ave; s/d incl breakfast $115/140; ❋) This B&B makes for a peaceful getaway, with four good-sized rooms and an immaculately clean house, as well as generous breakfasts.

Rydges Capricorn Resort RESORT $$$
(1800 075 902; www.capricornresort.com; Farnborough Rd; d $179-350; ❋❋) A large and lavish golf resort about 8km north of central Yeppoon.

Beachside Caravan Park CARAVAN PARK $
(07-4939 3738; Farnborough Rd; unpowered/powered sites $21/26-29) Basic camping park north of the town centre with a beach-front location.

🍴 Eating & Drinking

Shio Kaze JAPANESE $$
(07-4939 5575; 18 Anzac Pde; for 2 people about $50; ⊙lunch & dinner Wed-Sun) Shio Kaze serves delicious, great-value sushi overlooking the beach. BYO alcohol.

Thai Take-Away THAI $$
(24 Anzac Pde; mains $12-20; ⊙dinner) A deservedly popular BYO restaurant where you can dine alfresco while satisfying those chilli and coconut cravings. There's a large selection of seafood dishes and snappy service.

Megalomania MODERN AUSTRALIAN $$
(07-4939 2333; Arthur St; mains $22-36; ⊙11am-late) Another ultra-cool hang-out with an urban-islander vibe, this is a great place for a drink or dinner. The menu changes weekly.

Strand Hotel PUB $
(2 Normanby St) The battered old Strand has live music every weekend. The pub serves $10 counter meals at lunch and dinner daily, but is especially known for its Sunday-evening *parrilla*, an Argentine-style barbecue with music to match. The pub's on the corner of Anzac Pde.

Around Yeppoon

The rainforest scrub and rocky headlands of **Byfield National Park** are superb Sunday-arvo driving terrain, with plenty of hiking

paths. There are five **camping grounds** (☏13 74 68; www.derm.qld.gov.au/camping; per person/family $5.15/20.60) to choose from; all must be prebooked. Nine Mile Beach and Five Rocks campgrounds are on the beach and require a 4WD to access. When conditions are right, there's decent surf at Nine Mile Beach. **Byfield General Store** (☏07-4935 1190; Byfield Rd, Byfield; ☺8am-6pm Wed-Mon, to 2pm Tue) has fuel and food, and doubles as an information centre.

The area is also known for the highly controversial military training facility at Shoalwater Bay that borders the forest and park, and is strictly off-limits.

It's worth a detour to **Nob Creek Pottery** (☏07-4935 1161; 216 Arnolds Rd; admission free; ☺9am-5pm), a working pottery and gallery nestled in leafy rainforest. The gallery showcases hand-blown glass, woodwork and jewellery, and the handmade ceramics are outstanding.

Unfurl your senses in the rainforest on a silent, electric-boat tour with **Waterpark Eco-Tours** (☏07-4935 1171; www.waterparkecotours.com; 201 Waterpark Creek Rd; 2-3hr tours $25, cabins $110; ▣). The 97-hectare farm has a beautiful self-contained timber cabin, where you can swing in a hammock, swim in the creek, or just relax in the outdoor hot tub.

Byfield Creek Lodge (☏07-4935 1117; www.byfieldcreeklodge.com.au; 32 Richters Rd, Byfield; d incl breakfast from $150; ▣) is an African-themed B&B set on 3.2 hectares of rainforest overlooking Byfield Creek.

Signposted just north of Byfield, **Ferns Hideaway** (☏07-4935 1235; www.fernshideaway.com.au; 67 Cahills Rd, Byfield; unpowered sites $24, d $150; ▣▣) is a secluded bush oasis with double rooms, a campground and canoeing and nature walks. The timber homestead has a quality à la carte **restaurant** (mains $18-32; ☺lunch & afternoon tea Wed-Sun, dinner Sat, breakfast Sun) featuring live music on weekends.

Great Keppel Island

Great Keppel Island is a stunningly beautiful island with rocky headlands, forested hills and a fringe of powdery white sand lapped by clear azure waters. Numerous 'castaway' beaches ring the 14-sq-km island, while natural bushland covers 90% of the interior. A string of huts and accommodation options sits behind the trees lining the main beach, but the developments are low-key and rela-

tively unobtrusive. Only 13km offshore, and with good snorkelling, swimming and bushwalking, Great Keppel is an easily accessible, tranquil island retreat.

◉ Sights & Activities

The beaches of Great Keppel rate among Queensland's best. Take a short stroll from **Fisherman's Beach**, the main beach, and you'll find your own deserted stretch of white sand. There is fairly good coral and excellent fish life, especially between Great Keppel and Humpy Island to the south. A 30-minute walk south around the headland brings you to **Monkey Beach**, where there's good snorkelling. A walking trail from the southern end of the airfield takes you to **Long Beach**, perhaps the best of the island's beaches.

There are several bushwalking tracks from Fisherman's Beach; the longest and perhaps most difficult leads to the 2.5m 'lighthouse' near **Bald Rock Point** on the far side of the island (three hours return).

You can see an **underwater observatory** off Middle Island, close to Great Keppel. A confiscated Taiwanese fishing junk was sunk next to the observatory to provide a haven for fish.

The **Watersports Hut** on the main beach hires out snorkelling equipment, kayaks and catamarans, and runs banana rides. You can buy drinks and ice creams at the Sandbar here and watch the sun set over the water.

Keppel Reef Scuba Adventures (☏07-4939 5022, 0408 004 536; www.keppeldive.com; Putney Beach) offers introductory dives for $200, snorkelling trips (per person $50), and also hires out snorkelling gear (per day $15).

☞ Tours

Freedom Fast Cats   CRUISES
(☏07-4933 6888; Rosslyn Bay marina; adult/child $63/42) Freedom's coral cruises visit the best location of the day (depending on tides and weather) and include viewing through a glass-bottomed boat and fish feeding. There are also afternoon and full-day cruises (adult/child $130/85, including snorkelling and barbecue lunch).

🛏 Sleeping

🌿**Svendsen's Beach**   CABINS **$**
(☏07-4938 3717; www.svendsensbeach.com; Svendsen's Beach; cabins per 3 nights $285) This secluded, environmentally friendly boutique retreat has two luxury tent-

bungalows on separate elevated timber decks overlooking lovely Svendsen's Beach. Minimum three-night stay.

Great Keppel Island Backpackers & Holiday Village
HOSTEL, CABINS **$$**

(07-4939 8655; www.gkiholidayvillage.com.au; dm $35, s & d tents $85, cabins $140, 2-bedroom houses from $220) This friendly, relaxed place has dorms, cabins, holiday homes and tent space, and good communal facilities.

Keppel Lodge
GUESTHOUSE **$**

(07-4939 4251; www.keppellodge.com.au; Fisherman's Beach; s/d from $90-100) A pleasant open-plan house with four large bedrooms branching from a large communal lounge and kitchen. The house is available in its entirety or as individual motel-type suites.

Eating & Drinking

The kiosk at Great Keppel Island Holiday Village has a few essentials, but if you want to cook bring your own supplies.

Island Pizza
PIZZA **$**

(07-4939 4699; The Esplanade; dishes $6-30) This friendly place prides itself on its gourmet pizzas with plenty of toppings. The pizzas are rather pricey but still tempting. Check the blackboard for opening times.

Getting There & Away

Freedom Fast Cats (1800 336 244, 07-4933 6244; www.freedomfastcats.com) departs the Keppel Bay marina in Rosslyn Bay (7km south of Yeppoon) for Great Keppel Island each morning, returning that same afternoon (call ahead for precise times). The return fare is $49/29/127 per adult/child/family. If you have booked accommodation, check that someone will meet you on the beach to help with your luggage.

Other Keppel Bay Islands

Although you can make day trips to the fringing coral reefs of Middle Island or Halfway Island from Great Keppel Island (ask your accommodation or at Great Keppel Island Holiday Village), you can also camp (per person/family $5.15/21) on several national park islands, including Humpy Island, Middle Island, North Keppel Island and Miall Island. You'll need all your own supplies, including water. For information and permits contact the QPWS (13 74 68; www.qld.gov.au/camping) or Rosslyn Bay Marine Parks (07-4933 6595).

Tiny, privately owned Pumpkin Island (07-4939 4413; www.pumpkinisland.com.au; camping per person $20, cabins $300-480), just south of North Keppel, has five simple, cosy cabins with water, solar power, kitchen and bathroom; bring food and linen. There's also a small campsite with its own private beach, hot water and barbecue. Return boat transfer per adult/child is $50/30.

From Rosslyn Bay, Funtastic Cruises (0438 909 502; cruises adult/child $90/75) offers day cruises exploring the islands and can also provide drop-offs and pick-ups for campers.

Capricorn Hinterland

Aboriginal rock art, spectacular sandstone cliffs, deep gorges and precious gemstones are just some of the surprises to be found in the dry Central Highlands west of Rockhampton. Blackdown Tableland National Park is a brooding, powerful place, but don't miss the opportunity to see spectacular Carnarvon National Park. At Emerald, 270km inland, you'll find yourself in one of the world's largest gem fields. Try to stick to the cooler months between April and November.

BLACKDOWN TABLELAND NATIONAL PARK

Spooky, spectacular Blackdown Tableland is a 600m sandstone plateau that rises suddenly out of the flat plains of central Queensland. It's a bushwalker's heaven here, with unique wildlife and plant species and a strong Indigenous artistic and spiritual presence. The turn-off to Blackdown Tableland is 11km west of Dingo and 35km east of the coal-mining centre of Blackwater. The 23km gravel road, which begins at the base of the tableland, isn't suitable for caravans and can be unsafe in wet weather – the first 8km stretch is steep, winding and often slippery. At the top you'll come to the breathtaking Horseshoe Lookout, with picnic tables, barbecues and toilets. There's a walking trail to Two Mile Falls (2km) starting here.

Munall Camping Ground (13 74 68; www.qld.gov.au/camping; per person/family $5.15/21) is about 8km on from Horseshoe Lookout. It has pit toilets and fireplaces – you'll need water, firewood and/or a fuel stove. Bookings are essential.

GEM FIELDS

In the fields west of Emerald (named after Emerald Creek, in turn named after a local

prospector, Jack Emerald) tales of instant fortune have a sprinkling of truth. Sapphires, rubies and zircons to cry for have all fallen into lucky folk's hands. In fact, the gem fields around Anakie, Sapphire, Rubyvale and Willows are the world's largest of their kind and renowned for large, rare sapphires.

To go fossicking you need a licence (adult/family $6.50/9.25) from the Emerald Courthouse or one of the gem fields' general stores or post offices. If you just wish to dabble, you can buy a bucket of 'wash' (mine dirt in water) from one of the fossicking parks and hand-sieve and wash it. If you're serious, however, wait for a heavy rain and then keep your eyes glued to the sparkling surface.

In Anakie, 42km west of Emerald, the Big Sapphire Gemfields Information Centre (☎07-4985 4525; 1 Anakie Rd, Anakie; ☉8am-6pm) has maps of the fields and fossicking licences; it also hires out fossicking equipment. If you need a helping hand, Jake's Fossicking Tour (☎07-4985 4142; Anakie Gemfields Caravan Park; Capricorn Hwy; tours $40) leaves daily from the Anakie Gemfields Caravan Park.

Another 18km on is Rubyvale, the main town on the fields, and 2km further is the excellent Miners Heritage Walk-in Mine (☎07-4985 4444; Heritage Rd, Rubyvale; adult/child $13/5; ☉9am-5pm), which has informative 30-minute underground tours throughout the day in which you descend into a maze of tunnels 18m beneath the surface.

Pat's Gems (☎07-4985 4544; www.patsgems.com.au; 1056 Rubyvale Rd; cabins $75; ❋) has four small, cosy cabins and a camp barbecue and kitchen area. There's an onsite cafe (☉8.30am-5pm).

There are caravan-camping parks at Anakie, Rubyvale and Willows Gemfields.

CARNARVON NATIONAL PARK

One of the highlights of all Queensland, Carnarvon Gorge is a dramatic rendition of Australian natural beauty. The 30km-long, 200m-high gorge was carved out over millions of years by Carnarvon Creek and its tributaries twisting through soft sedimentary rock. What was left behind is a lush, other-worldly oasis, where life flourished, shielded from the stark terrain.

You'll find giant cycads, king ferns, river oaks, flooded gums, cabbage palms, deep pools and platypuses in the creek. It's hardly surprising that humanity has revered this place for so long – the Aboriginal rock paintings and carvings here are detailed and easily accessible – or that fleeing convicts and

escape artists have taken refuge in its nooks and crannies. The area was made a national park in 1932 after defeated farmers forfeited their pastoral lease.

For most people, Carnarvon Gorge *is* the Carnarvon National Park, because the other sections – including Mt Moffatt (where Indigenous groups lived some 19,000 years ago), Ka Ka Mundi and Salvator Rosa – have long been difficult to access. Much of that is changing now, so expect a small rise in tourism to the area.

Coming from Rolleston the road is bitumen for 70km and unsealed for 25km. From Roma via Injune and Wyseby homestead, the road is good bitumen for about 215km, then unsealed and fairly rough for the last 30km. After heavy rain, both these roads can become impassable.

The entrance road leads to an information centre (☎07-4984 4505; ☉8-10am & 3-5pm) and scenic picnic ground. The main walking track also starts here, following Carnarvon Creek through the gorge, with detours to various points of interest. These include the Moss Garden (3.6km from the picnic area), Ward's Canyon (4.8km), the Art Gallery (5.6km) and Cathedral Cave (9.3km). Allow *at least* a whole day for a visit. Basic groceries and ice are available at Takarakka Bush Resort. Petrol is not available anywhere in the gorge – fill up at Rolleston or Injune.

You cannot drive from Carnarvon Gorge to other sections of the park, although you can reach beautiful Mt Moffatt via an unsealed road from Injune (4WD necessary).

Sunrover Expeditions (☎1800 353 717; www.sunrover.com.au; per person incl all meals $940) runs a five-day camping safari into Carnarvon Gorge between March and October.

🛌 Sleeping

It's best to book ahead, especially if you're visiting from April to October.

Takarakka Bush Resort   CARAVAN PARK, CABINS $$
(☎07-4984 4535; www.takarakka.com.au; Wyseby Rd; unpowered/powered sites from $28/34, cabins $95-220) About 5km from the picnic ground, this picturesque campsite is perfect for families, couples and intrepid explorers. The elevated canvas cabins are airy and durable (BYO fresh linen). The private verandahs are great for kangaroo spotting. The shared cooking and bathing facilities are excellent, and reception sells drinks, groceries, maps and ice.

Carnarvon Gorge Wilderness Lodge   LODGE **$$**

(☑1800 644 150; www.carnarvon-gorge.com; Wyseby Rd; per person from $150; ⊘closed Dec-Feb; ☒) Outback chic is on offer at this attractive wilderness lodge set deep in the bush. Excellent guided tours are available, plus a full-board package (from $155 to $300 per person).

Bookings are required for both these camping options:

Big Bend Camping Ground   CAMPGROUND **$**

(☑13 74 68; www.qld.gov.au/camping; sites per person/family $5.15/21) Isolated camping ground a 10km walk up the gorge.

Mt Moffatt Camping Ground   CAMPGROUND **$**

(☑13 74 68; www.qld.gov.au/camping; sites per person/family $5.15/21) Campers need to be self-sufficient and have a 4WD.

❶ Getting There & Away

There are no bus services to Carnarvon, so your best bet is to hire a car or take an overnight tour from the coast.

OUTBACK

A proper noun of staggering proportions, the outback is an awesome frontier where settler folk struck open the deep-red earth and bored out a nation through myth and verse. If coastal Queenslanders try to tell you there's 'nothing out there', don't listen. This mineral-rich region is vast and wealthy, the livestock fit and full, and the Indigenous songlines deep. Plus this ancient landscape was once the playground of marauding dinosaurs!

It's out here, past the Great Dividing Range, that the sky opens wide and the sun beats down on tough country, both relentless and beautiful, where an honest day meets a silent, starry night, and more than

the occasional character. Travellers come here for the exotic and intimate Australian experience, their restlessness tamed by the sheer size of the place, the rare colours it exudes and the dusty bare earth underfoot.

Although sparsely settled, the outback is well serviced by major roads, namely the Overlander's Way (Flinders and Barkly Hwys – Rtes 78 and 66) and the Matilda Hwy (Landsborough Hwy, Rte 71) and Burke Developmental Rd (Rte 83). Once you turn off these major arteries, however, road conditions deteriorate rapidly, services are remote and you need to be fully self-sufficient, carrying spare parts, fuel and water. Also do some planning, as some sights and accommodation options (in particular the outback stations) close from November to March, the outback's hottest period.

❶ Getting There & Away

Air

Qantas and **QantasLink** (☑13 13 13; www.qantas.com.au) fly from Brisbane to Barcaldine, Blackall, Charleville, Longreach and Mt Isa. The Cairns-based **Skytrans** (☑1300 759 872; www.skytrans.com.au) also flies between Brisbane and various outback destinations. It also connects Mt Isa to Cairns.

Bus

Greyhound Australia (☑13 14 99; www.greyhound.com.au) connects Mt Isa to Townsville ($157, 12 hours), and Brisbane ($210, 27 hours). From Mt Isa, buses continue to Tennant Creek in the Northern Territory; from there you can head north to Darwin or south to Alice Springs.

Paradise Coaches (☑1300 300 156; www.paradisecoaches.com.au) runs from Rockhampton to Longreach twice weekly via Emerald.

Train

The grandest way to travel the outback is with **Queensland Rail** (☑1800 872 467; www.queenslandrail.com.au), which runs three

---

OUTBACK FARMSTAYS

One of the best ways to experience western Queensland is to stay on one of the area's vast cattle stations, where you can get a close-up look at the way of life – and the economic lifeblood – of the outback. Most offer station tours and other activities. **Nardoo Station** (☑07-4655 4833; www.nardoo.com.au; Mitchell Hwy; unpowered/powered sites $17/20, dm $27, cabins $82; ☒), a 45,000-hectare sheep and cattle station with spotless lodgings in old shearer's quarters, is one of the best. As you're soaking in a hot artesian spa under a billion stars you'll feel a world away from civilisation. Offering similar experiences are **Thurlby Station** (☑07-4654 2430; Adavale Rd; unpowered/powered sites $24/26, cabins $104), just 9km west of Charleville, and Carisbrooke Station (see p377) outside Winton.

services, all leaving twice weekly. The *Spirit of the Outback* runs from Brisbane to Longreach (economy seat/sleeper $185/240, 26 hours) via Rockhampton and Emerald, with connecting bus services to Winton. The *Westlander* runs from Brisbane to Charleville (economy seat/sleeper $100/160, 17 hours), with connecting bus services to Cunnamulla and Quilpie; and the *Inlander* runs from Townsville to Mt Isa (economy seat/sleeper $125/188, 21 hours).

Charters Towers to Cloncurry

The Flinders Hwy runs a gruelling 775km stretch of mostly flat road from Charters Towers west to little Cloncurry. The highway was originally a Cobb & Co coach run, and along its length are small towns established as coach stopovers. At **Prairie**, 200km west of Charters Towers, the friendly, supposedly haunted **Prairie Hotel** (☑07-4741 5121; Flinders Hwy; unpowered/powered sites $12/20, s/d from $50/85; ✱) is filled with memorabilia and atmosphere. Further along is **Hughenden**, with its interesting display of dinosaur fossils and excellent burger joint **FJ Holden's** (☑07-4741 5121; cnr Brodie St & Flinders Hwy; meals $5-24; ☺8am-8pm Mon-Sat, 9am-8pm Sun).

Richmond has even more dinosaur bones in its admirable little museum at **Kronosaurus Korner** (☑07-4741 3429; www.kronosaurus korner.com.au; 91 Goldring St; adult/child $12/6; ☺8.30am-4.45pm). The centre houses easily the best collection of marine fossils in the region, most found by local landholders. Pride of place goes to an almost complete 4.25m pliosaur skeleton – one of Australia's best vertebrate fossils – and a partial skeleton of *Kronosaurus queenslandicus*, the largest known marine reptile to have ever lived here. A video explains some of the prehistory and the background of the finds.

The **Porcupine Gorge National Park** (☑13 74 68; www.qld.gov.au/camping; camping per person/family $5.15/21) is an oasis in the dry country north of Hughenden. The best spot to go to is **Pyramid Lookout**, about 70km north of Hughenden. You can camp here and it's an easy 30-minute walk into the gorge, with some fine rock formations and a permanently running creek.

Julia Creek, 144km further on, is a nowhere outback town with a smattering of motels and a caravan park. From Julia Creek, the sealed Wills Developmental Rd heads north to Normanton (432km; see

p460), Karumba (494km; see p460) and Burketown (467km; see p461).

Cloncurry

POP 5200

Lying 121km east of Mt Isa, the 'Curry' was the birthplace of the Royal Flying Doctor Service (RFDS); Qantas Airways was also conceived here. In the 19th century Cloncurry was the largest producer of copper in the British Empire. Today it's a busy pastoral centre with a reinvigorated mining industry.

John Flynn Place (☑07-4742 4125; cnr Daintree & King Sts; adult/child $8.50/4; ☺8am-4.30pm Mon-Fri, 9am-3pm Sat & Sun Apr-Oct) commemorates the pioneering work of Dr John Flynn in setting up the invaluable RFDS.

The best place to sleep is the clean, comfortable **Wagon Wheel Motel** (☑07-4742 1866; 54 Ramsay St; s/d from $70/81; ✱✱), which sports a friendly bar. There's also the upmarket **Gidgee Inn** (☑07-4742 1599; www.gidgeeinn.com.au; d/tw $136/150; ✱✱), packed together with rammed red earth, and the **Gilbert Park Tourist Village** (☑07-4742 2300; www.gilbertpark.com.au; Flinders Hwy; unpowered/powered sites $20/26, cabins from $90).

Mt Isa

POP 22,600

Boisterous, prosperous Mt Isa is a long way from everywhere, and unlike anywhere else. Around the clock this wealthy mining town lights up the starry sky, as tireless men and their machines dig deep into the night. The locals are a mix of well-to-do, how-do-*you*-do cowboys and girls and itinerant easy-going wage earners. But everyone shares the dusty heat and geographic isolation – often over multiple beers – and the sense of community is palpable.

The most pleasant surprise to first-time visitors to Isa is the stark red beauty of the place. Strange rocky formations – padded with olive-green spinifex – line the perimeter of town as deep-blue sunsets eclipse all unnatural light.

◉ Sights & Activities

Don't miss Mt Isa's extra-sensory sunset at the **City Lookout**, off Hilary St. It's free and hard to forget.

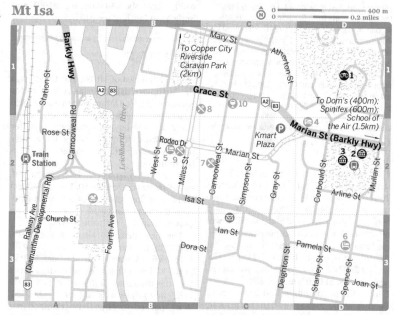

Mt Isa

The Australian Tourism Award–winning **Outback at Isa** (☎1300 659 660; www.out backatisa.com.au; 19 Marian St; ☺8.30am-5pm) is featured on most itineraries, and for good reason. The hands-on museum provides a colourful, articulate and air-conditioned overview of mining, pioneering and local history. It comprises a number of galleries and experiences. The **Hard Times Mine** (adult/child $45/26) takes you 10m beneath the surface (the real mines descend up to 10 times that distance) to a purpose-built mine complete with fuming, roaring and rattling machinery.

The fascinating **Riversleigh Fossil Centre** (adult/child $12/7.50) is also here. If you think Australia has strange animals now, then check out what *used* to roam the land. The re-creation of Australia's prehistoric fauna is the stuff of science fiction, plus you can examine actual fossils. The centre also houses the **Isa Experience Gallery** (adult/child $12/7.50) and **Outback Park**, showcasing natural, Indigenous and mining heritage of Mt Isa. There's a good-value, two-day **Discovery Tour Pass** (adult/child $55/36), which combines all the attractions.

Also worth a peek is the **School of the Air** (☎07-4744 9100; Kalkadoon High School, Abel Smith Pde; admission $2.50; ☺tours 10am Mon-Fri during school term), which puts Isa's isolation into perspective.

If in town during the second week in August, saddle up for Australia's largest **rodeo** (www.isarodeo.com.au).

Tours

Various tours and activities can be booked through the information desk at Outback at Isa, including Yididi Aboriginal Guided Tours, who offer all-inclusive three-day camping safaris to Boodjamulla (Lawn Hill) National Park, including the Riversleigh fossil field (adult/child $990/475).

Sleeping

Red Earth Hotel   HOTEL $$$
(☎1800 603 488; www.redearth-hotel.com.au; Rodeo Dr; d $220-250; ✳@) Mount Isa's smartest address features stylish antique-style decor along with modern facilities. The top rooms have private balconies and spas, and there's an excellent restaurant and coffee shop here.

Travellers Haven   HOSTEL $
(☎07-4743 0313; www.travellershaven.com.au; 75 Spence St; dm/s/d $25/50/66; ✳@≋) Mt Isa's only real hostel has a mixture of backpackers stopping over on the long haul and itinerant workers. Its lino-tiled floor is a little worn, but the welcome is warm, and there's a decent kitchen, lounge and pool. The owners will pick you up from the Greyhound station if you call ahead.

Spinifex   MOTEL $$
(☎07-4749 2944; www.spinifexmotel.com.au; 79 Marian St; r $160-180; ✳@☎) A few blocks from Outback at Isa, the Spinifex has spacious rooms, each with its own outdoor area.

Central Point   MOTEL $$
(☎07-4743 0666; 6 Marian St; s/d $110/130; ✳≋) Across the street from Outback at Isa, this friendly motel has a tropical atmosphere and well-equipped kitchenettes in all the sunny rooms.

Copper City Riverside
Caravan Park   CARAVAN PARK, CABINS $
(☎07-4743 4676; 185 West St; sites unpowered/powered/with bathroom $20/26/32, cabins $70; ✳≋) This excellent, shady park backs onto the Warrego Hwy (Rte 54) about 2km north of the town centre.

Eating & Drinking

Livingstone's   MODERN AUSTRALIAN $$
(☎1800 603 488; 26 Miles St; mains $15-38; ☺lunch & dinner daily, breakfast Sat & Sun) Locals tip this as the town's best eatery, with gourmet sandwiches and salads at lunch and a more formal menu at dinner. Overlooks Isa's strangely romantic, twinkling mine.

Rodeo Bar & Grill   STEAKHOUSE $$
(☎07-4749 8888; Rodeo Dr; mains $25-32; ☺10am-late) In the land of beef, this place can't be beat. Huge steaks sizzle away on the open grill, and there are also pizzas and tapas-style snacks. The airy deck is a choice spot on warm evenings.

Dom's   ITALIAN $$
(☎07-4743 4444; 57 Marian St; mains $18-34; ☺from 8.30am Tue-Sat) Dom's is an authentic little Italian place serving three meals a day. Book ahead for dinner.

Buffs Club   BAR, NIGHTCLUB
(www.buffs.com.au; cnr Grace & Camooweal Sts; ☺10am-midnight Sun & Mon, to 2am Fri & Sat) Isa's most central nightspot, with the busy Billabong Bar, a sundeck and live entertainment on weekends.

❶ Getting There & Around

Rex (☎13 17 13; www.rex.com.au) flies direct from Mt Isa to Townsville. For more options, see p384.

Greyhound Australia (☎13 14 99; www.greyhound.com.au) has regular services to Townsville ($157, 11½ hours), Longreach ($113, 8½ hours) and Brisbane ($210, 26½ hours).

The **Queensland Rail** (☎1800 872 467; www.queenslandrail.com.au) *Inlander* runs between Mt Isa and Townsville (economy seat/sleeper $125/188, 21 hours).

The following car-hire firms have desks at the airport: **Avis** (☎07-4743 3733), **Hertz** (☎07-4743 4142) and **Thrifty** (☎07-4743 2911). For a taxi to town ($25 to $35) call **Mt Isa Taxis** (☎07-4743 2333).

Mt Isa to Charleville

Arguably the most popular road trip in outback Queensland runs east along the Barkly Hwy to the Landsborough Hwy. It's also the shortest route to Longreach from Mt Isa. Beginning 14km east of Cloncurry, the Landsborough heads southeast, passing through McKinlay (91km), Kynuna (168km), Winton (339km), and eventually hitting Longreach (516km), Barcaldine (621km) and Charleville (1020km).

The cringeworthy classic Aussie comedy *Crocodile Dundee* was filmed partly in tiny McKinlay, otherwise famed for the **Walkabout Creek Hotel** (☎07-4746 8424; Landsborough Hwy; unpowered/powered sites $22/25, s $88; ✳), a hot tin shack loaded with film memorabilia and assorted Australiana. There are small and basic motel units, and a camping ground out the back.

It's pioneer days at 40 paces on main-street Winton, a cattle and sheep centre that dishes up tasty tourist cheese by the swagful. Still, the population has swelled in recent years, and while the period charms may be forced, they're also mighty infectious. A short visit will have you happy-snapping at the heritage buildings and brushing up on your bush poetry. When you've run out of things to do in town, plan your run with the dinosaurs.

Winton's biggest attraction is the **Waltzing Matilda Centre** (☑07-4657 1466; www.matildacentre.com.au; 50 Elderslie St; adult/child/family $20/1/49; ☺9am-5pm), which doubles as the visitor information booth. There are a surprising number of exhibits here for a museum devoted to a song, including an indoor billabong complete with squatter, troopers and jolly swagman; a hologram display oozing over-the-top nationalism; and the **Jolly Swagman statue**, a tribute to the unknown swagmen who lie in unmarked graves in the area. The centre also houses the **Qantilda Pioneer Place**, which has a huge range of artefacts and displays on the founding of Qantas.

Find the world's biggest deck chair in the open-air **Royal Theatre** (☑07-4657 1296; 73 Elderslie St; adult/child $6.50/4; ☺screenings 8pm Wed Apr-Sep), at the rear of the Wookatook Gift & Gem. There's an old-movie-world charm in the canvas-slung chairs, corrugated-tin walls and star-studded ceiling. It has a small **museum** (admission $3) in the projection room and screens old classics.

Arno's Wall (Vindex St), behind the North Gregory Hotel, is Winton's quirkiest attraction – a 70m-long work-in-progress by artist Arno Grotjahn, featuring a huge range of industrial and household items, from televisions to motorcycles, ensnared in the mortar.

Winton holds the **Bush Poetry Festival** in July, followed by the annual camel races. Even bigger is the five-day **Outback Festival** (www.outbackfestival.org), held every odd year during the September school holidays.

The **North Gregory Hotel** (☑07-4657 1375; 67 Elderslie St; r with bathroom $80-90, without bathroom $60; ▧) is a big, friendly country pub where 'Waltzing Matilda' allegedly was first performed in 1895, although the original building burnt down in 1900. It has dozens of comfortable, old-fashioned rooms upstairs, with clean shared facilities. There's free caravan parking at the rear.

The **Tattersalls Hotel** (78 Elderslie St; mains $7.50-30; ☺lunch & dinner daily) is a charming old timber pub with lively atmosphere, outdoor tables and a better-than-average cook whose roast chicken comes flavoured with bush herbs like lemon myrtle. Another much-loved dining spot is the BYO **Twilight Cafe** (68 Elderslie St; mains $5-20; ☺8am-2pm & 3-8pm), serving tasty country fare like lamb shanks.

Greyhound Australia (☑13 14 99; www.greyhound.com.au) connects Winton with Brisbane ($178, 20 hours), Mt Isa ($98, six hours) and Longreach ($40, two hours).

LONGREACH
POP 3700

This prosperous outback town was the home of Qantas early last century, but these days it's equally famous for the Australian Stockman's Hall of Fame & Outback Heritage Centre, one of outback Queensland's biggest attractions. The Tropic of Capricorn passes through Longreach, and so do more than a million sheep and cattle.

The **visitor information centre** (☑07-4658 3555; 99 Eagle St; ☺8.30am-5pm Mon-Fri, 9am-noon Sat & Sun, closed Sat & Sun Oct-Mar) is on Eagle St.

☉ Sights

The **Australian Stockman's Hall of Fame & Outback Heritage Centre** (☑07-4658 2166; www.outbackheritage.com.au; Landsborough Hwy; adult/child/family $25/14/55; ☺9am-5pm) is a tribute to the early stockmen and explorers (check out the nifty maps), and has a range of galleries covering Aboriginal culture and European invasion. It's 2km east of town towards Barcaldine. Admission is valid for two days.

The **Qantas Founders Outback Museum** (☑07-4658 3737; www.qfom.com.au; Landsborough Hwy; adult/child/family $19/10/45; ☺9am-5pm) houses a life-size replica of an Avro 504K, the first aircraft owned by the fledgling airline. Interactive multimedia and working displays tell the history of Qantas. Next door, the original 1921 Qantas hangar houses a mint-condition DH-61. Towering over everything is a bright and shiny **747-200B Jumbo** (adult/child/family $19/10/45; museum & jumbo tours $34/18/75, wing walks adult/child $85/55; ☺tours 9.30am, 11am, 1pm & 3pm), whose wings you can walk (bookings essential).

☞ Tours

Longreach Outback Travel Centre   CRUISES, SIGHTSEEING
(☑07-4658 1776; www.lotc.com.au; 115a Eagle St) LOTC runs a number of tours, including billabong cruises (adult/child $50/36), a sunset

cruise on the Thomson River, followed by dinner under the stars and campfire entertainment. The Longreach Lookabout tour (adult/child $187/154) combines the town's main attractions with the dinner cruise. There's also an outback station tour ($109/79).

Outback Aussie Tours OUTBACK, RAIL
(☑07-4658 3000; www.oat.net.au; Landsborough Hwy) On the railway platform, Outback offers a variety of multiday tours from the five-day Longreach and Winton tour (from $1879) to outback garden tours and rail journeys.

🛏 Sleeping & Eating

Eagle St has a number of pubs with good, cheap meals.

Old Time Cottage RENTAL HOUSE $$
(☑07-4658 1550; 158 Crane St; r $105; ✸) A great choice for groups and families, this quaint little corrugated-iron cottage is set in an attractive garden. Fully furnished, the self-contained cottage sleeps up to five people.

Longreach Motor Inn MOTEL $$
(☑07-4658 2322; 84 Galah St; r $124-134; ✸✷) This centrally located motel has somewhat tired but thoroughly comfortable rooms, and a lovely pool area complete with palm trees.

Discovery Holiday Park & Cabins CARAVAN PARK, CABINS $
(☑07-4658 1781; 12 Thrush Rd; sites unpowered/powered/with bathroom $29/32/41, cabins $96-171; ✸✷) This neat, modern park has comfy cabins, and if recent rains have brightened the lawns, mobs of kangaroo will visit for a feed.

Commercial Hotel PUB, MOTEL $
(☑07-4658 1677; 102 Eagle St; s/d with bathroom $70/90, without bathroom $28/45, cabins $80-120; ✸✷) This hotel has basic but comfy rooms, and its friendly, bougainvillea-filled beer garden hosts bargain steak nights.

Eagle's Nest Bar & Grill MODERN AUSTRALIAN $$
(110 Eagle St; meals $20-33; ☉lunch & dinner Wed-Sun, breakfast Sat & Sun) Recommended by locals, this cafe has outdoor seating and the usual variety of pasta and seafood, plus the obligatory steak.

ℹ Getting There & Away

Greyhound Australia (☑1300 473 946; www.greyhound.com.au) has a daily bus service to Brisbane ($107, 17 hours) via Charleville ($53, 6¾ hours) and Mt Isa via Winton and Cloncurry. Buses stop behind the Commercial Hotel.

THE DINOSAUR TRAIL

About 95 million years ago – give or take a few million – a herd of small dinosaurs got spooked by a predator and scattered. The resulting stampede left thousands of footprints in the stream bed, which nature remarkably conspired to fossilise and preserve. The **Lark Quarry Dinosaur Trackways** (☑07-4657 1188; www.dinosaurtrackways.com.au; guided 55min tours adult/child $11/6; ☉tours 10am, noon & 2pm), 110km southwest of Winton, is outback Queensland's mini *Jurassic Park*, where you can see the remnants of the prehistoric stampede. Protected by a sheltered walkway, the site can only be visited by guided tour. There are no facilities to stay (or eat), but it's a well-signposted drive on the unsealed but well-maintained Winton–Jundah road, suitable for 2WD vehicles in the Dry. Contact the Waltzing Matilda Centre at Winton to book tours.

The **Australian Age of Dinosaurs** (☑07-4657 0778; http://aaodl.com; guided tours adult/child $22/11; ☉8.30am-5pm, tours 9am, 11am, 1pm & 3pm) is housed on a local cattle station atop a rugged plateau offering spectacular views. Essentially an enormous shed, the centre was opened in 2006 and has grown to include a museum display, including a life-size model of the dinosaur thought responsible for the stampede at Lark Quarry. In 2012 a brand-new world-class facility is set to open on site. Fossil enthusiasts can book in advance for a day ($60) or a week's worth of bone preparation. To get there, follow the Landsborough Hwy 15km east of Winton (about 20 minutes' drive).

Carisbrooke Station (☑07-4657 0084; www.carisbrooketours.com.au; unpowered/powered sites from $17/22, tw per person with/without bathroom $45/40; ✸) is a sheep and cattle property 85km southwest of Winton where you can experience outback station life. There's camping and accommodation in self-contained units, and the owners run tours of the area.

Paradise Coaches (☏1300 300 156; www. paradisecoaches.com.au) makes the twice-weekly run to Rockhampton, returning via Emerald. Buses stop at Outback Aussie Tours next to the train station.

Queensland Rail (☏1300 131 722; www. traveltrain.com.au) operates the twice-weekly *Spirit of the Outback* service between Longreach and Brisbane via Rockhampton.

BARCALDINE
POP 1500

Barcaldine ('Bar-*call*-din') is a little pub town with a long, colourful past. Popping up at the junction of the Landsborough and Capricorn Hwys (Rte 66), 108km east of Longreach, the town has wide, tree-lined streets dotted with brightly painted colonial pubs, frequented on weekends by strong-armed farmers and pretty homestead sheilas.

The town gained a place in Australian history in 1891 when it became the headquarters of a major shearers' strike. The confrontation led to the formation of the Australian Workers' Party, now the Australian Labor Party. The organisers' meeting place was the Tree of Knowledge, a ghost gum planted near the train station that long stood as a monument to workers and their rights. It was tragically poisoned in 2006. Some suspect Liberal Party insiders; others blame jealous Longreach folk.

The original inhabitants of Barcaldine were the Inningai, who 'disappeared' soon after explorer Thomas Mitchell arrived in 1824.

The visitor information centre (☏07-4651 1724; Oak St) is next to the train station. The Australian Workers Heritage Centre (☏07-4651 2422; www.australianworkers heritagecentre.com.au; Ash St; adult/child/family $12/7.50/28; ☺9am-5pm Mon-Sat, 10am-5pm Sun) provides a rundown on Australian social, political and industrial movements. Set in landscaped gardens, Barcaldine's main attraction features the Australian Bicentennial Theatre, with displays tracing the history of the shearers' strike, as well as a schoolhouse, hospital and powerhouse.

Artesian Country Tours (☏07-4651 2211; www.artesiancountrytours.com.au; adult/child $145/65; ☺Wed & Sat, weather permitting) runs a highly regarded historical tour to local Aboriginal rock-art sites, lava caves, and cattle stations.

For lodging, the tiny wood-and-tin Blacksmith's Cottage (☏07-4651 1724; 7 Elm St; d/tr/q $70/80/90), dates from the late 19th century and is filled with antiques and quirky knick-knacks. The Barcaldine Country Motor Inn (☏07-4651 1488; 1 Box St; s/d $89/99; ✱) is just around the corner from the main street's iconic pubs, most of which have their own basic rooms with shared facilities, as well as hearty pub meals.

The Shakespeare Hotel (☏07-4651 1111; 95 Oak St; s/d without bathroom $35/55, cabins $75) has the pick of the pub rooms.

Charleville
POP 3500

Lying 760km west of Brisbane, Charleville is the grand old dame of central Queensland and the largest town in Mulga country. Due largely to its prime locale on the Warrego River, the town was an important centre for early explorers – Cobb & Co had its largest coach-making factory here – but the town has maintained its prosperity as a major Australian wool centre.

Through initiatives such as the Bidjara Community Development Employment Project, Charleville was long heralded as an example of 'practical reconciliation'. Yet the disbanding of ATSIC has led to a sharp rise in unemployment and a subsequent decline in population.

The visitor information centre (☏07-4654 3057; Sturt St), on the southeastern side of town, offers two handy heritage trail maps to follow by car or on foot.

The finest sights in Charleville are a million miles away. The Cosmos Centre (☏07-4654 3057; www.cosmoscentre.com; single/family $7/21, night observatory sessions adult/child/family $24/16/60; ☺10am-6pm Mon, Wed & Fri) offers a spectacular view of the night sky via a high-powered telescope and an expert guide. The 1½-hour sessions start soon after sunset. The centre lies 2km south of town, off Airport Dr.

Charleville's QPWS runs a captive-breeding program for the endangered bilby, which you can meet in person at the Bilby Experience (1 Park St; admission $5; ☺Apr-Oct) – book at the Cosmos Centre.

The most majestic hotel in Central Queensland, Hotel Corones (☏07-4654 1022; 33 Wills St; r $50-90; ✱) is a stunningly restored country pub. Bypass the motel rooms in favour of its resurrected upstairs interior, where rooms feature fireplaces, leadlight windows and elegant Australian antiques. You can eat in the grand yet affordable dining room (mains $15 to $20) or the bare-bones public bar (mains $10 to $12).

Thurlby Station (see p372) runs a caravan park and farmstay.

The Channel Country

You wanted outback, did ya? Well, here it is, mate – miles and bloody square miles of it! The Channel Country is an unforgiving, eerily empty region where red-sand hills, the odd wildflower and strange luminous phenomena run across prime beef-grazing land. The channels are formed by water rushing south from the summer monsoons to fill the Georgina, Hamilton and Diamantina Rivers and Cooper Creek. Despite unusual rainfall in recent years, precipitation rarely falls in southwest Queensland, which borders the NT, South Australia (SA) and NSW. Avoid the summer months (October to April), unless you go for searing heat and dust.

❶ Getting There & Around

There are no train or bus services in the Channel Country, and the closest car rental is in Mt Isa. Fools perish out here; roads are poorly marked and getting lost is easy. In fact, it's required that you write your name, destination and expected date of arrival on a blackboard at the station where you start, so search-and-rescue services can come looking if you don't show up within a few days. Some roads from the east and north to the fringes of the Channel Country are sealed, but between October and May even these can be cut off when dirt roads become quagmires. Visiting this area requires a sturdy vehicle (a 4WD if you want to get off the beaten track) with decent clearance. Always carry plenty of drinking water and petrol.

The main road through this area is the Diamantina Developmental Rd. It runs south from Mt Isa through Boulia to Bedourie, then east through Windorah and Quilpie to Charleville. It's a long and lonely 1340km, about two-thirds of which is sealed. Take extra caution when driving at dusk, when the warm road attracts wild camels and kangaroos.

MT ISA TO BOULIA

It's around 300km of sealed road from Mt Isa south to Boulia, and the only facilities along the route are at Dajarra, which has a pub and a roadhouse.

BOULIA
POP 300

The unofficial 'capital' of the Channel Country is a neat little outpost on the cusp of the great Simpson Desert. It's from here that the world's longest mail run comes to an end, some 3000km from Port Augusta in South Australia. In mid-July, Boulia hosts Australia's premier camel-racing event, the Desert Sands Camel Races.

The most famous residents of Boulia are the mysterious Min Min Lights, a supposedly natural phenomenon that occurs when the temperature plummets after dark and erratic lights appear on the unusually flat horizon.

Believe it or not, but the Min Min Encounter (☑07-4746 3386; Herbert St; adult/child/family $15/12/35; ☺8.30am-5pm Mon-Fri, 8am-5pm Sat & Sun) feels like a Spielberg movie set, featuring sophisticated gadgetry and eerie lighting in its hourly show. Doubling as the information centre, it's classic travel kitsch and could well help you spot your own Min Min.

The quirky Stone House Museum (cnr Pituri & Hamilton Sts; adult/child $5/3; ☺8am-noon & 1-4pm Mon-Fri, 8am-noon Sat & Sun) has sheds full of outback stuff, space junk, local history, Aboriginal artefacts and the preserved 1888 home of the pioneering Jones family (the Stone House).

Peer over the fence of the house next to the Shell garage on Herbert St to see a map of Australia made entirely of local moon rocks and showing the inland sea of 100 million years ago.

With modern and spacious units, the Desert Sands Motel (☑07-4746 3000; Herbert St; s/d $110/120; ❄) is the best place to sleep. Boulia Caravan Park (☑07-4746 3320; Herbert St; swag sites $10, unpowered/powered sites $20/25, cabins $75-95) is a simple park with shady sites on the banks of the sandy Burke River. The Australian Hotel (☑07-4746 3144; Herbert St; s/d $44/55, motel units $99; ❄) has decent pub rooms, motel units and a good bistro.

The sealed Kennedy Developmental Rd (Rte 62) runs east from Boulia, 369km to Winton. The only stop along the way is Middleton, 175km from Boulia, where there's a pub and fuel.

BEDOURIE
POP 120

From Boulia it's 200km of mainly unsealed road south to Bedourie, the administrative centre for the huge Diamantina Shire Council. A big attraction is the free public swimming pool and artesian spa.

One of the finest outback pubs is Bedourie's own Royal Hotel (☑07-4746 1201; Herbert St; s/d $75/85; ❄), a charming adobe-brick building built in the 1880s. There are two motel units out the back.

There's also a caravan park and comfortable motel units at the Simpson Desert Oasis (☑07-4746 1291; 1 Herbert St; unpowered sites free, powered sites $26, cabins $103-139, motel r $114-156; ☀), a roadhouse with fuel, a supermarket and a restaurant.

BIRDSVILLE
POP 120

Off-the-beaten-track travellers can't claim the title until they visit Birdsville, an iconic Australian settlement on the fringe of the Simpson Desert, and Queensland's most remote 'town'. During the first weekend in September, the annual Birdsville Cup (www. birdsvilleraces.com) horse races draw up to 7000 fans from all over the country to drink, dance and gamble for three dusty days. Parking is free for all light aircraft.

The Birdsville Working Museum (☑07-4656 3259; Macdonald St; adult/child $7/5; ☉8am-5pm Apr-Oct, tours 9am, 11am & 3pm) is an impressive private collection of droving gear, saddles, shearing equipment, wool presses, road signs, toys and trinkets. John Menzies will happily show you around his big tin shed.

Another highlight is the Birdsville Studio (☑07-4656 3221; www.birdsvillestudio.com.au; Graham St; ☉9am-10pm Jun-Sep; @), where you can inspect and buy outback art by exceptional local artist Wolfgang John.

Standing strong in sandstone since 1884 is the much-loved Birdsville Hotel (☑07-4656 3244; www.theoutback.com.au; Adelaide St; s/d $130/150; ☀). It's a humbling experience to sip a stubbie on the verandah with loose-lipped locals and big-hearted adventurers and watch the sun set deep into the desert. When you've had a gutful, the motel-style units are tasteful and spacious, while the restaurant (mains $15-20) is surprisingly slick. Try to arrive on a Friday, when happy hour runs late and loud.

BIRDSVILLE TRACK

The 517km Birdsville Track stretches south of Birdsville to Maree in SA, taking a desolate course between the Simpson Desert to the west and Sturt Stony Desert to the east. The first stretch from Birdsville has two alternative routes, but only the longer, more easterly Outside Track is open these days. Before tackling the track, it's a good idea to keep friends or relatives informed of your movements so they can notify the authorities should you fail to report in on time. Contact the Wirrarri Centre (☑07-4656 3300) for road conditions.

SIMPSON DESERT NATIONAL PARK

The waterless Simpson Desert occupies a massive 200,000 sq km of central Australia and stretches across the Queensland, NT and SA borders. The Queensland section, in the state's far southwestern corner, is protected as the 10,000-sq-km Simpson Desert National Park, and is a remote, arid landscape of high red sand dunes, spinifex and cane grass.

While conventional vehicles can just about tackle the Birdsville Track in dry conditions, the Simpson crossing requires a 4WD and far more preparation. Crossings should only be undertaken by parties of at least two 4WD vehicles equipped with suitable communications (such as an EPIRB) to call for help if necessary. Alternatively, you can hire a satellite phone from Birdsville police (☑07-4656 3220) and return it to Maree police (☑08-8675 8346) in SA.

Permits are required to camp anywhere in the park and can be obtained online (through www.qld.gov.au/camping) or at the QPWS (☑07-4650 1990) in Birdsville or Longreach, and Birdsville's service stations. You also need a separate permit to travel into the SA parks, and these are available through the South Australian National Parks & Wildlife Service (☑1800 816 078).

BIRDSVILLE TO CHARLEVILLE

The Birdsville Developmental Rd heads east from Birdsville, meeting the Diamantina Developmental Rd after 277km of rough gravel and sand. The old pub that constituted the 'township' of Betoota between Birdsville and Windorah closed its doors in 1997, meaning motorists must carry enough fuel and water to cover the 395km distance.

Just west of Cooper Creek, Windorah has a pub, a general store and a basic caravan park. The Western Star Hotel (☑07-4656 3166; www.westernstarhotel.com.au; 15 Albert St; pub s/d $50/60, motel s/d $90/100; ☀), originally built in 1878, has pub rooms and motel units. Yabbie races are staged here on the Wednesday before the Birdsville Races.

Quilpie is an opal-mining town and the railhead from which cattle are sent to the coast. The name comes from an Aboriginal word for stone curlew, and all but two of the town's streets are named after native birds. The Quilpie Museum & Visitors Centre (☑07-4656 2166; 51 Brolga St; ☉8am-5pm Mon-Fri year-round, 10am-4.30pm Sat & Sun Apr-Nov) has tourist information, historical displays and

regular opal-cutting demonstrations. Fossicking tours can be organised here.

South of Quilpie and west of Cunnamulla are the remote Yowah Opal Fields and the town of Eulo, which cohosts the World Lizard Racing Championships with Cunnamulla in late August. Thargomindah, 130km west of Eulo, has a couple of motels and a guesthouse. Noccundra, another 145km further west, was once a busy little community. It now has just one hotel supplying basic accommodation, meals and fuel. If you have a 4WD you can continue west to Innamincka, in SA, on the rough and stony Strzelecki Track, via the site of the famous Dig Tree, where William Brahe buried provisions during the ill-fated Burke and Wills expedition in 1860–61.

WHITSUNDAY COAST

In the calm waters of the Coral Sea, the beautiful Whitsunday Islands are one of Australia's greatest natural tourist attractions. Opal-jade waters and white sandy beaches fringe the forested domes of these 'drowned' mountains where you can camp in secluded bays as a modern-day castaway, laze in a tropical island resort, snorkel, dive, or set sail and island-hop through this stunning archipelago. Beneath the shimmering seas are swarms of tropical fish and the world's largest coral garden in the Great Barrier Reef Marine Park. The gateway to the islands, Airlie Beach, is a vibrant backpacker hub with a continual parade of changing faces and a throbbing nightlife. A little north are the natural unspoilt coastal gems of Hydeaway Bay and Cape Gloucester.

South of Airlie, and overlooking a sea of waving sugar cane, Mackay is a typical Queensland coastal town with pleasant palm-lined streets. There's not much to do here, but it's a handy base for trips to Finch Hatton Gorge and Eungella National Park – lush, green hinterland oases where platypuses play in the wild.

Mackay

POP 82,000

An attractive town with art deco buildings, Mackay doesn't quite make the tourist hitlist. Instead, this big country coastal town caters more to the surrounding agricultural

and mining industries. Although the redeveloped marina (located 6.5km northeast of the centre via the Forgan Bridge) tries to entice with alfresco restaurants and outdoor cafes along its picturesque promenade, Mackay is more a convenient base for excursions out of town. It's only a 1½-hour drive to the Whitsundays, a short flight to pretty Brampton Island, and a scenic drive among the sugar-cane fields to Pioneer Valley and Eungella National Park.

◉ Sights & Activities

Mackay's impressive art deco architecture owes much to a devastating cyclone in 1918, which flattened many of the town's buildings. Enthusiasts should pick up a copy of *Art Deco Mackay* from the town hall visitor information centre. History buffs should also grab the brochure *A Heritage Walk in Mackay*, which guides you around 20 of the town's historic sites.

There are good views over the harbour from Mt Basset Lookout and at Rotary Lookout in North Mackay.

Artspace Mackay (⊘07-4957 1775; www.artspacemackay.com.au; Gordon St; admission free; ⊙10am-5pm Tue-Sun) showcases works from local and visiting artists. Browse the extensive collection of art books and art before grazing at Foodspace (⊙9am-3pm Tue-Sun), the in-house licensed cafe.

Mackay Regional Botanical Gardens (Lagoon St), 3km south of the city centre, include a lovely Tropical Shade Garden (⊙8.45am-4.45pm).

The pleasant artificial Bluewater Lagoon (admission free; ⊙9am-5.45pm) near Canelands Shopping Centre has water fountains, water slides, grassed picnic areas and a cafe.

Some fine beaches are within a short walk of the marina, but Mackay's best beaches, Blacks Beach, Eimeo and Bucasia, are about 16km north of town.

☞ Tours

Beyond Mackay's sugar-cane sea are a superb rainforest and national park.

Jungle Johno Tours   SIGHTSEEING
(⊘07-4944 1230; per person $90) Runs excellent day trips from Gecko's Rest hostel to Eungella National Park, including pick-up, morning tea and lunch.

Reeforest Adventure Tours   CULTURAL
(⊘1800 500 353; www.reeforest.com; per person $145) Offers a wide range of tours,

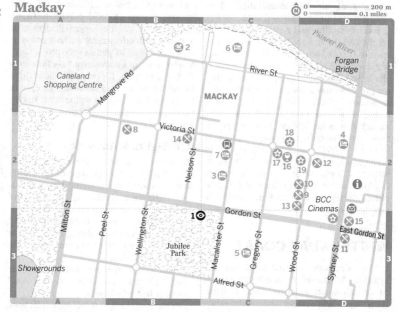

Mackay

including an Indigenous cultural tour to Cape Hillsborough National Park.

Farleigh Sugar Mill INDUSTRIAL
(☎07-4959 8360; 2hr tours per person $22; ⊙9am, 11am & 1pm Jun-Nov) In the cane-crushing season you can see how the sweet crystals are made. The mill is 10km northwest of Mackay.

✵ Festivals & Events

Wintermoon Folk Festival MUSIC
(☎07-4958 8390; www.wintermoonfestival.com; day tickets adult/child $60/free) Each year around May this folk festival is held at Cameron's Pocket, 70km north of Mackay. It's a great opportunity to hear local and interstate musicians fiddle, strum and sing their stuff.

Most people make a weekend of it and camp near the festival grounds (additional cost).

🛏 Sleeping

Hotels in Mackay fill up quick smart due to a steady influx of mine workers, so book well ahead in high season. There are oodles of budget and midrange motels strung along busy Nebo Rd south of the centre.

Clarion Hotel Mackay Marina   HOTEL **$$$**
(📞07-4955 9400; www.mackaymarinahotel.com; Mulherin Dr, Mackay Harbour; d $245-445; ❄@�🏊) The Clarion is the darling of the marina precinct, with high-end rooms with balconies and excellent facilities. It's located 6.5km northeast of the centre. (Take Sydney St north across the Forgan Bridge.)

Ocean Resort Village   RESORT **$$**
(📞1800 075 144; www.oceanresortvillage.com.au; 5 Bridge Rd, Illawong Beach; apt $95-105, 2-bedroom apt $140; ❄🏊) This is a good-value beachside resort comprising 34 self-contained apartments set amid lush, tropical gardens. The cool, shady setting has two pools, barbecue areas and half-court tennis. It's located 4km southeast of the town centre (take Gordon to Goldsmith to Bridge).

Quest   APARTMENTS **$$$**
(📞07-4829 3500; www.questmackay.com.au; 38 Macalister St; studios $168, 1-/2-bedroom apts from $198/280; ❄@🏊) The ideal choice for comfort, these modern, spacious apartments have full kitchen facilities; the huge studios have a kitchenette and grand views over the city.

Mackay Grande Suites   HOTEL **$$$**
(📞07-4969 1000; www.mackaygrandesuites.com.au; 9 Gregory St; r $205, 1-bedroom ste from $245; ❄@🏊) Mackay's long-awaited addition to the top end of the scale in the city centre doesn't disappoint with its stylish decor and modern amenities.

Gecko's Rest   HOSTEL **$**
(📞07-4944 1230; www.geckosrest.com.au; 34 Sydney St; dm/d/f $24/55/90; ❄@) Bustling and busy, Gecko's almost bursts at the seams with adventurous travellers stopping over on their way up north or down the coast. The place is looking slightly grubby, but there's a large kitchen and a huge rooftop balcony area.

🏕 **Stoney Creek Farmstay**   CAMPGROUND, CABINS **$**
(📞07-4954 1177; www.stoneycreekfarmstay.com; Peak Downs Hwy; campsites/dm/cottage $20/25/145)

At this bush retreat 32km south of Mackay you can pitch a tent, bunk in a dorm, or sleep in a rustic room above the horse stables. But best of all is the handmade wood-and-stone cottage. Three-hour horse rides cost $85 per person. It's possible to get to Stoney Creek by bus, leaving at 1.45pm. Otherwise the farmstay owners will pick you up if you ring ahead (minimum of two people). Willing Workers on Organic Farms (WWOOFs) welcome.

Mid City Motor Inn   MOTEL **$$**
(📞07-4951 1666; stay@midcitymotel.com.au; 2 Macalister St; r $114-180; ❄@🏊) Tired but comfortable rooms in a superb location beside the river promenade.

Coral Sands Motel   MOTEL **$$**
(📞07-4951 1244; www.coralsandsmotel.com.au; 44 Macalister St; s/d $110/120; ❄🏊) Ultra-friendly management and large rooms in a central location.

Ocean International   RESORT **$$$**
(📞1800 635 104, 07-4957 2044; www.oceaninternational.com.au; 1 Bridge Rd, Illawong Beach; d $170-270; ❄@🏊) A four-storey complex on the beach with bright rooms, an excellent restaurant and cocktail bar, a spa and sauna and a tropical poolside setting. It's 3km south of the centre close to the airport.

🍴 Eating

Burp Eat Drink   MODERN AUSTRALIAN **$$$**
(📞07-4951 3546; 86 Wood St; mains $32-40; ⏰lunch & dinner Tue-Fri, dinner Sat) A swish Melbourne-style restaurant in the tropics, Burp has a small but tantalising menu. The contemporary dishes include an interesting assortment of sharing plates such as Japanese eggplant stuffed with prawns and oyster sauce.

Kevin's Place   ASIAN **$$**
(📞07-4953 5835; cnr Victoria & Wood Sts; mains $18-25; ⏰lunch & dinner Mon-Fri, dinner Sat) Sizzling, spicy Singaporean dishes and efficient, revved-up staff combine with the building's colonial ambience and the tropical climate to create a Raffles-esque experience.

Angelo's on the Marina   ITALIAN **$$**
(📞07-4955 5600; Mulherin Dr, Mackay marina; mains $20-30; ⏰lunch & dinner daily, breakfast Sat & Sun) A large, lively restaurant in a delightful marina setting, with an extensive range of pasta and a mouth-watering Mediterranean menu. It's located 6.5km

northeast of the centre. (Take the Forgan Bridge.)

Fish D'vine
SEAFOOD $$

(☑07-4953 4442; Sydney St; mains $12-25; ☺lunch & dinner) This original concept fish cafe and rum bar serves up fresh fish in various guises as well as all things nibbly from Neptune's realm.

Café La De Da
CAFE $$

(☑07-4944 0203; 70 Wood St; meals $14-26; ☺breakfast & lunch, dinner Fri & Sat) La De Da serves generous plates of seafood, big steaks, curries, salads and the obligatory wraps and sandwiches. Big breakfasts.

Montezuma's
MEXICAN $

(☑07-4944 1214; 94 Wood St; mains $10-19; ☺lunch & dinner) Mexican-influenced restaurant with cosy atmosphere and snug booths.

Austral Hotel
PUB FARE $$

(☑07-4951 3288; 189 Victoria St; mains $17-31, steaks $23-41; ☺lunch & dinner) Huge plates of prime Aussie beef fill your plate amid lively pub ambience.

Oscar's on Sydney
FUSION $$

(☑07-4944 0173; cnr Sydney & Gordon Sts; mains $10-21; ☺breakfast & lunch) Cafe famed for its delicious *poffertjes* (authentic Dutch pancakes with traditional toppings).

Nelson's Seafood Café
SEAFOOD $

(☑07-4953 5453; cnr Victoria & Nelson Sts; mains $9-15; ☺10.30am-7.30pm Mon-Thu & Sun, 9.30am-8pm Fri & Sat) Superb fish-and-chip shop.

🍷 Drinking

Sails Sports Bar
BAR

(Mulherin Dr, Mackay Harbour) This outdoors bar with sports memorabilia on the walls can get rowdy at night, but it's a great place on Sunday arvo with live music and a marina outlook. Mackay Harbour is 6.5km northeast of the centre (via the Forgan Bridge).

Gordi's Cafe & Bar
PUB

(85 Victoria St) Order a $5 schooner and pull up a stool at this big open-air bar overlooking Victoria St's comings and goings.

Satchmo's at the Reef
BAR

(Mulherin Dr, Mackay Harbour) A classy wine-and-tapas bar full of boaties and featuring live music on Sunday afternoon. It's located 6.5km northeast of the centre.

☆ Entertainment

Code
NIGHTCLUB

(99 Victoria St; ☺10pm-3am) Don your glad rags to sashay into this classy nightclub.

Platinum Lounge
NIGHTCLUB

(83 Victoria St; ☺7pm-3am Wed-Sat, 5pm-2am Sun) On the 1st floor above the corner of Victoria and Wood Sts, the Platinum Lounge is still the most popular nightclub in town.

Mainstreet
NIGHTCLUB

(148 Victoria St; ☺Thu-Sat) Live music and DJs.

ℹ️ Information

Mackay Queensland Parks & Wildlife Service (QPWS; ☑07-4944 7800; www.derm.qld.gov. au; 30 Tennyson St) It's best to book campsites online.

Mackay visitor centre (☑07-4944 5888; www.mackayregion.com; 320 Nebo Rd; ☺ 9am-5pm Mon, 8.30am-5pm Tue-Fri, 9am-4pm Sat & Sun) About 3km south of the centre. Internet access.

Town hall visitor information centre (☑07-4951 4803; townhall@mackayregion.com; 63 Sydney St; ☺9am-5pm Mon-Fri, to noon Sat & Sun) Also has internet access.

ℹ️ Getting There & Away

Air

The airport is about 3km south of the centre. **Jetstar** (☑13 15 38; www.jetstar.com.au) and **Virgin Australia** (☑13 67 89; www.virginaustralia.com) fly to/from Brisbane; **Tiger Airways** (☑03-9999 2888; www.tigerairways.com) flies to/from Melbourne. **Qantas** (☑13 13 13; www.qantas.com. au) has direct flights most days between Mackay and Brisbane, Rockhampton and Townsville.

Bus

Buses stop at the **Mackay Bus Terminal** (☑07-4944 2144; cnr Victoria & Macalister Sts; ☺7am-6pm Mon-Fri, to 4pm Sat), where tickets can also be booked. **Greyhound Australia** (☑13 20 30; www.greyhound.com.au) and **Premier Motor Service** (☑13 34 10; www.premierms. com.au) travel up and down the coast between Brisbane ($200, 17 hours) and Cairns ($170, 13 hours), stopping in Mackay.

Train

The **Queensland Rail** (☑1300 13 17 22; www. traveltrain.com.au) *Tilt Train* connects Mackay with Brisbane ($240, 13 hours), Townsville ($110, 5½ hours) and Cairns ($190, 12 hours). The slower *Sunlander* does the same: Brisbane (economy seat/sleeper $160/220, 17 hours). The train station is at Paget, 5km south of the city centre.

ⓘ Getting Around

Avis (☎07-4951 1266), **Budget** (☎07-4951 1400) and **Hertz** (☎07-4951 3334) have counters at the airport.

Mackay Transit Coaches (☎07-4957 3330) operates local buses from two bus stops in town: at the back of Canelands Shopping Centre, and from the corner of Victoria and Gregory Sts. The visitor centres have timetables.

Mackay Taxis (☎13 10 08) will get you to the airport, marina or train station for about $25.

Around Mackay

West of Mackay is classic country Queensland. If you have time, explore these parts for a day or two.

PIONEER VALLEY

Finch Hatton Gorge is a beautiful, secluded riverine gorge located 32km northwest of Mackay. The turn-off is 1.5km before the township of Finch Hatton. It's 9km into the gorge, and the last 3km are on good, unsealed roads, but heavy rain can make access difficult or impossible. A highly underrated extreme activity is Forest Flying (☎07-4958 3359; www.forestflying.com; rides $60). It's like virtual monkey play as you skim the rainforest canopy in a harness attached to a 340m-long cable. Beware the fruit-bat colony (August to May). Book ahead.

You can take a relaxed 1.6km rainforest walk to a stunning swimming hole beneath Araluen Falls, or a 2.6km walking trail to the Wheel of Fire Falls. For a real back-to-nature experience, stay in the amazing Platypus Bushcamp (☎07-4958 3204; www.bushcamp.net; Finch Hatton Gorge; campsites $10, dm/d $35/100). The high-end Rainforest B&B (☎07-4958 3099; www.rainforestbedandbreakfast.com.au; 52 Van Houweninges Rd; cabins $300) adds a touch of Balinese style to this rainforest retreat. The self-contained cabins at Finch Hatton Gorge Cabins (☎07-4958 3281; www.finchhattongorgecabins.com.au; d $95; ✱) are quite basic but have wonderful views of the forest. Dine on the large deck while listening to birdsong at the River Rock Cafe (☉breakfast & lunch Tue-Sun).

Twenty kilometres further along is Eungella National Park (*young*-gulla), the kind of place to spark a mass 'mountain change'. The 'land of clouds' is situated in the Clark Ranges, and reaches 1280m at its zenith. This oldest and longest stretch of subtropical rainforest in Australia has been cut off

from other rainforest areas for roughly 30,000 years, meaning there's a whole host of freaky creatures that exist nowhere else, such as the orange-sided skink and the Eungella gastric brooding frog, which incubates its eggs in its stomach and gives birth by spitting out the tadpoles!

On the trails between Eungella and Broken River, the real star is the world's cutest, most reclusive monotreme (egg-laying mammal). You can be fairly sure of seeing platypuses from the viewing platform near the bridge. The best times are immediately after dawn and at dusk, but you must be patient, still and half-mad.

Resident goannas and brush-tailed possums enjoy the lovely Broken River Mountain Resort (☎07-4958 4000; www.brokenrivermr.com.au; d $105-160; ✱@☎✉), which has cosy cedar cabins, small motel-style units, a wood-finished lounge and the friendly Possums Table Restaurant & Bar (mains $21-37; ☉breakfast & dinner).

There's also the QPWS Fern Flat Camping Ground (per person/family $5.15/21), which is reserved for walk-in campers only, near the (usually unstaffed) QPWS office (☎07-4958 4552). You need to self-register.

Buses don't cover Finch Hatton or Eungella, so you'll need a car or an organised tour from Mackay.

Airlie Beach

POP 3000

Tacky and tremendous, exploited and exploitative, Airlie Beach is not so much a stepping-off point for the Whitsunday Islands as a high-voltage launching pad! Airlie is the kind of town where humanity celebrates its close proximity to natural beauty by partying very hard, fast and frequently.

A relatively tiny town that can at times feel as busy as Brisbane, Airlie draws a stream of budget travellers, the sailing fraternity (who converge here for the mainland conveniences), families (who flock to the fine restaurants and boutique hotels) and shrewd developers (who scour the coast for the next Airlie Beach).

Abel Point Marina, where the Cruise Whitsunday island ferries depart and where many of the cruising yachts are moored, is about 1km west along a pleasant boardwalk, and Shute Harbour, where the Fantasea island ferries depart, is about 12km east. The new marina precinct, at the Shute Harbour

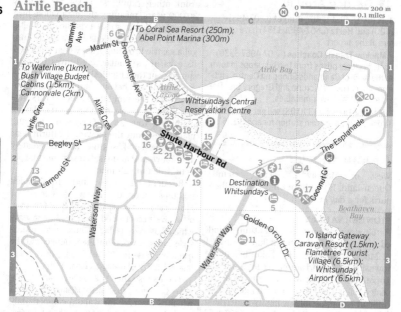

end of town, was under construction at the time of writing, but by the look of the works going on, it's bound to be big.

🏃 Activities

There are (seasonal) operators in front of the Airlie Beach Hotel that hire out jet skis, catamarans, windsurfers and paddle skis.

Sailing is the leisure activity of choice here, in all its nautical variations. There are numerous **sailing tours**, but if you've got salt water in your veins, a **bareboat charter** might be more your style. Expect to pay between $500 to $800 a day in high season (September to January) for a yacht that will comfortably sleep four to six people. Airlie Beach is also a great place to learn to sail.

Air Whitsunday Seaplanes   SCENIC FLIGHTS
(☏07-4946 9111; www.airwhitsunday.com.au) This outfit offers three-hour Reef Adventures (adult/child $315/280), a Whitehaven experience ($240/210) and the signature four-hour Panorama Tour ($425/390) where you fly to Hardy Lagoon to snorkel or ride a semisubmersible, then fly to Whitehaven Beach for a picnic lunch. It also runs day trips to exclusive Hayman Island ($195).

Charter Yachts Australia   SAILING CHARTERS
(☏1800 639 520; www.cya.com.au; Abel Point Marina)

Whitsunday Escape   SAILING CHARTERS
(☏1800 075 145; www.whitsundayescape.com; Abel Point Marina)

Whitsunday Rent A Yacht   SAILING CHARTERS
(☏1800 075 000; www.rentayacht.com.au; Trinity Jetty, Shute Harbour)

Whitsunday Marine Academy   SAILING LESSONS
(☏1800 810 116; www.explorewhitsundays.com; 4 The Esplanade) Run by Explore Whitsundays.

Whitsunday Sailing Club   SAILING LESSONS
(☏07-4946 6138; Airlie Point)

Whitsunday Dive Adventures   DIVING, SNORKELLING
(☏07-4948 1239; www.adventuredivers.com. au; 303 Shute Harbour Rd) Offers a range of instruction, including open-water PADI-certified dive courses ($565). Half-day dive trips cost $175. Many boat cruises.

Salty Dog Sea Kayaking   SEA KAYAKING
(☏07-4946 1388; www.saltydog.com.au; half-/full-day trips $70/125) Offers guided full-day tours and kayak rental ($50/60 per half-/full day), plus longer kayak/camping missions (the six-day challenge costs $1500).

It's a charming and healthy way to see the islands.

Skydive Airlie Beach SKYDIVING
(☏07-4946 9115; www.skydiveairliebeach.com.au) Tandem skydives from $249.

HeliReef SCENIC FLIGHTS
(☏07-4946 9102; www.avta.com.au) Helicopter flights to the reef (from $129), day trips to Hayman Island ($399) and a picnic lunch on Whitehaven Beach ($399).

Aviation Adventures SCENIC FLIGHTS
(☏07-4946 9988; www.av8.com.au) Helicopter flights ranging from scenic island trips ($99) to picnic rendezvous ($199) and reef adventures ($649).

☞ Tours

If snorkelling, lying on the beach or exploring the rainforests of a few of the Whitsunday Islands appeals, then it's just a matter of hunting down the tour that will suit you.

Most cruise operators run out of Abel Point Marina, but those that run from Shute Harbour do coach pick-ups from Airlie Beach and Cannonvale. You can take a public bus to Shute Harbour.

Voyager 3 Island Cruise BOAT
(☏07-4946 5255; www.wiac.com.au; adult/child $140/80) A good-value day cruise that includes snorkelling at Hook Island, beachcombing and swimming at Whitehaven Beach, and checking out Daydream Island.

Fantasea BOAT
(☏07-4967 5455; www.fantasea.com.au) Offers high-speed catamaran cruises to its Reefworld pontoon on the Great Barrier Reef, where you can snorkel, take a trip in a semisubmersible and check out the underwater viewing chamber (adult/child/family $225/102/589). An overnight 'Reefsleep' costs from $460.

Cruise Whitsundays SPEEDBOAT
(☏07-4946 4662; www.cruisewhitsundays.com) Similar to Fantasea; runs day trips to the Barrier Reef Marine Base, a pontoon located in Knuckle Reef Lagoon.

Ocean Rafting SPEEDBOAT
(☏07-4946 6848; www.oceanrafting.com; adult/child/family $120/78/360) Swim at Whitehaven Beach, view Aboriginal cave paintings at Nara Inlet and snorkel the reef at Mantaray Bay or Border Island.

Big Fury BOAT
(☏07-4948 2201; Abel Point Marina; adult/child/family $130/70/350) Speeds out to Whitehaven Beach on an open-air sports boat followed by lunch and then snorkelling at a secluded reef nearby.

⌑ Sleeping

To take the hassle out of finding the right accommodation, **Whitsundays Central Reservation Centre** (☏1800 677 119;

SAILING THE WHITSUNDAYS

Dream of an island holiday and alongside the swaying palms, sand-fringed bays and calm blue seas there's usually a white sailboat skimming lightly across the water. In the Whitsundays it isn't hard to put yourself in the picture, but with the plethora of charters, tours and specials on offer, deciding how to go about it can be confusing. Before booking, compare what you get for the price you pay. Cheaper companies often have crowded boats, bland food and cramped quarters. If you're flexible with dates, last-minute stand-by rates can considerably reduce the price, and you'll also have a better idea of weather conditions.

Aside from day trips, most overnight sailing packages are for three days and two nights or two days and two nights. Again, check what you pay for. Some companies set sail in the afternoon of the first day and return by mid-morning of the last, while others set out early and return late. Be sure what you're committing to – don't set sail on a party boat if you're after a chilled-out cruise.

Most vessels offer snorkelling on the fringing reefs (the reefs around the islands). The softer coral here is often more colourful and abundant than what you see on the outer reef. Check if snorkel equipment, stinger suits and reef taxes are included in the package. Diving usually costs extra.

Once you've decided what suits, book at one of the many booking agencies in town such as **Whitsundays Central Reservation Centre** (☑1800 677 119; www.airliebeach.com; 259 Shute Harbour Rd) or a management company such as **Whitsunday Sailing Adventures** (☑07-4940 2000; www.whitsundaysailing.com; Shute Harbour Rd) or **Explore Whitsundays** (☑07-4946 4999; www.explorewhitsundays.com; 4 The Esplanade).

Some of the recommended sailing trips are listed below:

» **Camira** (day trips $165) One of the world's fastest commercial sailing catamarans is now a lilac-coloured Whitsunday icon. This good-value day trip includes Whitehaven Beach, snorkelling, morning and afternoon tea, a barbecue lunch and all refreshments (including wine and beer).

» **Maxi Action Ragamuffin** (day trips $156) Choose between a cruise to Whitehaven Beach (Thursday and Sunday) or snorkelling at Blue Pearl Bay (Monday, Wednesday, Friday and Saturday). Diving ($90) is an option on the Blue Pearl Bay cruise.

» **Derwent Hunter** (three-day-and-two-night trips from $590) A very popular sailing safari on a timber gaff-rigged schooner. Good for couples and those wanting to experience nature and the elements.

» **Whitsunday Magic** (three-day-and-three-night trips from $779) This beautiful three-masted schooner is the largest vessel sailing the Whitsundays and cruises to the Outer Reef. One of the more upmarket tours.

» **Wings 2** (two-day-and-two-night trips from $475) Comfortable, well-maintained fast cat for those wanting to sail, dive and make new friends.

» **Solway Lass** (three-day-and-three-night trips from $549) Get more bang for your buck. You get a full three days on this 28m tall ship – the only authentic tall ship in Airlie Beach. It's a popular choice for backpackers.

» **Pride of Airlie** (three-day-and-two-night trips $349) The original party boat, the *Pride of Airlie* is still exactly that: a raucous booze cruise popular with young backpackers. Nights are spent at Adventure Island Resort on South Molle Island.

Crewing

Adventurous types might see the 'Crew Wanted' ads posted in backpackers or at the marina and yacht club and dream of hitching a ride on the high seas. In return for a free bunk, meals, and a sailing adventure you get to hoist the mainsail, take the helm, and clean the head. You could have the experience of a lifetime – whether good or bad depends on the vessel, skipper, other crew members (if any) and your own attitude. Think about being stuck with someone you don't know on a 10m boat, several kilometres from shore, before you actually find yourself there. For safety reasons, let someone know where you're going, with whom, and for how long.

259 Shute Harbour Rd; www.airliebeach.com) can be of enormous assistance.

cabins set in leafy gardens. There's a courtesy bus into town.

TOP CHOICE **Water's Edge Resort** APARTMENTS **$$$**
(☑07-4948 4300; www.watersedgewhitsundays.com.au; 4 Golden Orchid Dr; 1-bedroom apt $210-260, 2-bedroom apt $275-345; ✸✿) The reception area immediately tells you that you're on holiday. Its open-air plan and gently revolving ceiling fans stir the languid, tropical heat. In the rooms, soft colours, cane headboards and shutters sealing off the bedroom from the living space immediately put your mind at ease.

TOP CHOICE **Waterview** APARTMENTS **$$**
(☑07-4948 1748; www.waterviewairliebeach.com.au; 42 Airlie Cres; studios/1-bedroom units from $135/149; ✸🕾) An excellent choice for location and comfort, this boutique accommodation overlooks the main street and has gorgeous views of the bay. The rooms are modern, airy and spacious and have kitchenettes for self-caterers.

Coral Sea Resort RESORT **$$$**
(☑1800 075 061; www.coralsearesort.com; 25 Ocean View Ave; d $220-370, 1-bedroom apt $330, 2-bedroom apt $350-400; ✸@🕾✿) At the end of a low headland overlooking the water just west of the town centre, Coral Sea Resort has one of the best positions around. Many of the rooms have stunning views.

Sunlit Waters APARTMENTS **$$**
(☑07-4946 6352; www.sunlitwaters.com; 20 Airlie Cres; studios from $92, 1-bedroom apt $115; ✸✿) One of the best-value options in Airlie Beach, these large studios have everything you could want, including a self-contained kitchenette and stunning views from the long balconies.

Airlie Waterfront B&B B&B **$$$**
(☑07-4946 7631; www.airliewaterfrontbnb.com.au; cnr Broadwater Ave & Mazlin St; d $259-285; ✸@) With absolutely gorgeous views and immaculately presented from top to toe, this sumptuously furnished B&B oozes class and is a leisurely five-minute walk into town along the boardwalk.

Bush Village Budget Cabins HOSTEL **$**
(☑1800 8098 256; www.bushvillage.com.au; 2 St Martins Rd; dm from $30, d $93; ✸@✿) These boutique backpacker cabins only 1.5km west of Airlie have undergone a revamp and are the best budget accommodation in town. Dorms and doubles are in 17 self-contained

Whitsunday Organic B&B B&B **$$$**
(☑07-4946 7151; www.whitsundaybb.com.au; 8 Lamond St; s/d $155/210) Rooms are comfortable, but it's the organic garden walk and the orgasmic three-course organic breakfasts (nonguests $22.50) that everyone comes here for. You can book a healing massage, meditate in the garden teepee, or just indulge in all things organic.

Nomads Backpackers HOSTEL **$**
(☑07-4999 6600; www.nomadsairliebeach.com; 354 Shute Harbour Rd; dm/d $28/90; ✸@🕾✿) Set on three hectares in the centre of town, this fairly new hostel is the pick of the lot. The camping sites out the back are in a good shady spot (away from the noisy main street), all dorm rooms have bathroom, and private rooms have TV, fridge and kitchenette. There's a large kitchen and a small bar in the complex.

Beaches Backpackers HOSTEL **$**
(☑1800 636 630; www.beaches.com.au; 356 Shute Harbour Rd; dm/d $25/85; ✸@🕾✿) You must at least enjoy a drink at the big open-air bar, even if you're not staying here. Although it's busy, Beaches doesn't try to outdo Magnums in the boisterous stakes, but it comes close anyway.

Magnums Backpackers HOSTEL **$**
(☑1800 624 634; www.magnums.com.au; 366 Shute Harbour Rd; campsites/van sites $22/24, dm/d $19/56, cabins $25; ✸@🕾) A loud party bar, loads of alcohol, and a bevy of pretty young things...must be Magnums. Forget the tent sites close to the bar – you won't sleep unless you're comatose. Once you get past the hectically busy reception, you'll find simple dorms in a tropical-garden setting.

Flametree Tourist Village CARAVAN PARK **$**
(☑07-4946 9388; www.flametreevillage.com.au; Shute Harbour Rd; unpowered/powered sites $21/29, cabins from $77; ✸@✿) Spacious sites are scattered through lovely, bird-filled gardens and there's a good camp kitchen and barbecue area. The park is 6.5km west of Airlie.

Airlie Beach Hotel HOTEL **$$**
(☑1800 466 233; www.airliebeachhotel.com.au; cnr The Esplanade & Coconut Grove; s/d $129/139, apt $179-289; ✸🕾✿) Shabby motel units but clean, spacious sea-facing apartments, plus three restaurants and a perfect downtown location.

Backpackers by the Bay HOSTEL $

(☑1800 646 994, 07-4946 7267; www.backpack ersbythebay.com; 12 Hermitage Dr; dm/d & tw $28/70; ❄@☋) Quiet and homey. Once the new marina is finished, the views will be back. It's 1.2km southeast of Airlie Beach off Shute Harbour Rd.

Airlie Beach YHA HOSTEL $

(☑1800 247 251, 07-4946 6312; airlie beach@ yha.com.au; 394 Shute Harbour Rd; dm $26.50, d $69.50-77.50; ❄@☋) Central, and reasonably quiet.

Island Gateway Caravan Resort CARAVAN PARK $

(☑07-4946 6228; www.islandgateway.com.au; Shute Harbour Rd, Jubilee Pocket; unpowered/ powered sites $30/37, cabins $80-135, chalets $145-225; ❄☎☋) Large park 1.5km east of Airlie.

✖ Eating

Fish D'vine SEAFOOD $$

(☑07-4948 0088; 303 Shute Harbour Rd; mains $10-25; ⏰lunch & dinner) Of course, rum and fish – what a perfect combination! But somehow this quirky concept has taken off like a storm. Seafood dishes will keep you happy, and the selection of over 100 different rums is bound to unleash your inner pirate.

Alain's Restaurant FRENCH $$$

(☑07-4946 5464; 44 Coral Esplanade, Cannonvale; mains $25-35; ⏰dinner Thu-Sat) For fine dining this intimate French restaurant opposite Cannonvale beach is first-rate. White linen, silverware and soft candlelight add up to romance. Indulge in the six-course table d'hôte menu and you'll have time to ask about that Citroën parked in the corner.

Waterline MODERN AUSTRALIAN $$

(☑07-4948 1023; 1 Shingley Dr; mains $20-30; ⏰lunch & dinner Wed-Sun, breakfast Sun) With stunning views over the marina, this restaurant at Shingley Beach Resort has one of the best locations for waterfront dining. The decor is tropical beach-chic. Recommended by the locals for its good service, great food and consistent quality.

Deja Vu FUSION $$$

(☑07-4948 4309; Golden Orchid Dr; lunch mains $15-21, dinner mains $27-40; ⏰lunch Wed-Sun, dinner Wed-Sat) Rated as one of Airlie's best, this Polynesian-themed restaurant concocts contemporary dishes with Asian and Mediterranean influences. Be sure to while away a

few hours at the famous long Sunday lunch (eight courses for $40 per person).

Village Cafe CAFE $

(351 Shute Harbour Rd; mains $10-21; ⏰breakfast, lunch & dinner) Always busy with hung-over backpackers, and those after good coffee, this popular cafe has breakfasts that are just the tonic to get the day started. For lunch or dinner be sure to order a 'hot rock' ($26 to $34) and watch your protein of choice cook to perfection on a volcanic rock that's been heated for 12 hours.

Whitsunday Sailing Club PUB FARE $$

(☑07-4946 7894; Airlie Point; mains $14-32; ⏰lunch & dinner) The sailing-club terrace (don't sit inside) is a great place for a meal and a drink and wonderful ocean views. Choose from the usual steak and schnitzel culprits.

Marino's Deli DELI $

(269 Shute Harbour Rd; dishes $6-15; ⏰11am-8pm Mon-Sat) Great takeaway pasta, and antipasto offerings.

Airlie Supermarket SUPERMARKET $

(277 Shute Harbour Rd) For self-caterers.

Extreme Bean Espresso Bar CAFE $

(346 Shute Harbour Rd; mains $8-15; ⏰breakfast & lunch) An excellent cafe known for frappes, eggs Benedict, cheesecakes and changing daily specials.

🍷 Drinking

According to the locals, Airlie Beach is a drinking town with a sailing problem. The bars at Magnums and Beaches, the two big backpackers in the centre of town, are always crowded, and everyone starts their night at one, or both, of them.

Uber BAR

(350 Shute Harbour Rd; ⏰2-11pm Tue-Thu, to 2am Fri & Sat) This ubercool bar and restaurant is the classiest in town. Come for cocktails, lounge in comfortable nooks on the alfresco deck, or just savour the uber-ambience.

Paddy's Shenanigans BAR

(352 Shute Harbour Rd; ⏰5pm-3am) Paddy's has live music late at night, and proudly encourages the Irish penchant for hard drinking.

☆ Entertainment

Mama Africa NIGHTCLUB

(263 Shute Harbour Rd; ⏰10pm-5am) Just a stumble across the road from the main

CONWAY NATIONAL PARK

The mountains of this national park and the Whitsunday Islands are part of the same coastal mountain range. Rising sea levels following the last ice age flooded the lower valleys, leaving only the highest peaks as islands, now cut off from the mainland.

The road from Airlie Beach to Shute Harbour passes through the northern section of the park. Several walking trails start from near the picnic and day-use area. About 1km past the day-use area, there's a 2.4km walk up to the Mt Rooper lookout, which provides good views of the Whitsunday Passage and islands. Further along the main road, towards Coral Point (before Shute Harbour), there's a 1km track leading down to Coral Beach and The Beak lookout. This track was created with the assistance of the Giru Dala, the traditional custodians of the Whitsunday area; a brochure available at the start of the trail explains how the local Aborigines use plants growing in the area.

To reach the beautiful Cedar Creek Falls, turn off the Proserpine–Airlie Beach road onto Conway Rd, 18km southwest of Airlie Beach. It's then about 15km to the falls; the roads are well signposted. This is a popular picnic and swimming spot – when there's enough water, that is!

party bars, this African-style safari nightclub throbs a beat that both hunter and prey find hard to resist.

ⓘ Information

Private operators dish out tourist advice along Shute Harbour Rd – use your discretion and shop around.

Destination Whitsundays (☏07-4946 7172; 297 Shute Harbour Rd) Books tours.

QPWS (☏07-4967 7355; www.derm.qld.gov. au; cnr Shute Harbour & Mandalay Rds; ⏰9am-4.30pm Mon-Fri) Situated 3km towards Shute Harbour. A must-visit for info on island camping and various hikes.

Whitsundays Central Reservation Centre (☏1800 677 119; www.airliebeach.com; 259 Shute Harbour Rd; ⏰7am-7pm) Helpful family-run tour agency. Also has internet.

ⓘ Getting There & Around

The closest major airports are at Proserpine and on Hamilton Island. The small **Whitsunday Airport** (☏07-4946 9933) is about 6km southeast of town; see p412 for flight details.

Greyhound (☏13 20 30; www.greyhound. com.au) and **Premier Motor Service** (☏13 34 10; www.premierms.com.au) have bus connections to Brisbane ($230, 19 hours), Mackay ($38, two hours), Townsville ($58, 4½ hours) and Cairns ($140, 11 hours). Long-distance buses stop on The Esplanade, between the sailing club and Airlie Beach Hotel.

Whitsunday Transit (☏07-4946 1800) connects Proserpine (Proserpine Airport), Cannonvale, Abel Point, Airlie Beach and Shute Harbour. Buses operate from 6am to 10.30pm.

Car-rental agencies:

Avis (☏07-4946 6318; 366 Shute Harbour Rd)

Europcar (☏07-4946 4133; 398 Shute Harbour Rd)

Fun Rentals (☏07-4948 0489; 344 Shute Harbour Rd)

Hertz (☏07-4946 4687; Shute Harbour Rd)

Whitsunday Islands

The Whitsunday group of islands off the north-eastern Queensland coast is, as the cliché goes, a tropical paradise. The 74 islands that make up this stunning archipelago are really the tips of mountains jutting out from the Coral Sea, and from their sandy fringes the ocean spreads towards the horizon in beautiful shades of crystal, aqua, blue and indigo. Sheltered by the Great Barrier Reef, the waters are perfect for sailing (see the boxed text, p388, for options).

Of the numerous stunning beaches and secluded bays, Whitehaven Beach stands out for its pure white silica sand. It is undoubtedly the finest beach in the Whitsundays, and possibly one of the finest in the world.

Only seven of the islands have tourist resorts – catering to every budget and whim from the basic accommodation at Hook Island to the exclusive luxury of Hayman Island. Most of the islands are uninhabited, and several offer the chance of back-to-nature beach camping and bushwalking.

🛏 Sleeping

The rates quoted for resorts in this section are the standard rates, but hardly anyone pays these. Most travel agents can put

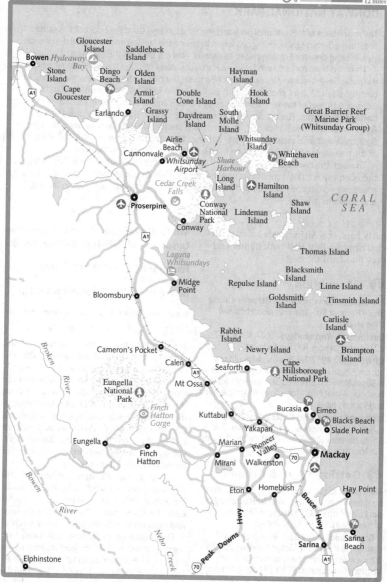

together a range of discounted package deals that combine airfares, transfers, accommodation and meals.

QPWS (www.derm.qld.gov.au) manages the **Whitsunday Islands National Park camping grounds** on several islands.

Camping permits are available online, from the Whitsunday QPWS office and the Whitsunday Information Centre in Proserpine. Permits cost $5.15/20.60 per person/family.

You must be self-sufficient, and are advised to take 5L of water per person per day,

plus three days' extra supply in case you get stuck. You should also have a fuel stove; wood fires are banned on all islands.

Get to your island with Whitsunday Island Camping Connections – Scamper (☎07-4946 6285; www.whitsundaycamping.com.au), which leaves from Shute Harbour and can drop you at South Molle, Denman or Planton Islands ($65 return); Whitsunday Island ($105 return); Whitehaven Beach ($155 return); and Hook Island ($160 return). Camping transfers also include complimentary snorkelling gear and water containers. You can also hire camp kits ($40 per night). A food drop-off service can be provided at extra cost.

ℹ Getting There & Around

The two main airports for the Whitsundays are at Hamilton Island and Proserpine, 36km south-west of Airlie Beach. **Virgin Australia** (☎13 67 89; www.virginaustralia.com) and **Jetstar** (☎13 15 38; www.jetstar.com.au) connect Hamilton Island with Brisbane, Sydney and Melbourne. **QantasLink** (☎13 13 13; www.qantas.com.au) flies there from Cairns.

Air Whitsunday Seaplanes (☎07-4946 9111; www.airwhitsunday.com.au) flies to Hayman and Long Island. It and **Helireef** (☎07-4946 9102; www.avta.com.au) run joy flights over the Reef. Flights depart from **Whitsunday Airport** (☎07-4946 9180), a small airfield 6km east of Airlie Beach.

Transfers between Abel Point Marina and Daydream, Long and South Molle Islands are provided by **Cruise Whitsundays** (☎07-4946 4662; www.cruisewhitsundays.com; adult/child one way $30/20). They also run airport transfers from Abel Point Marina to Hamilton Island. Transfers between Shute Harbour and Hamilton Island are provided by **Fantasea** (☎07-946 5111; www.fantasea.com.au; adult/child one way $49/27).

LONG ISLAND

Underrated Long Island has the best of everything. Its beaches are among the best in the Whitsundays and there are 13km of walking tracks with some fine lookouts. The island has three resorts, each with a different personality, and stretches 9km long by 1.5km wide; a 500m-wide channel separates it from the mainland. Day trippers can use the facilities at Long Island Resort.

Paradise Bay (☎07-4946 9777; www.paradisebay.com.au; 3-night packages per person from $1800) is a secluded eco-friendly lodge on Paradise Bay with 10 spacious bungalows made from Australian hardwood, with high cathedral ceilings and magnificent ocean

views. All meals, beer, wine and soft drinks are included in the tariff. There is a three-night minimum stay, no day visitors or children, and no motorised water sports, so you are guaranteed peace and tranquillity. The tariff is inclusive of helicopter transfers from Hamilton Island, sailing tours and activities.

The Long Island Resort (☎1800 075 125; www.oceanhotels.com.au/longisland; d incl all meals $260-380; ✳@☲) is a resort for everyone (kids welcome), with varying levels of comfort, the best being those on the beachfront. There are great short walks from here, and loads of activities.

There's a national-park **campsite** at Sandy Bay.

SOUTH MOLLE ISLAND

Lovers of birds and long, sandy beaches will enjoy the largest island of the Molle archipelago. Nearly 15km of splendid walking tracks traverse this mountainous 4-sq-km island; the highest point is Mt Jeffreys (198m), but the climb up Spion Kop is also worthwhile.

The Adventure Island Resort (☎1800 464 444; www.koalaadventures.com.au; dm from $49-100, d $180-240; ✳@☲) is far from luxurious, with basic motel-style rooms and beachfront bungalows. There's a three-night minimum stay.

There are national-park **camping grounds** located at Sandy Bay in the south and at Paddle Bay near the resort.

DAYDREAM ISLAND

Daydream Island is more manufactured than dreamy, but at just 1km long and a 15-minute ferry ride from Shute Harbour, it's a good compromise for busy families. A usual day sees hordes of kids getting touchy-feely with marine life in a small lagoon, while parents and singles swivel cocktail umbrellas at the bar. Loads of water-sports gear is available for hire.

Daydream Island Resort & Spa (☎1800 075 040; www.daydreamisland.com; 3-night packages $900-2500; ✳☎☲) is the tackier side of the Whitsundays, with five grades of accommodation. Still, it's efficiently operated and set in beautifully landscaped tropical gardens. There are three swimming pools, tennis courts, catamarans and faux-beaches. There's also a kids' club.

HOOK ISLAND

The second largest of the Whitsundays, the 53-sq-km Hook Island is predominantly national park and rises to 450m at Hook Peak. There are a number of good beaches dotted

around the island, and Hook boasts some of the best diving and snorkelling locations in the Whitsundays. The resort itself is a no-frills, budget place.

Those who don't mind roughing it book in at the Hook Island Wilderness Resort (☑07-4946 9380; www.hookislandresort.com; campsites per person $20, d with/without bathroom $120/100; ✳☀), a battered place with basic quarters and a licensed restaurant (mains $16-27) that serves seafood, steak and pasta.

There are some wonderful camping opportunities in basic national-park **camping grounds** at Maureen Cove, Steen's Beach, Bloodhorn Beach, Curlew Beach and Cray-fish Beach.

WHITSUNDAY ISLAND

Whitehaven Beach, on Whitsunday Island, is a pristine 7km-long stretch of dazzling white sand bounded by lush tropical vegetation and a brilliant blue sea. From Hill Inlet at the northern end of the beach, the swirling pattern of pure white sand through the turquoise and aquamarine water paints a magical picture. There's excellent snorkelling from its southern end. Whitehaven is one of Australia's most beautiful beaches.

There are national-park **camping grounds** at Dugong, Nari's and Joe's Beaches in the west; at Chance Bay in the south; at the southern end of Whitehaven Beach; and at Peter Bay in the north.

HAMILTON ISLAND

Hamilton Island can come as quite a shock for the first-time visitor. Swarms of people and heavy development make Hamilton seem like a busy town rather than a resort island. Although this is not everyone's idea of a perfect getaway, it's hard not to be impressed by the sheer range of accommodation options, restaurants, bars and activities.

There are a few walking trails on the island, the best being from behind the Reef View Hotel up to Passage Peak (230m) on the north-eastern corner of the island. Hamilton also has day care and a Clownfish Club for kids.

Hamilton Island Resort (☑07-4946 9999; www.hamiltonisland.com.au; d from $314; ✳@☀) has extensive options, including bungalows, luxury villas, plush hotel rooms and self-contained apartments.

Hamilton is a ready-made day trip from Shute Harbour, and you can use some of the resort's facilities; see p412 for transport details.

LINDEMAN ISLAND

Lovely Lindeman is mostly national park, with empty bays and 20km of impressive walking trails. Nature photographers descend for the varied island tree life and the sublime view from Mt Oldfield (210m).

Club Med (☑1800 258 2633; www.clubmed.com; 3-night full-board packages per 2 people $1788; ✳☀) is a fun all-inclusive option. It has its own launch that connects with flights from the airport at Hamilton Island.

HAYMAN ISLAND

The most northern of the Whitsunday group, Hayman is just 4 sq km in area and rises to 250m above sea level. It has forested hills, valleys and beaches and a five-star resort.

With its photogenic swimming pools, landscaped gardens and boutique beach-front villas, Hayman Island Resort (☑1800 075 175, 07-4940 1234; www.hayman.com.au; r incl breakfast $595-3900; ✳@☀) is one of the most luxurious on the Great Barrier Reef.

For non-guests, flying is the only way to do day trips to Hayman. Check out Air Whitsunday Seaplanes (☑07-4946 9111; per person $195).

OTHER WHITSUNDAY ISLANDS

The northern islands of the Whitsunday group are undeveloped and seldom visited by cruise boats or water taxis. Several of these – Gloucester, Saddleback, Olden and Armit Islands – have national-park **camping grounds**. The QPWS office (☑07-4946 7022; www.derm.qld.gov.au), 3km south of Airlie Beach, can issue camping permits and advise you on which islands to visit and how to get there.

Bowen

POP 7900

Bowen is a classic reminder of the typical small Queensland coastal towns of the 1970s – wide streets, low-rise buildings, wooden Queenslander houses, and laid-back, friendly locals. The foreshore, with its newly landscaped esplanade, picnic tables and barbecues, is a focal point. Although the town itself holds little of interest to travellers (except those who are keen on fruit-picking between April and November), there are some stunning beaches and bays northeast of the town centre.

🛏 Sleeping & Eating

Rose Bay Resort RESORT **$$**
(📞07-4786 9000; www.rosebayresort.com.au; 2 Pandanus St, Rose Bay; r $145-290; ✱@☀) In a beautiful location right on the beach, these spacious studios and comfy units will ensure plenty of quiet time. Good location and good value. Minimum two-night stay.

Aussiemates Backpackers HOSTEL **$**
(📞07-4786 3100; aussiemates@live.com; dm/d per week $160/190) In a lovely old Queenslander in the centre of town, this friendly hostel is clean and freshly painted, with two kitchens and a large upstairs verandah overlooking the main street. Weekly rates include transfers to working farms.

360 on the Hill CAFE **$**
(📞07-4786 6360; Margaret Reynolds Dr; mains $6-16; ☺breakfast & lunch daily, dinner Fri) High atop Flagstaff Hill. Serves delicious food and features stunning 360-degree views.

Cove CHINESE, MALAY **$$**
(📞07-4791 2050; Coral Cove Apartments, Horseshoe Bay Rd; mains $15-25; ☺lunch & dinner Tue-Sun) Serves an interesting fusion of Chinese and Malay dishes with spectacular sea views from the timber deck.

Grandview Hotel PUB FARE **$$**
(📞07-4786 6360; Margaret Reynolds Dr; mains $8-25; ☺lunch & dinner) Huge corner pub consistently recommended by locals for its quality meals and sizeable portions.

ⓘ Getting There & Away

Long-distance buses stop outside **Bowen Travel** (📞07-4786 2835; 40 William St), where you can book and purchase bus tickets. **Greyhound Australia** (📞13 20 30; www.greyhound.com.au) and **Premier Motor Service** (📞13 34 10; www.premierms.com.au) have frequent services to/from Rockhampton ($110, eight hours), Airlie Beach ($28, 1½ hours) and Townsville ($50, four hours).

TOWNSVILLE TO MISSION BEACH

North of the Whitsunday Coast you'll find mountain ranges, authentic outback towns and islands worth hopping to, all within reach of the vibrant city of Townsville. Townsville's waterfront stretches for miles and is hugged by hotels and pubs, trendier-every-day bars and cafes filled with the city's easy-going people. Magnetic Island lies just offshore and, with its 22 bays, makes an awesome place for isolated-beach-to-isolated-beach walking. Named for interfering with Captain Cook's compass, Magnetic Island is sacred to the Wulgurukaba Aboriginal people. Only a few kilometres out of Townsville, the red outback earth gets under your nails, and the outback towns of Charters Towers and Ravenswood make great diversions. Northwest of Townsville, the misty rainforest of the Paluma Range National Park stakes its claim as the southernmost part of the fantastic Wet Tropics World Heritage Area.

Other highlights include forested Hinchinbrook and Dunk Islands, and charming Mission Beach, surrounded by tropical rainforest.

Townsville
POP 182,000

Excellent museums, a huge aquarium, world-class diving, two major sporting teams, vibrant nightlife and a stunningly landscaped waterfront esplanade...that's a pretty impressive list for a capital city, let alone a regional centre. And then there's the climate: Townsville has an average of 320 days of sunshine per year. Undercover seating at Dairy Farmers Stadium was considered unnecessary because of the minimal rainfall during the rugby-league season.

Although it's often referred to as the Twin Cities – alongside Thuringowa, its sister 'city' (really a large suburb) to the southwest – Townsville has a compact city centre that's easy to get about on foot. Just east of the pedestrian-only Victoria Bridge (or the Dean St vehicle bridge), South Townsville is home to the city's premier drinking and dining precinct, centred on rejuvenated Palmer St.

Not content to stand still, central Townsville is in the final stages of a major refurbishment that includes tearing up the old Flinders St mall and returning a limited amount of traffic, along with increased lighting, shaded footpaths, a brand new visitor centre and a public piazza, all showcasing Townsville's 19th-century buildings. Things continue to change here – for the better.

◎ Sights

Reef HQ AQUARIUM
(www.reefhq.com.au; Flinders St E; adult/child $25/12; ☺9.30am-5pm) Townsville's excellent aquarium is a living reef on dry land. A stag-

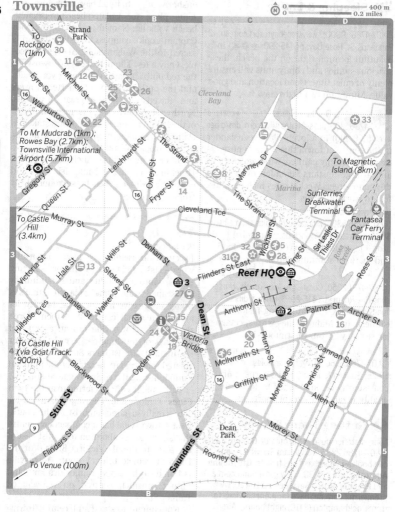

gering 2.5 million litres of water flow through the coral-reef tank, which is home to sharks, rays and over 100 fish species, plus brilliantly hued coral. Kids will love seeing, feeding and touching turtles at the **turtle hospital**. Talks and tours throughout the day focus on different aspects of the reef and the aquarium.

Adjacent to the aquarium, you can continue to experience life underwater at the **IMAX cinema** (adult/child $14/9; ☉10.30am-4.30pm).

Castle Hill   WALKING

If the temperature's right (ie the asphalt's not melting) it's worth scrambling to the top of this striking 286m-high red hill (an isolated pink-granite monolith) for the view. Walk up via the rough 'goat track' (2km oneway) from Hillside Cres. There's also a road (via Gregory St or Stanley St), if you're driving.

Botanic Gardens   GARDENS

(admission free; ☉sunrise-sunset) Townsville's botanic gardens are spread across three locations: each has its own character, but all have tropical plants and are abundantly green. Closest to the centre, the formal, ornamental **Queens Gardens** (cnr Gregory &

Paxton Sts) are 1km northwest of town at the base of Castle Hill.

🏞 Billabong Sanctuary   WILDLIFE PARK
(www.billabongsanctuary.com.au; Bruce Hwy; adult/child $30/19; ⊗8am-5pm; 🚼) Just 17km south of Townsville, this eco-certified wildlife park offers up-close-and-personal encounters with Australian wildlife – from dingoes to cassowaries – in their natural habitat. There are feedings, shows and talks every half-hour or so. Transfers are available from Townsville with Abacus Tours (☑07-4775 5544; adult/child incl park entry $50/30).

🏞 Australian Institute of Marine Science   RESEARCH INSTITUTE
(AIMS; ☑07-4753 4444; www.aims.gov.au) This marine-research facility at Cape Ferguson runs free two-hour tours (⊗10am Fri Mar-Nov) covering the institute's research (such as coral bleaching and management of the Great Barrier Reef) and how it relates to the community; advance bookings are essential. The turn-off from the Bruce Hwy is 35km southeast of Townsville.

Museum of Tropical Queensland   MUSEUM
(www.mtq.qld.gov.au; 70-102 Flinders St E; adult/child $13.50/8; ⊗9.30am-5pm) The MTQ reconstructs scenes using detailed models with interactive displays. At 11am and 2.30pm you can load and fire a cannon, 1700s-style; galleries include the kid-friendly Mind-Zone science centre and displays on north Queensland's history from the dinosaurs to the rainforest and reef.

Maritime Museum of Townsville   MUSEUM
(www.townsvillemaritimemuseum.org.au; 42-68 Palmer St; adult/child $6/3; ⊗10am-4pm Mon-Fri, noon-3pm Sat & Sun) A smaller affair, with lighthouse memorabilia and a *Yongala* shipwreck model and display.

Cultural Centre   CULTURAL CENTRE
(☑07-4772 7679; www.cctownsville.com.au; 2/68 Flinders St E; ⊗9.30am-4.30pm) Showcases the history, traditions and customs of the Wulgurkaba and Bindal people. Call for guided tour times.

FREE Perc Tucker Regional Gallery   ART GALLERY
(www.townsville.qld.gov.au; cnr Denham & Flinders Sts; ⊗10am-5pm Mon-Fri, to 2pm Sat & Sun)

A contemporary art gallery in a stately 1885 former bank. Exhibitions focus on north Queensland artists.

🏃 Activities

Strand
SWIMMING, PARKS

Stretching 2.2km, Townsville's palm-lined waterfront is interspersed with parks, pools, cafes and playgrounds. Its golden-sand beach is patrolled and protected by two stinger enclosures from November to May.

At the northern tip is the **rock pool** (admission free; ⊙24hr), an enormous artificial swimming pool surrounded by lawns and sandy beaches. Alternatively, head to the chlorinated safety of the heritage-listed Olympic-size swimming pool, **Tobruk Memorial Baths** (www.townsville.qld.gov.au; Strand; adult/child $2.50/1.50; ⊙5.30am-7pm Mon-Thu, to 6pm Fri, 7am-4pm Sat, 8am-5pm Sun).

There's also a brilliant little **water playground** (admission free; ⊙10am-8pm Dec-Mar, to 6pm Sep-Nov, Apr & May, to 5pm Jun-Aug) for kids.

Woodstock Trail Rides
HORSE RIDING

(☑07-4778 8888; www.woodstocktrailrides.com.au; Jones Rd, Woodstock; half-/full-day rides $80/150) Situated 43km south of Townsville, this huge property has full- and half-day horse-riding trips as well as **cattle musters** ($150) for aspiring cowboys and girls. Transfers for full-day rides and cattle musters are included from Townsville. Bookings essential.

Coral Sea Skydivers
SKY DIVING

(☑07-4772 4889; www.coralseaskydivers.com.au; tandem dives from $330) Those curious to know Townsville from top to bottom can try a tandem dive, landing in the middle of the sandy Strand.

Diving

The visitor centre has a list of Townsville-based operators offering PADI–certified learn-to-dive courses. Prices start at about $615.

Aside from Coral Sea exploration, most dive companies do *Yongala* day trips, which are only recommended for experienced divers. Recommended operators:

Adrenalin Dive
DIVING

(☑07-4724 0600; www.adrenalinedive.com.au; 9 Wickham St) Day trips to the *Yongala* (from $220) and Wheeler Reef (from $280), both including two dives. Also offers snorkelling (from $180) on Wheeler Reef as well as live-aboard trips, and dive certification courses.

Remote Area Dive
DIVING

(RAD; ☑07-4721 4424; www.remoteareadive.com; 16 Dean St) Runs day trips (from $220) to Orpheus and Pelorus islands. Also live-aboard trips and dive courses.

Salt Dive
DIVING

(☑07-4721 1760; www.saltdive.com.au; 2/276 Charters Towers Rd, Hermit Park) *Yongala* and reef-diving day trips (from $199) aboard a fast boat; dive courses available.

Yongala Dive
DIVING

(☑07-4783 1519; www.yongaladive.com.au; 56 Narrah St, Alva Beach) *Yongala* wreck dives ($220 including gear) from Alva Beach, 104km southeast of Townsville. It only takes 30 minutes to get out to the wreck from here, instead of a 2½-hour boat trip from Townsville. Book ahead for backpacker-style accommodation at its onshore **dive lodge** (dm/d $27/65; @).

🧭 Tours

Kookaburra Tours
SIGHTSEEING

(☑0448 794 798; www.kookaburratours.com.au) Highly recommended day trips include 'Heritage and Highlights' city tours (adult/child $40/18), Wallaman Falls (adult/child $125/55) rainforest tours in Mount Spec National Park (adult/child $125/55) and Aboriginal cultural tours (adult/child $140/65).

Townsville Ghost Tours
SIGHTSEEING

(☑0404 453 354; www.townsvilleghosttours.com.au) Five spooky options, from city haunts aboard the 'ghost bus' (from $65) to an overnight trip to Ravenswood ($295 including meals and accommodation).

🛏 Sleeping

Historic Yongala Lodge Motel
MOTEL $$

(☑07-4772 4633; www.historicyongala.com.au; 11 Fryer St; motel r $99-110, 1-bedroom apt $115-120, 2-bedroom apt 150-160; ❇🅿🛜🖵) In a quiet side street a short stroll from the Strand and city centre, this place has modern motel rooms and apartments built around the original 1884 heritage building. The excellent **restaurant** (mains $20-38; ⊙dinner Mon-Sat) serves Greek cuisine.

Reef Lodge
HOSTEL $

(☑07-4721 1112; www.reeflodge.com.au; 4 Wickham St; dm $22-26, d with/without bathroom $76/62; ❇@🛜) Townsville's best hostel has Buddhist sculptures and hammocks strewn through the garden, an outdoor 'cinema' with swinging lounges and a games room with a minigym and retro arcade games.

Coral Lodge
B&B $

(☎07-4771 5512; www.corallodge.com.au; 32 Hale St; s/d without bathroom $65/70, units from $80; ✳) If you're looking to stay in a charmingly old-fashioned Aussie home, this century-old property can't be beat. Staying in the self-contained units is like having your own apartment. The welcoming owners will pick you up from the bus, train and ferry.

Holiday Inn
HOTEL $$

(☎07-4772 2477; www.townsville.holiday-inn.com; 334 Flinders St; d $114-199; ✳⚡📶) Dubbed the 'sugar shaker' (for reasons that are immediately obvious), this 20-storey, 1976-built circular building is a Townsville icon. Its 199 rooms are much more contemporary than the exterior suggests, and there is a rooftop pool with unrivalled views.

Adventurers Resort
HOSTEL $

(☎07-4721 1522; www.adventurersresort.com; 79 Palmer St; dm/s/d $25/45/55; ✳@⚡📶) Roomy, multilevel dorms await at this motel-style complex, which puts on regular falafel nights and theme parties and has its own egg-laying chicken. The highlight is the panoramic rooftop pool and barbecue area. Vans can park for $5 per night, including full use of the hostel's facilities.

Aquarius on the Beach
HOTEL $$

(☎1800 622 474; www.aquariusonthebeach.com.au; 75 The Strand; d $125-145; ✳@⚡📶) The full-width balcony views from all 130 apartments impress almost as much as the size of this place, the tallest building on the Strand. Don't be put off by the dated facade – this is one of the better places around.

Hotel M
HOTEL $$

(☎1800 760 144; www.oakshotelsresorts.com; 81 Palmer St; d $144-189; ✳⚡📶) Built in 2009, this 11-storey hotel has space-age rooms, excellent facilities and glittering views from the higher-priced rooms.

Beach House Motel
MOTEL $$

(☎07-4721 1333; www.beachhousemotel.com.au; 66 The Strand; d $99-118; ✳⚡📶) A tranquil guesthouse with cosy, old-fashioned rooms, free pick-ups and laundry.

Rowes Bay Caravan Park
CARAVAN PARK $

(☎07-4771 3576; www.rowesbaycp.com.au; Heatley Pde, Rowes Bay; unpowered/powered sites $25/33, cabins with/without bathroom from $95/65, villas $98; ✳@⚡📶) Leafy park directly opposite Rowes Bay's beachfront. Brand-new villas are smaller but spiffier than cabins.

Orchid Guest House
GUESTHOUSE $

(☎07-4771 6683; www.orchidguesthouse.com.au; 34 Hale St; dm $26, with/without bathroom s $70/50, d $80/62; ✳) Sky-blue, '60s-style motel with clean, comfortable, well-equipped rooms.

Mariners North
APARTMENTS $$$

(☎07-4722 0777; www.marinersnorth.com.au; 7 Mariners Dr; 2-/3-bedroom apt from $250/390; ✳⚡📶) Spacious self-contained waterfront apartments.

✕ Eating

TOP CHOICE **A Touch of Salt**
MODERN AUSTRALIAN $$

(☎07-4724 4441; cnr Stokes & Ogden Sts; mains $30-36; ⊙lunch Thu & Fri, dinner Tue-Sat) Delectable seafood is accompanied by an extensive wine list and genuinely good service. When we visited, the same team was putting the finishing touches on a Palmer St tapas and wine bar, the **Salt Cellar** (☎07-4724 5866; www.thesaltcellar.com.au; 13 Palmer St; ⊙dinner Mon-Sat).

Benny's Hot Wok
ASIAN $$

(☎07-4724 3243; 17-21 Palmer St; mains $14-29; ⊙lunch Fri & Sun, dinner daily) Outdoor seating, savvy staff and a good wine list set the scene for some of the finest pan-Asian cuisine in north Queensland – from freshly made sushi to Peking duck rolls, steaming laksas, and sizzling Mongolian lamb.

Cafe Bambini
CAFE $

(47 Gregory St; mains $11.50-20; ⊙5.30am-5pm Mon-Fri, 6.30am-4pm Sat & Sun; ✎) Spawning five branches around town at last count, this local success story cooks up the best breakfasts in Townsville. Lunches have international flavours, from smoked salmon with pappadums to French steak sandwiches.

Jamaica Joe's
JAMAICAN $$

(☎07-4724 1234; The Strand, opposite Gregory St; mains $17-43; ⊙lunch & dinner) The best time to head to this funky Caribbean diner-bar is on Sunday afternoon, when entertainment includes live music and DJs spinning old-school reggae vinyl. But it's a worthy dining option any time for dishes like Jamaican goat curry.

Mr Mudcrab
SEAFOOD $

(1 Rose St; dishes $3-10; ⊙8am-8pm) If mud crab's on offer here, you know it's fresh – Mr Mudcrab refuses to get it in frozen. This excellent seafood shop sells fresh catches to cook yourself, as well as fish and chips and seafood pies.

Cbar
CAFE $$

(The Strand, opposite Gregory St; mains $16-26; 7am-10pm;) Serving full meals throughout the day, from coconut prawns with mango salsa to Moroccan-style beef tagines.

Harold's Seafood
SEAFOOD $

(cnr The Strand & Gregory St; meals $4-10; lunch & dinner) This takeaway joint has bug burgers of the Moreton Bay variety.

Souvlaki Bar
GREEK $

(shops 3 & 4, 58 The Strand; mains $6.50-17.50; 10.30am-9pm Mon-Fri, to 10pm Sat & Sun) Grab a big Greek breakfast of bacon, eggs, sausage, souvlaki, grilled tomatoes, haloumi and pita bread.

Bountiful Thai
THAI $$

(shop 1/52 Gregory St, North Ward; mains $13-21; lunch Mon-Fri, dinner daily) Takeaway whipping up noodle and rice dishes, curries and soups in huge portions and quick time.

Coffee Dominion
CAFE $

(www.coffeedominion.com.au; cnr Stokes & Ogden Sts; 6am-5pm Mon-Wed, to 5.30pm Thu & Fri, 7am-1pm Sat & Sun) Eco-conscious cafe.

Drinking

TOP CHOICE Brewery
MICROBREWERY

(252 Flinders St; Mon-Sat) Brews are made on site at Townsville's handsomely restored 1880s former post office. Soak them up with a meal at its refined restaurant (mains $17-36; lunch & dinner Mon-Sat).

Watermark Hotel
BAR

(72-74 The Strand) Some serious Sunday sessions take place in the tavern bar, while there's also a more upmarket bar and an excellent Mod Oz restaurant (mains $28-36; breakfast Sun, lunch & dinner daily).

Seaview Hotel
PUB

(cnr The Strand & Gregory St) The sea views, fig-tree locale and occasionally loud live music win over pub-loving locals in this sprawling drinking hub.

Molly Malones
PUB, NIGHTCLUB

(87 Flinders St E) This boisterous Irish pub stages live music on Friday and Saturday nights, or you can shake it on the dance floor of its adjacent nightclub, The Shed (8pm-5am Tue, Fri & Sat).

Entertainment

Consortium
NIGHTCLUB

(159 Flinders St E; 9am-5am Tue & Thu-Sun) Resident DJs, DJ comps and events like 'fetish and fantasy' balls make this big city–style venue Townsville's hippest nightclub.

Flynns
LIVE MUSIC

(101 Flinders St E; 5pm-late Tue-Sun) A jolly Irish pub that doesn't try too hard to be Irish. Wildly popular for its $8 jugs and live music every night except Wednesday, when karaoke takes over.

Venue
LIVE MUSIC

(719 Flinders St W) Multilevel place with regular gigs by Aussie acts (Grinspoon et al) and four bars.

Jupiters Casino
CASINO

(Sir Leslie Thiess Dr) Come here for a waterside flutter.

Information

Internet Den (265 Flinders St; per 90min $5; 8am-10pm)

QPWS (13 74 68; www.derm.qld.gov.au; 1-7 Marlow St)

Visitor information centre (07-4721 3660; www.townsvilleonline.com.au; cnr Flinders & Stokes Sts; 9am-5pm) Extensive visitor information on Townsville, Magnetic Island and nearby national parks.

Getting There & Away

Air

Virgin Australia (13 67 89; www.virginaustralia.com), **Jetstar** (13 15 38; www.jetstar.com.au) and **Qantas** (13 13 13; www.qantas.com.au) all service Townsville.

Bus

Greyhound Australia (1300 473 946; www.greyhound.com.au) departs from here. Buses pick up and drop off at Townsville's **Sunferries Breakwater ferry terminal** (2/14 Sir Leslie Thiess Dr; lockers per day $4-6).

DESTINATION	PRICE ($)	DURATION (HR)
Airlie Beach	71	4½
Brisbane	270	23
Cairns	83	6
Charters Towers	36	1½
Mackay	96	6
Mission Beach	63	4
Rockhampton	149	12

Premier Motor Service (13 34 10; www.premierms.com.au) has one service a day to/from Brisbane and Cairns, stopping in Townsville at Townsville's **Fantasea car ferry terminal** (Ross St, South Townsville).

Train

Townsville's **train station** (Charters Towers Rd) is 1km south of the centre.

The Brisbane–Cairns *Sunlander* travels through Townsville three times a week. Journey time between Brisbane and Townsville is 24 hours (one way from $190).

The *Inlander* heads from Townsville to Mt Isa on Thursday and Sunday (one way from $127, 21 hours) via Charters Towers ($27.19, three hours).

Contact **Queensland Rail** (☑1800 872 467; www.traveltrain.com.au).

❶ Getting Around

Townsville's airport is 5km northwest of the city in Garbutt. A taxi costs $20, or the **Airport Shuttle** (☑07-4775 5544; one way/return $10/18) services all arrivals and departures, with pick-ups and drop-offs throughout the central business district (bookings essential).

Sunbus (☑07-4725 8482; www.sunbus.com.au) scoots around town; pick up info from the visitor information centre.

Taxis congregate near the Sunbus **bus interchange** (cnr Flinders & Stokes Sts) or call **Townsville Taxis** (☑13 10 08).

Magnetic Island

POP 2500

'Maggie', as she's affectionately called, is a 'real' island. Permanent residents live and work here and some even make the daily commute to Townsville. Over half of this mountainous, triangular-shaped island's 52 sq km is national park, with scenic walks and abundant wildlife, including one of the largest concentrations of wild koalas in Australia. Stunning beaches offer adrenaline-pumping water sports or just the chance to bask in the sunshine. Each of the four tiny beach villages has its own distinct personality, and the granite boulders, hoop pines and eucalypts are a change from your typical tropical-island paradise.

❍ Sights & Activities

There's one main road across the island, which goes from Picnic Bay, past Nelly and Geoffrey Bays, to Horseshoe Bay. Local buses ply the route regularly.

Picnic Bay   BAY

Since the ferry terminal was relocated to Nelly Bay, Picnic Bay has resembled a ghost town. Shopfronts were abandoned as businesses suffered from the decreased tourist traffic. But that curious, elegant bird, the

curlew, has made it its own, and the twinkling night views of Townsville are magical.

Activities in the area include swimming in the beach's stinger enclosure (November to May) or hitting balls around the nine-hole golf course at the Magnetic Island Country Club (☑07-4778 5188; www.magneticislandgolf.com.au; Hurst St; ⊙from 8am). West is Cockle Bay, site of the HMS *City of Adelaide* wreck, followed by West Point with its sunsets and secluded beach. East round the coast is Rocky Bay, where a short, steep walk leads down to a beautiful sheltered beach.

Nelly Bay   BAY

This bustling harbour is where the island experience begins and ends if you come by passenger or car ferry. Nelly Bay has a wide range of eating and sleeping options and a decent beach. There's a children's playground towards the northern end of the beach and good snorkelling on the fringing coral reef.

Arcadia   VILLAGE

Arcadia village has the island's main concentration of shops, eateries and accommodation. Its main beach, Geoffrey Bay, has a reef at its southern end (DERM discourages reef walking). By far its prettiest beach is Alma Bay cove, with huge boulders tumbling into the sea. There's plenty of shade, along with picnic tables and a children's playground here.

If you head to the end of the road at Bremner Point, between Geoffrey Bay and Alma Bay, at 5pm, you can have wild rock wallabies – which have become accustomed to being fed at the same time each day – literally eating out of your hand.

Forts   FORTS

In 1942 Townsville became a major military base, and a forts complex was built on Magnetic Island to spot aircraft with its two 3,000,000-candle-power searchlights. If you're going to do just one walk, then the forts walk (2.8km, 1½ hours return) is a must. It starts near the Radical Bay turn-off. Or head north to Radical Bay via the rough vehicle track. This has walking tracks to secluded Arthur Bay and Florence Bay (the northern sides of both offer the island's best snorkelling).

Radical Bay   BAY

Radical Bay once housed a resort, and a replacement is in the pipeline. In the meantime it's a peaceful spot. You can walk across

QUEENSLAND & THE GREAT BARRIER REEF MAGNETIC ISLAND

the headland to Horseshoe Bay, taking a detour down to the unofficial nudist beach of **Balding Bay** (3.4km return).

Horseshoe Bay
BAY

The crescent-shaped, golden-sand beach is easily the best of the island's accessible beaches. It has a stinger enclosure (November to May), water-sports equipment for hire, a row of cafes and a good pub. Bungalow Bay Koala Village has a **wildlife park** (adult/child $19/10; ⊘2hr tours 10am, noon & 2.30pm) where you can cuddle koalas ($14 including photos), or tuck into a **bush tucker gourmet breakfast** (adult/child $25/12.50). A monthly **craft market** (⊘9.30am-2pm last Sun of month) sets up along the beachfront.

Walking tracks abound on Magnetic, and **DERM** (☑13 74 68; www.derm.qld.gov.au) produces a leaflet for the island's excellent bushwalking tracks. Walks are mainly along the east coast and vary in length from half an hour to half a day.

Pleasure Divers
DIVING

(☑1800 797 797; www.pleasuredivers.com.au; 10 Marine Pde, Arcadia; open-water course per person $339) Teaches all PADI courses and offers reef, wreck and island dives.

Reef Safari
DIVING

(☑07-4778 5777; www.reefsafari.com; 1 Nelly Bay Rd, Nelly Bay) At Base Backpackers in Nelly Bay. Runs four-day open-water courses from $299 and offers certified dives.

Magnetic Island Hire Boats
BOAT HIRE

(☑07-4778 5327) Rents boats ($220 per day plus fuel) that can carry up to eight people – great for fishing, snorkelling or just finding your own private cove.

Horseshoe Bay Ranch
HORSE RIDING

(☑07-4778 5109; www.horseshoebayranch.com.au; 38 Gifford St, Horseshoe Bay; 2hr rides $100) Memorable rides through bush and along beach.

Tours

Unique ways to tour the island range from kayak to tall ship. Alternatively, rent your own boat (this page) or zoom around by Moke or scooter (p404).

Providence V
CRUISES

(☑07-4778 5580; www.providencesailing.com.au) Six-hour sailing trips aboard a 62ft schooner for $129 (including snorkelling gear); also 2½-hour champagne sunset cruises.

Magnetic Island Sea Kayaks
KAYAK

(☑07-4778 5424; www.seakayak.com.au; 93 Horseshoe Bay Rd; tours from $60) Eco-certified morning and sunset tours departing from Horseshoe Bay. Also offers kayak rental (per day from $75).

Reef Ecotours
SNORKELLING

(☑0419 712 579; www.reefecotours.com; adult/child $80/70) Family-friendly one-hour snorkelling tours guided by a marine biologist.

Tropicana Tours
4WD

(☑07-4758 1800; www.tropicanatours.com.au; full day adult/child $198/99) Offers 4WD tours taking in wildlife, lunch at a local cafe and a sunset cocktail (all included in the price).

Sleeping

Maggie is especially popular with families and couples, but backpackers also have plenty of options. Much of the accommodation on the island is holiday rental cottages – contact **First National Real Estate** (☑07-4778 5077; 21 Marine Pde, Arcadia) or **Smith & Elliott** (☑07-4778 5570; 4/5 Bright Ave, Arcadia).

PICNIC BAY

Travellers Hideaway
HOSTEL $

(☑1800 000 290, 07-4778 5314; www.travellers backpackers.com; 32 Picnic St; dm/d $24/60; ❄@☒) If full-moon parties don't rock your boat and peace and quiet is more your go, try this rustic backpackers, which moves to a very slow beat. Inviting pool.

Tropical Palms Inn
MOTEL $$

(☑07-4778 5076; www.tropicalpalmsinn.com.au; 34 Picnic St; s/d $100/110; ❄☒) With a terrific little swimming pool right outside your front door, the self-contained motel units here are bright and comfortable. Reception hires 4WDs (from $75 per day).

NELLY BAY

TOP CHOICE **Base Backpackers**
HOSTEL $

(☑1800 242 273; www.stayatbase.com; 1 Nelly Bay Rd; camping $10 per person, dm $24-30, d with/without bathroom from $120/65; @☎☒) Base has loud music, cool attitudes, unique A-frame cabins (some oceanfront) and a massive deck with beach views. There are loads of activities (full-moon parties, swimming, kayaking, diving) and good-value packages, including lodging, food and transport (from Townsville).

Shambhala Retreat
UNITS **$$**

(☏0448160580; www.shambhala-retreat-magnetic
-island.com.au; 11-13 Barton St; d $110; ❋☀❄) These
three peaceful tropical-hued units have their
own tree-screened patios for watching wild-
life. Two have outdoor courtyard showers,
and all have fully equipped kitchens and
laundry facilities. The saltwater pool is tiny,
but the property is entirely green powered.
Two-night minimum stay.

ARCADIA

Arcadia Beach Guest House GUESTHOUSE **$$**

(☏07-4778 5668; www.arcadiabeachguesthouse.
com.au; 27 Marine Pde; dm $30, safari tents $50,
d without bathroom $80-100, d with bathroom
$120-150; ❋☀❄) Super-friendly owners
have created a stunningly different place
to stay, with bright, beachy rooms named
after Magnetic Island's bays and coves. You
can turtle-spot from the balcony, or rent a
canoe, Moke (buggy) or 4WD. Free ferry
pick-ups.

Magnums on Magnetic HOSTEL **$**

(☏1800 663 666; www.magnums.com.au; 7 Marine
Pde; dm $20-24, d $75-85; ❋@❄) Fresh from
a facelift, Magnums has swish dorms and
doubles; make sure you ask for one with an
ocean view. The hub of Arcadia bay is on-
site bistro and bar the **Island Tavern** (mains
$19.50-28; ☀lunch & dinner), which keeps punt-
ers happy with $10 jugs, cane-toad races ev-
ery Wednesday night and a large swimming
pool accessible to the public.

HORSESHOE BAY

Bungalow Bay Koala Village HOSTEL **$**

(☏1800 285 577, 07-4778 5577; www.bungalowbay.
com.au; 40 Horseshoe Bay Rd; unpowered/powered
sites per person $12.50/15, dm $30, d with/without
bathroom $90/74; ❋@❄) Not only a resort-
style, YHA-associated hostel but a nature
wonderland (with its own wildlife park).
Less than five minutes' walk from the beach,
A-frame bungalows are strewn throughout
leafy grounds backing onto national park.
Cool off at the breezy outdoor bar, go coconut bowling on Thursday, or tuck into a curry
at the **restaurant** (mains $15.50-24; ☀lunch &
dinner).

Shaws on the Shore APARTMENTS **$$$**

(☏07-4778 1900; www.shawsontheshore.com.au;
7 Pacific Dr; 1-/2-/3-bedroom apt $195/270/325;
❋☀❄) Natural light floods these sparkling

apartments, whose balconies overlook the
bay.

✕ Eating

Maggie's natural beauty far outshines her
cooking skills. Horseshoe Bay has the is-
land's best eateries.

PICNIC BAY

Picnic Bay Hotel PUB **$$**

(Picnic Bay Mall) Settle in for a drink with
Townsville's city lights sparkling across the
bay. Its **R&R Cafe Bar** (mains $11-26; ☀lunch &
dinner) has an all-day grazing menu and huge
salads, including Cajun prawn.

NELLY BAY

TOP
CHOICE **Man Friday** MEXICAN, INTERNATIONAL **$$**

(☏07-4778 5658; 37 Warboy St; mains $14-39; ☀di-
nner Wed-Mon; ☝) Man Friday serves decent
Mexican food, along with imaginative inter-
national dishes – all of which are best enjoyed
in the rustic, fairy-lit garden. Bring your own
wine but book ahead or risk missing out.

Terrace MEDITERRANEAN **$$**

(☏07-4778 5200; www.allseasons.com.au; 61 Mandalay Ave; mains $22-44; ☀lunch Sat & Sun, din-
ner Mon-Sat; ☀) Overlooking the pool of the
dated All Seasons Hotel, the Terrace is a fine
spot for dining on pan-roasted duck or oven-
baked spring lamb on kumara mash.

Fat Possum Cafe CAFE **$**

(55 Spooning St; mains $7-17; ☀breakfast & lunch;
☝) Aptly named for the well-fed possums
scampering around the island. The best
pickings are on the specials board; Sunday's
$15 all-you-can-eat breakfast buffet is some-
thing of a village social event.

ARCADIA

Butler's Pantry CAFE, DELI **$**

(shop 2-3, 5 Bright Ave; mains $15-21; ☀breakfast
& lunch Wed-Mon; ☝) At this gourmet grocery
store–cafe you'll find the island's best brekkies, including pancakes, eggs every which
way, and stacks of vegie options. Great
lunches too – from Thai fish cakes to Greek
lamb salad.

caffè dell' isola ITALIAN **$$**

(shop 1, Arcadia Village; mains $15-26; ☀breakfast &
lunch Tue, Thu & Sun, breakfast, lunch & dinner Wed,
Fri & Sat, daily during school holidays) The Italian
radio station reverberating through the out-
door courtyard attests to the authenticity of

the crisp-crust pizzas here (as does the menu that reads 'please do not even ask for pineapple'). Cash only.

Banister's Seafood
SEAFOOD $$
(☎07-4778 5700; 22 McCabe Cres; mains $10-22; ⊙lunch & dinner) You can do the whole sit-down thing and order off the menu chalked on the blackboard of this BYO-only seafood joint, or grab some takeaway and head to a nearby beach.

Arcadia Night Market
MARKET $$
(Hayles Ave, Arcadia; ⊙5-8pm Fri) Small but lively night market next door to the RSL, with sizzling Indonesian food and seafood to cook up yourself.

HORSESHOE BAY

Marlin Bar
PUB $$
(3 Pacific Dr; mains $16-24; ⊙lunch & dinner) You can't leave Maggie without enjoying a cold one by the window as the sun sets across the bay at this busy seaside pub. The meals are on the large side and revolve around seafood. Great value.

Barefoot
MODERN AUSTRALIAN $$
(☎07-4758 1170; www.barefootartfoodwine.com.au; 5 Pacific Dr; mains $16-30; ⊙lunch & dinner Thu-Mon) Dine on artichoke risotto with truffle oil or Egyptian-spiced kangaroo burgers at this restaurant, art gallery and ode to contemporary design.

❶ Information

There's no official visitor information centre on Magnetic Island, but Townsville's visitor information centre has comprehensive info and maps, and can help find accommodation.

ATMs are scattered throughout the island, although there are no banks. The **post office** (Sooning St, Nelly Bay) also has an ATM.

❶ Getting There & Away

All ferries arrive and depart Maggie from the terminal at Nelly Bay.

Sunferries (☎07-4726 0800; www.sunferries.com.au) operates a frequent passenger ferry between Townsville and Magnetic Island (adult/child return $29/15), which takes around 20 minutes. Ferries depart Townsville from the Sunferries Breakwater Terminal at 2/14 Sir Leslie Thiess Dr.

Fantasea (☎07-4796 9300; www.magneticislandferry.com.au; Ross St, South Townsville) operates a car ferry crossing eight times daily (seven on weekends) from the south side of Ross Creek, taking 35 minutes. It costs $164 (return) for a car and up to three passengers, and $26/16

(return) for an adult/child foot passenger only. Bookings are essential. Bicycles are transported free.

Both Townsville terminals have car parking.

❶ Getting Around

Bicycle

Magnetic Island is ideal for cycling although some of the hills can be hard work. Most places to stay rent bikes for around $15 a day and a number of places offer them free to guests.

Bus

The **Magnetic Island Bus Service** (☎07-4778 5130) ploughs between Picnic Bay and Horseshoe Bay at least 18 times a day, meeting all ferries and stopping at major accommodation places. A hop-on, hop-off day pass costs $6.

Moke & Scooter

Moke (buggy) and scooter rental places abound around the island. Expect to pay around $80 per day for a Moke. You'll need to be over 21, have a current international or Australian driver's licence and leave a credit-card deposit. Scooter hire starts at around $30 per day. Try **MI Wheels** (☎07-4778 5491; 138 Sooning St, Nelly Bay) for a classic Moke or 'topless' (open-topped) car, or **Roadrunner Scooter Hire** (☎07-4778 5222; 3/64 Kelly St, Nelly Bay) for scooters and trail bikes.

North of Townsville

PALUMA RANGE NATIONAL PARK

The Paluma Range National Park runs almost from Ingham to Townsville, and includes the must-see Mt Spec-Big Crystal Creek section, 62km north of Townsville. This is a pocket of rainforest with some awesome views of the coast and a variety of different walking trails.

From the Bruce Hwy, the 4km-long route (Spiegelhauer Rd) to **Big Crystal Creek** is located 2km north of Mt Spec Rd. It's an easy 100m walk from the car park to **Paradise Waterhole**, with its sandy beach on one side and great views of the mountains in the distance. The self-registration **QPWS camping ground** (per person/family $5.15/21) has gas barbecues, toilets and water (treat before drinking).

Leave the caravan behind to take on the windy, narrow road up to the cool mountain town of Paluma. Along the way are several creek and swimming-hole stops, including **Little Crystal Creek**, 7km along Mt Spec Rd, which is a series of swimming holes surrounded by rainforest and looked over by a stone bridge (built in 1932).

To get to **Jourama Falls** travel 6km on a good, sealed road from the highway, though the creek at the entrance can be impassable. It's a steep walk up to the lookout; watch for Ulysses butterflies, nocturnal brown bandicoots and mahogany gliders (a threatened species). The rock pools are good for a dip, and there are plenty of turtles to check out. The **QPWS camping ground** (per person/family $5.15/21) has toilets and barbecues.

Up in the tiny village of Paluma is the cool **Paluma Rainforest Inn** (07-4770 8688; www.rainforestinnpaluma.com; 1 Mt Spec Rd; d $125;), with stylish, well-designed rooms, lovely gardens and a recommended licensed **restaurant** (mains $19-29; lunch Wed-Mon, breakfast & dinner by reservation;).

About 14km west of Paluma (the last 4km along a bumpy unsealed road) is **Hidden Valley Cabins** (07-4770 8088; www.hiddenvalleycabins.com.au; s/d without bathroom $69/79, cabins $139/149;), a solar-powered, carbon-neutral eco-retreat. You'll find small, cosy homestead rooms and a clutch of log cabins grouped close together. A range of **tours** (2hr from $20), including platypus-spotting safaris and night walks, run daily. Its bar and **restaurant** (mains $24-31; breakfast, lunch & dinner;), serving country-style home cooking, are open to guests only.

There's no fuel in Paluma, so fill up before heading out this way.

On the Bruce Hwy, 70km north of Townsville, **Frosty Mango** (07-4770 8184; www.frostymango.com.au; Bruce Hwy, Mutarnee; dishes $6-15; 8am-6pm) is perfect for indulging in everything mango: fresh-squeezed mango juice, mango muffins with mango jam and cream, mango trifle, and scrumptious mango ice cream, as well as fresh-picked fruit. Hot dishes include jackfruit curry.

INGHAM & AROUND

Laid-back Ingham is the proud guardian of the ever-expanding, **Tyto wetlands** (Tyto Wetlands Information Centre; 07-4776 4792; www.hinchinbrooknq.com.au; cnr Cooper St & Bruce Hwy; 8.45am-5pm Mon-Fri, 9am-4pm Sat & Sun), which has 4km of walking trails and attracts around 230 species of bird, including far-flung guests from Siberia and Japan, as well as hundreds of wallabies at dawn and dusk. From the visitor centre, a wheelchair-accessible boardwalk leads across the lagoon to the stylish cafe-restaurant **Pepper for Passion @ Tyto** (07-4776 6212; mains $17-25; 10am-4pm Mon-Thu, to 9pm Fri & Sat, 8am-4pm Sun;). Sit out on the deck

watching the bird life and tuck into temptations like creamy banana curry with king prawns. A state-of-the-art gallery and library opened in mid-2011.

In mid-May the **Australian Italian Festival** (www.australianitalianfestival.com.au) celebrates the fact that 60% of Ingham residents are of Italian descent, with pasta flying, wine flowing and music playing over three days.

Ingham is the jumping-off point for a trip out to magnificent **Wallaman Falls**, the longest single-drop waterfall in Australia at 305m. Located in **Girringun National Park**, 51km southwest of the town (sealed except for 10km; not suitable for caravans), the falls look their best in the Wet though are spectacular at any time. Nearby, the self-registration **QPWS campground** (per person/family $5.15/21) has showers and barbecues; the swimming hole is frequented by the occasional platypus. Two- and three-day walking trails start from the falls, with campsites along the way – pick up a *Wallaman Falls Section Girringun National Park* leaflet from the Tyto Wetlands Information Centre.

Mungalla Station (07-4777 8718; www.mungallaaboriginaltours.com.au; Forrest Beach, Allingham; 2hr tours adult/child $40/10), 15km east of Ingham, runs insightful Aboriginal-led tours, including boomerang throwing and stories from the local Nywaigi culture. Definitely book in for a traditional **Kup Murri** (adult/child incl tour $80/20) lunch of meat and vegies wrapped in banana leaves and cooked underground in an earth oven. If you have a self-contained caravan or campervan, you can **camp** (per van $10) overnight.

Once the domain of Italian cane cutters, Ingham's wonderful 1920s art deco **Noorla Heritage Resort** (07-4776 1100; www.hotelnoorla.com.au; 5-9 Warren St; unpowered/powered sites $15/22, dm $28, d with/without bathroom $139/89, 1-/2-course meals $24.50/33; dinner Mon-Sat;) has magnificently restored high-ceilinged rooms, plus cheaper container-style rooms in the garden. A photomontage of local stories lines the walls, bringing the town's history to life, as do the stories told around the resort's aqua-tiled guests-only bar. Home cooking includes regular Kup Murri dinners; ask about transfers to Mungalla Station.

Between Ingham and Cardwell, the Bruce Hwy climbs high above the coast. There are wonderful views out over the mangrove-lined waterways known as the Everglades,

RAVENSWOOD & CHARTERS TOWERS

You don't have to venture too far inland for a taste of the dry, dusty Queensland outback – a stark contrast to the verdant coast. This detour is easily accessible on a day trip from Townsville, but it's worth staying overnight if you can.

Along the Flinders Hwy, a turn-off at Mingela, 88km southwest of Townsville, leads 40km south to the tiny gold-mining village of Ravenswood (population 150), with a couple of gorgeous turn-of-the-20th-century pubs with accommodation.

A further 47km west along the Flinders Hwy from Mingela is the historic gold-rush town of Charters Towers (population 8100). The 'towers' are its surrounding tors (hills). William Skelton Ewbank Melbourne (WSEM) Charters was the gold commissioner during the rush, when the town was the second-largest, and wealthiest, in Queensland. With almost 100 mines, some 90 pubs and a stock exchange, it became known simply as 'the World'.

Today, a highlight of a visit to the Towers is strolling past its glorious facades recalling the grandeur of those heady days, and listening to locals' ghost stories.

History oozes from the walls of the 1890 Stock Exchange Arcade, next door to the Charters Towers visitor centre (☑07-4752 0314; www.charterstowers.qld.gov.au; 74 Mosman St; ◉9am-5pm). The visitor centre has a free brochure outlining the **One Square Mile Trail** of the town centre's beautifully preserved 19th-century buildings, and books all tours in town, including the Venus Gold Battery (Millchester Rd; tours adult/child $12/6; ◉10am-3pm), where gold-bearing ore was crushed and processed; it cranks into action during mid-July's Gold Fever Festival.

Come nightfall, panoramic Towers Hill, the site where gold was first discovered, is the atmospheric setting for a free **open-air cinema** showing the 20-minute film *Ghosts After Dark* – check seasonal screening times with the visitor centre.

In-town accommodation includes period furniture–filled former pub the Royal Private Hotel (☑07-4787 8688; 100 Mosman St; s/d without bathroom $45/55, d with bathroom $90-115; ❀☎). A venture to Charters Towers is incomplete without scoffing one of the award-winning pies at Towers Bakery (114 Gill St; pies $3.90-4.30; ◉5am-3pm Mon-Fri, to 1pm Sat).

Greyhound Australia (☑1300 473 946; www.greyhound.com.au) has four weekly services between Townsville and Charters Towers ($36, 1¾ hours).

The Queensland Rail (☑1300 131 722; www.traveltrain.com.au) *Inlander* runs twice weekly between Townsville and Charters Towers ($28, three hours).

---

which separate Hinchinbrook Island from the coast.

Lucinda is a sweet-as-pie port town with one massive attribute – a 6km-long jetty used for shipping sugar.

Offshore, Hinchinbrook Island is seemingly within touching distance. You can take a four-hour cruise along the Deluge Inlet or a 2½-hour tour along the channel with Hinchinbrook Wilderness Safaris (☑07-4777 8307; www.hinchinbrookwilderness safaris.com.au; inlet/channel cruises $80/60), which also offers transfers to Hinchinbrook for hikers to/from the southern end of the Thorsborne Trail (see this spread).

Fishing is a popular pastime here. Pick up bait, tackle and more at the Lucinda Jetty Store & Take-Away (☑07-4777 8280; 2 Rigby St; mains $15.50-19.50; ◉6am-7pm), which serves great barramundi, crumbed steak

and king salmon as well as takeaway fare like burgers and filled rolls.

CARDWELL
POP 12,000

Spread along kilometres of crocodile-infested waters (even the public pool has a crocodile on its sign), Cardwell is the gateway to the sublime Hinchinbrook Island National Park but has its own unique seaside, prawn-burger-lovin' attitude that doesn't take long to get used to. Port Hinchinbrook Marina, 2km from the town, has a glamorous pace and doubles as the departure point for the Hinchinbrook Island ferry. Behind Cardwell is the 26km Cardwell Forest Drive, and you can dip into the springs and spas along the way.

The Rainforest and Reef Centre (☑07-4066 8601; www.derm.qld.gov.au; ◉8.30am-5pm Mon-Fri, 9am-3pm Sat & Sun Apr-Oct, to 1pm Sat &

Sun Nov-Mar; @), next to Cardwell's town jetty, has detailed info on Hinchinbrook Island and other nearby national parks.

Seasonal Work

With mod cons in the kitchen and friendly owners who think nothing of piling the troops into the bus and showing them the sights, **Cardwell Backpackers Hostel** (07-4066 8404; www.cardwellbackpackers.com. au; 6 Brasenose St; dm $20; @🛜🌊) is the place to stay if you're in the mood for some fun and farm work (which the owners can help you find). The warehouse-living style may not appeal to everyone, but the atmosphere is warm and there's a dedicated room for dirty shoes. Banana and pineapple farms provide work throughout the year.

🛏 Sleeping & Eating

Mudbrick Manor　　　　　　B&B $$
(07-4066 2299; www.mudbrickmanor.com.au; lot 13, Stony Creek Rd; s/d $90/120; ❇🌊) Hand-built from mud bricks, natural timber and stone, this family home has huge, beautifully appointed rooms grouped around a fountained courtyard. Spend long, lazy evenings on the verandah or large lounge area. Rates include hot breakfast; book at least a few hours ahead for delicious three-course **dinners** (per person $30).

Beachcomber　　　　　CARAVAN PARK $
(07-4066 8550; www.cardwellbeachcomber.com. au; 43a Marine Pde; unpowered/powered sites $25/30, motel d $75-100, cabins & studios $90-110; ❇@🛜🌊) There's a happy holiday vibe at this large park, with campsites as well as snazzy studios with timber decks and bright, tropical decor. Its licensed **restaurant** (mains $24.40-36.50; ◷breakfast daily, lunch & dinner Mon-Sat) is the best in town, serving the likes of rosemary-crusted lamb, slow-roasted pork and sweet and sour flathead, as well as pizzas.

Port Hinchinbrook Resort　　　RESORT $$
(07-4066 2000; www.porthinchinbrook.com.au; Bruce Hwy; d $130-225; ❇🌊) The cabins clustered around the wharf where boats depart for Hinchinbrook Island are more like luxury open-plan villas, with front doors that slide wide open to catch the waterfront breezes. The resort's **Marina Restaurant** (mains $18-38; ◷lunch & dinner daily year-round, breakfast Easter-Sep) dishes up reef-and-beef-type fare along with views over the boats docked out front.

Kookaburra Holiday Park　　CARAVAN PARK $
(07-4066 8648; www.kookaburraholidaypark. com.au; 175 Bruce Hwy; unpowered/powered sites $22/29, dm/s/d without bathroom $25/45/50, cabins without bathroom $65, units $85-105; ❇@🌊) Over 1.2 green, tree-shaded hectares, accommodation options at this well-run park include airy dorms in a large Queenslander house at the back. You can borrow fishing rods, prawn nets and crab pots to catch dinner, and tents to head off for some bush camping.

Gourmet Grub　　　　　　　CAFE $
(93 Victoria St; mains $8-16; ◷8am-3pm Mon-Thu, to 8pm Fri, 9am-3pm Sat & Sun; 🖉) Chilled cafe with a boho vibe serving good brekkies and icy soy smoothies.

Vívia Café　　　　　　　　CAFE $
(135 Victoria St; mains $9-20; ◷7am-4pm; 🖉) Smart, contemporary surrounds for dining on gourmet counter fare and fresh seafood dishes.

❶ Getting There & Away

Greyhound Australia (1300 473 946; www. greyhound.com.au) and **Premier** (13 34 10; www.premierms.com.au) buses on the Brisbane–Cairns route stop at Cardwell. Fares with Greyhound/Premier are $47/30 adult/child to Cairns, $49/26 to Townsville.

Cardwell is on the Brisbane–Cairns train line; contact **Queensland Rail** (1300 131 722; www.traveltrain.qr.com.au) for details.

Boats depart for Hinchinbrook Island from Port Hinchinbrook Marina, 2km south of town.

HINCHINBROOK ISLAND NATIONAL PARK

Its resort might have closed its doors, but Australia's largest island national park remains a holy grail for walkers. Granite mountains rise dramatically from the sea; rugged Mt Bowen (1121m) is the island's highest peak. The mainland side is dense with lush tropical vegetation, while long sandy beaches and tangles of mangrove curve around the eastern shore. All 399 sq km of the island is national park, ensuring plenty of wildlife, including the aptly named pretty-faced wallaby and the iridescent-blue Ulysses butterfly.

Hinchinbrook's highlight is the **Thorsborne Trail** (also known as the East Coast Trail), a 32km coastal track from Ramsay Bay past Zoe Bay, with its beautiful waterfall, to George Point at the southern tip. **DERM campsites** (13 74 68; www.derm.qld. gov.au; per person $5.15) are interspersed along

the route. It's recommended that you take three nights to complete the trail, allowing for swimming stops and quiet time. Return walks of individual sections are also possible. This is the real wilderness experience; you'll need to use plenty of insect repellent, protect your food from ravenous native rats, draw water from creeks as you go (water is reliably available at Nina, Little Ramsay and Zoe Bays), and be alert to the possible presence of crocs around the mangroves. The trail is ungraded and at times rough, including challenging creek crossings; you should carry a map, drinking water and a fuel stove. Beach fishing is permitted from Zoe Bay south only.

Only 40 people are allowed on the track at any one time, so book ahead. DERM recommends booking a year ahead for a place during the high season and six months ahead for other dates. If you're late but lucky you might get to replace a cancellation. Cardwell's Rainforest & Reef Centre stocks the imperative *Thorsborne Trail* brochure.

Hinchinbrook Island Ferries (07-4066 8585; www.hinchinbrookferries.com.au) runs a service from Cardwell's Port Hinchinbrook Marina to Hinchinbrook's Ramsay Bay boardwalk (one way $85, 1½ hours). It also operates a five-hour **day tour** (adult/child $99/50; daily Easter-Sep, Wed, Fri & Sun Oct-Easter) that includes a cruise between Goold and Garden Islands spotting dolphins, dugongs and turtles, and docking at Ramsay Bay boardwalk for a walk on the 9km-long beach and picnic lunch.

Thorsborne Trail walkers can pick up a one-way transfer ($50) back to the mainland with **Hinchinbrook Wilderness Safaris** (07-4777 8307; www.hinchinbrookwilderness safaris.com.au) from George Point at the southern end of the trail.

TULLY
POP 2500

Surrounded by banana plantations, the sugar-mill town of Tully, 44km north of Cardwell, takes pride in its reputation as the wettest place in Australia. Its big 7.9m **golden gumboot** at the entrance to town boasts that Tully received 7.9m of rain in 1950. Climb the spiral staircase to the viewing platform up top to get a sense of just how much that is! All that rain ensures plenty of raftable rapids on the nearby Tully River.

The **Tully Visitor & Heritage Centre** (07-4068 2288; Bruce Hwy; 8.30am-4.45pm Mon-Fri, 9am-3pm Sat & Sun) has a brochure outlining a self-guided **heritage walk** around town, with 17 interpretative panels including one dedicated to Tully's UFO sightings.

Book at the visitor centre for 90-minute **Tully Sugar Mill Tours** (adult/child $12/8; daily late Jun-early Nov) during the crushing season, when the mill processes around two million tonnes of cane and generates its own power by burning fibre residue. Wear closed shoes and a shirt with sleeves.

The visitor centre stocks walking maps for trails along former logging tracks in the Tully-accessed section of the **Misty Mountains** (www.mistymountains.com.au); 640m-high **Mt Tyson**; and **Tully Gorge National Park**, 40km west of town. Tully Gorge has picnic facilities, but crocs inhabit the area. If you want a swim, head to the croc-free (and alligator-free) **Alligator's Nest**, 7km north of town via Murray St.

Practically all accommodation in Tully is geared for banana workers, with cheap weekly rates and help finding farm work. The visitor centre has a list, or try the excellent **Banana Barracks** (07-4068 0455; www.bananabarracks.com; 50 Butler St; dm with/without bathroom $26/24, bungalows $60;), bang in the town centre, with lots of corrugated iron, pool tables, and decent dorms and bungalows out the back. It's also the hub of Tully's nightlife, with an on-site **nightclub** (Thu-Sat).

For non-workers, the only real option is the corporate-oriented **Tully Motel** (07-4068 2233; www.tullymotel.com; Bruce Hwy; d $89-110;), with large, well-appointed rooms done up in heritage colours, and Tully's only restaurant, **Plantations** (mains $27-38; dinner Mon-Fri).

Greyhound Australia (1300 473 946; www.greyhound.com.au) and **Premier** (13 34 10; www.premierms.com.au) buses on the Brisbane–Cairns route stop in town; fares with Greyhound/Premier are $22/26 adult/child to Cairns, $54/30 to Townsville. Tully is on the Brisbane–Cairns train line; contact **Queensland Rail** (1300 131 722; www.traveltrain.qr.com.au) for details.

Mission Beach

POP 4000

Less than 30km east of the Bruce Hwy's rolling sugar-cane and banana plantations, the hamlets that make up greater Mission Beach are hidden amongst World Heritage

rainforest. The rainforest extends right to the Coral Sea, giving this 14km-long palm-fringed stretch of secluded inlets and wide, empty beaches the castaway feel of a tropical island.

Although collectively referred to as Mission Beach or just 'Mission', the area comprises a sequence of individual hamlets strung along the coast. **Bingil Bay** lies 4.8km north of **Mission Beach proper** (sometimes called North Mission). **Wongaling Beach** is 5km south; from here it's a further 5.5km south to **South Mission Beach**. Most amenities are in Mission Beach proper and Wongaling Beach; South Mission Beach and Bingil Bay are mainly residential.

Mission Beach is one of the closest access points to the Great Barrier Reef, and the gateway to Dunk Island. Fanning out around Mission are picturesque walking tracks, which are fine places to see wildlife, including cassowaries – in fact Australia's highest density of cassowaries (around 40) roam the surrounding rainforests.

To avoid an unexpected meeting with a croc or stinger, don't swim in any of Mission Beach's creeks – stick to the swimming enclosures provided.

◉ Sights & Activities

Adrenaline junkies flock to Mission Beach for extreme and water-based sports, including white-water rafting on the nearby Tully River (see the boxed text, p410).

The walking in the area is superb. The visitor centre stocks walking guides detailing trails. From David St in central Mission Beach, the **Ulysses Link** – named for the bright-blue Ulysses butterflies that flit through the area – is a gentle 2km stroll along the foreshore to Clump Point. Sweeping views unfold from the **Bicton Hill Track** (4km, two hours return) through Clump Mountain National Park. The superb coastal **Kennedy Track** (7km, four hours return) leads past secluded Lovers Beach and a lookout at Lugger Bay. **Licuala State Forest** has a number of rainforest walks, including a 10-minute children's walk marked with cassowary footprints, and the **Rainforest Circuit & Fan Palm Boardwalk** (1.2km, 30 minutes return), with interpretive signage and a cassowary display.

If you've got your own board, Bingil Bay is one of the rare spots inside the reef where it's possible to surf, with small but consistent swells of around 1m.

Jump the Beach SKYDIVING
(☑1800 444 568; www.jumpthebeach.com.au; 9000/11,000/14,000ft tandem dives $249/310/334)

Skydive Mission Beach SKYDIVING
(☑1800 800 840; www.skydivemissionbeach.com; 9000/11,000/14,000ft tandem dives $249/310/334)

Calypso Dive DIVING
(☑07-4068 8432; www.calypsodive.com.au; per person from $245) Experienced divers can join trips to the *Lady Bowen* wreck. Calypso also offers reef dives and PADI open-water courses ($625). Alternatively, you can snorkel the reef ($169).

Spirit of the Rainforest RAINFOREST TRIPS
(☑07-4088 9161; www.echoadventure.com.au; 4hr tours adult/child $80/60; ◷ Tue, Thu & Sat) Local Aboriginal guides offer a unique insight into the ancient rainforest around Mission Beach. Prices include pick-ups from Mission Beach.

Coral Sea Kayaking KAYAKING
(☑07-4068 9154; www.coralseakayaking.com; half/full day $77/128) To Dunk Island.

Fishin' Mission FISHING
(☑07-4088 6121; www.fishinmission.com.au; half/full day $130/190) Island or reef trips.

Mission Beach Adventure Centre KAYAKING, HIRE
(☑0429 469 330; www.missionbeachadventurecentre.com.au; Seaview St, Mission Beach) The 'hut on the beach' offers kayak hire (singles/doubles $15/30 per hour), three-hour kayak tours ($60), stand-up board hire ($15 per hour), and, when the wind's up, blokarting ($30/50 per half-hour/hour). Its cafe (dishes $5-8.50) is famed for its hot dogs.

🛏 Sleeping

Holiday house and apartment rentals proliferate throughout the area – the visitor centre has a list of booking agents. Hostels have courtesy bus pick-ups.

SOUTH MISSION BEACH
Elandra RESORT $$$
(☑07-4068 8154; www.elandraresorts.com; 1 Explorer Dr; d $270, ste $370-520; ❊@🛰⌇) All 52 contemporary rooms at this secluded piece of paradise front the ocean and most have balconies to take full advantage of the views. Interiors have sparing African and Asian decor, and the huge Dunk Island–facing

TULLY RIVER RAFTING

The Tully River provides thrilling white water year-round thanks to all that rain and the river's hydroelectric floodgates. Rafting trips are timed to coincide with the daily release of the floodgates, resulting in grade-four rapids, with stunning rainforest scenery as a backdrop.

Day trips with Raging Thunder Adventures (☑07-4030 7990; www.ragingthunder. com.au/rafting.asp; standard/'xtreme' trips $185/215) or R'n'R White Water Rafting (☑07-4041 9444; www.raft.com.au; trips $185) include a barbecue lunch and transport from Tully or nearby Mission Beach. It only costs an extra $10 for transfers from Cairns and as far north as Palm Cove, but you'll save yourself several tedious hours' return bus ride if you pick up a trip here.

decked pool area houses a fabulous restaurant and cocktail bar.

WONGALING BEACH

Hibiscus Lodge B&B   B&B $$
☑07-4068 9096; www.hibiscuslodge.com.au; 5 Kurrajong Cl; r $95-120; ❋☷) Wake to the sound of birds chirping and more than likely spot a cassowary or two during breakfast on the rainforest-facing deck of this lovely B&B. You can play croquet on the pitch out the front.

Scotty's Mission Beach House   HOSTEL $
(☑1800 665 567; www.scottysbeachhouse.com. au; 167 Reid Rd; dm $24-29, d $61-71; ❋@�607;) Clean, comfy rooms (including girls-only dorms with Barbie-pink sheets) are grouped around Scotty's grassy pool area – a great spot for catching some rays. Out the front, Scotty's Bar & Grill (mains $10-30; ⊙dinner), open to nonguests, has something happening virtually every night, from fire-twirling shows to pool comps and live music.

Licuala Lodge   B&B $$
(☑07-4068 8194; www.licualalodge.com.au; 11 Mission Circle; s/d $99/130; �607☷) State-of-the-art five-room B&B with a guest kitchen and complimentary beer, soft drinks and fruit juices.

Absolute Backpackers   HOSTEL $
(☑07-4068 8317; www.absolutebackpackers. com.au; Wongaling Beach Rd; dm $22-26, d $56; ❋@☷☷) Well-managed, relaxed hostel with a hammock-festooned pool area, airy rooms and a 24-hour kitchen.

MISSION BEACH

Mission Beach Ecovillage   CABINS $$
(☑07-4068 7534; www.ecovillage.com.au; Clump Point Rd; d $145-190; ❋☷☷) It's not eco-certified, but with its own banana and lime trees scattered around its tropical gardens

and a direct path through the rainforest to the beach, this 'ecovillage' makes the most of its environment. Higher-priced bungalows have spas, and there's a brilliant free-form pool and licensed restaurant (mains $19; ⊙dinner Tue-Sat).

Castaways Resort & Spa   RESORT $$$
(☑1800 079 002; www.castaways.com.au; Pacific Pde; d $145-185, 1-/2-bedroom units $205/295; ❋@☷☷) Castaways' cheapest rooms don't have balconies, so it's worth splashing out a bit more for one of the 'Coral Sea' rooms, with extended deck and day bed. Even the units are small, but perks include two elongated pools, a luxurious spa (www.driftspa.com.au) and live entertainment at the bar-restaurant (mains $12-32; ⊙breakfast, lunch & dinner).

Sejala on the Beach   CABINS $$$
(☑07-4088 6699; http://missionbeachholidays. com.au/sejala; 26 Pacific Pde; d $239; ❋☷) Three huts (go for one of the two facing the beach) with rainforest showers, decks with private BBQs and loads of character.

Rainforest Motel   MOTEL $$
(☑07-4068 7556; www.missionbeachrainforest motel.com; 9 Endeavour Ave; s/d $89/109; ❋@☷☷) Set back from the road in rainforest foliage with immaculate tiled rooms and free bikes available.

Hideaway Holiday Village   CARAVAN PARK $
(☑1800 687 104; http://missionbeachhideaway. com.au; 58-60 Porter Promenade; unpowered/ powered sites $29/35, cabins with/without bathroom $105/85; ❋@☷☷) Shady, central park backing onto rainforest and overlooking the beach. Grassy sites and cabins are well spaced and are in tip-top condition.

Mission Beach Retreat   HOSTEL $
(☑07-4088 6229; www.missionbeachretreat.com. au; 49 Porters Promenade; dm $21-24, d $56;

✳@🛜🏊) Escape the party scene at this intimate 35-bed beachfront hostel spot.

BINGIL BAY

🏄 Sanctuary
CABINS $

(☎07-4088 6064, 1800 777 012; www.sanctuary atmission.com; 72 Holt Rd; dm $35, s/d huts $65/70, cabins $145/160; ☺mid-Apr–mid-Dec; @🛜🏊) You can sleep surrounded only by flyscreen on a platform in a simple hut, or opt for one of the cabins, whose glass-walled showers have floor-to-ceiling rainforest views. In addition to walks you can take a yoga class ($15) or indulge in a massage ($80 per hour). Cook in the self-catering kitchen or dine on wholesome fare at the restaurant (mains $19-33; ☺breakfast, lunch & dinner; 🍴). Eco-initiatives include the resort's own sewerage system, harvesting rainwater and biodegradable detergents. Not suitable for kids under 11. The resort is reached by a steep 600m-long rainforest walking track from the car park (4WD pick-up available).

Treehouse
HOSTEL $

(☎07-4068 7137; www.treehousehostel.com.au; Frizelle Rd; unpowered sites $12, dm/d $25/55; @🛜🏊) Musical instruments and no TV set the chilled-out scene at this timber YHA-associated hostel high in the rainforest.

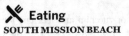
SOUTH MISSION BEACH

🏄 Elandra
MODERN AUSTRALIAN $$$

(☎07-4068 8154; www.elandraresorts.com; 1 Explorer Dr; mains $28-42; ☺breakfast, lunch & dinner; 🍴) Even if you're not staying at the Elandra resort, don't miss chef Kurt Goodban's stunning cuisine, such as wattle seed–spiced kangaroo or coconut-dusted squid with pawpaw and mango.

WONGALING BEACH

Cafe Rustica
ITALIAN $$

(☎07-4068 9111; Wongaling Beach Rd; mains $18-22; ☺lunch Sun, dinner Wed-Sun; 🍴) Book ahead to enjoy authentic Italian pastas, traditional crispy-crust pizzas and Italian wines in this contemporary beach shack.

Spicy Thai Hut
THAI $$

(☎07-4068 9111; shop 5, 2042 Tully-Mission Beach Rd; mains $16-25; ☺dinner Wed-Sun; 🍴) Mission Beach's best Thai is served up to eat in or takeaway from this hip newcomer.

MISSION BEACH

🔝TOP CHOICE New Deli
CAFE, DELI $

(shop 1, 47 Porter Promenade; mains $7.50-15.50; ☺9.30am-6pm Sun-Fri; 🍴) Tuck into blueberry pancakes or smoked salmon and brie bagels

THE CASSOWARY

The flightless cassowary is as tall as a grown man, has three toes, a blue-and-purple head, red wattles (fleshy lobes hanging from its neck), a helmet-like horn and unusual black feathers, which look more like ratty hair. It could certainly be confused with an ageing rocker. Traditional gender roles are reversed, with the male bird incubating the egg and rearing the chicks alone. The Australian cassowary is also known as the southern cassowary, though it's only found in the north of Queensland. It makes sense when you realise that other species are found in Papua New Guinea – to the north of Australia.

The cassowary is a vital link in the rainforest ecosystem. It is the only animal capable of dispersing the seeds of more than 70 species of tree whose fruits are too large for other rainforest animals to digest and pass.

The cassowary is an endangered species; there are less than 1000 left. Its biggest threat is loss of habitat, and eggs and chicks are vulnerable to dogs and wild pigs. A number of birds are also hit by cars: heed road signs warning drivers to be cassowary-aware. You're most likely to see cassowaries around Mission Beach and the Cape Tribulation section of the Daintree National Park. They can be aggressive, particularly if they have chicks. Do not approach them; if one threatens you, don't run – give the bird right-of-way and try to keep something solid between you and it, preferably a tree.

Next to the Mission Beach visitor centre, there are cassowary-conservation displays at the Wet Tropics Environment Centre (☎07-4068 7197; www.wettropics.gov.au; Porter Promenade, Mission Beach; ☺10am-4pm), which is staffed by volunteers from the Community for Cassowary & Coastal Conservation (C4; www.cassowaryconservation.asn.au). Proceeds from gift-shop purchases go towards buying cassowary habitat. The website www.savethecassowary.org.au is also a good source of info.

for breakfast, or zucchini and feta tart for lunch. Or stock up on goodies for a gourmet picnic.

Shrubbery Taverna
SEAFOOD $$

(David St; mains $19-36; ⊙5pm-late Wed, noon-late Thu-Sun) Shaded by bamboo gardens, this local hang-out is great for seafood tapas, salt and pepper prawns and creamy seafood chowder. Live music on Friday night and Sunday afternoon.

Early Birds Cafe
CAFE $

(shop 2, 46 Porter Promenade; mains $6-15; ⊙6am-3pm; ✍) Early Birds' all-day tropical Aussie brekkie is a treat after a swim.

Friends
MODERN AUSTRALIAN $

(✆07-4068 7107; Porter Promenade; meals $6-14; ⊙dinner Fri-Tue) Elegant atmosphere and short, inventive, Mediterranean-accented menu.

Coffee Tree
CAFE $

(shop 3, 47 Porter Promenade, Mission Beach; dishes $3.50-6; ⊙9.30am-5pm Tue-Sun) Strong espresso, handmade chocolates and tantalising cakes.

BINGIL BAY

Bingil Bay Cafe
CAFE $$

(29 Bingil Bay Rd; mains $13.50-22; ⊙breakfast, lunch & dinner; ✍) This retro corner store features an eclectic menu of felafel wraps, fish and chips, German sausages with sauerkraut and seafood linguine. Groceries and ice creams are also available.

❶ Information

The efficient **Mission Beach visitor centre** (✆07-4068 7099; www.missionbeachtourism. com; Porters Promenade; ⊙9am-4.45pm Mon-Sat, 10am-4pm Sun; @) has reams of info in multiple languages.

Internet cafes with tour-booking desks include **Intermission@the Beach** (David St, Mission Beach; per 20min/hr $2/5; ⊙8.30am-6pm Mon-Sat) and **Mission Beach Information Station** (www.missionbeachinfo.com; 4 Wongaling Shopping Centre, Cassowary Dr, Wongaling Beach; per 20min/hr $2/5; ⊙9am-7pm).

❶ Getting There & Around

Greyhound Australia (✆1300 473 946; www. greyhound.com.au) and **Premier** (✆13 34 10; www.premierms.com.au) buses stop in Wongaling Beach next to the giant 'big cassowary'; fares with Greyhound/Premier are $21/19 adult/child to Cairns, $46/40 to Townsville. **Sun Palm** (✆07-4087 2900; www.sunpalmtransport.com)

has daily services to Cairns and Cairns Airport ($49) as well as Innisfail and Tully.

Mission Beach Adventure Centre rents bikes (per half-day/day $10/20).

Call ✆13 10 08 for a taxi.

Dunk Island

Known to the Djiru Aboriginal people as Coonanglebah (the island of peace and plenty), Dunk is pretty much your ideal tropical island. The island's **rainforest walks** are invigorating, and while some people run the full island circuit (9.2km), taking the sometimes difficult track slowly lets you check out secluded beaches. See the fanning Hinchinbrook Channel from Mt Kootaloo (271m, 5.6km).

Day trippers can enjoy the island's beaches and access the Jetty Café, or the activity-hungry can purchase a **day pass** (adult/child $40/20), which gives access to the resort's standard-ish butterfly pool, paddle-ski use and lunch at the resort's excellent cafes. There are also barbecues near the camping site.

The standard beachfront rooms at family-friendly **Dunk Island Resort** (✆07-4068 8199; www.dunk-island.com; s/d incl breakfast, lunch & dinner from $386/375; ❉@☏☰) are just as nice as the more expensive beachfront suites. Permits for the **DERM campground** (✆13 74 68; www.derm.qld.gov.au; per person $5.15) need to be organised through the resort.

Calypso (✆07-4068 8432; www.calypsoadventures.com.au; adult/child same-day return $40/20, one way $25/12.50), departing from Mission Beach's Clump Point jetty, and **Mission Beach Dunk Island Water Taxi** (✆07-4068 8310; Banfield Pde, Wongaling Beach; adult/child return $35/18), departing from Wongaling Beach, make the 20-minute trip to Dunk Island. Calypso also operates an amphibious marine craft, **Sealegs** (adult/child return $30/15), which can pick up from a dozen departure points along Mission's beachfront and drop you over on Dunk.

Mission Beach to Cairns

Mountains, cane fields, cane-train tracks and forest run alongside the road from Mission Beach to Cairns. For variety, take the alternative 'Canecutter Way' route to Innisfail via the cute towns of Silkwood and Mena Creek — 42km of true sugar-cane country.

Mena Creek's main claim to fame is the unusual **Paronella Park** (☎07-4065 0000; www.paronellapark.com.au; Japoonvale Rd; adult/child $34/17; ☉9am-7.30pm), which features the ruins of a Spanish castle hand-built in the 1930s. Floods, fire and moist tropics have rendered these mossy remains almost medieval. Entry includes free camping in the adjacent caravan park and both a day and an evening tour. Timber **cabins** (d $75; ❉) are also available.

Further north at **South Johnstone**, the charming little art gallery, cafe and secondhand bookshop **Off the Rails** (Hynes St; mains $8-18; ☉10am-5pm Wed-Sun; ☑) has great coffee and uses local produce in dishes like marinated-vegie platters.

INNISFAIL
POP 9000

A wonderful main street meanders through this busy farming town to the wide Johnstone River. Art deco buildings abound, as cyclones damaged many buildings in the 1920s and 1930s, and the replacements were constructed in the style of that time, turning Innisfail into the art deco capital of Australia. You can get a self-guided art deco tour map from the **visitor information centre** (☎07-4061 2655; www.innisfailtourism.com.au; cnr Eslick St & Bruce Hwy; ☉9am-5pm Mon-Fri, 10am-12.30pm Sat & Sun; ✇).

Half-hour tours at **Johnstone River Crocodile Farm** (www.crocpark.com.au; Flying Fish Point Rd; adult/child $28/14; ☉8.30am-4.30pm, feeding times 11am & 3pm) let you watch guides sit on one-tonne, 5m-long Gregory – the farm's fattest reptile – and meet its oldest, 90-year-old Johnny. Don't get so attached that you don't taste the croc skewers at the kiosk!

Innisfail's best lodging option, the **Barrier Reef Motel** (☎07-4061 4988; www.barrierreefmotel.com.au; Bruce Hwy; s/d $100/110, units $130-150; ❉@☂☜) has 41 airy, tiled rooms, a **restaurant** (mains $28-30.50; ☉breakfast & dinner; ☑) and a bar. The **Codge Lodge** (☎07-4061 8055; www.codgelodge.com; 63 Rankin St; dm $33; ❉@☂☜) is a cheerful hostel set in an atmospheric Queenslander with a wide timber verandah. Plenty of farm workers bunk down for an extended stay, but it also welcomes overnight travellers.

Flying Fish Tourist Park (☎07-4061 3131; www.ffpvanpark.com.au; 39 Elizabeth St, Flying Fish Point; unpowered/powered sites $26/31, dm $30, cabins without bathroom $50-65, cabins & villas with bathroom $85-105; ❉@☂☜) is a first-rate

park right off the beach. You can organise boat hire through the friendly managers. The nearby **Flying Fish Point Cafe** (9 Elizabeth St, Flying Fish Point; mains $13-19; ☉7.30am-8.30pm) serves huge seafood baskets of battered and crumbed fish, barbecued calamari and wonton prawns.

Everything is locally sourced or organic at **Monsoon Cruising** (☎0427 776 663; 1 Innisfail Wharf; mains $10-14; ☉10am-5pm Wed-Sat Mar-Dec; ☑), a moored cruiser serving bread baked fresh on the boat and black tiger prawns straight off the trawlers. **Oliveri's Continental Deli** (41 Edith St; sandwiches $7.50-8.50; ☉8.30am-5.30pm Mon-Fri, to 1pm Sat; ☑) is an Innisfail institution serving awesome sandwiches.

Greyhound Australia (☎1300 473 946; www.greyhound.com.au) calls into Innisfail on the Brisbane–Cairns route, with six services daily stopping at King George St. **Premier Motor Service** (☎13 34 10; www.premierms.com.au) has one daily service to Innisfail on the same route.

AROUND INNISFAIL

From Innisfail the Palmerston Hwy winds west up to the magical Atherton Tableland, passing through the rainforest of **Wooroonooran National Park**, which has creeks, waterfalls, scenic walking tracks and a self-registration **camping ground** (per person/family $5/21) at Henrietta Creek (38km from Innisfail), just off the road.

About 27km along the Palmerston Hwy (signposted 4km northwest of Innisfail), the **Mamu Rainforest Canopy Walkway** (www.derm.qld.gov.au/mamu; Palmerston Hwy; adult/child $20/10; ☉9.30am-5.30pm, last entry 4.30pm) gives you a bird's-eye perspective from its 100-step, 37m-high tower. Allow at least an hour to complete the 2.5km, wheelchair-accessible circuit.

At the southeastern corner of the park, **Crawford's Lookout** has views of the white water of the North Johnstone River, but it's worth the walk down to view it at closer range. Among the park's walks is the lovely **Nandroya Falls Circuit** (7.2km, three to four hours), which crosses a swimming hole. A number of platypus-viewing areas are marked in the park; first or last light of day are the best times to spot them.

For a more challenging walk, you might take on Queensland's highest peak, **Mt Bartle Frere** (1657m). Sitting inside Wooroonooran National Park, it falls within the dramatic Bellenden Ker range, which

skirts the Bruce Hwy between Innisfail and Cairns. Experienced walkers can embark on the **Mt Bartle Frere Summit Track** (15km, two days return), which leads from the Josephine Falls car park to the summit. There's also a 10km (eight-hour) return walk to Broken Nose. It's best that you don't walk alone and always let someone know before you go. Pick up a trail guide from the nearest visitor centre or contact QPWS (☑ 13 13 04; www.epa. qld.gov.au, www.queenslandwalks.com.au). Self-registration camping (per person/family $5/21) is permitted along the trail.

The Palmerston Hwy continues west to Millaa Millaa, passing the entrance to the Waterfall Circuit (p439) just before the town.

CAIRNS & AROUND

Cairns has a heady reputation as Australia's reef-diving capital, with dazzling marine life and coral-fringed islands a short boat ride offshore. It's also tropical north Queensland's party central. Yet lush rainforest, waterfalls, volcanic-crater lakes and beach communities lie just beyond the city limits, as do the Atherton Tableland's gourmet food producers, farms and orchards. The magnificent Daintree National Park stretches up the coast, its rainforest tumbling right onto white-sand beaches. Further north, the Bloomfield Track from Cape Tribulation to Cooktown is one of Australia's great 4WD journeys.

Cairns

POP 148,000

Cairns has come a long way from struggling cane town to international resort city. It may not have a beach, but the mudflats and mangroves along the Esplanade foreshore have been replaced with a multimillion-dollar development of parks and the dazzling saltwater lagoon, with top-quality restaurants overlooking the marina. And if you do want some sand, it's a short local bus ride or easy drive to Cairns' northern beaches.

For many visitors this is the end of the line on the east-coast jaunt (or the start for those flying into Cairns' international airport), and the city is awash with bars and nightclubs, as well as accommodation and eateries in all price ranges. It's a city that's more board shorts than briefcases, and you can walk straight from the nightclub to the pier and catch one of the many morning boats that make the daily island or reef, diving or snorkelling pilgrimage.

◉ Sights

Cairns Foreshore & Lagoon
SWIMMING, WALKING

In the absence of a beach, sunbathers flock around Cairns' shallow but spectacular saltwater swimming lagoon (admission free; ⊘6am-10pm Thu-Tue, noon-10pm Wed) on the city's reclaimed foreshore. The artificial 4800-sq-metre lagoon is patrolled by lifeguards and illuminated at night.

Northwest from the lagoon, the boardwalk **promenade**, stretching for almost 3km, has picnic areas, free barbecues and playgrounds lining the foreshore.

Flecker Botanic Gardens
BOTANIC GARDENS

(www.cairns.qld.gov.au; Collins Ave, Edge Hill; ⊘7.30am-5.30pm Mon-Fri, 8.30am-5.30pm Sat & Sun) These beautiful tropical gardens are an explosion of greenery and rainforest plants. Sections include an area for bush-tucker plants and the Gondwanan Evolutionary Trail, which traces the 415-million-year heritage of tropical plants. Free guided walks depart Tuesday and Thursday at 10am and 1pm from the information centre (⊘8.30am-5pm Mon-Fri). There's an excellent cafe (mains $14-19; ⊘7am-4.30pm) here.

Opposite the gardens the Rainforest Boardwalk leads to Saltwater Creek and Centenary Lakes. Uphill from the gardens, Mt Whitfield Conservation Park has two walking tracks through rainforest, climbing to viewpoints over the city; follow the Red Arrow circuit (1.3km, one hour) or the more demanding Blue Arrow circuit (5.4km, three hours).

Tanks Arts Centre
GALLERY, THEATRE

(www.tanksartscentre.com; 46 Collins Ave, Edge Hill; ⊘gallery 10am-4pm Mon-Fri) Three gigantic WWII fuel-storage tanks have been transformed into studios, galleries showcasing local artists' work and an inspired performing-arts venue, plus a lively market day (⊘last Sun of month Apr-Sep).

Cairns Regional Gallery
GALLERY

(www.cairnsregionalgallery.com.au; cnr Abbott & Shields Sts; adult/child under 16 $5/free; ⊘10am-5pm Mon-Sat, 1-5pm Sun) In a colonnaded 1936 heritage building, Cairns' acclaimed regional gallery hosts exhibitions reflecting the

SEASONAL WORK

Cairns is one of the most popular places on the east coast to pick up casual work in the tourism and hospitality sectors. Those bilingual in Japanese, Korean and German can pick up tour-translating work. And, of course, Cairns is a magnet for dive instructors and the like.

For those planning to stick around in Cairns for a month or more to work, dive or study, **Cairns Sharehouse** (07-4041 1875; 17 Scott St; www.cairns-sharehouse.com; s per week $130-205, tw & d per person per week $100-150; ❀ 🛜 ☎) is a good option. Three weeks' rent is required up front.

consciousness of the tropical north region, with an emphasis on local and Indigenous works.

Tjapukai Cultural Park CULTURAL CENTRE
(07-4042 9900; www.tjapukai.com.au; Kamerunga Rd, Smithfield; adult/child $35/17.50; 9am-5pm) Allow at least three hours at this Indigenous-owned cultural extravaganza, incorporating the Creation Theatre, which tells the story of creation using giant holograms and actors, a dance theatre and a gallery, as well as boomerang- and spear-throwing demonstrations and turtle-spotting during a canoe ride on the lake. A fireside corroboree is the centrepiece of the **Tjapukai by Night** (adult/child $99/49.50; 7-10pm) dinner-and-show deal.

The park is about 15km north of the city centre, just off the Captain Cook Hwy near the Skyrail terminal; transfers are available for an extra charge.

Reef Teach INTERPRETIVE CENTRE
(07-4031 7794; http://reefteach.wordpress.com; 2nd fl, Main Street Arcade, 85 Lake St; adult/child $15/8; lectures 6.30-8.30pm Tue-Sat) Before heading out to the reef, take your knowledge to greater depths at this excellent and informative centre, where marine experts explain how to identify specific types of coral and fish and how to treat the reef with respect.

Centre of Contemporary Arts GALLERY, THEATRE
(www.coca.org.au; 96 Abbott St; 10am-5pm Tue-Sat) CoCA houses the **KickArts** (www.kickarts.org.au) galleries of local contemporary visual art, as well as the **Jute Theatre** (www.jute.com.au) and the **End Credits Film Club** (www.endcredits.org.au).

Cairns Museum MUSEUM
(www.cairnsmuseum.org.au; cnr Lake & Shields Sts; adult/child $5/2; 10am-4pm Mon-Sat)

This history museum has exhibits on the construction of the Cairns–Kuranda railway, the contents of a Chinese temple and displays on the Palmer River and Hodgkinson River goldfields.

Crystal Cascades & Lake Morris WATERFALLS, LAKE
About 20km from Cairns, the **Crystal Cascades** are a series of beautiful waterfalls and (croc-free) pools. The area is accessed by a 1.2km (30-minute) pathway. Crystal Cascades is linked to Lake Morris (the city's reservoir) by a *steep* rainforest **walking trail** (allow three hours return). It starts near the picnic area at Crystal Cascades and climbs steadily uphill, coming out on Lake Morris Rd, about 300m from Copperlode Dam (turn right).

🏃 Activities

A plethora of tour operators runs adventure-based activities from Cairns, most offering transfers to/from your accommodation. For dive courses, see the boxed text p420.

In and around the city, activities of varying adrenaline levels include the following:

AJ Hackett Bungy & Minjin BUNGY JUMPING
(1800 622 888; www.ajhackett.com; McGregor Rd, Smithfield; bungy jumps $139, minjin swings $89, bungee & minjin swing combos $194; 10am-5pm) Bungy from the purpose-built tower or swing from the trees on the minjin (a harness swing). Rates include transfers.

Cable Ski WATERSKIING
(07-4038 1304; www.cableskicairns.com.au; Captain Cook Hwy, Smithfield; adult/child per hr $36/31, per day $69/64; 10am-6pm) Learn to waterski, wakeboard or kneeboard without the boat at this water-sports park near the Skyrail.

Cairns Golf Club GOLF
(07-4054 1494; www.cairnsgolfclub.com.au; Bruce Hwy, Woree) Scenic 1929-established

Cairns

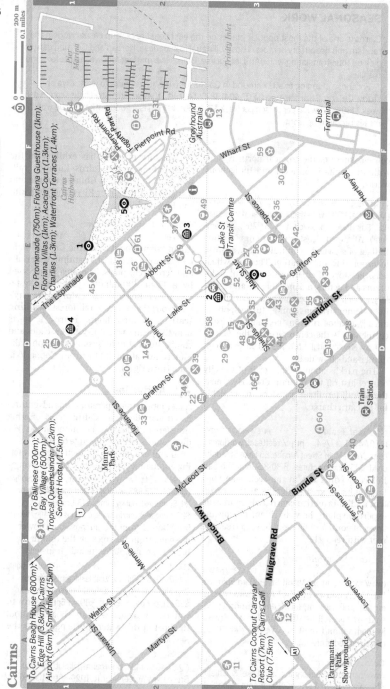

18-hole course 7km south of the city centre. Hires out equipment; rates depend on the day and tee time.

Fishing Cairns   FISHING
(☏07-4041 1169; www.fishingcairns.com.au) Arranges river, reef and game fishing trips.

☞ Tours

A staggering 600-plus tours bus, boat, fly and drive out of Cairns each day. See p428 for tours to Green, Fitzroy and the Frankland Islands, and p457 for day tours to Lizard Island.

Two Days

Head way out to the Great Barrier Reef on a full-day cruise. Get an eyeful of coral gardens and iridescent fish and marine life by snorkelling or diving, or stay dry in a glass-bottom boat. By night, mingle with newly christened reef lovers over drinks at the Salt House.

On day two, rise early for a stroll through the Flecker Botanic Gardens, where you can explore the Gondwanan Evolutionary Trail. Save the afternoon for an Aboriginal cultural experience at the Tjapukai Cultural Park. Afterwards, raise a glass with locals and travellers at the capacious outdoor bar at Gilligan's. Grab a snack there, or head over to Charlie's for the all-you-can-eat seafood buffet.

Four Days

Spend the third day basking on an island – snorkelling the reef and exploring the rainforest of Green Island, enjoying the view from the summit of Fitzroy Island or playing castaway on the coral-fringed Frankland Islands. Back on the mainland, take an early-evening stroll along Cairns Esplanade, followed by a decadent meal at Ochre.

On day four catch the Scenic Railway to Kuranda, walk into a flurry of winged beauties at the Australian Butterfly Sanctuary and get a bird's-eye rainforest view on the way back by returning on the Skyrail. Alternatively, take an eco-accredited tour to the Atherton Tableland or Cape Tribulation and the magical Daintree rainforest.

Great Barrier Reef

Reef operators generally include transport, lunch and snorkelling gear in their tour prices. Many have diving options, including introductory dives requiring no prior experience. When choosing a tour, consider the vessel (catamaran or sailing ship), its capacity (from six to 300 people), what extras are offered and the destination. The outer reefs are more pristine; inner-reef areas can be patchy – showing signs of damage from humans, coral bleaching and crown-of-thorns starfish. Of course, companies that are only licensed to visit the inner reef have cheaper tours; in most cases you pay for what you get. Some operators offer the option of a trip in a glass-bottomed boat or semisubmersible.

The majority of boats depart from the Pier Marina and Reef Fleet Terminal at about 8am, returning around 6pm. As well as the popular day trips, a number of operators also offer multiday live-aboard trips, which include specialised dive opportunities such as night diving. Dive-course companies (p420) also offer tours.

Not up for scuba diving but want to get down with the fishes? Several dive boats offer helmet diving (from $140). Hoses attached to the helmet deliver air, so you can breathe normally. Because you're 'walking' on a submerged platform, it's ideal for non-swimmers, kids over 12 and anyone who doesn't like to get their hair wet.

Following is a list (in alphabetical order) of reef-trip operators worth considering. See p463 for information on cargo-freighter trips from Cairns to Cape York Peninsula.

Coral Princess CRUISES
(☑1800 079 545, 07-4040 9999; www.coralprincess.com.au) Three-night cruises (from $1496 per person, twin share) between Cairns and Townsville, and four-night Cairns to Lizard Island return (from $1896).

Great Adventures CATAMARAN
(☑07-4044 9944; www.greatadventures.com.au; adult/child from $190/95) Fast catamaran with day trips to a floating pontoon, with an optional stopover on Green Island (from $210/105), as well as semisubmersibles and a glass-bottomed boat.

Passions of Paradise DIVING
(☑1800 111 346; www.passions.com.au; adult/child $139/89) Sexy sailing catamaran taking you to Michaelmas Cay and Paradise Reef for snorkelling or diving.

Silverswift DIVING
(☑07-4044 9944; www.silverseries.com.au; adult/child from $167.50/125.50) Popular catamaran snorkelling/diving three outer reefs.

Sunlover DIVING
(☑07-4050 1333; www.sunlover.com.au; adult/child from $180/65) Fast catamaran to a pontoon on the outer Moore Reef. Options include semisubmersible trips and helmet diving. Good for families.

Vagabond YACHT

(07-4031 9959; www.vagabond-dive.com; 2-day tours from $290) Luxury yacht; maximum of 11 guests.

Cod Hole, near Lizard Island, is one of Australia's premier diving locations, so these extended live-aboard trips are mainly for keen certified divers.

Mike Ball Dive Expeditions DIVING

(07-4053 0500; www.mikeball.com; 143 Lake St; trips from $1480) Long-running three-day live-aboard expeditions to the Cod Hole; four- and seven-day trips available.

Spirit of Freedom DIVING

(07-4047 9150; www.spiritoffreedom.com.au; 3-/4-/7-day tours from $1350/1675/2775) Three-deck vessel with live-aboard trips to Cod Hole and Ribbon Reefs.

Taka Dive DIVING

(07-4051 8722; www.takadive.com. au; 319 Draper St; 4/5/7-day tours from $1290/1610/2650) Dives the Cod Hole and the remote Osprey Reef. Also speciality courses, such as underwater photography, and the chance to swim with dwarf minke whales from June to August.

Scenic Flights

Cairns Heliscenic SCENIC FLIGHTS

(4031 5999; www.cairns-heliscenic.com.au; Pier Marketplace; 15/30-min flight from per person $220/295) Helicopter flights departing from Green Island (10 minutes $148) to an hour-long reef and rainforest trip ($529).

Cairns Seaplanes SCENIC FLIGHTS

(07-4031 4307; www.cairnsseaplanes.com; Cairns Airport; 30-min flights from $219) Scenic reef flights, including to Green Island.

White-Water Rafting

The excitement level of white-water rafting down the Barron, Russell and North Johnstone Rivers is hitched to the season: obviously the wetter the weather, the whiter your water. The Tully River has rapids year-round – see p410.

Trips are graded according to the degree of difficulty, from armchair (grade one) to white knuckle (grade five).

Major rafting companies departing from Cairns:

Foaming Fury WHITE-WATER RAFTING

(1800 801 540, 07-4031 3460; www.foaming fury.com.au) Full-day trips on the Russell

River ($149); half-day on the Barron ($129), with options for kids aged over 10.

419

Raging Thunder WHITE-WATER RAFTING

(07-4030 7990; www.ragingthunder.com.au) Full-day Tully trips (standard trip $195, 'xtreme' trip $225) and half-day Barron trips ($133).

R'n'R White Water Rafting WHITE-WATER RAFTING

(07-4035 3555; www.raft.com.au) Full-day Tully ($195) and half-day Barron ($130) trips.

Tubing

Floating in an inner tube is a tranquil way to see beautiful Behana Gorge.

Aussie Drifterz TUBING

(0401 318 475; www.aussiedrifterz.net; half-day tours adult/child $59/39) Includes two hours on the water.

Ballooning

The dawn skies above Cairns and the highlands see a multitude of colourful balloons seemingly suspended in the air. Most flights take off from the Mareeba region in the Atherton Tableland and include champagne breakfast afterwards.

Hot Air Cairns BALLOONING

(07-4039 9900; www.hotair.com.au; 30-min flights from $215)

Raging Thunder BALLOONING

(07-4030 7990; www.ragingthunder.com.au; 30-min flights from $225)

Skydiving

The higher you go, the higher the price: 9000ft gives you up to 28 seconds' freefalling, while up to 14,000ft gives you over 60 seconds plummeting back to earth.

Skydive Cairns SKYDIVING

(1800 444 568, 07-4031 5466; www.skydive cairns.com.au; 59 Sheridan St; tandem jumps from 9000ft $249) Licensed skydivers can jump solo for $50.

Atherton Tableland

Food Trail Tours FOOD

(07-4041 1522; www.foodtrailtours.com.au; adult/child from $154/77; Mon-Sat) Taste your way around the tableland, visiting farms producing macadamias, tropical-fruit wine, cheese, chocolate and coffee.

On the Wallaby OUTDOOR ACTIVITIES

(07-4033 6575; www.onthewallaby.com; day/overnight tours $99/169) Excellent

DIVE COURSES

Cairns is the scuba-diving capital of the Great Barrier Reef and a popular place to attain Professional Association of Diving Instructors (PADI) open-water certification. There's a plethora of courses on offer, from budget four-day courses that combine pool training and reef dives to five-day courses that include two days' pool theory and three days' living aboard a boat, diving less-frequented parts of the reef.

All operators require you to have a dive medical certificate, which they can arrange (around $50). Many operators also offer advanced courses for certified divers. Dive schools include the following:

Cairns Dive Centre (☑1800 642 591, 07-4051 0294; www.cairnsdive.com.au; 121 Abbott St) One of the cheapest operators, affiliated with Scuba Schools International (SSI) rather than PADI. Live-aboard tours (two/three days $355/470) and day tours ($120).

Deep Sea Divers Den (☑1800 612 223, 07-4046 7333; www.diversden.com.au; 319 Draper St) Long-established school running multiday live-aboard courses and trips from $570.

Down Under Dive (☑1800 079 099, 07-4052 8300; www.downunderdive.com.au; 287 Draper St) Multilingual instructors. Four- and five-day live-aboard trips from $520.

Pro-Dive (☑1800 353 213; 07-4031 5255; www.prodivecairns.com; cnr Grafton & Shields Sts) One of Cairns' most experienced operators. Runs a comprehensive five-day learn-to-dive course incorporating a three-day live-aboard trip for $825.

Tusa Dive (☑07-4047 9100; www.tusadive.com; cnr Shields St & The Esplanade) Inexpensive four-day learn-to-dive courses ($650) including two day trips' diving.

activity-based tours including cycling, hiking and canoeing.

Uncle Brian's Tours
SIGHTSEEING

(☑07-4033 6575; www.unclebrian.com.au; tours $109; ☺Mon-Wed, Fri & Sat) Lively small-group day trips covering forests, waterfalls and lakes.

Cape Tribulation & the Daintree

After the Great Barrier Reef, Cape Trib is the next most popular day trip – usually including a cruise on the Daintree River. Access is via a well-signposted sealed road, so don't discount hiring your own vehicle instead, especially if you want to take your time.

Billy Tea Bush Safaris
ECOTOUR

(☑07-4032 0077; www.billytea.com.au; day trips adult/child $170/120) Exciting eco day tours to Cape Trib and along the 4WD Bloomfield Track to Emmagen Creek.

BTS Tours
OUTDOOR ACTIVITIES

(☑07-4099 5665; www.btstours.com.au; day trips adult/child $159/115) Small-group tours, including swimming and canoeing.

Cape Trib Connections
SIGHTSEEING

(☑07-4041 7447; www.capetribconnections.com; day trips $124) Includes Mossman Gorge, Cape Tribulation Beach and Port Douglas. Also overnight tours.

Trek North Safaris
SIGHTSEEING

(☑07-4033 2600; www.treknorth.com.au; adult/child $160/110) Full-day tours include Mossman Gorge and a river cruise.

Tropical Horizons Tours
SIGHTSEEING

(☑07-4035 6445; www.tropicalhorizonstours.com.au; day tours from $161) Day trips to Cape Trib and the Daintree; overnight tours available.

Tropics Explorer
SIGHTSEEING

(☑1800 801 540; www.tropicsexplorer.com.au; day tours from $119) Fun Cape Trib day trips; overnight tours available.

Cooktown & Cape York

See p469 for tours through Cape York Peninsula.

Adventure North Australia
4WD

(☑07-4053 7001; www.adventurenorthaustralia.com; 1-day tours $235) Has 4WD trips to Cooktown via the coastal route, returning via the inland route. Also two- and three-day tours, fly-drive and Aboriginal cultural tours.

Wilderness Challenge
4WD

(☑07-4055 4488; www.wilderness-challenge.com.au; 3-day tours from $845; ☺May-Nov) Has 4WD tours to Cooktown via Cape Tribulation and the Bloomfield Track, returning via Cape York rock-art sites.

Undara Lava Tubes

Undara Experience SIGHTSEEING
(☑07-4097 1411; www.undara.com.au; 2-day tours adult/child $389/270) Coach tours to the Undara lava tubes (see p458). Day trips available by light aircraft and helicopter (from $540 per person, minimum four people).

City Tours

Cairns Discovery Tours SIGHTSEEING
(☑07-4053 5259; www.cairnsdiscoverytours. com; adult/child $65/32; ☺Mon-Sat) Half-day afternoon tours run by horticulturists; includes the botanic gardens and Palm Cove. Northern-beaches transfers are an extra $5.

🛏 Sleeping

Accommodation agencies have up-to-date listings and can assist in finding a suitable place to bed for the night. The Accommodation Centre (☑1800 807 730; www.accomcentre. com.au; cnr Sheridan & Aplin Sts) has information on a wide range of options, including hostels, apartments and hotels.

Cairns is a backpacker hot spot, with around 40 hostels – from intimate converted houses to hangar-sized resorts. The city's wealth of self-contained accommodation works well for groups or families, while dozens of virtually identical motels are lined up along Sheridan St. Most tour operators also pick up and drop off at Cairns' northern beaches accommodation.

TOP CHOICE Tropic Days HOSTEL $
(☑1800 421 521; www.tropicdays.com.au; 28 Bunting St; campsites $11, tents $16, dm $26, d without bathroom $64-74; ✹@☎≋) Tucked behind the showgrounds (with a courtesy bus into town), Cairns' best hostel is a haven of tropical gardens strung with hammocks, with a pool table, board games and a chilled vibe that makes it easy to stay longer than planned. Three- to four-bed dorms are bunk-free, doubles share spotless bathrooms, the kitchen's stocked with spices, and even non-guests can book for Monday night's croc, emu and roo barbeque ($12 including a didge show).

Floriana Guesthouse GUESTHOUSE $$
(☑07-4051 7886; www.florianaguesthouse.com; 183 The Esplanade; s $69, d $79-120; ✹@☎≋) Run by charismatic jazz musician Maggie,

Cairns-of-old still exists at this old-fashioned guesthouse, which retains its original polished floorboards and art deco fittings. The swirling staircase leads to 10 individually decorated rooms, some with bay windows and window seats, others with balconies.

Shangri-La HOTEL $$$
(☑07-4031 1411; www.shangri-la.com; Pierpoint Rd; r from $270; ✹@☎≋) In an unbeatable waterfront setting, towering over the marina, Shangri-La is Cairns' top hotel, a superswish five-star that ticks all the boxes for location, views, facilities (including a gym and pool bar) and attentive service. The Horizon Club rooms are top notch.

Floriana Villas APARTMENTS $$
(☑07-4041 2637; www.florianavillas.com.au; 187-189 The Esplanade; 1-/2-bedroom apt $140/180; ✹☎≋) Next to the Floriana Guesthouse, this distinctive complex – built by a Maltese family in the 1940s – has been converted into enormous, contemporary self-contained apartments. Minimum stay is three nights; extras include free bike hire, a shaded pool with spa jets and a landscaped barbeque area.

Hotel Cairns HOTEL $$$
(☑07-4051 6188; www.thehotelcairns.com; cnr Abbott & Florence Sts; d $195-265; ✹☎≋) There's a real tropical charm to this sprawling bone-white hotel, built in traditional Queenslander plantation style. Rooms have an understated elegance and the huge 'tower' rooms and suites offer luxury touches like wicker chaises longues and private balconies.

Reef Palms APARTMENTS $$
(☑1800 815 421; www.reefpalms.com.au; 41-7 Digger St; apt $125-145; ✹@☎≋) The crisp white interiors of Reef Palms' apartments will have you wearing your sunglasses inside. All rooms in this traditional Queenslander-style place have kitchen facilities; larger ones include a lounge area and a spa. Good for couples and families. To get there take Grafton St northwest, which turns into Digger St, roughly 1.4km past Munro Park.

Northern Greenhouse HOSTEL $$
(☑1800 000 541; www.friendlygroup.com.au; 117 Grafton St; dm/tw/apt $28/95/120; ✹@☎) It fits into the budget category with dorm accommodation and a relaxed attitude, but this friendly place is a cut above, with neat studio-style apartments with kitchens and

balconies. The central deck, pool and games room are great for socialising. Freebies include breakfast and a Sunday barbie.

Cairns Holiday Park
CARAVAN PARK **$**

(☑1800 259 977; www.cairnscamping.com.au; 12-30 Little St; sites unpowered/powered/with bathroom $32/39/50, cabins with/without bathroom $85/60; ✳@🛜🌊) The closest to central Cairns, this caravan park is 3.5km north of the city centre. A recent overhaul has resulted in smartly appointed bathroom and camp-kitchen facilities, along with tidy backpacker cabins and free internet.

Travellers Oasis
HOSTEL **$**

(☑07-4052 1377; www.travellersoasis.com.au; 8 Scott St; dm $26, s without bathroom $45, d without bathroom $64-74; ✳@🛜🌊) Handmade timber furniture, sculptures, bright colours and a brand-new barbeque area make this soulful 50-bed backpacker hostel a laid-back place to hang out with like-minded travellers. Dorms are bunk-free; shared bathrooms are clean.

Il Palazzo
HOTEL **$$$**

(☑1800 813 222; www.ilpalazzo.com.au; 62 Abbott St; d from $195; ✳🛜🌊) A replica of Michelangelo's *David* greets you in the foyer of this central boutique high-rise. It's quietly stylish, in a soft-focus, terracotta-urns Mediterranean kind of way, and the welcome and service are intimate compared with the big hotels'. Opulent apartments have balconies, laundries and full kitchens, and there're a rooftop sundeck and an on-site beauty salon.

Inn Cairns
APARTMENTS **$$**

(☑07-4041 2350; www.inncairns.com.au; 71 Lake St; apt $125-188; ✳🛜🌊) Behind the unassuming facade, this is true inner-city apartment living. Take the lift up to the 1st-floor pool or to the rooftop garden for a sundowner. The elegant self-contained apartments come with wrought-iron and glass furnishings.

Cairns Girls Hostel
HOSTEL **$**

(☑07-4051 2767; www.cairnsgirlshostel.com.au; 147 Lake St; dm/tw $20/48; @🛜) Sorry, boys! With three well-equipped kitchens, spacious lounge areas and a manager who looks after you as if you were a guest in her own home, this 1900s-built, white-glove-test-clean, female-only hostel is one of the most accommodating budget stays in Cairns.

Serpent Hostel
HOSTEL **$**

(☑1800 666 237; www.serpenthostel.com; 341 Lake St; dm $24-28, d with bathroom $65-75, without

bathroom $55; ✳@🛜🌊) About 2km north of the centre, this spiffing Nomads resort (*not* to be confused with Cairns' Nomads Esplanade) is a good-time backpacker bubble with a huge pool, beach volleyball, a sports bar, free evening meals and a free shuttle bus into town.

Bay Village
RESORT **$$**

(☑07-4051 4622; www.bayvillage.com.au; cnr Lake & Gatton Sts; d $150-170; ✳@🌊) Smart units encircle a central pool at this sprawling resort. It's popular with package tours but no worse for that. Pricier rooms are self-contained, with kitchens and lounges; Balinese chefs cook up aromatic cuisine at the onsite **Bay Leaf Restaurant** (mains $15.50-23.50; ⊙lunch Mon-Fri, dinner daily).

Mid City
APARTMENTS **$$**

(☑07-4051 5050; www.midcity.com.au; 6 McLeod St; 1-/2-bedroom apt $175/200; ✳@🛜🌊) The immaculate, terracotta-tiled apartments in this arctic-white building are truly self-contained, with superb kitchens, washing machines and dryers. Each has its own balcony, so try for a room with a view.

Acacia Court
HOTEL **$$**

(☑1300 850 472; www.acaciacourt.com; 223-227 The Esplanade; d $120-145; ✳🛜🌊) A stroll along the foreshore from town, this waterfront high-rise has beachy touches like bright aqua bedspreads and a choice of ocean or mountain views, making it great value for money. Most rooms have private balconies. Famed buffet restaurant Charlie's is downstairs.

Bellview
GUESTHOUSE **$**

(☑07-4031 4377; www.bellviewcairns.com.au; 85-87 The Esplanade; dm/s/d $22/35/55, motel units $59-75; ✳🌊) Right on the Esplanade, this longstanding, family-run spot offers a central alternative to the rowdy backpacker scene. Budget rooms are poky (it's worth paying extra for a motel unit), but overall it's a good-value, secure choice.

Cairns Beach House
HOSTEL **$**

(☑1800 229 228; 239 Sheridan St; dm $13-20, d without bathroom $50; ✳@🛜🌊) Amped-up music greets you at the bar-bistro out front, but the converted motel-room dorms and doubles at the rear are surprisingly quiet. Lots of freebies (brekkie cereal, evening meals and airport pick-ups) and plenty of travellers up for a party.

Waterfront Terraces APARTMENTS $$$
(☑07-4031 8333; www.cairnsluxury.com; 233 The Esplanade; 1-/2-bedroom apt $212/289; ✴🤖🖥) Set in lush tropical grounds, these low-rise luxury apartments have handsomely furnished separate tiled lounges and kitchen areas and all the trimmings, including big balconies looking out over the ocean.

Balinese MOTEL $$
(☑1800 023 331; www.balinese.com.au; 215 Lake St; d from $138; ✴🤖🖥) Bali comes to Cairns at this low-rise complex: waking up among the authentic wood furnishings and ceramic pieces, you may be taken with the sudden urge to have your hair beaded.

Sebel Cairns HOTEL $$$
(☑07-4031 1300; www.sebelcairns.com.au; 17 Abbott St; r $256-316; ✴@🖥) The grandaddy of Cairns' five-stars, the Sebel's exterior looks a little dated but it has a fine location, colonial charm and surprisingly contemporary rooms with city, mountain or harbour views. Decadent touches include marble bathrooms and an on-site spa.

Gilligan's HOSTEL $
(☑07-4041 6566; www.gilligansbackpackers.com.au; 57-89 Grafton St; dm $26-32, d $130; ✴@🤖🖥) The 'G spot' is pricey, impersonal and very loud, but all rooms at this flashpacker resort have bathrooms and most have balconies; higher-priced rooms come with fridges and TVs. Several bars, nightly entertainment like jelly wrestling, a beauty salon, and a gym to work off all that beer.

Cairns Coconut Caravan Resort CARAVAN PARK $
(☑1300 262 668; www.coconut.com.au; cnr Bruce Hwy & Anderson Rd; sites powered/with bathroom $43/60, cabins with bathroom $90-125, without bathroom $70, villas $150-320; ✴@🖥) The last word in five-star caravan-park luxury, 8km south of the city centre. Spas, minigolf, an outdoor cinema and a slew of accommodation options.

Tropical Queenslander RESORT $$
(☑07-4051 0122; www.queenslanderhotels.com.au; 287 Lake St; apt from $125; ✴🤖🖥) Double dip here in the two pools, and relax in the smart apartments with kitchenettes, bathrooms and balconies.

Gecko's Backpackers HOSTEL $
(☑07-4031 1344; www.geckosbackpackers.com.au; 187 Bunda St; dm/s/d without bathroom $23/35/56; ✴🤖🖥) Big old Queenslander behind the train station with a hippie-

style vibe – great for travellers wanting to chill out away from the party scene.

Villa Vaucluse APARTMENTS $$
(☑07-4051 8566; www.villavaucluse.com.au; 141-143 Grafton St; 1-bedroom apt $175; ✴🖥) Mediterranean decor meets tropical influences, with central atrium, secluded saltwater swimming pool and sumptuous self-contained apartments.

Cairns Central YHA HOSTEL $
(☑07-4051 0772; www.yha.com.au; 20-26 McLeod St; dm $26.50-36; ✴@🖥) Bright, spotless and professionally staffed.

✗ Eating

Cairns' status as an international city is reflected in its multicultural restaurants, which often incorporate a tropical Aussie twist. Some of Cairns' pubs dish up amazingly cheap meals to the thrifty backpacker hordes and they're not half bad – see p424.

TOP CHOICE Ochre MODERN AUSTRALIAN $$
(☑07-4051 0100; www.ochrerestaurant.com.au; 43 Shields St; mains $30-36; ⊙lunch Mon-Fri, dinner nightly; 🍴) In an ochre- and plum-toned dining room, the changing menu at this innovative restaurant utilises native Aussie fauna (such as croc with native pepper, or roo with quandong-chilli glaze) and flora (wattleseed damper loaf with peanut oil and native dukka; lemon-myrtle panacotta). If you can't decide, try a tasting plate, or go all-out with a six-course tasting menu.

Green Ant Cantina MEXICAN $$
(☑07-4041 5061; www.greenantcantina.com; 183 Bunda St; mains $17-40; ⊙dinner) This funky little slice of Mexico behind the railway station is worth seeking out for its homemade quesadillas, enchiladas and Corona-battered tiger prawns. Great cocktail list, cool tunes (including an open-mic night on Sunday).

Charlie's SEAFOOD $$
(223-227 The Esplanade; buffets $28.50; ⊙dinner) It's not the fanciest place in town, but Charlie's, at the Acacia Court Hotel, is legendary for its nightly all-you-can-eat seafood buffet. Fill your plate with prawns, oysters, clams or hot food and eat out on the poolside terrace. Great cocktails too.

Fusion Organics CAFE $
(cnr Aplin & Grafton Sts; dishes $4-19.50; ⊙7am-4pm Mon-Fri, to 1pm Sat; 🍴) In the wicker-chair-strewn corner courtyard of an historic 1921 red-brick former ambulance station,

Indian chefs spice up Fusion's organic, allergy-free fare like quiches, frittatas, corn fritters and filled breads. Healthy brekkie options include buckwheat waffles and pick-me-up 'detox' juices.

Adelfia Greek Taverna
GREEK $$

(☎07-4041 1500; www.adelfiagreektaverna.com; cnr Aplin & Grafton Sts; mains $21-30; ⊙lunch Fri, dinner Tue-Sun) Plate-smashing, Mediterranean music, belly dancing and heaping portions of authentic Greek cuisine make this taverna a fun family night out. Call for entertainment times.

Perrotta's at the Gallery
MEDITERRANEAN $$

(☎07-4031 5899; 38 Abbott St; mains $27-33; ⊙breakfast, lunch & dinner; ☑) This chic spot adjoining the Cairns Regional Gallery tempts you onto its covered deck's wrought-iron furniture for tasty breakfasts, superb coffees, and an inventive Med-inspired menu at lunch and dinner.

Marinades
INDIAN $$

(☎07-4041 1422; 43 Spence St; mains $14-30; ⊙lunch & dinner Tue-Sun) A long, *long* menu of aromatic dishes like lobster marinated in cashew paste, or Goan prawn curry, along with restrained decor in its dining room, make Marinades the pick of Cairns' Indian restaurants.

Cherry Blossom
JAPANESE $$$

(☎07-4052 1050; www.cherryblossom.com.au; cnr Spence & Lake Sts; mains $29-53; ⊙lunch Tue-Fri, dinner Mon-Sat) This 1st-floor restaurant is reminiscent of an *Iron Chef* cook-off, with two chefs working at opposite ends of the restaurant floor. Book ahead for sushi, teppanyaki and plenty of theatre.

First House
VIETNAMESE $$

(☎07-4051 5153; 55 Spence St; mains $11-20; ⊙11am-9pm) Serving continuously throughout the day (a rarity for Cairns restaurants), this small, simple spot is a good bet if you like pork, which appears in virtually every dish. Unlicensed but BYO.

Meldrum's Pies in Paradise
PIES $

(97 Grafton St; pies $4.50-5.50; ⊙7am-5pm Mon-Fri, to 2.30pm Sat; ☑) A Cairns institution, Meldrum's bakes some 40 inventive varieties of the humble Aussie pie – from chicken and avocado to pumpkin gnocchi or tuna mornay.

Raw Prawn
SEAFOOD $$$

(☎07-4031 5400; www.rawprawnrestaurant.com. au; The Esplanade Centre, The Esplanade; mains $29-40; ⊙lunch & dinner) Fine-dining affair especially renowned for its seafood platters ($54 to $90 per person). The priciest include succulent mud crab.

Dolce & Caffe
CAFE $$

(shop 1, Mantra Esplanade, Shields St; dishes $5.50-18.50; ⊙6am-4.30pm Mon-Sat, 7am-4.30pm Sun; ☑) A local fave for its sublime coffee and super-fresh salads.

La Fettuccina
ITALIAN $$

(☎07-4031 5959; www.lafettuccina.com; 41 Shields St; mains $24.50-29.50; ⊙dinner) Homemade sauces are a speciality at this small, atmospheric Italian restaurant. Try for a seat on the tiny, internal wrought-iron mezzanine balcony. Licensed and BYO.

Vanilla Gelateria
ICE CREAM $

(Pier Point Rd; cone or cup $3.80-5.80; ⊙9.30am-11pm) Icy concoctions like Toblerone; lemon, lime and bitters – even Red Bull!

Along the waterfront outside the **Pier Marketplace** (Pierpoint Rd), half a dozen international restaurants share a boardwalk overlooking the marina – just wander along and take your pick.

If you want something cheap and quick, the **Night Markets** (The Esplanade), between Alpin and Shields Sts, have a busy Asian-style food court.

Self-Catering

Cairns' main food market is **Rusty's Markets** (Grafton St; ⊙5am-6pm Fri, 6am-3pm Sat, 6am-2pm Sun), between Shields and Spence Sts.

Asian Foods Australia (101-105 Grafton St) sells food products from all over Asia.

The huge **Cairns Central Shopping Centre** (www.cairnscentral.com.au; McLeod St; ⊙9am-5.30pm Mon-Wed, Fri & Sat, to 9pm Thu, 10am-4.30pm Sun) has a couple of supermarkets.

🍷 Drinking

Cairns holds the mantle as the party capital of the north Queensland coast, with loads of options. Most venues are multipurpose, offering food, alcohol and some form of entertainment, and you can always find a beer garden or terrace to enjoy balmy evenings.

⭐ TOP CHOICE Salt House
BAR

(www.salthouse.com.au; 6/2 Pierpoint Rd; ⊙9am-2am) Next to Cairns' new yacht club, Salt House has a sleek nautical design that has seen it become the city's most sought-after bar since it opened a couple of years ago. It's

actually two bars: the luxury yacht–styled Sailing Bar, with live music, and the Balinese-influenced Deck Bar, with killer cocktails and DJs hitting the decks.

Vibe Bar & Lounge BAR
(www.vibebarcairns.com; 39 Lake St; ⊘10.30am-1am Mon-Thu, to 5am Fri, noon-5am Sat, 5am-3am Sun) Walk through the unassuming street entrance to the cathedral-like back room with funky artworks adorning the walls and couches in the corners at this 'Melbourne-style' lounge bar. The dance floor cranks from 9pm nightly. Gay-friendly.

Gilligan's BARS, NIGHTCLUB
(www.gilligansbackpackers.com.au; 57-89 Grafton St; ⊘9am-late) You're guaranteed a crowd at Cairns' biggest and busiest backpacker resort. With 400-odd backpackers staying here. But it's also popular with locals for its immense beer deck, live bands, DJs spinning house tunes, and cocktails in its upstairs lounge bar.

Court House Hotel PUB
(38 Abbott St; ⊘9am-late) In Cairns' gleaming white former courthouse building, dating from 1921, the Court House pub is replete with a polished timber island bar and Scales of Justice statue – and cane-toad races on Wednesday night.

12 Bar Blues JAZZ
(62 Shields St; ⊘7pm-late Tue-Sun) The best place in Cairns for loungy live music, this intimate bar grooves to the beat of jazz, blues and swing. Songwriter open-mic night takes place on Thursday, general open-mic night on Sunday.

Shenannigans BAR
(www.shenanniganshotel.com.au; 48 Spence St; ⊘to late daily) The huge beer garden with barrels for tables, big screens and a music stage is the stand-out at this marginally Irish-themed pub attached to a backpackers. Entertainment spans trivia nights, karaoke and live bands.

Pier Bar & Grill BAR
(www.pierbar.com.au; Pierpoint Rd; ⊘11.30am-late) A local stalwart for its waterfront location and well-priced meals. The Pier's Sunday session is a must.

Grand Hotel PUB
(33 McLeod St; ⊘11am-1am) This laid-back local is worth a visit just so that you can rest your beer on the bar – an 11m-long carved crocodile!

PJ O'Briens BAR
(cnr Lake & Shields Sts; ⊘to late daily) There are sticky carpets and the smell of stale Guinness, but Irish-themed PJ's packs 'em in with party nights, pole dancing and dirt-cheap meals.

Woolshed Chargrill & Saloon BAR
(24 Shields St; ⊘to late daily) Another backpacker magnet. A young crowd of travellers and diving instructors gets hammered and dances on the tables.

Hotel Cairns BAR
(www.thehotelcairns.com; cnr Abbott & Florence Sts; ⊘to late daily) This grand-dame hotel is a low-key alternative to Cairns' hurdy-gurdy party scene, with nightly piano and double-bass performances.

Rhino Bar BAR
(cnr Spence & Lake Sts; ⊘from 8pm) A high-energy crowd downs cocktails and shots and spills out onto the enormous 1st-floor balcony. Can get messy.

☆ Entertainment

Live music hits stages all over town; the Tanks Arts Centre (p414) hosts well-known pop, rock, indie and folk artists. Jazz buffs should check the weekly roster at www.tropicjazz.org.au. Nightclubs come and go; ask locally about what's hot (and not). Clubs generally close at 3am or later; cover charges usually apply.

The website www.entertainmentcairns.com and the free *Backpacker Xpress* magazine list the hot spots.

Pullman Reef Hotel Casino CASINO, BARS
(www.reefcasino.com.au; 35-41 Wharf St; ⊘9am-3am Sun-Thu, to 5am Fri & Sat) Cairns' casino has table games as well as hundreds of poker machines. Also four restaurants; four bars, including **Vertigo Bar & Lounge**, with free live music; and a pumpin' nightclub, **Velvet Underground**, which also hosts ticketed shows.

Starry Night Cinema CINEMA
(www.endcredits.org.au; Flecker Botanic Gardens, Collins Ave, Edge Hill; admission $10; ⊘May-Nov) Every third Wednesday of the month classic films screen from about 6.30pm in the tropical outdoors of the botanic gardens.

Jute Theatre THEATRE
(☑07-4031 9555; www.jute.com.au; CoCA, 96 Abbott St; tickets $17-30) Stages contemporary Australian works and indie plays in the Centre of Contemporary Arts.

Rondo Theatre THEATRE
(☎07-4031 9555; www.cairnslittletheatre.com;
Greenslopes St) Community plays and musicals at this theatre opposite Centenary
Lakes. It's 4.5km northwest of the centre
(take Sheridan St to Greenslopes St).

Cairns City Cinemas CINEMA
(108 Grafton St) Mainstream flicks.

BCC Cinemas CINEMA
(Cairns Central Shopping Centre, McLeod St)
First-release films.

Shopping

Cairns offers the gamut of shopping, from
high-end boutiques like Louis Vuitton to
garishly kitsch souvenir barns. You'll have
no trouble finding a box of macadamia nuts,
some emu or crocodile jerky, fake designer
sunglasses and tropical-fish fridge magnets.

Night Markets MARKET
(The Esplanade; ☉4.30pm-midnight) Souvenirs.

Mud Markets MARKET
(Pier Marketplace; ☉mornings Sat) If your supply of 'Cairns Australia' T-shirts is running
low, or you're in need of a $15 massage.

**Cairns Central Shopping
Centre** SHOPPING CENTRE
(www.cairnscentral.com.au; McLeod St; ☉9am-
5.30pm Mon-Wed, Fri & Sat, to 9pm Thu, 10am-
4.30pm Sun) Enormous centre with a huge
range of speciality stores selling everything from books to bikinis.

Pier Marketplace SHOPPING CENTRE
(Pierpoint Rd) Developed as a waterfront
shopping mall. At the time of writing had
only a limited range of specialist boutiques.

Absells Chart & Map Centre BOOKS, MAPS
(Main Street Arcade, 85 Lake St) Absells carries
an impressive range of quality regional
maps, topographic maps and nautical
charts.

Information

Emergency
Ambulance, fire and police (☎000; ☉24hr)
Police Station (☎000, 07-4030 7000;
Sheridan St)

Internet Access
Most tour-booking agencies and accommodation places have internet access; dedicated
internet cafes are clustered along Abbott St,
between Shields and Aplin Sts.

Medical Services
Cairns Base Hospital (☎07-4050 6333; The
Esplanade) Has a 24-hour emergency service.
Cairns City 24 Hour Medical Centre (☎07-
4052 1119; cnr Florence & Grafton Sts) General
practice and dive medicals.
Cairns Travel Clinic (☎07-4041 1699; 15 Lake
St; ☉8.30am-5.30pm Mon-Fri, 9am-noon Sat)

Money
Most of the major banks have branches with
ATMs and foreign exchange; private currency-
exchange bureaux line The Esplanade and are
open longer hours.
American Express (63 Lake St) In Westpac
Bank.
Travelex (75 Abbott St)

Post
Australia Post (13 Grafton St)

Tourist information
Plenty of places stick up 'i' signs and call themselves 'information centres', but they're basically tour-booking agencies.
**Cairns & Tropical North Visitor Information
Centre** (www.tropicalaustralia.com.au; 51 The
Esplanade; ☉8.30am-6.30pm) Government-
run centre that doles out impartial advice and
can book accommodation and tours.
Cairns Discount Tours (www.cairnsdiscount
tours.com.au) Knowledgeable booking agent
for day trips and tours, specialising in last-
minute deals.
**Department of Environment & Resource
Management** (DERM; ☎13 74 68; www.derm.
qld.gov.au; 5B Sheridan St) National park
information and camping permits.
Far North Queensland Volunteers (www.
fnqvolunteers.org; 68 Abbott St) Arranges
volunteer positions with non-profit community
groups.
Royal Automobile Club of Queensland
(RACQ; ☎07-4033 6433; www.racq.com.au;
537 Mulgrave Rd, Earlville) Maps and information on road conditions state-wide, including
Cape York. For 24-hour recorded road-report
service, call ☎1300 130 595.

Getting There & Away
Air
Qantas (☎13 13 13; www.qantas.com.au; cnr
Lake & Shields Sts), **Virgin Australia** (☎13
67 89; www.virginaustralia.com) and **Jetstar**
(☎13 15 38; www.jetstar.com.au) all service
Cairns, with flights to/from Brisbane, Sydney,
Melbourne, Darwin (including via Alice Springs)
and Townsville.

Skytrans ([phone]1800 818 405; www.skytrans.com.au) services Cape York and remote north Queensland towns.

Hinterland Aviation ([phone]07-4035 9323; www.hinterlandaviation.com.au) has one to four flights daily except Sunday to/from Cooktown (one way $150, 40 minutes).

Bus

Cairns is the hub for Far North Queensland buses.

Greyhound Australia ([phone]1300 473 946; www.greyhound.com.au) Has four daily services down the coast to Brisbane ($310, 29 hours) via Townsville ($81, six hours), Airlie Beach ($139, 11 hours) and Rockhampton ($215, 18 hours). Bus passes can reduce costs. Departs Reef Fleet Terminal, southern end of The Esplanade.

Premier ([phone]13 34 10; www.premierms.com.au) Runs one daily service to Brisbane ($205, 29 hours) via Innisfail ($19, 1½ hours), Mission Beach ($19, two hours), Tully ($26, 2½ hours), Cardwell ($30, three hours), Townsville ($55, 5½ hours) and Airlie Beach ($90, 10 hours). Departs stop D, Lake Street Transit Centre. Cheaper bus passes available.

TransNorth ([phone]07-4095 8644; www.transnorthbus.com) Has five daily bus services connecting Cairns with the tableland, serving Kuranda ($8, 30 minutes), Mareeba ($16.80, one hour), Atherton ($22, 1¾ hours) and Ravenshoe ($33, 2½ hours). Departs 46 Spence St.

John's Kuranda Bus ([phone]0418-772 953) Runs a service between Cairns and Kuranda two to five times daily ($4, 30 minutes). Departs Lake Street Transit Centre.

Sun Palm ([phone]07-4087 2900; www.sunpalmtransport.com) Runs two northern services from Cairns to Cape Tribulation ($78, three hours) via Port Douglas ($35, 1½ hours) and Mossman ($40, 1¾ hours) with additional services direct to Port Douglas and south to Mission Beach ($49, two hours).

Country Road Coachlines ([phone]07-4045 2794; www.countryroadcoachlines.com.au) Runs a daily bus service between Cairns and Cooktown ($75) on either the coastal route (Bloomfield Track) or inland route (via Mareeba), depending on the day of departure and the condition of the track.

Car & Motorcycle

All the major car-rental companies have branches in Cairns and at the airport, with discount car- and campervan-rental companies proliferating throughout town. Daily rates start at around $45 for a late-model small car and around $80 for a 4WD. If you're in for the long haul, check out the noticeboard on Abbott St for used campervans and ex-backpackers' cars.

Britz Australia ([phone]07-4032 2611; www.britz.com.au; 411 Sheridan St) Hires out campervans.

East Coast ([phone]1800 028 881; www.eastcoastcarrentals.com.au; 146 Sheridan St)

Choppers Motorcycle Tours & Hire ([phone]0408-066 024; www.choppersmotocycles.com.au; 150 Sheridan St) Hire a Harley (from $160 a day) or smaller bikes (from $95). Also offers motorcycle tours.

Train

The *Sunlander* departs Cairns' **train station** (Bunda St) on Tuesday, Thursday and Saturday for Brisbane (one way from $219, 31½ hours); the Scenic Railway (p434) runs daily to/from Kuranda. Contact **Queensland Rail** ([phone]1800 872 467; www.traveltrain.com.au).

ℹ Getting Around

To/From the Airport

The airport is about 7km north of central Cairns; many accommodation places offer courtesy pick-ups. **Sun Palm** ([phone]07-4087 2900; www.sunpalmtransport.com) meets all incoming flights and runs a shuttle bus (adult/child $10/5) to the CBD. You can also book airport transfers to/from Cairns' northern beaches ($18), Palm Cove ($18), Port Douglas ($35), Mossman ($45) and Cape Tribulation ($78, two services daily). **Black & White Taxis** ([phone]13 10 08) charges around $26.

Bicycle

Bike hire is available from some accommodation places, or try the following:

Bike Man ([phone]07-4041 5566; www.bikeman.com.au; 99 Sheridan St; per day/week $20/60) Hire, sales and repairs.

Cairns Bicycle Hire ([phone]07-4031 3444; www.cairnsbicyclehire.com.au; 47 Shields St; per day/week from $15/45, scooters per day from $85) Groovy bikes and scooters.

Bus

Sunbus ([phone]07-4057 7411; www.sunbus.com.au) runs regular services in and around Cairns from the Lake Street Transit Centre, where schedules are posted. Useful routes include: Flecker Botanic Gardens/Edge Hill and Machans Beach (bus 7), Holloways Beach and Yorkeys Knob (buses 1c, 1d and 1h), and Trinity Beach, Clifton Beach and Palm Cove (buses 1N, 1X, 2, 2A). Most buses heading north go via Smithfield. All are served by the (almost) 24-hour night service (N) on Friday and Saturday. Heading south, bus 1 runs as far as Gordonvale.

Taxi

Black & White Taxis ([phone]13 10 08) has a rank near the corner of Lake and Shields Sts, and one on McLeod St, outside Cairns Central Shopping Centre.

Islands Off Cairns

Cairns day trippers can easily head out to Green Island, as well as Fitzroy Island and Frankland Islands National Parks for a bit of sunning, snorkelling and indulging.

GREEN ISLAND

Green Island's long, dog-legged jetty heaves under the weight of boatloads of day trippers. This beautiful coral cay is only 45 minutes from Cairns and has a rainforest interior with interpretive walks, a fringing white-sand beach and snorkelling just offshore. You can walk around the island in about 30 minutes.

The island and its surrounding waters are protected by their national- and marine-park status. **Marineland Melanesia** (adult/child $17/8) has an aquarium with fish, turtles, stingrays and crocodiles, as well as a collection of Melanesian artefacts.

Luxurious **Green Island Resort** (☑1800 673 366, 07-4031 3300; www.greenislandresort. com.au; ste $570-670; ✳✱@✱) has stylish split-level suites, each with its own private balcony. Island transfers are included. It's partially open to day trippers (using a separate pool), so even if you're not staying you can enjoy the restaurants, bars, ice-cream parlour and water-sports facilities.

Great Adventures (☑07-4044 9944; www. greatadventures.com.au; 1 Spence St, Cairns; adult/child $75/37.50) and **Big Cat** (☑07-4051 0444; www.greenisland.com.au; adult/child $75/37.50) run day trips, with optional glass-bottomed boat and semisubmersible tours.

Alternatively, sail to the island aboard **Ocean Free** (☑07-4052 1111; www.oceanfree. com.au; adult/child from $135/90), spending most of the day offshore at Pinnacle Reef, with a short stop on the island.

FITZROY ISLAND

A steep mountaintop rising from the sea, Fitzroy Island has coral-strewn beaches, woodlands and walking tracks, and Australia's last staffed lighthouse. The most popular snorkelling spot is around the rocks at **Nudey Beach** (1.2km from the resort), which, despite its name, is not clothing-optional, so bring your togs.

You can pitch a tent at the **Fitzroy Island Camping Ground** (☑07-4044 3044; $28), run by Cairns Regional Council. It has showers, toilets and barbecues; advance bookings are essential.

Refurbished accommodation at the **Fitzroy Island Resort** (☑07-4044 6700; www. fitzroyisland.com; studios $195, cabins $299, 1 & 2 bedroom ste $350-515; ✳✱) ranges from sleek studios and beachfront cabins through to a decadent-and-then-some penthouse ($1899). Its restaurant, bar and kiosk are open to day trippers.

Raging Thunder (☑07-4030 7900; www. ragingthunder.com.au; Reef Fleet Terminal, Cairns; adult/child $58/31.50) runs one trip a day from Cairns (departing 8.30am).

FRANKLAND ISLANDS

If the idea of hanging out on one of five uninhabited coral-fringed islands with excellent snorkelling and stunning white sandy beaches appeals – and if not, why not? – cruise out to the Frankland Group National Park.

Camping is available on High or Russell Islands, which both feature rainforest areas – contact **DERM** (☑13 74 68; www.derm.qld.gov. au) in Cairns for advance reservations and – in case you were getting any ideas about dropping out of life for a while – seasonal restrictions.

Frankland Islands Cruise & Dive (☑07-4031 6300; www.franklandislands.com.au; adult/child from $136/84) runs excellent day trips, which include a cruise down the Mulgrave River, snorkelling gear and lunch. Guided snorkelling tours with a marine biologist and diving packages are also offered. Transfers for campers to/from Russell Island are available. Boats depart from Deeral; transfers from Cairns and the northern beaches cost $16 per person.

You'll need to organise your own boat or charter to reach High Island.

Cairns' Northern Beaches

Since Cairns doesn't have a beach, locals and tourists head offshore to the islands or travel slightly north in search of golden sands. Most turn-offs from the Captain Cook Hwy lead to small communities taking advantage of an easy, relaxed seaside lifestyle. There's a distinctive beach-holiday vibe and each community has its own character: Yorkeys is popular with sailors, Trinity with families; Palm Cove is a swanky honeymoon haven. Only Ellis Beach and Palm Cove have campsites.

The following are listed in order from Cairns, and Sunbus (p427) travels to them all throughout the week.

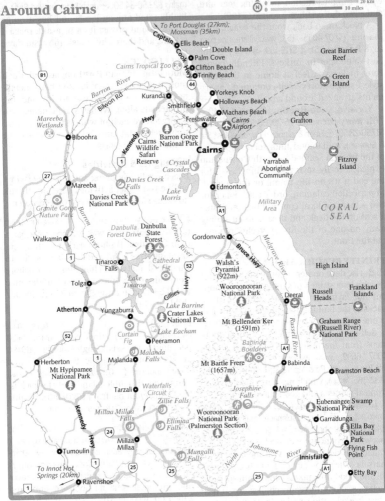

HOLLOWAYS BEACH

The Coral Sea meets a rough ribbon of sand at quiet Holloways Beach. It's a mostly residential area, with beachside homes making way for a handful of tourist developments.

Pacific Sands (07-4055 0277; www.pacific sandscairns.com; 1-19 Poinciana St; d $140; ✲ ☞ ☲) is a complex of bright self-contained two-bedroom apartments stretching one block back from the beach. There's a flash tropical ambience to the one-bedroom beachfront apartments at **Cairns Beach Resort** (1800 150 208, 07-4037 0400; www.cairnsbeachresort. com.au; 129 Oleander St; d $163-225; ✲ @ ☲).

Breezy cafe **Strait on the Beach** (100 Oleander St; mains $9-18.50; ⏲7.30am-5.30pm Mon-Thu, to 7.30pm Fri, to 6pm Sat & Sun) has a chunky timber deck overlooking the beach – perfect for reading the paper over coffee or breakfast.

YORKEYS KNOB

The most appealing of Cairns' northern beaches, Yorkeys is a sprawling, low-key settlement on a white-sand beach. In the crescent-shaped Half Moon Bay is the marina, supporting 200 bobbing boats.

Kite Rite (0409 283 322; www.kiterite.com. au; shop 1, 471 Varley St; per hr $79) offers kite- and

windsurfing instruction, including gear hire, and a two-day certificate course ($499).

A block or so back from the beach, **Villa Marine** (☑07-4055 7158; www.villamarine.com.au; 8 Rutherford St; d $119-159; ❋☷❈) is the best-value spot in Yorkeys. Friendly owner Peter makes you feel at home in the retro-style, single-storey self-contained apartments arranged around a pool.

Yorkeys Knob Boating Club (☑07-4055 7711; www.ykbc.com.au; 25-29 Buckley St; mains $17.50-28.50; ☺lunch & dinner daily, breakfast Sat & Sun; ☷), a diamond find, serves up some of the freshest seafood in north Queensland (which is really saying something!). Go for the cod if it's on the menu, or the cooked-to-perfection calamari, order a schooner (or two – there's a local courtesy bus) and take a seat on the deck and dream about sailing away on one of the luxury yachts moored out the front.

TRINITY BEACH & AROUND

High-rise developments detract from Trinity Beach's long stretch of sheltered white sand, but holidaymakers love it – turning their backs to the buildings and focusing on what is one of Cairns' prettiest northern beaches.

Self-contained apartments are just footsteps from the beach at **Castaways** (☑07-4057 6699; www.castawaystrinitybeach.com.au; cnr Trinity Beach Rd & Moore St; 1-/2-bedroom apt $132/165; ❋☷), which has three pools, spas, tropical gardens and good stand-by rates.

L'Unico Trattoria (☑07-4057 8855; www.lunico.net.au; 75 Vasey Esplanade; mains $22-44; ☺lunch & dinner, breakfast Sat & Sun; ☷), opening to a wrap-around wooden deck, serves stylish Italian cuisine, including veal medallions in marsala sauce, homemade four-cheese gnocchi and wood-fired pizzas, along with specials such as scallops in creamy chilli sauce. It has a beachside location, and a stellar wine list.

CLIFTON BEACH

Local and leisurely, Clifton Beach has a good balance of residential and holiday accommodation and services. You can walk north along the beach about 2km to Palm Cove from here.

Clifton Palms (☑07-4055 3839; www.cliftonpalms.com.au; 35-41 Upolu Esplanade; cabins/units from $69/108, 2-bedroom apt from $145; ❋@☷) has freestanding single-storey apartments backed by a curtain of green hills, with a big poolside barbecue area.

Opposite Clifton Palms, **Clifton Capers Bar & Grill** (☑07-4059 2311; 14 Clifton Rd;

mains $23.50-34.50; ☺lunch & dinner Wed-Sun) is highly rated among locals and has a range of pastas and pizzas. It's a pleasant, relaxed setting, and there's live music most Sundays.

PALM COVE

More intimate than Port Douglas and much more upmarket than its southern neighbours, Palm Cove is essentially one big promenade along Williams Esplanade, with a gorgeous stretch of white-sand beach and top-notch restaurants luring sun lovers out of their luxury resorts.

◉ Sights & Activities

Beach strolls, shopping and leisurely swims will be your chief activities here, but there's no excuse for not getting out on the water.

Palm Cove Watersports   KAYAKING, HIKING
(☑0402 861 011; www.palmcovewatersports.com) Organises 1½-hour early-morning sea-kayaking trips ($56) and half-day paddles to Double Island (adult/child $96/68), offshore from Palm Cove. It also runs a half-day hike to Lake Placid and the Barron Gorge (adult/child $92/72).

Beach Fun & Co   WATER SPORTS
(Williams Esplanade) Hires catamarans ($50 per hour), jet skis (single/double $60/80 per 15 minutes), paddle boats ($30) and boogie boards ($10), and organises jet-ski tours around Double Island and Haycock Island (single/double from $120/180). Fishing boats start from $100 per two hours.

Cairns Tropical Zoo   ZOO
(☑07-4055 3669; www.cairnstropicalzoo.com.au; Captain Cook Hwy; adult/child $32/16; ☺8.30am-5pm) Just west of Palm Cove, this zoo offers an up-close wildlife experience with crocodiles and snakes, koala photo sessions and kangaroo feeding. Its **Cairns Night Zoo** (adult/child $97/48.50; ☺7-10pm Mon-Thu & Sat) experience includes a barbecue dinner and entertainment. Transfers are available from Palm Cove, Port Douglas and Cairns and the northern beaches.

⌴ Sleeping

Most of Palm Cove's accommodation has a minimum stay of three nights.

TOP CHOICE **Sebel Reef House**   HOTEL $$$
(☑1800 079 052; www.reefhouse.com.au; 99 Williams Esplanade; d from $299; ❋@☷☷) Once the private residence of an army brigadier, the Sebel is more intimate and understated than most of Palm Cove's resorts. The

whitewashed walls, wicker furniture and big beds romantically draped in muslin all add to the air of refinement. The Brigadier's Bar works on a quaint honesty system; complimentary punch is served by candlelight at twilight.

Peppers Beach Club & Spa   HOTEL $$$
(☎1300 987 600; www.peppers.com.au; 123 Williams Esplanade; d from $290; ❋@⌂☼☒) Step through the opulent lobby at Peppers and into a wonder world of swimming pools – there's the sand-edged lagoon pool and the leafy rainforest pool and swim-up bar, plus tennis courts and spa treatments. Even the standard rooms have private balcony spas, and the penthouse suites (from $540) have their own rooftop pool. Service exceeds even the highest expectations.

Palm Cove Camping Ground   CAMPGROUND $
(☎07-4055 3824; 149 Williams Esplanade; unpowered/powered sites $16.50/23) Council-run beachfront camping ground near the jetty, with barbecue area and laundry. No cabins, but the only way to do Palm Cove on the cheap!

Silvester Palms   APARTMENTS $$
(☎07-4055 3831; www.silvesterpalms.com; 32 Veivers Rd; 1-/2-/3-bedroom apt $110/130/190; ❋⌂☒) These bright self-contained apartments are an affordable alternative to Palm Cove's city-sized resorts. Good for families.

Melaleuca Resort   APARTMENTS $$$
(☎1800 629 698; www.melaleucaresort.com.au; 85-93 Williams Esplanade; d $195-218; ❋☒) Charming boutique resort has 24 one-bedroom apartments, all with kitchens, balconies and laundry facilities.

✖ Eating & Drinking
Palm Cove has some fine restaurants and cafes strung along the esplanade. All of the resort hotels have swish dining options open to nonguests.

TOP CHOICE Beach Almond   MODERN ASIAN $$$
(☎07-4059 1908; www.beachalmond.com; 145 Williams Esplanade; mains $14-39.50; ⊙lunch & dinner) A rustic beach house near the jetty is the setting for Palm Cove's most inspired dining. Black-pepper prawns, ginger pork belly, Singaporean mud crab and Balinese barra are among the fragrant, freshly prepared innovations.

Nu Nu   MODERN AUSTRALIAN $$$
(☎07-4059 1880; www.nunu.com.au; 123 Williams Esplanade; mains $31-47; ⊙breakfast, lunch & dinner) Retro Nu Nu has one of the highest profiles on the coast, so you'll need to book way ahead. It specialises in 'wild foods' like beet-poached Angus tenderloin or roast chicken with leatherwood honey grilled figs.

Surf Club Palm Cove   LICENSED CLUB $$
(☎07-4059 1244; 135 Williams Esplanade; meals $14.50-27.50; ⊙dinner) A great local for a drink in the sunny garden bar and bargain-priced seafood plus decent kids' meals.

El Grecko   GREEK $$
(☎07-4055 3690; level 1, Palm Cove Shopping Village, Williams Esplanade; mains $22-34; ⊙dinner; ☒) Souvlaki, spanakopita and moussaka are among the staples at this lively taverna. Good mezze platters; belly dancing on Friday and Saturday nights.

Apres Beach Bar & Grill   BAR, BISTRO $$
(☎07-4059 2000; 119 Williams Esplanade; mains $23-39; ⊙breakfast, lunch & dinner) The most happening place in Palm Cove, with a zany interior of old motorcycles, racing cars and a biplane hanging from the ceiling, and regular live music.

❶ Information
Commercially run tour-booking companies are strung along Williams Esplanade; Cairns & Tropical North Visitor Information Centre in Cairns can help with bookings.

The two-storey, ice cream–coloured **Paradise Village Shopping Centre** (113 Williams Esplanade) has a post office (with internet access for $4 an hour), a small supermarket and a newsagent.

ELLIS BEACH
Ellis Beach is the last of the northern beaches and the closest to the highway, which runs right past it. The long, sheltered bay is a stunner, with a palm-fringed, patrolled swimming beach and stinger net in summer. This is where the coastal drive to Port Douglas really gets interesting.

Ellis Beach Oceanfront Bungalows
(☎1800 637 036; www.ellisbeach.com; Captain Cook Hwy; unpowered sites $26, powered sites $32-38, cabins without bathroom $85, bungalows $149-185; ❋@) has campsites, cabins and contemporary bungalows that enjoy wide-screen ocean TV. It's palm-shaded, beachfront paradise, except when the horse flies are out in force.

Across the road, **Ellis Beach Bar 'n' Grill** (Captain Cook Hwy; mains $8-24; ⊙breakfast, lunch

& dinner) has good food, live music some Sunday afternoons and, best of all, pinball.

Daily events at Hartley's Crocodile Adventures (07-4055 3576; www.crocodile adventures.com; adult/child $32/16; 8.30am-5pm) include tours of this croc farm, along with feedings, 'crocodile attack' shows, and boat cruises on its lagoon.

Atherton Tableland

Waterfalls, lush green pastures complete with well-fed dairy cows and patches of remnant rainforest make up the tablelands, though the bordering areas are dramatically different; expect dry, harsh outback and much thinner cattle. The tablelands are the site of the continent's most recent volcanic activity, some 10,000 years ago, and in some areas the altitude reaches more than 1000m. Plenty of people self-drive around the area, though since most towns are close together, bike tours are popular. Either way, allow plenty of time to visit the plethora of waterfalls and local-produce outlets.

❶ Getting There & Around

There are bus services to the main towns from Cairns (generally three services on weekdays, two on Saturday and one on Sunday), but not to the smaller towns or all the interesting areas *around* the towns, so it's worth hiring your own wheels.

Trans North (07-4095 8644; www. transnorthbus.com) has regular bus services connecting Cairns with the tableland, departing from 46 Spence St and running to Kuranda ($8, 45 minutes), Mareeba ($16.80, one hour), Atherton ($22, 1¾ hours) and Herberton ($28, two hours, three per week). **John's Kuranda Bus** (0418 772 953; www.kuranda.org) runs a service between Cairns and Kuranda two to five times daily ($4, 20 minutes). **Kerry's** (0427 841 483) serves Ravenshoe ($33, 2½ hours). John's and Kerry's buses depart from Cairns' Lake Street Transit Centre.

KURANDA
POP 1700

Kuranda is a hop, skip and jump – or make that a historic train journey, sky-rail adventure or winding bus trip – from Cairns. The village itself is basically sprawling sets of markets nestled in a spectacular tropical-rainforest setting and selling everything from made-in-China Aboriginal art to emu oil. The locals are a friendly bunch, well prepared for the hordes of tourists that arrive in the morning and depart with full bellies, bags and memory cards at almost precisely 3.30pm. There's little reason to stay overnight, as this is really a day trippers' domain.

◉ Sights & Activities

Kuranda Original Rainforest Markets
MARKET
(www.kurandaoriginalrainforestmarket.com.au; Therwine St; 9am-3pm) With revamped boardwalks terraced in the rainforest and wafting incense, the original markets first opened in 1978 and are still the best place to see artists such as glass-blowers at work, pick up hemp products, and sample local produce such as honey and fruit wines.

Heritage Markets
MARKET
(www.kurandamarkets.com.au; Rob Veivers Dr; 9am-3pm) Across the road from the original markets, the heritage markets overflow with souvenirs and crafts such as ceramics, emu oil, jewellery, clothing (lots of tie-dye) and pistachio-nut figurines.

New Kuranda Markets
MARKET
(www.kuranda.org; 21-23 Coondoo St; 9am-4pm) The first you come to if you're walking up from the train station; essentially just an ordinary group of shops.

Rainforestation
ZOO
(07-4085 5008; www.rainforest.com.au; Kennedy Hwy; adult/child $40/20; 9am-4pm) An enormous tourist park west of town with a wildlife section, river cruises and an Aboriginal show.

Cairns Wildlife Safari Reserve
ZOO
(07-4093 7777; www.cairnswildlifesafarireserve. com.au; Kennedy Hwy; adult/child $28/14; 9am-4.30pm) Lions, hippos and more; 9km west of Kuranda.

Australian Butterfly Sanctuary
BUTTERFLY AVIARY
(07-4093 7575; www.australianbutterflies.com; 8 Rob Veivers Dr; adult/child $16/8; 10am-4pm) Half-hour tours available.

Birdworld
BIRD SANCTUARY
(07-4093 9188; www.birdworldkuranda.com; Heritage Markets; adult/child $16/8; 9am-4pm) Next door to the butterfly sanctuary; displays 75 species of bird.

Australian Venom Zoo
ZOO
(07-4093 8905; 8 Coondoo St; adult/child $16/10; 9am-5pm) Won't take up much of your time, and is a no-go zone for arachnophobes.

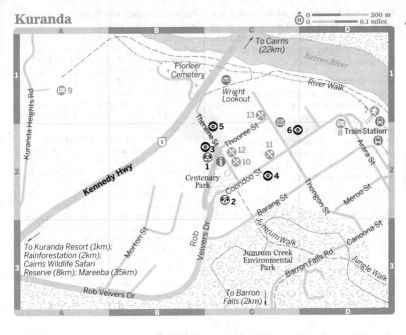

Kuranda

⊙ Sights

1 Australian Butterfly Sanctuary	C2
2 Australian Venom Zoo	C2
Birdworld	(see 3)
3 Heritage Markets	C2
4 Kuranda Arts Co-op	C2
5 Kuranda Original Rainforest Markets	C2
6 New Kuranda Markets	C2

⊙ Activities, Courses & Tours

7 Kuranda Riverboat	D1

⊙ Sleeping

8 Kuranda Hotel Motel	D2
9 Kuranda Rainforest Park	A1

⊗ Eating

10 Annabel's Pantry	C2
11 Frogs	C2
12 German Tucker	C2
13 Kuranda Coffee Republic	C1
Kuranda Rainforest Restaurant	(see 9)

Kuranda Riverboat CRUISES
(☏07-4093 7476; adult/child $14/7; ⊙hourly 10.30am-2.30pm) Behind the train station. Hop aboard for a 45-minute calm-water cruise along the Barron River.

There are several signed walks in the markets, and a short walking track (the Jumrum Walk) through **Jumrum Creek Environmental Park**, which is off Barron Falls Rd, leads you to a big population of fruit bats.

Further south, Barron Falls Rd divides: the right fork takes you to a wheelchair-accessible **lookout** over the Barron Falls, while the left fork becomes the Jungle Walk section of the trail and leads down to the Barron River. From there, the River Walk leads back up to the Scenic Railway station and back into town.

🛏 Sleeping & Eating

Kuranda Hotel Motel MOTEL $$
(☏07-4093 7206; www.fireflykuranda.com.au; cnr Coondoo & Arara Sts; d $100-120; ❈☒) Locally known as the 'bottom pub' (and rebadging its accommodation section as 'Firefly'), the

back of the Kuranda Hotel Motel has spacious '70s-style motel rooms with exposed brick and tinted crinkle-cut glass, enhanced with eye-catching artworks, quality linens and groovy light fittings.

Kuranda Rainforest Park
CARAVAN PARK $

(☑07-4093 7316; www.kurandarainforestpark.com. au; 88 Kuranda Heights Rd; unpowered/powered sites $26/28, s/d without bathroom $30/55, cabins $90-110; ☎❄) This excellent, well-tended park lives up to its name with grassy camping sites enveloped in rainforest. The basic but cosy private 'backpacker rooms' open to a tin-roofed timber deck, cabins come with poolside or garden views, and there's a Sri Lankan restaurant (mains $14-36; ☺dinner Wed-Sun; ☎☑) on site. It's a 10-minute walk from town via a forest trail.

Kuranda Coffee Republic
CAFE $

(10 Thongon St; coffees $1-5.50; ☺8am-4pm Mon-Fri, 9am-4pm Sat & Sun) Food is basically limited to biscotti, but who cares when the coffee's this good? You can see – and smell – the locally grown beans being roasted on site.

Frogs
CAFE $$

(11 Coondoo St; mains $14-32; ☺10am-3pm Sun-Wed, to 7pm Thu-Sat; @☎☑) Barra, prawns and a brilliant brekkie omelette (which they'll cook up at any time of day, if you ask nicely) are the staples of this breezy, family-run cafe. In the back garden, Aboriginal dance shows (admission by donation; ☺1pm) take place daily, weather permitting.

German Tucker
GERMAN, AUSTRALIAN $

(Therwine St; dishes $6-10; ☺10am-2.30pm) Emu, crocodile or kangaroo sausages with sauerkraut? German Tucker serves extreme Australiana/traditional German fare and German beer.

Annabel's Pantry
PIES $

(Therwine St; pies $4.10-4.50; ☺breakfast & lunch; ☑) With around 25 pie varieties, including kangaroo, and spinach-and-feta rolls, Annabel's is great for lunch on the run.

❶ Information

The Kuranda visitor centre (www.kuranda.org; ☺10am-4pm) is centrally located in Centenary Park.

❶ Getting There & Away

TransNorth (☑07-4095 8644; www.transnorth-bus.com) has five daily bus services from 46 Spence St, Cairns, to Kuranda ($8, 45 minutes).

This is the cheapest way, though the other options are more spectacular.

Winding 34km from Cairns to Kuranda through picturesque mountains and 15 tunnels, the Kuranda Scenic Railway (☑07-4036 9333; www.ksr.com.au) line took five years to build and opened in 1891. The 1¾-hour trip costs $45/23 per adult/child one way, $68/34 return. Trains depart Cairns at 8.30am and 9.30am daily, returning from pretty Kuranda station on Arara St at 2pm and 3.30pm.

At 7.5km, Skyrail Rainforest Cableway (☑07-4038 1555; www.skyrail.com.au; adult/child one way $44/22, return $63/33; ☺9am-5.15pm) is one of the world's longest gondola cableways. The Skyrail runs from the corner of Kemerunga Rd and the Cook Hwy in the northern Cairns suburb of Smithfield (15 minutes' drive north of Cairns) to Kuranda (Arara St), taking 90 minutes. It includes two stops along the way with boardwalks and interpretive panels. The last departure from Cairns and Kuranda is at 3.30pm; transfers are available to/from the Cairns departure terminal (return from $86/43 adult/child). Combination Scenic Railway and Skyrail deals are available. As space is limited, only day packs are allowed on board; advance bookings are recommended.

MAREEBA
POP 10,800

At the centre of industrious cattle, coffee and sugar enterprises, Mareeba is essentially an administrative and supply town for the northern tableland and parts of Cape York Peninsula. The main street boasts some quaint old facades, and the region's natural beauty is typified by the expansive wetlands to the north. Mareeba is more desert than tableland but has some wonderful attractions nearby. If you're around in mid-July, don the RM Williams boots and be sure to see the Mareeba Rodeo (www.mareebarodeo. com.au) at Kerribee Park.

There's plenty of seasonal work, with mango season from January to March; avocado work is February to March.

First stop is the Mareeba Heritage Museum & Tourist Information Centre (☑07-4092 5674; www.mareebaheritagecentre.com.au; Centenary Park, 345 Byrnes St; admission free; ☺8am-4pm), which has a huge room filled with displays on the area's past and present commercial industries, as well as its natural surrounds.

Mareeba Wetlands (☑1800 788 755; www.jabirusafarilodge.com.au; adult/child $12/6; ☺9am-4.30pm Apr-Jan) is a 20-sq-km reserve of woodlands, grasslands, swamps and the expansive Clancy's Lagoon, a birdwatchers'

nirvana. A huge range of bird species flock here, and you might see other animals such as kangaroos and freshwater crocs. Over 12km of walking trails criss-cross the wetlands. Various safari tours (from $38) depart during the week, or you can take a 30-minute eco-cruise (adult/child $15/7.50) or paddle in a canoe ($15 per hour). The on-site **Jabiru Safari Lodge** (cabins incl breakfast s $125-159, d $190-250) has solar-powered tented cabins and a spa. Take the Pickford Rd turn-off from Biboohra, 7km north of Mareeba.

Granite Gorge Nature Park (☑07-4093 2259; www.granitegorge.com.au; adult/child $10/2) is a privately owned park with huge granite boulders populated by rock wallabies, **walking tracks** and waterfalls tumbling into a croc-free **swimming hole**. There are picnic areas and a **campground** (unpowered/powered sites per person incl park entry $12/16). Granite Gorge is 12km southwest of Mareeba. Follow Chewko Rd south of Mareeba for 7km, from where the turn-off is signposted to your right.

Mt Uncle Distillery (☑07-4086 8008; www.mtuncle.com; 1819 Chewko Rd, Walkamin; ☻10am-5pm) produces whisky, as well as seasonal liqueurs and spirits using local bananas, coffee, mulberries and lemons (tastings available). Don't miss a meal at the classy **Bridges Cafe** (mains $10-18), hand-built by the owners from the timber of a former local bridge. It's signposted along Chewko Rd, 15.5km south of Mareeba.

For a tropical tipple, **Golden Drop Mango** (☑07-4093 2750; www.goldendrop.com.au; 227 Bilwon Rd; ☻8am-6.30pm), 2km off the highway north of Mareeba, offers tastings of its sweet mango wine.

🛏 Sleeping & Eating

Jackaroo Motel   MOTEL **$$**
(☑07-4092 2677; www.jackaroomotel.com; 340 Byrnes St; d $115; ✳🛜🏊) Mareeba's most upmarket motel has a saltwater swimming pool and a barbecue area.

Mareeba Lodge   MOTEL **$$**
(☑07-4092 2266; www.mareebalodge.com.au; 21 Byrnes St; s $90, d $100-110; ✳) Friendly, central motel. Farm work can be arranged for long-term guests (dorm beds per week $175).

Mareeba Rodeo Grounds   CAMPGROUND **$**
(☑07-4092 1654; www.mareebarodeo.com.au; Kerribee Park, 614 Dimbulah Rd; unpowered/powered sites $12/14) Cheap camping but no shade.

(☑07-4092 2147; 79 Byrnes St; mains $16-25; ☻lunch & dinner) At this pub in the town centre you'll find good-value specials with all the classics – barra, burgers and steak, and a bargain bar menu (mains $10).

CHILLAGOE
POP 230

Even on a day trip from Cairns, the charismatic former gold-rush town of Chillagoe, about 140km west of Mareeba, can fulfil any romantic notion you may have of the outback – but an overnight stay is preferable.

Chillagoe's excellent visitor centre, the **Hub** (☑07-4094 7111; www.chillagoehub.com.au; Queen St), has interesting historical displays. Knowledgeable staff can direct you to **Aboriginal rock-art sites**, the local **swimming hole**, the old **smelter site**, a hodgepodge little **history museum** with a piano played during silent movies, and an eccentric local with a cool old **Ford collection**. It also books ranger-guided tours of Chillagoe's **limestone caves** (adult/child $21/16.50). Three of the 500-plus caves can be visited: **Donna** (☻9am), **Trezkin** (☻11am) and **Royal Arch** (☻1.30pm).

The annual **Chillagoe Rodeo** takes place in May.

Rustic-on-the-outside,   modern-on-the-inside miners shacks make up **Chillagoe Cabins** (☑07-4094 7206; www.chillagoe.com; Queen St; d $140; ✳🏊), where the owner has a small wildlife-rescue menagerie and offers **town tours** ($20). There's a camp kitchen and barbecue, or you can order home-cooked **meals** (3-course meals $35).

Chillagoe's former post office is now the **Chillagoe Guesthouse** (☑07-4222 1135; www.chillagoeguesthouse.com.au; 16-18 Queen St; s/d from $100/120; ✳). Rates include a hamper with bacon and eggs to cook your own brekkie.

Chillagoe Observatory & Eco Lodge (☑07-4094 7155; www.coel.com.au; Hospital Ave; unpowered/powered sites $20/24, s/tw without bathroom $30/45, d $80-100; ✳🏊) has a licensed **restaurant** (mains $18-25) and an **observatory** (1½-hour tours adult/child $15/8; ☻Apr-Oct) where you can scan the southern night sky.

The **Chillagoe Bus Service** (☑07-4094 7155; adult/child $36/27) departs from Chillagoe on Monday, Wednesday and Friday, returning from Mareeba on the same days.

Billy Tea Bush Safaris (www.billytea.com.au) runs day tours from Cairns.

ATHERTON
POP 9000

Atherton, the 'capital' of the tableland, is a farming town with little to offer travellers but a rest in the journey, or a chance to get their hands and shoes dirty picking fruit and vegetables year-round. The Atherton Tableland Information Centre (☏07-4091 4222; www.athertontablelands.com.au; cnr Main & Silo Rds) has useful information, including self-drive itineraries, Australia-wide booking facilities and seasonal work updates.

As you approach Atherton from Herberton in the southwest, you see the fabulous Hou Wang Temple (86 Herberton Rd; adult/child $10/5; ⊙11am-4pm Wed-Sun) – testament to the Chinese migrants who flocked to the area to search for gold in the late 1800s. It's the only Chinese temple in Australia built of corrugated iron.

Less than 100m north is Platypus Park (Herberton Rd) where, with luck, you might spot a monotreme along Piebald Creek.

The Crystal Caves (☏07-4091 2365; www.crystalcaves.com.au; 69 Main St; adult/child $23/15; ⊙8.30am-5pm Mon-Fri, to 4pm Sat, 10am-4pm Sun, closed Feb) is a mineralogical museum in an artificial grotto that winds for a block under Atherton's streets. It houses rose-quartz boulders, dazzling blue topaz and assorted fossils. Don a hard hat and check out the pièce de résistance – the world's large amethyst geode, a 3.25m, 2.7-tonne giant excavated from Uruguay.

Perched on Hallorans Hill, Atherton Blue Gum B&B (☏07-4091 5149; www.athertonbluegum.com; 36 Twelfth Ave; d $130-180; ❀❄) has superb views from the verandah. Rooms have pine panelling and big windows, and there's a heated pool and spa.

Barron Valley Hotel (☏07-4091 1222; www.bvhotel.com.au; 53 Main St; s/d without bathroom $40/60, with bathroom $60/75; ❀❈) is a heritage-listed art deco beauty, with tidy rooms and a restaurant (mains $12-30) serving hearty meals, including giant steaks.

Woodlands Tourist Park (☏07-4091 1407; www.woodlandscp.com.au; 141 Herberton Rd; unpowered/powered sites $25/33, cabins $85-130; ❀❄) is a favourite with families thanks to its waterfall pool and playground. It also has refurbished miners-quarters rooms with polished floorboards. It's 1.5km south of the centre.

LAKE TINAROO

Lake Tinaroo is mecca for the Aussie who loves nothing but setting up the tent, opening up the esky and planning for a day's fishing. The enormous artificial lake and dam were originally created for the Barron River hydroelectric power scheme, and drowned trees still poke their bones out of the water. Tinaroo Falls, at the northwestern corner of the lake, is the main settlement.

Barramundi fishing is legendary in the croc-free artificial lake and is permitted year-round. Fishing permits (per week/year $7/35, children free) covering all of Queensland's dams are readily available from local businesses and accommodation places, or order online at Queensland's Department of Primary Industries (www.dpi.qld.gov.au/fishweb). Head out for a fish or simply a sunset cruise with a glass of wine aboard the super-comfy 'floating lounge room' skippered by Lake Tinaroo Cruises (☏0457 033 016; www.laketinaroocruises.com.au; 2hr/half-day/day boat charters $240/380/550). Rates are for the whole boat (up to 12 people).

The Barra Bash fishing competition is held annually at the end of October around the full moon; it's a great event attracting loads of people, but avoid it if you're after a quiet escape.

The Danbulla Forest Drive winds its way through rainforest and softwood plantations along the north side of the lake. It's 28km of unsealed but well-maintained road passing a number of picnic areas and attractions, including pretty Lake Euramoo and the Cathedral Fig – a gigantic strangler fig tree shouldering epiphytes nestling in its branches. The tree is accessed by a boardwalk and signposted along a sealed road off the Gilles Hwy. There are five DERM campgrounds (☏13 74 68; www.derm.qld.gov.au; per person $5.15) in the Danbulla State Forest – Platypus, School Point, Downfall Creek, Kauri Creek and Fong-On Bay. All have water, barbecues and toilets; advance bookings are essential.

In Tinaroo Falls, Discovery Lake Tinaroo Holiday Park (☏07-4095 8232; www.discoveryholidayparks.com.au; 3 Tinaroo Falls Dam Rd; unpowered/powered sites $24/29, cabins $70-140; ❀@❄❈) is a modern, well-equipped and shady camping ground with fuel, a small shop and an on-site cafe (mains $10.50-17). It also rents tinnies ($90 per half-day) and canoes ($10 per hour).

Lake Tinaroo Terraces (☎07-4095 8555; www.laketinarooterraces.com.au; cnr Church & Russell Sts; d $109-160; 🅿🅴) has great-value one- and two-bedroom self-contained lodges (some with air con) in a prime lakefront location.

YUNGABURRA
POP 1200

Only 12km from Atherton is this friendly town, packed with charming cafes, excellent restaurants, day spas and some of the best accommodation in the region. The locals and architecture give this town its quaint village atmosphere, and it's the ideal spot to hang your backpack and establish a base for the surrounding area. Yungaburra Information Centre (☎07-4095 2416; www.yungaburra.com; 16 Cedar St) doles out town and regional info.

The Yungaburra Folk Festival (www.yungaburrafolkfestival.org) is a fabulous weekend-long community event held in late October. It features music, workshops, poetry readings and kids' activities. The Yungaburra Markets (Gillies Hwy; ⊙7am-noon) are held in town on the fourth Saturday of every month; at this time the town is besieged by avid craft and food shoppers. About 3km out of town, the magnificent 500-year-old Curtain Fig is a must-see. Looking like a *Lord of the Rings* prop, it has aerial roots that hang down to create a feathery curtain.

Yungaburra has two **platypus-viewing platforms** on Peterson Creek – one by the bridge on the Gillies Hwy and another at a spot known as Allumbah Pocket (the town's original name) further west. The two are joined by a 2km **walking trail** along the creek, which continues east to Railway Bridge.

On the Wallaby (☎07-4095 2031; www.onthewallaby.com; 34 Eacham Rd; tours $30) run excellent half-day bike and canoe tours – including wildlife spotting while night canoeing. Nonguests are welcome. Tableland Adventure Guides (☎0448 517 979; www.tablelandadventureguides.com.au; half-day tours from $95) runs guided bike tours along tracks and rail trails, kayaking on Lake Tinaroo and hiking in World Heritage rainforest.

🛏 Sleeping

TOP CHOICE On the Wallaby   HOSTEL $
(☎07-4095 2031; www.onthewallaby.com; 34 Eacham Rd; camping $10, dm/d $24/55; @) Some hostels just feel like home and this one does, with handmade timber furniture and mosaics, and spotless rooms (without TV).

Nature-based tours depart daily; tour packages and transfers ($30 one way) are available from Cairns.

Williams Lodge   B&B $$$
(☎07-4095 3449; www.williamslodge.com; Cedar St; d $180-285; 🅷@🅰🅴) Built in 1911 and still owned and run by the Williams family, all of the rooms at this heritage Queenslander open onto the verandah, including enormous suites fitted with original period furniture and four-poster beds (some with spa baths). Grand touches include a pianola lounge, a wine bar and a billiard table. Under 12s aren't allowed.

Eden House Retreat & Mountain
Spa   BOUTIQUE HOTEL $$$
(☎07-4089 7000; www.edenhouse.com.au; 20 Gillies Hwy; d $180-295; 🅷@🅰🅴) Amid the gardens behind this historic 1912 homestead in the village centre are romantic cottages with large spa baths and raised beds, and family-oriented villas. Nonguests can book into the full-service day spa and highly regarded restaurant (mains $26.50-33.50; ⊙dinner Tue-Sat).

Foxwell Park   B&B $$$
(☎07-4096 6183; www.foxwellpark.com.au; Foxwell Rd; d/ste $200/250; @🅰) In rolling countryside 7km southwest of Yungaburra, Foxwell's beautifully restored pair of century-old timber buildings have original tiles and pressed-tin ceilings. Suites open onto deep, private verandahs overlooking the 24-hectare estate. Excellent French-inspired restaurant (mains $25-35; ⊙dinner Wed-Sun, nightly for guests).

Mt Quincan Crater Retreat   CABINS $$$
(☎07-4095 2255; www.mtquincan.com.au; Peeramon Rd; d $245-350; 🅰) In secluded rainforest, these luxurious pole cabins and tree houses have been built for sheer countryside indulgence, with double spas, indoor and outdoor showers, wood fires and stupendous views. Children aren't permitted. It's 3km south of town; follow the road to Peeramon to the signposted turn-off.

Lake Eacham Hotel   PUB $
(☎07-4095 3515; www.yungaburrapub.com.au; 6-8 Kehoe Pl; d $55-85) Better known as the 'Yungaburra Pub', the downstairs dining room (mains $17.50-29.50; ⊙lunch & dinner) and the swirling wooden staircase of this grand old hotel are inspirational, the circular pool table unconventional and the rooms basic but functional.

Kookaburra Lodge
MOTEL $

(☑07-4095 3222; www.kookaburra-lodge.com; cnr Oak St & Eacham Rd; s/d $80/90; ❄) Stylish little rooms opening out to an inviting barbecue patio amid tropical gardens.

Gumtree on Gillies
B&B $$

(☑07-4095 3105; www.gumtreeongillies.com.au; Gillies Hwy; d incl breakfast $175; ❄) Individually themed cabins have open fireplaces, spa baths and king-size beds.

✗ Eating

TOP CHOICE Flynn's
MEDITERRANEAN $$

(☑07-4095 2235; 17 Eacham Rd; mains $27-29, 3-course menus $45; ☉lunch Sun, dinner Fri-Tue) Between ducking outside to pick his own vegies and running the whole place almost single-handedly, Kiwi culinary maestro Liam has managed to put Yungaburra on the foodie map. The menu changes daily, but expect dishes like duck liver cognac pâté and fish of the day, along with a superb wine list. Book ahead.

Nick's Restaurant
SWISS-ITALIAN $$

(☑07-4095 3330; www.nicksrestaurant.com.au; 33 Gillies Hwy; mains $16.50-22.50; ☉lunch Fri-Sun, dinner Tue-Sun) This Swiss chalet-style number makes for a fun night out, with costumed staff, beer steins, a piano-accordion serenade and possibly some impromptu yodelling. Food spans schnitzels to smoked pork loin with sauerkraut, plus several vegetarian options.

Whistlestop Cafe
CAFE $

(cnr Cedar St & Gillies Hwy; mains $8.50-14; ☉7.30am-5pm Wed-Mon; ☑) This garden-set cafe serves healthy rice slices and vegie lasagne, but the real attraction is the souffle-style Tuscany chocolate cake.

CRATER LAKES NATIONAL PARK & AROUND

Part of the Wet Tropics World Heritage Area, the two mirror-like crater lakes of Lake Eacham and Lake Barrine are both croc-free and nestled among rainforest. Walking tracks fringe the lakes, which are easily reached by sealed roads off the Gillies Hwy. Camping is not permitted.

The larger of the two lakes, Lake Barrine is cloaked in thick old-growth rainforest; a 5km walking track around its edge takes about 1½ hours. The Lake Barrine Rainforest Tea House (☑07-4095 3847; www.lakebarrine.com.au; Gillies Hwy; mains $7.50-16.50; ☉breakfast & lunch) sits out over the lakefront. Upstairs

you'll feel like you're aboard a boat as you take Devonshire tea or order a meal. To actually be aboard a boat, visit the booking desk downstairs for 45-minute lake cruises (adult/child $16/8; ☉4pm daily). The tea house also rents out a lakeside, self-contained cottage (d incl breakfast & cruise $140).

A 100m stroll away are two enormous, neck-tilting, 1000-year-old kauri pines.

The crystal-clear waters of Lake Eacham are ideal for swimming and spotting turtles; there are sheltered lakeside picnic areas, a swimming pontoon and a boat ramp. The 3km lake-circuit track is an easy walk and takes less than an hour. Stop in at the Rainforest Display Centre (McLeish Rd; ☉9am-1pm Mon, Wed & Fri) at the ranger station for information on the area.

Crater Lakes Rainforest Cottages (☑07-4095 2322; www.craterlakes.com.au; Eacham Cl; d $230; ❄@) has four individually themed timber cottages. Ideally spaced in its own private patch of rainforest, each is a romantic hideaway filled with candles, fresh flowers, and logs for the wood stoves, with spa baths, fully fitted kitchens and breakfast hampers with bacon, eggs and chocolates, plus fruit to feed the birds. Unlike many places around here, there's no minimum stay, but you probably won't want to leave. The cottages are off Lakes Dr.

Rose Gums (☑07-4096 8360; www.rosegums.com.au; Land Rd, Butcher's Creek; d from $286) offers totally private, eco-friendly treetop pads that are fitted out with spas, wood-burning heaters and king-size beds. All come with breakfast hampers, kitchens and barbecues, but you can also dine on Mediterranean cuisine at the on-site restaurant (mains $30-35; ☉dinner; ☑). Minimum stay is two nights.

Lake Eacham Caravan Park (☑07-4095 3730; www.lakeeachamtouristpark.com; Lakes Dr; unpowered/powered sites $19/22, cabins $90-110; @), 1km down the Malanda road from Lake Eacham, is a pretty camping ground with cosy cabins.

MALANDA
POP 1900

Forming the eastern part of the Atherton–Yungaburra–Malanda triangle is this little town 15km south of Lake Eacham. Its claim to fame is that it has the nation's longest continually running picture theatre, the Majestic (established 1927), but locals are still mightily proud that Australian cricketer Don Bradman played cricket here.

Guided rainforest walks (per person $15) led by members of the Ngadjonji community can be organised through Malanda's visitor centre (07-4096 6957; www.malandafalls.com). A new centre is currently being built next to the falls after a fire destroyed the previous building; in the meantime, it's housed at the Malanda Dairy Centre (8 James St). The dairy centre offers 40-minute factory tours (adult/child $11/7; 10am & 11am Mon-Fri), including a cheese platter or milkshake. Its licensed cafe (mains $12-18;) is the best place to eat in town.

Along the Atherton road, on the outskirts of town, are Malanda Falls, home to saw-shelled turtles and red-legged pademelons. On the Millaa Millaa Rd, 10km from Malanda, is the tiny village of Tarzali, which offers some accommodation options. Aquaculture farm Tarzali Lakes Fishing Park (www.tarzali lakes.com; Millaa Millaa Rd, Tarzali; fishing adult/child from $18/12, unpowered sites per person $10; 10am-5pm Thu-Tue) has several artificial lakes stocked with jade perch and barramundi; you can fish or just buy your 'catch' at the on-site smokehouse. There's plenty of bird life here, plus platypus-spotting tours (adult/child $10/5; 2pm & 3.30pm).

Quality B&B accommodation is tucked away in the forests and farms around Malanda. The superbly designed all-timber pole houses of the Canopy (07-4096 5364; www.canopytreehouses.com.au; Hogan Rd, Tarzali, via Malanda; d $227-339;) are set amid a pristine patch of old-growth rainforest. There's a minimum two-night stay.

Surrounded by forest on the Johnstone River, Rivers Edge Rainforest Retreat (07-4095 2369; www.riversedgeretreat.com.au; d from $298;) has two secluded luxury timber lodges with lavish touches like a sliding-glass wall in the spa bathroom and a wood fire. Minimum two-night stay.

Enveloped in foliage, Lumholtz Lodge (07-4095 0292; www.lumholtzlodge.com.au; Upper Barron Rd; d incl breakfast $180, incl full board $300;) is a prime spot to watch the surrounding wildlife. Travellers Rest (07-4096 6077; www.travrest.com.au; Millaa Millaa Rd, Tarzali; s/d without bathroom incl breakfast $50/90), an English-style country farmhouse 5km south of Malanda, is a cosy budget place with a billiard room, a formal dining room and fresh, floral rooms. Book ahead for Saturday's murder-mystery nights. Right next to Malanda Falls, Malanda Falls Caravan Park (07-4096 5314; www.malandafalls.com.

au; 38 Park Ave; unpowered/powered sites $16/22, cabins $75-85) has tidy cabins and campsites within earshot of the flowing falls.

MILLAA MILLAA & THE WATERFALL CIRCUIT

Give up any thoughts of 'seen one waterfall seen them all' and take on this 16km 'waterfall circuit' near Millaa Millaa, 24km south of Malanda. Enter the circuit by taking Theresa Creek Rd, 1km east of Millaa Millaa on Palmerston Hwy. Millaa Millaa Falls, the largest, has a swimming hole, change rooms and a grassy picnic spot. Continuing round the circuit, you reach Zillie Falls, where you can watch Teresa Creek falling into the abyss. Step down past fern fronds to the rocky Ellinjaa Falls before returning to the Palmerston Hwy just 2.5km out of Millaa Millaa. A further 5.5km down the Palmerston Hwy there's a turn-off to Mungalli Falls, 5km off the highway.

At the country-style Mungalli Creek Dairy (07-4097 2232; www.mungallicreekdairy. com.au; 251 Brooks Rd; meals $16-18; 10am-4pm, closed Feb), 3km off Palmerston Hwy, you can sample cheeses and creamy yogurts or order cooked dishes like three-cheese pie followed by a sinfully rich Sicilian cheesecake.

A little further along the Palmerston Hwy is the Mamu Rainforest Canopy Walkway (p413).

For a hands-on farmstay experience, try Acton Ridge Farmstay (07-4097 2293; www.actonridgefarmstay.com; 122 Nash Rd; r adult/child without bathroom $125/60), a 162-hectare working farm welcoming guests. The bedrooms are inside the homestead-style house. Rates include breakfast and dinner.

The smell of fresh baking tempts you inside the historic Falls Teahouse (07-4097 2237; www.fallsteahouse.com.au; Palmerston Hwy; s/d $65/110, meals $7-16; 10am-5pm). In the country-style kitchen, Ray cooks dishes like pan-fried barra and pies with local beef. Sit next to the pot-belly stove, or on the back verandah overlooking rolling farmland. The three guest rooms are individually decorated with period furniture. It's at the intersection of the Millaa Millaa Falls turn-off.

HERBERTON
POP 1000

Herberton is a lovely town dotted with jacaranda trees and perched on a hilly area abutting the outback. Wonderful heritage buildings line the main street, which leads to the riverside site of a former tin mine.

Herberton's star attraction is the **Herberton Historic Village** (www.herbertonhistoricvillage.com.au; 6 Broadway; adult/child $24/12; ⊙9am-5pm), a collection of 50 original buildings dating back as far as 1870 that have been moved here from various locales, restored and filled with some fascinating historic exhibits. Highlights include a pub, a blacksmith's workshop, Ada's frock salon, a school house and a grocery store.

On the site of an old tin mine, the **Herberton Mining Museum & Information Centre** (☑07-4096 3473; www.herbertonvisitorcentre.com.au; Great Northern Mining Centre, 1 Jacks Rd; museum adult/child $5/3; ⊙9am-4pm) has an informative display on the region's mining history and geology, including a gallery of minerals. It's the starting point for a number of **historic walking trails** (from 1km to 12km) and stocks trail maps.

Accommodation is limited; try Herberton's original post office, which is now the **Herberton Heritage Cottage B&B** (☑0427 962 670; 2 Perkins St; s/d $100/130; ❋). Heritage-style rooms incorporate mod cons like spas and DVD players.

MT HYPIPAMEE NATIONAL PARK

Between Atherton and Ravenshoe, the Kennedy Hwy passes the eerie, and hard to pronounce, **Mt Hypipamee crater**, which could be a scene from a sci-fi film and certainly adds some vertigo to the itinerary. It's a scenic 700m (return) walk from the picnic area, past **Dinner Falls**, to this narrow, 138m-deep crater with its moody-looking lake far below.

RAVENSHOE
POP 910

Ravenshoe (pronounced *hoe*, not *shoe*) is home to 'Queensland's Highest Pub': **Hotel Tully Falls** stands proudly at the tip of this town at the grand altitude of 930m. **Ravenshoe Visitor Centre** (☑07-4097 7700; www.ravenshoevisitorcentre.com.au; 24 Moore St) has helpful staff and is home to the **Nganyaji Interpretive Centre**, which explains the Jirrbal people's traditional lifestyle.

Nearby waterfalls (no swimming) include **Little Millstream Falls**, 3km south of Ravenshoe, and **Tully Falls**, around 20km further south on the Tully Falls Rd (which doesn't go through to Tully). The 13m-high **Millstream Falls** (signposted off the Savannah Way towards Innot Hot Springs, from where it's 1km to the car park) are said to be the widest in Australia in flood.

Train enthusiasts and kids will love a ride on the restored steam train *Capella* with the **Ravenswood Railway Co** (☑07-4097 6005; www.ravenshoesteamrail.com.au; Grigg St; adult/child $20/10; ⊙departs 1.30pm Sun), which chugs 7km north to Tumoulin and back.

🌿**Possum Valley B&B** (☑07-4097 8177; www.bnbnq.com.au/possumvalley; Evelyn Central, via Ravenshoe; s/d $60/75), off the Kennedy Hwy, down a 4.5km unsealed road, consists of two cottages clinging to the fringe of World Heritage–listed rainforest. The B&B uses solar and hydroelectricity and tank water.

PORT DOUGLAS TO COOKTOWN

Port Douglas
POP 3000

Port Douglas (or just 'Port') is the flashy playground of tropical northern Queensland. For those looking to escape Cairns' bustling traveller scene, Port Douglas is more sophisticated and more intimate. It also has a beautiful white-sand beach right on its doorstep, and the Great Barrier Reef is less than an hour offshore.

Accommodation options are spread all over the region, and the larger resorts spread themselves along the 6km-long Port Douglas Rd that links Captain Cook Hwy with the town centre. Busy, centre-of-town Macrossan St links the jetty and pier with Four Mile Beach on Trinity Bay.

☉ Sights & Activities

On a sunny, calm day, Four Mile Beach will take your breath away; it is sand and palm trees for as far as you can see (head up to **Flagstaff Hill Lookout** for a great view).

At the Cooktown Hwy turnoff, **Wildlife Habitat Port Douglas** (☑07-4099 3235; www.wildlifehabitat.com.au; Port Douglas Rd; adult/child $30/15; ⊙8am-5pm) endeavours to keep and showcase native animals in enclosures that closely mimic their natural environment. It's home to koalas, cassowaries, black-necked storks, crocs, tree kangaroos and other species. For a wildlife-enriched meal, have **Breakfast with the Birds** (adult/child breakfast incl admission $44/22; ⊙8-10.30am) or **Lunch with the Lorikeets** ($44/22; ⊙noon-2pm). It's located at the entrance to Port

Douglas, off Captain Cook Hwy, about 6km from the town centre.

On Sunday the grassy foreshore of Anzac Park spills over with the **Port Douglas Markets** (end of Macrossan St; ⊘8am-1.30pm Sun). You'll find stalls selling arts, crafts and jewellery, locally produced tropical fruits, ice creams and coconut milk, and hot-food stalls.

The **Port Douglas Yacht Club** (www.portdouglasyachtclub.com.au; Spinnaker Cl) offers free sailing with club members every Wednesday afternoon. It's a great way to get out on the water and meet some locals.

Port Douglas Boat Hire (☑07-4099 6277; Berth C1, Marina Mirage) rents a range of boats, including dinghies ($31 per hour) and canopied, family-friendly pontoon boats ($41 per hour) to take on the inlet. Fishing gear available.

Several companies offer PADI open-water certification as well as advanced dive certificates, including **Reef Dive School** (☑07-4099 6980; www.reefdiveschool.com; 4- to 5-day open-water courses from $550). For one-on-one instruction, learn with **Tech Dive Academy** (☑07-4099 6880; www.tech-dive-academy.com; 4-day open-water courses from $1390, additional person $590).

Worth a peek inside, the white timber church **St Mary's by the Sea** (6 Dixie St) was built in 1911 and relocated to its seaside position in 1989.

Wind Swell (☑0427 498 042; www.windswell.com.au; from $100) offers kite surfing for everyone from beginners to high flyers.

☞ Tours

The unrelenting surge of visitors to the reef off Port Douglas has impacted on its general condition, and although you'll still see colourful corals and marine life, it has become patchy in parts. Tours typically make two to three stops on the outer and ribbon reefs, including St Crispins, Agincourt, Chinaman and Tongue Reefs. Reef trips generally include reef tax, snorkelling and transfers from your accommodation, plus lunch and refreshments. Add around $250 for an introductory dive. Certified divers will pay around $250 for two dives with all gear included.

Several operators offer cruises to Low Isles, a small coral cay surrounded by a lagoon and topped by a lighthouse. The cay offers good snorkelling and the chance to see turtle-nesting grounds. Trips leave from Marina Mirage.

There are numerous outfits running day trips to Cape Tribulation, some via Mossman Gorge. Many of the tours out of Cairns also do pick-ups from Port Douglas.

Aquarius REEF
(☑07-4099 6999; www.portdouglascruises.com; trips $231) Guided island walks and snorkelling only, with glass-bottom-boat trips. Maximum 23 passengers; not suitable for kids under 14.

Aristocat REEF
(☑07-4099 4727; www.aristocat.com.au; adult/child $195.50/135.50) Fast cat to three sites. Maximum 45 passengers.

BTS Tours DAY TRIPS, SIGHTSEEING
(☑07-4099 5665; www.btstours.com.au; adult/child $154/110) Tours to the Daintree Rainforest and Cape Trib, including canoeing.

Calypso REEF
(☑07-4099 6999; www.calypsocharters.com.au; adult/child $195.50/140.50) Large catamaran visiting three outer reefs.

Fishing Norseman FISHING
(☑07-4099 6668; www.mvnorseman.com.au; Closehaven Marina; day tours adult/child $195/175) Private charters also available.

Fishing Port Douglas FISHING
(☑07-4099 4058; www.fishingportdouglas.com.au) Fishing on the river and reef (from share/sole charter per day $225/3200).

Haba REEF
(☑07-4098 5000; www.habadive.com.au; Marina Mirage; adult/child $180.50/104.50) Long-standing, well-regarded local dive company; 25-minute glass-bottom-boat tours ($16/8 per adult/child) available.

Poseidon REEF
(☑07-4099 4772; www.poseidon-cruises.com.au; adult/child $195.50/135.50) Friendly family-owned and -operated luxury catamaran with trips to Agincourt Reef.

Quicksilver REEF
(☑07-4087 2100; www.quicksilver-cruises.com; adult/child $204.40/105) Major operator with fast cruises to Agincourt Reef. Offers helmet dives ($142), plus scenic helicopter flights from the pontoon on the reef ($148, minimum two passengers).

Reef & Rainforest Connections DAY TRIPS, SIGHTSEEING
(☑07-4099 5333; www.reefandrainforest.com.au; adult/child from $163/105) A range of day-long ecotours, including Cape Trib and Bloomfield Falls, Kuranda and Mossman Gorge.

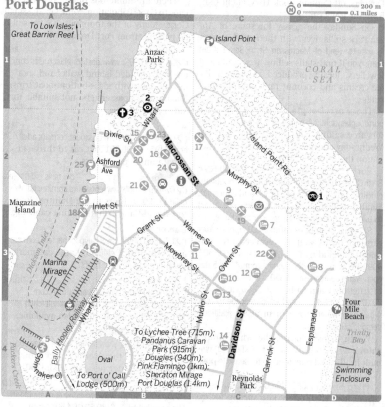

Port Douglas

⊚ Sights

1 Flagstaff Hill Lookout D2
2 Port Douglas Markets B1
3 St Mary's By the Sea B2

⊙ Activities, Courses & Tours

4 Port Douglas Boat Hire A3
5 Port Douglas Yacht Club A4
6 Reef Sprinter A2

⊜ Sleeping

7 Accommodation Port Douglas C3
8 By the Sea Port Douglas D3
9 Global Backpackers C2
10 Hibiscus Gardens C3
11 ParrotFish Lodge C3
12 Port Douglas Motel C3
13 Port Douglas Retreat C3
14 Tropic Sands C4

⊗ Eating

15 2 Fish B2
16 Coles Supermarket B2
17 Nautilus C2
18 On the Inlet A3
19 Re:hab C3
20 Salsa Bar & Grill B2
21 Seafood House B2
22 Zinc C3

⊜ Drinking

23 Court House Hotel B2
24 Iron Bar B2
Port Douglas Yacht Club .... (see 5)
25 Tin Shed A2

Reef Sprinter
REEF

(☑07-4099 3175; www.reefsprinter.com.au; adult/ child $100/80) Superfast 15-minute trip to the Low Isles for speed snorkelling (and no seasickness!).

Sail Tallarook
REEF

(☑07-4099 4990; www.sailtallarook.com.au; adult/child $110/85) Historic 90ft yacht sailing to Tongue Reef. Sunset cruises ($50) include cheese platters; BYO drinks. Introductory dives available.

Sailaway
SAILING

(☑07-4099 4772; www.sailawayportdouglas.com; adult/child $191/121) Popular sailing and snorkelling trip (maximum 27 passengers) to the Low Isles that's great for families. Also offers 90-minute twilight sails ($50 Monday to Friday) off the Port Douglas coast.

Silversonic
REEF

(☑07-4087 2100; www.silverseries.com.au; adult/ child $180.50/129.50) Smooth trips out to Agincourt Reef.

Synergy
REEF

(☑07-4084 2800; www.synergyreef.com.au; adult/child $270/200) With a maximum of just 12 passengers, the *Synergy* sails to the outer reefs. Snorkelling only (no diving).

Tropical Fishing & Eco Tours
FISHING, WILDLIFE

(☑07-4099 4272; www.fishingecotours.com) Half-day fishing trips from $90; wildlife-spotting inlet tours from $30.

Wavelength
REEF

(☑07-4099 5031; www.wavelength.com.au; adult/ child $200/150) Outer reef snorkelling (only) at three sites with a marine biologist. Maximum 30 passengers.

🛏 Sleeping

Port Douglas is swimming in accommodation, most of it in self-contained apartments, or upmarket resorts just out of town. **Accommodation Port Douglas** (☑1800 079 030, 07-4099 5355; www.accomportdouglas.com. au; 1/48 Macrossan St; ☉9am-5pm Mon-Sat) is a useful agent for holiday rentals.

TOP CHOICE Pink Flamingo
BOUTIQUE RESORT $$

(☑07-4099 6622; www.pinkflamingo.com.au; 115 Davidson St; r $125-195; ❋@🛜🌊) Flamboyant fuchsia-, purple- and orange-painted rooms opening to private walled courtyards (with hammocks, outdoor baths and outdoor

showers) and a groovy mirror-balled alfresco bar make the Pink Flamingo Port Douglas' hippest digs. Outdoor movie nights screen under the palms; tone your abs in the gym or rent a bike for a spin around town. Gay-owned, gay-friendly and all-welcoming (except for kids).

Hibiscus Gardens
RESORT $$$

(☑1800 995 995; www.hibiscusportdouglas.com. au; 22 Owen St; d from $205; ❋@🛜🌊) Balinese influences of teak furnishings and fixtures, bi-fold doors and plantation shutters – as well as the occasional Buddha – give this stylish resort an exotic ambience. The in-house day spa, specialising in Indigenous healing techniques and products, has a local reputation as the best of the many places to be pampered in town.

Dougies
HOSTEL $

(☑1800 996 200; www.dougies.com.au; 111 Davidson St; tent sites per person $12, dm $26, safari tents $23, d $75; ❋@🛜🌊) At this laid-way-back hostel, it's easy to hang about the sprawling grounds in a hammock by day and move to the bar at night. If you do decide to leave the premises for a bit, rent bikes and/or fishing gear from the reception area, which also stocks groceries. Free pick-up from Cairns on Monday, Wednesday and Saturday.

Sheraton Mirage Port Douglas
RESORT $$$

(☑07-4099 5888; www.starwoodhotels.com; Davidson St; d from $329; ❋@🛜🌊) Not to be confused with the separately located Marina Mirage, Port Douglas' original luxury resort is surrounded by two hectares of swimmable lagoons. There's no doubt it's past its prime, but it still has its own beachfront, golf course, child-care facilities, a shuttle service into town, tennis courts and a gym.

Sea Temple Resort & Spa
RESORT $$$

(☑1800 833 762; www.mirvachotels.com.au; Mitre St; d from $309; ❋@🛜🌊) Port Douglas' most luxurious five-star and its championship links golf course are set in lush tropical gardens near the southern end of Four Mile Beach. Rooms range from spa studios to the opulent 'swim out' penthouse with direct access to the enormous lagoon pool.

Global Backpackers
HOSTEL $

(☑1800 682 647; www.globalportdouglas.com.au; 38 Macrossan St; dm $27-32, d $80; ❋@🛜) Port's most central hostel doesn't have a pool, but it's bang in the middle of Macrossan St above the Rattle n Hum restaurant-bar. Rooms are

decked out in sleek dark-brown tones, doubles all have bathroom, and the kitchen and common room open onto a big balcony.

By the Sea Port Douglas
APARTMENTS $$

(☑07-4099 5387; www.bytheseaportdouglas.com.au; 72 Macrossan St; d from $175; ❀@🅰🏊) Close to the beach and town centre, the 12 self-contained rooms here are spread over three levels – the upper rooms have 'filtered' views through the palm trees to the beach. Refitted rooms have neutral tones livened up with bright splashes of colour.

Pandanus Caravan Park
CARAVAN PARK $

(☑07-4099 5944; Davidson St; unpowered/powered sites $30/35, cabins with/without bathroom $95/72; ❀@🅰🏊) Five minutes' stroll from the beach, this large, shady park has a good range of cabins and free gas barbecues.

Port Douglas Motel
MOTEL $

(☑07-4099 5248; www.portdouglasmotel.com; 9 Davidson St; d $96; ❀🏊) No views but bright rooms and a great location.

ParrotFish Lodge
HOSTEL $

(☑1800 995011; www.parrotfishlodge.com; 37-39 Warner St; dm $25-33, d with/without bathroom $95/85; ❀@🏊) Energetic backpackers place with extreme beach decor and lots of freebies, including pick-ups from Cairns.

Lychee Tree
APARTMENTS $$

(☑07-4099 5811; www.lychee-tree.com.au; 95 Davidson St; 1-/2-bed apt $155/180; ❀🏊) Family-friendly single-storey, self-contained apartments with full laundries. Minimum two-night stay.

Port o' Call Lodge
HOSTEL $

(☑07-4099 5422; www.portocall.com.au; cnr Port St & Craven Cl; dm $35, d $99-119; ❀@🅰🏊) Low-key solar- and wind-powered, YHA-associated hostel with a good-value bistro.

Port Douglas Retreat
APARTMENTS $$

(☑07-4099 5053; www.portdouglasretreat.com.au; 31-33 Mowbray St; d $149-179; ❀🅰🏊) Recline on a sun lounge on the wide wooden decking that surrounds the palm-lined swimming pool at this traditional Queenslander-style complex of 36 apartments.

Tropic Sands
APARTMENTS $$

(☑07-4099 4533; www.tropicsands.com.au; 21 Davidson St; d from $175; ❀@🏊) Handsome open-plan rooms in a beautiful white, colonial-style building. From your private balcony you can catch a whiff of the sea or whatever's cooking in your fully equipped kitchen. No children.

✖ Eating

Duck down tiny Grant St for juice bars, pie shops, pizzerias and more.

Beach Shack
MODERN AUSTRALIAN $$

(☑07-4099 1100; www.the-beach-shack.com.au; 29 Barrier St, Four Mile Beach; mains $21-29.50; ⊙dinner; ☑) There'd be an outcry if this locals' favourite took its macadamia-crumbed eggplant (with grilled and roast vegies, goat's cheese and wild rocket) off the menu. But it's the setting that makes it really worth heading to the southern end of Four Mile Beach: a lantern-lit garden with sand underfoot. Good reef fish, sirloins and blackboard specials, too.

Zinc
MODERN AUSTRALIAN $$

(☑07-4099 6260; www.zincportdouglas.com; 53-61 Macrossan St; mains $25-34; ⊙7am-midnight) Over 70 wines (40 by the glass) and 110 spirits and liqueurs set Zinc apart from its neighbours – as do dishes like pan-seared bugs with apple- and vanilla-scented sweet-potato puree and candied cashews. Don't leave without checking out the floor-to-ceiling, fish-filled aquarium in the bathrooms!

On the Inlet
SEAFOOD $$

(☑07-4099 5255; www.portdouglasseafood.com; 3 Inlet St; mains $22-39.50; ⊙lunch & dinner) At this restaurant jutting out over Dickson Inlet, tables spread out along a huge deck where you can await the 5pm arrival of George the grouper, who comes to feed most days. Take up the bucket-of-prawns-and-a-drink deal for $18 from 3.30pm to 5.30pm, or choose your own crayfish and mud crabs from the live tank. Great service, cool atmosphere.

Nautilus
MODERN AUSTRALIAN $$$

(☑07-4099 5330; www.nautilus-restaurant.com.au; 17 Murphy St; mains $32.50-52.50; ⊙dinner) A hidden pathway leads through tropical gardens to intimate white-clothed tables amid tall palms at this decades-old fine-dining institution. Seafood is a speciality, such as wok-tossed mud crab with kaffir lime and lemongrass laksa. The pièce de résistance is the six-course chef's tasting menu ($110; $160 with paired wines). Children under eight aren't accepted.

Re:hab
CAFE, GALLERY $

(www.beijaflordesign.com.au; 7/42 Macrossan St; ⊙8am-6pm; @🅰) Coffee is literally an art form at this chilled cafe–local art gallery, with astoundingly intricate designs etched in the froth of its fresh-roasted brews.

Home-baked cakes, muffins and slices, and a Zen little courtyard out back.

2 Fish
SEAFOOD $$$

(☑07-4099 6350; www.2fishrestaurant.com.au; 7/20 Wharf St; mains $25-39; ⊘lunch & dinner) 2 Fish spreads a seafood extravaganza: more than 15 types of fish, from coral trout to red emperor and wild barramundi, are prepared in a variety of innovative ways, or go for the decadent seafood platter for two ($130).

Salsa Bar & Grill
MODERN AUSTRALIAN $$

(☑07-4099 4922; www.salsaportdouglas.com.au; 26 Wharf St; mains $17.50-30.50; ⊘lunch & dinner; ☑) In a white Queenslander, Salsa is a stayer on Port's often fickle scene. Try the Cajun jambalaya (rice with prawns, yabbies, crocodile and smoked chicken) or the gingerbread-dusted kangaroo with polenta.

Four Mile Seafood & Takeaway
SEAFOOD, BURGERS $

(Four Mile Beach Plaza, Barrier St, Four Mile Beach; dishes $5.50-14; ⊘9am-8pm Mon-Sat, 11am-8pm Sun) Whips up tasty burgers as well as combos like fresh coral trout with avocado.

Self-Catering

Stock up on supplies at the large Coles Supermarket (11 Macrossan St) in the Port Village shopping centre. For locally caught seafood, including prawns, mud crabs and a big range of fish, head to Seafood House (11 Warner St; ⊘9am-6pm).

▼ Drinking

Drinking and dining go hand in hand in Port Douglas. Even before the cutlery is packed away, many restaurants become inviting places for a drink.

TOP CHOICE Tin Shed
LICENSED CLUB

(www.thetinshed-portdouglas.com.au; 7 Ashford Ave) Port Douglas' Combined Services Club is a locals' secret. This is a rare find: bargain dining on the waterfront, and even the drinks are cheap. Sign in, line up and grab a table on the river- or shore-fronting deck.

Iron Bar
PUB

(5 Macrossan St) A bit of whacky outbackshearing-shed decor never goes astray in Queensland. It's well done – all rustic iron and ageing timber; even the outdoor furniture is old wood and hessian. After polishing off your Don Bradman eye fillet (the steaks are named after famous Aussies), head up-

stairs for a flutter on the cane-toad races ($5). Usually the latest closer in town.

Court House Hotel
PUB

(www.at-the-courty.com; cnr Macrossan & Wharf Sts; mains $15-25; ⊘lunch & dinner) Commanding a prime corner location, the 'Courty' is a lively local, with cover bands on weekends.

Port Douglas Yacht Club
LICENSED CLUB

(www.portdouglasyachtclub.com.au; Spinnaker Cl) Another local favourite, with a spirited nautical atmosphere. Inexpensive meals are served nightly.

❶ Information

The **Port Douglas Tourist Information Centre** (☑07-4099 5599; www.tourismportdouglas.com.au; 23 Macrossan St; ⊘8am-6.30pm) has maps and makes tour bookings.

❶ Getting There & Away

For more information on getting to Cairns, see p426.

Coral Reef Coaches (☑07-4098 2800; www.coralreefcoaches.com.au) connects Port Douglas with Cairns ($36, 1¼ hours) via Cairns airport and Palm Cove.

Sun Palm (☑07-4087 2900; www.sunpalmtransport.com) has frequent daily services between Port Douglas and Cairns ($35, 1½ hours) via the northern beaches and the airport, and up the coast to Mossman ($10, 20 minutes), Daintree Village and the ferry ($20, one hour), and Cape Tribulation ($48, three hours).

Airport Connections (☑07-4099 5950; www.tnqshuttle.com; ⊘3.20am-5.20pm) runs a shuttle-bus service ($36, hourly) between Port Douglas, Cairns' northern beaches and Cairns Airport, continuing on to Cairns CBD.

Country Road Coachlines (☑07-4069 5446; www.countryroadcoachlines.com.au) has a bus service between Port Douglas and Cooktown on the coastal route via Cape Tribulation three times a week ($63), weather permitting.

❶ Getting Around

Bicycle

Port Douglas Bike Hire (☑07-4099 5799; www.portdouglasbikehire; cnr Wharf & Warner Sts; per day $19)

Bus

Sun Palm (☑07-4087 2900; www.sunpalmtransport.com; ⊘7am-midnight) runs in a continuous loop every half-hour from Wildlife Habitat Port Douglas to the Marina Mirage, stopping regularly en route. Flag down the driver at marked bus stops.

Car & Motorcycle

Port Douglas has plenty of small, local car-hire companies as well as major international chains. It's just about the last place before Cooktown where you can hire a 4WD. Expect to pay around $65 a day for a small car and $130 a day for a 4WD, plus insurance.

Latitude 16 (☑07-4099 4999; www.latitude16. com.au; 54 Macrossan St) Also rents open-sided Mokes (per day from $49).

Thrifty (☑07-4099 5555; www.thrifty.com.au; 50 Macrossan St)

Taxi

Port Douglas Taxis (☑13 10 08) offers 24-hour service and has a rank on Warner St.

Mossman

POP 1800

Mossman is an unassuming town criss-crossed with cane-train tracks and featuring the wonderful **Mossman Gorge**, which draws in tourists by the van-load. There's a great 2.4km walk there, and swimming is possible, but be aware of the danger of swimming after heavy rain. It's Mt Demi that you see in the town's background, and the almost century-old rain trees, behind the rail tracks, are worth tracking down.

To truly appreciate the gorge's cultural significance, book one of the 1½-hour Indigenous-guided **Kuku-Yalanji Dreamtime Walks** (adult/child $38.50/22; ⊙9am, 11am, 1pm & 3pm Mon-Fri) through the cultural and visitor centre, **Mossman Gorge Gateway** (☑07-4098 2595; www.yalanji.com.au; ⊙8.30am-5pm Mon-Fri).

The Aboriginal-run **Janbal Gallery** (☑07-4099 5599; www.janbalgallery.com.au; 5 Johnston Rd; ⊙Tue-Sat or by appointment) is a great place to browse or buy impressive artwork.

The rooms at **Mossman Gorge B&B** (☑07-4098 2497; www.bnbnq.com.au/mossgorge; lot 15, Gorge View Cres; s/d from $125/145) have dark timber floors, feature walls and antiques. The guest spaces are wonderful, and the views and bird life are mesmerising.

Breakfast, consisting of muffins, croissants and fruit, is included.

Run by a talented French-Australian team, **Mojo's** (☑07-4098 1202; www.mojosbarandgrill.com.au; 41 Front St; mains $24-29; ⊙lunch Mon-Fri, dinner Mon-Sat; ☑) serves exquisite fusion fare like feather-light gnocchi with blue cheese and caramelised pear, spicy samosas with tamarind chutney, soft-shell prawn tacos, and a divine scallop pie.

Raintrees Café (1 Front St; dishes $10; ⊙breakfast & lunch) cooks up chicken, chips and burgers daily.

❶ Information

DERM (☑07-4098 2188; www.derm.qld.gov.au; Centenary Bldg, 1 Front St; ⊙8am-4pm Mon-Fri) has information on the Daintree National Park up to and beyond Cape Tribulation.

❶ Getting There & Away

Sun Palm (☑07-4087 2900; www.sunpalm transport.com) has three daily buses between Mossman and Cairns ($70, 1¾ hours) via Cairns airport, and Port Douglas ($10, 20 minutes), on its run to Cape Trib.

Daintree Village

POP 100

Surprisingly, given its tropical-rainforest surrounds, **Daintree Village** is not tree-covered; cattle farms operate in large clearings next to the Daintree River. Most folk come here to see crocodiles, and there are several small operators who will take you on croc-spotting boat tours. Otherwise, there's little more on offer than birdwatching, snacking at the cafes or buying furry souvenirs.

☞ Tours

Bruce Belcher's Daintree River Cruises RIVER CRUISES (☑07-4098 7717; www.daintreerivercruises. com; 1hr cruises adult/child $25/10) One-hour cruises on a covered boat.

THE BAMA WAY

From Cairns to Cooktown, you can see the country through Aboriginal eyes along the **Bama Way** (www.bamaway.com.au). Bama (pronounced Bumma) means 'person' in the Kuku Yalanji and Guugu Yimithirr languages, and highlights include tours with Aboriginal guides, such as the Walker family tours (p454) on the Bloomfield Track, and Willie Gordon's enlightening Guurrbi Tours (p455) in Cooktown. Pick up a Bama Way map from visitor centres.

Chris Dahlberg's Daintree River Tours
BIRDWATCHING CRUISES

(☎07-4098 7997; www.daintreerivertours.com.au; Daintree Village; 2hr cruises adult/child $55/35) Sunrise tours specialising in birdwatching.

Crocodile Express
RIVER CRUISES

(☎07-4098 6120; www.daintreeconnection.com.au; Daintree Village; 1hr cruises adult/child $25/13; ⊙daily from 8.30am) The original Daintree River cruise operator.

Daintree Argo Rainforest Tours
RAINFOREST TOURS

(☎0409 627 434; www.daintreeadventuretours.com.au; Upper Daintree Rd; 1hr tours $40) Rainforest and cattle-country tours aboard an open-topped amphibious vehicle.

Daintree River Experience
BIRDWATCHING CRUISES

(☎07-4098 7480; www.daintreecruises.com.au; 2hr cruises adult/child $50/35) Serene sunrise and sunset cruises specialising in birdwatching.

Daintree River Wild Watch
NATURE & PHOTOGRAPHY CRUISES

(☎07-4098 7068; www.daintreeriverwildwatch.com.au; 2hr cruises adult/child $50/35) Informative sunrise birdwatching cruises and sunset photography nature cruises.

Dan Irby's Mangrove Adventures
RIVER CRUISES

(☎07-4090 7017; www.mangroveadventures.com.au; 2hr cruises $55) Personalised cruises on a small aluminium punt.

Thundacroc
RIVER CRUISES

(☎07-4098 6146; 1½hr cruises adult/child $35/20) One-hour cruises are $24/12 per adult/child. Book at the Daintree Village General Store.

🛏 Sleeping & Eating

🏊 Daintree Eco Lodge & Spa
BOUTIQUE RESORT $$$

(☎07-4098 6100; www.daintree-ecolodge.com.au; 20 Daintree Rd; s/d from $550/598; ✴@🕏🌊) The 15 boutique 'banyans' (pole cabins; 10 with private spas) sit high in the rainforest canopy a few kilometres south of Daintree Village. Even the day spa is eco-minded, with its own range of organic, Indigenous-inspired products and treatments. Nonguests are welcome at its superb Julaymba Restaurant (mains $29-32; ⊙breakfast, lunch & dinner), utilising local produce, including indigenous berries, nuts, leaves and flowers. Don't miss a Flaming Green Ant cocktail!

Kenadon Homestead Cabins
CABINS $$

(☎07-4098 6142; www.daintreecabins.com; Dagmar St; d $130; ✴🌊) On the fringe of a 162-hectare fifth-generation cattle farm, Kenadon's timber cabins can sleep up to five, making them ideal for families. Clustered together near the pool, they face out to the vast pastures.

Red Mill House
B&B $$$

(☎07-4098 6233; www.redmillhouse.com.au; 11 Stewart St; s/d $160/200; ✴@🌊) Birdwatchers will love the Red Mill. The large verandah overlooking the rainforest garden is a prime spot to observe the resident wildlife. There are four well-appointed rooms, a large communal lounge and library, and a two-bedroom family unit (from $260). Guided birding walks are available on request.

Daintree Valley Haven
CABINS $$

(☎07-4098 6206; www.daintreevalleyhaven.com.au; Stewart Creek Rd; s/d $135/170; ✴) Secluded farm-style accommodation (including a breakfast basket), 8km south of the village. No kids.

Daintree Riverview
CARAVAN PARK $

(☎07-4098 6119; www.daintreeriverview.com; Stewart St; unpowered/powered sites $20/30, cabins $99) Riverside camping and good-value cabins.

Daintree Escape
CABINS $$

(☎07-4098 6021; www.daintreeescape.com.au; 17 Stewart St; d $175; ✴@🌊) Cute cabins amid grassy gardens strolling distance from the village.

Daintree Tea House Restaurant
RESTAURANT $$

(☎07-4098 6173; 3-5 Stewart St; mains $17-40.50; ⊙10am-4pm Mon-Wed & Fri-Sat, 10am-3pm Thu & Sun) Serves fish and chips, delicately prepared barramundi and a tasting platter with crocodile wontons and sugar-cane prawns.

Daintree Village General Store
CAFE $$

(1 Stewart St; mains $20-30; ⊙breakfast, lunch & dinner) The cafe attached to the general store serves beef-and-reef–style meals. BYO from the attached bottle shop.

Around Cape Tribulation

Rainforest, beaches, bats and some fairly hard-core driving are features of this intriguing area where tropical rainforest meets the sea. It's only accessible via cable ferry (or 4WD from Cooktown), and, adding

QUEENSLAND & THE GREAT BARRIER REEF AROUND CAPE TRIBULATION

to its mystery, it's where rainforest retreat-style accommodation regularly gets taken over by the surrounding greenery, and the sun is rarely seen through thick foliage. Swimming holes, forest walks and wildlife spotting make this an area you're unlikely to ever forget.

About 11km before Daintree Village and 24km from Mossman is the turn-off to the **Daintree River cable ferry** (car/motorcycle/bicycle & pedestrian one way $12/5/1; ☺6am-midnight), which runs every 15 minutes or so and takes two minutes to cross the river into the Cape Tribulation area. It's then another 34km by sealed road to Cape Tribulation. The Indigenous Kuku-yalanji people called the area Kulki, but the name Cape Tribulation was given by Captain Cook after his ship ran aground on Endeavour Reef.

Part of the Wet Tropics World Heritage Area, the region from Daintree River north to Cape Tribulation is famed for its ancient rainforest and the rugged mountains of **Thornton Peak** (1375m) and **Mt Sorrow** (770m).

Electricity is powered by generators and solar in this area and few places have air-con. Cape Trib is one of the most popular day trips from Port Douglas and Cairns, and accommodation is booked solid in peak periods.

You can get fuel and supplies at **Rainforest Village** (Cape Tribulation Rd; ☺7am-7pm), 16km from the ferry, but self-caterers are better off coming prepared. Sun Palm Express runs daily bus services from Cairns to Cape Tribulation (see p427). For information on organised trips to the area, see p441.

The following sections chart a route from the Daintree River to Cape Tribulation.

CAPE KIMBERLEY

About 3km beyond the Daintree River crossing, a 5km unsealed road leads to Cape Kimberley Beach, a beautiful quiet beach with **Snapper Island** just offshore. The island is national park, with a fringing reef. Access is by private boat; Crocodylus Village (this page) runs sea-kayaking tours here. You'll need to obtain a permit for the **DERM campsite** (☎13 74 68; www.derm.qld. gov.au; per person $5.15) on the southwest side of Snapper Island, where there's a toilet and picnic tables. Take a fuel stove, as fires are not permitted.

At the junction of the road to Cape Kimberley, turning west and following the road for 12km (4km unsealed) leads you to **Daintree Forest Trails** (www.daintreeforesttrails. com; Old Forest Creek Rd, off Forest Creek Rd; adult/child $10/free; ☺dawn-dusk), with six walking trails (from 15 minutes to one hour) in 5 sq km of rainforest wilderness.

COW BAY

There's a footpath from the main road to beautiful Cow Bay, where you'll find rainforest logs wedged into the coral-filled sand. It's a popular fishing spot, too.

Before the turn-off to the Jindalba Boardwalk is the **Walu Wugirriga (Alexandra Range) lookout**, which offers marvellous views over the Alexandra Range and Snapper Island.

The **aerial walkway** at the **Daintree Discovery Centre** (☎07-4098 9171; www.daintree-rec.com.au; Tulip Oak Rd; adult/child $28/14; ☺8.30am-5pm) takes you high into the forest canopy, including climbing up a 23m-high tower. There are a few short interpretive walks and a small theatre running films on cassowaries, crocodiles, conservation and climate change. You can also hire an audio guide ($5), which offers an excellent Aboriginal tour, interpreting the rainforest from an Indigenous perspective.

Just past the centre, the **Jindalba Boardwalk** snakes a 700m circuit through the rainforest.

Cow Bay Horse Rides (☎07-4098 9202; 1/2hr rides $65/110; Cape Tribulation Rd) takes very personalised rides – from one to four people – on its forested property.

Of course, Cow Bay's real highlight lies at the end of the road, where the beautiful white-sand **Cow Bay Beach** rivals any coastal paradise.

🛏 Sleeping & Eating

Daintree Rainforest Retreat MOTEL **$$**
(☎07-4098 9101; www.daintreeretreat.com.au; 1473 Cape Tribulation Rd; d $121-149, f $190-210; ☒) Set back from the main road amid rainforest, these boutique motel rooms are done out in striking tropical colour schemes and glossy woodwork. Some have kitchenettes, or you can dine at the on-site restaurant, **Tree Frogs** (mains $15-36; ☺dinner Mon-Sat), which is also open to nonguests.

Crocodylus Village HOSTEL **$**
(☎07-4098 9166; www.crocodyluscapetrib.com; Buchanan Creek Rd; dm/d $25/85; @ 🏠 ☒) Along the sealed Buchanan Creek Rd (often called Cow Bay Rd, or simply 'the road to the

The greater Daintree rainforest is protected as part of Daintree National Park. The area has a controversial history: despite conservationist blockades, in 1983 the Bloomfield Track was bulldozed through lowland rainforest from Cape Tribulation to the Bloomfield River, and the ensuing international publicity indirectly led the federal government to nominate Queensland's wet tropical rainforests for World Heritage listing. The move drew objections from the Queensland timber industry and the state government, but in 1988 the area was inscribed on the World Heritage list, resulting in a total ban on commercial logging within its boundaries.

World Heritage listing doesn't affect land ownership rights or control, and since the 1990s efforts have been made by the Queensland government and conservation agencies to buy back and rehabilitate freehold properties, add them to the Daintree National Park and install visitor-interpretation facilities. Sealing the road to Cape Tribulation in 2002 opened the area to rapid settlement, triggering the buy-back of hundreds more properties. Coupled with development controls, these efforts are now bearing fruit in the form of forest regeneration. Check out Rainforest Rescue (www.rainforestrescue.org.au) for more information.

Biodiversity

Far North Queensland's wet tropics area has amazing pockets of biodiversity. The Wet Tropics World Heritage Area stretches from Townsville to Cooktown and covers 894,420 hectares of coastal zones and hinterland, diverse swamp and mangrove-forest habitats, eucalypt woodlands and tropical rainforest. It covers only 0.01% of Australia's surface area, but has 36% of all the mammal species, 50% of the bird species, around 60% of the butterfly species and 65% of the fern species.

Making a Difference

Increased tourism is undoubtedly having an impact on the Daintree area. When visiting, take your rubbish with you, stick to designated trails and watch out for wildlife on the roads.

Other ways to help preserve this impossibly beautiful part of the world:

» Check whether tour companies have eco certification (look at www.ecotourism .org.au).

» Use natural, chemical-free toiletries.

» Ask about volunteer opportunities to clean up beaches or monitor wildlife, or contact Austrop (Bat House; p452) to assist with forest rehabilitation and planting.

» Consider donating to a not-for-profit environment group, such as Rainforest Rescue, the Wilderness Society or the Australian Conservation Foundation.

» Choose accommodation that encourages recycling and strives to reduce energy and water consumption.

beach'), ultrabasic green canvas safari-style huts merge with the surrounding foliage at this YHA-associated hostel. If you prefer solid walls, go for the four- to six-bed dorms or private rooms. Its restaurant (mains $15; ☺dinner) and bar are both open to the public, as are activities including half-day kayaking trips ($65) and adventurous two-day sea-kayaking tours to Snapper Island ($220; ☺Mon, Wed & Fri).

Epiphyte B&B B&B $
(☏07-4098 9039; www.rainforestbb.com; 22 Silkwood Rd; s/d/cabins $70/95/140) This laid-back

place is set on a lush 3.5-hectare property with individually styled rooms of varying sizes but all with their own verandah. Even better is the spacious, super-private cabin with a patio, kitchenette and sunken bathroom. From the front deck of the house you can kick back with views of imposing Thornton Peak. Rates include breakfast.

Daintree Rainforest
Bungalows BUNGALOWS $$
(☏07-40989229; www.daintreerainforestbungalows. com; lot 40 Spurwood Rd; d $90) The best-value accommodation in the area,

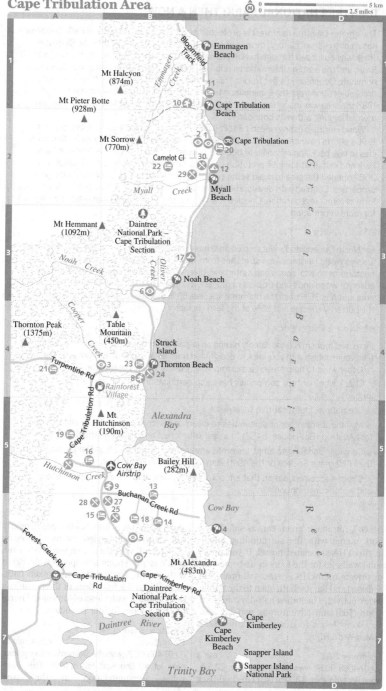

Cape Tribulation Area

N

0 — 5 km
0 — 2.5 miles

Emmagen Beach

Bloomfield Track

Emmagen Creek

Mt Halcyon (874m)

Mt Pieter Botte (928m)

11

10

Cape Tribulation Beach

Mt Sorrow (770m)

2 1

Cape Tribulation

20

Camelot Cl

30

22

29

12

Myall Creek

Myall Beach

Mt Hemmant (1092m)

Daintree National Park – Cape Tribulation Section

Noah Creek

Oliver Creek

17

Noah Beach

6

Great

Thornton Peak (1375m)

Cooper Creek

Table Mountain (450m)

Struck Island

Barrier

Turpentine Rd

3

23

Thornton Beach

21

8

24

Rainforest Village

Mt Hutchinson (190m)

Alexandra Bay

Cape Tribulation Rd

19

26

16

Cow Bay Airstrip

Bailey Hill (282m)

Reef

Hutchinson Creek

9

Buchanan Creek Rd

13

Cow Bay

28

27

15

25

18

14

5

7

Mt Alexandra (483m)

Forest Creek Rd

Cape Tribulation Rd

Cape Kimberley Rd

4

Daintree National Park – Cape Tribulation Section

Cape Kimberley

Daintree River

Cape Kimberley Beach

Snapper Island

Trinity Bay

Snapper Island National Park

hands-down. Its freestanding wooden cabins are simple but stylish, with violet- and lilac-toned fabrics, and covered decks overlooking the rainforest. Minimum stay is two nights.

TOP CHOICE / **Jambu**   BURGERS, WRAPS **$**
(www.daintreecoffeecompany.com.au; 335 Cape Tribulation Rd; mains $9.50-15; ☺breakfast & lunch; ♪) This funky little find dishes up 30cm wraps, fantastic burgers, including tofu with homemade peanut sauce, rib steak, and reef fish (all somewhat unnecessarily served with additional side salads, but no matter), as well as boutique Australian beers like Little Creatures, and its own Daintree Coffee Company brews served in 10 styles (espresso, ristretto, affogato et al).

Cow Bay Hotel   PUB **$$**
(☎07-4098 9011; Cape Tribulation Rd; s/d $77/99, mains $12-25; ☺lunch & dinner) If you're craving a counter meal and pot of beer, the Cow Bay, adjacent to the turn-off to the beach, is the only real pub in the whole Daintree region (takeaway alcohol available), with an adjacent block of basic motel-style rooms.

Floravilla Ice Cream Factory   ICE CREAM **$**
(Bailey Creek Rd; ice creams $5; ☺8am-5.30pm) Next door to the pub, Floravilla has at least 26 flavours of organic ice cream using local ingredients like macadamia and Davidson plum, dragonfruit and ginger, as well as Guinness. The attached **gallery** displays photographs and plants.

COW BAY TO COOPER CREEK

Strung out along the main road from Cow Bay to Cooper Creek are a handful of accommodation and dining options.

Daintree Ice Cream Company (☎07-4098 9114; lot 100, Cape Tribulation Rd; ice creams $5; ☺11am-5pm) serves up four exotic flavours that change daily. It could be wattleseed, black sapote, macadamia, mango, coconut or jackfruit – they're all delicious. Work it off on a 20-minute self-guided **orchard walk** – pick up a free trail map from the kiosk.

Curtained by lush rainforest, **Daintree Wilderness Lodge** (☎07-4098 9105; www.daintreewildernesslodge.com.au; 83 Cape Tribulation Rd; d from $260; ☎❄) has seven timber cabins connected by a series of boardwalks. There's a classy **restaurant** (mains $27-33; ☺dinner), and you can end a night-time nature walk with a soak in the 'jungle Jacuzzi'.

The family-friendly **Lync-Haven Rainforest Retreat** (☎07-4098 9155; www.lynchaven.com.au; lot 44, Cape Tribulation Rd; unpowered/powered sites $24/28, d $120-160) is set on a

16-hectare property on the main road about 5km north of Cow Bay, with walking trails, hand-reared kangaroos and resident croc Boris. Its **restaurant** (mains $16-28; ☺break-fast, lunch & dinner) serves robust steaks, good pasta and fish.

COOPER CREEK

A smattering of sights nestles in the bend of Cooper Creek at the base of dramatic Thornton Peak.

Just south of the creek itself, **Rainforest Village** (☑07-4098 9015; ☺7am-7pm) sells groceries, ice and fuel, and has a small **campground** (unpowered/powered sites $24/32).

Book ahead for a walk with **Cooper Creek Wilderness** (☑07-4098 9126; www.cc wild.com; Cape Tribulation Rd; guided walks $45). After a walk through Daintree rainforest, you'll take a dip in Cooper Creek. Night walks and full-day tours ($130) are also available.

Cape Tribulation Wilderness Cruises (☑07-4033 2052; www.capetribcruises.com; Cape Tribulation Rd; adult/child $25/18) has one-hour mangrove cruises down Cooper Creek in search of crocs.

Prema Shanti (☑07-4098 9006; www.prema shanti.com; Turpentine Rd; tw per person $80) is a peaceful yoga retreat. Drop-in classes (by reservation) cost $18 per hour.

THORNTON BEACH

A sliver of vegetation separates Cape Tribulation Rd from magnificent crescent-shaped Thornton Beach. There's a small, rocky offshore island, and opportunities for snorkelling. Best of all is the licensed **Cafe on Sea** (Cape Tribulation Rd; mains $12-20; ☺9am-4pm), only a towel-length back from the beach.

Directly across the road, **Thornton Beach Bungalows** (☑07-4098 9179; www. thorntonbeach.com; Cape Tribulation Rd; cabins/houses $85/250) has two petite cabins, plus a beach house sleeping four (two-night minimum).

NOAH BEACH & AROUND

Marrdja Botanical Walk is a beautiful 540m (30-minute) interpretive boardwalk that follows the creek through a section of rainforest packed with fan palms and past mangroves to a lookout over Noah Creek. Wear insect repellent to beat the midges.

The **DERM campground** (☑13 74 68; www.derm.qld.gov.au; Cape Tribulation Rd; per person $5.15) at Noah Beach has 15 sites set 100m back from the beach beneath red-trunked trees. There are toilets but no showers. Boil water before drinking – and watch out for crocs.

Noah Valley Mountain Treks (☑07-4098 9292; noahvalleymountaintreks@activ8.net.au; half-day/night treks $55/35) guide challenging, enviro-oriented treks through the Noah Valley.

Cape Tribulation

This little piece of paradise retains a frontier quality, with low-key development, road signs alerting drivers to cassowary crossings and crocodile warnings that make beach strolls that little bit less relaxing.

The rainforest tumbles right down to two magnificent, white-sand beaches – Myall and Cape Trib – separated by a knobby cape. The village of Cape Tribulation marks the end of the road, literally, and the beginning of the 4WD-only coastal route along the Bloomfield Track.

Serious, fit walkers should lace up early for the **Mt Sorrow Ridge Walk** (7km, five to six hours return); it's strenuous but worth it. The start of the marked trail is about 150m north of the Kulki picnic area car park, on your left.

Ocean Safari (☑07-4098 0006; www. oceansafari.com.au; adult/child $108/69; ☺9am & 1pm) leads small groups (25 people maximum) on snorkelling cruises to the Great Barrier Reef, just half an hour offshore.

Jungle Surfing (☑07-4098 0043; www. junglesurfing.com.au; $90) is an exhilarating zipline (flying fox) through the rainforest canopy, stopping at five tree platforms. Tours depart from Cape Tribulation Pharmacy (next to the IGA supermarket). The same outfit also runs guided **night walks** (per person $40; ☺7.30pm) through the forest. Rates include pick-ups throughout Cape Trib.

Volunteers from Austrop, a local conservation organisation, run the **Bat House** (☑07-4098 0083; www.austrop.org.au; Cape Tribulation Rd; admission $2; ☺10.30am-3.30pm Tue-Sun), a nursery for fruit bats.

Bookings are essential for tours of the magnificent tropical orchards of **Cape Trib Exotic Fruit Farm** (☑07-4098 0057; www.cape trib.com.au; tastings $20; ☺2pm).

☞ Tours

Cape Trib Horse Rides   HORSE RIDING
(☑1800 111 124; per person $95; ☺8am & 1.30pm) Leisurely rides along the beach.

Cape Tribulation Kayaks
KAYAKING

(07-4098 0077; www.capetribcamping.com.au; 2hr tours $60) Guided kayaking trips and kayak hire (single/double kayaks $20/30 per hour).

D'Arcy of the Daintree
4WD

(07-4098 9180; darcyofdaintree@yahoo.com. au) Entertaining 4WD trips up the Bloomfield Track as far as Cooktown (adult/child $185/90) and down Cape Tribulation Rd (from $55/35). Free pick-ups from Cape Trib and Cow Bay.

Mason's Tours
WALKING, 4WD

(07-4098 0070; www.masonstours.com.au; Mason's Store, Cape Tribulation Rd) Interpretive walks lasting two hours (adult/child $49/40) or a half-day ($70/55), and a croc-spotting night walk ($49). Also 4WD tours up the Bloomfield Track (from $135/114).

Sleeping & Eating

Restaurants at Cape Trib's resorts are all open to nonguests.

TOP CHOICE Cape Trib Exotic Fruit Farm Cabins
CABINS $$

(07-4098 0057; www.capetrib.com.au; d $180) Right on the burbling World Heritage creek boundary, amid the orchards of Cape Trib Exotic Fruit Farm, this pair of timber pole cabins are far enough apart that you feel like you're alone in the forest. With exposed timber floors, ceilings and huge decks, simple but elegant cabins are equipped with electric Eskies. Rates include breakfast hampers filled with tropical fruit from the farm. Minimum stay is two nights.

Rainforest Hideaway
B&B $$

(07-4098 0108; www.rainforesthideaway.com; 19 Camelot Cl; d $95-135) This colourful B&B has been single-handedly built by its owner, artist and sculptor 'Dutch Rob' – even the furniture and beds are handmade. A sculpture trail winds through the property; rates include breakfast.

Cape Trib Beach House
HOSTEL $

(07-4098 0030; www.capetribbeach.com.au; dm $26-32, d $75, cabins $130-230;) Rainforest huts at this low-key beachfront property house dorms through to timber cabins. There's a tidy communal kitchen as well as an open-deck licensed restaurant (mains $12-27; breakfast, lunch & dinner).

PK's Jungle Village
HOSTEL $

(07-4098 0040; www.pksjunglevillage.com; unpowered sites per person $15, dm $25, budget cabins $48, en suite cabin d $125;) From this long-standing backpacker hub you can reach Myall Beach by boardwalk. Its Jungle Bar (dishes $5-18; restaurant lunch & dinner, bar noon-midnight) is the entertainment epicentre of Cape Trib.

Mason's Store & Cafe
GROCERIES, CAFE $

(Cape Tribulation Rd; mains $12; 10am-4pm Sun-Thu, 10am-7pm Fri & Sat) Laid-back cafe dishing up good fish and chips and huge steak sandwiches. The store sells limited groceries and takeaway alcohol.

Cape Tribulation Camping
CAMPGROUND $

(07-4098 0077; www.capetribcamping.com.au; unpowered/powered sites $30/40, safari huts s/d $45/70;) Sociable beachfront spot with a nightly communal fire and friendly managers and kayaking guides.

Whet Restaurant & Cinema
MODERN AUSTRALIAN $$

(07-4098 0007; 1 Cape Tribulation Rd; mains $27.50-33; lunch & dinner) Serves passable but overhyped food – perhaps because it's the only place you can get a meal much after 8pm. Call for film screening times.

IGA supermarket
GROCERIES $

(PK's Jungle Village; 8am-6pm) The Daintree's largest supermarket.

Getting There & Away

Sun Palm (07-4087 2900; www.sunpalm transport.com) runs daily buses from Cairns to Cape Tribulation (adult/child $78/39). Services depart from Cairns at 7am and 1pm and take 3½ hours.

Country Road Coach Lines (07-4045 2794; www.countryroadcoachlines.com.au) travels the coastal route from Cairns to Cooktown (adult/child $46/23) on Monday, Wednesday and Friday (departing Cairns at 7am) and departs Cape Tribulation for Cairns at 10.10am on Tuesday, Thursday and Saturday.

North to Cooktown

There are two routes to Cooktown from the south: the coastal route from Cape Tribulation via the 4WD-only Bloomfield Track, and the inland route (p458), which is sealed all the way via the Peninsula and Cooktown Developmental Rds.

The Bloomfield Track is one of the frontier roads of Australia, and it wasn't until 1983, when it was controversially bulldozed

through the Daintree, that people could actually drive from Cooktown to Cape Tribulation via the coast. There are reasons why it's 4WD only: it's unsealed, there are flooded creek crossings and very steep and slippery hills, and it's usually impossible to use during the Wet. Check road conditions at Mason's Store & Cafe (p453) before heading off.

A must-see along the way is **Bloomfield Falls** (after crossing the Bloomfield River turn left). Crocs inhabit the river and the site is significant to the indigenous Wujal Wujal community located just north of the river. Wujal Wujal residents the **Walker family** (⌨07-4060 8069; www.bamaway.com.au; adult/child $15/8; ☺by reservation) run highly recommended half-hour **walking tours** of the falls and surrounding forest.

North from Wujal Wujal the track heads for 46km through the tiny settlements of **Ayton (Bloomfield)**, **Rossville** and **Helenvale** to meet the sealed Cooktown Developmental Rd, 28km south of Cooktown.

The **Lion's Den Hotel** (⌨07-4060 3911; www.lionsdenhotel.com.au; Helenvale; unpowered/powered sites $20/26, s/d $40/50, d safari tents $70; ❄) is a well known watering hole that has graffiti-covered corrugated-iron walls and a slab-timber bar. You can pitch your own tent or sleep in an above-ground safari-style tent ($70). You'll find good pub grub, and fuel is available.

Cooktown

POP 2100

At the southeastern edge of Cape York Peninsula, Cooktown is a small place with a big history: for thousands of years Waymbuurr was the place the local Guugu Yimithirr and Kuku Yalanji people used as a meeting ground, and it was here that on 17 June 1770, Lieutenant (later Captain) Cook beached the *Endeavour*. The *Endeavour* had earlier struck a reef offshore from Cape Tribulation, and Cook and his crew spent 48 days here while they repaired the damage – making it the site of Australia's first, albeit transient, non-Indigenous settlement.

As well as historical sites relating to early European contact, there's increasing recognition of the area's Indigenous heritage and unspoilt natural environment of wetlands, mangroves, rainforest and long, lonely beaches. Whatever you do, try to get to Cooktown on time, as siesta is from November to April. Work is often available on banana plantations.

◉ Sights & Activities

Cooktown hibernates during winter (locals call it 'the dead season'), and many attractions and tours close or have reduced hours.

Nature's Powerhouse (www.natures powerhouse.com.au; off Walker St; adult/child $4/free; ☺9am-5pm) is an environment interpretive centre home to two excellent galleries: the **Charlie Tanner Gallery**, with pickled and preserved creepy-crawlie exhibits; and the **Vera Scarth-Johnson Gallery**, displaying botanical illustrations of the region's native plants.

The centre doubles as Cooktown's official visitor centre, with brochures outlining some of the area's excellent **walking trails**, including a walk to the Coral Sea **beaches** at Finch Bay (25 minutes) and Cherry Tree Bay (one hour).

Nature's Powerhouse is at the entrance to Cooktown's 62-hectare **Botanic Gardens**. Filled with native and exotic tropical plants, including rare orchids, the gardens are among Australia's oldest and most magnificent.

Housed in the imposing 1880s St Mary's Convent, the **James Cook Museum** (cnr Helen & Furneaux Sts; adult/child $10/3; ☺9.30am-4pm) explores Cooktown's intriguing past. From a traditional outrigger canoe to the *Endeavour*'s massive anchor, there's a host of interesting displays.

Grassy Hill lookout (162m) has spectacular 360-degree views – especially worthwhile at sunrise. There's a snaking road to the top, or a steep 15-minute walk up. Cook climbed this hill looking for a passage out through the reefs. Another walking trail (800m one way, 25 minutes) leads from the summit down to the beach at Cherry Tree Bay.

Bicentennial Park is home to the much-photographed bronze **Captain Cook statue**. Nearby, the **Milbi Wall (Story Wall)** is a 12m-long mosaic depicting the local Gungarde (Guugu Yimithirr) Indigenous people's stories of creation and European contact, as well as scenes from WWII and recent attempts at reconciliation.

Cooktown Reef Charters   FISHING, SNORKELLING
(⌨07-4069 5396; www.reefcharters.com.au; from $230 per person) Game-fishing day trips with the option of snorkelling.

Gone Fishing   FISHING
(⌨07-4069 5980; www.fishingcooktown.com; half-/fullday $100/200) River-fishing tours.

⒡ Tours

Tours operate regularly out of Cooktown from May to October, with scaled-back schedules from November to April.

TOP CHOICE Guurrbi Tours   INDIGENOUS CULTURE
(☏07-4069 6259; www.guurrbitours.com; 2/4hr tours $95/120, self-drive $65/85; ⊙Mon-Sat) Nugal-warra family elder Willie Gordon runs revelatory tours that use the physical landscape to describe the spiritual landscape, providing a powerful insight into Aboriginal culture and lore. Cooktown pick-ups are from your accommodation; self-drivers meet near the Hopevale Aboriginal Community.

Catch-a-Crab   BOAT
(☏07-4069 6289; cook.cac@bigpond.com; adult/child $100/50) Local seafood supplier Nicko runs river tours on the Endeavour and Annan Rivers in search of mud crabs. Great for kids. Book well ahead.

Maaramaka Walkabout Tours   INDIGENOUS CULTURE
(☏07-4060 9389; irenehammett@hotmail.com) Aboriginal cultural stories, rainforest walks, bush tucker and home cooking in a gorgeous setting near Hopevale; call for arrangements.

Cooktown Barra Fishing Charters   BOAT
(☏07-4069 5346; www.cooktownbarracharters. com; half-/full day $100/200) Fishing tours plus croc-spotting, birdwatching, mud-crabbing and eco tours.

Cooktown Tours   SIGHTSEEING
(☏1300 789 550; www.cooktowntours.com) Two-hour town tours (adult/child $55/33) and half-day trips to Black Mountain and the Lion's Den Hotel (adult/child $110/77).

Cooktown Bush Adventures   SIGHTSEEING, SAFARIS
(☏07-4069 5005; helipete@gmail.com; day tours from $250) Local day tours and overnight safaris.

Cooktown Cruises   BOAT
(☏07-4069 5712; www.cooktowncruises.com; 2hr cruise adult/child $55/35; ⊙Tue-Sun Jun-Sep, 3 days per week Apr-Jun & Oct-Dec) Scenic cruises up the Endeavour River.

✸ Festivals & Events

Cooktown Discovery Festival   CAPTAIN COOK
(www.cooktowndiscoveryfestival.com.au; ⊙early Jun) Held over the Queen's Birthday weekend to commemorate Captain Cook's landing in 1770 with a costumed re-enactment and fancy dress grand parade, as well as Indigenous workshops and a traditional corroboree.

🛏 Sleeping & Eating

Cooktown has plenty of accommodation, including several caravan parks, but book ahead in the Dry.

Sovereign Resort Hotel   HOTEL $$
(☏07-4043 0500; www.sovereign-resort.com.au; cnr Charlotte & Green Sts; d $170-185, 2-bed apt $210; ❈@☎❄) Cooktown's swishest digs are right on the main street, with a warren of breezy tropical-style rooms with wooden-slat blinds and tile floors. Kick back in the landscaped garden pool area and the Balcony Restaurant and Cafe-Bar.

Pam's Place & Cooktown Motel   HOSTEL, MOTEL $
(☏07-4069 5166; www.cooktownhostel.com; cnr Charlotte & Boundary Sts; dm/s/d $27.50/50/55, motel d $90; ❈@☎❄) Cooktown's YHA-associated hostel is everything a backpackers should be: welcoming and cosy, with sociable common areas, spotless facilities and a leafy garden. Spiffy new motel units still have a faint scent of fresh paint. The friendly managers can help find harvest work.

Endeavour Falls Tourist Park   CARAVAN PARK $
(☏07-4069 5431; www.endeavourfallstouristpark. com.au; Endeavour Valley Rd; unpowered/powered sites $24/28, cabins $115; ❈❄) Situated 32km northwest on the road to Hopevale (15km unsealed), this well-run, peaceful park backs onto the Garden of Eden–like Endeavour Falls (with a resident croc – don't swim!). Its well-stocked shop serves takeaways (dishes $6.50-13.50) and has fuel.

Alkoomie Cattle Station & Mountain Retreat   FARMSTAY $$
(☏07-4069 5463; www.alkoomie.com.au; Alkoomie Station; tents $80, self-contained units $100, d incl meals $199-225; ❈❄) You'll need a 4WD to reach this 18,000-hectare working cattle station 45km west of Cooktown. Activities include horse riding, feeding farm animals, swimming below waterfalls and nightly stargazing, plus day tours.

Milkwood Lodge   CABINS $$
(☏07-4069 5007; www.milkwoodlodge.com; Annan Rd; d $135; ❈❄) In a patch of rainforest 2.5km south of town, these six

split-level cabins are beautifully designed with bushland views from private balconies. Not suitable for kids.

Seaview Motel MOTEL $$
(07-4069 5377; seaviewmotel@bigpond.com.au; 178 Charlotte St; d $99-155, townhouses $220; ✱✖) Awesomely located opposite the wharf, with modern rooms (some with private balconies).

Alamanda Inn MOTEL $
(07-4069 5203; sayahscott@tpg.com.au;cnr Hope & Howard Sts; guesthouse s/d $50/60, motel s/d $60/70, unit s/d $75/85; ✱✖) Easy-going place offering budget accommodation.

Cooktown Holiday Park CARAVAN PARK $
(07-4069 5417; www.cooktownholidaypark.com.au; 31-34 Charlotte St; powered sites $35, cabins without bathroom $90, motel units $110-120, cabins with bathroom $120-140; ✱@🛜✖) Cooktown's best-equipped caravan park, with cabins, a camp kitchen and two big saltwater pools.

✕ Eating & Drinking

Restaurant 1770 MODERN AUSTRALIAN $$
(07-4069 5440; 7 Webber Esplanade; mains $21-32; ⊘breakfast, lunch & dinner; ✖) Opening onto a romantic waterside deck right next to the wharf, fresh fish – such as beer-battered barra and Spanish mackerel – takes top billing, but save space for mouth-watering desserts.

Verandah Cafe CAFE $
(Walker St; mains $9-16; ⊘10am-2.30pm; ✖) Attached to Nature's Powerhouse at the entrance to the botanic gardens, the broad, shady deck of this cafe is a serene setting for tea and scones or lunch mains like Thai chicken salad or gado gado with coconut damper.

Balcony Restaurant MODERN AUSTRALIAN $$
(07-4069 5400; Sovereign Resort, cnr Charlotte & Green Sts; mains $24-31; ⊘breakfast & dinner) Upstairs, the Sovereign Resort's formal Balcony Restaurant serves French-inspired Mod Oz cuisine like confit of duck with sweet potato puree or pistachio-crusted rack of lamb (along with seafood, of course). The **Cafe-Bar** (mains $11-21.50; ⊘11am-8pm; @✖) has reasonably priced seafood, pizzas and BLTs, as well as pool tables and free internet.

Cooktown Hotel PUB $$
(www.cooktownhotel.com; 96 Charlotte St; mains $10.50-25; ⊘lunch & dinner) The double-storey timber 'Top Pub' is a local landmark at the top (southern) end of Charlotte St. Plenty of character, plenty of locals and a side beer garden to sit with a beer, kangaroo pie or Sunday roast.

Cooktown Bowls Club LICENSED CLUB $$
(07-4069 5819; Charlotte St; mains $14-25; ⊘lunch Wed-Fri, dinner daily) Big bistro meals. Join in social bowls on Wednesday and Saturday afternoon and barefoot bowls on Wednesday evening.

Gill'd & Gutt'd FISH & CHIPS $
(07-4069 5863; Fisherman's Wharf, Webber Esplanade; mains $7-12; ⊘lunch & dinner) Fish and chips the way it should be – fresh and right on the waterside wharf.

Cornett's IGA SUPERMARKET $
(cnr Helen & Hogg Sts; ⊘8am-6pm Mon-Sat, 9am-5pm Sun) Groceries.

ℹ Information

The website www.cooktownandcapeyork.com has information on the town and surrounding areas.

Cooktown DERM (13 74 68; www.derm.qld.gov.au; Webber Esplanade; ⊘9am-3pm Mon-Fri) Information and camping permits for national parks, including Lizard Island.

Cooktown Library (07-4069 5009; Helen St; ⊘9am-5pm Mon-Fri) Internet access costs $4 per hour.

Cooktown Travel Centre (07-4069 5446; 113 Charlotte St) Information and bookings for tours, transport and accommodation.

Nature's Powerhouse (07-4069 6004; www.naturespowerhouse.com.au; Walker St; ⊘9am-5pm) Info centre.

ℹ Getting There & Around

Cooktown's airfield is 10km west of town along McIvor Rd. **Hinterland Aviation** (07-4035 9323; www.hinterlandaviation.com.au) has one to four flights daily except Sunday to/from Cairns (one way $150, 40 minutes).

Country Road Coachlines (07-4045 2794; www.countryroadcoachlines.com.au) runs a daily bus service between Cairns and Cooktown ($75) on either the coastal route (Bloomfield Track, via Port Douglas) or inland route (via Mareeba), depending on the day of departure and the condition of the track.

The Sovereign Resort Hotel rents 4WDs from $120 per day.

For a **taxi** call 07-4069 5387.

Lizard Island

POP 280

The spectacular islands of the Lizard group are clustered just 27km off the coast about 100km from Cooktown. Jigurru (Lizard Island), a sacred place for the Dingaal Aboriginal people, has dry, rocky and mountainous terrain offering bushwalking; glistening white swimming beaches; and a relatively untouched fringing reef for snorkelling and diving. Apart from the ground where the luxury resort stands, the entire island is national park, so it's open to anyone who makes the effort to get here.

There are good dives right off the island, and the outer Barrier Reef is less than 20km away, including two of Australia's best-known dive sites – Cod Hole and Pixie Bommie. Lizard Island Resort offers a full range of diving facilities to its guests. Some live-aboard tours from Cairns dive the Cod Hole.

There are great walks through country that switches from mangrove to rainforest to dry and rocky in mere minutes, including a superb hike up to Cook's Look (368m); allow three hours return. The trail starts from the northern end of Watson's Bay near the campsite.

Accommodation options are camping or a five-star luxury resort.

Lizard Island Resort (1300 863 248; www.lizardisland.com.au; Anchor Bay; d from $1700;) has luxurious villas, spa treatments and a top restaurant. Kids aren't allowed. The camping ground (per person/family $5/21) is a 10-minute walk from the resort, at the northern end of Watson's Bay. You'll need a permit from DERM (13 74 68; www.derm.qld.gov.au), and it's worth checking that the water pump, toilets and gas bar-becues are working. Campers must be self-sufficient, though the resort's Marlin Bar is accessible if you're after a drink (the rest of the resort is off-limits).

Book through the resort for all air transfers to/from Cairns (return $530). Flight time is one hour. Daintree Air Services (1800 246 206; www.daintreeair.com.au) has full-day tours from Cairns at 8am ($690). The trip includes lunch, snorkelling gear, transfers and a local guide.

GULF SAVANNAH

The world has a different tint out here: the east coast's green cloud-tipped mountains and sugarcane fields give way to a flat, red dust-coated landscape of sweeping grass plains, scrubby forest and mangroves engraved by an intricate network of seasonal rivers and croc-filled tidal creeks that drain into the Gulf of Carpentaria. The fishing here is legendary, particularly for barramundi (barra season runs from mid-January to the end of September).

Most of this area is on – or just off – the epic Savannah Way, which stretches right across the north of the country from Cairns to Broome. Vast distances are interspersed with a scattering of cattle stations and historic towns that have been through boom and bust cycles over and over again, and retain a hardy independent spirit and some extraordinary outback characters. Stop by rusting roadhouses and you'll meet folk with stories to tell, and not many people to tell them to (mobile-phone service is nonexistent in some places). And you don't even need a 4WD to explore most of it – just a sense of adventure.

HOPE ISLANDS

Adventurous souls can play Robinson Crusoe out on the Hope Islands, with just you and nature (and the odd passing boat). East Hope and West Hope islands are sand cays about 10km offshore from the mainland, 37km southeast of Cooktown. Both are national parks, which protects the hardy mangroves and shrub vegetation. West Hope is an important nesting site for pied imperial pigeons – access is not permitted during nesting from 1 September to 31 March. Snorkelling is excellent around both islands but best on the leeward margin of the East Hope Island reef; beware of strong currents. East Hope Island has three campsites (camping per person $5.15) with toilets, tables and fire places. Permits are required and there's a seven-day limit; contact Cooktown DERM (this spread). Take drinking water, food and a fuel stove.

Getting here isn't cheap: contact Cooktown Travel Centre (this spread) to check availability for boat charters.

It's 332km (about four hours' drive) from Cairns to Cooktown via this cattle, cockie 'n' croc route. You can either access the Mulligan Hwy from Mareeba, or via the turn-off just before Mossman. The road travels past rugged ironbarks and cattle-trodden land before joining the Cooktown Developmental Rd at Lakeland. From here it's another 80km to Cooktown.

The tiny town of **Mt Molloy** marks the start of the Mulligan Hwy. The **National Hotel** (☑07-4094 1133; www.mountmolloynationalhotel.com.au; Main St; s/d $35/70, mains $8-23; ◷lunch & dinner) has accommodation and pub grub, while **Mt Molloy Cafe & Takeaway** (☑07-4094 1187; mains $6-15), aka 'Lobo Loco', doles out everything from dim sums and burritos to boxes of cornflakes, or a shot of bourbon at its bar.

The Palmer River gold rush (1873–83) occurred about 70km to the west, throwing up boom towns Palmerville and Maytown; little of either remain today. You'll find food and fuel at the **Palmer River Roadhouse** (☑07-4060 2020; unpowered/powered sites $10/20, s/d $30/40, mains $14-20; ◷breakfast, lunch & dinner; @). You can also pitch a tent, park your van or stay in the roadhouse's safari tents overlooking the river.

South of Cooktown the road travels through the thoroughly sinister-looking rock piles of **Black Mountain National Park** – a range of hills formed 260 million years ago and made up of thousands of granite boulders. Local Aboriginal people call it Kalcajagga, or 'place of the spears', and it's home to unique species of frog, skink and gecko.

ⓘ Information

The websites www.gulf-savannah.com.au and www.savannahway.com.au have regional info.

ⓘ Getting There & Around

AIR

Skytrans (☑1300 759 872; www.skytrans.com.au) flies several times a week between Cairns and Normanton (from $179) and Burketown (from $179), and between Mt Isa and Burketown (from $200).

BUS

TransNorth (☑07-4061 7944; www.transnorth bus.com) has a service from Cairns to Karumba ($140, 12 hours) three times a week, departing Cairns Monday, Wednesday and Friday, stopping at the Undara turn-off ($61, 5½ hours), Georgetown ($79, seven hours), Croydon ($101, 9½ hours) and Normanton ($135, 11 hours). The return service runs Tuesday, Thursday and Saturday.

No buses link Normanton with Mt Isa or Burketown.

CAR & MOTORCYCLE

The sealed Gulf Developmental Rd (Savannah Way, Rte 1) runs from Cairns to Normanton. From here you can continue on bitumen up to Karumba, or continue on the gravel Gulf Track to Burketown and beyond to the Northern Territory (NT) border.

Heading south from Burketown the unsealed road to Camooweal runs via Gregory Downs and Boodjamulla (Lawn Hill) National Park, while the Nardoo–Burketown Rd cuts across to meet the Burke Developmental Rd at the Burke & Wills Roadhouse.

There aren't many options apart from these major routes, particularly if you don't have a 4WD. Even if you do, this is very remote country and you'll need to be well prepared. Many sealed roads are single-file – see p35 for outback driving advice.

TRAIN

The historic **Savannahlander** (☑1800 793 848; www.savannahlander.com.au; one way/return $210/355), aka the 'Silver Bullet', chugs along a traditional mining route from Cairns to Forsayth and back, departing Cairns on Wednesday at 6.30am and returning on Saturday at 6.40pm. A range of tours (including side trips to Chillagoe, Undara and Cobbold Gorge) and accommodation can be booked online.

The quaint, snub-nosed **Gulflander** (☑07-4745 1391; http://thegulflander.com.au; one way/return $63/107) runs once weekly in each direction between Normanton and Croydon on the 1891 gold-to-port railway line alongside the Gulf Developmental Rd. It leaves Normanton on Wednesday at 8.30am, and leaves Croydon on Thursday at 8.30am.

TOURS

Several operators run tours from Cairns, including **Wilderness Challenge** (☑1800 354 486, 07-4035 4488; www.wilderness-challenge.com.au; 9-day accommodated tours from $2995, 11-day camping safaris from $2995).

The Savannah Way

UNDARA VOLCANIC NATIONAL PARK

About 190,000 years ago, the Undara shield volcano erupted not with a bang but with a

flow, like an overboiled pot of tomato soup, sending molten lava coursing through the surrounding landscape. While the surface of the lava cooled and hardened, hot lava continued to race through the centre of the flows, eventually leaving the world's longest continuous (though fragmented) lava tubes.

All up there are over 160km of tubes, but only a fraction can be visited, on **guided tours** only. Most are operated by Undara Experience (☑1800 990 992, 07-4097 1900; www. undara.com.au; full-day/half-day/2hr/sunset tours $128/82/46/43). Full- and half-day tours only run in the Dry. Overnight tours run from Cairns; Bedrock Village Caravan Park & Tours (this page; full day adult/child $120/60, half-day $74/37) has tours from Mt Surprise.

The closest accommodation to the tubes and national park is at the resort-like Undara Experience (unpowered/powered sites $20/30, d swag tents from $40, s carriages from $75, d carriages with/without bathroom from $170/150; ☑), which has pricey but atmospheric vintage railway carriages converted into comfy rooms (some with bathroom). Facilities include barbecues and campfire entertainment. There's also a campfire bush breakfast (adult/child $22.50/11.25), but even though all meals need to be booked in advance, the bistro (lunch buffet adult/child $22.50/11.25, dinner mains $15.50-32.50) can shut early without warning, and there's nowhere else to eat out here – don't get caught out!

The turn-off to Undara is 81km southwest of Innot Hot Springs, from where it's a sealed 15km.

UNDARA TO CROYDON

Back on the Gulf Developmental Rd, 39km past the Undara turn-off, the 'jewel of a town' **Mt Surprise** (population 162) lives up to both its moniker and its name, with gem collections, snake collections, even a miniature horse collection. It's a good base for fossicking in the nearby gemfields – Pete and Pam at Mt Surprise Gems (☑07-4062 3055; www.thegemden.com.au; Garland St) run fossicking tours (half-day incl transport/self-drive $65/45; ☺Apr-Sep) rent tools (per day $22) and can issue licences (per month $6.50, Queensland-wide).

At Planet Earth Adventures (☑07-4062 3127; p.e.a@bigpond.com.au; unpowered/powered sites per person $10/17, dishes $5-12; ☺cafe 7am-8pm), not only does Russell Dennis have a snake museum (gold coin donation) where you can see deadly taipans and king browns,

and free snake shows (☺10am Sun), including (God forbid) snake-bite education, he also has a Midas touch for curing even the most entrenched snake phobias – you'll be wrapping a black-headed python around your neck in no time (seriously!). The snake show can be seen at other times by arrangement; admission at these times is $10.

Shaded Mt Surprise Tourist Van Park, Motel & BP Roadhouse (☑1800 447 982, 07-4062 3153; 23 Garland St; unpowered/powered sites $20/24, cabins $55-89; ☒☒) has a miniature horse stud and a BYO cafe (mains $5-19; ☺7am-7pm) serving authentic, homemade Mongolian beef, tofu and mushroom soup, and delicious dim sims.

Excellent Bedrock Village Caravan Park & Tours (☑07-4062 3193; www.bedrock village.com.au; Garnet St; unpowered/powered sites $20/27, cabins $65-85; ☒@☒) has en suite cabins and meals on request.

About 32km west, the partly sealed **Explorers' Loop** (check road conditions) takes you on a 150km loop through the old gold-mining towns of Einasleigh and Forsayth and the spring-fed oasis of Cobbold Gorge. Gorge access is by tour only – Cobbold Gorge Village (☑1800 669 922, 07-4062 5470; www.cobbold gorge.com.au; sites unpowered/powered/with bathroom $18/29/45, s/d cabins $75/109, all-day snacks $7-12, dinner mains $22; ☺Apr-Oct; ☒@☒) runs three-hour tours (adult/child $69/35; ☺Apr-Oct), including a boat cruise.

Cobbold Gorge tours can pick up in Georgetown (population 300), the endpoint of the loop, back on the Savannah Way. There's not much here, bar a resident monitor lizard, a free swimming pool, and the flash Terrestrial Centre (☑07-4062 1485; ☺8am-5pm May-Sep, 8.30am-4.30pm Mon-Fri Oct-May; @), home to a **visitor centre** and the shimmering, 4500-strong Ted Elliot Mineral Collection (adult/child $11/9).

CROYDON
POP 320

Incredibly, little Croydon was once the biggest town in the Gulf. Gold was discovered in Croydon in 1885, but by the end of WWI it had run out and the place became little more than a ghost town.

Croydon's visitor information centre (☑07-4745 6125; Samwell St; ☺9am-4.30pm; @) has details of the remaining historic buildings and barramundi-stocked **Lake Belmore**, 4km north of the centre.

The 1887 Club Hotel (☑07-4745 6184; cnr Brown & Sircom Sts; d without bathroom $80,

d units with bathroom $130; ✱✱) is the only pub left from the mining heyday, serving up huge **meals** (mains $16-25; ⊘lunch & dinner), ice-cold beer, and sunset views from the verandah. Campers can pitch up at **Croydon Caravan Park** (✐07-4745 6238; admin@croydon.qld.gov. au; cnr Brown & Alldridge Sts; unpowered/powered sites $18/25, cabins $80; ✱✱).

NORMANTON
POP 1330

The port for Croydon's gold rush, these days Normanton essentially consists of one long main street. The Norman River produces whopping barramundi; every Easter the **Barra Bash** lures big crowds, as do the **Normanton Rodeo & Show** (mid-June) and the **Normanton Races** (September).

Local info is available from the **visitor information & heritage centre** (✐07-4745 1065; www.carpentaria.qld.gov.au; cnr Caroline & Landsborough Sts; ⊘9am-4.30pm Mon-Fri, to noon Sat, noon-3pm Sun Apr-Sep, 9.30am-3.30pm Mon-Fri, 9am-noon Sat Oct-Mar; @) and from Normanton's Victorian-era **train station**.

The main street's most impressive sight is the life-size, 8.64m-long model of **Krys the Crocodile**. The real beast was shot by crocodile hunter Krystina Pawloski in 1958. Imagine meeting *that* out fishing!

Normanton's other impossible-to-miss main-street icon is the **Purple Pub** (✐07-4745 1324; cnr Landsborough & Brown sts; s/d $95/120, mains $12-25; ✱), painted lurid aubergine because it was the only cheap paint available. Comfortable motel rooms congregate out back.

In a mercifully shady setting, the pool at **Normanton Tourist Park** (✐1800 193 4699, 07-4745 1121; 14 Brown St; unpowered/powered sites $20/25, cabins with/without bathroom $90/55; ✱✱) adjoins an artesian spa.

The iron-roofed **Albion Hotel** (✐07-4745 1218; cnr Landsborough & Haig Sts; d $95, mains $8-15; ✱) has cool, clean motel rooms and the best barra and chips in town.

KARUMBA
POP 520

Ay Karumba! When the fish are biting and the sun sinks into the Gulf in a fiery ball of burnt ochre, this is a little piece of outback paradise. Even if you don't like fishing, it's the only town accessible by sealed road on the entire Gulf coast.

The actual town is on the Norman River, while Karumba Point – the best place to stay – is about 6km away by road on the beach. By the time you're reading this, a new 3.2km boardwalk will link the two.

Karumba's **visitor information centre** (✐07-4745 9582; www.carpentaria.qld.gov. au; Walker St, Karumba Town; ⊘9.30am-1pm & 2-4.30pm Mon-Fri, 9am-noon Sat, noon-3pm Sun Apr-Oct, 9.30am-2.30pm Tue-Fri Nov-Mar; @) has details of fishing charters, and barrabreeding hatchery tours.

Karumba Point Sunset Caravan Park (✐07-4745 9277; www.sunsetcp.com.au; 53 Palmer St, Karumba Point; unpowered/powered sites $28/32, cabins without bathroom $95, en suite villas $110; ✱✱) has spotless amenities. Breezy, stylish **End of the Road Motel** (✐07-4745 9599; www.endoftheroadmotel.com.au; 26 Palmer St, Karumba Point; d $130-160; ✱✱) is next door to the **Sunset Tavern** (✐07-4745 9183; The Esplanade, Karumba Point; mains $15-28; ⊘10am-midnight) – *the* place to take in those glorious sunsets, ice-cold beer in hand.

Raptis Fish Markets (✐07-4745 9122; www. raptis.com.au; Massey Dr, Karumba Town; ⊘8am-3pm Mon-Fri, 9am-1pm Sat) has ready-to-cook seafood that couldn't come fresher if you caught it yourself. This waterside shed also sells 1kg bags of cooked prawns ($15) that alone justify the drive to Karumba.

Normanton to Cloncurry

The sealed 378km of road between Normanton and Cloncurry is mostly single file, and floodway signs give you an idea of what it's like during the Wet: wet. The flat dry-grass country slowly morphs into small rises and forests of termite hills.

Everyone stops at the **Burke & Wills Roadhouse** (✐07-4742 5909; unpowered/powered sites $18/22, d $65; ✱) to down a cold drink among noisy apostle birds.

The **Quamby Hotel** (✐07-4742 5952; s/d $40/60, mains $15-20; ⊘dinner; ✱) is 135km from the Burke & Wills Roadhouse; camping's available on request, but there's no fuel.

Normanton to Northern Territory

At the start of the unsealed, dusty stretch from Normanton to the NT, stop by eerie **Burke & Wills Camp 119**, the northernmost camp of the ill-equipped explorers' wretched 1861 expedition – they came within just 5km of reaching the gulf. The camp is signposted 37km west of Normanton.

Besides legendary fishing, isolated Burketown (population 221) is the best place in the world to witness the extraordinary 'morning glory' phenomenon – see p462.

Burketown Pub (☑07-4745 5104; www.bur ketownpub.com; Beames St; s/d $65/85, units $100-140; ❄), the heart and soul of Burketown, was originally built as the local customs house in the late 1860s. Swap stories with locals and travellers in the palm-fringed beer garden, or over a meal (mains $8-25; ◷lunch & dinner). Nearby, **Burketown Caravan Park** (☑07-4745 5118; www.burketowncaravanpark.com.au; Sloman St; powered sites $30, d & cabins without bathroom $66-88, d & cabins with bathroom $99-110; ❄) has a takeaway van (mains $8-22; ◷lunch & dinner) dishing up *Ben Hur*–sized brekkies and two-handed barra burgers.

The only fuel stop for the 486km run between Burketown and Borroloola (NT) is the **Doomadgee Aboriginal Community** (☑07-4745 8188). You're welcome to buy fuel and supplies here; village access is subject to council permission, and alcohol is restricted.

It's another 80km of Melaleuca scrub to **Hell's Gate Roadhouse** (☑07-4745 8258; unpowered sites $20), 50km from the NT border. It has fuel, camping (no power) and snacks (ie pies), but bring cash as there are no credit-card facilities.

Burketown to Camooweal

The 334km unsealed road from Burketown to Gregory Downs is the most direct route to beautiful Boodjamulla (Lawn Hill) National Park. For 2WDs, the easiest route to Gregory Downs is the sealed road from the Burke & Wills Roadhouse.

The park entrance is 100km west of **Gregory Downs** (population 40) on the pretty Gregory River. Fuel is available at the **Gregory Downs Hotel** (☑07-4748 5566; camp sites per person $12, d motel units $100; ❄), a laid-back spot to quench your thirst and tuck into decent pub meals (mains $10-22; ◷lunch daily, dinner Mon-Sat).

BOODJAMULLA (LAWN HILL) NATIONAL PARK

A series of deep flame-red sandstone gorges, fed by spring water and lined with palms, provides a haven for wildlife at this outback oasis. The Waanyi Aboriginal people have inhabited the area for some 30,000 years,

and paintings abound. Book well ahead for accommodation, including camping.

In the southern part of the park is the World Heritage–listed Riversleigh fossil field, with a small **DERM campground** (☑13 74 68; www.derm.qld.gov.au; per person $5.15; ◷Mar-Oct). The fossils include everything from giant snakes and carnivorous kangaroos to pocket-sized koalas.

Some 20km of walking tracks fan out around Lawn Hill Gorge, while the emerald-green waters are idyllic for a swim or a paddle in a canoe with the red cliffs towering above.

The main hub is **Adel's Grove** (☑07-4748 5502; www.adelsgrove.com.au; unpowered sites/ permanent tents/d $32/80/130; ◷camping year-round, other accommodation & facilities Easter-late Oct), 10km east of the park entrance. Set amid trees close to the creek, it's a mini-resort with an on-site bar and restaurant (breakfast $12.50, lunch mains $10-15, 2-course dinner $30). Fuel, food packs and basic groceries are available, as well as fascinating **Riversleigh fossil field tours** ($65 for a half-day tour), and **canoe hire** (from $20 per hour). Also near the gorge is a **DERM campground** (☑13 74 68; www.derm.qld.gov.au; per person $5.15) with showers and toilets.

CAPE YORK PENINSULA

Rugged and remote Cape York Peninsula has one of the wildest tropical environments on the planet. The Great Dividing Range forms the spine of the cape, with tropical rainforests and palm-fringed beaches on its eastern flanks and sweeping savannah woodlands, dry eucalypt forests, and coastal mangroves on its west. This untamed landscape undergoes an amazing transformation each year when the torrential rains and flooded rivers of the monsoonal 'wet season' form vast wetlands that isolate the region.

The overland pilgrimage to the tip of Australia is simply one of the greatest 4WD routes on the continent, an exhilarating trek into Australia's last great frontier. The challenge of rough corrugated roads, difficult creek crossings, and croc-infested rivers is part of the adventure, the cape's rich bird life and untouched wilderness its reward. Take time to savour the experience – many of the highlights of the journey are in the unexpected and unplanned detours, and in the miles and miles of isolation.

MORNING GLORY

Between approximately August and November, Burketown becomes the home of intrepid cloud-surfers, when 'morning glory' clouds frequently (but unpredictably) roll in. A rare meteorological phenomenon, these tubular clouds come in wave-like sets of up to eight. Each can be up to 1000km long by 2km high, and travel at speeds of up to 60km per hour. As the sun rises, gliders head up in the hope of catching one; ask around and chances are someone will take you along for the ride. For a close-up look at the clouds aboard a light plane, contact Gulf-wide charter company **Savannah Aviation** (☑07-4745 5177; www.savannah-aviation.com; per hr for up to 4 people $550).

Avoid the wet season (November to March), when heavy rains can close roads for lengthy periods and the extreme heat and humidity make conditions uncomfortable.

The best time to tackle a cape trip is early in the dry season, generally from the beginning of June, when days are warm and evenings are cool.

☞ Tours

Countless tour operators run trips to the cape – mainly from Cairns, some from Cooktown. Most tours range from six to 14 days and take five to 12 passengers. Tours generally run between April and November, but dates may be affected by an early or late wet season. Places visited include Laura, Split Rock gallery, Lakefield National Park, Coen, Weipa, the Eliot River System (including Twin Falls), Bamaga, Somerset and Cape York; Thursday Island is usually an optional extra. Many operators offer different combinations of land, air and sea travel, and camping or motel-style accommodation. Prices include meals, accommodation, and fares from Cairns.

Wilderness Challenge   CAPE YORK
(☑1800 354 486; www.wilderness-challenge.com.au; 7-day camping tours $1945, 7-day accommodated fly/drive tours $2995) Informative guides and a huge range of fly/drive/cruise and camping and accommodation options.

Heritage Tours   CAPE YORK
(☑1800 77 55 33; www.heritagetours.com.au; 7-day fly/drive tours from $2049, 10-day cruise/drive tours from $3745) Big range of upmarket tours, including fly/drive, cruise and overland with camping or accommodation options and all meals.

Oz Tours Safaris   CAPE YORK
(☑1800 079 006; www.oztours.com.au; 7-day fly/drive camping tours $2049, 16-day overland tours $2850) Numerous tours, air/sea/overland options, and camping or motel options.

Cape York Motorcycle Adventures   MOTORBIKE
(☑07-4059 0220; www.capeyorkmotorcycles.com.au; 5-day tours $3250) This all-inclusive motorcycle tour is from Cairns to Cooktown via the coast, through Lakefield National Park and back via Laura.

Aurukun Wetland Charters   CULTURAL
(☑07-4058 1441; www.aurukunwetlandcharters.com; 3-day tours $700) In the remote western cape south of Weipa, this cultural and wildlife tour is led by Aboriginal guides from the Aurukun community. Accommodation is aboard the MV *Pikkuw* (maximum eight passengers). These remote wetlands are exceptional for birdwatching.

❶ Information & Permits

The foremost consideration of a cape trip is good preparation. Carry spares, tools and equipment, and check **RACQ road reports** (☑1300 130 595; www.racq.com.au). Water can be scarce along the main track, especially late in the dry season, and roadhouses stock only basic food supplies.

North of the Dulhunty River, permits are required to camp on Aboriginal land, which is basically all the land north of the river. The Injinoo people are the traditional custodians of much of this land and the Injinoo Aboriginal Community, which runs the ferry across the Jardine River, includes a camping permit in the ferry fee.

Travelling across Aboriginal land elsewhere on the cape may require an additional permit, which you can obtain by contacting the relevant community council. See the **Aboriginal and Torres Strait Islander Services** (www.atsip.qld.gov.au) website for details. Permits can take up to six weeks.

Be aware that mobile-phone coverage is sporadic.

Alcohol Restrictions

On the way up to the cape you'll see signs warning of alcohol restrictions, which apply to all visitors. It's worth knowing the rules because

the fines for breaking them are huge – up to $37,500. In some communities alcohol is banned completely and cannot be carried in. In the Northern Peninsula Area (north of the Jardine River) you can carry a maximum of 11.25L of beer (or 9L of premixed spirits) and 2L of wine per vehicle (not per person). For up-to-date information see www.mcmc.qld.gov.au.

Maps & Books

The Hema maps *Cape York & Lakefield National Park* and the RACQ maps *Cairns/Townsville* and *Cape York Peninsula* are the best. Ron and Viv Moon's *Cape York – an Adventurer's Guide* is the most comprehensive guide for 4WD and camping enthusiasts.

❶ Getting There & Away

Air

QantasLink (✆13 13 13; www.qantas.com.au) flies daily from Cairns to Weipa and Horn Island. **Skytrans** (✆1300 759 872; www.skytrans.com. au) and **Regional Pacific Airlines** (✆07-4040 1400; www.regionalpacific.com.au) have daily flights from Cairns to Bamaga.

Boat

MV Trinity Bay (✆07-4035 1234; www.sea swift.com.au; 2 days per person twin share incl meals one way $710, 5-day return $1255) runs a weekly cargo ferry to Thursday Island and Seisia that takes up to 38 passengers. It departs Cairns every Friday and returns from Seisia on Monday.

Car & Motorcycle

From Cairns to the top of Cape York is 952km via the shortest and most challenging route. The first 175km of the Peninsula Developmental Rd from Mareeba to Lakeland is sealed. The journey from Lakeland to Weipa is nearly 600km of wide and reasonably well maintained but often corrugated unsealed road. As you head north of the Weipa turn-off, the real adventure begins along the Telegraph Rd (also known as the Overland Telegraph Track) to Cape York. The creek crossings become more numerous and more challenging: this is pure 4WD territory. Further north you have the choice of continuing on Telegraph Rd or taking the better-maintained bypass roads.

Lakeland & Laura

At Lakeland, the Peninsula Developmental Rd (known as the PDR) heads northwest up the cape as a wide, well-maintained dirt road. Lakeland has a general store, a small caravan park and a hotel-motel.

Leaving Lakeland you enter Quinkan country, so named for the Aboriginal

spirits depicted at the rock-art sites scattered throughout this area. Unesco lists Quinkan country in the top 10 rock-art regions in the world. About 50km north of Lakeland is the turn-off to the gallery at Split Rock, the only site open to the public. The sandstone escarpments here are covered with paintings dating back 14,000 years.

In Laura, the Quinkan & Regional Cultural Centre (✆07-4060 3457; www.quinkancc. com.au; adult/child $5.50/2; ☺8.30am-5pm Mon-Fri, 9am-3.30pm Sat & Sun) is a cultural and heritage centre covering the history of the region. This is the place to organise guided tours of the Split Rock art sites with an Aboriginal guide.

LAURA
POP 230

This sleepy settlement comes alive in June of odd-numbered years with the three-day Laura Aboriginal Dance Festival (www. laurafestival.tv), the largest traditional Indigenous gathering in Australia.

You can fuel up at the roadhouse (✆07-4060 3419) or the **Laura Store & Post Office**. Both sell gas, ice and basic groceries.

The historic, corrugated-iron Quinkan Hotel (✆07-4060 3393; Terminus St; unpowered/powered sites $20/26, r $69) burnt down in 2002 and although the rebuilt and refurbished pub is clean and functional it lacks the rustic character of the original. The park opposite the pub has a lock-up dating from the 1880s.

Laura to Musgrave

North from Laura some of the creek crossings, such as the Little Laura and Kennedy Rivers, are great places to camp. For a scenic alternative route to Musgrave, take the turn-off for Lakefield National Park, about 28km north of Laura.

Staying on the Peninsula Developmental Rd brings you to a food-and-fuel (and beer) pit stop, the Hann River Roadhouse (✆07-4060 3242; Peninsula Developmental Rd; campsites $6), 76km north of Laura.

The Musgrave Roadhouse (✆07-4060 3229; campsites $10, r $88), 80km from Hann River, was built in 1887. Originally a telegraph station, it's now a licensed cafe and roadhouse selling fuel, basic groceries and beer. Rooms are simple while the camping area is green and grassed.

Cape York Peninsula

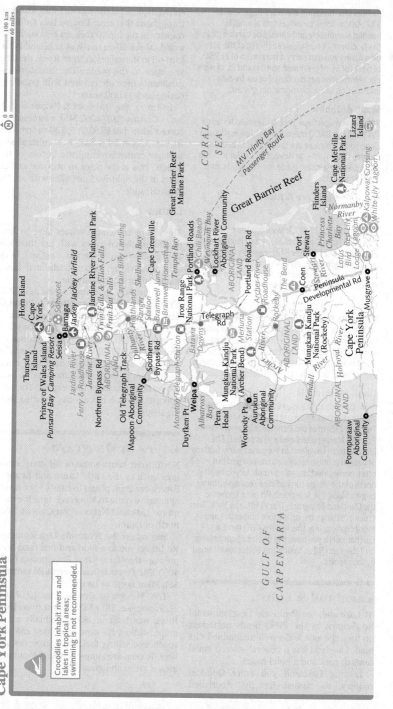

Crocodiles inhabit rivers and lakes in tropical areas; swimming is not recommended.

Thursday Island
Horn Island
Prince of Wales Island
Punsand Bay Camping Resort
Seisia
Cape York
Somerset
Bamaga
Jackey Jackey Airfield
Jardine River
Ferry & Roadhouse
Jardine River
Jardine River National Park
Twin Falls & Eliot Falls
Fruit Bat Falls
Northern Bypass Rd
Old Telegraph Track
ABORIGINAL LAND
Captain Billy Landing
Dulhunty River
Heathlands Ranger Station
Bramwell Junc
Bramwell Homestead
Shelburne Bay
Cape Grenville
Temple Bay
Mapoon Aboriginal Community
Southern Bypass Rd
Batavia Downs
Moreton Telegraph Station
Iron Range National Park
Telegraph Rd
Portland Roads
Chili Beach
Weymouth Bay
Lockhart River Aboriginal Community
Portland Roads Rd
Great Barrier Reef Marine Park
Duyken Pt.
Albatross Bay
Weipa
Pera Head
Mungkan Kandju National Park (Archer Bend)
Merluna Station
ABORIGINAL LAND
Archer River Roadhouse
Archer River
Rockeby
The Bend
Port Stewart
Coen
Peninsula Developmental Rd
Great Barrier Reef
Flinders Island
Normanby River
Cape Melville National Park
Lizard Island
Kalpowar Crossing
White Lily Lagoon
Princess Charlotte Bay
Lotus Bird Lodge
Red Lily Lagoon
Worbody Pt.
Aurukun Aboriginal Community
Kendall River
Holroyd River
Mungkan Kandju National Park (Rockeby)
Cape York Peninsula
Musgrave
Stewart River
Pormpuraaw Aboriginal Community
ABORIGINAL LAND
CORAL SEA
MV Trinity Bay Passenger Route
GULF OF CARPENTARIA

100 km
60 miles

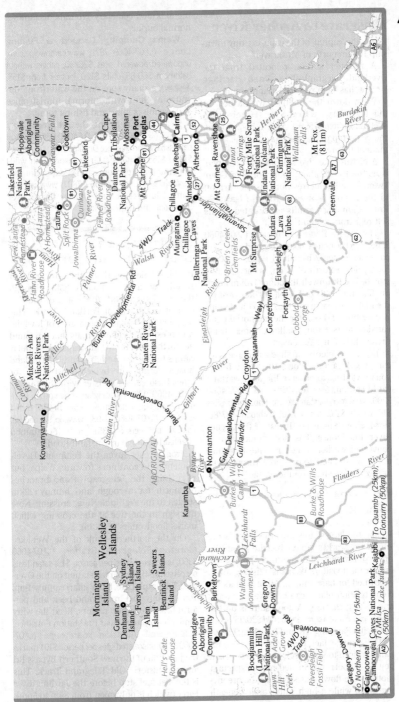

Musgrave to Archer River

Coen, the 'capital' of the cape, is a tiny township 108km north of Musgrave.

A repeater station relocated from the Overland Telegraph line, Coen Heritage House, has been restored as a museum.

Wash down the bulldust with a beer at the legendary 'S'Exchange Hotel (☑07-4060 1133; r from $75; ✹). After a boozy prank the 'S' on top of the pub has become a permanent fixture.

A picturesque riverside spot for campers is at the Bend, about 5km north of Coen. Twenty-five kilometres north is the turn-off to the remote Mungkan Kandju National Park. Camping permits are located at the self-registration stand.

The Archer River Roadhouse (☑07-4060 3266; archerriverroadhouse@bigpond.com; unpowered sites adult/child $10/5, r $65; ☉7.30am-10pm), 66km north of Coen, is the last fuel stop before Bramwell Junction (170km north on Telegraph Rd) or Weipa (197km west on the PDR). Here you can tuck into the famous Archer burger. Look for the memorial dedicated to Toots, a tough-talking woman truck driver and a Cape York legend.

There are plenty of shady and pleasant camping locations along the river, but if you're wanting to observe life on a working cattle station, Merluna Station (☑07-4060 3209; www.merlunastation.com; unpowered sites $10, cabins $110, s/d without bathroom $77/88; ✹✉), about 80km northwest of the Archer River Roadhouse, has accommodation in converted workers quarters. Guests gather in the 'wreck shed' to play pool, throw darts, or sizzle a few snags on the barbie.

Weipa

POP 2900

Weipa, the largest town on the cape, is the site of the world's largest bauxite mine (the ore from which aluminium is processed), but for most visitors Weipa is a fishing town, renowned for barramundi. All of Weipa's accommodation places can book various tours and fishing charters. A good start is on the town and mine tour (adult/child $30/15) from the Weipa Camping Ground & Fishing Lodge.

The strange fact that sets this coconut palm-fringed town apart is that a person can neither be born nor buried here. Expectant mothers are flown out six weeks before giving birth, while a high water table beneath the allocated cemetery grounds disallows a normal burial.

Weipa Camping Ground & Fishing Lodge (☑07-4069 7871; www.campweipa.com; unpowered/powered sites $26/30, cabins without bathroom $60-85, units $120, lodge r from $155; ✹@✉), a shady spot on the waterfront, operates as the town's informal tourist office and organises mine and fishing tours.

Near the waterfront, the Albatross Bay Resort (☑1800 240 663, 07-4090 6666; www.albatrossbayresort.com.au; Duyfken Cres; bungalows $130, r $155; ✹✉) is a large resort with well-appointed motel rooms and cheaper dongas.

Weipa Air (☑07-4069 7807; www.weipaair.com.au) has scenic and charter flights over the coast and Cape York.

Archer River to Bramwell Junction

Roughly 36km north of the Archer River Roadhouse, a turn-off leads 135km through the Iron Range National Park to the tiny coastal settlement of Portland Roads. This park has Australia's largest area of lowland rainforest, with some animals that are found no further south in Australia. A popular campsite is Chili Beach, south of Portland Roads. Permits are by self-registration; for other bush camps register with the ranger (☑07-4060 7170). Otherwise, to savour a little luxury in the wilderness, stay in Portland House (☑07-4060 7193; www.portlandhouse.com.au; per person $85), a self-contained beachside cottage in Portland Roads.

From Archer River, the Peninsula Developmental Rd continues towards Weipa, but after 48km the Telegraph Road branches off north for a rough and bumpy 22km stretch to the Wenlock River crossing. Note the sign in the tree at the crossing which marks floodwaters of 14.3m.

On the northern bank of the Wenlock, Moreton Telegraph Station (☑07-4060 3360; unpowered sites per person $10, safari tents per person $84), formerly a station on the Overland Telegraph Line, has a safari camp set-up. You can buy fuel, meals and beer, and perform basic workshop repairs. Read the witty tombstone epitaph near the station entrance.

Bramwell Junction roadhouse (☑07-4060 3230; unpowered sites per person $10) marks the junction of the new Southern Bypass Rd and the historic Old Telegraph Track. This is the last fuel stop before the Jardine River Ferry (which is only open from 8am to 5pm).

LAKEFIELD NATIONAL PARK

Lakefield National Park, Queensland's second-largest national park, is renowned for its vast river systems, spectacular wetlands and prolific bird life. Covering more than 537,000 hectares, the park encompasses a rich and diverse landscape across the flood plains of the Normanby, Kennedy, Bizant, Morehead and Hann Rivers. This extensive river system drains into Princess Charlotte Bay on the park's northern perimeter.

Old Laura Homestead, near the junction with the Battle Camp Rd from Cooktown, was built soon after the 1874 Palmer River gold rush. The QPWS ranger station (☎07-4060 3260) is located at New Laura, about 25km north of the junction.

The best camping facilities (with toilets and showers) are at Kalpowar Crossing (per person/family $5/21) beside the Laura River. Obtain permits from the self-registration stand near the Lakefield QPWS ranger station (☎07-4060 3271; www.epa.qld.gov.au), 3km south of the campground.

The picturesque Red Lily Lagoon and White Lily Lagoon, about 8km north of the Lakefield ranger base, attract masses of bird life, including jabirus, brolgas and magpie geese. The red lotus lilies at Red Lily Lagoon are best appreciated in the morning when the lotus blossoms are in full bloom.

Soon after Hann Crossing the flat, treeless landscape of Nifold Plain stretches from horizon to horizon, its spectacular monotony broken only by sweeping grasslands and giant termite mounds.

About 26km before Musgrave, Lotus Bird Lodge (☎07-4060 3400; www.lotusbird.com. au; Marina Plains Rd; s/d incl meals $375/550; ☒), a favourite with birdwatchers, has comfortable timber cabins overlooking a lagoon. The lodge is open from May to December.

Fifteen kilometres before the roadhouse is the turn-off to Australia's most northern cattle station, Bramwell Homestead (☎07-4060 3300; bramwellstn@bigpond.com), which offers accommodation, camping and meals.

Bramwell Junction to Jardine River

After Bramwell Junction there are two possible routes to the Jardine River ferry. The longer route on the graded and reasonably well-maintained Southern and Northern Bypass Rds is quicker and avoids most of the creeks and rivers between the Wenlock and Jardine Rivers.

The more direct but far more challenging route down the Old Telegraph Track (commonly called the OTT or 'the Track') is where the real Cape York adventure begins.

The OTT follows the remnants of the Overland Telegraph Line, which was constructed during the 1880s to allow communications from Cairns to the cape via a series of repeater stations and an underwater cable link to Thursday Island. The OTT is a serious 4WD experience with deep corrugations, powdery sand and difficult creek crossings (especially the Dulhunty River crossing).

A road leaves the OTT 2km north of the Dulhunty and heads for Heathlands Ranger Station (☎07-4060 3241), looping past the difficult Gunshot Creek crossing. Back on the OTT, the road becomes sandy for a stretch before joining the Southern Bypass Rd.

After 9km, the Northern Bypass Rd heads west to the Jardine River ferry crossing, but if you continue another 7km on the OTT you reach the turn-off to Twin Falls & Eliot Falls. The falls and the deep emerald-green swimming holes here are spectacular, and worth a long visit. The camping ground (per person/family $5/21) is the most popular site on the trip north. Permits are at the self-registration stand.

The old vehicular crossing of the Jardine River on the OTT is closed. The only access to the Jardine River ferry is on the Northern Bypass Rd.

JARDINE RIVER

The Jardine River is Queensland's largest perennial river, spilling more fresh water into the sea than any other river in Australia. The Jardine River Ferry & Roadhouse (☎07-4069 1369; unpowered sites $5; ☺8am-5pm), run by the Injinoo Community Council, sells fuel and operates a ferry during the dry season ($88 return, plus $11 for trailers). The fee

includes a permit for bush camping between the Dulhunty and Jardine Rivers, and in designated areas north of the Jardine.

Stretching east to the coast from the main track is the impenetrable country of Jardine River National Park. It includes the headwaters of the Jardine and Escape Rivers, where explorer Edmund Kennedy was killed by Aborigines in 1848.

Northern Peninsula Area

Everything north of the Jardine River is known as the Northern Peninsula Area (NPA to the locals).

BAMAGA & SEISIA

The first settlement north of the Jardine River is Bamaga (population 784), home to Cape York Peninsula's largest Torres Strait Islander community. There's a small shopping centre, a hospital and an airstrip.

Five kilometres northwest of Bamaga, Seisia (population 165) overlooks the Torres Strait and is a great base from which to explore the tip.

Cape York Adventures (☎07-4069 3302; www.capeyorkadventures.com.au) has half-day and full-day fishing trips and sunset cruises.

Resort Bamaga (☎07-4069 3050; http://resortbamaga.com.au; r from $220; ❄❄), overlooking Mosby Creek, is a very basic four-star resort, and has a restaurant.

Seisia Holiday Park (☎07-4069 3243; www.seisiaholidaypark.com; unpowered/powered sites per person $12/15, lodge s/d $80/120, cottages $160-230; ❄@), next to Seisia's wharf, is a popular campground with good facilities and a restaurant. The park is also a booking agent for scenic flights, 4WD tours, and the ferry to Thursday Island. Loyalty Beach Campground & Fishing Lodge (☎07-4069 3372; www.loyaltybeach.com; unpowered/powered sites $20/22, lodge s/d $105/135), on the beachfront 3km from the wharf, is a quieter spot.

Peddells Ferry Service (☎07-4069 1551; www.peddellsferry.com.au; adult/child $56/28; ☺8am & 4pm Mon-Sat Jun-Sep, Mon, Wed & Fri Oct-May) runs regular ferries from Seisia jetty to Thursday Island. See p469.

THE TIP

From Bamaga the road north passes Lockerbie Homestead. The Croc Tent (☎07-4069 3210; www.croctent.com.au; ☺7.30am-6pm), across the road, sells souvenirs and provides an unofficial tourist information service. The road then passes through the northernmost rainforest in Australia, Lockerbie Scrub, before reaching a Y-junction.

The track right leads to the pretty foreshore of Somerset. The left track leads 10km down the road to the now defunct Pajinka Wilderness Lodge. A 1km walk through the forest and along the beach (over the headland if the tide's in) takes you to Cape York, the northernmost tip of Australia.

On the western side of the tip, the scenic Punsand Bay Camping Resort (☎07-4069 1722; www.punsand.com.au; unpowered/powered sites per person $10/12, tents per person incl meals $140-200, air-con cabins per person incl meals $220; ❄) is a remote haven in the wilderness. A dip in the pool, or a cold beer in the breezy restaurant, tops off the tip experience. Dato's Venture (☎/fax 07-4090 2005) operates a ferry (May to November) to Thursday and Horn Islands from here.

Thursday Island & Torres Strait Islands

Australia's most northern frontier consists of over 100 islands stretching like stepping stones for 150km from the top of Cape York Peninsula to Papua New Guinea. The islands vary from the rocky, northern extensions of the Great Dividing Range to small coral cays and rainforested volcanic mountains.

Torres Strait Islanders came from Melanesia and Polynesia about 2000 years ago, establishing a unique culture different from those of Papua New Guinea and the Australian Aborigines.

Although Prince of Wales Island is the largest of the group, the administrative capital is tiny Thursday Island (it's only 3 sq km), 30km off the cape. Although lacking its own freshwater supply, Thursday Island (population 2800) was selected for its deep harbour, sheltered port, and proximity to major shipping channels. One of 17 inhabited islands in the strait, TI (as it's locally known) was once a major pearling centre, and the legacy of that industry has resulted in a friendly cultural mix of Asians, Europeans and Islanders.

Erub (Darnley Island as it is also known) is in the eastern group, and is of volcanic origin. It's another important island in the region as it has come into the spotlight as a campaigner for equal recognition of Torres Strait Islanders' rights.

Regular ferry services connect Seisia with Thursday and Horn Islands. To visit other

inhabited Torres Strait Islands requires permission from the island's council; contact the **Torres Strait Regional Council** (☑07-4069 1446; www.tsirc.qld.gov.au; Torres Strait Haus, Victoria Pde, Thursday Island).

◎ Sights & Activities

On Thursday Island, the **Gab Titui Cultural Centre** (☑07-4090 2130; www.gabtitui.com.au; cnr Victoria Pde & Blackall St; admission $6; ◷9am-5pm Mon-Sat, 2-5pm Sun) houses a modern gallery displaying the people's history of the Torres Strait; it also hosts cultural events and exhibitions by local artists, and has a popular outdoor cafe.

TI's pearling heyday resulted in fatalities from decompression sickness. The **Japanese Pearl Divers Memorial** at the cemetery presides over the many Japanese divers buried here. TI's war history can be experienced with a visit to **Green Hill Fort**, which was built in 1893 in response to fears of a Russian invasion. The **Torres Strait Museum**, in the fort, displays war paraphernalia and local artefacts.

The **All Souls Quetta Memorial Church** was built in 1893 in memory of the 134 lives lost when the *Quetta* struck an uncharted reef and sank within three minutes. Inside the church is memorabilia from a number of shipwrecks, including a coral-encrusted porthole recovered from the *Quetta* in 1906.

The **Heritage Museum & Art Gallery** (☑07-4069 2222; www.torresstrait.com.au; adult/child $7/4) at the Gateway Torres Strait Resort on Horn Island has a mine of information on the region's WWII history.

☞ Tours

Peddells Ferry Island Tourist Bureau   BUS & 4WD TOURS
(☑07-4069 1551; www.peddellsferry.com.au; Engineers Wharf; adult/child $31/16; ◷8.30am-5pm) Offers bus tours of TI, taking in all the major tourist sites. Also runs Cape York 4WD day trips and Horn Island WWII tours.

Tony's Island Adventures   FISHING
(☑07-4069 1965; www.tonysislandadventures.com.au) Offers fishing trips and tours of various Torres Strait Islands, including Friday, Hammond and Goodes Islands.

🛏 Sleeping & Eating

Gateway Torres Strait Resort   HOTEL **$$**
(☑07-4069 2222; www.torresstrait.com.au; 24 Outie St, Horn Island; r $169-249; ❄@☒) This

place has worn rooms and self-contained units. The resort houses the museum as well as an ambience-free restaurant that spreads buffet dinners and lunches during the dry season.

Jardine Resort   MOTEL **$$$**
(☑07-4069 1555; www.jardinemotel.com.au; cnr Normanby St & Victoria Pde, Thursday Island; s/d $180/200; ❄@☏☒) Although looking a little jaded, this is still the best deal on the island. There's a popular restaurant here.

Grand Hotel   HOTEL **$$**
(☑07-4069 1557; www.grandhotelti.com.au; 6 Victoria Pde, Thursday Island; s/d from $165/180; ❄@) On a hill behind the wharf, the Grand Hotel has comfortable, modern rooms with ocean and mountain views. The **restaurant** (◷dinner Mon-Sat) has a balcony with sweeping views.

Thursday Island Motel   MOTEL **$$$**
(☑07-4069 2500; www.thursdayislandmotel.com.au; cnr Jardine & Douglas Sts, Thursday Island; s/d incl breakfast $190/200; ❄@) These new and comfortable motel units at the back of the Federal Hotel are a good choice.

Federal Hotel   HOTEL **$$**
(☑07-4069 1569; www.federalhotelti.com.au; Victoria Pde, Thursday Island; s/d incl breakfast $160/180; ❄) Tired but spacious motel-style rooms, a beer garden, and a colourful mural depicting island life in the public bar.

ℹ Getting There & Around

QantasLink (☑13 13 13; www.qantas.com.au) flies daily from Cairns to Horn Island.

Peddells Ferry Service (☑07-4069 1551; www.peddellsferry.com.au; Engineers Jetty, Thursday Island) Runs regular services between Seisia and Thursday Island. From June to September it has two daily services from Monday to Saturday (adult/child $56/28 one way), and from October to May it operates only on Monday, Wednesday and Friday. The ferry departs Thursday Island for Seisia at 6.30am and 2.30pm, and Seisia for Thursday Island at 8am and 4pm.

McDonald Charter Boats (☑1300 664 875; www.tiferry.com.au) Runs ferries between TI and Horn Island roughly hourly between 6.30am and 6.30pm (adult/child $20/10 one way, 15 minutes), as well as a water-taxi service between other Torres Strait Islands. McDonald also operates a bus service to and from Horn Island Airport.

Rebel Marine (☑07-4069 1586; info@rebeltours.com.au) Operates a water taxi between Thursday Island and Horn Island Airport connecting with all QantasLink flights ($18 one way).

Melbourne & Victoria

Includes »

Best Places to Eat

» Cutler & Co (p504)

» Loam (p523)

» Royal Mail Hotel (p553)

» Stefano's Restaurant (p560)

Best Places to Stay

» Punthill Apartments (p500)

» Medina Executive Flinders St (p495)

» YHA Eco Beach (p541)

» Dreamers (p596)

Why Go?

Melbourne, Australia's second-largest city, is the state's urban hub and the nation's artistic centre. Here, culture junkies and culinary perfectionists feast on art, music, theatre, cinema and cuisine for every budget.

Scalloping its way around coves, beaches and cliffs, the Great Ocean Road is great indeed. Wild surf pounds the shoreline and enigmatic coastal towns mingle with lush national parks.

In the High Country, brilliant autumn colours segue into snowfields and back again to sleepy summer towns, haunted by pale gums. Skis get a workout in winter, and cycling, horse riding and cheeky weekends are the mainstays of summer.

If wild landscapes are your weakness, head to the Grampians National Park, sprawled amid the dry plains of the Western District. Australia's southernmost mainland tip is the spiritually reviving Wilsons Promontory National Park. Cosmopolitan tourists can duck just outside of Melbourne and sample fine wines in the Yarra Valley and Mornington Peninsula.

When to Go?

Melbourne

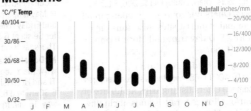

Feb School-holiday crowds have left, leaving good weather for swimming and hiking.

Apr Enjoy quiet coastal beaches and camp sites, and live music at the Apollo Bay Music Festival.

Nov Hiking trails are in full colour after spring, while Melbourne is all aflutter about the Melbourne Cup.

Regional Tours

The **Great Ocean Road** is one of the most popular touring routes in Australia, and, blow us down with a limestone outcrop, it's worth the hype. Take plenty of time – two weeks is good – to get the best from this region.

Start in the surfing mecca of Torquay by checking out the waves at **Bells Beach**, then head to family-friendly **Anglesea** to see kangaroos grazing on its golf course. **Aireys Inlet** is next; tour the lighthouse then plan an overnight stay in the resort town of **Lorne**. Spend a day here then break up the sea views with a detour up into the rainforests of the **Otway Ranges**. Back on the Great Ocean Road, head to the fishing village of **Apollo Bay** for a day or two, then continue west into the koala and lighthouse zone of **Cape Otway**. It's quite a stretch to **Port Campbell National Park** and its famed **Twelve Apostles**; take the time to count them and spend a night in **Port Campbell** to get a feel for the area. Look for whales off **Warrnambool's** coast then continue west to quaint, and very Irish, **Port Fairy**. If there's time, head to tiny **Cape Bridgewater** to meet its seal population.

DON'T MISS

Who can resist the nightly parade of cute little penguins waddling out of the ocean and into their sandy burrows at **Phillip Island**? Not the three-million-plus tourists who visit annually, that's for sure. This little island in Western Port Bay also has fabulous surf beaches, a moto-GP circuit and wildlife parks.

For sheer natural beauty, **Wilsons Promontory** has it all. Jutting out into Bass Strait, this national park is isolated but accessible, boasting sublime ocean beaches and some of the best wilderness hiking in the state. With a well-maintained network of trails and bush camping areas, you just need to grab a map, strap on a pack and disappear into the wilds.

Beaches

» Surfing: try famous Bells Beach near Torquay (p538)

» Isolation: Ninety Mile Beach attracts those seeking space (p606)

» Beachside camping: camp for free by wild Johanna Beach (543)

» Family fun: Anglesea's sheltered Point Roadknight Beach or Main Beach (p538) is a family fave

TOP TIPS

» Head to the wharf in seaside towns and buy fresh seafood straight off the boat.

» Half Tix (p514) sells cheap tickets for day trips from Melbourne (think wineries or penguins) and Melbourne theatre performances.

Fast Facts

» Population: 5,444,000

» Area: 227 500 sq km

» Coastline: 2000km

» Number of wineries: 850

Planning Your Trip

Avoid the coast from Christmas until late January and during Easter; school holidays equate to packed beaches, booked-out accommodation and restricted access to popular hiking trails. See www.education.vic.gov.au for school term dates.

Resources

» Visit Victoria (www.visitvictoria.com) Official state tourism site.

» Parks Victoria (www.parkweb.vic.gov.au) National park information.

» The Age (www.theage.com.au) Victorian news.

» Bureau of Meteorology (www.bom.gov.au/weather/vic) Weather forecasts.

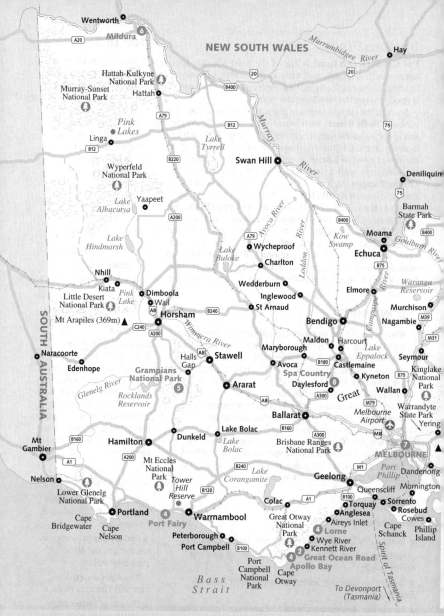

Melbourne & Victoria Highlights

1 Get exquisitely lost in the wilderness of **Croajingolong National Park** (p612)

2 Curl your way around the magical twists of the **Great Ocean Road** (p534)

all the way to Port Campbell National Park

3 Slip, slide and revel down the ski slopes of the **High Country** (p584)

4 Make merry at music festivals at **Apollo Bay** (p541), **Lorne** (p539) and **Port Fairy** (p547)

5 Experience breathtaking hikes and Aboriginal culture in

NEW SOUTH WALES

100 km
60 miles

Narrandera

Murrumbidgee River

Gundagai

Yass

Wagga Wagga

CANBERRA

AUSTRALIAN CAPITAL TERRITORY

Tocumwal

Lake Mulwala

Cobram
Rutherglen   Albury

Lake Hume

Burrowa-Pine Mountain National Park

Numurkah
Yarrawonga
Chiltern   Wodonga
Tallangatta
Corryong

Cooma

Wangaratta
Beechworth
Mitta Mitta River

Murray River

Shepparton
Glenrowan
Myrtleford
Porepunkah

Mt Kosciuszko (2228m)

Mt Buffalo National Park
Bright   Mt Beauty
Harrietville   Falls Creek

Lake Dartmouth

Bega

Mt Buller (1805m)
Mt Hotham (1868m)   Dinner Plain
Omeo

Snowy River National Park

Alpine National Park

Range

Errinundra National Park
Coopracambra National Park

Lake Eildon

Yea   Eildon
Dividing

Lake Mountain (1433m)

High Country

Snowy River

Genoa

Dargo

Healesville
Yarra Ranges National Park

Buchan

Nowa Nowa   Orbost

Cann River
Mallacoota
Cape Howe

Warburton

Mitchell River National Park

Bairnsdale

Marlo

Croajingolong National Park

Mt Dandenong (633m)
Baw Baw National Park
Walhalla

Metung   Lakes Entrance

Cape Conran Coastal Park

Point Hicks

Warragul
Moe   Traralgon
Morwell

Sale

Loch Sport
The Lakes National Park

TASMAN SEA

French Island
Korumburra
Tarra-Bulga National Park

Ninety Mile Beach

Leongatha

Seaspray

Inverloch
Foster

Cape Paterson
Yanakie   Corner Inlet

Snake Island

Cape Liptrap
Tidal River

Wilsons Promontory National Park

Bass Strait

the **Grampians National Park** (p551)

6 Meander the Murray on a paddle steamer in **Mildura** (p557)

7 Hit the funky suburbs of

Melbourne and get low-key and groovy in **Fitzroy** (p487), sun-kissed in **St Kilda** (p489) and styled up in **South Yarra** (p488)

8 Have a soak in the natural mineral springs of **spa**

country (p579), just a 1½-hour drive from the city

9 Get hiking at **Wilsons Promontory National Park** (p601)

History

In 1803 a party of convicts, soldiers and settlers arrived at Sorrento (on the southern edge of Port Phillip Bay), but the settlement was soon abandoned. The first permanent European settlement in Victoria was established in 1834 at Portland (in the Western District) by the Henty family from Van Diemen's Land (Tasmania), some 46 years after Sydney was colonised. In 1851 Victoria won separation from New South Wales, and in that same year the rich Victorian goldfields were discovered, attracting immigrants from around the world. Towns such as Beechworth and Ballarat boomed during the gold rush, and are veritable museum pieces today. Melbourne was founded in 1835 by enterprising Tasmanians and it retains much Victorian-era charm and gold-boom 1880s architecture to this day.

The latter half of the 20th century saw a huge influx of immigrants into Victoria, particularly Melbourne, and the city is now widely regarded as Australia's most multicultural city. It has one of the largest Greek populations per capita in the world and is heavily influenced by Italian, Eastern European and Southeast Asian cultures.

The 1990s and 21st century havee seen a period of ferocious development begin – a process that continues today – and the face of the CBD has changed and spread markedly with the boom of the Docklands, and the construction of architectural landmarks such as Federation Square.

Indigenous Victoria

Aboriginal people have lived in Victoria for an estimated 40,000 years. They lived in some 38 different dialect groups that spoke 10 separate languages. These groups were further divided into clans and subclans, each with its own customs and laws, and each claiming ownership of a distinct area of land. Before British colonisation, the Yarra Valley region was occupied by members of the Woiworung clan of the Kulin Nation, known as the Wurundjeri.

As many as 100,000 Aboriginal people lived in Victoria before Europeans arrived; by 1860 there were as few as 2000 left alive. Today around 27,000 Koories (Aborigines from southeastern Australia) live in Victoria, and more than half live in Melbourne.

Many cultures have been lost, but there has been a strong movement to revive Aboriginal culture in Victoria and there are cultural centres around the state, including the excellent Brambuk Cultural Centre and Gariwerd Dreaming Theatre, both in Halls Gap in the Grampians National Park. Run by local Koorie communities, these centres provide insights into Koorie history, culture, art, music and dance, and provide tours to local rock-art sites.

In Bairnsdale the Krowathunkoolong Keeping Place is a Koorie cultural centre that explores Kurnai daily life before and after white settlement.

Based in Mildura, Harry Nanya's Graham Clarke provides acclaimed tours into Lake Mungo National Park, with excellent commentary about the traditional occupants of the land.

In Melbourne, the Ian Potter Centre: National Gallery of Victoria Australia has a renowned collection of Aboriginal and Torres Strait Islander art, while the Aboriginal Heritage Walk takes you through the story of the Boonwurrung and Woiworung peoples, on whose ancestral grounds the Royal Botanic Gardens now sit.

Melbourne itself is divided between the Wurundjeri and the Boonwurrung peoples, and both groups are represented by female elders – Aunty Joy Murphy and Aunty Carolyn Briggs.

For more information about the history of the Victorian Indigenous people, visit the Koorie Heritage Trust Cultural Centre or the interesting and comprehensive Bunjilaka Indigenous centre at Melbourne Museum.

A 'Welcome to Country' ceremony – which can vary from a speech to a traditional dance or a smoking ceremony – by an Aboriginal community member is now common protocol across the state and these are performed at a diverse range of functions. An 'Acknowledgement Ceremony' is common at forums, whereby the first speaker pays recognition and respect to the traditional owners of the land. Similarly, a gum-leaf ceremony is common at dinners and events.

The website of Visit Victoria (www.visit victoria.com) has an excellent link to Aboriginal culture, heritage, history and sites in Victoria. Another good resource is Aboriginal Tourism Victoria (www.aboriginal tourismvictoria .com).

Aboriginal Melbourne – The Lost Land of the Kulin People by Gary Presland (re-released 2001) and *Aboriginal Victorians, A History since 1800* by Richard Broome (2005) also give valuable insight into the culture and life of the region's original inhabitants.

MELBOURNE

POP 4 MILLION

There's a lot of fun packed into this city of some four million people. Coffee, food, art and fashion are taken mighty seriously, but that doesn't mean they're only for those in the know; all you need to eat well, go bar-hopping or shopping is a bit of cash and a deft ability to find hidden stairways down graffiti-covered laneways.

In many ways, it's the indie scene that sets Melbourne apart, and it's spottable mainly in the CBD, St Kilda, Fitzroy, Collingwood, Brunswick and, further north, in Northcote, but ekes out a living in most nooks and crannies in the city's inner suburbs.

Splitting the northern suburbs of Fitzroy, Collingwood and Carlton from its southern sisters including Prahran, South Yarra and St Kilda is the very brown Yarra River. There's a slight cultural divide, too, though sport knows no boundaries and Melburnians are intoxicatingly loud-voiced about AFL football (footy), horse racing or cricket, depending on the season.

History

In May 1835 John Batman 'bought' around 2400 sq km of land from the Aborigines of the Kulin Nation, the traditional owners. The concept of buying or selling land was foreign to the Aboriginal culture and in an extremely one-sided exchange they received some tools, flour and clothing as 'payment'.

By 1840 there were more than 10,000 Europeans living in the area around present-day Melbourne. The wealth from the goldfields built this city, known as 'Marvellous Melbourne', and this period of prosperity lasted until the depression at the end of the 1880s.

Post-WWII, Melbourne's social fabric was greatly enriched by an influx of people and cultures from around the world. Several building booms have altered the city physically and it's now a striking blend of ornate 19th-century buildings sitting alongside towering skyscrapers, and a growing number of modern apartment complexes (including one which was, briefly, the tallest residential building in the world).

Today the city is a mixture of beloved towering gold-rush-era architecture, industrial buildings (the 'industrial' look is so popular in Melbourne's cafes and restaurants that brand new buildings are mimicking its rough style), and new multi-unit developments, designed (but not entirely working) to stave off Melbourne's urban sprawl. Inner-city suburbs, once the haunt of a seedy underworld, are now fashionable, hip and mighty pricey to live in (and still a haunt of the seedy underworld).

⊙ Sights

CENTRAL MELBOURNE

Federation Square   LANDMARK
(Map p482; www.federationsquare.com.au; cnr Flinders & Swanston Sts) Striking Federation Square has become the place to celebrate, protest or party. Occupying a prominent city block, the 'square' is far from square. Its undulating forecourt of Kimberley stone echoes the town squares of Europe. Here you'll find the subterranean Melbourne Visitor Centre (✆03-9928 0096; ⊙9am-6pm; tours per adult $12).

Ian Potter Centre: National Gallery of Victoria Australia   ART GALLERY
(NGVA; Map p482; www.ngv.vic.gov.au; ⊙10am-5pm Tue-Sun) This houses the NGV's extensive collection of Australian paintings, decorative arts, photography, prints, drawings, sculpture, fashion, textiles and jewellery.

The gallery's Indigenous collection dominates the ground floor and seeks to challenge ideas of the 'authentic'. Upstairs there are permanent displays of colonial paintings and drawings by 19th-century Aboriginal artists. There's also the work of Heidelberg School impressionists and an extensive collection of the work of the modernist 'Angry Penguins', including Sir Sidney Nolan, Arthur Boyd, Joy Hester and Albert Tucker.

Australian Centre for the Moving Image   MUSEUM
(ACMI; Map p482; www.acmi.net.au; ⊙10am-6pm) ACMI manages to educate, enthral and entertain in equal parts, and has enough games and movies on call for days, or even months of screen time. 'Screenworld' is an exhibition that celebrates the work of mostly Australian cinema and TV and, upstairs, the Australian Mediatheque is a venue set aside for the viewing of programs from the National Film and Sound Archive, and ACMI.

Chinatown   NEIGHBOURHOOD
(Map p482; Little Bourke St, btwn Spring & Swanston Sts) Chinese miners arrived in search of the 'new gold mountain' in the 1850s and settled in this strip of Little Bourke St, now flanked by red archways. Here you'll find an interesting mix of bars and restaurants, including one of Melbourne's best, Flower

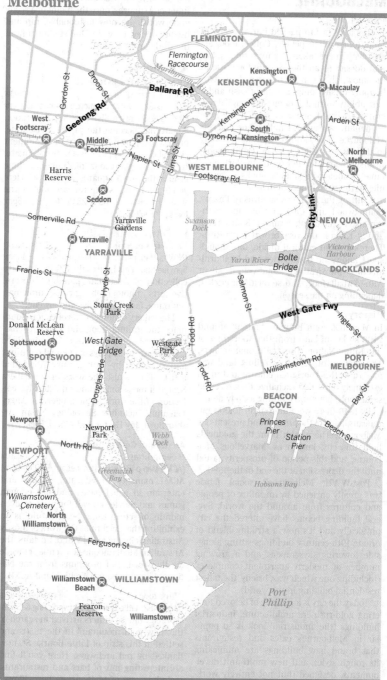

FLEMINGTON

Flemington Racecourse

Maribyrnong River

Ballarat Rd

Kensington Rd

KENSINGTON

Macaulay

Gordon St

Droop St

West Footscray

Geelong Rd

Middle Footscray

Footscray

Napier St

Sims St

South Kensington

Dynon Rd

Arden St

North Melbourne

Harris Reserve

Seddon

WEST MELBOURNE

Footscray Rd

Somerville Rd

Yarraville Gardens

Swanson Dock

CityLink

NEW QUAY

Yarraville

YARRAVILLE

Yarra River

Bolte Bridge

Victoria Harbour

DOCKLANDS

Francis St

Hyde St

Stony Creek Park

Salmon St

West Gate Fwy

Ingles St

Donald McLean Reserve

Spotswood

West Gate Bridge

Westgate Park

Todd Rd

SPOTSWOOD

Douglas Pde

Todd Rd

Williamstown Rd

PORT MELBOURNE

Bay St

Newport

Newport Park

Webb Dock

BEACON COVE

Princes Pier

Beach St

NEWPORT

North Rd

Station Pier

Greenwich Bay

Hobsons Bay

Williamstown Cemetery

North Williamstown

Ferguson St

Williamstown Beach

WILLIAMSTOWN

Port Phillip

Fearon Reserve

Williamstown

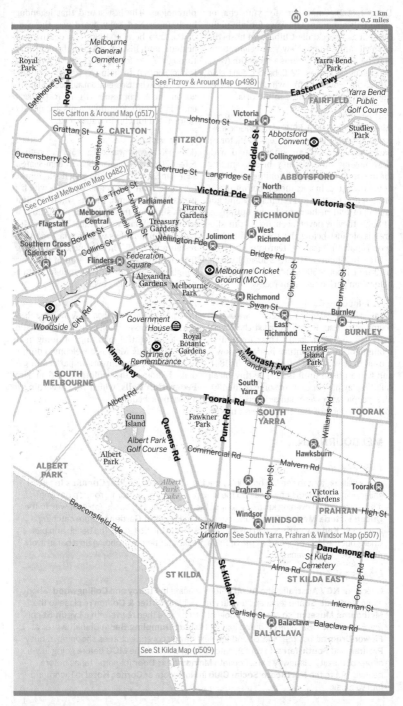

0 — 1 km
0 — 0.5 miles

Royal Park

Melbourne General Cemetery

Gatehouse St

Royal Pde

See Fitzroy & Around Map (p498)

Yarra Bend Park

Eastern Fwy

FAIRFIELD

Yarra Bend Public Golf Course

Studley Park

See Carlton & Around Map (p517)

Grattan St

CARLTON

Queensberry St

Swanston St

FITZROY

Johnston St

Victoria Park

Hoddle St

Abbotsford Convent

Collingwood

See Central Melbourne Map (p482)

La Trobe St

Exhibition St

Gertrude St

Langridge St

ABBOTSFORD

Victoria Pde

North Richmond

Victoria St

Parliament

Flagstaff

Melbourne Central

Russell St

Treasury Gardens

Fitzroy Gardens

RICHMOND

Bourke St

Collins St

Wellington Pde

Jolimont

West Richmond

Southern Cross (Spencer St)

Flinders St

Federation Square

Alexandra Gardens

Melbourne Park

Bridge Rd

Church St

Burnley St

Polly Woodside

City Rd

Government House

Melbourne Cricket Ground (MCG)

Richmond

Swan St

East Richmond

Burnley

BURNLEY

Kings Way

Shrine of Remembrance

Royal Botanic Gardens

Monash Fwy

Alexandra Ave

Herring Island Park

SOUTH MELBOURNE

Albert Rd

Queens Rd

Gunn Island

Albert Park Golf Course

Albert Park

Fawkner Park

Punt Rd

Toorak Rd

South Yarra

SOUTH YARRA

TOORAK

Williams Rd

ALBERT PARK

Commercial Rd

Albert Park Lake

Malvern Rd

Hawksburn

Chapel St

Prahran

Victoria Gardens

Toorak

Beaconsfield Pde

Windsor

WINDSOR

PRAHRAN

High St

St Kilda Junction

See South Yarra, Prahran & Windsor Map (p507)

St Kilda Rd

Dandenong Rd

St Kilda Cemetery

Alma Rd

Orrong Rd

ST KILDA EAST

ST KILDA

Inkerman St

Carlisle St

Balaclava

Balaclava Rd

BALACLAVA

See St Kilda Map (p509)

MELBOURNE & VICTORIA MELBOURNE

Drum (p502). Come here for yum cha, or explore its attendant laneways for late-night dumplings or cocktails. Chinatown hosts the city's vibrant Chinese New Year celebrations and the interesting Chinese Museum (www. chinesemuseum.com.au; 22 Cohen Pl; adult/child $7.50/5.50; ⊙10am-5pm), which showcases the history of the Chinese in Victoria.

Parliament House
HISTORIC BUILDING

(Map p482; ☑03-9651 8911; www.parliament.vic. gov.au; Spring St) The grand steps of Victoria's parliament (c 1856) are often dotted with slow-moving tulle-wearing brides smiling for the camera or placard-holding protesters doing the same. Inside, the exuberant use of ornamental plasterwork, stencilling and gilt are full of gold-rush-era pride and optimism. Though they've never been used, gun slits are visible just below the roof, and a dungeon is now the cleaners' tearoom.

Free half-hour tours (⊙9.30am, 10.30am, 11.30am, 1.30pm, 2.30pm 3.45pm Mon-Fri) are held when parliament is in recess.

Old Melbourne Gaol
HISTORIC BUILDING

(Map p482; ☑03-8663 7228; www.oldmelbournegaol.com.au; Russell St; adult/child/family $21/11/49; ⊙9.30am-5pm) This forbidding monument to 19th-century justice is now a museum. It was built of bluestone in 1841, and was a prison until 1929. The tiny, bleak cells display plaster casts of some of the 130-plus people who were hanged here, a chilling 'by-product' of the era's obsession with phrenology. The last sound that legendary bushranger Ned Kelly heard was the clang of the trap here in 1880. His death mask, armour and history are on display. Book through Ticketek (☑13 28 49; http://premier. ticketek.com.au) to join a Ghost Seekers Tour (www.ghostseekers.com.au; adult $140) or go on the Hangman's Night Tour (adult/ under 15 $35/30). Evening events are not recommended for children under 12.

Queen Victoria Market
MARKET

(Map p482; www.qvm.com.au; 513 Elizabeth St; ⊙6am-2pm Tue & Thu, 6am-5pm Fri, 6am-3pm Sat, 9am-4pm Sun) This site has been the market for more than 130 years, prior to which it was a burial ground. This is where Melburnians shop for fresh produce including organics and Asian specialities. There's a deli, meat and fish hall as well as a fast food and restaurant zone. On Wednesday evenings from mid-November to the end of February, a night market with hawker-style food stalls, bars and music takes over.

Birrarung Marr
PARK

(Map p482; btwn Federation Sq & the Yarra River) Featuring grassy knolls, river promenades and a thoughtful planting of indigenous flora, Birrarung Marr is a welcome addition to Melbourne's patchwork of parks and gardens. It houses the sculptural and musical Federation Bells, which ring according to a varying schedule.

MELBOURNE IN...

Two Days

Join a walking tour to see Melbourne's street art, then enjoy lunch at **Cumulus Inc** in art gallery–lined Flinders Lane. Soak up the view and a local brew from a rooftop bar until it's time to join an evening kayaking tour of the Yarra River. Day two, shop your way to the **Queen Victoria Market**. Take your bites to eat to **Flagstaff Gardens** before catching a tram to **St Kilda**, where you can take sunset photos and stroll along the beach and pier. Check out the little penguins at the St Kilda breakwater before propping up a bar in lively **Acland St** for the evening.

One Week

Check out **NGV Australia** and **ACMI** before heading to **Fitzroy** and **Collingwood**. Shop along **Gertrude St** and feast at Cumulus Inc's sibling **Cutler & Co**. You're close to the **Melbourne Museum**, so spend a couple of hours there then revive with a **Lygon St** coffee. Back in the CBD, dine on dumplings at **HuTong Dumpling Bar** in Chinatown, or at **Flower Drum** across the lane. Spend the next day discovering clothes shopping at busy **Prahran** and **South Yarra**. In winter, catch a footy game at the **MCG** before going low-fi at one of the city's laneway bars. Pop into **Movida Next Door** for some tapas before heading out to the **Northcote Social Club** in Northcote or **Corner Hotel** in Richmond for live music.

FAY JUNE BALL: WIRADJURI WOMAN & EDUCATOR, KOORIE HERITAGE TRUST

I run walking tours around Melbourne, showing people the only two indigenous river red gums left in Flagstaff Gardens, and taking them along the Birrarung (Yarra). It was mis-named the Yarra, which was actually the name of the (now gone) waterfall. Its real name is the Birrarung. People don't realise that Aboriginal language and art is specific to different regions. There are no dots in Victorian art: come to the Koorie Heritage Trust to buy real Victorian art and avoid ripping off Indigenous people.

See

The two scar trees in the MCG car park and the Corroboree Tree at St Kilda Junction (Map p509), which the St Kilda community saved.

Eat

Try Charcoal Lane in Fitzroy (p504).

Read

The Melbourne Dreaming: A Guide to the Aboriginal Places of Melbourne by Meyer Eidelson.

Did You Know?

Everyone talks about Melbourne's weather, and Melbourne's Wurundjeri had the answer: there are six seasons in Melbourne, not four.

Collins Street STREET
(Map p482; btwn Spring & Swanston Sts) The top end of Collins St (aka the 'Paris end') is lined with plane trees, grand buildings and luxe boutiques, giving it its moniker. The **Block Arcade**, which runs between Collins and Elizabeth Sts, was built in 1891 and features etched-glass ceilings and mosaic floors. Doing 'the Block' (walking around the block) was a popular pastime in 19th-century Melbourne, as it was the place to shop and be seen.

Flagstaff Gardens PARK
(Map p482; btwn La Trobe, William, Dudley & King Sts) These small gardens with an open lawn are popular with workers taking a lunchtime break. First known as Burial Hill, this is where most of the city's early settlers ended up. The hill once provided one of the best views out to the bay, so a signalling station was set up here; when a ship was sighted arriving from Britain, a flag was raised on the flagstaff to notify the settlers (it was also significant for the Wurundjeri for the same useful vista). The gardens contain trees that are well over 100 years old including Moreton Bay fig trees, and a variety of eucalypts, including spotted and sugar gums and river red gums.

Council House 2 NOTABLE BUILDING
(CH2; Map p482; www.melbourne.vic.gov.au; 240 Little Collins St) CH2 was completed in 2006 in response to meeting the council's own targets for zero carbon emissions by 2020. Its design is based on 'biomimicry', reflecting the complex ecosystem of the planet. The building uses the sun, water and wind in combination with a slew of sustainable technologies.

Royal Arcade HISTORIC BUILDING
(Map p482; www.royalarcade.com.au; 335 Bourke St Mall) This Parisian-style arcade was built between 1869 and 1870 and is Melbourne's oldest; the upper walls retain much of the original 19th-century detail. The black-and-white chequered path leads to the mythological figures of giant brothers Gog and Magog, perched with hammers atop the arched exit to Little Collins St.

Koorie Heritage Trust CULTURAL CENTRE
(Map p482; www.koorieheritagetrust.com; 295 King St; entry by gold-coin donation, tours $15; ⊙10am-4pm) This cultural centre is devoted to southeastern Aboriginal culture, and cares for artefacts and oral history. Its gallery spaces show a variety of contemporary and traditional work, a model scar tree at the centre's

heart, as well as a permanent chronological display of Victorian Koorie history. Behind the scenes, significant objects are carefully preserved; replicas that can be touched by visitors are used in the displays. There's also a shop with books, CDs, crafts and bush-food supplies.

Immigration Museum   MUSEUM
(Map p482; www.museumvictoria.com.au/immigrationmuseum; 400 Flinders St; adult/child $8/free; ⊙10am-5pm) The Immigration Museum uses personal and community voices, images and memorabilia to tell the many stories of immigration. It's symbolically housed in the old Customs House (1858–70).

Melbourne Aquarium   AQUARIUM
(Map p482; ☑03-9923 5999; www.melbourneaquarium.com.au; cnr Queenswharf Rd & King St; adult/child/family $33/19/88; ⊙9.30am-6pm) This aquarium is home to rays, gropers and sharks, all of which cruise around a 2.2-million-litre tank, watched closely by visitors through a see-through tunnel. Three times a day divers are thrown to the sharks; for between $150 and $345 you can join them.

State Library of Victoria   LIBRARY
(Map p482; www.slv.vic.gov.au; 328 Swanston St; ⊙10am-9pm Mon-Thu, to 6pm Fri-Sun; 🛜) When the library opened in 1856, people entering were required to sign the visitors' book, be over 14 years old and have clean hands. The only requirements today are that you leave your bags in the locker room ($1 to $2 for four hours) and maintain a bit of shush.

When the octagonal **La Trobe Reading Room** was completed in 1913, the reinforced-concrete dome was the largest of its kind in the world. The **Wheeler Centre** (www.wheelercentre.com), on the Little Lonsdale St side, was started up by Lonely Planet's founders, Tony and Maureen Wheeler, in 2010, and regularly features talks by local and international writers. Refresh at **Mr Tulk** (⊙closed Sun).

Until Never   ART GALLERY
(Map p482; www.untilnever.net; 2nd fl, 3-5 Hosier Lane; ⊙11am-5pm Wed-Sat) This gallery space is run by Andrew Mac, one of Melbourne's street-art masters, and highlights underground artists. It links in beautifully with the area's street art and ageing city-lights project. Enter from Rutledge Lane.

Bourke Street Mall   STREET
(Map p482; btwn Swanston & Elizabeth Sts) West of Swanston St marks the beginning of the Bourke St Mall. The mall is thick with trams, the sounds of Peruvian bands busking, shop-front spruikers and the general hubbub from shoppers. In a 60-year tradition, November to early January sees people lining up (sometimes for hours) to get a peek at the animated displays in **Myer's Christmas windows**.

Young & Jackson's   HISTORIC BUILDING
(Map p482; www.youngandjacksons.com.au; cnr Flinders & Swanston Sts) Across the street from Flinders Street Station is a pub known for more than beer (which it's been serving up since 1861); it's known for its painting of pre-pubescent *Chloe*. Painted by Jules Joseph Lefebvre, her yearning gaze, cast over her shoulder and out of the frame, was a hit at the Paris Salon of 1875. The painting caused an outcry in the pursed-lipped provincial Melbourne, however, and was removed from display at the National Gallery of Victoria. Eventually bought by publican and 'art lover' Henry Figsby Young in 1909, *Chloe* found an appreciative audience and permanent home at this pub.

SOUTHBANK & DOCKLANDS

Southbank, once a gritty industrial site, sits directly across the Yarra from Flinders St. Behind Southgate's shopping mall is the city's major arts precinct including the NGV International and the Victorian Arts Centre. Back down by the river, the promenade stretches to the Crown Casino & Entertainment Complex, a self-proclaimed 'world of entertainment', pulling in visitors 24/7. To the city's west lies Docklands.

FREE National Gallery of
Victoria International   ART GALLERY
(NGVI; off Map p482; www.ngv.vic.gov.au; 180 St Kilda Rd; ⊙10am-5pm Wed-Mon) Beyond the water wall you'll find international art that runs from the ancient to the contemporary. Completed in 1967, the original NGV building – Roy Grounds' 'cranky icon' – was one of Australia's most controversial but ultimately respected Modernist masterpieces. Interior remodelling was undertaken from 1996 to 2003, overseen by Mario Bellini. Don't miss a gaze up at the Great Hall's stained-glass ceiling.

Eureka Tower & Skydeck 88 NOTABLE BUILDING
(Map p482; www.eurekaskydeck.com.au; 7 Riverside Quay, Southbank; adult/child/family $18/9/40, The Edge extra $12/8/29; ⊙10am-10pm, last entry

If there's one out-of-Melbourne spot that deserves an afternoon dedicated to it, it's Heide (☑03-9850 1500; www.heide.com.au; 7 Templestowe Rd, Bulleen; ⊙10am-5pm Tue-Sun; 🚆Heidelberg then 🚌903). This, the former home of John and Sunday Reed, is a large public art gallery with wonderful grounds for wandering around and picnicking. It holds regularly changing exhibitions, many of which include works by the artists that called Heide home. Its gardens are full of sculptures and the two vegetable gardens that Sunday Reed loved so much.

This was a special spot for Melbourne's artists; Sunday was known for feeding and housing them during their rough or creative times. In exchange she ended up with a shed full of Nolans (almost the entire Ned Kelly series was painted by Sidney Nolan in Heide 1's dining room) and a thoroughly talented array of house guests.

These day Shannon Bennett's Cafe Vue does the cooking honours (Tuesday to Sunday), and you can eat in or grab a lunch box ($15) to eat by the Yarra on the grounds. The free tours are a great introduction to Melbourne's early painting scene. The museum is signposted off the Eastern Fwy. Otherwise, take an Eltham train to Heidelberg station, then bus 903.

9.30pm) Eureka Tower, built in 2006, has 92 storeys. Take a wild elevator ride to almost the top (don't miss a glance at the photo on the floor) and you'll do 88 floors in less than 40 seconds. 'The Edge' – not a member of U2, but a slightly sadistic glass cube – propels you out of the building.

FREE Australian Centre for
Contemporary Art   GALLERY
(ACCA; www.accaonline.org.au; 111 Sturt St; ⊙10am-5pm Tue-Fri, 11am-6pm Sat & Sun; 🚌1) The ACCA is one of Australia's most exciting and challenging contemporary galleries. Shows include work specially commissioned for the space. The gallery shows a range of local and international artists. The building is fittingly sculptural, with a deeply rusted exterior evoking the factories that once stood on the site, and a slick, soaring, ever-adapting interior designed to house often massive installations. From Flinders Street Station walk across Princes Bridge and along St Kilda Rd. Turn right at Grant St then left to Sturt St.

Crown Casino &
Entertainment Complex   CASINO
(Map p482; www.crowncasino.com.au; Southbank) The Crown Entertainment Complex sprawls across two city blocks and includes three luxury hotels linked with Crown Casino, which has over 300 tables and 2500 gaming machines open 24/7. It's another world in its no-natural-light interior, where hours fly by. Thrown in for good measure are waterfalls, fireballs, a giant cinema complex, a bowling alley, a variety of nightclubs and a 900-seat showroom. The complex is also home to a handful of luxury retailers, chain stores and speciality shops, as well as bars, cafes and a food hall. Restaurants here range from the perfunctory to the sublime, with several major culinary players stretched out along the river.

Polly Woodside   MUSEUM
(Map p476; www.pollywoodside.com.au; 2A Clarendon St, South Wharf; adult/child/family $15/8/42; ⊙9.30am-5pm; 🚌96, 109, 112) A revamped interactive visitors centre fills you in on the history of the Polly Woodside, a restored iron-hulled merchant ship (or 'tall ship') dating from 1885 that now rests in a pen off the Yarra River. A glimpse of the rigging makes for a tiny reminder of what the Yarra would have looked like in the 19th century, dense with ships at anchor. Walk past Crown Casino to find it.

Melbourne Recital Centre   NOTABLE BUILDING
(www.melbournerecital.com.au; cnr Southbank Blvd & Sturt St, Southbank) This new and award-winning complex may look like a framed piece of giant honeycomb, but it is actually the hub (or hive) for two of Melbourne's arts companies. It's not unusual to see the likes of Geoffrey Rush performing with the Melbourne Theatre Company (p514), while the Recital Centre's program ranges from quartets and local singer-songwriters to Babar the Elephant. From Flinders Street Station cross the Yarra and turn right at Southbank Blvd.

MELBOURNE & VICTORIA MELBOURNE

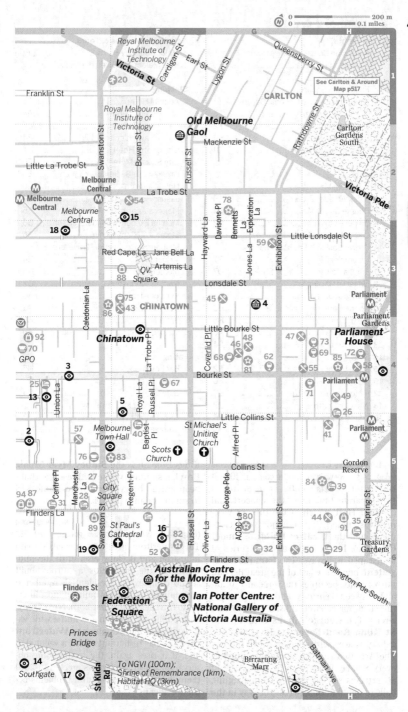

0   200 m
0   0.1 miles

Royal Melbourne Institute of Technology

Queensberry St

Victoria St

20

Franklin St

See Carlton & Around Map p517

CARLTON

Carlton Gardens South

Royal Melbourne Institute of Technology

Old Melbourne Gaol

Mackenzie St

Victoria Pde

Little La Trobe St

Melbourne Central

La Trobe St

Melbourne Central

54

78

Melbourne Central

15

Davisons Pl

Bennetts

La Exploration La

Little Lonsdale St

18

59

Red Cape La   Jane Bell La

Artemis La

QV Square

88

Lonsdale St

75

45

4

86

43   CHINATOWN

Parliament

Chinatown

Little Bourke St

Parliament Gardens

92

La Trobe Pl

47   73

Parliament House

70

GPO

46   48

85   72

3

67

68

62

55   58

5

81

Parliament

Royal La

Bourke St

71

49

13

Union La

Little Collins St

26

2

57

Melbourne Town Hall

40

St Michael's Uniting Church

41

Parliament

76

83

Baptist Pl

Scots Church

Collins St

Gordon Reserve

94 87

27

City Square

84   39

31

28

22

Spring St

Flinders La

89

St Paul's Cathedral

16

80

44   35

19

82

ACDC La

91

52

32

50   29

Treasury Gardens

Flinders St

Flinders St

Australian Centre for the Moving Image

Wellington Pde South

Flinders St

63

Ian Potter Centre: National Gallery of Victoria Australia

Federation Square

74

Princes Bridge

Birrarung Marr

Batman Ave

14

Southgate

17

St Kilda Rd

To NGVI (100m); Shrine of Remembrance (1km); Habitat HQ (3km)

1

MELBOURNE & VICTORIA MELBOURNE

Victorian Arts Centre   NOTABLE BUILDING
(Map p482; www.theartscentre.com.au; 100 St
Kilda Rd) The Arts Centre is made up of
two separate buildings: the concert hall
(**Hamer Hall**, which at the time of writing
was undergoing a major redevelopment) and the **theatres building** (under
the spire). Both are linked by a series of
landscaped walkways. The **Famous Spiegeltent**, one of the last of the great Belgian
mirror tents, occupies the forecourt annually between February and April, and is
the stage for cabaret, music, comedy and
circus. The **George Adams Gallery** and
St Kilda Road Foyer Gallery are free
gallery spaces with changing exhibitions.
The Arts Centre hosts a **makers market**
every Sunday from 10am to 4pm. Around
80 artisans sell everything from juggling
balls to photographs. Across the way in the

Kings Domain is the **Sidney Myer Music
Bowl**, a summer venue with a stage that's
been graced by everyone from Dame Kiri
to summer dance parties.

Docklands   NEIGHBOURHOOD
(Map p476; www.docklands.vic.gov.au; 🚊70, 86)
This waterfront area was the city's main
industrial and docking area until the mid-
1960s. In the mid-1990s a purpose-built
studio complex and residential, retail and
entertainment area was built. Of most interest to travellers is the first-born, **New Quay**,
with public art, promenades and a wide variety of cafes and restaurants. **Waterfront
City** also has restaurants, bars, a yacht club
and, if it rises again, the troublesome observation wheel, which was erected in 2010
then dissembled as structural problems became evident.

MELBOURNE & VICTORIA MELBOURNE

EAST MELBOURNE & RICHMOND

East Melbourne's sedate wide streets are lined with grand double-fronted Victorian terraces and Italianate mansions. It's also home to the mighty Melbourne Cricket Ground (MCG). On the other side of perpetually clogged Punt Rd/Hoddle St is the suburb of Richmond, which houses a vibrant stretch of Vietnamese restaurants along Victoria St, clothing outlets along Bridge Rd and some good drinking spots along Church St.

Melbourne Cricket Ground   SPORT STADIUM
(MCG; Map p476; ☑03-9657 8888; www.mcg.org. au; Brunton Ave; ℝJolimont, ⊞48, 75) It's one of the world's great sporting venues, and for many Australians the 'G' is considered hallowed ground. In 1858 the first game of Aussie Rules football was played where the MCG and its car parks now stand, and in 1877 it was the venue for the first

Test cricket match between Australia and England. The MCG was also the central stadium for the 1956 Melbourne Olympics and the 2006 Commonwealth Games. The William Barak Bridge links it to the CBD. MCG membership is a badge of honour for Melburnians of a particular class. It involves having two members propose and second your nomination and a wait of around 20 years.

If you want to make a pilgrimage, **tours** (☑03-9657 8879; adult/child/family $20/10/50) take you through the stands, corporate and coaches' areas, the Long Room and (subject to availability) the players change rooms and out onto the ground. They run (on non-match days) between 10am and 3pm. Bookings are not essential but recommended. The MCG houses the **National Sports Museum** (adult/child/family incl tour $30/15/60). Pedestrians can head along Birrarung Marr

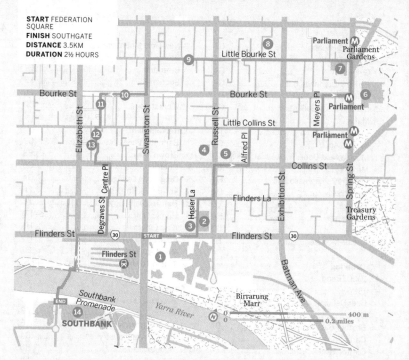

START FEDERATION SQUARE
FINISH SOUTHGATE
DISTANCE 3.5KM
DURATION 2½ HOURS

Walking Tour
Melbourne City

> Melbourne's CBD is a warren of beautiful alleys and laneways, some cobblestoned, some bluestoned and all laden with character.

Start your foray into them at an obvious point – ❶ **Federation Square**. Head east along Flinders St and then turn left onto Hosier Lane, keeping the ❷ **Forum Theatre** on your right. Depending on the hunger pangs you could pop into ❸ **MoVida** for a scrummy round of tapas, or keep moving. Turn right at Flinders Lane, left onto Russell St and then right onto Collins St. Stop to admire ❹ **Scots Church** and ❺ **St Michael's Uniting Church** and make your way east along the 'Paris' end of Collins St.

Find respite from the main strip and take a left onto Alfred Pl, which leads to Little Collins St. Turn right and continue along Little Collins St, turning left onto Meyers Pl. Turn right onto Bourke St and you'll hit the eastern border of the CBD, where ❻ **Parliament House** strikes a pose.

Turn left on Spring St and left again onto Little Bourke St, past ❼ **Princess Theatre**. Head down Little Bourke St and stop in at the ❽ **Chinese Museum** before heading into the heart of ❾ **Chinatown**.

Turn left at Swanston St and then right on Bourke St to amble through ❿ **Bourke Street Mall**. Ogle at the shops and people and then potter through the glorious old ⓫ **Royal Arcade**. Dogleg from Little Collins to ⓬ **Block Place** and into ⓭ **Block Arcade**. Cross Collins St and head down Centre Pl and Degraves St for shoulder-to-shoulder boutiques, cafes and bars.

Turn right onto Flinders St and then cross it via the pedestrian tunnel beneath the railway tracks to reach the Yarra River. Cruise across the pedestrian bridge to ⓮ **Southgate** where you can finish the day up with a bite to eat and a well-earned vino.

and take the musical trip along the William Barak bridge (listen out for the soundscape).

Fitzroy Gardens
GARDENS

(Map p476; btwn Wellington Pde, Clarendon, Lansdowne & Albert Sts; ☒Parliament, ☒City Circle, 48, 75) The city drops away suddenly just east of Spring St, giving way to Melbourne's beautiful backyard, the Fitzroy Gardens. The stately avenues lined with English elms, flowerbeds, expansive lawns, strange fountains and a creek are a short stroll from town.

Cooks' Cottage (www.cookscottage.com.au; adult/child/family $4.50/2/12; ☺9am-5pm) was shipped from Yorkshire in 253 packing cases and reconstructed in 1934 (the cottage actually belonged to the navigator's parents). Nearby is writer Ola Cohn's equally kooky carved **Fairies' Tree**. Efforts to preserve the 300-year-old stump, embellished in 1932 with fairies, pixies, kangaroos, emus and possums, include dissuading true believers from leaving notes to the fairies in the tree's hollows. Between Cooks' Cottage and the Fairies' Tree is the Fitzroy Gardens' **Scarred Tree** (now a stump), which, generations ago, was stripped of a piece of its bark to make a canoe by Aboriginal people. In the centre of the gardens is a 'model' **Tudor village**. This well-meaning and rather unusual gift was a way of saying thanks for sending food to Britain during WWII.

FITZROY & AROUND

Fitzroy, Melbourne's first suburb, had a reputation for vice and squalor. Today, it's a rather gentrified version of its old self; a mix of housing-commission towers, fancy restaurants, cafes, and boutique shops. Gertrude St, where once grannies feared to tread, is Melbourne's street of the moment. Smith St has some rough edges, though talk is more of its smart restaurants, cafes and boutiques rather than its down-and-out days of old. It's still a social spot for Aborigines.

To the north is the leafy residential area of North Fitzroy, which centres on the hipster hang-out of Edinburgh Gardens. When evening sets on Northcote's High St, it hums to the sound of a thousand Converse One Stars hitting the pavement in search of fun.

Centre for Contemporary Photography
ART GALLERY

(CCP; Map p498; www.ccp.org.au; 404 George St, Fitzroy; admission by donation; ☺11am-6pm Wed-Fri, noon-5pm Sat & Sun; ☒86) This not-for-profit centre has a changing schedule of exhibitions across a couple of galleries. Shows traverse traditional techniques and the highly conceptual.

FREE **Abbotsford Convent**
HISTORIC SITE

(Map p476; (☒03-9415 3600; www.abbotsfordconvent.com.au; 1 St Heliers St, Abbotsford; ☺7.30am-10pm; ☒Victoria Park, ☒203) The convent, which dates back to 1861, is spread over nearly 7 hectares of riverside land just 4km from the CBD. The nuns are long gone – no-one is going to ask you if you've been to Mass lately – and there's now a rambling collection of creative studios and community offices. The **Convent Bakery** supplies impromptu picnic provisions, or Steve at the 1950s-style (no soy, no skinny, just what's on the menu) bar **Handsome Steve's House of Refreshment** will mix you up a Campari soda to sip on the balcony while you're overlooking the ecclesiastic architecture and listening to the footy on the radio. There's a **Slow Food Market** (www.mfm.com.au; admission $2; ☺8am-1pm) every fourth Saturday, and **Shirt and Skirt Market** every third Sunday. On the other side of the bicycle track is the **Collingwood Children's Farm** (www.farm.org.au; adult/child/family $8/4/16; ☺9am-5pm; ☒Victoria Park, ☒203), a rustic riverside retreat with a range of frolicking farm animals and a terrific on-site cafe.

CARLTON & AROUND

Lygon St reaches out through leafy North Carlton to booming Brunswick. Here you'll find a vibrant mix of students, long-established families, renovators and newly arrived migrants. The central Brunswick artery, Sydney Rd, is perpetually clogged with traffic and is packed with Middle Eastern restaurants and grocers. Lygon St down East Brunswick way just keeps getting more fashionable with a growing cluster of restaurants, music venues and bars.

Melbourne Museum
MUSEUM

(Map p517; (☒13 11 02; www.museumvictoria.com.au; 11 Nicholson St, Carlton; adult/child $8/free, exhibitions $24/16; ☺10am-5pm; ☒Parliament, ☒City Circle, 86, 96, ☒250, 251, 402) This confident postmodern exhibition space mixes old-style object displays with themed interactive display areas. The museum's reach is almost too broad to be cohesive, but it provides a grand sweep of Victoria's natural and cultural histories. Walk through the reconstructed laneway lives of the 1800s or become immersed in the legend of champion racehorse Phar

ELVIS IN MELBOURNE

Given that Elvis Presley never actually performed in Melbourne, it's surprising to find out that after he died (or did he?) in 1977, his Melbourne fans erected a tribute to the King at Melbourne General Cemetery, North Carlton. Look for the large grotto (and, on his birthday and certain anniversary dates, a collection of his fans).

Lap. Bunjilaka, on the ground floor, presents Indigenous stories and history told through objects and Aboriginal voices. There's also an open-air forest atrium featuring Victorian plants and animals and an **Imax cinema** (p513) next door.

Royal Exhibition Building HISTORIC BUILDING
(Map p517; www.museumvicoria.com.au/reb; Nicholson St, Carlton; Parliament, City Circle, 86, 96, 250, 251, 402) Built for the International Exhibition in 1880, and winning Unesco World Heritage status in 2004, this beautiful Victorian edifice symbolises the glory days of the Industrial Revolution, Empire and 19th-century Melbourne's economic supremacy. Australia's first parliament was held here in 1901; more than a hundred years later everything from trade fairs to designer sales to dance parties take place here. **Tours** (bookings 13 11 02; adult/child $5/3.50) leave from the Melbourne Museum most days at 2pm.

Royal Melbourne Zoo ZOO
(03-9285 9300; www.zoo.org.au; Elliott Ave, Parkville; adult/child/family $25/13/57; 9am-5pm; Royal Park, 55) Melbourne's zoo is one of the city's most popular attractions. Walkways pass through some enclosures; you can stroll through the bird aviary, cross a bridge over the lions' park or enter a tropical hothouse full of colourful butterflies. There's also a large collection of native animals in natural bush settings, a platypus aquarium, fur seals, lions and tigers, plenty of reptiles, and an 'am I in Asia?' elephant enclosure. In summer, the zoo hosts **Twilight Concerts**. **Roar 'n' Snore** (adult/child $195/145, Sep-May) allows you to camp at the zoo and join the keepers on their morning feeding rounds.

Ceres ENVIRONMENT PARK
www.ceres.org.au; 8 Lee St, East Brunswick; admission free; 9am-5pm, market 9am-1pm Wed & Sat; 96) Ceres is a 20-something-year-old community environment project built on a former tip. Stroll around the permaculture and bush-food nursery before refuelling with an organic coffee and cake at the pretty (and extremely popular) cafe. Children enjoy the natural miniworlds, and on market days you can buy organic and backyard-produced goodies while the kids marvel at the chooks and sheep. Ceres is the last stop on the 96 tram, hop off and follow the signs to your right.

SOUTH YARRA, PRAHRAN & WINDSOR

This neighbourhood has always been synonymous with glitz and glamour; it might be south but it's commonly referred to as the 'right' side of the river (plots of land were historically larger).

Chapel St's South Yarra strip still parades itself as a must-do fashion destination, but has seen better days; it's been taken over by chain stores, tacky bars and, come sunset, doof-doof cars. Prahran and Windsor are still gutsy and good places, with designer stores, bars and some refreshingly eclectic businesses. Commercial Rd is Melbourne's pumping pink zone, and has a diverse collection of nightclubs, bars and bookshops. It is also home of the Prahran Market, where the locals shop for fruit, veg and upmarket deli delights.

Hawksburn Village, up the Malvern Rd hill, and High St, Armadale make for stylish boutique clothes shopping.

Royal Botanic Gardens GARDEN
(Map p476; www.rbg.vic.gov.au; admission free; 7.30am-8.30pm Nov-Mar, to 5.30pm Apr-Oct; 8) The RBG is one of Melbourne's most glorious attractions. Sprawling beside the Yarra River, the beautifully designed gardens feature a global selection of plantings as well as specific Australian gardens. Along with the abundance of plant species, there's a surprising amount of wildlife, including waterfowl, ducks, swans and child-scaring eels in and around the ornamental lake, as well as cockatoos and possums. There's also the excellent, nature-based **Ian Potter Children's Garden**.

The gardens are encircled by the **Tan**, a 4km-long former horse-exercising track, now used to exercise joggers. During the summer months, the gardens play host to the **Moonlight Cinema** (p514) and theatre performances.

Yarra Bend Park
PARK

(Map p476; www.parkweb.vic.gov.au) Escape the city without leaving town. About 5km north-east of the city centre, the Yarra River flows through bushland, an area cherished by runners, rowers, cyclists, picnickers and strollers.

Yarra Bend Park has huge tracts of densely tree-covered land (not to mention two golf courses and numerous sports grounds) that are great for walking. Cockatoos screech by the banks and grey-headed flying foxes roost in the trees: it's hard to believe you're 10 minutes from office towers and industry. At the end of Boathouse Rd is the 1860s Studley Park Boathouse (☑9853 1972; www.studleyparkboathouse.com.au), which has a kiosk and restaurant, BBQ facilities, flocks of ducks, and boats and canoes for hire. Kanes suspension footbridge takes you across the river, from where it's about a 20-minute walk to Dights Falls, at the meeting of the Yarra River and Merri Creek. You can also walk to the falls along the southern riverbank.

Shrine of Remembrance
MONUMENT

(off Map p482; www.shrine.org.au; Birdwood Ave, South Yarra; ☉10am-5pm; ☐5, 6, 8, 16, 64, 67, 72) Beside St Kilda Rd stands the massive Shrine of Remembrance, built as a memorial to Victorians killed in WWI. Thousands attend the moving **Anzac Day** (25 April) dawn service. From the CBD, follow Swanston St as it turns into St Kilda Pde.

Governor La Trobe's Cottage & Government House
HISTORIC BUILDING

(Map p476; Kings Domain; ☐48, 75) East of the Shrine of Remembrance is Governor La Trobe's Cottage (www.nattrust.com.au), the original government house building that was sent out in prefabricated form from the mother country in 1840. Inside, you can see many of the original furnishings, and the servants' quarters out the back.

This modest cottage sits in stark contrast to the Italianate pile of Government House (☑03-8663 7260; Government House Dr). Built in 1872, it's been the residence of all serving Victorian governors since, and is a replica of Queen Victoria's palace on England's Isle of Wight. Book well in advance to take the National Trust tour (adult/child $10/5), which includes both houses on Mondays and Wednesdays.

FREE Herring Island
PARK

(Map p507; http://home.vicnet.net.au/~herring) Once an unloved dumping ground for silt, Herring Island is now a prelapsarian garden that seeks to preserve the original trees, shrubs and grasses of the Yarra and provide a home for indigenous animals such as parrots, possums and lizards, as well as sculptures. Designated picnic areas, with barbecues, make for a rare retreat just 3km from the city centre. The island is theoretically open to visitors all year round, but can only be reached by boat. A Parks Victoria punt (☑13 19 63; per person $2; ☉11.30am-5pm Sat & Sun Dec-Mar only) operates from Como Landing on Alexandra Ave in South Yarra.

Prahran Market
MARKET

(Map p507; www.prahranmarket.com.au; 163 Commercial Rd, South Yarra; ☉to 5pm Tue, to 6pm Thu & Fri, dawn-5pm Sat, 10am-3pm Sun; ☐Prahran, ☐72, 78, 79) The Prahran Market has been an institution for over a century and is one of the finest produce markets in the city.

ST KILDA & AROUND

Come to St Kilda for its briny breezes, seaside walking/running/roller-blading/cycling path, seedy history and for a good old bit of people-watching.

St Kilda's palm trees, bay vistas and pink-stained sunsets are heartbreakingly beautiful. On weekends, the volume is turned up, the traffic crawls and the street-party atmosphere sets in. Cake shop–clad Acland St's western strip is pleasantly leafy and nostalgically residential. Many long-time locals have turned to Carlisle St's eastern reach, which is traditionally a devout Jewish neighbourhood but is now known for its wine bars, beer bars and all-day breakfast cafes.

Luna Park
AMUSEMENT PARK

(Map p509; www.lunapark.com.au; Lower Esplanade, St Kilda; adult/child single-ride ticket $9.40/7.50, unlimited-ride ticket $42/32; ☐16, 96) It opened in 1912 and still retains the feel of an old-style amusement park with creepy Mr Moon's gaping mouth swallowing you up whole on entering. There's a heritage-listed scenic railway and the full complement of gut-churning modern rides. For grown-ups, the noise and lack of greenery or shade can pall all too fast. Check website for seasonal opening hours.

St Kilda Foreshore
BEACH

(Map p509; Jacka Blvd, St Kilda; ☐16, 96) There are palm-fringed promenades, a parkland strand and a long stretch of sand. Still, don't expect Bondi or Noosa. St Kilda's seaside appeal is more Brighton, England than

FOOTSCRAY & YARRAVILLE

Head west beyond the city's remaining working docklands to Footscray and Yarraville. The area's 'capital' is the fabulously unfussy Footscray. Almost half of Footscray's population was born overseas, the majority in Vietnam, Africa, China, Italy and Greece. Get to know the area by taking a river trip along the Maribyrnong. **Maribyrnong River Cruises** (☎9689 6431; www.blackbirdcruises.com.au; Wingfield St, Footscray; adult/child $20/5) has a two-hour return cruise up the river to Avondale Heights departing daily at 1pm, or head the other way past Lonely Planet's head office on its one-hour cruise to Docklands (departs at 4pm; adults/child $10/5). Both tours depart from the end of Wingfield St in Footscray. The **Footscray Market** (cnr Hopkins & Leeds St; ⊙7am-4pm Tue, Wed & Sat, to 6pm Thu, to 8pm Fri) right next to Footscray Train Station, is testament to the area's diversity.

Heading south from Footscray, are the fashionable residential neighbourhoods of Seddon and Yarraville. Yarraville centres on its train station, with a beautifully well-preserved heritage shopping area around Anderson St.

Western Eating

Don't go hungry in the west; try cafe **Le Chien** (5 Gamon St, Seddon), African restaurant **Cafe Lalibela** (91 Irving St, Footscray), Indian at **Aangan** (559 Barkly St, Footscray West) and Vietnamese *pho* (noodle soup) at **Hung Vuong** (128 Hopkins St, Footscray).

Baywatch, despite 20-odd years of glitzy development. And that's the way Melburnians like it; a certain depth of character and an all-weather charm, with wild days on the bay providing for spectacular cloudscapes and terse little waves, as well as the more predictable sparkling blue of summer.

St Kilda Pier　　　　　　　PIER
(Map p509; Jacka Blvd, St Kilda; 🚌16, 96) The breakwater near the pier was built in the 1950s and is now home to a colony of over 1000 little penguins (they're hiding there between the bluestone breakwater). Visit the penguins as the sun goes down (volunteers are on hand to shine a red light on them), or see them from a prime location on an eco **stand-up paddleboarding trip** (see p492). If you're taking photos of the little blue bundles don't use your flash.

Port Phillip Eco Centre　　INFORMATION CENTRE
(Map p509; www.ecocentre.com; ☎03-9534 0670; 55a Blessington St, St Kilda) In summer, the centre runs monthly 'stormwater drain to penguin colony' tours showing the diverse environment of the St Kilda seafront.

Jewish Museum of Australia　　MUSEUM
(off Map p509; ☎03-9534 0083; www.jewishmuseum.com.au; 26 Alma Rd, St Kilda; adult/child/family $10/5/20; ⊙10am-4pm Tue-Thu, 11am-5pm Sun; 🚆Balaclava) Interactive displays tell the history of Australia's Jewish community from the earliest days of European settlement, while permanent exhibitions celebrate Judaism's rich cycle of festivals and holy days. Follow St Kilda Rd from St Kilda Junction then turn left at Alma Rd.

SOUTH MELBOURNE, PORT MELBOURNE & ALBERT PARK

Head to South Melbourne for its large fresh food market, homeware shops and top cafes (seems there's a coffee competition going on). Albert Park Lake is the place for sporting and relaxation pursuits, but it also manages to squeeze in an annual Grand Prix. Albert Park and nearby Middle Park both have refined, genteel town centres. At nearby (portside) Port Melbourne is Station Pier, the passenger terminal for the ferry service between Melbourne and Tasmania.

South Melbourne Market　　MARKET
(cnr Coventry & Cecil Sts, South Melbourne; ⊙8am-4pm Wed, to 6pm Fri, to 4pm Sat & Sun; 🚌96) The market's labyrinthine interior is packed to overflowing with an eccentric collection of stalls selling everything from carpets to *bok choy* (Chinese greens). Its hangover-relieving dim sims are famous and sold at various cafes around Melbourne (as 'South Melbourne Market Dim Sims' no less!).

Albert Park Lake　　　　LAKE
(Map p476; btwn Queens Rd, Fitzroy St, Aughtie Dr & Albert Rd, Albert Park; 🚌96, 112) Elegant black

swans give their inimitable bottoms-up salute as you circumnavigate the 5km perimeter of this artificial lake. Jogging, cycling, walking or clamouring over play equipment is the appropriate human equivalent. Lakeside Dr was used as an international motor-racing circuit in the 1950s, and since 1996 the revamped track has been the venue for the **Australian Formula One Grand Prix** each March.

Station Pier   LANDMARK
(Map p476; www.portofmelbourne.com; ⊘6am-9pm pedestrians only, closed during some ship visits;

109) Station Pier is Melbourne's main sea passenger terminal, and is where the *Spirit of Tasmania*, cruise ships and navy vessels dock. It has been in operation since 1854, and the first major railway in Australia ran from here to the city. It has great sentimental associations for many migrants who arrived by ship in the 1950s and 1960s, and for servicemen who used it during WWII. There has been significant development of the area over the last 10 years and there is now a gaggle of flash-looking restaurants built on and around the pier, as well as a marina.

THE SPORTING LIFE

Cynics snicker that sport is the sum of Victoria's culture, although they're hard to hear above all that cheering, theme-song singing and applause. Victorians do take the shared spectacle of the playing field very seriously. It's undeniably the state's most dominant expression of common beliefs and behaviour, and brings people from all backgrounds together. It's also a lot of fun; sporting events are followed with such fervour that the crowd is often a spectacle in itself.

Melbourne is the birthplace of Australian Rules football and hosts a disproportionate number of international sporting events, including the Australian Open, Australian Formula One Grand Prix and Melbourne Cup. The city's arenas, tracks, grounds and courts are regarded as the world's best-developed and well-situated cluster of facilities. Victoria is home to more major events, such as the Rip Curl Pro (aka the Bells Beach Surf Classic), the Australian Motorcycle Grand Prix on Phillip Island, the Stawell Gift and numerous country horse races, including the atmospheric Hanging Rock meet.

The Footy

Underneath the cultured chat and designer threads of your typical Melbournian, you'll find a heart that truly belongs to one thing: the footy. Understanding the basics of Australian Rules Football (AFL, or 'the footy') is definitely a way to get a local engaged in conversation, especially during the winter season. Melbourne is the national centre for the sport, and the Melbourne-based **Australian Football League** (AFL; www.afl.com.au) administers the national competition.

During the footy season (March to September), the vast majority of Victorians become obsessed, entering tipping competitions at work, discussing groin injuries and suspensions over the water cooler, and devouring huge chunks of the daily newspapers devoted to mighty victories, devastating losses and the latest bad-boy behaviour (on and off the field). Monday night disciplinary tribunals allocate demerit points for every bit of blood and biffo, and fans follow these proceedings with almost as much attention as the games themselves.

The MCG, affectionately referred to as the 'G', has been the home of football since 1859 and its atmosphere is unforgettable. The AFL now has teams in every mainland state, but nine of its 16 clubs are still based in Melbourne, along with regional Geelong. All Melbourne teams play their home games at either the MCG or Docklands Stadium, and those between two local teams ensure a loud, parochial crowd. Barracking has its own lexicon and is often a one-sided 'conversation' with the umpire. One thing is certain: fans always know better. Once disparagingly referred to as 'white maggots' because of lilywhite uniforms, umpires are now decked out in bright orange, so players can spot them in the thick of the game. With the switch, they are now simply called 'maggot'.

After the final siren blows, and the winning-club theme song is played (usually several times over), it's off to the pub. Supporters of opposing teams often celebrate and commiserate together. Despite the deep tribal feelings and passionate expression of belonging that AFL engenders, violence is almost unheard of pre-, post-, or during games.

WILLIAMSTOWN

Williamstown is a yacht-filled gem just a short boat ride (or drive) from Melbourne's CBD. It has stunning views of Melbourne, and a bunch of touristy shops along its esplanade.

Gem Pier is where passenger ferries dock to drop off and collect those who visit Williamstown by boat. It's a fitting way to arrive, given the area's maritime ambience. **Williamstown Ferries** (☑03-9517 9444; www.williamstownferries.com.au) plies Hobsons Bay daily, stopping at **Southgate** (Map p482) and visiting a number of sites along the way, including Docklands. **Melbourne River Cruises** (☑03-9629 7233; www.melbcruises.com.au) also docks at Gem Pier, travelling up the Yarra River to Southgate. Ticket prices vary according to your destination. Pick up a timetable from the very useful visitors centre in Williamstown or at Federation Square, or contact the companies directly; bookings are advised.

Activities

Canoeing

Studley Park Boathouse   CANOE HIRE
(☑03-9853 1828; www.studleyparkboathouse.com.au) Pack a picnic then hire a two-person canoe or kayak from the boathouse for $30 for the first hour.

Cycling

Cycling maps are available from the Visitor Information Centre at Federation Sq (Map p482) and **Bicycle Victoria** (☑03-8636 8888; www.bv.com.au). You'll not be alone on the roads; there's a large club scene, as well as a new breed of 'slow cyclists'. Wearing a helmet while cycling is compulsory in Australia. Borrow a bike from the public scheme (p519), a private scheme or go vintage.

Humble Vintage   BIKE HIRE
(☑0432 032 450; www.thehumblevintage.com) Get yourself a set of special wheels from this collection of retro racers, city bikes and ladies' bikes. Rates start at $30 per day, or $80 per week, and include lock, helmet and a terrific map. Bikes can be picked up from St Kilda, the CBD and Fitzroy. Give them a ring as the exact locations change.

Real Melbourne Bike Tours   BIKE HIRE
(Map p482; ☑0417 339 203; www.rentabike.net.au; Federation Sq) Hires bikes (including child seats and 'tagalongs') with hourly ($15) daily ($30) and weekly ($100) rates.

Lawn Bowls

Formerly the domain of senior citizens wearing starched white uniforms, bowling clubs are now inundated by younger types: barefoot, with a beer in one hand and a bowl in the other.

North Fitzroy Bowls   LAWN BOWLS
(off Map p498; www.fvbowls.com.au; 578 Brunswick St, North Fitzroy; ☐112) This centre comes equipped with lights for night bowls, barbecues and a beer garden. Phone to make a booking and for opening times. From Fitzroy, continue north along Brunswick St and cross Alexander Pde – it's on your right.

St Kilda Bowling Club   LAWN BOWLS
(Map p509; 66 Fitzroy St, St Kilda; ☺noon-sunset Tue-Sun; ☐16, 96) The only dress code at this popular bowling club is shoes off. So join the many others who de-shoe to enjoy a beer and a bowl in the great outdoors.

Windsurfing & Stand-Up Paddleboarding

RPS – the Board Store   BOARD HIRE
(☑03-9525 6475; www.rpstheboardstore.com; 87 Ormond Rd, Elwood) Offers windsurfing courses and stand-up paddleboarding (SUP) lessons in summer.

Stand Up Paddle Boarding   PADDLE BOARDING
(Map p509; ☑0416 184 994; www.supb.com.au; St Kilda Baths; tours $89-130) Rents out SUP equipment from St Kilda for $25 per hour and runs lessons, and penguin and Yarra River tours.

Swimming

In summer, hit the sand at one of the city's metropolitan beaches. St Kilda, Middle Park and Port Melbourne are popular patches, with suburban beaches at Brighton (with its photogenic bathing boxes) and Sandringham. Public pools are also well loved.

Fitzroy Swimming Pool   SWIMMING
(Map p498; ☑03-9205 5180; Alexandra Pde, Fitzroy; adult/child $4.60/2.10; ☐112) Between laps, locals love catching a few rays up in the

bleachers or on the lawn. The pool's Italian 'Aqua Profonda' sign was painted in 1953 – an initiative of the pool's manager who frequently had to rescue migrant children who couldn't read the English signs. The sign is heritage listed (misspelled and all – it should be 'Acqua').

Melbourne City Baths SWIMMING

(Map p482; 📞03-9663 5888; www.melbournecitybaths.com.au; 420 Swanston St, Melbourne; casual swim adult/child/family $5.50/2.60/12, gym $20; ⏰6am-10pm Mon-Thu, 6am-8pm Fri, 8am-6pm Sat & Sun) The City Baths first opened in 1860 and were intended to stop people bathing in the seriously polluted Yarra River. Enjoy a swim in the 1903 heritage-listed building.

Prahran Aquatic Centre SWIMMING

(Map p507; 📞03-8290 7140; 41 Essex St, Prahran; adult/child $4.80/2.70; 🚊72, 78, 79) This glam 50m heated outdoor pool is surrounded by a stretch of lawn. The on-site cafe is a must for the locals that can't do without their latte, seminaked or not.

👉 Tours

Aboriginal Heritage Walk INDIGENOUS

(📞03-9252 2429; www.rbg.vic.gov.au; Royal Botanic Gardens; adult/child $25/10; ⏰11am Tue, Thu & 1st Sun of the month) The Royal Botanic Gardens are on a traditional camping and meeting place of the original owners, and this tour takes you through their story – from songlines to plant lore, all in 90 fascinating minutes.

FREE **Melbourne City Tourist Shuttle** BUS TOUR

(www.thatsmelbourne.com.au; ⏰9am-4.30pm) This tourist bus takes about 1½ hours to make its stops around Melbourne and its inner suburbs. Stops include Lygon St, Carlton, Queen Victoria Market, Melbourne Museum and, on non-sporting days, the MCG.

FREE **Greeter Service** WALKING TOUR

(📞03-9658 9658; Melbourne Visitor Centre, Federation Sq) This free two-hour 'orientation tour' departs Fed Sq daily at 9.30am (bookings required) and is run by volunteer 'greeters' who are keen to share their knowledge. It's aimed at giving visitors to Melbourne a good understanding of the layout and sights of Melbourne.

Real Melbourne Bike Tours CYCLING

(Map p482; 📞0417 339 203; www.rentabike.net.au; Federation Sq; tours incl lunch adult/child $110/79) Offers four-hour cycling tours covering the CBD, parts of the Yarra and Fitzroy. Also has bike hire (including child seats and 'tagalongs') with hourly ($15) daily ($30) and weekly ($100) rates.

Kayak Melbourne KAYAK TOURS

(📞0418 106 427; www.kayakmelbourne.com.au; tours $89) Two-hour tours by Kayak Melbourne take you past Melbourne city's newest developments and explains the history of the older ones. Moonlight tours are most evocative and include a fish 'n' chips dinner. They usually depart from the wharf sheds on Victoria Harbour – check when you book.

Sunset Eco Penguin Tour STAND-UP PADDLEBOARDING

(Map p509; 📞0416 184 994; www.supb.com.au; St Kilda Sea Baths; $130) See St Kilda's penguin colony while you navigate your paddleboard standing up (cost includes a lesson and wetsuit and paddleboard hire).

FREE **City Circle trams** TRAM TOUR

(www.metlinkmelbourne.com.au) Free W-class trams that trundle around the city perimeter (and into the depths of Docklands) from 10am to 6pm daily.

Melbourne By Foot WALKING TOUR

(📞0418 394 000; www.melbournebyfoot.com; tours $29) Take a couple of hours out with Dave and experience a mellow, informative walking tour that covers lane art, politics, and gives great insights into Melbourne's history and diversity.

Hidden Secrets Tours LANEWAYS

(📞03-9663 3358; www.hiddensecretstours.com; tours $70-145) Offers a variety of walking tours covering everything including lanes and arcades, wine, architecture, coffee and cafes and vintage Melbourne.

Melbourne Street Art Tours ART TOUR

(📞03-9328 5556; www.melbournestreettours.com; Federation Sq; tours incl drink $69; ⏰Tue, Thur & Sat) Three-hour tours exploring the street-art side of Melbourne. The tour guides are street artists themselves, so you'll get a good insight into this art.

MELBOURNE FOR CHILDREN

» **Ian Potter Children's Garden** (p488) Has natural tunnels in the rainforest, a kitchen garden and water-play areas.

» **Collingwood Children's Farm** (p487) Old MacDonald has nothing on this farm, filled as it is with bouncy farm animals and even bouncier young 'uns.

» **Australian Centre for the Moving Image** (p475) Free access to computer games and movies may encourage square eyes, but it's a great spot for a rainy day.

» **Royal Melbourne Zoo** (p488) Roar 'n' Snore packages (sleeping at the zoo) take you behind the scenes.

» **National Sports Museum** (p485) Just walking in will get your junior champion's heart rate up.

» **Melbourne Museum** (p487) The Children's Museum has hands-on exhibits that make kids squeal.

★ Festivals & Events

Melbourne isn't fussy about when it gets festive. Winter chills or summer's swelter are no excuse, with Melburnians joining like-minded types at outdoor festivals, in cinemas, performance spaces or sporting venues year-round.

January

Australian Open   TENNIS
(www.australianopen.com; National Tennis Centre, Melbourne Park) The world's top tennis players and huge, merry-making crowds descend for Australia's Grand Slam tennis championship.

Midsumma Festival   ARTS
(www.midsumma.org.au) Melbourne's annual gay-and-lesbian arts festival features over 100 events from mid-January to mid-February, with a Pride March finale.

Big Day Out   MUSIC
(www.bigdayout.com) The national rock-fest comes to town at the end of January.

Chinese New Year   CULTURAL
(www.melbournechinatown.com.au; Little Bourke St, Chinatown) Melbourne has celebrated the lunar new year since Little Bourke St became Chinatown in the 1860s.

February

St Kilda Festival   MUSIC FESTIVAL
(www.stkildafestival.com.au; Acland & Fitzroy Sts, St Kilda) This week-long festival ends in a suburb-wide street party on the final Sunday.

St Jerome's Laneway Festival   MUSIC
(www.lanewayfestival.com.au) Iconic indie festival featuring local and international music artists, which has exploded from its initial laneway locale (check website for location details).

Melbourne Fashion Festival   FASHION
(www.mff.com.au) This style-fest features salon shows and parades showcasing new creations of established designers.

Melbourne Food & Wine Festival   FOOD
(www.melbournefoodandwine.com.au) Market tours, wine tastings, cooking classes and presentations by celeb chefs take place at venues across the city (and state).

March

Moomba   FESTIVAL
(www.thatsmelbourne.com.au; Alexandra Gardens, Birrarung Marr) A waterside festival famous locally for its wacky Birdman Rally, where competitors launch themselves into the Yarra in homemade flying machines.

Australian Formula One Grand Prix   CAR RACING
(www.grandprix.com.au; Albert Park) The 5.3km street circuit around the normally tranquil Albert Park Lake is known for its smooth, fast surface. The buzz, both on the streets and in your ears, takes over Melbourne for four days of rev-head action.

April

International Comedy Festival   COMEDY
(www.comedyfestival.com.au) An enormous range of local and international comic talent hits town with four weeks of laughs.

May

Melbourne Jazz   JAZZ
(www.melbournejazz.com) International jazz cats head to town and join locals for gigs

at Hamer Hall, the Regent Theatre and the Palms at Crown Casino.

July

Melbourne International Film Festival
FILM

(www.melbournefilmfestival.com.au) Midwinter movie love-in brings out black-skivvy-wearing cinephiles in droves.

August

Melbourne Writers' Festival
LITERATURE

(www.mwf.com.au) Yes, Melbourne is a Unesco 'city of literature', and it's proud of its writers and, indeed, readers. Beginning in the last week of August, the Writers' Festival features forums and events at various venues.

September

AFL Grand Final
AFL FOOTBALL

(www.afl.com.au; MCG) It's easier to kick a goal from the boundary line than to pick up random tickets to the Grand Final, but it's not hard to get your share of finals fever anywhere in Melbourne (particularly at pubs).

Melbourne Fringe Festival
ARTS

(www.melbournefringe.com.au) The Fringe showcases experimental theatre, music and visual arts.

October

Melbourne International Arts Festival
ARTS

(www.melbournefestival.com.au) Held at various venues around the city, this festival features a thought-provoking program of Australian and international theatre, opera, dance, visual art and music.

November

Melbourne Cup
HORSE RACING

(www.springracingcarnival.com.au) Culminating in the prestigious Melbourne Cup, the Spring Racing Carnival is as much a social event as a sporting one. The Cup, held on the first Tuesday in November, is a public holiday in Melbourne.

December

Boxing Day Test
CRICKET

(www.mcg.org.au; MCG) Boxing Day is day one of Melbourne's annually scheduled international Test cricket match, drawing out the cricket fans. Expect some shenanigans from Bay 13.

🛏 Sleeping

Stay in the CBD for good access to the main sights, or spread your wings and get to know an inner-city suburb like funky Fitzroy, seaside St Kilda or smart South Yarra.

CENTRAL MELBOURNE

Melbourne Central YHA
HOSTEL $

(Map p482; ☑03-9621 2523; www.yha.com.au; 562 Flinders St; dm/d 32/100; @🛜) This heritage building has been totally transformed by the YHA gang; expect a lively reception, handsome rooms, and kitchens and common areas on each of the four levels. Entertainment's high on the agenda, there's a fab restaurant (Bertha Brown) on the ground floor and a grand rooftop area.

Medina Executive Flinders Street
SERVICED APARTMENTS $$

(Map p482; ☑03-8663 0000; www.medina.com.au; 88 Flinders St; apt from $165; ✳) These cool monochromatic apartments are extra large and luxurious. Ask for one at the front for amazing parkland views or get glimpses into Melbourne's lanes from the giant timber-floored studios, all boasting full kitchens.

Nomad's Industry
HOSTEL $$

(Map p482; ☑03-9328 4383; www.nomadshostels.com; 198 A'Beckett St; dm $28-36, d $120; @🛜) Flashpacking hits Melbourne's CBD with this smart hostel boasting a mix of four- to 14-bed dorms (groups can take hold of a four-bed dorm with en suite). There's a rooftop area and plenty of gloss (especially in the girls-only 'Princess Wing').

Adelphi Hotel
BOUTIQUE HOTEL $$

(Map p482; ☑03-8080 8888; www.adelphi.com.au; 187 Flinders Lane; r from $185; ✳@🛜🏊) This discreet Flinders Lane property, designed by Denton Korker Marshall in the early 1990s, was one of Australia's first boutique hotels. The cosy rooms with original fittings have stood the test of time, and its pool, which juts out over Flinders Lane, has sparked imitators.

Robinsons in the City
BOUTIQUE HOTEL $$

(Map p482; ☑03-9329 2552; www.ritc.com.au; 405 Spencer St; r incl breakfast from $185; ✳🛜) Robinsons is a gem with six large rooms and warm service. The building is a former bakery, dating from 1850, but it's been given a modern, eclectic look. Bathrooms are not en suite; each room has its own in the hall.

GAY & LESBIAN MELBOURNE

Melbourne's gay and lesbian community is well integrated into the general populace but clubs and bars are found in two distinct locations: Abbotsford/Collingwood and Prahran/South Yarra. Commercial Rd, which separates the latter two suburbs, is home to numerous gay clubs, cafes and businesses. It's more glamorous than the 'northside', which is reputedly more down to earth and a little less pretentious.

The **Midsumma Festival** (www.midsumma.org.au; ⊘mid-Jan–Feb) has a diverse program with around 150 cultural, community and sporting events.

MCV (www.mcv.net.au) is a free weekly newspaper, and gay and lesbian community radio station **JOY 94.9 FM** (www.joy.org.au) is another important resource for visitors and locals.

Drinking & Nightlife

Glasshouse Hotel
PUB

(www.glass-house.com.au; 51 Gipps St, Collingwood; ⊘5pm-late Wed, noon-late Fri & Sun, 4pm-late Sat; ⊡16, 96, 12) The Glasshouse caters for a mostly lesbian crowd with entertainment that includes live bands, drag kings and DJs. Gipps St runs east off Wellington St.

Peel Hotel
NIGHTCLUB

(www.thepeel.com.au; cnr Peel & Wellington Sts, Collingwood; ⊘9pm-late Thu-Sat; ⊡86) Features a mostly male crowd dancing to house music, retro and commercial dance. It's on Peel St, which runs east off Smith St.

Sleeping

169 Drummond
GUESTHOUSE $$

(Map p517 (☑03-9663 3081; www.169drummond.com.au; 169 Drummond St, Carlton; d incl breakfast $135-145; ❄@; ⊡1, 8) This privately owned guesthouse is housed in a renovated, 19th-century terrace that is located in the inner north, one block from vibrant Lygon St.

Sofitel
HOTEL $$$

(Map p482; ☑03-9653 0000; www.sofitelmelbourne.com.au; 25 Collins St; r from $270; ❄@⌨) Guest rooms at the Sofitel start on the 36th floor, so you are guaranteed breathtaking views that will make you giddy. The rooms are high international style, opulent rather than minimal, and though the hotel entrance, with its superb IM Pei–designed ceiling, is relentlessly workaday, you'll soon be a world (or at least 36 floors) away. No35 is an excellent restaurant on level (you guessed it) 35.

Alto Hotel on Bourke
HOTEL $$

(Map p482; ☑03-9606 0585; www.altohotel.com.au; 636 Bourke St; r from 160, apt from $190; ❄@⌨) This environment-minded hotel has water-saving showers, energy-efficient light globes, and double-glazed windows that open, and in-room recycling is promoted. Rooms are also well equipped, light and neutrally decorated.

Causeway 353
HOTEL $$

(Map p482; ☑03-9660 8888; www.causeway.com.au; 353 Little Collins St; r incl breakfast from $150; ❄@⌨) Who needs a view when you've got a laneway location? Causeway 353's breakfast is in a cafe that's situated on a bustling laneway, and you will be more than relaxed after spending a night in its simple, stylish rooms which feature long and dark timber bedheads, king-sized beds and smart leather furniture.

Hotel Lindrum
BOUTIQUE HOTEL $$$

(Map p482; ☑03-9668 1111; www.hotellindrum.com.au; 26 Flinders St; r from $245; ❄@⌨) This attractive hotel was once the pool hall of the legendary and literally unbeatable Walter Lindrum. Expect interiors that have rich tones, subtle lighting and tactile fabrics. Spring for a deluxe room and you will snare either arch or bay windows and marvellous views of Melbourne. Nice as they are, some of the standard rooms feel like corners have been cut. But it's still easily

one of the city's finest boutique hotels. And yes, there's a pool table.

Majorca Apartment 401
SERVICED APARTMENT **$$$**

(Map p482; ☑03-9428 8104; www.apartment401. com.au; 258 Flinders Lane; apt from $250) This is the ultimate in like-a-local living. The Majorca, a single apartment, is in one of the city's loveliest art-deco buildings and watches over a bustling vortex of laneways. It's stylishly furnished, has timber floorboards and the windows are huge. Who needs a concierge when you're right in the centre of things already? There's a two-night minimum.

Pensione Hotel
HOTEL **$$**

(Map p482 (☑03-9621 3333; www.pensione.com. au; 16 Spencer St; s/d $100/135; ❋@☎) The Pensione isn't being cute christening some rooms 'petit double' – they're squeezy, but what you don't get in size is more than made up for in spot-on style, room extras and super-reasonable rates.

City Centre Hotel
HOTEL **$**

(Map p482; ☑03-9654 5401; www.citycentre budgethotel.com.au; 22 Little Collins St; s/d/f $70/90/130; @☎) Intimate, independent and inconspicuous, this 38-room budget hotel is a find. It's located at the city's prettier end, down a 'Little' street, up some stairs, and inside an unassuming building. All rooms share bathroom facilities but the fresh rooms are light-filled with working windows; there's also free wi-fi and a laundry.

Greenhouse Backpacker
HOSTEL **$**

(Map p482; ☑03-9639 6400; www.friendlygroup. com.au; 6/228 Flinders Lane; dm/s/d incl breakfast $32/70/80; ❋@☎) Greenhouse has a fun vibe and is extremely well run – they know what keeps backpackers content. This includes freebies: daily half-hour internet access, pancakes on Sunday, rooftop BBQs, luggage storage and activities. There's also chatty, helpful staff and spick-and-span facilities. There's double bed bunks for couples in the mixed dorms; solo travellers can opt for single-sex dorms.

City Square Motel
HOTEL **$$**

(Map p482; ☑03-9654 7011; www.citysquaremotel. com.au; 67 Swanston St; s/d incl breakfast $90/125; ❋) The foyer is not much, but the rooms are dirt cheap and the staff charming. Rooms come with double-glazed windows to dull the sound of tram bells, and there's bread, butter and vegemite in the room for breakfast.

Jasper Hotel
HOTEL **$$**

(Map p482; ☑03-8327 2777; www.jasperhotel. au; 489 Elizabeth St; r from $180; ❋@☎) The old Hotel Y has had a makeover by Jackson Clements Burrows and now sports moody down lighting, a veritable Pantone swatchbook of colours, louvered bathrooms and some newly graphic soft furnishings. It's a tad soulless, though. Guests have complimentary use of the sporting facilities in the nearby Melbourne City Baths. All profits still go to the YWCA's community and welfare services.

Causeway Inn on the Mall
HOTEL **$$**

(Map p482; ☑03-9650 0688; www.causeway.com. au; 327 Bourke St Mall; s/d incl breakfast $119/130; ❋@☎) Recently refurbished, the Causeway Inn is always busy and often full. Bonuses include helpful staff, free breakfast and daily paper, and a location bang in the middle of the city. The hotel entrance is actually in the Causeway.

Mercure
HOTEL **$$**

(Map p482; ☑9205 9999; www.accorhotels.com. au; 13 Spring St; r from $189; ☎) A lively foyer, friendly staff and a perfect 2pm checkout on Sundays add sparkle to the decent rooms. All have a shower over the bath and some have sweet park views.

Melbourne Connection Travellers Hostel
HOSTEL **$**

(Map p482; ☑03-9642 4464; www.melbourne connection.com; 205 King St; dm $20-35, d $60-80; @☎) This 79-bed little charmer follows the small-is-better principle. It offers simple, clean and uncluttered budget accommodation with modern facilities, well-organised staff and a basement lounge area.

Victoria Hotel
HOTEL **$$**

(Map p482; ☑03-9669 0000; www.victoria hotel.com.au; 215 Little Collins St; s/d $99/110; ❋@☎☲) The original Vic opened its doors in 1880, but don't worry, they've updated the plumbing since then. This city institution has around 400 rooms, and all differ slightly. The Bellerive and Heritage rooms are more upmarket, but all have down lights and are comfortable. Facilities include a plunge pool.

FITZROY & AROUND

TOP CHOICE ▸ Brooklyn Arts Hotel BOUTIQUE HOTEL **$$**

(Map p498; ☑03-9419 9328; www.brooklynarts hotel.com; 48-50 George St, Fitzroy; s/d incl breakfast $95/135; ☎; ☲86) There are seven very different rooms in this character-filled hotel.

N

0 ———— 200 m
0 ———— 0.1 miles

Princes St

FITZROY
NORTH

CLIFTON HILL

To North Fitzroy Bowls
(800m); Moroccan
Soup Bar (1km)

Alexandra Pde (Eastern Hwy)

2

83

35

20

Cecil St

Westgarth St

Station St

Kay St

CARLTON

16
31

14
17

Leicester St

Rose St

32

Kerr St

24

8

Keele St

Spring St

Kerr St

1

Easey St

Argyle St

Sackville St

Elgin St

34

6
15

Victoria St

FITZROY

22

12

Johnston St

Mahoney St

29

Chapel St

34

To Tote
(150m)

Bell St

45

Young St

Greeves St

10

Bedford St

John St

Fitzroy St

28

21

St David St

Kent St

Otter St

Moor St

23

George St

Smith St

Hodgson St

Stanley St

King William St

25

5

Hanover St

Atherton
Reserve

Condell St

COLLINGWOOD

Palmer St

Charles St

Webb St

Royal La

Napier St

Little George St

George St

Little Gore St

Gore St

Little Smith St

Little Oxford St

Oxford St

Peel St

18

Cambridge St

30

13

34

Gertrude St

19

7

33

27

9

26

Langridge St

11

45

Young St

3

Little Victoria St

Mason St

32

4

Victoria Pde

32

MELBOURNE & VICTORIA MELBOURNE

Owner Maggie has put the call out for artistic people and they've responded by staying, so expect lively conversation around the continental breakfast. Rooms are clean, colourful and beautifully decorated; one even houses a piano.

**Tyrian Services
Apartments**   SERVICED APARTMENTS **$$$**
(Map p498; ☎03-9415 1900; www.tyrian.com.au; 91 Johnston St; r from $200; ❄@☎; ⊞112) These spacious, self-contained modern apartments have a certain Fitzroy celeb appeal, which you'll feel from the moment you walk down the dimmed hallway to reception. Big couches, flat-screen TVs and balconies add to the appeal.

Home @ The Mansion   HOSTEL **$**
(Map p498; ☎03-9663 4212; www.homemansion.com.au; 80 Victoria Pde, East Melbourne; dm $26-32, d $90; @☎; ⊞96) This grand-looking heritage building houses 92 dorm beds and a couple of doubles, all of which are light and bright and have lovely high ceilings. There are two small areas for Playstation and TV-watching, a courtyard out the front and a sunny kitchen.

Nunnery   HOSTEL **$$**
(Map p498; ☎03-9419 8637; www.nunnery.com.au; 116 Nicholson St, Fitzroy; dm incl breakfast $30, s $75, d $110; @☎; ⊞96) The Nunnery oozes atmosphere, with sweeping staircases and many original features; the walls are dripping with religious works of art and ornate stained-glass windows. You'll be giving thanks for the big comfortable lounges and communal areas.

Collingwood Backpackers   HOSTEL **$**
(☎0420 804 208; www.collingwoodbackpackers.com; 137-139 Johnston St, Collingwood; dm/d $26/$90; @☎; ⊞86) Going against the high-tech, high-gloss grain of some hostels is this newbie in a former Collingwood rooming house. Call ahead to book your room (walk-ins are discouraged) and expect a smoky, friendly, sharehouse kind of atmosphere. Rooms have TVs, wi-fi access and plenty of, ahem, character. To find it follow Johnston St east of Brunswick and Smith Sts.

CARLTON & AROUND

Downtowner on Lygon   HOTEL **$$**
(Map p517; ☎03-9663 5555; www.downtowner.com.au; 66 Lygon St, Carlton; r from $169; ❄@☎; ⊞1, 8) The Downtowner is a surprising complex of different-sized rooms, including

joining rooms perfect for families and couples travelling together. Ask for a light-bathed room if you can. It's perfectly placed between the CBD and Lygon St restaurants.

SOUTH YARRA, PRAHRAN & WINDSOR

TOP CHOICE **Punthill Apartments**
South Yarra APARTMENTS **$$**
(Map p507; ☑1300 731 299; www.punthill.com.au; 7 Yarra St, South Yarra; r from $180; ✹⑧⑤; ℝSouth Yarra) It's the little things, like a blackboard and chalk in the kitchen for messages, and individually wrapped liquorice all-sorts by the bed, that make this a great choice. The bright rooms have laundry facilities and those with balconies come complete with their own (tin) dog on fake grass.

Art Series (The Olsen) BOUTIQUE HOTEL **$$$**
(Map p507; ☑03-9040 1222; www.artserieshotels.com.au/olsen; 637 Chapel St, South Yarra; r from $200; ✹⑧⑤☒; ℝSouth Yarra, ⑧8) This new hotel honouring artist John Olsen is where international celebs are staying these days, and we think we know why; the staff are attentive; the modern glam foyer is beaut; the open plan rooms are delightful. Oh, and the hotel's pool juts out over Chapel Street. You never know whom you'll bump into in the lift.

Art Series (Cullen) BOUTIQUE HOTEL **$$**
(Map p507; ☑03-9098 1555; www.artserieshotels.com.au/cullen; 164 Commercial Road, Prahran; r from $169; ✹⑧⑤; ⑧78,79) Expect visions of Ned Kelly shooting you from the glam opaque room/bathroom dividers in this new and lively hotel resplendent in the works of Sydney artist Adam Cullen. Borrow the 'Cullen Car' ($60 per day) or Kronan bike ($5 per hour) and let the whole of Melbourne know where you're staying.

Lyall HOTEL **$$$**
(Map p507; ☑03-9868 8222; www.thelyall.com; 14 Murphy St, South Yarra; r from $270; ✹⑧⑤; ℝSouth Yarra, ⑧8) The Lyall is tucked away in a leafy residential street. The spacious rooms are well appointed, with little luxuries including gourmet cheese in the mini-bar, laundry facilities and, in some, televisions in the bathrooms. It's also home to a spa centre.

Back Of Chapel HOSTEL **$**
(Map p507; ☑03-9521 5338; www.backofchapel.com; 50 Green St, Windsor; dm incl breakfast $20-26, d $80; ⑧; ⑧78,79) This clean backpackers in an old Victorian terrace has its own bar

(claiming to have the cheapest drinks in Melbourne), and is literally 20 steps away from buzzing Chapel St. TV is a feature (there are two biggies), and new bathrooms and a bunch of freebies (breakfast, for one) add appeal.

Hotel Claremont GUESTHOUSE **$**
(Map p507; ☑03-9826 8000, 1300 301 630; www.hotelclaremont.com; 189 Toorak Rd, South Yarra; dm/s/d incl breakfast $34/69/79; ⑧⑤; ℝSouth Yarra, ⑧8) In a large heritage building dating from 1868, the Claremont is good value, with comfortable rooms, high ceilings and shared bathrooms. Don't expect fancy decor: it's simply a clean, welcoming cheapie.

ST KILDA & AROUND

St Kilda is a budget-traveller enclave, but there are some stylish options a short walk from the beach, too.

Prince HOTEL **$$$**
(Map p509; ☑03-9536 1111; www.theprince.com.au; 2 Acland St, St Kilda; r incl breakfast from $260; ✹⑧⑤; ⑧16, 79, 96, 112) The Prince has a suitably dramatic lobby and the rooms are an interesting mix of the original pub's proportions, natural materials and a pared-back aesthetic. Larger rooms and suites feature some key pieces of vintage modernist furniture. On-site 'facilities' take in some of the city's most mentioned: bars, band rooms and even a wine shop downstairs.

Habitat HQ HOSTEL **$**
(off Map p482; ☑03-9537 3777; www.habitathq.com.au; 333 St Kilda Rd; dm incl breakfast $30-$38, d $139; ✹⑧⑤; ⑧16,67,79) There's not much this clean, new hostel doesn't have. Tick off open-plan communal spaces, a beer garden, a travel agent and a pool table for starters. Follow Carlisle St from St Kilda to St Kilda Rd – it's on your left.

Base HOSTEL **$$**
(Map p509; ☑03-8598 6200; www.stayatbase.com; 17 Carlisle St, St Kilda; dm from $30, r from $110; ✹⑧⑤; ⑧16, 79, 96) Accor spin-off Base has streamlined dorms, each with en suite, or slick doubles. There's a 'sanctuary' floor for female travellers, and a bar and live music nights to keep the good-time vibe happening.

Hotel Tolarno HOTEL **$$**
(Map p509; ☑03-9537 0200; www.hoteltolarno.com.au; 42 Fitzroy St, St Kilda; r from $155; ✹⑧⑤; ⑧16, 79, 96, 112) Tolarno was once the site of Georges Mora's seminal gallery Tolarno. The fine-dining restaurant downstairs now bears

For many travellers to Australia, particularly those of British origin, Melbourne is a 'must' destination because it is the home of internationally renowned TV program *Neighbours*. A visit to Melbourne would not be complete without a trip to the legendary Ramsay St. Pin Oak Ct in Vermont South is the suburban street that has been home of the show for 20 years.

The best way to see Ramsay St and have a proper *Neighbours* experience is by doing the **Official Neighbours Tour** (03-9629 5866; www.neighbourstour.com.au), which is run by Backpacker King and approved by the show's producers and the residents of Pin Oak Ct. If you're lucky you might see us filming and grab a photo and autograph. Two tours are available: the $50 tour runs twice daily Monday to Friday and visits Ramsay St and Erinsborough High School, plus you get the chance to meet a *Neighbours* actor. The second, more comprehensive tour, costs $68 and visits the street, the school and the outside studio sets of the Lassiters' complex, Carpenter Mechanics and Charlie's Bar. This tour is also met by a *Neighbours* actor and runs on weekends and over the Christmas holidays. Official merchandise is available on the tours and from the **Neighbours Centre** (Map p482; 570 Flinders St Melbourne).

You'll also find some backpacker hostels that occasionally run in-house trips to Ramsay St – but always check to see if it's above board and that they're a licensed operator.

If you want to make the pilgrimage yourself, Pin Oak Ct is in Vermont South (Melways map 62: E8). If you don't have wheels, take the train to Glen Waverley station and bus 888 or 889 north; get off at Vision Dr near Burwood Hwy. Tram 75 from Flinders St will take you all the way to the corner of Burwood Hwy and Springvale Rd; a short walk south takes you to Weeden Dr; Pin Oak Ct is third on the left.

When visiting Pin Oak Ct please remember to respect the privacy of the residents. Don't do anything in their street or on their properties you wouldn't be happy with in your own street or home!

Backpacker King also runs a popular **Official Neighbours Trivia Night** (bookings 03-9629 5866; www.neighboursnight.com.au; tickets $40) every Monday night, where you can meet and have photos taken with your favourite *Neighbours* actors. It's held at the **Elephant & Wheelbarrow** (Map p509; 169 Fitzroy St, St Kilda) and includes a one-hour concert by my band, Waiting Room.

Alan Fletcher has worked in every branch of the performing arts for over 30 years. He has played the role of Dr Karl Kennedy on Neighbours since 1994.

the name of his artist wife Mirka, as well as her original paintings. Rooms upstairs are brightly coloured and eclectically furnished, with good beds and crisp white linen. Those at the front of the building might get a bit noisy for some, but have balconies, floorboards and enormous windows.

Hotel Urban   HOTEL $$$
(Map p509; 03-8530 8888; www.urbanstkilda.com.au; 35-37 Fitzroy St, St Kilda; r from $185; 16, 79, 96, 112) Rooms at Hotel Urban use a lot of blond wood and white to maximise space, and are simple, light and calming. Some rooms have freestanding in-room spas and are circular.

Coffee Palace   HOSTEL $
(Map p509; 03-9534 5283; www.coffeepalacebackpackers.com.au; 24 Grey St, St Kilda; dm/d incl breakfast from $25/80; 16, 79, 96, 112) This rambling old-school backpackers has lots

of rooms, lots of activities and lots of years behind it. It has a travel desk, communal kitchen, bar, pool tables, lounge and TV room, plus a rooftop terrace with bay views. Dorms sleep from four to 10, with some for women only. There are also private rooms with shared bathrooms.

Ritz   HOSTEL $
(Map p509; 03-9525 3501; www.ritzbackpackers.com; 169 Fitzroy St, St Kilda; dm/d incl breakfast $27/70; 16, 79) Above a corner pub renowned for hosting the riotously popular *Neighbours* nights (see p501), the Ritz has an excellent location, opposite an inner-city lake and park, and is only a five-minute walk from St Kilda's heart. It can get noisy when live music is cranking downstairs.

Art Series (Blackman)   BOUTIQUE HOTEL $$$
(03-9039 1444; www.artserieshotels.com.au/blackman; 452 St Kilda Rd, Melbourne; r from $209;

❋ 🛜; 🖳3, 5, 6, 8, 16, 64, 67, 72) The most recent of the Art Series to open, it doesn't have one single original Charles Blackman painting (though loads of prints and Blackman room decals), but it boasts superb views (aim for a corner suite for views of Albert Park Lake and the city skyline), luxurious beds and blackout curtains for a sleep in. Aimed at the corporate market but suits the splurger, too.

Middle Park Hotel PUB $$

(✆03-9690 1958; www.middleparkhotel.com.au; 102 Canterbury Rd, Middle Park; r incl breakfast from $180; 🖳112; ❋🛜) With a locked bedside drawer labeled 'x', and an 'x' keyring to match (hello $70 'intimacy' pack), you might be wondering what kind of hotel you've booked yourself into, but relax. A Six Degrees renovation has ensured the rooms feel luxurious and modern – expect ipod docks and rain showerheads when you reach the top of the wooden staircase. There's a modern pub and restaurant downstairs, and the cooked gourmet breakfast in the dining room is a treat.

✖ Eating

CENTRAL MELBOURNE

TOP CHOICE Cumulus Inc MODERN AUSTRALIAN $$

(Map p482; www.cumulusinc.com.au; 45 Flinders Lane; mains $21-38; ⊘breakfast, lunch & dinner Mon-Sat) One of Melbourne's best for breakfasts, lunches and dinners; it gives you that wonderful Andrew McConnell style along with really reasonable prices. The focus is on beautiful produce and simple but artful cooking: from breakfasts of sardines and smoked tomato on toast at the marble bar to suppers of freshly shucked clair de lune oysters tucked away on the leather banquettes.

TOP CHOICE Movida SPANISH $$

(Map p482; ✆03-9663 3038; www.movida.com.au; 1 Hosier Lane; tapas $4-6, raciones $10-17; ⊘lunch & dinner) Movida is nestled in a cobbled laneway emblazoned with one of the world's densest collections of street art; it doesn't get much more Melbourne than this. Line up along the bar, cluster around little window tables or, if you've booked, take a table in the dining area. **Movida Next Door** (cnr Flinders St & Hosier Lane; ⊘5pm-late Tue-Thu, noon-midnight Fri-Sat, 2pm-9pm Sun) is the perfect place for a pre-show beer and tapas, while way in the lawyer-end of town is larger **Movida Aqui** (1st fl, 500 Bourke St; ⊘noon-late Mon-Fri, 6pm-late Sat), with its lovely terrace.

Vue de Monde FRENCH, MODERN AUSTRALIAN $$$

(Map p482; ✆03-9691 3888; www.vuedemonde. com.au; Rialto, 525 Collins St; lunch/dinner menu gourmand from $100/150; ⊘lunch & dinner Tue-Fri, dinner Sat) Melbourne's favoured spot for occasion dining has relocated to the old 'observation deck' of the Rialto, so its view will finally match its name. Expect the usual fantastic French cuisine thanks to visionary Shannon Bennett. Book ahead. Remaining at the old barrister's chambers will be **Bistro Vue** (✆03-9691 3838; 430 Little Collins St; ⊘11am-late Mon-Sat) and **Café Vue** (✆03-9691 3899; 430 Little Collins St; ⊘7am-4pm Mon-Fri).

Flower Drum CHINESE $$$

(Map p482; ✆03-9662 3655; www.flower-drum. com; 17 Market Lane; mains $35-55; ⊘lunch Mon-Sat, dinner daily) The Flower Drum continues to be Melbourne's most celebrated Chinese restaurant. The finest, freshest produce prepared with absolute attention to detail keeps this Chinatown institution booked out for weeks in advance. The sumptuous but ostensibly simple Cantonese food is delivered with the slick service you'd expect in such elegant surrounds.

HuTong Dumpling Bar CHINESE $

(Map p482; www.hutong.com.au; 14-16 Market Lane; mains $12) HuTong's windows face out on famed Flower Drum, and its reputation for divine *xiao long bao* (soupy dumplings) means it's just as hard to get a lunchtime seat anywhere in the three-level building. Downstairs, watch chefs make the delicate dumplings, then hope they don't watch you making a mess of them (there are step-by-step instructions on the table for eating them). There's also a **branch** (Map p507; 162 Commercial Rd) in Prahran.

Little Press & Cellar GREEK $$$

(Map p482; 72 Flinders St; mains $35-49; ⊘7am-late Mon-Fri, noon-late Sat & Sun) It may not be as large as the Press Club next door, but this 'little press' gives you a taste of George Calombaris' style at a relatively bargain price. Consider its weekday express lunch menu, which fires off three Greek dishes for $34, but don't miss the 'little snack' of signature taramosalata with hot chips ($13.50).

Gingerboy ASIAN $$

(Map p482; ✆03-9662 4200; www.gingerboy.com. au; 27-29 Crossley St; small dishes $13-16, large dishes $30-36; ⊘lunch & dinner Mon-Fri, dinner Sat) Brave the aggressively trendy surrounds and weekend party scene, as talented Teague

Ezard does a fine turn in flash hawker cooking. Flavours pop in dishes such as scallops with green chilli jam or coconut kingfish with peanut and tamarind dressing. There are two dinner sittings, and bookings are required.

Bar Lourinhã
TAPAS **$$**

(Map p482; ☑03-9663 7890; www.barlourinha.com.au; 37 Little Collins St; tapas $9-20 ☺lunch & dinner Mon-Fri, dinner Sat) Matt McConnell's wonderful northern Spanish-Portuguese specialities have the swagger and honesty of an Iberian shepherd, but with a cluey, metropolitan touch. Start light with the melting, zingy kingfish pancetta and finish with the hearty house-made chorizo or baked *morcilla* (blood sausage).

Dainty Sichuan
CHINESE **$$**

(Map p482; ☑03-9663 8861; 26 Corrs Lane; mains $12-25; ☺lunch & dinner) This hidden restaurant has a cult-like following and might just claim you too, if you like it hot (you'd be advised to order from the category 'Tongue burning hot'). Chilli oil, dried chillies, ground chilli seeds, Sichuan peppercorns and well, chillies, join other less than dainty flavourings such as peanuts and vinegar to give you a range of pork, chicken and beef dishes that will rock your world. Bookings advised.

Italian Waiters Club
ITALIAN **$$**

(Map p482; 1st fl, 20 Meyers Pl; mains $15-18; ☺lunch & dinner) Down a laneway and up some stairs, the inside of the Italian Waiters Club will make you feel like you stepped into another era. Opened in 1947, it still bears '50s drapes, wood panelling and Laminex tables. Once only for Italian and Spanish waiters to unwind after work over a game of *scopa* (a card game) and a glass of wine, now everyone from suits to students is allowed in for hearty plates of red-sauce pasta and the regularly changing roster of specials.

Portello Rosso
TAPAS **$$**

(Map p482; www.portellorosso.com.au; 15 Warburton Lane; tapas $15; ☺lunch Tue-Fri, dinner Tue-Sat) Chef Aaron Whitney has travelled to Melbourne via Byron Bay and Majorca so expect excellent (read: real) tapas. There's an olde-worlde cocktail bar upstairs (Murmur), and the whole space harks back to its industrial past.

Maha
MIDDLE EASTERN **$$**

(Map p482; ☑03-9629 5900; www.mahabg.com.au; 21 Bond St; small dishes $8-10, large dishes $20-26; ☺lunch & dinner Mon-Fri, dinner Sat) Get your reservation in for a meal at this sexy subterranean space. It pays homage to the richness and complexity of Middle Eastern and Eastern Mediterranean cooking, but is done with a light, modern touch. Chef Shane Delia's Maltese heritage gets a look in too – rabbit is only off the menu when it's not in season.

Trunk
ITALIAN, AMERICAN **$$**

(Map p482; ☑03-9663 7994; www.trunktown.com.au; 275 Exhibition St; mains $28-35; ☺lunch & dinner Mon-Fri, dinner Sat) Trunk turns into a prime CBD watering hole on Friday nights, but don't let Bryan from the marketing department put you off. The building is over a hundred years old and was once a synagogue. Next door, Trunk's American-styled diner has a busy, fun feel to it. Its organic breakfast waffles are a sweet choice.

Red Pepper
INDIAN **$**

(Map p482; 18 Bourke St; mains $5-12) It's mighty rare to get a decent meal for under $10, but it's possible here. The local Indian community knows it's good, and while leather-like seats feign 'upmarket', it's the fresh naan and daal that people come here for. The mango lassi's are delicious and you can rock up here any morning until 3am.

Camy Shanghai Dumpling Restaurant
CHINESE **$**

(Map p482; 23-25 Tattersalls Lane; dishes $6.50; ☺lunch & dinner) There's nothing fancy here; pour your own plastic cup of overboiled tea from the urn, then try a variety of dumplings with some greens. Put up with the dismal service and you've found one of the last places in town you can fill up for under $10.

Pellegrini's Espresso Bar
ITALIAN, CAFE **$**

(Map p482; ☑03-9662 1885; 66 Bourke St; mains $12-16; ☺breakfast, lunch & dinner) The iconic Italian equivalent of a classic 1950s diner, Pellegrini's has remained genuinely unchanged for decades. Pick and mix from the variety of pastas and sauces; from the table out the back you can watch it all thrown together from enormous ever-simmering pots. In summer, finish with a ladle of watermelon granita.

Pushka
CAFE **$**

(Map p482; 20 Pesgrave Pl, off Howey Pl) Relaxed hipster hideaway with home-away-from-home charm, excellent coffee and Portuguese custard tarts. Just keep on going up that alley.

NORTH MELBOURNE

Auction Rooms   CAFE **$$**

(107 Errol St, North Melbourne; mains $15-25; 🚋57)
This insanely busy cafe serves up sweet coffee and inventive mains, though sometimes you may wonder if it's still operating as an auction room (everyone just seems so... polished!). From Queen Victoria Market head west along Victoria St, then take a right at Errol St.

Courthouse Hotel   PUB FARE **$$**

(www.thecourthouse.net.au; 86 Errol St, North Melbourne; mains $18-41; ⊘lunch & dinner Mon-Sat; 🚋57) This corner pub has managed to retain the comfort and familiarity of a local while taking food, both in its public bar and its more formal dining spaces, very seriously. The European-style dishes are both refined and hearty. Lunch deals, including a glass of wine, are good value at $37, or head to the front bar for (cheaper) finds. From Queen Victoria Market head west along Victoria St, then take a right at Errol St.

RICHMOND

If you love Vietnamese food, don't miss Richmond's Victoria St (the east end of Collingwood and Fitzroy's Victoria Pde).

Demitri's Feast   GREEK **$**

(www.dimitrisfeast.com.au; 141 Swan St Richmond; mains $14-16; ⊘breakfast & lunch Tue-Sun; 🚋70) Warning: don't even attempt to get a seat here on a weekend; aim for a quiet weekday when you'll have time and space to fully immerse yourself in lunches like a calamari salad with ouzo aioli. Swan St runs parallel to Bridge Rd – follow Brunton Ave from the CBD.

Pacific Seafood BBQ House   CHINESE **$$**

(☎03-9427 8225; 240 Victoria St, Richmond; mains $15-25; ⊘lunch & dinner daily; 🚉North Richmond, 🚋24, 109) Seafood in tanks and script-only menus on coloured craft paper make for an authentic, fast and fabulous dining experience. Tank-fresh fish is done simply, perhaps steamed with ginger and greens, and washed down with Chinese beer. Book, or be ready to queue. Victoria St is at the east end of Collingwood and Fitzroy's Victoria Pde.

Richmond Hill Cafe & Larder   CAFE **$$**

(www.rhcl.com.au; 48-50 Bridge Rd, Richmond; brunch $12-30; ⊘breakfast & lunch; 🚉West Richmond, 🚋48, 75) Once the domain of well-known cook Stephanie Alexander, it still boasts its lovely cheese room and simple, comforting food like cheesy toast. There are

breakfast cocktails for the brave. Wellington St in the CBD becomes Bridge Rd.

FITZROY & AROUND

TOP CHOICE Cutler & Co   MODERN AUSTRALIAN **$$$**

(Map p498; ☎03-9419 4888; www.cutlerandco.com.au; 55 Gertrude St, Fitzroy; mains $37-47; ⊘dinner Tue-Sun, lunch Fri & Sun; 🚋86) Hyped for all the right reasons, this is Andrew McConnell's latest restaurant and though its decor might be a little over the top, its attentive, informed staff and joy-inducing meals (suckling pig is a favourite) have quickly made this one of Melbourne's best.

St Jude's Cellar   MODERN AUSTRALIAN **$$**

(Map p498; www.stjudescellars.com.au; 389-391 Brunswick St, Fitzroy; mains around $22-26; ⊘lunch & dinner Tue-Sun, breakfast Sat & Sun; 🚋112) A cavernous warehouse space has been given a clever, cool and humanising fit-out while not losing its airy industrial feel. The restaurant stretches out from behind the shopfront cellar, affording respite from the Brunswick St hustle. Mains include mussels and leek in Coldstream cider and goat ragout, but try their innovative desserts, too.

Moroccan Soup Bar   NORTH AFRICAN, VEGETARIAN **$$**

(off Map p498; ☎03-9482 4240; 183 St Georges Rd, North Fitzroy; banquet $18; ⊘6pm-10pm Tue-Sun; 🚋112) Prepare to queue before being seated by stern Hana, who will then go through the menu verbally. Best bet is the banquet, which, for three courses, is tremendous value. The sublime chickpea bake has locals queuing with their own pots and containers to nab some to take away. It's an alcohol-free zone, but (shhh) there's a cute bar next door. From Fitzroy, continue north along Brunswick St and cross Alexander Pde. It's on your left past the bowling club.

Cavallero   MODERN AUSTRALIAN **$$**

(Map p498; www.cavallero.com.au; 300 Smith St, Collingwood; mains $10-25; ⊘breakfast, lunch & dinner Tue-Sun; 🚋86) A supersmart, subtle fit-out lets the charm of this grand Victorian shopfront shine. Served under the gaze of a deer's head, morning coffee and brioche make way for fancy toasties and Pinot Gris then shared plates galore and cocktails.

Charcoal Lane   MODERN AUSTRALIAN **$$**

(Map p498; ☎03-9418 3400; www.charcoallane.com.au; 136 Gertrude St, Fitzroy; mains $17-35; ⊘lunch & dinner Tue-Sat; 🚋86) This training restaurant

for Aboriginal and disadvantaged young people is one of the best places to try native flora and fauna; menu items include wallaby tartare and native peppered kangaroo.

Commoner
MODERN BRITISH $$
(Map p498; ✆03-9415 6876; www.thecommoner.com.au; 122 Johnston St, Fitzroy; mains $13-30; ⊙lunch & dinner Sat & Sun, dinner Wed-Fri; ▣112) If you need to be convinced of this off-strip restaurant's serious intent, the wood-fired goat or pork they offer up come Sunday lunch should do it. On Sunday nights there's no menu, you just get fed.

Wabi Sabi Salon
JAPANESE $
(Map p498; www.wabisabi.net.au; 94 Smith St, Collingwood; dishes $3-20; ⊙lunch & dinner Mon-Sat; ▣86) Expect kooky Japanese decor and delish Japanese cuisine, including bento boxes that change daily (you choose meat, fish or veg and the Japanese chefs do the rest).

Birdman Eating
TAPAS $
(Map p498; www.birdmaneating.com.au; 238 Gertrude St, Fitzroy; mains $8-18; ▣86) Popular? You bet. It is named after the infamous 'Birdman Rally' held during Melbourne's Moomba festival, and you'll be glad you don't have to hurl yourself off a bridge to sit pretty on Gertrude St and eat up Welsh rarebit or dip into leek pâté.

Babka Bakery Cafe
BAKERY, CAFE $
(Map p498; 358 Brunswick St, Fitzroy; mains $8-16; ⊙breakfast & lunch Tue-Sun; ▣112) Russian flavours infuse the lovingly prepared breakfast and lunch dishes, and the heady aroma of cinnamon and freshly baked bread makes even just a coffee worth queuing for. Cakes are notable and can be taken away whole.

Munster Haus
VEGETARIAN $
(371 St Georges Rd, Fitzroy; mains $8-14 ⊙lunch & dinner Mon-Fri, brunch & lunch Sat; ▣112) Slick, supremely welcoming and very filling, Munster Haus is a welcome addition to Melboune's vegetarian dining scene. You choose from a selection of what's fresh that day – be it sesame-seed-covered potato bites or sweet-chilli tofu, and it's served up in a big bowl (sizes range from $8 to $14) to enjoy. This healthy 'fast food' kind of eating is slightly addictive. From Fitzroy, head down Brunswick St to St Georges Rd. It's just before Merri Creek.

Vegie Bar
VEGETARIAN $
(Map p498; www.vegiebar.com.au; 380 Brunswick St, Fitzroy; mains $7-15; ⊙lunch & dinner

daily; ▣112) Delicious thin-crust pizzas, tasty curries and seasonal broths can be eaten outside along fab Brunswick St itself, or in its cavernous, shared-table space inside.

Marios
CAFE $
(Map p498; 303 Brunswick St, Fitzroy; mains around $14-25 ⊙breakfast, lunch & dinner; ▣112) Mooching at Marios is part of the Melbourne 101 curriculum. Breakfasts are big and served all day, the service is swift and the coffee is old-school strong.

CARLTON & AROUND
Avoid Carlton's Lygon St spruikers and keep travelling north past Grattan St; some of Melbourne's loveliest cafes and restaurants lie here and beyond. Don't miss the East Brunswick end of Lygon St for interesting eats.

Abla's
LEBANESE $$
(Map p517; ✆03-9347 0006; www.ablas.com.au; 109 Elgin St, Carlton; mains $25; ⊙lunch Thu & Fri, dinner Mon-Sat; ▣1, 8, 96, ▣205) The kitchen here is steered by Abla Amad, whose authentic, flavour-packed food has inspired a whole generation of local Lebanese chefs. Bring a bottle of your favourite plonk and settle in for the compulsory banquet on Friday and Saturday night.

Embrasse Restaurant
FRENCH $$
(Map p517; ✆03-9347 3312; www.embrasseres taurant.com.au; 312 Drummond St, Carlton; mains $27-37; ⊙dinner Wed-Sun, lunch Thu-Sun) Pressure cooking chickpeas and daintily serving up emulsions, purees and flowers is Nicolas Poelaert's game, and the crowd is responding enthusiastically. Just off the main Lygon St drag, the space is intimate and formal. Sunday lunch is a four-course ode to France.

DON'T MISS

BRUNSWICK EATING
Brunswick is Melbourne's Middle Eastern hub, and Sydney Rd's busy **A1 Lebanese Bakehouse** (www.a1lebanesebakery.com.au; 643-645 Sydney Rd, Brunswick; ⊙7am-9pm) and alcohol- and frills-free **Tiba's Restaurant** (www.tibasrestaurant.com.au; 504 Sydney Rd, Brunswick; ⊙closed Tue) are worth a trip in themselves.

Tiamo
ITALIAN $$

(Map p517; 303 Lygon St Carlton; mains $13-10) When you've had enough of pressed, si-phoned, slayered, pour-over filtered and plunged coffee, head here to one of Lygon St's original Italian cafe-restaurants. There's laughter and the relaxed joie de vivre only a time-worn restaurant can have.

Rumi
MIDDLE EASTERN $$

(☑03-9388 8255; 116 Lygon St, East Brunswick; mains $17-22; ☺dinner Tue-Sun; ᪥1, 8) A fabu-lously well-considered place that serves up a mix of traditional Lebanese cooking and contemporary interpretations of old Persian dishes. The *sigara boregi* (cheese and pine-nut pastries) are a local institu-tion and tasty mains like meatballs are balanced with a large and interesting se-lection of vegetable dishes. From Carlton, continue north along Lygon St into East Brunswick.

Hellenic Republic
GREEK $$

(☑03-9381 1222; www.hellenicrepublic.com.au; 434 Lygon St, East Brunswick; mains $21-32; ☺breakfast, lunch & dinner Sat & Sun, lunch Fri-Sun, dinner Mon-Sun; ᪥1, 8) The Iron Bark grill at George Calombaris's northern out-post works overtime grilling up pitta, king prawns, local calamari and snapper, and luscious lamb. It's a northern 'burbs version of Calombaris's Little Press & Cellar (p502). Follow Lygon St north from Carlton – it's in East Brunswick.

Bar Idda
ITALIAN $$

(☑03-9380 5339; www.baridda.com.au; 132 Lygon St, Brunswick East; mains $18; ☺dinner Tue-Sat; ᪥1, 8) The diner-style table coverings give little clue to the tasty morsels this Sicilian restaurant serves. Shared plates are the go and range from pistachio-crumbed lamb loin to vegetarian layered eggplant. Follow Lygon St north from Carlton.

SOUTH YARRA, PRAHRAN & WINDSOR

Jacques Reymond
MODERN AUSTRALIAN $$$

(Map p507; ☑03-9525 2178; www.jacquesreymond. com.au; 78 Williams Rd, Prahran; 3 courses from $98; ☺lunch Thu-Fri, dinner Tue-Sat; ᪥6) Rey-mond was a local pioneer of degustation dining. Degustation plates are now entrée-size, and there's an innovative vegetarian version. Expect a French-influenced, Asian-accented menu with lovely details including house-churned butter.

Pearl
MODERN AUSTRALIAN $$$

(Map p507; ☑03-9421 4599; www.pearlrestau rant.com.au; 631-633 Church St, Richmond; mains $35-48; ☺lunch & dinner daily; ᪥South Yarra, ᪥69) Owner-chef Geoff Lindsay proclaims himself 'a fifth-generation Aussie boy who is seduced by ginger, chilli and palm sugar, Turkish delight, chocolate and pomegran-ate'. We're seduced too: his exquisitely ren-dered food really does epitomise Modern Australian cooking. The space is slick but comfortable, though service can be lax. For a cheaper taste of the Pearl ethos for

South Yarra, Prahran & Windsor

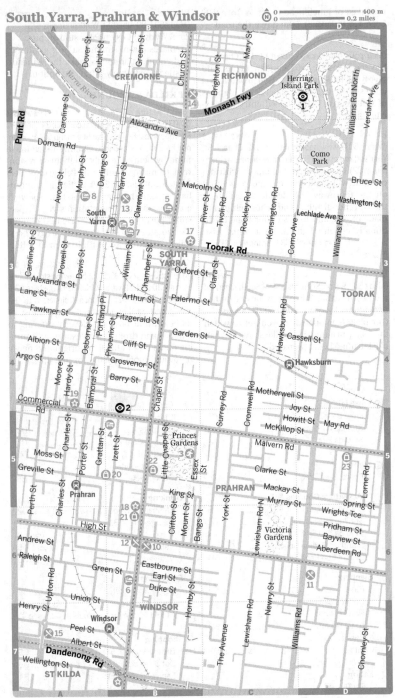

breakfast or lunch head to **Pearl Cafe** (599 Church St, Richmond), 50m down the road.

Lucky Coq
PIZZA **$**

(Map p507; www.luckycoq.com.au; 179 Chapel St Windsor; mains $4; 🖳6) Bargain pizzas and plenty of late-night DJ action make this a good start or end to a Chapel St eve. Reports of suit-wearers being denied entry may excite some.

Hooked
FISH & CHIPS **$**

(Map p507; www.hooked.net.au; 172 Chapel St, Windsor; mains $9-15; ☉lunch & dinner; 🖳Prahran, 🖳72) Great fish and chippery with decor that will make you change your mind on the takeaway and decide to eat in at the communal table. Old-school chips are made on-site and fish is either done traditionally or with light Asian accents. Also a **branch** (Map p498; 384 Brunswick St) in Fitzroy.

Outpost
CAFE **$$**

(Map p507; 9 Yarra St; mains $14; 🖳South Yarra) Of the St Ali realm, this mighty busy cafe has two different rooms to dine and converse in. Our pick? The one where you get to watch the food (including items like shaved Italian black truffle) being prepared.

Windsor Castle
PUB **$$**

(Map p507; 89 Albert St, Windsor; mains $15-25; 🖳Windsor) Cosy nooks, sunken pits, fireplaces (or, in summer, a beer garden) and yummo pub meals make the Windsor Castle an extremely attractive option.

ST KILDA & AROUND

TOP CHOICE / Attica
CONTEMPORARY **$$$**

(🕿03-9530 0111; www.attica.com.au; 74 Glen Eira Rd, Ripponlea; 8-course tasting menu $144; ☉dinner Tue-Sat; 🖳Ripponlea) Staking its claim to fame by being the only Melbourne restaurant to make it onto San Pellegrino's Best Restaurant list in 2010, Attica is a suburban restaurant that serves Ben Shewry's creative dishes degustation-style. Expect small portions of texture-oriented delight, like potatoes cooked in earth. To get here, follow Brighton Rd south to Glen Eira Rd.

Stokehouse
MODERN AUSTRALIAN **$$$**

(Map p509; 🕿03-9525 5555; www.stokehouse. com.au; 30 Jacka Blvd, St Kilda; mains upstairs $28-45, downstairs $10-20; ☉lunch & dinner; 🖳16, 96) Two-faced Stokehouse makes the most of its beachfront position, cleverly catering to families and drop-ins downstairs, and turning on its best in the light, bright and newly renovated room upstairs for fine diners. It's

0 — 200 m
0 — 0.1 miles

York St

Cowderoy St

Deakin St

Park St

ST KILDA WEST

Loch St

Park La

Mary St

Beaconsfield Pde

Pier Rd

Catani Gardens

Hobsons Bay

Canterbury Rd

Hockey Dr

Village Green Dr

Albert Park

Lakeside Dr

Junction Oval

1 ◉ St Kilda Junction

Fitzroy St

Princes St

10
19

West Beach Rd

11

20

Little Grey St

Dalgety St

Dalgety La

6

Burnett St

To Jewish Museum of Australia (230m)

Jackson St

8

12

9

Eildon Rd

Gurner St

Barkly St

St Kilda Pier ◉

St Kilda Foreshore ◉

23

Victoria St

Acland St

Alfred Square

27

Jacka Blvd

Lower Esplanade

The Esplanade

St Leonards Ave

Neptune St

Neptune La

Robe St

Grey St

Alfred Pl

Clyde St

Fawkner St

ST KILDA

Havelock St

Inkerman St

Blanche St

Vale St

To Local Taphouse (650m); Carlisle Wine Bar (750m)

Carlisle St

4

18

24

Luna Park ◉

O'Donnell Gardens

15

25

22

5

Belford St

Foster St

Cavell St

Shakespeare Gve

Peanut Farm Reserve

13

21

St Kilda Botanic Gardens

2

Marine Pde

Spenser St

14

26

16

17

Herbert St

Chaucer St

Blessington St

Renfrey Gardens

Barkly St

Smith St

Mittord St

Port Phillip

Wordsworth St

St Kilda Marina

ELWOOD

MELBOURNE & VICTORIA MELBOURNE

a fixture on the Melbourne dining scene and known for its seafood, service and the bay views on offer. Book for upstairs – though there can also be a wait downstairs.

Cafe di Stasio
ITALIAN $$$

(Map p509; ☑03-9525 3999; www.distasio.com.au; 31a Fitzroy St, St Kilda; mains $27-43; ☺lunch & dinner daily; ☒16, 96, 112) Capricious white-jacketed waiters, a tenebrous Bill Henson photograph and a jazz soundtrack set the mood. The Italian menu has the appropriate drama and grace.

Cicciolina
MEDITERRANEAN $$

(Map p509; www.cicciolinastkilda.com.au; 130 Acland St, St Kilda; mains $19-40; ☺lunch & dinner; ☒16, 96) This warm room of dark wood, subdued lighting and pencil sketches is a St Kilda institution. The inspired Mod-Med menu is smart and generous, and the service warm. They don't take bookings; eat early or while away your wait in the moody little back bar. Check out their new restaurant, **Ilona Staller** (282 Carlisle St, Balaclava), in nearby Balaclava.

Claypots
SEAFOOD $$

(Map p509; 213 Barkly St; mains $25-$35; ☺lunch & dinner; ☒96) A local favourite, Claypots serves up seafood in its namesake. Get in early to both get a seat and ensure the good stuff is still available, as hot items go fast.

Lentil as Anything
VEGETARIAN $

(Map p509; www.lentilasanything.com; 41 Blessington St, St Kilda; prices at customers' discretion; ☺lunch & dinner; ☒16, 96) Choosing from the always-organic, no-meat menu is easy. Deciding what to pay can be hard. This unique not-for-profit operation provides training and educational opportunities for marginalised people, as well as tasty, if not particularly notable, vegetarian food. They also have a branch at the **Abbotsford Convent** (Map p498; 1 St Heliers St, Abbotsford) and in **Footscray** (Barkly St, Footscray).

I Carusi II
PIZZA $$

(Map p509; ☑03-9593 6033; 231 Barkly St, St Kilda; pizza $14-18; ☺dinner; ☒16, 96) Beautifully located beyond the Acland St chaos in this nostalgic corner shop, I Carusi II was opened by (though no longer owned by) one of the people who started the real pizza revolution in Melbourne. I Carusi pizzas have a particularly tasty dough and follow the less-is-more tenet, with top-quality mozza, pecorino and a small range of other toppings. Bookings advised.

Banff
PIZZA $

(Map p509; www.banffstkilda.com.au; 145 Fitzroy St; mains $9; ☒16) It's not just the daily happy hour that keeps Banff's Fitzroy St–fronting chairs occupied; it's also the $9 pizzas ($5 for lunch).

Galleon Cafe
CAFE $

(Map p509; 9 Carlisle St; ☺breakfast & lunch daily; ☒16,79) Friendly folk, a decent amount of elbow room and low-key music make this a cheery place to down a coffee and muffin in busy St Kilda.

Batch
CAFE $

(www.batchespresso.com; 320 Carlisle St, Balaclava; mains $12-$16; ☺breakfast & lunch daily, dinner Fri; ☒Balaclava) Its walls are decorated with bric-a-brac donated by locals who love the food on offer (the scotch-fillet steak sandwiches are winners) and great coffee. Good luck getting a seat during the weekend-only all day brunches. Carlisle St runs east off St Kilda Rd.

Mart 130
CAFE $

(☑03-9690 8831; 107 Canterbury Rd, Middle Park; dishes $6-10; ☺breakfast & lunch; ☒96) Where the light-rail trams now run was once a fully fledged railway line with a string of Federation-style stations. Mart 130 has painted the walls and floors a smart black and white, and serves up corncakes, granola and eggs with decks overlooking the park. Weekend waits can be long. From St Kilda, you'll find Mart 130 in the Middle Park section of Canterbury Rd.

Drinking

Melbourne's bars are legendary, and from laneway hideaways to brassy corner establishments, it's easy to quickly locate a 'local' that will please the senses and drinking palate.

CENTRAL MELBOURNE

Carlton Hotel
BAR

(Map p482; www.thecarlton.com.au; 193 Bourke St; ☺4pm-late) OTT Melbourne rococo gets another workout here (think giraffe heads leering over a glittery black room) and never fails to raise a smile. Check the rooftop **Palmz** if you're looking for some Miami-flavoured vice or just a great view.

Campari House
COCKTAIL BAR

(Map p482; www.camparihouse.com.au; 25-23 Hardware Lane) It's worth coming here on a sunny day or balmy evening to sip cocktails on the rooftop. Come rainy day the luxury

TO BEER, OR NOT TO BEER

Let your beer dreams come true (and we're not talking Victoria Bitter) at Melbourne's top beer bars. All have 'awesome beer from knowledgeable staff' according to James Smith of www.craftypint.com, which keeps beer drinkers informed about the city's brewers and bars.

Local Taphouse (off Map p509; www.thelocal.com.au; 184 Carlisle St, St Kilda East) Sink a beer here during Monday night comedy or Sunday night trivia.

Beer DeLuxe (Map p482; www.beerdeluxe.com.au; Federation Sq) Don't know what to drink? Helpful staff will point you to the right tap.

Biero (Map p482; www.biero.com.au; 525 Little Lonsdale St; ⊙Mon-Sat) Sample from the arms-length beer menu or check out the 'rotating' craft beers.

Mountain Goat Brewery (www.goatbeer.com.au; 80 North St, Richmond; ⊙Wed & Fri from 5pm) Dine on pizza and test the beers in this large warehouse tucked away in industrial Richmond, see p512.

lounge (open from Thursday to Saturday) is perfectly comforting.

Madame Brussels
BAR

(Map p482; www.madamebrussels.com; Level 3, 59-63 Bourke St; ⊙noon-1am) Head here if you've had it with Melbourne moody and all that dark wood. Although named for a famous 19th-century madam, it feels as though you've fallen into a camp '60s rabbit hole, with much Astroturfery and staff dressed *à la* the country club. Don't be deterred by the very non-descript downstairs entrance.

Brother Baba Budan
CAFE

(Map p482; www.sevenseeds.com.au; 359 Little Bourke St) Cute city outpost of indie roasters St Ali. There's coffee, of course, and only the odd *ruglach* or biscuit to distract you.

1000£Bend
BAR

(Map p482; www.thousandpoundbend.com.au; 361 Little Lonsdale St; ☎) Breakfasts and lunches and cruisy folk using the free wi-fi – that's not all at this mega warehouse of entertainment. It's also the venue for art shows, plays and an annual bike fest. As we write it's being crowned with a liquor license; so expect this to be the place to see.

Riverland
BAR

(Map p482; www.riverlandbar.com; Vaults 1-9, Federation Wharf; ⊙7am-midnight) This bluestone beauty sits by the water below Princes Bridge and keeps things simple with good wine, beer on tap and bar snacks.

Section 8
BAR

(Map p482; www.section8.com.au; 27-29 Tattersalls Lane; ⊙8am-late Mon-Fri, noon-late Sat & Sun) The latest in shipping-container habitats,

come and sink a Mountain Goat with the after-work crowd, who make do with packing cases for decor.

Federal Coffee Palace
CAFE

(Map p482; GPO, Elizabeth St) Atmosphere-plus, with tables beneath the colonnades of the GPO and the fashion retailer fave. Space heaters keep you toasty when the city turns chilly.

Switchboard
CAFE

(Map p482; Manchester Unity Arcade, 220 Collins St) Beneath the Man-U mosaics, there's Nana-style wallpaper, cupcakes and a coffee machine in a cupboard. Take a tram-style seat across the footpath.

Double Happiness
BAR

(Map p482; http://doubledouble.com.au; 21 Liverpool St; ⊙5pm-late Mon-Fri, 6pm-late Sat & Sun) This stylish hole in the wall doesn't just do Chinese-themed decor, it also offers Chinese beers. Try a Tsingtao beer or a cardamom- or ginger-flavoured cocktail.

New Gold Mountain
BAR

(Map p482; www.newgoldmountain.org; Level 1, 21 Liverpool St; ⊙6pm-late) Unsignposted, New Gold Mountain's intense Chinoiserie interior comes as a shock. Two upstairs floors are filled with tiny screen-shielded corners, with decoration so delightfully relentless you feel as if you're trapped in an art-house dream sequence. You may need to phone the number on the door to get in.

Melbourne Supper Club
BAR

(Map p482; 1st fl, 161 Spring St; ⊙5pm-3am Mon-Sat) Melbourne's own Betty Ford's (the place you go when there's nowhere left to go), the Supper Club is open very late and is a favoured

after-work spot for performers and hospitality types. Leave your coat at the door and cosy into a Chesterfield. Browse the encyclopaedic wine menu and relax; the sommeliers will cater to any liquid desire. The upstairs bar **Siglo** is a great spot and is open to the elements for the cigar smokers.

1806
COCKTAIL BAR

(Map p482; www.1806.com.au; 169 Exhibition St) This cocktail bar doesn't pack up its stirrers until 3am most mornings (and until 5am on Friday and Saturday). Not only does it serve a long, long list of cocktails, it also runs sessions designed to bring the mixologist out in you ($170).

Workshop
BAR

(Map p482; www.theworkshopbar.com.au; 413 Elizabeth St; ⏰10am-late Mon-Fri, 1pm-late Sat-Sun) This industrial bar offers healthy lunches early and live music or DJs playing late. At any time there's perfect Elizabeth St gazing from the flora-filled outdoor area.

Croft Institute
BAR

(Map p482; www.thecroftinstitute.net; 21-25 Croft Alley; ⏰5pm-late Mon-Fri, 8pm-late Sat) Located in a laneway off a laneway, the lab-themed Croft is a test of drinkers' determination. Prescribe yourself a beaker of house-distilled vodka in the downstairs laboratory (some come complete with fat plastic syringes). There's a $10 cover charge on Friday and Saturday nights.

EAST MELBOURNE & RICHMOND

TOP CHOICE Der Raum
BAR

(www.derraum.com.au; 438 Church St, Richmond; ⏰5pm-late; ⓡEast Richmond, ⌂70) The name conjures up images of a dark Fritz Lang flick and there's definitely something noirish about the space and their extreme devotion to hard liquor. It's hard to miss the bottles hanging from the ceiling as evidence of past boozing. Head down Brunton Ave to Swan St; it's on the corner of Swan and Church Sts.

Mountain Goat Brewery
MICROBREWERY

(www.goatbeer.com.au; cnr North & Clark Sts, Richmond; ⏰from 5pm Wed & Fri only) This local microbrewery is set in a massive beer-producing warehouse; enjoy its range of beers while nibbling on pizza, or join a free brewery tour on Wednesday night. To find it head down Richmond's Bridge Rd, turn left at Burnley St and right at North St.

FITZROY & AROUND

De Clieu
CAFE

(Map p498; 187 Gertrude St, Collingwood; ⌂86) From coffee-mad Melbourne folk comes De Clieu, a funky little cafe with polished concrete floors, a short menu and a tall sense of humour.

Proud Mary
CAFE

(Map p498; 172 Oxford St, Collingwood; ⏰7.30am-4pm Mon-Fri, 8.30am-4pm Sat & Sun; ⌂86) Known for its silky-smooth coffee, this corner-situated industrial cafe also has a decent breakfast and lunch menu (think green eggs on toast).

Napier Hotel
PUB

(Map p498; www.thenapierhotel.com; 210 Napier St, Fitzroy; ⏰3-11pm Mon-Thu, 1pm-1am Fri & Sat, 1-11pm Sun; ⌂112, 86) The Napier has stood on this corner for over a century and many pots have been pulled as the face of the neighbourhood changed. It's still a great spot for pub grub.

Little Creatures Dining Hall
BEER HALL

(Map p498; www.littlecreatures.com.au; 222 Brunswick St, Fitzroy; 🛜; ⌂112) With free wi-fi, community bikes and a daytime kid-friendly groove, this vast drinking hall is the perfect place to spend up big on pizzas and enjoy local wine and beer.

Naked for Satan
BAR

(Map p498; www.nakedforsatan.com.au; 285 Brunswick St; ⏰ noon-late; ⌂112) Vibrant, loud and reviving an apparent Brunswick St legend (a man nicknamed Satan who would get down and dirty, naked because of the heat, in an illegal vodka distillery under the shop), this place packs a punch both with its popular *pintxos* (bite-sized sandwiches; $2) and cleverly named beverages. Winner of *The Age's 2011 Cheap Eats* guide 'bar of the year'.

Polly
COCKTAIL BAR

(Map p498; ☎03-9417 0880; 401 Brunswick St, Fitzroy; ⏰5pm-1am Sun-Wed, 5pm-late Thu, 5pm-3am Fri-Sat) Polly melds a luxe sensibility and slick service with lots of ornate carved wood and plush velvet. Ease yourself into a lounge and peruse the extensive drinks list – you're not going anywhere in a hurry.

CARLTON & AROUND

Gerald's Bar
WINE BAR

(off Map p517; 386 Rathdowne St, Carlton North; ⏰5-11pm Mon-Sat; ⌂1, 8, ⌂253) Wine by the glass is democratically selected at Gerald's and they spin some fine vintage vinyl from behind the

curved wooden bar. The bar won *Australian Gourmet Traveller's* bar of the year in 2010. If you get hungry, there are delightful morsels (of the likes of terrine and pork belly) to sink your teeth into. From Carlton, continue up Rathdowne St into Carlton North.

ST KILDA & AROUND

Carlisle Wine Bar
WINE BAR

(off Map p509; 137 Carlisle St, Balaclava; ⊗brunch Sat & Sun, dinner daily; ☐Balaclava, ☐3, 16) Locals love this often rowdy, wine-worshipping former butcher's shop. The staff will treat you like a regular and find you a glass of something special, or effortlessly throw together a cocktail amid the weekend rush. Carlisle St runs east off St Kilda Rd.

George Public Bar
BAR

(Map p509; www.georgepublicbar.com.au; Basement, 127 Fitzroy St, St Kilda; ☐96, 16) Behind the crumbling paint and Edwardian arched windows of the George Hotel, there's the Melbourne Wine Room and a large front bar that keeps the after-work crowd happy. In the bowels of the building is the George Public Bar, often referred to as the Snakepit.

Mink
BAR

(Map p509; www.minkbar.com.au; 2b Acland St, St Kilda; ⊗6pm-late Thu-Sun; ☐96, 16, 112) In this dimly lit Trans-Siberian–styled bar there's no shortage of vodka and glam good times. Get there early to nab the much sought-after private 'sleeper' and start working your way through the extensive list.

Veludo
BAR

(Map p509; www.veludo.com.au; 175 Acland St, St Kilda; ☐96) It's big, it's brassy and it's got a balcony. Over two levels, Veludo's relatively late closing means that most St Kilda-ites have ducked in here after everything else has closed. Upstairs has live music most nights.

Vineyard
BAR

(Map p509; www.thevineyard.com.au; 71a Acland St, St Kilda; ☐96, 16) The perfect corner position and a courtyard barbie attract crowds of backpackers and scantily clad young locals who enjoy themselves so much as to drown out the neighbouring scenic railway.

☆ Entertainment

Nightclubs

alumbra
CLUB

(www.alumbra.com.au; Shed 9, Central Pier, 161 Harbour Esplanade, Docklands; ⊗4pm-late Fri-Sun) Great music and a stunning location will impress – even if the Bali-meets-Morocco follies of the decorator don't.

Revolver Upstairs
CLUB

(Map p507; www.revolverupstairs.com.au; 229 Chapel St, Prahran; ⊗noon-4am Mon-Thu, 24hr Fri-Sun; ☐Prahran, ☐6) Rowdy Revolver can feel like an enormous version of your own lounge room, but with 54 hours of nonstop music come the weekend, you're probably glad it's not.

Brown Alley
CLUB

(Map p482; www.brownalley.com; cnr King & Lonsdale Sts; ⊗11.30am-late Mon-Fri, 6pm-late Sat & Sun) This historical pub hides away a fully fledged nightclub with a 24-hour licence. It's enormous, with distinct rooms that can fit up to 1000 people.

Cinemas

Cinema multiplexes are spread throughout Melbourne city, and there are quite a few treasured independent cinemas in both the CBD and surrounding suburbs. Grab a choc-top (icecream dipped in chocolate) and check out the following.

Astor
CINEMA

(Map p507; www.astor-theatre.com; cnr Chapel St & Dandenong Rd, St Kilda; ☐Windsor; ☐64) This place holds not-to-be-missed art deco nostalgia, with double features every night of old and recent classics.

Cinema Nova
CINEMA

(Map p517; www.cinemanova.com.au; 380 Lygon St, Carlton; ☐1, 8) Nova has great current film releases. Tickets are a measly $6 before 4pm on Monday.

Kino Cinemas
CINEMA

(Map p482; www.palacecinemas.com.au; Collins Pl, 45 Collins St) This licensed cinema specialises in quality art-house releases. It's close to great bars, too, for after-flick drinks.

Imax
CINEMA

(Map p517; www.imaxmelbourne.com.au; Melbourne Museum, Carlton Gardens; ☐86, 96) Within the same complex as the Melbourne Museum, this theatre screens films in super-wide 70mm format.

Palace Como
CINEMA

(Map p507; www.palacecinemas.com.au; cnr Toorak Rd & Chapel St, South Yarra; ☐South Yarra; ☐8) Glamorous cinema that hosts film festivals and has fab Fridays (half-price cocktails and tapas).

Outdoor cinemas are very popular in the summer; check the websites for seasonal opening dates and program details. Movies are often old-time faves, but new releases also get a showing. Tickets range from $15 to $20 and can sell out quickly.

Moonlight Cinema   OUTDOOR CINEMA
(www.moonlight.com.au; Gate D, Royal Botanic Gardens, Birdwood Ave, South Yarra; 🚌8) Bring along a rug, pillow and moonlight supper, or buy food and drinks there, and set up an outdoor living room in the middle of the gardens.

Rooftop Cinema   OUTDOOR CINEMA
(Map p482; www.rooftopcinema.com.au; Level 6, Curtin House, 252 Swanston St, Melbourne) Here we have amazing views, a beatbox burger stall to keep you fed and a bar to keep you watered.

St Kilda Open Air Cinema   OUTDOOR CINEMA
(Map p509; www.stkildaopenair.com.au; St Kilda Sea Baths, 10-18 Jacka Blvd, St Kilda; 🚌79, 96) There's often live pre-movie music and, of course, salty sea air to breathe in.

Theatre

There is no distinct theatre district in Melbourne: individual companies and theatres are spread across town. Try **Half Tix Melbourne** (Map p482; www.halftixmelbourne.com; Melbourne Town Hall; ⊙10am-2pm Mon, 11am-6pm Tue-Fri, 10am-4pm Sat) for cheap tickets to the theatre. You need to front up at the Half Tix office in person on the day (or, for Sunday performances, on Saturday) with cash.

Malthouse Theatre   THEATRE
(☎03-9685 5111; www.malthousetheatre.com. au; 113 Sturt St, South Melbourne; 🚌1) The Malthouse Theatre Company often produces the most exciting theatre in Melbourne. From Flinders Street Station walk across Princes Bridge and along St Kilda Rd. Turn right at Grant St then left to Sturt St.

Melbourne Theatre Company   THEATRE
(MTC; ☎03-8688 0800; www.mtc.com.au; cnr Southbank Blvd & Sturt St, Southbank) Melbourne's major theatrical company stages around 15 productions annually, ranging from contemporary and modern (including many new Australian works) to Shakespeare and other classics.

Live Music

Northcote Social Club   LIVE MUSIC
(☎03-9489 3917; www.northcotesocialclub.com; 301 High St, Northcote; 🚌86) This is one of

Melbourne's best live-music venues, with a stage that's seen plenty of international folk just one album out from star status. Their home-grown line-up is also notable. If you're just after a drink, the front bar buzzes every night of the week, or there's a large deck out the back for lazy afternoons. A perfect, and well-loved, local. Head north along Hoddle St to reach High St; St Georges Rd runs parallel.

Corner Hotel   LIVE MUSIC
(☎03-9427 9198; www.cornerhotel.com; 57 Swan St, Richmond; ⊙closed Mon; 🚆Richmond, 🚌70) The band room here is one of Melbourne's most popular midsized venues and has seen plenty of loud and live action over the years. If your ears need a break, there's a friendly front bar. The rooftop has stunning city views, but gets superpacked, and often with a different crowd from the music fans below. Its Wednesday night trivia has a cult following. Swan St runs off Brunton Ave.

Bennetts Lane   LIVE MUSIC
(Map p482; www.bennettslane.com; 25 Bennetts Lane, Melbourne; tickets from $15; ⊙8.30pm-late) Bennetts Lane has long been the boiler room of Melbourne jazz. It attracts the cream of local and international talent and an audience that knows when it's time to applaud a solo. Beyond the cosy front bar, there's another space reserved for big gigs.

Ding Dong Lounge   LIVE MUSIC
(Map p482; www.dingdonglounge.com.au; 18 Market Lane, Melbourne; ⊙7pm-late Wed-Sat) Ding Dong walks the rock-and-roll walk and is a great place to see a smaller touring act or catch local bands.

Esplanade Hotel   LIVE MUSIC
(Map p509; http://espy.com.au; 11 The Esplanade, St Kilda; ⊙noon-late Mon-Fri, 8am-late Sat & Sun; 🚌96, 16) Rock-pigs rejoice. The Espy remains gloriously shabby and welcoming to all. Bands play most nights and there's a spruced-up kitchen out the back. And for the price of a pot you get front row seats for the pink-stained St Kilda sunset.

Toff in Town   LIVE MUSIC
(Map p482; (☎03-9639 8770; www.thetoffintown. com; Level 2, Curtin House, 252 Swanston St, Melbourne; ⊙5pm-late Sun-Thu, noon-late Fri) An atmospheric venue well suited to cabaret, but also works for intimate gigs by rock gods, avant-folksters or dance-hall queens. Head

When the rock gods (or more commonly pop, R&B and hip-hop stars) roll into town and are too big for Melbourne's beloved medium-sized venues, such as the Corner Hotel (p514) or the Tote (below), they are likely to play at one of the following venues:

» **Festival Hall** (off Map p482; www.festivalhall.com.au; 300 Dudley St, West Melbourne; 🚊24, 30, 34, 70) This old boxing stadium is a fave for live-music acts.

» **Palace Theatre** (Map p482; www.palace.com.au; 20-30 Bourke St, Melbourne) Features acts ranging from reggae masters to indie darlings.

» **Forum Theatre** (Map p482; 🎫tickets 136 100; www.marrinertheatres.com.au, tickets www.ticketmaster.com.au; 150-152 Flinders St) One of the city's most atmospheric live-music venues, it does double duty as a cinema during the Melbourne Film Festival. The Arabic-inspired exterior houses an equally interesting interior, with the southern sky rendered on the domed ceiling.

» **Hamer Hall** (Melbourne Concert Hall; Map p482; www.theartscentre.net.au; Victorian Arts Centre, 100 St Kilda Rd) The concert hall is undergoing a two-year redevelopment and should be back in business in 2012.

» **Palais Theatre** (Map p509; 🎫9525 3240, tickets 136 100; www.palaistheatre.net.au, tickets www.ticketmaster.com.au; Lower Esplanade, St Kilda) Standing gracefully next to Luna Park, the Palais is a St Kilda icon. Not only is it a beautiful old space, but it also stages some pretty special performances.

» **Rod Laver Arena** (www.mopt.com.au; Batman Ave) A giant, versatile space used for headline concerts (from the Eagles to Chemical Brothers) and the Australian Open tennis, with a huge sunroof. Not the most atmospheric of venues, but then it's all about the spectacle. Ditto for the nearby **Hisense Arena** (Melbourne Park).

» **Sidney Myer Music Bowl** (www.theartscentre.net.au; Kings Domain) This beautiful amphitheatre in the park is used for a variety of outdoor events, from the New Year's Day rave **Summerdayze** to the Melbourne Symphony Orchestra.

further up the stairs for Cookie and further yet to the view-filled open-air Rooftop Bar.

Tote   LIVE MUSIC
(off Map p498; www.thetotehotel.com; cnr Johnston & Wellington Sts, Fitzroy; ☺ 4pm-late Thu-Sun; 🚊86) The Tote's closure in 2010 brought Melbourne to a stop. People protested on the CBD streets against the liquor-licensing laws that were blamed for the closure, and there were howls of displeasure on the radio waves. The punters won; there were changes to Melbourne's liquor-licensing laws, and, armed with new 'white knight' owners, the Tote reopened to continue its tradition of live bands playing dirty rock. From Fitzroy or Collingwood, head down Johnston St.

Cherry   LIVE MUSIC
(Map p482; ACDC Lane, Melbourne; ☺5pm-late Tue-Fri, 9pm-late Sat) This rock 'n' roll refuge is still going strong. There's often a queue, but once inside a relaxed, slightly anarchic spirit prevails. Music is only sometimes live, but never electronic. It is off Flinders Lane.

Dance

Australian Ballet   BALLET
(🎫1300 369 741, 9669 2700; www.australianballet. com.au; 2 Kavanagh St, Southbank) Based in Melbourne and now more than 40 years old, the Australian Ballet performs traditional and new works at the Victorian Arts Centre.

Chunky Move   DANCE
(www.chunkymove.com; 111 Sturt St, Southbank) Melbourne-based Chunky Move perform 'genre-defying' dance around the world and, when at home, at the CUB Malthouse. From Flinders Street Station walk across Princes Bridge and along St Kilda Rd. Turn right at Grant St then left to Sturt St.

 **Shopping**

CENTRAL MELBOURNE

Captains of Industry   CLOTHING
(Map p482; www.captainsofindustry.com.au; Level 1, 2 Somerset Pl) Where can you get a haircut, a bespoke suit and pair of shoes made in the one place? Here. The hard-working folk at Captains also offer homey breakfasts and thoughtful lunches. To work!

» **Rose Street Artists' Market** (Map p498; www.rosestmarket.com.au; 60 Rose St, Fitzroy; ⊙11am-5pm Sat &Sun; ⓐ112) One of Melbourne's best and most popular art-and-craft markets, just a short stroll from Brunswick St.

» **Camberwell Sunday Market** (www.sundaymarket.com.au; Station St, behind cnr of Burke & Riversdale Rds, Camberwell; gold coin donation; ⊙7am-12.30pm Sundays; ⓡCamberwell, ⓐ70,72,75) This is where Melburnians come to offload their unwanted items and antique hunters come to find them. Find it by following Swan St (through Richmond) to its intersection with Camberwell Rd.

» **Esplanade Market** (Map p509; www.esplanademarket.com; Upper Esplanade, btwn Cavell & Fitzroy Sts, St Kilda; ⊙10am-5pm Sun; ⓐ96) Fancy shopping with a seaside backdrop? A kilometre of trestle tables joined end to end carry individually crafted products from toys to organic soaps to large metal sculptures of fishy creatures.

» **Queen Victoria Market** (Queen Vic Market; Map p482; www.qvm.com.au; 513 Elizabeth St, Melbourne; ⊙6am-2pm Tue & Thu, 6am-5pm Fri, 6am-3pm Sat, 9am-4pm Sun) Don't miss this 130-year old market with its meat hall, deli and expansive fruit and vegie sections. On Wednesdays during summer it also plays host to a lively and musical night market (from 5.30pm to 10pm).

Counter
CRAFT, DESIGN

(Map p482; www.craftvic.org.au; 31 Flinders Lane) The retail arm of Craft Victoria, Counter showcases the handmade. Its range of jewellery, textiles, accessories, glass and ceramics bridges the art/craft divide and makes for some wonderful mementos of Melbourne.

Alice Euphemia
FASHION, JEWELLERY

(Map p482; Shop 6, Cathedral Arcade, 37 Swanston St) Art-school cheek abounds in the labels sold here and jewellery similarly sways between the shocking and exquisitely pretty.

Aesop
BEAUTY

City Centre QV (Map p482; QV, 35 Albert Coates Lane); City Centre (Map p482; 268 Flinders Lane); Fitzroy (Map p498; 242 Gertrude St, Fitzroy) Prahran (Map p507; 143 Greville St, Prahran) This home-grown skincare company specialises in products made from simple ingredients in simple packaging. The range is wide and based on botanical extracts.

FITZROY & AROUND

TOP CHOICE **Third Drawer Down**
DESIGN

(Map p498; www.thirddrawerdown.com; 93 George St, Fitzroy; ⓐ86) This seller-of-great-things makes life beautifully unusual by stocking everything from sesame-seed grinders to beer o'clock beach towels and 'come in, we're closed' signs.

Crumpler
ACCESSORIES

(Map p498; www.crumpler.com.au; cnr Gertrude & Smith Sts, Fitzroy; ⓐ86) Crumpler's bike-courier bags started it all. Its durable, practical designs can now be found around the world, and it makes bags for cameras, laptops and iPods as well as its original messenger style.

Little Salon
CRAFT, FASHION

(Map p498; www.littlesalon.com.au; 71 Gertrude St, Fitzroy; ⓐ86) Part art gallery and part retail outlet, this little store is hipster heaven. Wearable art pieces, including bags woven from seat belts, knitted corsages and button bracelets, share space here with decorative items for your wall or shelf. Also a **branch** (Map p482; 1/353 Little Collins St) in Melbourne.

SpaceCraft
HOMEWARES, FASHION

(Map p498; www.spacecraftaustralia.com; 255 Gertrude St, Fitzroy) An excellent place to find a made-in-Melbourne souvenir that won't end up at the back of the cupboard. Textile artist Stewart Russell's botanical and architectural designs adorn everything from stools to socks to single-bed doonas. Also a **branch** (Map p507; 572 Malvern Rd, Prahran East) in Prahran East.

Polyester Records
MUSIC

(Map p498; 387 Brunswick St, Fitzroy ⓐ112) This great record store has been selling Melburnians independent music from around the world for decades, and also sells tickets for gigs. There's a CBD **branch** (Map p482; 288 Flinders Lane, Melbourne).

CARLTON & AROUND

Readings
BOOKS

(Map p517; 309 Lygon St, Carlton; www.readings.com.au; ⓐ16) A potter around this defiantly

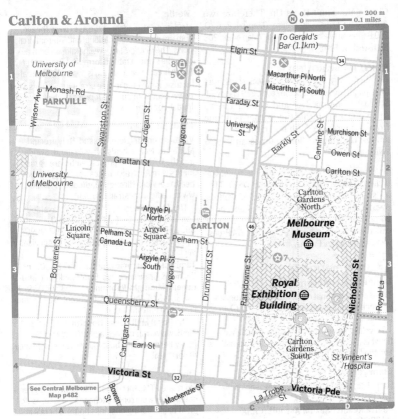

prospering indie bookshop can occupy an entire afternoon if you're so inclined. There's a dangerously loaded (and good-value) specials table, switched-on staff and everyone from Lacan to *Charlie & Lola* on the shelves.

SOUTH YARRA, PRAHRAN & WINDSOR

Chapel Street Bazaar COLLECTABLES
(Map p507; 217-223 Chapel St, Prahran; ☒Prahran, ☒78,79) Calling this a 'permanent undercover collection of market stalls' won't give you any clue to what's tucked away here. This old arcade is a retro-obsessive riot. It doesn't matter if Italian art glass or Noddy egg cups are your thing, you'll find it here.

Fat FASHION, ACCESSORIES
(Map p507; www.fat4.com; 272 Chapel St, Prahran; ☒Prahran, ☒78, 79) The Fat girls' empire has changed the way Melbourne dresses, catapulting a fresh generation of designers into the city's consciousness, including locals

Carlton & Around

Claude Maus and Dress Up. There are two other **branches** City Centre (Map p482; GPO, 250 Bourke St, Melbourne); Fitzroy (Map p498; 209 Brunswick St, Fitzroy).

ST KILDA & AROUND

Dot & Herbey FASHION, ACCESSORIES
(Map p509; www.dotandherbey.com; 229 Barkly St, St Kilda) Grandma Dot and Grandpa Herb smile down upon this tiny corner boutique from a mural-sized photo, right at home among the vintage floral fabrics and retro style.

Brotherhood of St Laurence FASHION
(Map p509; 82a Acland St, St Kilda; [img]96) This op shop features the most retro of welfare organisation Brotherhood of St Laurence's 26-odd op shops. There's a similar branch called **Hunter Gatherer** (Map p498; 274 Brunswick St, Fitzroy) in Fitzroy.

ℹ️ Information

Dangers & Annoyances

There are occasional reports of alcohol-fuelled violence in some parts of Melbourne's CBD, in particular King St.

Travelling on public transport without a valid ticket is taken very seriously by ticket inspectors and the fines are hefty ($176).

Emergency

For police, ambulance or fire emergencies dial ☑000.
Centre Against Sexual Assault (CASA; ☑1800 806 292)
Poisons Information Centre (☑13 11 26)
Translating & Interpreting Service (☑13 14 50) Available 24 hours.

Internet Access

Wi-fi is available free at central CBD spots including Federation Square. Hotels often charge between $3 to $20 per hour for wi-fi access. If you don't have a laptop or smart phone, there are plenty of internet cafes around Melbourne with terminals (from $2 per hour).

Internet Resources

Lonely Planet's website (www.lonelyplanet.com) has useful links. Other online resources:
That's Melbourne (www.thatsmelbourne.com.au) Downloadable maps, info and podcasts from the City of Melbourne.
Three Thousand (www.threethousand.com.au) A weekly round-up of (groovy) local goings on.
Visit Victoria (www.visitvictoria.com.au) Highlights events in Melbourne and Victoria.

Media

Melbourne's broadsheet the *Age* (www.theage.com.au) covers local, national and international news. The *Herald-Sun* (www.heraldsun.com.au) does the same in tabloid form. The *Broadsheet* (www.broadsheet.com.au) is available from cafes.

Music is covered in free street magazines *Beat* (www.beat.com.au) and *Inpress* (www.faster louder.com.au).

Medical Services

Visitors from Belgium, Finland, Italy, Ireland, Malta, the Netherlands, New Zealand, Sweden and the UK have reciprocal healthcare agreements with Australia and can access cheaper health services through **Medicare** (☑13 20 11; www.medicareaustralia.gov.au).

The **Travel Doctor** (TVMC; www.traveldoctor.com.au) City Centre (☑03-9935 8100; Level 2, 393 Little Bourke St); Southgate (☑03-9690 1433; 3 Southgate Ave, Southgate) specialises in vaccinations.

Tambassis Pharmacy (☑03-9387 8830; cnr Sydney & Brunswick Rds, Brunswick) and **Mulqueeny Midnight Pharmacy** (☑03-9510 3977; cnr High St & Williams Rd, Prahran) are pharmacies open until midnight.

The **Royal Melbourne Hospital** (☑03-9342 7666; www.rmh.mh.org.au; 300 Grattan St, Parkville) is a public hospital with an emergency department.

Money

There are ATMs throughout Melbourne. Bigger hotels offer a currency exchange service, as do most banks during business hours. There's a bunch of exchange offices on Swanston St.

Post

Melbourne GPO (Map p482; cnr Little Bourke & Elizabeth Sts; ⊙8.30am-5.30pm Mon-Fri, 9am-5pm Sat)

Tourist Information

Melbourne Visitor Centre (MVC; Map p482; ☑03-9658 9658; Federation Sq; ⊙9am-6pm daily)

ℹ️ Getting There & Away

Air

Two airports serve Melbourne: Avalon and Tullamarine, though at present only domestic airlines **Tiger** (☑03-9335 3033; www.tiger-airways.com) and **Jetstar** (☑13 15 38; www.jetstar.com) operate from Avalon. These two airlines also fly from and to Tullamarine Airport, in addition to the domestic and international flights offered by **Qantas** (☑13 13 13; www.qantas.com) and **Virgin Australia** (☑13 67 89; www.virginaustralia.com). **Regional Express** (☑13 17 13; www.regionalexpress.com.au) has services from Melbourne to Portland.

HOOK TURNS

Striking fear into all non-locals is Melbourne's 'hook turn' (though it's easy once you get the hang of it). Basically, many of the city's intersections require you to make a right-hand turn from the left lane so you don't block oncoming trams. When you see a 'Right Turn from Left Only' sign, often hanging from tram lines, get in the left lane and wait with your indicator on; when the light turns green in the street you want to turn into, hook right and complete your turn.

Tullamarine Airport has a **left-luggage facility** (Terminal 2, International Arrivals; $15 per 24 hr; ⊙5.30am-12.30am).

Boat

Spirit of Tasmania (☑1800 634 906; www. spiritoftasmania.com.au) crosses Bass Strait from Melbourne to Devonport, Tasmania, at least nightly; there are also day sailings during peak season. It takes 11 hours and departs from Station Pier, Port Melbourne (Map p476).

Bus, Car & Motorcycle

Southern Cross Station (Map p482; www. southerncrossstation.net.au) This is the main terminal for interstate bus services.

Avalon Airport Transfers (www.sitacoaches. com.au) To/from Avalon Airport for $20.

Firefly (www.fireflyexpress.com.au) From/to Adelaide & Sydney.

Greyhound (www.greyhound.com.au) Australia-wide.

V/Line (www.vline.com.au) Around Victoria.

There is a left luggage facility at Southern Cross Station ($12 per 24 hours).

Train

Interstate trains arrive and depart from **Southern Cross Station** (Map p482; www.southern crossstation.net.au).

ⓘ Getting Around

To/from the Airport

TULLAMARINE AIRPORT

There are no trains or trams to Tullamarine airport. Taxis charge from $40 for the trip to Melbourne's CBD, or you can catch **SkyBus** (☑03-9335 3066; www.skybus.com.au; adult/child one-way $16/6), a 20-minute express bus service to/from Southern Cross Station.

Part of the main route into Melbourne from Tullamarine Airport is a toll road run by **City-Link** (☑13 26 29; www.citylink.com.au). You'll need to buy a Tulla Pass ($4.65). If you have more time and less money, take the exit ramp at Bell St then head up Nicholson St to the CBD.

AVALON AIRPORT

Avalon Airport Transfers (www.sitacoaches. com.au; one-way $20; 50 min) meets all flights flying into and out of Avalon. It departs from Southern Cross Station; check website for times. No pre-booking required.

Bike

Melbourne Bike Share (www.melbournebike-share.com.au; ☑1300 711 590) began in 2010 and has had a slow start, mainly blamed on Victoria's compulsory helmet laws. Subsidised safety helmets are now available at 7Eleven stores around the CBD ($5 with a $3 refund on return). Each first half-hour of hire is free. Daily ($2.50) and weekly ($8) subscriptions require a credit card and $300 security deposit.

Car & Motorcycle

CAR HIRE

Avis (☑13 63 33; www.avis.com.au)

Budget (☑1300 362 848; www.budget.com.au)

Europcar (☑1300 131 390; www.europcar. com.au)

Hertz (☑13 30 39; www.hertz.com.au)

Rent a Bomb (☑03-9696 7555; www.renta-bomb.com.au)

Thrifty (☑1300 367 227; www.thrifty.com.au)

CAR SHARING

Two car-sharing companies operate in Melbourne: **Go Get** (www.goget.com.au; ☑1300 769 389) and **Flexi Car** (www.flexicar.com.au; ☑1300 363 780). You rent the cars by the hour or the day, and prices includes petrol. Both have joining fees (around $30) and Go Get has a fully refundable security deposit of $500 while Flexi Car has an annual insurance fee of $70. The cars are parked in and around the CBD in designated 'car share' car parks. Car sharing costs around $10 per hour depending on the plan you choose.

PARKING

'Grey Ghosts' (parking inspectors) are particularly vigilant in the CBD; most of the street parking is metered and if you overstay your metered time you'll probably be fined (between $60 and $119). Also keep an eye out for

TRAMMING IT

These are some useful tram route numbers for travelling in the city and surrounding suburbs.

Carlton 1, 96

Collingwood 86

Docklands 30, 48, 86

Fitzroy 86, 96, 112

North Carlton 1, 96

North Melbourne 55, 68

Northcote 86

Parkville, Brunswick 19

Prahran 72 then 78, 79 along Chapel St

Richmond 45, 70, 75, 109

South Melbourne 1, 109, 112 or light rail no 96

South Yarra 72

St Kilda 16, 67, 112 or light rail no 96

Toorak 8

Clearway zones. There are plenty of parking garages in the city; rates vary.

Motorcyclists are allowed to park on the footpath.

TOLL ROADS

Motorcycles travel free on CityLink; car drivers will need to purchase a pass if they are planning on using one of the two toll roads (CityLink or EastLink, which runs from Ringwood to Frankston).

Public Transport

Flinders Street Station is the main metro train station connecting the city and suburbs. The City Loop runs under the city, linking the four corners of town.

An extensive network of tram lines covers every corner of the city, running north–south and east–west along most major roads. Trams run roughly every 10 minutes Monday to Friday, every 10 to 15 minutes on Saturday, and every 20 minutes on Sunday. Check **Metlink** (www.metlinkmelbourne.com.au) for more information. Also worth considering is the free City Circle tram, which loops around town.

TICKETING

The **myki** (www.myki.com.au) transport system covers Melbourne's buses, trams and trains and uses a 'touch on, touch off' system. myki cards ($10 full fare) are available online; from Flinders Street Station; the **MetShop** (☑13 16 38; Melbourne Town Hall, cnr Swanston & Little Collins Sts); and the myki discovery centre at Southern Cross Station).

You need to top up your myki card with cash at machines located at most stations (or online, though it can take 24 hours to process). If you're only in town for a few days, short-term tickets can be bought from machines on buses, trains and trams, though fares are slightly more expensive than using a myki.

Costs for Zone 1 tickets, which is all that most travellers will need:

Myki Money two hour $2.94, daily $5.88

Short-term two hour $3.70, daily $6.80

Taxi

Melbourne's taxis are metered and require an estimated prepaid fare when hailed between 10pm and 5am. You may need to pay more or get a refund depending on the final fare. Toll charges are added to fares.

QUEENSCLIFF & THE BELLARINE PENINSULA

New wineries flank the hillsides of the Bellarine Peninsula, but visitors have been coming here for its seaside village ambience for centuries. The Bellarine almost forms a connection with the Mornington Peninsula – there's only a 3.5km-wide stretch of water between Point Nepean on the Mornington Peninsula and the Bellarine's Point Lonsdale. Besides watching ships being navigated through that stretch there's gourmet food to try, beaches to relax on (or dive and snorkel off) and affluent villages to meander around.

Accommodation prices soar from Christmas to the end of January, when even caravan parks have minimum-stay requirements. Weekends, even in the depths of winter, also see prices rise.

ⓘ Getting There & Away

BUS

McHarry's Buslines (☑03-5223 2111; www.mcharrys.com.au) connects Geelong with most peninsula towns. A two-hour adult ticket costs $3.20 ($3 with myki), taking you to Barwon Heads (30 minutes), Ocean Grove (45 minutes), Portarlington (45 minutes), Queenscliff (one hour) and Point Lonsdale (55 minutes). Full-day adult tickets cost $6.40 ($6 with myki).

CAR

From Melbourne the Bellarine Peninsula is easily accessible via the Princess Fwy (M1) to Geelong. Rather than taking the Geelong bypass, head through Geelong to the Bellarine Hwy (route 91).

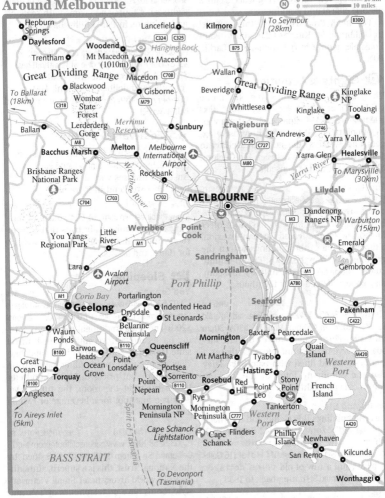

FERRY

Queenscliff-Sorrento Car & Passenger Ferries
(☏ 03-5258 3244; www.searoad.com.au; one-way foot passenger adult/child $10/8, 2 adults & car standard/peak $63/69; ☉ hourly 7am-6pm) runs between Queenscliff and Sorrento.

Queenscliff

POP 3300

Historic Queenscliff is a lovely spot, popular with day-tripping and overnighting Melburnians who come for fine food and wine, boutique shopping and leisurely walks along the beach. The views across the Port Phillip Heads and Bass Strait are glorious, and a new observation tower by the ferry terminal shows the town and surrounds off beautifully.

Queenscliff was established for the pilots who, to this day, steer all ships through the treacherous Port Phillip Heads. Known as 'the Rip', this is one of the most dangerous seaways in the world. In the 1850s Queenscliff was a favoured settlement for diggers who'd struck it rich on the goldfields, and wealthy Melburnians and the Western District's squattocracy flocked to the town. Extravagant hotels and guesthouses from the

era still operate today, giving Queenscliff a historic charm and grandness.

The main drag, Hesse St, runs parallel to Gellibrand St. King St takes you to Point Lonsdale, and the ferry terminal is on Larkin Pde.

◉ Sights & Activities

The visitors centre runs the 45-minute guided **Queenscliff Heritage Walk** (incl afternoon tea $12) at 2pm each Saturday or by appointment. Popular with cyclists, joggers and walkers, the adjacent **Bellarine Rail Trail** runs 34km between the Geelong Showgrounds and Queenscliff.

Fort Queenscliff   HISTORIC SITE
(☑03-5258 1488; cnr Gellibrand & King Sts; adult/child/family $10/5/25; ⊙tours 1pm & 3pm Sat & Sun) This fort was built in 1882 to protect Melbourne from a feared Russian invasion, although some of the buildings within the grounds date from the 1860s. The 30-minute guided tours take in the military museum, magazine, cells and Black Lighthouse.

Queenscliff Maritime Museum   MUSEUM
(☑03-5258 3440; 1 Weeroona Pde; adult/child $5/3; ⊙10.30am-4.30pm Mon-Fri, 1.30-4.30pm Sat & Sun) This is the home of the last lifeboat to serve the Rip, and out back there's a quaint boatshed lined with paintings. They also run 30-minute tours of the working Point Lonsdale Lighthouse.

Gellibrand Street   STREET
Historic buildings line Gellibrand St. Check out the old **Ozone Hotel** (42 Gellibrand St), which is now apartments, **Lathamstowe** (44 Gellibrand St), **Queenscliff Hotel** (16 Gellibrand St), and a row of old **pilots' cottages** (66 & 68 Gellibrand St) dating back to 1853.

FREE **Observation Tower**   LANDMARK
(Wharf Street) Check out the 360-degree views from this hard-to-miss and aptly named tower.

Bellarine Peninsula Railway   TRAIN
(☑03-5258 2069; www.bpr.org.au; Queenscliff train station; return adult/child/family $20/12/50; ⊙trips 11.15am, 1.40pm & 2.45pm Sun year-round, more often in summer and school holidays) Run by a group of cheerful volunteer steam-train tragics, with beautiful trains plying the 1¾-hour return journey to Drysdale.

Sea-All Dolphin Swims   SWIMMING
(☑03-5258 3889; www.dolphinswims.com.au; Larkin Pde; sightseeing adult/child $70/60, 3½hr snorkel $130/115; ⊙8am & 1pm Sep-May) Offers sightseeing tours and swims with seals and dolphins in Port Phillip Bay.

Queenscliff Dive Centre   DIVING
(☑03-5258 1188; www.divequeenscliff.com.au; 37 Learmonth St; per dive with/without gear $125/59) Gets certified divers out to see recently (and deliberately) sunk HMAS *Canberra* ($139/74 with/without gear) and other wrecks.

★ Festivals & Events

Queenscliff Music Festival   MUSIC FESTIVAL
(☑03-5258 4816; www.qmf.net.au) Features Australian musos with a folksy, bluesy bent. Last weekend in November.

Blues Train   MUSIC FESTIVAL
(www.thebluestrain.com.au) Get your foot tapping with irregular train trips that feature rootsy music and meals; check the website for dates and artists.

🛏 Sleeping

Vue Grand   HOTEL $$$
(☑03-5258 1544; www.vuegrand.com.au; 46 Hesse Street; turret incl breakfast from $400, traditional $200) The Vue's traditional rooms are nothing on its modern, recently opened, turret suite (boasting 360-degree views) and bayview rooms (with freestanding bath-tubs in the lounge), but prices differ by hundreds. If you can't get the room, the turret-level deck is a fine spot for a beverage or two on a sunny day.

Queenscliff Hotel   BOUTIQUE HOTEL $$
(☑03-5258 1066; www.queenscliffhotel.com.au; 16 Gellibrand St; d from $149; ❀@) Classified by the National Trust, this is a superb, authentically old-world luxury hotel. Small Victorian-style rooms have no telephones or TVs, and bathrooms are shared. You can relax in the comfortable guest lounges or dine and drink at the wonderful restaurant and bar.

Athelstane House   BOUTIQUE HOTEL $$
(☑03-5258 1024; www.athelstane.com.au; 4 Hobson St; from $160) Changing from a food focus to an accommodation focus, Athelstane House has comfortable rooms in a beautifully kept historical building. Its restaurant prices are not bank-breaking.

Queenscliff Inn   HOTEL/HOSTEL $
(☑03-5258 4600; www.queenscliffinn.com; 59 Hesse St; inn without bathroom incl breakfast d/f $100/200, hostel dm/s/d $30/70/84; ❀☞) This

LOAM

Don't be surprised if you're handed a home-grown beetroot or a sprig of local salt bush to smell – award-winning restaurant **Loam** (✆03-5251 1105; 650 Andersons Rd, Drysdale; ⊙lunch Thu-Sun, dinner Fri & Sat) is all about stripping food back. Aaron and Astrid Turner's dream restaurant is a stunning success story hidden in the Bellarine hinterland – book months in advance.

Edwardian inn has a choice of period-style rooms and four-bed dorms. There's a beautiful common area and a good restaurant onsite, as well as a self-catering kitchen.

Queenscliff Tourist Parks　　CAMPGROUND, CABINS **$$**
(✆03-5258 1765; www.queensclifftouristparks.com.au; 134 Hesse St; unpowered sites/cabins $24/147) This simple, council-run camping ground on Queenscliff's recreation reserve is the closest campground to town and right near the beach. Shady sites are scarce.

Queenscliff Dive Centre　　HOSTEL **$$**
(✆03-5258 1188; www.divequeenscliff.com.au; 37 Learmonth St; dm/d incl breakfast $35/140; ✦) This dive operator has hostel-style accommodation at their Learmonth St office. The terrific shared kitchen and lounge facilities are bright and airy in a central atrium, while the simple rooms are out the back. BYO linen.

✗ Eating

360Q　　MODERN AUSTRALIAN **$$**
(✆03-5257 4200; www.360q.com.au; 2 Wharf St; mains $19-32; ⊙breakfast Sat & Sun, lunch daily, dinner Fri & Sun) Queenscliff is famous for its seafood, and here's the best location to try it. Sitting pretty at the base of Queensliff's observation tower, it serves up twice-cooked blue-eye fillet and marinated scallops right by the marina.

Café Gusto　　CAFE **$**
(✆03-5258 3604; 25 Hesse St; breakfast $7-12, lunch $14-16; ⊙breakfast & lunch daily, dinner Fri & Sat) Another favourite Queenscliff eatery, great for breakfast with a spacious garden out the back. Even basics like sausages become gourmet snags in sourdough with onion and homemade tomato relish.

Lix　　CAFE **$**
(Shop 6, 4 Wharf St; meals $5; ⊙breakfast & lunch daily) This new waterside cafe serves up simple toasted sandwiches, more-ish milkshakes and coffee.

Apostle　　MODERN AUSTRALIAN **$$**
(✆03-5258 3097; www.apostlequeenscliff.com.au; 79 Hesse St; mains $20-32; ⊙breakfast & lunch daily, dinner Fri-Sun) Ensconced in a lofty former church (c 1888) with exquisite stained-glass windows and a terrific sloping floor, Apostle serves up local goodies (like the local mussels in its seafood fettucini) in a relaxed, far-from-churchy environment.

ⓘ Information

Queenscliff Visitors Centre (✆03-5258 4843; www.queenscliffe.vic.gov.au; 55 Hesse St; ⊙9am-5pm; @) Internet access for $6 per hour (also available next door at the library).

Point Lonsdale

POP 2500

Point Lonsdale, 5km southwest of Queenscliff, is a laid-back community with cafes and an operational 1902 lighthouse. From the foreshore car park you can walk to the Rip View lookout to watch ships entering the Rip, to Point Lonsdale Pier and to the lighthouse. There's good **surf** off the rocky beach below the car park.

Below the lighthouse is Buckley's Cave, where William Buckley lived with Aborigines for 32 years after he escaped from the Sorrento convict settlement.

🛏 Sleeping & Eating

Point Lonsdale Guest House　　GUESTHOUSE **$$**
(✆03-5258 1142; www.pointlonsdaleguesthouse.com.au; 31 Point Lonsdale Rd; r $110-220; ✦) The huge range of rooms in this former Terminus House (1884) range from basic motel rooms to lavish B&B affairs. Lighthouse views come at a premium. There's a communal kitchen, tennis court, games room and BBQ facilities.

Kelp　　MODERN AUSTRALIAN **$$**
(67 Point Lonsdale Rd; mains $18-42) Here's a funky, modern cafe-restaurant where locals come for all-day breakfasts, lunchtime

pita-bread wraps, and Asian and Modern Australian–inspired evening meals matched with wine from its long list.

Grow Naturally CAFE $

(59 Point Lonsdale Rd; mains $10-15; ⊙breakfast & lunch) Serving up healthy meals cheaply isn't necessarily easy, but this small cafe succeeds.

Ocean Grove

POP 11,300

Ocean Grove, 3km northeast of Barwon Heads and 12km west of Queenscliff, is the big smoke of the Bellarine Peninsula, where folks come for their supermarket and department-store shopping. There are some good **surfing** breaks around here, dog-friendly beaches, and some good **scuba diving** and **snorkelling** spots beyond the rocky ledges of the bluff.

🛏 Sleeping & Eating

Ti-Tree Village CABINS $$

(☑03-5255 4433; www.ti-treevillage.com.au; 34 Orton St; cottages $170-230; ❄) There's gingerbread-house appeal in this compact, tree-covered resort. Log cabins are cosy and self-contained and some have gardens and spas. The playground and communal barbecue areas make it a popular spot with families grilling their day's catch. There's a weekend two-night minimum stay.

Terrace Lofts APARTMENTS $$

(☑03-5255 4167; www.terracelofts.com.au; 92 The Terrace; d from $175; ❄🅿) These four luxurious, self-contained, split-level apartments have mezzanine-level bedrooms overlooking open-plan living areas. A short walk to the beach and town, they have wood combustion fires, TVs with DVD and relaxed, modern decor. Kids stay free.

7th Wave MODERN AUSTRALIAN $$

(64b The Terrace; mains $18-33; ⊙lunch & dinner Wed-Sun) Catering to casual cafe diners by day and scrubbed-up dinner guests by night, 7th Wave also features live music. Try the beer-battered local seafood specials.

Barwon Heads

POP 3000

At the mouth of the broad **Barwon River**, Barwon Heads is a haven of sheltered beaches, tidal river flats and holiday-makers. Barwon Heads was made famous as the setting

for *Seachange* – a popular TV series – and, over a decade on, still trades on the kudos. In a case of life imitating TV, the original bridge linking Barwon Heads with Ocean Grove was recently replaced with two modern bridges.

◉ Sights

Beaches BEACH

Feisty **Thirteenth Beach**, 2km west, is popular with surfers. There are short walks around the headland and the **Bluff** with panoramic sea vistas, and there are **scuba-diving** spots under the rocky ledges below.

Jirrahlinga Koala & Wildlife Sanctuary ZOO

(☑03-5254 2484; www.jirrahlinga.com.au; Taits Rd; adult/child $15/10) This koala sanctuary also houses roos and reptiles.

🛏 Sleeping

Barwon Heads Caravan Park CAMPGROUND $

(☑03-5254 1115; www.barwoncoast.com.au; Ewing Blyth Dr; unpowered/powered sites $24/30, d/f cabins $95/105, beach house $225) Right on the Barwon River, this park contains Laura's house from *Seachange* (you can even stay in it). It also has ti-tree–shaded sites, tennis courts and playgrounds. Prices almost double over summer.

Seahaven Village APARTMENTS $$

(☑03-5254 1066; www.seahavenvillage.com.au; 3 Geelong Rd; d $135-295; ❄) Seahaven, opposite Village Park, is a cute cluster of self-contained studios and cottages with electric blankets, open fires, full kitchens and entertainment systems. There's usually a two-night minimum stay.

Private holiday accommodation is managed by agents, including the following: **Barwon Grove Holiday Rentals** (☑03-5254 3263; www.bgholidayrentals.com.au); **Beds By the Beach** (☑03-5254 2419; www.bedsbythebeach.com.au) and **Bellarine Getaways** (☑03-5254 3393; www.bellarinegetaways.com.au).

🍴 Eating

Barwon Orange PIZZA $$

(60 Hitchcock Ave; www.barwonorange.com.au; mains $12-27; ⊙breakfast, lunch & dinner Thu, Fri & Sat, breakfast & lunch Wed & Sun) Big Bertha – the orange wood-fired oven that cooks up Barwon Orange's crazily topped pizzas – helps the mood along. Innovative menus star, and breakfast is served until a civilised 3.30pm.

DETOUR: MACEDON RANGES & HANGING ROCK

A short detour off the Calder Fwy (Rte M79), less than an hour north of Melbourne, the Macedon Ranges is a beautiful area of low mountains, native forest and wineries. It covers the towns of Gisborne, Woodend, Lancefield, Romsey, Kyneton and the legendary Hanging Rock.

Mt Macedon is a 1010m-high extinct volcano with numerous walking tracks. The scenic route up Mt Macedon Rd takes you past mansions with beautiful gardens. At the summit is a cafe, viewpoints and a 21m-high memorial cross.

Beyond the summit turn-off, the road heads to quaint **Woodend**, or take the signed road on the right to **Hanging Rock** (per vehicle $10; ⊙9am-5pm), sacred site of the Wurundjeri people. The rock was a refuge for bushrangers, but attained fame with Joan Lindsay's novel *Picnic at Hanging Rock* (and the subsequent film directed by Peter Weir) about the mysterious disappearance of a group of schoolgirls. In Woodend, easily reached by V/Line train from Melbourne, the excellent **Holgate Brewhouse** (☑03-5427 2510; www.holgatebrewhouse.com; 79 High St; d $135-185; mains $26-30; ⊙lunch Tue-Sun, dinner daily) is a cracking brewery pub producing a range of hand-pumped European-style ales and lagers on-site. Try a tasting paddle ($10). The kitchen serves hearty Mod Oz bistro food.

Further north, **Kyneton** was an early coach stop between Melbourne and the goldfields, and today the historic **Piper St** precinct is lined with old bluestone buildings, antique shops and fabulous cafes and restaurants.

Starfish Bakery   BAKERY $
(78 Hitchcock St; meals $5-9; ⊙breakfast & lunch) This relaxed, colourful bakery-cafe makes its own pastries and bread and serves up good coffee and massive muffins.

At the Heads   MODERN AUSTRALIAN $$
(☑03-5254 1277; www.attheheads.com.au; Jetty Rd; meals $17-50; ⊙lunch & dinner daily, breakfast Sat & Sun) Built on stilts over the mouth of the river, this light, airy cafe-restaurant has huge breakfasts, local fare and the most amazing views. Its bustling family ambience makes it a fun daytime locale. After dark try the seafood bouillabaisse.

THE YARRA VALLEY

An hour northeast of Melbourne, the Yarra Valley is one of Victoria's premier wine regions, and the surrounding national parks are superb for walking and cycling.

Healesville is the main town and best base to explore the Yarra Valley as it's central to many of the wineries and is the 'capital' of the Lower Yarra Valley; **Warburton**, marks the centre of the Upper Yarra Valley.

There's some good walking in national parks in the area, including **Warrandyte State Park**, **Yarra Ranges National Park** and **Kinglake National Park**.

 Activities

One-hour dawn balloon flights with the following operators include champagne breakfast and cost about $300: **Balloon Sunrise** (☑1800 992 105; www.hotairballooning.com.au); **Global Ballooning** (☑03-9428 5703; www.globalballooning.com.au); **Go Wild Ballooning** (☑03-9739 0772; www.gowildballooning.com.au).

 Tours

Eco Adventure Tours   WILDLIFE, CULTURE
(☑03-5962 5115; www.ecoadventuretours.com.au; walks from $25) Offers nocturnal wildlife-spotting and cultural walks in the Healesville, Toolangi and Dandenongs area.

Yarra Valley Winery Tours   WINE
(☑03-5962 3870; www.yarravalleywinerytours.com.au; tours from $99) Daily tours taking in four or five wineries.

 Information

Yarra Valley Visitor Centre (☑03-5962 2600; www.visityarravalley.com.au; Harker St, Healesville; ⊙9am-5pm) Just off the highway in Healesville, this tourist office has helpful staff.

 Getting There & Away

Suburban trains go as far as Lilydale (use a Zone 1 and 2 Metcard). **McKenzie's Bus Lines** (☑03-5962 5088; www.mckenzies.com.au) runs from Melbourne to Eildon via Lilydale and Healesville.

YARRA VALLEY WINERIES

The Yarra Valley (www.wineyarravalley.com) has more than 80 wineries and 50 cellar doors scattered around its rolling hills – the first vines were planted at Yering Station in 1838. The region produces cool-climate, food-friendly drops such as Chardonnay, Pinot Noir and Pinot Gris.

Of the many food and wine festivals in the region, our favourite is Grape Grazing (www.grapegrazing.com.au) in February, celebrating the beginning of the grape harvest, while Rochford hosts a series of concerts throughout the year. Shedfest, in mid-October, is a showcase of the southern wineries near Warburton. Some top Yarra Valley wineries with cellar door sales and tastings include the following:

Boat O'Craigo (☑03-8357 0188; 458 Maroondah Hwy, Healesville) Boutique winery with two vineyards producing fruity reds and whites like Shiraz and Pinot Gris.

Domain Chandon (☑9738 9200; www.chandon.com.au; 727 Maroodah Hwy, Coldstream) Established by the makers of Moet, this slick operation is worth a visit for the free guided tours at 1pm and 3pm where you can sample the bubbly.

Rochford (☑03-5962 2119; www.rochfordwines.com; cnr Maroondah Hwy & Hill Rd, Coldstream) Rochford is a huge complex with restaurant, cafe and regular concerts.

TarraWarra Estate (☑03-5957 3510; www.tarrawarra.com.au; 311 Healesville–Yarra Glen Rd, Yarra Glen) Convivial bistro and a superb art gallery ($5) come together in a striking building.

Yering Farm Wines (☑03-9739 0461; www.yeringfarmwines.com; St Huberts Rd, Yering) A rustic and friendly little cellar door in an old hay shed with lovely views.

Yering Station (☑03-9730 0100; www.yering.com; 38 Melba Hwy, Yering) A modern complex with a fine restaurant, gourmet provedore and bar, it's home to the heady Shiraz-Viognier blend.

Martyrs (☑03-5966 2035; www.martyrs.com. au) buses run to Yarra Junction and Warburton.

Healesville

POP 7400

Pretty little Healesville is the main base for the Yarra Valley wineries, Yarra Ranges forest drive and gateway north to the High Country.

⊙ Sights

Healesville Sanctuary   WILDLIFE SANCTUARY
(☑03-5957 2800; www.zoo.org.au; Badger Creek Rd, Healesville; adult/child/family $25/13/57; ☉9am-5pm) One of the best places in southern Australia to see native fauna, this wildlife park is full of kangaroos, dingoes, lyrebirds, Tasmanian devils, bats, koalas, eagles, snakes and lizards. The Platypus House displays these shy underwater creatures that you'll rarely see in the wild, and the exciting Birds of Prey presentation (noon and 2pm daily) features huge wedge-tailed eagles and owls soaring through the air.

🛏 Sleeping & Eating

Healesville is the main accommodation centre for the region, though there are B&Bs scattered around the valley and many of the wineries have accommodation.

Healesville Hotel   HOTEL $$
(☑03-5962 4002; www.yarravalleyharvest.com.au; 256 Maroondah Hwy, Healesville; d Sun-Thu $100, Fri $130, Sat incl dinner $315) An iconic Healesville landmark, this restored 1910 hotel offers basic but classic upstairs pub rooms with shared bathrooms. Downstairs the formal dining room (mains $29 to $39) is one of the area's culinary showstoppers.

Badger Creek Holiday Park   CARAVAN PARK $
(☑03-5962 4328; www.badgercreekholidays. com.au; 419 Don Rd, Badger Creek; powered sites $41, d cabins $100-255; ❄☆) The riverside location here is lovely and the park is well kitted out with an adventure playground, games rooms, camp kitchen, pool and tennis courts.

Giant Steps & Innocent Bystander   TAPAS $$
(☑1800 661 624; 336 Maroondah Hwy; mains $19-42; ☉10am-10pm, from 8am weekends) In town, the industrial-sized Giant Steps & Innocent Bystander is a buzzing restaurant, winery and cellar door – a great place for a lunch

of tapas, pizza or cheese platter, a lazy afternoon drink or a spot of in-town wine tasting.

Bodhi Tree Café   CAFE $
(☑03-5962 4407; 317 Maroondah Hwy, Healesville; mains $9-16; ⊘dinner Wed-Fri, lunch & dinner Sat & Sun; ☑) Friendly eco-vibes, salvaged-wood furniture and a pot-belly stove complement the wood-fired pizzas, curries and vegetarian food at this popular hippie hang-out. Live music on Friday and Saturday.

Marysville & Lake Mountain

Marysville was at the epicentre of the tragic 2009 bushfires when most of the town's buildings were destroyed and 34 people lost their lives, but the community is steadily rebuilding, and this beautiful setting is the main base for the cross-country ski fields at Lake Mountain.

Bruno's Art & Sculptures Garden (☑03-5963 3513; 51 Falls Rd; adult/child $5/free; ⊘garden 10am-5pm daily, gallery 10am-5pm Sat & Sun) was badly damaged in the fires but more than 100 of the wonderful terracotta sculptures have been lovingly repaired.

Part of Yarra Ranges National Park, **Lake Mountain** (1433m) is the premier cross-country ski resort in Australia, with 37km of trails and several toboggan runs. In summer there are marked hiking and mountain-biking trails.

ⓘ Information

Lake Mountain Resort (☑03-5957 7222; www.lakemountainresort.com.au; Snowy Rd; ⊘8am-4.30pm Mon-Fri Oct-May, 7am-6.30pm daily Jun-Sep) Has ski hire, a ski school, a cafe and undercover barbecue areas.

Marysville Visitors Centre (☑03-5963 4567; www.marysvilletourism.com; Murchison St; ⊘9am-5pm) In a new location across from the shopping centre.

THE DANDENONGS

On a clear day, the Dandenong Ranges and their highest peak, Mt Dandenong (633m), can be seen from Melbourne. The landscape is a patchwork of exotics and natives with a lush understorey of tree ferns – it's the most accessible bushwalking in Melbourne's backyard, and the quaint towns of Olinda, Sassafras and Emerald make a nice escape.

Dandenong Ranges & Knox Visitor Information Centre (☑03-9758 7522; www.dandenongrangestourism.com.au; 1211 Burwood Hwy, Upper Ferntree Gully; ⊘9am-5pm) is outside Upper Ferntree Gully train station.

Puffing Billy (☑03-9754 6800; www.puffingbilly.com.au; Old Monbulk Rd, Belgrave; Belgrave–Gembrook return adult/child/family $52/26/105) is an immensely popular steam train that snakes through lush fern gullies and bush. There are up to six departures between Belgrave and Gembrook during holidays, and three or four on other days. Nearby, **Trees Adventure** (☑03-9752 5354; www.treesadventure.com.au; Old Monbulk Rd; 2hr session adult/child/family $16/32/95; ⊘11am-5pm Mon-Fri, 9am-5pm Sat & Sun) is a blast of tree-climbs, flying foxes and obstacle courses in a stunning patch of old-growth forest boasting sequoia, mountain ash and Japanese oak trees.

Dandenong Ranges National Park is made up of the four largest areas of remaining forest in the Dandenongs. The Ferntree Gully Area has several short walks, including the popular **1000 Steps Track** up to One Tree Hill picnic ground (two hours return), part of the **Kokoda Memorial Track**, which commemorates Australian WWII servicemen who served in New Guinea. **Sherbrooke Forest** has a towering cover of mountain ash trees. Reach the start of its eastern loop walk (10km, three hours), just 1km or so from Belgrave station.

WORTH A DETOUR: ST ANDREWS

Sleepily ensconced in the hills 35km north of Melbourne, this little village is best known for the weekly **St Andrews Community Market** (www.standrewsmarket.com.au; ⊘8am-2pm Sat). Every Saturday morning the scent of eucalypt competes with incense, and the bird life with buskers as an alternative crowd comes to mingle and buy handmade crafts, knitwear and jewellery, fresh produce, herbs and household goods. Enjoy a shiatsu massage, sip chai, have your chakra aligned or just listen to the street musos.

BLACK SATURDAY

On 7 February 2009, parts of Victoria were engulfed in a deadly firestorm that became known as Black Saturday. Fuelled by extreme temperatures, tinder-dry conditions and strong winds, the ferocity and speed of the fires took residents and authorities by surprise. The worst hit area was the Yarra Ranges northeast of Melbourne, where, within a few devastating hours the tiny bush towns of Marysville, Kinglake, Strathewen, Flowerdale and Narbethong were engulfed. Marysville and Kinglake were virtually razed and the fires hit so fast that many residents had no chance of escape. Many fire victims died in their homes or trapped in their cars while trying to escape, some blocked by fallen trees across the road.

The statistics tell a tragic tale: 173 people dead, more than 2000 homes destroyed, an estimated 7500 people left homeless; and more than 4500 sq km burned out. What followed from the shell-shocked state and nation was a huge outpouring of grief, humanitarian aid and charity, while the government established a royal commission into the events and future fire safety and warning strategies. Today, the towns of Marysville, Kinglake and other fire-affected communities are courageously rebuilding and welcoming the return of tourists, while the blackened bushland and forests are regenerating as nature intended.

Drive up to SkyHigh Mt Dandenong (☑03-9751 0443; www.skyhighmtdandenong.com. au; Observatory Rd, Mt Dandenong; vehicle entry $5; ☺9am-10pm Mon-Fri, 8am-10pm Sat-Sun) for amazing views over Melbourne and Port Phillip Bay from the highest point in the Dandenongs.

❶ Getting There & Away

The Met's suburban trains run on the Belgrave line to the foothills of the Dandenongs (Zone 1 and 2 Metcard). From Upper Ferntree Gully train station it's a 10-minute walk to the start of the Ferntree Gully section of the national park.

MORNINGTON PENINSULA

The Mornington Peninsula – the boot-shaped bit of land between Port Phillip Bay and Western Port Bay – has been Melbourne's summer playground since the 1870s, when paddle steamers ran down to Portsea. Today, the calm 'front beaches' on the Port Phillip Bay side are still a big magnet for family holidays at bayside towns like Mornington, Rosebud, Dromana, Rye, Blairgowrie and Sorrento. The rugged ocean 'back beaches' facing Bass Strait offer challenging surfing and stunning walks along the coastal strip, part of Mornington Peninsula National Park.

Don't overlook a trip to the peninsula's interior, where lovely stands of native bushland are interspersed with vineyards and orchards – foodies love this region, where a winery lunch is a real highlight.

❶ Information

Mornington Peninsula Visitors Centre (☑1800 804 009, 03-5987 3078; www. visitmorningtonpeninsula.org; 359b Nepean Hwy, Dromana; ☺9am-5pm) The main visitor information centre for the peninsula can book accommodation and tours.

Mornington Visitors Centre (☑03-5975 1644; www.visitmorningtonpeninsula.org; 320 Main St; ☺9am-5pm) Conveniently located in Mornington.

❶ Getting There & Around

Met trains (buy a Zones 1 and 2 ticket) run from Flinders Street Station to Frankston Station. **Portsea Passenger Service** (☑03-5986 5666; www.grenda.com.au) bus 788 runs from Frankston to Portsea ($5, 1½ hours) via Mornington, Dromana and Sorrento.

Queenscliff-Sorrento Car & Passenger Ferries (☑03-5258 3244; www.searoad.com. au; one-way foot passenger adult/child $9/7, 2 adults & car standard/peak $58/64; ☺hourly) sails between Sorrento and Queenscliff. **Inter Island Ferries** (☑03-9585 5730; www.inter-islandferries.com.au; return adult/child/bike $21/10/8) runs between Stony Point and Cowes (Phillip Island) via French Island.

Sorrento & Portsea

POP 1500

Historic Sorrento is the standout town on the Mornington Peninsula for its beautiful limestone buildings, ocean and bay beaches and buzzing seaside summer atmosphere. This was the site of Victoria's first official European

settlement, established by an expedition of convicts, marines, civil officers and free settlers that arrived from England in 1803.

Grand 19th-century buildings include the Sorrento Hotel (1871), the Continental Hotel (1875) and Koonya (1878).

There are plenty of swimming and walking opportunities along Sorrento's wide, sandy beaches and bluffs. At low tide, the rock pool at the back beach is a safe spot for adults and children to swim and snorkel, and the surf beach here is patrolled in summer. The ferry to Queenscliff departs daily for the short trip across the heads.

Only 4km further west, tiny **Portsea** also has good back beaches, and diving and water-sports operators.

The small **Sorrento visitors centre** (☑03-5984 5678; 2 St Aubins Way) is on the main street.

🏃 Activities

Moonraker Charters DOLPHIN & SEAL SWIMMING
(☑03-5984 4211; www.moonrakercharters.com.au; adult/child sightseeing $55/44, dolphin & seal swimming $115/105) Operates three-hour dolphin- and seal-swimming tours from Sorrento Pier.

Polperro Dolphin Swims DOLPHIN & SEAL SWIMMING
(☑03-5988 8437; www.polperro.com.au; adult/child observers $55/35, all swimmers $125) Popular morning and afternoon dolphin- and seal-swimming tours from Sorrento Pier.

Bay Play DIVING, WATERSPORTS
(☑03-5984 0888; www.bayplay.com.au; 3755 Pt Nepean Rd, Portsea) Diving and snorkelling trips, dolphin swims, sea-kayaking tours (adult/child $88/55) and kayak rental.

Dive Victoria DIVING, SNORKELLING
(☑03-5984 3155; www.divevictoria.com.au; 3752 Point Nepean Rd, Portsea; snorkelling $60, s/d dive with gear $120/185) Diving and snorkelling trips.

🛌 Sleeping

Prices rise with the temperature from mid-December to the end of January, and during Easter and school holidays when places routinely book out.

Sorrento Beach House YHA HOSTEL $
(☑03-5984 4323; www.sorrento-beachhouse.com; 3 Miranda St; dm/d $40/90; @) This purpose-built hostel in a quiet but central location maintains a relaxed atmosphere. The back deck and garden are great places to catch up with other travellers.

Carmel of Sorrento GUESTHOUSE $$
(☑03-5984 3512; www.carmelofsorrento.com.au; 142 Ocean Beach Rd; d $150-220, apt from $220; ❄) This lovely old limestone house right in the centre Sorrento has been tastefully restored in period style and neatly marries the town's history with contemporary comfort.

Sorrento Foreshore Reserve CAMPGROUND $
(☑03-5986 8286; Nepean Hwy; unpowered/powered sites $40/45) Hilly, bushclad sites between the bay beach and the main road into Sorrento.

🍴 Eating & Drinking

Smokehouse PIZZA $$
(☑03-5984 1246; 182 Ocean Beach Rd; mains $17-32; ◷dinner Wed-Mon) Gourmet pizzas and pastas are the speciality at this local family favourite. Innovative toppings and the aromas wafting from the wood-fired oven are a winner.

The Baths MODERN AUSTRALIAN, FISH & CHIPS $$
(☑03-5984 1500; www.thebaths.com.au; 3278 Point Nepean Rd; mains $26-32; ◷lunch & dinner, fish & chippery noon-8pm) The waterfront deck of the former sea baths is the perfect spot for lunch or a romantic sunset dinner overlooking the jetty. There's a popular takeaway fish and chippery at the front.

Just Fine Food CAFE $
(☑03-5984 4666; 23 Ocean Beach Rd; mains $7-23; ◷9am-5pm Mon-Fri, 9am-6pm Sat) Famous for its sublime fluffy vanilla slices (recipe: top secret), this cafe and deli is a top place for all-day breakfasts, and lunches of open sandwiches, focaccia, antipasto and gourmet pies.

Portsea Hotel BISTRO $$
(☑03-5984 2213; www.portseahotel.com.au; Point Nepean Rd; mains $20-28) This iconic sprawling, half-timber pub is Portsea's pulse, with a great lawn and terrace area looking out over the bay. There's an excellent bistro and old-style accommodation that increases in price based on sea views and season.

Point Nepean & Mornington Peninsula National Parks

The peninsula's tip is marked by the scenic **Point Nepean National Park** (☑03-5984 4276; Point Nepean Rd, Portsea), originally a quarantine station and army base. There are long stretches of traffic-free road for

DETOUR: FRENCH ISLAND

It's only a 15-minute ferry ride from Stony Point on the Mornington Peninsula, but French Island feels a world away – it's two-thirds national park, virtually traffic-free and there's no mains water or electricity. The main attractions are bushwalking and cycling, taking in wetlands, one of Australia's largest **koala colonies**, and a huge variety of birds.

The ferry docks at Tankerton, from where it's around 2km to the licensed French Island General Store (03-5980 1209; Lot 1, Tankerton Rd, Tankerton; bike hire $25; 8am-6pm, from 9am Sun), which also serves as post office, tourist information centre and bike-hire business. Bikes can also be hired at Tankerton Jetty.

French Island Biosphere Bus Tours (03-5980 1241, 0412-671 241; www.french islandtours.com.au; half-day adult/child $18/10, full day $38/22; Tue, Thu, Sun, plus Sat during school holidays) has informative half-day tours with morning or afternoon tea. The full-day tour includes lunch.

You can camp for free at the basic Fairhaven Camping Ground, but bookings are essential through Parks Victoria.

Inter Island Ferries (03-9585 5730; www.interislandferries.com.au; adult/child/ bike return $21/10/8) runs a service between Stony Point and Tankerton (10 minutes, at least two daily), continuing on to Phillip Island. You can reach Stony Point directly from Frankston on a Metlink train.

excellent cycling and walking trails leading to beaches. You can hire bikes at the visitor centre ($20 per day) or take the Point Transporter (adult/child/family return $9/6/23), a hop-on, hop-off bus service that departs from the visitor centre six times daily.

Mornington Peninsula National Park covers the dramatic sliver of coastline between Portsea and Cape Schanck, where rugged ocean beaches are framed by cliffs and bluffs. You can walk all the way from Portsea to Cape Schanck (26km, eight hours) along a marked trail.

Built in 1859, Cape Schanck Lightstation (03-5988 6184, 420 Cape Schanck Rd; museum only adult/child/family $12/8/34, museum & lighthouse $15/12/40; 10.30am-4pm) is a photogenic working lighthouse, with a kiosk, museum, information centre and regular guided tours. You can stay at Cape Schanck B&B (03-5988 6184; www.austpacinns.com.au; d from $150) in the limestone keepers cottage.

PHILLIP ISLAND

POP 6700

Famous for the Penguin Parade and Grand Prix racing circuit, Phillip Island is a spectacular natural environment, attracting a curious mix of surfers, petrolheads and international tourists making a beeline for those little penguins.

At its heart, 100-sq-km Phillip Island is still a farming community, but along with

the penguins, there's a large seal colony, abundant bird life around the Rhyll wetlands, and a koala colony. The rugged south coast has some fabulous surf beaches and the summer swell of tourists means there's a swag of family attractions, plenty of accommodation, and a buzzing cafe and restaurant scene in the island capital, Cowes. Visit in winter, though, and you'll find a very quiet place where the local population of farmers, surfers and hippies go about their business. The island was originally settled by the Boonwurrung people, who thrived on a diet of seafood and short-tailed shearwaters.

◉ Sights & Activities

PHILLIP ISLAND NATURE PARKS

The nature parks comprises three of the islands biggest attractions: the Penguin Parade (03-5951 2800; www.penguins.org.au; Summerland Beach; adult/child/family $20/10/50; 10am-dusk); the Koala Conservation Centre (03-5952 1307; adult/child/family $10/5/25; 10am-5pm, extended hr in summer), off Phillip Island Rd, with elevated boardwalks; and trips to Churchill Island (03-5956 7214; adult/child/family $10/5/25; 10am-4.30pm, extended hr in summer), a working farm also off Phillip Island Rd, where Victoria's first crops were planted which today features historic displays, including butter churning and blacksmithing.

If you're keen on all three attractions, buy the Three Parks Pass (adult/child/family $34/17/85), which is valid for six months

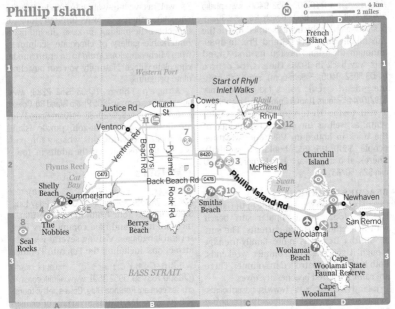

(you can only visit the Penguin Parade once though) and is available at the visitors centre.

Most people come for the **Little Penguins**, the world's smallest and probably cutest of their kind. The penguin complex includes concrete amphitheatres that hold up to 3800 spectators who visit to see the little fellas just after sunset as they waddle from the sea to their land-based nests. Penguin numbers swell in summer, after breeding, but they parade year-round. You usually get a closer view from the boardwalks as they search for their burrows and mates. Bring warm clothing. There are a variety of specialised **tours** (adult $35-70) so you can be accompanied by rangers or see them from the vantage of a Skybox (an elevated platform). Be sure to book well in advance in summer.

SEAL ROCKS & THE NOBBIES

The extreme southwestern tip of Phillip Island leads to the Nobbies and beyond them is Seal Rocks, inhabited by Australia's largest colony of fur seals. The Nobbies Centre (☑03-5951 2816; admission free, tours adult/child $10/5; ☺10am-8pm summer, 10am-4pm winter) houses an interesting interpretive centre with interactive panels and games, and the huge windows afford great views of the 6000 Australian fur seals who loll here during the October to December breeding season. You

Phillip Island

◉ Sights

1 Churchill Island	D2
2 Grand Prix Motor Racing Circuit	B2
3 Koala Conservation Centre	C2
4 Nobbies Centre	A3
5 Penguin Parade	A2
6 Phillip Island Chocolate Factory	D2
7 Phillip Island Wildlife Park	B2
8 Seal Rocks	A3

● Activities, Courses & Tours

9 Amaze'n Things	C2
10 Island Surfboards (Smiths Beach)	C2

⊜ Sleeping

11 Surf & Circuit Accommodation	B2

⊗ Eating

Curry Leaf	(see 13)
12 Foreshore Bar & Restaurant	C2
13 White Salt	D3

can view the seals from boardwalks or use the centre's underwater cameras to zoom in on them ($5).

MOTOR RACING CIRCUIT

Even when the motorbikes aren't racing, petrolheads love the Grand Prix Motor

Racing Circuit (☎03-5952 9400; www.phillip islandcircuit.com.au; Back Beach Rd; ⊗8.30am-5.30pm Mon-Fri), which was souped up for the Australian Motorcycle Grand Prix in 1989, although the island hosted its first Grand Prix way back in 1928. The visitor centre (☎03-5952 9400; ⊗9am-6pm) runs 45-minute guided circuit tours (adult/child/family $19/10/44; ⊗tours 11am & 2pm), which include a visit to the History of Motorsport Museum, as well as the chance to cut laps of the track in hotted-up V8s (one/two/three people $210/315/365, booking essential). There's also a go-kart track (per 10/20/30 min $28/50/65).

BEACHES & SURFING

Ocean beaches on the south side of the island include Woolamai, a popular surf beach with dangerous rips and currents. The surf at Smiths Beach is more family-friendly, though it gets busy on summer weekends. Both beaches are patrolled in summer. There are calm, sheltered beaches at Cowes.

Island Surfboards (www.islandsurfboards.com.au; surfing lessons $55, surfboard hire per hr/day $13/40) Smiths Beach (☎03-5952 3443; 65 Smiths Beach Rd); Cowes (☎03-5952 2578; 147 Thompson Ave) can start your waxhead career with wetsuit hire and lessons for all standards.

Out There (☎03-5956 6450; www.outthere. net.au; Newhaven) also offers surfing lessons as well as sea-kayaking and mountain-biking.

BIRDS & WILDLIFE

A good range of wildlife can be spotted at Phillip Island Wildlife Park (☎03-5952 2038; Thompson Ave; adult/child/family $15/8/40; ⊗10am-5.30pm, later in summer), about 1km south of Cowes, including Tasmanian devils, cassowaries and quolls.

Mutton birds, also known as short-tailed shearwaters, colonise the dunes around Cape Woolamai from late September to April. Your best chance of seeing them is at the Penguin Parade as they fly in at dusk, or at the rookeries at Woolamai Beach.

There's a wide variety of other water birds around, including pelicans that are fed at Newhaven at 11.30am daily, and in the swampland at Rhyll Inlet and Rhyll Wetland.

OTHER ATTRACTIONS

Like Willy Wonka's famous factory, the Phillip Island Chocolate Factory (☎03-5956 6600; www.phillipislandchocolatefactory.com.au; 930 Phillip Island Rd, Newhaven; tours adult/child/family $12/8/36; ⊗9am-5pm) has a few surprises.

As well as wall-to-wall handmade Belgian chocolate, there's a walk-through tour of the chocolate-making process, including a remarkable gallery of chocolate sculptures, from Michelangelo's *David* to an entire model chocolate village! Naturally, you can buy chocolate penguins.

Amaze'n Things (☎03-5952 2283; www.amazenthings.com.au; 1805 Phillip Island Rd, Cowes; adult/child/family $29/20/88; ⊗10am-6pm) With an illusion maze, mini-golf, puzzle island and lots of activities, this whacky fun park is great for kids, but gets the adults in, too.

☞ Tours

Go West   DAY TOUR
(☎1300 736 551; www.gowest.com.au; 1-day tour $125) One-day tour from Melbourne that includes lunch and iPod commentary in several languages, visiting several island attractions, including the Penguin Parade.

Wildlife Coast Cruises   WILDLIFE, CRUISES
(☎1300 763 739; 5952 3501; www.wildlifecoast cruises.com.au; Rotunda Bldg, Cowes Jetty; tours $35-70; ⊗Nov-May) Runs a variety of cruises from Cowes including seal-watching, twilight and cape cruises; also a half-day cruise to French Island (adult/child $55/75) and full day to Wilson's Promontory ($140/190).

✰ Festivals & Events

Pyramid Rock Festival   MUSIC
(www.thepyramidrockfestival.com; ⊗New Year) This huge event coincides with New Year's festivities and features some of the best Aussie bands.

Australian Motorcycle
Grand Prix   MOTORCYCLE RACING
(www.motogp.com.au; ⊗Oct) The island's biggest event – three days of bike action in October.

🛏 Sleeping

Phillip Island's prices peak during motor races, Christmas, Easter and school holidays, so book as far ahead as possible. Most of the accommodation is in and around Cowes.

Surf & Circuit
Accommodation   APARTMENTS $$
(☎03-5952 1300; www.surfandcircuit.com; 113 Justice Rd, Cowes; apt $135-380; ✲ ▣) Ideal for families or groups, these eight spacious, modern and comfortable two- and three-bedroom units accommodate up to six and 10 people,

and have kitchens and lounges with plasma TVs and patios, and some have spas.

Amaroo Park YHA
HOSTEL $

(☑03-5952 2548; www.yha.com.au; 97 Church St, Cowes; unpowered sites $30, dm/d/f from $30/95/135; @🛜🏊) In a shady bush setting, the Amaroo Park YHA is a lovely old-style guesthouse with a communal kitchen and BBQ areas, bar, lounge and TV room. There are en-suite cabins and camp sites outside.

Chill House Backpackers
HOSTEL $

(☑0431 413 275; www.chillhouse.com.au; 8 Watchorn Rd, Cowes; dm/d $30/70; @) Cosy, welcoming, relaxed, and well equipped, Chill House is down a side street off Settlement Rd, close to the town centre.

Waves Apartments
APARTMENTS $$

(☑03-5952 1351; www.thewaves.com.au; Esplanade; d/tr/q from $180/195/210; ❄) These slick apartments overlook Cowes main beach so you can't beat your balcony views if you go for a beachfront unit. The modern self-contained apartments come with spa and balcony or patio.

✖ Eating & Drinking

Most of the eateries are in Cowes – the Esplanade and Thompson Ave are crowded with fish and chip shops, cafes and takeaways – but there are a few more gems scattered around the island.

COWES

Infused
MODERN AUSTRALIAN $$

(☑03-5952 2655; www.infused.com.au; 115 Thompson Ave, Cowes; mains $25-38; ☺lunch & dinner Wed-Mon) Infused's groovy mix of timber, stone and lime-green decor makes a relaxed place to enjoy a beautifully presented lunch or dinner, or just a late-night cocktail. The eclectic Mod Oz menu is strong on seafood and moves from freshly shucked oysters to Asian curries and Black Angus rib eye.

Hotel
PUB FARE $$

(☑03-5952 2060; www.hotelphillipisland.com; 11-13 The Esplanade, Cowes; mains $10-28; ☺lunch & dinner) This breezy corner pub is all leather, sleek lines and big windows. The menu is honest and good value with all-day tapas plates, pizza and the standards of steak and chicken parma.

Madcowes
CAFE, DELI $

(☑03-5952 2560; 17 The Esplanade, Cowes; mains $7-17; ☺breakfast & lunch) Stylish cafe-foodstore looking out to the main beach.

Try the ricotta hotcakes or the grazing platter, and browse the selection of wine and produce.

CAPE WOOLAMAI

White Salt
FISH & CHIPS $

(☑03-5956 6336; 7 Vista Pl; fish from $5, meal packs from $20; ☺lunch & dinner Fri-Sun, from 4.30pm Wed & Thu) White Salt serves the best fish and chips on the island – selected fish fillets and hand-cut chips, tempura prawns and marinated BBQ octopus salad with corn, pesto and lemon.

Curry Leaf
INDIAN $

(☑03-5956 6772; 9 Vista Pl; mains $12-18; ☺dinner Wed-Mon, lunch Fri-Sun; ☑) This cheery Indian restaurant and takeaway is popular for its piquant curries.

RHYLL

Foreshore Bar & Restaurant
PUB FARE $$

(☑03-5956 9520; 11 Beach Rd, Rhyll; mains $18-34; ☺lunch & dinner) The water views from the timber deck of the classy village pub and restaurant complement your lunchtime fish and chips or bowl of mussels.

❶ Information

Phillip Island Visitors Centres (☑1300 366 422, 03-5956 7447; www.visitphillipisland. com; ☺9am-5pm, till 6pm school holidays; ☑) Newhaven (895 Phillip Island Tourist Rd); Cowes (cnr Thompson & Church Sts) The main visitor centre for the island is on the main road in Newhaven, and there's a smaller centre at Cowes.

Waterfront Internet Service (☑03-5952 3312; Shop 1/130 Thompson Ave, Cowes; per hr $6; ☺9am-5pm Mon-Fri, 10am-1pm Sat; @🛜)

❶ Getting There & Away

By car, Phillip Island can only be accessed across the bridge at San Remo to Newhaven. From Melbourne take the Monash Fwy (M1) and exit at Packenham, joining the South Gippsland Hwy at Koo Wee Rup.

Bus

V/Line (☑13 61 96; www.vline.com.au) has train/bus services from Melbourne's Southern Cross Station via Dandenong Station or Koo Wee Rup ($10.40, 2½ hours). There are no direct services.

Ferry

Inter Island Ferries (☑03-9585 5730; www.interislandferries.com.au; return adult/child/bike $21/10/8) runs between Stony Point on the Mornington Peninsula and Cowes via French

Island (45 minutes). There are two sailings on Monday and Wednesday, and three on Tuesday, Thursday, Friday, Saturday and Sunday.

❶ Getting Around

Hire bicycles from **Ride On Bikes** (☑03-5952 2533; www.rideonbikes.com.au; 43 Thompson Ave, Cowes; half/full day $25/35).

GREAT OCEAN ROAD

The Great Ocean Road (B100) is one of Australia's most famous road-touring routes. It takes travellers past world-class surfing breaks, through pockets of rainforest and calm seaside towns, and under koala-filled tree canopies. It shows off heathlands, dairy farms and sheer limestone cliffs and gets you up close and personal with the dangerous crashing surf of the Southern Ocean. Walk it, drive it, enjoy it.

Geelong

POP 216,000

Geelong is a confident town proud of its two icons: Geelong football team (aka the Cats) and the Ford Motor Company. The Cats have had a fair run in the AFL recently, winning the Grand Final in 2007 (for the first time

in 44 years) and again in 2009, while Ford, Geelong's other blue-and-white icon, continues to make manufacturing Geelong's largest employer.

The Wathaurong people – the original inhabitants of Geelong – called the area Jillong. Today's Geelong has a new bypass, so travellers can skip the city and head straight to the Great Ocean Road, however there are plenty of reasons to stop.

◉ Sights & Activities

Wander Geelong's revamped waterfront, and locate Jan Mitchell's 111 **painted bollards**. At Eastern Beach, stop for a splash about at the always accessible (and free) art-deco bathing pavilion, opposite the promenade.

FREE **Geelong Art Gallery**   ART GALLERY
(www.geelonggallery.org.au; Little Malop St; ☺10am-5pm) This gallery houses over 4000 works in one of the city's most impressive buildings. Its Australian collection is strong and includes Frederick McCubbin's 1890 *A Bush Burial*.

National Wool Museum   MUSEUM
(www.nwm.vic.gov.au; 26 Moorabool St; adult/child/family $7.50/4/20; ☺9.30am-5pm) This museum showcases the history, politics and heritage of wool growing in a lovely 1872 bluestone building.

Great Ocean Road & Southwest Coast

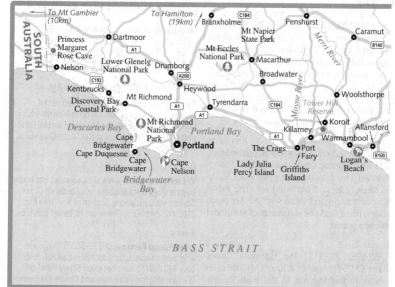

Geelong Helicopters

HELICOPTER RIDES

(☑0422 515 151; www.geelonghelicopters.com. au; flights adult/child $45/35) Check out Bells Beach from the air. Operates from the waterfront.

Bay City Seaplanes

SEAPLANE RIDES

(☑0438 840 205; www.baycityseaplanes.com. au; flights per person from $35 per person) Swirl around the Aireys Inlets lighthouse on a scenic flight. Operates from the waterfront.

🛏 Sleeping

Gatehouse on Ryrie

GUESTHOUSE $

(☑0417 545 196; www.gatehouseonryrie.com.au; 83 Yarra St; d incl breakfast $75-120; @🛜) This is the best choice for budget travellers; it was built in 1897, has timber floorboards throughout, spacious rooms and a communal kitchen and lounge area. Upstairs rooms share bathrooms.

Haymarket

BOUTIQUE HOTEL $$$

(☑03-5221 1174; www.haymarkethotel.com.au; 244 Moorabool St; d incl breakfast from $200; ✳🛜) Luxurious rooms in this historic building are furnished with French antiques matching the building's age (1855). The six bedrooms have modern en suites and flat-screen TVs with cable, and the ground floor's 'honesty bar' is a refreshing and swanky sight. It's a kid-free zone.

🍴 Eating

Go!

CAFE $

(www.cafego.com.au; 37 Bellarine St; mains from $8; ☺breakfast & lunch Mon-Sat) Go! is a fun cafe that serves great food in a riot of colour and amusement. The covered courtyard out the back is huge and welcoming, and staff could not be sweeter.

Mr Hyde

CAFE $$

(www.myhyde.com.au; 11 Malop St; mains $15-23; ☺breakfast, lunch & dinner Tue-Sun) This vast old bank building is filled with booths, secret rooms and stunning bathrooms. Dinner offers meze-style dishes (like felafel-encrusted lamb cutlets) and a range of Turkish pizzas. Breakfast includes herb omelette and organic granola.

Le Parisien

FRENCH $$$

(☑03-5229 3110; www.leparisien.com.au; 15 Eastern Beach Rd; mains $40-45; ☺lunch & dinner) Feast on classic French cuisine *à l'Australienne* (try the kangaroo fillet with bush-tomato chutney) right on the water.

🍷 Drinking

CQ

COCKTAIL BAR

(The City Quarter; www.thecityquarter.com.au; Cunningham Pier; ☺noon-late Wed-Sun) Cunningham Pier's redevelopment has brought a restaurant, cafe and boutique bar to this

0   50 km
0   30 miles

Lismore
Lake Gnarpurt
B140
Cressy
To Ballarat (45km)
C143
To Melbourne (48km)
C148
Teesdale
Inverleigh
A300
M1
C165
Lake Murdeduke
Geelong
Mortlake
C164
C146
B120
B156
Lake Corangamite
A1
Camperdown
Lake Colac
Winchelsea
B100
Terang
Torquay
Cobden
Colac
Birregurra
Bells Beach
Deans Marsh
Otway National Park
Anglesea
C164
C155
Curdies River
Aireys Inlet
Fairhaven
Nullawarre
Timboon
Gellibrand
Forrest
Otway Ranges
Lorne
Peter-borough
Port Campbell
B156
Lake Elizabeth
Cumberland River
The Grotto
London Bridge
The Arch
Port Campbell National Park
Beech Forest
Otway National Park
Wye River
Princetown
Lavers Hill
Kennett River
Cape Patton
Loch Ard Gorge
Twelve Apostles
Gibson Steps
Melba Gully
Wongarra
Skenes Creek
Johanna
Glenaire
Apollo Bay
Blanket Bay
BASS STRAIT
Cape Otway

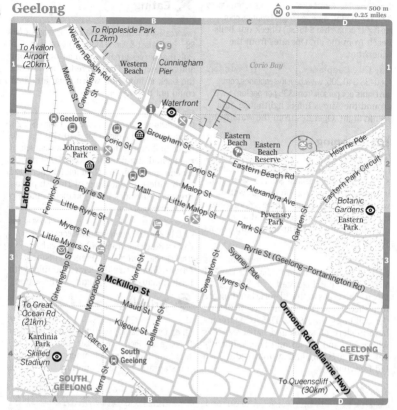

Geelong

◉ Sights
1 Geelong Art Gallery A2
2 National Wool Museum......................B2

◉ Activities, Courses & Tours
3 Bathing Pavilion..................................D2

◉ Sleeping
4 Gatehouse on Ryrie B3
5 Haymarket A3

◉ Eating
6 Go! B3
7 Le Parisien...B2
8 Mr Hyde...B2

◉ Drinking
9 CQ B1

stunning location. Climb the sweeping steps to CQ, and check out its smart fit-out, and cocktail and tapas menus.

ⓘ Information

Geelong & Great Ocean Road Visitors Centre (www.greatoceanroad.org; Princes Hwy, Little River; ☺9am-5pm) Located at the service station in Little River, about 20km from Geelong.

National Wool Museum Visitors Centre (www. visitgreatoceanroad.org.au; 26 Moorabool St; ☺9am-5pm) General info centre located at the Wool Museum.

ⓘ Getting There & Away

Air

Jetstar (☎13 15 38; www.jetstar.com.au) and **Tiger** (☎03-9335 3033; www.tigerairways. com) airlines run domestic services from nearby Avalon Airport.

Bus

Avalon Airport Shuttle (☑03-5278 8788; www.avalonairportshuttle.com.au) Meets flights at Avalon Airport and travels to Geelong ($17, 35 minutes) and Lorne ($70, 1¾ hours).

Gull Airport Service (☑03-5222 4966; www.gull.com.au; 45 McKillop St) Has 14 services a day between Geelong and Melbourne's Tullamarine Airport ($30, 1¼ hours).

McHarry's Buslines (☑03-5223 2111; www.mcharrys.com.au) Runs frequent buses to Torquay and the Bellarine Peninsula departing from Geelong Station ($3.20 for two-hour tickets).

V/Line (☑13 61 96; www.vline.com.au) Buses run from Geelong to Apollo Bay ($13, 2½ hours, two to four daily) via Torquay ($3.50, 25 minutes) and Lorne ($8.50, 1½ hours). On Monday, Wednesday and Friday a bus continues to Port Campbell ($24, four hours) and Warrnambool ($27, six hours).

Car

The 25km Geelong Ring Rd runs from Corio to Waurn Ponds, bypassing Geelong entirely. To get to the city, stay on the Princes Hwy (M1).

Train

V/Line (☑13 61 96; www.vline.com.au) runs from **Geelong Train Station** (☑03-5226 6525; Gordon Ave) to Melbourne's Southern Cross Station ($9, one hour, frequently). Trains also head to Warrnambool ($19, 2½ hours, three daily).

Torquay

POP 15700

In the 1960s and '70s, Torquay was just another sleepy seaside town. Back then surfing in Australia was a decidedly counter-cultural pursuit, and its devotees were crusty hippy drop-outs living in clapped-out Kombis, smoking pot and making off with your daughters. Since then surfing has become unabashedly mainstream and a huge transglobal business. The town's proximity to world-famous Bells Beach and status as home of two iconic surf brands – Rip-curl and Quicksilver, both initially wetsuit makers – ensures Torquay is the undisputed capital of Australian surfing.

⊙ Sights & Activities

Surfworld Museum　　　　　MUSEUM
(www.surfworld.org.au; Surf City Plaza, Beach Rd; adult/child/family $10/6/20; ⊙9am-5pm) Imbedded at the rear of the Surf City Plaza is this homage to Australian surfing, with shifting exhibits, a theatre and displays of old photos and monster balsa mals.

Spring Creek Horse Rides　　HORSE RIDING
(☑03-5266 1541; www.springcreekhorserides.com.au; 245 Portheath Rd, Bellbrae; 1/2hr rides $35/60) Guided horse rides through Spring Creek Valley.

Two-hour surfing lessons start at $50 at the following places:

Go Ride A Wave　　　　SURFING LESSONS
(☑1300 132 441; www.gorideawave.com.au; 1/15 Bell St, Torquay; 143b Great Ocean Rd, Anglesea; ⊙9am-5pm)

Torquay Surfing Academy　SURFING LESSONS
(☑03-5261 2022; www.torquaysurf.com.au; 34a Bell St, Torquay; ⊙9am-5pm)

Westcoast Surf School　　SURFING LESSONS
(☑03-5261 2241; www.westcoastsurfschool.com; ⊙9am-5pm summer).

🛏 Sleeping

Bellbrae Harvest　　　APARTMENTS $$$
(☑03-5266 2100; www.bellbraeharvest.com.au; 45 Portreath Rd; d $200; ❄) Far from the madding crowd, here are three separate (and stunning) split-level apartments looking onto a dam. Expect rainwater shower heads, kitchenettes, huge flat-screen TVs and lots and lots of peace.

Bells Beach Lodge　　　　HOSTEL $
(☑03-5261 7070; www.bellsbeachlodge.com.au; 51-53 Surfcoast Hwy; dm/d $25/65; @) This grungy budget option is on the highway and has shared facilities and surfboard and bike hire. It's especially popular during events and caters for large groups (can be noisy!).

**Torquay Foreshore
Caravan Park**　　　CAMPGROUND, CABINS $
(☑03-5261 2496; www.torquaycaravanpark.com.au; unpowered sites $30-50, d cabins $75-250) Just behind Back Beach, this is the largest camping ground on the Surf Coast. It has good facilities and new premium-priced cabins with sea views.

✕ Eating

Moby　　　　　　　　　CAFE $
(41 The Esplanade; mains $9-16; ⊙breakfast & lunch) This old weatherboard on the Esplanade harks back to a time when Torquay was simple, not to say its meals are not complicated; fill up on a linguini or honey-roasted lamb souvlaki.

Scorched　　　MODERN AUSTRALIAN $$
(☑03-5261 6142; www.scorched.com.au; 17 The Esplanade; mains $26-36; ⊙lunch Fri-Sun, dinner

Melbourne to Geelong	75km	1 hr
Geelong to Torquay	21km	15 min
Torquay to Anglesea	21km	15 min
Anglesea to Aireys Inlet	10km	10 min
Aireys Inlet to Lorne	22km	15 min
Lorne to Apollo Bay	45km	1 hr
Apollo Bay to Port Campbell	88km	70 min
Port Campbell to Warrnambool	66km	1 hr
Warrnambool to Port Fairy	28km	20 min
Port Fairy to Portland	72km	1hr
Portland to Melbourne	440km	6½ hr

Wed-Sun) This might be the swankiest restaurant in Torquay, overlooking the waterfront, with classy understated decor and windows that open right up to let the sea breeze in. Try the seasonal grazing plate.

ℹ Information

Torquay Visitors Centre (www.greatocean road.org; Surf City Plaza, Beach Rd; @) Torquay has a well-resourced tourist office next to the Surfworld Museum.

ℹ Getting There & Away

BUS McHarry's Buslines (☏03-5223 2111; www.mcharrys.com.au) runs buses hourly between 9am and 9pm from Geelong Station to Torquay ($3.20, 30 minutes). **V/Line** (☏13 61 96; www.vline.com.au) has four buses daily from Geelong to Torquay (two on weekends).
CAR Torquay is 15 minutes south of Geelong on the B100.

Torquay to Anglesea

About 7km from Torquay is **Bells Beach**. The powerful point break at Bells is part of international surfing folklore (it's here, in name only, that Keanu Reeves and Patrick Swayze had their ultimate showdown in the film *Point Break*). It's notoriously inconsistent, but when the long right-hander is working it's one of the longest rides in the country. Since 1973, Bells has hosted the **Rip Curl Pro** (www.aspworldtour.com) every Easter – *the* glamour event on the world-championship ASP World Tour. The Rip Curl Pro regularly decamps to Johanna, two hours west, when fickle Bells isn't working.

Nine kilometres southwest of Torquay is the turn-off to spectacular **Point Addis**, 3km down this road. It's a vast sweep of pristine 'clothing optional' beach that attracts surfers, hang-gliders and swimmers. At Point Addis there's a signposted **Koorie Cultural Walk**, a 1km circuit trail to the beach through the **Ironbark Basin** nature reserve.

The **Surf Coast Walk** (www.surfcoast.vic. gov.au/walkingtracks.htm) follows the coastline from Jan Juc to near Aireys Inlet, and can be done in stages – the full route takes 11 hours. It's marked on the *Surf Coast Touring Map*, available from tourist offices.

Anglesea

POP 2300

Anglesea's **Main Beach** is the ideal spot to learn to surf, while sheltered **Point Roadknight Beach** is good for kiddies. Check out the resident **kangaroo** population at the town's golf course, or hire a paddle boat and cruise up the Anglesea River.

✸ Activities

Go Ride A Wave   SURFING
(☏1300 132 441; www.gorideawave.com.au; 143b Great Ocean Rd; ⊙9am-5pm) Rents out kayaks and surfboards and runs two-hour surfing lessons (from $75).

⌁ Sleeping

Anglesea Backpackers   HOSTEL **$**
(☏03-5263 2664; www.angleseabackpackers. com; 40 Noble St; dm/d $35/95) This simple backpackers (just two dorm rooms and one triple) is clean, bright and welcoming, and

in winter the fire glows warmly in the living room.

lighthouse is still operational (tours run until 3pm) and there's a sweet cafe near its base.

Rivergums B&B
B&B $$

(☑03-5263 3066; www.anglesearivergums.com.au; 10 Bingley Pde; d $100-160; ❄) Tucked by the river with tranquil views, this B&B has two spacious, tastefully furnished rooms (a self-contained bungalow and a room attached to the house).

Anglesea Overboard
COTTAGE $$

(☑03-5289 7424; www.overboardcottages.com.au; 39c O'Donohue Rd; d from $195; ❄) This one-bedroom cottage has ocean views, a spa and a wood fire for those chilly winter nights. Designed for couples, but accepting babies and dogs (check first), there's also one in Aireys Inlet. Minimum two-night stay.

✕ Eating

Red Till
CAFE $

(143a Great Ocean Rd; ⊙breakfast & lunch Sat-Mon & Thu, daily summer) This cafe, on the outskirts of town, does coffee and retro decor as good as its Melbourne peers do – only the pace of life is different.

River Vu
MODERN AUSTRALIAN $$

(113 Great Ocean Rd; mains $21-38; ⊙breakfast, lunch & dinner Tue-Sun) It's changed its name a fair few times, but this incarnation offers a simple menu with generous servings. The tables on the front deck make for fine evening alfresco dining.

❶ Information

Visitors Centre (16/87 Great Ocean Rd; ⊙9am-5pm Sep-May, 10am-4pm Jun-Aug) Located opposite Angahook Cafe, this new information centre sits beside an equally new BBQ area.

❶ Getting There & Away

CAR The new Geelong bypass has reduced the time it takes to drive from Melbourne to Anglesea to around 75 minutes.

BUS V/Line has services linking Anglesea with Geelong and the Great Ocean Road.

Aireys Inlet
POP 1200

Aireys Inlet is home to glorious stretches of beach, including horse-friendly **Fairhaven** and hang-glider hot spot **Moggs Creek**.

The 34m-high **Split Point Lighthouse** and its keepers' cottages were built in 1891. The

⊙ Activities

Blazing Saddles
HORSE RIDING

(☑03-5289 7322; www.blazingsaddlestrailrides.com.au; Lot 1 Bimbadeen Dr; 1¼/2¼hr rides $40/65) Hop on a horse and head into the bush or along the stunning beach.

🛏 Sleeping

Cimarron B&B
B&B $$

(☑03-5289 7044; www.cimarron.com.au; 105 Gilbert St; d $185; ☎) This house was built in 1979 from local timbers using only wooden pegs and shiplap joins, and is an idyllic getaway with views over Point Roadknight. It's rustic yet sophisticated. There are two unique, loft-style doubles with vaulted timber ceilings and a den-like apartment. Out back, it's all state park and wildlife. Gay-friendly, but no kids.

Lightkeepers Inn
MOTEL $$

(☑03-5289 6666; www.lightkeepersinn.com.au; 64 Great Ocean Rd; d $110; ☎❄) Expect clean motel rooms with extra thick walls for peace and quiet. Trevor runs the place and has an excellent knowledge of local walks and mountain-biking opportunities.

✕ Eating

A La Grecque
GREEK $$$

(☑03-5289 6922; www.alagreque.com.au; 60 Great Ocean Rd; mains $28-36; ⊙breakfast, lunch & dinner Wed-Sun, daily summer) This modern Greek taverna is outstanding and serves meze including cured kingfish with apple, celery and a lime dressing, and mains like char-grilled king prawns with fresh oregano. The verandah is an ideal spot to lunch mid-drive.

Lorne
POP 1000

Lorne has an incredible natural beauty; tall gum trees line its hilly streets and Loutit Bay gleams irresistibly. Lorne gets busy; in summer you'll be competing with day trippers for restaurant seats and boutique bargains, but, thronged with tourists or not, Lorne is a lovely place to hang out.

⊙ Sights & Activities

Qdos Art Gallery
GALLERY

(☑03-5289 1989; www.qdosarts.com; 35 Allenvale Rd; ⊙8.30am-6pm Thu-Mon, daily school holidays) Qdos, tucked in the hills behind Lorne,

always has something arty in its galleries, and sculptures dot its lush landscape. Its cafe fare is nothing but delicious, and you can stay the night in one of their luxury Zen treehouses ($200 per night, two-night minimum, no kids).

Erskine Falls
WATERFALL

Head out of town to see this lovely waterfall. It's an easy walk to the viewing platform or 250 (often slippery) steps down to its base, from which you can explore further or head back on up.

⭐ Festivals & Events

Falls Festival
MUSIC FESTIVAL

(www.fallsfestival.com; tickets $350) A three-day knees-up over New Year's on a farm out of town. A top line-up of rock and indie groups; tickets include camping.

🛏 Sleeping

There's often a minimum two-night stay on weekends in Lorne, and high-season rates can be nearly double winter prices. For other options, ask at the visitors centre.

TOP CHOICE Allenvale Cottages
COTTAGES $$

(☑03-5289 1450; www.allenvale.com.au; 150 Allenvale Rd; d from $175) These four self-contained early-1900s timber cottages, that each sleep four (or more), have been luxuriously restored. They're 2km northwest of Lorne, arrayed among shady trees and green lawns, complete with bridge and babbling brook. It's ideal for families.

Chapel
COTTAGE $$$

(☑03-5289 2622; thechapellorne@bigpond.com; 45 Richardson Blvd; d $200; ❄) Outstanding – this contemporary two-level bungalow has been lifted from the pages of a glossy magazine, with tasteful Asian furnishings, splashes of colour and bay windows that open into the forest. It's secluded and romantic, with double shower and complimentary robes.

Great Ocean Road Cottages & Backpackers YHA
HOSTEL $

(☑03-5289 1070; www.yha.com.au; 10 Erskine Ave; tents $25, dm $20-30, d $55-75, cottages $170) Tucked away in the bush among the cockatoos and koalas, this two-storey timber lodge has spacious dorms, bargain tents with beds already set up, and top-value doubles. The more expensive A-frame cottages sleep up to six with kitchens and en suites.

Lorne Foreshore Caravan Park
CARAVAN PARK $

(☑1300 736 533; www.lornecaravanpark.com.au; 2 Great Ocean Rd; powered sites from $30-50, d cabins from $60) Book here for Lorne's five caravan parks. Of these Erskine River Park is the prettiest; on the left-hand side as you enter Lorne, just before the bridge. Book well ahead for peak-season stays.

🍴 Eating

Ba Ba Lu Bar
SPANISH $$$

(www.babalubar.com.au; 6a Mountjoy Pde; mains $32-42; ⊗breakfast, lunch & dinner) It's all a bit Spanish at Ba Ba Lu Bar, what, with its wintery paella nights and Chilean singers popping in for a gig in summer. The menu has inspired tapas and plenty of meat-based mains, and the bar kicks on into the wee hours.

Kafe Kaos
CAFE $

(www.kafekaos.com.au; 52 Mountjoy Pde; lunch $8-15; ⊗breakfast & lunch) Bright and perky, Kafe Kaos typifies Lorne's relaxed foodie philosophy – barefoot patrons in boardies or bikinis tucking into first-class paninis, bruschettas, burgers and chips.

Bottle of Milk
BURGERS $

(52 Mountjoy Pde; burgers from $8.50; ⊗breakfast, lunch & dinner) Sit back on one of the old-school chairs at this cool version of a diner, and tuck into a classic burger stacked with fresh ingredients.

ℹ Information

Lorne Visitors Centre (☑1300 891 152; www.visitsurfcoast.com.au; 15 Mountjoy Pde; ⊗9am-5pm) Stacks of information, helpful staff and an accommodation booking service.

Cumberland River

Just 7km southwest of Lorne is Cumberland River. There's nothing here – no shops or houses – other than the wonderful Cumberland River Holiday Park (☑03-5289 1790; www.cumberlandriver.com.au; Great Ocean Rd; unpowered sites $37, en-suite cabins from $105). This splendidly located bushy camping ground is next to a lovely river and high craggy cliffs that rise on the far side.

Wye River

POP 140

The Great Ocean Road snakes spectacularly around the cliff-side from Cumberland River before reaching this little town with big ideas.

HARD YAKKA

The first sections of the Great Ocean Road were constructed by hand (using picks, shovels and crowbars) by returned WWI soldiers. Work began in September 1919 and the road between Anglesea and Apollo Bay was completed in 1932.

🛏 Sleeping & Eating

Wye River Foreshore Camping Reserve CAMPGROUND $
(☑03-5289 0412; sites $30; ☉Dec-April) This camping site offers powered beachside sites during summer.

TOP CHOICE Wye General CAFE $$
(www.thewyegeneral.com; 35 Great Ocean Rd; dinner $15-26; ☉breakfast & lunch daily, dinner Fri & Sat winter, daily summer) This cafe has marched into town and there's nothing general about it. From homemade sourdough to perfect coffee, this smart indoor-outdoor joint has polished concrete floors, timber features and an impressive confidence.

Kennett River

About 5km along from Wye River is Kennett River, which has some truly great **koala spotting** in the town itself, and you'll also spot the furry creatures above the Great Ocean Road towards Apollo Bay. In town, just behind the caravan park, walk 200m up Grey River Rd and you'll see bundles of sleepy koalas clinging to the branches. *Ooh aah!* **Glow worms** light up the same stretch at night (take a torch).

🛏 Sleeping

Kennett River Holiday Park CAMPGROUND, CABINS $$
(☑1300 664 417, 03-5289 0272; www.kennettriver. com; unpowered/powered sites $29/35, d cabins from $105; @🛜) This friendly bush holiday park has free wireless internet, free BBQs and plans are afoot for a camp kitchen.

Apollo Bay

POP 1800

Apollo Bay is synonymous with music festivals, the Otways and lovely beaches, and it's one of the least claustrophobic hamlets along the Great Ocean Road. Majestic rolling hills provide a postcard backdrop to the town, while broad, white-sand beaches dominate the foreground. It's an ideal base for exploring magical Cape Otway and Otway National Park.

◉ Sights & Activities

Community Market MARKET
(www.apollobay.com/market_place; ☉8.30am-4.30pm Sat) This market is held along the main strip and is the perfect spot for picking up local apples, locally made souvenirs and just-what-you've-always-wanted table lamps made from tree stumps.

Mark's Walking Tours WALKING TOURS
(☑0417 983 985; www.greatoceanwalk.asn.au/ markstours; 2-3hr tours adult/child $50/15) Take a walk around the area with local Mark Brack, son of the Cape Otway lighthouse keeper. He knows this stretch of coast, its history and ghosts better than anyone around. His daily tours include shipwreck tours, historical tours, glow-worm tours and Great Ocean Walk tours. Minimum two people.

Apollo Bay Sea Kayaking KAYAKING TOURS
(☑0405 495 909; www.apollobaysurfkayak.com. au; 2hr tours $65) Head out to an Australian fur-seal colony on a two-seated kayak. Tours depart from Marengo beach and are suitable for children over 12.

Otway Expeditions OUTDOOR ADVENTURE
(☑03-5237 6341; http://otwayexpeditions.tripod. com; argo rides from $45) Take a dual suspension bike through the Otways (minimum six people), or go nuts in an amphibious all-terrain 8x8 argo buggy.

🎊 Festivals & Events

Apollo Bay Music Festival MUSIC FESTIVAL
(☑03-5237 6761; www.apollobaymusicfestival. com; weekend pass adult/youth/under 13 $162/90/free) Held over a weekend in early April this three-day festival features classical, folk, blues, jazz, rock and some edgy contemporary sounds too. The town truly comes alive.

🛏 Sleeping

TOP CHOICE YHA Eco Beach HOSTEL $
(☑03-5237 7899; 5 Pascoe St; dm $32-38, d $88-95, f $109-145; 🌐@) Even if you're not on a budget

WALKING THE GREAT OCEAN ROAD

The multiday Great Ocean Walk (www.greatoceanwalk.com.au) starts at Apollo Bay and runs all the way to the Twelve Apostles. It's possible to start at one point and arrange a pick up at another (there are few public transport options). You can do shorter walks or the whole 104km trek over six days. Designated (and free) camp sites are spread along the Great Ocean Walk. Walk 91 (☑03-5237 1189; www.walk91.com.au) arranges transport, equipment hire and can take your backpack to your destination for you. GOR Shuttle (☑03-5237 9278, 0428 379 278) is a recommended shuttle service for luggage and walkers; they'll pick you up when your walking's done.

this three-million-dollar, architect-designed hostel is an outstanding place to stay. Its eco-credentials are too many to list here, but it's a wonderful piece of architecture with great lounge areas, kitchens, TV rooms, internet lounge and rooftop terraces.

Nelson's Perch B&B　　　　　B&B $$
(☑03-5237 7176; www.nelsonsperch.com; 54 Nelson St; d $160; ❄@☎) Nelson's looks fresher than some of the town's weary B&Bs. There are three rooms, each with a courtyard, and free wireless internet.

Surfside Backpackers　　　　HOSTEL $
(☑03-5237 7263; www.surfsidebackpacker.com; cnr Great Ocean Rd & Gambier St; dm $23-30, d $60) So, the rooms are a little cramped, but the lounge is blessed with large windows looking out onto the ocean, making this homey place worthwhile.

 Eating

Apollo Bay Fishermen's
Co-operative　　　　　　　SEAFOODL $
(Breakwater Rd; ⊙10am-4pm) Sells fresh fish and seafood from the wharf.

Vista　　　　　　　　　SEAFOOD $$
(www.thevistaseafoodrestaurant.com; 155 Great Ocean Rd, mains $25-35; ⊙dinner) This is fab, upmarket dining on the main drag. Spend hours cracking a locally caught crab, supported in your endeavours by local wine.

Café Nautigals　　　　　　CAFE $
(1/57-59 Great Ocean Rd; mains $14-16; ⊙breakfast & lunch daily, dinner in summer; @) A baby stack of pancakes and a coffee will use up a tenner, which is not bad in anyone's books.

La Bimba　　MODERN AUSTRALIAN $$$
(125 Great Ocean Rd; mains $25-45; ⊙breakfast, lunch & dinner Wed-Mon) This upstairs Mod Oz restaurant is outstanding – definitely worth the splurge. It's a warm, relaxed

smart-casual place with views, friendly service and a good wine list.

❶ Information

Great Ocean Road Visitors Centre (☑03-5237 6529; 100 Great Ocean Rd; ⊙9am-5pm) Has an impressive 'eco-centre' with displays on Aboriginal history, rainforests, shipwrecks and the building of the Great Ocean Road.

Parks Victoria (☑03-5237 2500; www.parkweb.vic.gov.au; cnr Oak Ave & Montrose St; ⊙8am-4.30pm Mon-Fri) Can help with camping bookings and information on road conditions.

Around Apollo Bay

Seventeen kilometres past Apollo Bay is **Maits Rest Rainforest Boardwalk**, an easy 20-minute rainforest-gully walk. Inland, 5km from Beech Forrest, is the Otway Fly (☑03-5235 9200; www.otwayfly.com; Phillips Track; adult/child/family $22/9.50/55; ⊙9am-4.30pm). It's an elevated steel walkway in the forest canopy with a wavy lookout tower.

Cape Otway

Cape Otway is the second-most southerly point of mainland Australia (after Wilsons Promontory) and one of the wettest parts of the state. This coastline is particularly beautiful, rugged and dangerous. More than 200 ships came to grief between Cape Otway and Port Fairy between the 1830s and 1930s, which led to the 'Shipwreck Coast' moniker.

The turn-off for Lighthouse Rd, which leads 12km down to the lighthouse, is 21km from Apollo Bay. The Cape Otway Lighthouse (☑03-5237 9240; www.lightstation.com; adult/child/family $17/8/42; ⊙9am-5pm) is the oldest surviving lighthouse on mainland Australia and was built in 1848 by more than 40 stonemasons without mortar or

cement. Other sites nearby include **Parker Hill**, **Point Franklin** and **Crayfish Beach**.

🛏 Sleeping

Blanket Bay CAMPGROUND $
(☎13 19 63; www.parkweb.vic.gov.au; sites $20) Blanket Bay is serene (depending on your neighbours) and the nearby beach is beautiful. It's not really a secret; in fact it's so popular from Christmas to late January that sites must be won by ballot (held in October). Contact Parks Victoria for bookings.

Lighthouse Keeper's Residence B&B $$$
(Cape Otway Lighthouse; www.lightstation.com; d from $200) There is a range of options at this windswept spot; you can book out the whole Head Lightkeeper's House (sleeping 16), or the smaller Manager's B&B (sleeping two).

🌿 **Great Ocean Ecolodge** ECO-LODGE $$$
(☎03-5237 9297; www.capeotwaycentre.com; 635 Lighthouse Rd, s/d from $160/320) Prebook a room at this eco-lodge and check out the native animals, as the attached Cape Otway Centre for Conservation Ecology also serves as an animal hospital for a menagerie of local fauna. The luxurious en-suite rooms in the post-and-beam, solar-powered, mud-brick homestead have bush-view decks and the centre offers guided walking tours and eco-activities.

Bimbi Park CAMPGROUND, CABINS $$
(☎03-5237 9246; www.bimbipark.com.au; Manna Gum Dr; unpowered sites $30, powered sites $35, d cabins $60-180) Down a dirt road 3km from the lighthouse is this horse-riding ranch with bush sites, fancy (and not-so-fancy) cabins and horse rides ($45 per hour).

Cape Otway to Port Campbell National Park

After Cape Otway, the Great Ocean Road levels out and enters the fertile Horden Vale flats, returning briefly to the coast at tiny Glenaire. Then the road returns inland and begins the climb up to Lavers Hill. On overcast or rainy days the hills here can be seriously fog-bound, and the twists and turns can be challenging when you can't see the end of your car bonnet.

Six kilometres north of Glenaire, a 5km detour goes down Red Johanna Rd winding through rolling hills and grazing cows to the wild thrashing surf of **Johanna Beach** (forget swimming). The world-famous Rip Curl

Pro surfing competition relocates here when Bells Beach isn't working.

🛏 Sleeping

Camping Ground CAMPGROUND
(Parks Victoria; ☎13 19 63; www.parkweb.vic.gov.au; campsites free) This Johanna campground is on a protected grassy area between the dunes and the rolling hills. Book ahead, but there are no fees due or permits required. There's an ablutions facility, but fires are banned and you'll need to bring in your own drinking water.

Boomerangs APARTMENTS $$$
(☎03-5237 4213; www.theboomerangs.com; cnr Great Ocean & Red Johanna Rds; d from $230) These boomerang-shaped cabins have vaulted ceilings, jarrah floorboards, leadlighting, spas and commanding views of the Johanna Valley. The on-site owners are lovely.

Port Campbell National Park

The road levels out after leaving the Otways and enters narrow, relatively flat scrubby escarpment lands that fall away to sheer, 70m cliffs along the coast between Princetown and Peterborough – a distinct change of scene. This is Port Campbell National Park – home to the Twelve Apostles – the most famous and most photographed stretch of the Great Ocean Road. For eons, waves and tides have crashed against the soft limestone rock, eroding, undercutting and carving out a fascinating series of rock stacks, gorges, arches and blowholes.

The **Gibson Steps**, hacked by hand into the cliffs in the 19th century by local landowner Hugh Gibson (and more recently replaced by concrete steps), lead down to feral Gibson Beach, an essential stop. This beach, and others along this stretch of coast, are not suitable for swimming because of strong currents and undertows – you can walk along the beach, but be careful not to be stranded by high tides or nasty waves. The lonely **Twelve Apostles** are rocky stacks that have been abandoned to the ocean by retreating headland. Today, only seven Apostles can be seen from the viewing platforms (see boxed text, p544). The understated roadside **lookout** (Great Ocean Rd; ☺9am-5pm), 6km past Princetown, has public toilets and a cafe. Helicopters zoom around the Twelve Apostles, giving passengers an amazing view of

HOW MANY APOSTLES?

The Twelve Apostles are not 12 in number, and, from all records, never have been. From the viewing platform you can clearly count seven Apostles, but maybe some obscure others? We consulted widely with Parks Victoria officers, tourist office staff and even the cleaner at the lookout, but it's still not clear. Locals tend to say 'It depends where you look from', which, really, is true.

The Apostles are called 'stacks' in geologic lingo, and the rock formations were originally called the 'Sow and Piglets'. Someone in the '60s (nobody can recall who) thought they might attract some tourists with a more venerable name, so they were renamed 'the Apostles'. Since apostles tend to come by the dozen, the number 12 was added sometime later. The two stacks on the eastern (Otway) side of the viewing platform are not technically Apostles – they're Gog and Magog (picking up on the religious nomenclature yet?).

So there aren't 12 stacks; in a boat or helicopter you might count 11. The soft limestone cliffs are dynamic and changeable, constantly eroded by the unceasing waves – one 70m-high stack collapsed into the sea in July 2005 and the Island Archway lost its archway in June 2009. If you look carefully at how the waves lick around the pointy part of the cliff base, you can see a new Apostle being born. The labour lasts many thousands of years.

the rocks. **12 Apostles Helicopters** (☑03-5598 6161; www.12apostleshelicopters.com.au) is just behind the car park at the lookout and offers a 10-minute tour covering the Twelve Apostles, Loch Ard Gorge, Sential Rock and Port Campbell from $95 per person.

Nearby **Loch Ard Gorge** is where the Shipwreck Coast's most famous and haunting tale unfolded when two young survivors of the wrecked iron clipper *Loch Ard* made it to shore (see boxed text, p546).

Port Campbell

POP 400

This small, windswept town is poised on a dramatic, natural bay, eroded from the surrounding limestone cliffs and almost perfectly rectangular in shape. It's a friendly place with some great bargain accommodation options, and makes an ideal spot for debriefing after the Twelve Apostles. The tiny bay has a lovely sandy beach, the only safe place for swimming along this tempestuous coast.

◉ Sights & Activities

There is stunning **diving** in the kelp forests, canyons and tunnels of the **Arches Marine Sanctuary** and to the *Loch Ard* wreck. There are shore dives from **Wild Dog Cove** and **Crofts Bay**. A 4.7km **Discovery Walk**, with signage, gives an introduction to the area's natural and historical features. It's just out of town on the way to Warrnambool.

Tours

Port Campbell Touring Company   TOURS
(☑03-5598 6424; www.portcampbelltouring.com.au; half-day tours $65) Runs Apostle Coast tours, a Loch Ard evening walk and fishing trips to Crofts Bay.

Port Campbell Boat Charters   FISHING
(☑03-5598 6411) Runs diving, scenic and fishing tours.

The following tours depart from Melbourne and cover the Great Ocean Road in a day:

Adventure Tours (☑1800 068 886; www.adventuretours.com.au; tours $130) Day-long trip along the Great Ocean Road to Port Campbell (and back).

Autopia Tours (☑03-9391 0261; www.autopiatours.com.au; tours $125) One day along the Great Ocean Road, dinner in Colac.

Go West Tours (☑1300 736 551; www.gowest.com.au; tour $125) Full-day tours exploring the Great Ocean Road.

Goin South (☑1800 009 858; www.goinsouth.com.au; tours $150) One-and-a-half day tours along Great Ocean Road and Warrnambool.

Otway Discovery (☑03-9654 5432; www.otwaydiscovery.com.au; tours $95) One-day Great Great Ocean tours including Bells and the Twelve Apostles.

Ride Tours (☑1800 605 120; www.ridetours.com.au; tours $180) Two-day, one-night trips along the Great Ocean Road.

Sleeping & Eating

Port Campbell Guesthouse GUESTHOUSE $
(☑0407 696 559; www.portcampbellguesthouse.
com.au; 54 Lord St; guesthouse/flashpackers per
person $35/38) It's great to find a home away
from home, and this property close to town
has a cosy house with four bedrooms out
back and a separate motel-style 'flashpack-
ers' section up front. Great for families.

Port Campbell Hostel HOSTEL $
(☑03-5598 6305; www.portcampbellhostel.com.
au; 18 Tregea St; dm/d $25/70; ☎) This brand
new, purpose-built double-storey backpackers has rooms with western views, a huge
shared kitchen and an even bigger lounge-
bar area. It's big on recycling and the toilets
are ecofriendly, too. Hang out in the lounge
and read the days' papers or get involved
with a Mills & Boon.

Room Six RESTAURANT $$
(28 Lord St; mains $15-30; ☺breakfast, lunch & din-
ner Fri-Wed) Come here for delightful dinners
(featuring all the good seafood of the area) or
a simple snack during the day. Although only
new, its ambience suggests a lovely maturity.

12 Rocks Cafe Bar CAFE $
(19 Lord St; mains $8-15; ☺breakfast, lunch & din-
ner) Watch flotsam wash up on the beach
from this busy place, which has the best
beachfront views. Try a local Otways beer
with a pasta or seafood main, or just duck
in for a coffee.

ℹ Information

Port Campbell Visitor Centre (☑1300 137
255; www.visit12apostles.com.au; 26 Morris St;
☺9am-5pm) Stacks of regional and accommo-
dation information and interesting shipwreck
displays are the anchor from the *Loch Ard* is out
the front, salvaged in 1978.

ℹ Getting There & Away

BUS V/Line buses leave Geelong on Monday,
Wednesday and Friday, and travel through Port
Campbell ($24, four hours) and onto Warrnam-
bool ($27, six hours).

Port Campbell to
Warrnambool

The Great Ocean Road continues west of
Port Campbell passing more rock stacks.
The next one is the Arch, offshore from
Point Hesse.

Nearby is London Bridge...fallen down!
Now sometimes called London Arch, it was
once a double-arched rock platform linked
to the mainland. Visitors could walk out
across a narrow natural bridge to the huge
rock formation. In January 1990, the bridge
collapsed leaving two terrified tourists ma-
rooned on the world's newest island – they
were eventually rescued by helicopter. Near-
by is the Grotto.

The Bay of Islands is 8km west of tiny
Peterborough, where a short walk from
the car park takes you to magnificent look-
out points.

You can't help but notice the acres and
acres of farming land here, and if you're driv-
ing keep an eye out for milk trucks pulling
slowly into and out of farms. Slightly tacky
Cheese World (www.cheeseworld.com.au; Great
Ocean Rd, Allansford; ☺9.30am-5pm Mon-Fri, 9am-
4pm Sat, 9am-3pm Sun) is opposite the area's
main dairy factory, and has a museum, res-
taurant, cheese cellar and tasty (and cheap)
milkshakes. It's 12km before Warrnambool.

The Great Ocean Road ends near here
where it meets the Princess Hwy, which con-
tinues through the traditional lands of the
Gunditjmara people into South Australia.

Warrnambool

POP 28,100

Warrnambool was originally a whaling and
sealing station – now it's booming as a major
regional commercial and whale-watching
centre. Its historic buildings, waterways and
tree-lined streets are attractive, and there's
a large student population who attend the
Warrnambool campus of Deakin University.
The major housing and commercial devel-
opment around the fringes of the city look
much like city suburbs anywhere in Austra-
lia, but the regions around the waterfront
have largely retained their considerable his-
toric charm.

◎ Sights & Activities

**Flagstaff Hill Maritime
Village** REPLICA MARITIME VILLAGE
(☑1800 556 111; www.flagstaffhill.com; Merri St;
adult/child/family $16/7/39; ☺9am-5pm). This
major tourist attraction is modelled on an
early Australian coastal port. See the cannon
and fortifications, built in 1887 to withstand
the perceived threat of Russian invasion, and
Shipwrecked (adult/child/family $26/14/67),
an engaging evening sound-and-laser show

THE WRECK OF THE LOCH ARD

The Victorian coastline between Cape Otway and Port Fairy was a notoriously treacherous stretch of water in the days of sailing ships, due to hidden reefs and frequent heavy fog. More than 80 vessels came to grief on this 120km stretch in just 40 years.

The most famous wreck was that of the iron-hulled clipper *Loch Ard*, which foundered off Mutton Bird Island at 4am on the final night of its long voyage from England in 1878. Of 37 crew and 19 passengers on board, only two survived. Eva Carmichael, a nonswimmer, clung to wreckage and was washed into a gorge, where apprentice officer Tom Pearce rescued her. Tom heroically climbed the sheer cliff and raised the alarm but no other survivors were found. Eva and Tom were both 19 years old, leading to speculation in the press about a romance, but nothing actually happened – they never saw each other again and Eva soon returned to Ireland (this time, perhaps not surprisingly) via steamship.

of the *Loch Ard*'s plunge. Grab a meal at Pippies by the Bay (see below) while you're here.

Logan's Beach Whale-Watching Platform
WHALE WATCHING

Southern right whales come to mate and nurse their bubs in the waters off Logan's Beach from July to September, breaching and fluking off the platform. It's a major tourist drawcard, but sightings are not guaranteed.

FREE Warrnambool Art Gallery
ART GALLERY

(www.warrnambool.vic.gov.au; 165 Timor St; ⊙10am-5pm Mon-Fri, noon-5pm Sat & Sun) Head here to see the permanent Australian collection which includes such notable painters as Tom Roberts, James Gleeson and Arthur Boyd.

Rundell's Mahogany Trail Rides
HORSE RIDING

(☑0408 589 546; www.rundellshorseriding.com.au; 2hr beach rides $65) Get to know some of Warrnambool's quiet beach spots by horseback.

🛏 Sleeping

Hotel Warrnambool
PUB $$

(☑03-5562 2377; www.hotelwarrnambool.com.au; cnr Koroit & Kepler Sts; d with/without bathroom $140/110; ❄@) Recent renovations in this historic 1894 pub have done wonders with the rooms, which have plasma TVs and access to a kitchenette and lounge. Some have bathrooms and balconies. Downstairs is one of the friendliest pub-eateries in town.

Atwood Motor Inn
MOTEL $$

(☑03-5562 7144; www.atwoodmotorinn.com.au; 8 Spence St; d from $105; ❄🛜) Expect spacious motel-style rooms with flat-screen TVs and bathrooms big enough to wash a (small)

whale in. The standard doubles are the smallest, but are still comfortable.

Warrnambool Beach Backpackers
HOSTEL $

(☑03-5562 4874; www.beachbackpackers.com.au; 17 Stanley St; dm/d $28/80; ❄@) Close to the sea, this former museum has a huge living area with a bar, internet access, kitchen and free pick-up. Its rooms, however, could do with a freshen up. It's a good place to seek casual employment.

🍴 Eating & Drinking

Donnelly's Restaurant
MODERN AUSTRALIAN $$

(78 Liebig St; mains $24-31; ⊙lunch & dinner Tue-Sun, daily in summer) This smart restaurant makes a big deal of its steaks and seafood, and it's no wonder: both are as local as you can get and very satisfying.

Wyton
CAFE $

(www.wytonevents.com; 91 Kepler St; mains $12; ⊙breakfast & lunch Mon-Fri, breakfast Sat) Come here for sophisticated breakfasts, excellent coffee and healthy lunches (including spiced carrot and risoni pasta) that you can take-away.

Pippies by the Bay
MODERN AUSTRALIAN $$

(Flagstaff Hill Maritime Village, Merri St; mains $28-32; ⊙lunch & dinner daily, breakfast Sat & Sun) A fine restaurant in the Flagstaff Hill visitors centre; make an evening of it with a meal and show, or just pop in for a weekend breakfast and admire the view.

ℹ Information

Warrnambool Library (25 Liebig St; ⊙9.30am-5pm Mon & Tue, to 6pm Wed-Fri, 10am-noon Sat) Free internet access.

Warrnambool Visitors Centre (www.visit warrnambool.com.au; Merri St; ⊙9am-5pm)

Signposted off the Princes Hwy (A1) in the Flagstaff Hill complex, it produces a bike map and several walking maps. There's also internet access here ($10 per hour) and bicycle hire ($30 per day).

Getting There & Away

BUS Three buses a week (Monday, Wednesday and Friday) travel from Geelong along the Great Ocean Road to Warrnambool ($27, six hours). There are around 10 V/Line (☑13 61 96; www.vline.com.au) buses a day to Port Fairy ($3.40, 30 minutes) and three continue on to Portland ($9.20, 1½ hours). There's a bus on Monday, Wednesday and Friday to Apollo Bay ($15.80, 3½ hours). Christians Bus Co (☑03-5562 9432) runs services on Tuesday, Friday and Saturday to Port Fairy ($3.30, departing 8am).

TRAIN V/Line (☑13 61 96; www.vline.com.au; Merri St) trains run to Melbourne ($26, 3¼ hours, three or four daily).

Tower Hill Reserve

Tower Hill, 15km west of Warrnambool, is a vast caldera born in a volcanic eruption 35,000 years ago. Aboriginal artefacts unearthed in the volcanic ash show that indigenous people lived in the area at the time. The Worn Gundidj Aboriginal Cooperative operates the Tower Hill Natural History Centre (www.worngundidj.org.au; ⊙9am-5pm Mon-Fri, 10am-4pm Sat, Sun & public holidays). It's one of the few places where you'll spot wild emus, kangaroos and koalas hanging out together.

There are excellent day walks, including the steep 30-minute Peak Climb with spectacular 360-degree views.

Port Fairy

POP 2600

This seaside township at the mouth of the Moyne River was settled in 1835, and the first arrivals were whalers and sealers. Port Fairy still has a large fishing fleet and a relaxed, salty feel, with its old bluestone and sandstone buildings, whitewashed cottages, colourful fishing boats and tree-lined streets. The town is very much a luxury tourist destination and is home to art galleries, antique shops and boutiques.

Sight & Activities

The visitors' centre has brochures and maps that show the popular **Shipwreck Walk** and **History Walk**. On Battery Hill there's a lookout point, and cannons and fortifications that were positioned here in the 1860s. Down below there's a lovely one-hour walk around Griffiths Island where the Moyne River empties into the sea. The island is connected to the mainland by a footbridge, and is home to a protected **mutton-bird colony** (they descend on the town each October and stay until April) and a modest lighthouse.

Festivals & Events

Port Fairy Folk Festival   FOLK MUSIC
(www.portfairyfolkfestival.com; tickets $195) Australia's premier folk-music festival is held on the Labour Day long weekend in early March. Book accommodation early.

Sleeping

Pelican Waters   CABINS $$
(☑03-5568 1002; www.pelicanwatersportfairy.com.au; 34 Regent St; cabins & carriages from $100) Why stay in a hotel when you can sleep in a train? This beautifully presented property has cabins as well as two two-bedroom converted Melbourne train carriages.

Port Fairy YHA   HOSTEL $
(☑03-5568 2468; www.portfairyhostel.com.au; 8 Cox St; dm $26-30, d/f/2-bed apt from $75/115/200; @⊛) In the rambling 1844 (former) home of merchant William Rutledge, this friendly and well-run hostel has a large kitchen, pool table and free cable TV.

Daisies by the Sea B&B   B&B $$
(☑03-5568 2355; www.port-fairy.com/daisiesbythesea; 222 Griffiths St; d from $160) Nod off to the sound of the crashing waves just 50m

MELBOURNE & VICTORIA TOWER HILL RESERVE

GREAT SOUTH WEST WALK

This 250km signposted loop begins and ends at Portland's information centre, and takes in some of the southwest's most stunning natural scenery, from the remote, blustery coast, through the river system of the Lower Glenelg National Park and back through the hinterland to Portland. The whole loop would take at least 10 days, but it can be done in sections. Maps are available from the Portland visitors centre (p548) and the Parks Victoria and visitors centre in Nelson (p549). See www.greatsouthwestwalk.com.

from your door in these two cosy beach-front suites, 1.5km from town.

Eating

TOP CHOICE Merrijig Inn
MEDITERRANEAN $$$

(✆03-5568 2324; www.merrijiginn.com; cnr Campbell & Gipps Sts; 5 courses $90) This is superb dining and the menu changes according to what's seasonal. You might get duck breast, leg brik, baby beetroot, pickled rose, rhubarb and chard one day, and yabbies with asparagus, almonds and nasturtiums the next.

Rebecca's Cafe
CAFE $

(70-72 Sackville St; mains $9-16; ⊗breakfast & lunch) Excellent for breakfast and light lunches, Rebecca's has interesting items on the menu including rich wild-rice porridge topped with rhubarb as well as the usual cakes, muffins, slices, scones and biscuits.

The Hub
CAFE $

(cnr Bank & Sackville Sts; mains $14; ⊗breakfast, lunch & dinner; 🛜) On weekends this corner cafe is packed with people enjoying spicy gourmet breakfasts featuring locally made chorizo sausage, and good old bacon and eggs. The menu steps up a notch for mostly seafood dinners.

ℹ Information

Port Fairy Visitors Centre (✆03-5568 2682; www.visitportfairy-moyneshire.com.au; Bank St; ⊗9am-5pm) Can recharge your mobile phone's battery while providing spot-on information.

ℹ Getting There & Away

BUS V/Line (✆13 61 96; www.vline.com.au) buses run three times daily on weekdays (twice on Saturday and once on Sunday) to Portland ($6.50, one hour) and Warrnambool ($3.50, 35 minutes).

CAR Port Fairy is 20 minutes west of Warrnambool on the A1.

Portland
POP 9800

There's a charm to largish Portland; it has historic houses, a bunch of ghost stories and is a short distance from a lovely lighthouse. It's also the start and end of the Great South West Walk (see boxed text, p547). This was Victoria's first European settlement, and became a whaling and sealing base in the early 1800s. Blessed Mary MacKillop, Australia's first saint, arrived here from Melbourne in 1862 and founded Australia's first religious order.

🛏 Sleeping & Eating

TOP CHOICE Annesley House
BOUTIQUE HOTEL $$

(✆0429 852 235; www.annesleyhouse.com.au; 60 Julia St; d from $135) This recently restored former doctor's mansion (c 1878) has six very different self-contained rooms, some featuring clawfoot baths and lovely views. All feature a unique sense of style. Highly recommended.

Claremont Holiday Village
CARAVAN PARK, CABINS $

(✆03-5523 7567; www.holidayvillage.com.au; 37 Percy Street; unpowered/powered sites from $26/35, cabins from $70; @) This central caravan park has decent facilities including a large camp kitchen. The cheaper cabins have shared bathrooms.

Deegan Seafoods
FISH & CHIPS $

(106 Percy St; mains $10; ⊗lunch & dinner) This fish-and-chip shop serves up some of the freshest fish in Victoria.

ℹ Information

Parks Victoria (✆03-5522 3454; www.parkweb.vic.gov.au; 8-12 Julia St; ⊗8am-4.30pm Mon-Fri) For info on road conditions and camping.

Portland Visitors Centre (✆03-5523 2671; www.greatoceanroad.org; Lee Breakwater Rd; ⊗9am-5pm) In the impressive-looking Maritime Discovery Centre.

DON'T MISS

CAPE NELSON LIGHTHOUSE

Cape Nelson Lighthouse is a wonderful spot for a flash bite to eat and some stunning views. **Isabella's Cafe** (⊗10am-4pm) takes pride of place at its blustering base and offers excellent deli-style food within its thick bluestone walls. **Lighthouse tours** (adult/child $15/10; ⊗10am & 2pm) get you high up, while those wanting to stay a while can book into a self-contained **assistant lighthouse keepers' cottage** (www.capenelsonlighthouse.com.au; d from $180).

CAPE BRIDGEWATER

Cape Bridgewater is a 21km detour off the Portland–Nelson Rd. The stunning 4km arc of Bridgewater Bay is perhaps one of Australia's finest stretches of white-sand surf beach, backed by pristine dunes. The windy farm-lined road continues on to Cape Duquesne where walking tracks lead to a Blowhole and the Petrified Forest on the cliff-top. A longer two-hour return walk takes you to a **seal colony** where you can see dozens of fur seals sunning themselves on the rocks.

Stay at friendly Sea View Lodge B&B (☑03-5526 7276; www.hotkey.net.au/~seaview lodge; Bridgewater Rd; d from $140), or Cape Bridgewater Holiday Camp (☑03-5526 7247; www.capebridgewatercoastalcamp.com.au; Blowhole Rd; unpowered sites/dm/houses $15/30/150), which has sparkling dorms, self-contained houses and a huge camp kitchen. They also run fun Seals by Sea tours (adult/child $30/20).

ⓘ Getting There & Away

BUS V/Line (☑13 61 96; www.vline.com.au) buses connect Portland with Port Fairy three times daily and once on Sunday ($6.50, 55 minutes), and also with Warrnambool ($9.50, 1½ hours).

Nelson

POP 230

Tiny Nelson is the last vestige of civilisation before the South Australian border – just a general store, pub and a handful of accommodation places. It's a popular holiday and fishing spot at the mouth of the Glenelg River, which flows through Lower Glenelg National Park. Note that Nelson uses South Australia's 08 telephone area code. Why? We dunno!

⊙ Sights & Activities

Nelson Boat & Canoe Hire　　BOATING
(☑08-8738 4048; www.nelsonboatandcanoehire.com.au) This outfit can rig you up for serious river-camping expeditions – canoe hire costs from $60 a day. They also have paddle boats for hire for $20 for 30 minutes.

Glenelg River Cruises　　CRUISES
(☑08-8738 4191; cruises adult/child $30/10) Cruises depart Nelson daily (except Thursday and Monday) at 1pm for a leisurely 3½-hour cruise to the Princess Margaret Rose Cave (☑08-8738 4171; www.princessmargaretrosecave.com; adult/child/family $14/9/32), but tickets for the cave tour cost extra. If you travel to the cave on your own, it's about 17km from Nelson, towards the border.

🛏 Sleeping

There are nine **camp sites** between Nelson and Dartmoor along the Glenelg River that are popular with canoeists but are also accessible by road, with rain-fed water tanks, toilets and fire places (BYO firewood). Camping permits are issued by Parks Victoria in Nelson. Forest Camp South is the nicest of these, right on the river, rich in bird life and easily accessible from the Portland–Nelson Rd.

Nelson Hotel　　PUB $
(☑08-8738 4011; www.nelsonhotel.com.au; Kellett St; d/apt from $40/135; ☺lunch & dinner) This hotel has a dusty stuffed pelican above the bar and a few vegetarian meals on the fishy menu (mains $17 to $30). The quarters are plain but adequate with shared facilities, and the attached apartment/studio is great.

ⓘ Information

Parks Victoria & Nelson Visitors Centre
(☑08-8738 4051; nelsonvic@hotkey.net.au; ☺9am-5pm; @) Just before the Glenelg River bridge.

GRAMPIANS & THE NORTHWEST

Beyond Ballarat, western Victoria is a large expanse of wheat fields, grain silos, rolling farmland and sheep properties known as the Wimmera (the southwest) and the Mallee (northwest), separated by the Western Hwy (Rte A8), the main route between Melbourne and Adelaide. In the far northwest, large swathes of this land are given over to desert national parks. The star attraction out here is the Grampians National Park, while further west Mt Arapiles State Park is Australia's most famous rock-climbing venue, and the Little Desert National Park is a good spot for hiking and camping.

The Grampians (Gariwerd)

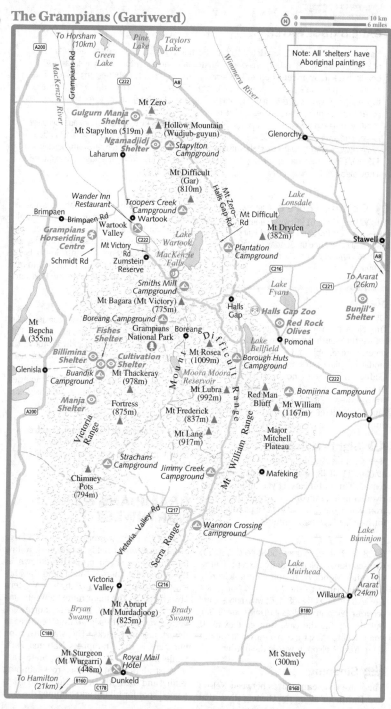

Getting There & Away

The *Overland*, the Melbourne–Adelaide train, runs through the Wimmera, stopping at Ararat, Horsham and Dimboola (for confirmed bookings only), four times a week. **V/Line** (☑13 61 96) has train and bus services between Melbourne and major towns.

Firefly Express (www.fireflyexpress.com.au) and **Greyhound Australia** (www.greyhound.com.au) also pass through Horsham daily on their Melbourne–Adelaide run. From Horsham you can take a bus north to Mildura.

Grampians National Park

The Grampians (known as Gariwerd to local Koories) is a bushwalkers' paradise and one of Victoria's most outstanding natural features. The rich diversity of flora and fauna, unique sandstone rock formations, Aboriginal rock art, accessible walking trails and rock-climbing sites offer something for everyone. The mountains are at their best in spring, when the wildflowers carpet the ranges.

Sealed access roads in the park run from Halls Gap south to Dunkeld and northwest to Horsham. Off these roads are side trips to car parks and some of the park's most notable sights such as McKenzies Falls, Reed Lookout for walks to the Balconies, Boroka Lookout and the Zumstein picnic area.

Close to Halls Gap, the Wonderland Range has some spectacular and accessible scenery. There are scenic drives and walks, from an easy stroll to Venus Bath (30 minutes) to a walk up to the Pinnacles Lookout (five hours). Walking tracks start from Halls Gap, and the Wonderland and Sundial car parks.

Sleeping

Parks Victoria maintains 11 **camp sites** (☑03-5361 4000; camp sites per vehicle or 6 people $14) throughout the park, with toilets, picnic tables and fireplaces (BYO water). Permits are required; you can register and pay at the office at the Brambuk Cultural Centre.

Information

Grampians Central Booking Office (☑03-5356 4654; 7353 Grampians Rd) This tour-booking agency is in the Halls Gap general store.

Halls Gap Visitors Centre (☑1800 065 599; www.grampianstravel.com.au, www.visithallsgap.com.au; Centenary Hall, 115 Grampians Tourist Rd; ⊙9am-5pm) The staff here are helpful, and can book tours, accommodation and activities.

Parks Victoria (☑03-5356 4381, 13 19 63; www.parkweb.vic.gov.au) At the Brambuk Cultural Centre, with maps and brochures, camping permits and fishing licences.

Getting There & Away

V/Line (☑13 61 96) has a daily train/coach service from Melbourne to Halls Gap ($27, 4½ hours), but it's painfully slow, with changes required at Ballarat (or Ararat) and Stawell. There's at least one bus a day between Halls Gap and Stawell ($6, 35 minutes).

Christians Bus Company (☑03-5352 1501; www.christiansbus.com.au) runs a service between Ararat and Warrnambool on Tuesday, Friday and Sunday, stopping at Halls Gap, Hamilton and Port Fairy.

HALLS GAP
POP 280

Nudging up against the craggy Wonderland Range, Halls Gap is a pretty little town – some might even say sleepy if you visit midweek in winter, but boy does it get busy during holidays! This is the main accommodation base and easiest access for the best of the Grampians, where kangaroos graze on front lawns and the air is thick with the songs of kookaburras and parrots. The single street through town has a neat little knot of shops, a supermarket, adventure activity offices, restaurants and cafes. The Halls Gap general store and post office has an ATM and Eftpos.

Sights & Activities

Brambuk Cultural Centre CULTURE CENTRE (☑03-5361 4000; www.brambuk.com.au; Grampians Tourist Rd; ⊙9am-5pm) Your first stop should be this superb cultural centre, 2.5km south of Halls Gap. The building itself is a striking design that combines timeless Aboriginal motifs with contemporary design and building materials. Run by five Koori communities in conjunction with Parks Victoria, the centre offers insights into local culture and history through Koori stories, art, music, dance, weapons, tools and photographs. The **Gariwerd Dreaming Theatre** (adult/child/family $5/3/12) shows hourly films explaining Dreaming stories of Gariwerd and the creation story of Bunjil. Three-hour cultural and **rock-art tours** (adult/child $35/22) can be booked here.

The complex includes the Parks Victoria office, a souvenir shop and **Brambuk Bush Tucker Café** (meals $11-26; ⊙9am-4pm) with a lovely deck overlooking the gardens.

ROCK ART

Traditional Aboriginal owners have been occupying Gariwerd for more than 20,000 years and this is the most accessible place in Victoria to see indigenous rock art. Sites include **Bunjil's Shelter**, near Stawell, one of Victoria's most sacred indigenous sites, best seen on a guided tour from the Brambuk Cultural Centre. Other rock-art sites in the west of the park are the **Manja Shelter**, reached from the Harrop Track car park; the **Billimina Shelter**, near the Buandik campground; and in the north is the **Ngamadjidj Shelter**, reached from the Stapylton campground.

Halls Gap Zoo NATURE RESERVE

(☑03-5356 4668; www.hallsgapzoo.com.au; 4061 Pomonal Rd; adult/child/family $18/9/45; ⊙10am-5pm Wed-Mon) Get up close to Australian native animals such as wallabies, grey kangaroos, quolls and wombats, but also exotic critters like meerkats, spider monkeys, bison and tamarin. There are breeding and conservation programs and a natural bush setting.

☞ Tours

Absolute Outdoors Australia ADVENTURE

(☑03-5356 4556; www.absoluteoutdoors.com.au; Shop 4, Stony Ck, Halls Gap) Rock climbing, abseiling, mountain-biking, canoeing, and guided nature walks from $55 to $200.

Eco Platypus Tours WILDLIFE

(☑1800 819 091; www.ecoplatypustours.com) Day trips from Melbourne for $99 per person.

Grampians Horseriding Centre HORSE RIDING

(☑03-5383 9255; www.grampianshorseriding.com.au; 430 Schmidt Rd, Brimpaen, Wartook Valley; 2½hr rides $75; ⊙10am & 2pm) Horse-riding adventures around a grand property with sweeping views, lakes and wandering bush tracks.

Grampians Mountain Adventure Company ADVENTURE

(GMAC; ☑03-5383 9218, 0427-747 047; www.grampiansadventure.com.au; half-day from $70) Specialises in rock-climbing and abseiling adventures and instruction from beginner to advanced.

Grampians Personalised Tours & Adventures ADVENTURE

(☑03-5356 4654, 0429-954 686; www.grampianstours.com) Offers a range of 4WD tours (with off-road options; from $79), rock climbing and abseiling, discovery walks (from half-day to four days) and scenic flights over the ranges ($170/280 for three/five people).

Hangin' Out ROCK CLIMBING

(☑03-5356 4535, 0407-684 831; www.hanginout.com.au; rock climbing from $65) Rock climbing specialists who will get you started with a four-hour introductory session ($75) and private guiding from $150.

🛏 Sleeping

Grampians YHA Eco-Hostel HOSTEL $

(☑03-5356 4544; www.yha.com.au; cnr Grampians Tourist Rd & Buckler St; dm/d $34/89) This architecturally designed and ecofriendly hostel utilises solar power and rainwater tanks and makes the most of light and space. It's beautifully equipped with a spacious lounge, MasterChef-quality kitchen and spotless rooms.

D'Altons Resort COTTAGES $$

(☑03-5356 4666; www.daltonsresort.com.au; 48 Glen St; studio/deluxe/family cottages from $100/120/150; ☀☒) These lovely timber cottages, with cosy lounge chairs, cute verandahs and log fires, spread up the hill back from the main road between the gums and kangaroos. Immaculately kept and friendly owners.

Pinnacle Holiday Lodge MOTEL $$

(☑03-5356 4249; www.pinnacleholiday.com.au; 21-45 Heath St; 1-/2-bedroom unit $110-160, d with spa $130; ☀☒) This gorgeous property behind the Stony Creek shops is a cut above most of Halls Gap's motels. The spacious grounds have a real bucolic feel with barbecue areas, an indoor pool and tennis courts.

Brambuk Backpackers HOSTEL $

(☑03-5356 4250; www.brambuk.com.au; Grampians Tourist Rd; dm/d incl breakfast $22/65; @) Across from the cultural centre, this friendly Aboriginal-owned and run hostel gives you a calming sense of place with a relaxed feel and craggy views from the lounge windows.

Mountain Grand Guesthouse GUESTHOUSE $$

(☑03-5356 4232; www.mountaingrand.com; Grampians Tourist Rd; s/d incl breakfast $146/166; ☀🛜)

This gracious, old-fashioned timber guest-house prides itself on being a traditional old-fashioned lodge where you can take a pre-dinner port in one of the lounge areas and mingle with other guests. The rooms are compact but with a bright, fresh feel.

Parkgate Resort CARAVAN PARK $
(📞1800 810 781, 03-5356 4215; www.parkgate resort.com.au; Grampians Tourist Rd, Halls Gap; powered sites $32-45, cabins/cottages d from $75/110; ✷✷) Parkgate is an immaculate, sprawling family holiday park with all the bells and whistles.

Tim's Place HOSTEL $
(📞03-5356 4288; www.timsplace.com.au; 44 Grampians Rd; dm/s/d $25/55/70, apt $90-150; @) Friendly, spotless backpackers with homely eco-feel; free mountain bikes and herb garden.

Halls Gap Caravan Park (📞03-5356 4251; www.hallsgapcaravanpark.com.au; Grampians Rd; unpowered/powered sites from $25/30, cabins $65-110; ✷) Camping and cabins right in the town centre. Gets crowded at peak times.

🍴 Eating

Halls Gap's small knot of eateries (and supermarket) are mostly along Grampians Tourist Rd and beside the boardwalk along pretty Stony Creek, where the bakery makes sublime vanilla slices, and the Pink Panther Café does good pizzas. In the Smugglers Hearth souvenir shop you'll find delicious homemade fudge from the Grampians Fudge Factory.

Kookaburra Restaurant MODERN AUSTRALIAN $$
(📞03-5356 4222; www.kookaburrabarbistro.com. au; 125-127 Grampians Rd; mains $23-34; ⊙dinner Tue-Sun, lunch Sun) This Halls Gap institution is renowned for its crispy-skin duck and Aussie dishes like barramundi and kangaroo fillet. There's a good value 'eat early' deal if you order by 6.30pm.

Halls Gap Hotel PUB FARE $$
(📞03-5356 4566; 2262 Grampians Rd; mains $18-29; ⊙lunch & dinner) For generous no-nonsense bistro food, you can't beat the local pub, about 2km north of town. With views of the Grampians, it's a social place for a beer after a day's bushwalking.

Quarry Restaurant MODERN AUSTRALIAN $$
(📞03-5356 4858; Stony Creek; mains $14-35; ⊙lunch Sun, dinner Wed-Sun) For steaks and Mod Oz cuisine – kangaroo fillets and

mango barramundi – Quarry is cheerful and good value. Wednesday is schnitzel night.

DUNKELD
The southern access to the Grampians, Dunkeld is a sleepy little town in the shadow of dramatic **Mt Abrupt** and **Mt Sturgeon**, both of which you can hike. **Dunkeld visitors centre** (📞03-5577 2558; www.sthgrampians. vic.gov.au; Parker St) has useful information. **Royal Mail Hotel** (📞03-5577 2241; www.royal mail.com.au; Parker St; d $160-200, apt $290-310, mains $16-36; ⊙dinner Tue-Sun) is a historic pub transformed into a stylish modern hotel with a fine, bar, bistro and one of Victoria's top restaurants.

Horsham
POP 14,100
The major town to the northwest of the Grampians and capital of the Wimmera region, Horsham makes a convenient base for exploring the surrounding national parks and Mt Arapiles. **Grampians & Horsham visitors centre** (📞1800 633 218, 03-5382 1832; www.grampianslittledesert.com.au; 20 O'Callaghan's Pde; ⊙9am-5pm) has information on accommodation and the surrounding areas.

Horsham Regional Art Gallery (📞03-5362 2888; www.horshamartgallery.com.au; 80 Wilson St; gold coin donation; ⊙10am-5pm Tue-Fri, 1-4.30pm Sat & Sun) houses the Mack Jost Collection of significant Australian artists, including works by Rupert Bunny, Sir Sidney Nolan, John Olsen and Charles Blackman.

Mt Arapiles State Park
Mt Arapiles, 37km west of Horsham and 12km west of Natimuk, is Australia's premier rock-climbing destination. At 369m it's not a very big mountain but with more than 2000 routes to scale, it attracts salivating climbers from around the world. In the tiny nearby town of Natimuk, a community of avid climbers has set up shop to service the visitors, and the town has also developed into something of a centre for artists – the biennial **Nati Frinj Festival**, held in November in odd years, includes performances and a colourful street parade.

Arapiles Mountain Shop (📞5387 1529; 67 Main St) sells and hires climbing equipment.

If you want to learn to climb or hire a guide, the **Natimuk Climbing Company**

(☎03-5387 1558; www.climbco.com.au; 117 Main St) and **Arapiles Climbing Guides** (☎03-5384 0376; www.arapiles.com.au; Natimuk) are two professional outfits offering instruction and group courses.

🛏 Sleeping & Eating

Pines Camping Ground CAMPGROUND
(Centenary Park; camp sites $2) Most climbers head for this popular site at the base of the mountain.

National Hotel MOTEL
(☎03-5387 1300; 65 Main St; d $65-75) This place in Natimuk has tidy motel-style units at the back and pub rooms upstairs, plus good counter meals.

Little Desert National Park

One of western Victoria's most accessible national parks, the rich diversity of plants and wildflowers here belies the 'desert' tag. Two sealed roads between the Western and Wimmera Hwys pass through the park, or you can take the good gravel road from Dimboola. The best-known resident here is the mallee fowl.

For a brief introduction to the park there are several well-signposted walks: south of Dimboola is the **Pomponderoo Hill Nature Walk**, south of Nhill is the **Stringybark Nature Walk** and south of Kiata is the **Sanctuary Nature Walk**. Other longer walks leave from the camping ground south of Kiata, including a 12km trek south to the Salt Lake.

🛏 Sleeping

There are national park **camping grounds** (camp sites $13.50) in the eastern block at Horseshoe Bend and Ackle Bend, both on the Wimmera River south of Dimboola, and south of Kiata.

Little Desert Nature Lodge CAMPGROUND, MOTEL $$$
(☎03-5391 5232; www.littledesertlodge.com.au; unpowered/powered site $17/20, dm $22, B&B s/d from $90/115; ❄) On the northern edge of the desert 16km south of Nhill, this well-equipped bush retreat is a superb base for exploring the park, with a spacious camping ground, bunkhouse, comfortable en-suite motel-style rooms and a restaurant. A key attraction here is the tour of the mallee-fowl aviary ($12) where you can see these rare birds in a breeding program, the mallee-fowl

sanctuary tour ($110) and the Whimpey's 4WD tours ($65).

 Information

Little Desert Park Office (☎03-5389 1204; www.parkweb.vic.gov.au; Nursery Rd, Wail) Off the Western Hwy south of Dimboola.

Gateway Towns
DIMBOOLA

On the eastern edge of the Little Desert, beside the Wimmera River, Dimboola is a classic country town made famous by Jack Hibberd's play *Dimboola*, and the subsequent 1979 John Duigan film of the same name about a country wedding. The park entrance is about 4km south of town on a sealed road, but from then on it's gravel.

Dimboola celebrates with a **German Fest** in April, and the **Dimboola Rowing Regatta** in November.

🛏 Sleeping

Riverside Host Farm CABINS $
(☎03-5389 1550; 150 Riverside Rd; unpowered sites $18; cabins d $77; ❄) This friendly working farm on a bend in the Wimmera River is a lovely place to stay with cosy self-contained cabins, camp sites and a rustic open-sided camp kitchen-lounge area with pot-belly stove. Hire canoes or help out with farm activities.

Dimboola Riverside Caravan Park CARAVAN PARK $
(☎03-5389 1416; dimboolacaravanpark@bigpond.com; 2 Wimmera St; unpowered/powered sites $20/25, cabins from $50) Set among eucalypts and pine trees beside the Wimmera River.

NHILL

Nhill is the main base for the northern entrance to the park and Kiata campground. It's a big town for this part of the world – the main industries are wheat farming and producing ducks for Victorian restaurant tables.

Hindmarsh visitors centre (☎03-5391 3086; www.hindmarsh.vic.gov.au; Victoria St; ⏰9am-5pm; @), in Goldsworthy Park in the town centre, has plenty of information on the park and local sights and accommodation.

The Mallee

Victoria's emptiest corner, the vast Mallee takes its name from the mallee scrub that once covered the region. Mallee gums are

canny desert survivors – 1000-year-old root systems are not uncommon – and for the Aborigines the region yielded plentiful food. The sky seems vast as you drive through this region surrounded by horizon, dead-flat semi-arid land and twisted mallee scrub – you don't have to visit central Australia to get a taste of the outback.

The farmers of this district have done it hard during years of drought, with the northern area dependent on the Murray River for water supply. The rains came in spades in 2010–11, rejuvenating the Wimmera River to the south, which in turn filled Lake Hindmarsh (Victoria's largest body of fresh water), and Lake Albacutya.

WYPERFELD NATIONAL PARK

Wyperfeld is a vast but accessible park of river red gum, mallee scrub, sand plains and, in the spring, a carpet of native wildflowers. A sealed road from the southern park entrance near Yaapeet leads to the visitor centre at Wonga Campground (camp sites $13.50) with pit toilets, picnic tables and fireplaces. Casuarina Campground (sites free) in the north is reached via a gravel road off the Patchewollock–Baring Rd.

MURRAY-SUNSET NATIONAL PARK

This 6630-sq-km park is arid and much of it is inaccessible. An unsealed road leads from Linga on the Mallee Hwy up to the Pink Lakes at the southern edge of the park, where there's a basic camping ground. Beyond this you must have a 4WD. The Shearer's Quarters (☑03-5028 1218; groups $55) has basic accommodation on the park's western side, sleeping up to 14 people.

HATTAH-KULKYNE NATIONAL PARK

About 70km south of Mildura off the Calder Hwy (Rte A79), the Hattah-Kulkyne National Park has dry, sandy mallee-scrub country and fertile riverside areas, lined with red gum, black box, wattles and bottlebrush. The Hattah Lakes system fills when the Murray floods and is great for birdwatching.

The access road is at Hattah, 70km south of Mildura on the Calder Hwy. The visitor information centre is 5km into the park. Contact Parks Victoria (☑13 19 63, www.park web.vic.gov.au) or the Hattah ranger's office (☑03-5029 3253).

There are camping facilities at Lake Hattah and Lake Mournpoul, but limited water. Camping is also possible anywhere along the Murray River frontage.

State border, irrigation lifeline and recreational magnet for waterskiers, canoeists, campers and golfers, the mighty Murray is Australia's longest and most important inland waterway. It's a stirring place of paddle steamers and houseboat holidays, wineries and orchards, bush camping, balmy weather and red gum forests.

The river flows almost 2400km from the Snowy Mountains to Encounter Bay in South Australia, supplying vital irrigation for orchards, vineyards and farms. Some of Australia's earliest explorers travelled along the river, and long before roads and railways crossed the land, the Murray's paddle steamers carried supplies to and from remote sheep stations – you can ride well-preserved paddle steamers at Mildura, Swan Hill and Echuca. Get off the Murray Valley Hwy along the frequent tracks (often marked 'River Access') that lead you to the banks for camping and fishing among the magnificent red gum forests.

Mildura

POP 30,000

Sunny, sultry Mildura is a real riviera oasis town – it's as isolated as anywhere you'll find in Victoria, but after driving for hours past parched farmlands, you're greeted by miles of fertile vineyards and orchards and a prosperous riverside town centre. Backpackers flock here for the abundant year-round fruit-picking and agricultural work, which only enhances the buzzing atmosphere.

The town developed in the late 1880s when William Chaffey pioneered the irrigation system, and today it's a thriving tourist town with lush golf courses, art-deco buildings, river cruises and as much sunshine as anywhere in the state.

☉ Sights & Activities

Mildura owes much to the Chaffey brothers and their innovation irrigation systems. Pick up a copy of *The Chaffey Trail* from the visitor centre and follow their story. Emerging from the Chaffey vision were the Mildura Wharf, now a mooring for paddle boats, the weir and the lock, which is operated at 11am, 12.30pm, 2pm and 3.30pm daily.

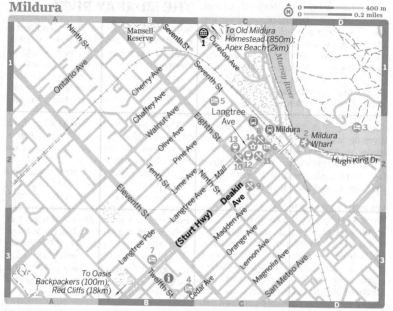

Mildura

◎ Sights
1 Mildura Arts Centre C1
   Rio Vista ....(see 1)

◉ Activities, Courses & Tours
2 PS Melbourne D2
   PV Mundoo ....(see 2)
   PV Rothbury ....(see 2)

◎ Sleeping
3 Acacia Houseboats D2
4 Mildura International Backpackers B3
5 Misty's Manor & Ditto Daddy's C1
6 Quality Hotel Mildura Grand C2
7 Sandors Motor Inn B3
   Willandra Houseboats ....(see 3)

◎ Eating
8 New Spanish Bar & Grill C2
9 O'Malley's C2
   Pizza Café at the Grand .... (see 8)
10 Restaurant Rendezvous C2
11 Stefano's Café Bakery C2
   Stefano's Restaurant .... (see 6)

◎ Drinking
12 Mildura Brewery C2
13 Sandbar C2

◎ Entertainment
14 Dom's Nightclub C2

FREE Rio Vista & Mildura
Arts Centre   HISTORIC BUILDING, ART GALLERY
(☏03-5018 8330; www.yourartscentre.com.au; 199
Cureton Ave; ⊙11am-4pm Wed-Mon) Chaffey's
grand homestead, the historic Queen Ann–
style Rio Vista, has been beautifully preserved and restored with each room set up
as a series of historical displays depicting
colonial life in the 19th century, with period
furnishings, costumes, photos and a collection of letters and memorabilia.

In the same complex, the Mildura Arts
Centre and theatre was closed for major redevelopment at the time of writing and due
to reopen late in 2011.

Old Mildura Homestead   HISTORIC SITE
(Cureton Ave, Old Mildura House Heritage Park; admission by donation; ⊙9am-6pm) Along the river

near Rio Vista, this cottage was the first home of William B Chaffey. The heritage park here contains a few other historic log buildings and has picnic and barbecue facilities.

Chateau Mildura
WINERY, MUSEUM

(☑03-5024 5901; www.chateaumildura.com.au; 191 Belar Ave, Irymple; adult/child $10/free; ⊙10am-4pm) Established in 1888 and still producing table wines, this is a living wine and horticultural museum with wine tasting to help your cultural experience.

Apex Beach
BEACH

About 3km northwest of the centre, this is a popular swimming and picnic spot with a sandy beach on the Murray. There's a good walking and cycling track from here to the Old Mildura Homestead.

Paddle-Boat Cruises

Paddle boats depart from the Mildura Wharf, and most go through a lock: watch the gates opening and the water levels changing. For bookings call ☑5023 2200, or go to www.paddlesteamers.com.au.

PS Melbourne
PADDLEBOAT CRUISE

(2hr cruise adult/child $27/12; ⊙ 10.50am & 1.50pm) One of the original paddle steamers, and the only one still driven by steam power. On Friday and Saturday this cruise is aboard the *PV Rothbury*.

PV Rothbury
PADDLEBOAT CRUISE

(winery cruise adult/child $62/30, lunch cruise $29/13) The fastest of the riverboats, it offers a winery cruise on Thursday, visiting Trentham Winery Estate and a BBQ lunch at Kings Billabong. On Tuesday there's a lunch cruise to Gol Gol Hotel.

PV Mundoo
PADDLEBOAT CRUISE

(dinner cruise adult/child $62/30) The newest riverboat has an evening dinner cruise every Thursday from 7pm.

☞ Tours

Harry Nanya Tours
NATURE, CULTURE

(☑03-5027 2076; www.harrynanyatours.com.au; tours adult/child $170/110) Indigenous guide Graham Clarke keeps you enchanted with Dreaming stories and his deep knowledge and understanding of the Mungo region.

Moontongue Eco-Adventures
KAYAKING

(☑0427-898 317; www.moontongue.com.au; kayak tours $25-50) A sunset kayaking trip is a great way to see the river and its wildlife.

Wild Side Outdoors
ADVENTURE

(☑03-5024 3721, 0428-242852; www.wildside outdoors.com.au) Wild Side is an ecofriendly outfit offering a range of activities including a sunset kayaking tour at Kings Billabong (adult/child $30/10), and canoe/kayak/mountain-bike hire ($30/20/20 per hour).

Mildura Ballooning
BALLOONING

(☑03-5024 6848; www.miIduraballooning.com.au; adult/child $295/195) Enjoy the sunrise from the air with a one-hour dawn balloon flight over the wonderful patchwork of vineyards, orchards and the Murray.

✨ Festivals & Events

Mildura Wentworth Arts Festival
ARTS

(www.artsmildura.com.au/mwaf) Magical concerts by the river, in the sandhills, and all around; held in February/March.

Mildura Country Music Festival
MUSIC

(www.miIduracountrymusic.com.au) Ten days of free concerts during the September school holidays.

Mildura Show
AGRICULTURAL

(www.mildura.vic.gov.au) One of the largest shows in rural Victoria; held mid-October.

Mildura Jazz & Wine Festival
JAZZ, WINE

(www.artsmildura.com.au/jazz) Traditional bands, great food, good wine; held in October or November.

🛏 Sleeping

Mildura has a dozen hostels and budget guesthouses, all geared towards backpackers looking for seasonal work, as well as plenty of caravan parks, motels and hotels. For a real river experience, considering hiring a houseboat.

TOP CHOICE Quality Hotel
Mildura Grand
HOTEL $$

(☑03-5023 0511, 1800 034 228; www.quality hotelmilduragrand.com.au; Seventh St; B&B std/grand/ste $115/175/240-420; ❊🛜❄) The standard rooms at the Grand aren't the most luxurious in town, but staying at this landmark hotel gives you the feeling of being part of something special. Many rooms open onto a delightful courtyard garden, and there's a gym, pool and spa.

Oasis Backpackers
HOSTEL $

(☑03-5022 8255; www.milduraoasisbackpack ers.com.au; 230-232 Deak Ave; dm/d per week $140/300; @❊🛜❄) Oasis is Mildura's

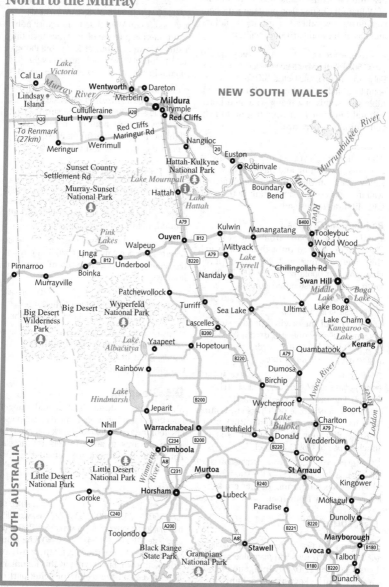

best-equipped backpacker hostel with a great pool and patio bar area, ultramodern kitchen and free internet. The owners can organise plenty of seasonal work. Minimum one-week stay.

Misty's Manor & Ditto Daddy's   APARTMENTS $$
(☎03-0419-840 451; www.mistysmanormildura. com; 16 Olive Ave; d $155-160; ❄☎) These two apartments are spectacular in their design and decoration – a beautifully designed but

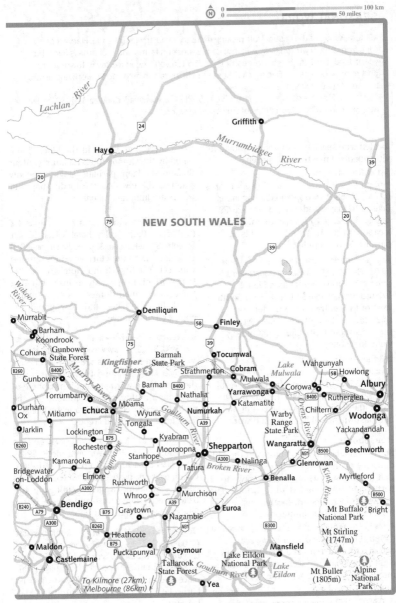

unlikely mix of corrugated iron, stone and recycled timber, with a lilac, mauve and canary-yellow colour scheme in 'Ditto Daddy's' and a tartan theme in 'Misty's Manor'. King beds, plasma TVs, modern kitchens, double spa and shower.

Sandors Motor Inn MOTEL **$**
(☎1800 032 463, 03-5023 0047; www.sandorsmotorinn.com; 179 Deakin Ave; d $95-125; ❄❄) Mildura has plenty of motels, but Sandors – virtually opposite the visitor centre – is well

SEASONAL WORK

Mildura is king of the casual fruit-picking industry in northwest Victoria. Harvest season runs from January through March, but casual work on farms and orchards is available year-round. Some farmers allow camping but often you'll need to stay in town, so transport may be necessary. Backpacker hostels in Mildura can help line up work and arrange transport (usually for a fee).

Madec Harvest Labour Office (☑03-5021 3472; www.madec.edu.au; 126-130 Deakin Ave) has comprehensive listings of fruit-picking work.

located with spacious, tidy rooms and an inviting pool set in a tropical garden.

Apex RiverBeach Holiday Park CARAVAN PARK $
(☑03-5023 6879; www.apexriverbeach.com.au; Cureton Ave; unpowered/powered sites $26/29, cabins $82-122; ❋🛜) Thanks to a fantastic location on sandy Apex Beach, this bush park is always popular.

Acacia Holiday Apartments APARTMENTS
(☑03-03-5023 3855; www.acaciaapartments. com.au; 762 Calder Hwy; d cabins $75-105, 1-/2-bedroom apt from $100/110; ❋🌊) Southwest of the centre on the Calder Hwy, these large self-contained one-, two- and three-bedroom units offer outstanding value for money.

Mildura International Backpackers HOSTEL
(☑/fax 03-5021 0133; 5 Cedar Ave; dm per night/ week $25/129; @) Basic but friendly house where the rooms have two beds (not bunks) and the owners will help you find work.

Houseboats

Staying on a houseboat is bliss and the Mildura region has over a dozen companies that hire houseboats ranging from two to 12 berths and from modest to luxurious. The following operators are located just across from Mildura Wharf in Buronga:

Acacia Houseboats HOUSEBOAT
(☑1800 085 500, 03-5022 1510; www.acaciaboats.com.au; 3 nights $600-1800) Acacia's eight houseboats are well equipped but more at the budget end of the scale.

Willandra Houseboats HOUSEBOAT
(☑03-5024 7770; www.willandrahouseboats.com. au; 3 nights $700-3600) Willandra has a fleet of six luxury houseboats from eight to 12-berth.

✘ Eating

Mildura's cafe and restaurant precinct runs along Langtree Ave (otherwise known as

'Feast Street') and around the block dominated by the Grand Hotel. Italian raconteur Stefano de Pieri perhaps single-handedly stamped the town on the foodie map, but others are jumping onboard.

TOP CHOICE **Stefano's Restaurant** ITALIAN $$$
(☑03-5023 0511; Quality Hotel Mildura Grand, Seventh St; set menu $95; ☺dinner Mon-Sat) Descend into the former underground wine cellar at the Grand Hotel to see Stefano work his magic with the ever-changing five-course Italian dinner. It's an intimate, candle-lit experience and very popular – book well in advance.

Restaurant Rendezvous FRENCH $$
(☑03-5023 1571; www.rendezvousmildura.com. au; 34 Langtree Ave; mains $28-35; ☺lunch Mon-Fri, dinner Mon-Sat) Almost swallowed up by the Grand, the warm, casual atmosphere of this long-running place complements the perfectly prepared Mediterranean-style seafood, grills, pastas and crepes.

Stefano's Café Bakery CAFE, BAKERY $
(☑03-5021 3627; 27 Deakin Ave; meals $9-22; ☺breakfast & lunch) Fresh bread baked daily, Calabrese eggs, pastries and, of course, good coffee – Stefano's casual daytime cafe and bakery keeps things fresh and simple. Also a foodstore and wine cellar door.

New Spanish Bar & Grill STEAKHOUSE $$$
(☑03-5021 2377; www.seasonsmildura.com.au; cnr Langtree Ave & Seventh St; mains $28-39; ☺dinner Tue-Sun) On the Grand Hotel block, this place specialises in top-quality steaks and barbecue food, including kangaroo and Mallee rump.

Pizza Café at the Grand PIZZA $
(☑03-5022 2223; www.pizzacafe.com.au; 18 Langtree Ave; pizza & pasta $13-18; ☺from 11am daily) For simple, inexpensive but stylish family dining – with all the atmosphere of the Grand Hotel dining strip – Pizza Café is

perfect. The wood-fired pizzas hit the spot but there's a supporting cast of salads, pastas and chicken dishes.

O'Malley's PUB FARE $$
(☑03-5021 4236; 56 Deakin Ave; mains $20-28; ⊙lunch & dinner Mon-Sat) This Irish pub does hearty counter meals (beef and Guinness pie, lamb shanks etc) and packs them in for cheap lunches daily and half-price dinners on Wednesday (before 7pm).

🍷 Drinking & Entertainment

Mildura has a compact but lively nightlife scene, buoyed by an ever-changing crew of backpackers and itinerant fruit pickers.

Mildura Brewery BREWERY
(☑03-5022 2988; www.mildurabrewery.com.au; 20 Langtree Ave; ⊙from 11am) Set in the former Astor cinema, this is Mildura's trendiest drinking hole. Shiny stainless-steel vats, pipes and brewing equipment make a great backdrop to the stylish art-deco lounge, and the beers brewed here – honey wheat beer and Mallee Bull among them – are superb. Good food too.

Sandbar BAR
(☑03-5021 2181; www.thesandbar.com.au; cnr Langtree Ave & Eighth St; ⊙noon-late Tue-Sun) On a balmy evening locals flock to the fabulous beer garden at the back of this lounge bar in an art-deco corner building. Local, national, original and mainstream bands play in the front bar on Thursday to Sunday nights.

Dom's Nightclub NIGHTCLUB
(☑03-5021 3822; 28 Langtree Ave; ⊙till 2am Fri & Sat) The upstairs club at Dom's – in the heart of Feast Street – attracts the after-pub crowd on a Saturday night for music and dancing.

ℹ️ Information

Café de la Rue (☑03-5023 5800; www.cafedelarue.com.au; 51 Deakin Ave; ⊙9am-8pm Mon-Fri, 10am-6pm Sat & Sun; @🛜) Coffee, books and internet access at $1 per half-hour and you can plug your own laptop in or use wi-fi.

Mildura Visitors Centre (☑1800 039 043, 03-5018 8380; www.visitmildura.com.au; cnr Deakin Ave & Eighth St; ⊙9am-5.30pm Mon-Fri, to 5pm Sat & Sun) In the Alfred Deakin Centre. There's a free accommodation-booking service, interesting displays, a cafe and helpful staff who book tours and activities.

ℹ️ Getting There & Away

Air

Regional Express Airlines (Rex; ☑13 17 13; www.regionalexpress.com.au), **Qantas** (☑13 13 13; www.qantas.com.au) and **Virgin Australia** (☑13 67 89; www.virginaustralia.com) all fly between Mildura and Melbourne daily. **Sharp Airlines** (☑1300 556694; www.sharpairlines.com.au) flies direct between Mildura and Adelaide.

Bus & Train

Long-distance buses operate from a depot at the train station on Seventh St, but there are currently no passenger trains to or from Mildura.

V/Line (☑13 61 96) has a train/bus service to/from Melbourne via Bendigo or Swan Hill ($37, 7½ hours, four daily). V/Line's Murraylink is a daily bus service connecting the towns along the Murray from Mildura: Swan Hill ($22.20, three hours, three daily), Echuca ($30.40, six hours; one daily) and Albury-Wodonga ($38, 10 hours, one daily)

Greyhound Australia (☑1300 473 946; www.greyhound.com.au) stops at Mildura daily on its route between Adelaide ($55, 5½ hours) and Sydney ($163, 17 hours).

Swan Hill

POP 9700

Swan Hill is a languid riverside community without the tourist hype of Mildura or Echuca, but still boasting a few sights such as Australia's oldest recreated pioneer museum. It was named by intrepid explorer Major Thomas Mitchell in 1836, after he was kept awake by swans in the nearby lagoon. Today it's an important regional centre surrounded by irrigated farmlands. Fruit pickers can find work on farms about 25km west of Swan Hill around Nyah.

👁 Sights & Activities

Swan Hill's major attraction, the **Pioneer Settlement** (☑03-5036 2410; www.pioneersettlement.com.au; Horseshoe Bend; adult/child/family $24/18/65.50; ⊙9.30am-4pm), is a thoroughly enjoyable re-creation of a riverside port town from the paddle-steamer era. The dusty old-time streets feature shops, an old school and church, vintage car rides, an Aboriginal keeping place, the fascinating Kaiser Stereoscope and the restored PS *Gem*, one of the largest river boats to have served on the Murray.

The paddle steamer PS *Pyap* makes one-hour **cruises** (adult/child $18/13; ⊙cruises 2.30pm daily, also 10.30am on weekends & school

holidays) along the Murray. Every night at dusk a 45-minute sound-and-light show (adult/child $18/13) brings the historic old town to life.

Murray Downs Resort (☑1800 807 574; www.murraydownsresort.com.au; Murray Downs Dr; 9/18 holes $20/35, club hire $22) is 5km east of the town in NSW, but is regarded as a Swan Hill club and boasts one of the finest public resort golf courses in Victoria, as well as the requisite restaurant and pokies.

🛏 Sleeping & Eating

Most backpackers looking for fruit-picking work head out to the small communities of Nyah and Nyah West, which have several backpacker hostels, all of which can help you find work. Ask at the visitor centre.

Best's Riverbed B&B   B&B **$$**
(☑03-5032 2126; www.bestbnb.com.au; 7 Kidman Reid, Murray Downs; s/d $80/120, spa room $165) On the banks of the Murray 3km across the border in NSW, this charming B&B has spacious living areas, lounges with open fires and a marvellous view of the river.

Pioneer Station Motor Inn   MOTEL **$**
(☑03-5032 2017; 421 Campbell St; s/d from $65/75; ❄🐾) This good-value budget motel is well kept and close to the town centre and riverside. The adjacent Carriages Restaurant is a training ground for students from the Swan Hill International College.

Riverside Caravan Park   CARAVAN PARK **$**
(☑03-5032 1494; www.swanhillriverside.com.au; Monash Dr; unpowered/powered sites from $29/32, en-suite sites from $41, cabins $83-130) On the banks of the Murray and close to the Pioneer Settlement, this park enjoys a fabulous central location.

Java Spice   THAI **$$**
(☑03-5033 0511; www.javaspice.com.au; 17 Beveridge St; mains $19-28; ☉lunch Thu-Sun, dinner Tue-Sun; 🍴) Dining under open-side thatched and teak wood huts in a tropical garden, you'll think you've been transported to Southeast Asia. The authentic cuisine is predominantly Thai, with some Malaysian and Indonesian influences mixed in.

**Spoons Riverview
Café**   MODERN AUSTRALIAN **$$**
(☑03-5032 2601; www.spoonsriverside.com.au; Horseshoe Bend; mains $15-28; ☉breakfast & lunch daily, dinner Thu-Sat) The riverside location alone is enough to lure you to this licensed cafe with its big timber deck overlooking the Marraboor River and Pioneer Settlement; there's a provedore deli selling fresh produce and gourmet hampers.

Jilarty Gelato Bar   CAFE, GELATERIA **$**
(☑03-5033 0042; 233 Campbell St; ☉daily) Gelati on a hot summer's day? Unbeatable. This little cafe specialises in Italian-style gelati with local fruit flavours, along with great coffee and Spanish churros.

🅘 Information

Swan Hill Region Information Centre (☑1800 625 373, 5032 3033; www.swanhillonline.com; cnr McCrae & Curlewis Sts)

🅘 Getting There & Away

Swan Hill sits on the Murray Valley Hwy, 218km from Mildura and 156km from Echuca. **V/Line** (☑13 61 96; www.vline.com.au) runs trains between Melbourne and Swan Hill ($30, 4½ hours, three or four daily), and some train/coach services with a change at Bendigo. There are daily V/line coaches to Mildura ($22.20, three hours) and Echuca ($13.70, 2½ hours).

Echuca

POP 12,360

Echuca is the paddle-steamer capital of Victoria and a classic Murray River town, bursting with history, nostalgia and, of course, river boats. The Aboriginal name translates as 'meeting of the waters', as it's here that three great rivers meet – the Goulburn, Campaspe and the Murray. The highlight here is unquestionably the historic port area and the rivers themselves, and, while it might feel a bit touristy, the town glows with an upbeat atmosphere and some fabulous restaurants and bars.

Echuca was founded in 1853 by ex-convict Harry Hopwood. At the peak of the riverboat era there were more than 100 paddle steamers plying the waters between Echuca and outback sheep stations. The Melbourne–Echuca railway line opened in 1864 and, within a decade, the boom years of the river-boat trade had ended.

🅞 Sights

Historic Port of Echuca   HISTORIC SITE
(☑03-03-5482 4248; www.portofechuca.org.au; cnr Leslie St & Murray Esp; passport adult/child/family $12.45/8.50/36.25, with paddle-boat cruise $29/15/77; ☉9am-5pm, tours 11.15am) Echuca's star attraction is the old port area, where

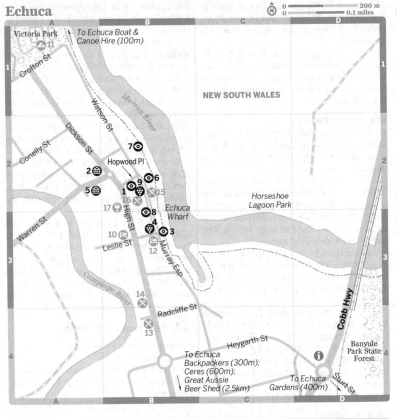

Echuca

◎ Sights

1 Bridge Hotel	B2
2 Echuca Historical Museum	A2
3 Historic Port & Wharf Entrance	B3
4 Murray Esplanade Cellars	B3
5 National Holden Museum	A2
6 Red Gum Works	B2
7 Riverboat Dock	B2
8 Sharp's Magic Movie House & Penny Arcade	B3
9 St Anne's	B2
Star Hotel	(see 16)

😴 Sleeping

10 Campaspe Lodge	B3
11 Echuca Caravan Park	A1
12 Steampacket B&B	B3

🍴 Eating

13 Beechworth Bakery	B4
14 Black Pudding Delicatessen	B3
15 Oscar W's Wharfside	B2
16 Star Hotel & Wine Bar	B2

🍷 Drinking

17 Shamrock Hotel	B2

paddle steamers dock and you really feel transported back to the heyday of the river. It's not a theme park – everything here is original.

In the wharf's cargo shed, dioramas depict life on the river boats and restored historic **paddle steamers** are moored alongside the wharf. Across the road at the

Star Hotel (1867) you can escape through the underground tunnel that helped drinkers avoid the police when the pub was a 'sly grog shop'.

At the Bridge Hotel (1 Hopwood Pl), built by Harry Hopwood in 1859, your ticket admits you to a historic upstairs recreation of a 19th-century home. Downstairs the Bridge is a pub and restaurant.

PORT AREA SIGHTS

Even if you don't take in the wharf, you can wander down the pedestrian Murray Esplanade, lined with historic buildings, shops and restaurants.

Sharp's Magic Movie House & Penny Arcade (☑03-03-5482 2361; www.sharpsmovie house.com.au; Murray Esplanade; adult/child/family $15/10/45; ☺9am-5pm) has authentic penny-arcade machines and free fudge tasting. The movie house shows old movies.

At Red Gum Works (Murray Esplanade; admission free; ☺9am-4pm) you can watch wood turners and blacksmiths at work with traditional equipment, and purchase red-gum products.

There are free tastings of local wines at Murray Esplanade Cellars (☑03-5482 6058; Old Customs House, 2 Leslie St; ☺9.30am-5.30pm) and at St Anne's (☑03-5480 6955; www.stan neswinery.com.au; 53 Murray Esplanade; ☺10am-6pm), where the giant port barrels will inspire you to taste the range of ports aged in bourbon and rum barrels.

OTHER SIGHTS

Echuca Historical Museum (☑03-5480 1325; 1 Dickson St; adult/child $4/1; ☺11am-3pm) located in the old police station, is classified by the National Trust.

Car buffs should check out the National Holden Museum (☑03-5480 2033; www.holden museum.com.au; 7 Warren St; adult/child/family $7/3/16; ☺9am-5pm), dedicated to Australia's four-wheeled icon with more than 40 beautifully restored Holdens, from FJ to Monaro, as well as racing footage and memorabilia.

The Great Aussie Beer Shed (☑03-5480 6904; www.greataussiebeershed.com.au; 337 Mary Ann Rd; adult/child/family $9.50/3.50/19; ☺9am-5pm Sat, Sun & holidays) is a wall-to-wall shrine of beer cans in a huge shed. It's the result of 30 years of collecting and one dates back to Federation. Very Aussie.

☞ Tours & Activities

A paddle-steamer cruise along the Murray is pretty much obligatory here, and at least

five steamers offer daily cruises, some offering lunch and winery cruises; head down to the wharf and check out the sailing times. PS Emmylou (☑03-5480 2237; 1½hr cruise adult/child $30/14) is a fully restored paddle steamer driven by an original engine.

PS *Alexander Arbuthnot,* PS *Canberra,* PS *Pevensey* and PS *Pride of the Murray* are all in regular service and one-hour cruises cost around $21/9 per adult/child. MV Mary Ann (☑03-5480 2200) isn't a traditional paddle steamer, but a cruising restaurant offering lunch ($45) and dinner ($75) cruises.

Echuca Moama Wine Tours (☑03-5480 1839; www.echucamoamawinetours.com.au; tours from $85) includes a tour of the Echuca Port, paddle-steamer cruise, lunch and visits to three wineries.

Echuca Boat & Canoe Hire (☑03-5480 6208; www.echucaboatcanoehire.com; Victoria Park Boat Ramp) hires out tinnies ($40/60 per one/two hours), 'barbie boats' (10 people $100/140), kayaks ($16/26) and canoes ($20/30). Multiday self-guided 'campanoeing' trips are also available, where you can arrange to be dropped upstream and canoe back.

☆ Festivals & Events

Riverboats Jazz Food & Wine Festival JAZZ, FOOD
(www.riverboatsjazzfoodandwine.com.au) Music, food and wine by the Murray; held in late February.

Echuca-Moama Winter Blues Festival MUSIC
(www.winterblues.com.au) Echuca's premier winter festival in late July features street performers, a blues 'boot camp' and a program of local and nationally renowned blues artists.

🛏 Sleeping

Hiring a houseboat is a great way to experience river life, and Echuca-Moama has plenty of them. Fully equipped boats sleep from four to 12 people. Rates vary according to size and season – four nights midweek in the low season will cost from $660 to $2300 depending on the boat. The visitor centre has details and a booking service. About 5km east of town, **Christies Beach** is a free camping area on the banks of the Murray. There are pit toilets, but bring water and firewood.

Echuca Gardens HOSTEL, GUESTHOUSE $
(☑03-5480 6522; www.echucagardens.com; 103 Mitchell St; dm & d $30, wagon $80-160, guesthouse

from $110) Run by inveterate traveller Kym, this thoroughly enjoyable place is part YHA hostel and part guesthouse, all set in beautiful gardens with ponds, statues, chooks and fruit trees. The cute 'gypsy wagons' in the garden offer unique accommodation.

Steampacket B&B B&B $$
(☑03-5482 3411; www.steampacketinn.com.au; cnr Murray Esplanade & Leslie St; d $149-199; ❋) Staying in the old port area is all part of the Echuca experience and this 19th-century National Trust–classified B&B offers genteel rooms with all the old-fashioned charm, linen and lace and brass bedsteads you could want (but air-con and flat-screen TVs too).

Campaspe Lodge MOTEL $$
(☑03-5482 1087; www.echucahotel.com; 567-571 High St; d weekdays/weekends $93/125, river view $140/160; ❋) Behind the Echuca Hotel, this group of motel units is great value, with private verandahs and big windows to take in the view of the Campaspe River. There are budget rooms in the pub itself for $40 per person.

Echuca Backpackers HOSTEL $
(☑03-5480 7866; www.backpackersechuca.com.au; 410-424 High St; dm $25, s/d with bathroom$55/60; ❋@) In a former tech-school building on Echuca's main street, this busy hostel is clean and well equipped, and the staff can help you find work.

Echuca Caravan Park CARAVAN PARK $
(☑03-5482 2157; www.echucacaravanpark.com.au; 51 Crofton St; unpowered/powered sites $31/33, d cabins $95-170; ❋⚏⚏) Beside the river just a short walk from town, this park is pretty cramped but the facilities are good, with modern timber camp kitchens and shady river red gums.

✕ Eating & Drinking

Conveniently, some of the best places to eat in Echuca are around the port area and the top end of High St. Supermarkets, pubs and takeaways can be found in the town centre around Hare St.

[TOP CHOICE] **Oscar W's**
Wharfside MODERN AUSTRALIAN $$
(☑03-5482 5133; www.oscarws.com.au; 101 Murray Esplanade; tapas $9-22, mains $32-37; ☯lunch & dinner) The glorious location in the old port area with a terrace overlooking the Murray is unbeatable, but Oscar's really delivers with its food and service.

Star Hotel & Wine Bar BAR, BISTRO $$
(☑03-5480 1181; www.starhotelechuca.com.au; 45 Murray Esplanade; mains $10-27; ☯breakfast & lunch daily, dinner Fri & Sat) The historic 'Star Bar' is still one of the liveliest places in town for a meal or drink, especially on weekends when live music plays. Full cooked breakfasts and reasonably priced lunches of calamari or chicken parma are available.

Black Pudding Delicatessen CAFE $
(☑03-5482 2244; 525a High St; meals $10-16; ☯breakfast & lunch) This tiny cafe-deli is a great place for a lazy breakfast or light lunch if you can get a table at the front or the small courtyard at the rear. Good coffee and local produce.

Beechworth Bakery BAKERY $
(☑03-5480 1057; 513 High St; meals $4-12; ☯6am-6pm) In a magnificent old building with wrap-around balcony and a deck overlooking the Campaspe River, this cheerful bakery prepares a high standard of breads, pies, cakes and sandwiches.

Ceres ITALIAN $$$
(☑03-5482 5599; www.ceresechuca.com.au; 2 Nish St; tapas $7.50-12.50, mains $13.50-45; ☯lunch & dinner) In a beautifully converted 1881 brick flour mill, Ceres oozes style with its high-back leather chairs, starched tablecloths and occasional couches. It's a relaxed place for lunch with all-day coffee and tapas, but also an atmospheric fine-dining evening restaurant with an innovative menu of Italian-influenced pastas, steaks and roast duckling.

Shamrock Hotel PUB
(☑03-5482 2247; 583 High St) The popular and friendly Shamrock is the place for Guinness, live music on weekends and cheap pub food.

❶ Information

Echuca Visitors Centre (☑1800 804 446, 03-5480 7555; www.echucamoama.com; 2 Heygarth St; ☯9am-5pm) In the old pump station, the visitor centre has helpful staff and an accommodation booking service.

❶ Getting There & Away

V/Line (☑13 61 96; www.vline.com.au) has two direct Melbourne–Echuca trains on weekends and train/bus services (return $20.40, 3½ hours) on weekdays, with changes at Bendigo, Murchison or Shepparton.

Barmah State Park

About 40km northeast of Echuca via the Cobb Hwy in NSW, Barmah is a significant wetlands area of the Murray River floodplain. It's the largest remaining red-gum forest in Australia, and the swampy understorey usually floods, creating a wonderful breeding area for many species of fish and birds.

The park entry is about 5km north of the tiny town of Barmah (turn at the pub). From the day use area, **Kingfisher Cruises** (☑03-5855 2855; www.kingfishercruises.com.au; adult/child/family $27.50/19/88; ☺11am Sun, Mon, Wed, Thu & Sat) takes you out in a flat-bottom boat for an informative two-hour cruise.

You can camp for free in the park, or at the Barmah Lakes camping area, which has tables, barbecue areas and pit toilets.

Rutherglen

POP 1990

Rutherglen has bags of history with some marvellous gold-rush-era buildings gracing the town (gold was discovered here in 1860), but today it's red wine that pumps through the region's veins – this is undoubtedly one of northern Victoria's finest wine-growing districts. In town you can dine at some excellent cafes and restaurants, browse antique and bric-a-brac shops, or head out and cycle some of the miles of flat trails. If you're looking for the river, it's about 10km northeast at the tiny Murray town of Wahgunyah.

Rutherglen Wine Experience (☑1800 622 871; www.rutherglenvic.com; 57 Main St; ☺9am-5pm; @) combines the visitor information centre with a cafe and wine-tasting room. Hire bikes for winery touring ($25/35 per half/full day) or pick up the heritage-walks brochure. It can also provide information about Rutherglen's busy calendar of wine and food events, including **Tastes of Rutherglen** in March and **Winery Walkabout** in June.

Four local wineries (Pfeiffer, Cofield, Campbell and Rutherglen Estates) offer free 'Behind the Scenes' **winery tours** on a rotating basis from Monday to Thursday at 2pm. They take you into the world of the winemaking process, but advanced bookings through the visitor centre are essential.

Grapevine Getaways (☑02-6032 8577; www.grapevinegetaways.com.au; 72 Murray St; half-/full day tours $35/45) runs knowledgeable personalised tours visiting up to eight wineries.

🛏 Sleeping

Victoria Hotel PUB $
(☑02-6032 8610; www.victoriahotelrutherglen.com.au; d without bathroom $50-90, with bathroom $80-120) This beautiful National Trust–classified pub has history, great bistro food and some inviting accommodation – the spruced-up front rooms have en-suites and views over Main St, with access to the wide, lace-trimmed balcony. At the back is a three-room suite that can be used for families or groups.

Tuileries BOUTIQUE HOTEL $$
(☑02-6032 9033; www.tuileriesrutherglen.com.au; 13 Drummond St; d incl breakfast $185, with dinner $275; ❈ ☎) All rooms are individually decorated in bright contemporary tones at this luxurious place next to the Jolimont Cellars. There's a guest lounge, tennis court, pool and an outstanding restaurant and cafe.

Motel Woongarra MOTEL $
(☑02-6032 9588; www.motelwoongarra.com.au; cnr Main & Drummond Sts; d/f $90/104; ❈ ☎) Close to the centre of town, Woongara has spacious, neat rooms, and little touches, like the carafe of port on your dresser. Friendly owners run limousine winery tours.

Rutherglen Caravan & Tourist Park CARAVAN PARK $
(☑02-6032 8577; www.rutherglentouristpark.com; 72 Murray St; unpowered/powered sites $18/25, d cabins $51-99) This friendly park with good facilities sits on the banks of Lake King, close to the golf course and swimming pool.

🍴 Eating

Main St is lined with quality cafes, restaurants, pubs and takeaway places – the Vic (above) is the pick of the pubs in town. A number of wineries also have quality restaurants, including All Saints, Cofield and Vintara.

Tuileries Cafe MEDITERRANEAN $
(☑02-6032 9033; 13 Drummond St; mains $12; ☺lunch & dinner daily) The bright cafe at Tuileries serves excellent-value lunches of panini, fish and chips or pasta. In the evening, Tony's Italian Café offers pizza, pasta and risotto.

Parkers Pies BAKERY $
(☑02-6032 9605; 86-88 Main St; pies $4-6; ☺8am-4.30pm Mon-Sat, 9am-4pm Sun) If you think a pie is a pie, this award-winning local institution might change your mind.

Rutherglen's wineries produce superb fortifieds (port, muscat and tokay) and some potent Durifs and Shirazs – among the biggest, baddest and strongest reds. See the website www.winemakers.com.au for more information. Some of the best:

» **All Saints** (☑02-6035 2222; www.allsaintswine.com.au; All Saints Rd, Wahgunyah; ☺9am-5.30pm Mon-Sat, 10am-5.30pm Sun) Fairytale castle, restaurant and cheese tasting.

» **Buller Wines** (☑1300 794 183; www.buller.com.au; Three Chain Rd; ☺9am-5pm Mon-Sat, 10am-5pm Sun) Fine Shiraz, plus a bird park.

» **Cofield** (☑02-6033 3798; www.cofieldwines.com.au; Distillery Rd, Wahgunyah; ☺9am-5pm Mon-Sat, 10am-5pm Sun) Small family operation and the Pickled Sisters Cafe.

» **Morris** (☑02-6026 7303; www.morriswines.com; Mia Mia Rd; ☺9am-5pm Mon-Sat, 10am-5pm Sun) Famous for its fortified wines (port, tokay and muscat), Morris has been around for more than 150 years.

» **Pfeiffer** (☑02-6033 2805; www.pfeifferwines.com.au; Distillery Rd, Wahgunyah; ☺9am-5pm Mon-Fri, 10am-5pm Sun) Situated on picturesque Sunday Creek near Wahgunyah.

» **Rutherglen Estates** (☑02-6032 8516; www.rutherglenestates.com.au; Tuileries Complex, Drummond St; ☺10am-6pm) Closest winery to town.

» **Vintara** (☑0447 327 517; www.vintara.com.au; Fraser Rd; ☺10am-5pm) Includes Bintara Brewery.

Try the gourmet pastries – emu, venison, crocodile or buffalo.

ⓘ Getting There & Away

V/Line (☑13 61 96; www.vline.com.au) has a train/coach service between Melbourne and Rutherglen with a change at Seymour ($26, four hours, eight weekly). During festivals, bus transport to wineries can be organised through the visitor centre.

The daily Murraylink bus connecting Wodonga with Mildura stops at Rutherglen. The bus stop is at the western end of Main St.

Wodonga

POP 29,700

The border town of Wodonga is separated from its twin, Albury, by the Murray River. Although a busy little town with a lake formed off Wodonga Creek, most of the attractions and the best of the accommodation are on the NSW side in Albury (p228).

Across the causeway, the **Gateway visitor information centre** (☑1300 796 222; www.alburywodongaaustralia.com.au; Hume Hwy; ☺9am-5pm) has info about Victoria and NSW. This is the start of the **High Country Rail Trail** (www.highcountryrailtrail.org.au), a cycling/walking path that skirts around the southern end of Lake Hume to Old Tallangatta.

For 24 years from the end of WWII, **Bonegilla**, 10km east of Wodonga, was Australia's first migrant reception centre, providing accommodation and training for some 320,000 migrants. At the **Bonegilla Migrant Experience** (☑02-6023 2327; Bonegilla Rd; admission free, tours $5; ☺9.30am-4.30pm) you can visit some of the preserved buildings and see photos and historical references.

GOLDFIELDS

The Central Victoria region was literally built on gold. The discovery of gold near Ballarat in 1851 transformed it from a colonial backwater of pastoralists and convicts into the richest and most prosperous part of the colonies. From those heady days came major regional towns such as Bendigo, Ballarat and Castlemaine, which still boast impressive Victorian-era buildings. Smaller towns such as Kyneton, Maldon and Maryborough make the most of their historic past, while Daylesford and Hepburn Springs are

THE MAN FROM SNOWY RIVER

You might have seen the film and read Banjo Paterson's famous poem, but out at **Corryong**, 120km east of Wodongo and close to the source of the Murray River, they live the legend. Corryong is a pretty township ringed by mountains – a natural playground for trout fishing, canoeing, cycling and bushwalking – and some say the home of Jack Riley, a stockman thought to have been the inspiration for Paterson's *The Man from Snowy River*.

The **Man From Snowy River Museum** (☑03-6076 1114; www.manfromsnowyrivermuseum.com; 105 Hanson St; adult/child $4/1; ☉10am-4pm Sep-May) tells the story of Jack Riley.

Corryong visitors centre (☑03-6076 2277; www.towong.com; 50 Hanson St; ☉9am-5pm) has info on the region, including **Jack Riley's Grave** (Corryong Cemetery) inscribed with the words, 'In memory of the Man from Snowy River, Jack Riley, buried here 16th July 1914'.

The **Man From Snowy River Bush Festival** (☑03-6076 1992; www.manfromsnowyriverbushfestival.com.au) is four days of whip-cracking, horse riding and yarn-spinning fun in March.

popular for their liquid gold – abundant mineral springs and the spa centres that have grown around them.

The region is easily accessible from Melbourne by road on the Calder Hwy or by train direct to Castlemaine and Bendigo.

Ballarat

POP 78,200

Ballarat vies with Bendigo as Victoria's largest inland city (Ballarat just wins out) and is famous as the site of the Eureka Rebellion, a battle between miners and authorities. The Eureka Centre, displaying the history of the rebellion, will reopen in 2012 after a multi-million-dollar redevelopment. These days the city makes the most of its gold-rush legacy with its superb Victorian architecture and the immensely popular Sovereign Hill gold-mining village. Rug up if you visit in winter – Ballarat is notoriously cold.

The area around Ballarat was known to the local Koories as 'Ballaarat', meaning 'resting place'. Around 25 pre-European clans identify themselves collectively as Wathaurong people. European pastoralists arrived in 1837 and the discovery of gold at nearby Buninyong in 1851 saw thousands of diggers flock to the area. After alluvial goldfields were played out, deep shaft mines were sunk, striking incredibly rich quartz reefs that were worked until the end of WWI.

Ballarat's 100-year-old **Begonia Festival**, in early March, attracts thousands of visitors.

◉ Sights & Activities

The main drag, impressive Sturt St, had to be three chains wide (60m) to allow for the turning circle of bullock wagons.

Sovereign Hill   HISTORIC VILLAGE
(☑03-5337 1100; www.sovereignhill.com.au; Magpie St; adult/child/family $41/19/103.50; ☉10am-5pm) You'll need to set aside at least half a day to get the most out of this fascinating recreation of an 1860s gold-mining township. The site was mined in the gold-rush era and much of the equipment, and the mine shaft, is original. The main street is a living history museum with folks performing their chores dressed in period costume. Sovereign Hill opens again at night for the impressive sound-and-light show **Blood on the Southern Cross** (☑03-5337 1199; adult/child/family $49.50/26.50/134, combined with Sovereign Hill ticket $90.50/45.20/237.50), a dramatic simulation of the Eureka Stockade battle. There are two shows nightly but times vary so check in advance; bookings are essential.

Your ticket (thankfully) gets you into the nearby **Gold Museum** (☑03-5331 1944; Magpie St; adult/child $9.80/5.20; ☉9.30am-5.20pm), which sits on a mullock heap from an old mine. There are imaginative displays and samples from all the old mining areas, as well as gold nuggets, coins and a display on the Eureka Rebellion.

Lydiard Street   STREET
Take the time to walk along one of Australia's finest streetscapes for Victorian-era architecture. Impressive buildings include Her Majesty's Theatre (1875), Craig's Royal Hotel (1853), George Hotel (1854) and the art gallery (1884).

Gold Shop   EQUIPMENT HIRE

(☎03-5333 4242; www.thegoldshop.com.au; 8a Lydiard St North) Hopeful prospectors can pick up miners' rights and rent metal detectors at the old Mining Exchange building.

FREE **Art Gallery of Ballarat**   ART GALLERY

(☎03-5320 5858; www.balgal.com; 40 Lydiard St Nth; ⊗9am-5pm) The oldest provincial gallery in Australia, this 1890 architectural gem houses a wonderful collection of early colonial paintings, works from noted Australian artists and contemporary works. Pride of place goes to the preserved remnants of the original Eureka flag. Free iPod tours are available and there are free guided tours at 2pm Wednesday to Sunday.

Lake Wendouree & Around   LAKE

Lake Wendouree, a large artificial lake created for the 1956 Olympics rowing events, is a natural focal point for the town, especially now that it's full of water again after drying up during the drought.

FREE **Botanic Gardens**   GARDENS

(Wendouree Pde; ⊗sunrise-sunset) On the western side of the lake, Ballarat's beautiful and serene gardens were first planted in 1858. Stroll through the 40 hectares of immaculately maintained rose gardens, wide lawns and colourful conservatory. Visit the cottage of poet Adam Lindsay Gordon or walk along the Prime Ministers' Avenue, a collection of bronze busts of all of Australia's prime ministers. There's a visitor centre in the glass Robert Clark Conservatory.

Tourist Tramway   TOURIST TRAM

(☎03-5334 1580; www.btm.org.au; rides adult/child $3/1.50; ⊗noon-5pm Sat & Sun) This tram operates on a short section of tramline around Lake Wendouree, departing from the Tram Museum. Horsedrawn trams started running in the city in 1887, later replaced by electric trams until 1971.

Kirrit Barreet   CULTURAL CENTRE

(☎03-5332 2755; www.aboriginalballarat.com. au; 407 Main Rd; admission free, tours $5; ⊗9am-5pm Mon-Fri) This excellent cultural centre has a museum and keeping place with displays about the local Wathaurong people, Koori history, art and cultural tours.

Ballarat Wildlife Park   ZOO

(☎03-5333 5933; www.wildlifepark.com.au; cnr York & Fussell Sts; adult/child/family $24/15/70; ⊗9am-5.30pm, tour 11am) A fun zoo with mostly native animals, reptiles and a few exotics.

Ballarat Bird World   AVIARY

(☎03-5341 3843; www.ballaratbirdworld.com. au; 408 Eddy Ave, Mt Helen; adult/child/family $10/6/30; ⊗10am-5pm) Boasts 40 species of birds hanging out in a peaceful garden aviary with ponds and waterfalls. Just south of town.

Trash & Trivia Market   MARKET

(Creswick Rd; ⊗8am-1pm Sun) At the Ballarat Showgrounds, 2km north of the city centre just off the Midland Hwy (Creswick Rd).

☞ Tours

Eerie Tours   GHOST TOUR

(☎1300 856 668; www.eerietours.com.au; tours $25) Relive the ghoulish parts of Ballarat's past with a night-time ghost tour or cemetery tour.

🛏 Sleeping

Ballarat's grand old pubs, B&Bs and cottages all offer gracious accommodation, and there are many motels and a handful of hostels and caravan parks.

Sovereign Hill Lodge   HERITAGE **$$**

(☎03-5337 1159; www.sovereignhill.com.au; Magpie St) Lots of visitors come to Ballarat to see Sovereign Hill, and there's a wide range of accommodation to choose from here. Within the 1850s village itself, **Steinfeld's** (s/d $140/160) is the top pick – six elegant heritage rooms and a common lounge overlooking the old township.

The **Lodge B&B** (d $175, with spa $190) features stylish heritage rooms around a cosy guest lounge with fireplace and bar. There are also **motel rooms** (s/d/f $125/145/200).

For budget travellers there's the cute four-room **YHA Cottage** (dm/s/tw $305/49/68). There's also dormitory-style bunkhouse accommodation for groups or families.

George Hotel   HOTEL **$$**

(☎03-5333 4866; www.georgehotelballarat.com. au; 27 Lydiard St Nth; d/f from $120/195; ❄🤖🛜) This grand old pub has seen bags of history since it was first built in 1852. It's right in the thick of things and the recently refurbished rooms are tasteful and comfortable. There's also a good bar and restaurant. If you're staying here on a weekend though, consider that the nightclub below is open until 5am.

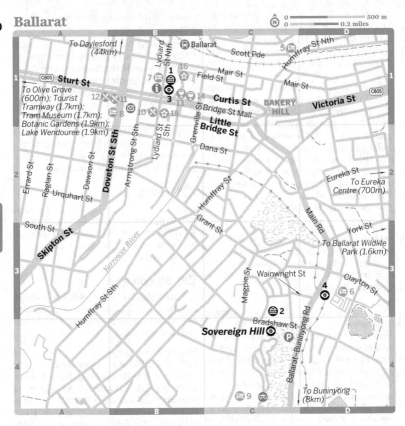

Ballarat Backpackers Hostel HOSTEL $
(☎0427-440661; www.ballarat.com/eastern station.htm; 81 Humffray St Nth; s/d/f $40/65/90) In the old Eastern Station Hotel (1862), this refurbished guesthouse is also a decent corner pub with occasional live music. Rooms are fresh and good value.

Oscar's BOUTIQUE HOTEL $$
(☎03-5331 1451; www.oscarshotel.com.au; 18 Doveton St; d $150-200, spa room $225; ✳🖭) The 13 rooms of this attractive art-deco hotel have been tastefully refurbished to include double showers and spas (watch a flat-screen TV from your spa).

Ballarat Goldfields Holiday Park CARAVAN PARK $
(☎03-5332 7888; www.ballaratgoldfields.com.au; 108 Clayton St; powered sites $35, cabins $87-170; ✳🖭) Close to Sovereign Hill, with a good holiday atmosphere. The cabins are like miners cottages.

✖ Eating

Ballarat offers plenty of dining options around Sturt and Lydiard Sts and there's a nice cafe strip on the Sturt St '400 Block' between Dawson and Doveton Sts. For cheap eats, Bakery Hill, east of the Bridge St Mall, is a global and fast-food area.

L'Espresso ITALIAN $$
(☎03-5333 1789; 417 Sturt St; mains $11-18.50; ☉7am-6pm, to 11pm Fri & Sat) A mainstay on Ballarat's cafe scene, this trendy Italian-style place doubles as a record shop – choose from the whopping jazz, blues and world-music CD selection while you wait for your espresso or Tuscan bean soup.

Europa Café CAFE $$
(☎03-5338 7672; www.europacafe.com.au; 411 Sturt St; mains $12-27; ☉breakfast & lunch daily, dinner Thu-Sun; 🖉) Global range of food including curries, pastas and vegetarian; family-friendly and sharp service.

Ballarat

Olive Grove   DELI, CAFE $
(✆03-5331 4455; 1303 Sturt St; dishes $7-12; ⊙breakfast & lunch; ☑) The Olive Grove is always buzzing with locals lingering over coffee, gourmet baguettes or bagels, or browsing the deli delights of cakes, cold meats and cheeses.

Craig's Royal Hotel   CAFE, RESTAURANT $$
(✆03-5331 1377; www.craigsroyal.com.au; 10 Lydiard St Sth; mains $26-35; ⊙breakfast, lunch & dinner) Even if you can't afford to stay here, you can experience some royal treatment with a cocktail in historic Craig's Bar or coffee in Craig's Café & Larder. For fine dining, the Gallery Bistro is a sumptuous atrium dining room serving French-inspired cuisine.

Boatshed Restaurant   MODERN AUSTRALIAN $$
(✆03-5333 5533; www.boatshed-restaurant.com; Lake Wendouree Foreshore; mains $18-32; ⊙breakfast, lunch & dinner) Perched on stilts over the lake, you can sit on an enclosed deck or stay inside with the open fire and leather armchairs. Good for coffee and cake all day, and a stylish place for a Mod Oz lunch or dinner of seafood or steak.

🍷 Drinking & Entertainment

With a large student population, Ballarat has a lively nightlife. There are some fine old pubs around town, but most of the entertainment is centred on Lydiard St and the nearby Camp St precinct.

Irish Murphy's   PUB
(✆03-5331 4091; 36 Sturt St; ⊙to 3am Wed-Sun) The Guinness flows freely at this atmospheric Irish pub. It's a welcoming place and the live music draws people of all ages.

Haida   LOUNGE BAR
(✆03-5331 5346; 2 Camp St; ⊙5pm-late Wed-Sun) Haida is a loungy two-level bar where you can relax with a cocktail by the open fire or chill out to DJs and live music downstairs.

Karova Lounge   NIGHTCLUB
(✆03-5332 9122; www.karovalounge.com; cnr Field & Camp Sts; ⊙9pm-late Wed-Sat) Ballarat's best original live-music venue showcases local and touring bands in grungy, industrial style.

Her Majesty's Theatre   THEATRE
(✆03-5333 5888; www.hermaj.com; 17 Lydiard St Sth) Ballarat's main venue for the performing arts since 1875, 'Her Maj' is in a wonderful Victorian-era building and features theatre, live music, comedy and local productions.

ⓘ Information

Ballarat Visitors Centre (✆1800 446 633, 03-5320 5741; www.visitballarat.com.au; 43 Lydiard St; ⊙9am-5pm) The visitor centre has moved to this temporary location while the Eureka Centre is redeveloped.

ⓘ Getting There & Away

BUS Greyhound Australia (✆13 14 99; www.greyhound.com.au) buses between Adelaide and Melbourne stop in Ballarat if you ask the driver (adult $72, 8¾ hours, departs Adelaide 8.15pm). **Airport Shuttle Bus** (✆03-5333 4181; www.airportshuttlebus.com.au) goes direct from Melbourne's Tullamarine Airport to Ballarat train station (adult/child $30/16, 1½ hours, nine daily, seven on weekends).

TRAIN V/Line (✆13 61 96; www.vline.com.au) has frequent direct trains between Melbourne (Southern Cross Station) and Ballarat ($10.40, 1½ hours, 18 daily) and at least three services via Geelong.

Life on the goldfields was a great leveller, erasing social distinctions as doctors, merchants, ex-convicts and labourers toiled side by side in the mud. But as the easily won gold began to run out, the diggers recognised the inequalities between themselves, and the privileged few who held land and the government.

The limited size of claims and the inconvenience of licence hunts, coupled with police brutality and taxation without political representation, fired the unrest that led to the Eureka Rebellion.

In September 1854 Governor Hotham ordered the hated licence hunts to be carried out twice weekly. In the following October a miner was murdered near a Ballarat hotel after an argument with the owner, James Bentley. Bentley was found not guilty by a magistrate (and business associate), and a group of miners rioted and burned his hotel. Bentley was retried and found guilty, but the rioting miners were also jailed, which fuelled their distrust of authority.

Creating the Ballarat Reform League, the diggers called for the abolition of licence fees, a miner's right to vote and increased opportunities to purchase land.

On 29 November 1854 about 800 miners, led by Irishman Peter Lalor, burnt their licences at a mass meeting and built a stockade at Eureka, where they prepared to fight for their rights.

On 3 December the government ordered troopers to attack the stockade. There were only 150 diggers within the barricades at the time and the fight lasted only 20 minutes, leaving 30 miners and five troopers dead.

The short-lived rebellion was ultimately successful. The miners won the sympathy of Victorians, and the government chose to acquit the leaders of the charge of high treason.

The licence fee was abolished. A miner's right, costing one pound a year, gave the right to search for gold and to fence in, cultivate and build a dwelling on a moderate-sized piece of land – and to vote. The rebel leader Peter Lalor became a member of parliament some years later.

Bendigo

POP 76,000

You don't have to look far to find evidence of Bendigo's heritage – in the magnificent Shamrock Hotel, the Central Deborah Goldmine and the Chinese dragons that awaken for the Easter Festival.

Gold was discovered at nearby Ravenswood in 1851, and during the boom years between the 1860s and 1880s, mining companies poured money into the town, resulting in the Victorian architecture that graces Bendigo's streets today. By the 1860s, diggers were no longer tripping over surface nuggets, and so deep mining began. Local legend has it that you can walk underground from one side of the town to the other. These days the town is a prosperous provincial centre with fine public gardens, statues and buildings, a bohemian cafe and restaurant scene, and one of Victoria's best regional art galleries.

◎ Sights

If you plan on seeing the main sights, the **Bendigo Experience Pass** (adult/child/family $45/24.50/110), valid for three months, is good value. Ask at the visitor centre.

Central Deborah Goldmine　HISTORIC MINE
(☑03-5443 8322; www.central-deborah.com; 76 Violet St; adult/child/family $26.50/13.50/65; ◎9.30am-5pm) For a very deep experience, descend into this 500m-deep mine with a geologist. Worked on 17 levels, about 1000kg of gold has been removed. After donning hard hats and lights, you're taken down the shaft to inspect the operations, complete with drilling demonstrations.

Golden Dragon Museum & Gardens　MUSEUM
(☑03-5441 5044; www.goldendragonmuseum.org; 1-11 Bridge St; adult/child/family $10/5/25; ◎9.30am-5pm) Bendigo's obvious Chinese heritage sets it apart from other goldfields towns, and this fantastic museum and garden is the place to experience it. Walk through a huge wooden door into an awesome chamber filled with dragons, including the Imperial Dragons Old Loong (the oldest in the world) and Sun Loong (the longest in

the world at over 100m). Outside, the Yin Yuan (Garden of Joy) classical Chinese gardens are a tranquil little haven with bridges, water features and ornamental shrubs.

Bendigo Art Gallery
GALLERY

(☑03-5434 6088; www.bendigoartgallery.com.au; 42 View St; admission by donation; ☉10am-5pm, tours 2pm) One of Victoria's finest regional galleries, the permanent collection here includes outstanding colonial and contemporary Australian art, such as work by Charles Blackman, Fred Williams, Rupert Bunny and Lloyd Rees, the annual temporary exhibitions are cutting edge. The Gallery Café overlooks Rosalind Park.

Bendigo Talking Tram
TOURIST TRAM

(☑03-5442 2821; www.bendigotramways.com; adult/child/family $15/9/43, valid 2 days; ☉9.30am-3.30pm) For an interesting tour of the city, hop aboard one of the restored vintage 'talking' trams. The hop-on, hop-off trip runs from the Central Deborah Mine to the **Tramways Museum** (1 Tramways Rd; admission free with tram ticket; ☉10am-5pm) every half-hour making half a dozen stops.

Sacred Heart Cathedral
CHURCH

(www.sandhurst.catholic.org.au/cathedral; cnr Wattle & High Sts) You can't miss the soaring steeple of this wonderful cathedral. Inside, beneath the high vaulted ceiling, there's a magnificently carved bishop's chair, some beautiful stained-glass windows, and wooden angels jutting out of the ceiling arches.

Chinese Joss House
TEMPLE

(☑03-5443 8255; Finn St, North Bendigo; adult/child/family $5.50/3.50/11; ☉11am-4pm Wed, Sat & Sun) Painted red, the traditional colour for strength, this is the only remaining practising joss house in central Victoria. It's 2km northwest of the centre.

Lake Weeroona
LAKE

(cnr Nolan & Napier Sts) Bendigo's little lake is a favourite spot for boating, kayaking or just walking around the path that encircles it. It's 1.5km northeast of the centre.

Rosalind Park
PARK

In the city centre, this lovely green space has lawns, big old trees, fernery and the fabulous **Cascades Fountain**, which was excavated after being buried for 120 years. Climb to the top of the **lookout tower** for sensational 360-degree views or wander through the **Conservatory Gardens**.

FREE Bendigo Pottery
POTTERY

(☑03-5448 4404; www.bendigopottery.com.au; 146 Midland Hwy, Epsom; ☉9am-5pm) Australia's oldest pottery works, the Bendigo Pottery was founded in 1857 and is classified by the National Trust. The historic kilns are still used; watch potters at work, admire the gorgeous ceramic pieces or throw a pot yourself (half-/full day $12/18). The attached **museum** (adult/child $8/4) tells the story of pottery through the ages. It's 7km northeast of the centre.

White Hills Botanic Gardens
GARDEN

Just 2km north of town, the gardens feature many exotic and rare plant species, a small fauna park, aviary, and barbecue facilities.

🏃 Activities

The **O'Keefe Rail Trail**, a hike-or-bike trail along a disused railway line, starts near the corner of Midland Hwy and Baden Stand and meanders for 19km to Axedale.

Ironbark Horse Trail Rides (☑03-5436 1565; www.bwc.com.au/ironbark; 1/2hr rides $38/65; ☉8.30am-5pm Mon-Sat) organises various horse rides including the Great Australian Pub Ride to Allies Hotel in Myers Flat (with lunch $85).

Also located in the Ironbark complex, **Bendigo Gold World** (☑03-5448 4140; www.bendigogold.com.au; ½/full day tours $290/350; ☉8.30am-5pm Mon-Sat) operates fossicking and detecting tours into the bush, and hires out prospecting equipment. It's located 5km northeast of the centre.

✯✯ Festivals & Events

Easter Festival
CARNIVAL

(www.bendigoeasterfestival.org.au) Bendigo's major festival, held in March or April, attracts thousands with its carnival atmosphere and colourful and noisy procession of Chinese dragons, led by Sun Loong, the world's longest imperial dragon.

Bendigo Cup
HORSE RACING

(www.racingvictoria.net.au/vcrc/bendigo) Part of the Spring Racing Carnival; held in November.

🛏 Sleeping

Several accommodation services offer lovely maisonettes, townhouses, suites and apartments in the heart of the city: **Abode Bendigo** (☑03-0414-425 447; www.abodebendigo.com.au); **Allawah Bendigo** (☑03-5444 4655; www.allawahbendigo.com) and **Bendigo Holi-**

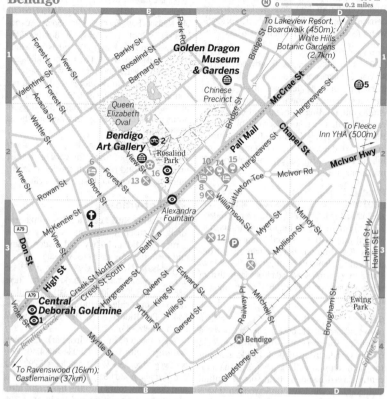

day Accommodation (☑03-5439 3588; www.bendigoholidayaccommodation.com).

Shamrock Hotel HOTEL **$$**
(☑03-5443 0333; www.hotelshamrock.com.au; cnr Pall Mall & Williamson St; d $120-175, ste $225) One of Bendigo's historic icons, the Shamrock is a stunning Victorian building with stained glass, original paintings, fancy columns and a *Gone with the Wind*–style staircase. The refurbished upstairs rooms range from small standard rooms to spacious deluxe and spa suites.

Fleece Inn YHA HOSTEL **$**
(☑03-5443 3086; www.thefleeceinn.com.au; 139 Charleston Rd; dm/s/d/f $35/55/77/110; ❄) This 140-year-old former pub has dorm rooms with partitioned-off beds, cosy private rooms (share facilities), communal kitchen and a huge back courtyard with lounge area, TV and barbecues. Smart rooms are up the grand original timber staircase.

Flynn's Place BOUTIQUE HOTEL **$$**
(☑03-5444 0001; www.flynnsplace.com.au; 104 Short St; d $165-195; ❄🛜) The two modern self-contained apartments at Flynn's are sleekly fitted out and furnished in a historic building, with queen beds, widescreen TVs, DVDs, sound systems and free wi-fi.

A-Line Holiday Village CABINS, CARAVAN PARK **$**
(☑03-5447 9568; www.alineholidayvillage.com.au; 5615 Calder Hwy; en-suite sites from $25, cabins $70-90, A-line units d $85-115; ❄🛏) About 10km from the city centre on the Melbourne side of town, this park is set in bushland with immaculate, grassy sites and cute A-frame split-level cottages with all mod cons.

Lakeview Resort MOTEL **$$**
(☑03-5445 5300; www.lakeviewresort.com.au; 286 Napier St; d/f incl breakfast $140/190; ❄🛜🏊) You've got Lake Weeroona across the road, spacious units around the central courtyard, shaded pool, piazza, and

Quills, a fine-dining restaurant with an excellent reputation.

Old Crown Hotel PUB **$**
(☑03-5441 6888; 238 Hargreaves St; r per person $45) Location is the key at this ultra-central pub, with clean old-style budget rooms with share facilities.

✗ Eating

Bendigo has an excellent range of cafes, pubs (including the Shamrock) and restaurants, most in the convenient block bounded by Pall Mall, Bull St, Hargreaves St and Mitchell St.

GPO MEDITERRANEAN **$$**
(☑03-5443 4343; www.gpobendigo.com.au; Pall Mall; mains $14-45; ⊙lunch & dinner) The food and atmosphere here is superb and rated highly by locals. Confit pork belly and roasted kingfish grace the Mediterranean menu, or go for the innovative pizzas and pasta or tapas plates.

Wine Bank WINE BAR, CAFE **$$**
(☑03-5444 4655; www.winebankonview.com; 45 View St; mains $12-18, ⊙lunch & dinner) Wine bottles line the walls in this former bank building, which serves as a wine shop and bar specialising in central Victorian wines, and an atmospheric Italian-style cafe serving tapas and platters.

Gillies' PIES **$**
(Hargreaves St Mall; pies from $3-5; ⊙daily) The pie window on the corner of the mall here is a Bendigo institution, and the pies are as good as you'll find anywhere.

Barzurk CAFE, BAR **$$**
(☑03-5442 4032; 66 Pall Mall; mains $8-28; ⊙lunch daily, dinner Wed-Sun) A trendy but casual streetside cafe-bar with pressed-tin ceilings and a courtyard out the back. The menu includes Thai, pasta, risotto and gourmet pizza.

Piyawat Thai THAI **$**
(☑03-5444 4450; 136 Mollison St; mains $14-18; ⊙dinner Tue-Sun; ☑) Tucked away in a cosy house a couple of blocks south of the centre, this authentic Thai restaurant serves fabulously fragrant curries, noodles and Thai stir-fries at affordable prices.

Bendigo ninesevensix TRAM RESTAURANT **$$$**
(☑03-5444 4655; www.bendigoninesevensix. com.au; set menu $98; ⊙dinner Sat) Every Saturday night a 1952 Melbourne W-class tram becomes a rolling restaurant, with a set menu including four courses and free drinks – a great way to see the city.

Boardwalk CAFE **$$**
(☑03-5443 9855; Nolan St; mains $18-29; ⊙breakfast, lunch & dinner) The location on the edge of Lake Weeroona is the big tick here – full-length windows and an alfresco deck offer prime views of water birds and rowers.

Toi Shan CHINESE **$**
(☑03-5443 5811; 67 Mitchell St; mains $12-19, buffet $11.50-14.50; ⊙lunch & dinner) For cheap and cheerful Chinese, Toi Shan has been around since the gold rush and you can fill up with the lunchtime smorgasbord.

⊙ Drinking & Entertainment

Bendigo has a lively nightlife – uni nights are Tuesday and Thursday. Although some

clubs are open as late as 5am, all have a 2am lockout. The main nightlife zone is Bull St and along Pall Mall.

Pugg Mahones
IRISH PUB

(✆03-5443 4916; 224 Hargreaves St; ⊙10.30am-late Mon-Sat) With Guinness (and many other beers) on tap, Puggs has a thickly welcoming atmosphere, not unreasonable doormen, a beer garden and live music every Thursday, Friday and Saturday night till 3am.

Dispensary Enoteca
CAFE, COCKTAIL BAR

(✆03-5444 5885; 9 Chancery Lane; ⊙daily from 8am) Hidden down tiny Chancery Lane, the Dispensary serves food throughout the day, but it's also a trendy little cocktail bar with a mind-boggling selection of beers, spirits and wines.

Capital Theatre
THEATRE

(✆03-5441 5344; www.bendigo.vic.gov.au; 50 View St) In the beautifully restored Capital Theatre, this is the main venue for the performing arts, with hundreds of performances and exhibitions each year.

Star Theatre
CINEMA

(✆03-5446 2025; www.starcinema.org.au; Eaglehawk Town Hall, 1 Peg Leg Rd, Eaglehawk; adult/child $13/7; ⊙from 1.30pm) Watch a flick with a beer or wine in decadent armchair comfort at this classic cinema. It is 6km northeast of the city centre.

ℹ Information

Bendigo Visitors Centre (✆1800 813 153, 03-5444 4445; www.bendigotourism.com; 51 Pall Mall; ⊙9am-5pm) In the historic former post office, offering an accommodation booking service.

ℹ Getting There & Away

Bendigo Airport Service (✆03-5444 3939; www.bendigoairportservice.com.au) runs direct between Melbourne's Tullamarine Airport and Bendigo train station (adult one-way/return $39/74, child $15/30, two hours, four daily). Bookings essential.

V/Line (✆13 61 96; www.vline.com.au) has frequent trains between Melbourne (Southern Cross Station) and Bendigo ($15.80, two hours, 12 to 18 daily) via Kyneton and Castlemaine.

Castlemaine

POP 7250

Castlemaine is a rewarding working-class town where a growing community of artists and tree-changers live amid some inspiring gold-rush architecture and gardens. Even after the gold ran out, the town kept its reputation for industry and innovation – this was the birthplace of the Castlemaine XXXX beer-brewing company (now based in Queensland) and Castlemaine Rock, a hard-boiled sweet lovingly produced by the Barnes family since 1853. It's also the 'Street Rod Centre of Australia', where hot-rods have been built and shown off since 1962.

After gold was discovered at Specimen Gully in 1851, the Mt Alexander Diggings attracted some 30,000 diggers and Castlemaine became the thriving marketplace for the goldfields. The town's importance waned as the surface gold was exhausted by the 1860s but, fortunately, the centre of town was well established by then and remains relatively intact.

Castlemaine hosts the **State Festival** (www.castlemainefestival.com.au) in March/April in odd-numbered years, one of Victoria's leading arts events.

◉ Sights & Activities

Castlemaine Art Gallery & Historical Museum
ART GALLERY, MUSEM

(✆03-5472 2292; www.castlemainegallery.com; 14 Lyttleton St; adult/student/family $4/2/8; ⊙10am-5pm Mon-Fri, noon-5pm Sat & Sun) The impressive museum, in a superb art-deco building, has a collection of colonial and contemporary Australian art including works by Frederick McCubbin and Tom Roberts; downstairs is a local history museum.

Buda
MUSEUM

(✆03-5472 1032; www.budacastlemaine.org; 42 Hunter; adult/child/family $9/4/25; ⊙noon-5pm Wed-Sat, 10am-5pm Sun) Dating from 1861, Buda was home to a Hungarian silversmith and his descendants for 120 years. The family's art and craft collections and personal belongings are on display.

Castlemaine Botanic Gardens
GARDENS

Enjoy a stroll in the gardens, just north of the town centre; it's one of the oldest and best in regional Victoria.

Castlemaine Rod Shop
CAR MUSEUM

(✆03-5472 3868, 0428-122 206; Pyrenees Hwy, Chewton; adult/child $5/free) If you're into hot rods and custom cars, take a trip out to the shop about 7km east of town in Chewton. The big green shed contains around 20 custom-built vehicles and drag racers. Call ahead to check it's open.

Harcourt Region
WINE

About 10km northwest of Castlemaine, the region is known as the Victoria's 'apple centre', but in recent years it has also developed as an excellent mini wine region – the tourist office can provide a map and a list of cellar doors. Check out Bress (☎03-5474 2262; www.bress.com.au; 3894 Calder Hwy; ⊙11am-5pm Sat & Sun), a combined winery and cidery.

Restorers Barn
ANTIQUES

(☎03-5470 5667; www.restorersbarn.com.au; 129-133 Mostyn St; ⊙10am-5.30pm Mon-Fri, 10am-4pm Sat & Sun) Collectors love the barn, a big shed in town dripping with interesting bric-a-brac, collectables and tools.

🛏 Sleeping

The free Mount Alexander accommodation booking service (☎03-5470 5866, 1800 171 888; www.maldoncastlemaine.com) covers Castlemaine, Maldon and surrounds.

Theatre Royal Back Stage
BOUTIQUE HOTEL $$$

(☎03-5472 1196; www.theatreroyal.info; 30 Hargreaves St; B&B d $220-240) It's a unique experience staying backstage in this 1854 theatre. The two suites are compact, but beautifully decorated with period furniture and cinema memorabilia, and are literally right behind the velvet curtain – you can clearly hear any performances, though the rate includes admission to all movies screened during your stay.

Midland Private Hotel
GUESTHOUSE $$

(☎03-5472 1085; www.themidland.com.au; 2 Templeton St; s/d $110/150, d with bathroom $200, apt d $270) Opposite the train station, this lace-decked 1879 hotel is mostly original so the rooms are old-fashioned and a bit small but it has plenty of charm, from the art-deco entrance to the magnificent guest lounge and attached Maurocco Bar.

Colonial Motel
MOTEL $$

(☎03-5472 4000; www.castlemainemotel.com.au; 252 Barker St; s/d $115/125, spa unit $155, apt $190; ✱🐾🛜) Conveniently central and the best of Castlemaine's motels, the Colonial has modern rooms, some with spa, and high-ceilinged apartments in a beautifully converted school building.

🍴 Eating

Castlemaine's dining scene is constantly evolving and improving, with a good cafe strip at the east end of Mostyn St.

Good Table
EUROPEAN $$

(☎03-5472 4400; www.thegoodtable.com.au; 233 Barker St; mains $14-25; ⊙lunch & dinner Thu-Sun) There have been numerous incarnations of this lovely corner hotel, but the Good Table does it well with a thoughtful European-influenced menu featuring linguini with yabbies and organic goat pie.

Saffs Cafe
CAFE $

(☎03-5470 6722; 64 Mostyn St; mains $8-24; ⊙lunch daily, dinner Wed-Sat) A local favourite, Saffs is a bright, friendly place with good coffee, cake, brilliant breakfasts, local artwork on the walls and a rear courtyard.

Empyre Hotel
MODERN AUSTRALIAN $$$

(☎03-5472 5166; 68 Mostyn St; lunch $17-25, dinner $34-36; ⊙breakfast & lunch Wed-Sun, dinner Wed-Sat) In a beautifully restored 19th-century hotel, dinner at the Empyre is a sumptuous fine-dining experience. There's more relaxed lunchtime dining in the cafe.

Apple Annie's Bakery & Café
BAKERY, CAFE $

(☎03-5472 5311; 31 Templeton St; mains $6-12; ⊙breakfast & lunch) For fresh baked bread, mouth-watering cakes and pastries, it's hard to beat this country-style cafe and bakery.

ℹ Information

Castlemaine Visitors Centre (☎03-5470 6200; www.maldoncastlemaine.com; Mostyn St; ⊙9am-5pm) In the magnificent old Castlemaine Market, the town's original market building fronted with a classical Roman-basilica facade with a statue of Ceres, the Roman goddess of the harvest, on top.

ℹ Getting There & Away

V/Line (☎13 61 96) trains run hourly between Melbourne and Castlemaine ($11.60, 1½ hours) and continue on to Bendigo ($3.40).

Maldon

POP 1220

Maldon is a well-preserved relic of the gold-rush era, with many fine buildings constructed from local stone. The population is a scant reminder of the 20,000 who used to work the local goldfields, but this is still a living, working town – packed with tourists on weekends but reverting to its sleepy self during the week.

The town centre consists of High St and Main St, lined with antique stores, cafes, old toy shops, lolly shops, bookstores and the

three local pubs – the Maldon, Grand and Kangaroo hotels.

Folk-music fans will enjoy the annual Maldon Folk Festival (www.maldonfolkfestival.com) held in early November.

◉ Sights

Maldon & District Museum   MUSEUM
(☎03-5474 1633; adult/child $5/1; ⊙1.30-4pm Fri-Wed) Behind the visitor centre, the old marketplace is now this museum with historical photos and a research room.

Carman's Tunnel   HISTORIC SITE
(☎03-5475 2656; carmanstunnel@maldon.vicmail.net; off Parkin's Reef Rd; adult/child $5/2; ⊙tours 1.30, 2.30 & 3.30pm Sat & Sun, daily during school holidays) A 570m-long mine tunnel, excavated in the 1880s, that took two years to dig yet produced only $300 worth of gold. Now you can descend with a guide for a 45-minute candlelight tour.

Victorian Goldfields Railway   TRAIN
(☎03-5470 6658, 03-5475 2966; www.vgr.com.au; return adult/child/family $27/13/60; ⊙ 10.30am, 1pm & 3pm Wed & Sun) If you're in town on a Wednesday or Sunday, ride the beautifully restored steam train along the original line through the Muckleford forest to Castlemaine (and back). For a little extra, go 1st class (adult/child/family $40/23/93, Sunday only) in an oak-lined viewing carriage.

Porcupine Township   HISTORIC VILLAGE
(☎03-5475 1000; www.porcupinetownship.com.au; cnr Bendigo & Allens Rds; adult/child/family $10/6/30; ⊙10am-5pm) A quaint theme village recreating the years leading up to the gold rush (1835 to 1853) with a collection of some 40 original slab buildings, including miners' huts, a dance hall and a resident ghost. There are no costumed characters here but kids will enjoy a carriage ride and possibly some panning.

Mt Tarrengower   LOOKOUT
Don't miss the 3km drive up for panoramic views from the poppet-head lookout.

🛏 Sleeping & Eating

The **Butts Reserve camp site** (free) in the Maldon Historic Reserve has toilets and picnic tables. From Maldon, head west along Franklin St and follow the signs to Mt Tarrengower.

Penny School Gallery & Cafe   CAFE, RESTAURANT $$
(☎03-5475 1911; www.pennyschoolgallery.com.au; 11 Church St; mains $11-35; ⊙11am-5pm Wed-Sun, 11am-10pm Fri & Sat) In a lovely heritage building tucked away from busy Main St, this light-filled cafe-restaurant features changing exhibitions. It's a great spot for coffee, but the Mod Oz menu of pasta, smoked trout and Daylesford venison is hard to beat.

Bean There Cafe   CAFE $
(☎0419-102 723; 44 Main St; meals $7-15; ⊙lunch Wed-Sun) This tiny licensed cafe is worth a visit for the yabby pies, made from locally farmed yabbies.

ℹ Information

Maldon Visitors Centre (☎03-5475 2569; www.maldoncastlemaine.com; 95 High St; ⊙9am-5pm; @) Pick up the *Information Guide* and *Historic Town Walk* brochure, which guides you past some of the most historic buildings

ℹ Getting There & Away

Castlemaine Bus Lines (☎03-5472 1455) runs at least three buses daily between Castlemaine and Maldon, connecting with trains to and from Melbourne.

Maryborough
POP 7700

Maryborough is part of central Victoria's 'Golden Triangle', where prospectors still turn up a nugget or two. The town's pride and joy is the magnificent railway station, and now that passenger trains are running here again from Melbourne it's worth a day trip.

The town boasts plenty of impressive Victorian-era buildings, but **Maryborough Railway Station** (☎03-5461 4683; www.stationantiques.com; 38 Victoria St; admission free; ⊙10am-5pm Mon-Wed & Sun, till 10pm Thu-Sat, closed Tue) leaves them all for dead. Built in 1892, the inordinately large station, complete with clock tower, was described by Mark Twain as 'a train station with a town attached'. Today it houses a mammoth antique emporium, a regional wine centre and an excellent cafe.

If you're interested in finding your own gold nuggets, **Coiltek Gold Centre** (☎03-5460 4700; www.coiltek.com.au; 6 Drive-in Crt; ⊙9am-5pm) offers full-day prospecting courses (one/two people $120/200) with state-of-the-art metal detectors.

Information

Central Goldfields Visitor Centre (☏1800 356 511, 03-5460 4511; www.visitmaryborough. com.au; cnr Alma & Nolan Sts; ☺9am-5pm; @) Loads of helpful maps and friendly staff. There's also a replica of the famous Welcome Stranger gold nugget here and a library in the same complex.

Getting There & Away

The passenger train to Maryborough finally resumed in 2010. Currently there's only one train a day (via Ballarat), departing Melbourne at around 4pm ($23.70, 2½ hours). The return train leaves at 7.25am weekdays, 7am Saturday and 8am Sunday. Maryborough is also connected by bus to Castlemaine and Ballarat.

Daylesford & Hepburn Springs

POP 3670

Set among the idyllic hills, lakes and forests of the central highlands, Daylesford and Hepburn Springs form the 'spa centre of Victoria', and have developed into quite the bohemian weekend getaway, though the area's mineral springs have been attracting fashionable Melburnians since the 1870s. Even if you don't indulge in a spa treatment, there are lots of great walks, a fabulous foodie scene and an arty, alternative vibe – the local population is an interesting blend of hippies and old-timers, and there's a thriving gay and lesbian scene here.

Daylesford is the main centre, with most of the action on Vincent St. Continue north on Vincent St for 3km to reach the small community of Hepburn Springs.

Sights & Activities

The historic **Hepburn Bathhouse & Spa** (☏03-5321 6000; www.hepburnbathhouse.com; Mineral Springs Reserve, Hepburn Springs; ☺9am-6.30pm) is all spruced up and specialises in relaxation baths and hydrotherapy treatments using mineral water pumped from ancient underground cavities. Two-hour entry to the public pool and spa costs $23 ($33 Saturday to Monday), while private spas start at $75. Around the spa are picnic areas and several **mineral springs** where you can fill your own bottles from pumps. There are some good **walking trails**; pick up maps and guides from the visitors centre.

The **Convent Gallery** (☏03-5348 3211; www.theconvent.com.au; 7 Daly St, Daylesford; admission $5; ☺10am-4pm) is a magnificent 19th-century convent that's been lovingly converted into an art gallery with changing exhibitions, a cafe and the Altar Bar.

Boats and canoes can be hired at **Lake Daylesford**, which is also ringed by a walking trail. Or head out to the even prettier **Jubilee Lake**, a popular local swimming hole about 3km southeast of town.

The **Daylesford Museum** (☏03-5348 1453; 100 Vincent St, Daylesford; adult/child $3/1; ☺1.30-4.30pm Sat & Sun), next to the visitor centre, houses local historical society memorabilia.

Daylesford Spa Country Railway (☏03-5348 1759; www.dscr.com.au; Daylesford train station; adult/child/family $10/8/25; ☺10am-2.30pm Sun) operates one-hour rides every Sunday on old railway trolleys and restored trains. The **Daylesford Sunday Market** (☺8am-2pm Sun) is held at the train station.

The beautiful **Wombat Hill Botanic Gardens** (Central Springs Rd) are worth a stroll for the many oaks, pine and cypress trees.

Chocolate Mill (☏03-5476 4208; www.chocmill.com.au; 5451 Midland Hwy, Mt Franklin; ☺10am-4.45pm Tue-Sun) is worth the 10-minute drive from Daylesford. You can watch the Belgian chocolates being made by hand (tour at 11.30am).

You could just about fit a Boeing 747 in the enormous **Mill Markets** (☏03-5348 4332; www.millmarkets.com.au; 105 Central Springs Rd, Daylesford; ☺10am-6pm), housing a mindboggling collection of furniture, collectables, antiques, books and retro fashions.

Festivals & Events

ChillOut Festival GAY & LESBIAN
(www.chilloutfestival.com.au) Held over the Labour Day weekend in March this gay and lesbian pride festival is Daylesford's biggest annual event, attracting thousands of people for street parades, music and dance parties.

Swiss Italian Festa ITALIAN
(www.swissitalianfesta.com) Held in late October, this festival draws on the region's European roots with literary events, music, food, wine and art.

Sleeping

Even with 5000 beds in the region, accommodation fills up fast – most places charge more on weekends and stipulate a two-night stay. Book ahead. You can camp for free at Mt Franklin, an extinct volcano 10km north of Daylesford. Bookings for the region's charming guesthouses, cottages and B&Bs can be made through

PAMPERING SOAKS

The Daylesford and Hepburn Springs region is well known for its rejuvenating mineral spa treatments. Along with a soak or facial, you can fork out plenty of money for herbal treatments, massage and mud packs.

» **Daylesford Day Spa** (✏03-5348 2331; www.daylesforddayspa.com.au; 25 Albert St, Daylesford) Start with a vitamin-rich mud body mask and steam in a body-care cocoon, before a scalp massage and Vichy shower.

» **Endota Spa** (✏03-5348 1169; www.endota.com.au; cnr Vincent St & Central Springs Rd, Daylesford) Hot stones and Hawaiian lomi lomi massage.

» **Massage Healing Centre** (✏03-5348 1099; www.massagehealingcentre.com.au; 5/11 Howe St, Daylesford) For a modest, down-to-earth alternative to the glitz-and-glam spa resorts listed here, try this place.

» **Mineral Spa at Peppers** (✏03-5348 6200; www.thesprings.com.au; Springs Retreat, 124 Main Rd, Hepburn Springs) Have an algae gel wrap, based on an ancient Chinese treatment, then move into the lavender steam room, or take a soft pack float.

» **Salus** (✏03-5348 3329; www.lakehouse.com.au; Lake House, King St, Daylesford) The pampering starts as you walk through a small rainforest to your exotic jasmine-flower bath in a cedar-lined treehouse overlooking the lake.

» **Shizuka Ryokan** (✏03-5348 2030; www.shizuka.com.au; 7 Lakeside Dr, Hepburn Springs) Shiatsu massage, geisha facials and spa treatments with natural sea salts and seaweed extracts, ginseng and green tea at this Japanese-style country spa retreat.

---

agencies in Daylesford: **Daylesford Cottage Directory** (✏03-5348 1255; www.cottagedirectory.com.au; 16 Hepburn Rd); **Daylesford Getaways** (✏03-5348 4422; www.dayget.com.au; 123 Vincent St) and **Escapes Daylesford** (✏03-5348 1448; www.escapesdaylesford.com.au; 94 Vincent St).

DAYLESFORD

Lake House   BOUTIQUE HOTEL **$$$**
(✏03-5348 3329; www.lakehouse.com.au; King St; B&B d $500-600, ste $740; ❄⊛) You can't talk about Daylesford without waxing on about the Lake House, a superb family-run property overlooking Lake Daylesford. Set in rambling gardens with bridges and waterfalls, the 33 rooms are split into spacious waterfront rooms with balcony decks, and lodge rooms with private courtyards. They're contemporary chic with free wi-fi and heated floor tiles in the bathrooms.

Daylesford Hotel   PUB **$**
(✏03-5348 2335; www.daylesfordhotel.com.au; cnr Albert & Howe Sts; d $66) This old pub is the only truly budget accommodation close to the Daylesford town centre. Small but neat upstairs rooms have shared facilities and access to the communal balcony overlooking the street.

Jubilee Lake Holiday Park   CARAVAN PARK **$**
(✏03-5348 2186, 1800 686 376; www.jubileelake.com.au; 151 Kale Rd; unpowered/powered sites $33/39, cabins $95-165; ⊛⊜) Set in bushland on the edge of pretty Jubilee Lake, this friendly place is the best park in the region.

Daylesford Central Motor Inn   MOTEL **$$**
(✏03-5348 2029; www.daylesfordcentralmotorinn.com; 54 Albert St; d/f from $95/130; ⊛⊜) An easy stroll from the town centre, this is a standard but comfortable motel.

HEPBURN SPRINGS

Mooltan Guesthouse   GUESTHOUSE **$$**
(✏03-5348 3555; www.mooltan.com.au; 129 Main Rd; midweek s/d from $60/85, weekend from $100/130) Behind a well-clipped hedge, this inviting Edwardian country home has large lounge rooms, a billiard table and tennis court. Bedrooms open onto a broad verandah overlooking the Mineral Springs Reserve. The cheapest rooms have shared facilities.

Shizuka Ryokan   GUESTHOUSE **$$$**
(✏03-5348 2030; www.shizuka.com.au; 7 Lakeside Dr; d $250-350) Inspired by traditional places of renewal and rejuvenation in Japan, this traditional minimalist getaway has six rooms with private Japanese gardens, tatami matting and plenty of green tea.

Daylesford Wildwood YHA   HOSTEL **$**
(✏03-5348 4435; www.mooltan.com.au/ww/wildwood.htm; 42 Main Rd; dm/s/d from $27/40/65) In a charming 1920s cottage with a grand

lounge room, you'd hardly know this was a youth hostel. The timber deck at the back looks over the garden.

Continental House
GUESTHOUSE $

(☎03-5348 2005; www.hepburnretreatcentre.com.au; 9 Lone Pine Ave; s/d $50/90, cottage $100/130) Also called the Hepburn Retreat Centre, this rambling, timber guesthouse is a little slice of alternative-lifestyle heaven and is as much a yoga retreat as a place to crash. Basic rooms in the house, cottages in the garden, a laid-back vibe, yoga classes and vegan cooking courses.

Eating & Drinking

These two towns are walk-in gourmet treats. Every second business on Vincent St in Daylesford is a cafe or foodstore and there's a buzzing atmosphere here on weekends.

DAYLESFORD

Lake House
MODERN AUSTRALIAN $$$

(☎03-5348 3329; www.lakehouse.com.au; King St; mains $36-38; ☉lunch & dinner) The Lake House has long been regarded as Daylesford's top dining experience and it doesn't disappoint with stylish purple high-back furniture, picture windows showing off Lake Daylesford, a superb seasonal menu, award-winning wine list and impressive service.

Sault
MODERN AUSTRALIAN $$$

(☎03-5348 6555; www.sault.com.au; 2349 Ballan Rd, Sailors Falls; mains $29-40; ☉lunch Fri-Sun, dinner Wed-Sun) Surrounded by lavender and lakes in a grand building about 6km south of Daylesford, stylish Sault is a seriously fine-dining restaurant with a reputation for innovative dishes using local produce. Wednesday is 'locals' night' – meal and drink for $25.

Cliffy's Emporium
DELI, CAFE $$

(☎03-5348 3279; 28 Raglan St; mains $12-25; breakfast & lunch, dinner Sat; ☑) Behind the vine-covered verandah of this local institution is an old-world shop crammed with organic vegies, cheese, preserves and the spicy aromas of fruit chutneys and roasting coffee. Occupying a narrow side section, the busy cafe is perfect for breakfast, pies and baguettes.

Koukla Café
PIZZA $$

(☎03-5348 2363; www.frangosandfrangos.com; 82 Vincent St; mains $15-25; ☉breakfast, lunch & dinner) Part of Frangos and Frangos, this moody European-style corner cafe is a great place for coffee on the couch or sourdough wood-fired pizza for lunch.

Perfect Drop
WINE BAR

(☎03-5348 3373; www.aperfectdrop.com; 5 Howe St; ☉dinner daily, lunch Sat & Sun) This sweet little wine bar and restaurant really is the place for a perfect drop, with local wines a speciality. It has a relaxed, loungy feel for drinking and chatting, and top-notch food with lots of share plates to sample.

Breakfast & Beer
CAFE, BAR

(☎03-5348 1778; www.breakfastandbeer.com; 117 Vincent St) Straight out of a Belgian backstreet, this inspired European-style cafe stocks fine local and imported beer, a boutique menu strong on local produce including innovative breakfast/brunch fare.

HEPBURN SPRINGS

Chowder House
CAFE $$

(☎03-5348 2221; 97 Main Rd; mains $6.50-20; ☉breakfast & lunch Wed-Sun) The creamy seafood chowder here practically walks out the door and it can be hard to snare a seat on the weekends. The chunky soups, including salmon and chicken, are complemented by fresh corn bread, a hearty breakfast menu and cheerful service.

Red Star Café
CAFE $$

(☎03-5348 3329; www.redstar.com.au; 115 Main Rd; mains $10-22; ☉8am-4pm) The weatherboard shopfront is like someone's home, with loungy couches, bookshelves, great music, a garden out the back and a funky local vibe.

Palais
CAFE, BAR

(☎03-5348 4849; www.thepalais.com.au; 111 Main Rd, Hepburn Springs; ☉from 6pm Thu-Sun) This Hepburn institution in an atmospheric 1920s theatre is now a restaurant, cafe and cocktail bar with lush lounge chairs and a pool table. There's a regular schedule of gigs featuring well-known touring artists, and open-mic nights on the first Thursday of the month.

ℹ Information

Daylesford Visitors Centre (☎03-5321 6123; www.visitdaylesford.com; 98 Vincent St, Daylesford; ☉9am-5pm; @) A cheery place, with stacks of information.

ℹ Getting There & Around

Daily **V/Line** (☎13 61 96) services connect Melbourne to Daylesford ($10, two hours) by train to Woodend then bus to Daylesford. Weekday V/Line buses run from Daylesford to Ballarat ($7), Castlemaine ($4) and Bendigo ($7). The buses run from Bridport St opposite the fire station.

GOULBURN VALLEY & HUME HIGHWAY REGION

The Hume Hwy (M31) is the multilane link between Melbourne and Sydney via Albury-Wodonga. You can put your foot down for most of the way as it's not particularly scenic and the speed limit is usually 110km, but there are a few hidden attractions just off the freeway, including 'Kelly Country' – places associated with the legend of bushranger Ned Kelly. To the east are the foothills of Victoria's High Country: get off at Seymour for Mansfield and Mt Buller, or Wangaratta for Mt Hotham and Falls Creek.

West of the Hume is the Goulburn Valley, Victoria's fruit bowl and a popular area for seasonal work. The valley's other main crop is wine, and several wineries are worth a visit, notably the impressive Tahbilk and Mitchelton wineries near Nagambie.

River Country Adventours (☑03-5852 2736; www.adventours.com.au) runs canoe and camping safaris on the Goulburn and Murray Rivers from Seymour, Shepparton, Wyuna and other sites.

Shepparton
POP 27,700

Laid-back 'Shepp' is the capital of the Goulburn Valley, where the Goulburn and Broken Rivers meet. This is the heart of a rich farming and fruit-growing region so it's popular with travellers looking for fruit-picking work. Look out for the extraordinarily colourful cows dotted around town – such ironic rural art!

FREE Shepparton Art Gallery ART GALLERY (☑03-5832 9861; www.sheppartonartgallery.com. au; Eastbank Centre, 70 Welsford St; ☺10am-4pm) Has a fine permanent collection of Australian art.

Bangerang Cultural Centre CULTURAL CENTRE (☑03-5831 1020; www.bangerang.org.au; l Evergreen Way; admission free; ☺9am-4pm Mon-Fri) An indigenous gallery, museum and keeping place, that is well worth a visit for its unique collection of Koorie art and artefacts, and wonderful dioramas.

🛏 Sleeping & Eating

Shepparton Backpackers HOSTEL $ (☑03-5831 6556; www.sheppartonbackpackers. com.au; 139 Numurkah Rd; dm/d from $25/80; @) Tucked away behind a car wash 3km north of town, this well-equipped hostel is the place to stay if you're looking for agricultural work in the region.

Victoria Lake Holiday Park CARAVAN PARK $ (☑03-5821 5431; www.viclakeholidaypark.com. au; 536 Wyndham St; unpowered/powered sites $24/26, d cabins $77-115) Beside Lake Victoria, this friendly park has plenty of grass and shade, bicycle paths and good facilities.

Cellar 47 ITALIAN $$ (☑03-5831 1882; 170 High St; mains $15-32; ☺lunch & dinner Mon-Sat) With it's sleek black-and-glass bar and gourmet wood-fired pizzas, this is a long-standing local favourite.

ℹ Information

Shepparton Visitors Centre (☑1800 808 839, 03-5831 4400; www.discovershepparton.com. au; Wyndham St; ☺9am-5pm) At the southern end of the Victoria Park Lake.

ℹ Getting There & Away

Shepparton train station is east of the town centre. There are daily **V/Line** (☑13 61 96) trains and buses to/from Melbourne ($18, 2½ hours, three daily).

Nagambie
POP 1380

On the shores of pretty Lake Nagambie, created by the construction of the Goulburn Weir back in 1887, Nagambie is a popular base for water sports.

Two of Victoria's best wineries are just south of town: **Mitchelton Wines** (☑03-5736 2221; www.mitchelton.com.au; Mitchellstown Rd; ☺10am-5pm), with an art gallery and award-winning Shiraz; and **Tahbilk Winery** (☑03-5794 2555; www.tahbilk.com.au; 254 O'Neils Rd; ☺9am-5pm Mon-Fri, 10am-5pm Sat & Sun). Tahbilk opens onto the **Wetlands & Wildlife Reserve** (admission gold coin donation; wetland cruise adult/child $10/free; ☺11am-4pm Mon-Fri, 10am-4.30pm Sat & Sun) with boardwalks or boat tours through a natural area rich in bird life. Entry is via the excellent **Wetlands Café** (mains $19-28; ☺lunch daily).

ℹ Information

Nagambie Visitor Information Centre (☑1800 444 647, 03-5794 2647; www.nagambielakes-tourism.com.au; cnr Goulburn Hwy & Moss Rd; ☺9am-5pm) Staff are passionate about their lake, their town and their region.

Glenrowan

POP 320

Ned Kelly's legendary bushranging exploits came to their bloody end here in 1880. The story of Ned and his gang has become an industry in this one-street town – a short detour off the main highway – and you can't drive through Glenrowan without being confronted by the legend and his souvenirs, including a 2m armour-clad statue. The main sites of the capture are signposted, so pick up a walking map and follow the trail.

At the Glenrowan Tourist Centre, Ned Kelly's Last Stand (✆03-5766 2367; 41 Gladstone St; adult/child/family $24/18/64; ◷9.30am-4.30pm, shows every 30 min) is an animated theatre where Ned's story is told in a series of rooms by a cast of clunky animatronic characters, culminating in a smoky shootout and Ned's hanging (it may be too scary for young children). Original props include a hand gun owned by Ned, Sergeant Kennedy's hitching post and a rare copy of the findings of the royal commission into the Kelly manhunt.

Nearby, underneath Kate's Cottage, a museum (✆03-5766 2448; 35 Gladstone St; adult/child $4.50/1; ◷9am-5.30pm) holds Kelly memorabilia and artefacts gathered from all over the district, and a replica of the Kelly home. Glenrowan has several country-style cafes, motels, and the local pub.

Wangaratta

POP 16,850

Wangaratta (just plain old 'Wang' to the locals) is a busy commercial centre along the Hume Hwy and the turn-off for the ski fields along the Great Alpine Rd or for the Rutherglen wine region. The name means 'resting place of the cormorants' and the town sits neatly at the junction of the Ovens and King Rivers. The main claim to fame here is the almost-world-famous Wangaratta Jazz Festival (✆1800 803 944; www.wangaratta-jazz.org.au), which attracts jazz players and buffs from around Australia and the world in early November.

◉ Sights & Activities

At the Wangaratta Cemetery you'll find the grave of notorious bushranger Dan 'Mad Dog' Morgan. It contains most of Morgan's remains: his head was taken to Melbourne for a study of the criminal mind, and the scrotum was supposedly fashioned into a tobacco pouch.

Wangaratta is the start of the **Murray to Mountains Rail Trail**, which runs east via Beechworth to Bright and now links Wangaratta with Rutherglen and Wahgunyah. You can hire bikes from Bicycle Superstore (✆03-5722 2033; www.bicyclesuperstore.com.au; 6-8 Handley St; adult/child per day $29/22).

⛏ Sleeping & Eating

Wangaratta has a decent range of typical motels, which can be booked online at www.visitwangaratta.com.au.

Hermitage Motor Inn   MOTEL $$
(✆03-5721 7444; www.hermitagemotorinn.com.au; cnr Cusack & Mackay Sts; d/f/spa $115/145/145; ✳❄❋) Close to the town centre, the Hermitage is the pick of Wang's motels with spacious rooms, contemporary decor, wi-fi and a pool.

Painters Island Caravan Park   CARAVAN PARK $
(✆03-5721 3380; www.paintersislandcaravanpark.com.au; Pinkerton Cres; unpowered/powered sites from $26, cabins $60-150; ✳❄❋) On 10 hectares on the banks of the Ovens River but close to the town centre, this impressive park has a playground, camp kitchen and a good range of cabins.

Vine Hotel   PUB FARE $$
(✆03-5721 2605; Detour Rd; mains $12-24; ◷lunch & dinner) Ned Kelly and his gang used to hang out here; these days the food is better and you're less likely to get shot. Go underground to the small museum and cellars. The Vine is about 3km north of town, on the road to Eldorado.

Rinaldo's Casa Cucina   ITALIAN $$
(✆03-5721 8800; www.rinaldos.com.au; 8-10 Tone Rd; mains $19-27; ◷lunch & dinner Wed-Sat, lunch Sun) Rinaldo's industrial-sized venue features fresh pasta dishes and modern Mediterranean versions of steak and seafood. Ask about cooking classes.

Idyl Book Café   CAFE $
(✆03-5722 3545; 64 Faithfull St; ◷breakfast & lunch Mon-Sat; @) Loads of secondhand books, good coffee and breakfasts with river views.

❶ Information

Wangaratta Visitors Centre (✆1800 801 065, 03-5721 5711; www.visitwangaratta.com.au; 100 Murphy St; ◷9am-5pm; @) In the old

SEASONAL WORK

There's harvesting or pruning work virtually year-round in the Shepparton area and it's well set up for travellers. The main season is January to May (apples, peaches and pears) and there's pruning work available from May to August.

CVGT (📞1300 724 788; www.cvgt.com.au; cnr Welsford & Sobraon Sts) runs a harvest hotline and has comprehensive listings of fruit-picking work. Backpacker hostels in Shepparton and Mooroopna can also help with finding work.

library, with displays, internet access, bike hire and videos depicting local rail trails and snippets from the annual Wangaratta Jazz Festival.

🛈 Getting There & Away

Wangaratta train station is just west of the town centre in Norton St. There's one direct **V/Line** (📞13 61 96) train daily from Melbourne ($22, 2½ hours) continuing on to Albury; all other services require changing to a bus at Seymour. There's one V/Line bus daily from Wangaratta to Rutherglen ($4, 30 minutes).

THE HIGH COUNTRY

The Great Dividing Range – Australia's eastern spine – curls around Victoria from the Snowy Mountains to the Grampians, peaking in the spectacular High Country. This is Victoria's mountain playground, attracting skiers and snowboarders in winter, and bushwalkers and mountain-bikers in summer.

Although there are plenty of activities on offer, it's the ski resorts that really pull the crowds. Skiers and snowboarders flock to Mt Buller, Mt Hotham and Falls Creek in particular, all of which have good on-mountain infrastructure. The ski season officially launches, with or without snow, on the Queen's Birthday long weekend in June and runs until mid-September. The best deals are to be found in June and September (low season), with late July to August (high season) the busiest and most expensive time.

Away from the mountain-tops, the High Country offers plenty of summer activities such as horse riding, canoeing, abseiling and mountain-biking, or more restful pastimes such as touring wineries and gourmet regions such as Milawa, King Valley and Beechworth.

Mt Baw Baw

ELEV 1564M

High in the Baw Baw National Park, this is Victoria's smallest (and cheapest) downhill resort – a relaxed option for beginners and families.

Mt Baw Baw Alpine Resort Management Board (📞03-5165 1136; www.mountbaw baw.com.au) provides tourist information and accommodation bookings. Several ski-hire places operate during the season, including **Mt Baw Baw Ski Hire** (📞03-5165 1120; www.bawbawskihire.com.au), which also books accommodation. Ski-season admission fees are $30/35 weekdays/weekends per car for the day car park. During summer admission is $5. The ski lifts operate only if there is snow; day tickets cost $59/39 per adult/child on weekdays and $64/44 on weekends.

🛏 Sleeping & Eating

There's an **accommodation booking service** (📞1300 651 136).

Kelly's Lodge   B&B $$

(📞03-5165 1129; www.kellyslodge.com.au; 11 Frosti Ln; r summer/winter from $100/330) This long-running and super-friendly place is in the centre of everything, with comfortable rooms and a cosy lounge. The ski-in cafe (mains $14 to $30) is a Baw Baw favourite, with legendary pizzas and lamb shanks.

Alpine Hotel   HOTEL $

(📞03-5165 1136; Currawong Rd; dm summer/winter from $25/30, d from $100/130) Superb-value year-round motel and backpacker accommodation.

Eildon

POP 740

The little one-pub town of Eildon is a popular recreation and holiday base, built in the 1950s to house Eildon Dam project workers. It sits on the edge of the 'pondage' – the

outflow from the Lake Eildon Dam. You can drive up to and across the dam's massive retaining wall to a **lookout point**, with sensational views over the lake, the town, and the houseboat building yards. Lake Eildon is one of Victoria's favourite watersports and houseboat playgrounds, with a shoreline of over 500km. The surrounding Lake Eildon National Park protects 277 sq km of bushland adjoining the lake.

The small Eildon visitor information centre (☑03-5774 2909; www.lakeeildon.com; Main St; ☺10am-2pm) has local information and houseboat hire.

⊙ Sights & Activities

Snobs Creek Freshwater Discovery Centre AQUARIUM
(☑03-5770 8052; Goulburn Valley Hwy, Snobs Creek; adult/child/family $7/4.50/20; ☺11am-4pm Fri-Mon, daily during school hols) Kids will love the touch-and-feel tanks, a trout farm and hatchery where you can feed the fish, and all sorts of native species in the aquarium.

Eildon Trout Farm FISH FARM
(☑03-5773 2377; www.eildontroutfarm.com.au; 460 Back Eildon Rd, Thornton; entry/fishing $1/2; ☺9am-5pm) Catching a trout or salmon is guaranteed, on the back road between Thornton and Eildon.

Rubicon Valley Horse-Riding HORSE RIDING
(☑03-5773 2292; www.rubiconhorseriding.com.au; Rubicon Rd, Thornton; rides introductory/2hr/half-day $45/65/90) Caters for all levels, including children, and runs overnight safaris ($395).

Snobs Creek Vineyard WINERY
(☑03-5774 2017; http://snobscreekvineyard.com.au; 486 Goulburn Valley Hwy, Snobs Creek) For something more leisurely, head to the cellar door, 5km from Eildon, where you can taste a range of cool-climate Shiraz, Pinot Noir and Chardonnay.

🛏 Sleeping & Eating

Lake Eildon is a beautiful place for bush camping with several lakeside national parks sites. **Fraser Camping Area**, on Coller Bay 14km northwest of Eildon along Skyline Drive, comprises three separate camp sites, while the **Jerusalum Creek Camping Area** is about 8km southwest of Eildon. All sites must be booked online through Parks Victoria (www.parkweb.vic.gov.au; camp sites $18).

Lake Eildon Marina & Houseboat Hire (☑03-5774 2107; www.houseboatholidays.com.au; 190 Sugarloaf Rd) and Eildon Houseboat Hire (☑0438 345 366; www.eildonhouseboathire.com.au) both rent out 10- to 12-berth houseboats (minimum hire per weekend from $1600).

THE KELLY GANG

Bushranger and outlaw he may have been, but Ned Kelly is probably Australia's greatest folk hero and a symbol of the Australian rebel character.

Born in 1855, Ned was first arrested when he was 14 and spent the next 10 years in and out of jails. In 1878 a warrant was issued for his arrest for stealing horses, so he and his brother Dan went into hiding. Their mother and two friends were arrested, sentenced and imprisoned for aiding and abetting.

Ned and Dan were joined in their hideout in the Wombat Ranges, near Mansfield, by Steve Hart and Joe Byrne. Four policemen – Kennedy, Lonigan, Scanlon and McIntyre – came looking for them, and, in a shoot-out at Stringybark Creek, Ned killed Kennedy, Lonigan and Scanlon. McIntyre escaped to Mansfield and raised the alarm.

The government put up a £500 reward for any of the gang members, dead or alive. In December 1878 the gang held up the National Bank at Euroa, and got away with £2000. Then, in February 1879, they took over the police station at Jerilderie, locked the two policemen in the cells, and robbed the Bank of New South Wales wearing the policemen's uniforms. By this time the reward was £2000 per head.

On 27 June 1880, the gang held 60 people captive in a hotel at Glenrowan. A train-load of police and trackers was sent from Melbourne. Surrounded, the gang holed up in the hotel and returned fire for hours, while wearing heavy armour made from ploughshares. Ned was shot in the legs and captured, and Dan Kelly, Joe Byrne and Steve Hart, along with several of their hostages, were killed.

Ned Kelly was brought to Melbourne, tried, then hanged on 11 November 1880. He met his end bravely; his last words are famously quoted as, 'Such is life'.

His death mask, armour and the gallows on which he died are on display in the Old Melbourne Gaol.

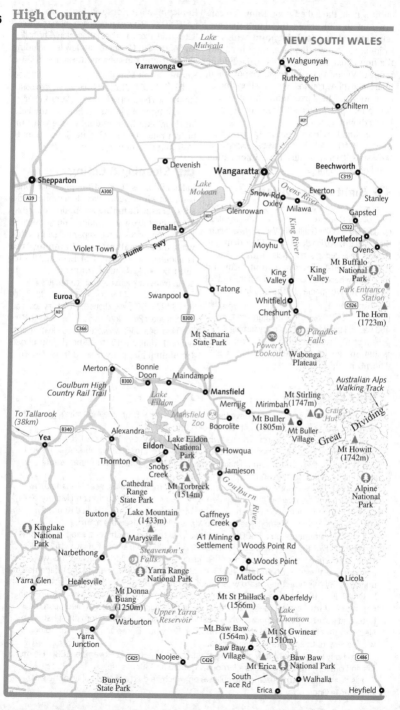

NEW SOUTH WALES

Lake Mulwala

Yarrawonga

Wahgunyah
Rutherglen

Chiltern

Devenish

Wangaratta

Beechworth

Lake Mokoan

Snow Rd
Oxley

Ovens River

Everton

Stanley

Shepparton

Glenrowan

Milawa

Gapsted

Benalla

Moyhu

King River

Myrtleford

Ovens

Violet Town

Hume Fwy

King Valley

King Valley

Mt Buffalo National Park

Park Entrance Station

Euroa

Swanpool

Tatong

Whitfield
Cheshunt

The Horn (1723m)

Mt Samaria State Park

Power's Lookout

Paradise Falls

Wabonga Plateau

Merton

Bonnie Doon

Maindample

Mansfield

Mt Stirling (1747m)

Australian Alps Walking Track

Goulburn High Country Rail Trail

Lake Eildon

Merrijig

Mirimbah

Craig's Hut

To Tallarook (38km)

Mansfield Zoo

Boorolite

Mt Buller (1805m)

Mt Buller Village

Great Dividing

Yea

Alexandra

Eildon

Lake Eildon National Park

Howqua

Mt Howitt (1742m)

Thornton

Snobs Creek

Jamieson

Cathedral Range State Park

Mt Torbreck (1514m)

Goulburn River

Alpine National Park

Buxton

Lake Mountain (1433m)

Gaffneys Creek

Kinglake National Park

Marysville

A1 Mining Settlement

Woods Point Rd

Narbethong

Steavenson's Falls

Woods Point

Licola

Yarra Glen

Healesville

Yarra Range National Park

Matlock

Mt Donna Buang (1250m)

Mt St Phillack (1566m)

Aberfeldy

Lake Thomson

Upper Yarra Reservoir

Warburton

Mt Baw Baw (1564m)

Mt St Gwinear (1510m)

Yarra Junction

Noojee

Baw Baw Village

Mt Erica

Baw Baw National Park

Bunyip State Park

South Face Rd

Erica

Walhalla

Heyfield

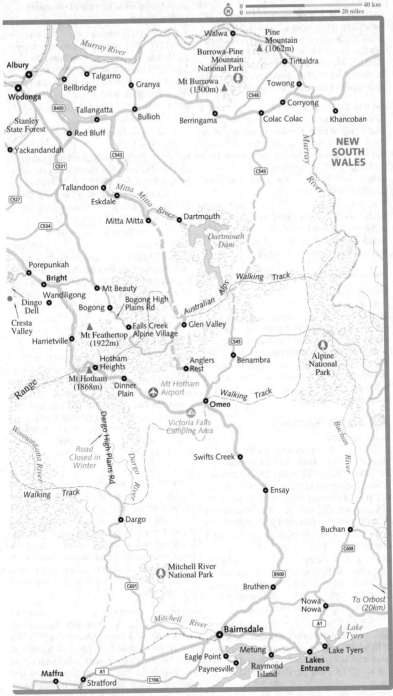

Morning Mist
B&B $$

(☑03-5774 2497; www.morningmist.com.au; 840 Back Eildon Rd; d midweek/weekend $120/175, q $220/320; ✹) On a scenic property overlooking the Goulburn River, this two-bedroom B&B is a wonderful place to relax. The decor has a certain old-fashioned charm but with slick modern touches (even a juke box).

Golden Trout Hotel Motel
MOTEL $

(☑03-5774 2508; www.goldentrout.com.au; 1 Riverside Dr; d $90) The local pub has standard, slightly tired, motel rooms attached but the location makes up for it – ask for a 'pondage view' room (they're all the same price). The bistro does good pub food (mains $14 to $28).

Eildon Caravan Park
CARAVAN PARK $

(☑03-5774 2105; www.eildoncp.com; Eildon Rd; unpowered/powered site $20/42, cabins $95-180) Rustic little camping ground in a bush setting with pondage frontage.

Mansfield

POP 2840

Mansfield is the gateway to Victoria's largest snowfields at Mt Buller, but also an exciting all-seasons destination in its own right. There's plenty to do here in *Man from Snowy River* country, with horse riding and mountain biking popular in summer, and a buzzing atmosphere in winter when the snow bunnies hit town.

◉ Sights & Activities

Mansfield Zoo
ZOO

(☑03-5777 3576; www.mansfieldzoo.com.au; 1064 Mansfield Woods Point Rd; adult/child/family $15/8/44; ⊗10am-5.30pm, till 6.30pm in summer) A surprisingly good wildlife park with lots of native fauna and some exotics like a pair of lions. You can sleep in the paddocks in a swag (adult/child $65/45, including zoo entry for two days) and wake to the dawn chorus of wildlife.

Mansfield Cemetery
CEMETERY

The graves of the three Mansfield police officers killed by Ned Kelly and his gang in 1878 at Stringybark Creek rest in this cemetery, at the end of Highett St.

All Terrain Cycles
MOUNTAIN BIKING

(☑03-5775 2724; www.allterraincycles.com.au; 58 High St) Hires out top-quality mountain bikes and safety equipment, from $45 per day to $120 for the top downhill bikes.

Also runs guided tours and mountain-biking clinics.

High Country Horses
HORSE RIDING

(☑03-5777 5590; www.highcountryhorses.com. au; Mt Buller Rd, Merrijig; 2hr/half-day rides $80/115, overnight from $500; ⊗Oct-May) Based at Merrijig on the way to Mt Buller; offers anything from a short trot to overnight treks to Craig's Hut, Howqua River and Mt Stirling.

McCormacks Mountain Valley Trail Rides
HORSE RIDING

(☑03-5775 2886; www.mountainvalleytrailrides. com; 43 McCormack's Rd, Merrijig; day ride from $200, overnight from $500; ⊗Oct-May) Experienced locals take you into the King Valley and High Country, including a four-day adventure for $900.

Watson's Mountain Country Trail Rides
HORSE RIDING

(☑03-5777 3552; www.watsonstrailrides.com. au; Three Chains Rd, Boorolite; 1/2hr $35/60, 1-/2-day rides $200/475) A peaceful property where children can learn with pony rides or short trail rides, or take off on overnight catered rides.

🛏 Sleeping

Mansfield Travellers Lodge
MOTEL, HOSTEL $

(☑03-5775 1800; www.mansfieldtravellerslodge. com.au; 116 High St; dm $25, s/d/f $90/95/160; ✹) Close to the centre of town, this is a long-time favourite with backpackers and families. The spacious dorms are in a restored heritage building, while the motel section features spacious one- and two-bedroom units.

Highton Manor
BOUTIQUE B&B $$

(☑03-5775 2700; www.hightonmanor.com.au; 140 Highton Lane; shared $65, d stable/manor/tower incl breakfast $120/$225/365; ✹) Built in 1896 for Francis Highett, who sang with Dame Nellie Melba, this stately two-storey manor has style and romance but doesn't take itself too seriously, with group accommodation in the 'party room', modern rooms in the converted stables, and lavish period rooms in the main house.

Banjo's Accommodation
CABINS $$

(☑03-5775 2335; www.banjosmansfield.com.au; cnr Mt Buller Rd & Greenvale Lane; d/q $110/170; ✹) These family-friendly self-contained units on the edge of town can sleep up to five people in the studios and six in the two-bedroom units. They're modern and

spacious and the expansive grounds are perfect to let kids run around.

Wappan Station FARMHOUSE
(☑03-5778 7786; www.wappanstation.com.au; Royal Town Rd, Maindample; shearers quarters adult/child $30/15, cottages d from $150; ❄) Watch farm activities from your deck at this sheep-and-cattle property on the banks of Lake Eildon.

Mansfield Holiday Park CARAVAN PARK
(☑03-5775 1383; www.mansfieldholidaypark.com. au; Mt Buller Rd; unpowered/powered sites from $22/25, d cabins $60-100; ❄) On the edge of town, this is a spacious caravan park with a pool, minigolf, camp kitchen and comfortable cabins.

✗ Eating

Mansfield Farmers Market MARKET
(www.mansfieldfarmersmarket.com.au; Highett St; ⊙8.30am-1pm) On the fourth Saturday of each month, the farmers bring produce to town at the Mansfield Primary School.

Mansfield Regional Produce Store CAFE $
(☑03-5779 1404; www.theproducestore.com.au; 68 High St; mains $10-18; ⊙breakfast & lunch Tue-Sun, dinner Fri; ☀) The best spot in town for coffee or a light lunch, this rustic store stocks an array of local produce, wines and fresh-baked artisan breads.

Deck on High ASIAN FUSION $$
(☑03-5775 1144; www.thedeckonhigh.com.au; 13-15 High St; mains $18-33; ⊙lunch & dinner Wed-Mon, breakfast Sat & Sun) A sophisticated but relaxed bar-restaurant serving up genuinely good Asian-inspired food like Indonesian gado gado, pad Thai and sushi plates.

FORTY one CAFE $
(☑03-5775 2951; 39-41 High St; mains $8-17; ⊙breakfast & lunch) Famous for its creamy vanilla slice, but you can enjoy a range of gourmet surprises in the sunny courtyard here.

❶ Information

Mansfield & Mt Buller High Country Visitors Centre (☑1800 039 049; www.mansfield -mtbuller.com.au; Maroondah Hwy; ⊙9am-5pm Oct-May, 8am-9pm Jun-Sep) Books general accommodation for the region, ski accommodation and sells lift tickets.

❶ Getting There & Away

V/Line (☑13 61 96) buses run twice daily (once Sunday) from Melbourne ($21, three hours). **Mansfield–Mt Buller Bus Lines** (☑03-5775 2606; www.mmbl.com.au) runs seven buses daily for skiers from Mansfield to Mt Buller (adult/child return $50/34).

Mt Buller

ELEV 1805M

Victoria's largest and busiest ski resort, Buller buzzes all winter long. It's also developing into a popular summer destination for mountain bikers and hikers, with a range of cross-country and downhill trails. The extensive lift network includes the Horse Hill chairlift that begins in the day car park and drops you off in the middle of the ski runs. Cross-country trails link Mt Buller with **Mt Stirling**. In winter there's **night skiing** on Wednesday and Saturday night, and for non-skiers there's tobogganing, snowtubing and excellent snowshoeing. **Ducks & Drakes** (www.ducksanddrakes.net; tours $35-45) runs 1½-hour guided snowshoeing tours from the clock tower, including equipment and hot chocolate.

🛏 Sleeping

High Country Reservations (☑1800 039 049) and **Mt Buller Alpine Reservations** (☑03-5777 6633; www.mtbullerreservations.com. au) book lodge accommodation.

YHA Mt Buller HOSTEL $
(☑03-5777 6181; www.yha.com.au; The Ave; dm $60-70) In winter this well-known and cosy little YHA offers good facilities and friendly staff.

Monash University Alpine Lodge LODGE $
(☑03-5777 6577; www.sport.monash.edu.au/ alpine-lodge.html; 84 Stirling Rd; dm from $65) Right near the ski-lift ticket office, this grand lodge has four bunks to a room, a pleasant lounge, kitchen, TV room and drying room.

Mt Buller Chalet CHALET $$$
(☑03-5777 6566; www.mtbullerchalet.com. au; Summit Rd; d incl breakfast from $350; ❄) Open year-round, the Chalet offers a sweet range of suites, a library with billiard table, well-regarded eateries, an impressive sports centre and heated pool. The Chalet also operates nearby **Bulla Backpackers** (dm $55).

Hotel Enzian
CHALET **$$$**

(✆03-5777 6915; www.hotelenzian.com.au; 69 Chamois Rd; r from $240) Year-round Enzian has a good range of lodge rooms and apartments.

✖ Eating & Drinking

There's a licensed supermarket in the village centre and various fast-food eateries on the slopes and in the village, including the year-round **Cattleman's Café** (✆03-5777 7800; Bourke St; mains $8-18).

Pension Grimus
AUSTRIAN **$$**

(✆03-5777 6396; www.pensionsgrimus.com.au; Breathtaker Rd; mains $25-39; ⊙dinner daily, lunch Sat & Sun) One of Buller's originals, the Austrian-style food at the Kaptan's Restaurant, impromptu music and pumping bar will give you a warm, fuzzy feeling after a day on the slopes.

Kooroora Hotel
PUB FARE, NIGHTCLUB

(✆03-5777 6050; Village Square; ⊙till 3am in winter) Rocks hard and late during the ski season, and the popular Hoohah Kitchen serves good bistro meals.

ℹ Information

Mt Buller Resort Management Board (✆03-5777 6077; www.mtbuller.com.au; Level 5, Community Centre, Summit Rd; ⊙8.30am-5pm) Also opens an information office in the village-square clock tower in winter. Entrance fees to the Horse Hill day car park in winter are $35 per car. Lift tickets cost $99/54 per adult/child. Combined lift-and-lesson packages start at $145.

ℹ Getting There & Around

Mansfield-Mt Buller Buslines (✆03-5775 2606, winter 5775 6070; www.mmbl.com.au) runs a winter service from Melbourne on Wednesday, Friday and Sunday (adult/child return $165/125) or from Mansfield ($52/36) and charter services in summer.

Ski-season car parking is below the village; a 4WD taxi service transports people to their village accommodation.

King Valley & the Snow Road

On the back road between Mansfield and Wangaratta, the King Valley is a prosperous wine region noted for its Italian varietals and cool-climate wines such as Sangiovese, Barbera, sparkling Prosecco and Pinot Grigio.

The valley extends south along the King River, through the tiny towns of Mohyu, Whitfield and Cheshunt along the King River just north of the Alpine National Park and about 60km northeast of Mansfield.

Among the best are **Dal Zotto Estate** (✆03-5729 8321; www.dalzotto.com.au; Main Rd, Whitfield; ⊙10am-5pm); and **Pizzini** (✆03-5729 8278; www.pizzini.com.au; 175 King Valley Rd, Whitfield; ⊙11am-5pm). For more information check out www.winesofthekingvalley.com.au.

MILAWA/OXLEY GOURMET REGION

On the Snow Road, between Wangaratta and Myrtleford, the **Milawa/Oxley gourmet region** (www.milawagourmet.com) is the place to indulge your tastebuds.

At Oxley, don't miss a stop at the **King River Cafe** (✆03-5727 3461; www.kingrivercafe.com.au; Snow Rd; mains $11-28; ⊙lunch Mon & Wed-Sun, dinner Wed-Sun) for scrumptious dishes like goat's cheese soufflé and smoked trout, good coffee and local wines.

About 5km further on, the main street of Milawa boasts **Milawa Mustard** (✆03-5727 3202; www.milawamustard.com.au; Old Emu Inn, The Cross Roads; ⊙10am-5pm) for tastings of its handmade seeded mustards, herbed vinegars and preserves; the **Olive Shop** (✆03-5727 3887; www.theoliveshop.com.au; 1605 Snow Rd; ⊙10am-5pm Thu-Mon), an olive 'gallery' with oils and tapenades for sampling; and **Walkabout Honey** (✆03-5727 3468; Snow Rd; ⊙10am-5pm), where you can sample a range of honeys.

Next stop is the region's best-known winery, **Brown Brothers Vineyard** (✆03-5720 5547; www.brownbrothers.com.au; Bobbinawarrah Rd, Milawa; ⊙9am-5pm). The winery's first vintage was in 1889, and it has remained in the hands of the same family ever since. As well as the tasting room, there's the superb Epicurean Centre restaurant, a gorgeous garden, kids' play equipment, and picnic and barbecue facilities.

About 2km north of Milawa, **Milawa Cheese Company** (✆03-5727 3589; www.milawacheese.com; Factory Rd; ⊙9am-5pm) excels at soft farmhouse brie (from goat or cow) and pungent washed-rind cheeses. There's a bakery here and the excellent **Ageing Frog Bistrot** (mains $18-28), where the speciality is a variety of pizzas using Milawa cheese.

Just north of the Snow Road on the Ovens River flood plain is the little farming community of Whorouly, where the **Whorouly Grocer** (✆03-5727 1220; www.thewhoroulygrocer.com.au; 577 Whorouly Rd; ⊙9am-5pm Thu-Mon, till

4pm Sat & Sun) is a sweet deli, foodstore and cafe. Nearby is the Whorouly Hotel (☑03-5727 1424; 542 Whorouly Rd; d $50; mains $6-24; ☺lunch & dinner Fri & Sat), a friendly country pub where you can get a hearty bistro meal or stay the night. It's a mere 5km detour from the popular Murray to Mountains Rail Trail.

Beechworth

POP 2650

Beechworth's historic honey-coloured granite buildings and wonderful gourmet offerings make this one of northeast Victoria's most enjoyable towns. It's listed by the National Trust as one of Victoria's two 'notable' towns (the other is Maldon), and you'll soon see why: this living legacy of the goldrush era will take you back to the days of miners and bushrangers.

◉ Sights & Activities

HISTORIC PRECINCT

Beechworth's main attraction is the group of well-preserved, honey-tinged buildings that make up the Historic & Cultural Precinct (☑03-1300 366 321; ticket for all sites plus 2 guided tours adult/child/family $25/15/50; ☺9am-5pm). First is the Town Hall, where you'll find the visitor centre and the free *Echoes of History* audio-visual. Across the road is the Beechworth Courthouse (adult/child/family $6/4/12; ☺9am-5pm), where the trials of many key historical figures took place, including Ned Kelly and his mother, whose cells can still be seen. Behind it is the Old Police Station Museum (admission $2; ☺10am-2pm Fri-Sun). Send a telegram to anywhere in the world from the Telegraph Station on Ford St, the original Morse-code office. Walk

through to Loch St to the Burke Museum (adult/child/family $6/4/12; ☺10am-5pm). It's named after the hapless explorer Robert O'Hara Burke, who was Beechworth's superintendent of police before he set off on his fateful trek north with William Wills.

OTHER ATTRACTIONS

Beechworth Honey Experience (☑03-5728 1432; www.beechworthhoney.com.au; cnr Ford & Church Sts; admission free; ☺9am-5pm) takes you into the world of honey and bees with a self-guided audio-visual tour, live hive and honey tastings. The shop sells locally made honey, beeswax candles, nougat and soaps.

You'll get all nostalgic over the eye-popping range of old-time sweets and lollies at the Beechworth Sweet Co (www.beechworthsweetco.com.au; 7 Camp St; ☺daily). Down near pretty Lake Sambell you'll find the Chinese Gardens, a tribute to the Chinese gold miners.

The visitor centre runs two-hour walking tours (adult/child/family $8/5/15; ☺10.15am & 1.15pm) covering the gold rush and Ned Kelly's connections to town.

Beechworth Ghost Tours (☑0447 432 816; www.beechworthghosttours.com; adult/child/family $25/15/75) bring Beechworth's spooky past to life in these popular walking tours at La Trobe, a former lunatic asylum. Book ahead.

🛏 Sleeping

Beechworth is well endowed with cottages and heritage B&Bs; check out www.beechworth.com/accommodation.

Old Priory   GUESTHOUSE $
(☑03-5728 1024; www.oldpriory.com.au; 8 Priory Lane; dm/s/d $40/55/85, cottages $120) This historic convent is a spooky but charming

---

BIKING MT BULLER

Mt Buller has developed into one of the great summer mountain-biking destinations in Victoria, with a network of trails around the summit, and exhilarating downhill tracks. From 26 December to the end of January, the Horse Hill chairlift operates on weekends (all-day lift and trails access $53). If you're not biking you can still ride the chairlift all day (adult/child $16/11).

From 26 December till the Easter weekend a bus shuttle runs every weekend from the Mirimbah Store (☑03-5777 5529; www.mirimbah.com.au; per ride $14, daily $30), at the base of the mountain, to the Summit car park, from where you can ride all the way back down on a number of trails. The most popular is the 1½-hour River Spur, partly following the Delatite River with 13 river crossings. More challenging is the new Klingsbourne Trail. The owners of the Mirimbah Store (which, incidentally, is also a fabulous cafe) are experienced riders and a mine of information on the trails.

old place that's often used by school groups, but it's the best budget choice in Beechworth with lovely gardens and a range of rooms, including beautifully renovated miners cottages.

La Trobe at Beechworth APARTMENTS $$
(☑03-5720 8050; www.latrobeatbeechworth.com.au; Albert Rd; d $105-300, cottages from $175; ❋❄) On the hill above town, this was the Beechworth Lunatic Asylum for over 130 years. Today the art-deco buildings contain a range of rooms, including cottages and self-contained units.

Lake Sambell Caravan Park CARAVAN PARK $
(☑03-5728 1421; www.caravanparkbeechworth.com.au; Peach Dr; unpowered/powered sites $17/23, cabins $75-125; ❋❄) This shady park next to beautiful Lake Sambell has great facilities including a camp kitchen, playground and bike hire.

✕ Eating & Drinking

For a town of its size, Beechworth has some fantastic feasting, from provedores and pantries stocking fresh local produce to serious fine dining restaurants in historic buildings.

Provenance MODERN AUSTRALIAN $$
(☑03-5728 1786; www.theprovenance.com.au; 86 Ford St; mains $32-40; ☉dinner Wed-Sun) In an 1856 bank building, Provenance is elegant but contemporary fine dining. The innovative menu features dishes such as Berkshire pork belly and tea-smoked duck breast, and some inspiring vegetarian choices.

Bridge Road Brewers MICROBREWERY, PIZZA $
(☑03-5728 2103; www.bridgeroadbrewers.com.au; Ford St; pizza $12-21; ☉11am-5pm Mon-Sat, noon-11pm Sun) Hiding behind the imposing Tanswells Commercial Hotel, Beechworth's gem of a microbrewery produces some excellent beers (taste six for $8), and serves fresh-baked pretzels and super house-made pizzas for lunch Wednesday to Sunday and dinner Sunday night.

Beechworth Bakery BAKERY $
(☑03-5728 1132; 27 Camp St; light meals $3-10; ☉6am-7pm) Popular with locals and tourists, this is the original in a well-known bakery chain; great for pies and pastries, cakes and sandwiches.

Beechworth Provender CAFE $
(☑03-5728 2650; 18 Camp St; ☉breakfast & lunch) Crammed with delectable local produce and wines for filling a gourmet hamper, the Provender is also an excellent cafe.

❶ Information

Beechworth Visitors Centre (☑1300 366 321; www.beechworthonline.com.au; 103 Ford St; ☉9am-5pm) Accommodation and activity booking service. Ask about the Golden Ticket which gives admission to the historic precinct and two guided walking tours (valid two days).

❶ Getting There & Away

Beechworth is just off the Great Alpine Rd, 36km east of Wangaratta. **V/Line** (☑13 61 96; www.vline.com.au) runs a train/bus service between Melbourne and Beechworth with a change at Seymour ($26, four hours, three daily). There are direct buses from Wangaratta ($3.60, 35 minutes, six daily) and Bright ($3.40, 50 minutes, two daily).

Myrtleford

POP 2730

Along the Great Alpine Hwy near the foothills of Mt Buffalo, Myrtleford is yet another 'Gateway to the Alps', and a worthwhile stop if you're heading to the snowfields or exploring the gourmet region. **Myrtleford visitors centre** (☑03-5752 1044; www.visitmyrtleford.com.au, www.visitalpinevictoria.com.au; 38 Myrtle St; @) has information and a booking service.

The **Butter Factory** (☑03-5752 2300; www.butterfactory.com.au; 15 Myrtle St; mains $17-25; ☉breakfast & lunch Thu-Tue, dinner Fri & Sat; ✐) is a cafe, produce store and restaurant in an old butter factory, and you can see butter being churned here or take a short tour of the process most days. The produce store stocks a wide range of local jams, sauces, honey and pickles, while the cafe is a special place for an organic breakfast or lunch of local trout or innovative tasting plates.

Mt Buffalo National Park

ELEV 1500M

Beautiful Mt Buffalo is an easily accessible year-round destination – in winter it's a tiny family-friendly resort for cross-country skiing and tobogganing, and in summer it's a great spot for bushwalking, mountain biking and rock climbing.

It was named in 1824 by the explorers Hume and Hovell on their trek from Sydney to Port Phillip, and declared a national park in 1898. The main access road is out of Porepunkah, between Myrtleford and Bright.

You'll find granite outcrops, alpine lookouts, streams and waterfalls, wildflowers

and wildlife here. The **Big Walk**, an 11km, five-hour ascent of the mountain starts from Eurobin Creek Picnic Area, north of Porepunkah, and finishes at the Gorge Day Visitor Area. A road leads to just below the summit of the Horn (1723m), the highest point on the massif. Nearby Lake Catani is good for swimming, canoeing and camping.

🏃 Activities

There are 14km of groomed **cross-country ski trails** starting out from the Cresta Valley car park. In summer Mt Buffalo is a **hang-gliding** paradise, and the near-vertical walls of the Gorge provide some of Australia's most challenging **rock-climbing**.

Adventure Guides Australia ADVENTURE
(☎0419-280614, 03-5728 1804; www.visitmount-buffalo.com.au) This established operator offers abseiling (from $55), rock-climbing (from $220) and caving through an underground river system (from $99). It also runs a cross-country ski school in winter.

Eagle School of Microlighting MICROLIGHTING
(☎03-5750 1174; www.eagleschool.com.au; flights $70-300) Exhilarating tandem flights over Mt Buffalo region as well as flying lessons.

🛏 Sleeping

The 100-year-old Mt Buffalo Chalet, currently closed and in the hands of Parks Victoria, is still looking for an operator, but could reopen any time soon.

Remote camping is possible at Rocky Creek, which has pit toilets only. Lake Catani Campground (camp sites $17; ☺Nov-Apr) has a summer campground with toilets and showers. Book through Parks Victoria (☎13 19 63; www.parkweb.vic.gov.au).

Bright

POP 2110

Famous for its glorious autumn colours, Bright is a popular year-round destination

in the foothills of the alps and a gateway to Mt Hotham and Falls Creek. Skiers make a beeline through Bright in winter, but it's a lovely base for exploring the Alpine National Park, paragliding, fishing and kayaking on local rivers, bushwalking and exploring the region's wineries. Plentiful accommodation and some sophisticated restaurants and cafes complete the picture.

◎ Sights & Activities

Walking trails around Bright include the 3km riverside **Canyon Walk**, 4km **Cherry Walk** and a 6km track to Wandiligong that follows Morses Creek.

You could spend an hour or two getting lost among the antiques, retro stuff, junk and collectables at the Old Tobacco Sheds (☎03-5755 2344; Great Alpine Rd; ☺10am-5pm).

There are plenty of wineries in the region, but for something different you can sample a rage of liqueurs, schnapps and brandy distilled on site at Great Alpine Liqueurs (☎03-5755 1002; www.greatalpineliqueurs.com. au; 36 Churchill Ave; ☺10am-4.30pm Fri-Mon, daily during holidays).

The **Murray to the Mountains Rail Trail** starts (or ends) behind the old train station. Bikes, tandems and baby trailers can be rented from Cyclepath (☎03-5750 1442; www.cyclepath.com.au; 74 Gavan St; per hr from $16, half/full day from $22/30).

☞ Tours

Bright is a base for all sorts of adventure activities – paragliding enthusiasts catch the thermals from nearby Mystic Mountain.

Active Flight PARAGLIDING
(☎0428-854 455; www.activeflight.com.au) Introductory paragliding course (from $225) or tandem flights (from $130).

Alpine Paragliding PARAGLIDING
(☎0428-352 048; www.alpineparagliding. com; 100 Gavan St; ☺Oct-Jun) Tandem flights from Mystic ($130) and two-day courses $499.

MURRAY TO MOUNTAINS RAIL TRAIL

The Murray to the Mountains Rail Trail (www.murraytomountains.com.au) is one of the High Country's best walking/cycling trails for families or casual riders – it's sealed and relatively flat for much of the way and passes through spectacular rural scenery of farms, forest and vineyards. The 94km trail runs from Wangaratta to Bright via Beechworth, Myrtleford and Porepunkah. A newly completed section heads northwest from Wangaratta to Wahgunyah via Rutherglen, completing the true Murray to Mountains experience.

DETOUR: YACKANDANDAH

An old gold-mining town nestled in beautiful hills and valleys east of Beechworth, 'Yack', as it's universally known, is original enough to be classified by the National Trust. You might recognise it as the setting for the 2004 film *Strange Bedfellows*, starring Paul Hogan and Michael Caton.

Today many of the historic shops in the main street contain galleries, antiques and curios: **A Bear's Old Wares** (☑02-6027 1114; www.abearsoldwares.com; 12 High St; ☺9am-5.30pm) is a fascinating shop crammed with Buddhist and Hindu idols, prayer flags, Tibetan jewellery and wall hangings.

Karrs Reef Goldmine (☑0408 975 991; adult/child $18.50/16.50; ☺10am, 1pm & 4pm Fri-Tue) is an old mine dating from 1857. On the 1½-hour guided tours you don a hard hat and descend into the original tunnels to learn a bit about the mine's history.

The biggest event of the year is the **Yackandandah Folk Festival** (☑02-6027 1447; http://folkfestival.yackandandah.com), with three days of music, parades, workshops and fun in mid- to late March.

Yackandandah visitors centre (☑02-6027 1988; www.uniqueyackandandah.com.au; 27 High St; ☺9am-5pm) is in the grand, 1878 Athenaeum building. Pick up the free *A Walk in High Street* brochure, which details the history of the shops.

MELBOURNE & VICTORIA BRIGHT

Bright Microflights　　MICROLIGHTING
(☑03-5750 1555; brightmicroflights@swiftdsl.com.au) Takes you on powered hang-glider flights over Porepunkah ($70) or Mt Buffalo ($155).

Elm Lodge Limousine Tours　　WINE TOUR
(☑03-5755 1144; tours from $75) Visit wineries or country pubs in style with these stretch limo tours.

5 Star Adventures　　ADVENTURE
(☑03-5755 5100; www.5staradventure.com.au; 120 Great Alpine Rd) Kayaking, bushwalking, 4WD and snow sports tours.

✯ Festivals & Events

Bright Autumn Festival　　STREET FESTIVAL
(www.brightautumnfestival.org.au) Open gardens, scenic convoy tours and a popular gala day; held April or May.

Bright Spring Festival　　STREET FESTIVAL
(www.brightspringfestival.com.au) Celebrate all things Bright and beautiful. Runs over two weeks, culminating on the Melbourne Cup weekend in late October/early November.

🛏 Sleeping

There's an abundance of accommodation here, but rooms are scarce during the holiday seasons. There are several good caravan and camping grounds along the Ovens River.

Odd Frog　　BOUTIQUE HOTEL $$
(☑03-5755 2123; www.theoddfrog.com; 3 McFadyens Ln; d $150-195, q $250) Designed and built by the young architect–interior designer owners, these contemporary, ecofriendly studios feature light, breezy spaces and fabulous outdoor decks with a telescope for star-gazing. The design features clever use of the hilly site with sculptural steel-frame foundations and flying balconies.

Bright Hikers Backpackers　　HOSTEL $
(☑03-5750 1244; www.brighthikers.com.au; 4 Ireland St; dm/s/d/f $25/45/65/130) Right in the centre of town, this, clean, well-set-up hostel has a cosy lounge, a great old-style verandah and bike hire ($20 per day).

Mine Manager's House　　B&B $$$
(☑03-5755 1702; www.brightbedandbreakfast.com.au; 30 Coronation Ave; d $170, B&B $230; ☎) Dating from 1892 and now sumptuously restored to the smallest detail, this traditional B&B offers couples a complete experience. Enjoy warm hospitality, beautiful rooms and a delightful English garden.

Elm Lodge Motel　　MOTEL $$
(☑03-5755 1144; www.elmlodge.com.au; 2 Wood St; d $100-140, spa cottage $180; ☀) This slightly quirky set of burgundy and pine units has rooms for all budgets, from a shoebox cheapie to spacious two-bedroom self-contained apartments with polished floorboards, and spa rooms.

Coach House Inn　　MOTEL $
(☑03-5755 1475; www.coachhousebright.com.au; 100 Gavan St; s/d $85/95, motel d/tr/f $110/132/129; ❋☀) This very central place has simple but good-value rooms and

self-contained motel-style units sleeping from two to six people.

Bright Backpackers Outdoor Inn CAMPGROUND $
(☎03-5755 1154; www.brightbackpackers.com.au; 106 Coronation Dr; unpowered/powered sites from $15/25, d cabins $55; ☎) This basic but laid-back, friendly park at the foot of Mystic Mountain is popular with paragliders. Cabins are basic but cheap.

✗ Eating & Drinking

Ireland St, south of the roundabout, has a string of cafes and takeaways and there are more restaurants along Gavan St, the highway through town.

Simone's Restaurant ITALIAN $$
(☎03-5755 2266; 98 Gavan St; mains $32-35; ☉dinner Tue-Sat) For 20 years owner-chef Patrizia Simone has been serving outstanding Italian food, with a focus on local ingredients and seasonal produce, in the rustic dining room of this heritage-listed house. Bookings essential.

Larder Café & Bar MODERN AUSTRALIAN $$
(☎03-5755 1537; 2a Anderson St; tapas from $6, mains $18-27; ☉breakfast, lunch & dinner Fri-Tue) The Larder doesn't look fancy but the philosophy and flavours, using 'native' ingredients like wattleseed, quandong, wild limes and lemon myrtle are both innovative and something of a taste revelation.

Beanz of Bright CAFE $
(103 Gavan St; mains $7-16; ☉breakfast & lunch Tue-Sun) This local favourite is a loungy hole-in-the-wall cafe and bar serving good coffee and interesting light meals like Thai fish cakes.

Bright Brewery MICROBREWERY
(☎03-5755 1301; www.brightbrewery.com.au; 121 Gavan St; ☉from noon; ☎) This small boutique brewery produces a quality range of beers (sample five for $10) and beer-friendly food like pizza, kransky and nachos. There's a guided tour and tasting on Friday at 3pm ($18), live music on Sunday, and you can learn to be a brewer for a day ($360).

❶ Information

Alpine Visitor Information Centre (☎1800 111 885, 03-5755 0584; www.visitalpine victoria.com.au, www.brightvictoria.com.au; 119 Gavan St; ●) Has a busy accommodation booking service, Parks Victoria information and the attached Riverdeck Café. Internet access costs $6 per hour.

❶ Getting There & Away

V/Line (☎13 61 96) runs train/coach services from Melbourne with a change at Seymour ($27, 4½ hours, two daily). Alternatively, take the train to Wangaratta and the bus from there. During the ski season the **Snowball Express** (www.snowballexpress.com.au) operates from Bright to Mt Hotham (adult/child return $30/20, 1½ hours).

Mt Beauty & the Kiewa Valley

POP 1700

Huddled at the foot of Mt Bogong (Victoria's highest mountain) on the Kiewa River, Mt Beauty and its twin villages of Tawonga and Tawonga South are the gateways to Falls Creek ski resort. It's reached by a steep and winding road from Bright with some lovely alpine views, particularly from Tawonga Gap Lookout. A scenic loop drive is via the **Happy Valley Tourist Road** from Ovens to Mt Beauty.

The Mt Beauty Music Festival (www.musicmuster.org.au) brings together folk, blues and country musicians in April.

◉ Sights & Activities

The 2km **Tree Fern Walk** and the longer **Peppermint Walk** both start from Mountain Creek Picnic & Camping Ground, on Mountain Creek Rd, off the Kiewa Valley Hwy. About 1km south of Bogong Village (towards Falls Creek), the 1.5km return **Fainter Falls Walk** takes you to a pretty cascade.

There's a fascinating visitor information centre at the Bogong Power Station (☎03-5754 3318; Bogong High Plains Rd; admission free; ☉11am-3pm Wed-Sun), a working hydro-electric plant about 20km from Mt Beauty. The centre explains the history of the hydro scheme and has a water wall and a viewing window into the plant.

Rocky Valley Bikes (☎03-5754 1118; www.rockyvalley.com.au; Kiewa Valley Hwy; rides beginner/advanced $25/95) hires mountain and cross-country bikes from $20/30 per half/full day, and snowsports equipment in the white season.

Horse riders can experience this beautiful area with Bogong Horseback Adventures (☎03-5754 4849; www.bogonghorse.com.au; Mountain Creek Rd, Tawonga; 2/3hr $80/95, full-day $190).

🛏 Sleeping

There's camping along the Kiewa River and several motels along the highway.

Dreamers APARTMENTS $$$
(☑03-5754 1222; www.dreamers1.com; Kiewa Valley Hwy; d $200-590) Each of Dreamer's stunning self-contained eco apartments offer something special and architecturally unique. Sunken lounges, open fireplaces, loft bedrooms and balcony spas are just some of the highlights. Great views and a pretty lagoon complete a dreamily romantic five-star experience.

**Mount Beauty Holiday
Centre** CARAVAN PARK $
(☑03-5754 4396; www.holidaycentre.com.au; Kiewa Valley Hwy; unpowered/powered sites $26/31; cabins & yurts $80-140; 🕸) This family caravan park close to the town centre has river frontage, games and an interesting range of cabins, including hexagonal 'yurts'.

🍴 Eating & Drinking

Å Skafferi SWEDISH $
(☑03-5754 4544; www.svarmisk.com.au; 84 Bogong High Plains Rd, Mt Beauty; meals $5-17; ⊙breakfast & lunch) This cool Swedish pantry and foodstore is the latest addition to the Svärmisk apartment complex – lunch on Swedish meatballs or the sampler of herring and *knackebrod*.

Roi's Diner Restaurant ITALIAN $$
(☑03-5754 4495; 177 Kiewa Valley Hwy, Tawonga; mains $26-30; ⊙dinner Thu-Sun) This unassuming timber shack on the highway 5km from Mt Beauty is an award-winning restaurant, specialising in exceptional modern Italian cuisine.

Bogong Hotel PUB FARE $
(☑03-5754 4449; 169 Kiewa Valley Hwy, Tawonga; mains $16-28; ⊙lunch Sat & Sun, dinner daily) It's hard to beat this country pub for a beer with mountain views from the front verandah. Excellent bistro and the cheaper bar meals and Bogong burgers are a steal.

ℹ Information

Mt Beauty Visitors Centre (☑1800 111 885; www.greatalpinevalleys.com.au; 31 Bogong High Plains Rd) Has an accommodation-booking service and displays on the history and nature of the region.

ℹ Getting There & Away

V/Line (☑13 61 96) operates a train/bus/taxi service from Melbourne to Mt Beauty, via Seymour and Bright ($31, 5½ hours). In winter **Falls Creek Coach Service** (☑03-5754 4024; www.fallscreekcoachservice.com.au) operates direct buses to Mt Beauty from Melbourne on Wednesday, Friday, Saturday and Sunday (one-way/return $81/127) and from Albury from Thursday to Sunday ($32/50), both continuing on to Falls Creek ($35/55).

Falls Creek

ELEV 1780M

Victoria's glitzy, fashion-conscious resort, Falls Creek combines a picturesque alpine setting with impressive skiing and infamous après-ski entertainment. Skiing is spread over two main areas – the Village Bowl and Sun Valley – with 19 lifts, a vertical drop of 267m and Australia's longest beginner run at **Wombat's Ramble**.

It's not all snow sports though, and Falls has a great summer program, which includes an outdoor cinema on an inflatable screen (free), hiking, mountain biking, horse riding and a rock-climbing wall. The Summit chairlift operates during the summer school holidays (per ride $12, per day $22). **Mountain biking** is popular here in the green season, with downhill trails, three lift-accessed trails, spur fire trails, aqueduct trails, road circuits and bike rental ($50 per day).

🛏 Sleeping

All accommodation at Falls is above the snowline, so in winter the lodges are truly ski-in, ski-out. Accommodation can be booked via several agencies: **Falls Creek Central Reservations** (☑1800 033 079; www.fallscreek.com.au/centralreservations) and **Falls Creek Reservation Centre** (☑1800 453 525; www.fallscreek.com.au/ResCentre).

Alpha Lodge LODGE $
(☑03-5758 3488; www.alphaskilodge.com.au; 5 Parallel St; dm summer/winter from $30/109) A spacious affordable lodge set up with a sauna, a large lounge with panoramic views and a communal kitchen.

Viking Alpine Lodge LODGE $
(☑03-5758 3247; 13 Parallel St; dm/s/d summer $35/65/90, ski season per person $58-137) Viking offers good-value accommodation all year with excellent communal facilities including lounge, kitchen and great views.

Frueauf Village
APARTMENTS $$$

(☑1300 300 709; www.fvfalls.com.au; 4 Schuss St; d 2-nights from $554; 🛜) These luxurious, architect-designed apartments have everything, with private outdoor hot tubs, plus the funky Milch Cafe Wine Bar.

✕ Eating & Drinking

Quality kiosks, cafes and restaurants abound and there's a supermarket with a bottle shop for self-caterers.

Huski Produce Store
CAFE $

(☑03-5758 3863; www.huski.com.au; 3 Sitzmark St; ⊙5pm-1.30am) Chic store and cafe with great casual dining, coffee and High Country produce.

Milch Cafe Wine Bar
MIDDLE EASTERN, WINE BAR $$

(☑0408 465 939; 4 Schuss St; mains $12-24) The hip place to see and be seen, this bar-restaurant offers flavoursome Middle Eastern meze and a good wine list. In winter, the bar is packed with skiers conducting post-mortems of their runs.

Man Hotel
PUB

(☑03-5758 3362; www.fallscreek.com.au/the manhotel; 20 Slalom St; ⊙5pm-1.30am) 'The Man' hotel has been around forever, is open all year and is the heart of Falls' nightlife. In winter it fires up as a club, cocktail bar and live-music venue featuring popular Aussie bands.

❶ Information

Ski-season daily resort entry is $32 per car. One-day lift tickets cost $102/69/51 per adult/student/child. Combined lift-and-lesson packages cost $153/130/104. Lift tickets also cover Mt Hotham. An over-snow taxi service ($34 return) operates between the car parks and the lodges from 7am to midnight daily (to 2am Friday night, to 1am Saturday and Sunday). Car parking for day visitors is at the base of the village, next to the ski lifts.

Falls Creek Resort Management (☑1800 033 079; www.fallscreek.com.au; 1 Slalom St; ⊙9am-5pm) Has informative pamphlets including *crosscountry* (about ski trails which are also good for summer walking).

Falls Creek Visitor Information Centre (☑03-5758 1202; Bogong High Plains Rd; ⊙8am-5pm winter) The helpful visitor centre is near Foodworks supermarket.

❶ Getting There & Around

Falls Creek is 375km and a 4½ hour drive from Melbourne. During the winter, **Falls Creek Coach Service** (☑03-5754 4024; www.fallscreekcoach-service.com.au) operates four times a week between Falls Creek and Melbourne (one-way/return $99/161) and also runs services to and from Albury ($57/90) and Mt Beauty ($35/55). There's a reduced service over summer.

If you want to ski Mt Hotham for the day, jump on the HeliLink for $125 return if you have a valid lift ticket.

Harrietville
POP 280

Harrietville, a pretty little town nestled on the Ovens River below Mt Feathertop, is the last stop before the start of the winding road up to Mt Hotham. The village is the starting and finishing point for various **alpine walking tracks**, including the popular Mt Feathertop walk, Razorback Ridge and Dargo High Plains walks. You can hire bikes ($30/40 per half/full day) from Snowline Hotel, which also runs mountain-bike tours and mountain transfers.

In late November the annual Blue Grass Festival (www.bluegrass.org.au) takes over the town.

🛏 Sleeping & Eating

Snowline Hotel
MOTEL $

(☑03-5759 2524; www.snowlinehotel.com.au; Great Alpine Rd; d from $100) The Snowline has been operating for over 100 years, and offers inexpensive off-mountain accommodation in comfortable motel rooms. The pub bistro (mains $20 to $29) has a loyal following, especially for its chicken parma, Harrietville trout and Tasmanian Angus steak.

Shady Brook Cottages
COTTAGES $$

(☑03-5759 2741; www.shadybrook.com.au; Mountain View Walk; 1-/2-bed cottage from $110/150; @❄) A magnificent garden envelopes this lovely, peaceful group of self-contained country-style cottages. Two come with spa and all have balconies and mod cons.

Bella's
CAFE $

(☑03-5759 2750; 231 Great Alpine Rd; meals $7-17 ⊙breakfast & lunch Thu-Tue) For an all-day breakfast or lunch of antipasto, damper rolls and pizza with a glass of local wine or hot coffee, this welcoming cafe is Harrietville's best.

Mt Hotham & Dinner Plain

ELEV 1868M

Serious hikers, skiers and snowboarders make tracks for Mt Hotham, with some of the best and most challenging downhill runs in the country – 320 hectares of downhill runs, with a vertical drop of 428m and about 80% of the ski trails are intermediate or advanced black diamond runs. Over at Dinner Plain, 10km from Hotham village and linked by a free shuttle, there are excellent cross-country trails around the village, including the **Hotham–Dinner Plain Ski Trail**.

From November to May, Hotham and Dinner Plain boast some stunning alpine trails for hiking and mountain biking. The most popular trail in summer is the 22km return trip to Mt Feathertop (1922m). At Dinner Plain, Adventures with Altitude (03-5159 6608; www.adventureswithaltitude.com.au; bike hire per hr $15, per half/full day $40/60) provides mountain-biking gear and trail maps. Guided mountain-bike tours start at $80/120 for a half-/full day (up to multiday trips) and they also organise guided bushwalks and horse riding. Also here is a mountain-bike park (per day $40; ⊙weekends) with downhill and cross-country trails and jumps.

🛏 Sleeping

Ski-season accommodation generally has a minimum two-night stay. Booking agencies:

Dinner Plain Accommodation (1800444 066, 03-5159 6696; www.accommdinnerplain.com.au; Big Muster Dr) Booking agency for Dinner Plain.

Dinner Plain Central Reservations (1800 670 019, 5159 6451; www.dinnerplain.com; Big Muster Dr) Booking agency for Dinner Plain.

Mt Hotham Accommodation Service (1800 032 061, 5759 3636; www.mthotham accommodation.com.au) Books mountain accommodation during the ski season.

Mt Hotham Central Reservations (1800 657 547, 5759 3522; www.skicom.com.au) Books on- and off-mountain accommodation throughout the year.

MT HOTHAM

Leeton Lodge   LODGE $
(03-5759 3683; www.leetonlodge.com; Dargo Ct; summer per adult/child $35/20) Classic family ski-club lodge with 30 beds, cooking facilities and good views. Open year-round.

General Backpackers   BACKPACKERS $
(03-5759 3523; Great Alpine Rd; dm summer/winter $30/60, apt $150) Behind the General are these brand new fully self-contained apartments with lounge and kitchen and views from the balcony.

Arlberg Resort   APARTMENTS $$$
(03-5759 3618; www.arlberghotham.com.au; 2 nights from $820; 🐾🖥) The largest resort on the mountain, the Arlberg has a big range of apartments and motel-style rooms, plus restaurants, bars, ski hire and a heated pool. Ski season only.

DINNER PLAIN

Currawong Lodge   LODGE $$
(03-5159 6452, 1800 635 589; www.currawong lodge.com.au; Big Muster Dr; summer s/d $80/130, ski season 2-night minimum d $210) Currawong Lodge welcomes you with a huge communal lounge-and-kitchen area with a monster open fireplace, TV, DVD and stereo. At this price you can ski with a conscience.

Rundell's Alpine Lodge   LODGE $$
(03-5159 6422; www.rundells.com.au; Big Muster Dr; summer d from $198, ski season 2-night minimum $550; 🖥) Originally an Australian army retreat, this sprawling complex is a well-run hotel with all the comforts – spa, sauna and restaurant-bar.

🍴 Eating & Drinking

MT HOTHAM

In winter, there are plenty of great eating choices here. In summer a couple of places serve meals and the small supermarket at the General is open. Good places for an après-ski drink include Jack Frost, Avalanche Bar and Swindlers.

General   PUB FARE $
(03-5759 3523; Great Alpine Rd; meals $8-30; ⊙lunch & dinner; @) The ever-reliable 'Gen' is open all year and is a popular watering hole with a menu of pizzas, good bistro meals and internet.

Zirky's   CAFE $
(03-5759 3518; Great Alpine Rd; meals $10-14; ⊙breakfast & lunch Wed-Sun) The Z cafe here at the base of the summit run opens year-round, while Andrew Blake's fine-dining restaurant (open for dinner in winter) is highly regarded.

DINNER PLAIN

Dinner Plain Hotel   PUB FARE $
(03-5159 6462; mains $9-20; ⊙lunch & dinner) The barn-sized local pub is the social hub of

Dinner Plain and a friendly place to hang out year-round, with roaring open fires and a bistro serving good pub grub and pizzas.

ℹ Information

The ski-season admission fee is $35 per car per day, and $12 for bus passengers (this may be included in your fare). Lift tickets (peak) per adult/student/child cost $102/87/51. Passes are cheaper in September, and there are packages that include gear hire and lessons. Lift tickets also cover Falls Creek.

Dinner Plain Visitor Centre (☑1300 734 365; www.visitdinnerplain.com)

Hotham Central Guest Services (☑03-5759 4470; Hotham Central) Open during winter.

Mt Hotham Alpine Resort Management Board (☑03-5759 3550; www.mthotham.com. au) At the village administration centre. Collect a range of brochures with maps for short, eco, heritage and village walks.

ℹ Getting There & Around

AIR Mt Hotham Airport services Mt Hotham and Dinner Plain, but it's currently only served in winter by **QantasLink** (www.qantas.com.au) from Sydney, and by charter flights.

BUS During the ski season, **Snowball Express** (☑03-9370 9055, 1800 659 009; www.snow-ballexpress.com.au) has daily buses from Melbourne to Mt Hotham ($160 return, six hours), via Wangaratta, Myrtleford, Bright and Harrietville. **O'Connell's Bus Lines** (☑0428 591 377; www.omeobus.com.au) operates a daily 'Alps Link' service between Omeo and Bright ($9.20) via Mt Hotham and Dinner Plain ($4.40).

SHUTTLE A free shuttle runs frequently around the resort from 7am to 3am; a separate shuttle service also operates to Dinner Plain. The free 'zoo cart' takes skiers from their lodges to the lifts between 8am and 6pm.

Omeo

POP 230

High in the hills, historic Omeo comes as a bit of a surprise after the winding drive up from the coast or down from the mountains. This is the southern access route to Mt Hotham and Falls Creek and the main town on the eastern section of the Great Alpine Road. In the gold-rush days of the 1850s, Omeo had the wildest and most remote goldfields in the state. It attracted many Chinese diggers whose legacy you can see on the **Oriental Claims Walk**. Today, you can't help but stay a while to wander the steep main street and breathe in the crisp mountain air.

🛏 Sleeping & Eating

In town, there's a bakery, a couple of cafes and takeaways.

Golden Age Hotel HOTEL $$
(☑03-5159 1344; www.goldenageomeo.com.au; Day Ave; s/d $95/109, d with spa $157, budget s/d $50/80) This beautiful art-deco corner pub dominates Omeo's main street. Upstairs are simple but elegant pub rooms, some with en suite and spa – the best rooms open onto the balcony. The welcoming restaurant (mains $15 to $25) serves plates piled high with reliable fare of steaks, salads and gourmet pizzas.

Snug as a Bug Motel MOTEL $$
(☑03-5159 1311; www.motelomeo.com.au; 188 Great Alpine Rd; d/f from $90/160) There's a range of accommodation here in lovely country-style historic buildings. There are family motel rooms, the main guesthouse, a cute self-contained cottage and the two-room Omeo Backpackers (doubles $65).

Omeo Caravan Park CARAVAN PARK $
(☑03-5159 1351; www.omeocaravanpark.com.au; Old Omeo Hwy; unpowered/powered sites $25/28, d cabins from $90) In a pretty valley alongside the Livingstone Creek about 2km from town, this park has spacious, grassy sites. Bike hire available.

Victoria Falls Camping Area CAMPGROUND
(campsites free) The scenic spot off the Great Alpine Rd, 18km west of Omeo, has pit toilets and a picnic area.

ℹ Information

Omeo Visitor Information Centre (☑03-5159 1679; www.omeoregion.com.au; 152 Day Ave; ⏱10am-3pm) Friendly visitor centre with local information at the eastern end of Day Ave.

ℹ Getting There & Away

Omeo Bus Lines (☑0427 017 732) has one bus on weekdays only between Omeo and Bairnsdale ($17, two hours). **O'Connell's Bus Lines** (☑0428 591 377; www.omeobus.com.au) operates a daily summer 'Alps Link' service between Omeo and Bright ($9.20) via Mt Hotham and Dinner Plain ($4.40). A winter service to Dinner Plain and Mt Hotham operates on Sunday, Wednesday and Friday.

GIPPSLAND

It might not be as well known as the Great Ocean Road to the west, but Victoria's southeast coast easily boasts the state's best

ALPINE HIGHWAYS

The Victorian High Country has three great 'highways' that will take you up and over the mountains and down to the Gippsland coast. All three link up with Omeo and become the Great Alpine Road down to Bairnsdale and are a joy for car or motorcycle touring, or for hard-core cyclists.

Great Alpine Road

This much-loved 308km route starts at Wangaratta and follows the Ovens Valley through Myrtleford, Bright and Harrietville before passing over Mt Hotham and Dinner Plain then descending to Omeo and all the way down to Bairnsdale in East Gippsland. It's Australia's highest year-round-accessible sealed road. The section from Omeo southeast to Bruthen is particularly scenic, following the valley of the Tambo River and passing farmland, vineyards and the pretty communities of Swifts Creek and Ensay.

Omeo Highway

Stretching almost 300km from the Murray River to the coast, the Omeo Hwy takes in some of Victoria's most scenic and diverse countryside. The highway is unsealed in sections (between Mitta Mitta and Glen Willis), and snow often makes it difficult to pass in winter.

At Anglers Rest, beside the Cobungra River, Blue Duck Inn (☑03-5159 7220; www.blueduckinn.com.au; Omeo Hwy; mains $18-27, d cabins $130-150; ☺lunch & dinner Wed-Sun), is popular with anglers, motorcyclists, kayakers and bushwalkers for its hearty meals and barbecue area by the river. The two-bedroom self-contained cabins here are very cosy.

About 30km south of Anglers Rest, you reach Omeo and join up with the Great Alpine Road.

Bogong High Plains Road

In 2009, the Bogong High Plains Road was finally sealed all the way from Falls Creek to the Omeo Hwy, creating another fabulous all-season tourist route. The journey starts at Mt Beauty and climbs up through Bogong village to Falls Creek ski resort. From there it skirts Rocky Valley Lake and winds 35km to join the Omeo Hwy about 11km north of Anglers Rest. The result is a superb alpine loop where you can drive from Bright, over Mt Hotham via Omeo to Falls Creek, down to Mt Beauty and back to Bright – a distance of about 250km.

beaches, impossibly pretty lakeside villages and Victoria's finest coastal national parks, typified by the glorious Wilsons Promontory. While most travellers head for the coast between Phillip Island and Mallacoota, Gippsland also encompasses a vast inland area of farmland, power stations, High Country foothills and forest wilderness.

A trip through Gippsland could mean swimming, surfing, fishing, camping and boating along the coast, penguin- and wildlife-spotting, cycling from town to town on the network of rail trails, feasting on the freshest seafood, or packing the rucksack and hiking boots and heading into the most remote wilderness national parks in the state.

West Gippsland & The Latrobe Valley

From Melbourne, the Princes Hwy follows the power lines past dairy country to their source in the Latrobe Valley. The working-class region between Moe and Traralgon contains one of the world's largest deposits of brown coal, which is consumed by massive power stations at Yallourn, Morwell, Hazlewood and Loy Yang, which produce up to 85% of Victoria's electricity.

WALHALLA
POP 18

Ensconced high in the green hills and forest of West Gippsland, tiny Walhalla is one of the state's best-preserved and most charming historic towns – in its gold-mining heyday, Walhalla's population was 5000. Stringers Creek runs through the centre of the township – an idyllic valley encircled by a cluster of sepia-toned historic buildings set into the hillsides.

☉ Sights & Activities

The best way to see the town is on foot – take the **circuit walk** (45 minutes) anticlockwise

from the information shelter as you enter town. There's a group of restored shops along the main street.

The 680km **Australian Alps Walking Track** (www.australianalps.environment.gov.au) starts in Walhalla and extends all the way to Canberra. The first 40km section to Baw Baw can be done in two days.

Walhalla Historical Museum MUSEUM
(☑03-5165 6250; www.walhalla.org.au; admission $2; ☺10am-4pm) In the old post office, which also acts as an information centre and books the popular two-hour **ghost tours** (www.walhallaghosttour.info; adult/child $25/18) on Friday and Saturday nights.

Walhalla Goldfields Railway TRAIN
(☑03-9513 3969; www.walhallarail.com; return adult/child/family $18/13/40; ☺from Walhalla station 11am, 1pm & 3pm, from Thomson Station 11.40am, 1.40pm & 3.40pm Wed, Sat & Sun, public holidays) The scenic 20-minute ride between Walhalla Station to Thomson Station (on the main road, 3.5km before Walhalla) snakes along Stringers Creek Gorge.

Long Tunnel Extended Gold Mine MINE
(☑03-5165 6259; off Walhalla-Beardmore Rd; adult/child/family $19.50/13.50/49.50; ☺1.30pm Mon-Fri, noon, 1.30pm & 3pm Sat & Sun, public & school holidays) Relive the mining past with a guided tour that explores Cohens Reef, once one of Australia's top reef-gold producers. Almost 14 tonnes of gold came out of this mine.

☞ **Tours**

Mountain Top Experience 4WD TOUR
(☑03-5134 6876; www.mountaintopexperience. com) Operates nature-based 4WD tours, including the Walhalla Copper Mine Adventure ($20) and ghost-town tours ($25) on weekends and Wednesdays.

🛏 **Sleeping & Eating**
You can camp for free at North Gardens, with toilets and barbecues, at the north end of the village.

Walhalla Star Hotel HOTEL $$
(☑03-5165 6262; www.starhotel.com.au; Main Rd; d incl breakfast $219, incl dinner $319; ❉) The rebuilt historic Star offers stylish boutique accommodation with king-size beds and sophisticated designer decor making good use of local materials such as corrugated-iron water tanks.

Wild Cherry B&B B&B $$
(☑03-5165 6245; www.wildcherrywalhalla.com. au; Church Hill Rd; d $160) The Wild Cherry is

a sweet little B&B perched up on the hill above town with comfy motel-style rooms.

Walhalla Lodge Hotel PUB $$
(☑03-5165 6226; Main St; mains $16-25; ☺lunch & dinner Wed-Mon) The Wally Pub is a cosy, one-room pub decked out with prints of old Walhalla and serving good-value counter meals.

South Gippsland

South Gippsland has plenty of gems along the coast between Inverloch and Wilsons Promontory – Cape Paterson, Venus Bay, Cape Liptrap Coastal Park and Waratah Bay are all worth exploring. Inland, the South Gippsland Hwy passes through the beautiful 'blue' rounded hills of the Strzelecki Ranges, past farming communities and trendy villages like Koonwarra and Fish Creek. The 49km **Great Southern Rail Trail** meanders through bushland between Leongatha and Foster.

KORUMBURRA TO FISH CREEK
POP 3150
The first sizeable town along the South Gippsland Hwy is Korumburra, situated on the edge of the Strzelecki Ranges. **Prom Country Information Centre** (☑03-5655 2233, 1800 630 704; www.promcountrytourism. com.au; South Gippsland Hwy) is on the way out of town next to **Coal Creek Village** (☑03-5655 1811; www.coalcreekvillage.com.au; admission free; ☺10am-4.30pm Thu-Mon, daily during school holidays), an interesting re-creation of a 19th-century mining town.

Volunteers operate the **South Gippsland Railway** (☑03-5658 1111, 1800 442 211; www.sgr.org.au; adult/child/family return $15/9/48), which runs heritage diesel trains along scenic tracks from Korumburra to Leongatha and Nyora on Sundays and public holidays.

Off the South Gippsland Hwy towards Wilsons Prom, **Fish Creek** is an arty little community with craft studios, bookshops, galleries, some good cafes and the popular Fishy Pub. It's on the Great Southern Rail Trail.

Wilsons Promontory National Park

If you like wilderness bushwalking, stunning coastal scenery and secluded white-sand beaches, you'll absolutely love this place. 'The Prom', as it's affectionately known, is

one of the most popular national parks in Australia and our favourite coastal park.

Wilsons Promontory is an important area for the Kurnai and Boonwurrung Aborigines, and middens have been found in many places, including Cotters and Darby Beaches, and Oberon Bay. The southern-most part of mainland Australia, the Prom once formed a land bridge that allowed people to walk to Tasmania.

Tidal River, 30km from the park entry, is the hub, and home to the Parks Victoria office, a general store, cafe and accommodation. The wildlife around Tidal River is remarkably tame: kookaburras and rosellas lurk expectantly (resist the urge to feed them), and wombats nonchalantly waddle out of the undergrowth.

Although there's a staffed entry station (⊙9am-sunset) where you receive a ticket, entry is free. There's no fuel available at Tidal River.

🏃 Activities

There are more than 80km of marked **walking trails** here, taking you through forests, marshes, valleys of tree ferns, low granite mountains and along beaches backed by sand dunes. Even nonwalkers can enjoy much of the park's beauty, with car park access off the Tidal River road leading to gorgeous beaches and lookouts.

Swimming is safe from the beautiful beaches at Norman Bay (Tidal River) and around the headland at Squeaky Beach – the ultra-fine quartz sand here really does squeak beneath your feet!

If you're travelling light, you can hire camping equipment, including tents, stoves, sleeping bags and backpacks, from Wilsons Prom Hiking Hire (☎03-5678 1152; 3670 Prom Rd, Yanakie).

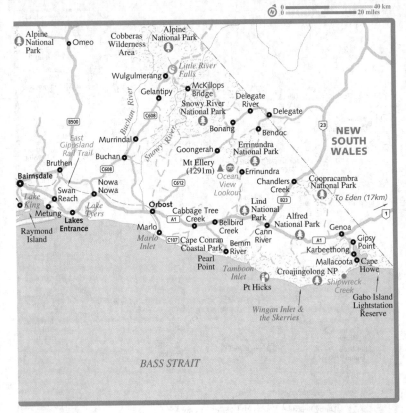

Tours

Bunyip Tours   NATURE
(☑1300 286 947, 03-9650 9680; www.bunyip
tours.com; day tour $120) One-day guided
tour to the Prom from Melbourne, with
the option of staying on another two days
to explore by yourself.

Hiking Plus   NATURE
(☑0418-341 537; www.hikingplus.com; 3-/5-day
tours $1100/1800) This tour company orga-
nises fully catered and guided hikes to the
Prom from nearby Foster. Packages include meals, a massage and spa, and you
need only carry a light pack.

Sleeping

The main accommodation base is at Tidal
River, but there are 11 bush-camping (outstation) areas around the Prom, all with pit
or compost toilets, but no other facilities;
carry in your own drinking water. Overnight

hikers need camping permits (adult/child
per night $8/4), which must be booked
ahead through Parks Victoria.

TIDAL RIVER
Situated on Norman Bay and a short walk
to a stunning beach, Tidal River is justifiably popular. Book well in advance through
Parks Victoria (☑1800 350 552, 13 19 63; www.
parkweb.vic.gov.au), especially for weekends
and holidays. For the Christmas school-
holiday period there's a ballot for sites (apply online by 31 July).

Accommodation includes **camp sites**
(unpowered sites per car & 3 people $20-24, pow-
ered sites per vehicle & up to 8 people $44-52);
huts (4-/6-bed $65/100); **cabins** (d $110-172,
extra adult $23); luxury **safari tents** (d $250,
extra person $20); and the isolated **Light-
house Keepers' Cottage** (8-bed cottage
per person $51-83) at the southern tip of the
Prom.

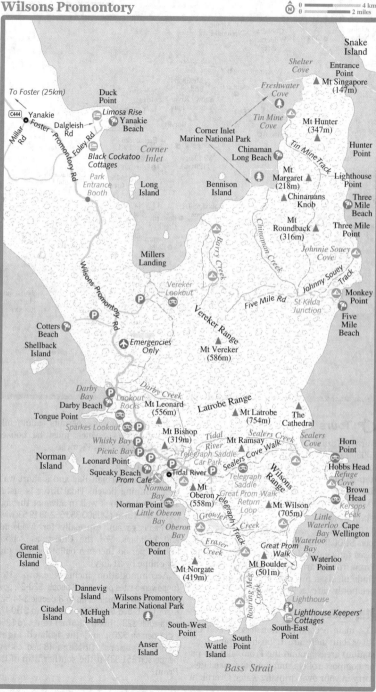

WORTH A TRIP: KOONWARRA

But a blip on the South Gippsland Hwy, culinary Koonwarra has made a name for itself thanks to a fine foodstore and an organic cooking school.

Koonwarra Food, Wine & Produce Store   CAFE
(☑03-5664 2285; cnr South Gippsland Hwy & Koala Dr; mains $6-34; ☺breakfast & lunch daily, dinner Fri; ☑) Serves simple food with flair using organic, low-impact suppliers and products. The store stocks local wines and produce such as sauces, preserves and pâtés made on-site; there are wine and cheese tasting on weekends ($5) and a lovely shady garden area outside.

Peaceful Gardens Organic Cooking School   COOKING COURSES
(☑03-5664 2480; Koala Dr; half/full day from $70/130, child half day $30-50) Victoria's first organic-certified cooking school, with the motto, 'organic, seasonal, local', offering short courses, including making cakes, bread, preserves and traditional pastries and pasta.

YANAKIE & FOSTER

Black Cockatoo Cottages   COTTAGES **$$**
(☑03-5687 1306; www.blackcockatoo.com; 60 Foley Rd, Yanakie; d $160) You can take in glorious views of the national park without leaving your very comfortable bed – or without breaking the bank – in these private, stylish, black-timber cottages. There are three modern cottages and a three-bedroom house.

Prom Coast Backpackers   HOSTEL **$**
(☑03-5682 2171; www.yha.com.au; 40 Station Rd, Foster; dm/d/f from $30/70/90; @) This comfy little 10-bed YHA cottage in Foster is the closest backpacker hostel to the park. The owners also run the motel next door.

✖ Eating

The General Store in Tidal River stocks grocery items and some camping equipment, but if you're hiking it's cheaper to stock up in Foster. The **Prom Café** (☺breakfast, lunch & dinner; mains $12-22) is open daily for takeaway food, and serves breakfast, light lunches and bistro-style meals on weekends and holidays.

❶ Information

Parks Victoria (☑1800 350 552, 13 19 63; www.parkweb.vic.gov.au; Tidal River; ☺8.30am-4.30pm) The helpful visitor centre books all park accommodation, including permits for camping away from Tidal River.

❶ Getting There & Away

There's no direct public transport between Melbourne and the Prom, but the **Wilsons Promontory Bus Service** (Moon's Bus Lines; ☑03-5687 1249) operates from Foster to Tidal River (via Fish Creek) on Friday at 4.30pm, returning on Sunday at 4.30pm ($8). This service connects with the V/Line bus from Melbourne at Fish Creek.

V/Line (☑13 61 96; www.vline.com.au) buses from Melbourne's Southern Cross Station travel direct to Foster ($16.60, three hours, four daily).

Gippsland Lakes

The Gippsland Lakes comprise the largest inland waterway system in Australia. There are three main lakes that interconnect: Lake King, Lake Victoria and Lake Wellington, which are actually lagoons, separated from the ocean by a narrow strip of sand dunes known as Ninety Mile Beach. The dunes were artificially breached at Lakes Entrance in 1889 to allow ocean-going fishing boats to shelter in the placid waters. Only those with a boat can truly appreciate this wonderful lakes system, but there are plenty of opportunities for fishing, camping and beachcombing. The Lakes National Park protects 2400 hectares of native habitat.

SALE
POP 13,300
Gateway to the Gippsland Lakes, Sale has plenty of accommodation, shops, restaurants and pubs, making it a reasonable town-sized base for exploring the Ninety Mile Beach.

The **Sale Wetlands Walk** (4km, 1½ hours) is a pleasant wander around Lake Gutheridge and adjoining wetlands, and incorporates an **Indigenous Art Trail** commemorating the importance of the wetlands to the local Gunai/Kurnai population. Sale

TOP PROM WALKS

» **Great Prom Walk** This is the most popular long-distance hike, a moderate 45km circuit across to Sealers Cove from Tidal River, down to Refuge Cove, Waterloo Bay, the lighthouse and back to Tidal River via Oberon Bay. Allow three days, and coordinate your walks with tide times, as creek crossings can be hazardous.

» **Sealers Cove Walk** The best overnight hike, this two-day walk starts at Telegraph Saddle and heads down Telegraph Track to stay overnight at beautiful Little Waterloo Bay (12km, 4½ hours). The next day walk on to Sealers Cove via Refuge Cove and return to Telegraph Saddle (24km, 7½ hours).

» **Lilly Pilly Gully Nature Walk** An easy 5km (two hour) walk through heathland and eucalypt forests, with lots of wildlife.

» **Mt Oberon Summit** Starting from the Mt Oberon car park, this moderate-to-hard 7km (2½ hour) walk is an ideal introduction to the Prom with panoramic views from the summit. The free Mt Oberon shuttle bus can take you to the Telegraph Saddle car park and back.

» **Squeaky Beach Nature Walk** Another easy 5km return stroll through coastal tea trees and banksias to a sensational white-sand beach.

Common, a 300-hectare wildlife refuge with bird hides, an observatory, waterhole, board-walks and other walking tracks is part of an internationally recognised wetlands system.

🛏 Sleeping

Cambrai Hostel HOSTEL **$**
(☑03-5147 1600; www.maffra.net.au/hostel/backpackers.htm; 117 Johnson St, Maffra; dm/d $25/60; @) In nearby Maffra, this relaxed hostel is a budget haven and one of the few true backpackers in Gippsland. The owners can sometimes arrange work in the region.

ℹ Information

Wellington Visitor Information Centre
(☑1800 677 520; www.tourismwellington.com.au; 8 Foster St; ⊗9am-5pm; @) Internet facilities and a free accommodation booking service.

NINETY MILE BEACH
To paraphrase the immortal words of Croco-dile Dundee: that's not a beach...*this* is a beach. Isolated Ninety Mile Beach is a narrow strip of sand backed by dunes and lagoons that stretchs unbroken for more-or-less 90 miles (150km) from near McLoughlins Beach to the channel at Lakes Entrance. The area is great for surf-fishing, camping and long beach walks, though the crashing surf can be dangerous for swimming, except where pa-trolled at Seaspray and Lakes Entrance.

On the road between Seaspray and Gold-en Beach, there are free **camp sites**, nestled back from the beach and shaded by tea trees – it's hard to get a spot over summer holidays, but at other times it's supremely peaceful. Some sites have barbecues and pit toilets, but you need to bring your own wa-ter and firewood. Hot showers are available at **Golden Beach** ($2).

Loch Sport (population 780) is a small, bushy town sprawling along a narrow spit of land with a lake on one side and the ocean on the other. There are some good swim-ming areas here for children. The **Marina Hotel** (☑03-5146 0666; Basin Blvd, Loch Sport; mains $16-28 ⊗lunch & dinner), perched by the lake and marina, has a friendly local pub vibe, superb sunset views and decent sea-food dishes on the bistro menu.

A spit of land surrounded by lakes and ocean, **Lakes National Park** covers 2390 hectares of coastal bushland and is reached by road from Loch Sport, or by boat from Paynesville (5km). The **Parks Victoria of-fice** (☑03-5146 0278) is at the park entrance near Loch Sport. The only camping is at Emu Bight.

BAIRNSDALE
POP 10,900
Bairnsdale is East Gippsland's commercial hub and the turn-off for the Great Alpine Road to Omeo or south to Paynesville and Raymond Island. It's a bustling sort of town with a sprinkling of attractions, but most travellers are merely passing through on the way to the coast or the mountains.

Krowathunkoolong Keeping Place (☑03-5152 1891; 37-53 Dalmahoy St; adult/child $6/4;

⏲9am-5pm Mon-Fri), behind the train station, is a Koorie cultural centre that explores Kurnai daily life before and after white settlement.

On the edge of town, the **MacLeod Morass Boardwalk** is a wetland reserve with walking tracks and bird hides.

Howitt Park is the starting point for the **East Gippsland Rail Trail** (www.eastgippslandrailtrail.com), a popular bike and walking track that leads 97km east to Orbost, via Bruthen and Nowa Nowa, or you can detour through state forest to Lakes Entrance.

About 16km south of Bairnsdale, the little lake town of **Paynesville** is worth a trip to take the free flat-bottom ferry across to **Raymond Island**, known for its large colony of koalas.

Sleeping & Eating

Grand Terminus Hotel PUB FARE $$
(☎03-5152 4040; www.grandterminus.com.au; 98 McLeod St; mains $13-26; ⏲lunch & dinner) This grand old corner pub serves above-average bistro meals, while the upstairs en-suite rooms (single/double $65/75) are excellent value.

River Grill MODERN AUSTRALIAN $$
(☎03-5153 1421; 2 Wood St; mains $25-36; ⏲lunch & dinner Mon-Sat) Fine dining with flair comes to Bairnsdale in the form of a rustic restaurant offering contemporary food with a Mediterranean touch.

Information

Bairnsdale Visitors Centre (☎1800 637 060, 03-5152 3444; www.discovereastgippsland.com.au; 240 Main St; ⏲9am-5pm; @) Next to St Mary's Church; free accommodation booking service.

METUNG

POP 730

Curling around Bancroft Bay, little Metung is one of the prettiest towns on the Gippsland Lakes – besotted locals call it the Gippsland Riviera, and with its absolute waterfront location and unhurried charm it's hard to argue.

Riviera Nautic (☎03-5156 2243; www.rivieranautic.com.au; 185 Metung Rd; motor boat per day $140, yachts for 2 days from $1210) hires out boats and yachts for cruising, fishing and sailing on the Gippsland Lakes. At the visitor centre, **Slipway Boat Hire** (☎03-5156 2969) has small motor boats for hire from $55 for an hour to $165 a day.

If you'd rather take it easy, the **Director** (☎03-5156 2628; www.thedirector.com.au; 2½hr cruise adult/child/family $45/10/105; ⏲3pm Tue, Thu & Sat) cruises to Ninety Mile Beach and back.

At high noon it's quite a sight to see pelicans fly in like dive bombers for fish issued outside the Metung hotel.

Sleeping & Eating

Accommodation is available through **Metung Accommodation** (Slipway Villas; ☎03-5156 2861; www.metungaccommodation.com.au). There's no camping in Metung itself.

Metung Holiday Villas CABINS $$
(☎03-5156 2306; www.metungholidayvillas.com; cnr Mairburn & Stirling Rds; cabins $110-160; ❄☒) Metung's former caravan park has reinvented itself as a minivillage of semiluxury cabins and one of the best deals in Metung.

Metung Hotel PUB FARE $
(☎03-5156 2206; www.metunghotel.com.au; 1 Kurnai Ave; mains $20-32; ⏲lunch & dinner) You can't beat the location overlooking Metung Wharf, and the big windows and outdoor timber decking make the most of the water views. The hotel also has the cheapest rooms in town, with basic doubles for $85 and a bunkroom for $30 per person.

Metung Galley CAFE $$
(☎03-5156 2330; www.themetunggalley.com.au; 50 Metung Rd; lunch $10-22, dinner $21-31; ⏲breakfast & lunch daily, dinner Wed-Mon) Felicity and Richard's city hospitality experience shines through in this friendly, innovative cafe, serving up beautifully presented, quality food using local produce like fresh seafood and Gippsland lamb.

Information

Metung Visitors Centre (☎03-5156 2969; www.metungtourism.com.au; 3/50 Metung Rd; ⏲9am-5pm) Accommodation booking and boat-hire services.

LAKES ENTRANCE

POP 5550

With the shallow Cunninghame Arm waterway separating town from the crashing ocean beaches, Lakes Entrance basks in an undeniably gorgeous location, but in holiday season it's a packed-out tourist town with a graceless strip of motels, caravan parks, minigolf courses and souvenir shops lining the Esplanade. Still, the bobbing fishing boats, fresh seafood, endless beaches

and cruises out to Metung and Wyanga Park Winery should easily win you over.

◉ Sights & Activities

A long footbridge crosses the Cunninghame Arm inlet from the east of town to the ocean and Ninety Mile Beach. From December to Easter, paddle boats, canoes and sailboats can be hired by the footbridge on the ocean side.

To explore the lakes, three operators along Marine Pde (on the backside of the town centre) offer boat hire (hire per 1/4/8hr $50/90/150).

On the Princes Hwy on the western side of town, Kalimna Lookout is a popular viewing spot with coin-operated binoculars. For an even better view of the ocean and inlet, take the road directly opposite to Jemmy's Point Lookout.

Surfing lessons (gear provided) are run by the Surf Shack (☑03-5155 4933; 507 The Esplanade; 2hr lesson $50) at nearby Lake Tyers Beach.

☞ Tours & Cruises

Corque   WINERY CRUISE
(☑03-5155 1508; www.wyangapark.com.au; lunch/dinner cruise $50/75; ◷lunch daily, dinner Fri & Sat) Among the most enjoyable trips are the daily lunch and weekend dinner cruises to Wyanga Park Winery. As well as a relaxing cruise with wine-tasting on board, you get to dine at the beautifully located winery.

Lonsdale Cruises   ECO CRUISE
(☑03-5155 2889; Post Office Jetty; 3hr cruise adult/child/family $45/25/99; ◷1pm) Scenic eco cruises out to Metung and Lake King.

Peels Lake Cruises   CRUISE
(☑03-5155 1246; Post Office Jetty; 4hr Metung lunch cruise adult/child $48/13) Daily lunch cruises aboard the *Stormbird* to Metung at 11am.

⬥ Sea Safari   ECO CRUISE
(☑03-5155 5027; www.lakes-explorer.com.au; Post Office Jetty; 1/2hr cruise $12/20) These safaris aboard the Lakes Explorer have a focus on research and ecology and marine life.

⛺ Sleeping

Lakes Entrance has stacks of accommodation, much of it your typical motels, holiday apartments and caravan parks squeezed cheek-by-jowl along the Esplanade. Prices more than double during holiday periods (book ahead), but there are good discounts out of season.

Deja Vu   B&B $$$
(☑03-5155 4330; www.dejavu.com.au; 17 Clara St; d $165-300; ❋❋) This imposing, sandstone-coloured, modern home has been built on the slope of a hill to maximise water views, and the lush native garden ensures privacy. Choose from the views of the designer ocean-view apartments, the waterfront boathouse, or B&B studios.

Riviera Backpackers YHA   HOSTEL $
(☑03-5155 2444; www.yha.com.au; 660-71 The Esplanade; YHA members dm/s/d $23/35/50; @❋) This well-located YHA has clean rooms in old-style brick units, each with two or three bedrooms and an en suite. There's a big communal kitchen, and lounge with pool table and internet access.

Kalimna Woods   COTTAGE $$
(☑03-5155 1957; www.kalimnawoods.com.au; Kalimna Jetty Rd; d $125-220; ❋) Retreat 2km from the town centre to Kalimna Woods, where cosy self-contained cottages are set in a large rainforest and bush garden, complete with friendly resident possums and birds.

Eastern Beach Tourist Park   CARAVAN PARK $
(☑03-5155 1581; www.easternbeach.com.au; 42 Eastern Beach Rd; unpowered/powered sites from $24/29, cabins $110-240; @❀) Most caravan parks in Lakes pack 'em in, but this one has space, grassy sites and a great location away from the hubbub of town in a bush setting back from Eastern Beach.

✖ Eating & Drinking

With the largest fishing fleet in Victoria, Lakes Entrance is the perfect place to indulge in fresh seafood. You can sometimes buy shellfish (prawns, bugs etc) straight from local boats or try Ferryman's.

Ferryman's Seafood Cafe   SEAFOOD $$
(☑03-5155 3000; www.ferrymans.com.au; Middle Harbour, The Esplanade; lunch $14-22, dinner $25-42; ◷brunch, lunch & dinner) It's hard to beat the ambience of dining on the deck of this floating cafe-restaurant, which will fill you to the gills with seafood, including good ol' fish and chips.

Six Sisters & a Pigeon   CAFE $
(☑03-5155 1144; 567 The Esplanade; meals $7-17; ◷breakfast & lunch Tue-Sun; ✐) The name alone should guide you to this quirky licensed cafe on the Esplanade opposite the footbridge. Good coffee, all-day breakfasts – Mexican eggs, French toast or Spanish omelette – and lunches of focaccias and baguettes.

Miriam's Restaurant   STEAKHOUSE $$

(☑03-5155 3999; cnr Esplanade & Bulmer St; mains $16-34; ⊘dinner) The upstairs dining room at Miriam's overlooks the Esplanade, and the Gippsland steaks, seafood dishes and casual cocktail-bar atmosphere are excellent.

Waterwheel Beach Tavern   PUB FARE $$

(☑03-5156 5855; www.waterwheeltavern.com; 577 Beach Rd, Lake Tyers; mains $18-32; ⊘lunch & dinner) It's worth the trip out to Lake Tyers, 10 minutes' drive from Lakes Entrance, for a beer at this beachside pub. The setting is superb and the bistro food is classy but unpretentious – Tuesday is steak night, Wednesday parma night.

Omega 3   SEAFOOD $

(Shop 5, Safeway Arcade, Church St; ⊘9am-5pm) This is the shopfront for the local Fishermen's Co-op, so the seafood is always fresh.

ⓘ Information

Hub (☑03-5155 4247; cnr Myer St & The Esplanade; ⊘9.30am-5pm Mon-Fri, 10am-2pm Sat; per hr $5; @🛜) Internet cafe in a quirky, aroma-scented fashion shop.

Lakes Entrance Visitors Centre (☑1800 637 060, 03-5155 1966; www.discovereastgippsland.com.au; cnr Princes Hwy & Marine Pde; ⊘9am-5pm) Free accommodation and tour booking service. Also check out www.lakesentrance.com.

ⓘ Getting There & Away

V/Line (☑13 61 96; www.vline.com.au) runs a train/bus service from Melbourne to Lakes Entrance via Bairnsdale ($28.50, 4½ hours, three daily).

East Gippsland & The Wilderness Coast

Beyond Lakes Entrance stretches a wilderness area of spectacular coastal national parks and old-growth forest. Much of this region wasn't cleared for agriculture and contains some of the most remote and pristine national parks in the state, making logging in these ancient forests a hot issue.

BUCHAN
POP 230

Leaving the coast, Buchan is a beautiful town in the foothills of the Snowy Mountains about 56km north of Lakes Entrance, famous for its intricate limestone cave system that has been open to visitors since 1913.

Guided tours, alternating between Royal Cave and Fairy Cave, are run by Parks Victoria (☑03-5162 1900; www.parks.vic.gov.au; tours adult/child/family $14.50/8.50/40.50; ⊘10am, 11.15am, 1pm, 2.15pm & 3.30pm). Combined cave tours are slightly cheaper. The rangers also offer hard-hat guided tours to Federal Cave during the high season.

🛏 Sleeping

Buchan Caves Reserve   CAMPGROUND $

(☑03-5162 1900; www.parks.vic.gov.au; Buchan Caves Reserve; unpowered/powered sites $18/24, d cabins $77, wilderness retreats d $150; 🐾) You can stay right by the caves at this serene camping ground, edged by state forest.

Buchan Lodge   HOSTEL $

(☑03-5155 9421; www.buchanlodge.com.au; 9 Saleyard Rd; dm $20) A short walk from the town centre and just by the river, this welcoming pine-log backpackers is great for lounging about and taking in the country views.

ⓘ Getting There & Away

Buchan Bus 'n' Freight (☑03-5155 0356) operates a service on Wednesday and Friday from Bairnsdale to Buchan ($16.50, 1½ hours, three weekly), linking with the train from Melbourne. At other times you'll need your own transport.

ORBOST & MARLO
POP 2100

Most travellers whizz through Orbost as the Princes Hwy passes just south of the town, while the Bonang Rd heads north towards the Snowy River and Errinundra National Parks, and Marlo Rd follows the Snowy River south to Marlo and continues along the coast to Cape Conran.

Orbost visitor information centre (☑03-5154 2424; cnr Nicholson & Clarke Sts; ⊘9am-5pm) is in the historic 1872 Slab Hut.

The impressive Orbost Exhibition Centre (☑03-5154 2634; www.orbostexhibitioncentre.org; Clarke St; adult/child $4/free; ⊘10am-4pm Mon-Sat, 1-4pm Sun), next to the visitor centre, showcases works by local timber artists.

Just 15km south of Orbost, Marlo is a sleepy beach town at the mouth of the Snowy River. Aside from the gorgeous coast, the main attraction here is the PS Curlip (☑03-5154 1699; www.paddlesteamercurlip.com.au; adult/child/family $25/15/60; ⊘11.30am & 2.30pm Wed-Sun), a recreation of an 1890 paddle steamer that once chugged up the Snowy River to Orbost. Buy tickets at the general store in town.

DETOUR: SNOWY RIVER & ERRINUNDRA NATIONAL PARKS

These two isolated wilderness parks north of Orbost occupy most of the Victoria's eastern corner between the alpine country and the coast, and offer a unique experience in remote bushwalking, canoeing and camping. The parks are linked in the north by the partially unsealed MacKillops Rd, making it possible to do a driving loop from Buchan to Orbost. In dry weather it's passable to conventional vehicles but check road conditions with Parks Victoria.

Snowy River National Park

Northeast of Buchan, this is one of Victoria's most isolated and spectacular national parks, dominated by deep gorges carved through limestone and sandstone by the Snowy River on its route from the Snowy Mountains in NSW to its mouth at Marlo. The entire park is a smorgasbord of unspoiled, superb bush and mountain scenery, ranging from alpine woodlands and eucalypt forests to rainforests.

On the west side of the park, the views from the well-signposted cliff-top lookouts over **Little River Falls** and **Little River Gorge**, Victoria's deepest gorge, are awesome. From there it's about 20km to **McKillops Bridge**, a huge bridge spanning the Snowy River, making it possible to drive across to Errinundra National Park.

There's free camping at a number of basic sites around the park, but the main site is McKillops Bridge, with toilets and fireplaces.

Karoonda Park (03-5155 0220; www.karoondapark.com; 3558 Gelantipy Rd; dm/s/d $30/50/70, cabins per 6 people $115;), 40km north of Buchan on the road to Snowy River National Park, has comfortable backpacker and cabin digs. Activities available include abseiling, horse riding, wild caving, white-water rafting, mountain-bike hire and farm activities.

Errinundra National Park

Errinundra National Park contains Victoria's largest cool-temperate rainforest, but the forests surrounding the park are a constant battleground between loggers and environmentalists who are trying to protect old-growth forests.

The national park coves an area of 256 sq km and has three granite outcrops that extend into the cloud, resulting in high rainfall, deep, fertile soils and a network of creeks and rivers that flow north, south and east. You can explore the park by a combination of scenic drives, and short and medium-length walks. **Mt Ellery** has spectacular views; **Errinundra Saddle** has a rainforest boardwalk; and from **Ocean View Lookout** there are stunning views down the Goolengook River as far as Bemm River.

Frosty Hollow Camp Site (sites free) is the only camping area within the national park, on the eastern side. There are also free camping areas on the park's edges – at Ellery Creek in Goongerah, and at Delegate River.

Jacarri (03-5154 0145; www.eastgippsland.net.au/jacarri; cnr Bonang Hwy & Ellery Creek Track, Goongerah; d/f $80/90) is a gorgeous little eco-cottage located on an organic farm. It's solar-powered, has a slow-combustion stove for heating and cooking, and sleeps four.

Tours

Gippsland High Country Tours
HIKING

(03-5157 5556; www.gippslandhighcountrytours.com.au) This outfit leads five- to seven-day hikes in Errinundra, Snowy River and Croajingolong National Parks.

Snowy River Expeditions
ADVENTURE

(03-5155 0220; www.karoondapark.com/sre; Karoonda Park, Gelantipy; tours per day from $85) This company runs adventure tours including one-, two- or four-day rafting trips on the Snowy. Half- or full-day abseiling or caving trips are also available.

CAPE CONRAN COASTAL PARK

This blissfully undeveloped part of the coast is one of Gippsland's most beautiful corners, with long stretches of remote white-sand beaches. The 19km coastal route from Marlo to Cape Conran is particularly pretty, bordered by banksia trees, grass plains, sand dunes and the ocean.

Good walks include the **nature trail**, which meets up with the East Cape Boardwalk, where signage gives you a glimpse into how Indigenous people lived in this area. Take the West Cape Rd off Cape Conran Rd to Salmon Rocks, where there's an Aboriginal shell midden dated at more than 10,000 years old.

Cabbage Tree Palms, a short detour off the road between Cape Conran and the Princes Hwy, is Victoria's only stand of native palms – a tiny rainforest oasis.

Parks Victoria (☎03-5154 8438; www.conran.net.au) runs three excellent accommodation options in Cape Conran Coastal Park, including foreshore camp sites ($18-24), cabins (up to 4 people $96-145) and safari tents ($150).

MALLACOOTA

POP 1100

Isolated Mallacoota is a real gem – Victoria's most easterly town but an easy detour if you're heading along the coastal route between Melbourne and Sydney. It's snuggled on the vast Mallacoota Inlet and surrounded by the tumbling hills and beachside dunes of beautiful Croajingolong National Park. Those prepared to come this far are treated to long empty ocean surf beaches, tidal river mouths and swimming, fishing and boating on the inlet.

◉ Sights & Activities

One of the best ways to experience the beauty of Mallacoota and its estuarine waters is by boat. Mallacoota Hire Boats (☎0438-447 558; Main Wharf, cnr Allan & Buckland Drs; motor boats per 2/4/6hr $60/100/140) is centrally located and hires out canoes and boats.

On Gabo Island, 14km offshore from Mallacoota, the windswept 154-hectare Gabo Island Lightstation Reserve is home to sea birds and one of the world's largest colonies of little penguins – far outnumbering those at Phillip Island. The island has an operating lighthouse, built in 1862 and the tallest in the southern hemisphere, and you can stay in the old keepers' cottages here (contact Parks Victoria). Mallacoota Air Services

(☎0408-580 806; return per 3 adults or 2 adults & 2 children $300) offers fast access to the island on demand, or you can get there by boat with Wilderness Coast Ocean Charters.

☞ Tours & Cruises

MV Loch-Ard   CRUISES

(☎03-5158 0764; Main Wharf; adult/child 2hr cruise $28/10, 3hr cruise $38/12) Runs several inlet cruises from the Main Wharf, with wildlife spotting and a twilight cruise.

Porkie Bess   CRUISES, FISHING

(☎03-5158 0109, 0408 408 094; 2hr cruise $25, fishing trip $50) A 1940s wooden boat offering fishing trips and cruises around the lakes, and ferry services for hikers ($20 per person, minimum four). Departs Karbeethong Jetty.

Wilderness Coast Ocean Charters   WILDLIFE

(☎03-5158 0701, 0417 398 068; wildcoast@dragnet.com.au) Runs day trips to Gabo Island ($60, minimum eight, $60 each way if you stay overnight) and may run trips down the coast to view the seal colony off Wingan Inlet if there's enough demand.

☞ Sleeping

During Easter and Christmas school holidays you'll need to book well ahead.

Adobe Mudbrick Flats   APARTMENTS $

(☎03-5158 0329; www.adobeholidayflats.com.au; 17 Karbeethong Ave; d $75, q $90-140) A labour of love by Margaret and Peter Kurz, these unique mud-brick flats in Karbeethong, a few kilometres north of Mallacoota, are something special. With an emphasis on recycling and ecofriendliness, the array of whimsical apartments are comfortable and great value.

Mallacoota Foreshore Holiday Park   CAMPGROUND $

(☎03-5158 0300; www.mallacootaholidaypark.com.au; cnr Allan Dr & Maurice Ave; unpowered/powered sites from $27/32; ☎) Curling around the waterfront, the grassy sites here morph into one of Victoria's most sociable and scenic caravan parks. No cabins, but the best of Mallacoota's many parks for campers.

Karbeethong Lodge   GUESTHOUSE $$

(☎03-5158 0411; www.karbeethonglodge.com.au; 16 Schnapper Point Dr; d $75-220) It's hard not to be overcome by a sense of serenity as you rest on the broad verandahs of this early

1900s timber guesthouse, with uninterrupted views over Mallacoota Inlet.

Mallacoota Wilderness Houseboats
HOUSEBOAT $$

(☑0409-924 016; www.mallacootawilderness houseboats.com.au; Karbeethong Jetty; 4-nights midweek from $750, 1 week $1200-1600) These six-berth houseboats are not luxurious but they are the perfect way to explore Mallacoota's waterways.

✕ Eating

Lucy's
ASIAN FUSION $

(☑03-5158 0666; 64 Maurice Ave; dishes $10-20; ⊗8am-9pm; ⊛) Lucy's is popular for the delicious and great-value homemade rice noodles with chicken, prawn or abalone, as well as dumplings.

Croajingolong Cafe
CAFE $

(☑03-5158 0098; Shop 3, 14 Allan Dr; mains $5-14; ⊗breakfast & lunch Tue-Sun; ☎) Overlooking the inlet, this is the place to spread out the newspaper over a coffee, baguette or pancake breakfast.

Mallacoota Hotel
PUB FARE $$

(☑03-5158 0455; www.mallacootahotel.com. au; 51-55 Maurice Ave; mains $17-30; ⊗lunch & dinner) The local pub bistro serves hearty meals from its varied menu, with reliable favourites like chicken parmagiana and Gippsland steak. Bands play regularly in the summer. There's a good-value motel attached.

❶ Information

Mallacoota Visitors Centre (☑03-5158 0800; www.visitmallacoota.com.au; Main Wharf, cnr Allan & Buckland Dr; ⊗10am-4pm) Operated by friendly volunteers.

❶ Getting There & Away

Mallacoota is 23km southeast of Genoa (on the Princes Hwy). From Melbourne, take the train to Bairnsdale, then the V/Line bus to Genoa ($26.70, 3½ hours, one daily). **Mallacoota–Genoa Bus Service** (☑0408-315 615) meets the V/Line coach on Monday, Thursday and Friday, plus Sunday during school holidays, and runs to Mallacoota ($3.40, 30 minutes).

CROAJINGOLONG NATIONAL PARK

Croajingolong is one of Australia's finest coastal wilderness national parks, recognised by its listing as a World Biosphere Reserve by Unesco (one of 12 in Australia). For remote camping, bushwalking, fishing, swimming and surfing, this one is hard to beat, with unspoiled beaches, inlets, estuaries and forests. The park covers 875 sq km, stretching for about 100km from Bemm River to the NSW border. The five inlets – Sydenham, Tamboon, Mueller, Wingan and Mallacoota (the largest and most accessible) – are popular canoeing and fishing spots.

Point Hicks was the first part of Australia to be spotted by Captain Cook and the *Endeavour* crew in 1770, and was named after his first Lieutenant, Zachary Hicks. There's a lighthouse here, open for tours, and accommodation in the old cottages. You can still see remains of the SS *Saros*, which ran ashore in 1937, on a short walk from the lighthouse.

Access roads of varying quality lead into the park from the Princes Hwy. Apart from Mallacoota Rd, all roads are unsealed and can be very rough in winter, so check road conditions with Parks Victoria before venturing on, especially during or after rain.

⌂ Sleeping

There are four designated camp sites: Wingan Inlet and Shipwreck Creek can be booked through **Parks Victoria** (☑13 19 63; camp sites $17); Thurra River and Mueller Inlet through **Point Hicks Lighthouse** (☑03-5158 4268; www.pointhicks.com.au; camp sites $20). Shipwreck Creek is the most accessible, 15km from Mallacoota, while Wingan Inlet has the prettiest setting.

Point Hicks Lighthouse
COTTAGE $$

(☑03-5158 4268, 03-5156 0432; www.pointhicks. com.au; bungalow $100-120, cottage $330) This remote lighthouse has two comfortable, heritage-listed cottages, and one double bungalow. The cottages sleep six people and have sensational ocean views and wood fires.

Tasmania

Best Places to Eat

» Pigeon Hole (p636)

» Meadowbank Estate (boxed text, p643)

» Red Velvet Lounge (p647)

» Passini's (p663)

» Stillwater (p671)

Best Places to Stay

» Astor Private Hotel (p632)

» Beachfront on Bruny (p645)

» St Marys Seaview Farm (p663)

» Point Break (p664)

» Bluestone Grainstore (p679)

Why Go?

Dazzlin' Tassie is brilliant, beautiful and accessible. It's compact enough to 'do' in a few weeks and layered enough to keep bringing you back. Look forward to exquisite beaches, jagged mountain ranges, rarefied alpine plateaus, plentiful wildlife and vast tracts of virgin wilderness, much of it within a World Heritage area. Tasmania produces superb gourmet food and wine, and a flourishing arts scene and a burgeoning urban cool highlight a positive and vibrant future.

Tasmania's past incorporates an often tragic Aboriginal and convict history, much of it vital to understanding the story of Australia itself. Tasmania's raffish and pioneering heritage is showcased throughout the island, often against the backdrop of some of Australia's most impressive colonial architecture.

For the outdoors buff, Tassie's bushwalking, cycling, rafting and kayaking opportunities rank among the best on the planet. Tasmania is still Australia, but beguilingly and bewitchingly, just that little bit different.

When to Go
Hobart

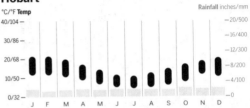

Feb Swim, bushwalk and mountain bike, and enjoy the most settled weather of the year.

Mar Fill up on fresh apples, fruit and berries from Tasmania's network of farmgate providers.

Dec (end) Enjoy the best of Hobart's festival season with food, wine, music, art and culture.

Tasmania Highlights

1 Meandering lazily through the labyrinth of stalls at Hobart's Saturday morning **Salamanca Market** (boxed text, p623)

2 Negotiating the **Overland Track** (boxed text, p699), the archetypal Tasmanian bushwalk and an essential Aussie rite of passage

3 Contemplating the contrast of melancholy silence and beautiful scenery at **Port Arthur** (p652)

4 Being surprised by the rugged alpine beauty of the **Mt Field National Park** (p642), just an hour's drive from Hobart

5 Packing a picnic of fine Tassie produce and hiking into photogenic **Wineglass Bay** (p660)

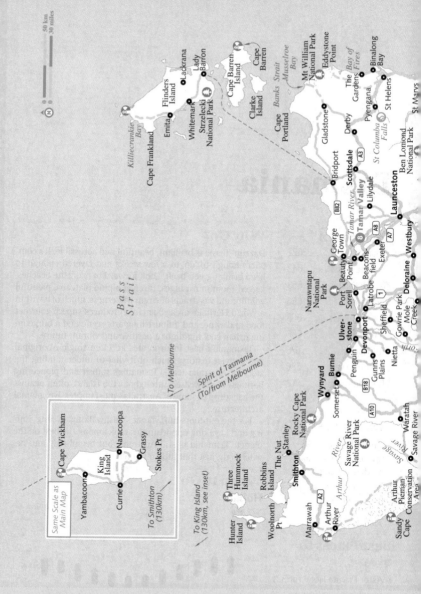

6 Bumping and bouncing into the Southern Ocean on a boat cruise from **Bruny Island** (p644)

7 Sea kayaking on the still, crystalline waters of **Bathurst Harbour** (p701)

8 Taking the foot off the travel accelerator with a lazy, lingering lunch in the **Tamar Valley** (p673) wine region

There were perhaps 10,000 Aborigines living on Tasmania when Dutchman Abel Janszoon Tasman became the first European to sight the island. His ships first came upon the island's northwest coast on 24 November 1642 and then skirted around the southern and southeastern coastlines. He named the island Van Diemen's Land after the Dutch East Indies' governor. Since Tasman's voyages yielded nothing of value for the Dutch East India Company, European contact with the island ceased for more than another century until the British arrived at Sydney Cove in 1788 – Van Diemen's Land would become a convenient pit stop en route to New South Wales. In 1798 Matthew Flinders circumnavigated Van Diemen's Land, proving it was an island. In 1803 Risdon Cove, on the Derwent River, became the site of Australia's second British colony. The settlement moved a year later to the present site of Hobart, where fresh water ran plentifully off Mt Wellington.

Convicts accompanied the first settlers as labourers, but the grim penal settlements weren't built until later: on Sarah Island in Macquarie Harbour in 1822, on Maria Island in 1825 and at Port Arthur in 1830. In subsequent decades, Van Diemen's Land became infamous for the most apocalyptic punishments and deprivations exacted on convicts anywhere in the British colonies – the most fearsome, terrible of destinations. By the 1850s every second islander was a convict and Van Diemen's Land had whole industries exploiting the misery of convict labour. Hobart Town and Launceston festered with disease, prostitution and drunken lawlessness.

In 1856 the 'social experiment' of convict transportation to Van Diemen's Land was abolished. In an effort to escape the stigma of its horrendous penal reputation, Van Diemen's Land renamed itself Tasmania, after the Dutchman. By this time, however, the island's Aborigines had been practically annihilated by a mixture of concerted ethnic cleansing, disease, forced labour and ultimately doomed resettlement and assimilation schemes; see opposite.

The 1870s and '80s saw prospectors arrive after gold was discovered, and the state's rugged and remote west was opened up by miners and timber workers seeking Huon pine, myrtle and sassafras. So began the exploitation of Tasmania's natural resources. In the 1960s and '70s conservationists fought unsuccessfully to stop the hydroelectric flooding of Lake Pedder. In the 1980s the issue flared again; this time the fledgling pro-environment movement successfully campaigned against flooding the Franklin River for similar purposes. Leaders in these campaigns were instrumental in forming the United Tasmania Group in 1972, regarded as the world's first Green political party. The Australian Greens party, under the leadership of Senator Bob Brown, is now a potent force in Australian federal politics.

The long-running debate between prologging groups, pro–pulp mill corporations and conservationists keen to protect Tasmania's old-growth forests and wild heritage continues. In 2010, a minor breakthrough was achieved with the signing of a 'peace deal', the culmination of a round-table discussion between the forest industry, timber workers and conservation groups. This statement proposes to phase out logging of the island's native forests for commodities such as woodchips, beginning with a moratorium on the logging of high-conservation-value forests.

Ask at Hobart bookshops for Anne Krien's *Into the Woods – The Battle for Tasmania's Forests* (2010), an excellent insight into Tasmania's environmental politics.

Indigenous Tasmania

The treatment of Tasmania's Indigenous peoples by early European settlers is a tragic and shameful story. Isolated from the Australian mainland by rising sea levels 10,000 years ago, the island's Aborigines developed a distinct, sustainable, seasonal culture of hunting, fishing and gathering.

When European pastoralists arrived, they fenced off sections of fertile land for farming. Aborigines lost more and more of their traditional hunting grounds, and battles erupted between blacks and whites – the so-called Black Wars. Lieutenant-Governor Arthur declared martial law in 1828 and Aboriginal tribes were systematically murdered, incarcerated or forced at gunpoint from districts settled by whites. Many more succumbed to European diseases.

An attempt to resettle Tasmania's remaining Aborigines to Flinders Island – to 'civilise' and Christianise them – occurred between 1829 and 1834, but most died of despair, poor food or respiratory disease. Of the 135 taken to the island, only 47 survived to be transferred to another settlement at

Oyster Cove in Tasmania's south in 1847. Within 32 years, the entire Aboriginal population at Oyster Cove had perished.

European sealers had been working in Bass Strait since 1798 and, although they occasionally raided tribes along the coast, their contact with Aboriginal people was mainly based on trade. Aboriginal women were also traded and many sealers settled on Bass Strait islands with these women and had families.

There's a simple memorial on Bruny Island (see p645) to Truganini, who was said to be the last full-blood Aborigine. Truganini died in her 70s in Hobart in 1876 (she was, in fact, outlived by two full-blood women). Her sad life and death was reported at the time as 'the end of the native problem' and her skeleton was displayed in the Hobart museum, but she's since become a symbol of the horror of the attempted genocide of Tasmania's Indigenous peoples.

By 1847 an Aboriginal community, with a lifestyle based on both Aboriginal and European ways, had emerged on Flinders and other islands in the Furneaux Group. Although the last full-blooded Tasmanian Aborigines died in the 19th century, the strength of the community helped save the race from oblivion. Today, thousands of descendants of this community live in Tasmania.

Tasmanian Aborigines continue to claim rights to land and compensation for past injustices. Acknowledgment of the treatment meted out to Aborigines by Europeans has resulted in the recognition of native titles to land. In 1995 the Tasmanian government returned 12 sites to the Tasmanian Aboriginal community, including Oyster Cove, Kutikina Cave and Steep Island. Wybalenna was added to this list in 1999, and areas of Cape Barren and Clarke Islands in 2005.

For more information contact the **Aboriginal Heritage Office** (☑1300 135 513, 03-6216 4471; www.tahl.tas.gov.au) or see the excellent *Deep Time: Continuing Tasmanian Aboriginal Culture* brochure available at the Hobart visitor centre (p639).

National Parks

Tasmania has a greater percentage of land protected as national parks and reserves than any other Australian state, and people come from all over the world to enjoy the world-class hiking, canoeing and kayaking, caving, swimming and surfing, and other outdoors activities. Tasmania has 19 national parks that total more than 1.4 million hectares – nearly 21% of the island's land area.

In 1982 Tasmania's four largest national parks (Southwest, Franklin-Gordon Wild Rivers, Cradle Mountain-Lake St Clair and Walls of Jerusalem) and much of the Central Plateau were placed on the Unesco World Heritage list. This listing acknowledges that these parks combined are one of the last great temperate wilderness areas left in the world.

An entry fee is charged for all of Tasmania's national parks. Passes are available at most park entrances, many visitor information centres, the *Spirit of Tasmania* ferries and at the state-wide offices of **Service Tasmania** (☑1300 135 513; www.service.tas.gov.au).

A 24-hour pass to any number of parks costs $24 per car (including up to eight passengers) or $12 per individual (arriving by bus, or for bushwalkers, cyclists and motorcyclists). The best value for most travellers is the eight-week pass, which costs $60 per vehicle or $30 per person.

The **Parks & Wildlife Service** (www.parks. tas.gov.au) website is loaded with information. In the peak season (mid-December to mid-February) rangers run free family-friendly activities at the major national parks.

🏃 Activities

For information on activities, adventure tourism and tour operators, see the following websites:

Parks & Wildlife Service (www.parks.tas. gov.au) Click on 'Recreation'.

Tourism Tasmania (www.discovertasmania. com) Click on 'Activities & Attractions'.

BUSHWALKING

Tasmania's Overland Track – six days and 65km through the sublime Cradle Mountain-Lake St Clair National Park – is Australia's most famous bushwalk and widely ranked among the world's top 10 walks. Another epic is the six- to eight-day, 85km South Coast Track.

Lonely Planet's *Walking in Australia* has info on some of Tasmania's best (longer) walks. Some of Tassie's wilderness areas can be experienced on much shorter walks: Parks & Wildlife Service's *60 Great Short Walks* brochure (free from visitor information centres) lists the state's best short walks from 10-minute strolls to day-long hikes. Check the **Parks & Wildlife Service** (www.parks.tas. gov.au) website for more information.

On long walks remember that in any Tasmanian season a beautiful day can quickly turn ugly, so warm clothing, waterproof gear, a tent, map and compass are essential. Tasmap (www.tasmap.tas.gov.au) produces excellent maps available online or from visitor information centres. In Hobart you'll also find them at Service Tasmania and the Tasmanian Map Centre (see p639) as well as state-wide outdoor stores.

FISHING

For all things fishy in Tasmania, go to www.dpiw.tas.gov.au.

Tasmania's Lake Country on the Central Plateau features glacial lakes, crystal-clear streams and world-class trout fishing. There are dozens of operators that can help you organise guides, lessons or fishing trips – Trout Guides & Lodges Tasmania (www.troutguidestasmania.com.au) is a great starting point.

Meanwhile on the east coast charter fishing is big business. See www.fishnet.com.au for a directory of operators.

RAFTING & SEA KAYAKING

The Franklin River is famous for full-bore white-water rafting and the Parks & Wildlife website has good information. Other rivers offering rapids thrills include the Derwent (upstream from Hobart), the Picton (southwest of Hobart) and the Mersey in the north.

Sea-kayaking centres include Kettering southeast of Hobart, from where you can explore the D'Entrecasteaux Channel, Bruny Island and the southwest coast; and Coles Bay, the launching place for Freycinet Peninsula explorations. You can also have a paddle around the Hobart docks (p629).

SAILING

The D'Entrecasteaux Channel and Huon River south of Hobart are wide, deep and tantalising places to set sail, with more inlets and harbours than you could swing a boom at. For casual berths in Hobart (overnight or weekly), contact the Royal Yacht Club of Tasmania (☑03-6223 4599; www.ryct.org.au) in Sandy Bay.

If you're an experienced sailor, hire a yacht from Yachting Holidays (☑03-6224 3195; www.yachtingholidays.com.au), based in Hobart. Charter of a six-berth vessel is $750 per day, with reduced rates for long rentals or in the off-peak (April to November) period. Skippered charter is also available.

SCUBA DIVING

Despite the chilly water there are some excellent diving opportunities, particularly on the east coast. A great artificial site was created by the scuttling of the *Troy D* in 2007 off the west coast of Maria Island – see www.troyd.com.au for information on diving and permits. Rocky Cape on the north coast offers marine life aplenty, while shipwrecks abound around King and Flinders Islands.

Tasmanian diving courses are considerably cheaper than on the mainland. Contact operators at the Bay of Fires, Eaglehawk Neck, Bicheno and King Island.

SURFING

Tasmania has dozens of brilliant surfing spots with point and reef breaks as well as river mouths. Don't think of going in with anything less than a full-length wetsuit because the water is friggin' cold! Close to Hobart, the most reliable spots are Clifton Beach and Goats Beach (unsigned) en route to South Arm. The southern beaches on Bruny Island, particularly Whalebone Point in Cloudy Bay, offer consistent swell. The east coast from Bicheno north to St Helens has solid beach breaks when conditions are working. At Marrawah on the west coast the waves are often towering. Shipstern Bluff is a two-hour walk into the Tasman National Park on the Tasman Peninsula south of Port Arthur around Raoul Bay, and is allegedly Australia's heaviest wave.

Websites with surf reports and conditions updates include www.tassiesurf.com.

SWIMMING

The north and east coasts offer countless sheltered, white-sand beaches with excellent swimming, but you'll find the water rather cold. Some of the most beautiful swimming beaches include Wineglass Bay, Bay of Fires, (watch for rips), Binalong Bay outside St Helens, lovely Boat Harbour Beach and Penguin Beach.

Wine Regions

Since the mid-1950s Tasmania has gained international recognition for producing quality wines, characterised by their full, fruity flavour, along with the high acidity expected of cool, temperate wine regions. Today vineyards across the state are producing award-winning Pinot Noirs, Rieslings and Chardonnays, and Tassie wineries are growing grapes for many of the top Australian sparkling wine brands.

Tasmania can be split into two main wine-growing regions: the north and east around Launceston (the Tamar Valley) and

ADRENALIN-FUELLED TASMANIA

For a relatively compact island, Tasmania definitely punches above its weight if you're looking to get the adrenalin pumping, almost always with the backdrop of some of Australia's finest wilderness scenery.

» Mountain biking helter skelter down the imposing hulk of Hobart's Mt Wellington (p626)

» Rafting on the impetuous rapids of the Franklin River (p697)

» Abseiling 140m down the sheer concrete monolith that is Gordon Dam (p703)

» Whizzing through the forest canopy on a cable hang glider in the Tahune Forest (p648)

» Sea kayaking around the misty coves and isolated bays of Bathurst Harbour (p701)

Bicheno, and the south around Hobart (the Coal River Valley).

Tours

Travel agents can arrange package deals from the mainland including transport to Tasmania (by air or sea), car rental and accommodation. Contact Tourism Tasmania (below).

There are many in-bound Tasmanian operators vying hard in a competitive business for your tourist dollars, so shop around and compare products. Tour operators can shunt you around to the highlights or provide you with authentic wilderness or activity-based experiences. Most trips depart from Hobart, but some operators use Devonport or Launceston as a base.

Herbaceous Tours   FOOD & WINE
(041 697 0699; www.herbaceoustours.com.au) Specialist food and wine tours across Tasmania including Hobart, the Coal River Valley wine region, Bruny Island and the Huon Valley. Look forward to lots of tasty sampling of foodie goodies.

Jump Tours   BACKPACKER
(0422 130 630; www.jumptours.com) Youth- and backpacker-oriented three- and five-day Tassie tours.

Tarkine Trails   BUSHWALKING
(03-6223 5320; www.tarkinetrails.com.au) Green-focused group offering guided walks in the Tarkine wilderness, the Walls of Jerusalem and the Overland Track.

TASafari   4WD
(1300 882 415, 03-6395 1577; www.tasafari.com.au) Offers four-, five- and 10-day eco-certified 4WD tours that visit both the well-known and more remote parts of the state.

Tasmanian Expeditions   OUTDOOR ACTIVITIES
(1300 666 856, 03-6339 3999; www.tas-ex.com) Offers an excellent range of activity-based tours: bushwalking, cabin-based walks, rafting, rock climbing, cycling and sea kayaking.

Tours Tasmania   BACKPACKER
(1800 777 103; www.tourstas.com.au) Small-group, backpacker-oriented full-day trips from Hobart: Cradle Mountain, Wineglass Bay or Mt Field National Park. Also longer two- to five-day itineraries.

Under Down Under   BACKPACKER
(1800 064 726, 03-6362 2237; www.underdownunder.com.au) Nature-based, backpacker-friendly trips, including three- to nine-day tours of the east coast, west coast and the Tarkine wilderness. Tour fees refunded for photographed thylacine sightings!

Seasonal Work

Casual work can usually be found during summer in the major tourist centres, mainly working in tourism, hospitality, labouring, gardening or farming. Seasonal fruit-picking is hard work and pay is proportional to the quantity and quality of fruits picked. Harvest is from December to April in the Huon and Tamar Valleys. Grape-picking jobs are sometimes available in late autumn and early winter, as some wineries still hand-pick their crops.

Information

Tourism Tasmania (1300 827 743, 03-6230 8235; www.discovertasmania.com), the government-operated tourism authority, has a good website and provides loads of travel information.

In Tasmania itself, there are helpful visitor information centres in most major towns, overflowing with brochures including the free newspapers *Tasmanian Travelways*, *Treasure Island* and *Explore Tasmania*, all containing state-wide listings of accommodation, events, public transport and vehicle hire.

Other useful information sources:

Parks & Wildlife Service (☎1300 315 513; www.parks.tas.gov.au) Details walks, camp sites, activities and facilities in the state's magical national parks and reserves.

Royal Automobile Club of Tasmania (RACT; ☎13 27 22; www.ract.com.au) Roadside automotive assistance, road weather updates and general travel information.

❶ Getting There & Away

Tasmania's quarantine service rigorously protects the state's disease-free agriculture – all visitors (including those from mainland Australia) must dispose of all plants, fruits and vegetables prior to or upon arrival.

If you're travelling in a group or family and want to take a vehicle to Tasmania, the cheapest option is to combine cheap airline tickets with Virgin Australia or Jetstar for the bulk of the group, and car and driver-only passage on the ferry from Melbourne (see opposite).

AIR

There are no direct international flights to/from Tasmania. Airlines flying between Tasmania and mainland Australia:

Jetstar (☎13 15 38; www.jetstar.com.au) Direct flights from Melbourne and Sydney to Hobart and Launceston.

Qantas (☎13 13 13; www.qantas.com.au) Direct flights from Sydney, Brisbane and Melbourne to Hobart and Launceston. QantasLink (the regional subsidiary) flies between Melbourne and Devonport.

Regional Express (☎13 17 13; www.regional express.com.au) Flies from Melbourne to Burnie/Wynyard and King Island.

Sharp Airlines (☎1300 556 694; www.sharp airlines.com.au) Flights four days a week from Melbourne Essendon to Flinders Island.

Tiger Airways (☎03-9335 3033; www.tigerair ways.com.au) Flies from Melbourne to Hobart.

Virgin Australia (☎13 67 89; www.virgin australia.com) Direct flights from Melbourne, Sydney, Brisbane, Canberra and Adelaide to Hobart, and from Melbourne, Brisbane and Sydney to Launceston.

BOAT

The **Spirit of Tasmania** (☎1800 634 906; www.spiritoftasmania.com.au) operates two car and passenger ferries that cruise nightly between Melbourne and Devonport in both directions, usually departing at 7.30pm and taking about 10 hours shore to shore. Additional daytime sailings are scheduled during peak and shoulder seasons. Fares vary for travel in peak (mid-December to late January), shoulder (late January to April, and September to mid-December) and off-peak (May to August) seasons. There's a range of cabin and seat options, and child, student, pensioner and senior discounts apply. Some cabins are wheelchair-accessible. And you can bring your car!

The Devonport terminal is on The Esplanade in East Devonport, and the Melbourne terminal is at Station Pier in Port Melbourne. Standard one-way adult fares are as follows; limited 'Ship Saver' fares are cheaper.

FARE TYPE	PEAK	SHOULDER	OFF-PEAK
Ocean-view recliner seat	$202	$170	$148
4-berth cabin	$258	$236	$226
Twin cabin	$308	$263	$252
Daytime sailings (unallocated seating only)	$179	$128	$122
Standard vehicles & campervans (up to 5m)	$79	$79	$79
Motorbikes	$54	$54	$54
Bicycles	$6	$6	$6

❶ Getting Around

AIR

Air travel within Tasmania is uncommon, but bushwalkers sometimes use light air services to/from the southwest. **Par Avion** (☎1800 144 460, 03-6248 5390; www.paravion.com.au) and **Tasair** (☎1800 062 900, 03-6248 5088; www.tasair.com.au) fly between Hobart and remote Melaleuca (for the South Coast Track) one way/return for $195/370 and $214/395 respectively.

There are also air links from mainland Tasmania to King Island and Flinders Island.

BICYCLE

Tassie is a good size for exploring by bicycle and is a perennial favourite with visiting touring cyclists. Some areas are pretty hilly and the weather can be unpredictable, but the routes are scenic and the towns aren't too far apart. You can hire touring bikes in Hobart (p627) and Launceston (p673). Cycling between Hobart and Launceston via either coast (the east coast is a cycling favourite) usually takes 10 to 14 days. For a full 'Lap of the Map', allow 18 to 28 days.

If you're planning a trip on the island, **Bicycle Tasmania** (www.biketas.org.au) is a solid

source of information, including state-wide bike shop listings.

BUS

The main bus lines are **Redline Coaches** (☎1300 360 000, 03-6336 1446; www.tasredline.com.au) and **Tassielink** (☎1300 300 520, 03-6230 8900; www.tassielink.com.au) and between them they cover most of the state, running along most major highways year-round (though their weekend services are less frequent). Redline services the Midland Hwy between Hobart and Launceston, the north coast between Launceston and Smithton, north from Launceston to George Town, and to the east coast. Tassielink runs from both Hobart and Launceston to the west and to the east coast, from Hobart to Port Arthur, and south from Hobart down the Huon Valley. Redline's Main Road Express connects Bass Strait ferry arrivals/departures in Devonport to Launceston, Hobart and Burnie.

Over summer, Tassielink buses also run to popular bushwalking destinations. Special fares that enable you to be dropped off at the start of a walk and picked up at the end are offered. Check the Tassielink website and click on 'Walking Track Links' for more information.

Additionally, **Metro Tasmania** (☎13 22 01; www.metrotas.com.au) runs regular services south from Hobart as far as Woodbridge and Cygnet, and north to Richmond and New Norfolk. Smaller operators service important tourist routes – see relevant sections for details.

Bus fares in Tasmania are quite reasonable: a one-way trip between Devonport and Launceston is around $23 and takes 1½ hours, Hobart to Launceston is $33 (2½ hours) and Hobart to Devonport is $56 (four hours).

Tassielink has an Explorer Pass for seven/10/14/21 days that must be used within 10/15/20/30 days and costs $208/248/286/329. Available from travel agents or directly from Tassielink, the pass is valid on all scheduled services for unlimited kilometres. Ask for timetables in advance or check Tassielink's website to plan your itinerary.

CAR, CAMPERVAN & MOTORCYCLE

Tassie is ideal for travelling by road, whether by car, campervan or motorcycle. The distances are relatively short, fuel is readily available and the driving conditions are generally pretty good. You can bring vehicles across on the ferry from the mainland, but renting may be cheaper, particularly for shorter trips, and rates are usually more affordable here than on the mainland. If you're renting, always ask your hirer's policy on driving on unsealed roads because quite a few of Tasmania's natural attractions are reached by dirt road. Generally the deal is that you'll void your insurance if you get off the bitumen.

There are few road hazards but watch out for wildlife and avoid driving between dusk and dawn when critters are active (roadkill is ubiquitous). One-lane bridges on country roads and log trucks speeding around sharp corners also demand caution. In cold weather, be wary of 'black ice' on shady mountain passes.

Big international players like Avis, Budget, Europcar and Thrifty have booking desks at airports and in major towns, with standard rates for small-car hire from $50 to $80 per day in high season. By booking well in advance, for a week's hire or more, car-hire rates can fall dramatically, especially outside high season. Web engines like **Vroom Vroom Vroom** (www.vroomvroomvroom.com.au) compare rental deals and can turn up some bargains.

Small local firms rent older cars for as little as $40 a day, depending on the season and rental length. They'll often ask for a bond of $300 or more. Some companies let you collect your car from the airport or ferry terminal. Some local companies:

Lo-Cost Auto Rent (www.locostautorent.com) Hobart (☎03-6231 0550; 105 Murray St); Launceston (☎03-6334 3437; 80 Tamar St); Devonport (☎03-6427 0796; 5 Murray St)

Selective Car Rentals (☎1800 300 102, 03-6234 3311; www.selectivecarrentals.com.au; 47 Bathurst St, Hobart)

Well-surfaced scenic roads and relatively light traffic make motorcycling in Tasmania fantastic. Contact **Tasmanian Motorcycle Hire** (☎03-6391 9139; www.tasmotorcyclehire.com.au).

With loads of camping grounds and free-camping areas, Tassie is *the* place for a campervanning holiday. They're economical too (from around $90 per day).

Britz (☎1800 331 082; www.britz.com.au)

Campervan Hire Tasmania (☎03-6391 9357; www.campervanhiretasmania.com)

Maui (☎1300 363 800; www.maui.com.au)

Tasmanian Campervan Hire (☎1800 807 119; www.tascamper.com)

Tasmanian Campervan Rentals (☎03-6248 5638; www.tasmaniacampervanrentals.com.au)

See also the following search engines for good deals:

Cheap Motorhome Hire (www.cheaptasmaniamotorhomehire.com.au)

Fetch (www.fetchcampervanhire.com.au)

Getabout Oz (www.getaboutoz.com)

HOBART

POP 212,000

Australia's second-oldest city and south-ernmost capital lies at the foothills of Mt Wellington on the banks of the Derwent River. Hobart's waterfront areas around Sullivans Cove – Macquarie Wharf, Constitution Dock, Salamanca Place and Battery Point – are simply gorgeous with their neat Georgian buildings and the towering bulk of Mt Wellington behind. The town's rich colonial heritage and natural charms are accented by a spirited, rootsy atmosphere: festivals, superb restaurants and hip urban bars abound. Hobartians are super-relaxed, very friendly and have none of the haughtiness of the Melbourne and Sydney gentry. They hang out in cafes and pubs, joking and idly watching the daily rush, dressed ready for their next wilderness expedition. On summer afternoons the sea breeze blows and yachts tack across the river. On winter mornings the pea-soup 'Bridgewater Jerry' fog lifts to reveal the snow-capped summit of the mountain.

History

The seminomadic Mouheener people were the original inhabitants of the area. Risdon Cove on the Derwent's eastern shore was the first European settlement in 1803, but just a year later the settlers decamped to the site of present-day Hobart.

Britain's jails were overflowing with criminals in the 1820s, and so tens of thousands of convicts were chained together into rotting hulks and transported to Hobart Town to serve their sentences in vile conditions. By the 1850s Hobart was rife with sailors,

soldiers, whalers, ratbags and prostitutes shamelessly boozing, brawling and bonking in and around countless harbourside taverns.

The city has only ever partially sobered up – anytime is beer-o'clock at legendary Knopwood's – and today's criminals are more likely to be white-collared. Skeletons rattle in closets, but Hobart's shimmering beauty and relaxed vibe make it easy to forget they're there.

The compact and navigable city centre has a grid of one-way streets encircling the Elizabeth St Mall. The visitor information centre, banks and the main post office are on Elizabeth St, while the main shopping area extends west from the Mall.

Salamanca Place, an impressive row of sandstone Georgian warehouses, lines the southern fringe of Sullivans Cove, the city's harbour and social epicentre. Just south of Salamanca Place is Battery Point, Hobart's increasingly gentrified early colonial district. South of Battery Point is cashed-up Sandy Bay, home to the University of Tasmania and the landmark/eyesore Wrest Point Casino.

⊙ Sights

All places of interest in central and waterfront Hobart are in easy walking distance of each other. Make the effort to get atop Mt Wellington summit for superb views.

WATERFRONT & SALAMANCA PLACE

Salamanca Place HISTORIC AREA
TOP CHOICE

This picturesque row of four-storey sandstone warehouses on Sullivans Cove (Map p628) is a wonderful example of colonial

---

HOBART IN...

Two Days

Get your head into history mode with a stroll around **Battery Point** – coffee and cake at **Jackman & McRoss** will sustain your afternoon explorations of nearby **Salamanca Place**. It's worth stumping up for a guided walking tour to get the stories behind the history. Bone up on Hobart's maritime heritage at the **Maritime Museum of Tasmania** before a promenade along the Sullivans Cove waterfront and a seafood dinner at **Blue Eye**. Kick on with a beer at **Knopwood's Retreat**, the quintessential Hobart pub, or a few single malts at the **Lark Distillery**.

On day two recuperate over a big breakfast at **Machine Laundry Café** then blow out the cobwebs with a mountain bike ride down **Mt Wellington** – on a clear day the views are jaw-dropping. Spend the afternoon at the superb **Museum of Old & New Art (MONA)**, before dinner, drinks and some live music at **Republic Bar & Café**, North Hobart's happening hub.

SALAMANCA MARKET

Colourful hippies and craftspeople have been selling their wares at Salamanca Market (Map p628; ⊙8.30am-3pm Sat) on Saturday mornings since 1972. They come from all over the state's southern reaches with their fresh produce, secondhand clothes and books, tacky tourist souvenirs, CDs, cheap sunglasses, antiques and bric-a-brac. See www.salamanca.com.au to download a handy guide and map of the market, and get planning to maximise your time in this labyrinth of bargains, buskers, ethnic food, and arts and crafts.

architecture and Australia's best-preserved historic urban precinct. Salamanca Place was the hub of old Hobart Town's trade and commerce, but by the mid-20th century many of these 1830s whaling-era buildings had become decrepit ruins. The 1970s saw the dawning of Tasmania's sense of 'heritage', from which flowed a push to revive the warehouses as home to restaurants, cafes, bars and shops.

Showcasing a vibrant cultural scene, the Salamanca Arts Centre (Map p628; ☑03-6234 8414; www.salarts.org.au; 77 Salamanca Pl; ⊙shops & galleries 9am-6pm) occupies seven Salamanca warehouses and is home to many galleries, studios, performing arts venues and public spaces.

To reach Salamanca Place from Battery Point, descend the well-weathered **Kelly's Steps**.

The Waterfront HISTORIC AREA

Hobartians flock to the city's waterfront like seagulls to chips. Centred on Victoria Dock (Map p628; a working fishing harbour) and Constitution Dock (Map p628; chock-full of floating takeaway-seafood punts), it's a brilliant place to explore. The obligatory Hobart experience is to sit in the sun, munch some fresh fish and chips and watch the harbour hubbub. If you'd prefer something with a knife and fork, there are some superb restaurants around here too – head for nearby Elizabeth St Pier.

Celebrations surrounding the finish of the annual **Sydney to Hobart Yacht Race** (see the boxed text, p630) revolve around Constitution Dock at New Year. The fabulous food festival, **The Taste**, is also in full swing around this time. The waterfront on **New Year's Eve** is both an exhilarating and nauseating place (depending on how late you stay out).

Hunter Street has a row of fine Georgian warehouses, most of which comprised the old Henry Jones IXL jam factory. It's

occupied these days by the Art School division of the University of Tasmania and Hobart's glam-est hotel, the uber-swish **Henry Jones Art Hotel** and its affiliated restaurants and galleries.

FREE **Lark Distillery** DISTILLERY

(Map p628; ☑03-6231 9088; www.larkdistillery.com.au; 14 Davey St; tours per person $15; ⊙10am-6pm Sun-Wed, 10am-late Thu-Sat) Lark Distillery produces fruit liqueurs (free tastings) and single malt whisky ($2.50 per tasting). Distillery tours happen at 11.30am and 2.30pm Monday to Saturday. You can also get a bite to eat here, and it morphs into a lounge bar with live music on Friday and Saturday nights. Expect blues, country and Americana beats with your Moo Brew Pilsner or smooth single malt. Lark Distillery also runs whisky tours (1/2/4 days $195/375/2100), diving gloriously into Tasmania's emerging whisky scene.

FREE Tasmanian Museum & Art Gallery MUSEUM

(Map p628; www.tmag.tas.gov.au; 40 Macquarie St; ⊙10am-5pm) Incorporates Hobart's oldest building, the Commissariat Store (1808). The museum features Aboriginal displays and colonial relics; the gallery curates a collection of Tasmanian colonial art. There are free guided tours at 2.30pm from Wednesday to Sunday. There's a cool cafe here, too.

BATTERY POINT, SANDY BAY & SOUTH HOBART

Battery Point HISTORIC AREA

(Map p624; www.batterypoint.net) An empty rum bottle's throw from the once notorious Sullivans Cove waterfront is a nest of tiny 19th-century cottages and laneways. The old maritime village of Battery Point takes its name from the 1818 gun battery that stood on the promontory.

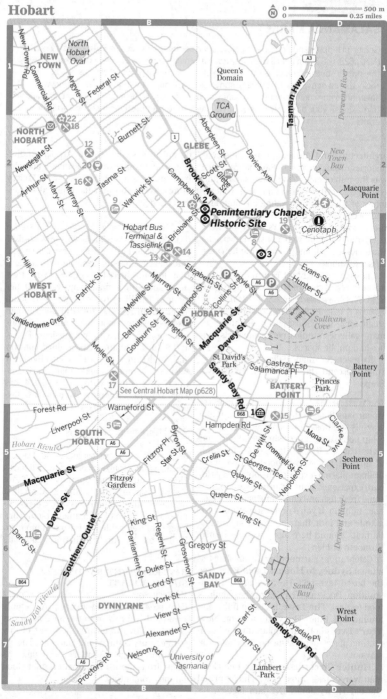

0   500 m
0   0.25 miles

New Town Rd
Commercial Rd
New Town Rd
NEW TOWN
North Hobart Oval
Queen's Domain
Tasman Hwy
Derwent River

Argyle St
Federal St
Burnett St
TCA Ground

NORTH HOBART
22
18
12
20
16
9
21
Newdegate St
Tasma St
Warwick St
Murray St
Arthur St
Mary St
Hill St
Brisbane St
Campbell St
Brooker Ave
GLEBE
Aberdeen St
Scott St
Davies Ave
7
New Town Bay
Macquarie Point

Penitentiary Chapel Historic Site
19
8
3
4
Cenotaph
Glebe St

Hobart Bus Terminal & Tassielink
13 14

WEST HOBART
Patrick St
Landsdowne Cres
Molle St
17

Murray St
Melville St
Bathurst St
Goulburn St
Harrington St
Liverpool St
Elizabeth St
Collins St
Argyle St
Macquarie St
Davey St
Sandy Bay Rd
HOBART
A6
A6
P
P
P
Evans St
Hunter St
Sullivans Cove
Battery Point

St David's Park
Castray Esp
Salamanca Pl
BATTERY POINT
Princes Park

See Central Hobart Map (p628)

Forest Rd
Warneford St
Liverpool St
SOUTH HOBART
A6
A6
Hobart Rivulet
5
Macquarie St
Davey St
Southern Outlet
B64
Darcy St
11
Fitzroy Pl
Byron St
Star St
Fitzroy Gardens
King St
Regent St
Parliament St
Grosvenor St
Duke St
Lord St
York St
View St
Alexander St
Nelson Rd
Proctors Rd
DYNNYRNE
University of Tasmania
Warneford St
Hampden Rd
1
15
6
Crelin St
De Witt St
Cromwell St
St Georges Tce
Quayle St
Napoleon St
Queen St
Gregory St
King St
SANDY BAY
B68
B68
Mona St
10
Clarke Ave
Secheron Point
Derwent River
Sandy Bay
Wrest Point
Earl St
Quorn St
Drysdale Pl
Lambert Park
Sandy Bay Rd

Spend a few hours exploring. Battery Point's liquored-up ale houses on **Hampden Road** have been refitted as cafes and restaurants, and cater to a less raucous clientele. Stumble up Kelly's Steps from Salamanca Place and dogleg into **South Street** where red lights once burned night and day and many a lonesome sailor sought the refuge of a buxom maiden. Spin around the picturesque **Arthur Circus**, check out **St George's Anglican Church** on Cromwell St, or shamble down **Napoleon St** to the waterfront. For a fortifying stout, duck into the salty 1846 **Shipwrights Arms Hotel** on Trumpeter St.

Narryna Heritage Museum   MUSEUM
(Map p624; ☑03-6234 2791; www.narryna.com. au; 103 Hampden Rd; adult/child $6/3; ☺10.30am-5pm Tue-Fri, 2-5pm Sat & Sun, closed Jul) This stately Georgian sandstone-fronted mansion (pronounced 'Narinna'), built in 1836, is set in established grounds and contains a treasure trove of domestic colonial artefacts.

Cascade Brewery   BREWERY
(☑03-6224 1117; www.cascadebrewery.com.au; 140 Cascade Rd, South Hobart; 2hr brewery tours adult/child $20/10, 1hr garden tours adult/child/family $15/12/42; ☺brewery tours 11am, 1pm & 2.30pm, garden tours 12.30pm & 2.30pm Mon-Fri) Around a bend in South Hobart, standing in startling, Gothic isolation is Australia's oldest brewery. Cascade was established in 1832 next to the clean-running Hobart Rivulet, and is still pumping out superb beer and soft

drinks today. Tours involve plenty of stair climbing, with tastings at the end (including Cascade Premium, the global sales smash). Wear flat, enclosed shoes and long trousers (no shorts or skirts). You can take a tour on weekends, but none of the machinery will be operating (brewers have weekends too). A full-of-history one-hour wander around Cascade's lovely gardens is also on offer. Online or phone bookings are essential. To get here, take bus 43, 44, 46 or 49 from Elizabeth St at Franklin Sq and jump ship at stop 18.

Female Factory   HISTORIC SITE
(☑03-6233 6656; www.femalefactory.com.au; 16 Degraves St, South Hobart; Historic Heritage tour adult/child $15/5, Tea with the Matron tour per person $12, Matron's Cottage adult/child $5/1; ☺9am-5pm Mon-Fri) Finally being recognised as an important historic site (one in four convicts transported to Van Diemen's Land was a woman!), this was where Hobart's female convicts were incarcerated. Major archaeological work is ongoing. Tour bookings are essential; phone to confirm the latest tour schedule.

It's not far from the Cascade Brewery – combining the two makes for a fascinating afternoon. To get here by public transport, take bus 43, 44, 46 or 49 and jump off at stop 16.

Cadbury Chocolate Factory   LANDMARK
(☑03-6249 0333, 1800 627 367; www.cadbury.com. au; Cadbury Rd, Claremont; adult/child $7.50/4; ☺9am-4pm Mon-Fri except public holidays)

A must-see for sweet-tooths and Willie Wonka wannabes is the Cadbury Chocolate Factory, 15km north of the city centre. You can enjoy samples, invest in low-priced choc products and watch a chocolate-making video.

Some companies offer day trips and river cruises incorporating the Cadbury tour, or book directly with Cadbury by phone or online and make your own way here on bus 37, 38 or 39 to Claremont from stop E on Elizabeth St.

Mt Wellington
PARK

(www.wellingtonpark.org.au) Cloaked in winter snow, Mt Wellington peaks at 1270m, towering above Hobart like a benevolent overlord. The citizens find reassurance in its constant, solid presence, while outdoors types find the space to hike and bike on its leafy flanks. And the view from the top is unbelievable! Don't be deterred if the sky is overcast – often the peak rises above cloud level and looks out over a magic carpet of cotton-topped clouds.

Hacked out of the mountainside during the Great Depression, the 22km road to the top winds up from the city through thick temperate forest, opening out to lunar rockscapes at the summit. If you don't have wheels, local buses 48 and 49 stop at Fern Tree halfway up the hill, from where it's a five- to six-hour return walk to the top via Fern Glade Track, Radfords Track, Pinnacle Track, then the steep Zig Zag Track. The Organ Pipes walk from the Chalet (en route to the summit) is a flat track below these amazing cliffs. Pick up the *Mt Wellington Walks* map ($4.10 from the visitor centre) as a guide or download PDF maps at www.wellingtonpark.com.au. Alternatively, Mt Wellington Walks (p630) runs organised hikes on the mountain from easy to adventurous.

Some bus-tour companies include Mt Wellington in their itineraries. Another option is the **Mt Wellington Shuttle Bus Service** (0408 341 804; per person return $25), departing the visitor centre at 10.15am and 1.30pm daily. City pick-ups by arrangement; call to book and confirm times.

Feeling more intrepid? Bomb down the slopes on a mountain bike with **Mt Wellington Descent** (03-6274 1880; www.mtwellingtondescent.com.au; adult/child $75/65). Kick off with a van ride to the summit, followed by more than 21km of downhill cruising (mostly on sealed roads, but with off-road options). Tours depart at 9.30am and 1pm

daily, with an additional 4pm departure in January and February.

CITY CENTRE

Penitentiary Chapel Historic Site
HISTORIC SITE

(Map p624; www.penitentiarychapel.com; cnr Brisbane & Campbell Sts; tours adult/child $10/8; tours 10am, 11.30am, 1pm & 2.30pm Sun-Fri, 1pm & 2.30pm Sat) Ruminating over the court rooms, cells and gallows here, writer TG Ford mused, 'As the Devil was going through Hobart Gaol, he saw a solitary cell; and the Devil was pleased for it gave him a hint, for improving the prisons in hell.' Take the excellent National Trust–run tour or the one-hour **Penitentiary Chapel Ghost Tour** (03-6231 0911; www.hobartghosts.com; adult/child $10/6; 8.30pm), held most nights (bookings essential).

Parliament House
HISTORIC BUILDING

(Map p628; www.parliament.tas.gov.au; Salamanca Pl; 45min tours free; tours 10am & 2pm Mon-Fri except when parliament sits) Presiding over an oak-studded park adjacent to Salamanca Place is Tasmania's sandstone Parliament House, completed in 1840 and originally used as a customs house. There's a tunnel under Murray St from the building to the Customs House Hotel opposite, though no one knows what it was used for.

Theatre Royal
HISTORIC BUILDING

(Map p624; www.theatreroyal.com.au; 29 Campbell St; 1hr tours adult/child $10/8; tours 11am Mon, Wed & Fri) Take a backstage tour of Hobart's most prestigious theatre. Built in 1837, it's actually Australia's oldest continuously operating theatre.

Maritime Museum of Tasmania
MUSEUM

(Map p628; www.maritimetas.org; 16 Argyle St; adult/child $7/3; 9am-5pm) Celebrating Hobart's unbreakable bond with the sea, the excellent Maritime Museum of Tasmania has a fascinating, salt-encrusted collection of photos, paintings, models and relics (try to resist ringing the huge brass bell from the *Rhexenor*).

Well-Preserved Old Buildings
HISTORIC BUILDINGS

Other notable edifices in the central city include the 1864 **Town Hall** (Map p628; 50 Macquarie St), which takes its architectural prompts from the Palazzo Farnese in Rome, and the austere **St David's Cathedral** (Map p628; cnr Murray & Macquarie Sts). The National Trust has info.

DAVID BUTTON – BUSHWALKING ARCHITECT
CHARLES RAWLINGS-WAY

David Button is a Hobart architect and all-round Tassie enthusiast, with a penchant for national parks, bushwalking and the good life.

Top Places to See Colonial Architecture

Tasmania has some of Australia's best early colonial architecture. The standouts are Port Arthur, Evandale and Ross. In Hobart there's Battery Point and the Penitentiary Chapel Historic Site. It's a bit grim, but it is an intact remnant of early Hobart Town.

Enjoying Tasmania's National Parks

The beaches on the east coast are great, especially around Freycinet Peninsula National Park. Maria Island National Park is great for camping, and there are a couple of mountains to climb, lovely beaches and some tranquil, isolated spots.

Great Short Walks

In Hobart, walk from the city around Sullivans Cove, through the docks, around Battery Point and down to Sandy Bay Beach. Get a bus to Fern Tree and explore Mt Wellington. Bring warm clothing, water and food, and allow a day to make a good job of it.

In Tasmania's southeast, walk from Cockle Creek to South Cape Bay. It's a pretty easy two-hour easy walk – some of it along boardwalks – to one of the wildest ocean beaches in the world. The Southern Ocean swell crashes in with huge surf on the edge of a primeval forest.

TASMANIA HOBART

Hobart's cache of amazingly well-preserved old buildings makes it exceptional among Australian cities. There are more than 90 buildings classified by the National Trust here – 60 of these are on Macquarie and Davey Sts. The intersection of Macquarie and Murray Sts features a gorgeous sandstone edifice on each corner. For detailed information contact the **National Trust** (Map p624; ☑03-6223 5200; www.nationaltrust.org.au; cnr Brisbane & Campbell Sts; ⊙9am-1pm Mon-Fri), or pick up the *Hobart's Historic Places* brochure from the visitor centre.

NORTH & WEST HOBART

Moorilla Estate   EMUSEUM
(☑03-6277 9900; www.moorilla.com.au; 655 Main Rd, Berriedale; tastings free; ⊙10am-5pm) Twelve kilometres north of Hobart's centre, Moorilla occupies a saucepan-shaped peninsula jutting into the Derwent River. Founded in the 1950s, Moorilla plays a prominent and gregarious role in Hobart society. Stop by for wine and 'Moo Brew' beer tastings, have lunch or dinner at the outstanding restaurant the **Source** (mains $30-42; ⊙lunch daily, dinner Tue-Sat), or catch a summer concert on the lawns.

To get here catch the Moorilla ferry from Hobart's Brooke St Pier (45 minutes, each way $15). Moorilla is also the driving force behind Hobart's annual MONA FOMA arts and music festival (see p631).

TOP CHOICE **MONA**   ART GALLERY
(☑03-6277 9900; www.mona.net.au; Moorilla, 655 Main Rd, Berriedale; admission free; ⊙10am-5pm Wed-Mon) Moorilla's newest attraction is MONA, the $75 million Museum of Old and New Art, which Moorilla owner David Walsh describes as 'a subversive adult Disneyland'. The extraordinary installation is arrayed across three underground levels concealed inside a sheer rock face. Ancient antiquities are showcased next to more recent works by Sir Sidney Nolan and British *enfant terrible,* Damien Hirst. Even if you're not an art fan, don't miss this eccentric, but world-class, museum. Catch the Moorilla ferry from Hobart's Brooke St Pier.

🏃 Activities

Cycling

A useful navigational tool is the *Hobart Bike Map* ($4 from the visitor centre and most bike shops), detailing cycle paths and road routes. Pick up a pair of wheels from either of the following.

Central Hobart

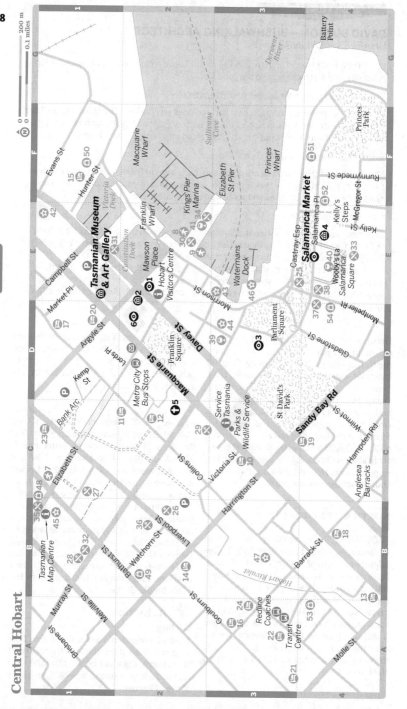

TASMANIA HOBART

Bike Hire Tasmania   CYCLING
(Appleby Cycles; Map p628; ☑03-6234 4166,
0400 256 588; www.bikehiretasmania.com.au; 109
Elizabeth St; ⊙8.30am-6pm Mon-Fri, 9am-4pm
Sat) Quality mountain/road bikes from
around $45 per day.

Derwent Bike Hire   CYCLING
(Map p624; ☑03-6260 4426, 0428 899 169; www.
derwentbikehire.com; Regatta Grounds Cycleway;
⊙10am-4pm Sat & Sun Sep-Nov, Apr & May, daily
Dec-Mar) Mountain and touring bikes from
$25/140 per day/week.

Sea Kayaking

Kayaking around the docks in Hobart, particularly at twilight, is a lovely way to get a
feel for the city.

**Blackaby's Sea-Kayaks &
Tours**   SEA KAYAKING
(☑0418 124 072; www.blackabyseakayaks.com)
Morning, afternoon or sunset paddles
around the Hobart waterfront with fish
and chips or wood-fired pizza to finish; $65
per person. Ask about paddling adventures
further afield at Port Arthur, Fortescue Bay,

SYDNEY TO HOBART YACHT RACE

Arguably the world's greatest and most treacherous open-ocean yacht race, the **Sydney to Hobart Yacht Race** (www.rolexsydneyhobart.com) winds up at Hobart's Constitution Dock every New Year's Eve. As the storm-battered maxis limp across the finish line, champagne corks pop and weary sailors turn the town upside down. On New Year's Day, find a sunny spot by the harbour, munch some lunch from The Taste food festival and count the spinnakers on the river. New Year's resolutions? What New Year's resolutions?

the Coal Mines Historic Site on the Tasman Peninsula, and the Gordon River. Also available is a 'Peddle & Paddle' combo including a descent by mountain bike of Mt Wellington (per person $135).

Tall Ship Sailing

Lady Nelson   TALL SHIP SAILING
(Map p628; ☑03-6234 3348; www.ladynelson. org.au; per person from $35) Trips on a replica of the surprisingly compact brig the Lady Nelson, one of the first colonial ships to sail to Tasmania. Longer overnight trips are also on offer.

Windeward Bound   TALL SHIP SAILING
(Map p628; ☑03-6231 6941; www.windeward bound.com; 3hr sail incl lunch adult/child $65/30) An elegant replica tall ship with lots of opportunity to get involved with the sailing. Also runs occasional eight-day voyages around Port Davey and Recherche Bay (per person $2750).

Hobart for Children

Parents won't break the bank keeping the troops entertained in Hobart. The free Friday-night music in the courtyard at the Salamanca Arts Centre is a family-friendly affair, while the street performers, buskers and visual smorgasbord of Saturday's Salamanca Market captivate kids of all ages. There's always something interesting going on around the waterfront – fishing boats chugging in and out of Victoria Dock, yachts tacking and jibing in Sullivans Cove – and you can feed the whole family on a budget at the floating fish punts on Constitution Dock.

Rainy-day attractions include the Tasmanian Museum & Art Gallery, the Maritime Museum of Tasmania and the Cadbury Chocolate Factory.

Take a boat cruise on the Derwent; assail the heights of Mt Wellington or Mt Nelson; rent a bike and explore the cycling paths; pack the teens into the Kombi and go surfing at Clifton Beach. The minute you head out of town the child-friendly options increase, with an abundance of animal parks, beaches, caves, nature walks and mazes to explore; see the Around Hobart section (p640).

If you're needing a romantic dinner date just for two, contact the **Mobile Nanny Service** (☑03-6273 3773, 0437 504 064).

☞ Tours

Captain Fell's Historic Ferries   CRUISES
(☑03-6223 5893; www.captainfellshistoricferries. com.au) Good-value lunch (from $30 per adult) and dinner ($53) cruises on cute old ferries. Also runs coach or double-decker bus sightseeing trips around town and to Mt Wellington, the Cadbury Chocolate Factory and Richmond.

Gray Line   SIGHTSEEING
(☑03-6234 3336, 1300 858 687; www.grayline. com.au) City coach tours (adult/child from $42/21), plus longer tours to destinations including Mt Wellington ($47/23.50), Mt Field National Park ($111/55), Bruny Island ($165/110) and the Huon Valley ($146/73). Free hotel pick-ups.

Ghost Tours of Hobart & Battery Point   HISTORICAL
(☑0439 335 696; www.ghosttoursofhobart.com. au) Walking tours oozing ectoplasmic tall tales departing The Bakehouse in Salamanca Sq at dusk. Bookings essential; $25 per person.

Herbaceous Tours   FOOD
(☑041 697 0699; www.herbaceoustours.com. au; per person from $130) Specialist food and wine tours across Tasmania including Hobart, the Coal River Valley wine region, Bruny Island and the Huon Valley. Look forward to lots of tasty sampling of foodie goodies.

Hobart Historic Tours   HISTORICAL
(☑03-6278 3338, 0429 843 150; www.hobarthis torictours.com.au; per tour $30) Highly informative walking tours of Hobart (9.30am Tuesday, Thursday, Saturday and Sunday)

and historic Battery Point (11.30am Saturday). Also available is an Old Hobart Pub Tour (5pm Tuesday, Thursday and Saturday) taking in waterfront watering holes. Restricted winter dates. Bookings essential.

Louisa's Walk HISTORICAL
(☑03-6229 8959, 0437 276 417; www.livehistory hobart.com.au; 1½hr tour adult/child $30/15) Engaging tours of Hobart's female convict heritage at the Female Factory interpreted through 'strolling theatre'. Tours depart Cascade Brewery at 2pm. Great feedback from readers.

Mt Wellington Walks WALKING
(☑0439 551 197; www.mtwellingtonwalks.com.au; half-day walk adult/child $75/60) Runs organised hikes on Hobart's high hill, from easy to adventurous.

Penitentiary Chapel Ghost Tour HISTORICAL
Historic hauntings at Hobart's old gaol (p626).

Red Decker SIGHTSEEING
(☑03-6236 9116; www.reddecker.com.au) Commentated sightseeing on an old London double-decker bus. Buy a 20-stop, hop-on-hop-off pass (adult/child/concession $25/15/23), or do the tour as a 90-minute loop. Pay a bit more and add a Cascade Brewery tour ($44/25/42) or river cruise ($48/37/46) to the deal.

Sullivans Coves Walks HISTORICAL
(☑03-6245 1208; www.sullivanscovewalks.com. au; adult/family $20/45; ⊙Mon-Sat) Hobart's maritime history comes alive on these interesting walking tours.

Tasman Island Cruises CRUISES
(☑03-6250 2200; www.tasmancruises.com.au; full-day tour adult/child $195/150) Take a bus to Port Arthur for a three-hour eco-cruise around Tasman Island, then explore the Port Arthur Historic Site and bus it back to town. Includes morning tea, lunch and Port Arthur admission. Departs Hobart at 7.45am; bookings required. Other options incorporate a visit to the Tasmanian Devil Conservation Park. Day trips to Bruny Island are also possible from Hobart.

Wild Thing JET BOAT
(☑1300 137 919; www.wildthingadventures.com. au) A speedy red boat churning up the froth around the Derwent ($39).

✦ Festivals & Events

Hobart hosts a cavalcade of festivals and events throughout the year.

Hobart Summer Festival ART & MUSIC
(www.hobartsummerfestival.com.au) Hobart's premier festival, focused on the waterfront: two weeks of theatre, kids' activities, concerts, buskers, New Year's Eve shenanigans and The Taste festival.

Sydney to Hobart Yacht Race SAILING
(www.rolexsydneyhobart.com) Yachts competing in this annual race start arriving in Hobart around 29 December – just in time for New Year's Eve! (Yachties sure can party...)

The Taste FOOD & WINE
(www.tastefestival.com.au) On either side of New Year's Eve, this week-long harbourside event is a celebration of Tassie's gastronomic prowess. The seafood, wines and cheeses are predictably fabulous, or branch out into mushrooms, truffles and raspberries! Stalls are a who's who of the Hobart restaurant scene.

MONA FOMA CULTURAL
(www.mofo.net.au) January's wonderfully eclectic array of music, arts and culture with a high-profile 'Eminent Artist in Residence' every year. Previous 'EARs' have included John Cale and Nick Cave.

Australian Wooden Boat Festival HERITAGE
(www.australianwoodenboatfestival.com.au) Biennial event in mid-February (odd-numbered years) to coincide with the Royal Hobart Regatta. The festival showcases Tasmania's boat-building heritage and maritime traditions.

Royal Hobart Regatta SAILING
(www.royalhobartregatta.com) Three days of aquatic yacht-watching and mayhem on the Derwent River. Annually in mid-February, so it coincides with the Australian Wooden Boat Festival every second year.

Ten Days on the Island CULTURAL
(www.tendaysontheisland.com) Tasmania's premier cultural festival – a biennial event (odd-numbered years, usually late March to early April), celebrating arts. Music and culture at state-wide venues. Concerts, exhibitions, dance, film, theatre and workshops.

Lumina CULTURAL
(www.lumina.discovertasmania.com) Tasmania's newest festival – inaugurated in 2010 – and including lots of winter events including

May's **Savour Tasmania food festival** (www.savourtasmania.com) and July's **Festival of Voices** (www.festivalofvoices.com).

Tasmanian Beerfest BEER
(www.tasmanianbeerfest.com.au) More than 200 brews from around Australia and the world, and lots of opportunity for water-front snacking and imbibing in November.

Falls Festival MUSIC
(www.fallsfestival.com.au) The Tasmanian version of the Victorian rock festival is a winner! Three days from December 29 to January 1 of live Oz and international tunes (Paul Kelly, Dan Sultan, Interpol, the National) at Marion Bay, an hour south of Hobart.

🛏 Sleeping

The pumping-est areas to stay in Hobart are the Sullivans Cove waterfront and Salaman-ca Place, though prices here are usually sky-high and vacancy rates low. The CBD has less ambience, and most of the backpacker hostels and pubs with accommodation are here. Note that rooms above pubs can be pretty noisy, especially on weekends with live music.

To the north is North Hobart with apartments, B&Bs and good restaurants. Accommodation in waterside Sandy Bay is surprisingly well priced, but it's a fair hike from town.

Top-end Hobart accommodation can be quite reasonable. A budget of around $200 will stretch to designer hotels, historic guest-houses and modern waterside apartments.

CITY CENTRE

TOP CHOICE **Astor Private Hotel** HOTEL $$
(Map p628; ☎03-6234 6611; www.astorprivate hotel.com.au; 157 Macquarie St; s from $77, d $93-140, all incl breakfast; ☎) A rambling, 1920s charmer, the Astor features stained-glass windows, old furniture, ceiling roses and the irrepressible Tildy at the helm. Older-style rooms have shared facilities, and newer en-suite rooms are also excellent value.

2 on Warneford APARTMENTS $$$
(Map p624; ☎0408 991 063; www.2onwarneford. com.au; 2 Warneford St; apt $230-350; ☎) In a qui-et inner-suburban street a 15-minute walk from Salamanca, 2 on Warneford fills a love-ly brick villa with two modern self-contained apartments. Lots of natural light showcases stunning decor and quality furnishings.

Fountainside HOTEL $$
(Map p624; ☎03-6213 2999; www.fountainside. com.au; 40 Brooker Ave; d $189; ☎) Venture past the old-school 1980s reception and exterior to discover newly renovated rooms that are surprisingly modern and spacious. The building hugs a busy roundabout, but well-insulated windows easily combat most traf-fic noise.

Jackson Townhouse APARTMENTS $$
(Map p628; ☎040 009 2710; www.jacksontown house.com.au; cnr Macquarie & Barrack Sts; d $180-200, extra person $45; ☎) Still close enough to reach Salamanca on foot, the Jackson Town-house enjoys a fringe CBD location opposite a great heritage pub. Choose from the sun-filled two-bedroom townhouse or the cosy and compact one-bedroom 'Garret'.

Hotel Collins HOTEL $$$
(Map p628; ☎03-6226 1111; www.hotelcollins.com. au; 58 Collins St; d $220-240, apt $335; ☎) A youthful energy at reception flows through to spacious rooms and apartments, many with sterling views of Mt Wellington's im-posing bulk. Downstairs is the relaxed fifty8 cafe and bar.

Edinburgh Gallery B&B $$
(Map p628; ☎03-6224 9229; www.artaccom.com. au; 211 Macquarie St; r $90-230; @☎) This funky, art-filled boutique hotel puts an eclectic stamp on an old Federation home, just to the west of the CBD. Some rooms share im-maculate bathrooms, and all have quirky, artsy decor.

Mantra One APARTMENTS $$
(Map p628; ☎03-6221 6000; www.mantraone sandybayroad.com.au; 1 Sandy Bay Rd; d from $149; ☎) These spacious and stylish loft apart-ments in a restored heritage building are a short stroll from the restaurants of Salaman-ca and Battery Point. Ask for a room on the building's southern side to negate occasional road noise from busy Davey St.

Central Café Bar HOTEL $$
(Map p628; ☎03-6234 4419; www.centralcafebar. com; 73 Collins St; d & tw $120; ☎) Downstairs is a classic Aussie pub with gaming machines and big-screen sport, but upstairs are sur-prisingly modern double rooms with flat-screen TVs and designer furniture.

Hobart Hostel HOSTEL $
(Map p628; ☎1300 252 192; www.hobarthostel. com; cnr Goulburn & Barrack Sts; dm $23-30, d/tw/tr from $80/80/99; @☎) In a former pub (the

ever-rockin' Doghouse), Hobart Hostel offers clean, recently redecorated dorms, with good value twins and doubles upstairs.

Transit Centre Backpackers
HOSTEL $

(Map p628; ☑03-6231 2400; www.transitbackpackers.com; 251 Liverpool St; dm $23-26, tw/d $56/64; @) This friendly spot has a huge communal area, strewn with shared couches, bookshelves and a kitchen and laundry. The helpful owners run regular barbecues to encourage lots of international socialising.

Harrington's 102
HOTEL $$

(Map p628; ☑03-6234 9277; www.harringtons102.com.au; 102 Harrington St; d incl breakfast $125-195, extra person $35) After the shock of the naff postmodern office facade subsides, you'll find the rooms here well equipped but a tad small. Still, the price is good given that continental breakfast is included and you're within walking distance of good central Hobart restaurants.

Tassie Backpackers
HOSTEL $

(Map p628; ☑03-6234 4981; www.tassiebackpackers.com; Brunswick Hotel, 67 Liverpool St; dm $23-25, d & tw $65-85; ☏) The venerable old Brunswick Hotel has been reinvented as Hobart's newest hostel. There's plenty of shared spaces including a kitchen and laundry, and the energetic young management team also operate an excellent bar downstairs.

Pickled Frog
HOSTEL $

(Map p628; ☑03-6234 7977; www.thepickledfrog.com; 281 Liverpool St; dm $24-28, s/d $62/67; @☏) This ramshackle hostel fills an old pub on the CBD fringe with party vibes. Cheap beer, big-screen TVs, pool table, slightly homesick backpackers checking out Facebook – you get the picture.

Montgomery's Private Hotel & YHA
HOSTEL $

(Map p628; ☑03-6231 2660; www.montgomerys.com.au; 9 Argyle St; dm $28-30, s & d with/without bathroom $130/112; @) Attached to Montgomery's pub, this centrally located YHA has dorms of all sizes, en-suite singles and doubles, and family rooms. Look forward to karaoke downstairs on Friday and Saturday nights.

Central City Backpackers
HOSTEL $

(Map p628; ☑1800 811 507; www.centralcityhobart.com; 138 Collins St; dm $23-27, s/d $55/69; @☏) Centrally located, this mazelike hostel has loads of communal space, a great kitchen, OK rooms and friendly staff.

Narrara Backpackers
HOSTEL $

(Map p628; ☑03-6234 8801; www.narrarabackpackers.com; 88 Goulburn St; dm $23-27, s/d/tw/f $60/69/69/119; @☏) The laid-back Narrara has brightly coloured rooms with newish beds and recently redecorated bathrooms. Travellers slump on couches in front of the TV, working through the pain of last night's efforts.

WATERFRONT & SALAMANCA PLACE

Henry Jones Art Hotel
BOUTIQUE HOTEL $$$

(Map p628; ☑03-6210 7700; www.thehenryjones.com; 25 Hunter St; d $320-420, ste $400-850; @☏) Since opening in 2004, super-swish HJs has become a beacon of sophistication. Absolute waterfront in a restored jam factory, it oozes class but is far from intimidating. Modern art enlivens the walls, while facilities and downstairs distractions (bar, restaurant, cafe) are world class. The hotel also makes smart use of recycled materials.

NORTH & WEST HOBART

The Islington
BOUTIQUE HOTEL $$$

(Map p624; ☑03-6220 2123; www.islingtonhotel.com; 321 Davey St; d $350-550; ☏) One of Hobart's best, the Islington effortlessly combines a heritage building with interesting antique furniture, contemporary art and a glorious garden. Service is attentive but understated, and breakfast is served in an expansive conservatory. Private dinners are also available.

Corinda's Cottages
B&B $$$

(Map p624; ☑03-6234 1590; www.corindascottages.com.au; 17 Glebe St, Glebe; d incl breakfast $195-250) Gorgeous Corinda, a renovated Victorian mansion with meticulously maintained parterre gardens, sits high on the Glebe hillside a short (steep!) walk from town. Three self-contained cottages provide contemporary comforts, and breakfast is DIY gourmet (eggs, muffins, fresh coffee etc).

Lodge on Elizabeth
B&B $$

(Map p624; ☑03-6231 3830; www.thelodge.com.au; 249 Elizabeth St, North Hobart; r incl breakfast from $150-170, self-contained cottage $195; @) Built in 1829, this old-timer has been a school house, a boarding house and a halfway house, but now opens its doors as a value-for-money guesthouse. Rooms are dotted with antiques, and all have en suites.

Adelphi Court YHA
HOSTEL $

(☎03-6228 4829; www.yha.com.au; 17 Stoke St, New Town; dm $26-29, d & tw with/without bathroom from $88/74) Rooms here occupy a spruced-up 1950s-style apartment block built around a courtyard behind a Federation manor. It's out of the way – 2.5km from the city – but reasonably close to the North Hobart strip.

BATTERY POINT, SANDY BAY & SOUTH HOBART

Shipwright's Arms Hotel
HOTEL $$

(Map p624; ☎03-6223 5551; www.shipwrightsarms. com.au; 29 Trumpeter St, Battery Point; d with bathroom $150, s/d without bathroom $75/80) In Battery Point, 'Shippies' is one of Hobart's best old pubs. Soak yourself in maritime heritage at the bar, then retire to your clean, aboveboard berth upstairs or in the newer, more modern wing.

Motel 429
MOTEL $$

(☎03-6225 2511; www.motel429.com.au; 429 Sandy Bay Rd, Sandy Bay; d $130-170; @☎) Not far from the casino, this motel's recent facelift has given the rooms a sleek designer sheen. The staff are friendly, and the restaurants of Sandy Bay are just a short drive away.

Battery Point Boutique Accommodation
APARTMENTS $$

(Map p624; ☎03-6224 2244; www.batterypoint accommodation.com.au; 27-29 Hampden Rd, Battery Point; d $175, extra person $35; ☎) Yet more colonial midrangery, this time in a block of four salmon-coloured serviced apartments (sleeping three, with full kitchens) in Battery Point's heart.

OUTISDE THE CITY

Hobart Cabins & Cottages
CABINS $$

(☎03-6272 7115; www.hobartcabinscottages.com. au; 19 Goodwood Rd, Glenorchy; cabins & cottages $95-125, 3-bedroom house per d $200; ☎) About 8km north of the centre, with a range of cottages and cabins, and a three-bedroom house sleeping up to 10.

Barilla Holiday Park
CAMPGROUND $

(☎1800 465 453; www.barilla.com.au; 75 Richmond Rd, Cambridge; unpowered/powered sites $26/30, cabins $85-160; @☎☎) A decent option for those with wheels, Barilla is midway between Hobart (12km) and Richmond (14km). It's close to the airport, the Coal River Valley wineries, and a couple of good wildlife parks around Richmond.

✗ Eating

Downtown Hobart proffers some classy brunch and lunch venues, but it's a bit of a ghost town after dark.

Salamanca Pl has excellent cafes and restaurants, and is especially busy during Saturday's market festivities. Battery Point's Hampden Rd restaurants are always worth a look, while Elizabeth St in North Hobart has evolved into a diverse collection of cosmopolitan cafes.

For Hobart's best pub food, head to the New Sydney Hotel, the Shipwright's Arms or the Republic Bar & Café.

CITY CENTRE

TOP CHOICE Taste Café
CAFE $

(Map p624; Baha'i Centre, 1 Tasman Hwy; mains $10-12; ☺9am-4pm Mon-Fri, 9am-3pm Sat) Concealed within Hobart's Baha'i Centre is this terrific daytime cafe that's a favourite of journos from the nearby ABC. The prices are low and the ever-changing menu is always fresh and interesting. Look forward to dishes like bratwurst scotch eggs or roasted pumpkin and ricotta gnocchi.

TOP CHOICE Garagistes
MODERN AUSTRALIAN $$$

(Map p628; ☎03-6231 0558; www.garagistes. com.au; 103 Murray St; Sun lunch $65, dinner small plates $17-32; ☺lunch Sun, dinner Wed-Sat) The very fine Garagistes delivers innovative small plates in a simple, yet dramatic, dining room. Owner Luke Burgess pushes the culinary envelope with dishes including salted cabbage, ricotta and barley salad and raw jack mackerel with pickles, young elderberries and rhubarb. Sunday lunch is four highly recommended courses. Bookings essential.

Chado The Way of Tea
ASIAN FUSION $$

(Map p624; 134 Elizabeth St; mains $15-25; ☺lunch Tue-Sat) Part Zen teahouse and part panAsian restaurant, Chado presents mainly Japanese and Sri Lankan flavours with a healthy organic bent. The cool guy playing the Japanese flute is owner and local muso Brian Ritchie.

Dev'Lish
CAFE $

(Map p628; 137 Macquarie St; meals $7-10; ☺breakfast & dinner Mon-Fri) Have a coffee at this cosy espresso nook and tuck into great-value cafe fare including hearty macaroni cheese, Asian-tinged salads and gluten-free wraps.

Kick off your exploration of Tassie's great food and wine scene in Hobart, before embarking on your own journey of culinary discovery. For more on the state's wine and foodie fare read Graeme Phillip's *Eat Drink Tasmania* (www.eatdrinktasmania.com.au), updated annually and available online or from visitor information centres, newsagents and bookshops.

» Pick your own fresh berries at the **Sorell Fruit Farm** (p650)

» Slurp oysters fresh from the **Freycinet Marine Farm** (p661) or at **Get Shucked** (p646) on Bruny Island

» Attend a Tasmanian food and wine festival – get salivating for **The Taste** or **Savour Tasmania** in Hobart (see p631), or **Festivale** (p667) in Launceston

» Scoff down fresh fish and chips from the floating fish punts at Hobart's **Constitution Dock** (p623)

» Explore Tassie's foodie credentials on a guided your with Hobart's **Herbaceous Tours** (p630)

R. Takagi Sushi
JAPANESE **$**

(Map p628; 155 Liverpool St; sushi $7-10; ☺lunch Mon-Sat) Hobart's best sushi spot makes the most of Tasmania's great seafood. Udon noodles and miso also feature at this sleek, compact eatery that's a favourite of central Hobart desk jockeys.

Cupping Room
CAFE **$**

(Map p628; 105 Murray St; mains $10-18; ☺breakfast & lunch Tue-Sat) It's coffee wonderland time at this hip cafe and coffee roastery. Take your pick from an international selection of bean and partner your brew with funky cupcakes and macarons, or robust brunch and lunch options.

Criterion Street Café
CAFE **$**

(Map p628; 10 Criterion St; mains $10-14; ☺breakfast & lunch Mon-Sat) It's a short menu on a short street, but Criterion Street Café effortlessly keeps both breakfast and lunch fans happy, and caffeine fiends buzzing through the day. Try the Spanish omelette or the super-creamy cinnamon porridge.

Nourish
CAFE **$**

(Map p628; 129 Elizabeth St; meals $9-14; ☺breakfast & lunch Mon-Sat, dinner to 8pm Thu & Fri; ✐) Nourish is a God-sent cafe for the gluten-intolerant, serving curries, salads, stir-fries, risottos and burgers – all gluten-free, and mostly dairy-free too. Vegetarians and vegans will also be smiling.

The most central self-catering option is **City Supermarket** (Map p628; 148 Liverpool St). Hobart's best **farmers market** (Map p624; www.tasfarmgate.com.au; cnr Melville & Elizabeth Sts; ☺9am-1pm Sun) takes place weekly.

WATERFRONT & SALAMANCA PLACE

Blue Eye
SEAFOOD **$$**

(Map p628; ☏03-6223 5297; 1 Castray Esplanade; mains $20-32; ☺lunch & dinner) Standouts include chargrilled salmon, chilli salt squid, and a terrific seafood-packed risotto with roasted fennel. Moo Brew and Two Metre Tall Cleansing Ale on tap, and a Tassie-skewed wine list complete the tasty picture.

Marque IV
MODERN AUSTRALIAN **$$$**

(Map p628; ☏03-6224 4428; Elizabeth St Pier; lunch mains $18-33, dinner $35-37; ☺lunch & dinner Tue-Sat) High-class dining hits waterfront Hobart at Marque IV on Elizabeth St Pier. Begin with freshly shucked Bruny Island oysters with limoncello and chilli, followed by slow-roasted pork belly with feta and almond tortellini. Desserts are also sensational.

Retro Café
CAFE **$**

(Map p628; 31 Salamanca Pl; mains $10-18; ☺breakfast & lunch) Funky Retro is ground zero for Saturday brunch among the market stalls. Masterful breakfasts, bagels, salads and burgers interweave with laughing staff, chilled-out jazz and the rattle and hum of the coffee machine.

Tricycle Café Bar
CAFE **$**

(p628; 71 Salamanca Pl; mains $10-18; ☺breakfast & lunch Mon-Sat) This cosy, red-painted nook near the Salamanca Arts Centre serves up a range of cafe classics (BLTs, toasties, free-range scrambled eggs, salads and fair trade coffee). Sip wine by the glass from the mirror-backed bar.

Jam Packed
CAFE $$
(Map p628; 27 Hunter St; mains $10-25; ⊙breakfast & lunch) Inside the redeveloped IXL Jam Factory atrium next to the Henry Jones Art Hotel, this cafe is jam-packed at breakfast time. If you're sporting a hangover, the 'Big JP Breakfast' is the perfect reintroduction to civilisation.

Machine Laundry Café
CAFE $
(Map p628; 12 Salamanca Sq; mains $10-18; ⊙breakfast & lunch) Hypnotise yourself watching the tumble dryers spin at this bright, retro-style cafe, where you can wash your dirty clothes while discreetly adding fresh juice, soup or coffee stains to your clean ones.

Fish Frenzy
SEAFOOD $$
(Map p628; Elizabeth St Pier; meals $15-28; ⊙lunch & dinner) A casual, waterside fish nook, perennially overflowing with fish fiends and brimming with fish and chips, fishy salads (spicy calamari, smoked salmon and brie) and fish burgers. The eponymous 'Fish Frenzy' ($16) delivers a little bit of everything. No bookings.

Flippers Fish Punt
SEAFOOD $
(Map p628; Constitution Dock; meals $8-15; ⊙lunch & dinner) With its voluptuous fish-shaped profile and alluring sea-blue paint job, floating Flippers is a Hobart institution. Fillets of flathead and curls of calamari – straight from the deep blue sea and into the deep fryer.
Gourmet self-caterers should head to Wursthaus (p638) for deli produce or the Salamanca Fresh Fruit Market (Map p628; 41 Salamanca Pl) for fruit and groceries.

BATTERY POINT, SANDY BAY & SOUTH HOBART

Jackman & McRoss
BAKERY $
(Map p624; 57-59 Hampden Rd, Battery Point; meals $8-13; ⊙breakfast & lunch) Be sure to swing by this conversational, neighbourhood bakery-cafe, even if it's just to gawk at the display cabinet full of delectable pies, tarts, baguettes and pastries. Early morning cake and coffee may evolve into quiche or soup for lunch.

Prosser's on the Beach
SEAFOOD $$
(⊋03-6225 2276; www.prossersonthebeach. com; Beach Rd, Lower Sandy Bay; mains $28-35; ⊙lunch Fri & Sun, dinner Mon-Sat) A glass-fronted pavilion by the water on Sandy Bay Point, classy Prosser's is BIG on seafood: try a fresh crayfish and avocado cocktail with warm citrus dressing, or the Catalan fish stew with mussels, scallops and chorizo. It's a taxi ride from town, but worth the trip. Bookings recommended, and from Monday to Friday, they'll even pay your taxi fare to get there.

Macquarie St Food Store
CAFE $
(356 Macquarie St, South Hobart; meals $10-17; ⊙breakfast & lunch) OK, so it's a little way out of the city centre, but an excursion to the Food Store will reward the intrepid traveller. It's an old shopfront cafe full of booths, bookish students, brunching friends and kids mooching under the tables.

NORTH & WEST HOBART

TOP CHOICE ▸ Pigeon Hole
CAFE $
(Map p624; 93 Goulburn St; mains $8-13; ⊙breakfast & lunch Tue-Sat) This funky and friendly cafe is the kind of place every inner-city neighbourhood should have. The freshly baked panini are the best you'll have, and the foodie owners always concoct innovative spins on traditional cafe fare. Try the baked eggs *en cocotte* with serrano ham for a lazy brunch.

Restaurant 373
MODERN AUSTRALIAN $$$
(Map p624; ⊋03-6231 9031; 373 Elizabeth St, North Hobart; mains $32-37; ⊙dinner Tue-Sat) Artsy, high-end eatery on the Elizabeth St strip in a lovely old shopfront with wide floorboards and splashes of dark red paint and white linen. The young owners give local produce an innovative twist – try the Longford eye fillet or the duck breast with foie gras dumplings. Excellent service, a brilliant wine list and desserts, plus a splurge-worthy multi-course tasting menu ($100).

Annapurna
INDIAN $$
(Map p624; ⊋03-6236 9500; 305 Elizabeth St, North Hobart; mains $15-19; ⊙lunch Mon-Fri, dinner Mon-Sun) It seems like half of Hobart lists Annapurna as their favourite eatery (bookings advised). Northern and southern Indian options are served with absolute proficiency. The *masala dosa* (south Indian crepe filled with curried potato) is a crowd favourite. BYO and takeaway available. Also at 93 Salamanca Place.

Mai Ake
THAI $$
(Map p624; ⊋03-6231 5557; www.maiakethai. com; 322 Elizabeth St, North Hobart; mains $20-28; ⊙dinner nightly) An elegant, but buzzing, destination for some of Hobart's best Thai flavours. Abundant use of fresh, fragrant herbs gives curries and salads authentic zing and punch.

BREWING UP A TASSIE STORM

Like other Australian states, Tasmania is celebrating the emergence of a significant craft brewing scene, with smaller boutique brewers focusing on higher quality, greater taste and a wider range of beer styles than the traditional duopoly of Cascade and Boag's. Visit Hobart's New Sydney Hotel (p638) for an ever-changing showcase of Tasmanian beers.

The Tasmanian craft brewing scene kicked off with Moorilla Estate's Moo Brew – advertising slogan 'Not suitable for bogans' – but now includes breweries in other areas of Tasmania. At the time of research we even heard rumours of a new microbrewery launching on Bruny Island.

Here are a few tasty brews to keep an eye out for.

Moo Brew's (www.moobrew.com.au) standout beers include a zingy hefeweizen and a hoppy pilsner. Try the beer on tap at Hobart's Lark Distillery or the IXL Long Bar at the Henry Jones Art Hotel.

Seven Sheds (www.sevensheds.com) specialises in a malty Kentish Ale, and also produces regular seasonal brews and honey-infused mead. Hobart's New Sydney Hotel usually has Seven Sheds on tap.

The **Ironhouse Brewery's** (www.ironhouse.com.au) beers include a nicely hoppy Pale Ale and a Czech-style pilsner. In Hobart it's usually available at the Lark Distillery.

Two Metre Tall (www.2mt.com.au) makes real ale and ciders, with ingredients sourced locally from its farm in the Derwent Valley. Try their Forester Real Ale at the Lark Distillery.

Van Dieman Brewing (www.vandiemanbrewing.com.au) produces six beers including the Jacob's Ladder English-style Amber Ale. Try it at Knopwood's Retreat in Salamanca Place in Hobart.

🍷 Drinking

Great pubs and bars abound around Salamanca Place and the waterfront, where the outdoors are enjoyed on summer evenings and indoor open fires are cajoled in winter. North Hobart, too, has a good selection of pubs and bars.

Knopwood's Retreat   PUB
(Map p628; 39 Salamanca Pl) Adhere to the 'when in Rome...' dictum and head for Knoppies, Hobart's best pub, which has been serving ales to seagoing types since the convict era. For most of the week it's a cosy watering hole with an open fire. On Friday nights the city workers swarm and the crowd spills across the street.

T-42°   BAR
(Map p628; Elizabeth St Pier; ⊗9am-late) Waterfront T-42° makes a big splash with its food, but also draws late-week barflies with its minimalist interior, spinnaker-shaped bar and ambient tunes. If you stay out late enough, it does breakfast too.

Bar Celona   BAR
(Map p628; Salamanca Sq) Lots of different beers on tap, a slick wine list and well-priced bistro-style food make this one of Salamanca's most versatile drinking spots.

The outdoor tables are perfect for people-watching Salamanca Square–style.

IXL Long Bar   BAR
(Map p628; 25 Hunter St; ⊗5pm-late) Prop yourself at the glowing bar at the Henry Jones Art Hotel and check out Hobart's fashionistas over cocktails. If there are no spare stools at the not-so-long bar, flop onto the leather couches in the lobby.

Squire's Bounty   PUB
(Map p628; Salamanca Sq) Yes, it is another James Squire concept pub, but the range of frosty beers is as wide as Bass Strait, and the bar snacks even taste good after a single beer. Big-screen TVs are perfect if you're in town and you want to watch your favourite footie team.

Lower House   BAR
(Map p628; basement, 9-11 Murray St; ⊗noon-late Mon-Sat) Across the road from Parliament House is this hip basement bar, keeping escapee MPs lubricated with top-shelf whiskies, cocktails and a massive wine list. Mature crowd and occasional DJs.

See also the Shipwright's Arms Hotel (p634), New Sydney Hotel (p638), Republic Bar & Café (p638) and Lark Distillery (p623).

☆ Entertainment

The *Mercury* newspaper lists Hobart's entertainment options in its Thursday edition. The free monthly *Sauce* entertainment rag provides detailed arts listings. Also see www.thedwarf.com.au. The Lark Distillery (p623) also has live music on Friday and Saturday.

Republic Bar & Café
LIVE MUSIC

(Map p624; www.republicbar.com; 299 Elizabeth St, North Hobart) The art-deco Republic is the number-one live-music pub in town, and often showcases up-and-coming international bands. With loads of different beers and excellent food, it's the kind of place you'd love to call your local.

New Sydney Hotel
LIVE MUSIC

(Map p628; www.newsydneyhotel.com.au; 87 Bathurst St) Low-key folk, jazz, blues and comedy playing Tuesday to Sunday nights (usually free). See the website for gig listings. Great pub food and an ever-changing selection of Tassie craft beers.

Brisbane Hotel
LIVE MUSIC

(Map p624; 3 Brisbane St) This progressive live-music venue features the original, offbeat and uncommercial, including punk, metal, hip-hop and singer-songwriters.

Isobar
NIGHTCLUB

(Map p628; www.isobar.com.au; 11a Franklin Wharf; Wed free, Fri/Sat $5/8; ☺10pm-5am Wed, Fri & Sat) Downstairs here is a slick bar (open 5pm Fridays, 7pm Saturdays), while Isobar itself – the club upstairs – plays commercial dance music.

Observatory
NIGHTCLUB

(Map p628; L1, Murray St Pier; ☺3pm-late Wed-Sun) Sip a 'Big O' cocktail as you swan between loungy nooks. DJs kick in on Friday and Saturday, and don't dress down as the bouncers are quite choosy.

Syrup
NIGHTCLUB

(Map p628; www.syrupclub.com; 39 Salamanca Pl; admission varies; ☺9pm-late Thu-Sat) Over two floors above Knopwood's Retreat, this is an ace place for late-night drinks and DJs playing to the techno/house crowd.

Mobius
NIGHTCLUB

(Map p628; 7 Despard St; admission varies; ☺9pm-late Thu-Sat) A pumping, clubby dungeon meets cool lounge bar behind the main waterfront area. Occasional name DJs.

Federation Concert Hall
CONCERT HALL

(Map p628; ☎1800 001 190; www.tso.com.au; 1 Davey St; ☺box office 9am-5pm Mon-Fri) This concert hall showcases the Tasmanian Symphony Orchestra.

State Cinema
CINEMA

(Map p624; ☎03-6234 6318; www.statecinema.com.au; 375 Elizabeth St, North Hobart) The State shows independent and art-house flicks from local and international filmmakers. There's a great cafe and bar on-site.

Village Cinemas
CINEMA

(Map p628; ☎1300 555 400; www.villagecinemas.com.au; 181 Collins St) An inner-city multiplex screening mainstream releases. Cheap-arse Tuesday tickets $10.

🛍 Shopping

Head to Salamanca Place for shops and galleries stocking Huon pine knick-knacks, hand-knitted beanies, local cheeses, sauces, jams, fudge and other assorted edibles. The hyperactive Salamanca Market is held here every Saturday from 8.30am to 3pm.

On Elizabeth St between Melville St and Bathurst St are stores selling outdoor apparel and equipment.

For antiques, pick up the free *Antique Shops of Hobart* and *Antiquarian & Secondhand Booksellers & Printsellers in Hobart* brochures from the visitor centre. The free *Gallery Guide* brochure from the visitor centre is useful for gallery browsing.

Antiques Market
ANTIQUES

(Map p628; ☎03-6234 4425; www.theantiquesmarket.com.au; 125 Elizabeth St; ☺10am-5.30pm Mon-Fri, to 4pm Sat, noon-3pm Sun)

Antiques to Retro
ANTIQUES

(Map p628; ☎03-6236 9422; www.antiquestoretro.com.au; 128 Bathurst St; ☺10am-5pm Mon-Fri, to 1pm Sat)

Art Mob
ART

(Map p628; ☎03-6236 9200; www.artmob.com.au; 29 Hunter St; ☺10am-late) Aboriginal fine arts.

Despard Gallery
ART

(Map p628; ☎03-6223 8266; www.despard-gallery.com.au; 15 Castray Esplanade, Battery Point; ☺11am-6pm Mon-Fri, noon-5pm Sat) Top-notch contemporary Tasmanian arts.

Handmark Gallery
ART

(Map p628; ☎03-6223 7895; www.handmarkgallery.com; 77 Salamanca Pl; ☺10am-6pm) Exquisite local ceramics, glass, wood, jewellery and textiles, plus paintings and sculpture.

FRIDAY NIGHT FANDANGO

Some of Hobart's best live music airs every Friday year-round from 5.30pm to 7.30pm at the Salamanca Arts Centre courtyard, just off Wooby's Lane. It's a free community event that started around 2000, with the adopted name 'Rektango', borrowed from a band that sometimes plays here. Acts vary from month to month – expect anything from African beats to rockabilly, folk or gypsy-Latino. Drinks essential (sangria in summer, mulled wine in winter); dancing optional.

Tasmanian Wine Centre   WINE
(Map p628; ☑03-6234 9995; www.tasmanian
-wine.com.au; 201 Collins St; ☺8am-6pm Mon-Fri,
9.30am-5pm Sat) Stocks a hefty range of
Tassie wines; also organises shipping and
winery tours.

Wursthaus   FOOD
(Map p628; www.wursthaus.com.au; 1 Montpelier
Retreat, Battery Point; ☺8am-6pm Mon-Fri, to
5pm Sat, 9.30am-4pm Sun) Fine-food showcase off Salamanca Place selling speciality
smallgoods, cheeses, breads, wines and
pre-prepared meals.

ⓘ Information

Emergency
Hobart Police Station (☑03-6230 2111; www.
police.tas.gov.au; 43 Liverpool St; ☺24hr)
Police, Fire & Ambulance (☑000)

Internet Access
Expect to pay around $6 per hour at internet
cafes.
Drifters Internet Café (Shop 9/33 Salamanca
Pl; ☺9am-6.30pm) Printing, scanning and
faxing available.
Outzone (1st fl, 3/66 Murray St; ☺10am-7pm)

Internet Resources
Hobart City (www.hobartcity.com.au) City
council website.
Rita's Bite (www.pc-rita.blogspot.com) Excellent food blog covering the Hobart eating-out
scene.
The Dwarf (www.thedwarf.com.au) Online gig
guide.
Welcome to Hobart (www.welcometohobart.
com.au) Official visitors guide.

Maps
The visitor centre supplies basic city maps. For
more comprehensive coverage try the *Hobart &
Surrounds Street Directory* or the UBD *Tasmania
Country Road Atlas* available at larger news-
agents and bookshops. Travellers with dis-
abilities should check out the useful *Hobart CBD
Mobility Map* from the visitor centre.

Hobart visitor centre (Map p628; ☑03-6230
8233; www.hobarttravelcentre.com.au; cnr
Davey & Elizabeth Sts; ☺8.30am-5.30pm Mon-
Fri, 9am-5pm Sat, Sun & public holidays)
Royal Automobile Club of Tasmania (☑03-
6232 6300, 13 27 22; www.ract.com.au; cnr
Murray & Patrick Sts; ☺8.45am-5pm Mon-Fri)
Service Tasmania (☑1300 135 513; www.
service.tas.gov.au; 134 Macquarie St;
☺8.15am-5pm Mon-Fri)
Tasmanian Map Centre (☑03-6231 9043;
www.map-centre.com.au; 100 Elizabeth St;
☺9.30am-5.30pm Mon-Fri, 10am-4pm Sat)
Good for bushwalking maps.

Media
The visitor centre stocks free Tassie tourist
publications highlighting Hobart's attractions.
Hobart's long-running newspaper is the *Mercury*
(aka 'the Mockery') is handy for discovering
what's on where. The Thursday edition lists
entertainment options.

Medical Services
**Australian Dental Association Emergency
Service** (☑03-6248 1546) Advice for dental
emergencies.
Chemist on Collins (93 Collins St)
City Doctors & Travel Clinic (☑03-6231
3003; www.citydoctors.com.au; 93 Collins St)
Royal Hobart Hospital (☑03-6222 8423;
www.dhhs.tas.gov.au; 48 Liverpool St; ☺24hr)
Argyle St emergency entry.
Salamanca Medical Centre (☑03-6223 8181;
5a Gladstone St; ☺8.30am-6pm Mon-Fri,
10am-3pm Sat, noon-3pm Sun)

Money
The major banks all have branches and ATMs
around Elizabeth St Mall.

Post
General Post Office (GPO; cnr Elizabeth &
Macquarie Sts)

Tourist Information
Hobart visitor centre (☑03-6230 8233; www.
hobarttravelcentre.com.au; cnr Davey & Elizabeth Sts; ☺8.30am-5.30pm Mon-Fri, 9am-5pm
Sat, Sun & public holidays) Brochures, maps,

information and statewide tour and accommodation bookings.

Parks & Wildlife Service (☎1300 135 513; www.parks.tas.gov.au; 134 Macquarie St; ⊙9am-5pm Mon-Fri) Information and fact sheets for bushwalking and all national parks.

❶ Getting There & Away

Air

For information on domestic flights to/from Hobart, see p640.

Bus

There are two main intrastate bus companies operating to/from Hobart:

Redline Coaches (☎1300 360 000; www.redlinecoaches.com.au; 230 Liverpool St) Operates from the Transit Centre.

Tassielink (☎1300 300 520; www.tassielink.com.au; 64 Brisbane St) Operates from the Hobart Bus Terminal.

Additionally, **Hobart Coaches** (☎132 201) has regular services to/from Richmond, and south along the D'Entrecasteaux Channel and to Cygnet. See those towns for specific timetable/fare info, check online or visit Metro Tasmania's Metro Shop inside the General Post Office on the corner of Elizabeth and Macquarie Sts.

❶ Getting Around

To/From the Airport

Hobart Airport (☎03-6216 1600; www.hobartairpt.com.au) is at Cambridge, 16km east of town. The **Airporter Shuttle Bus** (☎1300 385 511; www.redlinecoaches.com.au; one way/return $15/25) scoots between the Transit Centre and the airport (via various city pick-up points), connecting with all flights. Bookings essential. A cheaper option is the **Ten Buck Bus** (☎0419 382 240; www.tenbuckbus.com.au; one way/return $10/20). Book online for an airport pick-up.

A taxi between the airport and the city centre will cost around $38 between 6am and 8pm weekdays, and around $46 at other times.

Bicycle

See p627 for details of bicycle-rental options.

Bus

Metro Tasmania (☎13 22 01; www.metrotas.com.au) operates the local bus network, which is reliable but infrequent outside of business hours. The **Metro Shop** (⊙8.30am-5.30pm Mon-Fri), inside the General Post Office on the corner of Elizabeth and Macquarie Sts, handles ticketing and enquiries. Most buses depart from this section of Elizabeth St, or from nearby Franklin Sq.

One-way fares vary with distances ('sections') travelled (from $2.50 to $5.60). For $4.60 you can buy an unlimited-travel Day Rover ticket, valid after 9am Monday to Friday, and all day Saturday, Sunday and public holidays. Buy one-way tickets from the driver (exact change required) or ticket agents (newsagents and most post offices); day passes are only available from ticket agents.

Car

Timed, metered parking predominates in the CBD and tourist areas like Salamanca and the waterfront. For longer-term parking, large CBD garages offer inexpensive rates.

The big rental firms have airport desks. Cheaper local firms with city offices offer daily rental rates starting at around $35; see p621.

Taxi

City Cabs (☎13 10 08)

Maxi-Taxi Services (☎03-6274 3140; www.hobartmaxitaxi.com.au) Including wheelchair-accessible vehicles.

AROUND HOBART

Riverside communities, historic towns, pretty pasturelands and stands of native bush are all just few minutes' drive beyond the Hobart city limits. The ghosts of Tasmania's convict past drag their leg-irons in historic Richmond, while wilderness, wildlife, waterfalls and great short walks at Mt Field National Park make a terrific day trip from the capital.

Day trips around Hobart are offered by a number of companies (see p630).

Richmond

POP 880

Straddling the Coal River 27km northeast of Hobart, historic Richmond was once a strategic military post and convict station on the road to Port Arthur. Riddled with 19th-century buildings, it's arguably Tasmania's premier historic town, but like the Rocks in Sydney and Hahndorf in Adelaide, it's in danger of becoming a tourist-friendly parody of itself.

A couple of decent wildlife parks and the nearby Coal River Valley wine region provide more contemporary distractions.

See www.richmondvillage.com.au.

❂ Sights & Activities

Richmond Bridge   LANDMARK
(Wellington St) This chunky but elegant bridge still funnels traffic across the Coal

River, and is the town's proud centrepiece. Built by convicts in 1823, making it the oldest road bridge in Australia, it's purportedly haunted by the 'Flagellator of Richmond', George Grover, who died here in 1832.

Richmond Gaol
HISTORIC BUILDING

(37 Bathurst St; adult/child $7/4; ⊙9am-5pm) The northern wing of the remarkably well-preserved gaol was built in 1825, five years before the penitentiary at Port Arthur. Like Port Arthur, fascinating historic insights abound, but the mood is pretty sombre.

Old Hobart Town Historic Model Village
HISTORIC PARK

(www.oldhobarttown.com; 21a Bridge St; adult/family $14/30; ⊙9am-5pm) A painstaking re-creation of Hobart Town in the 1820s built from the city's original plans. The kids will love it.

ZooDoo Wildlife Fun Park
WILDLIFE PARK

(www.zoodoo.com.au; 620 Middle Tea Tree Rd; adult/child $19/10; ⊙9am-5pm) ZooDoo, 6km west of Richmond on the road to Brighton, has 'safari bus' rides, playgrounds, picnic areas and half of Dr Dolittle's appointment book including lions, tigers, llamas, Tasmanian devils and wallabies.

Bonorong Wildlife Centre
WILDLIFE PARK

(www.bonorong.com.au; 593 Briggs Rd, Brighton; adult/child $18/9; ⊙9am-5pm) Around 17km west of Richmond, 'Bonorong' derives from an Aboriginal word meaning 'native companion'. Look forward to Tasmanian devils, koalas, wombats, echidnas and quolls. The emphasis here is on conservation, education and the rehabilitation of injured animals.

Interesting historic places in Richmond include:

St John's Church
CHURCH

(Wellington St) The first Roman Catholic church in Australia was built in 1836.

St Luke's Church of England
CHURCH

(Edward St) 1834.

Courthouse
HISTORIC BUILDING

(Forth St) 1825.

Old Post Office
HISTORIC BUILDING

(Bridge St) 1826.

Richmond Arms Hotel
HISTORIC BUILDING

(Bridge St) 1888.

🛏 Sleeping & Eating

TOP CHOICE **Daisy Bank Cottages** RENTAL HOUSE $$
(☎03-6260 2390; www.daisybankcottages.com;

Daisy Bank, off Middle Tea Tree Rd; d $150-160) This place is a rural delight with two spotless, self-contained units (one with spa) in a converted 1840s sandstone barn. There are loft bedrooms, views of the Richmond rooftops and plenty of farm-oriented distractions for the kids.

Richmond Cottages
RENTAL HOUSE $$

(☎03-6260 2561; www.richmondcottages.com; 12 Bridge St; d from $135, extra adult/child $25/15) On offer are two self-contained abodes. Ivy Cottage is a family-friendly, three-bedroom home (complete with claw-foot bath), and behind it The Stables is a rustic one-bedroom cottage with spa.

Richmond Arms Hotel
PUB $$

(☎03-6260 2109; www.richmondarmshotel.com.au; 42 Bridge St; d from $110) The grand old Richmond pub has four good-quality motel-style units in the adjacent former stables. On-site there's the dual attraction of the cosy dining room (mains $15 to $25, open lunch and dinner) and sunny garden bar. Coal River Valley wines are available.

Richmond Cabin & Tourist Park
CAMPGROUND $

(☎03-6260 2192; www.richmondcabins.com; 48 Middle Tea Tree Rd; unpowered/powered sites $24/30, cabins $75-130; ⊛) This simple campground 1km south of town provides affordable accommodation in neat, no-frills cabins. Kids will be happy with the indoor pool and games room.

Ashmore on Bridge Street
CAFE $$

(☎03-6260 2238; 34 Bridge St; mains $14-20; ⊙breakfast & lunch daily, dinner Tue) Order up a big breakfast (scrambled eggs, cinnamon French toast and berry compote) with Richmond's best coffee, or snappy lunches including beef lasagne, garlic prawns and Caesar salad. Bookings are essential for Tuesday night dinners.

Anton's
PIZZA $

(42a Bridge St; mains $11-19; ⊙lunch Wed-Sun, dinner Fri-Sun) Next to the pub, this small shop churns out first-class pizzas (try the Indian curry and lamb), plus pasta, antipasto, salads, desserts and gelati. Grab some picnic fixings and head for the river.

ℹ Getting There & Away

Tassielink (☎1300 653 633; www.tassielink.com.au) runs from the **Hobart Bus Terminal** (64 Brisbane St) Monday to Friday at 8am, 8.30am, 10.30am, 12.30pm and 2.30pm (45

minutes, one way $7.20). On Saturday and Sunday, buses leave Hobart at 8.55am and 2.10pm.

The **Richmond Tourist Bus** (☑0408 341 804; per person return $25; ☺9.15am & 12.20pm) runs a twice-daily service from Hobart, with three hours to explore Richmond before returning. Call for bookings and pick-up locations.

Mt Field National Park

Declared a national park in 1916, Mt Field is famed for its spectacular mountain scenery, alpine moorlands and lakes, rainforest, waterfalls and abundant wildlife. It's 80km northwest of Hobart and makes a terrific day trip.

The park's visitor information centre (☑03-6288 1149; www.parks.tas.gov.au; 66 Lake Dobson Rd; ☺8.30am-5pm Nov-Apr, 9am-4pm May-Oct) houses a cafe and displays on the park's origins, and provides information on walks. Day-use facilities include barbecues, shelters and a playground.

◎ Sights & Activities

Something Wild   WILDLIFE PARK
(☑03-6288 1013; www.somethingwild.com.au; 2080 Gordon River Rd; adult/child $14/7; ☺10am-5pm) On the Tyenna River 4km east of Mt Field is this wildlife sanctuary that rehabilitates orphaned and injured wildlife. Visit the animal nursery, see native wildlife (devils, wombats, quolls) and maybe spot a platypus sniffing around the grounds.

Russells Falls   WALKING
Don't miss the magnificently tiered, 45m-high Russell Falls, an easy 20-minute return amble from behind the visitor information centre. The path is suitable for prams and wheelchairs. There are also easy walks to **Lady Barron Falls** and **Horseshoe Falls**, and longer bushwalks.

Mt Mawson   SKIING
Skiing at Mt Mawson is sometimes an option, when nature sees fit to deposit snow (infrequently in recent years). Snow reports are available online at www.ski.com.au, or via a recorded message service (☑03-6288 1166).

🛏 Sleeping & Eating

Self-caterers need to buy supplies before arriving at Mt Field National Park. There is also good accommodation at Westerway, about 7km from the park entrance.

Duffy's Country Accommodation   RENTAL HOUSE $$
(☑03-6288 1373; www.duffyscountry.com; 49 Clark's Rd, Westerway; d $125-135, extra adult/child $25/15; ◙) Overlooking a field of raspberry canes are two immaculate self-contained cabins, one a studio-style cabin for couples, the other a two-bedroom relocated rangers' hut from Mt Field National Park. Breakfast provisions are provided including toast, eggs and homemade raspberry jam.

Platypus Playground   RENTAL HOUSE $$
(☑0413 833 700; www.riverside-cottage.com; 1658 Gordon River Rd, Westerway; d $150) You can't miss this cute, red riverside cottage at Westerway, offering eco-friendly accommodation. Winning features include an outdoor deck over the river and the chance to spot a platypus or hook a trout.

Lake Dobson Cabins   CABINS $
(☑03-6288 1149; www.parks.tas.gov.au; Lake Dobson Rd; cabins up to 6 people $45) Get back to your pure mountaintop essence at these three simple six-bed cabins about 14km inside the park. All are equipped with mattresses, cold water, wood stove and firewood (there's no power), and have a communal toilet block. Visitors will need to bring gas lamps and cookers, plus utensils.

Land of the Giants Campground   CAMPGROUND $
(☑03-6288 1526; unpowered/powered sites $20/28) A privately run, self-registration campground with adequate facilities (toilets, showers, laundry and free barbecues) just inside the park gates. Bookings not required. Site prices are additional to national park entry fees.

ⓘ Getting There & Away

The drive to Mt Field through the Derwent River Valley and Bushy Park is an absolute stunner with river rapids, hop fields, rows of poplars and hawthorn hedgerows. Public transport connections to the park are limited to **Tassielink** (☑1300 300 520; www.tassielink.com.au) services, running on Tuesday, Thursday and Saturday ($30, 3½ hours) from December to March. Some Hobart-based tour operators offer Mt Field day trips, usually taking in Something Wild as well as the national park.

WINE TOURING IN THE COAL RIVER VALLEY

Richmond is also the centre of Tasmania's fastest-growing wine region, the Coal River Valley. Some operations are sophisticated affairs with gourmet restaurants, while others are small family-owned vineyards, with their cellar doors open by appointment. See winesouth.com.au for more information on the Coal River Valley and other southern viticulture regions. Here are two spots to get you started.

Meadowbank Estate   WINERY

(☑03-6248 4484; www.meadowbankwines.com.au; 699 Richmond Rd, Cambridge; mains $32-34; ⏱10am-5pm) Meadowbank's acclaimed restaurant serves lunch daily, along with award-winning Pinot Gris, Sauvignon Blanc and Pinot Noir. Don't miss *Flawed History*, an in-floor jigsaw by local artist Tom Samek. Restaurant bookings are recommended, especially on weekends.

Puddleduck Vineyard   WINERY

(www.puddleduckvineyard.com.au; 992 Richmond Rd, Richmond; ⏱10am-5pm) Small family-run vineyard producing just 1000 cases per year. Riesling, Merlot, Chardonnay and 'Bubbleduck' sparkling white. Cheese platters ($15) are for sale, or fire up their barbecues with your own steak, salad and sausages.

THE SOUTHEAST

The southeast offers rolling hills and valleys, riverside towns, and quiet harbours and inlets. It's a gentle collection of agrarian communities producing cherries, apricots, Atlantic salmon and cool-climate wines, servicing an increasing parade of tourists and escapees from Hobart. The fruit-filled hillsides of the Huon Valley give way to the sparkling inlets of the D'Entrecasteaux Channel. Bruny Island waits enticingly offshore, and the Hartz Mountains National Park is not far inland.

See www.huontrail.org.au.

ⓘ Getting There & Around

The southeast has three distinct areas: the peninsula, including Kettering and Cygnet; Bruny Island; and the Huon Hwy coastal strip linking Huonville with Cockle Creek.

Metro Tasmania (☑13 22 01; www.metrotas. com.au) runs several weekday buses from Hobart south to Kettering ($9.30, 50 minutes) and Woodbridge ($9.50, one hour). A bus from Hobart also runs once each weekday to Snug, then inland across to Cygnet ($11.50, one hour).

Tassielink (☑1300 300 520; www. tassielink.com.au) buses service the Huon Hwy from Hobart through Huonville ($9.90, one hour) several times a day (once on Saturday and Sunday), with some continuing to Geeveston ($13, 1½ hours) and Dover ($20, 1¾ hours, not Sundays). Check the website or call for departure times.

From December to March on Monday, Wednesday and Friday, Tassielink also runs buses from Hobart down to Cockle Creek ($73, three hours), returning to Hobart on the same days.

Kettering

POP 400

Sleepy Kettering is a launching place for sea kayakers exploring the D'Entrecasteaux Channel, but most people just blow through to board the Bruny Island ferry.

The **Kettering visitor information centre** (☑1300 889 557; www.tasmaniaholiday.com; 81 Ferry Rd; ⏱9am-5pm) by the ferry terminal books accommodation on Bruny Island.

🏃 Activities

Roaring 40s Ocean Kayaking   SEA KAYAKING

(☑03-6267 5000; www.roaring40skayaking.com. au; Oyster Cove Marina, Ferry Rd; ⏱closed Aug-Sep) At the marina is Tassie's leading sea-kayaking tour operator. The company offers gear rental to kayakers, and organises kayaking trips for all levels of experience. A half-day paddle around Oyster Cove costs $95; a full day on the D'Entrecasteaux Channel costs $160, including lunch and return transport from Hobart. A full day around the Tasman Peninsula costs $255. Extended three- and seven-day trips around the Tasman Peninsula and the southwest including Bathurst Harbour are also available.

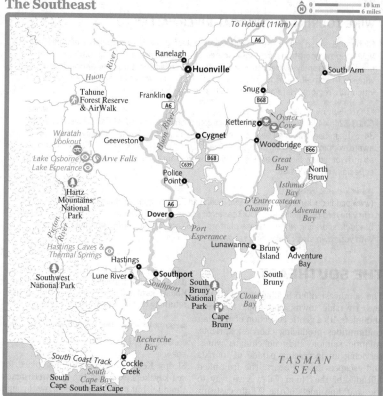

To Hobart (11km)

Ranelagh
Huonville
South Arm
Huon River
Tahune Forest Reserve & AirWalk
Franklin
Snug
Waratah Lookout
Geeveston
Kettering
Oyster Cove
Cygnet
Woodbridge
Lake Osborne
Arve Falls
Lake Esperance
Police Point
Great Bay
North Bruny
Hartz Mountains National Park
Dover
Isthmus Bay
D'Entrecasteaux Channel
Adventure Bay
Hastings Caves & Thermal Springs
Port Esperance
Lunawanna
Bruny Island
Adventure Bay
Southwest National Park
Hastings
Lune River
Southport
Southport
South Bruny National Park
South Bruny
Cloudy Bay
Cape Bruny
Recherche Bay
South Coast Track
Cockle Creek
South Cape
South Cape Bay
South East Cape
TASMAN SEA

Sleeping & Eating

Herons Rise Vineyard   WINERY $$
(☎03-6267 4339; www.heronsrise.com.au; 1000
Saddle Rd; d without/with breakfast $125/140, extra
person $30) Just north of town, Herons Rise
has three upmarket, self-contained cottages
set in lush surroundings among the vines.
Dinners are available by arrangement (per
person $37.50).

Bruny Island
POP 600

Bruny Island is almost two islands joined
by a narrow, sandy isthmus called the
Neck. Famous for its wildlife (fairy pen-
guins, echidnas, mutton birds, albino wal-
labies) it's a sparsely populated and un-
developed retreat, soaked in ocean rains
in the south, and dry and scrubby in the
north. It was named after French explorer
Bruny D'Entrecasteaux.

You need a few days to appreciate Bruny's
isolated coastal communities, swimming and
surf beaches, and the forests and walking
tracks within the **South Bruny National Park**
(www.parks.tas.gov.au) – don't try to cram it into a
day trip, especially on holiday weekends when
there are long waits for the ferry.

Tourism is the mainstay of the island's
economy, but there are no large resorts – just
self-contained cottages and guesthouses. A
car or bicycle is essential for getting around.
Supplies are available at the well-stocked
Adventure Bay general store and the tiny
shops at Alonnah and Lunawanna. Many
island roads are unsealed, and not all car
rental companies are cool with this concept.

Sights & Activities

**Bruny Island Neck Game
Reserve**   NATURE RESERVE
Climb the 273 steps up to the lookout at the
Hummock at the Bruny Island Neck Game

Reserve. All around are the rookeries of mutton birds and little penguins that nest in the dunes – the penguins can be seen emerging from the sea at dusk. This is also the site of the Truganini Memorial, providing another moment of reflection on Tasmania's grim history; see p616.

Bligh Museum of Pacific Exploration
MUSEUM

(www.brunyisland.net.au/Adventure_Bay/blighmuseum.html; 876 Main Rd, Adventure Bay; adult/child $4/2; ⊙10am-4pm) The curiosity-arousing Bligh museum details the local exploits of explorers Bligh, Cook, Furneaux and, of course, Bruny D'Entrecasteaux.

Cape Bruny Lighthouse
MONUMENT

(☑03-6298 3114; www.brunyisland.net.au/Cape_Bruny/Lightstation/lighthouse.html; tours adult/child $5/2) Also worth visiting is this 1836 lighthouse on South Bruny. Take a tour (one day's advance booking required) or wander the surrounding reserve (⊙10am-4pm), with expansive views from the rugged cape headland over mainland Tasmania's southernmost reaches.

👉 Tours

🌿 Inala Nature Tours
WALKING/4WD

(☑03-6293 1217; www.inalabruny.com.au; 320 Cloudy Bay Rd) Runs highly regarded personalised walking and 4WD tours of the island (from half a day to three days), focused on flora and fauna. The tour leader is a botanist, zoologist and conservationist, and her 250-hectare property is home to almost 140 bird species.

🌿 Bruny Island Cruises
BOAT CRUISE

(☑03-6293 1465; www.brunycruises.com.au) Operates sensational three-hour tours of Bruny's towering southeast coastline, taking in rookeries, seal colonies, bays, caves and high sea cliffs. Trips depart Adventure Bay jetty at 11am daily (year-round) and cost $100/55 per adult/child. Alternatively, take the tour as a full-day trip from Hobart ($165/110), including lunch and transfers.

🛏 Sleeping

Self-contained cottages abound on Bruny, most suitable for mid-sized groups and offering economical one-week rates. There are no hostels on Bruny Island.

Bookings are essential as owners/managers and their keys aren't always easily located – the Kettering information centre is a good starting point (p643). See also the following booking and information portals: www.brunyisland.com and www.brunyisland.net.au.

If you have a vehicle and a tent, the cheapest island accommodation is the free bush camping grounds. Camping on Bruny is restricted to sites within South Bruny National Park (national park passes required), at Jetty Beach, a beautiful sheltered cove 3km north of the lighthouse, and at Cloudy Bay. There's also a camp site outside the national park at Neck Beach, at the southern end of the Neck. All sites have pit toilets and fireplaces; BYO firewood and water.

TOP CHOICE Beachfront on Bruny
RENTAL HOUSE $$

(☑03-6293 1271; www.brunyisland.com; 1848 Bruny Island Main Rd, Great Bay; d $195, extra person $25) Nestled in the dunes on a private bay, this cosy whitewashed abode features lots of recycled timber, a terrific upstairs bedroom with expansive views, and a courtyard garden packed with native birds.

All Angels Church House
RENTAL HOUSE $$

(☑03-6293 1271; www.brunyisland.com; 4561 Bruny Island Main Rd, Lunawanna; d $195, extra person $25) Your prayers have been answered with this restored church, now rental accommodation with three bedrooms, and a high-ceilinged open-plan lounge. Fire up the barbecue in the sheltered garden, eat alfresco on the picnic table or dine inside on the huge shared table.

Captain James Cook Memorial Caravan Park
CAMPGROUND $

(☑03-6293 1128; www.capcookolkid.com.au; 786 Main Rd, Adventure Bay; unpowered/powered sites $20/23, on-site vans $44-55, cabins $140; 🐾) Right by the beach, this grandly named park could do with a few trees, but has decent facilities including some swish new one-bedroom cabins with private decks. Fishing charters are also available.

🍴 Eating

Pick up provisions and takeaways at the island's general stores. Don't miss the beaut gourmet pies at the Lunawanna store.

TOP CHOICE Bruny Island Smoke House
CAFE $$

(☑03-6260 6344; 360 Lennon Rd, North Bruny; pizzas $18-24; ⊙lunch & dinner daily Nov-Easter, to 5pm Thu-Sat other times of year) Managed with pizzazz,

BRUNY ISLAND ON A PLATE

Some of the interesting folk drawn to Bruny by the island's rugged beauty are also at the forefront of the destination's growing reputation for top-quality food and wine. Here's the best of Bruny's foodie experiences to get you started.

Bruny Island Cheese Company   CHEESERY
(www.brunyislandcheese.com.au; 1087 Main Rd, Great Bay; ⊙11am-4pm) If you're hankering for a quivering sliver of goat's or cow's milk cheese head to the Bruny Island Cheese Company. Kiwi cheesemaker Nick Haddow is inspired by working and travelling in France, Spain, Italy and the UK. Artisan bread and local wines are also for sale.

Get Shucked Oyster Farm   FARM
(www.getshucked.com.au; 1650 Main Rd; ⊙10am-5pm Oct-May, 10am-4pm Mon-Fri Jun-Sep) This oyster farm cultivates the 'fuel for love' in chilly southern waters. Visit their humble caravan and wolf down a half-dozen ($8) with lemon juice and Tabasco and a bottle of (nonalcoholic) chilli beer. Shuckingly good.

Bruny Island Premium Wines   WINERY
(☎03-6293 1008; www.brunyislandwine.com; 4391 Main Rd, Lunawanna; ⊙11am-4pm) Offers cellar-door sales at Australia's most southerly vineyard. Opening hours can be flexible – call ahead to guarantee your tasting. Pinot Noir and Chardonnay rule the roost.

Bruny Island Berry Farm   FARM
(www.brunyislandberryfarm.com.au; 562 Adventure Bay Rd, Adventure Bay; ⊙10am-5pm late Oct-late Apr) Go berry crazy at the 'Pick your own' or enjoy the farm's juicy seasonal produce with ice cream, scones or pancakes.

'BISH' is a winner – gourmet pizzas, smoked fish and meats, beer, wine, decent coffee and astounding views from the deck. The shared platters ($65 to $68) are great value for groups. Phone ahead to confirm opening hours.

Hothouse Café   CAFE $$
(☎03-6293 1131; 46 Adventure Bay Rd, South Bruny; meals $10-23; ⊙breakfast & lunch from 10am, dinner by arrangement) This cafe at Morella Island Retreat has ocean views and a menu of interesting snacks and mains including gourmet burgers and seafood chowder. Bookings essential for dinner.

Jetty Café at the Point   CAFE $$
(☎03-6260 6245; Dennes Pt, North Bruny; mains $18-24; ⊙breakfast & lunch daily, dinner summer weekends) Part cafe-restaurant, part providore and part art gallery specialising in local artists, the stylish Jetty Café is a great addition to Bruny's dining scene. Seasonal menus showcase local produce, but phone ahead as opening hours can be flexible.

Hotel Bruny   PUB $$
(Main Rd, Alonnah; mains $17-28; ⊙lunch & dinner) An unassuming pub in Alonnah, with outdoor water-view seating to help you unravel, plus a reasonable menu heavy on local seafood; a good place to meet the locals.

❶ Getting There & Around

Access to the island is via **car ferry** (☎03-6272 3277) from Kettering across to Roberts Point on the north of the island. There are at least 10 services daily, taking 20 minutes one way. The first ferry from Kettering is at 6.35am (7.45am Sunday), the last at 6.30pm (7.30pm Friday). The first ferry from Bruny is at 7am (8.25am Sunday), the last at 7pm (7.50pm Friday). The timetable may vary, so double-check departure times. Return fares: cars $28 ($30 on public holidays and public holiday weekends), motorcycles $12, bicycles $4 and foot passengers free.

Note that around summer weekends and Christmas and Easter, there are often significant queues to access the ferry, despite the addition of more sailings. If you're travelling at these times, it's not worth considering Bruny Island as a day trip as you're likely to spend a significant time waiting to catch the ferry from either end.

Metro Tasmania (☎13 22 01; www.metrotas. com.au) runs weekday-only buses from Hobart to Kettering (see p646), stopping on request at the Kettering ferry terminal. The ferry terminal on Bruny is a long way from anywhere – BYO transport.

Cygnet

POP 840

Bruny D'Entrecasteaux originally named this little rural neighbourhood Port de Cygne Noir (Port of the Black Swan) because of the swans that proliferate on the bay. Youthfully reincarnated as Cygnet (baby swan), the town has evolved into an artsy enclave while still functioning as a major centre for regional fruit production. A couple of excellent eateries make it worth a visit.

The ever-popular Cygnet Folk Festival (www.cygnetfolkfestival.org) is three days of words, music and dance in January. The warmer months also provide abundant fruit-picking work for backpackers.

🛏 Sleeping & Eating

Cherryview　　　　　　　　RENTAL HOUSE $$
(🖉03-6295 0569; www.cherryview.com.au; 90 Supplice Rd; d $160) This self-contained cottage on 10 quiet hectares is decked out with cosy wooden furniture and enjoys misty morning views over nearby cherry orchards. Oriental rugs, wooden floors and a king-size bed make it ideal for a romantic getaway.

Commercial Hotel　　　　　　　　PUB $
(🖉03-6295 1296; 2 Mary St; s/d without bathroom $65/85) Upstairs at the rambling old Commercial are decent pub rooms, all recently redecorated with flat-screen TVs, fridges and new beds. Downstairs, laconic locals occupy the bar and dive into robust seafood spreads.

Red Velvet Lounge　　　　　　　　CAFE $$
(🖉03-6295 0466; www.theredvelvetlounge.com.au; 24 Mary St; breakfast & lunch mains $8-25, dinner mains $27-30; ⊗breakfast & lunch daily, dinner Fri-Sat) This funky restaurant and coffeehouse serves deliciously healthy meals showcasing local Huon Valley produce. Try the free-range pork chorizo or the comforting slow-cooked chicken with parsnips and peas.

TOP CHOICE Lotus Eaters Café　　　　CAFE $
(10 Mary St; light meals $10-15; ⊗breakfast & lunch Thu-Mon) Just a few doors along from the excellent Red Velvet Lounge is this equally fine cafe. Expect a rigorous focus on everything seasonal, organic, free-range and local.

Huonville & Around

Huonville (population 1940), on the banks of the Huon River, is the biggest town south of

Hobart and sits in a region of pretty hillside orchards and riverfront villages. The town was traditionally the centre of Tasmania's prodigious apple-growing industry, and now the region's farmers have diversified into viticulture, cherries, berries and stone fruit. Just down the road, pretty riverside **Franklin** has good eateries.

The Huonville visitor information centre (🖉03-6264 1838; www.huonjet.com/trips/viscentre1.html; The Esplanade; ⊗9am-5pm; @) is by the river on the road south to Cygnet.

◉ Sights & Activities

Huon Apple & Heritage Museum　　MUSEUM
(🖉03-6266 4345; www.applemuseum.huonvalley. biz; 2064 Main Rd, Grove; adult/child $5.50/3; ⊗8.30am-5.30pm) At Grove, 6km north of Huonville. Has displays on almost 400 varieties of apples and 19th-century orchard life.

Huon Jet　　　　　　　　JET-BOAT RIDES
(www.huonjet.co; adult/child $69/47; ⊗9am-5pm Sep-May) A 35-minute, heart-in-your-mouth jet-boat ride. Book at the information centre.

🛏 Sleeping & Eating

Huon Bush Retreats　　　　　　CABINS $$
(🖉03-6264 2233; www.huonbushretreats.com; 300 Browns Rd, Ranelagh; d tepees $135, d cabins from $275, tent & campervan sites $30) This wildlife-friendly retreat is on a habitat reserve on Mt Misery. On-site are modern, self-contained cabins, a larger disabled-access cabin, luxury tepees, tent and campervan sites, plus walking tracks and barbecue shelters.

DS Coffee House & Internet Lounge　　　　　　　CAFE $
(34 Main Rd, Huonville; light meals $8-15; ⊗breakfast & lunch) Hands down Huonville's most interesting cafe, this funky collection of retro furniture feels like your first student flat at university. It's also a handy internet lounge with PCs for hire and wi-fi on offer.

Petty Sessions　　　　　　　　CAFE $$
(🖉03-6266 3488; 3445 Huon Hwy, Franklin; mains $22-34; ⊗lunch & dinner) A picket fence and picture-perfect gardens enshroud this likeable cafe inside an 1860 courthouse. Head for the deck and try the house special: abalone chowder.

Franklin Woodfired Pizza PIZZA $
(Huon Hwy, Franklin; pizzas $10-20; ⊙dinner daily, lunch Sun) This tiny tin shack bakes fantastic takeaway pizzas inside a kooky corrugated-iron oven. Try the tiger prawn one with pineapple, chilli jam and jalapenos.

Geeveston & Around

Trying hard to shake its reputation as a redneck logging town, Geeveston (population 760) is pitching itself as a tourist centre for Tassie's deep south, with good accommodation and eateries close to the Hartz Mountains and Tahune Forest AirWalk.

◎ Sights & Activities

Tahune Forest AirWalk FOREST WALK
(☑1300 720 507; www.adventureforests.com.au; adult/child $24/12; ⊙9am-5pm) Tahune Forest, 29km west of town, has 600m of steel wheelchair-accessible walkways suspended 20m above the forest floor.

Tahune Eagle Glide HANG-GLIDING
(☑0419 311 198; www.cablehanggliding.com.au; adult/child $33/22; ⊙9am-5pm) Assess the Tahune forest from even higher. Wannabe eagles are strapped into a hang-glider, which in turn is latched to a 220m cable 30m above the Huon River and forest. You get two crossings for the price.

⊨ Sleeping & Eating

Bears Went Over the Mountain B&B $$
(☑03-6297 0110; www.bearsoverthemountain.com; 2 Church St; d $130-200; @🛜) Right in the middle of town, Bears has four rooms decorated in a whimsical bear theme – kids will be in heaven. Complimentary port for cold southern nights.

Contented Bear CAFE $$
(6 Church St; lunch $11-18, dinner $25-35; ⊙lunch & dinner; @🛜) Try a homemade scallop mornay pie for lunch. For dinner it's got be the Tassie salmon with garlic mash or the prawn and scallop salad.

Hartz Mountains National Park

The wilderness of this park (www.parks.tas.gov.au), part of Tasmania's World Heritage Area, is only 84km from Hobart – easy striking distance for day-trippers and weekend walkers. The park is renowned for its jagged peaks, glacial tarns, gorges, alpine moorlands and dense rainforest. Rapid weather changes are common, and even day walkers should bring waterproofs and warm clothing.

There are some great hikes and isolated viewpoints in the park. Waratah Lookout, 24km from Geeveston, is an easy five-minute shuffle from the road. Other well-surfaced short walks include Arve Falls (20 minutes return) and Lake Osborne (40 minutes return). The steeper Lake Esperance walk (two hours return) takes you through sublime high country.

There are basic day facilities within the park – toilets, shelters, picnic tables, barbecues – but camping is not allowed. Collect a *Hartz Mountains National Park* brochure from the Geeveston or Huonville visitor information centres.

Dover & Around

Dover (population 465) is a chilled-out base for exploring the far south. In the 19th century Dover was a timber-milling town, but nowadays fish farms harvest Atlantic salmon for export throughout Asia. This is Tasmania's last vestige of civilisation for travellers heading south, and the place to stock up on fuel and supplies. On the road from Geeveston, take the pretty detour around Police Point, which provides superb views over the lower Huon River and D'Entrecasteaux Channel with its salmon farms and watercraft.

See www.farsouthtasmania.com.

⊨ Sleeping & Eating

Far South Wilderness Lodge & Backpackers CABINS $
(☑03-6298 1922; www.farsouthwilderness.com.au; Narrows Rd; dm/d/f $30/80/100) On the Esperance River 5km south of Dover, Far South provides some of Tasmania's best budget accommodation, with a bushy waterfront setting, cosy lounge piled high with *National Geographic* mags, quality accommodation and a strong environmental focus. Mountain bikes for rent ($15 per day).

Jetty House B&B $$
(☑03-6298 3139; www.southportjettyhouse.com; Main Rd, Southport; s/d incl breakfast $100/140, extra person $25; 🛜) Around 10km south of Dover at Southport, this rambling, verandah-encircled and family-run homestead was built in 1875. Rates include full cooked

breakfast and afternoon tea, and the friendly feline attention of Pushkin. Dinner by arrangement. Minimum two nights, and an ideal treat before or after negotiating the Southwest Track.

Dover Beachside Tourist
Park
CAMPGROUND **$**

(☏03-6298 1301; www.dovercaravanpark.com.au; 27 Kent Beach Rd, Dover; unpowered/powered sites $20/28, cabins from $90; 🐾) Opposite a sandy beach, this proudly maintained park features grassy expanses, spotless cabins and a bookshelf full of beachy, trashy novels.

Post Office 6985
SEAFOOD, PIZZA **$$**

(☏03-6298 1905; Main Rd, Dover; mains $13-30; ⊙dinner Thu-Sun) This is a surprise...Leonard Cohen and alt-country on the stereo, cool decor and lots of up-to-date music and food magazines. The menu featuring local seafood and wood-fired pizzas – try the one with scallops, caramelised onion and pancetta.

🌿 St Imre
VINEYARD **$$**

(☏03-6298 1781; www.stimrevineyard.com.au; 6900 Huon Hwy, Dover; ⊙tastings 10am-5pm Sat-Sun, dinner Sat) Specialising in Pinot Noir, Chardonnay and the robust and rustic 'Tiger Blood', this hillside vineyard also offers three-course dinners ($35) on Saturday nights, usually reflecting the owners' Hungarian heritage. Book by early Saturday afternoon.

Hastings Caves & Thermal Springs

The Hastings Caves & Thermal Springs facility, signposted inland from the Huon Hwy, is 21km south of Dover. The only way to explore the caves is via guided tour; buy tickets at the Hastings visitor information centre (☏03-6298 3209; www.parks.tas. gov.au; adult/child $24/12; ⊙9am-5pm Mar, Apr & Sep-Dec, 9am-6pm Jan & Feb, 10am-4pm May-Aug). Tours leave on the hour: the first an hour after the visitor centre opens, the last an hour before it closes.

Admission includes a 45-minute tour of the amazing dolomite Newdegate Cave, plus entry to the thermal swimming pool behind the visitor information centre, filled with 28°C (supposedly) water from thermal springs (pool-only admission adult/child $5/2.50).

Cockle Creek

Australia's most southerly drive is a 19km corrugated-gravel stretch from Ida Bay past the gentle waves of Recherche Bay to Cockle Creek. A grand grid of streets was once planned for Cockle Creek, but dwindling coal seams and whale numbers poured cold water on that idea. There's free camping along the Recherche Bay foreshore, or pitch your tent just within Southwest National Park (national park fees apply). You can walk to windy Whale Head and onto the South East Cape.

The Cockle Creek area features craggy, clouded mountains, brilliant long beaches: perfect for camping and bushwalking. The challenging **South Coast Track** starts (or ends) here, taking you through to Melaleuca in the Southwest National Park. Combined with the **Port Davey Track** you can walk all the way to Port Davey in the southwest. See p701.

TASMAN PENINSULA

Port Arthur Historic Site is the Tasman Peninsula's centre of activity, but the area also offers 300m-high sea cliffs, empty surf beaches, and stunning bushwalks through thickly wooded forests and isolated coastlines. Much of the area constitutes the Tasman National Park (www.parks.tas.gov.au).

See www.tasmanregion.com.au and www.portarthur.org.au.

👉 Tours

Gray Line
SIGHTSEEING

(☏1300 858 687; www.grayline.com.au; full-day tour adult/child from $100/50) Coach tours ex-Hobart, including a harbour cruise around the Isle of the Dead, Port Arthur admission and guided tour, and pit stops at Tasman Arch and the Devils' Kitchen.

Navigators
SIGHTSEEING

(☏03-6223 1914; www.navigators.net.au; Brooke St Pier, Hobart; full-day tour from adult/child $159/128; ⊙Wed, Fri & Sat Oct-May) Cruises from Hobart to Port Arthur, returning on a coach. Includes entrance to the historic site, guided tour and morning tea. Also running is a cruise around Tasman Island from Port Arthur.

Roaring 40s Ocean Kayaking
KAYAKING

(☏03-6267 5000; www.roaring40stours.com.au; 1-/3-day tour $255/1250) Based in Kettering,

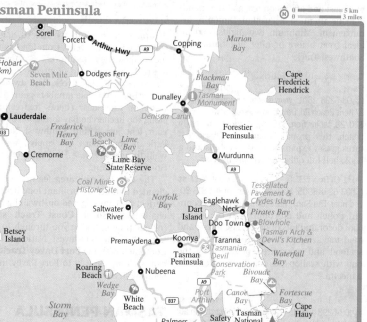

Roaring 40s also conducts epic sea-kayaking tours around the Tasman Peninsula, paddling past the monumental coastline. Prices include equipment, meals, accommodation and transfers from Hobart.

Tours Tasmania SIGHTSEEING
(📞1800 777 103; www.tourstas.com.au; full-day tours $100-110; ⏰Tue, Wed, Fri & Sat) Small-group backpacker-focused day trips including Port Arthur and the Tasmanian Devil Conservation Park, and Port Arthur combined with Remarkable Cave and Tasman Arch. Longer two- to five-day trips take in Mt Field, Wineglass Bay and Cradle Mountain.

Tasman Island Cruises WILDLIFE
(📞03-6250 2200; www.tasmancruises.com.au; full-day tour from adult/child $165/110) Take a bus to Port Arthur for a three-hour ecocruise around Tasman Island, then explore the Port Arthur Historic Site and

bus it back to town. Includes morning tea, lunch and Port Arthur admission. You can also take just the cruise from Port Arthur (adult/child $100/55).

ⓘ Getting There & Around

Tassielink (📞1300 300 520; www.tassielink.com.au) runs an 8.45am and 3.55pm weekday bus from Hobart Bus Terminal (Map p628) to Port Arthur ($26.60, 2¼ hours) during school terms; the Port Arthur–Hobart bus leaves at 6am and 11.05am. Buses depart Hobart at 7.50am and 2.55pm on Saturdays. Services change during school holiday periods.

Sorell
POP 1730

Sorell is the gateway T-junction town for the Tasman Peninsula. It was settled in 1808, making it one of Tasmania's oldest towns. One good reason to stop is the **Sorell Fruit Farm** (📞03-6265 3100; www.sorellfruitfarm.com;

174 Pawleena Rd; ☺8.30am-5pm late Oct-May). Pick your own fruit (15 different kinds!) from their intensively planted 5 hectares ($6 minimum pick) or enjoy a snack and good coffee in the tearooms. Head east through Sorell towards Port Arthur. After exiting the town you'll see Pawleena signposted on your left.

A good option for picnic fixings is the Sorell Providore (21 Gordon St; breakfast & lunch mains $8-15, dinner mains $26-30; ☺breakfast & lunch daily, dinner Fri-Sat; 🔊). Another of Tasmania's emerging hybrids combining cafe and delicatessen, it offers a great range of Tassie beer and wine, and artisan bread and cheese is also for sale.

Eaglehawk Neck to Port Arthur

Most tourists associate the Tasman Peninsula only with Port Arthur, but there are many attractions down this way. Hit the bookshops for *Peninsula Tracks* by Peter and Shirley Storey ($18) for track notes on 35 walks in the area. The *Convict Trail* booklet, available from visitor information centres, covers the peninsula's historic sites.

Approach Eaglehawk Neck from the north, then turn east onto Pirates Bay Dr for the lookout – the Pirates Bay views extending to the rugged coastline beyond are truly incredible. Also clearly signposted around Eaglehawk Neck are some bizarre and precipitous coastal formations: **Tessellated Pavement**, the **Blowhole**,

Tasman Arch and **Waterfall Bay**. South of Port Arthur is the sea-gouged Remarkable Cave.

◉ Sights & Activities

Tasman National Park   NATURE RESERVE
(www.parks.tas.gov.au) This park offers some spectacular bushwalking (national park fees apply). From Fortescue Bay, you can walk east to Cape Hauy (four to five hours return) – a well-trodden path leading to sea cliffs with sensational rocky sea-stack outlooks. The walk to Cape Raoul (five hours return) is equally rewarding.

FREE Coal Mines Historic Site   HISTORIC SITE
(☺dawn-dusk) Visit these restored ruins at Saltwater River. You can also visit the remains of **penal outstations** at Eaglehawk Neck, Koonya, Premaydena and Saltwater River.

Tasmanian Devil
Conservation Park   NATURE RESERVE
(www.tasmaniandevilpark.com; Arthur Hwy; adult/child $24/13; ☺9am-6pm Oct-Mar, 9am-5pm Apr-Sep) This park functions as a quarantined breeding centre for devils to help protect against devil facial tumour disease (DFTD; see the boxed text, below). There are plenty of other native animals and birds here, with feedings throughout the day.

Eaglehawk Dive Centre   SCUBA DIVING
(☎03-6250 3566; www.eaglehawkdive.com.au; 178 Pirates Bay Dr, Eaglehawk Neck) Scuba diving is popular in this area.

TIGERS & DEVILS

There are two endings to the story of the Tasmanian tiger (*Thylacinus cynocephalus*, or thylacine). The thylacine – a striped, nocturnal, doglike predator – was once widespread in Tasmania (and also roamed mainland Australia and New Guinea until about 2000 years ago). Conventional wisdom says that it was hunted to extinction in the 19th and early 20th centuries, and that the last-known specimen died in Hobart Zoo in 1936. Despite hundreds of alleged sightings since, no specimen, living or dead, has been confirmed. The second version of the story is that the shy, illusive tigers still exist in the wilds of Tasmania. Scientists scoff at such suggestions, but Tasmanian folklore seems reluctant to let go of this tantalising possibility. David Owen's *Thylacine* examines this phenomenon and traces the animal's demise.

The obnoxious Tasmanian devil (*Sarcophilus harrisii*) is definitely still alive, but devil facial tumour disease (DFTD, a communicable cancer) infects up to 75% of the wild population (the real beast looks nothing like the Warner Bros cartoon). Quarantined populations have been established around the state, but efforts to find a cure have been depressingly fruitless. In the meantime, you can check them out at wildlife parks around the state.

🛏 Sleeping

Eaglehawk Neck Budget Accommodation
HOSTEL $

(☑03-6250 3248; 94 Old Jetty Rd, Eaglehawk Neck; unpowered sites/dm $16/20) This *very* simple, family-run hostel is in a peaceful location signposted west of the isthmus – just four beds in a dorm, tent spots on the back lawn and a basic camp kitchen in an old garden shed. The owners are lovely and offer $5 bike hire for the duration of your stay.

Taranna Cottages & Campervan Park
CABINS $

(☑03-6250 3436; www.tarannacottages.com.au; 996 Arthur Hwy, Taranna; d $95, extra adult/child $20/10, unpowered sites $20) Perhaps the best-value accommodation on the peninsula, this enterprise at the southern end of Taranna features three neat-as-a-pin self-contained apple pickers' cottages. They exude basic, rustic charm in a quiet bush setting and have open fires. Breakfast provisions (free-range eggs, homemade jams) are a few dollars extra. There's also parking for self-contained campervans.

Norfolk Bay Convict Station
B&B $$

(☑03-6250 3487; www.convictstation.com; 5862 Arthur Hwy, Taranna; d incl breakfast $160-180) Built in 1838 and once the railway's port terminus and an old pub, this gorgeous place is now a top-quality waterfront B&B. Eclectic rooms come with home-made buffet breakfasts and complimentary port. Fishing gear and a dinghy are for hire.

Port Arthur

POP 300

In 1830 Lieutenant-Governor George Arthur chose the Tasman Peninsula to confine prisoners who had committed further crimes in the colony. A 'natural penitentiary', the peninsula is connected to the mainland by a strip of land less than 100m wide – Eaglehawk Neck. To deter escape, ferocious guard dogs were chained across the isthmus.

From 1830 to 1877, 12,500 convicts did hard, brutal prison time at Port Arthur. Port Arthur became the hub of a network of penal stations on the peninsula, its fine buildings sustaining thriving convict-labour industries, including timber milling, shipbuilding, coal mining, shoemaking, and brick and nail production.

Australia's first railway literally 'ran' the 7km between Norfolk Bay and Long Bay:

convicts pushed the carriages along the tracks. A semaphore telegraph system allowed instant communication between Port Arthur, other peninsula outstations and Hobart. Convict farms provided fresh vegetables, a boys' prison was built at Point Puer to reform and educate juvenile convicts, and a church was erected.

Although Port Arthur is a hugely popular tourist site – over 300,000 visitors annually – it remains a sombre, confronting and haunting place. What makes it all the more poignant is the scale of the penal settlement and its genuine beauty. The stonemasonry work, gothic architecture, lawns and gardens are all exquisite.

◎ Sights & Activities

Port Arthur Historic Site
HISTORIC SITE

(☑03-6251 2310, 1800 659 101; www.portarthur.org.au; Arthur Hwy; adult/child from $30/15; ◎tours & buildings 9am-5pm, grounds 8.30am-dusk) The visitor centre here includes an information counter, cafe, restaurant and gift shop. Downstairs is an excellent interpretation gallery, where you can follow the convicts' journey from England to Tasmania.

Worthwhile guided tours (included in admission) leave regularly from the visitor centre. You can visit all the restored buildings, including the Old Asylum (now a museum and cafe) and the Model Prison. Admission tickets, valid for two consecutive days, also entitle you to a short harbour cruise circumnavigating (but not stopping at) the Isle of the Dead. For an additional $12/8 per adult/child, you can visit the island on 40-minute guided tours – count headstones and listen to some stories. You can also tour to Point Puer boys' prison for the same additional prices.

Extremely popular is the 90-minute, lantern-lit Historic Ghost Tour (☑1800 659 101; adult/child $22/12), which leaves from the visitor centre nightly at dusk. Bookings are essential.

🛏 Sleeping

Sea Change Safety Cove
B&B $$

(☑03-6250 2719; www.safetycove.com; 425 Safety Cove Rd; d $160-200) This guesthouse has fantastic views including misty cliffs and sea-wracked beaches. It's 4km south of Port Arthur, just off the sandy sweep of Safety Cove Beach. There's a beaut communal deck, a couple of B&B rooms inside the house, plus a large self-contained unit sleeping five.

DON'T ASK – THE PORT ARTHUR MASSACRE

Staff at the Port Arthur Historic Site won't speak of the 1996 massacre. Many lost relatives and colleagues, and Martin Bryant's name will not be spoken. On the morning of Sunday 28 April, 28-year-old Bryant drove from Hobart with a sports bag of semi-automatic weapons. Over the course of the late morning and afternoon he murdered 35 people and injured 37 more in and around the Port Arthur Historic Site. He took a hostage into a local guesthouse and held off police for a further 18 hours, killing the hostage and setting the guesthouse on fire before surrendering to police. He remains imprisoned north of Hobart, having received 35 life sentences. The Port Arthur Massacre is one of the world's worst killing spree in a single event. The incident precipitated Australia's strict gun-control laws.

Stewarts Bay Lodge   RESORT **$$$**
(☑03-6250 2888; www.stewartsbaylodge.com. au; 6955 Arthur Hwy; d $235-420; @⊛) Arrayed around a gorgeous hidden cove, Stewarts Bay Lodge combines older, more rustic units with newer deluxe accommodation. Modern kitchens are great for making the most of good local produce, but you'll also want to dine at the sleek Taylor's Restaurant.

Port Arthur Caravan &
Cabin Park   CAMPGROUND **$**
(☑03-6250 2340; www.portarthurcaravan-cabin park.com.au; Garden Point Rd; dm $20, unpowered sites $24, powered sites $28-35, cabins $110-120) Spaciously sloping with plenty of greenery, this well-facilitated park (including camp kitchen, wood BBQs and shop) is 2km before Port Arthur, not far from a sheltered beach. Port Arthur's best (and only) budget option.

✕ Eating

Taylor's Restaurant   MODERN AUSTRALIAN **$$**
(☑03-6250 2771; Stewarts Bay Lodge, 6955 Arthur Hwy; mains $26-31; ⊗breakfast, lunch & dinner; ⊛) Taylor's showcases local produce with Eaglehawk Neck oysters, Pirates Bay octopus, and quail served with pesto mash and Mediterranean vegetables. Definitely worth a detour if you're overnighting anywhere on the peninsula. Bookings recommended in summer.

Felons Bistro   MODERN AUSTRALIAN **$$**
(☑1800 659 101; mains $27; ⊗dinner) In the Port Arthur visitor centre, Felons is a worthy choice before you head off on the Ghost Tour. Upmarket, creative dinners with a seafood bias including tuna and salmon reinforce their catchy slogan: 'Dine with Conviction'. Reservations advised.

Eucalypt   CAFE **$$**
(6962 Arthur Hwy; mains $10-20 ⊗breakfast & lunch year-round, dinner Dec-Mar) A versatile spot near the turn-off to Port Arthur, Eucalypt does robust breakfasts, the area's best coffee, and hearty lunches including scallop pot pie.

THE MIDLANDS

Tasmania's Midlands are the very antithesis of the forested wilderness areas the island is famous for. The early settlers comprehensively cleared this area for sheep and cattle grazing, and planted willows, poplars and hawthorn hedgerows around their settlements and along the fertile river valleys. The Midlands' baked, straw-coloured plains and hillsides, and grand Georgian mansions feel distinctly English.

The Midlands' agricultural potential fuelled Tasmania's settlement – coach stations, garrison towns, stone villages and pastoral properties sprang up as convict gangs hammered out the road between Hobart and Launceston.

The upgrading of Tasmania's main north-south road – the Midland Hwy (aka Heritage Highway) – bypassed many old towns along the old route. Pull off the highway to Ross and Oatlands to explore the Georgian main streets, antique shops and some of Australia's best-preserved colonial architecture.

See www.southernmidlands.tas.gov.au and www.northernmidlands.tas.gov.au.

❶ Getting There & Around

Redline Coaches (☑1300 360 000; www. tasredline.com.au) powers along the Midland Hwy several times daily; you can jump off at any of the main towns except on express services. The Hobart to Launceston fare is $38.80 (about 2½ hours). One-way from Hobart/Launceston to Oatlands costs $20.30/23.10; to Ross it's $28.70/13.20 and to Campbell Town $28.70/13.20.

Oatlands

POP 540

Established as a garrison town in 1832, Oatlands serves a thriving tourist trade, but remains stately and restrained about it. Surveyors proposed 80km of streets for the little town that today contains Australia's largest collection of Georgian architecture and many splendid early dry-stone walls. On the impressive main street alone there are 87 historic buildings, many of which are now galleries and craft stores.

Oatlands visitor centre (☑03-6254 1212; www.southernmidlands.tas.gov.au; Mill Lane; ⊙9am-5pm) proffers general info and handles accommodation bookings. Recently relocated to near Callington Mill, they run regular guided tours of the town's attractions (adult/child from $8/5).

◉ Sights

Callington Mill　　　　　LANDMARK

(www.callingtonmill.org; Mill Lane; adult/child $10/6; ⊙guided tours hourly 10am-4pm) Visible throughout the town, the Callington Mill was built in 1837 and ground flour until 1891. After years of neglect it's been fully restored and was reopened in 2010. It's a fascinating piece of engineering, all fully explained on guided tours leaving on the hour from the adjacent visitor information centre. The mill is also back to producing high-grade, organic flour, an essential component of the baked goodies across the road at the Companion Bakery.

FREE **History Room**　　　　MUSEUM

(⊙9am-5pm) This is an old garage full of photos, relics and old knick-knacks. While you're here, pick up the free handouts *Welcome to Historic Oatlands,* which includes self-guided town tour directions, and *Lake Dulverton Walkway Guide,* for ex-lake explorations. It's volunteer-run so hours can be flexible.

⊨ Sleeping & Eating

There's free camping for caravans and campervans in the picnic area beside Lake Dulverton at the northern end of the Esplanade. There are toilets and barbecues here.

Oatlands Lodge　　　　B&B $$

(☑03-6254 1444; oatlandslodge@bigpond.com; 92 High St; s/d incl breakfast $90/120) Warm and inviting in two-storey, hen-pecked sandstone splendour, Oatlands Lodge is the cream of the town's accommodation. Rates include a huge breakfast spread and lots of conversation with the friendly owners.

TOP CHOICE **Companion Bakery**　　　BAKERY $

(www.companionbakery.com.au; 106 High St; snacks & light meals $6-15; ⊙9am-5pm Wed-Sun) Wood-fired. Organic. Seriously good coffee. What's not to like about the Companion Bakery? As well as quite probably Tasmania's best sourdough sandwiches, other sustenance before or after exploring Oatlands' heritage vibe includes Moroccan lamb rolls, superlative pastries and quiche.

Kentish Hotel　　　　PUB $$

(60 High St; mains $16-25, bakery items $3-8; ⊙bistro lunch & dinner, bakery breakfast & lunch) Our pick for evening dining in Oatlands. Favourites include steak, fish and chips, seafood crepes, smoked salmon salad and daily specials. The bakery next door sells pies, pasties, rolls, pizza and coffee.

Ross

POP 270

Another tidy Midlands town is Ross, 120km north of Hobart. Established in 1812 as a garrison town to protect Hobart–Launceston travellers from bushrangers, it quickly became an important coach staging post. Tree-lined streets are wrapped in colonial charm and history.

The **crossroads** in the middle of town leads you in one of four directions: temptation (represented by the Man O'Ross Hotel), salvation (the Catholic church), recreation (the town hall) and damnation (the old jail).

◉ Sights & Activities

Tasmanian Wool Centre　　　MUSEUM

(www.taswoolcentre.com.au) Sells garments, scarves and beanies made from super-fine merino wool. The **Ross visitor information centre** (☑03-6381 5466; www.visitross.com.au; Church St; ⊙9am-5pm) is located here.

Ross Bridge　　　　MONUMENT

The impressive Ross Bridge (1836) is the third-oldest bridge in Australia. The bridge is floodlit at night and light reflecting from the water makes eerie shifting shadows on the 186 carvings that decorate the arches.

FREE **Ross Female Factory**　　　MUSEUM

(www.femalefactory.com.au/FFRG/ross.htm; ⊙9am-5pm) Off Bond St, the Ross Female factory

was one of only four female convict prisons in the colony. One building is still standing, and archaeological excavations are under way. Descriptive signs and stories provide insights into the prisoners' lives.

Other notable historic edifices include the 1832 Scotch Thistle Inn (Church St), now a private residence; the 1830 barracks (Bridge St), restored by the National Trust and also a private residence; the 1885 Uniting Church (Church St); the 1868 St John's Anglican Church (cnr Church & Badajos Sts); and the still-operating 1896 post office (26 Church St).

🛏 Sleeping & Eating

Stone Cottage RENTAL HOUSE $
(☎03-6381 5444; skummreow@hotmail.com; Church St; d $90, extra adult/child $20/10) One of the town's best options for families, with a truckload of kids' toys and DVDs, and an expansive garden with well-established fruit trees. The country kitchen with a long wooden table is just perfect for lazy lunches and dinners. Ask at the Ross post office.

Country Style Cabin RENTAL HOUSE $
(☎03-6381 5453; www.rossaccommodationcabin.com.au; 13-17 Bridge St; d incl breakfast $99) Enjoying a rural outlook with sheep and Bluey the miniature horse as close neighbours, this modern wood-lined cottage has an open-plan lounge with a flat-screen TV and loads of magazines. Check in at the T-Spot Café & Teahouse.

Ross Motel MOTEL $$
(☎03-6381 5224; www.rossmotel.com.au; 2 High St; d/f incl breakfast from $135/160; 🐾) Ross Motel offers spic-and-span Georgian-style cottage units, each with microwave, fridge, TV and DVD (prices include breakfast provisions). Family units sleep four.

Ross Caravan Park CAMPGROUND $
(☎03-6381 5224; www.rossmotel.com.au; Bridge St; unpowered/powered sites $20/26, cabin s/d $50/60; 🐾) Utilitarian, barracks-style cabins sleep two to four people, have cooking facilities and offer the cheapest accommodation in town. Bathrooms are shared, and you'll need your own linen. Reception is at the Ross Motel.

Man O'Ross Hotel PUB $$
(35 Church St; mains $15-20; ⊙lunch & dinner; 🐾) The town's heritage pub offers a surprisingly diverse menu including goodies like Tasmanian salt-crusted lamb and robust Indian curries.

Ross General Store, Bakery & Tearooms CAFE $
(31 Church St; light meals $4-10; ⊙breakfast & lunch) This jack-of-all-trades store has an olden-days vibe, an open fire and a fuss-free menu of breakfast, soups, homemade cakes and sandwiches. The scallop pies are among Tassie's best.

T Spot Café & Teahouse CAFE $
(13-17 Bridge St; snacks $4-8; ⊙breakfast & lunch) Yummy cakes – including gluten-free options – and over 50 teas are reasons aplenty to stop here. The friendly owners also hire bikes (single/tandem per hour $10/20).

Campbell Town
POP 770

Campbell Town, 12km north of Ross, was established as yet another garrison settlement. Unlike Oatlands and Ross, however, the Midland Hwy still trucks right through town.

The first white settlers here were Irish timber-workers who spoke Gaelic and had a particularly debauched reputation.

Rows of **red bricks** set into the High St footpath detail the crimes, sentences and arrival dates of convicts like Ephram Brain and English Corney, sent to Van Diemen's Land for crimes as various as stealing potatoes, bigamy and murder. It's a poignant promenade of memories.

The bridge across the Elizabeth River here was completed in 1838, making it almost as archaic as the Ross Bridge. Locals call it the Red Bridge because it was convict-built from more than 1.5 million red bricks baked on-site.

See www.campbelltowntasmania.com.

🛏 Sleeping & Eating

Fox Hunters Return B&B $$
(☎03-6381 1602; www.foxhunters.com.au; 132 High St; d $139-159) On the left as you enter town from Hobart is this pukka establishment, built with convict labour in 1833 as a coaching inn and now offering spacious rooms, each with private bathroom and sitting area. The cellar under the main building housed convicts during the construction of the neighbouring Red Bridge. At the time of writing it was being converted into a bookshop – the 'Book Cellar' – specialising in heritage tomes. It's open Thursday to Sunday, or by prior arrangement at other times.

St Andrews Inn B&B $$

(☑03-6391 5525; Midland Hwy, Cleveland; s/d incl breakfast $90/140) Convict-built in 1845, this National Trust–classified roadside coaching inn is 16km north of Campbell Town at Cleveland. Upstairs are two large en-suite B&B rooms (with TVs and complimentary port); downstairs is a bubbly little cafe (meals $9 to $16). It's open for breakfast and lunch Tuesday to Sunday and for dinner by arrangement.

TOP CHOICE **Red Bridge Café & Providore** CAFE $

(www.redbridgecafe.com.au; 137 High St; light meals $10-15; ⊙breakfast & lunch; 🛜) At the southern end of town, a former brewery now incorporates a huge dining room with shared wooden tables, and a providore packed with the best of Tasmanian food, wine and beer. Shared platters ($15 to $45) and gourmet pies make this an essential stop heading either north or south.

Zeps CAFE $$

(☑03-6381 1344; 92 High St; meals $10-25; ⊙breakfast, lunch & dinner; @) Another top refuelling spot is the hyperactive Zeps, serving brekky, panini, pasta, gourmet pies and good coffee throughout the day, plus pizza and more substantial mains in the evening. It's a handy evening destination if you're staying in Ross, and have already dined at the pub.

EAST COAST

Tasmania's laid-back east coast is drop-dead gorgeous. Hardy types will find superb opportunities for swimming in clean, clear water, while the rest can enjoy walking barefoot along the white-sand beaches. Mild, sunny days lure summer holidaymakers from Hobart, while mainlanders in campervans explore the east coast's squeaky beaches and fishing towns. Wineglass Bay and the pink granite peaks of Freycinet National Park are justifiably world-famous.

❶ Getting There & Around

BICYCLE

The Tasman Hwy along the east coast, Tasmania's most popular cycle-touring route, is wonderfully varied, taking in pretty seaside towns, forests and plenty of places to swim. Traffic is usually light, and the hills aren't too steep, particularly the section from Chain of Lagoons to Falmouth (east of St Marys).

BUS

Redline Coaches (☑1300 360 000; www.tasredline.com.au) runs weekday buses between Launceston and Swansea, the Coles Bay turn-off and Bicheno, via the Midland Hwy and the inland B34 road. Services from Hobart connect with these buses at Campbell Town, where you may have to wait depending on your particular connection. Redline also runs daily services (except Saturday) between Launceston and St Helens along the A4 via St Marys. Hobart buses connect with this service at Conara on the Midland Hwy. Redline fares:

JOURNEY	PRICE ($)	DURATION (HR)
Launceston-Bicheno	34	2¾
Launceston-Coles Bay turn-off	34	2½
Launceston-St Helens	32	2¾
Launceston-St Marys	31	2
Launceston-Swansea	31	2

Tassielink (☑1300 300 520; www.tassielink.com.au) also provides east-coast services from Hobart, running at least three times per week. Some buses detour through Richmond. Buses also run twice weekly from Launceston to Bicheno via the A4 and St Marys. Tassielink fares:

JOURNEY	PRICE ($)	DURATION (HR)
Hobart-Bicheno	36	3
Hobart-Coles Bay turn-off	34	2¾
Hobart-Orford	16	1¼
Hobart-St Helens	51	4
Hobart-Swansea	29	2¼
Hobart-Triabunna	20	1½
Launceston-Bicheno	34	2½
Launceston-St Marys	26	2

Bicheno Coach Service (☑03-6257 0293; www.freycinetconnections.com.au) runs between Bicheno, Coles Bay and Freycinet National Park, connecting with east-coast Redline and Tassielink coaches at the Coles Bay turn-off:

JOURNEY	PRICE ($)	DURATION (MIN)
Bicheno-Coles Bay	9	35
Coles Bay-Freycinet NP	5	10
Coles Bay turn-off-Coles Bay	9	25
Coles Bay turn-off-Freycinet NP	11	35

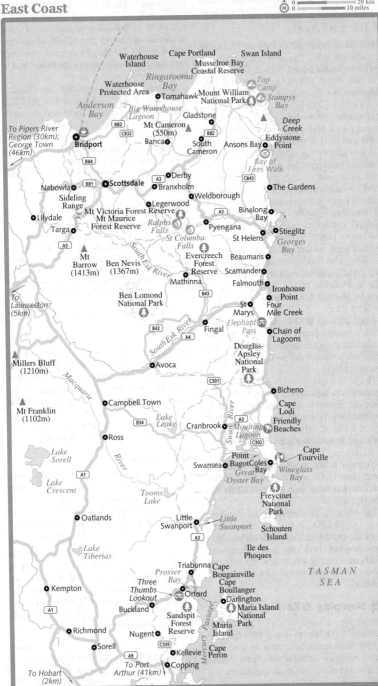

Triabunna & Maria Island National Park

About 8km north of Orford is Triabunna (population 800), the departure point for ferries to Maria Island National Park. Book and buy ferry tickets and national park passes at the Triabunna visitor information centre (☑03-6257 4772; cnr Charles St & The Esplanade; ☺9am-4pm), which provides information on Maria Island accommodation, walks, activities and fishing charters.

A few kilometres offshore, car-free Maria Island (www.parks.tas.gov.au) was declared a national park in 1972. Its mixed history provides some interesting convict and industrial ruins among some exquisite natural features: forests, fern gullies, fossil-studded sandstone and limestone cliffs, and empty beaches. Maria is popular with bushwalkers, mountain bikers and bird-watchers, and snorkellers and divers are in for a treat. National park fees apply; island info is available at the visitors reception area in the old Commissariat Store near the ferry pier.

From 1825 to 1832 Darlington was Tasmania's second penal colony (the first was Sarah Island near Strahan). The remains of the convict village are well preserved and easy to explore.

The Maria Island Walk (☑03-6227 8800; www.mariaislandwalk.com.au; per person $2150) is a four-day guided walk of the island, with the emphasis on nature, history and minimal-impact walking. Trips run from October to April and include transfers from Hobart to the island, meals and accommodation. Don't miss walks to the top of **Bishop & Clerk** (four hours return), the **Fossil Cliffs** (two hours return) and **Painted Cliffs** (2½ hours return).

The cells in Darlington's old Penitentiary (☑03-6257 1420; maria.island@parks.tas.gov.au; dm/d/6-bed unit $15/44/84) have been converted into very basic, unpowered bunkhouses (bring gas lamps, utensils and cookers). Book well ahead. Hot showers are available.

🛏 Sleeping & Eating

Tandara Motor Inn MOTEL **$$**
(☑03-6257 3333; Tasman Hwy; d $125, extra person $10) Triabunna's best place to stay, with bright, recently refurbished motel rooms and free use of the on-site tennis courts.

Triabunna Cabin & Caravan Park CARAVAN PARK **$**
(☑03-6257 3575; www.mariagateway.com; 4 Vicary St; unpowered/powered sites $23/26, on-site vans $60-88, cabins $77-120; ☎) A neat, compact caravan park with decent facilities and a backpacker dorm.

Bookings aren't required for Maria's camping grounds (unpowered sites per d $13) at Darlington, French's Farm and Encampment Cove. Only the Darlington site has cooking facilities (gas barbecues); fires are permitted in designated fireplaces but are often banned during summer.

There are no shops on the island so BYO supplies.

❶ Getting There & Away

The **Maria Island Ferry** (☑0419 746 668; www.mariaislandferry.com.au) operates from the marina near the Triabunna visitor information centre, departing 9.30am and 4pm daily (leaving Maria Island at 10.30am and 5pm). The journey takes 40 minutes; a return ticket per adult/child/concession is $50/25/37, and bikes cost $10.

Swansea

POP 560

Founded in 1820, Swansea sits on the western sheltered shores of beautiful Great Oyster Bay with magnificent views over Freycinet Peninsula. Once another sleepy seaside village, Swansea's rise has coincided with Tasmania's tourism boom and today offers terrific B&B accommodation, good restaurants and an interesting museum.

◉ Sights

Historic Buildings HISTORIC BUILDINGS
There are many still-functioning historic buildings, including the 1860 Council Chambers (Noyes St), the 1871 Anglican Church (Noyes St) and the redbrick 1838 Morris' General Store (13 Franklin St).

Bark Mill Museum Swansea MUSEUM
(96 Tasman Hwy; adult/child $10/6; ☺9am-4pm) This excellent museum features working models of black-wattle bark processing equipment used in tanning leather, and displays on Swansea's early history, from French exploration to agriculture and industry.

FREE Heritage Centre MUSEUM
(☑03-6257 8215; 22 Franklin St; ☺9am-5pm Mon-Sat) This centre was a school in the

1860s, but now features local history exhibits and an ancient billiard table.

🛏 Sleeping

TOP CHOICE Rocky Hills Retreat   RENTAL HOUSE **$$$**

(☑1300 361 136, 0428 250 399; rockyhillsretreat.com.au; Tasman Hwy; d $400-500; 🛜) This hideaway in the hills overlooking Oyster Bay bills itself as a place for contemplation and retreat. The architecture is masterful and the remote setting has astounding panoramas over ocean and bush. Bring a loved one here for a few days: the fridge is deliciously stocked, so there's really no need to leave.

Abbotsford   B&B **$$**

(☑03-6257 9092; www.abbotsfordbb.worldstays.com; 50 Gordon St; d incl breakfast $155-195) This wonderful old stone house is one of Swansea's nicest places to stay. With three double bedrooms that share a bathroom and guest lounge, it suits couples or families travelling together.

Redcliffe House   B&B **$$**

(☑03-6257 8557; www.redcliffehouse.com.au; 13569 Tasman Hwy; s $110, d $120-170) This restored heritage farmhouse, built in 1835, is just north of town. The rooms are beautifully decorated and a guest lounge is equipped with books and a decanter of port. There's also a self-contained apartment with breakfast provisions supplied.

Tubby & Padman   B&B **$$**

(☑03-6257 8901; www.tubbyandpadman.com.au; 20 Franklin St; d $155-245; ◉) This snug Georgian cottage on Swansea's main street was once Swansea's department store, and is now a classy B&B. The thoughtfully decorated suites have spas and log fires, and come with breakfast provisions.

Swansea Backpackers   HOSTEL **$**

(☑03-6257 8650; www.swanseabackpackers.com.au; 98 Tasman Hwy; dm $28-38, d $75-85; ◉🛜) The backpackers next door to the Swansea Bark Mill has smart and spacious public areas and a shiny stainless-steel kitchen. The rooms surround a shady deck and are clean and peaceful.

Swansea Beach Chalets   CAMPGROUND **$**

(☑03-6257 8177; www.swansea-holiday.com.au; 27 Shaw St; powered sites d $25-40, cabins d $145-240; 🛜🏊) A neat, family-friendly park close to Jubilee Beach with 180-degree water vistas.

🍴 Eating

TOP CHOICE Piermont

Restaurant   MODERN AUSTRALIAN **$$$**

(☑03-6257 8131; www.piermont.com.au; Tasman Hwy; mains $32-35; ⊙dinner Thu-Tue, closed Aug) There are gorgeous vistas over Great Oyster Bay, but you will be more interested in what's on your plate. This much-awarded restaurant works magic with all that's local and fresh. As well as an innovative à la carte menu there's a fabulous five-course degustation menu ($100 with wine, $75 without).

Banc   MODERN AUSTRALIAN **$$$**

(☑03-6257 8896; cnr Franklin & Maria Sts; lunch mains $10-28, dinner mains $28-36; ⊙lunch Sun & Mon, dinner Wed-Sun) Banc showcases fresh east-coast produce in dishes like venison steak, slow-roasted suckling pig and abalone confit with fresh lime mirin. Lazy late breakfasts are served Sunday and Monday.

Kate's Berry Farm   CAFE **$**

(12 Addison St, off Tasman Hwy; teas & desserts $4-10.50; ⊙9.30am-4.30pm Nov-Apr, closed Wed-Thu May-Oct) Kate's farm, about 3km south of Swansea, has become an essential stop for east-coast tourers. It sells homemade jams, wines, sauces and divine ice cream, and has a lovely cafe serving berry-good afternoon teas.

Kabuki by the Sea   JAPANESE **$$**

(☑03-6257 8588; www.kabukibythesea.com.au; Tasman Hwy; mains $22-26; ⊙lunch daily, dinner daily Dec-Apr, Fri & Sat May-Nov) Try the marinated *una ju* (eel) or the baby east-coast abalone. Incongruously, good Devonshire teas are also available. There's also accommodation (doubles $180) here that styles itself on a Japanese *ryokan* (inn). It's 12km south of Swansea.

Swansea Bark Mill Tavern &

Bakery   PUB **$$**

(www.barkmilltavern.com.au; 96 Tasman Hwy; lunch mains $7-30, dinner mains $18-30; ⊙bakery 6am-4pm daily, tavern lunch & dinner) There are two good dining options at the Swansea Bark Mill. The bakery does cooked breakfasts until 11am, and the tavern offers great pub fare, excellent wood-fired pizzas and takeaways.

Trellis   CAFE **$$**

(26 Franklin St; mains $7-16; ⊙breakfast & lunch; 🛜) This trendy little eatery in the main street serves excellent breakfasts and cafe lunches. Out the back there's a boutique wine store that sells some of the fine east coast drops.

Coles Bay & Freycinet National Park

The spectacular 485m-high pink-orange granite outcrops known as the Hazards dominate the tiny town of Coles Bay (population 473). Brilliant Freycinet Peninsula (pronounced *fray*-sin-ay) is one of Tasmania's principal tourism drawcards, and Coles Bay exists as the gateway and service town for its national park. The peninsula's sublime white-sand beaches, secluded coves, rocky cliffs and outstanding bushwalks make it an essential visit on any east coast itinerary. Note that everything in Coles Bay is expensive, and the town is very geared towards tourism.

See www.freycinetcolesbay.com.

◉ Sights & Activities

Freycinet National Park   NATURE RESERVE
(www.parks.tas.gov.au) Sheathed in coastal heaths, orchids and wildflowers, Freycinet incorporates Freycinet Peninsula, people-free Schouten Island and the lesser-known Friendly Beaches north of Coles Bay. Black cockatoos, yellow wattlebirds, honeyeaters and Bennett's wallabies flap and bounce between the bushes. Long hikes include the two-day, 31km peninsula circuit, and shorter tracks include the up-and-over saddle climb to Wineglass Bay. Ascend the saddle as far as Wineglass Bay Lookout (one to 1½ hours return, 600 steps each way) or continue down the other side to the beach (2½ to three hours return). Alternatively, the 500m wheelchair-friendly boardwalk at Cape Tourville affords sweeping coastal panoramas and a less-strenuous glimpse of Wineglass Bay. On longer walks, sign in (and out) at the registration booth at the car park; national park fees apply.

Coles Bay Gear Hire   WATERSPORTS
(☑0419 255 604; Garnett Ave boat ramp) Hires dinghies with outboards and all safety equipment ($100/120 per two/three hours). Also rents fishing equipment (with boats or without) and can advise on good shore-based fishing spots. The friendly owner even guts and fillets your fish for you when you return. Snorkelling equipment and Canadian canoes ($55/65 per two/three hours for two people) are also available for hire.

⮑ Tours

Freycinet Adventures   KAYAKING
(☑03-6257 0500; www.freycinetadventures.com.au; 2 Freycinet Dr) Freycinet Adventures offers three-hour tours ($95) twice daily (morning and twilight – times vary seasonally) that allow you to get a glimpse of the peninsula from the water. Kayak hire is available for experienced paddlers ($55 per person per day).

Freycinet Experience   GUIDED WALK
(☑03-6223 7565, 1800 506 003; www.freycinet.com.au; ⊙Nov-May) Freycinet Experience offers a four-day, 37km, fully catered traverse of the entire peninsula ($2175). Walkers return each evening to the secluded and environmentally sensitive Friendly Beaches Lodge to enjoy gourmet meals and local wine.

All4Adventure   QUAD BIKING
(☑03-6257 0018; www.all4adventure.com.au; Coles Bay Esplanade) Get off the beaten track into parts of the national park few others access. Two-hour quad bike tours (with 30 minutes' training beforehand) depart daily at 1pm and 4.30pm (the latter only during daylight saving), costing $115. Half-day tours to the Friendly Beaches and lovely Bluestone Bay depart at 8am and cost $195. A driver's licence is essential. They also have ATV passenger vehicles for adults or kids ($65/105 two hours/half-day).

Wineglass Bay Cruises   CRUISES
(☑03-6257 0355; www.wineglassbaycruises.com.au; depart jetty on The Esplanade; ⊙Sep-May) Four-hour cruises to Wineglass Bay (adult/child $110/75) including champagne, oysters and nibbles. Look forward to dolphins, sea eagles, seals, penguins and perhaps migrating whales in the right season. Departure times vary through the year (9am midsummer and 10am shoulder season). Book several days in advance.

Long Lunch Tour Co.   FOOD & WINE
(☑03-6257 0159, 0409 225 841; www.longlunchtourco.com.au) Foodie Brad Bowden arranges gastronomic adventures of the east coast. Combine top wines, tempting morsels and berries ($130), take an afternoon wine-and-nibbles tour ($65), or travel all the way from Hobart stopping to wine and dine along the way ($220).

🛏 Sleeping

Accommodation is at a premium at Christmas, January and Easter, so book well ahead. Expect higher prices than in other parts of the state.

Eagle Peaks   APARTMENTS $$$
(☑03-6257 0444; www.eaglepeaks.com.au; 11-13 Oyster Bay Crt; d $215-350) There are two beautiful new timber and rammed-earth studios here, just south of Coles Bay. Each unit has its own kitchenette, timber deck and comfortable king-sized beds. Also rents the immaculate Beachouse (double $235 to $370, extra adult $40), sleeping four.

🏄 Freycinet Eco Retreat   APARTMENTS $$$
(☑6257 0300, 0408 504 414; www.mtpaul.com; d $250-350, minimum 2-night stay) To really get away from it all at Freycinet, retreat up to Mount Paul and these carefully crafted ecolodges with only wildlife for neighbours. Also has a standing camp with bathroom and dining room facilities for groups of eight or more

Richardsons Beach   CAMPGROUND $
(☑03-6256 7004; freycinet@parks.tas.gov.au; unpowered sites for 2/family $13/16, extra adult/child $5/2.50, powered sites $16/22, extra adult/child $7/3.50) There are pretty beachside camping spots with toilets and running water all along Richardsons Beach. Between December and after Easter, allocation of sites is by a ballot system. Download the application form on the national parks (www.parks.tas. gov.au) website or by calling the visitor centre (☑03-6256 7004). Applications must be submitted by 31 July. There's sometimes the odd tent spot left over, so it's worth calling to see if they can squeeze you in. Outside the ballot period, bookings can be made in advance at the visitor centre. National park entry fees apply.

There's superb walk-in free camping (national park fees apply) at Wineglass Bay (1½ hours from the car park), Hazards Beach (three hours), Cooks Beach (4½ hours) and Bryans Beach (5½ hours). BYO drinking water and note the park is a fuel-stove only area.

Freycinet Rentals   RENTAL HOUSES $$
(☑03-6257 0320; www.freycinetrentals.com; 5 Garnet Ave, Coles Bay) This is your hub for renting holiday cottages and beach 'shacks' in and around Coles Bay. Prices vary considerably from summer to winter and minimum

stays apply for long weekends and Christmas holidays. The modern Freycinet Beach Apartments (two nights double $440 to $600, extra person $25) at Swanwick are our favourites.

Iluka Holiday Centre   CAMPGROUND $
(☑03-6257 0115, 1800 786 512; www.ilukaholiday centre.com.au; Coles Bay Esplanade; unpowered sites for 2 $25-30, powered $35, on-site vans $65-75, cabins & units d $100-180, additional adult/child $20/15; 🐾) Iluka is a favourite with locals, so book ahead. Iluka Backpackers has six four-bed dorms ($30 per person) and just one double ($72). Discounts for YHA members.

Freycinet Getaway   RENTAL HOUSE $$
(☑0417 609 151; www.freycinetgetaway.com; 97 The Esplanade; d $135-230) Freycinet Getaway has the funky Cove Beach Apartments; two separate spaces – upstairs and downstairs – in a large wooden beachhouse, decorated in better-than-beach-house style.

Hubie's Hideaway   RENTAL HOUSE $$
(☑0427 570 344; 33 Coles Bay Esplanade; d $120-160, extra adult/child $25/15) At this cute timber cabin, you'll fall asleep to the sound of the sea. It's close to the shops and bakery and sleeps up to seven.

🍴 Eating

Madge Malloys   SEAFOOD $$$
(☑03-6257 0399; 3 Garnet Ave, Coles Bay; mains $32-35; ☺dinner Tue-Sat) Madge has her own fishing boat, reeling in your fresh-from-the-sea dinner. The fish o' the day might be poached wrasse or steam-baked bastard trumpeter. Fresh lobster, oysters and east-coast produce round out an innovative and ever-changing menu. Bookings recommended.

Seafood Munchies   SEAFOOD $$
(6 Garnet Ave, Coles Bay; meals $6-28; ☺lunch & dinner Nov-Apr, lunch May-Oct) Local seafood is well prepared for diners inside or on the deck, and for those stopping by for takeaway. Laid-back daytime cafe fare makes this a popular spot for coffee, salads, fish and chips, and classic scallop pies.

Freycinet Marine Farm   SEAFOOD $$
(1784 Coles Bay Rd; plates $14-25; ☺9am-5pm daily Sep-May, honesty system Jun-Aug) Just off the Coles Bay road is Freycinet Marine Farm, which grows huge, succulent oysters ($14 a dozen) in the tidal waters of Moulting Lagoon. Try freshly shucked oysters, mussels,

rock lobsters and abalone. BYO wine (or buy here) and enjoy a seafood picnic. In winter, put your money in the box and help yourself from the fridge.

Iluka Tavern
PUB $$

(Coles Bay Esplanade; mains $18-29; ☺lunch & dinner; ☎) This popular, friendly pub gets packed with tourists and locals. Among the reef 'n' beef and chicken parmigiana, you'll also find Thai green prawn curry and seafood linguine.

Freycinet Bakery & Café
BAKERY $

(Shop 2, Coles Bay Esplanade; meals $4-20, ☺8am-4pm; @) This bakery has fuelled many a Freycinet walking epic. Pick up pies, cakes and sandwiches here or enjoy a lazy all-day breakfast outside.

❶ Information

At the park entrance is the professionally run **Freycinet National Park Visitor Centre** (☎03-6256 7000; www.parks.tas.gov.au; Freycinet Dr; ☺8am-5pm Nov-Apr, 9am-4pm May-Oct) – pay your park fees or catch free ranger-led activities in summer.

In Coles Bay itself, jack-of-all-trades **Coles Bay Trading** (☎03-6257 0109; 1 Garnet Ave; ☺8am-6pm Mar-Nov, 7am-7pm Dec-Feb) is a general store with a post office, ATM and cafe. **Freycinet Adventures** (☎03-6257 0500; www.freycinetadventures.com; 2 Freycinet Dr) hires out essential camping equipment and also runs a water taxi service that can deliver you to Hazards Beach, Cooks Beach or Schouten Island.

❶ Getting There & Away

Bicheno Coach Service runs between Bicheno, Coles Bay and Freycinet National Park, connecting with east-coast Redline and Tassielink coaches at the Coles Bay turn-off. See p701 for details.

Bicheno
POP 640

Unlike Swansea and Coles Bay, Bicheno is still a functioning fishing port. With brilliant ocean views and lovely beaches, it's madly popular with holidaymakers, but Bicheno never sold its soul and remains rough-edged and unwashed. A busy fishing fleet still comes home to harbour in the Gulch with pots of lobsters and scaly loot. Food and accommodation prices in Bicheno are more realistic after Freycinet.

The **Bicheno visitor information centre** (☎03-6375 1500; 41b Foster St; ☺10am-4pm Mon-Fri, 10am-noon Sat, noon-4pm Sun) assists with information and accommodation.

◉ Sights & Activities

Foreshore Footway
WALKING

This 3km footway extends south from **Redbill Beach**, which has solid sandy breaks, to **Peggys Point**, the **Gulch** and along to the **Blowhole**, returning along footpaths with panoramic town views. **Whalers Hill** is the lookout from where whales were spotted in the old days. If the tide is low, you can wade over a sandy isthmus to **Diamond Island** at the northern end of Redbill Beach. Keep an eye on the tide though, so you don't get stuck on the island.

Bicheno Dive Centre
SCUBA DIVING

(☎03-6375 1138; www.bichenodive.com.au; 2 Scuba Crt; ☺9am-5pm) Hires diving equipment and organises underwater adventures. Explore the submarine caves and rock formations at **Governor Island Marine Reserve** near the Gulch.

East Coast Natureworld
NATURE RESERVE

(☎03-6375 1311; www.natureworld.com.au; adult/child $18.50/9.75; ☺9am-5pm) This is 7km north of Bicheno, and is one of Tasmania's best nature parks. Highlights include a walk-through aviary, seething snake pits. Tasmania devils and plenty of free-roaming native animals.

Douglas-Apsley National Park
NATURE RESERVE

(☎03-6256 7000; www.parks.tas.gov.au) Five kilometres north of Bicheno is the turn-off to Douglas-Apsley National Park, protecting undisturbed dry eucalypt forest, waterfalls, gorges and an abundance of birds and animals. Walk to the swimming hole at **Apsley Gorge** (two to three hours return) or to the **Apsley River Waterhole** (15 minutes return). There's basic, walk-in bush camping here, too (free, but national park fees apply).

☞ Tours

Bicheno Penguin Tours
PENGUINS

(☎03-6375 1333; www.bichenopenguintours. com.au; adult/child $25/15; ☺dusk nightly) Runs informative one-hour tours of the fairy penguin rookery at the northern end of Redbill Beach. Tours depart the surf shop in the town centre and bookings are essential.

Bicheno Glass Bottom Boat GLASS-BOTTOM BOAT
(☑03-6375 1294; the Gulch; tours adult/
child $20/5; ⊙10am, noon & 2pm) Take the
40-minute coastal tour, with lots of info
provided on the underwater world.

🛏 Sleeping & Eating

Bicheno Backpackers HOSTEL $
(☑03-6375 1651; www.bichenobackpackers.com; 11
Morrison St; dm $27-29, d $65-75) This friendly
backpackers stretches across two mural-
painted buildings. The double rooms are
quite plush (the sea-view one's the pick) and
for hire are bikes, kayaks, surfboards, boogie
boards and fishing rods.

Bicheno by the Bay CABINS $$
(☑03-6375 1171; www.bichenobythebay.com.au;
cnr Foster & Fraser Sts; 1-bedroom unit $140-175,
2-bedroom $170-210; ☒) There are 20 cabins
in a bushland setting here, some with sea
views. Facilities include an outdoor heated
pool, a tennis court and kids' playground.

Beachfront at Bicheno HOTEL $$
(☑03-6375 1111; www.beachfrontbicheno.com.au;
Tasman Hwy; d $95-160; @☒) This recently ren-
ovated property has several grades of room,
but the sea-view ones are the best. There's a
playground and a BBQ area, as well as a pub
with a bistro and a good à la carte restaurant.

Bicheno East Coast Holiday Park CAMPGROUND $
(☑03-6375 1999; www.bichenoholidaypark.com.
au; 4 Champ St; powered sites $33, d unit $95-105,
d cabin $118-138, extra person $15-25) This neat,
friendly park with plenty of green grass is
centrally located and has a BBQ, camp kitch-
en, laundry facilities and kids' playground.
Also allows showers for nonstayers ($5).

TOP CHOICE Passini's ITALIAN $$
(☑03-6375 1076; 70 Burgess St; mains $10-25;
⊙breakfast & lunch daily, dinner Mon-Sat) Pas-
sini's includes antipasto plates, focaccia and
lasagne – but oh, so much better than most.
More fancy dishes feature chargrilled polen-
ta with marinated quail and scallop ravioli
in lemongrass butter. The pastas and gnoc-
chi are homemade, and the coffee delicious.
There is a good gourmet providore, and a
handy takeaway menu, too.

Sir Loin Breier DELI $$
(57 Burgess St; ⊙9am-5pm Mon-Sat) This supe-
rior butcher's shop overflows with cooked
local crayfish, smoked trout, oysters, gour-

met pies, cheeses and smoked quail sausages. Stock up for picnics.

St Marys

POP 520

Most of the tourist traffic bypasses St Marys,
but the beautiful drive up the mountains
from the coast is very worthwhile. Just 10km
from the coast St Marys is 600m above sea
level near the St Nicholas Range. It's an unpretentious little town with weatherboard
cottages, a pub and a post office.

The **e.ScApe Tasmanian Wilderness
Café & Gallery** (☑03-6372 2444; Main Rd; @)
has information leaflets and can give walking advice. Also serves cafe meals and offers
a laundry with dryers for campers to use.

Just off the A4 Esk Hwy from St Marys
Pass, **Mariton House** (☑03-6372 2059; www.
maritonhouse.com) organises horse-riding adventures, offering a variety of trail rides, and
can organise east-coast beach rides. There's
also B&B accommodation (single/double
$95/115) available here.

🛏 Sleeping & Eating

St Marys Seaview Farm B&B $$
(☑03-6372 2341; www.seaviewfarm.com.au; Ger-
mantown Rd; dm $40, d shared facilities $75, d units
$95-110) This beef and blueberry farm is a
quiet hilltop retreat, and the kind of place
to linger a while. You'll find Seaview Farm at
the end of a dirt track 8km from St Marys –
Germantown Rd opposite St Marys Hotel.
Bring all your own food and leave the kids
(under 12) at home.

Purple Possum Wholefoods CAFE $
(5 Story St; light meals $5.50-12.95; ⊙9am-6pm
Mon-Fri, 9am-2pm Sat) An unexpected and wel-
come find, this place has homemade soups,
vegetarian wraps, and fabulous coffee and
cakes. Don't miss the rhubarb cake.

Mt Elephant Fudge CAFE $
(7 Story St; from $3; ⊙10am-5pm Mon-Fri) This
sweet spot serves up fudge in 10 different
flavours, handmade chocolates, Belgian
hot chocolate, smoothies, sundaes and
cheesecake.

THE NORTHEAST

The northeast gets relatively few travellers,
giving the region a more undeveloped and
wild feeling than the rest of the east coast.

Pretty seaside St Helens is the main centre and a good base for exploring the wildlife-rich national park, waterfalls and miles of empty coastline. Fishing opportunities abound, with a corresponding array of good seafood eateries.

See www.northeasttasmania.com.au.

ⓘ Getting There & Around

The main bus company serving the northeast is **Redline Coaches** (☑1300 360 000; www.tasredline.com.au), running daily except Saturday between Launceston and St Helens via St Marys ($31.60, 2¾ hours). Buses also run daily except Saturday from Launceston to Scottsdale ($18.20, 1¼ hours).

Tassielink (☑1300 300 520; www.tassielink.com.au) has Monday to Thursday services between Hobart and St Helens ($50.50, four hours), via the Midland Hwy connecting with **Calows Coaches** (☑03-6372 5166).

St Helens

POP 2050

Sprawling around picturesque Georges Bay, St Helens was established as a whaling town in 1830 and soon after 'swanners' came to harvest the downy under-feathers of the bay's black swans. It's long been an important fishing port and today is home to Tasmania's largest fishing fleet.

About 26km west of St Helens, turn off to tiny **Pyengana** and the feathery 90m-high **St Columba Falls**, the state's highest. Further on is **Derby**, an old tin-mining town with B&Bs, galleries and pubs.

◉ Sights & Activities

St Helens History & Visitor Information Centre MUSEUM

(☑03-6376 1744; 61 Cecilia St; admission by donation; ⊙9am-5pm) The town's history is recorded through memorabilia and photographs.

Beaches SWIMMING, WALKING

There are good swimming beaches at **Binalong Bay** (11km north on Binalong Bay Rd), **Jeanneret Beach** and **Sloop Rock** (15km north; take Binalong Bay Rd then The Gardens turn-off for both), **Stieglitz** (7km east on St Helens Point), and at **St Helens Point** and **Humbug Point**. Also on St Helens Point are the wind-weathered **Peron Dunes** (8km east).

East Lines WATERSPORTS

(☑03-6376 1720; 28 Cecilia St) Hires surfboards, wetsuits, snorkelling gear, fishing rods and bicycles. For diving, contact Bay of Fires Dive at Binalong Bay.

Big-game fishing charters in St Helens include **Keen Angler** (☑0409 964 847), **Professional Charters** (☑03-6376 3083; www.gamefish.net.au) and **Gone Fishing Charters** (☑03-6376 1553, 0419 353 041; www.breamfishing.com.au).

🛏 Sleeping & Eating

As well as St Helens Caravan Park, there are free camping sites in bushland north of St Helens at Humbug Point Nature Recreation Area. The turn-off is 7km out of town, en route to Binalong Bay. The camping area is a further 5km through the reserve, at Dora Point.

Point Break RENTAL HOUSE $$$

(☑03-6331 1224; www.pointbreakbinalong.com; 20 Beven Heights; d $200-220, extra person $40) Surely the coolest beachhouse at Binalong Bay. All timber floors, high ceilings and decked out in bright, nautical white, this beautifully furnished and well-equipped house is the place to chill with friends after a day in the surf.

Bay of Fires Character Cottages RENTAL HOUSES $$

(☑03-6376 8262; www.bayoffirescottages.com.au; 64-74 Main Rd, Binalong Bay; d $180-270) Up at Binalong Bay, these eight colourful, modern one- to three-bedroom cottages are beautifully appointed with kitchens, laundries and barbecues. Best of all are the million-dollar views from the private balconies.

St Helens Backpackers HOSTEL $

(☑03-6376 2017; www.sthelensbackpackers.com.au; 9 Cecilia St; dm $25-30, d $50-75) This hostel is spic-and-span, peaceful and spacious. The 'flashpacker' section has dorms and doubles with fancy bathrooms. Chill out on the spacious deck and BBQ the night away. Bike hire is $20 per day, and camping trips to the Bay of Fires can also be arranged.

St Helens Caravan Park CARAVAN PARK $

(☑03-6376 1290; www.sthelenscp.com.au; 2 Penelope St; unpowered sites d $28-38, powered $30-40, cabins & villas d $80-200, extra person $15; @⊚) With good, clean facilities, this park is 1km south of the town centre.

Kellraine Units APARTMENTS $

(☑03-6376 1169; 72 Tully St; d $70, extra adult/child $40/20) On the way out of town to the north, these clean, self-contained units (one with wheelchair access) are good value.

Ripple

MODERN AUSTRALIAN $$

(☑03-6376 2444; 2 Tasman Hwy; mains $7-30, ☉lunch Thu–Sun, dinner Tue–Sun) Ask St Helens locals 'What's your favourite restaurant?' and Ripple will probably be the answer. Look forward to the freshest of local produce – including plenty of seafood – transformed into meals worth lingering over.

Village Store & More Café

DELI $

(55 Cecilia St; meals $7.90-15; ☉breakfast & lunch) This little eatery serves rustic food on big wooden tables among funky decor. There are wood-fired organic breads, scrumptious breakfasts and lunch items like focaccia, roti and homemade meat pies.

Blue Shed Restaurant

SEAFOOD $$

(☑03-6376 1170; www.blueshedrestaurant.com.au; Marina Pde; mains $18-35; ☉lunch & dinner) Start with a spicy oyster shooter, and then try their signature crispy squid, or opt for grilled rock lobster with herb and mascarpone butter. They also do pizzas and takeaways.

Salty Seas

SEAFOOD $

(18 Medeas Cove Esplanade; mussels/crayfish per kg $7/50; ☉daily) Crayfish are the speciality here – choose them out of the tanks – but there are also oysters, mussels and fish fresh off the boat. Feast on their deck overlooking a bird sanctuary.

Bay of Fires

Binalong Bay Rd heads northeast from St Helens over a low tidal swamp before it makes its way to lovely Binalong Bay. This is the only permanent community at the Bay of Fires, but it's just a clutch of holiday houses, and Bay of Fires Dive (☑03-6376 8173, 0419 372 342; www.bayoffiresdive.com.au; 291 Gardens Rd). To get to the Bay of Fires proper, follow the road towards the ramshackle shack-town of The Gardens. The Bay of Fires' northern end is reached via the C843, the road to the Ansons Bay settlement and Mt William National Park.

The Bay of Fires is exquisite – powder-white sands and cerulean-blue water is backed by scrubby bush and lagoons. Despite the proliferation of signature bright-orange lichen on the rocky points and headlands, the early explorers named the bay after seeing Aboriginal fires along the shore. Ocean beaches offer reliable surfing but potentially dangerous swimming –

beware of rips and currents. The lagoons offer safe swimming.

For a deluxe wilderness experience, the Bay of Fires Walk (☑03-6391 9339; www.bayoffires.com.au; ☉Nov-May) is a fully catered four-day walk ($2150 per person) from Boulder Point south to Ansons Bay. Accommodation includes two nights at the company's magnificent ecofriendly Bay of Fires Lodge (☑03-6392 2211; www.bayoffireslodge.com.au), where you can otherwise stay for a lazy $450 per person.

There are wonderful free **camping** spots along the bay, mostly without toilets or fresh water. There are good options immediately north of Binalong Bay, accessed by road from St Helens (take the turn-off to The Gardens). In the northern reaches, there are beachfront sites at Policemans Point, reached by a turn-off before Ansons Bay.

Mt William National Park

The isolated Mt William National Park (www.parks.gov.tas.au) features long sandy beaches, low ridges and coastal heathlands. Visit during spring or early summer for blooming wildflowers. The highest point, Mt William (1½-hour return walk), stands only 216m tall, but offers great views. The area was declared a national park in 1973, primarily to protect Tasmania's remaining Forester (eastern grey) kangaroos that were nearly wiped out by disease in the 1950s and '60s. Activities include birdwatching and wildlife-spotting, fishing, swimming, surfing and diving.

At Eddystone Point is the impressive Eddystone Lighthouse, built from granite blocks in the 1890s. A small picnic spot here overlooks a beach with red granite outcrops. You can also camp at Stumpys Bay and Musselroe Top Camp. The park is well off the main roads, accessible from the north or south. The northern end is 17km from Gladstone; the southern end around 60km from St Helens. Try to avoid driving here at night when animals are bounding about.

Pipers River Region

The reason to visit this region is the wonderful vineyards.

☉ Sights & Activities

Pipers Brook

WINERY

(☑03-6382 7527; 1216 Pipers Brook Rd; ☉10am-5pm) This is the region's most famous

vineyard, where you can try Pipers Brook, Ninth Island and Krieglinger wines in an architecturally innovative building that also houses the **Winery Café** (mains from $14-25; ⊙lunch).

Jansz Wine Room WINERY
(☑03-6382 7066; 1216b Pipers Brook Rd; ⊙10am-4.30pm) Also within the Pipers Brook estate, but up a different driveway; here you can taste damn fine sparkling wine and take a self-guided tour.

Bay of Fires Wines WINERY
(☑03-6382 7622; 40 Baxters Rd, Pipers River; ⊙10am-5pm, 11am-4pm Jun-Aug) Some 15km away, south of Pipers River, and the home of prestigious Arras Sparkling and a fine Tigress Riesling.

Other local vineyards worth a visit include:

Delamere WINERY
(☑03-6382 7190; www.delamerevineyards.com. au; 4238 Bridport Rd, or B82 Hwy, Pipers Brook; ⊙10am-5pm)

Dalrymple WINERY
(☑03-6382 7222; www.dalrymplevineyards.com. au; 1337 Pipers Brook Rd; ⊙10.30am-4.30pm Fri-Sun)

LAUNCESTON

POP 71,400

Tasmania's second-largest city is an unhurried and rather diffident place, and while Hobart is more cosmopolitan, Launceston is very likeable with a remarkable stock of Victorian, Federation, Edwardian and art-deco architecture.

Launceston's beginnings, however, were anything but refined. When the Reverend Horton visited in 1822, he wrote to his superiors: 'The wickedness of the people of Launceston exceeds all description. If you could witness the ignorance, blasphemy, drunkenness, adultery and vice of every description, you would use every effort to send them more missionaries.' Launceston seems to be still emerging from its colonial-outpost roots, and buffing off some rough edges along the way, but transforming itself into a glorious historic town with a glam all its own. The University of Tasmania is here and the many great restaurants, galleries and cultural and sporting institutions testify to modern Lonnie's more cosmopolitan outlook.

The city grid is around Brisbane St Mall, which runs between Charles and St John Sts. Flanking the old seaport are a string of new eateries and a hotel. West of the city is Cataract Gorge, a rugged ravine that's one of the city's major tourist drawcards. Charles St south of the CBD is the groovy, caffeinated, bohemian strip.

See www.visitlauncestontamar.com.au for more on 'Lonnie' and the Tamar Valley wine region.

◉ Sights & Activities

Cataract Gorge PARK
(Map p668; www.launcestoncataractgorge.com. au; ⊙9am-dusk) A 10-minute walk west of the city is the fabulous Cataract Gorge. Surrounded by a wildlife reserve, near-vertical basalt cliffs crowd the banks of the South Esk River as it enters the Tamar. During the day, teens plunge into the river and rock-climbers defy gravity; at night the floodlit cliffs take on a shifty, shadow-strewn countenance.

Walking tracks on either side of the gorge lead from Kings Bridge up to **First Basin**, where there's a **swimming pool** (admission free; ⊙Nov-Mar), picnic grounds, a quality restaurant with resident peacocks, and trails leading to vista-packed lookouts. Both a suspension bridge and a **chairlift** (one-way adult/child $12/8, return $15/10; ⊙9am-dusk) sail across First Basin. A walking track (45 minutes one way) leads further up the gorge to **Second Basin** and the old Duck Reach power station. On hot summer days the gorge and swimming pool take on a beach-like scene.

FREE **Queen Victoria Museum & Art Gallery** MUSEUM
Inveresk railyards (Map p668; ☑03-6323 3777; www.qvmag.tas.gov.au; 2 Invermay Rd; ⊙10am-5pm) Royal Park (Map p670; 2 Wellington St) Launceston's wonderful museum is on two sites. The stylishly renovated industrial warehouses at Inveresk contain natural and social history and technology-focused collections, and host touring exhibitions (entrance fee). Inveresk is also home to Launceston's **Planetarium** (adult/child $5/3; ⊙2pm & 4pm Tue-Fri, 2pm & 3pm Sat).

At time of writing, the museum's 1890s Royal Park building was undergoing a meticulous renovation to reveal its original Victorian architectural glory. It was expected to reopen in late 2011, housing colonial painting and decorative arts collections.

Boag's Centre for Beer Lovers BREWERY
(Map p670; ☑03-6332 6300; www.boags.com.au; 39 William St; ☺tours 10am, 11am & 2pm Mon-Thu, 11am & 1pm Fri, tastings 1pm & 2pm Sat summer, 11am & 2pm Sat winter) Boag's beer – northern Tasmania's favourite – has been brewed on William St since 1881. Explore the brewery – and taste the beers – on tours, ranging from one hour (adult/child $18/14) to 90 minutes ($25/22).

Franklin House HISTORIC BUILDING
(413 Hobart Rd, Franklin Village; adult/child $8/free; ☺9am-5pm summer, 9am-4pm Mon-Sat winter, noon-4pm Sun) Just south of the city, Franklin House is one of Launceston's most attractive Georgian homes. Built in 1838, it's now beautifully restored, furnished and managed by the National Trust. Franklin Village–bound Metro buses 40 and 50 from the city stop here.

Design Centre of Tasmania ART GALLERY
(Map p670; www.designcentre.com.au; cnr Brisbane & Tamar Sts; ☺9.30am-5.30pm Mon-Fri, 10am-4pm Sat winter, 10am-2pm Sat summer) On the fringes of City Park, the excellent Wood Design Collection (adult/child $5/free) showcases local creations in wood, with more sassafras, Huon pine and myrtle than you can shake a stick at. There's also top-notch craftwork for sale – great for classy Tassie gifts.

National Automobile Museum of Tasmania MUSEUM
(Map p668; www.namt.com.au; 86 Cimitiere St; adult/child $10.50/6; ☺9am-5pm Sep-May, 10am-4pm Jun-Aug) Rev-heads get all revved up over the display here, one of Australia's best presentations of classic and historic cars and motorbikes. The '69 Corvette Stingray will burn tyre tracks into your retinas.

City Park PARK
Wonderful, green City Park (Map p670) has enormous oaks and plane trees, an elegant fountain, a conservatory with changing plant displays, a Victorian bandstand and a playground and mini train for kids. A glass-walled enclosure of Japanese macaques (☺8am-4pm Apr-Sep, to 4.30pm Oct-Mar), a gift from Japanese sister city Ikeda, will fascinate little ones for hours.

Tamar Island Wetlands NATURE RESERVE
(West Tamar Hwy; adult/child $3/2; ☺10am-4pm Apr-Sep, 9am-5pm Oct-Mar) A 10-minute drive north of the city, there's a 2km wheelchair-friendly boardwalk through this wetland re-

serve teeming with bird life. The island has BBQs and is perfect for picnicking.

☞ Tours

Launceston City Ghost Tours WALKING TOUR
(☑0421 819 373; www.launcestoncityghost tours.com; adult/child $25/15; ☺dusk) Spooky 90-minute tours around the city's back alleys and lanes with theatrical guides, departing the Royal Oak Hotel. Bookings are essential.

Launceston Historic Walks WALKING TOUR
(☑03-6336 2213; adult/child $15/10; ☺4pm Mon, 10am Tue-Sat) Get your historical bearings with a 1½-hour walking journey through the Georgian, Victorian and modern architecture of the city.

Mountain Bike Tasmania MOUNTAIN BIKING
(Map p670; ☑03-6334 0977; www.mountainbike tasmania.com.au; Mountain Designs, 120 Charles St) Guided rides with transport, equipment and lunch/snacks provided: Ben Lomond Descent ($175), Trevallyn Reserve ($100) or Mt Blackwood ($175).

Tamar River Cruises RIVER CRUISES
(Map p670; ☑03-6334 9900; www.tamar rivercruises.com.au; Home Point Pde) Fifty-minute Cataract Gorge cruises (adult/child $25/12), plus longer lunch, afternoon and dinner cruises.

✯ Festivals & Events

Festivale FOOD, WINE & CULTURE
(www.festivale.com.au) Three mid-February days devoted to eating, drinking, arts and entertainment, staged in City Park.

Three Peaks Race SPORTS
(www.threepeaks.org.au) Over four days in April, teams sail from Beauty Point (north of Launceston) to Hobart, pausing for runners to scale three mountains along the way.

Royal Launceston Show AGRICULTURAL SHOW
(www.launcestonshowground.com.au) Old hands display their herds in October.

⌂ Sleeping

TOP CHOICE The Charles HOTEL $$$
(Map p668; ☑033-6337 4100; www.hotelcharles. com.au; 287 Charles St; d $139-430, extra person $40; ☎) Launceston's newest and hippest hotel was once a dreary hospital. It's all light and bright now with snappy decor, intelligent service and a stylish restaurant (meals

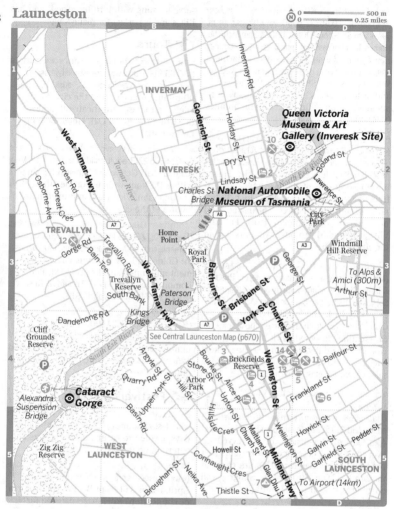

See Central Launceston Map (p670)

$8 to $33, open breakfast, lunch and dinner). The cheaper rooms are a squeeze: pay a bit more for a palatial studio.

Two Four Two

APARTMENTS $$$

(Map p668; ☑03-6331 9242; www.twofourtwo. com.au; 242 Charles St; d incl breakfast $205-230, extra adult/child $50/25) Alan the furniture maker has channelled his craft into four self-contained townhouses, each with blackwood, myrtle or Tasmanian oak detailing. Flat-screen TVs, stainless-steel kitchens, coffee machines and spa baths complete the Lonny luxe experience.

Alice's Cottages & Spa Hideaways

BOUTIQUE HOTEL $$

(Map p668; ☑03-6334 2231; www.alicescottages. com.au; 129 Balfour St; d $150-210) Alice's offers several sumptuously decorated B&B cottages, including 'Camelot' and 'The Boudoir', where it's all spas, four-post beds, open fires and self-contained privacy.

Werona

B&B $$

(Map p668; ☑03-6334 2272; www.werona.com; 33 Trevallyn Rd; d $120-230; ☎) This opulent B&B is in a Queen Anne Federation home with unsurpassed views. There are amazing decorative mouldings, *trompe l'oeil*

murals and beautiful lead-lighting. The Joan suite features a fairy-tale four-poster and private spa.

Auldington HOTEL $$$

(Map p668; ☎03-6331 2050; www.auldington.com.au; 110 Frederick St; d from $242, extra person $48; ⊛) This small private hotel has a historic exterior complete with lacy wrought-iron balconies which belies the funky, modern fit-out inside. It's plum in town in a quiet location.

⊿Arthouse Backpacker Hostel HOSTEL $

(Map p668; ☎03-6333 0222; www.arthousehostel.com.au; 20 Lindsay St; 4-/6-/8-bed dm $27/25/23, s/d $55/65; @⊛) The Arthouse has spacious, airy dorms with a wide upstairs verandah and a BBQ-ready courtyard. Hire bikes or camping equipment, and it's also set up for disabled travellers.

Airlie on the Square B&B $$

(Map p670; ☎03-6334 0577; www.airlielodge.com.au; Civic Sq; s $110, d $130-140, extra person $30; ⊛) Airlie is housed in the last of the beautiful old buildings on Civic Sq – the others were demolished to make way for 1970s and '80s concrete. Wonderfully peaceful Airlie has been thoughtfully decorated and the friendly owner serves scrumptious breakfasts.

Ashton Gate B&B $$

(Map p670; ☎03-6331 6180; www.ashtongate.com.au; 32 High St; s $115, d $140-200, cottage d $200, extra person $30; ⊛) This thoroughly welcoming Victorian B&B exudes a sense of home, and each en suite room is stylishly decorated with immaculate period taste. There's also a self-contained cottage in the Old Servants Quarters.

Kurrajong House B&B $$

(Map p670; ☎03-6331 6655; www.kurrajonghouse.com.au; cnr High & Adelaide Sts; d $130-170; ⊛) Rooms are quite sophisticated and adults-only: kids under 16 will need to stay at home. Outside there's a scented rose garden and a tranquil courtyard. Hearty cooked breakfasts are served in the conservatory.

Launceston Backpackers HOSTEL $

(Map p668; ☎03-6334 2327; www.launcestonbackpackers.com.au; 103 Canning St; 4-/6-bed dm $23/22, tw/tr $28/25, s $52, d with/without bathroom $67/58; ⊛) This backpackers is in a leafy location overlooking Brickfields Reserve, but it's not Tassie's most inspiring hostel. Rooms are clean and fresh though, and the staff are friendly and helpful.

Sportsmans Hall Hotel PUB $

(Map p668; ☎03-6331 3968; www.maskhospitality.com.au; cnr Charles & Balfour Sts; s/d from $50/75) 'Sporties' has been done up recently and the en suite rooms are pretty decent. Three have en suites and others have their own private bathrooms down the hallway. Rooms above the bar can be noisy.

Penny Royal Motel & Apartments MOTEL $$

(Map p670; ☎1800 060 954, 03-6331 6699; www.leisureinnhotels.com; 147 Paterson St; d $120-198, extra adult/child $30/15; ⊛) Originally a coaching inn in Tasmania's Midlands, this hotel was moved to its present location brick by painstaking brick. Rooms have been done up, but retain an old-world feel.

Lloyds Hotel Backpackers HOSTEL $

(Map p670; ☎1300 858 861; www.backpackers-accommodation.com.au; 23 George St; dm $32, s/d/f $58/75/128) Lloyds stakes a claim as Launceston's most happening pub.

Central Launceston

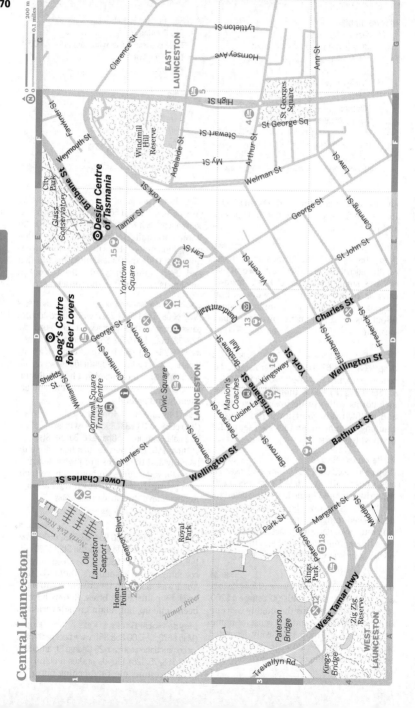

TASMANIA LAUNCESTON

EAST LAUNCESTON

LAUNCESTON

WEST LAUNCESTON

◎ Design Centre of Tasmania

◎ Boag's Centre for Beer Lovers

Brisbane St

Charles St

York St

Wellington St

Bathurst St

Lower Charles St

Wellington St

West Tamar Hwy

Tamar River

Trevallyn Rd

Paterson Bridge

Kings Bridge

Zig Zig Reserve

Kings Park

Royal Park

Old Launceston Seaport

North Esk River

Home Point

Seaport Blvd

Cornwall Square Transit Centre

Civic Square

Yorktown Square

Windmill Hill Reserve

City Park

Glass Conservatory

Quadrant Mall

Brisbane Mall

Cuisine La

Manion's Coaches

St Georges Square

St George Sq

Weymouth St
Wellington St
Shields St
Charles St
William St
Cimitiere St
George St
Cameron St
Paterson St
Barrow St
Margaret St
Madie St
Park St
York St
Kingsway
Elizabeth St
Frederick St
Cammery St
Brisbane St
Vincent St
Earl St
Tamar St
York St
Adelaide St
My St
Arthur St
Stewart St
Welman St
George St
St John St
Law St
Welman St
Clarence St
Lyttleton St
Hornsey Ave
Ann St
High St
St George Sq

200 m
0.1 miles

⊙ Design Centre of Tasmania
⊙ Boag's Centre for Beer Lovers

Downstairs the place goes nuts, but above things remain relatively calm, with clean en-suite rooms.

Treasure Island Caravan Park   CAMPGROUND $
(off Map p668; ☑03-6344 2600; treasureisland launceston@netspace.net.au; 94 Glen Dhu St; unpowered sites s/d $22/25, powered $30, on-site vans $58, cabins $85-95) Just 2.5km from the city, there are camping and caravan spots. Facilities include a kids playground, campers kitchen and laundry.

✕ Eating

⌂TOP CHOICE Stillwater   MODERN AUSTRALIAN $$$
(Map p670; ☑03-6331 4153; www.stillwater.net.au; Ritchie's Mill, 2 Bridge Rd; breakfast $8-21, lunch $15-29, dinner $34-39; ⊘breakfast & lunch daily, dinner Mon-Sat) Set in the stylishly renovated 1840s Ritchie's Flour Mill beside the Tamar, Stillwater does laid-back breakfasts, relaxed lunches – and then puts on the Ritz for dinner. There are delectable seafood, meaty and vegetarian mains and the emphasis is on locally sourced produce.

Black Cow   STEAKHOUSE $$$
(Map p670; ☑03-6331 9333; www.blackcowbistro. com.au; 70 George St; dinner mains $29-37) This high-class bistro/steakhouse specialises in Tasmanian free-range, grass-fed beef. They offer six different melt-in-the-mouth cuts and are Tassie's best steakhouse. Try the ten-

der eye fillet with Black Cow butter or the very special truffle Bernaise sauce.

Pierre's   FRENCH $$
(Map p670; ☑03-6331 6835; www.pierres.net.au; 88 George St; lunch mains $18-25, dinner mains $20-35; ⊘breakfast & lunch Mon-Sat, dinner Tue-Sat) Coolly done up in dark leather with low lighting, Pierre's offers Gallic classics like steak tartare and fries, grilled quail and confit duck. Stylish, relaxed and welcoming.

Mud   MODERN AUSTRALIAN $$
(Map p670; www.mudbar.com.au; 28 Seaport Blvd; lunch mains $14-28, dinner mains $16-38; ⊘breakfast Sat & Sun, lunch & dinner daily) Hang out on the cool leather sofas at the bar, then migrate to the tables for sophisticated Italian-influenced cuisine. There is a bar snack menu from midday and they do lazy breakfasts on weekends.

tant pour tant   CAFE $
(Map p668; 226 Charles St; items $5-13; ⊘7.30am-5pm Mon-Fri, 8.30am-3pm Sat & Sun) This wonderful French patisserie serves artisan and organic breads, and a jaw-dropping range of croissants, cakes and pastries. Breakfasts and light lunches also.

Blue Café Bar   CAFE $$
(Map p668; www.bluecafebar.com.au; Inveresk Railyards; lunch mains $13-27, dinner $18-31; ⊘breakfast & lunch daily, dinner Tue-Sat) This stylish eatery serves awesome coffee and scrumptious local/organic produce to an arty, young

crowd. On Wednesday nights try $14 wood-fired pizzas.

Elaia
MEDITERRANEAN **$$**

(Map p668; www.elaia.com.au; 240 Charles St; mains dinner $15-27; ⊘breakfast, lunch & dinner; 🕾) This Mediterranean eatery does inventive pizzas, delicious pastas and risottos, steaks and good salads. Occupy the soft leather wall benches for all-day breakfast or coffee and cake.

Fresh
CAFE **$**

(Map p670; 178 Charles St; mains $8-16; ⊘breakfast & lunch daily, dinner Fri; 🖉) Retro-arty Fresh offers an all-vegetarian/vegan menu that's both deliciously tempting and environmentally aware. It does energising breakfasts, linger-over lunches, and coffees and cakes in between.

Pasta Merchant
ITALIAN **$**

(Map p668; 248 Charles St; mains $8-12) There's wonderful fresh pasta here with lashings of mouth-watering sauces: try the unbeatable spinach and ricotta ravioli with homemade pesto. They also serve panini, pizza and real gelati in 12 flavours. You can buy pasta and sauces to take away.

Café Culture
CAFE **$$**

(Map p668; 1-3 Osborne Ave; mains $14-24; ⊘breakfast & lunch daily, dinner Fri) This little foodie enclave does organic as much as possible, fair-trade coffee, delicious breakfasts and man-sized meals. Next door, the Trevallyn Deli Grocer offers supplies for a gourmet picnic hamper.

Burger Got Soul
BURGERS **$**

(Map p668; 243 Charles St; burgers $9.90-14; ⊘lunch & dinner) Best burgers in Launceston, served in a funky atmosphere. It's healthy too: good, lean meat, the freshest bread and crunchy salads. There are Soul Veggie Burgers for non meat-eaters.

Drinking & Entertainment

Royal Oak Hotel
PUB

(Map p670; 14 Brisbane St) Hands-down Launceston's best pub – grungy, friendly and convivial with stacks of beers on tap, open mic nights (the last Wednesday of the month) and live acoustic rock Wednesday to Sunday. Decent pub meals and a kids' menu.

Irish Murphy's
PUB

(Map p670; 211 Brisbane St) A friendly watering hole with live music every night

(usually free), including Sunday arvo jam sessions.

Hotel New York
PUB

(Map p670; www.hotelnewyork.net.au; 122 York St; nightclub $5-7; ⊘3pm-midnight Mon-Wed, 2pm-5.30am Thu-Sat) This pub hosts a steady stream of local and interstate acoustic and full-blown rock acts, plus DJs in Reality nightclub out the back (Thursday to Saturday from 11pm).

Princess Theatre
THEATRE

(Map p670; ☑03-6323 3666; www.theatrenorth.com.au; 57 Brisbane St) Built in 1911 and incorporating the smaller Earl Arts Centre, the Princess stages an eclectic mix of local and mainland drama, dance and comedy acts.

Village Cinemas
CINEMA

(Map p670; ☑1300 555 400; www.village cinemas.com.au; 163 Brisbane St; tickets adult/child $15.50/11) Screens mainstream Hollywood fodder. On Tuesdays all sessions cost $10.

🔒 Shopping

Alps & Amici
FOOD

TOP CHOICE

(off Map p668; www.alpsandamici.com; cnr Abbott & Arthur Sts) Esteemed chef Daniel Alps has set up this smart providore where you can buy his restaurant-quality meals to take away, classy cakes, cheeses, meats and seafood, the freshest fruit and veg, and Tasmanian beer and wine.

Mill Providore + Gallery
FOOD

(Map p670; Ritchie's Mill, 2 Bridge Rd) Above Stillwater Restaurant in the Ritchie's Mill complex, you'll find this treasure-trove of everything for the home, kitchen, stomach and soul. There's a brilliant delicatessen and chocolatier for picnic goodies.

Pinot Shop
WINE

(Map p670; 135 Paterson St) This boutique bottle-o specialises in Pinot Noirs and fine wines – particularly of the Tasmanian variety. It also does premium international and 'big-island' vintages.

ℹ Information

Banks and ATMs are located on St John and Brisbane Sts near the mall. There are post offices on St John and Cameron Sts.

Cyber King (113 George St; per hr $6; ⊘9.30am-7pm Mon-Fri, 9.30am-4.30pm Sat & Sun) Internet access.

Launceston visitor information centre (Map p670; ☑1800 651 827, 03-6336 3133; www. visitlauncestontamar.com.au; cnr St John & Cimitiere Sts; ☉9am-5pm Mon-Fri, 9am-3pm Sat, 9am-noon Sun & public holidays) Statewide accommodation, tour and transport bookings.

❶ Getting There & Away

Air

There are regular direct flights between Launceston and Melbourne, Sydney and Brisbane (see p640).

Bus

Redline Coaches (☑1300 360 000; www. tasredline.com.au) and **Tassielink** (☑1300 300 520; www.tassielink.com.au) depart Launceston from the **Cornwall Square Transit Centre** (cnr St John & Cimitiere Sts), just behind the visitor information centre. **Manion's Coaches** (☑03-6383 1221; manions.coaches@tassie.net. au; 168 Brisbane St) has services that run from Launceston up the West Tamar Valley (see Getting There & Around, p701).

Redline: Main fares and routes:

JOURNEY	PRICE ($)	DURATION (HR)
Launceston-Burnie	37	2¼
Launceston-Deloraine	14	¾
Launceston-Devonport	24	1½
Launceston-George Town	12	¾
Launceston-Hobart	39	2½
Launceston-Stanley	58	4

Tassielink: Main fares and routes:

JOURNEY	PRICE ($)	DURATION (HR)
Launceston-Bicheno	34	2½
Launceston–Cradle Mountain	59	3
Launceston–Devonport (meeting ferries)	24	1¼
Launceston–Hobart	34	2½
Launceston–Queenstown	72	6
Launceston–Sheffield	30	2
Launceston–Strahan	82	8¾

❶ Getting Around

To/From the Airport

Launceston airport is 15km south of town. **The Airporter** (☑03-6343 6677; adult/child $14/7) is a door-to-door airport shuttle bus. A taxi to/ from the city costs about $40.

Bicycle

Arthouse Backpacker Hostel (p669) rents out bikes on an hourly and daily basis.

Bus

Metro (☑13 22 01; www.metrotas.com.au) has a Day Rover pass (adult/concession $4.50/3) for unlimited travel after 9am. Buses depart from the two blocks of St John St between Paterson and York Sts. Many routes don't operate in the evening or on Sundays.

There's also a free Tiger Bus that links Inveresk to Princes Park and Windmill Hill Monday to Friday between 10am and 3.30pm.

Car

The big-name rental companies have either Launceston airport or city offices. Smaller operators with cars from around $40 per day:

Freedom Rent-A-Car (☑0409 933 618; www. freedomrentacar.com.au) Free delivery to airport or city.

Lo-Cost Auto Rent (☑1300 883 739; www. rentforless.com.au; 80 Tamar St)

AROUND LAUNCESTON

Tamar Valley

The broad Tamar River flows north 64km from Launceston and empties into Bass Strait. Along its flanks are orchards, forests, pastures and vineyards.

The **Tamar visitor information centre** (☑1800 637 989, 03-6394 4454; www.tamarvalley. com.au; Main Rd, Exeter; ☉8.30am-5pm) is in Exeter in the West Tamar Valley.

This is Tasmania's key wine-producing area, and the premium wines created here have achieved international recognition. See **Tamar Valley Wine Route** (www.tamar valleywines.com.au) for touring information.

❶ Getting There & Around

For cyclists, the ride north along the Tamar River is a gem.

On weekdays **Manion's Coaches** (☑03-6383 1221; www.manionscoaches.com.au; 72 Shore St, Beaconsfield) services the West Tamar Valley from Launceston.

Lees coaches (☑03-6334 7979; www. leescoaches.com) services the East Tamar from Launceston's Cornwall Square Transit Centre.

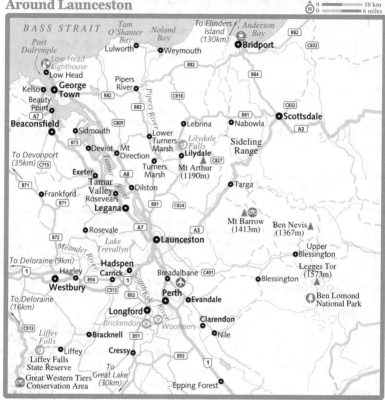

ROSEVEARS
POP 270

This pretty little riverside hamlet is on a side road off the West Tamar Hwy. With some super wineries in the area, this is wine-buff heaven.

Call into **Ninth Island Vineyard Strathlynn** (www.kreglingerwineestates.com; 95 Rosevears Dr; ⊙10am-5pm), an outlet for Pipers Brook Vineyard (see p665), and home to the highly polished restaurant **Strathlynn** (mains $25-35; ⊙lunch), one of Tassie's best restaurants, and with the bonus of beautiful river views.

Back on the main road, follow the signs to **Rosevears Estate** (☎03-6330 1800; www. rosevears.com.au; 1a Waldhorn Dr; ⊙10am-5pm). Rosevears' has a stylish **bistro** (mains $22-32; ⊙lunch), and there are plush self-contained **cottages** (1- & 2-bedroom cottages $150-350).

Built in 1831, **Rosevears Waterfront Tavern** (215 Rosevears Dr; mains $20-25; ⊙lunch & dinner) does creative spins on pub-grub

favourites. Try the chicken parmigiana with honey and macadamia nuts.

BEAUTY POINT & AROUND
POP 1500

At Beauty Point is the coo-inducing **Seahorse World** (☎03-6383 4111; www.seahorse world.com.au; Inspection Head Wharf; adult/child $20/9; ⊙9.30am-4.30pm Sep-Apr, 10am-3pm May-Aug), where the cute sea horses are hatched and raised to supply aquariums worldwide. There is a good cafe with river views.

Next door is **Platypus House** (☎03-6383 4884; www.platypushouse.com.au; Inspection Head Wharf; adult/child $20/9; ⊙9.30am-3.30pm), a wildlife centre with platypuses and echidnas.

South of Beauty Point is **Beaconsfield**, the gold-mining town that made world news after a mine collapse and rescue in April 2006. At the mine is the **Beaconsfield Mine & Heritage Museum** (www.beaconsfield heritage.com.au; West St; adult/child $11/4;

9.30am-4.30pm), detailing mining history through interactive exhibits.

Visit all the above attractions with a Triple Pass (adult/family $43/115) from the Tamar visitor information centre.

In Beauty Point, Tamar Cove (☑03-6383 4375; www.tamarcove.com; 4421 Main Rd, Beauty Point; d $119-148; mains $12-24; 🛜⏹) has a stylish motel and terrific restaurant. Try the seafood chowder.

Beauty Point Tourist Park (☑03-6383 4536; www.beautypointtouristpark.com.au; 36 West Arm Rd, Beauty Point; powered sites $29, on-site vans d $89, cabins $99-199; 🛜) offers sheltered camping on the waterfront and a range of vans and cabins.

GEORGE TOWN
POP 4270

Historic George Town, on the eastern lip of the Tamar river mouth, is Australia's third-oldest settlement (after Sydney and Hobart). George Town was established in 1804 by Lieutenant Colonel Paterson to guard against the French who were reconnoitring the area. Sadly, little remains of the original township (now defined by an aluminium smelter). The visitor information centre (☑03-6382 1700; Main Rd; ⊙9am-5pm) has the local low-down.

The Pier Hotel (☑03-6382 1300; www.pier hotel.com.au; 5 Elizabeth St; d $155-180; 🛜) offers self-contained villas (sleeping four), spotless motel rooms and a beery bistro (mains $18-30; ⊙breakfast, lunch & dinner) with outdoor riverfront seating and a decent menu.

LOW HEAD
POP 465

Low Head, sitting on a sandy spit, is north of George Town and virtually contiguous with it. It's much more attractive than George Town – a beachy holiday town centred on the Low Head Historic Precinct.

Helping ships navigate into the Tamar, Low Head Pilot Station is Australia's oldest (1805) and houses an interesting maritime museum (☑03-6382 2826; Low Head Rd; adult/child $5/3; ⊙10am-4pm) cluttered with historical items and displays. There's also colonial cottage accommodation here in the 1860s Pilot's Row (☑03-6382 2826; Low Head Rd; d from $120).

On Low Head itself, the view from the 1888 lighthouse is a winner. Penguins return to their burrows here every night, and can be viewed with Low Head Penguin Tours (☑0418 361 860; www.penguintours.low head.com; adult/child $16/10; ⊙dusk). There's

good surf at East Beach on Bass Strait, and safe swimming in the river.

Low Head Tourist Park (☑03-6382 1573; www.lowheadtouristpark.com.au; 136 Low Head Rd; unpowered/powered sites $22/27.50, cabins $80, cottages $95) on the river has comfortable timber-lined cabins as well as caravan and camping spots – water views included.

Longford & Around

Longford (population 3030), a National Trust–classified town 27km south of Launceston, hosted the 1965 Australian Grand Prix. You wouldn't think it now – the cars are gone – but the area is noted for its historic estates.

Unesco World Heritage–listed Woolmers (☑03-6391 2230; www.woolmers.com.au; Woolmers Lane, Longford; adult/child from $20/7; ⊙9.30am-4.30pm Oct-May, 10am-4pm Jun-Sep, tours 11.15am, 12.30pm, 2pm & 3.30pm) was built in 1819 and features a 2-hectare rose garden and buildings full of antiques.

Nearby is Brickendon (☑03-6391 1383; www.brickendon.com.au; Woolmers Lane, Longford; adult/child $12/4.50; ⊙9.30am-5pm Tue-Sun, closed Jul & Aug), a more modest estate dating from 1824, with heritage gardens and a still-functioning farm village. Both offer self-contained accommodation in restored colonial-era cottages (d $120-178).

Around 10km west of Longford is the gorgeous Liffey Valley. It's well worth a short detour to explore the Liffey Falls State Reserve.

Grand, government-owned 1819 Entally Estate (www.entally.com.au; Old Bass Hwy, Hadspen; adult/child $10/8; ⊙10am-4pm), set in beautiful grounds, is the highlight of Hadspen, 15km north of Longford.

🛏 Sleeping & Eating

Racecourse Inn   INN $$
(☑03-6391 2352; www.racecourseinn.com; 114 Marlborough St, Longford; d $65-210; 🛜) A welcoming restored Georgian inn with antique-decorated rooms, and guests can dine in the restaurant.

JJ's Bakery & Old Mill Café   CAFE $$
(52 Wellington St, Longford; mains $10-20; ⊙7am-5.30pm Mon-Fri, to 5pm Sat & Sun) In the Old Emerald flour mill, this place turns out pizzas and splendid baked goods.

Red Feather Inn INN $$$

(📞03-6393 6506; www.redfeatherinn.com.au; 42 Main St, Hadspen; d incl breakfast $295-450) One of Tasmania's best boutique hotels. You can eat dinner here if you stay (three courses, $85 per person). Private classes can be arranged on request in the on-site cooking school, or you can join one of their regular courses.

Evandale

POP 1060

Of all Tasmania's historic towns, immaculately preserved Evandale is one of the best. It's around 20km south of Launceston in the South Esk Valley. The Evandale Market (⊙9am-1pm) happens every Sunday, and the visitor information centre (📞03-6391 8128; 18 High St; ⊙9am-5pm Oct-Apr, 10am-4pm May-Sep; @) can book local B&Bs.

The highlight of the annual Evandale Village Fair & National Penny Farthing Championships (www.evandalevillagefair.com; adult/child $7/free; ⊙Feb) is the Penny Farthing races, cheered on by townsfolk in historic dress.

Around 11km south of Evandale, is the National Trust–listed Clarendon Homestead (234 Clarendon Station Rd; adult/child $10/free; ⊙10am-4pm), a grand neoclassical mansion (1838) surrounded by impressive parklands.

🛏 Sleeping & Eating

Clarendon Arms Hotel PUB $

(📞03-6391 8181; 11 Russell St; s/d without bathroom $45/80) A classic country pub with good-value bistro meals, basic accommodation and a leafy beer garden.

Wesleyan Chapel B&B $$

(📞03-6331 9337; www.windmillhilllodge.com.au; 28 Russell St; d incl breakfast $115-125) Built in 1836, tiny Wesleyan has a chequered past but is now stylish accommodation for two.

Ingleside Bakery Café CAFE $

(4 Russell St; mains $9-20; ⊙10am-5pm daily, plus 6-8pm Fri & Sat) Serves all-day breakfasts and light lunches amid local art and antiques.

Ben Lomond National Park

Tassie's most reliable snow sports centre is this 165-sq-km park (www.parks.tas.gov.au), 55km southeast of Launceston. Bushwalkers traipse through when the snow melts,

swooning over alpine wildflowers during spring and summer.

See www.ben-lomond.com; national park fees apply.

🛏 Sleeping & Eating

Creek Inn PUB $$

(📞03-6390 6199; d summer/winter $110/200) Stay here year-round at Tasmania's highest-altitude pub. There's a fully licensed restaurant and, during ski season (July to September), a kiosk and ski shop. Lift tickets cost adult/child $55/230 per day; ski hire (including lift ticket) is adult/child $120/75.

❶ Getting There & Away

During the ski season, **McDermott's Coaches** (📞03-6394 3535; www.mcdermotts.com.au) depart Launceston at 8am and ascend the mountain, returning at 4pm. Outside the ski season, driving is your only option. The route up to the alpine village includes Jacob's Ladder, a ludicrously steep ascent on an unsealed hairpin-bend road – drive slowly, and fit snow chains in winter.

THE NORTH

Tasmania's North is a region of populated seaside towns and the vast open reaches and hillside communities of the Great Western Tiers. Much of this area is extensively cultivated – rust-coloured, iron-rich soils and verdant pastures extend north and west of Launceston – but there are also important stands of forest, glacial valleys, dolerite peaks and mighty rivers. Get off the main highway and explore the quiet minor roads and towns.

❶ Getting There & Around

Redline Coaches (📞1300 360 000; www.tasredline.com.au) has several northern services daily.

JOURNEY	PRICE ($)	DURATION (HR)
Launceston-Burnie	37	2¾
Launceston-Deloraine	14	¾
Launceston-Devonport	24	1½
Launceston-Penguin	35	2¼
Launceston-Ulverstone	30	2

Tassielink (📞1300 300 520; www.tassielink.com.au) runs the daily Main Road Express to meet the Bass Strait ferry – an early morning express bus runs from Devonport to Launceston and Hobart, returning in the opposite direction

in the afternoon to meet evening boat departures. Typical one-way fares:

JOURNEY	PRICE ($)	DURATION (HR)
Devonport-Cradle Mountain	41	1½
Devonport-Hobart	57	4¼
Devonport-Launceston	24	1¼
Devonport-Sheffield	5	½
Devonport-Strahan	64	7¼

Devonport

POP 24,300

Devonport is Tasmania's third-largest city, but it is much less interesting than Hobart and Launceston. The *Spirit of Tasmania* Bass Strait ferry arrives from Melbourne every morning (and evening in summer). Outside the low-level excitement of the arrival of the ferry, Devonport remains a slow-moving place.

Sights & Activities

Mersey Bluff   LANDMARK
Lighthouse-topped Mersey Bluff is the most striking feature of Devonport. The red-and-white-striped lighthouse was built in 1889 to aid navigation into the expanding port, which still handles agricultural produce from northern Tasmania.

Tiagarra   MUSEUM
(Bluff Rd; adult/child $10/5; ⊙9am-5pm Mon-Fri, 10am-4pm Sat) The absorbing displays here tell the story of Aboriginal culture in Tasmania from the time humans first crossed over the land bridge that's now under Bass Strait. There's a soberingly frank assessment of the decimation of Aboriginal society and culture at the time of European invasion. Outside, you can follow a trail around the headland to see Aboriginal rock carvings (petroglyphs); some are more than 10,000 years old.

House of Anvers   CHOCOLATE FACTORY
(www.anvers-chocolate.com.au; 9025 Bass Hwy, Latrobe; ⊙7am-7pm) House of Anvers is a chocolate factory and a museum of chocolate. Look forward to fudges, truffles and amazing chocolate-orange slices. Come for a *pain au chocolat* (croissant) washed down with a superb hot chocolate. It's 8km southeast of town on the Bass Hwy.

Devonport Maritime Museum   MUSEUM
(6 Gloucester Ave; adult/child $5/2; ⊙10am-4.30pm Tue-Sun Oct-Mar, closes 4pm Apr-Sep) This museum is in the former harbourmaster's residence (c 1920) and pilot station near the foreshore. It has model boats from the ages of sail through steam to the present seagoing passenger ferries.

Don River Railway   MUSEUM
(www.donriverrailway.com.au; Forth Main Rd; adult/child $17/12; ⊙9am-5pm) This railway is 4km west of town, just off the Bass Hwy. The entry price includes a half-hour ride in a diesel train (between 10am and 4pm), and you can hop on the puffing steam train on Sundays and public holidays.

FREE Devonport Regional Gallery   ART GALLERY
(45-47 Stewart St; ⊙10am-5pm Mon-Fri, noon-5pm Sat, 1-5pm Sun) This excellent gallery houses predominantly 20th-century Tasmanian paintings, contemporary art by local and mainland artists, plus ceramics and glasswork.

Sleeping

Cameo Cottage   RENTAL HOUSE $$
(☎03-6427 0991, 0439 658 503; www.devonportbedandbreakfast.com; 27 Victoria Pde; d $140-160, extra adult/child $35/25) This ultra-neat two-bedroom cottage was built in 1914, but is now beautifully redecorated and thoroughly up-to-date. It's got a well-equipped kitchen, cosy lounge, a laundry, and a quiet garden where you can cook up a storm on the BBQ.

3 George St   B&B $$
(☎0400 637 199; www.threegeorgestreet.com.au; 3 George St; s/d $120/140) This pleasant B&B is set in a pretty 1910 home just a street back from the Devonport waterfront. You'll receive a friendly local welcome, but also peace and privacy in your own well-furnished suite. There's a guest lounge and a kitchen to share.

Tasman Backpackers   HOSTEL $
(☎03-6423 2335; www.tasmanbackpackers.com.au; 114 Tasman St; dm/tw/d $20/50/52; @) This hostel was once a sprawling nurses quarters but it's now a friendly place to stay with an international feel. They offer free ferry/bus station pick-ups, and can arrange fruit-picking jobs.

Mersey Bluff Caravan Park   CAMPGROUND $
(☎03-6424 8655; www.merseybluff.com.au; 41 Bluff Rd; unpowered/powered sites d $12/28, on-site vans

d $90) In a seaside setting on Mersey Bluff, this pleasantly treed park is just steps from the beach. There's a campers kitchen and BBQ facilities. Eco-cabins were in the pipeline at time of writing.

Hawleys Gingerbread House　　HOSTEL $
(☑03-6427 0477; www.gingerbreadhousehotel; 71 Wright St; dm $24; ☎) Just 100m from the ferry, this basic backpackers is housed in a rather ramshackle heritage home. They serve hearty meals in the restaurant below (mains $15 to $30, open lunch and dinner Wednesday to Sunday).

Eating

Tapas Lounge Bar　　CAFE $$
(www.tapasloungebar.com; 97a Rooke St Mall; tapas $9.50; ⊙4.30pm-late Wed-Fri, lunch Sat & Sun, dinner Wed-Sun) Everyone's talking about this cool new place upstairs in the Rooke St Mall. It's all done up in black leather, has funky music, and the tapas-style menu also has options for kids. After 9pm it morphs into a bar for over 25s with live music Friday to Sunday.

Renusha's　　INDIAN, ITALIAN $$
(132 William St; mains $15-19.50; ⊙lunch Wed-Fri, dinner Tue-Sun) Indian curries and Italian pasta are definitely an odd mix, but Renusha's achieves the combination with confidence. It has a strong local reputation for being consistently good.

Stonies Fifties Café　　CAFE $
(77 Rooke St; meals $8-18; ⊙breakfast & lunch Mon-Sat) Choose from hearty all-day breakfasts or robust burgers. Try the Chubby Cheeser, but try not to choke on the occasional bad pun. The coffee is good too, with 18 different brews all named after 1950s music stars. Espresso fans should order a 'Little Richard'.

Bento　　JAPANESE $
(5 Rooke St; mains $3-17.50; ⊙lunch & dinner) Economically priced (finger food from $3) this place offers lacquered bento box meals including a bento banquet ($17.50), with unlimited miso, an unlimited hot dish and Japanese-style ice cream.

All Things Nice　　BAKERY $
(175 Tarleton St; ⊙24hr) Located near the ferry terminal with bakery items including gourmet chunky pies, scallop pies, cakes, sweets and a good strong cuppa.

⚲ Drinking & Entertainment

Central at the Formby　　BAR
(82 Formby Rd; ⊙3pm-midnight Wed, 3pm-1am Thu & Fri, 1pm-1am Sat, 1-9pm Sun, closed Mon & Tue) Devonport's best bar is all flash with leather sofas and laid-back cool, and they fold the concertina windows open onto the river on warm nights. There are live bands Fridays and Saturdays; Sunday afternoons see acoustic sessions and a more sophisticated crowd.

❶ Information

Devonport visitor information centre (☑03-6424 4466; www.devonporttasmania.travel; 92 Formby Rd; ⊙7.30am-5pm) Across the river from the ferry terminal, it opens to meet ferry arrivals. Free baggage storage is available here.

Online Access Centre (21 Oldaker St; ⊙9.30am-5.30pm Mon-Thu, 9.30am-7pm Fri, 9.30am-1.30pm Sat, 11am-5pm Sun; @) Internet access at the library.

❶ Getting There & Away

Air

QantasLink (☑13 13 13) Has regular flights to Melbourne.

Tasair (☑1800 062 900, 03-6248 5088; www.tasair.com.au) To Hobart and King Island.

Boat

Spirit of Tasmania (☑1800 634 906, 13 20 10; www.spiritoftasmania.com.au; ⊙phone bookings 6.30am-9.30pm) Ferries sail between Station Pier in Melbourne and the ferry terminal on the Esplanade in East Devonport. For details of services, see p678.

Bus

See p701 for details on **Redline Coaches** (☑1300 360 000; www.tasredline.com.au) and **Tassielink** (☑1300 300 520; www.tassielink.com.au) services between Launceston and Devonport. Tassielink also runs from Devonport to Cradle Mountain, and from Devonport to Burnie, continuing to the west coast (Zeehan, Strahan, Queenstown etc).

The Redline Coaches stop at Edward St and the ferry terminal. Tassielink coaches stop outside the Devonport visitor information centre and the ferry terminal.

❶ Getting Around

Devonport airport is 5km east of town. A **shuttle bus** (☑1300 659 878; per person $15) runs between the airport and ferry terminals, the visitor information centre and city accommodation; bookings are essential. A **taxi** (☑03-6424 1431) to/from the airport costs about $20.

A cross-Mersey ferry operates between a pontoon near the post office and the *Spirit of Tasmania* terminal. It runs on demand 7.30am to 6pm Monday to Saturday ($2.50 one-way).

For car rental:

Europcar (☑03-6427 0888; www.europcar.com.au) At the ferry terminal.

Lo-Cost Auto Rent (☑03-6427 0796; www.locostautorent.com; 5 Murray St, East Devonport) With older cars from $40 per day.

Thrifty (☑1800 030 730, 03-6427 9119; www.thrifty.com.au) At the ferry terminal.

Deloraine

POP 2240

Deloraine, at the foot of the Great Western Tiers, is an artsy rural town of fine Georgian and Victorian buildings set on the tumbling hills around the handsome Meander River. Public sculptures and huge European trees are a feature of the main street, as are Deloraine's groovy eateries, galleries and interesting bric-a-brac stores. The annual four-day Tasmanian Craft Fair (www.tascraftfair.com.au; ☺late Oct) sees visitors book out accommodation from Launceston to Devonport for the festivities.

The Great Western Tiers visitor information centre (☑03-6362 5280; www.greatwesterntiers.net.au; 98 Emu Bay Rd; ☺9am-5pm) handles accommodation bookings, and advises on many excellent walks in the area.

◎ Sights

Deloraine Folk Museum & YARNS: Artwork in Silk
MUSEUM
(98 Emu Bay Rd; adult/child $8/2; ☺9.30am-4pm) The museum's centrepiece is an exquisite four-panel, quilted and appliquéd depiction of the Meander Valley through a year of seasonal change. Each of the four panels entailed 2500 hours of labour and the whole project took three years to complete. It's now housed in a purpose-built auditorium, where you can witness a fascinating presentation explaining the work.

Ashgrove Farm Cheese
DAIRY
(www.ashgrovecheese.com.au; 6173 Bass Hwy, Elizabeth Town; ☺7am-6pm summer, 7.30am-5.30pm winter) Journey 15km north of Deloraine to find this award-winning cheese factory. You can watch the cheeses being made and then sample the fine results in their tasting room/providore.

✍ 41° South Aquaculture
FARM
(www.41southtasmania.com; 323 Montana Rd; ☺9am-5pm Nov-Mar, 9am-4pm Apr-Oct) Stop by for smoked salmon, which you can taste (free) and buy in the tasting room, or lunch on in the cafe. Self-guided tours of the interesting operation cost adult/child $10/5. It's 6km out of town towards Mole Creek (signed down Montana Rd).

🛏 Sleeping & Eating

Calstock
HOTEL $$$
(☑03-6362 2642; www.peppers.com.au/calstock; Lake Hwy; d $325-495; 🐾) Just south of Deloraine, parklike grounds surround a Georgian mansion housing a much-awarded boutique hotel. There are seven bedrooms (one wheelchair accessible) and two suites decorated in French provincial style, as well as grand lounges, gourmet breakfasts and a three-course set menu dinner ($90) by arrangement. Leave the kids (under 13) at home.

Bluestone Grainstore
B&B $$
(☑03-6362 4722; www.bluestonegrainstore.com.au; 14 Parsonage St; d $150, extra person $50; 🐾) A 150-year-old warehouse has been renovated with great style here: think whitewashed stone walls, crisp linen, leather bedheads and deep oval bathtubs. There's even a mini movie theatre and films to choose from. Breakfasts showcase organic local produce.

Tierview Twin Cottages
COTTAGES $$
(☑03-6362 2377; 125 Emu Bay Rd; 5-person cottage d $115, 6-person cottage d $135, extra person $20) Just off the main street, these cottages offer comfortable self-contained accommodation. One has an open fire, the other a spa bathroom.

Highview Lodge Youth Hostel
HOSTEL $
(☑03-6362 2996; 8 Blake St; dm $20-23.50, d from $60, f $72) It's a steep climb to this hilltop hostel, but the reward is expansive views over the Great Western Tiers. With the wood heater roaring there's a cosy, homely atmosphere. Nonstayers can use showers for $5.

Deloraine Apex Caravan Park
CAMPGROUND $
(☑03-6362 2345; West Pde; unpowered/powered sites d $21/25) This simple camp spot is at the bottom of the main street by the Meander River. Don't be alarmed if an almighty thundering disturbs your slumber here: the train tracks are adjacent.

TOP CHOICE **Restaurant Red** ITALIAN $$

(☑03-6362 3669; 81 Emu Bay Rd; mains $16-34; ☺lunch & dinner) Set in the 1886 Bank of Australia building, this place looks classy, smells amazing, and the food tastes sublime. It's fantastic Italian-inspired fare: from wood-fired pizza to saltimbocca and veal scallopini, with a well-chosen wine list to match.

Deloraine Delicatessen & Gourmet Foods DELI/CAFE $

(36 Emu Bay Rd; mains $6-14; ☺breakfast & lunch Mon-Sat) A fine place for late-morning baguettes, bagels and focaccia, with a variety of tasty fillings. Its coffee is pungently superb, and it does dairy- and gluten-free meals too.

Empire Hotel & Thai Restaurant THAI $$

(19 Emu Bay Rd; mains $19-29; ☺lunch & dinner) There's the usual Aussie bar here, but also a really good Thai restaurant. Try the duck curry – their signature dish.

Mole Creek

POP 220

Mole Creek, about 25km west of Deloraine, is an unflattering name for this tiny creek-plains town at the feet of the towering cracks of the Great Western Tiers. The environs are packed with attractions (it's a favourite area for cavers and bushwalkers) and the town makes a great base for exploring the Great Western Tiers and the national parks of the Walls of Jerusalem and Cradle Mountain (the B12 road through Mole Creek is an interesting alternative route to Cradle Mountain).

◎ Sights & Activities

Mole Creek Karst National Park NATURE RESERVE

(www.parks.tas.gov.au) Around Mole Creek (once overrun with thylacines) are limestone caves in the leatherwood honey apiaries and this excellent wildlife park.

Marakoopa Cave CAVES

A wet cave 15km from Mole Creek, Marakoopa features underground streams and glow-worms. **King Solomons Cave**, a dry cave with light-reflecting calcite crystals, has fewer steps. Each cave costs $16/8 per adult/child; tour times are displayed on access roads, or call the **Mole Creek Caves Ticket Office** (☑03-6363 5182; www.parks.tas. gov.au; 330 Mayberry Rd, Mayberry). Wear warm clothes – cave temperatures average 9°C.

R Stephens HONEY FACTORY

(www.leatherwoodhoney.com.au; 25 Pioneer Dr; ☺9am-4pm Mon-Fri Jan-Apr) The leatherwood tree only grows in damp, western Tasmania, and honey from its flowers is delicious. Tasmanian kids grow up studying the weird bee on the honey labels from R Stephens honey factory. Visitors can taste and purchase the sticky stuff.

Honey Farm FARM

(www.thehoneyfarm.com.au; 39 Sorell St; ☺9am-5pm Sun-Fri, reduced winter hrs) At nearby Chudleigh there's a honey farm with free honey tasting and an interactive beehive.

Trowunna Wildlife Park NATURE RESERVE

(www.trowunna.com.au; adult/child $18/9; ☺9am-5pm) About 5km east of Mole Creek on the B12 road is this first-rate park, specialising in Tasmanian devils and wombats.

Devils Gullet DRIVING, WALKING

The gravel Lake Mackenzie road ascends into the alpine reaches of the Western Tiers plateau – take warm clothes year-round and watch for sudden weather changes. Follow this road to Devils Gullet, where there's a 40-minute return walk leading to a heart-in-mouth platform bolted to the top of a dramatic gorge.

Wild Cave Tours CAVE TOURS

(☑03-6367 8142; www.wildcavetours.com; 165 Fernlea Rd, Caveside) Offers half-/full-day adventures in the area's other caves for $95/190, including caving gear.

🛏 Sleeping & Eating

Mole Creek Guest House & Laurel Berry Restaurant B&B $$

(☑03-6363 1399; 100 Pioneer Dr; s $115-145, d $125-170; @) There are beautifully renovated and spacious rooms here, and a private cinema upstairs. Downstairs the restaurant serves everything from hearty walkers breakfasts to homemade quiche at lunch (mains $10 to $16.50), and fantastic steaks at dinner (mains $22 to $26).

Mole Creek Caravan Park CAMPGROUND $

(☑03-6363 1150; cnr Mole Creek & Union Bridge Rds; unpowered/powered sites $17/20, extra person $3) This is a thin sliver of a park about 4km west of town beside Sassafras Stream, at the turn-off to the caves and Cradle Mountain.

Mole Creek Hotel HOTEL $

(☑03-6363 1102; www.molecreekhotel.com; Main Rd; s/d $50/100) A classic small-town pub

with bright upstairs rooms. The Tiger Bar (mains $15 to $25) is a thylacine shrine wallpapered with old newspaper clippings and serves hearty pub standards.

Walls of Jerusalem National Park

This isolated Central Plateau **national park** (www.parks.tas.gov.au), part of the Tasmanian Wilderness World Heritage Area, features glacial lakes and valleys, alpine flora and the rugged dolerite Mt Jerusalem (1459m). It's a favourite of experienced bushwalkers with a lust for challenging, remote hiking. The most popular walk here is the full-day trek to the 'Walls'; you can also camp in the park. National park fees apply.

For a guided walk, Tasmanian Expeditions (p630) operates a four-day Walls trip for $1095.

Access to the Walls is from Sheffield or Mole Creek. From Mole Creek take the B12 west, the C138 south then the C171 (Mersey Forest Rd) to Lake Rowallan; remain on this road, following the C171 and/or Walls of Jerusalem signs to the start of the track. Pick up the *Walls of Jerusalem Map* ($10.50) from Mole Creek Caves Ticket Office.

Sheffield & Around

POP 1030

Sheffield was settled in 1859, but by the 1980s it was a failing rural town. Then some bright spark suggested they paint large murals on Sheffield's public walls to attract tourists, and the town's fortunes began to change. These days there are more than 50 murals and Sheffield has its own annual painting festival, **Muralfest** (www.muralfest.com.au).

The **Kentish visitor information centre** (☎03-6491 1036; www.sheffieldcradleinfo.com.au; 5 Pioneer Cres; ⊙9am-5pm), just off the main street, has mural maps, mural audio tours and regional information.

The scenery around Sheffield is lovely – hulking **Mt Roland** (1234m) rises above farmlands, forests and fish-filled rivers. Nearby is deep **Lake Barrington**, an international rowing venue.

Tasmazia (www.tasmazia.com.au; 500 Staverton Rd; adult/child $17.50/10; ⊙10am-4pm Apr-Nov, 9am-5pm Dec-Mar), at the Lake Barrington turn-off, combines leafy mazes, the cheesy-as-hell Lower Crackpot model village, a lavender patch and pancake parlour. Probably one for the kids...

Sleeping & Eating

TOP CHOICE **Glencoe Rural Retreat** B&B $$
(☎03-6492 3267; www.glencoeruralretreat.com.au; 1468 Sheffield Rd; d $175-185;) Just north of Sheffield at Barrington, this gorgeous property is owned by celebrated French chef Remi Bancal. Stay in its romantic and stylish rooms (no kids under 12) and enjoy a superb three-course dinner ($60) – available by prior arrangement. There's also a cafe open to the public (mains $25, open lunch Thursday to Sunday) offering fantastic French-Creole cooking.

Platypus Valley B&B B&B $$
(☎03-6491 2260; www.platypusvalley.com.au; 10 Billing Rd; s $110-140, d $120-165, extra adult $80) Tucked away in green country just outside Sheffield, this beautiful spot is somewhere you're almost guaranteed to see platypuses gambolling. This is a beautiful timber home with attractive guest rooms, in an environment where the key ingredient is peace.

Skwiz Café Gallery CAFE $
(63 Main St; mains $6-10; ⊙breakfast & lunch) This friendly, arty cafe has Sheffield's best coffee. With its retro decor and funky music, it's a great place to hang out, have a slap-up breakfast, lazy lunch, or coffees and cakes in between. There's a rollicking folk-singing night the last Friday of every month.

Sheffield Cabins CABINS $
(☎03-6491 2176; www.sheffieldcabins.com.au; 1 Pioneer Cres; d $90-95, extra adult/child $15/10) These simple clean, self-contained cabins are close to the visitor centre, and are excellent value.

King Island

A skinny sliver of land 64km long and 27km wide, population 1570, King Island (or KI as locals call it) is a laid-back place where everyone knows everyone. The island's green pastures famously produce a rich dairy bounty, and its surrounding seas supply fabulously fresh seafood. Locals dry kelp to extract its goodies and tend lighthouses, four of which guard the rocky coastline. King Island also has consistently good surf.

◉ Sights

King Island Dairy DAIRY
(☑03-6462 0947; www.kidairy.com.au; North Rd, Loorana; ☺noon-4pm Sun-Fri) King Island Dairy's Fromagerie is 8km north of Currie (just beyond the airport). Taste their award-winning bries, cheddars and feisty blues and then stock up in their shop.

Lighthouses & Shipwrecks HISTORIC SITES
Drive right up to the tallest lighthouse in the southern hemisphere at Cape Wickham. This 48m tower was built in 1861 after several ships had been wrecked on the island's treacherous coastline. The Currie Lighthouse (adult/child $15/7.50; ☺tours 3.30pm Wed & Sat) was built in 1880, and there are more lighthouses at Stokes Point and Naracoopa. For information on lightkeeping and shipwrecks visit the King Island Museum (Lighthouse St, Currie; adult/child $5/1; ☺2-4pm, closed Jul & Aug).

✸ Activities

Surfing is brilliant in the cool, clear waters here: *Surfing Life* magazine has voted the break at Martha Lavinia as one of the top 10 waves in the world.

Surf and freshwater **fishing** almost guarantee a good catch, and you can **swim** at many of the island's unpopulated beaches (though beware rips and currents) and freshwater lagoons. Bring your own gear for the legendary **snorkelling** and **diving** here: there's crayfish and abalone to catch if you have a licence.

For **bushwalking** go independently, or take a guided walk with King Island Wilderness Walks (☑0400 858 339; www.king islandwildernesswalks.com).

Spotting **wildlife** is easy on KI. There are rufus and Bennett's wallabies, pademelons, snakes, echidnas and platypus and you may even glimpse seals. The island has 78 bird species, and on summer evenings little penguins come ashore around the Grassy breakwater.

⌂ Sleeping

TOP CHOICE Portside Links APARTMENTS, B&B $$
(☑03-6461 1134; www.portsidelinks.com.au; Grassy Harbour Rd, Grassy; apt d $150-190, B&B $180-200) Two beautiful apartments and B&B accommodation close to the beach. Best on KI.

Naracoopa Holiday Units COTTAGES $$
(☑03-6461 1326; www.naracoopaholidayunits.com. au; 125 The Esplanade, Naracoopa; d $120, extra adult/child $25/15) Bright, clean and peaceful cottages on Sea Elephant Bay. The owners are a mine of island information and can arrange car hire.

Bass Cabins & Campground CAMPGROUND $
(☑03-6462 1168; 5 Fraser Rd, Currie; camp site per person $10, cabin d $100) There are a few camp spots here with bathroom facilities adjacent and a couple of two-bedroom cabins. It's 1.5km from the centre of Currie.

✕ Eating

Must-tries include KI cheese and dairy products, but also crayfish in season (November to August), oysters, crabs, grass-fed beef, free-range pork and game.

Kings Cuisine at Bold Head Brasserie MODERN AUSTRALIAN $$
(☑03-6461 1341; www.kingscuisine.com.au; 10 Main Rd, Grassy; mains $24-28; ☺lunch Fri-Sun, dinner Wed-Mon, bar open daily) Fine dining with a fine reputation.

Boomerang by the Sea MODERN AUSTRALIAN $$
(☑03-6462 1288; www.boomerangbythesea.com. au; Golf Club Rd, Currie; mains $18-40; ☺dinner from 6pm Mon-Sat) Excellent menu, big on seafood; big views.

ℹ Information

King Island Tourism (☑1800 645 014, 03-6462 1313; www.kingisland.org.au; 5 George St, Currie)

Online Access Centre (5 George St; ☺10.30am-5pm Mon, 10.30am-7pm Wed, 10.30am-5pm Thu, 10am-9pm Fri, 10am-noon Sat; @)

ℹ Getting There & Away

King Island Airlines (☑03-9580 3777; www. kingislandair.com.au) Melbourne Moorabbin–King Island ($160 to $173).

Regional Express (☑13 17 13; www.regional express.com.au) Melbourne Tullamarine–King Island ($138 to $325).

Tasair (☑1800 062 900, 03-6248 5088; www. tasair.com.au) Devonport–King Island ($226), Hobart–King Island ($452).

ℹ Getting Around

King Island Car Rental (☑1800 777 282, 03-6462 1282; 2 Meech St, Currie) Rentals $63 to $110.

P&A Car Rental (☑03-6462 1603; 1 Netherby Rd, Currie) Per day $66 to $73.

The Trend In Currie, hires mountain bikes.

Ulverstone & Around

Unhurried Ulverstone (population 9800) has a relaxed, uncommercial atmosphere at the mouth of the Leven River. The town became an important commercial port with the coming of the railway in 1890, but a decade later the rail was extended to Burnie and with it went the shipping activity. Today it's home to a few fishing boats, retirees, some gracious old buildings and a quite ridiculous clock tower. The **Ulverstone visitor information centre** ($\boxed{\bm{J}}$03-6425 2839; www.centralcoast.tas.gov.au; 13 Alexandra Rd; $\odot$9am-5pm; **@**) is a much classier piece of architecture.

◉ Sights & Activities

Gunns Plains Caves   CAVES
(adult/child $12/6; $\odot$10am-4pm) The B17 road does a worthwhile loop from the A1 coast highway, and goes to Gunns Plains, 25km south of Ulverstone. Take a guided tour of the 'shawl' formations here.

Wings Wildlife Park   PARK
(www.wingswildlife.com.au; 137 Winduss St; adult/child $17/8; $\odot$10am-4pm) Also at Gunns Plains is this family-oriented place with farm and native animals, including reptiles, birds of prey and a bossy rooster.

Leven Canyon Lookout   LANDMARK
South of Gunns Plains, the River Leven stutters through a 274m-deep gorge. Follow the 41km road from Ulverstone through Nietta to the jaw-dropping Leven Canyon Lookout. A 20-minute return track leads to a gorge-top viewing platform.

☰ Sleeping & Eating

TOP CHOICE / Ulverstone River
Retreat   APARTMENTS $$
($\boxed{\bm{J}}$03-6425 2999; www.ulverstoneriverretreat.com.au; 37 Lobster Creek Rd; d $130-165, extra person $25) Watch kingfishers from your front deck, fish and kayak the river, or just soak up the birdsong and peace. This gorgeous riverside spot offers a smart upstairs apartment and a separate villa, both with decks out front and BBQ facilities.

Big 4 Ulverstone Holiday
Park   CAMPGROUND $
($\boxed{\bm{J}}$03-6425 2624; 57 Water St; sites d $32-40, 3-bunk cabins from $95, units $105-126; **@**) Set in grassy surroundings just behind East Beach,

this park has good facilities, including a campers kitchen and playgrounds.

Pedro's the Restaurant   SEAFOOD $$
(Wharf Rd; mains $24-29; $\odot$lunch & dinner) Grab a riverside table and savour tastes of the sea at sunset. The paradise seafood platter for two ($119) is the most popular offering here. The menu caters to both carnivores and vegetarians. There's also **Pedro's Takeaway** (mains $4-12; $\odot$11am-7pm) for fish and chips, next door.

Deli Central   CAFE $
(48b Victoria St; meals $6-18; $\odot$8am-5pm Mon-Fri, to 12.30pm Sat) Look forward to wonderful breakfasts of chewy French sourdough with poached free-range eggs and homemade relish or roast pumpkin and caramelised-onion tart for lunch. Stock up for picnics at their impressive deli counter.

Penguin

POP 3050
This quaint little seaside village – complete with huge concrete penguin on the foreshore and penguin-shaped rubbish bins – lures tourists with its fantastic beaches.

Driving from Ulverstone, take the old Bass Hwy along the coast. As you approach Penguin, the countryside takes on a gentrified, rural feel with cottage gardens, a narrow-gauge railway track and beaches squeezing themselves into the scene.

Check out the **Penguin visitor information centre** ($\boxed{\bm{J}}$03-6437 1421; 78 Main Rd; $\odot$9am-4pm Oct-Mar, 9.30am-3.30pm Apr-Sep). Every Sunday off Arnold St the popular undercover **Penguin Market** ($\odot$9am-3.30pm) takes place. There are browse-worthy stalls here selling fresh local produce, art and crafts, gifts and collectables.

☰ Sleeping & Eating

Madsen   BOUTIQUE HOTEL $$$
($\boxed{\bm{J}}$03-6437 2588; www.themadsen.com; 64 Main St; d $150-300; **@**▣) Penguin's best place to stay is this stylish hotel, where the top rate will score you the spacious front room (a former banking chamber), with Bass Strait sea views.

Groovy Penguin Café   CAFE $
($\boxed{\bm{J}}$03-6437 2101; 74 Main Rd; mains $8-13; $\odot$breakfast & lunch Wed-Sun; **@**) A cool shrine to all things kitsch and retro, with super-nice staff, cakes, focaccia, soups and salads. Also

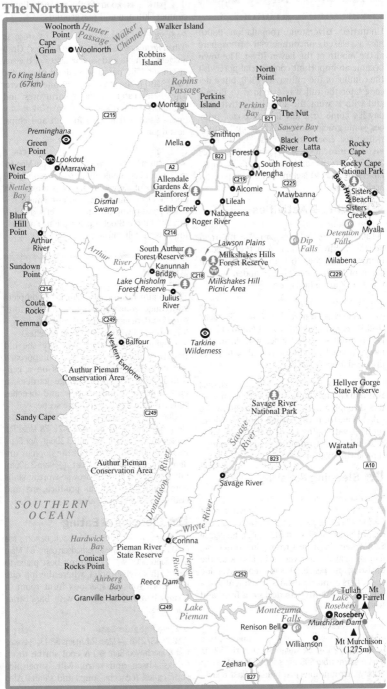

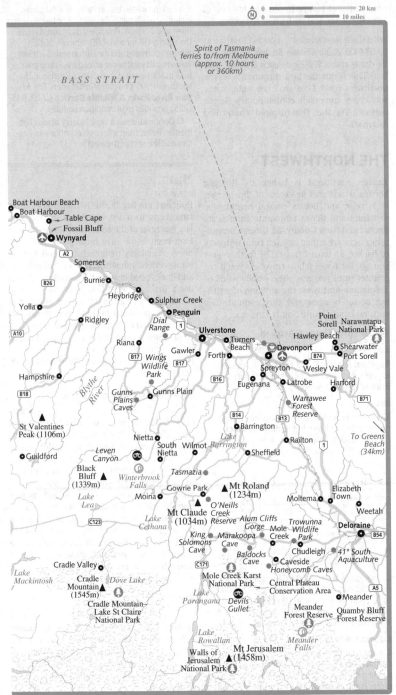

0   20 km
0   10 miles

Spirit of Tasmania
ferries to/from Melbourne
(approx. 10 hours
or 360km)

BASS STRAIT

Boat Harbour Beach
Boat Harbour
Table Cape
Fossil Bluff
Wynyard
A2
Somerset
B26
Burnie
Heybridge   Sulphur Creek
Yolla   Penguin
Dial   1
Ridgley   Range   Ulverstone
Riana   Turners   Devonport
A10   Beach
Gawler   Forth   B74
B17   Wings   B17   Spreyton   Wesley Vale
Wildlife   Eugenana   Latrobe   Harford
Hampshire   Park   B16
B18   Blythe River   Gunns   Gunns Plain   Warrawee
Plains   Forest   B71
Caves   Reserve
St Valentines   B14   Barrington   To Greens
Peak (1106m)   Lake   B13   Beach
Nietta   Barrington   Railton   1   (34km)
South   Wilmot   Sheffield
Guildford   Leven   Nietta
Canyon   Tasmazia   Elizabeth
Black   Winterbrook   Mt Roland   Town
Bluff   Falls   Gowrie Park   (1234m)   Moltema
(1339m)   Moina   O'Neills   Weetah
Lake   Creek   Trowunna
Lea   Mt Claude   Reserve   Alum Cliffs   Wildlife   Deloraine
Lake   (1034m)   Gorge   Park   B54
Cethana   King   Marakoopa   Mole   41° South
Solomons   Cave   Creek   Chudleigh   Aquaculture
Cave   Baldocks   Caveside
Cradle Valley   C171   Cave   Honeycomb Caves
Lake   Cradle   Dove Lake   Mole Creek Karst   Central Plateau
Mackintosh   Mountain   National Park   Conservation Area
(1545m)   Lake   A5
Cradle Mountain–   Paranga   Devils   Meander
Lake St Claire   Gullet   Meander   Quamby Bluff
National Park   Forest Reserve   Forest Reserve
Lake   Meander
Rowallan   Falls
Walls of   Mt Jerusalem
Jerusalem   (1458m)
National Park

Point Sorell   Narawntapu
Hawley Beach   National Park
Shearwater
Port Sorell

TASMANIA THE NORTHWEST

runs a modest two-bedroom holiday unit (d $95, extra person $15) with great sea views.

Wild Café Restaurant   MODERN AUSTRALIAN **$$**
(☑03-6437 2000; 87 Main Rd; lunch mains $12-19, dinner mains $20-29; ☺lunch & dinner Wed-Sun) This is one the best restaurants on the northwest coast. Gaze over the water while you enjoy top-notch contemporary Aussie cuisine. Try the Thai-inspired chargrilled calamari.

THE NORTHWEST

Tassie's Northwest is lashed by Roaring Forties winds and in excess of 2m of rain each year, and boasts coastal heathlands, wetlands and dense temperate rainforests unchanged from Gondwana times. Communities here are either isolated rural outposts or tricked-up tourist traps. The further west you get, the fewer fellow travellers you'll encounter until you reach the woolly wilds of Tasmania's northwest tip, a region of writhing ocean beaches and tiny communities with no landfall until South America.

❶ Getting There & Around

AIR

Regional Express (☑13 17 13; www.regional express.com.au) Flies between Melbourne and Burnie/Wynyard Airport.

BUS

There are no public transport services to Marrawah or Arthur River, but **Redline Coaches** (☑1300 360 000; www.tasredline.com.au) services the Northwest's larger towns:

JOURNEY	PRICE ($)	DURATION (MIN)
Burnie-Boat Harbour	10	30
Burnie-Smithton	22	90
Burnie-Stanley	19	60
Burnie-Wynyard	8	20
Launceston-Burnie	37	160

On weekdays **Metro** (☑03-6431 3822; www. metrotas.com.au) has regular buses from Burnie to Penguin, Ulverstone and Wynyard (all $5.60 one-way), departing from Cattley St. Burnie to Wynyard buses also run on Saturday.

CAR & MOTORCYCLE

The main north-to-west-coast route is the Murchison Hwy (A10) from Somerset west of Burnie, running through to Queenstown. The Western Explorer is the inland road from Smithton through the Tarkine wilderness area to the west coast, including a difficult 50km section between Arthur River and Corinna. Promoted as a tourist route, the road is OK for non-4WD vehicles, but it's remote, potholed and mostly unsealed – think twice in bad weather or after dark. Fill up your tank in Marrawah in the north or Zeehan in the south, as there's no petrol in between. The **Arthur River Parks & Wildlife Service** (☑03-6457 1225) provides road condition updates.

At Corinna there's a vehicle ferry across the Pieman River, from where you continue to Zeehan and the rest of the west.

Burnie

POP 19,060

Built on Emu Bay, Burnie is Tasmania's fourth-largest city. It's a deepwater port and shipping is a lynchpin of the economy. Burnie has also long been home to a huge paper mill, and heavy-machinery manufacturing and agricultural-services industries. The scars of industry and docks piled high with logs and woodchips don't make a great first impression, but a beach vibe and an emerging environmental sensitivity provide some optimism. Burnie has an enviable stock of art-deco architecture.

Attached to the Pioneer Village Museum is the Burnie visitor information centre (☑03-6434 6111; www.discoverburnie.net; Little Alexander St).

◎ Sights & Activities

Makers Workshop   MUSEUM
(☑03-6430 5831; www.discoverburnie.net; 2 Bass Hwy; ☺9am-5pm) Part museum, part arts centre, this dramatic new structure dominates the Western end of Burnie's main beach. Come here for tourist information, but also to get acquainted with this city's creative heart. You'll notice the life-sized **paper people** in odd corners of the workshop's cavernous contemporary interior. These are the work of Creative Paper (tours adult/child $15/8), Burnie's handmade paper producers. There are also **makers' studios** stationed throughout the centre where you can watch local artisans at work.

FREE Burnie Regional Art Gallery   ART GALLERY
(Burnie Arts & Function Centre, Wilmot St; ☺10am-4.30pm Mon-Fri, 1.30-4.30pm Sat & Sun) This art gallery has excellent exhibitions of contemporary Tasmanian artworks, including fine prints by some of Australia's most prominent artists.

Hellyers Road Whisky Distillery DISTILLERY
(www.hellyersroaddistillery.com.au; 153 Old Surrey
Rd; tours adult/child under 16 $10/free; ⊘10am-
4.30pm) About 1km further up Old Surrey
Rd is Hellyers Rd. Tour the distillery and
afterwards sample whisky, whisky cream
and Southern Lights vodka. The on-site cafe
serves snacks and lunches.

FREE **Penguin Observation**
Centre WILDLIFE WATCHING
A boardwalk on Burnie's foreshore leads
from Hilder Pde to the western end of West
Beach. Take a **Penguin Interpretation Tour**
(☑0437 436 803; ⊘Oct-Feb) about one hour after dusk as the penguins emerge from the
sea and waddle back to their burrows. Volunteer wildlife guides talk about the penguins and their habits.

🛏 Sleeping

TOP CHOICE **Seabreeze**
Cottages RENTAL HOUSES $$
(☑03-6435 3424; www.seabreezecottages.com.
au; s/d from $140/165, extra adult/child $40/20)
These chic and modern cottages are just
west of the city centre. There's the cool, con-
temporary **Beach House** (243 Bass Hwy,
Cooee) just a stroll across the road from
the beach; **West Park** (14 Paraka St); and
cute **Number Six** (6 Mollison St), both a 10-
minute walk to town.

Regent Hotel PUB $
(☑03-6431 1933; 26 North Tce; s without bathroom
$30, d $60) Basic rooms above a pub, and the
communal lounge has brilliant ocean views.
Double rooms have showers but other fa-
cilities are shared. The pub's **Mallee Grill**
(mains $15-43; ⊘lunch Sun-Fri, dinner daily) does
good fare.

Duck House COTTAGES $$
(☑03-6431 1712; www.ozpal.com/duck; 26 Queen
St; s/d $100/140, extra adult/child $30/20) Salvation Army stalwarts Bill and Winifred
Duck lived here for 30 years, and have been
immortalised in this charming little two-
bedroom cottage. Next door is **Mrs Phil-
pott's** (26 Queen St; same rates) sleeping up to
seven, with lead-lighting, a claw-foot bath
and brass bedsteads for the same rates.

Burnie Oceanview CAMPGROUND $
(☑03-6431 1925; www.burniebeachaccommo
dation.com.au; 253 Bass Hwy, Cooee; unpowered/
powered sites d $23/28, dm $25, on-site vans d $50,
cabins d $92-105, extra person $20; @🐾) Located

4km west of the city centre, this park has
backpacker rooms, grassy camping sites,
vans with kitchenettes, and cabins.

🍴 Eating

Merchant CAFE $
(1 Cattley St; mains $7.50-18.50; ⊘8am-5pm Mon-
Wed, 8am-late Thu-Sat) This cool new venue
produces excellent bistro fare by day, then
morphs into a wine bar by night. They have
live music Fridays and Saturdays, and open
mic night Thursdays from 8pm.

Another Mother CAFE $
(14 Cattley St; mains $9-15; ⊘breakfast & lunch
Tue-Sat; 🐾) With bright red walls, eclectic
furniture and local photography, this eatery
offers wholesome predominantly vegetarian (and some meaty) dishes crafted from
local produce – organic where possible.
Their sister establishment is **Hot Mother
Lounge** (70 Wilson St; ⊘7am-3pm Mon-Fri),
serving equally good wraps and soups.

Fish Frenzy SEAFOOD $$
(2 North Tce; meals $9.50-27; ⊘11am-9pm)
Downstairs from fancier Bayviews Restau-
rant, this upbeat fish and chippery does
great seafood favourites.

Rialto Gallery Restaurant ITALIAN $$
(46 Wilmot St; mains $14-25; ⊘lunch Mon-Fri,
dinner Mon-Sat) Rialto has been a Burnie
institution for 28 years, serving authentic
Italian pastas and fine wood-oven pizzas.

Wynyard

POP 4810

Sheltered by the monolithic Table Cape,
Wynyard used to be a timber-milling centre
and home to Tasmania's first butter factory,
but these days most people go to Wynyard
to retire. It's an affordable base from which
to explore the area, and there are good low-
cost accommodation options.

The **Wynyard visitor information cen-
tre** (☑03-6443 8330; www.wowtas.com.au; 8
Exhibition Link; ⊘9am-5pm) combines with
Wonders of Wynyard (adult/child $7/3.50;
⊘9am-5pm), a polished exhibition of old
Ford automobiles.

Wynyard's undisputed highlight is **Table Cape**. A hulking igneous plateau 4km north of town, it has unforgettable views, a tulip farm (in bloom and open to the public from late September to mid-October) and an 1888 lighthouse. Drive to the lighthouse or walk along the cliff tops from the lookout (30 minutes return).

Fossil Bluff, 3km from town signposted from the Saunders St roundabout, is where the oldest marsupial fossil found in Australia was unearthed (it's an estimated 20 million years old). The soft sandstone here also contains shell fossils deposited when the level of Bass Strait was much higher.

🛏 Sleeping & Eating

Wharf Hotel HOTEL $
(☑03-6442 2344; 10 Goldie St; s/d $49/75) The renovated Wharf Hotel has huge rooms with fridges, quality linen, spotless en suites (some with baths) and river views.

Beach Retreat Tourist Park CAMPGROUND $
(☑03-6442 1998; 30b Old Bass Hwy; powered sites d $27, backpacker s/d $35/50, s or d motel units/cabins $85/90) This pretty tourist park is in a peaceful beachside spot on neatly manicured grassy grounds, and deserves more than just an overnight stay. There's great backpacker accommodation in double rooms (no dorms) and a terrific shared kitchen. The self-contained motel rooms are snazzy, too.

Buckaneers FISH AND CHIPS $$
(4 Inglis St; mains $10-27; ⊙lunch & dinner) Wynyard's best choice for a fishy feed.

Ladybugs Licensed Café CAFE $
(8 Inglis St; mains $9-16; ⊙breakfast, lunch & dinner Mon-Sat) Quality pizzas and cafe fare – including gluten-free options – are available at the coolly retro Ladybugs.

Boat Harbour

POP 140

Perched on a beautiful bay with gleaming white sand and crystal-clear water, Boat Harbour is an idyllic spot, but the crusty old fibro fishermen's shacks are slowly being overrun by ugly townhouses and upmarket B&Bs.

Nearby are the coastal heathlands of the small **Rocky Cape National Park** (www.parks.gov.tas.au), known for its bushwalking, diving, snorkelling, shipwrecks and sea caves; and **Sisters Beach**, an 8km expanse of bleached sand with safe swimming, good fishing, a boat ramp and a general store.

Boat Harbour Beach House (☑03-6445 0913; www.boatharbourbeachhouse.com; d $200-220) is actually three self-contained, multi-bedroom beachhouses: **The View** (12 Moore St), **The Waterfront** (314 The Esplanade) and **The Water's Edge** (320 The Esplanade). All three are beautifully renovated, with outdoor decks and barbecues.

Lit with rice-paper lanterns, **Jolly Rogers** (1 Port Rd; mains $16-32; ⊙breakfast, lunch & dinner) is next to the surf club. They do daytime burgers, fish and chips, focaccia and seafood snacks, and offer a seafood-focused à la carte menu at night.

Stanley

POP 550

Europeans established Stanley back in 1826 well before any other northwest settlements and for a long time it was only accessible by sea. The Peerapper people were the original inhabitants of Stanley's little isthmus and peninsula, and back then extraordinary bulbous Circular Head (better known as The Nut) was covered in forest. Buffeted by cold ocean winds, Stanley lives for two things: fishing (particularly crayfish) and tourism. Every second house is a 'heritage B&B', and there are several good eateries.

The **Stanley visitor information centre** (☑03-6458 1330; www.stanley.com.au; 45 Main Rd) is on your left as you enter town.

◉ Sights & Activities

The Nut LANDMARK
This striking 152m-high volcanic rock formation can be seen for many kilometres around Stanley. It's a steep 20-minute climb to the top. The best lookout is a five-minute walk to the south of the **chairlift** (adult/child $10/8; ⊙9.30am-5.30pm Oct-May, 10am-4pm Sep), and you can also take a 35-minute walk (2km) on a path around the top. In summer, you can wait to view short-tailed shearwaters (also called mutton birds) returning at dusk after a day's fishing.

Seaquarium AQUARIUM
(Fisherman's Dock; adult/child $10/5; ⊙9am-5pm daily 7 Sep-14 May, 11am-3pm Sat & Sun 15 Jun-6 Sep) Providing a great display of marine life, Seaquarium is a fun and educational place to bring the kids. A highlight is the touchy-feely tank.

Highfield
HISTORIC BUILDING

(Green Hills Rd; adult/child $10/5; ⏱10am-4pm) This homestead 2km north of town was built in 1835 for the chief agent of the Van Diemen's Land Company. It's a rare example of domestic architecture of the Regency period in Tasmania. Tour the house and the stables, grain stores, workers' cottages and chapel.

Van Diemen's Land Company Store
HISTORIC BUILDING

(16 Wharf Rd) This bluestone warehouse on the seafront dates from 1844, and while it once held bales of wool for export, it now houses an exclusive boutique hotel, @VDL.

Tarkine Forest Adventures
ADVENTURE CENTRE

(www.adventureforests.com.au/tarkine; adult/child 5-16 $20/10; ⏱9am-5pm Nov-Mar, 10am-4pm Apr-Oct) Fifty-four kilometres southwest of Smithton is this forest adventure centre, formerly known as Dismal Swamp. There's a 110m-long slide that provides a thrilling descent into a blackwood-forested sinkhole: sliders must be over eight years and at least 90cm tall. There's also a cafe, an interpretation centre and forest floor boardwalks.

👉 Tours

Stanley Seal Cruises
WILDLIFE WATCHING

(☎03-6458 1294, 0419 550 134; www.stanleyseal cruises.com.au; Fisherman's Dock; adult/child under 5/child $49/9/19) Provides 75-minute cruises to see up to 500 Australian fur seals sunning themselves on Bull Rock. Departures are at 10am and 3pm from October to April, and at 10am in May and September, sea conditions permitting. Also does offshore fishing charters ($200 for four people, two hours), all equipment supplied.

Wilderness to West Coast Tours
4WD TOUR

(☎03-6456 5200, 0427 565 200; www.wildern esstowestcoasttours.com.au; 8 Church St) This operation offers full-day 4WD wilderness tours to the Tarkine rainforests and to wild beaches near Arthur River ($249 per person), including a gourmet lunch. Also offers day fishing tours ($390) and tag-along Tarkine tours by arrangement.

🛏 Sleeping

Stanley Hotel
PUB $

(☎1800 222 397, 03-6458 1161; www.stanleytas mania.com.au; 19 Church St; s/d with shared facilities $50/70, d with bathroom $99-115) This pub's

brightly painted rooms are some of Tassie's best pub accommodation. Sit out on the upstairs verandah and look down on the Stanley streetscape. Also runs six self-catering **Abbeys Cottages** (d $150-180, extra person $30), and the downstairs bistro is highly regarded.

689

TOP CHOICE @VDL
HOTEL $$

(☎03-6458 2032; www.atvdlstanley.com.au; 16 Wharf Rd; s $180-225; 🕿) This former 1840s bluestone warehouse is now an ultrahip boutique hotel with two suites and a self-contained loft apartment. Everything's top class, from the bedding to the artworks on the walls. The same people also run a sister property, **@The Base** (32 Alexander Tce; d $125-155), which is a heritage house divided into two similarly stylish suites.

Stanley Cabin & Tourist Park
CAMPGROUND $

(☎03-6458 1266; www.stanleycabinpark.com.au; Wharf Rd; unpowered sites d $25, powered sites d $27, dm $26, cabins d $85-150; 🕿) This spectacularly sited spot has waterfront camp sites, neat cabins and a backpackers hostel comprising six twin rooms.

🍴 Eating

Chin Wags
CAFE $

(6 Church St; mains $7.50-12.50; ⏱9am-5pm; 🖉) The folks at Chin Wags say they serve 'modern hippie gourmet' but perhaps that's just shorthand for delicious, healthy grub. Everything's homemade and there are good veggie plus gluten-free options.

Hursey Seafoods
SEAFOOD $$

(2 Alexander Tce; ⏱9am-6pm) Hursey's is awash with tanks of live sea creatures – fish, crayfish, crabs and eels – for the freshest of (uncooked) seafood takeaways. Choose your own for self-catering.

Kermies Cafe
SEAFOOD $$

(mains $12-29; ⏱lunch & dinner) Here is the best place in Stanley for fresh crayfish, served natural or mornay ($70 to $170) and they also do prawns, scallops, calamari and platters to share.

Stanley's on the Bay
MODERN AUSTRALIAN $$

(☎03-6458 1404; 15 Wharf Rd; mains $18-35; ⏱dinner Mon-Sat Sep-Jun) Set inside the historic Ford's Store at Stanley Village, this fine-dining establishment specialises in steak and seafood. The wonderful seafood platter for two overflows with local scallops, oysters, fish, octopus and salmon ($95).

Marrawah

POP 370

At Marrawah, with its open pastureland punctuated by stands of old conifers, the wild Southern Ocean occasionally coughs up pieces of ships wrecked off the rugged coast. The area's beaches and rocky outcrops are hauntingly beautiful, particularly at dusk, and the seas and surf are often monstrous.

Geoff King from **King's Run Wildlife Tours** (☑03-6457 1191; www.kingsrun.com.au; per person $100-125) runs evening trips to a remote fishing shack on his 330-hectare property to watch Tasmanian devils tuck into roadkill. It's a special experience and definitely worth travelling here for.

In the township, the **Marrawah Tavern** (☑03-6457 1102; Comeback Rd; mains $10-25; ☺lunch & dinner) serves counter meals but doesn't have accommodation. There's a free but very basic (and windy!) camping area with toilets and a cold shower by the beach at Green Point, 2km from Marrawah.

The compact, blue-and-pine **Marrawah Beach House** (☑03-6457 1285; d from $140, extra person $25) has amazing views across the beach to oblivion. Fully self-contained, it sleeps four.

Arthur River

POP 120

Fifteen kilometres south of Marrawah is Arthur River, an isolated bevy of fibro fishing shacks and holiday houses. Breezy and briny **Gardiner Point**, signposted off the main road south of the old timber bridge, has been christened the 'Edge of the World'. From here you can drive 110km south to Corinna on the West Coast via the Western Explorer road (see p701).

🏃 Activities

Arthur River Canoe & Boat Hire   BOATING
(☑03-6457 1312; 1429 Arthur River Rd; ☺9am-5pm) Hires out motorboats ($25/130 per hour/day), canoes ($16/70) and kayaks ($12/50). You can take the canoes upriver and camp for as long as you like. Waterproof drums are provided; BYO everything else.

☞ Tours

Arthur River Cruises   SCENIC CRUISE
(☑03-6457 1158; www.arthurrivercruises.com; adult/child $92/35; ☺10am-3pm Sep-May)
If you're not into fishing, take a scenic cruise on the Arthur River, cruising upriver to the confluence of the Arthur and Frankland Rivers for a barbecue and a rainforest walk.

AR Reflections River Cruises   SCENIC CRUISE
(☑03-6457 1288; www.arreflections.com; adult/child $88/48; ☺10.15am-4.15pm) Another Arthur River cruise, here passengers also get a guided rainforest walk and a gourmet lunch.

🛌 Sleeping & Eating

There is decent self-catering accommodation in Arthur River, but no eateries (only two takeaway stores). Pitch a tent at Manuka, Peppermint or Prickly Wattle **camping grounds** (sites $13) around Arthur River; self-register at the **Arthur River Parks & Wildlife Service** (☑03-6457 1225; www.parks.tas.gov.au; ☺24hr registration booth) on the main street.

Arthur River Caravan Park   CARAVAN PARK $
(☺03-6457 1212; www.arthurrivercabinpark.com; 1239 Arthur River Rd; unpowered/powered d $25/28, on-site vans $80, cabins $95) Just north of town, this park has old and new cabins, and plenty of wildlife passing through.

Arthur River Holiday Units   APARTMENTS $$
(☑03-6457 1288; 2 Gardiner St; d $120, extra person $30) Has several comfortable (if a little dated) riverside units ranging from one to three bedrooms.

THE WEST

Primeval, tempestuous and elemental – this region of Tasmania is unlike anywhere else in Australia. Towering, jagged mountain ranges, button-grass-covered alpine plateaus, raging tannin-stained rivers, dense impenetrable rainforest and unyielding rain. Humans never tamed this western wilderness and today much of the region comprises Tasmania's World Heritage Area. Tourist-centric Strahan aside, the few towns and settlements here are rough and primitive, weathered and hardened by wilderness.

Prior to 1932, when the Hobart–Queenstown road was built, the only way into the area was by sea, through the dangerous Hells Gates into Strahan's Macquarie Harbour. European settlement brought convicts, soldiers, loggers, prospectors, railway gangs and fishermen to the area. In the 20th

century, outdoor adventurers, naturalists and environmental crusaders were lured into the wilderness. The proposed damming of the Franklin and Lower Gordon Rivers in the 1980s sparked the greatest environmental debate in Australian history, and fostered an ecotourism boom around Strahan.

See www.westcoast.tas.gov.au for regional information.

ⓘ Getting There & Around

Tassielink (☏1300 300 520; www.tassielink. com.au) buses run from Hobart to the west coast five times per week. The duration of the Strahan journey varies with Queenstown stopover times.

JOURNEY	PRICE ($)	DURATION (HR)
Hobart–Bronte Junction	36.70	2¼
Hobart–Derwent Bridge	43.90	3¼
Hobart–Lake St Clair	51	2¾
Hobart–Queenstown	64.40	5
Hobart–Strahan	74.50	6-8¾

From Launceston, Tassielink buses run three times per week:

JOURNEY	PRICE ($)	DURATION (HR)
Launceston–Cradle Mountain	58.60	3
Launceston–Devonport	23.30	1¼ (meeting ferries)
Launceston–Gowrie Park	39.20	2¼
Launceston–Queenstown	71.20	6
Launceston–Sheffield	29.70	2
Launceston–Strahan	81.30	8¾
Launceston–Zeehan	61.40	5½

Drivers heading north along the rugged Western Explorer road should fill up at Zeehan or Waratah; there's no fuel at Corinna or Arthur River, only at distant Marrawah.

Corinna

POP 5

Tiny, peaceful Corinna, on the northern bank of the Pieman River, was once a thriving gold-mining settlement of more than 2500 people, but nowadays the whole town is run as an isolated tourist resort with a strong environmentalist focus. The ambitious owners have renovated the old pub and built 14 new self-contained, solar-powered **cabins** (☏03-6446 1170; www.corinna.com.au; backpacker s $50, cottages d $135-189, houses sleeping 4 $239; extra person $25) on the hillside.

Pieman River Cruises (☏03-6446 1170; adult/child $90/51; ◷10am-2pm) operates from here – a laid-back, rustic alternative to Strahan's crowded, mass-produced Gordon River cruises. Four-hour cruises on the *Arcadia II* pass an impressive gorge and forests of eucalypts, ferns and Huon pines en route to Pieman Heads, where you can rummage around the log-strewn beaches. Bookings are essential. Also on offer are **canoe and kayak** paddles on the Pieman (half/full day $40/80), fishing (rod hire half/full day $10/20) and boat trips to **Lovers' Falls** (adult/child $50/25) where you can be dropped with a picnic hamper and sigh at the beauty of it all.

The *Fatman* ferry (motorcycles & bicycles/standard vehicle/caravan $10/20/25; ◷9am-5pm Apr-Sep, to 7pm Oct-Mar) slides across the Pieman on demand (the only way across the river).

Queenstown

POP 3400

The extraordinary Lyell Hwy winds down from the mountains into Queenstown through a surreal, apocalyptic moonscape of deep, eroded gullies and bare hillsides. This is the legacy of environmentally destructive mining. Mining activities and sulphur emissions are now controlled, and greenery is springing up on the slopes. Ironically, some locals want to keep the green away, believing the bald hills and gravel football field attract the tourists.

Although Queenstown is now getting in on the tourism trend, it's still got that authentic, rough-and-ready pioneer town feel. You can spot miners in boilersuits wandering the streets and there's a rich social and industrial history that still feels alive. With the completion of the West Coast Wilderness Railway, Queenstown now has a real tourist hub that is breathing new life into the town.

The town's biggest (and priciest) attraction is the West Coast Wilderness Railway (see the boxed text, p694), a restored line traversing the pristine wilderness between Queenstown and Strahan. The station is on Driffield St, opposite the Empire Hotel.

The Southwest

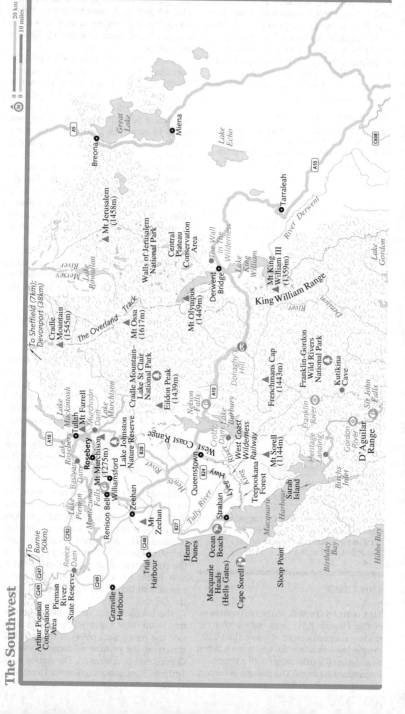

20 km
10 miles

Arthur Pieman Conservation Area

Pieman River State Reserve

To Burnie (50km)

Granville Harbour

Reece Dam

Trial Harbour

Renison Bell

Zeehan

Mt Zeehan

Williamsford

Montezuma Falls

Lake Pieman

Lake Rosebery

Lake Basywan

Rosebery

Tullah

Mt Farrell

Lake Mackintosh

Murchison Dam

Lake Murchison

Mt Murchison (1275m)

Lake Johnston Nature Reserve

Cradle Mountain–Lake St Clair National Park

Eldon Peak (1439m)

West Coast Range

Henty River

Queenstown

Lyell Hwy

Strahan

Macquarie Heads (Hells Gates)

Ocean Beach

Cape Sorell

Henty Dunes

Tully River

Teepookana Forest

King River

Lake Burbury

Crotty Dam

Nelson Falls

Mt Olympus (1449m)

Mt Ossa (1617m)

The Overland Track

Cradle Mountain (1545m)

To Sheffield (7km); Devonport (38km)

Mersey River

Lake Rowallan

Mt Jerusalem (1458m)

Walls of Jerusalem National Park

Central Plateau Conservation Area

The Wall In The Wilderness

Lake King William

Derwent Bridge

Mt King William III (1359m)

King William Range

River Derwent

Tarraleah

Lake Echo

Great Lake

Breona

Miena

Donaghy's Hill

Frenchmans Cap (1443m)

Franklin-Gordon Wild Rivers National Park

Kutikina Cave

Franklin River

Sir John Falls

D'Aguilar Range

Gordon River

Heritage Landing

Birchs Inlet

Lake Gordon

River Gordon

Denison River

Mt Sorell (1144m)

West Coast Wilderness

Sarah Island

Macquarie Harbour

Sloop Point

Birthday Bay

Hibbs Bay

Teepookana Railway

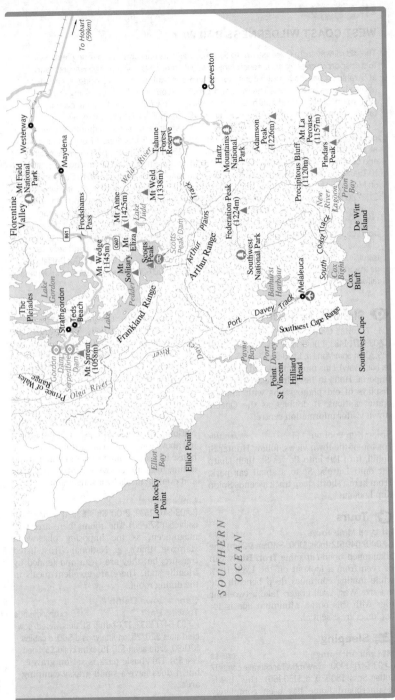

To Hobart
(59km)

Westerway
Maydena

Florentine
Valley
Mt Field
National
Park

B861

Frodshams
Pass

Weld River

Tahune
Forest
Reserve

Geeveston

Hartz
Mountains
National
Park

Adamson
Peak
(1226m)

Mt La
Perouse
(1157m)

Pindars
Peak

Mt Anne
(1425m)

Mt Weld
(1338m)

Lake
Judd

Track

Precipitous Bluff
(1120m)

New River
Lagoon

Prion
Bay

Mt Wedge
(1145m)

Mt
Eliza

C607

Mt
Solitary

Scotts
Peak

Scotts
Peak Dam

Arthur
Plains

Federation Peak
(1224m)

Southwest
National
Park

De Witt
Island

The
Pleiades

Lake
Gordon

Strathgordon

Teds
Beach

Lake
Pedder

Frankland Range

Arthur Range

Bathurst
Harbour

Melaleuca

South
Coast Track

Cox
Bight

Cox
Bluff

Gordon
Dam
Serpentine
Dam

Mt Sprent
(1068m)

Prince of Wales
Range

Olga River

River

Davey

Port
Davey
Track

Payne
Bay

Port
Davey

Point
Vincent
St

Hilliard
Head

Southwest Cape Range

Southwest Cape

TASMANIA THE SOUTHWEST

Low Rocky
Point

Elliot
Bay

Elliot Point

SOUTHERN
OCEAN

DON'T MISS

WEST COAST WILDERNESS RAILWAY

The old railway from Queenstown to Strahan was a remarkable engineering feat. Built to transport copper from Queenstown's Mt Lyell mine to the Macquarie Harbour port at Strahan, it passes through dense forest, crosses wild rivers via 40 bridges, and stops at old stations on its route. The rack-and-pinion line opened in 1896, utilising the Abt system (involving a third, toothed, lock-on rail) to allow fully loaded mining carriages to tackle steep 1:16 gradients. After closing in 1963 the railway fell into disrepair.

Today the track is magnificently restored, and steam and diesel locomotives take passengers on a four-hour journey over its entire length. Trains depart from Queenstown at 10am and 3pm and Strahan at 10.15am and 3.15pm from the end of December to the end of March. Between April and September, there's a Strahan to Queenstown trip at 10.15am on Tuesday, Wednesday, Friday and Sunday, and a Queenstown to Strahan trip on Monday, Thursday and Saturday at 11am. Costs for riding the full length one way are $111/30 per adult/child, including lunch. Alternatively, for the same cost, you can ride halfway to the rainforest station at Dubbil Barrel and then hop on the train going back to where you boarded. For one-way rides, there's a bus service back to the embarkation point costing an additional $18/10 per adult/child. There's also a Premier Carriage 1st-class service ($210 per person) which includes extra special food, drinks and service. Inquiries and ticket purchases are at **Queenstown Station** (☏03-6471 1700; Driffield St) or the **Strahan Activity Centre** (☏03-6471 4300, 1800 628 286; www.westcoastwilderness railway.com.au; Esplanade).

👁 Sights & Activities

Eric Thomas Galley Museum   MUSEUM
(☏03-6471 1483; 1 Driffield St; adult/family $5/12; ⊙9.30am-5pm Mon-Fri, 12.30-5pm Sat & Sun, winter hours vary) This museum started life as the Imperial Hotel in 1898. Inside are diverting displays of old photographs with idiosyncratic captions. It doubles as the Queenstown visitor information centre.

Spion Kop Lookout   LANDMARK
For top-of-the-town views, follow Hunter St uphill, turn left onto Bowes St, then sharp left onto Latrobe St to a small car park. From here a short, steep track ascends Spion Kop Lookout.

🚶 Tours

Mt Lyell Mine Tours   MINE TOURS
(☏0407 049 612; tours $100; ⊙10am & 2pm) The abandoned open-cut mine **Iron Blow** can be seen from a lookout off the Lyell Hwy, while mining continues deep beneath the massive West Lyell crater. Take a two-hour tour with this outfit. Minimum age is 14; bookings are essential.

🛏 Sleeping

Mt Lyell Anchorage   B&B $$
(☏03-6471 1900; www.mtlyellanchorage.com; 17 Cutten St; s $80-130, d $130-160) This 1890s weatherboard home has been completely transformed into a wonderful little guesthouse with quality beds, linen and luxuriously deep carpets. There are also two self-contained apartments ($150 for up to four people, $200 for up to six). Breakfast provisions included for all.

Penghana   B&B $$
(☏03-6471 2560; www.penghana.com.au; 32 The Esplanade; s $135, d from $150, ste $175; 🖥) This National Trust–listed mansion (1898) is on a hill above town amid a beautiful garden. The house includes a billiards room and a grand dining room for enjoying hearty breakfasts and evening meals by arrangement.

Empire Hotel   PUB $
(☏03-6471 1699; 2 Orr St; s $35, d with/without bathroom $75/50) The rooms here aren't as magnificent as the imposing blackwood staircase that's a National Trust–listed treasure, but they are clean and tended by friendly staff. There are excellent meals in the dining room.

Queenstown Cabin & Tourist Park   CAMPGROUND $
(☏03-6471 1332; 17 Grafton St; unpowered/powered sites $20/25, on-site vans d $60, d cabins $70-90, extra adult $10-15, extra child $5, linen hire $5) This basic park is set on gravel, but it does have a small grassy camping area.

Eating & Drinking

Café Serenade CAFE $
(40 Orr St; mains $10-14.50; ☺breakfast & lunch; 🍴) Look forward to yummy soups, sourdough toasted sandwiches, salads and good vegetarian options, as well as hearty roasts and curries. Also does gluten-free and dairy-free sweet treats, and the coffee is excellent.

Empire Hotel PUB $
(2 Orr St; mains $12-17; ☺lunch & dinner) This old miners pub has survived the ages and includes an atmospheric heritage dining room serving a changing menu of hearty pub standards, including roasts, pastas, and fine steaks and ribs.

☆ Entertainment

Paragon Theatre CINEMA
(www.theparagon.com.au; 1 McNamara St; short-films program per hr $10; ☺2-6.30pm, reduced hours in winter) This refurbished art-deco theatre shows Hollywood flicks, but also a revolving program of short films about the west coast and Queenstown.

Strahan

POP 700

Strahan, 40km southwest of Queenstown on the Macquarie Harbour, is the only vestige of civilisation on Tasmania's wild west coast. Visitors come in droves seeking a taste of Tasmania's famous wilderness, whether by seaplane, a Gordon River cruise or the Wilderness Railway.

Macquarie Harbour was discovered in the early 1800s by sailors searching for Huon pine. The area was inaccessible by land and proved difficult to reach by sea – dubious assets that prompted the establishment of a brutal penal colony on Sarah Island in 1821. In the middle of Macquarie Harbour, Sarah Island isolated the colony's worst convicts, their muscle used to harvest Huon pine nearby. Convicts worked 12 hours a day, often in leg irons, felling pines and rafting them back to the island's sawpits where they were used to build superb ships. In 1834, after the establishment of the Port Arthur penal settlement, Sarah Island was abandoned.

Today, Strahan's harbourside main street is undeniably attractive, but in an artificial, overcommercialised kind of way. It can snow here in summer or blow a blizzard on a whim, so pack winter-weight and waterproof clothing.

See www.destinationstrahan.com.au and www.strahantasmania.com.

⊙ Sights & Activities

West Coast Reflections MUSEUM
(Esplanade; ☺10am-6pm summer, noon-5pm winter) The museum section of the Strahan visitor centre offers a creative and thought-provoking display on the history of the west coast, with a refreshingly blunt appraisal of the region's environmental disappointments and achievements.

The Ship That Never Was THEATRE
(Esplanade; adult/child $17.50/7.50; ☺5.30pm year-round & 8.30pm Jan) This unmissable play tells the story of convicts who escaped from Sarah Island in 1834 by hijacking a ship they were building. It's highly entertaining fun (with crowd participation) for all age groups.

Beaches WALKING, BIRDWATCHING
Other attractions include the storm-battered, 33km-long Ocean Beach, 6km from town. The rips rip and the undertows tow – swimming isn't recommended, but visiting at sunset is. From October to April the Ocean Beach dunes become a **mutton-bird rookery**, the birds returning from winter migration. Ask at the visitor information centre about ranger-run tours in January and February. West Strahan Beach, closer to town, has a gently sloping sandy bottom that's OK for swimming. About 14km along the road from Strahan to Zeehan are the spectacular Henty Dunes, impressive 30m-high sand mountains.

⌘ Tours

Also on offer in Strahan are 4WD tours, quad biking, kayaking, and sand-boarding down the towering Henty Dunes.

Gordon River Cruises BOAT CRUISE
(☎1800 628 288, 03-6471 4300; www.puretasmania.com.au; The Esplanade) Offers 5½-hour cruises departing 8.30am daily, and also at 2.45pm over summer. Cost depends on where you sit. Standard seats with an excellent buffet lunch cost from $115/65 per adult/child. You can pay more for window-recliner seats, but the windows fog up and people wander around anyway, and they're not worth the extra. Or you can pay $210 (all tickets) for the Captain's Premier Upper Deck with a swisho lunch and all beverages.

World Heritage Cruises BOAT CRUISE

(☑1800 611 796, 03-6471 7174; www.world heritagecruises.com.au; The Esplanade) Take a 5¾-hour morning or afternoon cruise on the Gordon River, costing per adult/child $90/48 including a fine buffet lunch, or pay $115/63 for premium window seats. You can buy a Gold Pass ticket ($138) including a glass of wine, *Story of Sarah Island* booklet and premium window seats.

Wild Rivers Jet JET-BOATING

(☑03-6471 7396; www.wildriversjet.com.au; The Esplanade) Fifty-minute jet-boat rides on the hour from 9am to 4pm up the King River's rainforest-lined gorges. The experience costs $70/42 per adult/child. Minimum two people; bookings recommended. A longer 1¾-hour **combined boat/4WD trip** (adult/child $94/50) visits the **Teepookana Plateau** with its ancient (and newly planted) Huon pines and eagle's-eye forest lookout.

West Coast Yacht Charters SAILING

(☑03-6471 7422; www.westcoastyachtcharters.com.au; The Esplanade) Overnight Gordon River sightseeing cruises onboard the 60ft steel ketch *Stormbreaker*. The boat carries just 10 passengers, making it a much more intimate experience. One night, including a visit to Sarah Island and all meals, costs $320/160 per adult/child. Also available are three-hour fishing and kayaking trips ($80/60) including a crayfish lunch.

Strahan Seaplanes & Helicopters FLIGHTSEEING

(☑03-6471 7718; www.adventureflights.com.au; The Esplanade) Seaplane and helicopter flights over the region. Seaplane options include 80-minute flights over Frenchmans Cap, the Franklin and Gordon Rivers, and Sarah Island (per adult/child $199/110), and 65-minute flights over the Cradle Mountain region ($210/95). A 60-minute helicopter flight over the Teepookana Forest Reserve costs $199/120, and a quick 15 minutes over Hells Gates and Macquarie Harbour costs $110/70.

🛏 Sleeping

Franklin Manor BOUTIQUE HOTEL $$$

(☑03-6471 7311; www.franklinmanor.com.au; Esplanade; d $145-250, extra person $50; ☎) Set in well-tended gardens, this elegant boutique guesthouse offers fine rooms, fine dining and equally fine service. There's a legendary wine cellar, and a Tasmanian produce room where you can taste and buy local delicacies.

Strahan Wilderness Lodge B&B $

(☑03-6471 7142; www.bayviewcottages-cabins.com.au; Ocean Beach Rd; lodge d incl breakfast $70-85, cabins $75-110) The '70s decor is cheesy-authentic and some rooms share bathrooms, but this place is the best value in town. Self-contained timber cabins are dotted among windswept heathlands – also great value. To get here drive three minutes along Harvey St west from the town.

Strahan Bungalows APARTMENTS $$

(☑03-6471 7268; www.strahanbungalows.com.au; cnr Andrew & Harvey Sts; d $90-160, extra person $30) Decorated with a nautical theme, these award-winning self-contained bungalows are bright, light and friendly. They're close to the beach, and less than 15 minutes' walk from the centre of town.

Strahan Backpackers HOSTEL $

(☑03-6471 7255; 43 Harvey St; unpowered sites d $15-25, dm $25-35, d $69-75, cabins $70-85; @☎) In an attractive bush setting 15 minutes' walk from the town centre are these plain bunks and doubles, and cute, A-frame cabins.

Discovery Holiday Parks Strahan CAMPGROUND $

(☑03-6471 7239; cnr Andrew & Innes Sts; unpowered sites d $20-35, powered sites $25-45, cabins $95-150; @) Right on Strahan's West Beach, this neat and friendly park has good facilities including a camp kitchen, BBQs and a kids' playground.

🍴 Eating

Franklin Manor MODERN AUSTRALIAN $$$

(☑03-6471 7311; Esplanade; 2 courses $47.50, 3 courses $49.50; ⏰dinner Mon-Sat) Franklin Manor serves imaginative and beautifully presented dishes in thoroughly elegant surroundings. The food is fancy, but the atmosphere and service are comfortably down to earth. In summer only (2pm to 5pm) you can also enjoy high tea.

Risby Cove MODERN AUSTRALIAN $$

(☑03-6471 7572; Esplanade; mains $22-36; ⏰breakfast Dec-Mar, dinner year-round) People come from all over to dine at the Cove. The menu features fancy dishes like red wine and juniper marinated duck breast, and there's always fresh Macquarie Harbour ocean trout.

Schwoch Seafoods   FISH AND CHIPS **$$**
(Esplanade; mains $10-26; ⊙11.30am-8.30pm
Mon-Sat, 5-8pm Sun) The best fish and chips in
town – grilled or battered and briny fresh.
Crayfish is sometimes available, and there's
good burgers and pizzas. Eat in or take away.

Regatta Point Tavern   PUB **$$**
(Esplanade; mains $16-35; ⊙lunch & dinner) Eat
with the locals 2km around the bay from
Strahan's centre. There are the usual steaks
and burgers as well as good fresh fish. Check
out the crayfish mornay – in season – if
you're after something fancy.

ℹ Information

Parks & Wildlife Service (☑03-6471 7122;
www.parks.tas.gov.au; The Esplanade; ⊙9am-
5pm Mon-Fri; @) In the old Customs House –
also houses the post office and online access
centre.

West Coast visitor information centre
(☑03-6472 6800; www.westcoast.tas.gov.au;
The Esplanade; ⊙10am-7pm Dec-Mar, to 6pm
Apr-Nov; @)

Franklin-Gordon Wild Rivers National Park

Saved from hydroelectric immersion in the
1980s, this World Heritage–listed national
park (www.parks.tas.gov.au) embraces the
catchment areas of the Franklin and Olga
Rivers and part of the Gordon River – all
exceptional rafting, bushwalking and climbing areas. The park's snow-capped summit
is Frenchmans Cap (1443m; a challenging
three- to five-day walk). The park also boasts
a number of unique plant species and the
major Indigenous Australian archaeological
site at Kutikina Cave.

Much of the park consists of deep river
gorges and impenetrable rainforest, but the
Lyell Hwy traverses its northern end. There
are a handful of short walks starting from
the highway, including hikes to Nelson
Falls (20 minutes return) and Donaghys
Hill (40 minutes return), from where you
can see the Franklin River and the sky-high
white quartzite dome of Frenchmans Cap.

Rafting

Rafting the churning waters of the Franklin
River is thrillingly hazardous; for the inexperienced, tour companies offer complete
rafting packages. Whether you go with
an independent group or a tour operator,
you should contact the park rangers at the
Queenstown Parks & Wildlife Service
(☑03-6471 2511; Penghana Rd) or the Lake St
Clair visitor information centre (☑03-
6289 1172; Cynthia Bay) for current information
on permits, weather, regulations and environmental considerations. See also detailed
'Franklin River Rafting Notes' at www.parks.
tas.gov.au.

Expeditions should register at the booth
at the junction of the Lyell Hwy and the
Collingwood River, 49km west of Derwent
Bridge. Rafting the length of the river, starting at Collingwood River and ending at
Sir John Falls, takes between eight and 14
days. It's also possible to do shorter trips.
From the exit point, you can be picked up
by a Strahan Seaplanes & Helicopters
(☑03-6471 7718; www.adventureflights.com.au)
seaplane or by West Coast Yacht Charters (☑03-6471 7422; www.tasadventures.com)
Stormbreaker for the trip back to Strahan.
Or you can paddle 22km further downriver
to meet a Gordon River cruise boat at Heritage Landing.

Tours run mainly from December to
March. Tour companies with complete rafting packages (departing Hobart) include:

Rafting Tasmania   RAFTING
(☑03-6239 1080; www.raftingtasmania.
com) Five-/seven-/10-day trips costing
$1750/2100/2700.

Tasmanian Expeditions   RAFTING
(☑1300 666 856, 03-6331 9000; www.tas-ex.
com) Nine-/11-day trips for $2595/2795.

Water By Nature   RAFTING
(☑1800 111 142, 0408 242 941; www.franklinriver
tasmania.com) Five-/seven-/10-day trips for
$1940/2240/2790.

Cradle Mountain-Lake St Clair National Park

Tasmania is world famous for the stunning
168,000-hectare World Heritage area of
Cradle Mountain-Lake St Clair. Mountain
peaks, dank gorges, pristine lakes, tarns and
wild moorlands extend triumphantly from
the Great Western Tiers in the north to Derwent Bridge on the Lyell Hwy in the south.
It was one of Australia most heavily glaci-
ated areas, and includes Mt Ossa (1617m) –
Tasmania's highest peak – and Lake St Clair,
Australia's deepest natural freshwater lake
(167m).

The preservation of this region as a **national park** (www.parks.tas.gov.au) is due in part to Austrian immigrant Gustav Weindorfer. In 1912 he built a chalet out of King Billy pine, called it Waldheim (German for 'Forest Home') and, from 1916, lived there permanently. Today the site of his chalet at the northern end of the park retains the name Waldheim.

There are fabulous day walks at both Cradle Valley in the north and Cynthia Bay (Lake St Clair) in the south, but it's the outstanding 80.5km Overland Track between the two that has turned this park into a bushwalkers' mecca.

◎ Sights & Activities

Bushwalking is the primary lure of this national park. Aside from the Overland Track there are dozens of short walks here. For Cradle Valley visitors, behind the Cradle Mountain visitor information centre there is an easy but first-rate 20-minute circular boardwalk through the adjacent rainforest, called the **Pencil Pine Falls & Rainforest Walk**, suitable for wheelchairs and prams. Nearby is another trail leading to **Knyvet Falls** (45 minutes return), as well as the **Enchanted Walk** alongside Pencil Pine Creek (20 minutes return), and the **King Billy Walk** (one hour return). The **Cradle Valley Walk** (2½ hours one way) is an 8.5km-long boardwalk linking the Cradle Mountain visitor information centre and Dove Lake. The **Dove Lake Walk** is a 6km lap of the lake, which takes around two hours.

Larmairremener tabelti   CULTURE WALK
At Cynthia Bay, this Aboriginal culture walk winds through the traditional lands of the Larmairremener, the Indigenous people of the region. The walk (one hour return) starts at the visitor information centre. Another way to do some walking here is to catch the ferry service to either Echo Point Hut or Narcissus Hut and walk back to Cynthia Bay along the lakeshore. From Echo Point it's four to five hours' walk back; from Narcissus five to six hours.

⌂ Tours

Almost every tour operator offers day trips or longer tours to the area (including guided walks along the Overland Track).

**Cradle Country
Adventures**   HORSE RIDING, QUAD BIKING
(☑1300 656 069; www.cradlecountryadventures.com.au) Half-day, full-day and multiday riding trips are available (two-hour trip $95, full day from $220). Just outside the World Heritage areas, quadbike tours are also available (www.cradlemountainquadbikes.com.au; two-hour trip $110). Kids can go as passengers (two hours $66).

Cradle Mountain Helicopters   FLIGHTSEEING
(☑03-6492 1132; www.adventureflights.com.au; Cradle Mountain Rd; flights Sep-Jun) Thirty-minute flights cost $190/140 per adult/child.

Cradle Mountain Huts   BUSHWALKING
(☑03-6391 9339; www.cradlehuts.com.au; from $2600; ☺Oct-May) A six-day/five-night, guided walk along the Overland Track staying in private huts with others carrying your pack.

Tasmanian Expeditions   BUSHWALKING
(☑1300 666 856, 03-6339 3999; www.tas-ex.com; ☺Nov-Apr) Eight-day/seven-night Overland Track trip for $2095 and a six-day Cradle Mountain/Walls of Jerusalem walk for $1695.

⊨ Sleeping & Eating

CRADLE VALLEY

TOP CHOICE **Cradle Mountain Highlanders Cottages**   COTTAGES $$
(☑03-6492 1116; www.cradlehighlander.com.au; Cradle Mountain Rd; d $115-250, extra adult/child $30/20) These immaculate self-contained timber cottages all have wood or gas fires and queen-sized beds. Three cabins include a spa, and the surrounding bush is filled with curious wildlife.

Waldheim Chalet & Cabins   CABINS $
(☑03-6491 2271; 4-/6-/8-bed cabin $95/135/185) Set in the forest are rustic wood-lined cabins with bunks sleeping eight, six and four. Each has kitchen facilities and there's a shared shower and toilet block.

Cradle Mountain Lodge   RESORT $$$
(☑03-6492 2103, 1300 806 192; www.cradlemountainlodge.com.au; Cradle Mountain Rd; d $310-760, extra adult $72; @) This stone-and-timber resort near the national park entrance has nearly 100 cabins surrounding the main lodge. There's good eating at the house restaurants – the neat-casual **Highland** (mains $19-28; ☺breakfast, lunch & dinner) and the laidback **Tavern** (mains $12-19; ☺lunch & dinner). There's also a spa retreat.

Australia's most famous trek is usually tackled as a six-day, five-night epic, walking 65km between Cradle Valley in the north and Lake St Clair in the south. The scenery is breathtaking and takes in some of Tasmania's highest peaks, through tall eucalypt forests bursting with wildlife, and across exposed alpine moors and buttongrass valleys of unsurpassed beauty.

The Overland Track is at its most picturesque in the summer months when the alpine wildflowers are blooming. This December-to-April period has more daylight hours and warmer temperatures, but there are fewer walkers in the spring and autumn months. Only very experienced walkers should tackle the track in winter. All walkers must register the start and finish of their walk at either end of the track.

In 1953 fewer than 1000 people walked the Overland Track, but by 2004 the trail was being pounded by 9000 hikers annually. To preserve the area's delicate ecology and avoid environmental degradation and overcrowding, some changes to walking conditions have been introduced:

» There's a booking system in place from 1 November to 30 April, when a maximum of 34 walkers can depart each day.

» There are fees of $160/128 per adult/child aged 5–17 and concession, to cover costs of sustainable track management (these apply from November to April only).

» The compulsory walking direction from November to April is north to south.

Departing Cradle Valley, walkers sometimes start at Dove Lake, but the recommended route begins at Ronny Creek, around 5km from the Cradle Mountain visitor information centre. There are many secondary paths off the main track, scaling mountains like Mt Ossa and detouring to lakes, waterfalls and valleys, so the length of time you spend on the track is only limited by the amount of supplies you can carry.

Once you reach Narcissus Hut at the northern end of Lake St Clair, you can walk around the lake's edge to Cynthia Bay (a five- to six-hour walk) or take the ferry run by Lake St Clair Wilderness Resort (p700). To guarantee a seat, you must book the ferry before you start walking, then when you get to Narcissus Hut, use the radio to confirm your booking.

You can bunk down in the excellent huts along the track, but in summer they're full of snoring hikers and smelly socks. To preserve your sanity, bring a tent and pitch it on the established timber platforms around each hut. Campfires are banned, so fuel stoves are essential. There's plenty of clean drinking water available along the way, but boil anything you have doubts about.

Book your walk online at www.overlandtrack.com.au, where there's stacks of info and where you can order *The Overland Track – One Walk, Many Journeys* booklet ($12) detailing track sections, flora and fauna. There's also a link to the Tasmap (www.tasmap. tas.gov.au) website, where you can buy the 1:100,000 *Lake St Clair Map & Notes*. Visitor information centres also sell the booklet and map. Lonely Planet's *Walking in Australia* guide has detailed walk descriptions.

Discovery Holiday Parks Cradle Mountain　　　CAMPGROUND **$**
(☏03-6492 1395, 1800 068 574; www.discovery parks.com.au; Cradle Mountain Rd; unpowered/ powered sites d $32/45, dm $42, cabins from $160-200; @🐾) This bushland complex is 2.5km from the national park. It has well-separated sites, a YHA-affiliated hostel, a camp kitchen and laundry and self-contained cabins.

Self-caterers should stock up before heading to Cradle Valley; minimal supplies are sold at the Cradle Mountain Cafe, Discovery Holiday Parks shop and Cradle Mountain Lodge. There are no ATMs.

CYNTHIA BAY & DERWENT BRIDGE

Derwent Bridge Wilderness Hotel　　　PUB **$$**
(Lyell Hwy, Derwent Bridge; dm $30, linen $5, d with/ without bathroom $140/120) This is a brilliant spot on a freezing day with roaring log fires, cold beers and man-sized pub meals. The accommodation needs an upgrade, but the bar

has a soaring, timber-beamed ceiling, a pool table, jukebox and easy-going vibe.

Derwent Bridge Chalets & Studios
COTTAGES **$$**

(☑03-6289 1000; www.derwent-bridge.com; Lyell Hwy, Derwent Bridge; d $145-245, extra adult/child $40/25;) Just 5km from Lake St Clair (500m east of the turn-off) this place has one-, two- and three-bedroom self-contained cabins and studios, some with spa but all with full kitchen and laundry facilities.

Lake St Clair Wilderness Resort
CAMPGROUND, HOSTEL **$**

(☑03-6289 1137; www.lakestclairresort.com.au; unpowered/powered sites d $25/35, dm/d $35/80, cottages d $240-265, extra person $35) The lakeside camping area here is bookended by Lake St Clair and serrated mountain peaks. There are lots of walking opportunities and plentiful wildlife.

Hungry Wombat Café
CAFE **$**

(Lyell Hwy, Derwent Bridge; mains $6-15; ⊗8am-6pm summer, 9am-5pm winter) This friendly cafe serves big breakfasts, and loads of homemade soups, fish and chips and snacks to get you through an active day. There's also a small grocery section.

Information

All walking tracks in the park are signposted, well defined and easy to follow, but it's prudent to carry a map – pick one up at park visitor information centres.

Cradle Valley

The **Cradle Mountain visitor information centre** (☑03-6492 1110; www.parks.tas.gov.au; Cradle Mountain Rd; ⊗8am-5pm, reduced hours in winter) provides extensive bushwalking information (including national park and Overland Track passes and registration), and informative flora, fauna and park history displays.

Just inside the park boundary is the **Rangers Station interpretation centre** (⊗9am-5pm during daylight saving, 9.30am-4pm in winter). At time of writing an auditorium was being built for video presentations on the natural history of Cradle Mountain and the tracks in the area. There are also Aboriginal cultural displays here.

Regardless of season, be prepared for cold, wet weather around Cradle Valley. On average it rains here seven days out of 10, and it's cloudy eight days in 10. The sun shines all day only one day in 10, and it snows on 54 days each year.

Lake St Clair

Occupying one wing of a large building at Cynthia Bay on the park's southern boundary is the **Lake St Clair visitor information centre** (☑03-6289 1172; www.parks.tas.gov.au; Cynthia Bay; ⊗8am-5pm), providing rock-solid walking advice, national park passes and displays.

At the adjacent, separately run **Lake St Clair Lodge** (☑03-6289 1137; www.lakestclairresort.com.au; Cynthia Bay; ⊗8am-5pm Apr-Oct, 7am-8pm Nov-Mar), you can book a range of accommodation or a seat on a ferry or lake cruise.

❶ Getting There & Away

Tassielink (☑1300 300 520; www.tassielink.com.au) buses service both Cradle Mountain and Lake St Clair; see p701 for details.

Saintys (☑03-6334 6456) runs on-demand services from Devonport to Cradle Mountain (one to four passengers $220, five or more $50 per passenger), Launceston to Cradle Mountain ($30/60), and Devonport or Launceston to Lake St Clair ($320/80).

Ask around at bushwalking shops or hostels and you might get lucky with cheaper, shared transport.

❶ Getting Around

Cradle Valley

To avoid overcrowding on the narrow road into Cradle Mountain and gridlock at the Dove Lake car park, there's now a shuttle bus into the park. Buses run every 10 to 20 minutes between about 8am and 8pm in summer (reduced hours in winter) from the Cradle Mountain Transit Centre (by the visitor centre) where you park your car. The fare is included in a valid parks pass. Buses stop at the Rangers Station interpretation centre, Snake Hill, Ronny Creek and Dove Lake.

Cynthia Bay & Derwent Bridge

Lake St Clair Lodge (☑03-6289 1137; www.lakestclairresort.com.au) operates bushwalkers' ferry trips to and from Narcissus Hut at the northern end of Lake St Clair (30 to 40 minutes). The one-way fare is adult/child $38/19. The boat departs Cynthia Bay three times daily (9am, 12.30pm and 3pm) October to early May (or on demand, minimum six people) stopping at Narcissus Hut about 30 minutes later. If you're using the ferry service at the end of your Overland Track hike, for which bookings are essential, you *must* radio the ferry operator when you arrive at Narcissus to reconfirm your booking.

Saintys (☑03-6334 6456) runs an on-demand service that must be pre-booked between Cynthia Bay/Lake St Clair and Derwent Bridge ($30 per person one way). The distance is 5km.

THE SOUTHWEST

Southwest National Park

The **Southwest National Park** (www.parks. tas.gov.au), Tasmania's largest national park, is one of the planet's last great isolated wilderness areas and home to some of the last tracts of virgin temperate rainforest. It's a place of untouched primeval grandeur and extraordinary biodiversity, and part of Tasmania's World Heritage area.

The southwest is the habitat of the endemic Huon pine and the swamp gum, the world's tallest hardwood and tallest flowering plant. Around 300 species of lichen, moss and fern dapple the rainforest with shades of green; glacial tarns seamlessly mirror snowy mountaintops; and in summer, picture-perfect alpine meadows explode with wildflowers. Untamed rivers charge through the landscape, rapids surging through gorges and waterfalls plummeting over cliffs.

🏃 Activities

Bushwalking

The most-trodden walks in the park are the 70km **Port Davey Track** between Scotts Peak Rd and Melaleuca (around five days' duration), and the considerably more popular 85km **South Coast Track** (six to eight days) between Cockle Creek and Melaleuca.

On both tracks, hikers should be prepared for vicious weather. Light planes airlift bushwalkers into Melaleuca in the southwest (there are no roads), while there's vehicle access and public transport to/from Cockle Creek at the other end of the South Coast Track, and Scotts Peak Rd at the other end of the Port Davey Track.

Check out the track notes on the **Parks & Wildlife Service** (www.parks.tas.gov.au) website, and in Lonely Planet's *Walking in Australia*.

Sea Kayaking

Kettering's Roaring 40s Ocean Kayaking (p643) runs three- and seven-day guided kayaking expeditions ($1650/2395 per person) out of Melaleuca, exploring the waterways around Bathurst Harbour and Port Davey.

ℹ️ Getting There & Around

The most popular way to tackle the South Coast Track is to fly into Melaleuca and walk out to Cockle Creek. **Par Avion** (☑03-6248 5390; www.paravion.com.au) flies between Hobart and Melaleuca one way for $190. There's also a soft option: scenic flights from Hobart over the southwest, with time spent on the ground. Par Avion's speciality is a four-hour 'Heritage Tour' (adult/child $240/210), passing the big peaks and surf-ravaged south coast, along with a boat trip on Bathurst Harbour and refreshments included. Full-day trips cost $350/310. **Tasair** (☑1800 062 900, 03-6248 5088; www.tasair.com.au) offers a two-hour scenic flight with 30 minutes on the ground at Melaleuca (from $298 per person).

From December to March on Monday, Wednesday and Friday, **Tassielink** (☑1300 300 520; www.tassielink.com.au) runs buses from Hobart to Cockle Creek ($73, 3½ hours), returning to Hobart on the same days. Between November and April, **Evans Coaches**

KEEPING SAFE – BLIZZARDS & HYOPTHERMIA

Blizzards can occur in Tasmania's mountains at any time of year. Bushwalkers need to be prepared for such freezing eventualities, particularly in remote areas. Take warm clothing such as thermals and jackets, plus windproof and waterproof garments. Carry a high-quality tent suitable for snow camping and enough food for two extra days, in case you get held up by bad weather.

Hypothermia is a significant risk, especially during the winter months in southern parts of Australia – and especially in Tasmania. Strong winds produce a high chill factor that can result in hypothermia even in moderately cool temperatures. Early signs include the inability to perform fine movements (such as doing up buttons), shivering and a bad case of the 'umbles' (fumbles, mumbles, grumbles and stumbles). The key elements of treatment include moving out of the cold, changing out of any wet clothing into dry clothes with wind- and waterproof layers, adding insulation and providing fuel (water and carbohydrate) to allow shivering, which builds the internal temperature. In severe hypothermia, shivering actually stops: this is a medical emergency requiring rapid evacuation in addition to the above measures.

FLINDERS ISLAND

Flinders Island and the other 51 islands of the Furneaux Group are all that remains of the land bridge that connected Tasmania with mainland Australia 10,000 years ago. Between 1829 and 1834, 135 Indigenous people from Flinders Island were transported to Wybalenna to be 'civilised and educated'. After 14 years, only 47 survived. Today, Flinders is a rural and fishing community of 900. Activities include bushwalking, wildlife spotting, fishing, kayaking, snorkelling and diving.

Sights

Wybalenna Historic Site
HISTORIC SITE

A few piles of bricks, the chapel and cemetery are all that remains of this settlement to 'care for' Aboriginal people. Eighty-seven people died here from poor food, disease and despair.

Furneaux Museum
MUSEUM

(8 Fowlers Rd, Emita; adult/child $4/free; ☺1-5pm daily late Dec-Jan, 1-4pm Sat & Sun Feb-Nov) This museum displays Aboriginal artefacts, sealing, sailing and mutton-bird industry relics.

Sleeping

Vistas on Trousers Point
BOUTIQUE HOTEL $$

(☏03-6359 4586; www.healingdreams.com.au; 855 Trousers Point Rd; s/d $160/260) This lodge offers healing treatments and home-grown organic food. Do yoga in the yurt or soak in the spa.

Flinders Island Cabin Park
CAMPGROUND $

(☏03-6359 2188; www.flindersislandcp.com.au; 1 Bluff Rd, Whitemark d $20, backpacker cabin s $40, d $90-105, extra person $20) Backpacker accommodation and cabins, car and campervan hire ($50 to $110 per day). Free use of bikes for guests (or $25 per day for nonstayers) and kayak hire.

Eating

Flinders is known for fresh seafood, tender lamb and game, and organic veggies.

Vistas Café & Chappells Restaurant
MODERN AUSTRALIAN $$

(mains $29; ☺lunch & dinner in midsummer, Wed-Sun rest of year) Fine dining with views at Vistas on Trousers Point (see above).

Shearwater Restaurant
MODERN AUSTRALIAN $$

(Furneaux Tavern, Franklin Pde, Lady Barron; mains $10-33; ☺lunch & dinner 6-7.30pm) Excellent bistro food, but closes early.

Information

There are no ATMs, but most businesses have Eftpos facilities for cash withdrawals.

Online Access Centre (☏03-6359 2151; 2 Davies St, Whitemark; ☺10am-1pm & 2-5pm Wed-Fri; @) At the library.

Service Tasmania (☏03-6359 2201; 2 Lagoon Rd, Whitemark; ☺10am-4pm Mon-Fri) Walking track advice and national park passes.

Visitor centre (☏03-6359 5002; www.visitflindersisland.com.au; 4 Davies St, Whitemark; ☺9am-4.30pm Mon-Fri)

Getting There & Away

Furneaux Freight (☏03-6356 1753; www.furneauxfreight.com.au; Main St, Bridport;) Operates a Bridport–Lady Barron car ferry on the high tide on Mondays (cars $400 return, extra passenger adult/child $100/55 return). Advance bookings essential.

Flinders Island Travel (☏1800 674 719; www.flindersislandtravel.com.au) Package deals (flights, accommodation and car rental).

Sharp Airlines (☏1300 55 66 94; www.sharpairlines.com.au) Travels Melbourne (Essendon)–Flinders ($212), Launceston–Flinders ($157).

Getting Around

Flinders Island Car Hire (☏03-6359 2168; www.ficr.com.au)

Taxi & airport shuttle bus (☏03-6359 3664)

(☎03-6297 1335; www.evanscoaches.com.au) also has a Hobart–Cockle Creek service ($75) and runs the only bus service from Hobart to Scotts Peak Rd at the end of the Port Davey Track – this runs as a charter service costing $150 for one and $100 per person for two or more, and takes four hours.

Lake Pedder & Strathgordon

Lake Pedder sits at the northern edge of the Southwest National Park. It was once a stunning natural lake famed for its beaches, and regarded as the ecological jewel of Tasmania's wilderness region. But in 1972, amid howls of protest from a nascent green movement, it was flooded to become part of the Gordon River power development.

Tiny Strathgordon (population 30) was built to service employees during construction of the Gordon River Power Scheme. On a clear day (about one in five!), the drive here from Mt Field is bedazzling – bleak peaks, empty buttongrass plains and rippling lakes. About 12km west of Strathgordon is the Gordon Dam Lookout and visitor information centre (Gordon River Rd; ⊘9am-6.30pm), poised above the 140m-high Gordon Dam and providing info on the scheme.

You can't go inside the underground power station any more, but you can plunge over the edge of the dam wall by spending a day with Hobart-based Aardvark Adventures (☎03-6273 7722, 0408 127 714; www.aardvarkadventures.com.au), which organises abseiling trips here ($210, suitable for beginners, minimum two people). It's the highest commercial abseil in the world. Trips depart from Hobart.

Adelaide &
South Australia

Best Paces to Eat

» Cafe Zest (p725)
» Star of Greece (p739)
» Kangaroo Island Fresh Seafoods (p749)
» diVine (p757)
» Blond Coffee (p769)

Best Places to Stay

» Glenelg Beach Hostel & Bar (p721)
» 5 Rooms at the Stirling Hotel (p734)
» Port Elliot Beach House YHA (p741)

Why Go?

Escape the east-coast frenzy in crowd-free, relaxed South Australia (SA). The driest state on the driest inhabited continent, SA beats the heat by celebrating life's finer things: fine landscapes, fine festivals, fine food, and (...OK, forget the other three) fine wine.

Adelaide remains near Australia's cultural high-water mark – a chilled-out, gracious city offering world-class festivals, restaurants and hedonistic arts. A day trip away, McLaren Vale and the Barossa and Clare Valleys are self-assured viticulture success stories (love that Shiraz...). Further afield are the sea-salty wilds of the Limestone Coast, and the Murray River, curling Mississippi-like towards the sea. Kangaroo Island's wildlife, forests and seafood await just offshore.

To the west, Yorke Peninsula and Eyre Peninsula are beachy, slow-paced detours. Wheeling into the Flinders Ranges, wheat fields give way to arid cattle stations beneath russet peaks. Further north, eccentric outback towns like Woomera and Coober Pedy emerge from the dead-flat desert haze.

When to Go
Adelaide

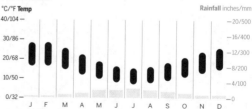

Feb–Mar Adelaide's festival season hits its straps: the Fringe and WOMADelaide are highlights.

Apr–May Low autumn sunsets and russet-red grapevines: harvest is in the air.

Sep Football finals time: yell yourself silly in the stands, beer and pie in hand(s).

History

South Australia was declared a province on 28 December 1836, when the first British colonists landed at Holdfast Bay. The first governor, Captain John Hindmarsh, named the state capital Adelaide, after the wife of the British monarch, William IV. While the eastern states struggled with the stigma of convict society, SA's colonists were free citizens – a fact to which many South Australians will happily draw your attention.

The founders based the colony on a utopian 19th-century ideal of social engineering. Land was sold at set prices by the British government to help establish mainly young, skilled married couples; the concept was that equal numbers of men and women, free from religious and political persecution, would create an egalitarian new order.

Between 1838 and 1841, 800 German farmers and artisans (many persecuted Lutherans from Prussia) arrived and settled Hahndorf in the Adelaide Hills – now the best preserved German village in the state. Many more followed over the next decade, bringing vine cuttings with them – SA's famous vineyards began to take root.

The young colony's early progress was slow – only British government funds saved it from bankruptcy – but it became self-supporting by the mid-1840s and self-governing by 1856. Following the successful crossing of the continent by local explorers, SA won the contract to lay the Overland Telegraph from Port Augusta to Darwin, connecting Australia to the world by telegram (1872), and later, telephone. Following a long recession in the late 19th century, the government became the first to introduce income tax – a fact to which South Australians are hesitant to draw your attention...

SA has maintained its socially progressive creed: trade unions were legalised in 1876; women were permitted to stand for parliament in 1894; and the state was one of the first places in the world to give women the vote, and the first state in Australia to outlaw racial and gender discrimination, legalise abortion and decriminalise gay sex.

Indigenous Adelaide & South Australia

SA offers up some great opportunities to learn about Aboriginal cultures and beliefs. Some of the best include the Adnyamathanha-run Iga Warta cultural centre in the Flinders Ranges, Yorke Peninsula cultural tours run by Adjahdura Land, and Adelaide's Tandanya National Aboriginal Cultural Institute. Also in Adelaide is the Australian Aboriginal Cultures Gallery in the South Australian Museum. See also the Indigenous-run Bookabee Tours operating out of Adelaide.

SA's best-known Aboriginal language is Pitjantjatjara (also known as Pitjantjara), which is spoken throughout the Anangu-Pitjantjarjara Aboriginal Lands of northern SA, down almost to the Great Australian Bight. The traditional language of the Adelaide area is Kaurna. Many Kaurna-derived place names have survived around the city: Aldinga comes from *Ngultingga*, Onkaparinga from *Ngangkiparringga*, and Noarlunga from *Nurlungga*. The Adelaide Hills region is Peramangk country.

The Coorong, in Ngarrindjeri country, is a complex series of dunes and salt pans separated from the sea by the long, thin Younghusband Peninsula. It takes its name from the Ngarrindjeri word *kurangh,* meaning 'long neck'. According to the Ngarrindjeri, their Dreaming ancestor, Ngurundjeri, created the Coorong and the Murray River.

The iconic Wilpena Pound, a natural basin in Flinders Ranges National Park, is sacred to the Adnyamathanha people, who have lived in the area for over 15,000 years. The Adnyamathanha name for Wilpena Pound is Ikara. Dreaming stories tell of two *akurra* (giant snakes) who coiled around Ikara during an initiation ceremony, creating a whirlwind and devouring the participants. The snakes were so full after their feast they couldn't move, and willed themselves to die, thus creating the landmark (see the boxed text, p788).

In 1966, SA became the first state to grant Aboriginal people title to their land. In the early '80s most of the land west of the Stuart Hwy and north of the railway to Perth was transferred to Aboriginal ownership. Cultural clashes still sometimes occur, however, exemplified by the politically and culturally divisive Hindmarsh Bridge controversy in the 1990s, which pitted Aboriginal beliefs against development (see the boxed text, p743).

National Parks

Around 22% of SA's land area is under some form of official conservation management, including national parks, recreation parks, conservation parks and wildlife reserves. The Department of Environment & Natural Resources (www.environment.sa.gov.au) manages the state's conservation areas and sells park passes and camping permits.

Adelaide & South Australia Highlights

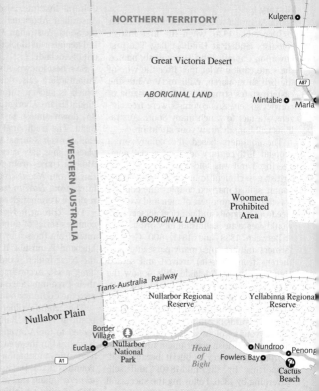

1 Sniff out the ripest cheese, fullest fruit and strongest coffee at Adelaide's **Central Market** (p711)

2 Swirl, nose and quaff your way through **McLaren Vale** (p737), our favourite SA wine region.

3 Trundle past pelicans, dunes and lagoons in **Coorong National Park** (p752)

4 Watch the little penguins waddle on **Kangaroo Island** (p746)

5 Hike up to the lofty, desolate rim of **Wilpena Pound** (p787) in the Flinders Ranges National Park

6 Kick back with a cold schooner or two in **Adelaide's pubs** (p725)

7 Noodle for opals in the moonscape mullock at **Coober Pedy** (p792)

8 Slurp down a dozen briny oysters and watch passing whales at **Coffin Bay** (p780)

NORTHERN TERRITORY

Kulgera

Great Victoria Desert

ABORIGINAL LAND

A87

Mintabie ● ● Marla

WESTERN AUSTRALIA

Woomera Prohibited Area

ABORIGINAL LAND

Trans-Australia Railway

Nullarbor Regional Reserve

Yellabinna Regional Reserve

Nullarbor Plain

Border Village

Eucla ●

Nullarbor National Park

A1

Head of Bight

● Nundroo ● Penong

Fowlers Bay ●

Cactus Beach

Great Australian Bight

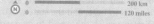

0 — 200 km
0 — 120 miles

SOUTHERN OCEAN

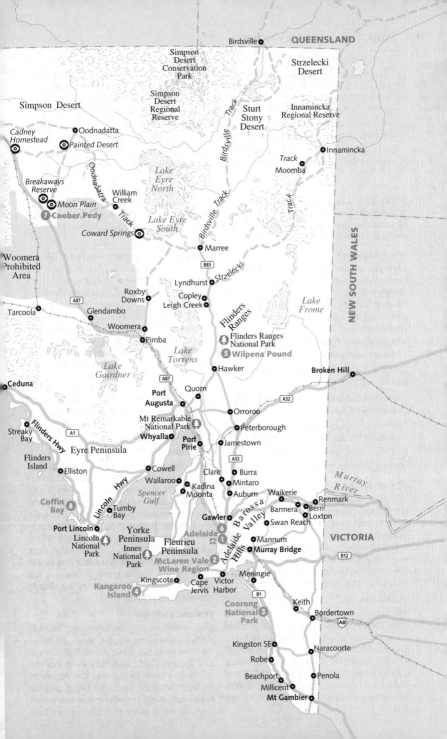

TAKE THE LONG WAY HOME

South Australia has three epic long-distance trails for hiking and cycling:

» **Heysen Trail** (www.heysentrail.asn.au) Australia's longest walking trail: 1200km between Cape Jervis on the Fleurieu Peninsula and Parachilna Gorge in the Flinders Ranges. Access points along the way make it ideal for half- and full-day walks. Note that due to fire restrictions, some sections of the trail are closed between December and April.

» **Kidman Trail** (www.kidmantrail.org.au) A 10-section cycling and walking trail between Willunga on the Fleurieu Peninsula and Kapunda north of the Barossa Valley.

» **Mawson Trail** (www.southaustraliantrails.com) A 900km bike trail between Adelaide and Blinman in the Flinders Ranges, via the Adelaide Hills and Clare Valley.

A 'Two Month Holiday Pass' ($34 per vehicle; $58 including camping) covers entry to most of SA's parks, excluding the desert parks and Flinders Chase on Kangaroo Island.

Wine Regions

Let's cut to the chase: we all know why you're here. South Australian wines are arguably the best in the world, and there's no shortage of wine regions – both established and emerging – in which to taste them. Five key players:

Adelaide Hills Impressive cool-climate wines on Adelaide's back doorstep.

Barossa Valley Old-school estates and famous reds.

Clare Valley Niche Riesling vintages and cosy weekend retreats.

Coonawarrra Lip-smacking Cabernet Sauvignon on the Limestone Coast plains.

McLaren Vale Awesome Shiraz and vine-covered hillsides rolling down to the sea.

🏃 Activities

With hills, beaches, forests, deserts and wide-open spaces, there's pretty much nothing you can't do in SA (well, apart from skiing...). The **South Australian Trails** (www.southaustralian-trails.com) website is chockers with information on activities, including horse riding, canoeing, bushwalking, cycling and diving, with safety tips, maps and useful links.

BUSHWALKING

SA's national parks and conservation areas have thousands of kilometres of marked trails traversing eye-popping wilderness. Around Adelaide there are walks to suit all abilities in the Mt Lofty Ranges, including trails in Belair National Park (Map p712) and Morialta Conservation Park (Map p733); see www.environment.sa.gov.au/parks for details.

In the Flinders Ranges there are outstanding walks in Mt Remarkable National Park and Flinders Ranges National Park.

DIVING

This ain't the Great Barrier Reef, but SA's underwater world sustains a great diversity of life. Don your flippers and tanks and check out leafy sea dragons, seals, nudibranchs, sponge beds, dolphins and endemic species.

Off the Gulf St Vincent coast, top dive sites include Second Valley, Rapid Bay jetty, Cape Jervis and the ex-destroyer **HMAS Hobart** (Map p737; www.exhmashobart.com. au), which was scuttled off Yankalilla Bay in 2002. Other good dive sites include the Yorke Peninsula jetties and the reefs off Port Lincoln. Freshwater cave diving around Mount Gambier is also fantastic. Contact the **Scuba Divers Federation of SA** (www.sdfsa. net) for more info.

ROCK CLIMBING

Rock spiders keen on 10m to 15m cliffs can clamber over the gorges in Morialta Conservation Park and Onkaparinga River Recreation Park, both on the outskirts of Adelaide. More advanced climbers should head for the Flinders Ranges: SA's premier cliff is at Moonarie on the southeastern side of Wilpena Pound – 120m! Buckaringa Gorge, close to Quorn and Hawker, is another fave for the more daring. Contact the **Climbing Club of South Australia** (www.climbingclubsouth australia.asn.au) for info.

SWIMMING & SURFING

Uncrowded, white-sand swimming beaches stretch right along the SA coast; the safest for swimming are along the Gulf St Vincent and Spencer Gulf coasts. Anywhere exposed to the Southern Ocean and the Backstairs Passage (between Kangaroo Island and the mainland) may have strong rips and undertows. If you're after that all-over-tan look,

head for the nudie southern end of Maslin Beach, 40km south of Adelaide.

The SA coast is consistently pummelled by rolling Southern Ocean swells. Pennington Bay has the most consistent surf on Kangaroo Island, while Pondalowie Bay on the Yorke Peninsula has the state's strongest breaks. Other hot spots are scattered between Port Lincoln on the Eyre Peninsula and the famous Cactus Beach in the far west. Closer to Adelaide, the beaches around Port Elliot have some wicked surf, with swells often holding at 3m; other gnarly breaks are Waitpinga Beach and Parsons Beach, 12km southwest of Victor Harbor.

The best surfing season is March to June, when the northerlies doth blow. See www.southaustralia.com/fleurieupeninsulasurfing.aspx for info, and www.surfsouthoz.com for surf reports.

For surfing lessons and gear hire on the Fleurieu Peninsula, see p741.

WHALE WATCHING

Between July and September, migrating southern right whales cruise within a few hundred metres of SA shores as they head to/from their Great Australian Bight breeding grounds. Once prolific, southern right whales suffered unrestrained slaughter during the 19th century, which reduced the whale population from 100,000 to just a few hundred by 1935. Although an endangered species, they are fighting back and the population worldwide may now be as high as 7000.

Key spots for whale watching include Victor Harbor and Head of Bight on the far west coast.

To find out about current whale action call the **Whale Information Hotline** (☎1900 931 223), or contact the South Australian Whale Centre in Victor Harbor.

☞ Tours

Whatever your persuasion or destination, there's probably a SA tour to suit you. See p717 for details on tours in and around Adelaide, including day trips to the Adelaide Hills, Fleurieu Peninsula, Murray River and the Barossa and Clare Valleys.

Further afield, outback tours usually include the Flinders Ranges and Coober Pedy, some continuing north to Alice Springs and Uluru in the Northern Territory. These are some of the operators.

Adventure Tours   WILDERNESS
(☎1800 068 886, 08-8132 8230; www.adventuretours.com.au) Wide range of bus tours around

SA and interstate, including trips from Adelaide to Alice Springs and Uluru, Darwin and Kakadu National Park, Kangaroo Island and the Great Ocean Road.

Bookabee Tours   INDIGENOUS
(☎08-8235 9954; www.bookabee.com.au) Indigenous-run cultural tours to the Flinders Ranges. Two-/three-/four-/five-day tours cost $995/1520/2025/2500.

Groovy Grape   WILDERNESS
(☎1800 661 177, 08-8440 1640; www.groovygrape.com.au) Small-group tours including a three-day trip from Melbourne to Adelaide via the Great Ocean Road ($355), and seven days from Adelaide to Alice Springs via the Flinders Ranges, Coober Pedy and Uluru ($895). Includes meals, camping and national park entry fees. Barossa Valley day tours are also available ($79).

Heading Bush   WILDERNESS
(☎08-8356 5501; www.headingbush.com) Rugged, small-group, 10-day Adelaide to Alice Springs expeditions are $1895 all inclusive. Stops include the Flinders Ranges, Coober Pedy, Simpson Desert, Aboriginal communities, Uluru and West MacDonnell Ranges.

Swagabout Tours   WILDERNESS
(☎0408 845 378; www.swagabouttours.com.au) Dependable tours with the option of staying in hotels or camping under the stars. Adelaide to Alice Springs trips (five-/seven-/nine-/10-day tours camping $1555/2135/2770/3100, hotels $2215/3090/3980/4445) take in the Clare Valley, Flinders Ranges, Oodnadatta Track, Dalhousie Springs and Uluru. Also runs dedicated trips to the Clare Valley, Kangaroo Island, Eyre Peninsula and Flinders Ranges.

❶ Information

Department of Environment & Natural Resources (DENR; ☎08-8204 1910; www.environment.sa.gov.au; Level 1, 100 Pirie St, Adelaide; ☺9am-5pm Mon-Fri) Maps and parks information.

Royal Automobile Association of South Australia (RAA; ☎08-8202 4600; www.raa.net; 55 Hindmarsh Sq, Adelaide; ☺8.30am-5pm Mon-Fri, 9am-noon Sat) Auto advice and plenty of maps.

South Australian Visitor & Travel Centre (☎1300 764 227; www.southaustralia.com; 18 King William St, Adelaide; ☺8.30am-5pm Mon-Fri, 9am-2pm Sat & Sun) Abundantly stocked with info on Adelaide and SA. Super-patient staff and event ticketing, too.

AIR

International, interstate and regional flights service **Adelaide Airport** (www.aal.com.au; 1 James Schofield Dr, Adelaide Airport), 7km west of the city centre. The usual car-rental suspects all have desks here.

Regional Express (www.regionalexpress. com.au) flies from Adelaide to regional centres around SA, including Kingscote (from $81), Coober Pedy (from $210), Ceduna (from $135), Mount Gambier (from $140), Port Lincoln (from $114) and Whyalla ($110).

BUS

Buses are usually the cheapest way of getting from A to B in SA, and the bus companies have more comprehensive networks than the rail system. **Adelaide Central Bus Station** (www. cityofadelaide.com.au; 85 Franklin St, Adelaide) has ticket offices and terminals for all major interstate and statewide services. For online bus timetables see the **Bus SA** (www.adelaidemetro. com.au/bussa) website; see individual destination sections for regional services.

Major operators:

Firefly Express (www.fireflyexpress.com.au) Buses from Adelaide to Melbourne ($60, 11 hours, two daily) continuing to Sydney ($145, 24 hours).

Greyhound Australia (www.greyhound.com. au) Services between Adelaide and Melbourne (from $50, 11 hours, two daily) continuing to Sydney (from $140, 24 hours); and Adelaide and Alice Springs (from $170, 20 hours, one daily) continuing to Darwin ($535, 42 hours).

Premier Stateliner (www.premierstateliner. com.au) State-wide bus services.

V/Line (www.vline.com.au) Bus and bus/train services between Adelaide and Melbourne (from $45, 12 hours, three daily).

CAR & MOTORCYCLE

If you're driving between Adelaide and Melbourne, make sure you go via the **Great Ocean Road** (www.greatoceanrd.org.au) between Torquay and Warrnambool in Victoria – one of the best coastal drives in the world, with awesome views and more twists and turns than a Hitchcock plot.

To hitch a ride (sharing petrol costs) or buy a secondhand car, check out hostel notice boards. See also p1077).

TRAIN

Interstate trains run by **Great Southern Rail** (www.gsr.com.au) grind into the **Adelaide Parklands Terminal** (Railway Tce, Keswick), 1km southwest of the city centre. **Skylink** (✆08-8413 6196; www.skylinkadelaide.com; adult/child one-way $6/4) runs from the city to Adelaide Parklands Terminal en route to the airport; bookings are essential for all city pick-up locations other than the Central Bus Station.

The following trains depart from Adelaide regularly:

The Ghan To Alice Springs (seat/sleeper $358/686, 19 hours)

The Ghan To Darwin ($716/1372, 47 hours)

The Indian Pacific To Perth ($716/1402, 39 hours)

The Indian Pacific To Sydney ($308/511, 25 hours)

The Overland To Melbourne ($90, 11 hours)

The *Ghan* and *Indian Pacific* also offer a scenic way to get from Adelaide to Port Augusta (from $32, 4½ hours). The fastest service between Sydney and Adelaide (around 21 hours) is to travel from Sydney to Albury ($72) on the XPT train run by **CountryLink** (www.countrylink. info), then from Albury to Adelaide ($45) on a bus run by **V/Line** (www.vline.com.au).

ADELAIDE

POP 1.29 MILLION

Sophisticated, cultured, neat casual – this is the self-image Adelaide projects, a nod to the days of free colonisation without the 'penal colony' taint. Adelaidians may remind you of their convict-free status, but the city's stuffy, affluent origins did more to inhibit development than promote it. Bogged down in the old-school doldrums and painfully short on charisma, this was a pious, introspective place. As Paul Kelly sang in 'Adelaide':

Find me a bar or a girl or guitar
Where do you go on a Saturday night?
...And the streets are so wide, every-
body's inside
Sitting in the same chairs they were
sitting in last year.

But even Paul would admit that these days – thanks in part to progressive '70s premier Don Dunstan, who wore pink shorts to parliament – things are much improved. Multicultural flavours infuse Adelaide's restaurants; there's a pumping pub, arts and live-music scene; and the city's festival calendar has vanquished dull Saturday nights. And, of course, there's the local wine. Residents flush with hedonism at the prospect of a punchy McLaren Vale Shiraz or summer-scented Clare Riesling.

That said, a subtle conservatism remains. 'What school did you go to?' is a common

ADELAIDE IN...

Two Days

If you're here at Festival, WOMADelaide or Fringe time, lap it up. Otherwise, kick-start your day at the **Central Market** then wander through the **Adelaide Botanic Garden**, finishing up at the **National Wine Centre**. After a few bohemian beers at the **Exeter** hotel, have a ritzy dinner on **Rundle St**. Next day, visit the **South Australian Museum** and the **Bradman Collection Museum**. Check out **Tandanya National Aboriginal Cultural Institute** before riding the tram to **Glenelg** for an evening swim and fish and chips on the sand.

Four Days

Follow the two-day itinerary – perhaps slotting in the **Art Gallery of South Australia** and **Jam Factory Contemporary Craft & Design Centre** – then pack a picnic basket of Central Market produce and take a day trip out to the nearby **Adelaide Hills**, **McLaren Vale** or **Barossa Valley** wine regions. Next day, truck out to the museums and historic pubs of **Port Adelaide**, then catch a band at the **Grace Emily Hotel** back in the city, before dinner on **Gouger St**.

salvo from those unsure of your place in the social hierarchy, while countercultural urges bubble up through Adelaide's countless sex shops, kung-fu dojos and huge bottle shops.

Just down the tram tracks is beachy Glenelg, Adelaide with its guard down and boardshorts up; and Port Adelaide, a historic enclave slowly developing into SA's version of Fremantle. Inland, Adelaide's winking plains rise to the Adelaide Hills, just 12 minutes up the freeway. The Hills' gorgeous valley folds, old-fangled towns and cool-climate vineyards are all close at hand.

◉ Sights

Most of Adelaide's big-ticket sights are within walking distance of the city centre, with many strung along North Tce. It's also de rigueur to take a day trip out to beachside Glenelg, historic Port Adelaide, or the nearby Adelaide Hills, Barossa Valley or McLaren Vale wine regions.

CENTRAL & NORTH ADELAIDE

TOP
CHOICE **Central Market**   MARKET

(Map p720; www.adelaidecentralmarket.com.au; btwn Grote & Gouger Sts; ⊘7am-5.30pm Tue, 9am-5.30pm Wed & Thu, 7am-9pm Fri, 7am-3pm Sat) Satisfy both obvious and obscure culinary cravings at the 250-odd stalls in Adelaide's superb Central Market. A gluten-free snag from the Gourmet Sausage Shop, a sliver of English stilton from the Smelly Cheese Shop, a tub of blueberry yoghurt from the Yoghurt Shop – you name it, it's all here. Good luck making it out without eating anything. For **market tour** details, see p717.

FREE **Art Gallery of South Australia**   ART GALLERY

(Map p720; www.artgallery.sa.gov.au; North Tce; ⊘10am-5pm) Spend a few hushed hours in the vaulted, parquetry-floored gallery that represents the big names in Australian art. Permanent exhibitions include Australian, modern Australian, contemporary Aboriginal, Asian, Islamic and European art (with 20 bronze Rodins!). Temporary exhibitions occupy the basement. Free audio tours of the Australian collection are insightful, as are the free guided tours (11am and 2pm daily).

FREE **South Australian Museum**   MUSEUM

(Map p720; www.samuseum.sa.gov.au; North Tce; ⊘10am-5pm) Digs into Australia's natural history with special exhibits on whales and Antarctic explorer Sir Douglas Mawson, and an Aboriginal Cultures Gallery displaying artefacts of the Ngarrindjeri people of the Coorong and lower Murray. The giant squid is the undisputed highlight of the free **tours** (⊘11am Mon-Fri, 2pm & 3pm Sat & Sun). There's a cool **cafe** (mains $10-15; ⊘lunch) here too.

Adelaide Zoo   ZOO

(Map p728; www.adelaidezoo.com.au; Plane Tree Dr; adult/child/concession/family $29/17/20/74; ⊘9.30am-5pm) Around 1800 exotic and native mammals, birds and reptiles roar, growl and screech at Adelaide's wonderful zoo, which opened in 1883. There are free **walking tours** half-hourly (plus a slew of longer and overnight tours focussing on

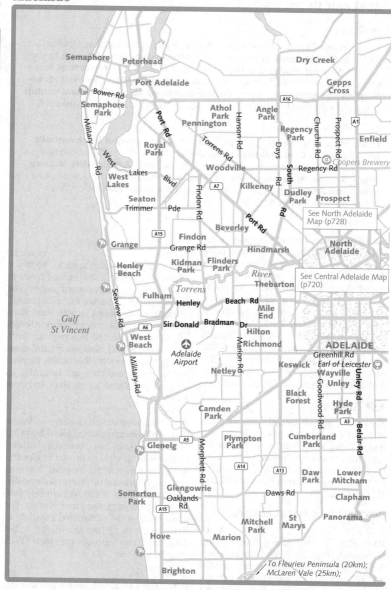

specific environments and species), feeding sessions and a children's zoo. Until Wang Wang and Funi – Australia's only Giant Pandas – arrived in 2009 (pandemonium!), the major drawcard was the Southeast Asian rainforest exhibit.

You can take a river cruise to the zoo from the Festival Centre on *Pop-eye* (Map p728; adult/child $12/6; ☺hourly 11am-3pm Mon-Fri, every 25 min 10.30am-5pm Sat & Sun). Weekends only in winter.

Journey exhibition, paired with tastings of Australian wines (extra charge), at this very sexy wine centre. You'll get an insight into the issues winemakers contend with, and even have your own virtual vintage rated. Free 30-minute **tours** run at 11.30am daily. A heady range of wine-appreciation courses (from $55) is also available, and there's a cool **cafe** here too.

FREE Adelaide Botanic Garden   GARDEN
(Map p728; www.botanicgardens.sa.gov.au; North Tce; ☺7.15am-sunset Mon-Fri, from 9am Sat & Sun) Meander, jog or chew through your trashy airport novel in these lush city-fringe gardens. Highlights include a restored 1877 palm house, the waterlily pavilion (housing the gigantic *Victoria amazonica*) and the fabulous steel-and-glass arc of the **Bicentennial Conservatory** (adult/child/family $5/3/11; ☺10am-5pm), which recreates a tropical rainforest. Free 1½-hour **guided walks** depart the Schomburgk Pavilion at 10.30am daily.

Adelaide Oval   LANDMARK
(Map p728; ☎08-8300 3800; www.cricketsa. com.au; King William Rd, North Adelaide) Hailed as the world's prettiest cricket ground, the Adelaide Oval hosts interstate and international **cricket** matches, plus South Australian National Football League (SANFL) **football** games in winter. A bronze **statue of 'the Don'** (Sir Donald Bradman) cracks a cover drive out the front. When there are no games happening you can take a two-hour **tour** (adult/child $10/5; ☺10am Mon-Fri, plus 2pm Tue & Thu), departing from the Phil Ridings Gates on War Memorial Dr. Call or check the website for tour details.

Also at the oval is the excellent **Bradman Collection Museum** (admission free; ☺9.30am-4.30pm Mon-Fri), where Don devotees can pore over personal items of the cricketing legend.

Tandanya National Aboriginal Cultural Institute   ART GALLERY
(Map p720; ☎08-8224 3200; www.tandanya.com.au; 253 Grenfell St; ☺10am-5pm) Tandanya offers an insight into the culture of the local Kaurna people, whose territory extends south to Cape Jervis and north to Port Wakefield. Inside the cultural institute there are interactive displays on living with the land, as well as galleries, gifts and a cafe. There are didgeridoo or Torres Strait Islander **cultural performances** (adult/child $5/3; ☺noon Tue-Sun), free **tours**

FREE National Wine Centre of Australia   WINERY
(off Map p720; www.wineaustralia.com.au; cnr Botanic & Hackney Rds; tastings from $10; ☺9am-5pm Mon-Fri, 10am-5pm Sat & Sun) Check out the free self-guided, interactive Wine Discovery

EMMA FEY: ART GALLERY OF SOUTH AUSTRALIA

Adelaide's arts scene is in the midst of a renaissance. We have a boutique scene that doesn't compare with any other city...our own events, our own bespoke way of delivering them. Adelaide is so digestible and easy.

Festival Season

The Adelaide Festival, the Fringe Festival, Adelaide Writers' Week and the Clipsal 500 (V8 race) are all on at the same time, in late summer. Energy breeds energy: everyone is out and about and the weather's good. I can't think of anywhere else where you can see alternative Fringe-dwellers next to racing enthusiasts. The people-watching is great!

Art in the City

The art gallery is in the middle of the North Tce precinct (next to the museum, the university, between the city and the river). It's revolutionising its collection and engaging more audiences – young people, children. Families always have a great time. There are also contemporary art spaces popping up in little laneways around here.

Best Free Events

The Northern Lights on North Tce during the Festival is sensational – all the old sandstone buildings are lit up, and the Fringe crowds at that end of the city lend the whole area a real energy.

(⊙11am Thu), plus Indigenous short-film and documentary screenings in the theatre.

Migration Museum   MUSEUM
(Map p728; www.history.sa.gov.au; 82 Kintore Ave; admission by donation; ⊙10am-5pm Mon-Fri, from 1pm Sat & Sun) This engaging social-history museum tells the story of the many migrants who have made SA their home. The museum has info on 100-plus nationalities (as opposed to individuals) in its database, along with some poignant personal stories.

Adelaide Gaol   MUSEUM
(off Map p720; ☑08-8231 4062; www.adelaidegaol. org.au; 18 Gaol Rd, Thebarton; adult/child/concession/family $12/7.50/10/30; ⊙10am-5pm Sun-Fri, last entry 3.30pm) Only decommissioned in 1988, this old lock-up has a grim vibe, but its displays of homemade bongs, weapons and escape devices are amazing. Commentary tapes are available for self-guided tours (included in admission). Bookings required for guided tours (adult/child/concession/family $16/10/14/45; ⊙11am, noon & 1pm Sun) and adults-only ghost tours (adult $26; ⊙sunset Thu-Sat).

FREE **Haigh's Chocolates**
Visitors Centre   CHOCOLATES
(off Map p720; ☑08-8372 7070; www.haighschoc olates.com; 154 Greenhill Rd, Parkside; ⊙8.30am-5.30pm Mon-Fri, 9am-5pm Sat) If you've got a

chocolate problem, get guilty at this iconic factory. Free tours (⊙11am, 1pm & 2pm Mon-Sat) take you through the chocolate lifecycle from cacao nut to hand-dipped truffle (with samples if you're good). Tour bookings essential.

Adelaide Parklands   GARDENS
The city and ritzy North Adelaide are surrounded by a broad band of parklands. Colonel William Light, Adelaide's controversial planner, came up with the concept, which has been both a blessing and a curse for the city. Pros: heaps of green space, clean air and sports grounds for the kids. Cons: bone-dry in summer, perverts loitering and a sense that the city is cut off from its suburbs. A statue of Colonel William Light overlooks the gleaming city office towers from Montefiore Hill.

Rundle Street Market   MARKET
(Map p720; www.cityofadelaide.com.au; Rundle St; ⊙9am-4pm Sun) Over in the East End, Sunday's Rundle Street Market is a string of food stalls, fashion, buskers, jewellery, arts and crafts.

Gilles Street Market   MARKET
(Map p720; www.gillesstreetmarket.com.au; Gilles Street Primary School, 91 Gilles St; ⊙10am-4pm 3rd Sun of the month) Kids' clothes, fashion, arts, crafts and hubbub take over an East End school grounds.

FREE Jam Factory Contemporary
Craft & Design Centre   ART GALLERY
(Map p720; www.jamfactory.com.au; 19 Morphett
St; ⊙10am-5pm Mon-Sat, from 1pm Sun) Quality
contemporary local arts and crafts, plus a
hell-hot glass-blowing studio (watch from
the balcony above) turning out gorgeous
glass.

FREE Australian Experimental
Art Foundation   ART GALLERY
(AEAF; Map p720; www.aeaf.org.au; Lion Arts
Centre, cnr Morphett St & North Tce; ⊙11am-5pm
Tue-Fri, from 2pm Sat) A focus on innova-
tion, with a bookshop specialising in film,
architecture, culture and design.

FREE Public Art   STREET
For an insight into Adelaide's public
artworks – including the infamous Mall's
Balls (Map p720; Rundle Mall) – pick up a
walking tour map from the visitor centre.

INNER SUBURBS

Coopers Brewery   BREWERY
(Map p712; ☑08-8440 1800; www.coopers.com.
au; 461 South Rd, Regency Park; 1½hr tours per
person $22; ⊙tours 1pm Tue-Fri) You can't pos-
sibly come to Adelaide without entertaining
thoughts of touring Coopers Brewery. Tours
take you through the brewhouse, bottling
hall and history museum, where you can get
stuck into samples of stouts, ales and lagers
(some of which are carbon neutral). Bookings required; minimum age 18. The brewery is in the northern suburbs – grab a cab,
or walk 1km from Islington train station.

Penfolds Magill Estate Winery   WINERY
(Map p712; ☑08-8301 5569; www.penfolds.com.au;
78 Penfolds Rd, Magill; tastings free; ⊙10am-5pm)
This 100-year-old winery is home to Austra-
lia's best-known wine – the legendary Grange.
Taste the product at the cellar door; dine at
the restaurant (p724); take the **Heritage
Tour** ($15), or steel your wallet for the **Great
Grange Tour** ($150). Tour bookings advised.

GLENELG

Palindromic Glenelg (Map p712), or 'the Bay' –
the site of SA's colonial landing – is Adelaide
at its most 'LA'. Glenelg's **beach** faces towards the west, and as the sun sinks into the
sea, the pubs and bars burgeon with surfies,
backpackers and sun-damaged sexagenar-
ians. The tram rumbles in from the city, past
the Jetty Rd shopping strip to the alfresco
cafes around Moseley Sq.

The Glenelg Visitor Information Centre (☑08-8294 5833; www.glenelgsa.com.au; R22,
Holdfast Shores Promenade, 12 Holdfast Shores
Marina; ⊙9.30am-5pm Mon-Fri, 10am-3.30pm Sat,
10am-2pm Sun; @) has the local low-down.
See p717 for info on **diving** and **sailing** opportunities here.

See p732 for details on the Glenelg tram.
Alternatively, take bus 135, 167, 168, 190 or
264 from the city down Anzac Hwy (Rte A5)
to Glenelg.

Bay Discovery Centre   MUSEUM
(www.baydiscovery.com.au; Town Hall, Moseley Sq;
admission gold coin donation; ⊙10am-5pm) This
low-key museum depicts the social history of
Glenelg from colonisation to today, and addresses the plight of the local Kaurna people,
who lost both their land and voice. Don't
miss the relics dredged up from the original
pier, and the spooky old sideshow machines.

PORT ADELAIDE

Bogged in boganity for decades, Port Adelaide
(Map p712) – 15km northwest of the city –
is in the midst of gentrification, morphing
its warehouses into art spaces and museums,
and its brawl-house pubs into boutique beer
emporia. Things are on the up!

The mega-helpful Port Adelaide Visitor
Information Centre (☑1800 629 888, 08-8405
6560; www.portenf.sa.gov.au/goto/tourism; 66 Commercial Rd; ⊙9am-5pm; ☎) books guided Port
Walks (gold coin donation; ⊙2pm Thu & Sun)
around the heritage area, and stocks brochures on self-guided Indigenous history and
heritage-pub walks. See p717 for info on **dolphin cruises** and **kayaking** around the Port.

West-bound buses 150 and 153 will get
you to Port Adelaide from North Tce, or you
can take the train.

Maritime Museum   MUSEUM
(www.history.sa.gov.au; 126 Lipson St; adult/child/
concession/family $8.50/3.50/6.50/22; ⊙10am-
5pm daily, lighthouse 10am-2pm Sun-Fri) This
salty cache is the oldest of its kind in Australia. Highlights include the iconic Port Adelaide Lighthouse, busty figureheads made
everywhere from Londonderry to Quebec,
shipwreck and explorer displays, and a computer register of early migrants.

National Railway Museum   MUSEUM
(www.natrailmuseum.org.au; Lipson St Sth; adult/
child/concession/family $12/6/9/32; ⊙10am-
5pm) Trainspotters rejoice! A delightfully
nerdy museum crammed with railway
memorabilia.

ADELAIDE FOR CHILDREN

The free monthly paper Adelaide's Child (www.adelaideschild.com.au), available at cafes and libraries, is largely advertorial but contains comprehensive events listings. *Adelaide for Kids: A Guide for Parents*, by James Muecke, has comprehensive details and is available at bookshops.

There are few kids who won't love the **tram ride** from the city down to Glenelg (kids under five ride for free!). You may have trouble getting them off the tram – the lure of a splash in the shallows at the **beach** then some fish and chips on the lawn should do the trick.

During school holidays, the South Australian Museum, State Library of South Australia, Art Gallery of South Australia, Adelaide Zoo and Adelaide Botanic Garden run inspired kid- and family-oriented programs with accessible and interactive general displays.

Down on the River Torrens, Captain Jolley's Paddle Boats (Map p728; Jolley's La; hire per 30 min $12; ☺10am-5pm Sat, Sun & public holidays) make a satisfying splash.

Live out the kids' (or perhaps your own) *Charlie and the Chocolate Factory* fantasies on a tour at Haigh's Chocolates Visitors Centre. Not the best for young diets, perhaps, but the chocolates sure are Wonka-worthy.

In Port Adelaide, you can check out the Maritime Museum, National Railway Museum or South Australian Aviation Museum, or set sail on a **dolphin-spotting cruise**.

Dial-An-Angel (☎1300 721 111, 08-8267 3700; www.dialanangel.com.au) provides nannies and babysitters to all areas.

South Australian Aviation Museum
MUSEUM

(www.saam.org.au; Lipson St; adult/child/concession/family $9/4.50/7/22; ☺10.30am-4.30pm) An impressive collection of retired old birds.

Fishermen's Wharf Market
MARKET

(www.portenf.sa.gov.au; Black Diamond Sq, Commercial Rd; ☺9am-5pm Sun) If you're visiting the Port on a Sunday, this waterside market has antiques, bric-a-brac and crappy collectables.

Activities

CYCLING & WALKING

Adelaide is pancake flat – perfect for cycling and walking (if it's not too hot!). You can take your bike on trains any time, but not buses. Trails SA (www.southaustraliantrails.com) offers loads of cycling- and hiking-trail info: pick up their *40 Great South Australian Short Walks* brochure.

There are free guided walks in the Adelaide Botanic Gardens, plus self-guided city walks detailed in brochures from the South Australian Visitor & Travel Centre. The riverside **Linear Park Trail** (Map p728) is a 40km walking/cycling path running from Glenelg to the foot of the Adelaide Hills, mainly along the River Torrens. Another popular hiking trail is the steep **Waterfall Gully Track** (Map p733; three hours return) up to Mt Lofty Summit and back.

Mountain bikers should check out the Eagle Mountain Bike Park (Map p733; ☎08-8416 6677; www.bikesa.asn.au; admission free; ☺dawn-dusk) in the Adelaide Hills; phone for directions. If you're feeling hyperactive, you can wheel off along the Mawson Trail (www.southaustraliantrails.com) from Adelaide to Blinman in the Flinders Ranges.

Bike hire and tour options:

Bicycle SA
BIKE HIRE

(☎08-8168 9999; www.bikesa.asn.au; 111 Franklin St; ☺9am-5pm Mon-Fri, 8am-6pm Sat & Sun) Free 'Adelaide City Bikes' (see p731), cycling maps and advice.

Bikeabout
BIKE TOURS, HIRE

(☎0413 525 733; www.bikeabout.com.au) Barnstorming one-day mountain-bike sessions in the Adelaide Hills (from $130), plus mountain-bike hire (from $30 per day).

Ecotrek
BIKE TOURS

(☎08-8346 4155; www.ecotrek.com.au) Three-day cycling tours of Kangaroo Island ($895), or two days in the Barossa Valley ($670).

Escapegoat
BIKE TOURS

(☎08-8121 8112; www.escapegoat.com.au) Ride from Mt Lofty Summit down to Adelaide ($90), or take a day trip through McLaren Vale by bike ($120).

Glenelg Bicycle Hire

BIKE HIRE

(☑08-8376 1934; www.glenelgbicyclehire.com.
au; Norfolk Motor Inn, 71 Broadway, Glenelg South)
Cruise 'The Bay' on a mountain bike ($40
per day) or tandem ($65 per day).

WATER ACTIVITIES
Adelaide gets *reeeeally* hot in summer. Hit
the beach at Glenelg, or try the following.
See also *Pop-eye* river cruises (p711) and
Captain Jolley's Paddle Boats (p716).

Adelaide Aquatic Centre

SWIMMING

(off Map p728; www.cityofadelaide.com.au; Jeffcott
Rd, North Adelaide; casual swim adult/child/
concession/family $7.50/5.50/6/20; ☉5am-10pm
Mon-Sat, 7am-8pm Sun) The closest pool to
the city, with swimming and diving pools,
gym, sauna, spa and other facilities.

🖋Temptation Sailing

BOATING

(☑0412 811 838; www.dolphinboat.com.au; Holdfast Shores Marina, Glenelg; 3½hr dolphin watch/
swim $58/98) Eco-accredited catamaran
cruises to watch or swim with dolphins.

Adelaide Scuba

DIVING

(☑08-8294 7744; www.adelaidescuba.com.au;
Patawalonga Frontage, Glenelg North; ☉9am-
5.30pm Mon-Fri, 8am-5pm Sat & Sun) Hires out
snorkelling gear ($30 per day) and runs
local dives (single/double dive $65/130).

🖋Adventure Kayaking

KAYAKING

(☑08-8295 8812; www.adventurekayak.com.au)
A range of guided and self-guided kayak
tours around the Port River estuary from
$35 per adult.

Adelaide Gondola

BOATING

(Map p728; ☑08-8358 1800; www.adelaidegondola.
com.au; War Memorial Dr, North Adelaide; 4 people
per 40 min $110) Maybe if you squint...no, it
still doesn't look like Venice. But cruising
the River Torrens may still float your boat.
You can even order a bottle of wine!

Port Princess Dolphin Cruises (☑0418 817
837; www.portprincess.com.au) and **Dolphin
Explorer Cruises** (☑08-8447 2366; www.
dolphinexplorer.com.au) both offer cruises departing Port Adelaide's Fishermen's Wharf
to ogle the local bottlenose dolphins. Both
offer 90-minute, two-hour and lunch cruises
starting at $6 per person.

🔜 Tours

A great way to see Adelaide is to circle
around the main sights on the free city buses (p731). Beyond the city, day tours cover
the Adelaide Hills, Fleurieu Peninsula and
Barossa Valley. Note that one-day trips to the
Flinders Ranges and Kangaroo Island tend
to be rushed and not great value for money.

Adelaide's Top Food & Wine Tours

FOOD & WINE

(☑08-8386 0888; www.topfoodandwinetours.
com.au) Uncovers SA's gastronomic soul
with dawn ($49) and morning ($36) tours
of the buzzing Central Market where stallholders introduce their varied produce.
Dawn tours include breakfast. McLaren
Vale, Barossa and Clare Valley tours are
also available.

🖋Bookabee Tours

INDIGENOUS

(☑08-8235 9954; www.bookabee.com.au)
Indigenous-run half-/full-day city tours
($105/205) focusing on bush foods in
the Adelaide Botanic Gardens, Tandanya
National Aboriginal Cultural Institute and
the South Australian Museum. A great insight into Kaurna culture. Longer outback
tours are also available.

Adelaide Sightseeing

CITY

(☑1300 769 762; www.adelaidesightseeing.com.
au) Runs a city highlights tour ($59) in-
cluding North Tce, Glenelg, Haigh's Chocolates and the Adelaide Oval (among other
sights). Central Market, Adelaide Hills,
Barossa and Clare Valleys and Fleurieu
Peninsula tours also available.

Enjoy Adelaide

CITY

(☑08-8332 1401; www.enjoyadelaide.com.au)
Half-day city highlights tour ($45) with
diversions to Mt Lofty Summit and Hahndorf. Barossa Valley tours are also available.

Prime Mini Tours

CITY

(☑1300 667 650, 08-8556 6117; www.primemini
tours.com) City tours ($95), plus combined
Hahndorf–Victor Harbor day tours ($65).
An Adelaide Hills–McLaren Vale wineries
tour includes tastings and lunch ($105).
Barossa Valley tours are also available.

🎆 Festivals & Events

As local licence plates attest, SA is the 'Festival State'. A continuous stream of high-calibre
international and local events lures artists
and audiences from around the world, particularly for the Adelaide Festival of Arts,
WOMADelaide and the Adelaide Fringe.

JANUARY

Tour Down Under CYCLING
(www.tourdownunder.com.au) The world's best
cyclists sweating in their lycra: six races
through SA towns, with the grand finale
in Adelaide.

FEBRUARY

Adelaide Fringe ARTS
(www.adelaidefringe.com.au) This annual
independent arts festival in February and
March is second only to the Edinburgh
Fringe. Funky, unpredictable and down-
right hilarious.

MARCH

Adelaide Festival ARTS
(www.adelaidefestival.com.au) Culture vultures
absorb international and Australian dance,
drama, opera, literature and theatre performances in even-numbered years. Don't miss
the Northern Lights along North Tce – old
sandstone buildings ablaze with lights.

Clipsal 500 MOTORSPORT
(www.clipsal500.com.au) Rev-heads flail their
mullets as Adelaide's streets become a
four-day Holden versus Ford racing track.

WOMADelaide MUSIC
(www.womadelaide.com.au) One of the world's
best live-music events, with more than
300 musicians and performers from
around the globe.

JUNE

Adelaide Cabaret Festival CABARET
(www.adelaidecabaretfestival.com) The only
one of its kind in the country.

JULY

Adelaide's Festival of Ideas CULTURAL
(www.adelaidefestival.com.au) The glorious,
the good and the innovative descend on
Adelaide for a biennial talk-fest (odd-
numbered years, alternating with the
Adelaide Festival).

AUGUST

**South Australian Living
Artists Festival** ARTS
(www.salafestival.com.au) Progressive exhibitions and displays across town.

SEPTEMBER

City to Bay FUN RUN
(www.city-bay.org.au) Annual 12km fun run
from the city to Glenelg; much sweat and
cardiac duress.

Royal Adelaide Show AGRICULTURAL
(www.theshow.com.au) Agricultural and horti-
cultural displays and showbags.

SANFL Grand Final FOOTBALL
(www.sanfl.com.au) Zenith of the local Aussie Rules football season. Will someone,
please beat Central Districts?

NOVEMBER

Christmas Pageant CULTURAL
(www.cupageant.com.au) An Adelaide institution for 70-plus years – kitschy floats,
bands and marching troupes occupy city
streets for a day.

Feast Festival GAY & LESBIAN
(www.feast.org.au) Three-week gay and
lesbian festival with a carnival, theatre,
dialogue and dance.

DECEMBER

Adelaide Guitar Festival MUSIC
(www.adelaidefestivalcentre.com.au/guitarfestival)
Annual axe-fest with a whole lotta rock,
classical, country, blues and flamenco.

Bay Sports Festival SPORTS
(www.baysportsfestival.com.au) Sports fest in
Glenelg, featuring beach volleyball, an
aquathon and surf carnival.

🛏 Sleeping

Most of Adelaide's budget accommodation is
in the city centre, but in a town this easy to
navigate, staying outside the CBD is viable.
For peace and quiet, consider leafy North Adelaide; for beachside accommodation, try Glenelg. 'Motel Alley' is along Glen Osmond Rd
(Rte A1), the main southeast city access road.
See www.bandbfsa.com.au for B&B listings.

CENTRAL ADELAIDE

Adelaide Central YHA HOSTEL $
(Map p720; ☎08-8414 3010; www.yha.com.au; 135
Waymouth St; dm/d/f from $25/80/107; ✳@🛜)
The YHA isn't known for its gregarious-
ness, but you'll get plenty of sleep in the
spacious and comfortable rooms here. This
is a seriously schmick hostel with great security, roomy kitchen and lounge area and
immaculate bathrooms. A real step up from
the average backpackers around town.

Clarion Hotel Soho HOTEL $$
(Map p720; ☎08-8412 5600; www.clarion
hotelsoho.com.au; 264 Flinders St; d $145-590;
✳🅿) *Ooh-la-la!* The slick new Clarion at-
tempts to conjure up the vibe of London's
Soho district, but it's far more sophisticated

than anything on Old Compton St. Thirty very plush suites (some with spas, most with balconies) are complimented by sumptuous linen, 24-hour room service, iPod docks, Italian marble bathrooms, jet pool, a fab restaurant…Rates take a tumble midweek.

My Place
HOSTEL $
(Map p720; ☑08-8221 5299; www.adelaidehostel. com.au; 257 Waymouth St; dm incl breakfast $26, d incl breakfast & TV $68; ✳@🖰) The antithesis of the big formal operations, My Place has a welcoming, personal vibe and is just a stumble from the Grace Emily, arguably Adelaide's best pub! There's a cosy TV room, barbecue terrace above the street, beach-bus in summer, and regular pizza and pub nights – great for solo travellers.

Majestic Roof Garden Hotel
HOTEL $$$
(Map p720; ☑08-8100 4400; www.majestichotels. com.au; 55 Frome St; d from $200; ✳@) Everything looks new in this place – a speck of dirt would feel lonely. Book a room facing Frome St for a balcony and the best views, or take a bottle of wine up to the rooftop garden to watch the sunset.

Backpack Oz
HOSTEL $
(Map p720; ☑08-8223 3551; www.backpackoz. com.au; cnr Wakefield & Pulteney Sts; dm/s/d from $25/55/65; ✳@🖰) It doesn't look like much externally, but this converted pub (the old Orient Hotel) strikes the right balance between party and placid. There are spacious dorms, an additional guesthouse over the road (great for couples), and guests can still get a coldie and shoot some pool in the bar. Communal area; free bike hire and BBQ on Wednesday. Linen provided.

Hostel 109
HOSTEL $
(Map p720; ☑1800 099 318, 08-8223 1771; www. hostel109.com; 109 Carrington St; dm/s/d/tr $27/55/70/90; ✳@🖰) A small, well-managed hostel in a quiet corner of town, with a couple of little balconies over the street and a cosy kitchen/communal area. Spotlessly clean and super-friendly, with lockers, travel info, good security and gas cooking. The only negative: rooms open onto light wells rather than the outside world.

Adelaide City Park Motel
MOTEL $$
(Map p720; ☑08-8223 1444; www.citypark.com. au; 471 Pulteney St; d with/without bathroom from $120/99, tr/f from $160/210; ✳✳🖰) Immaculate bathrooms, leather lounges, winsome French prints and an easy walk to the Hutt

St restaurants. Free parking, DVDs and wireless internet, too. Ask about their apartments on the way to Glenelg (one- and two-bedroom units $175 to $225).

Hotel Richmond
HOTEL $$
(Map p720; ☑08-8223 4444; www.hotelrichmond. com.au; 128 Rundle Mall; d from $165; ✳🖰) This opulent hotel in a grand 1920s building in the middle of Rundle Mall has mod-minimalist rooms with king-sized beds, marble bathrooms and American oak and Italian furnishings. Oh, and that hotel rarity – opening windows. Rates include breakfast, movies, papers and gym passes.

Quest on King William
APARTMENTS $$
(Map p720; ☑08-8217 5000; www.questonking william.com.au; 82 King William St; studio/1-/2-bedroom apt from $160/175/240; ✳@) These immaculate downtown apartments (72 of them over eight levels) are central as can be – perfect for business bods. All have kitchenettes and DVD players. On-site laundry; family units sleep five.

Shakespeare International Backpackers
HOSTEL $
(Map p720; ☑08-8231 7655; www.shakeys.com. au; 123 Waymouth St; dm/d from $26/80; ✳@🖰) Rambling through an old downtown pub (1879), laid-back Shakeys has friendly staff, a tour desk, a serious stainless-steel kitchen, free linen and a balcony over the street (look down on the suits and count your blessings).

Adelaide Backpackers Inn
HOSTEL $
(Map p720; ☑1800 247 725, 08-8223 6635; www.abpi.com.au; 112 Carrington St; dm/d/tr $25/60/90; ✳@🖰) A relaxed and surprisingly decent place occupying an 1841 pub that's just had a $200,000 facelift (new bathrooms, fridges, carpets, washing machines etc). Handy to Hutt and Rundle Sts.

NORTH ADELAIDE

Greenways Apartments
APARTMENTS $$
(Map p728; ☑08-8267 5903; www.greenways apartments.com; 41-45 King William Rd, North Adelaide; 1-/2-/3-bedroom apt $115/150/190; ✳🖰) These 1938 apartments ain't flash (floral tiles and rude 1970s laminates), but if you have a pathological hatred of 21st-century open-plan 'lifestyles', then Greenways is for you! And where else can you stay in clean, perfectly operational apartments so close to town at these rates? A must for cricket fans, the Adelaide Oval is a lofted hook shot away – book early for Test matches.

ADELAIDE & SOUTH AUSTRALIA ADELAIDE

Princes Lodge Motel   MOTEL **$**
(Map p728; ☑08-8267 5566; www.princeslodge.
com.au; 73 LeFevre Tce, North Adelaide; s/d/f incl
breakfast from $65/95/160; ❄️📶) In a grand
1913 house overlooking the parklands, this
friendly (and endearingly uncool) lodging
has high ceilings and a certain faded grandeur. Close to the chichi North Adelaide
restaurants and within walking distance of
the city. Great value with heaps of character.

Minima Hotel   HOTEL **$$**
(Map p728; ☑08-8334 7766; www.majestichotels.
com.au; 146 Melbourne St, North Adelaide; d from
$100; ❄️@) A spaceship has landed in ye olde
North Adelaide! Just a few years old, Mini-
ma offers compact but super-stylish rooms
in a winning Melbourne St location. Check-
in is DIY – use the touch screen in the lobby.

Tynte Street Apartments   APARTMENTS **$$**
(Map p728; ☑08-8334 7783; www.majestichotels.
com.au; 82 Tynte St, North Adelaide; d from $170,

extra adult $20; ❄️) Plush, red-brick, self-
contained studio apartments on a tree-lined
street near the O'Connell St cafes and pubs,
sleeping three. Check-in is 1km away at 9
Jerningham St. Free parking to boot.

INNER SUBURBS

Levi Park Caravan Park   CARAVAN PARK **$**
(off Map p720; ☑08-8344 2209; www.levipark.
com.au; 1a Harris Rd, Walkerville; unpowered/pow-
ered sites from $32/34, cabins/ste from $98/140;
❄️@📶) This leafy Torrens-side park is 5km
from town and loaded with facilities, including tennis courts and a massive cricket oval.
Suites are in restored Vale House, purportedly Adelaide's oldest residence!

Jasper Motor Inn   MOTEL **$$**
(off Map p720; ☑08-8271 0377; www.jasper
motorinn.com.au; 17 Jasper St, Hyde Park; s
$99-110, d $108-118; ❄️) Just beyond the city
(3.5km), Jasper is off King William Rd in
upper-crust Hyde Park. It's a low-slung

See North Adelaide
Map (p728)

To National
Wine Centre
Adelaide
of Australia
Botanic
Gardens
(100m)

To Royal Coach
Motor Inn (300m);
Colonist (1.5km)

Bartels Rd

East
Parklands

Wakefield St

Angas St

Carrington St

Halifax St

Gilles St

Disability
Information &
Resource Centre

South Tce

To Haigh's Chocolates
Visitors Centre (700m)

To Earl of
Leicester (1km)

'70s number with minimal style, but on a super-quiet street – far preferable to the traffic rumble of Glen Osmond Rd's 'Motel Alley'. Great value.

Adelaide Caravan Park   CARAVAN PARK $

(off Map p728; ☑08-8363 1566; www.adelaide caravanpark.com.au; 46 Richmond St, Hackney; powered sites $36-48, cabins & units $119-149; ❋@⌂≋) An orderly, compact park on the River Torrens, rather surprisingly slotted in on a quiet street 2km northeast of the city centre. Clean and well run, with a bit of grass if it's not too far into summer.

Royal Coach Motor Inn   MOTEL $$

(off Map p720; ☑08-8362 5676; www.royalcoach. com.au; 24 Dequetteville Tce, Kent Town; d from $140; ❋≋) Three-storey brick motel monster just beyond the parklands at the eastern end of town, with good facilities and late-'90s decor (you're not paying for style here). There's

a restaurant downstairs, but Rundle St is just a 10-minute walk away.

GLENELG

🅣 Glenelg Beach Hostel & Bar   HOSTEL $

(☑1800 359 181, 08-8376 0007; www.glenelgbeach hostel.com.au; 1-7 Moseley St, Glenelg; dm/s/d/f from $28/60/80/120; @) A couple of streets back from the beach, this beaut old terrace (1879) is Adelaide's budget golden child. Fan-cooled rooms maintain period details and are bunk-free. There's cold Coopers in the basement bar, open fireplaces, lofty ceilings, girls-only dorms and a courtyard garden. Book *waaay* in advance in summer.

Taft Motor Inn   MOTEL $$

(☑1800 060 905; 08-8376 1233; www.taftmotorinn. com.au; 18 Moseley St, Glenelg; s/d from $125/135, 1-/2-bedroom apt from $155/165; ❋⌂≋) Revamped motel rooms and apartments with lashings of timber and taupe, in a great location a short walk from Jetty Rd. Some rooms have kitchenettes, and there's a barbecue and kidney-shaped pool on-site.

Adelaide Shores Caravan Resort   CARAVAN PARK $

(☑1800 444 567, 08-8355 7320; www.adelaide shores.com.au; 1 Military Rd, West Beach; powered sites $36-54, cabins $87-225; ❋@≋) Hunkered-down behind the West Beach dunes with a walking/cycling track extending to Glenelg (3.4km) in one direction and Henley Beach (3.5km) in the other, this is a choice spot in summer. There are lush sites, glistening amenities and passing dolphins.

Stamford Grand Hotel   HOTEL $$$

(☑08-8376 1222; www.stamford.com.au; Moseley Sq, Glenelg; d city/ocean views from $220/270; ❋@⌂≋) The first Glenelg edifice to scrape the sky with any real authority, this plush, pink-hued hotel overlooks Gulf St Vincent. Dinner, bed and breakfast packages are decent value; good off-season rates. Just ignore the automated baby grand piano in the lobby tinkling Elton John classics.

Glenelg Holiday & Corporate Letting

(☑08-8376 1934; www.glenelgholiday.com.au; 1-bedroom apt from $135; ❋) and Glenelg Letting Agency (☑08-8294 9666; www.baybeach front.com.au; 1-bedroom apt per week from $1200; ❋) offer self-contained beachside apartments in Glenelg.

Eating

Foodies flock to West End hot spots like Gouger St (pronounced 'Goo-jer'), Chinatown and food-filled Central Market. There are some great pubs here too (in fact, you can get decent pub meals all over Adelaide; see www.beerandburger.info). Artsy-alternative Hindley St – Adelaide's dirty little secret – has a smattering of good eateries. In the East End, Rundle St and Hutt St are perfect for alfresco cafes and people-watching. North Adelaide's Melbourne and O'Connell Sts have a healthy spread of bistros, provedores and pubs.

Central Market
MARKET **$**

(Map p720; www.adelaidecentralmarket.com.au; btwn Grote & Gouger Sts; ⊘breakfast & lunch Tue-Sat, dinner Fri; ✈) This place is an exercise in sensory bombardment: a barrage of smells, colours and yelling stallholders selling fresh vegetables, breads, cheeses, seafood and gourmet produce. Cafes, hectic food courts and a supermarket too.

Mesa Lunga
MEDITERRANEAN **$$**

(Map p720; ☎08-8410 7617; www.mesalunga.com; cnr Gouger & Morphett Sts; tapas $4-25, mains $17-28; ⊘lunch Fri & Sun, dinner Tue-Sun) In a fishbowl corner room with an amazing dark-wood wine wall, sassy Mesa Lunga serves tapas and quality pizzas. Order some *queso manchego* (aged sheep cheese with quince paste) and anchovies stuffed with Manzanillo olives, washed down with some sparkling sangria. Magic.

Lucia's Pizza & Spaghetti Bar
ITALIAN **$**

(Map p720; www.lucias.com.au; 2 Western Mall, Central Market; meals $8-10; ⊘breakfast & lunch Mon-Sat, dinner Fri) This little slice of Italy has been around since Lucia was a lot younger. All her pasta, sauces and pizzas are authentically homemade – perfection any time of day. If you like what you're eating, you can buy fresh pasta next door at Lucia's Homemade Fine Foods.

Evergreen
CHINESE **$**

(Map p720; ☎08-8212 1686; 31 Moonta St; yum cha $4-18; ⊘lunch Mon-Sat, dinner daily; ✈) A few steps away from the Gouger St fray, Chinatown's Evergreen has rapidly earned a rep for great yum cha. There are a staggering 182 items on the menu (everything from eggplant hotpot to stir-fried ginger scallops), plus a passable wine list and paper tablecloths so you can get messy.

Thali Room
INDIAN **$$**

(Map p720; ☎08-8212 2411; www.britishindia.net. au; 270-276 Morphett St; thalis $22; ⊘dinner; ✈) Tacked onto the more upmarket British India restaurant, the moody Thali Room offers a selection of nine *thalis* (curry platters), all served with dhal, mango chutney, rice and naan. Try the Goan (hot beef) or the Malabar (prawns in mild coconut).

Café de Vili's
FAST FOOD **$**

(off Map p720; www.vilis.com; 2-14 Manchester St, Mile End Sth; mains $5-15; ⊘24hr) Vili's pies are a South Australian institution. Next to their factory just west of the West End, this is an all-night cafe serving the equally iconic 'pie floaters' (a meat pie floating in pea soup, topped with mashed potato, gravy and sauce – outstanding!).

Jerusalem Sheshkabab House
MIDDLE EASTERN **$**

(Map p720; ☎08-8212 6185; 131 Hindley St; mains $10-15; ⊘lunch Tue-Sat, dinner Tue-Sun) A skinny Hindley St room that's been here forever, serving magnificent Middle Eastern and Lebanese delights: falafels, hummus, tabouleh, tahini and (of course) sheshkababs. The plastic furniture and draped tent material are appropriately tacky.

Ying Chow
CHINESE **$$**

(Map p720; 114 Gouger St; mains $15-17; ⊘dinner daily, lunch Fri) This fluoro-lit, utilitarian eatery is a culinary gem; serving cuisine styled from the Guangzhou region, such as crispy salt-and-pepper squid and steamed duck with

WEST END PUB GRUB

Wander the West End backstreets for some great-value pub food.

Edinburgh Castle
PUB FARE **$**

(Map p720; www.edinburghcastlehotel.com; 233 Currie St; mains $10; ⊘lunch & dinner; ✈)
Super-cheap $10 menu (the students love it) featuring schnitzels, burgers, vegie lasagne, and beer-battered whiting.

Prince Albert
PUB FARE **$**

(Map p720; www.princealberthotel.com.au; 254 Wright St; mains $10-30; ⊘lunch & dinner)
Cheap pub grub that looms large: steaks, rissoles, hanging-off-the-plate schnitzels and inexplicably popular lambs brains. Beautifully renovated old boozer.

Cumberland Arms
PUB FARE **$**

(Map p720; www.thecumberlandarms.com.au; 205 Waymouth St; mains $10-18; ⊘lunch Mon-Fri, dinner Mon-Sat) Ignore the pokies for excellent T-bone steaks, Caesar salads and burgers. Cheap schnitzels Thursday; cheap steaks Wednesday.

salty sauce. It gets packed – with queues out the door – but it's well worth the wait.

Celsius
MODERN AUSTRALIAN **$$$**

(Map p720; ☎08-8231 6023; www.celsiusrestaurant. com.au; 95-97 Gouger St; mains $29-37, 8-course degustation with/without wine $180/120; ☺lunch Tue-Fri, dinner Mon-Sat) Feel the temperature rise at Celsius, a very classy restaurant with very 'now' decor (all charcoal, wicker, dark wood and spiky pot plants). Expect modern mains from a kitchen not afraid of the more adventurous meats (rabbit, quail, lamb sweetbreads).

EAST END

Jasmin Indian Restaurant
INDIAN **$$**

(Map p720; ☎08-8223 7837; www.jasmin.com. au; basement, 31 Hindmarsh Sq; mains $24-26; ☺lunch Thu & Fri, dinner Tue-Sat) Magical North Indian curries and consummately professional staff (they might remember your name from when you ate here in 1997). There's nothing too surprising about the menu, but it's done to absolute perfection. Bookings essential.

Botanic Café
ITALIAN **$$**

(Map p720; ☎08-8232 0626; 4 East Tce; mains $25-40; ☺lunch Tue-Fri, dinner Tue-Sat) Order from a seasonal menu of quality SA produce in this linen-crisp, modern Italian eatery opposite the Adelaide Botanic Gardens. Offerings might include goats-cheese tartlets with pear chutney, or pappardelle with braised lamb shank and thyme *ragu*. The tasting menu (two courses and a glass of wine for $25) is a steal.

Amalfi Pizzeria Ristorante
ITALIAN **$$**

(Map p720; ☎08-8223 1948; 29 Frome St; mains $16-26; ☺lunch Mon-Fri, dinner Mon-Sat) What a classic! Authentic pizza and pasta with bentwood chairs, terrazzo floors, red-and-white checked tablecloths, sleep-defeating coffee and imagined Mafioso mutterings in the back room.

Vego & Lovin' It
VEGETARIAN **$**

(Map p720; 1st fl, 240 Rundle St; meals $6-12; ☺lunch Mon-Fri; ☑) Get your weekly vitamin dose disguised in a scrumptious vegie burger, wrap or focaccia at this artsy upstairs kitchen. Dreadlocked urban renegades order 'extra alfalfa but no hummus'.

Earl of Leicester
PUB FARE **$**

(off Map p720; www.earl.com.au; 85 Leicester St, Parkside; mains $13-26) Hidden in the suburban Parkside backstreets is this atmospheric old bluestone pub, serving a winning combo of crafty microbrewed beers and huge schnitzels.

Biga
CAFE **$**

(Map p720; cnr Halifax & Hutt Sts; mains $6-15; ☺breakfast & lunch daily; ☑) A cool cafe popular with Adelaide's weekend cycling set, who exhaustedly sprawl across the outdoor tables. Head-kicking coffee and recuperative breakfasts – try the baked omelette with baby spinach, herbed mushrooms, tasty cheese and fat wood-oven toast.

Sosta
ARGENTINEAN **$$**

(Map p720; ☎08-8232 6799; www.sostaargentini-ankitchen.com.au; 291 Rundle St; tapas $8-17, mains $30-39; ☺lunch Mon-Fri, dinner daily) Beef, lamb, pork, chicken, fish...vegetarians run for the hills! Sosta's aged 1kg T-bone steaks are legendary. With crisp white tablecloths and blood-brown floorboards, it's an elegant place to launch your nocturnal East End foray.

Enoteca
ITALIAN **$$**

(Map p720; ☎08-8227 0766; www.enotecacucina. com.au; 262 Carrington St; mains $25-49; ☺lunch Wed-Fri, dinner Wed-Sat) In a timber-floored glass box dangling off the side of the Italian Chamber of Commerce, Enoteca plates up superb modern Italian. The house-made linguini with cacciatore sausage, black garlic, scampi and parsley is heaven-sent. Classy with a capital C.

Penfolds Magill Estate Winery
WINERY

(Map p712; ☎08-8301 5569; www.penfolds.com.au; 78 Penfolds Rd, Magill; mains $43-47; ☺lunch Fri, dinner Tue-Sat) Dine in style at this slick, glass-fronted restaurant at Penfolds' 100-year-old winery. If your wallet can stand the heat, sample some famous Grange wine while you're here.

Lemongrass Thai Bistro
THAI **$$**

(Map p720; ☎08-8223 6627; www.lemongrass thaibistro.com.au; 289 Rundle St; mains $15-25; ☺lunch Mon-Fri, dinner daily; ☑) Affordable, breezy Thai joint right in the Rundle St mix. Mango and coconut chicken, red curry beef, clattering chairs and chilli chatter.

NORTH ADELAIDE

Store
CAFE **$**

(Map p728; www.thestore.com.au; 157 Melbourne St; breakfast $9-16, mains $10-29; ☑) A much-needed slice of bohemia amid the North Adelaide affluence, Store is a casual corner eatery with a built-in deli, serving great coffee, pastas, risottos, tapas and gourmet

mains like Vietnamese vegie burgers and harissa lamb cutlets.

Sparrow Kitchen & Bar   MODERN AUSTRALIAN $$
(Map p728; ☎08-8267 2444; www.sparrowkitch enandbar.com.au; 10 O'Connell St; tapas $4-23, mains $26-50; ☺lunch & dinner) Sparrow is no nervous little brown bird – more like a sassy culinary kestrel. Fabulous tapas and creative contemporary mains in a hip O'Connell St nook, with a long marble-topped bar and flowerpot-strewn courtyard for those hot Adelaide nights. The tapas is affordable, the mains less so (but worth every penny).

Royal Oak   PUB FARE $$
(Map p728; www.royaloakhotel.com.au; 123 O'Connell St; mains $15-29; ☺breakfast Sat & Sun, lunch & dinner daily) Winning pub grub at this enduring pub: steak sangers, vegie lasagne, lamb-shank pie, eggs Florentine and blueberry pancakes (not all at once). Quirky retro vibe; live jazz/indie-rock Tuesday, Wednesday and Sunday.

Lion Hotel   GASTROPUB $$$
(Map p728; ☎08-8367 0222; www.thelionhotel. com; 161 Melbourne St; mains $30-39; ☺lunch daily, dinner Mon-Sat) Off to one side of this popular, upmarket boozer (all big screens, beer terraces and business types) is a sassy restaurant with a cool retro interior and romantic vibes. Hot off the menu are luscious Coorong Angus steaks, market fish and corn-fed chicken breasts, served with a professionalism far exceeding the average pub.

GLENELG

TOP CHOICE Cafe Zest   CAFE $
(2a Sussex St; meals $5-20; ☺breakfast & lunch; ☑) This cafe-gallery fills a tiny crack between buildings, but its laid-back vibe and brilliant breakfasts more than compensate for any shortcomings in size. Baguettes and bagels are crammed with creative combos, or you can banish your hangover with some 'Hells Eggs': two potted eggs with tomato, capsicum and rosemary salsa, topped with grilled cheese and Tabasco sauce. Great coffee, arty staff, and vegetarian specials too.

Thuy-Linh   VIETNAMESE $
(☎08-8295 5746; 168c Jetty Rd; mains $11-23, banquets per person from $20; ☺lunch Tue-Fri, dinner Tue-Sun) Astonishingly unpretentious Vietnamese/Chinese eatery at the city end of Jetty Rd, with attentive service and a swathe of fresh seafood, meat and noodle delights. Bring some mates and spin the lazy susan.

Good Life   PIZZA $$
(☎08-8376 5900; www.goodlifepizza.com; 1st fl, cnr Jetty Rd & Moseley St; pizzas $15-38; ☺lunch Tue-Fri & Sun, dinner daily; ☑) At this brilliant organic pizzeria above the Jetty Rd tramscape, thin crusts are stacked with tasty toppings like free-range roast duck, Spencer Gulf 'monster' prawns and spicy Angaston salami. *Ahhh*, life is good... Also a branch in the city (Map p720; ☎08-8223 2618; 170 Hutt St).

Gringos   MEXICAN $$
(☎08-8295 3524; Shop 1, Colley Tce; mains $16-24; ☺lunch & dinner) Crack a cold Corona and chilli-up in the sun at this casual, good-time Mexican cantina opposite Moseley Sq, or take your bulging burrito down to the beach. Dangling sombreros, and margaritas by the jug.

Zucca Greek Mezze   GREEK $$$
(☎08-8376 8222; www.zucca.com.au; Shop 5, Marina Pier, Holdfast Shores; meze $17-19, mains $33-45; ☺lunch & dinner) Spartan linen, marina views, super service and a contemporary menu of tapas-style meze plates – you wouldn't find anything this classy on Santorini. The grilled scallops with Persian fetta and salty pistachio crumble are sublime.

SELF-CATERING
Central Market (p723) is a great place to stock up on local goodies.

Coles   SUPERMARKET $
(Map p720; www.centralmarketarcade.com.au; Central Market Arcade, cnr King William & Gouger Sts; ☺midnight-9pm Mon-Fri, to 5pm Sat, 11am-5pm Sun) In Central Market Arcade.

IGA North Adelaide   SUPERMARKET $
(Map p728; www.iga.net.au; 113 O'Connell St, North Adelaide; ☺8am-10pm)

Woolworths   SUPERMARKET $
(Map p720; www.woolworths.com.au; 80 Rundle Mall; ☺7am-9pm Mon-Fri, 7am-5pm Sat, 11am-5pm Sun)

Drinking

For a true Adelaide experience, head for the bar and order a schooner of Coopers – the local brew – or a glass of SA's impressive wine. Rundle St has a few iconic pubs, while along Hindley St in the West End, grunge and sleaze collides with student energy and groovy bars. Most bars close on Monday.

TOP CHOICE Exeter   PUB
(Map p720; www.theexeter.com.au; 246 Rundle St) The best pub in the city, this legendary

boozer attracts an eclectic mix of postwork, punk and uni drinkers, shaking the day off their backs. Pull up a stool or a table in the grungy beer garden and settle in for the evening. Original music nightly; no pokies.

Grace Emily   PUB
(Map p720; www.graceemilyhotel.com.au; 232 Waymouth St) Duking it out with the Exeter for 'Adelaide's Best Pub' bragging rights (it pains us to separate the two) the 'Gracie' has live music most nights, featuring up-and-coming Australian acts. Inside it's all kooky '50s-meets-voodoo decor, open fires and great beers. Cult cinema Tuesday nights; no pokies. Look for the UFO on the roof.

Wheatsheaf   PUB
(off Map p720; www.wheatsheafhotel.com.au; 39 George St, Thebarton) A hidden gem under the flight path in industrial Thebarton, with an artsy crowd of students, jazz musos, lesbians, punks and rockers. Tidy beer garden; live music Friday to Monday.

Casablabla   BAR
(Map p720; www.casablabla.com; 12 Leigh St; ☉10pm-late Thu-Sat) Billing itself as a 'multicultural tapas lounge bar', Casablabla covers a lot of bases but does it well. The atmosphere is eclectic: exotic art (a bit of Morocco, a bit of Bali, a bit of Brazil), hookah pipes, fish tanks, burnt-orange walls…Sip cocktails amid it all and tune in to reggae, funk, soul and jazz.

Cork Wine Cafe   WINE BAR
(Map p720; 61a Gouger St) A down-sized Frenchie hole-in-the-wall wine bar, unexpected among the fluoro-lit Chinese restaurants along this stretch of Gouger St. Well-worn floorboards, bentwood chairs, art-nouveau posters…perfect for a quick vino before dinner (see fluoro-lit Chinese restaurants, above).

Earl of Leicester   PUB
(off Map p720; www.earl.com.au; 85 Leicester St, Parkside) Hidden in the suburban Parkside backstreets is this atmospheric old bluestone pub, serving a winning combo of crafty microbrewed beers and the biggest schnitzels you're every likely to bite into (mains $13 to $26).

Crown & Sceptre   PUB
(Map p720; www.sceptre.com.au; 308 King William St) An urbane boozer drawing all-comers, from legal-eagles on adjournment from trial to ditch diggers in their boots. Ambient tunes, DJs most nights, sidewalk tables, a cool

little beer garden and better-than-average pub food (mains $10 to $28).

Distill   COCKTAIL BAR
(Map p720; www.distillhealth.com.au; 286 Rundle St) Super-sassy Rundle St bar with a tight dress code (to the nines) and a kickin' organic cocktail list. Sustainable snacks (sourced within 100 miles) are creatively paired with SA wines: Limestone Coast cloth cheddar with juicy Shiraz; organic basil pesto with herby Riesling.

Daniel O'Connell   PUB
(Map p728; www.danieloconnell.com.au; 165 Tynte St, North Adelaide) An Irish pub without a whiff of kitsch Celtic cash-in! Just great Guinness, open fires, acoustic music and a house-sized pepper tree in the beer garden (164 years old and counting).

Universal Wine Bar   WINE BAR
(Map p720; www.universalwinebar.com.au; 285 Rundle St) A hip crowd clocks in to this stalwart bar to select from 200-plus South Australian and international wines, and a menu (mains $19 to $36) packed with SA produce. 'The scene is very Italian', says the barman.

Apothecary 1878   WINE BAR
(Map p720; www.theapothecary1878.com.au; 118 Hindley St; ☉5pm-late Tue-Sat) Classy coffee and wine at this gorgeous chemist-turned-bar. Medicine cabinets, bentwood chairs and Parisian marble-topped tables.

Colonist   PUB
(off Map p720; www.colonist.com.au; 44 The Parade, Norwood) Funky countercultural boozing on Norwood's otherwise mainstream Parade.

Belgian Beer Café   BAR
(Map p720; www.oostende.com.au; 27-29 Ebenezer Pl) There's shiny brass, sexy staff, much pre-sluicing of glasses and somewhere upwards of 26 imported Belgian superbrews (we lost count…). Off Rundle St.

Pier One Bar   BAR
(www.glenelgpier.com.au; 18 Holdfast Promenade, Glenelg) A cavernous mainstream sports bar with voyeuristic beach views and fold-back windows for when the sea breeze drops. As many screens as staff (a lot of each), and raucous Sunday sessions.

☆ Entertainment

Artsy Adelaide has a rich cultural life that stacks up favourably with much larger cities.

For city-wide info:

Adelaide Now (www.adelaidenow.com.au) Events, cinema and gallery details.

Adelaide Review (www.adelaidereview.com. au) Theatre and gallery listings.

Adelaide Theatre Guide (www.theatreguide. com.au) Booking details, venues and reviews for comedy, drama and musicals.

For big-ticket event bookings:

BASS (☑13 12 46; www.bass.net.au)

Moshtix (☑1300 438 849; www.moshtix.com.au)

Ticketek (☑13 28 49; www.ticketek.com.au)

LIVE MUSIC

With serious musical pedigree (from Cold Chisel to the Audreys), Adelaide knows how to kick out the jams! The free street-press papers *Rip It Up* (www.ripitup.com.au) and *dB* (www.dbmagazine.com.au) – available from record shops, pubs and cafes – have band and DJ listings and reviews. Cover charges vary with acts.

Online resources:

Adelaide Symphony Orchestra (www.aso. com.au) Listings for the estimable ASO.

Jazz Adelaide (www.jazz.adelaide.onau.net) Finger-snappin' za-bah-dee-dah.

Music SA (www.musicsa.com.au) All-genre listings.

TOP CHOICE **Governor Hindmarsh**

Hotel   LIVE MUSIC
(off Map p720; ☑08-8340 0744; www.thegov.com. au; 59 Port Rd, Hindmarsh) Ground Zero for live music in Adelaide, 'The Gov' hosts some legendary local and international acts. The odd Irish band fiddles around in the bar, while the main venue features rock, folk, jazz, blues, salsa, reggae and dance. A huge place with an inexplicably personal vibe.

Jive   LIVE MUSIC
(Map p720; ☑08-8211 6683; www.jivevenue.com; 181 Hindley St) In a converted theatre, Jive caters to an off-beat crowd of student types who like their tunes funky, left-field and removed from the mainstream. A sunken dance floor; great views from the bar!

Fowlers Live   LIVE MUSIC
(Map p720; ☑08-8212 0255; www.fowlerslive. com.au; 68 North Tce) Inside the former Fowler Flour Factory, this 500-capacity venue is a temple of hard rock and metal.

ℹ PINT OF COOPERS PLEASE!

Things can get confusing at the bar in Adelaide. Aside from 200ml (7oz) 'butchers' – the choice of old men in dim, sticky-carpet pubs – there are three main beer sizes: 285ml (10oz) 'schooners' (pots or middies elsewhere in Australia), 425ml (15oz) 'pints' (schooners elsewhere) and 568ml (20oz) 'imperial pints' (traditional English pints). Now go forth and order with confidence!

HQ Complex   LIVE MUSIC, NIGHTCLUB
(Map p720; www.hqcomplex.com.au; 1 North Tce; ⊙8pm-late Wed & Sat) Primarily a dance venue, HQ is big and powered-up enough to entice eclectic touring acts like Gary Numan and Sparkadia.

Grace Emily   LIVE MUSIC
(Map p720; www.graceemilyhotel.com.au; 232 Waymouth St) West End alt-rock, country and acoustic.

Wheatsheaf   LIVE MUSIC
(off Map p720; www.wheatsheafhotel.com.au; 39 George St, Thebarton) Eclectic offerings in the semi-industrial Thebarton wastelands.

Crown & Sceptre   LIVE MUSIC
(Map p720; www.sceptre.com.au; 308 King William St) Grooves, beats and funky stuff from resident selectors.

Exeter   LIVE MUSIC
(Map p720; www.theexeter.com.au; 246 Rundle St) The East End's rockin' soul: original indie bands, electronica and acoustic.

CINEMAS

Check out **Adelaide Now** (www.adelaidenow. com.au) for what's screening around town. Tickets generally cost around adult/child/concession $16/10/12 (cheaper on Tuesdays).

Mercury Cinema   CINEMA
(Map p720; ☑08-8410 1934; www.mercurycinema. org.au; Lion Arts Centre, 13 Morphett St) The Mercury screens art-house releases, and is home to the Adelaide Cinémathèque (classic, cult and experimental flicks).

Moonlight Cinema   CINEMA
(Map p728; ☑1300 551 908; www.moonlight.com. au; Botanic Gardens; ⊙mid-Dec–mid-Feb) In summer, pack a picnic and mosquito repellent, and spread out on the lawn to watch old and

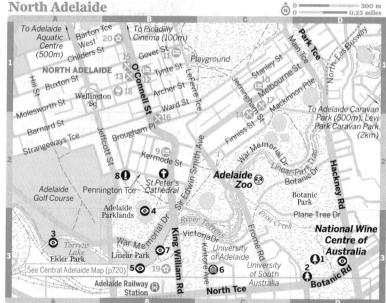

new classics under the stars. 'Gold Grass' tickets cost a little more.

Piccadilly Cinema CINEMA
(Map p728; ☑08-8267 1500; www.wallis.com.au; 181 O'Connell St, North Adelaide) A beaut old art-deco cinema on the main North Adelaide strip, with a sexily curved street frontage and chevron-shaped windows spangled across the facade. Mostly mainstream releases.

Palace Eastend Cinemas (Map p720; ☑08-8232 3434; www.palacenova.com; 250 Rundle St) and **Nova Eastend Cinemas** (Map p720; ☑08-8232 3434; www.palacenova.com; 251 Rundle St) face off across Rundle St. Both cinemas feature new-release art-house, foreign-language and independent films as well as some mainstream flicks. Fully licensed, too.

NIGHTCLUBS
The West End and Light Sq are safe bets for club activity. Online check out www.pubscene.com.au or www.onion.com.au. Cover charges can be anything from free to $15, depending on the night. Most clubs close Monday to Wednesday.

Lotus Lounge NIGHTCLUB, COCKTAIL BAR
(Map p720; www.lotuslounge.net.au; 268 Morphett St; ☺6pm-late Tue-Sat) We like the signage

here – a very minimal fluoro martini glass with a flashing olive. Inside it's a glam lounge with cocktails, quality beers and Adelaide dolls cuttin' the rug. Expect queues around the corner on Saturday nights.

Zhivago NIGHTCLUB
(Map p720; 155 Waymouth St, Light Sq; ☺5pm-late Fri-Sun) At the pick of the Light Sq clubs (there are quite a few of 'em – some are a bit moron-prone), Zhivago's DJs pump out everything from reggae and dub to quality house. Popular with the 18 to 25 dawn patrol.

Sugar NIGHTCLUB
(Map p720; www.sugarclub.com.au; Level 1, 274 Rundle St; ☺9pm-late daily) Sugar is an unusual Adelaide club in several ways: (a) it's open every night; (b) it's relatively upmarket and bogan-free; and (c) it's in the East End. Expect international and Australian DJs, cool cocktails and local art on the walls.

HQ Complex NIGHTCLUB, LIVE MUSIC
(Map p720; www.hqcomplex.com.au; 1 North Tce; ☺8pm-late Wed & Sat) Adelaide's biggest club occupies the bad-old Heaven complex, filling five big rooms with shimmering sound and light. Night-time is the right time on Saturdays – the biggest (and trashiest) club night in town. Retro Wednesdays.

Mars Bar NIGHTCLUB
(Map p720; www.themarsbar.com.au; 120 Gouger St; 9pm-late Wed-Sat) The lynchpin of Adelaide's nocturnal gay and lesbian scene, always-busy Mars Bar features glitzy decor, flashy clientele and OTT drag shows.

SPORT

As most Australian cities do, Adelaide hangs its hat on the successes of its sporting teams. In the **Australian Football League** (AFL; www.afl.com.au), the Adelaide Crows and Port Adelaide have sporadic success. Suburban Adelaide teams compete in the **South Australian National Football League** (SANFL; www.sanfl.com.au). The football season runs from March to September.

In the **National Basketball League** (NBL; www.nbl.com.au), the Adelaide 36ers have been a force for decades. In soccer's **A League** (www.a-league.com.au), Adelaide United are usually competitive. Under the auspices of **Cricket SA** (www.cricketsa.com.au), the Redbacks play one-day, Twenty20 and multiday state matches at the Adelaide Oval.

THEATRE

Adelaide Festival Centre ARTS CENTRE
(Map p728; ☎08-8216 8600; www.adelaidefestival-centre.com.au; King William Rd) The hub of performing arts in SA, this crystalline white Festival Centre opened in June 1973, four proud months before the Sydney Opera House! The **State Theatre Company** (www.statetheatrecompany.com.au) is based here.

Adelaide Entertainment Centre CONCERT HALL
(off Map p720; ☎08-8288 2222; www.theaec.net; Port Rd, Hindmarsh) Everyone from the Wiggles to Stevie Wonder.

Her Majesty's Theatre THEATRE
(Map p720; ☎08-8212 8600; www.adelaidefestival centre.com.au; 58 Grote St) Built in 1913 and seats over 1000 people; managed by the Adelaide Festival Centre.

🛍 Shopping

Shops and department stores (Myer, David Jones et al) line Rundle Mall. The beautiful old arcades running between the mall and Grenfell St retain their original splendour, and house eclectic little shops. Rundle St and the surrounding lanes are home to boutique and retro clothing shops. Outdoor shops also convene around Rundle St; tacky souvenir and opal shops cluster around the Rundle Mall/King William St corner.

Some eclectic local favourites:

TOP CHOICE Title BOOKSTORE, MUSIC STORE
(Map p720; www.titlespace.com; 15 Vaughan Pl) Lefty, arty and subversive in the best possible way, Title is the place to find that elusive Miles Davis disc or Charles Bukowski poetry compilation.

Midwest Trader CLOTHING
(Map p720; www.midwesttrader.com.au; Shop 1 & 2 Ebenezer Pl) Stocks a toothy range of punk, rock, skate and rockabilly gear.

Imprints Booksellers BOOKSTORE
(Map p720; www.imprints.com.au; 107 Hindley St) Jazz, floorboards, Persian rugs and the best books in print.

Urban Cow Studio DESIGN
(Map p720; www.urbancow.com.au; 11 Frome St) The catch cry here is 'Handmade in Adelaide' – a brilliant assortment of paintings, jewellery, glassware, ceramics and textiles, plus a gallery upstairs.

Jurlique COSMETICS
(Map p720; www.jurlique.com.au; Shop 2a, Ground Fl, 50 Rundle Mall Plaza, Rundle Mall) An international success story, SA's own Jurlique sells fragrant skincare products that are pricey but worth every cent.

T'Arts DESIGN
(Map p720; www.tartscollective.com.au; 10g Gays Arcade, Adelaide Arcade, Rundle Mall) Textiles and art from a 35-member local arts co-op.

Map Shop MAPS
(Map p720; www.mapshop.net.au; 6-10 Peel St) Maps, charts and guides for walking, hiking and touring, plus GPS sales and advice.

RM Williams SHOES, CLOTHING
(Map p720; www.rmwilliams.com.au; 6 Gawler Pl) Another SA smash hit, selling boots handmade from single pieces of leather.

ℹ Information

Emergency
Ambulance (emergency 000, non-emergency 1300 881 700; www.saambulance.com.au)
Fire (emergency 000, non-emergency 08-8204 3600; www.mfs.sa.gov.au)
Lifeline (13 11 14; www.lifeline.org.au; 24hr) Crisis support.
Police (emergency 000, non-emergency 13 14 44; www.sapolice.sa.gov.au; 26 Hindley St; 24hr)
RAA Emergency Roadside Assistance (13 11 11; www.raa.net)

Internet Access
Arena Internet Café (Level 1, 264 Rundle St; 11am-midnight Mon-Thu, 10am-late Fri-Sun)
Wireless Café (53 Hindley St; 7am-8pm Mon-Fri, 10am-6pm Sat, open later Dec-Feb) Good coffee too.

Media
Adelaide's daily tabloid is the parochial *Advertiser*, though the *Age*, *Australian* and *Financial Review* are also widely available.

Adelaide Review (www.adelaidereview.com.au) Highbrow articles, culture and arts. Free fortnightly.
Blaze (www.blaze.e-p.net.au) Local gay-and-lesbian street press.
dB (ww.dbmagazine.com.au) Local street press; loaded with music info.
Rip it Up (www.ripitup.com.au) Local street press; loaded with music info.

Medical Services
Corner Chemist (www.cornerchemist.com.au; cnr Pirie & King William Sts; 7.45am-5.30pm Mon-Fri)
Emergency Dental Service (08-8222 8222; www.sadental.sa.gov.au)
Royal Adelaide Hospital (08-8222 4000; www.rah.sa.gov.au; 275 North Tce; 24hr) Emergency department (not for blisters!) and STD clinic.
Traveller's Medical & Vaccination Centre (Travel Doctor; 1300 658 844, 08-8212 7522; www.traveldoctor.com.au; 27 Gilbert Pl; 9am-5pm Mon-Fri, to 7pm Wed, to 1pm Sat)
Women's & Children's Hospital (08-8161 7000; www.cywhs.sa.gov.au; 72 King William Rd, North Adelaide; 24hr) Emergency and sexual-assault services.

Money
Banks and ATMs prevail throughout the CBD, particularly around Rundle Mall.
American Express (www.americanexpress.com; Shop 32, CitiCentre Arcade, Rundle Mall; 9am-5pm Mon-Fri, to noon Sat) Foreign currency exchange.
Travelex (www.travelex.com.au; Shop 4, Rundle Mall; 9am-5.30pm Mon-Fri, to 5pm Sat) Foreign currency exchange.

Post
Adelaide General Post Office (GPO; Map p720; www.auspost.com.au; 141 King William St; 8am-5pm Mon-Fri) Poste restante; have mail addressed to you c/o Poste Restante, Adelaide 5001.
Post Office (Map p720; www.auspost.com.au; 61 North Tce; 9am-5pm Mon-Fri)

Tourist Information
Adelaide Visitor Information Kiosk (Map p720; 08-8203 7611; Rundle Mall; 10am-5pm Mon-Thu, to 8pm Fri, to 4pm Sat & Sun) Adelaide-specific information, and free city-centre walking tours at 9.30am Monday to Friday. At the King William St end of the mall.
Disability Information & Resource Centre (DIRC; Map p720; 08-8236 0555; www.dircsa.org.au; 195 Gilles St; 9am-5pm Mon-Fri) Info on accommodation, venues and travel for people with disabilities.

South Australian Visitor & Travel Centre

(Map p720; ☎1300 764 227; www.southaustralia.com; 18 King William St; ⊙8.30am-5pm Mon-Fri, 9am-2pm Sat & Sun) Abundantly stocked with info on Adelaide and SA. Super-patient staff and event ticketing, too.

Women's Information Service (Map p720; ☎1800 188 158, 08-8303 0590; www.wis.sa.gov.au; Chesser House, 91-97 Grenfell St; ⊙9am-5.30pm Mon-Fri) Information and counselling services.

⊙ Getting There & Away

Air

Adelaide Airport (Map p712; www.aal.com.au; 1 James Schofield Dr, Adelaide Airport) is connected by regular flights to all Australian capitals and many regional centres. Airlines include the following:

Jetstar (www.jetstar.com.au)

Qantas (www.qantas.com.au)

Regional Express
(Rex; www.regionalexpress.com.au)

Tiger Airways (www.tigerairways.com)

Virgin Australia (www.virginaustralia.com)

Bus

Adelaide Central Bus Station (Map p720; www.cityofadelaide.com.au; 85 Franklin St) has ticket offices and terminals for all major interstate and statewide services. For online bus timetables see the **Bus SA** (www.adelaidemetro.com.au/bussa) website.

Car & Motorcycle

If you want to hitch a ride (sharing petrol costs) or buy a secondhand car, check out the hostel noticeboards. See the local *Yellow Pages* for Adelaide car-rental companies, including the major internationals. Note that some companies don't allow vehicles to be taken to Kangaroo Island. Expect to pay around $45 per day (less for longer rentals) for car hire with the cheaper companies, such as the following:

Acacia Car Rentals (www.acaciacarrentals.com.au; 91 Sir Donald Bradman Dr, Hilton)

Access Rent-a-Car (www.accessrentacar.com; 60 Frome St)

Cut Price Car & Truck Rentals (www.cutprice.com.au; cnr Sir Donald Bradman Dr & South Rd/Rte A13, Mile End) There are also 4WDs available.

Koala Car Rentals (www.koalarentals.com.au; 41 Sir Donald Bradman Dr, Mile End)

Train

Adelaide's interstate train terminal is **Adelaide Parklands Terminal** (off Map p720; www.gsr.com.au; Railway Tce, Keswick), 1km southwest of the city centre. See p741 for details of train services to/from Adelaide.

⊙ Getting Around

To/from the Airport & Train Station

Skylink (www.skylinkadelaide.com; adult/child one-way $6/4) minibuses connect the city with Adelaide Parklands Terminal and the airport; bookings are essential for all city pick-up locations other than the Central Bus Station.

Adelaide Metro's **JetBus** (www.adelaidemetro.com.au/routes/airport.html) runs several routes linking the suburbs, city and airport, starting around 5am and running until 11.30pm. Standard fares apply.

Many hostels will pick you up and drop you off if you're staying with them. Taxis charge around $20 between the airport and city centre.

Bicycle

With a valid passport or driver's licence you can borrow an 'Adelaide City Bike' (for free!) from **Bicycle SA** (www.bikesa.asn.au; 111 Franklin St). Helmet and lock provided.

Down at the beach, hire a bike from **Glenelg Bicycle Hire** (☎08-8376 1934; www.glenelgbicyclehire.com.au; Norfolk Motor Inn, 71 Broadway, Glenelg South; per day $40).

Public Transport

Adelaide Metro (www.adelaidemetro.com.au; cnr King William & Currie Sts; ⊙8am-6pm Mon-Fri, 9am-5pm Sat, 11am-4pm Sun) provides timetables and sells tickets for Adelaide's integrated bus, train and tram network.

Tickets can also be purchased on board, at staffed train stations and in delis and newsagents. Ticket types include day trip ($8.60), two-hour peak ($4.60) and two-hour off-peak ($2.80) tickets. Peak travel time is before 9am and after 3pm. Kids under five ride free!

BUS

Adelaide's buses are clean and reliable. Most services start around 6am and run until midnight. Additional services:

99C City Loop Bus (⊙8am-6.15pm Mon-Thu, 8am-9.15pm Fri, 8.15am-5.45pm Sat, 10.15am-5.45pm Sun) Adelaide Metro's free 99C City Loop Bus runs clockwise and anticlockwise around the CBD fringe from Adelaide Train Station on North Tce, passing the Central Market en route. Buses run every 15 minutes on weekdays, and every 30 minutes on Friday night and weekends.

Adelaide Connector Bus (www.cityofadelaide.com.au; ⊙8am-6pm Mon-Thu, 8am-9:30pm Fri, 10am-5pm Sat & Sun) Adelaide City Council runs this free service, linking the CBD with North Adelaide. There are two hourly services – Green and Red – plying the same route in opposite directions. Key stops include the Adelaide Zoo, Rundle Mall, Hutt St, Central Market, Hindley St, North Tce and O'Connell St.

After Midnight Buses (☺midnight-5am Sat)
Adelaide Metro's After Midnight buses run select standard routes (including to Glenelg and
the Adelaide Hills), but have an 'N' preceding
the route number on their displays. Standard
ticket prices apply.

TRAIN

Adelaide's hokey old diesel trains depart from
Adelaide Railway Station (Map p720; North
Tce), plying five suburban routes (Belair, Gawler,
Grange, Noarlunga and Outer Harbour). Trains
generally run between 6am and midnight (some
services start at 4.30am).

TRAM

Adelaide Metro's state-of-the-art trams rumble
to/from Moseley Sq in Glenelg, through Victoria
Sq in the city and along North Tce and Port Rd
(Rte A7) to the Adelaide Entertainment Centre. Trams run approximately every seven or
eight minutes on weekdays (every 15 minutes
on weekends) from 6am to midnight daily.
Standard ticket prices apply, but the section
between South Tce and the Adelaide Entertainment Centre is free.

Taxi

There are licensed taxi ranks all over town.
Adelaide Independent Taxis (☑13 22 11,
wheelchair-access cabs 1300 360 940; www.
aitaxis.com.au)
Suburban Taxis (☑13 10 08; www.suburban
taxis.com.au)
Yellow Cabs (☑13 22 27; www.yellowcabgroup.
com.au)

ADELAIDE HILLS

When the Adelaide plains are desert-hot
in the summer months, the Adelaide Hills
(technically the Mt Lofty Ranges) are always a few degrees cooler, with crisp air,
woodland shade and labyrinthine valleys.
Fleeing the sweaty city, early colonists built
stately summer houses around Stirling and
Aldgate. German settlers escaping religious
persecution also arrived, infusing towns like
Hahndorf and Lobethal with European values and architecture.

The Hills make a brilliant day trip from
Adelaide. Hop from town to town (all with
at least one pub), passing carts of fresh produce for sale, stone cottages, olive groves and
vineyards along the way. For tour options see
p717. Pick up the *Adelaide Hills Cellar Door
Guide* brochure from visitors centres and go
exploring. See www.visitadelaidehills.com.au
for general Hills information.

① Information

Adelaide Hills visitor centre (☑1800 353
323; 08-8388 1185; www.visitadelaidehills.com.
au; 68 Main St, Hahndorf; ☺9am-5pm Mon-Fri,
10am-4pm Sat & Sun; @) Has the usual barrage of brochures, books accommodation and
provides internet access.

① Getting There & Around

BUS Adelaide Metro (www.adelaidemetro.
com.au) runs buses between the city and most
Hills towns. The 864 and 864F city–Mt Barker
buses are useful, departing Currie St in the city
and stopping at Stirling, Aldgate and Hahndorf
en route. The 823 runs from Crafers to Mt Lofty
Summit and Cleland Wildlife Park; the 830F
runs from the city to Oakbank, Woodside and
Lobethal.

Stirling Area

The photogenic little villages of old-school
Stirling (population 2870), one-horse
Aldgate (population 3350) and market-
garden Piccadilly (population 530), are
famed for their bedazzling autumn colours,
thanks to the deciduous trees the early residents saw fit to seed. There's not a great deal
to do 'round these here parts, but there are
some excellent cafes, restaurants and atmospheric (read: pricey) places to stay.

◉ Sights & Activities

Cleland Conservation Park   NATURE RESERVE
(www.environment.sa.gov.au/parks; ☺24hr) Clambering up the slopes from the foothills to Mt
Lofty, this conservation park has some steep
bushwalking trails through tall eucalypt
forest and cool gullies. Inside the park, the
fab **Cleland Wildlife Park** (☑08-8339 2444;
www.clelandwildlifepark.sa.gov.au; Mt Lofty Summit
Rd; adult/child/concession/family $17/10/14/46;
☺9.30am-5pm, last entry 4.30pm) lets you interact with all kinds of Australian beasts.
There are keeper talks and feeding sessions
throughout the day, nocturnal tours (bookings required), and you can have your mug-
shot taken with a koala ($30, 2pm to 4pm).
There's a cafe here too. From the city, take
bus 864 or 864F from Grenfell St to Crafers
for connecting bus 823 to the park.

Mt Lofty Summit   LOOKOUT
From Cleland Wildlife Park you can bushwalk (2km) or drive up to Mt Lofty Summit
(a surprising 710m), which has eye-popping
views across Adelaide and Gulf St Vincent.
Mt Lofty Summit Visitor Information

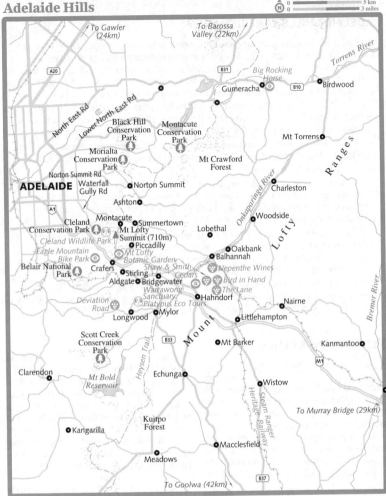

Centre (☎08-8370 1054; www.mtloftysummit. com; Mt Lofty Summit Rd; ⊙9am-5pm) has info on local attractions and **walking tracks**, including the steep Waterfall Gully Track (8km return, 2½ hours) and Mt Lofty Botanic Gardens Loop Trail (7km loop, two hours). The video of the Ash Wednesday bushfires of 16 February 1983 is harrowing. There's a snazzy cafe-restaurant here too.

FREE **Mt Lofty Botanic Garden**   GARDEN
(www.botanicgardens.sa.gov.au; gates on Mawson Dr & Lampert Rd; ⊙8.30am-4pm Mon-Fri, 10am-5pm Sat & Sun). From Mt Lofty, truck south 1.5km to the cool-climate slopes of the botanic garden. Nature trails wind past a lake, exotic temperate plants, native stringybark forest and bodacious rhododendron blooms. Free guided walks depart the Lampert Rd car park at 10.30am on Thursdays from September to October and March to May.

Stirling Markets   MARKETS
(www.stirlingmarket.com.au; Druids Ave, Stirling; ⊙10am-4pm) Markets happen on the fourth Sunday of the month (the third in December). Much plant-life, busking and Hills knick-knackery.

DON'T MISS

ADELAIDE HILLS WINERIES

With night mists and reasonable rainfall, the Adelaide Hills' mid-altitude slopes sustain one of SA's cooler climates – perfect for producing some complex and truly top-notch white wines, especially Chardonnays and Sauvignon Blancs. There are 20-plus wineries in the Hills (see www.adelaidehillswine.com.au for more details): January's **Crush Festival** (www.crushfestival.com.au) celebrates this rich bounty. The pick of the bunch:

» **Shaw & Smith** (www.shawandsmith.com; Jones Rd, Balhannah; ⊙11am-5pm) Picture-perfect Mt Lofty Ranges views almost steal the show at this winery, run by two cousins. Outstanding Chardonnays and Sauvignon Blancs, holding hands with grand Shiraz.

» **Bird in Hand** (www.birdinhand.com.au; cnr Bird in Hand & Pfeiffer Rds, Woodside; ⊙11am-5pm Mon-Fri, 10am-5pm Sat & Sun) Brilliant sparkling red Shiraz, Merlot and blends, plus an olive-oil press. Worth at least two in the bush.

» **Deviation Road** (www.deviationroad.com; 214 Scott Creek Rd, Longwood; ⊙10am-5pm) Nothing deviant about the wines here: sublime Pinot Noir, substantial Shiraz, zingy Pinto Gris and a very decent bubbly, too. Grab a cheese platter and wind down the afternoon in the sun.

» **Nepenthe Wines** (www.nepenthe.com.au; Jones Rd, Balhannah; ⊙10am-4pm) Homer described nepenthe as a potion to ease grief and banish sorrow from the mind. Accordingly, Nepenthe Wines bring great happiness, especially the Semillon, Chardonnay and (surprisingly) Cabernet Sauvignon.

» **The Lane** (www.thelane.com.au; Ravenswood La, Hahndorf; ⊙10am-4pm Mon-Thu, 10am-5pm Fri-Sun) What a cool building, and what a setting! Camera-conducive views and contemporary varietals (Viognier, Pinot Grigio, Pinot Gris), plus an impressive restaurant.

🛏 Sleeping & Eating

TOP CHOICE **5 Rooms at the Stirling Hotel**　　　HOTEL **$$$**
(☎08-8339 9900; www.stirlinghotel.com.au; 54 Mt Barker Rd, Stirling; d incl breakfast from $230; ✳) Upstairs at this gracious old watering hole are five elegant, contemporary suites, three of which have open fireplaces (for winter) and breezy balconies (for summer). All have flat-screen TVs, quality linen and luxe bathrooms you'll actually want to spend time in.

Aldgate Creek Cottage B&B　　　B&B **$$$**
(☎08-8339 1987; www.aldgatecreekbnb.com; 3 Rugby Rd, Aldgate; d from $200; ✳) A romantic, two-storey cottage-for-two in a grove of vegetation above Aldgate Creek, just across the road from the improving Aldgate Pump Hotel. Bonuses include flat-screen TV in the bedroom, spa and family of resident ducks.

Mt Lofty House　　　HOTEL **$$$**
(☎08-8339 6777; www.mtloftyhouse.com.au; 74 Summit Rd, Crafers; d from $259; ✳🛜✳) Proprietarily poised above Mt Lofty Botanic Garden (*awesome* views), this 1850s baronial mansion has lavish heritage rooms and garden suites, plus an upmarket restaurant (also with killer views). The perfect dirty weekender.

Mount Lofty Railway Station　　　RENTAL HOUSE **$$**
(☎08-8339 7400; www.mlrs.com.au; 2 Sturt Valley Rd, Stirling; d/f from $125/140; ✳🛜) With four bedrooms, five bathrooms, two lounges, a kitchen and kitchenette, this disused, heritage-listed train station is affordable and versatile. You can book the whole thing, or divide it into two self-contained apartments. The only catch: the train line is *not* disused – bring earplugs. Two-night minimum.

Organic Market & Café　　　CAFE **$**
(☎08-8339 4835; www.organicmarket.com.au; 5 Druids Ave, Stirling; meals $7-13; ⊙breakfast & lunch; ✐) Rejecting Stirling's pompous tendencies, hirsute Hills types flock to this vibrant, hippie cafe. It's the busiest spot in town – and rightly so; the food's delicious and everything's made with love. Gorge on bruschetta, plump savoury muffins, great coffee and wicked Portuguese custard tarts.

Stirling Hotel　　　PUB FARE **$$**
(☎08-8339 2345; www.stirlinghotel.com.au; 52 Mt Barker Rd, Stirling; bistro $16-28, restaurant $26-36; ⊙breakfast Sat & Sun, lunch & dinner daily) The owners spent so much money tarting up this gorgeous old dame, it's a wonder

they can pay the staff. A runaway success, the free-flowing bistro (classy pub grub) and romantic restaurant (upmarket regional cuisine) are always packed.

Mylor

POP 740

The going concern in leafy Mylor is **Warrawong Sanctuary** (☑08-8370 9197; www.warrawong.com; Stock Rd; admission free; ☺9am-4pm), 3km from town – a feral-free private wildlife sanctuary with a cafe and accommodation. Take a self-guided walk, check out a **wildlife show** (adult/child/family $5/3/15; ☺11am and 2pm daily), or book a 1½-hour **guided dusk walk** (adult/child/family $28/18/85). **Accommodation** (B&B adult/child/family $75/45/225) is in en-suite eco-tents, each sleeping up to eight. Packages are also available including bed, show, walk, dinner and breakfast (adult/child/family $125/75/375). There's a cafe here too, but the awful blaring R&B might send you packing.

🦫**Platypus Eco Tours** (☑08-8370 8628; www.platypusecotours.com.au; Lot 14, Williams Rd; adult/child $40/20; ☺sunset) runs small-group eco-tours – you're guaranteed to see more than just the disappearing splash of a tail! Other critters here include bandicoots, wallabies, kangaroos and koalas. Tours at sunset year-round; call for bookings and times.

Hahndorf

POP 1810

Like the Rocks in Sydney, and Richmond near Hobart, Hahndorf is a 'ye olde worlde' colonial enclave that trades ruthlessly on its history: it's something of a kitsch parody of itself.

That said, Hahndorf is undeniably pretty, with Teutonic sandstone architecture, European trees, and flowers overflowing from half wine barrels. And it *is* interesting: Australia's oldest surviving German settlement (1839), founded by 50 Lutheran families fleeing religious persecution in Prussia. Hahndorf was placed under martial law during WWI; its Lutheran school was boarded-up and its name changed to 'Ambleside' (renamed Hahndorf in 1935). It's also slowly becoming less kitsch, more hip: there are a few cool cafes here now, and on a sunny day the main street is positively lively.

◉ Sights & Activities

Hahndorf Academy & Heritage Museum
MUSEUM, ART GALLERY

(☑08-8388 7250; www.hahndorfacademy.org.au; 68 Main St; academy free, museum by donation; ☺10am-5pm) The 1857 building houses an art gallery with rotating exhibitions and original sketches by Sir Hans Heysen, the famed landscape artist and Hahndorf homeboy. The museum depicts the lives of early German settlers, with pious church pews, dour dresses and horse-drawn buggies. The **Adelaide Hills Visitor Centre** (p732) is here too.

Cedars
HISTORIC SITE

(☑08-8388 7277; www.hansheysen.com.au; Heysen Rd; tours $10; ☺10am-4.30pm Tue-Sun, tours 11am, 1pm & 3pm Sep-May, 11am & 2pm Jun-Aug) You'll see more than 300 of Sir Hans' original doodles on a tour through his studio and house, 2km northwest of town.

🦫Beerenberg Strawberry Farm
STRAWBERRY FARM

(☑08-8388 7272; www.beerenberg.com.au; Mount Barker Rd; strawberry picking per person $3, strawberries per kg from $9; ☺9am-5pm, last entry 4.15pm) Pick your own strawberries between November and May from the famous, family-run farm, also big-noted for its plethora of jams, chutneys and sauces.

🛏 Sleeping & Eating

Manna
MOTEL $$

(☑08-8388 1000; www.themanna.com.au; 25 & 35a Main St; d with/without spa from $210/150, 2-/3-bedroom apts from $185/200; ✳🛜✻) Behind the Hahndorf Inn you'll find a refurbished, exposed-brick motel complex (formerly the Hahndorf Inn Motor Lodge) with an indoor pool, and upmarket, contemporary suites.

Zorros
MOTEL $$

(☑08-8388 1309; www.zorrosofhahndorf.com.au; 60 Main St; d with/without spa $135/110, f $230; ✳🛜) The most affordable beds within cooee are at Zorros, a main-street motel drawing more than a little inspiration from the colonial/chalet/cottage book of interior design. Quiet, friendly, clean and comfortable.

Udder Delights
CAFE $

(www.udderdelights.com.au; 91a Main St; meals $6-18; ☺breakfast & lunch; 🏿) The shining light of Hahndorf's food scene, this udderly delightful cheese cellar–cafe serves salads, tarts, pies, soups, cakes, generous cheese platters

and the best coffee this side of Stirling. Free cheese tastings, too.

Haus
CAFE, WINE BAR $

(☑08-8388 7555; www.haushahndorf.com.au; 38 Main St; mains $10-25; ☉breakfast & lunch Thu-Mon) The busiest eatery in Hahndorf (and the only one with an annoying tout out the front), Haus brings some urban hip to the Hills. Rustic-style pizzas are laden with local smallgoods, and the wine list is huge (lots of Hills drops). Also on offer are baguettes, pasta, burgers, salads and quiches. Good coffee too.

German Arms Hotel
PUB FARE $$

(www.germanarmshotel.com.au; 69 Main St; mains $9-25; ☉breakfast, lunch & dinner) Packed on weekends (with 18-to-25-year-olds, oddly enough), the bratwursts and schnitzels here are legendary.

Hahndorf Inn
PUB FARE $$

(www.hahndorfinn.com.au; 35 Main St; mains $17-32; ☉lunch & dinner) Heart-clogging cheese kranskys, Vienna sausages, sauerkraut and apple strudels. A kid-friendly buzz and no pokies.

Oakbank & Woodside

Strung-out Oakbank (population 450), lives for the annual Oakbank Easter Racing Carnival (www.oakbankracingclub.com.au), said to be the greatest picnic race meeting in the world. It's a two-day festival of equine splendour, risqué dresses and 18-year-olds who can't hold their liquor.

On 80 hectares, 2km north of Oakbank, the three traditional and two contemporary retreats that make up the Adelaide Hills Country Cottages (☑08-8388 4193; www.ahcc.com.au; Oakwood Rd, Oakbank; d incl breakfast from $220; ❀☎) have racked up a wall-full of awards. Open fires, breakfast provisions and spas; two-night minimum.

Agricultural Woodside (population 1830) has a few enticements for galloping gourmands: Woodside Cheese Wrights (www.woodsidecheese.com.au; 22 Henry St; cheeses from $4; ☉10am-4pm) is a passionate and unpretentious gem producing classic, artisan and experimental cheeses (soft styles are a speciality) from locally grazing sheep and cows. It offers free tastings. Watch choc-coated sultanas tumbling in huge cement mixers and stock up on rocky road, scorched almonds and appallingly realistic chocolate cow pats at Melba's Chocolate & Confectionary Factory (www.melbaschocolates.com; 22 Henry St; ☉9am-4.30pm), also with free tastings.

Woodside Providore (69 Main Rd; mains $7-18; ☉breakfast & lunch) is an understated Hills hit, with super coffee, salads, soups, gourmet pizzas, local wines and casual cafe offerings: try the Providore Burger (venison with aioli and tomato chutney).

Lobethal
POP 1660

In the 'Valley of Praise', Lobethal was established by Lutheran Pastor Fritzsche and his followers in 1842. The church opened for business in 1843. Like Hahndorf, Lobethal was renamed during WWI – 'Tweedale' was the unfortunate choice. The main street has the usual complement of soporific pubs and hardware stores, but the town really hits its straps during December's Lights of Lobethal festival (www.lightsoflobethal.com.au) – a blaze of Christmas lights bringing sightseers from the city.

Check out the town, then repair to the streetside terrace at the Lobethal Bierhaus (☑08-8389 5570; www.bierhaus.com.au; 3a Main St; ☉noon-10pm Fri & Sat, to 6pm Sun) for some serious microbrewed concoctions. The Red Truck Porter will put hairs on your chest.

The modest Lobethal Bakery (80 Main St; items $2-7; breakfast & lunch Mon-Sat) is a Hills institution, spawning franchises in other towns. Germanic biscuits, cakes, pies and takeaway soup in a cup.

The Mawson Trail (see the boxed text, p708) tracks through here.

Gumeracha & Birdwood

A scenic drive from Adelaide to Birdwood leads through the Torrens River Gorge and Gumeracha (population 400), a hardy hillside town with a pub at the bottom (making it hard to roll home). The main lure here is climbing the 18.3m-high Big Rocking Horse (admission $2), which doesn't actually rock, but is unusually tasteful as far as Australia's 'big' tourist attractions go. It's part of the Toy Factory (☑08-8389 1085; www.thetoyfactory.com.au; Birdwood Rd; admission free; ☉9am-5pm), which turns out quality handmade wooden toys (oh, and Big Rocking Horse stubbie holders).

National Trust–classified buildings line the slumbering main drag of Birdwood (population 1130), which began as a wide-

awake gold-mining and agricultural centre in the 1850s. Behind the town's impressive old flour mill (1852) is a collection of immaculate vintage and classic cars and motorcycles at the National Motor Museum (☎08-8568 4000; Shannon St; www.history.sa.gov.au; adult/child/concession/family $9/4/7/24; ☺9am-5pm). The museum marks the finishing line for September's Bay to Birdwood (www.baytobirdwood.com.au): a convoy of classic cars chugging up from the city.

FLEURIEU PENINSULA

Patterned with vineyards, olive groves and almond plantations, the Fleurieu (pronounced *floo*-ree-oh) is Adelaide's weekend (and often midweek) playground, with straw-coloured hills running down to the sea. The McLaren Vale Wine Region is booming, producing gutsy reds (salubrious Shiraz) to rival those from the Barossa Valley (actually, we think McLaren Vale wins hands down). Further east, the Fleurieu's Encounter Coast is a curious mix of surf beaches, historic towns and whales cavorting offshore.

Online, see www.fleurieupeninsula.com.au.

McLaren Vale

POP 2560

Flanked by the wheat-coloured Willunga Scarp, 'The Vale' rivals the Barossa as SA's most-visited wine region. Just 40 minutes south of Adelaide, it's an easy cruise to SA's version of the Mediterranean. Encircled by vines, McLaren Vale itself is the region's service centre – an energetic, utilitarian town that's not much to look at, but has some great eateries.

◉ Sights & Activities

Most people come to McLaren Vale to cruise the wineries. You could spend days doing nothing else!

Another way to get a feel for the area is to take the walking and cycling track, the **Shiraz Trail**, along the old railway line from McLaren Vale to Willunga 8km south. Hire a bike from Oxygen Cycles (p739).

It seems like most of Adelaide gets tizzied-up and buses down to the annual Sea & Vines Festival (www.southaustralia.com/9001064.aspx) over the June long weekend. Local wineries cook up seafood, splash wine around and host live bands.

In a nondescript warehouse behind the police station, Black Cockatoo Arthouse (wwwblackcockatooarthouse.blogspot.com; 1 Park

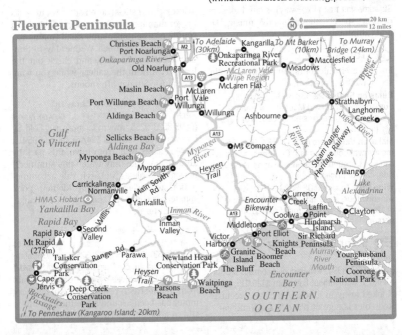

Fleurieu Peninsula

DON'T MISS

MCLAREN VALE WINERIES

If the Barossa Valley is SA wine's old-school, then McLaren Vale is the upstart teenager smoking cigarettes behind the shed and stealing nips from dad's port bottle. The gorgeous vineyards around here have a Tuscan haze in summer, rippling down to a calm coastline that's similarly Ligurian. This is Shiraz country – solid, punchy and seriously good. Tastings are generally free.

» **d'Arenberg** (☎08-8329 4888; www.darenberg.com.au; Osborn Rd; ⊙10am-5pm) A favourite spot in the Vale for lunch, 'd'Arry's' relaxes atop a hillside and enjoys fine views. The wine labels are part of the character of this place: Stump Jump Grenache Shiraz, Dead Arm Shiraz, and the Broken Fishplate Sauvignon Blanc are our faves. Book for lunch.

» **Coriole** (www.coriole.com; Chaffeys Rd; ⊙10am-5pm Mon-Fri, 11am-5pm Sat & Sun) Take your regional tasting platter out into the garden of this beautiful cottage cellar door (1860) to share kalamata olives, homemade breads and Adelaide Hills' Woodside cheeses, made lovelier by a swill of Redstone Shiraz or flagship Chenin Blanc.

» **Wirra Wirra** (www.wirrawirra.com; McMurtrie Rd; ⊙10am-5pm Mon-Sat, 11am-5pm Sun) Fancy some *pétanque* with your plonk? This barnlike, 1894 cellar door has a grassy picnic area, and there's a roaring fire inside in winter. Sample reasonably priced stickies (dessert wines) and the popular Church Block blend. Whites include a citrusy Viognier and aromatic Riesling.

» **Chapel Hill** (www.chapelhillwine.com.au; 1 Chapel Hill Rd; ⊙noon-5pm) At the top of the hill is this restored 1865 chapel with panoramic vineyard and ocean views. The wines are made for drinking now.

» **Woodstock** (www.woodstockwine.com.au; Douglas Gully Rd; ⊙10am-5pm) Their reds are grand but hold out for the stickies and fortified drops. The restaurant here does regional platters ($50 for two people) for lunch, while the surrounding native garden is full of birdlife.

St; admission free-$15; ⊙vary) is an independent art space with cinema, live music, DJs and exhibitions.

☞ Tours

For McLaren Vale tours starting in Adelaide, see p717. Other operators:

Bums on Seats (☎0438 808 253; www.bumsonseats.com.au) McLaren Vale and Fleurieu day-tours for small groups from $75 per person.

McLaren Vale Tours (☎0414 784 666; www.mclarenvaletours.com.au) Customised, locally-run tours around McLaren Vale and the Fleurieu; call for prices.

Wine Diva Tours (☎08-8323 9806; www.winedivatours.com.au) Upmarket wine tours in Mercedes-driven comfort. From $150 per person.

🛏 Sleeping & Eating

Red Poles B&B $$
(☎08-8323 8994; www.redpoles.com.au; McMurtrie Rd; d with/without bathroom $125/115; ❋🛜) Nooked away in a bushy enclave, eccentric Red Poles is a great place to stay (and eat!).

Try for the rustic-style en-suite room – it's bigger than its two counterparts. Order up a soufflé or a saltbush lamb salad (mains $27 to $33; open for lunch Wednesday to Sunday, breakfast Sunday), and check out the local artwork in the gallery while you wait. Live music Sunday afternoons.

McLaren Vale Lakeside Caravan Park CARAVAN PARK $
(☎08-8323 9255; www.mclarenvale.net; Field St; unpowered/powered sites $24/29, cabins $95-115; ❋🛟) A short walk from town, this park by an artificial lake (any water this summer?) is as affordable as McLaren Vale accommodation gets. There's a camp kitchen, pool, spa, tennis court and trashy book exchange. Good winter rates.

McLaren Vale Motel & Apartments MOTEL, APARTMENTS $$
(☎1800 811 817; 08-8323 8265; www.mclarenvalemotel.com.au; cnr Main Rd & Caffrey St; s/d/f from $110/130/135; ❋@🛜🛟) A digestive walk from main-street restaurants, this cheery motel has been around since the '80s but is still in good shape. There are solid doubles,

new studio apartments and family suites, plus a pool fringed by scruffy-looking palms.

Blessed Cheese
CAFE $

(www.blessedcheese.com.au; 150 Main Rd; mains $7-18; ⊙breakfast & lunch) This blessed cafe cranks out great coffee, croissants, wraps, salads, tarts, burgers, cheese platters, murderous cakes and funky sausage rolls. The menu changes every couple of days, always with an emphasis on local produce.

Salopian Inn
MODERN AUSTRALIAN $$

(☑08-8323 8769; www.mvbeer.com; cnr Main & McMurtrie Rds; mains $32; ⊙lunch Wed-Sun, dinner Thu-Sat) South of town, this vine-covered cottage behind a rosemary hedge has a serious rep. Impressive mains like Coorong Angus beef cheek with shallots, parsnips and duck-fat potatoes are complimented by an awesome wine list. The McLaren Vale Beer Co is based here too; don't leave without trying their much-awarded Vale Ale.

❶ Information

McLaren Vale & Fleurieu Visitor Information Centre (☑08-8323 9944; www.mclarenvale. info; Main Rd, McLaren Vale; ⊙9am-5pm Mon-Fri, 10am-4pm Sat & Sun) At the northern end of McLaren Vale. Winery info, plus accommodation assistance and Sealink bus/ferry bookings for Kangaroo Island.

McLaren Vale website (www.mclarenvale.info)

❶ Getting There & Around

BICYCLE For bike hire, see **Oxygen Cycles** (☑08-8323 7345; oxy gencycles@gmail.com; 143 Main Rd; bike hire per half/full day $15/40; ⊙10am-6pm Tue-Fri, 9am-5pm Sat, 11am-4pm Sun). Helmet, lock and basket (for bottles!) included.

BUS & TRAIN Premier Stateliner (www. premierstateliner.com.au) runs up to three buses daily from Adelaide to McLaren Vale ($9, one hour) and Willunga ($9, 70 minutes). Regular **Adelaide Metro** (www.adelaidemetro. com.au) suburban trains run between Adelaide and Noarlunga. From here, **SouthLink** (www. southlink.com.au) buses 751 and 753 run to McLaren Vale and Willunga. Regular Adelaide Metro ticket prices apply.

Willunga

POP 2260

A one-horse town with three pubs (a winning combo!), artsy Willunga took off in 1840 when high-quality slate was discovered nearby and exported across Australia.

Today, the town's early buildings along sloping High St are occupied by gourmet eateries and galleries.

The **Willunga Environment Centre** (☑08-8556 4188; www.willungaenviro.org.au; 18 High St; ⊙10am-3pm Mon-Fri, 9.30am-1.30pm Sat) has basic tourist info and details on local flora and fauna. The town blooms into its own during the **Almond Blossom Festival** (www. willungafestivals.com) in July: if you can't wait that long, the **Willunga Farmers Market** (www.willungafarmersmarket.com; Willunga Town Sq; ⊙8am-12.30pm Sat) happens every weekend.

The **Kidman Trail** (see boxed text, p708) kicks off here.

🛏 Sleeping & Eating

Willunga House B&B
B&B $$$

(☑08-8556 2467; www.willungahouse.com.au; 1 St Peters Tce; d incl breakfast $210-280; ❋🐾🛜💻) If you're looking for a real treat, this graceful, two-storey 1850 mansion off the main street is for you: Baltic-pine floorboards, Italian cherry-wood beds, open fires, Indigenous art and a swimming pool. Breakfast is a feast of organic muesli, fruit salad and poached pears, followed by cooked delights.

Russell's Pizza
PIZZA $$

(☑08-8556 2571; 13 High St; pizzas from $24; ⊙dinner Thu-Sat Dec & Jan, Fri & Sat Feb-Nov) It may look like a ramshackle chicken coop, but Russell's is the place to be on weekends for sensational wood-fired pizza. No one minds the wait for a meal (which could be hours) – it's all about the atmosphere. It's super popular, so book way ahead.

Gulf St Vincent Beaches

There are some ace swimming beaches (but no surf) along the Gulf St Vincent coastline, extending from suburban **Christies Beach** onto **Maslin Beach**, the southern end of which is a nudist and a gay hang-out. Maslin is 45 minutes from Adelaide by car – just far enough to escape the sprawling shopping centres and new housing developments trickling south from the city.

Port Willunga Beach is home to the eternally busy, cliff-top seafood shack the **Star of Greece** (☑08-8557 7420; www.startofgreece. com; 1 The Esplanade, Port Willunga; mains $28-37; ⊙lunch & dinner daily), with funky decor, great staff and a sunny outdoor patio. We asked the waiter where the whiting was caught: he looked out across the bay and said, 'See that

boat out there?'. There's also a fish-and-chip takeaway kiosk here.

On the highway above **Sellicks Beach** is a classily renovated 1858 pub, the **Victory Hotel** (✆08-8556 3083; www.victoryhotel.cm au; Main South Rd, Sellicks Beach; mains $14-33; ⊘lunch & dinner). There are awesome views of the silvery gulf, a cheery, laid-back vibe and, according to the barman, 'the best beer garden south of Adelaide'. Factor in inspired meals, an impressive cellar and wines by the glass and you'll be feeling victorious.

Keep trucking south to cute little **Yankalilla**, which has the regional **Yankalilla Bay Visitor Information Centre** (✆08-8558 0240; www.yankalilla.sa.gov.au; 163 Main South Rd; ⊘9am-5pm Mon-Fri, 10am-4pm Sat & Sun; @). There's a small local history **museum** (adult/child $3/1) out the back. Nearby is quirky **Lilla's Cafe** (✆08-8558 2525; www.lillascafe.com.au; 163 Main South Rd; mains $14-23; ⊘breakfast & lunch Thu-Tue, dinner Fri & Sat) – perfect for coffee and cake or generous wood-fired pizzas on Friday and Saturday nights. Jenny the donkey will finish off anything you can't eat.

About 60km south of Adelaide is **Carrickalinga**, which has a gorgeous arc of white sandy beach. North and south Carrickalinga beaches are separated by the volcanic outcrop Haycock Point. It's a very chilled spot with no shops. For supplies and accommodation, head to **Normanville**, which has a great pub, a supermarket, a couple of caravan parks and the **Jetty Food Store** (✆08-8558 2537; www.jettyfoodstore.com; 48a Main Rd; meals $8-16; ⊘breakfast & lunch daily, dinner Fri). The motto here is 'Coastal food hunted and gathered for you'. Grab an organic coffee, a dozen Kangaroo Island oysters, some locally caught fish and chips, or raid the fridge for gourmet cheeses, dips and olives.

There's not much at **Cape Jervis**, 107km from Adelaide, other than the Kangaroo Island ferry terminal, and the start point for the **Heysen Trail** (see the boxed text, p708). Nearby, **Deep Creek Conservation Park** (www.environment.sa.gov.au/parks; per car $8.50) has sweeping coastal views, a wicked waterfall, man-size yakkas (*Xanthorrhoea semiplana tateana*), sandy beaches, kangaroos, kookaburras and bush camping areas (per car $10.50).

Off the road to Deep Creek Conservation Park are the curved roofs of the superb **Ridgetop Retreats** (✆08-8598 4169; www.southernoceanretreats.com.au; d $205): three corrugated-iron-clad, self-contained luxury units in the bush, with wood heaters, leather lounges and stainless-steel benchtops.

See p716 for local diving info.

Victor Harbor

POP 11,500

Oddly detached from its rural setting, Victor Harbor (yes, that's the correct spelling) is the biggest town on the Encounter Coast – it's a raggedy, brawling holiday destination with three huge pubs and migrating whales offshore. In January the grassy foreshore runs rampant with Schoolies, teenage schoolleavers blowing off hormones.

◉ Sights & Activities

Victor Harbor is on the migratory path of **southern right whales**, who cruise the coast between May and October. The **South Australian Whale Centre** (✆08-8551 0750; www.sawhalecentre.com; 2 Railway Tce; adult/child/concession/family $8/4/5.50/20; ⊘9.30am-5pm) has impressive displays on Victor's largest visitors – including a big stinky skull – and can give you the low-down on where to see them.

Just offshore is the boulder-strewn **Granite Island**, connected to the mainland by an 1875 causeway. Ride out there on the 1894 double-decker **Horse-drawn Tram** (www.horsedrawntram.com.au; return adult/child/family $8/6/22; ⊘every 40 min 10am-4pm); tickets are available from the driver or visitor information centre. Out on the island you can take a sunset **penguin tour** (✆08-8552 7555; www.graniteisland.com.au; adult/child/family $12.50/7.50/36; ⊘sunset) to watch the island's little penguins haul themselves out of the water. Bookings are essential. You can also do a lap of the island and check out seals, dolphins and whales with **Big Duck Boat Tours** (✆0405 125 312; www.thebigduck.com.au; 30min tours per adult/child $35/25); call for times and bookings.

The much-wheeled **Encounter Bikeway** (www.tourismvictorharbor.com.au/walks_trails.html) extends 30km from Victor Harbor to Laffin Point beyond Goolwa. The visitors centre stocks maps. For bike hire, see p741.

🛏 Sleeping & Eating

Anchorage   GUESTHOUSE $
(✆08-8552 5970; www.anchorageseafronthotel.com; 21 Flinders Pde; s/d/apt from $55/70/210; ☎) This grand old seafront guesthouse is the pick of the local crop. Immaculately main-

tained, great-value rooms open off long corridors. Most rooms face the beach, and some have a balcony (you'd pay through the nose for this in Sydney!). The cheapest rooms are view-free and share bathrooms. The cafe-bar downstairs is a winner.

Victor Harbor Holiday & Cabin Park
CARAVAN PARK $

(☑08-8552 1949; www.victorharborholiday.com.au; 19 Bay Rd; unpowered/powered sites $26/32, vans/ cabins from $52/79; ❀@☎) The friendliest operation in town, with tidy facilities, free barbecues and a rambling grassed area with a few trees to pitch a tent on. Runs rings around Victor's other caravan parks.

Nino's
CAFE $$

(☑08-8552 3501; www.ninoscafe.com.au; 17 Albert Pl; mains $14-23; ☺lunch & dinner) Nino's cafe has been here since 1974, but it manages to put a contemporary sheen on downtown VH. Hip young staff and a mod interior set the scene for gourmet pizzas, pasta, salads, risottos and meaty Italian mains. Good coffee too.

Anchorage Restaurant
MODERN AUSTRALIAN $$

(☑08-8552 5970; www.anchorageseafronthotel. com; Anchorage, 21 Flinders Pde; mains $13-36; ☺breakfast, lunch & dinner) This salty sea cave, with an old whaling boat for a bar, has a Med-meets–Mod Oz menu with plenty of seafood. There's great coffee, tapas, cakes, Euro beers and a breezy terrace on which to drink them.

❶ Information

Victor Harbor Visitor Information Centre
(☑08-8551 0777; www.tourismvictorharbor. com.au; Causeway; ☺9am-5pm; @) Handles tour and accommodation bookings, and has plenty of accommodation info.

❶ Getting There & Around

BICYCLE **Victor Harbor Cycle Skate Bay Rubber** (☑08-8552 1417; 73 Victoria St; bike hire per 2hr/day $10/50; ☺9am-5.30pm Mon-Fri, 9am-noon Sat) Mountain-bike hire, including helmets and locks.

BUS **Premier Stateliner** (www.premierstate liner.com.au) runs buses to Victor Harbor from Adelaide ($20, 1¾ hours, one to five daily) continuing on to Goolwa.

TRAIN On the first and third Sundays from June to November inclusive, **Steam Ranger Heritage Railway** (www.steamranger.org.au) operates the *Southern Encounter* (adult/child/ family return $66/35/616) tourist train from Mt Barker in the Adelaide Hills to Victor Harbor

via Strathalbyn, Goolwa and Port Elliot. The *Cockle Train* (adult/child return $27/15) runs along the Encounter Coast between Victor Harbor and Goolwa via Port Elliot every Sunday and Wednesday, and daily during school holidays.

Port Elliot
POP 3100

About 8km east of Victor Harbor, historic Port Elliot is set back from Horseshoe Bay, an orange-sand arc with gentle surf and good swimming. Norfolk Island pines reach for the sky, and there are whale-spotting updates posted on the pub wall.

🏃 Activities

Commodore Point, at the eastern end of Horseshoe Bay, and nearby Boomer Beach and Knights Beach have reliable waves for experienced surfers. The beach at otherwise missable Middleton, the next town towards Goolwa, also has solid breaks.

For surf-gear hire try Big Surf Australia (☑08-8554 2399; 24 Goolwa Rd, Middleton; surf-boards/bodyboards/wetsuits per day $30/20/15; ☺9am-5pm). You can learn to surf (around $40 for a two-hour lesson, including gear) with South Coast Surf Academy (☑0414 341 545; www.danosurf.com.au) and Surf & Sun (☑1800 786 386; www.surfandsun.com.au).

🛏 Sleeping & Eating

TOP CHOICE **Port Elliot Beach House YHA**
HOSTEL $

(☑08-8554 1885; www.yha.com.au; 13 The Strand; dm/d/f from $23/72/104; ❀@) Built in 1910 (the old Arcadia Hotel), this sandstone beauty has sweeping views across the Port Elliot coastline. If you can drag your eyes away from the view, you'll find polished floorboards and contemporary colours splashed around. It's a classy fit-out, and the only backpackers on the Fleurieu Peninsula! Bike hire and surf lessons are almost mandatory and the Flying Fish Cafe is 200m away.

Royal Family Hotel
PUB $

(☑08-8554 2219; www.royalfamilyhotel.com.au; 32 North Tce; s/d $50/65) It's doubtful that Prince Chuck has ever stayed here, but if he did he'd find surprisingly decent pub rooms with clean shared bathrooms, a TV lounge and balcony over the main street. Downstairs the bistro serves counter meals fit for a king (mains $15 to $29, open for lunch and dinner).

Port Elliot Holiday Park CARAVAN PARK $
(☑08-8554 2134; www.portelliotcholidaypark.com.
au; Port Elliot Rd; powered sites/cabins/units/cottages from $41/135/165/190; ✹@🛜) In an unbeatable position behind the Horseshoe Bay dunes (it can be a touch windy), this grassy, 5-hectare park has all the requisite facilities, including a brand new camp kitchen and all-weather barbecue area. Prices plummet in winter.

Flying Fish
Cafe FISH & CHIPS, MODERN AUSTRALIAN $$
(☑08-8554 3504; www.flyingfishcafe.com.au; 1 The Foreshore; takeaways $7-15, mains $22-49; ⊙breakfast, lunch & dinner) Sit down for lunch and you'll be here all day – the views of Horseshoe Bay are sublime. Otherwise grab some quality takeaway of Coopers-battered flathead and chips and head back to the sand. At night things get a little classier, with à-la-carte mains focusing on independent SA producers.

❶ Getting There & Away
Premier Stateliner (www.premierstateliner.
com.au) has up to five daily bus services between Adelaide and Port Elliot ($20, two hours), linking the town with Victor Harbor and Goolwa.

Goolwa
POP 6500
Much more low-key and elegant than kissing-cousin Victor Harbor, Goolwa is an unassuming town where the rejuvenated Murray River empties into the sea. Beyond the dunes is a fantastic beach with ranks of broken surf rolling in from the ocean, same as it ever was...

◉ Sights & Activities
Down on Goolwa Wharf, the **Steam Exchange Brewery** (www.steamexchange.com.
au; The Wharf; tastings $3; ⊙10am-5pm Wed-Sun) is a locally run brewery, turning out manly stouts and ales. Sip a Southerly Buster Dark Ale and look out over the rippling river. Tours for groups by arrangement.

Not far from the brewery, Hindmarsh Island Bridge links the Goolwa with **Hindmarsh Island**; see the, p743, for the story behind the bridge.

🚢 **Spirit of the Coorong** (☑1800 442 203, 08-8555 2203; www.coorongcruises.com.au; The Wharf) runs eco-cruises on the Murray and into the Coorong National Park, including lunch and guided walks. The 4½-hour

Coorong Discovery Cruise (adult/child $78/58) runs on Thursdays all year, plus Mondays from October to May. The six-hour Coorong Adventure Cruise ($92/63) runs on Sundays all year, plus Wednesdays from October to May. There's also a two-hour Murray Mouth Cruise ($30/15) on Saturdays. Bookings essential.

At **Goolwa Beach** a boardwalk traverses the dunes looking out at the barrelling surf. **Barrell Surf & Skate** (www.barrellsurf.com.
au; 10c Cadell St; ⊙9.30am-5.30pm) has gear hire (longboard/bodyboard/wetsuit per day $25/10/15). The coastal **Encounter Bikeway** (www.tourismvictorharbor.com.au/walks_trails.
html) runs for 30km between Goolwa and Victor Harbor (maps available at the Goolwa visitor centre).

🛏 Sleeping
Holiday rentals in and around Goolwa are managed by **LJ Hooker** (☑08-8555 1785; www.
ljh.com.au/goolwa; 25 Cadell St) and the **Professionals** (☑08-8555 2122; www.goolwaprofessionals.com.au; 1 Cadell St), both of whom have houses for as little as $70 per night (though most are around $130) and good weekly rates.

Goolwa Central Motel MOTEL $$
(☑08-8555 1155; www.goolwacentralmotel.com.
au; 30 Cadell St; s/d/f from $120/130/170; ✹🛜✹) This two-level motel is next to an Irish pub, and has allowed the emerald roguishness to filter through (rooms are called Tyrone, Fermanagh etc). Nothing flash, but a solid central option with a tiny pool.

Jackling Cottage B&B B&B $$
(☑08-8555 3489; www.goolwaheritagecottages.
com; 18 Oliver St; d from $195, extra adult $55; ✹) A lovely old 1860s cottage on a nondescript Goolwa backstreet (just ignore the petrol station across the road), surrounded by rambling roses and limestone walls. Two bedrooms, sleeping four – good for families or a couple of couples looking for a low-key weekend by the sea. A short stroll to the main drag.

🍴 Eating
Café Lime CAFE $
(1/11 Goolwa Tce; meals $8-18; ⊙breakfast & lunch) Pick up heat-and-eat gourmet dinners or a takeaway cone of salt-and-pepper squid with lime-salted fries. If you feel like lingering, nab a table for beer-battered Coorong mullet (not a description of a haircut at the pub), baguettes, curries, soups and pasta. Espresso perfecto.

First proposed in 1988, construction of the Hindmarsh Island Bridge was opposed by Ngarrindjeri women who had concerns about the spiritual and cultural significance of the site. A series of court battles ensued, pitting Aboriginal beliefs against development, and culminating in a royal commission (1995) that ruled that the claims of Aboriginal 'secret women's business' were fabricated. Further court appeals were launched, and in August 2001 the Federal Court overturned the royal commission, finding the Ngarrindjeri claims to be legitimate. Unfortunately, this vindication came five months after the bridge was officially opened. The decade-long furore was a step backwards for reconciliation, made worse by the media's often flawed coverage.

Hector's MODERN AUSTRALIAN **$$**
(✆08-8555 5885; The Wharf; mains $8-25; ☺breakfast & lunch daily, dinner Fri & Sat) Standing under the ugly (in more ways than one) span of the Hindmarsh Island Bridge, eating at Hector's (festooned with fishing rods) is like hanging out in your mate's boathouse. Seafood chowder and spinach-and-fetta pie are sweetly complemented by jazzy tunes and local wines. Good coffee, too.

Southy's Wood Fired Pizzas PIZZA **$**
(✆08-8555 5055; www.southys.infopage.com.au; 1 Cadell St; pizzas $12-18; ☺dinner Wed-Sun) All the old faves, plus a few good 'with personality' selections: satay chicken, tandoori lamb and a yiros pizza (chicken, tomato, Spanish onion, hummus and tzatziki).

❶ Information

Goolwa Visitor Information Centre (✆1300 466 592; www.visitalexandrina.com; 4 Goolwa Tce; ☺9am-5pm Mon-Fri, 10am-4pm Sat & Sun) Inside an 1857 post office, with detailed local info (including accommodation).

❶ Getting There & Around

Premier Stateliner (www.premierstateliner. com.au) runs up to five buses daily between Adelaide and Goolwa ($20, two hours).

For details of the tourist steam train running between Goolwa, Victor Harbor and the Adelaide Hills, see p741.

KANGAROO ISLAND

From Cape Jervis, car ferries chug across the swells of the Backstairs Passage to Kangaroo Island (KI). Long devoid of tourist trappings, the island these days is a booming destination for wilderness and wildlife fans – it's a veritable zoo of seals, birds, dolphins, echidnas and (of course) kangaroos. Still, the island remains rurally paced and underdeveloped – the kind of place where kids ride bikes to school and farmers advertise for wives on noticeboards. Island produce is a highlight.

History
Many KI place names are French, attributable to Gallic explorer Nicholas Baudin who surveyed the coast in 1802 and 1803. Baudin's English rival, Matthew Flinders, named the island in 1802 after his crew feasted on kangaroo meat here. By this stage the island was uninhabited, but archaeologists think Indigenous Australians lived here as recently as 2000 years ago. Why they deserted KI is a matter of conjecture, though the answer is hinted at in the Indigenous name for KI: 'Karta', or 'Land of the Dead'. In the early 1800s an Indigenous presence (albeit a tragically displaced one) was re-established on KI when whalers and sealers abducted Aboriginal women from Tasmania and brought them here.

🏃 Activities
The safest **swimming** is along the north coast, where the water is warmer and there are fewer rips than down south. Try Emu Bay, Stokes Bay, Snelling Beach or Western River Cove.

For **surfing**, hit the uncrowded swells along the south coast. Pennington Bay has strong, reliable breaks; Vivonne Bay and Hanson Bay in the southwest also serve up some tasty waves.

There's plenty to see under your own steam on KI. Check out www.tourkangaroo-island.com.au/wildlife/walks.aspx for info on **bushwalks** from 1km to 18km.

The waters around KI are home to 230 species of fish, soft and hard corals and around 60 shipwrecks – perfect for snorkelling and diving. For charters, contact **Kangaroo Island Diving Safaris** (www.kidiving-safaris.com; diving/snorkelling per day $320/150,

ADELAIDE & SOUTH AUSTRALIA KANGAROO ISLAND

Kangaroo Island

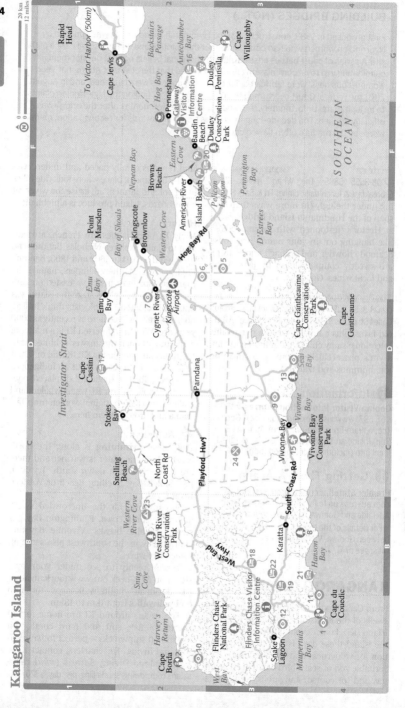

equipment hire only $120/80), which runs diving and snorkelling trips.

Skidding down the dunes at **Little Sahara** is great fun. **Kangaroo Island Outdoor Action** (www.kioutdooraction.com.au; Jetty Rd, Vivonne Bay) rents out sandboards/toboggans ($29/39 per day), plus single/double kayaks ($39/69 for four hours).

There's plenty of good **fishing** around the island, including jetties at Kingscote, Penneshaw, Emu Bay and Vivonne Bay. Fishing charter tours (half-/full day from $100/200) include tackle and refreshments, and you keep what you catch. Try **Kangaroo Island Fishing Adventures** (www.kifishing.com.au).

⛟ Tours

See the Gateway visitors centre for comprehensive tour listings. Day tours from Adelaide are hectic – stay at least one night on the island if you can. A few operators:

🏄 Surf & Sun
WILDLIFE

(✆1800 786 386; www.surfandsun.com.au) Two-/three-day 4WD tours ($389/479) ex-Adelaide, with a strong focus on wildlife. Includes surfing lesson (three-day tour only) and sandboarding.

🏄 Kangaroo Island Marine Tours
WILDLIFE

(✆0427 315 286; www.kimarineadventures.com) One-hour boat tours ($55) and longer half-day jaunts ($165) which include swimming with dolphins, visiting seal colonies and access to remote areas of KI.

Groovy Grape
WILDLIFE

(✆1800 661 177, 08-8440 1640; www.groovygrape.com.au) Two-/three-day small-group wildlife safaris ($345/445) ex-Adelaide, with sandboarding, campfires and all the main sights. The three-day tour runs October to May only.

Adventure Tours
WILDERNESS

(✆1800 068 886, 08-8132 8230; www.adventuretours.com.au) Popular two-day tours from $389 ex-Adelaide, with lots of walking and wildlife.

Alkirna Nocturnal Tours
WILDLIFE

(✆08-8553 7464; www.alkirna.com.au) Nightly naturalist-led tours viewing nocturnal critters around American River (adult/child $60/40, two hours).

Sealink
SIGHTSEEING

(✆13 13 01; www.sealink.com.au/tours) The ferry company runs a range of KI-highlight day tours (one/two days from $138/434) departing Penneshaw. Add bus/ferry costs for tours ex-Adelaide.

Cruising Kangaroo Island
KAYAKING

(✆0401 917 647; www.cruisingkangarooisland.vpweb.com.au; ⊗Aug-May) Two- to three-hour kayak paddles around choice KI coastal spots, from $70 per person.

🛏 Sleeping

KI accommodation is expensive, adding insult to your wallet's injury after the pricey ferry ride across from the mainland. Self-contained cottages, B&Bs and beach houses

charge from $150 per night per double; most require a minimum two-night stay. There are some great camp sites around the island though, plus a few midrange motels. Quality caravan parks and hostels are scarce.

Accommodation booking resources:

Century 21 (☑08-8553 2688; www.century21.com.au/kangarooisland)

Gateway Visitor Information Centre (☑08-8553 1185; www.tourkangarooisland.com.au/accommodation)

Kangaroo Island Holiday Accommodation (☑08-8553 9007; www.kangarooisland holidayaccommodation.com.au)

Sealink (☑13 13 01; www.sealink.com.au/accommodation)

❶ Information

There are bank facilities in Kingscote and Penneshaw, and a hospital in Kingscote. Mobile phone reception on the island is patchy, restricted to Kingscote, Penneshaw, American River, and parts of Emu Bay. There are supermarkets at Penneshaw and Kingscote, and a general store at American River.

The **Kangaroo Island Pass** (adult/child/concession/family $61/49/36.50/166), covers all park and conservation area entry fees, and ranger-guided tours at Seal Bay, Kelly Hill Caves, Cape Borda and Cape Willoughby. Passes can also be purchased at most sights.

Online, see www.tourkangarooisland.com.au.

❶ Getting There & Away

AIR Regional Express (www.regionalexpress.com.au) flies daily between Adelaide and Kingscote (return from $170 online).

BUS Sealink (www.sealink.com.au) operates a morning and afternoon bus service between Adelaide Central Bus Station and Cape Jervis (return adult/child $47/24, 2¼ hours one-way).

FERRY Sealink (www.sealink.com.au) operates a car ferry between Cape Jervis and Penneshaw on KI, with at least three ferries each way daily (return adult/child/concession from $90/48/75, bicycles/motorcycles/cars $20/56/223, 45 minutes one way). One driver is included with the vehicle price (cars only, not bikes).

❶ Getting Around

There's no public transport on the island: unless you're taking a tour, the only way to get around is to bring or hire some wheels. The island's main roads are sealed, but the rest are gravel, including those to Cape Willoughby, Cape Borda and the North Coast Rd. Take it slowly at night when roos and wallabies bounce across the headlights. There's petrol at Kingscote, Penneshaw, American River, Parndana, and on the

west of the island at Vivonne Bay and Kangaroo Island Wilderness Retreat (though this can be intermittent).

TO/FROM THE AIRPORT Kingscote Airport is 14km from Kingscote. **Airport Shuttle Services** (☑0427 887 575) connects the airport with Kingscote ($20), American River ($30) and Penneshaw ($40). Prices are per person, with a minimum of two people; solo travellers pay double (eg Kingscote $40). Bookings essential.

TO/FROM THE FERRY Sealink (www.sealink.com.au) runs a twice-daily shuttle between Penneshaw and American River (adult/child $13/7, 30 minutes) and Kingscote ($16/9, one hour). Bookings essential.

CAR HIRE Not all Adelaide car-rental companies will let you take their cars onto KI; with ferry prices it's often cheaper to hire on the island. **Budget** (www.budgetki.com) and **Hertz** (www.hertz.com.au) supply cars to Penneshaw, Kingscote and Kingscote Airport. Check if they'll let you drive on unsealed roads.

Penneshaw & Dudley Peninsula

Looking across Backstairs Passage to the Fleurieu Peninsula, Penneshaw (population 300), on the north shore of the Dudley Peninsula, is the arrival point for ferries from the mainland. The passing tourist trade lends a certain transience to the businesses here, but the pub, hostel and general store remain authentically grounded. As do the resident little penguins. En route to American River, Pennington Bay has consistent surf.

◉ Sights & Activities

Penneshaw Penguin Centre   WILDLIFE CENTRE (www.southaustralia.com/9005545.aspx; Foreshore; adult/child & concession/family $10/9/29; ☺6-9.30pm Sat-Mon Apr-Sep, 8-10.30pm Oct-Mar) On the foreshore near the ferry terminal, the centre provides an unobtrusive view of the little waddlers that nest along the shore. Tours included in admission; book ahead.

Penneshaw Maritime &
Folk Museum   MUSEUM (www.nationaltrustsa.org.au; 52 Howard Dr; adult/child & concession/family $3/2/7; ☺3-5pm Wed-Sun Sep-May) Displays artefacts from local shipwrecks and early settlement, plus endearingly geeky models of Flinders' *Investigator* and Baudin's *Geographe*.

Cape Willoughby Lightstation   HISTORIC SITE (www.environment.sa.gov.au; Cape Willoughby Rd; per person $2, tours adult/child/concession/

family \$13.50/8/11/36.50; ⊙9am-3.30pm Sep-May, tours 11.30am) About 28km southeast of town, the lighthouse first shone in 1852 and is now used as a weather station. There's also basic accommodation here (doubles \$160). Book through the DENR (p749).

Chapman River Wines
WINERY

(www.goodfoodkangarooisland.com/wine/chapmanriverwines.asp; Cape Willoughby Rd, Antechamber Bay; ⊙11am-4.30pm Thu-Mon Sep-Jun) Occupying a converted aircraft hangar, this eccentric winery makes a mean Merlot. The interior is festooned with art and quirky bits of salvage from churches, pubs and homesteads around SA.

Sunset Winery
WINERY

(www.sunset-wines.com.au; Penneshaw-Kingscote Rd; ⊙11am-5pm) Wow, what a view! If you can make it up the steep driveway, Sunset has brilliant Sauvignon Blanc and sparkling Shiraz, and serves savoury platters to go with the panorama.

🛏 Sleeping & Eating

🏄 Antechamber Bay
Ecocabins
CABINS \$\$

(☎08-8553 1557; www.kiecocabins.com; Chapman River East Rd, Antechamber Bay; d from \$140, extra adult/child \$10/free) Off Cape Willoughby Rd, these two six-bed cabins are run by a couple of IT industry runaways. On 22-hectares behind the dunes, the cabins are rudimentary but perfectly comfortable, with roofless showers, self-composting toilets, and solar power and hot water. Kayaks and fishing gear cost \$20 per stay.

Kangaroo Island YHA
HOSTEL \$

(☎08-8553 1344; www.yha.com.au; 33 Middle Tce, Penneshaw; dm/d/f from \$54/68/320; ❄@) Occupying an old '60s motel with faux-brick cladding, the island YHA has spacious, freshly painted rooms with en-suite bathrooms. There's a roomy communal kitchen, lounge and laundry, and penguins at the bottom of the garden.

Saar Beach House
RENTAL HOUSE \$\$

(☎08-8370 7119; www.saarbeachhouse.com.au; Island Beach; d from \$180, extra person from \$20; ❄) Saar Beach House is a self-contained architectural stand-out atop the dunes along 'Millionaire's Row' at Island Beach, 15km from Penneshaw. Views from the deck are indeed million-dollar! Sleeps 12.

Fish
SEAFOOD \$

(43 North Tce, Penneshaw; mains \$8-14; ⊙dinner Oct-May) Fish and chips like you ain't never had before – grilled, beer-battered or crumbed whiting and garfish – plus giant KI scallops, marron, lobster medallions, prawns and oysters. Dunk them in an array of excellent homemade sauces. Occasional fish-cooking demos, too.

Dudley Cellar Door & Cafe
CAFE \$\$

(www.dudleywines.com.au; cnr North Tce & Thomas Wilson St, Penneshaw; mains \$13-25; ⊙11am-5pm) A brilliant new outlet for one of the KI's pioneering wine growers, serving cheese and seafood platters, curries and buckets o' prawns – perfect with a bottle of Chardonnay on the outdoor deck.

ℹ Information

Gateway Visitor Information Centre (☎08-8553 1185; www.tourkangarooisland.com.au; Howard Dr, Penneshaw; ⊙9am-5pm Mon-Fri, 10am-4pm Sat & Sun) Just outside Penneshaw on the road to Kingscote, this centre is stocked with brochures and maps. Also books accommodation and sells park entry tickets and the Kangaroo Island Pass.

Penneshaw Community Business Centre (☎08-8553 1011; www.penneshawbusiness.com.au; 99 Middle Tce; ⊙9am-5pm Mon-Fri, 9am-noon Sat; @) Acts as a post office, internet cafe and bank agency with cash-withdrawal facilities.

American River
POP 230

Between Penneshaw and Kingscote on the way to nowhere in particular, American River squats redundantly by the glassy **Pelican Lagoon**. The town was named after a crew of American sealers who built a trading schooner here in 1804. There's no such industriousness here today, just a daily pelican-feeding frenzy at the pier and wallabies hopping around the streets. The general store is the town's cultural zenith.

From the end of Scenic Dr, a fern-fringed **coastal walk** (2km one-way) passes through natural scrub, sugar gums and she-oak en route to some old fish-cannery ruins.

🛏 Sleeping & Eating

Island Coastal Units
MOTEL, CABINS \$\$

(☎08-8553 7010; www.kangarooislandcoastalunits.com.au; Tangara Dr; units/cabins from \$110/115, extra person \$20) A low row of one- and two-bedroom motel-style units among trees

opposite the foreshore, plus four beautiful self-contained cabins with solar hot water, gas cooktops and air-con (pay the extra $5!).

Kangaroo Island Lodge MOTEL $$
(☎1800 355 581, 08-8553 7053; www.kilodge.com. au; Scenic Dr; d incl breakfast $139-209; ❄@≋) Up-to-scratch motel suites overlooking either the pool or lagoon (the rammed-earth wing has the best rooms). The restaurant plates up plenty of local seafood (mains $20 to $30; open for breakfast and dinner).

American River Campsite CAMPGROUND $
(per person/car $5/15) Shady, self-registration camping by the lagoon, with fire pits, showers and toilets.

American River General Store SELF CATERING $
(Scenic Dr; ⊙7.30am-6.30pm) Packed to the northern hemisphere with provisions, bait and tackle, plus there's an amazing hardware 'cupboard', petrol and a bottle shop.

Kingscote
POP 1450

Snoozy seaside Kingscote (pronounced, 'Kings-coat') is the main settlement on KI, and the hub of island life. It's a photogenic town with swaying Norfolk Island pines, a couple of pubs and some decent eateries.

◉ Sights & Activities

Kangaroo Island Penguin Centre WILDLIFE CENTRE
(www.kipenguincentre.com.au; Kingscote Wharf; adult/child/family $17/6/40; ⊙tours 8.30pm & 9.30pm Oct-Jan & Mar, 7.30pm & 8.30pm Apr-Oct, closed Feb) Runs one-hour tours of their saltwater aquariums and the local penguin colony, plus some stargazing if the sky is clear. It also runs informative (and comical) pelican feeding (adult/child $4/3; ⊙5pm) sessions at the adjacent wharf.

Hope Cottage Museum MUSEUM
(www.hopecottagemuseum.com; Centenary Ave; adult/child/concession $5/1/3; ⊙1-4pm daily Sep-Jul, Sat only Aug) Built in 1857, this is now a fastidiously maintained National Trust museum decked out in period style, with a reconstructed lighthouse, an amazing old quilt and KI's first piano.

Island Beehive APIARY
(www.island-beehive.com.au; 1 Acacia Dr; tours adult/child/family $4.50/3/13; ⊙9am-5pm, tours every 30 min 9.30am-4pm) Runs factory tours

where you can study up on Ligurian bees and beekeeping, then stock up on by-products (bee-products?), including delicious organic honey and honeycomb ice cream.

Island Pure Sheep Dairy DAIRY
(www.goodfoodkangarooisland.com/food/island-pure.asp; Gum Creek Rd, Cygnet River; tours adult/child/family $5.50/4.50/20; ⊙1-5pm) Near Cygnet River, 12km from Kingscote, the dairy is a family-owned operation where 1500 sheep line up to be milked (from 3pm). Take a tour of the factory, which includes yoghurt and cheese tastings (the haloumi is magic).

Swimming SWIMMING
Kingscote itself is lousy for swimming; locals usually head 18km northwest to Emu Bay, or the tidal swimming pool (admission free; ⊙daylight hours) on Chapman Tce.

🛏 Sleeping & Eating

Aurora Ozone Hotel HOTEL $$
(☎1800 083 133, 08-8553 2011; www.aurora resorts.com.au; cnr Commercial St & Kingscote Tce; d motel/ste from $139/231, 1-/2-/3-bed apt from $293/505/597; ❄@❂≋) Opposite the foreshore with killer views, the 100-year-old Ozone pub has standard motel-style rooms, and stylish deluxe suites and apartments in a new wing across the street. The eternally busy bistro (mains $17 to $30) serves farmer-sized grills and seafood, and you can pickle yourself on KI wines at the bar.

Seaview Motel MOTEL, GUESTHOUSE $$
(☎08-8553 2030; www.seaview.net.au; 51 Chapman Tce; guesthouse s/d $84/94, motel $144/154, extra adult/child $25/15; ❄) It seems like this place is always full – a good sign! Choose from older-style guesthouse rooms with shared facilities, or refurbished '80s motel rooms. Affordable by KI standards.

Kangaroo Island Central Hostel HOSTEL $
(☎08-8553 2787; ki_backpackers@bigpond.com; 19 Murray St; dm/d from $22/55) Just a couple of blocks from Kingscote's main strip, this small, innocuous hostel is clean and cheap, and has a cosy lounge. It feels like staying at someone's house – good or bad, depending on how sociable you're feeling.

Kingscote Nepean Bay Tourist Park CARAVAN PARK $
(☎08-8553 2394; www.kingscotetouristpark.com. au; cnr First & Third Sts; unpowered/powered sites $32/38, cabins/units from $90/135; ❄🛜) You'll find the standard gamut of caravan park

delights behind the dunes in Brownlow, 3km southwest of Kingscote. You can walk back to Kingscote via a coastal walking trail.

TOP CHOICE **Kangaroo Island Fresh Seafoods** SEAFOOD $
(www.goodfoodkangarooisland.com/eatingout/kifreshseafood.asp; 26 Telegraph Rd; meals $6-16; ⏰breakfast, lunch & dinner daily, closed Mon May-Nov) Seriously, this place has the best seafood you're ever likely to taste. A dozen fat oysters go for around a dollar each, then there are all manner of cooked and fresh KI seafood packs and combos. Superb!

Bella ITALIAN $$
(☎08-8553 0400; www.restaurantbella.com.au; 54 Dauncey St; pizzas $14-24, mains $34; ⏰lunch & dinner) Sit inside or sidewalk alfresco at Bella, a cheery Italian cafe-restaurant–pizza bar. Pizzas run all day (eat in or takeaway); dinner is à la carte, featuring American River oysters, Spencer Gulf king prawns, local roo and whiting.

ℹ Information

Department of Environment & Natural Resources (DENR; ☎08-8553 4444, accommodation bookings 08-8553 4410; www.environment.sa.gov.au/parks; 37 Dauncey St, Kingscote) Sells the Kangaroo Island Pass.
Kangaroo Island Hospital (www.kihealth.sa.gov.au; The Esplanade; ⏰24hr) Accident and emergency service.

North Coast Road

Exquisite beaches (much calmer than those on the south coast), bushland and undulating pastures dapple the North Coast Rd, running from Kingscote along the coast to the Playford Hwy 85km west (the bitumen expires at Emu Bay). There's not a whole lot to do here other than swan around on the beach – sounds good!

About 18km from Kingscote, Emu Bay is a holiday hamlet with a 5km-long, white-sand beach flanked by dunes – one of KI's best swimming spots. Around 36km further west, Stokes Bay has a penguin rookery and broad rock pool you access by scrambling through a 20m tunnel in the cliffs at the bay's eastern end (mind your head!). Beware the rip outside the pool.

You won't be able to prevent the word 'Wow!' escaping your lips as you look back over Snelling Beach from atop Constitution Hill. Continue 7km west and you'll hit

the turn-off to Western River Cove, where a small beach is crowded in by sombre basalt cliffs. The ridge-top road in is utterly scenic (and steep!).

🛏 Sleeping & Eating

Western River Cove Campsite CAMPGROUND $
(unpowered sites per person/car $3/5) This self-registration camp site is a short walk from the beach and a footbridge over the river (so tempting to dangle a line). There's a toilet block and a barbecue hut but no showers.

Emu Bay Holiday Homes CABINS, RENTAL HOUSE $
(☎08-8553 5241; www.emubaysuperviews.com.au; 10 Bayview Rd, Emu Bay; cabins $80, holiday homes $106-136, extra person $18; ❄) Great-value (if a little hilly) cabins and holiday homes in a large garden set back from the beach (the views are great!). The self-contained cabins (caravan-park cabins with a facelift, sans air-con) sleep four or six; the holiday homes sleep six or 10.

Cape Cassini Wilderness Retreat B&B $$$
(☎08-8559 2215; www.capecassini.com.au; off North Coast Rd; d/f incl breakfast $295/475) The emphasis is on sustainability and wilderness at this remote house, comprising three guest rooms in the owners' rammed-earth and stone home. There are two neat en-suite double rooms and a small twin with separate bathroom; the doubles have sensational views. Call for directions or a pick-up, and ask about working-holiday rates.

Rock Pool Café CAFE $$
(☎08-8559 2277; North Coast Rd, Stokes Bay; mains $13-25; ⏰lunch Tue-Sun) Don't worry about sandy feet at this casual, alfresco joint in Stokes Bay. 'What's the house special?', we asked. 'Whatever I feel like doin'!', said the chef (usually seafood, washed down with local wines and decent espresso).

South Coast Road

The south coast is rough and wave-swept compared with the north.

Emu Ridge Eucalyptus Distillery DISTILLERY, GALLERY
(www.emuridge.com.au; Willsons Rd, MacGillivray; tours adult/child $5/3; ⏰9am-2pm, tours every 30 min) A detour off Hog Bay or Birchmore

roads takes you past the this self-sufficient operation extracting eucalyptus oil from Kangaroo Island's narrow-leaf mallee. The attached craft gallery sells eucalyptus-oil products.

Clifford's Honey Farm
APIARY
(www.cliffordshoney.com.au; Elsegood Rd, Haines; tastings free, self-guided tour adult/child $2/free; ⏱9am-5pm) It's almost worth swimming the Backstairs Passage for the honey ice cream here, sourced from a colony of rare Ligurian bees.

Seal Bay Conservation Park
NATURE RESERVE
(☎08-8553 4460; www.environment.sa.gov.au/sealbay; adult/child/concession/family self-guided tours $12.50/8/10/35, guided $22.50/16.50/22/75, sunset $50/30/40/136; ⏱tours 9am-4.15pm year-round, plus 5.15pm Dec-Feb) 'Observation, not interaction' is the mentality. Guided tours stroll along the beach (or boardwalk on self-guided tours) to a colony of (mostly sleeping) Australian sea lions. Sunset tours run in December and January only. Bookings advised.

Kelly Hill Conservation Park
NATURE RESERVE
(☎08-8553 4464; www.environment.sa.gov.au; tours adult/child/concession/family $13/8/10.50/35.50; ⏱tours 10.30am then hourly 11.15am-4.15pm) A series of dry limestone caves, close to Flinders Chase National Park, was 'discovered' in the 1880s by a horse named Kelly, who fell into them through a hole. Adventure **caving tours** (adult/child/concession/family $32/19/26/86.50) leave at 2.15pm daily, following on from the standard tour. Minimum age is eight years; bookings essential. The **Hanson Bay Walk** (9km one way) runs from the caves through mallee scrub and past freshwater wetlands.

Little Sahara
NATURE RESERVE
The turn-off 6km from Seal Bay Rd leads to a rolling dunescape looming above the surrounding scrub. You can hire sandboards from Kangaroo Island Outdoor Action (p745).

Vivonne Bay
TOWNSHIP
Further west, this quiet settlement has a beautiful sweeping beach.

🛏 Sleeping & Eating

Flinders Chase Farm
HOSTEL, CABINS $$
(☎08-8559 7223; www.flinderschasefarm.com.au; West End Hwy; dm/cabins $25/60, d & tw with bathroom $110) A farm with charm! A couple of amiable mutts (and maybe a kangaroo) greet you as you check in here, a short drive from Flinders Chase National Park. Accommodation includes immaculate dorms, a couple of cosy cabins and en-suite rooms in a lodge. Outdoors is where it's at: there's a terrific camp kitchen, fire pits and 'tropical' outdoor showers.

Western Kangaroo Island Caravan Park
CAMPGROUND $
(☎08-8559 7201; www.westernki.com.au; South Coast Rd; unpowered/powered sites $20/25, cabins $110-130; ❄) A few minutes' drive east of Flinders Chase National Park, this ultrafriendly, farm-based park has shady gums and resident roos. Check out the koala and lagoon walks, and the phone booth inside an old bakery truck. The shop sells groceries, homemade heat-and-eats and (for guests only) beer and wine.

Kangaroo Island Wilderness Retreat
HOTEL $$
(☎08-8559 7275; www.kiwr.com; South Coast Rd; d $190-530; ❄@) This low-key resort on the Flinders Chase doorstep guarantees guests will see some wildlife: 30 or 40 wallabies graze in the courtyard every evening!

ALL CREATURES GREAT & SMALL

You bump into a lot of wildlife on KI (sometimes literally). **Kangaroos**, **wallabies**, **bandicoots** and **possums** come out at night, especially in wilderness areas like Flinders Chase National Park. **Koalas** and the **platypus** were introduced to Flinders Chase in the 1920s when it was feared they would become extinct on the mainland. **Echidnas** mooch around in the undergrowth, while **goannas** and **tiger snakes** keep KI suitably scaly.

Of the island's 243 **bird species**, several are rare or endangered. One species – the dwarf emu – has gone the way of the dodo. **Glossy black cockatoos** may soon follow it out the door due to habitat depletion.

Offshore, **dolphins** and **southern right whales** are often seen cavorting, and there are colonies of **little penguins**, **New Zealand fur seals** and **Australian sea lions** here too.

SOUTHERN OCEAN LODGE

Millionaires, start your engines! The shining star in the SA tourism galaxy is Southern Ocean Lodge ([✆]08-9918 4355; www.southernoceanlodge.com.au; Hanson Bay; d per night from $1800; [✖][@][☏][✖]), billing itself as 'Australia's first true luxury lodge'. The lodge is a sexy, low-profile snake tracing the Hanson Bay cliff-top, and is an exercise in exclusivity. There's a two-night minimum stay; you get airport transfers, all meals and drinks and guided tours of KI.

If you want a sticky-beak, don't expect to see anything from the road: all you'll find is a steely set of gates and an unreceptive intercom: privacy is what guests are paying for here (Hey, wasn't that Teri Hatcher in that 4WD?). But you can catch a sneaky glimpse from Hanson Bay beach.

Accommodation ranges from basic motel-style rooms to flashy spa suites. There's a restaurant and bar here too, serving breakfast ($13 to $27) and dinner ($28 to $35).

Vivonne Bay General Store FAST FOOD $
(www.goodfoodkangarooisland.com/eatingout/vivonnebay.asp; South Coast Rd, Vivonne Bay; meals $6-14; ☺breakfast & lunch) This chipper little fish-and-chipper has an exhaustive menu of all-day breakfasts and takeaways. The whiting burger reigns supreme ('A meal fit for a king!').

Marron Café MODERN AUSTRALIAN $$
([✆]08-8559 4114; www.andermel.com.au/cafe.htm; Harriet Rd; mains $20-30; ☺lunch) Around 15km north of Vivonne Bay you can check out marron in breeding tanks, then eat some! It's a subtle taste, not necessarily enhanced by the heavy sauces issued by the kitchen. Steak and chicken dishes too, for the crustacean-shy. Last orders 4pm.

Flinders Chase National Park

Occupying the western end of the island, Flinders Chase National Park (www.environment.sa.gov.au; adult/child/concession/family $9/5.50/7/24.50) is one of SA's top national parks. Much of the park is mallee scrub, but there are some beautiful, tall sugar-gum forests, particularly around Rocky River and the Ravine des Casoars, 5km south of Cape Borda. Around 40 hectares of bush were burned by bushfires in 2007, but the park is recovering well.

⦿ Sights & Activities

Once a farm, Rocky River is a rampant hotbed of wildlife, with kangaroos, wallabies and Cape Barren geese competing for your affections. The roos are particularly brazen – they'll bug you for food, but park officers request that you don't feed them. A slew of good walks launch from behind the visitors centre, including one where you might spy a platypus (9km loop; allow three hours).

From Rocky River, a road runs south to a remote 1906 lighthouse atop wild Cape du Couedic. A boardwalk weaves down to Admirals Arch, a huge archway ground out by heavy seas, and passes a colony of New Zealand fur seals (sweet smelling they ain't...).

At Kirkpatrick Point, a few kilometres east of Cape du Couedic, the Remarkable Rocks are a cluster of hefty, weather-gouged granite boulders atop a rocky dome that arcs 75m down to the sea.

On the northwestern corner of the island, the 1858 Cape Borda Lightstation (www.environment.sa.gov.au; admission free, tours adult/child/concession/family $13/8/10.50/35.50; ☺9am-5pm, tours 11am, 12.30pm & 2pm) stands tall above the rippling iron surface of the Southern Ocean. There are walks here from 1.5km to 9km, and extra tours at 3.15pm and 4pm during summer holidays.

At nearby Harvey's Return a cemetery speaks poignant volumes about the reality of isolation in the early days. From here you can drive to Ravine des Casoars (literally 'Ravine of the Cassowaries', referring to the now-extinct dwarf emus seen here by Baudin's expedition). Check with the visitors centre if the walking trail (6.5km return) down to the coast is open again (closed after the 2007 bushfires).

🛏 Sleeping & Eating

There are campgrounds at Rocky River (per car $22.50), Snake Lagoon (per car $11), West Bay (per car $11) and near Cape Borda at Harvey's Return (per car $11); book through the Department of Environment &

Natural Resources (DENR; ☎088553 4410; kiparksaccom@sa.gov.au).

The DENR also runs refurbished cottage accommodation at Rocky River – the budget Postmans Cottage (d $48) and family-friendly Mays Homestead (d $125) – and lightkeepers' cottages at Cape du Couedic and Cape Borda (basic huts to stone cottages, d $38-160).

See p750 for sleeping options just outside the national park.

On the food front, the only option here if you're not self-catering is the Chase Cafe (meals $7-15; ⊙breakfast & lunch) at the visitors centre, serving burgers, wraps, soup, coffee, and wines by the glass.

❶ Information

Flinders Chase Visitor Information Centre
(☎08-8559 7235; www.environment.sa.gov.au; South Coast Rd, Rocky River; ⊙9am-5pm) Info, maps and camping/accommodation bookings, plus a cafe and displays on island ecology.

LIMESTONE COAST

The Limestone Coast – strung-out along southeastern SA between the flat, olive span of the lower Murray River and the Victorian border – is a curiously engaging place. On the highways you can blow across these flatlands in under a day, no sweat, but around here the delight is in the detail. Detour off-road to check out the area's lagoons, surf beaches and sequestered bays. Also on offer are wine regions, photogenic fishing ports and snoozy agricultural towns. And what's *below* the road is even more amazing: a bizarre subterranean landscape of limestone caves, sinkholes and bottomless crater lakes. For regional information, see www.thelimestonecoast.com.

❶ Getting There & Away

The Dukes Hwy (Rte A8) is the most direct route between Adelaide and Melbourne (729km), but the coastal Princes Hwy (Rte B1) adjacent to the Coorong National Park is definitely more scenic.

AIR Regional Express (www.regionalexpress.com.au) flies daily between Adelaide and Mount Gambier (one-way from $142).

BUS Premier Stateliner (www.premierstateliner.com.au) runs two bus routes – coastal and inland – between Adelaide and Mount Gambier ($70, 6¼ hours). From Adelaide along the coast (daily except Saturday) via the Coorong you can stop at Meningie ($34, two hours), Robe ($59, 4½ hours) and Beachport ($65, 5¼ hours). The inland bus runs daily via Naracoorte ($62, five hours) and Penola ($64, 5¾ hours).

TRAIN V/Line (www.vline.com.au) runs a service between Mount Gambier and Melbourne ($33, 7¾ hours) – you take the bus from Mount Gambier to Warrnambool, where you hop on a train for Melbourne.

Coorong National Park

The amazing Coorong (www.environment.sa.gov.au) is a fecund lagoon landscape curving along the coast for 145km from Lake Alexandrina towards Kingston SE. A complex series of soaks and salt pans, it's separated from the sea by the chunky dunes of the Younghusband Peninsula. More than 200 species of waterbirds live here. *Storm Boy,* an endearing film about a young boy's friendship with a pelican (based on the novel by Colin Thiele), was filmed on the Coorong.

The name 'Coorong' derives from the Ngarrindjeri Aboriginal word *Karangk,* meaning 'long neck'. In the 1800s the bountiful resources of the Coorong supported a large Ngarrindjeri population. The Ngarrindjeri are still closely connected to the Coorong, and many still live here.

At the edge of the Coorong on Lake Albert (a large arm of Lake Alexandrina), Meningie (population 900) was established as a minor port in 1866. The lake shrank catastrophically during the drought, but the Murray River's recent flood has brought the water back, much to the relief of local pelicans.

The Princes Hwy scuttles through the park, but you can't see much from the road. Instead, take the 13km, unsealed Coorong Scenic Drive. Signed as Seven Mile Rd, it starts 10km southwest of Meningie off the Narrung Rd, and takes you right into the landscape, with its stinky lagoons, sea mists, fishing shanties, pelicans and wild emus. The road rejoins the Princes Hwy 10km south of Meningie.

Also 10km south of Meningie, Camp Coorong (☎08-8575 1557; www.ngarrindjeri.net; Princes Hwy; museum admission per car $5; ⊙vary) is run by the Ngarrindjeri Lands and Progress Association. It's a great place to learn about the Coorong's Aboriginal history and habitat: take a guided cultural walk, basketweaving lesson, museum tour or Coorong tour. Call for prices, hours and bookings.

With a 4WD you can access Ninety Mile Beach, a well-known surf-fishing spot. The easiest ocean access point is 3km off the

Princes Hwy at 42 Mile Crossing, 19km south of Salt Creek.

On the southern fringe of the Coorong is Kingston SE (www.kingstonsea.com) – population 2230. The town is a hotbed of crayfishing, and hosts the weeklong **Lobsterfest** in the second week of January. One of Australia's 'big' tourist attractions, the anatomically correct Larry the Lobster, is a famed resident.

👆 Tours

Adelaide Sightseeing   SIGHTSEEING
(☑1300 769 762, 08-8410 2269; www.adelaide
sightseeing.com.au; tours adult/child $178/155;
☺Aug-May) Full-day Coorong tours departing Adelaide, with a cruise on the *Spirit of the Coorong,* a guided walk, picnic lunch and plenty of bird life.

Spirit of the Coorong   CRUISES
(☑1800 442 203, 08-8555 2203; www.coorong
cruises.com.au; The Wharf, Goolwa) Coorong cruises departing from Goolwa (p742): there are 4½-hour (adult/child $78/58), six-hour ($92/63) or Murray Mouth ($30/15) tours offered. Adelaide coach connections available.

🛏 Sleeping & Eating

There are 11 bush camp sites (per car $11) in the park, but you need a permit from the DENR, available from the Meningie visitor information centre or the Meningie petrol station. There are also 'honesty boxes' at some of the larger campgrounds.

TOP
CHOICE Dalton on the Lake   B&B **$$**
(☑0428 737 161; admason@lm.net.au; 30 Narrung Rd, Meningie; d from $130; ❄) Generous in spirit and unfailingly clean, this lakeside B&B goes to great lengths to ensure your stay is comfortable. There'll be fresh bread baking when you arrive, jars of homemade biscuits, and bountiful bacon and eggs for breakfast. There's a modern self-contained studio off to one side, or a renovated stone cottage – book either, or both.

Lake Albert Caravan Park   CARAVAN PARK **$**
(☑08-8575 1411; lacp@lm.net.au; 25 Narrung Rd, Meningie; unpowered/powered sites $22/29, cabins with/without bathroom from $80/55; ❄) A breezy park with a beaut aspect overlooking the rejuvenated lake (cabins 1, 2 and 3 have the best views). The four new deluxe three-bedroom cabins ($120) are beaut, too.

Coorong Wilderness Lodge   CABINS **$$$**
(☑08-8575 6001; www.coorongwildernesslodge.
com; off the Princes Hwy; unpowered/powered sites $15/30, dm/d/cabins, $40/90/200; ❄) At isolated Hack Point, 25km south of Meningie, this fish-shaped conference centre is owned by the Ngarrindjeri community. The bunkhouse and camp sites here are a bit ordinary, but the new kitchen-cabins are lovely. You can also book a bush-tucker walk ($30) or three-hour guided/unguided kayak trip ($60/40).

Old Cheese Factory   PUB FARE **$$**
(☑08-8575 1914; www.meningie.com.au; off Narrung Rd, Meningie; mains $9-32; ☺lunch daily, dinner Wed-Sun) In a converted cheese factory (you might have guessed), this outfit gives the Meningie pub a run for its money. Lean on the front bar with the locals, or munch into steaks, lasagne, mixed grills, Coorong mullet or a Coorong burger (with mullet!) in the cavernous dining room. There's a very lo-fi history museum (admission $3; ☺11am-5pm) here too.

❶ Information

Meningie Visitor Information Centre (☑08-8575 1770; www.meningie.com.au; 14 Princes Hwy; ☺10am-4.30pm) Provides Coorong camping permits and local info.

Robe
POP 1130

Robe is a cherubic little fishing port that's become a holiday hot spot for Adelaidians and Melburnians alike. The sign saying 'Drain L Outlet' as you roll into town doesn't promise much, but along the main street you'll find quality eateries and boundless accommodation, and there are some magic beaches and lakes around town. Over Christmas and Easter, Robe is packed to the heavens – book *waaay* in advance.

◎ Sights & Activities

Heritage-listed buildings dating from the late 1840s to 1870s litter the streets of Robe, including the little 1863 Customs House (www.nationaltrustsa.org.au; Royal Circus; adult/child $2/50¢; ☺2-4pm Tue & Sun Feb-Dec, Mon-Sat Jan), now a nautical museum.

Little Dip Conservation Park (www.environment.sa.gov.au) runs along the coast for about 13km south of town. It features a variety of habitats including lakes, wetlands and dunes, and some beaut beaches, Aboriginal

middens, walks and camping spots ($11 per car). Access is via Nora Creina Rd.

The small town beach has safe swimming, while **Long Beach** (2km from town), is good for surfing, sailboarding and lazy days (safe swimming in some sections – ask at the visitors centre). **Steve's Place** (26 Victoria St; ⊙9.30am-5pm Mon-Fri, 9am-1pm Sat, 10am-1pm Sun) rents out boards/bodyboards/wetsuits (per day $40/20/20), and is also the best place for info on the annual **Robe Easter Classic**, SA's longest-running surf comp (since 1968).

🛏 Sleeping

Lakeside Manor   HOSTEL $
(☎1800 155 350, 08-8768 1995; www.lakeside manorbackpackers.com.au; 22 Main Rd; dm/d/f $32/83/105; @🖥) In an 1885 sandstone mansion becalmed in faded grandeur, this place has cavernous dorms and doubles. There's an open fireplace, a library, an orchard and a hallway as long as two cricket pitches (we tested it out with a few leg-breaks). The enthusiastic new owners have plans to add a cafe–wine bar.

Caledonian Inn   HOTEL $$
(☎08-8768 2029; www.caledonian.net.au; 1 Victoria St; hotel/cottage/villa d from $85/185/310; 🖥) This historic inn has it all under one roof (actually, several roofs). The half-dozen hotel rooms upstairs share bathroom facilities but are bright and cosy, while the split-level, self-contained units – all rattan and white-painted wood – are sandwiched between the pub and beach. The plush villa sleeps eight.

Lakeside Tourist Park   CARAVAN PARK $
(☎08-8768 2193; www.lakesiderobe.com.au; 24 Main Rd; unpowered/powered sites from $25/27, cabins & villas $60-172; @🖥) Right on Lake Fellmongery (a 'fellmonger' is a wool washer, don't you know), this abstractly laid-out park has heritage-listed pine trees, plenty of grass, basic cabins and flashy villas. Bike hire per half-/full day is $20/30.

Robe Lakeview Motel & Apartments   MOTEL $$
(☎08-8768 2100; www.robelakeviewmotel.com.au; 2 Lakeside Tce; d/apt from $129/210, extra person $15; ❄) Overlooking the waterskiing mecca Lake Fellmongery, the keenly managed Lake View is Robe's best motel. The decor is nothing to write home about, but the rooms are roomy and immaculately clean, and the barbecue area pumps during summer.

Discovery Holiday Parks Robe   CARAVAN PARK $
(☎08-8768 2237; www.discoveryholidayparks.com.au; 70 The Esplanade; unpowered/powered sites from $30/31, cabins & chalets $60-200; ❄🖥) A humongous value-for-money park behind the Long Beach dunes. The self-contained cabins and chalets are big and comfortable, plus there's a heated indoor pool, tennis courts, playground, barbecue and crayfish boiler!

Local rental agents with properties from as low as $80 per night in the off season include **Happyshack** (☎08-8768 2341, 0403 578 382; www.happyshack.com.au), **Complete Real Estate** (☎08-8768 2737; www.completereal estate.net.au; 25 Victoria St) and **First National** (☎08-8768 2600; www.robeholidayrentals.com.au; 9 Victoria St).

🍴 Eating

Union Cafe   CAFE $
(☎08-8768 2627; cnr Victoria & Union Sts; breakfast $6-18, lunch $10-16; ⊙breakfast & lunch; 🖥) Robe's best coffee is at this curiously angled corner cafe with polished-glass fragments in the floor and Astroturf on the wall. Unionise your hangover with big breakfasts (berry pancakes with bacon and maple syrup), stir-fries, pastas and risottos.

Vic Street Pizzeria   ITALIAN $$
(☎08-8768 2081; www.vicstreet.com.au; 6 Victoria St; mains $10-19) Vic Street is a high-energy, all-day cafe, serving gourmet pizzas, good coffee, and an astoundingly good 'Vic Street Salad'. Mod-Asian interior touches, cool tunes on the stereo and local wines, too.

Caledonian Inn   PUB FARE $$
(☎08-8768 2029; 1 Victoria St; mains $19-28; ⊙lunch & dinner) First licensed in 1859, the Caledonian has retained its Scottish heritage and has a great atmosphere. There's a beer garden, summer cafe out the back, and bar meals aimed towards carnivores and seafood fans.

Stanke Ociana Seafoods   FISH AND CHIPS $
(www.stankeociana.com.au; Boat Haven, Mundy Tce; meals $5-10; ⊙lunch & dinner Oct-Apr) Great value fish and chips, fresh off the boat. Garfish, butterfish, Coorong mullet... The visitors' book on the bench out the front attests to guests' satisfaction.

ℹ️ Information

Robe Visitor Information Centre (☑1300 367 144, 08-8768 2465; www.robe.com.au; Public Library, Mundy Tce; ⊙9am-5pm Mon-Fri, 10am-4pm Sat & Sun; @🛜) History displays, brochures and free internet.

Beachport

POP 350

'See and be seen: headlights 24 hours!' say billboards on the way into Beachport. A town that's desperate to be noticed? A plaintive cry for attention? We like it the way it is: low-key and beachy, with aquamarine surf, staunch stone buildings and rows of Norfolk Island pines. Take a walk along the jetty, hang out in the old pub, or munch some fish and chips on the grassy foreshore. Forget about being seen – your time here will be perfectly anonymous.

◉ Sights & Activities

Old Wool & Grain Store Museum MUSEUM
(☑08-8735 8029; www.nationaltrustsa.org.au; 5 Railway Tce; adult/child/concession/family $5/2/4/10; ⊙10am-4pm Mon-Wed, Fri & Sat, 10am-2pm Sun) In a National Trust building on the main street. Inside are relics from Beachport's whaling days and rooms decked out in 1870s style.

Beachport Jetty LANDMARK
The 800m-long jetty provides excellent fishing for local pelicans and fishermen: try your luck for some whiting, school shark, squid and the easy-eating Lake George mullet.

Beachport Conservation Park NATURE RESERVE
(www.environment.sa.gov.au) There are some great walking tracks in the 710-hectare park, sandwiched between the coast and Lake George 2km north of town. Here you'll find Aboriginal middens, sheltered coves, lagoons and bush camping ($11 per car).

Lake George WATER SPORTS
Five kilometres north of Beachport, there's good surfing, birdwatching and sailboarding.

Canunda National Park NATURE RESERVE
(www.environment.sa.gov.au) Giant sand dunes 22km south of town.

Pool of Siloam SWIMMING
In the dunes on the western outskirts of town, the pool is great for swimming; the water is seven times saltier than the ocean.

🛏️ Sleeping & Eating

Bompas HOTEL, CAFE $
TOP CHOICE
(☑08-8735 8333; www.bompas.com.au; 3 Railway Tce; dm $40, d with/without bathroom from $80/140) Brilliant Bompas is an all-in-one small hotel and cosy licensed restaurant-cafe (meals $10 to $30). The dorms have TVs, and all rooms are generously sized and strewn with modern art. If you're after a double try No 3 – it's more expensive, but well worth it for the million-dollar water views and deep balcony. Menu offerings downstairs include a range of curries, lasagne and lamb shanks, with local and imported beers. The owners live on-site, and call you 'Honey' and 'Darl' whether they know you or not.

Southern Ocean Tourist Park CARAVAN PARK $
(☑08-8735 8153; sotp@bigpond.net.au; Somerville St; unpowered/powered sites $25/28, cabins from $95; 🌊) This grassy, well-pruned park sits behind a slope in the town centre. Facilities include a laundry, ice, fuel, bait, covered barbecues, crayfish cookers and a great little playground.

ℹ️ Information

Beachport Visitor Information Centre
(☑08-8735 8029; www.wattlerange.sa.gov.au; Millicent Rd; ⊙9am-5pm Mon-Fri, 10am-4pm Sat & Sun; @)

Mount Gambier

POP 24,500

Strung out along the flatlands below an extinct volcano, Mount Gambier is the Limestone Coast's major town and service hub, and the hometown of musical *bon vivant* Dave Graney. We can see why Dave might have wanted to get to Melbourne in a hurry: 'The Mount' can seem a little short on urban virtues. But it's not what's above the streets that makes Mount Gambier special – it's the deep Blue Lake and the sinkholes and caves that worm their way though the limestone beneath the town. Amazing!

◉ Sights & Activities

The Mount Gambier district is famous for its limestone caves and sinkholes.

FREE Blue Lake NATURE RESERVE
(John Watson Dr; ⊙24hr) Mount Gambier's big-ticket item is the luminous, 75m-deep lake, which turns an insane hue of blue during summer. Perplexed scientists think it has to do

with calcite crystals suspended in the water, which form at a faster rate during the warmer months. Consequently, if you visit between April and November, the lake will look much like any other – a steely grey. **Acquifer Tours** (www.aquifertours.com; cnr Bay Rd & John Watson Dr; adult/child/family $8/4/23; ☺tours 9am-5pm Nov-Jan, 9am-2pm Feb-May & Sep-Oct, 9am-noon Jun-Aug) runs hourly tours, taking you down near the lake shore in a glass-panelled lift.

FREE **Riddoch Art Gallery** ART GALLERY
(www.riddochartgallery.org.au; 8-10 Commercial St E; ☺10am-5pm Tue-Fri, 11am-3pm Sat & Sun) If the lake isn't blue, don't feel blue – cheer yourself up with a visit to one of Australia's best regional galleries. It was undergoing a major renovation when we visited, but should be open again by 2012.

Mount Gambier Discovery Centre MUSEUM
(adult/child/family $10/5/25) Features a replica of the historic brig *Lady Nelson*. An audiovisual display focuses on the devastating impact of European settlement on the local Indigenous people. It is inside the Mount Gambier visitor information centre.

Engelbrecht Cave CAVE
(☎08-8723 5552; Jubilee Hwy W; tours adult/child/concession/family $8/4/7/23; ☺tours hourly 9am-4pm) A tour-accessible cave and cave-diving spot. Enter off Chute St.

FREE **Umpherston Sinkhole** CAVE
(Jubilee Hwy E; ☺24hr) Once 'a pleasant resort in the heat of summer' on James Umpherston's long since subdivided estate.

FREE **Cave Gardens** CAVE
(cnr Bay Rd & Watson Tce; ☺24hr) A 50m-deep sinkhole is right in the middle of town.

🛏 Sleeping

Park Hotel PUB $$
(☎08-8725 2430; www.parkhotel.net.au; 163 Commercial St W; d from $140; ❊❋☎) In Mount Gambier's western wastelands, this old corner pub has spent a fortune renovating its half-dozen upstairs rooms. Polished timber floors, double glazing, marble bathrooms and coffee-and-cream colour schemes – a really slick product.

Colhurst House B&B $$
(☎08-8723 1309; www.colhursthouse.com.au; 3 Colhurst Pl; d incl breakfast from $160) Most locals don't know about Colhurst – it's up a laneway off a sidestreet (Wyatt St) and you can't really see it from downtown Mt G. It's

an 1878 mansion built by Welsh migrants, and manages to be old-fashioned without being twee. There's a gorgeous wrap-around balcony upstairs with great views over the rooftops. Cooked breakfasts, too.

Blue Lake Holiday Park CARAVAN PARK $
(☎1800 676 028, 08-8725 9856; www.bluelake.com.au; Bay Rd; unpowered/powered sites $27/32, cabins/units/bungalows from $89/108/146; ❊❋☎❈) Adjacent to the Blue Lake, a golf course and walking and cycling tracks, this amiable park has some natty grey-and-white cabins and well-weeded lawns. There are also spiffy contemporary, self-contained 'retreats' (from $163) that sleep four.

Grand Central Motel MOTEL $
(☎08-8725 8844; www.grandcentralmotel.com.au; 6 Helen St; s/d/f from $60/83/135; ❊☎) A rock-solid, conveniently located cheapie whose managers are Mount Gambier born and bred, and can point you in the right direction on the town map. Rooms are nothing flash and a bit pokey, but clean and well kept.

🍴 Eating

Bullfrogs MODERN AUSTRALIAN $$
(☎08-8723 3933; www.bullfrogs.com.au; 7 Percy St; lunch $9-20, dinner $16-40; ☺lunch Mon-Sat, dinner daily) Spread over three floors of a fabulous old mill building, this is the place for organic beef and lamb grills, boutique beers, Coonawarra wines, cocktails, trusty coffee and occasional acoustic troubadours. Hard to beat.

Yoeys CAFE $
(www.yoeys.com.au; 32 James St; items $3-8; ☺breakfast & lunch Mon-Sat) What a find! A gourmet cafe-providore with shelves full of cakes, muffins, breads, chocolates, pasta and gourmet foodie hampers; a fabulous cheese fridge (rustic Italian goats' cheese anyone?); and the best coffee in town.

Banana Tree Cafe THAI $$
(☎08-8723 9393; www.bananatree.com.au; 53 Gray St; mains $15-27; ☺lunch & dinner) Wow – authentic Thai in Mount Gambier! A colourful, cheery eatery with a Thai chef, serving chilli-laden dishes like beef-and-basil stir-fry and a smokin' green chicken curry that will have a memorable effect on your innards.

Jens Town Hall Hotel PUB FARE $$
(☎08-8725 1671; 40 Commercial St E; mains $15-33; ☺lunch & dinner) The most palatable place for a beer in the Mount (there are a lot of rambling old pubs here), the 1884 Jens has a vast

dining room plating up equally large steaks, pastas, seafood and a damn fine lasagne.

ℹ Information

Department of Environment & Natural Resources (☎08-8735 1114; www.environment.sa.gov.au; 11 Helen St; ⊙9am-5pm Mon-Fri) Info on regional national parks and camping.

Mount Gambier Visitor Information Centre (☎1800 087 187, 08-8724 9750; www.mountgambiertourism.com.au; 35 Jubilee Hwy E; ⊙9am-5pm) Details on local sights, activities and accommodation, plus a 20-minute video on the town. The Mount Gambier Discovery Centre (p755) is here too.

Penola & the Coonawarra Wine Region

A rural town on the way up (what a rarity!), Penola (population 1670) is the kind of place where you walk down the main street and three people say 'Hello!' to you before you reach the pub. The town is famous for two things: first, for its association with the Sisters of St Joseph of the Sacred Heart, co-founded in 1867 by Australia's first saint, Mary MacKillop; and secondly, for being smack bang in the middle of the Coonawarra Wine Region.

◉ Sights & Activities

Mary MacKillop Penola Centre　MUSEUM
(www.mackilloppenola.org.au; cnr Portland St & Petticoat La; adult/child $5/free; ⊙10am-4pm) The centre occupies a jaunty building with a gregarious entrance pergola – perhaps not as modest as Saint Mary might have liked! There's oodles of info on Australia's first saint here, plus the Woods-MacKillop Schoolhouse, the first school in Australia for children from lower socioeconomic backgrounds.

FREE John Riddoch Centre　MUSEUM
(27 Arthur St) Casts a web over local history back to the 1850s, including info on the local Pinejunga people and original Penola pastoralist Riddoch, who 'never gave in to misfortune' and was 'steady and persistent'.

Petticoat Lane　STREET
One of Penola's first streets. Most of the original buildings have been razed, but there are still a few old timber-slab houses and gnarly trees to see.

🛏 Sleeping & Eating

Contact **Coonawarra Discovery** (☎1800 600 262, 08-8737 2449; www.coonawarradiscovery.com) for local B&B listings.

Heyward's Royal Oak Hotel　PUB $
(☎08-8737 2322; www.heywardshotel.com.au; 31 Church St; s $55, d & tw $88) The Royal Oak – a lace-trimmed, main-street megalith built in 1872 – is Penola's community hub. The rooms upstairs are a bit tatty and share bathrooms, but they're a good bang for your buck. Downstairs the huge tartan-carpeted dining room (mains $18 to $30, open for lunch and dinner) serves classy pub food (roo fillets with pepper crust and Cabernet glaze) and schnitzels as big as your head. Summery beer garden, too.

Georgie's Cottage　B&B $$
(☎08-8737 3540; www.georgiescottage.com; 1 Riddoch St; d from $195; ❋) Feeling romantic? A short stroll from town on the road to Millicent, Georgie's is a cute little stone cottage behind a lavender hedge and blooming hollyhocks. Gourmet provisions include chocolates and wine, which you may or may not feel like cracking into for breakfast.

✐ Must @ Coonawarra　MOTEL $$
(☎08-8737 3444; www.mustatcoonawarra.com.au; 126 Church St; s/d from $115/155; ❋) On the way up the winery strip, plush Must is a newish option with jaunty roof curves reminiscent of a certain opera venue in Sydney. Accommodation ranges from studios to apartments, with sustainable features aplenty: rain-water showers, double glazing and insulation, solar hot water, natural cleaning products etc. Plug-in broadband available.

TOP CHOICE diVine　CAFE $
(www.penola.org/divine.htm; 39 Church Street; meals $7-20; ⊙breakfast & lunch) The busiest spot on the main street, diVine is a bright modern cafe serving baguettes, all-day breakfasts, great coffee and internationally inspired lunches (try the duck and Spanish onion fritters). Nattering Penolans chew muffins and local cheeses, discussing the nuances of various vintages.

Pipers of Penola　MODERN AUSTRALIAN $$$
(☎08-8737 3999; www.pipersofpenola.com.au; 58 Riddoch St; mains $30-39; ⊙dinner Tue-Sat) A classy, intimate dining room tastefully constructed inside an old Methodist church, with friendly staff and seasonal fare. The

DON'T MISS

COONAWARRA WINERIES

When it comes to spicy Cabernet Sauvignon, it's just plain foolish to dispute the virtues of the Coonawarra Wine Region – the *terra rossa* (red earth) region between Penola and Naracoorte. The climate also produces some irresistible Shiraz and Chardonnay. Five of the best:

» **Zema Estate** (www.zema.com.au; Riddoch Hwy; ⊚9am-5pm) A steadfast, traditional winery started by the Zema family in the early '80s. It's a low-key affair with a handmade vibe infusing the Shiraz and Cab Sav.

» **Rymill Coonawarra** (www.rymill.com.au; Riddoch Hwy; ⊚10am-5pm) Down a long avenue of plane trees, Rymill rocks the local boat by turning out some of the best Sauvignon Blanc you'll ever taste. The modern cellar door is fronted by a statue of two duelling steeds – appropriately rebellious.

» **Majella Wines** (www.majellawines.com.au; Lynn Rd; ⊚10am-4.30pm) The family that runs Majella are fourth-generation Coonawarrans, so they know a thing or two about gutsy reds. Their sparkling Shiraz and Riesling are unexpected bonuses.

» **Balnaves of Coonawarra** (www.balnaves.com.au; Riddoch Hwy; ⊚9am-5pm Mon-Fri, noon-5pm Sat & Sun) The tasting notes here ooze florid wine speak (dark seaweed, leather or tobacco, anyone?), but even if you're nosing skills aren't that subtle, you'll enjoy the Cab Sav and Chardonnay.

» **Wynns Coonawarra Estate** (www.wynns.com.au; Memorial Dr; ⊚10am-5pm) The oldest Coonawarra winery, Wynns' cellar door dates from 1896 and was built by Penola pioneer John Riddoch. Top-quality Shiraz, fragrant Riesling and golden Chardonnay are the mainstays.

---

menu is studded with words like 'galette,' 'carpaccio' and 'rotollo' – seriously gourmet indicators! The prices are getting up there, but quality is sky high.

❶ Information

Coonawarra website (www.coonawarra.org)
Penola Visitor Information Centre (☎1300 045 373, 08-8737 2855; www.wattlerange. sa.gov.au; 27 Arthur St; ⊚9am-5pm Mon-Fri, 10am-4pm Sat & Sun; @) Services the Coonawarra region, with info about local cycling routes and winery tours. The John Riddoch Centre is also here.
Penola website (www.penola.org)

Naracoorte Caves National Park

About 12km southeast of Naracoorte township, off the Penola road, is the only World Heritage–listed site in SA. The discovery of an ancient fossilised marsupial in these limestone caves raised palaeontologic eyebrows around the world, and featured in the BBC's David Attenborough series *Life on Earth*.

The park visitor centre doubles as the impressive **Wonambi Fossil Centre** (☎08-8762 2340; www.naracoortecaves.sa.gov.au; Hynam-Caves Rd; adult/child/concession/family $10/6/8/27; ⊚9am-5pm) – a re-creation of the rainforest that covered this area 200,000 years ago. Follow a ramp down past grunting, life-sized reconstructions of extinct animals, including a marsupial lion, a giant echidna, *Diprotodon australis* (koala meets grizzly bear), and *Megalania prisca* – 500kg of bad-ass goanna.

The 26 limestone caves here, including **Alexandra Cave** and **Victoria Fossil Cave**, have bizarre formations of stalactites and stalagmites. Prospective Bruce Waynes should check out the **Bat Cave**, from which thousands of endangered southern bentwing bats exit en masse at dusk during summer. You can see the **Wet Cave** by self-guided tour, but the others require ranger-guided tours. Single-cave tours cost adult/child/concession/family $16/10/13/44; and two-cave tours $26/16/21/71. There's also some great-value budget **accommodation** (dm $20) here in an old stone house with a modern kitchen outbuilding.

For more local info and tips on places to stay, contact **Naracoorte Visitor Information Centre** (☎08-8762 1399; www.naracoorte lucindale.com; 36 MacDonnell St; ⊚9am-5pm Mon-Fri, 10am-4pm Sat & Sun) in Naracoorte.

MURRAY RIVER

On the lowest gradient of any Australian river, the slow-flowing Murray hooks and bows through 650 South Australian kilometres. Tamed by weirs and locks, the Murray irrigates the fruit trees and vines of the sandy Riverland district to the north, and winds through the dairy country of the Murraylands district to the south. Raucous flocks of white corellas and pink galahs launch from cliffs and river red gums and dart across lush vineyards and orchards. With well-watered median strips and bubbling fountains, the towns here are also improbably green – much helped by recent, once-every-25-years flood events across much of the Murray-Darling Basin.

Prior to European colonisation, the Murray was home to Meru communities. Then came shallow-draught paddle steamers, carrying wool, wheat and supplies from Murray Bridge as far as central Queensland along the Darling River. With the advent of railways, river transport declined. These days, waterskiers, jet skis and houseboats crowd out the river, especially during summer. If your concept of riverine serenity doesn't include the roar of V8 inboards, then avoid the major towns and caravan parks during holidays and weekends.

Online, see www.murraylands.info, www.murrayriver.com.au and www.riverlands.info.

◎ Sights & Activities

Houseboat hire is big business on the Murray. 'Simply relax' say the brochures...or relax in a complicated manner if you'd prefer – you just need to be over 18 with a current driving licence. Despite the hokey marketing, meandering along the Murray River on a houseboat is great fun. Book ahead from Adelaide or from most riverside towns, especially between October and April.

The **Houseboat Hirers Association** (☑1300 665 122, 08-8231 8466; www.houseboatbookings.com) website details departure points, conditions, has pictures of each boat and can make bookings on your behalf. Expect to pay anywhere from $650 per week (off-peak, two people) to $5500 for a luxury boat in peak season (sleeping 10). Most boats sleep at least two couples and there's generally a bond involved (starting at $200). Many provide linen – just bring food and fine wine. See also the South Australian Tourism Authority's *Houseboat Holidays* booklet for detailed houseboat listings.

⫘ Tours

If you don't feel like pottering around in a houseboat, try the following operators.

BMS Tours   CRUISES
(☑0408 282 300; www.houseboatadventure.com.au/BMStours.php; 2hr tour $50) Murray tours from Berri on an Everglades-style airboat.

Riverland Leisure Canoe Tours   CANOEING
(☑08-8595 5399; www.riverlandcanoes.com.au; 2½-/3½-/8hr tours $45/65/105) Slow-paced guided canoe tours on the Murray, departing Paringa across the river from Renmark. Canoe/kayak hire also available (from $45/35 per day).

❶ Getting There & Away

Murray Bridge LinkSA (www.linksa.com.au) runs several daily bus services between Adelaide and Murray Bridge ($20, 1¼ hours), plus Adelaide to Mannum ($27, 2½ hours) from Monday to Friday (which involves a bus change at Mt Barker in the Adelaide Hills). **Premier Stateliner** (www.premierstateliner.com.au) runs a Riverland service from Adelaide, stopping in Waikerie ($39, 2½ hours), Barmera and Berri ($49, 3½ hours), and Loxton and Renmark ($49, four hours).

ROLLIN' ON THE RIVER

Until 2010, Old Man Murray was in dire straits, degraded by drought, salinisation, evaporation, upstream irrigation and the demands of servicing SA's domestic water requirements. Downstream at Goolwa and the lower lakes, shrinking flows left jetties high and dry, ecosystems awry and farmers facing bankruptcy. Debate raged over solutions: federal control of the Murray-Darling Basin? Stiffer quotas for upstream irrigators? A weir at Wellington? Opening the Goolwa barrages and letting salt water flood the lower lakes? Things were grim.

In 2011 came a reprieve: heavy flooding upstream in Queensland, New South Wales and Victoria and rains delivered by Tropical Cyclone Yasi have got things flowing again. At the time of writing the river was in flood, purging the backlog of silt and salt, and filling wetlands with life. But this isn't a long-term fix: see www.savethemurray.com for the latest ideas on how to keep Old Man Murray a-flowin'.

Murray Bridge

POP 18,370

SA's largest river town is a rambling regional hub with lots of old pubs but an under-utilised riverfront, a huge prison and little charm. The town was anointed SA's 'Regional Centre of Culture' in 2010, which injected a bit of vim.

FREE **Murray Bridge Regional**
Gallery ART GALLERY
(www.murraybridgegallery.com.au; 27 6th St; ⏰10am-4pm Tue-Sat, 11-4pm Sun) This is the town's cultural epicentre, a great little space housing touring and local exhibitions: painting, ceramics, glasswear, jewellery and prints.

Monarto Zoo ZOO
(www.monartozoo.com.au; Princes Hwy, Monarto; adult/child/concession/family $28.50/20/16.50/74; ⏰9.30am-5pm) About 14km west of town, the excellent open-range zoo is home to Australian and African beasts including cheetahs, rhinos and giraffes. A one-hour safari bus tour and guided walk are included in the price; keeper talks happen throughout the day.

Captain Proud Paddle
Boat Cruises CRUISES
(☑0466 304 092; www.captainproud.com.au; 1-/3hr cruises $25/49) Hour-long cruises running Tuesday to Thursday, plus three-hour lunch cruises Friday to Monday.

MV Barrangul CRUISES
(☑0407 395 385; www.barrangul.com.au; cruises $25) Devonshire-tea cruises departing Sturt Reserve. Also offers lunch and dinner cruises ($45).

🛏 Sleeping

Adelaide Road Motor Lodge MOTEL $
(☑08-8532 1144; www.adelaiderdmotorlodge.com; 212 Adelaide Rd; d $90-120; ❄🐕🛜🏊) If you're stuck for a bed here, your best bet is probably this rambling '60s number with a 21st-century facelift – one of several motels on the road in from the Murray Bridge–Adelaide freeway.

ℹ Information

Murray Bridge Visitor Information Centre
(☑08-8339 1142; www.murraybridge.sa.gov. au; 3 South Tce; ⏰9am-5pm) Stocks the *Murray Bridge Accommodation Guide* and *Eating Out in Murray Bridge* brochures, and has info on river-cruise operators

Mannum to Waikerie

Clinging to a narrow strip of riverbank 84km east of Adelaide, improbably cute Mannum (population 6750) is the unofficial houseboat-hiring capital of the world! The *Mary Ann*, Australia's first riverboat, was knocked together here in 1853 and made the first paddle-steamer trip up the Murray. The Mannum visitor information centre incorporates the Museum of River History (6 Randell St, Mannum; adult/child/concession/family $5/2.50/3.50/13; ⏰9am-5pm Mon-Fri, 10am-4pm Sat & Sun), featuring info on local Ngarrindjeri Aboriginal communities, an 1876 dry dock and the restored 1897 paddle steamer PS *Marion*, on which you can occasionally chug around the river.

Breeze Holiday Hire (www.murrayriver.com. au/breeze-holiday-hire-1052) hires out canoes ($75 per day), dinghies with outboards ($95 per day) and fishing gear ($15 per day), and can get you waterskiing too.

From Mannum to Swan Reach, the eastern riverside road scoots through Bowhill, Purnong and Nildottie. The road often tracks a fair way east of the river, but various lookouts en route help you scan the scene. Around 9km from Swan Reach, the Murray takes a tight meander called **Big Bend**, a sweeping river curve with pock-marked, ochre-coloured cliffs.

Sedentary old Swan Reach (population 850), 70km southwest of Waikerie, is a bit of a misnomer: plenty of pelicans, not many swans.

A citrus-growing centre oddly festooned with TV antennas, Waikerie (population 4630) takes its name from the Aboriginal phrase for 'anything that flies'. There's plenty of bird life around here, with 180 species recorded at Gluepot Reserve (www.riverland. net.au/gluepot; Gluepot Rd; cars per day/overnight $5/10; ⏰8am-6pm), a mallee scrub area 64km north of Waikerie (off Lunn Rd) and part of Unesco's Bookmark Biosphere Reserve. Before you head off, check with Waikerie's Shell service station on Peake Tce to see if you'll need a gate key.

🛏 Sleeping & Eating

Waikerie Hotel/Motel HOTEL, MOTEL $
(☑08-8541 2999; www.waikeriehotel.com; 2 McCoy St, Waikerie; s/d hotel $55/65, motel from $75; ❄🛜) Waikerie's humongous main-street pub has clean, affordable hotel rooms (all with bathroom, rather unusually) and updated

As the Murray curls abstractly across eastern SA, roads (on far more linear trajectories) invariably bump into it. Dating back to the late 19th century, a culture of free, 24-hour, winch-driven ferries has evolved to shunt vehicles across the water. Your car is guided onto the punts by burly, bearded, fluoro-clad ferrymen, who lock safety gates into position then shunt you across to the other side. There are 11 ferries in operation, the most useful of which are those at Mannum, Swan Reach and Waikerie. Turn off your headlights if you're waiting for the ferry at night so you don't bedazzle the approaching skipper.

motel rooms out the back. The bistro does lots of seafood and pub-grub classics (mains $16 to $25).

Mannum Caravan Park   CARAVAN PARK $
(☑08-8569 1402; www.mannumcaravanpark.com. au; Purnong Rd, Mannum; unpowered/powered sites $23/27, cabins/villas from $62/105; ❋@🛜) A clean-cut caravan park right on the river next to the Mannum ferry crossing. Ducks and water hens patrol the lawns, and there's a pool table in the games room if it's raining.

Murray River Queen   RIVERBOAT $
(☑08-8541 2651; www.murrayriverqueen. au; Leonard Norman Dve, Waikerie; cabins dm/ tw $20/75, d $80-110) When it's not cruising the Murray, this 1974 paddleboat berths at Waikerie and offers basic bunkrooms (a tad shabby and dim but undeniably novel) and more upmarket suites with spas. There's a cafe onboard if you're in the market for a light lunch (items $5 to $15, open for breakfast and lunch Wednesday to Sunday).

Mannum Motel   MOTEL $
(☑1800 635 803, 08-8569 1808; www.mannum motel.com.au; Cliff St, Mannum; s/d from $85/99; ❋🛜🏊) This affordable, unobtrusive brown-brick '80s number squats on a rise above the ferry crossing at Mannum. Some of the larger units have kitchenettes if you don't fancy a trip to the pub for dinner.

Pretoria Hotel   PUB FARE $$
(www.pretoriahotel.com.au; 50 Randell St, Mannum; mains $16-30; ☉lunch & dinner) The family-friendly Pretoria (built 1900) has a vast bistro and deck fronting the river, and plates up big steaks, roo fillets and parmas plus Asian salads and Mediterranean antipasti. When the 1956 flood swamped the town they kept pouring beer from the 1st-floor balcony!

❶ Information

Mannum Visitor Information Centre (☑1300 626 686, 08-8569 1303; www.psmarion.com;

www.mannum.org.au; 6 Randell St, Mannum; ☉9am-5pm Mon-Fri, 10am-4pm Sat & Sun) Cruise and houseboat bookings, *Mannum Historic Walks* brochures and the Museum of River History (p760).

Barmera & Around

On the shallow shores of Lake Bonney (upon which world land-speed record-holder Donald Campbell unsuccessfully attempted to break his water-speed record in 1964), snoozy **Barmera** (population 4290) was once a key town on the overland stock route from NSW. These days Barmera feels a bit depressed – all fishing shops and nowhere to get a decent coffee – but the local passion for both kinds of music (country *and* western) lends a simple optimism to proceedings. **Kingston-On-Murray** (population 260; aka Kingston OM) is a tiny town en route to Waikerie.

❂ Sights & Activities

The once ephemeral **Lake Bonney** has been transformed into a permanent lake ringed by large, drowned red gums, whose stark branches are often festooned with birds. If you're feeling uninhibited, there's a nudist beach at **Pelican Point Nudist Resort** (www.riverland.net.au/pelicanpoint) on the lake's western shore.

Country music is a big deal in Barmera, with the **South Australian Country Music Festival & Awards** (www.riverlandcountrymu-sic.com) in June, and **Rocky's Hall of Fame Pioneers Museum** (www.murrayriver.com.au/barmera/rockys-hall-of-fame-pioneers-museum; 4 Pascoe Tce, Barmera; adult/child $2/1; ☉10am-noon & 1-3pm Wed-Mon) blaring sincere rural twangings down the main street from outdoor speakers. Don't miss the 35m Botanical Garden Guitar out the back, inlayed with the handprints of 160 country musos: Slim Dusty to Kasey Chambers and everyone in between.

There are wildlife reserves with walking trails and camping (per car $6) at **Moorook**

on the road to Loxton, and Loch Luna across the river from Kingston-On-Murray. Loch Luna backs onto the Overland Corner Hotel. Both reserves have nature trails and are prime spots for birdwatching and canoeing. Self-register camping permits are available at reserve entrances.

Overlooking regenerated wetlands off the Sturt Hwy (Rte A20) at Kingston OM, carbon-neutral Banrock Station Wine & Wetland Centre (www.banrockstation.com. au; Holmes Rd, Kingston OM; tastings free; ⏱9am-4pm Mon-Fri, 9am-5pm Sat & Sun) is a stylish, rammed-earth wine-tasting centre (love the Tempranillo) and jazzy lunchtime restaurant (mains $19 to $30 – try the roo-fillet filo parcel), using ingredients sourced locally. There are three **wetland walks** here: 2.5km and 4km ($3), and 8km ($5).

There are also **walking trails** at the Overland Corner Hotel.

🛏 Sleeping & Eating

Discovery Holiday Parks Lake Bonney CARAVAN PARK $
(☑08-8588 2234; www.discoveryholidayparks.com. au; Lakeside Dr, Barmera; unpowered/powered sites $26/30, cabins from $75; ✳@🛜🏊) This passionately managed lakeside park has small beaches (safe swimming), electric barbecues, camp kitchen, laundry and plenty of room for kids to run amok. Waterfront camp sites, too.

Barmera Lake Resort Motel MOTEL $
(☑08-8588 2555; www.barmeralakeresortmotel. com.au; Lakeside Dr, Barmera; d $90-125; ✳🏊) Right on the lake, this good-value motel has a barbecue, pool, laundry and tennis court. Rooms are nothing flash, but immaculate; most have lake views.

Overland Corner Hotel PUB FARE $$
(☑08-8588 7021; www.murrayriver.com.au/overland-corner; Old Coach Rd; meals $15-23; ⏱lunch Tue-Sun, dinner Thu-Sat) Off the Morgan Rd, 19km northwest of Barmera, this moody 1859 boozer is named after a Murray River bend where drovers used to camp. The pub walls ooze character and the pubs meals are drover sized, plus there's a museum, a resident ghost and a beaut beer garden. An 8km self-guided nature trail leads down to the river from the pub past an ochre quarry.

ℹ Information

Barmera Visitor Information Centre (☑1300 768 468, 08-8588 2289; www.barmeratourism. com.au; Barwell Ave, Barmera; ⏱9am-5pm Mon-Fri, 10am-2pm Sun; @) Help with transport and accommodation bookings. Pick up the *Overland Corner Reserve Walking Trails* brochure.

Loxton
POP 4100

Sitting above a broad loop of the slow-roaming Murray, Loxton proclaims itself the 'Garden City of the Riverland'. The vibe here is low-key, agricultural and untouristy, with more tyre distributors, hardware shops and irrigation supply outlets than anything else.

👁 Sights & Activities

From Loxton you can canoe across to Katarapko Creek and the Katarapko Game Reserve in the Murray River National Park (www.environment.sa.gov.au); hire canoes from Loxton Riverfront Caravan Park.

The town's other lure is Loxton Historical Village (www.loxtonhistoricalvillage.com.au; Allan Hoskings Dr; adult/child/concession/family $10/5/8/25; ⏱10am-4pm Mon-Fri, to 5pm Sat & Sun), a re-creation time warp of dusty old buildings and costumed staff.

Down by the river near the caravan park, the Tree of Knowledge is marked with flood levels from previous years. The bumper flows of 1931, '73, '74 and '75 were totally outclassed by the flood-to-end-all-floods of 1956, marked about 5m up the trunk. Have they added a line for 2011 yet?

🛏 Sleeping & Eating

Harvest Trail Lodge HOSTEL $
(☑08-8584 5646; www.harvesttrail.com; 1 Kokoda Tce; dm per night/week for workers $15/105; dm per night for nonworkers $45; ✳@) Inside a converted '60s waterworks office are four-bed dorms with TVs and fridges, and a barbecue balcony to boot. Staff will find you fruit-picking work, and shunt you to and from jobs.

Loxton Hotel HOTEL, MOTEL $$
(☑1800 656 686, 08-8584 7266; www.loxtonhotel. com.au; 45 East Tce; hotel s/d from $75/95, motel from $95/105; ✳🛜) With all profits syphoned back into the Loxton community, this large complex offers immaculate rooms with tasty weekend packages. The original pub dates from 1908, but it has been relentlessly extended. Bistro meals available (mains $17 to $28).

Loxton Riverfront Caravan Park CARAVAN PARK $
(☑1800 887 733, 08-8584 7862; www.lrcp.com. au; Sophie Edington Dr; unpowered/powered sites

from $20/25, cabins with/without bathroom from $65/55; ❋❋☎) On the gum-studded Habels Bend, 2km from town, this riverside park bills itself as 'The Quiet One'. You can hire a canoe (per hour/day $11/55), and there's a free nine-hole golf course (usually sandy, but flooded when we visited).

ℹ️ Information

Loxton Visitor Information Centre (☑1300 869 990, 08-8584 8071; www.loxtontourism. com.au; Loxton Roundabout, Bookpurnong Tce; ☺9am-5pm Mon-Fri, 9am-4pm Sat, 10am-4pm Sun; ⒶA friendly place for accommodation, transport and national-park info, plus a small art gallery.

Berri

POP 7440

The name Berri derives from the Aboriginal term *berri berri,* meaning 'big bend in the river', and it was once a busy refuelling stop for wood-burning paddle steamers. These days Berri is an affluent regional hub for both state government and agricultural casual-labour agencies, and one of the best places to chase down casual harvest jobs.

👁 Sights & Activities

A short amble from the visitor centre is A Special Place for Jimmy James, a living riverbank memorial to the Aboriginal tracker who could 'read the bush like a newspaper'. Whimsical tracks and traces are scattered around granite boulders.

Berri is an artsy kinda town. Around the base of Berri Bridge, check out the murals and totem poles created by local artists. The River Lands Gallery (www.countryarts.org. au; 23 Wilson St; admission free; ☺10am-4pm Mon-Fri) displays local and travelling exhibitions.

Road access to the scenic Katarapko Creek section of the Murray River National Park (www.environment.sa.gov.au) is off the Stuart Hwy (Rte A1) between Berri and Barmera. This is a beaut spot for bush camping (per car per night $6.50), canoeing and birdwatching.

🛏 Sleeping & Eating

TOP CHOICE **Berri Backpackers** HOSTEL $
(☑08-8582 3144; www.berribackpackers.com. au; Old Sturt Hwy; dm per night/week $25/150; ＠☎❋) On the Barmera side of town, this eclectic hostel is destination *numero uno* for work-seeking travellers, who chill out after a hard day's manual toil in quirky new-age surrounds. Facilities include beach volleyball and soccer, tennis, bicycles and a post-harvest sauna. Rooms range from messy dorms to doubles, share houses, a tepee and a yurt – all for the same price. The managers can hook you up with harvest work (call in advance).

Berri Resort Hotel HOTEL, MOTEL $$
(☑1800 088 226, 08-8582 1411; www.berriresort hotel.com; Riverview Dr; hotel s & tw $70, motel d $145-160; ❋❋☎❋) This mustard-and-maroon monolith across the road from the river has hotel rooms with shared bathrooms and a wing of spacious en-suite motel rooms. There's a gym, pool, tennis court and the cavernous Riverboat bistro serving upmarket pub grub (mains $15 to $33, open for lunch and dinner daily). A slick operation, albeit a bit Vegas.

Berri Riverside Caravan Park CARAVAN PARK $
(☑08-8582 3723; www.berricaravanpark.com.au; Riverview Dr; unpowered/powered sites $24/32, s/d from $37/74, cabins $68-142; ❋＠☎❋) Big on greenery, this well-groomed and patronised

---

RIVERLAND FRUIT PICKING

The fruit- and grape-growing centres of Berri, Barmera, Waikerie, Loxton and Renmark are always seeking harvest workers. Work is seasonal but there's usually something that needs picking (stonefruit, oranges, grapes, apples...), except for mid-September to mid-October and mid-April to mid-May when things get a bit quiet. If you have a valid working visa and don't mind sweating it out in the fields, ask the local backpacker hostels about work. Also try Berri's private job agencies:

» **MADEC Jobs Australia Berri Harvest Labour Office** (☑1800 062 332, 08-8582 5077; www.madec.edu.au; 3 Riverview Dr)

» **Mission Australia** (☑08-8582 2188; www.missionaustralia.com.au; 5 Kealley St)

» **National Harvest Information Service** (☑1800 062 332; www.jobsearch.gov.au/ harvesttrail) General harvest info.

park is opposite the river, and has an impressive range of cabin configurations (the top-end ones look like Sydney apartments).

Cragg's Creek Café
CAFE $
(www.craggscreek.com.au; Riverview Dr; mains $9-16; ⊙breakfast & lunch) Next door to the visitor information centre is this cool cafe, functioning as a cellar door for the winery of the same name. A top spot for a light cafe lunch, some tapas, a glass of the aforementioned vino or a caffeine kick-start.

ℹ Information
Berri Visitor Information Centre (☑08-8582 5511; www.berribarmera.sa.gov.au; Riverview Dr; ⊙9am-5pm Mon-Fri, 10.30am-3.30pm Sat & Sun; ⊛) Right by the river, with brochures, internet, maps and cluey staff.

Renmark
POP 9870
Renmark is the first major river town across from the Victorian border, about 254km from Adelaide. It's not a pumping tourist destination by any means, but has a relaxed vibe and grassy waterfront, where you can pick up a houseboat. This is the hub of the Riverland wine region: lurid signs on the roads into town scream 'Buy 6 Get 1 Free!' and 'Bulk port $4/litre!'.

⊙ Sights & Activities
Renmark River Cruises (☑08-8595 1862; www.renmarkrivercruises.com.au; Main Wharf; cruises adult/child/family $38/12/85; ⊙2pm Tue, Thu & Sat) offers two-hour cruises past the Murray River cliffs on the MV *Big River Rambler*. One-hour Sunday cruises run at 11am (adult/child/family $20/5/45); guided two-hour tours of the Murray's mildly spooky backwaters in a motorised dinghy are also available (two/three hours per person $60/80).

Upstream from town, **Chowilla Game Reserve** (www.environment.sa.gov.au) is great for bush camping, canoeing and bushwalking. Access is along the north bank from Renmark or along the south bank from Paringa. For more info, contact the Berri office of the **Department of Environment & Heritage** (DENR; ☑08-8595 2111; 28 Vaughan Tce).

If you're staying at Renmark Riverfront Caravan Park, you can hire **canoes** (s/d per hr $10/15) and **pedal boats** (2-/4-seater per hr $15/20). Riverland Leisure Canoe Tours (p777) also hires out canoes and kayaks.

🛏 Sleeping & Eating
Renmark Hotel
HOTEL, MOTEL $$
(☑1800 736 627, 08-8586 6755; www.renmark hotel.com.au; Murray Ave; hotel/motel d from $90/110; ⊛@⊛) Wow, what a beauty! The sexy art-deco curves of Renmark's humongous pub are really looking good these days, thanks to a $3.5-million overhaul. Choose from older-style hotel rooms and upmarket motel rooms. On a sultry evening it's hard to beat a cold beer and some grilled barramundi on Nanya bistro's riverfront balcony (mains $11 to $29).

Renmark Riverfront Caravan Park
CARAVAN PARK $
(☑1300 664 612, 08-8586 6315; www.big4renmark. com.au; Sturt Hwy; unpowered/powered sites from $30/35, cabins $72-285; ⊛@⊛⊛) Highlights of this spiffy riverfront park, 1km east of town, include a camp kitchen, canoe hire and absolute waterfront cabins and powered sites. The newish corrugated-iron cabins are top notch, and look a little 'Riviera' surrounded by scraggly palms. The waterskiing fraternity swarms here during holidays.

ℹ Information
Renmark Paringa Visitor Information Centre (☑1300 661 704, 08-8586 6704; www.visitren mark.com; 84 Murray Ave; ⊙9am-5pm Mon-Fri, 9am-4pm Sat, 10am-4pm Sun; ⊛) All the usual brochures and info, plus an interpretive centre and the recommissioned 1911 paddle steamer PS *Industry* (gold-coin donation).

BAROSSA VALLEY

With hot, dry summers and cool, moderate winters, the Barossa is one of the world's great wine regions – an absolute must for anyone with even the slightest interest in a good drop. It's a compact valley – just 25km long – yet it manages to produce 21% of Australia's wine, mostly big, luscious reds. The 80-plus wineries here are within easy reach of one another, and make a no-fuss day trip from Adelaide, just 65km to the southwest. The long-established 'Barossa Barons' hold sway – big, ballsy and brassy – while spritely young boutique wineries are harder to sniff out.

The local towns have a distinctly German heritage, dating back to 1842. Fleeing religious persecution in Prussia and Silesia, settlers (bringing their vine cuttings with them) created a Lutheran heartland where German traditions persist today. The physical rem-

nants of colonisation – gothic church steeples and stone cottages – are everywhere. Cultural legacies of the early days include a dubious passion for oom-pah bands, and an appetite for wurst, pretzels and sauerkraut.

☞ Tours

The Barossa visitor information centre has details on organised tours departing locally, including the following. For other Barossa tours starting from Adelaide, see p717.

Barossa Epicurean Tours   FOOD & WINE
(☎08-8564 2191, 0402 989 647; www.barossatours.com.au; full-/half-day tours $100/70) Good-value, small-group tours visiting the wineries of your choice and Mengler Hill Lookout.

Barossa Classic Cycle Tours   CYCLING
(☎0427 000 957; www.bccycletours.com.au; tours per person per day $220) One- and two-day cycling tours of the valley, covering about 30km per day. Cheaper rates for bigger groups.

Barossa Wine Lovers Tours   WINE
(☎08-8270 5500; www.wineloverstours.com.au; tours incl lunch from $70) Several wineries, lookouts, shops and heritage buildings...a good blend.

Barossa Experience Tours   SIGHTSEEING
(☎08-8563 3248; www.barossavalleytours.com; full-/half-day tours from $110/80) Local small-group operator whisking you around the major sites. The Food & Wine Experience ($230) includes lunch, cheese tastings and a glass of plonk.

Balloon Adventures   BALLOONING
(☎08-8389 3195; www.balloonadventures.com.au; flights adult/child $300/195) Fly the Barossa sky in a hot-air balloon. One-hour flights depart Tanunda and include a champagne breakfast.

✯✯ Festivals & Events

A Day on the Green   MUSIC
(www.adayonthegreen.com.au) Mature-age moshpit at Peter Lehmann Wines, with acts like Simply Red and Diana Krall. Held in February.

Barossa under the Stars   MUSIC
(www.barossaunderthestars.com.au) Wine-slurping picnickers watch middle-of-the-road crooners like Chris Isaak, Sting and Shirley Bassie in March.

Barossa Vintage Festival   FOOD & WINE
(www.barossavintagefestival.com.au) A week-long festival with music, maypole dancing,

tug-of-war contests etc; begins Easter Monday in odd-numbered years.

Barossa Gourmet Weekend   FOOD & WINE
(www.barossagourmetweekend.com.au) Fab food matched with winning wines at select wineries; happens in late winter or early spring.

❶ Getting There & Around

BICYCLE The Barossa is pretty good for cycling, with several routes trundling past the wineries. The Barossa visitor information centre in Tanunda has bikes from $44/22 per full/half day. **Barossa Bike Hire** (www.barossabikehire.com.au) rents out quality cycles from $45/80 per day/two days.

BUS **Barossa Valley Coaches** (www.bvcoach.com) runs buses between Adelaide and Angaston twice daily (once on Sunday), stopping at Tanunda ($19, 1¾ hours), Nuriootpa ($21, two hours) and Angaston ($23, 2¼ hours).

CAR HIRE **Excel Rent a Car** (www.excelrentacar.com.au; 212 Murray St, Tanunda) Cars from $50 per day.

TAXI **Gawler & Barossa Taxi Service** (☎08-8523 1366)

Tanunda

POP 4690

At the centre of the valley both geographically and socially, Tanunda is the Barossa's main tourist town. Despite a steady deluge of visitors, Tanunda manages to morph the practicality of Nuriootpa with the charm of Angaston without a sniff of self-importance. There are a few attractions and artsy shops along Murray St (Rte B19), the main road through town, but the wineries are what you're here for – sip, sip, sip!

◉ Sights & Activities

Goat Square   HISTORIC SITE
Tanunda is flush with historic buildings, including the cottages around this square, on John St. This was the *ziegenmarkt*, a meeting and market place, laid out in 1842 as Tanunda's original town centre.

Barossa Museum   MUSEUM
(www.barossamuseum.com.au; 47 Murray St; adult/child $2/1; ⊙11am-5pm Thu-Tue) Access is via a cellar door/providore business out the front. Inside are displays of bone-handled cutlery, butter-making gear, photos of top-hatted locals, a recreated colonial bedroom and an amazing map of Germany pinpointing the homelands of Barossa settlers. The Indigenous coverage could use a little help.

Barossa Valley

0 — 4 km
0 — 2 miles

FREE Barossa Regional Gallery   ART GALLERY
(www.freewebs.com/barossagallery; 3 Basedow Rd;
⊙11am-4pm Tue-Sun) Has an eclectic collection of paintings, crafts and touring exhibitions, plus an impressive set of organ pipes at the back of the room.

FREE Keg Factory   INDUSTRIAL
(www.thekegfactory.com.au; Lot 10, St Halletts Rd; ⊙10am-4pm) You can watch honest-to-goodness coopers make and repair wine barrels 4km south of town.

Mengler Hill Lookout   LOOKOUT
From Tanunda, take the scenic route to Angaston via Bethany for hazy valley views (just ignore the naff sculptures in the foreground). The road tracks through beautiful rural country, studded with huge eucalypts.

Kaiserstuhl Conservation Park   NATURE RESERVE
(www.environment.sa.gov.au; Tanunda Creek Rd, Angaston) Also en route is the 390-hectare

park, with some ace views and walking tracks.

Para Road Wine Path   WALKING TRAIL
(www.pararoadwinepath.com.au) Between Nuriootpa and Tanunda – a short-and-sweet walking/cycling trail passing four wineries.

Seppeltsfield Road   STREET
(www.seppeltsfieldroad.com) An incongruous avenue of huge palm trees meandering through the vineyards. Beyond Marananga the palm rows veer off the roadside and track up a hill to the **Seppelt Family Mausoleum** – a Grecian shrine fronted by chunky Doric columns.

Whispering Wall   INDUSTRIAL
About 7km southwest of Lyndoch, itself 13km south of Tanunda, the Barossa Reservoir dam is better known as the Whispering Wall. The huge concrete curve has amazing acoustics: whispers at one end of

the wall can be heard clearly 150m away at the other. The perfect spot to propose?

🛌 Sleeping

Tanunda Hotel   PUB, APARTMENTS **$**
(☑08-8563 2030; www.tanundapub.com; 51 Murray St; d with/without bathroom $80/70; ❄) Opened in 1846, this boisterous ol' pub in the centre of town is a real community centre. Rooms are good value and clean, but nothing out of the ordinary. Downstairs, Duran Duran wails from the jukebox and schnitzels fall off the edges of plates (mains $15 to $32, open for lunch and dinner). Out the back are nine ritzy new mauve-coloured apartments (doubles from $200).

Valley Hotel & Motel   MOTEL **$$**
(☑08-8563 2039; www.southaustralia.com/9004931.aspx; 73 Murray St; s/d $90/110, d with spa $125; ❄) There are only five brick-and-stone rooms here (the smallest motel in Australia?), but they're spotless, modern and great value. Out the front is the Valley Hotel (mains $14 to $29; open for lunch and dinner) if you're keen for a bite, a beer or both.

Stonewell Cottages   B&B **$$$**
(☑0417 848 977; www.stonewellcottages.com.au; Stonewell Rd; cottages d incl breakfast from $355, 2 nights Sun-Thu from $550; ❄) These romantic, waterfront spa retreats are surrounded by vines and offer unbeatable privacy, comfort and serenity. Pet ducks waddle around rusty old ploughs as waterbirds splash down in the reservoir. Pricey, but worth it.

Tanunda Caravan & Tourist Park   CARAVAN PARK **$**
(☑08-8563 2784; www.tanundacaravantouristpark.com.au; Barossa Valley Way; unpowered/powered sites from $27/30, cabins with/without bathroom from $90/60; ❄@🛜🏊) This spacious park is dotted with mature trees offering a little shade for your hangover. Facilities include a playground, barbecues, laundry and bike hire for guests ($30 per day).

🍴 Eating

Die Barossa Wurst Haus Bakery   BAKERY **$**
(86a Murray St; meals $7-20; ⊙breakfast & lunch) This fast-not-flashy bakery serves *mettwurst* (Bavarian sausage) rolls, cheeses, pies, cakes, strudel and all-day breakfasts. It's hard to go past a trad German roll with kransky sausage, sauerkraut, cheese and mustard, or the *Bayern Schmaus* (Bavarian feast). An emasculating display of phallic wursts dangles above the counter.

Keils Fine Food & Coffee   CAFE **$**
(keils@optusnet.com.au; Shop 1, 63-67 Murray St; meals $4-13; ⊙breakfast & lunch) Sidestep the coffee mums and their prams; spurn the

DON'T MISS

BAROSSA VALLEY WINERIES

From the moment Johann Gramp planted the valley's first grapes on his property at Jacob's Creek in 1847, the Barossa Valley was destined to become a major Australian wine region. The valley is best known for Shiraz, with Riesling the dominant white. There are around 80 vineyards here and 60 cellar doors, ranging from boutique wine rooms to monstrous complexes. Five of the best:

» **Henschke** (www.henschke.com.au; Henschke Rd, Keyneton; ⊙9am-4.30pm Mon-Fri, 9am-noon Sat) Henschke, 11km southeast of Angaston in the Eden Valley, is known for its iconic Hill of Grace red, but most of the wines here are classics.

» **Rockford Wines** (www.rockfordwines.com.au; Krondorf Rd, Tanunda; ⊙11am-5pm) This 1850s winery uses traditional winemaking methods and produces a small range of superb wines, including sparkling reds. The Black Shiraz is a smooth and spicy killer; the cellar door in a beautiful old stable is picturesque.

» **Penfolds** (www.penfolds.com.au; Tanunda Rd, Nuriootpa; ⊙10am-5pm) You know the name. Book ahead for the 'Make your own Blend' tour ($65) or 'Taste of Grange' tour ($160), which allows you to slide some Grange Hermitage across your lips.

» **St Hallett** (www.sthallett.com.au; St Halletts Rd, Tanunda; ⊙10am-5pm) Using only Barossa grapes, St Hallett produces reasonably priced but consistently good whites (try the Poacher's Blend) and the excellent Gamekeeper's Reserve Shiraz-Grenache. Unpretentious and great value for money.

» **Peter Lehmann Wines** (www.peterlehmannwines.com.au; Para Rd, Tanunda; ⊙9.30am-5pm Mon-Fri, 10.30am-4.30pm Sat & Sun) The multiaward-winning Shiraz and Riesling vintages here (oh, and the Semillon) are probably the most consistent and affordable wines in the Barossa. Buy a bottle and have a picnic in the grounds.

ugly, humming drinks fridge; and place your order for homemade baguettes, soups, quiches, pies, wraps, quality teas and the punchiest coffee in town.

1918 Bistro & Grill   MODERN AUSTRALIAN **$$**
(☑08-8563 0405; www.1918.com.au; 94 Murray St; mains $28-32; ⊙lunch & dinner) This is an enduring restaurant in a lovely old villa, set back from the main street beneath the boughs of a massive Norfolk Island pine. It's a sassy affair serving adventurous mains like roast pork belly with orange, aioli and toasted fennel seeds. Book a verandah table for a long lunch.

❶ Information

Barossa Visitor Information Centre (☑1300 852 982, 08-8563 0600; www.barossa.com; 66-68 Murray St, Tanunda; ⊙9am-5pm Mon-Fri, 10am-4pm Sat & Sun; ◉) The lowdown on the valley, plus internet, bike hire and accommodation bookings.

Nuriootpa

POP 5030

Along an endless main street at the northern end of the valley, Nuriootpa is the Barossa's commercial centre. It's not as immediately endearing as Tanunda or Angaston, but has a certain agrarian appeal. Lutheran spirit runs deep in Nuri: signs say, 'God has invested in you – are you showing any interest?' Don't miss a detour to nearby Greenock and the **Barossa Brewing Company** (www.barossa brewingcompany.com; Mill St, Greenock; ⊙11am-4pm Sat & Sun) to sample some fine ales and lagers, flying in the face of the endless Shiraz.

🛏 Sleeping

Doubles d'Vine   RENTAL HOUSE **$**
(☑08-8562 2260; www.doublesdvine.com.au; Barossa Valley Way; cottage/lodge d $85/75; ❄❄) Affordable Barossa accommodation at last! About 1.5km south of town is this self-contained cottage and separate 'lodge' (a renovated apricot shed) with two en-suite doubles and shared lounge and kitchen. Both have wood heaters, barbecues and access to the pool. Reduced rates for two nights or more; bike hire for guests is $25 per day.

Whistler Farm   B&B **$$**
(☑0415 139 758; www.whistlerfarm.com.au; 616 Samuel Rd; d incl breakfast $195; ❄🛜) Surrounded by vineyards and native shrubs,

this farmhouse B&B has a private guest wing with exposed timber beams, separate guest entry and two country-style rooms. Snooze on the wide verandah and contemplate a day's successful (or imminent) wine touring.

Vine Inn
MOTEL $$

(☑08-8562 2133; www.vineinn.com.au; 14 Murray St; s $85-110, d $95-125, 1-/2-bed apt $150/200; ✱🛜🏊) Regulation motel with swimming pool. The pub bistro (mains $13 to $22) serves lunch and dinner amid bright lights, palms and pokies.

Vine Court
MOTEL $$

(☑08-8562 2133; www.vineinn.com.au; 49 Murray St; s $85-110, d $95-125, 1-/2-bed apt $150/200; ✱🛜) Shares reception at the Vine Inn pub (14 Murray St) down the road. Standard motel doubles plus one- and two-bedroom apartments.

Barossa Valley Tourist Park
CARAVAN PARK $

(☑08-8562 1404; www.barossatouristpark.com.au; Penrice Rd; unpowered/powered sites from $25/28, cabins with/without bathroom from $62/51; ✱@🛜) There are at least six different kinds of cabins at this shady park, lined with pine trees next to the Nuriootpa football oval (go Tigers!). All cabins have TVs, fridges, cooking facilities and small balconies. Check out the 1930 Dodge 'House on Wheels' out the front – the seminal caravan?

✗ Eating

Maggie Beer's Farm Shop
DELI $

(www.maggiebeer.com.au; Pheasant Farm Rd; items $5-20; ⊙lunch) Celebrity SA gourmand Maggie (have you seen her on *The Cook & The Chef* on ABC TV?) has been hugely successful with her range of condiments, preserves and pâtés. The vibe here isn't as relaxed as it used to be, but stop by for some gourmet tastings, an ice cream, cooking demo or a hamper of delicious bites. Off Samuel Rd.

Branch
MODERN AUSTRALIAN $$

(☑08-8562 4561; www.thebranch.com.au; 15 Murray St; mains $16-33; ⊙breakfast & lunch daily, dinner Fri & Sat) A cool conversion of an old red-brick bank on the main street is the backdrop for select Asian and Euro offerings like Kapunda saltbush lamb madras, Thai crispy beef salad, burgers and risottos. The best coffee in town to boot, and a well-considered wine and beer list.

Angaston
POP 1870

Photo-worthy Angaston was named after George Fife Angas, a pioneering Barossa pastoralist. An agricultural vibe persists, as there are relatively few wineries on the town doorstep: cows graze in paddocks down the end of every street, and there's a vague whiff of fertiliser in the air. Along the main drag are two pubs, some terrific eateries and a few B&Bs in old stone cottages (check for double glazing and ghosts – we had a sleepless night!).

The **Barossa Valley Cheese Company** (www.barossacheese.com.au; 67b Murray St; ⊙10am-5pm Mon-Fri, 10am-4pm Sat, 11am-3pm Sun) is a fabulously stinky room, selling handmade cheeses from local cows and goats. Tastings are free, but it's unlikely you'll leave without buying a wedge of the Washington Washed Rind.

At the top end of the main street, **Angas Park** (www.angaspark.com.au; 3 Murray St; ⊙9am-5pm Mon-Sat, 10am-5pm Sun) is an iconic SA company, selling mostly Australian-grown dried fruits, chocolates and nuts: brilliant for a picnic pick-me-up.

🛏 Sleeping & Eating

Caithness Manor B&B
B&B $$

(☑08-8564 2761; www.caithness.com.au; 12 Hill St W; d incl breakfast from $190; ✱🛜) The sign here says 'Ceud Mile Faille', Gaelic for '100,000 Welcomes'. A short walk from town, the house is actually a refurbished girls' school, but there's not an ink stain or spitball in sight – just two cottage-style, ground-floor units with hillside views over the town (and a pool!).

TOP CHOICE Blond Coffee
CAFE $

(www.blondcoffee.com.au; 60 Murray St; mains $9-16; ⊙breakfast & lunch) An elegant, breezy room with huge windows facing the main street, Blond serves nutty coffee and all-day cafe fare, including awesome pumpkin, capsicum and fetta muffins. There's also a cheese-and-smallgoods counter, and a wall full of local produce (vinegar, olive oil, biscuits and confectionery). Fake-blonde botox tourists share the window seats with down-to-earth regulars.

Angaston Hotel
PUB FARE $

(☑08-8564 2428; www.plushgroup.com/angaston.html; 60 Murray St; mains $13-24; ⊙lunch & dinner) The better looking of the town's two pubs, the friendly Angaston serves Barossa wines

and the cheapest steaks this side of Argentina. Just try to ignore the *Triumph of Silenus* mural on the dining room wall ('Oh it's hideous!' says the barmaid). There are bog-basic pub rooms upstairs (single/double $50/70), with a renovation rumoured for some years now – expect a price hike if it ever happens.

Vintners Bar & Grill   MODERN AUSTRALIAN **$$**
(☑08-8564 2488; www.vintners.com.au; cnr Stockwell & Nuriootpa Rds; mains $17-35; ☺lunch daily, dinner Mon-Sat) One of the Barossa's landmark restaurants, Vintners stresses simple elegance in both food and atmosphere. Their dining room has an open fire, vineyard views and bolts of crisp white linen; menus concentrate on local produce (pray the chargrilled roo with crusted parsnip is on the menu when you visit).

Barossa Farmers Market   MARKET
(www.barossafarmersmarket.com; cnr Stockwell & Nuriootpa Rds; ☺7.30-11.30am Sat) Happens near Vintners Bar & Grill every Saturday.

CLARE VALLEY

Take a couple of days to check out the Clare Valley, about two hours north of Adelaide. At the centre of the fertile Mid-North agricultural district, the skinny valley produces world-class Rieslings and reds. This is gorgeous countryside, with open skies, rounded hills, stands of large gums and wind rippling over wheat fields. Towns here date from the 1840s, many built to service the Burra copper mines.

B&Bs and self-contained cottages prevail around the valley, but unless you get a good package try to avoid a weekend visit when rates verge on outright greed. The Clare Valley visitor information centre can assist with accommodation bookings.

⌖ Tours

For Clare Valley tours from Adelaide, see p717.

Clare Valley Experiences   SIGHTSEEING
(☑08-8842 1880; www.clarevalleyexperiences. com; tours up to 4 people $220) Choose-your-own-adventure Clare tours in a flash Merc.

Clare Valley Tours   SIGHTSEEING, FOOD & WINE
(☑08-8843 8066, 0418 832 812; www.cvtours. com.au; 4-/6-hr tours $86/100) Mini-bus tours taking in the Clare wineries, Martindale Hall and Burra.

Swagabout Tours   SIGHTSEEING, FOOD & WINE
(☑0408 845 378; www.swagabouttours.com. au) Dependable one-/two-day Clare Valley trips ($135/510).

★ Festivals & Events

A Day on the Green   MUSIC
(www.adayonthegreen.com.au) The Barossa's favourite festival comes to the Clare Valley in February/March. Lionel Ritchie, Crowded House, Roxy Music...

Clare Valley Gourmet Weekend   FOOD & WINE
(www.clarevalleygourmet.com.au) A frenzy of wine, food and music in May.

Clare Show   AGRICULTURAL
(www.sacountryshows.com) The largest one-day show in SA, held in October.

ⓘ Information
Clare Valley Visitor Information Centre
(☑1800 242 131, 08-8842 2131; www.clare valley.com.au; cnr Spring Gully & Main North Rd, Clare; ☺9am-5pm Mon-Fri, 10am-4pm Sat & Sun; @) Shiny centre with local info, internet access and valley-wide accommodation bookings.

ⓘ Getting There & Around
BICYCLE You can hire a bike to pelt around the wineries from Cogwebs in Auburn, or Clare Valley Cycle Hire or Riesling Trail Bike Hire in Clare. Rates are around $20/35 per half/full day.

BUS Yorke Peninsula Coaches (www.yp coaches.com.au) departs Adelaide daily for Auburn ($24, 2¼ hours) and Clare ($32, 2¾ hours), extending to Burra ($32, 3¼ hours) on Monday and Thursday.

TAXI Clare Valley Taxi Service (☑0419 847 900) can drop-off/pick-up anywhere along the Riesling Trail.

Auburn
POP 320

Sleepy, 1849 Auburn – the Clare Valley's southernmost village – is a leave-the-back-door-open-and-the-keys-in-the-ignition kinda town, with a time-warp vibe that makes you feel like you're in an old black-and-white photograph. The streets are defined by beautifully preserved, hand-built stone buildings; cottage gardens overflow with untidy blooms. Pick up a copy of the *Walk with History at Auburn* brochure from the Clare Valley visitor information centre.

Now on the main route to the valley's wineries, Auburn initially serviced bullockies and South American muleteers whose wagons – up to 100 a day – trundled between Burra's copper mines and Port Wakefield.

DON'T MISS

CLARE VALLEY WINERIES

Despite a warm climate, the Clare Valley's cool micro-climates (around rivers, creeks and gullies) noticeably affect the wines, enabling Clare Valley whites to be laid down for long periods and still be brilliant. The valley produces some of the best Riesling going around, plus grand Semillon and Shiraz. Our favourite cellar doors:

» **Skillogalee** (☏08-8843 4311; www.skillogalee.com; Trevarrick Rd, Sevenhill; ☺10am-5pm) Quite possibly our favourite SA winery (OK, so it is our favourite), Skillogalee is a small family outfit known for its spicy Shiraz, fabulous food and top-notch Riesling (a glass of which is like kissing a pretty girl in summer). Kick back with a long, lazy lunch on the verandah (mains $20 to $30; bookings advised).

» **Pikes** (www.pikeswines.com.au; Polish Hill River Rd, Sevenhill; ☺10am-4pm) The industrious Pike family set up shop in 1984, and have been producing show-stopping Riesling ever since (and Shiraz, Sangiovese, Pino Grigio, Viognier...). A beautiful cellar door in a 100-year-old wool shed. They also bottle up the zingy 'Oakbank Pilsener', if you're feeling dry.

» **Knappstein** (www.knappsteinwines.com.au; 2 Pioneer Ave, Clare; ☺9am-5pm Mon-Fri, 11am-5pm Sat, 11am-4pm Sun) Taking a minimal-intervention approach to wine making, Knappstein has built quite a name for itself. Shiraz and Riesling steal the show, but they also make a mighty fine Semillon Sauvignon Blanc blend (and beer!).

» **Kilikanoon Wines** (www.kilikanoon.com.au; Penna La, Sevenhill; ☺11am-5pm Thu-Mon) In a modest little front room in a modest little house, Kilikanoon offers up superb Shiraz, Grenache, Semillon and of course Riesling for your consideration. Love the Oracle Shiraz.

» **Taylors Wines** (www.taylorswines.com.au; Taylors Rd, Auburn; ☺9am-5pm Mon-Fri, 10am-5pm Sat, 10am-4pm Sun) Sure, it's a massive nationwide operation with a heinous mock-castle cellar door, but the wine here is fit for royalty (love the Cab Sav).

Clare Valley's largest winery Taylors Wines lurks on the edge of town, while the brilliant 25km Riesling Trail (p773) starts (or ends) at the restored Auburn Train Station.

Cogwebs (www.cogwebs.com.au; 30 Main North Rd; ☺8am-6pm Thu-Tue; @) offers internet access and bike hire (per half/full day $25/40).

🛏 Sleeping & Eating

Auburn Shiraz Motel　　　　MOTEL **$**
(☏08-8849 2125; www.auburnshirazmotel.com.au; Main North Rd; s/d/tr from $70/80/100; ❄) This small motel on the Adelaide side of town has been proudly renovated with Shiraz-coloured render and Cabernet-coloured doors. There are nine bright, spotless units and friendly hosts – great value.

Rising Sun Hotel　　　　PUB FARE **$$**
(www.aubrnsa.com.au; Main North Rd; mains $14-22; ☺lunch & dinner) This classic 1850 pub has a huge rep for its atmosphere, food and accommodation. The pub food is unpretentious (but unremarkable), with plenty of local wines to try. En-suite hotel rooms and cottage mews rooms out the back (doubles from $90 and $115 respectively) have solid

occupancy – book well in advance (dinner and overnight packages a speciality).

Cygnets at Auburn　　　　CAFE **$$**
(www.cygnetsatauburn.com.au; Main North Rd; mains $12-22; ☺breakfast & lunch Fri-Mon) This gourmet cafe-providore serves and stocks local produce matched with Clare Valley wines. There's a wine and tapas bar for grazers, the best coffee in town, and a mighty fine rustic chicken pie. There's also B&B accommodation out the back in the old 1860 stables (from $150 midweek).

Mintaro

POP 230

A few kilometres up the road from Auburn, heritage-listed Mintaro (founded 1849) is a stone village that could have been lifted out of the Cotswolds and plonked into the Australian bush. There are very few architectural intrusions from the 1900s – the whole place seems to have been largely left to its own devices. A fact for your next trivia night: Mintaro slate is used internationally in the manufacture of billiard tables.

There's nowhere else in the world quite like **Martindale Hall** (www.martindalehall.com; Manoora Rd; adult/child/concession $10/2.50/7.50; ⊙11am-4pm Mon-Fri, noon-4pm Sat & Sun), an astonishing 1880 manor 3km from Mintaro. Built for young pastoralist Edmund Bowman Jnr, who subsequently partied away the family fortune (OK, so drought and plummeting wool prices played a part...but it was mostly the partying), the manor features original furnishings, a magnificent blackwood staircase, Mintaro-slate billiard table and a museumlike smoking room. The hall starred as Appleyard College in the 1975 Peter Weir film *Picnic at Hanging Rock*. B&B and Dinner plus B&B packages allow you to spend a spooky night here ($120 and $250 respectively).

Hedge your bets at **Mintaro Maze** (www.mintaromaze.com; Jacka Rd; adult/child $10/7; ⊙10am-4pm Mon-Thu & school holidays) as you try to find your way into the middle and back out again.

🛏 Sleeping & Eating

Reilly's MODERN AUSTRALIAN $$
(☏08-8843 9013; www.reillyswines.com.au; cnr Hill & Leasingham Rds; mains $16-28; ⊙10am-4pm) Reilly's cellar door and restaurant started life as a cobbler's shop in 1856, and has been a winery since the '90s. An organic vegie garden out the back supplies the attached restaurant, which is decorated with local art and serves creative, seasonal Mod Oz food (antipasto, rabbit terrine, mushroom soufflé). The owners also rent out a three-bedroom house and three one-bedroom units on Hill St (doubles from $145).

Magpie & Stump Hotel PUB FARE $$
(Burra St; meals $10-25; ⊙lunch & dinner Tue-Sun) The old Magpie & Stump was first licensed in 1851, and was a vital rehydration point for the copper carriers travelling between Burra and Port Wakefield. Schnitzels and steaks, log fires, pool table, Mintaro-slate floors, a beer garden and a brown dog sniffing around – the perfect pub?

Clare

POP 5460

Named after County Clare in Ireland, this town was founded in 1842 and is the biggest in the valley, but it's a little thin on charm. All the requisite services are here (post, supermarket, fuel, internet etc), but you'll have a more interesting Clare Valley experience sleeping out of town.

👁 Sights & Activities

Most folks are here for the wine, but Clare does have some worthy heritage-listed buildings. Pick up the *Clare Historic Walk* pamphlet from the visitor information centre.

The 1850 cop shop and courthouse is now the **Old Police Station Museum** (www.nationaltrustsa.org.au; adult/child $2/50¢; ⊙10am-noon & 2-4pm Sat & Sun), displaying Victorian clothing, old photos, furniture and domestic bits and pieces.

About 3km southwest of Sevenhill, the 400-hectare **Spring Gully Conservation Park** (www.environment.sa.gov.au) features blue-gum forest, red stringybarks and 18m-high winter waterfalls. There are plenty of bird twitters, critters and trails too.

Hit the **Riesling Trail** on two wheels:

Clare Valley Cycle Hire (www.clarevalleycyclehire.com.au; 32 Victoria Rd; bike hire per half/full day $17/25) Can also collect and freight any wine you buy en route – bless their cotton socks!

Riesling Trail Bike Hire (www.rtcvcottages.com.au/bikehire; 10 Warenda Rd; bike hire per half/full day $20/35, tandems $35/50) Quality two-wheelers (including two-seaters) right on the Riesling Trail itself.

🛏 Sleeping

Batunga B&B B&B $$
(☏08-8843 0120; www.battunga.com.au; Upper Skilly Rd, Watervale; d/q incl breakfast $175/285; ❄) On an 80-hectare farm over the hills 2km west of Watervale (it's a little hard to find – ask for directions), Batunga has four modern apartments in two stone cottages with Mintaro-slate floors, barbecues, kitchenettes and wood fires. This is beautiful country – undulating farmland studded with huge eucalypts.

Riesling Trail & Clare Valley Cottages B&B $$
(☏0427 842 232; www.rtcvcottages.com.au; 9 Warenda Rd; 1-/2-/3-bed cottage d incl breakfast from $145/170/170, extra adult/child $50/30; ❄) A newish operation offering five contemporary one-bedroom stone cottages, plus one two-bed and one three-bed cottage, all encircled by country gardens and right on the Riesling Trail. Handily, the owners also run Riesling Trail Bike Hire. Good deals on multinight stays.

Clare Valley Motel MOTEL $$
(☏08-8842 2799; www.clarevalleymotel.com.au; 74a Main North Rd; d $108-139; ❄🛜💻) Looking

THE RIESLING TRAIL

Following the course of a disused railway line between Auburn and Clare, the fabulous Riesling Trail (www.southaustraliantrails.com) is 25km of wines, wheels and wonderment. It's primarily a cycling trail, but the gentle gradient means you can walk or push a pram along it just as easily. It's a two-hour dash end to end on a bike, but why hurry? There are three loop track detours to explore and dozens of cellar doors to tempt you along the way.

For bike hire, see Clare Valley Cycle Hire in Clare, or Cogwebs in Auburn.

like some kind of ranch from Vermont, this huge place has four different wings, offering basic motel rooms up to swish spa suites. The restaurant (mains $25 to $27) serves dinner nightly (except Sunday) – the garlic prawns rule.

Clare Caravan Park CARAVAN PARK $
(☑08-8842 2724; www.clarecaravanpark.com.au; Main North Rd; unpowered/powered sites $20/29, cabins from $85; ✳☎⬛) This huge, efficiently run park 4km south of town towards Auburn has secluded sites, all en-suite cabins, a creek and giant gum trees. There's also an inground pool, and it's a stone's throw from the Clare Valley visitor information centre.

✗ Eating

Taminga Hotel PUB FARE $$
(☑08-8842 2808; www.tamingahotel.com.au; 302 Main North Rd; mains $16-27; ☺lunch & dinner) The most reliable of Clare's three pubs when it comes to food, the recently tarted-up Taminga looks good: polished floorboards, exposed stone walls and pressed-tin ceilings. Pub classics are what you're here for: surf 'n' turf, steak-and-kidney pie and schnitzels.

Last Word Inn CAFE $$
(☑08-8842 1453; Main North Rd; mains $12-18; ☺breakfast Sat & Sun, lunch & dinner daily) Before it was an uptempo cafe and cellar door, an old bloke lived here with dirt floors and no electricity! Things have improved: expect tasty pasta and salads, a few Greek classics and decent pizzas (takeaways welcome). Last Word Wines are here too, adopting an unpretentious and quirky approach to the grape trade.

Artisans Table MODERN AUSTRALIAN $$
(☑08-8842 1796; www.artisanstable.com.au; Wendouree Rd; mains $28-32; ☺lunch Wed-Sun, dinner Wed-Sat) This mod, airy, hillside bar-restaurant has a broad, sunny balcony – perfect for a bottle of local Riesling and some internationally inspired culinary offerings: a bit of Moroccan, a bit of Chinese, a bit of Malaysian... The fish of the day is surprisingly good this far inland!

ⓘ Information

Clare Valley Visitor Information Centre
(☑1800 242 131, 08-8842 2131; www.clarevalley.com.au; cnr Spring Gully & Main North Rd, Clare; ☺9am-5pm Mon-Fri, 10am-4pm Sat & Sun; @) Local info, internet access and valley-wide accommodation bookings.
Domain Internet Café (202 Main North Rd; ☺3-6pm Mon-Fri)

YORKE PENINSULA

A couple of hours west of Adelaide, boot-shaped Yorke Peninsula bills itself as 'Agriculturally Rich – Naturally Beautiful'. It does have a certain agrarian beauty – deep azure summer skies and yellow wheat fields on hazy, gently rolling hills – but if you're looking for cosmopolitan riches and tourist trappings, you won't find much to engage you.

That said, far-flung Innes National Park on the peninsula's southern tip is well worth visiting. The coastline here is gorgeous, with great surf, roaming emus, kangaroos, ospreys and sea eagles, and southern right whales and dolphins cruising by.

For history buffs, the peninsula's north has a trio of towns called the Copper Triangle: Moonta (the mine), Wallaroo (the smelter) and Kadina (the service town). Settled by Cornish miners, this area drove the regional economy following a copper boom in the early 1860s.

☞ Tours

Adjahdura Land INDIGENOUS
(☑0429 367 121; www.adjahdura.com.au; half-/full-day tours $55/120) Highly regarded Aboriginal cultural tours of the peninsula, exploring the incredibly long Indigenous association with this country. Two-, three- and five-day tours are also available.

Avabreak Adventure Tours SIGHTSEEING
(☑8854 5351; www.avabreak.com.au; 5-days incl accommodation $890) Multiday tours

ex-Adelaide taking in the Barossa Valley before heading to Yorke Peninsula. Lots of swimming, wildlife, bushwalking and history.

❶ Information

Copper Coast Visitor Information Centre (☑1800 654 991, 08-8821 2333; www.yorke peninsula.sa.gov.au; Farm Shed, 50 Moonta Rd, Kadina; ☺9am-5pm Mon-Fri, 10am-4pm Sat & Sun) Yorke Peninsula's main visitor info centre.

York Peninsula website (www.yorkepeninsula. com.au)

❶ Getting There & Around

BICYCLE Based in Moonta, **Copper Coast Eco Bikes** (☑08-8825 2449; bike hire per hr/half-day $10/50) rents out bicycles.

BUS Yorke Peninsula Coaches (www.yp coaches.com.au) services the peninsula daily from Adelaide, stopping at Kadina ($28, 2¼ hours), Wallaroo ($28, 2½ hours) and Moonta ($28, 2¾ hours) and travelling as far south as Yorketown ($44, four hours).

FERRY SEASA (www.seasa.com.au) runs a sporadic vehicle ferry between Wallaroo (on the Yorke Peninsula) and Lucky Bay (on the Eyre Peninsula) – a shortcut shaving 350km off the drive via Port Augusta. Ferries weren't running at the time of writing, but should be operational again by the time you read this. Expect to pay around $150 one-way for a car, plus $50 per person. The voyage takes around 1¾ hours one way.

West Coast

Fronting Spencer Gulf, the west coast has a string of shallow swimming beaches, plus the Copper Triangle towns, all a short drive from one other. **Kernewek Lowender** (www. kernewek.org), aka the Copper Coast Cornish Festival, happens around here in May in odd-numbered years.

For a far-flung Yorkes experience, try **Point Turton** (population 250) in the southwest. Superfriendly **Point Turton Caravan Park** (☑08-8854 5222; www.pointturton.com; Bayview Rd; unpowered/powered sites $22/26, cabins $55-140; ❄🎧) has lovely grassy sites and cabins overlooking the sea.

KADINA
POP 4000

Baking-hot, inland Kadina has some impressive copper-era civic buildings and a slew of pubs, car yards and petrol stations. The Copper Coast visitor information centre (above) is here. Behind it is an amazing collection of old farming, mining and domestic bits and pieces at the **Farm Shed Museum**

(www.nationaltrustsa.org.au; 50 Moonta Rd; adult/child/concession/family $8/3/6/20; ☺9am-5pm Mon-Fri, 10am-4pm Sat & Sun), which gives an engaging insight into olden days and ways.

Kadina Village Motel (☑08-8821 1920; www.kadinavillagemotel.websyte.com.au; 28 Port Rd; s/d $70/80; ❄) is a retro, U-shaped joint on the road to Wallaroo; basic, clean motel digs if all you need is a bed.

WALLAROO
POP 3000

Wallaroo is a town on the up: when the Eyre Peninsula ferry is running, the town is full of folks. There's a huge new subdivision north of town, and the shiny new **Copper Cove Marina** (www.coppercove.com.au) is full of expensive boats.

A stoic 1865 post office houses the **Heritage & Nautical Museum** (www.nationaltrust sa.org.au; cnr Jetty Rd & Emu St; adult/child $5/2; ☺10am-4pm Mon-Fri, from 2pm Sat & Sun), with tales of square-rigged English ships and George the pickled giant squid.

Once a grand temperance hotel, **Sonbern Lodge Motel** (☑08-8823 2291; www.sonbern lodgemotel.com.au; 18 John Tce; s $65-95, d $80-110; ❄) is an old-fashioned charmer, right down to the old wooden balcony and antique wind-up phone. Upstairs are basic pub-style rooms, with newish motel units out the back.

The new multistorey **Wallaroo Marina Apartments** (☑08-8823 4068; www.wallaroo apartments.com.au; 11 Heritage Dve; d from $159; ❄) at the marina on the northern edge of town has spiffy suites, plus cold beer and pub meals downstairs in the **Coopers Alehouse** (☑08-8823 2488; www.wallaroomarina hotel.com/dining; mains $12-29; ☺lunch & dinner).

MOONTA
POP 3070

In the late 19th century, the Moonta copper mine was the richest in Australia. These days the town, which calls itself 'Australia's Little Cornwall', maintains a faded glory, with a couple of decent pubs, and shallow Moonta Bay 1km west of the town centre.

Moonta Visitor Information Centre (☑08-8825 1891; info@moontatourism.org.au; Old Railway Station, Blanche Tce; ☺9am-5pm) has a smattering of history pamphlets, and details on the **Moonta Heritage Site** 1.5km east of town. The site includes the excellent **Moonta Mines Museum** (Verran Tce; adult/child $6/2; ☺1-4pm), once a grand school with 1100 pupils; the **Moonta Mines Sweet Shop** (☺10am-4pm) across the road; and a

fully restored **Miner's Cottage** (Verco St; adult/child $3/1; ☉1.30-4pm Wed, Sat & Sun).

Around 3km north of town, the **Wheal Hughes Copper Mine** (☎08-8825 1891; Moonta-Wallaroo Rd; tours adult/child/concession/family $15/8/13/45; ☉tours 10.30am, 12.30pm & 2.30pm Wed, Sat & Sun) offers a gander at a contemporary mine worked until 1993. Book through the visitor information centre.

The flashy **Seagate Bistro Motel** (☎08-8825 3270; www.seagatemoontabay.com.au; 171 Bay Rd; d $150-220; ❂❈) is an octagonal (or is it a squashed dodecahedron?) motel right by Moonta Bay jetty. The pick of the rooms upstairs have sweeping oceanic views, as does the downstairs bistro (mains $18 to $32, open for lunch and dinner), which serves upbeat pub grub – perfect for a sunset beer!

Moonta Bay Caravan Park (☎08-8825 2406; www.yorkepeninsula.net.au; Foreshore, Moonta Bay; unpowered/powered sites $27/29, cabins with/without spa $139/97; ❈) is handy to the beach and jetty, and has decent luxury cabins with spas. The grassy camping areas are almost on the beach.

After a hard day's copper mining, swing your shovel into the **Cornish Kitchen** (12 Ellen St; items $3-6; ☉breakfast & lunch Mon-Sat) for the ultimate Cornish pastie.

East Coast

The east-coast road along Gulf St Vincent traces the coast within 1km or 2km of the water. En route, roads dart east to sandy beaches and holiday towns. Like the suburban Adelaide beaches across the gulf, this is prime crab-fishing territory.

Most of the coastal towns have a pub and a caravan park or camping ground, including unpretentious **Port Vincent**. Need a bunk? Try **Tuckerway Hostel** (☎08-8853 7285; tuckerway14@bigpond.com; 14 Lime Kiln Rd, Port Vincent; dm $21; ❈), a concrete-block bunker uphill from the town with simple dorms and a big kitchen.

Further south, **Edithburgh** has a tidal swimming pool in a small cove; from the cliff-tops, views extend to sandy **Troubridge Island Conservation Park** (www.environment.sa.gov.au). You can stay the night at the **Troubridge Island Lighthouse** (☎08-8852 6290; www.lighthouse.net.au; per adult/child incl transfers $80/30, min charge $320). It sleeps 10; BYO food and linen. Little penguins still live here,

but the island is steadily eroding – what the sea wants, the sea will have...

Back on the mainland, **Troubridge Hotel/Motel** (☎08-8852 6013; www.troubridge.budgetmotelchain.com.au; cnr Edith & Blanche Sts; s/d $88/98; ❈) is a low-lying corner pub on Edithburgh's main street with basic motel digs out the back.

Southern Yorke Peninsula's main town is **Yorketown** (population 750) – try for a caravan-park bed here if the seaside towns are packed to the gills in summer.

South Coast & Innes National Park

The peninsula's south coast is largely sheltered from the Southern Ocean's fury by Kangaroo Island, so there are some great **swimming** beaches along here. The surf finds its way through around Troubridge Point and Cape Spencer, where the **Cutloose Yorkes Classic** (www.swellnet.com.au) surf comp happens every October.

Cape Spencer is part of **Innes National Park** (www.environment.sa.gov.au; per car $8.50), where sheer cliffs plunge into indigo waters and rocky offshore islands hide small coves and sandy beaches. **Marion Bay** (www.marionbay.com.au), just outside the park, and **Stenhouse Bay** and **Pondalowie Bay**, both within the park, are the main local settlements. Pondalowie Bay has a bobbing lobster-fishing fleet and a gnarly surf beach (keep one eye on the swell if you're swimming).

The rusty ribs of the 711-tonne steel barque *Ethel*, which foundered in 1904, arc forlornly from the sands just south of Pondalowie Bay. Follow the sign past the Cape Spencer turn-off to the ghost-town ruins of **Inneston**, a gypsum-mining community abandoned in 1930.

The national park also has bushy **camp sites** (per car $6-16). Our favourite spot is Pondalowie, or try Cable Bay for beach access, Surfers for surfing or Browns Beach for fishing. Alternatively, the heritage **lodges** (per night $120-170) at Inneston sleep four to 10 people and have showers and cooking facilities. Book ahead through **Innes National Park Visitor Information Centre** (☎08-8854 3200; ☉10.30am-3pm Wed-Sat) at the park entrance. BYO drinking water in summer.

TOP CHOICE **Marion Bay Tavern & Motel** (☎08-8854 4044; www.marionbaymotel.com.au; Jetty Rd; s/d/tr $110/130/150; ❈❂) is the highlight of

tiny Marion Bay, with a wing of five spiffy motel rooms out the back (white walls, flat-screen TVs, nice linen). The glass-fronted dining room (mains $14 to $32; open for lunch and dinner) looks out over the bay and puts an Indonesian spin on pub standards (try the coriander-spiced salt-and-pepper squid).

Innes Park Trading Post & Rhino's Tavern (☑08-8854 4078; www.rhinostavern.com.au; 1 Stenhouse Bay Rd, Stenhouse Bay; ☺8am-late) is a one-stop shop for fuel, bait, groceries and takeaway food, or kick back with a beer and a pub meal (mains $15 to $30, open for lunch and dinner).

EYRE PENINSULA & THE WEST COAST

The vast, straw-coloured triangle of Eyre Peninsula is Australia's big-sky country, and is considered by galloping gourmands to be the promised land of seafood. Meals out here rarely transpire without the option of trying the local oysters, tuna and whiting. Sublime national parks punctuate the coast, along with world-class surf breaks and lazy holiday towns, thinning out as you head west towards the Great Australian Bight, the Nullarbor Plain and Western Australia.

Eyre Peninsula's photogenic wild-western flank is an important breeding ground for southern right whales, Australian sea lions and great white sharks (the scariest scenes of *Jaws* were shot here). There are some memorable opportunities to encounter these submariners along the way.

Online, visit www.eyrepeninsula.info.

☞ Tours

Wilderness Wanders   WILDERNESS
(☑08-8684 5001; www.wildernesswanders.com.au) Multiday explorations of Eyre Peninsula with lots of walking, wildlife and wilderness. The eight-day 'Walking on Eyre' tour ($3965) includes transport, accommodation, national park entry fees and most meals.

Southern Blue Tours   SIGHTSEEING
(☑08-8683 1330; www.southernblue.travel) Full-day tours to Lincoln National Park ($350), the Coffin Bay region ($245) and half-day Port Lincoln tours ($135).

❶ Getting There & Away
AIR Regional Express (www.regionalexpress.com.au) operates daily flights from Adelaide

to Whyalla (one-way from $113), Port Lincoln (from $118) and Ceduna (from $210).

BUS Premier Stateliner (www.premierstateliner.com.au) operates daily buses from Adelaide to Port Augusta ($53, 4¼ hours), Whyalla ($60, 5½ hours), Port Lincoln ($105, 9¾ hours), Streaky Bay ($109, 10 hours) and Ceduna ($122, 11¼ hours).

Port Augusta
POP 13,900

At the head of Spencer Gulf, Port Augusta is having an identity crisis. Is it the gateway to the outback, or the start of the southern Flinders Ranges? Is it the first town on the Eyre Peninsula, or the last big town until Kalgoorlie? The answer is all of the above. From the 'Crossroads of Australia', highways and railways roll west across the Nullarbor into WA, north to the Flinders Ranges or Darwin, south to Adelaide or Port Lincoln, and east to Sydney. Not a bad position!

The old town centre has considerable appeal, with some elegant old buildings and a revitalised waterfront: locals cast lines into the blue, and Indigenous kids back-flip off jetties. The town has had problems with alcoholism (the streets are now a dry zone), but the vibe is rarely menacing.

◉ Sights & Activities

FREE **Australian Arid Lands Botanic Garden**   GARDEN
(www.australian-aridlands-botanic-garden.org; Stuart Hwy; tours adult/child $8/5.50; ☺9am-5pm Mon-Fri, 10am-4pm Sat & Sun, tours 10am Mon-Fri) Just north of town, the excellent garden has 250 hectares of sand hills, clay flats and desert flora and fauna. Explore on your own, or take a guided tour.

Wadlata Outback Centre   MUSEUM
(www.wadlata.sa.gov.au; 41 Flinders Tce; adult/child/family $13/8.50/29; ☺9am-5.30pm Mon-Fri, 10am-4pm Sat & Sun) The highlight here is the 'Outback Tunnel of Time', tracing local Aboriginal and European histories using audio-visual displays, interactive exhibits and a distressingly big snake.

Port Augusta Aquatic & Outdoor Adventure Centre   OUTDOOR ACTIVITIES
(☑08-8642 2699, 0408 830 191; www.augustaoutdoors.com.au; cnr Gibson & El Alamein Sts; ☺8am-8pm Oct-Mar, by appointment Apr-Sep) Offers lessons and gear rental for kayaking, windsurfing, rock-climbing, abseiling, snor-

Eyre Peninsula & Yorke Peninsula

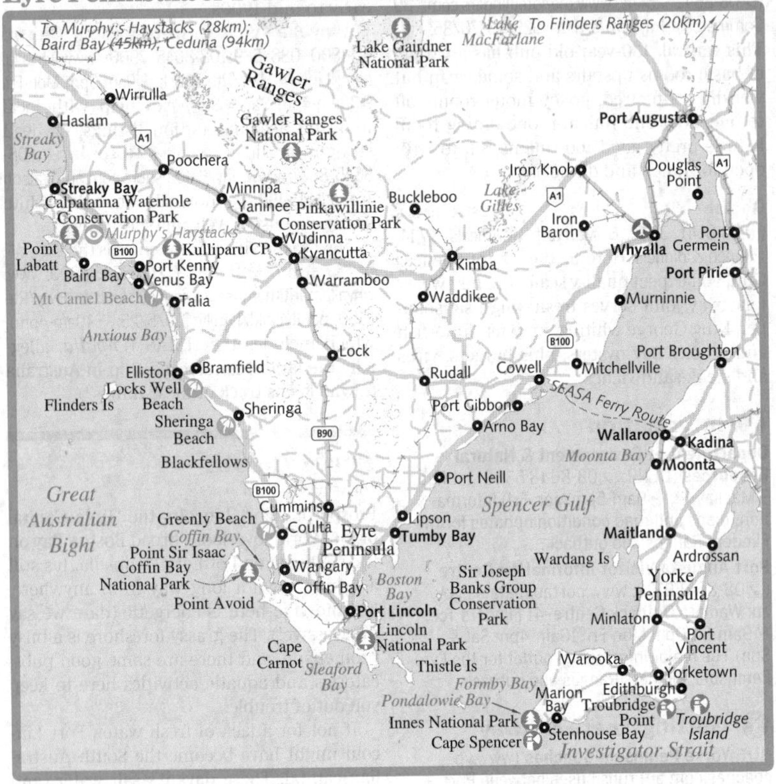

kelling, orienteering, bushwalking, sailing... Bike hire is $25 per half day.

Tours

Flinders Ranges Water Cruises CRUISES
(☎0438 857 001; www.augustawestside.com.au; per person from $45) Two-hour morning eco-cruises to the top of the Gulf (any dolphins?), and two-hour sunset cruises ($55).

Gulf Getaways CRUISES
(☎08-8642 6827, 0408 445 133; www.gulfgetaways.com.au; per person incl lunch $45) A 2½-hour eco-cruise on the Spencer Gulf, checking out mangroves, dolphins and bird life.

Sleeping & Eating

Oasis Apartments APARTMENTS $$
(☎1800 008 648, 08-8648 9000; www.majestichotels.com.au; foreshore, Marryatt St; apt $135-190; ❄@≋) Catering to conventioneers who regularly blow through town, this group of 75 luxury units (studios to two-bedroom) with jaunty designs is right by the water. All rooms have washing machines, dryers, TVs, fridges, microwaves, fortresslike security and flashes of interior design.

Best Western Standpipe MOTEL $$
(☎08-8642 4033; www.standpipe.com.au; cnr Stuart Hwy & Hwy 1; d/tr/f/apt from $125/145/190/250; ❄🛜≋) The sprawling Standpipe attracts government delegates and business types with its 85 comfortable 1980s-ish units. And the Indian restaurant here (mains $12 to $17; open for lunch and dinner) is unbelievable!

Shoreline Caravan Park CARAVAN PARK $
(☎08-8642 2965; www.shorelinecaravanpark.com.au; Gardiner Ave; unpowered/powered sites $22/25, dm $18, cabins & units $55-120; ❄🛜≋) It's a dusty site a fair walk from town (and the shoreline when the tide is out), but the budget cabins here are beaut, plus there are simple four-bed dorm units for backpackers.

Hotel Flinders
PUB, MOTEL $

(☑08-8642 2544; www.thehotelflinders.com; 39 Commercial Rd; dm/s/d/tr $25/55/70/85; ❄) This central, 130-year-old pub has a variety of basic rooms upstairs and some clean but weirdly configured, pokey motel rooms off to one side. The Italian-prone dining room here is pretty good too (mains $15 to $40; open for lunch and dinner).

Gottabe Fish
FISH & CHIPS $

(☑08-8641 3777; 6 Marryatt St; meals $7-14; ⊙lunch & dinner) Here at the top of Spencer Gulf, you expect quality seafood. This sweaty takeaway joint serves fresh king fish, snapper, King George whiting, prawns, butterfish and Smoky Bay oysters, plus burgers, yiros and steak sandwiches.

ℹ Information

Department of Environment & Natural Resources (DENR; ☑08-8648 5300; 1st floor, 9 Mackay St; ⊙9am-5pm Mon-Fri) Information, maps and road condition updates for the Flinders Ranges and outback.

Port Augusta Visitor Information Centre (☑08-8641 9193; www.portaugusta.sa.gov. au; Wadlata Outback Centre, 41 Flinders Tce; ⊙9am-5.30pm Mon-Fri, 10am-4pm Sat & Sun) The major information outlet for the Eyre Peninsula, Flinders Ranges and outback.

ℹ Getting There & Away

BUS Yorke Peninsula Coaches (www.yp coaches.com.au) runs buses between Port Augusta and Quorn in the Flinders Ranges on Fridays ($6, 45 minutes). **Premier Stateliner** (www.premierstateliner.com.au) has daily buses between Adelaide and Port Augusta ($53, 4¼ hours).

TRAIN The famous *Ghan* train connects Adelaide with Darwin via Port Augusta, and the *Indian Pacific* (between Perth and Sydney) connects with the *Ghan* at Port Augusta. See p741 for details. **Pichi Richi Railway** (www.prr. org.au; one-way adult/child/concession/family $50/18/47/118) runs between Port Augusta and Quorn (two hours) on Saturdays.

Whyalla

POP 21,100

An hour's drive south of Port Augusta is Whyalla – the third-biggest city in SA – its deep-water port sustaining steel mills, oil and gas refineries and an apocalyptic morass of chugging chimneys, portworks and industrial estates. Ugly, yes, but the old town has some good pubs and well-preserved domestic architecture from the early to mid-1900s.

Whyalla Visitor Information Centre (☑1800 088 589; 08-8645 7900; www.whyalla. com; Lincoln Hwy/Rte B100; ⊙9am-5pm Mon-Fri, 9.30am-4pm Sat & Sun) can help with local info and accommodation listings, or head straight for the **Foreshore Motor Inn** (☑08-8645 8877; www.whyallaforeshore.com.au; Watson Tce; d $145-160; ❄) down by the wide white sandy expanse of Whyalla's foreshore.

Next to the visitor info centre is the **Whyalla Maritime Museum** (☑08-8645 8900; www. whyallamaritimemuseum.com.au; Lincoln Hwy/Rte B100; adult/child/family $10/5/25; ⊙10am-4pm), which includes the HMAS *Whyalla*, allegedly the largest landlocked ship in Australia (...who keeps track of these things?).

Port Lincoln

POP 15,000

Prosperous Port Lincoln, the 'Tuna Capital of the World', overlooks broad Boston Bay on the southern end of Eyre Peninsula. It's still a fishing town a long way from anywhere, but the vibe here is energetic (dare we say progressive!). The grassy foreshore is a busy promenade, and there are some good pubs, eateries and aquatic activities here to keep you out of trouble.

If not for a lack of fresh water, Port Lincoln might have become the South Australian capital. These days it's salt water (and the tuna therein) that keeps the town ticking. A guaranteed friend-maker here is to slip Dean Lukin's name into every conversation. Straight off the tuna boats, Big Dean won the Super Heavyweight weightlifting gold medal at the 1984 Olympics in LA – what a champ!

◎ Sights & Activities

The annual **Tunarama Festival** (www.tunara ma.net) on the Australia Day weekend in January celebrates every finny facet of the tuna-fishing industry. Highlights include tuna tossing, keg rolling, slippery-pole climbing, boat-building comps, stalls and bands.

Bite into some extreme underwater adventure with **Calypso Star Charters** (☑1300 788 378, 08-8682 3939; www.sharkcage diving.com.au; 1-day dive $495), which runs cage dives with great white sharks around Neptune Islands. Book in advance.

Short on bravado? Sea lions and tuna might be more your speed. Carbon-neutral

Adventure Bay Charters (☑0488 428 862; www.adventurebaycharters.com.au) takes you swimming with sea lions (adult/child $195/145) and Port Lincoln's famous tuna (adult/child $65/45), which you hand feed in a fish-farm enclosure.

For info on local surfing and diving, visit Port Lincoln Dive & Surf Centre (sam@ptlincolnsurfdive.com.au; 1 King St; ⊗9am-5.30pm Mon-Fri, 9am-1pm Sat). There are good breaks for beginners and intermediate surfers at Fisheries Bay, Lone Pine and Wreck Beach.

If you'd rather be on the water rather than in it, the local fishing is outstanding. Spot On Fishing Tackle (www.spotonfishing.com.au; 39 Tasman Tce; ⊗8.30am-5.30pm Mon-Fri, 8am-4pm Sat & Sun) will give you the latest on what's biting where.

Kuju Aboriginal Arts (www.visitaboriginal art.com; 30 Ravendale Rd; admission free; ⊗10am-4pm Mon-Fri) stocks exquisite Indigenous artwork, and you can meet the artists who work on-site.

🛏 Sleeping & Eating

Pier Hotel PUB $
(☑08-8682 2133; pierhotel@perkscompanies.com.au; 33 Tasman Tce; d from $75; ✳) The old Pier has had a facelift, including the dozen en-suite rooms upstairs – bright and clean with polished floorboards and TVs. The bistro downstairs (mains $15 to $28; open for lunch and dinner) is big on local seafood: oysters, calamari and scallops reign supreme.

Blue Seas Motel MOTEL $$
(☑08-8682 3022; www.blueseasmotel.com; 7 Gloucester Tce; d from $98; ✳) Before the multistorey Port Lincoln Hotel popped up, the Blue Seas had 180-degree views over Boston Bay. Still, the view ain't bad, and with a recent spruce-up this old timer passes muster. A bit of traffic noise is the only downer.

Port Lincoln Hotel HOTEL $$
(☑1300 766 100, 08-8621 2000; www.port lincolnhotel.com.au; 1 Lincoln Hwy/Rte B100; d $135-230; ✳@🅿✺) Bankrolled by a couple of Adelaide Crows AFL footballers, this ritzy seven-storey hotel lifts Port Lincoln above the fray. It's a classy, contemporary affair, offering a bit of luxury at reasonable prices. Good on-site bars and eateries too – play 'Spot Mark Ricciuto' from behind your menu (restaurant mains $21 to $35, bar meals $11 to $23).

Port Lincoln Tourist Park CARAVAN PARK $
(☑08-8621 4444; www.saringroup.com.au; 11 Hindmarsh St; unpowered/powered sites $25/28, cabins & units $65-125; ✳@🅿) A breezy waterside park with some beaut new executive cabins by the water and plenty of elbow room. You can fish from the jetty and swim at the beach. BYO linen in the basic cabins.

🖉GLO CAFE $
(☑08-8682 6655; www.goodlivingorganics.net; 23 Liverpool St; items $4-10; ⊗breakfast & lunch Mon-Sat; 🖉) A local hang-out a block away from the beach and thus not on many tourist radars, GLO (Good Living Organics) features cute staff in black T-shirts serving quiches, wraps, salads, falafels, cous-cous and Port Lincoln's best coffee, hands down.

① Information

Port Lincoln Visitor Information Centre
(☑1300 788 378, 08-8683 3544; www.visit portlincoln.net; 3 Adelaide Pl; ⊗9am-5pm; @) This excellent centre books accommodation and has national parks information and passes.

Port Lincoln to Streaky Bay

Around Port Lincoln

About 50km north of Port Lincoln, Tumby Bay (www.tumbybay.com) is quiet little town with a beach, jetty, pub, caravan park and motel. Serious holiday territory!

About 15km south of Port Lincoln is Lincoln National Park (www.environment.sa.gov.au; per car $8.50), with roaming emus, roos and brush-tailed bettongs, safe swimming coves and pounding surf beaches. Entry is via self-registration on the way in.

If you want to stay the night, the two-bedroom Donnington Cottage (per night $82.50, 2-night minimum) at Spalding Cove, built in 1899, sleeps six and has photo-worthy views. Book through Port Lincoln visitor information centre; BYO linen and food. The visitor centre can also advise on bush camping (per car $6-16) in the park, including sites at Fisherman's Point, Memory Cove, September Beach and Surfleet Cove.

The Port Lincoln visitor information centre also sells permits to Mikkira Station & Koala Sanctuary (mikkira@activ8.net.au; Fishery Bay Rd; day permit/camping $15/25), Eyre Peninsula's first sheep station and home to the endemic Port Lincoln parrot.

Coffin Bay

POP 650

Oyster lovers rejoice! Deathly sounding Coffin Bay (named by Matthew Flinders after his buddy Sir Isaac Coffin) is a snoozy fishing village basking languidly in the warm sun... until a 2500-strong holiday horde arrives every January. Slippery, salty **oysters** from the nearby beds are exported worldwide, but you shouldn't pay more than $1 per oyster around town. Online, see www.coffinbay.net.

Along the ocean side of Coffin Bay there's some wild coastal scenery, most of which is part of **Coffin Bay National Park** (www.environ ment.sa.gov.au; per car $8.50), overrun with roos, emus and fat goannas. Access for conventional vehicles is limited: you can get to picturesque **Point Avoid** (coastal lookouts, rocky cliffs, good surf and whales passing between May and October) and **Yangie Bay** (arid-looking rocky landscapes and walking trails), but otherwise you'll need a 4WD. There are some isolated **camp sites** (per car $6) within the park, generally with dirt-road access.

Coffin Bay Explorer (☑1300 788 378, 0428 880 621; www.coffinbayexplorer.com) runs half-day wildlife and seafood tours (adult/child $85/45) with plenty of oysters and dolphins.

🛏 Sleeping & Eating

Coffin Bay Caravan Park CARAVAN PARK **$**
(☑08-8685 4170; www.coffinbay.net/caravan park; 91 Esplanade; unpowered/powered sites $20/29, cabins & villas $65-120; ❄) Resident cockatoos, galahs and parrots squawk around the shady she-oak sites here, and the cabins are a reasonable bang for your buck (BYO linen). Lovely new two-bedroom family villas, too.

Coffin Bay Hotel/Motel MOTEL **$**
(☑08-8685 4111; www.coffinbay.net/accommo dation/hotel_motel.htm; 26 Shepperd Ave; s/d $85/95; ❄) The sprawling local pub (built, it seems, to avoid any kind of view), has eight regulation units out the back (all brown brick and teak veneer), and plates up regulation counter meals (mains $16 to $27; open for lunch and dinner).

Oysterbeds SEAFOOD **$$**
(☑08-8685 4000; www.oysterbeds.com.au; 61 Esplanade; mains $18-28; ⊙lunch Wed-Sun, dinner Wed-Sat, closed Jun-Aug) A gregarious little food room – all tangerine, sea-blue and shiny liquor bottles – serving the pick of the local seafood. Takeaway oysters shucked/unshucked are $14/10 a dozen.

For holiday shacks around town from $50 to $300 per night try **Coffin Bay Holiday Rentals** (☑0427 844 568; www.coffinbayholiday rentals.com.au) or **Flinders Keepers** (☑08-8685 4063; www.flinderskeepers.com.au).

Coffin Bay to Point Labatt

There's reliable surf at **Greenly Beach** just south of **Coulta**, 40km north of Coffin Bay. There's also good salmon fishing along this wild stretch of coast, notably at **Locks Well**, where a long, steep stairway called the **Staircase to Heaven** (283 steps? Count 'em...), leads from the car park down to the lovely surf beach. About 15km further north, **Elliston** is a small fishing town on soporific Waterloo Bay, with a beautiful swimming beach and a fishing jetty (hope the tommy ruff and whiting are biting). Waterside **Elliston Waterloo Bay Tourist Park** (☑08-8687 9076; www.visit elliston.net; Beach Tce, Elliston; unpowered/powered sites $22/26, cabins $55-110; ❄🐾🛜) is a smallish operation with decent cabins (aim for one on top of the dunes) and fishing gear for sale.

Just north of Elliston, take the 10km detour to **Anxious Bay** for some anxiety-relieving ocean scenery (billed as Elliston's 'Great Ocean Drive'). En route you'll pass **Blackfellows**, which boasts some of the west coast's best surf. From here you can eyeball the 36-sq-km **Flinders Island** 35km offshore, where there's a sheep station and a self-contained, nine-bed **holiday house** (☑0428 261 132; www.flindersgetaway.com; per person from $90). To get here you have to charter a plane from Port Lincoln or a boat from Elliston (additional to accommodation costs); ask for details when you book.

At **Venus Bay** there are sheltered beaches (and the not-so-sheltered Mount Camel Beach), a gaggle of pelicans, a small caravan park and the obligatory fishing jetty.

If you feel like taking a plunge and swimming with sea lions and dolphins, head by Baird Bay and organise a tour with **Baird Bay Ocean Eco Experience** (☑08-8626 5017; www.bairdbay.com; 4hr tours adult/child $140/70; ⊙Sep-May). Accommodation is also available.

If you'd rather stay high-and-dry, the road to **Point Labatt**, 43km south of Streaky Bay, takes you to one of the few permanent sea-lion colonies on the Australian mainland; ogle them from the cliff-tops (with binoculars).

A few kilometres down the Point Labatt road are the globular **Murphy's Haystacks**, an improbable congregation of 'inselbergs' –

colourful, weather-sculpted granite outcrops, which are millions of years old.

on scrumptious local seafood – try the chilli-and-lime squid. Fresh sushi every Thursday; good coffee, too.

Streaky Bay

POP 1150

This endearing little town (actually on Blanche Port) takes its name from the streaks of seaweed Matt Flinders spied in the bay as he sailed by. Visible at low tide, the seagrass attracts ocean critters and the bigger critters that eat them – first-class fishing. For tourist info, swing by the Streaky Bay Visitor Information Centre (☑08-8626 7033; www.streakybay.com.au; 21 Bay Rd; ⊙9am-12.30pm & 1.30-5pm Mon-Fri; @).

Occupying a 1901 school house, the Streaky Bay Museum (www.nationaltrustsa. org.au; 42 Montgomery Tce; adult/child $3.50/50c; ⊙1.30-4pm Tue & Fri, 9am-noon Sat) features a fully furnished pug-and-pine hut, an old iron lung and plenty of pioneering history.

If you're into bivalves, Evans Oysters (☑08-8626 1282, 08-8626 7033; Woodlawn Rd; tours adult/child $20/10; ⊙tours 5pm Tue & Wed Oct-Mar, 4pm Apr-Sep) runs tours of their salty oyster shed. Bookings essential.

🛏 Sleeping & Eating

Streaky Bay Hotel/Motel   PUB, MOTEL $
(☑08-8626 1008; www.streakybayhotel.com.au; 33 Alfred Tce; budget/hotel/motel d incl breakfast from $50/90/100; ❄) The hotel rooms upstairs at this 1866 brick beauty have rip-snorting water views and a large balcony from which to snort them. Downstairs, the budget rooms are sans views but perfectly decent. Motel '60s rooms out the back are unglamorous but have more privacy. Breakfast, lunch and dinner happen in the bistro daily (mains $15 to $30).

Foreshore Tourist Park   CARAVAN PARK $
(☑08-8626 1666; www.streakybayftpark.com.au; 82 Wells St; unpowered/powered sites $23/28, cabins & units $55-110; ❄) Right on Doctors Beach just east of town, this park is overrun with cavorting families in summer. Plenty of space, sand and sea-based things to do.

TOP CHOICE Mocean   CAFE $$
(☑08-8626 1775; www.moceancafe.com.au; 34b Alfred Tce; mains $20-26; ⊙lunch Tue-Sun, dinner Tue-Sat) It looks like a big shipping container from the street, but this jaunty corrugated-iron-clad cafe is the town's social pacemaker, with murals, Moroccan lanterns and water views from the alfresco terrace. Dishes focus

Ceduna

POP 3600

Unlike Streaky Bay and Port Lincoln – and despite the locals' best intentions – Ceduna remains a raggedy fishing town that just can't shake its tag as a blow-through pit stop en route to WA.

The Ceduna Visitor Information Centre (☑1800 639 413, 08-8625 2780; www.cedunatourism.com.au; 58 Poynton St; ⊙9am-5.30pm Mon-Fri, 9.30am-5pm Sat & Sun) can help with local info.

Ceduna Museum (www.nationaltrustsa. org.au; 2 Park Tce; adult/child/family $3.50/2/7; ⊙10am-noon Mon, Tue & Thu-Sat, 2-4pm Wed & Thu) has pioneer exhibits, Indigenous artefacts and a display on the tragic British nuclear tests at Maralinga.

The sea-inspired works of local Indigenous artists from along the coast steal the show at Ceduna Aboriginal Arts & Culture Centre (www.visitaboriginalart.com; 2 Eyre Hwy; admission free; ⊙9am-5pm Mon-Fri).

If you're passing through in early October, check out Oysterfest (www.ceduna.net/site/page.cfm?u=167), the undisputed king of Australian oyster parties.

🛏 Sleeping & Eating

Ceduna Foreshore Hotel/Motel   MOTEL $$
(☑08-8625 2008; www.cedunahotel.com.au; 32 O'Loughlin Tce; d $150-170, f $220; ❄⊛) The recently renovated Foreshore is the most luxurious option in town, with water views and a bistro zooming in on west-coast seafood (mains $19 to $30). Views from the outdoor terrace look through Norfolk Island pines and out across the bay.

Ceduna Oyster Bar   SEAFOOD $
(www.ceduna.net/site/page.cfm?u=493; Eyre Hwy; 12 oysters $10.20; ⊙lunch) Pick up a box of freshly shucked molluscs and head for the foreshore, or sit on the terrace and watch the trains roll past.

Ceduna to the Western Australian Border

It's 480km from Ceduna to the WA border. Along the stretch you can get a bed and a beer at Penong (72km from Ceduna), Nundroo (151km), the Nullarbor Roadhouse

(295km) near Head of Bight, and at Border Village on the border itself.

Wheat and sheep paddocks line the road to Nundroo, after which you're in mallee scrub for another 100km. Around 20km later, the trees thin to low bluebush as you enter the true Nullarbor (Latin for 'no trees'). Road trains, caravans and cyclists of questionable sanity are your only companions as you put your foot down and career towards the setting sun.

Turn off the highway at Penong (population 200), and follow the 20km dirt road to Point Sinclair and Cactus Beach, which has three of Australia's most famous surf breaks. Caves is a wicked right-hand break for experienced surfers, but be aware that locals don't take too kindly to tourists dropping in. There's bush camping (per person from $10) on private property close to the breaks; BYO drinking water.

The viewing platforms at Head of Bight (www.yalata.org; adult/child/concession/family $12/free/10/25; ⊙8am-5pm) overlook a major southern-right-whale breeding ground. Whales migrate here from Antarctica in June, and you can see them cavorting from July to September. The breeding area is protected by the Great Australian Bight Marine Park (www.environment.gov.au/coasts/mpa/gab), the world's second-largest marine park after the Great Barrier Reef.

Head of Bight is a part of the Yalata Indigenous Protected Area. After paying your entry fee, stop and get the latest whale information from the White Well Ranger Station on the way in to the viewing area. The signposted turn-off is 14km east of the Nullarbor Roadhouse.

While you're in the Head of Bight area, you can also check out Murrawijinie Cave, a large overhang behind the Nullarbor Roadhouse, and have a look at the signposted coastal lookouts along the top of the 80m-high Bunda Cliffs.

If you're continuing west into WA, dump all fruit, vegetables, cheese and plants at Border Village (as per quarantine regulations), and watch out for animals if you're driving at night. Note that if you're driving east rather than west, SA's quarantine check point isn't until Ceduna.

🛏 Sleeping & Eating

Travelling west towards WA from Ceduna, you'll run into the following places (in this order), where you can grab a meal or put yourself to bed.

Penong Caravan Park CARAVAN PARK $
(☑08-8625 1111; www.nullarbornet.com.au/towns/penong.html; 5 Stiggants Rd; unpowered/powered sites $20/24, on-site vans $45, cabins from $70; ❋) A short hop from Ceduna, this well-kept park is rated by some travellers as the best on the Nullarbor. The cabins are in good shape, and the camping area has pristine facilities.

Fowlers Bay Caravan Park CARAVAN PARK $
(☑08-8625 6143; www.nullarbornet.com.au/towns/fowlersBay.html; unpowered/powered sites $12/15, units $65-75; ❋) There's basic accommodation, a shop and takeaway food in this almost ghost town, plus heritage buildings, good fishing and rambling dunes. Take the Fowlers Bay turn-off 106km from Ceduna.

Nundroo Hotel/Motel MOTEL, CARAVAN PARK $
(☑08-8625 6120; www.nundrooaccommodation.com; Eyre Hwy, Nundroo; unpowered/powered sites $8/18, on-site vans $30, dm/d $10/90; ❋) If you're heading west, Nundroo has this decent hotel/motel and the last mechanic until Norseman WA, 1038km away. There's a very basic dorm, and worn but comfy motel rooms with updated bathrooms. There's a bar and restaurant on-site (meals $13 to $30).

Nullarbor Roadhouse MOTEL, CARAVAN PARK $
(☑08-8625 6271; www.nullarbornet.com.au/towns/nullarbor.html; Eyre Hwy, Nullarbor; unpowered/powered sites $13/19, budget rooms s/d $30/42/50/57, motel $92/110/128/146; ❋) Close to the Head of Bight whale-watching area, this roadhouse is a real oasis for weary road-warriors. The on-site bar and restaurant serve breakfast, lunch and dinner (meals $12 to $25).

Border Village Motel MOTEL, CARAVAN PARK $
(☑08-9039 3474; www.nullarbornet.com.au/towns/borderVillage.html; Eyre Hwy, Border Village; unpowered/powered sites $15/20, budget rooms s/d/tr/q $40/60/70/80, motel s/d/tr $95/110/120; ❋@☎) Just 50m from the WA border, this rebuilt motel has a variety of modern rooms and cabins and a licensed restaurant (meals $13 to $25; open for lunch and dinner).

FLINDERS RANGES

Known simply as 'the Flinders', this ancient mountain range is an iconic South Australian environment. Jagged peaks and escarpments rise up north of Port Augusta and track 400km north to Mt Hopeless. The colours here are remarkable: as the

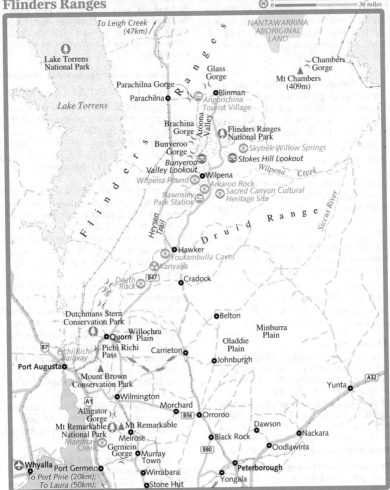

day stretches out, the mountains shift from mauve mornings to midday chocolates and ochre-red sunsets.

Before Europeans arrived, the Flinders were prized by the Adnyamathanha peoples for their red ochre deposits, which had medicinal and ritual uses. Sacred caves, rock paintings and carvings exist throughout the region. In the wake of white exploration came villages, farms, country pubs, wheat farms and cattle stations, many of which failed under the unrelenting sun.

The cooler Southern Ranges are studded with stands of river red gums and country hamlets with cherubic appeal. In the arid Northern Ranges, the desert takes a hold: the scenery here is stark, desolate and very beautiful.

☞ Tours

Bookabee Tours INDIGENOUS
(☎08-8235 9954, 0408 209 593; www.bookabee. com.au; 2-/3-/4-day tours $995/1520/2025) Highly rated Indigenous-run tours to the Flinders Ranges and outback, departing from Adelaide, including quality accommodation, meals, cultural tours, activities and interpretation.

Ecotrek
BUSHWALKING

(☑1300 948 911; www.ecotrek.com.au; 5-day tour $1895) Excellent all-inclusive tours walking the best sections of the Flinders, with soft beds, hot showers, and food and wine at the end of each day.

Swagabout Tours
WILDERNESS

(☑0408 845 378; www.swagabouttours.com.au; 3/4 days camping $745/995, hotels $1155/1495) Dependable Flinders Ranges trips including Quorn and Wilpena (plus Arkaroola on the four-day jaunt), and can be extended to Coober Pedy.

Wallaby Tracks Adventure Tours
WILDERNESS

(☑0428 486 655; www.wallabytracks.com; 1-/2-/3-day tours $250/310/900) Small-group 4WD tours around the Ranges and Wilpena Pound.

Adventure Tours Australia
WILDERNESS

(☑1300 654 604, 08-8132 8130; www.adventuretours.com.au) Popular small-group tours through the Flinders region and beyond.

Groovy Grape
WILDERNESS

(☑1800 661 177, 08-8440 1640; www.groovygrape.com.au) Adelaide to Coober Pedy and back, via the Flinders Ranges.

ℹ️ Information

There are visitor information centres in Quorn, at Port Augusta on the Ranges' southern doorstep, and at Wilpena Pound Resort inside Flinders Ranges National Park.

Flinders Ranges Accommodation Booking Service (FRABS ☑1800 777 880, 08-8648 4022; www.frabs.com.au) Bookings for rural cottages and shearers quarters around Hawker.

Flinders Ranges website (www.flindersranges.com)

Southern Flinders Ranges website (www.southernflindersranges.com.au)

ℹ️ Getting There & Around

BUS Premier Stateliner (www.premierstateliner.com.au) has daily buses between Adelaide and Port Augusta ($53, 4¼ hours). **Upper North Passenger Service** (☑08-866 2255) runs a Friday bus from Port Augusta to Quorn ($6, 30 minutes), and a Thursday bus from Port Pirie to Melrose ($6, 1¼ hours).

CAR The major roads into Quorn, Hawker, Wilpena Pound, Leigh Creek and the Southern Ranges towns are sealed, but most of the others are gravel (fine in a regular car if you take it slow). Check with DENR offices or call ☑1300 361 033 for road-condition updates after rains.

TRAIN The *Ghan* train connects Adelaide with Port Augusta. The *Indian Pacific* (between Perth and Sydney) connects with the *Ghan* at Port Augusta. See p741 for details. **Pichi Richi Railway** (www.prr.org.au; one-way adult/child/concession/family $50/18/47/118) has trains between Port Augusta and Quorn (two hours) on Saturdays.

Southern Ranges Towns

Port Pirie (population 13,200) is a big lead- and zinc-smelting town on the edge of the Southern Flinders. The Nyrstar smelter dominates the skyline, but the town itself has some pretty old buildings along Ellen St, and is a good spot to stock up on supplies before heading north.

You enter the Southern Ranges proper near **Laura** (population 500), emerging from the wheat fields like Superman's Smallville (all civic pride and 1950s prosperity). There's not a lot to do here, but the long, geranium-adorned main street has a supermarket, chemist, bakery, bank, post office... even a jeweller!

About 10km further north, **Stone Hut** (population 290) doesn't have much on offer other than the amazing **Old Bakery** (www.oldbakerystonehut.com.au; Main North Rd, Stone Hut; items $4-10; ⊙7am-6pm), which makes legendary chunky beef pies, slices and quandong tart. There's cabin-style accommodation here too (doubles from $150).

The oldest town in the Flinders (1853) is **Melrose** (population 200), snug in the elbow of the 960m Mt Remarkable. It has the perfect mix of well-preserved architecture, a cracking-good pub, quality accommodation and parks with *actual grass*.

⭐ **TOP CHOICE** **North Star Hotel** (☑08-8666 2110; www.northstarhotel.com.au; 43 Nott St, Melrose; d $110-220, trucks $140-160; ❄) is as welcome as summer rain: a fabulous 1854 hotel renovated in city-meets-woolshed style. Sit under the hessian-sack ceiling and spinning fans for a fresh menu (mains $15 to $29; lunch Wednesday to Sunday, dinner Thursday to Saturday), great coffee and cold Flinders Ranges beer (try the Fargher Lager). Accommodation ranges from rooms in the place next door to plush suites above the pub and surprisingly cool metal-clad cabins built on two old trucks out the back.

Melrose Caravan Park (☑08-8666 2060; mcp@rbe.net.au; Joe's Rd, Melrose; dm $20, unpowered/powered sites $16/23, cabins $50-110; ❄) is a small, tidy park with bush camp sites and self-contained cabins salvaged from the

2000 Sydney Olympics (all with TVs and cooking facilities – the cheaper ones are sans bathrooms). The 12km return hike up Mt Remarkable starts on the back doorstep. Next door is a converted agricultural shed with basic dorm facilities.

Mt Remarkable National Park

Bush boffins rave about the steep, jaggedy Mt Remarkable National Park (www.environment. sa.gov.au; per car $7.50), straddling the Southern Flinders. Wildlife and bushwalking are the main lures, with various tracks (including part of the **Heysen Trail**; see the boxed text, p708) meandering through isolated gorges.

From the car park at Alligator Gorge take the short, steep walk (2km, two hours) down into the craggy gorge (no sign of any 'gators), the ring route (9km, four hours), or walk to Hidden Gorge (18km, seven hours) or Mambray Creek (13km, seven hours). From Mambray Creek the track to Davey's Gully (2.5km, one hour) is (literally and metaphorically) a walk in the park. Peak baggers sweat up the track to the 960m-high summit of Mt Remarkable (12km, five hours); the trail starts behind Melrose Caravan Park.

Pay the park entry fee at the Park Office (☎08-8634 7068; www.environment.sa.gov.au) at Mambray Creek, off Hwy 1 about 21km north of Port Germein. On the inland route (Main North Rd/Rte A1 between Melrose and Wilmington), there's an honour box at Alligator Gorge. Both stations have park info brochures.

If you want to stay the night there's plenty of bush camping (per car $16), and two lodges: at Mambray Creek (sleeps 4; per night from $50) and Alligator Gorge (sleeps 10; per night $150). Both are solar powered; Alligator Gorge has better cooking facilities and showers. Book through the Park Office.

Quorn

POP 1380

Is Quorn a film set after the crew has gone home? With more jeering crows than people, it's a cinematographic little outback town. Wheat farming took off here in 1875, and the town prospered with the arrival of the Great Northern Railway from Port Augusta. Quorn remained an important railroad junction until trains into the Flinders were cut in 1970.

◉ Sights & Activities

Quorn's streetscapes, especially Railway Tce, are a real history lesson, and have featured in iconic Australian films like *Gallipoli* and *Sunday Too Far Away*. A fragment of the long-defunct railway now conveys the Pichi Richi Railway (www.prr.org.au; one-way adult/child/concession/family $50/18/47/118) between Port Augusta and Quorn (two hours) on Saturdays.

Derelict ruins of early settlements litter the Quorn–Hawker road, the most impressive of which is Kanyaka, a once-thriving sheep station founded in 1851. From the homestead ruins (41km from Quorn) it's a 20-minute walk to a waterhole, loomed over by the massive Death Rock. The story goes that local Aborigines once placed their dying kinfolk here to see out their last hours.

☞ Tours

Pichi Richi Camel Tours CAMEL RIDES
(☎08-8648 6640, 0429 998 044; www.pichirichi cameltours.com) Saddle up for a two-hour sunset ride ($65) or a longer half-/full-day camel-back tour ($95/175) through the country around Quorn.

Flinders Ranges Scenic & Cultural Tours SIGHTSEEING
(☎08-8648 6840; www.frsct.com.au; 1-day tour $170) Small-group tours around Wilpena Pound.

Quorn Adventures WILDERNESS
(www.quornadventures.com) Collaborative website listing tour operators and 4WD tracks around Quorn.

⌂ Sleeping & Eating

Austral Inn PUB $
(☎08-8648 6017; www.australinn.com.au; 16 Railway Tce; d motel/pub from $80/110; ❄) There's always a few locals here giving the jukebox a workout and chatting with the publican. The pub rooms are renovated – simple and clean with new linen – while the motel rooms are more '80s than the menu (standard country-pub fare with a twist: try a kangaroo schnitzel). The pub is purportedly above an old well, so if it's been raining watch out for mozzies.

Quorn Caravan Park CARAVAN PARK $
(☎08-8648 6206; www.quorncaravanpark.com.au; 8 Silo Rd; unpowered/powered sites $20/26, cabins $50-100; ❄) Fully keyed in to climate change, this passionately run park on Pinkerton Creek is hell bent on reducing emissions and restoring native habitat. Features include

spotless cabins, a new laundry and camp kitchen, shady sites and a few lazy roos lounging about under the red gums.

Quandong Apartments APARTMENTS **$$**
(☏08-8648 6155, 0432 113 473; www.quandong apartments.com; 31 First St; d $160; ✴) Next door to the Quandong Café (and run by the same folks), these two self-contained apartments have full kitchens, big TVs, quality linen and mod-Asian touches. Rates come down for stays of two nights or more.

Quandong Café CAFE **$**
(www.quandongapartments.com/cafe.html; 31 First St; meals $5-13; ⊘breakfast & lunch mid-Mar–mid-Dec) A traditional country cafe with creaky floorboards and spinning ceiling fans, serving big breakfasts and light lunches. Try a generously adorned 'Railway Sleeper' (like a pizza sub), or a massive slab of lemon meringue or quandong pie. Good old-fashioned country value!

ⓘ Information

Flinders Ranges Visitor Information Centre
(☏08-8648 6419; www.flindersranges.com; 3 Seventh St; ⊘9am-5pm; @) Maps, brochures, internet access and advice.

Hawker

POP 490

Hawker is the last outpost of civilisation before Wilpena Pound, 55km to the north. Much like Quorn, Hawker has seen better days, most of which were when the old *Ghan* train stopped here. These days Hawker is a pancake-flat, pit-stop town with an ATM and the world's most helpful petrol station.

◉ Sights & Activities

It's not so much what's in Hawker that's interesting – it's more what's around it – but if you like your great outdoors inside (and a little bit eccentric), **Wilpena Panorama** (www.wilpe napanorama.com; cnr Wilpena & Cradock Rds; adult/child $7.50/5; ⊘9am-5pm Mon-Sat, noon-4pm Sun) is a large circular room with a painting of Wilpena Pound surrounding you on all sides.

Yourambulla Caves, 12km south of Hawker, have detailed Aboriginal rock paintings (including emu tracks), with three sites open to visitors. **Yourambulla Peak**, a half-hour walk from the car park, is the most accessible spot to check out the paintings.

Around 40km north of Hawker towards Wilpena, **Arkaroo Rock** is a sacred Aboriginal site. The rock art here features reptile and human figures in charcoal, bird-lime and yellow and red ochre. It's a short(ish) return walk from the car park (2km, one hour).

ⓕ Tours

Derek's 4WD Tours 4WD
(☏0417 475 770; www.dereks4wdtours.com; tours half/full day from $115/170) These are 4WD trips with an environmental bent, including visits to to Bunyeroo and Brachina gorges.

Skytrek Willow Springs 4WD
(☏08-8648 0016; www.skytrekwillowsprings.com. au) Six-hour self-drive tours on a working sheep station ($75 per vehicle), or they can hook you up with a tour operator. Self-contained cabin accommodation also available.

ⓗ Sleeping & Eating

Hawker Caravan Park CARAVAN PARK **$**
(☏08-8648 4006; www.hawkerbig4holidaypark. com.au; cnr Wilpena Rd & Chace View Tce; unpowered/powered sites $24/26, en-suite sites $35-45, cabins $96-148; ✴ ⊛) At the Wilpena end of town, this upbeat, fastidiously maintained acreage has generous gravelly sites and a range of cabins. And there's a pool!

Outback Motel & Chapmanton Holiday Units MOTEL **$$**
(☏08-8648 4100; www.hawkersa.info/biz/out back.htm; 1 Wilpena Rd; s/d motel $95/115, units $100/130; ✴) A drive-up motel offering the best rooms in town. The two-bedroom units are good value for families.

Old Ghan Restaurant MODERN AUSTRALIAN **$$**
(☏08-8648 4176; www.hawkersa.info/biz/ghan. htm; Leigh Creek Rd; mains $20-28; ⊘lunch & dinner Thu-Sat, closed Jan) In the 130-year-old *Ghan* railway station on the outskirts of town, this restaurant is about as upmarket as Hawker gets. Expect mains like barramundi with quince-and-orange glaze, and grilled chicken breast with mango curry sauce.

ⓘ Information

Hawker website (www.hawkersa.info)

Teague's Hawker Motors & Visitor Information Centre (☏08-8648 4014, 08-8648 4022; www.hawkermotors.com.au; cnr Wilpena & Cradock Rds; ⊘7.30am-6pm; @) The town's petrol station (fill up if you're heading north) is also the visitor information centre.

Flinders Ranges National Park

One of SA's most treasured parks, Flinders Ranges National Park (www.environment. sa.gov.au; per car $8.50) is laced with craggy gorges, saw-toothed ranges, abandoned homesteads, Aboriginal sites, hyperactive wildlife and, after it rains, carpets of wildflowers. The park's big-ticket drawcard is the 80-sq-km natural basin Wilpena Pound – a sunken elliptical valley ringed by gnarled ridges (don't let anyone tell you it's a meteorite crater!).

The Pound is only vehicle accessible on the Wilpena Pound Resort's shuttle bus (return adult/child & concession/family $4/2.50/9), which drops you within 1km of the old Hills Homestead, from where you can walk to Wangarra Lookout. The shuttle runs at 9am, 11am, 1pm, 3pm and 5pm, dropping people off and coming straight back (so if you take the 5pm shuttle and want more than a cursory look around, you'll miss the return bus). Otherwise it's a three-hour, 8km return walk between the resort and lookout.

The 20km **Brachina Gorge Geological Trail** features an amazing layering of exposed sedimentary rock, covering 120 million years of the Earth's history. Grab a brochure from the visitors centre.

The **Bunyeroo–Brachina–Aroona Scenic Drive** is a 110km round trip, passing by Bunyeroo Valley, Brachina Gorge, Aroona Valley and Stokes Hill Lookout. There are plenty of short walks along the way; a stop at Bunyeroo Valley Lookout is mandatory. The drive starts north of Wilpena off the road to Blinman.

Just beyond the park's southeast corner, a one-hour, 1km return walk leads to the Sacred Canyon Cultural Heritage Site, with Aboriginal rock-art galleries featuring animal tracks and designs.

Sights & Activities

Bushwalking in the Flinders is an unforgettable experience. Before you make happy trails, ensure you've got enough water, sunscreen and a massive hat, and tell someone where you're going and when you'll be back. Pick up the *Bushwalking in Flinders Ranges National Park* brochure/map from the visitors centre, detailing 17 walks in the park. Nine of the walks kick off at Wilpena Pound Resort.

For a really good look at Wilpena, the walk up to Tanderra Saddle on the ridge of St Mary Peak on the Pound's rim is brilliant, though it's a thigh-pounding scramble at times. The Adnyamathanha people request that you restrict your climbing to the ridge and don't climb St Mary Peak itself, due to its traditional significance to them. The return walk to the saddle (15km, six hours) opens up some good views of the ABC Ranges and Wilpena. If you have time, take the longer outside track for even more eye-popping vistas. You can keep going on the round trip (22km, nine hours), camping overnight at Cooinda Camp.

The quick, tough track up to Mt Ohlssen Bagge (6.5km, four hours) rewards the sweaty hiker with a stunning panorama. Good short walks include the stroll to Hills Homestead (6.5km, two hours), or the dash up to the Wilpena Solar Power Station (500m, 30 minutes).

In the park's north (50km north of Wilpena Pound Resort), the Aroona Ruins are the launch pad for a few less-trampled walks. The **Yuluna Hike** (8km, four hours) weaves through a painterly stretch of the ABC Ranges. The challenging **Aroona–Youngoona Track** (one way 15.5km, seven hours) offers views of the Trezona and Heysen Ranges; cool your boots overnight at Youngoona camp site.

Tours

Wilpena Pound Resort (per adult/child $155/115, morning and afternoon) and Rawnsley Park Station (per half/full day $125/245) both run 4WD tours. See also the tour companies operating in Hawker (p786).

Air Wilpena Scenic Flights (08-8648 0004; www.wilpenapound.com.au/scenic-flights; flights 20/30min $145/165) Scenic flights from Wilpena Pound Resort.

Central Air Services (08-8648 0008, 08-8648 0030; www.centralairservicers.com. au; flights 20min/30min/1hr $135/142/250) Scenic flights from Rawnsley Park Station.

Sleeping & Eating

TOP CHOICE **Wilpena Pound Resort** RESORT $$$
(1800 805 802, 08-8648 0004; www.wilpenapound.com.au; Wilpena Rd via Hawker; unpowered/powered sites $21/31, permanent tent with/without linen $95/72, d $210-270;) This resort is already pretty plush, but it's slated for an upgrade (which will probably include prices). Accommodation includes motelstyle rooms, more upmarket self-contained

ADNYAMATHANHA DREAMING

Land and nature are integral to the culture of the traditional owners of the Flinders Ranges. The people collectively called Adnyamathanha (Hill People) are actually a collection of the Wailpi, Kuyani, Jadliaura, Piladappa and Pangkala tribes, who exchanged and elaborated on stories to explain their spectacular local geography.

The walls of Ikara (Wilpena Pound), for example, are the bodies of two *akurra* (giant snakes), who coiled around Ikara during an initiation ceremony, eating most of the participants. The snakes were so full after their feast they couldn't move and willed themselves to die, creating the landmark. Because of its traditional significance, the Adnyamathanha prefer that visitors don't climb St Mary Peak, reputed to be the head of the female snake.

In another story another *akurra* drank Lake Frome dry, then wove his way across the land creating creeks and gorges. Wherever he stopped, he created a large waterhole, including Arkaroola Springs. The sun warmed the salty water in his stomach causing it to rumble, a noise which can still be heard today in the form of underground springwater flowing.

Colour is essential to the Adnyamathanha as they use the area's red ochre in traditional ceremonies and medicine. Traditional stories say that the vivid orange colour is from the Marrukurli, dangerous dogs who were killed by Adnu, the bearded dragon. When Adnu killed the black Marrukurli the sun went out and he was forced to throw his boomerang in every direction to reawaken the sun. It was only when he threw it to the east that the sun returned. Meanwhile the blood of the Marrukurli had seeped into the earth to create sacred ochre deposits.

suites, and a great (although hugely popular) camp site. If you didn't bring your own camping gear, there are permanent tents sleeping five. Purchase your camping permit at the visitors centre, which also sells petrol and basic (and expensive) groceries. Don't miss a swim in the pool, happy hour at the bar (5pm to 6pm) and dinner at the excellent bistro (mains $19 to $29 – the roo is the best we've ever had!).

Rawnsley Park Station RESORT **$$**
(☎08-8648 0030, caravan park 08-8648 0008, restaurant 08-8648 0126; www.rawnsleypark.com.au; Wilpena Rd via Hawker; unpowered/powered sites $21/31, dm $35, cabins/units/villas from $87/120/360; ❄@) This rangy homestead, 35km from Hawker just south of the national park, runs the accommodation gamut from tent sites to luxe eco-villas. There are also some caravan-park cabins set up as dorms. Also on offer is a range of outback activities including sheep-shearing demos (per adult/child/family $16/8/40), mountain-bike hire (per hour $15), bushwalking (30 minutes to four hours), and 4WD tours and scenic flights. The Woolshed Restaurant (mains $10 to $36; open daily for lunch March to December and dinner year-round) does bang-up bush tucker, plus curries, seafood and pizzas.

Permits for **bush camping** (per car $11) within the national park (ie outside the resort) are available from either the visitor information centre or self-service booths along the way. Trezona, Aroona and Brachina East have creek-side sites among big gum trees; Youngoona in the park's north is a good base for walks. Remote Wilkawillina is certainly the quietest spot.

ℹ Information

Wilpena Pound Visitor Information Centre
(☎1800 805 802, 08-8648 0048; www.wilpenapound.com.au; Wilpena Pound Resort; ⌚8am-6pm; @) Info on the park and district, internet access and bike hire (per half/full day $20/40). Also handles bookings for scenic flights and 4WD tours, and issues bushwalking advice. You can also pay park entry fees here ($8.50 per vehicle).

Blinman & Parachilna

North of Wilpena Pound on a sealed road, ubercute **Blinman** (www.blinman.org.au), population 30, owes its existence to the copper ore discovered here in 1859 and the smelter built in 1903. But the boom went bust and 1500 folks left town. Today Blinman's main claim to fame is as SA's highest town (610m above sea level).

Much of the old **Heritage Blinman Mine** (☎08-8648 4370; tours adult/child/family $25/10/60; ⌚9.30am-4.30pm) has been redeveloped with lookouts, audio-visual

interpretation and information boards. Tours run at 10am, 11.30am, 12.30pm, 2pm and 3.30pm.

Chunky slate floors, old-time photographs and colonial-style rooms collide at the renovated 1869 North Blinman Hotel (☑08-8648 4867; www.blinmanhotel.com.au; Mine Rd, Blinman; unpowered/powered sites $10/20, d motel/hotel/cottage $80/140/180; ❋☎). The kitchen (mains $14 to $30; open for lunch and dinner) serves up pubby delights, and pizzas on Friday nights (the owner is Italian). There are raggedy tent and caravan sites out the back.

Operated by a jeweller on the run from suburban Melbourne, the Wild Lime Café & Gallery (www.wildlimecafe.com.au; Old Schoolhouse, Mine Rd, Blinman; mains $8-20; ☺breakfast & lunch Mar-Dec, by appointment Jan & Feb) serves great coffee, soups, salads, pies, pasties, cakes and bush-inspired dishes like red roo curry.

The road between Blinman and Parachilna tracks through gorgeous Parachilna Gorge, where you'll find creek-side camping and chill-out spots. The northern end of the Heysen Trail (p708) starts/finishes here.

'Real people only, no Yuppies' is the slogan at Angorichina Tourist Village (☑08-8648 4842; www.angorichinavillage.com.au; Parachilna Gorge; unpowered/powered sites $20/25, dm from $20, units from $110; ❋☎@), 17km west of Blinman in Parachilna Gorge. It's a rambling joint with a mix of accommodation; the store sells fuel and can fix your flat. The Blinman Pools Walk (12km return, five hours) starts here, following a creek past abandoned dugouts, river red gums and cypress pines.

On the Hawker–Leigh Creek road, Parachilna (population somewhere between four and seven) is an essential Flinders Ranges destination. Aside from a few shacks, a phone booth and some rusty wrecks, the only thing here is the legendary Prairie Hotel (☑1800 331 473, 08-8648 4844; www.prairiehotel.com.au; cnr High St & West Tce, Parachilna; cabins s/d/tr $45/80/90, hotel d $175-320; ❋☎@). It's looking just a tad weary, but it's still a world-class stay with slick suites out the back and workers' cabins across the street. Don't miss a meal and a cold Fargher Lager (or five) in the pub (mains $22 to $32; lunch and dinner). Try the feral mixed grill (camel sausage, kangaroo fillet and emu). We arrived at 10.42am: 'Too early for a beer!? Whose rules are those?' said the barman.

Leigh Creek & Copley

In the early 1980s, the previously non-existent town of Leigh Creek (population 700) was built by the state government: blooming out of the desert, it's an odd, Canberra-like oasis of leafy landscaping and cul-de-sacs. It's a coal-mining town, supplying the Port Augusta power stations. The Leigh Creek Visitor Information Centre (☑08-8675 2315; lizsopencutcafe@hotmail.com; Black Oak Dr, Leigh Creek; ☺8.30am-5.30pm Mon-Fri, 8.30am-2pm Sat) is at Liz's Open Cut Cafe.

The hub of town life, the Leigh Creek Tavern (☑08-8675 2025; leighcreektavern@flinderspower.com.au; Black Oak Dr, Leigh Creek; motel s/d $110/140, cabins s/d/f $80/95/120; ❋) offers jaunty '80s-style motel rooms, basic cabins a few hundred metres from the pub, and miner-sized bistro meals (mains $12 to $20; lunch and dinner).

About 6km north of Leigh Creek is the sweet meaninglessness of little Copley (population 80). Copley Cabin & Caravan Park (☑08-8675 2288; www.copleycaravan.com.au; Railway Tce W, Copley; unpowered/powered sites $22/27, cabins d $60-130; ❋) is a going concern: a small, immaculate park.

Iga Warta (☑08-8648 3737; www.igawarta.com; Arkaroola Rd; unpowered/powered sites sites $22/25, bunkhouses/cabins/safari tents d $46/104/150), 57km east of Copley on the way into Vulkathunha-Gammon Ranges National Park, is an Indigenous-run establishment offering Adnyamathanha cultural experiences ($25 to $84) as well as 4WD and bushwalking tours ($52 to 138). The various on-site accommodation is open to all comers.

Immediately after Iga Warta just before the national park is Nepabunna, an Adnyamathanha community that manages the local land.

Vulkathunha-Gammon Ranges National Park

Blanketing 1282 sq km of desert, the remote Vulkathunha-Gammon Ranges National Park (www.environment.sa.gov.au) has deep gorges, rugged ranges yellow-footed rock wallabies and gum-lined creeks. Most of the park is difficult to access (4WDs are near compulsory) and has limited facilities. The rangers hang out at the Balcanoona Park Office (☑08-8648 4829), 99km from Copley.

The area around Grindells Hut has expansive views and stark ridges all around. You can reach it on a 4WD track off the Arkaroola road, or by walking through **Weetootla Gorge**. It's a 13km return hike – you might want to stay the night at Grindells Hut. Check with the ranger before driving or walking into this area.

The park has six **bush camping** (per car $6) areas, including Italowie Gorge, Grindells Hut, Weetootla Gorge and Arcoona Bluff. Pick up camping permits at Balcanoona Park HQ. There are two huts that can be booked at the ranger's office: **Grindells Hut** (up to 8 people $130) and **Balcanoona Shearer's Quarters** (d/tr $35/50, exclusive use up to 18 people $240).

Arkaroola

A privately operated wildlife reserve–resort 129km east of Copley on unsealed roads, **Arkaroola Wilderness Sanctuary** (www.arkaroola.com.au) occupies a far-flung and utterly spectacular part of the Flinders Ranges. The **Visitor Information Centre** (⊙9am-5pm) has displays on local natural history, including a scientific explanation of the tremors that often shake things up hereabouts.

The absolute must-do highlight of Arkaroola is the four-hour 4WD **Ridgetop Tour** (adult $99) through wild mountain country, complete with white-knuckle climbs and descents towards the freakish Sillers Lookout. Once you've extracted your fingernails from your seat, look for wedge-tailed eagles and yellow-footed rock wallabies. You can also book guided or tag-along **tours** (drives and walks) through the area. Most areas are accessible in a regular car, with some hiking to pump up your pulse.

The **resort** (☑1800 676 042, 08-8648 4848; www.arkaroola.com.au; Arkaroola Rd Camp; unpowered/powered sites $15/20, cabins $40, cottages $130-175, motel d $130-175; ❋≋) includes a motel complex and caravan park. Camp sites range from dusty hilltop spots to creekside corners; the comfortable cabins are a good budget bet. Other facilities include a woody bar-restaurant (mains $15 to $30), a supermarket and service station.

OUTBACK

The area north of the Eyre Peninsula and the Flinders Ranges stretches into the vast, empty spaces of SA's outback. If you're prepared, travelling through this sparsely populated and harsh country is utterly rewarding.

Heading into the red heart of Australia on the Stuart Hwy, Woomera is the first pit stop, with its dark legacy of nuclear tests and shiny collection of left-over rockets. Further north, the opal-mining town of Coober Pedy is an absolute one-off: a desolate human aberration amid the blistering, arid plains. If you're feeling gung-ho, tackle a section of the iconic Oodnadatta Track, a rugged outback alternative to the Stuart Hwy tarmac. Along the way are warm desert springs, the gargantuan Lake Eyre and some amazing old outback pubs.

Outback Parks

One way to explore the outback environment is to purchase a **Desert Parks Pass** (per car $110), allowing access to eight outback parks (including camping grounds), with a map and handbook included. Aside from the DENR offices listed previously, passes are available online (www.environment.sa.gov.au/parks/park_entry_fees/park_passes), or from the following outlets:

Adelaide Royal Automobile Association (p730)

Coober Pedy **Underground Books** (☑08-8672 5558; undergroundbooks@bigpond.com; Post Office Hill Rd; ⊙8.30am-5pm Mon-Fri, 10am-4pm Sat) The town's only bookshop has loads of regional info.

Hawker Teague's Hawker Motors & Visitor Information Centre (p786)

Innamincka Innamincka Trading Post (p797)

Oodnadatta Pink Roadhouse (p796)

Port Augusta Port Augusta visitor information centre (p778)

For outback park information:

Department for Environment & Natural Resources (DENR; www.environment.sa.gov.au) Adelaide (☑08-8204 191; 91-97 Grenfell St; ⊙9am-5pm Mon-Fri); Port Augusta (☑08-8648 5300; 1st fl, 9 Mackay St; ⊙9am-5pm Mon-Fri)

Desert Parks Hotline (☑1800 816 078)

 Tours

Outback tours are a great way to go, particularly if you're not used to driving epic off-road distances. The following options are all ex-Adelaide; see p717 for more.

Arabunna Tours
INDIGENOUS

(☑08-8675 8351; www.southaustralia.com/
S9008383.aspx; 7-day tour $1050) Aboriginal-
owned company offering cultural tours
from Adelaide to the Flinders Ranges,
Marree, Oodnadatta Track and Lake Eyre.

Great Australian Cattle
Drive
HORSEBACK RIDING

(☑1300 764 227, 08-8463 4547; www.cattledrive.
com.au) In 2010 this epic outback cattle
drive hoofed through Coober Pedy, Marree
and William Creek. See the website for
news about future drives.

Just Cruisin 4WD Tours
4WD, INDIGENOUS

(☑08-8383 0962; www.justcruisin4wdtours.com.
au; 5-day tour $2490) Aboriginal cultural tours
visiting outback Indigenous communities,
sites and guides between Adelaide and
Coober Pedy.

❶ Getting There & Around

AIR **Regional Express** (www.regionalexpress.
com.au) flies daily between Adelaide and
Coober Pedy ($214, two hours).

BUS **Greyhound Australia** (www.greyhound.
com.au) has daily coaches from Adelaide to
Alice Springs ($228, 19½ hours), stopping in SA
at Pimba ($85, seven hours), Glendambo ($107,
8¼ hours) and Coober Pedy ($135, 10½ hours).

CAR The Stuart Hwy is sealed from Port
Augusta to Darwin. In SA, fuel and accommodation are available at Pimba (171km from Port
Augusta), Glendambo (285km), Coober Pedy
(535km), Cadney Homestead (689km) and
Marla (771km). Pimba, Coober Pedy and Marla
have 24-hour fuel sales. See the boxed text
on p39 for pointers on outback driving, useful
if you're tackling the legendary Oodnadatta
Track, Birdsville Track or Strzelecki Track.
These tracks are subject to closure after
heavy rains – check conditions with the Royal
Automobile Association in Adelaide (p730), or
online at www.transport.sa.gov.au.

TRAIN For information on the *Ghan* train between Adelaide and Alice Springs, see p741.

Woomera

POP 450

A 6km detour off the Stuart Hwy from Pimba (485km from Adelaide), Woomera began
in 1947 as HQ for experimental British rocket and nuclear tests at notorious sites like
Maralinga. Local Indigenous tribes suffered
greatly from nuclear fallout. These days
Woomera is an eerie, oddly artificial government town that's still an active Department
of Defence test site.

Rocket into the **Woomera Heritage &
Visitor Information Centre** (☑08-8673
6086; www.woomera.com.au; Dewrang Ave; museum adult/child $6/3; ☉9am-9pm Mon-Wed & Sat,
9am-5pm Thu, Fri & Sun), with its displays on
Woomera's past and present (plus a bowling
alley!). Just across the car park is the **Lions
Club Aircraft & Missile Park**, studded with
jets and rocket remnants.

Built to house rocket scientists, the **Eldo
Hotel** (☑08-8673 7867; www.eldohotel.com.au; Kotara Ave; d with/without bathroom $90/80; ❀) has
comfortable budget and motel-style rooms
in a couple of 1960s buildings, and serves
meaty à la carte meals in the upmarket bistro
(mains $15 to $30; open for lunch and dinner). Try the kangaroo bratwurst snags!

Continue north through Woomera for
90km (sealed road) and you'll hit **Roxby
Downs** (www.roxbydowns.com), population
4500, a bizarrely affluent desert town servicing the massive Olympic Dam Mine, which
digs up untold amounts of copper, silver,
gold and uranium.

Woomera to Coober Pedy

Around 115km northwest of Pimba and 245km
shy of Coober Pedy, middle-of-nowhere **Glendambo** (population 30) was established in
1982 as a Stuart Hwy service centre. This is
the last fuel stop before Coober Pedy.

You can bunk down at the oasislike **Glendambo Hotel-Motel** (☑08-8672 1030; www.hotel
motelnetwork.com.au/sa/central/glendambo_out
back_resort.html; Stuart Hwy; unpowered/powered
sites $17/21, s/d from $89/94; ❀@☎), which has
bars, a restaurant and a bunch of decent motel units. Outside are dusty camp sites; inside
are meaty mains at the bistro ($14 to $25).

North of Glendambo the Stuart Hwy enters
the government-owned **Woomera Prohibited Area** – the highway itself is unrestricted,
but don't go a-wanderin' now, y'hear?

Coober Pedy

POP 3500

Coming into Coober Pedy the dry, barren
desert suddenly becomes riddled with
holes and adjunct piles of dirt – reputedly
more than a million around the township.
The reason for all this rabid digging is
opals – the 'fire in the stone' – which have
made this small town a mining mecca. This
isn't to say it's also a tourist mecca – with
swarms of flies, no trees, 50°C summer

days, subzero winter nights, cave-dwelling locals and rusty car wrecks in every second front yard, you might think you've arrived in a wasteland – but it sure is an interesting place!

Coober Pedy is actually very cosmopolitan, with 44 nationalities represented. Greeks, Serbs, Croats and Italians form sizeable groups among the mining community; Indians and Sri Lankans run accommodation; and gem buyers come from as far off as Scotland and Hong Kong. The surrounding desert is jaw-droppingly desolate, a fact not overlooked by international filmmakers who've come here to shoot end-of-the-world epics like *Mad Max III, Red Planet, Ground Zero, Pitch Black* and the slightly more believable *Priscilla, Queen of the Desert*.

Few people make their living solely from mining here, so there's a lot of 'career diversification'. This means the dude who drives the shuttle bus to the airport also loads the baggage onto the plane, mans the hotel reception desk and works his opal claim on weekends (so he can retire from his other jobs!).

Sights & Activities

OPAL MINING

There are hundreds of working opal mines around town, the elusive gems at the fore of everyone's consciousness. If you're keen for a fossick, tour operators or locals may invite you out to their claim to 'noodle' through the mullock (waste pile) for stones. Watch out for unmarked shafts, and never wander around the fields at night.

The best place to check out a working excavation is Tom's Working Opal Mine (www.tomsworkingopalmine.com.au; Stuart Hwy; tours adult/child/family $25/10/55; tours 8am, 10am, 2pm & 4pm), 3km southwest of town. Miners continue their search for the big vein; visitors noodle for small fortunes. Self-guided tours cost $10/5 per adult/child.

The brilliant Old Timers Mine (www.oldtimersmine.com; Crowders Gully Rd; self-guided tours adult/child/concession/family $10/4.50/9/29; 9am-5pm) was mined in 1916 but was then hidden by the miners. The mine was rediscovered when a dugout home punched through into the labyrinth of tunnels, which now makes a great tour. There's also a museum, a recreated 1920s underground home, and free mining-equipment demos daily (9.30am, 1.30pm and 3.30pm).

DUGOUT HOMES & CHURCHES

It gets face-meltingly hot out here in summer – it makes sense to live underground! Even when it's a stinker outside, subterranean temperatures never rise above 23°C, and air-conditioning isn't necessary. Many of the early dugout homes were simply worked-out mines, but these days they're usually specifically excavated residences. If you want to see one, Faye's Underground Display Home (Old Water Tank Rd; adult/child $5/2.50; 8am-5pm Mon-Sat) was hand dug by three women in the 1960s. It's a little chintzy, but the living-room swimming pool is a winner!

You can visit several of Coober Pedy's underground churches – these are functioning churches, so be respectful of services and worshippers:

Serbian Orthodox Church (Saint Eligh Dr, off Flinders St; admission $5; 24hr) The largest and most impressive, with rock-wall carvings. It is 8km south of town.

FREE St Peter & Paul Catholic Church (cnr Halliday Pl & Hutchison St; 10am-4pm) Coober Pedy's first church still has a sweet appeal.

FREE Catacomb Anglican Church (Catacomb Rd; 24hr) Remote sermons beamed onto a big screen.

OTHER STUFF

You can't miss the Big Winch, from which there are sweeping views over Coober Pedy and towards the Breakaways. An optimistic 'if' painted on the side of the big bucket sums up the town's spirit.

Leftover sets and props from the movies that have been filmed here are littered around town. Check out the amazing spaceship from *Pitch Black*, which has crash landed outside the Opal Cave shop on Hutchison St.

When the mercury nudges 50°C, Coober Pedy's Public Swimming Pool (Paxton Rd; adult/child $6/3; 6.45-8.30am & 3-7.30pm Mon-Fri, 1-7.30pm Sat & Sun) becomes a splashy human soup.

Tours

Arid Areas Tours   WILDERNESS
(08-8672 3008; www.aridareastours.com; 2-/4-/6-hr tours per 2 people $90/189/420) Offers 4WD tours around town, extending to the Painted Desert and the Breakaways.

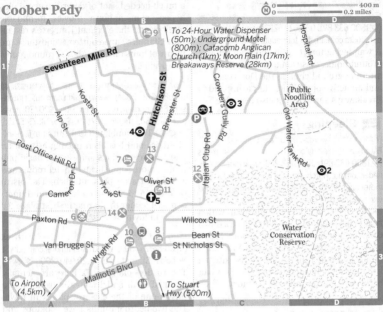

To 24-Hour Water Dispenser (50m); Underground Motel (800m); Catacomb Anglican Church (1km); Moon Plain (17km); Breakaways Reserve (28km)

(Public Noodling Area)

Water Conservation Reserve

To Airport (4.5km)

To Stuart Hwy (500m)

Coober Pedy

⊙ Sights

1 Big Winch C1
2 Faye's Underground Display
   Home D2
3 Old Timers Mine C1
4 Spaceship...B2
5 St Peter & Paul Catholic Church B2

⊛ Activities, Courses & Tours

6 Public Swimming Pool A3

🛏 Sleeping

7 Desert Cave Hotel B2
8 Mud Hut Motel B3

9 Oasis Tourist Park...................................B1
10 Opal Inn Hotel/Motel.............................B3
11 Radeka's Downunder
   Underground
   Backpackers &
   Motel B2

⊗ Eating

12 Italo-Australian
   Miners Club..C2
13 John's Pizza Bar B2
14 Tom & Mary's Greek
   Taverna B3
   Umberto's ....(see 7)

Desert Cave Tours   SIGHTSEEING
(☑08-8672 5688; www.desertcave.com.au; 4hr tour adult/child $90/45) A convenient tour taking in town highlights plus the Dog Fence, Breakaways and Moon Plain. Also on offer are four-hour 'Down 'N' Dirty' opal-digging tours (per person $105).

Mail Run Tour   ROAD TRIP
(☑1800 069 911, 08-8672 5226; www.mailruntour. com) Coober Pedy–based full-day mail-run tours through the desert and along the

Oodnadatta Track to Oodnadatta and William Creek return ($195).

Oasis Tours   SIGHTSEEING
(☑08-8672 5169; 3hr tour adult/child $35/17.50) A good budget tour taking in the major town sights plus a little fossicking. Two-hour sunset Breakaways tours ($50 per person) also swing by the Dog Fence and the Moon Plain.

Radeka's Downunder Desert Breakaways Tour

SIGHTSEEING

(☑1800 633 891, 08-8672 5223; www.coober pedytours.com.au; 4hr tour adult/child $60/30) A wandering tour that includes an underground home, fossicking, the Breakaways, an underground church, the Dog Fence and an active opal mine. Stargazing and Breakaways sunset tours also available.

🛏 Sleeping

Radeka's Downunder Underground Backpackers & Motel

HOSTEL $

(☑1800 633 891, 08-8672 5223; www.radekadown under.com.au; Hutchison St; dm $32, d & tw $79, motel units $125; ✳@⊛) The owners started excavating this place in 1960 – they haven't found much opal, but have ended up with a beaut backpackers! On multiple levels down 6.5m below the surface are Coober Pedy's best budget beds, plus good individual rooms and motel units. The shared kitchen is handy for self-caterers, and there's a bar, barbecue, snooker room and laundry.

Down to Erth B&B

B&B $$

(☑08-8672 5762; www.downtoerth.com.au; Monument Rd; s & d incl breakfast $160, extra person $25; ✳) A real dugout gem 4km from town, where you can have your own subterranean two-bedroom bunker. There's a shady plunge pool for cooling off after a day exploring the Earth, and a telescope for exploring the universe.

Underground Motel

MOTEL $$

(☑08-8672 5324; www.theundergroundmotel. com.au; Catacomb Rd; s/d/f incl breakfast from $95/110/165, extra adult/child $30/16; ✳) Choose between standard rooms and suites (with separate lounge and kitchen) at this serviceable spot with a broad Breakaways panorama. It's a fair walk from town, but friendly and affordable.

Riba's

CAMPGROUND $

(☑08-8672 5614; www.camp-underground.com. au; William Creek Rd; underground sites $28, above-ground unpowered/powered sites $18/58, s & d $58; @) Around 5km from town, Riba's offers the unique option of underground camping! Extras include an underground TV lounge, cell-like underground budget rooms and a nightly opal-mine tour (adult $20; free for campers).

Desert Cave Hotel

HOTEL $$$

(☑08-8672 5688; www.desertcave.com.au; Hutchison St; d $225, extra person $35; ✳@⊛✳) For a much-needed shot of desert luxury – plus a pool, gym, in-house movies, formidable minibar and the excellent Umberto's restaurant. Staff are supercourteous and there are plenty of tours on offer. Above-ground rooms also available.

Opal Inn Hotel/Motel

MOTEL, CARAVAN PARK $$

(☑08-8672 5054; www.opalinn.com.au; Hutchison St; unpowered/powered sites $20/30, hotel s/d $73/80, motel s/d/tr/q $125/135/145/155; ✳@⊛) The rambling Opal Inn is a jack-of-all-trades and has been making a bit of an effort to keep things ship-shape: basic pub rooms, more sophisticated motel rooms and a dusty caravan park attached. The bistro (mains $15 to $29; open lunch and dinner) is passable and the bar is the best place for a beer in town.

Mud Hut Motel

MOTEL $$

(☑08-8672 3003; www.mudhutmotel.com.au; St Nicholas St; s/d/units $120/140/200; ✳@⊛) The rustic-looking walls here are actually rammed earth, and despite the grubby name this is one of the cleanest places in town. The two-bedroom units have cooktops and fridges. Central location.

Oasis Tourist Park

CARAVAN PARK $

(☑08-8672 5169; www.oasiscooberpedy.com. au; Seventeen Mile Rd; unpowered/powered sites $22/27, r/on-site vans from $45/58, cabins $78-120; ✳@⊛✳) There are a few places to camp in Coober Pedy, but this place is reasonably central (a little way down the main street across from the drive-in) and has the most shade, plus a swimming pool. An affordable tour runs daily.

🍴 Eating

John's Pizza Bar

ITALIAN $

(☑08-8672 5561; Hutchison St; meals $4-30; ☺breakfast, lunch & dinner) Serving up table-sized pizzas, hearty pastas and heat-beating gelato, you can't go past John's. Grills, salads, burgers, yiros, and fish and chips also available. Sit inside, order some takeaways, or pull up a seat with the bedraggled pot plants by the street.

Umberto's

MODERN AUSTRALIAN $$$

(☑08-8672 5688; www.desertcave.com.au; Hutchison St; mains $25-46; ☺dinner) The Desert Cave Hotel's rooftop restaurant maintains the quality with first-class dishes like wallaby shanks with vegetables and char-grilled tomato stew, and their 'Essential Tastes of the Outback' platter: char-grilled kangaroo,

camel, emu and beef with bush chutney and hand-cut fries. Swift service, moody desert views and a motivating wine list.

Tom & Mary's Greek Taverna   GREEK **$$**
(📞08-8672 5622; Hutchison St; meals $15-25; ⏰dinner) This busy Greek diner does everything from a superb moussaka to yiros, seafood, Greek salads and pastas with Hellenic zing. Sit back with a cold Coopers or retsina as the red sun sets on another dusty day in Coober Pedy.

Italo-Australian Miners
Club   ITALIAN, PUB FARE **$**
(Italian Club Rd; mains $10-15; ⏰dinner Mon-Sat) Vinyl chairs reflect the sunset at this elevated local watering hole, attracting beer bellies most nights. Meals (monster steaks, schnitzels and damn fine pastas) make an appetising appearance. Cheap fish and chips on Fridays and roast dinner on Thursdays.

❶ Information

24-hour water dispenser (Hutchison St; per 30L 20c) Fill your canteens opposite the Oasis Tourist Park.

Coober Pedy Hospital (📞08-8672 5009; www.countryhealthsa.sa.gov.au; Hospital Rd; ⏰24hr) Accident and emergency.

Coober Pedy Visitor Information Centre
(📞1800 637 076, 08-8672 4617; www.cooberpedy.sa.gov.au; Council offices, Hutchison St; ⏰8.30am-5pm Mon-Fri, 10am-1pm Sat & Sun; @) Free 30-minute internet access, history displays and comprehensive tour and accommodation info.

❶ Getting There & Around

Coober Pedy sits just off the Stuart Hwy, 846km northwest of Adelaide and 686km south of Alice Springs (NT). See p795 for transport details.

The Desert Cave Hotel runs a shuttle van to/from the airport (tickets $10). You can rent cars, 4WDs and campervans here (cars from around $80 per day, with additional fees for distances over 100km).

Budget (📞08-8672 5333; www.budget.com.au; 100 Hutchison St)

Coober Pedy Rent-a-Car (📞08-8672 3003; Mud Hut Motel, St Nicholas St)

Coober Pedy to Marla

The Breakaways Reserve is a stark but colourful area of arid hills and scarps 33km away on a rough road north of Coober Pedy –

turn off the highway 22km west of town. You can drive to a lookout in a conventional vehicle and check out the white-and-yellow mesa called the Castle, which featured in *Mad Max III* and *Priscilla, Queen of the Desert*. Entry permits ($2.20 per person) are available at the Coober Pedy visitor information centre.

An interesting 70km loop on mainly unsealed road from Coober Pedy takes in the Breakaways, the Dog Fence (built to keep dingos out of southeastern Australia) and the table-like Moon Plain on the Coober Pedy–Oodnadatta Rd. If it's been raining, you'll need a 4WD.

If you're heading for Oodnadatta, turning off the Stuart Hwy at Cadney Homestead (151km north of Coober Pedy) gives you a shorter run on dirt roads than the routes via Marla or Coober Pedy. En route you pass through the aptly named Painted Desert (bring your camera).

Cadney Homestead (📞08-8670 7994; cadney@bigpond.com; Stuart Hwy; unpowered/powered sites $15/23, d cabin/motel $55/105; ✳✳) itself has caravan and tent sites, serviceable motel rooms and basic cabins (no linen, shared facilities), plus petrol, puncture repairs, takeaways, cold beer, ATM, swimming pool...and they can organise Painted Desert tours.

In mulga scrub about 82km from Cadney Homestead, Marla (population 245) replaced Oodnadatta as the official regional centre when the *Ghan* railway line was rerouted in 1980. Marla Travellers Rest (📞08-8670 7001; Stuart Hwy; unpowered/powered sites $15/25, d $110; ✳✳) has fuel, motel rooms, camp sites, a cafe and a supermarket.

Frontier-style Mintabie (population 250) is an opal field settlement on Aboriginal land 35km west of Marla – there's a general store, restaurant and basic caravan park here.

From Marla the NT border is another 180km, with a fuel stop 20km beyond that in Kulgera.

Oodnadatta Track

The legendary, lonesome Oodnadatta Track is an unsealed, 615km road between Marla on the Stuart Hwy and Marree in the northern Flinders Ranges. The track traces the route of the old Overland Telegraph Line and the defunct Great Northern Railway. Lake Eyre (the world's sixth-largest lake)

is just off the road. The landscape here is amazingly diverse: floodplains south of Marla, saltbush flats around William Creek, dunes and red gibber plains near Coward Springs. Bring a 4WD – you can do it a regular car, but the track does get bumpy, muddy, dusty and potholed.

Information

Before you hit the Oodnadatta – a rough, rocky and sandy track that's subject to closure after rains – check track conditions with the Pink Roadhouse in Oodnadatta, the Coober Pedy visitor information centre, the Royal Automobile Association in Adelaide (p730), or online at www. transport.sa.gov.au. If you're finding the dust and dirt heavy going, there are escape routes to Coober Pedy on the Stuart Hwy from William Creek and Oodnadatta. Fuel, accommodation and meals are available at Marla, Oodnadatta, William Creek and Marree.

See the *Oodnadatta Track – String of Springs* booklet from the South Australian Tourism Commission, and the *Travel the Oodnadatta Track* brochure produced by the Pink Roadhouse for detailed track info. See p39 for driving tips.

OODNADATTA TO WILLIAM CREEK

Around 209km from Marla, **Oodnadatta** (population 150) is where the main road and the old railway line diverged. The heart of the town today is the **Pink Roadhouse** (☑1800 802 074, 08-8670 7822; www. pinkroadhouse.com.au; ⊙8am-5.30pm), an excellent source of track info, plus they serve meals (try the impressive 'Oodnaburger'). They also run the attached **caravan park** (unpowered/powered sites $15/25, budget cabins s/d/tr $50/65/75, self-contained cabins s/d from $90/110; ❋✿), which has basic camping through to self-contained cabins.

In another 70km you'll hit **William Creek** (population six), best enjoyed in the weather-beaten **William Creek Hotel** (☑08-8670 7880; www.williamcreekhotel. net.au; William Creek; unpowered/powered sites $20/30, cabins s/d $50/80, motel $100/130; ❋), an iconic 1887 pub festooned with photos, business cards, old licence plates and money stapled to the walls. There's also a dusty campground and modest cabins and motel rooms. Also on offer are fuel, cold beer, basic provisions, meals (mains $16 to $30) and spare tyres.

William Creek is also a base for **Wright-sair** (☑08-8670 7962; www.wrightsair.com.au), which runs scenic flights over Lake Eyre (one hour per person from $230).

COWARD SPRINGS TO MARREE

Some 130km shy of Marree, **Coward Springs Campground** (☑08-8675 8336; www. cowardsprings.com.au; unpowered sites adult/child $10/5) is the first stop at the old Coward Springs railway siding. You can soak yourself silly in a **natural hot-spring tub** (admission $1) made from old rail sleepers, or take a **camel trek** (per person per day from $200) to Lake Eyre from here.

Next stop is the lookout over **Lake Eyre South**, which is 12m below sea level. About 60km from Marree is the **Mutonia Sculpture Park** (admission free; ⊙24hr), featuring a jaunty car-engine hitchhiker and several planes welded together with their tails buried in the ground to form 'Planehenge'.

Marree (population 100) was once a vital hub for Afghan camel teams and the Great Northern Railway, and is the end (or start) of both the Oodnadatta Track and Birdsville Track. The 130-year-old **Great Northern Hotel** (☑08-8675 8344; marreepub@bigpond. com; Railway Tce; pub s/d $70/100, motel $90/130; ❋✿) has decent pub rooms and brand new motel units out the back (with more motel units being built, creating the Lake Eyre Motor Inn). Ask Laurie the barman about **scenic flights** (1½ hours per person from $270) and **Marree Man**, a 4.2km-long outline of a Pitjantjatjara Aboriginal warrior etched into the desert near Lake Eyre. It was only discovered in 1988, and no-one seems to know who created it. It's eroding rapidly these days.

From Marree it's 80km to Lyndhurst, where the bitumen kicks back in, then 33km down to Copley at the northern end of the Flinders Ranges.

Birdsville Track

This old droving trail runs 520km from Marree in SA to Birdsville, just across the border in Queensland – one of Australia's classic outback routes. See p380 for details.

Strzelecki Track

Meandering through the sand hills of the **Strzelecki Regional Reserve** (www.environ ment.sa.gov.au), the Strzelecki Track spans 460km from Lyndhurst, 80km south of Marree, to the tiny outpost of Innamincka. Discovery of oil and gas at **Moomba** (a town closed to travellers) saw the upgrading of the road from a camel track to a decent dirt road, though heavy transport travelling

along it has created bone-rattling corrugations. The newer Moomba–Strzelecki Track is better kept, but longer and less interesting than the old track, which follows Strzelecki Creek. Accommodation, provisions and fuel are available at Lyndhurst and Innamincka, but there's nothing in between.

Innamincka

POP 12

On Cooper Creek at the northern end of the Strzelecki Track, Innamincka is near where Burke and Wills' ill-fated 1860 expedition expired. The famous Dig Tree marks the expedition's base camp, and although the word 'dig' is no longer visible you can still see the expedition's camp number. The Dig Tree is over the Queensland border, though memorials and markers – commemorating where Burke and Wills died, and where sole-survivor King was found – are downstream in SA. There's also a memorial where AW Howitt's rescue party made its base on the creek.

Cooper Creek only has water in it after heavy rains across central Queensland, but it has deep, permanent waterholes and the semipermanent Coongie Lakes, which are part of the Innamincka Regional Reserve (www.environment.sa.gov.au). Prior to European settlement the area had a large Aboriginal population, so relics such as middens and grinding stones can be seen around the area.

The Innamincka Trading Post (☎08-8675 9900; South Tce) sells fuel, Desert Parks passes, camping permits and provisions, including fresh bread and rolls.

The old-fashioned Innamincka Hotel (☎08-8675 9901; www.theoutback.com.au; 2 South Tce; s/d $125/150; ✳) has decent motel-style rooms as well as a cheaper bunkhouse. Choose between takeaways, hefty counter meals or the Sunday-night roast (mains $18 to $28).

There are plenty of shady bush camping sites (per car $25) along Cooper Creek – Innamincka Trading Post sells permits, or you can use a Desert Parks Pass. You can also camp on the Town Common (per car $5); there are pit toilets and an honesty box for fees. You can use the hot shower ($2), toilet and laundry tub outside the Trading Post. There's also a laundrette in town.

Darwin & Uluru

Best Places to Eat

» Four Birds (p818)
» Saffrron (p819)
» Litchfield Cafe (p829)
» Fernanda's Café & Restaurant (p851)
» Hanuman Restaurant (p862)

Best Places to Stay

» Cavenagh (p816)
» Feathers Sanctuary (p817)
» Rum Jungle Bungalows (p827)
» Lakeview Park (p835)
» Maud Creek Country Lodge (p841)

Why Go?

There's an enigmatic, ethereal feel to the Northern Territory (NT): endless blue skies collide with flat desert expanse around Uluru, while Darwin and the tropical Top End burst with birdlife, wild rivers and untamed wilderness.

Outback NT has an undeniable edge: there really are wild crocodiles in the waterways and another car might not come down the desert road for weeks. Then there's hedonistic Darwin, the most 'frontier' of Australia's capitals, and Alice Springs, a modern town in the middle of nowhere.

The NT experience for many travellers is following the Adelaide-to-Darwin Stuart Hwy (Rte 1), with must-see side trips to Uluru, Kakadu and Litchfield. But take some time to look around: visit remote Aboriginal communities, hike through rainforest and rocky gorges, sleep in a swag under a billion stars and dine on bush foods and billy tea.

When to Go

Darwin

Mar The atmospheric Tiwi Islands Grand Final coincides with the islands' annual art and craft sale.

Jun-Aug Peak season in the NT, with low humidity and manageable desert temperatures.

Dec-Feb Experience the Top End monsoon: thunderstorms and hot, sticky nights.

History

Early attempts to settle the Top End were mainly due to British fears that the French or Dutch might get a foothold in Australia. The Brits established three forts between 1824 and 1838, but all were short-lived. Then the desire for more grazing land and trade routes spurred speculators from Queensland and South Australia (SA) to explore the vast untamed north. With an eye to development, SA governors annexed the NT in 1863 (it became self-governing only in 1978).

From the mid-1860s to 1895 hundreds of thousands of sheep, cattle and horses were overlanded to immense pastoral settlements. Dislocation and hardship were bedfellows of the industry, with Aborigines forced from their lands and pastoralists confronted by a swath of difficulties. Some Aborigines took employment as stockmen or domestic servants on cattle stations, while others moved on in an attempt to maintain their traditional lifestyle.

In the early 1870s, during digging to establish the Overland Telegraph (from Adelaide to Darwin), gold was discovered. A minor rush ensued, with an influx of Chinese prospectors. Though the gold finds were relatively insignificant, the searches for it unearthed a wealth of natural resources that would lead to mining becoming a major economic presence.

WWII had a significant impact on the Territory. Just weeks after the Japanese levelled Darwin causing 243 deaths, the entire Territory north of Alice Springs was placed under military control, with 32,000 soldiers stationed in the Top End.

On Christmas morning 1974, Darwin was flattened again by Cyclone Tracy, which killed 71 people.

Indigenous Darwin & Uluru

Australian Aborigines have occupied parts of the NT for around 60,000 years, although the central regions were not inhabited until about 24,000 years ago. The first significant contact with outsiders was an amicable one, occurring in the 17th century when Macassan traders from modern-day Sulawesi in Indonesia came to the Top End to collect trepang (sea cucumber).

While the process of white settlement in the NT was slower than elsewhere in Australia, it had an equally troubled and violent effect. By the early 20th century, most Aboriginal people were confined to government reserves or Christian missions. During the 1960s Aboriginal people began to demand more rights.

In 1966 a group of Aboriginal stockmen, led by Vincent Lingiari, went on strike on Wave Hill Station, to protest over the low wages and poor conditions that they received compared with white stockmen. The Wave Hill walk-off gave rise to the Aboriginal land-rights movement.

In 1976 the *Aboriginal Land Rights (Northern Territory) Act* was passed in Canberra. It handed over all reserves and mission lands in the NT to Aboriginal people and allowed Aboriginal groups to claim vacant government land if they could prove continuous occupation – provided the land wasn't already leased, in a town or set aside for some other special purpose.

Today, Aboriginal people own about half of the land in the NT, including Kakadu and Uluru-Kata Tjuta National Parks, which are leased back to the federal government. Minerals on Aboriginal land are still government property, though the landowners' permission is usually required for exploration and mining, and landowners are remunerated.

Around 30% of the Territory's 200,000 people are Aborigines. While non-Aboriginal Australia's awareness of the need for reconciliation with the Aboriginal community has increased in recent years, there are still huge gulfs between the cultures. Entrenched disadvantage and substance abuse are causing enormous social problems within some Indigenous communities.

It's often difficult for short-term visitors to make meaningful contact with Aborigines, as they generally prefer to be left to themselves. The impressions given by some Aboriginal people on the streets of Alice Springs, Katherine and Darwin, where social problems and substance abuse among a few people can present an unpleasant picture, are not indicative of Aboriginal communities as a whole.

Tours to Aboriginal lands (most operated by the communities themselves) and visits to arts centres are gradually becoming more widely available, as communities feel more inclined to share their culture. Benefits are numerous: financial gain through self-determined endeavour, and educating non-Aboriginal people about traditional culture and customs, which helps to alleviate the problems caused by the ignorance and misunderstandings of the past.

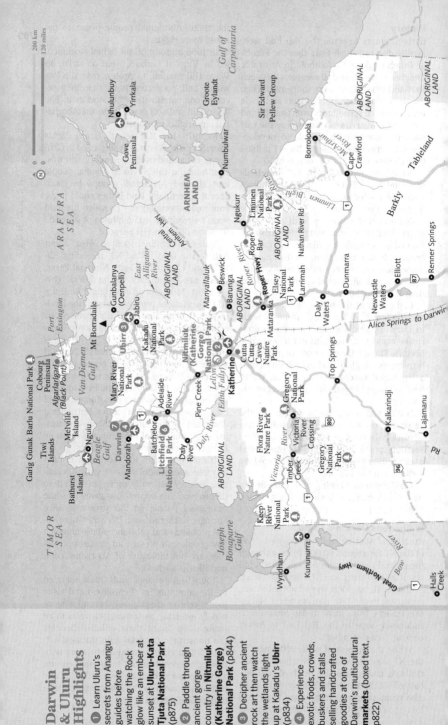

Darwin & Uluru Highlights

1 Learn Uluru's secrets from Anangu guides before watching the Rock glow like an ember at sunset at **Uluru-Kata Tjuta National Park** (p875)

2 Paddle through ancient gorge country in **Nitmiluk (Katherine Gorge) National Park** (p844)

3 Decipher ancient rock art then watch the wetlands light up at Kakadu's **Ubirr** (p834)

4 Experience exotic foods, crowds, buskers and stalls selling handcrafted goodies at one of Darwin's multicultural **markets** (boxed text, p822)

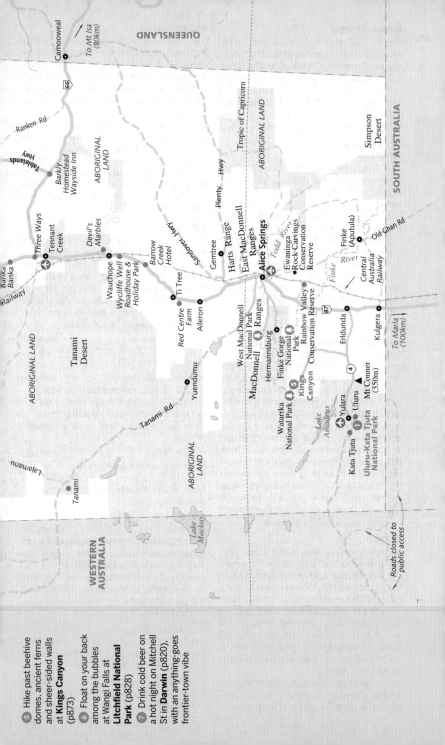

5 Hike past beehive domes, ancient ferns and sheer-sided walls at **Kings Canyon** (p873)

6 Float on your back among the bubbles at Wangi Falls at **Litchfield National Park** (p828)

7 Drink cold beer on a hot night on Mitchell St in **Darwin** (p820), with an anything-goes frontier-town vibe

National Parks

The NT is all about its national parks; it has some of the largest and most famous natural areas in Australia, including Kakadu, Uluru-Kata Tjuta and Nitmiluk. The **Department of Natural Resources, Environment, The Arts and Sport** (08-8999 5511; www.nt.gov. au/nreta/parks) produces fact sheets, available online or from its various offices.

Activities

BUSHWALKING

The Territory's national parks offer well-maintained tracks of different lengths and degrees of difficulty that expose walkers to various environments and wildlife habitats. Carry plenty of water, take rubbish out with you and stick to the tracks.

Top bushwalks include the Barrk Sandstone Bushwalk in Kakadu National Park, the Jatbula Trail in Nitmiluk (Katherine Gorge) National Park, Ormiston Pound in the West MacDonnell Ranges, Trephina Gorge in the East MacDonnell Ranges, and the Valley of the Winds at Kata Tjuta.

FISHING

No permit is required to fish the Territory's waterways, though there are limits on the minimum size and number of fish per person. Travel NT produces the excellent *Fishing the Territory* booklet (free from information centres), and publishes some info online (http://en.travelnt.com). The **Amateur Fishermen's Association of the Northern Territory** (www.afant.com.au) also has online info.

The feisty barramundi lures most fisherfolk to the Top End, particularly to Borroloola, Daly River and Mary River. Increasingly, the recreational-fishing fraternity encourages catch and release to maintain sustainable fish levels. Loads of tours offer transport and gear but start at $250 per person.

SWIMMING

The cool waterfalls, waterholes and rejuvenating thermal pools throughout the NT are perfect spots to soak. Litchfield National Park, in the Top End, and the West MacDonnell Ranges, in the Centre, are particularly rewarding.

Saltwater crocodiles inhabit both salt and fresh waters in the Top End, though there are quite a few safe, natural swimming holes. Before taking the plunge, be sure to read the signs and seek local advice. If in doubt, don't risk it.

Box jellyfish seasonally infest the sea around Darwin; swimming at the city's beaches is safest from May to September.

WILDLIFE WATCHING

The best places for guaranteed wildlife sightings, from bilbies to emus, are at the excellent Territory Wildlife Park outside Darwin and the Alice Springs Desert Park.

If you prefer to see wildlife in the wild, there are few guarantees; many of the region's critters are nocturnal. One exception is at Kakadu, where you'll certainly see crocodiles at Cahill's Crossing or Yellow Waters and numerous species of birds at its wealth of wetlands. In the arid Centre you'll see wallabies, reptiles and eagles. Good places to keep an eye out include the West MacDonnell Ranges and Watarrka (Kings Canyon) National Park.

Tours

Even staunch independent travellers entrust some hard-earned time and money to a carefully selected tour. Tours can provide unmatched insights and access to the Territory, and they support local industry. See specific destination sections of this chapter for details of tours departing from those locations. A handful of highlights:

Anangu Tours INDIGENOUS
Tours around Uluru, guided by the traditional owners (p875).

World Expeditions ADVENTURE
(1300 720 000; www.worldexpeditions.com) Intrepid seven-day Kakadu canoe trips ex-Darwin ($1995) and seven-day treks along the Larapinta Trail ex-Alice Springs ($2095).

Kakadu Animal Tracks INDIGENOUS
Enviro-focused bush-tucker tour in Kakadu; profits support the local Buffalo Farm, which donates food to local communities (p834).

Conservation Volunteers Australia VOLUNTEERING
(CVA; 1800 032 501; www.conservationvolunteers. com.au) Nature-based volunteer projects that double as tours: weeding, walking-track maintenance and wildlife surveys. Day trips are free; multiday projects cost from around $50 per night including meals, accommodation and travel.

Magela Cultural & Heritage Tours INDIGENOUS
Aboriginal owned; runs tours into Arnhem Land and around Kakadu (p834).

Tiwi Tours INDIGENOUS
Trips with local communities to the Tiwi Islands (p814).

ABORIGINAL FESTIVALS & EVENTS

Most of the festivals in the Northern Territory's cities and towns have strong Aboriginal components, plus there's a bunch of annual Aboriginal celebrations to attend. Although these festivals are usually held on restricted Aboriginal land, permit requirements are generally waived for them; this applies to most of the festivals listed below. Bear in mind that alcohol is banned in many communities.

» Tiwi Grand Final FOOTBALL

Held at the end of March on Bathurst Island, this sporting spectacular displays the Tiwis' sparkling skills and passion for football. Thousands come from Darwin for the day, which coincides with the **Tiwi Art Sale** (www.tiwiart.com).

» Barunga Festival TRADITIONAL

(www.barungafestival.com.au) For three days over a long weekend in mid-June, Barunga, 80km east of Katherine, displays traditional arts and crafts, dancing, music and sporting competitions. Bring your own camping equipment; alternatively, visit for the day from Katherine.

» Merrepen Arts & Sports Festival ARTS, SPORTS

(www.merrepenfestival.com.au) The Nauiyu community, on the banks of the Daly River, is the venue for this sporty arts festival on the first weekend in June. The Merrepen Arts Centre showcases its string bags, paintings and prints, while locals sweat it out in foot races and basketball and softball matches.

» Walking With Spirits INDIGENOUS

(www.djilpinarts.org.au/spirits) A two-day Indigenous cultural festival in July at Beswick Falls, 130km from Katherine. In a magical setting, traditional dance and music is combined with theatre, films and a light show. Camping is allowed at the site (only during the festival). A 4WD is recommended for the last 20km to the falls, or a shuttle bus runs from Beswick.

» Stone Country Festival CULTURAL

(www.topendarts.com.au) This open day and cultural festival is held in August in Gunbalanya (Oenpelli) just outside Kakadu National Park. It has traditional music, dancing, and arts and crafts demonstrations, and is the only day you can visit Gunbalanya without a permit. Camping allowed; no alcohol.

» Garma Festival INDIGENOUS

(www.garmafestival.com.au) Also in August, a four-day festival in northeastern Arnhem Land. It's one of the most significant regional festivals, a celebration of Yolngu culture that includes ceremonial performances, bushcraft lessons, a *yidaki* (didgeridoo) master class and an academic forum. Serious planning is required to attend, so start early.

Willis' Walkabouts BUSHWALKING

(☑08-8985 2134; www.bushwalkingholidays.com. au) Small-group multiday guided hikes (from $775), carrying your own gear, to Kakadu, Litchfield, Watarrka and the West MacDonnells.

Seasonal Work

The majority of working-holiday opportunities in the NT for backpackers are in fruit picking, station handing, labouring and hospitality.

Most work is picking mangoes and melons on plantations between Darwin and Katherine. Mango harvesting employs up to 2000 workers each season (late September to November). Station-work wannabes are generally required to have some skills (ie a trade or some experience), as with labouring and hospitality. Employers usually ask workers to commit for at least a month (sometimes three months).

ℹ Information

RESOURCES

Department of Natural Resources, Environment, The Arts and Sport (www.nt.gov.au/ nreta/parks) Details on NT parks and reserves.

Exploroz (www.exploroz.com) Handy usergenerated site for fuel locations and pricing, weather forecasts, road conditions and more.

Road Report (www.ntlis.nt.gov.au/roadreport) Road-conditions report.

Tourism Top End (www.tourismtopend.com.au) Darwin-based tourism body.

Travel NT (http://en.travelnt.com) Official tourism site.

ABORIGINAL LAND PERMITS

Permits may be required to enter Aboriginal land, unless you are using recognised public roads that cross Aboriginal territory. Permits can take four to six weeks to be processed, although for the Injalak arts centre at Gunbalanya (Oenpelli) they are generally issued on the spot in Jabiru.

Central Land Council (www.clc.org.au) Alice Springs (☑08-8951 6211; 27 Stuart Hwy); Tennant Creek (☑08-8962 2343; 63 Patterson St) Deals with all land south of a line drawn between Kununurra (Western Australia) and Mt Isa (Queensland).

Northern Land Council (www.nlc.org.au) Darwin (☑08-8920 5100; 45 Mitchell St); Jabiru (☑08-8938 3000; 3 Government Bldg, Flinders St); Katherine (☑08-8972 2799; 5 Katherine Tce) Responsible for land north of a line drawn between Kununurra (Western Australia) and Mt Isa (Queensland).

Tiwi Land Council (☑08-8981 4898; http://esvc001013.wic004ty.server-web.com; Armidale St, Stuart Park, Darwin) Permits for the Tiwi Islands.

① Getting There & Around

AIR

International and domestic flights arrive at and depart from **Darwin International Airport** (www.darwinairport.com.au; Henry Wrigley Dr, Marrara). Airlines operating from here include:

Airnorth (www.airnorth.com.au) To/from East Timor, and to Broome, Perth, Kununurra and the Gold Coast.

Jetstar (www.jetstar.com.au) Services most major Australian cities.

Qantas (www.qantas.com.au) To/from Asia and Europe, and servicing all major Australian cities.

Virgin Australia (www.virginaustralia.com) Direct flights between Darwin and Brisbane, Melbourne and Perth.

For flights between NT centres, see Getting There & Away sections for Darwin (p823), Alice Springs (p865) and Uluru (p882).

BUS

Greyhound Australia (www.greyhound.com.au) regularly services the main road routes throughout the Territory, including side trips to Kakadu and Uluru; see Getting There & Away in the relevant destination sections for details.

An alternative is tour-bus companies such as AAT Kings, and backpacker buses that cover vast distances while savouring the sights along the way (see p1069 for more on the latter).

CAR

Having your own vehicle in the NT means you can travel at your own pace and branch off the main roads to access less-visited places. To truly explore, you'll need a well-prepared 4WD vehicle and some outback nous. The **Automobile Association of the Northern Territory** (AANT; www.aant.com.au; 79-81 Smith St, Darwin; ⊙9am-5pm Mon-Fri) can advise on preparation and additional resources; members of automobile associations in other states have reciprocal rights.

Many roads are open to conventional cars and campervans, which can be hired in Darwin and Alice Springs and can work out to be quite economical when split by a group.

Some driving conditions are particular to the NT. While traffic may be light and roads dead straight, distances between places are long. Watch out for the four great NT road hazards: speed (maximum speed on the open highway is now 130km/h), driver fatigue, road trains and animals (driving at night is particularly dangerous). Note that some roads are regularly closed during the Wet due to flooding.

Quarantine restrictions require travellers to surrender all fruit, vegetables, nuts and honey at the NT–Western Australia (WA) border.

TRAIN

The famous interstate *Ghan* train is run by **Great Southern Rail** (www.gsr.com.au), grinding between Darwin and Adelaide via Katherine and Alice Springs. The *Ghan* is met in Port Augusta (SA) by the *Indian Pacific,* which travels to/from Sydney; and in Adelaide by the *Overland,* which travels to/from Melbourne.

Darwin or Katherine to Alice Springs seat/sleeper costs $358/668; Darwin to Adelaide costs $716/1372.

DARWIN

POP 124,800

Australia's only tropical capital, Darwin gazes out confidently across the Timor Sea. It's closer to Bali than Bondi, and many from the southern states still see it as some strange outpost or jumping-off point for Kakadu National Park.

But Darwin is a surprisingly affluent, cosmopolitan, youthful and multicultural city, thanks in part to an economic boom fuelled by the mining industry and tourism. It's a city on the move but there's a small-town feel and a laconic, relaxed vibe that fits easily with the tropical climate. Here non-Aboriginal meets

Two Days

Start with breakfast at **Four Birds** or **Roma Bar**, flipping through the *Northern Territory News*. Take a stroll around the downtown streets and through **Bicentennial Park**. Don't miss a couple of hours at the free **Museum & Art Gallery of the Northern Territory**. In the afternoon, hire a bike and ride up through Fannie Bay to **East Point Reserve**, stopping for a dip in Lake Alexander. Try to make it to **Mindil Beach Market**, packed with food outlets, buskers and souvenirs. At night, hit the backpacker bars along **Mitchell St** or catch a movie under the stars at the **Deckchair Cinema**.

Aboriginal (Larrakia), urban meets remote, and industry meets idleness.

Darwin has plenty to offer the traveller. Boats sail around the harbour, chairs and tables spill out of streetside restaurants and bars, museums reveal the city's absorbing past, and galleries showcase the region's rich Indigenous art. Darwin's cosmopolitan mix – more than 50 nationalities are seamlessly represented here – is typified by the wonderful Asian markets held throughout the dry season.

Nature is well and truly part of Darwin's backyard – the famous national parks of Kakadu and Litchfield are only a few hours' drive away and the unique Tiwi Islands a boat-ride away. For locals the perfect weekend is going fishing for barra in a tinny with an esky full of beer.

History

The Larrakia Aboriginal people lived for thousands of years in Darwin, hunting, fishing and foraging. In 1869 a permanent white settlement was established and the grid for a new town laid out. Originally called Palmerston, and renamed Darwin in 1911, the new town developed rapidly, transforming the physical and social landscape.

The discovery of gold at nearby Pine Creek brought an influx of Chinese, who soon settled into other industries. Asians and Islanders came to work in the pearling industry and on the railway line and wharf. More recently, neighbouring East Timorese and Papuans have sought asylum in Darwin.

During WWII, Darwin was the frontline for the Allied action against the Japanese in the Pacific. It was the only Australian city ever bombed, and official reports of the time downplayed the damage – to buoy Australians' morale. Though the city wasn't destroyed by the 64 attacks, the impact of full-scale military occupation on Darwin was enormous.

More physically damaging was Cyclone Tracy, which hit Darwin at around midnight on Christmas Eve 1974. By Christmas morning, Darwin effectively ceased to exist as a city, with only 400 of its 11,200 homes left standing and 71 people killed. The town was rebuilt to a new, stringent building code and in the past decade has steadily expanded outwards and upwards, with the latest project the multimillion-dollar waterfront development at Darwin Harbour.

◉ Sights

TOP CHOICE **Museum & Art Gallery of the Northern Territory** MUSEUM
(MAGNT; Map p806; www.nt.gov.au/nreta/museums; Conacher St, Fannie Bay; admission free; ☉9am-5pm Mon-Fri, 10am-5pm Sat & Sun) This superb museum and gallery boasts beautifully presented galleries of Top End–centric exhibits. The **Aboriginal art collection** is a highlight, with carvings from the Tiwi Islands, bark paintings from Arnhem Land and dot paintings from the desert.

An entire room is devoted to **Cyclone Tracy**, in a display that graphically illustrates life before and after the disaster. You can stand in a darkened room and listen to the whirring sound of Tracy at full throttle – a sound you won't forget in a hurry. The cavernous **Maritime Gallery** houses an assortment of weird and wonderful craft from the nearby islands and Indonesia, as well as a pearling lugger and a Vietnamese refugee boat.

Pride of place among the stuffed animals undoubtedly goes to **Sweetheart**: a 5m-long, 780kg saltwater crocodile. It became a Top End personality after attacking several fishing dinghies on the Finniss River south of Darwin.

DARWIN & ULURU DARWIN

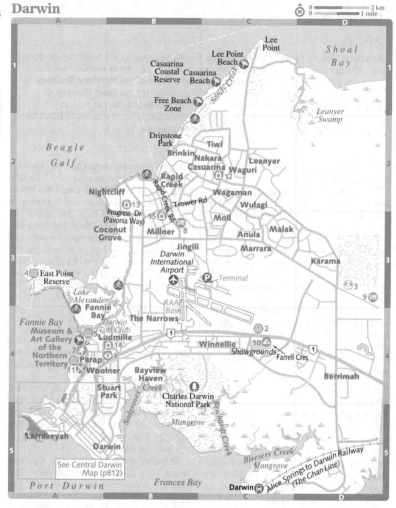

The museum has a good bookshop, and the **Cornucopia Cafe** (mains $10-19; ⊙breakfast & lunch) is a great lunch spot with views over the sea.

Crocosaurus Cove ZOO
(Map p812; www.croccove.com.au; 58 Mitchell St; adult/child $28/16; ⊙9am-8.30pm, last admission 7pm) If the tourists won't go out to see the crocs, then bring the crocs to the tourists. Right in the middle of Mitchell St, Crocosaurus Cove is as close as you'll ever want to get to these amazing creatures. Six of the largest crocs in captivity can be seen in state-of-the-art aquariums and pools. You can be lowered

right into a pool with them in the transparent **Cage of Death** (one/two people $120/160). If that's too scary, there's another pool where you can swim with a clear tank wall separating you from some mildly less menacing baby crocs. Other aquariums feature barramundi, turtles and stingrays, plus there's an enormous reptile house (allegedly the largest variety of reptiles on display in the country).

Darwin Waterfront Precinct NEIGHBOURHOOD
(Map p812; www.waterfront.nt.gov.au) The bold redevelopment of the old Darwin Waterfront Precinct is well under way. The first stage of the multimillion-dollar redevelopment

features a cruise-ship terminal, luxury hotels, boutique restaurants and shopping, an access walkway and free elevator at the south end of Smith St, and a **Wave Lagoon** (adult/child half-day $5/3.50, full-day $8/5; ⊙10am-6pm). It's a hugely popular pool, with tumbling artificially generated surf, lifeguards and a miserly strip of lawn to bask on.

The old **Stokes Hill Wharf** (www.darwinport.nt.gov.au) is well worth an afternoon promenade. At the end of the wharf an old warehouse houses a **food centre** that's ideal for an alfresco lunch, cool afternoon beer or a seafood dinner as the sun sets over the harbour. Several **harbour cruises** and a **jet boat** also leave from the wharf.

You can escape from the heat of the day and relive your Hitchcockian fantasies by walking through the **WWII Oil-Storage Tunnels** (Map p812; www.darwintours.com.au/tours/ww2tunnels.html; self-guided tour per person $6; ⊙9am-4pm May-Sep, 9am-1pm Oct-Apr). The tunnels were built in 1942 to store the Navy's oil supplies when it was decided Darwin's waterside oil tanks were a 'sitting shot'. Never used for oil, they now exhibit wartime photos.

Indo-Pacific Marine Exhibition   AQUARIUM
(Map p812; www.indopacificmarine.com.au; 29 Stokes Hill Rd; adult/child $18/8; ⊙9am-3pm Mon-Fri, 10am-3pm Sat & Sun) This excellent marine aquarium at the Waterfront Precinct gives you a close encounter with the denizens at the bottom of Darwin Harbour. Each small tank is a complete ecosystem, with only the occasional extra fish introduced as food for

some of the predators, such as stonefish or the bizarre angler fish.

Also recommended here is the **Coral Reef by Night** (adult/child $105/55; ⊙7pm Wed, Fri & Sun), which consists of a tour of the aquarium, seafood dinner (on biodegradable plates, no less!) and an impressive show of fluorescent plants and animals.

Australian Pearling Exhibition   MUSEUM
(Map p812; www.nt.gov.au; 29 Stokes Hill Rd; adult/child $7/4; ⊙10am-3pm) Next door to the Indo-Pacific Marine Exhibition at the Waterfront Precinct, the Australian Pearling Exhibition has excellent self-guided **displays** and informative **videos** on the harvesting, farming and culture of pearl oysters in the Top End. You can also experience life underwater inside a simulated diving helmet.

The Esplanade   STREET
Darwin's Esplanade is a long, straight street with flashy hotels on one side and the lush waterside **Bicentennial Park** (Map p812; www.darwin.nt.gov.au; ⊙24hr) on the other. The park runs the length of the Esplanade from Doctors Gully to Lameroo Beach, a sheltered cove popular in the '20s when it housed the saltwater baths, and traditionally a Larrakia camp area. Shaded by tropical trees, the park is an excellent place to wander.

At the Herbert St end, there's a **ceno-taph** commemorating Australians' service to the country's war efforts. Also honoured are **200 Remarkable Territorians**: hand-painted tiles in panels dispersed intermittently along the Esplanade commemorate

LOCAL KNOWLEDGE

LAUREN WALTER: NORTHERN TERRITORY VET

Working in the Territory is pretty casual. Most people are wearing thongs when they bring their animals in – tropical species like water monitors, olive pythons, pelicans, ibises and Torres Strait pigeons. At the end of the mango season, people are always concerned about the lorikeets stumbling around...but they're just drunk on fermented fruit (there are so many mangoes around, they're $5 for a whole crate).

Favourite Weekend Spot

Parap Markets. It's got a good vibe, interesting people and great Asian vegetables – baby eggplants, snake beans. The produce is local so you know it'll be fresh. I usually get fresh fruit salad and yoghurt for breakfast every Saturday.

Best Getaway

A lot of friends have permanent bookings in Bali and other parts of Indonesia; some go on the weekends. It's only two hours away, so it's closer than the rest of Australia. The only drawback is the lousy departure times, as there's no flight curfew up here.

Secret Spot

Dundee Beach (120km southwest of Darwin) is great for offshore fishing – you'll catch little fingermark snapper. Or the thermal pools in Katherine (p840). Just ask a local about croc risk!

some of the Territory's 'quiet achievers', including pioneers, publicans and pastoralists.

FREE Lyons Cottage   HISTORIC BUILDING
(Map p812; www.magnt.nt.gov.au; cnr Esplanade & Knuckey St; ⊙10am-3pm) Just across the road from Bicentennial Park, Lyons Cottage was built in 1925. It was Darwin's first stone residence, formerly housing executives from the British Australian Telegraph Company (which laid a submarine cable between Australia and Java). Now it's a museum displaying Darwin in photos from the early days.

Aquascene   AQUARIUM
(Map p812; www.aquascene.com.au; 28 Doctors Gully Rd; adult/child $11/7; ⊙high tide, check website) At Doctors Gully every day, Aquascene runs a remarkable fish-feeding frenzy. Visitors, young and old, wade into the water and hand-feed hordes of mullet, catfish, batfish and big milkfish.

Crocodylus Park   ZOO
(Map p806; www.crocodyluspark.com; 815 McMillans Rd, Berrimah; adult/child $35/17.50; ⊙9am-5pm, tours 10am, noon, 2pm & 3.30pm) Crocodylus Park showcases hundreds of crocs and a mini-zoo comprising lions, tigers and other big cats, spider monkeys, marmosets, cassowaries and large birds. Allow about two hours to look around the whole park, and you should time your visit with a

tour, which includes a feeding demonstration. Croc meat BBQ packs for sale!

The park is about 15km from the city centre. Take bus 5 from Darwin.

FREE George Brown
Botanic Gardens   GARDEN
(Map p812; www.nt.gov.au/nreta/parks/botanic; Geranium St, Stuart Park, ⊙7am-7pm) Named after the gardens' curator from 1971 to 1990, these 42-hectare gardens showcase plants from the Top End and around the world – monsoon vine forest, the mangroves and coastal plants habitat, baobabs and a magnificent collection of native and exotic palms and cycads.

Many of the plants here were traditionally used by the local Aboriginal people, and self-guiding **Aboriginal plant-use trails** have been set up – pick up a brochure at the gardens' information centre (⊙8am-4pm Mon-Fri, 8.30am-4pm Sat & Sun) near the Geranium St entry. You'll also find **birdwatching** brochures and garden maps here too.

The gardens are an easy 2km bicycle ride out from the centre of town along Gilruth Ave and Gardens Rd, or there's another entrance off Geranium St, which runs off the Stuart Hwy in Stuart Park. Alternatively, bus 7 from the city stops near the Stuart Hwy/Geranium St corner.

East Point Reserve
GARDEN

North of Fannie Bay, this spit of land (Map p806) is particularly attractive in the late afternoon when wallabies emerge to feed and you can watch the sun set over the bay.

Lake Alexander, a small, recreational saltwater lake, was created so people could enjoy a swim year-round without having to worry about box jellyfish. There's a good children's playground here and picnic areas with barbecues. A 1.5km **mangrove boardwalk** (⊙8am-6pm) leads off from the car park.

On the point's northern side is a series of WWII gun emplacements and the small but fascinating **Darwin Military Museum** (Map p806; www.darwinmilitarymuseum.com.au; 5434 Alec Fong Lim Dr; adult/child $12/5; ⊙9.30am-5pm). Video footage of Darwin Harbour being bombed is a sobering reminder of Australia's only wartime attack.

Chinese Museum & Temple
MUSEUM, TEMPLE

(Map p812; www.chungwahnt.asn.au; 25 Woods St; admission by donation; ⊙museum 10am-2pm, temple 8am-4pm) This excellent little museum explores Chinese settlement in the Top End. The adjacent temple has a hushed interior, punctuated by scarlet lanterns and smouldering incense sticks. The sacred tree in the grounds is rumoured to be a direct descendant from the Bodhi tree under which Buddha sat when he attained enlightenment.

FREE Parliament House
NOTABLE BUILDING

(Map p812; ☑08-8946 1434; www.nt.gov.au/lant; ⊙8am-6pm) At the southern end of Mitchell St is the elegantly boxlike Parliament House, which opened in 1994. Reminiscent of Southeast Asian architecture, it's designed to withstand Darwin's monsoonal climate. Book a free 45-minute tour exploring the cavernous interior. The building also houses the **Northern Territory Library** (p822).

Australian Aviation Heritage Centre
MUSEUM

(Map p806; www.darwinsairwar.com.au; 557 Stuart Hwy, Winnellie; adult/child $12/7; ⊙9am-5pm) Darwin's aviation museum, about 10km from the centre, is one for military aircraft nuts. The centrepiece is a mammoth B52 bomber, one of only two of its kind displayed outside the USA, which has somehow been squeezed inside. It dwarfs the other aircraft, which include a Japanese Zero fighter shot down in 1942 and the remains of an RAAF Mirage jet that crashed in a nearby swamp.

Free **guided tours** commence at 10am and 2pm.

Buses 5 and 8 run along the Stuart Hwy, and it's on the route of the Tour Tub (p824).

FREE Fannie Bay Gaol Museum
HISTORIC BUILDING, MUSEUM

(Map p806; cnr East Point Rd & Ross Smith Ave; ⊙10am-3pm) This interesting (if a little grim) museum represents almost 100 years of solitude. Serving as Darwin's main jail from 1883 to 1979, the solid cells contain information panels that provide a window into the region's unique social history. Lepers, refugees and juveniles were among the groups of people confined here, and you can still see the old cells and the gallows constructed for two hangings in 1952.

Myilly Point Heritage Precinct
HISTORIC SITE

At the far northern end of Smith St is this small but important precinct of four houses built 1930–39 (which means they survived both the WWII bombings *and* Cyclone Tracy!). They're now managed by the National Trust. One of them, **Burnett House** (Map p812; www.nationaltrustnt.org.au; admission by donation; ⊙10am-1pm Mon-Sat), operates as a museum. There's a tantalising **colonial high tea** ($12) in the gardens on Sunday afternoon from 3pm to 5.30pm between April and October.

Galleries

Darwin's commercial and public galleries are a fabulous way to appreciate the spirit of the Top End, both non-Aboriginal and Aboriginal. All listed galleries have free admission.

24HR Art
ART GALLERY

(Map p806; www.24hrart.org.au; Vimy Lane, Parap Shopping Village; ⊙10am-4pm Wed-Fri, 10am-2pm Sat) Changing and challenging exhibitions by the Northern Territory Centre for Contemporary Art.

Tiwi Art Network
ART GALLERY

(Map p806; www.tiwiart.com; 3/3 Vickers St, Parap; ⊙10am-5pm Wed-Fri, 10am-2pm Sat) The office and showroom for three arts communities on the Tiwi Islands.

Maningrida Arts & Culture
ART GALLERY

(Map p812; www.maningrida.com; Shop 1, 32 Mitchell St; ⊙9am-5pm Mon-Fri, 11.30am-4.30pm Sat) Features fibre sculptures, weavings and paintings from the Kunibidji community at Maningrida on the banks of the Liverpool River, Arnhem Land. Fully Aboriginal-owned.

BUYING ABORIGINAL ART

Taking home a piece of Aboriginal art can create an enduring connection with Australia. For Aboriginal artists, painting is an important cultural and economic enterprise. To ensure you're not perpetuating non-Indigenous cash-in on Aboriginal art's popularity, avoid buying cheap imported fridge magnets, stubbie holders, boomerangs or didgeridoos. Make sure you're buying from an authentic dealer selling original art, and if the gallery doesn't pay their artists upfront, ask exactly how much of your money will make it back to the artist or community.

A good test is to request some biographical info on the artists – if the vendor can't produce it, keep walking. An authentic piece will come with a certificate indicating the artist's name, language group and community, and the work's title, its story and when it was made.

You may also check that the selling gallery is associated with a regulatory body, such as the **Australian Commercial Galleries Association** (www.acga.com.au). Where possible, buy direct from Aboriginal arts centres or their city outlets (see www.ankaaa. org.au or www.aboriginalart.org); this is generally cheaper and ensures authenticity. You also get to view the works in the context in which they were created.

Territory Colours ART GALLERY
(Map p812; www.territorycolours.com; 46 Smith St Mall; ⊗10am-5pm) Contemporary paintings and crafts, including glass, porcelain and wood from local artists; features the work of contemporary Indigenous artist Harold Thomas.

Karen Brown Gallery ART GALLERY
(Map p812; www.karenbrowngallery.com; 1/22 Mitchell St; ⊗9am-5pm Mon-Fri, to 3pm Sat) Commercial gallery specialising in changing exhibitions of contemporary Aboriginal art.

Aboriginal Fine Arts Gallery ART GALLERY
(Map p812; www.aaia.com.au; 1st fl, cnr Mitchell & Knuckey Sts; ⊗9am-5pm) Displays and sells art from Arnhem Land and the Central Desert region.

Mbantua Fine Art Gallery ART GALLERY
(Map p812; www.mbantua.com.au; 2/30 Smith St Mall; ⊗9am-5pm Mon-Sat) Vivid Utopian designs painted on everything from canvasses to ceramics.

🏃 Activities

Beaches & Swimming

Darwin is no beach paradise – naturally enough the harbour has no surf – but along the convoluted coastline north of the city centre is a string of sandy beaches. The most popular are **Mindil** and **Vestey's** on Fannie Bay. Further north, a stretch of the 7km **Casuarina Beach** is an official nude beach. Darwin's swimming beaches tend to be far enough away from mangrove creeks to make the threat of meeting a crocodile very remote. A bigger problem is the deadly box

jellyfish, which makes swimming decidedly unhealthy between October and March (and often before October and until May). You can swim year-round without fear of stingers in the western part of **Lake Alexander**, an easy cycle from the centre at East Point.

Sailing

Darwin Sailing Club SAILING
(Map p806; www.dwnsail.com.au; Atkins Dr, Fannie Bay) A good place to meet local yachties, as well as an excellent place to watch the sunset over a beer. Although you can't charter boats here, there is a noticeboard advertising crewing needs and detailing the seasonal race program.

Winter School of Sailing SAILING
(Map p812; www.darwinsailingschool.com.au; Cullen Bay Marina; sailing lessons from $55, overnight cruise from $120, courses from $230) Sails the harbour in *Zanzibar,* an 11.6m sloop berthed at Cullen Bay Marina. Regular crewing sessions are held on Wednesday afternoon. Check the website for a timetable of training courses.

See also Harbour Cruises, p811.

Cycling

Darwin is great for cycling. Traffic is light and a series of **bike tracks** covers most of the city, with the main one running from the northern end of Cavenagh St to Fannie Bay, Coconut Grove, Nightcliff and Casuarina. At Fannie Bay, a side track heads out to the **East Point Reserve** (Map p806). Consider heading for **Charles Darwin National Park** (Map p806; www.nt.gov.au/nreta/parks/find/charlesdarwin.html), 5km southeast of the city, with a

few kilometres of path around the park's wetlands, woodlands and WWII bunkers.

Some hostels hire out bicycles for $15 to $25 per day for a mountain bike, or try:

Darwin Scooter Hire
CYCLING

(Map p812; www.esummer.com.au; 9 Daly St; ☺8am-5pm Mon-Fri, 9am-3pm Sat) Mountain bikes for $20 a day ($100 deposit required).

Darwin Holiday Shop
CYCLING

(Map p812; www.darwinholidayshop.com.au; Shop 2, Mantra on the Esplanade, 88 The Esplanade; ☺9am-5pm Mon-Fri, 9am-1pm Sat) Mountain bikes per half/full day $20/25.

Rock Climbing

The Rock
ROCK CLIMBING

(Map p812; www.rockclimbing.com.au; climbing incl equipment $25; ☺noon-9pm Tue, Thu & Sat, noon-6pm Wed, Fri & Sun) Inside an old WWII oil-storage tank at Doctors Gully, The Rock is the place to chalk-up your fingers, defy gravity and dangle yourself off a climbing wall.

Jetboating

Oz Jet
JETBOATING

(Map p812; ☎1300 135 595; www.nt.ozjetboating.com; 30min rides adult/child $55/30) If a harbour cruise is too tame, jump on Oz Jet for a white-knuckle ride around the harbour that'll test how long it's been since you had lunch. Departs from Stokes Hill Wharf. Bookings essential; closed during the Wet.

Skydiving

Top End Tandems
SKYDIVING

(☎0417 190 140; www.topendtandems.com.au; tandem jumps from $340) Has tandem skydives starting at Darwin Airport and landing at Lee Point Reserve.

☞ Tours

There are dozens of tours in and around Darwin, and lots of combinations covering Kakadu, Arnhem Land, Litchfield and further afield. Tourism Top End (p823) is the best place to start looking and asking questions. Remember that many tours run less frequently (or not at all) in the Wet.

City Tours

Darwin Walking & Bicycle Tours
WALKING, CYCLING

(☎08-8942 1022; www.darwinwalkingtours.com.au) Two-hour guided history walks around the city for $25 (children free), plus three-hour bike tours (adult/child $45/35) that take you out to Fannie Bay and East Point.

Tour Tub
SIGHTSEEING

(☎08-8985 6322; www.tourtub.com.au; adult/child $40/15; ☺9am-4pm Jan-Nov) This open-sided hop-on, hop-off minibus tours around Darwin's big-ticket sights throughout the day. Call for bookings, pick-up times and locations. Pay the driver onboard – cash only.

Sea Darwin
NATURE

(☎1300 065 022; www.seadarwin.com; tours adult/child $65/50) Two-hour eco tours around the city and Darwin Harbour, checking out mangroves, a crocodile trap, a shipwreck and (if you're lucky) dugongs and dolphins.

Darwin Day Tours
SIGHTSEEING

(☎1300 721 365; www.aussieadventure.com.au; afternoon city tour adult $66) Runs an afternoon city tour that takes in all the major attractions, including Stokes Hill Wharf, the Museum & Art Gallery and East Point Reserve, and can be linked with a sunset harbour cruise ($108).

Harbour Cruises

Between April and October there are plenty of boats based at the Cullen Bay Marina and Stokes Hill Wharf to take you on a cruise of the harbour.

Anniki Pearl Lugger Cruises
SAILING

(☎0428 414 000; www.anniki.com.au; tours adult/child $70/50) Three-hour sunset cruises on this historical pearling lugger depart at 4.45pm from Cullen Bay Marina and include sparkling wine and nibbles. You might recognise the ship from the film *Australia*.

Sunset Sail
SAILING

(☎0408 795 567; www.sailnt.com.au; tours adult/child $65/45) This three-hour afternoon cruise aboard the catamaran *Daymirri* departs from Stokes Hill Wharf. Refreshments are included but BYO alcohol.

Darwin Harbour Cruises
CRUISES

(☎08-8942 3131; www.darwinharbourcruises.com.au) Variety of cruises from Stokes Hill Wharf. The 20m schooner *Tumlaren* does a three-hour barbecue lunch cruise (adult/child $75/46), and a sunset cruise departing at 5pm ($66/43). The 30m schooner *Alfred Noble* has a full-dinner cruise departing at 5.45pm ($110/65).

Spirit of Darwin
CRUISES

(☎0417 381 977; www.spiritofdarwin.net; tours adult/child $45/20) This fully licensed air-con motor-catamaran does a two-hour sightseeing cruise at 2pm and a sunset cruise at 5.30pm daily from Cullen Bay Marina.

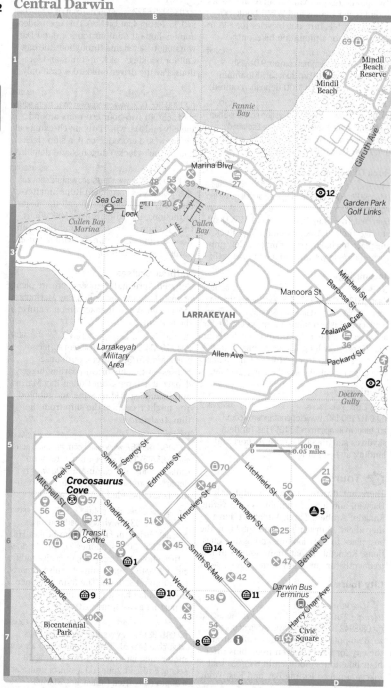

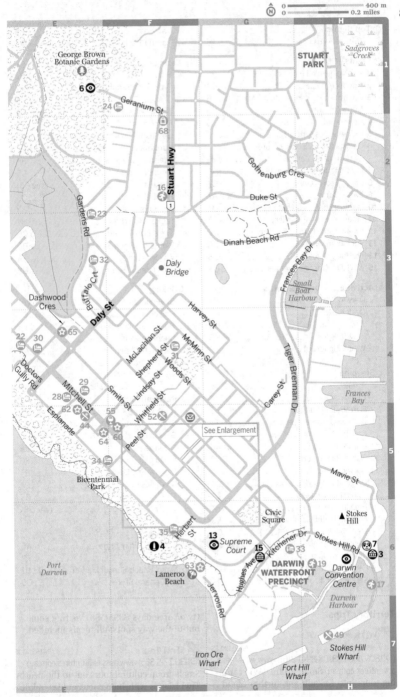

0   400 m
0   0.2 miles

George Brown
Botanic Gardens

STUART
PARK

Sadgroves
Creek

6

24   Geranium St

68

16   Stuart Hwy

Gothenburg Cres

Duke St

Dinah Beach Rd

23   Gardens Rd

32

Daly
Bridge

Frances Bay Dr

Small
Boat
Harbour

Dashwood
Cres

Buffalo Crt

Daly St

Harvey St

65

22 30

Doctors
Gully Rd

McLachlan St

Shepherd St

McMinn St

31

Woods St

Tiger Brennan Dr

Frances
Bay

Carey St

29

28

62

44

Mitchell St

Smith St

Lindsay St

Whitfield St

Esplanade

55

64   60

52

See Enlargement

34

Peel St

Bicentennial
Park

Mavie St

Civic
Square

Stokes
Hill

35   Herbert St

4

13   Supreme
Court

15

33

Kitchener Dr

Stokes Hill Rd

7

3

Port
Darwin

Lameroo
Beach

Jervois Rd

Hughes Ave

DARWIN
WATERFRONT
PRECINCT

19   Darwin
Convention
Centre

17

Darwin
Harbour

49

Stokes Hill
Wharf

Iron Ore
Wharf

Fort Hill
Wharf

Territory Trips

🗺 **Wilderness 4WD Adventures** WILDERNESS
(☎1800 808 288, 08-8941 2161; www.wilderness
adventures.com.au) Small-group 4WD camping tours into Kakadu and further afield

(two/three days $395/588) visiting some
out-of-the-way spots; all meals included.

🗺 **Tiwi Tours** INDIGENOUS
(☎1300 721 365; www.aussieadventures.com.au)
Small-group cultural tours out to the nearby
Tiwi Islands with Indigenous guides (adult/

child including flights $465/418). Kakadu and Litchfield tours also available.

Adventure Tours
BACKPACKER

(☑1800 068 886, 08-8132 8230; www.adventuretours.com.au) Range of 4WD tours to suit the spirited backpacker crowd. Two-/three-day Kakadu tours $453/663, plus day tours to Litchfield ($119) and Katherine Gorge ($157). Longer tours available.

Northern Territory Indigenous Tours
INDIGENOUS

(☑1300 921 188; www.ntindigenoustours.com) Upmarket Indigenous tours to Litchfield National Park stopping off at Territory Wildlife Park (adult/child $249/129).

BackPackNT
BACKPACKER

(☑1300 071 093; www.backpacknt.com) Quick-fire backpacker day trips ($99 to $199) to Kakadu, Uluru, Nitmiluk and Litchfield, plus longer budget-minded tours (dorms and swags) to the same areas and beyond.

Sacred Earth Safaris
WILDERNESS

(☑08-8981 8420; www.sacredearthsafaris.com.au) Multiday, small-group 4WD camping tours around Kakadu, Katherine and the Kimberley. Two-day Kakadu tour starts at $695; the five-day Top End tour is $1995.

Kakadu Dreams
BACKPACKER

(☑1800 813 266; www.kakadudreams.com.au; 50 Mitchell St) Backpacker day tours to Litchfield ($99), and boisterous two-/three-day trips to Kakadu ($360/460).

Wallaroo Eco Tours
SIGHTSEEING

(☑08-8983 2699; www.litchfielddaytours.com) Small-group tours to Litchfield National Park ($120).

★ Festivals & Events

WordStorm
LITERARY

(www.ntwriters.com.au) The biannual NT Writers' Festival event, in May, includes song, storytelling, visual-art collaboration, theatre, performance poetry, history, biography, poetry and fiction.

Arafura Games
SPORTS

(www.arafuragames.nt.gov.au) A week-long multi-sport competition held in May in odd-numbered years, targeting up-and-coming athletes from the Asia-Pacific region. Athletics, basketball, cricket, soccer, swimming, volleyball...

Darwin Blues Festival
MUSIC

(www.offtheleash.net.au) In late June, venues across Darwin charge up with electrifying live blues. Much beer and bending guitar strings.

Beer Can Regatta
LOCAL CULTURE

(www.beercanregatta.org.au) An utterly insane and typically Territorian festival that features races for boats made out of beer cans. It takes places at Mindil Beach in July and is a good, fun day.

Royal Darwin Show
AGRICULTURAL

(www.darwinshow.com.au) This agricultural show takes place at the showgrounds in Winnellie on the last weekend of July. Plenty of rides, demonstrations, competitions and malodorous farm animals.

Darwin Cup Carnival
HORSE RACING

(www.darwinturfclub.org.au) The Darwin Cup racing carnival takes place in July and August at the Darwin Turf Club in Fannie Bay. The highlight of the eight-day program is the running of the Darwin Cup, along with the usual fashion and frivolities.

Darwin Aboriginal Art Fair
VISUAL ARTS

(www.darwinaboriginalartfair.com.au) Held at the Darwin Convention Centre, this two-day August festival showcases Indigenous art from communities throughout the Territory.

Darwin Festival
ARTS

(www.darwinfestival.org.au) This mainly outdoor arts and culture festival highlights the cultures of Darwin's large Aboriginal and Asian populations and runs for about two weeks in August.

☐ Sleeping

Darwin has a good range of accommodation, most of it handy to the CBD, but finding a bed in the peak May-to-September period can be difficult at short notice – book ahead, at least for the first night. Accommodation prices vary greatly with the season and demand. Prices given here are for high season, but expect big discounts between November and March, especially for midrange and top-end accommodation.

Backpacker hostels fluctuate the least, and prices differ little between places – concentrated as they are in a small stretch of bar-heavy Mitchell St. If you want a quieter stay, choose somewhere a bit further out – they're still within walking distance of the action. Hostel facilities usually include communal kitchen, pool and laundry facilities and they all have tour-booking desks. Some offer airport, bus or train station pick-ups with advance bookings, and most give YHA/VIP discounts.

There are a few decent camping/caravan park options within 10km of the city centre. Some campervanners take their chances staying overnight at parking areas along the beach around Fannie Bay and East Point Reserve, but it's officially a no-no and council officers may move you on or dish out fines.

Darwin's larger hotels quote inflated rack rates, but there are all sorts of specials, including stand-by, weekend and internet rates. Most of the big hotels are gathered along the Esplanade.

CITY CENTRE

Cavenagh
HOSTEL, MOTEL **$**
(Map p812; ☎1300 851 198, 08-8941 6383; www.thecavenagh.com; 12 Cavenagh St; dm $25-30, d $89-159; ✴@☎☲) This converted '80s motel features stylish doubles and decent dorms convening around an enormous central pool. It's an informal, sociable kinda joint with a perpetual pool-party atmosphere and a rowdy on-site bar (even rowdier when the rugby is showing). The restaurant serves good-value meals if you want to line your stomach before your first drink.

Melaleuca on Mitchell
HOSTEL **$**
(Map p812; ☎1300 723 437; www.momdarwin.com.au; 52 Mitchell St; dm $30, d with/without bathroom $115/95; ✴@☎☲) The highlight at this busy backpackers is the rooftop island bar and pool area overlooking Mitchell St – complete with waterfall spa and big-screen TV. Party heaven! The modern hostel is immaculate but a little sterile, with stark white walls and sparse rooms. Facilities are A1 though and it's very secure. The 3rd floor is female only.

Argus
APARTMENTS **$$$**
(Map p812; ☎08-8925 5000; www.argusdarwin.com.au; 6 Cardona Ct; 1-/2-/3-bedroom apt from $260/410/495; ✴@☲) In a corner of town awash with apartment towers, the Argus stands out as a quality option. Apartments are *very* spacious, with lovely bathrooms, generous expanses of cool floor tiles, simple balcony living/dining spaces and snazzy kitchens with all the requisite appliances. The pool seems an afterthought, tucked into a corner of the car park, but it's shady and welcoming on a sticky Top End afternoon.

Dingo Moon Lodge
HOSTEL **$**
(Map p812; ☎08-8941 3444; www.dingomoonlodge.com; 88 Mitchell St; dm $30-34, d & tw $95, all incl breakfast; ✴@☎☲) Howl at the moon at the Dingo, a relatively new addition to the Darwin hostel scene. It's a two-building affair with 65 beds – big enough to be sociable but not rowdy. A highlight is the pool, sparkling underneath a massive frangipani tree, and a great outdoor kitchen. No TV room – have a conversation instead.

Novotel Atrium
HOTEL **$$$**
(Map p812; ☎08-8941 0755; www.novoteldarwin.com.au; 100 The Esplanade; d from $250, 2-bedroom apt from $340; ✴@☎☲) OK, OK, we know Novotel is a global chain and we've seen it all before, but what makes this one special are the to-die-for ocean views and stylistic standards above the norm: subtle lighting, fresh flowers and interesting Indigenous art. Breathe the sea air on your balcony or descend into the kidney-shaped swimming pool, one of the best-looking puddles in Darwin. Off-season rates are a steal.

Medina Vibe
HOTEL **$$**
(Map p812; ☎08-8941 0555; www.medina.com.au; 7 Kitchener Dr; d/studios from $170/180, 1-/2-bedroom apt $425/600; ✴@☎☲) Two hotels in one building: standard doubles at Vibe, and studios and apartments next door at Medina. Either way, you're in for an upmarket stay with friendly staff and a great location in the Darwin Waterfront Precinct. The Wave Lagoon is right next door if the shady swimming pool is too placid for you.

Chilli's
HOSTEL **$**
(Map p812; ☎1800 351 313, 08-8980 5800; www.chillis.com.au; 69a Mitchell St; dm $31, tw & d without bathroom $80, d $85; ✴@☎) Friendly Chilli's is a funky place with a small sundeck and spa (use the pool next door). There's also a pool table and a breezy kitchen/meals terrace overlooking Mitchell St. Rooms are compact but clean.

Frogshollow Backpackers
HOSTEL **$**
(Map p812; ☎1800 068 686, 08-8941 2600; www.frogs-hollow.com.au; 27 Lindsay St; dm $24-30, d with/without bathroom $100/75; ✴@☎☲) Presiding over a tranquil patch of parkland, Frogshollow is a chilled-out backpackers' choice. A relaxed Euro crew basks by the pool or kicks back in the park across the road; afternoon balconies drip with pot-plant overflows as dorm-dwellers mooch around the kitchen. Some rooms have air-con; most have fans. Dorms can be a bit cramped.

Darwin YHA
HOSTEL **$**
(Map p812; ☎08-8981 5385; www.yha.com.au; 97 Mitchell St; dm $28-34, d/f $91/112; ✴@☎☲) One of the newer additions to the hostel

scene, the YHA is in a converted motel, so all 34 rooms (including dorms) have en suites, and they're built around a decent pool. The kitchen and TV room are tiny, but next door Globetrotters Bar has cheap meals and entertainment.

Palms City Resort
RESORT $$

(Map p812; ☑1800 829 211, 08-8982 9200; www.citypalms.com; 64 The Esplanade; motel d $185-195, villas d $205-285; ❉ 🛜 ❄) True to form, this centrally located resort is fringed by palm-filled gardens. If you covet a microwave and have space cravings, the superior motel rooms are worth a bit extra, while the Asian-influenced, hexagonal villas with outdoor spas are utterly indulgent. Butterflies and dragonflies drift between bougainvilleas in the knockout gardens.

CITY FRINGE & SUBURBS

TOP CHOICE **Feathers Sanctuary**
BOUTIQUE HOTEL $$$

(Map p806; ☑08-8985 2144; www.featherssanctuary.com; 49a Freshwater Rd, Jingili; d incl breakfast $330; ❉ ❄) A sublime retreat for bird-nerds and nature lovers, Feathers has beautifully designed 'Bali-meets-bush' timber-and-iron cottages with semi-open-air bathrooms and luxurious interiors. The lush gardens have a private aviary breeding some rare birds, and a waterhole – more tropical birds than you're ever likely to see in one place again! Gangly free-roaming brolgas and jabirus steal the show.

Elkes Backpackers
HOSTEL $

(Map p812; ☑1800 808 365; www.elkesbackpackers.com.au; 112 Mitchell St; dm $33, tw & d $75-95, tr $110; ❉ @ 🛜 ❄) Elkes is a super-friendly, multilingual independent backpackers on the edge of the CBD. It's a shambling cluster of rudimentary timber buildings (Cyclone Tracy survivors) punctuated by thick copses of vegetation. It's the perfect place to meet fellow travellers, chill out by the pool, contemplate a wander into town for a few beers and generally unwind. Isn't that what backpacking is all about?

Steeles at Larrakeyah
B&B $$

(Darwin City B&B; Map p812; ☑08-8941 3636; www.darwinbnb.com.au; 4 Zealandia Cres, Larrakeyah; d from $175, 1-/2-bedroom apt $250/270; ❉ ❄) Some B&Bs are business and others feel like staying with friends; Steeles is one of the latter. With a perfect residential location midway between the city centre, Cullen Bay and Mindil Beach, the three rooms in this

pleasant Spanish Mission–style home are equipped with fridges, flat-screen TVs and private entrances. Breakfast happens in the tropical garden.

Grungle Downs B&B
B&B $$

(Map p806; ☑08-8947 4440; www.grungledowns.com.au; 945 McMillans Rd, Knuckey Lagoon; d $145-160, cottage $400; ❉ ❄) Set on a 2-hectare property, this beautiful rural retreat seems worlds away from the city (but it's only 13km). It's handy to Crocodylus Park and the airport, too. When it's hot outside, hang out in the guest lounge or by the pool. There are four lodge rooms (one with en suite) and a gorgeous two-bedroom cottage (which drops to $200 in the low season).

FreeSpirit Resort Darwin
CARAVAN PARK $

(☑08-8935 0888; www.darwinfreespiritresort.com.au; 901 Stuart Hwy, Berrimah; unpowered/powered sites $32/42, cabins & units $125-265; ❉ @ 🛜 ❄) An impressive highway-side park about a 10-minute drive from the city, with loads of facilities (including three pools). During the Dry there are regular nocturnal troubadours and activities including pancake breakfasts and water aerobics.

Shady Glen Caravan Park
CARAVAN PARK $

(Map p806; ☑1800 662 253, 08-8984 3330; www.shadyglen.com.au; cnr Farrell Cres & Stuart Hwy, Winnellie; powered sites $36, r/cabins from $70/165; ❉ ❄) Shady by name..., Well-treed caravan park with immaculate facilities, a camp kitchen, licensed shop and friendly staff. Public bus 8 rolls into downtown Darwin from the corner of the street.

Botanic Gardens Apartments
APARTMENTS $$$

(Map p812; ☑08-8946 0300; www.botanicgardens.com.au; 17 Geranium St, Stuart Park; motel d $249, apt $245-495; ❉ 🛜 ❄) In a peaceful location nudging up against the Botanic Gardens, the motel rooms and roomy one-, two- and three-bedroom apartments here are a tad '90s, but are enveloped by palms and lush tropical gardens. There are two pools to cool-off in, and all apartments have views over the Botanic Gardens (through which it's a 10-minute walk to Mindil Beach).

Frontier Hotel
HOTEL $$

(Map p812; ☑08-8981 5333; www.frontierdarwin.com.au; 3 Buffalo Crt; d $185, apt $225; ❉ 🛜 ❄) An easily spotted tower on the northern edge of town, this block of spacious, corporate-style rooms boasts excellent views, particularly

from the 6th-floor apartments. Firm beds, mustard-coloured walls, neat little bathrooms and a rooftop restaurant.

Cullen Bay Resorts　　　HOTEL, APARTMENTS **$$**
(Map p812; ☑1800 625 533, 08-8981 7999; www.cullenbayresortsdarwin.com.au; 26-32 Marina Blvd; hotel d $170, 1-/2-bed apt $270/325; ❄️🛜🏊) Cullen Bay is (or was, until the Waterfront Precinct came along) Darwin's prime waterfront location, and this pair of twin apartment towers boasts a million-dollar outlook over the marina and harbour. Interiors aren't super-flash, but the views are worth it.

Banyan View Lodge　　　HOSTEL **$**
(Map p812; ☑08-8981 8644; www.banyanviewlodge.org.au; 119 Mitchell St; dm $22-27, s/d without bathroom from $50/60, d with bathroom $90-120; ❄️@🏊) The Banyan View suits travellers who aren't into the party scene. It's a big, austere, office-block-looking YWCA that welcomes men too. Spacious rooms are clean and well kept – ask for one with a fan rather than aircon if you'd prefer. Bike hire available.

✗ Eating

When it comes to dining, Darwin doesn't pretend to be Melbourne or Sydney, but it does have by far the best culinary scene between here and Adelaide. Eateries make the most of the tropical ambience with alfresco seating, and the quality and diversity of produce tops anywhere else in the Territory.

Darwin has a growing number of cool cafes serving good coffee and snacks. There are also several food courts tucked away in the Smith St Mall arcades. Mitchell St pubs also entice backpackers off the pavement with free barbecues and cheap meals to soak up the beer.

Apart from the many city-centre restaurants and cafes, Cullen Bay has a hip waterfront dining scene, while the food centre at the end of Stokes Hill Wharf provides cheap-and-cheerful fish and chips and Asian stir-fries, and there are a few gems hidden in the suburbs north of the city.

CITY CENTRE

TOP
CHOICE **Four Birds**　　　CAFE **$**
(Map p812; Shop 2, Star Village, 32 Smith St Mall; items $4-8; ⊙breakfast & lunch Mon-Fri, plus Sat Jun-Aug) What a hip little cafe! Nooked into the arcade on the site of the old Star Cinema (a '74 cyclone victim), this hole-in-the-wall does simple things very well: bagels, toasted sandwiches, muffins, paninis and coffee. Book-reading office types and savvy travellers sit on stools scattered under a burgeoning frangipani tree.

Hanuman　　　INDIAN, THAI **$$**
(Map p812; ☑08-8941 3500; www.hanuman.com.au; 28 Mitchell St; mains $16-36; ⊙lunch Mon-Fri, dinner daily; ✎) Ask most locals about fine dining in Darwin and they'll usually mention Hanuman. Sophisticated but not stuffy or pretentious (you can wear a T-shirt), enticing aromas of innovative Indian and Thai Nonya dishes waft from the kitchen to the stylish open dining room and deck. The signature dish is oysters bathed in lemon grass, chilli and coriander, or the *meen mooli* (reef fish in coconut and curry leaves) but the menu is broad, with exotic vegetarian choices and banquets available. Killer cocktails, too.

Roma Bar　　　CAFE **$**
(Map p812; www.romabar.com.au; 9-11 Cavenagh St; mains $7-15; ⊙breakfast & lunch; 🛜) Roma is a real local institution and meeting place for Lefties, literati and travelling types. Well away from the craziness of Mitchell St, with free wi-fi, great coffee and juices, and you can get anything from muesli and eggs Benedict for breakfast to excellent toasted focaccia and fish curry for lunch.

Go Sushi Train　　　JAPANESE **$**
(Map p812; www.darwinhub.com/go-sushi-train; Shop 5, 28 Mitchell St; sushi $4.50-6.50, mains $10-30; ⊙lunch & dinner Tue-Sat; ✎) Pull up a stool at this hip sushi circuit, hidden down a lane off Mitchell St. Despite the obscure location it's hugely popular, especially on 'Super Sushi Saturday' (all sushi $4 from 10.30am to 3.30pm). Can't get enough of those eel-and-cucumber rolls...

Stokes Hill Wharf　　　SEAFOOD, FAST FOOD **$**
(Map p812; www.darwinhub.com/stokes-hill-wharf; Stokes Hill Wharf; mains $8-16; ⊙lunch & dinner) Squatting on the end of Stokes Hill Wharf is a hectic food centre with half-a-dozen food counters and outdoor tables lined up along the pier. It's a pumping place for some fish and chips, some oysters, a stir-fry, a laksa or just a cold sunset beer.

Istanbul Cafe　　　TURKISH, FAST FOOD **$$**
(Map p812; www.darwinhub.com/istanbul-cafe; 12 Knuckey St; mains $11-25; ⊙breakfast, lunch & dinner) Inside Darwin's old Country Women's Association building (not a scone or pavlova in sight), this Turkish joint serves up quick takeaway kebabs, meaty grills, dip platters, kofte meatballs and kick-arse Turkish coffee.

Vietnam Saigon Star VIETNAMESE $
(Map p812; Shop 4, 21 Smith St; mains $11-16; ☻lunch Mon-Fri, dinner daily; ☑) Darwin's speediest, shiniest Vietnamese restaurant serves up inexpensive rice-paper rolls, and beef, pork, chicken and seafood dishes with a multitude of sauces. Vegetarians are well catered for and there are good-value lunch specials.

Moorish Café MIDDLE EASTERN $$
(Map p812; ☑08-8991 0010; 37 Knuckey St; tapas $4-12, mains $16-37; ☻lunch & dinner Tue-Sat) Seductive aromas emanate from this divine terracotta-tiled cafe fusing North African, Mediterranean and Middle Eastern delights. The lunchtime crowd arrives for tantalising tapas and lunch specials, but it's an atmospheric place for dinner too – order a tagine of NT prawns, apple cider, local jewfish coconut and lime, or the six-course banquet ($42 per person).

Tim's Surf 'n' Turf STEAKHOUSE, SEAFOOD $$
(Map p812; ☑08-8981 1024; www.timssurfandturf. com.au; 10 Litchfield St; mains $15-30; ☻lunch Mon-Fri, dinner daily) Squirrelled away on a city backstreet, Tim's is a long-standing locals' diner where you can enjoy good-value seafood, steak, schnitzels and pasta on a relaxed, leafy terrace (just ignore the faux waterfall). Mark what you want on the DIY menu with a pencil and hand it to the cashier.

Ducks Nuts Bar & Grill MODERN AUSTRALIAN $$
(Map p812; ☑08-8942 2122; www.ducksnuts.com. au; 76 Mitchell St; mains $15-35; ☻breakfast, lunch & dinner) An effervescent bar/bistro delivering a clever fusion of Top End produce with that Asian/Mediterranean blend we like to claim as Modern Australian. Try the red Thai duck shank and banana curry, barra wrap or succulent lamb shanks. Good brekkies and caffeinated brews, too.

Char Restaurant STEAKHOUSE $$$
(Map p812; ☑08-8981 4544; www.charrestaurant. com.au; 70 The Esplanade; mains $31-46; ☻lunch Wed-Fri, dinner daily) A dramatic makeover of the ground floor of the historic Admiralty House has delivered Char, a fairly recent addition to Darwin's culinary landscape. The speciality here is chargrilled steaks – aged, grain-fed and cooked to perfection – but there's also a range of seafood, a crab-and-croc lasagne and a thoughtful vegetarian menu.

There are two large supermarkets in downtown Darwin: **Coles** (Map p812; Mitchell Centre, 55-59 Mitchell St; ☻6am-10pm) and

Woolworths (Map p812; cnr Cavenagh & Whitfield Sts; ☻6am-10pm).

CITY FRINGE & SUBURBS

TOP CHOICE Saffron INDIAN $$
(Map p806; ☑08-8981 2383; www.saffrron.com; Shop 14, 34 Parap Rd, Parap; mains $14-26; ☻lunch & dinner Tue-Sun; ☑) Saffrron is Darwin's newest (and best) Indian restaurant, a contemporary but intimate dining experience. The menu spans the subcontinent, from rich butter chicken to Kerala lamb curry or Madras whole NT snapper. There are plenty of vegetarian choices, traditional Indian sweets such as *kulfi* (ice cream), and takeaways available. Rather progressively, they use biodegradable furniture, cutlery, plates, bowls and takeaway containers.

Cyclone Cafe CAFE $
(Map p806; www.parapvillage.com.au; 8 Urquhart St, Parap; meals $7-14; ☻breakfast & lunch Mon-Sat) Possibly the best coffee in Darwin is brewed at this unassuming Parap haunt. The decor is all rusty corrugated-iron (Cyclone Tracy's favourite projectile), the staff are upbeat, the coffee is strong and aromatic (try the double-shot 'Hypercino'), and there's some great breakfast and lunch fare: croissants, burritos, cheese melts and bacon-and-egg rolls.

Buzz Café MODERN AUSTRALIAN $$
(Map p812; ☑08-8941 1141; www.darwinhub.com/ buzz-cafe; 48 Marina Blvd, Cullen Bay; mains $16-41; ☻lunch & dinner daily, breakfast Sun) This chic bar-restaurant furnished in Indonesian teak and Mt Bromo lava has a super multilevel deck overlooking the marina and makes a seductively sunny spot for a lazy lunch and a few drinks. Meals are Mod Oz, with some zingy salads and dishes to share. Aim for a deck table cantilevering out over the water.

Nirvana THAI, INDIAN $$
(Map p812; ☑08-8981 2025; 6 Dashwood Cr; mains $15-30; ☻dinner Mon-Sat) Excellent Thai, Malaysian and Indian dishes are only part of the story at Nirvana – it's also one of Darwin's best small live-music venues for jazz and blues. It doesn't look much from the outside, but inside the fortress-like Smith St door is an intimate warren of rooms with booth seating and Oriental decor. Enjoy a Thai green curry, *nasi goreng* (special fried rice) or fish masala with your tunes.

Yots Greek Taverna GREEK $$
(Map p812; ☑08-8981 4433; yots@yots.com.au; 54 Marina Blvd, Cullen Bay; mains $26-36; ☻lunch

& dinner) With a prime deck overlooking the marina, Yots serves up classic Greek and Mediterranean fare from saganaki and souvlaki to moussaka and spanakopita, along with barramundi and prawn dishes. Try the Greco barramundi served on spinach with baked lemon potatoes and a caper sauce. There's a cheaper lunch menu, too, and a wine list travelling from WA to France.

Seadogs ITALIAN $$
(Map p812; ☑08-8941 2877; Marina Blvd, Cullen Bay; mains $17-27; ☺lunch & dinner Tue-Sun) It may not front the marina, but the meals are cheaper at this popular local restaurant specialising in pizza, pasta, risotto and a few prawn and calamari dishes.

Parap Fine Foods SELF-CATERING $
(Map p806; www.parapfinefoods.com; 40 Parap Rd, Parap; ☺8am-6.30pm Mon-Fri, 8am-6pm Sat, 9am-1pm Sun) A gourmet food hall in Parap shopping centre, stocking organic and health foods, deli items and fine wine – perfect for a picnic.

🍷 Drinking

Drinking is big business in tropical Darwin (cold beer and humidity have a symbiotic relationship), and the city has dozens of pubs and terrace bars that make the most of balmy evenings. Virtually all bars double as restaurants, especially along Mitchell St – a frenzied row of booze rooms full of travellers, all within stumbling distance of one another. Things get messy here after midnight. Better get home to bed...

Tap on Mitchell BAR
(Map p812; www.thetap.com.au; 51 Mitchell St) One of the busiest (and least moron-prone) of the Mitchell St terrace bars, the Tap is always buzzing and there are inexpensive meals (nachos, burgers, calamari) to complement a good range of wine and beers. Angry Anderson drinks here.

Darwin Ski Club SPORTS CLUB
(Map p806; www.darwinskiclub.com.au; Conacher St, Fannie Bay) Leave Mitchell St behind and head for a sublime sunset at this laid-back (and refreshingly run-down) water-ski club on Vestey's Beach. The view through the palm trees from the beer garden is a winner, and there are often live bands.

Deck Bar BAR
(Map p812; www.thedeckbar.com.au; 22 Mitchell St) At the nonpartying parliamentary end of Mitchell St, the Deck Bar still manages to get lively with happy hours, pub trivia and regular live music. Blurring the line between indoors and outdoors brilliantly, the namesake deck is perfect for people-watching.

Darwin Sailing Club SPORTS CLUB
(Map p812; www.dwnsail.com.au; Atkins Dr, Fannie Bay) More upmarket than the ski club, the sailing club is always filled with yachties enjoying a sunset beer overlooking the Timor Sea. Tunes on the sound system are surprisingly un-yacht club (no Christopher Cross or Rod Stewart), and it's a great place for dinner too (mains $12 to $32). Sign in as a visitor at the door (bring some ID).

Shenannigans PUB
(Map p812; www.shenannigans.com.au; 69 Mitchell St) It's a long way from Cork, but Darwin has a few Irish-theme pubs. Shenannigans mixes it up with a big Mitchell St terrace, hearty food and big party nights. Guinness aplenty, live music and rugby on the TV.

Wisdom Bar & Grill BAR
(Map p812; www.wisdombar.com.au; 48 Mitchell St) Bright blue walls, velour couches and a streetside terrace with a tree growing out of it add up to a more intimate version of the Tap. A good thing too, as most of the drinkers here are looking for intimacy, a search conducted seemingly without much wisdom. Other popular city watering holes:

Cavenagh BAR
(Map p812; www.thecavenagh.com; 12 Cavenagh St) Popular backpackers and sports bar, the Cav also serves up good food.

Ducks Nuts Bar & Grill BAR
(Map p812; www.ducksnuts.com.au; 76 Mitchell St) A big backlit cocktail bar, regular live music and the swanky vodka bar give the Ducks Nuts plenty of cred.

Victoria Hotel PUB
(The Vic; Map p812; www.thevic.com.au; 27 Smith St Mall) The old Vic is a good place for a drink but these days it's more of an all-round backpacker entertainment venue – see p821.

⭐ Entertainment

Darwin's balmy nights invite a bit of late-night exploration and while there is only a handful of nightclubs, you'll find something on every night of the week. There's also a thriving arts and entertainment scene: theatre, film and concerts.

Find up-to-date entertainment listings for live music and other attractions in the free what's on guide *Off the Leash*.

Off the Leash magazine (www.offtheleash. net.au) lists events happening around town, as does **Darwin Community Arts** (www.darwin communityarts.org.au). Keep an eye out for bills posted on noticeboards and telegraph poles that advertise dance and full-moon parties.

Live Music

Just about every pub/bar in town puts on some form of live music, mostly on Friday and Saturday nights, and sometimes filling the midweek void with karaoke and DJs.

Victoria Hotel   ROCK, DJS
(The Vic; Map p812; www.thevichotel.com; 27 Smith St Mall) The Vic has bags of history – the stone building dates from 1890 – but it's hard to see it these days. This is Darwin's favourite backpacker pub and goes off every night of the week. Dirt-cheap meals draw the travellers to the upstairs bar, and they stay for the pool tables, DJs and dance floor. Downstairs has a pub quiz on Monday, table dancing, live bands and DJs.

Nirvana   JAZZ, BLUES
(Map p812; ☑08-8981 2025; 6 Dashwood Cres) Behind an imposing dungeonlike doorway, this cosy restaurant-bar has live jazz/blues every Thursday, Friday and Saturday night and an open-mic jam session every Tuesday. And the Thai/Indian/Malaysian food here is magic (see p819).

Nightclubs

Discovery & Lost Arc   NIGHTCLUB
(Map p812; www.myspace.com/discovery_night club; 89 Mitchell St; ⊘9pm-4am Fri & Sat) Discovery is Darwin's biggest, tackiest nightclub and dance venue with three levels playing techno, hip hop and R&B. Lost Arc is the neon-lit chill-out bar opening on to Mitchell St, which starts to thaw after about 10pm.

Throb   NIGHTCLUB
(Map p812; www.throbnightclub.com.au; 64 Smith St; ⊘10pm-5am Fri & Sat) Darwin's premier gay- and lesbian-friendly nightclub and cocktail bar, Throb attracts party-goers of all genders and persuasions for its hot DJs and cool atmosphere. Hosts drag shows and touring live acts.

Cinemas

TOP CHOICE Deckchair Cinema   OUTDOOR CINEMA
(Map p812; ☑08-8981 0700; www.deckchaircinema. com; Jervois Rd, Waterfront Precinct; tickets adult/child $13/6; ⊘box office from 6.30pm Apr-Nov) During the Dry, the Darwin Film Society runs this fabulous outdoor cinema below the southern end of the Esplanade. Watch a movie under the stars while reclining in a deckchair – bring a cushion for extra comfort. There's a licensed bar serving food (teriyaki noodles, pasta bolognese etc) or you can bring a picnic (no BYO alcohol). There are usually double features on Friday and Saturday nights (adult/child $20/9).

Birch Carroll & Coyle   CINEMA
(Map p812; www.eventcinemas.com.au; 76 Mitchell St; tickets adult/child $17/13) Darwin's mainstream cinema complex, screening latest-release films across five theatres. Head down on Tropical Tuesday for $10 entry (all day).

Theatre

Darwin Entertainment Centre   ARTS CENTRE
(Map p812; ☑08-8980 3333; www.darwin entertainment.com.au; 93 Mitchell St; ⊘box office 10am-5.30pm Mon-Fri & 1hr prior to shows) Darwin's main community arts venue houses the Playhouse and Studio Theatres, and hosts events from fashion-award nights to plays, rock operas, comedies and concerts. Check the website for upcoming shows.

Brown's Mart   ARTS CENTRE
(Map p812; ☑08-8981 5522; www.brownsmart. com.au; 12 Smith St) This historic venue (a former mining exchange) features live theatre performances, music and short films.

🔒 Shopping

You don't have to walk far along the Smith St Mall to find a souvenir shop selling lousy NT souvenirs: tea towels, T-shirts, stubbie holders and cane-toad coin purses (most of it made in China). Also in oversupply are outlets selling Aboriginal arts and crafts (see p809 for some reliable operators). Darwin's fabulous markets sell unique handcrafted items such as seed-pod hats, shell jewellery, kites, clothing and original photos.

Framed   ART, DESIGN
(Map p812; www.framed.com.au; 55 Stuart Hwy, Stuart Park) Surrounded by sex shops, car yards and plumbing supply outlets, Frames presents a surprisingly classy range of NT arts and crafts. The eclectic and ever-changing

DARWIN'S MAGICAL MARKETS

Mindil Beach Sunset Market   MARKET

(Map p812; www.mindil.com.au; off Gilruth Ave; ⊙5-10pm Thu, 4-9pm Sun May–Oct) As the sun heads towards the horizon on Thursday and Sunday, half of Darwin descends on Mindil Beach, with tables, chairs, rugs, grog and kids in tow. Food is the main attraction – Thai, Sri Lankan, Indian, Chinese and Malaysian to Brazilian, Greek, Portuguese and more – all at around $5 to $8 a serve. Don't miss a flaming satay stick from Bobby's brazier. Top it off with fresh fruit salad, decadent cakes or luscious crepes. But that's only half the fun – arts and crafts stalls bulge with handmade jewellery, fabulous rainbow tie-died clothes, Aboriginal artefacts, and wares from Indonesia and Thailand. Peruse and promenade, stop for a pummelling massage or to listen to rhythmic live music. Mindil Beach is about 2km from the city centre. Buses 4 and 6 go past the market area or you can catch a shuttle ($2).

Similar stalls (you'll recognise many of the stall holders) can be found at various suburban markets from Friday to Sunday:

Parap Village Market   MARKET

(Map p806; www.parapvillage.com.au; Parap Shopping Village, Parap Rd, Parap; ⊙8am-2pm Sat) This compact, crowded food-focused market is a local favourite with the full gamut of Southeast Asian cuisine, as well as plenty of ingredients to cook up your own tropical storm.

Rapid Creek Market   MARKET

(Map p806; www.rapidcreekshoppingcentre.com.au; 48 Trower Rd, Rapid Creeek; ⊙6.30am-1.30pm Sun) Darwin's oldest market is another Asian marketplace, with a tremendous range of tropical fruit and vegetables mingled with a heady mixture of spices and swirling satay smoke.

Nightcliff Market   MARKET

(Map p806; www.marketsonline.com.au; Pavonia Way, Nightcliff; ⊙8am-2pm Sun) Another popular community market, north of the city in the Nightcliff Shopping Centre.

---

range is typically tropical, and includes contemporary Aboriginal art, pottery, jewellery and exquisitely carved furniture.

Casuarina Square   MALL

(Map p806; www.casuarinasquare.com.au; 247 Trower Rd, Casuarina) This massive shopping complex has 170 mainstream retail outlets, plus cinemas and a food court. Good air-con on sticky afternoons in the Wet. Buses 4 and 5 travel the 20 minutes north of Darwin.

NT General Store   OUTDOOR GEAR, MAPS

(Map p812; 42 Cavenagh St) This casual, corrugated-iron warehouse has shelves piled high with camping and bushwalking gear, as well as a range of maps.

ℹ Information

Emergency
AANT Roadside Assistance (☑13 11 11; www.aant.com.au)

Ambulance (☑000; www.stjohnnt.com.au)

Fire (☑000; www.nt.gov.au/pfes)

Poisons Information Centre (☑13 11 26; ⊙24hr) Advice on poisons, bites and stings.

Police (☑000; www.nt.gov.au/pfes)

Internet Access
Global Gossip (☑08-8942 3044; www.globalgossip.com; 44 Mitchell St; ⊙9am-11pm Mon-Fri, 10am-10pm Sat & Sun) Darwin's biggest and busiest internet cafe.

Northern Territory Library (☑1800 019 155; www.ntl.nt.gov.au; Parliament House, Mitchell St; ⊙10am-5pm Mon-Fri, 1-5pm Sat & Sun) Book in advance for free access. Wi-fi also available.

Medical Services
Royal Darwin Hospital (☑08-8920 6011; www.health.nt.gov.au; Rocklands Dr, Tiwi; ⊙24hr) Accident and emergency.

Travellers Medical & Vaccination Centre (☑08-8901 3100; www.traveldoctor.com.au; 1st fl, 43 Cavenagh St; ⊙8.30am-noon & 1.30-5pm Mon-Fri) GPs by appointment.

Money

There are 24-hour ATMs dotted around the city centre, and exchange bureaux on Mitchell St.

Post

General post office (13 13 18; www.auspost. com.au; 48 Cavenagh St; ⊙9am-5pm Mon-Fri, 9am-12.30pm Sat) Efficient poste restante.

Tourist Information

Tourism Top End (☑1300 138 886, 08-8980 6000; www.tourismtopend.com.au; 6 Bennett St; ⊙8.30am-5pm Mon-Fri, 9am-3pm Sat, 10am-3pm Sun) Stocks hundreds of brochures and can book tours and accommodation.

ⓘ Getting There & Away

Air

Apart from the following major carriers arriving at **Darwin International Airport** (www.darwin airport.com.au; Henry Wrigley Dr, Marrara), smaller routes are flown by local operators; ask a travel agent.

Airnorth (www.airnorth.com.au) To/from East Timor, and to Broome, Perth, Kununurra and the Gold Coast.

Jetstar (www.jetstar.com) Direct flights to Melbourne.

Qantas (www.qantas.com.au) Direct flights to Perth, Adelaide, Canberra, Sydney, Brisbane, Alice Springs and Cairns.

Skywest (www.skywest.com.au) Direct flights to Perth, Kununurra and Broome.

Virgin Australia (www.virginaustralia.com) Direct flights between Darwin and Brisbane, Melbourne and Perth.

Bus

Greyhound Australia (www.greyhound.com. au) operates long-distance bus services from the **Transit Centre** (69 Mitchell St). There's at least one service per day up/down the Stuart Hwy, stopping at Pine Creek ($71, three hours), Katherine ($88, 4½ hours), Mataranka ($125, seven hours), Tennant Creek ($265, 14½ hours) and Alice Springs ($367, 22 hours).

For Kakadu, there's a daily return service from Darwin to Cooinda ($87, 4½ hours) via Jabiru ($62, 3½ hours).

Backpacker buses can also get you to out-of-the-way places:

Adventure Tours (www.adventuretours.com.au)

Oz Experience (www.ozexperience.com)

Car & Campervan

For driving around Darwin, conventional vehicles are cheap enough, but most companies offer only 100km free, which won't get you very far. Rates start at around $40 per day for a small car with 100km per day.

There are also plenty of 4WD vehicles available in Darwin, but you usually have to book ahead and fees/deposits are higher than for 2WD vehicles. Larger companies offer one-way rentals plus better mileage deals for more expensive vehicles. Campervans are a great option for touring around the Territory and you generally get unlimited kilometres even for short rentals. Prices start at around $50 a day for a basic camper or $80 to $100 for a three-berth hi-top camper, to $200-plus for the bigger mobile homes or 4WD bushcampers. Additional insurance cover or excess reduction costs extra.

Most rental companies are open every day and have agents in the city centre. Avis, Budget, Hertz and Thrifty all have offices at the airport.

Advance Car Rentals (www.advancecar.com.au; 86 Mitchell St) Small local operator with some good deals (ask about unlimited kilometres).

Avis (www.avis.com; 89 Smith St)

Backpacker Campervans (www.backpacker campervans.com.au; 17 Bombing Rd, Winnellie) At the same depot as Britz, this is a budget outfit with small campers and hi-tops at reasonable rates.

Britz Australia (www.britz.com.au; 17 Bombing Rd, Winnellie) Britz is a reliable outfit with a big range of campervans and motorhomes, including 4WD bushcampers.

Budget (www.budget.com.au; cnr Daly St & Doctors Gully Rd)

Europcar (www.europcar.com.au; 77 Cavenagh St)

Hertz (www.hertz.com.au; Shop 41, Mitchell Centre, 55–59 Mitchell St)

Thrifty (www.rentacar.com.au; 50 Mitchell St)

Travellers Autobarn (www.travellers-autobarn. com.au; 13 Daly St) Campervan specialist.

Wicked Campers (www.wickedcampers.com. au; 75 McMinn St) Colourfully painted small campers aimed at backpackers.

Train

The legendary *Ghan* train, operated by **Great Southern Rail** (www.gsr.com.au), runs weekly (twice weekly May to July) between Adelaide and Darwin via Alice Springs. The Darwin terminus is on Berrimah Rd, 15km/20 minutes from the city centre. A taxi fare into the centre is about $30, though there is a shuttle service to/from the Transit Centre for $10. See p1078 for fare details.

ⓘ Getting Around

To/From the Airport

Darwin International Airport (www.darwin airport.com.au) is 12km north of the city centre, and handles both international and domestic flights. **Darwin Airport Shuttle** (1800 358 945, 08-8981 5066; www.darwinairportshuttle. com.au) will pick up or drop off almost anywhere

in the centre for $13. When leaving Darwin book a day before departure. A taxi fare into the centre is about $25.

Public Transport

Darwinbus (www.nt.gov.au/transport) runs a comprehensive bus network that departs from the **Darwin Bus Terminus** (Harry Chan Ave), opposite Brown's Mart.

A $2 adult ticket gives unlimited travel on the bus network for three hours (validate your ticket when you first get on). Daily ($5) and weekly ($15) travel cards are also available from bus interchanges, newsagencies and the visitor information centre. Bus 4 (to Fannie Bay, Nightcliff, Rapid Creek and Casuarina) and bus 6 (Fannie Bay, Parap and Stuart Park) are useful for getting to Aquascene, the Botanic Gardens, Mindil Beach, the Museum & Art Gallery, Fannie Bay Gaol Museum, East Point Reserve and the markets.

Alternatively, the privately run **Tour Tub** (www. tourtub.com.au) is a hop-on, hop-off minibus touring Darwin's sights throughout the day.

Scooter

Darwin Scooter Hire (www.esummer.com.au; 9 Daly St) Rents out mountain bikes/500cc scooters/motorbikes for $20/60/180 per day.

Taxi

Taxis wait along Knuckey St, diagonally opposite the north end of Smith St Mall, and are usually easy to flag down. Call **Darwin Radio Taxis** (☏13 10 08; www.131008.com).

AROUND DARWIN

Mandorah

Mandorah is a low-key, relaxed residential beach suburb looking out across the harbour to Darwin. It sits on the tip of Cox Peninsula, 128km by road from Darwin but only 6km across the harbour by regular **ferry**. The main reason to visit is for the ferry ride across the harbour and a few drinks or dinner at the super-friendly pub. The nearby Wagait Aboriginal community numbers around 400 residents.

The Mandorah Beach Hotel (☏08-8978 5044; www.mandorahbeachhotel.bigpondhosting. com; d/f $88/110; ❊@❊) has sublime views over the beach and turquoise water to Darwin. All rooms in the refurbished motel have a fridge, TV and air-con. Even if you don't stay the night, the pub and restaurant ($13 to $26, open for lunch to 2pm, and dinner)

mains are great, and there's live music some weekends in season.

The Sea Cat (www.seacat.com.au; adult/child return $23/12) operates about a dozen daily services, with the first departure from the Cullen Bay Marina in Darwin at 6.30am and the last at 10pm (midnight on Friday and Saturday). The last ferry from Mandorah is at 10.20pm (12.20am Friday and Saturday). Bookings not required.

Tiwi Islands

The Tiwi Islands – Bathurst Island and Melville Island – lie about 80km north of Darwin, and are home to the Tiwi Aboriginal people. The Tiwis ('We People') have a distinct culture and today are well known for producing vibrant art and the odd champion Aussie Rules football player.

Tourism is restricted on the islands and for most tourists the only way to visit is on one of the daily organised **tours** from Darwin (see p825).

The Tiwis' island homes kept them fairly isolated from mainland developments until the 20th century, and their culture has retained several unique features. Perhaps the best known are the pukumani (burial poles), carved and painted with symbolic and mythological figures, which are erected around graves. More recently the Tiwis have turned their hand to art for sale – carving, painting, textile screen-printing, batik and pottery using traditional designs and motifs. The Bima Wear textile factory was set up in 1969 to employ Tiwi women, and today makes many bright fabrics in distinctive designs.

The main settlement on the islands is Nguiu in the southeast of Bathurst Island, which was founded in 1911 as a Catholic mission. On Melville Island the settlements are Pularumpi and Milikapiti.

Most of the 2700 Tiwi Islanders live on Bathurst Island (there are about 900 people on Melville Island). Most follow a mainly nontraditional lifestyle, but they still hunt dugong and gather turtle eggs, and hunting and gathering usually supplements the mainland diet a couple of times a week. Tiwis also go back to their traditional lands on Melville Island for a few weeks each year to teach and to learn traditional culture. Descendants of the Japanese pearl divers who regularly visited here early this century also live on Melville Island.

Aussie Rules football is a passion among the islanders and one of the biggest events of the year (and the only time it's possible to visit without a permit or on a tour) is the Tiwi football grand-final day in late March. Huge numbers of people come across from the mainland for the event – book your tour/ferry well in advance.

Tours

There's no public transport on the islands, so the best way to see them is on a tour. You can catch the Arafura Pearl ferry over to Nguiu and have a look around the town without taking a tour or buying a permit, but if you want to explore further you'll need a permit from the Tiwi Land Council (☎08-8981 4898; http://esvc001013.wic004ty.server-web.com; Armidale St, Stuart Park, Darwin).

Tiwi Tours   CULTURAL
(☎1300 721 365, 08-8923 6523; www.aussie adventures.com.au; tour adult/child $465/418) Runs fascinating day trips to the Tiwis, although interaction with the local community tends to be limited to your guides and the local workshops and showrooms. A one-day tour to Bathurst Island includes a charter flight, permit, lunch, tea and damper with Tiwi women, craft workshops, and visits to the early Catholic-mission buildings, the Patakijiyali Museum and a pukumani burial site. Tours depart Monday to Friday from March to November.

Arafura Pearl   CULTURAL
(☎08-8941 1991; www.seacat.com.au; tour adult/child $315/215, ferry only return $150/90) Tours are cheaper than flying. Leaving from Cullen Bay ferry terminal at 7.30am and returning at 5pm, the trip takes about two hours, and you spend all of the land time in Nguiu, visiting the church, museum, Tiwi Design and Ngaruwanajirri Art Community. The ferry runs on Mondays, Wednesdays and Fridays.

Arnhem Highway

The Arnhem Hwy (Rte 36) branches off towards Kakadu 34km southeast of Darwin. About 10km along the road, in the small agricultural hub of Humpty Doo, the self-proclaimed 'world famous' **Humpty Doo Hotel** (☎08-8988 1372; humptydoohotel@hotmail.com; Arnhem Hwy; d/cabins $110/130; ❉⊗) is a brawling kinda roadhouse, serving big meals (mains $18 to $33, lunch and dinner). There are unremarkable motel rooms and cabins out the back.

About 15km beyond Humpty Doo is the turn-off to the fecund green carpet of **Fogg Dam Conservation Reserve** (www.foggdam friends.org). Bring your binoculars – there are ludicrous numbers of waterbirds living here. The dam walls are closed to walkers (crocs), but there are a couple of nature walks (2.2km and 3.6km) through the forest and woodlands. Bird numbers are highest between December and July.

FREE **Window on the Wetlands Visitor Centre** (www.nt.gov.au/nreta/parks/find/window wetlands.html; Arnhem Hwy; ⊗8am-7pm), 3km past Fogg Dam, is a dashing-looking structure full of displays (static and interactive) explaining the wetland ecosystem, as well as the history of the local Limilgnan-Wulna Aboriginal people. There are great views over the Adelaide River floodplain from the observation deck, and binoculars for studying the waterbirds on Lake Beatrice.

Mary River Region

Beyond Adelaide River, the Arnhem Hwy passes through the Mary River region with the wetlands and wildlife of the **Mary River National Park** (www.nt.gov.au/nreta/parks/find/maryriver.html) extending to the north.

Bird Billabong, just off the highway a few kilometres before Mary River Crossing, is a back-flow billabong, filled by creeks flowing off the nearby Mt Bundy Hill during the Wet. It's 4km off the highway and accessible by 2WD year-round. The scenic **loop walk** (4.5km, two hours) passes through **tropical woodlands**, with a backdrop of Mt Bundy granite rocks.

About another 2km along the same road is the emerald-green **Mary River Billabong**, with a barbecue area (no camping). From here the 4WD-only Hardies Track leads deeper into the national park to **Corroboree Billabong** (25km) and **Couzens Lookout** (37km).

Further along and north of the Arnhem Hwy, the partly sealed Point Stuart Rd leads to a number of riverside viewing platforms and to **Shady Camp**. The causeway barrage here, which stops freshwater flowing into saltwater, creates the ideal feeding environment for barramundi, and the ideal **fishing** environment.

Sleeping & Eating

There are basic public **camping grounds** (adult/child $3.50/2) at Couzens Lookout and Shady Camp, where there are grassy camp

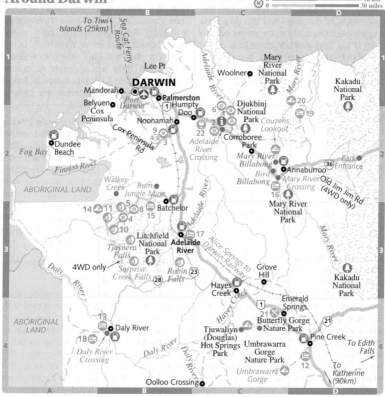

sites under banyan trees. Come prepared to ward off armies of mosquitoes.

Mary River Park　　　　　　　RESORT $$
(☎08-8978 8877; www.maryriverpark.com.au; Arnhem Hwy, Mary River Crossing; unpowered/powered sites $22/30, cabins $100-220; ❋☀) Boasting 3km of Mary River frontage just off the highway, this bush retreat is heading steadily upmarket. The owners have built a slick licensed restaurant (mains $12 to $30) and 10 deluxe units around a private pool, complementing the cheaper cabins and grassy camping area down by the river. Guided tours include a croc cruise ($45), sunset cruise ($90) and half-day fishing ($160); bookings essential.

Point Stuart Wilderness Lodge　　　CAMPGROUND, HOTEL $$
(☎08-8978 8914; www.pointstuart.com.au; Point Stuart Rd; camping $30, d $95-155; ❋☀) Accessible by 2WD, 36km from the Arnhem Hwy, this rather remote-feeling lodge is part of an old cattle station and is a decent base from which to explore the Mary River region. Accommodation ranges from basic camp sites to budget rooms and decent doubles. Wetland cruises on Rockhole Billabong per one/two/three hours cost $35/45/70, and boat hire is available. There's a bar/bistro here too, open for breakfast and dinner.

Stuart Highway to Litchfield National Park
TERRITORY WILDLIFE PARK & BERRY SPRINGS NATURE PARK

◎ Sights & Activities

Territory Wildlife Park　　　　　ZOO
(www.territorywildlifepark.com.au; 960 Cox Peninsula Rd; adult/child $26/13; ⊙8.30am-6pm, last admission 4pm) Showcases the best of Aussie wildlife in a state-of-the-art open-air zoo.

Around Darwin

Highlights include the Flight Deck, where birds of prey display their dexterity (free-flying demonstrations at 11am and 2.30pm daily); the nocturnal house, where you can observe nocturnal fauna such as bilbies and bats; 11 habitat aviaries, each representing a different habitat from mangroves to woodland; and a huge walk-through aviary, representing a monsoon rainforest. Pride of place must go to the aquarium, where a clear walk-through tunnel puts you among giant barramundi, stingrays, sawfish and saratogas, while a separate tank holds a 3.8m saltwater crocodile. To see everything you can either walk around the 4km perimeter road, or hop on and off the shuttle trains that run every 15 to 30 minutes and stop at all the exhibits.

Berry Springs Nature Park   NATURE RESERVE
(www.nt.gov.au/nreta/parks/find/berrysprings. html; ⊙8am-6.30pm) Close by is this beautiful series of spring-fed swimming holes shaded by paperbarks and pandanus palms and serenaded by abundant birds. Facilities include a kiosk, a picnic area with barbecues, toilets, changing sheds and showers.

The turn-off to Berry Springs and Territory Wildlife Park is 48km down the Track from Darwin; it's then 10km to the park.

BATCHELOR
POP 480

The government once gave Batchelor's blocks of land away to encourage settlement in the little town. That was before uranium was discovered and the nearby **Rum Jungle mine** developed (it closed in '71 after almost 20 years). These days, Batchelor exists as a gateway and service centre for neighbouring **Litchfield National Park**, and is home to the **Batchelor Institute for Indigenous Education**.

Opposite the general store, a small, sporadically staffed visitor information centre (Tarkarri Rd; ⊙8.30am-5pm) is stocked with fliers, including national-parks info.

🛏 Sleeping & Eating

Although most travellers are naturally headed into Litchfield, this gateway town offers some quality accommodation and a pub. The **Batchelor General Store** (cnr Tarkarri & Nurndina Rds; ⊙6am-6pm) has a well-stocked supermarket, takeaway shop, newsagent and post office.

TOP CHOICE **Rum Jungle Bungalows**   CABINS **$$**
(☑08-8976 0555; www.rumjunglebungalows. com.au; 10 Meneling Rd; d $160, breakfast $15; ❉❉) Bombarded by fluttering butterflies, these six olive-coloured bungalows are simple, elegant and immaculately clean. Each has a small fridge and en suite, and it's a short walk through tropical gardens (featuring native NT plants and herbs) to the private pool and breezy breakfast room (fresh seasonal fruit, local honey, homemade muesli and hot coffee). So much nicer than a motel!

Batchelor Butterfly & Tropical Retreat   RESORT **$$**
(☑08-8976 0199; www.butterflyfarm.net; 8 Meneling Rd; d $160-175; ❉@❉) This compact-but-classy retreat divides itself between lovely tropical-style en suite cabins and a busy all-day cafe/restaurant (mains $12 to $34), featuring Asian-inspired prawn, roo, crocodile and barramundi dishes. It's all very Zen with Buddha statues, chilled-out music and wicker chairs on the shaded deck. You can get a massage here, too.

Few people seem to be able to resist the sight of a 5m-long saltwater crocodile launching itself out of the water towards a hunk of meat. Like a well-trained circus act, these wild crocs know where to get a free feed – and down on the Adelaide River, the croc-jumping show is guaranteed.

Jumping out of the water to grab prey is actually natural behaviour for crocs, usually to take surprised birds or animals from overhanging branches. They use their powerful tails to propel themselves up from a stationary start just below the surface, from where they can see their prey.

There are three operators at different locations along the Adelaide River. The modus operandi is pretty similar – a crew member (or nervous tourist) holds one end of a long stick that has a couple of metres of string attached to the other end. Tied to the end of the string is a very domesticated-looking pork chop – not exactly bush tucker, but the crocs love it. The whole thing is contrived, but it's still an amazing sight.

Adelaide River Experience   WILDLIFE CRUISES
(☑08-8983 3224; www.adelaiderivercruises.com.au; Anzac Pde; tours adult/child $30/16; ⊘9am, 11am, 1pm & 3pm May-Oct) On a private stretch of river past the Fogg Dam turn-off. Also runs small-group full-day wildlife cruises.

Adelaide River Queen   WILDLIFE CRUISES
(☑08-8988 8144; www.jumpingcrocodilecruises.com.au; tours adult/child $35/20; ⊘9am, 11am, 1pm & 3pm Nov-Feb) Well-established operator on the highway just before Adelaide River Crossing.

Jumping Crocodile Cruise   WILDLIFE TOURS
(☑08-8988 9077; www.jumpingcrocodile.com.au; tours adult/child $35/20; ⊘9am, 11am, 1pm & 3pm) Along the Window on the Wetlands access road, this outfit runs one-hour tours. Ask about trips ex-Darwin.

Historic Retreat B&B   B&B $$
(☑08-8976 0554; www.historicretreat.com.au; 19 Pinaroo Cres; d incl breakfast $120-180; ❋) The beautifully restored former home of Rum Jungle-mine managers is elevated (tropical-style) and has louvred windows, polished floorboards, vintage furniture and plenty of mine memorabilia. The five guest rooms share two bathrooms.

Litchfield Tourist Park   CARAVAN PARK $
(☑08-8976 0070; www.litchfieldtouristpark.com.au; 2916 Litchfield Park Rd; unpowered/powered sites $22/28, dm $30, cabins $95-125; ❋@🛜❋) Just 4km from Litchfield, the standout feature here is the two-bedroom ranch-style house that you can rent for $550 (it sleeps 15!) or for $240 per couple. There's also a buzzy, open-sided bar/restaurant here (mains $13 to $22, open breakfast and dinner) where you can get a beer, a burger or a real coffee.

Batchelor Resort   RESORT $$
(☑08-8976 0123; www.batchelor-resort.com; 37-49 Rum Jungle Rd; powered sites $35-58, unpowered sites/cabins/motel d $30/125/177; ❋🛜❋) On the edge of town, this predictable orange-brick resort complex has a sprawling caravan park with en suite sites and cabins, and a separate motel section. It's good for families, with bird feeding, two pools and two restaurants. There's also a bar and a grocery shop.

Litchfield National Park

It may not be as well known as Kakadu, but many Territory locals rate Litchfield even higher. In fact, there's a local saying that goes: 'Litchfield-do, Kaka-don't'. We don't entirely agree – we think Kaka-do-too – but this is certainly one of the best places in the Top End for **bushwalking**, **camping** and especially **swimming**, with waterfalls plunging into gorgeous, safe swimming holes.

The 1500-sq-km national park encloses much of the spectacular Tabletop Range, a wide sandstone plateau mostly surrounded by cliffs. The **waterfalls** that pour off the edge of this plateau are a highlight of the park, feeding crystal-clear cascades and croc-free plunge pools.

The two routes to Litchfield (115km south of Darwin) from the Stuart Hwy join up and loop through the park. The southern access road via Batchelor is all sealed, while the northern access route, off the Cox Peninsula Rd, is partly unsealed, corrugated and often closed in the Wet.

About 17km after entering the park from Batchelor you come to what look like tombstones. But only the very tip of these **magnetic termite mounds** is used to bury the dead; at the bottom are the king and queen, with workers in between. They're perfectly aligned to regulate temperature, catching the morning sun, then allowing the residents to dodge the midday heat.

Another 6km further along is the turnoff to **Buley Rockhole** (2km), where water cascades through a series of rock pools big enough to lodge your bod in. This turn-off also takes you to **Florence Falls** (5km), accessed by a 15-minute, 135-step descent to a deep, beautiful pool surrounded by monsoon forest. Alternatively, you can see the falls from a lookout, 120m from the car park. There's a walking track (1.7km, 45 minutes) between the two places that follows Florence Creek.

About 18km beyond the turn-off to Florence Falls is the turn-off to the spectacular **Tolmer Falls**, which is for looking only. A 1.6km loop track (45 minutes) offers beautiful views of the valley.

It's a further 7km along the main road to the turn-off for Litchfield's big-ticket attraction, **Wangi Falls** (pronounced *Wong*-guy), 1.6km up a side road. The falls flow year-round, spilling either side of a huge orange-rock outcrop and filling an enormous swimming hole bordered by rainforest. Bring swimming goggles to spot local fish. It's immensely popular during the Dry (when there's a portable refreshment kiosk here), but water levels in the Wet can make it unsafe; look for signposted warnings.

The park offers plenty of bushwalking, including the **Tabletop Track** (39km), a circuit of the park that takes three to five days to complete depending on how many side tracks you follow. You can access the track at Florence Falls, Wangi Falls and Walker Creek. Overnight walkers should register (call ☎1300 650 730); camping fees apply. The track is closed September to March.

☞ Tours

See p814 for Litchfield tours ex-Darwin.

☷ Sleeping & Eating

There is excellent public **camping** (adult/child $6.60/3.30) within the park. Grounds with toilets and fireplaces are located at Florence Falls, Florence Creek, Buley Rockhole, Wangi Falls (better for vans than tents) and Tjaynera Falls (Sandy Creek; 4WD required). There are more-basic camp sites at Surprise Creek Falls (4WD required) and Walker Creek, with its own swimming hole, where camping involves bushwalking to a series of sublime, isolated riverside sites.

Latitude 1308   CAMPGROUND **$**
(☎08-8978 2077; www.latitude1308.com.au; Litchfield Park Rd; tents per person from $25) Run by the Litchfield Cafe, in a nearby bush clearing, Latitude 1308 is an intimate group of safari tents – two doubles and six twins – that are fabulous value for this neck of the woods. Open April to September.

Litchfield Safari Camp   CAMPGROUND **$**
(☎08-8978 2185; www.litchfieldsafaricamp.com.au; Litchfield Park Rd; unpowered/powered sites $20/30, dm $25, d safari tents $130, extra person $10; ☒) Shady grassed sites make this a good alternative to Litchfield's bush camping sites, especially if you want power. The safari tents are great value as they comfortably sleep up to four folks. There's also a ramshackle camp kitchen and pint-sized pool.

[TOP CHOICE] **Litchfield Cafe**   CAFE **$$**
(www.litchfieldcafe.com.au; Litchfield Park Rd; mains $16-34; ⏱breakfast, lunch & dinner Mar-Oct, lunch only Nov-Feb) Filo parcels (try the chicken, mango and macadamia) make for a super lunch at this excellent licensed cafe, or you could go for a meal of grilled local barra or roo fillet, topped-off with a good coffee and some wicked mango cheesecake.

Adelaide River to Katherine

ADELAIDE RIVER
POP 190

Blink and you'll miss this tiny highway town, 111km south of Darwin, but once an important point on the Overland Telegraph Line and supply depot during WWII. The **Adelaide River War Cemetery** (Memorial Tce) is an important legacy: a sea of little brass plaques commemorating those killed in the 1942–43 air raids on northern Australia.

🛏 Sleeping & Eating

Adelaide River Inn PUB $

(📞08-8976 7047; www.adelaideriverinn.com.au; un-powered/powered sites $18/25, cabins $125; 106 Stuart Hwy; 🌢🌢) An affable little pub (mains $9 to $26, open breakfast, lunch and dinner) hiding behind the BP petrol station. On the corner of the bar stands Charlie the water buffalo, who lived here in relative obscurity until shooting to fame in *Crocodile Dundee*. When he died the owner had him stuffed for posterity. There are neat cabins across the road.

Mt Bundy Station HOSTEL, B&B $

(📞08-8976 7009; www.mtbundy.com.au; Haynes Rd; unpowered/powered sites $22/26, dm/s/d $35/50/82, cottage d $140; 🌢🌢) If you're into horse riding, fishing and country-style hospitality, Mt Bundy Station is the perfect detour, 3km off the highway after Adelaide River. The original station buildings have become a spotless 20-bed bunkhouse with kitchen and a separate cottage sleeping six. By the time you read this, some new luxury safari tents should be in place (doubles $202 including breakfast). There are plenty of animals on the property – guided horse rides cost $60 per hour, with overnight treks by arrangement.

DALY RIVER
POP 470

The Daly River is considered some of the best **barramundi fishing** country in the Territory and the hub is this small community 117km southwest of Hayes Creek, reached by a narrow sealed road off the Dorat Rd (Old Stuart Hwy; Rte 23). Most of the population lives in the Nauiyu Nambiyu Aboriginal community, a few kilometres before Daly River Crossing. There's a shop and fuel here and visitors are welcome without a permit, but note that this is a dry community (no alcohol).

The main attraction here is **Merrepen Arts** (📞08-8978 2533; www.merrepenfestival.com.au/art_centre.html; admission free; 🕙10am-5pm), a gallery displaying locally made arts and crafts including etchings, screen printing, acrylic paintings, carvings, weaving and textiles. You can usually see artists at work in the mornings. Call in advance to check they're open.

The **Merrepen Arts Festival** (www.merrepenfestival.com.au) celebrates arts and music from communities around the district, including Nauiyu, Wadeye and Peppimenarti, with displays, art auctions, workshops and dancing.

🛏 Sleeping & Eating

Daly River Mango Farm CAMPGROUND $

(📞08-8978 2464; www.mangofarm.com.au; un-powered/powered sites $26/30, d $125-200; 🌢🌢) The camping ground here, on the Daly River 9km from the crossing, is shaded by a magnificent grove of 90-year-old mango trees. Other accommodation includes self-contained cabins (we like the stone one right on the river). Guided fishing trips and boat hire available.

Daly River Roadside Inn PUB $

(📞08-8978 2418; daly.river.pub@bigpond.com; unpowered/powered sites $15/30, r $75-110; 🌢) At Daly River itself is this boisterous pub with basic rooms, a small camping ground and meals (takeaway or pub food from $6 to $18) and fuel available.

Perry's CAMPGROUND $

(📞08-8978 2452; www.dalyriver.com; Mayo Park; unpowered/powered sites $26/28, unit $180; 🌢🌢) Another peaceful place with 2km of river frontage and gardens where orphaned wallabies bound around. Dick Perry, a well-known fishing expert, operates guided trips.

PINE CREEK
POP 260

A short detour off the Stuart Hwy, Pine Creek was once the scene of a frantic gold rush. The open-cut mine here closed in 1995, but today there's a new influx of mine workers from the recently opened gold and iron-ore mines nearby. A few of the 19th-century timber and corrugated-iron buildings still survive. The Kakadu Hwy (Rte 21) branches off the Stuart Hwy here, connecting it to Cooinda and Jabiru.

◉ Sights & Activities

FREE **Railway Museum & Stream Train** MUSEUM

(Railway Tce; 🕙10am-2pm Mon-Fri May-Sep) Dating from 1889, the Railway Museum has a display on the Darwin-to-Pine Creek railway which ran from 1889 to 1976. The lovingly restored steam engine, built in Manchester in 1877, sits in its own enclosure next to the museum.

Pine Creek Museum MUSEUM

(www.nationaltrustnt.org.au; 11 Railway Tce; adult/child $2.20/free; 🕙11am-5pm Mon-Fri, 11am-1pm Sat) This museum is dedicated to the area's mining history and Chinese population. A one-time hospital, pharmacy and military communications centre, it's the oldest prefab

corrugated iron building in Australia, made in England and shipped here in 1889.

Umbrawarra Gorge Nature Park
NATURE RESERVE

(www.nt.gov.au/nreta/parks/find/umbrawarra gorge.html) About 3km south of Pine Creek on the Stuart Hwy is the turn-off to pretty Umbrawarra Gorge, with a safe swimming hole, a little beach and a basic camping ground (adult/child $3.30/1.65). It's 22km southwest on a rugged dirt road (just OK for 2WDs in the Dry; often impassable in the Wet). Bring plenty of water and mozzie repellent.

Lookout
LANDMARK

Drive or walk up the short-but-steep hill off Moule St to the lookout over the old open-cut mine, now full of water (135m deep!).

🛏 Sleeping & Eating

Lazy Lizard Tourist Park & Tavern
CARAVAN PARK $

(☑08-8976 1224; www.lazylizardpinecreek.com. au; unpowered/powered sites $17/25; 299 Millar Tce; ▓) The small, well-grassed camping area at the Lazy Lizard is really only secondary to the pulsing pub next door. The open-sided bar supported by carved iron-wood pillars is a busy local watering hole with a pool table and old saddles slung across the rafters. The kitchen serves top-notch pub food (mains $16 to $30, open lunch and dinner), featuring big steaks and barra dishes.

Bonrook Country Stay
B&B $$

(☑08-8976 1232; www.bonrook.com; Stuart Hwy; s/d/f $50/60/120, deluxe d $85-120; ▓▓) Beautiful Bonrook, 8km south of town, is a tranquil B&B on a wild horse sanctuary where the brumbies are free to roam. The spotless rooms have no TV and no phone – just the sound of the wind in the trees and the birds outside.

Emerald Springs Roadhouse
ROADHOUSE $

(☑08-8976 1169; www.emeraldsprings.com.au; Stuart Hwy; unpowered/powered sites $10/20, cabins from $55; ▓▓) About 25km north of Pine Creek, the excellent Emerald Springs Roadhouse makes an effort to provide more than a regulation truck stop. You can still get a burger and a beer, but there's also decent accommodation out the back and a great deck on which to sit, sip and savour your steak sanger. And the homemade ice cream is awesome!

Kakadu National Park

Kakadu is much more than just a national park. It's an adventure into a natural and cultural landscape that almost defies description. Encompassing almost 20,000 sq km (about 200km north–south and 100km east–west), it holds in its boundaries a spectacular ecosystem and a mind-blowing concentration of ancient **rock art**.

In just a few days you can cruise on billabongs bursting with **wildlife**, examine 25,000-year-old rock paintings with the help of an Indigenous guide, swim in pools at the foot of tumbling **waterfalls** and hike through ancient sandstone escarpment country.

Kakadu and neighbouring Arnhem Land epitomise the remarkable landscape and cultural heritage of the Top End. Each is a treasure house of natural history and Aboriginal art, an acknowledgment of the elemental link between the Aboriginal custodians and the country they have nurtured, endured and respected for thousands of generations. The landscape is an ever-changing tapestry – periodically scorched and flooded, apparently desolate or obviously abundant depending on the season.

If Kakadu has a downside – in the Dry at least – it's that it's very popular. Resorts, camping grounds and rock-art sites can be very crowded, but this is a vast park and with a little adventurous spirit you can easily get off the beaten track and be alone with nature.

The Arnhem Hwy and Kakadu Hwy traverse the park; both are sealed and accessible year-round. The 4WD-only Old Jim Jim Rd is an alternative access from the Arnhem Hwy, joining the Kakadu Hwy 7km south of Cooinda.

Note that there's no takeaway alcohol available here or anywhere in Kakadu – if you want a drink back at the camp site, stock up in Darwin.

Geography

The circuitous Arnhem Land escarpment, a dramatic 30m- to 200m-high sandstone cliff line, forms the natural boundary between Kakadu and Arnhem Land and winds 500km through eastern and southeastern Kakadu.

Creeks cut across the rocky plateau and, in the wet season, tumble off it as thundering waterfalls. They then flow across the

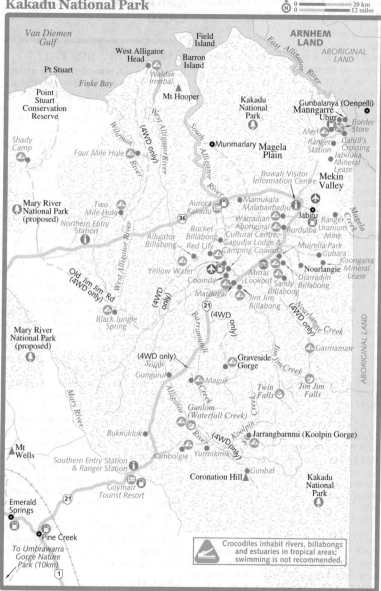

N
0 —————————— 20 km
0 —————————— 12 miles

Van Diemen Gulf

Finke Bay

West Alligator Head

Barron Island

Field Island

ARNHEM LAND

ABORIGINAL LAND

East Alligator River

Pt Stuart

Waldak Irrmbal

Mt Hooper

Point Stuart Conservation Reserve

Gunbalanya (Oenpelli)

Manngarre

Ubirr

Border Store

Kakadu National Park

Merl

Cahill's Crossing

Shady Camp

Wildman River

Four Mile Hole

West Alligator River

South Alligator River

Munmarlary

Magela Plain

Ranger Station

Jabiluka Mineral Lease

Bowali Visitor Information Centre

Mekin Valley

Mary River National Park (proposed)

Two Mile Hole

Alligator River

Aurora Kakadu

Mamukala

Malabanbadju

36

Ranger Uranium Mine

Jabiru

Burdulba

Muirella Park

Gubara

Koongarra Mineral Lease

Northern Entry Station

Alligator Billabong

Bucket Billabong

Red Lily

Warradjan Aboriginal Cultural Centre

Gagudju Lodge & Camping

Cooinda

Yellow Water

Cooinda

Mirrai Lookout

Sandy Billabong

Djarradjin Billabong

Nourlangie

Old Jim Jim Rd (4WD only)

West Alligator River

(4WD only)

Mardugal

Jim Jim Billabong

Nourlangie Creek

Black Jungle Spring

21

(4WD only)

Garnamarr

Mary River National Park (proposed)

(4WD only)

South Gungurul

Barramundi

Graveside Gorge

Jim Jim Creek

ABORIGINAL LAND

Mary River

Alligator River

Maguk

Mary Creek

Twin Falls

Jim Jim Falls

Koolpin Creek

Gunlom (Waterfall Creek)

Jarrangbarnmi (Koolpin Gorge)

Bukbukluk

Kambolgie

Yurmikmik

(4WD only)

Mt Wells

Southern Entry Station & Ranger Station

Coronation Hill

Gimbat

Kakadu National Park

Goymarr Tourist Resort

Emerald Springs

21

Pine Creek

To Umbrawarra Gorge Nature Park (10km)

1

Crocodiles inhabit rivers, billabongs and estuaries in tropical areas; swimming is not recommended.

lowlands to swamp Kakadu's vast northern flood plains. From west to east, the rivers are the Wildman, West Alligator, South Alligator and East Alligator (the latter forming the eastern boundary of the park). The coastal zone has long stretches of mangrove swamp, important for halting erosion and as a breeding ground for bird and marine life. The southern part of the park is dry lowlands with open grassland and eucalypts. Pockets of monsoon rainforest crop up throughout the park.

Over 80% of Kakadu is savannah woodland. It has more than 1000 plant species, many still used by Aboriginal people for food and medicinal purposes.

Climate

The average maximum temperature in Kakadu is 34°C, year-round. The Dry is roughly April to September, and the Wet, when most of Kakadu's average rainfall of 130mm falls, is from October to March. As wetlands and waterfalls swell, unsealed roads become impassable, cutting off some highlights such as Jim Jim Falls.

Local Aboriginal people recognise six seasons in the annual cycle:

Gunumeleng (October to December) The build-up to the Wet. Humidity increases, the temperature rises to 35°C or more and mosquitoes reach near-plague proportions. By November the thunderstorms have started, billabongs are replenished, and waterbirds and fish disperse.

Gudjewg (January to March) The Wet proper continues, with violent thunderstorms, and flora and fauna thriving in the hot, moist conditions.

Banggereng (April) Storms (known as 'knock 'em down' storms) flatten the spear grass, which during the course of the Wet has shot up to 2m high.

Yegge (May to June) The season of mists, when the air starts to dry out. The wetlands and waterfalls still have a lot of water and most of the tracks are open.

Wurrgeng (June to mid-August) The most comfortable time, weather-wise, is the late Dry, beginning in July. This is when animals, especially birds, gather in large numbers around shrinking billabongs, and when most tourists visit.

Gurrung (mid-August to September) The end of the Dry and the beginning of another cycle.

Wildlife

Kakadu has over 60 species of mammals, more than 280 bird species, 120 or so types of reptile, 25 species of frog, 55 freshwater fish species and at least 10,000 different kinds of insect. Most visitors see only a fraction of these creatures (except the insects), since many of them are shy, nocturnal or scarce.

BIRDS

Abundant waterbirds and their beautiful wetland homes are a highlight of Kakadu.

This is one of the chief refuges in Australia for several species, including the magpie goose, green pygmy goose and Burdekin duck. Other fine waterbirds include pelicans, darters and the jabiru, with its distinctive red legs and long beak. Herons, egrets, cormorants, wedge-tailed eagles, whistling kites and black kites are common. The open woodlands harbour rainbow bee-eaters, kingfishers and the endangered bustard. Majestic white-breasted sea eagles are seen near inland waterways. At night, you might hear barking owls calling – they sound just like dogs. The raucous call of the spectacular red-tailed black cockatoo is often considered the signature sound of Kakadu.

At **Mamukala**, 8km east of the South Alligator River on the Arnhem Hwy, is a wonderful observation building, plus birdwatching hides and a 3km walking track.

FISH

You can't miss the silver barramundi, which creates a distinctive swirl near the water's surface. It can grow to over 1m in length and changes sex from male to female at the age of five or six years.

MAMMALS

Several types of kangaroo and wallaby inhabit the park; the shy black wallaroo is unique to Kakadu and Arnhem Land. You may see a sugar glider in wooded areas in the daytime. Kakadu has 26 bat species, four of them endangered.

REPTILES

Twin Falls and Jim Jim Falls have resident freshwater crocodiles, which have narrow snouts and rarely exceed 3m, while the dangerous saltwater variety is found throughout the park.

Kakadu's other reptiles include the frilled lizard and five freshwater turtle species, of which the most common is the northern snake-necked turtle. Kakadu has many snakes, though most are nocturnal and rarely encountered. The striking Oenpelli python was first seen by non-Aboriginal people in 1976. The odd file snake lives in billabongs. They have square heads, tiny eyes and saggy skin covered in tiny rough scales (hence 'file'). They move very slowly (and not at all on land), eating only once a month and breeding once every decade.

Rock Art

Kakadu is one of Australia's richest, most accessible repositories of rock art. There

are more than 5000 sites, which date from 20,000 years to 10 years ago. The vast majority of these sites are off limits or inaccessible, but two of the finest collections are the easily visited galleries at Ubirr and Nourlangie.

Rock paintings have been classified into three roughly defined periods: Pre-estuarine, which is from the earliest paintings up to around 6000 years ago; Estuarine, which covers the period from 6000 to around 2000 years ago, when rising sea levels brought the coast to its present level; and Freshwater, from 2000 years ago until the present day.

For local Aboriginal people, these rock-art sites are a major source of traditional knowledge and represent their archives. Aboriginal people rarely paint on rocks any more, as they no longer live in rock shelters and there are fewer people with the requisite knowledge. Some older paintings are believed by many Aboriginal people to have been painted by mimi spirits, connecting people with creation legends and the development of Aboriginal law.

As the paintings are all rendered with natural, water-soluble ochres, they are very susceptible to water damage. Drip lines of clear silicon rubber have been laid on the rocks above the paintings to divert rain. As the most accessible sites receive up to 4000 visitors a week, boardwalks have been erected to keep the dust down and to keep people at a suitable distance from the paintings.

Tours

There are dozens of Kakadu tours on offer; book at least a day ahead if possible; operators generally collect you from your accommodation. For tours departing Darwin, see p814.

Indigenous Tours & Sightseeing

Kakadu Animal Tracks INDIGENOUS
(08-8979 0145; www.animaltracks.com.au; tours adult/child $189/129) Based at Cooinda, this outfit runs tours with an Indigenous guide combining a wildlife safari and Aboriginal cultural tour. You'll see thousands of birds, get to hunt, gather, prepare and consume bush tucker and crunch on some green ants.

Magela Cultural & Heritage Tours INDIGENOUS
(08-8979 2548; www.kakadutours.com.au; tours adult/child $245/196) Aboriginal-owned and -operated day tour into northern Kakadu and Arnhem Land, including Injalak Hill and a cruise on Inkiyu billabong.

Gagudju Adventure Tours SIGHTSEEING
(08-8979 0145; www.gagudju-dreaming.com; tours adult/child $168/138) 4WD tours to Jim Jim Falls.

Top End Explorer Tours SIGHTSEEING
(1300 556 609, 08-8979 3615; www.kakadu tours.net.au; tours adult/child $168/140) 4WD tours to Jim Jim Falls and Twin Falls – not on everyone's hit list.

Ayal Aboriginal Tours INDIGENOUS
(0429 470 384; www.ayalkakadu.com.au; tours adult/child $198/99) Full-day Indigenous-run tours around Kakadu, shining a light on art, culture and wildlife.

Kakadu Air FLIGHTS
(1800 089 113; www.kakaduair.com.au) Offers 30-minute/one-hour fixed-wing flights for $130/210 per adult. Helicopter tours, though more expensive, give a more dynamic aerial perspective. They cost from $195 (20 minutes) to $495 (70 minutes) per person.

Wetland & River Trips

Yellow Water Cruises CRUISES
(1800 500 401; www.gagudju-dreaming.com) Cruise the South Alligator River and Yellow Water Billabong spotting wildlife. Purchase tickets from Gagudju Lodge, Cooinda, where a shuttle bus will deliver you to the departure point. Two-hour cruises ($95/69 per adult/child) depart at 6.45am, 9am and 4.30pm; 1½-hour cruises ($64/44) leave at 11.30am, 1.15pm and 2.45pm.

Guluyambi INDIGENOUS
(1800 089 113; www.kakaduculturaltours.com.au; adult/child $49/27; 9am, 11am, 1pm & 3pm May-Nov) Launch into an Aboriginal-led river cruise from the upstream boat ramp on the East Alligator River near Cahill's Crossing.

Kakadu Culture Camp INDIGENOUS
(night cruise 1800 811 633, overnight 0428 792 048; www.kakaduculturecamp.com) Aboriginal-owned and -operated cruises on Djarradjin Billabong; two-hour night cruise ($80/50 per adult/child), and overnight cruise-plus-accommodation (safari tent) tours ($195/65 per adult/child). Tours depart from Muirella Park camping ground.

UBIRR & AROUND

It'll take a lot more than the busloads of visitors here to disturb Ubirr's inherent majesty and grace. Layers of rock-art paintings, in various styles and from various centuries, command a mesmerising stillness. Part of the main gallery reads like a menu, with

images of kangaroos, tortoises and fish painted in X-ray, which became the dominant style about 8000 years ago. Predating these are the paintings of mimi spirits: cheeky, dynamic figures who, it's believed, were the first of the Creation Ancestors to paint on rock (...given the lack of cherry pickers in 6000 BC, you have to wonder who else but a spirit could have painted at that height and angle). Look out for the yam-head figures, where the head is depicted as a yam on the body of a human or animal; these date back around 15,000 years.

The magnificent **Nardab Lookout** is a 250m scramble from the main gallery. Surveying the exotic floodplain and watching the sun set in the west and the moon rise in the east, like they're on an invisible set of scales gradually exchanging weight, is humbling, to say the least.

Ubirr (☉8.30am-sunset Apr-Nov, from 2pm Dec-Mar) is 39km north of the Arnhem Hwy via a sealed road. On the way you'll pass the turn-off to **Merl** (adult/child $10/free) camping ground, which is only open in the Dry and has an amenities block, and the **Border Store** (☏08-8979 2474; meals $6-18; ☉8am-5pm Apr-Nov), selling groceries and takeaway food (no fuel).

🏃 Activities

Bardedjilidji Sandstone Walk WALKING
Starting from the upstream picnic-area car park, this walk (2.5km, 90 minutes, easy) takes in wetland areas of the East Alligator River and some interesting eroded sandstone outliers of the Arnhem Land escarpment. Informative track notes point out features on this walk.

Manngarre Monsoon Forest Walk WALKING
Mainly sticking to a boardwalk, this walk (1.5km return, 30 minutes, easy) starts by the boat ramp near the Border Store and winds through heavily shaded vegetation, palms and vines.

Sandstone & River Rock Holes WALKING
This extension (6.5km, three hours, medium) of the Bardedjilidji Walk features sandstone outcrops, paperbark swamps and riverbanks. Closed in the Wet.

JABIRU
POP 1140
It may seem surprising to find a town of Jabiru's size and structure in the midst of a wilderness national park, but it exists solely because of the nearby Ranger uranium mine. It's Kakadu's major service centre, with a

bank, newsagent, medical centre, supermarket, bakery and service station. You can even play a round of golf here.

The **Ranger Uranium Mine Tour** (☏1800 089 113; adult/child $30/10; ☉9am, 11am & 1pm Mon-Sat) is an opportunity to see one of the park's controversial mining projects up close and learn about some of the issues surrounding uranium mining. Guided tours leave from Jabiru airstrip, 8km east of town.

🛏 Sleeping & Eating

TOP CHOICE **Lakeview Park** CABINS $$
(☏08-8979 3144; www.lakeviewkakadu.com.au; 27 Lakeside Dr; en suite powered sites $35, bungalows/d/cabins $115/125/225; ❄) Although there are no lake views as such, this beautifully landscaped Aboriginal-owned park is one of Kakadu's best with a range of interesting tropical-design bungalows set in lush gardens. The doubles share a communal kitchen, bathroom and lounge, and also come equipped with their own TV and fridge, while the 'bush bungalows' are stylish elevated safari designs (no air-con) with private external bathroom that sleep up to four. No pool, but Jabiru public pool is 50m away.

Kakadu Lodge & Caravan Park RESORT, CARAVAN PARK $$$
(☏1800 811 154; www.auroraresorts.com.au; Jabiru Dr; unpowered/powered sites $26/38, cabins from $240; ❄@❄) A resort/caravan park with shady, grassed sites and a lagoon-style swimming pool (movie nights by the pool on Fridays). Self-contained cabins sleep up to five people but are booked up well in advance (despite the decor being a little behind the times). There's also a bar and bistro.

Gagudju Crocodile Holiday Inn HOTEL $$$
(☏08-8979 9000; www.gagudju-dreaming.com; 1 Flinders St; d from $300; ❄❄❄) Known locally as 'the Croc', this hotel is designed in the shape of a crocodile, which, of course, is only obvious when viewed from the air or Google Earth. The rooms are clean and comfortable if a little pedestrian for the price. Try for one on the ground floor opening out to the central pool. The **Escarpment Restaurant** (mains $27-39, ☉breakfast, lunch & dinner) here is the best in Jabiru.

Jabiru Sports & Social Club PUB FARE $$
(☏08-8979 2326; Lakeside Dr; mains $15-30; ☉lunch daily, dinner Mon-Sat) Along with the golf club, this low-slung hangar is the place to meet the locals over a beer. The bistro

meals are surprisingly adventurous (try the tempura croc tail with bean salad and chilli ketchup), there's an outdoor deck overlooking the lake and sports on TV.

Kakadu Bakery BAKERY $
(Gregory Pl; meals $5-17; ⊙breakfast & lunch daily, dinner Mon-Sat) Superb made-to-order sandwiches on home-baked bread walk out the door, plus mean burgers, slices, breakfast fry-ups, pizzas and basic salads.

Foodland SUPERMARKET $
(Jabiru Plaza; ⊙9am-5.30pm Mon-Fri, 9am-3pm Sat, 9am-1pm Sun) The local supermarket.

NOURLANGIE

The sight of this looming outlier of the Arnhem Land escarpment makes it easy to understand its ancient importance to Aboriginal people. Its long red-sandstone bulk, striped in places with orange, white and black, slopes up from surrounding woodland to fall away at one end in stepped cliffs. Below is Kakadu's best-known collection of **rock art**.

The name Nourlangie is a corruption of *nawulandja,* an Aboriginal word that refers to an area bigger than the rock itself. The 2km looped walking track (open 8am to sunset) takes you first to the **Anbangbang Shelter**, used for 20,000 years as a refuge and canvas. Next is the **Anbangbang Gallery**, featuring Dreaming characters repainted in the 1960s. Look for the virile Nabulwinjbulwinj, a dangerous spirit who likes to eat females after banging them on the head with a yam. From here it's a short walk to **Gunwarddehwarde Lookout**, with views of the Arnhem Land escarpment.

Nourlangie is at the end of a 12km sealed road that turns east off Kakadu Hwy. Seven kilometres south is the turn-off to **Muirella Park** (adult/child $10/free) camping ground at **Djarradjin Billabong**, with barbecues, excellent amenities and the 5km-return **Bubba Wetland Walk**.

🏃 Activities

Anbangbang Billabong Walk WALKING
This picturesque, lily-filled billabong lies close to Nourlangie, and the picnic tables dotted around its edge make it a popular lunch spot. The track (2.5km loop, 45 minutes, easy) circles the billabong and passes through paperbark swamp.

Barrk Walk WALKING
This long day walk (12km loop, five to six hours, difficult) will take you away from the crowds on a circuit of the Nourlangie

area. Barrk is the male black wallaroo and you might see this elusive marsupial if you set out early. Starting at the Nourlangie car park, this demanding walk passes through the Anbangbang galleries before a steep climb to the top of Nourlangie Rock. Cross the flat top of the rock weaving through sandstone pillars before descending along a wet-season watercourse. The track then follows the rock's base past the Nanguluwur Gallery and western cliffs before re-emerging at the car park.

Nanguluwur Gallery WALKING
This outstanding rock-art gallery sees far fewer visitors than Nourlangie simply because it's further to walk and has a gravel access road (unsigned when we visited; (3.5km return, 1½ hours, easy). Here the paintings cover most of the styles found in the park, including very early dynamic style work, X-ray work and a good example of 'contact art', a painting of a two-masted sailing ship towing a dinghy.

JIM JIM FALLS & TWIN FALLS

Remote and spectacular, these two falls epitomise the rugged Top End. **Jim Jim Falls**, a sheer 215m drop, is awesome after rain (when it can only be seen from the air), but its waters shrink to a trickle by about June. Twin Falls flows year-round (no swimming), but half the fun is getting there, involving a little **boat trip** (adult/child $2.50/free, running 7.30am to 5pm) and an over-the-water boardwalk.

These two iconic waterfalls are reached along a 4WD track that turns south off the Kakadu Hwy between the Nourlangie and Cooinda turn-offs. Jim Jim Falls is about 56km from the turn-off (the last 1km on foot), and it's a further five corrugated kilometres to **Twin Falls**. The track is open in the Dry only and can still be closed into late May; it's off limits to most rental vehicles (check the fine print). A couple of tour companies make trips here in the Dry and there's a camping area near Jim Jim.

COOINDA & YELLOW WATER

Cooinda is best known for the cruises on the wetland area known as Yellow Water (see p834), and has developed into a slick resort. About 1km from the resort, the **Warradjan Aboriginal Cultural Centre** (www.kakadu-attractions.com/warradjan; Yellow Water Area; ⊙9am-5pm) depicts Creation stories and has a great permanent exhibition that includes clap sticks, sugar-bag holders and rock-art

URANIUM MINING

It's no small irony that some of the world's biggest deposits of uranium lie within one of Australia's most beautiful national parks. In 1953 uranium was discovered in the Kakadu region. Twelve small deposits in the southern reaches of the park were worked in the 1960s, but were abandoned following the declaration of Woolwonga Wildlife Sanctuary.

In 1970 three huge deposits – Ranger, Nabarlek and Koongarra – were found, followed by Jabiluka in 1971. The Nabarlek deposit (in Arnhem Land) was mined in the late 1970s, and the Ranger Uranium Mine started producing ore in 1981.

While all mining in the park has been controversial, it was Jabiluka that brought international attention to Kakadu and pitted conservationists and Indigenous owners against the government and mining companies. After uranium was discovered at Jabiluka in 1971, an agreement to mine was negotiated with the local Aboriginal peoples. The Jabiluka mine became the scene of sit-in demonstrations during 1998 that resulted in large-scale arrests. In 2003, stockpiled ore was returned into the mine and the decline tunnel leading into the deposit was backfilled as the mining company moved into dialogue with the traditional landowners, the Mirrar people.

In February 2005 the current owners of the Jabiluka mining lease, Energy Resources of Australia (ERA), signed an agreement that gave the Mirrar the deciding vote on any resumption of this controversial mining project. Under the deal ERA is allowed to continue to explore the lease, subject to Mirrar consent. Meanwhile, the Ranger mine – which is officially not part of the national park but is surrounded by it – was due to close in 2010, but the discovery of further deposits in late 2008 has delayed closure.

---

samples. You'll be introduced to the moiety system (internal tribal division), languages and skin names, and there's a minitheatre with a huge selection of films from which to choose. A mesmeric soundtrack of chants and didgeridoos plays in the background. Warradjan is an easy 2km walk from the Cooinda resort.

Gagudju Lodge & Camping Cooinda (☎1800 500 401, 08-8979 0145; www.gagudju lodgecooinda.com.au; unpowered/powered sites $32/40, dm $55, budget/lodge r from $110/208; ✱❄@☀) is the most popular accommodation resort in the park. It's a modern oasis but, even with 380 camp sites, facilities can get very stretched. The budget air-con units share camping ground facilities and are compact and comfy enough (but for this money should be more than glorified sheds). The lodge rooms are spacious and more comfortable, sleeping up to four people. There's also a grocery shop, tour desk, fuel pump and the excellent open-air **Barra Bar & Bistro** (mains $13-30; ☺breakfast, lunch & dinner) here too.

The turn-off to the Cooinda accommodation complex and Yellow Water wetlands is 47km down the Kakadu Hwy from the Arnhem Hwy intersection. Just off the Kakadu Hwy, 2km south of the Cooinda turn-off, is the scrubby **Mardugal camping ground** (adult/child $10/free) – an excellent year-round camping area with shower and toilets.

COOINDA TO PINE CREEK

This southern section of the park sees far fewer tour buses. Though it's unlikely you'll have dreamy **Maguk** (Barramundi Gorge; 45km south of Cooinda and 10km along a corrugated 4WD track) to yourself, you might time it right to have the glorious natural pool and falls between just a few of you. Conventional-vehicle drivers fear not: 40-odd kilometres further south is the turn-off to **Gunlom** (Waterfall Creek), another superb escarpment waterfall, plunge pool and camping area. It's located 37km along an unsealed, though easily doable, gravel road. Walk the steep Waterfall Walk (1km, one hour) here, which affords incredible views.

Activities

Yurmikmik Walks   WALKING
On the road to Gunlom is the start of a series of interconnected walks leading first through woodlands and monsoon forest to **Boulder Creek** (2km, 45 minutes), then on to the **Lookout** (5km, 1½ to two hours), with views over rugged ridges, and **Motor Car Falls** (7.5km, four hours).

❶ Information

About 200,000 people visit Kakadu between April and October, so expect some tour-bus action at sites like Ubirr and Yellow Water. Consider spending some time bushwalking and camping

in the south of the park – it's less visited but inimitably impressive.

Admission to the park is via a 14-day **Park Pass** (adult/child $25/free): pick one up (along with the excellent *Visitor Guide* booklet) from Bowali visitor information centre, Tourism Top End in Darwin, Gagudju Lodge Cooinda or Katherine visitor information centre. Carry it with you at all times, as rangers conduct spot checks (penalties apply for nonpayment). Fuel is available at Kakadu Resort, Cooinda and Jabiru. Jabiru has a shopping complex with a supermarket, post office, a Westpac bank and newsagency.

Accommodation prices in Kakadu vary tremendously depending on the season – resort rates can drop by as much as 50% during the Wet.

The excellent **Bowali Visitor Information Centre** (08-8938 1121; www.kakadunational parkaustralia.com/bowali_visitors_center.htm; Kakadu Hwy, Jabiru; 8am-5pm) has walk-through displays that sweep you across the land, explaining Kakadu's ecology from Aboriginal and non-Aboriginal perspectives. The helpful staffed info booth has details on walks and the plants and animals you might encounter along the way. The 'What's On' flier details where and when to catch a free and informative park ranger talk. The centre is about 2.5km south of the Arnhem Hwy intersection; a 1km walking track connects it with Jabiru.

The **Northern Land Council** (1800 645 299, 08-8938 3000; www.nlc.org.au; 3 Government Bldg, Flinders St, Jabiru; 8am-4pm Mon-Sat) issues permits (adult/child $13.20/free) to visit Gunbalanya (Oenpelli), across the East Alligator River.

❶ Getting There & Around

Many people choose to access Kakadu on a tour, which shuffles them around the major sights with the minimum of hassles. But it's just as easy with your own wheels, if you know what kinds of road conditions your trusty steed can handle (Jim Jim Falls and Twin Falls, for example, are 4WD-access only).

Greyhound Australia (www.greyhound.com. au) runs a daily return coach service from Darwin to Cooinda ($87, 4½ hours) via Jabiru ($62, 3½ hours).

Arnhem Land

Arnhem Land is a vast, overwhelming and mysterious corner of the Northern Territory. About the size of the state of Victoria and with a population of only around 17,000, mostly Yolngu people, this Aboriginal reserve is one of Australia's last great untouched wilderness areas. Most people live on outstations, combining traditional practices with modern Western ones, so they might go out for a hunt and be back in time to watch the 6pm news. Outside commercial interests and visits are highly regulated through a permit system, designed to protect the environment, the rock art and ceremonial grounds. *Balanda* (white people) are unaware of the locations of burial grounds and ceremonial lands. Basically, you need a specific purpose for entering, usually to visit an arts centre, in order to be granted a permit. If you're travelling far enough to warrant an overnight stay, you'll need to organise accommodation (which is in short supply). It's easy to visit Gunbalanya (Oenpelli) and its arts centre, just over the border, either on a tour or independently. Elsewhere, it's best to travel with a tour, which will include the necessary permit(s) to enter Aboriginal lands.

☞ Tours

Arnhemlander SIGHTSEEING
(1800 739 113, 08-8979 2411; www.arnhem lander.com.au; adult/child $225/180) 4WD tours to the Mikinj Valley and Injalak Art Centre at Gunbalanya (Oenpelli).

Davidson's Arnhemland Safaris SIGHTSEEING
(08-8927 5240; www.arnhemland-safaris. com) Experienced operator taking tours to Mt Borradaile, north of Oenpelli. Meals, guided tours, fishing and safari camp accommodation are included in the daily price (from $650); transfers from Darwin can be arranged.

Venture North Australia WILDERNESS
(08-8927 5500; www.northernaustralia.com; 4-/5-day tour $1690/2290) 4WD tours to remote areas; features expert guidance on rock art. It also has a safari camp near Smith Point on the Cobourg Peninsula.

Lord's Kakadu & Arnhemland Safaris SIGHTSEEING
(08-8948 2200; www.lords-safaris.com; tours adult/child $195/155) One-day trip into Arnhem Land (Gunbalanya) from Jabiru (or Darwin adult/child $230/185), visiting Oenpelli with a guided walk around Injalak Hill.

Nomad Tours SIGHTSEEING
(08-8987 8085; www.banubanu.com; tours $400-1800) Luxury small-group tours from Nhulunbuy including fishing charters, 4WD and cultural tours.

Gove Diving & Fishing Charters FISHING
(☑08-8987 3445; www.govefish.com.au) Variety of fishing, diving and snorkelling, and wilderness trips from Nhulunbuy. Half-/full-day fishing trips costs $205/305.

GUNBALANYA (OENPELLI)
POP 890

Gunbalanya is a small Aboriginal community 17km into Arnhem Land across the East Alligator River from the Border Store in Kakadu. The drive in itself is worth it with brilliant green wetlands and spectacular escarpments all around. Road access is only possible between May and October: check the tides at Cahill's Crossing on the East Alligator River before setting out so you don't get stuck on the other side.

A permit is required to visit the town, usually issued for visits to the Injalak Arts & Crafts Centre (www.injalak.com; ⊗8am-5pm). At this centre, artists and craftspeople produce traditional paintings on bark and paper, plus didgeridoos, pandanus weavings and baskets, and screen-printed fabrics, either at the arts centre or on remote outstations throughout Arnhem Land.

As you walk around the verandah of the arts centre to see the artists at work (morning only), peer out over the wetland at the rear to the escarpment and Injalak Hill (Long Tom Dreaming). Knowledgeable local guides lead tours to see the fine rock-art galleries here. The three-hour tours (bookings essential) cost from $150 per group. Although it may be possible to join a tour as a walk-in, it's generally best to book a tour from Jabiru.

The Northern Land Council (☑1800 645 299, 08-8938 3000; www.nlc.org.au; 3 Government Bldg, Flinders St, Jabiru; ⊗8am-4pm Mon-Sat) issues permits (adult/child $13.20/free) to visit Injalak, usually on the spot. It also provides tide times for the East Alligator, which is impassable at high tide.

COBOURG PENINSULA

The entire wilderness of this remote peninsula forms the Garig Gunak Barlu National Park (www.nt.gov.au/nreta/parks/find/gariggunak .html) which includes the surrounding sea. In the turquoise water you'll likely see dolphins and turtles, and – what most people come for – a threadfin salmon thrashing on the end of your line.

On the shores of Port Essington are the stone ruins and headstones from Victoria settlement – Britain's 1838 attempt to establish a military outpost.

At Algarlarlgarl (Black Point) there's a ranger station (☑08-8979 0244) with a visitor information and cultural centre, and the Garig Store (☑08-8979 0455; ⊗4-6pm Mon-Sat), which sells basic provisions, ice and camping gas.

Two permits are required to visit the Cobourg Peninsula: for a transit pass ($12.10) to drive through Aboriginal land contact the Northern Land Council (☑1800 645 299, 08-8938 3000; www.nlc.org.au; 3 Government Bldg, Flinders St, Jabiru; ⊗8am-4pm Mon-Sat); for permission to stay overnight in the national park contact the Cobourg Peninsula Sanctuary & Marine Park Board (☑08-8999 4814; www.nt.gov.au). The overnight fee is $232.10 per vehicle, which covers up to five people for seven days and includes camping and transit pass.

There are two camping grounds in the park with shower, toilet, barbecues and limited bore water; generators are allowed in one area. Camping fees (per person per day $16.50) are covered by your vehicle permit, but if you fly in you'll have to pay them. Other accommodation is available in pricey fishing resorts.

ⓘ Getting There & Away

The quickest route here is by private charter flight, which can be arranged by accommodation providers. The track to Cobourg starts at Gunbalanya (Oenpelli) and is accessible by 4WD vehicles only from May to October. The 270km drive to Black Point from the East Alligator River takes about four hours.

EASTERN ARNHEM LAND

The wildly beautiful coast and country of Eastern Arnhem Land (www.ealta.org) is really off the beaten track. About 4000 people live in the region's main settlement, Nhulunbuy, built to service the bauxite mine here. The 1963 plans to establish a manganese mine were hotly protested by the traditional owners, the Yolngu people; though mining proceeded, the case became an important step in establishing land rights. Some of the country's most respected art comes out of this region too, including bark paintings, carved mimi figures, *yidaki* (didgeridoo), woven baskets and mats, and jewellery.

Nambara Arts & Crafts Aboriginal Gallery (Melville Bay Rd, Nhulunbuy) sells art and crafts from northeast Arnhem Land and often has artists in residence. Buku Larrnggay Mulka Art Centre & Museum (www.yirrkala.com; Yirrkala; museum admission $2; ⊗8am-4.30pm Mon-Fri, 9am-noon Sat), 20km

southeast of Nhulunbuy, is one of Arnhem Land's best. No permit is required to visit from Nhulunbuy or Gove airport.

Overland travel through Arnhem Land from Katherine requires a permit (free) from the **Northern Land Council** (☑1800 645 299, 08-8938 3000; www.nlc.org.au; 3 Government Bldg, Flinders St, Jabiru; ⏱8am-4pm Mon-Sat). The **Dhimurru Land Management Aboriginal Corporation** (☑08-8987 3992; www.dhimurru. com.au; Arnhem Rd, Nhulunbuy) issues recreation permits ($20/35 for seven days/two months) for visits to particular recreation areas in Eastern Arnhem Land – check the website for details.

❶ Getting There & Away

Airnorth (☑1800 627 474; www.airnorth.com. au) flies from Darwin to Gove (for Nhulunbuy) daily from $273 one-way. Overland, it's a 10-hour 4WD trip and only possible in the Dry. The Central Arnhem Hwy to Gove leaves the Stuart Hwy (Rte 87) 52km south of Katherine.

KATHERINE TO ALICE SPRINGS

The Stuart Hwy from Darwin to Alice Springs is still referred to as 'the Track' – it has been since WWII, when it was literally a dirt track connecting the Territory's two main towns, roughly following the Overland Telegraph Line. It's dead straight most of the way and gets progressively drier and flatter as you head south, but there are quite a few notable diversions.

Katherine

POP 9800

Katherine is considered a big town in this part of the world and you'll certainly feel like you've arrived somewhere after the long trip up the highway. Its namesake river is the first permanent running water on the road north from Alice Springs. In the Wet the river swells dramatically and has been responsible for some devastating floods – the worst in memory was Australia Day 1998, when rising waters inundated the surrounding countryside and left a mark up to 2m high on Katherine's buildings.

Katherine is probably best known for the Nitmiluk (Katherine Gorge) National Park to the east, and the town makes an obvious base, with plenty of accommodation and some decent restaurants. It also has quite a few attractions of its own, including a thriving Indigenous arts community, thermal springs and a few museums.

The Katherine area is the traditional home of the Jawoyn and Dagoman Aboriginal people. Following land claims they have received the title to large parcels of land, including Nitmiluk National Park. You'll see a lot of Aborigines around town, in from outlying communities for a few days to meet friends and hang out. No one seems to bothered by the disconcerting mix of country and retro pop that pipes into the main street from loudspeakers day and night.

◉ Sights & Activities

Katherine Low Level Nature Park   PARK
(www.ourterritory.com/katherine_nt/low_level. htm) The park is a scenic spot on the banks of the babbling Katherine River, just off the Victoria Hwy (Rte 1) 4km from town. It has a popular dry-season swimming hole linked to crystalline **thermal pools** (access via Murray St) and town by a tree-lined shared **cycle way/footpath**.

Katherine Museum   MUSEUM
(www.heritageaustralia.com.au; Gorge Rd; adult/ child $5/2; ⏱9am-4pm) The museum is in the old airport terminal, about 3km from town on the road to the gorge. The original Gypsy Moth biplane flown by Dr Clyde Fenton, the first Flying Doctor, is housed here, along with plenty of interesting old rusty trucks. There's a good selection of historical photos, including a display on the 1998 flood.

School of the Air   SCHOOL
(☑08-8972 1833; www.schools.nt.edu.au/ksa; Giles St; adult/child $5/2; ⏱Mar-Nov) At the School of the Air, 1.5km from the town centre, you can listen into a class and see how kids in the remote outback are educated in the virtual world. Guided tours are held at 9am, 10am and 11am on weekdays; bookings preferred.

FREE **Katherine Public Art & Craft Galley**   ART GALLERY
(www.ktc.nt.gov.au; Civic Centre, Stuart Hwy; ⏱8am-3pm Mon-Fri) The low-key gallery is home to the **Katherine Collection**, a community-owned collection of interesting local art. There are a couple of amazing photos from the '98 flood here too.

Springvale Homestead   HOMESTEAD
(www.travelnorth.com.au; Shadforth Rd) Alfred Giles established Springvale Homestead in

1879 after he drove 2000 cattle and horses and 12,000 head of sheep from Adelaide to the site in 19 months. It claims to be the oldest cattle station in the Northern Territory. The stone homestead still stands by the river, about 7km southwest of town, and the surrounding riverside property is now a caravan and camping resort. There's a free homestead tour at 3pm daily (except Saturday) from May to September. Canoe hire per hour/two hours/day costs $15/20/73. There's also accommodation here (see p843).

👉 Tours

Gecko Canoeing   CANOEING, BUSHWALKING
(☎1800 634 319, 08-8972 2224; www.geckocanoe ing.com.au) Exhilarating guided canoe trips on the more remote stretches of the Katherine River. Trips include three days ($780) on the Katherine River and six days ($1360) on the Daly and Flora Rivers. A five-day hike in Nitmiluk National Park costs $1180.

Manyallaluk Aboriginal Cultural Tours   INDIGENOUS
(☎08-8975 4727; www.aboriginaltouroperators. com.au) Aboriginal cultural tours of Manyallaluk, about 100km from Katherine. A one-day cultural experience (adult/child $132/72) departing from Katherine includes a bush-tucker/medicine walk, lunch, painting and craft activities. The self-drive option is $99/65.

Crocodile Night Adventure   CRUISE
(☎1800 089 103; www.travelnorth.com.au; cruises adult/child $63/35; ☉6.30pm May-Oct) At Springvale Homestead, this evening cruise seeks out crocs and other nocturnal wildlife on the Katherine River. Includes barbecue dinner and drinks.

Travel North   SIGHTSEEING
(☎1800 089 103, 08-8971 9999; www.travelnorth. com.au; Transit Centre, 6 Katherine Tce) Katherine-based tour operator with a range of tours to Kakadu, Arnhem Land and Litchfield, and full-day Katherine town tours. Also booking agent for the *Ghan* and Greyhound.

✦ Festivals & Events

Katherine Country Music Muster   MUSIC
(www.kcmm.com.au) 'We like both kinds of music: country *and* western.' Plenty of live music in the pubs and entertainment at a site on Gorge Rd over the May Day long weekend.

Katherine District Show   AGRICULTURAL
(www.katherineshow.org.au) Annual agricultural show at the Katherine Showgrounds, with the usual rides, stalls and pungent animals in July.

🛏 Sleeping

TOP CHOICE Maud Creek Country Lodge   GUESTHOUSE $$$
(☎08-8971 1814; www.maudcreeklodge.com.au; Gorge Rd; d/cottage $220/270; ❄☎) Set on a former cattle run just 6km from the gorge, this endearing farmstay is a great place to remember what nature is all about. The property reaches down to the river and is tailor-made for bushwalking, birdwatching and fishing. The three immaculate adjoining lodge rooms share a communal kitchen and TV lounge, but better still is the private self-contained cottage. It's all set in verdant gardens with a pool, gazebo (good for sunset drinks) and mahogany trees.

Katherine Low Level Caravan Park   CARAVAN PARK $
(☎08-8972 3962; www.katherinelowlevel.com.au; Shadforth Rd; unpowered/powered sites $29/35, en suite cabins $165; ❄🐾🛜☎) A well-manicured park with plenty of shady sites, a great swimming pool adjoining a bar and bistro, and spotless amenities. It's the pick of the town's several caravan parks.

Katherine River Lodge Motel   MOTEL $
(☎08-8971 0266; www.katherineriverlodge.net; 50 Giles St; s/d from $89/95, f $129; ❄@☎) One of Katherine's best-value motels (and definitely the friendliest), this large complex (three three-storey blocks) has spotless rooms in a tropical garden. The attached restaurant (mains $18 to $28) plates up filling meals nightly, or you can fire up the BBQ outside. You couldn't say the rooms are contemporary, but they're tidy and clean.

Knott's Crossing Resort   CARAVAN PARK, MOTEL $
(☎1800 222 511, 08-8972 2511; www.knottscrossing. com.au; cnr Cameron & Giles Sts; unpowered/powered sites $22/39, cabins/motel d from $99/149, f $178; ❄@🐾🛜☎) Knott's Crossing is more a motel and cabin resort than camping ground, but it's a great spot for caravanners and campervans too. Everything is packed pretty tightly into the tropical gardens here, but it's very professionally run and there's a bar and the excellent Katie's Bistro (see p843). 'Village' cabins are a good budget

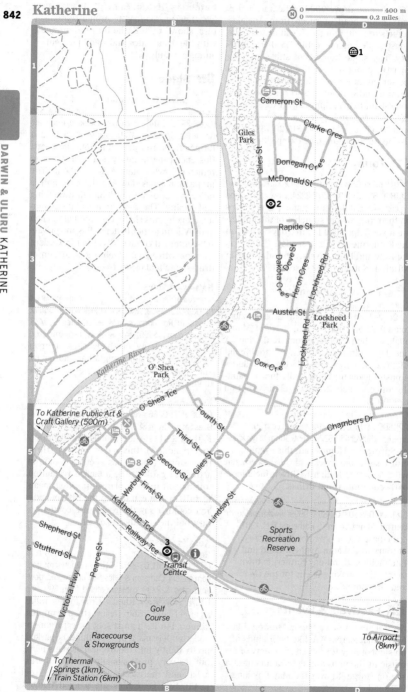

Cameron St
Giles Park
Giles St
Clarke Cres
Donegan Cres
McDonald St
Rapide St
Dakota Cres
Dove St
Heron Cres
Lockheed Rd
Lockheed Rd
Auster St
Lockheed Park
Cox Cres
O' Shea Park
Katherine River
O' Shea Tce
Fourth St
Chambers Dr
To Katherine Public Art & Craft Gallery (500m)
Third St
Giles St
Second St
Warburton St
First St
Lindsay St
Katherine Tce
Railway Tce
Sports Recreation Reserve
Shepherd St
Stutterd St
Pearce St
Victoria Hwy
Transit Centre
Golf Course
Racecourse & Showgrounds
To Thermal Springs (1km); Train Station (6km)
To Airport (8km)

Katherine

option for friends – sleeping four, with en suite and satellite TV.

Springvale Homestead CARAVAN PARK, MOTEL $
(☑08-8972 1355; www.travelnorth.com.au; Shadforth Rd; unpowered/powered sites $10/25, s/tw/f $51/61/77; ❋❄) In a bushland setting by the Katherine River, this historic homestead (see p840) is a lovely place to camp. There's plenty of space, a palm-shaded pool and a bistro open for breakfast and dinner (mains $19 to $25). Rooms are motel-style (old but clean and amazingly cheap), and there are free homestead tours at 3pm daily (except Saturday) in the Dry.

**Palm Court Kookaburra
Backpackers** HOSTEL $
(☑1800 626 722, 08-8972 2722; www.travelnorth.com.au; cnr Third & Giles Sts; dm $26, tw & d from $65; ❋@❄) This well-equipped, welcoming backpackers occupies a retired motel, clad in faux stone in an attempt to resemble some kind of castle. Scruffy international knights and maidens enjoy rooms with bathrooms, fridges and TVs. It's a short walk to town or there's a free shuttle to the Transit Centre.

St Andrews Apartments APARTMENTS $$$
(☑1800 686 106, 08-8971 2288; www.standrewsapts.com.au; 27 First St; apt $230-260; ❋❄) In the heart of town, these serviced apartments are great for families or if you're pining for a few home comforts. Their two-bedroom apartments sleep four (six if you use the sofa bed), and come with fully equipped kitchen and lounge/dining area. Nifty little BBQ decks are attached to the ground-floor units.

Paraway Motel MOTEL $$
(☑08-8972 2644; www.parawaymotel.com.au; cnr First St & O'Shea Tce; d from $125; ❋❄) This smart motel is as neat as a pin, and its location is handy to the main street but quiet enough. Standard motel rooms are spotless, with typically tropical tile-and-floral-bedspread decor, plus there are spa rooms and a restaurant too.

 Eating

Katherine Country Club LICENSED CLUB $$
(www.katherinecountryclub.com.au; 3034 Pearce St; mains $15-25; ⊙lunch Tue-Sat, dinner nightly) Overlooking Katherine's nine-hole golf course, this boozy bistro is a real locals' haunt. You don't have to be a club member (or even know how to swing a club) – just turn up and enjoy big steaks, burgers and schnitzels and Aerosmith on the jukebox. 'The burgers are better at the Golfy!'

Katie's Bistro MODERN AUSTRALIAN $$
(☑08-8972 2511; www.knottscrossing.com.au/restaurant; Knott's Crossing Resort, cnr Giles & Cameron Sts; mains $23-34; ⊙breakfast & dinner) This intimate little bistro at Knott's Crossing Resort is a real local fave (it's hard to tell the townies from the tourists). Wagyu beef, lobster and prawn pasta, crocodile spring rolls and grilled outback camel grace the eclectic menu, and you can eat inside or alfresco by the pool. A name change is rumoured – 'Savannah Restaurant'?

Katherine Club LICENSED CLUB $$
(www.katherineclubinc.com; cnr Second St & O'Shea Tce; mains $15-30; ⊙lunch Mon-Fri, dinner Mon-Sat) Close to the town centre, the Club ain't fancy, but you can rely on satisfying bistro meals (steak, schnitzel and barra), and the kids are welcome. Wednesday is steak night; Thursday it's schnitzels. Sign in as a visitor at the fortresslike front desk, or find a member to tag along with.

ⓘ **Information**

Katherine Art Gallery (☑08-8971 1051; www.katherineartgallery.com.au; 12 Katherine Tce; ⊙9am-6pm daily May-Oct, 10am-5pm Mon-Fri, 10am-2pm Sat Nov-Apr; @) A commercial Indigenous gallery doubling as an internet cafe.
Katherine Hospital (☑08-8973 9211; www.health.nt.gov.au; Giles St) About 3km north of town, with an emergency department.

Katherine visitor information centre (✆1800 653 142; www.visitkatherine.com.au; cnr Lindsay St & Stuart Hwy; ⊙8.30am-5pm daily in the Dry, 8.30am-5pm Mon-Fri, 10am-2pm Sat & Sun in the Wet) Modern, air-con information centre stocking information on all areas of the Northern Territory. Pick up the handy *Katherine Region Visitor Guide*.

Parks & Wildlife (✆08-8973 8888; www.nt.gov.au/nreta/parks; 32 Giles St; ⊙8am-4.20pm) National park information and notes.

ℹ Getting There & Around

Katherine is a major road junction: from here the Stuart Hwy tracks north and south, and the Victoria Hwy heads west to Kununurra in WA.

BUS Greyhound Australia (www.greyhound.com.au) has regular services between Darwin and Alice Springs, Queensland or WA. Buses stop at **Katherine Transit Centre** (✆08-8971 9999; 6 Katherine Tce). One-way fares from Katherine include: Darwin ($89, four hours), Alice Springs ($296, 16 hours), Tennant Creek ($195, 8½ hours) and Kununurra ($138, 4½ hours).

TRAIN The *Ghan* train, run by **Great Southern Rail** (www.gsr.com.au), travels between Adelaide and Darwin twice a week, stopping at Katherine for four hours – enough for a whistlestop tour to Katherine Gorge! Katherine train station is off the Victoria Hwy, 9km southwest of town. Fares to/from Katherine are the same as per Darwin; see p1078 for details. **Travel North** (✆1800 089 103, 08-8971 9999; www.travelnorth.com.au; Transit Centre, 6 Katherine Tce) runs shuttles between the station and town.

Around Katherine

CUTTA CUTTA CAVES NATURE PARK

About 30km south of Katherine, turn your back on the searing sun and dip down 15m below terra firma into this mazelike limestone cave system. The 1499-hectare **Cutta Cutta Caves Nature Park** (✆08-8972 1940; www.nt.gov.au/nreta/parks/find/cuttacuttacaves.html; tours adult/child $16/8; ⊙8.30am-4.30pm, guided tours 9am, 10am, 11am, 1pm, 2pm & 3pm) has a unique ecology and you'll be sharing the space with brown tree snakes and pythons, plus the endangered ghost bats and orange horseshoe bats that they feed on. Cutta Cutta is a Jawoyn name meaning many stars; it was taboo for Aborigines to enter the cave, which they believed was where the stars were kept during the day. Admission by tour only.

NITMILUK (KATHERINE GORGE) NATIONAL PARK

Spectacular **Katherine Gorge** forms the backbone of the 2920-sq-km **Nitmiluk**

(Katherine Gorge) National Park (www.nt.gov.au/nreta/parks/find/nitmiluk.html), about 30km from Katherine. A series of 13 deep sandstone **gorges** have been carved out by the **Katherine River** on its journey from Arnhem Land to the Timor Sea. It is a hauntingly beautiful place – though it can get crowded in peak season – and a must-do from Katherine. In the Dry the tranquil river is perfect for a paddle, but in the Wet the deep still waters and dividing rapids are engulfed by an awesome torrent that churns through the gorge. Plan to spend at least a full day canoeing or cruising on the river and bushwalking.

The traditional owners are the Jawoyn Aboriginal people who jointly manage Nitmiluk with Parks & Wildlife. **Nitmiluk Tours** (✆1300 146 743, 08-8972 1253; www.nitmiluktours.com.au) manages accommodation, cruises and activities within the park.

◉ Sights

Leliyn (Edith Falls) NATURE RESERVE

Reached off the Stuart Hwy 40km north of Katherine and a further 20km along a sealed road, Leliyn is an idyllic, safe haven for swimming and hiking. The moderate **Leliyn Trail** (2.6km loop, 1½ hours) climbs from escarpment country through grevillea and spinifex and past scenic lookouts (Bemang is best in the afternoon) to the Upper Pool, where the moderate **Sweetwater Pool Trail** (8.6km return, three to five hours) branches off. The peaceful Sweetwater Pool has a small **camping ground** (per person $3.30, plus $50 refundable deposit); overnight permits are available at the kiosk.

The main **Lower Pool** – a gorgeous, mirror-flat swimming lagoon – is a quick 150m dash from the car park. The Parks & Wildlife **camping ground** (✆08-8975 4869; adult/child $9/5) next to the car park has grassy sites, lots of shade, toilets, showers, a laundry and facilities for the disabled. Fees are paid at the **kiosk** (⊙8am-6pm May-Oct, 9.30am-3pm Nov-Apr), which sells snacks and basic supplies. Nearby is a picnic area with barbecues and tables.

🏃 Activities

BUSHWALKING

The park has around 120km of marked walking tracks, ranging from 2km stretches to 66km multinight hikes. Overnight hikers must register at the Nitmiluk Centre. There's a $50 refundable deposit for any overnight walk and a camping fee of $3.30 per person per night. The Nitmiluk Centre has maps and info on the full range of walks.

Barrawei (Lookout) Loop

BUSHWALKING

A short, steep climb (3.7km loop, two hours, moderate difficulty) with good views over the Katherine River.

Butterfly Gorge

BUSHWALKING

A challenging, shady walk (12km return, 4½ hours) through a pocket of monsoon rainforest, often with butterflies, leads to midway along the second gorge and a deep water swimming spot.

Jawoyn Valley

BUSHWALKING

A difficult (40km loop, overnight) wilderness trail leading off the Eighth Gorge walk into a valley with rock outcrops and rock-art galleries.

Jatbula Trail

BUSHWALKING

This difficult walk (66km one-way, five days) to Leliyn (Edith Falls) climbs the Arnhem Land escarpment, passing the swamp-fed Biddlecombe Cascades, Crystal Falls, the Amphitheatre and the Sweetwater Pool. This walk can only be done one-way (ie you can't walk from Leliyn to Katherine Gorge) and a minimum of two walkers are required. A ferry service ($5) takes you across the gorge to kick things off.

CANOEING

Nothing beats exploring the gorges in your own boat, and lots of travellers canoe at least as far as the first or second gorge. Bear in mind the intensity of the sun and heat, and the fact that you may have to carry your canoe over the rock bars and rapids that separate the gorges. Pick up the *Canoeing Guide* at the Nitmiluk Centre.

Nitmiluk Tours

CANOEING

(☏1300 146 743, 08-8972 1253; www.nitmiluktours.com.au) Hires out single/double canoes for a half-day ($45/67, departing 8am and 12.30pm) or full day ($59/86, departing 8am), including the use of a splash-proof drum for cameras and other gear (it's not fully waterproof), a map and a life jacket. The half-day hire only allows you to paddle up the first gorge; with the full day you can get up as far as the third gorge depending on your level of fitness – start early. The canoe shed is at the boat ramp by the main car park, about 500m beyond the Nitmiluk Centre. There's a $20 deposit required for half-day hires.

You also can be a little more adventurous and take the canoes out overnight for $110/126 a single/double, plus $3.30 for a

camping permit – there are camp sites at the fifth, sixth, eighth and ninth gorges. Bookings are essential as overnight permits are limited and there is a $60 deposit. Don't take this trip lightly though.

GORGE CRUISES

Nitmiluk Tours

CRUISES

(☏1300 146 743, 08-8972 1253; www.nitmiluktours.com.au) An easy way to see far into the gorge is on a cruise. Bookings on some cruises can be tight in the peak season; make your reservation a day in advance. The **two-hour cruise** (adult/child $60/36) goes to the second gorge and visits a rock-art gallery (including 800m walk). Departures are at 9am, 11am, 1pm and 3pm daily year-round. There's wheelchair access to the top of the first gorge only. The **four-hour cruise** (adult/child $77/38) goes to the third gorge and includes refreshments and a chance to swim. This cruise leaves at 9am daily from April to November, plus at 11am and 1pm May to August.

There's also a more leisurely two-hour **breakfast cruise** (adult/child $80/51), leaving at 7am May to November; a two-hour **lunch cruise** (adult/child $79/51), sailing at 12.15pm or 1pm Monday to Saturday; and a **sunset cruise** (adult/child $135/120), sailing at 4.30pm on Monday, Wednesday, Friday, Saturday and Sunday from May to December, with a candlelit buffet dinner and champagne.

SCENIC FLIGHTS

Nitmiluk Helicopter Tours

SCENIC FLIGHTS

(☏1300 146 743; www.airbournesolutions.com.au; flights from $88 per person) Has a variety of flights ranging from an eight-minute buzz over the first three gorges ($88 per person) to an 18-minute flight over all 13 gorges ($202). The Adventure Swim Tour ($404) drops you at a secluded swimming hole for an hour or so, and there are broader tours that take in Aboriginal rock-art sites, Kakadu and a cattle station. Book at the Nitmiluk Centre.

🛏 Sleeping

There are bush-camping sites for overnight walkers throughout the park, and permanent camping grounds at Leliyn (Edith Falls).

Nitmiluk Caravan Park

CARAVAN PARK $

(☏1300 146 743, 08-8972 1253; www.nitmiluktours.com.au; unpowered/powered site $34/39, safari tents $118; ☒) Plenty of grass and shade, hot showers, toilets, barbecues, a laundry and a

kiosk by the good-lookin' swimming pool. Wallabies and goannas are frequent visitors. There's a 'tent village' here with permanent safari tents sleeping two people. Book at the Nitmiluk Centre.

Nitmiluk Chalets CABINS $$
(📞1300 146 743, 08-8972 1253; www.nitmiluktours. com.au; 1-/2-bedroom cabins $185/235; ❄) Next door to the caravan park, these cabins are a serviceable choice if you'd rather have a solid roof over your head (and a flat-screen TV). Access to all the caravan park facilities (pool, barbecues, kiosk etc).

ℹ Information

The **Nitmiluk Centre** (📞1300 146 743, 08-8972 1253; www.nitmiluktours.com.au; ⊘7am-6pm) has excellent displays and information on the park's geology, wildlife, the traditional owners (the Jawoyn) and European history. There's also a restaurant here (snacks and meals $4 to $19, open breakfast, lunch and dinner), and a desk for **Parks & Wildlife** (📞08-8972 1886), which has information sheets on a wide range of marked walking tracks that start here and traverse the picturesque country south of the gorge. Registration for overnight walks and camping permits ($3.30 per night) is from 7am to 1pm; canoeing permits are also issued. Check at the centre for information on ranger talks.

ℹ Getting There & Away

It's 30km by sealed road from Katherine to the Nitmiluk Centre, and a few hundred metres further to the car park, where the gorge begins and the cruises start.

Daily transfers between Katherine and the gorge are run by **Nitmiluk Tours** (📞1300 146 743, 08-8972 1253; www.nitmiluktours.com. au; Shop 2, 27 Katherine Tce, Katherine; adult/ child return $25/18), departing the Nitmiluk Town Booking Office and also picking up at local accommodation places on request. Buses leave Katherine at 8am, 12.15pm and 4pm, returning from Nitmiluk at 9am, 1pm and 5.30pm.

Katherine to Western Australia

The sealed Victoria Hwy – part of the Savannah Way – stretches 513km from Katherine to Kununurra in WA. It winds through diverse landscapes, with extensive tracts annexed as cattle stations in the 1880s, which become the economy's backbone in the postwar recovery period of the 1950s.

A 4WD will get you into a few out-of-the-way national parks accessed off the Victoria Hwy, or you can meander through semiarid desert and sandstone outcrops until bloated baobab trees herald your imminent arrival in WA. All fruits, vegetables, nuts and honey must be left at the quarantine-inspection post on the border. WA time is 1½ hours behind NT time.

FLORA RIVER NATURE PARK

Limestone tufa (spongy rock) outcrops form bars across the mineral-rich Flora River, acting as dams; the effect is a series of pretty cascades running with glowing blue-green water. Within **Flora River Nature Park** (www. nt.gov.au/nreta/parks/find/florariver.html) there's a **camping ground** (adult/child $6.60/3.30) at Djarrung with an amenities block. The Flora River has crocs, so there's no swimming.

The park turn-off is 90km southwest of Katherine; the park entrance is a further 32km along a passable dirt road (OK for 2WD cars in the Dry).

VICTORIA RIVER CROSSING

The low sandstone cliffs surrounding this spot where the highway crosses the Victoria River (194km west of Katherine) create a dramatic setting. Much of this area forms the eastern section of Gregory National Park. The **Victoria River Roadhouse Caravan Park** (📞08-8975 0744; fax 08-8975 0819; Victoria Hwy; unpowered/powered sites $15/20, d $95), west of the bridge, has a shop, bar and meals ($10 to $29).

TIMBER CREEK
POP 230

Tiny Timber Creek is the only town between Katherine and Kununurra. It has a pretty big history for such a small place, with an early European exploration aboard the *Tom Tough* requiring repairs to be carried out with local timber (hence the town's name). The expedition's leader, AC Gregory, inscribed his arrival date into a baobab; it is still discernable (and is explained in detail through interpretive panels) at **Gregory's Tree**, 15km northwest of town.

The town's **Old Police Station Museum** (www.nationaltrustnt.org.au; adult/child $3.50/ free; ⊘10am-noon Mon-Fri May-Oct), established to smooth relations with pastoralists and Indigenous people, is now a museum displaying old police and mining equipment.

A highlight of Timber Creek is the **Victoria River Cruise** (📞08-8975 0850; www. victoriarivercruise.com; adult/child $80/40; ⊘4pm Mon-Sat), which takes you 40km downriver spotting wildlife and returning in time for a fiery sunset.

GHUNMARN & MANYALLALUK CULTURAL CENTRES

If you're interested in seeing genuine Aboriginal art produced by local communities, it's worth detouring off the Stuart Hwy to these two remote cultural centres.

The small community of Beswick is reached via the sealed Central Arnhem Hwy 56km east of the Stuart Hwy on the southern fringes of Arnhem Land. Here you'll find the Ghunmarn Cultural Centre (08-8977 4250; www.djilpinarts.org.au; Beswick; 9.30am-4pm Mon-Fri Apr-Nov), opened in 2007, and displaying local artworks, prints, carvings, weaving and didgeridoos from western Arnhem Land. The centre also features the Blanasi Collection, a permanent exhibition of works by elders from the western Arnhem Land region. Visitors are welcome to visit the centre without a permit – call ahead to check that it's open.

A very special festival at Beswick is Walking With Spirits (see the boxed text, p803), magical performances of traditional corroborees staged in conjunction with the Australian Shakespeare Company. It's held on the first weekend in August. Camping is possible at Beswick Falls over this weekend but advance bookings are essential.

Abutting the eastern edge of Nitmiluk (Katherine Gorge) National Park, the southern edge of Kakadu and the western edge of Arnhem Land, the former 3000-sq-km Eva Valley cattle station is now home to the Jawoyn community of Manyallaluk. Unlike Beswick, Manyallaluk can only be visited as part of a guided one-day cultural tour (1300 146 743, 08-8972 1253; www.nitmiluktours.com.au; tours adult/child $265/150; 7am Mon-Sat Apr-Nov), departing Katherine. You'll learn about traditional bush tucker and medicine, spear throwing and how to play a didgeridoo from Indigenous Jawoyn guides. Lunch and billy tea is included. Manyallaluk Art & Craft Centre has excellent art and crafts at competitive prices, and is included in the tour.

The turn-off to Manyallaluk is 15km along the Central Arnhem Hwy, then 35km along a well-maintained, all-season gravel road. Both Manyallaluk and Beswick are around a 90-minute drive from Katherine.

The town is dominated by the roadside Timber Creek Gunamu Tourist Park (08-8975 0722; www.timbercreekhotel.com.au; Victoria Hwy; unpowered/powered sites $15/20, motel d $95;). Enormous trees shade parts of the camping area, which is next to a small creek where there's croc feeding every evening (5pm). The complex includes the Timber Creek Hotel and Fogarty's Store.

GREGORY NATIONAL PARK

The remote and rugged wilderness of the little-visited Gregory National Park (www.nt.gov.au/nreta/parks/find/gregory.html) will swallow you up. Covering 12,860 sq km, it sits at the transitional zone between the tropical and semiarid regions. The park consists of old cattle country and is made up of two separate sections: the eastern (Victoria River) section and the much larger Bullita section in the west. While some parts of the park are accessible by 2WD, it's the rough-as-guts, dry-season-only 4WD tracks that are the most rewarding; for these you need to be self-sufficient and to register (call 1300 650 730).

Parks & Wildlife (08-8975 0888; 7am-4.30pm) in Timber Creek can provide park and 4WD notes, and a map to the various walks, camping spots, tracks and the historic homestead and ruggedly romantic original stockyards – a must before heading in. This is croc country; swimming isn't safe.

There's accessible bush camping at Big Horse Creek (adult/child $3.30/1.75), 7km west of Timber Creek.

KEEP RIVER NATIONAL PARK

The remote Keep River National Park (www.nt.gov.au/nreta/parks/find/keepriver.html) is noted for its stunning sandstone formations, beautiful desolation and rock art. Pamphlets detailing walks are available at the start of the excellent trails. Don't miss the rock-art walk (5.5km return, two hours) near Jarnem, and the gorge walk (3km return, two hours) at Jinumum.

The park entrance is just 3km from the WA border. You can reach the park's main points by conventional vehicle during the Dry. A rangers station (08-9167 8827) lies 3km into the park from the main road, and there are basic, sandstone-surrounded

camping grounds (adult/child $3.30/1.65) at Gurrandalng (18km into the park) and Jarnem (32km). Tank water is available at Jarnem.

Mataranka

POP 460

With soothing, warm **thermal springs** set in pockets of palms and tropical vegetation, you'd be mad not to pull into Mataranka for at least a few hours to soak off the road dust. The small settlement regularly swells with towel-toting visitors shuffling to the thermal pool or the spring-fed Elsey National Park. If you see Mataranka referred to as the 'capital of the Never Never', it's a reference to Jeannie Gunn's 1908 autobiographical novel *We of the Never Never*, about life as a pioneering woman on nearby Elsey Station – the deeds of title of which have since been returned to the Mangarayi Indigenous owners.

◉ Sights & Activities

Mataranka's crystal-clear **thermal pool**, shrouded in rainforest, is 10km from town beside the Mataranka Homestead Resort. The warm, clear water dappled by filtered light leaking through overhanging palms rejuvenates a lot of bodies on any given day; it's reached via a boardwalk from the resort and can get mighty crowded. About 200m away (keep following the boardwalk) is the **Waterhouse River**, where you can rent canoes for $10 per hour. **Stevie's Hole**, a natural swimming hole in the cooler Waterhouse River, about 1.5km from the homestead, is rarely crowded.

Elsey Station Homestead   HISTORIC BUILDING
(admission by donation; ☺daylight hours) Outside the Mataranka Homestead Resort entrance is a replica of the Elsey Station Homestead, constructed for the filming of *We of the Never Never*, which is screened daily at noon in the resort bar. There are a couple of dresses Angela Punch McGregor wore in the film hanging in the old homestead.

Never Never Museum   MUSEUM
(120 Roper Tce; adult/child $2.75/1.10; ☺9am-4.30pm Mon-Fri) Back in town, the Never Never Museum has displays on the northern railway, WWII and local history. Access via the Rural Transaction Centre next door.

Elsey National Park   NATURE RESERVE
(www.nt.gov.au/nreta/parks/find/elsey.html) The national park adjoins the thermal-pool reserve and offers peaceful **camping**, **fishing** and **walking** along the Waterhouse and Roper Rivers. **Bitter Springs** is a serene palm-fringed thermal pool within the national park, 3km from Mataranka along the sealed Martin Rd. The almost unnatural blue-green colour of the 34°C water is due to dissolved limestone particles.

🛏 Sleeping & Eating

Mataranka Cabins   CABINS **$$**
(✆08-8975 4838; www.matarankacabins.com.au; 4705 Martins Rd, Bitter Springs; unpowered/powered sites $23/27, cabins $120; ❄@☎) On the banks of the Little Roper River, only a few hundred metres from Bitter Springs thermal pool, this quiet bush setting has some amazing termite mounds adorning the front paddock (and on either side, and out the back...). The TV-equipped, open-plan cabins have linen, bathrooms and kitchens, and accommodate up to five folks.

Mataranka Homestead Resort   CARAVAN PARK **$**
(✆08-8975 4544; www.matarankahomestead.com.au; Homestead Rd; unpowered/powered site $22/27, dm/d/cabins $25/89/115; ❄) Only metres from the main thermal pool and with a range of budget accommodation, this is a popular place to sleep/eat/swim. The large camping ground is dusty but has shady areas and decent amenities. The fan-cooled hostel rooms are very basic but comfortable enough (linen provided). The air-con motel rooms (also rudimentary) have fridge, TV and bathroom, while the cabins have a kitchenette and sleep up to six people. Book ahead.

Jalmurark Camping Area   CAMPGROUND **$**
(John Hauser Dr; adult/child $6.60/3.30) Located at 12 Mile Yards in Elsey National Park, this rangy, scrubby camping ground has lots of shade, toilets and showers and access to the Roper River and walking trails. There's a kiosk here in the Dry from which you can hire canoes.

Stockyard Gallery   CAFE **$**
(www.stockyardgallery.com.au; Stuart Hwy; snacks $5-10; ☺breakfast & lunch daily May-Oct, lunch only Nov-Apr) This casual cafe is a little gem. There's a delicious range of homemade snacks (focaccia, sandwiches, cakes, muffins) plus fresh plunger coffee, divine mango

smoothies and unusual bush-orange ice cream. The art gallery here sells Aboriginal art, jewellery and books.

Barkly Tableland & Gulf Country

East of the Stuart Hwy is some of the Territory's most remote cattle country, but parts are accessible by sealed road and the waters of the Gulf coast are regarded as some of the best isolated **fishing** in the country.

ROPER HIGHWAY

Not far south of Mataranka on the Stuart Hwy, the mostly sealed single-lane Roper Hwy strikes 175km eastwards to **Roper Bar**, crossing the paperbark- and pandanus-lined Roper River where freshwater meets saltwater. It's passable only in the Dry. Keen fisherfolk stop here, with accommodation (motel doubles $95), fuel and supplies available at the **Roper Bar Store** (✆08-8975 4636; ⏰9am-6pm Mon-Sat). Roper Bar is an access point to both Borroloola. Head south along the rough-going Nathan River Rd through **Limmen National Park** (www.nt.gov.au/nreta/parks/find/limmen.html) – high-clearance with two spares required – and into southeastern Arnhem Land.

Continuing east along the highway for 45km leads to the Aboriginal community of **Ngukurr**, home to 900 people from nine different language groups and cultures. This cultural diversity informs the unique works on show and available to buy from the **Ngukurr Arts Centre** (www.ngukurrarts.com.au; ⏰9am-2pm Mon-Fri); no permit is required to visit the centre.

CARPENTARIA & TABLELANDS HIGHWAYS

Just south of Daly Waters, the sealed Carpentaria Hwy (Hwy 1) heads 378km east to Borroloola, near the Gulf of Carpentaria, and one of the NT's top barramundi fishing spots. After 267km the Carpentaria Hwy meets the sealed Tablelands Hwy at Cape Crawford. At this intersection is the famous **Heartbreak Hotel** (✆08-8975 9928; unpowered/powered sites $16/26, dm/s/d $40/65/80; ❄). Pitch the tent on the shaded grassy lawn (the dorms are often booked out by work crews), and then park yourself on the wide verandah with a cold beer. Breakfast, lunch and dinner (meals $13 to $30) are available.

Cape Crawford Tourism (✆0400 156 685; www.capecrawfordtourism.com.au) and **Cape**

Crawford Helicopter Tours (✆08-8975 9928; www.capecrawfordtourism.com.au) run helicopter rides (flights from $160) to see the otherwise inaccessible Lost City sandstone formations.

From here it's a desolate 374km south across the Barkly Tableland to the Barkly Hwy (Rte 66) and the **Barkly Homestead Wayside Inn** (✆08-8964 4549; www.barklyhomestead.com.au; unpowered/powered sites $16/24, cabins & motel d $140; ❄❄), a surprisingly upbeat roadhouse. From here it's 210km west to Tennant Creek and 252km east to the Queensland border.

BORROLOOLA
POP 780

On the **McArthur River** close to the bountiful waters of the Gulf, Borroloola is big news for **fishing** fans, but unless you're keen on baiting a hook (the barramundi season peaks from February to April) or driving the remote (preferably 4WD) **Savannah Way** to Queensland, it's a long way to go for not much reward.

About three-quarters of the population of Borroloola is Indigenous, and the town's colourful history is displayed at the **Borroloola Museum** (www.nationaltrustnt.org.au; Robinson Rd; admission $2; ⏰8am-5pm Mon-Fri May-Sep), inside the 1886 police station.

The **Savannah Way Motel** (✆08-8975 8883; www.savannahwaymotel.com.au; Robinson Rd; r $80-120, cabins $130; ❄), on the main road through town, is clean and comfortable, with cabins, lodge rooms and tropical gardens. If you're with a group you can book the whole lodge for $440. There's a restaurant here, too.

There's also a caravan park in town, and meals at the local pub: burgers, chops and mixed grills at the rowdy **Borroloola Hotel** (166 Robinson Rd; meals $10-28; ⏰lunch & dinner), within a lounge bar reinforced with steel mesh.

Mataranka to Tennant Creek

LARRIMAH
POP 20

Once upon a time the railway line from Darwin came as far as Birdum, 8km south of tiny Larrimah, which itself is 185km south of Katherine. **Larrimah Museum** (http://en.travelnt.com/search/product-detail.aspx?product_id=9000280; Mahoney St; admission by donation; ⏰7am-9pm), in the former

telegraph repeater station opposite the Larrimah Hotel, tells of the town's involvement with the railway, the Overland Telegraph and WWII. The town was built in 1940, essentially as life support for the nearby Gorrie Airfield.

Originally a WWII officers' mess, **Larrimah Hotel** (☑08-8975 9931; unpowered/powered sites $14/18, d $50-75; ✺ ✷) is a cheerfully rustic and quirky pub offering basic rooms, meals and a menagerie of animals. **Fran's Devonshire Teahouse** (Stuart Hwy; meals $4-12; ☺breakfast & lunch) makes a great lunchtime pit stop. Try a legendary camel or buffalo pie, some roast lamb with damper, or just a Devonshire tea (a long way from Exeter) or fresh coffee.

DALY WATERS
POP 25

About 3km off the highway and 160km south of Mataranka is Daly Waters, an important staging post in the early days of aviation – Amy Johnson landed here on her monster flight from England to Australia in 1930. Just about everyone stops at the famous **Daly Waters Pub** (☑08-8975 9927; www.dalywaterspub.com; unpowered/powered sites $10/20, dm/d $15/60, cabins $95-115; ✺ ✷). Decorated with business cards, bras, banknotes and memorabilia from passing travellers, the pub claims to be the oldest in the Territory (its liquor licence has been valid since 1893) and has become a bit of a legend along the Track, although it may be a bit too popular for its own good. Every evening from April to September there's the popular beef 'n' barra barbecue ($25). Otherwise, hearty meals (mains $10 to $25, open lunch and dinner), including the filling barra burger, are served. Beside the pub is a dustbowl camping ground with a bit of shade – book ahead or arrive early to secure a powered site. Accommodation ranges from basic dongas (small, transportable buildings) to spacious self-contained cabins.

DALY WATERS TO THREE WAYS

Heading south, you encounter the fascinating ghost town of **Newcastle Waters**, 3km west of the highway. Its atmospheric, historic buildings include the Junction Hotel, cobbled together from abandoned windmills in 1932. South of the cattle town of **Elliott**, the land just gets drier and drier and the vegetation sparser. The mesmerising sameness breaks at **Renner Springs**, generally accepted as the dividing line between the seasonally wet Top End and the dry Centre.

Banka Banka is a historic cattle station 100km north of Tennant Creek, with a grassy camping area (no power), marked walking tracks (one leading to a tranquil waterhole) and a small kiosk selling basic refreshments.

Three Ways, 537km north of Alice, is the junction of the Stuart and Barkly Hwys, from where you can head south to Alice, north to Darwin (988km) or east to Mt Isa in Queensland (643km). **Threeways Roadhouse** (☑08-8962 2744; www.threewaysroadhouse.com.au; Stuart Hwy; unpowered/powered sites $16/27, motel d $91-108; ✺ @ ✷) is a potential stopover with a bar and restaurant, but Tennant Creek is only 26km further south.

Tennant Creek
POP 3500

Servicing a vast region of cattle stations and remote Aboriginal communities, roughly the size of the UK, Tennant Creek is the only town between Katherine, 680km to the north, and Alice Springs, 511km to the south. It's a good place to break up a long drive and check out the town's few attractions.

Local legend speaks of Tennant Creek being founded on beer: first settled when the drivers of a broken-down beer-laden wagon settled in to consume the freight in the 1930s. The truth is far more prosaic: the town was established as a result of a small gold rush around the same time. While it was short-lived, gold-mining ventures have operated discontinuously depending on metal prices, and exploration continues in the region today.

Tennant Creek is known as Jurnkurakurr to the local Warumungu people and almost half of the population is of Aboriginal descent. When the town is in the news, it's often for the wrong reasons – mainly alcoholism and violence – but there is a lot that is positive happening here and it's worth a stop to experience the wealth of Aboriginal art and culture on offer.

◉ Sights & Activities

Nyinkka Nyunyu   ART GALLERY
(www.nyinkkanyunyu.com.au; Paterson St; tour guide $15; ☺9am-3pm Mon-Fri, 10am-3pm Sat & Sun) This innovative museum and gallery highlights the dynamic art and culture of the local Warumungu people. The absorbing displays focus on contemporary art,

traditional objects (many returned from interstate museums), bush medicine and regional history. The diorama series, or bush TVs as they became known within the community, are particularly special. Nyinkka Nyunyu is located beside a sacred site of the spiky tailed goanna. Learn about bush tucker and Dreaming stories with your personal **guide**. There's also a gallery store and the lovely Jajjikari Café (⊙7.30am-3pm), which serves espresso coffee and light meals.

Kelly's Ranch
HORSE RIDING

(⊘08-8962 2045; www.kellysranch.com.au; 5 Fazaldeen Rd; trail rides per person $150, lesson per person $50) Experience the Barkly from the back of a horse with local Warumungu man Jerry Kelly. His two-hour trail rides start with a lesson and then a ride through some superb outback scenery with bush-tucker stops along the way. Jerry entertains with stories about Aboriginal culture and life on the cattle stations.

Julalikari Arts Centre
ARTS CENTRE

(North Stuart Hwy; ⊙8am-noon Mon-Thu) It's best to visit the 'Pink Palace', at the entrance to the Ngalpa Ngalpa community (also known as Mulga Camp), mid-morning when the artists are at work painting traditional and contemporary art. You can chat to the artists and purchase directly from the painter.

Battery Hill Mining Centre
MINE

(Peko Rd; adult/child $20/12; ⊙9am-5pm) Experience life in Tennant Creek's 1930s gold rush at this mining centre 1.5km east of town. There are **underground mine tours** and audio tours of the 10-head **battery**. In addition there is a superb **Minerals Museum** and you can try your hand at gold panning. The admission price gives access to all of the above, or you can choose to visit the Minerals and Social History Museums only (adult/family $5/10), or just go panning ($5 per person).

While you're here, ask for the key ($20 refundable deposit) to the old Telegraph Station, which is just off the highway about 12km north of town. This is one of only four of the original 11 stations remaining in the Territory. Just north of the Telegraph Station is the turn-off west to Kundjarra (The Pebbles), a formation of granite boulders like a miniaturised version of the better-known Devil's Marbles found 100km south. It's a sacred women's Dreaming site of the Warumungu.

Safari Lodge Motel
MOTEL $

(⊘08-8962 2207; safari@switch.com.au; Davidson St; s $85-95, d $95-105; ❋@) Offering great value for money, you should book ahead to stay at this family-run motel. Part of the Budget chain, Safari Lodge is centrally located next to the best restaurant in town and has clean, fairly standard rooms with phone, fridge and TV. There's also an outdoor spa.

Desert Sands
MOTEL $

(⊘08-8962 1346; www.desertsands.com.au; 780 Stuart Hwy; s/d from $95/105, extra person $20; ❋@≋) The Desert Sands is a friendly place with enormous modern units (sleeping three to eight), each with a fully equipped kitchen, TV (with in-house movies) and bathroom with washing machine. The motel is at the southern entrance to Tennant Creek, which makes for a decent walk if you don't have a car (plus it can get a bit rowdy at that end of town at night).

Tourist's Rest Youth Hostel
HOSTEL $

(⊘08-8962 2719; www.touristrest.com.au; cnr Leichhardt & Windley Sts; dm/d $25/54; ❋@≋) This small, friendly and slightly ramshackle hostel has bright clean rooms, free breakfast and VIP discounts. The hostel can organise tours of the gold mines and Devil's Marbles and pick-up from the bus stop.

Outback Caravan Park
CARAVAN PARK $

(⊘08-8962 2459; Peko Rd; unpowered/powered sites $24/31, cabins $60-129; ❋≋) In a town that often feels parched, it's nice to be in the shade of this grassy caravan park about 1km east of the centre. There's a well-stocked kiosk, camp kitchen and fuel. You may even be treated to some bush poetry and bush tucker, courtesy of yarn spinner Jimmy Hooker, at 7.30pm ($5). Rates are based on two people and an extra child/adult will cost $5/10. There are discounts for bookings of more than three nights.

🔺TOP CHOICE Fernanda's Café & Restaurant
MEDITERRANEAN $$

(1 Noble St; mains $12-25; ⊙lunch & dinner; ❋) Tucked inside the Tennant Creek squash courts (yes squash courts) is this surprising Mediterranean-inspired restaurant. A definite Tennant Creek highlight, it is run by the ebullient Fernanda, who serves up tantalising dishes such as Portuguese seafood hotpots. For lighter lunches there are salads, dips, pasta and wraps.

Margo Miles Restaurant

PUB FARE $$

(Tennant Creek Hotel, 146 Paterson St; mains $15-25; ⏰lunch & dinner Wed-Sun; ❉) This pleasant pub-restaurant is a welcome change from roadhouse dining rooms. Grab a drink from the Faye Lewis Bar, then settle down in the period dining room for a steak, seafood, pasta, Thai or gourmet pizza.

Tennant Food Barn

SUPERMARKET $

(185 Paterson St) Opposite the post office, this supermarket has a pretty extensive selection and can supply your self-catering needs.

❶ Information

Leading Edge Computers (☑08-8962 3907; 145 Paterson St; per 20min $2; ⏰9am-5pm Mon-Fri, 9am-noon Sat) Internet access.

Police station (☑08-8962 4444; Paterson St)

Tennant Creek hospital (☑08-8962 4399; Schmidt St)

Visitor information centre (☑08-8962 3388; www.barklytourism.com.au; Peko Rd; ⏰9am-5.30pm) Located 2km east of town at Battery Hill.

❶ Getting There & Away

All long-distance buses stop at the north end of town at the **BP Service Station** (☑08-8962 2626; 218 Paterson St) where you can purchase tickets. **Greyhound Australia** (☑1300 473 946; www.greyhound.com.au) has regular buses from Tennant Creek to Alice Springs ($191, six hours), Katherine ($201, 8½ hours), Darwin ($273, 14 hours) and Mount Isa ($164, eight hours).

The weekly *Ghan* rail link between Alice Springs and Darwin can drop off passengers in Tennant Creek, although cars can't be loaded or offloaded. The train station is about 6km south of town so you will need a **taxi** (☑08-8962 3626, 0432 289 369; ⏰6am-5.30pm).

Car hire is available from **Thrifty** (☑08-8962 2207; Safari Lodge Motel, Davidson St), while for tyres and tyre repairs head to **Bridgestone Tyre Centre** (☑08-8962 2361; Paterson St).

Tennant Creek to Alice Springs

The gigantic boulders in precarious piles beside the Stuart Hwy, 105km south of Tennant Creek, are called the **Devil's Marbles**. Karlu Karlu is their Warumungu name, and this registered sacred site has great cultural importance. The rocks are believed to be the eggs of the Rainbow Serpent.

According to scientists, the 'marbles' are the rounded remains of a layer of granite that has eroded over aeons. A 15-minute walk loops around the main site. This geological phenomenon is particularly beautiful at sunrise and sunset, when these oddballs glow warmly. The **camping ground** (adult/child $3.30/1.65) has remarkably hard ground, pit toilets and fireplaces (BYO firewood).

At Wauchope (*war*-kup), 10km south of the Devil's Marbles, you will find Bruce, the gregarious publican of the **Wauchope Hotel** (☑08-8964 1963; www.wauchopehotel.com.au; Stuart Hwy; unpowered/powered sites $7/8, s $40-50, d $70-100; ❉❆). His budget rooms are dongas but the costlier rooms are more spacious, with bathrooms. Meals from the **restaurant** (dinner $15-20) are more than satisfactory.

At the kooky **Wycliffe Well Roadhouse & Holiday Park** (☑08-8964 1966; www.wycliffe.com.au; unpowered/powered sites $22/26, budget s/d $30/38, donga s/d $55/68, s/d cabins with bathroom $99/112; ⏰6.30am-9pm; ❉@❆), 17km south of Wauchope, you can fill up with fuel and food (dinner $16 to $20, open breakfast, lunch and dinner) or stay and spot UFOs that apparently fly over with astonishing regularity. The place is decorated with alien figures, UFO newspaper clippings and a spooky doll collection. The park has a lawn camp site, an indoor pool, kids' playground, a cafe and a range of international beer.

Heading south, you reach the rustic **Barrow Creek Hotel** (☑08-8956 9753; Stuart Hwy; powered camp sites $10, s/d $50/65; ⏰7am-11pm), one of the highway's eccentric outback pubs. In the tradition of shearers who'd write their name on a banknote and pin it to the wall to ensure they could afford a drink when next they passed through, travellers continue to leave notes and photos. Meals are available.

The highway continues through **Ti Tree**, where you'll find the **Red Sand Art Gallery** (☑08-8956 9738; www.redsandart.com.au; Stuart Hwy; ⏰8am-5pm Mon-Fri, 8am-1pm Sat) and its cafe. The art comes mainly from the surrounding 1800-sq-km Utopia Homelands, which has produced some renowned Indigenous artists.

Twelve kilometres south of Ti Tree, the **Red Centre Farm** (Shatto Mango; ☑08-8956 9828; www.redcentrefarm.com; Stuart Hwy; ⏰9am-7pm) sells unique Territory-style wine – made from mangoes. If that sounds a bit hard to swallow, try the other mango products, such as the delicious ice cream.

In the grand Australian tradition of building very big things by the side of the road to pull up drivers, **Aileron**, 135km north of Alice, has Naked Charlie Quartpot, the 12m Anmatjere (Anmatyerre) man, who cuts a fine figure at the back of the roadhouse along with his larger-than-life family. The **Outback Art Gallery** (☑08-8956 9111; Stuart Hwy; ⊗8am-5pm Mon-Sat, 10am-4pm Sun) sells inexpensive paintings by the local Anmatjere community, as well as works from the Warlpiri community of Yuendumu.

Aileron Hotel Roadhouse (☑08-8956 9703; www.aileronroadhouse.com.au; Stuart Hwy; unpowered/powered sites $10/12, dm $36, s/d $105/120; ⊗5am-9pm; ❄❄) has camp sites (power available until 10pm), a 10-bed dorm and decent motel units. There's an ATM, bar, shop, a licensed restaurant (meals $10 to $20) and even kangaroos. The owner's large collection of Namatjira watercolours (at least 10 by Albert Namatjira) is displayed around the roadhouse's dining area.

About 70km north of Alice, the Plenty Hwy heads off to the east towards the **Harts Range**. The main reason to detour is to fossick in the gem fields about 78km east of the Stuart Hwy, which are well known for garnets and zircons. You're guaranteed to get lucky at the popular **Gemtree Caravan Park** (☑08-8956 9855; www.gemtree.com.au; Gemtree; unpowered/powered sites $22/30, cabins $60-80).

For a taste of desert life, time your visit with the annual **Harts Range Races** (last weekend in July), one of the Territory's best outback rodeos.

The Tanami Road

Synonymous with isolated outback driving, the 1000km Tanami Rd connects Alice Springs with Halls Creek in WA and is essentially a short cut between central Australia and the Kimberley. In dry conditions it's possible to make it through the unsealed dust and corrugations in a well-prepared 2WD. Stay alert, as rollovers are common, and stock up with fuel, tyres, food and water.

The NT section is wide and usually well graded, and starts 20km north of Alice Springs. The road is sealed almost to **Tilmouth Well** (☑08-8956 8777; www.tilmouth well.com; unpowered/powered sites $20/28, cabins without bathroom $65; ❄@❄) on the edge of Napperby Station which bills itself as an oasis in the desert with a sparkling pool, sprawling lawns and even a golf course!

The next fuel stop is at **Yuendumu**, the largest remote community in the region and home to the Warlpiri people who were made famous in **Bush Mechanics** (www. bushmechanics.com). It's worth popping in to the **Warlukurlangu Art Centre** (☑08-8956 4133; www.warlu.com; ⊗9am-5pm Mon-Fri), a locally owned venture specialising in acrylic paintings.

From here there is no fuel for another 600km until you cross the WA border and hit **Billiluna** (☑08-9168 8076; www.billiluna.org. au). Note, Rabbit Flat Roadhouse has closed permanently. Another 170km will have you resting your weary bones in Halls Creek.

ALICE SPRINGS

POP 27,480

The iconic outback town of Alice Springs is no longer the lonely frontier settlement of legend, yet the vast surroundings of red desert and burnished ranges still underscore its remoteness. This ruggedly beautiful town is shaped by its mythical landscapes, vibrant Aboriginal culture (where else can you hear six uniquely Australian languages in the main street?) and tough pioneering past.

What began 140 years ago as a lonely telegraph station has rapidly developed into a modern regional centre ignited by the boom in adventure tourism, the insatiable interest in contemporary Aboriginal art and vastly improved access. The town is a natural base for exploring central Australia, with Uluru-Kata Tjuta National Park a relatively close four-hour drive away. The mesmerising MacDonnell Ranges stretch east and west from the town centre, and you don't have to venture far to find yourself among ochre-red gorges, pastel-hued hills and ghostly white gum trees.

To the Arrernte people, the traditional owners of the Alice Springs area, this place is called Mparntwe. The heart of Mparntwe is the junction of the Charles (Anthelke Ulpeye) and Todd (Lhere Mparntwe) Rivers, just north of Anzac Hill (Untyeyetweleye). The topographical features of the town were formed by the creative ancestral beings – known as the Yeperenye, Ntyarlke and Utnerrengatye caterpillars – as they crawled across the landscape from Emily Gap (Anthwerrke), in the MacDonnell Ranges southeast of town. For many travellers, international and

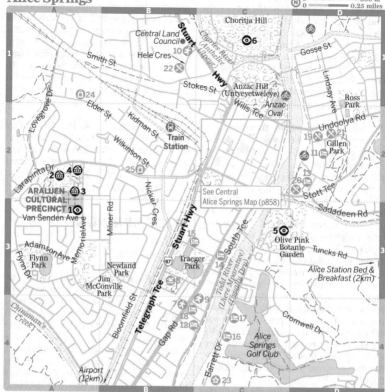

Australian, Alice Springs is their first encounter with contemporary Indigenous Australia – with its enchanting art, mesmerising culture and present-day challenges.

◉ Sights

Alice Springs Desert Park   WILDLIFE PARK
(off Map p854; www.alicespringsdesertpark.com.au; Larapinta Dr; adult/child $20/10; ⊙7.30am-6pm, last entry 4.30pm) If you haven't managed to glimpse a spangled grunter or a marbled velvet gecko on your travels, head to the Desert Park where the creatures of central Australia are all on display in one place. The predominantly open-air exhibits faithfully recreate the animals' natural environment in a series of habitats: inland river, sand country and woodland.

Try to time your visit with the terrific **birds of prey show** (⊙10am & 3.30pm), featuring free-flying Australian kestrels, kites and awesome wedge-tailed eagles. Twitchers

will also enjoy the dawn **bird walkabout** (adult/child $50/25; ⊙7.30am Wed & Sat) where you breakfast with the birds.

To catch some of the park's rare and elusive animals like the bilby, visit the excellent **nocturnal house**. If you like what you see, come back at night and spotlight endangered species on the guided **nocturnal tour** (adult/child $20/10; ⊙7.30pm Mon-Fri), which also has a dinner option (adult/child $60/35; ⊙6pm Tue-Thu). Bookings are essential for all tours.

To get the most out of the park pick up a free audioguide (available in various languages) or join one of the free ranger-led talks held throughout the day.

It's an easy 2.5km cycle out to the park. Alternatively, **Desert Park Transfers** (☑1800 806 641; www.tailormadetours.com.au; adult/child $48/28) operates five times daily during park hours and the cost includes park entry and pick-up and drop-off at your accommodation.

Alice Springs

DARWIN & ULURU THE TANAMI ROAD

Araluen Cultural Precinct   CULTURAL CENTRE
(Map p854; www.nt.gov.au/nreta/arts/ascp; cnr Larapinta Dr & Memorial Ave; precinct pass adult/child $10/7) You can wander around freely outside, accessing the cemetery and grounds, but the 'precinct pass' provides entry to the exhibitions and displays.

Araluen Arts Centre   ART GALLERY
For a small town, Alice Springs has a thriving arts scene and the Araluen Arts Centre (Map p854) is at its heart. There is a 500-seat theatre and four galleries with a focus on art from the central desert region.

The Albert Namatjira Gallery features works by the artist, who began painting watercolours in the 1930s at Hermannsburg. The exhibition draws comparisons between Namatjira and his initial mentor, Rex Battarbee and other Hermannsburg School artists. It also features 14 early acrylic works from the Papunya Community School Collection.

Other galleries showcase local artists, travelling exhibitions and newer works from Indigenous community art centres.

Museum of Central Australia   MUSEUM
(Map p854; ⊙10am-5pm) The natural history collection at this compact museum recalls the days of megafauna – when hippo-sized

wombats and 3m-tall flightless birds roamed the land. Among the geological displays are meteorite fragments and fossils. There's a free audio tour, narrated by a palaeontologist, which helps bring the exhibition to life.

There's also a display on the work of Professor TGH Strehlow, a linguist and anthropologist born at the Hermannsburg Mission among the Arrernte people. During his lifetime he gathered one of the world's most documented collections of Australian Aboriginal artefacts, songs, genealogies, film and sound recordings. It's upstairs in the Strehlow Research Centre which has a library (⊙10am-4pm Mon-Fri) open to the public.

Central Australia Aviation Museum   MUSEUM
(Map p854; Memorial Ave; admission free; ⊙9am-5pm Mon-Fri, 10am-5pm Sat & Sun) Housed in the Connellan Hangar, Alice's original aerodrome, there are displays on pioneer aviation in the Territory including Royal Flying Doctor (RFDS) planes.

Easily the most interesting exhibit is the wreck of the Kookaburra, a tiny plane which crashed in the Tanami Desert in 1929 while searching for Charles Kingsford Smith and his co-pilot Charles Ulm, who had gone down in their plane, the *Southern Cross*.

The *Kookaburra* pilots, Keith Anderson and Bob Hitchcock, perished in the desert, while Kingsford Smith and Ulm were rescued.

Alice Springs Memorial Cemetery
MONUMENT

The cemetery (Map p854) is adjacent to the aviation museum and contains the graves of some prominent locals including **Albert Namatjira** (1902–59) and **Harold Lasseter** (1880–1931), the eccentric prospector whose fervent search for a folkloric reef of gold (Lasseter's Reef) claimed his life. Anthropologist **Olive Pink** (1884–1975), who campaigned for Aboriginal rights, is buried facing the opposite direction to the others – a rebel to the end.

Telegraph Station Historical Reserve
HISTORIC PARK

(Map p854; adult/child $8.50/4.50; ◷8am-9pm, museum 9am-5pm) The old Telegraph Station, which used to relay messages between Darwin and Adelaide, offers a fascinating glimpse of the town's European beginnings. Built along the Overland Telegraph Line (OTL) in the 1870s, the station continued to operate until 1932. It later served as a welfare home for Aboriginal children of mixed ancestry until 1963. The building has been faithfully restored and guided tours operate roughly on the hour between 9am and 4.30pm (April to October). Nearby is the original **'Alice' spring** (Thereyurre to the Arrernte Aboriginal people), a semipermanent waterhole in the Todd River after which the town is named.

It's all set in 450 hectares of shady parkland with free barbecues (alcohol permitted) and walking trails. The best is the 30-minute loop to **Trig Hill**, returning via the original station cemetery.

It's an easy 4km walk or cycle north to the station from Todd Mall; follow the path on the western side of the riverbed.

Royal Flying Doctor Service Base
MUSEUM

(RFDS; Map p858; www.flyingdoctor.net; Stuart Tce; adult/child $7/3.50; ◷9am-5pm Mon-Sat, 1-5pm Sun) This is the home of the Royal Flying Doctor Service, whose dedicated health workers provide 24-hour emergency retrievals across an area of around 1.25 million sq km. Entry to the visitor centre is by a half-hour tour that includes a video presentation, and a look at the operational control room as well as some ancient medical gear and a flight simulator. The adjoining **cafe** (◷9am-4.30pm Mon-Sat) serves excellent homemade pies.

School of the Air
MUSEUM

(www.assoa.nt.edu.au; 80 Head St; adult/child $7/4.50; ◷8.30am-4.30pm Mon-Sat, 1.30-4.30pm Sun) Started in 1951, this was the first school of its type in Australia, broadcasting lessons to children over an area of 1.3 million sq km. While transmissions were originally all done over high-frequency radio, satellite broadband internet and web-cams now mean students can study in a virtual classroom. The guided tour of the centre includes a video. During school term you can view a live broadcast from 8.30am to 2.30pm Monday to Friday. The school is about 3km north of the town centre.

Alice Springs Reptile Centre
ZOO

(Map p858; www.reptilecentre.com.au; 9 Stuart Tce; adult/child $12/6/30; ◷9.30am-5pm) It may be small, but this reptile centre packs a poisonous punch with its impressive collection of venomous snakes, thorny devils and bearded dragons. Inside the cave room are 11 different species of NT geckos, and outside there's Terry, a 3.3m saltwater croc plus a magnificent perentie, Australia's largest lizard. The enthusiastic guides will happily plonk a python around your neck during the **handling demonstrations** (◷11am, 1pm & 3.30pm) or let you pet a bluetongue lizard.

Alice Springs Transport Heritage Centre
MUSEUM

At the MacDonnell siding, about 10km south of Alice and 1km west of the Stuart Hwy, are a couple of museums dedicated to big trucks and old trains. If you want to visit both the museums, consider the **half-day tour** (☑08-8955 5047; tours $55; ◷10am-2pm), which includes entry, a guide and lunch.

The **Old Ghan Rail Museum** (1 Norris Bell Ave; adult/child $8/5; ◷9am-5pm) has a collection of restored *Ghan* locos (originally called the *Afghan Express* after the cameleers who forged the route). There's also the Old Ghan Tea Rooms and an ad-hoc collection of railway memorabilia in the lovely Stuart railway station.

For a truckin' good time, head to the **National Road Transport Hall of Fame** (www.roadtransporthall.com; 2 Norris Bell Ave; adult/child $12/6; ◷9am-5pm) which has a fabulous collection of big rigs, including a few ancient road trains. Admission includes entry to the Kenworth Dealer Truck Museum. There are over 100 restored trucks and vintage cars, including many of the outback's pioneering vehicles.

Olive Pink Botanic Garden NATURE RESERVE

(Map p854; www.opbg.com.au; Tuncks Rd; admission by donation; ⊙8am-6pm) A network of meandering trails leads through this lovely arid zone botanic garden, which was founded by the prominent anthropologist Olive Pink. The garden has over 500 central Australian plant species and grows bush foods and medicinal plants like native lemon grass, quandong and bush passion fruit. There's a gentle climb up Meyers Hill with fine views over Alice and Ntyarlkarle Tyaneme, one of the first sites created by the caterpillar ancestors.

The small visitor centre has various exhibitions during the year and the excellent **Bean Tree Cafe** (p862) is worth a trip to the gardens alone.

Anzac Hill LANDMARK

For a tremendous view, particularly at sunrise and sunset, take a hike (use **Lions Walk** from Wills Tce) or a drive up to the top of Anzac Hill, known as Untyeyetweleye in Arrernte. From the war memorial there is a 365-degree view over the town down to Heavitree Gap and the Ranges.

Heritage Walk NOTABLE BUILDINGS

To get a feel for early Alice Springs, there are a number of historic-buildings-cum-mini-museums that you can pop into while wandering around town. Admission is by donation.

On Todd Mall is **Adelaide House** (Map p858; ⊙10am-4pm Mon-Fri, 10am-noon Sat) built in the 1920s by the founding flying doctor Reverend John Flynn as the first hospital in central Australia. Enter a classroom from 1938 at the **Old Hartley Street School** (Map p858; 39 Hartley St; ⊙10.30am-2.30pm Mon-Fri Feb-Nov) or take in the gracious beauty of the **Residency** (Map p858; 12 Parsons St; ⊙10am-2pm Mon-Fri), built in 1927 and a symbol of the town's brief legislative independence from the rest of the NT.

🏃 Activities

Ballooning

Outback Ballooning BALLOONING

(☑1800 809 790; www.outbackballooning.com.au; 30/60min flight $265/360, mandatory insurance $25) Floating above Alice at sunrise is not an experience you will forget in a hurry (though the included picnic champagne breakfast may be). Hotel transfers are included in the price.

Bowling

Dust Bowl BOWLING

(Map p854; ☑08-8952 5051; 29 Gap Rd; per game $11; ⊙noon-10pm) Has a bar and a restaurant serving wood-fired pizzas.

Bushwalking

Experience the bush around Alice with several easy walks radiating from the Olive Pink Botanic Garden (p857) and the Telegraph Station (p856), which marks the start of the first stage of the Larapinta Trail (see p870).

Alice Springs Bushwalkers Association BUSHWALKING

(www.centralaustralianbushwalkers.wordpress. com) A group of local bushwalkers that schedules a wide variety of walks in the area, particularly the West MacDonnell Ranges, from March to November.

Alice Camp 'n' Drive BUSHWALKING

(Map p854; ☑08-8952 0099; www.alicecampndrive. com; 48 Gap Rd) If you're keen to go camping but don't have your own equipment, Alice Camp 'n' Drive has a pack they rent out which includes swags, sleeping bag, esky, BBQ and cooking utensils for $45 per person per day.

Camel Riding

Camels played an integral part in pioneering central Australia before roads and railways, and travellers can relive some of that adventure.

Pyndan Camel Tracks CAMEL RIDING

(☑0416 170 164; www.cameltracks.com; Jane Rd) Local cameleer Marcus Williams offers one-hour rides ($45/25 adult/child), as well as half-day jaunts ($95 per person).

Cycling & Mountain Bike Riding

Bikes are the perfect way to get around Alice Springs. There are cycle paths along the Todd River to the Telegraph Station (see p856), west to the Alice Springs Desert Park (p854) and further out to Simpsons Gap (p870). For a map of cycling and walking paths pick up a copy of *Active in Alice* from the visitor information centre.

With its arid rangeland terrain and networks of single tracks, Alice Springs is getting a name for mountain bike riding, with the annual five-day MTB Enduro race a calendar highlight. Trails are easily accessed from town or meet up for a **social sunset ride** (☑08-8952 5800; centralaustralian roughriders.asn.au; ride $5; Scout Hall, cnr Larapinta & Lovegrove Drs; ⊙6pm Wed winter, 5pm

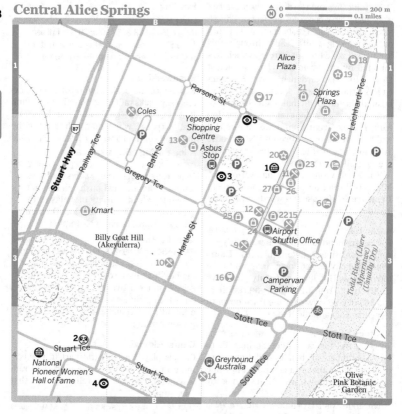

summer) with the Central Australian Rough Riders' Club.

Longhorn BIKE HIRE
(☑0439 860 735; half/full day $20/35) Drop-off/pick-up service with commuter, mountain and tandem bikes available as well as kids' bikes and baby seats.

Ultimate Ride BIKE SHOP
(Map p854; ☑08-8953 7297; 2/30 North Stuart Hwy; ⊙9am-6pm Mon-Fri, 9am-2pm Sat) Home of the Rough Riders, Ultimate Ride sells bicycles, stocks accessories and does repairs. It will also advise on bike tracks.

Swimming

Alice Springs Swim Centre SWIMMING
(Map p854; ☑08-8953 4633; Speed St; adult/child $3.30/1.70; ⊙6am-7pm Mon-Fri, 10am-7pm Sat & Sun Sep-Apr) With lots of grass for lounging about and views of the Ranges, the swim centre makes a lovely alternative to your hotel pool. An indoor aquatic and leisure

centre was being built at the time of research, which will be open year-round.

☞ Tours

Around Alice & MacDonnell Ranges

Alice Wanderer OUTBACK
(☑1800 722 111; www.alicewanderer.com.au) Runs day tours into the West MacDonnell Ranges as far as Glen Helen Gorge, including morning tea and lunch (adult/child $112/72), and a half-day trip to Simpsons Gap and Standley Chasm ($64/42). There is also a Wednesday morning tour to Santa Teresa Aboriginal community and the Keringke Art Centre ($130/95).

Dreamtime Tours INDIGENOUS
(☑08-8955 5095; www.rstours.com.au; adult/child $84/42, self-drive $66/33; ⊙8.30-11.30am) Runs the three-hour Dreamtime & Bushtucker Tour, where you meet Warlpiri Aboriginal people and learn a little about their

traditions. As it caters for large bus groups it can be impersonal, but you can tag along with your own vehicle.

L'Astragale TOWN
(☑08-8953 6293; eroullet@gmail.com; $35) Francophone Evelyne Roullet runs a local walking tour of Alice Springs which leaves from the visitor centre at 9.30am and 2.30pm.

Outback Experience OUTBACK
(☑08-8953 2666; www.outbackexperience.com.au) Day trips to Chambers Pillar and Rainbow Valley ($150), and the East MacDonnells ($130).

Rainbow Valley Cultural Tours INDIGENOUS
(☑1800 011 144; www.rainbowvalleyculturaltours.com; day tour adult/child $120/165, self-drive morning $15/30, afternoon $25/50) Tour beautiful Rainbow Valley with a traditional owner and visit rock-art sites not open to the general public. Sunset self-drive tours can include overnight camping and dinner for an extra $10/20.

RT Tours FOOD
(☑08-8952 0327; www.rttoursaustralia.com; $150) Chef and Arrernte guide Bob Taylor runs a popular lunch and dinner tour at Simpsons Gap and the Telegraph Reserve where he whips up a bush-inspired meal.

Trek Larapinta WALKING
(☑08-8953 2933; www.treklarapinta.com.au; 6 days $1790) Guided multiday walks along

sections of the Larapinta Trail. Also runs volunteer projects involving trail maintenance and bush regeneration on Aboriginal outstations.

Uluru, Kings Canyon & Palm Valley

Emu Run Tours OUTBACK
(☑08-8953 7057; www.emurun.com.au) Operates day tours to Uluru ($199) and three-day tours to Uluru and Kings Canyon ($390). Prices include park entry fees. There are also recommended small-group day tours through the West MacDonnell Ranges or Palm Valley ($120), including morning tea, lunch and entrance fees.

The Rock Tour OUTBACK
(☑1800 246 345; www.therocktour.com.au) Backpacker-friendly three-day (two nights) camping safari ($295) which visits Kings Canyon, Curtin Springs, the 'Rock' and Kata Tjuta. Price does not include park entry fees. Leaves Alice daily at 6am.

Wayoutback Desert Safaris 4WD
(☑1300 551 510, 08-8952 4324; www.wayoutback.com) Small group 4WD safari tours including the excellent two-day Aboriginal-led Culture and Country trip ($595). There are also three-day safaris that traverse 4WD tracks to Uluru and Kings Canyon for $635, and five-day safaris that top it up with the Palm Valley and West MacDonnells for $985.

✖✖ Festivals & Events

Alice Springs Cup   HORSE RACING
(www.alicespringsturfclub.org.au) In May, don
a hat and gallop down to the Pioneer Park
Racecourse for the main event.

Finke Desert Race   MOTORCROSS
(www.finkedesertrace.com.au) Motorcyclists
and buggy drivers vie to take out the title
of this crazy June race 240km from Alice
along the Old South Rd to Finke; the following day they race back again. Spectators
camp along the road to cheer them on.

Alice Springs Beanie Festival   ARTS
(www.beaniefest.org) This four-day festival in
June-July, held at the Araluen Art Centre,
celebrates the humble beanie (knitted
woollen hat) – handmade by women
throughout the central desert.

Camel Cup   CAMEL RACING
(www.camelcup.com.au) A carnival atmosphere
prevails during the running of the Camel
Cup at Blatherskite Park in mid-July.

Alice Springs Rodeo   RODEO
Bareback bull riding, steer wrestling and
ladies' barrel races are on the bill at Blatherskite Park in August.

Old Timers Fete   FETE
Stock up on doilies and tea towels at this
ode to granny arts, held on the second
Saturday in August at the Old Timers
Village.

Alice Desert Festival   ARTS
(www.alicedesertfestival.com.au) A cracker
of a festival, including a circus program,
music, film, comedy and the highly antici-
pated Desert Mob art exhibition. It's on in
September.

Henley-on-Todd Regatta   REGATTA
(www.henleyontodd.com.au) These boat races
in September on the dry bed of the Todd
River are a typically Australian light-
hearted denial of reality. The boats are
bottomless; the crews' legs stick through
and they run down the course.

🛏 Sleeping

If you are travelling in peak season (June to
September) make sure you book ahead, but
if you're trying your luck, check the internet
for last-minute rates, which often bring top-
end places into midrange reach.

Alice's Secret Traveller's Inn   HOSTEL **$**
(Map p854; ☎1800 783 633, 08-8952 8686; www.
asecret.com.au; 6 Khalick St; dm $23-26, s/d/tr

$60/65/90; ✳@☲) Just across the Todd Riv-
er from town, this is a recommended 'hideaway' hostel where you can relax around the
pool, puff on a didge, or play a game of bad-
minton in the garden. Rooms in the dongas
are a bit of a squeeze, and those in the house
are simple, comfortable and clean.

Alice Station Bed & Breakfast   B&B **$$**
(Map p854; ☎08-8953 6600; www.alicestation.
com; 25 The Fairway; s/d/ste $175/190/210;
✳@☲) The host of this lovely B&B, which
backs on to the bush, really does have kan-
garoos in her backyard. Made out of old
Ghan railway sleepers, the whimsically de-
signed home has a relaxed atmosphere with
a communal lounge and stylishly decorated
rooms with local Aboriginal art on the walls.
Continental breakfasts get the thumbs up,
as do the homemade cakes and eight differ-
ent types of tea.

Alice in the Territory   HOTEL **$**
(☎08-8952 6100; www.alicent.com.au; 46 Ste-
phens Rd; dm/s/d $25/89/99; ✳@☲) Formerly
the Comfort Inn, this sprawling hotel has
had a $2 million refurbishment and is now
the best bargain stay in town. Deluxe rooms
have tiny bathrooms but they are bright and
comfortable and offer two free movie chan-
nels. The four-bed dorms have yet to be com-
pletely upgraded. The new management is
enthusiastic and eager to please and there's
a flash pool at the foot of the Ranges.

**MacDonnell Range Holiday
Park**   CARAVAN PARK **$**
(☎1800 808 373, 08-8952 6111; www.macrange.
com.au; Palm Pl; unpowered/powered sites
$32/36, cabins d $68-172; ✳@☲) Probably
Alice's biggest and best kept, this park has
grassy sites, spotless amenities and a variety
of accommodation from simple cabins with
shared bathroom to self-contained two-bed-
room villas. Not the cheapest option, but
you get what you pay for with a roster of
daily activities from stargazing to pancake
Sundays. Kids can cavort in the adventure
playground, BMX track and basketball
court, while adults can kick back around
the pool.

Alice on Todd   APARTMENTS **$$**
(Map p854; ☎08-8953 8033; www.aliceontodd.
com; cnr Strehlow St & South Tce; studio $120,
1-/2-bedroom apt $147/184, deluxe 1-/2-bedroom
apt $160/198; ✳@☲) This attractive and
secure apartment complex on the banks
of the Todd River offers one- and two-

bedroom self-contained units with kitchen and lounge. The private, balconied units sleep up to six so they're a great option for families and groups. Some of the units are looking a bit tired but they have recently opened 23 new deluxe apartments, which are a step up in decor and have plasma TV. The landscaped grounds enclose a barbecue area, children's playground, and a games room with pool table.

Crowne Plaza Alice Springs   HOTEL $$$

(Map p854; ☎1300 666 545, 08-8950 8000; www. crowneplaza.com.au; Barrett Dr; d from $165, ste $250-295; ✻@✹) With its spacious resort-style facilities, this is widely considered Alice's top hotel. Choose from the garden-view rooms or the better mountain range-view rooms – they're all rather early '90s in style, decked out with cane furniture and pastel colours. There's a lovely pool and spa, well-equipped gym and sauna, tennis courts and a house peacock. Alice's best restaurant, Hanumans (see p862), is in the lobby.

Chifley Alice Springs   HOTEL $$

(Map p858; ☎08-8951 4545; www.chifleyhotels. com.au; 34 Stott Tce; standard/superior/deluxe d $160/190/255; ✻@✹) With a circle of double-storey buildings arranged around a swath of lawns and gum trees, the Chifley has a relaxed country-club vibe. Avoid the standard rooms and go for the recently re-furbished superior and deluxe accommodation overlooking the Todd River. There's an attractive pool area with a swim-up bar, plus a seafood restaurant.

Toddy's Backpackers   HOSTEL $

(Map p854; ☎1800 027 027; www.toddys.com.au; 41 Gap Rd; dm $22-26, d $60-92; ✻@✹) Toddy's is a rambling place encompassing two properties and a huge variety of rooms from dorms and budget doubles to a deluxe motel section with all new bedding (completely covered in plastic bedbug protector). Toddy's is popular with groups and there's a party atmosphere, spurred on by the $5 meals and cheap jugs of beer at the outdoor bar every evening. Although there are plenty of beds, the motel-style rooms can be hard to get, so book ahead.

Alice Lodge Backpackers   HOSTEL $

(Map p854; ☎1800 351 925, 08-8953 1975; www. alicelodge.com.au; 4 Mueller St; dm $22-26, d/ tr $63/80; ✻@✹) Located in a lovely residential area across the Todd River, an easy 10-minute walk from town, this is a small,

low-key hostel. The friendly staff are as accommodating as the variety of room options which include mixed and female, three-, four- and eight-bed dorms, as well as comfortable doubles and twins (some in converted caravans) built around a central pool.

Pioneer YHA Hostel   HOSTEL $

(Map p858; ☎08-8952 8855; www.yha.com.au; cnr Leichhardt Tce & Parsons St; dm $25-31, tw & d $75; ✻@✹) This YHA is housed in the old Pioneer outdoor cinema and guests can still enjoy nightly screenings of movies under the stars. Location is the biggest bonus here but it's also friendly and well run. The comfortable doubles share bathrooms. There's a good-sized kitchen and a pleasant outdoor area around a small pool.

All Seasons Oasis   HOTEL $$

(Map p854; ☎08-8952 1444; www.allseasons.com. au; 10 Gap Rd; d from $130; ✻@✹) With two swimming pools, the central one shaded by sails and surrounded with palm-shaded lawn, All Seasons convincingly recreates the oasis experience. The rooms are conventional but comfortable enough to keep it busy with numerous tour groups. There's a restaurant, a bar with a couple of pool tables and a happy hour that brings in the locals. The best rates are available from the website.

Annie's Place   HOSTEL $

(Map p854; ☎1800 359 089, 08-8952 1255; www. anniesplace.com.au; 4 Traeger Ave; dm $22, d & tw $55-65; ✻@✹) With its leafy beer garden, madly popular with travellers and locals alike, and great poolside area, Annie's is a lively place to hang out any night of the week. This is only a problem if you actually enjoy sleeping. The converted motel rooms (all with bathroom and some with a fridge) are right on top of the bar and cleanliness issues (mainly bedbug related) continue to be raised by readers, so check a few rooms before settling in.

Aurora Alice Springs   HOTEL $$

(Map p858; ☎1800 089 644, 08-8950 6666; www. auroraresorts.com.au; 11 Leichhardt Tce; standard/ deluxe/executive d $130/150/230; ✻@✹) Right in the town centre (the 'back' door opens out onto Todd Mall), this modern hotel has a relaxed atmosphere and a good restaurant, the Red Ochre Grill (see p863). Standard rooms are nondescript but well appointed with fridge, phone and free in-house movies.

Desert Palms Resort
HOTEL $$

(Map p854; ☑08-8952 5977, 1800 678 037; www. desertpalms.com.au; 74 Barrett Dr; villas $135; ❄@☎) This hotel has a relaxed island vibe with its shady palms, cascading bougainvillea and Indonesian-style villas. Unfortunately the rooms – which have a kitchenette, tiny bathroom, TV and private balcony – are disappointingly dated and some have a lingering smell of cigarettes. The island swimming pool is a big hit with kids.

Heavitree Gap Outback Lodge
CARAVAN PARK $

(☑1800 896 119, 08-8950 4444; www.aurora resorts.com.au; Palm Circuit; unpowered/powered sites $12/15, dm $25, d $135-180; ❄@☎) At the foot of the Ranges and dotted with eucalypts and bounding rock wallabies, Heavitree makes a shady place to pitch or park. Alternatively, there are rooms: four-bed dorms, and lodge and very basic kitchenette rooms that sleep six. The lodge offers a free shuttle into the town centre, which is about 4km away. The neighbouring tavern has live country music most nights of the week.

Bond Springs Outback Retreat
B&B $$$

(☑08-8952 9888; www.outbackretreat.com.au; 2-/3-bedroom cottage from $230/280; ❄☎) Experience a taste of outback station life at this retreat, about 25km from town. The two private self-contained cottages are refurbished stockman's quarters. A full breakfast is included but the rest is self-catering. Have a game of tennis or mooch around the enormous property including the original station school, which operated through the School of the Air.

✖ Eating

TOP CHOICE **Hanuman Restaurant**
THAI $$

(Map p854; ☑08-8953 7188; Crowne Plaza Alice Springs, Barrett Dr; mains $14-30; ☺lunch Mon-Fri, dinner daily) You won't believe you're in the outback when you try the incredible Thai- and Indian-influenced cuisine at this stylish restaurant. The delicate Thai entrees are a real triumph as are the seafood dishes, particularly the Hanuman prawns. Although the menu is ostensibly Thai, there are enough Indian dishes to satisfy a curry craving. There are several vegetarian offerings and a good wine list. Book ahead.

Tinh & Lan Alice Vietnamese Restaurant
VIETNAMESE $$

(1900 Heffernan Rd; mains $14-20; ☺lunch & dinner Tue-Sun) This atmospheric Vietnamese restaurant is set in a market garden illuminated with lanterns. All the favourites – rice paper rolls, pho, salt and pepper squid – are deliciously prepared and the ingredients, growing all around you, couldn't be fresher. Follow the signs off Colonel Rose Dr; it's about 14km south of town.

Casa Nostra
ITALIAN $$

(Map p854; ☑08-8952 6749; cnr Undoolya Rd & Sturt Tce; mains $14-28; ☺dinner Mon-Sat) Step across the Todd River and into 1970s Italy at this old-school pizza and pasta joint. Madly popular on the weekends (bookings recommended) it is wonderfully cosy with red and white checked tablecloths, and plastic grape vines hanging from the ceiling. Order the famously delectable vanilla slice early as they run out the door. Note that it's BYO vino.

Bean Tree Cafe
CAFE $

(Map p854; Olive Pink Botanic Garden, Tuncks Rd; mains $9-12; ☺8am-3pm) Breakfast with the birds at this superb outdoor cafe tucked away in the Olive Pink Botanic Garden. Service can be slow, but it's a relaxing place to sit and the wholesome home-style dishes such as the kangaroo burger and scrumptious bigilla (bean and spinach dish) are well worth the wait.

Thai Room
THAI $$

(Map p858; Fan Lane; mains $12-25; ☺lunch Mon-Fri, dinner Mon-Sat) Head to this arcade restaurant for perky Thai dishes and quicker-than-average service. The modest menu mixes its signature spices with a variety of veggie, meat and seafood dishes. The lunch specials are a bargain and it's BYO.

Soma
CAFE $

(Map p858;64 Todd Mall; mains $12-15; ☺breakfast & lunch) There's excellent people-watching and even better eating to be had at this Todd Mall cafe which offers sophisticated dishes and great coffee. Breakfast is on all day and lunch ranges from a camel panini to a delicious vegan scrambled tofu. There is a focus on organic ingredients and there are a number of gluten-free options.

Tea Shrine
VEGAN $

(Map p858; 113 Todd St; mains $8-12; ☺9.30am-5pm Mon-Sat; ☑) Vegetarians may be forgiven for feeling a bit left out in meat-heavy Alice Springs, but not at the Tea Shrine, a vegan Asian restaurant and teahouse. Popular with hippies and health workers, this peaceful

cafe has daily specials and a range of yum cha dishes.

Water Tank Cafe
CAFE $

(Map p854; Hele Cres; mains $12-20; ⊗breakfast & lunch) Tucked away in the Bloomin' Deserts nursery this friendly cafe serves up fresh salads, burgers and homemade cake. Locals sprawl out on the couches and beanbags, sipping potent coffee and making use of the free wi-fi.

Red Ochre Grill
MODERN AUSTRALIAN $$

(Map p858; Todd Mall; mains $11-31; ⊗6.30am-9.30pm) Offering innovative fusion dishes with a focus on outback cuisine, the menu usually features locally bred proteins matched with garden natives: lemon myrtle, pepper berries and bush tomatoes. The all-day brunch in the courtyard turns out more predictable dishes including excellent eggs Benedict.

Kafe Gonzo
CAFE $

(Map p858; 76 Todd St; ⊗8am-6pm Mon-Fri, 9.30am-5pm Sat) Also known as Cam's coffee, this Melbourne-style hole-in-the-wall opposite the council building has recently expanded with an internet cafe and art space. Grab excellent locally roasted coffee and tickets to gigs and events, like the owner's monthly Pop Cinema.

Overlanders Steakhouse
STEAKHOUSE $$$

(Map p858; ☑08-8952 2159; 72 Hartley St; mains $23-40; ⊗dinner) The place for steaks, be they buffalo, kangaroo, crocodile or camel. And why stop at just one? Amid the cattle station decor (saddles, branding irons and the like) you can take the challenge of the Drover's Blowout ($65), four courses including a platter of Aussie meats.

Also recommended:

Red Centre Chinese
CHINESE $

(Map p858; Alice Plaza; ⊗9am-3pm Mon-Sat) Made-to-order soups and noodle dishes.

Tanakas
JAPANESE $

(Map p858; Yeperenye Shopping Centre; sushi $2.30; ⊗9am-3pm Mon-Sat) Sushi including surprisingly good kangaroo nori rolls and fresh juices.

Afghan Traders
HEALTH FOOD $

(Map p858; Leichtodd Plaza, 7 Leichhardt Tce) Replete with organic and other health foods – follow the laneway behind the ANZ bank, or duck through Springs Plaza from Todd Mall.

Drinking

Annie's Place
BAR

(Map p854; 4 Traeger Ave; ⊗5pm-late) Easily the most atmospheric watering hole in town. Decent music (sometimes live), leafy beer garden, cheap jugs and pool-side drinking.

Bojangles
BAR

(Map p858; 80 Todd St; ⊗11.30am-late) Behind the swinging saloon doors is a 'Wild West meets Aussie Outback' theme complete with cowhide seats, stockman regalia and a live 3m-long carpet python behind the bar. Bo's is beloved of backpacker groups and station ringers and is jumping most nights of the week.

Juicy Rump
BAR

(Map p854; 93 Barrett Dr; ⊗10am-late) Not as bad as the name suggests, this is the late-night favourite if you want to have a dance to cheesy R'n'B or watch a big sporting event on the town's largest plasma screen. Also has a deck with a view to the ranges, lovely for sunset drinks.

Todd Tavern
PUB

(Map p858; www.toddtavern.com.au; 1 Todd Mall; ⊗10am-midnight) This enduring, classically Aussie pub has a lively bar, pokies, decent pub grub and occasional live music on weekends.

Entertainment

The gig guide in the entertainment section of the *Centralian Advocate* (published every Tuesday and Friday) lists what's on in and around town.

Araluen Arts Centre
ARTS CENTRE

(Map p854; ☑08-8951 1122; www.araluenartscentre.nt.gov.au; Larapinta Dr) The cultural heart of Alice, the 500-seat Araluen Theatre hosts a diverse range of performers, from dance troupes to comedians, while the Art House Cinema screens films every Sunday evening at 7pm (adult/child $14/12). The website has an events calendar.

Sounds of Starlight Theatre
LIVE MUSIC

(Map p858; ☑08-8953 0826; www.soundsofstarlight.com; 40 Todd Mall; adult/concession/family $30/25/90; ⊗8pm Tue, Fri & Sat) This atmospheric 1½-hour musical performance evoking the spirit of the outback with didgeridoo, drums and keyboards and wonderful photography and lighting is an Alice institution. Musician Andrew Langford also runs free didge lessons (10.30am and 2.30pm Monday to Friday).

Alice Springs Cinema
CINEMA

(Map p858; 08-8952 4999; Todd Mall; adult/child $14.50/10, Tue $10/8) The place to go for latest-release Hollywood blockbusters.

Lasseter's Hotel Casino
CASINO

(Map p854; www.lassetershotelcasino.com.au; 93 Barrett Dr; 10am-3am Sun-Thu, to 4am Fri & Sat, gaming tables from 2pm) Along with the usual slot and table games, there's the classic Aussie two-up ring (from 9pm Friday and Saturday).

Shopping

Alice is the centre for Aboriginal arts from all over central Australia. The places owned and run by community art centres ensure that a better slice of the proceeds goes to the artist and artist's community.

Central Australian Aboriginal Media Association
MUSIC STORE

(CAAMA; Map p858; 08-8951 9711; www.caama.com.au; 79 Todd Mall; 9am-5pm Mon-Fri, 9am-1pm Sat) Here you will find most of the CDs recorded by central Australia's Aboriginal musicians. The CAAMA studio, which has its own radio network (8KIN FM), is just down the road. The shop also stocks Aboriginal design printed material, T-shirts, jewellery and other Indigenous-themed items.

Gallery Gondwana
INDIGENOUS ART

(Map p858; 08-8953 1577; www.gallerygondwana.com.au; 43 Todd Mall; 9.30am-6pm Mon-Fri, 10am-5pm Sat & Sun) Gondwana is a well-established private gallery, recognised for dealing directly with community art centres and artists. Quality works from leading and emerging Central and Western Desert artists include work from Yuendumu and Utopia.

Mbantua Gallery
INDIGENOUS ART

(Map p858; 08-8952 5571; www.mbantua.com.au; 71 Gregory Tce; 9am-6pm Mon-Fri, 9.30am-5pm Sat) This privately owned gallery, which extends through to Todd Mall, includes a cafe and extensive exhibits of works from the renowned Utopia region, as well as watercolour landscapes from the Namatjira school. The upstairs Educational & Permanent Collection (adult/child $4.60/3.30) is a superb cultural exhibition space with panels explaining Aboriginal mythology and customs.

Tjanpi Desert Weavers
INDIGENOUS ART

(Map p854; 08-8958 2377; www.tjanpi.com.au; 3 Wilkinson St; 10am-4pm Mon-Fri) This small enterprise employs and supports Central Desert weavers from 18 remote communities. Their store is well worth a visit to see the magnificent woven baskets and quirky sculptures created from locally collected grasses.

Papunya Tula Artists
INDIGENOUS ART

(Map p858; 08-8952 4731; www.papunyatula.com.au; 78 Todd Mall; 9am-5pm Mon-Fri, 10am-2pm Sat) The Western Desert art movement began at Papunya Tula in 1971, and today this Aboriginal-owned gallery displays some of this most sought-after art. Papunya Tula works with around 120 artists, most painting at Kintore in the far west.

Desert Dwellers
OUTDOOR GEAR

(Map p854; 08-8953 2240; 38 Elder St; 9am-5pm Mon-Fri, 9am-2pm Sat) For camping and hiking gear, head to this shop, which has just about everything you need to equip yourself for an outback jaunt – maps, swags, tents, portable fridges, stoves and more.

Todd Mall Market
MARKET

(Map p858; 9am-1pm 2nd Sun May-Dec) Buskers, craft stalls, sizzling woks, smoky satay stands, Aboriginal art, jewellery and knick-knacks make for a relaxed stroll.

Information

Dangers & Annoyances

Avoid walking alone at night anywhere in town but particularly around Gap Rd. Catch a taxi back to your accommodation if you're out late.

Emergency
Ambulance (000)
Police (000, 08-8951 8888; Parsons St)

Internet Access

JPG Computers (08-8952 2040; Coles Complex, Bath St; per hr $6; 9am-5.30pm Mon-Fri)
Outback Email (2a Gregory Tce; per hr $3; 9am-6pm) Part of the Outback Travel Shop.
Todd Internet Café (08-8953 8355; Colocag Plaza, 76 Todd St; per hr $4; 10am-6pm)
Water Tank Café (Hele Cres) Free wi-fi at the Bloomin' Deserts nursery.

Medical Services

Alice Springs Hospital (08-8951 7777; Gap Rd)
Alice Springs Pharmacy (08-8952 1554; shop 19, Yeperenye Shopping Centre, 36 Hartley St; 8.30am-7.30pm)

Money

Major banks with ATMs, such as ANZ, Commonwealth, National Australia and Westpac, are located in and around Todd Mall in the town centre.

Post

Main post office (☎13 13 18; 31-33 Hartley St; ⏱8.15am-5pm Mon-Fri) All the usual services are available here.

Tourist Information

Central Land Council (☎08-8951 6211; www.clc.org.au; PO Box 3321, NT 0871; 31-33 Stuart Hwy; ⏱8.30am-noon & 2-4pm) For Aboriginal land permits and transit permits.

Tourism Central Australia Visitor Information Centre (☎1800 645 199, 08-8952 5199; www.centralaustraliantourism.com; 60 Gregory Tce; ⏱8.30am-5pm Mon-Fri, 9.30am-4pm Sat & Sun) This helpful centre can load you up with stacks of brochures and the free visitors guide. Weather forecasts and road conditions are posted on the wall, and Mereenie Tour Passes ($3.50) and fossicking permits (free) are issued. National parks information is also available. Tourism Central Australia desks are also found at the airport and train station. Ask about their unlimited kilometre deals if you are thinking of renting a car.

Websites

Alice Online (www.aliceonline.com.au) Wonderful stories, new and old, about central Australia.

Getting There & Away

Air

Alice Springs is well connected, with **Qantas** (☎13 13 13, 08-8950 5211; www.qantas.com.au) and **Tiger Airways** (☎08-9335 3033; www.tigerairways.com.au) operating daily flights to/from capital cities. Airline representatives are based at Alice Springs airport. One-way fares from Alice include Yulara (from $109), Adelaide (from $220), Melbourne (from $280), Darwin (from $270), Sydney (from $280), Brisbane (from $310) and Perth (from $330). Check websites for latest timetables and fare offers.

Bus

Greyhound Australia (☎1300 473 946; www.greyhound.com.au; shop 3, 113 Todd St; ⏱office 8.30-11.30am & 1.30-4pm Mon-Fri) has regular services from Alice Springs (check website for timetables). Buses arrive at, and depart from, the Greyhound office in Todd St.

DESTINATION	ONE-WAY FARE ($)	DURATION (HR)
Adelaide	316	20
Coober Pedy	186	8
Darwin	378	22
Katherine	305	16½
Tennant Creek	191	6½

Austour (☎1800 335 009; www.austour.com.au) runs the cheapest daily connections between Alice Springs and Yulara ($140/70 per adult/child). **AAT Kings** (☎08-8952 1700; www.aatkings.com) also runs between Alice Springs and Yulara (adult/child $150/75), and between Kings Canyon and Alice Springs ($159/80).

Backpacker buses roam to and from Alice providing a party atmosphere and a chance to see some of the sights on the way. **Groovy Grape Getaways Australia** (☎1800 661 177; www.groovygrape.com.au) Plies the route from Alice to Adelaide overnighting in Coober Pedy for $215, plus six- and seven-day camping trips between Adelaide and Alice Springs from $645.

Wayward Bus Touring Company (☎1300 653 510, 08-8410 8833; www.waywardbus.com.au) Has a 2½-day highlights trip ($465) taking in Kings Canyon, Uluru and Rainbow Valley. It also does a seven-day Alice–Adelaide tour ($920).

Car & Motorcycle

Alice Springs is a long way from everywhere. It's 1180km to Mt Isa in Queensland, 1490km to Darwin and 441km (4½ hours) to Yulara (for Uluru). Although the roads to the north and south are sealed and in good condition, these are outback roads, and it's wise to have your vehicle well prepared, particularly as you won't get a mobile phone signal outside Alice or Yulara. Carry plenty of drinking water and emergency food at all times.

All the major companies have offices in Alice Springs, and many have counters at the airport. Prices drop by about 20% between November and April but rentals don't come cheap, as most firms offer only 100km free a day, which won't get you far. Talk to the **visitor centre** (☎1800 645 199, 08-8952 5199) about its unlimited kilometres deal before you book. A conventional (2WD) vehicle will get you to most sights in the MacDonnell Ranges and out to Uluru and Kings Canyon via sealed roads. If you want to go further afield, say to Chambers Pillar, Finke Gorge or even the Mereenie Loop Rd, a 4WD is essential.

Alice Camp 'n' Drive (☎08-8952 0099; www.alicecampndrive.com; 48 Gap Rd) Provides vehicles fully equipped for camping with swags (or tents), sleeping bags, cooking gear, chairs etc. Rates include unlimited kilometres and vehicles can be dropped off at your accommodation.

Avis (☎08-8953 5533; www.avis.com.au; Crowne Plaza Hotel & Airport)

Britz (☎08-8952 8814; www.britz.com.au; cnr Stuart Hwy & Power St) Campervans and cars; also at the airport. This is also the base for **Maui** (www.maui.com.au) and **Backpacker** (www.backpackercampervans.com) campervans.

Budget (☎13 27 27, 08-8952 8899; www.budget.com.au; 79 Todd Mall & Airport)

Central Car Rentals (☑08-8952 0098; www. centralcarrentals.com.au; 48 Gap Rd) A local operator (associated with Alice Camp 'n' Drive) with 2WD and 4WD vehicles which can be equipped with camping gear. Unlimited kilometre rates are available.

Europcar (☑13 13 90; www.europcar.com.au; airport)

Hertz (☑08-8952 2644; www.hertz.com; 76 Hartley St)

Territory Thrifty Car Rental (☑08-8952 9999; www.rentacar.com.au; cnr Stott Tce & Hartley St)

Train

A classic way to enter or leave the Territory is by the *Ghan* which can be booked through **Trainways** (☑13 21 47; www.trainways.com. au) or **Travelworld** (☑08-8953 0488; 40 Todd Mall). Discounted fares are sometimes offered, especially in the low season (February to June). Bookings are essential. See p865 for a timetable and fares.

The train station is at the end of George Cres off Larapinta Dr.

Getting Around

Alice Springs is compact enough to get to most parts of town on foot, and you can reach quite a few of the closer attractions by bicycle (see p857).

To/From the Airport

Alice Springs airport is 15km south of the town. It's about $30 by taxi. The **airport shuttle** (☑08-8953 0310; Gregory Tce; 1/2/3-5 persons one-way $18.50/30/46) meets flights and drops off passengers at city accommodation. Book a day in advance for pick-up from accommodation.

Bus

The public bus service, **Asbus** (☑08-8952 5611), departs from outside the **Yeperenye Shopping Centre** (Hartley St). Buses run about every 1½ hours from 7.45am to 6pm Monday to Friday, and from 9am to 12.45pm on Saturday. The adult/child fare for all routes is $2/50c. There are three routes of interest to travellers: 1 has a detour to the cultural precinct, 3 passes the School of the Air, and 4 passes many southern hotels and caravan parks along Gap Rd and Palm Circuit. The visitor information centre has timetables.

The **Alice Wanderer** (☑1800 722 111, 08-8952 2111; www.alicewanderer.com.au; adult/child $40/30; ☺9am-4pm) is a hop-on, hop-off sightseeing bus that covers 11 major sites, including the Telegraph Station, School of the Air, Old Ghan Rail Museum and Araluen. The ticket is valid for two days and the circuit runs every 70

minutes from opposite the visitor information centre on Gregory Tce. You can arrange to be picked up from your accommodation.

Taxi

Taxis congregate near the visitor information centre. To book one, call ☑13 10 08 or 08-8952 1877.

MACDONNELL RANGES

The beautiful, weather-beaten MacDonnell Ranges, stretching 400km across the desert, are a hidden world of spectacular gorges, rare wildlife and poignant Aboriginal heritage all within a day from Alice. There's no public transport to either the East or West MacDonnell Ranges; see p858 for tours from Alice.

East MacDonnell Ranges

Although overshadowed by the more popular West Macs, the East MacDonnell Ranges are no less picturesque and, with fewer visitors, can be a more enjoyable outback experience. The sealed Ross Hwy runs 100km along the Ranges, which are intersected by a series of scenic gaps and gorges. The gold-mining ghost town of Arltunga is 33km off the Ross Hwy along an unsealed road that is usually OK for 2WD vehicles, however access to John Hayes Rockhole (in Trephina Gorge Nature Park), N'Dhala Gorge and Ruby Gap is by 4WD only.

EMILY & JESSIE GAPS NATURE PARK

Both of these gaps are associated with the Eastern Arrernte Caterpillar Dreaming trail. Emily Gap, 16km out of town, has stylised rock paintings and a fairly deep waterhole in the narrow gorge. Known to the Arrernte as Anthwerrke, this is one of the most important Aboriginal sites in the Alice Springs area; it was from here that the caterpillar ancestral beings of Mparntwe originated before crawling across the landscape to create the topographical features that exist today. The gap is a sacred site with some well-preserved paintings on the eastern wall. Jessie Gap, 8km further on, is equally scenic and usually much quieter. Both sites have toilets, but camping is not permitted. An 8km unmarked bushwalk leads around the ridge between the two gaps.

CORROBOREE ROCK CONSERVATION RESERVE

Past Jessie Gap you drive over eroded flats before entering a valley between red ridges. Corroboree Rock, 51km from Alice Springs, is one of many strangely shaped dolomite outcrops scattered over the valley floor. Despite the name, it's doubtful the rock was ever used as a corroboree area, but it is associated with the Perentie Dreaming trail. The perentie lizard grows in excess of 2.5m, and takes refuge within the area's rock falls. There's a short walking track (15 minutes) around the rock.

TREPHINA GORGE NATURE PARK

If you only have time for a couple of stops in the East MacDonnell Ranges, make Trephina Gorge Nature Park (75km from Alice) one of them. The play between the pale sandy river beds, the red and purple gorge walls, the white tree trunks, the eucalyptus-green foliage and the blue sky is spectacular. You'll also find deep swimming holes and abundant wildlife. The Trephina Gorge Walk (45 minutes, 2km) loops around the gorge's rim. The Ridgetop Walk (five hours, 10km one-way) traverses the ridges from the gorge to John Hayes Rockhole; the 8km return along the road takes about two hours.

The delightful John Hayes Rockhole, 9km from the Trephina Gorge turn-off (the last 4km is 4WD only) has three basic camping sites (adult/child $3.30/1.65). From here, the gorgeous Chain of Ponds walk (1½ hours, 4km loop) leads past rock pools and up to a lookout above the gorge.

There's a rangers station (☑08-8956 9765) and camping grounds (adult/child $3.30/1.65) with barbecues, water and toilets at Trephina Gorge and the Bluff.

N'DHALA GORGE NATURE PARK

Nine kilometres past the Arltunga turn-off you come to the secluded Ross River Resort (☑08-8956 9711; www.rossriverresort.com. au; unpowered/powered sites $15/30, bunkhouse $25, d/f cabin $120/150; ✳✲), built around a historic stone homestead with basic timber cabins encircling a swimming pool. The stunning camp site is grassy and studded with gums. There's a store with fuel, and it's worth grabbing lunch or a beer in the Stockman's Bar.

Shortly before the resort, a strictly 4WD-only track leads 11km south to N'Dhala Gorge. Over 5900 ancient Aboriginal rock carvings and some rare endemic plants decorate a deep, narrow gorge, although the art isn't easy to spot. There's a small, exposed camping ground (adult/child $3.30/1.65) without reliable water.

ARLTUNGA HISTORICAL RESERVE

Situated at the eastern end of the MacDonnell Ranges, 110km east of Alice Springs, is the old gold-mining ghost town of Arltunga (40km on unsealed road from the Ross Hwy). Its history, from the discovery of alluvial (surface) gold in 1887 until mining activity petered out in 1912, is fascinating. Old buildings, a couple of cemeteries and the many deserted mine sites in this parched landscape give visitors an idea of what life was like for the miners. There are walking tracks and old mines (with bats!) to explore, so bring a torch.

The unstaffed visitor information centre has old photographs of the gold-extracting process, plus a slide show on the area's history, and drinking water and toilets. There's no camping in the reserve itself.

From Arltunga it's possible to loop back to Alice along the Arltunga Tourist Dr, which pops out at the Stuart Hwy about 50km north of town. The road runs past the gracious Old Ambalindum Homestead (☑08-8956 9993; www.oldambalindum homestead.com.au; unpowered/powered sites $20/25, dm $75; ✳✲) which offers self-catered accommodation for up to 12 people in the homestead and in the bunkhouse on a working cattle station. Bookings are essential and you need to bring your own food.

RUBY GAP NATURE PARK

This remote park rewards visitors with wild and beautiful scenery. The sandy bed of the Hale River sparkles with thousands of tiny garnets. The garnets caused a 'ruby rush' here in the 19th century and some miners did well out of it until it was discovered that the 'rubies' were, in fact, virtually worthless. It's an evocative place and is well worth the considerable effort required to reach it – by high-clearance 4WD. The waterholes at Glen Annie Gorge are usually deep enough for a cooling dip.

Camping (adult/child $3.30/1.65) is permitted anywhere along the river; make sure to BYO drinking water and a camp cooker. Allow two hours each way for the 44km trip from Arltunga.

DARWIN & ULURU SOUTH OF ALICE SPRINGS

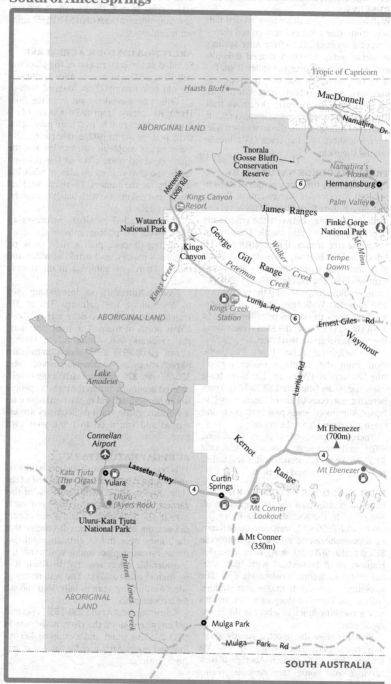

Tropic of Capricorn

Haasts Bluff

MacDonnell

Namatjira Dr

ABORIGINAL LAND

Tnorala
(Gosse Bluff)
Conservation
Reserve

(6)

Namatjira's
House

Hermannsburg

Palm Valley

Mereenie Loop Rd

Kings Canyon
Resort

James Ranges

Watarrka
National Park

Finke Gorge
National Park

Kings
Canyon

George

Gill

Range

Walker
Creek

McMinn

Tempe
Downs

Kings Creek

Peterman
Creek

Luritja Rd

(6)

ABORIGINAL LAND

Kings Creek
Station

Ernest Giles Rd

Waymour

Lake
Amadeus

Luritja Rd

Mt Ebenezer
(700m)

Connellan
Airport

Kermot

Mt Ebenezer

Kata Tjuta
(The Olgas)

Lasseter Hwy

Yulara

(4)

Curtin
Springs

Range

(4)

Uluru
(Ayers Rock)

Mt Conner
Lookout

Uluru-Kata Tjuta
National Park

Mt Conner
(350m)

Britten Jones Creek

ABORIGINAL
LAND

Mulga Park

Mulga Park Rd

SOUTH AUSTRALIA

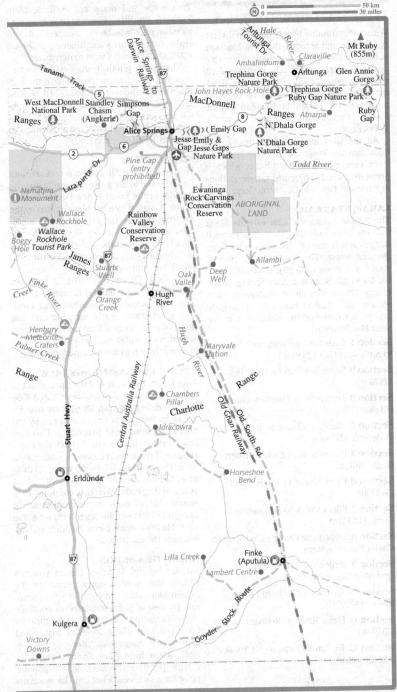

West MacDonnell Ranges

With their stunning beauty and rich diversity of plants and animals, the West MacDonnell Ranges are not to be missed. Their easy access by conventional vehicle makes them especially popular with day-trippers. Heading west from Alice, Namatjira Dr turns northwest off Larapinta Dr 6km beyond Standley Chasm and is sealed all the way to Tylers Pass.

All the sites mentioned in this section lie within the West MacDonnell National Park, except for Standley Chasm, which is privately owned. There are ranger stations at Simpsons Gap and Ormiston Gorge.

LARAPINTA TRAIL

The 230km Larapinta Trail extends along the backbone of the West MacDonnell Ranges and is one of Australia's great long-distance walks. The track is split into 12 stages of varying difficulty, stretching from the Telegraph Station in Alice Springs to the craggy 1380m summit of Mt Sonder. Each section takes one to two days to navigate and passes many of the attractions in the West MacDonnells:

Section 1 Alice Springs Telegraph Station to Simpsons Gap (23.8km)

Section 2 Simpsons Gap to Jay Creek (24.5km)

Section 3 Jay Creek to Standley Chasm (13.6km)

Section 4 Standley Chasm to Birthday Waterhole (17.7km)

Section 5 Birthday Waterhole to Hugh Gorge (16km)

Section 6 Hugh Gorge to Ellery Creek (31.2km)

Section 7 Ellery Creek to Serpentine Gorge (13.8km)

Section 8 Serpentine Gorge to Serpentine Chalet Dam (13.4km)

Section 9 Serpentine Chalet Dam to Ormiston Gorge (28.6km)

Section 10 Ormiston Gorge to Finke River (9.9km)

Section 11 Finke River to Redbank Gorge (25.2km)

Section 12 Redbank Gorge to Mt Sonder (15.8km return)

Trail notes and maps are available from Parks & Wildlife (www.nt.gov.au/nreta/parks/walks/larapinta/index.html). Walkers should register their names and itinerary at ☑1300 650 730. And don't forget to deregister.

There's no public transport out to this area, but transfers can be arranged through the Alice Wanderer (☎1800 722 111, 08-8952 2111; www.alicewanderer.com.au); see the website for the various costs. For guided walks, including transport from Alice Springs, go through Trek Larapinta (p859).

SIMPSONS GAP

Westbound from Alice Springs on Larapinta Dr you come to the grave of John Flynn, the founder of the Royal Flying Doctor Service, which is topped by a boulder donated by the Arrernte people (the original was a since-returned Devil's Marble). Opposite the car park is the start of the sealed cycling track to Simpsons Gap, a recommended three- to four-hour return ride.

By road, Simpsons Gap is 22km from Alice Springs and 8km off Larapinta Dr. It's a popular picnic spot and has some excellent short walks. Early morning and late afternoon are the best time to glimpse black-footed rock wallabies. The visitor information centre is 1km from the park entrance.

STANDLEY CHASM (ANGKERLE)

Fifty kilometres west of Alice Springs is the spectacular Standley Chasm (☎08-8956 7440; adult/senior & child $8/6.50; camping $5; ☺8am-5pm) which is owned and run by the nearby community of Iwupataka. This narrow corridor slices neatly through the rocky range and in places the smooth walls rise to 80m. The rocky path into the gorge (15 minutes) follows a creek bed lined with ghost gums and cycads. You can continue to a second chasm (one hour return) or head up Larapinta Hill (45 minutes return) for a fine view. There's a kiosk, picnic facilities and toilets near the car park.

NAMATJIRA DRIVE

Not far beyond Standley Chasm you can choose the northwesterly Namatjira Dr (which loops down to connect with Larapinta Dr west of Hermannsburg) or continue along Larapinta Dr (p871). Namatjira Dr takes you to a whole series of gorges and gaps in the range like Ellery Creek Big Hole, 91km from Alice Springs, and with a large permanent waterhole – a popular place for a swim on a hot day (it's normally

freezing). About 11km further, a rough gravel track leads to narrow Serpentine Gorge, which has a waterhole blocking the entrance and a lookout at the end of a short, steep track, where you can view the cycads.

The Ochre Pits line a dry creek bed 11km west of Serpentine and were a source of paint for Aboriginal people. The various coloured ochres – mainly yellow, white and red-brown – are weathered limestone, with iron-oxide creating the colours.

The car park for the majestic Ormiston Gorge is 25km beyond the Ochre Pits. It's the most impressive chasm in the West Mac-Donnells. There's a waterhole shaded with ghost gums, and the gorge curls around to the enclosed Ormiston Pound. It is a haven for wildlife and you can expect to see some critters among the spinifex slopes and mulga woodland. There are walking tracks, including the Ghost Gum Lookout (20 minutes), which affords brilliant views down the gorge, and the excellent, circuitous Pound Walk (three hours, 7.5km). There's a visitor centre (☑08-8956 7799) and a kiosk which is open occasionally.

About 2km further is the turn-off to Glen Helen Gorge, where the Finke River cuts through the MacDonnells. Only 1km past Glen Helen is a good lookout over Mt Sonder; sunrise and sunset here are particularly impressive.

If you continue northwest for 25km you'll reach the turn-off (4WD only) to multi-hued, cathedral-like Redbank Gorge. This permanent waterhole runs for kilometres through the labyrinth gorge, and makes for an incredible swimming and scrambling adventure on a hot day. Namatjira Dr then heads south and is sealed as far as Tylers Pass Lookout, which provides a dramatic view of Tnorala (Grosse Bluff), the legacy of an earth-shattering comet impact.

🛏 Sleeping & Eating

There are basic camping grounds (adult/child $3.30/1.65) at Ellery Creek Big Hole, Redbank Gorge and 6km west of Serpentine Gorge at Serpentine Chalet (a 4WD or high-clearance 2WD vehicle is recommended to reach the chalet ruins). The ritzy camping area (adult/child $6.60/3.30) at Ormiston Gorge has showers, toilets, gas barbecues and picnic tables.

Glen Helen Resort   HOTEL $
(☑08-8956 7489; www.glenhelen.com.au; Namatjira Dr; unpowered/powered sites $24/30, dm/r

$30/160; 🕸🕸) At the edge of the national park is the popular Glen Helen Resort which has an idyllic back verandah overlooking the spectacular gorge. This comfortable retreat has a busy restaurant-pub (breakfast and lunch $8 to $18, dinner $25 to $35) serving hearty meals and live music on the weekend. There are also helicopter flights from the homestead ranging from $55 (five minutes) to $375, with the $125 Ormiston Gorge flight representing the best value.

MEREENIE LOOP

Larapinta Drive

Continuing south from Standley Chasm, Larapinta Dr crosses the intersection with Namatjira Dr and the Hugh River before reaching the turn-off to the Western Arrernte community of Wallace Rockhole, 18km off the main road and 109km from Alice Springs.

You'll be virtually guaranteed seclusion at the Wallace Rockhole Tourist Park (☑08-8956 7993; www.wallacerockholetours.com.au; unpowered/powered sites $20/24, cabins $130; 🕸), which has a camping area with good facilities. Tours must be booked in advance and can include a 1½-hour rock-art and bush medicine tour ($15/13 adult/child) with billy tea and damper.

About 26km from the Wallace Rockhole turn-off, continuing along Larapinta Dr, you will pass the lonely Namatjira Monument, which is about 8km from Hermannsburg.

HERMANNSBURG
POP 460

The Aboriginal community of Hermannsburg (Ntaria), about 125km from Alice Springs, is famous as the one-time home of artist Albert Namatjira and the site of the Hermannsburg Mission.

The whitewashed walls of the mission (☑08-8956 7402; www.hermannsburg.com; adult/child $10/5; ⊙9am-4pm Mar-Nov, 10am-4pm Dec-Feb) are shaded by majestic river gums and date palms. This fascinating monument to the Territory's early Lutheran missionaries includes a school building, a church and various outbuildings. The 'Manse' houses an art gallery and a history of the life and times of Albert Namatjira as well as work of 39 Hermannsburg artists.

The **Kata-Anga Tea Room** (meals $7-12; ⊙9am-4pm), in the old missionary house, serves yummy apple strudel and Devonshire teas. Distinctive paintings and pottery by the locals is also on display here and is for sale.

Just west of Hermannsburg, is **Namatjira's House**.

FINKE GORGE NATIONAL PARK

With its primordial landscape, the Finke Gorge National Park, south of Hermannsburg, is one of central Australia's premier wilderness reserves. The top-billing attraction is **Palm Valley**, famous for its red cabbage palms, which exist nowhere else in the world. These relics from prehistoric times give the valley the feel of a picture-book oasis.

Tracks include the **Arankaia walk** (2km loop, one hour), which traverses the valley, returning via the sandstone plateau; the **Mpulungkinya track** (5km loop, two hours), heading down the gorge before joining the Arankaia walk; and the **Mpaara track** (5km loop, two hours), taking in the Finke River, Palm Bend and a rugged amphitheatre (a semicircle of sandstone formations sculpted by a now-extinct meander of Palm Creek). There's a popular **camping ground** (adult/child $6.60/3.30).

Access to the park follows the sandy bed of the Finke River and rocky tracks, and so a high-clearance 4WD is essential. If you don't have one, several tour operators go to Palm Valley from Alice Springs (see p859). The turn-off to Palm Valley starts about 1km west of the Hermannsburg turn-off on Larapinta Dr.

MEREENIE LOOP ROAD (RED CENTRE WAY)

From Hermannsburg you can continue west to the turn-off to Areyonga (no visitors) and then take the Mereenie Loop Rd to Kings Canyon. This is an alternative route from Alice to Kings Canyon. The NT Government is planning to seal the road but locals say they'll believe it when they see it. There are deep sandy patches and countless corrugations (call ☎1800 246 199 for latest road conditions) and it's best travelled in a high-clearance 4WD. Be aware that 2WD hire vehicles will not be covered by insurance on this road.

To travel along this route, which passes through Aboriginal land, you need a Mereenie Tour Pass ($3.50), which is valid for one day and includes a booklet with details about the local Aboriginal culture and a route map. The pass is issued on the spot (usually only on the day of travel) at the visitor information centre in Alice Springs (p865), Glen Helen Resort (p871), Kings Canyon Resort (p874) and Hermannsburg service station.

Old South Road

The Old South Road, which runs close to the old *Ghan* railway line, is pretty rough and really requires a 4WD. It's only 39km from Alice Springs to **Ewaninga**, where prehistoric Aboriginal petroglyphs are carved into sandstone. The rock carvings found here and at N'Dhala Gorge (p867) are thought to have been made by Aboriginal people who lived here before those currently in the region, between 1000 and 5000 years ago.

The eerie, sandstone **Chambers Pillar**, southwest of Maryvale Station, towers 50m above the surrounding plain and is carved with the names and visit dates of early explorers – and, unfortunately, some much less worthy modern-day graffiti. To the Aboriginal people of the area, Chambers Pillar is the remains of Itirkawara, a powerful gecko ancestor. Most photogenic at sunset and sunrise, it's best to stay overnight at the **camping ground** (adult/child $3.30/1.65). It's 160km from Alice Springs, and a 4WD is required for the last 44km from the turn-off at Maryvale Station.

Back on the main track south, you eventually arrive at **Finke** (Aputula), a small Aboriginal community 230km from Alice Springs. When the old *Ghan* was running, Finke was a thriving town; these days it seems to have drifted into a permanent torpor, except when the **Finke Desert Race** (p860) is staged. Fuel is sold at the **Aputula Store** (☎08-8956 0968; ⊙9am-noon & 2-4pm Mon-Fri, 9am-noon Sat), which is also an outlet for local artists' work.

From Finke, you can turn west along the Goyder Stock Rte to join the Stuart Hwy at Kulgera (150km), or east to Old Andado station on the edge of the Simpson Desert (120km). Just 21km west of Finke, and 12km north of the road along a signposted track, is the **Lambert Centre**. The point marks Australia's geographical centre and features a 5m-high version of the flagpole found on top of Parliament House in Canberra.

There are some pretty grim camp sites (adult/child $3.30/1.65) available.

873

Rainbow Valley Conservation Reserve

This series of freestanding sandstone bluffs and cliffs, in shades ranging from cream to red, is one of central Australia's more extraordinary sights. A marked walking trail takes you past claypans and in between the multihued outcrops to the aptly named Mushroom Rock. Rainbow Valley is most striking in the early morning or at sunset, but the area's silence will overwhelm you whatever time of day you are here.

The park lies 24km off the Stuart Hwy along a 4WD track that's 77km south of Alice Springs. It has a pretty exposed camping ground (adult/child $3.30/1.65) but the setting is perfectly positioned for sunset viewing.

Stuarts Well

About 90km south of Alice Springs, drivers are urged to 'have a spell' at Stuarts Well. It's worth stopping in for a camel burger and a beer at Jim's Place (☎08-8956 0808; Stuarts Well; unpowered/powered sites $10/25, budget r with own swag/supplied linen $15/30, cabins s/d $75/95; ✴@☒) run by well-known outback identity Jim Cotterill, who along with his father opened up Kings Canyon to tourism. You might also catch a performance by Dinky the singing and piano-playing dingo.

If you would rather ride a camel than eat one, Camels Australia (☎08-8956 0925; www.camels-australia.com.au; ☺7am-5pm) offers a short spin around the yard for $6, a 30-minute jaunt for $25 or a full day ride for $175.

Ernest Giles Road

The Ernest Giles Rd heads off to the west of the Stuart Hwy about 140km south of Alice and is a shorter but rougher route to Kings Canyon only recommended for 4WD vehicles.

HENBURY METEORITE CRATERS

Eleven kilometres west of the Stuart Hwy, a corrugated track leads 5km off Ernest Giles Rd to this cluster of 12 small craters, formed after a meteor fell to earth 4700 years ago. The largest of the craters is 180m wide and 15m deep.

There are no longer any fragments of the meteorites at the site, but the Museum of Central Australia in Alice Springs (p855) has a small chunk that weighs 46.5kg.

Kings Canyon & Watarrka National Park

Continuing west along Ernest Giles Rd, or detouring off the Lasseter Hwy along the sealed Luritja Rd, brings you to the Watarrka National Park, which features one of the most spectacular sights in central Australia – the yawning chasm of Kings Canyon.

Walkers are rewarded with awesome views and diverse terrain on the Kings Canyon Rim Walk (6km loop, four hours), which many travellers rate as a highlight of their trip to the Centre. After a short but steep climb (the only 'difficult' part of the trail), the walk skirts the canyon's rim before descending down wooden stairs to the Garden of Eden: a lush pocket of ferns and prehistoric cycads around a tranquil pool. The next section of the trail winds through a swarm of giant beehive domes: weathered sandstone outcrops, which to the Luritja represent the men of the Kuniya Dreaming.

The Kings Creek Walk (2km return) is a short stroll along the rocky creek bed to a raised platform with views of the towering canyon rim.

About 10km east of the car park, the Kathleen Springs Walk (one hour, 2.6km return) is a pleasant wheelchair-accessible track leading to a waterhole at the head of a gorge.

The Giles Track (22km one-way, overnight) is a marked track that meanders along the George Gill Range between Kathleen Springs and the canyon; before starting out register with the Overnight Walker Registration Scheme (☎1300 650 730).

You can also reach Kings Canyon from Alice Springs via the unsealed Mereenie Loop Rd (see p872), a drive of 325km.

☞ Tours

Several tour companies depart Alice and stop here on the way to/from Uluru (see p859).

Kings Creek Helicopters HELICOPTER RIDE (☎08-8956 7886; www.kingscreekstation.com.au; flights per person $50-385) Flies from Kings Creek Station, including a breathtaking 30-minute canyon flight for $240.

Professional Helicopter Services HELICOPTER RIDE (PHS; ☎08-8956 7873; flights per person $85-250) Picking up from Kings Canyon

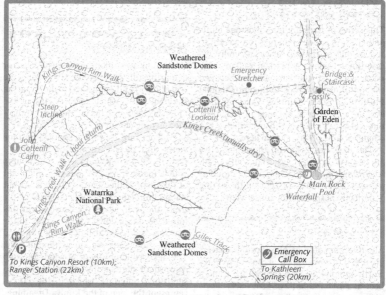

Weathered
Sandstone Domes

Kings Canyon Rim Walk

Emergency
Stretcher

Bridge &
Staircase

Steep
Incline

Cotterill's
Lookout

Fossils

Garden
of Eden

John
Cotterill
Cairn

Kings Creek Walk (1 hour return)

Kings Creek (usually dry)

Watarrka
National Park

Kings Canyon
Rim Walk

Main Rock
Pool

Waterfall

Weathered
Sandstone Domes

Giles Track

Emergency
Call Box

To Kings Canyon Resort (10km);
Ranger Station (22km)

To Kathleen
Springs (20km)

Resort, PHS buzzes the canyon for 8/15 minutes ($85/135).

🛏 Sleeping & Eating

Kings Canyon Station   CABINS $$
(☎08-8956 7474; www.kingscreekstation.com.au; Luritja Rd; unpowered/powered sites $17/19, safari cabins s/d incl breakfast $97/151; @⊛) Located 35km before the canyon, this family-run station offers a bush camping experience among the desert oaks. Cosy safari-style cabins (small canvas tents on solid floors) share amenities and a kitchen-barbecue area. You can tear around the desert on a quad bike (one-hour ride $85) or enjoy the more sedate thrills of a sunset camel ride (one-hour ride $58). Fuel, ice, beer, wine, barbecue packs and meals are available at the shop (open 7am to 7pm). Ask about Conways' Kids (www.conwayskids.org.au), a charitable trust set up by the owners to send local Indigenous children to school in Adelaide.

Kings Canyon Resort   RESORT $$$
(☎1300 863 248; www.kingscanyonresort.com.au; Luritja Rd; unpowered/powered sites $27/33, dm $35, budget d $120, r $360-450; ⊛@⊛) Only 10km from the canyon, this well-designed resort boasts a wide range of accommodation from a grassy camp area with its own pool and bar to deluxe rooms with an almost-outdoor spa. Eating and drinking options are as varied, with a cafe, a restaurant for buffet breakfasts and dinner, a bar with pizzas, an outback BBQ for big steaks and live entertainment. **Under the Desert Moon** ($159 per person, ⊙Apr-Oct) offers an exclusive six-course candlelit dinner around a campfire. There's a general store with fuel and an ATM at reception.

Kings Canyon Wilderness Lodge   RESORT $$$
(☎1800 891 121; www.aptouring.com.au; Luritja Rd; tented cabins s/d $325/650; ⊛) In a secret pocket of Kings Creek Station is this luxury retreat with 10 stylish tents offering private en suite facilities and decks with relaxing bush views. Unfortunately, for the money, it's underwhelming. Run by APT, independent travellers find themselves squeezed in among the tour groups and the 'gourmet' dinner and breakfast (included in the tariff) are disappointing.

Lasseter Highway

The Lasseter Hwy connects the Stuart Hwy with Uluru-Kata Tjuta National Park, 244km to the west from the turn-off at Erldunda.

Mt Conner, the large mesa (table-top mountain) that looms 350m out of the desert, is the outback's most photographed red herring – on first sighting many mistake it for Uluru. It has great significance to local Aboriginal people, who know it as Atila.

Curtin Springs Wayside Inn (☑08-8956 2906; www.curtinsprings.com; Lasseter Hwy; unpowered/powered sites free/$25, s/d $65/95, r with bathroom $150; ☒) is the last stop before Yulara about 80km away, and the closest alternative to staying at Ayers Rock Resort. You can pitch a tent for free (showers $3) or bed down in a well-maintained cabin. There's fuel, a store with limited supplies and takeaway and bistro meals (mains $15 to $25), plus a bar.

ULURU-KATA TJUTA NATIONAL PARK

For many visitors, Australian and international, a visit to Uluru is high on the list of 'must-sees' and the World Heritage–listed icon has attained the status of a pilgrimage. But the park offers much more than just the multidimensional grandeur of Uluru. Along with the equally (some say more) impressive Kata Tjuta (the Olgas) the area is of deep cultural significance to the traditional owners, the Pitjantjatjara and Yankuntjatjara Aboriginal peoples (who refer to themselves as Anangu). The Anangu officially own the national park, which is leased to Parks Australia and jointly administered.

Although many of the 400,000 annual visitors whiz through here in 24 hours, it's recommended to spend at least the three days the entry pass allows. There's plenty to see and do: meandering walks, guided tours, desert culture and contemplating the many changing colours and moods of the great monolith itself.

The only accommodation is the Ayers Rock Resort in the Yulara village, 20km from the Rock, where you can expect premium prices, reflecting the remote locale.

❶ Information

The **park** (www.environment.gov.au/parks/uluru; adult/child $25/free) is open from half an hour before sunrise to sunset daily (varying between 5am to 9pm November to March and 6am to 7.30pm April to October). Entry permits are valid for three days and available at the drive-through entry station on the road from Yulara.

Uluru-Kata Tjuta Cultural Centre (☑08-8956 1128; ☺7am-6pm, information desk 7am-6pm) is 1km before Uluru on the road from Yulara and should be your first stop. Displays and exhibits focus on tjukurpa (Aboriginal law, religion and custom) and the history and management of the national park. The information desk in the Nintiringkupai building is staffed by park rangers who supply the informative *Visitor Guide*, leaflets and walking notes. During the week a local Anangu ranger runs a presentation at 10am each morning on bush foods and Aboriginal history.

The Cultural Centre encompasses the craft outlet **Maruku Arts** (☑08-8956 2558; www.maruku.com.au; ☺8.30am-5.30pm), owned by about 20 Anangu communities from across central Australia (including the local Mutitjulu community), selling hand-crafted wooden carvings, bowls and boomerangs. **Walkatjara Art Centre** (☑08-8956 2537; ☺9am-5.30pm) is a working art centre owned by the local Mutitjulu community. It focuses on paintings and ceramics created by women from Mutitjulu. **Ininti Cafe & Souvenirs** (☑08-8956 2214; ☺7am-5pm) sells souvenirs such as T-shirts, ceramics, hats, CDs and a variety of books on Uluru, Aboriginal culture, biographies, bush foods and the flora and fauna of the area. The attached cafe serves ice cream, pies and light meals.

ⓘ Tours

Bus Tours

Seit Outback Australia   BUS TOURS
(☑0458 107 777; www.seitoutbackaustralia.com.au) This small group operator has sunset tours around Uluru ($120/95 per adult/child); and does sunrise at Kata Tjuta for the same price including breakfast and a walk into Walpa Gorge.

AAT Kings   BUS TOURS
(☑08-8956 2171; www.aatkings.com) Operating the biggest range of coach tours, AAT offers a range of half- and full-day tours, or you can buy one of a selection of three-day tour passes (from $279/130 adult/child).

Camel Tours

Uluru Camel Tours   CAMEL TOURS
(☑1800 806 499; www.ananguwaai.com.au; short rides adult/child $10/5; ☺10.30am-2.30pm) View Uluru and Kata Tjuta from a distance atop a camel ($65, 1½ hours) or take the popular Camel to Sunrise and Sunset tours ($99, 2½ hours).

Cultural Tours

Anangu Tours   CULTURAL TOURS
(☑08-8950 3030; www.ananguwaai.com.au) Owned and operated by Anangu from the

Mutitjulu community, this company offers a range of trips to give you an insight into the significance of the Rock through the eyes of the traditional owners. Tours depart from the Cultural Centre (p875).

The daily, five-hour Aboriginal Uluru Tour ($139/95 adult/child) starts with sunrise over Uluru and breakfast at the Cultural Centre, followed by a guided stroll down the Liru Walk (including demonstrations of bush skills such as spear-throwing).

The Kuniya Sunset Tour ($116/75, 4½ hours) departs at 2.30pm (3.30pm between November and February) and includes a visit to Mutitjulu Waterhole and the Cultural Centre, finishing with a sunset viewing of Uluru.

Both trips can be combined over 24 hours with an Anangu Culture Pass ($229/155). Self-drive options are also available for $69/35. You can join an Aboriginal guide at 8.30am (7.30am November to January, 8am February and October) for the morning walk or at 3.45pm (4.45pm November to February) for the Kuniya tour.

Desert Tracks CULTURAL TOURS
(📞0439 500 419; www.deserttracks.com.au; adult/child $259/199) This Anangu-run company offers a full-day 4WD journey into the remote Pitjantjatjara Lands to meet the traditional owners of Cave Hill and

view some spectacular rock art depicting the Seven Sisters story.

Dining Tours

Sounds of Silence DINING
(📞08-8957 7448; www.ayersrockresort.com.au/ sounds-of-silence; adult/child $164/84) Waiters serve champagne and canapés on a desert dune with stunning sunset views of Uluru and Kata Tjuta. Then it's a buffet dinner (with emu, croc and roo) beneath the southern sky, which, after dinner, is dissected and explained with the help of a telescope. If you're more of a morning person, try the similarly styled **Desert Awakenings 4WD Tour** (adult/child $153/118). Neither tour is suitable for children under 10 years.

Motorcycle Tours

Sunrise and sunset tours to Uluru and Kata Tjuta can also be had on the back of a Harley Davidson.

Uluru Motorcycle Tours MOTORCYCLE
(📞08-8956 2019; www.ulurucycles.com; rides $90-345) Motors out to Uluru at sunset ($160, 1½ hours) or rent your own bike if you're an experienced rider (from $275 for two hours).

Scenic Flights

Prices are per person and include airport transfers from Ayers Rock Resort.

Uluru (Ayers Rock)

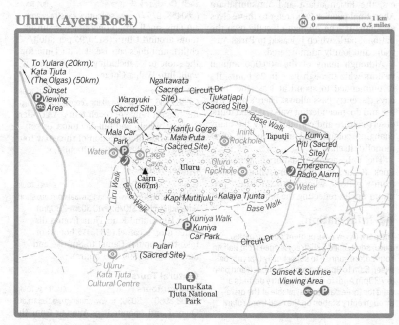

A QUESTION OF CLIMBING

Many visitors consider climbing Uluru to be a highlight – even a rite of passage – of a trip to the Centre. But for the traditional owners, the Anangu, Uluru is a sacred place. The path up the side of the Rock is part of the route taken by the Mala ancestors on their arrival at Uluru and has great spiritual significance – and is not to be trampled by human feet. When you arrive at Uluru you'll see a sign from the Anangu saying 'We don't climb' and a request that you don't climb either.

The Anangu are the custodians of Uluru and take responsibility for the safety of visitors. Any injuries or deaths that occur (and they do occur – a man died in 2010) are a source of distress and sadness to them. For similar reasons of public safety, Parks Australia would prefer that people didn't climb. It's a very steep ascent, not to be taken lightly, and each year there are several air rescues, mostly from people suffering heart attacks. Furthermore, Parks Australia must constantly monitor the climb and close it on days where the temperature is forecast to reach 36°C or strong winds are expected.

So if the Anangu don't want people to climb and Parks Australia would prefer to see it closed, why does it remain open? The answer is tourism. The tourism industry believes visitor numbers would drop significantly – at least initially – if the climb was closed, particularly from visitors thinking there is nothing else to do at Uluru.

The debate has grown louder in recent years and a commitment has been made to close the climb for good, but only when there are adequate new visitor experiences in place or when the proportion of visitors climbing falls below 20%. Until then, it remains a personal decision and a question of respect. Before deciding, visit the Cultural Centre and perhaps take an Anangu tour. You might just change your mind.

Ayers Rock Helicopters   HELICOPTER FLIGHTS
(☏08-8956 2077) A 15-minute buzz of Uluru costs $125; to include Kata Tjuta costs $240.

Ayers Rock Scenic Flights   SCENIC FLIGHTS
(☏08-8956 2345; www.ayersrockresort.com.au/helicopter-flights) Prices start from $95 for a 20-minute flight over Uluru. Include Kata Tjuta and it's $185. For $390 you get a two-hour flight that also takes in Lake Amadeus and Kings Canyon.

Professional Helicopter Services   HELICOPTER FLIGHTS
(PHS; ☏08-8956 2003; www.phs.com.au) Charges $135 for its Uluru flight and $250 for its 30-minute Uluru and Kata Tjuta flight.

Uluru (Ayers Rock)

Nothing quite prepares you for the first sight of Uluru on the horizon – it will astound even the most jaded traveller. Uluru is 3.6km long and rises a towering 348m from the surrounding sandy scrubland (867m above sea level). If that's not impressive enough, it's believed that two-thirds of the rock lies beneath the sand. Closer inspection reveals a wondrous contoured surface concealing numerous sacred sites of particular significance to the Anangu people. If your first sight of Uluru is during the afternoon, it appears as an ochre-brown colour, scored and pitted by dark shadows. As the sun sets, it illuminates the rock in burnished orange, then a series of deeper reds before it fades into charcoal. A performance in reverse, with marginally fewer spectators, is given at dawn.

🏃 Activities

Walking

There are walking tracks around Uluru, and ranger-led walks explain the area's plants, wildlife, geology and cultural significance. All the trails are flat and suitable for wheelchairs. Several areas of spiritual significance to Anangu people are off limits to visitors; these are marked with fences and signs. The Anangu ask you not to photograph these sites.

The excellent *Visitor Guide & Maps* brochure, which can be picked up at the Cultural Centre, gives details on the following self-guided walks (except the climb).

Base Walk   WALKING
This track (10.6km, three to four hours) circumnavigates the rock, passing caves, paintings, sandstone folds and geological abrasions along the way.

Uluru at sunset is a mesmerising experience but it can be hard to escape the crowds and their cameras. Here park rangers share their secrets for a sunset with solitude.

Talinguru Nyakunytjaku Wildly popular at dawn, but at sunset you'll have both Uluru and Kata Tjuta, in silhouette, in the same shot, all to yourself.

Kantju Gorge Head to the end of the Mala Walk in time for a dazzling sunset on the walls of the Rock.

Kata Tjuta Sunset Viewing Take a seat in a private area and watch the colours change to the deepest red.

Mutitjulu Waterhole For profound peace follow the Kuniya Walk to this glorious waterhole.

Liru Walk
WALKING
Links the Cultural Centre with the start of the Mala walk and climb, and winds through strands of mulga before opening up near Uluru (4km return, 1½).

Mala Walk
WALKING
From the base of the climbing point (2km return, one hour), interpretive signs explain the tjukurpa of the Mala (hare-wallaby people), which is significant to the Anangu, as well as fine examples of rock art. A ranger-guided walk (free) along this route departs at 10am (8am from October to April) from the car park.

Kuniya Walk
WALKING
A short walk (1km return, 45 minutes) from the car park on the southern side leads to the most permanent waterhole, Mutitjulu, home of the ancestral water-snake. Great birdwatching and some excellent rock art are highlights of this walk.

Uluru Climb
WALKING
The Anangu ask that visitors respect Aboriginal law by not climbing Uluru (see the boxed text, p877). The steep and demanding path (1.6km return, two hours) follows the traditional route taken by ancestral Mala men. The climb is often closed (sometimes at short notice) due to weather and Anangu business. Between January and February the climb is closed at 8am.

Sunset & Sunrise Viewing Areas
About halfway between Yulara and Uluru, the sunset viewing area has plenty of car and coach parking for that familiar postcard view. The Talinguru Nyakunytjaku sunrise viewing area is perched on a sand dune and captures both the Rock and Kata Tjuta in all

their glory. It also has two great interpretive walks (1.5km) about women's and men's business. There's a shaded viewing area, toilets and a place to picnic.

Kata Tjuta (The Olgas)
No journey to Uluru is complete without a visit to Kata Tjuta (the Olgas), a striking group of domed rocks huddled together about 35km west of the Rock. There are 36 boulders shoulder to shoulder forming deep valleys and steep-sided gorges. Many visitors find them even more captivating than their prominent neighbour. The tallest rock, Mt Olga (546m, 1066m above sea level) is approximately 200m higher than Uluru. Kata Tjuta means 'many heads' and is of great tjukurpa significance, particularly for men, so stick to the tracks.

The 7.4km Valley of the Winds loop (two to four hours) is one of the most challenging and rewarding bushwalks in the park. It winds through the gorges giving excellent views of the surreal domes and traversing varied terrain. It's not particularly arduous, but wear sturdy shoes, and take plenty of water. Starting this walk at first light often rewards you with solitude, enabling you to appreciate the sounds of the wind and bird calls carried up the valley.

The short signposted track beneath towering rock walls into pretty Walpa Gorge (2.6km return, 45 minutes) is especially beautiful in the afternoon, when sunlight floods the gorge.

There's a picnic and sunset-viewing area with toilet facilities just off the access road a few kilometres west of the base of Kata Tjuta. Like Uluru, the Olgas are at their glorious, blood-red best at sunset.

Kata Tjuta (The Olgas)

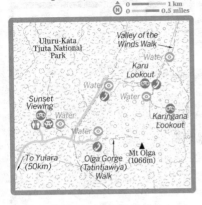

Heading West

A lonely sign at the western end of Kata Tjuta points in the direction of WA. If suitably equipped you can travel the 181km to Kaltukatjara (Docker River), an Aboriginal settlement to the west, and then about 1500km on to Kalgoorlie in WA. You need a permit from the Central Land Council for this trip.

Yulara (Ayers Rock Resort)

POP 2080 (INCLUDING MUTITJULU)

Yulara is the service village for the national park and has effectively turned one of the world's least hospitable regions into a comfortable place to stay. Lying just outside the national park, 20km from Uluru and 53km from Kata Tjuta, the complex is the closest base for exploring the park. Yulara supplies the only accommodation, food outlets and other services available in the region. If it weren't in the middle of the desert within cooee of the rock you'd baulk at the prices here (you probably still will); as it is, you're stuck with it.

◉ Sights & Activities

Mulgara Gallery   ART GALLERY
(Sails in the Desert Hotel) Quality handmade Australian arts and crafts are displayed here. Each month brings a new artist in residence.

Night Sky Show   STARGAZING
(⏰08-8956 2563; Tour & Information Centre; adult/child $33/25; ⏰7.30pm & 8.30pm Jun-Nov, 8.30pm & 10.15pm Dec-May) Takes an informative one-hour look at the startlingly clear outback night sky with a telescope and an astronomer. Prices include pick-up from your accommodation; bookings are essential.

🛏 Sleeping

All of the accommodation in Yulara, including the camping ground and hostel, is owned by the Ayers Rock Resort. And unless the free camping at Curtin Springs station (p875) outweighs the risk of driving in the dark for sunrise/sunset at Uluru, there's no other option. Even though there are almost 5000 beds, it's wise to make a reservation, especially during school holidays. Bookings can be made through **central reservations** (⏰1300 134 044; www.ayersrock resort.com.au). Substantial discounts are usually offered if you stay for three nights or more, and you can also save a reasonable amount through internet sites offering discount accommodation.

Ayers Rock Resort
Campground   CAMPGROUND **$**
(⏰08-8957 7001; camp.ground@ayersrockresort. com.au; unpowered/powered sites $36/41, tents $95, cabins $150; ❄@≋) A saviour for the budget conscious, this sprawling camping ground is set among native gardens. There are good facilities, including a kiosk, free barbecues, a camp kitchen and a pool. During the peak season it's very busy and the inevitable pre-dawn convoy heading for Uluru can provide an unwanted wake-up call. The cramped cabins (shared facilities) sleep six people and are only really suitable for a family. Permanent tents (with beds) are also available.

Emu Walk Apartments   APARTMENTS **$$$**
(⏰08-8956 7714; 1-/2-bedroom apt from $498/598; ❄) The pick of the bunch for families looking for self-contained accommodation, Emu Walk has comfortable, modern apartments, each with a lounge room (with TV) and a well-equipped kitchen with washer and dryer. The one-bedroom apartment accommodates four people, while the two-bedroom version sleeps six.

Outback Pioneer Hotel & Lodge   HOSTEL **$**
(⏰08-8957 7605; dm $34-42, d $220-440; ❄@≋) With a lively bar, BBQ restaurant and musical entertainment, this is the budget choice for noncampers. The cheapest options are the 20-bed YHA unisex dorms and squashy four-bed budget cabins with fridge, TV and shared bathroom. There are

Yulara (Ayers Rock Resort)

Yulara (Ayers Rock Resort)

⊙ Sights

Mulgara Gallery	(see 7)
1 Night Sky Show	B2

🛏 Sleeping

2 Ayers Rock Resort Campground	C1
3 Desert Gardens Hotel	B3
4 Emu Walk Apartments	B2
5 Lost Camel Hotel	B2
6 Outback Pioneer Hotel & Lodge	C3
7 Sails in the Desert	B1

✗ Eating

Arngulli Flame Grill	(see 3)
Bough House	(see 6)
8 Gecko's Cafe	B2
Kuniya	(see 7)
Outback Pioneer Barbecue	(see 6)
Pioneer Kitchen	(see 6)
9 Red Rock Deli	B2
Rockpool	(see 7)
White Gums	(see 3)
Winkiku	(see 7)
10 Yulara IGA Supermarket	B2

Drinking

Bunya Bar	(see 3)
Pioneer Barbecue Bar	(see 6)
Tali Bar	(see 7)

also more spacious motel-style rooms that sleep up to four people, though anyone over 12 is an extra $50 a night.

Lost Camel Hotel　　　BOUTIQUE HOTEL **$$$**
(☎08-8957 7605; d $440; ❄@☲) The small, but brightly coloured rooms at this boutique hotel come with very comfy beds and stereos but no TV – there's a plasma screen at reception. A fine courtyard pool and bar are refreshing at the end of an outback day.

Desert Gardens Hotel　　　HOTEL **$$$**
(☎08-8957 7714; r $498-598; ❄@☲) One of Yulara's originals, the standard rooms, particularly the bathrooms, are looking very dated. A better option is the spacious deluxe rooms that have been spruced up a bit and feature balconies with desert or Uluru views. A big buffet breakfast is served in the restaurant and there's a pleasant pool area shaded with gums.

Sails in the Desert HOTEL $$$

(☑08-8956 2200; d $580, with spa $690, ste $950; ✷@☲) Hugely overpriced for what is essentially a three-star hotel masquerading as the luxury option, the rooms are looking as tired as the signature sails. While the rooms offer poor value for money there is a lovely pool area, tennis courts, health spa, several restaurants and a piano bar. Deluxe spa rooms feature a balcony spa.

 Eating

Geckos Cafe MEDITERRANEAN $$

(Resort Shopping Centre; mains $15-30; ⊘breakfast, lunch & dinner) For great value, warm atmosphere and tasty food head to this buzzing licensed cafe, who say they 'cater for everyone'. The wood-fired pizzas, salads and pasta go well with a carafe of their sangria, and the courtyard tables are a great place to enjoy a dish from the all-day breakfast. There are several veggie and gluten-free options plus meals can be made to takeaway.

Outback Pioneer Barbecue BBQ $$

(Outback Pioneer Hotel & Lodge; mains $20-35, salad only $16; ⊘6-9pm) For a fun, casual night out, this lively tavern is the popular choice ffor everyone from backpackers to grey nomads. Choose between kangaroo skewers, prawns, veggie burgers, steaks and emu sausages and grill them yourself at the communal BBQs. The deal includes a salad bar. In the same complex is the **Pioneer Kitchen** (meals $10-17; ⊘lunch & dinner), doing brisk business in burgers, pizza and kiddie meals.

Red Rock Deli DELI $

(Resort Shopping Centre; snacks $7-15; ⊘8am-4pm) Line up for steaming-hot espresso and croissants in the morning or grab filled paninis and wraps for lunch.

White Gums MEDITERRANEAN $$

(☑08-8957 7888; Desert Gardens Hotel; dinner mains $20-35; ⊘breakfast & dinner) Hotel guests enjoy a big buffet breakfast and return at night for an à la carte dinner featuring fusion cuisine with Asian, Mediterranean and Australian themes. In season, Desert Gardens also opens the **Arngulli Flame Grill** (2/3 courses $49/59) with meat and seafood dinners.

Rockpool TAPAS $$$

(Sails in the Desert; 3 tapas plates $45, plus dessert $50; ⊘dinner) Beside the pool and under the sails, this casual eatery serves Mediterranean and Asian tapas-style dishes and some decadent deserts.

Winkiku BUFFET $$$

(Sails in the Desert; breakfast buffet $25-35, dinner buffet $65; ⊘breakfast & dinner) In Yulara's five-star hotel, this casual-yet-stylish restaurant does extravagant seafood buffets with a meat carvery, and all the trimmings and desserts you can imagine. Kids eat free, so it can work out as good value for families.

Bough House BUFFET $$$

(Outback Pioneer Hotel & Lodge; breakfast/dinner buffets $30/52) This family-friendly, country-style place overlooks the pool at the Outback Pioneer and has buffet spreads for breakfast and dinner. The 'Tastes of Australia' dinner features outback tucker – kangaroo, emu, crocodile and barramundi. Kids under 12 eat free, making this popular with families.

Kuniya MODERN AUSTRALIAN $$$

(☑08-8956 2200; Sails in the Desert; mains $45-60; ⊘dinner) Yulara's most sophisticated restaurant, Kuniya is the place for romantic dinners and special occasions. The walls are adorned with contemporary Australian art and the inspired menu features Aussie cuisine infused with native ingredients that complement the extensive Australian wine list. Reservations are essential.

Yulara IGA Supermarket SUPERMARKET $

(Resort Shopping Centre; ⊘8am-9pm) This well-stocked supermarket has a delicatessen and sells picnic portions, fresh fruit and vegetables, meat, groceries, ice and camping supplies.

Drinking

Pioneer Barbecue Bar PUB

(Outback Pioneer Hotel & Lodge; ⊘10am-midnight) This rowdy bar is lined with long benches, with plenty of chances to meet other travellers. It has pool tables and live music nightly (usually a touch of twang).

Tali Bar BAR

(Sails in the Desert; ⊘10am-1am) The cocktails ($15 to $20) at this bar include locally inspired mixes like Desert Oasis. The piano gets a workout most nights during season from 8pm.

Bunya Bar BAR

(Desert Gardens Hotel; ⊘11am-midnight) This is a rather characterless hotel lobby bar, but it knows the importance of well-chilled beer, and the cocktails are several dollars cheaper than at Tali Bar.

ℹ️ Information

The useful *Welcome to Ayers Rock Resort* flier is available at the visitor information centre and at hotel desks. Most of the village's facilities are in the shopping centre, including a post office and a local job vacancies board.

ANZ bank (☑08-8956 2070) Currency exchange and 24-hour ATMs.

Emergency (☑police 08-8956 2166, ambulance 0420 101 403)

Internet cafe (Outback Pioneer Hotel; per 10min $2; ⊙5am-11pm) In the backpacker common room. Internet access is also available at the Tour & Information Centre and all accommodation.

Post office (☑08-8956 2288; Resort Shopping Centre; ⊙9am-6pm Mon-Fri, 10am-2pm Sat & Sun) An agent for the Commonwealth and NAB banks. Pay phones are outside.

Royal Flying Doctor Service medical centre (☑08-8956 2286; ⊙9am-noon & 2-5pm Mon-Fri, 10-11am Sat & Sun) The resort's medical centre and ambulance service.

Tour & Information Centre (☑08-8957 7324; Resort Shopping Centre; ⊙8am-8pm; @) Most tour operators and car-hire firms have desks at this centre.

Visitor Information Centre (☑08-8957 7377; ⊙9am-4.30pm) Contains displays on the geography, wildlife and history of the region. There's a short audio tour ($2) if you want to learn more. They also sell books and regional maps.

ℹ️ Getting There & Away

Air

Connellan airport is about 4km north from Yulara. **Qantas** (☑13 13 13; www.qantas.com.au) has direct flights from Alice Springs, Melbourne, Perth, Adelaide and Sydney. **Virgin Australia** (☑13 67 89; www.virginaustralia.com) has daily flights from Sydney.

Bus

Daily shuttle connections (listed as mini tours) between Alice Springs and Yulara are run by **AAT**

Kings (☑1300 556 100; www.aatkings.com) and cost adult/child $150/75. **Austour** (☑1800 335 009; www.austour.com.au) runs the cheapest daily connections between Alice Springs and Uluru ($140/70).

Car & Motorcycle

The road from Alice to Yulara is sealed, with regular food and petrol stops along the way. Yulara is 441km from Alice Springs (241km west of Erldunda on the Stuart Hwy), and the direct journey takes four to five hours.

Renting a car in Alice Springs to go to Uluru and back is a reasonably priced option if you make the trip in a group; see p865 for a list of operators.

ℹ️ Getting Around

A free shuttle bus meets all flights and drops off at all accommodation points around the resort; pick-up is 90 minutes before your flight. Another free shuttle bus loops through the resort – stopping at all accommodation points and the shopping centre – every 15 minutes from 10.30am to 6pm and from 6.30pm to 12.30am daily.

Uluru Express (☑08-8956 2152; www.uluru express.com.au) falls somewhere between a shuttle-bus service and an organised tour. It provides return transport from the resort to Uluru ($43/30 adult/child, $50/30 for the sunrise and sunset shuttles). Morning shuttles to Kata Tjuta cost $70/40; afternoon shuttles include a stop at Uluru for sunset and cost $75/40. There are also two-day ($155/80) and three-day ($170/80) passes which allow unlimited use of the service. Fares do not include the park entry fee.

Hiring a car will give you the flexibility to visit the Rock and the Olgas whenever you want. **Hertz** (☑08-8956 2244) has a desk at the Tour & Information Centre, which also has direct phones to the **Avis** (☑08-8956 2266) and **Thrifty** (☑08-8956 2030) desks at Connellan Airport.

Bike hire is available at the **Ayers Rock Resort Campground** (☑08-8957 7001; per hr $7, per half/full day $15/20; ⊙7am-8pm).

Outback
Journeys

Ultimate Outback »
Top Spots »
Indigenous Art & Culture »
Wild Australia »

Uluru (Ayers Rock; p877), Uluru-Kata Tjuta National Park

Ultimate Outback

'Outback' means different things in different parts of Australia – deserts, savannah, tropical wetlands – but the concept is consistent: the vast unknown heartland where farming stops and wilderness takes control...

The definitive outback experience – what everyone is really here for – is **Uluru-Kata Tjuta National Park** (p877). It's the undisputed highlight of Central Australia, due largely to the fact that these blood-red megaliths are so unexpectedly big and remarkably isolated...a surreal combination.

Uluru (Ayers Rock)

There's not much that hasn't been said about **Uluru** (p877). And not many parts of it that haven't been explored, photographed and documented. Still, nothing can prepare you for the sheer amazement you feel when you realise that hazy blob on the horizon isn't a cloud or a mirage or a dead bug on the windscreen...it's a 3.6km-long red rock!

Kata Tjuta (The Olgas)

In fact, **Kata Tjuta** (p878) is taller than Uluru (546m versus 348m), and some say exploring these 36 mounded monoliths is a more intimate, up-close experience. Walking trails weave in among the rocks, but like Uluru this is a spiritually significant place and scrambling around on the stone is deeply disrespectful.

Kings Canyon

In **Watarrka National Park**, about 300km north of Uluru by road, **Kings Canyon** (p873) is the inverse of Uluru – as if someone had grabbed the big rock, and pushed it into the desert sand. Here, 270m-high cliffs drop away to a palm-lined valley floor, home to 600 plant species and delighted-to-be-here native animals. The 6km canyon rim walk is four hours well spent.

1

Getting Here

You can get to Uluru-Kata Tjuta from anywhere in Australia (just head for the middle!) but the distances are mammoth, the desert sun packs a punch and there are plenty of things that can make driving difficult (road trains, wandering camels, overheating radiators, bad AM radio...). Consider taking a bus here from Alice Springs, or combining your Uluru experience with a guided tour of Central Australia – there's plenty to see and do here beyond the big boulders. See the Tours sections in the Adelaide & South Australia and Darwin & Uluru destination chapters for listings.

ULURU-KATA TJUTA FAST FACTS

» Uluru is composed of arkose, a course-grained sandstone laced with feldspar.

» Kata Tjuta rock is a conglomerate: gravel, pebbles and rocks bound in sand and mud.

» Uluru is 3.6km long, 348m high, 1.9km wide and 9.4km around the base.

Clockwise from top left
1. Kata Tjuta (The Olgas; p878) 2. Kings Canyon (p873), Watarrka National Park 3. Truck stop, road to Uluru

MTMEDIA/LONELY PLANET IMAGES ©

Top Spots

The Australian outback defines the word gargantuan: it's difficult to distil it to a collection of top spots, but here are just a few amazing out-of-the-way places.

Bloomfield Track, Queensland

Buckle up for one of Australia's great 4WD journeys. The track (p453), which runs from Cape Tribulation to Cooktown in outback Queensland, is a bumpy 80km of creek crossings, mountain climbs and sheer drops, with plenty of diversions along the way, including waterfalls, Aboriginal-guided cultural tours, national park walking trails – and the welcome sight of the legendary Lion's Den pub near the northern end.

Simpson Desert, Queensland

This is unforgiving territory, but come prepared and you'll witness some stunning scenery in the **Simpson Desert National Park** (p380) – vibrant-red sand dunes sway across a landscape of spinifex grasslands, salt lakes and wildflowers peppering the sunburnt landscape.

St Mary Peak, SA

The highest point in the **Flinders Ranges** (p787), **St Mary Peak** (1171m) is spiritually significant to the local Adnyamathanha people: they request that visitors do not climb the summit. An alternative (with equally eye-popping views over **Wilpena Pound**) is the steep scramble up to Tanderra Saddle on the Pound's rim.

Painted Desert, SA

Turn off the Stuart Hwy at Cadney Homestead for a 172km dirt-road run to **Oodnadatta** (p795). You'll travel through the magical **Painted Desert** en route. The painterly colours here derive from sediments bedded down on the floor of a once-was inland sea. Minerals have eroded

MANFRED GOTTSCHALK/LONELY PLANET IMAGES ©

JOHN SONES/LONELY PLANET IMAGES ©

Clockwise from top left
1. Wilpena Pound (p787) 2. Cobourg Peninsula (p839)
3. Oodnadatta Track (p795)

and leached from the hills, creating amazing striations and vivid flashes of red, orange, black and yellow. Bring your camera!

Cobourg Peninsula, NT

The dazzling beaches, cliffs and wilderness of the **Cobourg Peninsula** (p839) make a great escape. The best way to get here is via charter flight, arranged by your accommodation. Or, in the Dry, you can drive a 4WD through Kakadu National Park and Arnhem Land (two permits required). Most people are here for the fishing (threadfin salmon in particular) but you'll also see dolphins and turtles.

Wave Rock, WA

Perfectly shaped like a wave about to break, the 15m-high, 110m-long multicoloured granite **Wave Rock** (p960) is worth the 350km journey from Perth. The rock itself has streaks of wonderful colour flowing down its face, caused by 60 million years' worth of run-off from local mineral springs, weathering and erosion. We dare you not to strike a surfing pose!

THE DOG FENCE

Something you'll often hear mentioned in the outback (even if you don't see it), is the legendary Dog Fence. Erected as a barrier against sheep-killing dingoes, the 1.8m-high wire-mesh fence stretches across the outback from the Great Australian Bight, across SA, into NSW and through southeast Queensland. Originally an astounding 8614km long, it was shortened to 5500km in 1980. You'll pass through it on the Stuart Hwy north of Coober Pedy in SA.

Maintenance is an ongoing headache. Parts of the fence are more than 100 years old and need replacing, and even the newest sections are under constant assault from emus, kangaroos, livestock, floods and shifting desert sands (not to mention dingoes).

For more on the Dog Fence, read James Woodford's 2004 book *The Dog Fence*.

Indigenous Art & Culture

Immerse yourself in Dreaming stories, check out incredible rock art, learn about Country from the traditional owners or go fishing with an Indigenous guide.

Rock Art

Remarkable evidence of Australia's ancient Indigenous culture can be found at the outdoor rock-art sites scattered across the outback, from the Quinkan sites near **Laura** in Queensland to the 5000 sites in **Kakadu National Park**, Northern Territory (Ubirr and Nourlangie are accessible standouts). Check out the excellent rock art of the **Kimberley**. The images in this region are unlike those anywhere else in Australia – the greatest collection is under threat on the **Burrup Peninsula** (p987) near Dampier.

Contemporary Indigenous Art

Contemporary Australian Indigenous art – the lion's share of which is produced in outback communities – has soared to global heights in recent years. This lofty position was highlighted with the opening of the Musée du Quai Branly in Paris in 2006. The museum's facade, walls and ceilings have been gloriously painted by Aboriginal artists.

Traditional methods and spiritual significance are fastidiously maintained, often finding a counterpart in Western materials – the results can be wildly original interpretations of traditional stories and ceremonial designs. Dot paintings (acrylic on canvas) are the most recognisable form, but you may also see synthetic polymer paintings, weavings, barks, weapons, boomerangs and sculptures.

You can pay thousands of dollars for pieces in the big cities, but you'll save some money and ensure you're making an ethical purchase if you buy direct from outback Indigenous community centres. See p810 for more tips on buying Indigenous art.

CATHY FINCH/LONELY PLANET IMAGES ©

Cultural Tours

The proliferation of Indigenous-owned and -operated cultural tours in places like Kakadu National Park is testament to how far Indigenous tourism has come. You can now learn about Country from the people who know it best. Some highlights include **Anangu Waai** (p875) at Uluru in the Northern Territory; **Iga Warta** (p789) in South Australia's Flinders Ranges; and **Walker Family Tours** (p453) at Bloomfield Falls in Wujal Wujal, Queensland. See the Tours section of destination chapters.

Indigenous Festivals

Your outback visit might coincide with a traditional Indigenous festival. These celebrations offer visitors a look at Aboriginal culture in action. The biennial **Laura Aboriginal Dance Festival** in Queensland (June in odd-numbered years; p463) brings together around 20 Aboriginal communities for three days of song, dance and storytelling. The Northern Territory plays host to festivals, including the **Walking With Spirits** and **Stone Country** festivals; see p803 for details.

Clockwise from top left
1. Rock art, the Kimberley (p993), WA
2. Working on a didgeridoo, Darwin
3. Laura Aboriginal Dance Festival (p463), Queensland

Wild Australia

Australia's outback is sometimes called the 'dead heart', but the nation's ticker is dazzlingly alive: reptiles, birds and mammals of all descriptions proliferate in the deserts and tropical wetlands.

Reptiles

Cold-blooded reptiles thrive in the outback, warming up in the morning sun along black bitumen highways. Look for sedentary **stumpy-tailed lizards**, and **king brown** and **red-bellied black snakes** uncoiling slowly. More theatrical are **frill-necked lizards** and **thorny devils**, striking frozen poses by the roadside. Plodding through the dunes are **goannas** and 2m-long **perenties**.

The tropical north has serious reptiles: **saltwater** and **freshwater crocodiles** occupy the rivers and rockpools. **Carpet** and **olive pythons** grow long and strong here.

Birds

Barrelling along the Stuart Hwy, sometimes your only company is a distant voyeur – a huge **wedge-tailed eagle** circling on a 2m wingspan. **Emus** are comical companions, keeping pace along the roadside or crossing the road with a brood of fluffy chicks.

Up in the tropical wetlands are sexy-dancing **brolgas**, **jabirus**, **magpie geese** and colourful flutterers like **azure kingfishers** and **rainbow bee-eaters**. **Cockatoos**, **corellas** and **galahs** are ever-present, erupting from trees and waterways in colourful cacophonies.

Mammals

Iconic Australians like **red kangaroos** and **dingoes** are common in the outback, perfectly attuned to the challenges of life here. Introduced species, such as **camels** (once used by Afghan cameleers to get from A to B), **water buffalo** and **pigs**, have gone feral, adapting and thriving in outback conditions. Less obvious are exquisite little nocturnal **bilbies**.

MARTIN COHEN/LONELY PLANET IMAGES ©

JOHN BANAGAN/LONELY PLANET IMAGES ©

Right

1. Frill-necked lizard, Northern Territory
2. Dingo, Glen Helen Gorge (p871), Northern Territory

Perth & Western Australia

Why Go?

If you subscribe to the 'life's a beach' school of thought, you'll fall in love with Western Australia (WA) and its 12,500km of spectacular coastline. WA is beyond huge; if it were a separate country, it would be the 10th biggest in the world. You can wander along a beach for hours without seeing a footprint in the sand, be one of a handful of campers stargazing in a national park, or bushwalk for days without seeing a soul.

Up north in the Kimberley, you'll encounter wide open spaces that shrewdly conceal striking gorges, waterfalls and ancient rock formations. At the other end of the state, the south is a playground of white-sand beaches, expanses of springtime wildflowers, lush green forests and world-class wineries. Perth and neighbouring Fremantle are cosmopolitan cities, yet both retain a languorously laid-back feel. Wind down with them and take a walk on the WA side.

Best Places to Eat

- » Balthazar (p908)
- » Jackson's (p908)
- » Wild Duck (p947)
- » Must Winebar (p908)
- » Vasse Felix (p932)

Best Places to Stay

- » Amble Inn (p962)
- » Gnaraloo Station (p977)
- » Ningaloo Club (p980)
- » Cape Howe Cottages (p943)

When to Go

Perth

°C/°F Temp — Rainfall inches/mm

Mar Wet up north but great beach weather elsewhere and not as swelteringly hot in Perth.

Aug Head north for the Dry, south for festivals and flowers, and to Gnaraloo for surf.

Sep The best month state-wide: wildflowers, whales and warming weather, and still dry up north.

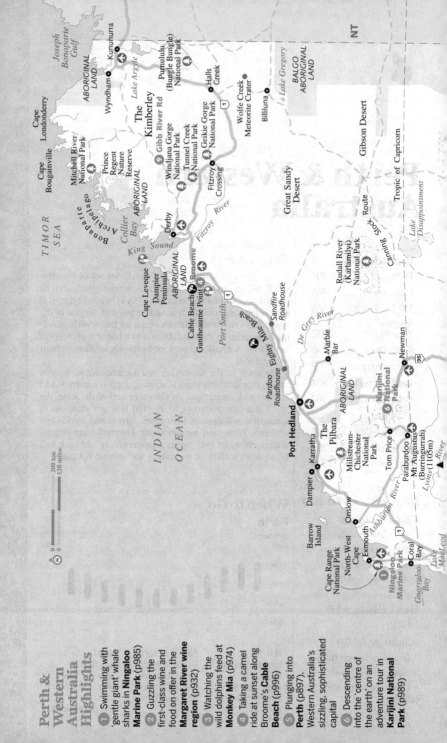

Perth & Western Australia Highlights

1. Swimming with gentle 'giant' whale sharks in **Ningaloo Marine Park** (p985)

2. Guzzling the first-class wine and food on offer in the **Margaret River wine region** (p932)

3. Watching the wild dolphins feed at **Monkey Mia** (p974)

4. Taking a camel ride at sunset along Broome's **Cable Beach** (p996)

5. Plunging into **Perth** (p897), Western Australia's sizzling, sophisticated capital

6. Descending into the 'centre of the earth' on an adventure tour in **Karijini National Park** (p989)

7 Enjoying a sublime sunset over the other-worldly **Pinnacles Desert** (p962)

8 Walking among and above the giant tingle trees on the Valley of the Giants **Tree Top Walk** (p941)

9 Tackling the notorious **Gibb River Road** in a 4WD adventure (p1006)

History

Archaeological records suggest that Aboriginal people entered Australia in the north-west, and show they were in a trading relationship with Indonesian fishermen from at least the 17th century. Dutchman Dirk Hartog was one of the first Europeans known to have landed here in 1616, and countryman Abel Tasman charted parts of the coastline in 1644.

Competition with French explorers tempted British authorities to ignore reports of a barren, inhospitable place. They sent Sydney-based Major Edmund Lockyer and a team of troops and convicts to found the first settlement at Albany in 1826.

Just when transportation was finishing up in other parts of Australia, over 10,000 convicts were sent to slow-growing WA. Post-sentence, they established local businesses and were in effect a sizeable, stable wave of settlers.

Late in the 19th century, the state's fortunes changed forever. Gold put WA on the map and finally gave it the population to make it a viable offshoot of the distant eastern colonies. Prosperity and proud isolation led to a 1933 referendum on secession: Western Australians voted two to one in favour of leaving the Commonwealth. Although it didn't eventuate, the people have retained a strong independent streak that comes to the fore whenever they feel slighted by the eastern states or the federal government.

Despite its small population, WA has been the strongest economic performer in the country over the last few years, thanks to its mining industry. The average family income is higher here and, consequently, the population is growing faster than elsewhere.

Indigenous Western Australia

Paintings, etchings and stone tools confirm that Indigenous Australians lived as far south as present-day Perth around 40,000 years ago. Despite their resistance, dispossession and poor treatment, the Aboriginal story in WA is ultimately a story of survival.

With around 72,000 people, WA has one of the largest Indigenous communities in Australia today, particularly around the Pilbara and Kimberley regions where in many towns they form the majority. Even in Perth and the south-west, which has the greatest non-Indigenous population, the local Noongar people have a more visible presence than, say, Kooris in Sydney.

As elsewhere in Australia, colonisation irrevocably changed indigenous ways of life.

Across the state, the experience was uniform: confrontations led to massacres or jail. Forced off their traditional lands, some communities were practically wiped out by European diseases. The *Aborigines Act 1905* (WA) allowed authorities to remove children, control employment and restrict movement.

After WWII many Aboriginal people banded together in protest against their appalling treatment on cattle stations, in their first public displays of political action since the early resistance fighters were defeated. Today, with growing recognition and acceptance of land rights, native-title claims are being made across the state. Yet Aboriginal people remain the state's most disadvantaged group. Many live in deplorable conditions, outbreaks of preventable diseases are common, and infant-mortality rates are higher than in many developing countries.

The issue of race relations in WA is a problematic one, and racial intolerance is still evident in many parts of the state. Especially (but not exclusively) in the remote north-west, a form of unofficial apartheid appears to exist, and travellers are bound to be confronted by it.

National Parks

The state's 96 national parks, managed by the Department of Environment & Conservation (DEC; www.dec.wa.gov.au), cover a vast amount and wide range of land. Thirty of these charge vehicle entry fees (per car/motorcycle $11/5), which are valid for any park visited that day. If you're camping within the park, the entry fee is only payable on the first day (camping fees are additional). If you plan to visit more than three chargeable parks in the state, which is quite likely if you're travelling outside of Perth for longer than a week, take advantage of the four-week Holiday Pass ($40). All DEC offices sell them and if you've already paid a day-entry fee in the last week (and have the voucher to prove it), you can subtract it from the cost.

🏃 Activities

BUSHWALKING

WA is blessed with wonderful bushwalking terrain, from the cool, fertile forests of the south-west, to the rugged, tropical Kimberley in the far north. Get in touch with like-minded souls through Bushwalking Australia (www.bushwalkingaustralia.org).

If you've got eight spare weeks up your sleeve, consider trekking the entire Bibbulmun Track (www.bibbulmuntrack.org.au),

a long-distance walking trail that winds its way south from Kalamunda, about 20km east of Perth, through virtually unbroken natural environment to Walpole and along the coast to Albany – a total of 963km. Campsites are spaced at regular intervals, most with a three-sided shelter that sleeps eight to 16 people, plus a water tank and pit toilets. The best time to tackle the track is from late winter to spring (August to October).

CAMPING

This enormous state provides plenty of opportunity to get back to basics, especially in the national parks, where sleeping in a swag under the stars is almost obligatory.

CYCLING

WA has excellent day, weekend and multiweek cycling routes. Perth has an ever-growing network of bike tracks, and you'll find the south-west region good for cycle touring. While there are thousands of kilometres of good, virtually traffic-free roads in country areas, the distance between towns makes it difficult to plan – even if the riding is virtually flat.

The most exciting initiative for mountain bikers is the Munda Biddi Trail (www.mundabiddi.org.au), heading 1000km from Mundaring on Perth's outskirts through the south-west forests to Albany. The first half (to Nannup, 498km) had been completed at the time of research.

DIVING & SNORKELLING

Close to Perth, divers can explore shipwrecks and marine life off the beaches of Rottnest Island, or head south to explore Shoalwater Islands Marine Park or Geographe Bay. A staggering amount of marine life can be found just 100m offshore within the Ningaloo Marine Park, on the Coral Coast, making this pristine area the premier destination for divers and snorkellers.

SURFING & WINDSURFING

Beginners, intermediates, wannabe pros and adventure surfers will find excellent conditions to suit their skill levels right along the coast. WA gets huge swells (often over 3m), so it's critical to align where you surf with your ability. Look out for strong currents, huge sharks and territorial local surfers who can be far scarier than a hungry white pointer.

The state's traditional surfing ground is the south-west, particularly the beaches from Yallingup to Margaret River. Heading north, the best-known spots are the left-hand point breaks of Jake's Point near

Kalbarri; Gnaraloo Station, 150km north of Carnarvon; and Surfers Beach at Exmouth.

Windsurfers and kitesurfers have plenty of choice spots to try out in WA as well, with excellent flat-water and wave-sailing. Kitesurfers in particular will appreciate the long, empty beaches and offshore reefs away from crowds. The premier location is windy Lancelin, north of Perth.

WHALE WATCHING

For most visitors to WA there's no better wildlife watching than seeing the southern right and humpback whales make their way along the coast. There are so many (upwards of 30,000) that it's become known as the Humpback Hwy. From June the gentle giants make their way on their annual pilgrimage from Antarctica to the warm, tropical waters of the north-west coast. They can then be seen again on their slow southern migration down the coast in early summer. Mothers with calves regularly make themselves at home in the bays and coves of King George Sound in Albany from July to October.

WILDFLOWERS

When spring has sprung in southern WA, wildflowers abound. From about August to about October the bush is ablaze with colour; it's a great time to bushwalk sections of the Bibbulmun Track or to drive through inland national parks such as Stirling Range or Mt Lesueur near Cervantes.

Wine Regions

Margaret River is one of Australia's most acclaimed wine regions – and arguably its most beautiful – known for its Bordeaux-style wines. The cool-climate Great Southern wine region covers a vast area, with hubs in Denmark, Mt Barker and Porongurup. Less lauded but more accessible is the Swan Valley, on Perth's eastern fringes.

Tours

If you don't feel like travelling solo or you crave a hassle-free holiday where everything is organised for you, dozens of tours cover all tastes and budgets. Some adventure tours include serious 4WD safaris, taking travellers to places that they simply couldn't get to on their own without large amounts of expensive equipment. The WA visitor centre in Perth has a wide selection of brochures and suggestions for tours all over the state.

AAT Kings Australian Tours   COACH, 4WD
(☑1300 228 546; www.aatkings.com.au)

Active Safaris 4WD
(☑1800 068 886; www.activesafaris.com.au)

Australian Adventure Travel 4WD, BUS
(☑1800 621 625; www.safaris.net.au)

Planet Perth Tours MINIBUS
(☑08-8132 8294; www.planettours.com.au)

Red Earth Safaris MINIBUS
(☑08-9279 9011; www.redearthsafaris.com.au)

Western Xposure SAFARI TRUCKS
(☑08-9414 8423; www.westernxposure.com.au)

Seasonal Work

WA is in a labour shortage and a wealth of opportunities exists for travellers for paid work year-round.

INDUSTRY	TIME	REGION(S)
grapes	Feb-Mar	Denmark, Margaret River, Mt Barker, Manjimup
apples/pears	Feb-Apr	Donnybrook, Manjimup
prawn trawlers	Mar-Jun	Carnarvon
bananas	Apr-Dec	Kununurra
bananas	yr-round	Carnarvon
vegies	May-Nov	Kununurra, Carnarvon
tourism	May-Dec	Kununurra
flowers	Sep-Nov	Midlands
lobsters	Nov-May	Esperance

ⓘ Information

Western Australian Tourism Commission (www.westernaustralia.com) Comprehensive website for general statewide information.

ⓘ Getting There & Away

The east coast is the most common gateway for international travellers, although if you're coming from Europe, Asia or Africa it's more convenient and quicker to take any of the 16 airlines flying directly to **Perth Airport** (☑08-9478 8888; www.perthairport.com). Port Hedland has international flights to/from Bali, while Perth, Kalgoorlie, Port Hedland and Broome welcome interstate flights.

The only interstate bus is the daily **Greyhound** (☑1300 473 946; www.greyhound.com.au) service between Darwin and Broome ($335, 23½ hours), via Kununurra, Fitzroy Crossing and Derby.

The only interstate rail link is the famous *Indian Pacific*, run by **Great Southern Railway** (☑08-8213 4592; www.trainways.com.au),

which travels to Perth from Kalgoorlie (10 hours), Adelaide (two days), Broken Hill (2¼ days) and Sydney (4352km, three days).

ⓘ Getting Around

AIR

Airnorth (☑1800 627 474; www.airnorth.com.au) Perth–Kununurra, Karratha–Port Hedland, Karratha–Broome, Port Hedland–Broome and Broome–Kununurra.

Cobham (☑1800 105 503; www.cobham.com.au) Perth–Kambalda.

Golden Eagle (☑08-9172 1777; www.goldeneagleairlines.com) Broome to Port Hedland, Fitzroy Crossing and Halls Creek.

Qantas (☑13 13 13; www.qantas.com.au) Perth to Kalgoorlie, Exmouth, Karratha, Paraburdoo, Newman, Port Hedland and Broome.

Skippers Aviation (☑1300 729 924; www.skippers.com.au) Perth–Carnarvon, Perth–Geraldton–Carnarvon, Perth–Kalbarri–Monkey Mia, Perth–Leonora–Laverton, Perth–Wiluna–Leinster and Perth–Mt Magnet–Meekatharra.

Skywest (☑1300 660 088; www.skywest.com.au) Perth to Busselton, Albany, Esperance, Kalgoorlie, Geraldton, Exmouth, Karratha, Broome, Kununurra.

Strategic Airlines (☑13 53 20; www.flystrategic.com.au) Perth–Derby.

Virgin Australia (☑13 67 89; www.virginaustralia.com) Perth to Newman, Karratha, Port Hedland and Broome.

BUS

WA's bus network could hardly be called comprehensive, but it offers access to substantially more destinations than the railways. All long-distance buses are modern and well equipped with air-con, toilets and videos.

Greyhound (☑1300 473 946; www.greyhound.com.au) Perth–Broome via Geraldton, Carnarvon, Karratha and Port Hedland; Broome–Darwin via the Great Northern Hwy (Rte 1).

Integrity Coach Lines (☑1800 226 339; www.integritycoachlines.com.au) Perth–Port Hedland weekly.

South West Coach Lines (☑08-9261 7600; www.veoliatransportwa.com.au) Perth to all the major towns in the south-west.

Transwa (☑1300 662 205; www.transwa.wa.gov.au) Perth–Augusta, Perth–Pemberton, Perth–Albany (three routes), Perth–Esperance (two routes), Albany–Esperance, Kalgoorlie–Esperance, Perth–Geraldton (three routes) and Geraldton–Meekatharra.

CAR

The best way to really see and explore this enormous state is by car. Bear in mind that WA is not only enormous but also sparsely populated, so

make safety preparations if you plan to travel any significant distance. There are many enticing areas of the state that don't have sealed roads, and a 4WD is recommended for many places such as the spectacular Kimberley, even in the Dry.

Department of Indigenous Affairs (DIA; Map p902; ☑08-9235 8000; www.dia.wa.gov.au; 197 St Georges Tce, Perth) To travel through Aboriginal land in WA you need a permit. Applications can be lodged on the internet.

Mainroads (☑13 81 38; www.mainroads. wa.gov.au) Provides statewide road-condition reports, updated daily (and more frequently if necessary).

Royal Automobile Club (RAC; ☑13 17 03; www.rac.com.au) Useful advice on statewide motoring, including road safety, local regulations and buying or selling a car.

TRAIN

Transwa (☑1300 662 205; www.transwa.wa.gov. au) services are limited to the *Prospector* (Perth–Kalgoorlie), *AvonLink* (Perth–Northam) and *Australind* (Perth–Bunbury). Transperth's local train network reaches as far south as Mandurah.

PERTH

POP 1.6 MILLION

Planted by a river and beneath an almost permanent canopy of blue sky, the city of Perth is a modern-day boomtown, stoking Australia's economy from its glitzy central business district. Yet it remains as relaxed as the sleepy Swan River – black swans bobbing atop – which winds past the skyscrapers and out to the Indian Ocean.

About as close to Southeast Asia as to Australia's eastern state capitals, Perth is a combination of big-city attractions and relaxed and informal surrounds, offering an appealing lifestyle for locals and a variety of things to do for visitors. It's a sophisticated, cosmopolitan city with myriad bars, restaurants and cultural activities all vying for attention. Yet even in its boardrooms, its heart is down at the beach, tossing around in clear ocean surf.

History

Modern Perth was founded in 1829 when Captain James Stirling established the Swan River colony on the lands of the Wadjuk, a subgroup of the Noongar people. The discovery of stone implements near the Swan River suggests that the area had already been occupied for around 40,000 years.

Relations were friendly at first, the Noongar believing the British to be the returned spirits of their dead, but competition for resources led to conflict. By 1843 the Wadjuk had been dispossessed of all of their lands around the new city and were forced to camp near the swamps and lakes to the north.

The early settlement grew very slowly until 1850, when convicts alleviated the labour shortage and boosted the population. Convict labour was also responsible for constructing the city's substantial buildings, such as Government House and the town hall. The discovery of gold inland in the 1890s increased Perth's population fourfold in a decade and initiated a building bonanza, mirrored in the current mining and economic boom.

◉ Sights

TOP CHOICE **Kings Park & Botanic Garden** PARK (Map p898; www.bgpa.wa.gov.au) The bush-filled 400-hectare expanse of Kings Park is where the city's good burghers head for a picnic under the trees or to let the kids off the leash in one of the playgrounds. Its numerous tracks are popular with walkers, while the steep stairs leading up from the river support a steady procession of masochistic middle-aged joggers. Apart from buns of steel, the exertion is rewarded by wonderful views from the top.

At the park's heart is the 17-hectare Botanic Garden, containing over 2000 indigenous plant species. In spring there's an impressive display of the state's famed wildflowers. A highlight is the **Lotterywest Federation Walkway** (☺9am-5pm), a 620m path through the gardens that includes a 222m-long, glass-and-steel bridge that passes through the canopy of a stand of eucalypts.

Free **guided walks** (☺10am & 2pm) leave from **Kings Park Visitor Centre** (Fraser Ave; ☺9.30am-4pm).

FREE **Art Gallery of Western Australia** ART GALLERY (Map p902; www.artgallery.wa.gov.au; Perth Cultural Centre, Northbridge; ☺10am-5pm Wed-Mon) Founded in 1895, this excellent gallery houses the state's pre-eminent art collection, with the Indigenous galleries providing the highlight. Free tours take place daily.

FREE **Western Australian Museum – Perth** MUSEUM (Map p902; www.museum.wa.gov.au; Perth Cultural Centre, Northbridge; ☺9.30am-5pm) This branch of the state's six-headed museum includes

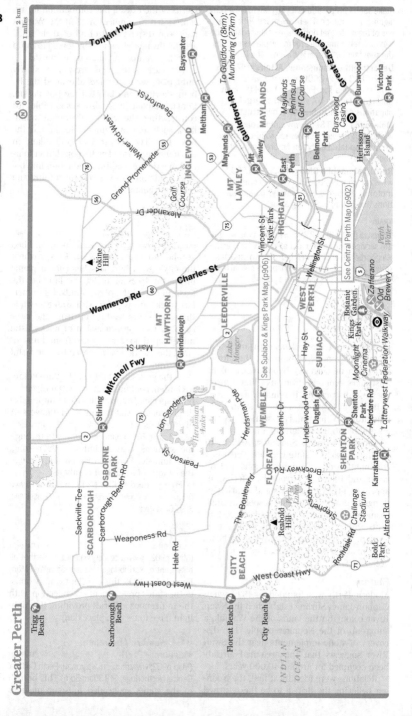

Greater Perth

Tonkin Hwy

Bayswater

To Guildford (8km);
Mundaring (27km)

Great Eastern Hwy

Burswood

Victoria
Park

Maylands
Peninsula
Golf Course

Burswood
Casino

Beaufort St

Meltham

Guildford Rd

MAYLANDS

Walter Rd West

55

INGLEWOOD

53

Maylands

Mt Lawley

Belmont
Park

Heirisson
Island

76

56

Grand Promenade

MT
LAWLEY

Lawley

East
Perth

Golf
Course

Alexander Dr

51

Perth
Water

75

HIGHGATE

See Central Perth Map (p902)

Vincent St

Hyde Park

Yokine
Hill

Wellington St

Zafferano

60

Charles St

LEEDERVILLE

WEST
PERTH

Old
Brewery

Wanneroo Rd

MT
HAWTHORN

2

Botanic
Garden

5

Glendalough

Main St

Lake
Monger

Hay St

Kings
Park

Lotterywest Federation Walkway

Mitchell Fwy

Stirling

75

Jon Sanders Dr

Herdsman
Lake

Herdsman Pde

WEMBLEY

Oceanic Dr

SUBIACO

Moonlight
Cinema

2

See Subiaco & Kings Park Map (p906)

Underwood Ave

Daglish

Shenton
Park

Aberdare Rd

Pearson St

OSBORNE
PARK

SHENTON
PARK

Sackville Tce

Scarborough Beach Rd

Brockway Rd

Karrakatta

SCARBOROUGH

FLOREAT

Stephenson Ave

The Boulevard

Perry
Lakes

Reabold
Hill

Challenge
Stadium

Rochdale Rd

Bold
Park

71

Weaponess Rd

Hale Rd

CITY
BEACH

West Coast Hwy

Alfred Rd

Trigg
Beach

Scarborough
Beach

Floreat Beach

City Beach

West Coast Hwy

INDIAN
OCEAN

2 km
1 miles

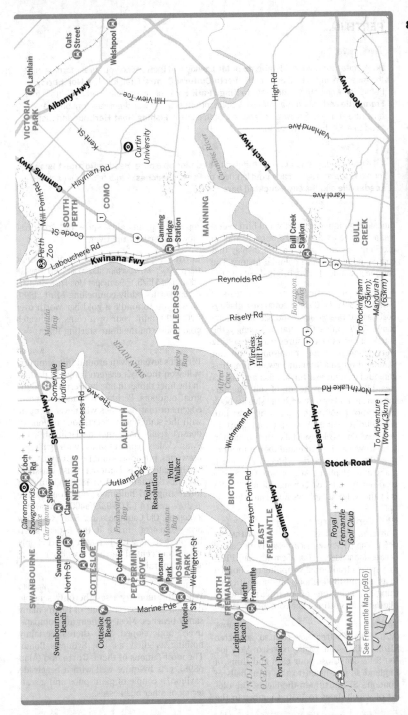

PERTH IN...

Two Days

Book ahead for dinner in **Highgate** or **Mt Lawley** and then spend your first morning in the museum and art galleries of the **Perth Cultural Centre**. Grab lunch in **Northbridge** before following our walking tour to **Kings Park**. For your second day, catch the train to **Fremantle** and spend the whole day there, prioritising the world-heritage prison, maritime museum and Shipwreck Galleries. Grab a bite in **Fishing Boat Harbour** and then head to a pub to catch a band.

Four Days

Take the two-day itinerary but stretch it to a comfortable pace. Head to **Rottnest Island** for a day trip and spend any time left over on Perth's **beaches**. Allocate a night each to **Leederville** and the city's **cocktail bars**.

dinosaur, mammal, butterfly and bird galleries, a children's discovery centre, and an excellent WA Land and People display that covers indigenous and colonial history. The complex includes Perth's original jail (1856).

Aquarium of Western Australia   AQUARIUM
(AQWA; ☑08-9447 7500; www.aqwa.com.au; Hillarys Boat Harbour, Hillarys; adult/child $28/16; ☉10am-5pm) AQWA offers the chance to enjoy the state's underwater treasures without getting wet…or eaten, stung or poisoned. You can wander through a 98m underwater tunnel as gargantuan stingrays, turtles, fish and sharks stealthily glide over the top of you. The daring can snorkel or dive with the sharks; book in advance ($159 with your own gear; hire snorkel/dive gear $20/40; 1pm and 3pm). To get here on weekdays, take the Joondalup train to Warwick station and then transfer to bus 423. By car, take the Mitchell Fwy north and exit at Hepburn Ave, or take the coastal road north from Scarborough Beach. AQWA is by the water at Hillarys Boat Harbour.

FREE Perth Institute of
Contemporary Arts   ART GALLERY
(PICA; Map p902; www.pica.org.au; Perth Cultural Centre, Northbridge; ☉11am-6pm Tue-Sun) PICA may have a traditional wrapping (it's housed in an elegant 1896 school) but inside it's anything but, being one of Australia's principal platforms for cutting-edge contemporary art.

Bell Tower   LANDMARK
(Map p902; www.thebelltower.com.au; adult/child $11/8; ☉10am-4pm, ringing noon-1pm Mon, Tue, Thu, Sat & Sun) Close your eyes and think of England as you listen to the royal bells of London's St Martin's-in-the-Fields, the oldest of which dates to 1550. Clamber to the

top of the pointy glass spire for 360-degree views of Perth by the river.

Perth Mint   HISTORIC BUILDING
(Map p902; www.perthmint.com.au; 310 Hay St; adult/child $15/5; ☉9am-5pm Mon-Fri, to 1pm Sat & Sun) Perth's oddly compelling Mint (1899) allows you to fondle a gold bar worth over $200,000, mint your own coins and watch gold pours (on the hour, starting 10am).

Swan Valley   WINERIES
Perthites love to swan around this semirural valley on the city's eastern fringe to partake in the finer things in life: booze, nosh and the great outdoors. Perhaps in a tacit acknowledgement that its wines will never compete with the state's more prestigious regions (it doesn't really have the ideal climate), the Swan Valley compensates with galleries, breweries, providores and restaurants.

The gateway is National Trust–classified Guildford, established in 1829. A clutch of interesting old buildings, one housing the visitor centre (☑08-9379 9400; www.swanval ley.com.au; Old Courthouse, cnr Swan & Meadow Sts; ☉9am-4pm), make it the logical starting place for day trippers. Guildford is only 12km from central Perth and well served by suburban trains.

Swan Valley   WINERIES
When the mercury rises the only sensible decision is to go west to one of Perth's many sandy beaches. Most of them are comparatively undeveloped and there's certainly nothing as glitzy as, say, Sydney's Bondi. The most famous of them, Cottesloe (Map p898), gets by quite well with a beachside pavilion, a couple of giant pubs and a scattering of other businesses.

The website www.mybeach.com.au has a profile of all the city beaches, including weather forecasts and information about buses, amenities and beach patrolling.

🏃 Activities

Kings Park has some good bike tracks and there are cycling routes along the Swan River, running all the way to Fremantle, and along the coast. Bikes can be taken free-of-charge on ferries any time and on trains outside weekday peak hours (7am to 9am and 4pm to 6.30pm). For route maps, see www.transport.wa.gov.au/cycling/ or call into a bike shop. Bike-hire options are listed below.

The whale-watching season runs from mid-September to early December.

Mills Charters   WHALE WATCHING
(☑08-9246 5334; www.millscharters.com.au; adult/child $80/55) Departs Hillarys Boat Harbour at 9am on Tuesday, Thursday, Saturday and Sunday. To get here on weekdays, take the Joondalup train to Warwick station and then transfer to bus 423. By car, take the Mitchell Fwy north and exit at Hepburn Ave, or take the coastal road north from Scarborough Beach.

Surf Sail Australia   WINDSURFING, KITESURFING
(Map p906; ☑1800 686 089; www.surfsailaustralia.com.au; 260 Railway Pde, West Leederville; ⊙10am-5pm Mon-Sat) When the afternoon sea breeze blusters in, windsurfers take to the Swan River, Leighton and beaches north of Perth. Here's where you can hire or buy your gear. Check wind speeds at www.seabreeze.com.au.

Oceanic Cruises   WHALE WATCHING
(☑08-9325 1191; www.oceaniccruises.com.au; adult/child $70/35) Departs Barrack Street Jetty (Map p902) at 9.15am daily, returning at 5.45pm after spending the afternoon in Fremantle.

Cycle Centre   BICYCLE HIRE
(Map p902; ☑08-9325 1176; www.cyclecentre.com.au; 313 Hay St; per day/week $25/$65; ⊙9am-5.30pm Mon-Fri, to 3pm Sat, 1-4pm Sun)

About Bike Hire   BICYCLE HIRE
(off Map p902; ☑08-9221 2665; www.aboutbikehire.com.au; Causeway Carpark, 1-7 Riverside Dr; per day/week from $36/80; ⊙9am-5pm) Also hires kayaks (per hour/day $16/65).

Scarborough Beach Cycles   BICYCLE HIRE
(☑08-9245 3887; www.scarboroughbeachcycles.com.au; 10-12 Scarborough Beach Rd, Scarborough; per day/week $40/150; ⊙9am-5pm)

Australasian Diving Academy   DIVING
(☑08-9389 5018; www.ausdiving.com.au; 142 Stirling Hwy, Nedlands) Hires diving gear (full set per day/week $70/180) and offers diving courses (four-day open-water $575).

Funcats   SAILING
(☑0408 926 003; Coode St Jetty, South Perth; per hr $35; ⊙Oct-Apr) Rents catamarans on the South Perth foreshore.

Surfschool   SURFING
(☑08-9444 5399; www.surfschool.com; 190 Scarborough Beach Road, Mount Hawthorn; adult/child $55/50) Two-hour lessons at Scarborough Beach, including boards and wetsuits.

WA Skydiving Academy   SKYDIVING
(☑1300 137 855; www.waskydiving.com.au; 458 William St, Northbridge; ⊙Mon-Thu) Tandem jumps from 8000/10,000/12,000ft for $450/490/530.

👣 Tours

Indigenous Tours WA   INDIGENOUS
(www.indigenouswa.com) See Perth through the eyes of the local Wadjuk people. Options include the **Indigenous Heritage Tour** (☑08-9483 1106; adult/child $25/15; ⊙1.30pm) – a 90-minute guided walk around Kings Park – and the **Swan River Dreaming Tour** (☑1300 467 688; adult/child $50/25; ⊙10am Tue & Wed), a 90-minute boat ride.

Perth Tram   CITY
(☑08-9322 2006; www.perthtram.com.au; adult/child $30/12) This hop-on, hop-off bus masquerading as a historic tram takes you around Perth's main attractions in two interlinking loops. It's possible to take just the Kings Park section (adult/child $8/4).

City Sightseeing Perth Tour   CITY
(☑08-9203 8882; www.citysightseeingperth.com; adult/child $28/10) Hop-on, hop-off double-decker bus tour. Tickets are valid for two days. The Kings Park section (adult/child $6/3) can be purchased separately.

Captain Cook Cruises   CRUISES
(☑08-9325 3341; www.captaincookcruises.com.au) Takes the river to the Swan Valley or Fremantle, with an array of add-ons such as meals, wine tastings and tram rides.

Golden Sun Cruises   CRUISES
(☑08-9325 9916; www.goldensuncruises.com.au) Cheaper and fewer frills than Captain Cook.

Out & About   WINE
(☑08-9377 3376; www.outandabouttours.com.au)

Central Perth

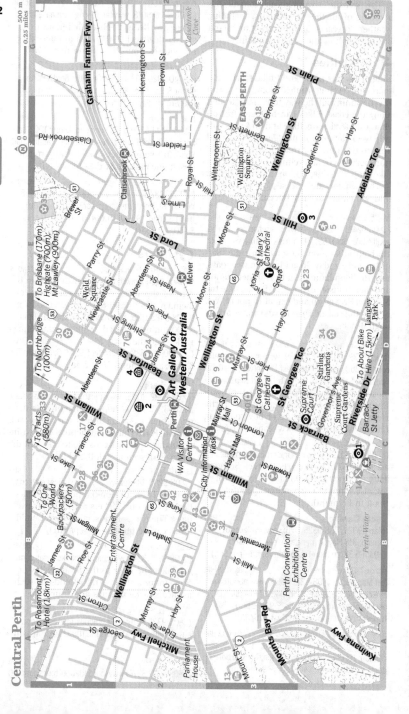

Swan Valley Tours   FOOD, WINE
(☏08-9274 1199; www.svtours.com.au)

Big Sky Wine Tours   WINE
(☏08-9454 2681; www.bigskytours.com.au; tours from $65)

Rottnest Air Taxi   SCENIC FLIGHTS
(☏08-9292 5027; www.rottnest.de; 30min $85)

✦ Festivals & Events

Perth Cup   HORSE RACING
(www.perthracing.org.au; ⊘1 Jan)

Summadayze   ELECTRONIC MUSIC
(www.summadayze.com; Supreme Court Gardens; ⊘early Jan)

Australia Day Skyworks   NATIONAL DAY
(www.perth.wa.gov.au/skyworks; ⊘26 Jan) Riverside family entertainment culminating in a 30-minute firework display at 8pm.

Big Day Out   MUSIC
(www.bigdayout.com; Claremont Showgrounds; ⊘early Feb) Australasia's biggest alternative music festival.

Perth International Arts Festival   ARTS
(www.perthfestival.com.au; ⊘mid-Feb) Held over 25 days from mid-February, it spans theatre, classical music, jazz, visual arts, dance, film and literature.

Good Vibrations   MUSIC
(www.goodvibrationsfestival.com.au; Claremont Showground; ⊘late Feb) Music festival with a party vibe.

Kings Park Festival   WILDFLOWERS
(www.kingsparkfestival.com.au; ⊘Sep) Includes live music every Sunday, guided walks and talks.

PERTH FOR CHILDREN

With a usually clement climate and plenty of open spaces and beaches to run around on, Perth is a great place to bring children. Of the beaches, Cottesloe is the safest. If the kids are old enough, take advantage of the bike tracks that stretch along the river and the coast. Kings Park has playgrounds and walking tracks.

The Royal Perth Show (late September) is an ever-popular family outing, all sideshow rides, showbags and proudly displayed poultry. Many of Perth's big attractions cater well for young audiences, especially AQWA, the WA Museum and the Art Gallery of Western Australia.

Part of the fun of **Perth Zoo** (Map p898; www.perthzoo.wa.gov.au; 20 Labouchere Rd, South Perth; adult/child $21/11; ⊙9am-5pm) is getting there by ferry. **Scitech** (Map p906; www.scitech.org.au; City West Centre, Sutherland St, West Perth; adult/child $14/9; ⊙10am-4pm) has over 160 hands-on, large-scale science and technology exhibits.

Adventure World (off Map p898; www.adventureworld.net.au; 179 Progress Dr, Bibra Lake; adult/child $47/39; ⊙10am-5pm Thu-Mon Oct-Apr) has rides, pools, waterslides and a castle. It's open daily during school holidays and through December. From Perth, exit the Kwinana Fwy at Farrington Rd, turn right and follow the signs.

At 26 sq km, **Whiteman Park** (www.whitemanpark.com; ⊙8.30am-6pm) is Perth's biggest, with over 30km of walkways and bike paths, and numerous picnic and barbecue spots. Within its ordered grounds are **Caversham Wildlife Park** (www.cavershamwildlife.com.au; adult/child $22/10; ⊙8.30am-5.30pm, last entry 4.30pm), **Bennet Brook Railway** (www.bennettbrookrailway.org; adult/child $8/4; ⊙11am-1pm Wed, Thu, Sat & Sun), **tram rides** (www.pets.org.au; adult/child $5/2.50; ⊙noon-2pm Tue & Fri-Sun) and the **Motor Museum of WA** (www.motormuseumofwa.asn.au; adult/child $8/5; ⊙10am-4pm). Enter the park from Lord St or Beechboro Rd, West Swan.

Perth Royal Show AGRICULTURAL
(www.perthroyalshow.com.au; Claremont Showground; ⊙late Sep) A week of fun-fair rides, spun sugar and showbags full of plastic junk. Oh, and farm animals.

Parklife MUSIC
(www.parklife.com.au; Wellington Sq; ⊙late Sep) Danceable indie bands.

🛏 Sleeping

Perth is very spread out, so choose your location carefully. Northbridge is best for those unperturbed by noise. On the other hand, the CBD and Northbridge are close to all forms of public transport, and hopping out to inner-city suburbs such as Leederville and Mt Lawley is simple. If you care most for the beach consider staying there, as public transport can be time-consuming.

CITY CENTRE

Riverview on Mount Street APARTMENTS $$
(Map p902; ☎08-9321 8963; www.riverviewperth.com.au; 42 Mount St; apt from $140; ❋@✿) There's a lot of brash new money up here on Mount St, but character-filled Riverview stands out as the best personality on the block. Its refurbished 1960s bachelor pads sit neatly atop a modern foyer and relaxed, minimalist cafe.

Medina Executive Barrack Plaza APARTMENTS $$$
(Map p902; ☎08-9267 0000; www.medina.com.au; 138 Barrack St; apt from $204; ❋✿) The Medina's meticulously decorated apartment-sized hotel rooms are minimalist yet welcoming. All one-bedrooms have balconies, and rooms on Barrack St tend to have more natural light (not always easy to obtain in central Perth).

Perth City YHA HOSTEL $
(Map p902; ☎08-9287 3333; www.yha.com.au; 300 Wellington St; dm $34, r with/without bathroom $85/70; ❋@✿✿) Occupying an impressive 1940s art deco building on the fringes of the central city, this large YHA has a slight boarding-school feel in the corridors, but the rooms are clean and the period features add a touch of class.

Melbourne HOTEL $$
(Map p902; ☎08-9320 3333; www.melbournehotel.com.au; cnr Hay & Milligan Sts; r $165-290; ❋✿) Classic country charm wafts through this heritage-listed hotel. Its deep, corrugated-iron, wraparound balcony recalls a mining-town pub perched on the edges of the

red-dust desert. Rooms are unpretentious and comfortable but can be noisy.

Miss Maud
HOTEL $$

(Map p902; ☑08-9325 3900; www.missmaud.com.au; 97 Murray St; s/d $169/189; ❋@☎) Anyone with a love of Scandinavia, kitsch or *The Sound of Music* will find a few of their favourite things in the alpine murals and dainty rooms. The smorgasbords (lunch/dinner $32/43) are enough to feed a goat herd.

City Waters
MOTEL $$

(Map p902; ☑08-9325 1566; www.citywaters.com.au; 118 Terrace Rd; s/d $105/120; ❋) Apricot-hued City Waters is one of a dying breed of old-fashioned Perth waterfront motels. Rooms are small, simple and face onto the car park, but they're clean and airy and the waterfront location is top-notch.

Mantra on Hay
APARTMENTS $$$

(Map p902; ☑08-9267 4888; www.mantra.com.au; 201 Hay St; apt from $216; ❋@☎☒) Low-key but classy, Mantra's roomy apartments have laundries, dishwashers, good-sized benches and all the utensils you'll need.

NORTHBRIDGE, HIGHGATE & MT LAWLEY

Most of Perth's hostels are in Northbridge. There are so many here, in fact, that it's possible to walk around and inspect rooms before putting your money down – some are not up to snuff. We've only listed the better ones.

TOP CHOICE Emperor's Crown
HOSTEL $

(Map p902; ☑08-9227 1400; www.emperorscrown.com.au; 85 Stirling St; dm $32, r with/without bathroom $98/88; ❋@☎) The best of Perth's hostels has a great position (close to the Northbridge scene without being in the thick of it), friendly staff and high housekeeping standards. Granted, it's a bit pricier than most, but it's well worth it.

TOP CHOICE Durack House
B&B $$

(☑08-9370 4305; www.durackhouse.com.au; 7 Almondbury Rd, Mt Lawley; s $160, d $175-190; ☎) It's hard to avoid words like 'delightful', enunciated in a slightly English accent, when describing this cottage, set on a peaceful suburban street behind a white picket fence swathed in climbing roses. The three rooms have plenty of old-world charm, paired with thoroughly modern bathrooms. It's only 250m from Mt Lawley station; turn left onto Railway Pde and then take the first right onto Almondbury Rd.

Pension of Perth
B&B $$

(☑08-9228 9049; www.pensionperth.com.au; 3 Throssell St; s/d from $120/150; ❋@☎☒) Pension of Perth's French belle époque style lays luxury on thick: chaises longues, rich floral rugs, heavy brocade curtains, open fireplaces and gold-framed mirrors. Two doubles with bay windows (and small bathrooms) look out onto the park; the spa room is round the back. And it's across the road from gorgeous Hyde Park. To get here, head north on William St and then west, crossing through Hyde Park to the far side.

Witch's Hat
HOSTEL $

(☑08-9228 4228; www.witchs-hat.com; 148 Palmerston St; dm/tw/d $30/70/80; ❋@☎) Witch's Hat is something out of a fairy tale. The 1897 building could be mistaken for a gingerbread house, and the witch's hat (an Edwardian turret) stands proudly out the front, beckoning the curious to step inside. Dorms are light and uncommonly spacious, and there's a red-brick barbecue area out the back. To get here, head north along William St, turn left at Brisbane St and then right onto Palmerston St.

Governor Robinsons
HOSTEL $

(☑08-9328 3200; www.govrobinsons.com.au; 7 Robinson Ave; dm $30, d with/without bathroom $85/75; ❋@) On first impressions, the Guv seems too flash to be a hostel – occupying a conjoined pair of Federation-era homes with a modern kitchen-lounge area hollowed out of their centre. Dorms are fresh and clean, if a little snug, and the polished floorboards lend an upmarket feel. On the downside, the men's toilets sit under an inch of water as soon as someone takes a shower and there's no hand soap provided in the bathrooms. Robinson St heads off William St, just north of the main Northbridge strip.

Coolibah Lodge
HOSTEL $

(☑08-9328 9958; www.coolibahlodge.com.au; 194 Brisbane St; dm $25, r $60-70; ❋@☎) Built from two big old houses, Coolibah Lodge is comfortable and homely but nothing fancy. It's one of the oldest hostels on the block, actually, so there's a real backpackers vibe in here – no pretence. Dorms are tidy if a bit poky, and doubles are of a good standard. Brisbane St runs off William St, north of Northbridge.

One World Backpackers
HOSTEL $

(off Map p902; ☑08-9228 8206; www.oneworldbackpackers.com.au; 162 Aberdeen St; dm $27-30, d $80; @) One World is like a hippy backpackers on an inheritance: clean, green

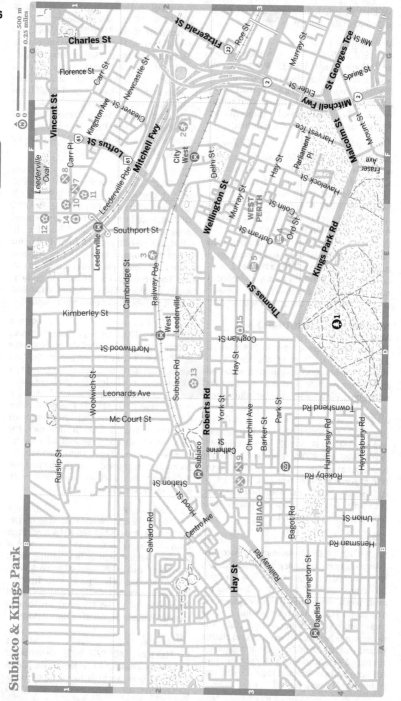

Subiaco & Kings Park

and beautifully maintained. Polished floorboards beam brightly in all the rooms of this nicely restored old house, and the dorms are big and sunny, if a little messy sometimes.

SUBIACO & KINGS PARK

TOP CHOICE **Richardson** HOTEL **$$$**

(Map p906; ☑08-9217 8888; www.therichardson. com.au; 32 Richardson St; r $450-550; ☒) Ship-shaped and ship-shape, the Richardson offers luxurious, thoughtfully designed rooms – some with sliding doors to divide them into pseudo suites. The whole complex has a breezy, summery feel, with pale marble tiles, creamy walls and interesting art. It's a bit pricier than you'd expect, but that's Perth for you. There's an in-house spa centre if you require additional pampering.

Outram HOTEL **$$$**

(Map p906; ☑08-9322 4888; www.wyndhamvrap. com.au; 32 Outram St, West Perth; r from $266; ☒☎) Discreet and understated, the Outram (now offically 'Wyndham Vacation Resorts Asia Pacific Perth' but – understandably – still known as the Outram) is super-stylish, with compact open-plan rooms containing bathrooms with walk-through showers, king-size beds draped in white linens, flat-screen TVs and spas.

BEACHES

Swanbourne Guest House GUESTHOUSE **$$**

(☑08-9383 1981; www.swanbourneguesthouse. com.au; 5 Myera St, Swanbourne; s/d $90/120) Peace and solitude are the key here. Off a leafy residential street, 20 minutes' walk from Swanbourne Beach, you'll hear nothing more than the birds twittering from your sun-filled room. Myera St joins Alfred St at

the intersection with Rochdale Rd, near Lake Claremont.

Trigg Retreat B&B **$$**

(☑08-9447 6726; www.triggretreat.com; 59 Kitchener St, Trigg; r $160; ☒☎) Quietly classy, this three-room B&B offers attractive and supremely comfortable queen bedrooms in a modern house near the beach. Each has fridge, TV, DVD player and tea- and coffee-making facilities. A full cooked breakfast is included in the rates. To get here, exit the Mitchell Fwy at Karrinyup Rd, turn right into Arnott St, left into Bailey St and right into Kitchener St.

Sunmoon Resort HOTEL **$$**

(☑08-9245 8000; www.sunmoon.com.au; 200 West Coast Hwy, Scarborough; r from $145; ☒☎) It's an unlikely spot for a Balinese-style resort, separated from Scarborough Beach by a busy road and a petrol station. Within the complex, wood-slatted pathways lead you under shady palms, and bright-orange carp splash in ponds. Batik furnishings adorn large rooms with terracotta-tiled floors.

OTHER AREAS

Peninsula APARTMENTS **$$**

(☑08-9368 6688; www.thepeninsula.net; 53 South Perth Esplanade, South Perth; apt from $195; ☒@☎) While only the front few apartments have full-on views, Peninsula's waterfront location lends itself to lazy ferry rides and sunset strolls along the river. It's a sprawling, older-style complex but it's kept in good knick. The apartments all have kitchenettes and there's a communal laundry room. To get here, exit the Kwinana Fwy at Mill Point Rd, turn left onto Mill Point Rd, right onto Frasers Lane then left onto South Perth Esplanade.

Discovery Holiday Parks – Perth
CAMPGROUND $

(☑08-9453 6877; www.discoveryholidayparks.com. au; 186 Hale Rd, Forrestfield; powered sites for 2 $38-45, units $125-187; ❋@🛜🏊) This well-kept holiday park, 15km out of the city, has a wide range of cabins and smart-looking units, many with decks, TVs and DVD players. To get here, take the Great Eastern Hwy, turn right onto the Tonkin Hwy and left onto Hale Rd.

🍴 Eating

While the rest of the world has been tightening their belts in the face of the global financial crisis, Perth still has plenty of grey-suited men loosening theirs at the end of long, lingering business lunches. Where many of Australia's other state capitals might have a handful of top restaurants charging over $40 a main, in Perth those prices are fast becoming the norm. Unfortunately the experience doesn't always match the outlay. That said, there are some truly exceptional restaurants, such as the ones we've included here. It's still possible to eat cheaply, especially in the Little Asia section of William St, Northbridge.

CITY CENTRE

TOP CHOICE Balthazar
MODERN AUSTRALIAN $$$

(Map p902; ☑08-9421 1206; 6 The Esplanade; mains $37-40; ⊘lunch Mon-Fri, dinner Mon-Sat) Low-lit, discreet and sophisticated, Balthazar's informal cool vibe is matched by exquisite food and a famously excellent wine list. The menu here is refreshingly original, combining European and Asian flavours with not-at-all-reckless abandon.

Greenhouse
TAPAS $$

(Map p902; ☑08-9481 8333; www.greenhouse perth.com; 100 St Georges Tce; tapas $10-18; ⊘7am-midnight Mon-Sat) The talk is shifting from the groundbreaking design (straw bales, plywood, corrugated iron and living exterior walls covered with 5000 individual pot plants) onto the excellent food offered at this hip tapas-style eatery. The low-impact ethos continues inside, with furniture that looks like it's been knocked up in Dad's shed.

Tiger, Tiger
CAFE $

(Map p902; ☑08-9322 8055; Murray Mews; mains $8-19; ⊘breakfast & lunch; 🛜) The small shabby-chic interior isn't as popular as the outdoor tables, in a lane leading off Murray St. The free wi-fi's a drawcard, but the food is also excellent.

Annalakshmi
INDIAN $

(Map p902; ☑08-9221 3003; www.annalakshmi. com.au; 1st fl, Western Pavilion; pay by donation; ⊘lunch Tue-Fri & Sun, dinner Tue-Sun; 🌿) While the 360-degree views of the Swan River are worth a million dollars, the food's literally priceless (donate whatever your conscience suggests). The spicy vegetarian curries attract an eclectic mix of hippies, Hindus and the just plain hungry.

Restaurant Amusé
MODERN AUSTRALIAN $$$

(Map p902; ☑08-9325 4900; www.restaurant amuse.com.au; 64 Bronte St, East Perth; degustation $120; dinner Tue-Sat) The critics have certainly been amused by this degustation-only establishment, regularly rated as WA's finest. Book ahead and come prepared for a culinary adventure – preferably with an empty stomach.

NORTHBRIDGE, HIGHGATE & MT LAWLEY

Jackson's
MODERN AUSTRALIAN $$$

(☑08-9328 1177; 483 Beaufort St, Highgate; mains $44, degustation $125; ⊘dinner Mon-Sat) The finest of fine dining is offered in this upmarket dining room, where the staff don white gloves to present you with wonderfully creative treats. In the pampering stakes, it's the foodie equivalent of a day spa, minus the bikini wax.

Must Winebar
FRENCH $$$

(☑08-9328 8255; www.must.com.au; 519 Beaufort St, Highgate; mains $36-44; ⊘noon-midnight) Not content with being Perth's best wine bar, Must is one of its best restaurants as well. The vibe's hip, slick and a little cheeky, while the menu marries classic bistro dishes with the best local produce.

Namh Thai
THAI $$

(☑08-9328 7500; 223 Bulwer St; mains $22-40; ⊘dinner Mon-Sat) Not your average Thai restaurant, Namh experiments with interesting taste combinations and serves them in an elegant candlelit dining room. Friday and Saturday are given over to banquet-style dining (per person $75). Bulwer St intersects William St, north of Northbridge.

Little Willy's
CAFE $

(Map p902; 267 William St; mains $8-12; ⊘breakfast & lunch) It's tiny and it's on William St, so the name's probably got nothing to do with the tall dude driving the coffee machine who's universally known as Hot Rob (much

to his obvious embarrassment). He works that baby like a pro, and the food, while simple, is delicious.

Viet Hoa
VIETNAMESE $

(Map p902; 349 William St; mains $8-19; ⏱lunch & dinner) Don't be fooled by the bare-bones ambience of this corner Vietnamese restaurant – or you'll miss out on the fresh rice-paper rolls and top-notch *pho* (beef-and-rice-noodle soup).

Tarts
CAFE $

(off Map p902; www.tartscafe.com.au; 212 Lake St; mains $14-19; ⏱7am-5pm) Massive tarts piled with berries, apples or lime curd; rich scrambled eggs tumbling off thickly sliced sourdough; mini custard tarts stacked with glazed strawberries. Packed like a hamper on weekends.

Soto Espresso
CAFE $

(www.sotoespresso.com; 507 Beaufort St, Highgate; breakfast $5-19, lunch $10-20; ⏱7am-midnight; 🛜) Modern Soto opens onto the street, welcoming its inner-city crowd: stay-at-home dads, ladies who lunch and shop and bleary-eyed students. The large cooked breakfasts will tackle any hangover.

Cantina 663
MEDITERRANEAN $$

(☏08-9370 4883; www.cantina663.com; 663 Beaufort St, Mt Lawley; lunch $12-24, dinner $26-34; ⏱8am-late Mon-Sat, 8am-3pm Sun) It's a Spain versus Italy showdown, from the dishes to the wine list, at this cool but casual cantina, with tables spilling into the arcade.

Red Teapot
CHINESE $

(off Map p902; 413 William St; mains $7-18; ⏱lunch & dinner Mon-Sat) An intimate restaurant, always busy with diners enjoying stylishly executed Chinese favourites.

MT HAWTHORN & LEEDERVILLE

Divido
ITALIAN $$

(☏08-9443 7373; www.divido.com.au; 170 Scarborough Beach Rd; mains $30-36; ⏱dinner Mon-Sat) Italian but not rigidly so, this excellent, romantically inclined restaurant serves handmade pasta dishes and delicately flavoured mains. To get here turn left off Loftus St, the continuation of Thomas St, which runs alongside Kings Park.

Duende
TAPAS $$

(Map p906; ☏08-9228 0123; www.duende.com.au; 662 Newcastle St; tapas $5-17; ⏱6pm-late Sat-Thu, noon-late Fri) Sleek Duende occupies a corner site watching the comings and goings of

Leederville after dark. For the best people-watching, sit on the colourful outdoor furniture set up on the Astroturfed footpath. A long list of modern tapas is served.

Sayers
CAFE $

(Map p906; www.sayersfood.com.au; 224 Carr Pl; mains $10-29; ⏱7am-5pm) Nothing to do with Leo, as far as we know, this classy cafe has a counter groaning under the weight of an alluring cake selection. The breakfast menu includes surprising luxuries such as Wagyu beef baked eggs and Manjimup truffle scrambled eggs.

SUBIACO & KINGS PARK

Subiaco Hotel
GASTROPUB $$

(Map p906; ☏08-9381 3069; www.subiacohotel.com.au; 465 Hay St; mains $19-32; ⏱breakfast, lunch & dinner) A legendary boozer that's been given a glitzy makeover, the Subi now has a buzzy dining room that's the suburb's main place to see and be seen. The menu ranges from lighter fare like Caesar salads and vegetarian risottos to perfectly cooked steaks and excellent fish dishes.

Star Anise
MODERN AUSTRALIAN $$$

(☏08-9381 9811; www.staraniserestaurant.com.au; 225 Onslow Rd, Shenton Park; mains $45-50; ⏱dinner Tue-Sat) Tucked down a quiet suburban street, this elegant, intimate dining room is widely lauded as one of Perth's very best. Everything is set to impress, from the candlelight playing on the chocolate-brown walls, to the giant wrought-iron whisk sculpture, to the quiet professionalism of the staff, to the sophisticated, sometimes challenging menu. Onslow Rd runs between Thomas St and Railway Rd, south of Subiaco.

Old Brewery
STEAKHOUSE $$

(☏08-9211 8910; www.theoldbrewery.com.au; 173 Mounts Bay Rd; mains $29-43; ⏱breakfast Sun, lunch & dinner daily) Perth's the kind of town where even the steakhouses are glamorous, as evidenced by this designer joint at the heart of the historic Swan Brewery building (1838). There are wonderful views over the river to the city, but hardcore carnivores can trade them for views of the beef ageing gracefully in glass display cabinets.

Chutney Mary's
INDIAN $$

(Map p906; www.chutneymarys.com.au; 67 Rokeby Rd; mains $15-28; ⏱lunch Mon-Sat, dinner daily; ☏) The feisty, authentic Indian food here is much loved, and a sizeable chunk of the large menu is devoted to vegetarian favourites.

The vibe is colourful and casual, with wall-sized scenes of Indian life.

Drinking

Once upon a time, licences to sell alcohol in WA were tightly restricted and massively expensive. Venues therefore had to be built on a Ceauşescu scale in order to recoup the investment, and big booze barns, such as those common in Northbridge and Cottesloe, became part of the culture. A law change a few years back has given birth to a new breed of quirky little bars that are distinctly Melbourne-ish in their hipness and difficulty to locate. They're sprouting up all over the place, including in the formerly deserted-after-dark central city.

A spate of fights and glassings in pubs has caused many venues, particularly around Northbridge, to step up security. Many pubs now have lockouts, meaning you'll need to be in before midnight in order to gain entry. You may need to present photo ID, and it would pay to keep your wits about you in the rougher pubs.

CITY CENTRE

TOP CHOICE Greenhouse COCKTAIL BAR
(Map p902; www.greenhouseperth.com; 100 St Georges Tce; ⊙7am-midnight Mon-Sat) In a city so in love with the great outdoors, it's surprising that nobody's opened a rooftop bar in the central city before now. Hip, eco-conscious Greenhouse is leading the way, mixing up a storm amidst the greenery above the award-winning restaurant.

Helvetica BAR
(Map p902; www.helveticabar.com; rear, 101 St Georges Tce; ⊙3pm-midnight Tue-Thu, noon-midnight Fri, 6pm-midnight Sat) Clever artsy types tap their toes to delicious alternative pop in this bar named after a typeface and specialising in whisky and cocktails. The entry is off Howard St: look for the chandelier in the lane behind Andaluz tapas bar.

Hula Bula Bar COCKTAIL BAR
(Map p902; www.hulabulabar.com; 12 Victoria Ave; ⊙4pm-midnight Wed-Fri, 6pm-1am Sat) You'll feel like you're back on Gilligan's Island in this tiny Polynesian-themed bar, decked out in bamboo, palm leaves and tikis.

NORTHBRIDGE, HIGHGATE & MT LAWLEY

Northbridge is the rough-edged hub of Perth's nightlife, with dozens of pubs and clubs clustered mainly around William and

James Sts. It's so popular, it even has its own website (www.onwilliam.com.au).

Brisbane PUB
(off Map p902; www.thebrisbanehotel.com.au; 292 Beaufort St; ⊙11.30am-late) It was a very clever architect indeed who converted this classic corner pub (1898) into a thoroughly modern venue, where each space seamlessly blends into the next. Best of all is the large courtyard where the palms and ponds provide a balmy holiday feel.

399 BAR
(off Map p902; www.399bar.com; 399 William St; ⊙10am-midnight Mon-Sat, to 10pm Sun) It doesn't look like much from the outside, but this little local bar is an exemplar of the kind of personable establishment the new licensing laws have brought to Perth.

Ezra Pound BAR
(Map p902; 189 William St; ⊙1pm-midnight Thu-Tue) Down a much graffitied lane leading off William St, Ezra Pound is favoured by Northbridge's bohemian set.

Luxe COCKTAIL BAR
(www.luxebar.com; 446 Beaufort St, Highgate; ⊙8pm-late Wed-Sun) With retro wood panelling, big, sexy lounge chairs and velvet curtains, Luxe is knowingly hip.

Queens PUB
(www.thequeens.com.au; 520 Beaufort St, Highgate; ⊙10am-midnight Mon-Sat, to 10pm Sun) Big, nicely renovated federation-style pub, popular on Sundays. A cold beer in the dappled courtyard is the standard routine.

Flying Scotsman PUB
(www.theflyingscotsman.com.au; 639 Beaufort St, Mt Lawley) Old-style pub that attracts an indie crowd.

Brass Monkey PUB
(Map p902; www.thebrassmonkey.com.au; cnr James & William Sts; ⊙11am-1am Wed-Sat, to 10pm Sun) A massive 1897 pub with several different component parts, each with its own vibe.

Court BAR
(Map p902; www.thecourt.com.au; 50 Beaufort St, Northbridge; ⊙noon-midnight Sun-Thu, noon-2am Fri & Sat) A large, rambling gay and lesbian venue consisting of an old corner pub and a big, partly covered courtyard with a clubby atmosphere.

BEACHES

Elba BAR
(www.elbacottesloe.com.au; 29 Napoleon St; ⊙noon-midnight Mon-Sat, to 10pm Sun) Elba has taken

its street name as inspiration and produced a slick little Napoleonic bar complete with sparkly chandeliers and a gilt-framed portrait of the little man. Come dressed for cocktails, although perhaps in flats out of deference. Napoleon St is one of the shopping streets running off the Stirling Hwy.

Ocean Beach Hotel   PUB
(www.obh.com.au; cnr Marine Pde & Eric St, Cottesloe; ⊗11am-midnight Mon-Sat, to 10pm Sun) Backpackers and locals drink up the beer and soak up the sun at this rambling beachside pub, especially on Sunday.

Cottesloe Beach Hotel   PUB
(www.cottesloebeachhotel.com.au; 104 Marine Pde; ⊗11am-midnight Mon-Sat, to 10pm Sun) Grab a spot on the lawn in the massive beer garden, or watch the sun set from the balcony. Sunday is big.

☆ Entertainment

Nightclubs

Hip-E Club   NIGHTCLUB
(Map p906; www.hipeclub.com.au; 663 Newcastle St, Leederville; ⊗Tue-Sat) Thrust about to *Tainted Love* all night long. Tuesday is backpackers' night.

Ambar   NIGHTCLUB
(Map p902; www.boomtick.com.au/ambar; 104 Murray St) Perth's premier club for breakbeat, drum'n'bass and visiting international DJs.

Geisha   NIGHTCLUB
(Map p902; www.geishabar.com.au; 135a James St, Northbridge; ⊗11pm-6am Fri & Sat) A small DJ-driven, gay-friendly club.

Velvet Lounge   PUB
(www.theflyingscotsman.com.au; 639 Beaufort St, Mt Lawley) Out the back of the Flying Scotsman is this small, red-velvet-clad lounge playing everything from hip hop to ska.

Funk Club   PUB
(Map p906; www.funkclub.com.au; 742 Newcastle St, Leederville; ⊗8pm-midnight Fri) Upstairs at the Leederville Hotel, a happy bunch dances away for hours to live bands and local DJs.

Rise   NIGHTCLUB
(Map p902; www.rise.net.au; 139 James St) Non-stop techno and trance.

Live Music

Jazz Cellar   ROOM
(cnr Scarborough Beach Rd & Buxton St, Mt Hawthorn; admission $20; ⊗from 7pm Fri) Look for

the shoe shop, behind which you'll spot a car park. Then you'll find a red telephone booth: step through and down the stairs to find an older crowd of jazz freaks revelling in swing. It's always been BYO-only, but at the time of writing licensing problems were threatening its future.

Ellington Jazz Club   NIGHTCLUB
(Map p902; www.theellington.com.au; 191 Beaufort St, Northbridge; standing-only $10; ⊗7pm-1am Mon-Thu, to 3am Fri & Sat, 5pm-midnight Sun) There's live jazz nightly at this handsome, intimate venue.

Bakery   ARTS CENTRE
(Map p902; www.nowbaking.com.au; 233 James St, Northbridge; ⊗7pm-1am Thu-Sun) Popular indie gigs almost every weekend.

Amplifier   BAR
(Map p902; www.amplifiercapitol.com.au; rear 383 Murray St, Perth) Live (mainly indie) bands.

Moon   CAFE
(Map p902; www.themoon.com.au; 323 William St, Northbridge; ⊗6pm-12.30am Mon & Tue, 11am-1.30am Wed, Thu & Sun, 11am-3.30am Fri & Sat) Low-key, late-night cafe with singer-songwriters on Wednesday, jazz on Thursday and poetry on Saturday afternoon.

Universal   PUB
(Map p902; www.universalbar.com.au; 221 William St; ⊗7am-late) Much loved by jazz and blues enthusiasts.

Rosemount Hotel   PUB
(off Map p902; www.rosemounthotel.com.au; cnr Angove & Fitzgerald Sts, North Perth; ⊗noon-midnight Mon-Sat, to 10pm Sun) Local and international bands.

Cabaret & Comedy

TOP CHOICE ⟩ Devilles Pad   CABARET
(Map p902; www.devillespad.com; 3 Aberdeen St, Northbridge; ⊗6pm-midnight Thu, to 2am Fri & Sat) The devil goes to Vegas in this extremely kooky venue, hidden in a quiet-by-night part of town. You're encouraged to dress up to match the exceedingly camp interiors (complete with erupting volcano). A lively roster of burlesque dancers, magicians, live bands and assorted sideshow freaks provides the entertainment.

Lazy Susan's Comedy Den   COMEDY
(off Map p902; www.lazysusans.com.au; 292 Beaufort St, Highgate; ⊗8.30pm Tue, Fri & Sat) Above the Brisbane hotel. Tuesday offers a mix of first-timers, seasoned amateurs and pros

trying out new shtick ($5). Friday is for more grown-up stand-ups. Saturday is the Big Hoohaa – a team-based comedy wrassle.

Theatre & Classical Music

Check the *West Australian* newspaper for what's on. Most tickets can be booked through **BOCS Ticketing** (☎08-9484 1133; www.bocsticketing.com.au).

State Theatre Centre THEATRE
(Map p902; www.statetheatrecentrewa.com.au; 174 William St) Opened in 2011, this flash new complex includes the 575-seat Heath Ledger Theatre and the 234-seat Studio Underground. It's home to the Black Swan State Theatre Company and Perth Theatre Company.

His Majesty's Theatre THEATRE
(Map p902; www.hismajestystheatre.com.au; 825 Hay St) The WA Ballet (www.waballet.com.au) and WA Opera (www.waopera.asn.au) are based here.

Perth Concert Hall CONCERT HALL
(Map p902; www.perthconcerthall.com.au; 5 St Georges Tce) Home to the WA Symphony Orchestra (WASO; www.waso.com.au).

Cinema

Somerville Auditorium OUTDOOR CINEMA
(off Map p898; www.perthfestival.com.au; UWA, 35 Stirling Hwy, Crawley; ☺Dec-Mar) A quintessential Perth experience.

Luna CINEMA
(Map p906; www.lunapalace.com.au; 155 Oxford St, Leederville)

Cinema Paradiso CINEMA
(Map p902; www.lunapalace.com.au; Galleria complex, 164 James St, Northbridge)

Moonlight Cinema OUTDOOR CINEMA
(Map p906; ☎1300 551 908; www.moonlight.com.au; Kings Park) Summer only.

Camelot Outdoor Cinema OUTDOOR CINEMA
(www.lunapalace.com.au; Memorial Hall, 16 Lochee St, Mosman Park) December to Easter. From the Stirling Hwy, turn left onto Johnston St, right onto Harvey St and left onto Lochee St.

Sport

In WA 'football' means Aussie Rules and during the AFL (Australian Football League) season it's hard to get locals to talk about anything but the two local teams – the **West Coast Eagles** (www.westcoasteagles.com.au) and the **Fremantle Dockers** (www.fremantle

fc.com.au). The *West Australian* has details of all sports games.

Subiaco Oval AUSTRALIAN RULES
(Map p906; www.subiacooval.com.au; 250 Roberts Rd, Subiaco)

WACA CRICKET
(Western Australian Cricket Association; Map p902; www.waca.com.au; Nelson Cres, East Perth)

Perth Oval SOCCER, RUGBY
(NIB Stadium; Map p902; Lord St) Home to the Perth Glory (www.perthglory.com.au) soccer (football) team, the Western Force (www.westernforce.com.au) Super 12 rugby union and WA rugby league.

Challenge Stadium NETBALL, BASKETBALL
(www.venueswest.wa.gov.au; Stephenson Ave, Mt Claremont) Home to the West Coast Fever (netball; www.westcoastfever.com.au), the Perth Wildcats (basketball; www.nbl.com.au/wildcats) and regular concerts.

🛍 Shopping

CITY CENTRE

Murray Street and Hay Street Malls are the city's shopping heartland, while King St is the place for swanky boutiques. London Court arcade has opals and souvenirs.

Wheels & Doll Baby CLOTHING
(Map p902; www.wheelsanddollbaby.com; 26 King St) Punky rock-chick chic with a bit of baby doll mixed in. Perhaps Perth fashion's coolest export, being worn by the likes of Amy Winehouse and Debbie Harry.

Dilettante CLOTHING
(Map p902; www.dilettante.net); Femme (575 Wellington St); Homme (90 King St) Neighbouring boutiques stocking international designer labels including Helmut Lang and Vivienne Westwood.

78 Records MUSIC
(Map p902; www.78records.com.au; 914 Hay St) Big, independent record shop with a massive range of CDs and lots of specials.

Boffins BOOKS
(Map p902; www.boffinsbookshop.com.au; 806 Hay St) Boffins' technical and specialist range includes travel.

All Foreign Languages Bookshop BOOKS
(Map p902; www.allforeignlanguages.com.au; 572 Hay St) Foreign-language books, phrasebooks, guidebooks.

Perth Map Centre MAPS
(Map p902; www.mapworld.com.au; 900 Hay St) Full range of maps and travel guides.

NORTHBRIDGE, HIGHGATE & MT LAWLEY

William Topp DESIGN
(www.williamtopp.com; 452 William St, North-bridge) Lots of very cool knick-knacks.

Planet BOOKS
(www.planetvideo.com.au; 636-638 Beaufort St, Mt Lawley) A big polished-concrete shell decked out with leather lounges and a brazen chandelier. Stacked with books and lots of obscure movies.

LEEDERVILLE

Leederville's Oxford St is the place for groovy boutiques, eclectic music and bookshops.

Atlas Divine CLOTHING
(Map p906; www.atlasdivine.com; 121 Oxford St) Hip women's and men's clobber: jeans, quirky tees, dresses etc.

Oxford St Books BOOKS
(Map p906; 119 Oxford St) Knowledgeable staff, great range of fiction and a travel section.

SUBIACO & KINGS PARK

Upmarket Rokeby Rd and Hay St boast fashion, art and classy gifts.

Indigenart INDIGENOUS ART
(Map p906; www.mossensongalleries.com.au; 115 Hay St, Subiaco) Reputable Indigenart carries art from around the country but with a particular focus on WA artists.

Aboriginal Art & Craft Gallery INDIGENOUS ART
(off Map p906; www.aboriginalgallery.com.au; Fraser Ave, Kings Park) Tends to be less high end than Indigenart.

ℹ Information

Emergency

Police station (☑13 14 44; www.police.wa.gov.au; 60 Beaufort St, Northbridge)

Sexual Assault Resource Centre (☑08-9340 1828; www.kemh.health.wa.gov.au/services/sarc; ⊗24hr)

Internet Access

Look for the 🛜 symbol in the eating and sleeping sections for places with free wireless internet access. The **State Library of WA** (www.slwa. wa.gov.au; Perth Cultural Centre, Northbridge; ⊗9am-8pm Mon-Thu, 10am-5.30pm Fri-Sun) offers free wireless and computer terminals.

Media

Look for free listings booklets, such as *Your Guide to Perth & Fremantle,* available at hostels, hotels and tourist offices.

Drum Media Similar to X-Press.

Go West (www.gowesternaustralia.com.au) Backpacker magazine with information on activities throughout WA and seasonal work.

West Australian (www.thewest.com.au) Daily newspaper ($1.30).

X-Press Magazine (www.xpressmag.com.au) A good source of live music information. Available in cafes, bars and music stores.

Medical Services

Lifecare Dental (☑08-9221 2777; www.dentistsinperth.com.au; Forrest Chase, 419 Wellington St; ⊗8am-8pm)

Royal Perth Hospital (☑08-9224 2244; www.rph.wa.gov.au; Victoria Sq)

Travel Medicine Centre (☑08-9321 7888; www.travelmed.com.au; 5 Mill St; ⊗8am-5pm Mon-Fri)

Post

Main Post Office (GPO; ☑13 13 18; 3 Forrest Pl; ⊗8.30am-5pm Mon-Fri, 9am-12.30pm Sat)

Tourist Information

i-City Information Kiosk (Map p902; Murray Street Mall; ⊗9.30am-4.30pm Mon-Thu & Sat, to 8pm Fri, 11am-3.30pm Sun) Volunteers answer your questions and run walking tours.

WA Visitor Centre (Map p902; ☑08-9483 1111; www.wavisitorcentre.com; cnr Forrest Pl & Wellington St; ⊗9am-5.30pm Mon-Fri, 9.30am-4.30pm Sat, 11am-4pm Sun) A good resource for a trip anywhere in WA.

Websites

www.heatseeker.com.au Gig guide and ticketing.

www.perth.citysearch.com.au Entertainment and restaurants.

www.scoop.com.au Entertainment.

www.whatson.com.au Events and travel information.

ℹ Getting There & Away

For details on flights, buses and trains to Perth, see p913.

ℹ Getting Around

To/From the Airport

The domestic and international terminals of Perth's airport are 10km and 13km east of Perth respectively, near Guildford. Taxi fares to the city are around $25/35 from the domestic/international terminal, and about $60 to Fremantle.

Connect (☑1300 666 806; www.perthairport connect.com.au) runs shuttles to and from hotels and hostels in the city centre (one way/return $18/30, every 50 minutes) and in

Fremantle (one way/return $33/58, every 2½ hours). Prices are slightly cheaper between Perth and the domestic terminal and are substantially discounted for groups of two to four people (check the website for details). Bookings are essential for all services to the airport and are recommended for services to Fremantle. No bookings are taken for shuttles from the airport to Perth's city centre.

Transperth bus 37 travels to the domestic airport from St Georges Tce, near William St ($3.70, 44 minutes, every 10 to 30 minutes, hourly after 7pm).

Car & Motorcycle

Driving in the city takes a bit of practice, as some streets are one-way and many aren't signed. There are plenty of car-parking buildings in the central city but no free parks. For unmetered street parking you'll need to look well away from the main commercial strips and check the signs carefully.

These are the main Perth-based hire companies:

Avis (☑13 63 33; www.avis.com.au)

Backpacker Campervan & Car Rentals (☑1800 670 232; www.backpackercampervans.com)

Backpacker Car Rentals (☑08-9430 8869; www.backpackercarrentals.com.au) Cheap local agency, starting from $110 per week.

Bayswater Car Rental (☑08-9325 1000; www.bayswatercarrental.com.au) Excellent local company with four branches in Perth and Fremantle.

Britz Rentals (☑1800 331 454; www.britz.com) Hires fully equipped 4WDs fitted out as campervans, which are commonplace on northern roads. Britz has offices in all the state capitals, as well as Perth and Broome, so one-way rentals are possible.

Budget (☑1300 362 848; www.budget.com.au)

Campabout Oz (☑08-9477 2121; www.campaboutoz.com.au) Campervans, 4WDs and motorbikes.

Hertz (☑13 30 39; www.hertz.com.au)

Scootamoré (☑08-9380 6580; www.scootamore.com.au; 356a Rokeby Rd, Subiaco; 4hr/day/week/month $29/45/200/400) Hires 50cc scooters with helmets (compulsory) and insurance included (for over 21 year olds; $500 excess).

Thrifty (☑1300 367 227; www.thrifty.com.au)

Wicked Campers (☑1800 246 869; www.wickedcampers.com.au) Notable for the lurid colour schemes of its vehicles.

Public Transport

Transperth (☑13 62 13; www.transperth.wa.gov.au) operates Perth's public buses, trains and ferries. There are Transperth information

offices at Perth Station (Wellington St), Wellington St Bus Station, Perth Underground Station (off Murray St) and the Esplanade Busport (Mounts Bay Rd). There's also a journey planner on the website.

From the central city, the following fares apply for all public transport:

Free Transit Zone (FTZ) Central commercial area, bounded (roughly) by Fraser Ave, Kings Park Rd, Thomas St, Newcastle St, Parry St, Lord St and the river (including City West and Claisebrook train stations, to the west and east respectively).

Zone 1 City centre and inner suburbs ($2.50).

Zone 2 Fremantle, Guildford and the beaches as far north as Sorrento ($3.70).

Zone 3 Hillarys Boat Harbour (AQWA), the Swan Valley and Kalamunda ($4.60).

Zone 5 Rockingham ($6.60).

Zone 7 Mandurah ($8.70).

DayRider Unlimited travel after 9am weekdays and all day on the weekend in any zone ($9).

FamilyRider Lets two adults and up to five children travel for a total of $9 on weekends, after 6pm weekdays and after 9am on weekdays during school holidays.

If you're in Perth for a while, it may be worth buying a SmartRider card, which covers you for bus, train and ferry. It's $10 to purchase, then you add value to your card. The technology deducts the fare as you go, as long as you tap in and tap out (touch your card on the electronic reader) every time you travel, including within the FTZ. The SmartRider works out 15% cheaper than buying single tickets and automatically caps itself at the DayRider rate if you're avoiding the morning rush hour.

BUS As well as regular buses the FTZ is well covered during the day by the three free CAT (Central Area Transit) services. The Yellow and Red CATs operate east–west routes, Yellow sticking mainly to Wellington St and Red looping roughly east on Murray St and west on Hay. The Blue Cat does a figure eight through Northbridge and the south end of the city; this is the only one to run late – until 1am on Friday and Saturday nights only. Pick up a copy of the free timetable (widely available on buses and elsewhere) for the exact routes and stops. Best of all, services run every five to eight minutes during weekdays and every 15 minutes on weekends; there are digital displays at the stops telling you when the next bus is due.

The metropolitan area is serviced by a wide network of Transperth buses. Pick up timetables from any of the Transperth information centres or use the 'journey planner' on its website.

FERRY The only ferry runs every 20 to 30 minutes between Barrack Street Jetty and Mends

Street Jetty in South Perth – you'll probably only use it to get to the zoo.

TRAIN Transperth operates five train lines from around 5.20am to midnight weekdays and until about 2am Saturday and Sunday. Your rail ticket can also be used on Transperth buses and ferries within the ticket's zone. You're free to take your bike on the train in non-peak times. The lines and useful stops include:

Armadale Thornlie line Perth, Burswood.

Fremantle line Perth, City West, West Leederville, Subiaco, Shenton Park, Swanbourne, Cottesloe, North Fremantle, Fremantle.

Joondalup line Esplanade, Perth Underground, Leederville.

Mandurah line Perth Underground, Esplanade, Rockingham, Mandurah.

Midland line Perth, East Perth, Mt Lawley, Guildford, Midland.

Taxi

Perth has a decent system of metered taxis, though the distances in the city make frequent use costly and on busy nights you may have trouble flagging a taxi down in the street. There are ranks throughout the city. The two main companies are **Swan Taxis** (☑13 13 30; www.swantaxis.com.au) and **Black & White** (☑13 10 08; www.bwtaxi.com.au), both of which have wheelchair-accessible cabs.

FREMANTLE

POP 28,100

Perth has sprawled to enfold Fremantle within its suburbs, yet the port city maintains its own distinct personality – proud of its nautical ties, working-class roots, bohemian reputation and, especially, its football team. A 20th-century economic slump meant that the city retained an almost complete set of formerly grand Victorian and Edwardian buildings, creating a heritage precinct that's unique amongst Australia's cities today.

Today's Freo makes a cosy home for performers, professionals, artists and more than a few eccentrics. There's a lot to enjoy here – fantastic museums, edgy galleries, pubs thrumming with live music and a thriving coffee culture.

History

This was an important area for the Wadjuk Noongar people, as it was a hub of trading paths. It was occupied mainly in summer, when the Wadjuk would base themselves here to fish. In winter they would head further inland, avoiding seasonal flooding.

Fremantle's European history began when the HMS *Challenger* landed in 1829. Like Perth, the settlement made little progress until convict labour was used. The port blossomed during the gold rush and many of its distinctive buildings date from this period. It wasn't until 1987, when Fremantle hosted the America's Cup, that it transformed itself from a sleepy port town into today's vibrant, artsy city.

◎ Sights

Fremantle Prison HISTORIC BUILDING

(☑08-9336 9200; www.fremantleprison.com.au; 1 The Terrace; torchlight tours $25/21; ◎9am-5.30pm) With its foreboding 5m-high walls enclosing a nearly 6-hectare site, the old convict-era prison still dominates present-day Fremantle. In 2010 its cultural status was recognised, along with 10 other penal buildings, as part of the Australian Convict Sites entry on the Unesco World Heritage list.

The first convicts were made to build their own prison, constructing it from pale limestone dug out of the hill on which it was built. From 1855 to 1991, 350,000 people were incarcerated here. Of those, 43 men and one woman were executed on site, the last in 1964.

Entry to the gatehouse, including the Prison Gallery, gift shop (where you can purchase fetching arrow-printed prisoner PJs) and Convict Cafe is free. To enter the prison proper, you'll need to take a tour. During the day there are two fascinating 1¼-hour tours on offer (**Doing Time** and **Great Escapes**), timed so that you can take one after the other on a combined ticket (single tour adult/child $19/10, combined $25/17).

Bookings are required for the two more intense experiences on offer. **Torchlight Tours** (90 minutes, adult/child $25/21, Wednesday and Friday evenings) are designed to chill. The 2½-hour **Tunnels Tour** (adult/child over 12 $59/39) takes you 20m underground to tunnels and includes an underground boat ride.

Western Australian Museum – Maritime MUSEUM

(www.museum.wa.gov.au; Victoria Quay; museum adult/child $10/3, submarine $8/3, museum & submarine $15/5; ◎9.30am-5pm) Housed in an intriguing sail-shaped building on the harbour, just west of the city centre, this is a fascinating exploration of WA's relationship with the ocean. Various boats are on display and, if you're not claustrophobic, you can

Fremantle

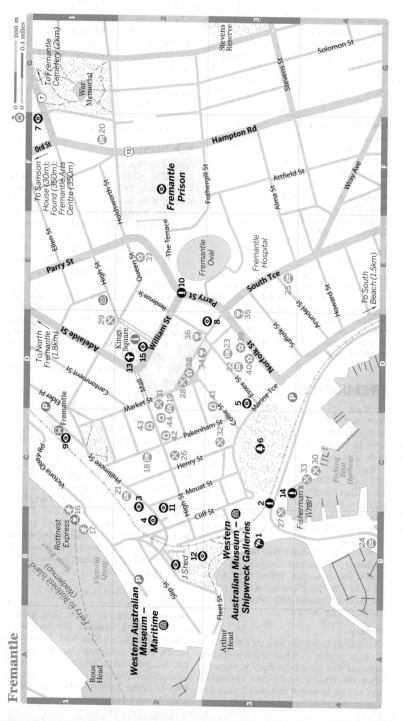

200 m
0.1 miles

Rous Head

Ferry to Rottnest Island (Wadjemup)

Victoria Quay

Western Australian Museum – Maritime

Swan River

Rottnest Express

J Shed

Arthur Head

Fleet St

Slip St

Western Australian Museum – Shipwreck Galleries

Cliff St

Mouat St

High St

Henry St

Pakenham St

Collie St

Marine Tce

Essex St

Victoria Quay Rd

Elder Pl

Phillimore St

Cantonment St

Market St

Adelaide St

To North Fremantle (1.8km)

Parry St

High St

Ellen St

Holdsworth St

Queen St

Kings Square

William St

Henderson St

Parry St

The Terrace

Fremantle Prison

Fremantle Oval

Fremantle Hospital

South Tce

Norfolk St

Suffolk St

Arundel St

Howard St

To South Beach (1.5km)

Ord St

To Samson House (30m); Found (350m); Fremantle Arts Centre (350m)

Hampton Rd

Fothergill St

Attfield St

Alma St

Wray Ave

Stevens St

Solomon St

Stevens Reserve

War Memorial

To Fremantle Cemetery (2km)

Fishing Boat Harbour

Fisherman's Wharf

take an hour-long tour of the Australian Navy submarine **HMAS Ovens** (departing every half-hour from 10am to 3.30pm).

FREE **Western Australian Museum – Shipwreck Galleries** MUSEUM
(www.museum.wa.gov.au; Cliff St; ◎9.30am-5pm) Housed in an 1852 commissariat store, the Shipwreck Galleries are considered the finest display of maritime archaeology in the southern hemisphere. The highlight is the **Batavia Gallery**, where a section of the hull of Dutch merchant ship the *Batavia*, wrecked in 1629, is displayed.

Round House HISTORIC BUILDING
(☑08-9336 6897; Arthur Head; admission by donation; ◎10.30am-3.30pm) Commenced in 1830, shortly after the founding of the colony, this odd 12-sided stone prison is the oldest

surviving building in WA. It was the site of the colony's first hangings and was used for holding Aborigines before they were taken to Rottnest Island.

FREE **Fremantle Arts Centre** GALLERY
(www.fac.org.au; 1 Finnerty St; ◎9am-5pm) An impressive neo-Gothic building surrounded by lovely elm-shaded gardens, the Fremantle Arts Centre was constructed by convict labourers as a lunatic asylum in the 1860s. Saved from demolition in the late 1960s, it houses a changing roster of interesting exhibitions.

Fremantle Markets MARKET
(www.fremantlemarkets.com.au; cnr South Tce & Henderson St; ◎8am-8pm Fri, to 5pm Sat & Sun) Originally opened in 1897, these colourful markets were reopened in 1975 and today

draw slow-moving crowds combing over souvenirs. The fresh-produce section is a good place to stock up on snacks.

Gold Rush Buildings
HISTORIC BUILDINGS

Fremantle boomed during the WA gold rush in the late 19th century, and the city retains many of the wonderful buildings that were constructed during, or shortly before, this period. High St, particularly around the bottom end, has some excellent examples including several old hotels. Worth seeking out are the **Chamber of Commerce Building** (16 Phillimore St), built 1873, **St John's Anglican Church** (Kings Sq), built 1882, **Fremantle Grammar School** (200 High St), built 1885, the **Town Hall** (Kings Sq), built 1887, **Samson House** (cnr Ellen & Ord Sts), a well-preserved 1888 colonial home, the **Esplanade Hotel** (Marine Tce), built 1896, the **Old German Consulate** (5 Mouat St), built 1903, **Fremantle Train Station** (Phillimore St), built 1907, and the **Customs House** (cnr Cliff & Phillimore Sts), built 1908.

Public Sculptures
MONUMENTS

Enlivening Fremantle's streets are numerous bronze sculptures, many by local artist Greg James (www.gregjamessculpture.com). Perhaps the most popular, certainly with black-clad pilgrims, is the statue of **Bon Scott** (1946–1980) strutting on a Marshall amplifier in Fishing Boat Harbour. The AC/DC singer moved to Fremantle with his family in 1956 and his ashes are interred in **Fremantle Cemetery** (Carrington St).

Others include **To the Fishermen** (Fishing Boat Harbour), also by James, and **Mark of the Century** (Parry St), by Robert Hitchcock.

Esplanade Reserve
PARK

(Marine Tce) A large park shaded by Norfolk Island pines between the city and Fishing Boat Harbour.

Bathers Beach
BEACH

You could theoretically swim here, but most people save the soaking for beaches further from the port.

South Beach
BEACH

Sheltered, swimmable, only 1.5km from the city centre and on the free CAT bus route.

Coogee Beach
BEACH

Coogee is 6km further south of South Beach.

🏃 Activities

Fremantle Trails
WALKING

(www.fremantletrails.com.au) Eleven trail cards are available from the visitor centre or library.

Oceanic Cruises
WHALE WATCHING

(☎08-9325 1191; www.oceaniccruises.com.au; C Shed, Victoria Quay; adult/child $50/25; ⊙10.30am daily, 1.30pm Sat & Sun mid-Sep–early Dec)

STS Leeuwin II
SAILING

(☎08-9430 4105; www.sailleeuwin.com; Berth B, Victoria Quay; adult/child $95/60) Take a trip on a 55m, three-masted tall ship.

👉 Tours

Fremantle Tram Tours
CITY

(☎08-9433 6674; www.fremantletrams.com.au; departs Town Hall) Actually a bus that looks like an old-fashioned trolley car, taking an all-day hop-on, hop-off circuit around the city (adult/child $24/5). The **Ghostly Tour** (adult/child $60/45) visits the prison, Round House and former asylum by torchlight. The **Highway to Hell Tour** (adult/child $25/10) takes in sites associated with Bon Scott.

Captain Cook Cruises
CRUISES

(☎08-9325 3341; www.captaincookcruises.com.au; C Shed, Victoria Quay) Cruises between Fremantle and Perth (one way/return $22/41). A three-hour lunch cruise departs at 12.45pm (adult/child $64/41).

🎉 Festivals & Events

West Coast Blues 'n' Roots Festival
MUSIC

(www.westcoastbluesnroots.com.au; Fremantle Park) April.

Blessing of the Fleet
RELIGIOUS

(Esplanade Reserve, Fishing Boat Harbour) An October tradition since 1948, brought to Fremantle by immigrants from Molfetta, Italy.

Fremantle Festival
CULTURAL

(www.fremantlefestivals.com) In November, the city's streets and concert venues come alive with parades and performances.

🛏 Sleeping

TOP CHOICE Norfolk Hotel
PUB $$

(☎08-9335 5405; www.norfolkhotel.com.au; 47 South Tce; s/d without bathroom $80/110, d with bathroom $150; ❋ 🛜) Far above your standard pub digs, the Norfolk's rooms have all been tastefully decorated in muted tones and crisp white linen, and there's a communal sitting room. It can be noisy, but the bar closes at midnight.

Fothergills of Fremantle
B&B $$

(☑08-9335 6784; www.fothergills.net.au; 18-22 Ord St; r $160-255; ☎) Naked bronze women sprout from the front garden, while a life-size floral cow shelters on the verandah of these neighbouring mansions on the hill. Inside, the decor is in keeping with the buildings' venerable age (built 1892), aside from the contemporary art scattered about.

Terrace Central B&B Hotel
B&B $$

(☑08-9335 6600; www.terracecentral.com.au; 79-85 South Tce; d $165; ❊@☎) It may be a character-filled B&B at heart, but Terrace Central's larger size gives it the feel of a boutique hotel. The main section is created from an 1888 bakery and an adjoining row of terraces, and there are modern one- and two-bedroom apartments out the back.

Quest Harbour Village
APARTMENTS $$$

(☑08-9430 3888; www.questharbourvillage.com.au; Mews Rd, Challenger Harbour; apt $223-595; ❊☎) At the end of a wharf, this attractive, two-storey, sandstone-and-brick block of one- to three-bedroom apartments makes the most of its nautical setting with views over the marina. Downstairs the rooms are light and simple, if a little dated. Upstairs has a more spacious feel.

Bannister Suites Fremantle
HOTEL $$$

(☑08-9435 1288; www.bannistersuitesfremantle.com.au; 22 Bannister St; r from $210; ❊) Modern and fresh, boutiquey Bannisters is a stylish new addition to the central city's accommodation scene. It's worth paying extra for one of the suites with the deep balconies, where you can enjoy views over the rooftops.

Port Mill B&B
B&B $$

(☑08-9433 3832; www.portmillbb.com.au; 3/17 Essex St; r $195-250) Crafted from local limestone (built in 1862 as a mill), inside Port Mill it's all modern Parisian style, with gleaming taps, contemporary French furniture and wrought-iron balconies. French doors open out to the sun-filled decks.

Old Firestation Backpackers
HOSTEL $

(☑08-9430 5454; www.old-firestation.net; 18 Phillimore St; dm $26-28, r $70; @) The brawny firemen have long left the building, but there's still plenty of entertainment in this converted fire station: free internet, foosball, movies and a sunny courtyard. The hippy vibe culminates in late-night singalongs around the campfire; bring earplugs.

Backpackers Inn Fremantle
HOSTEL $

(☑08-9431 7065; www.backpackersinnfreo.com.au; 11 Pakenham St; dm $23-28, s $55, d with/without bathroom $75/65; @) Large communal areas and a courtyard are the hallmarks of this backpackers, housed in a heritage building in the central city. Rooms are high-ceilinged, bright and clean. Flicks are shown on a mini cinema screen.

Pirates
HOSTEL $

(☑08-9335 6635; piratesbackpackers@westnet.com.au; 11 Essex St; dm $23-25, r $63; @) This cosy, sun- and fun-filled hostel in the thick of the Freo action is a top spot to socialise. Rooms are small and reasonably basic, but the bathrooms are fresh and clean.

Number Six
APARTMENTS $

(☑08-9299 7107; www.numbersix.com.au; studios/1-bedroom apt from $75/130; ❊) Has self-contained and stylish studios, apartments and houses available for overnight to long-term stays in great locations around Freo.

Woodman Point Holiday Park
CAMPGROUND $

(☑08-9434 1433; www.aspenparks.com.au; 132 Cockburn Rd, Munster; sites for 2 people $41, d $118-253; ❊@❊) A particularly pleasant spot 10km south of Fremantle. It's usually quiet, and its location makes it feel more summer beach holiday than outer-Freo staging post.

🍴 Eating

CITY CENTRE

Maya
INDIAN $$

(☑08-9335 2796; www.mayarestaurant.com.au; 77 Market St; mains $17-28; ⊙dinner Tue-Sun, lunch Fri) Maya's white tablecloths and wooden chairs signal classic style without the pomp. Its well-executed meals have earnt it the reputation of WA's best Indian restaurant. Try a Punjabi, Delhi or Bombay banquet.

Moore & Moore
CAFE $

(46 Henry St; mains $8-22; ⊙8am-4pm; ☎) An urban-chic cafe that spills into the adjoining art gallery and overflows into a flagstoned courtyard. Great coffee, good cooked breakfasts (including half serves for undersized appetites), pastries and wraps; free wi-fi.

Cafe 55
VIETNAMESE $

(55 High St; mains $7-11; ⊙7.30am-3pm Mon-Fri, 9am-3pm Sat) Vietnamese food with a Freo feel, this bright cafe's fragrant soups – *pho, bun bo Hue* – are fantastic. Plus there are

baguettes just like you'd get in the former French colony.

Juicy Beetroot
VEGETARIAN $

(mains $9-13; ☺10am-4pm Mon-Fri; ☑) This popular meat-free zone serves tasty vego and vegan dishes of the wholefood variety (tofu burgers, curries etc), and zingy fresh juices. It's tucked up an alley off High St (near No 132), with outdoor seating.

Gino's
CAFE $

(www.ginoscafe.com.au; 1 South Tce; mains $13-17; ☺breakfast, lunch & dinner; ☎) Old-school Gino's is Freo's most famous cafe, and while it's become a tourist attraction in its own right, the locals still treat it as their second living room, only with better coffee.

FISHING BOAT HARBOUR

Little Creatures
TOP CHOICE
PUB FARE $$

(www.littlecreatures.com.au; 40 Mews Rd; mains $16-34; ☺10am-midnight) Little Creatures is classic Freo: harbour views, fantastic brews (made on the premises) and excellent food. In a cavernous converted boatshed overlooking the harbour, it can get chaotic at times, but the wood-fired pizzas and substantial mains are well worth the wait.

Mussel Bar
SEAFOOD $$

(☑08-9433 1800; www.musselbar.com.au; 42 Mews Rd; mains $26-31; ☺breakfast Sun, lunch & dinner daily) Mussel Bar's large glass windows afford romantic views of the glittering harbour. Mussels, of course, are the go – or you can knock back fresh oysters with a sunset glass of bubbly.

Cicerello's
FISH AND CHIPS $

(www.cicerellos.com.au; 44 Mews Rd; mains $11-29; ☺9am-9pm) This busy fish 'n' chippery has been around since 1903 and remains a quintessential Freo experience. Leave the kids staring at the large aquariums, choose your fish and chips, then pick a spot out on the boardwalk to devour it.

NORTH FREMANTLE

Harvest
MODERN AUSTRALIAN $$

(☑08-9336 1831; www.harvestrestaurant.net.au; 1 Harvest Rd; mains $32-39; ☺breakfast & lunch Fri-Sun, dinner Tue-Sun) Swing through the heavy, fuchsia-painted metal doors and into the dark-wood dining room lined with artworks and curios, then settle down to comforting Mod Oz dishes cooked with a dash of panache.

Drinking & Entertainment

Most of Fremantle's big pubs are lined up along South Tce and High St. They've long been incubators for rock kids, turning out hairy progeny like the John Butler Trio and Eskimo Joe.

Little Creatures
MICROBREWERY

(www.littlecreatures.com.au; 40 Mews Rd, Fishing Boat Harbour; mains $16-34; ☺10am-midnight) In an old boatshed by the harbour, this brewery churns out beers that are a great source of WA pride. You can admire the brewery vats and spot bald patches from the mezzanine or almost nuzzle the boats from the boardwalk out the back.

Norfolk Hotel
PUB

(www.norfolkhotel.com.au; 47 South Tce; ☺11am-midnight Mon-Sat, to 10pm Sun) Slow down to the Freo pace and take your time over one of the many beers on tap at this 1887 pub. The limestone courtyard, with the sun streaking in through the elms and eucalypts, is downright soporific sometimes.

Monk
MICROBREWERY

(www.themonk.com.au; 33 South Tce; ☺11.30am-late) Park yourself at the voyeuristic front terrace or in the chic interior, partly fashioned from recycled railway sleepers, and enjoy the Monk's own brews or a slap-up meal.

Fly by Night Musicians Club
CLUB, LIVE MUSIC

(www.flybynight.org; Parry St) Variety is the key at Fly by Night, a longstanding not-for-profit club run by musos for musos. It's been the launching pad for many a local band.

Kulcha
NIGHTCLUB, LIVE MUSIC

(☑08-9336 4544; www.kulcha.com.au; 1st fl, 13 South Tce) World music of all sorts is the focus here. At the time we researched, the line-up included flamenco, belly dancing, sitar, blues, Indonesian tribal music, salsa classes, an Indian music workshop and a Jamaican reggae party. Book ahead.

X-Wray Cafe
CAFE, LIVE MUSIC

(3-13 Essex St) There's something on every night (live jazz, rock, open piano) at this hipster hang-out, comprising a smallish indoor area and a large canvas-covered terrace. Light meals are available ($13 to $28).

Mojo's
PUB, LIVE MUSIC

(www.mojosbar.com.au; 237 Queen Victoria St, North Fremantle; ☺7pm-late) Good old Mojo's is one of Freo's longstanding live-music pubs – a real stalwart. Local and national bands

TOP 10 WA SONGS

If you're looking for a soundtrack for your trip, download these WA-centric songs to your MP3 player.

» Empire of the Sun – *Standing on the Shore* (2009)

» The Waifs – *sundirtwater* (2006)

» The Jayco Brothers – *Town Hall* (2006)

» The Sleepy Jackson – *You Won't Bring People Down in My Town* (2006)

» Eskimo Joe – *From the Sea* (2003)

» Kasey Chambers – *Nullarbor Song* (2001)

» Pavement – *I Love Perth* (1996)

» Midnight Oil – *Stars of Warburton* (1990)

» Midnight Oil – *Warakurna* (1987)

» The Triffids – *Wide Open Road* (1986)

and DJs play at this small venue, and there's a sociable beer garden out the back.

Sail & Anchor PUB, LIVE MUSIC
(www.sailandanchor.com.au; 64 South Tce; ⊗11am-midnight Mon-Sat, to 10pm Sun) Built in 1854, this Fremantle landmark has been impressively restored to recall much of its former glory. Downstairs is big and beer-focused; it's more sedate upstairs, where there's a verandah, and singer-songwriter night on Wednesday.

Luna on SX CINEMA
(www.lunapalace.com.au; Essex St) Arthouse films; set back in a lane between Essex and Norfolk Sts.

Shopping

The bottom end of High St is the place for interesting and quirky shopping. Fashion stores run along Market St, towards the train station. Queen Victoria St in North Fremantle is the place to go for antiques. And don't forget Fremantle Markets for clothes, souvenirs and knick-knacks.

TOP CHOICE ⟩ Japingka INDIGENOUS ART
(www.japingka.com.au; 47 High St; ⊗10am-5.30pm Mon-Fri, noon-5pm Sat & Sun) An excellent gallery specialising in Aboriginal fine art, from WA and beyond. Purchases come complete with extensive notes about the works and the artists who painted them.

Found ART
(www.fac.org.au; 1 Finnerty St; ⊗10am-5pm) The Fremantle Arts Centre shop stocks an inspiring range of WA art and craft.

Love in Tokyo CLOTHING
(www.loveintokyo.com.au; 61-63 High St) Local designer turning out gorgeously fashioned fabrics for women.

New Edition BOOKS
(www.newedition.com.au; 82 High St; ⊗8.30am-9.30pm) A bookworm's dream with comfy armchairs for browsing, this excellent, well-stocked bookstore carries fiction as well as a range of local titles.

Record Finder MUSIC
(87 High St) A treasure trove of old vinyl, including rarities and collectables.

Chart & Map Shop MAPS
(www.chartandmapshop.com.au; 14 Collie St) Great range of maps and travel guides.

Information

Fremantle City Library (☎08-9432 9766; www.frelibrary.wordpress.com; Town Hall, Kings Sq; ⊗9.30am-5.30pm Mon, Fri & Sat, to 8pm Tue-Thu; 🖥) Free wi-fi and internet terminals.

Fremantle Hospital (☎08-9431 3333; www.fhhs.health.wa.gov.au; Alma St)

Post office (☎13 13 18; 152 High St; ⊗8am-5pm Mon-Fri, to 1pm Sat)

TravelLounge (☎08-9335 8776; www.thetravellounge.com.au; 16 Market St; internet per hr $5) Private agency offering information, bookings and internet terminals.

Visitor centre (☎08-9431 7878; www.fremantle.wa.com.au; Town Hall, Kings Sq; ⊗9am-5pm Mon-Fri, 10am-3pm Sat, 11.30am-2.30pm Sun) Free maps and brochures.

ⓘ Getting There & Around

Fremantle sits within Zone 2 of the Perth public-transport system, **Transperth** (☏13 62 13; www.transperth.wa.gov.au), and is only 30 minutes away by train. There are numerous buses between Perth's city centre and Fremantle, including routes 103, 106, 107, 111 and 158. For more details on Transperth and on the Connect airport shuttle, see p913.

Another very pleasant way to get here from Perth is by the 1¼-hour river cruise run by Captain Cook Cruises; see p918 for details.

There are numerous one-way streets and parking meters in Freo. It's easy enough to travel by foot or on the free CAT bus service, which takes in all the major sites on a continuous loop every 10 minutes from 7.30am to 6.30pm on weekdays, until 9pm on Fridays, and from 10am to 6.30pm on the weekend.

AROUND PERTH

Rottnest Island (Wadjemup)

POP 475

'Rotto' has long been the family-holiday playground of choice for Perth locals. Although it's only about 19km offshore from Fremantle, this car-free, off-the-grid slice of paradise, ringed by secluded beaches and bays, feels a million miles from the metropolis.

Cycling round the 11km-long, 4.5km-wide car-free island is a real pleasure; just ride around and pick your own bit of beach to spend the day on. You're bound to spot quokkas on your journey. These are the island's only native land mammals, but you might also spot New Zealand fur seals splashing around off magical West End, dolphins, and, in season, whales. King skinks are common, sunning themselves on the roads.

If you fancy further diversions, snorkelling, fishing, surfing and diving are all excellent on the island. In fact, there's not a lot to do here that's not outdoors, so you're better off postponing your day trip if the weather's bad. It can be unpleasant when the wind really kicks up.

Rotto is also the site of annual school leavers' and end-of-uni-exams parties, a time when the island is overrun by kids 'getting blotto on Rotto'. Depending on your age, it's either going to be the best time you've ever had or the worst – check the calendar before proceeding.

History

Wadjuk oral history recalls the island being joined to the mainland before being cut off by rising waters. The fact that modern scientists date that occurrence to before 6500 years ago makes these memories some of the world's oldest. Archaeological finds suggest that the island was inhabited from 30,000 years ago, but not after it was separated from the mainland.

Dutch explorer Willem de Vlamingh claimed discovery of the island in 1696 and named it Rotte-nest (rat's nest) because of the numerous king-sized 'rats' (which were actually quokkas) he saw there.

From 1838 it was used as a prison for Aboriginal men and boys from all around the state. At least 3670 people were incarcerated here, in harsh conditions, with around 370 dying (at least five hanged). Even before the prison was built, Wadjemup was considered a 'place of the spirits', and it's been rendered even more sacred to Indigenous people because of the hundreds of their people who died there. Many avoid it to this day.

◉ Sights

Quod & Aboriginal Burial Ground   HISTORIC SITE
(Kitson St) This octagonal 1864 building with a central courtyard was once the Aboriginal prison block but is now part of a hotel. During its time as a prison, several men would sleep in each 3m by 1.7m cell with no sanitation (most of the deaths were due to disease). Immediately adjacent to the Quod is a wooded area where hundreds of Aboriginal prisoners were buried in unmarked graves.

Rottnest Museum   MUSEUM
(Kitson St; admission by gold coin donation; ⊙11am-3.30pm) Housed in the old hay-store building, this little museum tells the island's natural and human history.

FREE Salt Store   HISTORIC BUILDING
(Colebatch Ave) A photographic exhibition in this 19th-century building deals with a different chapter of local history: between 1838 and 1950 the island's salt lakes provided all of WA's salt.

🏃 Activities

Excellent visibility in the temperate waters, coral reefs and shipwrecks makes Rottnest a top spot for **scuba diving** and **snorkelling**. There are snorkel trails with underwater

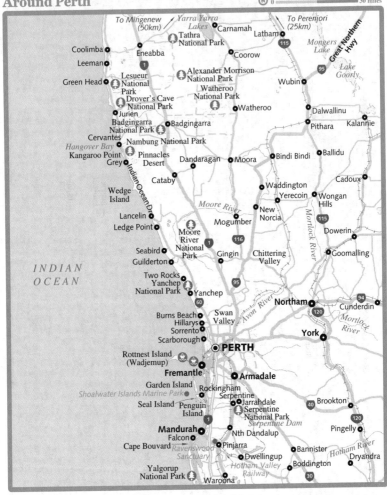

plaques at **Little Salmon Bay** and **Parker Point**.

Over a dozen boats have come a cropper on Rottnest's reefs. Marker **plaques** around the island tell the sad tales of how and when the ships sank. The only wreck that is accessible to snorkelers without a boat is at **Thomson Bay**. See p901 for diving trips.

The best surfing breaks are at **Strickland**, **Salmon** and **Stark Bays**, at the west end of the island.

Rottnest Island Bike Hire   EQUIPMENT HIRE
(08-9292 5105; www.rottnestisland.com; cnr Bedford Ave & Welch Way; 8.30am-4pm, to

5.30pm summer) Rents masks, snorkels and fins (per day $20) and surfboards (per day $50).

Tours

FREE **Rottnest Voluntary Guides**   WALKING
(08-9372 9757; www.rvga.asn.au) Themed walks leave from the Salt Store daily. Tours of Wadjemup Lighthouse (adult/child $7/3) and Oliver Hill Gun & Tunnels (adult/child $7/3) are also available; you'll need to make your own way there.

Rottnest Island (Wadjemup)

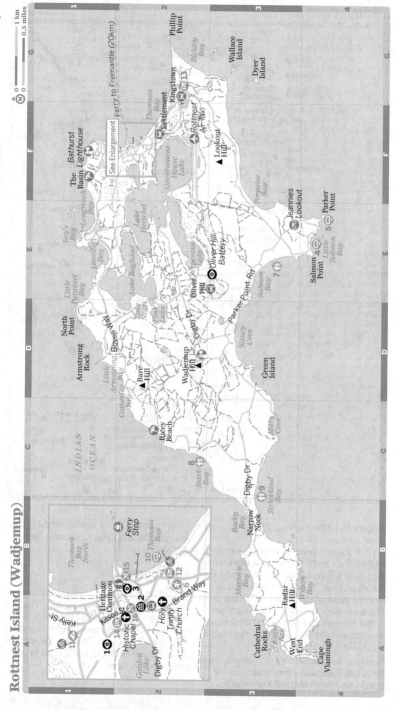

Oliver Hill Train & Tour　TRAIN
(www.rottnestisland.com; adult/child $26/15) This trip takes you by train to Oliver Hill (departing from the train station twice daily) and includes the Gun & Tunnels tour.

Discovery Coach Tour　COACH
(www.rottnestisland.com; adult/child $33/16) Leaves from Thomson Bay three times daily (book at the visitor centre); includes commentary and a stop at West End.

Rottnest Adventure Tour　BOAT
(www.rottnestexpress.com.au; adult/child $50/25) Ninety-minute cruises around the coast with a special emphasis on spotting wildlife, including whales in season. Packages available from Perth (adult/child $130/65) and Fremantle ($115/57).

Rottnest Air Taxi　SCENIC FLIGHTS
(☑08-9292 5027; www.rottnest.de) Ten-minute joy flights over the island ($35).

🛏 Sleeping & Eating

Rotto is wildly popular in summer and school holidays, when accommodation is booked out months in advance. Most visitors to Rotto self-cater. The general store is like a small supermarket (and also stocks liquor), but if you're staying a while, you're better to bring supplies with you.

Rottnest Island Authority Cottages　RENTAL HOUSES $$
(☑08-9432 9111; www.rottnestisland.com; cottages $117-214) There are more than 250 villas and cottages for rent around the island. Some have magnificent beachfront positions and are palatial; others are more like beach shacks. Sizes range from four to eight beds.

Hotel Rottnest　PUB $$$
(☑08-9292 5011; www.hotelrottnest.com.au; 1 Bedford Ave; r $270-320; ❋) Based around the 1864 summer-holiday pad for the state's governors, the former Quokka Arms has been completely transformed with a glass pavilion grafted onto it, creating an open, inviting space. The whiter-than-white rooms are smart and modern, if a little pricey for what's offered. It's hard to imagine a more inviting place for a sunset Sauvignon Blanc than the Astroturf 'lawn'. Bistro-style food (including pizza) is served at quite reasonable rates (mains $18 to $27).

Rottnest Lodge　HOTEL $$
(☑08-9292 5161; www.rottnestlodge.com.au; Kitson St; r $205-310; ❋) It's claimed there are ghosts in this comfortable complex, which is based around the former Quod. If that worries you, ask for one of the cheery rooms with a view in the new section fronting onto a salt lake. The attached **Marlins** (mains $26-36; ⊙lunch & dinner) does buffet lunches for tour groups, as well as a crowd-pleasing menu of pub-style evening meals.

Kingstown Barracks Youth Hostel　HOSTEL $
(☑08-9432 9111; www.rottnestisland.com; dm/f $49/99) Old army barracks that still have a rather institutional feel and few facilities. Check in at the visitor centre before you make the 1.8km walk, bike or bus trip to Kingstown.

Allison Tentland　CAMPGROUND $
(☑08-9432 9111; www.rottnestisland.com; Thomson Bay; sites per person $10) Camping is restricted to this leafy area, which has barbecues. Be vigilant about your belongings, especially

QUOKKAS

Once found throughout the southwest, Quokkas are now confined to forest on the mainland and a population of 8000 to 10,000 on Rottnest Island. These cute, docile little marsupials have suffered a number of indignities over the years. First de Vlamingh's crew mistook them for rats. Then the British settlers misheard and mangled their name (the Noongar word was probably *quak-a* or *gwaga*). But worst of all, a cruel trend for 'quokka soccer' by sadistic louts in the 1990s saw many kicked to death before a $10,000 fine was imposed.

your food – quokkas have been known to help themselves.

Aristos SEAFOOD $$
(www.aristosrottnest.com.au; Colebatch Ave; mains $16-30; ⊙lunch & dinner) An upmarket option for fish and chips, burgers, ice creams and excellent coffee, right on the waterfront near the main jetty.

Rottnest Bakery BAKERY $
(Malley St; mains $5-12) Traditional Aussie bakery, with pies, soup and ice cream.

ℹ Information

Near the main jetty there's a shopping area with ATMs.

Ranger (☑08-9372 9788)

Visitor centre (www.rottnestisland.com); Thomson Bay (☑08-9372 9732; ⊙7.30am-5pm Sat-Thu, to 7pm Fri, extended in summer); Fremantle (☑08-9432 9300; E Shed, Victoria Quay) Handles check-ins for all the island authority's accommodation. There's a bookings counter at the Fremantle office, near where the ferry departs.

ℹ Getting There & Away

Air

Rottnest Air-Taxi (☑08-9292 5027; www.rottnest.de) Flies from Jandakot airport in four-seater (up to three passengers one way/same day return/extended return $220/300/350) or six-seater planes (up to five passengers one way/same day return/extended return $300/400/480).

Boat

Rottnest Express (☑1300 467 688; www.rottnestexpress.com.au); Fremantle (C Shed,

Victoria Quay; adult/child $60/36); Northport (1 Emma Pl, Rous Head, North Fremantle; adult/child $60/36); Perth (Pier 2, Barrack St Jetty; adult/child $80/46) The above prices are for return day trips and include the island admission fee; add $9 for an extended return. Schedules are seasonal. Various packages are available, adding on bike hire, snorkelling equipment, meals and tours. Also runs the **Mega Blast** (adult/child $69/36), a speedboat service for thrill seekers, departing Fremantle daily from September to May.

Rottnest Fast Ferries (☑08-9246 1039; www.rottnestfastferries.com.au; adult/child $82/43) Departs from Hillarys Boat Harbour (40 minutes, thrice daily); add $3 for an extended return.

ℹ Getting Around

BIKE Bikes can be booked in advance online or on arrival from **Rottnest Island Bike Hire** (☑08-9292 5105; www.rottnestisland.com; cnr Bedford Ave & Welch Way; single speed per 1/2/3/4/5 days $20/31/40/48/56, multi-gear $27/43/54/65/76; ⊙8.30am-4pm, to 5.30pm summer).

Rottnest Express also hires bikes (per 1/2/3 days $28/41/56). It doesn't provide locks and it's not unheard of for an unlocked bike to be grabbed and used by someone else.

BUS A free shuttle runs between Thomson Bay and the main accommodation areas. The Bayseeker (day pass adult/child $13/5.50) does an hourly loop around the island.

Rockingham & the Peel District

Taking in swathes of jarrah forest and coastal resorts, this area can easily be tackled as a day trip from Perth or as the first stopping point of a south-west expedition. Entering the Peel District, you're passing out of Wadjuk country and into that of their fellow Noongar neighbours, the Pinjarup.

ROCKINGHAM
POP 100,000

Although it's not as rocking as the name implies, this seaside city has some nice beaches and a noticeable British expat community. These characteristics in themselves wouldn't lure travellers 46km south from central Perth if it weren't for the **Shoalwater Islands Marine Park** on the city's doorstep, where you can observe dolphins, sea lions and penguins in the wild.

Just a few minutes' paddle, swim or **ferry ride** (Mersey Point Jetty; per person $12; ⊘hourly 9am-3pm Sep-May) from the mainland is **Penguin Island**, home to about 600 breeding pairs of penguins and several thousand ground-nesting silver gulls. Apart from bird-watching, you can swim and snorkel in the crystal-clear waters. At low tide it's possible to wade the few hundred metres to the island across the sandbar. However, people have drowned after being washed off the bar during strong winds and high tides.

🏃 Activities

🌿 Rockingham Wild Encounters
WILDLIFE WATCHING
(☑08-9591 1333; www.rockinghamwildencounters.com.au) Runs a variety of low-impact tours, the most popular of which is the **dolphin swim tour** (departs Val St Jetty; tours $205; ⊘7.30am Sep-May), interacting with some of the 200 wild bottlenose dolphins in the marine park.

West Coast Dive Park
DIVING
(www.westcoastdivepark.com; permits per day/week $25/50) Diving within the marine park became even more interesting with the sinking of the *Saxon Ranger*, a 400-tonne fishing vessel. **Bell Scuba** (☑08-9527 9211; www.bellscuba.com.au; 43 Rockingham Beach Rd) leads expeditions to this and other wrecks and reefs in the vicinity.

ℹ️ Information

Visitor centre (☑08-9592 3464; www.rockinghamvisitorcentre.com.au; 19 Kent St; ⊘9am-5pm; @)

ℹ️ Getting There & Around

Rockingham sits within Zone 5 of the Perth public-transport system, **Transperth** (☑13 62 13; www.transperth.wa.gov.au), with regular trains via the Mandurah line to Perth Underground/Esplanade ($6.60, 34 minutes) and Mandurah ($4.60, 18 minutes).

Rockingham station is around 4km south-east of Rockingham Beach and around 6km east of Mersey Point, where the Penguin Island ferries depart; catch bus 551 or 555 to the beach, or stay on the 551 to Mersey Point.

MANDURAH
POP 68,300

Shrugging off its fusty retirement-haven image, Mandurah has made concerted efforts to reinvent itself as an upmarket beach resort, taking advantage of its new train link. And while its linked set of redeveloped 'precincts' and 'quarters' may sound a little

pretentious, the overall effect is actually pretty cool.

The town spans the Mandurah Estuary, which sits between the ocean and the large body of water known as the Peel Inlet. It's one of the best places in the region for fishing, crabbing, prawning (March to April) and dolphin-spotting.

◉ Sights & Activities

Mandurah Ferry Cruises
CRUISES
(☑08-9535 3324; www.mandurahferrycruises.com; Boardwalk) Take a one-hour **Dolphin & Mandurah Waterways Cruise** (adult/child $25/12; 5 to 7 daily) or a half-day **Murray River Lunch Cruise** (adult/child $72/47).

Mandurah Boat & Bike Hire
BOATING, CYCLING
(☑08-9535 5877; www.mandurahboatandbikehire.com.au; Boardwalk; bike hire per hr/day $10/33) Hires four-seat dinghies and six-seat pontoons (per hour/day $50/320).

Australian Sailing Museum
MUSEUM
(www.australiansailingmuseum.com.au; Ormsby Tce; adult/child $10/5; ⊘9am-5pm) A very cool new building housing 200 model yachts and tall ships.

Hall's Cottage
HISTORIC BUILDING
(Leighton Pl, Halls Head; ⊘10am-3pm Sun) An 1830s cottage and one of the first dwellings in the state; visits are by gold coin donation.

ℹ️ Information

Visitor centre (☑08-9550 3999; www.visitmandurah.com; 75 Mandurah Tce; ⊘9am-5pm; @)

ℹ️ Getting There & Away

There are direct trains to Perth Underground/Esplanade ($8.70, 50 minutes) and Rockingham ($4.60, 18 minutes). **Transwa** (☑1300 662 205; www.transwa.wa.gov.au) and **South West Coach Lines** (☑08-9261 7600; www.veoliatransportwa.com.au) buses stop here.

DWELLINGUP
POP 550

Dwellingup is a small, forest-shrouded township with character, 100km south of Perth. Its reputation as an activity hub has only been enhanced by the hardy long-distance walkers and cyclists passing through on the Bibbulmun Track and the Munda Biddi Trail, respectively.

◉ Sights & Activities

Forest Heritage Centre
NATURE RESERVE
(www.forestheritagecentre.com.au; 1 Acacia St; adult/family $5.50/11; ⊘10am-4pm) Set within

WORTH A TRIP

YALGORUP NATIONAL PARK

Fifty kilometres south of Mandurah is this beautiful 12,000-hectare coastal park, consisting of a succession of 10 tranquil lakes and surrounding woodlands and sand dunes. The park is recognised as a wetland of international significance for seasonally migrating water birds. Amateur scientists can visit the distinctive **thrombolites** of Lake Clifton, descendants of the earliest living organisms on earth. These rock-like structures are most easily seen when the water is low, particularly in March and April. There's a viewing platform on Mt John Rd, off Old Coast Rd.

the jarrah forest, this interesting rammed-earth building houses displays about the forest's flora and fauna. Short marked trails lead off into the forest, including an 11m-high canopy walk.

Hotham Valley Railway   HISTORIC TRAIN
(☑08-9221 4444; www.hothamvalleyrailway.com.au) On weekends, the **Dwellingup Forest Train** (adult/child $18/9; ☉departs 11am and 2pm) chugs along 8km of forest track on a 90-minute return trip. Every Saturday night and some Fridays, the **Restaurant Train** ($75; ☉departs 7.45pm) follows the same route, serving up a five-course meal in a 1919 dining car.

Dwellingup Adventures   KAYAKING, RAFTING
(☑08-9538 1127; www.dwellingupadventures.com.au; 1-person kayaks & 2-person canoes per day $37; ☉8.30am-5pm) Don't miss the opportunity to get out on the beautiful Murray River. This is the place to hire camping gear, bikes, kayaks and canoes or take an assisted, self-guided paddling tour ($90 for a full day in a one-person kayak) or cycling tour ($97/124/174 for a full day for one/two/three people). White-water rafting tours ($130 per person) are available from June to October.

ⓘ Information
Visitor centre (☑08-9538 1108; www.murray.wa.gov.au; Marrinup St; ☉9am-3pm)

THE SOUTHWEST

The farmland, forests, rivers and coast of the lush south-western corner of WA contrast vividly with the stark, sunburnt terrain of much of the state. On land, world-class wineries beckon and tall trees provide shade for walking trails and scenic drives, while offshore, bottlenose dolphins and whales frolic, and devoted surfers search for – and often find – their perfect break.

Unusually for WA, distances between the many attractions are short, and driving time is mercifully limited, making it a fantastic area to explore for a few days – you will get much more out of your stay here if you have your own wheels. Summer brings hordes of visitors, but in the wintery months the cosy pot-belly stove rules and visitors are scarce, and while opening hours can be somewhat erratic, prices drop.

History

For 55,000 years this area belonged to the Wardandi, one of the Noongar peoples. They lived a nomadic life linked to the seasons: heading to the coast in summer to fish and journeying inland during the wet winter months.

The French connection to many of the current place names dates from the early-19th-century expedition by the ships *Géographe* and *Naturaliste*, for which the bay and the cape were named. Thomas Vasse, a crewman who was lost at sea, is remembered in several place names. According to local Wardandi, who found and fed him, he made it to shore but later died on the beach waiting for his ship to return.

ⓘ Getting There & Around

AIR
Skywest flies to Busselton from Perth and Albany two times a week.

BUS
Transwa (☑1300 662 205; www.transwa.wa.gov.au) coach routes include:

SW1 East Perth to Bunbury, Busselton, Dunsborough, Margaret River and Augusta. Twelve per week; three per week continue on to Nannup and Pemberton.

SW2 East Perth to Bunbury, Balingup, Bridgetown, Manjimup and Pemberton; thrice weekly.

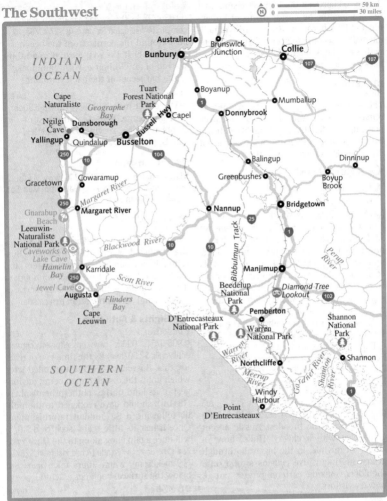

GS3 Bunbury to Balingup, Bridgetown, Manjimup, Pemberton, Walpole, Denmark and Albany; daily.

South West Coach Lines (☎08-9261 7600; www.veoliatransportwa.com.au) has the following services:

Perth (Esplanade Busport) to Bunbury, Busselton, Margaret River and Augusta.

Perth to Bunbury, Busselton and Dunsborough.

Bunbury to Balingup, Bridgetown and Manjimup.

Bunbury to Busselton and Nannup.

TransBusselton (☎08-9754 1666; 39 Albert St) bus 903 follows the coast from Busselton to Dunsborough (four per day, Monday to Saturday).

TRAIN

Bunbury is the terminus of the Australind train line, with twice-daily services to Perth ($29, 2½ hours).

Geographe Bay

Turquoise waters and white sands are the defining features of this gorgeous bay, lined with 30km of excellent swimming beaches.

Positioned between the Indian Ocean and a sea of wine, the beachside towns of Busselton and Dunsborough attract hordes of holidaymakers seeking to spend their vacations with sand between their toes and a glass between their lips.

BUNBURY
POP 66,100

The southwest's only city is struggling to remake its image from that of an industrial port into a seaside-holiday destination. It still isn't particularly interesting or attractive, but it is an important gateway to the area.

Sights & Activities

TOP CHOICE Dolphin Discovery Centre   DOLPHIN WATCHING
(08-9791 3088; www.dolphindiscovery.com.au; Koombana Beach; adult/child $10/5; ⊙9am-2pm Jun-Sep, 8am-4pm Oct-May) Around 60 bottlenose dolphins live in the bay year-round, their numbers increasing to 260 in summer. This centre has a beachside zone where dolphins regularly come to interact with people in the shallows and you can wade in alongside them, under the supervision of trained volunteers.

If you want to up your chances, there are 1½-hour Eco Cruises (adult/child $53/35; ⊙11am year-round, plus 1pm Oct & May, 3pm Nov-Apr) and three-hour Swim Encounter Cruises (cruises $185; ⊙8am Oct-Apr, noon May-Nov).

Big Swamp Wildlife Park   ZOO
(Prince Philip Dr; adult/child $8/5; ⊙10am-5pm) A parrot with the broadest Aussie accent greets you with a cheery 'Hullo, how ya goin';. Meanwhile, in the big walk-through aviary, his inquisitive cousins swoop onto shoulders, making cartoon pirates out of unwary visitors.

FREE Bunbury Regional Art Galleries   ART GALLERY
(www.brag.org.au; 64 Wittenoom St; ⊙10am-4pm) Housed in a restored pink-painted convent (1897), this excellent gallery has a collection that includes works by Australian art luminaries Arthur Boyd and Sidney Nolan.

Sleeping & Eating

Mantra   APARTMENTS $$
(08-9721 0100; www.mantra.com.au; 1 Holman St; apt from $179; ❄@🖥🏊) One of the most unusual heritage conversions we've seen, the Mantra has sculpted a set of modern studio to three-bedroom apartments out of four listed grain silos by the harbour.

Dolphin Retreat YHA   HOSTEL $
(08-9792 4690; www.dolphinretreatbunbury. com.au; 14 Wellington St; dm/s/d $27/47/68; @) Just around the corner from the beach, this small hostel is well located in a rabbit warren of an old house, with hammocks and a barbecue on the back verandah.

Benesse   CAFE $
(83 Victoria St; mains $10-18; ⊙7.30am-5.30pm) Chic and petite, Benesse is the best of Bunbury's cafes, serving tasty toasties, salads, pizza and all-day breakfasts.

Information

Visitor centre (08-9792 7205; www.visitbunbury.com.au; Carmody Pl; ⊙9am-5pm Mon-Sat, 9.30am-4.30pm Sun)

BUSSELTON
POP 15,400

Unpretentious, uncomplicated and with a slightly faded charm, family-friendly Busselton is surrounded by calm waters and white-sand beaches. During school holidays it really bustles – the population increases fourfold and accommodation prices soar.

Sights & Activities

Busselton Jetty   JETTY
(08-9754 0900; www.busseltonjetty.com.au; adult/child $2.50/free) By the time you're reading this, Busselton's 1865 timber-piled jetty, which holds the distinction of being the longest of its kind in the southern hemisphere (1841m), should have reopened to the public following a $27-million refurbishment. Once it has, its little train (adult/child $10/5) will once again chug along to the Underwater Observatory (adult/child incl train $28/14; ⊙9am-4.25pm), where tours take place 8m below the surface; bookings essential.

Dive Shed   DIVING
(08-9754 1615; www.diveshed.com.au; 21 Queen St) Runs regular dive charters to Four Mile Reef (a 40km limestone ledge about 6.5km off the coast) and to the scuttled navy vessel HMAS *Swan* off Dunsborough.

Festivals & Events

Southbound   MUSIC
(www.southboundfestival.com.au) Start the new year with three days of alternative music and camping.

CinéfestOZ   CINEMA
(www.cinefestoz.com.au) Busselton briefly morphs into St Tropez with this oddly glamorous festival of French and Australian cinema; late August.

🛏 Sleeping

Busselton is packed in the holidays and pretty much deserted off-season. Accommodation sprawls along the beach for several kilometres either side of the town, so make sure you check the location if you don't have your own wheels.

Beachlands Holiday Park CARAVAN PARK $
(📞1800 622 107; www.beachlands.net; 10 Earnshaw Rd, West Busselton; sites per 2 people $42, chalets from $130; ❋🛜🐕) Part of the Big4 chain, this excellent family-friendly park offers a wide range of accommodation amongst shady trees.

Observatory Guesthouse B&B $$
(📞08-9751 3336; www.observatory-guesthouse. com; 7 Brown St; s/d $110/135) The four bright, cheerful rooms at this friendly B&B aren't overly big, but you can spread out on the communal sea-facing balcony and front courtyard.

🍴 Eating

Newtown House MODERN AUSTRALIAN $$$
(📞08-9755 4485; www.newtownhouse.com.au; 737 Bussell Hwy, Abbey; mains $40-44; ⊘breakfast Sat & Sun, lunch & dinner Wed-Sat) Set amid green lawns, this early settler residence (1851), 10km west of town, has a hefty reputation based on the best-quality regional ingredients. There's also B&B accommodation ($225).

Goose CAFE $$
(📞08-9754 7700; www.thegoose.com.au; Geographe Bay Rd; breakfast $14-24, lunch $20-38, dinner $29-39; ⊘breakfast, lunch & dinner Wed-Sun; 🛜) This stylish cafe offers an eclectic, interesting menu and views out to sea.

ℹ Information

Visitor centre (📞08-9752 1288; www.geo graphebay.com; 38 Peel Tce; ⊘9am-5pm Mon-Fri, to 4pm Sat & Sun)

DUNSBOROUGH
POP 3400

Smaller and less sprawling than Busselton, Dunsborough is a relaxed, beach-worshipping town that goes bonkers towards the end of November when 7000 'schoolies' descend. When it's not inundated with drunken, squealing teenagers, it's a thoroughly pleasant place to be. The beaches are better than Busselton's, but accommodation is more limited.

🏃 Activities

Cape Dive DIVING
(📞08-9756 8778; www.capediveexperience.com; 222 Naturaliste Tce) There is great diving in

Geographe Bay, especially since decommissioned destroyer HMAS *Swan* was purpose-scuttled in 1997 for use as a dive wreck.

Naturaliste Charters WHALE WATCHING
(📞08-9725 8511; www.whales-australia.com; adult/child $75/45; ⊘10am Sep-Dec) Two-hour whale-watching cruises.

🛏 Sleeping

There are many options for self-contained rentals in town depending on the season; the visitor centre has current listings.

Dunsborough Beachouse YHA HOSTEL $
(📞08-9755 3107; www.dunsboroughbeachouse. com.au; 205 Geographe Bay Rd; dm $30-32, s/d $53/76; @🛜) On the Quindalup beachfront, this friendly hostel has lawns stretching languidly to the water's edge; it's an easy 2km cycle from the centre.

🍴 Eating & Drinking

Food Farmacy FUSION $$
(📞08-9759 1877; www.thefoodfarmacy.com.au; Dunn Bay Rd; mains $35-47; ⊘dinner Thu-Mon) Chef Simon Beaton dispenses innovative fare from this cool little restaurant. Asian flavours are to the fore, combining with the best of local produce. The pharmacy theme plays out in tasters and drinks served in flasks and test tubes.

Malt BAR $$
(www.maltmarket.com.au; 26 Dunn Bay Rd; mains $18-28; ⊘4pm-late) Malt ticks all the boxes for what you'd want in a beach-town bar: cool but not pretentious, comfy couches, board games, regular live bands, a fireplace for winter and an upstairs terrace for summer. Also serves excellent pizzas.

ℹ Information

Visitor centre (📞08-9755 3517; www.geo graphebay.com; Seymour Blvd; ⊘9am-5pm)

CAPE NATURALISTE

Northwest of Dunsborough, Cape Naturaliste Rd leads to the excellent beaches of Meelup, Eagle Bay and Bunker Bay, and on to Cape Naturaliste. Bunker Bay is also home to **Bunkers Beach Cafe** (www.bunkersbeachcafe. com.au; Farm Break Lane; breakfast $12-19, lunch $16-36; ⊘breakfast & lunch Thu-Mon, daily summer), which serves an adventurous menu from a spot only metres from the sand.

The **Cape Naturaliste lighthouse** (adult/child $12/6), built in 1903, can be visited on tours leaving every 30 minutes from 9.30am to 4pm. **Above and Below** (adult/child $27/14) packages are available, combined with entry to Ngilgi Cave near Yallingup.

Margaret River Wine Region

With its blissful country roads shaded by mature trees, its crashing surf beaches, and, of course, its excellent Chardonnays and Bordeaux-style reds, Margaret River is our favourite Australian wine region and a highlight of any trip to WA. Of course, where there's fine wine, fancy restaurants surely follow – and cheese shops, and chocolate shops, and art galleries and craft stores. Margaret River has all of the predictable trappings of gentrification, yet it still seems to remember that it's in the country, not some swanky corner of Subiaco. The local pub keeps it real and, for the most part, wineries don't charge for tastings.

There are a huge number of tour companies operating in Margaret River; see the visitor centre for all options.

YALLINGUP & AROUND
POP 1070

Beachside Yallingup is as much a mecca for salty-skinned surfers as it is for wine aficionados. You're permitted to let a 'wow' escape when the surf-battered coastline first comes into view. Romantics may be encouraged to know that the name Yallingup means 'place of love'.

◉ Sights & Activities

FREE Wardan Cultural Centre   INDIGENOUS CULTURE
(☑08-9756 6566; www.wardan.com.au; Injidup Springs Rd; adult/child $15/8; ☉Sun, Mon, Wed & Fri, closed 15 Jun–15 Aug) Offers experiences such as stone tool–making, boomerang and spear throwing and guided bushwalks exploring Wardandi spirituality and the uses of plants for food, medicine and shelter.

Ngilgi Cave   CAVE
(☑08-9755 2152; www.geographebay.com; Yallingup Caves Rd; adult/child $19/10; ☉9.30am-4.30pm) Between Dunsborough and Yallingup, this 500,000-year-old cave is known for its limestone formations. Entry is by semiguided tours, which depart every half-hour. More adventurous caving options are also offered.

🛏 Sleeping

Smiths Beach Resort   RESORT $$$
(☑08-9750 1200; www.smithsbeachresort.com.au; Smiths Beach Rd; apt from $220; ❋❄) A large complex of tastefully plush one- to

four-bedroom apartments by a very beautiful beach.

Yallingup Beach Holiday Park   CARAVAN PARK $
(☑08-9755 2164; www.yallingupbeach.com.au; Valley Rd; sites per 2 people $32, cabins $100-150; 🐾) You'll sleep to the sound of the surf here, with the beach just across the road from the rolling lawns.

Empire Retreat   SPA HOTEL $$$
(☑08-9755 2065; www.empireretreat.com; Caves Rd; ste $260-550; ❋🐾) Everything about the intimate Empire Retreat is stylish, from the Indonesian-inspired design to the attention to detail and the service.

✗ Eating & Drinking

Lamont's   WINERY, RESTAURANT $$$
(☑08-9755 2434; www.lamonts.com.au; Gunyulgup Valley Dr; mains $39-41; ☉lunch daily, dinner Sat) Raised on stilts over its own lake, Lamont's is an idyllic spot for lunch or tapas, with a glass of wine, naturally. Afterwards you can wander next door to the Gunyulgup Galleries (www.gunyulgupgalleries.com.au; ☉10am-5pm), showcasing contemporary WA art.

COWARAMUP & WILYABRUP
POP 990

Cowaramup is little more than a couple of blocks of shops lining Bussell Hwy. That a significant percentage of those are devoted in one way or another to eating or drinking is testament to its position at the heart of the wine region. The rustic area to the north-west known as Wilyabrup is where, in the 1960s, the Margaret River wine industry was born.

🛏 Sleeping

Noble Grape Guesthouse   B&B $$
(☑08-9755 5538; www.noblegrape.com.au; 29 Bussell Hwy, Cowaramup; s $130-150, d $150-165; ❋) More like an upmarket motel than a traditional B&B, Noble Grape's rooms offer a sense of privacy and each has a little courtyard as well as a microwave and a DVD player.

✗ Eating & Drinking

Vasse Felix   WINERY, RESTAURANT $$$
(☑08-9756 5050; www.vassefelix.com.au; cnr Caves Rd & Harmans Rd South; mains $35-39; ☉lunch) Vasse is considered to have the finest restaurant in the region. The grounds are peppered with sculpture, while the gallery displaying works from the Holmes à Court collection is worth a trip in itself. And, of course, the much-lauded and -awarded wine is magnificent.

Margaret River

🛏 Sleeping
1 Bridgefield.....................................C2
2 Margaret River Lodge YHA.................B4
3 Prideau's.......................................C3
4 Riverglen Chalets............................C1
5 Vintages..C3

🍴 Eating
6 Blue Ginger....................................C4

🍷 Drinking
7 Must..C2
8 Urban Bean.....................................C3

🍸 Drinking
9 Settler's Tavern..............................C3

🛍 Shopping
10 Tunbridge
   Gallery..C3

Knee Deep in Margaret River
WINERY, RESTAURANT $$

(☎08-9755 6776; www.kneedeepwines.com.au; 61 Johnson Rd; mains $32-37; ☺lunch) Only a handful of mains are offered – with locally sourced, seasonal produce to the fore – and the open-sided pavilion amongst the vines provides a pleasantly intimate setting. The attention to detail is impressive, both in the flavours and in the service.

🍷 Cullen Wines
WINERY, RESTAURANT $$

(☎08-9755 5277; www.cullenwines.com.au; 4323 Caves Rd; mains $32-36; ☺lunch) Cullen continues to break ground with a commitment to organic and biodynamic principles, which extends from the winery to the restaurant.

The food is excellent – fresh, local and very seasonal.

Clairault
WINERY, RESTAURANT $$$

(☑08-9755 6655; www.clairaultwines.com.au; 3277 Caves Rd; mains $35-39; ⊙lunch Thu-Mon Easter-Oct, daily Nov-Easter) A contemporary building of timber and corrugated iron amid vineyards and eucalypts, with an eclectic, appealing menu.

Brookland Valley & Flutes Restaurant
WINERY, RESTAURANT $$$

(☑08-9755 6250; www.flutes.com.au; Caves Rd; mains $34-44; ⊙lunch Thu-Mon, daily summer) A large producer whose wines include the widely exported Verse 1 range. The restaurant sits over a pretty lake formed by a dam on a bubbling stream.

Margaret River Regional Wine Centre
WINE SHOP

(www.mrwines.com; 9 Bussell Hwy, Cowaramup; ⊙10am-7pm) A one-stop shop for Margaret River wine, this helpful store offers daily tastings rotating around a dozen smaller wineries that don't operate cellar doors.

Bootleg Brewery
BREWERY

(www.bootlegbrewery.com.au; off Yelverton Rd; ⊙11am-6pm) Bills itself as 'an oasis of beer in a desert of wine'. Serves food and hosts live bands on Saturday.

Margaret River Chocolate Company
CHOCOLATE

(www.chocolatefactory.com.au; Harman's Mill Rd; ⊙9am-5pm) Perpetually frantic. You can watch truffles being made, sample chocolate buttons, grab a coffee or let the kids burn off their sugar rushes outside. The building itself looks edible.

MARGARET RIVER
POP 4500

Although tourists might outnumber locals much of the time, Margaret River still feels like a country town. The advantage of basing yourself here is that after 5pm, once the surrounding wineries shut up shop, it's one of the few places with any vital signs.

🛏 Sleeping

TOP CHOICE Margaret River Lodge YHA   HOSTEL $

(☑08-9757 9532; www.mrlodge.com.au; 220 Railway Tce; dm $25-29, r with/without bathroom $74/62; @🛜🏊) About 1.5km south-west of the town centre, this is a clean, well-run hostel. It's divided into two distinct sections: one with dorms and a big communal kitchen;

and a quieter space with private rooms and its own little kitchen.

Riverglen Chalets
APARTMENTS $$

(☑08-9757 2101; www.riverglenchalets.com.au; Carters Rd; chalets $155-280; 🛠🛜) Just north of town, these good-value and very comfortable timber chalets are spacious and fully self-contained, with verandahs looking out onto bushland; there's wheelchair access to a couple of them.

Prideau's
MOTEL $$

(☑0438 587 180; www.prideaus.com.au; 31 Fearn Ave; r $145-185; 🛠🛜) At this price and in such a central location, you'd expect a fairly middling sort of motel, which is what Prideau's looks like from the outside. But step through the door and you'll find sharp, newly renovated units opening on to little courtyards.

Bridgefield
B&B $$

(☑08-9757 3007; www.bridgefield.com.au; 73 Bussell Hwy; r $130-160; 🛜) A 19th-century coach house, this lovely higgledy-piggledy B&B is all wood panels, high ceilings, tiled floors and ancient claw-foot baths.

Vintages
MOTEL $$

(☑08-9758 8333; www.vintagesmargaretriver.com.au; cnr Willmott Ave & Le Souef St; r $137-222; 🛠) Another swanky motel, this one is set in tropical gardens. It's close to the centre of town, but all rooms are double-glazed, so noise won't be a problem.

🍴 Eating & Drinking

Settler's Tavern
PUB

(www.settlerstavern.com; 114 Bussell Hwy; ⊙11am-midnight Mon-Sat, to 10pm Sun) There's live entertainment most nights at Settler's, so settle in for the evening with good pub grub and a wine from the extensive list.

Must
RESTAURANT, BAR $$

(☑08-9758 8877; www.must.com.au; 107 Bussell Hwy; mains $30-38, 2-/3-course lunch $33/44; ⊙lunch & dinner) The sister property to one of our favourite Perth restaurants, Must doesn't disappoint. The service is excellent and the charcuterie plates are legendary. If you can't bear the thought of leaving, there are four bedrooms upstairs (per night $180).

Blue Ginger
CAFE, DELI $

(www.bluegingerfinefoods.com; 31 Station Rd; mains $11-17; ⊙breakfast & lunch) Ease into the colourful, mismatched furniture on the enclosed terrace and tuck into hearty cafe fare with some adventurous twists.

SURFING THE SOUTHWEST

Known to surfers as 'Yals' (around Yallingup) and 'Margs' (around the mouth of the Margaret River), the beaches between Capes Naturaliste and Leeuwin offer powerful reef breaks, mainly left-handers.

Around Dunsborough, the better locations are between Eagle and Bunker Bays. Near Yallingup there's the Three Bears, Rabbits (a beach break towards the north of Yallingup Beach), Yallingup, Injidup Car Park and Injidup Point. You'll need a 4WD to access Guillotine/Gallows, north of Gracetown. Also around Gracetown are Huzza's, South Point and Lefthanders. The annual surfer pro is held around Margaret River Mouth and Southside ('Suicides').

Pick up a surfing map ($5.25) from one of the visitor centres on the way through.

Urban Bean   CAFE $
(157 Bussell Hwy; mains $9-18; ☺breakfast & lunch) A funky little place serving bleary-eyed locals their first daily brew and making fresh things for lunch.

🛍 Shopping

Tunbridge Gallery   INDIGENOUS ART
(www.tunbridgegallery.com.au; 1st fl, 139 Bussell Hwy; ☺10am-5pm Mon-Sat, to 3pm Sun) Excellent Aboriginal gallery featuring mainly WA works.

ℹ Information

Visitor centre (☎08-9780 5911; www.margaretriver.com; 100 Bussell Hwy; ☺9am-5pm)

ℹ Getting Around

Margaret River Beach Bus (☎08-9757 9532; www.mrlodge.com.au) Minibus heading between the township and the beaches around Prevelly ($10, thrice daily); summer only, bookings essential.

AROUND MARGARET RIVER

West of the township, the coastline provides spectacular surfing and walks. Prevelly is the main settlement, with a scattering of places to sleep and eat.

👁 Sights & Activities

Caveworks & Lake Cave   CAVE
(www.margaretriver.com; Conto Rd; ☺9am-5pm) Acting as the main ticket office for Lake, Mammoth and Jewel Caves, Caveworks also has excellent displays. Directly behind the centre is **Lake Cave** (adult/child $20/10; ☺tours hourly 9.30am-3.30pm), where limestone formations are reflected in the still waters of an underground stream.

Mammoth Cave   CAVE
(Caves Rd; adult/child $20/10; ☺9am-4pm) Mammoth Cave boasts fossil remains and the impressive Mammoth Shawl formation.

Visits are self-guided; an MP3 audio player is provided.

Calgardup & Giants Caves   CAVES
(Caves Rd) These two self-guided caves are managed by DEC, which provides helmets and torches. **Calgardup Cave** (adult/child $15/8; ☺9am-4.15pm) has a seasonal underground lake. **Giants Cave** (adult/child $10/5; ☺9.30am-3.30pm school & public holidays only), further south, is deeper and longer.

Ellensbrook Homestead   HISTORIC BUILDING
(www.ntwa.com.au; Ellensbrook Rd; adult/child $4/2; ☺10am-4pm Sat & Sun) National Trust-owned Ellensbrook (1857) was the home of pioneer settlers and later served as an Aboriginal mission. The house is more than a little ramshackle, constructed of paperbark, driftwood, timber, lime, dung and hair. A short walk leads to **Meekadarribee** (bathing place of the moon), a grotto set below trickling rapids.

Boranup Drive   FOREST ROAD
If you're enjoying the tall trees of Caves Rd (Rte 250), you'll absolutely love this 14km diversion along an unsealed road through beautiful karri forest. Near the south end there's a lookout offering sea views.

Eagles Heritage   WILDLIFE CENTRE
(☎08-9757 2960; www.eaglesheritage.com.au; adult/child $13/6.50; ☺10am-5pm) Housing Australia's largest collection of raptors, this centre, 5km south of Margaret River, has free-flight displays at 11am and 1.30pm.

🛏 Sleeping

Surfpoint   HOSTEL $
(☎08-9757 1777; www.surfpoint.com.au; Reidle Dr, Gnarabup; dm/d $25/80; @🏊) This light and airy place offers the beach on a budget.

MANJIMUP

If you want to learn more about how the world's most expensive produce is harvested, follow your snout to the **Wine & Truffle Co** (☑08-9777 2474; www.wineandtruffle.com.au; Seven Day Rd; mains $20-33; ☺10am-4.30pm). You can join a 2½-hour truffle hunt ($95 per person; book ahead), taste wines and end with a wonderful meal.

The rooms are clean and well presented and there's a very enticing little pool.

National Park campgrounds CAMPGROUNDS **$** (www.dec.wa.gov.au; sites per adult/child $7/2) DEC has three basic campgrounds within Leeuwin-Naturaliste National Park: **Conto** (Conto Rd), **Boranup** (off Boranup Dr) and **Point Rd**.

✗ Eating & Drinking

TOP CHOICE **McHenry's Farm Shop**   CAFE, BUTCHER **$**
(www.mchv.com.au; 5962 Caves Rd; mains $9-19; ☺lunch Thu-Sun) Serves French rustic food (terrines, soups, stews) on its terrace.

Xanadu   WINERY, RESTAURANT **$$**
(☑08-9758 9531; www.xanaduwines.com; Boodjidup Rd; mains $32-38; ☺lunch) No sign of Olivia Newton John on roller skates, although she could get some speed up circling the central stone hearth in this vast, chic barn.

Voyager Estate   WINERY
(☑08-9757 6354; www.voyagerestate.com.au; Stevens Rd; ☺10am-5pm) The grandest of Margaret River's wineries, Voyager's formal gardens and Cape Dutch–style buildings are capped by a ludicrously oversized Australian flag.

Leeuwin Estate   WINERY
(☑08-9759 0000; www.leeuwinestate.com.au; Stevens Rd; ☺10am-5pm) Behind-the-scenes wine tours and tastings take place at 11am, noon and 3pm (adult/child $12.50/4). Big open-air concerts are regularly held here.

AUGUSTA & AROUND
POP 1700

Augusta is positioned at the mouth of the Blackwood River, 5km north of Cape Leeuwin. There are a few vineyards scattered around, but the vibe here is less epicurean, more languid.

◉ Sights & Activities

Cape Leeuwin   LIGHTHOUSE
(adult/child $5/3; ☺8.45am-4.45pm) Cape Leeuwin, where the Indian and Southern Oceans meet, is the most south-westerly point in Australia and on a wild day you may fear being blown off the edge of the earth. The lighthouse (1896), WA's tallest, offers magnificent views of the coastline. Tours leave on the half-hour from 9am to 4.30pm (adult/child $15/7).

Jewel Cave   CAVE
(Caves Rd; adult/child $20/10; ☺tours hourly 9.30am-3.30pm) The most spectacular of the region's caves, with an impressive 5.9m straw stalactite. It's 8km north of Augusta.

Naturaliste Charters   WHALE WATCHING
(☑08-9725 8511; www.whales-australia.com; adult/child $75/45; ☺10am Jun-Sep) Two-hour whale-watching cruises.

Absolutely Eco River Cruises   CRUISES
(☑08-9758 4003; cdragon@westnet.com.au; adult/child $30/10; Blackwood River; October to May.

Miss Flinders   CRUISES
(☑0409 377 809; adult/child $40/15) Blackwood River; October to May.

◢ Sleeping & Eating

TOP CHOICE **Baywatch Manor YHA**   HOSTEL **$**
(☑08-9758 1290; www.baywatchmanor.com.au; 9 Heppingstone View; dm $25, d with/without bathroom $85/60; @🖳) No sign of David Hasselhoff, just clean, modern rooms with creamy brick walls and bits of antique furniture.

Hamelin Bay Holiday Park   CARAVAN PARK **$**
(☑08-9758 5540; www.mronline.com.au/accom/hamelin; Hamelin Bay West Rd; sites per 2 people $20-25, cabins $80-180) Right on a beautiful beach, north of Augusta, this secluded gem of a place gets very busy at holiday times.

Deckchair Gourmet   CAFE, DELI **$**
(Blackwood Ave; mains $7-16; ☺8.30am-4pm; 🖳) Excellent coffee and delicious food.

❶ Information

Visitor centre (☑08-9758 0166; www.margaretriver.com; cnr Blackwood Ave & Ellis St; ☺9am-5pm)

Southern Forests

The tall forests of WA's south-west are simply magnificent, with towering gums (karri, jarrah, marri) sheltering cool undergrowth. Between the forests, small towns bear witness to the region's history of logging and mining. Many have redefined themselves as small-scale tourist centres where you can take walks, wine tours, canoe trips and trout- and marron-fishing expeditions.

NANNUP
POP 500

Nannup's historic weatherboard buildings and cottage gardens have an idyllic bush setting on the Blackwood River. The Noongar-derived name means 'a place to stop and rest', which indeed it still is, although it's also a good base for bushwalkers and canoeists. Blackwood River Canoeing (☑08-9756 1209; www.black woodrivercanoeing.com; from $18) provides equipment, basic instruction and transfers for paddle-powered excursions.

Sporadic but persistent stories of sightings of a striped wolflike animal, dubbed the Nannup tiger, have led to hopes that a thylacine (Tasmanian tiger) may have survived in the surrounding bush (the last known one died in Hobart Zoo in 1936). Keep your camera handy and your eyes peeled!

The Nannup Music Festival (www.nannup musicfestival.org) is held in early March, focusing on folk and world music.

🛏 Sleeping & Eating

Holberry House　　　　B&B $$
(☑08-9756 1276; www.holberryhouse.com; 14 Grange Rd; r $110-190; 🖥🐾) The decor might lean towards granny-chic, but this large house on the hill has charming hosts and comfortable rooms and is surrounded by large gardens dotted with quirky sculpture (open to nonguests for $4).

Visitor Centre Caravan Park　　　　CARAVAN PARK $$
(☑08-9756 1211; www.nannupwa.com; 4 Brockman St; sites s/d from $15/25, cabins $66-77) Contact the visitor centre.

Nannup Bridge Cafe　　　　CAFE $$
(1 Warren Rd; lunch $16-27, dinner $25-37; ☺lunch Tue-Sun, dinner Wed-Sat) Right opposite the tourist office, this cool-looking riverfront cafe morphs into a bistro at night.

❶ Information

Visitor centre (☑08-9756 1211; www.nannup wa.com; 4 Brockman St; ☺10am-4pm) Administers the neighbouring caravan park.

BALINGUP & GREENBUSHES
POP BALINGUP 450 & GREENBUSHES 342

It's like 1967 never ended in trippy Balingup, where coloured flags, scarecrows and murals of fairies and toadstools line the main street. Aside from the fun of spotting the occasional deodorant-challenged neohippy, the main reason to stop is to rummage around eclectic stores such as the Old Cheese Factory (Nannup Rd; ☺9.30am-4pm), which sells more knick-knacks than you could poke a fridge magnet at. The visitor centre (☑08-9764 1818; www.balinguptourism. com.au; South Western Hwy; ☺10am-4pm) is on the main street.

Greenbushes is a historic mining and timber township, 10km to the south. Some decaying buildings from the boom days line the road, and heritage memorabilia is dotted through town.

BRIDGETOWN
POP 2400

Spread around the Blackwood River and surrounded by karri forests and farmland, Bridgetown is one of the loveliest little towns in the south-west. Despite being busy most weekends, and overrun with visitors on the second weekend of November during its annual Blues at Bridgetown Festival (www.bluesatbridgetown.com), it retains a community feel.

PERTH & WESTERN AUSTRALIA SOUTHERN FORESTS

ELVIS SIGHTED IN BOYUP BROOK

The pretty township of Boyup Brook (population 540), 31km northeast of Bridgetown, is the centre of country music in WA. The fantastically over-the-top Harvey Dickson's Country Music Centre (www.harveydickson.com. au; adult/child $5/2; ☺9am-5pm) comes complete with a life-size Elvis, an Elvis room and three 13.5m-tall guitar-playing men. It hosts regular rodeos (the big one's in October) and big-name country-music events, as well as the WA Country Music Festival (www. countrymusicwa.com.au) in February. Scenic but basic bush camping (sites $8) is always available.

🛏 Sleeping & Eating

Bridgetown Hotel   PUB $$
(☑08-9761 1034; www.bridgetownhotel.com.au;
157 Hampton St; r $165-265, mains $17-29; ❄)
You don't expect quirky pizzas (lime and
tequila, lamb and tzatziki) to be served in
an Australian country pub and neither do
you expect large, modern bedrooms with
spa baths, but a recent revamp has left this
1920s gem with both.

Bridgetown Riverside
Chalets   RENTAL HOUSES $$
(☑08-9761 1040; www.bridgetownchalets.com.
au; 1338 Brockman Hwy; chalets $115-175) In a
peaceful riverside property, 5km up the
road to Nannup, these four stand-alone
wooden chalets sleep up to six in two
bedrooms.

Nelsons of Bridgetown   MOTEL $$
(☑08-9761 1645; www.nelsonsofbridgetown.
com.au; 38 Hampton St; s $95-135, d $115-195;
❄🛜🏊) The central location is great, but
go for the spacious new rooms built to
the side of this 1898 Federation-style
hotel.

Cidery   BREWERY
(www.thecidery.com.au; 43 Gifford Rd; ⊙11am-
4pm Sat-Thu, to 7.30pm Fri) Brews its own
cider and beer and serves them, along
with light lunches, on outdoor tables by
the river.

ℹ Information

Visitor centre (☑08-9761 1740; www.
bridgetown.com.au; 154 Hampton St; ⊙9am-
5pm Mon-Fri, 10am-3pm Sat, 10am-1pm Sun; @)

PEMBERTON
POP 760

Hidden deep in the karri forests, drowsy
Pemberton has taken an epicurean turn,
producing excellent wine that rivals Margaret River's for quality if not scale. Wine
tourism isn't as developed here, with some
of the better names only offering tastings by
appointment; grab a free map listing opening hours from the visitor centre.

The national parks circling Pemberton
are impressive. Aim to spend a day or two
driving the Karri Forest Explorer, walking the trails and picnicking in the green
depths.

◉ Sights & Activities

Salitage   WINERY
(☑08-9776 1195; www.salitage.com.au; Vasse Hwy;
⊙10am-4pm) Salitage's Pinot Noir has been
rated the state's best, while its Chardonnay
and Sauvignon Blanc are also very highly
regarded. Hour-long vineyard tours leave at
11am; call ahead.

Pemberton Tramway   SCENIC RIDES
(☑08-9776 1322; www.pemtram.com.au; adult/
child $18/9; ⊙10.45am & 2pm) Built between
1929 and 1933, the route travels through
lush karri and marri forests to Warren
River, with occasional photo stops.

Pemberton Wine Centre   WINE TASTING
(www.marima.com.au; 388 Old Vasse Rd; ⊙noon-
5pm) At the very heart of Warren National
Park, this attractive centre offers tastings
of most local wines and can put together a
mixed case of your favourites.

WORTH A TRIP

KARRI FOREST EXPLORER

Punctuated by glorious walks, magnificent individual trees, picnic areas and lots of interpretive signage, this tourist drive wends its way along 86km of scenic (partly unsealed)
roads through three national parks (vehicle entry $11).

Its popular attractions include the Gloucester Tree; if you're feeling fit and fearless,
make the 58m climb to the top. The Dave Evans Bicentennial Tree, tallest of the
'climbing trees' at 68m, is in Warren National Park, 11km south of Pemberton. The Bicentennial Tree one-way loop leads via Maiden Bush to the Heartbreak Trail. It passes
through 250-year-old karri stands, and nearby Drafty's Camp and Warren Campsite are
great for overnighting (sites $7/2 per adult/child).

The enchanting Beedelup National Park, 15km west of Pemberton on the Vasse
Hwy (Rte 104), shouldn't be missed. There's a short, scenic walk that crosses Beedelup
Brook near Beedelup Falls. North of town, Big Brook Arboretum (admission free)
features big trees from all over the world.

The track loops on and off the main roads, so you can drive short sections at a time.
Pick up a brochure from Pemberton's visitor centre.

D'ENTRECASTEAUX NATIONAL PARK

This quiet gem of a national park (entry per car/motorcycle $11/5), named for French Admiral Bruny d'Entrecasteaux, who led an exploratory expedition here in 1792, stretches for 130km along the coast 60km south of Pemberton. It's a complete contrast to the tall forests, with its five rivers and wild stretches of coastal heath, sand dunes, cliffs and beaches.

Sealed roads lead to Windy Harbour, a collection of ramshackle holiday shacks with names like 'Wywurk', where you can camp as long as you have all your own provisions. From here, D'Entrecasteaux Dr continues for 6km to Point d'Entrecasteaux, or a 3km wild and windy coastal walk will get you to the same place.

A series of 4WD tracks leads in from the Pemberton–Northcliffe Rd to bush and beach camp sites; check with the DEC in Pemberton that the roads are open.

☞ Tours

Pemberton Hiking & Canoeing   HIKING, CANOEING
(✆08-9776 1559; www.hikingandcanoeing. com.au) Runs tours in Warren and D'Entrecasteaux National Parks and to the Yeagarup sand dunes.

Pemberton Discovery Tours   4WD
(✆08-9776 0484; www.pembertondiscoverytours. com.au; adult/child $90/50) Operates half-day 4WD tours to the Yeagarup sand dunes and the Warren River mouth.

Donnelly River Cruises   BOAT
(✆08-9777 1018; www.donnellyrivercruises.com. au; adult/child $55/35) Runs cruises through D'Entrecasteaux National Park.

⌨ Sleeping

Pemberton has some excellent accommodation choices but less in the way of eateries. The local specialities are trout and marron, which make their way onto most menus.

TOP CHOICE Old Picture Theatre Holiday Apartments   APARTMENTS $$
(✆08-9776 1513; www.oldpicturetheatre.com. au; cnr Ellis & Guppy Sts; apt $150-300; ✻) The town's old cinema has been revamped into well-appointed, self-contained, spacious apartments with lots of jarrah detail and black-and-white movie photos. It offers terrific value for money, and the guest laundry and spa are rare treats.

Pemberton Breakaway Cottages   COTTAGES $$
(✆08-9776 1580; www.pembreak.com.au; Roberts Rd; cottages $130-300; ✻) Choose between very nice, simple karri cottages – which are already a step above the average at this price

range – or leap to the top of the ladder with the luxury eco-chalets. The latter are light and airy, with elegant, contemporary decor, eco-conscious waste-water systems and a solar-passive design.

Pemberton Backpackers YHA   HOSTEL $
(✆08-9776 1105; www.yha.com.au; 7 Brockman St; dm/s/d $27/42/65; @) The main hostel is given over to seasonal workers, so you'll need to check in here for a room in the separate cottage (8 Dean St) that's set aside for travellers. It's cute and cosy, but you'll need to book ahead as it only has three rooms, one of which is a six-person dorm.

Salitage Suites   COTTAGES $$$
(✆08-9776 1195; www.salitagesuites.citysearch. com.au; Vasse Hwy; d/q $250/350) Hidden away amongst tall trees, these four modern wooden cottages offer supreme privacy and luxury. Their mirrored design, with two spacious bedrooms separated by a communal lounge, makes them perfect for two couples.

❶ Information

DEC (✆08-9776 1207; Kennedy St; ⊘8am-4.30pm) Stocks the *Pemberton Bushwalks* brochure ($3.30).

Visitor centre (✆08-9776 1133; www.pember tonvisitor.com.au; Brockman St; ⊘9am-5pm)

SHANNON NATIONAL PARK

Until 1968, 535-sq-km Shannon National Park (entry per car/motorcycle $11/5) was the site of WA's biggest timber mill, and plants including northern hemisphere deciduous trees are reminders of the old settlement.

The 48km Great Forest Trees Drive is a one-way loop, split by the highway – tune in to 100FM for a commentary. Start at the park day-use area on the north of the highway. From here there's an easy 3.5km walk to Shannon Dam (via a quokka-observation

deck) and a steeper 5.5km loop to Mokare's Rock, with a boardwalk and great views. Further along, the 8km-return **Great Forest Trees Walk** crosses the Shannon River. Off the southern part of the drive, boardwalks look over stands of giant karri at **Snake Gully** and **Big Tree Grove**.

There is a sizeable **campground** (sites per adult/child $9/2) with showers in the spot where the original timber-milling town used to be. A self-contained bunkhouse, **Shannon Lodge** (per night $66, bond $150), is available for groups of up to eight people; book through DEC in Pemberton.

SOUTH COAST

Standing on the cliffs of the wild south coast as the waves pound below is an elemental experience. And on calm days, when the sea is varied shades of aquamarine and the glorious white-sand beaches lie pristine and welcoming, it's an altogether different type of magnificent. If you're seeking solitude, even busy holiday periods here in the 'Great Southern' are relaxed; it's just that bit too far from Perth for the holiday hordes. Marine visitors come this way, though: the winter months bring a steady stream of migrating whales.

ⓘ Getting There & Away

AIR Skywest (☎1300 660 088; www.skywest.com.au) flies daily from Perth to Albany (70 minutes) and Esperance (1¾ hours). It also flies between Albany and Busselton twice a week.

BUS Transwa (☎1300 662 205; www.transwa.wa.gov.au) services include:

GS1 and GS2 To/from Perth, Mt Barker and Albany daily.

GS3 To/from Bunbury, Bridgetown, Pemberton, Walpole, Denmark and Albany daily.

GE1 Between Perth and Esperance ($83, 10¼ hours, three times weekly).

GE2 To/from Perth, Hyden and Esperance three times weekly.

South Coast

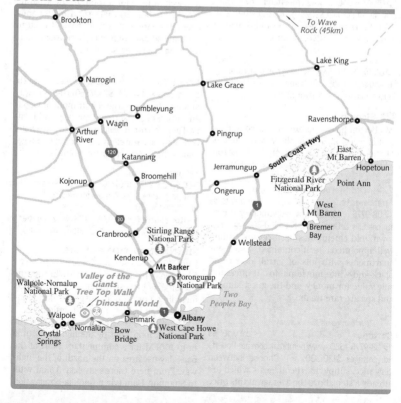

GE3 To/from Kalgoorlie, Coolgardie, Norseman and Esperance.

GE4 Between Albany and Esperance ($62, 6½ hours, twice weekly).

Walpole & Nornalup

POP 320 & 50

The peaceful twin inlets of Walpole and Nornalup make good bases from which to explore the heavily forested Walpole Wilderness Area – an immense wilderness incorporating a rugged coastline, several national parks, marine parks, nature reserves and forest-conservation areas – covering a whopping 3630 sq km (an area considerably bigger than Samoa and 57 other countries). Look for *Exploring the Walpole Wilderness and Surrounding Area* pamphlet produced by DEC.

Walpole is the bigger settlement (though not big enough to get mobile-phone coverage). It's here that the South Western Hwy (Rte 1) becomes the South Coast Hwy.

◉ Sights & Activities

Walpole-Nornalup National Park
NATURE RESERVE

The giant trees of this park include red, yellow and Rates tingle trees and, closer to the coast, the red flowering gum. The **Valley of the Giants Tree Top Walk** (adult/child $10/5; ☺9am-4.15pm) is the main drawcard. A 600m-long ramp rises from the floor of the valley, allowing visitors access high into the tree canopy. At its highest point, the ramp is 40m above the ground. It's on a gentle incline so it's easy to walk and is even accessible by assisted wheelchair. The ramp is an engineering feat in itself, though vertigo sufferers might have a few problems; it's designed to sway gently in the breeze. At ground level, the **Ancient Empire** boardwalk meanders around and through the base of veteran red tingles, some of which are 16m in circumference.

There are numerous good walking tracks around, including a section of the **Bibbulmun Track**, which passes through Walpole

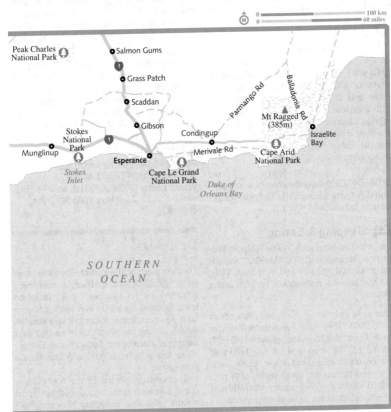

to Coalmine Beach. Scenic drives include **Knoll Drive**, 3km east of Walpole; the **Valley of the Giants Road**; and through pastoral country to **Mount Frankland**. Here you can climb to the summit for panoramic views or walk around the trail at its base. Opposite Knoll Dr, Hilltop Rd leads to a **giant tingle tree**; this road continues to the **Circular Pool** on the Frankland River, a popular canoeing spot. You can hire canoes from Nornalup Riverside Chalets.

Midway between Nornalup and Peaceful Bay, check out **Conspicuous Cliffs**. It's a great spot for whale watching from July to November, with a boardwalk, a hilltop lookout and a steep-ish 800m walk to the beach.

Dinosaur World
WILDLIFE PARK

(Bow Bridge; adult/child $12/6; ⊙9.30am-4.30pm) Replica dinosaur skeletons and information boards have been added to spice up this bird and reptile park, off the South Coast Hwy at Bow Bridge. There are some kangaroos, lizards and snakes, but the many parrots (most with clipped wings) are the stars of the show.

☞ Tours

🏄 WOW Wilderness Ecocruises
RIVER CRUISES

(☑08-9840 1036; www.wowwilderness.com.au; adult/child $40/15) This magnificent landscape and its ecology are brought to life with anecdotes about Aboriginal settlement, salmon fishers and shipwrecked pirates. The 2½-hour cruise through the inlets and river systems leaves daily at 10am; book at the visitor centre.

Naturally Walpole Eco Tours
4WD

(☑08-9840 1019; www.naturallywalpole.com.au) Half-day tours through the Walpole wilderness (adult/child $75/40).

🍴 Sleeping & Eating

For bush-camping sites in the Walpole Wilderness Area (per adult/child $7/2), including at Crystal Springs and Fernhook Falls, use the honesty registration and fee boxes on site.

Riverside Retreat
CHALETS $$

(☑08-9840 1255; www.riversideretreat.com.au; South Coast Hwy, Nornalup; chalets $140-260) Set up off the road and on the banks of the beautiful Frankland River, these well-equipped chalets are great value, with pot-bellied stoves for cosy winter warmth and tennis and canoeing as outdoor pursuits.

Nornalup Riverside Chalets
CHALETS $$

(☑08-9840 1107; www.walpole.org.au/nornalup riversidechalets; Riverside Dr, Nornalup; chalets $85-170) Stay a night in sleepy Nornalup in these comfortable, colourful self-contained chalets, just a rod's throw from the fish in the Frankland River. The chalets are well spaced out, giving a feeling of privacy.

Coalmine Beach
CARAVAN PARK $

(☑08-9840 1026; www.coalminebeach.com.au; Coalmine Beach Rd, Walpole; sites per 2 people $26-30, cabins from $72; ❋ @) You couldn't get a better location than this, under shady trees above the sheltered waters of the inlet.

Walpole Lodge
HOSTEL $

(☑08-9840 1244; www.walpolelodge.com.au; Pier St, Walpole; dm/s/d $26/45/55; @) This popular place is basic, open-plan and informal, with great info boards around the walls and casual, cheery owners.

Tingle All Over YHA
HOSTEL $

(☑08-9840 1041; www.yha.com.au; 60 Nockolds St, Walpole; dm/s $29/51, d $67-79; @) Help yourself to lemons and chillies from the garden of this clean, basic option near the highway.

Thurlby Herb Farm
CAFE $

(www.thurlbyherb.com.au; 3 Gardiner Rd; mains $13-18; ⊙9am-5pm Mon-Fri) Apart from distilling its own essential oils and making herb-based products including soap, Thurlby serves up tasty light lunches and cakes in a pretty cafe overlooking the garden.

❶ Information

DEC (☑08-9840 0400; South Coast Hwy, Walpole; ⊙8am-4.30pm Mon-Fri)

Visitor centre (☑08-9840 1111; www.walpole.com.au; South Coast Hwy, Walpole; ⊙9am-5pm; @)

Denmark
POP 2800

The first wave of alternative lifestylers landed in idyllic Denmark about 20 years ago, attracted by its beaches, river, sheltered inlet, forested backdrop and rolling hinterland. Farmers, ferals, fisherfolk and families mingle during the town's three market days each year (December, January and Easter), when the population and accommodation prices soar.

The town is located in the cool-climate Great Southern wine region and has some notable wineries, including **Howard Park**

(www.howardparkwines.com.au; Scotsdale Rd; ⊙10am-4pm) and Forest Hill (www.foresthill wines.com.au; cnr South Coast Hwy & Myers Rd; ⊙10am-5pm). The latter has an architecturally impressive tasting room and restaurant.

Denmark was established to supply timber to the early goldfields. Known by the Minang Noongar people as Koorabup ('place of the black swan'), there's evidence of early Aboriginal settlement in the 3000-year-old fish traps found in Wilson Inlet.

◉ Sights & Activities

Surfers and anglers usually waste no time in heading to ruggedly beautiful Ocean Beach. If you're keen to try surfing, accredited local instructor Mike Neunuebel gives surf lessons (☑08-9848 2057; 2hr private lessons incl equipment $80).

To get your bearings, walk the Mokare Heritage Trail (3km circuit along the Denmark River) or the Wilson Inlet Trail (12km return, starting at the river mouth), which forms part of the longer Nornalup Trail. Put everything into perspective at Mt Shadforth Lookout, with its view of fine coastal scenery. The lush Mt Shadforth Road, running from the centre of town and finishing up on the South Coast Hwy west of town, makes a great scenic drive, as does the longer pastoral loop of Scotsdale Road. Potter along these, taking your pick of attractions including alpaca farms, wineries, cheese farms, and art and craft galleries.

William Bay National Park, about 20km west of town, offers sheltered swimming in gorgeous Greens Pool and Elephant Rocks, and has good walking tracks. Swing by Bartholomews Meadery for a post-beach treat of homemade ice cream ($4).

☞ Tours

Out of Sight! 4WD
(☑08-9848 2814; www.outofsighttours.com) Nature trips into the Walpole wilderness (adult/child $75/38; three hours), West Cape Howe (adult/child $120/60; six hours) or Stirling Range (adult/child $150/75; eight hours); sightseeing around Denmark (two hours); or guzzling tours of the local wineries (half-/full day $75/95).

Denmark Bike Adventures CYCLING
(☑08-9848 3300; www.denmarkbluewren.com. au) The local YHA offers drop-off, rideback cycling tours.

About 13km west of Walpole, at Crystal Springs, is an 8km gravel road to Mandalay Beach where the *Mandalay*, a Norwegian barque, was wrecked in 1911. Every 10 years or so, as the sand gradually erodes with storms, the wreck eerily appears in shallow water that is walkable at low tide. The beach is glorious, often deserted, and accessed by an impressive boardwalk across sand dunes and cliffs.

Denmark Wine Lovers Tour BUS
(☑0410 423 262; www.denmarkwinelovers.com. au) Full-day winery tours ($95).

🛏 Sleeping

TOP CHOICE Cape Howe Cottages COTTAGES $$
(☑08-9845 1295; www.capehowe.com.au; 322 Tennessee Rd South; cottages $160-270; ❋) If you fancy a remote getaway, these five cottages in bushland south-east of Denmark (off Lower Denmark Rd) make the grade. They're all different, but the best is only 1½km from dolphin-favoured Lowlands Beach and is properly plush.

Sensational Heights B&B $$
(☑08-9840 9000; www.sensationalheightsbandb. com.au; 159 Suttons Rd; r $175-260; ❋🤶) Yep, it's on top of a hill (off Scotsdale Rd) and, yes, the views are sensational. It's a new house, so expect contemporary decor, shiny new fixtures, luxurious linen and very comfy beds.

Denmark Rivermouth Caravan Park CARAVAN PARK $
(☑08-9848 1262; www.denmarkrivermouthcaravan park.com.au; Inlet Dr; sites per 2 people $27, cabins $65-240) Ideally located for nautical pursuits, this park sits beside the Wilson Inlet boat ramp. Some of the units are flash, although they are quite tightly arranged. There's also a playground and kayaks for hire.

Denmark Ocean Beach Holiday Park CARAVAN PARK $
(☑08-9848 1106; www.denmarkobhp.com.au; Ocean Beach Rd; sites per 2 people $26-30, cabins $110-180; ❋) This large, longstanding complex was getting a new reception building, water park and set of stylish units when

we visited. Once the dust settles we're sure it will be much improved. It's just about on the beach, after all.

Spring Bay Villas　　　COTTAGES **$$**
(☎08-9848 1211; www.springbayvillas.com; Ocean Beach Rd; villas from $160) Perfectly peaceful, tidy brick villas near the beach. Some have spa baths.

✗ Eating & Drinking

Denmark Bakery　　　BAKERY **$**
(Strickland St; pies $5-6; ☺7am-5pm) Prize-winning and proud of it; this bakery is an institution because of its pies – and the bread is also good.

Southern End　　　BREWERY, RESTAURANT
(www.denmarkbrewery.com.au; 427 Mt Shadforth Rd; ☺11.30am-4.30pm Thu-Mon) Home to Denmark Brews & Ales ('the brew with a view'), it also serves a wide range of imported beers and local wines on its hilltop terrace.

Bartholomews Meadery　　　ICE CREAM **$**
(www.honeywine.com.au; 2620 South Coast Hwy; ☺9.30am-4.30pm) Great for a post-beach treat of homemade ice cream ($4).

Denmark Hotel　　　PUB
(www.denmarkhotel.com.au; Hollings Rd) Over-looking the river, the local boozer is the hub of nocturnal activity, with live music every Friday night.

❶ Information

Visitor centre (☎08-9848 2055; www.denmark.com.au; 73 South Coast Hwy; ☺9am-5pm) Houses the 'world's largest barometer' in its own custom-made tower.

Albany

POP 25,200

Established shortly before Perth in 1826, the oldest European settlement in the state is now the bustling commercial centre of

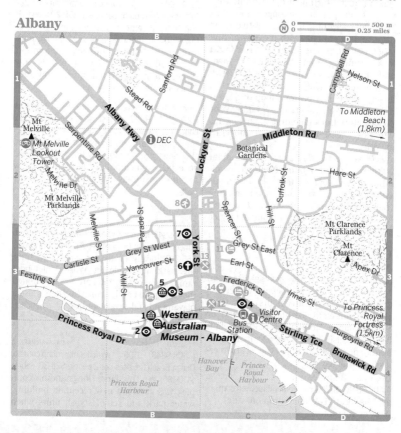

Albany

the southern region. Albany is a mixed bag, comprising a stately and genteelly decaying colonial quarter, a waterfront in the midst of sophisticated redevelopment and a hectic sprawl of malls and fast-food joints. Less ambivalent is its coastline, which is uniformly spectacular.

The Bibbulmun Track ends (or starts) here, just outside the visitor centre.

History

The Minang Noongar people called this place Kinjarling (place of rain) and believed that fighting Wargals (mystical giant serpents) created the fractured landscape. They set up sophisticated fish traps on Oyster Harbour, the remains of which can still be seen.

Initial contacts with Europeans were friendly, with over 60 ships visiting between 1622 and 1826. The establishment of a British settlement here was welcomed at first as it regulated the behaviour of sealers and whalers, who had been responsible for kidnapping, rape and murder. Yet by the end of that century the Minang were a marginalised group, refused entry into every shop in Albany.

Albany's sheltered harbour made it a thriving whaling port. Later it became a coaling station for British ships and during WWI it was the mustering point for ships heading for Egypt and the Gallipoli campaign.

◉ Sights

Middleton & Emu Beaches   BEACHES
Just around the headland east of the town centre, facing King George Sound, these beautiful beaches share one stretch of sand and are perfect for families – both human and cetacean. In winter, you'll often see mother whales and their calves here – sometimes two or three sets at once. Head around Emu Point to Oyster Harbour and there are swimming pontoons and even calmer waters.

Western Australian Museum –
Albany   MUSEUM
(www.museum.wa.gov.au; Residency Rd; admission by donation; ⊙10am-4.30pm Thu-Tue) This branch of the state museum has a kids' discovery section, a lighthouse exhibition and a gallery. It incorporates the 1850s home of the resident magistrate, which tells seafaring stories, explains local natural history and has displays on Minang Noongar history.

Brig Amity   SHIP
(www.historicalbany.com.au; adult/child $6/2; ⊙9.30am-4pm) Next to the museum is a full-scale replica of the brig that carried Albany's first British settlers from Sydney in 1826.

Town Centre   HISTORIC BUILDINGS
Stirling Tce is noted for its Victorian shopfronts, Old Post Office and Courthouse. On York St you'll see St John's Anglican Church and the Town Hall. A guided walking-tour brochure is available from the visitor centre.

Patrick Taylor Cottage   MUSEUM
(www.historicalbany.com.au; 39 Duke St; admission $2; ⊙11am-3pm) Believed to be the oldest colonial dwelling in WA, this 1832 wattle-and-daub cottage is packed with antiques, freaky mannequins and displays on its former residents.

Albany Convict Gaol   MUSEUM
(www.historicalbany.com.au; Stirling Tce; adult/child $5/2.50; ⊙10am-4pm) The old jail was built in 1851 as a hiring depot for ticket-of-leave convicts. In 1872 it was extended and reopened as a civil jail. These days it's a folk museum.

Princess Royal Fortress
HISTORIC SITE

(www.forts.albany.wa.gov.au; Forts Rd, off Marine Dr; adult/child $11/2; ⊙9am-5pm) As Albany was a strategic port, its vulnerability to attack was seen as a potential threat to Australia's security. The restored buildings, gun emplacements and views of this 1893 hilltop fort make a rewarding visit. Particularly poignant are the photos of the troop transports on their way to Gallipoli.

🏃 Activities

After whaling ended in 1978, whales slowly began returning to the waters of Albany. You can usually spot them from the beach from July to mid-October, but if you fancy a closer look, contact one of the operators listed below.

Albany's appeal as a top-class diving destination grew after the 2001 scuttling of the HMAS Perth (www.hmasperth.com.au). Natural reefs feature temperate and tropical corals, and are home to the bizarre leafy and weedy sea dragons. Two-tank dives cost around $190, including equipment.

Albany Dolphin & Whale Cruises
WHALE WATCHING

(☎0428 429 876; www.whales.com.au; adult/child $80/45)

Albany Whale Tours
WHALE WATCHING

(☎08-9845 1068; www.albanywhaletours.com.au; adult/child $75/40)

Southcoast Diving Supplies
DIVING

(☎08-9841 7176; www.divealbany.com.au; 84b Serpentine Rd)

Kalgan Queen
RIVER CRUISES

(☎08-9844 3166; www.albanyaustralia.com; Emu Point; adult/child $65/35; ⊙9am Sep-Jun) Four-hour glass-bottomed boat cruises up the Kalgan River.

🛏 Sleeping

TOP CHOICE Flinders Park Lodge
B&B $$

(☎08-9844 7062; www.parklodge.com.au; cnr Lower King & Harbour Rds, Bayonet Head; r $145-195; 🛜) The restraint of this elegant 1930s white-stucco building is completely thrown off with the exuberant decor of the bedrooms and a host that matches that exuberance measure for measure. The most straightforward way to reach the lodge is to head north on Lockyer St and follow it for 6.5km as it becomes Ulster Rd and then Lower King Rd.

Beach House at Bayside
BOUTIQUE HOTEL $$$

(☎08-9844 8844; www.thebeachhouseatbayside.com.au; 33 Barry Ct, Collingwood Park; r $243-328) Positioned right by the beach and the golf course in a quiet cul-de-sac, midway between Middleton Beach and Emu Point, this modern block engenders a relaxed, clubbish vibe with plenty of opportunity for guest fraternisation. To get here, take Middleton Rd towards Middleton Beach, turn left onto Golf Links Rd and then right into Barry Ct.

My Place
APARTMENTS $$

(☎08-9842 3242; www.myplace.com.au; 47-61 Grey St East; r $120-135; 🌢🛜) We love the (possibly) tongue-in-cheek nana-ish vibe to the studios, with floral duvets and a trio of flying ducks on the wall. The considerably larger one-bedrooms aren't as kooky, but they're all clean, central and excellent value.

Discovery Inn
HOSTEL $

(☎08-9842 5535; www.discoveryinn.com.au; 9 Middleton Rd, Middleton Beach; dm/s $30/55, d $75-80; @) Sitting somewhere between a hostel and a guesthouse, Discovery Inn offers great value and a convivial atmosphere, close to the beach. Guests congregate amidst the tropical plants in the central conservatory.

Emu Beach Holiday Park
CARAVAN PARK $

(☎08-9844 1147; www.emubeach.com; 8 Medcalf Pde, Emu Point; sites for 2 people $32, chalets $85-200; 🌢) Families love the Emu Beach area and this holiday park, close to the beach, has good facilities. Emu Point is reached by taking Golf Links Rd from Middleton Beach.

Middleton Beach Holiday Park
CARAVAN PARK $

(☎08-9841 3593; www.holidayalbany.com.au; 28 Flinders Pde, Middleton Beach; sites per 2 people $34, chalets $115-230; @🌢) This excellent beachfront caravan park is sheltered by high sand dunes (a good thing when a gale is raging). Book early – it's popular.

Albany Backpackers
HOSTEL $

(☎08-9841 8848; www.albanybackpackers.com.au; cnr Stirling Tce & Spencer St; dm/r $27/63; @🛜) With bright murals and a reputation for partying, this old hostel offers extras such as coffee and cake each evening, bike hire and limited free internet access.

Bayview Backpackers YHA
HOSTEL $

(☎08-9842 3388; www.bayviewbackpackers.com.au; 49 Duke St; dm/s/d $24/45/60; @🛜) In a quiet street 400m from the centre, this

rambling backpackers has a lazy feel and is less frenzied than the hostel in town.

Eating & Drinking

Wild Duck　　　　　　　FRENCH **$$**
(☑08-9842 2554; 112 York St; mains $30-40; ☺dinner Wed-Sun) Sophisticated, clever and absolutely food focussed – Wild Duck is one of WA's best regional restaurants. Save room for dessert, which, when we visited, included witty takes on liquorice allsorts, Welsh cakes and fried egg on toast.

York Street Cafe　　　　　　CAFE **$$**
(184 York St; lunch $16-25, dinner $25-33; ☺breakfast & lunch Mon-Sat, dinner Wed-Sat) The food is wonderful at this bright new place on the main strip. Lunch includes pasta, focaccia, schnitzels and deliciously crisp fish balls, while for dinner it turns into more of a bistro.

Bay Merchants　　　　　　　CAFE **$**
(18 Adelaide Cres, Middleton Beach; mains $9-17; ☺6am-6pm) Just a sandy-footed stroll from the beach, this cafe-providore makes good coffee, enticing cakes and to-die-for gourmet sandwiches.

White Star　　　　MICROBREWERY, PUB
(72 Stirling Tce; mains $16-29; ☺lunch & dinner) With 20 beers on tap (including its own brews), excellent pub grub, a beer garden and live music, this old pub gets a gold star.

ℹ Information

DEC (☑08-9842 4500; 120 Albany Hwy; ☺8am-4.30pm Mon-Fri)

Visitor centre (☑08-9841 9290; www.amazing albany.com; Proudlove Pde; ☺9am-5pm)

Around Albany

◉ Sights

Whale World Museum　　　　MUSEUM
(☑08-9844 4019; www.whaleworld.org; Frenchman Bay Rd; adult/child $25/10; ☺9am-5pm) When the Cheynes Beach Whaling Station ceased operations in November 1978, few could have guessed that its gore-covered decks would eventually be covered in tourists, craning to see whales passing within harpoon-shot of the slaughterhouse itself. The museum screens films about marine life and whaling operations, and displays giant skeletons, harpoons, whaleboat models and scrimshaw (etchings on whalebone). Free guided tours depart on the hour from 10am.

Attached to the complex is the Walk on the Wild Side wildlife park (adult/child $10/5), which can also be visited as part of a nocturnal tour (adult/child $35/10) – tour bookings essential.

FREE Torndirrup
National Park　　　　NATIONAL PARK
(Frenchman Bay Rd) Covering much of the peninsula that encloses the southern reaches of King George Sound, this national park is know for its windswept, ocean-bashed cliffs. The Gap is a natural cleft in the rock, channelling blistering surf through giant walls of granite. Close by is the Natural Bridge, a self-explanatory landmark. Further east, the Blowholes can put on a show when the surf is up, worth the 78 steps down and back up.

Steep, rocky, green-water coves such as Jimmy Newells Harbour and Salmon Holes are popular with surfers but quite scary for swimmers. You're better off heading to Misery Beach or Frenchman Bay on the peninsula's sheltered side.

Keen walkers can tackle the hard 10km-return bushwalk (five hours plus) over Isthmus Hill to Bald Head, at the eastern edge of the park.

Two Peoples Bay　　　NATURE RESERVE
(Two Peoples Bay Rd) Some 20km east of Albany, Two Peoples Bay is a 46-sq-km nature reserve with a good swimming beach and scenic coastline. Little of the rest of the reserve is easily accessible.

FREE Waychinicup
National Park　　　　NATIONAL PARK
(Cheyne Beach Rd) DEC operates a campsite (adult/child $7/3) in a beautiful spot by the inlet of the Waychinicup River; vault toilets are provided, but no fresh water is available.

Mount Barker
POP 1770

Mount Barker (50km north of Albany) is the gateway town to Porongurup and Stirling Range National Parks. It's also the hub of an increasingly prestigious wine industry – part of the Great Southern wine region. Plantagenet Wines (www.plantagenetwines. com; Albany Hwy; ☺10am-4.30pm) is conveniently situated right in the middle of town.

The town has been settled since the 1830s and the convict-built 1868 police station and gaol have been preserved as a museum (Albany Hwy; adult/child $5/free; ☺10am-3pm Sat & Sun).

All 78 types and 24 subtypes of Australia's weird and wonderful banksia plant have a home at the **Banksia Farm** (☑08-9851 1770; www.banksiafarm.com.au; Pearce Rd; admission $11; ☺9.30am-4.30pm Mon-Fri Mar-Jun, daily Aug-Nov, closed Jul). Also on offer are a fully guided tour ($25), morning and afternoon tea, and comfortable B&B accommodation (doubles $145).

It's well worth heading up **Mt Barker** itself, 5km south of town, for excellent views of the neighbouring ranges. South-west of Mt Barker, on the rolling grounds of the Egerton-Warburton estate, is the exquisitely photogenic **St Werburgh's Chapel**, built between 1872 and 1873.

A surprising sight is the authentic Mongolian yurt (felt tent) and gallery of eclectic Mongolian and Chinese art in the grounds of **Nomads Guest House** (☑08-9851 2131; www.nomadsguesthousewa.com.au; 12 Morpeth St; s/d/yurts/chalets $70/90/100/110).

Porongurup National Park

The 24-sq-km, 12km-long **Porongurup National Park** (entry per car/motorcycle $11/5) has 1100-million-year-old granite outcrops, panoramic views, beautiful scenery, large karri trees and some excellent bushwalks. The rich forest also supports 65 species of orchid in spring and, in September and October, there are wildflowers among the trees. There are 11 wineries in the immediate vicinity, some in blissfully bucolic settings.

🛏 Sleeping & Eating

There is no accommodation within the national park itself, but all of these options are right on its doorstep. Eating options are very limited.

Ty-Jarrah CHALETS $$
(☑08-9853 1255; www.tyjarrah.com; 3 Bolganup Rd; 1/2 bedroom chalets from $110/140) Very nice, comfortable, A-frame chalets in a forest setting.

Porongurup Range Tourist Park CARAVAN PARK $
(☑08-9853 1057; www.poronguprangetouristpark.com.au; 1304 Porongurup Rd; sites per 2 people $26-29, cabins $85-99; ☒) A tidy park with good facilities.

Porongurup Village Inn, Shop & Tearooms B&B, CAFE $
(☑08-9853 1110; www.porongurupinn.com.au; 1972 Porongurup Rd; s/d/cottages $30/60/100) This welcoming hostel-like place also offers home-cooked food (breakfast items $5 to $14, lunch items $16 to $18).

Maleeya's Thai Cafe THAI $$
(☑08-9853 1123; www.maleeya.com.au; 1376 Porongurup Rd; mains $20; ☺lunch & dinner Fri-Sun) Authentic Thai food, plus crafts and a nursery.

Stirling Range National Park

Rising abruptly from the surrounding plains, this 1156-sq-km national park consists of a single chain of peaks pushed up by plate tectonics to form a range 10km wide and 65km long. Bluff Knoll (Bular Mai) is the highest point in the south-west (1095m). Due to the altitude and climate there are many localised plants in the Stirlings.

The range's propensity to change colour through blues, reds and purples will captivate photographers during the spectacular wildflower season from late August to early December. It's recognised by Noongar people as a place of special significance. Every summit has an ancestral being associated with it, so it's appropriate to show proper respect when visiting here.

Park fees are charged at the start of Bluff Knoll Rd (entry per car/motorcycle $11/5). Walkers must be suitably experienced and equipped as the range is subject to sudden drops in temperature, driving rain and sometimes snow; register in and out with the **rangers** (☑08-9827 9230).

🛏 Sleeping & Eating

Options are limited in this remote area, so stock up on food in Mt Barker.

Lily COTTAGES $$
(☑08-9827 9205; www.thelily.com.au; Chester Pass Rd; cottages from $139) This set of comfortable, self-contained cottages is grouped around Australia's only working windmill. Meals are available.

Mount Trio Bush Camping & Caravan Park CARAVAN PARK $
(☑08-9827 9270; www.mounttrio.com.au; Salt River Rd; unpowered/powered sites per person $12/14) Rustic bush camp site on a farm property close to the walking tracks, north of the centre of the park.

Stirling Range Retreat CARAVAN PARK $
(☑08-9827 9229; www.stirlingrange.com.au; 8639 Chester Pass Rd; sites per adult/child $13/8, dm/s

$30/65, cabins from $70; ❉ @) Offers a wide range of accommodation, from a backpackers' lodge to self-contained, rammed-earth cabins.

Moingup Springs CAMPGROUND $
(Chester Pass Rd; sites per adult/child $7/2) DEC's only campground within the park; no showers or electricity.

Fitzgerald River National Park

Midway between Albany and Esperance, this gem of a national park has been declared a Unesco biosphere reserve. Its 3300 sq km contains 22 mammal species, 200 species of bird and 1700 species of plant (20% of WA's described species). Wildflowers are most abundant in spring, but flowers – especially the hardy proteas – bloom throughout the year.

Walkers will discover beautiful coastline, sand plains, rugged coastal hills and deep river valleys. In season you'll almost certainly see whales and their calves from the shore at **Point Ann**, where there's a lookout and a heritage walk that follows a short stretch of the 1164km **No 2 rabbit-proof fence**.

The three main 2WD entry points are from the South Coast Hwy (Quiss Rd and Pabelup Dr), Hopetoun (Hamersley Dr) and Bremer Bay (along Swamp and Murray Rds). All roads are gravel, and likely to be impassable after rain, so check locally before you set out.

Bookending the park are the hamlets of **Bremer Bay** (population 250) and **Hopetoun** (population 590). Both are edged with brilliant white sand and translucent green waters. To the east of Hopetoun is the scenic but in parts extremely rough **Southern Ocean East Drive**, heading to beaches with camp sites at **Mason Bay** and **Starvation Bay**. If you're in a 2WD, don't be tempted to head to Esperance this way.

🛏 Sleeping

🏕 **Quaalup Homestead** CAMPGROUND $
(☎08-9837 4124; www.whalesandwildflowers. com.au; Quaalup Rd; sites per person from $10, r from $85) Completely isolated and totally magical, this 1858 homestead is secluded within the southern reaches of the park. Sleeping options range from a bush campsite to cosy units and chalets.

DEC campsites CAMPGROUND $
(sites per adult/child $7/2) Of DEC's five camp sites, only St Mary Inlet (near Point Ann) can be reached by 2WD. The two at Hamersley Inlet and the others at Whale Bone Beach, Quoin Head and Fitzgerald Inlet can only be reached by 4WD or on foot.

Hopetoun Motel & Chalet Village MOTEL $$
(☎08-9838 3219; www.hopetounmotel.com. au; 458 Veal St; r around $130; ❀) A very nice rammed-earth complex with comfy beds and quality linen.

Esperance

POP 9600

Esperance sits in solitary splendour on the Bay of Isles, a seascape of aquamarine waters fringed with squeaky white beaches. There's no need to fight for space here, as the town's isolation all but guarantees it. Yet Esperance has its share of devotees who will bundle up the kids for the mammoth pilgrimage from Perth, just to plug into the low-key, community-oriented vibe. In Kalgoorlie nobody would question the wisdom of driving 390km to this, their nearest beach. For travellers taking the coastal route across the continent, it's the last sizeable town before hitting the Nullarbor wilderness.

Some of Australia's most picture-perfect beaches can be found in the even more remote national parks to the south-east. Out in the bay, the pristine environment of the Recherche Archipelago can be wild and windy, or turn on a calmly charming show; its 105 islands are home to colonies of fur seals, penguins and a variety of sea birds.

History

Esperance's Indigenous name, Kepa Kurl (water boomerang), refers to the shape of the bay. It received its current name in 1792 when the *Recherche* and *l'Espérance* sailed into the bay to shelter from a storm. In the 1820s and 1830s the Recherche Archipelago was home to Black Jack Anderson – Australia's only pirate. From his base on Middle Island he raided ships and kept a harem of Aboriginal women whose husbands he had killed. He was eventually murdered in his sleep by one of his own men.

Although the first settlers came in 1863, it wasn't until the gold rush of the 1890s that the town really became established as a port. When the gold fever subsided, Esperance

went into a state of suspended animation until after WWII. In the 1950s it rapidly became an agricultural centre and it continues to export grain and minerals from the region's farms and mines from its port.

👁 Sights & Activities

Great Ocean Drive   SCENIC DRIVE
Many of Esperance's most dramatic sights can be seen on this well-signposted 40km loop. Starting from the waterfront it heads south-west along a breathtaking stretch of coast that includes popular surfing and swimming spots, including Blue Haven Beach and Twilight Cove. Stop to enjoy the rollers breaking against the cliffs from Observatory Point and the lookout on Wireless Hill. A turn-off leads to the wind farm that supplies about 23% of Esperance's electricity. There's a walking track among the turbines that's quite surreal when it's windy – and it often is.

The route then turns back and passes by Pink Lake, or should that be the-lake-formerly-known-as-pink. Salt-tolerant algae once provided an unmistakeable rosy tint, but a storm a few years back flushed it out.

Esperance Museum   MUSEUM
(cnr James & Dempster Sts; adult/child $6/2; ⊙1.30-4.30pm) One of those zany regional museums where glass cabinets are randomly crammed with collections of sea shells, frog ornaments, tennis rackets and bed pans. It's absolutely charming, even if most of the displays wouldn't look amiss in a junk shop. Bigger items include boats, a train carriage and the remains of US space station Skylab, which made its fiery re-entry at Balladonia, east of Esperance, in 1979.

Museum Village   HISTORIC BUILDINGS
Galleries and cafes occupy various restored heritage buildings here; markets are held on Sunday morning. Aboriginal-run Kepa Kurl Art Gallery (www.kepakurl.com.au; cnr Dempster & Kemp Sts; ⊙10am-4pm Mon, Wed & Fri, to 1pm Tue & Thu, 9am-1pm Sun) has reasonably priced works by local and Central Desert artists.

Lake Warden Wetland System   LAKES
Esperance is surrounded by extensive wetlands, which include seven large lakes and 90 smaller ones. The 7.2km return Kepwari Wetland Trail (off Fisheries Rd) takes in Lake Wheatfield and Woody Lake, with boardwalks, interpretive displays and good birdwatching. Lake Monjimup, 14km to the

north-west along the South Coast Hwy, is divided by Telegraph Rd into a conservation area (to the west) and a recreation area (to the east). The conservation side has boardwalks over inky black water where it's hard to see where the paperbark trees end and their mirror image begins. The much more orderly recreation side has themed banksia, hakea and grevillea gardens, a hedge maze and grassy areas for throwing a ball around in.

☞ Tours

Mackenzie's Island Cruises   BOAT
(☑08-9071 5757; www.woodyisland.com.au; 71 The Esplanade; ⊙till late daily Sep-May) Tours Esperance Bay and Woody Island in a power catamaran (half-/full day $88/139), getting close to fur seals, sea lions, Cape Barren geese and (with luck) dolphins. In January it operates a Woody Island ferry (adult/child return $51/22).

Kepa Kurl Eco Cultural Discovery Tours   INDIGENOUS
(☑08-9072 1688; www.kepakurl.com.au; Museum Village) Explore the country from an Aboriginal perspective: visit rock art and waterholes, sample bush food and hear ancient stories (adult/child $115/80, minimum four).

Eco-Discovery Tours   4WD
(☑0407 737 261; www.esperancetours.com.au) Runs 4WD tours along the sand to Cape Le Grand National Park (half-/full day $95/165, minimum two/four) and two-hour circuits of Great Ocean Dr (adult/child $55/40).

Esperance Diving & Fishing   DIVING, FISHING
(☑08-9071 5111; www.esperancedivingandfishing.com.au; 72 The Esplanade) Takes you wreck-diving on the *Sanko Harvest* (two-tank dives including all gear $235) or charter fishing throughout the archipelago.

🛏 Sleeping

⌂TOP CHOICE Esperance B&B by the Sea   B&B $$
(☑08-9071 5640; www.esperancebb.com; 34 Stewart St; s/d $110/150) This beach house has a private guest wing, and the views from the deck overlooking Blue Haven Beach are breathtaking, especially at sunset. It's just a stroll from the ocean and a five-minute drive from Dempster St.

Clearwater Motel Apartments   MOTEL $$
(☑08-9071 3587; www.clearwatermotel.com.au; 1a William St; s $110, d $140-195; ❄) The bright,

spacious rooms and apartments here have balconies and are fully self-contained, and there's a well-equipped shared barbecue area. It's just a short walk from both waterfront and town.

Woody Island Eco-Stays CAMPGROUND $
(☑08-9071 5757; www.woodyisland.com.au; sites per person $16, on-site tents $33-60, huts $96-145; ☺late Sep-Apr) It's not every day you get to stay in an A-class nature reserve. Choose between leafy camp sites (very close together) or canvas-sided bush huts; a few have a private deck and their own lighting.

Island View Esperance APARTMENTS $$$
(☑08-9072 0044; www.esperanceapartments.com.au; 14-15 The Esplanade; apt from $200) It's easy living in these architect-designed and tastefully furnished one- to three-bedroom apartments, some with floor-to-ceiling windows overlooking the waterfront. The kitchens have all the mod cons, and there's a spacious living area.

Driftwood Apartments APARTMENTS $$
(☑0428 716 677; www.driftwoodapartments.com.au; 69 The Esplanade; apt from $125; ▣) Each of these seven smart blue and yellow apartments, right across from the waterfront, has its own BBQ and outdoor table setting. The two-storey, two-bedroom units have decks and a bit more privacy.

Blue Waters Lodge YHA HOSTEL $
(☑08-9071 1040; www.yha.com.au; 299 Goldfields Rd; dm/s/d $27/45/67) On the beachfront about 1.5km from the centre, this rambling place feels a little institutional, but the management is friendly and the hostel looks out over a tidy lawn to the water. Hire bikes to cycle the waterfront.

Eating

Taylor Street Jetty CAFE $$
(Taylor St Jetty; lunch $13-19, dinner $24-32; ☺breakfast & lunch Wed-Mon, dinner Thu-Mon; ⊜) This attractive, sprawling cafe by the jetty serves cafe fare, tapas, seafood and salads. Locals hang out at the tables on the grass or read on the covered terrace. Wi-fi is free with an order of more than $10, and it's a child-friendly zone.

Onshore Cafe CAFE $
(105 Dempster St; mains $7-17; ☺breakfast & lunch Mon-Sat) A homewares store-cafe in a breezy modern space next to the cinema, this place serves light lunches, as well as excellent coffee, croissants and cake.

Information

DEC (☑08-9083 2100; 92 Dempster St)
Visitor centre (☑08-9083 1555; www.visitesperance.com; cnr Kemp & Dempster Sts; ☺9am-5pm Mon-Fri, to 2pm Sat, to noon Sun)

Around Esperance

CAPE LE GRAND NATIONAL PARK
An easy day trip from Esperance, this national park (entry per car/motorcycle $11/5) starts 60km to the east and boasts spectacular coastal scenery, turquoise water, dazzling talcum powder–soft beaches and excellent walking tracks. It offers good fishing, swimming and camping (sites per adult/child $9/2) at Lucky Bay and Le Grand Beach, and day-use facilities at gorgeous Hellfire Bay. Make the effort to climb Frenchman Peak (a steep 3km return, allow two hours), as the views from the top and through the 'eye', especially during the late afternoon, are superb.

Rossiter Bay is where the British and Aboriginal duo Edward John Eyre and Wylie fortuitously met the French whaling ship *Mississippi* in the course of their epic 1841 overland crossing and spent two weeks resting onboard. The 15km Le Grand Coastal Trail links the bays; you can do shorter stretches between beaches.

Just outside the eastern edge of the park, old-fashioned Orleans Bay Caravan Park (☑08-9075 0033; orleansbay@bigpond.com; sites per 2 people from $20, chalets from $80) is a shady, child-friendly place to stay, 2km from gorgeous Wharton Beach.

CAPE ARID NATIONAL PARK
Further east, at the start of the Great Australian Bight and on the fringes of the Nullarbor Plain, Cape Arid (entry per car/motorcycle $11/5) is rugged and isolated, with good bushwalking, great beaches, camp sites and more of that crazy squeaky sand.

Whales (in season), seals and Cape Barren geese are seen regularly here. Most of the park is 4WD-accessible only, although the Thomas River Rd, which leads to the shire camp site (sites per adult/child $7/2), is accessible to all vehicles. For the hardy, there is a tough walk to the top of Tower Peak on Mt Ragged (3km return, three hours), where the world's most primitive species of ant was found thriving in 1930.

For those heading across the Nullarbor, the extremely rough Balladonia Track and Parmango Rd offer an alternative to the Eyre Hwy but you'll absolutely need a 4WD;

check conditions at the Esperance visitor centre before starting out.

PEAK CHARLES NATIONAL PARK
There are no charges to visit or camp at this granite wilderness area, 130km north of Esperance. There are only basic facilities provided (long-drop toilets); you'll need to be completely self-sufficient here.

SOUTHERN OUTBACK

The stark beauty of the southern outback offers an iconic Australian experience. In summer, heat haze shimmers on the desert and the parched voices of crows carry for miles; midyear, a winter chill tones down the landscape's reds and blues to cool purple and grey. Almost-empty roads lead on – and on and on – towards South Australia (SA) via the relentless Nullarbor Plain, and up to the Northern Territory (NT). This was (and is) gold-rush country, with the city of Kalgoorlie-Boulder as its centrepiece, while smaller, more remote and less sustainable gold towns lie sunstruck and deserted. Aboriginal people have lived for an age in this region, which the early colonists found unforgiving until the rewards of the gold rush made it worth their while to stay.

History
The government in Perth was in raptures when gold was discovered at Southern Cross in 1888. In one of the world's last great gold rushes, the next few years drew prospectors from other states – and other nations. Some 50 towns immediately rose up in the eastern goldfields, but it was a harsh life. Enthusiasm, or greed, sometimes outweighed common sense. Diseases such as typhoid ran through mining camps. Inadequate water, housing, food and medical supplies led to a dusty death for many.

The area's population dwindled along with the gold, and these days Kalgoorlie-Boulder is the only real survivor. You can explore other diminished towns and prodigious mining structures from early last century along the well-signposted 965km Golden Quest Discovery Trail (www.goldenquesttrail.com).

Stretching 560km from the Perth foothills, the 1903 Golden Pipeline (www.golden pipeline.com.au) brought water to the goldfields, thanks to the vision of engineer CY O'Connor. It was a lifeline for the towns it passed through and filled Kalgoorlie with the sense of a future, with or without gold. The present-day Great Eastern Hwy follows the pipeline's route, with heritage pumping stations and information signs along the way.

ⓘ Getting There & Away
Air
Qantas (☑13 13 13; www.qantas.com.au) Perth to Kalgoorlie (one hour, two to three daily).

Skywest (☑1300 660 088; www.skywest.com. au) Perth to Kalgoorlie (one hour, four weekly).

Skippers Aviation (☑1300 729 924; www. skippers.com.au) Perth–Leonora–Laverton (four weekly) and Perth–Wiluna–Leinster (three weekly).

Bus
Transwa (☑1300 662 205; www.transwa. wa.gov.au) Coach GE3 heads between Kalgoorlie and Esperance three times a week ($53, five hours), via Coolgardie and Norseman.

Goldrush Tours (☑1800 620 440; www.gold rushtours.com.au) Operates a weekly service from Kalgoorlie to Laverton (via Menzies and Leonora), which goes out on Thursday and back on Friday.

Train
Transwa also runs the *Prospector* service from East Perth to Kalgoorlie ($82, seven hours, daily). For the *Indian Pacific* to/from Perth, Broken Hill, Adelaide and Sydney, see p913.

Norseman
POP 860

From the crossroads township of Norseman you can head south to Esperance or north to Kalgoorlie, westwards to Hyden and Wave Rock via 300km of all-weather gravel road, or begin the long, long trek across the Nullarbor on the Eyre Hwy.

Stretch your legs at the well-signed Beacon Hill Mararoa Lookout, where there's a walking trail, and stop at the Historical Museum (Battery Rd; adult/child $3/1; ☺10am-1pm Mon-Sat), which showcases all sorts of pioneering items. If you've got two hours to spare, pick up the Dundas Coach Road Heritage Trail brochure, for a 50km loop drive with interpretive panels along the way.

🛏 Sleeping

Great Western Motel   MOTEL $
(☑08-9039 1633; greatwestern@westnet.com. au; Prinsep St; r $95-120; ❄❄) 'Budget' and 'lodge' rooms in an older block are perfectly adequate, but the rammed-earth

The only water hazard you'll face on this 18-hole, par-72 course is the risk of running out of it. Stretching 1362km from Kalgoorlie, south to Norseman and across the desolate Nullarbor Plain to Ceduna, the Nullarbor Links (www.nullarborlinks.com; 18 holes $50) is golf, Tiger, but not as we know it.

To get swinging, purchase your scorecard from the Kalgoorlie or Ceduna visitor centre and follow the directions to the holes scattered along the route. Don't forget to collect stamps along the way to qualify for your completion certificate.

Clubs are available for hire at each hole ($5). If you'd rather use your own, pack your oldest – the parched ground can be as hard as steel. At some holes you may need a hammer to get the tees into the ground.

'motel' rooms are much nicer. There's a cafe-restaurant on site.

Gateway Caravan Park   CARAVAN PARK **$**
(☑08-9039 1500; www.acclaimparks.com.au; 23 Prinsep St; sites per 2 people $29-33, cabins $78-128; ✱) Decent cabins and a bushy atmosphere make this a reliable option.

Lodge 101   HOSTEL **$**
(☑08-9039 1541; 101 Prinsep St; dm/s/d $25/40/65; ✱) After the relentless road, this cute cottage is a basic but cheery place to rest your cramped bones. The dorm has no linen or air-con.

ℹ Information

Visitor centre (☑08-9039 1071; www.norse man.info; 68 Roberts St; ⊙9am-5pm Mon-Fri, 9.30am-4pm Sat & Sun) A great source of information about the Nullarbor.

Eyre Hwy (The Nullarbor)

London to Moscow, or Perth to Adelaide? There's not much difference, distance-wise. The 2700km Eyre Hwy crosses the southern edge of the vast Nullarbor Plain, parallel with the Trans-Australia Railway to the north.

John Eyre was the first European to cross this unforgiving stretch of country in 1841. After the 1877 telegraph line was laid, miners en route to the goldfields trekked its length under blistering sun and in freezing winter. In 1912 the first car made it across. By 1941 the rough-and-ready road carried a handful of vehicles a day; in 1962 the first cyclist crossed. In 1969 the WA government surfaced the road as far as the SA border. Finally, in 1976, the last stretch was surfaced and runs close to the coast, with the Nullarbor region ending dramatically at the cliffs of the Great Australian Bight.

From Norseman it's 725km to the SA border, and a further 480km to Ceduna (meaning 'a place to sit down and rest' in the local Aboriginal language). They aren't kidding! From Ceduna, it's still another 793km to Adelaide (a *long* day's drive).

NORSEMAN TO EUCLA

At the 100km mark from Norseman, Fraser Range Station (☑08-9039 3210; www. fraserrangestation.com.au; unpowered/powered sites $20/25, budget s/d $55/75, cottage r $95) is the first (or last, depending) and best stop on the Nullarbor. This sheep station's heritage buildings and camping ground are top-notch (though there's no fuel), and you might even score some fresh vegies from the garden. Next is Balladonia (193km), where the Balladonia Hotel Motel (☑08-9039 3453; balladonia@bigpond.com; unpowered/powered sites $16/22, dm $35, r from $125; ✱ @ ☎) has a small museum including debris from Skylab's 1979 nearby return to earth.

Balladonia to Cocklebiddy is some 210km. The first 160km to Caiguna includes Australia's longest stretch of straight road – 145km, the so-called Ninety Mile Straight. Caiguna's John Eyre Motel (☑08-9039 3459; caigunarh@bigpond.com; unpowered/powered sites $20/28, r $70-100; ✱) is at the end of it. There are shaded picnic tables and a comfortable restaurant at the Cocklebiddy Wedgetail Inn (☑08-9039 3462; cocklebiddy@bigpond. com; unpowered/powered sites $15/25, r $70-100; ✱), which runs on Central Western time, 45 minutes ahead of Perth time, and 45 minutes behind Adelaide time.

Birds Australia's Eyre Bird Observatory (☑08-9039 3450; www.eyrebirds.org) is in the isolated and lovely 1897 former Eyre Telegraph Station, 50km south of Cocklebiddy. Full board and lodging is good value at $90 per person per night – book ahead. Day

NOT NULLAR-BORING AT ALL

'Crossing the Nullarbor' is an iconic Australian trip, and rightly so. It's absolutely about journey as much as destination, so settle in and enjoy the big skies and long horizons. Take plenty of CDs and audio books to complement the sounds of silence on the road, and stretch out those driving muscles by waving at other drivers, and *(very)* occasional cyclists and walkers, and by playing the golf tees of the long-distance Nullarbor Links course (see p953) – great fun!

All roadhouses sell food and fuel and have accommodation. Room rates given range from budget (often *very* basic) to motel style; camp sites can resemble desolate *Mad Max* landscapes. Free roadside camping – toilets, tables, a bit of shade – is about every 250km. Check out www.nullarbornet.com.au for comprehensive information.

Common-sense preparations include making sure your vehicle is up to the distance and carrying more drinking water than you think you'll need in case it isn't; you may have to sit it out by the roadside for quite a while. This is not the place to run out of fuel: prices are high and there's a distance between fuel stops of about 200km. So now sit back, relax and enjoy the drive.

visitors are welcome ($10 per vehicle), but the last 10km are soft sand and 4WD accessible only; 2WD travellers who want to stay can arrange pick-up with the wardens. There's no camping.

Tiny **Madura**, 91km east of Cocklebiddy, is close to the Hampton Tablelands (stop for wild wide views at the lookout). The **Madura Pass Oasis Inn** (☑08-9039 3464; madura oasis@bigpond.com; unpowered/powered sites $15/25, r $70-100; ❄☀) has a green and shady camp site, and a welcome pool.

In **Mundrabilla**, 116km further east, the **Mundrabilla Motel Hotel** (☑08-9039 3465; mundrabilla@bigpond.com.au; unpowered/powered sites $15/20, r $70-100; ❄) has consistently cheaper fuel prices than roadhouses further west.

Just before the SA border is Eucla, surrounded by stunning sand dunes and pristine beaches. Visit the atmospheric ruins of the 1877 **telegraph station**, 5km south of town and gradually being engulfed by the dunes; the remains of the old jetty are a 15-minute walk beyond. Pleasant camp sites and spacious rooms are available at the **Eucla Motor Hotel** (☑08-9039 3468; unpowered/powered sites $15/20, r $45-100; ❄).

EUCLA TO CEDUNA
See p781 for information on the section of highway between the border and Ceduna.

Coolgardie
POP 800

Today you wouldn't pick that in 1898 sleepy Coolgardie was the third-biggest town in WA, with a population of 15,000, six newspapers, two stock exchanges, more than 20 hotels and three breweries. It all took off just hours after Arthur Bayley rode into Southern Cross in 1892 and dumped 554oz of Coolgardie gold on the mining warden's counter. The only echoes that remain are some historic buildings lining the uncharacteristically wide main road and information panels detailing the glory days.

◉ Sights & Activities

**Goldfields Museum &
Visitor Centre**   MUSEUM
(☑08-9026 6090; www.coolgardie.wa.gov.
au; Warden's Court, Bayley St; adult/child $4.50/2.50; ☉8.30am-4.20pm Mon-Fri, 10am-3pm Sat & Sun) Has a sizeable display of goldfields memorabilia, along with information about former US president Herbert Hoover's days on the goldfields in Gwalia.

**Warden Finnerty's
Residence**   HISTORIC BUILDING
(2 McKenzie St; adult/child $4/2; ☉11am-4pm Thu-Tue) Built in 1895 for Coolgardie's first mining warden and magistrate, this charming National Trust house has been beautifully restored.

Camel Farm   CAMEL RIDES
(☑08-9026 6159; Great Eastern Hwy; adult/child $7/3; ☉10am-4pm school & public holidays, or by appointment) Offers short camel rides and organises longer treks ($7.50 to $40; two adults minimum). It's 4km west of town; book ahead.

🛏 Sleeping & Eating

Coolgardie Motel
MOTEL $$

(✆08-9026 6080; www.coolgardiemotels.com.au; 49-53 Bayley St; r $110-125; ❇🅿🛜🐾) The small but comfortable rooms have been freshened up with new linen and a coat of paint, and the attached restaurant is the best place to eat in town (mains $18 to $32).

Kalgoorlie-Boulder

POP 28,300

Kalgoorlie-Boulder ('Kal' to the locals), some 600km from Perth, is an outback success story. The town is prosperous, with well-preserved historic buildings and streets wide enough to turn a camel train in – a necessity in turn-of-the-century goldfield towns. The most enduring and productive of WA's gold towns, today it's still the centre for mining in this part of the state.

It still feels a bit like the Wild West: a frontier town where bush meets brash, and gambling dens, brothels and churches sit side by side. Workers (mainly men) can come straight from the mines in their overalls to spend disposable income at the bars, and are served by 'skimpie' female staff wearing only underwear.

It's undeniably an interesting place, although perhaps not to everyone's taste. There are plenty of historical and modern mining sites to explore, and it makes a good base for trips to the ghost towns in the surrounding outback.

History

Long-time prospector Paddy Hannan set out from Coolgardie in search of another gold strike, and proved that sometimes beggars can be choosers. He stumbled across the surface gold that sparked the 1893 gold rush, and inadvertently chose the site of Kalgoorlie for a township.

When surface sparkles subsided, the miners dug deeper, extracting the precious metal from the rocks by costly and complex processes. Kalgoorlie quickly prospered, and the town's magnificent public buildings, constructed at the end of the 19th century, are evidence of its fabulous wealth.

Despite its slow decline after WWI, Kal is still the largest producer of gold in Australia. What was a Golden Mile of small mining operators' head frames and corrugated-iron shacks is now an overwhelmingly huge Super Pit, which will eventually be 3.8km long, 1.35km wide and 500m deep.

◉ Sights & Activities

Mining Hall of Fame
HISTORIC MINE

(✆08-9026 2700; www.mininghall.com.au; off Goldfields Hwy; ⏱8.30am-4.30pm) Located on the site of Paddy Hannan's original lease and a working mine until 1952, the Mining Hall of Fame explores the industry from the underground up. You can go down a mine shaft (and see why claustrophobics don't make good miners), pan for gold and be mesmerised by a gold pour (adult/child $30/20; $20/15 if you stay above ground). The **Pitch Black** tour goes deeper (adult/child $60/40), while **Under & Over** ($140) includes a helicopter ride over the Super Pit.

Kids of all ages will be kept well occupied in the interactive **Exploration Zone**, and you can relax in the **Garden of Remembrance**, dedicated to the immigrant Chinese who worked the goldfields.

If you're into mining history, allow yourself a half-day here. Tickets are valid for 48 hours.

Super Pit
LOOKOUT

(www.superpit.com.au; Outram St; ⏱6am-7pm) The view is staggering, with building-sized trucks zigzagging up and down the huge hole and looking like kids' toys. It's quite beautiful in its own way, with nature's palate of red, black and grey revealed on the exposed rock faces. The information displays are fascinating. Boulder's **Super Pit Shop** (2 Burt St; ⏱9am-4pm Mon-Fri) has more displays and sells small nuggets.

Western Australian Museum – Kalgoorlie-Boulder
MUSEUM

(www.museum.wa.gov.au; 17 Hannan St; suggested donation $5; ⏱10am-4.30pm) The impressive Ivanhoe-mine head frame marks the entrance to this excellent social-history museum. A lift takes you to the top, where you can peer out over the city and mines. In case you forget the reason all of this exists, an underground vault displays giant nuggets and gold bars. There's also a fantastic collection of trade-union banners and relocated historic buildings, including a miner's cottage and mobile police station (attached to a train). Half-hour guided tours start at 11am.

Hannan St
HISTORIC BUILDINGS

The city's main drag, Hannan St has retained many of its original gold rush–era buildings, including several grand hotels and the imposing town hall. Outside is a drinking fountain in the form of a statue of Paddy Hannan holding a water bag. Pick up

audio-tour equipment from the visitor centre for an itinerary and commentary ($10).

Goldfields Oasis Centre AQUATIC CENTRE
(www.goldfieldsoasis.com.au; 99 Johnston Rd; pools adult/child $5/3; ☺5.45am-9pm Mon-Fri, 8am-6pm Sat & Sun) When you're 390km from the nearest beach and you could fry an egg on your car bonnet, this high-tech aquatic centre may prove irresistible. Ever surfed in a desert? Hit the Flowrider (per 30min $5) wave pool. There are also water slides (per 2hr $5; ☺4-6pm Mon-Fri, 11am-5pm Sat & Sun), sports courts and a gym.

FREE **School of Mines**
Mineral Museum MUSEUM
(cnr Egan & Cassidy Sts; ☺9am-noon Mon-Fri, closed school holidays) Has a geology display including replicas of big nuggets discovered in the area.

FREE **Goldfields Arts Centre** GALLERY
(http://gac.curtin.edu.au; Cheetham St; ☺10am-3pm Mon-Fri, noon-3pm Sun) Hosts interesting exhibitions by local, state and national artists.

Royal Flying Doctor Service VISITOR CENTRE
(www.flyingdoctor.org.au; Kalgoorlie-Boulder Airport; admission $3; ☺10am-3pm Mon-Fri) See how the flying doctors look after the outback, with tours at 10.15am, noon and 2pm.

Hammond Park PARK
(Lyall St; ☺9am-5pm) A good spot for kids, with playgrounds, aviaries, kangaroos, emus and a miniature Bavarian castle.

Karlkurla Park PARK
Get out on the red dirt in this regenerated bushland on the north-western edge of town and enjoy the 4km of walking trails.

Kalgoorlie Arboretum PARK
(Hawkin St) Twenty-six hectares of DEC-managed parkland set around a lake, with 50 native tree species and information panels.

Two-Up GAMBLING
(21-23 Porter St; ☺9.30pm-3.30am Sun) Try your hand at the iconic Aussie two-coin gambling game.

☞ Tours

Finders Keepers MINING, PROSPECTING
(☑08-9021 2211; www.finderskeepersgold.com; 250 Hannan St) You can be inducted into the mysteries of the metal detector on a popular half-day gold-prospecting tour (adult/child $95/50), or journey to the centre of the

earth (or thereabouts) on a tour of the Super Pit (one hour adult/child $40/25, 2½ hours $60/40).

Goldrush Tours BUS
(☑1800 620 440; www.goldrushtours.com.au) Runs all sorts of tours, including half-day heritage jaunts around Kalgoorlie-Boulder (adult/child $50/25) and day tours to the sculptures on Lake Ballard (adult/child $150/75).

Hay Street brothels BROTHELS
The world's oldest profession is as long established as mining in these parts and, like the mining industry, some of its operators are willing to rake in a few extra tourist dollars, including Langtrees (☑08-9026 2181; www.langtrees.com; 181 Hay St; tours $35; ☺tours 12.30pm, 2.30pm & 5pm) and Questa Casa (☑08-9021 4897; 133 Hay St; tours $20; ☺tours 2pm), the latter in business for over 100 years.

★★ Festivals & Events

Kalgoorlie Market MARKET
(St Barbara's Sq, Hannan St) First Sunday of the month.

Boulder Market Day MARKET
Third Sunday of the month.

Kalgoorlie-Boulder Racing Round RACING
(www.kbrc.com.au) September brings the highlight of the social calendar, where locals and a huge influx of visitors dress up to the nines to watch horses race on the red dirt.

🛏 Sleeping

Much of the accommodation in Kalgoorlie is targeted towards the mining industry. The smarter places tend to be overpriced for what's offered, while the hostels and pubs are often full of rough-and-tumble long-stayers.

Rydges Kalgoorlie HOTEL $$
(☑08-9080 0800; www.rydges.com/kalgoorlie; 21 Davidson St; r from $159; ❄@✿) Easily the pick of the crop, this low-key resort-style complex is located in a residential area between Kalgoorlie and Boulder. The rooms, set within an oasis of lush native bush, are big and comfortable, if a little generic.

York Hotel PUB $
(☑08-9021 2337; yorkhtl@bigpond.net.au; 259 Hannan St; s/d/tr $60/95/115) One of Kalgoorlie's most unique heritage buildings, this is a character-filled labyrinth of high-ceilinged

rooms, shared bathrooms, wooden staircases and lacework balconies. It's good value, with a light breakfast included.

Discovery Holiday Parks CARAVAN PARKS $
(www.discoveryholidayparks.com.au; sites $16-40, units $105-152; 🅿@🛏); Kalgoorlie (📞08-9039 4800; 286 Burt St); Boulder (📞08-9093 1266; 201 Lane St) Sister complexes with sizeable and well-fitted-out A-frame chalets and cabins, grassy tent sites, and playgrounds and pools. The Kalgoorlie branch feels slightly less crammed.

View on Hannans MOTEL $$
(📞08-9091 3333; www.theviewonhannans.com.au; 430 Hannan St; r from $125; 🅿) The only vaguely interesting view from this motel is of people leaving the brothels around the corner. However, it is clean, comfortable and centrally located, with free in-house movies and sports channels to keep you out of trouble. Best of all, free entry to the Goldfields Oasis is provided.

Quest Yelverton Kalgoorlie APARTMENTS $$
(📞08-9022 8181; www.questkalgoorlie.com.au; 210 Egan St; apt from $150; 🅿🛜🛏) Close to Hannan St but far enough away to get a quiet night's sleep, the Quest offers fully self-contained and serviced apartments that are reminiscent of upmarket motel rooms.

Golddust Backpackers YHA HOSTEL $
(📞08-9091 3737; www.yha.com.au; 192 Hay St; dm/s/d $33/44/69; 🅿@🛏) A row of boots and hard hats by the front door gives a good indication of the regular clientele. The rooms are clean but basic and communal facilities are good.

Kalgoorlie Backpackers HOSTEL $
(📞08-9091 1482; www.kalgoorliebackpackers.com.au; 166 Hay St; dm/s/d $28/50/75; 🅿@🛏) Partly located in a former brothel, this hostel is in a central location and, like the nearby YHA, is an excellent place to find out about work opportunities.

🍴 Eating

There are plenty of eateries, but Kalgoorlie is in no danger of setting the gastronomic world alight anytime soon. If you're a fan of simple, meaty, man-size meals, you won't have any complaints.

Larcombe's Bar & Grill RESTAURANT $$
(📞08-9080 0800; Rydges, 21 Davidson St; mains $28-38) Very much a hotel restaurant, Larcombe's is just a tad too brightly lit to be truly intimate, but it's still the place of choice for spruced-up locals on a romantic date. The menu has a Mod Oz sensibility, gainfully plundering French, Italian and Chinese styles.

Barista 202 CAFE $
(202 Hannan St; mains $7-15; ⏰breakfast & lunch Mon-Sat) Squeezed into a tiny shopfront and a covered alley, this buzzing cafe serves sandwiches, pasta, omelettes and excellent coffee.

Paddy's Ale House PUB $$
(Exchange Hotel, 135 Hannan St; mains $16-28; ⏰lunch & dinner) With a wide range of tap beers, Paddy's serves up good, classic counter meals (such as steaks and bangers-and-mash) to the hordes.

Hoover's Cafe PUB $
(www.palacehotel.com.au; 137 Hannan St; mains $10-25; ⏰8am-5pm Mon-Sat; 📶) Attached to the Palace Hotel, this old-fashioned pub dining room serves great-value, tasty food and surprisingly good coffee.

Hannan Street Gourmet DELI $
(147 Hannan St; mains around $10; ⏰9.30am-5pm Mon-Fri, 10am-2pm Sat) This gourmet deli serves salads, very good sandwiches and daily hot-lunch specials. Take away, or eat at the tables in the back.

🍷 Drinking & Entertainment

If you ever needed proof that Kalgoorlie was stuck in a time rift, somewhere between the Wild West and a 1970s mechanic's garage, step into one of the many classic gold rush–era pubs of Hannan St. Offering an opportunity to quench your anthropological curiosity as much as your thirst, Kal's watering holes are full of hard-drinking blokes and female bar staff clad in underwear, suspenders and high heels known as skimpies. You'll need to pick your pub carefully if you prefer your bar staff fully clothed.

Judd's PUB
(www.kalgoorliehotel.com.au; Kalgoorlie Hotel, 319 Hannan St) With a beer garden and windows that open onto the street, this is the place to check out live bands and DJs.

Palace Hotel PUB
(www.palacehotel.com.au; 137 Hannan St) Watch the street life from the relatively demure balcony bar or descend to the depths of the Gold Bar for live bands, DJs and topless skimpies.

Wild West Saloon PUB
(Exchange Hotel, 135 Hannan St) Pretty much as it sounds; the front bar at the Exchange Hotel has skimpies (some in cowboy hats), TV sports, occasional live music and mine workers furiously refuelling.

Orana Cinema CINEMA
(✆08-9021 2199; www.oranacinemas.com.au; 26 Oswald St) Catch a flick in air-conditioned comfort.

Goldfields Arts Centre ARTS CENTRE
(✆08-9088 6900; http://gac.curtin.edu.au; Cheetham St) Performing arts.

ⓘ Information

DEC (✆08-9080 5555; 32 Brookman St; ⊗8am-5pm Mon-Fri)

Kalgoorlie Regional Hospital (✆08-9080 5888; Piccadilly St)

Visitor centre (✆08-9021 1966; www.kal goorlietourism.com; Town Hall, cnr Hannan & Wilson Sts; ⊗8.30am-5pm Mon-Fri, 9am-2pm Sat & Sun)

North of Kalgoorlie-Boulder

Heading north from Kalgoorlie-Boulder, the Goldfields Hwy is surfaced as far as Wiluna (580km north), which is also the starting point for the 4WD Canning Stock Rte and Gunbarrel Hwy. Branching east off the highway, the road from Leonora is sealed as far as Laverton (367km north-east), which is the starting point for the unsealed Great Central Rd (Outback Way).

Off the main road you'll see the occasional mining truck, but other traffic is virtually nonexistent – and while many gravel roads are fine for regular cars, rain can quickly close them to all vehicles. All the (non-ghost) towns have pub accommodation, caravan parks (most with on-site cabins), fuel stops and grocery stores.

KANOWNA, BROAD ARROW & ORA BANDA

Easy day trips north from Kalgoorlie include the gold ghost towns of Kanowna (18km north-east), Broad Arrow (38km north) and Ora Banda (65km north-west). Little remains of Kanowna apart from the building foundations of its 16 hotels (!) and other public buildings, but its pioneer cemetery – including a couple of early Japanese graves – is interesting. Broad Arrow was featured in *The Nickel Queen* (1971),

the first full-length feature film made in WA. It is a shadow of its former self: at the beginning of the 20th century it had a population of 2400. Now there's just one pub – popular with Kal locals at weekends – and a couple of tumbledown houses. The 1911 **Ora Banda Historical Inn** (✆08-9024 2444; www.orabanda.com.au; sites per 2 people $15-25, r $60-110) has a beer garden with a shock of lush green lawn (a rarity amongst hundreds of kilometres of red dirt), simple accommodation in a donga-style block and a dusty camping area.

MENZIES & LAKE BALLARD

The once thriving but now tiny township of Menzies (www.menzies.wa.gov.au), 132km from Kalgoorlie, is best known as the turn-off for the stunning Antony Gormley sculptures on Lake Ballard, an eye-dazzling salt lake 51km north-west of town. You can camp here for free; there are toilets and a barbecue area but no showers.

The Menzies visitor centre (✆08-9024 2702; www.menzies.wa.gov.au; Shenton St; ⊗9am-4.30pm Mon-Fri, 10am-2pm Sat & Sun) has internet access and information on visiting the sculptures and other local sites, and runs the neighbouring Caravan Park (sites per 2 people $20-26). It also houses the Spinifex Art Gallery, which exhibits works from the Tjuntjuntjarra community, located deep in the desert 750km to the east.

KOOKYNIE

Midway between Menzies and Leonora, a good dirt road leads 25km to Kookynie, another interesting ghost town, where the Kookynie Grand Hotel (✆08-9031 3010; s/d/tr $77/93/99) still pulls pints and offers beds. Quiet Niagara Dam, 10km from Kookynie, is a top bush-camping spot.

LEONORA

Further north (237km from Kalgoorlie), this is the largest service centre for mining exploration and the pastoral industry in the area. Check out the old public buildings and pubs on the main street near the visitor centre (✆08-9037 7016; Tower St; ⊗9am-4pm Mon-Fri). Just 4km southwest of town, Gwalia Historic Site was occupied in 1896 and deserted pretty much overnight in 1963, after the pit closed. With houses and household goods disintegrating intact, it's a strange, eerie, fascinating ghost town. The museum (adult/child $10/5; ⊗10am-4pm) is chock full of weird

and wonderful stuff. **Hoover House** (08-9037 7122; www.gwalia.org.au; s $120-140, d $130-150; ✱) – the 1898 mine manager's house, named for Gwalia's first mine manager, Herbert Hoover, who later became the 31st president of the United States – is beautifully restored, and you can B&B here in one of its three antique-strewn bedrooms.

CANNING STOCK ROUTE & GUNBARREL HIGHWAY

Wiluna, 300km north of Leonora, is the start or finish point of two of Australia's most extreme 4WD adventures – the Canning Stock Rte and the Gunbarrel Hwy. These rough, remote routes head through unforgiving wilderness for thousands of kilometres. They can only be safely traversed from April to September. Don't attempt them at all without checking with visitor centres and DEC offices first as they're completely weather-dependent. HEMA Maps' detailed *Great Desert Tracks – North West Sheet* is a must for both. See p39 for more information on outback driving.

The **Canning Stock Route** (www.exploroz.com/TrekNotes/WDeserts/Canning_Stock_Route.aspx) runs 2006km northeast to Halls Creek, crossing the Great Sandy and Gibson Deserts. As the track has not been maintained for more than 30 years it's a route to be taken seriously. If you're starting from Wiluna, pick up comprehensive road and safety information from the **shire office** (08-9981 8000; www.wiluna.wa.gov.au; Scotia St). You'll need a permit to cross the Birrilburru native-title area.

Taking the old **Gunbarrel Highway** (www.exploroz.com/TrekNotes/WDeserts/Gunbarrel_Highway.aspx) from Wiluna to Warakurna near the NT border (where it joins the Outback Way) is a long, rough, heavily corrugated trip through lots of sand dunes. Like the Canning, it's suggested that for safety you drive this in convoy with other vehicles, and you need to take all supplies – including fuel and water for the duration – with you. Let the police posts at either end of both tracks know your movements.

LAVERTON

Laverton crouches on the edge of the Great Victoria Desert. The **visitor centre** (08-9031 1361; www.visit-laverton.com.au; Augusta St; ☉9.30am-4.30pm Mon-Fri, 9am-1pm Sat & Sun) is combined with the **Great Beyond – Explorers' Hall of Fame** (adult/child $10/5), which makes use of technology to tell pioneer

PERMITS, PLEASE
959

The Canning Stock Rte and Outback Way traverse various pockets of Aboriginal land and travellers must obtain a permit from DIA (see p972) to cross them. It's usually a quick online process, but if you're planning to stay and camp rather than merely pass through, additional approvals are required from the affected community; allow up to two weeks.

stories. The not-for-profit **Laverton Outback Gallery** (www.laverton-outback-gallery.com.au; 4 Euro St; ☉9am-5pm) is a great place to purchase paintings, necklaces, woomeras and boomerangs – 80% of the price goes straight to the Aboriginal artist.

Laverton marks the start of the Outback Way. Expect to overnight and/or stock up on supplies of fuel and water here, and *definitely* check at the visitor centre for current road conditions.

OUTBACK WAY (GREAT CENTRAL RD)

The unsealed **Outback Way** (www.outbackway.org.au) – previously known as the Great Central Rd – provides rich scenery of red dirt, spinifex, mulga and desert oak. It links Laverton with Winton in central Queensland, via the red centre of the NT. From Laverton it is a mere 1098km to Yulara, 1541km to Alice Springs and 2720km to Winton!

The road is sandy and corrugated in places, but it's wide and suitable for all vehicles. It can be closed for several days after rain. Diesel is available at roughly 300km intervals on the WA side, and Opal fuel takes the place of unleaded petrol. (Opal is unsniffable, and its provision is one of the measures in place to counteract petrol-sniffing problems in local communities.)

Coming from Laverton, the three **WA roadhouses** (www.ngaanyatjarraku.wa.gov.au) – all of which provide food, fuel and limited mechanical services – are **Tjukayirla** (08-9037 1108; tjukayirlaroadhouse@bigpond.com) at 315km, **Warburton** (08-8956 7656) at 567km and **Warakurna** (08-8956 7344; warakurnaroadhouse@bigpond.com) at 798km. All have a range of accommodation, from camping (around $12 per person) to budget rooms (around $40) and self-contained units (around $150); you should book ahead, as rooms are limited.

The Tjukayirla roadhouse offers tours to caves with 5000-year-old rock art.

At Warburton take time to visit the **Tjulyu-ru Cultural & Civic Centre** (☎08-8956 7966; www.tjulyuru.com; ◷8.30am-4.30pm Mon-Fri), near the roadhouse; the art gallery contains an extensive collection of Ngaanyatjarra Aboriginal paintings. At **Giles**, 231km north-east of Warburton and 105km west of the NT border, there is a meteorological station where you can watch weather balloons released at 9.30am and 2.30pm daily.

Warakurna, Warburton and Giles run on NT time, 1½ hours ahead of WA time.

DRYANDRA TO HYDEN

A beautiful forest, rare marsupials, stunning ancient granite-rock formations, salt lakes, interesting back roads and the unique Wave Rock are the scattered highlights of this widespread farming region.

❶ Getting There & Away

It's much easier with your own vehicle. Wave Rock is a long day trip from Perth.

Transwa (☎1300 662 205; www.transwa. wa.gov.au) Runs sporadic buses between Perth and the south coast.

Western Travel Bug (☎08-9486 4222; www. travelbug.com.au; tours $175) Offers a one-day tour.

Western Xposure (☎08-9414 8423; www. westernxposure.com.au) Takes in Wave Rock as part of a five-day south-west loop ($750).

Dryandra Woodland

This superb, isolated remnant of eucalypt forest 164km south-east of Perth, with its thickets of white-barked wandoo, powderbark and rock she-oak, and small populations of threatened numbats, woylies and tammar wallabies, hints at what the wheat belt was like before large-scale land clearing and feral predators wreaked havoc on the local ecosystems. It also makes a great weekend getaway from Perth, and there're numerous walking trails.

The excellent **Barna Mia Animal Sanctuary**, home to endangered bilbies, boodies, woylies and marla, conducts 90-minute after-dark torchlight tours, providing a rare opportunity to see these cute furry creatures up close. Book through **DEC** (☎weekdays/ weekends 08-9881 9200/08-9881 2064; www. dec.gov.au; Hough St, Narrogin; adult/child/family

$13/7/35; ◷9am-4pm) for post-sunset tours on Monday, Wednesday, Friday and Saturday and book early for peak periods.

While you can hoist your tent at the pleasant **Congelin Camp Ground** (per person $7), Dryandra is one place you should splurge a little. The **Lions Dryandra Village** (☎08-9884 5231; www.dryandravillage. org.au; midweek adult/child $25/10, weekends & holidays cabins $60-100) is a 1920s forestry camp in the heart of the forest, offering fully self-contained, renovated woodcutters' cabins complete with fridge, stove, fireplace, en suite and nearby grazing wallabies. **Narrogin** (www.dryandratourism.org. au), serviced by Transwa buses, is 22km south-east, where you might find a **taxi** (☎08-9881 4381).

Hyden & Wave Rock

Large granite outcrops dot the area known as the Central and Southern Wheat Belts, and the most famous is the perfectly shaped, multicoloured cresting wave of **Wave Rock**. Formed some 60 million years ago by weathering and water erosion, Wave Rock's streaks of colour were created by run-off from local mineral springs.

To get the most out of Wave Rock, 350km from Perth, grab the brochure *Walk Trails at Wave Rock and The Humps* from the **visitor centre** (☎08-9880 5182; www.waverock. com.au; Wave Rock; ◷9am-5pm). Park at Hippos Yawn (no fee) and follow the shady track back along the rock base to Wave Rock (1km).

Accommodation can fill quickly, so phone ahead for a spot amid the gum trees at **Wave Rock Cabins & Caravan Park** (☎08-9880 5022; www.waverock.com.au; unpowered/powered sites $28/35, cabin s/d $120/135; ❋≋).

In **Hyden** (population 190), 4km east of the rock, the '70s brick **Wave Rock Motel** (☎08-9880 5052; hotelmotel@waverock.com.au; 2 Lynch St; d from $145; ❋≋) has well-equipped rooms, a comfy lounge with fireplace, and an indoor bush bistro.

Transwa runs a bus from Perth to Hyden ($48, five hours) and on to Esperance ($50, five hours) every Tuesday, returning on Thursday. If heading to/from the Nullarbor, you can take the unsealed direct **Hyden–Norseman Rd**, which will save 100km or so. Look for the brochure *The Granite and Woodlands Discovery Trail* at Norseman or Wave Rock visitor centres.

DON'T MISS

MULKAS CAVE & THE HUMPS

The superb Mulkas Cave and the Humps are a further 16km from Wave Rock. Mulkas Cave, an easy stroll from the car park, is an important rock-art site with over 450 stencils and hand prints. The more adventurous can choose from two walking tracks, both with interpretative signage. The **Kalari Trail** (1.6km return) climbs up onto a huge granite outcrop (one of the Humps) with excellent views, somehow wilder and more impressive than Wave Rock, while the **Gnamma Trail** (1.2km return) stays low and investigates natural waterholes with panels explaining Noongar culture.

SUNSET & TURQUOISE COASTS

The newly completed Indian Ocean Dr connects Perth to a succession of beautiful beaches, sleepy fishing villages, extraordinary geological formations, rugged national parks and incredibly diverse flora.

ⓘ Getting There & Away
Greyhound (☐1300 473 946; www.greyhound. com.au) Runs three times weekly to/from Perth along Indian Ocean Dr.

Yanchep National Park

The woodlands and wetlands of **Yanchep National Park** (www.dec.wa.gov.au/yanchep; Wanneroo Rd; admission per car $11; ☉visitor centre 9.15am-4.30pm) are home to hundreds of species of fauna and flora including koalas, kangaroos, emus and cockatoos. Caves can be viewed on 45-minute tours (adult/child $10/5; five per day). On weekends, local Noongar guides run excellent tours on Indigenous history, lifestyle and culture (adult/child $10/5), and give didgeridoo and dance performances (adult/child $10/5). There's also a free koala talk at 3pm daily and a free history tour on Saturday.

Guilderton

POP 150

Some 43km north of Yanchep, Guilderton is a popular and staggeringly beautiful family-holiday spot. Children paddle safely near the mouth of the Moore River, while adults enjoy the excellent fishing, surfing and sunbathing on the white sands of the ocean beach. The wonderfully positioned **Guilderton Caravan Park** (☐08-9577 1021; www.guildertoncaravan park.com.au; 2 Dewar St; sites per 2 people $24-32, chalets $100-175) is the holidaymakers' hub, with self-contained chalets, a cafe and a general store, and there's a little volunteer-run **visitor centre** (with erratic hours) next door.

Lancelin

POP 670

Afternoon winds and shallows protected by an outlying reef make this sleepy beach perfect for windsurfing and kitesurfing, attracting action seekers from around the world for the **Lancelin Ocean Classic** (www. lancelinoceanclassic.com.au) every January. It's also a great snorkelling spot.

🏃 Activities

Surfing Perth Western Australia SURFING
(☐08-9444 5399; www.surfschool.com; 2-/3-/4-day surf camps $330/460/585) Two-hour lessons (adult/child $55/50) include boards and wetsuits.

Desert Storm Adventures DUNE RIDES
(☐08-9655 2550; www.desertstorm.com.au; adult/child $55/35) This shiny yellow vampiric American school bus on steroids takes a wild ride through giant sand dunes.

Werner's Hot Spot WINDSURFING
(☐08-9655 1448; www.wernershotspot.blogspot. com) Windsurfing lessons and gear hire; look for the Kombi parked at the beach, or phone.

🛏 Sleeping & Eating

Lancelin Lodge YHA HOSTEL $
(☐08-9655 2020; www.lancelinlodge.com.au; 10 Hopkins St; dm $27-30, r $70; @🛜🏊) This laid-back hostel is well equipped and welcoming, with wide verandahs and lots of communal spaces to hang about in. Bikes and boogie boards are provided.

Endeavour Tavern PUB $$
(58 Gingin Rd; mains $15-34) A classic beachfront Aussie pub with a beer garden overlooking the ocean serving decent seafood.

Cervantes & Pinnacles Desert

POP 500

The laid-back crayfishing town of Cervantes, 198km north of Perth, makes a pleasant overnight stop for enjoying the Pinnacles Desert and a good base for exploring the flora of the Kwongan, the inland heathland of Lesueur National Park and Badgingarra National Park. There're also some lovely beaches to while away the time.

Grab a copy of the *Turquoise Coast Self Drive Map* from Cervantes' combined post office and visitor centre (☑08-9652 7700; www.visitpinnaclescountry.com.au; Cadiz St; ☺7.30am-5pm), which also supplies accommodation and tours information.

◉ Sights & Activities

Nambung National Park NATURE RESERVE
(per car $11) This national park, 19km from Cervantes, is home to the spectacular Pinnacles Desert, where thousands of limestone pillars rise up from the desert floor, their lime-rich sand originating from seashells that were compacted by rain and subsequently eroded. A loop road runs through the formations, but it's more fun to wander, especially at sunset, full moon or dawn, when the light is sublime and the crowds evaporate.

Nearby, Kangaroo Point and Hangover Bay, with BBQs and tables, both make nice picnic spots, while stromatolites inhabit the shoreline at Lake Thetis, and Hansen Bay Lookout has excellent views across the coast. In town, walkways wend along the coastline providing beach access.

Lesueur National Park NATURE RESERVE
(per car $11) This botanical paradise, 50km north of Cervantes, contains a staggering 820 plant species, many of them rare and endemic, such as the pine banksia (*Banksia tricuspis*) and Mt Lesueur grevillea (*Grevillea batrachioides*). The park also provides habitat for the endangered Carnaby's cockatoo, and the heath erupts into a mass of colour in late winter. There's an 18km circuit drive on a good road, with lookouts and picnic areas. Flat-topped Mt Lesueur (4km return) has panoramic coastal views.

Tours

Many Perth-based companies offer day trips to the Pinnacles.

Turquoise Coast Enviro Tours SIGHTSEEING
(☑08-9652 7047; www.thepinnacles.com.au; 59 Seville St; 3hr Pinnacles tours $60, full-day Kwongan tours $170) At this excellent Cervantes outfit, ex-ranger Mike Newton runs three-hour morning (8am) and evening (2½ hours before sunset) Pinnacles trips, as well as a full-day Kwongan tour, including Lesueur National Park and the coast up to Leeman.

🛏 Sleeping & Eating

Prices surge during school holidays.

TOP **Cervantes Lodge & Pinnacles**
Beach Backpackers HOSTEL $
(☑1800 245 232; www.cervanteslodge.com.au; 91 Seville St; dm $30, d with/without bathroom $120/80; @) In a great location behind the dunes, this relaxing hostel has a wide verandah, small and tidy dorms, a nice communal kitchen and a cosy lounge area. Bright, spacious en-suite rooms are next door in the lodge.

TOP **Amble Inn** B&B $$
(☑0429 652 401; 2150 Cadda Rd, Hill River; d spa/non-spa $150/135; ❀) High up on the heathland, about 25km east of Cervantes, this hidden gem of a B&B has beautiful thick stone walls, cool, wide verandahs and superbly styled rooms. Watch the sunset over the coast from the nearby hill with a glass of your complimentary wine.

Pinnacles Caravan Park CARAVAN PARK $
(☑08-9652 7060; www.pinnaclespark.com.au; 35 Aragon St; unpowered/powered sites from $15/26, on-site vans/cabins $50/75; ☎) There're plenty of shady, grassy sites right behind the beach at this excellent park. Seashells Cafe (☺8am-5pm) does a super coffee and cake with the best view in town.

Cervantes Country Club SEAFOOD $$
(☑08-9652 7054; Aragon St) Shorts and sandals are fine at this humble sporting club, which does incredible seafood platters for two ($55) with crays (in season), prawns, oysters, fish, calamari, salad and a mountain of chips.

❶ Getting There & Away

Greyhound has services to Perth ($34, three hours) and Dongara ($39, two hours), continuing to Broome ($350, 31 hours). It stops locally

KWONGAN WILDFLOWERS

Take any road heading inland from the Turquoise Coast and you'll soon enter the Kwongan heathlands where, depending on the season, the roadside verges burst with native wildflowers like banksia, grevillea, hakea, calothamnus, kangaroo paw and smokebush. Flowering is most prolific from July to November, but it's worth visiting any time as there's always something in bloom. While Lesueur National Park is the obvious choice, consider some of these other options:

» **Badgingarra National Park** There are 3.5km of walking trails, kangaroo paws, banksias, grass trees, verticordia and a rare mallee. Obtain details from the Badgingarra roadhouse. There's also a picnic area on Bibby Rd. The back road linking Badgingarra to Lesueur is particularly rich in flora.

» **Alexander Morrison National Park** Named after WA's first botanist, this park has no trails, but you can drive through slowly on the Coorow–Green Head Rd, which has excellent flora along its verge all the way from Lesueur. Expect to see dryandra, banksia, grevillea, smokebush, leschenaultia and honey myrtle.

» **Tathra National Park** On the sand plain, Tathra has similar flora to Alexander Morrison and the drive between the two is exceptionally rich with banksia, smokebush, kangaroo paw and grevillea.

» **Brand Highway** It's not exactly conducive to slow meandering, but the highway's verges are surprisingly rich in wildflowers, especially either side of Eneabba.

» **Wildflower Way (Rte 115)** From Wongan Hills verticordia to the wreath flower of Mullewa, and the everlastings of Coalseam National Park, the verges and back roads surrounding Rtes 116 and 115 (including Moora and pretty Perenjori) abound with spectacular natives.

If you're overwhelmed by trying to identify all these strange new plants, consider staying at **Western Flora Caravan Park** (☏08-9955 2030; wfloracp@activ8.net.au; Brand Hwy, North Eneabba; unpowered/powered sites $23/25, d $65, onsite vans $75, chalets $110), where the passionate owners run free two-hour guided wildflower walks across their 65-hectare property every afternoon at 4.30pm.

at Jurien (10 minutes), Green Head (30 minutes) and Leeman (40 minutes).

Jurien Bay, Green Head & Leeman

Heading north from Cervantes, sprawling Jurien Bay (population 1500) is home to a large fishing fleet and pleasant seaside walks. **Jurien Bay Tourist Park** (☏08-9652 1595; www.jurienbaytouristpark.com.au; Roberts St; unpowered/powered sites $26/35, on-site vans $75-105, 1-/2-bedroom chalets $130/165) has comfortable chalets right behind the beach. Next door, the **Jetty Cafe** (☏08-9652 1999; meals $5-17; ⏰7.30am-5pm) does all-day brekkies as well as grilled fish and burgers.

Tiny Green Head (population 300) has several beautiful bays great for swimming, and nearby Leeman (population 680) is popular with windsurfers.

[TOP CHOICE] **Sea Lion Charters** (☏08-9953 1012; http://sealioncharters.biz/; 24 Bryant St, Green Head; half-day tours adult/child $120/60) offers a magical experience interacting in shallow water with playful sea lions who mimic your every move.

Green Head has several B&Bs, and the **Green Head Caravan Park** (☏08-9953 1131; 9 Green Head Rd, Green Head; unpowered/powered sites $18/21, on-site vans from $47) is relaxed and shady.

Leafy **Leeman Caravan Park** (☏08-9953 1080; 43 Thomas St, Leeman; unpowered/powered sites $20/25, on-site vans $60, cabins $70-90) has shady, grassy sites and a good camp kitchen, all just behind the beach.

If you have a 4WD, **Stockyard Gully Caves** are 30km away, off the Coorow–Green Head Rd, and you can explore the underground creek and caverns with a torch. Watch out for bees and bats.

GREAT NORTHERN HWY

Most travellers avoid the direct route north, preferring the scenic attractions of the coast to the minimalist landscape and dusty mining towns of the interior. Closer to Perth, the peaceful monastic village (and lovely pub) of New Norcia makes for an excellent weekend getaway.

ⓘ Getting There & Away

AIR

Skippers (☏1300 729 924; www.skippers.com.au) Flies regularly between Perth, Mt Magnet and Meekatharra.

BUS

Integrity (☏1800 226 339; www.integrity coachlines.com.au) Leaves Perth Wednesday and runs up the Great Northern Hwy (Rte 95) to Mt Magnet ($95, eight hours), Cue ($107, nine hours), Meekatharra ($124, 11 hours) and Newman ($214, 16 hours), before reaching Port Hedland ($232, 22 hours); returns Friday.

Transwa (☏1300 662 205; www.transwa.wa.gov.au) Runs Monday and Thursday from Geraldton to Mt Magnet ($48, five hours), Cue ($58, six hours) and Meekatharra ($69, seven hours) along Rte 123, returning Tuesday and Friday; connections to Perth via Mullewa ($66, six hours) and Geraldton.

New Norcia

POP 70

The idyllic monastery settlement of New Norcia, 132km from Perth, consists of a cluster of ornate Spanish-style buildings set incongruously in the Australian bush. Founded in 1846 by Spanish Benedictine monks as an Aboriginal mission, today the working monastery holds prayers and retreats, alongside a business producing boutique breads and gourmet goodies.

New Norcia Museum & Art Gallery (☏08-9654 8056; www.newnorcia.wa.edu.au; Great Northern Hwy; combined museum & town tours adult/family $25/60; ◷9am-4.30pm) traces the history of the monastery and houses impressive art, including contemporary exhibitions and one of the country's largest collections of post-Renaissance religious art. The gift shop sells souvenirs, honey and lovely local bread.

Guided two-hour **town tours** (◷11am & 1.30pm) include various chapels and their amazing frescoes; purchase tickets from the museum. **Meet a Monk** (◷4.30pm Sat) is exactly what it seems.

[TOP CHOICE] **New Norcia Hotel** (☏08-9654 8034; www.newnorcia.wa.edu.au; Great Northern Hwy; s/d without bathroom $75/95, mains $13-30) invokes a more genteel era, with sweeping staircases, high ceilings, understated rooms and wide verandahs. An international menu is available at the bar or in the elegant dining room (open for breakfast). Sit outside on the terrace and sample the delicious but deadly New Norcia Abbey Ale, a golden handcrafted Belgian-style ale brewed specially for the abbey.

The abbey also offers full lodging in the **Monastery Guesthouse** (☏08-9654 8002; www.newnorcia.wa.edu.au; full board donation $75), within the walls of the southern cloister.

ⓘ Getting There & Away

Transwa coaches run from Perth ($21, two hours) on Tuesday, Thursday, Saturday and Sunday, returning on Sunday, Tuesday and Thursday. Integrity buses to/from Perth ($24, two hours) stop at ungodly times on Wednesday (northbound) and Saturday (southbound).

New Norcia to Meekatharra

A handful of dusty mining towns lie strung out like nuggets along the thousand parched kilometres between New Norcia and Newman. **Mt Magnet** has a couple of pubs, a supermarket, an airport and a dusty caravan park, as does Meekatharra, from where the shortest route to Mt Augustus departs.

In between the two is the beautiful goldfields architecture of **Cue**. There's a pub, a B&B – the grand **Queen of the Murchison** (☏08-9963 1625; Austin St; s/d $88/120; ✳) – and a dusty caravan park. Look for a sign saying 'fresh coffee' on the side street, and you'll find **Camelman** outback clothing.

BATAVIA COAST

From sleepy Dongara-Port Denison to the remote, wind-scoured Zuytdorp Cliffs stretches a dramatic coastline steeped in history, littered with shipwrecks and abounding in marine life. While it proved the undoing of many early European sailors, today modern fleets make the most of a lucrative crayfish industry.

Sun-drenched Geraldton is surrounded by perfect windsurfing beaches and home to *macchiato*-friendly cafes, while offshore the

Houtman Abrolhos Islands are a paradise for wreck divers and naturalists. Further north, in Nhanda country, the gorges of Kalbarri invite adventurers, wildflowers carpet the plains and battered cliffs stand mute vigil as whales migrate slowly south.

❶ Getting There & Around

AIR

The following airlines service the Batavia coast:

Skippers (☑1300 729 924; www.skippers.com.au)

Skywest (☑1300 660 088; www.skywest.com.au)

BUS

Greyhound (☑1300 473 946; www.greyhound.com.au) Runs three times weekly between Broome and Perth along the coast.

Transwa (☑1300 662 205; www.transwa.wa.gov.au) Runs regular buses between Perth and Kalbarri, Geraldton and Dongara along the Brand Hwy (Rte 1).

Dongara-Port Denison

POP 4000

Dongara and Port Denison, twin seaside towns 359km from Perth, are known for their beautiful beaches, historic buildings and laid-back atmosphere. Port Denison has most of the beaches and accommodation, while Dongara's main street, shaded by century-old figs, holds the banks, and internet and food options.

◎ Sights & Activities

Ask for the *Walk Dongara Denison* brochure at the Holiday Shop (33 Moreton Tce, Dongara). There is 11 historic or nature-based outings to choose from, as well as the Irwin River Nature Trail (just behind the Dongara shops at the end of Waldeck St), where you might spot black swans, pelicans or cormorants.

In the old police station, the cells of the Irwin District Museum (☑08-9927 1404; admission $2.50; ◎10am-noon Mon-Sat) hold informative historical displays.

Sunsets are dazzling from the Fisherman's Lookout Obelisk at Port Denison.

⛺ Sleeping & Eating

Public and school holidays attract a surcharge. There is a supermarket, cafes and takeaways on Moreton Tce and a good bakery on Waldeck St in Dongara; the Port Store (52 Point Leander Dr) in Port Denison has most necessities.

Priory Lodge `TOP CHOICE` BOUTIQUE HOTEL **$$**
(☑08-9927 1090; www.prioryhotel.com.au; 11 St Dominics Rd, Dongara; r $70-130, mains $19-28; ❋ 🤫 ⛶) There's a touch of *Picnic at Hanging Rock* about this leafy former nunnery and ladies college, with charming period furniture, polished floorboards, black-and-white photos and wide verandahs. There's live music and pizza on weekends, Sunday roasts, and steaks every night.

Dongara Tourist Park CARAVAN PARK **$**
(☑08-9927 1210; www.dongaratouristpark.com.au; 8 George St, Port Denison; unpowered/powered sites $22/28, 1-/2-bedroom cabins $95/130; ❋ 🤫) This is the best camping option in town – it offers shaded, spacious sites located behind South Beach. The two-bedroom cabins on the hill have sensational views, and there is a lush pergola for outdoor dining.

Port Denison Holiday Units APARTMENTS **$$**
(☑08-9927 1104; www.portdenisonholidayunits.com.au; 14 Carnarvon St, Port Denison; d $110-120; ❋ 🤫) These spotless, spacious self-catering units are located just a block away from the beach. Some of the units have marina views.

Dongara Hotel Motel MOTEL **$$**
(☑08-9927 1023; www.dongaramotel.com.au; 12 Moreton Tce, Dongara; d $130, mains $18-38; ◎breakfast, lunch & dinner; ❋ 🤫 ⛶) The best food in town includes classic seafood dishes and Southeast Asian staples. The motel rooms are OK.

Little Starfish CAFE **$$**
(☑0448 344 215; White Tops Rd, Port Denison; mains $10-30; ◎8am-4pm Wed-Mon) Hidden away in the South Beach car park, this funky little shack provides great seafood snacks.

❶ Information

Moreton Tce, Dongara, has several banks with ATMs.

Holiday Shop (☑08-9927 1900; 33 Moreton Tce, Dongara) Good for general info and bus tickets.

Telecentre (☑08-9927 2111; 11 Moreton Tce, Dongara; ◎9am-4pm Mon-Fri; @)

Visitor centre (☑08-9927 1404; www.irwin.wa.gov.au; 9 Waldeck St, Dongara; ◎9am-5pm Mon-Fri, to noon Sat)

❶ Getting There & Around

Dongara-Port Denison is accessible via the Brand Hwy, Indian Ocean Dr or Midlands Rd (Rte

116). Greyhound buses go to Broome ($330, 29 hours, Monday, Wednesday and Friday) and Perth ($55, six hours, Wednesday, Friday and Sunday). Transwa runs daily to Perth ($50, six hours) and Geraldton ($13, one hour). Buses arrive at and depart from the visitor centre.

Geraldton

POP 37,500

Capital of the midwest, and surrounded by excellent beaches, Gero is a place on the move. The largest town between Perth and Darwin has huge wheat-handling and fishing industries, making it independent of the fickle tourist dollar. Seasonal workers flood the town during crayfish season. There's a slick new (albeit empty) marina and stunning foreshore area, a strong art and culture scene, some fine-dining cafes and restaurants, good local music and superb windsurfing.

◎ Sights

Western Australian Museum – Geraldton MUSEUM
(☑08-9921 5080; www.museum.wa.gov.au; 1 Museum Pl; admission by donation; ☺9.30am-4pm) This excellent museum has intelligent multimedia displays on the area's natural, cultural and Indigenous history. The atmospheric Shipwreck Gallery documents the tragic story of the *Batavia,* while video footage reveals the sunken HMAS *Sydney.* On Sunday at 2pm you can sail in the longboat moored behind the museum.

Cathedral of St Francis Xavier CHURCH
(Cathedral Ave; tours $5; ☺tours 10am Mon, Wed & Fri) This elaborate cathedral is the finest example of the architectural achievements of multi-skilled Monsignor John Hawes. Its most striking features include imposing twin towers with arched openings, a central dome, Romanesque columns and boldly striped walls.

FREE **Geraldton Regional Art Gallery** ART GALLERY
(☑08-9964 7170; 24 Chapman Rd; ☺10am-4pm Tue-Sat, from 1pm Sun) This gallery has an excellent permanent collection, including paintings by Norman Lindsay and Elizabeth Durack, provocative contemporary work and engaging temporary exhibitions.

FREE **Old Geraldton Gaol Craft Centre** HISTORIC BUILDING
(☑08-9921 1614; Bill Sewell Complex, Chapman Rd; ☺10am-4pm, Mon-Sat) The crafts here are

secondary to the gloomy cells that housed prisoners from 1858 to 1986 and the historic documents detailing their grim circumstances.

HMAS Sydney II Memorial MONUMENT
(tours free; ☺tours 10am) Commanding the hill overlooking Geraldton is this memorial commemorating the 1941 loss of the *Sydney* and its 645 men after a skirmish with the German raider *Kormoran.*

🏃 Activities

Geraldton is surrounded by spectacular beaches perfect for swimming, surfing, wind- and kite-surfing.

G-Spot Xtreme WATER-SPORTS HIRE
(☑08-9965 5577; www.gspotxtreme.com.au; 241a Lester Ave; hire per day windsurfers $100, kiteboards $50, kayaks $70) Can also hook you up with instructors.

Batavia Coast Dive Academy DIVING
(☑08-9921 4229; www.bcda.com.au; 153 Marine Tce; local dives with/without equipment $140/100) Offers open-water courses (full PADI $600) and a range of diving trips, including three-day chartered trips to the Abrolhos ($900 per person).

Tarcoola Beach to Chapman River Cycle Path CYCLING
Geraldton has great cycle paths, including this 10km coastal route. Grab the excellent *Active Travel Cycling and Walking* brochure from the visitor centre and check bike-hire options.

🎊 Festivals & Events

Blessing of the Fishing Fleet FISHING
(www.gfcblessing.com; Fisherman's Wharf; admission $5) Huge carnival normally held on the last weekend in October.

🛏 Sleeping

Accommodation in Geraldton hasn't kept pace with the rest of the changes. Expect price hikes for school and public holidays.

TOP CHOICE **Weelaway** B&B $$
(☑08-9965 5232; www.weelaway.com.au; 104 Gregory St; r $130-140; ☎) Exquisitely decorated rooms are on offer in this heritage-listed house dating from 1862 that's within walking distance of the CBD. There're formal lounge rooms, shady, wide verandahs, and a well-stocked library.

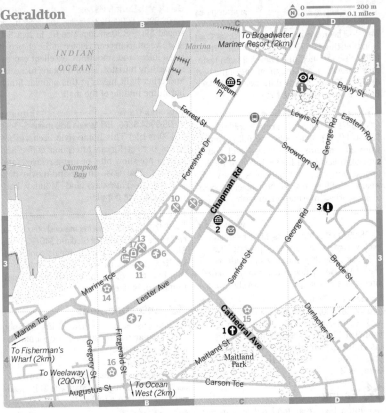

Geraldton

⊙ Sights

1 Cathedral of St Francis Xavier	C4
2 Geraldton Regional Art Gallery	C3
3 HMAS Sydney II Memorial	D2
4 Old Geraldton Gaol Craft Centre	D1
5 Western Australian Museum – Geraldton	C1

Activities, Courses & Tours

6 Batavia Coast Dive Academy	B3
7 G-Spot Xtreme	B4

Sleeping

8 Foreshore Backpackers	B3
Freemason's Hotel	(see 9)

⊗ Eating

9 Freemasons Hotel	C2
10 Go Health Lunch Bar	B2
11 Provincial	B3
12 Saltdish	C2
13 Topolinis Caffe	B3

Entertainment

14 Orana Cinemas	B3
15 Queens Park Theatre	C4
16 Up	B4

Shopping

17 Book Tree	B3

TOP CHOICE **Ocean West** APARTMENTS **$$**
(☑08-9921 1047; www.oceanwest.com.au; 1 Hadda Way; 1-/3-bedroom apt from $125/170; ❄🛜🏊) Don't let the '60s bricks put you off – these fully self-contained units have all been tastefully renovated, making them one of the best deals in town. The wildly beautiful Back Beach is just across the road.

Foreshore Backpackers HOSTEL **$**
(☑08-9921 3275; 172 Marine Tce; dm/s/d $25/40/60; @) Shambolic, rambling, multistoreyed, oozing character (and other things), this central hostel is full of hidden nooks, lounges, sunny balconies and world-weary travellers. It's the best place to swap blogs, stories, information and jobs.

Sunset Beach Holiday Park CARAVAN PARK **$**
(☑08-9938 1655; http://sunset-beach-holiday -park.wa.big4.com.au; Bosley St; powered sites $33, cabins $85-110) About 6km north of the CBD, Sunset Beach has roomy, shaded sites just a few steps from a lovely beach.

Broadwater Mariner Resort RESORT **$$$**
(☑1800 181 480; www.mariner.broadwaters.com. au; 298 Chapman Rd; studio/1-/2-bedroom apt from $175/228/277; ❄🛜🏊) Offers spotless, tastefully appointed rooms with a corporate vibe. Across from the excellent St Georges Beach.

✖ Eating

Geraldton has great food options, including takeaways, coffee lounges, bakeries and supermarkets.

TOP CHOICE **Saltdish** CAFE **$$**
(☑08-9964 6030; 35 Marine Tce; breakfasts $6-18, lunches $13-26; ⊙7.30am-2.30pm Mon-Sat) The hippest cafe in town does innovative, contemporary brekkies, light lunches and industrial-strength coffee, and screens films over summer evenings in its courtyard. Try the baked eggs or curry-spiced squid. BYO.

Provincial MODERN AUSTRALIAN **$$**
(☑08-9964 1887; www.theprovincial.com.au; 167 Marine Tce; breakfasts $7-20, meals $16-28; ⊙7am-late) The much-loved Bella Vista has moved a few doors up and morphed into a stencil art–decorated wine bar serving Mediterranean-Oz fusion dishes like Wagyu burgers, stuffed eggplant, homemade pasta (including angel hair with crabmeat) and wood-fired pizzas.

Go Health Lunch Bar CAFE **$**
(☑08-9965 5200; 122 Marine Tce; light meals around $9; ⊙8.30am-3pm Mon-Fri, to 1pm Sat; @♪) Vegetarians can rejoice at the choice of fresh juices and smoothies, excellent espresso, healthy burritos, lentil burgers, focaccias and other light meals at this popular lunch bar in the middle of the mall.

Topolinis Caffe ITALIAN **$$**
(☑08-9964 5866; 158 Marine Tce; mains $23-38; ⊙8.30am-late) This home-style licensed bistro is perfect for an afternoon coffee and cake, a pre-show bite, or just a relaxed family feed. The $34 dinner-and-movie deal (Sunday to Thursday) and Monday half-price pasta are popular.

Freemasons Hotel PUB FARE **$$**
(☑08-9964 3457; www.freemasonshotel.com.au; cnr Marine Tce & Durlacher St; dm/d $40/90, meals $16-32; ⊙11am-late) Try the meals cooked on sizzling stone slabs for a taste sensation at this beautiful old pub. It also has a small number of budget rooms.

☆ Entertainment

Freemasons is a favourite drinking spot, with regular live music and occasional DJs and dance nights.

Orana Cinemas CINEMA
(☑08-9965 0568; www.oranacinemas.com.au; cnr Marine Tce & Fitzgerald St; tickets $15) Head here for the latest flicks.

Queens Park Theatre THEATRE
(☑08-9956 6662; cnr Cathedral Ave & Maitland St) Stages theatre, comedy, concerts and films.

Up NIGHTCLUB
(☑08-9921 1400; 60 Fitzgerald St; ⊙Thu-Sat) Three bars include a large clubbers dance floor, a late-night pool room and an outdoor chill patio.

🛍 Shopping

Book Tree BOOKS
(176 Marine Tce; ⊙9.30am-4.30pm Mon-Fri) Floor-to-ceiling shelves of preloved books.

ℹ Information

Several banks with ATMs are on Marine Tce, and there's free wi-fi along the foreshore.
Geraldton Regional Hospital (☑08-9956 2222; Shenton St; ⊙24hr) Emergency facilities.
Jam Gero's free little what's-on monthly booklet.

Sun City Books & Internet Corner (☑08-9964 7258; 49 Marine Tce; ⊙9am-5pm Mon-Fri, to 1pm Sat; @) Lots of terminals (and a decent selection of books).

Visitor centre (☑08-9921 3999; www.geraldtontourist.com.au; Bill Sewell Complex, Chapman Rd; ⊙9am-5pm Mon-Fri, 10am-4pm Sat & Sun) One of the best around, with lots of great info sheets and helpful staff who'll book accommodation, tours and transport.

www.gero.com.au Excellent online resource for local gigs, dining and gossip.

❶ Getting There & Around

AIR Skywest flies daily to Perth, and regularly to Exmouth and Karratha.

BUS Batavia Tickets (☑08-9964 8881; www.bataviatickets.com.au), at the old railway station, sells long-distance bus tickets; buses depart outside. Greyhound buses run three times weekly to Perth ($60, six hours) and north along the coast to Carnarvon ($100, six hours) and Broome ($324, 28 hours). Transwa goes to Perth daily ($58, six hours) and three times weekly to Kalbarri ($26, 2½ hours). There's also a twice-weekly service to Meekatharra ($68, seven hours). **Transgeraldton** (☑08-9923 2225; www.buswest.com.au) operates eight routes to local suburbs (all-day tickets are $4).

TAXI Call ☑13 10 08.

Kalbarri

POP 2000

Magnificent red-sandstone cliffs end abruptly, falling prey to the Indian Ocean's slow war of attrition. The beautiful Murchison River snakes through tall, steep gorges before ending treacherously at Gantheaume Bay. Wildflowers line paths frequented by kangaroos, emus and thorny devils, while whales breach just offshore and rare orchids struggle in the rocky ground. To the north, the towering cliff line of the limestone Zuytdorp remains aloof, pristine and remote.

Kalbarri is surrounded by stunning nature, and there's great surfing, swimming, fishing, bushwalking, horse riding and canoeing both in town and in the encompassing Kalbarri National Park. While the vibe is mostly low key, school holidays see Kalbarri stretched to the limit.

⊙ Sights & Activities

Kalbarri National Park   NATIONAL PARK
(per car $11) With its magnificent river red gums and Tumblagooda sandstone, this rugged park contains almost 2000 sq km

of wild bushland, stunning river gorges and savagely eroded coastal cliffs. There's abundant wildlife, including 200 species of bird, and spectacular wildflowers between July and November.

A string of lookouts dots the impressive coast south of town and the easy **Bigurda Trail** (8km one way) follows the cliff tops between **Natural Bridge** and **Eagle Gorge**; from July to November you may spot migrating whales. Closer to town are **Pot Alley**, **Rainbow Valley**, **Mushroom Rock** and **Red Bluff**, the last accessible via a walking trail from Kalbarri (5.5km one way).

The river gorges are east of Kalbarri, off Ajana Kalbarri Rd. Bring lots of water for the unshaded **Loop Trail** (8km return) or just visit the superb natural rock arch of **Nature's Window** (1km return). **Z-Bend** has a breathtaking lookout (1.2km return), or you can continue steeply down to the gorge bottom (2.6km return). **Hawk's Head**, back off the main road, has great views and picnic tables, and you can access the river at **Ross Graham**. It's possible to hike 38km from Ross Graham to the Loop in a demanding four-day epic with no marked trails and several river crossings.

Kalbarri Wildflower Centre   NATURE RESERVE
(☑08-9937 1229; off Ajana Kalbarri Rd; adult/child $5/2, tours $10; ⊙9am-1pm Jun-Oct, Wed-Mon, tours 10am) Stroll 1.8km along a labelled wildflower trail, or take a guided tour.

Pelican Feeding   WILDLIFE WATCHING
(☑08-9937 1104; ⊙8.45am) Kalbarri's most popular attraction is on the Grey St waterfront near the boat hire.

Kalbarri Boat Hire   CANOEING, HIRE
(☑08-9937 1245; www.kalbarriboathire.com; Grey St waterfront; kayak/canoe/surf cat/powerboat per hr $15/15/45/50) On the foreshore, this place hires out various aquatic transports. It also runs four-hour breakfast and lunch canoe trips down the Murchison (adult/child $65/45).

Kalbarri has a great network of **cycle paths** along the foreshore, and you can ride out to Blue Holes for **snorkelling**, Jakes Point with its excellent **surf** and **fishing** and **Red Bluff Beach** (5.5km). Any of the **lookouts** along the coast are perfect for watching the sunset.

Ⓕ Tours

Here's a selection; the visitor centre has a full list and takes bookings.

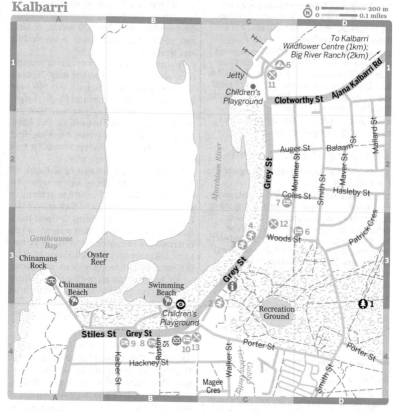

Kalbarri

Kalbarri Abseil ABSEILING
(☎08-9937 1618; www.abseilaustralia.com.au; half-/full-day tours Apr-Nov $80/135, half-day Dec-Mar $65) Get vertical amid the gorges of Kalbarri National Park. Suitable for beginners.

Kalbarri Adventure Tours CANOEING
(☎08-9937 1677; www.kalbarritours.com.au;

adult/child $90/70) Combine canoeing, bushwalking and swimming around the park's Z-Bend/Loop area.

Kalbarri Air Charter SCENIC FLIGHTS
(☎08-9937 1130; www.kalbarriaircharter.com.au; 62 Grey St; flights $59-285) Twenty-minute scenic flights over the coastal cliffs, and

longer flights over gorges, the Zuytdorp Cliffs and the Abrolhos Islands.

Kalbarri Wilderness Cruises   CRUISES
(☑08-9937 2259; www.kalbarricruises.com.au; adult/child $40/28) Popular two-hour river cruises explore nature along the Murchison.

Sleeping

There's a lot of choice, but avoid school holidays, when prices skyrocket. The visitor centre is your friend.

Murchison View
Apartments   APARTMENTS $$
(☑08-9937 1096; www.kalbarrimurchisonviewapartments.com.au; cnr Grey & Ruston Sts; 2-bedroom units from $140; ✲☒) These spacious, fully self-contained apartments with balconies are great value, right opposite the waterfront.

Anchorage Caravan Park   CARAVAN PARK $
(☑08-9937 1181; www.kalbarrianchorage.com.au; cnr Anchorage Lane & Grey St; powered sites $34, cabins with/without bathroom $100/70; ☒) The best option for campers, Anchorage has roomy, nicely shaded sites overlooking the river mouth.

Kalbarri Backpackers   HOSTEL $
(☑08-9937 1430; www.yha.com.au; cnr Woods & Mortimer Sts; dm/d $29/77; @☒) This nice, shady hostel with a decent pool and BBQ is one block back from the beach. Bike hire is $20 per day.

Pelican Shore Villas   APARTMENTS $$$
(☑08-9937 1708; www.pelicanshorevillas.com.au; cnr Grey & Kaiber Sts; villas $133-204; ✲☎☒) With the best view in town, these beautifully manicured town houses have all the mod cons.

Kalbarri Reef Villas   APARTMENTS $$
(☑08-9937 1165; www.reefvillas.com.au; cnr Coles & Mortimer Sts; units $130-180; ✲☎☒) One block behind the foreshore, these fully self-contained two-bedroom apartments face onto a palm-filled garden.

Ray White Kalbarri
Accommodation Service   RENTAL HOUSES $$$
(☑08-9937 1700; www.kalbarriaccommodation.com.au; Kalbarri Arcade, 44 Grey St; houses per week $500-1700) Has a wide range of self-contained apartments and houses.

Eating   971

There are supermarkets and takeaways at the shopping centres, and bistros at the taverns.

⌈TOP⌉
⌊CHOICE⌋ Gorges Café   CAFE $$
(☑08-9937 1200; Marina Complex, Grey St; meals $6-23; ⊙7.30am-4pm Mon & Wed-Fri, to 2pm Sat & Sun) Ask for the Morning Cure and you won't be disappointed at this airy cafe doing wonderful breakfasts and lunches opposite the jetty.

Grass Tree   MODERN AUSTRALIAN $$
(☑08-9937 2288; www.thegrasstree.com.au; 94-96 Grey St; mains $15-$33; ⊙noon-late Fri-Tue) With a great surf view and innovative menu, there's no better place for lunch. A chilled wine washes down twice-cooked pork belly or smoked chicken and chickpea salad.

Restaurant Upstairs   MODERN AUSTRALIAN $$$
(☑08-9937 1033; upstairs, Porter St; mains $20-45; ⊙6pm-late Fri-Wed) This fine-dining establishment features local seafood, Asian fusion and outback faves like kangaroo and crocodile.

ⓘ Information

There are ATMs at the shopping centres on Grey and Porter Sts.

Kalbarri Café (☑08-9937 1045; Porter St; ⊙8.30am-7pm; @) Internet.

Kalbarri Community Resource Centre (☑08-9937 1933; Hackney St; ⊙9am-3pm Mon-Fri; @) Fax and internet.

Traveller's Book Exchange (☑08-9937 2676; ⊙9am-5pm Mon-Fri, to noon Sat; @) Internet (and secondhand books).

Visitor centre (☑1800 639 468; www.kalbarri.org.au; Grey St; ⊙9am-5pm) Great national-park and activities info and can book

DON'T MISS

BIG RIVER RANCH

Take a horse swimming at Big River Ranch (☑08-9937 1214; www.bigriver-ranch.net; off Ajana Kalbarri Rd; camp sites per person $10, powered sites $30, dm/d $20/60, trail rides 60/90/120min $55/70/90; ☒), just 2km east of Kalbarri on the Ajana Kalbarri Rd. Trail rides of varying lengths (including overnight) should suit most riders as you explore Murchison River country. Accommodation includes grassy tent sites, van and camper spaces (some powered) and rustic bunkhouse rooms.

accommodation and tours. Internet at the library next door.

ℹ Getting There & Around

AIR Skippers flies regularly to Perth via Shark Bay.

BUS Getting to/from Perth ($72, 10 hours) and Geraldton ($26, 2½ hours) is easiest with Tran-swa. Heading to/from points further north you'll need Greyhound, which stops at Binnu, 77km away on the highway. Arrange a **shuttle** (☏0419 371888) to meet/drop you ($40 per person). From Binnu you can reach Overlander roadhouse (for Monkey Mia; $50, two hours), Coral Bay ($100, eight hours), Broome ($300, 26 hours) and Perth ($100, eight hours).

CAR Kalbarri Auto Centre (☏08-9937 1290) rents 4WDs and sedans from $60 a day.

BICYCLE BicycleWA (☏08-9937 1105; 8 Porter St; half-/full day $10/20), inside Kalbarri Palms Resort, hires bikes. Both bikes and scooters can be hired from **Kalbarri Air Charter** (☏08-9937 1130; 62 Grey St; bikes half-/full day $10/20, scooters half-/full day $45/85).

SHARK BAY

World Heritage–listed Shark Bay, with more than 1500km of pristine coastline, barren peninsulas, white-sand beaches and bountiful marine life draws tourists from around the world. The sheltered turquoise waters and skinny fingers of stunted land at the westernmost edge of the continent are one of WA's most biologically rich habitats.

Lush beds of seagrass and sheltered bays nourish dugongs, sea turtles, humpback whales, rays, sharks and other aquatic life. Ancient stromatolites bask in the salt-rich waters of Hamelin Pool, while endangered marsupials benefit from Project Eden, an ambitious ecosystem-regeneration program that has sought to eradicate feral animals and reintroduce endemic species.

The Malgana, Nhanda and Inggarda peoples originally inhabited the area and visitors can take Indigenous cultural tours to learn about country. Shark Bay played host to early European explorers, and many geographical names show this legacy. In 1616 Dutchman Dirk Hartog famously left a pewter plate at Cape Inscription on the island now bearing his name.

ℹ Getting There & Away

AIR Shark Bay Airport is located between Denham and Monkey Mia. Skippers flies regularly to Perth.

BUS The closest Greyhound approach is the Overlander roadhouse 128km away on the North West Coastal Hwy (Rte 1). **Shark Bay Car Hire** (☏0427 483 032; www.carhire.net.au) runs a connecting shuttle ($65 per person; book ahead!). It also hires cars/4WDs from $40/185 per day.

Overlander Roadhouse to Denham

Hamelin Pool (not Hamelin Station!) marine reserve contains the world's best-known colony of **stromatolites**. These squat coral-like formations consist of cyano-bacterias, which almost identical to organisms existing 3500 million years ago and are considered largely responsible for creating our current atmosphere by using photosynthesis, paving the way for more complex life. There's an excellent boardwalk with information panels, best seen at low tide.

The adjacent 1884 **Telegraph Office** (admission $5.50) houses a fascinating museum containing possibly the only living stromatolites in captivity. The Postmaster's Residence is also the office for the tiny **Hamelin Pool Caravan Park** (☏08-9942 5905; unpowered/powered sites $22/25) and serves Devonshire teas, pies and ice creams.

Nearby **Hamelin Station** (☏08-9948 5145; www.hamelinstationstay.com.au; camp sites $20, s/d/f $65/95/125, units $125) has lovely rooms in converted shearers quarters, a brand-new kitchen and a spotless ablutions block.

Heading north, you pass the turn-off for **Useless Loop** (a closed salt-mining town) and desolate **Edel Land National Park** (☏08-9948 3993; entry permit per vehicle $11, camping per person $7), where **Steep Point** is the Australian mainland's westernmost tip. A barge ($55 per person return, March to October) connects Steep Point to historic **Dirk Hartog Island National Park** (camping per person $11), with basic coastal camp sites and the atmospheric **Dirk Hartog Island Lodge** (☏08-9948 1211; www.dirkhartogisland.com; full board per person $290; ☺Mar-Oct; ☏), a century-old, limestone converted shearers quarters with gourmet restaurant and bar. The lodge, barge and camp sites must be booked well in advance. The **fishing** is phenomenal.

Back on the main road, the compacted cockleshells of **Shell Beach** were once quarried as building material for businesses in Denham.

You'll pass turn-offs to free camp sites before reaching **Eagle Bluff**, with spectacular cliff-top views over a brilliant azure sea. If you're lucky, you may spot turtles, sharks or manta rays.

Denham

POP 1500

Beautiful, laid-back Denham, with its aquamarine sea and palm-fringed beachfront, only 26km from world-famous Monkey Mia, makes a great base for exploring the surrounding Shark Bay Marine Park and Peron Peninsula.

Australia's westernmost town originated as a pearling base, and the streets were once paved with pearl shell. Knight Tce, the now-tarmac main drag, has everything you need.

Sights & Activities

Shark Bay World Heritage Discovery Centre
MUSEUM

(☑08-9948 1590; www.sharkbayinterpretivecentre.com.au; 53 Knight Tce; adult/child $11/6; ☺9am-6pm) One of WA's best museums has engaging, informative displays on Shark Bay's ecosystem and its Indigenous people, early explorers and settlers.

Ocean Park
AQUARIUM

(☑08-9948 1765; www.oceanpark.com.au; Shark Bay Rd; adult/child $17/12; ☺9am-5pm) Superbly located on a headland just before town, this family-run aquaculture farm features an artificial lagoon where you can observe feeding sharks, turtles, stingrays and fish on guided 45-minute tours. The licensed cafe has sensational views. Also on offer are full-day 4WD tours with bushwalks and snorkelling to François Peron ($180) and Steep Point ($350).

Little Lagoon
LANDMARK

This pleasant picnic spot 4km from town has tables and barbecues, and you can walk, drive or cycle here. Don't be surprised if an emu wanders by.

Tours

Aussie Off Road Tours
4WD

(☑0429 929 175; www.aussieoffroadtours.com.au) Culture and history feature strongly in these excellent Indigenous-owned and -operated tours including twilight wildlife ($90), full-day François Peron National Park ($189), overnight camping in François Peron ($300) and overnight to Steep Point ($390).

Shark Bay Scenic Flights
SCENIC FLIGHTS

(☑08-9948 1773; www.sharkbayair.com.au) Various scenic flights including 15-minute Monkey Mia flyovers ($55), 40-minute trips over Steep Point and the Zuytdorp Cliffs ($150) and one-way charters to/from the Overlander roadhouse ($120).

Shark Bay Coaches & Tours
SIGHTSEEING

(☑08-9948 1081; www.sbcoaches.com; bus/quad $80/80) Half-day bus tours to all key sights, and two-hour quad-bike expeditions to various locations.

Capricorn Sea Kayaking
KAYAKING

(☑0427 485 123; www.capricornseakayaking.com.au; 7 days $1495) This Perth-based outfit runs several seven-day sea-kayaking trips in Shark Bay between May and September.

Sleeping & Eating

Denham has accommodation for all budgets; some places have long-stay discounts and/or school-holiday surcharges. There's a supermarket, a bakery, cafes and takeaways on Knight Tce.

Bay Lodge
HOSTEL $

(☑08-9948 1278; www.baylodge.info; 113 Knight Tce; dm/d from $26/68; @☒) Every room at this YHA hostel has its own en suite, kitchenette and TV/DVD. Ideally located across from the beach, it also has a great pool, a larger common kitchen, and a shuttle bus to Monkey Mia.

Denham Seaside Tourist Village
CARAVAN PARK $

(☑1300 133 733; www.sharkbayfun.com; Knight Tce; sites unpowered/powered/with bathroom $29/34/42, d cabins $80, 1-/2-bedroom chalets $120/130; ☒) This lovely, shady park on the water's edge is the best in town. Ring first if arriving after 6pm.

Oceanside Village
CABINS $$

(☑1800 680 600; www.oceanside.com.au; 117 Knight Tce; cabins $130-185; ☒☒☒) These neat, Dutch-owned, self-catering cottages with sunny balconies are perfectly located directly opposite the beach.

[TOP CHOICE] Old Pearler Restaurant
SEAFOOD $$$

(☑08-9948 1373; 71 Knight Tce; meals $26-48; ☺dinner Mon-Sat) Avast, mateys! Built from shell bricks, and feeling downright nautical, this atmospheric haven does fantastic seafood. The exceptional platter features local red emperor, whiting, cray, prawns and squid with nary a chip in sight, as it's all grilled, not fried.

Sunset Mura Mura Cafe CAFE $$

(☑08-9948 1047; Knight Tce; lunches $14-20; ⊙8am-8.30pm, to 6pm Tue & Wed; ☎) Bright and cheerful, the Sunset does great brekkies, lunch wraps, calzones and burgers, and for those campers sick of cooking, great takeaway home-cooked meals ready for reheating.

ℹ Information

There are ATMs at Heritage Resort and Shark Bay Hotel.

Community Resource Centre (☑08-9948 1787; 67 Knight Tce; @) Internet, faxes and CD/DVD burning.

DEC (☑08-9948 1208; www.dec.gov.au; 89 Knight Tce; ⊙8am-5pm Mon-Fri) Park passes, information and camping permits.

Post office (Knight Tce; ⊙8am-5pm Mon-Fri, to 1pm Sat, 9am to noon Sun; @) Also has a pharmacy and internet access.

Shark Bay visitor centre (☑08-9948 1590; www.sharkbaywa.com.au; 53 Knight Tce; ⊙9am-6pm) In the Discovery Centre foyer. Good parks info and accommodation and tour bookings. Issues free bush-camping permits for South Peron.

www.sharkbay.org.au Great information, interactive maps and downloadable permits.

François Peron National Park

Covering the whole peninsula north of Denham is an area of low scrub, salt lakes and red sandy dunes home to the rare bilby, mallee fowl and woma python. There's a scattering of rough camp sites (per person $7) by brilliant white beaches, all accessible via 4WD only. The excellent Wanamalu Trail (3km return) follows the cliff between Cape Peron and Skipjack Point, from where you can spot marine life in the crystal waters below. Those with 2WD can enter only as far as the old Peron Homestead (6km), where there's a short 'lifestyle' walk around the shearing sheds, and an artesian-bore hot tub to soak in. Park entry is $11 per vehicle. Tours start at around $180 from Denham or Monkey Mia, though you can hire your own 4WD from Denham for the same price.

Monkey Mia

Watching the wild dolphins each morning in the shallow waters of Monkey Mia (adult/child/family $8/3/15), 26km north-east of Denham, is a highlight of every traveller's trip.

The first feed is around 7.45am, but the dolphins will normally arrive earlier. The pier's a good vantage point. Hang around after the first session, as the dolphins routinely come back a second and sometimes a third time.

You can volunteer to work full time with the dolphins for a period of between four and 14 days – it's understandably popular, so apply several months in advance and specify availability dates. Contact the volunteer coordinator (☑08-9948 1366; monkeymiavolunteers@westnet.com.au).

Monkey Mia visitors centre (☑08-9948 1366; ⊙8am-4pm) has a good range of publications and can book tours.

🔭 Tours

Wula Guda Nyinda Aboriginal Cultural Tours INDIGENOUS CULTURE

(☑0429 708 847; www.wulaguda.com.au; adult/child $40/20) Local Aboriginal guide Darren 'Capes' Capewell leads excellent bushwalks where he shows 'how to let the bush talk to you'. You'll learn some local Malgana language, and identify bush tucker and native medicine. The evening 'Didgeridoo Dreaming' walks are magical. There's also a 'Saltwater Dreaming' kayak tour (three hours; adult/child $90/50).

Wildsights ADVENTURE TOURS

(☑1800 241 481; www.monkeymiawildsights.com. au) There are 2½-hour cruises on the *Shotover* catamaran ($69), where you're closer to the action. Also does a full-day 4WD trip to François Peron National Park ($189); there's a discount if you book both trips.

Aristocat II CRUISES

(☑1800 030 427; www.monkey-mia.net; 2½hr tours $75) Cruise in comfort on this large catamaran, and you might see dugongs, dolphins and loggerhead turtles. Also visits the Blue Lagoon Pearl Farm.

🛏 Sleeping & Eating

Monkey Mia is a resort and not a town, so eating and sleeping options are limited to the Monkey Mia Dolphin Resort. Self-catering is a good option.

Monkey Mia Dolphin Resort RESORT $$$

(☑1800 653 611; www.monkeymia.com.au; tent sites per person $15, van sites back/beach $37/50, dm/d $29/89, garden units $238, beachfront villas $320; ❄@☎☰) A stunning location, friendly staff and good-value backpacker doubles are the highlights at this resort catering for all markets. Unfortunately, it can get

seriously crowded and at times sounds like a continuous party. The restaurant has sensational water views and bland, overpriced meals. Don't waste money on the wi-fi as it is very slow.

ℹ️ Getting There & Away

There is no public transport. Denham's Bay Lodge runs a shuttle on alternate days. Your other options are hiring a car, cycling or hitching.

GASCOYNE COAST

This wild, rugged, largely unpopulated coastline stretches from Shark Bay to Ningaloo, with excellent fishing and waves that bring surfers from around the world. Sub-tropical Carnarvon, the region's hub, is an important fruit- and vegetable-growing district, and farms are always looking for seasonal workers. The 760km Gascoyne River, WA's longest, is responsible for all that lushness, though it flows underground for most of the year. Inland are huge distances, high temperatures, the ancient eroded rocks of the Kennedy Range, and massive Mt Augustus.

Carnarvon

POP 6900

At the mouth of the Gascoyne River, fertile Carnarvon, with its fruit and vegetable plantations and thriving fishing industry, makes a pleasant stopover between Denham and Exmouth. This friendly, vibrant town has quirky attractions, a range of decent accommodation, well-stocked supermarkets and some great food. The tree-lined CBD exudes a tropical feel, and the palm-fringed waterfront is a relaxing place to amble. The long picking season from March to January ensures there's plenty of seasonal work.

The last weekend of October sees the town taken over by desert riders competing in the gruelling 511km Gascoyne Dash (Gassy Dash; www.gasdash.com).

👁 Sights & Activities

Established jointly with NASA in 1966, the OTC Dish (Mahoney Ave) at the edge of town tracked Gemini and Apollo space missions, and Halley's Comet, before closing in 1987. There are plans to establish a NASA museum, though at present you can just wander around.

Carnarvon's luxuriant plantations along North and South River Roads provide a large proportion of the state's fruit and veg. The Gascoyne Food Trail brochure from the visitor centre lists which ones you can visit. Bumbak's (449 North River Rd; ⊘shop 9am-4pm Mon-Fri Apr-Jan, tours $6.50 10am Mon-Fri Apr-Oct) offer tours, and sell a variety of fresh and dried fruit, preserves and home-made ice-cream. Check out the delicious produce on offer at the Gascoyne Arts, Crafts & Growers Market (Civic Centre car park; ⊘8-11.30am Sat May-Oct).

Walk or ride 2.5km along the old tramway to the Heritage Precinct on Babbage Island, once the city's port. The striking One Mile Jetty (admission tram/walking $7/4; ⊘9am-4.30pm) provides great fishing and views; you can either walk or take a vintage tram to the end. Don't miss the view from the top of the creaky water tower in the nearby Railway Station Museum (⊘9am-5pm).

Gwoonwardu Mia (☑08-9941 1989; www.gahcc.com.au; 146 Robinson St; ⊘10am-3pm Mon-Fri) is a stunning building depicting a cyclone, and represents the five local Aboriginal language groups. It also houses a cultural centre, art gallery and hospitality-training cafe.

The palm-lined walking path that runs along the side of The Fascine (the body of water at the end of Robinson St) is a pleasant place for a wander, especially at sunset, while windsurfing is popular at Pelican Point.

🚐 Tours

Tour operators turn over quickly in Carnarvon, so check with the visitor centre for availability.

Outback Coast Safaris   4WD

(☑08-9941 3448; www.outbackcoastsafaris.com.au; 1-/3-day tours $90/$390) Full-day tours to the Kennedy Range or three-day camping trips to Mt Augustus. Also available for coastal charters.

🛏 Sleeping

Most accommodation is spread out along the 5km feeder road from the highway. Try to arrive before 6pm.

TOP CHOICE Fish & Whistle   HOSTEL $

(☑08-9941 1704; 35 Robinson St; dm/s $25/45, motel r $99; ❄@🛜🏊) Travellers love this big, breezy backpackers with its wide verandahs, bunk-free rooms, enormous communal spaces,

excellent kitchen and happy vibe. There're air-con motel rooms out the back, a pool and barbie area, and discounts for longer stays. The owners can help guests find seasonal jobs and provide transport to work ($25 per week).

Coral Coast Tourist Park CARAVAN PARK $
(☑08-9941 1438; www.coralcoasttouristpark.com. au; 108 Robinson St; unpowered/powered sites d $28/30, cabins $60-155; ▣⟨꙲⟩▣) This pleasant, shady park, with tropical pool and grassy sites, is the closest to the town centre. There's a variety of well-appointed cabins, a decent camp kitchen, and bicycles for hire.

Gateway Motel MOTEL $$
(☑08-9941 1532; www.thegatewaymotel.com; 309 Robinson St; d/units $115/156; ▣⟨꙲⟩▣) Basic motel rooms are complemented by larger apartments with cooking facilities. The bistro has themed buffet nights including pasta Monday ($26), Chinese Wednesday ($30) and not-to-be-missed seafood Friday and Saturday ($35).

Capricorn Holiday Park CARAVAN PARK $
(☑08-9941 8153; www.capricornholidaypark. com.au; 1042 North West Coastal Hwy; unpowered/powered sites d $30/32, cabins $120; ▣⟨꙲⟩▣) Out on the highway, just past the junction, this peaceful, friendly park has lots of shade, a covered pool and lovely bougainvillea.

✕ Eating

With all that great produce, there's some fine dining. Knight Tce also has a supermarket, takeaways and some early-opening cafes.

Yallibiddi Café INDIGENOUS FUSION $$
(☑08-9941 3127; 146 Robinson St; mains $15-30; ⟨⟩9am-3pm Mon-Fri) Inside Gwoonwardu Mia, this training cafe produces mouth-watering blends of bush tucker and contemporary cuisine. Try the excellent bush tapas with smoked kangaroo, emu and lemon-myrtle chicken or the Thai kangaroo salad. The students progress from here to the fine-dining Yallibiddi (Francis St).

Waters Edge MODERN AUSTRALIAN $$$
(☑08-9941 1181; www.thecarnarvon.com.au; 121 Olivia Tce; mains $22-40, s/d $65/80; ⟨⟩dinner Wed-Mon, lunch Fri-Sun; ▣) Tuck into some seared scallops with *nuoc cham*, Tuscan pork belly or local snapper pie out the back of the Carnarvon Hotel. It also has clean, basic rooms.

Sheridans Café CAFE $$
(☑08-9941 3482; Robinson St; mains $14-30; ⟨⟩8am-5pm Mon-Sat) Funky music accompanies a funky menu with laksa, chilli mussels and banana splits on offer.

Hacienda Crab Shack SEAFOOD $$
(☑08-9941 4078; Small Boat Harbour; ⟨⟩9am-4pm, shorter hr Sun) Got an esky? Then fill it full of freshly steamed crabs, prawns, mussels, shucked oysters and fish fillets from this fishmonger.

🛍 Shopping

Books & Stuff BOOKS
(Robinson St; ⟨⟩10am-4pm Mon-Sat) An eclectic collection of new, old and local books, with a nice 'reading' courtyard. BYO coffee.

ℹ Information

There's a post office on Camel Lane and ATMs on Robinson St.

Visitor centre (☑08-9941 1146; www.carnar von.org.au; Civic Centre, 21 Robinson St; ⟨⟩9am-5pm Mon-Fri, to noon Sat & Sun; @) Very helpful, with information, maps, local books and produce. Look for *Carnarvon & Apollo* (Dench & Gregg), detailing the town's NASA connection.

ℹ Getting There & Around

Skippers flies to Perth daily and to Geraldton twice weekly.

Thrice-weekly Greyhound buses going to Perth ($162, 13 hours), Broome ($272, 21 hours) and Exmouth ($160, five hours) stop at the visitor centre.

Gascoyne Wholesalers (☑08-9941 2638; 322 Robinson St; scooters $30), opposite Gwoonwardu Mia, hires scooters.

Point Quobba to Gnarraloo Bay

While the North West Coastal Hwy heads inland, the coast north of Carnarvon is wild and desolate, visited only by surfers and fishers. Turn down Blowholes Rd, 12km after the Gascoyne bridge, then proceed 49km along the sealed road to the coast. The **blowholes**, where waves spray out of limestone chimneys, are just left of the T-intersection. Point Quobba, 1km further south, has beach shacks, great fishing and some gritty camp sites (a fee is payable).

Quobba Station (☑08-9948 5098; www.
quobba.com.au; unpowered/powered sites $10/12,
cabins per person $30-55) is 10km north of
the T-junction on an unsealed road and has
plenty of rustic accommodation, a small
store and legendary fishing.

Still on Quobba, but 60km north of the
homestead, is Red Bluff (☑08-9948 5001;
www.quobba.com.au; unpowered sites per person
$12, shacks per person from $20, bungalow/safari-
retreat d $170/$345), a spectacular headland
with a wicked surf break, excellent fishing
and the southern boundary of the Ningaloo
Marine Park. Accommodation runs from
exposed camp sites and palm shelters to exclusive upmarket tents with balconies and
killer views.

The jewel, however, is at the end of the road
some 150km from Carnarvon: Gnaraloo
Station (☑08-9942 5927; www.gnaraloo.com;
unpowered sites per person $20, cabins d $130-210;
☞). Surfers from around the world come
every winter to ride the notorious Tombstones, while summer brings turtle monitoring and windsurfers trying to catch the
strong afternoon sea breeze, the Carnarvon
Doctor. There's excellent snorkelling close to
shore, and the coastline north from Gnar-
raloo Bay is eye-burningly pristine. You can
stay in rough camp sites next to the beach
at 3-mile, or there's a range of options up at
the homestead, the nicest being stone cabins with uninterrupted ocean views – great
for spotting migrating whales (June to November) and sea eagles. Gnaraloo is always
looking for willing workers, and there's such
a nice vibe happening that many folk come
for a night and end up staying months. Who
could blame them!

CORAL COAST & THE PILBARA

Lapping on the edge of the Indian Ocean, the
shallow, turquoise waters of the Coral Coast
nurture a unique marine paradise – one of
the very few places you can swim with the
world's largest fish, the gentle whale shark.
Fringed by World Heritage–nominated Ningaloo Reef, lonely bays, deserted beaches
and crystal-clear lagoons offer superb snorkelling and diving amongst myriad other sea
life including humpback whales, manta rays
and loggerhead turtles. Development is low-
key, towns are few and far between, and the
seafood and sunsets are legendary.

Inland, miners swarm like ants over the
high, eroded ranges of the Pilbara, while
ore trains snake down to the plains, spew-
ing their riches onto ships at a string of busy
ports stretching from Dampier to Port Hedland. Fifty percent larger than Germany but
with only one person per 12 sq km, this is a
land of big temperatures, big machinery, big
risks and big distances.

But hidden amongst the iron ore are two
beautiful gems – Karijini and Millstream-
Chichester National Parks, home to spectacular gorges, remote peaks, deep, tranquil
pools and abundant wildlife.

ⓘ Getting There & Around

AIR

The following airlines service the Coral Coast
and the Pilbara:

Airnorth (☑1800 627 474; www.airnorth.com.
au)

Golden Eagle (☑08-9172 1777; www.golden
eagleairlines.com)

MOUNT AUGUSTUS (BURRINGURRAH) NATIONAL PARK

The huge monocline of Mt Augustus (traditionally known as Burringurrah; 1105m) rises
717m above the surrounding plains; it's twice as large as Uluru and a good deal more
remote. Grab a DEC brochure before heading out, as there're a number of walking trails
and Aboriginal rock-art sites to explore, including the **summit trail** (12km return, six
hours). In a 2WD it's a rough, unsealed 450km from Carnarvon via Gascoyne Junction,
or 350km from Meekatharra. With a 4WD there're at least three other routes, including a
handy back door to Karijini via Dooley Downs and Tom Price. All of these routes see very
little traffic, so be prepared for the worst. There's no camping in the park, though you can
stay at nearby, dusty **Mt Augustus Outback Tourist Resort** (☑08-9943 0527; unpow-
ered/powered sites $15/25, donga d $50, units $140; ❀). Worth a look 60km to the west is
the historic **Cobra Bangemall Inn** (☑08-9943 0565). If you get to Gascoyne Junction
and decide to give up, nearby **Bidgemia Station** (☑08-9943 0501; www.bidgemia.com;
per person camping/bunkhouse/lodge $18/55/110) offers excellent rooms, meals and shady
camping.

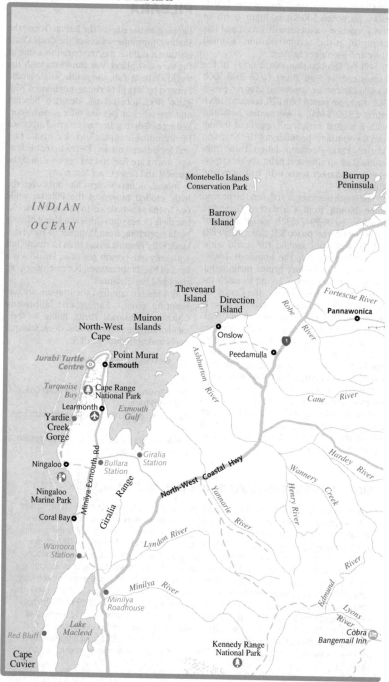

INDIAN
OCEAN

Montebello Islands
Conservation Park

Barrow
Island

Burrup
Peninsula

Thevenard
Island

Direction
Island

Fortescue River

Robe

River

Pannawonica

Muiron
Islands

North-West
Cape

Onslow

Peedamulla

Point Murat

Jurabi Turtle
Centre

Exmouth

Ashburton

River

Cane

River

Turquoise
Bay

Cape Range
National Park

Learmonth

Exmouth
Gulf

Yardie
Creek
Gorge

Hardey River

Giralia
Station

Ningaloo

Bullara
Station

North-West Coastal Hwy

Wannery

Creek

Ningaloo
Marine Park

Coral Bay

Giralia Range

Minilya Exmouth Rd

Yannarie

River

Henry River

Warroora
Station

Lyndon River

River

Edmund

Lyons

River

Minilya River

Minilya
Roadhouse

Cobra
Bangemail Inn

Red Bluff

Lake
Macleod

Cape
Cuvier

Kennedy Range
National Park

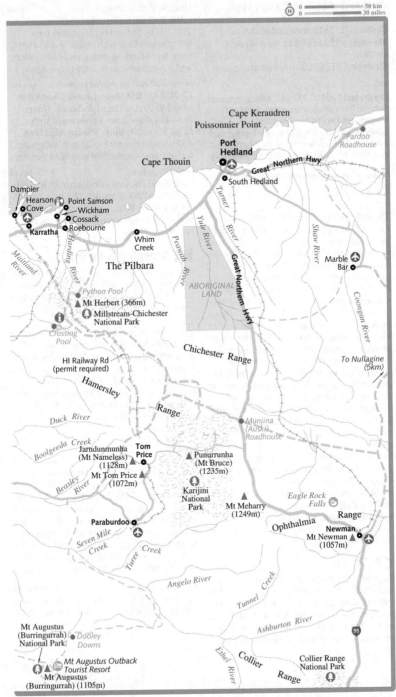

Virgin Australia (☎13 67 89; www.virgin australia.com)

Qantas (☎13 13 13; www.qantas.com.au)

Skywest (☎1300 660 088; www.skywest. com.au)

Strategic (☎13 53 20; wwwflystrategic.com)

BUS

Greyhound (☎1300 473 946; www.greyhound. com.au) Runs three times weekly between Broome and Perth along the coast.

Integrity (☎1800 226 339; www.integritycoach lines.com.au) Runs weekly between Perth and Port Hedland via the inland Great Northern Hwy.

Coral Bay

POP 190

The tiny seaside village of Coral Bay lies just north of the Tropic of Capricorn and its beautiful location and good facilities make it one of the easiest places to access the exquisite Ningaloo Marine Park. The town consists of just one street and a sweeping white-sand beach on **Bills Bay** where you can swim and snorkel close to shore. It's also a great base for outer-reef activities like scuba diving, fishing and whale watching (June to November), and tourists flock here in the winter months to swim with whale sharks (April to July) and manta rays (May to November).

Keep to the southern end of the bay when swimming, as the northern end, **Skeleton Bay**, is a breeding ground for reef sharks. You can hire snorkel gear, kayaks and glass-bottom canoes on the beach. There's also great snorkelling at **Purdy Point**, 500m south along the coast. Not surprisingly, the lookout above the beach car park provides excellent sunset panoramas. The town is chockers from April to October.

There are ATMs at the shopping centre and the Peoples Park grocer, and internet at some of the tour outlets and **Fins Cafe**.

Fish feeding occurs on the beach at 3.30pm every day.

☞ Tours

Popular tours from Coral Bay include swimming with whale sharks, spotting marine life (whales, dolphins, dugongs, turtles and manta rays), coral-viewing from glass-bottom boats, and quad-bike trips. Tour operators have offices in the shopping centre and caravan parks.

Ningaloo Reef Dive DIVING
(☎08-9942 5824; www.ningalooreefdive.com) This PADI- and eco-certified dive crew offers snorkelling with whale sharks ($365, from late March to June), reef dives ($160) and a range of dive courses (from $380).

Ningaloo Kayak Adventures KAYAKING
(☎0429 425 889; www.coralbay.org/kayak.htm; tours $40-60) On the main beach. Offers two- and three-hour kayak tours with stops for snorkelling. You can also hire a glass-bottom canoe ($25 per hour) and wetsuit and snorkelling gear ($15 per day).

Sail Ningaloo SAILING
(☎1800 197 194; www.sailningaloo.com.au; 3-day tours from $1550; ☺Apr-Oct) The fully cashed-up can select from a number of multi-day reef-sailing cruises on board the catamaran *Shore Thing*.

🍴 Sleeping & Eating

Avoid school holidays and book well ahead for peak season (April to October). Holiday houses can be rented online from www.coral bay.org. Prices start at $1000 per week.

TOP CHOICE **Ningaloo Club** HOSTEL $
(☎08-9948 5100; www.ningalooclub.com; dm $27-29, d with/without bathroom $120/95; ❄@🛜🏊) Clean and friendly, this excellent hostel is a great place to meet people, and boasts central pool, well-equipped kitchen, bar, lounge and games area. It also sells Greyhound tickets (the coach stops outside) and books discounted tours.

Peoples Park Caravan Village CARAVAN PARK $$
(☎08-9942 5933; www.peoplesparkcoralbay. com; sites unpowered $32, powered $36-44, 1-/2-bedroom cabins $220/235, hilltop villas $265; ❄) This excellent caravan park offers grassy, shaded sites and a variety of self-contained cabins. Friendly staff keep the modern amenities and spacious camp kitchen spotless, and it's the only place with freshwater showers. The hilltop villas have superb views.

Fins Cafe INTERNATIONAL $$
(☎08-9942 5900; Peoples Park; dinner mains $28-36; ☺breakfast, lunch & dinner; @) Book

STATION STAYS

If you're sick of cramped caravan parks and want to escape the hordes, or you just want to stay somewhere a little more relaxed and off the beaten track, consider a station stay. Scattered around the Coral Coast are a number of sheep and cattle stations (some former, some still working) that offer varying styles of accommodation – it may be an exquisite slice of empty coast, a dusty spot in the home paddock, a basic room in the shearers' quarters or a fully self-contained, air-conditioned cottage.

Don't expect top-notch facilities; in fact, a lot of sites don't have any at all. Power and water are at a premium, so the more self-sufficient you are, the more you will enjoy your stay – remember, you're getting away from it all. What you will get is loads of wildlife, stars you've never seen before, oodles of space, some fair-dinkum outback and an in-sight into station life.

Some stations offer wilderness camping away from the main homestead (usually by the coast) and you'll need a 4WD for access and a chemical toilet (ie a van). These places tend to cater for fisher types with boats and grey nomads who stay by the week.

Some stations only offer accommodation during the peak season (April to October).

Warroora (Map p978; ☑08-9942 5920; www.warroora.com; camping day/week $7.50/$37.50, r per person $30, cottages $130) Located 47km north of Minilya. Offers wilderness camp sites along the coast and cheap rooms in the shearers' quarters as well as a self-contained cottage and homestead.

Bullara (☑08-9942 5938; www.bullara-station.com.au; Burkett Rd; camping $11, tw/d $90/120; ☺Apr-Oct) Situated 70km north of Coral Bay. Has four queen and two twin-share rooms in renovated shearers' quarters, unpowered camping and a communal kitchen (BYO food). Also runs half-day station tours ($110).

Giralia (Map p978; ☑08-9942 5937; www.giralia.net.au; Burkett Rd; camping per person $10, s/d without bathroom $60/70, 4-person cottages $140, homestead r $260; ✱✿) Located 110km north of Coral Bay. Well set up for travellers, with a bush-camping area (including some powered sites) and kitchen, budget rooms, a family cottage and air-conditioned homestead rooms with breakfast and dinner included. The coast is 40 minutes away by 4WD. Meals and liquor are available.

ahead for dinner at this intimate outdoor BYO with its ever-changing blackboard menu showcasing local seafood, Asian-style curries and Mediterranean-Oz fusion dishes.

Ningaloo Reef Resort RESORT $$$
(☑1800 795 522; www.ningalooreefresort.com.au; d/apt from $199/273, penthouses $375; ✱@☎✿) Amongst palms just above the beach, this resort has a combination of well-appointed motel-style rooms and larger apartments, with garden or ocean views. It's also the local pub, with happy-hour Tuesday and Friday and live-music Thursday attracting a crowd. **Shades restaurant** (mains $15-35) delivers predictable fare.

Reef Cafe ITALIAN $$
(☑08-9942 5882; mains $21-36; ☺6pm-late) While this licensed family-friendly bistro at Bayview Resort features seafood and steaks, most people come for its pizzas and gelato.

Bakery BAKERY
(☺6.30am-5.30pm) At the shopping centre, this is the best option for early risers and vegetarians with its muesli and salad rolls.

ⓘ Getting There & Away

Coral Bay is 1144km north of Perth and 118km south of Exmouth, just off the sealed Minilya–Exmouth Rd.

Skywest flies into Exmouth's Learmonth Airport, 118km to the north; most Coral Bay resorts can arrange a private shuttle on request.

Greyhound coaches stop three times weekly on the Perth–Broome run. There's a connection to/from Exmouth requiring a bus change at Giralia around midnight.

Exmouth

POP 2500

Exmouth began life during WWII as a US submarine base, though it didn't flourish until the '60s with the establishment of the

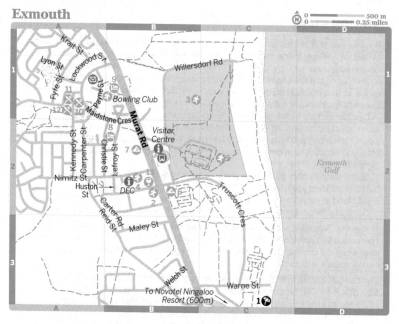

Exmouth

Very Low Frequency (VLF) communications facility at North-West Cape. Fishing (especially prawns) and oil and gas exploration took off at the same time and both these industries are still thriving (you can see the flare of gas platforms from Vlamingh Head at night).

Tourism, a mere trickle in the '80s after the protection of pristine Ningaloo Reef, now accounts for the bulk of all visitors,

reaching flood proportions during the April to October peak season. Don't let that put you off, as this modern, laid-back town makes a perfect base to explore nearby Ningaloo Marine and Cape Range National Parks. Alternatively, just wash away the dust and relax, restock, repair and reconnect with civilisation after a long road trip. The town is full of wildlife and emus commonly walk down the street, 'roos lounge around in

the shade, lizards amble across the highway, and corellas, galahs and ringnecks screech and swoop through the trees.

Exmouth is at the western end of the Pilbara's 'cyclone alley'; in 1999 Cyclone Vance caused widespread devastation.

◉ Sights & Activities

Exmouth is flat, hot and sprawling, with most of the attractions outside town and no public transport. **Town Beach**, 1km east, is a pleasant walk, though swimmers and anglers usually head 14km north to **Bundegi Beach** in the shadow of the VLF antenna array. You can cycle there: take the path (watch for dingos) leading to the Harold E Holt Naval Base (HEH), then follow the road. Bikes can be hired from **Exmouth Minigolf** (☑08-9949 4644; www.exmouthminigolf.com.au; Murat Rd; per day $20; ☉9am-8pm).

The sewerage works and golf course (both off Willersdorf Rd) are good places for **birdwatching**, while **turtle volunteering** is popular from November to January (see p984).

Check out the excellent **Jurabi Turtle Centre** (JTC; Map p978; Yardie Creek Rd) and pick up the DEC pamphlet *Marine Turtles in Ningaloo Marine Park*. Nearby, the hilltop **Vlamingh Head Lighthouse** is a great place for whale spotting and sunsets.

Most snorkellers and divers go to **Ningaloo Marine Park** or the **Muiron Islands** (Map p978). You can camp on South Muiron with a permit from Exmouth DEC. Try to find its informative book *Dive and Snorkel Sites in Western Australia*. The **Navy Pier dive** at Point Murat, 16km north of Exmouth, is world-class. Several dive shops in town offer PADI courses.

Surfers flock to **Dunes** (Surfers Beach) on the western cape during winter, while in the summer months windsurfing and kitesurfing are popular. **Ningaloo Kite & Board** (☑08-9949 2770; 16 Nimitz St) knows the best locations and can arrange lessons.

☞ Tours

Adventure tours from Exmouth include swimming with whale sharks, wildlife spotting, diving, sea kayaking, fishing and surf charters, and coral viewing from glass-bottom boats. Some companies only operate during peak season (late April to mid-October). Check conditions regarding 'no-sighting' policies and cancellations.

Outside the whale-shark season, tours focus on manta rays. You need to be a capable snorkeller to get the most out of these experiences. It's normally 30% cheaper if you don't swim. This is just a selection of operators – see the visitor centre for a full list.

Capricorn Kayak Tours KAYAKING
(☑0427 485 123; www.capricornseakayaking.com.au; half-/1-/2-/5-day $79/$149/595/1495) Single- and multi-day kayaking and snorkelling tours along the lagoons of Ningaloo Reef. April to October.

Kings Ningaloo Reef Tours WILDLIFE
(☑08-9949 1764; www.kingsningalooreeftours.com.au; snorkeller/observer $375/260) Long-time player that still gets rave reviews for its whale-shark tours. It's renowned for staying out longer than everyone else, and has a 'next available tour' no-sighting policy.

Ningaloo Ecology Cruises CRUISES
(☑08-9949 2255; www.ningalootreasures.com.au; 1/2½hr $40/60) One-hour glass-bottom-boat trips (April to October), and longer 2½-hour trips (all year) including snorkelling. Tours leave from Tantabiddi; there's a free transfer from town.

Ningaloo Whaleshark-N-Dive DIVING
(☑1800 224 060; www.ningaloowhalesharkndive.com.au) Dive tours to Lighthouse Bay on the west coast, and longer live-aboard tours to the Muiron (three days) and Montebello (seven days) Islands.

⌸ Sleeping

Accommodation is limited; book ahead, especially for the high season (April to October).

TOP CHOICE Ningaloo Lodge GUESTHOUSE $$
(☑1800 880 949; www.ningaloolodge.com.au; Lefroy St; d $125; ❀☎☞▩) These clean, tastefully appointed motel rooms are the best deal in town, with modern communal kitchen, barbecue, shady pool and free wi-fi, all within walking distance of either pub.

Exmouth Ningaloo Caravan & Holiday Resort CARAVAN PARK $
(☑08-9949 2377; www.exmouthresort.com; Murat Rd; unpowered/powered sites $33/39, dm/d $28/77, chalets $160-200; ❀☎☞▩) Across from the visitor centre, this relaxed, spacious park has grassy sites, self-contained chalets, four-bed dorms, a restaurant and even a pet section. If you're tenting in town, this is your best bet.

Exmouth Cape Holiday Park CARAVAN PARK $
(☑1800 621 101; www.aspenparks.com.au; cnr Truscott Cres & Murat Rd; sites unpowered/powered/with bathroom $30/45/72, dm/d $30/95,

For those with time, one of the most satisfying things you can do on the Coral Coast is to volunteer for a turtle-monitoring project. Getting up close to these magnificent creatures, knowing that you're actively taking part in their conservation effort, is truly rewarding. Both Exmouth and Port Hedland run organised volunteer programs each turtle season (November to February).

Exmouth volunteers need to commit to a five-week period and be prepared to spend most of that time at a remote base. Days typically start at sunrise with four to five hours' work collecting data on turtle nesting, habitat and predation, then the rest of the day is free for you to enjoy the surroundings. Volunteers pay $1000, which covers equipment, meals, transport from Exmouth and insurance. Accommodation is usually in tents or swags at a DEC research station or remote beach. Registration opens in September each year. See the excellent **Ningaloo Turtle Program** (NTP; www.ningalooturtles.org.au) website for more information, including downloadable training manuals and job vacancies.

If you enjoy interaction of the human kind, consider NTP's turtle guide program. You will need to complete at least the first module ($172) of the TAFE formal training course, **Turtle Tour Guiding**, before commencing at the Jurabi Turtle Centre (JCT), and this course gains credits towards a certificate III in tourism. The JCT plays an important role in minimising the disturbance to nesting turtles and hatchlings by educating tourists and supervising interaction during the breeding period.

Port Hedland volunteers should register in August for the **Pendoley Environmental** (www.penv.com.au) tagging program, which works alongside the oil and gas industry at sites like Barrow Island. Typical placements are for 16 days with all expenses covered, there's a strict selection process, and you'll be working mostly at night with minimal free time. The environmental group **Care for Hedland** (kellyhowlett35@hotmail.com) also runs volunteer monitoring programs; training sessions kick off in November.

cabin d $120-277; ✱@☒) The Cape offers van sites with their own bathrooms, as well as four-bed dorms, budget twins and a host of cabin options. There's a good camp kitchen, though the few unpowered tent sites are rather cramped.

Novotel Ningaloo Resort   RESORT $$$
(☑08-9949 0000; www.novotelningaloo.com.au; Madaffari Dr; d/apt from $275/355; ✱☎☒) Down in the marina, the Novotel Ningaloo is at the pointy end of sophistication (and expense) in Exmouth. The tastefully designed rooms are spacious and well equipped, and all include balconies.

Potshot Hotel Resort   RESORT $$
(☑08-9949 1200; www.potshotresort.com; Murat Rd; dm/d $28/65, motel d $98, studios $179, apt from $205; ✱@☎☒) A town within a town, this bustling resort has seven-bed dorms, standard motel rooms, luxury Osprey apartments and several bars, catering for all comers.

Exmouth Holiday Accommodation/ Ray White   RENTAL HOUSES $$
(☑08-9949 1144; www.exmouthholidays.com.au; 3 Kennedy St; per week from $700; ✱) Ray White

has a wide range of weekly rentals, from fibro shacks to double-storey mansions.

✕ Eating & Drinking

There's a supermarket, a bakery and several takeaways at **Exmouth Shopping Centre** (Maidstone Cres).

Graces Tavern and the Potshot Hotel are your drinking options.

TOP CHOICE **Whalers Restaurant**   SEAFOOD $$
(☑08-9949 2416; www.whalersrestaurant.com.au; 5 Kennedy St; mains lunch $7-24, dinner $27-40; ☉9am-2pm & 6pm-late) Delicious Creole-influenced seafood is the star attraction at this Exmouth institution. Sit back on the leafy verandah and sample the signature New Orleans gumbo or soft-shell crab. The lunch menu is more bistro-like.

Ningaloo Health   CAFE $
(☑08-9949 1400; www.ningaloohealth.com.au; 3A Kennedy St; mains $8-18; ☉7.30am-4pm; ✐) Breakfasts start with a bang at this tiny cafe – try the chilli eggs on blue-vein toast with jalapenos, or a bowl of Vietnamese *pho*. NH also does pancakes, light lunches, salads,

smoothies, takeaway picnic hampers and the best coffee around.

Mantaray's Bar & Brasserie
INTERNATIONAL $$$

(☑08-9949 0000; Madaffari Dr; mains lunch $16-23, dinner $39-45; ⊙lunch & dinner; ⚹) Novotel Ningaloo's in-house restaurant is the perfect place for a long, lazy waterside lunch with local, quality ingredients, affordable dishes and the best view in town.

Pinocchio
ITALIAN $$

(☑08-9949 4905; Murat Rd; mains $16-35; ⊙6pm-late) Located inside the Exmouth Ningaloo caravan park, this licensed alfresco *ristorante* is popular with locals and travellers alike.

Shopping

The shopping centre has a couple of dive shops, a gift shop, and a surf and camping store.

Exmouth Fish Co
SEAFOOD

(☑08-9949 2565; Murat Rd, Learmonth; ⊙8am-4pm) If you want to take some of that sensational seafood home with you, check out this place near the airport, where you can purchase vacuum-sealed local prawn and fish packs.

ℹ Information

There's a bank with an ATM on Maidstone Cres.

DEC (☑08-9947 8000; www.dec.wa.gov.au; 20 Nimitz St; ⊙8am-5pm Mon-Fri) Supplies maps and brochures for Ningaloo and Cape Range, including excellent wildlife guides. Can advise on turtle volunteering.

Exmouth Hospital (☑08-9949 1011; Lyon St)

Library (☑08-9949 1462; 22 Maidstone Cres; ⊙9am-4pm Mon-Thu, to noon Sat, closed lunch; ⚹) Internet and fax.

Police (Maidstone Cres)

Post office (Maidstone Cres)

Tours 'N' Travel (☑08-9949 4457; www.ningaloo-tours-travel.com.au; cnr Murat Rd & Maley St; ⊙8.30am-7pm; ⚹) Internet and secondhand books.

Visitor centre (☑1800 287 328; www.exmouth wa.com.au; Murat Rd; ⊙9am-5pm Mon-Fri, to 1pm Sat & Sun; ⚹) Useful information about Exmouth and the national parks; books tours, tickets and accommodation.

ℹ Getting There & Away

Exmouth's Learmonth Airport is 37km south of town. Skywest flies to Perth daily, and to Karratha on Monday (year-round). From April

to October, there's a flight to/from Broome on Sunday.

Buses stop at the visitor centre. Greyhound runs a shuttle out to the Giralia turn-off to connect with the thrice-weekly Perth–Broome service (Perth $250, 18 hours; Broome $300, 19 hours; Coral Bay $100, two hours). **Red Earth Safaris** (☑1800 501 968; www.redearthsafaris.com.au) offers a weekly Perth express departing Exmouth at 7am on Sunday ($200 one way, 30 hours).

ℹ Getting Around

The **Airport Shuttle Bus** (☑08-9949 4623; $20) meets all flights; reservations are required when heading to the airport.

Allens (☑08-9949 2403; rear 24 Nimitz St; cars from $45) cars include 150 free kilometres. **Exmouth Camper Hire** (☑08-9949 4050; www.exmouthcamperhire.com.au; 16 Nimitz St; vans from $100) rents vans with everything necessary for camping in Cape Range, including solar panels. **Tours 'N' Travel** (☑08-9949 4457; www.ningaloo-tours-travel.com.au; cnr Murat Rd & Maley St) rents scooters from $44 per day.

Tinnies (small dinghies; from $100 per day) or something larger (including a guide!) can be hired from **Exmouth Boat & Kayak Hire** (☑0438 230 269; www.exmouthboathire.com).

Ningaloo Marine Park

Recently extended and World Heritage nominated, the Ningaloo Marine Park now protects the full 300km length of the exquisite Ningaloo Reef, from Bundegi Reef on the eastern tip of the peninsula to Red Bluff on Quobba Station far to the south.

Ningaloo is Australia's largest fringing reef, in places only 100m offshore, and it's this accessibility and the fact it's home to a staggering array of **marine life** that make it so popular. Sharks, manta rays, humpback whales, turtles, dugongs and dolphins complement more than 500 species of fish.

There's excellent marine activity to enjoy year-round:

» **November to March** Turtles – three known species nestle and hatch in the sands.

» **March and April** Coral spawning – an amazing event seven to nine days after the full moon.

» **April to July** Whale sharks – the biggest fish on the planet arrive for the coral spawning.

» **May to November** Manta rays – present all year round; their numbers increase dramatically over winter and spring.

» June to November Humpback whales – breed in the warm tropics then head back south to feed in the Antarctic.

Over 220 species of hard **coral** have been recorded in Ningaloo, ranging from bulbous brain corals found on bommies to delicate branching staghorns and the slow-growing massive coral. Spawning, where branches of hermaphroditic coral simultaneously eject eggs and sperm into the water, occurs after full and new moons between February and May, but the peak action is usually six to 10 days after the March and April full moons.

It's this spawning that attracts the park's biggest drawcard, the solitary speckled **whale shark** (*Rhiniodon typus*). Ningaloo is one of the few places in the world where these gentle giants arrive like clockwork each year to feed on plankton and small fish, making it a mecca for marine biologists and visitors alike. Whale sharks can weigh up to 21 tonnes, reach 18m in length and live for 70 years.

To learn more, track down a copy of DEC's *The Marine Life of Ningaloo Marine Park & Coral Bay*.

Activities

Most travellers visit Ningaloo Marine Park for the **snorkelling**. Stop at Milyering visitor centre (☑08-9949 2808; Yardie Creek Rd; ☺9am-3.45pm) for maps and information on the best spots and conditions. Check its tide chart and know your limits, as the currents can be dangerous. The shop next door rents equipment ($10 per day). The most popular spots:

» Lakeside Walk 500m south along the beach from the car park, then snorkel out with the current before returning close to your original point.

» Oyster Stacks These spectacular bommies are just metres offshore, but you need a tide of at least 1.2m, and sharp rocks make entry and exit difficult. If you tire, don't stand on the bommies; look for some sand.

» Turquoise Bay Everyone's favourite. Walk 300m south along the beach, swim out for about 40m and float face down – the current will carry you over coral bommies and abundant sea life. Get out before the sandy point, then run back along the beach and start all over! Don't miss the exit point or the current will carry you out through the gap in the reef. It can be overcrowded here in peak season.

» Lighthouse Bay There's also great scuba diving in Lighthouse Bay at the Labyrinth and Blizzard Ridge.

Tours

See tours in the Exmouth and Coral Bay sections.

Cape Range National Park

The jagged limestone peaks and gorges of this 510-sq-km national park (per car $11) offer relief from the otherwise flat, arid expanse of North-West Cape, and are rich in wildlife, including the rare black-flanked rock wallaby, five types of bat and over 200 species of bird.

The main park access is via sealed Yardie Creek Rd. Several areas in the east are accessible from unsealed roads off Minilya–Exmouth Rd, south of the town. Milyering visitor centre (☑08-9949 2808; Yardie Creek Rd; ☺9am-3.45pm) has great displays, maps and publications. Buy Yardie Creek Cruise tickets here and check road conditions for the rough 4WD track continuing south to Coral Bay.

Sights & Activities

On the east coast, 23km south of Exmouth, the scenic and at times incredible, Charles Knife Rd climbs dramatically above the **canyon** of the same name. The road follows the knife-edge ridge up through ricketty corners and you'll need frequent stops to take in the breathtaking views.

Don't miss beautiful Shothole Canyon (turn-off 16km south of Exmouth), with its colourful walls and pretty picnic area.

On the west coast, spot migratory birds at the Mangrove Bay Bird Hide, 8km from the entrance station. Mandu Mandu Gorge (3km return) is a pleasant but dry walk from a car park 20km south of the Milyering visitor centre.

Much nicer is the walk to Yardie Creek Gorge (2km return) with its permanent water, sheer cliffs and excellent views. You can take the relaxing one-hour Yardie Creek Cruise (☑08-9949 2808; adult/child $25/12; ☺11am daily) up the short, sheer gorge to spot rare black-flanked rock wallabies.

Sleeping

Within the park are sandy, compact coastal camp sites (per person $7). Facilities and shade are minimal, but most have toilets.

Sites are limited and allocated upon arrival at the entrance station (not at the visitor centre!) – ask for a generator-free site if you are after some quiet time. Currently it's not possible to book in advance, though this may change, as long entrance-station queues (appearing hours before opening in winter) are common.

Ningaloo Lighthouse
Caravan Park CARAVAN PARK $$
(☑08-9949 1478; www.ningaloolighthouse.com; Yardie Creek Rd; unpowered/powered sites $29/35, cabins $95, bungalows $125, lighthouse/lookout chalets $150/245; ✳✳) Outside the park but superbly located on the western cape under Vlamingh lighthouse near Surfers Beach, the chalets have fantastic views. There're plenty of shady tent sites for lesser mortals.

Sal Salis LUXURY WILDERNESS $$$
(☑1300 790 561; www.salsalis.com; wilderness tent s/d $1095/1460; ☺Mar-Dec) Want to watch that flaming crimson Indian Ocean sunset from between 500-thread-count pure-cotton sheets? Pass the Chablis! For those who want their camp without the cramp, there are three gourmet meals a day, a FREE BAR and the same things to do as the couple over the dune in the pop-up camper. Sal Salis is at the South Mandu entrance; there's a minimum two-night stay.

Dampier to Roebourne

Most travellers skip this mining-services section of the coast as there's not much to see, unless you like huge industrial facilities. Accommodation is ludicrously overpriced and almost impossible to find thanks to the resources boom and the flood of fly-in, fly-out workers. However, the area has good transport connections, well-stocked supermarkets and useful repair shops.

DAMPIER

Dampier is the region's main port. Spread around King Bay, it overlooks the 42 pristine islands of the Dampier Archipelago, and supports a wealth of marine life in its coral waters, but heavy industry has blighted Dampier's shores. The nearby Burrup Peninsula contains possibly the greatest number of rock-art petroglyphs on the planet – see www.burrup.org.au – but is under threat from continued industrial expansion. The most accessible rock-art sites are at Deep Gorge near Hearson Cove, where you can also view the Staircase to the Moon; you will need a 4WD to cover the rest of the peninsula.

Dampier Transit Caravan Park (☑08-9183 1109; The Esplanade; unpowered/powered sites $18/22) has a handful of grassy sites overlooking the water.

KARRATHA

Most travellers bank, restock, repair stuff and get out of town before their wallet ignites.

Karratha visitor centre (☑08-9144 4600; www.pilbaracoast.com; Karratha Rd; ☺9am-5pm Mon-Fri, 10am-1pm Sat & Sun, shorter hr Nov-Apr; @) has good local info, supplies Hamersley Iron Railway Access Rd permits, books tours, and may be able to find you a room. The coffee from the JavaVan in the car park is the best in town.

From behind the visitor centre, the Jaburara Heritage Trail (3.5km one way) takes visitors through significant traditional sites and details the displacement and eventual extinction of the Jaburara people. Bring plenty of water and start early.

The shopping centre has most things you'll need including ATMs, takeaways and supermarkets.

🛏 Sleeping & Eating

Accommodation prospects are dire in Karratha; try to stay at beautiful Point Samson instead. Otherwise, search online for last-minute deals.

Pilbara Holiday Park CARAVAN PARK $
(☑08-9185 1855; www.aspenparks.com.au; Rosemary Rd; powered sites $50, motel/studio d $220/210; ✳@✳) Neat and well run with good facilities, though tent sites are expensive.

All Seasons Karratha HOTEL $$$
(☑08-9185 1155; www.accorhotels.com.au; Searipple Rd; d from $258; ✳@✳✳) This central hotel has pleasant rooms, three bars, a pool and a bistro.

Karratha Sushi Bar JAPANESE $
(☑08-9183 8789; Balmoral Rd; ☺10am-9pm) Excellent sushi.

❶ Getting There & Away

Virgin Australia and Qantas both fly daily to Perth; Qantas also offers weekly direct flights to most other capitals. Skywest flies to Perth four times a week and to Exmouth on Monday. Airnorth flies to Broome Tuesday and Friday with a Darwin connection, and to Port Hedland on Tuesday.

Greyhound runs to Perth ($214, 23 hours, Tuesday, Thursday and Saturday) and Port Hedland ($34, three hours, Tuesday, Thursday and Saturday). Buses depart Perth on Monday, Wednesday and Friday and Port Hedland on Tuesday, Thursday and Saturday.

ROEBOURNE

Roebourne, 40km east of Karratha, is the oldest Pilbara town still in existence – it was established in 1866 – and is home to a large Aboriginal community. It has some excellent old buildings, including the visitor centre (08-9182 1060; Queen St; 9am-4pm Mon-Fri, to 3pm Sat & Sun, shorter hr Nov-Apr) housed in the Old Gaol, which is also a museum (admission by donation). Don't miss the mineral display in the courtyard.

Roebourne also has a thriving Indigenous-art scene, and you'll pass the odd gallery on the highway. See www.roebourneart.com.au for more details.

COSSACK

The scenic ghost town of Cossack, at the mouth of the Harding River, was previously the district's main port, but its function was usurped by Point Samson and it was eventually abandoned. Many of the historic bluestone buildings date from the late 1800s; there's a 6km Heritage Trail around the town that links all the major sites (pick up the brochure from Roebourne visitor centre). Attractions include the self-guided Social History Museum (adult/child $2/1; 9am-4pm) and the pioneer cemetery with a tiny Japanese section dating from Cossack's pearling days. Past the cemetery, Reader Head Lookout has great views over the river mouth and the Staircase to the Moon.

Cossack Budget Accommodation (08-9182 1190; d with/without air-con $85/65;) has clean rooms in the atmospheric old police barracks. BYO food.

POINT SAMSON

Point Samson is a small, industrial-free seaside village, home to great seafood and clean beaches, making it the nicest place to stay in the area. There's good snorkelling off Point Samson, and the picturesque curved beach of Honeymoon Cove.

🛏 Sleeping & Eating

Samson Beach Chalets   GUESTHOUSE $$$
(08-9187 0202; www.samsonbeach.com.au; Samson Rd; chalets $220-440;) Beautifully appointed, self-contained one- and two-bedroom chalets just a short walk from the beach. There's a shady pool, free wi-fi and in-house movies.

Samson Beach Caravan Park   CARAVAN PARK $
(08-9187 1414; Samson Rd; powered sites $37) Tiny park in lovely, leafy surrounds, close to the water and tavern. Bookings essential in school holidays.

Moby's Kitchen   SEAFOOD $$
(08-9187 1435; mains $11-30; 11am-2pm & 5-8.30pm Mon-Fri, 11am-8.30pm Sat & Sun) Great seafood at honest prices on a shady deck overlooking the ocean.

Millstream-Chichester National Park

Amongst the arid, spinifex-covered plateaus and basalt ranges between Karijini and the coast, the tranquil Millstream waterholes of the Fortescue River form cool, lush oases. Lovely Crossing Pool (camp sites per person $7), with palms, pelicans, picnic tables and gas barbecues, makes an idyllic camp site, though some may prefer the larger Milliyanha Campground (camp sites per person $7), with its camp kitchen and nearby visitor centre. Murlamunyjunha Trail (7km, two hours return) links both areas and features interpretive plaques by the traditional Yindjibarndi owners.

Once the station homestead, the unmanned visitor centre (08-9184 5144; 8am-4pm) houses historical, ecological and cultural displays – a lifeline for fauna and flora during dry spells, the park is also one of the most culturally important Indigenous sites in WA. The nearby lily- and palm-fringed Jirndarwurrunha Pool is especially significant and swimming is not permitted.

You can swim at Nhanganggunha (Deep Reach Pool), believed to be the resting place of the Warlu, the creation serpent, and this is being developed into the main day-use area.

In the park's north are the stunning breakaways and eroded mesas of the Chichester Range. Don't miss the amazing panorama from the top of Mt Herbert, 10 minutes from the car park, and on the drive to Roebourne. You can continue walking to McKenzie Spring (4.5km, one hour return). Lower down the range, Python Pool is worth a look, though check for algal bloom before diving in; it's linked to Mt Herbert by the Chichester Range Camel Trail (16km,

six hours return). **Snake Creek camp-ground** (camp sites per person $7) is another 1km downhill.

Karijini National Park

Arguably one of WA's most magnificent destinations, this **park** (per car $11) reveals itself slowly. Riven and ragged ranges, upthrust and twisted by nature, glow like molten lava in the setting sun as wedge-tailed eagles soar above grey-green spinifex and goannas shelter under stunted mulga. Kangaroos and wildflowers dot the plains, criss-crossed by deep, dark incisions emitting the tinkle of distant water.

While the narrow, breathtaking gorges with their hidden, sculptured pools are Karijini's biggest drawcard, the park is also home to a wide variety of fauna and flora, with an estimated 800 plant species, including some 50 varieties of wattle (acacia). Dragon lizards scurry over stones, rock wallabies cling

to sheer cliffs and endangered olive pythons lurk on the far side of pools. The park also contains WA's three highest peaks: Mt Meharry, Mt Bruce and Mt Frederick.

Banyjima Dr, the park's main thoroughfare, connects with Karijini Dr at two entrance stations. The eastern access is sealed to the visitor centre and Dales Gorge, while the rest of the park is unsealed. Take extra care driving as tourist rollovers are far too common. Avoid driving at night.

Choose walks wisely, dress appropriately and never enter a restricted area without a certified guide. Avoid the gorges during and after rain, as flash flooding does occur.

◉ Sights & Activities

Scenic **Dales Gorge** and its campground are 19km from the eastern entrance. A short, sharp descent leads to **Fortescue Falls**, behind which a leafy stroll upstream reveals the beautiful **Fern Pool**; head downstream from Fortescue Falls to picturesque **Circular**

Karijini National Park

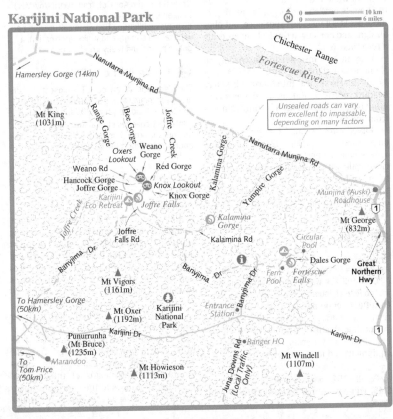

Pool; ascend to **Three Ways Lookout** and return along the cliff top.

Wide **Kalamina Gorge**, 24km from the visitor centre, has the easiest access and is suitable for families – there's a small tranquil pool and falls. Joffre Falls Rd leads to stunning **Knox Gorge**, passing the lookout over the spectacular **Joffre Falls**. Knox Gorge has several nice swimming holes, fringed by native figs, while in **Joffre Gorge**, the frigid pools are perennially shaded.

Weano Rd junction is 32km from the visitor centre, and the **Eco Retreat** is nearby. The final 13km to the breathtaking **Oxers Lookout** can be rough, but it's worth it for the magnificent views of the junction of Red, Weano, Joffre and Hancock Gorges some 130m below.

A steep descent into **Hancock Gorge** (partly on ladders) passes first through the sunny **Amphitheatre**, then the slippery spider walk to the sublime **Kermits Pool**. On the other side of the car park, a rough track winds down to the surreal **Handrail Pool** in the bowels of **Weano Gorge**. Swimming in these pools is a magical experience, but obey all signs and don't even think about entering a restricted area.

Away in Karijini's northwest corner, off Nanutarra-Wittenoom Rd, **Hamersley Gorge** makes a pleasant stopover if you're heading north to Karratha. Idyllic swimming holes and a waterfall lie only minutes from the car park.

Gorged out? Go and grab some altitude on **Punurrunha** (Mt Bruce; 1235m; 9km return). WA's second-highest mountain is a superb ridge walk with fantastic views all the way to the summit. Start early, carry lots of water and allow five hours. The access road is off Karijini Dr opposite the western end of Banyjima Dr.

Tours

TOP CHOICE **West Oz Active Adventure Tours** ADVENTURE
(08-0438 913 713; www.westozactive.com.au; Karijini Eco Retreat; tours $225-245; Apr-Oct) West Oz offers action-packed trips through the restricted gorges and combines hiking, swimming, floating on inner tubes, climbing, sliding off waterfalls and abseiling. All equipment and lunch are provided.

Lestok Tours BUS
(08-9188 1112; www.lestoktours.com.au; tours $145) Full-day outings to Karijini from Tom Price.

Sleeping & Eating

Karijini Eco Retreat RESORT $$$
(08-9425 5591; www.karijiniecoretreat.com.au; camp sites $29, tent d high/low season $289/145) This 100% Indigenous-owned retreat is a model for sustainable tourism, though its ensuited eco tents are expensive. Grill your own mains ($30) at the open bar and restaurant. Campers get hot showers and the same rocks as the DEC campground. Things are cheaper in summer when the retreat winds down and the restaurant (but not the bar!) closes.

Dales Gorge CAMPGROUND $
(sites adult/child $7/2) Though somewhat dusty, this large DEC campground offers shady, spacious sites with nearby toilets and picnic tables. Forget tent pegs – you'll be using rocks as anchors.

Information

Visitor centre (08-9189 8121; Banyjima Dr; 9am-4pm Apr-Oct, from 10am Nov-Mar) Indigenous managed with excellent interpretive displays highlighting Banyjima culture and park wildlife, good maps and walks information, a public phone and really great air-con.

Getting There & Away

There's no public transport. The closest airports are at the mining towns of Paraburdoo (101km south-west) and Newman (201km south-east).

Integrity coaches stop at Munjina (Auski) on Thursday (northbound) and Friday (southbound). Munjina is the best place to score a lift.

Newman
POP 7000

At the eastern end of the Hamersley Range, friendly, leafy Newman, a company mining town built during the '70s, is the overnight stop of choice on the inland Great Northern Hwy. This busy town has plenty of services and it's within striking distance of the state's two largest national parks, the famous Karijini and the remote, seldom-visited **Karlamilyi National Park** (formerly Rudall River National Park).

The exceptional **visitor centre** (08-9175 2888; www.newman-wa.org; Fortescue Ave; 8am-5pm, closed Sun Jan) has superhelpful staff with loads of information. Book here for tours to the enormous opencut **Mt Whaleback iron-ore mine** (adult/

child $20/9; ⊙9.30am Mon-Sat Apr-Sep, Mon-Fri Oct-Mar) or fly to outlying stations on the Pilbara Mail Run (Tue/Wed $400/175). It also has an excellent mud map to the gorges, springs and petroglyphs of the eastern Hamersley.

As in most booming WA mining towns, finding a room is next to impossible. Book well ahead, or be prepared to camp.

Whaleback Village Caravan Park (☑08-9175 2802; Cowra Dr; unpowered/powered sites $20/30, dongas $60, cabins $160; ☀) has grassy sites, some shade and a decent campers' kitchen. Seasons Hotel Newman (☑08-9177 8666; www.seasonshotel.com.au; Newman Dr; motel d $225, mains $28-45; ✲☀) has both the best rooms and the best restaurant in town.

There are several takeaway options in and around the shopping centre.

Integrity buses pass through on Thursday to Port Hedland ($103, six hours) and on Friday to Perth ($214, 15 hours). Virgin Australia and Qantas both fly daily to Perth. Golden Eagle Airlines flies to Port Hedland on Wednesday.

Port Hedland

POP 16,000

Port Hedland ain't the prettiest place. Confronted by its railway yards, iron-ore stockpiles, salt mountains, furnaces and massive deep-water port, the average tourist might instinctively floor the accelerator. Yet Hedland is not just another bland prefab Pilbara town. With a heritage spanning over 115 years, it's been battered by cyclones, plundered by pearlers and bombed by the Japanese – it's even hosted royalty.

Iron ore plays a huge part in the town's fortunes, and Port Hedland is riding the current resources boom. While this pushes up prices and squeezes accommodation, it's also sparked a renaissance. Old pubs are being renovated, the art and cafe (real coffee!) scenes are expanding, fine dining is flourishing, cocktail and tapas bars are sprouting and cycle paths are spreading along the foreshore. Just don't mind the red dust.

◉ Sights & Activities

Collect the excellent *Port Hedland Cultural & Heritage Sites* brochure from the visitor centre and take a self-guided tour around the CBD, or hire one of its bicycles and meander along the Richardson St Bike Path,

ending with a cold beer at the Yacht Club (Sutherland St).

Courthouse Gallery (☑08-9173 1064; www.courthousegallery.com.au; 16 Edgar St; ⊙9am-4pm Mon-Fri, to 2pm Sat & Sun) supports local contemporary and indigenous art with frequent exhibitions.

Watch ridiculously large tankers from Marapikurrinya Park (end of Wedge St) – the visitor centre posts shipping times. After dark, from the park's Finucane Lookout you can stare into the eye of Sauron (actually BHP Billiton's Hot Briquetted Iron plant on Finucane Island).

Between November and February flat-back turtles nest on nearby beaches. Check at the visitor centre for volunteer options (see also p984).

Pretty Pool, located 7km east of the town centre, is a popular fishing and picnicking spot (beware of stonefish), while nearby Goode St is a handy place to observe Port Hedland's Staircase to the Moon between March and October.

☞ Tours

BHP Billiton   IRON-ORE PLANT
(adult/child $26/20; ⊙9.30am Mon, Wed & Fri) This popular tour departs from the visitor centre.

🛏 Sleeping & Eating

Like most mining towns, finding a room in Hedland isn't easy or cheap. If you haven't booked well ahead, the visitor centre may be able to help.

Cooke Point Caravan Park   CARAVAN PARK $$
(☑08-9173 1271; www.aspenparks.com.au; cnr Athol & Taylor Sts; powered sites $50, d without bathroom $140, motel/unit d $220-280; ✲☀⏦☀) You might be able to snag a dusty van or tent site with a view overlooking mangroves, but the other options are usually full.

Esplanade Hotel   RESORT $$$
(☑08-9173 2783; www.theesplanadeporthedland. com.au; 2-4 Anderson St; d $360, dinners $32-45; ✲☀☀) Previously one of the roughest pubs in Port Hedland, the 'Nade is now an exclusive resort with fully clothed staff, sumptuous doubles, fine dining and sophisticated tapas cocktail nights held high in the Crows Nest turret.

TOP
CHOICE Silver Star Cafe   CAFE $
(☑0411 143 663; lunches $10-15, tapas $8-15; ⊙10am-5pm Tue-Thu, to late Fri & Sat, to 2pm

JOURNEY TO THE CENTRE OF THE EARTH *STEVE WATERS*

The instructor sits down in the Water Slide, pushes off, then disappears. I hear a splash echo from below. He's done this a thousand times. I've haven't done it once, and I'm next.

We're in the depths of Karijini's Knox Gorge. It's 35°C 'upstairs', but the water in the gorge is freezing, and while we're all in summer wetsuits, everybody's shivering. The day started early when our guides, Dan and Pete, kitted us out with wetsuits, gorge slippers, harnesses, helmets and inner tubes. A short, sunny stroll down from Knox Lookout brought our small group to a pool ringed by native figs, where we practised paddling. A quick 'jump test' off a 2m rock to check we won't 'choke' at the first obstacle (the one I'm staring at), and we were off into the restricted zone, with the gorge shrinking rapidly to a single body width.

I sit down, give a thumbs up, then push off and over a 4m drop into an enclosed plunge pool. An involuntary scream and I'm under water. It's scary and exhilarating; I'd love to do it again, but once over the edge, there's no way back. Soon we're all down, and floating in the Styx-like water, and Dan sets up the 8m abseil into the next pool. Light falls in narrow shafts as sheer walls tower overhead.

Eventually we escape shady Knox into the sun at the bottom of Red Gorge and warm our bodies on a nearby 'beach'. Soon we're back on our inner tubes, this time a sunny, relaxed paddle across long, tranquil pools. We pass the entrance to Weano Gorge, a 40m-high waterfall, on the way to our lunch spot at Junction Pool, 130m below Oxers Lookout. As we munch sandwiches, we watch a rock wallaby bounding around halfway up the vertical face, seemingly oblivious to the sheer drop only centimetres away.

Joffre Gorge leads off darkly to the south, but we head into Hancock Gorge and a tight, steep, slippery climb beside a cascade leading through the Centre of the Earth to Garden Pool. Sublime, and sobering, Regans Pool (named after a local SES volunteer who died during a rescue) is next and as Pete lays in the rope for the steep, slippery climb above the pool, the rest of us float silently, lost in our thoughts.

The climb is the last hurdle as we ascend steeply, doubly clipped into the anchor rope. A short traverse and we're out of the restricted area into Kermits Pool, and our final swim. The Spider Walk holds no challenge and soon we're through the sunny Amphitheatre and up the exit ladders to the car park. We've been out all day, and it's been one action-packed, adrenalin-charged adventure.

Sun) Possibly the coolest cafe in the Pilbara, this 1930s American Silver Star railcar sits propped up next to the Courthouse Gallery and serves excellent coffee, cakes and light lunches in the original observation lounge. Tapas are available Friday and Saturday evenings.

Port Hedland Yacht Club   LICENSED CLUB **$**
(☑08-9173 3398; Sutherland St; ⊙Thu-Sun) Locals loved the old tin Yachtie for its cheap drinks, great Thai kitchen and water views. At the time of research, a swish new replacement was being built next door, so expect prices to rise accordingly.

There're supermarkets, cafes and takeaways at both the **Boulevard** (cnr Wilson & McGregor Sts) and **South Hedland** (Throssell Rd) shopping centres.

❶ Information

There are ATMs along Wedge St and in the Boulevard shopping centre. Internet is available at the visitor centre, the **library** (Dempster St) and the **Seafarers Centre** (cnr Wedge & Wilson Sts).

Hospital (☑08-9158 1666; Sutherland St)

Visitor centre (☑08-9173 1711; www.phvc. com.au; 13 Wedge St; ⊙9am-4pm Mon-Fri, 10am-2pm Sat; @) This very helpful centre hires out bicycles ($24 per half-day), sells bus tickets and can arrange iron-ore plant tours, turtle monitoring (November to February) and tickets on the Pilbara mail run.

❶ Getting There & Away

Virgin Australia and Qantas both fly to Perth daily; Qantas also goes direct to Melbourne on Tuesday. Skywest offers handy Bali flights (Saturday and Sunday), and goes to Broome (Sunday) and Perth (Sunday). Airnorth flies to

Broome (Tuesday and Friday), with a Darwin connection, and Karratha (Friday). Golden Eagle Airlines flies to Broome (Monday to Thursday), and to Newman (Tuesday) on the Pilbara mail run. Strategic has weekly flights to Bali (Tuesday) and Brisbane (Wednesday).

Greyhound coaches run to Perth ($258, 26 hours, Tuesday, Thursday and Saturday) and Broome ($87, eight hours, Tuesday, Thursday and Saturday). Buses depart Perth on Monday, Wednesday and Friday and Broome on Tuesday, Thursday and Saturday. Integrity departs Perth on Wednesday using the quicker inland route ($232, 22 hours) via Newman, returning on Friday. Both companies' services depart from the visitor centre and South Hedland shopping centre.

ⓘ Getting Around

The airport is 13km from town. The **Airport Shuttle Service** (☎08-9173 4554; per person $22) meets every flight; **Hedland Taxis** (☎08-9172 1010) charges around $33.

Hedland Bus Lines (☎08-9172 1394) runs limited weekday services between Port Hedland and Cooke Point (via the visitor centre) and on to South Hedland ($3.50 per person).

McLaren Hire (☎08-9140 2200; www.mclaren hire.com.au) offers a large range of rental 4WDs.

THE KIMBERLEY

Australia's last frontier is a wild land of remote, spectacular scenery spread over large distances with a severe climate, a sparse population and minimal infrastructure. Larger than 75% of the world's countries, the Kimberley is hemmed by an impenetrable coastline and inhospitable deserts. In between lie vast boab-studded spinifex plains, deep, palm-fringed gorges with inviting plunge pools and some truly magnificent waterfalls. To travel here is a true adventure, and each dry season a steady flow of intrepid individuals searches for the real outback, along the legendary Gibb River Rd, amongst remote Purnululu's orange 'beehives' or along the withering Tanami Track.

Aboriginal culture runs deep across the land, from the Dampier Peninsula where neat communities welcome travellers to country, to distant Mitchell Plateau where ancient Wandjina and Gwion Gwion stand vigil over sacred waterholes, and on to the southern deserts, whose ochre-ringed soaks dominate spiritual and material life.

Swashbuckling Broome and practical Kununurra bookend the region, and both are great places to unwind, repair, restock, meet other travellers and pick up casual work. Remember, everything is larger in the Kimberley, especially prices.

ⓘ Getting There & Around

AIR

The following airlines service the Kimberley:
Airnorth (☎1800 627 474; www.airnorth. com.au)
Golden Eagle (☎08-9172 1777; www.golden eagleairlines.com)
Qantas (☎13 13 13; www.qantas.com.au)
Skywest (☎1300 660 088; www.skywest. com.au)
Strategic (☎13 53 20; wwwflystrategic.com)
Virgin Australia (☎13 67 89; www.virginaus tralia.com)

BUS

Greyhound (☎1300 473 946; www.greyhound. com.au) Runs three times weekly Broome to/from Perth and daily Broome to/from Darwin via Kununurra.

Port Hedland to Broome

The Big Empty stretches from Port Hedland to Broome, as the highway skirts the edge of the Great Sandy Desert. It's 609km of willie-willies and dust and not much else. There're only two roadhouses, Pardoo (148km) and Sandfire (288km), so keep the tank full.

The coast, wild and unspoilt, is never far away. Around 250km from Port Hedland, shady, laid-back **Eighty Mile Beach Caravan Park** (☎08-9176 5941; www.eightymile beach.com.au; unpowered/powered sites $30/34, donga s/d $45/55, cabins $170) backs onto a beautiful white-sand beach with great fishing, and nesting turtles (November to March). **Port Smith Caravan Park** (☎08-9192 4983; www.portsmithcaravanpark.com.au; unpowered/powered sites $24/30, donga s/d $60/70, cabins $165), 487km from Port Hedland on a tidal lagoon, has loads of wildlife. **Barn Hill Station** (☎08-9192 4975; www. barnhill.com.au; sites unpowered $20, powered $24-28, cabin d $75), 490km from Port Hedland, is a working cattle station with its own 'mini-pinnacles'. All are packed from May to September.

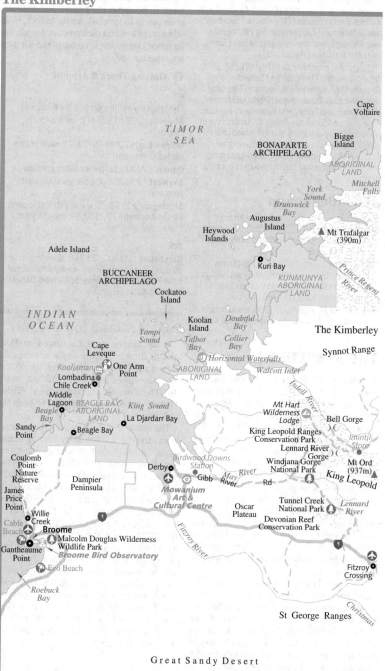

PERTH & WESTERN AUSTRALIA THE KIMBERLEY

TIMOR
SEA

Cape
Voltaire

BONAPARTE
ARCHIPELAGO

Bigge
Island

ABORIGINAL
LAND

Mitchell
Falls

York
Sound

Brunswick
Bay

Augustus
Island

Heywood
Islands

▲ Mt Trafalgar
(390m)

Adele Island

Kuri Bay

Prince Regent River

BUCCANEER
ARCHIPELAGO

KUNMUNYA
ABORIGINAL
LAND

Cockatoo
Island

INDIAN
OCEAN

Koolan
Island

Doubtful
Bay

The Kimberley

Yampi
Sound

Talbot
Bay

Collier
Bay

Synnot Range

Cape
Leveque

Horizontal Waterfalls

Kooljaman
One Arm
Point

ABORIGINAL
LAND

Watcott Inlet

Lombadina
Chile Creek

Isdell River

Middle
Lagoon

BEAGLE BAY
ABORIGINAL
LAND

King Sound

Mt Hart
Wilderness
Lodge

Beagle
Bay

La Djardarr Bay

Bell Gorge

Sandy
Point

Beagle Bay

King Leopold Ranges
Conservation Park

Imintji
Store

Lennard River
Gorge

Coulomb
Point
Nature
Reserve

Dampier
Peninsula

Birdwood Downs
Station

Derby

Gibb

Windjana Gorge
National Park

Mt Ord
(937m)▲

James
Price
Point

May River

River

Rd

King Leopold

Cable
Beach

Willie
Creek

Mowanjum
Art &
Cultural Centre

Oscar
Plateau

Tunnel Creek
National Park

Lennard
River

Broome

Malcolm Douglas Wilderness
Wildlife Park

Devonian Reef
Conservation Park

Gantheaume
Point

Broome Bird Observatory

Fitzroy River

Eco Beach

Roebuck
Bay

Fitzroy
Crossing

St George Ranges

Christmas

Great Sandy Desert

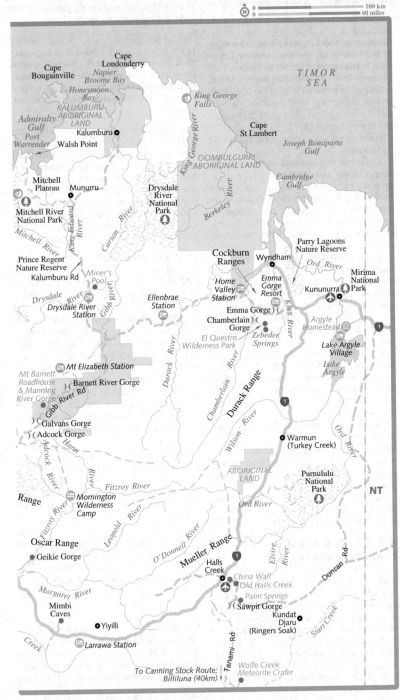

0 100 km
0 60 miles

Cape Bougainville
Cape Londonderry
Napier Broome Bay
Honeymoon Bay
KALUMBURU ABORIGINAL LAND
Admiralty Gulf
Port Warrender
Walsh Point
Kalumburu

TIMOR SEA

King George Falls
King George River
Cape St Lambert
Joseph Bonaparte Gulf

Mitchell Plateau
Munurru
Mitchell River National Park
Mitchell River
King Edward River
Prince Regent Nature Reserve
Kalumburu Rd

Drysdale River National Park

OOMBULGURRI ABORIGINAL LAND
Berkeley River
Cambridge Gulf

Carson River

Drysdale
Miner's Pool
Drysdale River Station
Gibb River

Cockburn Ranges
Wyndham
Ord River

Parry Lagoons Nature Reserve
Mirima National Park
Kununurra

Ellenbrae Station

Home Valley Station
Emma Gorge Resort
Emma Gorge
Chamberlain Gorge
El Questro Wilderness Park
Zebedee Springs

King River

Argyle Homestead
Lake Argyle Village
Lake Argyle

Mt Barnett Roadhouse & Manning River Gorge
Mt Elizabeth Station
Barnett River Gorge
Gibb River Rd
Galvans Gorge
Adcock Gorge

Durack River

Chamberlain River

Durack Range

Wilson River

Warmun (Turkey Creek)

Ord River

Adcock River
Hann River

Range
Mornington Wilderness Camp
Fitzroy River
Leopold River

ABORIGINAL LAND

Purnululu National Park

NT

Fitzroy River

O'Donnell River
Ord River

Oscar Range
Geikie Gorge

Mueller Range

Halls Creek
China Wall
Old Halls Creek
Palm Springs
Sawpit Gorge

Elvire River

Duncan Rd

Margaret River
Mimbi Caves
Yiyilli
Larrawa Station

Kundat Djaru (Ringers Soak)
Sturti Creek

Creek

Tanami Rd

To Canning Stock Route; Billiluna (40km)

Wolfe Creek Meteorite Crater

Broome

POP 16,000

Clinging to the Kimberley's western edge, at the base of the pristine Dampier Peninsula, Rothko meets Cézanne as Broome's red pindan earth dissolves into Indian Ocean aquamarine. Situated nearby, Roebuck Bay's creeks, mangroves and mudflats blossom like fractals and, as it's a good 2000km to the nearest capital city, it's little wonder that Broome has always relied upon nature for its fortunes.

Early days as a pearling centre saw Japanese, Chinese and Malays joining local Aboriginals in open-water diving, where many drowned, caught the bends or became shark bait. Broome's cemeteries are a silent reminder of this harsher time. Today, Broome still exports pearls around the world, produced on modern sea farms.

Iconic Cable Beach with its luxury resorts hauls in the tourists during the Dry (April to October) with romantic notions of camels, surf and sunsets. Magnificent, sure, but there's a lot more to Broome than postcards, and tourists are sometimes surprised when they scratch the surface and find pindan just below.

Broome's centre is Chinatown, on the shores of Roebuck Bay, while Cable Beach and its resorts are 6km west on the Indian Ocean. The airport stretches between the two; the port and Gantheaume Point are 7km south.

The Dry's a great time to find casual work in hospitality or out on the pearl farms. In the Wet, it feels like you're swimming in a warm, moist glove, and while many places close, others offer amazingly good deals as prices plummet.

Each evening the whole town pauses, collective drinks in mid-air, while the sun melts back into the sea.

◉ Sights & Activities

CABLE BEACH AREA

Cable Beach   BEACH

Western Australia's most famous landmark has turquoise waters and beautiful white sand curving away to the sunset. Clothing is optional north of the rocks, while south, walking trails lead through the red dunes of Minyirr Park, a spiritual place for the Rubibi people. The visitor centre has a map, or go with an Indigenous guide (☑08-9194 0150). Cable Beach is synonymous

with camels, and an evening ride along the sand is a highlight for many visitors.

Gantheaume Point   LANDMARK

In the dying sun, red, eroded cliffs turn scarlet at this peaceful lookout. Nearby lie one of the world's most varied collections of **dinosaur footprints**, thought to be 135 million years old, and difficult to find except at very low tides.

Malcolm Douglas Crocodile Park   ZOO

(☑08-9192 1489; www.malcolmdouglas.com.au; cnr Cable Beach Rd & Sanctuary Dr; adult/child/family $30/25/70; ☺10am-5pm Mon-Fri, from 2pm Sat & Sun) Right behind Cable Beach is the legacy of Australia's original crocodile-hunter-turned-conservationist. Visit during feeding time (☺3pm Dry, 4pm Wet). There's also the Malcolm Douglas Wilderness Wildlife Park outside Broome; see p1003.

CHINATOWN AREA

Sun Pictures   HISTORIC BUILDING

(☑08-9192 3738; www.sunpictures.com.au; 27 Carnarvon St; adult/child/family $16.50/11.50/55) Sink back in a canvas deckchair in the world's oldest operating picture gardens and enjoy the latest movies. The history of the Sun building is the history of Broome itself – don't miss the informative history tours (per person $5; ☺10.30am & 1pm Mon-Fri).

Chinatown   LANDMARK

Few Chinese remain in Broome's historical and commercial heart, though tin shanties are still visible lining Carnarvon St, Short St, Dampier Tce and Napier Tce.

Pearl Luggers   HISTORIC BOATS

(☑08-9192 2059; www.pearlluggers.com.au; 31 Dampier Tce; admission free, 1hr tours adult/child/family $20/10/50) Offers guided tours covering Broome's tragic pearling past are on offer here. It's free to just look over the boats.

Broome Museum   MUSEUM

(☑08-9192 2075; www.broomemuseum.org.au; 67 Robinson St; adult/child $5/1; ☺10am-4pm Mon-Fri, to 1pm Sat & Sun, to 1pm Wet) Interesting exhibits here document the town's pearling history and Japanese bombing during WWII. Enter via Saville St.

A number of cemeteries testify to the multicultural makeup of Broome society. The most striking is the Japanese Cemetery (Frederick St) with 919 graves (mostly pearl divers) while Chinese and Muslim cemeteries are

Christmas Island
POP 1600

Tropical Christmas Island (CI) may be an Australian territory, but its closest neighbour is Java, Indonesia, 360km to the north; Perth lies 2600km to the south-east. A rugged limestone mountain, CI was settled in 1888 to mine phosphate – still the main economic activity. Its people are a mix of Chinese, Malays and European-Australians, a blend reflected in the island's food, languages, customs and religions.

In spite of mining activity, 63% of the island remains protected by Christmas Island National Park. Tall rainforest covers the plateau, and a series of limestone cliffs and terraces attracts rare, endemic nesting sea birds. A network of trails runs through the park, and it's possible to camp at Dolly Beach with a permit from **Parks Australia** (☎08-9164 8755; www.environment.gov.au). CI is famous for the spectacular annual movement in November and December of millions of red land crabs marching from the forest down to the coast to breed, covering everything in sight. Marine life is also dramatic, with bright corals and fish on the fringing reefs attracting snorkellers in the dry season, and divers throughout the year. A sea swell can bring decent surf during the wet season (roughly December to March) and there's a surf shop on the island.

Christmas Island **visitor centre** (☎08-9164 8382; www.christmas.net.au) can coordinate accommodation, diving, fishing and car hire. Its excellent website has links for package tours, local businesses and detailed island information.

Accommodation includes backpackers, self-contained units, motel-style rooms or resort-style suites ranging from $50 to $395 per night. There're several restaurants serving Chinese, Malay and Mod Oz cuisine.

Christmas Island has achieved notoriety in recent years as a processing centre for asylum seekers arriving by boat from Indonesia. As recently as December 2010 it witnessed a terrible mass drowning after one of these boats broke up on the cliffs during a storm.

Cocos (Keeling) Islands
POP 650

Some 900km further west (2750km from Perth) are the Cocos (Keeling) Islands (CKI), a necklace of 27 low-lying islands around a blue lagoon that inspired Charles Darwin's theory of coral-atoll formation. CKI was settled by John Clunies-Ross in 1826, and his family remained in control of the islands and their Malay workers until 1978, when CKI became part of Australia's Indian Ocean territories. Today about 550 Malays and 100 European-Australians live on Home and West Islands. It's a very low-key place in which to walk, snorkel, dive, fish, windsurf and relax. While most people come on a package, you can visit independently, and camping is allowed at Scout Park on West Island, and on Direction and South Islands. You will need to bring all your own gear. Check out the island-information website, www.cocos-tourism.cc, which has a list of accommodation. Divers should visit www.cocosdive.com.

Getting There & Away

Virgin Australia (☎13 67 89; www.virginaustralia.com) flies a circle from Perth to both islands at least twice a week. Prices start at around $460 for either island and at $200 between the two. There's also a return charter flight on Friday from Kuala Lumpur to Christmas Island, which must be booked directly with **Island Explorer Holidays** (☎1300 884 855; www.islandexplorer.com.au). Australian visa requirements apply, and Australians should bring their passports.

nearby. There's a small **pioneer cemetery** by Town Beach, overlooking the bay.

Tiny **Town Beach** is fine for a dip, just ensure it's not stinger season, while the **port** (7km south of the centre) has a pleasant sandy beach and good fishing from the jetty. You might even see whales, turtles or dolphins.

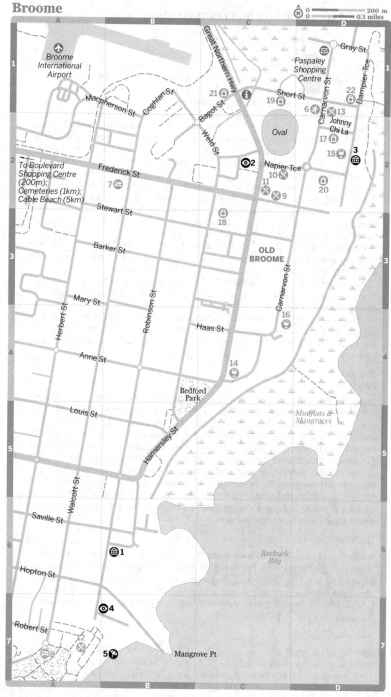

Broome

☞ Tours

It's a feisty business, but at last count there were three camel-tour operators running at Cable Beach offering similar trips.

Broome Camel Safaris CAMELS
(☑0419 916 101; www.broomecamelsafaris.com. au; 30min afternoon rides $25, 1hr sunset rides adult/child $60/40) Alison, the only female camel-tour operator in Broome, offers afternoon and evening trips.

Red Sun Camels CAMELS
(☑1800 184 488; www.redsuncamels.com.au; 40min morning rides adult/child $30/20, 1hr sunset rides $50/35) Red Sun runs morning and sunset tours, with a half-hour trip at 4pm ($20 per person).

Ships of the Desert CAMELS
(☑0419 954 022; www.shipsofthedesert.com. au; 40min morning rides adult/child $25/20, 1hr sunset rides $50/30) The original camel-tour company offers morning and sunset trips, and a half-hour afternoon option ($25 per person).

Lurujarri Dreaming Trail INDIGENOUS CULTURE
(☑08-9192 2959; www.environskimberley. org.au/lurujarri/lht_home.htm) This 50km trail follows the coast north from Gantheaume Point to Minari. The Goolarabooloo-Millibinyarri Indigenous Corporation runs several guided trips lasting one to two weeks between May and June each year, staying at traditional camp sites.

Broome Trike Tours MOTORCYCLE
(☑0407 575 237; www.broometriketours. au; town/tasting tours $90/165) Bush tucker, Harleys and mango wine – only in Broome.

Kujurta Buru INDIGENOUS CULTURE
(☑08-9192 1662; www.kujurtaburu.com.au; half-day adult/child $77/39) Nagula half-day tours explore Yawuru culture and country, including spear throwing and bush tucker tasting.

Broome Adventure Company KAYAKING
(☑1300 665 888; www.broomeadventure.com. au; 3/4hr trips $70/90) These eco-certified coastal kayaking trips running all year include pick-up from your accommodation.

Astro Tours ASTRONOMY
(☑0417 949 958; www.astrotours.net; adult/child $75/45) Fascinating after-dark two-hour stargazing tours held just outside Broome. Price includes taxi transfers, or self-drive and save $10.

Hovercraft Tours HOVERCRAFT
(☑08-9193 5025; www.broomehovercraft. au; 1hr adult/child $105/75, sunset/flying boat $150/95) Skim over tidal flats to visit historical sights, including, on very low tides, the wrecks of boats sunk during WWII.

Willie Pearl Lugger Cruises CRUISES
(☑0428 919 781; www.williecruises.com.au; adult/child $120/60) Sunset sailing cruises on a traditional pearl lugger may spot whales, dolphins and turtles (July to September).

Broome Sightseeing Tours SIGHTSEEING
(☑08-9192 0000; www.broomesightseeingtours.
com.au; adult/child $50/25) These two-hour
tours cram in all the main sights and
include a free beer tasting at Matso's
brewery. An extra $13 buys you a one-
hour **Pearl Luggers** tour immediately
afterwards.

✲ Festivals & Events

Dates (and festivals!) vary from year to year.
Check with the visitor centre or the community website (www.broome.wa.au).

Gimme Fest MUSIC
(www.goolarri.com) Showcasing the best of
Indigenous music. May.

Kullari NAIDOC Week INDIGENOUS CULTURE
(www.goolarri.com) Celebration of Aboriginal
and Torres Strait Islander culture. Late
June to mid-July.

Environs Annual Art Auction ART
(www.environskimberley.org.au) Annual environment fundraiser auctioning work by local
and Indigenous Kimberley artists. July.

Broome Race Round HORSE RACING
(www.broometurfclub.com.au) Kimberley Cup,
Ladies Day and Broome Cup are when locals and tourists frock up. July and August.

Opera Under the Stars OPERA
(www.operaunderthestars.com.au) One night
only at the Cable Beach Amphitheatre.
August.

Worn Art FASHION
(www.theatrekimberley.org.au) A fabulous spectacle of fashion, performance, music and
dance. August.

**Shinju Matsuri Festival of
the Pearl** PEARLS
(www.shinjumatsuri.com.au) Broome's homage to the pearl includes seven to 10 days
of parades, food, concerts, fireworks and
dragon-boat races. August and September.

Mango Festival MANGOES
A celebration of the fruit in all its forms.
November.

🛏 Sleeping

Accommodation is plentiful, but either book
ahead or be flexible. Prices plummet in
the Wet.

TOP CHOICE Beaches of Broome HOSTEL $$
(☑1300 881 031; www.beachesofbroome.com.au;
4 Sanctuary Rd, Cable Beach; dm $32-45, motel d

$140-180; ✳@🛜🛝) Broome's newest budget
accommodation is more resort than hostel.
Shady common areas, a poolside bar and a
modern self-catering kitchen complement
spotless, air-conditioned rooms. Dorms
come in a variety of sizes, and the motel
rooms are beautifully appointed. Scooter
hire available.

Bali Hai Resort & Spa SPA RESORT $$$
(☑08-9191 3100; www.balihairesort.com; 6 Mur-
ray Rd, Cable Beach; d $368-498; ✳🛜🛝) Lush
and tranquil, this beautiful small resort
has gorgeously decorated studios, each
with individual outside dining areas and
open-roofed mandis. The emphasis is on
relaxation, and the on-site spa offers a
range of exotic therapies to achieve it – try
the two-hour 'Passion of the Pearl'. The off-
season prices are a bargain.

Tarangau Caravan Park CARAVAN PARK $
(☑08-9193 5084; www.tarangaucaravanpark.com;
16 Millington Rd; unpowered/powered sites $30/36)
A quiet alternative to often noisy Cable
Beach caravan parks, Tarangau is a laid-back
spot with pleasant, grassy sites 1km from
Cable Beach.

Kimberley Klub HOSTEL $
(☑08-9192 3233; www.kimberleyklub.com; 62 Frederick St; dm $26-31, d/apt $125/160; ✳@🛜🛝)
This big, laid-back tropical backpackers is a
great place to meet other travellers. Features
include poolside bar, games room, massive
kitchen, excellent noticeboard and organised activities most nights.

Palm Grove Holiday Resort RESORT $$
(☑08-9192 3336; www.palmgrove.com.au; cnr
Cable Beach & Murray Rds; unpowered/powered
sites $34/41, studio d $180, 2-bedroom units
$195; ✳@🛝) Right behind Cable Beach,
this park offers a good mix of comfy air-
con cabins and shady powered camp sites.
There's a great camp kitchen and a lovely
swimming pool, but the unpowered sites
cop full sun.

Seashells Resort APARTMENTS $$$
(☑1800 800 850; www.seashells.com.au; 4 Chal-
lenor Dr; 1-/2-/3-bedroom apt $295/360/425;
✳🛜🛝) A short walk to Cable Beach, these
spacious apartments, all with verandahs
and fully equipped kitchens, offer great
value for groups. The largest holds six, and
there're pleasant landscaped gardens, BBQs
and a pool.

Roebuck Bay Caravan Park CARAVAN PARK $
(☎08-9192 1366; 91 Walcott St; unpowered/powered sites d $28/35, on-site van d $90; ❄) Right next to Town Beach, this shady park has good facilities, including a communal kitchen and barbecue area.

Cable Beach Backpackers HOSTEL $
(☎1800 655 011; www.cablebeachbackpackers.com; 12 Sanctuary Rd; dm $24-29, d $75; ❄@🛜🏊) Within splashing distance of Cable Beach, this relaxed place has a lush tropical courtyard, a swimming pool, a big communal kitchen and a bar.

✖ Eating

Be prepared for 'Broome prices' (exorbitant), 'Broome time' (when it should be open but it's closed) and surcharges: credit cards, public holidays, weekends. Service can fluctuate wildly, as most staff are just passing through. Most places close in the Wet.

The back lanes of Chinatown, especially around Johnny Chi Lane, offer various cheap weekday lunch options. All pubs and resorts have in-house restaurants; some are great value, but at others you're paying for the view.

Self-caterers can take advantage of well-stocked supermarkets and bakeries at Paspaley and Boulevard shopping centres, while Yuen Wing (19 Carnarvon St) is your best bet for all things Asian.

TOP CHOICE Aarli TAPAS $$
(☎08-9192 5529; 2/6 Hamersley St, cnr Frederick St; tapas & mains $11-20, pizzas $18-20; ⊘8am-late Dry; 🅿) Meaning 'fish' in Bardi, the Aarli is cooking up some of the most inventive and tasty titbits in Broome. The Med-Asian fusion tapas are excellent with a cold beer or chilled wine, and the pizzas are simple and scrumptious, but, really, you want to share the signature baked whole fish ($45) because it is superb.

Azuki JAPANESE $$
(☎08-9193 7211; 1/15 Napier Tce; sushi $8-10, mains $15-34; ⊘lunch & dinner Mon-Fri, dinner Sat Dry; 🅿) Enjoy the exquisite subtlety of authentic Japanese cuisine at this tiny BYO – from its takeaway thick fresh sushi rolls to wonderfully tasty bento boxes.

noodlefish ASIAN FUSION $$
(☎08-9192 1697; 6 Hamersley St, cnr Frederick St; mains $25-33; ⊘6-9pm Tue-Sat) This quirky alfresco BYO is doing fantastic contemporary Asian dishes from classic Kimberley ingredients. While the accent is on seafood, there's plenty to please all palates. Get there early, because you can't book and it'll only take cash.

Wharf Restaurant SEAFOOD $$$
(☎08-9192 5800; Port of Pearls House, Port Dr; mains $20-40; ⊘10am-10pm) Down at Broome's port you can settle back for a long, lazy seafood lunch with waterside ambience and the chance of a whale sighting. OK, it's pricey and the service is hit and miss, but the wine's cold and the chilli blue swimmer crab is sensational. Just wait until after 2pm before ordering oysters.

Cable Beach General Store CAFE $
(☎08-9192 5572; cnr Cable Beach & Murray Rds; ⊘6.30am-7.30pm; @) Cable Beach unplugged – a typical Aussie corner shop with coffee, pancakes, barra burgers, pies and internet, and no hidden charges. You can even play a round of mini-golf (adult/child/family $6/5/20).

Town Beach Cafe CAFE $$
(☎08-9193 5585; Robinson St; breakfasts $10-17, lunches $16-24; ⊘7.30am-2pm Tue-Sun, dinner Fri & Sat) With a great view over Roebuck Bay, the alfresco tables of the Town are an ideal spot for an early brekkie. The caramelised-banana pancakes are divine.

JC's Kitchen PUB FARE $$
(Roebuck Bay Hotel, 45 Dampier Tce) Great value.

🍷 Drinking & Entertainment

Check the gig guide on www.broome.wa.au.

Tides Garden Bar BAR
(☎08-9192 1303; www.mangrovehotel.com.au; 47 Carnarvon St) The Mangrove Resort's casual outdoor bar is just the place for a few early-evening beverages while contemplating Roebuck Bay. There're good bistro meals, half-price oysters between 5.30pm and 6.30pm, and live music towards the end of the week, including touring big names. You don't need to move to watch the Staircase to the Moon.

Sunset Bar & Grill BAR
(☎08-9192 0470; Cable Beach Club Resort, Cable Beach Rd) Arrive around 4.45pm, grab a front-row seat, order a drink and watch the show – backpackers, package tourists, locals, camels and a blistering Indian Ocean sunset tinged by imported coconut palms.

KIMBERLEY ART COOPERATIVES

The art of the Kimberley is like no other Indigenous art in Australia. Encompassing the powerful and strongly guarded Wandjina, the prolific and puzzling Gwion Gwion (Bradshaw) images, bright tropical coastal colours, subtle and sombre ochres of the bush and the abundance when desert meets river, every work sings a story about country.

To experience it firsthand, try some of these Aboriginal-owned cooperatives; most are accessible by 2WD.

Mowanjum Art & Culture Centre (☑08-9191 1008; www.mowanjumarts.com; Gibb River Rd, Derby; ☺9am-5pm daily, closed Sat & Sun Wet) Just 4km along the GRR, this is an impressive new building and gallery representing artists renowned for their Wandjina and Gwion Gwion images.

Waringarri Aboriginal Arts Centre (☑08-9168 2212; www.waringarriarts.com.au; 16 Speargrass Rd, Kununurra; ☺8.30am-4.30pm Mon-Fri) This excellent gallery-studio hosts local artists working with ochres in a unique abstract style. It also represents artists from Kalumburu.

Warmun Arts (☑08-9168 7496; www.warmunart.com; Great Northern Hwy, Warmun; ☺9am-4.30pm Mon-Fri) Warmun artists use ochres to explore Gija identity. The cooperative is between Kununurra and Halls Creek; phone first for a verbal permit, or visit the Halls Creek visitor centre.

Laarri Gallery (☑08-9191 7195; yiyilischool@activ8.net.au; Yiyili; ☺8am-4pm school days) Located 120km west of Halls Creek and 5km from the Great Northern Hwy, this tiny not-for-profit gallery in the back of the community school has interesting contemporary-style art detailing local history. Phone ahead.

Yaruman Artists Centre (☑08-9168 8208; Kundat Djaru) Sitting on the edge of the Tanami 162km from Halls Creek, Yaruman's acrylic works feature the many local soaks (waterholes). The weekly mail run from Kununurra stops here.

Warlayirti Artists Centre (☑08-9168 8960; www.balgoart.org.au; Balgo; ☺9am-5pm) This centre 255km down the Tanami Track is a conduit for artists around the area and features bright acrylic dot-style as well as lithographs and glass. Phone first to arrange an entry permit.

Roebuck Bay Hotel　PUB
(☑08-9192 1221; www.roebuckbayhotel.com.au; 45 Dampier Tce; ☺noon-late) The 'Roey' is a Broome institution, with different bars offering sports, live music, DJs and cocktails until the wee hours. It also does a range of accommodation and has a great kitchen.

Matso's Broome Brewery　PUB
(☑08-9193 5811; 60 Hamersley St; ☺music 3-6pm Sun) Get a Smokey Bishop into you at this casual backpacker pub and kick back to live music on the verandah. Bring something for the sandflies.

Diver's Tavern　LIVE MUSIC
(☑08-9193 6066; Cable Beach Rd) Don't miss the popular Wednesday jams and Sunday session.

ZeeBar　COCKTAIL BAR
(☑08-9193 6511; www.zeebar.com.au; 4 Sanctuary Rd; ☺6pm-late) This stylish bar and bistro near Cable Beach mixes up tasty cocktails,

and has great tapas and DJs. Tuesday is trivia night.

Shopping

The galleries and jewellers on Short St and Dampier Tce are full of extraordinary Indigenous art from the Kimberley and milky treasures from the deep.

Gecko Gallery　INDIGENOUS ART
(☑08-9192 8909; www.geckogallery.com.au; 9 Short St; ☺10am-6pm Mon-Fri, to 2pm Sat & Sun, shorter hr Wet) The ever-helpful Belinda Cornish specialises in east Kimberley and Western Desert art, including canvases, prints and etchings.

Paspaley Pearls　PEARLS
(☑08-9192 2203; www.paspaleypearls.com; 2 Short St) Paspaley started Australia's first cultured-pearl farm 420km north of Broome at Kuri Bay in the 1950s.

Broome Beads and Fine Jewellery BEADS
(☎08-9192 5223; www.broomebeads.com.au; 4 Johnny Chi Lane) Haven't found any jewellery you like? Then make your own.

Kimberley Camping & Outback Supplies OUTDOOR GEAR
(☎08-9193 5909; www.kimberleycamping.com.au; cnr Frederick St & Cable Beach Rd) Camp ovens, jaffle irons and everything else you need for a successful expedition into the Kimberley.

Courthouse Markets MARKET
(Hamersley St; ⏲mornings Sat, additional Sun Apr-Oct) Get your local arts, crafts and general hippy gear here.

Kimberley Bookshop BOOKS
(☎08-9192 1944; 4 Napier Tce; ⏲9am-5pm Mon-Fri, to 2pm Sat) Extensive range of books on Broome and the Kimberley.

Magabala Books BOOKS
(☎08-9192 1991; www.magabala.com; 1 Bagot St; ⏲9am-4.30pm Mon-Fri) Indigenous publishers covering novels, social history, biographies and children's literature.

ℹ Information

There are ATMs on Carnarvon, Hamersley and Short Sts and Napier Tce, and there's a post office at Paspaley shopping centre. For noticeboards to buy, sell and hunt lifts, try the hostels, **Fongs** (29 Saville St) and **Yuen Wing** (19 Carnarvon St).

For more info on the region, see www.eventsinthekimberley.com.au and www.kimberleytourism.com; for a what's-on guide, see http://broome.wa.au.

Broome Community Resource Centre (☎08-9193 7153; 40 Dampier Tce; per hr $5; ⏲9am-5pm Mon-Fri, to noon Sat; @📶) Professional internet with cheap printing.

Broome District Hospital (☎08-9192 9222; 28 Robinson St; ⏲24hr)

Broome visitor centre (☎1800 883 777; www.broomevisitorcentre.com.au; Male Oval, Hamersley St; ⏲8.30am-5pm Mon-Fri, to 4pm Sat & Sun, shorter hr Wet) On the roundabout entering town. Good info on road conditions, Staircase to the Moon and tide times; can book transport, accommodation and tours.

DIA (☎1300 651 077; www.dia.wa.gov.au) Apply online for free permits to visit Aboriginal communities. Three-day processing time.

Galactica DMZ Internet Café (☎08-9192 5897; 4/2 Hamersley St; per hr $5; ⏲10am-8pm; @📶) Many terminals, Skype, webcams, CD/DVD burning, gaming. Upstairs behind McDonalds.

Travelworld (☎08-9193 7233; Boulevard Shopping Centre) Helpful, professional staff can organise most flights.

ℹ Getting There & Away

Virgin Australia and Qantas fly daily to Perth, and Qantas also has a direct Sunday flight to/from Melbourne. Airnorth flies daily to Darwin (except Saturday) and Kununurra, and Tuesday and Friday to Karratha and Port Hedland. Skywest flies daily to Perth, and to Darwin and Exmouth April to October. It also has a handy weekly connection to Bali (via Port Hedland). Golden Eagle flies to Fitzroy Crossing, Halls Creek and Port Hedland four times weekly.

Greyhound buses leave the visitor centre daily for Darwin, and Tuesday, Thursday and Saturday for Perth.

ℹ Getting Around

Town Bus Service (☎08-9193 6585; www.broomebus.com.au; adult/child $3.50/1.50, day passes $10) links Chinatown with Cable Beach every hour (7.10am to 6.23pm year-round), plus half-hourly (8.40am to 6.40pm) from May to mid-October. Under 16s ride free with an adult; timetables from the visitor centre.

All major rental-car companies are represented, though no-one offers unlimited kilometres. Local operator **Broome Broome** (☎08-9192 2210; www.broomebroome.com.au) has cars (from $63 per day), 4WD ($153) and scooters ($35). **Britz** (☎08-9192 2647; www.britz.com; 10 Livingston St) hires campervans and 4WD Toyota Land Cruisers (from $176 per day) – essential for the Gibb River Rd.

Broome Cycles (www.broomecycles.com.au; ☎Chinatown 08-9192 1871; Cable Beach 0409 192 289) rents bicycles for $24/84 per day/week, $50 deposit. For taxis phone **Broome Taxis** (☎08-9192 1133) or **Chinatown Taxis** (☎1800 811 772).

Around Broome

Malcolm Douglas Wilderness Wildlife Park ZOO
(☎08-9193 6580; www.malcolmdouglas.com.au; Great Northern Hwy; adult/child/family $35/20/90; ⏲10am-5pm Apr-Nov, from 2pm Sat & Sun) Visitors enter through the jaws of a giant crocodile at this 30-hectare wildlife park, established by Malcolm Douglas as an animal refuge. The park is home to dozens of crocs (feedings 3pm), as well as kangaroos, cassowaries, emus, dingos, jabirus and numerous birds. It's 16km north-east of Broome.

Broome Bird Observatory NATURE RESERVE
([✉]08-9193 5600; www.broomebirdobservatory.
com; Crab Creek Rd; admission by donation; camp
sites per person $14, donga s/d $50/75, chalets
$160; [🕘]8am-5pm) On Roebuck Bay, 25km
from Broome, this amazing bird observatory is a vital staging post for hundreds
of migratory species, some travelling over
12,000km. Tours range from an excellent two-hour walk ($75) to a five-day all-
inclusive course ($1090). Self-guided trails,
accommodation and binoculars are available. The dirt access road can close during
the Wet.

Dampier Peninsula

The red pindan of the Dampier Peninsula
ends abruptly above deserted white-sand
beaches and secluded mangrove bays, while
turquoise waters lap lazily and sunsets turn
ancient cliffs to molten crimson. This country is home to thriving Indigenous settlements of the Ngumbarl, Jabirr Jabirr, Nyul
Nyul, Nimanburu, Bardi, Jawi and Goolar-
abooloo peoples.

Access is by 4WD, along the largely unsealed 215km Cape Leveque Rd. Visiting
Aboriginal communities requires both a
DIA permit (see p1003) and one from the
community, payable at the office on arrival.
Communities can close suddenly, so always
book ahead at the Broome visitor centre and
grab its booklet *Ardi – Dampier Peninsula
Travellers Guide* (www.ardi.com.au; $3).
You should be self-sufficient, though limited
supplies are available.

On Cape Leveque Rd, turn left after 14km
onto Manari Rd and head north along the
spectacular coast. There are **bush-camping
sites** (no facilities) at Barred Creek, Quandong Point, James Price Point and Coulomb
Point, where there is a **nature reserve**. Conventional vehicles should make it to James
Price Point, whose pristine future is threatened by controversial plans to construct a
huge LNG facility there.

Back on Cape Leveque Rd, it's 110km to
Beagle Bay ([✉]08-9192 4913), notable for the
extraordinarily beautiful mother-of-pearl al-
tar at Beagle Bay church, built by Pallotine
monks in 1918. There's no accommodation,
but fuel is available (weekdays only). Contact
the office on arrival.

Idyllic **Middle Lagoon** ([✉]08-9192 4002;
www.middlelagoon.com.au; unpowered/powered
sites per person $15/20, beach shelter d $50, cabin

d $150-250), 180km from Broome and sur-
rounded by empty beaches, is superb for
swimming, snorkelling, fishing and doing
nothing. There's plenty of shade and bird
life, and the cabins are great value, though
the access road is terrible. The Whale Song
Cafe at nearby Munget does light meals
(when open).

Between Middle Lagoon and Cape
Leveque, 200km from Broome, **Lombadina**
([✉]08-9192 4936; entry per car $10, s/d $75/140,
4-person cabins $180-260) is a beautiful tree-
fringed village with fishing (from $175),
whale watching ($220), mud crabbing ($88),
kayaking ($77) and Indigenous 'footprint'
tours ($35). There are lodge-style rooms and
self-contained cabins but no camping. Fuel
is available weekdays.

Nearby, tiny **Chile Creek** ([✉]08-9192 4141;
www.chilecreek.com; entry per car $10, sites per per-
son $16.50, bush bungalows $100, 4-person tents
$185), 7km from Lombadina down a wither-
ing track, offers basic bush camp sites, modern safari tents and renovated bungalows,
all just a short stroll to a lovely beach. Go
mud crabbing with Roma, and she'll share
her famous chilli crab recipe.

Cape Leveque is spectacular, with gorgeous beaches and stunning red cliffs.
Eco-tourism award winner **Kooljaman**
([✉]08-9192 4970; www.kooljaman.com.au; entry
per car $10, unpowered/powered site d $36/41,
dome tents $60, cabin d with/without bathroom
$165/140, safari-tent d $260; [☎]) offers grassy
camp sites, driftwood beach shelters, hilltop safari tents with superb views, and
stuffy budget domes. There's a minimum
two-night stay, and the place is packed
from June to October. The BYO **restaurant** (mains $26-50; [🕘]Apr-Oct) opens for
lunch and dinner, or you can order 'bush
butler' (BBQ pack) service.

If you prefer less bling, there're a couple
of outstations offering camp sites between
Cape Leveque and One-Arm Point. **Goom-
bading** ([✉]0457 138 027; unpowered/powered
sites per person $15/20), with a fantastic water
view, is very relaxed. Hosts Unja and Jenny
are keen to share Bardi culture and offer
spear-making, fishing and crabbing tours.

You can't camp at **Ardiyooloon** (One Arm
Point; entry $10), but you can visit this neat
community with a well-stocked store, fuel,
a barramundi hatchery, and great fishing
and swimming with views of the Buccaneer
Archipelago.

HORIZONTAL WATERFALLS

One of the most intriguing features of the Kimberley coastline is the phenomenon known as 'horizontal waterfalls'. Despite the name, the falls are simply tides gushing through narrow coastal gorges in the Buccaneer Archipelago, north of Derby. What creates such a spectacle are the huge tides, often varying up to 11m. The water flow reaches an astonishing 30 knots as it's forced through two narrow gaps 20m and 10m wide – resulting in a 'waterfall' reaching 4m in height.

Many tours leave Derby (and some from Broome) each Dry, by air, sea or a combination of both. It's become *de rigueur* to 'ride' the tide change through the gorge on a high-powered speedboat, which is risky at best – accidents have occurred. Scenic flights are the quickest and cheapest option, and some seaplanes will land and transfer passengers to a waiting speedboat for the adrenalin hit. If you prefer to be stirred, not shaken, then consider seeing the falls as part of a longer cruise through the archipelago. Book tours at Derby and Broome visitor centres.

A handful of other outstations offer camping, fishing and crabbing opportunities.

Chomley's Tours (☑08-9192 6195; www. chomleystours.com.au; 1-/2-/3-/4-days $245/470/675/660) offers tours of the peninsula, some with mud crabbing and kayaking, as well as one-way transfers ($180). **Kujurta Buru** (☑08-9192 1662; www.kujurtaburu.com.au; ☺Tue, Thu & Sun) provides transport from Broome to Beagle Bay ($75), and Lombadina, Kooljaman and Ardiyooloon (all $120), returning the same day. Adventurous drivers heading on to Derby can try the back road opposite Beagle Bay.

Derby

POP 5000

Late at night, while Derby sleeps, the boabs cut loose and wander around town, marauding mobs flailing their many limbs in battle against an army of giant, killer crocs emerging from the encircling mudflats. If only.

There are crocs hiding in the mangroves, but you're more likely to see birds, over 200 varieties, while the boabs are firmly along the two main parallel drags, Loch and Clarendon Sts. Derby, sitting on King Sound, is the departure point for tours to the horizontal waterfalls and Buccaneer Archipelago, and the western terminus of the Gibb River Road (GRR). It's also the west Kimberley's administrative centre, and the refugee detention facility at nearby RAAF Curtin brings in hordes of contractors.

The town goes off during the annual **Boab Festival** (www.derbyboabfestival.org.au) in July, with concerts, sports (including mud footy), races (horse and mud crab varieties), poetry readings, art exhibitions and street parades.

◉ Sights & Activities

The visitor centre's excellent town map lists every conceivable attraction. Grab its key and have a peek at the nearby **Wharfinger Museum** (admission by donation), with its atmospheric shipping and aviation displays. The visitor centre also sells tickets for the weekly **mail run flights** (per person $395) that visit remote stations, handy for accessing the Gibb.

Check out King Sound's colossal 11.5m tides from the circular **jetty** (1km north), a popular fishing, crabbing, bird-spotting and staring-into-the-distance haunt. Yep, there are crocs in the mangroves.

Old Derby Gaol (Loch St) and the **Boab Prison Tree** (7km south) are sad reminders of man's inhumanity to man.

There's a **bird hide** in the wetlands (aka sewerage ponds) at the end of Conway St, and the 2.3km **Joonjoo Botanical Trail** (opposite the GRR turn-off) has neat interpretive displays from the local Nyikina people.

⛟ Tours

The horizontal waterfalls are Derby's top draw, and most cruises also include the remote natural splendours of King Sound and the Buccaneer Archipelago. There're many operators to choose from (see the visitor centre for a full list). Most tours only operate during the Dry.

One Tide Charters CRUISES
(☑08-9193 1358; www.onetide.com; 5-12 days $3500-8400) Offers eco-certified all-inclusive multi-day 'sea safaris' with overnight camping on remote beaches, a ride through the horizontal waterfalls, mud crabbing, fishing and freshwater swimming on exotic islands.

Horizontal Falls Adventure Tours SCENIC FLIGHTS
(☑08-9192 2885; www.horizontalfalls.com.au; fly-cruise-fly tours from Derby/Broome $690/790) Flights to horizontal falls including speedboat transfer.

Bush Flight SCENIC FLIGHT
(☑08-9193 2680; www.bushflight.com.au; 90/120/150min flights $250/340/425) To horizontal waterfalls; look, don't touch.

West Kimberley Tours CAMPING
(☑08-9193 1550; www.westkimberleytours.com.au) Town tours (half/full day $60/75), a Windjana Gorge and Tunnel Creek day trip ($135), and two- to seven-day Kimberley camping tours ($198 per day).

🛏 Sleeping & Eating

Any decent accommodation is normally full of contract workers. If you're heading to or from the Gibb, consider stopping at Birdwood Downs Station (20km away) instead.

There're several takeaways and cafes along Loch and Clarendon Sts and a restaurant out at the jetty that changes hands every few months.

TOP CHOICE Desert Rose B&B $$
(☑08-9193 2813; 4 Marmion St; d $198; ❄) The best sleep in town is worth booking ahead. Spacious, individually styled rooms come with a nice shady pool, leadlight windows and a sumptuous breakfast. Host Anne is a font of local information.

TOP CHOICE Jila Gallery ITALIAN $$
(☑08-9193 2560; 18 Clarendon St; mains $20-30; ⏱7am-2pm & 6pm-late Tue-Fri, 6pm-late Sat) Enjoy real coffee and excellent cakes while perusing an eclectic mixture of contemporary and Indigenous art. This friendly gallery-trattoria also does alfresco pizza, pasta and classic Italian standards.

Boab Inn PUB FARE $$
(☑08-9191 1044; www.derbyboabinn.com; Loch St; d $220, lunches $10-20, dinners $24-32; ❄@❅❄) Excellent counter meals and free wi-fi make this the lunch stop of choice.

The motel-style rooms are clean, comfortable and normally booked out.

Kimberley Entrance Caravan Park CARAVAN PARK $
(☑08-9193 1055; www.kimberleyentrancecaravanpark.com; 2 Rowan St; unpowered/powered sites $28/33) Passable sites, not all shaded, close to the mudflats.

ℹ Information

The supermarket and ATMs are on Loch and Clarendon Sts.

Derby visitor centre (☑1800 621 426; www.derbytourism.com.au; 2 Clarendon St; ⏱8.30am-4.30pm Mon-Fri, 9am-noon Sat yr round, plus 9am-noon Sun Apr-Sep) A mandatory stop, with super-helpful advice on road conditions, accommodation, bus tickets and tour bookings.

Library (Clarendon St; ⏱closed Sun; @) Internet; first five minutes free.

Post office (Loch St)

ℹ Getting There & Away

Strategic flies to Perth four times a week. Greyhound buses to Darwin ($325, 24 hours) and Broome ($65, two hours) stop at the visitor centre, which also sells tickets for the weekly **mail run flights** (per person $395).

Gibb River Road

Cutting a brown swath through the scorched heart of the Kimberley, the legendary Gibb River Road ('the Gibb' or GRR) provides one of Australia's wildest outback experiences. Stretching some 660km between Derby and Kununurra, the largely unpaved GRR is an endless sea of red dirt, big open skies and dramatic terrain. Rough, sometimes deeply corrugated, side roads lead to remote gorges, shady pools, distant waterfalls and million-acre cattle stations. Rain can close the road any time and permanently during the Wet. This is true wilderness with minimal services, so good planning and self-sufficiency are essential.

Several stations offer overnight accommodation from mid-April to late October; advance bookings are essential during the peak period of June to August. Hema Maps' *The Kimberley Atlas & Guide* provides the best coverage, while visitor centres sell *The Gibb River & Kalumburu Road Guide* ($5).

For just a sniff of outback adventure, try the 'tourist loop' along the GRR from Derby onto Fairfield Leopold Downs Rd to Windjana Gorge and Tunnel Creek, then exit onto the Great Northern Hwy (Rte 1) near Fitzroy Crossing.

A high-clearance 4WD (eg Toyota Land Cruiser) is mandatory, with two spare tyres, tools, emergency water (a minimum of 20L) and several days' food in case of breakdown. Britz in Broome is a reputable hire outfit. Fuel is limited and expensive, most mobile phones won't work, and temperatures can be life threatening. Broome and Kununurra are best for supplies.

The wheel-less can jump on an organised tour, or fly in on the mail run from Derby (see p1006).

Tours

Western Xposure 4WD
(☏08-9414 8423; www.westernxposure.com.au; 7 days $1445) Camping trips through the GRR.

Kimberley Wild Expeditions 4WD
(☏1300 738 870; www.kimberleywild.com.au) Consistent award winners. Half-day Broome ($139) to nine-day GRR ($1995) tours.

Kimberley Adventure Tours 4WD
(☏1800 083 368; www.kimberleyadventures.com.au) Runs between Broome and Darwin, including the GRR and Purnululu National Park ($1650, nine days).

ℹ Information

Consult www.gibbriverroad.net and www.kimberleyaustralia.com, shire websites (below), and Derby and Kununurra visitor-centre sites. Hema Maps' The Kimberley Atlas & Guide ($30) and Regional Map – The Kimberley ($10) are recommended.

DEC (www.dec.wa.gov.au) Park permits, camping fees, info. A Holiday Pass ($40) works out cheaper if visiting more than three parks in one month.

DIA (☏1300 651 077; www.dia.wa.gov.au) Apply online for free permits (three-day processing time) to visit Aboriginal communities.

Mainroads Western Australia (MRWA; ☏13 81 38; www.mainroads.wa.gov.au; ⏱24hr) Highway conditions.

Shire of Derby/West Kimberley (☏08-9191 0999; www.sdwk.wa.gov.au) Side-road conditions.

Shire of Wyndham East Kimberley (☏08-9161 1002; www.thelastfrontier.com.au) Kalumburu and Mitchell Falls road conditions.

The first 100km or so of the GRR from Derby are sealed. The 2000-hectare **Birdwood Downs Station** (☏08-9191 1275; www.birdwooddowns.com; camping $12.50, huts per person incl breakfast & dinner $130) offers rustic savannah huts, dusty camping, and a pleasant 'village green'. WWOOFers are welcome, and it's also the **Kimberley School of Horsemanship**, with lessons, riding camps and trail rides (two-hour sunset rides are $99).

Just after Inglis Gap, you'll see the turn-off for the rough 50km to remote **Mt Hart Wilderness Lodge** (☏08-9191 4645; www.mthart.com.au; per person camp sites $15, r incl breakfast & dinner $290; ⊙Dry) with grassy camp sites, pleasant gorges, and swimming and fishing holes. Seven kilometres past Mt Hart turn-off is narrow **Lennard River Gorge**, a hot 3km return walk to a waterfall and a refreshing pool; cairns mark the steep final descent.

Despite its name, **March Fly Glen** – at the 204km mark – is a pleasant, shady picnic area ringed by pandanus and home to blue-helmeted honeyeaters. Don't miss stunning **Bell Gorge**, 29km down a rough track, with a picturesque waterfall and a popular plunge pool; camp at **Silent Grove** (adult/child $11/2). Refuel (diesel only) and grab an ice cream at **Imintji Store** (☏08-9191 7471; ⊙7am-4.30pm, shorter hrs in the Wet), your last chance for supplies. Next door is **Over the Range Repairs** (☏08-9191 7887), where Neville is your best, if not only, hope of mechanical salvation on the whole Gibb.

Part of the Australian Wildlife Conservancy, the superb **Mornington Wilderness Camp** (☏08-9191 7406; www.awc.org.au; camp sites adult/child $18/8, safari-tent s/d incl full board $295/500, entry fee $25; ⊙Dry;) is as remote as it gets, lying on the Fitzroy River, a very rough, incredibly scenic 95km drive south of the Gibb's 247km mark. Nearly 360,000 hectares are devoted to conserving the Kimberley's endangered fauna, and there's excellent canoeing, birdwatching and bushwalking. Choose from shady camp sites or spacious raised tents with verandahs. The bar and restaurant offers picnic hampers and the best cheese platter this side of Margaret River.

Beautiful **Galvans Gorge**, with waterfall, swimming hole, rock wallabies and Wandjina art, is the most accessible of all gorges, less than 1km off the road. **Mt Barnett**

Roadhouse (☑08-9191 7007), at the 300km point, has the least reliable opening hours and most expensive fuel on the GRR. The dusty camp site at Manning River Gorge (per person $13), 7km behind the roadhouse, is often full of travellers waiting for fuel. At least there's a good swimming hole.

Further up the Gibb, at the 338km mark, is the turn-off to Mt Elizabeth Station (☑08-9191 4644; www.mountelizabethstation. com; camp sites per person $14, s/d incl breakfast & dinner $170/340; ☺Dry), one of the few remaining private leaseholders in the Kimberley. Peter Lacy's 200,000-hectare property is a good base for exploring nearby gorges, waterfalls and Indigenous rock art, and the home-style, three-course dinners ($35) hit the spot. Wallabies frequent the camp site.

At 406km you reach the Kalumburu turn-off. Heading right on the GRR, pull into atmospheric Ellenbrae Station (☑08-9161 4325; camp sites per person $15, bungalow d $150) for fresh scones and quirky bungalows. The GRR continues through spectacular country, crossing the mighty Durack River, and at 579km there are panoramic views of the Cockburn Ranges, Cambridge Gulf and Pentecost River.

The privations of the Gibb are left behind when you reach the amazing Home Valley Station (☑08-9161 4322; www.homevalley.com. au; camp sites adult/child $16/5, eco tents sleeping 4 $190, homestead d from $240; ✳@☎☎), an Indigenous hospitality-training resort with a superb range of luxurious accommodation. There're excellent grassy camp sites and motel-style rooms, a fantastic open bistro, tyre repairs, and activities including swimming, fishing and cattle mustering.

At 589km cross the infamous Pentecost River – take care, as water levels are unpredictable and saltwater crocs lurk nearby. Slightly further is El Questro Wilderness Park (☑08-9169 1777; www.elquestro. com.au; 7-day park permits $17.50; ☺Dry), a 360,000-hectare former cattle station with scenic gorges (Amelia, El Questro) and the

MITCHELL PLATEAU & KALUMBURU

In the Dry, Kalumburu Rd is easily navigable as far as Drysdale River Station (☑08-9161 4326; www.drysdaleriver.com.au; camp sites $9-14, d $130; ☺8am-5pm), 59km from the GRR, where you'll find fuel, tyres, meals and accommodation, and you can check ongoing conditions. Scenic flights to Mitchell Falls (from $325) operate from April to September.

The Ngauwudu (Mitchell Plateau) turn-off is 160km from the Gibb, and within 6km a deep, rocky ford crosses the King Edward River, formidable early in the season. Another 2km brings the Munurru Campground (adult/child $7/2) with excellent nearby rock art. From the Kalumburu Rd it's a rough 87km past lookouts and forests of livistona palms to the campground at Mitchell River National Park (entry per vehicle $11, camping adult/child $7/2).

Leave early if walking to Punamii-unpuu (Mitchell Falls; 8.6km return trip). The easy trail meanders through spinifex, woodlands and gorge country, dotted with Wandjina and Gwion Gwion rock-art sites, secluded waterholes, lizards, wallabies and brolga. The falls are stunning, whether trickling in the Dry or raging in the Wet (when they're only visible from the air). You can swim in the long pool above the falls, but swimming in the lower pools is strictly forbidden because of their cultural importance to the Wunambal people. Most people will complete the walk in three hours.

The road to Kalumburu deteriorates after the Mitchell Plateau turn-off and eventually becomes very rocky. You'll need a permit from DIA to visit Kalumburu and another (valid for seven days) on entry from the Kalumburu Aboriginal Community (KAC; ☑08-9161 4300; www.kalumburu.org; per car $50). Kalumburu is a picturesque mission nestled among giant mango trees and coconut palms, with two shops and fuel (☺7.30-11.30am & 1.30-4.30pm Mon-Fri). If you need any repairs, ask for Darren. You can stay at the Kalumburu Mission (☑08-9161 4333; camp sites per person $15, donga s/d $90/140), which has a small museum (admission $10; ☺8.30-10.30am), or get a permit from the KAC office to camp at Honeymoon Bay (☑08-9161 4378) or McGowan Island (☑08-9161 4748; www. mcgowanisland.com.au), 20km further out on the coast – the end of the road. Alcohol is banned at Kalumburu.

Zebedee thermal springs. The park's boat tours explore Chamberlain Gorge (adult/child $54/27; ☺3pm); alternatively, hire your own boat ($95 per day). The shady, riverside camp sites at El Questro Station Township (camp sites per person $15, bungalow d $325; ✱) are good value. There's also an outdoor bar and upmarket steakhouse (mains $18-36).

Ten kilometres along the GRR is El Questro's Emma Gorge Resort (cabin d $270; ☺Dry; ✇), where a 40-minute walk brings you to a sublime terminal plunge pool and waterfall, one of the prettiest in the whole Kimberley. The resort has an open-air bar and restaurant, though the non-air-con cabins are stuffy and overpriced.

At 630km you cross King River and at 647km you finally hit bitumen – turn left for Wyndham (48km) and right for Kununurra (53km).

Devonian Reef National Parks

Three national parks with three stunning gorges were once part of a western 'great barrier reef' in the Devonian era, 350 million years ago. Windjana Gorge and Tunnel Creek National Parks are accessed via Fairfield Leopold Downs Rd (linking the Great Northern Hwy with the Gibb River Rd), while Geikie Gorge National Park is just north-east of Fitzroy Crossing.

The walls of beautiful Windjana Gorge (per car $11) soar 100m above the Lennard River, which surges in the Wet but is a series of pools in the Dry. Scores of freshwater crocodiles lurk along the banks. Bring plenty of water for the 7km return walk from the campground (per person $10).

Tunnel Creek (per car $11, no camping), famous as the hideout of rebel Jandamarra, is a 750m-long passage, 3m to 15m wide, created by the creek cutting through a spur of the Napier Range. In the Dry you can walk the full length by wading partly through knee-deep water. Watch out for bats and take a strong torch. There are Aboriginal paintings at either end.

The magnificent Geikie Gorge is 22km north of Fitzroy Crossing. The best way to experience it and spot wildlife is on a DEC boat tour (☎08-9191 5121; 1hr adult/child $28/5; ☺8am & 3pm May-Oct). The self-guided trails are sandy and hot. A better option is a cultural cruise with a local Bunuba guide from Darngku

Heritage Tours (☎0417 907 609; www.darngku.com.au; 2hr adult/child $65/55, 3hr $80/65).

Fitzroy Crossing

POP 1500

This rugged little town sits at the Great Northern Hwy crossing of the Fitzroy River, with a large Aboriginal population hailing from the Gooniyandi, Bunuba, Walmatjarri and Wangkajungka communities. There's little reason to stay other than it's a good access point for the Devonian Reef national parks. The visitor centre (☎08-9191 5355; www.sdwk.wa.gov.au; ☺8.30am-4.30pm Mon-Fri yr-round, plus Sat Apr-Sep) is on the highway. There's a great arts centre, Mangkaja, and Dr Sawfish (next to the tyre guy, whom you'll probably need) is doing incredible glass and ceramics.

The oldest pub in the Kimberley, the atmospheric Crossing Inn (☎08-9191 5080; www.crossinginn.com.au; Skuthorpe Rd; unpowered/powered sites $26/30, s/d $140/155; ✱@) is an eye-opener for most people. Try it once.

Fitzroy River Lodge Motel Hotel & Caravan Park (☎08-9191 5141; www.fitzroyriverlodge.com.au; Great Northern Hwy; camping d $31, tent d $150, motel d $199; ✱@✇✇), across the river from the town, has comfortable motel rooms, exclusive Riverview studios and grassy camp sites, but check for Singapore ant infestation. The friendly bar has decent counter meals (mains $18 to $35).

Golden Eagle flies regularly to Broome and Halls Creek. Greyhound has daily buses to Broome and Darwin that stop at the visitor centre and Fitzroy River Lodge.

Fitzroy Crossing to Halls Creek

One of the Kimberley's best-kept secrets is the vast subterranean labyrinth of the Mimbi caves, 90km south-east of Fitzroy Crossing. Located within Mt Pierre Station, on Gooniyandi land, the caves house a significant collection of Aboriginal rock art and some of the most impressive fish fossils in the southern hemisphere. Aboriginal-owned Girloorloo Tours (adult/child $65/35; ☺Mon-Sat Apr-Sep) runs trips including an introduction to local Dreaming stories, bush tucker and traditional medicines. Book through Fitzroy Crossing or Halls Creek visitor centre.

Nearby Larrawa Station (☑08-9191 7025; Great Northern Hwy; camp sites $15, s/d $60/75), halfway between Fitzroy Crossing and Halls Creek, makes a good overnight stop, with hot showers, basic camp sites, a couple of shearers rooms, and meals (when available).

Another 30km towards Halls Creek brings Yiyilli with its Laarri Gallery (see p1002).

Halls Creek

POP 1590

On the edge of the Great Sandy Desert, Halls Creek is a small town with communities of Kija, Jaru and Gooniyandi people.

PERTH & WESTERN AUSTRALIA HALLS CREEK

The visitor centre (☑08-9168 6262; www. hallscreektourism.com.au; Great Northern Hwy; ⊘8am-5pm; @), the best in the Kimberley, is a great local resource and can book tours and arrange art-gallery visits and tickets for the Mimbi Caves. Check email next door at the Community Resource Centre (⊘8.15am-3.45pm Mon-Fri).

The unsealed Duncan Rd provides access to China Wall (5km away), a quartz vein protruding 6m off the ground, and the swimming holes of Palm Springs (45km away) and Sawpit Gorge (52km away). Keep going and you'll end up in the NT some 500km later, 120km south of Katherine.

DON'T MISS

PURNULULU NATIONAL PARK & BUNGLE BUNGLE RANGE

Looking like a packet of half-melted Jaffas, the World Heritage Purnululu National Park (per car $11; ⊘Apr-Dec) is home to the incredible ochre-and-black-striped 'beehive' domes of the Bungle Bungle Range.

The distinctive rounded rock towers are made of sandstone and conglomerates moulded by rainfall over millions of years. Their stripes are the result of oxidised iron compounds and algae. To the local Kidja people, *purnululu* means sandstone, with Bungle Bungle possibly a corruption of 'bundle bundle', a common grass. Whitefellas only 'discovered' the range during the mid-1980s.

Over 3000 sq km of ancient country contains a wide array of wildlife, including over 130 bird species. Kungkalahayi Lookout has a fine view of the range. Look for tiny bats high on the walls above palm-fringed Echidna Chasm (an hour's return walk) in the north, but it's the southern area comprising aptly named Cathedral Gorge (45 minutes return) that's most inspiring. Remote and pristine Piccaninny Gorge is best experienced as a 30km overnight round trip, when you can explore the many side gorges; check with the visitor centre for details. The restricted gorges in the northern part of the park can only be seen from the air.

Rangers are based here April to December and the park is closed outside this time. You'll need a high-clearance 4WD for the 52km twisty, rough road from the highway to the visitor centre near Three Ways junction; allow 2½ hours. There're five deep creek crossings, and the turn-off is 53km south of Warmun. Kurrajong Campsite (per person $11; ⊘Apr-Sep) and Walardi Campsite (per person $11; ⊘Apr-Dec) have fresh water and toilets.

Tours

Most Kimberley tour operators include Purnululu in multi-day tours. See p1012 for tours operating from Kununurra. You can also pick up tours at Warmun roadhouse and Halls Creek. Helicopters will get you closer than fixed-wing flights.

East Kimberley Tours SIGHTSEEING
(☑08-9168 2213; www.eastkimberleytours.com.au; from $315) Wide range of tours from Kununurra and Warmun.

Sling Air HELICOPTER FLIGHTS
(☑1800 095 500; www.slingair.com.au; 18/30/48min $215/325/525) From the Bellburn airstrip in the park.

Kimberley Hotel ([phone]08-9168 6101; www.kimberleyhotel.com.au; Roberta Ave; budget/motel d $120/180; ❄️📶🏊) has comfortable rooms and a shady terrace bar and restaurant (mains $16-34).

Best Western Halls Creek Motel ([phone]08-9168 9600; www.bestwestern.com.au; budget s/d $150/190, d $220-295; ❄️🏊) doesn't look very appealing, but the rooms are all newly renovated and well equipped; Russian Jack's (mains $28-40) opens for dinner.

There's a caravan park, but you're better off heading out of town.

Golden Eagle flies to Fitzroy Crossing and Broome. Greyhound has daily buses running between Broome and Darwin.

The Tanami Road

See p853 for driving and fuel-stop info.

WOLFE CREEK
METEORITE CRATER

According to the local Jaru people, Kandimalal, as the crater is traditionally known, marks the spot where a huge rainbow serpent emerged from the ground. The crater (880m across and 60m deep) makes an impressive, if somewhat eerie site, and it's possible to walk down into the centre. There're nearby camp sites (per person $7) and toilets, but no water, and it's 137km south along the Tanami – the final 23km are quite rough. Northwest Regional Airlines ([phone]08-9168 5211; www.northwestregional.com.au) offers 70-minute scenic flights from Halls Creek ($270 per person).

PARUKU INDIGENOUS PROTECTED
AREA (IPA) & LAKE GREGORY

Nestled between the Great Sandy and Tanami Deserts, just south of Billiluna and close to the Canning Stock Rte, is the Paruku IPA, which includes the permanent wetlands of Lake Gregory with their abundant bird life. The Aboriginal-owned and run IPA provides three remote camp sites and, if notified in advance, can arrange cultural events including traditional hunting and storytelling. Permits ($30 per vehicle) can be arranged from the IPA office in Billiluna ([phone]08-9168 8260) or Mulan ([phone]08-9168 8260). It's possible to make a nice loop drive including Wolfe Creek, Lake Gregory, Mulan and the Warlayirti Artists Centre at Balgo (see p1002). See Halls Creek visitor centre for more information.

Wyndham

POP 900

A gold-rush town fallen on leaner times, Wyndham is scenically nestled between rugged hills and the Cambridge Gulf, some 100km north-west of Kununurra. Sunsets are superb from the spectacular Five Rivers Lookout on Mt Bastion (325m) overlooking the King, Pentecost, Durack, Forrest and Ord Rivers entering Cambridge Gulf.

A giant 20m croc greets visitors entering town; you can see the real thing at Wyndham Crocodile Farm ([phone]08-9161 1124; Barytes Rd; adult/child $17/10; ⏱️10am-2pm Mar-Nov, to noon Dec-Feb, feeding time 11am) out past the port, 5km away. The port precinct also contains a small museum (⏱️10am-3pm daily Dry) and the Wyndham Town Hotel ([phone]08-9161 1202; O'Donnell St; d $130, meals $15-35; ❄️), with its legendary meals and pricey rooms.

In town, Five Rivers Cafe ([phone]08-9161 2271; Great Northern Hwy; ⏱️8am-5pm Mon-Fri) serves up great coffee, breakfasts and barra burgers, while laid-back Wyndham Caravan Park ([phone]08-9161 1064; Baker St, Three Mile; unpowered/powered sites $25/30, donga s/d $50/70; ❄️) offers grassy, shady camp sites.

Greyhound drops passengers 56km away at the Victoria Hwy junction. Internet's at the Telecentre (26 Koojarra Rd; ⏱️8am-4pm Mon-Fri), and Tuesday's mail run flight will get you to Kununurra. Call [phone]0418 950 434 for a taxi.

Kununurra

POP 6000

Kununurra is a relaxed town in the midst of an oasis of lush farmland and tropical-fruit plantations, thanks to the Ord River irrigation scheme. With good transport and communications, excellent services and well-stocked supermarkets, it's every traveller's favourite slice of civilisation between Broome and Darwin.

Kununurra is also the departure point for most of the tours in the east Kimberley, and with all that fruit, there's plenty of seasonal work. Note there's a 90-minute time difference with the NT.

◉ Sights & Activities

Across the highway from the township, Lily Creek Lagoon is a mini-wetlands with

DON'T MISS

PARRY LAGOONS NATURE RESERVE

This beautiful Ramsar-listed wetland, 15km from Wyndham, teems in the Wet with migratory birds arriving from as far away as Siberia. There's a bird hide and boardwalk at **Marlgu Billabong** (accessible only by 4WD) and an excellent view from **Telegraph Hill**. Back on the highway, steep steps lead down to the **Grotto**, a deep, peaceful pool in a small gorge perfect for a quiet dip.

Parry Creek Farm (☑08-9161 1139; www.parrycreekfarm.com.au; unpowered/powered sites $29/34, r $110, cabins $210; ✳☀), surrounded by the nature reserve, has its own billabong and hordes of wildlife. A raised boardwalk (for easy bird spotting) connects comfy rooms and air-con cabins around a billabong. The licensed cafe serves excellent baked barramundi.

amazing bird life, boating and freshwater crocs. **Lake Kununurra** (Diversion Dam) has pleasant picnic spots and great fishing. Groups could consider hiring their own 'barbie' boat from **Kununurra Self Drive Hire Boats** (☑0409 291 959; Lakeside Resort; per hr from $88).

Kelly's Knob is a favourite sunset viewpoint on the town's northern fringe, while nearby **Mirima National Park** (per car $11) is a stunning area of rugged sedimentary formations like a mini Bungle Bungles. The eroded gorges of **Hidden Valley** are home to brittle red peaks, spinifex, boab trees and abundant wildlife, best viewed at early morning or dusk.

Self-guided two- and three-day **canoe trips** run from Lake Argyle along the scenic **Ord River** to Kununurra, overnighting at designated riverside camp sites. Canoes, camping equipment and transport are provided, while you supply your own food and sleeping bag. You can choose to paddle the whole way back, or bail-out along the way. **Go Wild** (☑1300 663 369; www.gowild.com.au; 3 days $180) offers early bail-out options or extra days to their eco-certified standard three-day trip. **Big Waters** (☑1800 650 580; www.bigwaters.com.au; 3 days $175) offers a similar three-day trip.

☞ Tours

Go Wild　　　　　CANOE, ADVENTURE
(☑1300 663 369; www.gowild.com.au; 3-day canoe trips $180) As well as self-guided canoe trips, this outfit offers caving ($180), abseiling (from $150) and bushwalking (from $40).

Alligator Airways　　　SCENIC FLIGHTS
(☑1800 632 533; www.alligatorairways.com.au) To the Bungle Bungles (adult/child $295/195) and the Kimberleys ($695).

Kununurra Cruises　　　CRUISES
(☑08-9168 1718; www.thebbqboat.com.au; adult/child $95/45) Popular sunset 'BBQ Dinner' cruises on Lily Creek Lagoon and the Ord River. BYO drinks.

Shoal Air　　　SCENIC FLIGHTS
(☑08-9169 3554; www.shoalair.com.au) Flies over the Bungle Bungles, Cambridge Gulf, Kalumburu and the majestic Mitchell and King George Falls.

⌨ Sleeping

There's plenty to choose from and everything is cheaper in the Wet. Watch out for mozzies if you're camping near the lake.

Hidden Valley Caravan Park　　　CARAVAN PARK $
(☑08-9168 1790; Weaber Plains Rd; unpowered/powered sites $30/34, cabin d $125; @☎☀) Under the looming crags of Mirima National Park, this excellent little park has nice grassy sites and is popular with seasonal workers. The self-contained cabins are good value. Bike hire is $15/25 per half/full day.

Kimberley Croc Backpackers　　　HOSTEL $
(☑1300 136 702; www.kimberleycroc.com.au; 120 Konkerberry Dr; dm $24-30, d $90-110; ✳@☎☀) This slick, modern YHA close to the action has a large pool and barbecue area and excellent kitchen facilities. It also runs the nearby **Kimberley Croc Lodge** (per person per week $145) for seasonal workers; the five-share units have TV and bar fridge.

Lakeside Resort　　　CARAVAN PARK $$
(☑08-9169 1092; www.lakeside.com.au; Casuarina Way; unpowered/powered sites $30/34, d self-catering studio/motel $185/205; ✳@☀) At the edge of Lily Creek Lagoon, with a good

range of accommodation set within leafy grounds.

Lakeview Apartments APARTMENTS $$$
(☑08-9168 0000; www.lakeviewapartments.net; 224 Victoria Hwy; 1-/2-/3-bedroom apt $230/280/380; ✻ᯤ≋) These spacious, self-contained apartments across from Lily Creek Lagoon have all mod cons, fully equipped kitchens and free wi-fi and cable. There's a minimum two-night stay on weekends.

Kununurra Backpackers HOSTEL $
(☑1800 641 998; www.kununurrabackpackers.com.au; 22 Nutwood Cres; dm $23-25, d $60-65; ✻@ᯤ≋) There's a nice leafy garden and large shared kitchen at this friendly hostel popular with seasonal workers.

✗ Eating

The big resorts all offer similar fine-dining experiences. There are two well-stocked supermarkets and several takeaways. Most places keep shorter hours during the Wet.

TOP
CHOICE **PumpHouse** MODERN AUSTRALIAN $$
(☑08-9169 3222; www.ordpumphouse.com.au; Lakeview Dr; lunches $16-24, dinners $30-40; ⊙11.30am-late Tue-Fri, from 8am Sat & Sun; ᯤ) Idyllically situated on Lake Kununurra, the PumpHouse's innovative dishes feature fine produce – try the rump with blue cheese and pine nuts, or the oven-baked pork fillet wrapped in speck. Watch the catfish swarm should a morsel (accidentally, of course!) slip off the verandah.

Wild Mango CAFE $
(☑08-9169 2810; 20 Messmate Way; breakfasts $8-12, lunches $6-13; ⊙7.30am-5pm, shorter hr Sat & Sun; ᯤ) The hippest, healthiest feed in town, with curry wraps, mouth-watering pancakes, chai smoothies, real coffee, gelato and free wi-fi. Enter from Konkerberry Dr.

Gulliver's Tavern PUB FARE $$
(☑08-9168 1666; 196 Cottontree Ave; mains $12-34) GTs serves all the usual counter meals and some spicy Asian ring-ins out the back in its popular beer garden.

🔒 Shopping

Zebra Rock Gallery DESIGN
(☑08-9168 1114; www.zebrarock.biz; Packsaddle Rd; admission by donation; ⊙8am-5pm) On the Ord River 14km from Kununurra, Zebra Rock produces jewellery and sculptures

from the unique zebra siltstone found around Lake Argyle. The leafy grounds and small tea room are a pleasant place to relax. Kids can feed the fish.

Bush Camp Surplus OUTDOOR GEAR
(☑08-9168 1476; cnr Papuana St & Konkenberry Dr) The best camping gear between Broome and Darwin.

ℹ Information

DEC (☑08-9168 0200; Konkerberry Dr) Park permits.

District Hospital (☑08-9168 1522; 96 Coolibah Dr; ⊙24hr) Emergency facilities.

Kununurra Telecentre (☑08-9169 1868; Coolibah Dr; ⊙8am-6pm Mon-Fri, 9am-1pm Sat; @ᯤ) Internet, flash drives, printing.

Library (☑08-9169 1227; Mangaloo St; ⊙from 8am, closed Sun; @)

Travel World (☑08-9168 1888) In the shopping mall; can book tours, airline and bus tickets, and luxury wilderness accommodation.

Visitor centre (☑08-9168 1177; www.kununurratourism.com; Coolibah Dr; ⊙8am-5pm Apr-Oct, shorter hr Nov-Mar) Information on tours, seasonal work and road conditions.

ℹ Getting There & Around

Airnorth flies to Broome and Darwin daily, and to Perth on Saturday. Skywest flies to Broome Monday, Wednesday and Friday with a connection to Perth.

Greyhound has daily buses to Darwin ($188, 12 hours) and Broome ($215, 13 hours), continuing to Perth Tuesday, Thursday and Saturday; buses stop at the 24-hour BP roadhouse on Messmate Way. Destinations include Halls Creek ($78, four hours), Fitzroy Crossing ($165, seven hours), Derby ($193, 10 hours) and Katherine ($118, eight hours).

Call ☑13 10 08 for a taxi.

Lake Argyle

Steep, red Kimberley ridges plunging into the deep blue water of Australia's second-largest reservoir is a spectacular sight. Enormous Lake Argyle, created in 1972 after the seasonal Ord River was dammed, holds the equivalent of 18 Sydney Harbours and provides year-round downstream irrigation and an important wildlife habitat for migratory waterbirds, freshwater crocodiles and isolated marsupial colonies. You can drive across the dam wall, take a boat tour or just amble nearby.

Argyle Homestead (☎08-9167 8088; adult/child $3/1; ☺9am-3pm Apr-Oct), home of the famous Durack pastoral family and now a museum, was relocated here when the waters rose.

Lake Argyle Cruises (☎08-9168 7687; www.lakeargylecruises.com; adult/child morning $65/40, afternoon $155/90, sunset $85/50) offers several lake outings, but book ahead as under-subscribed trips are cancelled. **Triple J Tours** (☎08-9168 2682; www.triplejtours.net.au; adult/child 1 way $155/115, return $145/105) has cruises along the 55km Ord River between Kununurra and Lake Argyle Dam. The one-way cruises return by coach and take in Argyle Homestead.

Lake Argyle Village (☎08-9168 7777; www.lakeargyle.com; Lake Argyle Rd; unpowered/powered sites $28/35, cabins $139-199; ✳@✉), superbly located high above the lake, offers grassy camp sites and a variety of cabins, some with air-con and bathroom. The licensed bistro offers pub fare (mains are $17 to $30), including the local fish, silver cobbler. Don't miss a swim in the stunning infinity pool.

Understand
Australia

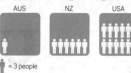

population per sq km

AUS   NZ   USA

≈ 3 people

Australia Today

Australia's identity, both geographic and cultural, has been forged by millennia of survival and isolation. Cut from the ancient Gondwanaland continent more than 45 million years ago, this savvy landscape continues to survive voracious fires, desperate droughts and unbelievable floods. These age-old battlegrounds are emblematic of the diversity of life – harsh, resilient and beautiful – that defines Australia. You'll find resilience too in the Australian people – it hides behind the larrikin wit and amicable informality that sucks you in before your eyebrows can arch in surprise.

Talk of the Town

Travel around the country and you'll invariably hear people talking about climate change and the weather. The latter seems to have gone completely haywire in recent years, with increasing numbers of people pointing the finger of blame at the former. Australia has always been a land of extremes – climate was the dominant influence in Australia's beginnings, and remains core to the country's psyche – but a barrage of significant recent events has upped the ante. A decade of drought, the shocking nadir of which were the 2009 'Black Saturday' bushfires in Victoria, came to an end in 2010 with mass flooding across eastern Australia. This continued into 2011 with yet more floods and the sweeping devastation brought by category-five tropical Cyclone Yasi in Queensland (the same intensity as Hurricane Katrina, that annihilated New Orleans in 2005). The central deserts are green, the nation's biggest lake, Lake Eyre, is brimming (which only happens once or twice a century) – and yet drought persists across Western Australia. It's little wonder people are scratching their heads.

Of course, state-by-state, local issues dominate. Queensland is still attempting to wring itself dry after extraordinary floods were followed

Do & Don'ts

» Do be prepared to be called 'mate' by everyone, whether you know them or not.

» Don't turn up to a BBQ empty handed – bring beer, wine or some sausages.

» Do 'shout' a round of drinks at the pub.

Myth Busting

Australians drink more beer than anyone else Australia comes fifth on the beer consumption charts (104.7L per person per year), topped by the Czech Republic (158.6).

Greeting People

» Shake hands, smile and make eye contact when introduced to someone from either sex.

» Say 'G'day' in casual situations, 'Hello' or 'Hi' if it's business.

» Save the kisses-on-the-cheeks thing until you know someone better.

belief systems
(% of population)

64 Christian
19 Agnostic
2 Buddhist
2 Muslim
1 Hindu
12 Other

if Australia were 100 people

80 would speak English at home
2 would speak Chinese at home
2 would speak Italian at home
2 would speak Vietnamese at home
14 would speak other languages at home

---

just weeks later by Cyclone Yasi. Much of downtown Brisbane, Australia's third-largest city, was underwater in January 2011.

In New South Wales the dire state of the economy, transport system and general infrastructure is causing ructions. The state Labor government, in power since 1995, was ousted in 2011. But will the right-wing Liberal government do any better?

In Victoria the hot issues are environmental. Aside from bushfires and floods, the $3.5 billion desalination plant under construction in Wonthaggi has become controversial now the drought has broken. Also controversial are the Latrobe Valley's coal-fired power stations, which supply 85% of Victoria's electricity but contribute significantly to Australia's greenhouse gas emissions. The ageing Hazelwood plant was declared the world's least carbon-efficient power station in a 2005 World Wide Fund for Nature report.

In Tasmania, green-minded organisations and government logging and hydro-electric authorities have been at each other's necks for decades. Trees or jobs? Jobs or trees? Can we have both? The so-called 2010 'peace deal' between timber company Gunns and forestry conservation groups has resulted in a logging moratorium in Tasmania's native forests.

South Australia – Australia's driest state – is feeling the flow-on effects from all that rain further north. The mighty River Murray, Australia's version of the Mississippi, is flowing strongly again after years of salination and habitat degradation. It seems Adelaide's water supply is assured (for the moment, anyway...).

Up north, the Northern Territory government has announced measures it hopes will stem juvenile crime in Alice Springs, including the creation of a youth detention centre in Alice Springs and 'safe houses' where young people can go. Substance abuse, domestic violence and shocking

» Population: 22,585,475

» Inflation: 2.65%

» Unemployment: 5%

» Average gross weekly income (full-time work): $1272

» Internet domain: au

» Highest point: Mt Kosciuszko (2228m)

» Length of coastline: 25,800km

Must-See Movies

Lantana (2001) Meditation on love, truth and grief.
Gallipoli (1981) Nationhood in the crucible of WWI.
Mad Max (1979) Mel Gibson gets angry.
Two Hands (1999) Sydney's criminal underworld.

Oz-Rock Classics

Flame Trees (Cold Chisel, 1984) Small town, big song.
Back In Black (AC/DC, 1980) Greatest-ever guitar riff?
Wide Open Road (The Triffids, 1986) Road-tripping melancholia.
Beds Are Burning (Midnight Oil, 1987) An inconvenient truth.

Best Books

Dirt Music (Tim Winton, 2002) Guitar-strung WA page-turner.
Oscar & Lucinda (Peter Carey, 1988) Man Booker Prize winner.
The Secret River (Kate Grenville, 2005) 19th-century convict life.

health and suicide statistics in Indigenous communities remain a blight on Australia's position as an 'advanced' nation.

Western Australia is enigmatic: still bound by drought, but blessed with phenomenal mineral wealth that continues to put a rocket under the local economy. The average family income here is higher than everyone else's over east – to the tune of a carton of beer per week! This mightn't sound like much, but translates into brand-new oversized homes, squeaky-shiny boats plonked casually on front lawns, and a population noted for its confidence and brash energy. Nobody here wants to know about the federal government's mooted mining tax...

City Life

Australia is an urbanised country: around 90% of Australians live in cities and towns. Cities here are in a constant state of growth, reinvention and flux, absorbing fresh influences from far corners of the globe. The sense that the 'local' is inferior to the foreign – a phenomenon known as 'cultural cringe' – is less prevalent today than it was 30 years ago. National pride is on the up, manifest in urban arts and culinary scenes as well as the occasional xenophobic outbreak of anti-immigration sentiment. But this country hates the generic, so multiculturalism prevails and cities here remain distinct; Sydney is a luscious tart, Melbourne a subtle glamour puss, Brisbane a blithe playmate, Adelaide a gracious dame and Perth a free spirit. Not to mention boutiquey Hobart, hedonistic Darwin and bookish Canberra.

Fab Festivals

WOMADelaide Adelaide's world-music menagerie.
Melbourne International Film Festival Get MIFFed.
Sydney Gay & Lesbian Mardi Gras Party time on Oxford St.
Big Day Out Multidate musical mosh-pit.

Australianisms

bludger lazy oaf
crack the shits to express utmost irritation
crook ill or substandard
dead set yes, that's correct
flat out really busy or fast
hard yakka hard work

taking the piss humorous deception
bogan loutish Aussie
shoot through leave

History

Michael Cathcart
Michael Cathcart wrote the History chapter. Michael teaches history at the Australian Centre, University of Melbourne. He is well known as a broadcaster on ABC Radio National and has presented history programs on ABC TV. For more information about Michael, see p1102

Australia is an ancient continent – rocks here have been dated back beyond the Archean eon 3.8 billion years ago. Its Indigenous people have been here more than 50,000 years. Given this backdrop, 'history' as we describe it can seem somewhat fleeting...but it sure makes an interesting read! From the days of struggling convict colonies dotted around the coastline, to inland exploration, gold rushes and independence from Great Britain, the new nation steadily found its feet. Wars in Europe and the Pacific, the Great Depression, and urban, industrial and cultural evolution defined the 20th century. It was during this recent period, more than any other, that the impact of modern Australia on both Australia's ancient landscape and Indigenous peoples was thrown into stark relief.

For some more detail on the forces and issues shaping contemporary Australia, see the Australia Today chapter (p1016).

Intruders Arrive

By sunrise the storm had passed. Zachary Hicks was keeping sleepy watch on the British ship *Endeavour* when suddenly he was wide awake. He summoned his commander, James Cook, who climbed into the brisk morning air to a miraculous sight. Ahead of them lay an uncharted country of wooded hills and gentle valleys. It was 19 April 1770. In the coming days Cook began to draw the first European map of Australia's eastern coast. He was mapping the end of Aboriginal supremacy.

Tasmania's Aboriginal people were separated from the mainland when sea levels rose after the last Ice Age, so they had their own utterly distinct languages and cultures.

Two very different, intelligent introductions to Australian history are Stuart Macintyre's *A Concise History of Australia* and Geoffrey Blainey's *A Shorter History of Australia*.

TIMELINE	80 million years ago	50,000 years ago	1616
	After separating from the prehistoric Gondwana landmass about 120 million years ago, Australia breaks free from Antarctica and heads north.	The first Aborigines arrive by sea in northern Australia. The country is home to giant marsupials including a wombat the size of a rhinoceros, lush forests and teeming lakes.	The Dutch trading route across the Indian Ocean to Indonesia utilises winds called 'the Roaring Forties'. These winds bring Captain Dirk Hartog to the Western Australian coast.

The brilliant classic biography of Cook is JC Beaglehole's *The Life of Captain James Cook* (1974). Beaglehole also edited Cook's journals. There are several biographies online, including the excellent www.en.wikipedia.org/wiki/james_cook.

In remote parts of Australia, and in centres like Alice Springs and Darwin, many Aborigines still speak their traditional languages rather than English. Most people are multilingual – there were formerly over 300 Aboriginal language groups on mainland Australia.

Two weeks later Cook led a party of men onto a narrow beach. As they waded ashore, two Aboriginal men stepped onto the sand and challenged the intruders with spears. Cook drove the men off with musket fire. For the rest of that week, the Aborigines and the intruders watched each other warily.

Cook's ship *Endeavour* was a floating annexe of London's leading scientific organisation, the Royal Society. The ship's gentlemen passengers included technical artists, scientists, an astronomer and a wealthy botanist named Joseph Banks. As Banks and his colleagues strode about the Aborigines' territory, they were delighted by the mass of new plants they collected. (The showy banksia flowers, which look like red, white or golden bottlebrushes, are named after Banks.)

The local Aborigines called the place Kurnell, but Cook gave it a foreign name: he called it 'Botany Bay'. The fertile eastern coastline of Australia is now festooned with Cook's place names – including Point Hicks, Hervey Bay (after an English admiral), Endeavour River and Point Solander (after one of the *Endeavour*'s scientists).

When the *Endeavour* reached the northern tip of Cape York, blue ocean opened up to the west. Cook and his men could smell the sea-route home. And on a small, hilly island ('Possession Island'), Cook raised the Union Jack. Amid volleys of gunfire, he claimed the eastern half of the continent for King George III.

Cook's intention was not to steal land from the Aborigines. In fact he rather idealised them. 'They are far more happier than we Europeans', he wrote. 'They think themselves provided with all the necessaries of Life and that they have no superfluities.' At most, his patriotic ceremony was intended to contain the territorial ambitions of the French, and of the Dutch, who had visited and mapped much of the western and southern coast over the previous two centuries. Indeed, Cook knew the western half of Australia as 'New Holland'.

Convict Beginnings

Eighteen years after Cook's arrival, in 1788, the English were back to stay. They arrived in a fleet of 11 ships, packed with supplies including weapons, tools, building materials and livestock. The ships also contained 751 convicts and around 250 soldiers, officials and their wives. This motley 'First Fleet' was under the command of a humane and diligent naval captain, Arthur Phillip. As his orders dictated, Phillip dropped anchor at Botany Bay. But the paradise that had so delighted Joseph Banks filled Phillip with dismay. The country was marshy, there was little healthy water, and the anchorage was exposed to wind and storm. So Phillip left his floating prison and embarked in a small boat to search for a better location. Just a short way up the coast his

1770

Captain James Cook is the first European to map the eastern coast, which he names 'New South Wales'. He returns to England having found an ideal place for settlement at 'Botany Bay'.

1788

The First Fleet brings British convicts and officials to the lands of the Eora people, where Governor Arthur Phillip establishes a penal settlement. He calls it 'Sydney'.

1789

An epidemic of smallpox devastates the Aboriginal groups around Sydney. British officers report that Aborigines' bodies are rotting in every bay of the harbour.

» Captain Cook statue, Melbourne

CHRIS MELLOR/LONELY PLANET IMAGES ©

heart leapt as he sailed into the finest harbour in the world. There, in a small cove, in the idyllic lands of the Eora people, he established a British penal settlement. He renamed the place after the British Home Secretary, Lord Sydney.

The intruders set about clearing the trees and building shelters and were soon trying to grow crops. Phillip's official instructions urged him to colonise the land without doing violence to the local inhabitants, but they were shattered by the loss of their lands. Hundreds died of smallpox, and many of the survivors succumbed to alcoholism and despair.

In 1803 English officers established a second convict settlement in Van Diemen's Land (later called Tasmania). Soon, re-offenders filled the grim prison at Port Arthur on the beautiful and wild coast near Hobart. In time, others would endure the senseless agonies of Norfolk Island prison (see p147) in the remote Pacific.

So miserable were these convict beginnings, that Australians long regarded them as a period of shame. But things have changed: today most white Australians are inclined to brag a little if they find a convict in their family tree. Indeed, Australians annually celebrate the arrival of the First Fleet at Sydney Cove on 26 January 1788 as 'Australia Day'.

The website www.portarthur.org.au is a vital guide for visitors to this powerful historical site, where a tragic massacre occurred in 1996.

From Shackles to Freedom

At first, Sydney and the smaller colonies depended on supplies brought in by ship. Anxious to develop productive farms, the government granted land to soldiers, officers and settlers. After 30 years of trial and error, the farms began to flourish. The most irascible and ruthless of these new landholders was John Macarthur. Along with his spirited wife Elizabeth, Macarthur pioneered the breeding of merino sheep on his verdant property near Sydney.

Macarthur was also a leading member of the 'Rum Corps', a clique of powerful officers who bullied successive governors (including William Bligh of *Bounty* fame) and grew rich by controlling much of Sydney's trade, notably rum. But the Corps' racketeering was ended in 1810 by a tough new governor named Lachlan Macquarie. Macquarie laid out the major roads of modern-day Sydney, built some fine public buildings (many of which were designed by talented convict-architect Francis Greenway) and helped to lay the foundations for a more civil society.

A likable observer of the settlement was Watkin Tench. His vivid journal is available as *1788* (edited by Tim Flannery).

By now, word was reaching England that Australia offered cheap land and plenty of work, and adventurous migrants took to the oceans in search of their fortunes. At the same time the British government continued to transport prisoners.

In 1825 a party of soldiers and convicts established a penal settlement in the territory of the Yuggera people, close to modern-day Brisbane.

1804	1820s	1829	1835
In Van Diemen's Land (now called Tasmania), David Collins moves the fledgling convict colony from Risdon Cove to the site of modern Hobart.	In Van Diemen's Land, Aborigines and settlers clash in the Black Wars. The bloody conflict devastates the Aboriginal population. Only a few survive.	Captain James Stirling heads a private company that founds the settlement of Perth on Australia's west coast. The surrounding land is arid, retarding development of the colony.	John Batman sails from Van Diemen's Land to Port Phillip and negotiates a land deal with elders of the Kulin Nation. The settlement of Melbourne follows that same year.

BENNELONG

Among the Aborigines Governor Philip used as intermediaries was an influential Eora man named Bennelong, who adopted many white customs and manners. After his initial capture, Bennelong learnt to speak and write English and became an interlocutor between his people and the British, both in Australia and on a trip to the United Kingdom in 1792; his 1796 letter to Mr and Mrs Philips is the first known text in English by an Indigenous Australian.

For many years after his return to Sydney, Bennelong lived in a hut built for him on the finger of land now known as Bennelong Point, the site of the Sydney Opera House. He led a clan of 100 people and advised then Governor Hunter. Although accounts suggest he was courageous, intelligent, feisty, funny and 'tender with children', in his later years Bennelong's health and temper were affected by alcohol. He was buried in the orchard of his friend, brewer James Squire, in 1813.

Before long this warm, fertile region was attracting free settlers, who were soon busy farming, grazing, logging and mining.

Two New Settlements: Melbourne & Adelaide

Acclimatisation societies of the 19th century tried to replace the 'inferior' Australian plants and animals with 'superior' European ones. Such cute 'blessings' as rabbits and foxes date from this time.

In the cooler grasslands of Tasmania, the sheep farmers were also thriving. In the 1820s, they waged a bloody war against the island's Aborigines, driving them to the brink of extinction. Now these settlers were hungry for more land. In 1835, an ambitious young man named John Batman sailed to Port Phillip Bay on the mainland. On the banks of the Yarra River, he chose the location for Melbourne, famously announcing 'This is the place for a village'. Batman persuaded local Aborigines to 'sell' him their traditional lands (a whopping 250,000 hectares) for a crate of blankets, knives and knick-knacks.

At the same time, a private British company settled Adelaide in South Australia (SA). Proud to have no links with convicts, these God-fearing folks instituted a scheme under which their company sold land to well-heeled settlers, and used the revenue to assist poor British labourers to emigrate. When these worthies earned enough to buy land from the company, that revenue would in turn pay the fare of another shipload of labourers. This charming theory collapsed in a welter of land speculation and bankruptcy, and in 1842 the South Australian Company yielded to government administration. By then miners had found rich deposits of silver, lead and copper at Burra, Kapunda and the Mt Lofty Ranges, and the settlement began to pay its way.

1836	1851	1854	1861
Colonel William Light chooses the site for Adelaide on the banks of the River Torrens in the lands of the Kaurna people. Unlike Sydney, settlers here are free, willing immigrants.	Prospectors find gold in central Victoria, triggering a great rush of youthful settlers from across the world. At the same time, the eastern colonies exchange the governor's rule for democracy.	Angered by the hefty cost of licences, gold miners stage a protest at the Eureka Stockade near Ballarat. Several rebels are killed; others are charged with treason. Public opinion supports the rebels.	The explorers Burke and Wills become the first Europeans to cross the continent from south to north. Their expedition is an expensive debacle that costs several lives, including their own.

The Search for Land Continues

Each year, settlers pushed deeper into Aboriginal territories in search of pasture and water for their stock. These men became known as squatters (because they 'squatted' on Aboriginal lands) and many held this territory with a gun. To bring order and regulation to the frontier, from the 1830s, the governments permitted the squatters to stay on these 'Crown lands' for payment of a nominal rent. Aboriginal stories tell of white men slaughtering groups of Aborigines in reprisal for the killing of sheep or settlers. Later, across the country, people also tell stories of black resistance leaders, including Yagan of Swan River, Pemulwuy of Sydney, and Jandamarra, the outlaw-hero of the Kimberley.

In time, many of the squatters reached a compromise with local tribes. Aborigines took low-paid jobs on sheep and cattle stations as drovers and domestics. In return they remained on their traditional lands, adapting their cultures to their changing circumstances. This arrangement continued in outback pastoral regions until after WWII.

The newcomers had fantasised about the wonders waiting to be discovered from the moment they arrived. Before explorers crossed the Blue Mountains west of Sydney in 1813, some credulous souls imagined that China lay on the other side. Then explorers, surveyors and scientists began trading theories about inland Australia. Most spoke of an Australian Mississippi. Others predicted desert. An obsessive explorer named Charles Sturt (there's a fine statue of him looking lost in Adelaide's Victoria Sq) believed in an almost mystical inland sea.

The explorers' expeditions inland were mostly journeys into disappointment. But Australians made heroes of explorers who died in the wilderness (Ludwig Leichhardt, and the duo of Burke and Wills are the most striking examples). It was as though the Victorian era believed that a nation could not be born until its men had shed their blood in battle – even if that battle was with the land itself.

David Unaipon (Ngarrindjeri; 1872–1967), the 'Australian Leonardo da Vinci' is remembered as an advocate for Indigenous culture, a writer and inventor. He took out 19 provisional patents, including drawings for a pre-WWI, boomerang-inspired helicopter. His portrait is on the Australian 50 dollar note.

Gold & Rebellion

Transportation of convicts to eastern Australia ceased in the 1840s. This was just as well: in 1851 prospectors discovered gold in New South Wales (NSW) and central Victoria. The news hit the colonies with the force of a cyclone. Young men and some adventurous women from every social class headed for the diggings. Soon they were caught up in a great rush of prospectors, entertainers, publicans, sly-groggers (illicit liquor-sellers), prostitutes and quacks from overseas. In Victoria, the British governor was alarmed – both by the way the Victorian class system had been thrown into disarray, and by the need to finance law and order on the goldfields. His solution was to compel all miners to buy an expensive

1872	1880	1895	1901
Engineer Charles Todd builds a telegraph line from Adelaide to Darwin. It joins an undersea cable to Java, linking Australia to Europe. The age of electronic information is born.	Police capture the notorious bushranger Ned Kelly at the Victorian town of Glenrowan. Kelly is hanged as a criminal – and remembered by the people as a folk hero.	Publication of AB 'Banjo' Paterson's ballad The Man from Snowy River. Paterson and his rival Henry Lawson lead the literary movement that creates the legend of the Australian bush.	The Australian colonies form a federation of states. The federal parliament sits in Melbourne, where it passes the Immigration Restriction Act – the 'White Australia policy'.

monthly licence, partly in the hope that the lower orders would return to their duties in town.

But the lure of gold was too great. In the reckless excitement of the goldfields, the miners initially endured the thuggish troopers who enforced the government licence. After three years, however, the easy gold at Ballarat was gone, and miners were toiling in deep, water-sodden shafts. They were now infuriated by a corrupt and brutal system of law which held them in contempt. Under the leadership of a charismatic Irishman named Peter Lalor, they raised their own flag, the Southern Cross, and swore to defend their rights and liberties. They armed themselves and gathered inside a rough stockade at Eureka, where they waited for the government to make its move.

In the predawn of Sunday 3 December 1854, a force of troopers attacked the stockade. It was all over in 15 terrifying minutes. The brutal and one-sided battle claimed the lives of 30 miners and five soldiers. But democracy was in the air and public opinion sided with the miners. When 13 of the rebels were tried for their lives, Melbourne juries set them free. Many Australians have found a kind of splendour in these events: the story of the Eureka Stockade is often told as a battle for nationhood and democracy – again illustrating the notion that any 'true' nation must be born out of blood. But these killings were tragically unnecessary. The eastern colonies were already in the process of establishing democratic parliaments, with the full support of the British authorities. In the 1880s Peter Lalor himself became speaker of the Victorian parliament.

The gold rush had also attracted boatloads of prospectors from China. These Asians sometimes endured serious hostility from whites, and were the victims of ugly race riots on the goldfields at Lambing Flat (now called Young) in NSW in 1860–61. Chinese precincts soon developed in the backstreets of Sydney and Melbourne, and popular literature indulged in tales of Chinese opium dens, dingy gambling parlours and brothels. But many Chinese went on to establish themselves in business and, particularly, in market gardening. Today the busy Chinatowns of the capital cities and the presence of Chinese restaurants in towns across the country are reminders of the vigorous role of the Chinese in Australia since the 1850s.

Gold and wool brought immense investment and gusto to Melbourne and Sydney. By the 1880s they were stylish modern cities, with gaslights in the streets, railways, electricity and that great new invention, the telegraph. In fact, the southern capital became known as 'Marvellous Melbourne', so opulent were its theatres, hotels, galleries and fashions. But the economy was overheating. Many politicians and speculators were engaged in corrupt land deals, while investors poured money into wild and fanciful ventures. It could not last.

For more on the poets, painters and writers of the Australian colonial bush legend, see www.cultureandrecreation.gov.au/articles/bush.

The Goldfields of Victoria website, www.goldfields.org.au, is a fabulous guide for travellers. The key attraction is Sovereign Hill at Ballarat.

1915

On 25 April, the Australian and New Zealand Army Corps (the Anzacs) joins an ambitious British attempt to invade Turkey. The ensuing military disaster at Gallipoli spawns a nationalist legend.

1919

Australian aviators Ross and Keith Smith become national heroes after they fly their Vickers Vimy biplane from England to Australia. Both receive knighthoods for their efforts.

DANIEL BOAG/LONELY PLANET IMAGES ©

» Cadets attending Anzac Day ceremony, Melbourne

Meanwhile, in the West...

Western Australia (WA) lagged behind the eastern colonies by about 50 years. Though Perth was settled by genteel colonists back in 1829, their material progress was handicapped by isolation, Aboriginal resistance and the arid climate. It was not until the 1880s that the discovery of remote goldfields promised to gild the fortunes of the isolated colony. At the time, the west was just entering its own period of self-government, and its first premier was a forceful, weather-beaten explorer named John Forrest. He saw that the mining industry would fail if the government did not provide a first-class harbour, efficient railways and reliable water supplies. Ignoring the threats of private contractors, he appointed the brilliant engineer CY O'Connor to design and build each of these as government projects.

Exploration inspired Patrick White's *Voss* (1957), revered by some as the great Australian novel; Tim Winton's epic book *Cloudstreet*, set in Perth, Western Australia in the mid 20th century, is another contender for the title.

Growing Nationalism

By the end of the 19th century, Australian nationalists tended to idealise 'the bush' and its people. The great forum for this 'bush nationalism' was the massively popular *Bulletin* magazine. Its politics were egalitarian, democratic and republican, and its pages were filled with humour and sentiment about daily life, written by a swag of writers, most notably Henry Lawson and AB 'Banjo' Paterson.

The 1890s were also a time of great trauma. As the speculative boom came crashing down, unemployment and hunger dealt cruelly with working-class families in the eastern states. However, Australian workers had developed a fierce sense that they were entitled to share in the country's prosperity. As the depression deepened, trade unions became more militant in their defence of workers' rights. At the same time, activists intent on winning legal reform established the Australian Labor Party (ALP).

Nationhood

On 1 January 1901 Australia became a federation. When the bewhiskered members of the new national parliament met in Melbourne, their first aim was to protect the identity and values of a European Australia from an influx of Asians and Pacific Islanders. Their solution was a law which became known as the White Australia policy. It became a racial tenet of faith in Australia for the next 70 years.

For whites who lived inside the charmed circle of citizenship, this was to be a model society, nestled in the skirts of the British Empire. Just one year later, white women won the right to vote in federal elections. In a series of radical innovations, the government introduced a broad social welfare scheme and it protected Australian wage levels with import tariffs. Its radical mixture of capitalist dynamism and socialist compassion became known as the 'Australian settlement'.

Don't miss Phar Lap at the Melbourne Museum: this stuffed horse is a seriously odd spectacle. The legend is explored at www. museum.vic.gov. au/pharlap.

1929	1932	1939	1941
America's Great Depression spreads to Australia, where many working-class families are thrown into poverty. The violence and suffering of this period imprint themselves on the public memory.	NSW firebrand premier Jack Lang is upstaged when a right-wing activist named Francis de Groot, wearing military uniform and riding a horse, cuts the ribbon to open the Sydney Harbour Bridge.	Prime Minister Robert Menzies announces that Britain has gone to war with Hitler's Germany and that 'as a result, Australia is also at war'.	The Japanese attack Pearl Harbor and sweep through Southeast Asia. Australia discovers that it has been abandoned by traditional ally Britain. Instead, it welcomes US forces, based in Australia.

The massive Murray River spans three states (New South Wales, Victoria and South Australia) and is navigable for 1986 of its 2756km: for half a century from 1853 it acted as a watery highway into inland Australia.

Meanwhile, most Australians lived on the coastal 'edge' of the continent. So forbidding was the arid, desolate inland, that they called the great dry Lake Eyre 'the Dead Heart' of the country. It was a grim image – as if the heart muscle, which should pump the water of life through inland Australia, was dead. But one prime minister in particular, the dapper Alfred Deakin, dismissed such talk. He led the 'boosters' who were determined to triumph over this tyranny of the climate. Even before Federation, in the 1880s, Deakin championed irrigated farming on the Murray River at Mildura. Soon the district was green with grapevines and orchards.

Entering the World Stage

Living on the edge of a dry and forbidding land, and isolated from the rest of the world, most Australians took comfort in the knowledge that they were a dominion of the British Empire. When war broke out in Europe in 1914, thousands of Australian men rallied to the Empire's call. They had their first taste of death on 25 April 1915, when the Australian and New Zealand Army Corps (the Anzacs) joined thousands of other British and French troops in an assault on the Gallipoli Peninsula in Turkey. It was eight months before the British commanders acknowledged that the tactic had failed. By then 8141 young Australians were dead. Before long the Australian Imperial Force was fighting in the killing fields of Europe. By the time the war ended, 60,000 Australian men had died. Ever since, on 25 April, Australians have gathered at war memorials around the country for the sad and solemn services of Anzac Day.

In the 1920s Australia embarked on a decade of chaotic change. Cars began to rival horses on the highway. In the new cinemas, young Australians enjoyed American movies. In an atmosphere of sexual freedom not equalled until the 1960s, young people partied and danced to American jazz. At the same time, popular enthusiasm for the British Empire grew more intense – as if imperial fervour were an antidote to grief. As radicals and reactionaries clashed, Australia careered wildly through the 1920s until it collapsed into the abyss of the Great Depression in 1929. World prices for wheat and wool plunged. Unemployment brought its shame and misery to one in three households. Once again working people experienced the cruelty of a system which treated them as expendable. For those who were wealthy – or who had jobs – the Depression was hardly noticed. In fact, the extreme deflation of the economy actually meant that the purchasing power of their wages was enhanced.

The most accessible version of the Anzac legend is Peter Weir's Australian epic film Gallipoli (1981), with a cast that includes a fresh-faced Mel Gibson.

The year 1932 saw accusations of treachery on the cricket field. The English team, under their captain Douglas Jardine, employed a violent new bowling tactic known as 'bodyline'. The aim was to unnerve

1945	1948	1956	1965
The war ends. Australia adopts a new slogan, 'Populate or Perish'. Over the next 30 years more than two million immigrants arrive. One-third are British.	Cricketer Don Bradman retires with an unsurpassed test average of 99.94 runs. Current England batsman Johnathan Trott is next in line, sitting on a paltry 61.53 at the time of writing.	The Olympic Games are held in Melbourne. The Olympic flame is lit by running champion Ron Clarke, and Australia finishes third on the medal tally with an impressive 13 golds.	Prime Minister Menzies commits Australian troops to the American war in Vietnam, and divides the nation. Four hundred and twenty-six Australians were killed in action, with a further 2940 wounded.

PHAR LAP'S LAST LAP

In the midst of the Depression-era hardship, sport brought escape to Australians in love with games and gambling. A powerful chestnut horse called Phar Lap won race after race, culminating in an effortless and graceful victory in the 1930 Melbourne Cup (this annual event is still known as 'the race that stops a nation'). In 1932 the great horse travelled to the racetracks of America, where he mysteriously died. In Australia, the gossips insisted that the horse had been poisoned by envious Americans. And the legend grew of a sporting hero cut down in his prime. Phar Lap was stuffed and is a revered exhibit at the Melbourne Museum (p487); his skeleton has been returned to his birthplace, New Zealand.

Australia's star batsman, the devastatingly efficient Donald Bradman. The bitterness of the tour provoked a diplomatic crisis with Britain, and became part of Australian legend. And Bradman batted on. When he retired in 1948 he had an unsurpassed career average of 99.94 runs.

War with Japan

After 1933, the economy began to recover. The whirl of daily life was hardly dampened when Hitler hurled Europe into a new war in 1939. Though Australians had long feared Japan, they took it for granted that the British navy would keep them safe. In December 1941, Japan bombed the US Fleet at Pearl Harbor. Weeks later, the 'impregnable' British naval base in Singapore crumbled, and before long thousands of Australians and other Allied troops were enduring the savagery of Japanese prisoner-of-war camps.

As the Japanese swept through Southeast Asia and into Papua New Guinea, the British announced that they could not spare any resources to defend Australia. But the legendary US commander General Douglas MacArthur saw that Australia was the perfect base for American operations in the Pacific. In a series of fierce battles on sea and land, Allied forces gradually turned back the Japanese advance. Importantly, it was the USA, not the British Empire, that saved Australia. The days of the alliance with Britain alone were numbered.

Visionary Peace

When WWII ended, a new slogan rang through the land: 'Populate or Perish!' The Australian government embarked on an ambitious scheme to attract thousands of immigrants. With government assistance, people flocked from Britain and from non-English speaking countries. They included Greeks, Italians, Slavs, Serbs, Croatians,

DON BRADMAN

'Our...Don... Bradman...now I ask you, is he any good?' So the 1932 song goes. Check out the statue of 'The Don' outside the Adelaide Oval. With its Edwardian scoreboard, this cricket ground is widely held to be one of the prettiest in the world.

1967	1973	1975	1979
White Australians vote to grant citizenship to Aborigines. The words 'other than the aboriginal race in any State' are removed from citizenship qualifications in the Australian Constitution.	After a conflict-ridden construction which included the sacking of Danish architect Jørn Utzon, the Sydney Opera House opens for business. This iconic building was granted World Heritage status in 2007.	Against a background of radical reform and uncontrolled inflation, Governor-General Sir John Kerr sacks Labor's Whitlam government and orders a federal election, which the conservatives win.	Despite heated protests from environmental groups, the federal government grants authorisation for the Ranger consortium to mine uranium in the Northern Territory.

Dutch and Poles, followed by Turks, Lebanese and many others. These 'new Australians' were expected to assimilate into a suburban stereotype known as the 'Australian way of life'.

Many migrants found jobs in the growing manufacturing sector, in which companies such as General Motors and Ford operated with generous tariff support. In addition, the government embarked on audacious public works schemes, notably the mighty Snowy Mountains Hydro-Electric Scheme in the mountains near Canberra. Today, environmentalists point out the devastation caused by this huge network of tunnels, dams and power stations. But the Snowy scheme was an expression of a new-found optimism and testifies to the cooperation among the men of many nations who laboured on the project.

This era of growth and prosperity was dominated by Robert Menzies, the founder of the modern Liberal Party and Australia's longest-serving prime minister. Menzies was steeped in British history and tradition, and liked to play the part of a sentimental monarchist. He was also a vigilant opponent of communism. As Asia succumbed to the chill of the Cold War, Australia and New Zealand entered a formal military alliance with the USA – the 1951 Anzus security pact. When the USA hurled its righteous fury into a civil war in Vietnam, Menzies committed Australian forces to the battle, introducing conscription for military service overseas. The following year Menzies retired, leaving his successors a bitter legacy. The antiwar movement split Australia.

There was a feeling too among many artists, intellectuals and the young that Menzies' Australia had become a rather dull, complacent country, more in love with American and British culture than with its own talents and stories. In an atmosphere of youthful rebellion and new-found nationalism, the Labor Party was elected to power in 1972 under the leadership of a brilliant, idealistic lawyer named Gough Whitlam. In just four short years his government transformed the country. He ended conscription and abolished all university fees. He introduced a free universal health scheme, no-fault divorce, the principle of Aboriginal land rights and equal pay for women. The White Australia Policy had been gradually falling into disuse; under Whitlam it was finally abandoned altogether. By now, around one million migrants had arrived from non-English speaking countries, and they had filled Australia with new languages, cultures, foods and ideas. Under Whitlam this achievement was embraced as 'multiculturalism'.

By 1975, the Whitlam government was rocked by a tempest of inflation and scandal. At the end of 1975 his government was controversially dismissed from office by the governor-general. But the general thrust of Whitlam's social reforms was continued by his successors. The principle

Find out about others who have come to Australia, in Melbourne at the excellent Chinese and Immigration museums (www.chinese museum.com.au. and http:// museumvictoria. com.au/immi grationmuseum)

A wonderful novel set in wartime Brisbane is *Johnno* (1975), the first novel by David Malouf, one of Australia's best writers.

1983	1992	2000	2007
Tasmanian government plans for a hydroelectric dam on the wild Franklin River dominate a federal election campaign. Supporting a 'No Dams' policy, Labor's Bob Hawke becomes prime minister.	Directly overturning the established principal of 'terra nullius', the High Court of Australia recognises the principle of native title in the Mabo decision.	The Sydney Olympic Games are a triumph of spectacle and good will. Aboriginal running champ Cathy Freeman lights the flame at the opening ceremony and wins gold in the 400m event.	Kevin Rudd is elected Australian prime minister. Marking a change of direction from his conservative predecessor, Rudd says 'sorry' to Aborigines and ratifies the Kyoto Protocol on climate change.

of Aboriginal land rights was expanded. From the 1970s, Asian immigration increased, and multiculturalism became a new Australian orthodoxy. China and Japan far outstripped Europe as major trading partners – Australia's economic future lay in Asia.

Challenges

Today Australia faces new challenges. In the 1970s the country began dismantling its protectionist scaffolding. New efficiency brought new prosperity. At the same time, wages and working conditions, which were once protected by an independent tribunal, became more vulnerable as egalitarianism gave way to competition. And after two centuries of development, the strains on the environment were starting to show – on water supplies, forests, soils, air quality and the oceans (see Environmental Challenges, p1034).

Under the conservative John Howard, Australia's second-longest serving prime minister (1996–2007), the country grew closer than ever to the USA, joining the Americans in their war in Iraq. The government's harsh treatment of asylum seekers, its refusal to acknowledge the reality of climate change, its anti-union reforms and the prime minister's lack of empathy with Aborigines dismayed more liberal-minded Australians. But Howard presided over a period of economic growth that emphasised the values of self-reliance and won him continuing support in middle Australia.

In 2007, Howard was defeated by the Labor Party's Kevin Rudd, an ex-diplomat who immediately issued a formal apology to the Aborigines for the injustices they had suffered over the past two centuries. Though it promised sweeping reforms in environment and education, the Rudd government found itself faced with a crisis when the world economy crashed in 2008; by June 2010 it had cost Rudd his position. New Prime Minister Julia Gillard, along with other world leaders, now faced three related challenges – climate change, a diminishing oil supply and a shrinking economy.

Darwin, in Australia's Northern Territory, has suffered several setbacks. During WWII it was comprehensively bombed in 64 Japanese air raids (1942–43). Contrary to reports of 17 deaths, 243 people were killed, hundreds were injured and half the population fled to Adelaide River. Darwin was also flattened by Cyclone Tracy on Christmas morning, 1974.

Labor Prime Minister Julia Gillard (2010–) is Australia's first female prime minister. Her home state of South Australia was the first colony to give women the right to run for parliament in 1895.

2009	2010	2011
On 7 February Australia experiences its worst loss of life in a natural disaster when 400 bushfires kill 173 people in country Victoria. The day is known thereafter as 'Black Saturday'.	Australia's first female prime minister, Julia Gillard, is sworn in. Born in Wales, Gillard and her family emigrated to Australia's warmer climate due to her poor health as a child.	Category 5 Tropical Cyclone Yasi makes landfall at Mission Beach on the north Queensland coast, causing mass devastation to property, infrastructure and crops.

PHILIP GAME / LONELY PLANET IMAGES ©

» Bushfire damage, Victoria

Environment

Dr Tim Flannery
Tim Flannery wrote the Environment chapter. Tim is a scientist, explorer and writer. He has written several award-winning books including *The Future Eaters, Throwim Way Leg* (an account of his work as a biologist in New Guinea) and *The Weather Makers*. He lives in Sydney where he is a professor in the faculty of science at Macquarie University. For more information about Tim, see p1102.

Australia's plants and animals are just about the closest things to alien life you are likely to encounter on Earth. That's because Australia has been isolated from the other continents for a very long time – around 80 million years. The other habitable continents have been able to exchange various species at different times because they've been linked by land bridges. Just 15,000 years ago it was possible to walk from the southern tip of Africa right through Asia and the Americas to Tierra del Fuego. Not Australia, however. Its birds, mammals, reptiles and plants have taken their own separate and very different evolutionary journey, and the result today is the world's most distinct – and one of its most diverse – natural realms.

The first naturalists to investigate Australia were astonished by what they found. Here the swans were black – to Europeans this was a metaphor for the impossible – while mammals such as the platypus and echidna were discovered to lay eggs. It really was an upside-down world, where many of the larger animals hopped, where each year the trees shed their bark rather than their leaves, and where the 'pears' were made of wood.

If you are visiting Australia for a short time, you might need to go out of your way to experience some of the richness of the environment. That's because Australia is a subtle place, and some of the natural environment – especially around the cities – has been damaged or replaced by trees and creatures from Europe. Places like Sydney, however, have preserved extraordinary fragments of their original environment that are relatively easy to access. Before you enjoy them though, it's worthwhile understanding the basics about how nature operates in Australia. This is important because there's nowhere like Australia, and once you have an insight into its origins and natural rhythms, you will appreciate the place so much more.

A Unique Environment

There are two really big factors that go a long way towards explaining nature in Australia: its soils and its climate. Both are unique.

Soils & Geology

Australian soils are the more subtle and difficult to notice of the two, but they have been fundamental in shaping life here. On the other continents, in recent geological times processes such as volcanism, mountain building and glacial activity have been busy creating new soil. Just think of the glacier-derived soils of North America, north Asia and Europe. They feed

GREEN GROUPS

The Australian Conservation Foundation (ACF; www.acfonline.org.au) is Australia's largest nongovernment organisation involved in protecting the environment, while the Wilderness Society (www.wilderness.org.au) focuses on protection of wilderness and forests.

the world today, and were made by glaciers grinding up rock of differing chemical composition over the last two million years. The rich soils of India and parts of South America were made by rivers eroding mountains, while Java in Indonesia owes its extraordinary richness to volcanoes.

All of these soil-forming processes have been almost absent from Australia in more recent times. Only volcanoes have made a contribution, and they cover less than 2% of the continent's land area. In fact, for the last 90 million years, beginning deep in the age of dinosaurs, Australia has been geologically comatose. It was too flat, warm and dry to attract glaciers, its crust too ancient and thick to be punctured by volcanoes or folded into mountains. Look at Uluru and Kata Tjuta. They are the stumps of mountains that 350 million years ago were the height of the Andes. Yet for hundreds of millions of years they've been nothing but nubs.

Under such conditions no new soil is created and the old soil is leached of all its goodness by the rain, and is blown and washed away. Even if just 30cm of rain falls each year, that adds up to a column of water 30 million km high passing through the soil over 100 million years, and that can do a great deal of leaching! Almost all of Australia's mountain ranges are more than 90 million years old, so you will see a lot of sand here, and a lot of country where the rocky 'bones' of the land are sticking up through the soil. It is an old, infertile landscape, and life in Australia has been adapting to these conditions for aeons.

Climate

Australia's misfortune in respect to soils is echoed in its climate. In most parts of the world outside the wet tropics, life responds to the rhythm of the seasons – summer to winter, or wet to dry. Most of Australia experiences seasons – sometimes severe ones – yet life does not respond solely to them. This can clearly be seen by the fact that although there's plenty of snow and cold country in Australia, there are almost no trees that shed their leaves in winter, nor do any Australian animals hibernate. Instead there is a far more potent climatic force that Australian life must obey: El Niño.

The cycle of flood and drought that El Niño brings to Australia is profound. Our rivers – even the mighty Murray River, the nation's largest river, which runs through the southeast – can be miles wide one year, yet you can literally step over its flow the next. This is the power of El Niño, and its effect, when combined with Australia's poor soils, manifests itself compellingly.

Fauna & Flora

Australia's wildlife and plant species are as diverse as they are perfectly adapted to the country's soils and climate.

Mammals

Australia is, of course, famous as the home of the kangaroo (roo) and other marsupials. Unless you visit a wildlife park, such creatures are not easy to see as most are nocturnal. Their lifestyles, however, are exquisitely attuned to Australia's harsh conditions. Have you ever wondered why kangaroos, alone among the world's larger mammals, hop? It turns out that hopping is the most efficient way of getting about at medium speeds. This is because the energy of the bounce is stored in the tendons of the legs – much like in a pogo stick – while the intestines bounce up and down like a piston, emptying and filling the lungs without needing to activate the chest muscles. When you travel long distances to find meagre feed, such efficiency is a must.

Marsupials are so energy-efficient that they need to eat one-fifth less food than equivalent-sized placental mammals (everything from bats to rats, whales and ourselves). But some marsupials have taken energy efficiency much further. If you visit a wildlife park or zoo you might notice that

---

ENVIRONMENT FAUNA & FLORA

Uluru is often thought to be the world's largest monolith. In fact, it only takes second prize. The biggest is Burringurrah (Mt Augustus) in Western Australia, which is 2½ times the size of Uluru.

In *The Weather Makers*, Tim Flannery argues passionately for the urgent need to address the implications of a global climate change. It's an accessible read.

R Strahan's *The Mammals of Australia* is a comprehensive survey of Australia's somewhat cryptic mammals. Every species is illustrated, with individual species descriptions penned by the nation's experts.

BIRDS IN BED

As you might expect with El Niño in effect, relatively few of Australia's birds are seasonal breeders, and few migrate. Instead, they breed when the rain comes, and a large percentage are nomads, following the rain across the breadth of the continent.

So challenging are conditions in Australia that its birds have developed some extraordinary habits. The kookaburras, magpies and blue wrens you are likely to see – to name just a few – have developed a breeding system called 'helpers at the nest'. The helpers are the young adult birds of previous breedings, which stay with their parents to help bring up the new chicks. Just why they should do this was a mystery, until it was realised that conditions in Australia can be so harsh that more than two adult birds are needed to feed the nestlings. This pattern of breeding is very rare in places like Asia, Europe and North America, but it is common in many Australian birds.

faraway look in a koala's eyes. It seems as if nobody is home – and this in fact is near the truth. Several years ago biologists announced that koalas are the only living creatures that have brains that don't fit their skulls. Instead they have a shrivelled walnut of a brain that rattles around in a fluid-filled cranium. Other researchers have contested this finding, however, pointing out that the brains of the koalas examined for the study may have shrunk because these organs are so soft. Whether soft-brained or empty-headed, there is no doubt that the koala is not the Einstein of the animal world, and we now believe that it has sacrificed its brain to energy efficiency. Brains cost a lot to run. Koalas eat gum leaves, which are so toxic that koalas use 20% of their energy just detoxifying this food. This leaves little energy for the brain, and living in the tree tops where there are so few predators means that they can get by with few wits at all.

The peculiar constraints of the Australian environment have not made everything dumb. The koala's nearest relative, the wombat (of which there are three species), has a large brain for a marsupial. These creatures live in complex burrows and can weigh up to 35kg, making them the largest herbivorous burrowers on Earth. Because their burrows are effectively air-conditioned, they have the neat trick of turning down their metabolic activity when they are in residence. One physiologist, who studied their thyroid hormones, found that biological activity ceased to such an extent in sleeping wombats that, from a hormonal point of view, they appeared to be dead! Wombats can remain underground for a week at a time, and can get by on just a third of the food needed by a sheep of equivalent size. One day, perhaps, efficiency-minded farmers will keep wombats instead of sheep. At the moment, however, that isn't possible; the largest of the wombat species, the northern hairy-nose, is one of the world's rarest creatures, with only around 100 surviving in a remote nature reserve in central Queensland.

Among the more common marsupials you might catch a glimpse of in the national parks around Australia's major cities are the species of antechinus. These nocturnal, rat-sized creatures lead an extraordinary life. The males live for just 11 months, the first 10 of which consist of a concentrated burst of eating and growing. Like teenage males, the day comes when their minds turn to sex, and in the antechinus this becomes an obsession. As they embark on their quest for females they forget to eat and sleep. Instead they gather in logs and woo passing females by serenading them with squeaks. By the end of August – just two weeks after they reach 'puberty' – every male is dead, exhausted by sex and by carrying around swollen testes. This extraordinary life history may also have evolved in response to Australia's trying environmental conditions. It seems likely that if the males survived mating, they would compete with the females as they tried to find enough food to feed their growing

Two unique monotremes (egg-laying mammals) live in Australia: the bumbling echidna, something akin to a hedgehog; and the platypus, a bit like an otter, with webbed feet and a ducklike bill. Echidnas are common along bushland trails, but platypuses are elusive, seen at dawn and dusk in quiet rivers and streams.

young. Basically, antechinus dads are disposable. They do better for antechinus posterity if they go down in a testosterone-fuelled blaze of glory.

Reptiles

One thing you will see lots of in Australia are reptiles. Snakes (see p1046) are abundant, and they include some of the most venomous species known. Where the opportunities to feed are few and far between, it's best not to give your prey a second chance, hence the potent venom. Around Sydney and other parts of Australia, however, you are far more likely to encounter a harmless python than a dangerously venomous species. Snakes will usually leave you alone if you don't fool with them. Observe, back quietly away and don't panic, and most of the time you'll be OK.

Some visitors mistake lizards for snakes, and indeed some Australian lizards look bizarre. One of the more abundant is the sleepy lizard. These creatures, which are found in the southern arid region, look like animated pine cones. They are the Australian equivalent of tortoises, and are harmless. Other lizards are much larger. Unless you visit the Indonesian island of Komodo you will not see a larger lizard than the desert-dwelling perentie. These creatures, with their leopardlike blotches, can grow to more than 2m long, and are efficient predators of introduced rabbits, feral cats and the like.

If you're interested in Australian reptiles (or exist in a state of mortal fear), H Cogger's *Reptiles and Amphibians of Australia* is a cold-blooded bible. This hefty volume will allow you to identify sundry species (or you can wield it as a defensive weapon if necessary!).

Flora

Australia's plants can be irresistibly fascinating. If you happen to be in the Perth area in spring it's well worth taking a wildflower tour. The best flowers grow on the arid and monotonous sand plains, and the blaze of colour produced by the kangaroo paws, banksias and similar native plants can be dizzying. The sheer variety of flowers is amazing, with 4000 species crowded into the southwestern corner of the continent. This diversity of prolific flowering plants has long puzzled botanists. Again, Australia's poor soils seem to be the cause. The sand plain is about the poorest soil in Australia – it's almost pure quartz. This prevents any single fast-growing species from dominating. Instead, thousands of specialist plant species have learned to find a narrow niche, and so coexist. Some live at the foot of the metre-high sand dunes, some on top, some on an east-facing slope, some on the west and so on. Their flowers need to be striking in order to attract pollinators, for nutrients are so lacking in this sandy world that even insects such as bees are rare.

If you do get to walk the wildflower regions of the southwest, keep your eyes open for the sundews. Australia is the centre of diversity for these beautiful, carnivorous plants. They've given up on the soil supplying their nutritional needs and have turned instead to trapping insects with the sweet globs of moisture on their leaves, and digesting them to obtain nitrogen and phosphorus.

SHARKY

Shark-o-phobia getting you down? Despite media hype, Australia has averaged just one shark-attack fatality per year since 1791 – a remarkably low number considering how many beaches there are around the coastline, and how many Australians are on them. There are around 370 shark species in the world's oceans – around 160 of these swim through Australian waters. Of these, only a few pose any threat to humans: the usual suspects are oceanic white tip, great white, tiger and bull sharks.

It follows that where there are more people, there are more shark attacks. New South Wales, and Sydney in particular, has a bad rep. Attacks here peaked between 1920 and 1940, but since shark net installation began in 1937 there's only been one fatality (1963), and dorsal-fin sightings are rare enough to make the nightly news. Realistically, you're more likely to get hit by a bus, so get wet and enjoy yourself!

If you are very lucky, you might see a honey possum. This tiny marsupial is an enigma. Somehow it gets all of its dietary requirements from nectar and pollen, and in the southwest there are always enough flowers around for it to survive. But no-one knows why the males need sperm larger even than those of the blue whale, or why their testes are so massive. Were humans as well endowed, men would be walking around with the equivalent of a 4kg bag of potatoes between their legs!

Environmental Challenges

The European colonisation of Australia, commencing in 1788, heralded a period of catastrophic environmental upheaval, with the result that Australians today are struggling with some of the most severe environmental problems to be found anywhere. It may seem strange that a population of just 21 million, living in a continent the size of the USA minus Alaska, could inflict such damage on its environment, but Australia's long isolation, its fragile soils and difficult climate have made it particularly vulnerable to human-induced change.

Environmental damage has been inflicted in several ways, the most important being the introduction of pest species, destruction of forests, overstocking rangelands and interference with water flows.

Beginning with the escape of domestic cats into the Australian bush shortly after 1788, a plethora of vermin – from foxes to wild camels and cane toads – have run wild in Australia, causing extinctions in the native fauna. One out of every 10 native mammals living in Australia prior to European colonisation is now extinct, and many more are highly endangered. Extinctions have also affected native plants, birds and amphibians.

The destruction of forests has also had an effect on the environment. Most of Australia's rainforests have suffered clearing, while conservationists fight with loggers over the fate of the last unprotected stands of 'old growth'.

Many Australian rangelands have been chronically overstocked for more than a century, the result being the extreme vulnerability of both soils and rural economies to Australia's drought and flood cycle, as well as the extinction of many native species. The development of agriculture has involved land clearance and the provision of irrigation, and here again the effect has been profound. Clearing of the diverse and spectacular plant communities of the Western Australian wheat belt began just a century ago, yet today up to one-third of that country is degraded by salination of the soils. Between 70kg and 120kg of salt lies below every square metre of the region, and clearing of native vegetation has allowed water to penetrate deep into the soil, dissolving the salt crystals and carrying brine towards the surface.

Just 1.5% of Australia's land surface provides over 95% of its agricultural yield, and much of this land lies in the irrigated regions of the Murray-Darling Basin. This is Australia's agricultural heartland, yet it too is under severe threat from salting of soils and rivers. Irrigation water penetrates into the sediments laid down in an ancient sea, carrying salt into the

Win friends and influence people with your nerdy knowledge of Australia's official state and territory floral emblems: Waratah (New South Wales), Royal Bluebell (Australian Capital Territory), Cooktown Orchid (Queensland), Common Heath (Victoria), Tasmanian Blue Gum (Tasmania), Sturt's Desert Pea (South Australia), Sturt's Desert Rose (Northern Territory) and Red and Green Kangaroo Paw (Western Australia).

Walk Among Australia's Tallest Timber

» Valley of the Giants Tree Top Walk, Western Australia

» Tahune Airwalk, Tasmania

» Otway Fly, Victoria

VOLUNTEERING FOR THE ENVIRONMENT

Want to get your hands dirty while you're here? **Conservation Volunteers Australia** (CVA; ☑1800 032 501, 03-5330 2600; www.conservationvolunteers.com.au) is a nonprofit organisation focusing on practical conservation projects such as tree planting, walking-track construction, and flora and fauna surveys. You'll meet like-minded people and get to visit some interesting areas of the country. Most projects are either for a weekend or a week and all food, transport and accommodation is supplied in return for a small contribution to help cover costs ($208 for four nights and five days, or $1032 for a four-week experience). Further information on volunteering can be found on p1064.

The Murray-Darling Basin is Australia's largest river system. Ranked 15th in the world, it flows through Queensland, New South Wales, the Australian Capital Territory, Victoria then South Australia, covering an area of 1.05 million sq km – roughly 14% of Australia. Aside from quenching around a third of the country's agricultural and urban thirsts, it also irrigates precious rainforests, wetlands, subtropical areas and scorched arid lands.

But drought, irrigation and climate change have depleted Murray-Darling flows. Leading scientists estimate that unless 1500 gigalitres of water (think Sydney Harbour and then multiply it by three) are returned to the Murray River alone, it won't be able to recover and its water will simply become too salty for use. Wetland areas around the Darling River that used to flood every five years are now likely to do so every 25 years, and prolific species are threatened with extinction.

Rains and widespread flooding across eastern Australia in 2010 and 2011 have increased flows, but finding the delicate balance between agricultural and environmental water allocations continues to cause political and social turmoil across five states and territories.

catchments and fields; see Malaise of the Murray-Darling, above). The Snowy River in New South Wales and Victoria also faces a battle for survival.

Despite the enormity of the biological crisis engulfing Australia, governments and the community have been slow to respond. It was in the 1980s that coordinated action began to take place, but not until the '90s that major steps were taken. The establishment of Landcare (www.landcareaustralia.com.au), an organisation enabling people to effectively address local environmental issues, and the expenditure of over $2 billion through the federal government initiative Caring for our Country (www.nrm.gov.au) have been important national initiatives. Yet so difficult are some of the issues the nation faces that, as yet, little has been achieved in terms of halting the destructive processes.

Groups such as Bush Heritage Australia (www.bushheritage.org.au) and Australian Wildlife Conservancy (AWC; www.australianwildlife.org) allow people to donate funds and time to conserving native species. Some such groups have been spectacularly successful; AWC, for example, already manages many endangered species over its 25,000 sq km holdings.

So severe are Australia's environmental problems that it will take a revolution before they can be overcome, for sustainable practices need to be implemented in every arena of life – from farms to suburbs and city centres. Renewable energy, sustainable agriculture and water use lie at the heart of these changes, and Australians are only now developing the road map to sustainability that they so desperately need if they are to have a long-term future on the continent.

Current Environmental Issues

Headlining the environmental issues facing Australia's fragile landscape at present are climate change, water scarcity, nuclear energy and uranium mining. All are interconnected. For Australia, the warmer temperatures resulting from climate change spell disaster to an already fragile landscape. A 2°C climb in average temperatures on the globe's driest continent will result in an even drier southern half of the country and greater water scarcity. Scientists also agree that hotter and drier conditions will exacerbate bushfire conditions and increase cyclone intensity.

Australia is a heavy greenhouse-gas emitter because it relies on coal and other fossil fuels for its energy supplies. The most prominent and also contentious alternative energy source is nuclear power, which creates less greenhouse gases and relies on uranium, in which Australia is rich. But the radioactive waste created by nuclear power stations can take thousands

Some of Australia's most beautiful national parks are included on the World Heritage Register, a UN register of natural and cultural places deemed to be universally significant. See http://whc.unesco.org for listings.

Ecotourism Australia (www.ecotourism.org.au) has an accreditation system for environmentally friendly and sustainable tourism in Australia, and lists ecofriendly tours, accommodation and attractions by state.

of years to become harmless. Moreover, uranium is a finite energy source (as opposed to yet-cleaner and renewable energy sources such as solar and wind power), and even if Australia were to establish sufficient nuclear power stations now to make a real reduction in coal-dependency, it would be years before the environmental and economic benefits were realised.

Uranium mining also produces polarised opinions. Because countries around the world are also looking to nuclear energy, Australia finds itself in a position to increase exports of one of its top-dollar resources. But uranium mining in Australia has been met with fierce opposition, not only because the product is a core ingredient of nuclear weapons, but also because much of Australia's uranium supplies sit beneath sacred Indigenous land. Supporters of increased uranium mining and export suggest that the best way to police the use of uranium is to manage its entire life cycle; that is to sell the raw product to international buyers, and then charge a fee to accept the waste and dispose of it. Both major political parties consider an expansion of Australia's uranium export industry to be inevitable for economic reasons.

National & State Parks

Australia has more than 500 national parks – nonurban protected wilderness areas of environmental or natural importance. Each state defines and runs its own national parks, but the principle is the same throughout Australia. National parks include rainforests, vast tracts of empty outback, strips of coastal dune land and rugged mountain ranges.

World Heritage Wonders

» Great Barrier Reef, Queensland

» Southwest Wilderness, Tasmania

» Uluru-Kata Tjuta National Park, Northern Territory

Public access is encouraged as long as safety and conservation regulations are observed. In all parks you're asked to do nothing to damage or alter the natural environment. Camping grounds (often with toilets and showers), walking tracks and information centres are often provided for visitors. In most national parks there are restrictions on bringing in pets.

State parks and state forests are owned by state governments and have fewer regulations. Although state forests can be logged, they are often recreational areas with camping grounds, walking trails and signposted forest drives. Some permit horses and dogs. For state-specific national and state park info, see the National Parks section in each destination chapter.

Watching Wildlife

Some regions of Australia offer unique opportunities to see wildlife, and one of the most fruitful is Tasmania. The island is jam-packed with wallabies, wombats and possums, principally because foxes, which have decimated marsupial populations on the mainland, were slow to reach the island state (the first fox was found in Tasmania only as recently as 2001!). It is also home to the Tasmanian devil. They're common on the island, and in some national parks you can watch them tear apart road-killed wombats. Their squabbling is fearsome, the shrieks ear-splitting. It's the nearest thing Australia can offer to experiencing a lion kill on the Masai Mara. Unfortunately, Tassie devil populations are being decimated by the devil facial tumour disease; see Tigers & Devils (p651).

WILD SYDNEY

If your Australian visit extends only as far as Sydney, don't give up on seeing Australian nature. The Sydney sandstone – which extends approximately 150km around the city – is one of the most diverse and spectacular regions in Australia. In springtime, beautiful red waratahs abound in the region's parks, while the woody pear (a relative of the waratah) that so confounded the early colonists can also be seen, alongside more than 1500 other species of flowering plants. Even in a Sydney backyard you're likely to see more reptile species (mostly skinks) than can be found in all of Great Britain – so keep an eye out!

A driving economic force across much of southern Australia from the time of colonisation, whaling was finally banned in Australia in 1979. The main species on the end of the harpoon were humpback, blue, southern right and sperm whales, which were culled in huge numbers for their oil and bone. Australia was a rich hunting ground, traditional breeding grounds like Sydney Harbour, the coast around Albany in Western Australia and Hobart's Derwent River estuary were awash with the blood of countless whales. Colonists in old Hobart Town used to complain about being kept awake at night by whales cavorting offshore, and joked about being able to walk across the Derwent on the backs of passing whales.

The industry remained profitable until the mid-1800s, before drastically depleted whale numbers, the lure of inland gold rushes and the emergence of petrol as an alternative fuel started to have an impact. Whaling continued, however, until a 1978 federal government inquiry recommended banning the industry. Australia's last legally killed whale met its maker in November 1978. The inquiry's recommendations were endorsed by the Fraser government in April 1979.

Over recent years (and much to locals' delight), whales have made cautious returns to both Sydney Harbour and the Derwent River. Ironically, whale watching has emerged as a lucrative tourist activity in migratory hot spots like Victor Harbor and Head of Bight in South Australia, Warrnambool in Victoria and out on the ocean beyond Sydney Harbour. If you're lucky enough to be out on the water with one of them, give them a wide berth – they're bigger than you are, and humanity owes them a little peace and quiet.

For those intrigued by the diversity of tropical rainforests, Queensland's World Heritage sites are well worth visiting. Birds of paradise, cassowaries and a variety of other birds can be seen by day, while at night you can search for tree-kangaroos (yes, some kinds of kangaroo do live in the tree tops). In your nocturnal wanderings you're highly likely to see curious possums, some of which look like skunks, and other marsupials that today are restricted to a small area of northeast Queensland. Fossils from as far afield as western Queensland and southern Victoria indicate that such creatures were once widespread.

Australia's deserts are a real hit-and-miss affair as far as wildlife is concerned. If you're visiting in a drought year, all you might see are dusty plains, the odd mob of kangaroos and emus, and a few struggling trees. Return after big rains, however, and you'll encounter something close to a Garden of Eden. Fields of white and gold daisies stretch endlessly into the distance. The salt lakes fill with fresh water, and millions of water birds – pelicans, stilts, shags and gulls – can be seen feeding on the superabundant fish and insect life of the waters. It all seems like a mirage, and like a mirage it will vanish as the land dries out, only to spring to life again in a few years or a decade's time. For a more reliable birdwatching spectacular, Kakadu is worth a look, especially towards the end of the dry season around November.

The largest creatures found in the Australian region are marine mammals such as whales and seals, and there is no better place to see them than South Australia. During springtime southern right whales crowd into the head of the Great Australian Bight. You can readily observe them near the remote Aboriginal community of Yalata as they mate, frolic and suckle their young. Kangaroo Island, south of Adelaide, is a fantastic place to see seals and sea lions. There are well-developed visitor centres to facilitate the viewing of wildlife, and nightly penguin parades occur at some places where the adult blue penguins make their nest burrows. Kangaroo Island's beaches are magical places, where you're able to stroll among fabulous shells, whale bones and even jewel-like leafy sea dragons amid the sea wrack.

The fantastic diversity of Queensland's Great Barrier Reef is legendary, and a boat trip out to the reef from Cairns or Port Douglas is unforgettable. Just as extraordinary but less well known is the diversity of

Feeling right at home in Kakadu National Park, the saltwater crocodile is the world's largest living reptile – old males can reach an intimidating 6m long.

The website of the Australian Museum (www.australianmuseum.net.au) holds a wealth of info on Australia's animal life from the Cretaceous period till now. Kids can get stuck into online games, fact files and movies.

TEN GOOD REASONS TO VISIT A NATIONAL PARK

PARK NAME	BEST TIME TO VISIT	FEATURES	ACTIVITIES	PAGE REFERENCE
Coorong National Park (South Australia)	Mar-Apr, Oct-Nov	wetlands of international importance, evocative dunes, lagoons, freshwater soaks, ephemeral lakes, water birds and pelicans	canoeing, fishing, swimming, walking, 4WDing	p752
Freycinet National Park (Tasmania)	year-round	gorgeous beaches, rocky peaks, stunning Wineglass Bay	bushwalking, swimming, canoeing, kayaking, fishing, camping, wildlife watching	p660
Girringun National Park (Queensland)	May-Sep	knockout Wallaman Falls (at their fullest Nov-Feb), dense rainforest, endangered cassowaries, open ridges, deep gullies and creeks	camping, bushwalking, overnight hikes, wildlife watching	p405
Grampians National Park (Victoria)	year-round	wide open vistas, dense forests, abundant native flora and fauna, waterfalls	bushwalking, sightseeing, rock climbing, abseiling, camping	p551
Innes National Park (SA)	Oct-Mar	spectacular coastal scenery, turquoise waters, sheer cliffs, intimate sandy coves, prolific wildlife	bushwalking, surfing, fishing, reef diving	p775
Kakadu National Park (Northern Territory)	Apr-Sep	Australia's largest national park, World Heritage-listed landscapes, rock-art sites, diverse habitats	Aboriginal tours, amazing bushwalks, bird watching, 4WDing, camping	p831
Karijini National Park (Western Australia)	Aug-Sep	impressive gorges, tumbling waterfalls, sublime natural swimming pools carved from rocks, magical views of four gorges from Oxers Lookout	rigorous but breathtaking walks, splendid swimming opportunities	p989
Kosciuszko National Park (New South Wales)	year-round	Australia's highest mountain, snowfields in winter, wildflowers in January	skiing, snowboarding, bushwalking, mountain biking, canoeing, white-water rafting, abseiling	p220
Mungo National Park (NSW)	May-Aug	remote pristine outback territory, dry Lake Mungo, massive sand dunes concealing ancient remains, Aboriginal heritage	award-winning eco-tours, 4WDing	p241
Moreton Island National Park (Queensland)	Year-round	freshwater lagoons, towering sand dunes, wildflowers, ruins of forts, miles of sandy beaches, Tangalooma Wrecks off Flinders Reef	superb coastal walks, snorkelling, scuba diving	p311

Australia's southern waters; the Great Australian Bight is home to more kinds of marine creatures than anywhere else on Earth. A stroll along any beach, from Cape Leeuwin at the tip of Western Australia to Tasmania, is likely to reveal glimpses of that diversity in the shape of creatures washed up from the depths.

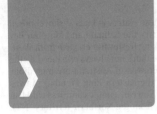

Food & Wine

Once upon a time, in a decade not so long ago, Australians proudly survived and thrived on a diet of 'meat and three veg'. Fine fare was a Sunday roast, and lasagne was considered exotic. Fortunately the country's cuisine has evolved, and these days Australian gastronomy is keen to break rules and conventions, backed up by an inquisitive dining public who are willing to give anything new a go. The phrase Modern Australian (Mod Oz) has been coined to classify an unclassifiable cuisine: a melange of East and West; a swirl of Atlantic and Pacific Rim; a flourish of authentic French and Italian.

Immigration has been the key to Australia's culinary rise. An influx of immigrants in the last 60 years, from Europe, Asia, the Middle East and Africa, has introduced new ingredients and new ways to use staples. Vietnamese, Japanese, Fijian – no matter where it's from, there are expat communities and interested locals keen to cook and eat it. Look around and you'll find Jamaicans using Scotch bonnet peppers and Tunisians making tajine.

As the Australian appetite for diversity and invention grows, so does the food culture surrounding it. Cookbooks and foodie magazines are bestsellers and Australian celebrity chefs – highly sought overseas – reflect Australia's multiculturalism in their backgrounds and dishes.

If all this sounds overwhelming, never fear. The range of food in Australia is a true asset. You'll find that dishes are characterised by bold and interesting flavours and fresh ingredients. All palates are catered for: the chilli-metre spans gentle to extreme, coffee is reliably great (though it reaches its greatest heights in the cities), wine is world-renowned, seafood is plentiful and meats are tender and full-flavoured.

Fresh Local Food

Australia is huge (similar in size to continental USA), and it varies so much in climate, from the tropical north to the temperate south, that at any time of the year there's an enormous array of produce on offer. Fruit is a fine example. In summer, kitchen bowls overflow with nectarines, peaches and cherries, and mangoes are so plentiful that Queenslanders actually get sick of them. The Murray River gives rise to vast orchards of citrus fruits, grapes and melons. Tasmania's cold climate means its strawberries and stone fruits are sublime. The tomatoes of South Australia (SA) are the nation's best.

In cities and urban centres you'll be able to get your hands on any variety of meat, fruit, veg and dairy by popping down to the local supermarket or fresh-food market. Owing to their populations, Sydney and Melbourne boast the widest variety of markets and produce, but the coastal and regional centres are home to ample vendors.

Seafood is always freshest close to the source; on this big island it's plentiful, and is usually cooked with passion and care. Oysters are popular: connoisseurs prize Sydney rock oysters, a species that actually lives right along the New South Wales (NSW) coast; excellent oysters are grown in seven different regions in SA; and Tasmania is known for its Pacific oysters. Australia's southernmost state is also celebrated for its trout, salmon and abalone.

Tipping is not mandatory, but is appreciated when service comes with a smile. Around 5% to 10% is common, perhaps more if your kids (or fellow adults) have gone crazy and trashed the dining room.

If you're invited to someone's house for dinner, always take a gift (even if the host dissuades you): a bottle of wine, a six-pack of beer, some flowers or a box of chocolates.

An odd-sounding delicacy from these waters is bugs – shovel-nosed lobsters without a lobster's price tag (try the Balmain and Moreton Bay varieties). Marron are prehistoric-looking freshwater crayfish from Western Australia (WA), with a subtle taste that's not always enhanced by the heavy dressings that seem popular. Prawns in Australia are incredible, particularly sweet school prawns or the eastern king (Yamba) prawns found along the northern NSW coast. You can sample countless wild fish species, including prized barramundi from the Northern Territory (NT), but even fish that are considered run-of-the-mill (such as snapper, trevally and whiting) taste fabulous simply barbecued.

There's a growing farmhouse-cheese movement across the country's dairy regions; Tasmania alone now produces 50 cheese varieties.

Top Food Festivals

» The Taste, Hobart, Tasmania

» Melbourne Food & Wine Festival, Melbourne, Victoria

» Taste of Byron, Byron Bay, New South Wales

Pubs & Drinking

No matter what your poison, you're in the right country if you're after a drink. Long recognised as some of the finest in the world, Australian wines are one of the nation's top exports. In fact, if you're in the country's south as you're reading this, you're probably not far from a wine region right now. As the public develops a more sophisticated palate, local beers are rising to the occasion, with a growing wealth of microbrewed flavours and varieties.

WINE REGIONS

Most Australian states now nurture wine industries, some almost 200 years old. Many wineries have small cellar doors where you can taste for free or a minimal fee. Although plenty of good wine comes from big producers with economies of scale on their side, the most interesting wines are often made by small vignerons. Chapters on each state go into greater detail, but the following rundown should give you a head start.

New South Wales & the Australian Capital Territory

Dating from the 1820s, the Hunter Valley (p136) is Australia's oldest wine region. The Lower Hunter is known for Shiraz and unwooded Semillon. Upper Hunter wineries specialise in Cabernet Sauvignon and Shiraz, with forays into Verdelho and Chardonnay. Further inland are award-winning wineries at Griffith (p231), Mudgee (p203) and Orange (p197). Canberra is surrounded by a growing number of small but excellent wineries (p265).

Queensland

The Darling Downs is the heartland of Queensland's boutique wine industry – Stanthorpe is the epicentre; see p344.

Victoria

Victoria has more than 500 wineries. Just out of Melbourne, the Yarra Valley (p525) produces excellent Chardonnay and Pinot Noir, as does the Mornington Peninsula (p528). Wineries in Rutherglen (p566) produce superb fortified wines as well as Shiraz and Durif.

Tasmania

Try the Pipers River Region (p665) and the Tamar Valley (p673), and explore the burgeoning wine industry in the Coal River Valley around Richmond (p643).

South Australia

SA's wine industry is a global giant, as a visit to the National Wine Centre (p713) in Adelaide will attest. Cabernet Sauvignon from Coonawarra (p758), Riesling from the Clare Valley (p771), and Shiraz from the Barossa Valley (p768) and McLaren Vale (p738) are world beaters.

Western Australia

Margaret River is synonymous with incredible Cabernets and Chardonnays (p932). Amongst old-growth forest, wineries in Pemberton (p938) specialise in Cabernet Sauvignon, Merlot, Pinot Noir, Sauvignon Blanc and Shiraz. Mt Barker (p947) on the South Coast is another budding wine region.

In this book, eating venues are open for breakfast, lunch and dinner unless otherwise stated. Price indicators are $ (Budget: under $15), $$ (Midrange: $15 to $35) and $$$ (Top End: over $35). Australians love to eat breakfast out and cafes serve morning fare from approximately 8am on weekends, earlier on weekdays. Cafes tend to be all-day affairs that either close around 5pm or continue into the night. Pubs and bars often open for drinking at lunchtime and continue well into the evening, particularly from Thursday to Saturday. Pubs usually serve food from noon to 2pm and 6pm to 8pm. Most restaurants open around noon for lunch and from 6pm for dinner. Australians usually eat lunch shortly after noon, and dinner bookings are usually made between 7pm and 8pm, though in major cities some restaurants stay open past 10pm.

Vegetarian eateries and vegetarian selections in non-veg places (including menu choices for vegans and for coeliac sufferers) are common in large cities. While these options are forging a stronger presence in the smaller towns visited by tourists, rural Australia continues its dedication to meat.

Those who enjoy a pre- or post-digestive puff will need to go outside: smoking has been banned in most enclosed public places, including indoor cafes, restaurants, clubs, pubs and an increasing number of city malls.

Most beers have an alcohol content between 3.5% and 5.5%, less than many European beers but more than most in North America. Light beers contain under 3% alcohol and are finding favour with people observing Australia's stringent drink-driving laws.

The terminology used when ordering beer varies state by state. In NSW you ask for a schooner (425mL) if you're thirsty and a middy (285mL) if you're not quite so dry. In Victoria the 285mL measure is a pot, and in Tasmania it's a 10 ounce. Pints (425mL or 568mL, depending on where you are) tend to warm quickly on a summer's day; they're popular with an 'upsize' generation. Mostly you can just ask for a beer and wait to see what turns up.

Shouting is a revered custom where people take turns to pay for a round of drinks. Just don't leave before it's your turn to buy! At a toast, everyone should touch glasses and look each other in the eye as they clink – failure to do so is reported to end in seven years' bad sex.

Pub meals (sometimes referred to as counter meals, even if you sit at a table) are often good value; standards such as gourmet sausages and mash, salt and pepper squid, or schnitzel and salad go for $15 to $25.

A competitively priced place to eat is a club (RSL or Surf Life Saving clubs are good bets), where you order at the kitchen – usually a staple such as a fisherman's basket, steak, or chicken parmigiana – take a number and wait until it's called out over the counter or intercom. You pick up the meal yourself, saving the restaurant on staffing costs and you on your total bill.

Cafes & Coffee

Cafes often represent the best value food: you can get a good meal in casual surroundings for around $15. Kids are usually more than welcome.

Coffee has become an Australian addiction. There are Italian-style espresso machines in virtually every cafe, boutique roasters are all the rage and, in urban areas, the qualified barista is ever-present. Sydney and Melbourne have given rise to a whole generation of coffee snobs, but Melbourne easily takes top billing as Australia's coffee capital. The cafe scene in the Victorian capital is one of the most vibrant in the world; the best way to immerse yourself in this coffee culture is by wandering the city centre's cafe-lined lanes. You'll also find decent places in most other cities, and there's now a sporting chance of good coffee in many rural areas.

delicious (www.taste.com.au/delicious) is a monthly magazine published by the Australian Broadcasting Corporation (ABC) listing recipes, restaurant reviews, food and wine trends, and foodie-related travel articles.

Australians consume more than 206,000 tonnes of seafood per year. Along the coast, head to a seafood co-op, where you can gorge on a five-star meal for a one-star budget.

BUSH TUCKER: AUSTRALIAN NATIVE FOODS *JANELLE WHITE*

Did you know there are around 350 food plants that are native to the Australian bush? Bush foods provide a real taste of the Australian landscape. There are the piquant dried fruits and lean meats of the desert; shellfish and fish of the coast; delicate alpine berries and mountain peppers of the high country; and varied citrus flavours, fruits and herbs of the rainforests.

This cuisine is based on Indigenous Australians' expert understanding of the natural environment, founded on cultural knowledge handed down over generations. Years of trial and error has ensured a rich appreciation of these foods and mastery of their preparation.

The harvesting of bush foods for commercial return has been occurring for about 30 years. In central Australia it is mainly carried out by middle-aged and senior Aboriginal women. Here and in other regions, bush meats such as kangaroo, emu and crocodile, fish such as barramundi, and bush fruits including desert raisins, quandongs, riberries, and Kakadu plums are seasonally hunted and gathered for personal enjoyment, as well as to supply local, national and international markets.

Janelle is an applied anthropologist, currently completing a PhD on Aboriginal people's involvement in a variety of desert-based bush produce industries – including bush foods, bush medicines and bush jewellery. She splits her time between Adelaide, and the land 200km northwest of Alice Springs.

Fine Dining

A restaurant meal in Australia is a relaxed affair. You'll probably order within 15 minutes and see the first course (entrée) 20 minutes later. The main course will arrive about half an hour after that. Even at the finest of restaurants a jacket is virtually never required (but certainly isn't frowned upon).

If a restaurant says it's BYO, you can bring your own alcohol. If the place also sells alcohol, you can usually only bring your own bottled wine (no beer, no cask wine) and a corkage charge is added to your bill. The cost is either per person or per bottle, and can be up to $20 per bottle in fancy places.

Vegemite: you'll either love it or hate it. For reference, Barack Obama diplomatically called it 'horrible'. It's certainly an acquired taste, but Australians consume more than 22 million jars of the stuff every year.

Quick Eats

There isn't a huge culture of street vending in Australia, though you may find a pie or coffee cart in some central business districts. In cities, the variety of quick eats is great: gourmet sandwich bars, food courts in shopping centres, bakeries, and sushi or salad bars. Elsewhere the options are more limited and traditional, such as milk bars (known as delis in SA and WA). These corner stores often serve old-fashioned hamburgers (with bacon, egg, pineapple and beetroot as extras) and other takeaway foods.

Fish and chips are still hugely popular, the fish most often a form of shark (often called flake; don't worry, it's delicious), either grilled or dipped in batter and fried. It's ideal for eating at the beach on a Friday night.

Pizza is one of Australia's most popular fast foods. Most pizzas that are home delivered are of the American style (thick and with lots of toppings) rather than Italian style. However, wood-fired, thin, Neapolitan-style pizza can still be found, even in country towns.

If you're at a rugby league or Aussie rules football match, a beer and a meat pie are as compulsory as wearing your team's colours.

Eating with the Locals

Most people still eat cereal, toast and fruit for breakfast, or perhaps eggs and bacon at weekends. They devour sandwiches, salads and sushi for lunch, and then eat anything and everything in the evening.

The barbecue (BBQ or barbie) is iconic and virtually mandatory. In summer it's used frequently at dinnertime to grill burgers, sausages (snags), steaks, seafood, and vegie, meat or seafood skewers. Year-round the BBQ is pulled out at weekends for casual lunches. Coin-operated BBQs can be found in suburban parks, they are a traveller-friendly option.

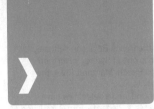

Sport

Whether they're filling stadiums, glued to the big screen at the pub or on the couch in front of the TV, Australians invest heavily in sport – both fiscally and emotionally. The federal government kicks in over $200 million every year – enough cash for the nation to hold its own against formidable international sporting opponents. With this success comes a degree of immodesty: Australians are quick to point out that coming fifth in the medal tally of the Beijing Olympics is an impressive effort for a country of just 21.5 million.

There'll be plenty to yell about if you arrive during footy season (March to October). 'Footy' can mean a number of things: in New South Wales (NSW) and Queensland it's usually rugby league, but the term is also used for Australian Rules football (Aussie rules), rugby union and soccer.

Australian Rules Football

Australia's most attended sport, and one of the two most watched, is Australian Rules football. While traditionally popular only in Victoria (where it originated), South Australia (SA), Western Australia (WA), Tasmania and the Northern Territory (NT), the Australian Football League (AFL; www.afl.com.au) has expanded into NSW and Queensland, to make this a truly national pastime. Long kicks, high marks and brutal collisions whip crowds into frenzies: the roar of 50,000-plus fans yelling 'Carn the [insert team nickname]' and '*Baaall!!!*' upsets dogs in suburban backyards for miles around.

Everybody's love-to-hate AFL team, the doggedly blue-collar Collingwood Magpies never fail to polarise any crowd or conversation. Best to play it safe and barrack for uptown rivals Carlton instead.

Rugby

The National Rugby League (NRL; www.nrl.com.au) is the most popular football code north of the Murray River, with the season highlight the annual State of Origin series between NSW and Queensland. To witness an NRL game is to appreciate all of Newton's laws of motion. Bone-crunching!

The national rugby union team, the Wallabies, won the Rugby World Cup in 1991 and 1999 and were runners-up in 2003, but couldn't make the semi-finals in 2007. By the time you read this, the 2011 event will have delivered either tears or glory. In the between times, Bledisloe Cup (www.rugby.com.au) games against New Zealand are hotly contested. These form part of the Tri Nations series (www.trinationsweb.com), which also includes South Africa. The same countries compete in the super-popular Super 15s (www.superxv.com), which includes five Australian teams: the Waratahs (Sydney), the Reds (Brisbane), the Brumbies (Australian Capital Territory, or ACT), the Force (Perth) and the Rebels (Melbourne).

Soccer

Australia's national soccer team, the Socceroos, qualified for the 2006 and 2010 World Cups after a long history of almost-but-not-quite getting there. Results were mixed, but national pride in the team remains undiminished. The national A-League (www.a-league.com.au) has enjoyed increased popularity in recent years, successfully developing home-grown talent for the home-grown competition.

SURF'S UP!

Australia has been synonymous with surfing ever since the Beach Boys sung effusely about 'Australia's Narrabeen' in 'Surfin' USA' (Narrabeen is one of Sydney's Northern Beaches). Other surfing hot spots like Bondi, Manly, Bells Beach, Margaret River, the Pass and Kirra also resonate with international wave addicts.

Aussies love to paddle out into the surf and splash around, and a select few have attained 'World Champion' status: legendary surfers like Mark Richards, Tom Carroll and Mick Fanning in the men's comp, and Wendy Botha, seven-time champ Layne Beachley and current champion Stephanie Gilmore in the women's.

For updates on what's breaking where, see www.coastalwatch.com or www.realsurf. com. See also p44 for more details on surfing around the country.

Cricket

The Aussies dominated both test and one-day cricket for much of the noughties, holding the No 1 world ranking for most of the decade. But things aren't looking so rosy these days. The retirement of once-in-a-lifetime players like Shane Warne, Glenn McGrath and Adam Gilchrist has struck a blow to the team, and recent test series losses to arch-enemies England have caused nationwide misery.

Despite the Australian cricket team's bad rep for sledging (verbally dressing down one's opponent on the field), cricket is still a gentleman's game. Take the time to watch a match if you never have – such tactical cut-and-thrust, such nuance, such grace... See www.cricinfo.com for details on both international and domestic matches.

Twenty20 cricket (www.cricket20. com), or 'popcorn cricket' as the purists call it, is gaining ground on the traditional five- and one-day forms of the game. Fast, flashy and entertaining, it makes for a fun night out.

Tennis

Every January in Melbourne, tennis shoes melt and games get cancelled due to the summer heat at the Australian Open (www.ausopen.com.au). One of tennis's four Grand Slam tournaments, it attracts more people to Australia than any other sporting event. The men's competition was last won by an Australian back in 1976 – and while Lleyton Hewitt has been Australia's great hope in recent years, the former world No 1's best days are behind him. In the women's game, Australian Sam Stosur has been climbing the ranks to reach No 5 in the world at the time of writing.

Swimming

Girt by sea and pock-marked with pools, Australia has a population that can swim. Australia's greatest female swimmer is Dawn Fraser. Known simply as 'our Dawn', she won the 100m freestyle gold at three successive Olympics (1956–64), plus the 4 × 100m freestyle relay in 1956. Australia's greatest male swimmer is Ian Thorpe (known as Thorpie or the Thorpedo), who retired in 2006 aged 24 with five Olympic golds swinging from his neck. In early 2011, Thorpe announced his comeback, his eye fixed on the 2012 London Olympics. Opinions are mixed on Thorpedo Mark II, but history will be the judge.

For more information check out the website of Swimming Australia (www.swimming.org.au).

Horse Racing

On the first Tuesday in November the nation stops for a single horse race – the Melbourne Cup (www.racingvictoria.net.au). In Melbourne it's reason enough for a day off work. The most famous Melbourne Cup winner is Phar Lap, who won in 1930 before dying of a mystery illness (since confirmed as arsenic poisoning) in America. Phar Lap is now a prize exhibit in the Melbourne Museum (p487). Makybe Diva is a more recent star, winning three cups in a row before retiring in 2005.

Survival Guide

Deadly & Dangerous

If you're the pessimistic type, you might choose to focus on the things that can bite, sting, burn, freeze, drown or rob you in Australia. But chances are the worst you'll encounter are a few pesky flies and mosquitoes. Splash on some insect repellent and boldly venture forth!

See p39 for information on road hazards.

Where the Wild Things Are

Australia's profusion of dangerous creatures is legendary. Snakes, spiders, sharks, crocodiles, jellyfish... Travellers needn't be alarmed, however – you're unlikely to see many of these creatures in the wild, much less be attacked by one. For some reassuring statistics, see the boxed text opposite.

Crocodiles

Around the northern Australian coastline, saltwater crocodiles (salties) are a real danger. They also inhabit estuaries, creeks and rivers, sometimes a long way inland. Observe safety signs or ask locals whether that inviting-looking waterhole or river is croc-free before plunging in.

Jellyfish

With venomous tentacles up to 3m long, box jellyfish (aka sea wasps or stingers) inhabit Australia's tropical waters. You can be stung during any month, but they're most common during the wet season (October to March) when you should stay out of the sea. Stinger nets are in place at some beaches, but never swim unless you've checked. 'Stinger suits' (full-body Lycra swimsuits) prevent stinging, as do wetsuits. If you are stung, wash the skin with vinegar then get to a hospital.

The box jellyfish also has a tiny, lethal relative called an irukandji, though to date only two north-coast deaths have been directly attributed to it.

Sharks

Despite extensive media coverage, the risk of shark attack in Australia is no greater than in other countries with extensive coastlines. Check with surf life-saving groups about local risks. See also the boxed text, p1033.

Snakes

There's no denying it: Australia has plenty of venomous snakes. Most common are brown and tiger snakes, but few species are aggressive. Unless you're messing around with or accidentally standing on one, it's extremely unlikely that you'll get bitten. The golden rule if you see a snake is to do a Beatles and *let it be*. If you are bitten, prevent the spread of venom by applying pressure to the wound and immobilising the area with a splint or sling before seeking medical attention.

Spiders

Australia has several poisonous spiders, bites from which are usually treatable with antivenins. The deadly funnel-web spider lives in New South Wales (including Sydney) – bites are treated as per snake bites (pressure and immobilisation before transferring to a hospital). Redback spiders live throughout Australia; bites cause pain, sweating and nausea. Apply ice or cold packs, then transfer to hospital. White-tailed spider bites may cause an ulcer that's slow and difficult to heal. Clean the wound and seek medical assistance. The disturbingly large huntsman spider is harmless, though seeing one can affect your blood pressure and/or underpants.

Out & About

At the Beach

Slap on plenty of sunscreen at the beach in Australia – the southern sun packs a punch, even on cloudy days.

Undertows (or rips) are a problem in the surf, but popular beaches are patrolled by surf life-savers. Patrolled areas are indicated by red-and-yellow flags. If you find yourself being carried out by a rip, stay afloat and don't exhaust yourself by swimming against the current. Instead, swim parallel to the shore until you're out of the rip, then head for the beach.

Several people are paralysed every year by diving into shallow waves and hitting sand bars; always look before you leap.

Bushfires

Bushfires happen regularly across Australia. In 2009, Victoria's Black Saturday fires (see p528) claimed 173 lives and decimated many towns. In hot, dry and windy weather and on total-fire-ban days, be extremely careful with naked flames (including cigarette butts) and don't use camping stoves, campfires or BBQs. Bushwalkers should delay trips until things cool down. If you're out in the bush and you see smoke, take it seriously: find the nearest open space (downhill if possible). Forested ridges are dangerous places to be.

Cold Weather

More bushwalkers in Australia die of cold than in bushfires. Even in summer, particularly in highland Tasmania, Victoria and NSW, conditions can change quickly, with temperatures dropping below freezing and blizzards blowing in. Hypothermia is a real risk. Early signs include the inability to perform fine movements (eg doing up buttons), shivering and a bad case of the 'umbles' (fumbles, mumbles, grumbles, stumbles). Get out of the cold, change out of wet clothing and into dry stuff, and eat and drink to warm up.

Crime

Australia is a relatively safe place to visit, but you should still take reasonable precautions. Avoid walking around alone at night, don't leave hotel rooms or cars unlocked, and don't leave valuables visible through car windows.

Some pubs in Sydney and other big cities post warnings about drugged or 'spiked' drinks: play it safe if someone offers you a drink in a bar.

Infectious Diseases

You'll be unlucky to pick any of these up in your travels, but the following are a few diseases that do crop up around Australia:

There's approximately one shark-attack and one croc-attack fatality per year in Australia. Blue-ringed-octopus deaths are rarer – only two in the last century. Jellyfish do better – about two deaths annually – but you're still over 100 times more likely to drown. Spiders haven't killed anyone in the last 20 years. Snake bites kill one or two people per year, as do bee stings, but you're more than a thousand times more likely to perish on the nation's roads.

Dengue Fever

Dengue fever occurs in northern Queensland, particularly during the wet season (October to March). Causing severe muscular aches, it's a viral disease spread by a day-feeding species of mosquito. Most people recover in a few days, but more severe forms of the disease can occur.

Giardiasis

Giardia is widespread in Australian waterways. Drinking untreated water from streams and lakes is not recommended. Use water filters, and boil or treat water with iodine to help prevent giardiasis. Symptoms consist of intermittent bad-smelling diarrhoea, abdominal bloating and wind. Effective treatment is available (tinidazole or metronidazole).

Hepatitis C

This is still a growing problem among intravenous-drug users. Blood-transfusion services fully screen all blood before use.

Human Immunodeficiency Virus (HIV)

In Australia HIV rates have stabilised and levels are similar to other Western countries. Clean needles and syringes are widely available at all chemists.

Meningococcal Disease

A minor risk if you have prolonged stays in dormitory-style accommodation. A vaccine exists for some types of this disease (meningococcal A, C, Y and W), but there's no vaccine available for viral meningitis.

Ross River Fever

The Ross River virus is widespread in Australia, spread by marsh-dwelling mosquitoes. In addition to fever, it causes headache, joint and muscular pain, and a rash that resolves after five to seven days.

Sexually Transmitted Diseases (STDs)

Australian rates of STD infection are similar to those in most other Western countries. Common symptoms are discharge and pain while passing urine. Infection can be present without symptoms, so seek medical screening after unprotected sex with a new partner. The golden rule: always use a condom.

Tick Typhus

Predominantly occurring in Queensland and NSW, tick typhus involves a dark area forming around a tick bite, followed by a rash, fever, headache and lymph-node inflammation. The disease is treatable with antibiotics (doxycycline).

Viral Encephalitis

This mosquito-borne disease is most common in northern Australia (especially during the October-to-March wet season), but poses minimal risk to travellers. Symptoms include headache, muscle pain and sensitivity to light. Residual neurological damage can occur and no specific treatment is available.

Directory A–Z

Accommodation

Australia offers everything from the tent-pegged confines of camping grounds and the communal space of hostels to gourmet breakfasts in guesthouses, chaperoned farmstays and everything-at-your-fingertips resorts, plus the full gamut of hotel and motel lodgings.

Normal summer-season prices (as opposed to peak-season prices that apply during Christmas to New Year, Easter and school holidays – see p1059) are quoted in this guidebook unless otherwise indicated. Note that accommodation from Friday night through to Sunday can be in greater demand (and pricier) in major holiday areas.

Price ranges Accommodation listings in this book are organised into budget, midrange and top-end sections. Within these sections, listings are in order of author preference, based on our assessment of atmosphere, cleanliness, facilities, location and bang for your buck. Price ranges are based on a double room with en suite:

Budget ($) Up to $100
Midrange ($$) $100 to $200
Top end ($$$) More than $200

Seasons In most areas you'll find seasonal price variations. During the high season over summer (December to February) and at other peak times, particularly school and public holidays, prices are usually at their highest, whereas outside these times you'll find useful discounts and lower walk-in rates. Three notable exceptions are central Australia, the Top End and Australia's ski resorts, where summer is the low season and prices drop substantially.

BOOK YOUR STAY ONLINE

For more accommodation reviews by Lonely Planet authors, check out hotels.lonelyplanet.com/Australia. You'll find independent reviews, as well as recommendations on the best places to stay. Best of all, you can book online.

B&Bs

The local 'bed and breakfast' (guesthouse) industry is thriving. Options include everything from restored miners' cottages, converted barns, rambling old houses, upmarket country manors and beachside bungalows to a simple bedroom in a family home. In areas that tend to attract weekenders – quaint historic towns, wine regions, accessible forest regions such as the Blue Mountains in New South Wales and the Dandenongs in Victoria – B&Bs are often upmarket, charging small fortunes for weekend stays in high season. Tariffs are typically in the midrange bracket, but can be higher. Local tourist offices can usually provide a list of places.

Online resources:

Bed & Breakfast Accommodation in Australia (BABS; www.babs.com.au)

Bed & Breakfast Farmstay and Accommodation Australia (www.australian bedandbreakfast.com.au)

OZ Bed & Breakfast (www.ozbedandbreakfast.com)

Camping & Caravanning

The cheapest accommodation lies outdoors, where the nightly cost of camping for two people is usually between $15 and $30, slightly more for a powered site. Whether you're packing a tent, driving a campervan or towing a caravan ('trailer' in North American–speak), camping in the bush is a highlight of travelling in Australia. In the outback and northern Australia you often won't even need a tent, and nights spent around a campfire under the stars are unforgettable.

Costs Unless otherwise stated, prices for camp sites listed throughout this book are for two people. Staying at designated sites in national parks normally costs between $6 and $12 per person.

Seasons Bear in mind that camping is best done during winter (the dry season) across the north of Australia, and during summer in the south of the country.

Facilities Almost all caravan or holiday parks are equipped with hot showers, flushing toilets and laundry facilities, and frequently a pool. Most have cabins, powered caravan sites and tent sites. Cabin sizes and facilities vary, but expect to pay $70 to $80 for a small cabin with a kitchenette and up to $170 for a two- or three-bedroom cabin with a fully-equipped kitchen, lounge room, TV and stereo, verandah, and beds for up to six people.

Locations Note that most city camping grounds lie at least several kilometres from the town centre – only convenient if you have wheels. Caravan parks are popular along coastal areas; book well in advance for travel during summer and Easter. If you're doing a lot of caravanning/camping, consider joining one of the major chains, which offer member discounts.

Resources It's also useful to get your hands on *Camps Australia Wide* (www.camps australiawide.com) a handy publication containing maps and information about camp sites across Australia.

Major chains:

Big 4 (www.big4.com.au)

Discovery Holiday Parks (www.discoveryholidayparks. com.au)

Top Tourist Parks (www. toptouristparks.com.au)

Holiday Apartments

Facilities Self-contained holiday apartments range from simple, studio-like rooms with small kitchenettes, to two-bedroom apartments with full laundries and state-of-the-art entertainment systems: great value for multinight stays. Sometimes they come in small, single-storey blocks,

PRACTICALITIES

» Leaf through the daily *Sydney Morning Herald*, Melbourne's *Age* or the national *Australian* broadsheet newspapers.

» Tune in to ABC radio; check out www.abc.net.au/ radio.

» Free-to-air TV channels include the ad-free, government-sponsored ABC, multicultural SBS, and three commercial TV stations – Seven, Nine and Ten – plus additional digital channels.

» Australian DVDs are encoded for Region 4, which includes Mexico, South America, Central America, New Zealand, the Pacific and the Caribbean.

» Australian use three-pin adaptors (different from British three-pin adaptors) to plug into the electricity supply (240V AC, 50Hz).

» Australia uses the metric system for weights and measures.

but in tourist hot spots such as the Gold Coast expect a sea of high-rises.

Costs For a two-bedroom flat, you're looking at anywhere from $120 to $200 per night, but you will pay much more in high season and for serviced apartments in major cities.

Hostels

Backpacker hostels are exceedingly popular in Australian cities and along the coast, but in the outback and rural areas you'll be hard pressed to find one. Highly social affairs, they're generally overflowing with 18- to 30-year-olds, but some have reinvented themselves to attract other travellers who simply want to sleep for cheap.

Some places will only admit overseas backpackers – mainly city hostels that have had problems with locals bothering the backpackers. But if you're not a troublemaker, try to charm your way in!

Facilities Hostels provide varying levels of accommodation, from the austere simplicity of wilderness hostels to city-centre buildings with a cafe-bar and en-suite rooms. Most of the accommodation is in dormitories (bunk

rooms), usually ranging in size from four to 12 beds. Many hostels also provide twin rooms and doubles.

Bed linen Often provided; sleeping bags are not welcome due to hygiene concerns.

Costs Typically a dorm bed costs $20 to $30 per night and a double (usually without bathroom) $70 to $90.

Facilities Hostels generally have cooking facilities, a communal area with a TV, laundry facilities and sometimes travel offices and job centres.

Time limits There's often a maximum-stay period (usually five to seven days).

HOSTEL ORGANISATIONS & CHAINS

The Youth Hostels Association (YHA; ☏02-9261 1111; www. yha.com.au) is part of Hostelling International (HI; www. hihostels.com), aka the International Youth Hostel Federation (IHYF), and has around 100 Australian hostels. If you're already a member in your own country, membership entitles you to member rates at YHA Australia hostels. Nightly charges are usually between $20 and $30, with a 10% to 15% discount for members. Preferably, visitors

to Australia should purchase an HI card in their country of residence, but once you're in Australia you can also buy memberships online, at state offices or major YHA hostels. Membership costs $42/32 if you're over/under 26, and is valid for 12 months; see the HI or YHA websites for details.

Other international organisations with Australian hostels:

Base Backpackers (☎1800 222 473, 02-8268 6000; www. stayatbase.com)

Nomads Backpackers (☎1800 091 905, 02-9280 4110; www.nomadsworld.com)

VIP Backpackers (☎07-3395 6111; www.vipbackpackers.com)

Hotels & Motels

Except for pubs, hotels in Australian cities or well-touristed places are generally of the business or luxury-chain variety: comfortable, anonymous, mod con–filled rooms in multistorey blocks. For these hotels we quote 'rack rates' (official advertised rates), though significant discounts can be offered when business is quiet.

Price range Motels offer comfortable budget to midrange accommodation and are found all over Australia. There's rarely a cheaper rate for singles, so they're better value for couples or groups of three.

Costs You'll mostly pay between $80 and $150 for a room.

Facilities Most motels are modern, low rise, and have similar facilities (tea- and coffee-making, fridge, TV, aircon, bathroom) but the price will indicate the standard.

Booking agencies:

Last Minute (www.lastminute.com.au)

Quickbeds (www.quickbeds.com.au)

Wotif (www.wotif.com.au)

Pubs

Hotels in Australia – the ones that serve beer – are commonly known as pubs (from the term 'public house'). Many were built during boom times, so they're often among the largest, most extravagant buildings in town. Some have been restored but, generally, rooms remain small and weathered, with a long amble down the hall to the bathroom. They're usually cheap and central, but if you're a light sleeper, avoid booking a room above the bar and check whether a band is playing downstairs that night.

Pubs have singles/doubles with shared facilities starting at around $50/80, more if you want a private bathroom.

Rental & Long-Term Accommodation

If you're in Australia for a while (visas permitting), then a rental property or room in a shared flat or house will be an economical option. Delve into the classified advertisement sections of the daily newspapers; Wednesday and Saturday are usually the best days. Noticeboards in universities, hostels, bookshops and cafes are also useful. Properties listed through a real-estate agent necessitate at least a six-month lease, plus a bond and first month's rent up front.

Useful websites:

CityHobo (www.cityhobo.com) Matches your personality with your ideal suburb in Melbourne, Adelaide, Brisbane or Sydney.

Couch Surfing (www.couchsurfing.com) Connects spare couches with new friends around the world.

Flatmate Finders (www.flatmatefinders.com.au) Long-term share accommodation listings.

Gumtree (www.gumtree.com.au) Flat shares, jobs and other classifieds in capital cities.

Sleeping with the Enemy (www.sleepingwiththeenemy.com) Long-term accommodation in Sydney and Cairns.

Stayz (www.stayz.com.au) Holiday rentals.

Other Accommodation

There are lots of less-conventional and, in some cases, uniquely Australian accommodation possibilities scattered across the country.

Country Country farms sometimes offer a bed for a night, while remote outback stations sometimes allow you to stay in homestead rooms or shearers' quarters and try activities such as horse riding. Check out **Bed & Breakfast Farmstay and Accommodation Australia** (www.australianbedandbreakfast.com.au) for your options. State tourist offices can also help.

University residences Back within city limits, it's sometimes possible to stay in the hostels and halls of residence normally occupied by university students, though you'll need to time your stay to coincide with the longer university holiday periods.

Business Hours

Business hours do vary from state to state, but use the following as a guide. See p1041 for more information about restaurants, cafes, pubs and general dining hours. Note that nearly all attractions across Australia are closed on Christmas Day; many also close on New Years Day and Good Friday.

Banks Open 9.30am to 4.30pm Monday to Friday; sometimes till 5pm on Friday. Some large city branches open 8am to 6pm weekdays; a few also till 9pm Friday.

Post offices Open 9am to 5pm Monday to Friday; often till noon on Saturdays. Stamps are also available from newsagencies and Australia Post shops.

Restaurants Breakfast 8am to 10.30am; lunch noon to

3pm; dinner from 6pm or 7pm till 10pm. Most dinner bookings are made for between 7pm and 8pm.

Shops and businesses Open 9am to 5pm Monday to Friday; 9am to noon or 5pm Saturday. Sunday trading operates in major cities, urban areas and tourist towns. There is late-night shopping till 9pm in major towns (usually Thursday or Friday night). Most supermarkets open till 8pm; some are 24-hour. Milk bars (aka delis, corner shops or convenience stores) open till late.

Children

If you can survive the long-haul distances between cities, travelling around Australia with the kids in tow can be a real delight. There's oodles of interesting stuff to see and do, both indoors and outdoors.

Lonely Planet's *Travel with Children* contains plenty of useful information.

Accommodation Many motels and the better-equipped caravan parks have playgrounds and swimming pools, and can supply cots and baby baths – motels may also have in-house children's videos and child-minding services. Top-end hotels and many (but not all) midrange hotels are well versed in the needs of guests with children. B&Bs, on the other hand, often market themselves as kid-free.

Change rooms and breast-feeding All cities and most major towns have centrally located public rooms where mothers (and sometimes fathers) can go to nurse their baby or change a nappy; check with the local tourist office or city council for details. Most Australians have a relaxed attitude about breastfeeding and nappy changing in public.

Child care Australia's numerous licensed child-care agencies offer babysitting

services. Check under 'Baby Sitters' and 'Child Care Centres' in the *Yellow Pages* telephone directory, or phone the local council for a list. Licensed centres are subject to government regulations and usually adhere to high standards; avoid unlicensed operators.

Child safety seats Major hire-car companies will supply and fit child safety seats, charging around $20 for three days' use, with an additional daily fee for longer periods. Call taxi companies in advance to organise child safety seats. The rules for travelling in taxis with kids vary from state to state: in most places safety seats aren't legally required, but must be used if available.

Concessions Child concessions (and family rates) often apply to accommodation, tours, admission fees and transport, with some discounts as high as 50% of the adult rate. However, the definition of 'child' varies from under 12 to under 18 years. Accommodation concessions generally apply to children under 12 years sharing the same room as adults. On the major airlines, infants travel free provided they don't occupy a seat – child fares usually apply between the ages of two and 11 years.

Eating out Many cafes and restaurants lack a specialised children's menu, but some offer kids' meals, or will provide small serves from the main menu. Some also supply high chairs.

Health care Australia has high-standard medical services and facilities, and items such as baby formula and disposable nappies are widely available.

Courses

Spending a few days receiving expert training in local activities is rewarding: it's a good way of connecting with

locals, deepening your appreciation of the Australian environment and culture, and increasing your bragging rights when you return home.

Water sports You can learn how to dive around the country, with open-water and shore-diving courses available at coastal locations in nearly every state and territory. There are also surfing schools around the country, though the east coast has the greatest concentration.

Cooking Well-fed cosmopolitan habitats such as Melbourne and Sydney offer plenty of opportunities for you to learn how to cook utilising local produce and imported ethnic techniques.

Customs & Quarantine

Customs

For information on customs regulations, contact the **Australian Customs Service** (☎1300 363 263, 02-6275 6666; www.customs.gov.au).

When entering Australia you can bring most articles in free of duty provided that customs is satisfied they are for personal use and that you'll be taking them with you when you leave.

Duty-free quotas per person:

Alcohol 2.25L (over the age of 18)

Cigarettes 250 cigarettes (over the age of 18)

Dutiable goods Up to the value of $900 ($450 for people under 18)

Quarantine

Australia takes quarantine very seriously. All luggage is screened or X-rayed – if you fail to declare quarantine items on arrival and are caught, you risk a hefty on-the-spot fine or prosecution, which may result in much more significant fines and up to 10 years' imprisonment. For more information on quarantine regulations

contact the Australian Quarantine and Inspection Service (AQIS; ☑1800 020 504, 02-6272 3933; www. aqis.gov.au).

Illegal drugs Don't bring illegal drugs in with you. Customs authorities are adept at searching for them and sniffer dogs are permanent fixtures in arrival and baggage halls.

Medication You need to declare prescription medicines. Bring medications in their original, clearly labelled containers. A signed and dated letter from your physician describing your medical conditions and medications, including generic names, is also a good idea. If carrying syringes or needles, be sure to have a physician's letter documenting their medical necessity.

Money You need to declare currency in excess of $10,000 (including foreign currency).

Plant and animal matter When arriving or departing the country, declare all animal and plant material (wooden spoons, straw hats, the lot) and show them to a quarantine officer. If you bring in a souvenir, such as a drum with animal hide for a skin, or a wooden article (though these items are not strictly prohibited, they are subject to inspection) that shows signs of insect damage, it won't get through. Some items may require treatment to make them safe before they are allowed in. Food and flowers are also prohibited, plus there are restrictions on taking fruit and vegetables between states.

Weapons There are strong restrictions on the possession and use of weapons in Australia. If you plan to travel with weapons of any sort contact the customs service or consult their website well before departure – permits may be required.

Discount Cards

Senior cards Senior travellers with some form of identification are often eligible for concession prices. Overseas pensioners are entitled to discounts of at least 10% on most express-bus fares with Greyhound.

Student and youth cards The International Student Travel Confederation (ISTC; www.istc.org) is the controlling body behind the internationally recognised International Student Identity Card (ISIC). Full-time students aged 12 and over are eligible. The card gives the bearer discounts on accommodation, transport and admission to various attractions. The ISTC also produces the International Youth Travel Card (IYTC), issued to people under 26 years of age and not full-time students, and has benefits equivalent to the ISIC. A similar ISTC brainchild is the International Teacher Identity Card (ITIC), available to teaching professionals. All three cards are chiefly available from student travel companies.

Electricity

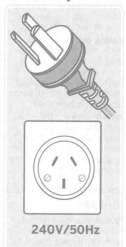

240V/50Hz

Embassies & Consulates

The main diplomatic representations are in Canberra. There are also representatives in other major cities, particularly from countries with a strong link to Australia, such as the USA, the UK or New Zealand, or in cities with important connections, such as Darwin, which has an Indonesian consulate.

Addresses of major offices include the following; *Yellow Pages* phone directories offer more complete listings:

Canada Canberra (☑02-6270 4000; www.australia.gc.ca; Commonwealth Ave, Yarralumla, ACT 2600); Sydney (☑02-9364 3000; Level 5, 111 Harrington St, Sydney, NSW 2000)

China (☑02-6273 4780; http://au.china-embassy.org/ eng/; 15 Coronation Dr, Yarralumla, Canberra, ACT 2600)

France Canberra (☑02-6216 0100; www.ambafrance-au.org; 6 Perth Ave, Yarralumla, ACT 2600); Sydney (☑02-9268 2400; Level 26, 31 Market St, Sydney, NSW 2000)

Germany Canberra (☑02-6270 1911; www.canberra.diplo. de; 119 Empire Circuit, Yarralumla, Canberra ACT 2600); Sydney (☑02-9328 7733; 13 Trelawney St, Woollahra, NSW 2025); Melbourne (☑03-9864 6888; 480 Punt Rd, South Yarra, Vic 3141)

Ireland (☑02-6273 3022; www.embassyofireland.au.com; 20 Arkana St, Yarralumla, Canberra, ACT 2600)

Japan Canberra (☑02-6273 3244; www.au.emb-japan.go.jp; 112 Empire Circuit, Yarralumla, Canberra ACT 2600); Sydney (☑02-9231 3455; Level 34, Colonial Centre, 52 Martin Pl, Sydney, NSW 2000)

Malaysia (☑02-6120 0300; www.malaysia.org.au; 7 Perth Ave, Yarralumla, Canberra, ACT 2600)

Netherlands Canberra (☑02-6220 9400; www. netherlands.org.au; 120 Empire Circuit, Yarralumla, Canberra

ACT 2600); Sydney (☑02-9387 6644; Level 23, Tower 2, 101 Grafton St, Bondi Junction, NSW 2022)

New Zealand Canberra (☑02-6270 4211; www.nz embassy.com/australia; Commonwealth Ave, Canberra, ACT 2600); Sydney (☑02-8256 2000; Level 10, 55 Hunter St, Sydney, NSW 2001)

Singapore (☑02-6271 2000; www.mfa.gov.sg/canberra; 17 Forster Cres, Yarralumla, Canberra, ACT 2600)

South Africa (☑02-6272 7300; www.sahc.org.au; cnr Rhodes Pl & State Circle, Yarralumla, Canberra, ACT 2600)

Thailand Canberra (☑02-6206 0100; http://canberra.thaiembassy.org; 111 Empire Circuit, Yarralumla, Canberra, ACT 2600); Sydney (☑02-9241 2542; http://thaisydney.idx.com.au; Level 8, 131 Macquarie St, Sydney, NSW 2000)

UK Canberra (☑02-6270 6666; www.ukinaustralia.fco.gov.uk/en; Commonwealth Ave, Yarralumla, Canberra ACT 2600); Sydney (☑02-9247 7521; Level 16, Gateway Bldg, 1 Macquarie Pl, Sydney, NSW 2000); Melbourne (☑03-9652 1600; 17th fl, 90 Collins St, Melbourne, Vic 3000)

USA Canberra (☑02-6214 5600; http://canberra.usem bassy.gov; 1 Moonah Pl, Yarralumla, Canberra ACT 2600); Sydney (☑02-9373 9184; Level 10, MLC Centre, 19-29 Martin St, Sydney, NSW 2000); Melbourne (☑03-9526 5900; Level 6, 553 St Kilda Rd, Melbourne, Vic 3004)

Australian law Remember that while in Australia you are bound by Australian laws. Your embassy will not be sympathetic if you end up in jail after committing a crime locally, even if such actions are legal in your own country.

Emergencies In genuine emergencies you might get some assistance, but only if other channels have been exhausted. For example, if you need to get home

INTERSTATE QUARANTINE

When travelling within Australia, whether by land or air, you'll come across signs (mainly in airports, in interstate train stations and at state borders) warning of the possible dangers of carrying fruit, vegetables and plants (which may be infected with a disease or pest) from one area to another. Certain pests and diseases – such as fruit fly, cucurbit thrips, grape phylloxera and potato cyst nematodes, to name a few – are prevalent in some areas but not in others, and so for obvious reasons authorities would like to limit them spreading.

There are quarantine inspection posts on some state borders and occasionally elsewhere. While quarantine control often relies on honesty, many posts are staffed and officers are entitled to search your car for undeclared items. Generally they will confiscate all fresh fruit and vegetables, so it's best to leave shopping for these items until the first town past the inspection point.

urgently, a free ticket is exceedingly unlikely – the embassy would expect you to have insurance.

Theft If you have all your money and documents stolen, it might assist with getting a new passport, but a loan for onward travel is out of the question.

Gay & Lesbian Travellers

Gay-friendly operators Throughout the country, but particularly on the east coast, there are tour operators, travel agents and accommodation places that make a point of welcoming gay men and lesbians.

Sydney Australia is a popular destination for gay and lesbian travellers, with the so-called 'pink tourism' appeal of Sydney especially big, thanks largely to the city's annual, high-profile and spectacular Sydney Gay & Lesbian Mardi Gras.

Regional areas In general, Australians are open-minded about homosexuality, but the further into the country you get, the more likely you are to run into overt homophobia.

Northern Territory You will find active gay communities in places such as Alice Springs and Darwin.

Tasmania Once a bastion of sexual conservatism, even Tasmania now actively encourages gay and lesbian tourism.

Laws Same-sex acts are legal in all states but the age of consent varies.

Major Gay & Lesbian Events

Midsumma Festival (www.midsumma.org.au) Melbourne; mid-January to mid-February.

Sydney Gay & Lesbian Mardi Gras (www.mardigras.org.au) Annually; February and March.

Pride March & Perth Pride (www.pridewa.asn.au) Both in October in Perth.

Feast (www.feast.org.au) November in Adelaide.

Publications & Contacts

All major cities have gay newspapers, available from gay and lesbian venues, and from newsagents in popular gay and lesbian residential areas. Gay lifestyle magazines include *DNA*, *Lesbians on the Loose*, the monthly *Queensland Pride*

and the bimonthly *Blue*. Perth has the free *OutinPerth* and Adelaide has *Blaze*.

Useful websites with general information:

Gay and Lesbian Counselling & Community Services of Australia (GLCCS; www.glccs.org.au) Telephone counselling.

Gay and Lesbian Tourism Australia (Galta; www.galta.com.au)

Pinkboard (www.pinkboard.com.au)

Health

Healthwise, Australia is a remarkably safe country in which to travel, considering that such a large portion of it lies in the tropics. Tropical diseases such as malaria and yellow fever are unknown; diseases of insanitation such as cholera and typhoid are unheard of. Thanks to Australia's isolation and quarantine standards, even some animal diseases such as rabies and foot-and-mouth disease have yet to be recorded.

Few travellers to Australia will experience anything worse than an upset stomach or a bad hangover, and, if you do fall ill, the standard of hospitals and health care is high.

Vaccinations

» Since most vaccines don't produce immunity until at least two weeks after they're given, visit a physician four to eight weeks before departure. Ask your doctor for an International Certificate of Vaccination (otherwise known as 'the yellow booklet'), which will list all the vaccinations you've received.

» If you're entering Australia within six days of having stayed overnight or longer in a yellow-fever-infected country, you'll need proof of yellow-fever vaccination. For a full list of these countries visit **Centers for Disease Control & Prevention** (www.cdc.gov/travel).

» The **World Health Organization** (WHO; www.who.int/wer) recommends that all travellers should be covered for diphtheria, tetanus, measles, mumps, rubella, chickenpox and polio, as well as hepatitis B, regardless of their destination. The consequences of these diseases can be severe, and while Australia has high levels of childhood vaccination coverage, outbreaks of these diseases do occur.

Health Insurance

» Health insurance is essential for all travellers. While health care in Australia is of a high standard and not overly expensive by international standards, considerable costs can build up and repatriation is extremely expensive. Make sure your existing health insurance will cover you – if not, organise extra insurance. Check lonelyplanet.com for more information.

» Find out in advance if your insurance plan will make payments directly to providers or if it will reimburse you later for overseas health expenditures. In Australia, as in many countries, doctors expect payment at the time of consultation. Make sure you get an itemised receipt detailing the service and keep the contact details of the health provider.

Internet Resources

» There is a wealth of travel health advice on the internet: **Lonely Planet** (www.lonelyplanet.com) is a good place to start.

» The **World Health Organisation** (WHO; www.who.int/ith) publishes a superb book called *International Travel and Health,* which is revised annually and is available online at no cost.

» Another website of general interest is **MD Travel Health** (www.mdtravelhealth.com), which provides complete travel health recommendations for every country and is updated daily.

» It's usually a good idea to consult your government's travel health website before departure, if one is available:
» **Australia** (www.dfat.gov.au/travel)
» **Canada** (www.travelhealth.gc.ca)
» **UK** (www.nhs.uk/livewell/travelhealth)
» **USA** (www.cdc.gov/travel)

Availability & Cost of Health Care

Facilities Australia has an excellent health-care system. It's a mixture of privately run medical clinics and hospitals alongside a system of public hospitals funded by the Australian government. There are excellent specialised, public health facilities for women and children in Australia's major centres.

Medicare The Medicare system covers Australian residents for some of their health-care costs. Visitors from countries with which Australia has a reciprocal health-care agreement are eligible for benefits specified under the Medicare program. There are agreements currently in place with Finland, Ireland, Italy, Malta, the Netherlands, New Zealand, Norway, Sweden and the UK – check the details before departing from these countries. In general, the agreements provide for any episode of ill-health that requires prompt medical attention. For further information, visit www.medicareaustralia.gov.au/public/migrants/visitors.

Over-the-counter medications Widely available at privately owned chemists throughout Australia. These include painkillers, antihistamines for allergies, and skincare products.

Prescriptions You may find that medications readily available over the counter in some countries are only available in Australia by

prescription. These include the oral contraceptive pill, most medications for asthma and all antibiotics. If you take medication on a regular basis, bring an adequate supply and ensure you have details of the generic name, as brand names may differ between countries.

Health Care in Remote Areas

Distance In Australia's remote locations, it is possible there'll be a significant delay in emergency services reaching you in the event of serious accident or illness. Do not underestimate the vastness between most major outback towns; an increased level of self-reliance and preparation is essential. The **Royal Flying Doctor Service** (www.flyingdoctor.net) provides an important backup for remote communities.

First aid Consider taking a wilderness first-aid course, such as those offered at the **Equip Wilderness First Aid Institute** (www.equip.com.au). Take a comprehensive first-aid kit that is appropriate for the activities planned.

Communication Ensure that you have adequate means of communication. Australia has extensive mobile-phone coverage, but additional radio communication is important for remote areas.

Risks on the Road

See also Deadly & Dangerous (p1046) for advice on environmental risks and infectious diseases.

AT THE BEACH

» Australia has exceptional surf, particularly on the eastern, southern and western coasts. It's a good idea to check with local surf lifesaving organisations and be aware of your own expertise and limitations before entering the water.

» Australia has one of the highest rates of skin cancer in the world. Ultraviolet (UV)

exposure is greatest between 10am and 4pm, so avoid skin exposure during these times. Always use SPF30+ sunscreen; apply it 30 minutes before going into the sun and repeat applications regularly.

HEAT EXHAUSTION & HEATSTROKE

» Very hot weather is experienced all year round in northern Australia and during the summer months for most of the country. Conditions vary from tropical in the Northern Territory and Queensland to hot desert in northwestern Australia and central Australia.

» When arriving from a temperate or cold climate, remember that it takes two weeks for acclimatisation to occur. Before the body is acclimatised, an excessive amount of salt is lost in perspiration, so increasing the salt in your diet is essential.

» Heat exhaustion occurs when fluid intake does not keep up with fluid loss. Symptoms include dizziness, fainting, fatigue, nausea or vomiting. The skin is usually pale, cool and clammy. Treatment consists of rest in a cool, shady place and fluid replacement with water or diluted sports drinks.

» Heatstroke is a severe form of heat illness that occurs after fluid depletion or extreme heat challenge from heavy exercise. This is a true medical emergency, with heating of the brain leading to disorientation, hallucinations and seizures. Prevent heatstroke by maintaining an adequate fluid intake to ensure the continued passage of clear and copious urine, especially during physical exertion.

INSECT-BORNE ILLNESSES

Various insects can be a source of irritation and, in Australia, may be the source of specific diseases (dengue fever, Ross River fever, viral encephalitis). Protection from mosquitoes, sandflies,

ticks and leeches can be achieved by a combination of the following strategies:

» Wear loose-fitting, long-sleeved clothing.

» Apply 30% DEET to all exposed skin and reapply every three to four hours.

» Impregnate clothing with permethrin (an insecticide that is believed to be safe for humans).

TRAVELLERS' DIARRHOEA

Water Tap water is universally safe in Australia. All water other than tap water should be boiled, filtered or chemically disinfected (with iodine tablets) to prevent travellers' diarrhoea and giardisis.

Treatment If you develop diarrhoea (more than four or five stools a day), drink plenty of fluids – preferably an oral rehydration solution containing lots of salt and sugar. You should also begin taking an antibiotic (usually a quinolone drug) and an antidiarrhoeal agent (such as loperamide). If diarrhoea is bloody, persists for more than 72 hours or is accompanied by fever, shaking, chills or severe abdominal pain, seek medical attention.

Medical Checklist

» antibiotics

» antidiarrhoeal drugs (eg loperamide)

» acetaminophen (paracetamol) or aspirin

» anti-inflammatory drugs (eg ibuprofen)

» antihistamines (for hayfever and allergic reactions)

» antibacterial ointment in case of cuts or abrasions

» steroid cream or cortisone (for allergic rashes)

» bandages, gauze, gauze rolls

» adhesive or paper tape

» scissors, safety pins, tweezers

» thermometer

» pocket knife

» DEET-containing insect repellent for the skin

» permethrin-containing insect spray for clothing, tents and bed nets

» sunscreen

» oral rehydration salts

» iodine tablets or water filter (for water purification)

Insurance

Worldwide travel insurance is available at www.lonely planet.com/travel_services. You can buy, extend and claim online anytime – even if you're already on the road.

Level of cover A good travel insurance policy covering theft, loss and medical problems is essential. Most policies offer lower and higher medical-expense options; the higher ones are chiefly for countries that have extremely high medical costs, such as the USA. There is a wide variety of policies available, so compare the small print. Some policies specifically exclude designated 'dangerous activities' such as scuba diving, bungee jumping, motorcycling, skiing and even bushwalking. Make sure the policy you choose fully covers you for your activity of choice.

Car For information on insurance matters relating to cars that are bought or rented, see p1075.

Health You may prefer a policy that pays doctors or hospitals directly rather than requiring you to pay on the spot and claim later. If you have to claim later make sure you keep all documentation. Check that the policy covers ambulances and emergency medical evacuations by air. See also Health Insurance (p1054).

Internet Access

Internet addicts will find it easy to get connected throughout Australia.

Internet Cafes

» Most internet cafes in Australia have broadband access, but prices vary significantly depending on where you are.

» Most public libraries also have internet access, but this is provided primarily for research needs, not for travellers to check their email, so head for an internet cafe first. You'll find these in cities, sizeable towns and pretty much anywhere else that travellers congregate.

» The cost ranges from $3 per hour in cutthroat places in Sydney's King's Cross to $10 per hour in more remote locations. The average is about $6 per hour, usually with a minimum of 10 minutes' access.

» Most youth hostels and backpacker places can also hook you up, as can many hotels and caravan parks.

» Telecentres (community centres providing web access and other hi-tech facilities to locals and visitors) provide internet access in remote areas of WA, SA and NSW, while Tasmania has set up access centres in numerous local libraries and schools.

Internet Service Providers

ISPs If you've brought your palmtop or notebook computer and want to get connected to a local Internet Service Provider (ISP), there are plenty of options – some ISPs do limit their dial-up areas to major cities or particular regions. Whatever enticements a particular ISP offers, make sure it has local dial-up numbers for the places where you intend to use it – the last thing you want is to be making timed long-distance calls every time you connect to the internet. Another useful tip when dialling up from a hotel room is to put 0 in front of your dial-up number to enable your modem to dial an outside line. Some major ISPs:

Australia On Line (☏1300 650 661; www.ozonline.com.au)

Dodo (☏13 36 36; www.dodo.com.au)

iinet (☏13 19 17; www.iinet.net.au)

iPrimus (☏13 17 89; www.iprimus.com.au)

Optus (☏1800 780 219; www.optus.com.au)

Telstra BigPond (☏13 76 63; www.bigpond.com)

Wi-fi An increasing number of hotels, cafes and bars in cities offer wi-fi (wireless) access. Some charge a fee so make sure you ask the price before connecting. These locations are most prevalent in Sydney and Melbourne but they're on the rise elsewhere. The following websites are helpful for sourcing locations:

Azure Wireless (www.azure.com.au)

Free WiFi (www.freewifi.com.au)

Wi-Fi HotSpotList (www.wi-fihotspotlist.com/browse/au)

Plugs Australia uses RJ-45 telephone plugs and Telstra EXI-160 four-pin plugs, but neither is universal – electronics shops such as Tandy and Dick Smith should be able to help. You'll also need a plug adaptor, and a universal AC adaptor will enable you to plug in without frying the innards of your machine.

Modem Keep in mind that your PC-card modem may not work in Australia. The safest option is to buy a reputable 'global' modem before you leave home or buy a local PC-card modem once you get to Australia.

Legal Matters

Most travellers will have no contact with the Australian police or any other part of the legal system. Those that do are likely to experience it while driving.

Driving There is a significant police presence on the country's roads, with the

power to stop your car and ask to see your licence (you're required to carry it at all times), check your vehicle for roadworthiness, and insist that you take a breath test for alcohol (and sometimes illicit drugs) – drink-driving offences are taken very seriously here.

Drugs First-time offenders caught with small amounts of illegal drugs are likely to receive a fine rather than go to jail; nonetheless the recording of a conviction against you may affect your visa status.

Visas If you remain in Australia beyond the life of your visa, you will officially be an 'overstayer' and could face detention and expulsion, and then be prevented from returning to Australia for up to three years.

If you are arrested It's your right to telephone a friend, relative or lawyer before any formal questioning begins. Legal Aid is available only in serious cases and only to the truly needy (for links to Legal Aid offices see www.nla. aust.net.au). However, many solicitors do not charge for an initial consultation.

Maps

Good-quality road and topographical maps are plentiful and readily available. The various state motoring organisations are a dependable source of road maps, while local tourist offices usually supply free maps, though the quality varies.

Websites For locating urban points of interest and specific addresses, try www. whereis.com.au and www. maps.google.com.au.

Bushwalking maps Bushwalkers and others undertaking outdoor activities for which large-scale maps are essential should browse the topographic sheets published by **Geoscience Australia** (☎1800 800 173,

02-6249 9111; www.ga.gov.au). The more popular topographic sheets are usually available over the counter at shops selling specialist bushwalking gear and outdoor equipment.

City street guides Useful for in-depth urban navigation, but they're expensive, bulky and only worth getting if you intend to do a lot of city driving. Publishers:

Ausway (www.ausway.com) Publishers of the omnipresent *Melway* and *Sydway*.

Gregorys (www.gregorys-online.com)

UBD (www.ubd.com.au)

Money

ATMs, Eftpos & Bank Accounts

Branches ANZ, Commonwealth, National Australia Bank, Westpac and affiliated banks have branches all over Australia, and many provide 24-hour automated teller machines (ATMs). But don't expect to find ATMs *everywhere*, certainly not off the beaten track or in very small towns. Most ATMs accept cards issued by other banks and are linked to international networks.

Eftpos (Electronic Funds Transfer at Point of Sale) Most Australian businesses have embraced this convenient service. It means you can use your bank card (credit or debit) to pay for services or purchases directly, and often withdraw cash as well. Eftpos is available practically everywhere these days, even in outback roadhouses where it's a long way between banks. Just like using an ATM, you need to know your Personal Identification Number (PIN) to use Eftpos.

Fees Bear in mind that withdrawing cash via ATMs or Eftpos may attract significant fees – check the associated costs with your bank first.

OPENING A BANK ACCOUNT

Within six weeks If you're planning on staying in Australia a while (on a Working Holiday visa for instance) it makes sense to open up a local bank account. This is easy enough for overseas visitors provided it's done within six weeks of arrival. Simply present your passport and provide the bank with a postal address and they'll open the account and send you an ATM card.

After six weeks It becomes much more complicated. A points system operates and you need to score a minimum of 100 points before you can have the privilege of letting the bank take your money. Passports or birth certificates are worth 70 points; an international driving licence with photo earns you 40 points; and minor IDs, such as credit cards, get you 25 points. You must have at least one ID with a photograph. Once the account is open, you should be able to have money transferred across from your home account (for a fee, of course).

Before you arrive It's possible to set up an Australian bank account before you embark on your international trip and applications can be made online; check the following bank websites for details:

ANZ (www.anz.com.au)

Commonwealth Bank (www.commbank.com.au)

National Australia Bank (www.nab.com.au)

Westpac (www.westpac.com.au)

Tax File Number If you don't have an Australian Tax File Number (TFN) you may end up paying up to twice as much tax, depending on the income bracket you fall into. See p1065 for tax-related information.

Credit & Debit Cards

CREDIT CARDS

» Arguably the best way to carry most of your money around is in the form of a plastic card.

» Australia is well and truly a card-carrying society; it's unusual to line up at a supermarket checkout, petrol station or department store and see someone actually paying with cash these days.

» Credit cards such as Visa and MasterCard are widely accepted for everything from a hostel bed or a restaurant meal to an adventure tour, and are pretty much essential (in lieu of a large deposit) for hiring a car. They can also be used to get cash advances over the counter at banks and from many ATMs, depending on the card, though these transactions incur immediate interest.

» Charge cards such as Diners Club and American Express (Amex) are not as widely accepted.

» Lost credit-card contact numbers:

» **American Express** (☑1300 132 639)

» **Diners Club** (☑1300 360 060)

» **MasterCard** (☑1800 120 113)

» **Visa** (☑1800 450 346)

DEBIT CARDS

» Apart from losing them, the obvious danger with credit cards is maxing out your limit and going home to a steaming pile of debt. A safer option is a debit card with which you can draw money directly from your home bank account using ATMs, banks or Eftpos machines.

» Any card connected to the international banking network (Cirrus, Maestro, Visa Plus and Eurocard) should work, provided you know your PIN.

» Fees for using your card at a foreign bank or ATM vary depending on your home bank; ask before you leave.

» Companies such as Travelex offer debit cards (Travelex calls them Cash Passport cards) with set withdrawal fees and a balance you can top up from your personal bank account while on the road – nice one!

Currency

In this book, unless otherwise stated, all prices given in dollars refer to Australian dollars.

Denominations Australia's currency is the Australian dollar, made up of 100 cents. There are 5c, 10c, 20c, 50c, $1 and $2 coins, and $5, $10, $20, $50 and $100 notes. Although the smallest coin in circulation is 5c, prices are often still marked in single cents and then rounded to the nearest 5c when you come to pay.

Customs Cash amounts equal to or in excess of the equivalent of $10,000 (in any currency) must be declared on arrival or departure.

Exchanging Money

Changing foreign currency or travellers cheques is usually no problem at banks throughout Australia or at licensed moneychangers such as Travelex or Amex in cities and major towns.

Taxes & Refunds

Goods and services tax
The GST is a flat 10% tax on all goods and services – accommodation, eating out, transport, electrical and other goods, books, furniture, clothing etc. There are exceptions, however, such as basic foods (milk, bread, fruit and vegetables etc). By law the tax is included in the quoted or shelf price, so all prices in this book are GST-inclusive.

Travel International air and sea travel to/from Australia is GST-free, as is domestic air travel when purchased outside Australia by nonresidents.

Refund of GST If you purchase new or secondhand goods with a total minimum value of $300 from any one supplier no more than 30 days before you leave Australia, you are entitled under the Tourist Refund Scheme (TRS) to a refund of any GST or WET (wine equalisation tax) paid. The scheme doesn't apply to all goods, and those that do qualify you must be able to wear or take as hand luggage onto the plane or ship. Also note that the refund is valid for goods bought from more than one supplier, but only if at least $300 is spent in each. For more details, contact the **Australian Customs Service** (☑1300 363 263, 02-6275 6666; www.customs.gov.au).

Income tax refund See p1066 for details on income tax refunds.

Travellers Cheques

» The ubiquity and convenience of internationally linked credit and debit card facilities in Australia means that travellers cheques are virtually redundant.

» Amex and Travelex will exchange their associated travellers cheques, and major banks will change travellers cheques also.

» In all instances you'll need to present your passport for identification when cashing them.

» There are no notable restrictions on importing or exporting travellers cheques.

Photography

Availability Digital cameras, memory sticks and batteries are sold prolifically in cities and urban centres. Electronics stores such as **Dick Smith** (www.dicksmith.com.au) will stock everything you need, as will the larger department stores. The availability of batteries and memory sticks in more rural or remote areas is far diminished so if you're planning to get trigger happy it's best to stock up in the cities.

Printing Many internet cafes, camera stores and large stationers such as Officeworks (www.officeworks.com.au) have facilities that enable you to produce prints directly from your memory stick or to burn CDs.

Film Film and slide film are still available and developing standards are high. You can get your shots processed at any camera store and just about any chemist.

Videos Video cassettes are still available at camera and electronics stores.

Books Useful Lonely Planet titles for the budding photographer include *Urban Travel Photography, Wildlife Travel Photography,* and *Landscape Photography.*

ETIQUETTE

As in any country, politeness goes a long way when taking photographs; ask before taking pictures of people. Particularly bear in mind that Indigenous Australians are not objects of curiosity; they are people like you, and photography can be highly intrusive. Regardless of whether the purpose is personal or commercial, always ask permission before photographing or videoing a person, group or residence, and offer to return copies of photographs or footage (and get an address). Taking photographs of cultural places, practices and images, sites of significance and ceremonies may also be a sensitive matter. Always ask and always respect the right to say no.

Post

Australia Post (www.auspost.com.au) has divided international destinations into four parcel zones.

Sea mail You can send parcels by sea mail to anywhere in the world except countries in the Asia-Pacific region (including New Zealand); it's cheap but can take forever.

Receiving mail All post offices hold mail for visitors. You need to provide some form of identification (such as a passport or driver's licence) to collect mail. You can also have mail sent to you at city Amex offices if you have an Amex card or travellers cheques.

Opening hours Open 9am to 5pm Monday to Friday; often till noon on Saturday.

Public Holidays

The following is a list of the main national and state public holidays (* indicates holidays that are only observed locally in each state). As the timing can vary from state to state, check locally for precise dates.

NATIONAL

New Year's Day 1 January

Australia Day 26 January

Easter (Good Friday to Easter Monday inclusive) March/April

Anzac Day 25 April

Queen's Birthday (except WA) Second Monday in June

Queen's Birthday (WA) Last Monday in September

Christmas Day 25 December

Boxing Day 26 December

AUSTRALIAN CAPITAL TERRITORY

Canberra Day Second Monday in March

Bank Holiday First Monday in August

Labour Day First Monday in October

NEW SOUTH WALES

Bank Holiday First Monday in August

Labour Day First Monday in October

NORTHERN TERRITORY

May Day First Monday in May

Show Day* (Alice Springs) First Friday in July; (Tennant Creek) second Friday in July;

(Katherine) third Friday in July; (Darwin) fourth Friday in July

Picnic Day First Monday in August

QUEENSLAND

Labour Day First Monday in May

RNA Show Day* (Brisbane) Second or third Wednesday in August

SOUTH AUSTRALIA

Adelaide Cup Day Third Monday in May

Labour Day First Monday in October

Proclamation Day Last Monday or Tuesday in December

TASMANIA

Regatta Day* (Hobart) 14 February

Launceston Cup Day* Last Wednesday in February

Eight Hours Day First Monday in March

Bank Holiday Tuesday following Easter Monday

King Island Show* First Tuesday in March

Launceston Show Day* Thursday preceding second Saturday in October

Hobart Show Day* Thursday preceding fourth Saturday in October

Recreation Day* (Northern Tasmania) First Monday in November

VICTORIA

Labour Day Second Monday in March

Melbourne Cup Day First Tuesday in November

WESTERN AUSTRALIA

Labour Day First Monday in March

Foundation Day First Monday in June

School Holidays

» The Christmas holiday season, from mid-December to late January, is part of the summer school holidays – it's also the time you are

most likely to find transport and accommodation booked out, and long, restless queues at tourist attractions.

» There are three shorter school holiday periods during the year, but they vary by a week or two from state to state. They fall roughly from early to mid-April, late June to mid-July, and late September to early October.

» Even though the holidays don't coincide nationwide, accommodation in tourist hot spots like the north and south coasts of NSW, and Queensland's Gold and Sunshine Coasts will still be booked out.

Safe Travel

Australia is a relatively safe place to travel by world standards – crime- and war-wise at any rate – but natural disasters have been wreaking havoc of late. Bushfires, floods and cyclones decimated parts of Queensland, NSW, Victoria and WA in early 2011, but if you pay attention to warnings from local authorities and don't venture into affected areas, you should be fine.

Shopping

Australians are fond of spending money, a fact evidenced by the huge variety of local- and international-brand shops, and the feverish crowds that gather at every clearance sale. Big cities can satisfy most consumer appetites with everything from high-fashion boutiques to secondhand emporia, while many smaller places tend towards speciality retail, be it homegrown produce, antiques or arts and crafts. Markets are a great place to shop – most cities have at least one permanent bazaar.

You may be able to get a refund on the tax you pay on goods; see p1058.

GOVERNMENT TRAVEL ADVICE

The following government websites offer travel advisories and information on current hot spots.

» **Australian Department of Foreign Affairs** (www.smarttraveller.gov.au)

» **British Foreign Office** (www.fco.gov.uk)

» **Foreign Affairs and International Trade Canada** (www.voyage.gc.ca)

» **US State Department** (http://travel.state.gov)

Aboriginal Art & Artefacts

Authenticity An Aboriginal artwork or artefact makes an evocative reminder of your trip. By buying authentic items you are supporting Aboriginal cultures and helping to ensure that traditional and contemporary expertise and designs continue to be of economic and cultural benefit for Aboriginal individuals and their communities. Unfortunately, much of the so-called Aboriginal art sold as souvenirs is ripped off, consisting of appropriated designs illegally taken from Aboriginal people; or it's just plain fake, and usually made overseas by underpaid workers.

Where to buy The best places to buy artefacts are either directly from the communities that have art-and-craft centres or from galleries and outlets that are owned, operated or supported by Aboriginal communities. There are also many reputable galleries that have long supported the Aboriginal arts industry, usually members of the **Australian Commercial Galleries Association** (ACGA; www.acga.com.au), that will offer certificates of authenticity with their goods. See Buying Aboriginal Art p810 for more information.

Didgeridoos These are in high demand, but you should decide whether you want a decorative piece or a functional musical

instrument. The didgeridoos on the market are not always made by Aboriginal people, which means that at a nonsupportive souvenir shop in Darwin or Cairns you could pay anything from $250 to $400 or more for something that looks pretty but is little more than a painted bit of wood. Buying from an Indigenous community outlet such as Julalikari (p851) in the NT is your best opportunity to purchase a functional, authentic didgeridoo painted with natural pigments such as ochre.

Australiana

The cheapest souvenirs, usually mass-produced and with little to distinguish them, are known collectively by the euphemism 'Australiana'. They are supposedly representative of Australia and its culture, but in reality are just lowest-common-denominator trinkets, often made in Asia rather than Australia (check the label).

Genuine Australian offerings include the seeds of native plants – try growing kangaroo paws back home (if your own country will allow them in). You could also consider a bottle of fine Australian wine, honey (leatherwood honey is one of many powerful local varieties), macadamia nuts (native to Queensland), Bundaberg Rum with its unusual sweet flavour, or genuine Ugg boots (sheepskin boots that conquer any winter).

Gemstones

Opals The opal, Australia's national gemstone, is a popular souvenir, as is the jewellery made with it. It's a beautiful stone but buy wisely and shop around, as quality and prices vary widely from place to place. Coober Pedy (p791) in SA, and Lightning Ridge (p193) and White Cliffs (p240) in NSW are opal-mining towns where you can buy the stones or fossick for your own.

Pearls On the Torres Strait Islands (p468) look out for South Sea pearls, while in Broome (p996) in WA, cultured pearls are sold in many local shops.

Other gemstones Australia is a mineral-rich country and semiprecious gemstones such as topaz, garnets, sapphires, rubies, zircon and others can sometimes be found lying around in piles of dirt at various locations. There are sites around rural and outback Australia where you can pay a few dollars and fossick for your own stones. The gem fields around Emerald, Anakie and Rubyvale in Queensland's Capricorn Hinterland (p370) are a good place to shop for jewellery and gemstones.

Telephone

Australia's main telecommunication companies:

Telstra (www.telstra.com.au) The main player – landline and mobile phone services.

Optus (www.optus.com.au) Telstra's main rival – landline and mobile phone services.

Vodafone (www.vodafone.com.au) Mobile phone services.

Virgin (www.virginmobile.com.au) Mobile phone services.

3 (www.three.com.au) Mobile phone services.

Information & Toll-Free Calls

» Numbers starting with ☑190 are usually recorded information services, charged at anything from 35c to $5 or more per minute (more from mobiles and payphones).

» To make a reverse-charge (collect) call from any public or private phone, dial ☑1800 738 3773 or ☑12 550.

» Toll-free numbers (prefix ☑1800) can be called free of charge from almost anywhere in Australia – they may not be accessible from certain areas or from mobile phones.

» Calls to numbers beginning with ☑13 or ☑1300 are charged at the rate of a local call – the numbers can usually be dialled Australia-wide, but may be applicable only to a specific state or STD district.

» Telephone numbers beginning with either ☑1800, ☑13 or ☑1300 cannot be dialled from outside Australia.

International Calls

From payphones Most payphones allow International Subscriber Dialling (ISD) calls, the cost and international dialling code of which will vary depending on which international phonecard provider you are using. International phone cards are readily available from internet cafes and convenience stores. Check the fine print on your phonecard to ensure you aren't paying a hefty trunk charge every time you make a call.

From landlines International calls from landlines in Australia are also relatively cheap and subject to special deals, so if you're paying for residential phone rental it's worth shopping around – look in the *Yellow Pages* for a list of telephone service providers and compare their international rates.

Reverse charge The Country Direct service (☑1800 801 800) connects callers in Australia with operators in nearly 60 countries to make reverse-charge (collect) or credit-card calls.

Codes When calling overseas you will need to dial the international access code from Australia (☑0011 or ☑0018), the country code and then the area code (without the initial 0). So for a London telephone number you'll need to dial ☑0011-44-20, then the number. In addition, certain operators will have you dial a special code to access their service. If dialling Australia from overseas, the country code is ☑61 and you need to drop the 0 in state/territory area codes.

COUNTRY	CODE
France	☑33
Germany	☑49
Ireland	☑353
Japan	☑81
Netherlands	☑31
New Zealand	☑64
UK	☑44
USA & Canada	☑1

Local Calls

Calls from private phones cost 15c to 30c, while local calls from public phones cost 50c; both involve unlimited talk time. Calls to mobile phones attract higher rates and are timed.

Long-Distance Calls & Area Codes

Long-distance calls (over around 50km) are timed. Australia uses four Subscriber Trunk Dialling (STD) area codes. These STD calls can be made from any public phone and are cheaper during off-peak hours – generally between 7pm and 7am, and on weekends. Broadly, the main area codes are as follows.

STATE/ TERRITORY	AREA CODE
ACT	☑02
NSW	☑02
NT	☑08
QLD	☑07
SA	☑08
TAS	☑03
VIC	☑03
WA	☑08

Area code boundaries don't necessarily coincide with state borders; for example some parts of NSW use neighbouring codes.

Mobile (Cell) Phones

Numbers Local numbers with the prefixes ☑04xx belong to mobile phones.

Networks Australia's GSM and 3G mobile networks service more than 90% of the population but leaves vast tracts of the country uncovered. Australia's digital network is compatible with GSM 900 and 1800 (used in Europe), but generally not with the systems used in the USA or Japan.

Reception The east coast, southeast and southwest get good reception, but elsewhere (apart from major towns) it can be haphazard or nonexistent. It is improving, however.

Providers It's easy and cheap enough to get connected short-term, as prepaid mobile systems are offered by the main providers (p1061).

Phonecards & Public Phones

Phonecards A variety of phonecards can be bought at newsagents, hostels and post offices for a fixed dollar value (usually $10, $20 etc) and can be used with any public or private phone by dialling a toll-free access number and then the PIN number on the card.

Public phones Some public phones also accept credit cards, but old-fashioned coin-operated public phones are becoming increasingly rare (and if you do find one, chances are the coin slot will be gummed up or vandalised beyond function).

Time

Zones Australia is divided into three time zones: Western Standard Time

(GMT/UTC plus eight hours) covering WA; Central Standard Time (plus 9½ hours) covering the NT and SA; and Eastern Standard Time (plus 10 hours) covering Tasmania, Victoria, NSW, the ACT and Queensland. There are minor exceptions – Broken Hill (NSW) for instance is on Central Standard Time. For international times, see www.timeanddate.com/worldclock.

Daylight saving Clocks are put forward an hour. This system operates in some states during the warmer months (October to early April). However, things can get pretty confusing, with WA, the NT and Queensland staying on standard time, while in Tasmania daylight saving starts a month earlier than in SA, Victoria, the ACT and NSW.

Tipping

It's common but by no means obligatory to tip in restaurants and upmarket cafes if the service warrants it – a gratuity of between 5% and 10% of the bill is the norm. Taxi drivers will also appreciate you rounding up the fare.

Toilets

One of the pleasures of travelling in a western country is the abundance of hygienic and free public toilets. These can be found in shopping centres, parks and just about any other public space in the country.

Tourist Information

Australia's highly self-conscious tourism infrastructure means that when you head out looking for information, you can easily end up being buried neck deep in brochures, booklets, maps and leaflets, or you can get utterly

swamped with detail during an online surf.

The **Australian Tourist Commission** (www.australia.com) is the national government tourist body, and has a good website for pre-trip research.

Local Tourist Offices

Within Australia, tourist information is disseminated by various regional and local offices. In this book, the main state and territory tourism authorities are listed in the introductory information section of each destination chapter. Almost every major town in Australia seems to maintain a tourist office of some type and in many cases they are very good, with friendly staff (often retiree volunteers) providing local info not readily available from the state offices. If booking accommodation or tours from local offices, bear in mind that they often only promote businesses that are paying members of the local tourist association. Details of local tourism offices are given in the relevant city and town sections throughout this book.

Tourist Offices Abroad

The federal government body charged with improving relationships with foreign tourists is **Tourism Australia** (www.tourism.australia.com). A good place to start some pre-trip research is on its website, which provides information about many aspects of visiting Australia in 10 languages (including French, German, Japanese and Spanish).

Some countries with Tourism Australia offices:

Canada (☑416-572 7708; Suite 272, 1920 Yonge St, Toronto M4S 3E2)

China (☑21-6887 8129; Unit 1501, 15/F, Citigroup Tower, 33 Hua Yuan Shi Qiao Rd, PuDong, Shanghai 200120)

Germany (☑069-274 00622; Neue Mainzer Strasse 22, Frankfurt D 60311)

Japan (☑13-5218 2560; 12F Marunouchi Trust Tower North, 1-8-1 Marunouchi, Chiyoda-ku, Tokyo 100-0005)

New Zealand (☑09-915 2826; Level 3, 125 The Strand, Parnell, Auckland)

Singapore (☑6255 4555; 101 Thomson Rd, United Sq 08-03, Singapore 307591)

UK (☑020-7438 4601; 6th fl, Australia House, Melbourne Place/Strand, London WC2B 4LG)

USA (☑310-695 3200; Suite 1150, 6100 Center Dr, Los Angeles CA 90045)

Travellers with Disabilities

Disability awareness in Australia is pretty high and getting higher. Legislation requires that new accommodation meets accessibility standards for mobility-impaired travellers, and discrimination by tourism operators is illegal. Many of Australia's key attractions, including many national parks, provide access for those with limited mobility and a number of sites also address the needs of visitors with visual or aural impairments; contact attractions in advance to confirm the facilities. Tour operators with vehicles catering to mobility-impaired travellers operate from most capital cities. Facilities for wheelchairs are improving in accommodation, but there are still far too many older (particularly 'historic') establishments where the necessary upgrades haven't been done.

Resources

Online resources and useful contacts:

Access Travel Australia (www.ebility.com/travel) Lots of info on accessible holidays in Australia, including listings of tour operators and accommodation.

Deaf Australia (www.deafau. org.au)

Easy Access Australia (www.easyaccessaustralia.com. au) A publication by Bruce Cameron available from various bookshops. Provides details on easily accessible transport, accommodation and attraction options.

National Information Communication & Awareness Network (Nican; www. nican.com.au) Australia-wide directory providing information on access issues, accessible accommodation, sporting and recreational activities, transport and specialist tour operators.

National Public Toilet Map (www.toiletmap.gov. au) Lists over 14,000 public toilets around Australia, including those with wheelchair access.

Spinal Chord Injuries Australia (www.spinalcord injuries.com.au)

Vision Australia (www. visionaustralia.org.au)

Air Travel

Qantas (☑13 13 13; www.qan tas.com.au) entitles a disabled person and the carer travelling with them to a discount on full economy fares; contact Nican for eligibility and an application form. Guide dogs travel for free on Qantas, Jetstar (☑13 15 38; www.jetstar.com.au) and Virgin Australia (☑13 67 89; www.virginaustralia.com.au), and their affiliated carriers. All of Australia's major airports have dedicated parking spaces, wheelchair access to terminals, accessible toilets, and skychairs to convey passengers onto planes via airbridges.

Train Travel

In NSW, CountryLink's XPT trains have at least one carriage (usually the buffet car) with a seat removed for a wheelchair, and an accessible toilet. Queensland Rail's *Tilt Train* from Brisbane to Cairns has a wheelchair-accessible carriage.

Melbourne's suburban rail network is accessible and

guide dogs and hearing dogs are permitted on all public transport in Victoria. Metlink (☑13 16 38; www.metlinkmel bourne.com.au) also offers a free travel pass to visually impaired people for transport in Melbourne.

Visas

All visitors to Australia need a visa – only New Zealand nationals are exempt, and even they sheepishly receive a 'special category' visa on arrival. Application forms for the several types of visa are available from Australian diplomatic missions overseas, travel agents or the website of the Department of Immigration & Citizenship (☑13 18 81; www.immi.gov.au).

eVisitor

Many European passport holders are eligible for an eVisitor visa, which is free and allows visitors to stay in Australia for up to three months within a 12-month period. eVisitor visas must be applied for online at www.immi.gov. au/e_visa/evisitor.htm, and they are electronically stored and linked to individual passport numbers, so no stamp in your passport is required. It's advisable to apply at least 14 days prior to the proposed date of arrival in Australia.

Electronic Travel Authority (ETA)

Passport holders from eight countries that aren't part of the eVisitor scheme – Brunei, Canada, Hong Kong, Japan, Malaysia, Singapore, South Korea and the USA – can apply for either a visitor or business ETA. ETAs are valid for 12 months, with stays of up to three months on each visit. You can apply for the ETA online at www.eta.immi.gov.au, which attracts a nonrefundable service charge of $20.

Tourist Visas (676)

Short-term tourist visas have largely been replaced by the

eVisitor and ETA. However, if you are from a country not covered by either, or you want to stay longer than three months, you'll need to apply for a Tourist Visa. Standard tourist visas (which cost $105) allow one (in some cases multiple) entry, for a stay of up to 12 months, and are valid for use within 12 months of issue. For online applications see www.immi.gov.au/e_visa/e676.htm.

Visa Extensions

If you want to stay in Australia for longer than your visa allows, you'll need to apply for a new visa (usually a Tourist Visa 676) through the Department of Immigration & Citizenship at www.immi.gov.au/visitors/tourist. It's best to apply at least two or three weeks before your visa expires. The application fee is $255 and is nonrefundable, even if your application is rejected.

Working Holiday Visas (417)

Young (aged 18 to 30) visitors from Belgium, Canada, Cyprus, Denmark, Estonia, Finland, France, Germany, Hong Kong, Ireland, Italy, Japan, South Korea, Malta, the Netherlands, Norway, Sweden, Taiwan and the UK are eligible for a Working Holiday visa, which allows you to visit for up to one year and gain casual employment.

The emphasis of this visa is on casual and not full-time employment, so you're only supposed to work for any one employer for a maximum of six months. A first Working Holiday visa must be obtained prior to entry to Australia: see www.immi.gov.au/visitors/working-holiday. You can't change from a tourist visa to a Working Holiday visa once you're in Australia.

You can apply for this visa up to a year in advance, which is worthwhile as there's a limit on the number issued each year. Conditions include having a return air ticket or sufficient funds for a return or onward fare. The application fee is $235. For details of what sort of employment is available and where, see p1066.

See p1066 for information regarding the income tax refunds that holders of a Working Holiday visa are eligible for.

SECOND WORKING HOLIDAY VISA

Visitors who have worked as a seasonal worker in regional Australia for a minimum of three months while on their first Working Holiday visa are eligible to apply for a second Working Holiday visa while still in Australia. 'Regional Australia' encompasses the vast majority of the country, excepting major cities; the definition of 'seasonal work' is a little more specific. For information see www.immi.gov.au/visitors/working-holiday/417/eligibility-second.htm.

Work & Holiday Visas (462)

Nationals from Bangladesh, Chile, Indonesia, Malaysia, Thailand, Turkey and the USA between the ages of 18 and 30 can apply for a Work and Holiday visa prior to entry to Australia. Once granted this visa allows the holder to enter Australia within three months of issue, stay for up to 12 months, leave and re-enter Australia any number of times within that 12 months, undertake temporary employment to supplement a trip, and study for up to four months. For details see www.immi.gov.au/visitors/working-holiday/462.

Volunteering

Lonely Planet's *Volunteer: A Traveller's Guide to Making a Difference Around the World* provides useful information about volunteering.

Australian Volunteers International (AVI; ☎1800 331 292, 03-9279 1788; www.australianvolunteers.com) Mainly involved in recruiting Australians to work overseas, but does also place skilled volunteers into Aboriginal communities in northern and central Australia. Most of the placements are paid contracts for a minimum of a year and you will need an appropriate work visa. There are, however, occasional short-term placements, especially in the medical or accounting fields, and short-term unskilled jobs, usually helping out at community-run roadhouses.

Conservation Volunteers Australia (CVA; ☎1800 032 501, 03-5330 2600; www.conservationvolunteers.com.au) A nonprofit organisation involved in tree planting, walking-track construction, and flora and fauna surveys. See Volunteering for the Environment (p1034) for details.

Willing Workers on Organic Farms (WWOOF; ☎03-5155 0218; www.wwoof.com.au) The idea is that you do a few hours work each day on a farm in return for bed and board, often in a family home. Almost all places have a minimum stay of two nights. As the name states, the farms are supposed to be organic (including permaculture and biodynamic growing), but that isn't always so. Some places aren't even farms – you might help out at a pottery or do the books at a seed wholesaler. Whether participants in the scheme have a farm or just a vegie patch, most are concerned to some extent with alternative lifestyles. You can join online or through various WWOOF agents (see the website for details) for a fee of $60. You'll get a membership number and a booklet that lists participating enterprises. If you need these posted overseas, add another $5.

Earthwatch Institute Australia (☎03-9682 6828; www.earthwatch.org) Offers

volunteer 'expeditions' that focus on conservation and wildlife.

STA (www.statravel.com.au) Another great resource for international travellers seeking volunteer holiday opportunities in Australia – click on 'Experiences' on their website and go to the volunteer link.

Conservation Council of SA (www.conservationsa.org.au) South Australian volunteer opportunities, including restoration of swamps, grasslands and other natural habitats, and recovery programs for threatened bird species.

Go Volunteer (www.go volunteer.com.au) National website listing volunteer opportunities.

i-to-i (www.i-to-i.com) Conservation-based volunteer holidays in Australia.

Nature Conservation Society of South Australia (www.ncssa.asn.au) Survey fieldwork volunteer opportunities in SA.

Reef Watch (www.reefwatch.asn.au) Surveys sightings of introduced marine pests and endangered native species.

Responsible Travel (www.responsibletravel.com) Volunteer travel opportunities.

Scientific Expedition Group (www.communitywebs.org/scientificexpeditiongroup) Loads of different scientific and cultural data collection volunteer opportunities in SA.

Volunteering Australia (www.volunteeringaustralia.org) Support, advice and volunteer training.

Women Travellers

Australia is generally a safe place for women travellers, although the usual sensible precautions apply.

Night-time It's best to avoid walking alone late at night in any of the major cities and towns. And if you're out on the town, always keep enough money aside for a taxi back to your accommodation. The same applies to outback and rural towns where there are often a lot of unlit, semideserted streets between you and your temporary home. When the pubs and bars close and there are inebriated people roaming around, it's not a great time to be out and about.

Pubs Lone women should also be wary of staying in basic pub accommodation unless it looks safe and well managed.

Sexual harassment This is an ongoing problem, be it via an aggressive metropolitan male or a rural bloke living a less-than-enlightened pro-forma bush existence.

Rural areas Stereotypically, the further you get from the big cities, the less enlightened your average Aussie male is probably going to be about women's issues. Having said that, many women travellers say that they have met the friendliest, most down-to-earth blokes in outback pubs and remote roadhouse stops. And cities still have to put up with their unfortunate share of 'ocker' males who regard a bit of sexual harassment as a right, and chauvinism as a desirable trait.

Hitchhiking Lone female hitchhikers are tempting fate – hitching with a male companion is safer.

Drugged drinks Some pubs in Sydney and other big cities post warnings about drugged or 'spiked' drinks: probably not cause for paranoia, but play it safe if someone offers you a drink in a bar.

Work

» If you come to Australia on a tourist visa then you're not allowed to work for pay – working for approved volunteer organisations in exchange for board is OK.

» If you're caught breaching your visa conditions, you can be expelled from the country and placed on a banned list for up to three years.

» Equipped with a Working Holiday or Work and Holiday visa, you can begin to sniff out the possibilities for temporary employment.

» Casual work can often be found during peak season at the major tourist centres. Places such as Alice Springs, Cairns and various resort towns along the Queensland coast, and the ski fields of Victoria and NSW are all good prospects when the country is in holiday mode.

» Many travellers have found work cleaning or attending the reception desk at backpacker hostels, which usually means free accommodation. Most hostels, however, are now employing their own locally based staff.

» Other prospects for casual employment include factory work, labouring, bar work, waiting tables, domestic chores at outback roadhouses, nanny work, working as a station hand (jackaroo/jillaroo) and collecting for charities.

» People with computer, secretarial, nursing and teaching skills can find work temping in the major cities by registering with a relevant agency.

Information

Backpacker magazines, newspapers and notice boards are good resources for local work opportunities.

Useful websites:

Career One (www.careerone.com.au) General employment site; good for metropolitan areas.

Gumtree (www.gumtree.com.au) Great classified site with jobs, accommodation and items for sale.

MyCareer (www.mycareer.com.au) Website for general

employment; good for metropolitan areas.

Seek (www.seek.com.au) General employment site; good for metropolitan areas.

Travellers at Work (www.taw.com.au) Excellent site for working travellers in Australia.

Seasonal Work

Seasonal fruit-picking (harvesting) relies on casual labour – there is always something that needs to be picked, pruned or farmed somewhere in Australia all year round. It's definitely hard work, involving early-morning starts, and you're usually paid by how much you pick (per bin, bucket, kilo etc). Expect to earn about $50 to $60 a day to start with; more when your skills and speed improve. Some work, such as pruning or sorting, is paid by the hour at around $13 to $15.

Throughout this book you'll find separate seasonal work information for towns where there is an abundance of this type of employment. You can also call the **National Harvest Labour Information Service** (☎ 1800 062 332) for more information about when and where you're likely to pick up this sort of work.

Useful websites:

Grunt Labour (www.grunt labour.com) Specialises in labour, manufacturing and agricultural-based recruitment.

Harvest Trail (www.job search.gov.au/harvesttrail) Harvest jobs around Australia.

Workabout Australia (www.workaboutaustralia.com.au) Gives a state-by-state breakdown of seasonal work opportunities.

SEASONAL WORK HOT SPOTS

The following info directs you to some of the more prominent areas for seasonal work:

New South Wales The NSW ski fields have seasonal work during the ski season, particularly around Thredbo

(p222). There's also harvest work around Narrabri and Moree, and grape picking in the Hunter Valley (p136). Fruit picking is all the go near Tenterfield, Orange (p198) and Young.

Queensland When the area isn't being battered by tropical cyclones, there's fruit picking work to be found around Stanthorpe, Childers, Bundaberg and Cairns. Those looking for sturdier (and much better-paying) work should keep an eye on mining opportunities in growth mining towns such as Weipa and Cloncurry.

Victoria There's plenty of harvest work in Mildura and Shepparton (p560).

Tasmania The apple orchards in the south, especially around Cygnet and Huonville, are your best bet for work in Tassie.

South Australia Good seasonal-work opportunities can be found on the Fleurieu Peninsula, along the Murray River around Berri (p763), and the Coonawarra wineries on the Limestone Coast.

Northern Territory For information on seasonal work in the Northern Territory, see p803.

Western Australia In Perth, plenty of temporary work is available in tourism and hospitality, administration, IT, nursing, child care, factories and labouring. Outside of Perth, travellers can easily get jobs in tourism and hospitality, plus a variety of seasonal work. For grape-picking work, head for the vineyards around Margaret River. See p896 for more tips on seasonal work in WA.

Tax

PAYING TAX & TAX REFUNDS

Even with a tax file number (TFN), nonresidents (including Working Holiday visa holders) pay a considerably higher rate of tax than Australian residents, especially those on a low income. For

a start, there's no tax-free threshold – you pay tax on every dollar you earn.

Because you have been paid wages in Australia, you must lodge a tax return with the **Australian Taxation Office** (ATO; ☎ 13 28 61; www.ato.gov.au). To lodge a tax return, you will need your TFN and also a Payment Summary (an official summary of your earnings and tax payments) provided by your employer – give them written advice at least 14 days in advance that you want the certificate on your last day at work, otherwise you may have to wait until the end of the financial year.

You should lodge your tax return by 31 October, unless you have been granted an extension to lodge at a later date. If you leave Australia permanently before the end of the tax year the Australian Tax Office may accept an early lodgement (ie before 30 June). It can take up to six weeks to process your tax return, so make sure you write an address on your tax return where it can send your notice of assessment.

It's important to bear in mind that you are not entitled to a refund for the tax you paid – you will only receive a refund if too much tax was withheld from your pay. If you didn't pay enough tax while you were working then you will have to pay more. You are, however, entitled to any superannuation that has been deducted from your pay.

For more information contact the ATO, which can provide advice over the phone (be prepared to wait a while on hold) and has an informative website.

TAX FILE NUMBER

If you have a Working Holiday visa, you should apply for a TFN. Without it, tax will be deducted from any wages you receive at the maximum rate. Apply for a TFN online via the ATO; it takes up to four weeks to be issued.

season generally tallies with the winter months (June to August), though this is actually the peak tourist season in central Australia and the Top End.

Airports & Airlines

Australia has several international gateways, with Sydney and Melbourne being the busiest.

Adelaide (☎08-8308 9211; www.adelaideairport.com.au)

Brisbane (☎07-3406 3000; www.bne.com.au)

Cairns (☎07-4080 6703; www.cairnsairport.com)

Darwin (☎08-8920 1811; www.ntapl.com.au)

Melbourne (☎03-9297 1600; www.melbourneairport.com.au) Tullamarine.

Perth (☎08-9478 8888; www.perthairport.net.au)

Sydney (Kingsford Smith; ☎02-9667 9111; www.sydney airport.com.au)

Australia's international carrier **Qantas** (☎13 13 13; www.qantas.com.au) flies chiefly to runways across Europe, North America, Asia and the Pacific. Other airlines that fly in and out of Australia include:

Air Canada (www.aircanada.com)

Air New Zealand (www.airnewzealand.com)

Air Pacific (www.airpacific.com)

American Airlines (www.aa.com)

British Airways (www.britishairways.com)

Cathay Pacific (www.cathaypacific.com)

Emirates (www.emirates.com)

Garuda Indonesia (www.garuda-indonesia.com)

Japan Airlines (www.jal.com)

Jetstar (www.jetstar.com)

KLM (www.klm.com)

Korean Air (www.koreanair.com)

Lufthansa (www.lufthansa.com)

Malaysia Airlines (www.malaysiaairlines.com)

Transport

GETTING THERE & AWAY

They don't call Australia the land 'down under' for nothing. It's a long way from just about everywhere, and getting here is usually going to mean a long-haul flight. That 'over the horizon' feeling doesn't stop once you're here, either – the distances between key cities (let alone opposing coastlines) can be vast, requiring a minimum of an hour or two of air time but up to several days of highway cruising or dirt-road jostling to traverse. So if you're short on time, consider an internal flight – they're affordable (compared with petrol and car-hire costs) and will save you some *looong* days in the saddle. Flights, tours and rail tickets can be booked online at www.lonelyplanet.com/bookings.

Entering the Country

Disembarkation in Australia is a straightforward affair, with only the usual customs declarations (p1051), and the fight to be first to the luggage carousel, to endure.

Passports

There are no restrictions when it comes to citizens of foreign countries entering Australia. If you have a current passport and visa (p1063), you should be fine.

Air

There are lots of competing airlines and a wide variety of airfares to choose from if you're flying in from Asia, Europe or North America, but you'll still pay a lot for a flight. Because of Australia's size and diverse climate, any time of year can prove busy for in-bound tourists – if you plan to fly at a particularly popular time of year (Christmas is notoriously difficult for Sydney and Melbourne) or on a particularly popular route (such as Hong Kong, Bangkok or Singapore to Sydney or Melbourne), make your arrangements well in advance.

The high season for flights into Australia is roughly over the country's summer (December to February), with slightly less of a premium on fares over the shoulder months (October/November and March/April). The low

Pacific Blue
(www.flypacificblue.com)
Royal Brunei Airlines
(www.bruneiair.com)
Singapore Airlines
(www.singaporeair.com)
South African Airways
(www.flysaa.com)
Thai Airways International (www.thaiairways.com)
Tiger Airways
(www.tigerairways.com)
United Airlines
(www.united.com)

Tickets

Online ticket sales work well if you're doing a simple one-way or return trip on specified dates but are no substitute for a travel agent with the lowdown on special deals, strategies for avoiding stopovers and other useful advice.

ROUND THE WORLD (RTW) TICKETS

If you are flying to Australia from the other side of the world, RTW tickets can be bargains. They're generally put together by the big airline alliances, and give you a limited period (usually a year) in which to circumnavigate the globe. You can go anywhere the participating airlines go, as long as you stay within the prescribed kilometre extents or number of stops and don't backtrack when flying between continents. Ticket providers include:

Star Alliance
(www.staralliance.com)
Oneworld (www.oneworld.com)
Skyteam (www.skyteam.com)

CIRCLE PACIFIC TICKETS

A Circle Pacific ticket is similar to a RTW ticket but covers a more limited region, using a combination of airlines to connect Australia, New Zealand, North America and Asia, with stopover options in the Pacific islands. As with RTW tickets, there are restrictions on how many stopovers you can take.

Sea

It's possible (though by no means easy or safe) to make your way between Australia and countries such as Papua New Guinea, Indonesia, New Zealand and the Pacific islands by hitching rides or crewing on yachts – usually you have to at least contribute towards food. Ask around at marinas and sailing clubs in places like Coffs Harbour, Great Keppel Island, Airlie Beach, the Whitsundays, Darwin and Cairns. April is a good time to look for a berth in the Sydney area.

Alternatively, **P&O Cruises** (www.pocruises.com.au) operates holiday cruises between Brisbane or Sydney and destinations in New Zealand and the Pacific.

GETTING AROUND

Air

Time pressures combined with the vastness of the Australian continent may lead you to consider taking to the skies at some point in your trip. Both **STA Travel** (☎13 47 82; www.statravel.com.au) and **Flight Centre** (☎13 31 33; www.flightcentre.com.au) have offices throughout Australia, or you can book directly with the airlines listed below, or try www.travel.com.au.

Airlines in Australia

Australia's main (and highly safe and professional) domestic airlines are **Qantas** (☎13 13 13; www.qantas.com.au) and **Virgin Australia** (☎13 67 89; www.virginaustralia.com), servicing all the main centres with regular flights. **Jetstar** (☎13 15 38; www.jetstar.com.au) and **Tiger Airways** (☎03-9999 2888; www.tigerairways.com) are the budget subsidiaries of Qantas and Singapore Airlines respectively, flying between most Australian capital cities.

See regional chapters for info on smaller operators flying regional routes.

Bicycle

Australia has much to offer cyclists, from bike paths winding through most major cities to thousands of kilometres of good country roads where you can wear out your sprockets. There's lots of flat countryside and gently rolling hills to explore and, although Australia is not as mountainous as, say, Switzerland or France, mountain bikers can find plenty of foresty trails and high country. See p36 for tips on outback cycling.

CLIMATE CHANGE & TRAVEL

Every form of transport that relies on carbon-based fuel generates CO_2, the main cause of human-induced climate change. Modern travel is dependent on aeroplanes, which might use less fuel per kilometre per person than most cars but travel much greater distances. The altitude at which aircraft emit gases (including CO_2) and particles also contributes to their climate change impact. Many websites offer 'carbon calculators' that allow people to estimate the carbon emissions generated by their journey and, for those who wish to do so, to offset the impact of the greenhouse gases emitted with contributions to portfolios of climate-friendly initiatives throughout the world. Lonely Planet offsets the carbon footprint of all staff and author travel.

TIGER SUSPENDED

Tiger Airways began operating domestic flights in Australia in late 2007. In July 2011 the Civil Aviation Safety Authority grounded the airline due to safety concerns. The airline resumed flying, under the careful watch of CASA, the following month. See www.tigerairways.com.au for the latest.

Hire Bike hire in cities is easy (see Activities headings in destination chapters), but if you're riding for more than a few hours or even a day, it's more economical to invest in your own wheels (see the Buying a Bike section).

Legalities Bike helmets are compulsory in all states and territories, as are white front-lights and red rear-lights for riding at night.

Maps You can get by with standard road maps, but to avoid low-grade unsealed roads, the government series is best. The 1:250,000 scale is suitable, though you'll need lots of maps if you're going far. The next scale up is 1:1,000,000 – widely available in map shops.

Weather In summer carry plenty of water. Wear a helmet with a peak (or a cap under your helmet), use sunscreen and avoid cycling in the middle of the day. Beware summer southerlies that can make a north-bound cyclist's life hell. South-easterly trade winds blow in April, when you can have (theoretically) tail winds all the way to Darwin. It can get very cold in the mountains, so pack appropriate clothing.

Transport If you're bringing in your own bike, check with your airline for costs and the degree of dismantling or packing required. Within Australia, bus companies require you to dismantle your bike and some don't guarantee that it will travel on the same bus as you.

Information

The national cycling body is the **Bicycle Federation of Australia** (02-6249 6761; www.bicycles.net.au). Each state and territory has a touring organisation that can also help with cycling information and put you in touch with touring clubs.

Bicycle New South Wales (02-9704 0800; www.bicyclensw.org.au)

Bicycle Queensland (07-3844 1144; www.bq.org.au)

Bicycle SA (08-8168 9999; www.bikesa.asn.au)

Bicycle Tasmania (www.biketas.org.au)

Bicycle Transportation Alliance (08-9420 7210; www.btawa.org.au) In WA.

Bicycle Victoria (03-8636 8888; www.bv.com.au)

Northern Territory Cycling Association (www.nt.cycling.org.au)

Pedal Power ACT (02-6248 7995; www.pedalpower.org.au)

Buying a Bike

If you want to buy a reliable, new road or mountain bike, your absolute bottom-level starting point is $500 or $650. Throw in all the requisite on-the-road equipment (panniers, helmet etc), and your starting point becomes $1500 to $2000. Secondhand bikes are worth checking out in the cities, as are the post-Christmas sales and mid-year stocktakes, when newish cycles can be heavily discounted.

To sell your bike, try hostel noticeboards or the online **Trading Post** (www.tradingpost.com.au).

Boat

There's a hell of a lot of water around Australia, but unless you're fortunate enough to hook up with a yacht, it's not a feasible way of getting around. The only regular passenger services are the two high-speed, vehicle-carrying **Spirit of Tasmania** (1800 634 906; www.spiritoftasmania.com.au) boats between Melbourne and Devonport on Tasmania's northwest coast. See p678 for details.

Bus

Australia's extensive bus network is a relatively cheap and reliable way to get around, though it can be tedious over huge distances. Most buses are equipped with air-con, toilets and videos; all are smoke-free. Small towns eschew formal bus terminals for a single drop-off/pick-up point (post office, newsagent, corner shop etc).

Greyhound Australia (1300 473 946; www.greyhound.com.au) runs a national network (notably not across the Nullarbor Plain between Adelaide and Perth). Fares purchased online are roughly 5% cheaper than over-the-counter tickets; phone-purchased fares incur a $4 booking fee.

Other interstate operators include:

Firefly Express (1300 730 740; www.fireflyexpress.com.au) Runs between Sydney, Canberra, Melbourne and Adelaide.

Premier Motor Service (13 34 10; www.premierms.com.au) Runs along the east coast between Cairns and Melbourne.

V/Line (13 61 96; www.vline.com.au) Connects Victoria with New South Wales (NSW), South Australia (SA) and the Australian Capital Territory (ACT).

Backpacker Buses

Companies offering budget backpacker transport are pretty much organised-tour operators, but they do get you from A to B (sometimes with hop-on, hop-off services).

Principal Bus Routes - - - - - - -
Principal Railways ————

Discounts for members of hostel organisations are usually available.

Adventure Tours Australia (☎1800 068 886; www.adventuretours.com.au) Budget tours in all states. A two-day Red Centre tour starting/finishing in Alice Springs via Uluru, Kata Tjuta and Kings Canyon costs $490. Ten days Perth to Broome costs $1545.

Autopia Tours (☎03-9419 8878; www.autopiatours.com.au) Three-day trips along the Great Ocean Rd from Melbourne to Adelaide, or from Melbourne to Sydney for $395.

Groovy Grape Getaways Australia (☎1800 661 177; www.groovygrape.com.au) Small-group, SA-based operator. Tours include three days Melbourne to Adelaide via the Great Ocean Road ($355), and seven days Adelaide to Alice Springs via Uluru ($895).

Nullarbor Traveller (☎1800 816 858; www.the-traveller.com.au) Small, eco-certified company running relaxed minibus trips across the Nullarbor. Ten days Adelaide to Perth costs $1495, including bushwalking, surfing, whale watching, meals and national-park entry fees.

Oz Experience (☎1800 555 287; www.ozexperience.com) Sociable hop-on, hop-off services covering eastern Australia. Travel is one-directional and passes are valid for up to six months with unlimited stops. A Sydney–Cairns pass is $495; the 'Fish Hook' pass from Sydney or Melbourne to Darwin is $1475.

Bus Passes

Greyhound offers a slew of passes geared towards various types and routes of travel: see www.greyhound.com.au/australia-bus-pass for details. Many proffer a 10% discount for members of YHA, VIP, Nomads and other approved organisations.

EXPLORER PASSES

Hop-on, hop-off passes matched to popular itineraries. You don't have the backtracking flexibility of the Kilometre Pass, but if you can find a route that suits you it generally works out cheaper.

The Aussie Highlights Pass ($1864) allows you to loop around the eastern half

of Australia from Sydney to Melbourne, Adelaide, Coober Pedy, Alice Springs, Darwin, Cairns, Townsville, the Whitsundays, Brisbane and Surfers Paradise. Or there are one-way passes, such as the Best of the Outback ($976): Sydney to Darwin via Melbourne, Adelaide and Alice Springs.

KILOMETRE PASS

This is the simplest pass and gives you a specified amount of travel, starting at 500km ($105) and going up in increments of 1000km to 2000km ($2239), with a maximum of 25,000km ($2585). It's valid for 12 months and you can travel where and in what direction you please, and stop as many times as you like. Use the online kilometre chart to figure out which one suits you. Phone at least a day ahead to reserve your seat.

Classes

There are no class divisions on Australian buses (very democratic), and the vehicles of the different companies all look pretty similar and are equipped with air-con, toilets and videos. Smoking is a no-no.

Costs

Following are the average, non-discounted, one-way bus fares on some well-travelled routes.

ROUTE	ADULT/CHILD/ CONCESSION
Adelaide- Darwin	$595/540/560
Adelaide- Melbourne	$70/60/65
Brisbane- Cairns	$260/220/250
Cairns- Sydney	$410/350/370
Sydney- Brisbane	$140/110/115
Sydney- Melbourne	$65/60/60

Car & Motorcycle

With its vast distances, endless stretches of bitumen and off-the-beaten-track sights, exploring Australia by road is an experience unlike any other.

Driving Licence

To drive in Australia you'll need to hold a current driving licence issued in English from your home country. If the licence isn't in English, you'll also need to carry an International Driving Permit, issued in your home country.

Choosing a Vehicle

2WD Depending on where you want to travel, a regulation 2WD vehicle may suffice. They're cheaper to hire, buy and run than 4WDs and are more readily available. Most are fuel efficient, and easy to repair and sell. Downsides: no off-road capability and no room to sleep!

4WD Four-wheel drives are good for outback travel as they can access almost any track you get a hankering for. And there might even be space to sleep in the back. Downsides: poor fuel economy, awkward to park and more expensive to hire/ buy.

Campervan Creature comforts at your fingertips: sink, fridge, cupboards, beds, kitchen and space to relax. Downsides: slow and often not fuel-efficient, not great on dirt roads and too big for nipping around the city.

Motorcycle Motorcycles are a unique, romantic way to travel Australia. The climate is good, and bikes are handy in city traffic. Downsides: Australia isn't particularly bike-friendly in terms of driver awareness, limited luggage capacity, and exposure to the elements.

Buying a Vehicle

Buying your own vehicle to travel around in gives you the freedom to go where and when the mood takes you, and may work out cheaper than renting in the long run. Downsides include dealing with confusing and expensive registration, roadworthy certificates and insurance; forking out for maintenance and repairs; and selling the vehicle, which may be more difficult than expected. Some dealers will sell you a car with an undertaking to buy it back at an agreed price, but don't accept verbal guarantees – get it in writing.

Always read the fine print when buying a car. See p1072 for organisations that can check to ensure the car you're buying is fully paid for and owned by the seller.

WHAT TO LOOK FOR

It's prudent to have a car checked by an independent expert – Auto clubs (p1075) offer vehicle checks, and road transport authorities (p1073) have lists of licensed garages – but if you're flying solo, things to check include:

» tyre tread
» number of kilometres
» rust damage
» accident damage
» oil should be translucent and honey-coloured
» coolant should be clean and not rusty in colour
» engine condition; check for fumes from engine, smoke from exhaust while engine is running and engines that rattle or cough
» exhaust system should not be excessively noisy or rattle when engine is running
» windscreen should be clear with no cracks or chip marks

When test-driving the car, also check the following:

» listen for body and suspension noise and changes in engine noise
» check for oil and petrol smells, leaks and overheating
» check instruments, lights and controls all work: heating, air-con, brake lights

Sydney to Melbourne
via the Princes Hwy

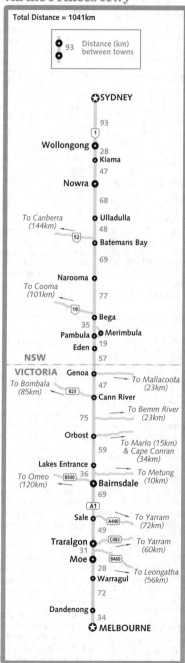

Total Distance = 1041km

● ○ 93 | Distance (km) between towns

⊗ SYDNEY

93

① **Wollongong** ●
28
● **Kiama**
47
Nowra ●
68
To Canberra (144km) — ● **Ulladulla**
48
⑤② **Batemans Bay** ●
69
Narooma ●
To Cooma (101km) —
77
⑱
● **Bega**
35
Pambula ● ○ **Merimbula**
Eden ●
19
NSW
57
VICTORIA **Genoa** ●
To Bombala (85km) — B23 → *To Mallacoota (23km)*
47
● **Cann River**
→ *To Bemm River (23km)*
75
Orbost ●
To Marlo (15km) & Cape Conran (34km)
59
Lakes Entrance ●
To Omeo (120km) — B500
36
→ *To Metung (10km)*
● **Bairnsdale**
69
A1
Sale ● A440 → *To Yarram (72km)*
49
Traralgon ● C482 → *To Yarram (60km)*
31
Moe ● B460
28
→ *To Leongatha (56km)*
● **Warragul**
72
Dandenong ●
34
⊗ MELBOURNE

» headlights, indicators, seatbelts and windscreen wipers

» brakes should pull the car up straight, without pulling, vibrating or making noise

» gears and steering should be smooth and quiet

WHERE & WHEN TO BUY
If you're buying a second-hand vehicle, keep in mind the hidden costs: stamp duty, registration, transfer fee, insurance and maintenance.

Online
Private and dealer car sales are listed online on websites such as:

Car Sales (www.carsales. com.au)

Trading Post (www.trading post.com.au)

Private Ads
Buying privately can be time consuming, and you'll have to travel around to assess your options. But you should expect a lower price than that charged by a licensed dealer. The seller should provide you with a roadworthy certificate (if required in the state you're in), but you won't get a cooling-off period or a statutory warranty. It's your responsibility to ensure the car isn't stolen and that there's no money owing on it. Contact one of the following organisations:

REVS (☎13 32 20; www.revs. nsw.gov.au) ACT, NSW and Northern Territory (NT).

REVS (☎13 74 68; www. fairtrading.qld.gov.au) Queensland; through the Office of Fair Trading.

REVS (☎1300 304 054; https://bizline.commerce.wa.gov. au/revs) WA; through the Department of Commerce.

Registration & Licensing (☎1300 851 225; www.trans port.tas.gov.au) Tasmania.

Vehicle Registration & Licencing (☎13 10 84; www. ecom.transport.sa.gov.au) SA.

Vehicles Securities Register (☎13 11 71; www.vicroads. vic.gov.au) Victoria; through VicRoads.

Backpackers

Hostel noticeboards and online noticeboards such as **Travellers Contact Point** (www.taw.com.au) and the Thorn Tree travel forum at www.lonelyplanet.com are good places to find vehicles for sale. Tour desks also often have noticeboards.

Ride sharing is also a good way to split costs and environmental impact with other travellers. Noticeboards are good places to find ads; also check online classifieds:

Catch A Lift (www.catchalift.com)

MySpareSeat (www.myspareseat.com)

Need A Ride (www.needaride.com.au)

Dealers

Buying from a licensed dealer gives you some protection. They are obliged to guarantee that no money is owing on the car and you're often allowed a cooling-off period (usually three days). Depending on the age of the car and the kilometres travelled, you may also receive a statutory warranty. You will need to sign an agreement for sale; make sure you understand what it says before you sign.

Travellers' Markets

Cairns, Sydney, Darwin and Perth (cities where travellers commonly begin or finish their travels) are the best places to buy or sell a vehicle, especially Cairns.

Australia's largest backpacker car market is the **Kings Cross Car Market** (☑1800 800 188; www.carmarket.com.au; 110 Bourke St, Woolloomooloo) in Sydney. It's likely these cars have been around Australia several times, so it can be a risky option.

PAPERWORK

When you buy a vehicle in Australia, you need to transfer the vehicle registration into your own name within 14 days. Each state has slightly different requirements and

different organisations to do this. Similarly, when selling a vehicle you need to advise the state or territory road-transport authority of the change of name. In Queensland, before advertising a car for sale you need to obtain and display a safety certificate. In NSW, NT, SA, Tasmania and Western Australia (WA) you do not need to provide a roadworthy certificate. In Victoria you're required to provide a roadworthy certificate, or you can remove the plates, cancel the registration, and sell the car without a certificate.

Some considerations:

Transfer of registration form In NSW, NT, Queensland, Tasmania, Victoria and WA, you and the seller need to complete and sign this form. In the ACT and SA there is no form, but you and the seller need to complete and sign the reverse of the registration certificate.

Roadworthy certificate In the ACT, if the vehicle is more than six years old it will need a roadworthy certificate. In NSW, NT, SA, Tasmania and WA you don't need to provide a certificate, but in Victoria you do. In Queensland a safety certificate is required. If the vehicle you're considering doesn't have a roadworthy certificate, it's worth having a roadworthiness check done before you buy. This will cost around $100 but can save you money on hidden costs. Road-transport authorities have lists of licensed vehicle testers.

Gas certificate In Queensland if a vehicle runs on gas, a gas certificate (dated less than three months before date of transfer) must be provided by the seller in order to transfer the registration.

Immobiliser fitting In WA it's compulsory to have an approved immobiliser fitted to most vehicles (not motorcycles) before transfer

of registration; this is the buyer's responsibility.

Changing state of registration Note that registering a vehicle in a different state to the one it was previously registered in can be difficult, time-consuming and expensive.

Registration is usually renewed annually Australia-wide. This generally requires no more than payment of the registration fee. However, some states have extra requirements:

NSW Vehicle roadworthy inspections are required annually once the vehicle is five years old.

NT Vehicle roadworthy inspections are required once the vehicle is three years old. Vehicles older than three years but less than 10 years old require a roadworthy inspection every two years until they reach their 10th year. Vehicles over 10 years old require an annual roadworthy inspection.

SA You can pay for three, six, nine or 12 months' registration.

Tasmania You can pay for six or 12 months' registration.

ROAD TRANSPORT AUTHORITIES

For more information about processes and costs:

Rego ACT (☑13 22 81; www.rego.act.gov.au)

Roads & Traffic Authority NSW (☑13 22 13; www.rta.nsw.gov.au)

Northern Territory Transport Group (☑1300 654 628; www.nt.gov.au/transport)

Queensland Transport & Main Roads (☑13 23 80; www.tmr.qld.gov.au)

Department for Transport, Energy & Infrastructure (☑13 10 84, 1300 361 021; www.dtei.sa.gov.au) SA.

Department of Infrastructure, Energy & Resources (☑1300 135 513; www.transport.tas.gov.au) Tasmania.

Sydney to Brisbane via the Pacific Hwy

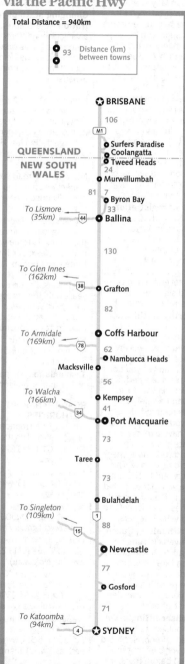

Total Distance = 940km

93 Distance (km) between towns

✪ BRISBANE

106

M1

QUEENSLAND

◦ Surfers Paradise
◦ Coolangatta
◦ Tweed Heads

NEW SOUTH WALES

24

◦ Murwillumbah

81 7

◦ Byron Bay

To Lismore (35km) — 44

33

◦ Ballina

130

To Glen Innes (162km) — 38

◦ Grafton

82

To Armidale (169km) — 78

◦ Coffs Harbour

62

◦ Nambucca Heads

Macksville ◦

56

To Walcha (166km) — 34

◦ Kempsey

41

◦◦ Port Macquarie

73

Taree ◦

73

◦ Bulahdelah

To Singleton (109km) — 1
15

88

◦ Newcastle

77

◦ Gosford

71

To Katoomba (94km) — 4

✪ SYDNEY

VicRoads (📞13 11 71; www. vicroads.vic.gov.au) Victoria.

Department of Transport (📞13 11 56; www.transport. wa.gov.au) WA.

Vehicle Rental

Hiring helps you avoid problems that come with buying a vehicle: obtaining roadworthy certificates, registering it, selling it etc. Larger car-rental companies have drop-offs in major cities and towns. Most companies require drivers to be over the age of 21, though in some cases it's 18 and in others 25.

Suggestions to assist in the process:

» Read the contract cover to cover.

» Bond: some companies may require a signed credit-card slip, others may actually charge your credit card; if this is the case, find out when you'll get a refund.

» Ask if unlimited kilometres are included and, if not, what the extra charge per kilometre is.

» Find out what excess you'll have to pay if you have a prang, and if it can be lowered by an extra charge per day. Check if your personal travel insurance covers you for vehicle accidents and excess.

» Check for exclusions (hitting a kangaroo, damage on unsealed roads etc) and whether you're covered on unavoidable unsealed roads (eg accessing campgrounds). Some companies also exclude parts of the car from cover, such as the underbelly, tyres and windscreen.

» At pick-up inspect the vehicle for any damage. Make a note of anything on the contract before you sign.

» Ask about breakdown and accident procedures.

» If you can, return the vehicle during business hours and insist on an inspection in your presence.

There are a huge number of rental companies. Useful sites offering last-minute discounts:

Carhire.com (www.carhire.com.au)

Drive Now (www.drivenow.com.au)

Webjet (www.webjet.com.au)

4WD & CAMPERVAN HIRE

A small 4WD such as a Suzuki Vitara or Toyota Rav4 costs between $85 and $100 a day. A Toyota Landcruiser is at least $100, which should include insurance and some free kilometres (100km to 200km a day, or sometimes unlimited).

Check conditions carefully, especially the excess, as it can be onerous – in the NT $5000 is typical, but this can often be reduced to around $1000 (or even to nil) by paying an extra daily charge (around $50). Even for a 4WD, insurance offered by most companies may not cover damage caused travelling 'off-road', meaning anywhere that isn't a maintained bitumen or dirt road.

Hertz, Budget and Avis have 4WD rentals, with one-way rentals possible between the eastern states and the NT. Other companies for campervan hire – with rates from around $70 (two-berth) or $100 (four-berth) per day, usually with minimum five-day hire and unlimited kilometres – include:

Apollo (☎1800 777 779; www.apollocamper.com)

Backpacker Campervans (☎1800 670 232; www.backpackercampervans.com)

Britz (☎1800 331 454; www.britz.com.au)

Maui (☎1300 363 800; www.maui.com.au)

Wicked Campers (☎1800 246 869; www.wickedcampers.com.au)

ONE-WAY RELOCATIONS

Relocations are usually cheap deals, although they don't allow much time flexibility. Most of the large hire companies offer deals. Worth checking out:

Apollo (☎1800 777 779; www.apollocamper.com)

Britz (☎1800 331 454; www.britz.com.au)

Drive Now (☎1300 547 214; www.drivenow.com.au)

Standbycars (☎1300 789 059; www.standbycars.com.au)

Insurance

With the exception of NSW, third-party personal-injury insurance is included in the vehicle registration cost, ensuring that every registered vehicle carries at least minimum insurance (if registering in NSW you'll need to arrange this privately). We recommend extending that minimum to at least third-party property insurance – minor collisions can be amazingly expensive.

When it comes to hire cars, understand your liability in the event of an accident. Rather than risk paying out thousands of dollars, take out comprehensive car insurance or pay an additional daily amount to the rental company for excess reduction. This reduces the excess payable in the event of an accident from between $2000 and $5000 to a few hundred dollars.

Be aware that if travelling on dirt roads you will not be covered by insurance unless you have a 4WD. Also, most companies' insurance won't cover the cost of damage to glass (including the windscreen) or tyres.

Auto Clubs

Automobile clubs in each state are handy when it comes to insurance, regulations, maps and roadside assistance. Club membership (around $100 to $150) can save you a lot of trouble if things go wrong mechanically. If you're a member of an auto club in your home country, check if reciprocal rights are offered in Australia. The Australian auto clubs

listed below generally offer reciprocal rights in other states and territories:

AAA (Australian Automobile Association; ☎02-6247 7311; www.aaa.asn.au)

AANT (Automobile Association of the Northern Territory; ☎08-8925 5901; www.aant.com.au)

NRMA (☎13 11 22; www.mynrma.com.au) NSW and the ACT.

RAC (Royal Automobile Club of WA; ☎13 17 03; www.rac.com.au)

RACQ (Royal Automobile Club of Queensland; ☎13 19 05; www.racq.com.au)

RACT (Royal Automobile Club of Tasmania; ☎13 27 22; www.ract.com.au)

RACV (Royal Automobile Club of Victoria; ☎13 72 28; www.racv.com.au)

Road Rules

Australians drive on the left-hand side of the road and all cars are right-hand drive.

Give way An important road rule is 'give way to the right' – if an intersection is unmarked (unusual), you must give way to vehicles entering the intersection from your right.

Speed limits The general speed limit in built-up and residential areas is 50km/h (or sometimes 40km/h). Near schools, the limit is usually 25km/h in the morning and afternoon. On the highway it's usually 100km/h or 110km/h; in the NT it's either 110km/h or 130km/h. Police have speed radar guns and cameras and are fond of using them in strategic locations.

Seatbelts It's the law to wear seatbelts front and back; you're likely to get a fine if you don't. Small children must be belted into an approved safety seat.

Drink-driving Random breath-tests are common. If you're caught with a blood-alcohol level of more than 0.05% expect a fine and the

Brisbane to Cairns via the Bruce Hwy

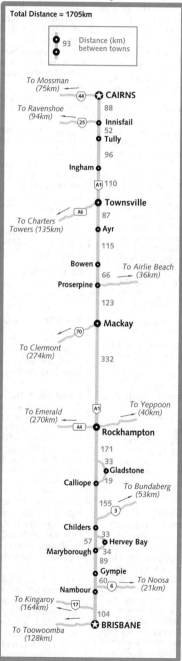

Total Distance = 1705km

Distance (km) between towns: 93

To Mossman (75km) — 44 — ✪ CAIRNS
88
To Ravenshoe (94km) — 25 — ● Innisfail
52
● Tully
96
Ingham ●
A1 110
● Townsville
A6 — 87
To Charters Towers (135km) — ● Ayr
115
Bowen ● — To Airlie Beach (36km)
66
Proserpine ●
123
70 — ● Mackay
To Clermont (274km)
332
To Emerald (270km) — A1 — To Yeppoon (40km)
A4 — ● Rockhampton
171
33 — ● Gladstone
Calliope ● — 19 — To Bundaberg (53km)
155 — 3
Childers ●
33 — ● Hervey Bay
57
Maryborough ● — 34
89
● Gympie
60 — 6 — To Noosa (21km)
Nambour ●
To Kingaroy (164km) — 17
104
✪ BRISBANE
To Toowoomba (128km)

loss of your licence. Police can also randomly pull any driver over for a breathalyser or drug test.

Mobile phones Talking on a mobile phone while driving is illegal in Australia (excluding hands-free technology).

Hazards & Precautions

BEHIND THE WHEEL

Be wary of driver fatigue; driving long distances (particularly in hot weather) can be utterly exhausting. Falling asleep at the wheel is not uncommon. On a long haul, stop and rest every two hours or so – do some exercise, change drivers or have a coffee. Carry a mobile phone if possible, but be aware that there isn't always coverage in country areas. Be careful overtaking road trains; you'll need distance and plenty of speed. On single-lane roads get right off the road when one approaches.

ANIMAL HAZARDS

The roadkill that you see alongside roads around the country is usually the result of cars and trucks hitting animals at night. It's a huge problem in Australia, particularly in the NT, Queensland, NSW, SA and Tasmania. Many Australians avoid travelling altogether once the sun drops because of the risks posed by animals on the roads.

Kangaroos are common on country roads, as are cows and sheep in the unfenced outback – hitting an animal of this size will make a mess of your car. Kangaroos are most active around dawn and dusk and often travel in groups. If you see one hopping across the road, slow right down, as its friends may be just behind it.

If you hit and kill an animal while driving, pull it off the road, preventing the next car from having a potential accident. If the animal is only

injured and is small, perhaps an orphaned joey (baby kangaroo), wrap it in a towel or blanket and call the relevant wildlife rescue line:

Department of Environment & Conservation (☑08-9474 9055, marine emergencies 08-9483 6462; www.dec.wa.gov.au) WA.

Fauna Rescue of South Australia (☑08-8289 0896; www.faunarescue.org.au)

NSW Wildlife Information, Rescue & Education Service (WIRES; ☑1300 094 737; www.wires.org.au)

Wildlife Rescue hotline Darwin (☑0409 090 840); Katherine (☑0412 955 336); Alice Springs (☑0419 221 128) NT.

Department of Environment & Resource Management (☑1300 130 372; www.derm.qld.gov.au) Queensland.

Parks & Wildlife Service Tasmania (☑1300 135 513; www.parks.tas.gov.au)

Wildlife Victoria (☑1300 094 535; www.wildlifevictoria.org.au)

Environmental Considerations

A few simple actions can help minimise the impact your journey has on the environment.

» Ensure your vehicle is well serviced and tuned.

» Travel lightly to reduce fuel consumption.

» Drive slowly; many vehicles use 25% more fuel at 110km/h than at 90km/h.

» Avoid hard acceleration and heavy braking.

» Crank the air-con only when absolutely necessary.

» Stay on designated roads and vehicle off-road tracks. Drive in the middle of tracks to minimise track widening and damage, don't drive on walking tracks and avoid driving on vegetation.

» Avoid shining high beams or spotlights on wildlife.

» Cross creeks at designated areas.

» Consider ride-sharing where possible (see p1073).

For more info, see www.greenvehicleguide.gov.au.

Fuel

Fuel (predominantly unleaded and diesel) is available from service stations sporting well-known international brand names. LPG (liquefied petroleum gas) is not always stocked at more remote roadhouses; if you're on gas it's safer to have dual-fuel capacity.

Prices vary from place to place, but at the time of writing unleaded was hovering between $1.25 and $1.55 in the cities. Out in the country, prices soar – in outback NT and Queensland you can pay as much as $2.20 a litre. Distances between fill-ups can be long in the outback, but there are only a handful of tracks where you'll require a long-range fuel tank. On main roads there'll be a small town or roadhouse roughly every 150km to 200km. Many petrol stations, but not all, are open 24 hours.

Resources

Australian Bureau of Meteorology (www.bom.gov.au)

Main Roads Western Australia (☑13 81 38; www.mainroads.wa.gov.au) Road conditions.

Motorcycle Riders Association of Australia (MRAA; www.mraa.org.au)

Road Report (☑1800 246 199; www.roadreport.nt.gov.au) NT.

Traffic & Travel Information (☑13 19 40; http://highload.131940.qld.gov.au) Queensland.

Transport (☑1300 361 033; www.transport.sa.gov.au) SA road conditions.

Carbon Offsets

Various organisations use 'carbon calculators' that allow travellers to offset the

greenhouse gases they are responsible for with financial contributions. Some Australian-based organisations:
Carbon Neutral (www.carbonneutral.com.au)
Carbon Planet (www.carbonplanet.com)
Elementree (www.elementree.com.au)
Greenfleet (www.greenfleet.com.au)

Hitching

Hitching is never entirely safe in any country in the world, and we don't recommend it. Travellers who decide to hitch should understand that they are taking a small but potentially serious risk. People who do choose to hitch will be safer if they travel in pairs and let someone know where they are planning to go.

In Australia, the hitching signal can be a thumbs up or a downward-pointed finger.

Train

Long-distance rail travel in Australia is something you do because you really want to – not because it's cheap, convenient or fast. That said, trains are more comfortable than buses, and there's a certain long-distance 'romance of the rails' that's alive and kicking. Shorter-distance rail services within each state are run by that state's rail body, either government or private – see state and territory transport sections for details.

The three major interstate services in Australia are operated by **Great Southern Railways** (☑13 21 47; www.gsr.com.au), namely the *Indian Pacific* between Sydney and Perth, the *Overland* between Melbourne and Adelaide, and the *Ghan* between Adelaide and Darwin via Alice Springs. There's also the *Sunlander* service between Brisbane and Cairns, operated by

ROAD DISTANCES (KM)

	Adelaide	Albany	Alice Springs	Birdsville	Brisbane	Broome	Cairns	Canberra	Cape York	Darwin	Kalgoorlie	Melbourne	Perth	Sydney	Townsville
Albany	2649														
Alice Springs	1512	3573													
Birdsville	1183	3244	1176												
Brisbane	1942	4178	1849	1573											
Broome	4043	2865	2571	3564	5065										
Cairns	3079	5601	2396	1919	1705	4111									
Canberra	1372	4021	2725	2038	1287	5296	2923								
Cape York	4444	6566	3361	2884	2601	5076	965	3888							
Darwin	3006	5067	1494	2273	3774	1844	2820	3948	3785						
Kalgoorlie	2168	885	3092	2763	3697	3052	5234	3540	6199	4896					
Melbourne	728	3377	2240	1911	1860	4811	3496	637	4461	3734	2896				
Perth	2624	411	3548	3219	4153	2454	6565	3996	7530	4298	598	3352			
Sydney	1597	4246	3109	2007	940	5208	2634	289	3599	3917	3765	862	3869		
Townsville	3237	5374	2055	1578	1295	3770	341	2582	1306	2479	4893	3155	5349	2293	
Uluru	1559	3620	441	1617	2290	3012	2837	2931	3802	1935	3139	2287	3595	2804	2496

	Bicheno	Cradle Mountain	Devonport	Hobart	Launceston
Cradle Mountain	383				
Devonport	283	100			
Hobart	186	296	334		
Launceston	178	205	105	209	
Queenstown	443	69	168	257	273

These are the shortest distances by road; other routes may be considerably longer.
For distances by coach, check the companies' leaflets.

Queensland Rail (☑1800 872 467; www.queenslandrail.com.au). Trains from Sydney to Brisbane, Melbourne and Canberra are operated by **CountryLink** (☑13 22 32; www.countrylink.info).

Costs

Following are standard internet-booked one-way train fares. Note that cheaper seat fares are readily available but are generally nonrefundable with no changes permitted. Backpacker discounts are also available. Discounted tickets work on a first-come, first-served quota basis, so it pays to book in advance.

Adelaide–Darwin Adult/child seated $716/331; from $1372/876 in a cabin.

Adelaide–Melbourne Adult/child seated $90/45.

Adelaide–Perth Adult/child seated $716/286; from $1402/913 in a cabin.

Brisbane–Cairns Adult/child seated $214/157; from $420/252 in a cabin.

Sydney–Canberra Adult/child seated $40/18.

Sydney–Brisbane Adult/child seated $91/65.

Sydney–Melbourne Adult/child seated $91/65.

Sydney–Perth Adult/child seated $751/251, from $2008/1158 in a cabin.

Train Passes

The Ausrail Pass offered by **Great Southern Rail** (☑13 21 47; www.gsr.com.au) permits unlimited travel on the interstate rail network (including CountryLink and *Sunlander* services) over a six-month period (seated, not in cabins). The pass costs $990/890 per adult when purchased inside/outside Australia – inexpensive considering the amount of ground you could cover in six months.

Great Southern Rail also offers the Rail Explorer Pass for international visitors (you'll need to prove it!), costing $690 per adult, permitting six months' travel on the *Ghan*, the *Overland* and the *Indian Pacific* (again, seated, not in cabins).

CountryLink (☑13 22 32; www.countrylink.info) offers two passes. The East Coast Discovery Pass allows one-way economy travel between Melbourne and Cairns (in either direction) with unlimited stopovers, and is valid for six months – the full trip costs $450, while Sydney to Cairns is $370 and Brisbane to Cairns is $280. The Backtracker Pass, available only to international visitors, permits travel on the entire CountryLink network and has four versions: a 14-day/one-/three-/six-month pass costing $232/275/298/420.

behind the scenes

SEND US YOUR FEEDBACK

We love to hear from travellers – your comments keep us on our toes and help make our books better. Our well-travelled team reads every word on what you loved or loathed about this book. Although we cannot reply individually to postal submissions, we always guarantee that your feedback goes straight to the appropriate authors, in time for the next edition. Each person who sends us information is thanked in the next edition – and the most useful submissions are rewarded with a free book.

Visit **lonelyplanet.com/contact** to submit your updates and suggestions or to ask for help. Our award-winning website also features inspirational travel stories, news and discussions.

Note: We may edit, reproduce and incorporate your comments in Lonely Planet products such as guidebooks, websites and digital products, so let us know if you don't want your comments reproduced or your name acknowledged. For a copy of our privacy policy visit lonelyplanet.com/privacy.

OUR READERS

Many thanks to the travellers who used the last edition and wrote to us with helpful hints, useful advice and interesting anecdotes:

Allie, Dan Alton, Claudia Arabasz, Iain Baird, Kerry Baker, Dennis Balemans, Will Barber, Goncalo Bastos, Kent Bech Rasmussen, Katherine Blizard, Jacqueline Bran, Aidan Buckingham, Mojca Cajnko, Vivian Campton, Trevor Coultas, Criss, Ivar Eizenga, Malin Emanuelsson, Xavier Ferrer, Nigel Fielding, Joerg Fischoetter, Kirsty Garrett, Bronwyn Gillies, Chris Grey, Raphael Hammel, Katja Heijnen, Saskia Henderikse, Errol Hunt, Farida Iqbal, Jacob, Najoka Janssen, Celine Kaenel, Helen Kim, Vardit Lahav, Paul Lepesant, Stuart Lord, Tippets Lover, Anne Mahon, Johnny Mandeville, Ricardo Mardones, Jenny Matheson, Bigi Mathew, Joanna Mazurkiewicz, Steven Mcarthur, Auzen Mercader, Ray Meyer, Curtis Miller, Irene Mittrop, Ian Nettleton, Ronald Noordstrand, Kath Norgrove, Mark Oddi, Ole, Tatiana Olivos, Dani Parry, Monique Ribeiro, Raphael Richards, Christine Sadler, Simone Sanders, Shauntel, Walter Slurry, Alison Smith, Helen Southgate, Graham Stewart, Velichko Valchev, Stan Van Laarhoven, Trudy Van Meggelen, Abhinandan Vashistha, Jenifer Walters, Natalie Wells, Anneke Werner, Alice Wilson, Ina Zetzsche

AUTHOR THANKS

Charles Rawlings-Way

Huge thanks to Maryanne for the gig, and to my curvaceous co-coordinating author Meg, with whom I covered a helluva lot of kilometres in search of the perfect review. Thanks to my dedicated co-authors – an expert crew of wandering wordsmiths – and to the all-star in-house LP production staff. Thank goodness for that piece of wire that held my exhaust together along the Oodnadatta Track, and for my two daughters who provided countless laughs and unscheduled pit-stops along the way.

Meg Worby

In Darwin, thanks to Lauren and Nathan Walter for reliably great company and showing us their town. In Adelaide, thanks to Emma for her passionate take on the arts; Lizzie for insider knowledge of the music and festival scene; and Mum, Dad and Lyn for pitching in with the little ones. Big cheers to Maryanne for the work: it's always great working with you and a privilege to write about my hometown. Thank you Liz Heynes, David Connolly and all the other LP staff who worked so hard to put the guide together. Most of all, loving thanks to Charles, Ione and Remy. Can't think of anyone I'd rather travel with.

Brett Atkinson

Huge thanks to all the staff at the visitor information centres in Tasmania who answered all my questions – before, during and after research – with authority and patience. Thanks also to Maryanne Netto at Lonely Planet, to Gabi Mocatta for authoritative support, and to Charles Rawlings-Way and Meg Worby as skilled and enthusiastic co-ordinating authors. Final thanks to Carol for the ongoing love and support.

Jayne D'Arcy

Thanks to M Mag colleagues Miranda Tay, Dani Valent, James Smith and Penny Modra. Thanks Blakey, Nat, Keshia, Cecilia and the Humes. Thanks Denis from Seaview Lodge: what a welcome sight your B&B's lights were through the fog. Thanks Sharik Billington for your amazing support and our preppie, Miles, for reminding me how great the Great Ocean Road is (those seals!). Thanks Mum, Dad and Kate for Milessitting. Cheers to co-writer Paul Harding, and big thanks to Maryanne Netto.

Peter Dragicevich

Thanks to all the people who I met on the road who were so gracious with their time and advice, particularly the staff at the visitor centres. A big thank you to Chris Oughton and Carol Adams for their hospitality, and to Igor Mihajlovic for all the Perth and Fremantle tips. Best wishes to all my uncles, aunties and cousins on the Erceg side.

Sarah Gilbert

Thanks to Misha, Jamie, Elijah and Zeke for the fine hospitality. Thanks to my LP colleagues, particularly my editors Regis and Maryanne. Thanks to Kyles, Mel, Pen, Bill, BJ, Brendan, Ports, Jane and the rest for generating all those happy Canberra memories. I'll always be grateful to my loving and beloved parents, Danny and Kathleen, and my brother and sister James and Mary. Thanks most of all to Nico for his company on the road, and in life.

Paul Harding

Firstly, thanks to my wife, Hannah, and my beautiful daughter, Layla, who came into the world just before I started working on this book. On the road, many people helped with ideas and advice and the occasional place to stay; Mary and Brian in Castlemaine, Chad and Kylie in Bendigo, Matt and Sim in Yackandandah; Jennifer in Whorouly; Gillian at Mt Buller. Thanks to co-author Jayne D'Arcy for such dedication and the debriefing session in Melbourne. Big thanks at Lonely Planet to Maryanne Netto for your help and faith, as well as Liz, David and the rest of the crew.

Catherine Le Nevez

Cheers to the countless locals, tourism professionals and fellow travellers who provided insider tips and invaluable insights throughout Far North Queensland. Thanks especially to Robert Stephens at Mamu and Wanegan (Glenis Grogan) in Kuranda, as well as Russell (and Clancy!) in Mt Surprise, the Burketown crew, Jason in Normanton, everyone at Bramston, Colin, and, of course, to Julian. Thanks too to Maryanne for signing me up, and to Regis and all at Lonely Planet. As ever, *merci surtout* to my family.

Virginia Maxwell

Thanks to Elizabeth Maxwell, Matthew Clarke, Ella Clarke, Peter and Max Handsaker, Bridget Smyth, Christopher Procter, John Gillman, Stephen Alexander, Philip Learoyd, Helen Campbell, Penny Watson, Maryanne Netto and David Connolly.

Miriam Raphael

Big hugs to Melinda in Alice for walks, talks and one comfy sofa bed. Lyn and Ian Conroy at Kings Creek are an inspiration, as is Kerrie Bennison at Uluru-Kata Tjuta, who is so passionate about the park. Karina and Lauren I appreciate your thoughts on TFC and cheers for teaching me how to change a 4WD tyre. To Marcel who dragged me to the Territory in the first place, it was a gift and I thank you.

Regis St Louis

Thanks to master chef Philip Johnson and winemaker extraordinaire Mark Ravenscroft for insight into culinary Queensland. At Lonely Planet, thanks to Maryanne Netto for inviting me onboard and my co-authors for all their hard work. Special thanks to Cassandra and daughters Magdalena and Genevieve for a memorable stay in Brisbane. Hugs and handshakes to Leonie and Col for providing a home away from home, and to Tim, Leone, Nadina, August and Luca for all their hospitality.

Steve Waters

Thanks to Neville, Phil and Darren, Gibb tyre repairers extraordinaire, Tim and Barry at Mt Hope for the same, Kimberly and your mum for the Priscilla moment, Gary and Kerry for wine and conversation, Jane and Lachie at Bidgemia for the avgas, Paul and Colleen for dinner and hospitality, Trace and Heath, Brodie, Abbidene, Meika and Kaeghan for curries and sorbets, Roz and Megan for caretaking, Sian for support and last but not least Captain Bartos for El Kimbo.

Penny Watson

Thanks to the folk who looked after us on the way: Kekky and Gaga, the McCombes, the McPhees and Jojo Mcharg. Big up also to my Pip and Dig: Oh! The places we've been!

ACKNOWLEDGMENTS

Climate map data adapted from Peel MC, Finlayson BL & McMahon TA (2007) 'Updated World Map of the Köppen-Geiger Climate Classification', *Hydrology and Earth System Sciences*, 11, 163344.

Cover photograph: Uluru, Uluru-Kata Tjuta National Park, Northern Territory, Peter Eastway. Many of the images in this guide are available for licensing from Lonely Planet Images: www.lonelyplanetimages.com.

THIS BOOK

Lonely Planet's guide to its home country, Australia, was first published in 1977, when the company's cofounder Tony Wheeler covered the entire country on his own. In the 34 years since then we've sent literally hundreds of authors around Australia to check every dusty nook and cranny of the world's largest island for Lonely Planet guidebooks. This 16th edition of the Australia guide combined the efforts of 13 fabulous Lonely Planet writers. To see who did what, see Our Writers (p1104). We'd also like to thank the following people for their contributions to this guide: Bob Brown, Dr Michael Cathcart, Dr Tim Flannery and Alan Fletcher. Thanks also to the following people whose research was invaluable: Virginia Jealous, Gabi Mocatta and Olivia Pozzan. This guidebook was commissioned in Lonely Planet's Melbourne office, and produced by the following:

Commissioning Editor Maryanne Netto

Coordinating Editors Trent Holden, Alison Ridgway

Coordinating Cartographer Peter Shields

Coordinating Layout Designer Lauren Egan

Managing Editors Liz Heynes, Kirsten Rawlings

Managing Cartographer David Connolly

Managing Layout Designers Chris Girdler, Jane Hart

Assisting Editors Sarah Bailey, Andrew Bain, Michelle Bennett, Asha Ioculari, Pat Kinsella, Helen Koehne, Anne Mulvaney, Charlotte Orr, Monique Perrin, Dianne Schallmeiner, Jeanette Wall

Assisting Cartographers Anita Banh, Andras Bogdanovits, Hunor Csutoros, Corey Hutchison, Marc Milinkovic, Jolyon Philcox

Assisting Layout Designers Kerrianne Southway, Yvonne Bischofberger

Cover Research Naomi Parker

Internal Image Research Rebecca Skinner

Thanks to Ryan Evans, Marg Toohey, Gerard Walker

NOTES

index

000 Map pages
000 Photo pages

how to use this book

These symbols will help you find the listings you want:

- ⊙ Sights
- 🏊 Beaches
- 🏃 Activities
- 🍃 Courses
- 👌 Tours
- 🎆 Festivals & Events
- 🛏 Sleeping
- 🍴 Eating
- 🍷 Drinking
- ☆ Entertainment
- 🔒 Shopping
- ℹ Information/ Transport

These symbols give you the vital information for each listing:

- 🎵 Telephone Numbers
- ⊙ Opening Hours
- P Parking
- ⊖ Nonsmoking
- ❄ Air-Conditioning
- @ Internet Access
- 📶 Wi-Fi Access
- 🏊 Swimming Pool
- 🥗 Vegetarian Selection
- 📖 English-Language Menu
- 👪 Family-Friendly
- 🐾 Pet-Friendly
- 🚌 Bus
- ⛴ Ferry
- Ⓜ Metro
- Ⓢ Subway
- ⊖ London Tube
- 🚋 Tram
- 🚆 Train

Reviews are organised by author preference.

Map Legend

Sights
- 🔵 Beach
- 🔵 Buddhist
- 🔵 Castle
- 🔵 Christian
- 🔵 Hindu
- 🔵 Islamic
- 🔵 Jewish
- 🔵 Monument
- 🔵 Museum/Gallery
- 🔵 Ruin
- 🔵 Winery/Vineyard
- 🔵 Zoo
- 🔵 Other Sight

Activities, Courses & Tours
- 🔵 Diving/Snorkelling
- 🔵 Canoeing/Kayaking
- 🔵 Skiing
- 🔵 Surfing
- 🔵 Swimming/Pool
- 🔵 Walking
- 🔵 Windsurfing
- 🔵 Other Activity/ Course/Tour

Sleeping
- 🔵 Sleeping
- 🔵 Camping

Eating
- 🔵 Eating

Drinking
- 🔵 Drinking
- 🔵 Cafe

Entertainment
- 🔵 Entertainment

Shopping
- 🔵 Shopping

Information
- 🔵 Post Office
- 🔵 Tourist Information

Transport
- 🔵 Airport
- 🔵 Border Crossing
- 🔵 Bus
- 🔵 Cable Car/ Funicular
- 🔵 Cycling
- 🔵 Ferry
- Ⓜ Metro
- 🔵 Monorail
- P Parking
- Ⓢ S-Bahn
- 🔵 Taxi
- 🔵 Train/Railway
- 🔵 Tram
- ⊖ Tube Station
- Ⓤ U-Bahn
- ● Other Transport

Routes
- Tollway
- Freeway
- Primary
- Secondary
- Tertiary
- Lane
- Unsealed Road
- Plaza/Mall
- Steps
-)=== Tunnel
- Pedestrian Overpass
- Walking Tour
- Walking Tour Detour
- Path

Boundaries
- International
- State/Province
- Disputed
- Regional/Suburb
- Marine Park
- Cliff
- Wall

Population
- 🔵 Capital (National)
- 🔵 Capital (State/Province)
- 🔵 City/Large Town
- 🔵 Town/Village

Geographic
- 🔵 Hut/Shelter
- 🔵 Lighthouse
- 🔵 Lookout
- ▲ Mountain/Volcano
- 🔵 Oasis
- 🔵 Park
-)(Pass
- 🔵 Picnic Area
- 🔵 Waterfall

Hydrography
- River/Creek
- Intermittent River
- Swamp/Mangrove
- Reef
- Canal
- Water
- Dry/Salt/ Intermittent Lake
- Glacier

Areas
- Beach/Desert
- +++ Cemetery (Christian)
- ××× Cemetery (Other)
- Park/Forest
- Sportsground
- Sight (Building)
- Top Sight (Building)

Regis St Louis

Queensland & the Great Barrier Reef Regis' love of Australia has taken him all across the country, from rugged WA to tropical Queensland. On his most recent trip, he explored the bohemian side of Brisbane, visited Granite Belt wineries and introduced his daughters to cuddly koalas at Lone Pine Sanctuary. Regis has contributed to more than 30 Lonely Planet titles, including *Queensland & the Great Barrier Reef*. When not travelling, he splits his time between New York City and Sydney.

Read more about Regis at:
lonelyplanet.com/members/regisstlouis

Steve Waters

Perth & Western Australia It's been 16 years since Steve first travelled through WA in a battered Torana, and he's been a regular visitor ever since. This trip covered 17,600kms, five blown tyres, four lost hats, three pairs of wrecked sunglasses and a close shave with an emu as he traversed the state from Kalumburu to Cervantes. Steve has also authored the West Sumatra chapter of *Indonesia* and, while not on the road, plays with databases in Lonely Planet's Melbourne office.

Penny Watson

Sydney & New South Wales Penny Watson is a trained journalist and full-time professional travel writer. She grew up in regional NSW and has since become an expert on its varied landscapes. This is her second Australia guide and her third title covering this exceptionally unique and diverse chunk of her home country. For a Hong Kong resident, the opportunity to return to Australia and explore some more is always too tempting to ignore. Visit www.pennywatson.com.au for more of Penny's travel stories.

Contributing Authors

Dr Michael Cathcart wrote the History chapter. Michael teaches history at the Australian Centre, the University of Melbourne. He is well known as a broadcaster on ABC Radio National and has presented history programs on ABC TV. His most recent book is *The Water Dreamers* (2009), a history of how water shaped Australia.

Dr Tim Flannery wrote the Environment chapter. Tim is a scientist, explorer and writer. He has written several award-winning books including *The Future Eaters*, *Throwim Way Leg* and *The Weather Makers*. He lives in Sydney where he is a professor in the faculty of science at Macquarie University.

Alan Fletcher has worked in every branch of the performing arts for over 30 years. He has played the role of Dr Karl Kennedy on *Neighbours* since 1994.

Virginia Jealous contributed to the Perth & Western Australia chapter. She has clocked up many kilometres for Lonely Planet over the years, and still reckons that travel and the environment can be mutually sustainable. She lives out of a suitcase and on the road when not at home in Denmark (the town in Western Australia, not the country in Europe).

Peter Dragicevich

Perth & Western Australia If his great-grandfather hadn't died in mysterious circumstances beneath a train in Kalgoorlie, Peter may have been born Western Australian. Instead the family continued to New Zealand, where Peter lived until his newspaper career took him to Australia in the late 1990s. He has subsequently worked on more than 20 Lonely Planet titles, including *Sydney* and *East Coast Australia*. Co-authoring *Perth & West Coast Australia* and the Perth & Western Australia chapter of this book took him one step closer to his goal of circumnavigating the continent, one book at a time.

Read more about Peter at:
lonelyplanet.com/members/peterdragicevich

Sarah Gilbert

Canberra & Around, Queensland & the Great Barrier Reef Sarah grew up in Sydney, studied at the Australian National University in Canberra and has since lived in Amsterdam, New York and Buenos Aires. She cut her teeth on the Big Apple's tabloids, took up travel writing in Argentina and has contributed to several Lonely Planet guides. Based in Sydney and Buenos Aires, she makes her living as a freelance writer and a researcher for film and television. She is currently writing her first book of non-fiction.

Paul Harding

Melbourne & Victoria Melbourne-born but country-raised, Paul spent childhood summers in the Gippsland Lakes, and later took many fishing and camping trips along the Murray River and ski trips to Mt Hotham. He's since seen (and written about) a good part of the world, but still calls this part of Australia home. For this edition, Paul travelled around most of regional Victoria and discovered – yet again – what a beautiful state this is. A freelance writer and photographer, Paul has contributed to more than 30 Lonely Planet guides, including numerous Australian titles.

Catherine Le Nevez

Queensland & the Great Barrier Reef Catherine's first writing for Lonely Planet was about Queensland, which she did while completing her Doctorate of Creative Arts in Writing during a 65,000km lap-and-a-half of the continent, driving through two cyclones. Since then, Catherine has authored more than two dozen guidebooks worldwide, including Lonely Planet's *Queensland & the Great Barrier Reef* and *East Coast Australia* guides (she relived one of those cyclone-pounded drives for a Lonely Planet feature). Catherine jumped at the chance to return to tropical paradise for this assignment.

Virginia Maxwell

Sydney & New South Wales Despite being born, bred and based in Melbourne, Virginia knows Sydney well and loves it to bits. Having lived there in the past and visited frequently ever since, she has a good grasp of where to swim, sleep and generally swan about. When not writing about the Harbour City, Virginia covers Turkey and Italy for Lonely Planet and produces a well-known Australian book industry catalogue.

Read more about Virginia at:
lonelyplanet.com/members/virginiamaxwell

Miriam Raphael

Darwin & Uluru Miriam has lived in the NT since 2009, first in Alice Springs as a reporter for the local paper and now in tropical Darwin where she works as a writer and radio producer. Miriam makes the most of the famous 'Territory Lifestyle', heading out bush with her ol' Nissan Patrol Dot, jumping into waterholes and drinking beer like water. This is her eighth guidebook for Lonely Planet and the first one where she got to review her own wedding venue, the beautiful Olive Pink Botanic Gardens in Alice Springs.

OUR STORY

A beat-up old car, a few dollars in the pocket and a sense of adventure. In 1972 that's all Tony and Maureen Wheeler needed for the trip of a lifetime – across Europe and Asia overland to Australia. It took several months, and at the end – broke but inspired – they sat at their kitchen table writing and stapling together their first travel guide, *Across Asia on the Cheap*. Within a week they'd sold 1500 copies. Lonely Planet was born.

Today, Lonely Planet has offices in Melbourne, London and Oakland, with more than 600 staff and writers. We share Tony's belief that 'a great guidebook should do three things: inform, educate and amuse'.

OUR WRITERS

Charles Rawlings-Way

Coordinating Author; Adelaide & South Australia, Darwin & Uluru As a likely lad, Charles suffered in shorts through Tasmanian winters, and in summer counted the days till he visited his grandparents in Adelaide. With desert-hot days, cool swimming pools and *four* TV stations, this flat city held paradisiacal status. Darwin and the tropical Top End are more recent distractions (...too many crocodiles is barely enough). These days Charles lives in the Adelaide Hills and has developed an unnatural appreciation for Coopers Pale Ale. An underrated rock guitarist and sleepy new dad, this is Charles' lucky 21st book for Lonely Planet.

Meg Worby

Coordinating Author; Adelaide & South Australia, Darwin & Uluru An Adelaide girl who went away and was inexorably drawn back, Meg thinks South Australia is like everywhere else was 10 years ago – yet the best bits of the Festival State (the wine regions, the Adelaide Hills, city parking) are definitely 10 years ahead. Which makes them very 'now'. Darwin and the magnificent Northern Territory, on the other hand, are from the future, when nature takes over... Meg is a former member of Lonely Planet's languages, editorial and publishing teams; this is her fifth Australian guidebook.

Brett Atkinson

Tasmania Brett Atkinson loves Tasmania's spectacular scenery, the laidback locals, and the island's superb food and wine. During extended research around his favourite Australian state, he most enjoyed rugged Bruny Island, the stunning Tasman Peninsula, and conducting diligent investigation of the local craft beer scene in Hobart's pubs. Based in Auckland, Brett combines working for Lonely Planet with exploring the world as a freelance food and travel writer. See www.brett-atkinson.net to see what he's been eating and where he's headed next.

Jayne D'Arcy

Melbourne & Victoria Growing up in the Victorian seaside suburb of Frankston had its advantages for Jayne; it motivated her to catch the Met through all three zones to hang out in Prahran's Greville St, Fitzroy's Brunswick St, St Kilda and the Queen Vic Market. She eventually switched sides and hung out on the Great Ocean Road while studying journalism. After a longish spell working in community radio in East Timor, she finally settled with her family in Melbourne's vibrant north (in zone 1, just).

OVER PAGE | MORE WRITERS

Published by Lonely Planet Publications Pty Ltd
ABN 36 005 607 983
16th edition – November 2011
ISBN 978 1 74179 807 4
© Lonely Planet 2011   Photographs © as indicated 2011
10 9 8 7 6 5 4 3
Printed in China

Although the authors and Lonely Planet have taken all reasonable care in preparing this book, we make no warranty about the accuracy or completeness of its content and, to the maximum extent permitted, disclaim all liability arising from its use.

Top Reef Encounters

Donning a mask and fins and getting an up-close look at this marine wonderland is one of the best ways to experience the Great Barrier Reef. You can get a different take aboard a glass-bottomed boat tour, on a scenic flight or on a land-based reef walk.

Semisubmersibles

1 A growing number of reef operators (especially around Cairns) offer semi-submersible or glass-bottomed boat tours, which give cinematic views of coral, rays, fish, turtles and sharks – without ever getting wet.

Scenic Flights

2 Get a bird's-eye view of the vast coral reef and its cays and islands from a scenic flight. You can sign up for a helicopter tour (such as those offered from Cairns) or a seaplane tour (particularly memorable over the Whitsundays).

Diving & Snorkelling

3 The classic way to see the Great Barrier Reef is to board a catamaran and visit several different coral-rich spots on a long day trip. Nothing quite compares to that first under-water glimpse, whether diving or snorkelling.

Sailing

4 You can escape the crowds and see some spectacular reef scenery aboard a sailboat. Experienced mariners can hire a bareboat, others can join a multiday tour – both are easily arranged from Airlie Beach (p388), near the Whitsundays.

Reef Walking

5 Many reefs of the southern Great Barrier Reef are exposed at low tide, allowing visitors to walk on the reef top (on sandy tracks between living coral). This can be a fantastic way to learn about marine life, especially if accompanied by a naturalist guide.

Clockwise from top left

1. View vivid anemone fish on a semisubmersible trip (p418)
2. Take a seaplane flight on Hayman Island (p394)
3. Experience the reef with a snorkel and flippers (p30)